DEPARTMENT OF COMMERCE
BUREAU OF THE CENSUS
SAM. L. ROGERS, DIRECTOR

NEGRO POPULATION
1790–1915

WASHINGTON
GOVERNMENT PRINTING OFFICE
1918

CONTENTS.

SUMMARY OF CHAPTERS.

(3)

CONTENTS.

CONTENTS OF CHAPTERS.

INTRODUCTION.

PART I.—GROWTH AND GEOGRAPHIC DISTRIBUTION: 1790–1910.

CHAPTER I.—THE STATES AND OUTLYING POSSESSIONS.

CHAPTER II.—GROWTH IN THE STATES: 1790–1910—NUMBER, INCREASE, AND PROPORTION OF NEGROES IN THE TOTAL POPULATION.

CHAPTER III.—GEOGRAPHIC DISTRIBUTION AND INCREASE, BY STATES: 1790–1910.

CHAPTER III.—GEOGRAPHIC DISTRIBUTION AND INCREASE, BY STATES: 1790–1910—Continued.

GENERAL TABLE.

CHAPTER IV.—PROPORTION NEGRO IN THE POPULATION AT EACH CENSUS, BY STATES: 1790–1910.

GENERAL TABLES.

CHAPTER V.—FREE COLORED AND SLAVE POPULATION: 1790–1860.

GENERAL TABLE.

PART II.—MIGRATORY DISPLACEMENT AND SEGREGATION.

CHAPTER VI.—NATIVITY—PLACE OF BIRTH, PARENTAGE, AND INTERSTATE MIGRATION.

CHAPTER VI.—NATIVITY—PLACE OF BIRTH, PARENTAGE, AND INTERSTATE MIGRATION—Continued.

CONTENTS.

PART II.—MIGRATORY DISPLACEMENT AND SEGREGATION—Continued.

PART III.—PHYSICAL CHARACTERISTICS.

CONTENTS.

PART III.—PHYSICAL CHARACTERISTICS—Continued.

PART IV.—VITAL STATISTICS.

8 CONTENTS.

PART IV.—VITAL STATISTICS—Continued.

PART V.—EDUCATIONAL AND SOCIAL STATISTICS.

CONTENTS.

PART V.—EDUCATIONAL AND SOCIAL STATISTICS—Continued.

PART VI.—ECONOMIC STATISTICS.

PART VI.—ECONOMIC STATISTICS—Continued.

PART VI.—ECONOMIC STATISTICS—Continued.

LETTER OF TRANSMITTAL.

DEPARTMENT OF COMMERCE,
BUREAU OF THE CENSUS,
Washington, D. C., June 5, 1918.

SIR:

I transmit herewith a report on the Negro population of the United States, prepared by Dr. John Cummings in the Division of Revision and Results, under the general supervision of Dr. Joseph A. Hill. This report is based upon publications, schedules, and manuscript tables of this bureau and covers a period of 125 years, from 1790 to 1915. I believe, therefore, that it is the most comprehensive statistical report ever published on the subject to which it relates, and I feel confident that it will prove to be a very valuable source of information regarding the progress of the Negro race in this country.

It is worthy of note that the tabulations for this report were made by a corps of Negro clerks working under the efficient direction of three men of their own race, namely, Robert A. Pelham, Charles E. Hall, and William Jennifer.

Respectfully,

SAM. L. ROGERS,
Director of the Census.

Hon. WILLIAM C. REDFIELD,
Secretary of Commerce.

(13)

NEGRO POPULATION: 1790-1915

PERCENTAGE NEGRO IN THE POPULATION OF THE UNITED STATES, BY COUNTIES· 1910.

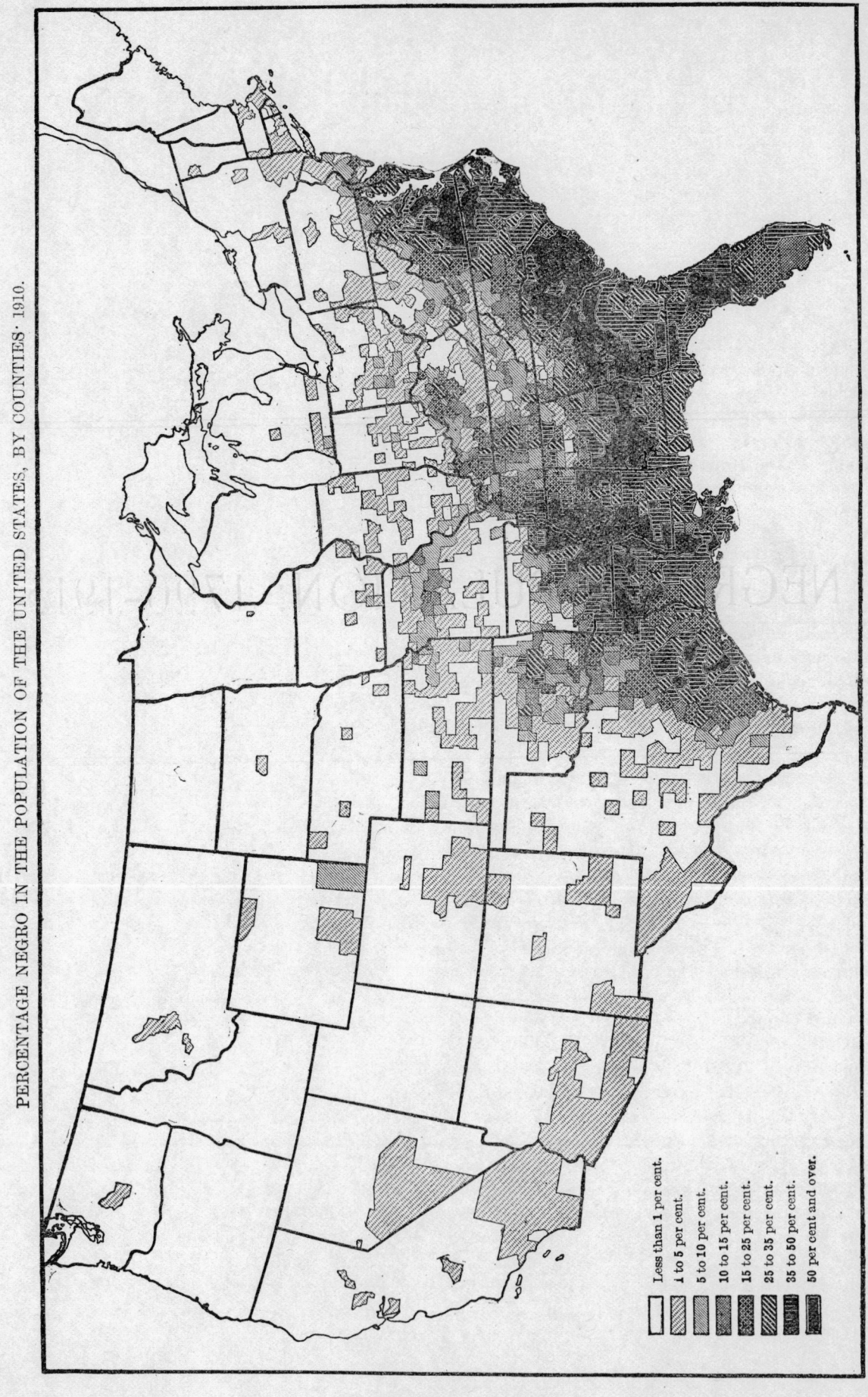

Less than 1 per cent.
1 to 5 per cent.
5 to 10 per cent.
10 to 15 per cent.
15 to 25 per cent.
25 to 35 per cent.
35 to 50 per cent.
50 per cent and over.

NEGRO POPULATION: 1790-1915.

By JOHN CUMMINGS, Ph. D.,

Expert Special Agent, Bureau of the Census.

INTRODUCTION.

SOURCES AND SCOPE OF COMPILATIONS.

Statistics relating to the Negro population have been compiled in the present report from publications, schedules, and unpublished manuscript tables of the Census Bureau, covering the period of 125 years from 1790 to 1915. In part, therefore, the tabulations of the report are compilations which assemble and reorganize material previously published, and in part they are entirely original from records, manuscripts, and schedules.

Voluminous and fugitive records of a century and a quarter are summarized in these compilations, which in the aggregate present a statistical account of the Negro population, covering its racial experience under the conditions imposed by slavery and under the no less difficult conditions imposed by emancipation and freedom.

Specifically this statistical account comprehends the growth of the Negro population from decade to decade; its geographical distribution at each decennial enumeration; its migratory drift westward in the early decades of the last century, when Negroes and whites were moving forward into the East and West South Central states as cultivators of virgin soil; its drift northward and cityward, and in more recent decades southward out of the "black belt," in response to the universal gravity pull of complex economic and social forces; its widespread dispersion on the one hand, and on the other its segregation with reference to the white population; its sex and age composition and marital condition; its fertility, as indicated by the proportion of children to women of childbearing age in different periods—again, under social conditions varying from the irresponsible relations of slavery to the more exacting institutions of freedom; its intermixture with other races, as shown by the increase in the proportion mulatto; its annual mortality in the registration area; its educational progress since emancipation, in so far as this can be measured by elementary schooling and by increasing literacy; its criminality, dependency, and physical and mental defectiveness—those characteristics of individual de-

generacy which Negroes manifest in common with other racial classes in all civilized communities; finally, its economic progress, as indicated by increasing ownership of homes, by entrance into skilled trades and professions, and primarily and fundamentally by the rapid development of Negro agriculture.

Entirely new compilations have been made from manuscript tables and directly from schedules and records, relating especially to mortality, ownership of homes, and agriculture. The rapid development of Negro agriculture, as demonstrated in the statistics which show an increasing acreage and value for Negro farms, and an increasing value of live stock, crops, and farm property on such farms, seems extremely significant. This progress has provided a substantial basis for general social improvement in the recent past, and it is a sure guaranty of further improvement in the future.

DETAIL OF TABULATIONS FOR DIFFERENT YEARS.

As is true in the case of the white population, the statistics of the Negro population in the decennial census reports have tended to become, from census to census, more comprehensive and detailed, not only as regards diversity of topics covered by schedule inquiries, but also as regards completeness of compilation of the returns.

At the earlier censuses, returns relating to the slave and to the free colored population were generally restricted to a few simple inquiries. At the census of 1790, for example, the number of slaves was ascertained without distinction of either sex or age, and at each of the five succeeding censuses, 1800–1840, age was recorded for Negroes, free and slave, in less detail than for whites. At the censuses of 1850 and 1860, also, the returns for the slave population, which were made upon special schedules, were less detailed than were those secured for the free colored and white population. In 1870, however, since all Negroes were free, the returns for the total Negro population were made upon the schedule provided for all free inhabitants, and at this census as at each succeeding census they were made in the same detail for Negroes as for whites.

It is true generally, also, that in the published population reports of the census, beginning with that of 1870, so far as the schedule inquiries are applicable to Negroes, practically the same detail is shown for Negroes as for whites.

REORGANIZATION OF MATERIAL.

The compilations for Negroes of the returns at the census of 1910 are in fact scattered through the seven quarto volumes constituting the general report of the Thirteenth Census on Population, Occupations, and Agriculture, averaging more than a thousand pages per volume. Similarly, for other census years, also, returns relating to Negroes are scattered through volumes of general reports. Data relating to mortality of Negroes in the registration area are contained in the annual mortality reports compiled by the Bureau of the Census, which constitute a series of publications entirely separate from the reports of the decennial census.

It will be apparent that the process of assembling these data itself involves original compilations and rearrangements of statistical material, since the figures relating to Negroes can not generally be mechanically cut out of tables which present statistics for the Negro population as a component element in the total population. A mechanical excision of the data for Negroes from these tables would yield an aggregation of statistical fragments more or less unrelated, unintelligible, and insignificant.

The assembling and presentation of statistics for Negroes clearly involves a selection of such numbers, proportions, and ratios for other classes as are required for interpretation of figures specifically for Negroes and the rejection of all other data. It is, however, seldom the case that any important series of figures for another class is entirely without significance when it is related to a similar series for Negroes. Generally such totals, and especially all derived figures, are of greater or less significance, and selections must be made accordingly, in each case by the exercise of judgment as to what numbers, proportions, and ratios are of sufficient import specifically for Negroes to justify quotation. Finally, new analyses are frequently required to insure a fair degree of comparability of data for different years.

Consistently with the purpose of the report to present the economic and social progress of the Negro population, in so far as that progress can be statistically determined, practically all of the tabulations included institute comparisons, either of present conditions with those obtaining in the past among Negroes, or of Negro characteristics and tendencies with those of other racial classes—comparisons, it may be noted, which have frequently involved new combinations of data for classes other than Negro and the computation of new percentages and ratios.

EMANCIPATION AND SOCIAL PROGRESS.

The compilations of the report for the most part relate to the period since emancipation, but in some detail the statistical record embraces also the period of slavery. Where it does so bridge the gap between slavery and freedom, not the least interesting fact established by the record is the unbroken persistence and gradual modification of racial characteristics and tendencies in the face of extreme social changes. No very extraordinary irregularities in the series of figures extending back into the first half of the nineteenth century mark the years of transition from slavery to freedom. Social betterment has been, not an immediate and direct consequence of a boon conferred upon the race in a given year, but rather a somewhat deferred and indirect consequence which appears in the record as an achievement of the race from decade to decade. Aggregate improvement has been substantial and progress from decade to decade has been at an accelerating rate.

Slavery, emancipation, and a half-century experience of freedom are the large facts in the history of the Negro population, and although the statistical evidence of racial progress are relatively few in the earlier decades of the period following emancipation—chiefly, it may be, because of incompleteness of the record for those years—and although these evidences are largely cumulated in recent decades, it is nevertheless important in interpreting the whole record that the date of the great event, which is still a living memory in the minds of both Negroes and whites, be kept in mind. For, however much deferred, the whole amount of racial progress must be measured by reference to the original status under slavery, and by taking account of the extreme brevity of the period comprehending this progress, when the period is measured in terms of racial rather than of individual improvement.

PART I.—GROWTH AND GEOGRAPHIC DISTRIBUTION: 1790–1910.

Chapter I.—THE STATES AND OUTLYING POSSESSIONS.

NEGRO POPULATION AND INCREASE: 1900–1910.

The great mass of the Negro population under the jurisdiction of the United States is resident in the states. In 1910 Negroes resident in the outlying possessions constituted only 3.8 per cent of the aggregate Negro population within the area of census enumeration, and practically this entire Negro population of the outlying possessions was in Porto Rico.

The area of census enumeration does not as a whole constitute a unit of area which may advantageously be used to any considerable extent as a basis of statistical tabulation. In this report the more detailed compilations are restricted to the population of the states, and in some cases to the population of the Southern states, in which Negroes constitute a relatively large element in the population. Some general data may, however, be introduced at the outset, relative to the number, increase, and proportion of the Negro population of these outlying areas, in comparison with corresponding data for the states, and with corresponding data for other principal classes of population.

For the areas enumerated at the Thirteenth Census, the Negro population in 1910 and in 1900, and the increase during the decade 1900–1910 was as given in Table 1.

Table 1	NEGRO POPULATION.				PERCENTAGE DISTRIBUTION, BY AREA.	
			Increase,[1] 1900–1910.			
AREA.	1910	1900[1]	Number.	Per cent.	Negro population, 1910.	Negro increase, 1900–1910.
Area of enumeration...	10,215,482	9,204,531	1,010,951	11.0	100.0	100.0
United States...........	9,827,763	8,833,994	993,769	11.2	96.2	98.3
Porto Rico..............	385,437	363,742	21,695	6.0	3.8	2.1
Hawaii.................	695	233	462	198.3	(3)	(3)
Alaska.................	209	168	41	24.4	(3)	(3)
Military and naval service abroad...........	1,378	6,394	−5,016	−78.4	(3)	−0.5

[1] A minus sign (−) denotes decrease. [2] In the case of Porto Rico, 1899.
[3] Less than one-tenth of 1 per cent.

Of the total Negro population enumerated in 1910, numbering 10,215,482, for the areas specified in Table 1, 9,827,763, or 96.2 per cent, were returned from the states, and 385,437, or 3.8 per cent, from Porto Rico, the numbers returned from Hawaii and Alaska, being relatively insignificant.[1]

During the decade 1900–1910, the Negro population of the United States, including that of the outlying territories, increased by more than a million, and of this increase, as of the population in 1910, only a small proportion was in the outlying possessions—98.3 per cent of the increase, as compared with 96.2 per cent of the population in 1910, being in the states. The rate of increase in the states, 11.2 per cent, considerably exceeded the corresponding rate of 6 per cent in Porto Rico, while the higher rates shown in the table for Hawaii and Alaska represent very small absolute population changes.

NEGRO AND OTHER RACIAL CLASSES: 1910.

Table 2 (p. 22) gives the number of Negroes and of other principal racial classes composing the populations enumerated in 1910, together with the number in each class per 1,000 population, and the percentage distribution of each class, by areas.

In Porto Rico the number of Negroes per 1,000 population was 345; in the states, 107; in Hawaii, 4; and in Alaska, 3. The population other than Negro in the states was 99.5 per cent white, although the colored other than Negro—including Indians, Chinese, and Japanese—numbered, in 1910, 412,546. In Porto Rico, also, the population other than Negro is practically all of it white.

While, as has been noted, the great mass of the Negro population was resident in the states, the proportion living in the outlying possessions, in 1910, somewhat exceeded the corresponding proportion for whites, being 3.8 per cent for Negroes, as compared with 1 per cent for whites; 1 in 26 of the Negro population, therefore, and less than 1 in 100 of the white population were living in the outlying possessions, enumerated in 1910. In the case of Negroes, however, the proportion does not to any considerable extent represent emigration from the states. The Negro populations of Hawaii and Alaska are insignificant,

[1] The Thirteenth Census did not cover the Philippine Islands, the Panama Canal Zone, Guam, or Samoa. In 1903, according to a census of the Philippine Islands, taken under direction of the Philippine Commission, the civilized blacks in a total population of 7,635,426, numbered 1,019 (males 767, females 252); the total number of blacks, including Negritos, was 24,530. A census of the Canal Zone, taken in 1912 by the Department of Civil Administration, reported the number of blacks, in a total population of 61,279, to be 30,948 (males 22,427, females 8,521). No enumerations have been made in Guam or in Samoa, except of persons included in the military and naval service of the United States.

and only an inconsiderable number of Porto Rico's black and mulatto population were born in the states.[1]

Table 2

CLASS.	POPULATION: 1910.					
	Area of enumeration.	United States.	Porto Rico.	Hawaii.	Alaska.	Military and naval service abroad.
	NUMBER IN EACH CLASS.					
All classes...	93,402,151	91,972,266	1,118,012	191,909	64,356	55,608
Negro..........	10,215,482	9,827,763	385,437	695	209	1,378
White..........	82,598,168	81,731,957	732,555	44,048	36,400	53,208
Indian.........	291,018	265,683	....	....	25,331	4
Chinese........	94,648	71,531	12	21,674	1,209	222
Japanese.......	152,956	72,157	8	79,675	913	203
Other..........	49,879	3,175	....	45,817	294	593
	PERCENTAGE IN EACH CLASS.					
All classes...	100.0	100.0	100.0	100.0	100.0	100.0
Negro..........	10.9	10.7	34.5	0.4	0.3	2.5
White..........	88.4	88.9	65.5	23.0	56.6	95.7
Indian.........	0.3	0.3	....	....	39.4	(1)
Chinese........	0.1	0.1	(1)	11.3	1.9	0.4
Japanese.......	0.2	0.1	(1)	41.5	1.4	0.4
Other..........	0.1	(1)	....	23.9	0.5	1.1
	PERCENTAGE IN EACH AREA, BY CLASSES.					
All classes...	100.0	98.5	1.2	0.2	0.1	0.1
Negro..........	100.0	96.2	3.8	(1)	(1)	(1)
White..........	100.0	99.0	0.9	0.1	(1)	0.1
Indian.........	100.0	91.3	....	....	8.7	(1)
Chinese........	100.0	75.6	(1)	22.9	1.3	0.2
Japanese.......	100.0	47.2	(1)	52.1	0.6	0.1
Other..........	100.0	6.4	....	91.9	0.6	1.2

[1] Less than one-tenth of 1 per cent.

INCREASE, BY CLASSES: 1900–1910.

The population increase during the decade 1900–1910 is given in Table 3 for the classes shown in Table 2. In the case of each class the increase includes increase by net immigration from foreign countries, as well as by excess of births over deaths; but foreign immigration has contributed little to the Negro increase, which, both in the states and in Porto Rico, is almost entirely a natural growth by excess of births over deaths. On the other hand, immigration has contributed largely to the growth of the white population in the states, and accounts in part for the excess of the percentage increase of the white population in the entire area of enumeration over that of the Negro population. For the aggregate area enumerated in 1910, the increase of the Negro population during the decade 1900–1910 amounted to 1,010,951, or 11 per cent., and the increase of the white population to 15,056,025, or 22.3 per cent.

[1] The number can not be precisely determined from census returns, but in the population of Porto Rico, white and colored—numbering, in 1910, 1,118,012—there were only 2,303 natives of the states. In the 1910 census report these immigrants from the states are not classified by color. In 1899, however, only 97 of the 1,069 natives of the states resident at that time in Porto Rico were colored. Exclusive of foreign-born persons the population of Porto Rico, white and colored, in 1910, was 99.8 per cent native of Porto Rico.

Table 3

CLASS.	POPULATION INCREASE:[1] 1900–1910.				
	Area of enumeration.[2]	United States.	Porto Rico.	Hawaii.	Alaska.
	NUMBER.				
All classes.........	16,145,521	15,977,691	164,769	37,908	764
Negro..............	1,010,951	993,769	21,695	462	41
White..............	15,056,025	14,922,761	143,129	15,229	5,907
Indian.............	24,258	28,487	....	....	−4,205
Chinese............	−24,477	−18,332	−63	−4,093	−1,907
Japanese...........	66,956	47,831	8	18,564	634
Other..............	11,808	3,175	....	7,746	294
	PER CENT.				
All classes.........	20.9	21.0	17.3	24.6	1.2
Negro..............	11.0	11.2	6.0	198.3	24.4
White..............	22.3	22.3	24.3	52.8	19.4
Indian.............	9.1	12.0	....	....	−14.2
Chinese............	−20.5	−20.4	(3)	−15.9	−61.2
Japanese...........	77.9	196.6	....	30.4	227.2

[1] A minus sign (−) denotes decrease.
[2] Includes military and naval service abroad.
[3] Percentage not shown, base being less than 100.

PROPORTION NEGRO: 1910 AND 1900.

The proportion Negro declined during the decade in Porto Rico from 382 to 345 per 1,000 population, and in the states from 116 to 107 per 1,000 population. The number of Negroes per 1,000 population other than Negro, in 1910, was 526 in Porto Rico and 120 in the states, the corresponding numbers for 1900 being 617 and 132. These proportions are shown in Table 4.

Table 4

AREA.	NEGROES.			
	Per 1,000 population of all classes.		Per 1,000 population other than Negro.	
	1910	1900[1]	1910	1900[1]
Area of enumeration................	109	119	123	135
United States.....................	107	116	120	132
Porto Rico........................	345	382	526	617
Hawaii............................	4	2	4	2
Alaska............................	3	3	3	3

[1] In the case of Porto Rico, 1899.

BLACK AND MULATTO POPULATION: 1910.

The Negro population of the states and outlying possessions are classified as black and mulatto, in Table 5, Negroes showing a perceptible trace of white blood being classified as mulatto.

Of the black population 99.3 per cent, and of the mulatto, 85.9 per cent were resident in the states, the proportions resident in the three outlying possessions enumerated in 1910, being 0.6 per cent for the black population, and 14.1 per cent for the mulatto. The relatively larger proportion in the outlying possessions for mulattoes is accounted for by the mulatto population native of, and resident in Porto Rico. The colored population of Porto Rico in 1910 was more than six-sevenths mulatto, the proportion mulatto being much greater in the colored population of

Porto Rico than it was in that of the states. Per 1,000 blacks in the population, there were in Porto Rico 6,671 mulattoes, and in the states, 264.

Table 5	NEGRO POPULATION: 1910.						
AREA.	Total.	Black.	Mulatto.		Percentage in each area.		Mulattoes per 1,000 blacks, 1910.
			Number.	Per cent.	Black population.	Mulatto population.	
Area of enumeration.........	10,215,482	7,828,695	2,386,787	23.4	100.0	100.0	305
United States......	9,827,763	7,777,077	2,050,686	20.9	99.3	85.9	264
Porto Rico.........	385,437	50,245	335,192	87.0	0.6	14.0	6,671
Hawaii............	695	158	537	77.3	(1)	(1)	2 3,399
Alaska............	209	124	85	40.7	(1)	(1)	2 685
Military and naval service abroad....	1,378	1,091	287	20.8	(1)	(1)	263

¹ Less than one-tenth of 1 per cent.   ² Number of blacks less than 1,000.

NATIVITY AND PARENTAGE: 1910.

In the census classification, persons born in the United States or in any of its outlying territories are classified as native, all other persons being classified as foreign born. Natives are further classified as natives of native parentage (i. e., both parents native); natives of mixed parentage (i. e., one parent native and one foreign born); and natives of foreign parentage (i. e., both parents foreign born). So classified, as shown in Table 6, the Negro population enumerated in 1910 was 99.6 per cent native, the corresponding percentage for the white population being 83.8. The Negro population was 99.1 per cent, and the white population 60.8 per cent, native of native parentage. The percentages given in Table 6 may be read as follows: Per 1,000 persons enumerated in 1910, 991 Negroes, and 608 whites were natives, born of native parents; 3 Negroes, and 73 whites were natives, having one parent foreign born; 2 Negroes, and 157 whites were natives of foreign parentage, and 4 Negroes and 162 whites were foreign born. It will be understood that as regards any single area shown in Table 6, Porto Rico, for example, the class of natives includes not only residents born in Porto Rico, but, also, those born in the states, or in some outlying possession other than Porto Rico.

NATIVITY AND PARENTAGE OF THE NEGRO AND OF THE WHITE POPULATION BY AREAS OF ENUMERATION: 1910.

Table 6	POPULATION: 1910.										
NATIVITY AND PARENTAGE CLASS.	Area of enumeration.	United States.	Porto Rico.	Hawaii.	Alaska.	Military and naval service abroad.	Percentage in each class.				
							Area of enumeration.	United States.	Porto Rico.	Hawaii.	Alaska.
NEGRO.											
All classes.....................	10,215,482	9,827,763	385,437	695	209	1,378	100.0	100.0	100.0	100.0	100.0
Native¹..........................	10,172,974	9,787,424	383,451	602	168	1,329	99.6	99.6	99.5	86.6	80.4
Both parents native............	10,127,805	9,748,439	377,547	337	154	1,278	99.1	99.2	98.0	55.7	73.7
One parent foreign born........	28,969	24,425	4,388	107	9	40	0.3	0.2	1.1	15.4	4.3
Both parents foreign born......	16,200	14,560	1,516	108	5	11	0.2	0.1	0.4	15.5	2.4
Foreign born....................	42,508	40,339	1,986	93	41	49	0.4	0.4	0.5	13.4	19.6
WHITE.											
All classes.....................	82,598,168	81,731,957	732,555	44,048	36,400	53,208	100.0	100.0	100.0	100.0	100.0
Native¹..........................	69,203,955	68,386,412	722,791	28,930	18,426	47,396	83.8	83.7	98.7	65.7	50.6
Both parents native............	50,239,453	49,488,575	696,699	10,689	10,993	32,497	60.8	60.5	95.1	24.3	30.2
One parent foreign born........	6,014,468	5,981,526	21,838	3,380	2,673	5,051	7.3	7.3	3.0	7.7	7.3
Both parents foreign born......	12,950,034	12,916,311	4,254	14,861	4,760	9,848	15.7	15.8	0.6	33.7	13.1
Foreign born....................	13,394,213	13,345,545	9,764	15,118	17,974	5,812	16.2	16.3	1.3	34.3	49.4

¹ Born in the United States or in any of its outlying possessions.

CHAPTER II.—GROWTH IN THE STATES: 1790–1910.—NUMBER, INCREASE, AND PROPORTION OF NEGROES IN THE TOTAL POPULATION.

POPULATION AND INCREASE, BY CLASSES: 1900–1910.

The increase of the Negro population during the decade 1900–1910 was very nearly equal to the total Negro population of the country, as returned in the year 1800 at the second census enumeration. It fell little short of an annual average increase of 100,000. This decennial increase, and the population as returned at each of the last two censuses is shown in Table 1, with corresponding data for other principal classes.

Table 1	POPULATION.				PERCENTAGE DISTRIBUTION.		
RACIAL CLASS.	1910	1900	Increase,[1] 1900–1910.		Population.		Increase,[1] 1900–1910.
			Number.	Per cent.	1910	1900	
All classes....	91,972,266	75,994,575	15,977,691	21.0	100.0	100.0	100.0
Negro............	9,827,763	8,833,994	993,769	11.2	10.7	11.6	6.2
White............	81,731,957	66,809,196	14,922,761	22.3	88.9	87.9	93.4
Indian...........	265,683	237,196	28,487	12.0	0.3	0.3	0.2
Chinese.........	71,531	89,863	−18,332	−20.4	0.1	0.1	−0.1
Japanese........	72,157	24,326	47,831	196.6	0.1	(2)	0.3
Other classes.....	3,175	....	3,175	....	(2)	....	(2)

[1] A minus sign (−) denotes decrease.   [2] Less than one-tenth of 1 per cent.

While the Negro increase of 993,769, or 11.2 per cent, for the decade may be regarded as a natural increase by excess of births over deaths, the white increase of 14,922,761, or 22.3 per cent, covered a considerable gain—estimated to be approximately 5,000,000, or one-third of the total white increase— by net immigration of whites from foreign countries. This net gain by immigration accounts in part, but it would appear, not entirely, for the difference between the rate of growth shown for the Negro, and that for the white population. For the aggregate white population the natural increase in the period from 1900 to 1910 by excess of births over deaths is estimated to have amounted to between 14 and 15 per cent. (See Thirteenth Census Reports, Vol. I, p. 127.) As indicating natural increase this estimated rate, rather than the enumerated increase of 22.3 per cent shown in Table 1 for the white population, is comparable with the Negro increase of 11.2 per cent. The aggregate white population, however, includes the foreign white stock, whose rate of natural increase undoubtedly exceeded, as that of the native white stock of native parentage undoubtedly fell short of the estimated natural increase per cent for the aggregate white population. From the census data, rates of natural increase can not be precisely determined for the native white stock separately, or specifically for any of the several nativity and parentage classes of the whites. No census classification is sufficiently detailed, for example, to eliminate the effects of intermarriage between the classes, or to separate out the children of recent immigrants from the children of older immigrants, or the children of natives of native parentage from the children of natives of foreign parentage. But it seems probable that the rate of natural increase of the native white population, and more particularly that of the native white population of native parentage, during the decade 1900–1910, did not very materially, if at all, exceed the rate of increase of the Negro population.

The increase shown for the Negro population in the decade 1900–1910 is equivalent to a constant annual increase of 1.07 per cent, at which rate, if it should be maintained, the Negro population would double its numbers in a period of approximately 65 years. There is, however, no statistical basis for the assumption, in the case either of the Negro or of the white population—whose corresponding doubling period would be between 30 and 40 years—that the rate of increase during the decade 1900–1910 will be maintained for any definite period. Rather it would seem probable since, as regards both Negroes and whites, the rate of growth has retarded in recent decades, that this retardation will continue more or less uninterruptedly in the future.

As enumerated at the Thirteenth Census, the Negro population—including with persons of unmixed Negro parentage persons of mixed Negro and white parentage—constituted in 1910, somewhat over one-tenth of the total population of the states. The proportion Negro in this total population fell off from 11.6 per cent in 1900 to 10.7 per cent in 1910 in consequence of the higher rate of natural increase of the white population and of the large gain by net immigration of whites.

Of the total population increase for the decade, 6.2 per cent was Negro and 93.4 per cent was white, less than one-half of 1 per cent being Indian, Chinese, Japanese, or of other racial character.

NEGRO, WHITE, AND OTHER POPULATION AT EACH
CENSUS: 1790–1910.

In Table 2 is given a summary of the returns for
Negroes, whites, and persons of other racial character,
at each of the 13 decennial censuses.

The Negro population increased from three-quarters
of one million to nearly ten million in the period of 120
years from 1790 to 1910. Of this increase, approximately one-half was in the four decades 1870–1910.
The white population increased from 3,172,006 in
1790, to 81,731,957 in 1910, and for this larger population group, nearly one-half of the increase for the
period of 120 years was in the three decades 1880–1910.
In other words the increase of the Negro population
in the 40 years 1870–1910 was approximately equal to
the increase of this class in the 80 years preceding;
while in the case of the white population, the increase
in the 30 years 1880–1910 was equal nearly to the increase of the preceding 90 years.

The proportion Negro in the total population decreased from 19.3 per cent, nearly one-fifth, in 1790,
to 10.7 per cent, a little more than one-tenth, in 1910.

NEGRO, WHITE, AND OTHER POPULATION AT EACH CENSUS, AND DECENNIAL INCREASE IN EACH DECADE:
1790—1910.

Table 2	POPULATION.[1]											
YEAR.	All classes.	Negro.		White	All other.	Increase during preceding 10 years.						
						Number.			Per cent.			
		Number.	Per cent.			All classes.	Negro.	White.	All classes.	Negro.	White.	
1910	91,972,266	9,827,763	10.7	81,731,957	412,546	15,977,691	993,769	14,922,761	21.0	11.2	22.3	
1900	75,994,575	8,833,994	11.6	66,809,196	351,385	13,046,861	1,345,318	11,707,938	20.7	18.0	21.2	
1890	62,947,714	7,488,676	11.9	55,101,258	357,780	12,791,931	907,883	11,698,288	25.5	13.8	27.0	
1880	50,155,783	6,580,793	13.1	43,402,970	172,020	11,597,412	1,700,784	9,813,593	30.1	34.9	29.2	
1870	38,558,371	4,880,009	12.7	33,589,377	88,985	7,115,050	438,179	6,666,840	22.6	9.9	24.8	
1860	31,443,321	4,441,830	14.1	26,922,537	78,954	8,251,445	803,022	7,369,469	35.6	22.1	37.7	
1850	23,191,876	3,638,808	15.7	19,553,068		6,122,423	765,160	5,357,263	35.9	26.6	37.7	
1840	17,069,453	2,873,648	16.8	14,195,805		4,203,433	545,006	3,658,427	32.7	23.4	34.7	
1830	12,866,020	2,328,642	18.1	10,537,378		3,227,567	556,986	2,670,581	33.5	31.4	33.9	
1820	9,638,453	1,771,656	18.4	7,866,797		2,398,572	393,848	2,004,724	33.1	28.6	34.2	
1810	7,239,881	1,377,808	19.0	5,862,073		1,931,398	375,771	1,555,627	36.4	37.5	36.1	
1800	5,308,483	1,002,037	18.9	4,306,446		1,379,269	244,829	1,134,440	35.1	32.3	35.8	
1790	3,929,214	757,208	19.3	3,172,006								

[1] For a revision of figures in accordance with estimates of population for 1870 and 1890, and with reference to extensions of the area of census enumeration, see Table 3.

Diagrams I, II, and III (p. 26) illustrate the data
of Table 2, as regards growth of the Negro population
from census to census absolutely and relatively to
the white population.

FLUCTUATION IN THE RATES OF INCREASE.

As regards the Negro population, the returns of the
several censuses taken since 1860 have been admittedly less accurate than they have been as regards the
white population, and, in consequence of these inaccuracies, erroneous conclusions in respect to the rate
of growth of the Negro population have been derived
from the data; as, for example, that this class of the
population was increasing much more rapidly than any
other class, and, again, upon publication of new data,
that its rate of growth was rapidly declining to a stationary state of population, and even to a state of
numerical decline. None of these extravagant conclusions have been in fact justified, but it was not possible
prior to publication of the Thirteenth Census data, to
determine with any high degree of certainty the actual
trend of the rate of growth of the Negro population in
the past five decades.

It will be noted that the decennial increases of the
Negro population, as shown in Table 2, and in the
accompanying diagrams, for the four decades 1860–
1900, are exceedingly irregular, and it should be explained that these irregularities result undoubtedly
from defective enumerations at two censuses—that of
1870, and that of 1890. Some correction of the population figures for these two years, and of the dependent
increases and proportions, is undertaken in Table 3.

The fluctuations in the decennial rates of increase
since 1860, where these rates have been figured, as in
Table 2, upon the enumerated populations returned at
the several censuses, have been so considerable as to
be in themselves improbable. The changes have,
moreover, been in successive decades contrary in direction. Since, however, the increase of the Negro population is essentially a natural increase, any advance or
decline in the rate of growth should tend in the absence
of extraordinary influences to be fairly persistent, re-
flecting relatively permanent tendencies in the rates of
natality and of mortality. Both of these rates tend,
in fact, if they are changing, to move upward or downward over any long period by fairly even gradations,
and such violent and contrary fluctuations in the rate
of growth as are indicated for the Negro population by
the decennial percentage increases, 22.1, 9.9, 34.9, 13.8,
18.0, and 11.2, in successive decades during the period
extending from 1850 to 1910, imply abrupt and inconsistent changes in the birth rate or in the death
rate, or in both rates conjointly, which are highly
improbable.

DIAGRAM I.—NEGRO AND WHITE POPULATION AT EACH CENSUS: 1790–1910.

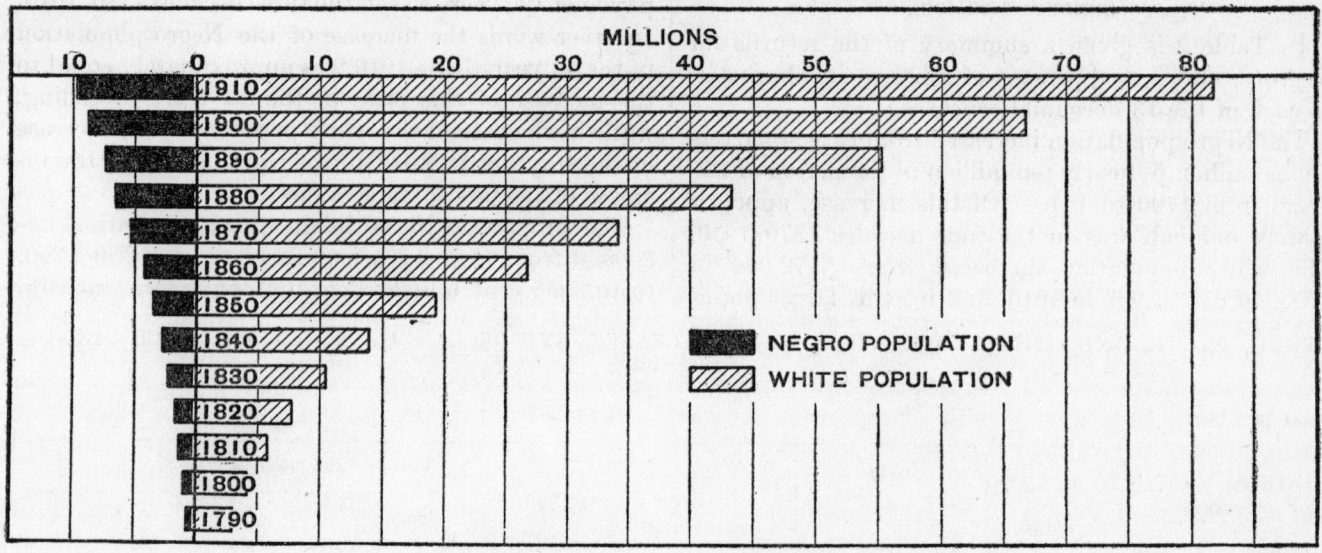

DIAGRAM II.—DECENNIAL INCREASE OF THE NEGRO POPULATION: 1790–1910.

DIAGRAM III.—DECENNIAL PERCENTAGE INCREASE OF THE NEGRO AND OF THE WHITE POPULATION: 1790–1910.

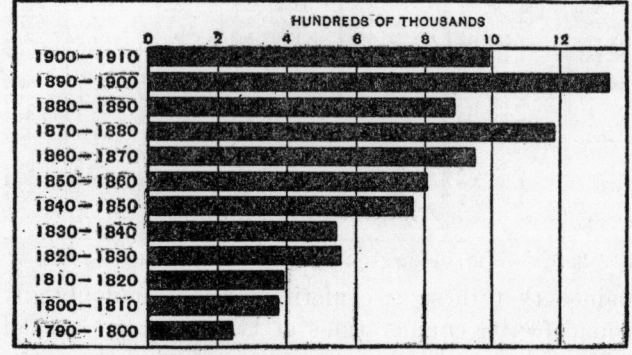

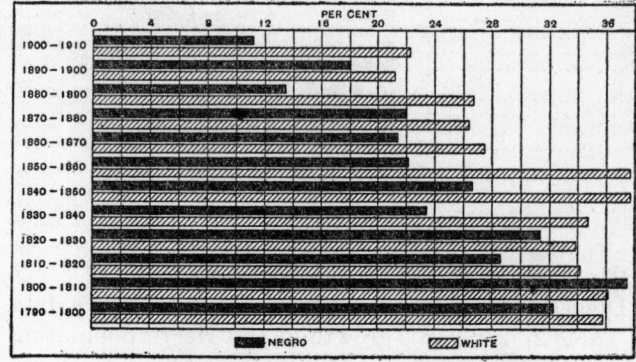

THE UNDERCOUNT OF 1870.

It should be borne in mind that an undercount at any census necessarily affects the rates of increase for two decades, depressing the rate for the decade preceding the defective census below, and raising the rate for the decade following above, the true rate. In the case of the Negro population, the depression of its rate of increase to 9.9 per cent for the decade 1860–1870, followed in the succeeding decade by the advance to 34.9 per cent, undoubtedly resulted from an undercount at the census of 1870; and, similarly, in the absence of any extraordinary social conditions affecting the Negro population during the decade 1880–1890, the depression of the rate of increase for this decade to 13.8 per cent, followed by the advance in the succeeding decade to 18 per cent, indicates as at least highly probable an undercount at the census of 1890. The returns at these two censuses affect the rates of increase for the four decades 1860–1900, a period, it may be noted, which is of special interest in the history of the Negro race, since it is the period in which the race was adjusting itself to a new social status. Some estimate of the number of omissions in 1870 and in 1890 is, therefore, required to develop clearly the trend of the rate of growth of the Negro population during the past half century of social adjustment and emergence.

In the South the confusion consequent upon the war was sufficient in 1870 to interfere seriously with the Federal census enumeration of that year, and it is estimated that the returns of the Ninth Census understated the population of this section of the country by at least 1,250,000. According to this estimate—which is figured upon a somewhat arbitrary distribution of the population increase in the South during the 20-year period 1860–1880—the Negro population in the country as a whole increased 21.4 per cent in the decade 1860–1870 and 22 per cent in the decade 1870–1880.[1] In the case of the Negro

[1] The census estimate that 512,163 Negroes were omitted from enumeration in 1870 is based upon the assumption that in the Southern states the rate of increase of the Negro population in the decade 1860–1870 was the same as in the decade 1870–1880, i. e., that the Negro population of the Southern states in 1870 was the geometric mean of the Negro populations of these states as returned in 1860 and in 1880, respectively. Outside of these states the returns of the census are accepted as correct. These assumptions give a rate of increase for the aggregate Negro population during the decade 1860–1870 which is slightly below that during the decade 1870–1880 (21.4 as compared with 22 per cent). This slight depression of the rate in 1860–1870 does not seem in itself improbable, although any considerable depression in the rate for the decade 1860–1870 below that for 1870–1880 would be inconsistent with the general tendency which has been in evidence during recent decades of the rate of growth to retard—even the depression from 21.4 to 21 per cent would give a rate for the decade 1870–1880 higher than the enumerated rate for the decade 1850–1860.

population the number of omissions at the census of 1870, as estimated, exceeded 500,000 and in the case of the white population amounted nearly to 750,000.[1] The number of omissions thus constituted over 12 per cent of the Negro and over 10 per cent of the white population of the South. Since, however, the proportion living in the South was much greater in the case of the Negro than it was in the case of the white population of the country as a whole, the omissions in the Southern states constituted a much larger proportion of the total Negro than of the total white population. Relatively to the total estimated population of each class in the country as a whole, the omissions in the case of Negroes amounted nearly to 10 per cent, as compared with a proportion of somewhat over 2 per cent in the case of the whites. As regards the Negro element, therefore, the deficiencies of the census of 1870 were so considerable and with respect to different localities so indeterminable as practically to destroy the significance of the data, although the total number of omissions of Negroes at this census can be estimated for the South as a whole with a fair degree of accuracy. No attempt is made in the present report to apportion these omissions to the several states, and it would certainly be impossible to correct the data for smaller areas generally.

THE UNDERCOUNT OF 1890.

In the 20 years 1860–1880 the Negro population increased 48.2 per cent, and in the following period of 20 years, 1880–1900, 34.2 per cent. These rates are equivalent to decennial increases of 21.7 per cent for the earlier period and of 15.9 per cent for the later period. For the decade 1900–1910 the enumerated increase was 11.2 per cent. A declining rate of increase for the Negro population is clearly indicated in the data. According to the returns at the census of 1890, however, as has been noted, the Negro population increased only 13.8 per cent in the decade 1880–1890, while the percentage increase for the decade following advanced to 18. The absolute increase of 907,883, shown in the returns for the decade 1880–1890, was 280,738 less than the estimated increase in the decade immediately preceding, and 437,435 less than the enumerated increase in the decade immediately following. It seems impossible to account for the drop in the absolute and in the percentage increase for the decade 1880–1890 on any assumption other than that of an undercount at the census of 1890.

Some indirect evidence of an undercount at this census is found in the age returns. If the Negro population were in fact increasing much more rapidly in the decade 1890–1900 than it was in the decade immediately preceding, the proportion of children in this class of the population must under normal conditions, and in the absence of highly improbable changes in the incidence of mortality by age, have increased during the decade 1890–1900. According to the census, however, the proportion of children under 10 years of age decreased from 288 per 1,000 population in 1890 to 275 per 1,000 in 1900. This decline in the proportion of children is inconsistent with a marked advance in the rate of increase. In the decade 1900–1910 the proportion of children declined further to 256 per 1,000, coincidently with a retardation in the rate of growth. The decline in the proportion of children at each census, 1880–1910, would indicate as probable a more or less continuous retardation in the rate of natural growth.

Evidence of an undercount in 1890 may be found also in what may be called the decennial mortality rate for the several decades, as indicated by census returns of age. The Negro population 10 years of age and over, as enumerated at the census of 1890, was 5,293,159. This was approximately the number of survivors in 1890 of the total Negro population enumerated in 1880, and indicates a gross mortality for the decade of 1,287,634, or 19.6 per cent. The corresponding mortality rate for the decade 1890–1900 was 15 per cent; and for the decade 1900–1910, 17.5 per cent. This crude census mortality rate for the decade 1880–1890 is, therefore, nearly one-third higher than that for the decade 1890–1900, while the rate for the decade 1900–1910 is approximately midway between the rates for the two preceding decades, as it would normally be if the rates for the two preceding decades had been materially affected by an undercount in 1890. It is, moreover, entirely improbable that the mortality rate for the Negro population was markedly higher in the decade 1900–1910, than it was in the decade preceding. It is probable rather that the rate has either remained fairly constant or decreased in each decade 1880–1910. The only plausible explanation of the variation in the rate from decade to decade, is an undercount in 1890, which indicated an improbably high mortality rate for the decade 1880–1890, and an improbably low mortality rate for the decade 1890–1900.

The presumption of an undercount at the census of 1890, therefore, rests upon the improbability of the decennial rates of increase themselves, as developed from the census returns, the inconsistency of the indicated changes in the rates from decade to decade with the changes in the proportion of children in the Negro population, and upon the improbability of the decennial mortality indicated for the decades 1880–1890 and 1890–1900.

---

[1] See census of 1890, Population, Part 1, pp. XI, XII, and XVI. In this report the following statement is made: "These omissions were not the fault of the Census Office, nor within its control. The census of 1870 was taken under a law which the superintendent, Francis A. Walker, characterized as 'clumsy, antiquated, and barbarous.' The Census Office had no power over its enumerators save a barren protest, and even this right was questioned in some quarters."

The number of omissions at the census of 1890 can not be accurately determined, but it would seem to be a fair assumption—in consideration especially of the decrease in the proportion of children from census to census—that the decline in the rate of increase from decade to decade was constant, and that the rate fell off in each of the two decades 1880–1890 and 1890–1900 by approximately the same amount. If the Negro increase of 34.2 per cent in the 20-year period 1880–1900 be so distributed as to give equal decreases in each decade from the estimated rate of 22 per cent in the decade 1870–1880, the increase for the decade 1880–1890 was 17.9 per cent, and for the decade 1890–1900, 13.8 per cent, those rates being equivalent to the enumerated increase of 34.2 per cent for the 20 years 1880–1900. On this assumption, the probable rates of increase for the four decades 1870–1910 are 22, 17.9, 13.8, and 11.2 per cent. Although the rate of 11.2 per cent, for the decade 1900–1910, is the enumerated increase per cent for that decade, and is, therefore, in no way affected by the distribution of the increase in the preceding 20-year period, it will be noted, that it is, nevertheless, entirely consistent with the assumption of a constantly decreasing rate for the four decades. A rate of 17.9 per cent for the decade 1880–1890 would give a Negro population in 1890 of nearly 7,760,000, which in round numbers exceeds the population as enumerated at the census of 1890 by 270,000. This is approximately the number of omissions of Negroes at the census of 1890, on the assumption that the retardation in the rate of growth in the 20 years 1880–1900 was constant.

It is not improbable that at other recent censuses the proportion of omissions has been higher, and the proportion of duplications lower in the enumeration of the Negroes than it has been in the enumeration of the whites; and that in general the margin of error has been greater in the case of Negroes. The percentage increase of the Negro population would not, however, be affected by this undercounting in so far as the population was understated at the several censuses by any constant percentage. If, for example, the census of 1900 and that of 1910 each of them understated the Negro population by 1 per cent, or by any greater proportion, the percentage increase figured upon the census returns would, nevertheless, be the true percentage increase for the decade, and it would be entirely comparable with the percentage increase for other classes, whatever the proportion of omissions or duplications for those other classes, provided only that the proportions should be as regards each class unvarying from census to census. Where, however, the proportion of omissions at any census is exceptionally large, as at the census of 1890, the decennial percentage increase for two decades will be materially affected.

INCREASE AFFECTED BY EXTENSION OF AREA.

In considering the increase of population from decade to decade, it should be noted that the area of census enumeration in the states has been considerably extended at several censuses. At the census of 1890, for example, the population of Indian Territory and on Indian reservations was enumerated for the first time, and in Table 2 this population—aggregating 325,464 persons, among whom were 18,636 Negroes, and 117,368 whites—is included in the increase for the decade 1880–1890. It will be obvious, however, that only a portion of the population enumerated in these areas is properly classified as increase for the decade, and that that portion representing the growth of population during the decade, if it could be determined, could not all of it be properly regarded as constituting a portion of the increase of the population enumerated at the census of 1880. By excluding the population of the added areas from the total population enumerated in 1890, the population increase within the area enumerated at the census of 1880 may be determined. The exclusion of areas representing extension of the area of enumeration at the census of 1890 reduces slightly the decennial increase per cent both for Negroes and for whites. In the case of Negroes the reduction is from 13.8 to 13.5 per cent and in the case of whites, from 27 to 26.7.

At other censuses, also, as well as at the census of 1890, the area of census enumeration has been extended to embrace new territory, and these accidental extensions have tended in each case to raise the percentage increase somewhat above that which would represent the growth of population during the decade. At the census of 1850, for example, the areas enumerated first in that year aggregated 335,300 square miles, representing an increase for the decade 1840–1850 of more than one-fourth in the area of census enumeration. This added area returned a population in 1850 of 391,410 persons, among whom were 59,799 Negroes and 331,611 whites. The exclusion of this population from the increase for the decade 1840–1850 reduces the percentage increase for the Negroes from 26.6 to 24.5, and for the whites from 37.7 to 35.4. Undoubtedly the population of the areas enumerated first in 1850 embraces a considerable number of migrants who had entered these areas during the decade, coming in from other sections of the country, and the increase in the area enumerated in 1840 is reduced by the number of such migrants.

REVISED FIGURES OF INCREASE 1790–1910.

In Table 3 the increase of the Negro population is shown for each decade, exclusive of the population of areas which represent extensions of the area of census enumeration in the given decade, and the increases and proportions given in the table, in so far as they pertain to the years 1870 and 1890, are figured upon the estimated populations for these years.

Table 3	NEGRO POPULATION.					White population increase per cent within area enumerated at preceding census.	Percentage Negro in the total population.	Negroes per 1,000 white population.
		Increase during preceding 10 years.						
YEAR.	Number.	Total.	Population of area enumerated first in year specified.	Increase within area enumerated at preceding census.				
				Number.	Per cent.			
1910.......	9,827,763	993,769	....	993,769	11.2	22.3	10.7	120
1900 [1].......	8,833,994	1,073,994		1,073,994	13.8	21.2	11.6	132
1890 [1].......	7,760,000	1,179,207	18,636	1,160,571	17.6	26.7	12.3	142
1880 [1].......	6,580,793	1,188,621		1,188,621	22.0	26.4	13.1	152
1870 [1].......	5,392,172	950,342		950,342	21.4	27.5	13.5	157
1860........	4,441,830	803,022	800	802,222	22.0	36.8	14.1	165
1850........	3,638,808	765,160	59,799	705,361	24.5	35.4	15.7	186
1840........	2,873,648	545,006	188	544,818	23.4	34.3	16.8	202
1830........	2,328,642	556,986	16,345	540,641	30.5	33.7	18.1	221
1820........	1,771,656	393,848	....	393,848	28.6	34.2	18.4	225
1810........	1,377,808	375,771	45,863	329,908	32.9	34.9	19.0	235
1800........	1,002,037	244,829	[2] 4,480	240,349	31.7	34.0	18.9	233
1790........	757,208						19.3	239

[1] Figures in italics are estimates.
[2] Includes slaves only for western Georgia.

Fluctuations in the percentage increase are markedly reduced in Table 3, as compared with those shown in Table 2, even for the earlier decades. According to Table 2, for example, the Negro population in the two decades 1790–1800 and 1800–1810 increased 32.3 and 37.5 per cent, respectively, the corresponding increases according to Table 3 being 31.7 and 32.9 per cent. In the case of the white population, fluctuations in the rates for the five decades 1790–1840 almost entirely disappear in Table 3, the rates being 34, 34.9, 34.2, 33.7, and 34.3 per cent, respectively. In both tables the maximum rate of increase for the Negro population is that for the decade 1800–1810 and the next highest that for the decade 1790–1800; but the maximum rate is reduced from 37.5 to 32.9 per cent by excluding from the increase the population of areas enumerated first in 1810.

The increase of the Negro population in the two decades 1790–1810, the period of its most rapid rate of growth, is in part attributable to the continued importation of slaves during the years 1790–1808, but for the period of 100 years, from 1810 to 1910, net immigration or emigration of Negroes has been inconsiderable. In the case of the white population, on the other hand, immigration has contributed largely to its increase not only in the last decade, but in each preceding decade.

During the four decades 1790–1830 there was no considerable change from decade to decade in the percentage increase of the Negro population. As shown in Table 3, the increases for these decades were 31.7, 32.9, 28.6, and 30.5 per cent, respectively. For the five decades 1830–1880, also, the decennial percentage increases—i. e., 23.4, 24.5, 22, 21.4, 22—remained fairly constant without any marked fluctuations or persistent tendency upward or downward, although the percentages indicate clearly a retardation of the rate growth in this period as compared with the rate maintained in the earlier period. The minimum rate for the period 1790–1830, 28.6 per cent, is considerably above the maximum rate, 24.5 per cent, for the later period, while the average of the decennial rates dropped from 30.9 per cent for the four decades 1790–1830 to 22.7 per cent for the five decades 1830–1880.

If the increases shown in Table 3 be accepted as accurate, it appears that the growth of the Negro population, considered by decades, was greatest in the decade 1870–1880, the estimated addition to the population in this decade being 1,188,621. In the period from 1790 to 1880 the absolute growth of the Negro population increased from decade to decade, with exception that the growth in the decade ending in 1840 was practically the same as in the decade preceding. In each decade since 1880, however, the absolute increase, as well as the percentage increase, has tended to fall off.

The proportion Negro in the population has decreased in each decade, with exception of a slight increase for the decade 1800–1810. During the first four decades, however, although the total population more than trebled, the decrease in the proportion Negro, from 19.3 per cent in 1790 to 18.1 per cent in 1830, was inconsiderable, amounting to an average decrease in the percentage per decade of only 0.3; in other words, the number of Negroes per 1,000 population decreased on the average by 3 in the course of each 10 years. In the period 1830 to 1910 the decennial decreases in the percentage Negro were generally greater than those for the earlier period, the decrease from 18.1 per cent in 1830 to 10.7 in 1910 being equivalent to an average decrease per decade for these eight decades of 0.9, or 9 per 1,000 population. This is the amount of the decrease in the last decade—from 11.6 per cent in 1900 to 10.7 per cent in 1910.

The proportion of Negroes to whites was somewhat less than 1 to 4 in 1790, and 1 to 8 in 1910, the number of Negroes per 1,000 whites being as shown in Table 3, in the two years, respectively 239 and 120.

INCREASE BY 30, 50, AND 60 YEAR PERIODS: 1790–1910.

In Table 4, on the following page, the increase of the population, Negro and white, is shown by 30, 50, and 60 year periods.

In each of the two 30-year periods, 1790–1820 and 1820–1850, the Negro population more than doubled its numbers, the increase amounting to 134 per cent in the earlier period and to 105.4 per cent in the later. For the two succeeding 30-year periods the percentage increase fell off to 80.9 for the period 1850–1880 and to 49.3 for the period 1880–1910. The percentage increase from 1790 to 1820 was thus nearly three times as great as the percentage increase from 1880 to 1910. The corresponding percentages for the white population in the several periods are 148, 148.6, 122, and 88.3.

Although the percentage increase of the Negro population fell off from period to period, the lower percentages for the later periods represent larger absolute additions to the population. In the 30-year period 1790–1820, with a percentage increase of 134, the growth of the Negro population amounted to a little over one million, while in the period 1880–1910, with a percentage increase of 49.3, the growth of population exceeded three million. In the 50 years 1860–1910 the increase of 121.3 per cent amounted to 5,385,933 persons, while the increase of 222.4 per cent for the 50 years preceding the war, in terms of population, was less than three-fifths as great, the absolute increase for the earlier period being 3,064,022. If the period 1790–1910 be divided into two periods of 60 years each, the percentage increase in the period 1790–1850 is more than twice the corresponding percentage for the period 1850–1910, while the absolute increase in the earlier period is less than one-half that in the later period.

Table 4 PERIOD.	POPULATION AT BEGINNING OF PERIOD.		INCREASE DURING PERIOD.				Negroes per 1,000 whites in the increase.
			Number.		Per cent.		
	Negro.	White.	Negro.	White.	Negro.	White.	
1910............	9,827,763	81,731,957	......	......	......	......	......
30-year periods:							
1880–1910.....	6,580,793	43,402,970	3,246,970	38,328,987	49.3	88.3	85
1850–1880.....	3,638,808	19,553,068	2,941,985	23,849,902	80.9	122.0	123
1820–1850.....	1,771,656	7,866,797	1,867,152	11,686,271	105.4	148.6	160
1790–1820.....	757,208	3,172,006	1,014,448	4,694,791	134.0	148.0	216
50-year periods:							
1860–1910.....	4,441,830	26,922,537	5,385,933	54,809,420	121.3	203.6	98
1810–1860.....	1,377,808	5,862,073	3,064,022	21,060,464	222.4	359.3	145
60-year periods:							
1850–1910.....	3,638,808	19,553,068	6,188,955	62,178,889	170.1	318.0	100
1790–1850.....	757,208	3,172,006	2,881,600	16,381,062	380.6	516.4	176

CHAPTER III.—GEOGRAPHIC DISTRIBUTION AND INCREASE, BY STATES: 1790-1910.

AREAS.

State areas, and combinations of state areas into geographic divisions and sections, are the units of area with reference to which the Negro population is classified in the tables following. These tables, therefore, do not comprehend the distribution of that population in detail with reference to urban and rural communities, or by county areas. In subsequent chapters statistics are given relating to the distribution within the several states—by urban and rural communities in Chapter VII and by county areas in Chapter VIII.[1]

For the Negro population statistical interest attaches largely to compilations relating to the South as a whole, in which this class constitutes a considerable population element, and to the South in comparison with the North and the West, since the natural, social, and economic environmental conditions in the several sections are more or less dissimilar. The Negro population living in the North and West has increased by migration from the South in recent decades, as well as by natural growth, and in 1910 exceeded one million— a number sufficient to provide, in comparison with the South, significant data relative to progress achieved by the race under diverse conditions of living.

RACIAL CLASSES, BY SECTIONS AND DIVISIONS: 1910.

The geographic distribution of the Negro, white, and other population classes in 1910 is shown in Table 1, by sections and divisions.

The Negro population of the South in 1910 numbered 8,749,427, and amounted to 89 per cent, or approximately nine-tenths of the total Negro population of the country. The white population of the South numbered 20,547,420, and amounted to 25 per cent, or one-fourth, of the total white population.

---

[1] The primary areas of census enumeration are the enumeration districts—of which there were approximately 70,000 at the census of 1910—devised at each census for administrative purposes, and representing in themselves no permanent civil divisions. The returns of population from these districts are compiled into totals for the minor civil divisions of counties and cities, and these totals into totals for the counties and cities themselves, and further into aggregates for states. The states are grouped to compose the nine geographic divisions, and for certain tabulations the divisions are combined into sections—the South, the North, and the West. In those tables which give statistics by states (see, for example, Table 13 of this chapter), with few exceptions the states are arranged geographically under the divisional headings. In the published reports of the census the population is not classified by race or other characteristic for county or minor civil divisions. Urban communities and counties are therefore the primal areas of compilation in the present report.

Thus the great mass of the Negro population was in the South, and to a somewhat less degree it is true that the great mass of the white population was in the North and West.

In the North the Negro population numbered 1,027,674, and in the West 50,662, the white populations for these two sections being, respectively, 54,640,209 and 6,544,328.

Considering the nativity and parentage classes of the white population, it appears that a much larger proportion of the native white of native parentage, than of the white population of foreign birth or parentage was resident in the South. The proportion in the South for the native white of native parentage (i. e., both parents native), was 37.5 per cent; for the native white of foreign parentage (i. e., both parents foreign born), 5.9 per cent; for the native white of mixed parentage (i. e., one parent native, one foreign born), 8.3 per cent; and for the foreign-born white, 5.4 per cent. For the Negro population the proportion living in the South—89 per cent—was much higher than the corresponding proportion for any other race or nativity class.

In 1910 the Negro population of the South Atlantic division numbered 4,112,488; that of the East South Central, 2,652,513; and that of the West South Central, 1,984,426—more than two-fifths of the total Negro population of the country being in the South Atlantic division.

Except in Oklahoma the colored population of the South is almost entirely Negro, the colored, other than Negro—including Indian, Chinese, and Japanese —constituting a very inconsiderable factor in the total colored population. Of this other colored population in the South, numbering 92,483 in 1910, 88,433 were Indian; 3,299 were Chinese; 610 Japanese; and 141 of other racial character. As may be seen by reference to Table 13 (p. 43), a large proportion of the Indian population of the South—74,825 out of 88,433— was in Oklahoma. In the South, exclusive of Oklahoma, the Negro population numbered 8,611,815 and the other colored only 17,471. The colored other than Negro constituted a more considerable element in the total colored population of the North, and was largely in the majority in the colored population of the West. The proportion Negro in the colored population was 99 per cent in the South as a whole, and

99.8 per cent in the South, exclusive of Oklahoma. It was 92 per cent in the North, and in the West only 18 per cent.

Diagram I (p. 33) distributes the population of divisions in 1910, by color, nativity, and parentage, combinations having been made of certain classes shown separately in Table 1. The population of each division is classified in the diagram as Negro, native white of native parentage, native white of foreign or mixed parentage, foreign-born white, and all other. The areas of the bars are proportional to the populations of the divisions, and the areas shaded for the several classes are proportional to the numbers in those classes. By a comparison of areas, therefore, the relative numerical importance of the classes in the divisions and in the country as a whole becomes apparent.

GEOGRAPHIC DISTRIBUTION OF RACE, NATIVITY, AND PARENTAGE CLASSES, BY SECTIONS AND DIVISIONS: 1910.

Table 1

SECTION AND DIVISION.	POPULATION: 1910.											
	Total.	Negro.	White.						Indian.	Chinese.	Japanese.	Other.
			Total.	Native.				Foreign born.				
				Total.	Native parentage.	Foreign parentage.	Mixed parentage.					
	NUMBER.											
United States	91,972,266	9,827,763	81,731,957	68,386,412	49,488,575	12,916,311	5,981,526	13,345,545	265,683	71,531	72,157	3,175
The South	29,389,330	8,749,427	20,547,420	19,821,249	18,561,146	762,398	497,705	726,171	88,433	3,299	610	141
South Atlantic	12,194,895	4,112,488	8,071,603	7,781,048	7,341,205	274,451	165,392	290,555	9,054	1,582	156	12
East South Central	8,409,901	2,652,513	5,754,326	5,667,469	5,452,492	123,915	91,062	86,857	2,612	414	26	10
West South Central	8,784,534	1,984,426	6,721,491	6,372,732	5,767,449	364,032	241,251	348,759	76,767	1,303	428	119
The North	55,757,115	1,027,674	54,640,209	43,319,193	27,352,035	11,126,359	4,840,799	11,321,016	69,454	16,298	3,397	83
New England	6,552,681	66,306	6,480,514	4,666,128	2,613,419	1,460,565	592,144	1,814,386	2,076	3,499	272	14
Middle Atlantic	19,315,892	417,870	18,880,452	14,054,273	8,462,961	4,113,076	1,478,236	4,826,179	7,717	8,189	1,643	21
East North Central	18,250,621	300,836	17,927,622	14,860,402	9,751,968	3,450,015	1,658,419	3,067,220	18,255	3,415	482	11
West North Central	11,637,921	242,662	11,351,621	9,738,390	6,523,687	2,102,703	1,112,000	1,613,231	41,406	1,195	1,000	37
The West	6,825,821	50,662	6,544,328	5,245,970	3,575,394	1,027,554	643,022	1,298,358	107,796	51,934	68,150	2,951
Mountain	2,633,517	21,467	2,520,455	2,083,545	1,466,624	370,009	246,912	436,910	75,338	5,614	10,447	196
Pacific	4,192,304	29,195	4,023,873	3,162,425	2,108,770	657,545	396,110	861,448	32,458	46,320	57,703	2,755
	PER CENT.											
United States	100.0	100.0	100.0	100.0	100.0	100.0	100.0	100.0	100.0	100.0	100.0	100.0
The South	32.0	89.0	25.1	29.0	37.5	5.9	8.3	5.4	33.3	4.6	0.8	4.4
South Atlantic	13.3	41.8	9.9	11.4	14.8	2.1	2.8	2.2	3.4	2.2	0.2	0.4
East South Central	9.1	27.0	7.0	8.3	11.0	1.0	1.5	0.7	1.0	0.6	(1)	0.3
West South Central	9.6	20.2	8.2	9.3	11.7	2.8	4.0	2.6	28.9	1.8	0.6	3.7
The North	60.6	10.5	66.9	63.3	55.3	86.1	80.9	84.8	26.1	22.8	4.7	2.6
New England	7.1	0.7	7.9	6.8	5.3	11.3	9.9	13.6	0.8	4.9	0.4	0.4
Middle Atlantic	21.0	4.3	23.1	20.6	17.1	31.8	24.7	36.2	2.9	11.4	2.3	0.7
East North Central	19.8	3.1	21.9	21.7	19.7	26.7	27.7	23.0	6.9	4.8	0.7	0.3
West North Central	12.7	2.5	13.9	14.2	13.2	16.3	18.6	12.1	15.6	1.6	1.4	1.2
The West	7.4	0.5	8.0	7.7	7.2	8.0	10.8	9.7	40.6	72.6	94.4	92.9
Mountain	2.9	0.2	3.1	3.0	3.0	2.9	4.1	3.3	28.4	7.8	14.5	6.2
Pacific	4.6	0.3	4.9	4.6	4.3	5.1	6.6	6.5	12.2	64.8	80.0	86.8

¹Less than one-tenth of 1 per cent.

NEGRO AND WHITE POPULATION, BY SECTIONS AND DIVISIONS: 1790–1910.

In Table 2 is given the total, the Negro, and the white population at each census, 1790–1910, by geographic sections and divisions.

At the date of the first census, in 1790, the Negro population of the South numbered 689,784. Of this population, 673,462 were resident in the South Atlantic states, and 16,322 in the East South Central region. The Negro population of the North numbered 67,424, and this population was all of it returned from the New England and Middle Atlantic states. The entire Negro population, therefore, except the 16,322 re- turned from the East South Central region, was resi- dent in the states of the Atlantic seaboard. The entire white population, also, was returned from these states, with exception of 93,046 enumerated in the East South Central region, although undoubtedly some white population was at this date settled in the terri- tory north of the Ohio River, which was not embraced in the area of census enumeration. No population whatever was returned prior to 1850 from any portion of the region now included in the West (the Mountain and Pacific divisions). The greater portion of this far western region was, in fact, brought under the jurisdiction of the United States in the decade preced- ing the census of 1850.

TOTAL, NEGRO, AND WHITE POPULATION AT EACH CENSUS, BY SECTIONS AND SOUTHERN DIVISIONS: 1790–1910.

Table 2 SECTION AND DIVISION.	POPULATION AT EACH CENSUS.												
	1910	1900	1890	1880	1870	1860	1850	1840	1830	1820	1810	1800	1790
	TOTAL.												
United States.......	91,972,266	75,994,575	62,947,714	50,155,783	38,558,371	31,443,321	23,191,876	¹17,069,453	¹12,866,020	9,638,453	7,239,881	5,308,483	3,929,214
The South.............	29,389,330	24,523,527	20,028,059	16,516,568	12,288,020	11,133,361	8,982,612	6,950,729	5,707,848	4,419,232	3,461,099	2,621,901	1,961,174
South Atlantic........	12,194,895	10,443,480	8,857,922	7,597,197	5,853,610	5,364,703	4,679,090	3,925,299	3,645,752	3,061,063	2,674,891	2,286,494	1,851,806
East South Central....	8,409,901	7,547,757	6,429,154	5,585,151	4,404,445	4,020,991	3,363,271	2,575,445	1,815,969	1,190,489	708,590	335,407	109,368
West South Central....	8,784,534	6,532,290	4,740,983	3,334,220	2,029,965	1,747,667	940,251	449,985	246,127	167,680	77,618	....	....
The North.............	55,757,115	47,379,699	39,817,386	31,871,518	25,279,841	19,690,984	14,030,446	10,112,624	7,152,854	5,219,221	3,778,782	2,686,582	1,968,040
The West..............	6,825,821	4,091,349	3,102,269	1,767,697	990,510	618,976	178,818	....	....	....	....	....	....
	NEGRO.												
United States.......	9,827,763	8,833,994	7,488,676	6,580,793	4,880,009	4,441,830	3,638,808	2,873,648	2,328,642	1,771,656	1,377,808	1,002,037	757,208
The South.............	8,749,427	7,922,969	6,760,577	5,953,903	4,420,811	4,097,111	3,352,198	2,641,977	2,161,885	1,642,672	1,268,499	918,336	689,784
South Atlantic........	4,112,488	3,729,017	3,262,690	2,941,202	2,216,705	2,058,198	1,860,871	1,597,317	1,529,283	1,273,399	1,080,800	859,690	673,462
East South Central....	2,652,513	2,499,886	2,119,797	1,924,996	1,464,252	1,394,360	1,122,790	830,306	501,587	288,057	145,454	58,646	16,322
West South Central....	1,984,426	1,694,066	1,378,090	1,087,705	739,854	644,553	368,537	214,354	131,015	81,216	42,245	....	....
The North.............	1,027,674	880,771	701,018	615,038	452,818	340,240	285,369	231,671	166,757	128,984	109,309	83,701	67,424
The West..............	50,662	30,254	27,081	11,852	6,380	4,479	1,241	....	....	....	....	....	....
	WHITE.												
United States.......	81,731,957	66,809,196	55,101,258	43,402,970	33,589,377	26,922,537	19,553,068	¹14,195,805	¹10,537,378	7,866,797	5,862,073	4,306,446	3,172,006
The South.............	20,547,420	16,521,970	13,193,453	10,555,427	7,863,209	7,033,973	5,630,414	4,308,752	3,545,963	2,776,560	2,191,538	1,703,565	1,271,390
South Atlantic........	8,071,603	6,706,058	5,592,149	4,654,112	3,635,238	3,305,107	2,818,219	2,327,982	2,116,469	1,787,664	1,594,091	1,426,804	1,178,344
East South Central....	5,754,326	5,044,847	4,305,668	3,657,593	2,939,091	2,626,376	2,240,481	1,745,139	1,314,382	902,432	563,136	276,761	93,046
West South Central....	6,721,491	4,771,065	3,295,636	2,243,722	1,288,880	1,102,490	571,714	235,631	115,112	86,464	34,311	....	....
The North.............	54,640,209	46,413,758	39,035,798	31,235,267	24,815,772	19,337,997	13,745,077	9,880,953	6,986,097	5,090,237	3,670,535	2,602,881	1,900,616
The West..............	6,544,328	3,873,468	2,872,007	1,612,276	910,396	550,567	177,577	....	....	....	....	....	....

¹ Includes white persons (6,100 in 1840 and 5,318 in 1830) on public ships in the service of the United States, not credited to any division or state.

The percentage distribution of the Negro population, by sections and divisions, at each census, 1790–1910, is shown in Table 3.

Table 3	PERCENTAGE DISTRIBUTION OF THE NEGRO POPULATION, BY AREAS.						
YEAR.	United States	The South.				The North.	The West.
		Total.	South Atlantic division.	East South Central division.	West South Central division.		
1910..........	100.0	89.0	41.8	27.0	20.2	10.5	0.5
1900..........	100.0	89.7	42.2	28.3	19.2	10.0	0.3
1890..........	100.0	90.3	43.6	28.3	18.4	9.4	0.4
1880..........	100.0	90.5	44.7	29.3	16.5	9.3	0.2
1870..........	100.0	90.6	45.4	30.0	15.2	9.3	0.1
1860..........	100.0	92.2	46.3	31.4	14.5	7.7	0.1
1850..........	100.0	92.1	51.1	30.9	10.1	7.8	(¹)
1840..........	100.0	91.9	55.6	28.9	7.5	8.1	....
1830..........	100.0	92.8	65.7	21.5	5.6	7.2	....
1820..........	100.0	92.7	71.9	16.3	4.6	7.3	....
1810..........	100.0	92.1	78.4	10.6	3.1	7.9	....
1800..........	100.0	91.6	85.8	5.9	....	8.4	....
1790..........	100.0	91.1	88.9	2.2	....	8.9	....

¹ Less than one-tenth of 1 per cent.

As regards the Negro population, the proportion resident in the South has not varied greatly from census to census. In 1790 the proportion living in the South was 91.1 per cent, and this proportion increased slightly in succeeding decades, to a maximum proportion of 92.8 per cent in 1830. It was 91.9 in 1840; 92.1 in 1850; and 92.2 in 1860. It fell off to 90.6 in 1870; and thereafter declined slightly, from census to census, to 89 in 1910. Conversely, the proportion living in the North and West, which was 8.9 per cent in 1790, fell off to 7.2 per cent in 1830, and in succeeding decades, with some fluctuation, increased to 11 per cent in 1910.

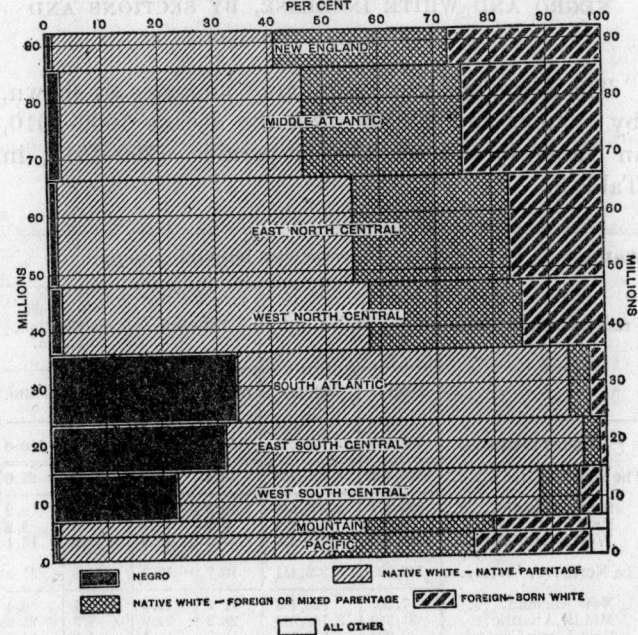

DIAGRAM I.—COLOR, NATIVITY, AND PARENTAGE OF THE POPULATION BY DIVISIONS: 1910.

As between the South and the North, therefore, the net changes in the geographic distribution of the Negro population have not been very considerable over an extended period, although the proportion in the North has tended in recent decades to increase.

During the entire period 1790–1910 the principal direction of migration and growth for the Negro population of the South, as for the white, has been westward. In 1790, of the total Negro population, 88.9 per cent was resident in the South Atlantic states. This population increased in each decade, from 673,462 in 1790 to 4,112,488 in 1910, but at each census, notwithstanding its rapid increase, the population of this division constituted a smaller proportion of the total Negro population in the country as a whole. In the period from 1790 to 1860 the percentage living in this division decreased from 88.9 to 46.3, and the decline in the proportion has been continuous since 1860, although the aggregate change in the period of 50 years, from 46.3 per cent in 1860 to 41.8 per cent in 1910, was less than the average change per decade for the period from 1790 to 1860.

At each census, 1790–1860, the proportion living in the East South Central division increased, the increase being from 2.2 per cent in 1790 to 31.4 per cent in 1860. At each census since 1860 the proportion in this division has decreased, to 27 per cent in 1910. The proportion living in the West South Central division has increased continuously from 3.1 per cent in 1810, to 20.2 per cent, or approximately one-fifth, in 1910.

NEGRO AND WHITE INCREASE, BY SECTIONS AND DIVISIONS: 1790–1910.

The Negro and white population increases are shown, by sections and divisions, for the decade 1900–1910, in Table 4, and by 30-year periods, 1790–1910, in Table 5.

Table 4	POPULATION INCREASE: 1900–1910.					
SECTION AND DIVISION.	Number.		Per cent.		Percentage distribution, by area.	
	Negro.	White.	Negro.	White.	Negro.	White.
United States......	993,769	14,922,761	11.2	22.3	100.0	100.0
The South...............	826,458	4,025,450	10.4	24.4	83.2	27.0
South Atlantic........	383,471	1,365,545	10.3	20.4	38.6	9.2
East South Central...	152,627	709,479	6.1	14.1	15.4	4.8
West South Central ..	290,360	1,950,426	17.1	40.9	29.2	13.1
The North...............	146,903	8,226,451	16.7	17.7	14.8	55.1
New England.........	7,207	953,488	12.2	17.3	0.7	6.4
Middle Atlantic......	91,949	3,769,590	28.2	24.9	9.3	25.3
East North Central...	42,994	2,217,569	16.7	14.1	4.3	14.9
West North Central..	4,753	1,285,804	2.0	12.8	0.5	8.6
The West...............	20,408	2,670,860	67.5	69.0	2.1	17.9
Mountain.............	5,877	940,600	37.7	59.5	0.6	6.3
Pacific...............	14,531	1,730,260	99.1	75.4	1.5	11.6

In the decade 1900–1910 the Negro population of the South increased by 826,458, or 10.4 per cent; the white population by 4,025,450, or 24.4 per cent. The Negro population of the North increased by 146,903, or 16.7 per cent; the white population by 8,226,451, or 17.7 per cent. In the West the Negro increase amounted to 20,408, or 67.5 per cent; and the white increase, to 2,670,860, or 69 per cent.

The percentage increase of the Negro population in the South was slightly below, and the percentages for the North and West were considerably above the rate of 11.2 per cent shown for the Negro population of the country as a whole. The relatively high percentage increases for the North and West indicate some gain by net migration of Negroes into these sections from the South during the decade; not, however, a gain so considerable in dimensions, when measured against the aggregate Negro population of the South, as to constitute anything in the nature of a general exodus from the South. Such a gain is indicated clearly for the Middle Atlantic division, in which the Negro population increased by 91,949, or 28.2 per cent, and for the smaller populations of the Mountain and Pacific divisions, in which the percentage increases were 37.7 and 99.1, respectively. In the West, where the Negro population is numerically inconsiderable, it is clear that a comparatively small gain by migration— measured in thousands of migrants—would be sufficient to produce the high rate of increase shown in the table. As between the North and the South it should be borne in mind that the net migration of any given number would affect the rate of increase more in the North than in the South, owing to the fact that the Negro population resident in the North is smaller than that resident in the South. In a subsequent chapter statistics are presented which indicate the extent to which the several sections of the country have gained or lost by interstate migration (see Chapter VI).

The Negro population of the South Atlantic division increased in the decade 1900–1910 by 383,471, nearly two-fifths of the total Negro increase being in this division; that of the East South Central division increased by 152,627; and that of the West South Central division by 290,360.

The percentage increase in the South Atlantic division was 10.3 for the Negroes and 20.4 for the whites; in the East South Central division it was 6.1 for Negroes and 14.1 for whites; and in the West South Central division 17.1 for Negroes and 40.9 for whites. Thus in each of those divisions, the percentage increase for whites considerably exceeded that for Negroes. The divisional increases of both Negroes and whites were obviously affected by migration during the decade, since the percentage increases in several of the divisions depart widely from the average for the country as a whole.

INCREASE BY 30-YEAR PERIODS FOR NEGRO AND WHITE POPULATION, BY SECTIONS AND DIVISIONS: 1790-1910.

Table 5

PERIOD.	United States.		The South.								The North.		The West.	
			Total.		South Atlantic division.		East South Central division.		West South Central division.					
	Negro.	White.	Negro.	White.	Negro.	White.	Negro.	White.	Negro.	White.	Negro.	White.	Negro.	White.
	NUMBER.													
1880–1910	3,246,970	38,328,987	2,795,524	9,991,993	1,171,286	3,417,491	727,517	2,096,733	896,721	4,477,769	412,636	23,404,942	38,810	4,932,052
1850–1880	2,941,985	23,849,902	2,601,705	4,925,013	1,080,331	1,835,893	802,206	1,417,112	719,168	1,672,008	329,669	17,490,190	10,611	1,434,699
1820–1850	1,867,152	11,686,271	1,709,526	2,853,854	587,472	1,030,555	834,733	1,338,049	287,321	485,250	156,385	8,654,840	1,241	177,577
1790–1820	1,014,448	4,694,791	952,888	1,505,170	599,937	609,320	271,735	809,386	81,216	86,464	61,560	3,189,621	......	......
	PER CENT.													
1880–1910	49.3	88.3	47.0	94.7	39.8	73.4	37.8	57.3	82.4	199.6	67.1	74.9	327.5	305.9
1850–1880	80.9	122.0	77.6	87.5	58.1	65.1	71.4	63.3	195.1	292.5	115.5	127.2	855.0	807.9
1820–1850	105.4	148.6	104.1	102.8	46.1	57.6	289.8	148.3	353.8	561.2	121.2	170.0	......	......
1790–1820	134.0	148.0	138.1	118.4	89.1	51.7	1,664.8	869.9	......	......	91.3	167.8	......	......

During the 30 years 1880–1910, as shown in Table 5, in the South the Negro increase amounted to 2,795,524 and the white increase to 9,991,993; in the North the Negro increase amounted to 412,636 and the white increase to 23,404,942; in the West the Negro increase amounted to 38,810 and the white increase to 4,932,052. The percentage increase in the South was 47 for the Negro population and 94.7 for the white population; in the North 67.1 for Negroes and 74.9 for whites; and in the West 327.5 for Negroes and 305.9 for whites. In the 30 years 1790–1820 the Negro population at the South increased at a more rapid rate than the white population, the percentage increases being, respectively, 138.1 and 118.4. In the following period the percentages were more nearly equal, the percentage for Negroes being somewhat higher than that for whites. In the two succeeding periods the percentage increase for Negroes fell below that for whites. Nearly one-half of the total Negro increase in the South from 1820 to 1850 was in the East South Central division, in which the increase amounted to 834,733, or 289.8 per cent. This increase was largely by migration from the South Atlantic division, in which the rate of growth was reduced far below the rate for the South as a whole.

NEGRO AND WHITE POPULATION, BY STATES: 1790–1910.

The Negro and the white population of the states and divisions at each census, 1790–1910, is given in Table 13, pages 43 to 45, which gives also, for 1910 and for 1900, the Indian and all other population. The Negro populations of the states in 1910 and in 1900 are also represented by the diagram on page 36.

At the date of the First Census, in 1790, Virginia's Negro population of 305,493 greatly exceeded that of any other state. Two-fifths of the total Negro population of the country were resident in this state, although three other states reported populations in excess of 100,000—Maryland, 111,079; North Carolina, 105,547; and South Carolina, 108,895. The fifth largest Negro population was that of Georgia, 29,662, and the sixth largest that of New York, 25,978. Negroes were reported from every state enumerated, the number returned from New Hampshire, 788, being greater than the number returned from that state at the census of 1910.

Throughout the period from 1790 to 1860, Virginia maintained her preeminence as regards Negro population over all other states. At the census of 1860, 5 Southern states reported Negro populations in excess of 400,000—Virginia, 548,907; Georgia, 465,698; Alabama, 437,770; Mississippi, 437,404; South Carolina, 412,320—and 7 other Southern states reported Negro populations in excess of 100,000. At the census of 1870 and at each succeeding census Georgia's Negro population exceeded that of any other state. In 1910 its Negro population numbered 1,176,987. One other state, Mississippi, in 1910, reported a Negro population in excess of 1,000,000. Six states besides Georgia and Mississippi, reported Negro populations in excess of 500,000, and 11 other states, of which 5 were Northern, Negro populations in excess of 100,000.

The rank of the states, as regards Negro, white, and total population in 1910, is shown in Table 6, in which the states are arranged in order, according to their Negro population, these populations being also cumulated by states.

Of the 13 states reporting Negro population in excess of 200,000 in 1910, all were Southern. The aggregate Negro population of these states was 8,422,015, amounting to 85.7 per cent, or six-sevenths of the total Negro population of the country. The remaining one-seventh of the Negro population was reported from 35 states—of which 3 (Oklahoma, West Virginia, and Delaware), were Southern—and the District of Columbia, whose populations ranged from 513 in Nevada to 193,919 in Pennsylvania. The 13 states reporting six-sevenths of the Negro population reported approximately one-fifth of the white population of the country.

Table 6 STATE.	Negro population: 1910.	RANK OF STATE.			NEGRO POPULATION, 1910, CUMULATED BY STATES.	
		By Negro population.	By white population.	By total population.	Number.	Per cent.
United States.....	9,827,763	......	......	......	9,827,763	100.0
Georgia............	1,176,987	1	20	10	1,176,987	12.0
Mississippi........	1,009,487	2	30	21	2,186,474	22.2
Alabama...........	908,282	3	22	18	3,094,756	31.5
South Carolina....	835,843	4	33	26	3,930,599	40.0
Louisiana.........	713,874	5	29	24	4,644,473	47.3
North Carolina....	697,843	6	18	16	5,342,316	54.4
Texas.............	690,049	7	6	5	6,032,365	61.4
Virginia..........	671,096	8	21	20	6,703,461	68.2
Tennessee.........	473,088	9	16	17	7,176,549	73.0
Arkansas..........	442,891	10	25	25	7,619,440	77.5
Florida...........	308,669	11	38	33	7,928,109	80.7
Kentucky..........	261,656	12	15	14	8,189,765	83.3
Maryland..........	232,250	13	28	27	8,422,015	85.7
Pennsylvania......	193,919	14	2	2	8,615,934	87.7
Missouri..........	157,452	15	7	7	8,773,386	89.3
Oklahoma..........	137,612	16	19	23	8,910,998	90.7
New York..........	134,191	17	1	1	9,045,189	92.0
Ohio..............	111,452	18	4	4	9,156,641	93.2
Illinois..........	109,049	19	3	3	9,265,690	94.3
District of Columbia.....	94,446	20	45	43	9,360,136	95.2
New Jersey........	89,760	21	10	11	9,449,896	96.2
West Virginia.....	64,173	22	24	28	9,514,069	96.8
Indiana...........	60,320	23	9	9	9,574,389	97.4
Kansas............	54,030	24	17	22	9,628,419	98.0
Massachusetts.....	38,055	25	5	6	9,666,474	98.4
Delaware..........	31,181	26	47	47	9,697,655	98.7
California........	21,645	27	12	12	9,719,300	98.9
Michigan..........	17,115	28	8	8	9,736,415	99.1
Connecticut.......	15,174	29	27	31	9,751,589	99.2
Iowa..............	14,973	30	13	15	9,766,562	99.4
Colorado..........	11,453	31	31	32	9,778,015	99.5
Rhode Island......	9,529	32	37	38	9,787,544	99.6
Nebraska..........	7,689	33	23	29	9,795,233	99.7
Minnesota.........	7,084	34	14	19	9,802,317	99.7
Washington........	6,058	35	26	30	9,808,375	99.8
Wisconsin.........	2,900	36	11	13	9,811,275	99.8
Wyoming...........	2,235	37	48	48	9,813,510	99.9
Arizona...........	2,009	38	46	46	9,815,519	99.9
Montana...........	1,834	39	41	40	9,817,353	99.9
New Mexico........	1,628	40	44	44	9,818,981	99.9
Vermont...........	1,621	41	42	42	9,820,602	99.9
Oregon............	1,492	42	34	35	9,822,094	99.9
Maine.............	1,363	43	32	34	9,823,457	100.0
Utah..............	1,144	44	40	41	9,824,601	100.0
South Dakota......	817	45	36	36	9,825,418	100.0
Idaho.............	651	46	43	45	9,826,069	100.0
North Dakota......	617	47	35	37	9,826,686	100.0
New Hampshire.....	564	48	39	39	9,827,250	100.0
Nevada............	513	49	49	49	9,827,763	100.0

Georgia, which ranked first in Negro population in 1910, ranked twentieth in white population and tenth in total population. Mississippi, the second most populous state as regards Negro population, ranked thirtieth in white population and twenty-first in total population. Alabama ranked third in Negro population, twenty-second in white population, and eighteenth in total population. New York, which ranked first in total and in white population, ranked seventeenth in Negro population. Pennsylvania, which ranked second in total and in white population, ranked fourteenth in Negro population.

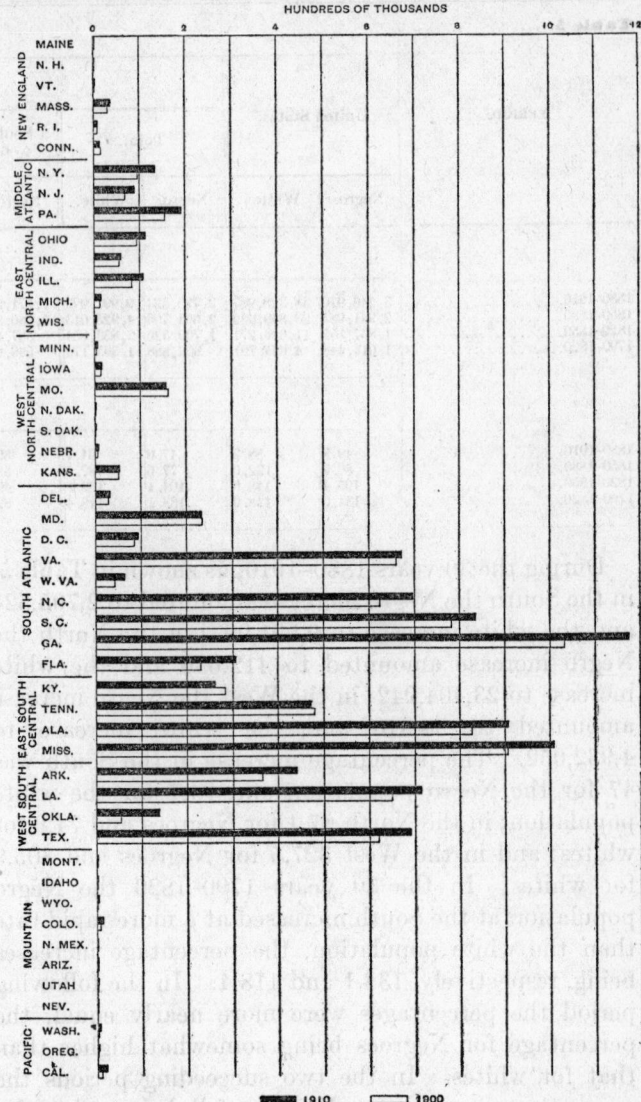

DIAGRAM II.—NEGRO POPULATION, BY STATES: 1910 AND 1900.

NEGRO AND WHITE INCREASE, BY STATES: 1790–1910.

The increase of the Negro and of the white population, during the decade 1900–1910, and by 30-year periods, 1790–1910, is given for states and divisions in Table 7, on the following page. These increases are figured upon the populations of Table 13.

During the decade 1900–1910 the Negro populations increased in 42 states and in the District of Columbia, and decreased in 6 states, of which 3 were Southern and 3 Northern.

In each of the nine geographic divisions the percentage increase for this class of the population varied greatly from state to state. In the case of no one of these divisions, in fact, is the rate of increase for the division as a whole even approximately indicative of the several rates for the states composing the divisions. In New England, for example, the Negro population increased 12.2 per cent, but this average for the

NEGRO AND WHITE INCREASE, BY DIVISIONS AND STATES: DECENNIAL, 1900–1910, AND BY 30-YEAR PERIODS, 1790–1910.

[A minus sign (−) denotes decrease.]

Table 7 — INCREASE OF NEGRO AND WHITE POPULATION.

DIVISION AND STATE.	1900–1910 Negro Number.	Negro Per cent.	1900–1910 White Number.	White Per cent.	1880–1910 Negro.	1880–1910 White.	1850–1880 Negro.	1850–1880 White.	1820–1850 Negro.	1820–1850 White.	1790–1820 Negro.	1790–1820 White.
UNITED STATES	993,769	11.2	14,922,761	22.3	3,246,970	38,328,987	2,941,985	23,849,902	1,867,152	11,686,271	1,014,448	4,694,791
GEOGRAPHIC DIVISIONS:												
New England	7,207	12.2	953,488	17.3	26,381	2,511,725	16,904	1,263,694	2,094	1,065,951	3,940	646,723
Middle Atlantic	91,949	28.2	3,769,590	24.9	228,378	8,575,397	62,751	4,533,061	36,944	3,161,946	39,360	1,701,853
East North Central	42,994	16.7	2,217,569	14.1	117,538	6,915,575	138,103	6,533,982	37,504	3,693,037	7,691	785,028
West North Central	4,753	2.0	1,285,804	12.8	40,339	5,402,245	111,911	5,159,453	79,843	733,906	10,569	56,017
South Atlantic	383,471	10.3	1,365,545	20.4	1,171,286	3,417,491	1,080,331	1,835,893	587,472	1,030,555	599,937	609,320
East South Central	152,627	6.1	709,479	14.1	727,517	2,096,733	802,206	1,417,112	834,733	1,338,049	271,735	809,386
West South Central	290,360	17.1	1,950,426	40.9	896,721	4,477,769	719,168	1,672,008	287,321	485,250	81,216	86,464
Mountain	5,877	37.7	940,600	59.5	16,445	1,905,634	4,950	541,966	72	72,855		
Pacific	14,531	99.1	1,730,260	75.4	22,365	3,026,418	5,661	892,733	1,169	104,722		
NEW ENGLAND:												
Maine	44	3.3	47,769	6.9	−88	93,143	95	65,039	427	284,407	391	201,404
New Hampshire	−98	−14.8	19,115	4.7	−121	83,677	165	28,773	−266	74,081	−2	102,278
Vermont	795	96.2	11,527	3.4	564	23,080	339	17,816	−185	78,324	632	149,924
Massachusetts	6,081	19.0	555,162	20.0	19,358	1,561,144	9,633	778,332	2,324	468,903	1,277	143,223
Rhode Island	437	4.8	113,442	27.1	3,041	262,553	2,818	126,064	68	64,418	−753	14,987
Connecticut	−52	−0.3	206,473	23.1	3,627	488,128	3,854	247,670	−274	95,818	2,395	34,907
MIDDLE ATLANTIC:												
New York	34,959	35.2	1,809,964	25.3	69,087	3,950,823	16,035	1,967,697	9,702	1,714,880	13,389	1,019,303
New Jersey	19,916	28.5	633,577	35.0	50,907	1,353,877	14,807	626,508	4,029	207,951	5,832	87,604
Pennsylvania	37,074	23.6	1,326,049	21.6	108,384	3,270,697	31,909	1,938,856	23,213	1,239,115	20,139	594,946
EAST NORTH CENTRAL:												
Ohio	14,551	15.0	594,693	14.6	31,552	1,536,977	54,621	1,162,870	20,556	1,378,339	4,723	576,711
Indiana	2,815	4.9	181,459	7.4	21,092	701,163	27,966	961,644	9,842	831,396	1,420	145,758
Illinois	23,971	28.2	792,089	16.7	62,681	2,495,811	40,932	2,185,117	4,062	792,197	1,374	53,837
Michigan	1,299	8.2	386,684	16.1	2,015	1,170,687	12,517	1,219,489	2,409	386,349	174	8,722
Wisconsin	358	14.1	262,644	12.8	198	1,010,937	2,067	1,004,862	635	304,756		
WEST NORTH CENTRAL:												
Minnesota	2,125	42.9	322,191	18.5	5,520	1,282,343	1,525	770,846	39	6,038		
Iowa	2,280	18.0	−9,476	−0.4	5,457	594,591	9,183	1,422,719	333	191,881		
Missouri	−3,782	−2.3	190,089	6.5	12,102	1,112,106	55,310	1,430,822	79,471	535,987	10,569	56,017
North Dakota	331	115.7	258,143	82.8	504	533,663	[1]401	[1]133,147				
South Dakota	352	75.7	183,057	48.1	529	466,816	}					
Nebraska	1,420	22.7	123,767	11.7	5,304	730,529	2,385	449,764				
Kansas	2,027	3.9	218,033	15.4	10,923	682,197	43,107	952,155				
SOUTH ATLANTIC:												
Delaware	484	1.6	17,125	11.1	4,739	50,942	6,079	48,991	2,896	15,887	4,681	8,972
Maryland	−2,814	−1.2	110,215	11.6	22,020	337,946	45,139	306,750	17,964	157,720	36,048	51,574
District of Columbia	7,744	8.9	44,596	23.3	34,850	118,122	45,850	80,065	3,321	15,327	10,425	22,614
Virginia	10,374	1.6	196,954	16.5	39,480	508,951	104,755	−13,942	64,830	291,465	156,538	161,218
West Virginia	20,674	47.5	241,584	26.4	38,287	564,280	25,886	592,537				
North Carolina	73,374	11.7	236,908	18.7	166,566	633,269	215,266	314,214	96,382	133,828	114,082	130,996
South Carolina	53,522	6.8	121,354	21.8	231,511	288,056	210,388	116,542	128,642	37,123	156,406	97,262
Georgia	142,174	13.7	250,508	21.2	451,854	614,896	340,520	295,334	233,194	332,002	121,757	136,684
Florida	77,939	33.8	146,301	49.2	181,979	301,029	86,448	95,402	40,242	47,203		
EAST SOUTH CENTRAL:												
Kentucky	−23,050	−8.1	165,642	8.9	−9,795	650,772	50,459	615,766	91,501	326,587	116,947	373,693
Tennessee	−7,155	−1.5	171,246	11.1	69,937	572,601	157,270	381,995	163,037	416,857	79,066	308,066
Alabama	80,975	9.8	227,680	22.7	308,179	566,647	254,994	235,671	302,659	341,063	42,450	85,451
Mississippi	101,857	11.2	144,911	22.6	359,196	306,713	339,483	183,680	277,536	253,542	33,272	42,176
WEST SOUTH CENTRAL:												
Arkansas	76,035	20.7	186,446	19.7	232,225	539,495	162,958	429,342	182,731	181,624	1,676	12,597
Louisiana	63,070	9.7	211,474	29.0	230,219	486,132	221,384	199,463	46,032	149,592	79,540	73,867
Oklahoma	81,928	147.1	774,327	115.5	137,612	1,444,531						
Texas	69,327	11.2	778,179	32.1	296,665	2,007,611	334,826	1,043,203	58,558	154,034		
MOUNTAIN:												
Montana	311	20.4	134,297	59.3	1,488	325,195	346	35,385				
Idaho	358	122.2	164,726	106.6	598	290,208	53	29,013				
Wyoming	1,295	137.8	51,267	57.6	1,937	120,881	298	19,437				
Colorado	2,883	33.6	254,369	48.1	9,018	592,289	2,435	191,126				
New Mexico	18	1.1	124,387	69.0	613	195,873	993	47,196	22	61,525		
Arizona	161	8.7	78,565	84.6	1,854	136,308	155	35,160				
Utah	472	70.2	94,118	34.5	912	224,160	182	131,093	50	11,330		
Nevada	379	282.8	38,871	109.8	25	20,720	488	53,556				
PACIFIC:												
Washington	3,544	141.0	612,807	123.5	5,733	1,041,912	325	67,199				
Oregon	387	35.0	260,508	66.0	1,005	492,015	280	149,988	207	13,087		
California	10,600	96.0	856,945	61.1	15,627	1,492,491	5,056	675,546	962	91,635		

[1] Dakota Territory.

division covers state rates ranging from a decrease of 14.8 per cent in New Hampshire, to an increase of 96.2 per cent in Vermont; the state rate most nearly approaching the average is that of 19 per cent for Massachusetts. The increase for the South Atlantic division was 10.3 per cent, but in this division the state increases range from a decrease of 1.2 per cent in Maryland, to an increase of 47.5 per cent in West Virginia. In the East South Central division a divisional increase of 6.1 per cent covers state rates ranging from a decrease of 8.1 per cent in Kentucky to an increase of 11.2 per cent in Mississippi. In the West South Central division a rate of 17.1 per cent covers state rates ranging from 9.7 in Louisiana to 147.1 per cent in Oklahoma. In the West North Central a divisional rate of 2 per cent increase covers state rates ranging from a decrease of 2.3 per cent in Missouri to an increase of 115.7 per cent in North Dakota. In the four other divisions the divergences of the state rates from the divisional rates are equally marked.

The wide range of variation in the state rates of increase is apparent in Table 8, in which the states are ranged in order according to the percentage increase of the Negro population, the percentage increase for the white population being given for comparison.

More than one-half of the total Negro population in 1910 and more than one-half of the increase during the decade 1900–1910 was in the 6 Southern states, in which the percentage increase during the decade ranged from 9.7 to 13.7. These states and their percentage increases were: Georgia, 13.7; North Carolina, 11.7; Mississippi, 11.2; Texas, 11.2; Alabama, 9.8; and Louisiana, 9.7. The aggregate Negro population of these 6 states in 1910 was 5,196,522, and the aggregate increase in the preceding decade amounted to 530,777, or 11.4 per cent. Although the 26 states, with higher rates of increase, reported less than one-fifth of the total Negro population in 1910, the increase in these states exceeded two-fifths of the total Negro increase for the decade. In 1910 these 26 states reported a Negro population of 1,712,497, and an aggregate increase of 421,018, or 32.6 per cent. Only 3 of this group of states were Southern—Oklahoma, increase 81,928, or 147.1 per cent; West Virginia, increase 20,674, or 47.5 per cent; and Florida, increase 77,939, or 33.8 per cent. In 16 states and in the District of Columbia, the Negro population increased at rates below 9.7 per cent, or decreased. Four of the 6 states in which the Negro population fell off during the decade, namely, Maryland, Tennessee, Kentucky, and Missouri were states with a considerable Negro population. In Virginia the increase amounted to only 1.6 per cent; and in South Carolina, to 6.8 per cent.

While approximately one-half of the Negro population in 1910 was living in states in which the percentage increase was near the average for the Negro population as a whole, the increases in the states generally are characterized by wide divergencies from the average—ranging from a decrease of 14.8 per cent to an increase of 282.8 per cent.

The Negro increase of two states in the decade 1900–1910 exceeded 100,000. In Georgia the increase amounted to 142,174 and in Mississippi to 101,857. Georgia's Negro increase in this decade and in each of the three 30-year periods 1820 to 1910 exceeded that of any other state. In the 30 years 1790–1820, the Negro population of Georgia increased by 121,757; in the 30 years 1820–1850, by 233,194; in the 30 years 1850–1880, by 340,520; and in the 30 years ending in 1910, by 451,854. In this latter period the Negro population of Mississippi increased by 359,196; that of Alabama, by 308,179; that of Texas, by 296,665; that of Arkansas, by 232,225; that of South Carolina, by 231,511; that of Louisiana, by 230,219; and that of 3 other states—Florida, North Carolina, and Oklahoma—by more than 100,000.

Table 8 STATE.	Negro population, 1910.	Negro increase,[1] 1900–1910.	PERCENTAGE INCREASE:[1] 1900–1910.	
			Negro population.	White population.
Total	9,827,763	993,769	11.2	22.3
Nevada	513	379	282.8	109.8
Oklahoma	137,612	81,928	147.1	115.5
Washington	6,058	3,544	141.0	123.5
Wyoming	2,235	1,295	137.8	57.6
Idaho	651	358	122.2	106.6
North Dakota	617	331	115.7	82.8
Vermont	1,621	795	96.2	3.4
California	21,645	10,600	96.0	61.1
South Dakota	817	352	75.7	48.1
Utah	1,144	472	70.2	34.5
West Virginia	64,173	20,674	47.5	26.4
Minnesota	7,084	2,125	42.9	18.5
New York	134,191	34,959	35.2	25.3
Oregon	1,492	387	35.0	66.0
Florida	308,669	77,939	33.8	49.2
Colorado	11,453	2,883	33.6	48.1
New Jersey	89,760	19,916	28.5	35.0
Illinois	109,049	23,971	28.2	16.7
Pennsylvania	193,919	37,074	23.6	21.6
Nebraska	7,689	1,420	22.7	11.7
Arkansas	442,891	76,035	20.7	19.7
Montana	1,834	311	20.4	59.3
Massachusetts	38,055	6,081	19.0	20.0
Iowa	14,973	2,280	18.0	−0.4
Ohio	111,452	14,551	15.0	14.6
Wisconsin	2,900	358	14.1	12.8
Georgia	1,176,987	142,174	13.7	21.2
North Carolina	697,843	73,374	11.7	18.7
Mississippi	1,009,487	101,857	11.2	22.6
Texas	690,049	69,327	11.2	32.1
Alabama	908,282	80,975	9.8	22.7
Louisiana	713,874	63,070	9.7	29.0
District of Columbia	94,446	7,744	8.9	23.3
Arizona	2,009	161	8.7	84.6
Michigan	17,115	1,299	8.2	16.1
South Carolina	835,843	53,522	6.8	21.8
Indiana	60,320	2,815	4.9	7.4
Rhode Island	9,529	437	4.8	27.1
Kansas	54,030	2,027	3.9	15.4
Maine	1,363	44	3.3	6.9
Delaware	31,181	484	1.6	11.1
Virginia	671,096	10,374	1.6	16.5
New Mexico	1,628	18	1.1	69.0
Connecticut	15,174	−52	−0.3	23.1
Maryland	232,250	−2,814	−1.2	11.6
Tennessee	473,088	−7,155	−1.5	11.1
Missouri	157,452	−3,782	−2.3	6.5
Kentucky	261,656	−23,050	−8.1	8.9
New Hampshire	564	−98	−14.8	4.7

[1] A minus sign (−) denotes decrease.

The white increase exceeded the Negro increase in each state during the decade 1900–1910 and in the 30-year period 1880–1910. In the preceding 30-year period 1850–1880, the Negro increase exceeded the white in South Carolina, Georgia, Alabama, Mississippi, and Louisiana.

NEGRO AND FOREIGN-BORN WHITE POPULATION: 1900–1910.

Some interest attaches to the increase in recent decades of the foreign-born white population in the South, since this class competes more directly than other classes with the Negro population in certain lines of employment.

The Negro and the foreign-born white population in 1910 and in 1900, and the increase 1900–1910 of these classes of the population, with the number of foreign-born whites to 1,000 Negroes, are given in Table 9, for sections and southern divisions and states. Only a small proportion of the foreign-born white population is resident in the South. In 1910 the number of this class in the South was 726,171, or 5.4 per cent of the total foreign-born white population of the country. In this year foreign-born whites constituted only 2.5 per cent of the total population of the South. The increase during the decade 1900–1910 in the South amounted to 163,596, or 29.6 per cent, the corresponding increase for the Negro population being 826,458, or 10.4 per cent. According to these figures the absolute increase of the foreign-born whites was approximately one-fifth as great as that of the Negroes, although in the increase of adults, the proportion foreign-born white was undoubtedly greater than in the increase of the population of all ages, because the foreign-born whites are largely in the adult ages.

NEGRO AND FOREIGN-BORN WHITE POPULATION, BY SECTIONS, SOUTHERN DIVISIONS, AND STATES: 1900–1910.

Table 9	POPULATION.										FOREIGN-BORN WHITES TO 1,000 NEGROES.	
	1910		1900		Increase,[1] 1900–1910.				Percentage distribution, 1910.			
					Number.		Per cent.					
SECTION, DIVISION, AND STATE.	Negro.	Foreign-born white.	Negro.	Foreign-born white.	Negro.	Foreign-born white.	Negro.	Foreign-born white.	Negro.	Foreign-born white.	1910	1900
United States	9,827,763	13,345,545	8,833,994	10,213,817	993,769	3,131,728	11.2	30.7	100.0	100.0	1,358	1,156
The South	8,749,427	726,171	7,922,969	562,575	826,458	163,596	10.4	29.6	89.0	5.4	83	71
South Atlantic division	4,112,488	290,555	3,729,017	208,883	383,471	81,672	10.3	39.1	41.8	2.2	71	56
East South Central division	2,652,513	86,857	2,499,886	89,682	152,627	−2,825	6.1	−3.2	27.0	0.7	33	36
West South Central division	1,984,426	348,759	1,694,066	264,010	290,360	84,749	17.1	32.1	20.2	2.6	176	156
The North	1,027,674	11,321,016	880,771	8,890,390	146,903	2,430,626	16.7	27.3	10.5	84.8	11,016	10,094
The West	50,662	1,298,358	30,254	760,852	20,408	537,506	67.5	70.6	0.5	9.7	25,628	25,149
THE SOUTH.												
South Atlantic division:												
Delaware	31,181	17,420	30,697	13,729	484	3,691	1.6	26.9	0.3	0.1	559	447
Maryland	232,250	104,174	235,064	93,144	−2,814	11,030	−1.2	11.8	2.4	0.8	449	396
District of Columbia	94,446	24,351	86,702	19,520	7,744	4,831	8.9	24.7	1.0	0.2	258	225
Virginia	671,096	26,628	660,722	19,068	10,374	7,560	1.6	39.6	6.8	0.2	40	29
West Virginia	64,173	57,072	43,499	22,379	20,674	34,693	47.5	155.0	0.7	0.4	889	514
North Carolina	697,843	5,942	624,469	4,394	73,374	1,548	11.7	35.2	7.1	(2)	9	7
South Carolina	835,843	6,054	782,321	5,371	53,522	683	6.8	12.7	8.5	(2)	7	7
Georgia	1,176,987	15,072	1,034,813	12,021	142,174	3,051	13.7	25.4	12.0	0.1	13	12
Florida	308,669	33,842	230,730	19,257	77,939	14,585	33.8	75.7	3.1	0.3	110	83
East South Central division:												
Kentucky	261,656	40,053	284,706	50,133	−23,050	−10,080	−8.1	−20.1	2.7	0.3	153	176
Tennessee	473,088	18,459	480,243	17,586	−7,155	873	−1.5	5.0	4.8	0.1	39	37
Alabama	908,282	18,956	827,307	14,338	80,975	4,618	9.8	32.2	9.2	0.1	21	17
Mississippi	1,009,487	9,389	907,630	7,625	101,857	1,764	11.2	23.1	10.3	0.1	9	8
West South Central division:												
Arkansas	442,891	16,909	366,856	14,186	76,035	2,723	20.7	19.2	4.5	0.1	38	39
Louisiana	713,874	51,782	650,804	51,853	63,070	−71	9.7	−0.1	7.3	0.4	73	80
Oklahoma	137,612	40,084	55,684	20,390	81,928	19,694	147.1	96.6	1.4	0.3	291	366
Texas	690,049	239,984	620,722	177,581	69,327	62,403	11.2	35.1	7.0	1.8	348	286

[1] A minus sign (−) denotes decrease.   [2] Less than one-tenth of 1 per cent.

In the South Atlantic division the foreign-born white population increased by 81,672, or 39.1 per cent; the Negro population by 383,471, or 10.3 per cent. In the East South Central division the foreign-born white population decreased by 2,825, or 3.2 per cent, and the Negro population increased by 152,627, or 6.1 per cent. In the West South Central division the foreign-born white increase amounted to 84,749, or 32.1 per cent, and the Negro increase to 290,360, or 17.1 per cent.

Nearly one-third of the total foreign-born white population of the South in 1910 and more than one-third of the foreign-born white increase for the decade 1900–1910 in the South was in the state of Texas. The percentage increase for this class during the decade 1900–1910 exceeded that for the Negro population in all but four Southern states. In three Southern states—Alabama, Maryland, and West Virginia—the absolute as well as the percentage increase of the foreign-born whites exceeded that of the Negro population, and in Tennessee the foreign-born white population increased by 873, while the Negro population decreased by 7,155.

The number of foreign-born whites to 1,000 Negroes in the South in 1910 was 83; in the North, 11,016; and in the West, 25,628. In each section the proportion of foreign-born whites to Negroes increased during the decade 1900–1910. Among Southern states in 1910 the proportion was highest in West Virginia—889 foreign-born whites to 1,000 Negroes—and lowest in South Carolina—7 foreign-born whites to 1,000 Negroes.

DENSITY OF NEGRO AND WHITE POPULATION, TOTAL AND RURAL: 1910.

Tables 10 and 11 give the density of the Negro and white population and of the Negro and white rural[1] population in 1910, as indicated by the average population of each class per square mile of area— Table 10 for sections and southern divisions; and Table 11 for the states.

Table 10	Area in square miles.	POPULATION PER SQUARE MILE: 1910.				
		Total.			Rural.	
SECTION AND DIVISION.		All classes.	Negro.	White.	Negro.	White.
The South..............	878,326	33.5	10.0	23.4	7.9	18.0
South Atlantic..........	269,071	45.3	15.3	30.0	11.9	21.9
East South Central.....	179,509	46.8	14.8	32.1	11.9	26.1
West South Central.....	429,746	20.4	4.6	15.6	3.6	12.1
The North.............	918,344	60.7	1.1	59.5	0.3	24.8
The West.............	1,177,220	5.8	....	5.6	....	2.8

These densities are averages for state areas and combinations of state areas, and do not necessarily indicate conditions prevailing within any subdivision of the state. Where, for example, the total population, urban and rural, is related to the total area, the density figure for a state with any considerable urban population does not necessarily represent conditions prevailing anywhere in the state, either in urban communities or in rural districts. A somewhat closer approximation may be made to conditions prevailing outside of urban communities by relating the rural population to total area, although the density of the rural population itself may vary markedly from one rural district to another within any given state. Moreover, the Negro population may be resident predominantly in one rural section and the white population in another, and in such cases the averages for the state would not represent accurately the density of either class or the relative number of Negroes and whites in any section. The averages represent the condition which would prevail generally were each class of the population distributed evenly over the territory of the state, or division, or section, and to

[1] The rural population is the total population living outside of cities and other incorporated places of 2,500 or more inhabitants.

the extent that the distribution of the population approximates such a distribution, the averages represent conditions actually prevailing.

In the South as a whole the Negro population averaged 10 per square mile; in the North, 1.1; and in the West, less than 1 in 20 square miles. The corresponding densities for the white population were 23.4, 59.5, and 5.6 persons per square mile. The rural Negro population averaged 7.9 persons per square mile in the South, and the rural white, 18. The population per square mile, Negro and white, total and rural, was much less in the West South Central division than it was in the South Atlantic or East South Central divisions.

In Table 11 the states are arranged in order, according to the density of the Negro population. The Negro population of South Carolina in 1910 averaged 27.4 per square mile. This density exceeded the corresponding density for any other state, and exceeded the density of the white population in South Carolina, which amounted to 22.3.

Table 11	Area in square miles.	POPULATION PER SQUARE MILE: 1910.				
		Total.			Rural.	
STATE.[1]		Negro.	White.	All classes.	Negro.	White.
United States......	2,973,890	3.3	27.5	30.9	2.4	14.1
District of Columbia......	60	1,574.1	3,935.5	5,517.8	....	....
South Carolina............	30,495	27.4	22.3	49.7	24.1	18.2
Maryland................	9,941	23.4	106.9	130.3	13.4	50.7
Mississippi..............	46,362	21.8	17.0	38.8	19.7	14.5
Georgia................	58,725	20.0	24.4	44.4	16.2	19.0
Alabama................	51,279	17.7	24.0	41.7	14.7	19.8
Virginia................	40,262	16.7	34.5	51.2	12.7	26.6
Delaware................	1,965	15.9	87.1	103.0	10.2	43.4
Louisiana..............	45,409	15.7	20.7	36.5	12.2	13.3
North Carolina.........	48,740	14.3	30.8	45.3	11.9	26.6
New Jersey.............	7,514	11.9	325.5	337.7	3.2	80.6
Tennessee.............	41,687	11.3	41.1	52.4	7.7	34.1
Rhode Island..........	1,067	8.9	499.1	508.5	0.4	16.4
Arkansas..............	52,525	8.4	21.5	30.0	7.3	18.8
Kentucky..............	40,181	6.5	50.5	57.0	3.9	39.3
Florida................	54,861	5.6	8.1	13.7	4.0	5.7
Massachusetts........	8,039	4.7	413.6	418.8	0.3	29.6
Pennsylvania..........	44,832	4.3	166.6	171.0	0.8	66.8
Connecticut..........	4,820	3.1	228.0	231.3	0.3	23.6
New York..............	47,654	2.8	188.2	191.2	0.4	40.0
Ohio..................	40,740	2.7	114.3	117.0	0.7	50.9
West Virginia.........	24,022	2.7	48.2	50.8	2.0	39.3
Texas................	262,398	2.6	12.2	14.8	1.9	9.3
Missouri..............	68,727	2.3	45.6	47.9	0.8	26.8
Oklahoma.............	69,414	2.0	20.8	23.9	1.4	16.8
Illinois...............	56,043	1.9	98.6	100.6	0.4	38.2
Indiana..............	36,045	1.7	73.2	74.9	0.3	42.9

[1] States having Negro population less than 1 per square mile are omitted. These states are as follows: Arizona, California, Colorado, Idaho, Iowa, Kansas, Maine, Michigan, Minnesota, Montana, Nebraska, Nevada, New Hampshire, New Mexico, North Dakota, Oregon, South Dakota, Utah, Vermont, Washington, Wisconsin, Wyoming.

GEOGRAPHIC CENTER OF THE NEGRO POPULATION: 1790, 1880–1910.

The center of population is the point to which the population in the aggregate is nearest—the point at which the population could assemble by traveling in the aggregate the least number of miles, assuming that each individual could travel in a direct line from his place of residence to the point.

Theoretically, the point responds to each change in residence on the part of individuals composing the population, and to the growth or decline of population in any community. Its movement in any direction from census to census is a resultant of the local growth or decline, and the net drift of population during the intervening decade.

By analogy it may be described as the center of gravity of population. If the surface of the United States be conceived as being a rigid plane without weight, capable of sustaining the population distributed thereon—individuals being assumed to be of equal weight, and each, therefore, to exert a gravity pull with reference to any supporting pivotal point directly proportional to his distance from the point—the pivotal point on which the plane balanced, that is to say, its center of gravity—would be the center of population.

It will be obvious that the center is not necessarily located in a region of great density of population. It may, on the contrary, be located in a region of relatively low density. The density of population in the

[1] For an account of the method of determining the center of population, see Thirteenth Census report, Vol. I, p. 46.

region immediately surrounding the center is in fact a very inconsiderable factor in determining the location of the point, which by the general geographic disposition of the aggregate population of the country may be brought indifferently into a desert, a wilderness, or a relatively populous community.

The center of the Negro population in 1790 and at each of the four censuses 1880–1910 is indicated on the accompanying map by stars.

As a consequence of changes in the geographic distribution of the Negro population, due to growth and migration during the period of 90 years 1790–1880, the center moved from a point in Dinwiddie County, Va., to a point 443 miles southwest, located in Walker County, in northwestern Georgia. During the three decades 1880–1910 it progressed farther in a southwesterly direction, a distance of approximately 36 miles, to a point in Dekalb County in northeastern Alabama.

The latitude and longitude of the center of the Negro population at each of the five censuses for which its location has been determined, and the progression of the point in miles during the periods intervening between the censuses, is given in Table 12.

CENTER OF THE NEGRO POPULATION: 1790, 1880–1910.

Table 12 CENSUS YEAR.	North latitude.			West longitude.			LOCATION OF CENTER. Approximate location by important towns.	DECENNIAL MOVEMENT IN MILES.
	°	′	″	°	′	″		
1790	37	4	8	77	51	21	25 miles west-southwest of Petersburg, Dinwiddie County, Va.	
1880	34	42	14	85	6	56	10.4 miles east of Lafayette, Walker County, Ga	443 miles southwest.
1890	34	36	18	85	26	49	15.7 miles southwest of Lafayette, Walker County, Ga	20.5 miles southwest.
1900	34	31	16	85	34	35	10.7 miles northeast of Fort Payne, Dekalb County, Ala.	9.5 miles southwest.
1910	34	30	0	85	40	43	5.4 miles north-northeast of Fort Payne, Dekalb County, Ala.	5.8 miles west-southwest.

The average decennial movement for the nine decades 1790–1880 was 49.2 miles. In the decade 1880–1890 the center progressed 20.5 miles; in the decade following 9.5 miles; and in the decade ending in 1910, 5.8 miles. It will be noted that the progression of the point has retarded from decade to decade, that the advance made in the decade 1900–1910 was very inconsiderable, and that the direction of the movement veered from southwest to a course more nearly westerly.

Migration of Negroes from the South to Northern and Eastern states, in recent decades, as well as the large increases in certain eastern states of the South has retarded the movement of the center southward and westward. In general the retardation indicates

that the westward drift which, during the past century has characterized the Negro as well as the white population, has become less considerable, relatively to the settled population, although it does not necessarily follow from this that the number of migrants, or the volume of migration westward has declined.

It is undoubtedly true, also, that counter currents of migration have in recent decades partially neutralized the westward drift. The retardation in movement of the center is not inconsistent with an increasing proportion of migrants in the Negro population, but would indicate rather that the net result of migratory displacement in the Negro population is a dispersion of the population about the center rather than a mass drift in any one direction,

ARKANSAS

MISSOURI

ILLINOIS

INDIANA

OHIO

KENTUCKY

TENNESSEE

MISSISSIPPI

ALABAMA

GEORGIA

FLORIDA

SOUTH CAROLINA

NORTH CAROLINA

VIRGINIA

WEST VIRGINIA

MARYLAND

DELAWARE

LITTLE ROCK

JACKSON

MEMPHIS

ST. LOUIS

SPRINGFIELD

INDIANAPOLIS

NASHVILLE

LOUISVILLE

CINCINNATI

CLARKSBURG

RICHMOND

BIRMINGHAM

HUNTSVILLE

ATLANTA

ASHEVILLE

CHARLESTON

SAVANNAH

JACKSONVILLE

MISSISSIPPI RIVER

OHIO RIVER

1910 1890 1900 1880 1790

CENTER OF NEGRO POPULATION
1790 AND 1880 TO 1910

★ Center of Negro Population

TABLE 13.—POPULATION BY STATES: NEGRO AND WHITE, AT EACH CENSUS, 1790–1910; INDIAN AND OTHER, 1910 AND 1900.

| DIVISION AND STATE. | NEGRO, WHITE, INDIAN, AND OTHER POPULATION, 1910 AND 1900. | | | | | | | | | |
| | 1910 | | | | | 1900 | | | | |
	Total.	Negro.	White.	Indian.	Other.[1]	Total.	Negro.	White.	Indian.	Other.[1]
UNITED STATES	91,972,266	9,827,763	81,731,957	265,683	146,863	75,994,575	8,833,994	66,809,196	237,196	114,189
GEOGRAPHIC DIVISIONS:										
New England	6,552,681	66,306	6,480,514	2,076	3,785	5,592,017	59,099	5,527,026	1,600	4,292
Middle Atlantic	19,315,892	417,870	18,880,452	7,717	9,853	15,454,678	325,921	15,110,862	6,959	10,936
East North Central	18,250,621	300,836	17,927,622	18,255	3,908	15,985,581	257,842	15,710,053	15,027	2,659
West North Central	11,637,921	242,662	11,351,621	41,406	2,232	10,347,423	237,909	10,065,817	42,339	1,358
South Atlantic	12,194,895	4,112,488	8,071,603	9,054	1,750	10,443,480	3,729,017	6,706,058	6,585	1,820
East South Central	8,409,901	2,652,513	5,754,326	2,612	450	7,547,757	2,499,886	5,044,847	2,590	434
West South Central	8,784,534	1,984,426	6,721,491	76,767	1,850	6,532,290	1,694,066	4,771,065	65,574	1,585
Mountain	2,633,517	21,467	2,520,455	75,338	16,257	1,674,657	15,590	1,579,855	66,155	13,057
Pacific	4,192,304	29,195	4,023,873	32,458	106,778	2,416,692	14,664	2,293,613	30,367	78,048
NEW ENGLAND:										
Maine	742,371	1,363	739,995	892	121	694,466	1,319	692,226	798	123
New Hampshire	430,572	564	429,906	34	68	411,588	662	410,791	22	113
Vermont	355,956	1,621	354,298	26	11	343,641	826	342,771	5	39
Massachusetts	3,366,416	38,055	3,324,926	688	2,747	2,805,346	31,974	2,769,764	587	3,021
Rhode Island	542,610	9,529	532,492	284	305	428,556	9,092	419,050	35	379
Connecticut	1,114,756	15,174	1,098,897	152	533	908,420	15,226	892,424	153	617
MIDDLE ATLANTIC:										
New York	9,113,614	134,191	8,966,845	6,046	6,532	7,268,894	99,232	7,156,881	5,257	7,524
New Jersey	2,537,167	89,760	2,445,894	168	1,345	1,883,669	69,844	1,812,317	63	1,445
Pennsylvania	7,665,111	193,919	7,467,713	1,503	1,976	6,302,115	156,845	6,141,664	1,639	1,967
EAST NORTH CENTRAL:										
Ohio	4,767,121	111,452	4,654,897	127	645	4,157,545	96,901	4,060,204	42	398
Indiana	2,700,876	60,320	2,639,961	279	316	2,516,462	57,505	2,458,502	243	212
Illinois	5,638,591	109,049	5,526,962	188	2,392	4,821,550	85,078	4,734,873	16	1,583
Michigan	2,810,173	17,115	2,785,247	7,519	292	2,420,982	15,816	2,398,563	6,354	249
Wisconsin	2,333,860	2,900	2,320,555	10,142	263	2,069,042	2,542	2,057,911	8,372	217
WEST NORTH CENTRAL:										
Minnesota	2,075,708	7,084	2,059,227	9,053	344	1,751,394	4,959	1,737,036	9,182	217
Iowa	2,224,771	14,973	2,209,191	471	136	2,231,853	12,693	2,218,667	382	111
Missouri	3,293,335	157,452	3,134,932	313	638	3,106,665	161,234	2,944,843	130	458
North Dakota	577,056	617	569,855	6,486	98	319,146	286	311,712	6,968	180
South Dakota	583,888	817	563,771	19,137	163	401,570	465	380,714	20,225	166
Nebraska	1,192,214	7,689	1,180,293	3,502	730	1,066,300	6,269	1,056,526	3,322	183
Kansas	1,690,949	54,030	1,634,352	2,444	123	1,470,495	52,003	1,416,319	2,130	43
SOUTH ATLANTIC:										
Delaware	202,322	31,181	171,102	5	34	184,735	30,697	153,977	9	52
Maryland	1,295,346	232,250	1,062,639	55	402	1,188,044	235,064	952,424	3	553
District of Columbia	331,069	94,446	236,128	68	427	278,718	86,702	191,532	22	462
Virginia	2,061,612	671,096	1,389,809	539	168	1,854,184	660,722	1,192,855	354	253
West Virginia	1,221,119	64,173	1,156,817	36	93	958,800	43,499	915,233	12	56
North Carolina	2,206,287	697,843	1,500,511	7,851	82	1,893,810	624,469	1,263,603	5,687	51
South Carolina	1,515,400	835,843	679,161	331	65	1,340,316	782,321	557,807	121	67
Georgia	2,609,121	1,176,987	1,431,802	95	237	2,216,331	1,034,813	1,181,294	19	205
Florida	752,619	308,669	443,634	74	242	528,542	230,730	297,333	358	121
EAST SOUTH CENTRAL:										
Kentucky	2,289,905	261,656	2,027,951	234	64	2,147,174	284,706	1,862,309	102	57
Tennessee	2,184,789	473,088	1,711,432	216	53	2,020,616	480,243	1,540,186	108	79
Alabama	2,138,093	908,282	1,228,832	909	70	1,828,697	827,307	1,001,152	177	61
Mississippi	1,797,114	1,009,487	786,111	1,253	263	1,551,270	907,630	641,200	2,203	237
WEST SOUTH CENTRAL:										
Arkansas	1,574,449	442,891	1,131,026	460	72	1,311,564	366,856	944,580	66	62
Louisiana	1,656,388	713,874	941,086	780	648	1,381,625	650,804	729,612	593	616
Oklahoma [2]	1,657,155	137,612	1,444,531	74,825	187	790,391	55,684	670,204	64,445	58
Texas	3,896,542	690,049	3,204,848	702	943	3,048,710	620,722	2,426,669	470	849
MOUNTAIN:										
Montana	376,053	1,834	360,580	10,745	2,894	243,329	1,523	226,283	11,343	4,180
Idaho	325,594	651	319,221	3,488	2,234	161,772	293	154,495	4,226	2,758
Wyoming	145,965	2,235	140,318	1,486	1,926	92,531	940	89,051	1,686	854
Colorado	799,024	11,453	783,415	1,482	2,674	539,700	8,570	529,046	1,437	647
New Mexico	327,301	1,628	304,594	20,573	506	195,310	1,610	180,207	13,144	349
Arizona	204,354	2,009	171,468	29,201	1,676	122,931	1,848	92,903	26,480	1,700
Utah	373,351	1,144	366,583	3,123	2,501	276,749	672	272,465	2,623	989
Nevada	81,875	513	74,276	5,240	1,846	42,335	134	35,405	5,216	1,580
PACIFIC:										
Washington	1,141,990	6,058	1,109,111	10,997	15,824	518,103	2,514	496,304	10,039	9,246
Oregon	672,765	1,492	655,090	5,090	11,093	413,536	1,105	394,582	4,951	12,898
California	2,377,549	21,645	2,259,672	16,371	79,861	1,485,053	11,045	1,402,727	15,377	55,904

[1] Chinese, Japanese, and all other.　　　　[2] Includes Indian Territory for 1900 and 1890.

TABLE 13.—POPULATION BY STATES: NEGRO AND WHITE, AT EACH CENSUS, 1790–1910; INDIAN AND OTHER, 1910 AND 1900—Continued.

DIVISION AND STATE.	NEGRO AND WHITE POPULATION AT EACH CENSUS, 1790 TO 1910.									
	1890 [1]		1880		1870		1860		1850	
	Negro.	White.	Negro.	White.	Negro.	White.	Negro.	White.	Negro.	White.
UNITED STATES	7,488,676	55,101,258	6,580,793	43,402,970	4,880,009	33,589,377	4,441,830	26,922,537	3,638,808	19,553,068
GEOGRAPHIC DIVISIONS:										
New England	44,580	4,653,191	39,925	3,968,789	31,705	3,455,043	24,711	3,110,480	23,021	2,705,095
Middle Atlantic	225,326	12,468,794	189,492	10,305,055	148,033	8,662,226	131,290	7,327,548	126,741	5,771,994
East North Central	207,023	13,253,725	183,298	11,012,047	130,497	8,987,512	63,699	6,855,644	45,195	4,478,065
West North Central	224,089	8,660,088	202,323	5,949,376	142,583	3,710,991	120,540	2,044,325	90,412	789,923
South Atlantic	3,262,690	5,592,149	2,941,202	4,654,112	2,216,705	3,635,238	2,058,198	3,305,107	1,860,871	2,818,219
East South Central	2,119,797	4,305,668	1,924,996	3,657,593	1,464,252	2,939,091	1,394,360	2,626,376	1,122,790	2,240,481
West South Central	1,378,090	3,295,636	1,087,705	2,243,722	739,854	1,288,880	644,553	1,102,490	368,537	571,714
Mountain	12,971	1,117,363	5,022	614,821	1,555	301,848	235	164,092	72	72,855
Pacific	14,110	1,754,644	6,830	997,455	4,825	608,548	4,244	386,475	1,169	104,722
NEW ENGLAND:										
Maine	1,190	659,263	1,451	646,852	1,606	624,809	1,327	626,947	1,356	581,813
New Hampshire	614	375,840	685	346,229	580	317,697	494	325,579	520	317,456
Vermont	937	331,418	1,057	331,218	924	329,613	709	314,369	718	313,402
Massachusetts	22,144	2,215,373	18,697	1,763,782	13,947	1,443,156	9,602	1,221,432	9,064	985,450
Rhode Island	7,393	337,859	6,488	269,939	4,980	212,219	3,952	170,649	3,670	143,875
Connecticut	12,302	733,438	11,547	610,769	9,668	527,549	8,627	451,504	7,693	363,099
MIDDLE ATLANTIC:										
New York	70,092	5,923,955	65,104	5,016,022	52,081	4,330,210	49,005	3,831,590	49,069	3,048,325
New Jersey	47,638	1,396,581	38,853	1,092,017	30,658	875,407	25,336	646,699	24,046	465,509
Pennsylvania	107,596	5,148,258	85,535	4,197,016	65,294	3,456,609	56,949	2,849,259	53,626	2,258,160
EAST NORTH CENTRAL:										
Ohio	87,113	3,584,805	79,900	3,117,920	63,213	2,601,946	36,673	2,302,808	25,279	1,955,050
Indiana	45,215	2,146,736	39,228	1,938,798	24,560	1,655,837	11,428	1,338,710	11,262	977,154
Illinois	57,028	3,768,472	46,368	3,031,151	28,762	2,511,096	7,628	1,704,291	5,436	846,034
Michigan	15,223	2,072,884	15,100	1,614,560	11,849	1,167,282	6,799	736,142	2,583	395,071
Wisconsin	2,444	1,680,828	2,702	1,309,618	2,113	1,051,351	1,171	773,693	635	304,756
WEST NORTH CENTRAL:										
Minnesota	3,683	1,296,408	1,564	776,884	759	438,257	259	169,395	39	6,038
Iowa	10,685	1,901,090	9,516	1,614,600	5,762	1,188,207	1,069	673,779	333	191,881
Missouri	150,184	2,528,458	145,350	2,022,826	118,071	1,603,146	118,503	1,063,489	90,040	592,004
North Dakota	373	182,407	[2] 113	[2] 36,192	} [2] 94	[2] 12,887	(2)	[2] 2,576		
South Dakota	541	328,010	[2] 288	[2] 96,955						
Nebraska	8,913	1,047,096	2,385	449,764	789	122,117	82	28,696		
Kansas	49,710	1,376,619	43,107	952,155	17,108	346,377	627	106,390		
SOUTH ATLANTIC:										
Delaware	28,386	140,066	26,442	120,160	22,794	102,221	21,627	90,589	20,363	71,169
Maryland	215,657	826,493	210,230	724,693	175,391	605,497	171,131	515,918	165,091	417,943
District of Columbia	75,572	154,695	59,596	118,006	43,404	88,278	14,316	60,763	13,746	37,941
Virginia	635,438	1,020,122	631,616	880,858	512,841	712,089	548,907	1,047,299	526,861	894,800
West Virginia	32,690	730,077	25,886	592,537	17,980	424,033				
North Carolina	561,018	1,055,382	531,277	867,242	391,650	678,470	361,522	629,942	316,011	553,028
South Carolina	688,934	462,008	604,332	391,105	415,814	289,667	412,320	291,300	393,944	274,563
Georgia	858,815	978,357	725,133	816,906	545,142	638,926	465,698	591,550	384,613	521,572
Florida	166,180	224,949	126,690	142,605	91,689	96,057	62,677	77,746	40,242	47,203
EAST SOUTH CENTRAL:										
Kentucky	268,071	1,590,462	271,451	1,377,179	222,210	1,098,692	236,167	919,484	220,992	761,413
Tennessee	430,678	1,336,637	403,151	1,138,831	322,331	936,119	283,019	826,722	245,881	756,836
Alabama	678,489	833,718	600,103	662,185	475,510	521,384	437,770	526,271	345,109	426,514
Mississippi	742,559	544,851	650,291	479,398	444,201	382,896	437,404	353,899	310,808	295,718
WEST SOUTH CENTRAL:										
Arkansas	309,117	818,752	210,666	591,531	122,169	362,115	111,259	324,143	47,708	162,189
Louisiana	559,193	558,395	483,655	454,954	364,210	362,065	350,373	357,456	262,271	255,491
Oklahoma [3]	21,609	172,554								
Texas	488,171	1,745,935	393,384	1,197,237	253,475	564,700	182,921	420,891	58,558	154,034
MOUNTAIN:										
Montana	1,490	127,690	346	35,385	183	18,306				
Idaho	201	82,117	53	29,013	60	10,618				
Wyoming	922	59,324	298	19,437	183	8,726				
Colorado	6,215	404,534	2,435	191,126	456	39,221	46	34,231		
New Mexico	1,956	142,918	1,015	108,721	172	90,393	85	82,924	22	61,525
Arizona	1,357	55,734	155	35,160	26	9,581				
Utah	588	205,925	232	142,423	118	86,044	59	40,125	50	11,330
Nevada	242	39,121	488	53,556	357	38,959	45	6,812		
PACIFIC:										
Washington	1,602	340,829	325	67,199	207	22,195	30	11,138		
Oregon	1,186	301,982	487	163,075	346	86,929	128	52,160	207	13,087
California	11,322	1,111,833	6,018	767,181	4,272	499,424	4,086	323,177	962	91,635

[1] Includes persons specially enumerated in 1890 in Indian Territory and on Indian reservations—Negroes, 18,636; whites, 117,368.
[2] Dakota Territory.
[3] Includes Indian Territory for 1900 and 1890.

TABLE 13.—POPULATION BY STATES: NEGRO AND WHITE, AT EACH CENSUS 1790–1910: INDIAN AND OTHER, 1910 AND 1900—Continued.

DIVISION AND STATE.	NEGRO AND WHITE POPULATION AT EACH CENSUS, 1790 TO 1910.											
	1840		1830		1820		1810		1800		1790	
	Negro.	White.	Negro.	White.	Negro.	White.	Negro.	White.	Negro.	White.	Negro.	White.
UNITED STATES	2,873,648	14,189,705	2,328,642	10,532,060	1,771,656	7,866,797	1,377,808	5,862,073	1,002,037	4,306,446	757,208	3,172,006
GEOGRAPHIC DIVISIONS:												
New England	22,657	2,212,165	21,379	1,933,338	20,927	1,639,144	19,906	1,452,067	18,652	1,214,359	16,987	992,421
Middle Atlantic	119,667	4,406,593	103,835	3,483,829	89,797	2,610,048	82,331	1,932,371	64,414	1,338,151	50,437	908,195
East North Central	29,345	2,895,383	15,883	1,454,135	7,691	785,028	3,454	268,870	635	50,371		
West North Central	60,002	366,812	25,660	114,795	10,569	56,017	3,618	17,227				
South Atlantic	1,597,317	2,327,982	1,529,283	2,116,469	1,273,399	1,787,664	1,080,800	1,594,091	859,690	1,426,804	673,462	1,178,344
East South Central	830,306	1,745,139	501,587	1,314,382	288,057	902,432	145,454	563,136	58,646	276,761	16,322	93,046
West South Central	214,354	235,631	131,015	115,112	81,216	86,464	42,245	34,311				
Mountain												
Pacific												
NEW ENGLAND:												
Maine	1,355	500,438	1,192	398,263	929	297,406	969	227,736	818	150,901	538	96,002
New Hampshire	538	284,036	607	268,721	786	243,375	970	213,490	860	182,998	788	141,097
Vermont	730	291,218	881	279,771	903	235,078	750	217,145	557	153,908	271	85,154
Massachusetts	8,669	729,030	7,049	603,359	6,740	516,547	6,737	465,303	6,452	416,393	5,463	373,324
Rhode Island	3,243	105,587	3,578	93,621	3,602	79,457	3,717	73,214	3,684	65,438	4,355	64,470
Connecticut	8,122	301,856	8,072	289,603	7,967	267,281	6,763	255,179	6,281	244,721	5,572	232,374
MIDDLE ATLANTIC:												
New York	50,031	2,378,890	44,945	1,873,663	39,367	1,333,445	40,350	918,699	31,320	557,731	25,978	314,142
New Jersey	21,718	351,588	20,557	300,266	20,017	257,558	18,694	226,868	16,824	194,325	14,185	169,954
Pennsylvania	47,918	1,676,115	38,333	1,309,900	30,413	1,019,045	23,287	786,804	16,270	586,095	10,274	424,099
EAST NORTH CENTRAL:												
Ohio	17,345	1,502,122	9,574	928,329	4,723	576,711	1,899	228,861	337	45,028		
Indiana	7,168	678,698	3,632	339,399	1,420	145,758	630	23,890	298	5,343		
Illinois	3,929	472,254	2,384	155,061	1,374	53,837	781	11,501				
Michigan	707	211,560	293	31,346	174	8,722	144	4,618				
Wisconsin	196	30,749										
WEST NORTH CENTRAL:												
Minnesota												
Iowa	188	42,924										
Missouri	59,814	323,888	25,660	114,795	10,569	56,017	3,618	17,227				
North Dakota												
South Dakota												
Nebraska												
Kansas												
SOUTH ATLANTIC:												
Delaware	19,524	58,561	19,147	57,601	17,467	55,282	17,313	55,361	14,421	49,852	12,786	46,310
Maryland	151,815	318,204	155,932	291,108	147,127	260,223	145,429	235,117	125,222	216,326	111,079	208,649
District of Columbia	13,055	30,657	12,271	27,563	10,425	22,614	7,944	16,079	4,027	10,066		
Virginia	498,829	740,968	517,105	694,300	462,031	603,335	423,086	551,514	365,920	514,280	305,493	442,117
West Virginia												
North Carolina	268,549	484,870	265,144	472,843	219,629	419,200	179,090	376,410	140,339	337,764	105,547	288,204
South Carolina	335,314	259,084	323,322	257,863	265,301	237,440	200,919	214,196	149,336	196,255	108,895	140,178
Georgia	283,697	407,695	220,017	296,806	151,419	189,570	107,019	145,414	60,425	102,261	29,662	52,886
Florida	26,534	27,943	16,345	18,385								
EAST SOUTH CENTRAL:												
Kentucky	189,575	590,253	170,130	517,787	129,491	434,826	82,274	324,237	41,082	179,873	12,544	61,133
Tennessee	188,583	640,627	146,158	535,746	82,844	339,979	45,852	215,875	13,893	91,709	3,778	31,913
Alabama	255,571	335,185	119,121	190,406	42,450	85,451						
Mississippi	196,577	179,074	66,178	70,443	33,272	42,176	17,328	23,024	3,671	5,179		
WEST SOUTH CENTRAL:												
Arkansas	20,400	77,174	4,717	25,671	1,676	12,597						
Louisiana	193,954	158,457	126,298	89,441	79,540	73,867	42,245	34,311				
Oklahoma [1]												
Texas												
MOUNTAIN:												
Montana												
Idaho												
Wyoming												
Colorado												
New Mexico												
Arizona												
Utah												
Nevada												
PACIFIC:												
Washington												
Oregon												
California												

[1] Includes Indian Territory for 1900 and 1890.

CHAPTER IV.—PROPORTION NEGRO IN THE POPULATION AT EACH CENSUS, BY STATES: 1790-1910.

PERCENTAGE DISTRIBUTION, BY RACIAL CLASSES, FOR SECTIONS AND DIVISIONS: 1910.

The percentage distribution of the population of divisions and sections in 1910, by racial classes, is shown in Table 1.

Table 1 — PERCENTAGE IN EACH CLASS OF POPULATION: 1910.

| SECTION AND DIVISION. | All classes. | Negro. | White. | | | Indian. | Chinese, Japanese, and all other. |
			Total.	Native.	Foreign born.		
United States........	100.0	10.7	88.9	74.4	14.5	0.3	0.2
The South.................	100.0	29.8	69.9	67.4	2.5	0.3	(1)
South Atlantic.........	100.0	33.7	66.2	63.8	2.4	0.1	(1)
East South Central.....	100.0	31.5	68.4	67.4	1.0	(1)	(1)
West South Central.....	100.0	22.6	76.5	72.5	4.0	0.9	(1)
The North.................	100.0	1.8	98.0	77.7	20.3	0.1	(1)
New England..........	100.0	1.0	98.9	71.2	27.7	(1)	0.1
Middle Atlantic........	100.0	2.2	97.7	72.8	25.0	(1)	0.1
East North Central.....	100.0	1.6	98.2	81.4	16.8	0.1	(1)
West North Central.....	100.0	2.1	97.5	83.7	13.9	0.4	(1)
The West.................	100.0	0.7	95.9	76.9	19.0	1.6	1.8
Mountain...............	100.0	0.8	95.7	79.1	16.6	2.9	0.6
Pacific.................	100.0	0.7	96.0	75.4	20.5	0.8	2.5

¹ Less than one-tenth of 1 per cent.

In the South, as a whole, 29.8 per cent of the total population in 1910 was Negro; in the North, 1.8 per cent; and in the West, 0.7. The proportion Negro was highest in the South Atlantic division, in which 33.7 per cent, or one-third of the population, was Negro. In the East South Central division the proportion was 31.5 per cent and in the West South Central, 22.6 per cent. The highest percentage in any northern or western division was 2.2, the lowest 0.7, these being the percentages for the Middle Atlantic and the Pacific divisions, respectively.

From these proportions it will be apparent that the Negro population is a much larger factor in the total population of the South Atlantic and East South Central states than it is in the West South Central states, and that in the North and West as a whole this class of the population is numerically relatively unimportant. It will be found, however, by reference to state tables (see, for example, Table 5, p. 51) that the proportion Negro in the population of certain Northern and Western states approaches the proportion in some Southern states much more nearly than the average for any

northern division approaches that for any southern division.

The Negro and white population combined constituted, in 1910, 99.7 per cent of the total population of the South, 99.8 per cent of the total population of the North, and 96.6 per cent of the total population of the West.

PERCENTAGE NEGRO, AND NEGROES TO 1,000 WHITES, BY SECTIONS AND DIVISIONS: 1790–1910.

In Table 2 the percentage Negro in the total population and the number of Negroes per 1,000 whites, at each census 1790–1910, is given by sections and southern divisions.

Table 2 — UNITED STATES.

| YEAR. | Total. | The South. | | | | The North. | The West. |
		Total.	South Atlantic division.	East South Central division.	West South Central division.		
			PERCENTAGE NEGRO IN THE POPULATION.				
1910...............	10.7	29.8	33.7	31.5	22.6	1.8	0.7
1900...............	11.6	32.3	35.7	33.1	25.9	1.9	0.7
1890...............	11.9	33.8	36.8	33.0	29.1	1.8	0.9
1880...............	13.1	36.0	38.7	34.5	32.6	1.9	0.7
1870...............	12.7	36.0	37.9	33.2	36.4	1.8	0.6
1860...............	14.1	36.8	38.4	34.7	36.9	1.7	0.7
1850...............	15.7	37.3	39.8	33.4	39.2	2.0	0.7
1840...............	16.8	38.0	40.7	32.2	47.6	2.3	....
1830...............	18.1	37.9	41.9	27.6	53.2	2.3	....
1820...............	18.4	37.2	41.6	24.2	48.4	2.5	....
1810...............	19.0	36.7	40.4	20.5	54.4	2.9	....
1800...............	18.9	35.0	37.6	17.5	....	3.1	....
1790...............	19.3	35.2	36.4	14.9	....	3.4	....
			NUMBER OF NEGROES PER 1,000 WHITES.				
1910...............	120	426	510	461	295	19	8
1900...............	132	480	556	496	355	19	8
1890...............	136	512	583	492	418	18	9
1880...............	152	564	632	526	485	20	7
1870...............	145	562	610	498	574	18	7
1860...............	165	582	623	531	585	18	8
1850...............	186	595	660	501	645	21	7
1840...............	203	613	686	476	910	23	....
1830...............	221	610	723	382	1,138	24	....
1820...............	225	592	712	319	939	25	....
1810...............	235	579	678	258	1,231	30	....
1800...............	233	539	603	212	....	32	....
1790...............	239	543	572	175	....	35	....

The percentage Negro in the total population of the South was lower in 1910 than at any preceding census. Making allowance for the omissions of 1870, the proportion Negro in the population of the South decreased, in each of the seven decades 1840–1910, from 38 per cent in 1840 to 29.8 per cent in 1910. In the period preceding 1840 the proportion increased in each of the four decades 1800–1840 from 35 per cent to 38 per cent, the proportion for 1790, 35.2 per cent, being slightly higher than that for 1800.

At each census the percentage Negro in the population of the South Atlantic division exceeded that in the population of the South, as a whole. In this division the percentage increased from 36.4 in 1790 to 41.9 in 1830 and fell off in subsequent decades to 33.7 in 1910. In the East South Central division the percentage increased from 14.9 in 1790 to 34.7 in 1860 and declined to 31.5 in 1910. In the West South Central division the decline in the proportion has been continuous since 1810, except for an increase in the decade 1820–1830.

In the North the proportion Negro in the population has not changed materially since 1850, and it has not at any census since that date amounted to so much as 2 per cent. In this section the percentage declined from 3.4 in 1790 to 2 in 1850. At no census has the proportion in the West amounted to more than a fraction of 1 per cent.

PERCENTAGE NEGRO IN THE POPULATION, BY STATES: 1910.

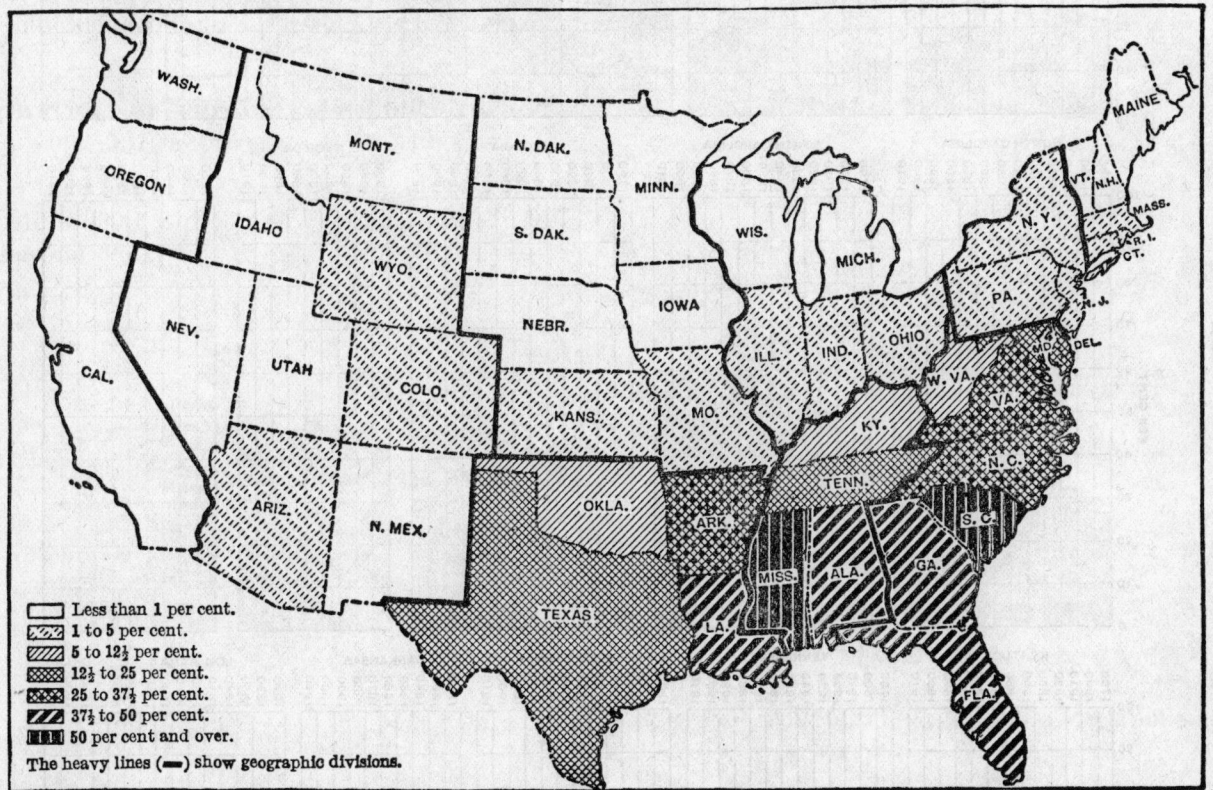

The number of Negroes per 1,000 whites in the population of the South, as a whole, was 543 in 1790, it was 613 in 1840, and fell off in subsequent decades to 426 in 1910. In the population of the South Atlantic division there were 572 Negroes per 1,000 whites in 1790. The proportion rose to 723 in 1830 and declined to 510 in 1910. In the East South Central division the proportion rose from 175 per 1,000 in 1790 to 531 per 1,000 in 1860 and declined to 461 in 1910. At two of the earlier censuses the number of Negroes in the East South Central division exceeded the number of whites. The proportion for 1810 of 1,231 Negroes to 1,000 whites in this section is, however, in fact, the proportion for Louisiana, the only state or territory in the section for which returns of population were made in this year. At the following census returns were made from Arkansas and in 1850 from Texas. In these states and in Oklahoma the growth of the white population has been exceptionally rapid, and the decrease in the proportion of Negroes to whites has been more marked than in either of the other two southern divisions.

In the North the number of Negroes per 1,000 whites was 35 in 1790 and 19 in 1910. In the West it has not at any census exceeded 9 to 1,000. In no northern or western division did the proportion of Negroes to whites in the population in 1910 exceed 22 to 1,000, the lowest proportion among the southern divisions being that for the West South Central division, of 295 per 1,000.

DIAGRAM **I.**—PERCENTAGE NEGRO IN THE POPULATION OF THE SOUTHERN STATES AT EACH
CENSUS: 1790–1910.

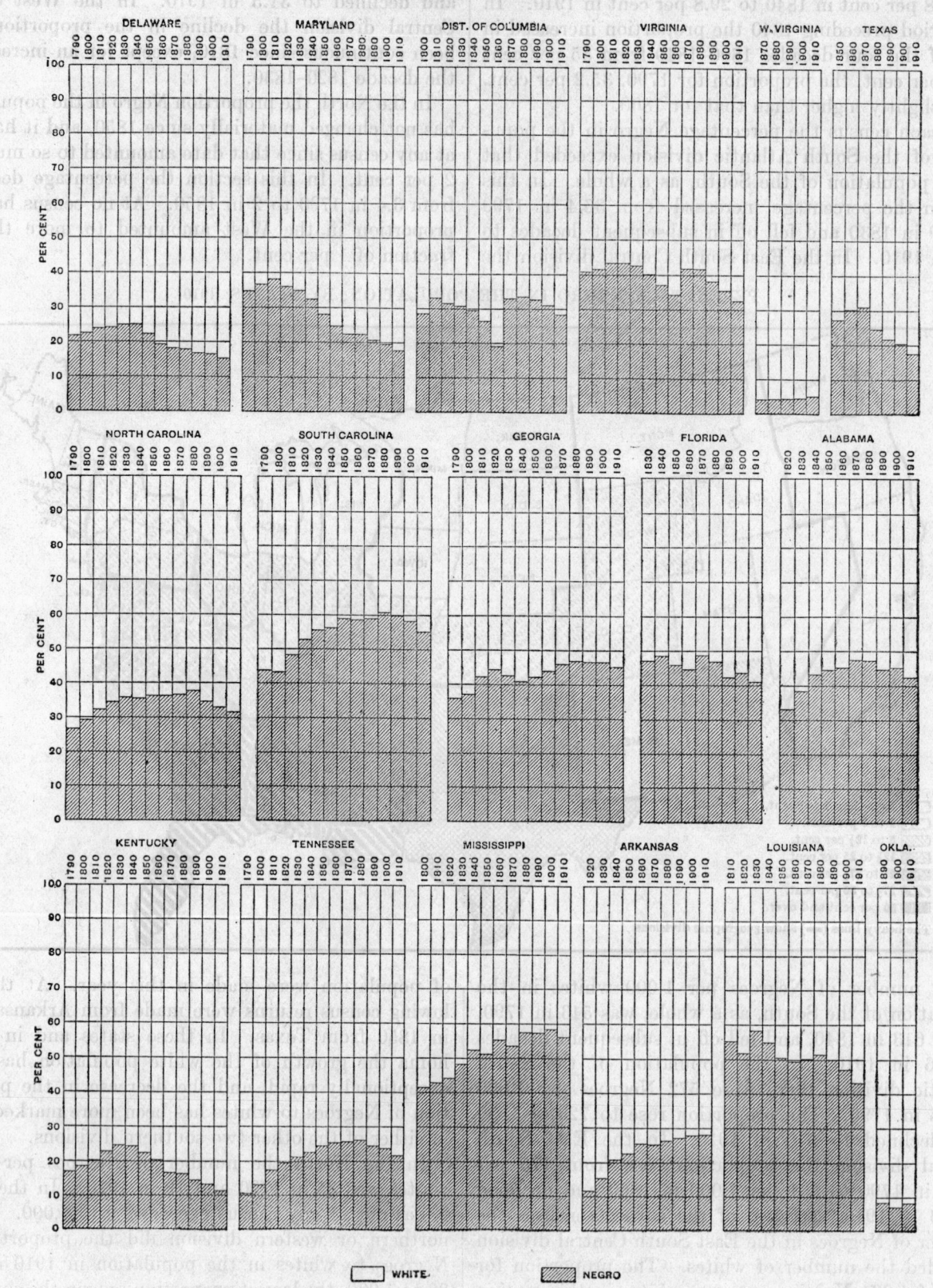

PERCENTAGE NEGRO AT EACH CENSUS, BY STATES: 1790–1910.

The percentage Negro in the population at each census 1790–1910 is given, for divisions and states, in Table 5. For states, in 1910, the percentage Negro in the population is presented graphically by the map on page 47, and for each of the Southern states at each census 1790–1910 by the diagram on page 48.

In Table 3 the percentage Negro in the population of the states is given, the states being ranged in order according to this percentage, and the Negro and white population cumulated by states.

The percentage Negro in the population of the Southern states in 1910 ranged from 5.3 per cent in West Virginia to 56.2 per cent in Mississippi. The second highest percentage was that for South Carolina, in which state the percentage had declined during three decades from 60.7 in 1880—the maximum percentage shown for any state at any census in the period from 1790 to 1910—to 55.2 per cent in 1910.

NEGROES TO 100,000 WHITES AT EACH CENSUS, BY STATES: 1790–1910.

The number of Negroes per 100,000 whites at each census, 1790 to 1910, is given in Table 6, by divisions and states, the proportions shown in this table being derived from the populations given in Table 13 of Chapter III.

In 1910 the Negro population exceeded the white population in two states, namely, South Carolina and Mississippi. The number of Negroes to 100,000 whites was 123,070 in South Carolina and 128,415 in Mississippi. In South Carolina the Negro population has exceeded the white at each census, beginning with that of 1820, in which year the number of Negroes to 100,000 whites was 111,734. In the 60 years, 1820 to 1880, the proportion of Negroes to whites in the population of this state increased continuously from census to census, except for a slight decline in the decade 1850–1860, the number of Negroes to 100,000 whites in 1880 being 154,519. At each census since 1880 the proportion has declined. In Mississippi Negroes have constituted a majority of the population at each census, beginning with that of 1840. In the period of 60 years, 1840 to 1900, the proportion advanced with some fluctuation from 109,774 to 141,552. In Louisiana the proportion in 1830 was 141,208; it declined to 98,018 in 1860; increased to 106,309 in 1880; and decreased to 75,856 in 1910.

The proportion of Negroes to whites increased during the decade 1900–1910 in 20 states—3 Southern and 17 Northern or Western—it decreased in 28 states—13 Southern and 15 Northern or Western, and in the District of Columbia. Considered by states, the proportion of Negroes to whites in the South decreased generally during this decade, except in West Virginia, Arkansas, and Oklahoma. In partial explanation of these decreases in Southern states and of the increases in Northern states, it may be noted that there has been in recent decades some net migration of Negroes out of the South into the North, and some net migration of whites, native and foreign born, into the South. Interstate migration of both Negroes and whites within the South, as well as between the South and other sections of the country, is undoubtedly an important factor underneath changes in the proportion of Negroes to whites in the population of the several states.

STATE.	Percentage Negro.	Negro.			White.		
		Number.	Cumulated by states.		Number.	Cumulated by states.	
			Number.	Per cent.		Number.	Per cent.
Mississippi	56.2	1,009,487	1,009,487	10.3	786,111	786,111	1.0
South Carolina	55.2	835,843	1,845,330	18.8	679,161	1,465,272	1.8
Georgia	45.1	1,176,987	3,022,317	30.8	1,431,802	2,897,074	3.5
Louisiana	43.1	713,874	3,736,191	38.0	3,838,160	3,838,160	4.7
Alabama	42.5	908,282	4,644,473	47.3	1,228,832	5,066,992	6.2
Florida	41.0	308,669	4,953,142	50.4	443,634	5,510,626	6.7
Virginia	32.6	671,096	5,624,238	57.2	1,389,809	6,900,435	8.4
North Carolina	31.6	697,843	6,322,081	64.3	1,500,511	8,400,946	10.3
Dist. Columbia	28.5	94,446	6,416,527	65.3	236,128	8,637,074	10.6
Arkansas	28.1	442,891	6,859,418	69.8	1,131,026	9,768,100	12.0
Tennessee	21.7	473,088	7,332,506	74.6	1,711,432	11,479,532	14.0
Maryland	17.9	232,250	7,564,756	77.0	1,062,639	12,542,171	15.3
Texas	17.7	690,049	8,254,805	84.0	3,204,848	15,747,019	19.3
Delaware	15.4	31,181	8,285,986	84.3	171,102	15,918,121	19.5
Kentucky	11.4	261,656	8,547,642	87.0	2,027,951	17,946,072	22.0
Oklahoma	8.3	137,612	8,685,254	88.4	1,444,531	19,390,603	23.7
West Virginia	5.3	64,173	8,749,427	89.0	1,156,817	20,547,420	25.1
Missouri	4.8	157,452	8,906,879	90.6	3,134,932	23,682,352	29.0
New Jersey	3.5	89,760	8,996,639	91.5	2,445,894	26,128,246	32.0
Kansas	3.2	54,030	9,050,669	92.1	1,634,352	27,762,598	34.0
Pennsylvania	2.5	193,919	9,244,588	94.1	7,467,713	35,230,311	43.1
Ohio	2.3	111,452	9,356,040	95.2	4,654,897	39,885,208	48.8
Indiana	2.2	60,320	9,416,360	95.8	2,639,961	42,525,169	52.0
Illinois	1.9	109,049	9,525,409	96.9	5,526,962	48,052,131	58.8
Rhode Island	1.8	9,529	9,534,938	97.0	532,492	48,584,623	59.4
New York	1.5	134,191	9,669,129	98.4	8,966,845	57,551,468	70.4
Wyoming	1.5	2,235	9,671,364	98.4	140,318	57,691,786	70.6
Colorado	1.4	11,453	9,682,817	98.5	783,415	58,475,201	71.5
Connecticut	1.4	15,174	9,697,991	98.7	1,098,897	59,574,098	72.9
Massachusetts	1.1	38,055	9,736,046	99.1	3,324,926	62,899,024	77.0
Arizona	1.0	2,009	9,738,055	99.1	171,468	63,070,492	77.2
California	0.9	21,645	9,759,700	99.3	2,259,672	65,330,164	79.9
Iowa	0.7	14,973	9,774,673	99.5	2,209,191	67,539,355	82.6
Michigan	0.6	17,115	9,791,788	99.6	2,785,247	70,324,602	86.0
Nebraska	0.6	7,689	9,799,477	99.7	1,180,293	71,504,895	87.5
Nevada	0.6	513	9,799,990	99.7	74,276	71,579,171	87.6
Montana	0.5	1,834	9,801,824	99.7	360,580	71,939,751	88.0
New Mexico	0.5	1,628	9,803,452	99.8	304,594	72,244,345	88.4
Vermont	0.5	1,621	9,805,073	99.8	354,298	72,598,643	88.8
Washington	0.5	6,058	9,811,131	99.8	1,109,111	73,707,754	90.2
Minnesota	0.3	7,084	9,818,215	99.9	2,059,227	75,766,981	92.7
Utah	0.3	1,144	9,819,359	99.9	366,583	76,133,564	93.2
Idaho	0.2	651	9,820,010	99.9	319,221	76,452,785	93.5
Maine	0.2	1,363	9,821,373	99.9	739,995	77,192,780	94.4
Oregon	0.2	1,492	9,822,865	100.0	655,090	77,847,870	95.2
New Hampshire	0.1	564	9,823,429	100.0	429,906	78,277,776	95.8
North Dakota	0.1	617	9,824,046	100.0	569,855	78,847,631	96.5
South Dakota	0.1	817	9,824,863	100.0	563,771	79,411,402	97.2
Wisconsin	0.1	2,900	9,827,763	100.0	2,320,555	81,731,957	100.0

More than one-half of the Negro population lived in states in which the proportion Negro in the population exceeded 40 per cent. These states reported only 6.7 per cent of the white population.

Among the Southern states the proportion of Negroes to whites was lowest in West Virginia—5,547 Negroes to 100,000 whites—and highest in Mississippi—128,415. Among Northern and Western states it was highest in Missouri—5,022—whose proportion approached nearly to that of West Virginia. In 18 Northern and Western states the number of Negroes to 100,000 whites was less than 1,000, and in 10 of these states it was less than 500.

The Negro and white populations of the states in 1910 are classified in Table 4 with reference to the proportion of Negroes to whites in their populations.

NEGRO AND WHITE POPULATION OF STATES CLASSIFIED ACCORDING TO NUMBER OF NEGROES PER 100,000 WHITES: 1910 AND 1900.

Table 4 — STATES HAVING SPECIFIED NUMBER OF NEGROES TO 100,000 WHITES IN THE POPULATION.

NEGROES TO 100,000 WHITES.	Number of states.		Population.				Percentage distribution.			
			1910		1900		1910		1900	
	1910	1900	Negro.	White.	Negro.	White.	Negro.	White.	Negro.	White.
Total	49	49	9,827,763	81,731,957	8,833,994	66,809,196	100.0	100.0	100.0	100.0
Under 1,000	18	18	89,708	18,661,465	64,733	14,769,385	0.9	22.8	0.7	22.1
1,000 to 5,000	13	14	831,176	39,388,140	728,557	33,488,231	8.5	48.2	8.2	50.1
5,000 to 10,000	3	2	359,237	5,736,280	216,918	3,615,047	3.7	7.0	2.5	5.4
10,000 to 20,000	2	2	292,837	2,199,053	315,403	2,016,286	3.0	2.7	3.6	3.0
20,000 to 30,000	3	2	1,395,387	5,978,919	855,786	3,379,093	14.2	7.3	9.7	5.1
30,000 to 40,000	2	2	537,337	1,367,154	847,099	2,484,766	5.5	1.7	9.6	3.7
40,000 to 50,000	2	2	1,368,939	2,890,320	711,171	1,455,135	13.9	3.5	8.1	2.2
50,000 to 75,000	2	1	1,216,951	1,672,466	660,722	1,192,855	12.4	2.0	7.5	1.8
75,000 to 100,000	2	4	1,890,861	2,372,888	2,743,654	3,209,391	19.2	2.9	31.1	4.8
100,000 and over	2	2	1,845,330	1,465,272	1,689,951	1,199,007	18.8	1.8	19.1	1.8
Total	49	49	9,827,763	81,731,957	8,833,994	66,809,196	100.0	100.0	100.0	100.0
Under 1,000	18	18	89,708	18,661,465	64,733	14,769,385	0.9	22.8	0.7	22.1
1,000 or more	31	31	9,738,055	63,070,492	8,769,261	52,039,811	99.1	77.2	99.3	77.9
Under 5,000	31	32	920,884	58,049,605	793,290	48,257,616	9.4	71.0	9.0	72.2
5,000 or more	18	17	8,906,879	23,682,352	8,040,704	18,551,580	90.6	29.0	91.0	27.8
Under 10,000	34	34	1,280,121	63,785,885	1,010,208	51,872,663	13.0	78.0	11.4	77.6
10,000 or more	15	15	8,547,642	17,946,072	7,823,786	14,936,533	87.0	22.0	88.6	22.4
Under 20,000	36	36	1,572,958	65,984,938	1,325,611	53,888,949	16.0	80.7	15.0	80.7
20,000 or more	13	13	8,254,805	15,747,019	7,508,383	12,920,247	84.0	19.3	85.0	19.3
Under 30,000	39	38	2,968,345	71,963,857	2,181,397	57,268,042	30.2	88.0	24.7	85.7
30,000 or more	10	11	6,859,418	9,768,100	6,652,597	9,541,154	69.8	12.0	75.3	14.3
Under 40,000	41	40	3,505,682	73,331,011	3,028,496	59,752,808	35.7	89.7	34.3	89.4
40,000 or more	8	9	6,322,081	8,400,946	5,805,498	7,056,388	64.3	10.3	65.7	10.6
Under 50,000	43	42	4,874,621	76,221,331	3,739,667	61,207,943	49.6	93.3	42.3	91.6
50,000 or more	6	7	4,953,142	5,510,626	5,094,327	5,601,253	50.4	6.7	57.7	8.4
Under 75,000	45	43	6,091,572	77,893,797	4,400,389	62,400,798	62.0	95.3	49.8	93.4
75,000 or more	4	6	3,736,191	3,838,160	4,433,605	4,408,398	38.0	4.7	50.2	6.6
Under 100,000	47	47	7,982,433	80,266,685	7,144,043	65,610,189	81.2	98.2	80.9	98.2
100,000 or more	2	2	1,845,330	1,465,272	1,689,951	1,199,007	18.8	1.8	19.1	1.8

Of the total Negro population, 18.8 per cent, or nearly one-fifth, in 1910 was living in the 2 states in which the number of Negroes to 100,000 whites in the population exceeded 100,000. These states reported 1.8 per cent, or less than one-fiftieth of the white population. One-half, or 50.4 per cent, of the Negro population in 1910 was living in the 6 states in which the number of Negroes per 100,000 whites exceeded 50,000. The aggregate Negro population of these 6 states in 1910 was 4,953,142, which slightly exceeded the Negro population of the 42 states and the District of Columbia, in which a lower proportion of Negroes to whites prevailed. The aggregate white population of these two groups of states was 5,510,626 and 76,221,331, respectively. Of the white population in 1910, 22.8 per cent, or more than one-fifth, lived in the 18 states in which the number of Negroes per 100,000 whites was less than 1,000. Less than 1 per cent of the Negro population lived in these states. It may be noted that in 1900, 50.2 per cent, or one-half of the Negro population, was living in the 6 states in which the number of Negroes to 100,000 whites exceeded 75,000.

TABLE 5.—PERCENTAGE NEGRO IN THE POPULATION AT EACH CENSUS, BY DIVISIONS AND STATES: 1790–1910.

DIVISION AND STATE.	PERCENTAGE NEGRO IN THE POPULATION.												
	1910	1900	1890	1880	1870	1860	1850	1840	1830	1820	1810	1800	1790
UNITED STATES	10.7	11.6	11.9	13.1	12.7	14.1	15.7	16.8	18.1	18.4	19.0	18.9	19.3
GEOGRAPHIC DIVISIONS:													
New England	1.0	1.1	0.9	1.0	0.9	0.8	0.8	1.0	1.1	1.3	1.4	1.5	1.7
Middle Atlantic	2.2	2.1	1.8	1.8	1.7	0.8	2.1	2.6	2.9	3.3	4.1	4.6	5.3
East North Central	1.6	1.6	1.6	1.6	1.4	0.9	1.0	1.0	1.1	1.0	1.3	1.2	
West North Central	2.1	2.3	2.5	3.3	3.7	5.6	10.3	14.1	18.3	15.9	17.4		
South Atlantic	33.7	35.7	36.8	38.7	37.9	38.4	39.8	40.7	41.9	41.6	40.4	37.6	36.4
East South Central	31.5	33.1	33.0	34.5	33.2	34.7	33.4	32.2	27.6	24.2	20.5	17.5	14.9
West South Central	22.6	25.9	29.1	32.6	36.4	36.9	39.2	47.6	53.2	48.4	54.4		
Mountain	0.8	0.9	1.1	0.8	0.5	0.1	0.1						
Pacific	0.7	0.6	0.7	0.6	0.7	1.0	1.1						
NEW ENGLAND:													
Maine	0.2	0.2	0.2	0.2	0.2	0.2	0.2	0.3	0.3	0.3	0.4	0.5	0.6
New Hampshire	0.1	0.2	0.2	0.2	0.2	0.2	0.2	0.2	0.2	0.3	0.5	0.5	0.6
Vermont	0.5	0.2	0.3	0.3	0.3	0.2	0.2	0.3	0.3	0.4	0.3	0.4	0.3
Massachusetts	1.1	1.2	1.0	1.1	1.0	0.8	0.9	1.2	1.2	1.3	1.4	1.5	1.4
Rhode Island	1.8	2.1	2.1	2.4	2.3	2.3	2.5	3.0	3.7	4.3	4.8	5.3	6.3
Connecticut	1.4	1.7	1.6	1.8	1.8	1.9	2.1	2.6	2.7	2.9	2.6	2.5	2.3
MIDDLE ATLANTIC:													
New York	1.5	1.4	1.2	1.3	1.2	1.3	1.6	2.1	2.3	2.9	4.2	5.3	7.6
New Jersey	3.5	3.7	3.3	3.4	3.4	3.8	4.9	5.8	6.4	7.2	7.6	8.0	7.7
Pennsylvania	2.5	2.5	2.1	2.0	1.9	2.0	2.3	2.8	2.8	2.9	2.9	2.7	2.4
EAST NORTH CENTRAL:													
Ohio	2.3	2.3	2.4	2.5	2.4	1.6	1.3	1.1	1.0	0.8	0.8	0.7	
Indiana	2.2	2.3	2.1	2.0	1.5	0.9	1.1	1.0	1.1	1.0	2.6	5.3	
Illinois	1.9	1.8	1.5	1.5	1.1	0.4	0.6	0.8	1.5	2.5	6.4		
Michigan	0.6	0.6	0.7	0.9	1.0	0.9	0.6	0.3	0.9	2.0	3.0		
Wisconsin	0.1	0.1	0.1	0.2	0.2	0.2	0.2	0.6					
WEST NORTH CENTRAL:													
Minnesota	0.3	0.3	0.3	0.2	0.2	0.1	0.6						
Iowa	0.7	0.6	0.6	0.6	0.5	0.2	0.2	0.4					
Missouri	4.8	5.2	5.6	6.7	6.9	10.0	13.2	15.6	18.3	15.9	17.4		
North Dakota	0.1	0.1	0.2	[1]0.3	[1]0.7								
South Dakota	0.1	0.1	0.2										
Nebraska	0.6	0.6	0.9	0.5	0.6	0.3							
Kansas	3.2	3.5	3.5	4.3	4.7	0.6							
SOUTH ATLANTIC:													
Delaware	15.4	16.6	16.9	18.0	18.2	19.3	22.2	25.0	24.9	24.0	23.8	22.4	21.6
Maryland	17.9	19.8	20.7	22.5	22.5	24.9	28.3	32.3	34.9	36.1	38.2	36.7	34.7
District of Columbia	28.5	31.1	32.8	33.6	33.0	19.1	26.6	29.9	30.8	31.6	33.1	28.6	
Virginia	32.6	35.7	38.4	41.8	41.9	34.4	37.1	40.2	42.7	43.4	43.4	41.6	40.9
West Virginia	5.3	4.5	4.3	4.2	4.1								
North Carolina	31.6	33.0	34.7	37.9	36.6	36.4	36.4	35.6	35.9	34.4	32.2	29.4	26.8
South Carolina	55.2	58.4	59.9	60.7	58.9	58.6	58.9	56.4	55.6	52.8	48.4	43.2	43.7
Georgia	45.1	46.7	46.7	47.0	46.0	44.0	42.4	41.0	42.6	44.4	42.4	37.1	35.9
Florida	41.0	43.6	42.4	47.0	48.8	44.6	46.0	48.7	47.1				
EAST SOUTH CENTRAL:													
Kentucky	11.4	13.3	14.4	16.5	16.8	20.4	22.5	24.3	24.7	22.9	20.2	18.6	17.0
Tennessee	21.7	23.8	24.4	26.2	25.6	25.5	24.5	22.7	21.4	19.6	17.5	13.2	10.6
Alabama	42.5	45.2	44.8	47.5	47.7	45.4	44.7	43.3	38.5	33.2			
Mississippi	56.2	58.5	57.6	57.5	53.7	55.3	51.2	52.3	48.4	44.1	42.9	41.5	
WEST SOUTH CENTRAL:													
Arkansas	28.1	28.0	27.4	26.3	25.2	25.6	22.7	20.9	15.5	11.7			
Louisiana	43.1	47.1	50.0	51.5	50.1	49.5	50.7	55.0	58.5	51.8	55.2		
Oklahoma	8.3	[2]7.0	[2]8.4										
Texas	17.7	20.4	21.8	24.7	31.0	30.3	27.5						
MOUNTAIN:													
Montana	0.5	0.6	1.1	0.9	0.9								
Idaho	0.2	0.2	0.2	0.1	0.4								
Wyoming	1.5	1.0	1.5	1.4	2.0								
Colorado	1.4	1.6	1.5	1.3	1.1	0.1							
New Mexico	0.5	0.8	1.2	0.9	0.2	0.1	(3)						
Arizona	1.0	1.5	1.5	0.4	0.3								
Utah	0.3	0.2	0.3	0.2	0.1	0.2	0.4						
Nevada	0.6	0.3	0.5	0.8	0.8	0.7							
PACIFIC:													
Washington	0.5	0.5	0.5	0.4	0.9	0.2							
Oregon	0.2	0.3	0.4	0.3	0.4	0.3	1.6						
California	0.9	0.7	0.9	0.7	0.8	1.1	1.0						

[1] Dakota Territory. [2] Includes population of Indian Territory for 1900 and 1890. [3] Less than one-tenth of 1 per cent.

TABLE 6.—NUMBER OF NEGROES TO 100,000 WHITES, AT EACH CENSUS, BY DIVISIONS AND STATES: 1790 TO 1910.

DIVISION AND STATE.	NUMBER OF NEGROES TO 100,000 WHITES.												
	1910	1900	1890	1880	1870	1860	1850	1840	1830	1820	1810	1800	1790
UNITED STATES	12,024	13,223	13,591	15,162	14,528	16,499	18,610	20,252	22,110	22,521	23,504	23,268	23,872
GEOGRAPHIC DIVISIONS:													
New England	1,023	1,069	958	1,006	918	794	851	1,024	1,106	1,277	1,371	1,536	1,712
Middle Atlantic	2,213	2,157	1,807	1,839	1,709	1,792	2,196	2,716	2,980	3,440	4,261	4,814	5,554
East North Central	1,678	1,641	1,562	1,665	1,452	929	1,009	1,014	1,092	980	1,285	1,261	
West North Central	2,138	2,364	2,588	3,401	3,842	5,896	11,446	16,358	22,353	18,867	21,002		
South Atlantic	50,950	55,607	58,344	63,196	60,978	62,273	66,030	68,614	72,256	71,233	67,800	60,253	57,153
East South Central	46,096	49,553	49,233	52,630	49,820	53,091	50,114	47,578	38,161	31,920	25,829	21,190	17,542
West South Central	29,524	35,507	41,816	48,478	57,403	58,463	64,462	90,970	113,815	93,930	123,124		
Mountain	852	987	1,161	817	515	143	99						
Pacific	726	639	804	685	793	1,098	1,116						
NEW ENGLAND:													
Maine	184	191	181	224	257	212	233	271	299	312	425	542	560
New Hampshire	131	161	163	198	183	152	164	189	226	323	454	470	558
Vermont	458	241	283	319	280	226	229	251	315	384	345	362	318
Massachusetts	1,144	1,154	1,000	1,060	966	786	920	1,189	1,168	1,305	1,448	1,549	1,463
Rhode Island	1,790	2,170	2,188	2,404	2,347	2,316	2,551	3,071	3,822	4,533	5,077	5,630	6,755
Connecticut	1,381	1,706	1,677	1,891	1,833	1,911	2,119	2,691	2,787	2,981	2,650	2,567	2,398
MIDDLE ATLANTIC:													
New York	1,497	1,387	1,183	1,298	1,203	1,279	1,610	2,103	2,399	2,952	4,392	5,616	8,270
New Jersey	3,670	3,854	3,411	3,558	3,502	3,918	5,166	6,177	6,846	7,772	8,240	8,658	8,346
Pennsylvania	2,597	2,554	2,090	2,038	1,889	1,999	2,375	2,859	2,926	2,984	2,960	2,776	2,423
EAST NORTH CENTRAL:													
Ohio	2,394	2,387	2,430	2,563	2,429	1,593	1,293	1,155	1,031	819	830	748	
Indiana	2,285	2,339	2,106	2,023	1,483	854	1,153	1,056	1,070	974	2,637	5,577	
Illinois	1,973	1,797	1,513	1,530	1,145	448	643	832	1,537	2,552	6,791		
Michigan	614	659	734	935	1,015	924	654	334	935	1,995	3,118		
Wisconsin	125	124	145	206	201	151	208	637					
WEST NORTH CENTRAL:													
Minnesota	344	285	284	201	173	153	646						
Iowa	678	572	562	589	485	159	174	438					
Missouri	5,022	5,475	5,940	7,185	7,365	11,143	15,209	18,467	22,353	18,867	21,002		
North Dakota	108	92	204	[1] 301	[1] 729								
South Dakota	145	122	165										
Nebraska	651	593	851	530	646	286							
Kansas	3,306	3,672	3,611	4,527	4,939	589							
SOUTH ATLANTIC:													
Delaware	18,224	19,936	20,266	22,006	22,299	23,874	28,612	33,340	33,241	31,596	31,273	28,928	27,610
Maryland	21,856	24,681	26,093	29,010	28,966	33,170	39,501	47,710	53,565	56,539	61,854	57,886	53,237
District of Columbia	39,998	45,268	48,852	50,503	49,167	23,560	36,230	42,584	44,520	46,100	49,406	40,006	
Virginia	48,287	55,390	62,290	71,705	72,019	52,412	58,880	67,321	74,479	76,580	76,714	71,152	69,098
West Virginia	5,547	4,753	4,478	4,369	4,240								
North Carolina	46,507	49,420	53,158	61,261	57,725	57,390	57,142	55,386	56,074	52,392	47,578	41,549	36,622
South Carolina	123,070	140,249	149,117	154,519	143,549	141,545	143,480	129,423	125,385	111,734	93,801	76,093	77,683
Georgia	82,203	87,600	87,781	88,766	85,322	78,725	73,741	69,586	74,128	79,875	73,596	59,089	56,087
Florida	69,577	77,600	73,875	88,840	95,453	80,618	85,253	94,958	88,904				
EAST SOUTH CENTRAL:													
Kentucky	12,902	15,288	16,855	19,711	20,225	25,685	29,024	32,118	32,857	29,780	25,375	22,839	20,519
Tennessee	27,643	31,181	32,221	35,400	34,433	34,234	32,488	29,437	27,281	24,367	21,240	15,149	11,838
Alabama	73,914	82,636	81,381	90,625	91,201	83,183	80,914	76,248	62,562	49,678			
Mississippi	128,415	141,552	136,287	135,647	116,011	123,596	105,103	109,774	93,945	78,888	75,261	70,882	
WEST SOUTH CENTRAL:													
Arkansas	39,158	38,838	37,755	35,614	33,738	34,324	29,415	26,434	18,375	13,305			
Louisiana	75,856	89,199	100,143	106,309	100,592	98,018	102,654	122,402	141,208	107,680	123,124		
Oklahoma [2]	9,526	8,309	12,523										
Texas	21,531	25,579	27,960	32,858	44,887	43,460	38,016						
MOUNTAIN:													
Montana	509	673	1,167	978	1,000								
Idaho	204	190	245	183	565								
Wyoming	1,593	1,056	1,554	1,533	2,097								
Colorado	1,462	1,620	1,536	1,274	1,163	134							
New Mexico	534	893	1,369	934	190	103	36						
Arizona	1,172	1,989	2,435	441	271								
Utah	312	247	286	163	137	147	441						
Nevada	691	378	619	911	916	661							
PACIFIC:													
Washington	546	507	470	484	933	269							
Oregon	228	280	393	299	398	245	1,582						
California	958	787	1,018	784	855	1,264	1,050						

[1] Dakota Territory.   [2] Includes Indian Territory in 1900 and 1890.

CHAPTER V.—FREE COLORED AND SLAVE POPULATION: 1790-1860.

NUMBER AND INCREASE: 1790–1860.

Returns of free colored[1] persons and slaves were made at each decennial census from 1790 to 1860. This classification was essential to the observance of that article of the Constitution, which directed that representation in the House should be apportioned to the several states according to their population, including in the apportionment population all free persons except Indians not taxed, and "three-fifths of all other persons." In the first eight census reports data for the slave and for the free colored population were compiled in greater or less detail, the amount of detail shown for each class increasing from census to census, as the schedule inquiries and the compilations of the returns became more elaborate. At the censuses of 1850 and 1860, returns for the free colored were made in the same detail as for whites, a separate schedule carrying fewer inquiries than that pertaining to free persons being used in securing returns of slaves. With the abolition of slavery in the decade 1860–1870, the class of free persons came to embrace the entire Negro population, and at the census of 1870 the distinction relating to the status of the individual as being free or slave, which had characterized the returns of the Negro population at each preceding census, lapsed.

At the census of 1790 slaves were reported from all the states and territories enumerated with the exception of Vermont and Massachusetts—Maine being at that time a district of Massachusetts.

The number of free colored persons and slaves as returned at the first eight censuses is given, by states, in Table 6, on page 57. Tables 21 and 22 of Chapter XI, classify the free and slave population of divisions and states in 1860 and 1850, as black and mulatto, the distinction of sex being shown on the table for 1860.

For the country as a whole, the free and slave population at each census is given in Table 1 following, together with decennial increases.[2]

Table 1	NEGRO POPULATION.							
CENSUS YEAR.	Free.			Slave.	Decennial increase.			
	Total.	Number.	Per cent.		Number.		Per cent.	
					Free.	Slave.	Free.	Slave.
1860......	4,441,830	488,070	11.0	3,953,760	53,575	749,447	12.3	23.4
1850......	3,638,808	434,495	11.9	3,204,313	48,202	716,958	12.5	28.8
1840......	2,873,648	386,293	13.4	2,487,355	66,694	478,312	20.9	23.8
1830......	2,328,642	319,599	13.7	2,009,043	85,965	471,021	36.8	30.6
1820......	1,771,656	233,634	13.2	1,538,022	47,188	346,660	25.3	29.1
1810......	1,377,808	186,446	13.5	1,191,362	78,011	297,760	71.9	33.3
1800......	1,002,037	108,435	10.8	893,602	48,908	195,921	82.2	28.1
1790......	[1]757,181	59,557	7.9	697,624	......	......	......	......

[1] In other sections of this report and in census reports generally the total Negro population in 1790 is given as 757,208. The population given in Table 1 is taken from "A Century of Population Growth in the United States, 1790–1900," and is a revised figure.

The number of free colored persons increased in each decade of the period covered by Table 1. During the two decades 1790–1810 the rate of increase for this class exceeded that for slaves, and the proportion free

---

[1] In the earlier censuses the term "colored" is used to designate the Negro population.

[2] Slavery was introduced into the colonies in August, 1619, when African Negroes were brought to Jamestown by Dutch traders and sold to the planters of Virginia. At that time the sale of Africans who had been captured or purchased was sanctioned by the leading European nations and formed a very profitable business. The slave traders, taking advantage of the new field opened to them by the colonization of the coast of North America, introduced slavery into most of the colonies soon after they were founded. The only colony established with ordinances against this institution was Georgia; and this state also was soon forced, by social contact and business competition with the neighboring settlements, to legalize the holding of slaves.

The actual importations of slaves can only be estimated. Mr. Carey, author of a work on the slave trade, is the authority for the following estimate of the number of slaves imported:

PERIOD.	Number of slaves.	PERIOD.	Number of slaves.
Total..............	333,000	1751 to 1760..............	35,000
		1761 to 1770..............	74,000
Prior to 1715..............	30,000	1771 to 1790..............	34,000
1715 to 1750..............	90,000	1791 to 1808..............	70,000

It is claimed, however, that this total is too small, and that a closer estimate would bring the number to 370,000, or even 400,000. Mr.

Carey's figures indicate that the average annual importation was about 2,500 between 1715 and 1750 and 3,500 for the period from 1751 to 1760. The following decade was the period of greatest activity, the importation reaching an average of 7,400 a year. For the 20 years from 1771 to 1790 the average fell to 1,700, but for the period immediately preceding the legal abolition of the slave traffic in the United States it was more than double that number. By 1790 the survivors and descendants of the African slaves imported numbered 757,208, according to the Federal census of that year.

Early in the history of the Southern colonies the planters realized that slave labor could be utilized to good advantage in the cultivation of tobacco and some other crops. (The cotton crop, which later furnished an extensive field for slave labor, did not assume great importance until the invention of the cotton gin in 1793. After that date the employment of slaves in the cultivation of cotton became especially profitable, since this crop furnishes work for a considerable portion of the year and makes it possible to utilize to advantage the services of women and children.) At the beginning of the eighteenth century Negro slavery was considered by the settlers of all of the colonies as a usual and routine matter, and in the New England and Middle colonies, as well as in the South, the possession of slaves was generally accepted as an evidence of wealth and of importance in the community.

By 1750 Negro slavery was recognized by law in every North American colony. At the time of the Declaration of Independence the British possessions had local enactments protecting slave property and providing special codes and tribunals for slaves. Some of

in the Negro population accordingly rose, from 7.9 per cent in 1790, to 13.5 per cent in 1810. Although the Negro population more than doubled during the 30 years, 1810–1840, the proportion free in this population remained nearly constant. This proportion, however, fell off in each of the two decades 1840–1860, to 11.9 per cent in 1850, and to 11 per cent in 1860.

Of the total Negro increase during the decade 1790–1800, 20.8 per cent, or more than one-fifth, was in the free population, the proportion free in the increase of the decade following also being approximately one-fifth. In succeeding decades, free colored persons constituted a less considerable factor in the Negro increase, only 6.7 per cent, or one-fifteenth of the Negro increase in the decade 1850–1860, being in the free population.

The increase of the free colored population during this period of 70 years was in part a natural increase by excess of births over deaths among the free colored; in part, an increase by accessions from the class of slaves, through private or general-law manumission, purchase, and escape of slaves to free territory; and for several decades, in part, an increase by extension of the area of census enumeration. Only 7,011 free colored persons in 1860 were foreign born—3,700 or more than one-half of these being in the state of New York—and it seems probable from such data as are available that neither the net immigration nor the net emigration of free Negroes in the immediately preceding decades had been so considerable as materially to affect the rate of increase for this class.

The number of slaves manumitted during the year preceding the census of 1850, as returned on the census schedules, was 1,467; the number becoming fugitive in this year was 1,011; the number of manu-missions reported for 1860 was about 3,000, and the number becoming fugitive during that year, 803. The census of 1860 states that 20,000 manumissions "are believed to have occurred in the past 10 years."

The increase of the free colored population, although in this class natural growth was continuously supplemented by accessions from the slave population, was nevertheless insufficient in the decades immediately preceding the Civil War to produce a rate of growth equal to the natural increase of the Negro population as a whole. In the decade 1840 to 1850, the percentage increase of the slave population was more than double and in the decade following nearly double that of the free colored. The Compendium of the Seventh Census (1850) commented upon the "declining ratio of the increase of the free colored in every section," which in New England "is now almost nothing," and in the Southern states "only one-fourth as great as between 1800 and 1810." The report of 1860, also, noted that the rate of increase of the free colored had been gradually declining for several decades, "to 1860, when the increase throughout the United States was but 1 per cent per annum."

Census data do not very clearly account for this decline in the rate of increase of the free element in the Negro population, so far below the rate for the slave population, but it may be noted that, as compared with the slave population, the free colored were somewhat older, and on that account naturally subject to a higher mortality rate, and somewhat less normally distributed by sex, and, therefore, probably characterized by a marital condition less favorable to rapid natural increase. Among the free colored at each of the five censuses 1820 to 1860 there were fewer

---

the slave codes were extremely severe, because of the fear of Negro insurrections.

Although slavery became the presumptive status of every Negro, most of the colonies recognized the status of free Negroes. But the presence of a free Negro was believed to have an unfavorable influence on the slaves in the neighborhood, and hence many of the colonies made the conditions surrounding manumission so exacting that slave owners seldom took advantage of the legal right to free their slaves. There are, however, numerous instances of Negroes who were freed by their masters, and some cases of Negroes who were given their freedom by the state on account of some public service performed by them; but no data are available as to the aggregate number of slaves manumitted.

Free Negroes were allowed property rights, and, consequently, some of them became slave owners. Often a manumitted Negro would purchase the freedom of the members of his family or of friends, and unless he went through the formality of manumission these persons were legally his slaves.

*   *   *   *   *   *

The first petition against slavery recorded in American history was made in 1688, by Friends, in Germantown, Pa. The agitation against slavery was continued by other Quakers, by the Puritans, and by groups of individuals here and there. As the direct result of this movement, prohibitive duties on the importation of slaves were imposed by Pennsylvania in 1712, and also by other colonies from time to time. (In some colonies the duty on a slave brought from another colony was several times that on a slave imported directly from Africa or from the West Indies; the impression appears to have existed that slaves were sent from one colony to another because of undesirable qualities, or because they had committed crimes, and that the colony which deported them was taking this way of ridding itself of their presence.)

Since the slave trade was a source of revenue to British merchants, and even to the Crown, legislation against it was distasteful to the British Government, and objections were raised on account of the legislative action of the colonies. The governors sent to South Carolina in 1756 and 1761 bore instructions prohibiting the enactment of any law imposing duties on imported Negroes.

By 1778 legislative measures prohibiting the slave trade had been passed by all of the New England and Middle states, and by Maryland and Virginia; by 1798, similar action had been taken by every other state, although the trade was afterwards revived in South Carolina.

The first assumption of national control of the slave trade came in 1774, when the Continental Congress passed a resolution to abolish it. In 1789 the convention that framed the Constitution made plans for the abolition of this traffic in 1808, and later the first day of 1808 was chosen as the time when the slave trade should become illegal.

The first action against the ownership of slaves was taken by Vermont. In its Declaration of Rights, in 1777, this colony declared for the freedom of all persons at the age of maturity; a few years later it took a more definite stand, abolishing slavery outright. By 1783 slavery had been prohibited in Massachusetts and New Hampshire. Gradual emancipation was provided for in acts passed by Pennsylvania in 1780 and by Connecticut and Rhode Island in 1784. In 1787 slavery was forbidden in the Northwest Territory by congressional legislation, although the courts held that the ordinance did not free the slaves already held in the territory. By the date of the first Federal census laws providing for the extinction of slavery had been put into operation in all states north of Maryland, with the exception of New York and New Jersey.—A Century of Population Growth, pp. 36–37, Bureau of the Census: 1909.

males than females, while in the slave population, on the other hand, at each of these censuses the number of males exceeded the number of females. In 1850, however, the slave population of over 3,000,000 was so evenly divided by sex that the excess of males over females amounted to less than 1 in 4,000 population. In this year the sex ratio in the free colored population was 924 males to 1,000 females, the relative deficiency of males being practically confined to the population 15 years of age and over; in the slave population it was 1,000 males to 1,000 females; in 1860 the ratio was 922 males to 1,000 females in the free colored, and 1,006 males to 1,000 females in the slave population. The disparity of numbers between the sexes was thus in both years much greater in the free colored population.

DISTRIBUTION BY SECTIONS AND SOUTHERN DIVISIONS: 1790–1860.

In Table 2 the free colored and slave population at each census from 1790 to 1860 is given, by sections and southern divisions.

SLAVE AND FREE COLORED POPULATION AT EACH CENSUS BY SECTIONS AND SOUTHERN DIVISIONS: 1790–1860.

Table 2	NEGRO POPULATION.													
	Number.							Percentage distribution by area.						
CENSUS YEAR.		The South.				The North.	The West.		The South.				The North.	The West.
	United States.	Total.	South Atlantic division.	East South Central division.	West South Central division.			United States.	Total.	South Atlantic division.	East South Central division.	West South Central division.		
SLAVE.														
1860	3,953,760	3,838,765	1,840,445	1,372,913	625,407	114,966	29	100.0	97.1	46.5	34.7	15.8	2.9	(1)
1850	3,204,313	3,116,629	1,663,397	1,103,162	350,070	87,658	26	100.0	97.3	51.9	34.4	10.9	2.7	(1)
1840	2,487,355	2,427,986	1,425,539	814,060	188,387	59,369	....	100.0	97.6	57.3	32.7	7.6	2.4	....
1830	2,009,043	1,980,384	1,376,196	490,024	114,164	28,659	....	100.0	98.6	68.5	24.4	5.7	1.4	....
1820	1,538,022	1,508,692	1,156,479	281,532	70,681	29,330	....	100.0	98.1	75.2	18.3	4.6	1.9	....
1810	1,191,362	1,160,841	983,997	142,184	34,660	30,521	....	100.0	97.4	82.6	11.9	2.9	2.6	....
1800	893,602	857,097	799,681	57,416	....	36,505	....	100.0	95.9	89.5	6.4	....	4.1	....
1790	697,624	657,538	641,691	15,847	....	40,086	....	100.0	94.3	92.0	2.3	....	5.7	....
FREE.														
1860	488,070	258,346	217,753	21,447	19,146	225,274	4,450	100.0	52.9	44.6	4.4	3.9	46.2	0.9
1850	434,495	235,569	197,474	19,628	18,467	197,711	1,215	100.0	54.2	45.4	4.5	4.3	45.5	0.3
1840	386,293	213,991	171,778	16,246	25,967	172,302	....	100.0	55.4	44.5	4.2	6.7	44.6	....
1830	319,599	181,501	153,087	11,563	16,851	138,098	....	100.0	56.8	47.9	3.6	5.3	43.2	....
1820	233,634	133,980	116,920	6,525	10,535	99,654	....	100.0	57.3	50.0	2.8	4.5	42.7	....
1810	186,446	107,658	96,803	3,270	7,585	78,788	....	100.0	57.7	51.9	1.8	4.1	42.3	....
1800	108,435	61,239	60,009	1,230	....	47,196	....	100.0	56.5	55.3	1.1	....	43.5	....
1790	59,557	32,523	32,048	475	....	27,034	....	100.0	54.6	53.8	0.8	....	45.4	....

[1] Less than one-tenth of 1 per cent.

At the census of 1790, 92 per cent of the slave population was in the South Atlantic division; 2.3 per cent was in the East South Central division; and 5.7 per cent were in the North. At succeeding censuses the proportion in the South Atlantic division fell off, with the growth of population in the East South Central and West South Central divisions. In 1860, 46.5 per cent of the slave population was in the South Atlantic division; 34.7 per cent in the East South Central division; 15.8 per cent in the West South Central division; and 2.9 per cent in the North. The Northern and Western states reporting slaves in 1860, and the number of slaves reported were as follows: New Jersey, 18; Missouri, 114,931; Nebraska, 15; Kansas, 2; Utah, 29.

Of the free colored population in 1860, 46.2 per cent was in the North and 44.6 per cent in the South Atlantic division. The proportion in the East and West South Central divisions—4.4 and 3.9 per cent, respectively—was much smaller than the proportion of slaves in these divisions.

FREE AND SLAVE POPULATION OF FOUR CITIES: 1790.

The Negro population of New York, Philadelphia, Boston, and Baltimore in 1790 is classified as free and slave in Table 3.

Table 3	POPULATION: 1790.				
CITY.	Total.	Negro.			White.
		Total.	Free.	Slave.	
New York	32,305	3,262	1,078	2,184	29,043
Philadelphia	28,522	1,630	1,420	210	26,892
Boston	18,038	761	761	....	17,277
Baltimore	13,503	1,578	323	1,255	11,925

In 1790, of the 3,252 Negroes reported from New York City and constituting 10.1 per cent of the total population of the city, 2,184 were slaves and 1,078 free colored. Philadelphia reported in this year a Negro population of 1,630, the number of slaves being 210 and of free colored 1,420; Baltimore, a Negro population of 1,578, the number of slaves being 1,255, and of free colored 323; Boston, a Negro population of 761, all free. The slave population of New York City in 1790 exceeded that of Baltimore, and the proportion slave in the population of Baltimore was not materially greater than in that of New York City, being 9.3 in Baltimore, as compared with 6.8 per cent in New York City.

SLAVEHOLDING AND NONSLAVEHOLDING FAMILIES: 1790 AND 1850.

On the schedules of the census of 1790, which are in existence, there is reported a total of 5,161 free colored families, of which 195 are designated as slaveholding families.[1]

The following table gives a summary of the data available for 1790, as regards the number of slaveholding and of nonslaveholding families, in the free colored and the white population.

Table 4

PRIVATE FAMILIES: 1790.[1]

DIVISION AND STATE.	Free colored.			White.		
	Total number.	Slaveholding.	Nonslaveholding.	Total number.	Slaveholding.	Nonslaveholding.
Area covered by 1790 schedules in existence	5,161	195	4,966	405,475	47,664	357,811
New England	1,634	6	1,628	172,383	2,141	170,242
Maine	37	....	37	16,972	....	16,972
New Hampshire	83	....	83	23,982	123	23,859
Vermont	23	....	23	14,969	....	14,969
Massachusetts	630	....	630	65,149	....	65,149
Rhode Island	442	....	442	10,854	461	10,393
Connecticut	419	6	413	40,457	1,557	38,900
Middle states	1,245	16	1,229	127,507	9,638	117,869
New York	693	9	684	54,185	7,787	46,398
Pennsylvania	552	7	545	73,322	1,851	71,471
Southern states	2,282	173	2,109	105,585	35,885	69,700
Maryland [2]	1,282	84	1,198	32,012	12,142	19,870
North Carolina [3]	680	28	652	48,021	14,945	33,076
South Carolina	320	61	259	25,552	8,798	16,754

[1] Data not available for New Jersey, Delaware, Virginia, Georgia, Kentucky, or Southwest Territory.
[2] Data not available for Allegany, Calvert, or Somerset Counties.
[3] Data not available for Caswell, Granville, or Orange Counties, except the total number of families.

The average number of slaves per slaveholding family was 7.3 in 1790 and 9.2 in 1850. The number of slaveholding families and of slaves and the average number of slaves per slaveholding family are given in Table 5, by states, for these two years.

[1] Data are not available as to the number of free colored slaveholding families in the states of New Jersey, Delaware, Virginia, Georgia, Kentucky, or the Southwest Territory.

Table 5

DIVISION AND STATE.	NUMBER OF SLAVEHOLDING FAMILIES.		NUMBER OF SLAVES.		Average per slaveholding family.	
	1850	1790	1850	1790	1850	1790
United States	347,725	96,168	3,204,313	697,624	9.2	7.3
New England	....	2,147	....	3,763	....	1.8
Maine	....	....	....	....	....	....
New Hampshire	....	123	....	157	....	1.3
Vermont	....	....	....	....	....	....
Massachusetts	....	....	....	....	....	....
Rhode Island	....	461	....	958	....	2.1
Connecticut	....	1,563	....	2,648	....	1.7
Middle Atlantic	200	14,414	236	36,323	1.2	2.5
New York	....	7,796	....	21,193	....	2.7
New Jersey	200	[1] 4,760	236	11,423	1.2	2.4
Pennsylvania	....	1,858	....	3,707	....	2.0
South Atlantic	169,264	77,242	1,663,397	641,691	9.8	8.3
Delaware	809	[1] 1,851	2,290	8,887	2.8	4.8
Maryland	16,040	13,777	90,368	103,036	5.6	7.5
Dist. Columbia	1,477	....	3,687	....	2.5	....
Virginia [2]	55,063	[1] 34,026	472,528	292,627	8.6	8.5
North Carolina	28,303	16,310	288,548	100,783	10.2	6.7
South Carolina	25,596	8,859	384,984	107,094	15.0	12.1
Georgia	38,456	[1] 2,419	381,682	29,264	9.9	12.1
Florida	3,520	....	39,310	....	11.2	....
East South Central	124,660	2,365	1,103,162	15,847	8.8	6.7
Kentucky	38,385	[1] 1,855	210,981	12,430	5.5	6.7
Tennessee	33,864	[1] 510	239,459	3,417	7.1	6.7
Alabama	29,295	....	342,844	....	11.7	....
Mississippi	23,116	....	309,878	....	13.4	....
West South Central	34,416	....	350,070	....	10.2	....
Arkansas	5,999	....	47,100	....	7.9	....
Louisiana	20,670	....	244,809	....	11.8	....
Texas	7,747	....	58,161	....	7.5	....
West North Central	19,185	....	87,422	....	4.6	....
Missouri	19,185	....	87,422	....	4.6	....
Mountain	(3)	....	26	....	....	....
Utah	(3)	....	26	....	....	....

[1] Estimated.   [2] Includes area now West Virginia.   [3] Data not available.

The figures given for 1790 in Table 5 include estimates for certain areas for which data gathered in 1790 are not now available.

In the 60 years, 1790 to 1850, the number of slaveholding families in the United States increased from 96,168 to 347,725. At the First Census, New England reported 2,147 slaveholding families and the three Middle Atlantic states, 14,414. No slaveholding families were reported from the states of these divisions in 1850, except for 200 such families in New Jersey, and none from any other Northern states, except Missouri, which in this year reported 19,185 holders of slaves. A few slaves were, however, held in Utah, although the number of slaveholding families is not given.

TABLE 6.—NEGRO POPULATION, SLAVE AND FREE, AT EACH CENSUS BY DIVISIONS AND STATES: 1790–1860.

DIVISION AND STATE.	NEGRO POPULATION. 1860		1850		1840		1830		1820		1810		1800		1790	
	Slave.	Free.	Slave.	Free.	Slave.	Free.	Slave.	Free.	Slave.	Free.	Slave.	Free.	Slave.	Free.	Slave.	Free.
UNITED STATES.....	3,953,760	488,070	3,204,313	434,495	2,487,355	386,293	2,009,043	319,599	1,538,022	233,634	1,191,362	186,446	893,602	108,435	697,624	59,557
GEOGRAPHIC DIVISIONS:																
New England........		24,711		23,021	23	22,634	48	21,331	145	20,782	418	19,488	1,339	17,313	3,763	13,059
Middle Atlantic.......	18	131,272	236	126,505	742	118,925	2,732	101,103	17,856	71,941	26,663	55,668	35,031	29,383	36,323	13,975
East North Central....		63,699		45,195	348	28,997	788	15,095	1,107	6,584	429	3,025	135	500		
West North Central....	114,948	5,592	87,422	2,990	58,256	1,746	25,091	569	10,222	347	3,011	607				
South Atlantic.........	1,840,445	217,753	1,663,397	197,474	1,425,539	171,778	1,376,196	153,087	1,156,479	116,920	983,997	96,803	799,681	60,009	641,691	32,048
East South Central....	1,372,913	21,447	1,103,162	19,628	814,060	16,246	490,024	11,563	281,532	6,525	142,184	3,270	57,416	1,230	15,847	475
West South Central....	625,407	19,146	350,070	18,467	188,387	25,967	114,164	16,851	70,681	10,535	34,660	7,585				
Mountain..............	29	206	26	46												
Pacific................		4,244		1,169												
NEW ENGLAND:																
Maine...............		1,327		1,356		1,355	2	1,190		929		969		818		536
New Hampshire......		494	1	520		537	3	604		786		970	8	852	157	630
Vermont.............		709		718		730		881		903		750		557		269
Massachusetts.......		9,602		9,064		8,669	1	7,048		6,740		6,737		6,452		5,369
Rhode Island........		3,952	5	3,670	5	3,238	17	3,561	48	3,554	108	3,609	380	3,304	958	3,484
Connecticut.........		8,627		7,693	17	8,105	25	8,047	97	7,870	310	6,453	951	5,330	2,648	2,771
MIDDLE ATLANTIC:																
New York...........		49,005		49,069	4	50,027	75	44,870	10,088	29,279	15,017	25,333	20,903	10,417	21,193	4,682
New Jersey..........	18	25,318	236	23,810	674	21,044	2,254	18,303	7,557	12,460	10,851	7,843	12,422	4,402	11,423	2,762
Pennsylvania........		56,949		53,626	64	47,854	403	37,930	211	30,202	795	22,492	1,706	14,564	3,707	6,531
EAST NORTH CENTRAL:																
Ohio................		36,673		25,279	3	17,342	6	9,568		4,723		1,899		337		
Indiana.............		11,428		11,262	3	7,165	3	3,629	190	1,230	237	393	135	163		
Illinois.............		7,628		5,436	331	3,598	747	1,637	917	457	168	613	24	120		
Michigan............		6,799		2,583		707	32	261		174		120				
Wisconsin...........		1,171		635	11	185										
WEST NORTH CENTRAL:																
Minnesota...........		259		39												
Iowa................		1,069		333	16	172										
Missouri............	114,931	3,572	87,422	2,618	58,240	1,574	25,091	569	10,222	347	3,011	607				
North Dakota........																
South Dakota........																
Nebraska............	15	67														
Kansas..............	2	625														
SOUTH ATLANTIC:																
Delaware............	1,798	19,829	2,290	18,073	2,605	16,919	3,292	15,855	4,509	12,958	4,177	13,136	6,153	8,268	8,887	3,899
Maryland............	87,189	83,942	90,368	74,723	89,737	62,078	102,994	52,938	107,397	39,730	111,502	33,927	105,635	19,587	103,036	8,043
District of Columbia..	3,185	11,131	3,687	10,059	4,694	8,361	6,119	6,152	6,377	4,048	5,395	2,549	3,244	783		
Virginia.............	490,865	58,042	472,528	54,333	448,987	49,842	469,757	47,348	425,148	36,883	392,516	30,570	345,796	20,124	292,627	12,866
West Virginia........																
North Carolina.......	331,059	30,463	288,548	27,463	245,817	22,732	245,601	19,543	204,917	14,712	168,824	10,266	133,296	7,043	100,783	5,041
South Carolina.......	402,406	9,914	384,984	8,960	327,038	8,276	315,401	7,921	258,475	6,826	196,365	4,554	146,151	3,185	107,094	1,801
Georgia.............	462,198	3,500	381,682	2,931	280,944	2,753	217,531	2,486	149,656	1,763	105,218	1,801	59,406	1,019	29,264	398
Florida.............	61,745	932	39,310	932	25,717	817	15,501	844								
EAST SOUTH CENTRAL:																
Kentucky............	225,483	10,684	210,981	10,011	182,258	7,317	165,213	4,917	126,732	2,759	80,561	1,713	40,343	739	12,430	114
Tennessee...........	275,719	7,300	239,459	6,422	183,059	5,524	141,603	4,555	80,107	2,737	44,535	1,317	13,584	309	3,417	361
Alabama.............	435,080	2,690	342,844	2,265	253,532	2,039	117,549	1,572	41,879	571						
Mississippi..........	436,631	773	309,878	930	195,211	1,366	65,659	519	32,814	458	17,088	240	3,489	182		
WEST SOUTH CENTRAL:																
Arkansas............	111,115	144	47,100	608	19,935	465	4,576	141	1,617	59						
Louisiana...........	331,726	18,647	244,809	17,462	168,452	25,502	109,588	16,710	69,064	10,476	34,660	7,585				
Oklahoma...........																
Texas...............	182,566	355	58,161	397												
MOUNTAIN:																
Montana.............																
Idaho...............																
Wyoming............																
Colorado............		46														
New Mexico.........		85		22												
Arizona.............																
Utah................	29	30	26	24												
Nevada..............		45														
PACIFIC:																
Washington..........		30														
Oregon..............		128		207												
California...........		4,086		962												

PART II.—MIGRATORY DISPLACEMENT AND SEGREGATION.

THE NATIVITY INQUIRY.

The nativity inquiry of the population schedule calls for a statement of place of birth of persons enumerated, and of their parents. In the case of natives the state or territory of birth is designated, and in the case of foreign-born persons the country of birth.

Upon the basis of the returns under this inquiry the population is classified as native and foreign born and the native population is further classified as of native, foreign, or mixed parentage. Finally the foreign-born population is classified by country of birth, and the native population by state or territory of birth.

Data relating to nativity have been returned at each census beginning with that of 1850, at which census the state or country of birth of each free inhabitant was recorded for the first time at any decennial enumeration. The place of birth of parents was called for first at the census of 1870.

NATIVE AND FOREIGN BORN: 1850–1910.

At the censuses of 1850 and 1860 the nativity inquiry was included in the schedule for free inhabitants only, embracing free colored persons (Negroes) to the number of 434,495 in 1850 and 488,070 in 1860. For nearly nine-tenths of the total Negro population no nativity data are available covering these years.

In Table 1, classifying the Negro population as native and foreign born, the entire slave population of 1850 and 1860 is classified as native, together with the free colored returned as native on the schedule for free inhabitants.

Table 1	NEGRO POPULATION.				WHITE POPULATION.	
YEAR.	Total.	Native.[1]	Foreign born.		Number foreign born.	Percentage foreign born.
			Number.	Per cent.		
1910	9,827,763	9,787,424	40,339	0.4	13,345,545	16.3
1900	8,833,994	8,813,658	20,336	0.2	10,213,817	15.3
1890	7,488,676	7,468,697	19,979	0.3	9,121,867	16.6
1880	6,580,793	6,566,776	14,017	0.2	6,559,679	15.1
1870	4,880,009	4,870,364	9,645	0.2	5,493,712	16.4
1860	4,441,830	[1]4,437,467	4,363	0.1	4,099,401	15.2
1850	3,638,808	[1]3,634,741	4,067	0.1	2,240,535	11.5

[1] Includes all slaves and native free colored.

The 40,339 foreign-born Negroes in 1910 constituted 0.4 per cent of the total Negro population. In 1900 the foreign-born Negro population numbered 20,336, the increase for the decade being 20,003. At no census for which data are available has the foreign-born element in the Negro population amounted to so much as one-half of 1 per cent.

In Table 2 the native and foreign-born Negro population of the United States is given, by sections and divisions, for 1910.

Table 2	NEGRO POPULATION: 1910.			PERCENTAGE DISTRIBUTION: 1910.		PERCENTAGE FOREIGN BORN: 1910.	
SECTION AND DIVISION.	Total.	Native.	Foreign born.	Foreign-born Negro population.	Foreign-born white population.	Negro population.	White population.
United States	9,827,763	9,787,424	40,339	100.0	100.0	0.4	16.3
The South	8,749,427	8,738,858	10,569	26.2	5.4	0.1	3.5
South Atlantic	4,112,488	4,104,413	8,075	20.0	2.2	0.2	3.6
East South Central	2,652,513	2,651,888	625	1.5	0.7	(1)	1.5
West South Central	1,984,426	1,982,557	1,869	4.6	2.6	0.1	5.2
The North	1,027,674	999,451	28,223	70.0	84.8	2.7	20.7
New England	66,306	58,596	7,710	19.1	13.6	11.6	28.0
Middle Atlantic	417,870	401,548	16,322	40.5	36.2	3.9	25.6
East North Central	300,836	297,452	3,384	8.4	23.0	1.1	17.1
West North Central	242,662	241,855	807	2.0	12.1	0.3	14.2
The West	50,662	49,115	1,547	3.8	9.7	3.1	19.8
Mountain	21,467	21,094	373	0.9	3.3	0.2	17.3
Pacific	29,195	28,021	1,174	2.9	6.5	4.0	21.4

[1] Less than one-tenth of 1 per cent.

As is true in the case of the white population, the foreign-born Negro population in 1910 was largely resident in the North, the proportion living in the North being 84.8 per cent for the foreign-born white population and 70 per cent for the foreign-born Negro population.

Of the Negro population in the South, only one-tenth of 1 per cent was foreign born, the corresponding proportion for the North being 2.7 per cent, and for the West, 3.1 per cent. The highest proportion foreign born for the Negro population is that of 11.6 per cent for New England.

Table 3 gives the foreign-born Negro population by states, in 1910 and in 1900, with the increase for the decade 1900–1910.

FOREIGN-BORN NEGRO POPULATION: 1910 AND 1900.

Table 3

DIVISION AND STATE.	FOREIGN-BORN NEGROES.			DIVSION AND STATE.	FOREIGN-BORN NEGROES.		
	1910	1900	Increase:[1] 1900–1910.		1910	1900	Increase: 1900–1910.
UNITED STATES	40,339	20,336	20,003	WEST NORTH CENTRAL—Continued.			
				Nebraska	97	53	44
GEOGRAPHIC DIVISIONS:				Kansas	118	64	54
New England	7,710	4,368	3,342	SOUTH ATLANTIC:			
Middle Atlantic	16,322	4,875	11,447	Delaware	35	29	6
East North Central	3,384	2,316	1,068	Maryland	451	303	148
West North Central	807	412	395	District of Columbia	238	174	64
South Atlantic	8,075	5,495	2,580	Virginia	296	152	144
East South Central	625	512	113	West Virginia	82	24	58
West South Central	1,869	1,556	313	North Carolina	88	54	34
Mountain	373	217	156	South Carolina	72	97	−25
Pacific	1,174	585	589	Georgia	228	202	26
				Florida	6,585	4,460	2,125
NEW ENGLAND:				EAST SOUTH CENTRAL:			
Maine	237	218	19	Kentucky	66	72	−6
New Hampshire	40	29	11	Tennessee	99	92	7
Vermont	40	18	22	Alabama	282	195	87
Massachusetts	6,152	3,475	2,677	Mississippi	178	153	25
Rhode Island	872	392	480	WEST SOUTH CENTRAL:			
Connecticut	369	236	133	Arkansas	80	54	26
MIDDLE ATLANTIC:				Louisiana	575	490	85
New York	12,851	3,552	9,299	Oklahoma	123	41	82
New Jersey	1,487	459	1,028	Texas	1,091	971	120
Pennsylvania	1,984	864	1,120	MOUNTAIN:			
EAST NORTH CENTRAL:				Montana	61	20	41
Ohio	655	483	172	Idaho	28	9	19
Indiana	97	64	33	Wyoming	38	9	29
Illinois	928	610	318	Colorado	130	54	76
Michigan	1,640	1,103	537	New Mexico	34	22	12
Wisconsin	64	56	8	Arizona	31	84	−53
WEST NORTH CENTRAL:				Utah	32	14	18
Minnesota	200	82	118	Nevada	19	5	14
Iowa	55	39	16	PACIFIC:			
Missouri	326	153	173	Washington	238	108	130
North Dakota	2	7	−5	Oregon	62	44	18
South Dakota	9	14	−5	California	874	433	441

[1] A minus sign (−) denotes decrease.

PARENTAGE: 1910 AND 1900.

In Table 4 the native and the foreign-born Negro population in 1910 and in 1900 is classified according to parentage, data for the white population being introduced for comparison.

Of the total Negro population in 1910, 9,787,424 or 99.6 per cent were native, and 9,748,439 or 99.2 per cent were native of native parents, the number born of foreign parents being in both years inconsiderable. In 1910 the number born with one or both parents foreign born was 38,985, or 0.4 per cent.

PARENTAGE OF THE NEGRO AND THE WHITE POPULATION: 1910 AND 1900.

Table 4

NATIVITY AND PARENTAGE.	POPULATION.											
	Number.				Per cent distribution.				Increase:[1] 1900–1910.			
	1910		1900		1910		1900		Number.		Per cent.	
	Negro.	White.	Negro.	White.	Negro.	White.	Negro.	White.	Negro.	White.	Negro.	White.
Total	9,827,763	81,731,957	8,833,994	66,809,196	100.0	100.0	100.0	100.0	993,769	14,922,761	11.2	22.3
Native	9,787,424	68,386,412	8,813,658	56,595,379	99.6	83.7	99.8	84.7	973,766	11,791,033	11.0	20.8
Both parents native	9,748,439	49,488,575	8,779,267	40,949,362	99.2	60.5	99.4	61.3	969,172	8,539,213	11.0	20.9
One or both parents foreign born	38,985	18,897,837	34,391	15,646,017	0.4	23.1	0.4	23.4	4,594	3,251,820	13.4	20.8
One parent foreign born, one native	24,425	5,981,526	25,193	5,013,737	0.2	7.3	0.3	7.5	−768	967,789	−3.0	19.3
Father foreign born	15,332	3,923,845		3,346,652	0.2	4.8		5.0		577,193		17.2
Mother foreign born	9,093	2,057,681		1,667,085	0.1	2.5		2.5		390,596		23.4
Both parents foreign born	14,560	12,916,311	9,198	10,632,280	0.1	15.8	0.1	15.9	5,362	2,284,031	58.3	21.5
Foreign-born	40,339	13,345,545	20,336	10,213,817	0.4	16.3	0.2	15.3	20,003	3,131,728	98.4	30.7
Both parents native[1]	(2)	(2)	538	8,854	(2)	(2)	(3)	(3)	[2]−538	[2]−8,854	(2)	(2)
One or both parents foreign born	40,339	13,345,545	19,798	10,204,963	0.4	16.3	0.2	15.3	20,541	3,140,582	103.8	30.8
One parent foreign born, one native	1,452	83,879		61,356	(3)	0.1		0.1		22,523		36.7
Father foreign born	703	48,594		45,340	(3)	0.1		0.1		3,254		7.2
Mother foreign born	749	35,285		16,016	(3)	(3)		(3)		19,269		120.3
Both parents foreign born	38,887	13,261,666		10,143,607	0.4	16.2		15.2		3,118,059		30.7

[1] A minus sign (−) denotes decrease. [2] Classified as native of native parentage in 1910. [3] Less than one-tenth of 1 per cent.

COUNTRY OF BIRTH.

The 40,339 foreign-born Negroes in 1910 are classified by country of birth in Table 5.

Table 5 COUNTRY OF BIRTH.	Foreign-born Negroes: 1910.	COUNTRY OF BIRTH.	Foreign-born Negroes: 1910.
All foreign countries.......	40,339	Asia....................	100
		China..................	10
America..................	33,233	Japan..................	2
Canada and Newfoundland	6,775	All other..............	88
Mexico...................	1,184		
Central America..........	215	Africa..................	473
Cuba and other West Indies [1]	24,426	Australia...............	94
		Atlantic Islands.........	2,478
South America............	633	Pacific Islands [2].......	61
		All other..............	39
Europe...................	3,861		

[1] Except Porto Rico.   [2] Except Hawaii and Philippine Islands.

More than half of the foreign-born Negroes were natives of Cuba and other West Indies; 6,775 were natives of Canada and Newfoundland; and 1,184 were natives of Mexico. The total from North and South American countries was 33,233, and for European countries 3,861.

NATIVE POPULATION REPORTING STATE OF BIRTH.

Of the 9,787,424 native Negroes resident in the States in 1910, 9,783,986 were born in the States and 3,438 in outlying possessions, or at sea under the flag, or abroad of American parents. Of those born in the States, state of birth was reported by 9,746,043, leaving 37,943 for whom no report of state of birth was made. The tabulations following, classifying the population in 1910 by state of birth, relate to this aggregate Negro population which embraces the small number born outside of the States but does not include the foreign-born resident in the States.

In Table 6 this native Negro population is shown for sections and southern divisions.

Table 6 DIVISION AND SECTION.	Total.	Born in the United States.			Born in outlying possessions.[2]
		Total.	State of birth reported.	State of birth not reported.[1]	
United States.....	9,787,424	9,783,986	9,746,043	37,943	3,438
The South.............	8,738,858	8,738,162	8,710,108	28,054	696
South Atlantic......	4,104,413	4,104,020	4,094,486	9,534	393
East South Central.	2,651,888	2,651,797	2,643,722	8,075	91
West South Central.	1,982,557	1,982,345	1,971,900	10,445	212
The North.............	999,451	997,017	988,126	8,891	2,434
The West.............	49,115	48,807	47,809	998	308

[1] Includes those for whom no report of place of birth was made.
[2] Includes 4 persons born in Alaska, 1 in Guam, 58 in Hawaii, 119 in the Philippine Islands, 173 in Port Rico, 217 born at sea under the United States flag, and 2,866 American citizens born abroad.

CLASSIFICATION BY STATE OF BIRTH: 1850.

As has been noted, state of birth was recorded first at the census of 1850. Tables 7 and 8 are reproduced from the Compendium of the 1850 census as being the first state of birth tables prepared by the Census Bureau relating to the Negro population. In Table 7 the free colored population is classified by sex, and as born in the state of residence, born out of the state of residence in the United States, and born in foreign countries. In Table 8 the nativities of the free colored population of Connecticut and Louisiana, and of the cities of New York and New Orleans, are shown, the state and country of birth being designated for the black and mulatto population of these two states and two cities—a northern state and city in comparison with a southern.

The data given in Tables 7 and 8 are, of course, not comparable with the data given for succeeding census years, since the return of nativity in 1850, as has been noted, embraced only a small proportion of the Negro population.

Table 7 STATE AND TERRITORY.	FREE COLORED POPULATION: 1850.							
	Born in the state.		Born out of the state and in the United States.		Born in foreign countries.		Unknown.	
	Males.	Females.	Males.	Females.	Males.	Females.	Males.	Females.
Alabama............	758	883	279	310	5	6	14	10
Arkansas...........	165	128	138	159	1	2	10	5
California..........	60	9	641	68	161	12	10	1
Connecticut........	2,945	3,132	685	666	127	40	63	35
Delaware...........	8,467	8,465	559	570	7	3	2	......
District of Columbia.	2,580	3,417	1,655	2,386	3	2	10	6
Florida.............	357	447	46	53	15	14	......	......
Georgia.............	1,223	1,358	133	170	12	24	7	4
Illinois.............	1,308	1,356	1,396	1,267	16	16	57	20
Indiana.............	2,593	2,556	3,073	2,958	19	16	30	17
Iowa...............	24	28	140	140	1	......	17	15
Kentucky...........	3,732	3,936	1,106	1,186	8	11	11	15
Louisiana...........	6,821	8,381	387	892	238	687	33	23
Maine..............	449	479	178	98	81	49	18	4
Maryland...........	34,485	38,871	571	531	103	95	33	34
Massachusetts......	2,719	2,980	1,348	1,339	232	194	125	127
Michigan...........	452	338	898	745	53	57	28	12
Mississippi.........	317	323	144	121	3	3	10	9
Missouri............	842	788	492	451	15	7	12	11
New Hampshire.....	165	174	84	83	8	......	3	3
New Jersey.........	9,978	10,451	1,655	1,454	86	58	79	49
New York..........	17,680	19,895	5,089	5,277	379	326	304	119
North Carolina.....	12,939	13,879	333	275	13	3	13	8
Ohio...............	6,093	6,293	6,451	6,211	57	37	90	47
Pennsylvania.......	17,603	20,165	7,367	7,796	151	161	248	135
Rhode Island.......	1,129	1,377	563	520	42	28	4	7
South Carolina.....	3,994	4,623	68	74	69	130	......	2
Tennessee..........	2,500	2,640	584	634	7	8	26	23
Texas..............	92	71	79	92	39	22	1	1
Vermont............	234	218	117	103	14	13	10	9
Virginia............	25,710	28,090	266	218	15	17	11	6
Wisconsin..........	100	67	255	199	3	3	7	1
Territories:								
Minnesota.......	7	7	14	11	......	......	......	......
New Mexico.....	7	4	10	1	......	......	......	......
Oregon..........	47	62	23	12	50	13	......	......
Utah............	2	2	12	8	......	......	......	......
Total..........	168,577	185,893	36,839	37,078	2,033	2,057	1,275	743

FREE COLORED BLACK AND MULATTO POPULATION OF SELECTED AREAS CLASSIFIED BY STATE AND COUNTRY OF BIRTH: 1850.

Table 8 — FREE COLORED POPULATION: 1850.

PLACE OF BIRTH.	Connecticut.			Louisiana.			New York City.			New Orleans.		
	Blacks.	Mulattoes.	Total.	Blacks.	Mulattoes.	Total.	Blacks.	Mulattoes.	Total.	Blacks.	Mulattoes.	Total.
Alabama	2	....	2	16	46	62	4	1	5	13	41	54
Arkansas				4	....	4						
Connecticut	4,671	1,406	6,077	....	3	3	242	77	319			
Delaware	9	1	10	....	1	1	159	30	189	....	1	1
District of Columbia	5	....	5	7	23	30				6	21	27
Florida	1	3	4	8	26	34	4	7	11	8	20	28
Georgia	11	8	19	5	13	18	18	14	32	2	11	13
Indiana				....	1	1	....	1	1	....	1	1
Illinois				6	11	17				....	5	5
Kentucky	1	....	1	31	77	108	10	4	14	21	57	78
Louisiana	2	....	2	2,488	12,714	15,202	22	5	27	1,303	6,820	8,123
Maine	1	....	1	....	1	1	10	4	14			
Maryland	67	14	81	56	45	101	580	170	750	27	47	74
Massachusetts	141	47	188	4	7	11	111	30	141	2	7	9
Mississippi	1	....	1	30	59	89	8	3	11	9	50	59
Missouri				3	16	19	2	....	2	3	14	17
New Hampshire				....	1	1	4	....	4	....	1	1
New Jersey	80	15	95	2	....	2	1,234	246	1,480	1	....	1
New York	447	125	572	12	32	44	6,469	1,887	8,356	10	31	41
North Carolina	13	4	17	22	41	63	81	23	104	10	10	20
Ohio		1	1	3	20	23	7	9	16	3	19	22
Pennsylvania	75	38	113	10	33	43	513	169	682	9	33	42
Rhode Island	118	41	159	....	1	1	46	9	55	....	1	1
South Carolina	6	5	11	40	47	87	62	33	95	17	32	49
Tennessee				17	27	44	2	....	2	8	20	28
Texas				8	15	23						
Vermont	2	1	3				6	7	13			
Virginia	53	13	66	226	223	449	712	166	878	153	225	378
Germany				1	4	5				1	3	4
Mexico	1	....	1	3	33	36				2	31	33
South America	2	....	2	....	2	2	2	2	4	....	2	2
West Indies	41	11	52	167	494	661	93	54	147	151	496	647
England	2	1	3	....	3	3	16	9	25	....	3	3
France	2	....	2	9	17	26	5	11	16	6	13	19
Ireland				6	....	6				....	6	6
Spain				7	....	7	8	2	10	....	7	7
Portugal	2	....	2				3	5	8			
China	1	....	1	....	1	1				....	1	1
Africa	4	1	5	146	10	156	17	....	17	114	7	121
Other countries and unknown	134	63	197	59	19	78	299	88	387	24	22	46
Total	5,895	1,798	7,693	3,379	14,083	17,462	10,749	3,066	13,815	1,903	8,058	9,961

Out of 7,693 free colored persons in Connecticut, 1,798 were mulattoes, of whom 48 were born in the slave States. Out of 13,815 free colored in New York City, 3,066 were mulattoes. Thus, in both instances, the mulattoes constituted less than one-fourth of the free colored population. About one-fifth of the free colored in New York were born in the present slave States.—*Compendium of the Seventh Census, p. 80.*

POPULATION BORN IN THE SOUTH: 1870–1910.

In Table 9 the native Negro population is classified as born in the South and born in the North and West, at each census, 1870 to 1910. The proportion of the total native Negro population born in the South in 1910 was practically the same as in 1870, the percentage in 1870 being 93.4 and in 1910, 93.1. A nearly identical proportion obtained at each of the five censuses covered by Table 9, the percentages for the several years being 93.4, 93.3, 92.5, 93.2, and 93.1. The proportion born in the North and West ranged from 6.4 to 6.7.

Certain of the figures given in Table 9 are estimates. This is true of the number born in the South and in the North and West for 1890 and for 1880, and of the percentages based upon these populations. For these years statistics are available for the aggregate colored population only. The process of estimating is explained in a note attached to Table 12 (p. 66). It may be observed that while the process of estimating involves a number of small eliminations of Indians, Chinese, and Japanese from the aggregate colored,

Table 9 — NATIVE POPULATION.

YEAR.	Total.	Born in the South.	Born in the North and West.	Other.[1]	Percentage—	
					Born in the South.	Born in the North and West.
NEGRO.						
1910	9,787,424	9,109,153	636,890	41,381	93.1	6.5
1900	8,813,658	8,216,458	570,089	27,111	93.2	6.5
1890[2]	7,468,697	*6,908,869*	*481,101*	78,727	*92.5*	*6.4*
1880[2]	6,566,776	*6,124,351*	*442,357*	68	*93.3*	*6.7*
1870	4,870,364	4,548,991	319,897	1,476	93.4	6.6
COLORED.						
1890	7,718,763	6,915,715	534,474	268,174	89.6	6.9
1880	6,632,549	6,130,710	501,771	68	92.4	7.6

[1] Includes persons born in the United States, state of birth not reported; born in outlying possessions; born at sea under the United States flag; American citizens born abroad; and, for 1890, the colored population specially enumerated in Indian Territory and on Indian reservations, for whom no return of state of birth was made.
[2] Figures in italics are estimates. (See Note 2, Table 12, p 66.)

the numbers in these several classes are so inconsiderable, relatively to the total Negro population, that the error in the estimates for Negroes is negligible. The principal effect of the estimating for each year is exclusion of the native Indian population of the North and West from the aggregate native colored population of these sections. Data for the colored in 1890 and in 1880, upon which the estimates for Negroes are based, are given in Table 9.

MIGRATION FROM AND TO THE SOUTH.

Table 10 shows for each of the five census years, 1870 to 1910, the number of Negroes born in the South living in the North and West, and the number born in the North and West, living in the South. In this table, as in Table 9, figures for Negroes in 1890 and in 1880 are estimates, the margin of error in the estimates being probably no greater than the error in enumeration of the Negro population in other census years.

Table 10	NATIVE NEGRO POPULATION.					
	Born in the South.			Born in the North and West.		
YEAR.	Total.	Living in the North and West.		Total.	Living in the South.	
		Number.	Per cent.		Number.	Per cent.
1910	9,109,153	440,534	4.8	636,890	41,489	6.5
1900	8,216,458	349,651	4.3	570,089	30,397	5.3
1890[1]	*6,908,869*	*241,855*	*3.5*	*481,101*	*23,268*	*4.8*
1880[1]	*6,124,351*	*198,029*	*3.2*	*442,357*	*22,039*	*5.0*
1870	4,548,991	149,100	3.3	319,897	15,583	4.9

[1] Figures in italics are estimates. See Note 2, Table 12 (p. 66).

Of the Negro population born in the South, 440,534, or 4.8 per cent, were living in the North and West in 1910. This number indicates a very considerable dispersion of the Negro population born in the South through other sections of the country.

The migration to the South of Negroes born in the North and West, while it is less considerable in volume than the migration out of the South, is, relatively to the Negro population born in the North and West, somewhat greater than the migration out of the South, relatively to the Negro population born in the South. The 41,489 Negroes born in the North and West and living in the South in 1910 constituted 6.5 per cent of the total Negro population born in the North and West, the corresponding proportion for migrants born in the South being, as noted above, 4.8 per cent.

Each decennial period covered by Table 10 shows a substantial increase in the number of natives of the South living in the North and West. In the period of 40 years, 1870-1910, this number increased from 149,100 in 1870 to 440,534 in 1910. In the same period the number born in the North and West living in the South increased from 15,583 to 41,489.

It should be understood that the 440,534 natives of the South living in the North and West in 1910 do

not embrace the total number of migrants out of the South during any given period. Among migrants leaving the South during any period prior to the Census of 1910 a certain number died before the taking of the 1910 census, and of the survivors those only were returned as migrants out of the South who had not returned to the South or migrated from the North or West to an outlying possession or to a foreign country. It is clear, therefore, that the number of migrants leaving the South in recent years very considerably exceeds the number found living in the North and West at the last census. Similarly, it is true that the number of migrants to the South in recent years exceeds the number of natives of the North and West enumerated in the South.

The net gain of the North and West and loss of the South by interstate migration of Negroes is shown for each of the last five census years in Table 11.

Table 11	NATIVE NEGRO POPULATION.					
	Born in the South and living in the North and West.		Born in the North and West and living in the South.		Net gain of the North and West and loss of the South.	
YEAR.	Number.	Increase.	Number.	Increase.	Number.	Increase.
1910	440,534	90,883	41,489	11,092	399,045	79,791
1900[1]	349,651	*107,796*	30,397	*7,129*	319,254	*200,667*
1890[1]	*241,855*	*43,826*	*23,268*	*1,229*	*118,587*	*−57,403*
1880[1]	*198,029*	*48,929*	*22,039*	*6,456*	*175,990*	*42,473*
1870	149,100	....	15,583	....	133,517	....

[1] Figures in italics are estimates. See Note 2, Table 12 (p. 66).

The net migration out of the South to the North and West amounted in 1910 to 399,045. That is to say, if every Negro inhabitant born in the United States and living in the United States in 1910 had returned to his or her state of birth, the North and West would have lost the 440,534 natives of the South and would have gained the 41,489 natives of the North and West living in the South, suffering a net loss equal to the difference between these two numbers, 399,045. The net gain of the North and West in 1900 was 319,254, the increase in the net gain during the decade 1900–1910 being 79,791. In the successive decades the net gain of the North and West and loss of the South has increased from 133,517 in 1870 to 399,045 in 1910.

The increase in the number of migrants shown for each of the four decades should not be confused with the volume of migration as between the North and West, and the South. The increase for the decade 1900–1910, for example, of 90,883 in the number of Negroes born in the South living in the North and West is the excess of 1910 over 1900 in the number of such migrants reported. Migration during the decade must have been sufficient to cover (1) mortality during the decade among migrants living in these sections of the country in 1900; (2) returns of migrants to the South, and (3) emigration of migrants to foreign countries and to outlying possessions. Under any assumption of a constant stream of migration from the South to the North and West during any considerable period of time, the population living in the North and West born in the South would tend to become stationary, and the increase in the number born in the South would disappear at that point where the number of migrants entering a section exactly equaled the mortality during the period covered. If, therefore, the number of natives of the South living in the North and West were to become stationary, the implication would be not that migration had ceased but that a condition had been reached in which the continuing migration exactly offset the mortality in the migrant population resident in the North. Obviously the volume of migration required merely to offset mortality without providing any increase, increases as the population native of the South and resident in the North and West increases.

The number of migrants in the Negro population as in other classes of the population tends to increase with population, that is to say, the number of natives of the North and West living in the South, for example, tends to increase as the population living in the North and West increases, and the population native of the South living in the North and West tends to increase with the population of the South. This would be true unless the tendency on the part of the Negro population to migrate from state to state was itself diminishing, the fact being that this tendency is rather increasing, as is shown by the percentages of Table 10.

The net gain of the North and West by interstate migration, as shown in the census returns, does not of course measure the full population gain of the North and West directly and indirectly attributable to migration in recent years, since that full gain must include not only migrants themselves but, as well, the children of migrants born subsequently to migration. It should be borne in mind also that the increase in the net gain shown for the several decades does not equal the net migration in these decades. The increase of 79,791 for the decade 1900–1910, for example, does not indicate a net migration of 79,791 during this decade, since the net migration into this section during this decade must have been sufficient to cover not only the net gain shown, but also deaths among the migrants during the decade, and deaths, returns to the South, and migrants among the population returned in 1900 as resident in the North and West and born in the South.

PROPORTION OF MIGRANTS IN THE SOUTH AND IN THE NORTH AND WEST.

In Table 12 statistics similar to those given in Table 9 for the United States as a whole are given for the South and for the North and West. This table shows, for example, that of the total native Negro population of 8,738,858 living in the South in 1910, 8,668,619 were born in the South and 41,489 were born in the

North and West. Of this Southern native Negro population, therefore, 99.2 per cent were born in the South and only 0.5 in the North and West. Of the 1,048,566 native Negroes living in the North and West in this year, 440,534 were born in the South and 595,401 in the North and West, the percentage born in the South being 42 and the percentage born in the North and West 56.8. Corresponding data are given for each of the last five censuses.

It may be noted as regards the Negro population of the North and West that the percentage born in the South increased from 33.8 in 1890 to 42 in 1910, the proportion for the earlier years being approximately the same as in 1890.

Table 12	NATIVE NEGRO POPULATION.						
					Percentage.		
YEAR.	Total.	Born in the South.	Born in the North and West.	Other.[1]	Born in the South.	Born in the North and West.	Other (1).
LIVING IN THE SOUTH.							
1910	8,738,858	8,668,619	41,489	28,750	99.2	0.5	0.3
1900	7,915,406	7,866,807	30,397	18,202	99.4	0.4	0.2
1890 [2]	6,753,917	6,667,014	23,268	63,635	98.7	0.3	0.9
1880 [2]	5,948,406	5,926,322	22,039	45	99.6	0.4	(3)
1870	4,416,788	4,400,132	15,583	1,073	99.6	0.4	(3)
LIVING IN THE NORTH AND WEST.							
1910	1,048,566	440,534	595,401	12,631	42.0	56.8	1.2
1900	898,252	349,651	539,692	8,909	38.9	60.1	1.0
1890 [2]	714,780	241,855	457,833	15,092	33.8	64.1	2.1
1880 [2]	618,370	198,029	420,318	23	32.1	68.0	(3)
1870	453,576	149,100	304,073	403	32.9	67.0	(3)

[1] See Note 1, Table 9 (p. 64).

[2] Figures in italics are estimates. It is assumed that in 1890 two-thirds—approximately the proportion in 1880—of the foreign-born Negro population of 19,979 lived in the North and West, and one-third in the South; that of the Indians, Chinese, and Japanese, the same proportion of the native as of the total in each class lived in the North and West, and in the South, respectively, and that the natives of these classes resident in the North and West were born in the North and West, and the natives resident in the South were born in the South. As practically all—i. e., 57,571 out of 58,806—of the native civilized Indians included in the aggregate colored distributed by state of birth, were native, the error in the assumption that the same proportion of the natives as of the total lived in the South and in the North and West is immaterial. The great mass of the Indian population in 1890—189,447 out of 248,253—were specially enumerated, and for these state of birth was not reported. They are included under "Other colored" in Table 9. The number of native Chinese and Japanese is so small—i. e., 2,930 Chinese and 118 Japanese—that any error in distributing them as living in and born in the North and West, or South, is immaterial in its effects upon the figures for the native Negro population of 7,468,697. In the 57,571 civilized native Indian population, 2,930 Chinese and 118 Japanese included in the aggregate native colored population of 7,510,680 in 1890, there were undoubtedly a few migrants into and out of the South. These are not taken into account in the estimate, but their number could not have been sufficiently large materially to affect the figures for the aggregate Negro. Similar assumptions are made for 1880, except that for this year the number of native Negroes, Indians, Chinese, and Japanese, living in each state is given in the report for 1880, and the number living in the South and in other sections is, therefore not as regards natives in these classes an estimated number, as it is for 1890. For 1880, therefore, it is assumed in the estimate that the 6,269 native Indians, Chinese, and Japanese returned as resident in the South were natives of the South, and that the 59,504 resident in the North and West were native of the North and West.

[3] Less than one-tenth of 1 per cent.

INTERSECTIONAL MIGRATION.

In Table 13 the native Negro and the native white population are classified according to section of residence and section of birth.

As regards the Negro population, Table 13 is to be read as follows: In the total native Negro population in 1910, numbering 9,787,424, there were returned 9,109,153 as born in the South, 621,286 as born in the North, and 15,604 as born in the West; the remaining

41,381 includes those for whom state of birth was not reported, those born in outlying possessions, born at sea under the United States flag, and American citizens born abroad; of the 9,109,153 born in the South 8,668,619 were living in the South; 415,533 were living in the North, and 25,001 in the West. Similar data are given for the white population, and for each of the three geographical sections.

Of the native Negro population of the South 99.2 per cent were born in the South; of the native Negro population of the North, 41.6 per cent were born in the South; and of the native Negro population of the West, 50.9 per cent were born in the South, and 24.3 per cent in the North.

Of the native Negro population born in the South, 95.2 per cent were living in the South, 4.6 per cent in the North, and 0.3 per cent in the West; of the native Negro population born in the North, 91.8 per cent were living in the North, 6.3 per cent in the South, and 1.9 per cent in the West; of the native Negro population born in the West, 69.8 per cent were living in the West, 15.5 per cent in the South, and 14.7 per cent in the North. The proportion of intersectional migrants is, it appears, somewhat smaller for Negroes born in the South (4.9 per cent), than it is for Negroes born in the North (8.2 per cent), the proportion of such migrants being greatest (30.2 per cent) among the small number of Negroes born in the West.

In Table 14, on the following page, the migration of Negroes out of and into the South is shown by divisions and states for each of the five census years, 1870 to 1910.

The table shows, for example, for the state of Maine, that there were living in the state, in 1910, 178 Negroes born in the South; the number born in the South living in this state decreased by 34 during the decade 1900–1910, and was less in 1910 than it was in 1870, in which year there were living in the state 366 Negroes who were natives of the South.

Among the Northern states Pennsylvania showed, in 1910, the largest Negro population born in the South, the number of Negroes born in the South living in this state being 97,020. New York showed the second largest population born in the South, with 60,494; Illinois the third largest, with 50,314; Ohio the fourth, with 44,439; and New Jersey the fifth, with 40,987.

Except in five Northern states the Negro population born in the South increased during the decade 1900–1910. Of these five states in which the number decreased, four are New England states (Maine, New Hampshire, Massachusetts, Rhode Island) and one (Kansas) is in the West North Central division. The largest increases are in the Middle Atlantic states and in Illinois.

The distribution of the Negro population born in the North and West among the Southern states is shown in the lower portion of Table 14. The Southern state reporting the largest number of Negroes born in the North and West was Oklahoma, the number of such natives being 6,096; Texas reported 4,158; Kentucky, 3,735; and Arkansas, 3,690. In every Southern state during the decade 1900–1910 the number of Negroes native of the North and West increased, the aggregate increase being 11,092.

NATIVE NEGRO AND WHITE POPULATION CLASSIFIED BY SECTION OF RESIDENCE, AND BY SECTION OF BIRTH: 1910.

Table 13	NATIVE POPULATION: 1910.									
SECTION OF RESIDENCE.	Total.		Born in—						State of birth not reported, or born in outlying possessions.[1]	
			The South.		The North.		The West.			
	Negro.	White.	Negro.	White.	Negro.	White.	Negro.	White.	Negro.	White.
	NUMBER.									
United States	9,787,424	68,386,412	9,109,153	19,814,860	621,286	45,488,942	15,604	2,766,492	41,381	316,118
The South	8,738,858	19,821,249	8,668,619	18,326,236	39,077	1,407,262	2,412	34,523	28,750	53,228
The North	999,451	43,319,193	415,533	1,110,245	570,298	41,891,353	2,295	116,939	11,325	200,656
The West	49,115	5,245,970	25,001	378,379	11,911	2,190,327	10,897	2,615,030	1,306	62,234
	PERCENTAGE DISRIBUTION BY SECTION OF BIRTH.									
United States	100.0	100.0	93.1	29.0	6.3	66.5	0.2	4.0	0.4	0.5
The South	100.0	100.0	99.2	92.5	0.4	7.1	(²)	0.2	0.3	0.3
The North	100.0	100.0	41.6	2.6	57.1	96.7	0.2	0.3	1.1	0.5
The West	100.0	100.0	50.9	7.2	24.3	41.8	22.2	49.8	2.7	1.2
	PERCENTAGE DISTRIBUTION BY SECTION OF RESIDENCE.									
United States	100.0	100.0	100.0	100.0	100.0	100.0	100.0	100.0	100.0	100.0
The South	89.3	29.0	95.2	92.5	6.3	3.1	15.5	1.2	69.5	16.8
The North	10.2	63.3	4.6	5.6	91.8	92.1	14.7	4.2	27.4	63.5
The West	0.5	7.7	0.3	1.9	1.9	4.8	69.8	94.5	3.2	19.7

[1] Includes also persons born at sea under the United States flag and American citizens born abroad.   ² Less than one-tenth of 1 per cent.

MIGRATION OF NEGROES OUT OF AND INTO THE SOUTH, BY STATES: 1870–1910.

Table 14 SECTION, DIVISION, AND STATE.	1910	1900	1890[1]	1880[1]	1870	INCREASE.[2]			
						1900–1910	1890–1900	1880–1890	1870–1880
			NEGRO POPULATION BORN IN THE SOUTH.						
THE NORTH AND WEST	440,534	349,651	241,855	198,029	149,100	90,883	107,796	43,826	48,929
THE NORTH	415,533	336,076	230,931	194,630	146,490	79,457	105,145	36,301	48,140
New England	22,600	22,279	13,848	10,824	8,269	321	8,431	3,024	2,555
Middle Atlantic	198,501	150,399	78,579	48,332	33,754	48,102	71,820	30,247	14,578
East North Central	128,547	102,917	78,567	75,217	63,856	25,630	24,350	3,350	11,361
West North Central	65,885	60,481	59,937	60,257	40,611	5,404	544	−320	19,646
NEW ENGLAND:									
Maine	178	212	177	227	366	−34	35	−50	−139
New Hampshire	169	298	158	162	173	−129	140	−4	−11
Vermont	779	190	111	142	199	589	79	−31	−57
Massachusetts	13,064	13,080	7,744	5,851	4,347	−16	5,336	1,893	1,504
Rhode Island	3,191	3,423	2,558	2,013	1,385	−232	865	545	628
Connecticut	5,219	5,076	3,100	2,429	1,799	143	1,976	671	630
MIDDLE ATLANTIC:									
New York	60,494	42,985	21,694	14,373	8,147	17,509	21,291	7,321	6,226
New Jersey	40,987	29,491	14,669	7,401	5,166	11,496	14,822	7,268	2,235
Pennsylvania	97,020	77,923	42,216	26,558	20,441	19,097	35,707	15,658	6,117
EAST NORTH CENTRAL:									
Ohio	44,439	34,848	32,280	31,880	31,378	9,591	2,568	400	502
Indiana	30,123	27,711	21,315	20,355	13,459	2,412	6,396	960	6,896
Illinois	50,314	36,976	21,647	19,150	14,408	13,338	15,329	2,497	4,742
Michigan	2,897	2,647	2,725	3,282	3,752	250	−78	−557	−470
Wisconsin	774	735	600	550	859	39	135	50	−309
WEST NORTH CENTRAL:									
Minnesota	2,502	1,901	1,355	558	391	601	546	797	167
Iowa	4,452	3,690	3,512	2,919	2,258	762	178	593	661
Missouri	36,329	32,376	28,665	30,785	30,754	3,953	3,711	−2,120	31
North Dakota	223	110	105	[3]120	[3]62	113	5	199	58
South Dakota	249	171	214			78	−43		
Nebraska	2,327	1,854	2,983	1,035	353	473	−1,129	1,948	682
Kansas	19,803	20,379	23,103	24,840	6,793	−576	−2,724	−1,737	18,047
THE WEST	25,001	13,575	10,924	3,399	2,610	11,426	2,651	7,525	789
Mountain	10,140	7,294	5,855	1,606	754	2,846	1,439	4,249	852
Pacific	14,861	6,281	5,069	1,793	1,856	8,580	1,212	3,276	−63
MOUNTAIN:									
Montana	682	652	795	80	71	30	−143	715	9
Idaho	248	109	77	22	26	139	32	55	−4
Wyoming	1,210	398	528	108	96	812	−130	420	12
Colorado	5,212	3,789	2,423	942	248	1,423	1,366	1,481	694
New Mexico	889	880	725	187	80	9	155	538	107
Arizona	1,251	1,054	989	65	18	197	65	924	47
Utah	397	356	233	60	38	41	123	173	22
Nevada	251	56	85	142	177	195	−29	−57	−35
PACIFIC:									
Washington	2,992	1,225	803	99	33	1,767	422	704	66
Oregon	620	419	278	63	102	201	141	215	−39
California	11,249	4,637	3,988	1,631	1,721	6,612	649	2,357	−90
			NEGRO POPULATION BORN IN THE NORTH AND WEST.						
THE SOUTH	41,489	30,397	23,268	22,039	15,583	11,092	7,129	1,229	6,456
South Atlantic	15,651	9,297	6,388	5,207	2,425	6,354	2,909	1,181	2,782
East South Central	9,808	8,098	6,686	7,017	4,564	1,710	1,412	−331	2,453
West South Central	16,030	13,002	10,194	9,815	8,594	3,028	2,808	379	1,221
SOUTH ATLANTIC:									
Delaware	1,397	1,167	919	772	429	230	248	147	343
Maryland	2,894	2,019	1,453	999	677	875	566	454	322
District of Columbia	2,542	1,781	1,529	960	279	761	252	569	681
Virginia	3,151	1,408	741	530	207	1,743	667	211	323
West Virginia	2,127	1,211	681	477	224	916	530	204	253
North Carolina	911	404	195	438	122	507	209	−243	316
South Carolina	429	202	174	231	127	227	28	−57	104
Georgia	1,146	573	319	390	211	573	254	−71	179
Florida	1,054	532	377	410	149	522	155	−33	261
EAST SOUTH CENTRAL:									
Kentucky	3,735	3,244	2,089	1,622	977	491	1,155	467	645
Tennessee	2,676	2,233	1,733	1,653	1,231	443	500	80	422
Alabama	1,412	691	869	1,455	358	721	−178	−586	1,097
Mississippi	1,985	1,930	1,995	2,287	1,998	55	−65	−292	289
WEST SOUTH CENTRAL:									
Arkansas	3,690	2,918	3,149	2,806	2,032	772	−231	343	774
Louisiana	2,086	1,818	1,975	2,686	2,497	268	−157	−711	189
Oklahoma	6,096	4,225	870	[4]	[4]	1,871	3,355	870	....
Texas	4,158	4,041	4,200	4,323	4,065	117	−159	−123	258

[1] Colored.   [2] A minus sign (−) denotes decrease.   [3] Dakota Territory in 1880 and 1870.   [4] No enumeration for Oklahoma and Indian Territory in 1880 and 1870.

INTERDIVISIONAL MIGRATION.

In Table 15 the migration of the Negroes is tabulated by geographic divisions. This table shows, for example, that in 1910 of the 37,799 Negroes born in New England, 30,815 were living in New England, and 6,984, or 18.5 per cent, were living in other divisions; that of the 58,109 Negroes living in New England, 27,294, or 47 per cent, were born in other divisions; that the net gain of the New England states through interdivisional migration in 1910 amounted to 20,310.

INTERDIVISIONAL MIGRATION OF THE NEGRO POPULATION.

Table 15	NEGROES BORN IN AND LIVING IN THE UNITED STATES AND WITH STATE OF BIRTH REPORTED: 1910.								
	Born in the specified division.				Living in the specified division.				Net gain (+) or loss (−) through interdivisional migration (col.7—col.3).
DIVISION.	Total.	Living in the same division.	Living in other divisions.		Total.	Born in the same division.	Born in other divisions.		
			Number.	Per cent of total.			Number.	Per cent of total.	
	1	2	3	4	5	6	7	8	9
United States...........	9,746,043	8,782,890	963,153	9.9	9,746,043	8,782,890	963,153	9.9	....
New England...........	37,799	30,815	6,984	18.5	58,109	30,815	27,294	47.0	+20,310
Middle Atlantic........	212,145	189,962	22,183	10.5	398,529	189,962	208,567	52.3	+186,384
East North Central.....	173,226	145,187	28,039	16.2	292,875	145,187	147,688	50.4	+119,649
West North Central....	198,116	162,054	36,062	18.2	238,613	162,054	76,559	32.1	+40,497
South Atlantic.........	4,487,313	4,039,173	448,140	10.0	4,094,486	4,039,173	55,313	1.4	−392,827
East South Central.....	2,844,598	2,491,607	352,991	12.4	2,643,722	2,491,607	152,115	5.8	−200,876
West South Central....	1,777,242	1,713,888	63,354	3.6	1,971,900	1,713,888	258,012	13.1	+194,658
Mountain..............	7,342	4,122	3,220	43.9	20,571	4,122	16,449	80.0	+13,229
Pacific................	8,262	6,082	2,180	26.4	27,238	6,082	21,156	77.7	+18,976

The number of Negroes born in the South Atlantic division living in other divisions in 1910 was 448,140, or 10 per cent of the total Negro population born in the South Atlantic division. Of Negroes born in the East South Central division 352,991, or 12.4 per cent, were living in other divisions. The largest proportion living in other divisions was shown by the Mountain division, with 43.9 per cent of its native Negro population living in other divisions.

Seven of the nine geographic divisions had gained by migration from other divisions and two, namely, the South Atlantic and the East South Central, had lost population as the result of interdivisional migration. The net loss of the South Atlantic division amounted in 1910 to 392,827 and the net loss of the East South Central division to 200,876. The losses of these two divisions, of course, exactly equaled the gains of the other seven divisions.

Turning to that portion of the table which shows the proportion of interdivisional migrants in the resident population it will be noted that the proportion of such migrants is very high in the two far western divisions, being 80 per cent in the Mountain division and 77.7 per cent in the Pacific. More than half of the Negro population of the Middle Atlantic and East North Central divisions (52.3 and 50.4 per cent) and nearly half (47 per cent) of that of New England were born outside the division of residence.

Table 16 shows for 1910 and 1900 the native Negro population classified according to division of nativity. It shows, for example, that the Negro population native of the South Atlantic division and resident in the United States increased in the decade 1900–1910 from 4,125,476 to 4,487,313, the increase amounting to 361,837. The corresponding increase for the East South Central division was 219,705 and for the West South Central division 311,153. In 1910 per 1,000 native Negroes resident in the United States 458 were born in the South Atlantic division, the proportion born in this division having decreased during the decade from 468 per 1,000.

Table 16	NEGRO POPULATION RESIDENT IN THE STATES, BORN IN SPECIFIED SECTION OR DIVISION.					
SECTION AND DIVISION OF BIRTH.	Number.		Increase:[1] 1900–1910.		Per 1,000 of total.	
	1910	1900	Number.	Per cent.	1910	1900
Total...............	9,787,424	8,813,658	973,766	11.0	1,000	1,000
Born in the United States.	9,783,986	8,810,029	973,957	11.1	1,000	1,000
In the South..........	9,109,153	8,216,458	892,695	10.9	931	932
South Atlantic......	4,487,313	4,125,476	361,837	8.8	458	468
East South Central...	2,844,598	2,624,893	219,705	8.4	291	298
West South Central..	1,777,242	1,466,089	311,153	21.2	182	166
In the North..........	621,286	560,166	61,120	10.9	63	64
New England........	37,799	32,662	5,137	15.7	4	4
Middle Atlantic......	212,145	177,492	34,653	19.5	22	20
East North Central...	173,226	154,222	19,004	12.3	18	17
West North Central..	198,116	195,790	2,326	1.2	20	22
In the West..........	15,604	9,923	5,681	57.2	2	1
Mountain...........	7,342	4,063	3,279	80.7	1	(2)
Pacific.............	8,262	5,860	2,402	41.0	1	1
State of birth not reported	37,943	23,482	14,461	61.6	4	3
Born in outlying possessions [3].............	3,438	3,629	−191	−5.3	(2)	(2)

[1] A minus sign (−) denotes decrease.
[2] Less than 1.
[3] Includes also persons born at sea under United States flag and American citizens born abroad.

Although the number born in any division is not affected directly by interdivisional migration, the increase of the population native of any division is affected indirectly by such migration—the percentage increase tending to be relatively high in divisions in which population is increasing by net immigration from other divisions—since the children born of migrants in any divisions are natives of the division, as well as children born of natives of the division. The two divisions which showed for the decade 1900–1910 a net loss of Negro population by interdivisional migration showed percentages of increase below the average for the Negro population as a whole—the increase being 8.8 per cent for the South Atlantic division, and 8.4 for the East South Central—while the number of Negroes born in the Mountain division increased in the same period by 80.7 per cent.

INTERSTATE MIGRATION.

The preceding tables have classified the Negro population by nativity and residence, with reference to the several geographic sections or divisions of the country, showing for these large areas the displacement of population by migration. The full detail of nativity by state of birth and of residence in 1910 is given in Table 20 (p. 75), which by lines, distributes the native Negro population living in each division or state by division and state of birth, and, by columns, the Negro population born in each division or state by division or state of residence. From the detailed distributions of Table 20 the 1910 aggregates of the preceding tables, for the country as a whole, and for the several sections and divisions have been composed, no account being taken in them of intradivisional migration; that is to say, of migration from state to state within the several geographic divisions. Table 17, which classifies the Negro population born in each state as living in the state or in other states, and the native Negro population living in each state as born in the state or in other states, covering the years 1910 and 1900, embraces this intradivisional, together with the interdivisional migration.

As regards the state of Delaware, for example—and similar data are given for each of the other states—Table 17 shows that there were, in 1910, living in the United States 32,664 Negroes who were natives of the state of Delaware; that of this population native of Delaware 9,996, or 30.6 per cent, were living in other states, and 22,668 were living in Delaware; that the native Negro population of Delaware numbered 31,067, of whom 8,399, or 27 per cent, were born in other states, and 22,668, as already noted, were born in Delaware; that the net loss of the state by interstate migration—i. e., the excess of the population born in the state over the population living in the state, or of the population born in Delaware and living in other states, over the population born in other states and living in Delaware—was 1,597; that the number of Negroes native of Delaware decreased during the decade from 33,050 in 1900 to 32,664 in 1910; that both the number and the proportion living in other states among natives of Delaware increased during the decade; that the number of

natives of the state living in the state decreased; that, nevertheless, the total native Negro population increased, in consequence of an increase in the number of natives of other states living in Delaware—the proportion of such natives in the total native population of the state having increased from 23.9 per cent in 1900 to 27 per cent in 1910; and that the net loss by interstate migration decreased from 2,479 in 1900 to 1,597 in 1910.

Turning to Table 20, it may be seen where the 9,996 natives of Delaware living in other states were living—in Pennsylvania 5,798, in New Jersey 2,102, in Maryland 840, in New York 463, in Virginia 130, in Massachusetts 122, and in each of 36 other states numbers ranging from 1 to 80. Table 20 shows also, in which states were born the 8,399 Negroes native of other states living in Delaware—in Maryland 5,440, in Virginia 1,206, in Pennsylvania 952, in New Jersey 226, in North Carolina 142, in New York 126, and in 27 other states numbers ranging from 1 to 40.

In Table 21 (p. 80) are given for each state the principal states of residence for natives of the state living in other states, and in Table 22 (p. 83) for each state the principal states of birth for natives of other states. These tables show for each state where natives leaving the state have chiefly gone, and whence natives entering the state have chiefly come. The tables present a rearrangement of totals selected from Tables 17 and 20, pages 71 and 75.

In each of 42 states and in the District of Columbia the number of resident Negroes native of other states increased during the decade 1900–1910. It thus appears that in the case of each of these states immigration of Negroes native of other states was, during the decade, more than sufficient to cover the mortality among immigrants living in the state in 1900, or entering the state during the decade, and also the emigration of natives of other states during the decade.

In the same period for each state and the District of Columbia, with the single exception of Vermont, the number of Negroes native of the state living in other states had increased.

The state showing the highest percentage of its Negro natives resident in other states in 1910 was Nevada. Of the 376 Negroes born in Nevada 332, or 88.3 per cent, were living in other states, only 44 of the 484 native Negro residents of Nevada being natives of the state. The state showing the smallest proportion of its natives living in other states was Florida. Of the 215,110 Negroes native of Florida only 16,614, or 7.7 per cent, were living in other states. Of the 664,823 Negroes born in Texas, 62,062, or 9.3 per cent, were living in other states. Among the Southern states the percentage "living in other states" was relatively high for the northern border states lying east of the Mississippi (Delaware 30.6 per cent, Virginia 28.9, Kentucky 27.9, West Virginia 25.4, Tennessee

NEGROES BORN IN EACH STATE, WITH NUMBER AND PERCENTAGE LIVING IN OTHER STATES, AND NEGROES LIVING IN EACH STATE, WITH NUMBER AND PERCENTAGE BORN IN OTHER STATES: 1910 AND 1900.

Table 17 STATE.	NEGROES BORN IN AND LIVING IN THE UNITED STATES FOR WHOM STATE OF BIRTH WAS REPORTED: 1910.								NEGROES BORN IN AND LIVING IN THE UNITED STATES FOR WHOM STATE OF BIRTH WAS REPORTED: 1900.							
	Born in the specified state.			Born in and living in the specified state.	Living in the specified state.			Gain (+) or loss (−) through interstate migration.	Born in the specified state.			Born in and living in the specified state.	Living in the specified state.			Gain (+) or loss (−) through interstate migration.
	Total.	Living in other states.			Total.	Born in other states.			Total.	Living in other states.			Total.	Born in other states.		
		Number.	Per cent.			Number.	Per cent.			Number.	Per cent.			Number.	Per cent.	
UNITED STATES	9,746,043	1,616,608	16.6	8,129,435	9,746,043	1,616,608	16.6		8,786,547	1,373,996	15.6	7,412,551	8,786,547	1,373,996	15.6	
NEW ENGLAND:																
Maine	1,585	783	49.4	802	1,112	310	27.9	−473	1,321	573	43.4	748	1,076	328	30.5	−245
New Hampshire	506	272	53.8	234	515	281	54.6	+9	444	229	51.6	215	627	412	65.7	+183
Vermont	1,045	608	58.2	437	1,546	1,109	71.7	+501	1,204	753	62.5	451	802	351	43.8	−402
Massachusetts	19,078	4,125	21.6	14,953	31,641	16,688	52.7	+12,563	15,031	3,284	21.8	11,747	28,198	16,451	58.3	+13,167
Rhode Island	5,401	1,317	24.4	4,084	8,597	4,513	52.5	+3,196	4,778	908	19.0	3,870	8,656	4,786	55.3	+3,878
Connecticut	10,184	2,888	28.4	7,296	14,698	7,402	50.4	+4,514	9,884	2,337	23.6	7,547	14,934	7,387	49.5	+5,050
MIDDLE ATLANTIC:																
New York	61,580	11,830	19.2	49,750	120,029	70,279	58.6	+58,449	54,574	9,960	18.3	44,614	94,642	50,028	52.9	+40,068
New Jersey	45,312	8,295	18.3	37,017	87,762	50,745	57.8	+42,450	38,119	6,456	16.9	31,663	68,628	36,965	53.9	+30,509
Pennsylvania	105,253	20,293	19.3	84,960	190,738	105,778	55.5	+85,485	84,799	14,434	17.0	70,365	155,207	84,842	54.7	+70,408
EAST NORTH CENTRAL:																
Ohio	76,044	16,850	22.2	59,194	109,643	50,449	46.0	+33,599	70,081	13,849	19.8	56,232	95,654	39,422	41.2	+25,573
Indiana	34,794	9,570	27.5	25,224	59,812	34,588	57.8	+25,018	32,141	7,107	21.9	25,304	57,059	31,755	55.7	+24,648
Illinois	48,564	12,647	26.0	35,917	106,141	70,224	66.2	+57,577	38,761	8,739	22.5	30,022	83,514	53,492	64.1	+44,753
Michigan	11,576	3,384	29.2	8,192	14,516	6,324	43.6	+2,940	10,951	3,036	27.7	7,915	13,469	5,554	41.2	+2,518
Wisconsin	2,248	1,077	47.9	1,171	2,763	1,592	57.6	+515	2,018	1,026	50.8	992	2,418	1,426	59.0	+400
WEST NORTH CENTRAL:																
Minnesota	2,738	1,182	43.2	1,556	6,688	5,132	76.7	+3,950	1,665	569	34.2	1,096	4,690	3,594	76.6	+3,025
Iowa	8,736	3,483	39.9	5,253	14,702	9,449	64.3	+5,966	6,836	2,225	32.5	4,611	12,503	7,892	63.1	+5,667
Missouri	149,218	39,269	26.3	109,949	155,248	45,299	29.2	+6,030	155,029	34,503	22.3	120,526	159,981	39,455	24.7	+4,952
North Dakota	297	195	65.7	102	592	490	82.8	+295	143	74	51.7	69	273	204	74.7	+130
South Dakota	495	356	71.9	139	782	643	82.2	+287	191	87	45.5	104	444	340	76.6	+253
Nebraska	2,846	1,189	41.8	1,657	7,397	5,740	77.6	+4,551	2,129	707	33.2	1,422	6,168	4,746	76.9	+4,039
Kansas	33,786	10,852	32.1	22,934	53,204	30,270	56.9	+19,418	29,797	7,960	26.7	21,837	51,626	29,789	57.7	+21,829
SOUTH ATLANTIC:																
Delaware	32,664	9,996	30.6	22,668	31,067	8,399	27.0	−1,597	33,050	9,776	29.6	23,274	30,571	7,297	23.9	−2,479
Maryland	262,540	60,946	23.2	201,594	231,363	29,769	12.9	−31,177	266,637	57,965	21.7	208,672	234,318	25,646	10.9	−32,319
District of Columbia	52,282	11,823	22.6	40,459	93,517	53,058	56.7	+41,235	45,704	9,364	20.5	36,340	86,446	50,106	58.0	+40,742
Virginia	876,806	253,334	28.9	623,472	670,042	46,570	7.0	−206,764	878,104	252,560	28.8	625,544	659,674	34,130	5.2	−218,430
West Virginia	36,417	9,257	25.4	27,160	63,733	36,573	57.4	+27,316	29,013	7,593	26.2	21,420	43,056	21,636	50.3	+14,043
North Carolina	806,537	143,143	17.7	663,394	696,786	33,392	4.8	−109,751	733,359	136,468	18.6	596,891	623,238	26,347	4.2	−110,121
South Carolina	956,605	135,547	14.2	821,058	835,126	14,068	1.7	−121,479	881,495	113,897	12.9	767,598	781,867	14,269	1.8	−99,628
Georgia	1,248,352	151,095	12.1	1,097,257	1,173,078	75,821	6.5	−75,274	1,089,474	131,229	12.0	958,245	1,032,809	74,564	7.2	−56,665
Florida	215,110	16,614	7.7	198,496	299,774	101,278	33.8	+84,664	168,640	11,625	6.9	157,015	225,217	68,202	30.3	+56,557
EAST SOUTH CENTRAL:																
Kentucky	323,794	90,340	27.9	233,454	260,916	27,462	10.5	−62,878	344,789	84,764	24.6	260,025	283,784	23,759	8.4	−61,005
Tennessee	517,072	123,899	24.0	393,173	470,878	77,705	16.5	−46,194	508,067	103,060	20.3	405,007	478,883	73,876	15.4	−29,184
Alabama	971,167	131,346	13.5	839,821	905,802	65,981	7.3	−65,365	873,184	120,089	13.8	753,095	825,489	72,394	8.8	−47,695
Mississippi	1,032,565	132,875	12.9	899,690	1,006,126	106,436	10.6	−26,439	898,853	108,166	12.0	790,687	906,081	115,394	12.7	+7,228
WEST SOUTH CENTRAL:																
Arkansas	334,589	38,549	11.5	296,040	440,105	144,065	32.7	+105,516	267,405	27,140	10.1	240,265	364,968	124,703	34.2	+97,563
Louisiana	726,496	83,763	11.5	642,733	710,755	68,022	9.6	−15,741	632,020	52,020	8.2	580,189	649,329	69,140	10.6	+17,120
Oklahoma[1]	51,334	5,358	10.4	45,976	136,396	90,420	66.3	+85,062	24,984	1,981	7.9	23,003	55,306	32,303	58.4	+30,322
Texas	664,823	62,062	9.3	602,761	684,644	81,883	12.0	+19,821	541,491	24,577	4.5	516,914	616,168	99,254	16.1	+74,677
MOUNTAIN:																
Montana	665	326	49.0	339	1,706	1,367	80.1	+1,041	344	122	35.5	222	1,469	1,247	84.9	+1,125
Idaho	468	399	85.3	69	608	539	88.7	+140	104	74	71.2	30	278	248	89.2	+174
Wyoming	314	161	51.3	153	2,146	1,993	92.9	+1,832	176	79	44.9	97	925	828	89.5	+749
Colorado	3,513	1,357	38.6	2,156	11,096	8,940	80.6	+7,583	2,165	644	29.7	1,521	8,319	6,798	81.7	+6,154
New Mexico	941	531	56.4	410	1,577	1,167	74.0	+636	605	271	44.8	334	1,553	1,219	78.5	+948
Arizona	538	251	46.7	287	1,945	1,658	85.2	+1,407	325	61	18.8	264	1,744	1,480	84.9	+1,419
Utah	527	365	69.3	162	1,009	847	83.9	+482	252	129	51.2	123	642	519	80.8	+390
Nevada	376	332	88.3	44	484	440	90.9	+108	92	64	69.6	28	124	96	77.4	+32
PACIFIC:																
Washington	1,546	1,012	65.5	534	5,591	5,057	90.4	+4,045	923	625	67.1	307	2,300	1,993	86.7	+1,368
Oregon	398	204	51.3	194	1,387	1,193	86.0	+989	330	117	35.5	213	1,046	833	79.6	+716
California	6,318	1,258	19.9	5,060	20,260	15,200	75.0	+13,942	4,598	720	15.7	3,878	10,374	6,496	62.6	+5,776

[1] Includes population of Indian Territory for 1900.

24, Maryland 23.2), and relatively low in the states lying farther to the south and west (North Carolina 17.7 per cent, South Carolina 14.2, Alabama 13.5, Mississippi 12.9, Georgia 12.1, Arkansas 11.5, Louisiana 11.5, Oklahoma 10.4, Texas 9.3, and Florida 7.7). In 20 of the 32 Northern and Western states the percentage "living in other states" exceeded the maximum percentage shown for any Southern state (namely, 30.6 for Delaware).

Table 17 shows also the net gain or loss through interstate migration of each state for the two years 1900 and 1910. In 1910 it is shown that the state of Virginia had lost on account of interstate migration of Negroes, 206,764 in population. For this state there were reported as born in the state and living in other states 253,334, and as living in the state and born in other states 46,570, the difference between these numbers giving the net loss of the state on account of interstate migration. The corresponding net loss in 1900 was somewhat greater than in 1910, being in 1900 218,430. Generally, it is true of the Northern and Western states that they have gained by interstate migration, the only exception among these states being in fact Maine, and generally the Southern states have lost, although in the case of six Southern states, three being in the West South Central division, the population has increased on account of interstate migration.

The total number of interstate migrants in 1910, as shown in Table 17 (1,616,608), exceeded the number of interdivisional migrants, as shown in Table 15 (963,153), by 653,455, which was the number of intradivisional migrants among native Negroes, i. e., the number of Negroes who had migrated from their native state and were in 1910 living in some other state in the same geographic division. This total embraces, as is shown by the more detailed classification of Table 20, 91,333 natives of the state of Virginia who were living in other states of the South Atlantic division, since as is shown in Table 20, in the Negro population native of Virginia (numbering in 1910, 876,806) the number living in the South Atlantic division (714,805) exceeded the number living in Virginia (623,472) by 91,333. Similar aggregates may be determined for each other state of this division and of other divisions, the sum of these aggregates giving the total of 653,455, as the number of intradivisional migrants in the native Negro population.

While this intradivisional migration may properly be characterized as being in large part short-distance migration across common boundaries of contiguous states, it undoubtedly embraces cases of migrants who have moved very considerable distances, the areas of the several geographic divisions being in each case sufficient to embrace extensive migratory shiftings of population. It is possible, for example, to travel directly west from the lower Mississippi River for a distance of more than 700 miles without leaving the West South Central division, and undoubtedly there is a considerable Negro migration westward within this division. Some of this movement is indicated in Table 20, which shows that 10,771 natives of Arkansas and 8,498 natives of Louisiana were living in Oklahoma in 1910 and that 6,328 natives of Arkansas and 19,703 natives of Louisiana were living in Texas. It may be noted incidentally that there had been within this division also a considerable Negro migration northward and eastward out of the state of Texas, as is shown by the number of native Texans living in Oklahoma (35,397), Arkansas (5,383), and Louisiana (8,058).

Although the intradivisional shiftings of population embrace migrations for distances amounting in individual cases to hundreds of miles, it will be apparent that migration for a very short distance may in other cases carry the migrant across a divisional or sectional boundary, and bring him into the class of interdivisional or intersectional migrants. Migration from the South into the North may be effected by crossing the Ohio River from Kentucky into Illinois, Indiana, or Ohio, or by crossing the Mississippi into Missouri, or by simply moving across any common boundary separating a Southern from a Northern state.

On the other hand, a very considerable amount of short-distance migration is intrastate, and is, therefore, not at all in evidence even in Table 20, classifying the population by state of birth and by state of residence. This table can not take account, for example, of the very considerable and persistent migration out of rural districts into urban communities where the rural district and the urban community both lie within the boundaries of a single state.

It should be borne in mind further that the number of interstate migrants as it is figured from the census returns, is determined by the place of residence at the date of the census. A native of Georgia or of any other Southern state who had lived during the greater portion of his life in New York City, but had prior to the census returned to his native state would not be distinguished in the census returns as a migrant.

It will be clear also that a tabulation by state of birth affords no indication of the number of migrants or of migrations in any given period, because the migration revealed by the fact that the person enumerated in the census was living in a different state from that in which he was born may have occurred at any period during his lifetime. It may therefore be a very recent event or it may have occurred many years ago.

Table 18 covering the two years 1910 and 1900 summarizes data for the South, the North, and the West. It shows for the Negro population born in the South the number and proportion living in the state of birth and the number and proportion living in some other state in the South, in the North, and in the West; and for the Negro population living in the South the number and proportion born in the state of residence and the number and proportion born in some other state in the South, in the North, and in the West— corresponding data being shown for the North, and for the West. As regards the population figures of Table 18, the lower half of the table is a rearrangement of the detail of the upper half, although the bases upon which the percentages are figured are different in the two halves of the table. For the Negro population born in and living in the United States the aggregate born in the several sections combined is of course identical with the aggregate living in the several sections combined (9,746,043 in 1910, and 8,786,547 in 1900, which aggregates are distributed twice in Table 18). The slight differences in certain of the percentages of Table 18 from similar percentages shown in Tables 12 and 13 are accounted for by the inclusion in Tables 12 and 13 of Negroes for whom state of birth was not reported and native Negroes born outside the United States.

The distributions of Table 18 indicate a general though not very marked increase in intrasectional as well as in intersectional migration during the decade 1900–1910. The tendency among Negroes born in the South to migrate from the state of birth to another Southern state, increased slightly, the percentage living in the South outside the state of birth among natives of the South increasing from 11 in 1900 to 11.2 in 1910, and similarly the tendency among Negroes born in the North to migrate to a Northern state, and among Negroes born in the West to migrate to a Western state increased (the percentage change for these natives being from 14.5 to 16 in the North and from 8.2 to 9.5 in the West). The proportion living in the state of birth accordingly decreased among those born in each section (among natives of the South from 84.8 per cent in 1900 to 84 per cent in 1910, among natives of the North from 78.8 to 75.8 and among natives of the West from 70.7 to 60.3). Among natives of the South the proportion living in the North increased from 4.1 to 4.6 per cent, and the proportion living in the West from 0.2 to 0.3.

The small proportion born in the North among Negroes living in the South (0.4 per cent) remained unchanged and among Negroes living in the West decreased (from 27.3 to 24.9 per cent). The proportion born in the West is inconsiderable among Negroes living in the South and in the North.

Reference has already been made to Table 20, in which the Negro population is classified according to division and state in which born and by division or state of residence, this being, as regards 1910, the basic state of birth table for Negroes; to Table 21, which shows for Negroes born in each state the number living in selected states of residence; and to Table 22, which shows the number of natives and of foreign-born Negroes resident in each state, and for the natives the number born in selected states.

INTERSTATE MIGRANTS IN URBAN COMMUNITIES.

Table 19 classifies by nativity for 1910 the Negro and white population of cities of 50,000 or more inhabitants having a Negro population of 5,000 or more, the cities being grouped as northern and western and as southern cities, and arranged in order in each group according to their Negro populations. In this table it is shown that of the 91,709 Negroes living in New York City in 1910, 26,977 were born in the state of New York, and 52,202, or 56.9 per cent, in other states. The 773 "other native" include those born in the United States, state of birth not reported, born in outlying possessions, or at sea under the United States flag, and American citizens born abroad. The number foreign born in the Negro population of New York City was 11,757. Similar data are shown for the white population.

Among Negroes the percentage born in a state other than that in which the city of residence was located was highest for Los Angeles, of whose Negro population 83.4 per cent were born outside of California. The second highest proportion was that for Oklahoma City, 82.6 per cent; the third, that for Jersey City, 71.8 per cent. In 22 of the 41 cities listed in Table 19 the proportion born outside of the state exceeded one-half, the proportion being generally much higher in the northern and western than it was in the southern cities. Exceptions among southern cities were Oklahoma City, Washington, and Jacksonville, each of which showed a high percentage of migrants. In the aggregate population for northern and western cities 60.9 per cent of the Negro as compared with 13.9 per cent for the white population was born outside the state in which the city of residence was located, the proportion being much higher for Negroes than for whites. In the southern cities as a group the proportion "Born outside the state" was much lower for Negroes and higher for whites than in the northern and western cities, the proportion for Negroes of 26.1 per cent being only slightly above that of 24.8 per cent for whites.

Table 18	NEGROES BORN IN AND LIVING IN THE UNITED STATES FOR WHOM STATE OF BIRTH WAS REPORTED.			
NATIVITY AND RESIDENCE.	Number.		Per cent.	
	1910	1900	1910	1900
Total....................	9,746,043	8,786,547	....	....
Born in the South....................	9,109,153	8,216,458	100.0	100.0
Living in the state of birth.........	7,649,206	6,964,184	84.0	84.8
Living outside the state of birth....	1,459,947	1,252,274	16.0	15.2
In the South......................	1,019,413	902,623	11.2	11.0
In the North......................	415,533	336,076	4.6	4.1
In the West......................	25,001	13,575	0.3	0.2
Born in the North....................	621,286	560,166	100.0	100.0
Living in the state of birth.........	470,821	441,350	75.8	78.8
Living outside the state of birth....	150,465	118,816	24.2	21.2
In the North......................	99,477	81,118	16.0	14.5
In the South......................	39,077	29,650	6.3	5.3
In the West......................	11,911	8,048	1.9	1.4
Born in the West....................	15,604	9,923	100.0	100.0
Living in the state of birth.........	9,408	7,017	60.3	70.7
Living outside the state of birth....	6,196	2,906	39.7	29.3
In the West......................	1,489	812	9.5	8.2
In the South......................	2,412	746	15.5	7.5
In the North......................	2,295	1,348	14.7	13.6
Total....................	9,746,043	8,786,547	....	....
Living in the South....................	8,710,108	7,897,204	100.0	100.0
Born in the state of residence.......	7,649,206	6,964,184	87.8	88.2
Born outside the state of residence..	1,060,902	933,020	12.2	11.8
In the South......................	1,019,413	902,623	11.7	11.4
In the North......................	39,077	29,650	0.4	0.4
In the West......................	2,412	747	(1)	(1)
Living in the North....................	988,126	859,891	100.0	100.0
Born in the State of residence.......	470,821	441,350	47.6	51.3
Born outside the state of residence..	517,305	418,541	52.4	48.7
In the North......................	99,477	81,118	10.1	9.4
In the South......................	415,533	336,076	42.1	39.1
In the West......................	2,295	1,347	0.2	0.2
Living in the West....................	47,809	29,452	100.0	100.0
Born in the state of residence.......	9,408	7,017	19.7	23.8
Born outside the state of residence..	38,401	22,435	80.3	76.2
In the West......................	1,489	812	3.1	2.8
In the South......................	25,001	13,575	52.2	46.1
In the North......................	11,911	8,048	24.9	27.3

[1] Less than one-tenth of 1 per cent.

The proportion born in the South increased among Negroes living in the North (from 39.1 to 42.1 per cent) and in the West (from 46.1 to 52.2 per cent).

MIGRANTS AND IMMIGRANTS IN NEGRO AND WHITE POPULATION OF CITIES OF 50,000 OR MORE INHABITANTS, HAVING 5,000 OR MORE NEGROES: 1910.

CITY.[1]	All classes.	Negro. Total.	Negro. Born in the state.	Negro. Born in other states. Number.	Negro. Born in other states. Per cent.	Negro. Other native.[2]	Negro. Foreign born.	White. Total.	White. Born in the state.	White. Born in other states. Number.	White. Born in other states. Per cent.	White. Other native.[2]	White. Foreign born.	Indian, Chinese, Japanese, and other colored.
All cities [1]	17,025,664	1,228,509	719,566	479,793	39.1	9,300	19,850	15,774,773	8,580,586	2,420,968	15.3	66,138	4,707,081	22,382
NORTHERN AND WESTERN CITIES: Total	14,123,471	456,653	155,046	278,066	60.9	5,414	18,127	13,646,530	7,224,187	1,893,441	13.9	56,033	4,472,869	20,288
New York, N. Y.	4,766,883	91,709	26,977	52,202	56.9	773	11,757	4,669,162	2,414,318	311,477	6.7	15,664	1,927,703	6,012
Mahattan Borough	2,331,542	60,534	14,309	37,001	61.1	485	8,739	2,266,578	991,167	159,438	7.0	11,954	1,104,019	4,430
Bronx Borough	430,980	4,117	1,484	2,266	55.0	23	344	426,650	249,388	27,278	6.4	1,049	148,935	213
Brooklyn Borough	1,634,351	22,708	8,768	11,182	49.2	254	2,504	1,610,487	937,250	99,849	6.2	2,032	571,356	1,156
Queens Borough	284,041	3,198	1,805	1,284	40.2	7	102	280,691	184,628	16,502	5.9	446	79,115	152
Richmond Borough	85,969	1,152	611	469	40.7	4	68	84,756	51,885	8,410	9.9	183	24,278	61
Philadelphia, Pa	1,549,008	84,459	29,686	53,161	62.9	455	1,157	1,463,371	951,780	126,692	8.7	2,321	382,578	1,178
Chicago, Ill.	2,185,283	44,103	8,519	34,017	77.1	903	664	2,139,057	1,008,868	337,253	15.8	11,719	781,217	2,123
St. Louis, Mo	687,029	43,960	20,782	22,593	51.4	465	120	642,488	377,039	137,181	21.4	2,562	125,706	581
Pittsburgh, Pa.	533,905	25,623	8,810	16,289	63.6	258	266	508,008	323,773	42,093	8.3	1,706	140,436	274
Kansas City, Mo	248,381	23,566	12,887	9,976	42.3	653	50	224,677	93,696	100,497	44.7	5,157	25,327	138
Indianapolis, Ind.	233,650	21,816	7,200	14,434	62.2	151	31	211,780	142,005	49,141	23.2	867	19,767	54
Cincinnati, Ohio	363,591	19,639	5,575	13,658	69.5	361	45	343,919	232,018	53,871	15.7	1,238	56,792	33
Boston, Mass.	670,585	13,564	3,961	7,759	57.2	90	1,754	655,696	342,995	69,827	10.6	2,152	240,722	1,325
Columbus, Ohio	181,511	12,739	6,705	5,912	46.4	81	41	168,709	128,314	22,979	13.6	1,131	16,285	63
Newark, N. J.	347,469	9,475	3,931	5,331	56.3	66	147	337,742	179,529	46,441	13.8	1,117	110,655	252
Kansas City, Kans.	82,331	9,286	3,057	6,098	65.7	115	16	72,996	27,159	34,743	47.6	750	10,344	49
Cleveland, Ohio	560,663	8,448	3,015	4,885	57.8	256	292	551,925	292,747	61,667	11.2	1,808	195,703	290
Los Angeles, Cal	319,198	7,599	1,050	6,341	83.4	103	105	305,307	62,084	180,590	59.1	2,049	60,584	6,292
Evansville, Ind.	69,647	6,266	2,010	4,235	67.6	19	2	63,377	43,081	15,738	24.8	96	4,462	4
Camden, N. J.	94,538	6,076	2,540	3,463	57.0	28	45	88,391	45,229	27,339	30.9	141	15,682	71
Jersey City, N. J.	267,779	5,960	1,500	4,278	71.8	27	155	261,659	129,879	53,489	20.4	594	77,697	160
East St. Louis, Ill.	58,547	5,882	1,933	3,907	66.4	35	7	52,646	27,948	15,123	28.7	175	9,400	19
Detroit, Mich.	465,766	5,741	1,850	2,575	44.9	412	904	459,926	243,383	57,929	12.6	2,049	156,565	99
Denver, Colo.	213,381	5,426	973	4,277	78.8	130	46	207,071	53,781	112,193	54.2	2,156	38,941	884
Providence, R. I.	224,326	5,316	2,085	2,675	50.3	33	523	218,623	104,561	37,178	17.0	581	76,303	387
SOUTHERN CITIES: Total	2,902,193	771,856	564,520	201,727	26.1	3,886	1,723	2,128,243	1,356,399	527,527	24.8	10,105	234,212	2,094
Washington, D. C.	331,069	94,446	40,459	53,058	56.2	691	238	236,128	98,843	111,452	47.2	1,482	24,351	495
New Orleans, La.	339,075	89,262	76,383	12,169	13.6	333	377	249,403	193,787	25,539	10.2	2,391	27,686	410
Baltimore, Md.	558,485	84,749	64,872	19,240	22.7	274	363	473,387	347,168	48,359	10.2	817	77,043	349
Memphis, Tenn.	131,105	52,441	26,044	25,595	48.8	778	24	78,590	36,167	35,008	44.5	948	6,467	74
Birmingham, Ala.	132,685	52,305	39,593	12,419	23.7	271	22	80,369	45,744	28,621	35.6	304	5,700	11
Atlanta, Ga.	154,839	51,902	45,683	6,071	11.7	114	34	102,861	72,815	25,277	24.6	359	4,410	76
Richmond, Va.	127,628	46,733	42,926	3,705	7.9	62	40	80,879	67,177	9,448	11.7	169	4,085	16
Louisville, Ky.	223,928	40,522	33,143	7,229	17.8	120	30	183,390	135,577	30,086	16.4	291	17,436	16
Nashville, Tenn.	110,364	36,523	33,443	2,991	8.2	73	16	73,831	58,531	12,223	16.6	84	2,993	10
Savannah, Ga.	65,064	33,246	21,614	11,499	34.6	45	88	31,784	20,313	8,097	25.5	42	3,332	34
Charleston, S. C.	58,833	31,056	30,423	579	1.9	23	31	27,764	22,335	2,976	10.7	49	2,404	13
Jacksonville, Fla.	57,699	29,293	13,430	15,630	53.4	81	152	28,329	10,352	15,020	53.0	469	2,488	77
Norfolk, Va.	67,452	25,039	16,728	8,204	32.8	38	69	42,353	26,724	11,998	28.3	67	3,564	60
Houston, Tex.	78,800	23,929	19,313	4,399	18.4	155	62	54,832	30,467	17,628	32.1	419	6,318	39
Mobile, Ala.	51,521	22,763	19,974	2,451	10.8	258	80	28,737	19,791	6,623	23.0	115	2,208	21
Dallas, Tex.	92,104	18,024	14,318	3,565	19.8	127	14	74,043	38,283	30,147	40.7	394	5,219	37
Fort Worth, Tex.	73,312	13,280	10,759	2,263	17.0	232	26	59,960	31,559	23,552	39.3	640	4,209	72
San Antonio, Tex.	96,614	10,716	9,219	1,324	12.4	141	32	85,801	48,870	18,983	22.1	541	17,407	
Wilmington, Del.	87,411	9,081	5,107	3,932	43.3	28	14	78,309	44,108	20,349	26.0	174	13,678	97
Oklahoma City, Okla.	64,205	6,546	1,089	5,404	82.6	42	11	57,493	7,788	46,141	80.3	350	3,214	166

[1] Cities of 50,000 or more inhabitants, having 5,000 or more Negroes.
[2] Includes persons born in the United States, State of birth not reported; persons born in outlying possessions, at sea under the United States flag, and American citizens born abroad.

In the South and in the North and West, for the aggregate Negro population of the cities, the proportion born outside the state of residence was considerably above the corresponding proportion for the Negro population as a whole in these sections— 26.1, as compared with 12.2 per cent in the South, and 60.9 as compared with 53.6 per cent in the North and West.

It should be borne in mind that the proportion born outside the state in the case of any individual city is materially affected by the location of the city. A city located on the boundary of two states may draw population from the neighboring state in much larger proportion than a city located in the interior of the state, remote from the territory of other states.

TABLE 20.—NATIVE NEGRO POPULATION, CLASSIFIED ACCORDING TO DIVISION AND STATE IN WHICH BORN, BY DIVISIONS AND STATES: 1910.

[Table continued on page 76.]

| DIVISION AND STATE OF RESIDENCE. | Total native Negro population: 1910. | United States. | NEGRO POPULATION BORN IN— | | | | | | | | | United States (state not reported). | Outlying possessions.[1] |
			New England.	Middle Atlantic.	East North Central.	West North Central.	South Atlantic.	East South Central.	West South Central.	Mountain.	Pacific.		
UNITED STATES	9,787,424	9,783,986	37,799	212,145	173,226	198,116	4,487,313	2,844,598	1,777,242	7,342	8,262	37,943	3,438
GEOGRAPHIC DIVISIONS:													
New England	58,596	58,407	30,815	3,952	398	206	21,353	966	281	56	82	298	189
Middle Atlantic	401,548	400,879	3,877	189,962	4,259	997	191,438	5,769	1,294	338	595	2,350	669
East North Central	297,452	296,038	586	4,967	145,187	13,110	35,242	88,337	4,968	262	216	3,163	1,414
West North Central	241,855	241,693	244	1,144	8,540	162,054	12,568	39,937	13,380	554	192	3,080	162
South Atlantic	4,104,413	4,104,020	1,401	9,154	3,150	1,127	4,039,173	37,491	2,171	448	371	9,534	393
East South Central	2,651,888	2,651,797	185	953	5,126	3,064	108,702	2,491,607	33,605	319	161	8,075	91
West South Central	1,982,557	1,982,345	339	953	3,442	10,183	70,311	171,671	1,713,888	764	349	10,445	212
Mountain	21,094	21,019	100	355	1,342	4,298	2,672	4,341	3,127	4,122	214	448	75
Pacific	28,021	27,788	252	705	1,782	3,077	5,854	4,479	4,528	479	6,082	550	233
NEW ENGLAND:													
Maine	1,126	1,123	890	31	7	2	158	9	11	2	2	11	3
New Hampshire	524	520	318	24	2	....	155	14	....	....	2	5	4
Vermont	1,581	1,553	504	113	64	75	402	309	68	6	5	7	28
Massachusetts	31,903	31,785	16,360	1,812	233	92	12,438	476	150	35	45	144	118
Rhode Island	8,657	8,637	4,842	505	26	16	3,112	62	17	3	14	40	20
Connecticut	14,805	14,789	7,901	1,467	66	21	5,088	96	35	10	14	91	16
MIDDLE ATLANTIC:													
New York	121,340	120,923	2,352	55,056	1,198	478	57,585	2,255	654	164	287	894	417
New Jersey	88,273	88,205	700	45,396	387	129	40,014	741	232	50	113	443	68
Pennsylvania	191,935	191,751	825	89,510	2,674	390	93,839	2,773	408	124	195	1,013	184
EAST NORTH CENTRAL:													
Ohio	110,797	110,489	164	2,670	61,711	545	20,308	23,572	559	58	56	846	308
Indiana	60,223	60,177	47	238	28,787	577	3,186	26,618	319	25	15	365	46
Illinois	108,121	107,866	239	1,371	42,449	11,499	9,999	36,437	3,878	154	115	1,725	255
Michigan	15,475	14,694	110	600	10,616	255	1,449	1,296	152	20	18	178	781
Wisconsin	2,836	2,812	26	88	1,624	234	300	414	60	5	12	49	24
WEST NORTH CENTRAL:													
Minnesota	6,884	6,841	58	189	1,167	2,727	790	1,423	289	25	20	153	43
Iowa	14,918	14,907	24	145	1,117	8,909	2,303	1,811	338	30	25	205	11
Missouri	157,126	157,080	79	431	4,241	113,886	5,685	23,636	7,008	196	86	1,832	46
North Dakota	615	613	9	23	98	232	91	109	23	3	4	21	2
South Dakota	808	807	5	24	105	383	97	122	30	12	4	25	1
Nebraska	7,592	7,564	29	103	464	4,399	633	1,218	476	62	13	167	28
Kansas	53,912	53,881	40	229	1,348	31,518	2,969	11,618	5,216	226	40	677	31
SOUTH ATLANTIC:													
Delaware	31,146	31,141	45	1,304	26	12	29,626	30	14	6	4	74	5
Maryland	231,799	231,752	247	2,220	243	86	227,879	441	149	30	68	389	47
District of Columbia	94,208	94,162	301	1,512	485	183	89,441	1,155	379	37	24	645	46
Virginia	670,800	670,740	337	1,967	448	136	664,024	2,687	180	133	130	698	60
West Virginia	64,091	64,080	40	642	1,296	92	59,807	1,712	87	24	33	347	11
North Carolina	697,755	697,730	84	507	121	136	694,612	1,116	147	32	31	944	25
South Carolina	835,771	835,758	93	175	41	73	833,987	605	105	40	7	632	13
Georgia	1,176,759	1,176,629	121	375	236	269	1,155,923	15,479	530	103	42	3,551	130
Florida	302,084	302,028	133	452	254	140	283,874	14,266	580	43	32	2,254	56
EAST SOUTH CENTRAL:													
Kentucky	261,590	261,569	24	230	2,731	675	5,602	251,012	567	40	35	653	21
Tennessee	472,989	472,966	75	278	1,173	982	436,423	5,335	110	58	2,088	23
Alabama	908,000	907,974	48	279	576	397	47,201	855,654	1,535	80	32	2,172	26
Mississippi	1,009,309	1,009,288	38	166	646	1,010	29,455	948,518	26,168	89	36	3,161	21
WEST SOUTH CENTRAL:													
Arkansas	442,811	442,793	41	177	1,183	2,090	29,533	79,269	327,613	123	76	2,688	18
Louisiana	713,299	713,220	113	279	615	889	14,229	38,631	655,809	129	61	2,465	79
Oklahoma	137,489	137,465	33	148	897	4,864	7,190	22,468	100,642	108	46	1,069	24
Texas	688,958	688,867	152	349	747	2,340	19,359	31,303	629,824	404	166	4,223	91
MOUNTAIN:													
Montana	1,773	1,761	10	58	181	371	254	307	121	382	22	55	12
Idaho	623	616	5	21	64	135	78	103	67	115	20	8	7
Wyoming	2,197	2,189	16	38	202	451	460	532	218	215	14	43	8
Colorado	11,323	11,295	44	148	621	2,723	1,306	2,600	1,306	2,311	37	199	28
New Mexico	1,594	1,593	3	17	57	133	166	284	439	459	19	16	1
Arizona	1,978	1,971	6	36	86	184	223	262	766	331	51	26	7
Utah	1,112	1,108	11	25	83	223	106	172	119	249	21	99	4
Nevada	494	486	5	12	48	78	79	81	91	60	30	2	8
PACIFIC:													
Washington	5,820	5,770	52	171	682	881	1,226	1,238	528	140	673	179	50
Oregon	1,430	1,406	12	69	153	233	236	223	161	35	265	19	24
California	20,771	20,612	188	465	947	1,963	4,392	3,018	3,839	304	5,144	352	159

[1] Includes also persons born at sea under United States flag and American citizens born abroad.

TABLE **20.**—NATIVE NEGRO POPULATION, CLASSIFIED ACCORDING TO DIVISION AND STATE IN WHICH BORN, BY DIVISIONS AND STATES: 1910—Continued.

[Table continued on page 77.]

DIVISION AND STATE OF RESIDENCE.	NEGRO POPULATION BORN IN—													
	New England division.						Middle Atlantic division.			East North Central division.				
	Maine.	New Hampshire.	Vermont.	Massachusetts.	Rhode Island.	Connecticut.	New York.	New Jersey.	Pennsylvania.	Ohio.	Indiana.	Illinois.	Michigan.	Wisconsin.
UNITED STATES	1,585	506	1,045	19,078	5,401	10,184	61,580	45,312	105,253	76,044	34,794	48,564	11,576	2,248
GEOGRAPHIC DIVISIONS:														
New England	1,094	382	641	15,975	4,553	8,170	2,169	731	1,052	214	57	67	52	8
Middle Atlantic	147	24	257	1,629	472	1,348	54,777	42,763	92,422	2,962	393	533	304	67
East North Central	60	13	21	293	51	148	1,386	239	3,342	65,326	30,178	38,038	10,086	1,559
West North Central	33	5	19	115	25	47	387	100	657	1,586	1,166	5,033	402	353
South Atlantic	120	21	62	661	222	315	2,038	1,248	5,868	2,201	293	418	190	48
East South Central	36	4	6	86	22	31	209	61	683	1,603	1,645	1,703	125	50
West South Central	56	47	25	139	27	45	224	78	651	1,018	551	1,651	152	70
Mountain	15	4	7	47	7	20	99	39	217	499	210	509	88	36
Pacific	24	6	7	133	22	60	291	53	361	635	301	612	177	57
NEW ENGLAND:														
Maine	802	10	1	64	8	5	13	3	15	6				1
New Hampshire	13	234	13	45	5	8	15	4	5	2				
Vermont	3	7	437	49	3	5	62	12	39	30	15	13	4	2
Massachusetts	254	122	145	14,953	335	551	889	341	582	123	28	39	38	5
Rhode Island	14	6	14	419	4,084	305	230	94	181	14	4	6	2	
Connecticut	8	3	31	445	118	7,296	960	277	230	39	10	9	8	
MIDDLE ATLANTIC:														
New York	75	13	184	917	264	899	49,750	2,617	2,689	638	129	246	156	29
New Jersey	36	3	30	301	96	234	3,606	37,017	4,773	215	56	78	24	14
Pennsylvania	36	8	43	411	112	215	1,421	3,129	84,960	2,109	208	209	124	24
EAST NORTH CENTRAL:														
Ohio	25	4	6	65	18	46	476	91	2,103	59,194	1,375	430	669	43
Indiana	3		4	21	3	16	65	21	152	1,934	25,224	1,206	405	18
Illinois	20	5	5	140	24	45	524	82	765	2,766	2,731	35,917	750	285
Michigan	7	4	5	53	4	37	274	42	284	1,332	774	276	8,192	42
Wisconsin	5		1	14	2	4	47	3	38	100	74	209	70	1,171
WEST NORTH CENTRAL:														
Minnesota	7	1	7	25	3	15	92	15	82	291	170	421	111	174
Iowa	5		2	10	1	6	36	10	99	160	126	746	38	47
Missouri	7		3	45	11	13	139	31	261	561	515	3,006	103	56
North Dakota	3		1	1	1	3	12	2	9	33	8	37	6	14
South Dakota				3	1	1	11	4	9	23	12	58	3	9
Nebraska	4	3	2	13	3	4	35	9	59	110	74	217	39	24
Kansas	7	1	4	18	5	5	62	29	138	408	261	548	102	29
SOUTH ATLANTIC:														
Delaware	2			23	8	12	126	226	952	16		6	3	1
Maryland	51	3	12	101	35	45	343	256	1,621	130	13	38	59	3
District of Columbia	16	3	17	166	29	70	435	229	848	285	52	101	41	6
Virginia	5	3	14	182	38	95	570	305	1,092	283	46	69	26	24
West Virginia	3		6	16	4	11	63	25	554	1,176	65	31	23	1
North Carolina		1	3	43	10	27	161	82	264	82	20	11	5	3
South Carolina	4	1	1	18	62	7	48	20	107	27	1	6	6	1
Georgia	7	4	5	60	20	25	101	42	232	104	39	73	16	4
Florida	32	6	4	52	16	23	191	63	198	98	57	83	11	5
EAST SOUTH CENTRAL:														
Kentucky	2			13	4	5	49	20	161	805	1,239	642	34	11
Tennessee	20	3	3	33	5	11	79	20	179	366	211	542	36	18
Alabama	3	1	2	20	11	11	53	13	213	229	89	219	31	8
Mississippi	11		1	20	2	4	28	8	130	203	106	300	24	13
WEST SOUTH CENTRAL:														
Arkansas	10	1	3	15	5	7	47	12	118	266	166	696	36	19
Louisiana	10	6	6	71	7	13	71	30	178	230	106	233	35	11
Oklahoma	5	5	3	11	2	7	32	15	101	285	134	427	41	10
Texas	31	35	13	42	13	18	74	21	254	237	145	295	40	30
MOUNTAIN:														
Montana	4		1	3	1	1	13	5	40	60	25	65	20	11
Idaho	2			2		1	8	2	11	21	11	25	4	3
Wyoming	2	1	1	8	2	2	8	3	27	85	39	65	8	5
Colorado	4	2	2	23	2	11	42	22	84	231	87	258	33	12
New Mexico	1			2			9	1	7	17	13	21	6	
Arizona	1	1	1	1	1	1	6	4	26	39	15	24	5	3
Utah	1		2	4		4	8	1	16	22	16	36	7	2
Nevada				4	1		5	1	6	24	4	15	5	
PACIFIC:														
Washington	7	1	2	26	3	13	60	7	104	223	141	233	52	33
Oregon		1		7	2	2	35	3	31	54	19	56	21	3
California	17	4	5	100	17	45	196	43	226	358	141	323	104	21

TABLE 20.—NATIVE NEGRO POPULATION, CLASSIFIED ACCORDING TO DIVISION AND STATE IN WHICH BORN, BY DIVISIONS AND STATES: 1910—Continued.

[Table continued on page 78.]

DIVISION AND STATE OF RESIDENCE.	NEGRO POPULATION BORN IN—															
	West North Central division.							South Atlantic division.								
	Minnesota.	Iowa.	Missouri.	North Dakota.	South Dakota.	Nebraska.	Kansas.	Delaware.	Maryland.	District of Columbia.	Virginia.	West Virginia.	North Carolina.	South Carolina.	Georgia.	Florida.
UNITED STATES	2,738	8,736	149,218	297	495	2,846	33,786	32,664	262,540	52,282	876,806	36,417	806,537	956,605	1,248,352	215,110
GEOGRAPHIC DIVISIONS:																
New England	10	19	104	4	2	27	40	237	1,894	930	10,218	147	4,599	1,746	1,280	302
Middle Atlantic	118	97	534	33	21	58	136	8,363	29,814	6,208	98,862	2,843	26,252	10,744	6,319	2,033
East North Central	209	976	10,733	19	12	165	996	104	1,598	645	15,156	2,801	6,705	2,620	5,116	497
West North Central	1,748	6,445	124,080	124	192	2,083	27,382	25	664	275	5,812	395	1,463	1,119	2,551	264
South Atlantic	106	258	451	33	56	100	123	23,793	225,837	43,602	714,805	29,492	734,184	910,771	1,150,165	206,524
East South Central	206	178	2,194	26	157	44	259	38	935	172	17,962	341	16,723	14,065	55,046	3,420
West South Central	172	300	6,742	21	35	111	2,802	59	1,337	206	11,796	220	15,360	14,760	24,792	1,781
Mountain	67	251	2,459	20	11	174	1,316	13	199	106	919	88	304	186	769	88
Pacific	102	212	1,921	17	9	84	732	32	262	138	1,276	90	947	594	2,314	201
NEW ENGLAND:																
Maine	1						1		22	8	64	2	36	14	10	2
New Hampshire								1	13	4	74	1	32	19	6	5
Vermont	1	5	30	1		18	20		41	26	98	9	56	51	113	8
Massachusetts	6	12	55	2		4	13	122	953	528	5,750	67	2,991	1,060	798	169
Rhode Island	1	1	8	1	2	3		34	546	184	1,611	12	309	203	168	45
Connecticut	1	1	11			2	6	80	319	180	2,321	56	1,175	399	185	73
MIDDLE ATLANTIC:																
New York	81	42	232	7	9	32	75	463	3,510	2,080	29,157	345	10,283	6,698	3,792	1,257
New Jersey	11	10	73	9	3	6	17	2,102	6,274	1,191	20,710	238	6,234	1,933	949	383
Pennsylvania	26	45	229	17	9	20	44	5,798	20,030	2,937	48,995	2,260	9,735	2,113	1,578	393
EAST NORTH CENTRAL:																
Ohio	16	56	353	4	3	27	86	35	737	284	10,195	2,358	3,884	1,102	1,549	164
Indiana	19	46	388	1	2	16	105	7	80	38	938	93	1,320	195	468	47
Illinois	120	797	9,732	12	5	105	728	24	643	268	3,326	229	1,175	1,217	2,874	243
Michigan	15	25	144	1	1	12	57	37	111	47	597	110	301	77	138	31
Wisconsin	39	52	116	1	1	5	20	1	27	8	100	11	25	29	87	12
WEST NORTH CENTRAL:																
Minnesota	1,556	258	683	12	12	45	161	7	76	50	267	34	77	53	200	26
Iowa	42	5,253	3,272	1	16	106	219	4	95	17	1,588	117	208	82	177	15
Missouri	60	374	109,949	3	5	119	3,376	11	278	60	2,583	102	606	523	1,372	150
North Dakota	39	16	66	102	3	1	5		10	3	44	6	6	10	9	3
South Dakota	19	59	112		139	25	29		5	1	35	6	21	5	23	1
Nebraska	11	323	1,736	1	13	1,657	658		47	19	244	38	82	45	142	16
Kansas	21	162	8,262	5	4	130	22,934	3	153	125	1,051	92	463	401	628	53
SOUTH ATLANTIC:																
Delaware	2	1	8	1				22,668	5,440	87	1,206	19	142	40	12	12
Maryland	5	26	45	2	3		5	840	201,594	1,603	20,151	682	2,127	484	304	94
District of Columbia	8	28	94	1	13	10	29	71	15,632	40,459	28,051	430	2,754	1,088	839	117
Virginia	12	21	66	10	1	13	13	130	2,033	1,054	623,472	962	33,513	1,750	875	235
West Virginia	6	15	39	7	4		21	5	526	143	26,565	27,160	4,622	461	275	50
North Carolina	2	17	18	5	8	59	27	12	184	52	7,957	98	663,394	21,650	1,105	160
South Carolina	22	20	14	5	9	3		14	52	23	897	62	7,769	821,058	3,799	313
Georgia	35	102	97	1	8	8	18	14	229	132	4,294	38	10,173	36,739	1,097,257	7,047
Florida	14	28	70	1	10	7	10	39	147	49	2,212	41	9,690	27,501	45,699	198,496
EAST SOUTH CENTRAL:																
Kentucky	14	23	503	12	5	13	105	5	86	34	2,749	159	987	448	1,034	100
Tennessee	60	45	727	2	50	12	86	10	156	41	4,825	56	4,783	3,207	13,075	291
Alabama	9	32	207	5	93	9	42	12	261	59	4,569	65	3,658	5,179	31,202	2,196
Mississippi	123	78	757	7	9	10	26	11	432	38	5,819	61	7,295	5,231	9,735	833
WEST SOUTH CENTRAL:																
Arkansas	54	63	1,753	9	5	23	183	5	261	30	2,921	43	7,471	8,482	10,013	307
Louisiana	62	42	729	4	3	10	39	17	613	79	3,931	42	2,571	1,952	4,270	754
Oklahoma	20	104	2,382	4	8	48	2,298	6	91	19	1,017	68	1,633	1,427	2,791	138
Texas	36	91	1,878	4	19	30	282	31	372	78	3,927	67	3,685	2,899	7,718	582
MOUNTAIN:																
Montana	27	25	214	12	6	6	81	1	34	20	80	5	33	26	47	8
Idaho	6	17	78	4		5	25	1	9	2	23	4	14	2	19	4
Wyoming	7	37	222	3	2	57	123	1	36	26	153	14	54	32	131	13
Colorado	13	122	1,617	1		71	899	5	74	38	498	46	138	76	396	35
New Mexico	3	9	73		1	5	42	1	7	1	54	5	20	11	56	11
Arizona	5	9	102		1	7	60	3	24	3	38	11	29	25	78	12
Utah	2	24	112		1	20	64		6	9	43	3	11	7	24	3
Nevada	4	8	41			3	22	1	9	7	30		5	7	18	2
PACIFIC:																
Washington	63	78	476	9	4	35	216	13	66	34	412	36	219	119	282	45
Oregon	7	26	148			12	40	1	14	5	91	4	32	20	64	5
California	32	108	1,297	8	5	37	476	18	182	99	773	50	696	455	1,968	151

TABLE 20.—NATIVE NEGRO POPULATION, CLASSIFIED ACCORDING TO DIVISION AND STATE IN WHICH BORN, BY DIVISIONS AND STATES: 1910—Continued.

[Table concluded on page 79.]

DIVISION AND STATE OF RESIDENCE.	NEGRO POPULATION BORN IN—															
	East South Central division.				West South Central division.				Mountain division.							
	Kentucky.	Tennessee.	Alabama.	Mississippi.	Arkansas.	Louisiana.	Oklahoma.	Texas.	Montana.	Idaho.	Wyoming.	Colorado.	New Mexico.	Arizona.	Utah.	Nevada.
UNITED STATES...	323,794	517,072	971,167	1,032,565	334,589	726,496	51,334	664,823	665	468	314	3,513	941	538	527	376
GEOGRAPHIC DIVISIONS:																
New England	333	281	269	83	51	115	12	103	11	1	7	15	4	2	2	14
Middle Atlantic	2,120	1,944	1,261	444	227	572	52	443	30	62	13	77	53	22	30	51
East North Central	53,882	24,299	4,660	5,496	1,644	2,030	218	1,076	22	19	12	141	28	15	15	10
West North Central	13,152	15,552	4,540	6,693	4,421	2,545	2,161	4,253	29	14	30	358	56	33	25	9
South Atlantic	2,517	5,295	27,495	2,184	433	927	99	712	53	91	17	71	48	20	65	83
East South Central	241,884	425,243	889,162	935,318	8,772	22,419	313	2,101	70	49	8	88	3	42	25	34
West South Central	7,273	41,485	41,746	81,167	318,032	696,316	47,941	651,599	35	121	13	232	138	52	107	66
Mountain	1,328	1,477	1,063	473	432	389	314	1,992	362	85	199	2,339	553	310	221	53
Pacific	1,305	1,496	971	707	577	1,183	224	2,544	53	26	15	192	58	42	37	56
NEW ENGLAND:																
Maine	2	3	2	2	1	6	1	3	2							
New Hampshire	5	3	5	1												
Vermont	107	126	66	10	10	6	5	47	4		1			1		
Massachusetts	159	111	150	56	35	71	4	40	2	1	3	12	3	1	1	12
Rhode Island	22	13	25	2	2	8		7	1			2	1			
Connecticut	38	25	21	12	3	24	2	6	2		3	1			1	2
MIDDLE ATLANTIC:																
New York	873	648	536	198	97	290	22	245	17	13	4	35	37	8	15	35
New Jersey	255	231	180	75	68	81	13	70	7	6	1	15	6	3	3	9
Pennsylvania	992	1,065	545	171	62	201	17	128	6	43	8	27	10	11	12	7
EAST NORTH CENTRAL:																
Ohio	18,835	3,481	781	475	121	233	65	140	7	7	5	21	6	3	7	2
Indiana	20,756	5,073	499	290	99	112	18	90	1	1	2	16	3	2		
Illinois	13,314	15,303	3,208	4,612	1,354	1,609	126	789	13	8	4	89	18	8	8	6
Michigan	781	329	116	70	48	56	8	40	1	1	1	13	1	1		2
Wisconsin	196	113	56	49	22	20	1	17		2		2		1		
WEST NORTH CENTRAL:																
Minnesota	579	418	199	227	75	124	18	72	4	2		16	2	1		
Iowa	713	473	398	227	73	58	91	116	3		5	13	4	2	1	2
Missouri	6,903	9,814	2,412	4,507	2,958	1,631	512	1,907	9	6	4	135	18	14	8	2
North Dakota	48	44	7	10	6	7	1	9	1	2						
South Dakota	35	54	19	14	9	6	1	14	1		1	9		1		
Nebraska	516	362	176	164	92	100	56	228	5	1	11	32	6	1	5	1
Kansas	4,358	4,387	1,329	1,544	1,208	619	1,482	1,907	6	3	9	153	26	14	11	4
SOUTH ATLANTIC:																
Delaware	12	10	3	5		9	1	4	1	1		3		1		
Maryland	125	155	105	56	25	66	9	49	2	8	2	8	9		1	
District of Columbia	255	303	330	267	53	117	18	191	12	2	3	12	3	5		
Virginia	593	1,545	415	134	38	64	15	63	6	25	6	12	27	4	52	1
West Virginia	907	554	206	45	11	41	8	27	3	4	2	6	4	2	2	1
North Carolina	76	486	340	214	43	49	7	48	1	16	3	2		2	2	6
South Carolina	31	141	322	111	38	20	3	44	2	16	1	3	1	2	2	13
Georgia	243	1,482	13,101	653	158	212	24	136	22	14		19	1	4	4	39
Florida	275	619	12,673	699	67	349	14	150	4	5		6	3		2	23
EAST SOUTH CENTRAL:																
Kentucky	233,454	15,672	1,160	726	156	240	26	145	5	11	2	10	2	4	2	4
Tennessee	6,062	393,173	11,127	26,061	3,377	1,224	107	627	9	14	3	41	1	16	10	16
Alabama	655	6,337	839,821	8,841	305	816	77	337	2	16	2	26		12	10	12
Mississippi	1,713	10,061	37,054	899,690	4,934	20,139	103	992	54	8	1	11		10	3	2
WEST SOUTH CENTRAL:																
Arkansas	1,936	24,875	12,991	39,467	296,040	25,382	808	5,383	7	16	1	42	5		21	31
Louisiana	1,424	1,826	8,755	26,626	4,893	642,733	125	8,058	7	37		46	5	11	7	16
Oklahoma	1,884	6,864	6,720	7,000	10,771	8,498	45,976	35,397	4	5	4	59	13	10	7	6
Texas	2,029	7,920	13,280	8,074	6,328	19,703	1,032	602,761	17	63	8	85	115	31	72	13
MOUNTAIN:																
Montana	114	120	42	31	29	24	12	56	339	2	3	17	5	6	8	2
Idaho	34	34	23	12	14	15	5	33	3	69	6	9	1	1	25	1
Wyoming	206	163	118	45	44	32	19	123	3		153	38	14	4	1	2
Colorado	734	910	689	267	235	189	198	684	6	4	35	2,156	85	5	18	2
New Mexico	73	67	89	55	26	43	30	340	2			45	410	2		
Arizona	72	94	60	36	48	42	32	644	1	1		21	16	287	4	1
Utah	68	59	25	20	18	23	11	67	6	9	2	45	20	4	162	1
Nevada	27	30	17	7	18	21	7	45	2			8	2	1	3	44
PACIFIC:																
Washington	395	439	224	180	74	132	39	283	28	6	5	81	7	2	8	3
Oregon	76	73	47	27	40	47	17	57	8	11		8		2	5	1
California	834	984	700	500	463	1,004	168	2,204	17	9	10	103	51	38	24	52

TABLE 20.—NATIVE NEGRO POPULATION, CLASSIFIED ACCORDING TO DIVISION AND STATE IN WHICH BORN, BY DIVISIONS AND STATES: 1910—Concluded.

| DIVISION AND STATE OF RESIDENCE. | NEGRO POPULATION BORN IN— | | | | | | | | | Born at sea under United States flag. | American citizens born abroad. |
| | Pacific division. | | | United States (state not reported). | Outlying possessions. | | | | | | |
	Washington.	Oregon.	California.		Alaska.	Guam.	Hawaii.	Philippine Islands.	Porto Rico.		
UNITED STATES	1,546	398	6,318	37,943	4	1	58	119	173	217	2,866
GEOGRAPHIC DIVISIONS:											
New England	41	2	39	298			3	17	6	3	160
Middle Atlantic	420	24	151	2,350	1		7	8	77	9	567
East North Central	63	13	140	3,163			2	15	4	4	1,389
West North Central	37	19	136	3,080	1			10	3	5	143
South Atlantic	204	28	139	9,534			2	12	24	134	221
East South Central	50	8	103	8,075				6		18	67
West South Central	91	30	228	10,445			2	12	7	42	149
Mountain	31	10	173	448			6	6	3		60
Pacific	609	264	5,209	550	2	1	36	33	49	2	110
NEW ENGLAND:											
Maine			2	11							3
New Hampshire	1		1	5							4
Vermont		1	4	7				16	2		10
Massachusetts	22	1	22	144			2		2	2	112
Rhode Island	10		4	40			1		1	1	17
Connecticut	8		6	91				1	1		14
MIDDLE ATLANTIC:											
New York	193	9	85	894	1		4	5	63	5	339
New Jersey	81	4	28	443					1	2	65
Pennsylvania	146	11	38	1,013			3	3	13	2	163
EAST NORTH CENTRAL:											
Ohio	17	6	33	846			1	2	2		303
Indiana	2		13	365			1	1		1	43
Illinois	32	6	77	1,725				5	2	1	247
Michigan	6	1	11	178				7		2	772
Wisconsin	6		6	49							24
WEST NORTH CENTRAL:											
Minnesota	8	6	6	153					1		42
Iowa	8	3	14	205						2	9
Missouri	9	5	72	1,832	1			5	2		38
North Dakota	1		3	21				1			1
South Dakota	1		3	25							1
Nebraska	3	1	9	167				1			27
Kansas	7	4	29	677				3		3	25
SOUTH ATLANTIC:											
Delaware	2		2	74							5
Maryland	44	1	23	389				2	4	7	34
District of Columbia	13		11	645				2	5	1	38
Virginia	96	8	26	698			1	4	6	10	39
West Virginia	12	12	9	347						1	10
North Carolina	21	1	9	944				2		3	20
South Carolina	1	1	5	632						4	9
Georgia	6	2	34	3,551			1	1	1	108	19
Florida	9	3	20	2,254				1	8		47
EAST SOUTH CENTRAL:											
Kentucky	15	1	19	653						4	17
Tennessee	24	1	33	2,088						4	19
Alabama	7	2	23	2,172				4		7	15
Mississippi	4	4	28	3,162				2		3	16
WEST SOUTH CENTRAL:											
Arkansas	13	8	55	2,688			1			5	12
Louisiana	13	6	42	2,465			1	10	7	9	52
Oklahoma	10	4	32	1,069						3	21
Texas	55	12	99	4,223				2		25	64
MOUNTAIN:											
Montana	11	2	9	55			1	2	1		8
Idaho	7	5	8	8							7
Wyoming	2		12	43			1		1		6
Colorado	6	1	30	199			3	3			22
New Mexico	1	1	17	16							1
Arizona	3		48	26			1				6
Utah	1	1	19	99				1			3
Nevada			30	2					1		7
PACIFIC:											
Washington	534	37	102	179	1		5	6	1		37
Oregon	24	194	47	19			10	4	1		9
California	51	33	5,060	352	1	1	21	23	47	2	64

TABLE **21.**—NEGRO POPULATION BORN IN EACH STATE DISTRIBUTED ACCORDING TO SELECTED STATES OF RESIDENCE: 1910.

STATE.	Number.	Per cent.
NEW ENGLAND.		
MAINE, persons born in........	1,585	100.0
Living in Maine....	802	50.6
Living in other states....	783	49.4
Massachusetts....	254	16.0
New York....	75	4.7
Maryland....	51	3.2
New Jersey....	36	2.3
Pennsylvania....	36	2.3
Florida....	32	2.0
Texas....	31	2.0
Ohio....	25	1.6
Illinois....	20	1.3
Tennessee....	20	1.3
All other....	203	12.8
NEW HAMPSHIRE, persons born in....	506	100.0
Living in New Hampshire....	234	46.2
Living in other states....	272	53.8
Massachusetts....	122	24.1
Texas....	35	6.9
New York....	13	2.6
Maine....	10	2.0
All other....	92	18.2
VERMONT, persons born in....	1,045	100.0
Living in Vermont....	437	41.8
Living in other states....	608	58.2
New York....	184	17.6
Massachusetts....	145	13.9
Pennsylvania....	43	4.1
Connecticut....	31	3.0
New Jersey....	30	2.9
District of Columbia....	17	1.6
Virginia....	14	1.3
Rhode Island....	14	1.3
All other....	130	12.4
MASSACHUSETTS, persons born in....	19,078	100.0
Living in Massachusetts....	14,953	78.4
Living in other states....	4,125	21.6
New York....	917	4.8
Connecticut....	445	2.3
Rhode Island....	419	2.2
Pennsylvania....	411	2.2
New Jersey....	301	1.6
Virginia....	182	1.0
District of Columbia....	166	0.9
Illinois....	140	0.7
Maryland....	101	0.5
California....	100	0.5
All other....	943	4.9
RHODE ISLAND, persons born in....	5,401	100.0
Living in Rhode Island....	4,084	75.6
Living in other states....	1,317	24.4
Massachusetts....	335	6.2
New York....	264	4.9
Connecticut....	118	2.2
Pennsylvania....	112	2.1
New Jersey....	96	1.8
South Carolina....	62	1.1
Virginia....	38	0.7
Maryland....	35	0.6
District of Columbia....	29	0.5
All other....	228	4.2
CONNECTICUT, persons born in..	10,184	100.0
Living in Connecticut....	7,296	71.6
Living in other states....	2,888	28.4
New York....	899	8.8
Massachusetts....	551	5.4
Rhode Island....	305	3.0
New Jersey....	234	2.3
Pennsylvania....	215	2.1
Virginia....	95	0.9
District of Columbia....	70	0.7
Ohio....	46	0.5
All other....	473	4.6
MIDDLE ATLANTIC.		
NEW YORK, persons born in...	61,580	100.0
Living in New York....	49,750	80.8
Living in other states....	11,830	19.2
New Jersey....	3,606	5.9
Pennsylvania....	1,421	2.3
Connecticut....	960	1.6
Massachusetts....	889	1.4

STATE.	Number.	Per cent.
MIDDLE ATLANTIC—Continued.		
NEW YORK—Continued.		
Living in other states—Continued.		
Virginia....	570	0.9
Illinois....	524	0.9
Ohio....	476	0.8
District of Columbia....	435	0.7
Maryland....	343	0.6
Michigan....	274	0.4
Rhode Island....	230	0.4
All other....	2,102	3.4
NEW JERSEY, persons born in....	45,312	100.0
Living in New Jersey....	37,017	81.7
Living in other states....	8,295	18.3
Pennsylvania....	3,129	6.9
New York....	2,617	5.8
Massachusetts....	341	0.8
Virginia....	305	0.7
Connecticut....	277	0.6
Maryland....	256	0.6
District of Columbia....	229	0.5
Delaware....	226	0.5
All other....	915	2.0
PENNSYLVANIA, persons born in....	105,253	100.0
Living in Pennsylvania....	84,960	80.7
Living in other states....	20,293	19.3
New Jersey....	4,773	4.5
New York....	2,689	2.6
Ohio....	2,103	2.0
Maryland....	1,621	1.5
Virginia....	1,092	1.0
Delaware....	952	0.9
District of Columbia....	848	0.8
Illinois....	765	0.7
Massachusetts....	582	0.6
West Virginia....	554	0.5
All other....	4,314	4.1
EAST NORTH CENTRAL.		
OHIO, persons born in....	76,044	100.0
Living in Ohio....	59,194	77.8
Living in other states....	16,850	22.2
Illinois....	2,766	3.6
Pennsylvania....	2,109	2.8
Indiana....	1,934	2.5
Michigan....	1,332	1.8
West Virginia....	1,176	1.5
Kentucky....	805	1.1
New York....	638	0.8
Missouri....	561	0.7
Kansas....	408	0.5
Tennessee....	366	0.5
California....	358	0.5
All other....	4,397	5.8
INDIANA, persons born in....	34,794	100.0
Living in Indiana....	25,224	72.5
Living in other states....	9,570	27.5
Illinois....	2,731	7.8
Ohio....	1,375	4.0
Kentucky....	1,239	3.6
Michigan....	774	2.2
Missouri....	515	1.5
Kansas....	261	0.8
Tennessee....	211	0.6
Pennsylvania....	208	0.6
Minnesota....	170	0.5
Arkansas....	166	0.5
All other....	1,920	5.5
ILLINOIS, persons born in....	48,564	100.0
Living in Illinois....	35,917	74.0
Living in other states....	12,647	26.0
Missouri....	3,006	6.2
Indiana....	1,206	2.5
Iowa....	746	1.5
Arkansas....	696	1.4
Kentucky....	642	1.3
Kansas....	548	1.1
Tennessee....	542	1.1
Ohio....	430	0.9
Oklahoma....	427	0.9
Minnesota....	421	0.9
California....	323	0.7
Mississippi....	300	0.6
Texas....	295	0.6
Michigan....	276	0.6
Colorado....	258	0.5
All other....	2,531	5.2

STATE.	Number.	Per cent.
EAST NORTH CENTRAL—Con.		
MICHIGAN, persons born in....	11,576	100.0
Living in Michigan....	8,192	70.8
Living in other states....	3,384	29.2
Illinois....	750	6.5
Ohio....	669	5.8
Indiana....	405	3.5
New York....	156	1.3
Pennsylvania....	124	1.1
Minnesota....	111	1.0
California....	104	0.9
Missouri....	103	0.9
Kansas....	102	0.9
Wisconsin....	70	0.6
Maryland....	59	0.5
All other....	731	6.3
WISCONSIN, persons born in....	2,248	100.0
Living in Wisconsin....	1,171	52.1
Living in other states....	1,077	47.9
Illinois....	285	12.7
Minnesota....	174	7.7
Missouri....	56	2.5
Iowa....	47	2.1
Ohio....	43	1.9
Michigan....	42	.1.9
Washington....	33	1.5
Texas....	30	1.3
Kansas....	29	1.3
New York....	29	1.3
Nebraska....	24	1.1
Pennsylvania....	24	1.1
Virginia....	24	1.1
California....	21	0.8
All other....	216	9.6
WEST NORTH CENTRAL.		
MINNESOTA, persons born in....	2,738	100.0
Living in Minnesota....	1,556	56.8
Living in other states....	1,182	43.2
Mississippi....	123	4.5
Illinois....	120	4.4
New York....	81	3.0
Washington....	63	2.3
Louisiana....	62	2.3
Missouri....	60	2.2
Tennessee....	60	2.2
Arkansas....	54	2.0
Iowa....	42	1.5
All other....	517	18.9
IOWA, persons born in....	8,736	100.0
Living in Iowa....	5,253	60.1
Living in other states....	3,483	39.9
Illinois....	797	9.1
Missouri....	374	4.3
Nebraska....	323	3.7
Minnesota....	258	3.0
Kansas....	162	1.9
Colorado....	122	1.4
California....	108	1.2
Oklahoma....	104	1.2
Georgia....	102	1.2
Texas....	91	1.0
All other....	1,042	11.9
MISSOURI, persons born in....	149,218	100.0
Living in Missouri....	109,949	73.7
Living in other states....	39,269	26.3
Illinois....	9,732	6.5
Kansas....	8,262	5.5
Iowa....	3,272	2.2
Oklahoma....	2,382	1.6
Texas....	1,878	1.3
Arkansas....	1,753	1.2
Nebraska....	1,736	1.2
Colorado....	1,617	1.1
California....	1,297	0.9
Mississippi....	757	0.5
Louisiana....	729	0.5
Tennessee....	727	0.5
Minnesota....	683	0.5
All other....	4,444	3.0
NORTH DAKOTA, persons born in	297	100.0
Living in North Dakota....	102	34.3
Living in other states....	195	65.7
Pennsylvania....	17	5.7
Illinois....	12	4.0
Kentucky....	12	4.0
Minnesota....	12	4.0
Montana....	12	4.0
Virginia....	10	3.4
All other....	120	40.4

TABLE 21.—NEGRO POPULATION BORN IN EACH STATE DISTRIBUTED ACCORDING TO SELECTED STATES OF RESIDENCE: 1910—Continued.

STATE.	NEGROES: 1910. Number.	NEGROES: 1910. Per cent.
WEST NORTH CENTRAL—Contd.		
SOUTH DAKOTA, persons born in	495	100.0
Living in South Dakota	139	28.1
Living in other states	356	71.9
Alabama	93	18.8
Tennessee	50	10.1
Texas	19	3.8
Iowa	16	3.2
District of Columbia	13	2.6
Nebraska	13	2.6
Minnesota	12	2.4
Florida	10	2.0
All other	130	26.3
NEBRASKA, persons born in	2,846	100.0
Living in Nebraska	1,657	58.2
Living in other states	1,189	41.8
Kansas	130	4.6
Missouri	119	4.2
Iowa	106	3.7
Illinois	105	3.7
Colorado	71	2.5
North Carolina	59	2.1
Wyoming	57	2.0
Oklahoma	48	1.7
Minnesota	45	1.6
California	37	1.3
Washington	35	1.2
All other	377	13.2
KANSAS, persons born in	33,786	100.0
Living in Kansas	22,934	67.9
Living in other states	10,852	32.1
Missouri	3,376	10.0
Oklahoma	2,298	6.8
Colorado	899	2.7
Illinois	728	2.2
Nebraska	658	1.9
California	476	1.4
Texas	282	0.8
Iowa	219	0.6
Washington	216	0.6
Arkansas	183	0.5
All other	1,517	4.5
SOUTH ATLANTIC.		
DELAWARE, persons born in	32,664	100.0
Living in Delaware	22,668	69.4
Living in other states	9,996	30.6
Pennsylvania	5,798	17.8
New Jersey	2,102	6.4
Maryland	840	2.6
New York	463	1.4
Virginia	130	0.4
Massachusetts	122	0.4
Connecticut	80	0.2
District of Columbia	71	0.2
Florida	39	0.1
All other	351	1.1
MARYLAND, persons born in	262,540	100.0
Living in Maryland	201,594	76.8
Living in other states	60,946	23.2
Pennsylvania	20,030	7.6
District of Columbia	15,632	6.0
New Jersey	6,274	2.4
Delaware	5,440	2.1
New York	3,510	1.3
Virginia	2,033	0.8
Massachusetts	953	0.4
Ohio	737	0.3
Illinois	643	0.2
Louisiana	613	0.2
Rhode Island	546	0.2
West Virginia	526	0.2
Mississippi	432	0.2
Texas	372	0.1
Connecticut	319	0.1
Missouri	278	0.1
Alabama	261	0.1
Arkansas	261	0.1
All other	2,086	0.8
DISTRICT OF COLUMBIA, persons born in	52,282	100.0
Living in District of Columbia	40,459	77.4
Living elsewhere	11,823	22.6
Pennsylvania	2,937	5.6
New York	2,080	4.0
Maryland	1,603	3.1

STATE.	NEGROES: 1910. Number.	NEGROES: 1910. Per cent.
SOUTH ATLANTIC—Continued.		
DISTRICT OF COLUMBIA—Con.		
Living elsewhere—Continued.		
New Jersey	1,191	2.3
Virginia	1,054	2.0
Massachusetts	528	1.0
Ohio	284	0.5
Illinois	268	0.5
Rhode Island	184	0.4
Connecticut	180	0.3
West Virginia	143	0.3
Georgia	132	0.3
Kansas	125	0.2
California	99	0.2
All other	1,015	1.9
VIRGINIA, persons born in	876,806	100.0
Living in Virginia	623,472	71.1
Living in other states	253,334	28.9
Pennsylvania	48,995	5.6
New York	29,157	3.3
District of Columbia	28,051	3.2
West Virginia	26,565	3.0
New Jersey	20,710	2.4
Maryland	20,151	2.3
Ohio	10,195	1.2
North Carolina	7,957	0.9
Mississippi	5,819	0.7
Massachusetts	5,750	0.7
Tennessee	4,825	0.6
Alabama	4,569	0.5
Georgia	4,294	0.5
Louisiana	3,931	0.4
Texas	3,927	0.4
Illinois	3,326	0.4
Arkansas	2,921	0.3
Kentucky	2,749	0.3
Connecticut	2,621	0.3
Missouri	2,583	0.3
Florida	2,212	0.3
Rhode Island	1,611	0.2
Iowa	1,588	0.2
Delaware	1,206	0.1
Kansas	1,051	0.1
Oklahoma	1,017	0.1
All other	5,553	0.6
WEST VIRGINIA, persons born in	36,417	100.0
Living in West Virginia	27,160	74.6
Living in other states	9,257	25.4
Ohio	2,358	6.5
Pennsylvania	2,260	6.2
Virginia	962	2.6
Maryland	682	1.9
District of Columbia	430	1.2
New York	345	0.9
New Jersey	238	0.7
Illinois	229	0.6
Kentucky	159	0.4
Iowa	117	0.3
Michigan	110	0.3
Missouri	102	0.3
North Carolina	98	0.3
Indiana	93	0.3
Kansas	92	0.3
Oklahoma	68	0.2
All other	914	2.5
NORTH CAROLINA, persons born in	806,537	100.0
Living in North Carolina	663,394	82.3
Living in other states	143,143	17.7
Virginia	33,513	4.2
New York	10,283	1.3
Georgia	10,173	1.3
Pennsylvania	9,735	1.2
Florida	9,690	1.2
South Carolina	7,769	1.0
Arkansas	7,471	0.9
Mississippi	7,295	0.9
New Jersey	6,234	0.8
Tennessee	4,783	0.6
West Virginia	4,622	0.6
Ohio	3,884	0.5
Texas	3,685	0.5
Alabama	3,658	0.5
Massachusetts	2,991	0.4
District of Columbia	2,754	0.3
Louisiana	2,571	0.3
Maryland	2,127	0.3
Oklahoma	1,633	0.2
Indiana	1,320	0.2
Connecticut	1,175	0.1
Illinois	1,175	0.1
All other	4,602	0.6

STATE.	NEGROES: 1910. Number.	NEGROES: 1910. Per cent.
SOUTH ATLANTIC—Continued.		
SOUTH CAROLINA, persons born in	956,605	100.0
Living in South Carolina	821,058	85.8
Living in other states	135,547	14.2
Georgia	36,739	3.8
Florida	27,501	2.9
North Carolina	21,650	2.3
Arkansas	8,482	0.9
New York	6,698	0.7
Mississippi	5,231	0.5
Alabama	5,179	0.5
Tennessee	3,207	0.3
Texas	2,899	0.3
Pennsylvania	2,113	0.2
Louisiana	1,952	0.2
New Jersey	1,933	0.2
Virginia	1,750	0.2
Oklahoma	1,427	0.1
All other	8,786	0.9
GEORGIA, persons born in	1,248,352	100.0
Living in Georgia	1,097,257	87.9
Living in other states	151,095	12.1
Florida	45,699	3.7
Alabama	31,202	2.5
Tennessee	13,075	1.0
Arkansas	10,013	0.8
Mississippi	9,735	0.8
Texas	7,718	0.6
Louisiana	4,270	0.3
South Carolina	3,799	0.3
New York	3,792	0.3
Illinois	2,874	0.2
Oklahoma	2,791	0.2
California	1,968	0.2
New Jersey	1,578	0.1
All other	12,581	1.0
FLORIDA, persons born in	215,110	100.0
Living in Florida	198,496	92.3
Living in other states	16,614	7.7
Georgia	7,047	3.3
Alabama	2,196	1.0
New York	1,257	0.6
Mississippi	833	0.4
Louisiana	754	0.4
Texas	582	0.3
Pennsylvania	393	0.2
New Jersey	383	0.2
South Carolina	313	0.1
All other	2,856	1.3
EAST SOUTH CENTRAL.		
KENTUCKY, persons born in	323,794	100.0
Living in Kentucky	233,454	72.1
Living in other states	90,340	27.9
Indiana	20,756	6.4
Ohio	18,835	5.8
Illinois	13,314	4.1
Missouri	6,903	2.1
Tennessee	6,062	1.9
Kansas	4,358	1.3
Texas	2,029	0.6
Arkansas	1,936	0.6
Oklahoma	1,884	0.6
Mississippi	1,713	0.5
Louisiana	1,424	0.4
Pennsylvania	992	0.3
West Virginia	907	0.3
New York	873	0.3
California	834	0.3
Michigan	781	0.2
Colorado	734	0.2
Iowa	713	0.2
Alabama	655	0.2
Virginia	593	0.2
Minnesota	579	0.2
Nebraska	516	0.2
Washington	395	0.1
All other	2,554	0.8
TENNESSEE, persons born in	517,072	100.0
Living in Tennessee	393,173	76.0
Living in other states	123,899	24.0
Arkansas	24,875	4.8
Kentucky	15,672	3.0
Illinois	15,303	3.0
Mississippi	10,061	1.9
Missouri	9,814	1.9
Texas	7,920	1.5
Oklahoma	6,864	1.3
Alabama	6,337	1.2

Table 21.—NEGRO POPULATION BORN IN EACH STATE DISTRIBUTED ACCORDING TO SELECTED STATES OF RESIDENCE: 1910—Concluded.

STATE.	Number.	Per cent.
EAST SOUTH CENTRAL—Contd.		
TENNESSEE—Continued.		
Living in other states—Continued.		
Indiana	5,073	1.0
Kansas	4,387	0.8
Ohio	3,481	0.7
Louisiana	1,826	0.4
Virginia	1,545	0.3
Georgia	1,482	0.3
Pennsylvania	1,065	0.2
California	984	0.2
Colorado	910	0.2
New York	648	0.1
All other	5,652	1.1
ALABAMA, persons born in	971,167	100.0
Living in Alabama	839,821	86.5
Living in other states	131,346	13.5
Mississippi	37,054	3.8
Texas	13,280	1.4
Georgia	13,101	1.3
Arkansas	12,991	1.3
Florida	12,673	1.3
Tennessee	11,127	1.1
Louisiana	8,755	0.9
Oklahoma	6,720	0.7
Illinois	3,208	0.3
Missouri	2,412	0.2
Kansas	1,329	0.1
All other	8,696	0.9
MISSISSIPPI, persons born in	1,032,565	100.0
Living in Mississippi	899,690	87.1
Living in other states	132,875	12.9
Arkansas	39,467	3.8
Louisiana	26,626	2.6
Tennessee	26,061	2.5
Alabama	8,841	0.9
Texas	8,074	0.8
Oklahoma	7,000	0.7
Illinois	4,612	0.4
Missouri	4,507	0.4
Kansas	1,544	0.1
All other	6,143	0.6
WEST SOUTH CENTRAL.		
ARKANSAS, persons born in	334,589	100.0
Living in Arkansas	296,040	88.5
Living in other states	38,549	11.5
Oklahoma	10,771	3.2
Texas	6,328	1.9
Mississippi	4,934	1.5
Louisiana	4,893	1.5
Tennessee	3,377	1.0
Missouri	2,958	0.9
Illinois	1,354	0.4
Kansas	1,208	0.4
California	463	0.1
All other	2,263	0.7
LOUISIANA, persons born in	726,496	100.0
Living in Louisiana	642,733	88.5
Living in other states	83,763	11.5
Arkansas	25,382	3.5
Mississippi	20,139	2.8
Texas	19,703	2.7
Oklahoma	8,498	1.2
Missouri	1,631	0.2
Illinois	1,609	0.2
Tennessee	1,224	0.2
California	1,004	0.1
All other	4,573	0.6
OKLAHOMA, persons born in	51,334	100.0
Living in Oklahoma	45,976	89.6
Living in other states	5,358	10.4
Kansas	1,482	2.9
Texas	1,032	2.0
Arkansas	808	1.6
Missouri	512	1.0
Colorado	198	0.4
California	108	0.3
Illinois	126	0.2
Louisiana	125	0.2
Tennessee	107	0.2
Mississippi	103	0.2
Iowa	91	0.2
Alabama	77	0.2
All other	529	1.0

STATE.	Number.	Per cent.
WEST SOUTH CENTRAL—Contd.		
TEXAS, persons born in	664,823	100.0
Living in Texas	602,761	90.7
Living in other states	62,062	9.3
Oklahoma	35,397	5.3
Louisiana	8,058	1.2
Arkansas	5,383	0.8
California	2,204	0.3
Kansas	1,907	0.3
Missouri	1,907	0.3
Mississippi	992	0.1
All other	6,214	0.9
MOUNTAIN.		
MONTANA, persons born in	665	100.0
Living in Montana	339	51.0
Living in other states	326	49.0
Mississippi	54	8.1
Washington	28	4.2
Georgia	22	3.3
California	17	2.6
New York	17	2.6
Texas	17	2.6
Illinois	13	2.0
All other	158	23.8
IDAHO, persons born in	468	100.0
Living in Idaho	69	14.7
Living in other states	399	85.3
Texas	63	13.5
Pennsylvania	43	9.2
Louisiana	37	7.9
Virginia	25	5.3
Alabama	16	3.4
Arkansas	16	3.4
North Carolina	16	3.4
South Carolina	16	3.4
All other	167	35.7
WYOMING, persons born in	314	100.0
Living in Wyoming	153	48.7
Living in other states	161	51.3
Colorado	35	11.1
Nebraska	11	3.5
California	10	3.2
All other	105	33.4
COLORADO, persons born in	3,513	100.0
Living in Colorado	2,156	61.4
Living in other states	1,357	38.6
Kansas	153	4.4
Missouri	135	3.8
California	103	2.9
Illinois	89	2.5
Texas	85	2.4
Washington	81	2.3
Oklahoma	59	1.7
Louisiana	46	1.3
New Mexico	45	1.3
Utah	45	1.3
Arkansas	42	1.2
Tennessee	41	1.2
All other	433	12.3
NEW MEXICO, persons born in	941	100.0
Living in New Mexico	410	43.6
Living in other states	531	56.4
Texas	115	12.2
Colorado	85	9.0
California	51	5.4
New York	37	3.9
Virginia	27	2.9
Kansas	26	2.8
Utah	20	2.1
Illinois	18	1.9
Missouri	18	1.9
Arizona	16	1.7
All other	118	12.5
ARIZONA, persons born in	538	100.0
Living in Arizona	287	53.3
Living in other states	251	46.7
California	38	7.1
Texas	31	5.8
Tennessee	16	3.0
Kansas	14	2.6
Missouri	14	2.6
Alabama	12	2.2

STATE.	Number.	Per cent.
MOUNTAIN—Continued.		
ARIZONA—Continued.		
Living in other states—Continued.		
Louisiana	11	2.0
Pennsylvania	11	2.0
All other	104	19.3
UTAH, persons born in	527	100.0
Living in Utah	162	30.7
Living in other states	365	69.3
Texas	72	13.7
Virginia	52	9.9
Idaho	25	4.7
California	24	4.6
Arkansas	21	4.0
Colorado	18	3.4
New York	15	2.8
Pennsylvania	12	2.3
Kansas	11	2.1
All other	115	21.8
NEVADA, persons born in	376	100.0
Living in Nevada	44	11.7
Living in other states	332	88.3
California	52	13.8
Georgia	39	10.4
New York	35	9.3
Arkansas	31	8.2
Florida	23	6.1
Louisiana	16	4.3
Tennessee	16	4.3
South Carolina	13	3.5
Texas	13	3.5
Alabama	12	3.2
Massachusetts	12	3.2
All other	70	18.6
PACIFIC.		
WASHINGTON, persons born in	1,546	100.0
Living in Washington	534	34.5
Living in other states	1,012	65.5
New York	193	12.5
Pennsylvania	146	9.4
Virginia	96	6.2
New Jersey	81	5.2
Texas	55	3.6
California	51	3.3
Maryland	44	2.8
Illinois	32	2.1
Oregon	24	1.6
Tennessee	24	1.6
Massachusetts	22	1.4
North Carolina	21	1.4
Ohio	17	1.1
Kentucky	15	1.0
All other	191	12.4
OREGON, persons born in	398	100.0
Living in Oregon	194	48.7
Living in other states	204	51.3
Washington	37	9.3
California	33	8.3
Texas	12	3.0
West Virginia	12	3.0
Pennsylvania	11	2.8
All other	99	24.9
CALIFORNIA, persons born in	6,318	100.0
Living in California	5,060	80.1
Living in other states	1,258	19.9
Washington	102	1.6
Texas	99	1.6
New York	85	1.3
Illinois	77	1.2
Missouri	72	1.1
Arkansas	55	0.9
Arizona	48	0.8
Oregon	47	0.7
Louisiana	42	0.7
Pennsylvania	38	0.6
Georgia	34	0.5
Ohio	33	0.5
Tennessee	33	0.5
All other	493	7.8

TABLE 22.—NEGRO POPULATION OF EACH STATE CLASSIFIED AS NATIVE AND FOREIGN BORN, AND THE NATIVE POPULATION DISTRIBUTED ACCORDING TO SELECTED STATES OF BIRTH: 1910.

STATE.	NEGROES: 1910. Number.	Per cent.
NEW ENGLAND.		
MAINE, persons living in.......	1,363	100.0
Native population.................	1,126	82.6
With state reported:		
Born in Maine.................	802	58.9
Born in other states...........	310	22.7
Massachusetts.............	64	4.7
Virginia..................	64	4.7
North Carolina............	36	2.6
Maryland.................	22	1.6
Pennsylvania.............	15	1.1
South Carolina............	14	1.0
New York.................	13	1.0
All other states...........	82	6.0
Other native[1].............	14	1.0
Foreign born.................	237	17.4
NEW HAMPSHIRE, persons living in.	564	100.0
Native population.................	524	92.9
With state reported:		
Born in New Hampshire........	234	41.5
Born in other states...........	281	49.8
Virginia..................	74	13.1
Massachusetts.............	45	8.0
North Carolina............	32	5.7
South Carolina............	19	3.4
New York.................	15	2.6
Maine....................	13	2.3
Maryland.................	13	2.3
Vermont..................	13	2.3
Connecticut...............	8	1.4
Georgia..................	6	1.1
All other states...........	43	7.6
Other native[1].............	9	1.6
Foreign born.................	40	7.1
VERMONT, persons living in....	1,621	100.0
Native population.................	1,581	97.5
With state reported:		
Born in Vermont.............	437	27.0
Born in other states...........	1,109	68.4
Tennessee................	126	7.8
Georgia..................	113	7.0
Kentucky.................	107	6.6
Virginia..................	98	6.0
Alabama.................	66	4.1
New York.................	62	3.8
North Carolina............	56	3.4
South Carolina............	51	3.2
Massachusetts.............	49	3.0
Texas...................	47	2.9
Maryland.................	41	2.5
Pennsylvania.............	39	2.4
All other states...........	254	15.6
Other native[1].............	35	2.2
Foreign born.................	40	2.5
MASSACHUSETTS, persons living in.	38,055	100.0
Native population.................	31,903	83.8
With state reported:		
Born in Massachusetts.........	14,953	39.3
Born in other states...........	16,688	43.9
Virginia..................	5,750	15.1
North Carolina............	2,991	7.9
South Carolina............	1,060	2.8
Maryland.................	953	2.5
New York.................	889	2.3
Georgia..................	798	2.1
Pennsylvania.............	582	1.5
Connecticut...............	551	1.4
District of Columbia........	528	1.4
New Jersey...............	341	0.9
Rhode Island..............	335	0.9
Maine....................	254	0.7
All other states...........	1,656	4.4
Other native[1].............	262	0.7
Foreign born.................	6,152	16.2
RHODE ISLAND, persons living in.	9,529	100.0
Native population.................	8,657	90.8
With state reported:		
Born in Rhode Island........	4,084	42.9
Born in other states...........	4,513	47.4
Virginia..................	1,611	16.9
Maryland.................	546	5.7
Massachusetts.............	419	4.4
North Carolina............	309	3.2
Connecticut...............	305	3.2
New York.................	230	2.4
South Carolina............	203	2.1

STATE.	NEGROES: 1910. Number.	Per cent.
NEW ENGLAND—Continued.		
RHODE ISLAND—Continued.		
Native population—Continued.		
With state reported:		
Born in other states—Con.		
District of Columbia........	184	1.9
Pennsylvania.............	181	1.9
Georgia..................	168	1.8
New Jersey...............	94	1.0
All other states...........	263	2.8
Other native[1].............	60	0.6
Foreign born.................	872	9.2
CONNECTICUT, persons living in.	15,174	100.0
Native population.................	14,805	97.6
With state reported:		
Born in Connecticut............	7,296	48.1
Born in other states...........	7,402	48.8
Virginia..................	2,621	17.3
North Carolina............	1,175	7.7
New York.................	960	6.3
Massachusetts.............	445	2.9
South Carolina............	399	2.6
Maryland.................	319	2.1
New Jersey...............	277	1.8
Pennsylvania.............	230	1.5
Georgia..................	185	1.2
District of Columbia........	180	1.2
Rhode Island..............	118	0.8
All other states...........	493	3.2
Other native[1].............	107	0.7
Foreign born.................	369	2.4
MIDDLE ATLANTIC.		
NEW YORK, persons living in...	134,191	100.0
Native population.................	121,340	90.4
With state reported:		
Born in New York............	49,750	37.1
Born in other states...........	70,279	52.4
Virginia..................	29,157	21.7
North Carolina............	10,283	7.7
South Carolina............	6,698	5.0
Georgia..................	3,792	2.8
Maryland.................	3,510	2.6
Pennsylvania.............	2,689	2.0
New Jersey...............	2,617	2.0
District of Columbia........	2,080	1.6
Florida..................	1,257	0.9
Massachusetts.............	917	0.7
Connecticut...............	899	0.7
Kentucky.................	873	0.7
Tennessee................	648	0.5
Ohio....................	638	0.5
Alabama.................	536	0.4
All other states...........	3,685	2.7
Other native[1].............	1,311	1.0
Foreign born.................	12,851	9.6
NEW JERSEY, persons living in.	89,760	100.0
Native population.................	88,273	98.3
With state reported:		
Born in New Jersey...........	37,017	41.2
Born in other states...........	50,745	56.5
Virginia..................	20,710	23.1
Maryland.................	6,274	7.0
North Carolina............	6,234	6.9
Pennsylvania.............	4,773	5.3
New York.................	3,606	4.0
Delaware.................	2,102	2.3
South Carolina............	1,933	2.2
District of Columbia........	1,191	1.3
Georgia..................	949	1.1
Florida..................	383	0.4
Massachusetts.............	301	0.3
Kentucky.................	255	0.3
All other states...........	2,034	2.3
Other native[1].............	511	0.6
Foreign born.................	1,487	1.7
PENNSYLVANIA, persons living in.	193,919	100.0
Native population.................	191,935	99.0
With state reported:		
Born in Pennsylvania.........	84,960	43.8
Born in other states...........	105,778	54.5
Virginia..................	48,995	25.3
Maryland.................	20,030	10.3
North Carolina............	9,735	5.0
Delaware.................	5,798	3.0
New Jersey...............	3,129	1.6
District of Columbia........	2,937	1.5

STATE.	NEGROES: 1910. Number.	Per cent.
MIDDLE ATLANTIC—Continued.		
PENNSYLVANIA—Continued.		
Native population—Continued.		
With state reported:		
Born in other states—Cont'd.		
West Virginia.............	2,260	1.2
South Carolina............	2,113	1.1
Ohio....................	2,109	1.1
Georgia..................	1,578	0.8
New York.................	1,421	0.7
Tennessee................	1,065	0.5
Kentucky.................	992	0.5
Alabama.................	545	0.3
All other states...........	3,071	1.6
Other native[1].............	1,197	0.6
Foreign born.................	1,984	1.0
EAST NORTH CENTRAL.		
OHIO, persons living in.	111,452	100.0
Native population.................	110,797	99.4
With state reported:		
Born in Ohio...............	59,194	53.1
Born in other states...........	50,449	45.3
Kentucky.................	18,835	16.9
Virginia..................	10,195	9.1
North Carolina............	3,884	3.5
Tennessee................	3,481	3.1
West Virginia.............	2,358	2.1
Pennsylvania.............	2,103	1.9
Georgia..................	1,549	1.4
Indiana..................	1,375	1.2
South Carolina............	1,102	1.0
Alabama.................	781	0.7
Maryland.................	737	0.7
Michigan.................	669	0.6
New York.................	476	0.4
Mississippi...............	475	0.4
Illinois..................	430	0.4
Missouri.................	353	0.3
All other states...........	1,646	1.5
Other native[1].............	1,154	1.0
Foreign born.................	655	0.6
INDIANA, persons living in......	60,320	100.0
Native population.................	60,223	99.8
With state reported:		
Born in Indiana.............	25,224	41.8
Born in other states...........	34,588	57.3
Kentucky.................	20,756	34.4
Tennessee................	5,073	8.4
Ohio....................	1,934	3.2
North Carolina............	1,320	2.2
Illinois..................	1,206	2.0
Virginia..................	938	1.6
Alabama.................	499	0.8
Georgia..................	468	0.8
Michigan.................	405	0.7
Missouri.................	388	0.6
Mississippi...............	290	0.5
All other states...........	1,311	2.2
Other native[1].............	411	0.7
Foreign born.................	97	0.2
ILLINOIS, persons living in......	109,049	100.0
Native population.................	108,121	99.1
With state reported:		
Born in Illinois.............	35,917	32.9
Born in other states...........	70,224	64.4
Tennessee................	15,303	14.0
Kentucky.................	13,314	12.2
Missouri.................	9,732	8.9
Mississippi...............	4,612	4.2
Virginia..................	3,326	3.1
Alabama.................	3,208	2.9
Georgia..................	2,874	2.6
Ohio....................	2,766	2.5
Indiana..................	2,731	2.5
Louisiana................	1,609	1.5
Arkansas................	1,354	1.2
South Carolina............	1,217	1.1
North Carolina............	1,175	1.1
Iowa....................	797	0.7
Texas...................	789	0.7
Pennsylvania.............	765	0.7
Michigan.................	750	0.7
Kansas..................	728	0.7
Maryland.................	643	0.6
New York.................	524	0.5
All other states...........	2,007	1.8
Other native[1].............	1,980	1.8
Foreign born.................	928	0.9

[1] Includes persons born in the United States, state of birth not reported; persons born in outlying possessions, or at sea under United States flag; and American citizens born abroad.

TABLE 22.—NEGRO POPULATION OF EACH STATE CLASSIFIED AS NATIVE AND FOREIGN BORN, AND THE NATIVE POPULATION DISTRIBUTED ACCORDING TO SELECTED STATES OF BIRTH: 1910—Continued.

STATE.	Negroes: 1910. Number.	Per cent.
EAST NORTH CENTRAL—Contd.		
MICHIGAN, persons living in....	17,115	100.0
Native population	15,475	90.4
With state reported:		
Born in Michigan	8,192	47.9
Born in other states	6,324	36.9
Ohio	1,332	7.8
Kentucky	781	4.6
Indiana	774	4.5
Virginia	597	3.5
Tennessee	329	1.9
North Carolina	301	1.8
Pennsylvania	284	1.7
Illinois	276	1.6
New York	274	1.6
Missouri	144	0.8
Georgia	138	0.8
Alabama	116	0.7
Maryland	111	0.6
West Virginia	110	0.6
All other states	757	4.4
Other native[1]	959	5.6
Foreign born	1,640	9.6
WISCONSIN, persons living in...	2,900	100.0
Native population	2,836	97.8
With state reported:		
Born in Wisconsin	1,171	40.4
Born in other states	1,592	54.9
Illinois	209	7.2
Kentucky	196	6.8
Missouri	116	4.0
Tennessee	113	3.9
Ohio	100	3.4
Virginia	100	3.4
Georgia	87	3.0
Indiana	74	2.6
Michigan	70	2.4
Alabama	56	1.9
Iowa	52	1.8
Mississippi	49	1.7
New York	47	1.6
Minnesota	39	1.3
Pennsylvania	38	1.3
South Carolina	29	1.0
All other states	217	7.5
Other native[1]	73	2.5
Foreign born	64	2.2
WEST NORTH CENTRAL.		
MINNESOTA, persons living in...	7,084	100.0
Native population	6,884	97.2
With state reported:		
Born in Minnesota	1,556	22.0
Born in other states	5,132	72.4
Missouri	683	9.6
Kentucky	579	8.2
Illinois	421	5.9
Tennessee	418	5.9
Ohio	291	4.1
Virginia	267	3.8
Iowa	258	3.6
Mississippi	227	3.2
Georgia	200	2.8
Alabama	199	2.8
Wisconsin	174	2.5
Indiana	170	2.4
Kansas	161	2.3
Louisiana	124	1.8
Michigan	111	1.6
All other states	849	12.0
Other native[1]	196	2.8
Foreign born	200	2.8
IOWA, persons living in	14,973	100.0
Native population	14,918	99.6
With state reported:		
Born in Iowa	5,253	35.1
Born in other states	9,449	63.1
Missouri	3,272	21.9
Virginia	1,588	10.6
Illinois	746	5.0
Kentucky	713	4.8
Tennessee	473	3.2
Alabama	398	2.7
Mississippi	227	1.5
Kansas	219	1.5
North Carolina	208	1.4
Georgia	177	1.2
Ohio	160	1.1
Indiana	126	0.8
West Virginia	117	0.8
Texas	116	0.8
Nebraska	106	0.7
Pennsylvania	99	0.7
Maryland	95	0.6

STATE.	Negroes: 1910. Number.	Per cent.
WEST NORTH CENTRAL—Contd.		
IOWA—Continued.		
Native population—Continued.		
With state reported:		
Born in other states—Contd.		
Oklahoma	91	0.6
South Carolina	82	0.5
All other states	436	2.9
Other native[1]	216	1.4
Foreign born	55	0.4
MISSOURI, persons living in....	157,452	100.0
Native population	157,126	99.8
With state reported:		
Born in Missouri	109,949	69.8
Born in other states	45,299	28.8
Tennessee	9,814	6.2
Kentucky	6,903	4.4
Mississippi	4,507	2.9
Kansas	3,376	2.1
Illinois	3,006	1.9
Arkansas	2,958	1.9
Virginia	2,583	1.6
Alabama	2,412	1.5
Texas	1,907	1.2
Louisiana	1,631	1.0
Georgia	1,372	0.9
North Carolina	606	0.4
Ohio	561	0.4
South Carolina	523	0.3
Indiana	515	0.3
Oklahoma	512	0.3
Iowa	374	0.2
All other states	1,739	1.1
Other native[1]	1,878	1.2
Foreign born	326	0.2
NORTH DAKOTA, persons living in	617	100.0
Native population	615	99.7
With state reported:		
Born in North Dakota	102	16.5
Born in other states	490	79.4
Missouri	66	10.7
Kentucky	48	7.8
Tennessee	44	7.1
Virginia	44	7.1
Minnesota	39	6.3
Illinois	37	6.0
Ohio	33	5.3
Iowa	16	2.6
Wisconsin	14	2.3
New York	12	1.9
Maryland	10	1.6
Mississippi	10	1.6
South Carolina	10	1.6
All other states	107	17.3
Other native[1]	23	3.7
Foreign born	2	0.3
SOUTH DAKOTA, persons living in	817	100.0
Native population	808	98.9
With state reported:		
Born in South Dakota	139	17.0
Born in other states	643	78.7
Missouri	112	13.7
Iowa	59	7.2
Illinois	58	7.1
Tennessee	54	6.6
Kentucky	35	4.3
Virginia	35	4.3
Kansas	29	3.5
Nebraska	25	3.1
Georgia	23	2.8
Ohio	23	2.8
North Carolina	21	2.6
Alabama	19	2.3
Minnesota	19	2.3
Mississippi	14	1.7
Texas	14	1.7
Indiana	12	1.5
All other states	91	11.1
Other native[1]	26	3.2
Foreign born	9	1.1
NEBRASKA, persons living in...	7,689	100.0
Native population	7,592	98.7
With state reported:		
Born in Nebraska	1,657	21.6
Born in other states	5,740	74.6
Missouri	1,736	22.6
Kansas	658	8.6
Kentucky	516	6.7
Tennessee	362	4.7
Iowa	323	4.2

STATE.	Negroes: 1910. Number.	Per cent.
WEST NORTH CENTRAL—Contd.		
NEBRASKA—continued.		
Native population—Continued.		
With state reported:		
Born in other states—Contd.		
Virginia	244	3.2
Texas	228	3.0
Illinois	217	2.8
Alabama	176	2.3
Mississippi	164	2.1
Georgia	142	1.8
Ohio	110	1.4
Louisiana	100	1.3
All other states	764	9.9
Other native[1]	195	2.5
Foreign born	97	1.3
KANSAS, persons living in	54,030	100.0
Native population	53,912	99.8
With state reported:		
Born in Kansas	22,934	42.4
Born in other states	30,270	56.0
Missouri	8,262	15.3
Tennessee	4,387	8.1
Kentucky	4,358	8.1
Texas	1,907	3.5
Mississippi	1,544	2.9
Oklahoma	1,482	2.7
Alabama	1,329	2.5
Arkansas	1,208	2.2
Virginia	1,051	1.9
Georgia	628	1.2
Louisiana	619	1.1
Illinois	548	1.0
North Carolina	463	0.9
Ohio	408	0.8
South Carolina	401	0.7
Indiana	261	0.5
All other states	1,414	2.6
Other native[1]	708	1.3
Foreign born	118	0.2
SOUTH ATLANTIC.		
DELAWARE, persons living in..	31,181	100.0
Native population	31,146	99.9
With state reported:		
Born in Delaware	22,668	72.7
Born in other states	8,399	26.9
Maryland	5,440	17.4
Virginia	1,206	3.9
Pennsylvania	952	3.0
New Jersey	226	0.7
North Carolina	142	0.5
New York	126	0.4
All other states	307	1.0
Other native[1]	79	0.3
Foreign born	35	0.1
MARYLAND, persons living in...	232,250	100.0
Native population	231,799	99.8
With state reported:		
Born in Maryland	201,594	86.8
Born in other states	29,769	12.8
Virginia	20,151	8.7
North Carolina	2,127	0.9
Pennsylvania	1,621	0.7
District of Columbia	1,603	0.7
Delaware	840	0.4
West Virginia	682	0.3
South Carolina	484	0.2
New York	343	0.1
All other states	1,918	0.8
Other native[1]	436	0.2
Foreign born	451	0.2
DISTRICT OF COLUMBIA, persons living in	94,446	100.0
Native population	94,208	99.7
With state reported:		
Born in the District of Columbia	40,459	42.8
Born elsewhere	53,058	56.2
Virginia	28,051	29.7
Maryland	15,632	16.6
North Carolina	2,754	2.9
South Carolina	1,088	1.2
Pennsylvania	848	0.9
Georgia	839	0.9
New York	435	0.5
West Virginia	430	0.5
Alabama	330	0.4
Tennessee	303	0.3
Ohio	285	0.3
Mississippi	267	0.3
Kentucky	255	0.3
New Jersey	229	0.2
All other states	1,312	1.4
Other native[1]	691	0.7
Foreign born	238	0.3

[1] Includes persons born in the United States, state of birth not reported; persons born in outlying possessions, or at sea under United States flag; and American citizens born abroad.

TABLE 22.—NEGRO POPULATION OF EACH STATE CLASSIFIED AS NATIVE AND FOREIGN BORN, AND THE NATIVE POPULATION DISTRIBUTED ACCORDING TO SELECTED STATES OF BIRTH: 1910—Continued.

STATE.	NEGROES: 1910. Number.	NEGROES: 1910. Per cent.
SOUTH ATLANTIC—Continued.		
VIRGINIA, persons living in....	671,096	100.0
Native population....	670,800	100.0
With state reported:		
Born in Virginia....	623,472	92.9
Born in other states....	46,570	6.9
North Carolina....	33,513	5.0
Maryland....	2,033	0.3
South Carolina....	1,750	0.3
Tennessee....	1,545	0.2
Pennsylvania....	1,092	0.2
District of Columbia....	1,054	0.2
West Virginia....	962	0.1
All other states....	4,621	0.7
Other native [1]....	758	0.1
Foreign born....	296	(2)
WEST VIRGINIA, persons living in....	64,173	100.0
Native population....	64,091	99.9
With state reported:		
Born in West Virginia....	27,160	42.3
Born in other states....	36,573	57.0
Virginia....	26,565	41.4
North Carolina....	4,622	7.2
Ohio....	1,176	1.8
Kentucky....	907	1.4
Pennsylvania....	554	0.9
Tennessee....	554	0.9
Maryland....	526	0.8
South Carolina....	461	0.7
Georgia....	275	0.4
Alabama....	206	0.3
District of Columbia....	143	0.2
All other states....	584	0.9
Other native [1]....	358	0.6
Foreign born....	82	0.1
NORTH CAROLINA, persons living in....	697,843	100.0
Native population....	697,755	100.0
With state reported:		
Born in North Carolina....	663,394	95.1
Born in other states....	33,392	4.8
South Carolina....	21,650	3.1
Virginia....	7,957	1.1
Georgia....	1,105	0.2
Tennessee....	486	0.1
All other states....	2,194	0.3
Other native [1]....	969	0.1
Foreign born....	88	(2)
SOUTH CAROLINA, persons living in....	835,843	100.0
Native population....	835,771	100.0
With state reported:		
Born in South Carolina....	821,058	98.2
Born in other states....	14,068	1.7
North Carolina....	7,769	0.9
Georgia....	3,799	0.5
Virginia....	897	0.1
All other states....	1,603	0.2
Other native [1]....	645	0.1
Foreign born....	72	(2)
GEORGIA, persons living in....	1,176,987	100.0
Native population....	1,176,759	100.0
With state reported:		
Born in Georgia....	1,097,257	93.2
Born in other states....	75,821	6.4
South Carolina....	36,739	3.1
Alabama....	13,101	1.1
North Carolina....	10,173	0.9
Florida....	7,047	0.6
Virginia....	4,294	0.4
Tennessee....	1,482	0.1
All other states....	2,985	0.3
Other native [1]....	3,681	0.3
Foreign born....	228	(2)
FLORIDA, persons living in....	308,669	100.0
Native population....	302,084	97.9
With state reported:		
Born in Florida....	198,496	64.3
Born in other states....	101,278	32.8
Georgia....	45,699	14.8
South Carolina....	27,501	8.9
Alabama....	12,673	4.1
North Carolina....	9,690	3.1

STATE.	NEGROES: 1910. Number.	NEGROES: 1910. Per cent.
SOUTH ATLANTIC—Continued.		
FLORIDA—Continued.		
Native population—Continued.		
With state reported—Continued.		
Born in other states—Contd.		
Virginia....	2,212	0.7
Mississippi....	699	0.2
Tennessee....	619	0.2
Louisiana....	349	0.1
All other states....	1,836	0.6
Other native [1]....	2,310	0.7
Foreign born....	6,585	2.1
EAST SOUTH CENTRAL.		
KENTUCKY, persons living in..	261,656	100.0
Native population....	261,590	100.0
With state reported:		
Born in Kentucky....	233,454	89.2
Born in other states....	27,462	10.5
Tennessee....	15,672	6.0
Virginia....	2,749	1.0
Indiana....	1,239	0.5
Alabama....	1,160	0.4
Georgia....	1,034	0.4
North Carolina....	987	0.4
Ohio....	805	0.3
Mississippi....	726	0.3
Illinois....	642	0.2
Missouri....	503	0.2
South Carolina....	448	0.2
Louisiana....	240	0.1
All other states....	1,257	0.5
Other native [1]....	674	0.3
Foreign born....	66	(2)
TENNESSEE, persons living in..	473,088	100.0
Native population....	472,989	100.0
With state reported:		
Born in Tennessee....	393,173	83.1
Born in other states....	77,723	16.4
Mississippi....	26,061	5.5
Georgia....	13,075	2.8
Alabama....	11,127	2.4
Kentucky....	6,062	1.3
Virginia....	4,825	1.0
North Carolina....	4,783	1.0
Arkansas....	3,377	0.7
South Carolina....	3,207	0.7
Louisiana....	1,224	0.3
Missouri....	727	0.2
Texas....	627	0.1
All other states....	2,628	0.6
Other native [1]....	2,111	0.4
Foreign born....	99	(2)
ALABAMA, persons living in....	908,282	100.0
Native population....	908,000	100.0
With state reported:		
Born in Alabama....	839,821	92.5
Born in other states....	65,981	7.3
Georgia....	31,202	3.4
Mississippi....	8,841	1.0
Tennessee....	6,337	0.7
South Carolina....	5,179	0.6
Virginia....	4,569	0.5
North Carolina....	3,658	0.4
Florida....	2,196	0.2
Louisiana....	816	0.1
All other states....	3,183	0.4
Other native [1]....	2,198	0.2
Foreign born....	282	(2)
MISSISSIPPI, persons living in..	1,009,487	100.0
Native population....	1,009,309	100.0
With state reported:		
Born in Mississippi....	899,690	89.1
Born in other states....	106,436	10.5
Alabama....	37,054	3.7
Louisiana....	20,139	2.0
Tennessee....	10,061	1.0
Georgia....	9,735	1.0
North Carolina....	7,295	0.7
Virginia....	5,819	0.6
South Carolina....	5,231	0.5
Arkansas....	4,934	0.5
Kentucky....	1,713	0.2
Texas....	992	0.1
All other states....	3,463	0.3
Other native [1]....	3,183	0.3
Foreign born....	178	(2)

STATE.	NEGROES: 1910. Number.	NEGROES: 1910. Per cent.
WEST SOUTH CENTRAL.		
ARKANSAS, persons living in...	442,891	100.0
Native population....	442,811	100.0
With state reported:		
Born in Arkansas....	296,040	66.8
Born in other states....	144,065	32.5
Mississippi....	39,467	8.9
Louisiana....	25,382	5.7
Tennessee....	24,875	5.6
Alabama....	12,991	2.9
Georgia....	10,013	2.3
South Carolina....	8,482	1.9
North Carolina....	7,471	1.7
Texas....	5,383	1.2
Virginia....	2,921	0.7
Kentucky....	1,936	0.4
Missouri....	1,753	0.4
Oklahoma....	808	0.2
Illinois....	696	0.2
Florida....	307	0.1
All other states....	1,580	0.4
Other native [1]....	2,706	0.6
Foreign born....	80	(2)
LOUISIANA, persons living in...	713,874	100.0
Native population....	713,299	99.9
With state reported:		
Born in Louisiana....	642,733	90.0
Born in other states....	68,022	9.5
Mississippi....	26,626	3.7
Alabama....	8,755	1.2
Texas....	8,058	1.1
Arkansas....	4,893	0.7
Georgia....	4,270	0.6
Virginia....	3,931	0.6
North Carolina....	2,571	0.4
South Carolina....	1,952	0.3
Tennessee....	1,826	0.3
Kentucky....	1,424	0.2
Florida....	754	0.1
All other states....	2,962	0.4
Other native [1]....	2,544	0.4
Foreign born....	575	0.1
OKLAHOMA, persons living in...	137,612	100.0
Native population....	137,489	99.9
With state reported:		
Born in Oklahoma....	45,976	33.4
Born in other states....	90,420	65.7
Texas....	35,397	25.7
Arkansas....	10,771	7.8
Louisiana....	8,498	6.2
Mississippi....	7,000	5.1
Tennessee....	6,864	5.0
Alabama....	6,720	4.9
Georgia....	2,791	2.0
Missouri....	2,382	1.7
Kansas....	2,298	1.7
Kentucky....	1,884	1.4
North Carolina....	1,633	1.2
South Carolina....	1,427	1.0
Virginia....	1,017	0.7
Illinois....	427	0.3
All other states....	1,311	1.0
Other native [1]....	1,093	0.8
Foreign born....	123	0.1
TEXAS, persons living in......	690,049	100.0
Native population....	688,958	99.8
With state reported:		
Born in Texas....	602,761	87.4
Born in other states....	81,883	11.9
Louisiana....	19,703	2.9
Alabama....	13,280	1.9
Mississippi....	8,074	1.2
Tennessee....	7,920	1.1
Georgia....	7,718	1.1
Arkansas....	6,328	0.9
Virginia....	3,927	0.6
North Carolina....	3,685	0.5
South Carolina....	2,899	0.4
Kentucky....	2,029	0.3
Missouri....	1,878	0.3
Oklahoma....	1,032	0.2
All other states....	3,410	0.5
Other native [1]....	4,314	0.6
Foreign born....	1,091	0.2

[1] Includes persons born in the United States, state of birth not reported; persons born in outlying possessions, or at sea under United States flag; and American citizens born abroad.

[2] Less than one-tenth of 1 per cent.

TABLE 22.—NEGRO POPULATION OF EACH STATE CLASSIFIED AS NATIVE AND FOREIGN BORN, AND THE NATIVE POPULATION DISTRIBUTED ACCORDING TO SELECTED STATES OF BIRTH: 1910—Continued.

STATE.	Number.	Per cent.
MOUNTAIN.		
MONTANA, persons living in...	1,834	100.0
Native population	1,773	96.7
With state reported:		
Born in Montana	339	18.5
Born in other states	1,367	74.5
Missouri	214	11.7
Tennessee	120	6.5
Kentucky	114	6.2
Kansas	81	4.4
Virginia	80	4.4
Illinois	65	3.5
Ohio	60	3.3
Texas	56	3.0
Georgia	47	2.6
Alabama	42	2.3
Pennsylvania	40	2.2
All other states	448	24.4
Other native[1]	67	3.7
Foreign born	61	3.3
IDAHO, persons living in	651	100.0
Native population	623	95.7
With state reported:		
Born in Idaho	69	10.6
Born in other states	539	82.8
Missouri	78	12.0
Kentucky	34	5.2
Tennessee	34	5.2
Texas	33	5.1
Illinois	25	3.8
Kansas	25	3.8
Utah	25	3.8
Alabama	23	3.5
Virginia	23	3.5
Ohio	21	3.2
All other states	218	33.5
Other native[1]	15	2.3
Foreign born	28	4.3
WYOMING, persons living in	2,235	100.0
Native population	2,197	98.3
With state reported:		
Born in Wyoming	153	6.8
Born in other states	1,993	89.2
Missouri	222	9.9
Kentucky	206	9.2
Tennessee	163	7.3
Virginia	153	6.8
Georgia	131	5.9
Kansas	123	5.5
Texas	123	5.5
Alabama	118	5.3
Ohio	85	3.8
Illinois	65	2.9
Nebraska	57	2.6
North Carolina	54	2.4
Mississippi	45	2.0
Arkansas	44	2.0
All other states	404	18.1
Other native[1]	51	2.3
Foreign born	38	1.7
COLORADO, persons living in	11,453	100.0
Native population	11,323	98.9
With state reported:		
Born in Colorado	2,156	18.8
Born in other states	8,940	78.1
Missouri	1,617	14.1
Tennessee	910	7.9
Kansas	899	7.8
Kentucky	734	6.4
Alabama	689	6.0
Texas	684	6.0
Virginia	498	4.3
Georgia	396	3.5
Mississippi	267	2.3
Illinois	258	2.3
Arkansas	235	2.1
Ohio	231	2.0
Oklahoma	198	1.7
Louisiana	189	1.7
All other states	1,135	9.9
Other native[1]	227	2.0
Foreign born	130	1.1

STATE.	Number.	Per cent.
MOUNTAIN—Continued.		
NEW MEXICO, persons living in.	1,628	100.0
Native population	1,594	97.9
With state reported:		
Born in New Mexico	410	25.2
Born in other states	1,167	71.7
Texas	340	20.9
Alabama	89	5.5
Kentucky	73	4.5
Missouri	73	4.5
Tennessee	67	4.1
Georgia	56	3.4
Mississippi	55	3.4
Virginia	54	3.3
All other states	360	22.1
Other native[1]	17	1.0
Foreign born	34	2.1
ARIZONA, persons living in	2,009	100.0
Native population	1,978	98.5
With state reported:		
Born in Arizona	287	14.3
Born in other states	1,658	82.5
Texas	644	32.1
Missouri	102	5.1
Tennessee	94	4.7
Georgia	78	3.9
Kentucky	72	3.6
Alabama	60	3.0
Kansas	60	3.0
Arkansas	48	2.4
California	48	2.4
Louisiana	42	2.1
All other states	410	20.4
Other native[1]	33	1.6
Foreign born	31	1.5
UTAH, persons living in	1,144	100.0
Native population	1,112	97.2
With state reported:		
Born in Utah	162	14.2
Born in other states	847	74.0
Missouri	112	9.8
Kentucky	68	5.9
Texas	67	5.9
Kansas	64	5.6
Tennessee	59	5.2
Colorado	45	3.9
Virginia	43	3.8
Illinois	36	3.1
Alabama	25	2.2
Georgia	24	2.1
Iowa	24	2.1
Louisiana	23	2.0
Ohio	22	1.9
All other states	235	20.5
Other native[1]	103	9.0
Foreign born	32	2.8
NEVADA, persons living in	513	100.0
Native population	494	96.3
With state reported:		
Born in Nevada	44	8.6
Born in other states	440	85.8
Texas	45	8.8
Missouri	41	8.0
California	30	5.8
Tennessee	30	5.8
Virginia	30	5.8
Kentucky	27	5.3
Ohio	24	4.7
Kansas	22	4.3
Louisiana	21	4.1
Arkansas	18	3.5
Georgia	18	3.5
Alabama	17	3.3
Illinois	15	2.9
All other states	102	19.9
Other native[1]	10	1.9
Foreign born	19	3.7

STATE.	Number.	Per cent.
PACIFIC.		
WASHINGTON, persons living in.	6,058	100.0
Native population	5,820	96.1
With state reported:		
Born in Washington	534	8.8
Born in other states	5,057	83.5
Missouri	476	7.9
Tennessee	439	7.2
Virginia	412	6.8
Kentucky	395	6.5
Texas	283	4.7
Georgia	282	4.7
Illinois	233	3.8
Alabama	224	3.7
Ohio	223	3.7
North Carolina	219	3.6
Kansas	216	3.6
Mississippi	180	3.0
Indiana	141	2.3
Louisiana	132	2.2
South Carolina	119	2.0
Pennsylvania	104	1.7
California	102	1.7
All other states	877	14.5
Other native[1]	229	3.8
Foreign born	238	3.9
OREGON, persons living in	1,492	100.0
Native population	1,430	95.8
With state reported:		
Born in Oregon	194	13.0
Born in other states	1,193	80.0
Missouri	148	9.9
Virginia	91	6.1
Kentucky	76	5.1
Tennessee	73	4.9
Georgia	64	4.3
Texas	57	3.8
Illinois	56	3.8
Ohio	54	3.6
Alabama	47	3.2
California	47	3.2
Louisiana	47	3.2
Arkansas	40	2.7
Kansas	40	2.7
New York	35	2.3
North Carolina	32	2.1
Pennsylvania	31	2.1
Mississippi	27	1.8
Iowa	26	1.7
All other states	202	13.5
Other native[1]	43	2.9
Foreign born	62	4.2
CALIFORNIA, persons living in..	21,645	100.0
Native population	20,771	96.0
With state reported:		
Born in California	5,060	23.4
Born in other states	15,200	70.2
Texas	2,204	10.2
Georgia	1,968	9.1
Missouri	1,297	6.0
Louisiana	1,004	4.6
Tennessee	984	4.5
Kentucky	834	3.9
Virginia	773	3.6
Alabama	700	3.2
North Carolina	696	3.2
Mississippi	500	2.3
Kansas	476	2.2
Arkansas	463	2.1
South Carolina	455	2.1
Ohio	358	1.7
Illinois	323	1.5
All other states	2,165	10.0
Other native[1]	511	2.4
Foreign born	874	4.0

[1] Includes persons born in the United States, state of birth not reported; persons born in outlying possessions, or at sea under United States flag; and American citizens born abroad.

CHAPTER VII.—URBANIZATION—URBAN AND RURAL CLASSIFICATION, AND POPULATION OF CITIES.

POPULATION, URBAN AND RURAL, AND IN CLASSES OF CITIES, BY RACIAL CLASSES: 1910.

In the census tabulations the population living in cities and towns of 2,500 or more inhabitants is classified as urban, and the population living in smaller villages and towns and in open country districts as rural.

Under this classification the urban population, although it is purely urban in the sense that it is entirely a city or town population, does not embrace the entire population gathered into cities, towns, and villages. The rural population, on the other hand, is not purely a scattered population, since it embraces a semiurban element in the population of many small rural towns and villages. Undoubtedly the conditions obtaining in these small population centers differ materially from those obtaining in the open country. The small village may be primarily commercial or industrial, while the open country is primarily agricultural. It would, however, be exceedingly difficult, if not impossible, to separate accurately this small village population from the population of the open country, since the rural village communities are in many cases unincorporated, and without definitely established boundaries. In such cases the rural village may graduate by imperceptible degrees of population density into the surrounding country with which it is more or less intimately affiliated by economic interests.

Urbanization as defined in the census figures relates, therefore, as has been stated, to an arbitrarily determined population limit. It does not comprehend the growth of the small village population in the rural districts, but only that urban growth which is located in the larger towns and cities.

So defined, the proportions urban and rural, and the changes in these proportions from decade to decade, indicate conditions and tendencies for the several classes of the population which are of social significance.

In Table 1, on the following page, the urban and rural population, and the population of urban communities of specified size in 1910, is given for each racial class.

The proportion urban in 1910 was lowest among Negroes and highest among foreign-born whites, the percentage living in urban communities being 27.4 for Negroes and 72.2 for foreign-born whites. This proportion varies greatly from one white class to another, even among natives. Of native whites of native parentage, 36.1 per cent were in urban communities; of native whites of mixed parentage (one parent native, one foreign born), 59.4 per cent; and of native whites of foreign parentage (both parents foreign born), 68.1 per cent.

A much larger proportion of the white population of foreign birth and parentage than of the Negro, or of the native white population of native parentage, were in the larger cities. Of the foreign-born whites, for example, 29 per cent, and of the native whites of foreign parentage, 25.4 per cent, or more than one-fourth of each class, were in cities of 500,000 or more in 1910, the proportion in such cities for Negroes being 4 per cent and for native whites of native parentage, 6 per cent.

Of the Negroes, 72.6 per cent were living in rural communities, the corresponding proportion for native whites being 55.8 per cent and for foreign-born whites 27.8 per cent.

The several racial classes thus contribute in varying proportions to the urban and rural population aggregates, and it follows necessarily that the racial composition of the urban population differs from that of the rural. Of the total urban population in 1910, 6.3 per cent was Negro, and of the total rural, 14.5 per cent. The urban population was 41.9 per cent native white of native parentage, the rural 64.1 per cent. More than one-half of the urban population and approximately one-fifth of the rural was of foreign birth or of foreign or mixed parentage.

In the aggregate population of cities of 500,000 or more, in which more than 70 per cent of the population was of foreign birth or of foreign or mixed parentage, Negroes constituted only 3.4 per cent. The percentage Negro for classes of cities having less than 500,000 population was higher than for the class of larger cities, and was almost unvarying from one class to another, the range of variation being from 7.1 per cent in cities of 100,000 to 500,000 to 7.7 per cent in cities of 2,500 to 10,000. Geographic location rather than size is of course the determining factor as regards proportion Negro in the population, and the low percentage Negro for the cities of 500,000 and over is explained by the fact that these eight cities are none of them, except Baltimore, located in Southern states.

(87)

POPULATION, URBAN AND RURAL, AND IN CLASSES OF CITIES, BY RACIAL CLASSES: 1910.

Table 1

CLASS OF COMMUNITY.	POPULATION: 1910.							
	All classes.	Negro.	White.					Foreign born.
			Total.	Native.				
				Total.	Native parentage.	Mixed parentage.	Foreign parentage.	
	NUMBER.							
United States	91,972,266	9,827,763	81,731,957	68,386,412	49,488,575	5,981,526	12,916,311	13,345,545
Urban communities	42,623,383	2,689,229	39,831,913	30,196,544	17,849,644	3,554,980	8,791,920	9,635,369
Cities of 2,500 to 10,000	8,470,359	655,266	7,798,201	6,620,540	4,872,584	614,978	1,132,978	1,177,661
Cities of 10,000 to 25,000	5,609,208	408,362	5,186,578	4,207,860	2,827,915	446,063	933,882	978,718
Cities of 25,000 to 100,000	8,241,678	602,040	7,626,923	5,963,109	3,779,057	665,863	1,518,189	1,663,814
Cities of 100,000 to 500,000	8,790,297	626,946	8,117,117	6,173,049	3,422,040	821,365	1,929,644	1,944,068
Cities of 500,000 and over	11,511,841	396,615	11,103,094	7,231,986	2,948,048	1,006,711	3,277,227	3,871,108
Rural communities	49,348,883	7,138,534	41,900,044	38,189,868	31,638,931	2,426,546	4,124,391	3,710,176
	PERCENTAGE DISTRIBUTION, BY CLASS OF COMMUNITY.							
United States	100.0	100.0	100.0	100.0	100.0	100.0	100.0	100.0
Urban communities	46.3	27.4	48.7	44.2	36.1	59.4	68.1	72.2
Cities of 2,500 to 10,000	9.2	6.7	9.5	9.7	9.8	10.3	8.8	8.8
Cities of 10,000 to 25,000	6.1	4.2	6.3	6.2	5.7	7.5	7.2	7.3
Cities of 25,000 to 100,000	9.0	6.1	9.3	8.7	7.6	11.1	11.8	12.5
Cities of 100,000 to 500,000	9.6	6.4	9.9	9.0	6.9	13.7	14.9	14.6
Cities of 500,000 and over	12.5	4.0	13.6	10.6	6.0	16.8	25.4	29.0
Rural communities	53.7	72.6	51.3	55.8	63.9	40.6	31.9	27.8
	PERCENTAGE DISTRIBUTION, BY RACIAL CLASS.							
United States	100.0	10.7	88.9	74.4	53.8	6.5	14.0	14.5
Urban communities	100.0	6.3	93.5	70.8	41.9	8.3	20.6	22.6
Cities of 2,500 to 10,000	100.0	7.7	92.1	78.2	57.5	7.3	13.4	13.9
Cities of 10,000 to 25,000	100.0	7.3	92.5	75.0	50.4	8.0	16.6	17.4
Cities of 25,000 to 100,000	100.0	7.3	92.5	72.4	45.9	8.1	18.4	20.2
Cities of 100,000 to 500,000	100.0	7.1	92.3	70.2	38.9	9.3	22.0	22.1
Cities of 500,000 and over	100.0	3.4	96.4	62.8	25.6	8.7	28.5	33.6
Rural communities	100.0	14.5	84.9	77.4	64.1	4.9	8.4	7.5

RACIAL COMPOSITION OF THE URBAN AND RURAL POPULATION: 1910, 1900, 1890.

In Table 2 the urban and rural population and the percentage urban and rural is shown by racial classes for the three years, 1910, 1900, and 1890, together with the percentage distribution of the urban and rural population by racial classes in each of these years.

The percentage urban in the Negro population increased from 19.8 in 1890 to 22.7 in 1900 and to 27.4 in 1910; in the native white population of native parentage the corresponding increase was from 26.2 to 30.9 and to 36.1 per cent.

In each of the classes shown in Table 2 the proportion urban increased during each decade in approximately the same degree, so that only slight changes were effected in the racial composition either of the urban or of the rural population. Although, for example, the percentage urban in the Negro population increased from 19.8 in 1890 to 27.4 in 1910, the percentage Negro in the urban and in the rural population was almost unvarying, being in the urban 6.5 in 1890, 6.5 in 1900, and 6.3 in 1910; and in the rural population, 14.9 in 1890, 15.1 in 1900, and 14.5 in 1910.

Table 2

CLASS AND YEAR.	POPULATION.					
	Number.		Percentage.		Percentage in each racial class.	
	Urban.	Rural.	Urban.	Rural.	Of total urban.	Of total rural.
All classes:						
1910	42,623,383	49,348,883	46.3	53.7	100.0	100.0
1900	30,797,185	45,197,390	40.5	59.5	100.0	100.0
1890	22,720,223	40,227,491	36.1	63.9	100.0	100.0
Negro:						
1910	2,689,229	7,138,534	27.4	72.6	6.3	14.5
1900	2,005,972	6,828,022	22.7	77.3	6.5	15.1
1890	1,481,142	6,007,534	19.8	80.2	6.5	14.9
White:						
1910	39,831,913	41,900,044	48.7	51.3	93.5	84.9
1900	28,717,990	38,091,206	43.0	57.0	93.2	84.3
1890	21,173,685	33,927,573	38.4	61.6	93.2	84.3
Native—						
1910	30,196,544	38,189,868	44.2	55.8	70.8	77.4
1900	21,895,860	34,699,519	38.7	61.3	71.1	76.7
1890	15,538,263	30,441,128	33.8	66.2	68.4	75.7
Native parentage—						
1910	17,849,644	31,638,931	36.1	63.9	41.9	64.1
1900	12,380,669	28,568,693	30.9	69.8	40.2	63.2
1890	9,022,289	25,453,427	26.2	73.8	39.7	63.3
Foreign or mixed parentage—						
1910	12,346,900	6,550,937	65.3	34.7	29.0	13.3
1900	9,515,191	6,130,826	60.8	39.2	30.9	13.6
1890	6,515,974	4,987,701	56.6	43.4	28.7	12.4
Foreign born—						
1910	9,635,369	3,710,176	72.2	27.8	22.6	7.5
1900	6,822,130	3,391,687	66.8	33.2	22.2	7.5
1890	5,635,422	3,486,445	61.8	38.2	24.8	8.7

The native white of native parentage, in which the percentage urban increased from 26.2 in 1890 to 36.1 in 1910, constituted 39.7 per cent of the urban population in 1890, 40.2 per cent in 1900, and 41.9 per cent in 1910; the percentage in this class of the total rural population being in these years 63.3, 63.2, and 64.1, respectively.

URBAN AND RURAL INCREASE: 1890–1910.

Three factors may be indicated in the growth of the urban population: (1) The natural increase by excess of births over deaths in urban communities; (2) the increase by net migration to the cities from the country districts; and (3) the growth by extension of urban territory, that is to say, by the growth of rural into urban communities.

Even if population were increasing at the same rate in all communities, both urban and rural, the aggregate urban population would increase faster than the aggregate rural, since in any period a certain number of rural communities would in consequence of the normal population growth become urban, and their total populations would thereby be added to the urban increase and subtracted from the rural. The rates of growth characteristic of urban and rural communities are, therefore, not accurately represented by the rates of growth of the urban and rural population aggregates, since the increases for these aggregates do not, in fact, relate to a specific group of urban communities on the one hand, or on the other to a specific rural area. The increase of the urban population by the growth of rural into urban communities is, however, relatively small as compared with the total urban increase in any decade. Increases figured upon the populations of Table 2 may, therefore, be regarded as indicating approximately the rates of urban and rural population growth in the two decades 1890–1900 and 1900–1910. Such increases are presented in Table 3.

Table 3	POPULATION INCREASE.[1]			
RACIAL CLASS AND DECADE.	Number.		Per cent.	
	Urban.	Rural.	Urban.	Rural.
All classes:				
1900–1910	11,826,198	4,151,493	38.4	9.2
1890–1900	8,076,962	4,469,899	35.6	12.4
Negro:				
1900–1910	683,257	310,512	34.1	4.5
1890–1900	524,830	820,488	35.4	13.6
White:				
1900–1910	11,113,923	3,808,838	38.7	10.0
1890–1900	7,544,305	4,163,633	35.6	12.3
Native—				
1900–1910	8,300,684	3,490,349	37.9	10.1
1890–1900	6,357,597	4,255,391	40.9	14.0
Native parentage—				
1900–1910	5,468,975	3,070,238	44.2	10.8
1890–1900	3,358,380	3,115,266	37.2	12.2
Foreign or mixed parentage—				
1900–1910	2,831,709	420,111	29.8	6.9
1890–1900	2,999,217	1,143,125	46.0	22.9
Foreign born—				
1900–1910	2,813,239	318,489	41.2	9.4
1890–1900	1,186,708	−94,758	21.1	−2.7

[1] A minus sign (−) denotes decrease.

The urban Negro population in 1910 exceeded the urban Negro population in 1900 by 683,257, or 34.1 per cent, and the rural Negro in 1910 exceeded the rural Negro in 1900 by 310,512, or 4.5 per cent. The corresponding percentage increases for the preceding decade were 35.4 for the urban and 13.6 for the rural population. In each class of the population the percentage increase of the urban aggregate greatly exceeded that of the rural aggregate. In the Thirteenth Census report the increase of the total population in the area classified as urban in 1910 and in the area classified as rural in 1910 was figured, but not by racial classes. The population increase in the 1910 urban territory was 34.8 per cent and in the 1910 rural territory 11.2 per cent. The differences between these percentages and the percentages shown in Table 3 for the total population—i. e., the difference between 34.8 and 38.4 per cent for the urban and between 11.2 and 9.2 for the rural—are accounted for by the net growth of rural into urban communities during the decade 1900–1910. The percentages for Negro increase were undoubtedly similarly affected, and a calculation similar to that made for the total population, if it could have been made for the Negro element, would undoubtedly have shown a Negro increase for territory classified as urban in 1910 somewhat below 34.1 per cent and an increase for territory classified as rural in 1910 somewhat above 4.5 per cent. The difference between the rate of growth of the urban and of the rural element would thus have been somewhat less than the difference indicated by the per- **centages** of Table 3.

SECTIONS AND SOUTHERN DIVISIONS.

The number and percentage urban and rural in the Negro and white population classes in 1910 is given in Table 4 for sections and southern divisions.

The percentage urban for the Negro population in the North and West greatly exceeded the corresponding percentage for that population class in the South. The Negro population in the North was 77.4 per cent urban; in the West, 78.6; and in the South, 21.2. Conversely, 78.8 per cent of the Negro population in the South was rural, the percentage rural for the North being 22.6, and for the West, 21.4. It is clear from these figures that the Negro migration to the North and West has been largely to urban centers, since more than three-fourths of this class in the North are in such centers, while in the South more than three-fourths are in rural communities.

In the South the percentage urban was somewhat higher, although the difference is not considerable, for Negroes than for native whites of native parentage— 21.2 as compared with 19.8 per cent—but was very much lower for Negroes than for whites of foreign birth or parentage. In the North and West, however, the Negro percentage urban exceeded that for any other racial class in these sections, even that for the foreign-born whites, who are largely concentrated in urban centers, the percentage urban for Negroes in the North being 77.4, and for foreign-born whites 75.5. While, therefore, in the South the Negro population is largely rural in character, in the North this class is the most urban of the racial classes.

NUMBER AND PERCENTAGE, URBAN AND RURAL, IN THE NEGRO AND WHITE POPULATION CLASSES, BY SECTIONS AND SOUTHERN DIVISIONS: 1910.

Table 4

RACIAL CLASS.	POPULATION: 1910.												
	United States.	The South.				The North.	The West.	United States.	The South.				The North.	The West.
		Total.	South Atlantic division.	East South Central division.	West South Central division.				Total.	South Atlantic division.	East South Central division.	West South Central division.		
	URBAN.							PERCENTAGE URBAN.						
All classes.............	42,623,383	6,623,838	3,092,153	1,574,229	1,957,456	32,669,705	3,329,840	46.3	22.5	25.4	18.7	22.3	58.6	48.8
Negro....................	2,689,229	1,854,455	909,520	509,097	435,838	794,966	39,808	27.4	21.2	22.1	19.2	22.0	77.4	78.6
White....................	39,831,913	4,761,463	2,180,990	1,064,740	1,515,733	31,851,632	3,218,818	47.8	23.2	27.0	18.5	22.6	58.3	49.2
Native.................	30,196,544	4,374,967	1,989,234	1,006,808	1,378,925	23,304,578	2,516,999	44.2	22.1	25.6	17.8	21.6	53.8	48.0
Native parentage.......	17,849,644	3,675,281	1,675,819	856,826	1,142,636	12,564,943	1,609,420	36.1	19.8	22.8	15.7	19.8	45.9	45.0
Mixed parentage........	3,554,980	263,411	108,506	58,820	96,085	2,956,676	334,893	59.4	52.9	65.6	64.6	39.8	61.1	52.8
Foreign parentage......	8,791,920	436,275	204,909	91,162	140,204	7,782,959	572,686	68.1	57.2	74.7	73.6	38.5	70.0	55.7
Foreign born..............	9,635,369	386,496	191,756	57,932	136,808	8,547,054	701,819	72.2	53.2	66.0	66.7	39.2	75.5	54.1
	RURAL.							PERCENTAGE RURAL.						
All classes.............	49,348,883	22,765,492	9,102,742	6,835,672	6,827,078	23,087,410	3,495,981	53.7	77.5	74.6	81.3	77.7	41.4	51.2
Negro....................	7,138,534	6,894,972	3,202,968	2,143,416	1,548,588	232,708	10,854	72.6	78.8	77.9	80.8	78.0	22.6	21.4
White....................	41,900,044	15,785,957	5,890,613	4,689,586	5,205,758	22,788,577	3,325,510	51.3	76.8	73.0	81.5	77.4	41.7	50.8
Native.................	38,189,868	15,446,282	5,791,814	4,660,661	4,993,807	20,014,615	2,728,971	55.8	77.9	74.4	82.2	78.4	46.2	52.0
Native parentage.......	31,638,931	14,885,865	5,665,386	4,595,666	4,624,813	14,787,092	1,965,974	63.9	80.2	77.2	84.3	80.2	54.1	55.0
Mixed parentage........	2,426,546	234,294	56,886	32,242	145,166	1,884,123	308,129	40.6	47.1	25.3	35.4	60.2	38.9	47.2
Foreign parentage......	4,124,391	325,123	69,542	32,753	223,828	3,343,400	454,868	31.9	42.8	34.4	26.4	61.5	30.0	44.3
Foreign born..............	3,710,176	339,675	98,799	28,925	211,951	2,773,962	596,539	27.8	46.8	34.0	33.3	60.8	24.5	45.9

DIAGRAM I.—PERCENTAGE URBAN AND RURAL IN THE NEGRO AND WHITE POPULATION, BY SECTIONS: 1910.

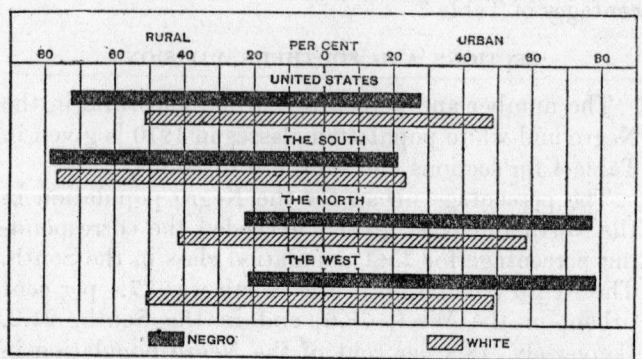

Since, however, the great mass of the Negro population is in the South, the extremely high percentage urban applies to a relatively small proportion of this racial class.

In Table 5 the percentage urban and rural in the Negro population of the South and North is shown for the years 1910, 1900, and 1890. In each section and division the proportion of the Negro population living in urban communities increased during each of the two decades covered by the table. In the South the increase was from 15.3 per cent in 1890, to 17.2 per cent in 1900, and 21.2 per cent in 1910; in the North from 61.8 per cent in 1890, to 70.5 per cent in 1900, and to 77.4 per cent in 1910; and in the West from 54 per cent in 1890 to 67.4 per cent in 1900, and to 78.6 per cent in 1910. Corresponding decreases are shown for the proportion living in rural communities in each section and division. These proportions for sections are illustrated in Diagram II.

Table 5

SECTION AND DIVISION.	NEGRO POPULATION.					
	Percentage urban.			Percentage rural.		
	1910	1900	1890	1910	1900	1890
United States....................	27.4	22.7	19.8	72.6	77.3	80.2
The South.....................	21.2	17.2	15.3	78.8	82.8	84.7
South Atlantic...............	21.1	18.7	17.4	77.9	81.3	82.6
East South Central...........	19.2	15.5	12.9	80.8	84.5	87.1
West South Central...........	22.0	16.7	14.0	78.0	83.3	86.0
The North.....................	77.4	70.5	61.8	22.6	29.5	38.2
The West......................	78.6	67.4	54.0	21.4	32.6	46.0

The geographic distribution of the urban and rural Negro and white population in 1910 is shown in Table 6. Of the Negro urban, 69 per cent was in the South; of the native white urban, 14.5 per cent; and of the foreign-born white urban, 4 per cent. Of the rural Negro population, 96.6 per cent was in the South; of the rural native white, 40.4 per cent; and of the rural foreign-born white, 9.2 per cent. Only 3.4 per cent of the rural Negro population was in the North and West.

Table 6	PERCENTAGE DISTRIBUTION, BY AREA: 1910.				
SECTION AND DIVISION.	Total population.	Negro population.	White population.		
			Total.	Native.	Foreign born.
URBAN.					
United States..........	100.0	100.0	100.0	100.0	100.0
The South.................	15.5	69.0	12.0	14.5	4.0
South Atlantic...........	7.3	33.8	5.5	6.6	2.0
East South Central......	3.7	18.9	2.7	3.3	0.6
West South Central......	4.6	16.2	3.8	4.6	1.4
The North.................	76.6	29.6	80.0	77.2	88.7
The West..................	7.8	1.5	8.1	8.3	7.3
RURAL.					
The United States.....	100.0	100.0	100.0	100.0	100.0
The South.................	46.1	96.6	37.7	40.4	9.2
South Atlantic...........	18.4	44.9	14.1	15.2	2.7
East South Central......	13.9	30.0	11.2	12.2	0.8
West South Central......	13.8	21.7	12.4	13.1	5.7
The North.................	46.8	3.3	54.4	52.4	74.8
The West..................	7.1	0.2	7.9	7.1	16.1

DIAGRAM II.—PERCENTAGE URBAN AND RURAL IN THE NEGRO POPULATION, BY SECTIONS: 1910, 1900, AND 1890,

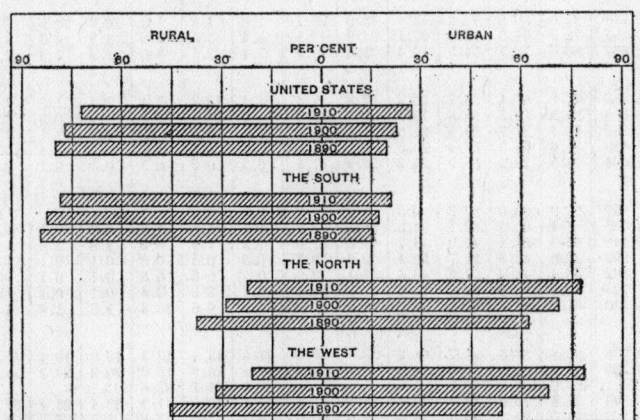

The percentage Negro in the urban and rural population of the North and South is given in Table 7 for 1910, 1900, and 1890.

Table 7	PERCENTAGE NEGRO IN THE POPULATION.					
SECTION AND DIVISION.	Urban.			Rural.		
	1910	1900	1890	1910	1900	1890
United States.......................	6.3	6.5	6.5	14.5	15.1	14.9
The South..........................	28.0	30.9	31.7	30.3	32.6	34.2
South Atlantic....................	29.4	31.2	32.8	35.2	36.9	37.8
East South Central...............	32.3	34.2	33.5	31.4	32.9	32.9
West South Central...............	22.3	26.7	26.9	22.7	25.8	29.4
The North.........................	2.4	2.5	2.4	1.0	1.1	1.2
The West..........................	1.0	1.2	1.3	0.3	0.4	0.6

Of the urban population in 1910, 28 per cent was Negro in the South; 2.4 per cent in the North; and 1 per cent in the West. Of the rural population, 30.3 per cent was Negro in the South; 1 per cent, in the North; and 0.3 per cent, in the West. In the South as a whole, the percentage Negro in the urban population decreased from 31.7 per cent in 1890, to 30.9 in 1900, and to 28 in 1910; and in the rural population from 34.2 per cent in 1890, to 32.6 in 1900, and to 30.3 in 1910.

THE STATES.

Table 8 gives the Negro and white urban and rural population in 1910 and the percentage urban in the Negro and white population, by states.

Table 8	POPULATION: 1910.					
DIVISION AND STATE.	Urban.		Rural.		Percentage urban.	
	Negro.	White.	Negro.	White.	Negro.	White.
UNITED STATES...	2,689,229	39,831,913	7,138,534	41,900,044	27.4	48.7
GEOGRAPHIC DIVISIONS:						
New England.......	60,877	5,389,967	5,429	1,090,547	91.8	83.2
Middle Atlantic....	339,246	13,373,921	78,624	5,506,531	81.2	70.8
East North Central.	230,542	9,381,652	70,294	8,545,970	76.6	52.3
West North Central.	164,301	3,706,092	78,361	7,645,529	67.7	32.6
South Atlantic.....	909,520	2,180,990	3,202,968	5,890,613	22.1	27.0
East South Central.	509,097	1,064,740	2,143,416	4,689,586	19.2	18.5
West South Central.	435,838	1,515,733	1,548,588	5,205,758	22.0	22.6
Mountain...........	15,446	924,291	6,021	1,596,164	72.0	36.7
Pacific.............	24,362	2,294,527	4,833	1,729,346	83.4	57.0
NEW ENGLAND:						
Maine...............	924	380,292	439	359,703	67.8	51.4
New Hampshire....	356	254,664	208	175,242	63.1	59.2
Vermont............	1,341	167,579	280	186,719	82.7	47.3
Massachusetts......	35,243	3,087,146	2,812	237,780	92.6	92.8
Rhode Island.......	9,055	515,011	474	17,481	95.0	96.7
Connecticut........	13,958	985,275	1,216	113,622	92.0	89.7
MIDDLE ATLANTIC:						
New York..........	117,486	7,061,043	16,705	1,905,802	87.6	78.7
New Jersey.........	65,427	1,840,560	24,333	605,334	72.9	75.3
Pennsylvania.......	156,333	4,472,318	37,586	2,995,395	80.6	59.9
EAST NORTH CENTRAL:						
Ohio................	82,282	2,582,143	29,170	2,072,754	73.8	55.5
Indiana.............	48,425	1,095,026	11,895	1,544,935	80.3	41.5
Illinois.............	85,538	3,388,881	23,511	2,138,081	78.4	61.3
Michigan...........	12,156	1,314,186	4,959	1,471,061	71.0	47.2
Wisconsin..........	2,141	1,001,416	759	1,319,139	73.8	43.2
WEST NORTH CENTRAL:						
Minnesota..........	6,518	843,322	566	1,215,905	92.0	41.0
Iowa................	9,786	670,035	5,187	1,539,156	65.4	30.2
Missouri............	104,462	1,293,554	52,990	1,841,378	66.3	41.3
North Dakota......	306	62,765	311	507,090	49.6	11.0
South Dakota......	412	76,070	405	487,701	50.4	13.5
Nebraska...........	6,621	303,767	1,068	876,526	86.1	25.7
Kansas.............	36,196	456,579	17,834	1,177,773	67.0	27.9
SOUTH ATLANTIC:						
Delaware..........	11,157	85,903	20,024	85,199	35.8	50.2
Maryland..........	99,230	558,582	133,020	504,057	42.7	52.6
District of Columbia	94,446	236,128	....	....	100.0	100.0
Virginia...........	158,218	318,159	512,878	1,071,650	23.6	22.9
West Virginia......	15,380	212,783	48,793	944,034	24.0	18.4
North Carolina....	115,975	202,438	581,868	1,298,073	16.6	13.5
South Carolina.....	101,702	123,089	734,141	556,072	12.2	18.1
Georgia............	224,826	313,606	952,161	1,118,196	19.1	21.9
Florida.............	88,586	130,302	220,083	313,332	28.7	29.4
EAST SOUTH CENTRAL:						
Kentucky..........	106,631	448,727	155,025	1,579,224	40.8	22.1
Tennessee..........	150,506	290,431	322,582	1,421,001	31.8	17.0
Alabama...........	156,603	213,756	751,679	1,015,076	17.2	17.4
Mississippi........	95,357	111,826	914,130	674,285	9.4	14.2
WEST SOUTH CENTRAL:						
Arkansas..........	59,147	143,326	383,744	987,700	13.4	12.7
Louisiana..........	160,845	335,175	553,029	605,911	22.5	35.6
Oklahoma..........	36,982	278,698	100,630	1,165,833	26.9	19.3
Texas..............	178,864	758,534	511,185	2,446,314	25.9	23.7
MOUNTAIN:						
Montana...........	1,455	130,531	379	230,049	79.3	36.2
Idaho..............	426	68,604	225	250,617	65.4	21.5
Wyoming...........	1,041	41,444	1,194	98,874	46.6	29.5
Colorado...........	9,359	394,156	2,094	389,259	81.7	50.3
New Mexico.......	795	45,588	843	259,006	48.8	15.0
Arizona............	1,310	60,355	699	111,113	65.2	35.2
Utah...............	959	170,884	185	195,699	83.8	46.6
Nevada............	101	12,729	412	61,547	19.7	17.1
PACIFIC:						
Washington........	4,699	590,181	1,359	518,930	77.6	53.2
Oregon.............	1,254	297,095	228	357,995	84.7	45.4
California..........	18,399	1,407,251	3,246	852,421	85.0	62.3

Table 9 relates to the Negro population alone, giving by states the urban and rural Negro population, the percentage urban and rural in the Negro population, and the percentage Negro in the urban and rural population, for the three years, 1910, 1900, and 1890.

NEGROES IN URBAN AND RURAL COMMUNITIES, BY DIVISIONS AND STATES: 1910, 1900, AND 1890.

[Urban includes population living in places of 2,500 or more inhabitants; rural includes all other.]

Table 9

DIVISION AND STATE.	NEGRO POPULATION. Urban. 1910	1900	1890	Rural. 1910	1900	1890	Percentage. Urban. 1910	1900	1890	Rural. 1910	1900	1890	PERCENTAGE NEGRO. In total urban population. 1910	1900	1890	In total rural population. 1910	1900	1890
UNITED STATES	2,689,229	2,005,972	1,481,142	7,138,534	6,828,022	6,007,534	27.4	22.7	19.8	72.6	77.3	80.2	6.3	6.5	6.5	14.5	15.1	14.9
GEOGRAPHIC DIVISIONS:																		
New England	60,877	53,530	39,567	5,429	5,569	5,013	91.8	90.6	88.8	8.2	9.4	11.2	1.1	1.2	1.1	0.5	0.5	0.4
Middle Atlantic	339,246	247,769	153,346	78,624	78,152	71,980	81.2	76.0	68.1	18.8	24.0	31.9	2.5	2.5	2.1	1.4	1.5	1.3
East North Central	230,542	180,121	124,213	70,294	77,721	82,810	76.6	69.9	60.0	23.4	30.1	40.0	2.4	2.5	2.4	0.8	0.9	1.0
West North Central	164,301	139,363	116,145	78,361	98,546	107,944	67.7	58.6	51.8	32.3	41.4	48.2	4.2	4.7	5.0	1.0	1.3	1.6
South Atlantic	909,520	696,372	566,519	3,202,968	3,032,645	2,696,171	22.1	18.7	17.4	77.9	81.3	82.6	29.4	31.2	32.8	35.2	36.9	37.8
East South Central	509,097	386,268	273,971	2,143,416	2,113,618	1,845,826	19.2	15.5	12.9	80.8	84.5	87.1	32.3	34.2	33.5	31.4	32.9	32.9
West South Central	435,838	282,156	192,745	1,548,588	1,411,910	1,185,345	22.0	16.7	14.0	78.0	83.3	86.0	22.3	26.7	26.9	22.7	25.8	29.4
Mountain	15,446	9,834	6,733	6,021	5,756	6,238	72.0	63.1	51.9	28.0	36.9	48.1	1.6	1.8	1.9	0.4	0.5	0.7
Pacific	24,362	10,559	7,903	4,833	4,105	6,207	83.4	72.0	56.0	16.6	28.0	44.0	1.0	0.9	1.0	0.3	0.3	0.6
NEW ENGLAND:																		
Maine	924	918	792	439	401	398	67.8	69.6	66.6	32.2	30.4	33.4	0.2	0.3	0.3	0.1	0.1	0.1
New Hampshire	356	419	300	208	243	314	63.1	63.3	48.9	36.9	36.7	51.1	0.1	0.2	0.2	0.1	0.1	0.2
Vermont	1,341	444	460	280	382	477	82.7	53.8	49.1	17.3	46.2	50.9	0.8	0.3	0.4	0.1	0.2	0.2
Massachusetts	35,243	29,867	20,427	2,812	2,107	1,717	92.6	93.4	92.2	7.4	6.6	7.8	1.1	1.2	1.0	1.2	0.9	0.7
Rhode Island	9,055	8,423	7,014	474	669	379	95.0	92.6	94.9	5.0	7.4	5.1	1.7	2.1	2.1	2.6	3.2	2.0
Connecticut	13,958	13,459	10,574	1,216	1,767	1,728	92.0	88.4	86.0	8.0	11.6	14.0	1.4	1.7	1.7	1.1	1.5	1.4
MIDDLE ATLANTIC:																		
New York	117,486	81,356	51,364	16,705	17,876	18,728	87.6	82.0	73.3	12.4	18.0	26.7	1.6	1.5	1.3	0.9	0.9	0.9
New Jersey	65,427	46,128	25,043	24,333	23,716	22,595	72.9	66.0	52.6	27.1	34.0	47.4	3.4	3.5	2.9	3.9	4.3	4.0
Pennsylvania	156,333	120,285	76,939	37,586	36,560	30,657	80.6	76.7	71.5	19.4	23.3	28.5	3.4	3.5	3.0	1.2	1.3	1.1
EAST NORTH CENTRAL:																		
Ohio	82,282	64,986	51,124	29,170	31,915	35,989	73.8	67.1	58.7	26.2	32.9	41.3	3.1	3.3	3.4	1.4	1.5	1.7
Indiana	48,425	42,274	28,839	11,895	15,231	16,376	80.3	73.5	63.8	19.7	26.5	36.2	4.2	4.9	4.9	0.8	0.9	1.0
Illinois	85,538	60,993	34,076	23,511	24,085	22,952	78.4	71.7	59.8	21.6	28.3	40.2	2.5	2.3	2.0	1.1	1.1	1.1
Michigan	12,156	10,009	8,734	4,959	5,807	6,489	71.0	63.3	57.4	29.0	36.7	42.6	0.9	1.1	1.2	0.3	0.4	0.5
Wisconsin	2,141	1,859	1,440	759	683	1,004	73.8	73.1	58.9	26.2	26.9	41.1	0.2	0.2	0.3	0.1	0.1	0.1
WEST NORTH CENTRAL:																		
Minnesota	6,518	4,495	3,286	566	464	397	92.0	90.6	89.2	8.0	9.4	10.8	0.8	0.8	0.7	(1)	(1)	(1)
Iowa	9,786	8,097	6,635	5,187	4,596	4,050	65.4	63.8	62.1	34.6	36.2	37.9	1.4	1.4	1.6	0.3	0.3	0.3
Missouri	104,462	89,247	70,636	52,990	71,987	79,548	66.3	55.4	47.0	33.7	44.6	53.0	7.5	7.9	8.2	2.8	3.6	4.4
North Dakota	306	125	81	311	161	292	49.6	43.7	21.7	50.4	56.3	78.3	0.5	0.5	0.1	0.1	0.1	0.2
South Dakota	412	195	149	405	270	392	50.4	41.9	27.5	49.6	58.1	72.5	0.5	0.5	0.5	0.1	0.1	0.1
Nebraska	6,621	5,441	7,188	1,068	828	1,725	86.1	86.8	80.6	13.9	13.2	19.4	2.1	2.2	2.5	0.1	0.1	0.2
Kansas	36,196	31,763	28,170	17,834	20,240	21,540	67.0	61.1	56.7	33.0	38.9	43.3	7.3	9.6	10.3	1.5	1.8	1.9
SOUTH ATLANTIC:																		
Delaware	11,157	11,537	9,428	20,024	19,160	18,958	35.8	37.6	33.2	64.2	62.4	66.8	11.5	13.5	13.3	19.0	19.4	19.5
Maryland	99,230	93,849	79,392	133,020	141,215	136,265	42.7	39.9	36.8	57.3	60.1	63.2	15.1	15.9	16.0	20.9	23.7	24.9
District of Columbia	94,446	86,702	75,572				100.0	100.0	100.0				28.5	31.1	32.8			
Virginia	158,218	124,799	117,092	512,878	535,923	518,346	23.6	18.9	18.4	76.4	81.1	81.6	33.2	36.7	41.4	32.4	35.4	37.7
West Virginia	15,380	8,761	6,327	48,793	34,738	26,363	24.0	20.1	19.4	76.0	79.9	80.6	6.7	7.0	7.8	4.9	4.2	3.9
North Carolina	115,975	76,169	55,695	581,868	548,300	505,323	16.6	12.2	9.9	83.4	87.8	90.1	36.4	40.8	48.1	30.8	32.1	33.6
South Carolina	101,702	84,358	64,049	734,141	697,963	624,885	12.2	10.8	9.3	87.8	89.2	90.7	45.2	49.3	55.1	56.9	59.7	60.4
Georgia	224,826	161,061	123,862	952,161	873,752	734,953	19.1	15.6	14.4	80.9	84.4	85.6	41.7	46.5	48.1	46.0	46.7	46.5
Florida	88,586	49,136	35,102	220,083	181,594	131,078	28.7	21.3	21.1	71.3	78.7	78.9	40.4	45.9	45.4	41.2	43.1	41.7
EAST SOUTH CENTRAL:																		
Kentucky	106,631	100,145	75,274	155,025	184,561	192,797	40.8	35.2	28.1	59.2	64.8	71.9	19.2	21.4	21.1	8.9	11.0	12.8
Tennessee	150,506	131,144	94,898	322,582	349,099	335,780	31.8	27.3	22.0	68.2	72.7	78.0	34.1	40.1	39.8	18.5	20.6	22.0
Alabama	156,603	98,154	69,607	751,679	729,153	608,882	17.2	11.9	10.3	82.8	88.1	89.7	42.3	45.3	45.7	42.5	45.2	44.7
Mississippi	95,357	56,825	34,192	914,130	850,805	708,367	9.4	6.3	4.6	90.6	93.7	95.4	46.0	47.3	48.9	57.5	59.4	58.1
WEST SOUTH CENTRAL:																		
Arkansas	59,147	37,171	25,491	383,744	329,685	283,626	13.4	10.1	8.2	86.6	89.9	91.8	29.2	33.3	34.8	28.0	27.5	26.9
Louisiana	160,845	116,954	87,094	553,029	533,850	472,099	22.5	18.0	15.6	77.5	82.0	84.4	32.4	31.9	30.7	47.7	52.6	56.6
Oklahoma [2]	36,982	8,702	679	100,630	46,982	20,930	26.9	15.6	3.1	73.1	84.4	96.9	11.6	14.9	7.2	7.5	6.4	8.4
Texas	178,864	119,329	79,481	511,185	501,393	408,690	25.9	19.2	16.3	74.1	80.8	83.7	19.1	22.9	22.7	17.3	19.8	21.7
MOUNTAIN:																		
Montana	1,455	931	628	379	592	862	79.3	61.1	42.1	20.7	38.9	57.9	1.1	1.1	1.6	0.2	0.4	0.8
Idaho	426	71		225	222	201	65.4	24.2		34.6	75.8	100.0	0.6	0.7		0.1	0.1	0.2
Wyoming	1,041	489	327	1,194	451	595	46.6	52.0	35.5	53.4	48.0	64.5	2.4	1.8	1.5	1.2	0.7	1.4
Colorado	9,359	7,052	5,009	2,094	1,518	1,206	81.7	82.3	80.6	18.3	17.7	19.4	2.3	2.7	2.7	0.5	0.5	0.5
New Mexico	795	581	274	833	1,029	1,682	48.8	36.1	14.0	51.2	63.9	86.0	1.7	2.1	2.7	0.3	0.6	1.1
Arizona	1,310	330	94	699	1,518	1,263	65.2	17.9	6.9	34.8	82.1	93.1	2.1	1.7	1.1	0.5	1.5	1.6
Utah	959	343	294	185	329	294	83.8	51.0	50.0	16.2	49.0	50.0	0.6	0.3	0.4	0.1	0.2	0.2
Nevada	101	37	107	412	97	135	19.7	27.6	44.2	80.3	72.4	55.8	0.8	0.5	0.7	0.6	0.3	0.4
PACIFIC:																		
Washington	4,699	1,606	978	1,359	908	624	77.6	63.9	61.0	22.4	36.1	39.0	0.8	0.8	0.8	0.3	0.3	0.3
Oregon	1,264	878	597	228	227	589	84.7	79.5	50.3	15.3	20.5	49.7	0.4	0.7	0.7	0.1	0.1	0.3
California	18,399	8,075	6,328	3,246	2,970	4,994	85.0	73.1	55.9	15.0	26.9	44.1	1.3	1.0	1.1	0.4	0.4	0.8

[1] Less than one-tenth of 1 per cent. [2] Includes population of Indian Territory for 1900 and 1890.

Excepting Massachusetts, Rhode Island, and New Jersey, the percentage urban in each Northern and Western state was higher in 1910 among Negroes than among whites. In these states the percentage urban in the Negro population ranged from 46.6 per cent in Wyoming to 95 per cent in Rhode Island. In the Southern states the proportion ranged from 9.4 per cent in Mississippi to 42.7 per cent in Maryland.

The highest percentage Negro in both the urban and the rural population in 1910 was that of Mississippi, in which state 46 per cent of the urban and 57.5 of the rural population were Negroes. Consistently with changes in the proportion Negro in the total population, the proportion Negro in the urban and in the rural population tended to decline in the Southern states, in the two decades 1890–1910, although in some instances the proportion increased.

URBAN COMMUNITIES.

Table 10 gives the Negro population in 1910 and in 1900, and the Negro increase 1900–1910, for the 43 cities having in 1910 a Negro population of 10,000 or more, the cities being arranged in order according to the 1910 Negro population. Ten of these cities lie outside the Southern states. The total Negro population of the 43 cities in 1910 was 1,341,468, or 13.6 per cent of the Negro population of the United States.

The city of Washington reported the largest Negro population of any city in 1910, and New York City the second largest. Birmingham, Ala., reported the largest increase during the decade 1900–1910, 35,730, or 215.6 per cent, and New York City, the second largest increase, 31,043, or 51.2 per cent. The Negro population of Fort Worth, Tex., increased 212.5 per cent; of Jackson, Miss., 137.3 per cent, and of Portsmouth, Va., 106.5 per cent. Charleston, S. C., Augusta, Ga., and Little Rock, Ark., showed slight decreases.

In Table 11 the Negro and white population of the 50 cities having in 1910 a population of 100,000 or more is given, together with the percentage Negro and the percentage foreign-born white. The cities are arranged in order according to the percentage foreign-born white. The aggregate population of these 50 cities was 20,302,138, of which 1,023,561, or 5 per cent, were Negroes and 5,815,176, or 25 per cent, were foreign-born whites. The 5 cities in this group in which the percentage foreign-born white was lowest were Nashville, Atlanta, Richmond, Birmingham, and Memphis.

Table 10

CITY.	NEGRO POPULATION. 1910	NEGRO POPULATION. 1900	NEGRO INCREASE:[1] 1900 TO 1910. Number.	NEGRO INCREASE:[1] 1900 TO 1910. Per cent.	PERCENTAGE NEGRO IN TOTAL POPULATION. 1910	PERCENTAGE NEGRO IN TOTAL POPULATION. 1900
Washington, D. C.	94,446	86,702	7,744	8.9	28.5	31.1
New York, N. Y.	91,709	60,666	31,043	51.2	1.9	1.8
New Orleans, La.	89,262	77,714	11,548	14.9	26.3	27.1
Baltimore, Md.	84,749	79,258	5,491	6.9	15.2	15.6
Philadelphia, Pa.	84,459	62,613	21,846	34.9	5.5	4.8
Memphis, Tenn.	52,441	49,910	2,531	5.1	40.0	48.8
Birmingham, Ala.	52,305	16,575	35,730	215.6	39.4	43.1
Atlanta, Ga.	51,902	35,727	16,175	45.3	33.5	39.8
Richmond, Va.	46,733	32,230	14,503	45.0	36.6	37.9
Chicago, Ill.	44,103	30,150	13,953	46.3	2.0	1.8
St. Louis, Mo.	43,960	35,516	8,444	23.8	6.4	6.2
Louisville, Ky.	40,522	39,139	1,383	3.5	18.1	19.1
Nashville, Tenn.	36,523	30,044	6,479	21.6	33.1	37.2
Savannah, Ga.	33,246	28,090	5,156	18.4	51.1	51.8
Charleston, S. C.	31,056	31,522	−466	−1.5	52.8	56.5
Jacksonville. Fla.	29,293	16,236	13,057	80.4	50.8	57.1
Pittsburgh, Pa.	25,623	20,355	5,268	25.9	4.8	4.5
Norfolk, Va.	25,039	20,230	4,809	23.8	37.1	43.4
Houston, Tex.	23,929	14,608	9,321	63.8	30.4	32.7
Kansas City, Mo.	23,566	17,567	5,999	34.1	9.5	10.7
Mobile, Ala.	22,763	17,045	5,718	33.5	44.2	44.3
Indianapolis, Ind.	21,816	15,931	5,885	36.9	9.3	9.4
Cincinnati, Ohio.	19,639	14,482	5,157	35.6	5.4	4.4
Montgomery, Ala.	19,322	17,229	2,093	12.1	50.7	56.8
Augusta, Ga.	18,344	18,487	−143	−0.8	44.7	46.9
Macon, Ga.	18,150	11,550	6,600	57.1	44.6	49.6
Dallas, Tex.	18,024	9,035	8,989	99.5	19.6	21.2
Chattanooga, Tenn.	17,942	13,122	4,820	36.7	40.2	43.5
Little Rock, Ark.	14,539	14,694	−155	−1.1	31.6	38.4
Shreveport, La.	13,896	8,542	5,354	62.7	49.6	53.3
Boston, Mass.	13,564	11,591	1,973	17.0	2.0	2.1
Fort Worth, Tex.	13,280	4,249	9,031	212.5	18.1	15.9
Columbus, Ohio.	12,739	8,201	4,538	55.3	7.0	6.5
Wilmington, N. C.	12,107	10,407	1,700	16.3	47.0	49.6
Vicksburg, Miss.	12,053	8,147	3,906	47.9	57.9	54.9
Charlotte, N. C.	11,752	7,151	4,601	64.3	34.6	39.5
Portsmouth, Va.	11,617	5,625	5,992	106.5	35.0	32.3
Columbia, S. C.	11,546	9,858	1,688	17.1	43.9	46.7
Petersburg, Va.	11,014	10,751	263	2.4	45.7	49.3
Lexington, Ky.	11,011	10,130	881	8.7	31.4	38.4
San Antonio, Tex.	10,716	7,538	3,178	42.2	11.1	14.1
Jackson, Miss.	10,554	4,447	6,107	137.3	49.6	56.9
Pensacola, Fla.	10,214	8,561	1,653	19.3	44.4	48.2

[1] A minus sign (−) denotes decrease.

Table 11

CITY.	POPULATION: 1910. All classes.[1]	Negro.	White. Total.	White. Native.	White. Foreign born.	Percentage. Negro.	Percentage. Foreign born white.
Total	20,302,138	1,023,561	19,220,211	13,405,035	5,815,176	5.0	25.0
Nashville, Tenn.	110,364	36,523	73,831	70,838	2,993	33.1	2.7
Atlanta, Ga.	154,839	51,902	102,861	98,451	4,410	33.5	2.8
Richmond, Va.	127,628	46,733	80,879	76,794	4,085	36.6	3.2
Birmingham, Ala.	132,685	52,305	80,369	74,669	5,700	39.4	4.3
Memphis, Tenn.	131,105	52,441	78,590	72,123	6,467	40.0	4.9
Washington, D. C.	331,069	94,446	236,128	211,777	24,351	28.5	7.4
Louisville, Ky.	223,928	40,522	183,390	165,954	17,436	18.1	7.8
New Orleans, La.	339,075	89,262	249,403	221,717	27,686	26.3	8.2
Indianapolis, Ind.	233,650	21,816	211,780	192,013	19,767	9.3	8.5
Columbus, Ohio.	181,511	12,739	168,709	152,424	16,285	7.0	9.0
Kansas City, Mo.	248,381	23,566	224,677	199,350	25,327	9.5	10.2
Dayton, Ohio.	116,577	4,842	111,707	97,860	13,847	4.2	11.9
Baltimore, Md.	558,485	84,749	473,490	396,344	77,043	15.2	13.8
Cincinnati, Ohio.	363,591	19,639	343,919	287,127	56,792	5.4	15.6
Albany, N. Y.	100,253	1,037	99,171	81,006	18,165	1.0	18.1
Denver, Colo.	213,381	5,426	207,071	168,130	38,941	2.5	18.2
St. Louis, Mo.	687,029	43,960	642,488	516,782	125,706	6.4	18.3
Los Angeles, Cal.	319,198	7,599	305,307	244,723	60,584	2.4	19.0
Toledo, Ohio.	168,497	1,877	166,567	134,530	32,037	1.1	19.0
Spokane, Wash.	104,402	723	103,071	81,851	21,220	0.7	20.3
Portland, Oreg.	207,214	1,045	198,952	155,172	43,780	0.5	21.1
Omaha, Nebr.	124,096	4,426	119,580	92,512	27,068	3.6	21.8
Syracuse, N. Y.	137,249	1,124	136,101	105,320	30,781	0.8	22.4
Oakland, Cal.	150,174	3,055	141,958	105,134	36,822	2.0	24.5
Philadelphia, Pa.	1,549,008	84,459	1,463,371	1,080,793	382,578	5.5	24.7
Grand Rapids, Mich.	112,571	665	111,879	83,544	28,335	0.6	25.2
Seattle, Wash.	237,194	2,296	227,753	166,918	60,835	1.0	25.6
Pittsburgh, Pa.	533,905	25,623	508,008	367,572	140,436	4.8	26.3
St. Paul, Minn.	214,744	3,144	211,516	154,992	56,524	1.5	26.3
Rochester, N. Y.	218,149	879	217,205	158,212	58,993	0.4	27.0
Scranton, Pa.	129,867	567	129,288	94,176	35,112	0.4	27.0
Buffalo, N. Y.	423,715	1,773	421,809	303,365	118,444	0.4	28.0
Minneapolis, Minn.	301,408	2,592	298,672	212,734	85,938	0.9	28.5
Jersey City, N. J.	267,779	5,960	261,659	183,962	77,697	2.2	29.0
Milwaukee, Wis.	373,857	980	372,809	261,353	111,456	0.3	29.8
San Francisco, Cal.	416,912	1,642	400,014	269,140	130,874	0.4	31.4
Newark, N. J.	347,469	9,475	337,742	227,087	110,655	2.7	31.8
New Haven, Conn.	133,605	3,561	129,944	87,160	42,784	2.7	32.0
Cambridge, Mass.	104,839	4,707	100,017	65,409	34,608	4.5	33.0
Worcester, Mass.	145,986	1,241	144,664	96,172	48,492	0.9	33.2
Detroit, Mich.	465,766	5,741	459,926	303,361	156,565	1.2	33.6
Providence, R. I.	224,326	5,316	218,623	142,320	76,303	2.4	34.0
Cleveland, Ohio.	560,663	8,448	551,925	356,222	195,703	1.5	34.9
Bridgeport, Conn.	102,054	1,332	100,650	64,470	36,180	1.3	35.5
Chicago, Ill.	2,185,283	44,103	2,139,057	1,357,840	781,217	2.0	35.7
Boston, Mass.	670,585	13,564	655,696	414,974	240,722	2.0	35.9
Paterson, N. J.	125,600	1,539	123,969	78,571	45,398	1.2	36.1
New York, N. Y.	4,766,883	91,709	4,669,162	2,741,459	1,927,703	1.9	40.4
Lowell, Mass.	106,294	133	106,102	62,645	43,457	0.1	40.9
Fall River, Mass.	119,295	355	118,857	67,983	50,874	0.3	42.6

[1] Includes Indians, Chinese, Japanese, and other colored.

These were also the 5 cities having the highest percentage Negro in the population. In these cities the percentages were, for foreign-born whites, 2.7, 2.8, 3.2, 4.3, and 4.9; and for Negroes, 33.1, 33.5, 36.6, 39.4, and 40. The 5 cities in which the percentage foreign-born white was highest were Boston, Paterson, New York, Lowell, and Fall River, the percentages for this class being 35.9, 36.1, 40.4, 40.9, and 42.6; and for Negroes, 2, 1.2, 1.9, 0.1, and 0.3. The conditions obtaining in the cities generally reflect those obtaining in the states in which the cities are located, the percentage foreign-born white being generally low in the South, and high in the North in the cities as in the states.

The Negro population for the two years 1910 and 1900, in cities of 100,000 or more, is represented by Diagram III on this page, cities having a Negro population of less than 1,000 being omitted.

Table 12 gives the Negro population in 1910 and 1900 of all urban communities—that is to say, of all cities, towns, and villages having in 1910 a population of 2,500 or more.

WARDS OF CITIES.

The Negro population in 1910, and the percentage Negro in the population, is given in Table 13, for wards or equivalent subdivisions, of each city having, in 1910, a total population of at least 50,000 and a Negro population of at least 5,000. While the range of variation from ward to ward in the percentage Negro is very considerable in the cities shown in Table 13, it is nevertheless true of the southern cities that the Negro population is generally distributed throughout these urban communities, constituting in the case of each city a considerable element in the population of the several wards.

CHARACTERISTICS OF URBAN COMMUNITIES.

Statistics for urban communities, showing for the Negro population number of males 21 years of age and over, number of illiterates in the population

10 years of age and over, and number attending school in the population 6 to 14 years of age, are given in General Table I. Statistics of sex and age composition, marital condition, school attendance, illiteracy, nativity (state of birth), and color (black and mulatto), are given for urban communities, in sections of the chapters dealing with these characteristics.

DIAGRAM III.—NEGRO POPULATION IN CITIES HAVING 100,000 POPULATION OR MORE AND A NEGRO POPULATION OF MORE THAN 1,000: 1910 AND 1890.

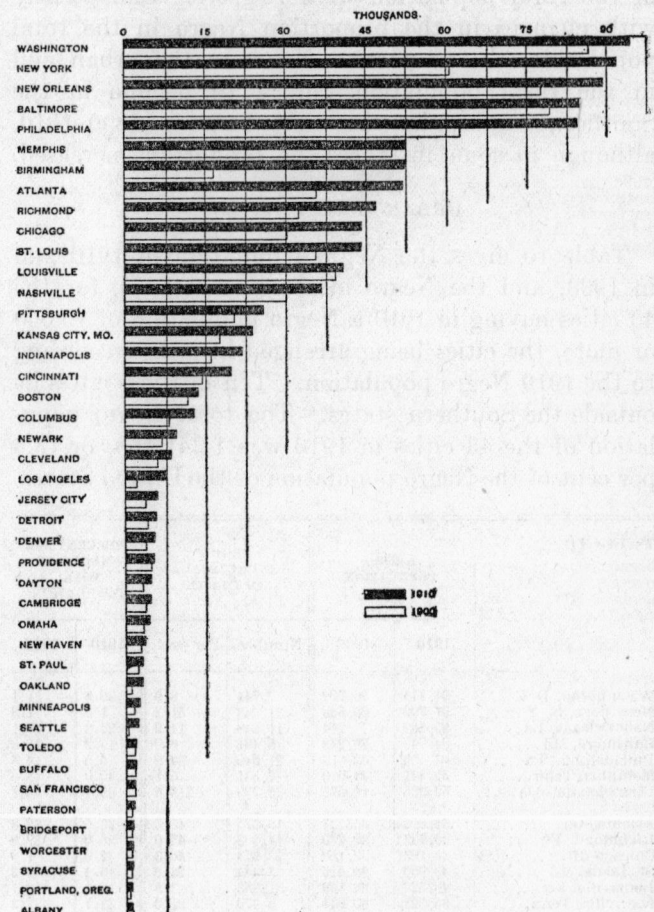

TABLE **12.**—NEGRO POPULATION OF URBAN COMMUNITIES: 1910 AND 1900.

CITY, TOWN, VILLAGE, AND BOROUGH.	POPULATION.			CITY, TOWN, VILLAGE, AND BOROUGH.	POPULATION.			CITY, TOWN, VILLAGE, AND BOROUGH.	POPULATION.		
	Total, 1910	Negro.			Total, 1910	Negro.			Total, 1910	Negro.	
		1910	1900			1910	1900			1910	1900
ALABAMA.				CALIFORNIA—Con.				COLORADO—Con.			
Alabama City	4,313	57	(¹)	Eureka	11,845	19	4	Monte Vista	2,544	2	(¹)
Anniston	12,794	4,570	3,669	Fresno	24,892	250	291	Montrose	3,254	2	(¹)
Attalla	2,513	896	(¹)	Glendale	2,746			Pueblo	44,395	1,498	1,213
Bessemer	10,864	6,210	3,695	Grass Valley	4,520	2	4	Rocky Ford	3,230	34	(¹)
Birmingham	132,685	52,305	16,575	Hanford	4,829	128	54				
								Salida	4,425	40	38
Decatur	4,228	2,499	1,518	Hayward	2,746	2	(¹)	Sterling	3,044	20	(¹)
Dothan	7,016	3,483	1,497	Lodi	2,697	14		Trinidad	10,204	180	125
Eufaula	4,259	2,155	2,365	Long Beach	17,809	100	(¹)	Victor	3,162	23	43
Florence	6,689	1,798	1,952	Los Angeles	319,198	7,599	2,131				
Gadsden	10,557	3,435	1,569	Marysville	5,430	188	147	**CONNECTICUT.**			
Girard	4,214	1,472	1,348	Merced	3,102	30	(¹)	Ansonia	15,152	413	501
Greenville	3,377	1,918	1,573	Mill Valley	2,551			Berlin	3,728	35	28
Huntsville	7,611	3,309	3,709	Modesto	4,034	78	(¹)	Bethel town	3,792	70	(³)
Jasper	2,509	609	(¹)	Monrovia	3,576	121	(¹)	*Bethel borough*	*3,041*	*63*	*38*
Lanett	3,820	832	880	Monterey	4,923	44	(·)	Branford town	6,047	19	20
								Branford borough	*2,560*	*2*	
Mobile	51,521	22,763	17,045	Napa	5,791	20	14	Bridgeport	102,054	1,332	1,149
Montgomery	38,136	19,322	17,229	Nevada City	2,689	2	19				
New Decatur	6,118	902	1,095	Oakland	150,174	3,055	1,026	Bristol town	13,502	7	(³)
Opelika	4,734	2,228	2,544	Ocean Park	3,119	33		*Bristol borough*	*9,527*	*4*	*19*
Phenix	4,555	612	673	Ontario	4,274	8	(¹)	Canton	2,732	32	32
								Danbury town	23,502	230	(³)
Selma	13,649	7,863	4,429	Orange	2,920		(¹)	*Danbury city*	*20,234*	*197*	*241*
Sheffield	4,865	1,766	1,415	Oroville	3,859	33		Danielson borough (see			
Talladega	5,854	2,793	2,687	Oxnard	2,555	38		Killingly town).			
Troy	4,961	2,543	2,140	Palo Alto	4,486	25	(¹)				
				Pasadena	30,291	744	218	Darien	3,946	37	52
Tuscaloosa	8,407	4,148	2,508					Derby	8,991	70	159
Tuscumbia	3,324	1,259	(¹)	Petaluma	5,880	2	6	East Hartford	8,138	72	78
Tuskegee	2,803	2,137	(¹)	Pomona	10,207	27	27	East Windsor	3,362	46	28
Union Springs	4,055	2,719	1,495	Porterville	2,696	21	(¹)	Enfield	9,719	22	30
				Red Bluff	3,530	39	95				
ARIZONA.				Redding	3,572	114	122	Essex	2,745	11	18
								Fairfield	6,134	87	84
Bisbee	9,019	195		Redlands	10,449	130	58	Farmington	3,478	25	42
Clifton	4,874	52		Redondo Beach	2,935	14	(¹)	Glastonbury	4,796	84	54
Douglas	6,437	158		Richmond	6,802	29		Greenwich town	16,463	429	356
Globe	7,083	188		Riverside	15,212	421	195	*Greenwich borough*	*3,886*	*115*	*(¹)*
Nogales	3,514	30	(¹)	Roseville	2,608	9					
								Griswold town	4,233	46	66
Phoenix	11,134	328	148	Sacramento	44,696	486	402	*Jewett City borough*	*3,023*	*20*	*(¹)*
Prescott	5,092	113	77	Salinas	3,736	21	28	Groton	6,495	89	96
Tucson	13,193	222	86	San Bernardino	12,779	177	84	Guilford	3,001	37	38
Yuma	2,914	24		San Diego	39,578	597	313	Hamden	5,850	190	213
				San Francisco	416,912	1,642	1,654				
ARKANSAS.								Hartford	98,915	1,745	1,887
				San Jose	28,946	182	209	Huntington town	6,545	43	(³)
Argenta	11,138	4,210		San Leandro	3,471		(¹)	*Shelton borough*	*4,807*	*14*	*27*
Arkadelphia	2,745	744	904	San Luis Obispo	5,157	17	1	Jewett City borough			
Batesville	3,399	673	(¹)	San Mateo	4,384	27	(¹)	(see Griswold town).			
Blytheville	3,849	691	(¹)	San Rafael	5,934	24	20				
Camden	3,995	1,980	1,422					Killingly town	6,564	42	(³)
				Santa Ana	8,429	38	8	*Danielson borough*	*2,934*	*27*	*18*
Conway	2,794	568	(¹)	Santa Barbara	11,659	77	19	Litchfield	3,005	23	58
El Dorado	4,202	1,455	(¹)	Santa Clara	4,348	4	2	Manchester	13,641	22	43
Eureka Springs	3,228	52	142	Santa Cruz	11,146	58	29	Meriden town	32,066	133	208
Fayetteville	4,471	278	367	Santa Monica	7,847	191	60	*Meriden city*	*27,265*	*133*	*207*
Fordyce	2,794	1,239	(¹)								
				Santa Rosa	7,817	12	13	Middletown town	20,749	177	(³)
Fort Smith	23,975	4,456	2,407	South Pasadena	4,649	19	(¹)	*Middletown city*	*11,851*	*73*	*127*
Helena	8,772	5,596	3,400	Stockton	23,253	196	213	Milford	4,366	143	173
Hope	3,639	1,275	(¹)	Tulare	2,758	5	(¹)	Montville	2,804	3	(¹)
Hot Springs	14,434	3,827	3,102	Vallejo	11,340	224	39	Naugatuck	12,722	22	31
Jonesboro	7,123	979	861								
				Ventura	2,945	21	(¹)	New Britain	43,916	94	118
Little Rock	45,941	14,539	14,694	Visalia	4,550	39	40	New Canaan	3,667	40	33
Malvern	2,778	939	(¹)	Watsonville	4,446	7	25	New Haven	133,605	3,561	2,887
Marianna	4,810	2,991	(¹)	Whittier	4,550		(¹)	New London	19,659	379	378
Mena	3,953	16	88	Woodland	3,187	93	100	New Milford	5,010	144	150
Newport	3,557	1,544	1,334								
				COLORADO.				Newtown	3,012	34	67
Paragould	5,248	37	68					Norwalk town	24,211	497	( )
Pine Bluff	15,102	6,124	5,771	Alamosa	3,013	36	(¹)	*Norwalk city*	*6,954*	*185*	*189*
Prescott	2,705	1,187	(¹)	Boulder	9,539	166	96	*South Norwalk city*	*8,968*	*184*	*88*
Rogers	2,820		(¹)	Canon City	5,162	168	117	Norwich town	28,219	627	633
				Colorado City	4,333	32	17	*Norwich city*	*20,367*	*528*	*544*
Russellville	2,936	378	(¹)	Colorado Springs	29,078	1,107	875				
Stuttgart	2,740	533	(¹)					Orange town	11,272	113	(³)
Texarkana ²	5,655	2,101	2,078	Cripple Creek	6,206	99	188	*West Haven borough*	*8,543*	*62*	*59*
Van Buren	3,878	735	533	Denver	213,381	5,426	3,923	Plainfield	6,719	52	45
				Durango	4,686	55	17	Plainville	2,882	153	(¹)
CALIFORNIA.				Englewood	2,983	44		Plymouth	5,021	16	8
				Florence	2,712	33	22	Portland	3,425	5	7
Alameda	23,383	211	144								
Alhambra	5,021	18		Fort Collins	8,210	32	15	Putnam town	7,280	60	(³)
Anaheim	2,628		(¹)	Fort Morgan	2,800	7	(¹)	*Putnam city*	*6,637*	*42*	*81*
Bakersfield	12,727	262	151	Grand Junction	7,754	106	52	Ridgefield	3,118	25	31
Berkeley	40,434	247	66	Greeley	8,179	35	3	Rockville city (see Ver-			
				La Junta	4,154	110	42	non town).			
Chico	3,750	53	37								
Coalinga	4,199	2		Lamar	2,977	32	(¹)	Salisbury	3,522	68	93
Colton	3,980	11	(¹)	Leadville	7,508	64	195	Seymour	4,786	24	39
Corona	3,540	15	(¹)	Longmont	4,256	8	(¹)	Shelton borough (see			
Emeryville	2,613	84	(¹)	Loveland	3,651		(¹)	Huntington town).			

¹ Data not available, total population in 1900 being less than 2,500.
² Joint population of Texarkana, Miller County, Ark., and Texarkana, Bowie County, Tex.: 1910, 15,445; Negro, 5,319 in 1910, and 4,042 in 1900.
³ Data not available for the town.

TABLE 12.—NEGRO POPULATION OF URBAN COMMUNITIES: 1910 AND 1900—Continued.

CITY, TOWN, VILLAGE, AND BOROUGH.	Total, 1910	Negro.		CITY, TOWN, VILLAGE, AND BOROUGH.	Total, 1910	Negro.		CITY, TOWN, VILLAGE, AND BOROUGH.	Total, 1910	Negro.	
		1910	1900			1910	1900			1910	1900
CONNECTICUT—Con.				GEORGIA—Con.				ILLINOIS—Con.			
Simsbury	2,537	19	(1)	Cedartown	3,551	978	753	Duquoin	5,454	584	499
South Norwalk city (see Norwalk town).				Columbus	20,554	7,644	7,267	East Moline	2,665	16	(1)
				Cordele	5,883	3,209	1,973	East St. Louis	58,547	5,882	1,799
Southington town	6,516	36	(2)	Covington	2,697	1,040	(1)	Edwardsville	5,014	368	315
Southington borough	*3,714*	*21*	*2*	Cuthbert	3,210	2,113	1,771	Effingham	3,898	3	3
Sprague	2,551	3	(1)	Dalton	5,324	952	957	Eldorado	3,366		(1)
Stafford town	5,233	7		Dawson	3,827	2,216	1,702	Elgin	25,976	171	187
Stafford Springs borough	*3,059*	*6*	*(1)*	Douglas	3,550	1,515	(1)	Evanston	24,978	1,160	737
Stamford town	28,836	343	275	Dublin	5,795	2,769	1,151	Fairbury	2,505	67	(1)
Stamford city	*25,138*	*332*	*266*	East Point	3,682	903	(1)	Flora	2,704		(1)
Stonington	9,154	127	141	Elberton	6,483	2,919	1,609	Forest Park	6,594	8	107
Stratford	5,712	133	180	Fitzgerald	5,795	2,151	(1)	Freeport	17,567	68	46
Suffield	3,841	98	123	Fort Valley	2,697	1,370	(1)	Galena	4,835	13	18
Thomaston	3,533	6	8	Gainesville	5,925	1,629	1,186	Galesburg	22,089	701	738
Thompson	4,804	7	10	Griffin	7,478	3,425	3,258	Geneseo	3,199		8
Torrington town	16,840	88	(2)	Hawkinsville	3,420	1,846	(1)	Granite	9,903	18	154
Torrington borough	*15,483*	*78*	*67*	La Grange	5,587	2,063	1,725	Greenville	3,178	65	114
Vernon town	9,087	56	(2)	Macon	40,665	18,150	11,550	Harrisburg	5,309	262	(1)
Rockville city	*7,977*	*44*	*28*	Marietta	5,949	2,192	1,928	Harvard	3,008	6	1
Wallingford town	11,155	25	(2)	Milledgeville	4,385	2,560	2,663	Harvey	7,227	215	83
Wallingford borough	*8,690*	*16*	*21*	Monroe	3,029	951	(1)	Havana	3,525	7	12
Waterbury	73,141	775	540	Moultrie	3,349	1,329	(1)	Herrin	6,861		(1)
Waterford	3,097	23	15	Newnan	5,548	2,180	1,511	Highland	2,675		(1)
Watertown	3,850	41	45	Quitman	3,915	1,801	(1)	Highland Park	4,209	34	12
West Hartford	4,808	88	92	Rome	12,099	3,758	2,830	Hillsboro	3,424	75	(1)
West Haven borough (see Orange town).				Sandersville	2,641	1,391	(1)	Hoopeston	4,698	47	37
				Savannah	65,064	33,246	28,090	Jacksonville	15,326	1,245	997
Westport	4,259	35	46	Statesboro	2,529	871	(1)	Jerseyville	4,113	72	107
Wethersfield	3,148	95	89	Summerville	4,361	1,586	1,304	Johnston	3,248		(1)
Willimantic city (see Windham town).				Thomasville	6,727	3,789	3,296	Joliet	34,670	497	650
Winchester town	8,679	71	(2)	Toccoa	3,120	888	(1)	Kankakee	13,986	204	175
Winsted borough	*7,754*	*50*	*63*	Valdosta	7,656	3,844	2,958	Kewanee	9,307	85	57
				Washington	3,035	1,865	2,163	La Grange	5,282	98	47
				Waycross	14,485	6,729	2,899	La Salle	11,537		
Windham town	12,604	88	(2)	Waynesboro	2,729	1,706	(1)	Lake Forest	3,349	145	(1)
Willimantic city	*11,230*	*86*	*74*					Lawrenceville	3,235	41	(1)
Windsor	4,178	166	168	IDAHO.				Lincoln	10,892	278	238
Windsor Locks	3,715		37	Boise	17,358	135	36	Litchfield	5,971	106	156
Winsted borough (see Winchester town).				Caldwell	3,543	5	(1)	Lockport	2,555	94	130
				Coeur d'Alene	7,291	26	(1)	Macomb	5,774	109	154
DELAWARE.				Idaho Falls	4,827	34	(1)	Madison	5,046	381	(1)
Dover	3,720	978	772	Lewiston	6,043	32	(1)	Marion	7,093	263	93
Milford	2,603	546	506	Moscow	3,670	6	(1)	Marseilles	3,291	2	
New Castle	3,351	552	523	Nampa	4,205	20	(1)	Marshall	2,569	38	(1)
Wilmington	87,411	9,081	9,736	Pocatello	9,110	127	35	Mattoon	11,456	166	227
DISTRICT OF COLUMBIA.				Sandpoint	2,993	3		Maywood	8,033	86	19
Washington	331,069	94,446	86,702	Twin Falls	5,258	26		Melrose Park	4,806	36	7
				Wallace	3,000	6	(1)	Mendota	3,806	34	49
FLORIDA.				Weiser	2,600	6	(1)	Metropolis	4,655	926	823
Apalachicola	3,065	1,525	1,589					Moline	24,199	281	268
Bartow	2,662	1,137	(1)	ILLINOIS.				Monmouth	9,128	537	321
Daytona	3,082	1,605	(1)	Alton	17,528	1,160	896	Morgan Park	3,694	99	(1)
De Land	2,812	1,107	(1)	Anna	2,809	3	4	Morris	4,563	17	20
Fernandina	3,482	2,407	1,902	Aurora	29,807	293	211	Mound City	2,837	1,065	1,165
Gainesville	6,183	3,079	1,803	Averyville	2,668	5	(1)	Mount Carmel	6,934	24	32
Jacksonville	57,699	29,293	16,236	Batavia	4,436	56	62	Mount Olive	3,501		
Key West	19,945	5,515	5,562	Beardstown	6,107		1	Mount Vernon	8,007	328	190
Lake City	5,032	1,564	2,159	Belleville	21,122	216	230	Murphysboro	7,485	692	456
Lakeland	3,719	1,048	(1)	Belvidere	7,253	41	50	Naperville	3,449		1
Live Oak	3,450	1,768	(1)	Benton	2,675	9	(1)	Normal	4,024	204	252
Miami	5,471	2,258	(1)	Berwyn	5,841	7		North Chicago	3,306	15	(1)
Ocala	4,370	2,179	1,642	Bloomington	25,768	809	599	Oak Park	19,444	116	
Orlando	3,894	1,416	1,810	Blue Island	8,043	13	1	Olney	5,011	3	8
Palatka	3,779	2,239	1,810	Bridgeport	2,703	20	(1)	Ottawa	9,535	30	34
Pensacola	22,982	10,214	8,561	Bushnell	2,619	12	(1)	Pana	6,055	4	11
Quincy	3,204	2,150	(1)	Cairo	14,548	5,434	5,000	Paris	7,664	289	277
St. Augustine	5,494	2,116	1,735	Canton	10,453	103	38	Paxton	2,912	16	9
St. Petersburg	4,127	1,100	(1)	Carbondale	5,411	1,140	586	Pekin	9,897	8	4
Sanford	3,570	1,592	(1)	Carlinville	3,616	51	49	Peoria	66,950	1,569	1,402
Tallahassee	5,018	3,237	1,755	Carmi	2,833	250	290	Peru	7,984	3	
Tampa	37,782	8,951	4,382	Carterville	2,971		(1)	Petersburg	2,587	88	107
West Tampa	8,258	1,086	(1)	Centralia	9,680	593	418	Pinckneyville	2,722	11	(1)
GEORGIA.				Champaign	12,421	759	404	Pontiac	6,090	301	168
Albany	8,190	4,812	2,903	Charleston	5,884	25	45	Portland	3,194	2	
Americus	8,063	4,574	4,661	Chester	2,747	165	158	Princeton	4,131	51	64
Athens	14,913	6,316	5,190	Chicago	2,185,283	44,103	30,150	Quincy	36,587	1,596	2,029
Atlanta	154,839	51,902	35,727	Chicago Heights	14,525	104	47	Robinson	3,863	31	(1)
Augusta	41,040	18,344	18,487	Cicero	14,557	7		Rochelle	2,732	2	(1)
Bainbridge	4,217	2,314	1,471	Clinton	5,165	43	69	Rock Falls	2,657	4	(1)
Barnesville	3,068	1,158	1,440	Coal City	2,667	3		Rock Island	24,335	397	282
Brunswick	10,182	5,567	5,184	Collinsville	7,478	250	204	Rockford	45,401	197	212
Carrollton	3,297	684	(1)	Danville	27,871	1,465	638	St. Charles	4,049	26	35
Cartersville	4,067	1,577	1,454	Decatur	31,140	776	620	Salem	2,669	9	(1)
				Dekalb	8,102	13	11	Sandwich	2,557	7	17
				Dixon	7,216	43	59	Savanna	3,691	8	22
				Downers Grove	2,601	4	(1)				

[1] Data not available, total population in 1900 being less than 2,500.   [2] Data not available for the town.

TABLE 12.—NEGRO POPULATION OF URBAN COMMUNITIES: 1910 AND 1900—Continued.

CITY, TOWN, VILLAGE, AND BOROUGH.	POPULATION.			CITY, TOWN, VILLAGE, AND BOROUGH.	POPULATION.			CITY, TOWN, VILLAGE, AND BOROUGH.	POPULATION.		
	Total, 1910	Negro.			Total, 1910	Negro.			Total, 1910	Negro.	
		1910	1900			1910	1900			1910	1900
ILLINOIS—Con.				**INDIANA—Con.**				**IOWA—Con.**			
Shelbyville	3,590	69	67	New Castle	9,446	213	181	Pella	3,021	2	4
Sparta	3,081	437	454	Noblesville	5,073	294	226	Perry	4,630	37	4
Spring Valley	7,035	84	135	North Vernon	2,915	134	114	Red Oak	4,830	38	46
Springfield	51,678	2,961	2,227	Peru	10,910	75	67	Sheldon	2,941		(1)
Staunton	5,048			Plymouth	3,838	3	2	Shenandoah	4,976	16	7
Sterling	7,467	24	23	Portland	5,130	111	89	Sioux City	47,828	305	280
Streator	14,253	196	100	Princeton	6,448	683	628	Spencer	3,005		1
Sullivan	2,621		(1)	Richmond	22,324	1,191	1,009	Valley Junction	2,573		(1)
Sycamore	3,926	50	14	Rochester	3,364	3	14	Vinton	3,336	1	8
Taylorville	5,446	78	75	Rockport	2,736	359	564	Washington	4,380	81	59
Upper Alton	2,918	218	(1)	Rushville	4,925	206	254	Waterloo	26,693	24	20
Urbana	8,245	117	71	Seymour	6,305	124	204	Waverly	3,205	4	3
Vandalia	2,974	1	1	Shelbyville	9,500	386	257	Webster City	5,208	32	24
Venice	3,718	229	(1)	South Bend	53,684	604	572	Winterset	2,818	3	3
Virden	4,000	9	(1)	Sullivan	4,115	53	44				
Waukegan	16,069	101	44	Tell City	3,369	33	83	**KANSAS.**			
West Hammond	4,948	1		Terre Haute	58,157	2,593	1,520	Abilene	4,118	110	154
Westville	2,607	74	(1)	Tipton	4,075	3	4	Anthony	2,669	34	(1)
Wheaton	3,423	43	(1)	Union City [2]	3,209	15	10	Arkansas City	7,508	297	302
White Hall	2,854	3	(1)	Valparaiso	6,987	1	5	Atchison	16,429	2,618	2,508
Wilmette	4,943	25	(1)	Vincennes	14,895	413	432	Beloit	3,082	5	(1)
Winnetka	3,168	25	(1)	Wabash	8,687	152	134	Caney	3,597	1	(1)
Woodstock	4,331	8	6	Warsaw	4,430	22	30	Chanute	9,272	255	171
Zion City	4,789	108		Washington	7,854	129	255	Cherryvale	4,304	312	180
				West Lafayette	3,867	42	(1)	Clay Center	3,438	103	154
INDIANA.				West Terre Haute	3,083	25	(1)	Coffeyville	12,687	1,309	803
Alexandria	5,096	125	396	Whiting	6,587	7	2	Columbus	3,064	110	(1)
Anderson	22,476	532	680	Winchester	4,266	24	58	Concordia	4,415	57	42
Angola	2,610	14	(1)					Council Grove	2,545	68	(1)
Attica	3,335	4	7	**IOWA.**				Dodge	3,214	81	(1)
Auburn	3,919	8	7	Albia	4,969	131	108	Eldorado	3,129	83	71
Aurora	4,410			Algona	2,908	3		Emporia	9,058	533	663
Bedford	8,716	74	101	Ames	4,223	5	(1)	Fort Scott	10,463	1,047	1,205
Bicknell	2,794			Anamosa	2,983	74	55	Fredonia	3,040	11	(1)
Bloomington	8,838	402	396	Atlantic	4,560	21	4	Frontenac	3,396	3	(1)
Bluffton	4,987	2	1	Belle Plaine	3,121	6	7	Galena	6,096	239	580
Boonville	3,934	155	199	Boone	10,347	86	61	Garden City	3,171	158	(1)
Brazil	9,340	212	320	Burlington	24,324	398	403	Great Bend	4,622	255	(1)
Clarksville	2,743	264	(1)	Carroll	3,546	28	21	Herington	3,273	2	(1)
Clinton	6,229	103	51	Cedar Falls	5,012	1		Hiawatha	2,974	190	226
Columbia City	3,448	12		Cedar Rapids	32,811	213	230	Holton	2,842	96	136
Columbus	8,813	217	224	Centerville	6,936	285	149	Horton	3,600	106	80
Connersville	7,738	423	394	Chariton	3,794	59	92	Humboldt	2,548	85	(1)
Crawfordsville	9,371	238	230	Charles City	5,892	6	5	Hutchinson	16,364	840	442
Crown Point	2,526	7	(1)	Cherokee	4,884	4	10	Independence	10,480	733	331
Decatur	4,471	2		Clarinda	3,832	175	133	Iola	9,032	573	207
Dunkirk	3,031	41	16	Clinton	25,577	432	180	Junction	5,598	389	292
East Chicago	19,098	28	1	Colfax	2,524	117	(1)	Kansas City	82,331	9,286	6,509
Elkhart	19,282	81	35	Council Bluffs	29,292	320	240	Kingman	2,570	32	(1)
Elwood	11,028	1	5	Cresco	2,658	12	15	Larned	2,911	44	(1)
Evansville	69,647	6,266	7,518	Creston	6,924	44	44	Lawrence	12,374	1,764	2,032
Fairmount	2,506	32	47	Davenport	43,028	569	488	Leavenworth	19,363	2,477	2,925
Fort Wayne	63,933	572	276	Decorah	3,592			McPherson	3,546	1	30
Frankfort	8,634	83	90	Denison	3,133	1	8	Manhattan	5,722	303	301
Franklin	4,502	270	272	Des Moines	86,368	2,930	1,675	Neodesha	2,872	7	(1)
Garrett	4,149	3		Dubuque	38,494	96	115	Newton	7,862	383	251
Gary	16,802	383		Eaglegrove	3,387		1	Olathe	3,272	179	249
Gas City	3,224	1	5	Estherville	3,404	18	7	Osawatomie	4,046	255	277
Goshen	8,514	2	14	Fairfield	4,970	69	54	Ottawa	7,650	363	550
Greencastle	3,790	191	155	Fort Dodge	15,543	73	112	Paola	3,207	449	466
Greenfield	4,448	88	87	Fort Madison	8,900	290	230	Parsons	12,463	999	807
Greensburg	5,420	71	107	Glenwood	4,052	47	29	Pittsburg	14,755	500	365
Hammond	20,925	40	17	Grinnell	5,036	38	31	Pratt	3,302	118	(1)
Hartford City	6,187	28	12	Hampton	2,617	10	4	Rosedale	5,960	497	379
Huntington	10,272	7	8	Harlan	2,570		(1)	Salina	9,688	484	356
Indianapolis	233,650	21,816	15,931	Independence	3,517	13	22	Topeka	43,684	4,538	4,807
Jasonville	3,295			Indianola	3,283	25	32	Wellington	7,034	185	141
Jeffersonville	10,412	1,535	1,818	Iowa City	10,091	57	61	Wichita	52,450	2,457	1,389
Kendallville	4,981	7	6	Iowa Falls	2,797	7	14	Winfield	6,700	172	282
Kokomo	17,010	388	359	Keokuk	14,008	1,016	1,192				
Lafayette	20,081	338	344	Knoxville	3,190	27	26	**KENTUCKY.**			
Laporte	10,525	30	59	Le Mars	4,157	4		Ashland	8,688	505	489
Lawrenceburg	3,930	31	72	Manchester	2,758	1		Bellevue	6,683	19	21
Lebanon	5,474	77	46	Maquoketa	3,570		1	Bowling Green	9,173	2,486	2,593
Linton	5,906	1		Marion	4,400	29	14	Catlettsburg	3,520	186	239
Logansport	19,050	177	167	Marshalltown	13,374	128	148	Central City	2,545	256	(1)
Madison	6,934	413	570	Mason City	11,230	142	55	Corbin	2,589	61	(1)
Marion	19,359	836	650	Missouri Valley	3,187	11	6	Covington	53,270	2,899	2,487
Martinsville	4,529	22	49	Mount Pleasant	3,874	217	311	Cynthiana	3,603	851	1,050
Michigan City	19,027	285	197	Muscatine	16,178	122	125	Danville	5,420	1,991	1,913
Mishawaka	11,886	25	21	Mystic	2,663	42	(1)	Dayton	6,979	41	63
Mitchell	3,438	204	(1)	Newton	4,616	45	72	Earlington	3,931	1,393	986
Montpelier	2,786	11	7	Oelwein	6,028	9	7	Frankfort	10,465	2,851	3,316
Mount Vernon	5,563	761	892	Oskaloosa	9,466	254	344	Franklin	3,063	964	(1)
Muncie	24,005	1,005	739	Ottumwa	22,012	533	598	Fulton	2,575	427	818
New Albany	20,629	1,583	1,905					Georgetown	4,533	1,624	1,677

[1] Data not available, total population in 1900 being less than 2,500.
[2] Joint population of Union City, Randolph County, Ind., and Union City village, Darke County, Ohio: 1910, 4,804; Negro population, 43.

TABLE 12.—NEGRO POPULATION OF URBAN COMMUNITIES: 1910 AND 1900—Continued.

CITY, TOWN, VILLAGE, AND BOROUGH.	POPULATION.		
	Total, 1910	Negro. 1910	Negro. 1900

KENTUCKY—Con.

City	Total, 1910	Negro 1910	Negro 1900
Harrodsburg	3,147	1,074	1,150
Henderson	11,452	3,016	4,029
Hickman	2,736	893	(¹)
Hopkinsville	9,419	4,187	3,243
Lebanon	3,077	899	1,051
Lexington	35,099	11,011	10,130
Louisville	223,928	40,522	39,139
Ludlow	4,163	29	25
Madisonville	4,966	1,860	1,367
Mayfield	5,916	1,233	869
Maysville	6,141	1,167	1,155
Middlesboro	7,305	1,441	891
Morganfield	2,725	487	(¹)
Mount Sterling	3,932	1,264	1,212
Newport	30,309	569	424
Nicholasville	2,935	975	(¹)
Owensboro	16,011	3,115	3,061
Paducah	22,760	6,047	5,814
Paris	5,859	1,764	1,646
Princeton	3,015	1,003	1,049
Richmond	5,340	1,917	2,087
Russellville	3,111	1,031	1,055
Shelbyville	3,412	1,366	1,407
Somerset	4,491	519	561
Winchester	7,156	2,688	3,128

LOUISIANA.

City	Total, 1910	Negro 1910	Negro 1900
Abbeville	2,907	1,198	(¹)
Alexandria	11,213	5,854	3,142
Baton Rouge	14,897	7,899	6,596
Covington	2,601	729	(¹)
Crowley	5,099	1,963	1,759
Donaldsonville	4,090	1,813	1,951
Franklin	3,857	1,717	1,172
Hammond	2,942	962	(¹)
Houma	5,024	1,794	1,263
Jennings	3,925	1,197	(¹)
Kentwood	3,609	1,181	(¹)
Lafayette	6,392	2,792	1,542
Lake Charles	11,449	4,437	2,407
Minden	3,002	1,562	(¹)
Monroe	10,209	5,320	2,734
Morgan City	5,477	2,351	(¹)
Natchitoches	2,532	1,226	(¹)
New Iberia	7,499	3,480	3,309
New Orleans	339,075	89,262	77,714
Opelousas	4,623	2,491	1,593
Patterson	2,998	1,810	
Plaquemine	4,955	2,673	1,869
Ruston	3,377	1,095	(¹)
Shreveport	28,015	13,896	8,542
Thibodaux	3,824	1,281	1,361
Winnfield	2,925	862	

MAINE.

City	Total, 1910	Negro 1910	Negro 1900
Auburn	15,064	12	2
Augusta	13,211	53	51
Bangor	24,803	205	176
Bath	9,396	53	40
Belfast	4,618	9	12
Biddeford	17,079	1	1
Brewer	5,667	1	12
Bridgton	2,660	1	
Brunswick town	6,621	34	(²)
Brunswick village	*5,341*	*28*	*13*
Calais	6,116	8	21
Camden	3,015	1	
Caribou	5,377	2	6
Chelsea	3,216	12	5
Dexter	3,530	3	
East Livermore	2,641		(¹)
Eastport	4,961	5	4
Eden	4,441	5	20
Ellsworth	3,549	3	4
Fairfield town	4,435	3	
Fairfield village	*2,801*	*2*	*(¹)*
Farmington	3,210	1	4
Fort Fairfield	4,381		3
Fort Kent	3,710	2	
Gardiner	5,311	13	20
Gorham	2,822	2	2
Hallowell	2,864	3	1

MAINE—Con.

City	Total, 1910	Negro 1910	Negro 1900
Houlton	5,845	35	14
Jay	2,987	6	3
Kennebunk	3,099	1	8
Kittery	3,533	6	6
Lewiston	26,247	47	47
Lisbon	4,116	1	1
Lubec	3,363	3	
Madison	3,379		1
Millinocket	3,368		
Milo	2,556		(¹)
Norway	3,002	13	11
Old Town	6,317	2	2
Orono	3,555		2
Paris	3,436	5	3
Pittsfield	2,891	3	
Portland	58,571	273	291
Presque Isle town	5,179	2	1
Presque Isle village	*2,938*		*(¹)*
Rockland	8,174	31	31
Rumford town	6,777	5	(²)
Rumford Falls village	*5,427*	*2*	*1*
Saco	6,583	5	7
Sanford	9,049	6	1
Skowhegan	5,341		
South Berwick	2,935	6	11
South Portland	7,471	12	1
Van Buren	3,065		(¹)
Waldoboro	2,656		3
Waterville	11,458	11	15
Westbrook	8,281	13	11
Winslow	2,709	4	(¹)
York	2,802	2	5

MARYLAND.

City	Total, 1910	Negro 1910	Negro 1900
Annapolis	8,609	3,184	3,002
Baltimore	558,485	84,749	79,258
Brunswick	3,721	192	(¹)
Cambridge	6,407	2,000	1,958
Chestertown	2,735	988	1,220
Crisfield	3,468	870	799
Cumberland	21,839	1,067	1,100
Easton	3,083	872	1,024
Frederick	10,411	1,468	1,535
Frostburg	6,028	237	236
Hagerstown	16,507	1,125	1,277
Havre de Grace	4,212	680	563
Salisbury	6,690	1,404	1,006
Westernport	2,702	58	(¹)
Westminster	3,295	336	355

MASSACHUSETTS.

City	Total, 1910	Negro 1910	Negro 1900
Abington	5,455	19	5
Adams	13,026	4	18
Agawam	3,501	18	8
Amesbury	9,894	10	23
Amherst	5,112	146	199
Andover	7,301	144	98
Arlington	11,187	67	75
Athol	8,536	15	9
Attleborough	16,215	138	111
Ayer	2,797	12	(¹)
Barnstable	4,676	138	88
Barre	2,957		(¹)
Belmont	5,542	15	4
Beverly	18,650	51	50
Billerica	2,789	22	37
Blackstone	5,648		
Boston	670,585	13,564	11,591
Braintree	8,066	10	22
Bridgewater	7,688	126	52
Brockton	56,878	531	310
Brookline	27,792	221	161
Cambridge	104,839	4,707	3,888
Canton	4,797	17	22
Chelmsford	5,010	8	1
Chelsea	32,452	242	731
Chicopee	25,401	7	10
Clinton	13,075	12	24
Cohasset	2,585	26	34
Concord	6,421	28	41
Dalton	3,568	46	50
Danvers	9,407	6	10
Dartmouth	4,378	24	79
Dedham	9,284	54	65
Dracut	3,461	6	4
Dudley	4,267	6	11

MASSACHUSETTS—Con.

City	Total, 1910	Negro 1910	Negro 1900
East Bridgewater	3,363	3	8
Easthampton	8,524	8	42
Easton	5,139	16	19
Everett	33,484	795	634
Fairhaven	5,122	48	41
Fall River	119,295	355	324
Falmouth	3,144	160	79
Fitchburg	37,826	42	65
Foxborough	3,863	31	12
Framingham	12,948	69	38
Franklin	5,641	6	6
Gardner	14,699	34	53
Gloucester	24,398	12	39
Grafton	5,705	33	13
Great Barrington	5,926	104	138
Greenfield	10,427	61	17
Hardwick	3,524		1
Haverhill	44,115	397	373
Hingham	4,965	75	85
Holbrook	2,816		(¹)
Holliston	2,711	1	
Holyoke	57,730	45	40
Hudson	6,743	15	11
Hyde Park	15,507	87	116
Ipswich	5,777	8	17
Lawrence	85,892	265	87
Lee	4,106	87	83
Leicester	3,237	1	1
Lenox	3,060	52	83
Leominster	17,580	91	75
Lexington	4,918	25	13
Lowell	106,294	133	136
Ludlow	4,948	5	2
Lynn	89,336	700	784
Malden	44,404	486	446
Manchester	2,673	1	11
Mansfield	5,183	15	5
Marblehead	7,338	14	23
Marlborough	14,579	26	31
Maynard	6,390	2	
Medfield	3,466	42	18
Medford	23,150	431	244
Medway	2,696	6	7
Melrose	15,715	110	130
Methuen	11,448	11	17
Middleborough	8,214	100	60
Milford	13,055	28	24
Millbury	4,740	1	2
Milton	7,924	44	64
Monson	4,758	42	42
Montague	6,866		1
Nantucket	2,962	35	46
Natick	9,866	29	52
Needham	5,026	25	19
New Bedford	96,652	2,885	1,685
Newburyport	14,949	98	97
Newton	39,806	467	505
North Adams	22,019	88	90
North Andover	5,529	1	8
North Attleborough	9,562	66	59
North Brookfield	3,075	29	15
Northampton	19,431	75	108
Northbridge	8,807	2	4
Norton	2,544	14	(¹)
Norwood	8,014	18	19
Orange	5,282	1	1
Oxford	3,361	5	26
Palmer	8,610	31	29
Peabody	15,721	21	38
Pepperell	2,953	30	15
Pittsfield	32,121	320	277
Plymouth	12,141	145	146
Provincetown	4,369	70	54
Quincy	32,642	45	27
Randolph	4,301	14	2
Reading	5,818	21	6
Revere	18,219	33	43
Rockland	6,928	23	6
Rockport	4,211	3	4
Salem	43,697	163	156
Saugus	8,047	55	27
Somerset	2,798	2	(¹)
Somerville	77,236	217	140
South Hadley	4,894	2	3
Southbridge	12,592	17	29

¹ Data not available, total population in 1900 being less than 2,500. ² Data not available for the town.

Table 12.—NEGRO POPULATION OF URBAN COMMUNITIES: 1910 AND 1900—Continued.

CITY, TOWN, VILLAGE, AND BOROUGH.	Total, 1910	Negro 1910	Negro 1900
MASSACHUSETTS—Con.			
Spencer	6,740	1	5
Springfield	88,926	1,475	1,021
Stoneham	7,090	25	21
Stoughton	6,316	9	9
Sutton	3,078	....	3
Swampscott	6,204	14	44
Taunton	34,259	297	226
Templeton	3,756	10	11
Tewksbury	3,750	23	43
Uxbridge	4,671	4	14
Wakefield	11,404	31	25
Walpole	4,892	13	11
Waltham	27,834	62	51
Ware	8,774	2	....
Wareham	4,102	440	187
Warren	4,188	7	18
Watertown	12,875	44	53
Webster	11,509	16	32
Wellesley	5,413	29	17
West Springfield	9,224	21	16
Westborough	5,446	32	26
Westfield	16,044	40	81
Westford	2,851	....	1
Westport	2,928	20	24
Weymouth	12,895	26	40
Whitman	7,292	53	38
Williamstown	3,708	122	138
Winchendon	5,678	3	8
Winchester	9,309	281	140
Winthrop	10,132	47	43
Woburn	15,308	242	261
Worcester	145,986	1,241	1,104
MICHIGAN.			
Adrian	10,763	164	243
Albion	5,833	8	27
Allegan	3,419	48	47
Alma	2,757	17	(1)
Alpena	12,706	2	1
Ann Arbor	14,817	515	359
Battle Creek	25,267	575	527
Bay City	45,166	160	143
Belding	4,119	4	8
Benton Harbor	9,185	302	.
Bessemer	4,583	....	14
Big Rapids	4,519	2	14
Boyne City	5,218	49	(1)
Cadillac	8,375	14	....
Charlotte	4,886	15	16
Cheboygan	6,859	19	9
Coldwater	5,945	15	19
Crystal Falls	3,775	3	4
Detroit	465,766	5,741	4,111
Dowagiac	5,088	159	125
East Jordan	2,516	6	(1)
Escanaba	13,194	22	25
Flint	38,550	397	257
Gladstone	4,211	10	....
Grand Haven	5,856	30	18
Grand Ledge	2,893	3	(1)
Grand Rapids	112,571	665	604
Greenville	4,045	12	9
Hamtramck	3,559	85	....
Hancock	8,981	12	4
Hastings	4,383	1	....
Highland Park	4,120	15	(1)
Hillsdale	5,001	4	14
Holland	10,490	5	2
Houghton	5,113	23	22
Ionia	5,030	18	25
Iron Mountain	9,216	4	5
Ironwood	12,821	4	1
Ishpeming	12,448	....	....
Jackson	31,433	354	473
Kalamazoo	39,437	685	471
Lansing	31,229	354	323
Lapeer	3,946	15	18
Laurium	8,537	....	1
Ludington	9,132	....	5
Manistee	12,381	3	8
Manistique	4,722	3	....
Marine City	3,770	....	....
Marquette	11,503	66	62
Marshall	4,236	23	42

CITY, TOWN, VILLAGE, AND BOROUGH.	Total, 1910	Negro 1910	Negro 1900
MICHIGAN—Con.			
Menominee	10,507	2	....
Midland	2,527	16	(1)
Monroe	6,893	3	27
Mount Clemens	7,707	39	18
Mount Pleasant	3,972	3	11
Munising	2,952	11	(1)
Muskegon	24,062	50	23
Negaunee	8,460	1	....
Niles	5,156	152	137
Norway	4,974	....	....
Onaway	2,702	....	(1)
Otsego	2,812	5	(1)
Owosso	9,639	7	22
Petoskey	4,778	17	24
Pontiac	14,532	192	151
Port Huron	18,863	62	69
Red Jacket	4,211	....	14
River Rouge	4,163	313	(1)
Saginaw	50,510	313	348
St. Clair	2,633	2	1
St. Johns	3,154	9	16
St. Joseph	5,936	82	103
Sault Ste. Marie	12,615	38	22
South Haven	3,577	45	52
Sturgis	3,635	11	(1)
Three Rivers	5,072	17	36
Traverse City	12,115	12	8
Wyandotte	8,287	2	1
Ypsilanti	6,230	434	608
MINNESOTA.			
Albert Lea	6,192	6	8
Alexandria	3,001	3	3
Anoka	3,972	30	10
Austin	6,960	13	3
Bemidji	5,099	4	(1)
Brainerd	8,526	1	4
Chisholm	7,684	....	....
Cloquet	7,031	....	....
Crookston	7,559	12	1
Detroit	2,807	....	....
Duluth	78,466	410	357
East Grand Forks	2,533	10	(1)
Ely	3,572	....	....
Eveleth	7,036	3	....
Fairmont	2,958	2	2
Faribault	9,001	16	11
Fergus Falls	6,887	34	56
Hastings	3,983	19	35
Hibbing	8,832	1	(1)
Lake City	3,142	3	6
Little Falls	6,078	1	1
Luverne	2,540	1	(1)
Mankato	10,365	3	7
Melrose	2,591	3	(1)
Minneapolis	301,408	2,592	1,548
Montevideo	3,056	1	(1)
Moorhead	4,840	8	3
New Ulm	5,648	2	3
Northfield	3,265	4	11
Owatonna	5,658	15	19
Red Wing	9,048	20	14
Richfield	2,673	2	....
Rochester	7,844	27	10
St. Cloud	10,600	12	18
St. Paul	214,744	3,144	2,263
St. Peter	4,176	11	3
South St. Paul	4,510	5	(1)
Staples	2,558	....	(1)
Stillwater	10,198	56	53
Thief River Falls	3,714	6	(1)
Two Harbors	4,990	....	3
Virginia	10,473	13	1
Wabasha	2,622	4	....
Waseca	3,054	1	3
West Minneapolis	3,022	....	(1)
West St. Paul	2,660	....	(1)
Willmar	4,135	2	1
Winona	18,583	18	30

CITY, TOWN, VILLAGE, AND BOROUGH.	Total, 1910	Negro 1910	Negro 1900
MISSISSIPPI.			
Aberdeen	3,708	1,960	1,924
Bay St. Louis	3,388	1,014	979
Biloxi	8,049	1,436	949
Brookhaven	5,293	2,732	1,168
Canton	3,929	2,398	1,985
Clarksdale	4,079	2,478	(1)
Collins	2,581	1,036	....
Columbus	8,988	4,401	3,366
Corinth	5,020	1,563	1,174
Greenville	9,610	6,010	4,987
Greenwood	5,836	3,062	1,884
Grenada	2,814	1,227	1,336
Gulfport	6,386	1,703	(1)
Hattiesburg	11,733	4,357	1,687
Jackson	21,262	10,554	4,447
Laurel	8,465	3,103	1,428
McComb	6,237	1,140	829
Meridian	23,285	9,321	5,787
Moss Point	3,054	1,591	(1)
Natchez	11,791	6,700	7,090
Okolona	2,584	1,386	(1)
Pascagoula	3,379	1,220	(1)
Starkville	2,698	1,438	(1)
Tupelo	3,881	1,883	(1)
Vicksburg	20,814	12,053	8,147
Water Valley	4,275	1,460	1,378
West Point	4,864	2,772	1,647
Winona	2,512	1,205	(1)
Yazoo City	6,796	4,154	2,886
MISSOURI.			
Aurora	4,148	1	9
Boonville	4,252	910	1,111
Brookfield	5,749	261	299
Butler	2,894	205	188
Cameron	2,980	114	159
Cape Girardeau	8,475	875	719
Carrollton	3,452	565	716
Carterville	4,539	5	12
Carthage	9,483	454	539
Caruthersville	3,655	697	(1)
Charleston	3,144	719	(1)
Chillicothe	6,265	444	538
Clinton	4,992	374	470
Columbia	9,662	2,246	1,916
De Soto	4,721	339	364
Eldorado Springs	2,503	....	(1)
Excelsior Springs	3,900	222	(1)
Farmington	2,613	340	(1)
Fayette	2,586	855	897
Festus	2,556	253	(1)
Flat River	5,112	....	....
Fredericktown	2,632	246	(1)
Fulton	5,228	1,134	1,167
Hannibal	18,341	1,846	1,836
Higginsville	2,628	434	482
Independence	9,859	1,031	937
Jefferson City	11,850	1,924	1,822
Joplin	32,073	801	773
Kansas City	248,381	23,566	17,567
Kennett	3,033	49	(1)
Kirksville	6,347	190	291
Kirkwood	4,171	690	528
Lexington	5,242	1,319	1,170
Liberty	2,980	475	(1)
Louisiana	4,454	705	1,075
Macon	3,584	544	741
Maplewood	4,976	10	....
Marceline	3,920	137	104
Marshall	4,869	698	724
Maryville	4,762	138	98
Mexico	5,939	853	948
Moberly	10,923	988	923
Monette	4,177	1	....
Neosho	3,661	204	193
Nevada	7,176	87	168
Poplar Bluff	6,916	858	800
Rich Hill	2,755	10	61
Richmond	3,664	633	734
St. Charles	9,437	708	719
St. Joseph	77,403	4,249	6,260
St. Louis	687,029	43,960	35,516
Sedalia	17,822	1,871	1,725
Sikeston	3,327	71	(1)
Slater	3,238	491	506

[1] Data not available, total population in 1900 being less than 2,500.

TABLE 12.—NEGRO POPULATION OF URBAN COMMUNITIES: 1910 AND 1900—Continued.

CITY, TOWN, VILLAGE, AND BOROUGH.	Total, 1910	Negro. 1910	Negro. 1900	CITY, TOWN, VILLAGE, AND BOROUGH.	Total, 1910	Negro. 1910	Negro. 1900	CITY, TOWN, VILLAGE, AND BOROUGH.	Total, 1910	Negro. 1910	Negro. 1900
MISSOURI—Con.				**NEW HAMPSHIRE—Con.**				**NEW JERSEY—Con.**			
Springfield	35,201	1,995	2,265	Portsmouth	11,269	117	101	Summit	7,500	273	129
Trenton	5,656	147	200	Rochester	8,868	3	3	Tenafly	2,756	40	(1)
Warrensburg	4,689	411	556	Somersworth	6,704	......	......	Trenton	96,815	2,581	2,096
Washington	3,670	191	251	Walpole	2,668	......	1	Union	21,023	29	7
								Vineland	5,282	197	191
Webb City	11,817	45	26	**NEW JERSEY.**							
Webster Groves	7,080	413	(1)	Asbury Park	10,150	1,934	273	Wallington	3,448	17	(1)
Wellston	7,312	376	......	Atlantic City	46,150	9,834	6,513	Washington	3,567	157	187
West Plains	2,914	84	92	Bayonne	55,545	561	335	West Hoboken	35,403	56	22
				Bloomfield	15,070	490	329	West New York	13,560	147	87
MONTANA.				Boonton	4,930	31	25				
Anaconda	10,134	124	135					West Orange	10,980	64	60
Billings	10,031	144	89	Bordentown	4,250	213	191	Westfield	6,420	466	......
Bozeman	5,107	38	33	Bound Brook	3,970	33	55	Wharton	2,983	......	(1)
Butte	39,165	240	248	Bridgeton	14,209	801	701	Woodbury	4,642	564	517
Deer Lodge	2,570	39	(1)	Burlington	8,336	538	590				
				Camden	94,538	6,076	5,576	**NEW MEXICO.**			
Great Falls	13,948	116	128					Albuquerque	11,020	244	226
Havre	3,624	35	(1)	Cairstadt	3,807	31	2	Clovis	3,255	2	......
Helena	12,515	420	228	Cliffside Park	3,394	3	(1)	Las Cruces	3,836	51	......
Kalispell	5,549	23	28	Collingswood	4,795	72	(1)	Las Vegas city (East Las Vegas P. O.)	3,755	94	116
Lewistown	2,992	54	(1)	Dover	7,468	43	53	Las Vegas town	3,179	9	(2)
				East Newark	3,163	3	3				
Livingston	5,359	16	8					Raton	4,539	89	26
Miles City	4,697	81	(1)	East Orange	34,371	1,907	1,420	Roswell	6,172	165	(1)
Missoula	12,869	120	34	East Rutherford	4,275	147	166	Santa Fe	5,072	69	87
Red Lodge	4,860	5	(1)	Edgewater	2,655	1	(1)	Silver City	3,217	60	76
				Elizabeth	73,409	1,381	1,139	Tucumcari	2,526	12	......
NEBRASKA.				Englewood	9,924	777	386				
Alliance	3,105	45	68					**NEW YORK.**			
Auburn	2,729	3	......	Flemington	2,693	65	(1)	Albany	100,253	1,037	1,178
Aurora	2,630	16	(1)	Fort Lee	4,472	3	......	Albion	5,016	52	43
Beatrice	9,356	54	27	Freehold	3,233	139	126	Amityville	2,517	80	(1)
Benson	3,170	8	(1)	Garfield	10,213	6	15	Amsterdam	31,267	118	94
				Glen Ridge	3,260	165	(1)	Auburn	34,668	527	507
Blair	2,584	2	4								
Chadron	2,687	22	(1)	Gloucester	9,462	6	5	Babylon	2,600	93	(1)
Columbus	5,014	15	15	Guttenberg	5,647	1	1	Baldwinsville	3,099	8	14
Fairbury	5,294	30	5	Hackensack	14,050	773	515	Ballston Spa	4,138	10	24
Falls City	3,255	65	69	Hackettstown	2,715	5	(1)	Batavia	11,613	44	32
				Haddonfield	4,142	352	236	Bath	3,884	79	133
Fremont	8,718	55	62								
Grand Island	10,326	117	38	Haledon	2,560	15	......	Binghamton	48,443	635	501
Hastings	9,338	82	58	Hammonton	5,088	24	21	Brockport	3,579	20	16
Havelock	2,680	......	(1)	Harrison	14,498	84	49	Buffalo	423,715	1,773	1,698
Holdrege	3,030	4	12	Hawthorne	3,400	12	(1)	Canandaigua	7,217	96	110
				Hoboken	70,324	120	101	Canastota	3,247	42	40
Kearney	6,202	43	19								
Lincoln	43,973	733	814	Irvington	11,877	76	42	Canton	2,701	4	......
McCook	3,765	3	(1)	Jersey City	267,779	5,960	3,704	Carthage	3,563	11	19
Nebraska City	5,488	81	142	Kearny	18,659	61	58	Catskill	5,296	226	304
				Keyport	3,554	152	170	Clyde	2,695	10	21
Norfolk	6,025	49	40	Lambertville	4,657	110	125	Cohoes	24,709	16	15
North Platte	4,793	8	11								
Omaha	124,096	4,426	3,443	Little Ferry	2,541	30	(1)	Cold Springs	2,549	3	(1)
Plattsmouth	4,287	5	13	Lodi	4,138	18	(1)	Corning	13,730	99	119
				Long Branch	13,298	1,248	987	Cornwall	2,658	287	(1)
South Omaha	26,259	717	571	Madison	4,658	393	300	Cortland	11,504	29	51
University Place	3,200	9	(1)	Millville	12,451	116	139	Dansville	3,938	......	3
Wymore	2,613	1	......								
York	6,235	28	30	Montclair	21,550	2,485	1,344	Depew	3,921	8	1
				Morristown	12,507	991	815	Dobbs Ferry	3,455	61	23
NEVADA.				New Brunswick	23,388	690	755	Dolgeville	2,685	9	(1)
Reno	10,867	93	28	Newark	347,469	9,475	6,694	Dunkirk	17,221	9	10
Sparks	2,500	8	......	Newton	4,467	46	53	East Aurora	2,781	6	(1)
NEW HAMPSHIRE.				North Plainfield	6,117	212	182	East Syracuse	3,274	9	18
				Nutley	6,009	126	......	Ellenville	3,114	25	54
Berlin	11,780	10	......	Orange	29,630	2,479	1,903	Elmira	37,176	513	803
Claremont	7,529	18	23	Passaic	54,773	535	443	Elmira Heights	2,732	2	(1)
Concord	21,497	56	58	Paterson	125,600	1,539	1,182	Fairport	3,112	13	(1)
Conway	3,413	......	4								
Derry	5,123	4	7	Perth Amboy	32,121	165	89	Fishkill Landing	3,902	108	112
				Phillipsburg	13,903	64	36	Fort Edward	3,762	4	3
Dover	13,247	13	15	Plainfield	20,550	1,833	1,450	Fort Plain	2,762	18	(1)
Exeter	4,897	11	31	Pleasantville	4,390	619	(1)	Frankfort	3,303	23	8
Farmington	2,621	......	(1)	Princeton	5,136	1,148	899	Fredonia	5,285	7	17
Franklin	6,132	11	14								
Goffstown	2,579	12	19	Prospect Park	2,719	......	......	Freeport	4,836	219	67
				Rahway	9,337	393	349	Fulton	10,480	20	3
Haverhill	3,498	2	2	Raritan	3,672	2	1	Geneva	12,446	153	193
Keene	10,068	12	5	Red Bank	7,398	844	620	Glens Falls	15,243	22	33
Laconia	10,183	7	21	Ridgewood	5,416	247	105	Gloversville	20,642	194	216
Lancaster	3,054	6	8								
				Roosevelt	5,786	22	......	Goshen	3,081	299	313
Lebanon	5,718	11	5	Roselle	2,725	157	(1)	Gouverneur	4,128	2	1
Littleton town	4,069	3	3	Roselle Park	3,138	34	......	Granville	3,920	2	4
Littleton village	3,059	2	......	Rutherford	7,045	149	105	Green Island	4,737	2	1
Manchester	70,063	36	28	Salem	6,614	1,015	809	Greenport	3,089	75	(1)
Milford	3,939	2	3								
				Secaucus	4,740	43	(1)	Hastings-upon-Hudson	4,552	50	(1)
Nashua	26,005	15	62	Somerville	5,060	434	450	Haverstraw	5,669	315	568
Newmarket	3,348	......	......	South Amboy	7,007	4	7	Hempstead	4,964	242	304
Newport	3,765	6	4	South Orange	6,014	253	151	Herkimer	7,520	8	26
Pembroke	3,062	1	......	South River	4,772	22	26	Homer	2,695	11	(1)

1 Data not available, total population in 1900 being less than 2,500.   2 Data not available for the town.

TABLE 12.—NEGRO POPULATION OF URBAN COMMUNITIES: 1910 AND 1900—Continued.

CITY, TOWN, VILLAGE, AND BOROUGH.	Total, 1910	Negro 1910	Negro 1900
NEW YORK—Con.			
Hoosick Falls	5,532	10	10
Hornell	13,617	51	69
Hudson	11,417	417	424
Hudson Falls	5,189	25	42
Ilion	6,588	30	47
Ithaca	14,802	470	364
Jamestown	31,297	108	77
Johnstown	10,447	101	108
Kingston	25,908	630	545
Lackawanna	14,549	197	....
Lancaster	4,364	2	3
Leroy	3,771	36	71
Lestershire	3,775	9	1
Little Falls	12,273	52	66
Lockport	17,970	126	160
Lowville	2,940	....	(1)
Lyons	4,460	16	38
Malone	6,467	4	18
Mamaroneck	5,699	231	....
Massena	2,951	3	(1)
Matteawan	6,727	53	70
Mechanicville	6,634	17	8
Medina	5,683	50	30
Middletown	15,313	317	380
Mount Kisco	2,802	46	(1)
Mount Morris	2,782	8	(1)
Mount Vernon	30,919	896	516
New Rochelle	28,867	1,754	777
New York City [2]	4,766,883	91,709	60,666
Manhattan Borough	*2,331,542*	*60,534*	*36,246*
Bronx Borough	*430,980*	*4,117*	*2,370*
Brooklyn Borough	*1,634,351*	*22,708*	*18,367*
Queens Borough	*284,041*	*3,198*	*2,611*
Richmond Borough	*85,969*	*1,152*	*1,072*
Newark	6,227	20	13
Newburgh	27,805	604	558
Niagara Falls	30,445	266	344
North Tarrytown	5,421	268	242
North Tonawanda	11,955	6	....
Norwich	7,422	133	120
Nyack	4,619	332	247
Ogdensburg	15,933	34	23
Olean	14,743	161	122
Oneida	8,317	53	82
Oneonta	9,491	28	20
Ossining	11,480	631	308
Oswego	23,368	364	57
Owego	4,633	144	214
Patchogue	3,824	56	53
Peekskill	15,245	346	243
Penn Yan	4,597	60	67
Perry	4,388	21	13
Plattsburg	11,138	9	9
Port Chester	12,809	237	97
Port Jervis	9,564	74	119
Potsdam	4,036	....	2
Poughkeepsie	27,936	699	623
Rensselaer	10,711	21	18
Rochester	218,149	879	601
Rockville Center	3,667	89	(1)
Rome	20,497	136	89
Rye	3,964	283	....
Sag Harbor	3,408	119	(1)
St. Johnsville	2,536	5	(1)
Salamanca	5,792	16	21
Saranac Lake	4,983	56	18
Saratoga Springs	12,693	555	619
Saugerties	3,929	31	61
Schenectady	72,826	274	127
Scotia	2,957	1	....
Seneca Falls	6,588	19	9
Sidney	2,507	4	(1)
Silver Creek	2,512	....	(1)
Solvay	5,139	1	3
Southampton	2,509	91	(1)
Suffern	2,663	10	(1)
Syracuse	137,249	1,124	1,034
Tarrytown	5,600	237	191
Tonawanda	8,290	1	....
Troy	76,813	651	400
Tuckahoe	2,722	52	....
Tupper Lake	3,067	1	....
Utica	74,419	357	244
NEW YORK—Con.			
Walden	4,004	7	4
Walton	3,103	24	23
Wappingers Falls	3,195	19	19
Warsaw	3,206	12	20
Waterford	3,245	20	15
Waterloo	3,931	17	40
Watertown	26,730	76	75
Watervliet	15,074	26	59
Watkins	2,817	96	91
Waverly	4,855	60	55
Wellsville	4,382	55	32
Westfield	2,985	2	(1)
White Plains	15,949	858	369
Whitehall	4,917	10	8
Yonkers	79,803	1,549	1,005
NORTH CAROLINA.			
Asheville	18,762	5,359	4,724
Belhaven	2,863	1,439	(1)
Burlington	4,808	491	454
Charlotte	34,014	11,752	7,151
Concord	8,715	1,831	1,789
Durham	18,241	6,869	2,241
Edenton	2,789	1,669	2,090
Elizabeth City	8,412	3,977	3,164
Fayetteville	7,045	3,293	2,221
Gastonia	5,759	1,320	1,108
Goldsboro	6,107	2,521	2,520
Graham	2,504	464	(1)
Greensboro	15,895	5,710	4,086
Greenville	4,101	2,221	1,472
Henderson	4,503	2,484	2,194
Hendersonville	2,818	737	(1)
Hickory	3,716	907	698
High Point	9,525	2,099	928
Kinston	6,995	3,027	1,528
Lenoir	3,364	819	(1)
Lexington	4,163	858	(1)
Monroe	4,082	1,264	(1)
Mooresville	3,400	543	(1)
Morganton	2,712	802	(1)
Mount Airy	3,844	625	691
Newbern	9,961	5,649	5,878
Oxford	3,018	1,392	(1)
Raleigh	19,218	7,372	5,721
Reidsville	4,828	1,903	1,206
Rocky Mount	8,051	3,069	1,505
Salem	5,533	1,259	488
Salisbury	7,153	2,432	2,408
Shelby	3,127	743	(1)
Statesville	4,599	805	773
Tarboro	4,129	1,569	(1)
Thomasville	3,877	696	(1)
Washington	6,211	3,072	2,550
Wilmington	25,748	12,107	10,407
Wilson	6,717	2,998	1,131
Winston	17,167	7,828	5,043
NORTH DAKOTA.			
Bismarck	5,443	30	42
Devils Lake	5,157	42	(1)
Dickinson	3,678	....	(1)
Fargo	14,331	99	54
Grand Forks	12,478	49	28
Jamestown	4,358	2	1
Mandan	3,873	4	(1)
Minot	6,188	58	(1)
Valley City	4,606	2	(1)
Williston	3,124	20	(1)
OHIO.			
Akron	69,067	657	525
Alliance	15,083	116	98
Ashland	6,795	12	7
Ashtabula	18,266	69	75
Athens	5,463	245	278
Barberton	9,410	3	7
Barnesville	4,233	232	254
Bellaire	12,946	355	428
Bellefontaine	8,238	355	326
Bellevue	5,209	18	18
Berea	2,609	1	....
Bowling Green	5,222	49	37
OHIO—Con.			
Bridgeport	3,974	206	248
Bryan	3,641	1	37
Bucyrus	8,122	24	22
Byesville	3,156	9	(1)
Cambridge	11,327	343	279
Canal Dover	6,621	18	10
Canton	50,217	291	135
Carthage	3,618	305	22
Celina	3,493	2	1
Chicago Junction	2,950	4	(1)
Chillicothe	14,508	948	986
Cincinnati	363,591	19,639	14,482
Circleville	6,744	376	551
Cleveland	560,663	8,448	5,988
Cleveland Heights	2,955	37	....
Clyde	2,815	....	23
Columbus	181,511	12,739	8,201
Conneaut	8,319	27	12
Coshocton	9,603	91	71
Crestline	3,807	14	11
Crooksville	3,028	1	(1)
Cuyahoga Falls	4,020	17	11
Dayton	116,577	4,842	3,387
Defiance	7,327	16	39
Delaware	9,076	485	432
Delphos	5,038	49	59
Dennison	4,008	7	18
East Cleveland	9,179	30	15
East Liverpool	20,387	315	219
East Palestine	3,537	7	(1)
East Youngstown	4,972	2	....
Eaton	3,187	60	115
Elmwood Place	3,423	119	91
Elyria	14,825	235	201
Findlay	14,858	193	294
Fostoria	9,597	128	169
Franklin	2,659	111	136
Fremont	9,939	119	137
Galion	7,214	14	18
Gallipolis	5,560	684	852
Girard	3,736	11	2
Glouster	2,527	207	(1)
Greenfield	4,228	247	312
Greenville	6,237	38	31
Hamilton	35,279	725	347
Hartwell	2,823	217	(1)
Hillsboro	4,296	696	748
Ironton	13,147	1,046	924
Jackson	5,468	126	140
Kent	4,488	2	3
Kenton	7,185	263	271
Lakewood	15,181	43	4
Lancaster	13,093	223	212
Lebanon	2,698	274	272
Leetonia	2,665	3	7
Lima	30,508	978	731
Lisbon	3,084	73	103
Lockland	3,439	853	480
Logan	4,850	10	42
London	3,530	326	361
Lorain	28,883	375	359
Madisonville	5,193	375	240
Mansfield	20,768	105	123
Marietta	12,923	270	361
Marion	18,232	193	112
Martins Ferry	9,133	227	253
Marysville	3,576	66	106
Massillon	13,879	197	83
Medina	2,734	7	(1)
Miamisburg	4,271	9	9
Middleport	3,194	241	409
Middletown	13,152	405	314
Mingo Junction	4,049	48	54
Montpelier	2,759	3	(1)
Mount Vernon	9,087	289	239
Napoleon	4,007	2	6
Nelsonville	6,082	160	204
New Comerstown	2,943	46	72
New Lexington	2,559	1	(1)
New Philadelphia	8,542	35	36
Newark	25,404	346	300
Newburgh	5,813	98	12
Niles	8,361	1	1

[1] Data not available, total population in 1900 being less than 2,500.　　[2] Population of New York and its boroughs as now constituted.

TABLE 12.—NEGRO POPULATION OF URBAN COMMUNITIES: 1910 AND 1900—Continued.

CITY, TOWN, VILLAGE, AND BOROUGH.	Total, 1910	Negro 1910	Negro 1900
OHIO—Con.			
North Baltimore	2,503	3	4
Norwalk	7,858	109	101
Norwood	16,185	99	80
Oberlin	4,365	789	641
Orrville	3,101	.....	(1)
Painesville	5,501	165	179
Piqua	13,388	527	487
Pomeroy	4,023	191	280
Port Clinton	3,007	.....	(1)
Portsmouth	23,481	772	947
Ravenna	5,310	152	190
Reading	3,985	.....	.....
Rockport	3,179	7	(1)
St. Bernard	5,002	11	7
St. Marys	5,732	28	9
Salem	8,943	235	227
Sandusky	19,989	172	295
Shelby	4,903	7	12
Sidney	6,607	106	108
Springfield	46,921	4,933	4,253
Steubenville	22,391	677	736
Struthers	3,370	41	44
Tiffin	11,894	36	44
Toledo	168,497	1,877	1,710
Toronto	4,271	3	.....
Troy	6,122	353	391
Uhrichsville	4,751	51	70
Upper Sandusky	3,779	8	37
Urbana	7,739	851	796
Van Wert	7,157	146	183
Wadsworth	3,073	85	(1)
Wapakoneta	5,349	3	3
Warren	11,081	70	137
Washington Court House	7,277	704	708
Wauseon	2,650	3	(1)
Wellston	6,875	19	29
Wellsville	7,769	204	113
Wilmington	4,491	465	575
Woodsfield	2,502	.....	(1)
Wooster	6,136	52	42
Xenia	8,706	2,052	1,988
Youngstown	79,066	1,936	915
Zanesville	28,026	1,384	1,012
OKLAHOMA.			
Ada	4,349	159	.....
Altus	4,821	104	.....
Alva	3,688	1	(1)
Anadarko	3,439	323	.....
Ardmore	8,618	1,628	1,153
Bartlesville	6,181	212	(1)
Blackwell	3,266	.....	(1)
Chickasha	10,320	1,265	239
Claremore	2,866	316	(1)
Clinton	2,781	69	.....
Coalgate	3,255	221	209
Durant	5,330	13	2
El Reno	7,872	688	223
Elk City	3,165	1	.....
Enid	13,799	661	140
Frederick	3,027	142	.....
Guthrie	11,654	2,976	3,036
Hartshorne	2,963	517	(1)
Hobart	3,845	21	.....
Hugo	4,582	512	.....
Kingfisher	2,538	410	(1)
Krebs	2,884	101	.....
Lawton	7,788	542	.....
McAlester	12,954	2,997	[2] 592
Mangum	3,667	48	.....
Miami	2,907	.....	(1)
Muskogee	25,278	7,831	1,120
Norman	3,724	.....	(1)
Nowata	3,672	456	(1)
Oklahoma City	64,205	6,546	1,219
Okmulgee	4,176	1,376	.....
Pauls Valley	2,689	330	(1)
Pawhuska	2,776	70	(1)
Perry	3,133	347	399
Ponca	2,521	41	163
Purcell	2,740	422	(1)
Sapulpa	8,283	406	(1)
Shawnee	12,474	828	207

CITY, TOWN, VILLAGE, AND BOROUGH.	Total, 1910	Negro 1910	Negro 1900
OKLAHOMA—Con.			
Stillwater	3,444	105	(1)
Sulphur	3,684	164	(1)
Tahlequah	2,891	316	(1)
Tulsa	18,182	1,959	(1)
Vinita	4,082	518	(1)
Wagoner	4,018	1,038	(1)
Waurika	2,928	300	.....
Woodward	2,696	2	.....
OREGON.			
Albany	4,275	1	16
Ashland	5,020	1	.....
Astoria	9,599	22	8
Baker City	6,742	23	47
Corvallis	4,552	1	(1)
Eugene	9,009	6	3
Grants Pass	3,897	1	(1)
Klamath Falls	2,758	12	(1)
La Grande	4,843	6	1
Marshfield	2,980	8	(1)
Medford	8,840	9	(1)
Oregon City	4,287	.....	3
Pendleton	4,460	40	16
Portland	207,214	1,045	775
Roseburg	4,738	6	(1)
St. Johns	4,872	9	.....
Salem	14,094	47	5
The Dalles	4,880	27	4
PENNSYLVANIA.			
Allentown	51,913	134	85
Altoona	52,127	453	406
Ambler	2,649	266	(1)
Ambridge	5,205	29	.....
Apollo	3,006	86	77
Archbold	7,194	.....	.....
Ashland	6,855	2	1
Ashley	5,601	1	.....
Aspinwall	2,592	25	(1)
Athens	3,796	38	51
Austin	2,941	4	(1)
Avalon	4,317	58	(1)
Avoca	4,634	.....	.....
Bangor	5,369	5	14
Barnesboro	3,535	2	(1)
Beaver	3,456	60	(1)
Beaver Falls	12,191	161	161
Bellefonte	4,145	136	191
Bellevue	6,323	251	154
Berwick	5,357	4	.....
Bethlehem	12,837	100	[3] 111
Birdsboro	2,930	8	(1)
Blairsville	3,572	82	97
Blakeley	5,345	2	.....
Bloomsburg	7,413	80	96
Brackenridge	3,134	2	.....
Braddock	19,357	421	558
Bradford	14,544	135	177
Bridgeport	3,860	6	12
Bristol	9,256	286	290
Brookville	3,003	34	(1)
Butler	20,728	159	86
Canonsburg	3,891	240	378
Carbondale	17,040	9	4
Carlisle	10,303	1,119	1,148
Carnegie	10,009	310	273
Carrick	6,117	4	.....
Catasauqua	5,250	.....	10
Chambersburg	11,800	744	769
Charleroi	9,615	220	197
Chester	38,537	4,795	4,403
Clairton	3,326	63	.....
Clarion	2,612	10	(1)
Clearfield	6,851	95	51
Clifton Heights	3,155	28	(1)
Coaldale	5,154	.....	.....
Coatesville	11,084	1,520	431
Columbia	11,454	417	421
Connellsville	12,845	558	362
Conshohocken	7,480	80	78
Coplay	2,670	.....	(1)
Coraopolis	5,252	292	138
Corry	5,991	8	15
Coudersport	3,100	12	19
Crafton	4,583	56	(1)

CITY, TOWN, VILLAGE, AND BOROUGH.	Total, 1910	Negro 1910	Negro 1900
PENNSYLVANIA—Con.			
Curwensville	2,549	77	(1)
Danville	7,517	54	68
Darby	6,305	676	318
Derry	2,954	115	(1)
Dickson City	9,331	2	.....
Donora	8,174	359	.....
Dorranceton	4,046	.....	(1)
Downingtown	3,326	264	(1)
Doylestown	3,304	93	74
Dubois	12,623	26	24
Dunmore	17,615	7	2
Duquesne	15,727	246	192
Duryea	7,487	.....	.....
East Conemaugh	5,046	1	(1)
East Mauch Chunk	3,548	2	2
East Pittsburgh	5,615	52	112
East Stroudsburg	3,330	40	5
Easton	28,523	284	325
Edgewood	2,596	40	(1)
Edwardsville	8,407	1	.....
Elizabethtown	2,587	4	(1)
Ellwood City	3,902	6	(1)
Emaus	3,501	1	(1)
Emporium	2,916	30	(1)
Ephrata	3,192	2	(1)
Erie	66,525	340	244
Etna	5,830	6	45
Exeter	3,537	.....	(1)
Ford City	4,850	26	48
Forest City	5,749	3	1
Frackville	3,118	1	.....
Franklin	9,767	288	264
Freedom	3,060	19	(1)
Freeland	6,197	2	1
Galeton	4,027	2	(1)
Gallitzin	3,504	4	4
Gettysburg	4,030	259	234
Gilberton	5,401	1	.....
Girardville	4,396	1	1
Glassport	5,540	25	.....
Greater Punxsutawney	9,058	9	[4] 5
Greensburg	13,012	180	128
Greenville	5,909	31	34
Grove City	3,674	2	(1)
Hanover	7,057	11	32
Harrisburg	64,186	4,535	4,107
Hazleton	25,452	19	14
Hollidaysburg	3,734	109	116
Homestead	18,713	867	640
Honesdale	2,945	6	2
Huntingdon	6,861	102	122
Indiana	5,749	19	17
Irwin	2,886	49	(1)
Jeannette	8,077	109	65
Jenkintown	2,968	246	(1)
Jermyn	3,158	1	1
Jersey Shore	5,381	68	44
Johnsonburg	4,334	2	1
Johnstown	55,482	442	314
Juniata	5,285	4	(1)
Kane	6,626	62	54
Kingston	6,449	9	13
Kittanning	4,311	116	85
Knoxville	5,651	29	55
Lancaster	47,227	803	777
Lansford	8,321	5	1
Lansdale	3,551	2	2
Lansdowne	4,066	214	143
Larksville	9,288	14	.....
Latrobe	8,777	50	31
Lebanon	19,240	84	61
Leechburg	3,624	.....	(1)
Lehighton	5,316	2	2
Lewisburg	3,081	44	53
Lewistown	8,166	145	132
Lock Haven	7,772	83	122
Luzerne	5,426	2	10
Lykens	2,943	.....	.....
McAdoo	3,389	.....	(1)
McDonald	2,543	133	(1)
McKees Rocks	14,702	23	20
McKeesport	42,694	799	748
Mahanoy City	15,936	14	4
Mauch Chunk	3,952	3	3
Mayfield	3,662	2	(1)

1 Data not available, total population in 1900 being less than 2,500.
2 Population of South McAlester only in 1900.
3 Includes population of West Bethlehem borough in 1900.
4 Does not include Clayville borough in 1900.

TABLE 12.—NEGRO POPULATION OF URBAN COMMUNITIES: 1910 AND 1900—Continued.

First column group

CITY, TOWN, VILLAGE, AND BOROUGH.	Total, 1910	Negro 1910	Negro 1900
PENNSYLVANIA—Con.			
Meadville	12,780	187	173
Mechanicsburg	4,469	86	106
Media	3,562	542	469
Meyersdale	3,741	119	90
Middletown	5,374	244	289
Millvale	7,861	7	9
Milton	7,460	90	97
Miners Mills	3,159	1	[1]
Minersville	7,240	3	....
Monaca	3,376	28	[1]
Monessen	11,775	232	[1]
Monongahela City	7,598	463	345
Moosic	3,964	2	[1]
Mount Carmel	17,532	6	10
Mount Oliver	4,241	1	[1]
Mount Pleasant	5,812	144	173
Mount Union	3,338	51	[1]
Munhall	5,185	22	....
Nanticoke	18,877	2	1
Nazareth	3,978	5	[1]
New Brighton	8,329	175	179
New Castle	36,280	529	463
New Kensington	7,707	63	86
New Philadelphia	2,512	....	[1]
Norristown	27,875	1,015	728
North Braddock	11,824	287	167
North East	2,672	6	....
Northampton	8,729	9	....
Northumberland	3,517	8	4
Oakmont	3,436	70	[1]
Oil City	15,657	187	184
Old Forge	11,324	....	....
Olyphant	8,505	8	....
Parkesburg	2,522	161	[1]
Parnassus	2,578	26	[1]
Parsons	4,338	....	3
Patton	3,907	....	3
Pen Argyl	3,967	18	26
Perkasie	2,779	2	[1]
Philadelphia	1,549,008	84,459	62,613
Philipsburg	3,585	66	92
Phoenixville	10,743	191	278
Pitcairn	4,975	2	4
Pittsburgh[2]	533,905	25,623	20,355
Pittston	16,267	25	22
Plymouth	16,996	13	25
Port Carbon	2,678	6	[1]
Portage	2,954	1	[1]
Pottstown	15,599	341	292
Pottsville	20,236	93	168
Quakertown	3,801	12	9
Rankin	6,042	443	274
Reading	96,071	787	534
Renovo	4,621	10	13
Reynoldsville	3,189	2	8
Ridgway	5,408	7	3
Rochester	5,903	225	116
Royersford	3,073	21	3
St. Clair[3]	5,640	7	....
St. Clair[4]	6,455	9	7
St. Marys	6,346	....	1
Sayre	6,426	3	3
Schuylkill Haven	4,747	1	....
Scottdale	5,456	119	63
Scranton	129,867	567	521
Sewickley	4,479	428	367
Shamokin	19,588	52	65
Sharon	15,270	194	113
Sharpsburg	8,153	209	258
Sharpsville	3,634	2	19
Shenandoah	25,774	8	2
Shippensburg	3,457	183	158
Slatington	4,454	....	4
Somerset	2,612	17	[1]
South Bethlehem	19,973	128	115
South Brownsville	3,943	332	[1]
South Fork	4,592	2	4
South Sharon	10,190	185	....
South Williamsport	3,734	18	32
Spangler	2,700	5	[1]
Spring City	2,880	2	....
Steelton	14,246	1,234	1,508
Stroudsburg	4,379	120	121
Summit Hill	4,209	....	3
Sunbury	13,770	32	12

Second column group

CITY, TOWN, VILLAGE, AND BOROUGH.	Total, 1910	Negro 1910	Negro 1900
PENNSYLVANIA—Con.			
Susquehanna	3,478	1	7
Swissvale	7,381	93	[1]
Swoyersville	5,396	1	[1]
Tamaqua	9,462	2	13
Tarentum	7,414	3	....
Taylor	9,060	4	1
Throop	5,133	1	[1]
Titusville	8,533	87	106
Towanda	4,281	41	94
Turtle Creek	4,995	19	22
Tyrone	7,176	121	115
Union City	3,684	2	10
Uniontown	13,344	1,280	803
Vandergrift	3,876	28	[1]
Vandergrift Heights	3,438	18	[1]
Verona	2,849	4	[1]
Warren	11,080	33	1
Washington	18,778	1,471	984
Waynesboro	7,199	119	89
Waynesburg	3,545	190	152
Weatherly	2,501	1	[1]
Wellsboro	3,183	35	30
West Berwick	5,512	1	....
West Chester	11,767	1,868	1,777
West Hazleton	4,715	....	....
West Homestead	3,009	21	....
West Newton	2,880	33	[1]
West Pittston	6,848	101	77
Wickboro	2,775	1	....
Wilkes-Barre	67,105	673	680
Wilkinsburg	18,924	428	275
Williamsport	31,860	957	1,142
Williamstown	2,904	....	....
Wilmerding	6,133	20	17
Windber	8,013	13	....
Winton	5,280	31	14
Wyoming	3,010	....	[1]
York	44,750	1,231	776
RHODE ISLAND.			
Bristol	8,565	43	129
Burrillville	7,878	26	3
Central Falls	22,754	11	62
Coventry	5,848	2	16
Cranston	21,107	245	216
Cumberland	10,107	1	....
East Greenwich	3,420	91	136
East Providence	15,808	435	369
Johnston	5,935	7	20
Lincoln	9,825	42	16
Newport	27,149	1,600	1,613
North Kingstown	4,048	106	83
North Providence	5,407	13	9
North Smithfield	2,699	8	[1]
Pawtucket	51,622	234	173
Portsmouth	2,681	65	[1]
Providence	224,326	5,316	4,817
Scituate	3,493	4	6
Smithfield	2,739	16	[1]
South Kingstown	5,176	267	298
Tiverton	4,032	40	26
Warren	6,585	97	14
Warwick	26,629	173	183
Westerly	8,696	193	185
Woonsocket	38,125	20	6
SOUTH CAROLINA.			
Abbeville	4,459	2,122	1,830
Aiken	3,911	2,289	2,131
Anderson	9,654	3,370	1,744
Bennettsville	2,646	1,133	[1]
Camden	3,569	1,858	[1]
Charleston	58,833	31,056	31,522
Cheraw	2,873	1,546	[1]
Chester	4,754	2,041	1,931
Clinton	3,272	1,033	[1]
Columbia	26,319	11,546	9,858
Darlington	3,789	1,720	1,274
Easley	2,983	599	[1]
Florence	7,057	3,536	2,603
Gaffney	4,767	1,152	1,005
Georgetown	5,530	3,650	2,718
Greenville	15,741	6,319	5,414
Greenwood	6,614	2,943	2,288

Third column group

CITY, TOWN, VILLAGE, AND BOROUGH.	Total, 1910	Negro 1910	Negro 1900
SOUTH CAROLINA—Con.			
Laurens	4,818	1,923	1,605
Marion	3,844	1,959	[1]
Newberry	5,028	1,698	1,861
Orangeburg	5,906	3,017	2,518
Rock Hill	7,216	2,167	1,706
Spartanburg	17,517	6,873	4,269
Sumter	8,109	4,125	3,160
Union	5,623	2,027	1,701
SOUTH DAKOTA.			
Aberdeen	10,753	67	12
Brookings	2,971	2	[1]
Deadwood	3,653	100	47
Huron	5,791	29	5
Lead	8,392	28	19
Madison	3,137	1	2
Mitchell	6,515	17	6
Pierre	3,656	6	[1]
Rapid City	3,854	26	[1]
Redfield	3,060	....	[1]
Sioux Falls	14,094	63	30
Watertown	7,010	23	4
Yankton	3,787	50	70
TENNESSEE.			
Bristol[5]	7,148	1,073	954
Brownsville	2,882	1,286	1,335
Chattanooga	44,604	17,942	13,122
Clarksville	8,548	4,285	5,094
Cleveland	5,549	846	815
Columbia	5,754	2,336	2,716
Covington	2,990	1,132	1,146
Dyersburg	4,149	1,756	1,778
Fayetteville	3,439	1,213	1,176
Franklin	2,924	1,417	[1]
Harriman	3,061	521	516
Humboldt	3,446	1,448	1,432
Jackson	15,779	5,719	6,108
Johnson City	8,502	1,441	985
Knoxville	36,346	7,638	7,359
La Follette	2,816	453	[1]
Lebanon	3,659	1,195	[1]
Lenoir City	3,392	20	....
Memphis	131,105	52,441	49,910
Morristown	4,007	771	706
Murfreesboro	4,679	2,030	2,248
Nashville	110,364	36,523	30,044
Paris	3,881	1,405	[1]
Park City	5,126	531	....
Pulaski	2,928	1,242	1,420
Rockwood	3,660	718	616
Shelbyville	2,869	901	[1]
Tullahoma	3,049	640	702
Union City	4,389	1,583	962
TEXAS.			
Abilene	9,204	602	169
Amarillo	9,957	123	[1]
Austin	29,860	7,478	5,822
Ballinger	3,536	83	[1]
Bay City	3,156	852	....
Beaumont	20,640	6,896	2,953
Beeville	3,269	346	....
Belton	4,164	842	705
Big Spring	4,102	....	....
Bonham	4,844	903	1,223
Bowie	2,874	1	2
Brady	2,669	101	....
Brenham	4,718	2,129	2,701
Brownsville	10,517	43	18
Brownwood	6,967	500	182
Bryan	4,132	1,701	1,515
Calvert	2,579	1,461	1,764
Cameron	3,263	1,043	1,040
Childress	3,818	....	[1]
Cleburne	10,364	891	611
Coleman	3,046	96	[1]
Comanche	2,756	6	[1]
Commerce	2,818	154	....
Corpus Christi	8,222	436	460
Corsicana	9,749	2,842	2,399
Crockett	3,947	2,254	1,208
Cuero	3,109	701	894
Dalhart	2,580	2	....
Dallas	92,104	18,024	9,035
Denison	13,632	2,799	2,251

[1] Data not available, total population in 1900 being less than 2,500.
[2] Includes population of Allegheny in 1900.
[3] Allegheny County.
[4] Schuylkill County.
[5] Joint population of Bristol, Sullivan County, Tenn., and Bristol, Va.: Total, 1910, 13,395; Negro, 2,217 in 1910 and 1,981 in 1900.

NEGRO POPULATION.

TABLE 12.—NEGRO POPULATION OF URBAN COMMUNITIES: 1910 AND 1900—Continued.

CITY, TOWN, VILLAGE, AND BOROUGH.	Total, 1910	Negro. 1910	Negro. 1900
TEXAS—Con.			
Denton	4,732	556	514
Dublin	2,551	53	(1)
Eagle Pass	3,536	82	(1)
El Paso	39,279	1,452	466
Ennis	5,669	1,557	1,057
Fort Worth	73,312	13,280	4,249
Gainesville	7,624	1,269	1,201
Galveston	36,981	8,036	8,291
Georgetown	3,096	712	608
Gonzales	3,139	755	1,228
Greenville	8,850	1,887	1,751
Hillsboro	6,115	1,084	1,077
Houston	78,800	23,929	14,608
Houston Heights	6,984	719	(1)
Jacksonville	2,875	741	(1)
Jefferson	2,515	1,336	1,473
Laredo	14,855	32	87
Lockhart	2,945	540	(1)
Longview	5,155	2,253	1,761
Lufkin	2,749	521	(1)
McKinney	4,714	762	917
Marlin	3,878	1,511	1,235
Marshall	11,452	4,997	3,769
Mart	2,939	708	(1)
Mexia	2,694	972	(1)
Mineral Wells	3,950	489	(1)
Mount Pleasant	3,137	1,133	(1)
Nacogdoches	3,369	1,076	(1)
Navasota	3,284	1,588	2,105
New Braunfels	3,165	121	(1)
Orange	5,527	1,519	970
Palestine	10,482	3,554	2,872
Paris	11,269	3,131	3,061
Plainview	2,829		
Port Arthur	7,663	1,493	(1)
Quanah	3,127	32	(1)
San Angelo	10,321	652	
San Antonio	96,614	10,716	7,538
San Marcos	4,071	892	(1)
Seguin	3,116	876	(1)
Sherman	12,412	2,220	2,131
Smithville	3,167	713	657
Snyder	2,514		
Stamford	3,902	150	
Stephenville	2,561	166	(1)
Sulphur Springs	5,151	1,449	1,280
Sweetwater	4,176	86	(1)
Taylor	5,314	1,878	1,260
Teague	3,288	564	
Temple	10,993	2,814	1,425
Terrell	7,050	1,617	1,517
Texarkana [2]	9,790	3,218	1,964
Tyler	10,400	2,954	2,693
Uvalde	3,998	178	(1)
Vernon	3,195	54	(1)
Victoria	3,673	742	978
Waco	26,425	6,067	5,826
Waxahachie	6,205	1,592	1,178
Weatherford	5,074	512	515
Wichita Falls	8,200	578	(1)
Yoakum	4,657	984	641
UTAH.			
American Fork	2,797		
Bingham	2,881	1	
Brigham	3,685	2	
Eureka	3,416		1
Lehi	2,964		
Logan	7,522	6	9
Murray	4,057	4	
Nephi	2,759	1	(1)
Ogden City	25,580	203	43
Park	3,439		6
Provo	8,925	2	3
Richfield	2,559		(1)

CITY, TOWN, VILLAGE, AND BOROUGH.	Total, 1910	Negro. 1910	Negro. 1900
UTAH—Con.			
Salt Lake City	92,777	737	278
Spanish Fork	3,464		2
Springville	3,356		1
Tooele	2,753	3	(1)
VERMONT.			
Barre city	10,734	2	3
Barre town	4,194	10	2
Barton	3,346	2	
Bennington town	8,698	33	(3)
Bennington village	6,211	22	38
Brandon	2,712	19	13
Brattleboro town	7,541	9	(3)
Brattleboro village	6,517	9	16
Burlington	20,468	115	115
Colchester town	6,450	653	(3)
Winooski village	4,520	87	2
Derby	3,639	2	
Essex	2,714	317	(1)
Fair Haven town	3,095	7	1
Fair Haven village	2,554	7	(1)
Hardwick	3,201	5	(1)
Hartford	4,179	7	3
Lyndon	3,204	2	3
Middlebury	2,848	5	5
Montpelier	7,856	9	8
Morristown	2,652		1
Newport town	3,684	8	3
Newport village	2,548	8	(1)
Northfield	3,226		1
Poultney	3,644	8	1
Proctor town	2,871	1	(1)
Proctor village	2,756	1	(1)
Randolph	3,191	3	2
Richford	2,907	1	(1)
Rockingham town	6,207	14	(3)
Bellow Falls village	4,883	5	7
Rutland	13,546	18	54
St. Albans	6,381	40	57
St. Johnsbury town	8,098	2	(3)
St. Johnsbury village	6,693	2	
Springfield town	4,784	2	8
Springfield village	3,250	1	(1)
Swanton	3,628	7	6
Waterbury	3,273	11	5
West Rutland	3,427	2	13
Woodstock	2,545	27	33
VIRGINIA.			
Alexandria	15,329	4,188	4,533
Bedford City	2,508	851	(1)
Big Stone Gap	2,590	396	(1)
Bristol [4]	6,247		
Buena Vista	3,245	416	(1)
Charlottesville	6,765	2,524	2,613
Clifton Forge	5,748	1,092	695
Covington	4,234	1,000	838
Danville	19,020	6,207	6,515
Farmville	2,971	1,598	(1)
Fredericksburg	5,874	1,480	1,621
Hampton	5,505	2,182	1,249
Harrisonburg	4,879	941	971
Lexington	2,931	1,173	1,252
Lynchburg	29,494	9,466	8,254
Marion	2,727	324	(1)
Martinsville	3,368	1,475	(1)
Newport News	20,205	7,259	6,798
Norfolk	67,452	25,039	20,230
Petersburg	24,127	11,014	10,751
Portsmouth	33,190	11,617	5,625
Pulaski	4,807	1,221	944
Radford	4,202	665	456
Richmond	127,628	46,733	32,230
Roanoke	34,874	7,924	5,834
Salem	3,849	849	798
South Boston	3,516	1,441	(1)
Staunton	10,604	2,476	1,828
Suffolk	7,008	2,806	1,310
Williamsburg	2,714	897	(1)
Winchester	5,864	1,038	1,105
Wytheville	3,054	782	883

CITY, TOWN, VILLAGE, AND BOROUGH.	Total, 1910	Negro. 1910	Negro. 1900
WASHINGTON.			
Aberdeen	13,660	45	13
Anacortes	4,168	4	(1)
Bellingham [5]	24,298	44	30
Bremerton	2,993	14	
Centralia	7,311	23	(1)
Chehalis	4,507	4	(1)
Cle Elum	2,749	21	
Colfax	2,783	3	(1)
Ellensburg	4,209	63	(1)
Everett	24,814	185	54
Hillyard	3,276		
Hoquiam	8,171	9	14
North Yakima	14,082	176	41
Olympia	6,996	21	8
Port Townsend	4,181	5	7
Pullman	2,602		(1)
Puyallup	4,544	9	(1)
Renton	2,740	1	
Roslyn	3,126	111	317
Seattle	237,194	2,296	406
Snohomish	3,244	9	(1)
South Bend	3,023	3	(1)
Spokane	104,402	723	376
Tacoma	83,743	778	307
Vancouver	9,300	34	7
Walla Walla	19,364	114	25
Wenatchee	4,050	4	(1)
WEST VIRGINIA.			
Benwood	4,976		
Bluefield	11,188	2,238	754
Charles Town	2,662	883	(1)
Charleston	22,996	3,086	1,787
Chester	3,184	11	
Clarksburg	9,201	847	574
Davis	2,615	94	(1)
Elkins	5,260	215	(1)
Fairmont	9,711	458	283
Grafton	7,563	166	162
Hinton	3,656	274	541
Huntington	31,161	2,140	1,212
Keyser	3,705	64	157
McMechen	2,921	1	(1)
Mannington	2,672	42	(1)
Martinsburg	10,698	992	678
Morgantown	9,150	214	(1)
Moundsville	8,918	544	468
Parkersburg	17,842	869	783
Princeton	3,027	389	
Richwood	3,061	21	
Sistersville	2,684	73	67
Wellsburg	4,189	92	102
Wheeling	41,641	1,201	1,066
Williamson	3,561	466	
WISCONSIN.			
Antigo	7,196	1	
Appleton	16,773	9	18
Ashland	11,594	3	12
Baraboo	6,324	26	25
Beaver Dam	6,758	2	1
Beloit	15,125	94	66
Berlin	4,636	5	1
Burlington	3,212		1
Chippewa Falls	8,893	2	1
Columbus	2,523	1	(1)
Cudahy	3,691		(1)
De Pere	4,477		7
Eau Claire	18,310	32	11
Edgerton	2,513	9	(1)
Fond du Lac	18,797	47	136
Fort Atkinson	3,877	6	9
Grand Rapids	6,521		
Green Bay	25,236	45	33
Hartford	2,982	2	(1)
Hudson	2,810		2
Janesville	13,894	37	18
Jefferson	2,582		
Kaukauna	4,717	14	3
Kenosha	21,371	33	32
La Crosse	30,417	59	56

[1] Data not available, total population in 1900 being less than 2,500.
[2] Joint population of Texarkana, Bowie County, Tex., and Texarkana, Miller County, Ark.: 1910, 15,445; Negro, 5,319 in 1910 and 4,042 in 1900.
[3] Data not available for the town.
[4] Joint population of Bristol, Va., and Bristol, Sullivan County, Tenn., total, 1910, 13,395; Negro, 2,217 in 1910 and 1,981 in 1900.
[5] Fairhaven and New Whatcom consolidated under the name of Bellingham in 1903.

TABLE 12.—NEGRO POPULATION OF URBAN COMMUNITIES: 1910 AND 1900—Continued.

CITY, TOWN, VILLAGE, AND BOROUGH.	Total, 1910	Negro 1910	Negro 1900
WISCONSIN—Con.			
Lake Geneva	3,079	4	......
Madison	25,531	143	69
Manitowoc	13,027	11	3
Marinette	14,610	1	1
Marshfield	5,783	3	3
Menasha	6,081	5	2
Menomonie	5,036	......	......
Merrill	8,689	3	......
Milwaukee	373,857	980	862
Mineral Point	2,925	15	15
Monroe	4,410	......	2
Neenah	5,734	3	2
New London	3,383	1	1
Oconomowoc	3,054	1	1
Oconto	5,629	......	7
Oshkosh	33,062	98	52
Platteville	4,452	1	1
Plymouth	3,094	1	(1)
Port Washington	3,792	......	......
Portage	5,440	8	11
WISCONSIN—Con.			
Prairie du Chien	3,149	......	87
Racine	38,002	112	(1)
Reedsburg	2,615	1	(1)
Rhinelander	5,637	1	1
Rice Lake	3,968	6	......
Richland Center	2,652	......	(1)
Ripon	3,739	......	......
Shawano	2,923	......	(1)
Sheboygan	26,398	9	......
South Milwaukee	6,092	1	......
Sparta	3,973	16	33
Stanley	2,675	......	(1)
Stevens Point	8,692	1	......
Stoughton	4,761	8	1
Sturgeon Bay	4,262	3	3
Superior	40,384	182	186
Tomah	3,419	2	5
Tomahawk	2,907	2	(1)
Two Rivers	4,850	......	......
Washburn	3,830	......	......
WISCONSIN—Con.			
Watertown	8,829	4	......
Waukesha	8,740	47	47
Waupaca	2,789	2	6
Waupun	3,362	27	17
Wausau	16,560	9	1
Wauwatosa	3,346	1	......
West Allis	6,645	......	......
Whitewater	3,224	2	8
WYOMING.			
Casper	2,639	17	(1)
Cheyenne	11,320	653	295
Evanston	2,583	......	(1)
Laramie	8,237	52	90
Rawlins	4,256	86	(1)
Rock Springs	5,778	80	104
Sheridan	8,408	153	(1)

[1] Data not available, total population in 1900 being less than 2,500.

TABLE 13.—NEGRO POPULATION BY WARDS OR EQUIVALENT SUBDIVISIONS OF CITIES HAVING 50,000 OR MORE INHABITANTS OF WHOM AT LEAST 5,000 ARE NEGROES: 1910.

[Per cent not shown for wards having less than one-tenth of 1 per cent.]

STATE, CITY, AND WARD.	Number.	Per cent of total population.
ALABAMA.		
Birmingham	52,305	39.4
Ward 1	1,322	45.1
Ward 2	4,712	58.8
Ward 3	3,358	45.1
Ward 4	2,586	37.7
Ward 5	2,184	35.2
Ward 6	2,489	47.9
Ward 7	3,467	42.7
Ward 8	3,266	43.1
Ward 9	4,082	45.2
Ward 10	986	25.1
Ward 11	3,997	49.8
Ward 12	3,086	21.4
Ward 13	3,511	48.6
Ward 14	4,441	47.7
Ward 15	5,390	41.4
Ward 16	3,428	22.3
Mobile	22,763	44.2
Ward 1	2,088	55.2
Ward 2	151	8.8
Ward 3	261	12.9
Ward 4	942	19.0
Ward 5	1,387	36.7
Ward 6	3,950	48.6
Ward 7	11,262	79.3
Ward 8	632	14.0
Ward 9	1,266	24.6
Ward 10	824	25.4
CALIFORNIA.		
Los Angeles	7,599	2.4
Assembly district 67	22	2.1
Assembly district 69	451	1.7
Assembly district 70	1,409	1.9
Assembly district 71	2,696	7.1
Assembly district 72	656	1.7
Assembly district 73	1,210	3.2
Assembly district 74	579	1.0
Assembly district 75	576	1.2
COLORADO.		
Denver	5,426	2.5
Ward 1	41	0.8
Ward 2	54	0.7
Ward 3	299	3.8
Ward 4	1,098	12.6
Ward 5	940	12.0
Ward 6	68	0.3
Ward 7	288	2.5
Ward 8	556	3.0
Ward 9	806	4.3
Ward 10	321	1.4
Ward 11	333	2.7
Ward 12	78	0.5
Ward 13	85	0.5
Ward 14	237	2.7
Ward 15	68	0.4
Ward 16	154	1.1
DELAWARE.		
Wilmington	9,081	10.4
Ward 1	425	16.2
Ward 2	757	14.6
Ward 3	277	5.1
Ward 4	443	11.6
Ward 5	1,202	12.0
Ward 6	2,218	36.7
Ward 7	1,249	8.3
Ward 8	1,221	13.6
Ward 9	647	6.1
Ward 10	58	0.9
Ward 11	45	0.7
Ward 12	536	8.7
DISTRICT OF COLUMBIA.		
Washington	94,446	28.5
District 1	43,195	35.9
District 2	6,486	15.8
District 3	13,336	41.0
District 4	8,009	21.7
District 5	3,922	24.4
DISTRICT OF COLUMBIA—Continued.		
Washington—Con.		
District 6	1,220	18.3
District 7	10,367	21.1
District 8	1,904	15.7
District 9	6,005	36.3
FLORIDA.		
Jacksonville	29,293	50.8
Ward 1	1,968	28.3
Ward 2	4,311	63.4
Ward 3	1,290	33.7
Ward 4	779	20.1
Ward 5	1,569	43.9
Ward 6	5,743	68.9
Ward 7	6,346	66.2
Ward 8	6,591	70.3
Ward 9	696	13.0
GEORGIA.		
Atlanta	51,902	33.5
Ward 1	12,180	63.6
Ward 2	4,143	19.8
Ward 3	7,193	28.6
Ward 4	12,575	57.2
Ward 5	2,314	18.4
Ward 6	6,895	27.6
Ward 7	738	10.3
Ward 8	1,152	15.2
Ward 9	1,814	20.6
Ward 10	2,898	43.7
Savannah	33,246	51.1
ILLINOIS.		
Chicago	44,103	2.0
Ward 1	2,603	8.8
Ward 2	10,709	25.0
Ward 3	11,081	24.0
ILLINOIS—Continued.		
Chicago—Contd.		
Ward 4	167	0.3
Ward 5	38	......
Ward 6	1,962	2.6
Ward 7	1,903	2.1
Ward 8	95	0.1
Ward 9	19	......
Ward 10	12	......
Ward 11	13	......
Ward 12	176	0.2
Ward 13	212	0.4
Ward 14	2,409	4.6
Ward 15	23	......
Ward 16	18	......
Ward 17	49	......
Ward 18	798	3.1
Ward 19	62	0.1
Ward 20	369	0.6
Ward 21	721	1.5
Ward 22	524	1.1
Ward 23	141	0.3
Ward 24	20	......
Ward 25	419	0.4
Ward 26	77	0.1
Ward 27	167	0.1
Ward 28	26	......
Ward 29	124	0.2
Ward 30	6,431	12.5
Ward 31	1,806	2.3
Ward 32	514	0.7
Ward 33	101	0.1
Ward 34	72	0.1
Ward 35	242	0.4
East St. Louis	5,882	10.0
Ward 1	697	15.6
Ward 2	1,931	25.2
Ward 3	881	16.3
Ward 4	1,071	14.5
Ward 5	559	8.6
Ward 6	119	1.2
Ward 7	288	3.5
Ward 8	336	3.7

TABLE **13.**—NEGRO POPULATION BY WARDS OR EQUIVALENT SUBDIVISIONS OF CITIES HAVING 50,000 OR MORE INHABITANTS OF WHOM AT LEAST 5,000 ARE NEGROES: 1910—Continued.

[Per cent not shown for wards having less than one-tenth of 1 per cent.]

STATE, CITY, AND WARD.	Number.	Per cent of total population.
INDIANA.		
Evansville	6,266	9.0
Ward 1	565	5.8
Ward 2	717	16.6
Ward 3	582	10.4
Ward 4	906	5.9
Ward 5	403	3.8
Ward 6	460	3.4
Ward 7	2,633	25.1
Indianapolis	21,816	9.3
Ward 1	2,941	14.7
Ward 2	899	6.1
Ward 3	3,920	27.8
Ward 4	3,141	13.7
Ward 5	3,497	32.4
Ward 6	2,549	25.6
Ward 7	788	6.1
Ward 8	1,053	9.3
Ward 9	500	2.1
Ward 10	851	4.2
Ward 11	291	2.1
Ward 12	296	2.8
Ward 13	272	1.4
Ward 14	300	2.7
Ward 15	518	2.8
KANSAS.		
Kansas City	9,286	11.3
Ward 1	776	19.7
Ward 2	2,782	30.1
Ward 3	3,824	16.5
Ward 4	626	6.2
Ward 5	361	2.0
Ward 6	299	1.9
Ward 7	708	10.6
KENTUCKY.		
Louisville	40,522	18.1
Ward 1	1,250	6.8
Ward 2	820	4.5
Ward 3	4,161	15.4
Ward 4	3,261	28.5
Ward 5	3,980	21.1
Ward 6	1,981	17.2
Ward 7	1,122	10.1
Ward 8	3,059	27.6
Ward 9	4,038	41.3
Ward 10	7,999	58.2
Ward 11	6,526	20.4
Ward 12	2,325	5.7
LOUISIANA.		
New Orleans	89,262	26.3
Ward 1	3,260	21.2
Ward 2	4,733	27.4
Ward 3	12,145	31.5
Ward 4	4,539	27.6
Ward 5	6,852	26.7
Ward 6	3,578	21.5
Ward 7	10,165	31.2
Ward 8	2,106	14.7
Ward 9	2,932	11.5
Ward 10	5,755	24.8
Ward 11	9,986	36.4
Ward 12	5,732	26.8
Ward 13	3,976	23.3
Ward 14	1,987	12.9
Ward 15	5,760	37.2
Ward 16	3,300	42.1
Ward 17	2,456	28.1
MARYLAND.		
Baltimore	84,749	15.2
Ward 1	180	0.8
Ward 2	364	1.6
Ward 3	1,624	7.3
Ward 4	4,119	24.5
Ward 5	5,350	26.3
Ward 6	2,839	10.1
Ward 7	2,768	10.4
Ward 8	1,156	3.6
Ward 9	1,095	4.8

STATE, CITY, AND WARD.	Number.	Per cent of total population.
MARYLAND—Con.		
Baltimore—Con.		
Ward 10	3,160	14.7
Ward 11	6,673	32.9
Ward 12	4,523	16.4
Ward 13	604	2.4
Ward 14	8,392	37.4
Ward 15	6,473	21.5
Ward 16	4,852	19.0
Ward 17	12,738	61.5
Ward 18	4,498	22.4
Ward 19	2,652	11.6
Ward 20	643	2.3
Ward 21	2,744	13.5
Ward 22	4,958	28.2
Ward 23	2,327	12.8
Ward 24	17	......
MASSACHUSETTS.		
Boston	13,564	2.0
Ward 1	9	......
Ward 2	87	0.3
Ward 3	26	0.2
Ward 4	131	1.0
Ward 5	71	0.6
Ward 6	25	......
Ward 7	357	2.4
Ward 8	233	0.7
Ward 9	859	3.3
Ward 10	1,998	7.9
Ward 11	1,084	3.9
Ward 12	1,702	7.0
Ward 13	1	......
Ward 14	13	......
Ward 15	15	......
Ward 16	40	0.2
Ward 17	615	2.3
Ward 18	5,122	22.5
Ward 19	218	1.0
Ward 20	109	0.2
Ward 21	79	0.3
Ward 22	433	1.4
Ward 23	70	0.2
Ward 24	65	0.2
Ward 25	202	0.8
MICHIGAN.		
Detroit	5,741	1.2
Ward 1	550	2.1
Ward 2	96	0.6
Ward 3	2,744	11.7
Ward 4	100	0.4
Ward 5	1,177	4.0
Ward 6	29	0.1
Ward 7	399	1.8
Ward 8	39	0.2
Ward 9	202	0.5
Ward 10	29	0.1
Ward 11	67	0.3
Ward 12	65	0.3
Ward 13	37	0.1
Ward 14	62	0.3
Ward 15	20	0.1
Ward 16	36	......
Ward 17	50	0.1
Ward 18	39	0.1
MISSOURI.		
Kansas City	23,566	9.5
Ward 1	1,412	11.7
Ward 2	1,253	7.8
Ward 3	794	7.2
Ward 4	546	2.2
Ward 5	345	2.8
Ward 6	3,392	23.1
Ward 7	2,234	10.6
Ward 8	2,969	11.1
Ward 9	2,437	10.0
Ward 10	316	1.9
Ward 11	6,392	48.9
Ward 12	675	4.9
Ward 13	208	2.2
Ward 14	364	2.4
Ward 15	189	1.9
Ward 16	40	0.6

STATE, CITY, AND WARD.	Number.	Per cent of total population.
MISSOURI—Continued.		
St. Louis	43,960	6.4
Ward 1	638	2.8
Ward 2	119	0.6
Ward 3	107	0.5
Ward 4	1,602	4.2
Ward 5	5,149	19.7
Ward 6	6,310	31.5
Ward 7	1,809	8.9
Ward 8	381	1.5
Ward 9	1	......
Ward 10	83	0.4
Ward 11	301	1.2
Ward 12	1,063	4.2
Ward 13	105	0.4
Ward 14	72	0.3
Ward 15	713	3.5
Ward 16	4,182	20.0
Ward 17	6,851	27.8
Ward 18	254	1.2
Ward 19	3,319	15.3
Ward 20	844	3.7
Ward 21	365	1.6
Ward 22	3,108	14.0
Ward 23	2,852	12.3
Ward 24	652	2.0
Ward 25	636	2.4
Ward 26	1,522	6.7
Ward 27	305	0.9
Ward 28	617	2.4
NEW JERSEY.		
Camden	6,076	6.4
Ward 1	74	0.9
Ward 2	271	3.2
Ward 3	261	5.4
Ward 4	129	2.8
Ward 5	787	8.3
Ward 6	701	8.8
Ward 7	1,878	12.9
Ward 8	1,548	17.7
Ward 9	139	2.0
Ward 10	19	0.2
Ward 11	42	0.7
Ward 12	227	3.5
Jersey City	5,960	2.2
Ward 1	576	2.8
Ward 2	87	0.4
Ward 3	404	2.0
Ward 4	579	3.4
Ward 5	483	2.5
Ward 6	928	5.3
Ward 7	81	0.4
Ward 8	1,677	5.4
Ward 9	921	4.1
Ward 10	87	0.4
Ward 11	100	0.4
Ward 12	37	0.1
Newark	9,475	2.7
Ward 1	615	4.4
Ward 2	1,577	11.5
Ward 3	1,356	3.7
Ward 4	1,037	7.5
Ward 5	33	0.2
Ward 6	212	1.0
Ward 7	1,441	6.4
Ward 8	698	3.5
Ward 9	313	2.0
Ward 10	624	2.6
Ward 11	450	2.0
Ward 12	22	0.1
Ward 13	26	0.1
Ward 14	275	0.8
Ward 15	647	3.3
Ward 16	149	0.5
NEW YORK.		
New York City	91,709	1.9
Manhattan Borough	60,534	2.6
Assembly dist. 1	529	0.7
Assembly dist. 2	65	......
Assembly dist. 3	85	......
Assembly dist. 4	31	......

STATE, CITIY, AND WARD.	Number.	Per cent of total population
NEW YORK—Con.		
New York City—Continued.		
Manhattan Borough—Contd.		
Assembly dist. 5	1,066	1.9
Assembly dist. 6	28	......
Assembly dist. 7	1,850	3.5
Assembly dist. 8	28	......
Assembly dist. 9	5,361	9.8
Assembly dist. 10	27	......
Assembly dist. 11	1,269	2.4
Assembly dist. 12	91	0.1
Assembly dist. 13	9,273	17.7
Assembly dist. 14	86	0.1
Assembly dist. 15	1,865	2.6
Assembly dist. 16	693	1.1
Assembly dist. 17	3,074	4.9
Assembly dist. 18	38	......
Assembly dist. 19	1,690	2.1
Assembly dist. 20	723	1.1
Assembly dist. 21	10,921	14.9
Assembly dist. 22	181	0.3
Assembly dist. 23	2,092	1.7
Assembly dist. 24	2,051	2.4
Assembly dist. 25	1,407	2.6
Assembly dist. 26	893	1.1
Assembly dist. 27	3,548	6.4
Assembly dist. 28	283	0.3
Assembly dist.(pt.of)30	7,556	8.2
Assembly dist. 31	1,779	2.8
Bronx Borough	4,117	1.0
Assembly dist.(pt.of)30	308	1.2
Assembly dist. 32	1,364	1.0
Assembly dist. 33	1,589	2.0
Assembly dist. 34	274	0.3
Assembly dist. 35	582	0.7
Brooklyn Borough	22,708	1.4
Assembly dist. 1	3,110	6.2
Assembly dist. 2	946	1.8
Assembly dist. 3	50	......
Assembly dist. 4	321	0.6
Assembly dist. 5	653	1.2
Assembly dist. 6	449	0.6
Assembly dist. 7	48	
Assembly dist. 8	1,424	2.6
Assembly dist. 9	185	0.2
Assembly dist. 10	2,889	5.4
Assembly dist. 11	2,009	3.5
Assembly dist. 12	210	0.4
Assembly dist. 13	37	......
Assembly dist. 14	42	......
Assembly dist. 15	15	
Assembly dist. 16	1,314	1.5
Assembly dist. 17	2,109	4.2
Assembly dist. 18	1,281	1.5
Assembly dist. 19	20	
Assembly dist. 20	19	
Assembly dist. 21	267	0.3
Assembly dist. 22	1,337	1.0
Assembly dist. 23	3,973	2.5
Queens Borough	3,198	1.1
Assembly dist. 1	321	0.6
Assembly dist. 2	1,140	1.9
Assembly dist. 3	320	0.3
Assembly dist. 4	1,417	1.9
Richmond Borough	1,152	1.3
OHIO.		
Cincinnati	19,639	5.4
Ward 1	456	2.0
Ward 2	619	3.1
Ward 3	2,636	19.3
Ward 4	975	8.1
Ward 5	215	1.9
Ward 6	1,202	11.9
Ward 7	351	2.6
Ward 8	898	8.5
Ward 9	407	3.1
Ward 10	74	0.5
Ward 11	19	0.1
Ward 12	116	0.7

TABLE 13.—NEGRO POPULATION BY WARDS OR EQUIVALENT SUBDIVISIONS OF CITIES HAVING 50,000 OR MORE INHABITANTS OF WHOM AT LEAST 5,000 ARE NEGROES: 1910—Continued.

[Per cent not shown for wards having less than one-tenth of 1 per cent.]

STATE, CITY, AND WARD.	Number.	Per cent of total population.
OHIO—Continued.		
Cincinnati—Contd.		
Ward 13	1,007	4.8
Ward 14	185	1.2
Ward 15	1,001	7.0
Ward 16	2,602	16.0
Ward 17	1,058	7.8
Ward 18	3,986	26.6
Ward 19	191	1.2
Ward 20	116	0 7
Ward 21	263	1.9
Ward 22	379	3.0
Ward 23	622	3.2
Ward 24	261	1.8
Cleveland	8,448	1.5
Ward 1	37	0.2
Ward 2	13	......
Ward 3	13	......
Ward 4	35	0.2
Ward 5	5	......
Ward 6	18	......
Ward 7	18	......
Ward 8	62	0.4
Ward 9	371	4.7
Ward 10	315	2.2
Ward 11	13	......
Ward 12	2,792	16.3
Ward 13	1,360	6.0
Ward 14	1,126	6.4
Ward 15	421	1.7
Ward 16	12	......
Ward 17	6	......
Ward 18	87	0.3
Ward 19	254	0.8
Ward 20	87	0.5
Ward 21	206	1.4
Ward 22	78	0.4
Ward 23	20	......
Ward 24	51	0.2
Ward 25	328	1.9
Ward 26	705	1.7
Not returned by wards.	15	2.3
Columbus	12,739	7.0
Ward 1	249	1.3
Ward 2	1,535	9.7
Ward 3	697	4.3
Ward 4	3,332	18.6
Ward 5	1,172	8.8
Ward 6	1,213	13.3
Ward 7	256	2.6
Ward 8	1,020	9.9
Ward 9	599	2.9
Ward 10	730	6.0
Ward 11	1,066	7.4
Ward 12	870	3.9
OKLAHOMA.		
Oklahoma City	6,546	10.2
Ward 1	293	4.4
Ward 2	283	3.4
Ward 3	879	6.9
Ward 4	944	14.9
Ward 5	3,111	39.5
Ward 6	651	6.9
Ward 7	307	3.7
Ward 8	78	1.6
PENNSYLVANIA.		
Philadelphia	84,459	5.5
Ward 1	208	0.4
Ward 2	689	1.7
Ward 3	1,501	5.8
Ward 4	2,542	11.4
Ward 5	763	4.5
Ward 6	73	1.1

STATE, CITY, AND WARD.	Number.	Per cent of total population.
PENNSYLVANIA—Continued.		
Philadelphia—Contd.		
Ward 7	11,553	42.1
Ward 8	1,839	13.2
Ward 9	844	16.6
Ward 10	593	3.1
Ward 11	99	0.9
Ward 12	249	1.6
Ward 13	670	3.4
Ward 14	3,085	15.8
Ward 15	2,698	5.7
Ward 16	50	0.3
Ward 17	143	0.8
Ward 18	14	......
Ward 19	185	0.4
Ward 20	4,500	9.9
Ward 21	679	1.9
Ward 22	4,799	6.8
Ward 23	868	2.7
Ward 24	3,958	7.3
Ward 25	100	0.2
Ward 26	5,191	9.5
Ward 27	3,195	13.2
Ward 28	1,074	2.2
Ward 29	818	2.7
Ward 30	9,999	34.2
Ward 31	20	......
Ward 32	1,517	3.8
Ward 33	192	0.4
Ward 34	997	2.0
Ward 35	296	2.8
Ward 36	5,840	9.5
Ward 37	608	2.6
Ward 38	1,356	2.8
Ward 39	906	1.7
Ward 40	1,307	3.1
Ward 41	552	3.5
Ward 42	498	2.1
Ward 43	762	1.8
Ward 44	1,463	3.7
Ward 45	181	0.7
Ward 46	1,105	2.9
Ward 47	3,880	12.9
Pittsburgh	25,623	4.8
Ward 1	166	1.4
Ward 2	330	2.3
Ward 3	4,608	17.4
Ward 4	703	2.8
Ward 5	6,146	25.1
Ward 6	1,644	6.3
Ward 7	768	5.8
Ward 8	618	3.4
Ward 9	272	1.5
Ward 10	1,083	5.1
Ward 11	1,043	6.1
Ward 12	2,219	9.9
Ward 13	973	4.0
Ward 14	369	2.8
Ward 15	142	0.7
Ward 16	37	0.2
Ward 17	177	0.7
Ward 18	498	2.8
Ward 19	294	1.3
Ward 20	272	1.5
Ward 21	569	2.5
Ward 22	582	3.7
Ward 23	286	1.3
Ward 24	55	0.3
Ward 25	984	6.1
Ward 26	356	2.3
Ward 27	429	1.8
RHODE ISLAND.		
Providence	5,316	2.4
Ward 1	1,652	7.9
Ward 2	540	2.8
Ward 3	229	0.8
Ward 4	634	3.2
Ward 5	145	0.7

STATE, CITY, AND WARD.	Number.	Per cent of total population.
RHODE ISLAND—Continued.		
Providence—Contd.		
Ward 6	355	1.6
Ward 7	1,308	7.2
Ward 8	16	......
Ward 9	418	1.5
Ward 10	19	......
SOUTH CAROLINA.		
Charleston	31,056	52.8
Ward 1	1,553	52.8
Ward 2	709	30.5
Ward 3	1,568	40.7
Ward 4	2,937	57.0
Ward 5	2,241	45.2
Ward 6	1,436	34.2
Ward 7	2,719	60.5
Ward 8	2,689	55.0
Ward 9	2,144	45.7
Ward 10	3,376	52.8
Ward 11	5,966	60.8
Ward 12	3,718	72.3
TENNESSEE.		
Memphis	52,441	40.0
Ward 1	1,797	46.0
Ward 2	491	16.0
Ward 3	260	9.5
Ward 4	328	13.9
Ward 5	4,134	54.8
Ward 6	1,401	32.2
Ward 7	3,626	47.2
Ward 8	2,004	32.6
Ward 9	3,117	43.1
Ward 10	2,753	56.6
Ward 11	4,628	68.3
Ward 12	1,605	48.7
Ward 13	2,692	34.1
Ward 14	2,167	57.2
Ward 15	1,223	29.6
Ward 16	533	16.1
Ward 17	1,088	19.3
Ward 18	2,514	41.1
Ward 19	3,773	47.8
Ward 20	378	24.9
Ward 21	2,213	55.7
Ward 22	1,258	47.0
Ward 23	1,126	32.5
Ward 24	3,615	64.6
Ward 25	1,741	25.4
Ward 26	977	32.8
Ward 27	654	18.3
Ward 28	69	4.5
Ward 29	276	22.3
Nashville	36,523	33.1
Ward 1	599	12.1
Ward 2	873	10.9
Ward 3	4,243	70.8
Ward 4	2,963	72.1
Ward 5	336	30.4
Ward 6	566	17.5
Ward 7	737	18.5
Ward 8	2,263	52.6
Ward 9	2,387	39.5
Ward 10	587	15.4
Ward 11	1,046	34.3
Ward 12	1,546	58.9
Ward 13	1,882	36.2
Ward 14	3,276	62.3
Ward 15	1,681	30.2
Ward 16	3,206	53.6
Ward 17	817	18.9
Ward 18	837	17.6
Ward 19	2,377	43.5
Ward 20	898	16.1
Ward 21	325	9.4

STATE, CITIY, AND WARD.	Number.	Per cent of total population.
TENNESSEE—Contd.		
Nashville—Contd.		
Ward 22	587	23.1
Ward 23	96	3.8
Ward 24	1,099	35.3
Ward 25	1,296	24.0
TEXAS.		
Dallas	18,024	19.6
Ward 1	1,263	27.3
Ward 2	912	19.4
Ward 3	5,413	36.7
Ward 4	1,421	20.8
Ward 5	2,903	30.5
Ward 6	2,471	15.7
Ward 7	1,458	13.4
Ward 8	785	7.3
Ward 9	1,189	11.7
Ward 10	209	4.9
Fort Worth	13,280	18.1
Ward 1	1,358	33.1
Ward 2	884	15.1
Ward 3	3,492	45.6
Ward 4	773	13.7
Ward 5	799	13.6
Ward 6	1,124	16.5
Ward 7	1,945	23.6
Ward 8	807	10.4
Ward 9	565	13.4
Ward 10	57	4.5
Ward 11	1,185	17.3
Ward 12	254	4.4
Ward 13	37	1.1
Houston	23,929	30.4
Ward 1	1,390	20.0
Ward 2	2,335	30.8
Ward 3	7,662	31.0
Ward 4	6,366	38.0
Ward 5	4,967	29.5
Ward 6	1,209	20.3
San Antonio	10,716	11.1
Ward 1	227	2.2
Ward 2	1,052	7.1
Ward 3	1,495	12.7
Ward 4	1,335	8.1
Ward 5	931	12.0
Ward 6	3,013	20.2
Ward 7	2,513	17.0
Ward 8	150	2.6
VIRGINIA.		
Norfolk	25,039	37.1
Ward 1	1,577	21.2
Ward 2	4,316	49.8
Ward 3	2,298	34.7
Ward 4	12,770	92.6
Ward 5	43	0.5
Ward 6	835	7.6
Ward 7	53	1.3
Ward 8	3,147	40.9
Richmond	46,733	36.6
Clay ward	3,287	14.6
Henry ward	9,413	62.8
Jefferson ward	2,779	17.2
Lee ward	7,454	45.7
Madison ward	6,399	43.7
Marshall ward	6,424	35.6
Monroe ward	7,814	53.6
Washington ward	3,163	30.5

THE COUNTY AS A UNIT AREA OF COMPILATION.

The county areas, which are the units of compilation in the present chapter, embrace, as subdivisions of the states, in the aggregate, the entire area of the states, including urban communities as well as country districts.

The population of a county may be largely or entirely urban, or, on the other hand, largely or entirely rural in character. It may be primarily industrial or commercial, or primarily agricultural; and the character of its industry, commerce or agriculture, may differ materially from that of other counties in the same state, or in other states. Generally it is true of the county population, as of the state population, that it is partly urban and partly rural, partly industrial or commercial, and partly agricultural.

These characteristics affect variously the number and increase of county populations. A county, for example, in which a large city is located, may be attracting population from neighboring counties and may show in consequence a rapid increase in population, while the populations of the neighboring counties themselves are, on the other hand, reduced, or at least prevented from increasing normally. Within any given county all of the increase may be localized in one or two urban cummunities, while in an adjoining county the increase may be distributed throughout the entire area.

As regards the diversity of their characteristics the counties resemble in miniature the states. The areas of certain counties, however, exceed the areas of some states, and there are a number of urban counties of comparatively small area, each of whose populations exceed the population of several states combined. Besides the state of New York, for example, there were in 1910 only seven states which reported populations greater than that reported by the single county of New York, whose population in fact exceeded the combined population of the eight states constituting the Mountain division, and there were in New York state alone 20 other counties whose populations severally exceeded that of the state of Nevada.

Compilations which deal with county aggregates of population do not distinguish the urban from the rural elements, but they do determine by relatively small areas the geographic distribution of the population within the several states. As regards the Negro population, this distribution, taken in conjunction with the corresponding distribution of the white population, is a fact of considerable interest, especially when conditions obtaining in one census year are compared with those obtaining in a subsequent year, to determine to what extent, if at all, the Negro population is massing in certain areas, and is diffusing itself throughout other areas.

By a composition of county areas, independently of state boundaries, it is possible to determine for the Negro population, the areas of high density, and those of rapid or slow increase or decrease. These composed areas are defined in the following tables, and are developed graphically upon several maps.

CLASSIFICATION OF COUNTIES BY NEGRO POPULATION: 1910.

The aggregate number of counties in the United States in 1910 was 2,953, of which 1,351 were in the South, 1,265 in the North, and 337 in the West.

Negro population was reported from 2,843 of these counties, the number reporting no Negro population being 110, of which 32 were in the South and 78 in the North and West. Of the 32 southern counties which reported no Negro population, 28 were in Texas, 2 in Oklahoma, 1 in Arkansas, and 1 in North Carolina. Outside of Texas, therefore, there were in the South only 4 counties which reported no Negro population in 1910. The average Negro population per county in the South was 6,476, and the average white population 15,209; the corresponding averages for the North were 812 Negroes and 43,194 whites, and for the West 150 Negroes and 19,419 whites. There was, however, in every section of the country a wide range of variation in the Negro population of counties, as is shown in Table 1, in which the counties are classified with reference to their Negro population in 1910.

The District of Columbia is classified in Table 1 and in other county tables as a county, and its Negro population of 94,446 exceeded that of any other county. Shelby County, Tenn., in which is located the city of Memphis, reported the second largest Negro population, 91,719, and Jefferson County, Ala., which includes Birmingham city, the third largest, 90,617. Of the 2,843 counties reporting Negroes in 1910, 1,088 reported in each case fewer than 100. The Negro population in 1910 of the 2,843 counties reporting Negroes, is given in General Table III which presents, by counties, general statistics relating to number, color, sex, males 21 years of age and over, illiteracy, and school attendance, for the Negro population of all states, Northern and Western as well as Southern.

It will be apparent from Table 1 that the Negro populations (as well as the total populations) of many counties exceeded the Negro populations of a number of states. There were, for example, 53 counties which reported Negro populations in excess of 25,000, and 23 states whose Negro populations were less than 25,000. The aggregate Negro population of these 53 counties was 2,203,951, or nearly one-fourth of the total Negro population of the country. They reported a population greater than the aggregate Negro population of the 32 Northern and Western states, combined with that of 6 Southern states—Florida, Kentucky, Maryland, Oklahoma, West Virginia, and Delaware—and the District of Columbia.

COUNTIES CLASSIFIED ACCORDING TO NEGRO POPULATION, BY SECTIONS AND SOUTHERN DIVISIONS: 1910.

Table 1				NUMBER OF COUNTIES: 1910.											
				Reporting Negro population—											
SECTION AND DIVISION.	Total.	Report-ing no Negro popula-tion.	Total.	Under 1,000.				1,000 or more.							
				Total.	Under 100.	100 to 500.	500 to 1,000.	Total.	1,000 to 5,000.	5,000 to 10,000.	10,000 to 25,000.	25,000 to 50,000.	50,000 to 75,000.	75,000 to 100,000.
United States	2,953	110	2,843	1,735	1,088	446	201	1,108	494	302	259	43	4	6
The South	1,351	32	1,319	391	152	133	106	928	355	277	248	40	3	5
South Atlantic	534	1	533	92	19	44	29	441	157	144	120	16	2	2
East South Central	361		361	103	21	41	41	258	109	59	69	18	1	2
West South Central	456	31	425	196	112	48	36	229	89	74	59	6		1
The North	1,265	62	1,203	1,033	684	260	89	170	131	23	11	3	1	1
The West	337	16	321	311	252	53	6	10	8	2				

Of the 1,602 northern and western counties, only 180 reported Negro populations of 1,000 or more, the Negro population in the case of 936 of these counties being less than 100.

Statistics for individual southern counties, showing the Negro population in each of the four years, 1910, 1900, 1890, and 1880; the decennial increase in each of the three decades 1880–1910; the percentage Negro, at each of the four censuses noted; the number of Negroes to 1,000 whites in the population, in 1910; the area of the county; and the Negro population per square mile in 1910—will be found in General Table II. The statistics given in the following sections of this chapter relate generally to county areas and populations grouped with reference to the number and increase of the Negro population as shown in this county table.

AREA OF RELATIVELY HIGH DENSITY: 1910.

A glance at accompanying Map I will reveal an area of relatively high density of Negro population, extending south from New York City along the Atlantic seaboard, broadening to the southward, through portions of New Jersey, Pennsylvania, Delaware, Maryland, Virginia, North Carolina, and South Carolina, and continuing westward from South Carolina through central Georgia, Alabama, and Mississippi to the Mississippi River, where it expands north along the Mississippi River, into southwestern Tennessee, and south into Louisiana.

Even within this belt, however, the Negro population does not in itself constitute a population of high density; nor is the region generally one of high density of total population, Negro and white, as compared with the density of population in some other sections of the country. In portions of the belt which have been indicated the density of the Negro population, figured by counties, ranges as low as 10 and even 5 or less per square mile. The area in which it exceeds on the average 30 per square mile is not, as compared with the total area, very extensive, and is much broken into by areas of lower density.

The average density of population of all classes for the country as a whole in 1910 was 30.9 persons per square mile; for New England, where the population was practically all of it white, it was 105.7, and for the Middle Atlantic states, 193.2. It rose to 418.8 in Massachusetts, and to 508.5 in Rhode Island; and exceeded 100 in eight other states, only two of which were Southern. In the Middle Atlantic states the average density of the rural white population was 55; in the East North Central division, 34.8; in the South Atlantic, 21.9; and in the East South Central, 26.1. In these divisions and states there were of course county areas in which the white population per square mile greatly exceeded the average for the division or state as a whole. In the case of the Negro population the average density for the total Negro population was 15.3 in the South Atlantic division, and 14.8 in the East South Central division. The average density for

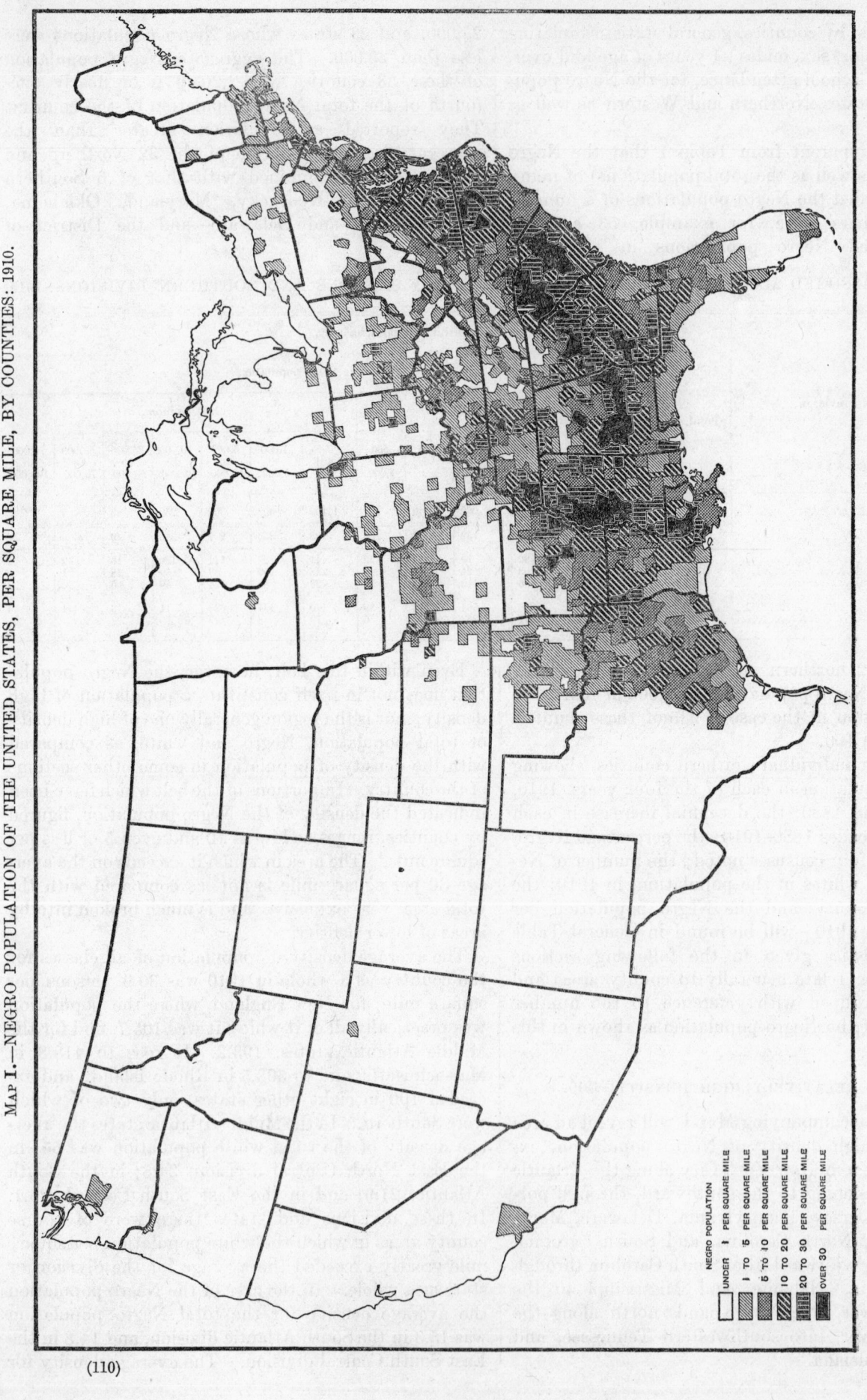

MAP I.—NEGRO POPULATION OF THE UNITED STATES, PER SQUARE MILE, BY COUNTIES: 1910.

NEGRO POPULATION

UNDER 1 PER SQUARE MILE
1 TO 5 PER SQUARE MILE
5 TO 10 PER SQUARE MILE
10 TO 20 PER SQUARE MILE
20 TO 30 PER SQUARE MILE
OVER 30 PER SQUARE MILE

the rural Negro population in each of these divisions was 11.9. In a number of counties which were almost entirely rural, however, as shown by the map, the density of the Negro population exceeded 30. By comparison with general averages for the white population in certain sections of the country the Negro densities appear relatively low, even in the area of maximum Negro population per square mile.

The belt of maximum Negro density of population, it will be noted, lies in the central portions of South Carolina, Georgia, Alabama, and Mississippi; somewhat removed from the Atlantic and Gulf coasts. As compared with this central region, the density of the Negro population in the coast counties, and in the region lying to the north between the Appalachian Mountains and the Ohio River—embracing the states of West Virginia, Kentucky, and Tennessee; the northern portions of Alabama and Georgia; and the western portions of North Carolina, and Virginia—are regions of relatively low density of Negro population.

AREA OF INCREASING, DECREASING, AND STATIONARY NEGRO POPULATION: 1900–1910.

The number of counties in which the Negro population increased, decreased, or remained unchanged during the decade, and the number reporting no Negro population either in 1900 or in 1910, is shown in Table 2. In this table, however, and in other tables where increases or decreases of population are figured by county areas, it has been necessary, on account of changes in county boundaries, to make in certain cases combinations of two or more counties in order to get population figures for identical areas in 1910 and in 1900. These combinations account for the difference between the number of areas for which increases or decreases have been found, and the total number of counties in 1910. The number of counties (2,953) exceeded the number of county areas for which increases or decreases were found (2,751) by 202, which is the reduction in the number of areas resulting from combinations of counties.

It should be noted that the state of Oklahoma, in which there were 76 counties in 1910, is treated as one area, since changes in county boundaries in this state were so general during the decade that accurate comparisons by county areas of 1910 with 1900 were impossible. Except for these combinations, increases and decreases have been figured for single county areas, as defined in 1910.

The Negro population increased during the decade 1900–1910 in 1,433 county or combination-county areas, decreased in 1,229 areas, and remained unchanged in 44 areas, there being 45 areas which reported no Negro population either at the beginning or at the end of the decade. As has been noted in the preceding section, the Negro population of many northern and western counties was very small, and

it is chiefly among such counties that cases of no change in Negro population, or of inconsiderable changes are found. In general, however, it will be apparent that there was in each section of the country a very considerable area in which the Negro population, classified by counties, decreased during this decade.

Table 2	Number of counties, 1910.	NUMBER OF COUNTIES OR COMBINATIONS OF COUNTIES.[1]				
			In which the Negro population—			Having no Negro population in 1910 or in 1900.
SECTION OR DIVISION.		Total.	Increased, 1900– 1910.	Decreased, 1900– 1910.	Did not change, 1900– 1910.	
United States.......	2,953	2,751	1,433	1,229	44	45
The South..............	1,351	1,214	662	533	4	15
South Atlantic..........	534	491	298	192	1	....
East South Central......	361	347	138	208	1	....
West South Central.....	456	376	226	133	2	15
The North..............	1,265	1,236	582	603	29	22
The West..............	337	301	189	93	11	8

[1] In cases where boundaries of counties were changed during the decade 1900–1910, county areas and populations have been combined and computations made for the combined area. The entire state of Oklahoma is classified as a single area. See text.

It is equally true of the total population of the country, all classes combined, that it decreased during the decade 1900–1910 in a large number of counties, including counties in those sections in which the total population is almost entirely white. According to the Thirteenth Census, for example, the total population decreased in 769 out of 2,841 county or combination-county areas.[1] The decreasing counties embraced in the aggregate 472,462 square miles, or approximately one-sixth of the total land area of the country. Of this decreasing area, 338,334 square miles was in the North and West, and 134,128 square miles was in the South, the area of decreasing population in the South constituting 15.3 per cent of the total area, or approximately one-sixth in the South as in the country as a whole. In the South Atlantic division the decreasing area amounted to 36,830 square miles, or 13.7 per cent of the total area of the division; in the East South Central, to 45,339 square miles, or 25.3 per cent; and in the West South Central, to 51,959, or 12.1 per cent. Even in the West, in which section the population increase amounted to 66.8 per cent, the area of counties in which population decreased amounted to 59,379 square miles. In the northern divisions the decreasing area amounted to from 19.2 per cent, or nearly one-fifth, in New England 37.6 per cent; or nearly two-fifths, in the East North Central division.

[1] The number of counties or combinations of counties considered in the Thirteenth Census report exceeds somewhat the number used in this report. The discrepancies are in the Southern states, and are chiefly accounted for by the fact that in the Thirteenth Census report comparison for Oklahoma counties is based upon the census of 1907, whereas in this report comparison for Oklahoma as for other states is with 1900, the state being treated as one area, owing to the general rearrangement of county boundaries. In several other Southern states a few additional combinations have been made in the present report.

Areas of decreasing population were defined in 1910 in 43 of the 48 states. It will be clear from these figures that population decreases over considerable areas are not peculiar to any one class of population.

In Table 3 the number, area, and Negro population of southern counties or combinations of counties are classified in detail with reference to specific percentages of Negro increase or decrease during the decade 1900–1910. The purpose of these classifications is to determine for the South as a whole the area of rapid, of average, and of slow increase; of relatively stationary population, and of slow, and of relatively rapid decrease. These areas are represented also by hachures on Map II. Counties or combinations of counties having a Negro population of less than 100 at each census are not classified in Table 3 according to percentage increase. There were 143 such county units, with an aggregate area of 136,973 square miles, or 15.6 per cent of the total area of the South.

COUNTY AREAS AND NEGRO POPULATIONS CLASSIFIED ACCORDING TO RATES OF NEGRO INCREASE OR DECREASE, FOR SOUTHERN STATES: 1900–1910.

Table 3

SOUTHERN COUNTIES OR COMBINATIONS [1] OF COUNTIES.

RATE OF INCREASE, 1900–1910.	Number.	Area.		Negro population.						
		Square miles.	Per centage distribution.	Number.		Percentage distribution.		Increase,[2] 1900–1910.	
				1910	1900	1910	1900	Number.	Per cent.
Total, all counties...	1,214	878,326	100.0	8,749,427	7,922,969	100.0	100.0	826,458	10.4
Counties having less than 100 Negroes at each census....................	143	136,973	15.6	2,690	2,775	(2)	(3)	−85	−3.1
Area of increasing Negro population..................................	603	493,058	56.1	6,491,951	5,435,313	74.2	68.6	1,056,638	19.4
Increase above average—									
Increase 18 per cent or more...............................	254	287,685	32.8	2,531,665	1,781,533	28.9	22.5	750,132	42.1
Increase 13 to 18 per cent.................................	82	48,162	5.5	994,647	860,391	11.4	10.9	134,256	15.6
Increase 10.5 to 13 per cent...............................	40	20,561	2.3	352,822	315,894	4.0	4.0	36,928	11.7
Increase below average—									
Increase 8 to 10.5 per cent................................	47	29,050	3.3	669,329	614,958	7.6	7.8	54,371	8.8
Increase 2.5 to 8 per cent.................................	117	72,410	8.2	1,459,576	1,384,180	16.7	17.5	75,396	5.4
Increase 0.0 to 2.5 per cent...............................	63	35,190	4.0	483,912	478,357	5.5	6.0	5,555	1.2
Area of decreasing Negro population.................................	468	248,295	28.3	2,254,786	2,484,881	25.8	31.4	−230,095	−9.3
Decrease 0.0 to 2.5 per cent....................................	56	30,748	3.5	390,999	395,961	4.5	5.0	−4,962	−1.3
Decrease 2.5 to 7.5 per cent...................................	106	61,310	7.0	801,504	843,396	9.2	10.6	−41,892	−5.0
Decrease 7.5 per cent or more.................................	306	156,237	17.8	1,062,283	1,245,524	12.1	15.7	−183,241	−14.7
Area increasing more than the average (10.5 per cent or more)............	376	356,408	40.6	3,879,134	2,957,818	44.3	37.3	921,316	31.1
Area increasing less than the average, or decreasing.....................	695	384,945	43.8	4,867,603	4,962,376	55.6	62.6	−94,773	−1.9
Area of relatively rapid increase (13 per cent or more)...................	336	335,847	38.2	3,526,312	2,641,924	40.3	33.3	884,388	33.5
Area of approximately average increase (8 to 13 per cent)	87	49,611	5.6	1,022,151	930,852	11.7	11.7	91,299	9.8
Area of low increase (less than 8 per cent) or decrease...................	648	355,895	40.5	4,198,274	4,347,418	48.0	54.9	−149,144	−3.4
Area of approximately stationary population (increase or decrease less than 2.5 per cent)...	119	65,938	7.5	874,911	874,318	10.0	11.0	593	0.1
Area decreasing more than 2.5 per cent...............................	412	217,547	24.8	1,863,787	2,088,920	21.3	26.4	−225,133	−10.8

[1] See note to Table 2.   [2] A minus sign (−) denotes decrease.   [3] Less than one-tenth of 1 per cent.

Considering counties having a Negro population in 1910 or in 1900, of at least 100, the Negro population decreased during the decade 1900–1910 in 468 southern counties or combinations of counties, aggregating 248,295 square miles in area. This decreasing area amounted to 28.3 per cent, or more than one-fourth of the total area of the South. As may be seen by reference to the map, this area of decreasing Negro population embraces a very large proportion of the region lying between the Appalachian Mountains and the Ohio River, and specifically of four southern states, namely, Maryland, Virginia, Kentucky, and Tennessee. The areas of the 603 county units in which the Negro population increased aggregated 493,058 square miles, or 56.1 per cent of the total area of the South.

In the decreasing area the Negro population fell off from 2,484,881 in 1900, to 2,254,786 in 1910, the decrease amounting to 230,095, or 9.3 per cent. In 1900, 31.4 per cent, and in 1910, 25.8 per cent of the total Negro population of the South lived in this area.

The increase of the increasing counties aggregated 1,056,638, or 19.4 per cent.

The Negro increase of 10.4 per cent in the South as a whole may be taken as representing the natural increase of this class in the South, less a certain number to cover the effect upon population in 1910, of net migration during the decade to the North and West. Making due allowance for variation in the rate of natural increase from county to county, it may fairly be assumed that, in general, counties in which the Negro population increased at a rate above 10.4 per cent, increased in part by a net immigration of Negroes from other counties; and that counties in which the Negro increase was less than 10.4 per cent and those in which the Negro population decreased, lost population during the decade by net emigration to other counties—not necessarily, of course, to other southern counties. The area described in Table 3 as the "area increasing more than the average" may, therefore, be fairly characterized as being the area gaining by a migratory assembling or concentration of Negro population within the South, and the area described as the "area increasing less than the average, or decreasing," as the area losing by net emigration to other counties in the South or to other sections of the country.

Counties in which the Negro population increased at a rate above the average for the southern Negro population as a whole, aggregated 356,408 square miles, or 40.6 per cent of the total area of the South.

Within this area the Negro population increased by 921,316, or 31.1 per cent. The Negro increase in these counties, constituting approximately two-fifths of the total area of the South, thus exceeded the total Negro increase in the South as a whole by 94,858, which is the net decrease of the Negro population in the "area increasing less than the average, or decreasing."

MAP II.—PERCENTAGE INCREASE OR DECREASE OF THE NEGRO POPULATION, BY COUNTY AREAS FOR SOUTHERN STATES (EXCLUSIVE OF OKLAHOMA): 1910–1900.

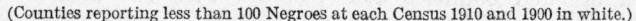

(Counties reporting less than 100 Negroes at each Census 1910 and 1900 in white.)

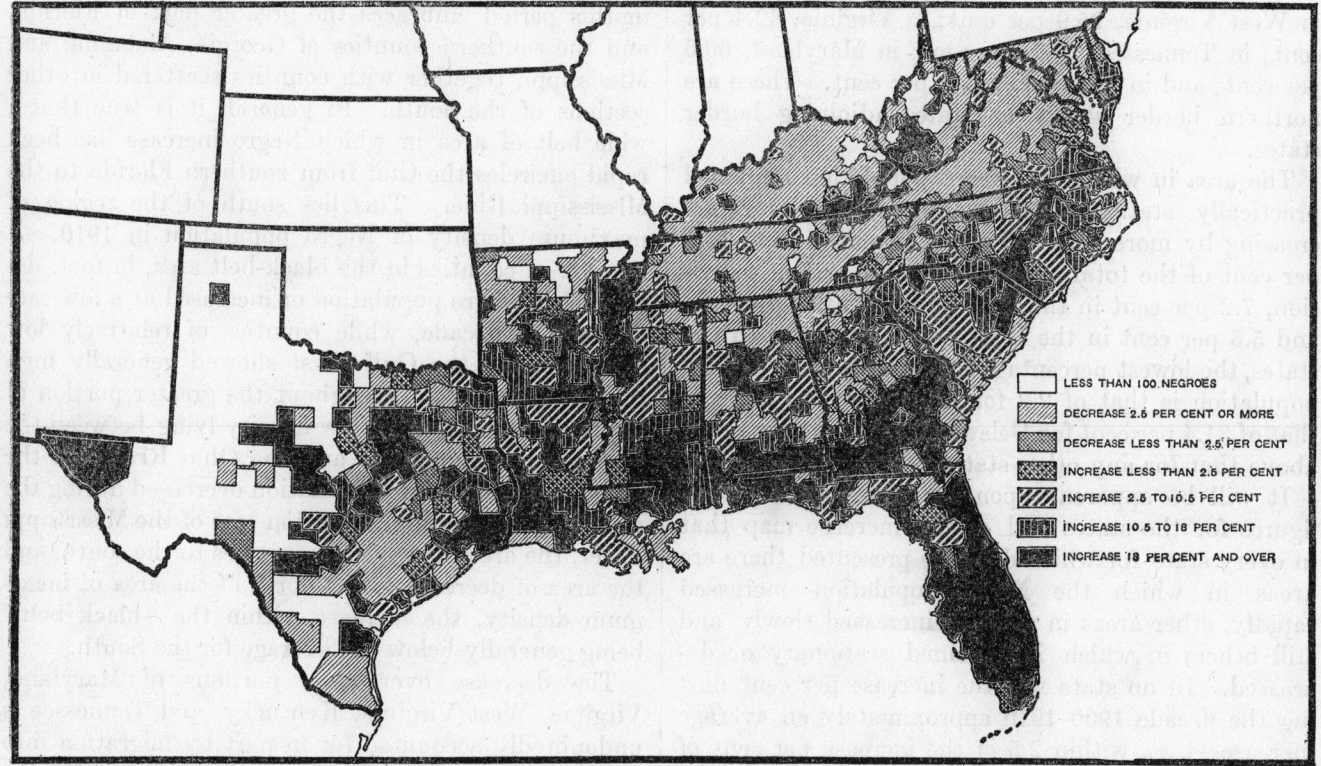

LESS THAN 100 NEGROES
DECREASE 2.5 PER CENT OR MORE
DECREASE LESS THAN 2.5 PER CENT
INCREASE LESS THAN 2.5 PER CENT
INCREASE 2.5 TO 10.5 PER CENT
INCREASE 10.5 TO 18 PER CENT
INCREASE 18 PER CENT AND OVER

In Table 3 an "area of approximately average increase (8 to 13 per cent)" is shown in comparison with the area of "relatively rapid increase (13 per cent or more)," and the "area of low increase (less than 8 per cent) or decrease." The area of relatively rapid increase amounted to 335,847 square miles, or 38.2 per cent of the total area of the South. In this area the Negro increase amounted to 884,388, or 33.5 per cent. In the area of low increase or of decrease, aggregating 355,895 square miles, or 40.5 per cent of the total area, the net decrease of population amounted to 149,144, or 3.4 per cent. The area of "approximately average increase" amounted to 49,611 square miles, and in this area population increased by 91,299 or 9.8 per cent. The area of approximately average increase thus constituted a comparatively small portion (5.6 per cent) of the total area.

Counties in which the Negro increase amounted to 18 per cent or more aggregated 287,685 square miles, or nearly one-third—32.8 per cent—of the total area of the South; and counties in which the decrease amounted to 7.5 per cent or more aggregated 156,237 square miles, or 17.8 per cent of the total area.

Data similar to those given in Table 3 for the South as a whole, are given in Table 4 for each southern division, and southern state.

The Negro population decreased during the decade 1900–1910 in counties aggregating in the South Atlantic division 29.2 per cent of the total area of the division; in the East South Central division, 49.6 per cent; and in the West South Central division, 18.8 per cent.

In Delaware the decreasing area amounted to 53.5 per cent or more than one-half of the total area of the state; in Virginia to 67.6 per cent or more than two-thirds of the total area of the state; in Kentucky, and in Tennessee to 74.2 per cent or nearly three-fourths of the total area in each case; and in Maryland to 81.2 per cent, or more than four-fifths of the total area.

In every Southern state for which county increases are shown in Table 4, except Delaware, there were counties in which the decrease of the Negro population during the decade amounted to 7.5 per cent or more. In Arkansas the area of such counties constituted 20.9 per cent of the total area of the state; in West Virginia, 25.9 per cent; in Virginia, 42.4 per cent; in Tennessee, 53.1 per cent; in Maryland, 60.6 per cent; and in Kentucky, 62.2 per cent. These are northern border states or states adjoining border states.

The area in which the Negro population remained practically stationary, neither increasing nor decreasing by more than 2.5 per cent, constituted 10.9 per cent of the total area in the South Atlantic division, 7.2 per cent in the East South Central division, and 5.5 per cent in the West South Central. In the states, the lowest percentage for the area of stationary population is that of 2.2 for Kentucky; the highest, that of 31.4 per cent for Delaware, which is very much above that for any other state.

It will be apparent upon an examination of the figures for the states and of the increase map that in every state for which data are presented there are areas in which the Negro population increased rapidly, other areas in which it increased slowly, and still others in which it remained stationary or decreased. In no state was the increase per cent during the decade 1900–1910 approximately an average increase—i. e., within 2.5 of the increase per cent of the Negro population in the South as a whole—over more than 14.9 per cent of the total area of the state. In the South as a whole this area of average increase amounted, as has been noted, to only 5.6 per cent of the total area of the South. The increase throughout 94.4 per cent of the area of the South was either distinctly above or distinctly below the average of 10.4, being either above 13 or below 8 per cent. These

variations are, of course, too considerable to be covered by variations in the rates of natural increase from county to county. They indicate clearly a migratory shifting of the Negro population during the decade, within the Southern states and across state borders, as characteristic of Negro population growth generally throughout the South.

A comparison of the density and increase maps will reveal the fact that the area of rapid increase during the decade 1900–1910 does not generally correspond with the area of maximum density of Negro population. The area of most rapid Negro increase in this period embraces the greater part of Florida, and the southern counties of Georgia, Alabama, and Mississippi, together with counties scattered in other sections of the South. In general, it is true that a wide belt of area in which Negro increase has been rapid encircles the Gulf from southern Florida to the Mississippi River. This lies south of the region of maximum density of Negro population in 1910. A number of counties in the black-belt area, in fact, decreased in Negro population or increased at a low rate during the decade, while counties of relatively low density along the Gulf coast showed generally high rates of increase. Throughout the greater portion of the region of relatively low density lying between the Appalachian Mountains and the Ohio River, on the other hand, the Negro population decreased during the decade. Considering the region east of the Mississippi River, the area of rapid increase lies to the south, and the area of decrease to the north of the area of maximum density, the increase within the "black belt" being generally below the average for the South.

The decrease over large portions of Maryland, Virginia, West Virginia, Kentucky, and Tennessee is undoubtedly accounted for in part by migration into northern states, but the population changes for the decade in the South as a whole indicate for the Negro population of this section a decided drift southward. Considerable areas of rapid increase are scattered, also, in the region to the west of the lower Mississippi, in Louisiana, Texas, and Arkansas, indicating a net Negro migration westward across the Mississippi during the decade.

SOUTHERN COUNTIES IN WHICH THE PROPORTION NEGRO IN THE POPULATION WAS 50 TO 75 PER CENT, AND 75 PER CENT AND OVER:
1910, 1900, 1880, AND 1860.

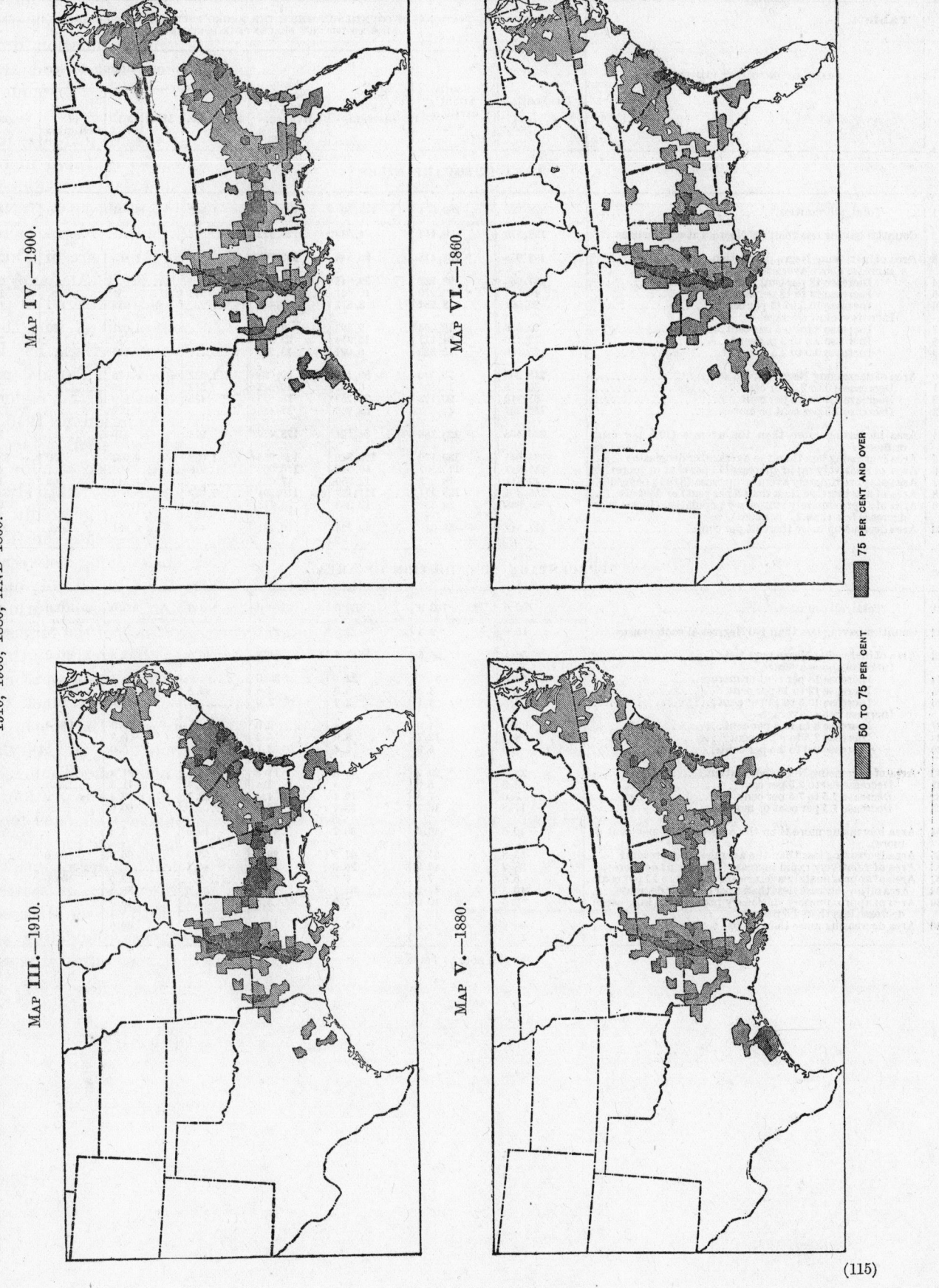

MAP III.—1910.

MAP IV.—1900.

MAP V.—1880.

MAP VI.—1860.

50 TO 75 PER CENT

75 PER CENT AND OVER

AREA OF COUNTIES, AND NUMBER AND INCREASE OF NEGRO POPULATION, BY PERCENTAGE

Table 4 RATE OF INCREASE: 1900–1910.	COUNTIES OR COMBINATIONS[1] OF COUNTIES IN WHICH THE NEGRO POPULATION INCREASED OR DECREASED, 1900 TO 1910, BY PERCENTAGE SPECIFIED.							
	The South.	South Atlantic division.	East South Central division.	West South Central division.	South Atlantic division.			
					Delaware.	Maryland.	District of Columbia.	Virginia.

AREA IN SQUARE MILES.

		The South.	South Atlantic division.	East South Central division.	West South Central division.	Delaware.	Maryland.	District of Columbia.	Virginia.
1	Total, all counties	878,326	269,071	179,509	429,746	1,965	9,941	60	40,262
2	Counties having less than 100 Negroes at each census	136,973	6,113	4,538	126,322				839
3	Area of increasing Negro population	493,058	184,418	85,849	222,791	913	1,865	60	12,216
	Increase above average—								
4	Increase 18 per cent or more	287,685	93,237	39,647	154,801				2,762
5	Increase 13 to 18 per cent	48,162	22,270	10,631	15,261	913			1,801
6	Increase 10.5 to 13 per cent	20,561	8,281	3,873	8,407		319		1,296
	Increase below average—								
7	Increase 8 to 10.5 per cent	29,050	10,696	9,693	8,661		1,021	60	
8	Increase 2.5 to 8 per cent	72,410	34,111	15,914	22,385		30		3,563
9	Increase 0.0 to 2.5 per cent	35,190	15,823	6,091	13,276		495		2,794
10	Area of decreasing Negro population	248,295	78,540	89,122	80,633	1,052	8,076		27,207
11	Decrease 0.0 to 2.5 per cent	30,748	13,509	6,897	10,342	617	1,125		3,606
12	Decrease 2.5 to 7.5 per cent	61,310	20,198	22,259	18,853	435	929		6,511
13	Decrease 7.5 per cent or more	156,237	44,833	59,966	51,438		6,022		17,090
14	Area increasing more than the average (10.5 per cent or more).	356,408	123,788	54,151	178,469	913	319		5,859
15	Area increasing less than the average, or decreasing	384,945	139,170	120,820	124,955	1,052	9,622	60	33,564
16	Area of relatively rapid increase (13 per cent or more)	335,847	115,507	50,278	170,062	913			4,563
17	Area of approximately average increase (8 to 13 per cent)	49,611	18,977	13,566	17,068		1,340	60	1,296
18	Area of low increase (less than 8 per cent) or decrease	355,895	128,474	111,127	116,294	1,052	8,601		33,564
19	Area of approximately stationary population (increase or decrease less than 2.5 per cent).	65,938	29,332	12,988	23,618	617	1,620		6,400
20	Area decreasing more than 2.5 per cent	217,547	65,031	82,225	70,291	435	6,951		23,601

PERCENTAGE DISTRIBUTION OF AREA.

		The South.	South Atlantic division.	East South Central division.	West South Central division.	Delaware.	Maryland.	District of Columbia.	Virginia.
21	Total, all counties	100.0	100.0	100.0	100.0	100.0	100.0	100.0	100.0
22	Counties having less than 100 Negroes at each census	15.6	2.3	2.5	29.4				2.1
23	Area of increasing Negro population	56.1	68.5	47.8	51.8	46.5	18.8	100.0	30.3
	Increase above average—								
24	Increase 18 per cent or more	32.8	34.7	22.1	36.0				6.9
25	Increase 13 to 18 per cent	5.5	8.3	5.9	3.6	46.5			4.5
26	Increase 10.5 to 13 per cent	2.3	3.1	2.2	2.0		3.2		3.2
	Increase below average—								
27	Increase 8 to 10.5 per cent	3.3	4.0	5.4	2.0		10.3	100.0	
28	Increase 2.5 to 8 per cent	8.2	12.7	8.9	5.2		0.3		8.8
29	Increase 0.0 to 2.5 per cent	4.0	5.9	3.4	3.1		5.0		6.9
30	Area of decreasing Negro population	28.3	29.2	49.6	18.8	53.5	81.2		67.6
31	Decrease 0.0 to 2.5 per cent	3.5	5.0	3.8	2.4	31.4	11.3		9.0
32	Decrease 2.5 to 7.5 per cent	7.0	7.5	12.4	4.4	22.1	9.3		16.2
33	Decrease 7.5 per cent or more	17.8	16.7	33.4	12.0		60.6		42.4
34	Area increasing more than the average (10.5 per cent or more).	40.6	46.0	30.2	41.5	46.5	3.2		14.6
35	Area increasing less than the average, or decreasing	43.8	51.7	67.3	29.1	53.5	96.8	100.0	83.4
36	Area of relatively rapid increase (13 per cent or more)	38.2	42.9	28.0	39.6	46.5			11.3
37	Area of approximately average increase (8 to 13 per cent)	5.6	7.1	7.6	4.0		13.5	100.0	3.2
38	Area of low increase (less than 8 per cent), or decrease	40.5	47.7	61.9	27.1	53.5	86.5		83.4
39	Area of approximately stationary population (increase or decrease less than 2.5 per cent).	7.5	10.9	7.2	5.5	31.4	16.3		15.9
40	Area decreasing more than 2.5 per cent	24.8	24.2	45.8	16.4	22.1	69.9		58.6

[1] See note to Table 2.

INCREASE OF COUNTY POPULATION, 1900 TO 1910, BY BY SOUTHERN DIVISIONS AND STATES.

COUNTIES OR COMBINATIONS[1] OF COUNTIES IN WHICH THE NEGRO POPULATION INCREASED OR DECREASED, 1900 TO 1910, BY PERCENTAGE SPECIFIED.

	South Atlantic division.				East South Central division.				West South Central division.				
West Virginia.	North Carolina.	South Carolina.	Georgia.	Florida.	Kentucky.	Tennessee.	Alabama.	Mississippi.	Arkansas.	Louisiana.	Oklahoma.	Texas.	

AREA IN SQUARE MILES.

West Virginia.	North Carolina.	South Carolina.	Georgia.	Florida.	Kentucky.	Tennessee.	Alabama.	Mississippi.	Arkansas.	Louisiana.	Oklahoma.	Texas.	
24,022	48,740	30,495	58,725	54,861	40,181	41,687	51,279	46,362	52,525	45,409	69,414	262,398	1
4,355	298	....	621	....	2,732	1,176	630	....	5,961	....	....	120,361	2
11,034	35,883	26,580	44,743	51,124	7,634	9,598	32,151	36,466	31,266	36,228	69,414	85,883	3
6,357	11,276	4,215	26,672	41,955	4,690	1,773	17,776	15,408	14,732	14,680	69,414	55,975	4
994	7,396	5,048	5,153	965	....	933	2,048	7,650	6,526	4,272	....	4,463	5
609	1,131	2,987	1,398	541	731	468	1,519	1,155	1,726	1,919	....	4,762	6
505	3,721	1,563	1,549	2,277	239	2,303	4,678	2,473	1,250	4,727	....	2,684	7
699	9,628	9,964	7,203	3,024	1,239	3,015	5,375	6,285	3,992	7,110	....	11,283	8
1,870	2,731	2,803	2,768	2,362	735	1,106	755	3,495	3,040	3,520	....	6,716	9
8,633	12,559	3,915	13,361	3,737	29,815	30,913	18,498	9,896	15,298	9,181	....	56,154	10
358	2,870	592	3,758	583	163	2,612	2,553	1,569	1,422	1,304	....	7,616	11
2,053	3,440	1,575	4,210	1,045	4,666	6,175	8,245	3,173	2,882	3,788	....	12,183	12
6,222	6,249	1,748	5,393	2,109	24,986	22,126	7,700	5,154	10,994	4,089	....	36,355	13
7,960	19,803	12,250	33,223	43,461	5,421	3,174	21,343	24,213	22,984	20,871	69,414	65,200	14
11,707	28,639	18,245	24,881	11,400	32,028	37,337	29,306	22,149	23,580	24,538	....	76,837	15
7,351	18,672	9,263	31,825	42,920	4,690	2,706	19,824	23,058	21,258	18,952	69,414	60,438	16
1,114	4,852	4,550	2,947	2,818	970	2,771	6,197	3,628	2,976	6,646	....	7,446	17
11,202	24,918	16,682	23,322	9,123	31,789	35,034	24,628	19,676	22,330	19,811	....	74,153	18
2,228	5,601	3,395	6,526	2,945	898	3,718	3,308	5,064	4,462	4,824	....	14,332	19
8,275	9,689	3,323	9,603	3,154	29,652	28,301	15,945	8,327	13,876	7,877	....	48,538	20

PERCENTAGE DISTRIBUTION OF AREA.

West Virginia.	North Carolina.	South Carolina.	Georgia.	Florida.	Kentucky.	Tennessee.	Alabama.	Mississippi.	Arkansas.	Louisiana.	Oklahoma.	Texas.	
100.0	100.0	100.0	100.0	100.0	100.0	100.0	100.0	100.00	100.0	100.00	100.0	100.0	21
18.1	0.6	....	1.1	....	6.8	2.8	1.2	....	11.3	....	....	45.9	22
45.9	73.6	87.2	76.2	93.2	19.0	23.0	62.7	78.7	59.5	79.8	100.0	32.7	23
26.5	23.1	13.8	45.4	76.5	11.7	4.3	34.7	33.2	28.0	32.3	....	21.3	24
4.1	15.2	16.6	8.8	1.8	....	2.2	4.0	16.5	12.4	9.4	....	1.7	25
2.5	2.3	9.8	2.4	1.0	1.8	1.1	3.0	2.5	3.3	4.2	....	1.8	26
2.1	7.6	5.1	2.6	4.2	0.6	5.5	9.1	5.3	2.4	10.4	....	1.0	27
2.9	19.8	32.7	12.3	5.5	3.1	7.2	10.5	13.6	7.6	15.7	....	4.3	28
7.8	5.6	9.2	4.7	4.3	1.8	2.7	1.5	7.5	5.8	7.8	....	2.6	29
35.9	25.8	12.8	22.8	6.8	74.2	74.2	36.1	21.3	29.1	20.2	....	21.4	30
1.5	5.9	1.9	6.4	1.1	0.4	6.3	5.0	3.4	2.7	2.9	....	2.9	31
8.5	7.1	5.2	7.2	1.9	11.6	14.8	16.1	6.8	5.5	8.3	....	4.6	32
25.9	12.8	5.7	9.2	3.8	62.2	53.1	15.0	11.1	20.9	9.0	....	13.9	33
33.1	40.6	40.2	56.6	79.2	13.5	7.6	41.6	52.2	43.8	46.0	100.0	24.8	34
48.7	58.8	59.8	42.4	20.8	79.7	89.6	57.2	47.8	44.9	54.0	....	29.3	35
30.6	38.3	30.4	54.2	78.2	11.7	6.5	38.7	49.7	40.5	41.7	100.0	23.0	36
4.6	10.0	14.9	5.0	5.1	2.4	6.6	12.1	7.8	5.7	14.6	....	2.8	37
46.6	51.1	54.7	39.7	16.6	79.1	84.0	48.0	42.4	42.5	43.6	....	28.3	38
9.3	11.5	11.1	11.1	5.4	2.2	8.9	6.5	10.9	8.5	10.6	....	5.5	39
34.4	19.9	10.9	16.4	5.7	73.8	67.9	31.1	18.0	26.4	17.3	....	18.5	40

AREA OF COUNTIES, AND NUMBER AND INCREASE OF NEGRO POPULATION, CLASSIFIED BY PERCENTAGE

Table 4 / RATE OF INCREASE: 1900–1910.	COUNTIES OR COMBINATIONS[1] OF COUNTIES IN WHICH THE NEGRO POPULATION INCREASED OR DECREASED, 1900 TO 1910, BY PERCENTAGE SPECIFIED.				South Atlantic division.			
	The South.	South Atlantic division.	East South Central division.	West South Central division.	Delaware.	Maryland.	District of Columbia.	Virginia.

NEGRO POPULATION: 1910.

		The South.	South Atlantic division.	East South Central division.	West South Central division.	Delaware.	Maryland.	District of Columbia.	Virginia.
1	Total, all counties	8,749,427	4,112,488	2,652,513	1,984,426	31,181	232,250	94,446	671,096
2	Counties having less than 100 Negroes at each census	2,690	423	596	1,671	....	....	....	11
3	Area of increasing Negro population	6,491,951	3,240,172	1,655,540	1,596,239	7,938	115,472	94,446	376,934
	Increase above average—								
4	Increase 18 per cent or more	2,531,665	1,171,386	623,883	736,396	....	....	....	114,236
5	Increase 13 to 18 per cent	994,647	482,847	193,235	318,565	7,938	....	....	34,999
6	Increase 10.5 to 13 per cent	352,822	226,038	48,443	78,341	....	4,787	....	76,949
	Increase below average—								
7	Increase 8 to 10.5 per cent	669,329	275,969	286,478	106,882	....	18,911	94,446	....
8	Increase 2.5 to 8 per cent	1,459,576	798,959	427,147	233,470	....	84,749	....	86,470
9	Increase 0.0 to 2.5 per cent	483,912	284,973	76,354	122,585	....	7,025	....	64,280
10	Area of decreasing Negro population	2,254,786	871,893	996,377	386,516	23,243	116,778	....	294,151
11	Decrease 0.0 to 2.5 per cent	390,999	205,582	105,220	80,197	7,561	23,943	....	48,867
12	Decrease 2.5 to 7.5 per cent	801,504	296,825	392,750	111,929	15,682	13,499	....	100,868
13	Decrease 7.5 per cent or more	1,062,283	369,486	498,407	194,390	....	79,336	....	144,416
14	Area increasing more than the average (10.5 per cent or more)	3,879,134	1,880,271	865,561	1,133,302	7,938	4,787	....	226,184
15	Area increasing less than the average, or decreasing	4,867,603	2,231,794	1,786,356	849,453	23,243	227,463	94,446	444,901
16	Area of relatively rapid increase (13 per cent or more)	3,526,312	1,654,233	817,118	1,054,961	7,938	....	....	149,235
17	Area of approximately average increase (8 to 13 per cent)	1,022,151	502,007	334,921	185,223	....	23,698	94,446	76,949
18	Area of low increase (less than 8 per cent), or decrease	4,198,274	1,955,825	1,499,878	742,571	23,243	208,552	....	444,901
19	Area of approximately stationary population (increase or decrease less than 2.5 per cent)	874,911	490,555	181,574	202,782	7,561	30,968	....	113,147
20	Area decreasing more than 2.5 per cent	1,863,787	666,311	891,157	306,319	15,682	92,835	....	245,284

PERCENTAGE DISTRIBUTION OF NEGRO POPULATION: 1910.

		The South.	South Atlantic division.	East South Central division.	West South Central division.	Delaware.	Maryland.	District of Columbia.	Virginia.
21	Total, all counties	100.0	100.0	100.0	100.0	100.0	100.0	100.0	100.0
22	Counties having less than 100 Negroes at each census	(2)	(2)	(2)	0.1	....	....	....	(2)
23	Area of increasing Negro population	74.2	78.8	62.4	80.4	25.5	49.7	100.0	56.2
	Increase above average—								
24	Increase 18 per cent or more	28.9	28.5	23.5	37.1	....	....	....	17.0
25	Increase 13 to 18 per cent	11.4	11.7	7.3	16.1	25.5	....	....	5.2
26	Increase 10.5 to 13 per cent	4.0	5.5	1.8	3.9	....	2.1	....	11.5
	Increase below average—								
27	Increase 8 to 10.5 per cent	7.6	6.7	10.8	5.4	....	8.1	100.0	....
28	Increase 2.5 to 8 per cent	16.7	19.4	16.1	11.8	....	36.5	....	12.9
29	Increase 0.0 to 2.5 per cent	5.5	6.9	2.9	6.2	....	3.0	....	9.6
30	Area of decreasing Negro population	25.8	21.2	37.6	19.5	74.5	50.3	....	43.8
31	Decrease 0.0 to 2.5 per cent	4.5	5.0	4.0	4.0	24.2	10.3	....	7.3
32	Decrease 2.5 to 7.5 per cent	9.2	7.2	14.8	5.6	50.3	5.8	....	15.0
33	Decrease 7.5 per cent or more	12.1	9.0	18.8	9.8	....	34.2	....	21.5
34	Area increasing more than the average (10.5 per cent or more)	44.3	45.7	32.6	57.1	25.5	2.1	....	33.7
35	Area increasing less than the average, or decreasing	55.6	54.3	67.3	42.8	74.5	97.9	100.0	66.3
36	Area of relatively rapid increase (13 per cent or more)	40.3	40.2	30.8	53.2	25.5	....	....	22.2
37	Area of approximately average increase (8 to 13 per cent)	11.7	12.2	12.6	9.3	....	10.2	100.0	11.5
38	Area of low increase (less than 8 per cent), or decrease	48.0	47.6	56.5	37.4	74.5	89.8	....	66.3
39	Area of approximately stationary population (increase or decrease less than 2.5 per cent)	10.0	11.9	6.8	10.2	24.2	13.3	....	16.9
40	Area decreasing more than 2.5 per cent	21.3	16.2	33.6	15.4	50.3	40.0	....	36.5

[1] See note to Table 2.

INCREASE OF COUNTY POPULATION, 1900 TO 1910, BY SOUTHERN DIVISIONS AND STATES—Continued.

COUNTIES OR COMBINATIONS[1] OF COUNTIES IN WHICH THE NEGRO POPULATION INCREASED OR DECREASED, 1900 TO 1910, BY PERCENTAGE SPECIFIED.

NEGRO POPULATION: 1910.

South Atlantic division.					East South Central division.				West South Central division.				
West Virginia.	North Carolina.	South Carolina.	Georgia.	Florida.	Kentucky.	Tennessee.	Alabama.	Mississippi.	Arkansas.	Louisiana.	Oklahoma.	Texas.	
64,173	697,843	835,843	1,176,987	308,669	261,656	473,088	908,282	1,009,487	442,891	713,874	137,612	690,049	1
326	....	....	86	....	355	187	54	....	257	....	....	1,414	2
54,217	596,110	693,537	1,022,978	278,540	76,022	241,311	574,638	763,569	417,933	579,655	137,612	461,039	3
44,798	217,824	103,268	506,521	184,739	14,073	32,655	272,785	304,370	264,873	94,072	137,612	239,839	4
1,930	138,163	164,617	120,946	14,254	....	1,583	51,849	139,803	92,124	196,615	....	29,826	5
1,494	16,305	87,473	36,543	2,487	3,667	819	19,701	24,256	6,704	43,180	....	28,457	6
1,510	42,218	35,286	61,669	21,929	7,934	99,600	102,648	76,296	9,626	67,761	....	29,495	7
132	149,729	235,698	211,984	30,197	48,906	105,177	109,390	163,674	26,255	118,128	....	89,087	8
4,353	31,871	67,195	85,315	24,934	1,442	1,477	18,265	55,170	18,351	59,899	....	44,335	9
9,630	101,733	142,306	153,923	30,129	185,279	231,590	333,590	245,918	24,701	134,219	....	227,596	10
294	37,914	19,140	65,608	2,255	3,228	23,899	45,411	32,682	5,808	29,499	....	44,890	11
2,274	37,217	80,680	44,252	2,353	50,640	75,787	183,966	82,357	11,363	26,613	....	73,953	12
7,062	26,602	42,486	44,063	25,521	131,411	131,904	104,213	130,879	7,530	78,107	....	108,753	13
48,222	372,292	355,358	664,010	201,480	17,740	35,057	344,335	468,429	363,701	333,867	137,612	298,122	14
15,625	325,551	480,485	512,891	107,189	243,561	437,844	563,893	541,058	78,933	380,007	....	390,513	15
46,728	355,987	267,885	627,467	198,993	14,073	34,238	324,634	444,173	356,997	290,687	137,612	269,665	16
3,004	58,523	122,759	98,212	24,416	11,601	100,419	122,349	100,552	16,330	110,941	....	57,952	17
14,115	283,333	445,199	451,222	85,260	235,627	338,244	461,245	464,762	69,307	312,246	....	361,018	18
4,647	69,785	86,335	150,923	27,189	4,670	25,376	63,676	87,852	24,159	89,398	....	89,225	19
9,336	63,819	123,166	88,315	27,874	182,051	207,691	288,179	213,236	18,893	104,720	....	182,706	20

PERCENTAGE DISTRIBUTION OF NEGRO POPULATION: 1910.

West Virginia.	North Carolina.	South Carolina.	Georgia.	Florida.	Kentucky.	Tennessee.	Alabama.	Mississippi.	Arkansas.	Louisiana.	Oklahoma.	Texas.	
100.0	100.0	100.0	100.0	100.0	100.0	100.0	100.0	100.0	100.0	100.0	100.0	100.0	21
0.5	....	....	(²)	....	0.1	(²)	(²)	....	0.1	....	....	0.2	22
84.5	85.4	83.0	86.9	90.2	29.1	51.0	63.3	75.6	94.4	81.2	100.0	66.8	23
69.8	31.2	12.4	43.0	59.9	5.4	6.9	30.0	30.2	59.8	13.2	100.0	34.8	24
3.0	19.8	19.7	10.3	4.6	....	0.3	5.7	13.8	20.8	27.5	....	4.3	25
2.3	2.3	10.5	3.1	0.8	1.4	0.2	2.2	2.4	1.5	6.0	....	4.1	26
2.4	6.0	4.2	5.2	7.1	3.0	21.1	11.3	7.6	2.2	9.5	....	4.3	27
0.2	21.5	28.2	18.0	9.8	18.7	22.2	12.0	16.2	5.7	16.5	....	12.9	28
6.8	4.6	8.0	7.2	8.1	0.6	0.3	2.0	5.5	4.1	8.4	....	6.4	29
15.0	14.6	17.0	13.1	9.8	70.8	49.0	36.7	24.4	5.6	18.8	....	33.0	30
0.5	5.4	2.3	5.6	0.7	1.2	5.1	5.0	3.2	1.3	4.1	....	6.5	31
3.5	5.3	9.7	3.8	0.8	19.4	16.0	20.3	8.2	2.6	3.7	....	10.7	32
11.0	3.8	5.1	3.7	8.3	50.2	27.9	11.5	13.0	1.7	10.9	....	15.8	33
75.1	53.3	42.5	56.4	65.3	6.8	7.4	37.9	46.4	82.1	46.8	100.0	43.2	34
24.3	46.7	57.5	43.6	34.7	93.1	92.6	62.1	53.6	17.8	53.2	....	56.6	35
72.8	51.0	32.0	53.3	64.5	5.4	7.2	35.7	44.0	80.6	40.7	100.0	39.1	36
4.7	8.4	14.7	8.3	7.9	4.4	21.2	13.5	10.0	3.7	15.5	....	8.4	37
22.0	40.6	53.3	38.3	27.6	90.1	71.5	50.8	46.0	15.6	43.7	....	52.3	38
7.2	10.0	10.3	12.8	8.8	1.8	5.4	7.0	8.7	5.5	12.5	....	12.9	39
14.5	9.1	14.7	7.5	9.0	69.6	43.9	31.7	21.1	4.3	14.7	....	26.5	40

[2] Less than one-tenth of 1 per cent.

AREA OF COUNTIES, AND NUMBER AND INCREASE OF THE NEGRO POPULATION, CLASSIFIED BY PERCENTAGE

Table 4	CPUNTIES OR COMBINATIONS[1] OF COUNTIES IN WHICH THE NEGRO POPULATION INCREASED OR DECREASED, 1900 TO 1910, BY PERCENTAGE SPECIFIED.							
RATE OF INCREASE: 1900–1910.	The South.	South Atlantic division.	East South Central division.	West South Central division.	South Atlantic division.			
					Delaware.	Maryland.	District of Columbia.	Virginia.

NEGRO POPULATION: 1900.

		The South.	South Atlantic division.	East South Central division.	West South Central division.	Delaware.	Maryland.	District of Columbia.	Virginia.
1	Total, all counties	7,922,969	3,729,017	2,499,886	1,694,066	30,697	235,064	86,702	660,722
2	Counties having less than 100 Negroes at each census	2,775	609	578	1,588	....	....	....	5
3	Area of increasing Negro population	5,435,313	2,785,079	1,392,575	1,257,659	6,762	107,812	86,702	339,183
	Increase above average—								
4	Increase 18 per cent or more	1,781,533	873,721	436,007	471,805	....	....	....	94,071
5	Increase 13 to 18 per cent	860,391	417,830	167,450	275,111	6,762	....	....	29,957
6	Increase 10.5 to 13 per cent	315,894	202,364	43,556	69,974	....	4,237	....	69,197
	Increase below average—								
7	Increase 8 to 10.5 per cent	614,958	253,462	263,342	98,154	....	17,446	86,702	....
8	Increase 2.5 to 8 per cent	1,384,180	755,974	406,701	221,505	....	79,258	....	82,703
9	Increase 0.0 to 2.5 per cent	478,357	281,728	75,519	121,110	....	6,871	....	63,255
10	Area of decreasing Negro population	2,484,881	943,329	1,106,733	434,819	23,935	127,252	....	321,534
11	Decrease 0.0 to 2.5 per cent	395,961	208,515	106,499	80,947	7,738	24,160	....	49,765
12	Decrease 2.5 to 7.5 per cent	843,396	313,296	412,223	117,877	16,197	14,128	....	106,565
13	Decrease 7.5 per cent or more	1,245,524	421,518	588,011	235,995	....	88,964	....	165,204
14	Area increasing more than the average (10.5 per cent or more.)	2,957,818	1,493,915	647,013	816,890	6,762	4,237	....	193,225
15	Area increasing less than the average, or decreasing	4,962,376	2,234,493	1,852,295	875,588	23,935	230,827	86,702	467,492
16	Area of relatively rapid increase (13 per cent or more)	2,641,924	1,291,551	603,457	746,916	6,762	....	....	124,028
17	Area of approximately average increase (8 to 13 per cent)	930,852	455,826	306,898	168,128	....	21,683	86,702	69,197
18	Area of low increase (less than 8 per cent), or decrease	4,347,418	1,981,031	1,588,953	777,434	23,935	213,381	....	467,492
19	Area of approximately stationary population (increase or decrease less than 2.5 per cent)	874,318	490,243	182,018	202,057	7,738	31,031	....	113,020
20	Area decreasing more than 2.5 per cent	2,088,920	734,814	1,000,234	353,872	16,197	103,092	....	271,769

PERCENTAGE DISTRIBUTION OF NEGRO POPULATION: 1900.

		The South.	South Atlantic division.	East South Central division.	West South Central division.	Delaware.	Maryland.	District of Columbia.	Virginia.
21	Total, all counties	100.0	100.0	100.0	100.0	100.0	100.0	100.0	100.0
22	Counties having less than 100 Negroes at each census	(2)	(2)	(2)	0.1	....	....	....	(2)
23	Area of increasing Negro population	68.6	74.7	55.7	74.2	22.0	45.9	100.0	51.3
	Increase above average—								
24	Increase 18 per cent or more	22.5	23.4	17.4	27.9	....	....	....	14.2
25	Increase 13 to 18 per cent	10.9	11.2	6.7	16.2	22.0	....	....	4.5
26	Increase 10.5 to 13 per cent	4.0	5.4	1.7	4.1	....	1.8	....	10.5
	Increase below average—								
27	Increase 8 to 10.5 per cent	7.8	6.8	10.5	5.8	....	7.4	100.0	...
28	Increase 2.5 to 8 per cent	17.5	20.3	16.3	13.1	....	33.7	....	12.5
29	Increase 0.0 to 2.5 per cent	6.0	7.6	3.0	7.2	....	2.9	....	9.6
30	Area of decreasing Negro population	31.4	25.3	44.3	25.7	78.0	54.1	....	48.7
31	Decrease 0.0 to 2.5 per cent	5.0	5.6	4.3	4.8	25.2	10.3	....	7.5
32	Decrease 2.5 to 7.5 per cent	10.6	8.4	16.5	7.0	52.8	6.0	....	16.1
33	Decrease 7.5 per cent or more	15.7	11.3	23.5	13.9	....	37.8	....	25.0
34	Area increasing more than the average (10.5 per cent or more.)	37.3	40.1	25.9	48.2	22.0	1.8	....	29.2
35	Area increasing less than the average, or decreasing	62.6	59.9	74.1	51.7	78.0	98.2	100.0	70.8
36	Area of relatively rapid increase (13 per cent or more)	33.3	34.6	24.1	44.1	22.0	....	....	18.8
37	Area of approximately average increase (8 to 13 per cent)	11.7	12.2	12.3	9.9	....	9.2	100.0	10.5
38	Area of low increase (less than 8 per cent), or decrease	54.9	53.1	63.6	45.9	78.0	90.8	....	70.8
39	Area of approximately stationary population (increase or decrease less than 2.5 per cent)	11.0	13.1	7.3	11.9	25.2	13.2	....	17.1
40	Area decreasing more than 2.5 per cent	26.4	19.7	40.0	20.9	52.8	43.9	....	41.1

[1] See note to Table 2.

INCREASE OF COUNTY POPULATION, 1900 TO 1910, BY SOUTHERN DIVISIONS AND STATES—Continued.

COUNTIES OR COMBINATIONS[1] OF COUNTIES IN WHICH THE NEGRO POPULATION INCREASED OR DECREASED, 1900 TO 1910, BY PERCENTAGE SPECIFIED.

South Atlantic division.					East South Central division.				West South Central division.				
West Virginia.	North Carolina.	South Carolina.	Georgia.	Florida.	Kentucky.	Tennessee.	Alabama.	Mississippi.	Arkansas.	Louisiana.	Oklahoma.	Texas.	

NEGRO POPULATION: 1900.

WV	NC	SC	GA	FL	KY	TN	AL	MS	AR	LA	OK	TX	
43,499	624,469	782,321	1,034,813	230,730	284,706	480,243	827,307	907,630	366,856	650,804	55,684	620,722	1
430	26	....	148	....	401	170	7	....	353	....	....	1,235	2
31,296	516,219	627,577	871,660	197,868	69,013	217,852	471,282	634,428	338,481	502,046	55,684	361,448	3
22,477	170,680	83,993	392,982	109,518	10,112	22,792	192,685	210,418	201,120	59,830	55,684	155,171	4
1,685	119,011	142,950	105,189	12,276	....	1,368	44,594	121,488	79,594	169,748	....	25,769	5
1,345	14,580	78,275	32,488	2,242	3,311	729	17,655	21,861	5,949	38,634	....	25,391	6
1,391	38,611	32,346	56,827	20,139	7,283	91,991	93,970	70,098	8,825	62,340	....	26,989	7
123	141,931	223,304	199,715	28,940	46,871	99,507	104,155	156,168	24,838	112,266	....	84,401	8
4,275	31,406	66,709	84,459	24,753	1,436	1,465	18,223	54,395	18,155	59,228	....	43,727	9
11,773	108,224	154,744	163,005	32,862	215,292	262,221	356,018	273,202	28,022	148,758	....	258,039	10
299	38,437	19,372	66,464	2,280	3,282	24,172	46,015	33,030	5,861	29,866	....	45,220	11
2,344	39,648	85,728	46,214	2,472	53,092	79,804	192,292	87,035	12,082	28,118	....	77,677	12
9,130	30,139	49,644	50,327	28,110	158,918	158,245	117,711	153,137	10,079	90,774	....	135,142	13
25,507	304,271	305,218	530,659	124,036	13,423	24,889	254,934	353,767	286,663	268,212	55,684	206,331	14
17,562	320,172	477,103	504,006	106,694	270,882	455,184	572,366	553,863	79,840	382,592	....	413,156	15
24,162	289,691	226,943	498,171	121,794	10,112	24,160	237,279	331,906	280,714	229,578	55,684	180,940	16
2,736	53,191	110,621	89,315	22,381	10,594	92,720	111,625	91,959	14,774	100,974	....	52,380	17
16,171	281,561	444,757	447,179	86,555	263,599	363,193	478,396	483,765	71,015	320,252	....	386,167	18
4,574	69,843	86,081	150,923	27,033	4,718	25,637	64,238	87,425	24,016	89,094	....	88,947	19
11,474	69,787	135,372	96,541	30,582	212,010	238,049	310,003	240,172	22,161	118,892	....	212,819	20

PERCENTAGE DISTRIBUTION OF NEGRO POPULATION: 1900.

WV	NC	SC	GA	FL	KY	TN	AL	MS	AR	LA	OK	TX	
100.0	100.0	100.0	100.0	100.0	100.0	100.0	100.0	100.0	100.0	100.0	100.0	100.0	21
1.0	(2)	....	(2)	....	0.1	(2)	(2)	....	0.1	....	....	0.2	22
71.9	82.7	80.2	84.2	85.8	24.2	45.4	57.0	69.9	92.3	77.1	100.0	58.2	23
51.7	27.3	10.7	38.0	47.5	3.6	4.7	23.3	23.2	54.8	9.2	100.0	25.0	24
3.9	19.1	18.3	10.2	5.3	....	0.3	5.4	13.4	21.7	26.1	....	4.2	25
3.1	2.3	10.0	3.1	1.0	1.2	0.2	2.1	2.4	1.6	5.9	....	4.1	26
3.2	6.2	4.1	5.5	8.7	2.6	19.2	11.4	7.7	2.4	9.6	....	4.3	27
0.3	22.7	28.5	19.3	12.5	16.5	20.7	12.6	17.2	6.8	17.3	....	13.6	28
9.8	5.0	8.5	8.2	10.7	0.5	0.3	2.2	6.0	4.9	9.1	....	7.0	29
27.1	17.3	19.8	15.8	14.2	75.6	54.6	43.0	30.1	7.6	22.9	....	41.6	30
0.7	6.2	2.5	6.4	1.0	1.2	5.0	5.6	3.6	1.6	4.6	....	7.3	31
5.4	6.3	11.0	4.5	1.1	18.6	16.6	23.2	9.6	3.3	4.3	....	12.5	32
21.0	4.8	6.3	4.9	12.2	55.8	33.0	14.2	16.9	2.7	13.9	....	21.8	33
58.6	48.7	39.0	51.3	53.8	4.7	5.2	30.8	39.0	78.1	41.2	100.0	33.2	34
40.4	51.3	61.0	48.7	46.2	95.1	94.8	69.2	61.0	21.8	58.8	....	66.6	35
55.5	46.4	29.0	48.1	52.8	3.6	5.0	28.7	36.6	76.5	35.3	100.0	29.1	36
6.3	8.5	14.1	8.6	9.7	3.7	19.3	13.5	10.1	4.0	15.5	....	8.4	37
37.2	45.1	56.9	43.2	37.5	92.6	75.6	57.8	53.3	19.4	49.2	....	62.2	38
10.5	11.2	11.0	14.6	11.7	1.7	5.3	7.8	9.6	6.5	13.7	....	14.3	39
26.4	11.2	17.3	9.3	13.3	74.5	49.6	37.5	26.5	6.0	18.3	....	34.3	40

[2] Less than one-tenth of 1 per cent.

AREA OF COUNTIES, AND NUMBER AND INCREASE OF THE NEGRO POPULATION, CLASSIFIED BY PERCENTAGE

[A minus sign (−) denotes decrease.]

Table 4 RATE OF INCREASE: 1900–1910.	COUNTIES OR COMBINATIONS[1] OF COUNTIES IN WHICH THE NEGRO POPULATION INCREASED OR DECREASED, 1900 TO 1910, BY PERCENTAGE SPECIFIED.							
					South Atlantic division.			
	The South.	South Atlantic division.	East South Central division.	West South Central division.	Delaware.	Maryland.	District of Columbia.	Virginia.

INCREASE OF NEGRO POPULATION: 1900 TO 1910.

		The South.	South Atlantic division.	East South Central division.	West South Central division.	Delaware.	Maryland.	District of Columbia.	Virginia.
1	Total, all counties	826,458	383,471	152,627	290,360	484	−2,814	7,744	10,374
2	Counties having less than 100 Negroes at each census	−85	−186	18	83				6
3	Area of increasing Negro population	1,056,638	455,093	262,965	338,580	1,176	7,660	7,744	37,751
	Increase above average—								
4	Increase 18 per cent or more	750,132	297,665	187,876	264,591				20,165
5	Increase 13 to 18 per cent	134,256	65,017	25,785	43,454	1,176			5,042
6	Increase 10.5 to 13 per cent	36,928	23,674	4,887	8,367		550		7,752
	Increase below average—								
7	Increase 8 to 10.5 per cent	54,371	22,507	23,136	8,728		1,465	7,744	
8	Increase 2.5 to 8 per cent	75,396	42,985	20,446	11,965		5,491		3,767
9	Increase 0.0 to 2.5 per cent	5,555	3,245	835	1,475		154		1,025
10	Area of decreasing Negro population	−230,095	−71,436	−110,356	−48,303	−692	−10,474		−27,383
11	Decrease 0.0 to 2.5 per cent	−4,962	−2,933	−1,279	−750	−177	−217		−898
12	Decrease 2.5 to 7.5 per cent	−41,892	−16,471	−19,473	−5,948	−515	−629		−5,697
13	Decrease 7.5 per cent or more	−183,241	−52,032	−89,604	−41,605		−9,628		−20,788
14	Area increasing more than the average (10.5 per cent or more).	921,316	386,356	218,548	316,412	1,176	550		32,959
15	Area increasing less than the average, or decreasing	−94,773	−2,699	−65,939	−26,135	−692	−3,364	7,744	−22,591
16	Area of relatively rapid increase (13 per cent or more)	884,388	362,682	213,661	308,045	1,176			25,207
17	Area of approximately average increase (8 to 13 per cent)	91,299	46,181	28,023	17,095		2,015	7,744	7,752
18	Area of low increase (less than 8 per cent), or decrease	−149,144	−25,206	−89,075	−34,863	−692	−4,829		−22,591
19	Area of approximately stationary population (increase or decrease less than 2.5 per cent).	593	312	−444	725	−177	−63		127
20	Area decreasing more than 2.5 per cent	−225,133	−68,503	−109,077	−47,553	−515	−10,257		−26,485

PERCENTAGE INCREASE OF NEGRO POPULATION: 1900 TO 1910.

		The South.	South Atlantic division.	East South Central division.	West South Central division.	Delaware.	Maryland.	District of Columbia.	Virginia.
21	Total, all counties	10.4	10.3	6.1	17.1	1.6	−1.2	8.9	1.6
22	Counties having less than 100 Negroes at each census	−3.1	−30.5	3.1	5.2				(2)
23	Area of increasing Negro population	19.4	16.3	18.9	26.9	17.4	7.1	8.9	11.1
	Increase above average—								
24	Increase 18 per cent or more	42.1	34.1	43.1	56.1				21.4
25	Increase 13 to 18 per cent	15.6	15.6	15.4	15.8	17.4			16.8
26	Increase 10.5 to 13 per cent	11.7	11.7	11.2	12.0		13.0		11.2
	Increase below average—								
27	Increase 8 to 10.5 per cent	8.8	8.9	8.8	8.9		8.4	8.9	
28	Increase 2.5 to 8 per cent	5.4	5.7	5.0	5.4		6.9		4.6
29	Increase 0.0 to 2.5 per cent	1.2	1.2	1.1	1.2		2.2		1.6
30	Area of decreasing Negro population	−9.3	−7.6	−10.0	−11.1	−2.9	−8.2		−8.5
31	Decrease 0.0 to 2.5 per cent	−1.3	−1.4	−1.2	−0.9	−2.3	−0.9		−1.8
32	Decrease 2.5 to 7.5 per cent	−5.0	−5.3	−4.7	−5.0	−3.2	−4.5		−5.3
33	Decrease 7.5 per cent or more	−14.7	−12.3	−15.2	−17.6		−10.8		−12.6
34	Area increasing more than the average (10.5 per cent or more).	31.1	25.9	33.8	38.7	17.4	13.0		17.1
35	Area increasing less than the average, or decreasing	−1.9	−0.1	−3.6	−3.0	−2.9	−1.5	8.9	−4.8
36	Area of relatively rapid increase (13 per cent or more)	33.5	28.1	35.4	41.2	17.4			20.3
37	Area of approximately average increase (8 to 13 per cent)	9.8	10.1	9.1	10.2		9.3	8.9	11.2
38	Area of low increase (less than 8 per cent), or decrease	−3.4	−1.3	−5.6	−4.5	−2.9	−2.3		−4.8
39	Area of approximately stationary population (increase or decrease less than 2.5 per cent).	0.1	0.1	−0.2	0.4	−2.3	−0.2		0.1
40	Area decreasing more than 2.5 per cent	−10.8	−9.3	−10.9	−13.4	−3.2	−9.9		−9.7

[1] See note to Table 2.

INCREASE OF COUNTY POPULATION, 1900 TO 1910, BY SOUTHERN DIVISIONS AND STATES—Continued.

[A minus sign (−) denotes decrease.]

COUNTIES AND COMBINATIONS[1] OF COUNTIES IN WHICH THE NEGRO POPULATION INCREASED OR DECREASED, 1900 TO 1910, BY PERCENTAGE SPECIFIED.

INCREASE OF NEGRO POPULATION: 1900 TO 1910.

West Virginia.	North Carolina.	South Carolina.	Georgia.	Florida.	Kentucky.	Tennessee.	Alabama.	Mississippi.	Arkansas.	Louisiana.	Oklahoma.	Texas.	
20,674	73,374	53,522	142,174	77,939	−23,050	−7,155	80,975	101,857	76,035	63,070	81,928	69,327	1
−104	−26	....	−62	....	−46	17	47	....	−96	....	....	179	2
22,921	79,891	65,960	151,318	80,672	7,009	23,459	103,356	129,141	79,452	77,609	81,928	99,591	3
22,321	47,144	19,275	113,539	75,221	3,961	9,863	80,100	93,952	63,753	34,242	81,928	84,668	4
245	19,152	21,667	15,757	1,973	....	215	7,255	18,315	12,530	26,867	....	4,057	5
149	1,725	9,198	4,055	245	356	90	2,046	2,395	755	4,546	....	3,066	6
119	3,607	2,940	4,842	1,790	651	7,609	8,678	6,198	801	5,421	....	2,506	7
9	7,798	12,394	12,269	1,257	2,035	5,670	5,235	7,506	1,417	5,862	....	4,686	8
78	465	486	856	181	6	12	42	775	196	671	....	608	9
−2,143	−6,491	−12,438	−9,082	−2,733	−30,013	−30,631	−22,428	−27,284	−3,321	−14,539	....	−30,443	10
−5	−523	−232	−856	−25	−54	−273	−604	−348	−53	−367	....	−330	11
−70	−2,431	−5,048	−1,962	−119	−2,452	−4,017	−8,326	−4,678	−719	−1,505	....	−3,724	12
−2,068	−3,537	−7,158	−6,264	−2,589	−27,507	−26,341	−13,498	−22,258	−2,549	−12,667	....	−26,389	13
22,715	68,021	50,140	133,351	77,444	4,317	10,168	89,401	114,662	77,038	65,655	81,928	91,791	14
−1,937	5,379	3,382	8,885	495	−27,321	−17,340	−8,473	−12,805	−907	−2,585	....	−22,643	15
22,566	66,296	40,942	129,296	77,199	3,961	10,078	87,355	112,267	76,283	61,109	81,928	88,725	16
268	5,332	12,138	8,897	2,035	1,007	7,699	10,724	8,593	1,556	9,967	....	5,572	17
−2,056	1,772	442	4,043	−1,295	−27,972	−24,949	−17,151	−19,003	−1,708	−8,006	....	−25,149	18
73	−58	254	....	156	−48	−261	−562	427	143	304	....	278	19
−2,138	−5,968	−12,206	−8,226	−2,708	−29,959	−30,358	−21,824	−26,936	−3,268	−14,172	....	−30,113	20

PERCENTAGE INCREASE OF NEGRO POPULATION: 1900 TO 1910.

West Virginia.	North Carolina.	South Carolina.	Georgia.	Florida.	Kentucky.	Tennessee.	Alabama.	Mississippi.	Arkansas.	Louisiana.	Oklahoma.	Texas.	
47.5	11.7	6.8	13.7	33.8	−8.1	−1.5	9.8	11.2	20.7	9.7	147.1	11.2	21
−24.2	(2)	....	−41.9	....	−11.5	10.0	(2)	....	−27.2	....	....	14.5	22
73.2	15.5	10.5	17.4	40.8	10.2	10.8	21.9	20.4	23.5	15.5	147.1	27.6	23
99.3	27.6	22.9	28.9	68.7	39.2	43.3	41.6	44.7	31.7	57.2	147.1	54.6	24
14.5	16.1	15.2	15.0	16.1	15.8	15.7	16.3	15.1	15.7	15.8	....	15.7	25
11.1	11.8	11.8	12.5	10.9	10.8	12.3	11.6	11.0	12.7	11.8	....	12.1	26
8.6	9.3	9.1	8.5	8.9	8.9	8.3	9.2	8.8	9.1	8.7	....	9.3	27
7.3	5.5	5.6	6.1	4.3	4.3	5.7	5.0	4.8	5.7	5.2	....	5.6	28
1.8	1.5	0.7	1.0	0.7	0.4	0.8	0.2	1.4	1.1	1.1	....	1.4	29
−18.2	−6.0	−8.0	−5.6	−8.3	−13.9	−11.7	−6.3	−10.0	−11.9	−9.8	....	−11.8	30
−1.7	−1.4	−1.2	−1.3	−1.1	−1.6	−1.1	−1.3	−1.1	−0.9	−1.2	....	−0.7	31
−3.0	−6.1	−5.9	−4.2	−4.8	−4.6	−5.0	−4.3	−5.4	−6.0	−5.4	....	−4.8	32
−22.7	−11.7	−14.4	−12.4	−9.2	−17.3	−16.6	−11.5	−14.5	−25.3	−14.0	....	−19.5	33
89.1	22.4	16.4	25.1	62.4	32.2	40.9	35.1	32.4	26.9	24.5	147.1	44.5	34
−11.0	1.7	0.7	1.8	0.5	−10.1	−3.8	−1.5	−2.3	−1.1	−0.7	....	−5.5	35
93.4	22.9	18.0	26.0	63.4	39.2	41.7	36.8	33.8	27.2	26.6	147.1	49.0	36
9.8	10.0	11.0	10.0	9.1	9.5	8.3	9.6	9.3	10.5	9.9	....	10.6	37
−12.7	0.6	0.1	0.9	−1.5	−10.6	−6.9	−3.6	−3.9	−2.4	−2.5	....	−6.5	38
1.6	−0.1	0.3	....	0.6	−1.0	−1.0	−0.9	0.5	0.6	0.3	....	0.3	39
−18.6	−8.6	−9.0	−8.5	−8.9	−14.1	−12.8	−7.0	−11.2	−14.7	−11.9	....	−14.1	40

[2] Per cent not shown where base is less than 100.

PROPORTION NEGRO IN THE POPULATION, BY COUNTIES.

It will be clear from the data presented in preceding sections, that the Negro population, although it is largely massed in the South, is nevertheless widely distributed throughout every section of the country, and that within the South it is so distributed that there are areas of relatively dense, and other areas, much more extensive, of relatively sparse Negro population. It has been shown, also, that in certain regions the Negro population has been increasing rapidly, in other regions slowly, and that in still other regions of great extent in the South, it has been decreasing. The various rates of growth and decrease in the different areas have necessarily modified the geographic distribution of the Negro population in recent decades, and seem to indicate, as has been noted, for the decade 1900–1910, a general drift southward from the central area of greatest density, and depletion of the Negro population over an extensive area lying between the Appalachian Mountains and the Ohio River.

Of the white population, also, as well as of the Negro, it is true that over extensive areas it has increased rapidly, increased slowly, and decreased, and that its geographic distribution has been modified by its various rates of growth and decrease in different areas.

The racial composition of the population resident in these areas has necessarily been affected in varying degrees, by the changes in the geographic distribution of the Negro and white elements in the population which have taken place in recent decades. These changes have been largely in response to local or sectional economic developments, which have induced migratory shiftings of population more or less selective as regards racial elements, within the South and in the country as a whole.

The more rapid increase of the white, as compared with the Negro element, by natural growth and by immigration, during this period has tended to lower the proportion Negro in the population generally throughout the country, but this general decline has been obscured by local variations. In the South the proportion Negro in the population declined from 32.3 per cent in 1900 to 29.8 per cent in 1910, and if the population increase, Negro and white, during the decade had been distributed proportionally to the population of each class, the proportion Negro in the population of each southern community would have shown a decline.

While, however, the proportion Negro has in fact declined over considerable areas in the South, it has coincidently increased over other areas of large extent. Diverse influences have affected the increase of the Negro and white elements in varying degrees locally, and it would be exceedingly difficult to determine by any statistical analysis the single effect of any one tendency, such as, for example, the tendency toward racial agglomeration or segregation, on the one hand,

or on the other hand toward more even diffusion of racial elements. It would not be difficult to devise an index of segregation, and by the employment of such an index to arrive at a statistical conclusion that the Negro and white elements were in some definite degree more or less separated from one another in 1910 than they were in 1900, that these elements had in the aggregate in some degree either drawn apart, or become more evenly diffused with reference to one another during the decade. An accurate statistical measurement of the relative dispersion of the Negro and white elements, would undoubtedly demonstrate that relatively to one another the geographic distribution of these elements had changed during the decade, but such a change might be due to accidental causes, quite independent of any tendency of the population to segregate along racial lines, or of the racial elements in the population to diffuse, and it is certain that any index of segregation would yield very different results, according as it was applied to the population growth and distribution in different sections of the country. The aggregate tendency represented by any statistical summarization would not be a tendency prevailing generally throughout the country, but would be merely an artificial resultant of very uncertain significance.

If the racial elements composing the population of the South had been evenly diffused throughout that section of the country in 1910, the proportion Negro in the population of each county would have been, as it was in the South as a whole, 29.8 per cent. Under this assumption, the proportion white in the population would have been 69.9 per cent, leaving a small fraction of 1 per cent to represent population of other racial character. In fact, however, the proportion Negro in the population of southern counties varied in 1910 from zero to 94.2 per cent, and conversely the proportion white varied from 100 to 5.8 per cent. This wide range of variation from county to county indicates that the geographic distribution of the Negro population in the South differed materially from that of the white population, and that in this sense at least a considerable degree of segregation or separation of Negro and white elements obtained as a present condition.

Statistics showing the proportion Negro by counties do not uncover that segregation of elements which obtains more or less generally within the counties themselves—in urban communities by wards or city blocks, and in rural subdivisions by neighborhoods. No tabulation has been made from census schedules to cover this neighborhood grouping of racial elements, but such a tabulation could not materially increase the significance of the data as regards the relative geographic distribution of these elements, or changes in that distribution, since the disposition of the racial elements within county areas by small neighborhood communities is determined by factors quite independent of those which determine the geographic distribution and drift of these elements in the country as a whole.

It may be remarked that migration northward in recent decades has depleted the Negro population in certain sections of the South and has in consequence accentuated the relative concentration of the Negro element in other sections. A decline in the proportion Negro in any section does not, however, of course necessarily imply emigration of Negroes from that section either to the North or to any other southern community. Such a decline is, on the contrary, entirely consistent with, and is in fact, frequently associated with rapid growth of both Negro and white elements, by natural increase supplemented by immigration. Obviously increase or decrease in the proportion Negro is dependent not upon the increase or decrease of the Negro element alone, but upon the increase or decrease of the Negro and white elements relatively to one another.

In the following sections of this chapter the areas and Negro populations of counties and the Negro-population increases are classified with reference to the proportion Negro in the population, and with reference to changes in this proportion from census to census. The areas within which the proportion Negro in the population is relatively high, and within which it is relatively low, and the areas within which the proportion is increasing and within which it is decreasing are determined. Analysis of these data indicates that the relative increase of the Negro and white elements has been determined locally by diverse factors, which can not be summarized as constituting in the aggregate any simple tendency, either of segregation or of diffusion of racial elements.

THE "BLACK BELT" COUNTIES.

In the four maps on page 115, the geographic distribution of the counties in which the proportion Negro in the population was 50 per cent or more is shown for the four census years 1860, 1880, 1900, and 1910, the counties in which the proportion Negro amounted to 75 per cent or more being also indicated.

It will be apparent upon examination of these maps that the area within which Negroes constituted a majority of the population in 1910 was in general largely coextensive with the corresponding area at each of the earlier censuses. At each census the area embraced a group of counties in eastern Virginia and North Carolina; a belt of counties extending from the South Carolina coast through South Carolina, central Georgia, and Alabama; and a detached area embracing a portion of the lower Mississippi River Valley. The general contour and extent of these areas has shown remarkably little change in a period of 50 years. It may be noted that this area of relatively high proportion Negro in the population corresponds generally with the area of relatively high density of Negro population, and it is the area popularly designated as the "black belt."

The number and area of counties in which the population was half or more Negro are shown in Table 5 for four census years, by divisions and states, together with decennial increases and decreases, and the percentage of total area embraced within these counties.

NUMBER AND AREA OF SOUTHERN COUNTIES IN WHICH THE PROPORTION NEGRO IN THE POPULATION WAS 50 PER CENT OR MORE, BY DIVISIONS AND STATES: 1910, 1900, 1890, AND 1880.

Table 5	COUNTIES IN WHICH THE PROPORTION NEGRO IN THE POPULATION IN THE YEAR SPECIFIED WAS 50 PER CENT OR MORE.																		
	Number of counties.							Area of counties in square miles.											
DIVISION AND STATE.					Increase or decrease.[1]							Increase or decrease.[1]			Percentage of total area of specified section, division, or state.			
	1910	1900	1890	1880	1900–1910	1890–1900	1880–1890	1910	1900	1890	1880	1900–1910	1890–1900	1880–1890	1910	1900	1890	1880
The South	264	286	282	300	−22	4	−18	147,219	166,742	167,230	176,764	−19,523	−488	−9,534	16.8	19.0	19.0	20.2
South Atlantic	156	165	156	168	−9	9	−12	76,584	83,485	80,067	87,093	−6,901	3,418	−7,026	28.5	31.1	29.8	32.4
East South Central	61	63	62	69	−2	1	−7	40,721	42,936	41,960	46,340	−2,215	976	−4,380	22.7	23.9	23.4	25.8
West South Central	47	58	64	63	−11	−6	1	29,914	40,321	45,203	43,331	−10,407	−4,882	1,872	7.0	9.4	10.5	10.2
South Atlantic:																		
Delaware																		
Maryland	1	2	2	3	−1	……	−1	464	673	678	1,070	−209	−5	−392	4.7	6.8	6.9	10.9
District of Columbia																		
Virginia	32	36	39	46	−4	−3	−7	11,375	12,705	12,669	15,293	−1,330	36	−2,624	28.3	31.7	31.6	38.1
West Virginia																		
North Carolina	14	18	16	22	−4	2	−6	6,044	8,453	7,844	12,230	−2,409	609	−4,386	12.4	17.4	16.1	25.2
South Carolina	33	30	26	25	3	4	1	23,316	23,090	23,450	23,710	226	−360	−260	76.5	76.5	77.7	78.6
Georgia	66	67	63	63	−1	4	……	27,418	28,577	26,262	26,460	−1,159	2,315	−198	46.7	48.5	44.5	44.9
Florida	10	12	10	9	−2	2	1	7,967	9,987	9,164	8,330	−2,020	823	834	14.5	18.4	16.9	15.4
East South Central:																		
Kentucky																		
Tennessee	2	3	3	5	−1	……	−2	1,126	1,907	1,928	2,810	−781	−21	−882	2.7	4.6	4.6	6.7
Alabama	21	22	20	24	−1	2	−4	16,678	17,648	16,056	19,160	−970	1,592	−3,104	32.5	34.2	31.2	37.2
Mississippi	38	38	39	40	……	−1	−1	22,917	23,381	23,976	24,370	−464	−595	−394	49.4	50.5	51.7	52.6
West South Central:																		
Arkansas	14	15	15	13	−1	……	2	9,556	10,529	10,385	8,790	−973	144	1,595	18.2	19.8	19.6	16.6
Louisiana	25	31	33	36	−6	−2	−3	15,207	20,058	21,148	22,961	−4,851	−1,090	−1,813	33.5	44.2	46.6	50.6
Oklahoma																		
Texas	8	12	16	14	−4	−4	−2	5,151	9,734	13,670	11,580	−4,583	−3,936	2,090	2.0	3.7	5.2	4.4

[1] Minus sign (−) denotes decrease.

In 1910 Negroes constituted 50 per cent or more of the total population in 264 counties, whose areas aggregated 147,219 square miles. The area of these counties constituted 16.8 per cent, or one-sixth of the total area of the South. In the South Atlantic division the majority-Negro counties constituted 28.5 per cent of the total area, in the East South Central 22.7 per cent, and in the West South Central 7 per cent.

In each of the Southern states except Delaware, West Virginia, Kentucky, and Oklahoma, there were counties in 1910 in which Negroes constituted 50 per cent or more of the population. In each of these states, however, except South Carolina and Mississippi, the number of such counties fell off during the decade 1900–1910—in South Carolina the number increased from 30 in 1900 to 33 in 1910, and in Mississippi it was 38 in each year. In the South as a whole the number of these majority-Negro counties

decreased from 286 to 264, or by 22; the area from 166,742 to 147,219 square miles, or by 19,523 square miles.

The figures for 1890 and the increases and decreases for the two decades, 1880–1890 and 1890–1900, are probably affected by the undercount at the census of 1890, which by understating the Negro population may have reduced the number of counties in which the proportion Negro amounted to 50 per cent or more.

In Table 13 (p. 134) the percentage Negro in the population of each of the 264 counties covered by Table 5 is shown for 1910 and for 1900, and also the number of Negroes per 1,000 whites. The total Negro and white populations of these counties are given by divisions and states for four census years in Table 6, with the percentages which these populations respectively form of the total Negro and white population of the state or division.

NEGRO AND WHITE POPULATION OF COUNTIES IN WHICH THE PROPORTION NEGRO IN THE POPULATION WAS 50 PER CENT OR MORE, BY DIVISIONS AND STATES: 1910, 1900, 1890 AND 1880.

Table 6	COUNTIES IN WHICH THE NEGRO POPULATION CONSTITUTED 50 PER CENT OR MORE OF THE TOTAL POPULATION.															
	Negro population.								White population.							
DIVISION AND STATE.	1910	1900	1890	1880	Percentage of total Negro population of division or state.				1910	1900	1890	1880	Percentage of total white population of division or state.			
					1910	1900	1890	1880					1910	1900	1890	1880
The South	3,932,484	4,057,619	3,555,970	3,392,235	44.9	51.2	52.6	57.0	2,094,964	2,163,731	1,876,611	1,862,669	10.2	13.1	14.2	17.6
South Atlantic	1,988,088	2,006,301	1,790,847	1,790,391	48.3	53.8	54.9	60.9	1,236,542	1,219,672	1,062,175	1,082,551	15.3	18.2	19.0	23.3
East South Central	1,277,080	1,325,226	1,101,348	1,071,915	48.1	53.0	52.0	55.7	498,985	546,196	476,088	513,478	8.7	10.8	11.1	14.0
West South Central	667,316	726,092	663,775	529,929	33.6	42.9	48.2	48.7	359,437	397,863	338,348	266,640	5.3	8.3	10.3	11.9
South Atlantic:																
Delaware																
Maryland	8,572	14,791	13,200	25,234	3.7	6.3	6.1	12.0	7,813	13,094	11,850	20,786	0.7	1.4	1.4	2.9
District of Columbia																
Virginia	271,097	286,733	292,784	366,750	40.4	43.4	46.1	58.1	201,575	202,027	197,553	254,099	14.5	16.9	19.4	28.8
West Virginia																
North Carolina	166,520	198,237	175,255	235,290	23.9	31.7	31.2	44.3	123,841	152,251	120,609	164,799	8.3	12.0	11.4	19.0
South Carolina	699,471	662,991	594,257	533,648	83.7	84.7	86.3	88.3	403,227	342,669	297,562	269,149	59.4	61.4	64.4	68.8
Georgia	735,972	708,765	610,733	541,269	62.5	68.5	71.1	74.6	434,209	423,042	370,291	329,297	30.3	35.8	37.8	40.3
Florida	106,456	134,784	104,618	88,200	34.5	58.4	63.0	69.6	65,877	86,589	64,310	44,421	14.8	29.1	28.6	31.1
East South Central:																
Kentucky																
Tennessee	40,412	123,535	97,674	109,707	8.5	25.7	22.7	27.2	15,742	84,882	67,475	78,526	0.9	5.5	5.0	6.9
Alabama	487,399	505,576	405,941	435,795	53.7	61.1	59.8	72.6	198,572	205,486	157,755	199,004	16.2	20.5	18.9	30.1
Mississippi	749,269	696,115	597,733	526,413	74.2	76.7	80.5	81.0	284,671	255,828	250,858	235,948	36.2	39.9	46.0	49.2
West South Central:																
Arkansas	226,145	187,866	161,188	97,559	51.1	51.2	52.1	46.3	104,389	90,336	79,681	49,277	9.2	9.6	9.7	8.3
Louisiana	356,707	418,148	376,273	334,550	50.0	64.3	67.3	69.2	194,319	220,339	176,349	156,653	20.6	30.2	31.6	34.4
Oklahoma																
Texas	84,464	120,078	126,314	97,820	12.2	19.3	25.9	24.9	60,729	87,188	82,318	60,710	1.9	3.6	4.7	5.1

The Negro population living in counties in which Negroes constituted a majority of the population in 1910 amounted to 3,932,484, or 44.9 per cent of the total Negro population of the South. In 1900 the population of majority Negro counties amounted to 4,057,619, or 51.2 per cent of the Negro population of the South; in 1890 to 3,555,970, or 52.6 per cent; and in 1880 to 3,392,235, or 57 per cent. While, therefore, the population aggregate for counties in which the population was 50 per cent or more Negro was greater in 1900 than in 1880, this aggregate constituted in 1900, as compared with 1880, a smaller proportion of the total Negro population. In the decade 1900–1910 the population aggregate for the black belt

counties decreased absolutely as well as relatively to the total Negro population of the South, the population aggregate for this class of counties being 3.1 per cent less and for other counties 24.6 per cent greater in 1910 than in 1900. The areas compared are, of course, as regards each class of counties in the several census years, not entirely identical.

In 1910 the white population of the majority-Negro counties was 2,094,964, or 10.2 per cent of the total white population of the South. The average number of Negroes per 1,000 whites in these counties, which occupied one-sixth of the total area of the South, was 1,877, and the proportion Negro in the total population approximately 65 per cent.

In each of the Southern states in which there were counties having a population more than one-half Negro the proportion of the total Negro population living in such counties was smaller in 1910 than it was in 1900, although in the case of four states the Negro population living in this class of counties was greater in 1910. In the case of the white population, a smaller proportion was in every southern state, without exception, living in the majority Negro counties in 1910 than in 1900.

AREA OF SPECIFIC PROPORTION NEGRO IN THE POPULATION: 1880–1910.

In Table 7 southern counties and their areas are classified according to the percentage Negro in their populations in 1910, the number of counties and the aggregate areas in square miles and in percentage of total area being shown for classes of counties in which the proportion Negro in the population was, respectively, less than 12.5 per cent—in which class are included counties reporting no Negro population—12.5 to 24.9 per cent, 25 to 49.9 per cent, 50 to 74.9 per cent, and 75 per cent or more.

In 540 southern counties, with an aggregate area of 391,273 square miles, or 44.5 per cent of the total area of the South, the percentage Negro in the population in 1910 was less than 12.5. The aggregate area of the 202 counties in which the percentage Negro was 12.5 to 24.9 per cent amounted to 14.1 per cent of the total area of the South; that of the 345 counties with a percentage Negro ranging from 25 to 49.9, amounted to 24.6 per cent of the total area; that of the 211 counties with a percentage Negro of 50 to 74.9, amounted to 12.9 per cent of the total area; and that of the 53 counties in which the percentage Negro was 75 or more, to 3.9 per cent of the total area.

SOUTHERN COUNTY AREAS CLASSIFIED ACCORDING TO SPECIFIC PERCENTAGE NEGRO IN THE POPULATION BY DIVISIONS AND STATES: 1910.

Table 7 — SOUTHERN STATES: 1910.

DIVISION AND STATE.	All counties.	Counties in which the percentage Negro was—					All counties.	Counties in which the percentage Negro was—					All counties.	Counties in which the percentage Negro was—				
		Less than 12.5.[1]	12.5 to 24.9.	25 to 49.9.	50 to 74.9.	75 or more.		Less than 12.5.[1]	12.5 to 24.9.	25 to 49.9.	50 to 74.9.	75 or more.		Less than 12.5.[1]	12.5 to 24.9.	25 to 49.9.	50 to 74.9.	75 or more.
	NUMBER OF COUNTIES.						AREA IN SQUARE MILES.						PERCENTAGE OF TOTAL AREA OF DIVISION OR STATE.					
The South......	1,351	540	202	345	211	53	878,326	391,273	123,581	216,253	113,138	34,081	100.0	44.5	14.1	24.6	12.9	3.9
South Atlantic......	534	124	73	181	143	13	269,071	52,484	41,564	98,439	68,972	7,612	100.0	19.5	15.4	36.6	25.6	2.8
East South Central...	361	153	75	72	32	29	179,509	59,559	34,278	44,951	21,112	19,609	100.0	33.2	19.1	25.0	11.8	10.9
West South Central..	456	263	54	92	36	11	429,746	279,230	47,739	72,863	23,054	6,860	100.0	65.0	11.1	17.0	5.4	1.6
South Atlantic:																		
Delaware.........	3		3				1,965		1,965				100.0		100.0			
Maryland.........	24	6	6	11	1		9,941	3,347	1,789	4,341	464		100.0	33.7	18.0	43.7	4.7	
Dist. Columbia...	1			1			60			60			100.0			100.0		
Virginia.........	117	22	22	41	32		40,262	10,161	6,838	11,888	11,375		100.0	25.2	17.0	29.5	28.3	
West Virginia....	55	51	3	1			24,022	22,192	1,297	533			100.0	92.4	5.4	2.2		
North Carolina...	98	25	17	42	14		48,740	10,841	8,066	23,789	6,044		100.0	22.2	16.5	48.8	12.4	
South Carolina...	43		2	8	29	4	30,495		1,687	5,492	19,975	3,341	100.0		5.5	18.0	65.5	11.0
Georgia.........	146	19	12	49	59	7	58,725	5,485	4,472	21,350	24,447	2,971	100.0	9.3	7.6	36.4	41.6	5.1
Florida.........	47	1	8	28	8	2	54,861	458	15,450	30,986	6,667	1,300	100.0	0.8	28.2	56.5	12.2	2.4
East South Central:																		
Kentucky.........	119	82	31	6			40,181	27,798	10,337	2,046			100.0	69.2	25.7	5.1		
Tennessee.........	96	59	20	15	1	1	41,687	23,633	9,451	7,477	508	618	100.0	56.7	22.7	17.9	1.2	1.5
Alabama.........	67	10	13	23	10	11	51,279	7,171	8,654	18,776	8,315	8,363	100.0	14.0	16.9	36.6	16.2	16.3
Mississippi......	79	2	11	28	21	17	46,362	957	5,836	16,652	12,289	10,628	100.0	2.1	12.6	35.9	26.5	22.9
West South Central:																		
Arkansas.........	75	36	6	19	9	5	52,525	25,554	3,790	13,625	6,327	3,229	100.0	48.7	7.2	25.9	12.0	6.1
Louisiana.........	60		10	25	19	6	45,409		12,660	17,542	11,576	3,631	100.0		27.9	38.6	25.5	8.0
Oklahoma.........	76	62	8	6			69,414	58,036	7,317	4,061			100.0	83.6	10.5	5.9		
Texas.........	245	165	30	42	8		262,398	195,640	23,972	37,635	5,151		100.0	74.6	9.1	14.3	2.0	

[1] Includes counties reporting no Negro population.

The area of counties in which the percentage Negro was less than 12.5 constituted 19.5 per cent, or nearly one-fifth of the total area of the South Atlantic division; 33.2 per cent or nearly one-third of the area of the East South Central division, and 65 per cent, or nearly two-thirds of the area of the West South Central division. In Mississippi such counties constituted only 2.1 per cent of the total area of the state, while in West Virginia they constituted 92.4 per cent.

In eight Southern states in 1910 counties were reported in which the Negro population amounted to 75 per cent or more of the total population, and in Mississippi such counties constituted 22.9 per cent of the total area of the state.

The proportion Negro in the population is represented graphically, by counties, in the frontispiece map and in the series of state maps introduced at the close of this chapter.

Data relating to the area of counties, classified as in Table 7, according to percentage Negro in the population, are given in Table 8 for southern divisions, covering the last four censuses.

Counties in which the percentage Negro was less than 12.5 per cent, including in this class counties reporting no Negro population, constituted a slightly smaller proportion of the total area of the South in 1910 than such counties did in 1900, and a somewhat larger proportion than they did in 1880. In the South Atlantic and in the West South Central divisions the percentage for this class of counties fell off, and in the East South Central division it increased during the decade 1900–1910. In each division there was a slight decrease in the area of counties in which the percentage Negro was 75 or more, and also in the area of counties in which the percentage Negro was from 50 to 74.9. In each division the area of counties in which the percentage Negro was 12.5 to 24.9 per cent increased during the decade.

SOUTHERN COUNTY AREAS CLASSIFIED ACCORDING TO SPECIFIC PERCENTAGE NEGRO IN THE POPULATION, BY DIVISIONS: 1910, 1900, 1890, AND 1880.

Table 8

DIVISION AND YEAR.	All counties.	Counties in which the percentage Negro was—					All counties.	Counties in which the percentage Negro was—					All counties.	Counties in which the percentage Negro was—				
		Less than 12.5.[1]	12.5 to 24.9.	25 to 49.9.	50 to 74.9.	75 or more.		Less than 12.5.[1]	12.5 to 24.9.	25 to 49.9.	50 to 74.9.	75 or more.		Less than 12.5.[1]	12.5 to 24.9.	25 to 49.9.	50 to 74.9.	75 or more.
	AREA IN SQUARE MILES.						PERCENTAGE DISTRIBUTION OF AREA.						INCREASE OR DECREASE OF AREA IN SQUARE MILES.[2]					
The South:																		
1910	878,326	391,273	123,581	216,253	113,138	34,081	100.0	44.5	14.1	24.6	12.9	3.9	−509	−8,385	17,803	9,596	−16,812	−2,711
1900	878,835	399,658	105,778	206,657	129,950	36,792	100.0	45.5	12.0	23.5	14.8	4.2	−5,024	5,845	−333	−221	−267
1890	878,835	404,682	99,933	206,990	130,171	37,059	100.0	46.0	11.4	23.6	14.8	4.2	5,740	35,823	−28,245	7,696	−13,704	4,170
1880	873,095	368,859	128,178	199,294	143,875	32,889	100.0	42.2	14.7	22.8	16.5	3.8						
South Atlantic:																		
1910	269,071	52,484	41,564	98,439	68,972	7,612	100.0	19.5	15.4	36.6	25.6	2.8	451	−6,625	5,629	8,348	−6,407	−494
1900	268,620	59,109	35,935	90,091	75,379	8,106	100.0	22.0	13.4	33.5	28.1	3.0	−6,683	−25	3,290	3,789	−371
1890	268,620	65,792	35,960	86,801	71,590	8,477	100.0	24.5	13.4	32.3	26.7	3.2	5,558	−1,607	3,075	−8,183	1,157
1880	268,620	60,234	37,567	83,726	79,773	7,320	100.0	22.4	14.0	31.2	29.7	2.7						
East South Central:																		
1910	179,509	59,559	34,278	44,951	21,112	19,609	100.0	33.2	19.1	25.0	11.8	10.9	−121	5,248	3,923	−7,077	−1,103	−1,112
1900	179,630	54,311	30,355	52,028	22,215	20,721	100.0	30.2	16.9	29.0	12.4	11.5	983	−2,905	946	−1,430	2,406
1890	179,630	53,328	33,260	51,082	23,645	18,315	100.0	29.7	18.5	28.4	13.2	10.2	5,358	−2,630	1,652	−7,195	2,815
1880	179,630	47,970	35,890	49,430	30,840	15,500	100.0	26.7	20.0	27.5	17.2	8.6						
West South Central:																		
1910	429,746	279,230	47,739	72,863	23,054	6,860	100.0	65.0	11.1	17.0	5.4	1.6	−839	−7,008	8,251	8,325	−9,302	−1,105
1900	430,585	286,238	39,488	64,538	32,356	7,965	100.0	66.5	9.2	15.0	7.5	1.8	676	8,775	−4,569	−2,580	−2,302
1890	430,585	285,562	30,713	69,107	34,936	10,267	100.0	66.3	7.1	16.0	8.1	2.4	5,740	24,907	−24,008	2,969	1,674	198
1880	424,845	260,655	54,721	66,138	33,262	10,069	100.0	61.4	12.9	15.6	7.8	2.4						

[1] Includes counties reporting no Negro population.   [2] Minus sign (−) denotes decrease.

The Negro population of southern counties classified as in Table 8, according to percentage Negro in the population is given in Table 9 for southern divisions and states, covering the last four censuses.

Table 9

DIVISION, STATE, AND YEAR.	All counties.	Counties in which the percentage Negro was—				
		Less than 12.5.	12.5 to 24.9.	25 to 49.9.	50 to 74.9.	75 or more.
	NUMBER.					
The South:						
1910	8,749,427	401,024	1,013,764	3,402,155	2,870,001	1,062,483
1900	7,922,969	345,797	726,179	2,793,374	2,966,976	1,090,643
1890	6,760,577	260,889	584,976	2,358,742	2,603,400	952,570
1880	5,953,903	186,630	499,348	1,875,690	2,674,953	717,282
South Atlantic:						
1910	4,112,488	119,336	385,290	1,619,774	1,800,468	187,620
1900	3,729,017	87,556	294,219	1,340,941	1,811,166	195,135
1890	3,262,690	71,415	252,193	1,148,235	1,584,487	206,360
1880	2,941,202	58,603	210,857	881,351	1,634,306	156,085
East South Cent.:						
1910	2,652,513	31,209	347,831	896,393	571,531	705,549
1900	2,499,886	116,958	264,157	793,545	604,890	720,336
1890	2,119,797	101,938	236,593	679,918	544,538	556,810
1880	1,924,996	180,111	217,372	555,598	649,936	421,979
West South Cent.:						
1910	1,984,426	150,479	280,643	885,988	498,002	169,314
1900	1,694,066	141,283	167,803	658,888	550,920	175,172
1890	1,378,090	87,536	96,190	530,589	474,375	189,400
1880	1,087,705	47,916	71,119	438,741	390,711	139,218
South Atlantic:						
Delaware—						
1910	31,181		31,181			
1900	30,697		30,697			
1890	28,386		28,386			
1880	26,442		26,442			
Maryland—						
1910	232,250	23,743	108,049	91,886	8,572	
1900	235,064	12,438	100,535	107,300	14,791	
1890	215,657	6,256	94,216	101,985	13,200	
1880	210,230	7,013	82,922	95,061	25,234	
District of Columbia—						
1910	94,446		94,446			
1900	86,702		86,702			
1890	75,572		75,572			
1880	59,596		59,596			
Virginia—						
1910	671,096	23,358	61,753	314,888	271,097	
1900	660,722	18,947	48,499	306,543	283,004	3,729
1890	635,438	16,768	31,886	294,000	292,784	
1880	631,616	13,157	26,605	225,104	366,750	

DIVISION, STATE, AND YEAR.	All counties.	Counties in which the percentage Negro was—				
		Less than 12.5.[1]	12.5 to 24.9.	25 to 49.9.	50 to 74.9	75 or more.
South Atlantic—Continued.						
West Virginia—						
1910	64,173	30,736	18,770	14,667		
1900	43,499	24,830	12,700	5,969		
1890	32,690	21,907	6,667	4,116		
1880	25,886	19,860	1,981	4,045		
North Carolina—						
1910	697,843	29,001	87,104	415,218	166,520	
1900	624,469	19,616	43,702	362,914	198,237	
1890	561,018	15,811	48,651	321,301	175,255	
1880	531,277	10,509	34,935	250,543	235,290	
South Carolina—						
1910	835,843		12,098	124,274	619,748	79,723
1900	782,321		4,801	114,529	566,999	95,992
1890	688,934			94,677	476,833	117,424
1880	604,332			70,684	468,890	64,758
Georgia—						
1910	1,176,987	11,304	39,944	389,767	655,915	80,057
1900	1,034,813	9,969	33,834	282,245	641,970	66,795
1890	858,815	8,452	31,923	207,707	548,627	62,106
1880	725,133	6,763	31,786	145,315	479,450	61,819
Florida—						
1910	308,669	1,194	26,391	174,628	78,616	27,840
1900	230,730	1,756	19,451	74,739	106,165	28,619
1890	166,180	2,221	10,464	48,877	77,788	26,830
1880	126,690	1,301	6,186	31,003	58,692	29,508
East South Cent.:						
Kentucky—						
1910	261,656	58,799	153,160	49,697		
1900	284,706	57,460	121,495	105,751		
1890	268,071	50,402	101,556	116,113		
1880	271,451	42,801	93,577	135,073		
Tennessee—						
1910	473,088	58,061	89,796	284,819	17,710	22,702
1900	480,243	43,938	84,529	228,241	123,535	
1890	430,678	37,477	80,300	215,227	97,674	
1880	403,151	27,429	72,137	193,878	109,707	
Alabama—						
1910	908,282	12,062	69,266	339,555	200,208	287,191
1900	827,307	13,167	43,363	265,201	206,845	298,731
1890	678,489	12,083	33,219	227,246	147,745	258,196
1880	600,103	8,414	32,127	123,767	217,193	218,602

[1] Includes counties reporting no Negro population.

Table 9—Con.

NEGRO POPULATION.

DIVISION, STATE, AND YEAR.	All counties.	Counties in which the percentage Negro was—				
		Less than 12.5.[1]	12.5 to 24.9.	25 to 49.9.	50 to 74.9.	75 or more.
South Atlantic—Continued.						
Mississippi—						
1910	1,009,487	2,287	35,609	222,322	353,613	395,656
1900	907,630	2,393	14,770	194,352	274,510	421,605
1890	742,559	1,976	21,518	121,332	299,119	298,614
1880	650,291	1,467	19,531	102,880	323,036	203,377
West South Cent.:						
Arkansas—						
1910	442,891	25,387	19,000	172,359	131,977	94,168
1900	366,856	28,026	14,163	136,801	117,539	70,327
1890	309,117	22,110	14,635	111,184	97,250	63,938
1880	210,666	17,411	5,114	90,582	64,537	33,022
Louisiana—						
1910	713,874	....	51,260	305,907	281,561	75,146
1900	650,804	1,279	20,937	210,440	313,303	104,845
1890	559,193	2,169	10,467	170,284	265,911	110,362
1880	483,655	377	6,728	142,000	247,017	87,533
Oklahoma—						
1910	137,612	58,004	26,908	52,700	....	....
1900	55,684	38,628	16,075	981	....	....
1890	21,609	14,882	1,300	5,427	....	....
1880						
Texas—						
1910	690,049	67,088	183,475	355,022	84,464	....
1900	620,722	73,350	116,628	310,666	120,078	....
1890	488,171	48,375	69,788	243,694	111,214	15,100
1880	393,384	30,128	59,277	206,159	79,157	18,663

PER CENT.

	All counties.	Less than 12.5.[1]	12.5 to 24.9.	25 to 49.9.	50 to 74.9.	75 or more.
The South:						
1910	100.0	4.6	11.6	38.9	32.8	12.1
1900	100.0	4.4	9.2	35.3	37.4	13.8
1890	100.0	3.9	8.7	34.9	38.5	14.1
1880	100.0	3.1	8.4	31.5	44.9	12.0
South Atlantic:						
1910	100.0	2.9	9.4	39.4	43.8	4.6
1900	100.0	2.3	7.9	36.0	48.6	5.2
1890	100.0	2.2	7.7	35.2	48.6	6.3
1880	100.0	2.0	7.2	30.0	55.6	5.3
East South Cent.:						
1910	100.0	4.9	13.1	33.8	21.5	26.6
1900	100.0	4.7	10.6	31.7	24.2	28.8
1890	100.0	4.8	11.2	32.1	25.7	26.3
1880	100.0	4.2	11.3	28.9	33.8	21.9
West South Cent.:						
1910	100.0	7.6	14.1	44.6	25.1	8.5
1900	100.0	8.3	9.9	38.9	32.5	10.5
1890	100.0	6.4	7.0	38.5	34.4	13.7
1880	100.0	4.4	6.5	40.3	35.9	12.8
South Atlantic:						
Delaware—						
1910	100.0	....	100.0	....		
1900	100.0	....	100.0	....		
1890	100.0	....	100.0	....		
1880	100.0	....	100.0	....		
Maryland—						
1910	100.0	10.2	46.5	39.6	3.7	....
1900	100.0	5.3	42.8	45.6	6.3	....
1890	100.0	2.9	43.7	47.3	6.1	....
1880	100.0	3.3	39.4	45.2	12.0	....
District of Columbia—						
1910	100.0	....	....	100.0		
1900	100.0	....	....	100.0		
1890	100.0	....	....	100.0		
1880	100.0	....	....	100.0		

NEGRO POPULATION.

DIVISION, STATE, AND YEAR.	All counties.	Counties in which the percentage Negro was—				
		Less than 12.5.[1]	12.5 to 24.9.	25 to 49.9.	50 to 74.9.	75 or more.
South Atlantic—Continued.						
Virginia—						
1910	100.0	3.5	9.2	46.9	40.4	....
1900	100.0	2.9	7.3	46.4	42.8	0.6
1890	100.0	2.6	5.0	46.3	46.1	....
1880	100.0	2.1	4.2	35.6	58.1	....
West Virginia—						
1910	100.0	47.9	29.2	22.9	....	....
1900	100.0	57.1	29.2	13.7	....	....
1890	100.0	67.0	20.4	12.6	....	....
1880	100.0	76.7	7.7	15.6	....	....
North Carolina—						
1910	100.0	4.2	12.5	59.5	23.9	....
1900	100.0	3.1	7.0	58.1	31.7	....
1890	100.0	2.8	8.7	57.3	31.2	....
1880	100.0	2.0	6.6	47.2	44.3	....
South Carolina—						
1910	100.0	....	1.4	14.9	74.1	9.5
1900	100.0	....	0.6	14.6	72.5	12.3
1890	100.0	....	....	13.7	69.2	17.0
1880	100.0	....	....	11.7	77.6	10.7
Georgia—						
1910	100.0	1.0	3.4	33.1	55.7	6.8
1900	100.0	1.0	3.3	27.3	62.0	6.5
1890	100.0	1.0	3.7	24.2	63.9	7.2
1880	100.0	0.9	4.4	20.0	66.1	8.5
Florida—						
1910	100.0	0.4	8.5	56.6	25.5	9.0
1900	100.0	0.8	8.4	32.4	46.0	12.4
1890	100.0	1.3	6.3	29.4	46.8	16.1
1880	100.0	1.0	4.9	24.5	46.3	23.3
East South Cent.:						
Kentucky—						
1910	100.0	22.5	58.5	19.0	....	....
1900	100.0	20.2	42.7	37.1	....	....
1890	100.0	18.8	37.9	43.3	....	....
1880	100.0	15.8	34.5	49.8	....	....
Tennessee—						
1910	100.0	12.3	19.0	60.2	3.7	4.8
1900	100.0	9.1	17.6	47.5	25.7	....
1890	100.0	8.7	18.6	50.0	22.7	....
1880	100.0	6.8	17.9	48.1	27.2	....
Alabama—						
1910	100.0	1.3	7.6	37.4	22.0	31.6
1900	100.0	1.6	5.2	32.1	25.0	36.1
1890	100.0	1.8	4.9	33.5	21.8	38.1
1880	100.0	1.4	5.4	20.6	36.2	36.4
Mississippi—						
1910	100.0	0.2	3.5	22.0	35.0	39.2
1900	100.0	0.3	1.6	21.4	30.2	46.5
1890	100.0	0.3	2.9	16.3	40.3	40.2
1880	100.0	0.2	3.0	15.8	49.7	31.3
West South Cent.:						
Arkansas—						
1910	100.0	5.7	4.3	38.9	29.8	21.3
1900	100.0	7.6	3.9	37.3	32.0	19.2
1890	100.0	7.2	4.7	36.0	31.5	20.7
1880	100.0	8.3	2.4	43.0	30.6	15.7
Louisiana—						
1910	100.0	....	7.2	42.9	39.4	10.5
1900	100.0	0.2	3.2	32.3	48.1	16.1
1890	100.0	0.4	1.9	30.5	47.6	19.7
1880	100.0	0.1	1.4	29.4	51.1	18.1
Oklahoma—						
1910	100.0	42.2	19.6	38.3	....	....
1900	100.0	69.4	28.9	1.8	....	....
1890	100.0	68.9	6.0	25.1	....	....
1880						
Texas—						
1910	100.0	9.7	26.6	51.4	12.2	....
1900	100.0	11.8	18.8	50.0	19.3	....
1890	100.0	9.9	14.3	49.9	22.8	3.1
1880	100.0	7.7	15.1	52.4	20.1	4.7

[1] Includes counties reporting no Negro population.

Of the total Negro population of the South in 1910 only 4.6 per cent lived in counties in which the proportion Negro in the population was less than 12.5 per cent, while 12.1 per cent lived in counties in which the proportion Negro was 75 per cent or more. The corresponding percentages for the South Atlantic division were 2.9 and 4.6, for the East South Central division 4.9 and 26.6, and for the West South Central 7.6 and 8.5. Of Mississippi's Negro population 39.2 per cent, or nearly two-fifths, were in 1910 living in counties in which the proportion Negro in the population was 75 per cent or more.

It may be noted, in comparing the figures given for population in Table 9 with those for areas given in Table 8, that in the South as a whole 44.5 per cent, or more than two-fifths, of the area, and 4.6 per cent, or less than one-twentieth, of the Negro population was in counties in which the proportion Negro was less than 12.5 per cent. On the other hand, 12.1 per cent, nearly one-eighth, of the Negro population was living in 3.9 per cent of the total area of the South—this being the 1910 population and the area of counties in which the percentage Negro was 75 per cent or more.

Comparing 1880 with 1910 it will be found that the proportion of the Negro population living in each class of counties in which the percentage Negro was less than 50 has increased; the proportion living in counties in which the percentage Negro was 50 to 74.9 has decreased very considerably—from 44.9 to 32.8 per cent; while the proportion living in counties in which the percentage Negro was 75 or more was practically the same in 1910 as in 1880, though lower than in 1900. Corresponding changes have taken place in each of the three southern divisions, although it may be noted that in the East South Central division the proportion living in counties in which the percentage Negro was 75 per cent or more increased from 21.9 per cent of the total Negro population in 1880 to 26.6 per cent in 1910. The proportion living in such counties increased in Mississippi from 31.3 per cent in 1880 to 39.2 per cent in 1910, and in Arkansas from 15.7 to 21.3 per cent.

It decreased in South Carolina, Georgia, Florida, Alabama, and Louisiana.

INCREASE AND PROPORTION NEGRO, BY COUNTIES.

A comparison of the rates of growth of the Negro population during the decade 1900-1910 in the several classes of counties for which data are presented in the tables preceding is made in Table 10. In determining the increases and decreases shown in this table, the counties have been classified according to the percentage Negro in the population in 1910, and the Negro populations in 1910 and in 1900 of the counties so grouped have been compared. The increase or decrease pertains in each case, therefore, to a specific group of counties, and indicates population change within a specific aggregate area, characterized as having in 1910 a given proportion of Negroes in the enumerated population.

INCREASE OR DECREASE OF NEGRO POPULATION IN SOUTHERN STATES CLASSIFIED BY PROPORTION NEGRO IN THE POPULATION IN 1910, BY SOUTHERN DIVISIONS AND STATES: 1900-1910.

Table 10	INCREASE OR DECREASE OF NEGRO POPULATION IN SOUTHERN STATES: 1900-1910.											
			Counties or combinations[1] of counties in which the percentage Negro in 1910 was—										
DIVISION OR STATE.	All counties.		Less than 12.5.		12.5 to 24.9.		25 to 49.9.		50 to 74.9.		75 or more.	
	Increase.	Decrease.	Increase.	Decrease.	Increase.	Decrease.	Increase.	Decrease.	Increase.	Decrease.	Increase.	Decrease.
NUMBER.												
The South..................	826,458	....	73,077	....	93,886	....	418,229	....	199,001	....	42,265	....
South Atlantic..............	383,471	....	2,404	....	34,301	....	216,745	....	132,743	....	....	2,722
East South Central..........	152,627	....	18,266	....	60,581	996	116,228	....	25,472	....	30,189	....
West South Central..........	290,360	....	88,939	....	60,581	....	85,256	....	40,786	....	14,798	....
South Atlantic:												
Delaware................	484	....	....	....	484	....	....	....	....	....	....	....
Maryland................	....	2,814	....	313	4,662	....	....	6,087	....	1,076	....	....
District of Columbia.....	7,744	....	....	....	....	....	7,744	....	....	....	....	....
Virginia.................	10,374	....	....	1,954	....	1,785	6,027	....	8,086	....	....	....
West Virginia............	20,674	....	5,906	....	6,070	....	8,698	....	....	....	....	....
North Carolina..........	73,374	....	52	....	5,369	....	51,910	....	16,043	....	....	....
South Carolina..........	53,522	....	....	....	977	....	14,730	....	43,574	....	....	5,759
Georgia.................	142,174	....	....	1,200	5,150	....	78,971	....	55,437	....	3,816	....
Florida.................	77,939	....	....	87	13,374	....	54,752	....	10,679	....	....	779
East South Central:												
Kentucky................	....	23,050	7,941	....	....	10,339	....	4,770	....	....	....	....
Tennessee...............	....	7,155	9,010	....	....	6,160	6,365	....	630	....	1,020	....
Alabama................	80,975	....	1,209	....	15,152	....	66,986	....	11,586	....	....	11,540
Mississippi.............	101,857	....	106	....	351	....	47,647	....	13,256	....	40,709	....
West South Central:												
Arkansas................	76,035	....	1,033	....	3,231	....	27,932	....	22,064	....	23,841	....
Louisiana...............	63,070	....	....	....	18,907	....	33,924	....	19,282	....	....	9,043
Oklahoma...............	81,928	....	81,928	....	....	....	....	....	....	....	....	....
Texas...................	69,327	....	8,044	....	38,443	....	23,400	....	....	560	....	....
PER CENT.												
The South..................	10.4	....	18.0	....	10.5	....	13.8	....	7.6	....	4.4	....
South Atlantic..............	10.3	....	2.1	....	9.9	....	14.6	....	8.1	....	....	2.0
East South Central..........	6.1	....	12.3	....	....	0.3	14.8	....	4.7	....	4.5	....
West South Central..........	17.1	....	63.0	....	31.7	....	11.3	....	9.1	....	9.6	....
South Atlantic:												
Delaware................	1.6	....	....	....	1.6	....	....	....	....	....	....	....
Maryland................	....	1.2	....	1.3	4.5	....	....	6.2	....	11.2	....	....
District of Columbia.....	8.9	....	....	....	....	....	8.9	....	....	....	....	....
Virginia.................	1.6	....	....	7.7	....	2.8	1.8	....	3.5	....	....	....
West Virginia............	47.5	....	23.8	....	47.8	....	145.7	....	....	....	....	....
North Carolina..........	11.7	....	0.2	....	6.6	....	14.3	....	10.7	....	....	....
South Carolina..........	6.8	....	....	....	8.8	....	15.0	....	7.0	....	....	10.6
Georgia.................	13.7	....	....	10.2	15.8	....	21.4	....	9.8	....	7.1	....
Florida.................	33.8	....	....	6.8	110.1	....	45.3	....	15.7	....	....	2.7
East South Central:												
Kentucky................	....	8.1	11.9	....	....	6.3	....	8.8	....	....	....	....
Tennessee...............	....	1.5	13.4	....	....	6.4	2.3	....	3.7	....	4.7	....
Alabama................	9.8	....	9.6	....	24.7	....	25.2	....	6.1	....	....	3.9
Mississippi.............	11.2	....	4.4	....	1.1	....	25.7	....	4.0	....	11.5	....
West South Central:												
Arkansas................	20.7	....	....	....	3.9	....	20.5	....	18.4	....	21.5	....	33.9	....
Louisiana...............	9.7	....	....	....	62.2	....	12.4	....	7.4	....	....	10.7
Oklahoma...............	147.1	....	147.1	....	....	....	....	....	....	....	....	....
Texas...................	11.2	....	13.6	....	26.5	....	7.1	....	....	0.7	....	....

[1] See note to Table 2.

While the percentages of Table 10 do not indicate that the rate of growth of the Negro population varies in any regular or close correspondence with the proportion Negro in the population, the aggregates for the South as a whole and for southern divisions would seem to justify the generalization that the rate of increase of the Negro population is relatively low in counties in which the percentage Negro is high. In the South, as a whole, the percentage increase was lowest during the decade 1900–1910 in that class of counties in which the proportion Negro was highest, and increased from class to class as the proportion Negro declined—except that the percentage increase was somewhat higher for the 25 to 49.9 per cent counties than it was for the 12.5 to 24.9 per cent counties. The percentage increases for the several classes of counties, beginning with the class having the highest proportion of Negroes in the population, ran as follows: 4.4, 7.6, 13.8, 10.5, and 18.

It should be noted, however, that the percentage for the class of counties having less than 12.5 per cent Negro in the population is largely determined by Oklahoma's increase, which as has been explained is not figured by counties. If the increase in Oklahoma could have been figured by counties some of it would have been thrown into classes of counties with a percentage Negro higher than 12.5, since in 14 of the state's 76 counties in 1910 the percentage Negro exceeded 12.5.

In each division the percentage increase for each of the two classes of counties in which the proportion Negro exceeded 50 per cent was below the average increase per cent of the Negro population in the South as a whole, while for counties having a percentage Negro of 25 to 49.9 per cent the percentage increase in each division exceeded the average for the population as a whole.

Arkansas is the only state in which the percentage increase for counties having, in 1910, a proportion Negro of 75 per cent or more exceeded the percentage increase for each class of counties with a lower proportion Negro. In nine Southern states, counties having a proportion Negro of less than 12.5 per cent showed a decrease of Negro population during the decade 1900–1910, the decrease amounting in the case of Tennessee to 13.4 per cent. In only three states was the increase for this class of counties as great as the average increase of the Negro population as a whole in the South. More than one-half of the total Negro increase in the South—418,229 out of 826,458—was in counties in which the proportion Negro was 25 to 49.9 per cent. The increase in these counties amounted to 13.8 per cent, and was accordingly considerably above the percentage increase of 10.4 for the South as a whole. For counties in which the proportion Negro was 50 to 74.9 per cent the increase amounted to 198,659, or 7.5 per cent, the rate of growth in these counties being considerably below the rate for the South as a whole. These two classes of counties account for approximately three-fourths of the total Negro increase at the South.

It will be obvious that increase of the Negro population in counties in which the proportion is low has a significance entirely different from that of an increase in proportion pertaining to counties in which the proportion is high, the tendency being in the one case toward more even dispersion of the Negro element and in the other toward further agglomeration.

PROPORTION NEGRO AND DENSITY OF NEGRO POPULATION.

While in general it is true, as has been noted, that the counties with a high proportion Negro in the population are characterized also by a relatively high density of Negro population, there is no close correlation of proportion Negro and density of population in detail. This will be apparent in Table 11, in which are shown the proportion Negro and the Negro population per square mile for each of the 53 counties with a proportion Negro in the population of 75 per cent or more in 1910, the counties being arranged in order according to the proportion Negro.

PROPORTION NEGRO AND NEGRO POPULATION PER SQUARE MILE FOR THE 53 COUNTIES IN WHICH THE PROPORTION NEGRO WAS 75 PER CENT: 1910.

Table 11 COUNTIES IN ORDER OF DECREASING PERCENTAGE NEGRO.	NEGRO POPULATION. Per cent in total population.	Number per square mile.	COUNTIES IN ORDER OF DECREASING PERCENTAGE NEGRO.	NEGRO POPULATION. Per cent in total population.	Number per square mile.	COUNTIES IN ORDER OF DECREASING PERCENTAGE NEGRO.	NEGRO POPULATION. Per cent in total population.	Number per square mile.
Issaquena, Miss	94.2	24.5	Concordia, La	83.6	16.7	Russell, Ala	77.9	30.8
Tensas, La	91.5	24.7	Burke, Ga	82.4	23.5	Stewart, Ga	77.8	25.2
Tunica, Miss	90.7	40.4	West Feliciana, La	81.9	31.3	Berkley, S. C	77.6	14.7
East Carroll, La	89.3	24.7	Wilcox, Ala	81.6	30.8	Marengo, Ala	77.3	31.9
Sharkey, Miss	89.0	31.4	Dallas, Ala	81.5	45.5	McIntosh, Ga	77.3	10.6
Coahoma, Miss	88.8	57.3	Madison, Miss	81.5	37.6	Bossier, La	77.0	19.4
Madison, La	88.6	14.5	Sumter, Ala	81.3	25.7	Wilkinson, Miss	76.9	20.8
Lowndes, Ala	88.2	38.0	Sunflower, Miss	80.9	33.7	Calhoun, S. C	76.6	32.6
Bolivar, Miss	87.4	48.6	Chicot, Ark	80.4	29.1	Quitman, Miss	76.5	22.4
Beaufort, S. C	86.9	28.7	Holmes, Miss	79.8	37.4	Jefferson, Fla	76.2	22.4
Greene, Ala	86.7	31.0	Desha, Ark	79.4	16.2	Yazoo, Miss	76.1	34.2
Lee, Ga	85.6	30.6	Hale, Ala	78.9	34.0	De Soto, Miss	76.0	37.0
Washington, Miss	85.0	47.4	Phillips, Ark	78.6	38.1	Fairfield, S. C	76.0	28.2
Macon, Ala	84.6	35.9	Perry, Ala	78.5	33.2	Leon, Fla	75.8	20.6
Crittenden, Ark	84.6	32.6	Lee, Ark	78.4	31.6	Terrell, Ga	75.5	51.6
Leflore, Miss	84.4	53.5	Jefferson, Miss	78.4	28.2	Dougherty, Ga	75.1	35.2
Bullock, Ala	84.0	41.6	Claiborne, Miss	78.2	27.8	Fayette, Tenn	75.0	36.7
Noxubee, Miss	84.0	35.1	Quitman, Ga	78.1	24.9			

In this group of counties the largest Negro population per square mile was that of 51.6 in Terrell County, Ga., whose proportion Negro was 75.5 per cent. The smallest population per square mile was that of 10.6 in McIntosh County, Ga., whose proportion Negro was 77.3 per cent. In Issaquena County, Miss., whose proportion Negro of 94.2 per cent exceeded that of any other county, the Negro population per square mile was 24.5.

AREA OF INCREASING AND DECREASING PROPORTION NEGRO: 1900–1910.

Southern counties and county areas have been classified in Table 12 according to increase or decrease of the percentage Negro in the population during the decade 1900–1910. The aggregate area within which the proportion Negro in the population increased, and within which it decreased in this decade is given, in square miles and in percentage of total area, for the South as a whole, and for each southern division and state.

The percentage Negro increased during the decade 1900–1910 in 276 county areas and decreased in 807, there being in the case of 143 areas either no Negro population or a Negro population of less than 100 reported in both 1900 and 1910. The area of counties in which the proportion Negro increased amounted to 275,908 square miles, or 31.4 per cent of the total area of the South; that of counties in which it decreased to 465,445 square miles, or 53 per cent of the total area.

In the West South Central division the proportion Negro in the population decreased in counties whose aggregate areas constituted 37.3 per cent of the total area of the division; the counties of decreasing proportion Negro constituted 64.8 per cent, or nearly two-thirds, of the total area in the South Atlantic division; and 72.9 per cent, or nearly three-fourths, of the total area in the East South Central division.

Except in the case of Florida, the area of counties in which the proportion Negro in the population decreased in the several Southern states, exceeded that of the counties in which the proportion increased. In Florida the counties in which the proportion Negro decreased embraced 28.2 per cent of the total area of the state; the corresponding percentage for Texas being 33.7; for Delaware and Maryland, 53.5; for West Virginia, 60; for Georgia, 62.1; for Alabama, 62.4; for Mississippi, 62.8; for Arkansas, 69.5; for North Carolina, 73.7; for Louisiana, 77.9; for Kentucky, 81.1; for South Carolina, 83.7; for Virginia, 88.4; for Tennessee, 89.

NUMBER AND AREA OF COUNTIES IN WHICH THE PERCENTAGE NEGRO INCREASED AND IN WHICH IT DECREASED: 1900–1910.

Table 12

	COUNTIES OR COMBINATIONS[1] OF COUNTIES.									
	Number.			Area.						
				Square miles.				Percentage distribution.		
DIVISION AND STATE.	Total	Percentage Negro increased, 1900–1910.	Percentage Negro decreased, 1900–1910.	No Negro population or less than 100, 1900–1910.	Total.	Percentage Negro increased, 1900–1910.	Percentage Negro decreased, 1900–1910.	No Negro population or less than 100, 1900–1910.	Total.	Percentage Negro increased, 1900–1910.	Percentage Negro decreased, 1900–1910.	No Negro population or less than 100, 1900–1910.
The South	1,214	276	795	143	878,326	275,908	465,445	136,973	100.0	31.4	53.0	15.6
South Atlantic	491	131	343	17	269,071	88,525	174,433	6,113	100.0	32.9	64.8	2.3
East South Central	347	68	264	15	179,509	44,176	130,795	4,538	100.0	24.6	72.9	2.5
West South Central	376	77	188	111	429,746	143,207	160,217	126,322	100.0	33.3	37.3	29.4
South Atlantic:												
Delaware	3	1	2	....	1,965	913	1,052	....	100.0	46.5	53.5	....
Maryland	24	....	24	....	9,941	....	9,941	....	100.0	....	100.0	....
District of Columbia	1	....	1	....	60	....	60	....	100.0	....	100.0	....
Virginia	110	12	96	2	40,262	3,830	35,593	839	100.0	9.5	88.4	2.1
West Virginia	55	12	31	12	24,022	5,256	14,411	4,355	100.0	21.9	60.0	18.1
North Carolina	96	24	71	1	48,740	12,526	35,916	298	100.0	25.7	73.7	0.6
South Carolina	34	7	27	....	30,495	4,985	25,510	....	100.0	16.3	83.7	....
Georgia	123	48	73	2	58,725	21,648	36,456	621	100.0	36.9	62.1	1.1
Florida	45	27	18	....	54,861	39,367	15,494	....	100.0	71.8	28.2	....
East South Central:												
Kentucky	119	11	98	10	40,181	4,871	32,578	2,732	100.0	12.1	81.1	6.8
Tennessee	95	10	81	4	41,687	3,406	37,105	1,176	100.0	8.2	89.0	2.8
Alabama	62	23	38	1	51,279	18,641	32,008	630	100.0	36.4	62.4	1.2
Mississippi	71	24	47	....	46,362	17,258	29,104	....	100.0	37.2	62.8	....
West South Central:												
Arkansas	73	15	49	9	52,525	10,066	36,498	5,961	100.0	19.2	69.5	11.3
Louisiana	59	9	50	....	45,409	10,035	35,374	....	100.0	22.1	77.9	....
Oklahoma	1	1	....	....	69,414	69,414	....	....	100.0	100.0	....	....
Texas	243	52	89	102	262,398	53,692	88,345	120,361	100.0	20.5	33.7	45.9

[1] See note to Table 2.

The map on page 133 represents the distribution of those counties in the country as a whole, having a Negro population in 1910 of at least 1,000, and showing a proportion Negro in the population higher in 1910 than in 1900. In this map the comparison as regards Oklahoma is of 1910 with 1907, comparable data for 1900 not being available. It will be noted that in a number of northern counties, including some of the larger urban communities, the proportion Negro increased.

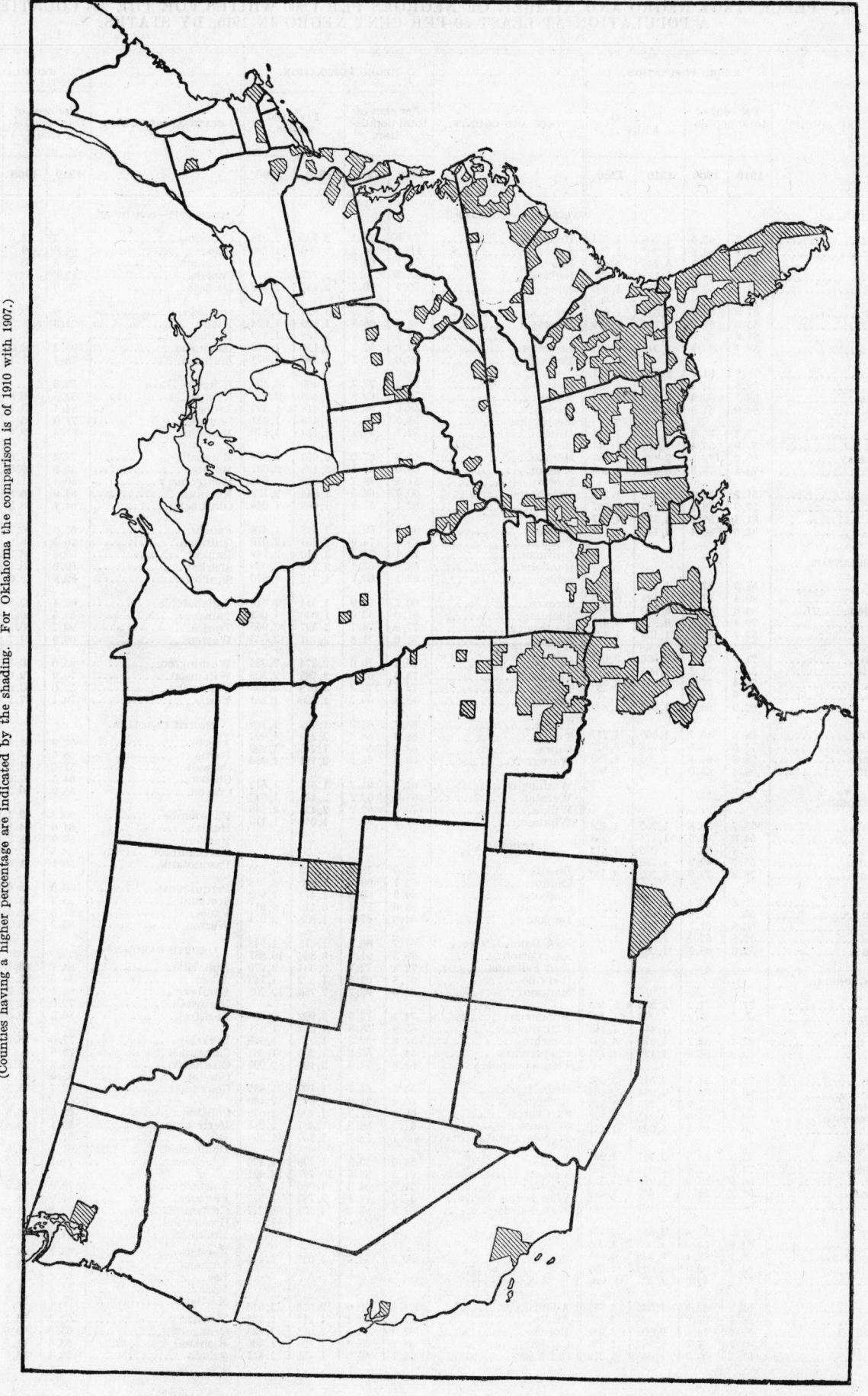

MAP VII.—COUNTIES HAVING AT LEAST 1,000 NEGROES IN 1910, AND A PERCENTAGE NEGRO IN THE POPULATION HIGHER IN 1910 THAN IN 1900.

(Counties having a higher percentage are indicated by the shading. For Oklahoma the comparison is of 1910 with 1907.)

TABLE 13.—PERCENTAGE NEGRO AND NUMBER OF NEGROES PER 1,000 WHITES FOR THE 264 COUNTIES HAVING A POPULATION AT LEAST 50 PER CENT NEGRO IN 1910, BY STATES.

STATE AND COUNTY.	NEGRO POPULATION.			
	Per cent of total population.		Per 1,000 whites.	
	1910	1900	1910	1900
ALABAMA.				
Autauga	58.5	62.4	1,408	1,657
Barbour	62.5	63.6	1,667	1,750
Bullock	84.0	81.7	5,248	4,464
Butler	53.0	51.4	1,126	1,058
Chambers	51.8	53.5	1,073	1,150
Choctaw	62.2	56.7	1,648	1,308
Clarke	55.9	57.0	1,267	1,324
Dallas	81.5	83.0	4,399	4,887
Greene	86.7	86.3	6,542	6,312
Hale	78.9	81.7	3,730	4,475
Lee	59.8	59.9	1,485	1,494
Lowndes	88.2	86.6	7,462	6,487
Macon	84.6	81.6	5,500	4,439
Marengo	77.3	76.9	3,401	3,334
Monroe	57.9	55.4	1,412	1,246
Montgomery	69.2	72.5	2,248	2,633
Perry	78.5	78.5	3,641	3,660
Pickens	51.7	57.0	1,070	1,328
Russell	77.9	78.1	3,523	3,567
Sumter	81.3	82.7	4,337	4,767
Wilcox	81.6	80.4	4,446	4,105
ARKANSAS.				
Ashley	52.5	53.7	1,107	1,160
Chicot	80.4	87.1	4,124	6,743
Crittenden	84.6	84.6	5,520	5,489
Desha	79.4	81.7	3,862	4,470
Drew	53.7	52.9	1,159	1,123
Jefferson	71.5	72.8	2,506	2,675
Lafayette	52.3	61.2	1,095	1,579
Lee	78.4	77.8	3,634	3,510
Lincoln	65.9	63.1	1,935	1,711
Monroe	62.9	65.4	1,697	1,889
Ouachita	56.6	55.7	1,306	1,257
Phillips	78.6	78.6	3,673	3,677
St. Francis	68.8	64.1	2,203	1,789
Woodruff	58.4	61.0	1,403	1,565
FLORIDA.				
Alachua	55.7	58.8	1,255	1,428
Citrus	54.0	48.9	1,174	958
Gadsden	67.4	64.4	2,070	1,812
Hernando	55.7	49.9	1,255	996
Jefferson	76.2	77.9	3,202	3,530
Leon	75.8	80.4	3,135	4,117
Madison	55.6	57.6	1,253	1,361
Marion	60.8	61.7	1,550	1,608
Nassau	52.8	52.7	1,117	1,117
Putnam	52.0	48.3	1,082	934
GEORGIA.				
Baker	71.7	71.2	2,536	2,466
Baldwin	60.0	63.3	1,498	1,729
Brooks	59.1	58.6	1,445	1,416
Burke	82.4	81.7	4,675	4,463
Butts	52.8	53.2	1,121	1,135
Calhoun	73.8	74.1	2,812	2,866
Camden	66.5	68.4	1,984	2,165
Chatham	55.2	57.9	1,233	1,378
Chattahoochee	69.2	68.0	2,244	2,126
Clarke	50.6	53.5	1,023	1,151
Clay	73.3	66.6	2,747	1,991
Columbia	74.6	72.8	2,944	2,673
Coweta	56.5	56.9	1,298	1,322
Crawford	59.2	56.1	1,453	1,279
Crisp	52.5	......	1,104	......
Decatur	57.6	53.6	1,360	1,154
Dooly	61.9	55.3	1,626	1,236
Dougherty	75.1	82.1	3,025	4,581
Early	62.2	60.5	1,646	1,529
Elbert	50.1	49.6	1,003	986
Glynn	62.2	63.6	1,646	1,751
Greene	62.9	67.8	1,693	2,106
Hancock	74.4	74.6	2,902	2,931
Harris	71.9	67.7	2,562	2,093
Henry	51.1	50.5	1,045	1,019

STATE AND COUNTY.	NEGRO POPULATION.			
	Per cent of total population.		Per 1,000 whites.	
	1910	1900	1910	1900
GEORGIA—continued.				
Houston	73.6	75.1	2,795	3,018
Jasper	69.4	64.2	2,266	1,790
Jefferson	60.7	63.6	1,545	1,745
Jenkins	63.3	......	1,727	......
Jones	70.9	70.7	2,435	2,418
Lee	85.6	85.4	5,923	5,864
Liberty	64.6	65.8	1,829	1,923
Lincoln	59.4	59.7	1,462	1,482
Lowndes	53.0	53.3	1,128	1,143
McDuffie	58.0	62.7	1,380	1,678
McIntosh	77.3	77.7	3,400	3,490
Macon	70.5	69.5	2,386	2,276
Marion	58.6	58.0	1,418	1,382
Meriwether	58.5	59.2	1,410	1,451
Mitchell	52.7	54.1	1,113	1,179
Monroe	66.8	67.0	2,010	2,034
Morgan	68.0	67.1	2,128	2,037
Newton	51.3	48.7	1,052	948
Oglethorpe	60.7	68.5	1,544	2,172
Pike	52.1	51.2	1,088	1,048
Pulaski	59.1	59.7	1,448	1,478
Putman	73.3	74.9	2,753	2,976
Quitman	78.1	73.3	3,610	2,749
Randolph	68.9	67.1	2,218	2,035
Schley	63.1	65.2	1,712	1,870
Screven	60.2	56.9	1,514	1,318
Spalding	51.0	52.0	1,039	1,081
Stewart	77.3	74.7	3,397	2,945
Sumter	73.0	71.8	2,707	2,543
Talbot	70.4	70.0	2,374	2,334
Taliaferro	73.6	69.8	2,785	2,309
Terrell	75.5	70.2	3,078	2,353
Thomas	58.8	56.2	1,426	1,281
Troup	58.7	63.9	1,422	1,769
Twiggs	68.9	66.6	2,214	1,994
Upson	54.9	54.7	1,215	1,209
Warren	68.6	66.5	2,181	1,984
Washington	61.7	61.7	1,613	1,612
Webster	68.0	62.2	2,124	1,643
Wilkes	70.8	69.2	2,426	2,248
Wilkinson	51.2	52.7	1,047	1,115
LOUISIANA.				
Bossier	77.0	78.2	3,345	3,590
Caddo	62.1	68.9	1,640	2,218
Claiborne	59.6	60.0	1,477	1,503
Concordia	83.6	87.4	5,110	6,911
De Soto	64.8	67.4	1,838	2,071
East Baton Rouge	61.7	66.1	1,615	1,948
East Carroll	89.3	91.6	8,366	10,857
East Feliciana	72.5	72.7	2,634	2,670
Iberville	61.8	63.5	1,622	1,743
Madison	88.6	92.7	7,750	12,705
Morehouse	74.4	76.5	2,902	3,253
Natchitoches	55.8	58.8	1,262	1,431
Ouachita	54.8	62.5	1,213	1,669
Plaquemines	54.7	55.8	1,206	1,263
Pointe Coupee	67.8	74.4	2,106	2,905
Red River	54.5	64.7	1,197	1,832
Richland	66.4	71.0	1,973	2,449
St. Charles	60.0	67.3	1,498	2,055
St. James	57.2	56.2	1,337	1,285
St. John the Baptist	56.7	58.3	1,309	1,396
St. Mary	54.0	59.3	1,179	1,470
Tensas	91.5	93.5	10,797	14,491
Webster	51.6	54.6	1,066	1,204
West Baton Rouge	73.0	77.1	2,703	3,375
West Feliciana	81.9	86.2	4,521	6,227
MARYLAND.				
Charles	52.3	54.6	1,097	1,204
MISSISSIPPI.				
Adams	74.8	78.6	2,976	3,676
Amite	54.8	59.4	1,215	1,465
Bolivar	87.4	88.1	7,013	7,433
Carroll	58.2	58.4	1,394	1,405
Chickasaw	55.7	59.0	1,255	1,441

STATE AND COUNTY.	NEGRO POPULATION.			
	Per cent of total population.		Per 1,000 whites.	
	1910	1900	1910	1900
MISSISSIPPI—continued.				
Claiborne	78.2	78.0	3,595	3,552
Clay	69.8	69.7	2,314	2,300
Coahoma	88.8	88.2	7,983	7,525
Copiah	55.6	52.4	1,255	1,103
De Soto	76.0	74.8	3,163	2,970
Grenada	71.0	72.9	2,445	2,686
Hinds	71.3	75.2	2,479	3,032
Holmes	79.8	77.9	3,954	3,535
Issaquena	94.2	94.0	16,278	15,709
Jefferson	78.4	81.1	3,632	4,296
Jefferson Davis	52.5	......	1,107	......
Kemper	57.5	56.8	1,367	1,343
Leflore	84.4	88.2	5,422	7,522
Lowndes	71.0	75.5	2,442	3,086
Madison	81.5	79.8	4,406	3,943
Marshall	72.2	67.6	2,595	2,087
Monroe	55.5	59.8	1,249	1,486
Montgomery	50.4	51.8	1,017	1,077
Noxubee	84.0	84.8	5,257	5,564
Oktibbeha	64.4	68.5	1,811	2,172
Panola	67.9	66.7	2,112	2,005
Quitman	76.5	76.9	3,253	3,320
Rankin	59.5	58.5	1,470	1,414
Sharkey	89.0	88.1	8,116	7,400
Sunflower	80.9	75.0	4,237	3,013
Tallahatchie	69.4	67.8	2,269	2,105
Tate	58.5	59.1	1,410	1,443
Tunica	90.7	90.5	9,786	9,566
Warren	69.9	74.7	2,320	2,953
Washington	85.0	89.7	5,706	8,825
Wilkinson	76.9	79.6	3,333	3,893
Yalobusha	52.0	53.0	1,082	1,126
Yazoo	76.1	77.1	3,182	3,376
NORTH CAROLINA.				
Anson	52.3	53.4	1,098	1,145
Bertie	58.6	57.6	1,416	1,356
Caswell	51.5	54.6	1,062	1,201
Chowan	54.5	57.0	1,197	1,328
Craven	55.9	60.2	1,269	1,513
Edgecombe	60.8	62.4	1,549	1,658
Halifax	64.6	64.1	1,827	1,784
Hertford	58.9	58.7	1,435	1,423
Northampton	58.5	57.3	1,410	1,342
Pasquotank	50.1	51.4	1,003	1,060
Perquimans	50.6	49.6	1,023	983
Scotland	55.2	53.5	1,243	1,175
Vance	51.5	58.5	1,062	1,408
Warren	65.2	68.2	1,877	2,149
SOUTH CAROLINA.				
Abbeville	64.7	66.1	1,834	1,948
Aiken	54.6	55.4	1,203	1,245
Bamberg	69.4	67.3	2,271	2,057
Barnwell	72.0	71.6	2,578	2,519
Beaufort	86.9	90.5	6,656	9,596
Berkeley	77.6	78.7	3,469	3,699
Calhoun	76.6	......	3,271	......
Charleston	63.2	68.5	1,722	2,182
Chester	65.0	67.7	1,861	2,096
Clarendon	72.7	71.5	2,660	2,509
Colleton	63.0	66.6	1,703	1,990
Darlington	59.1	59.6	1,444	1,476
Dillon	51.0	......	1,049	......
Dorchester	61.4	61.9	1,590	1,627
Edgefield	71.1	71.2	2,463	2,468
Fairfield	76.0	76.0	3,167	3,174
Florence	57.0	58.5	1,327	1,409
Georgetown	72.3	76.6	2,616	3,281
Greenwood	62.2	66.7	1,648	2,003
Hampton	64.2	65.3	1,790	1,882
Kershaw	60.7	59.5	1,544	1,469
Laurens	54.8	59.3	1,211	1,459
Lee	68.1	......	2,139	......
Marion	54.4	51.6	1,194	1,069
Marlboro	60.7	59.4	1,462	
Newberry	63.7	65.7	1,757	1,916
Orangeburg	65.8	69.5	1,927	2,275
Richland	53.6	61.6	1,153	1,603
Saluda	53.4	53.5	1,147	1,151

TABLE 13.—PERCENTAGE NEGRO AND NUMBER OF NEGROES PER 1,000 WHITES FOR THE 264 COUNTIES HAVING A POPULATION AT LEAST 50 PER CENT NEGRO IN 1910, BY STATES—Continued.

STATE AND COUNTY.	NEGRO POPULATION.				STATE AND COUNTY.	NEGRO POPULATION.				STATE AND COUNTY.	NEGRO POPULATION.			
	Per cent of total population.		Per 1,000 whites.			Per cent of total population.		Per 1,000 whites.			Per cent of total population.		Per 1,000 whites.	
	1901	1900	1910	1900		1910	1900	1910	1900		1910	1900	1910	1900
SOUTH CAROLINA—con.					VIRGINIA.					VIRGINIA—continued.				
Sumter	73.0	74.9	2,743	2,977	Amelia	63.0	66.2	1,700	1,961	Lunenburg	53.3	56.1	1,141	1,280
Union	51.7	57.1	1,071	1,330	Brunswick	59.1	59.5	1,443	1,470	Mecklenburg	56.6	61.0	1,305	1,565
Williamsburg	61.7	62.7	1,611	1,681	Caroline	52.7	54.1	1,115	1,179	Middlesex	52.4	55.2	1,100	1,231
York	53.0	52.4	1,132	1,104	Charles City	71.7	73.3	2,738	2,750	Nansemond	57.8	56.2	1,369	1,281
					Charlotte	52.8	55.7	1,119	1,257	New Kent	59.6	65.9	1,569	1,930
TENNESSEE.														
Fayette	75.0	73.0	3,010	2,704						Norfolk	60.3	62.2	1,520	1,653
Haywood	68.4	67.8	2,160	2,106	Cumberland	65.8	69.0	1,926	2,223	Northampton	55.9	55.4	1,266	1,242
					Dinwiddie	60.7	61.8	1,542	1,617	Nottoway	54.6	59.8	1,201	1,490
TEXAS.					Essex	58.4	63.1	1,402	1,713	Powhatan	59.6	65.7	1,473	1,913
Fort Bend	62.9	65.4	1,693	1,889	Goochland	56.6	58.4	1,305	1,403	Prince Edward	59.3	64.9	1,456	1,852
Gregg	55.0	55.9	1,227	1,268	Greensville	62.2	65.1	1,644	1,868	Prince George	58.0	62.7	1,380	1,683
Harrison	63.6	68.1	1,750	2,133						Princess Anne	50.5	50.8	1,019	1,033
Marion	64.2	66.5	1,796	1,982	Halifax	50.0	51.8	999	1,075	Southampton	61.2	59.9	1,576	1,493
Robertson	53.1	53.2	1,131	1,139	Isle of Wight	50.3	47.8	1,013	917	Surry	61.8	61.2	1,619	1,577
San Jacinto	54.4	53.8	1,194	1,172	King and Queen	56.1	56.8	1,278	1,313	Sussex	65.6	65.9	1,906	1,932
Walker	52.1	52.6	1,086	1,110	King William	56.8	59.2	1,382	1,519	Warwick	71.7	76.3	2,539	3,217
Waller	55.3	55.3	1,237	1,235	Lancaster	52.7	54.7	1,114	1,205	Westmoreland	50.1	52.6	1,005	1,110

PERCENTAGE NEGRO IN THE POPULATION OF GEORGIA AND FLORIDA, BY COUNTIES: 1910.

Map VIII.—GEORGIA.

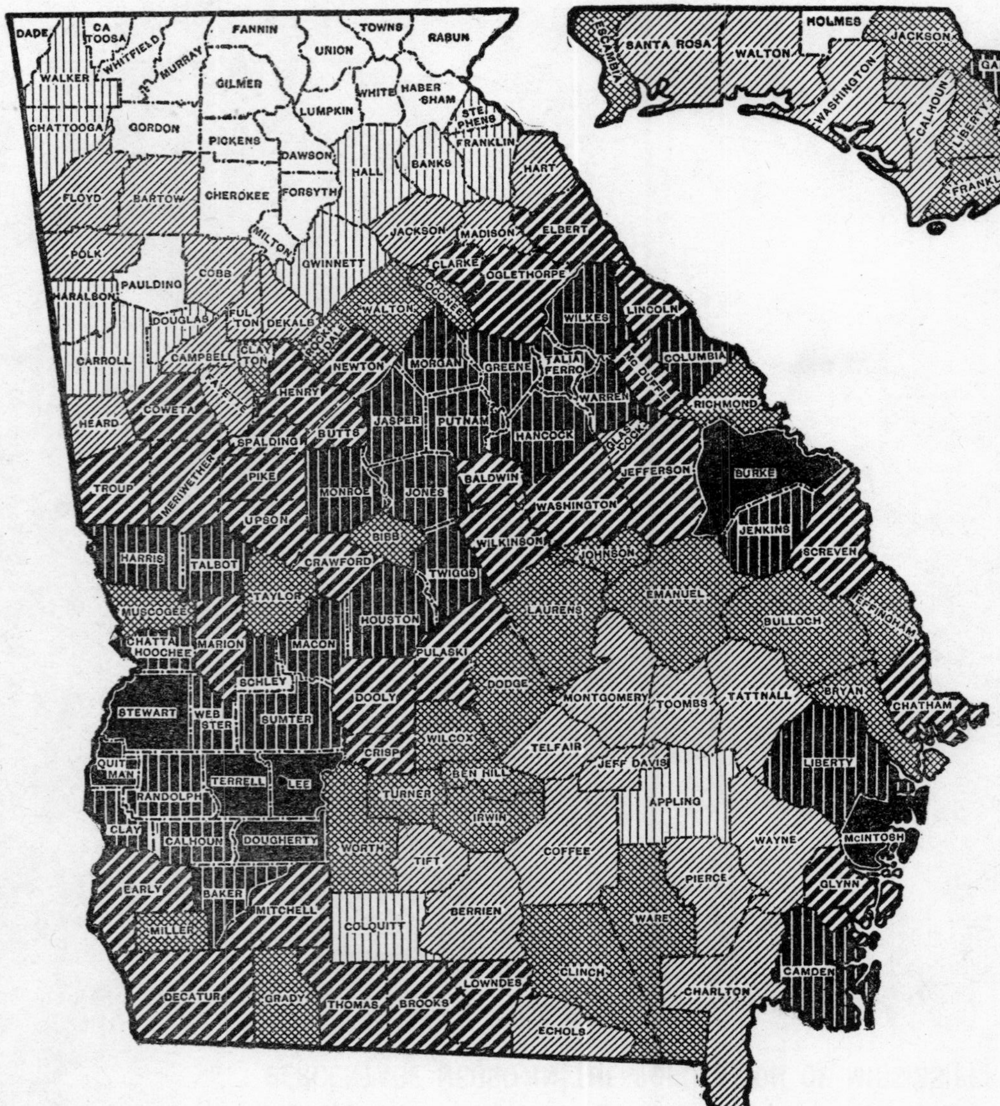

Map IX.—FLORIDA.

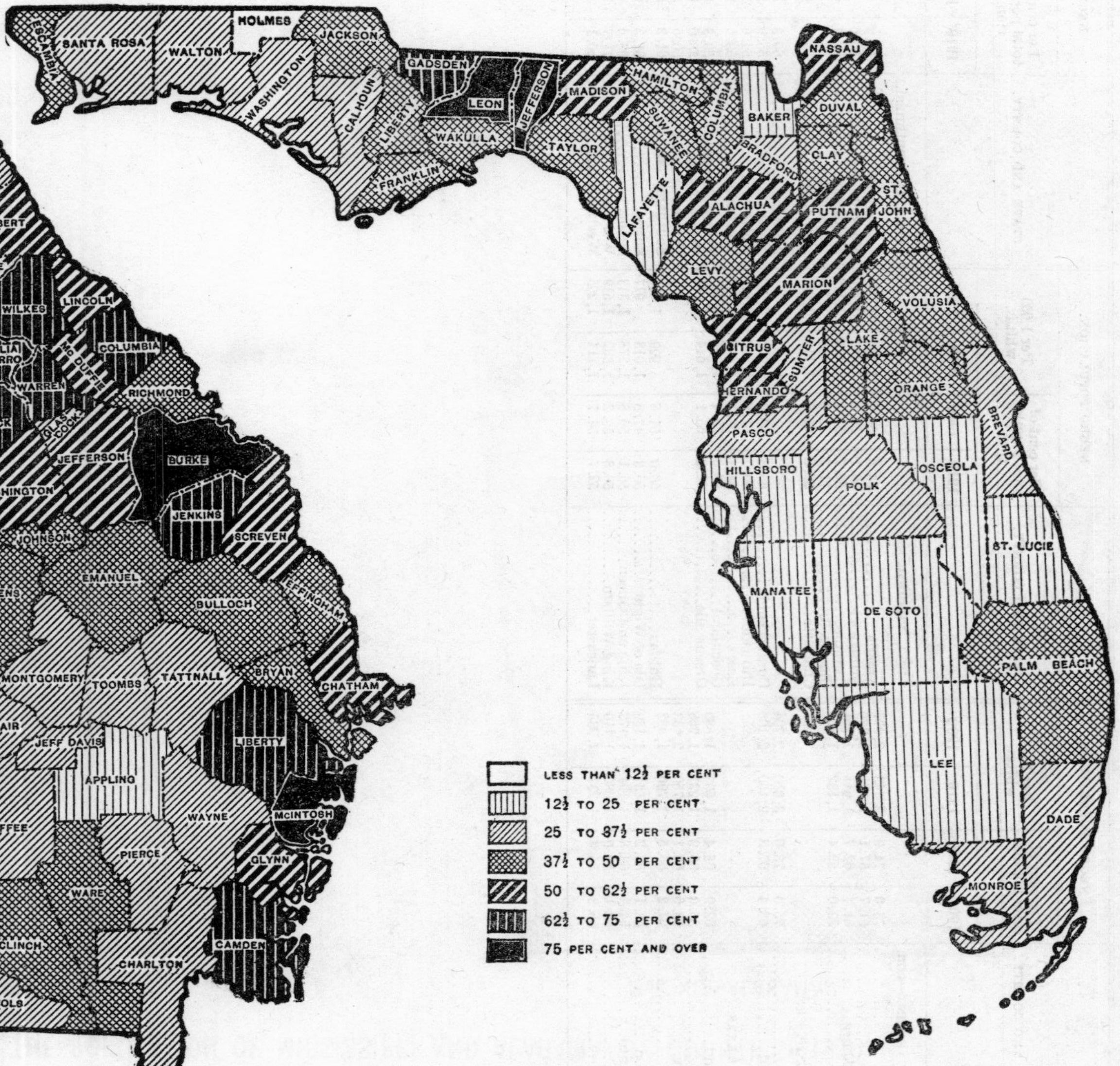

LESS THAN 12½ PER CENT
12½ TO 25 PER CENT
25 TO 37½ PER CENT
37½ TO 50 PER CENT
50 TO 62½ PER CENT
62½ TO 75 PER CENT
75 PER CENT AND OVER

PERCENTAGE NEGRO IN THE POPULATION OF ARKANSAS AND MARYLAND, BY COUNTIES: 1910.

Map XII. ARKANSAS.

PERCENTAGE NEGRO IN THE POPULATION OF MISSISSIPPI AND ALABAMA, BY COUNTIES: 1910.

Map XI.—ALABAMA.

Map X.—MISSISSIPPI.

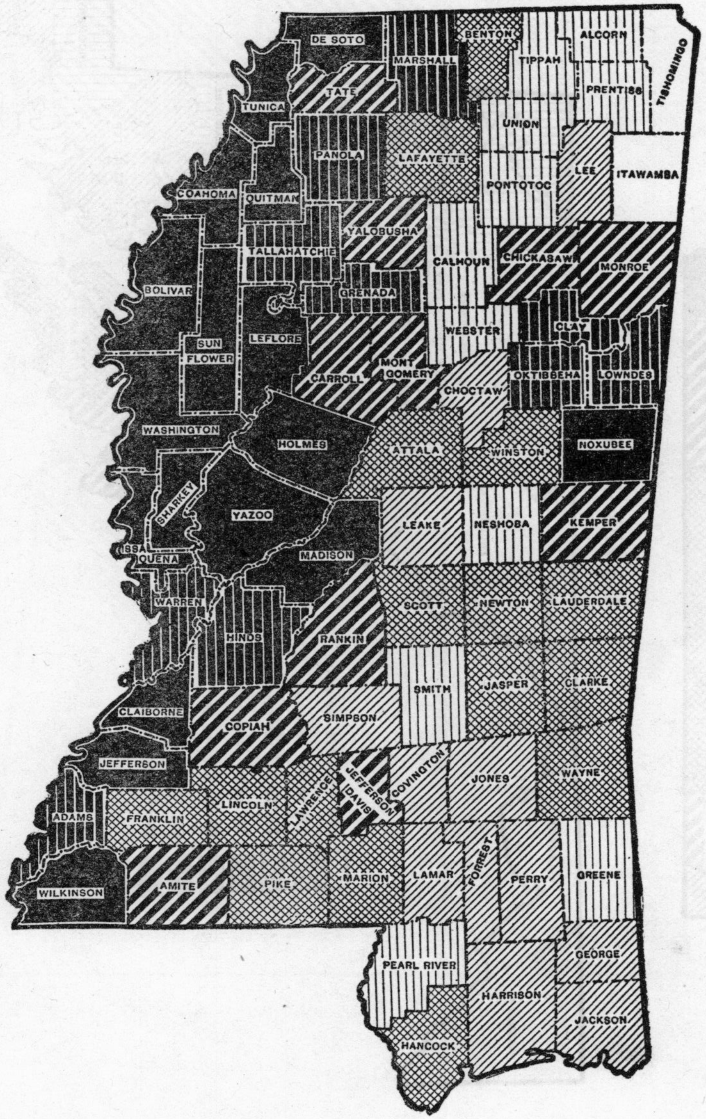

LESS THAN 12½ PER CENT
12½ TO 25 PER CENT
25 TO 37½ PER CENT
37½ TO 50 PER CENT
50 TO 62½ PER CENT
62½ TO 75 PER CENT
75 PER CENT AND OVER

(137)

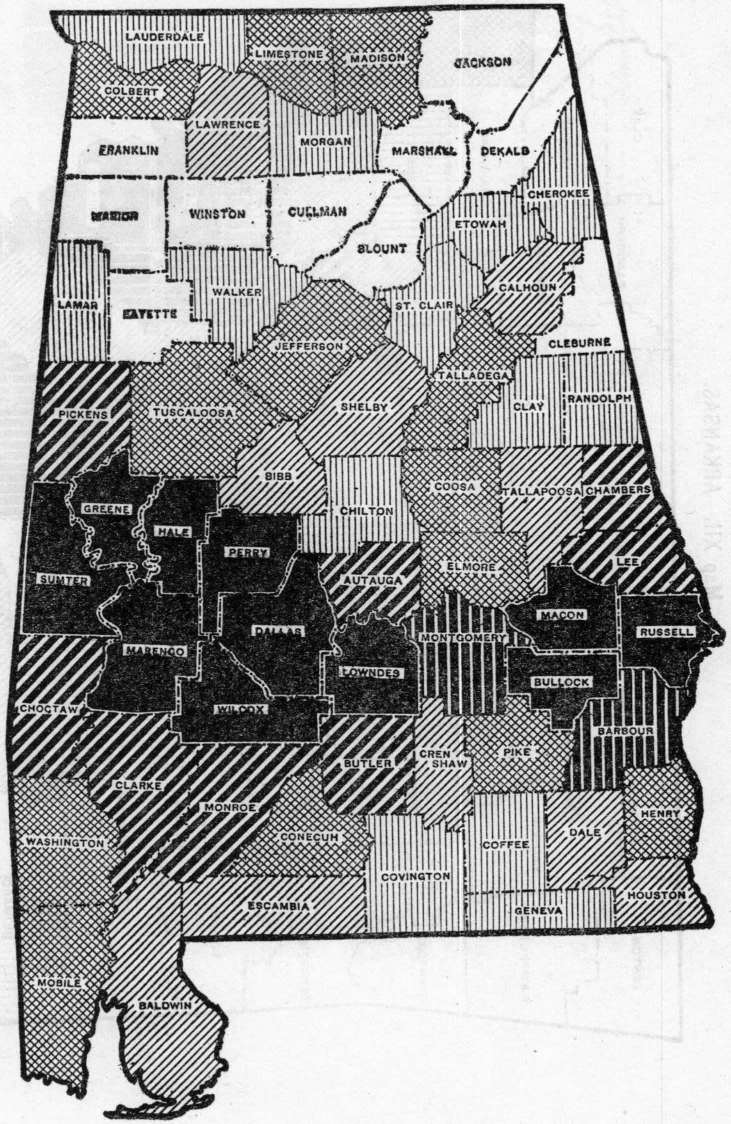

PERCENTAGE NEGRO IN THE POPULATION OF ARKANSAS AND MARYLAND, BY COUNTIES: 1910.

Map XII.—ARKANSAS.

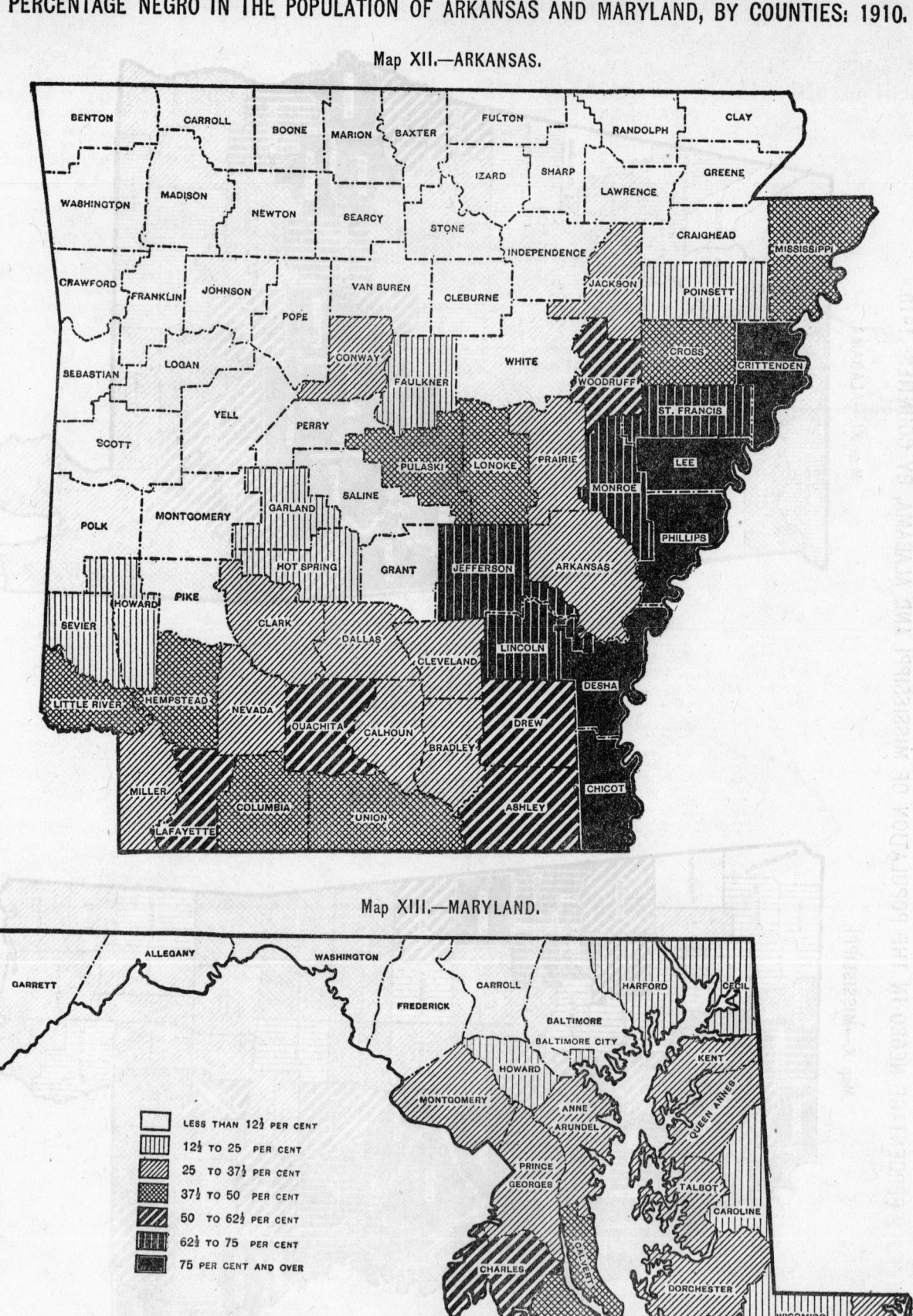

Map XIII.—MARYLAND.

LESS THAN 12½ PER CENT
12½ TO 25 PER CENT
25 TO 37½ PER CENT
37½ TO 50 PER CENT
50 TO 62½ PER CENT
62½ TO 75 PER CENT
75 PER CENT AND OVER

PERCENTAGE NEGRO IN THE POPULATION OF LOUISIANA, BY PARISHES, AND OKLAHOMA, BY COUNTIES, 1910.

PERCENTAGE NEGRO IN THE POPULATION OF NORTH CAROLINA AND SOUTH CAROLINA, BY COUNTIES; 1910.

Map XIV.—NORTH CAROLINA.

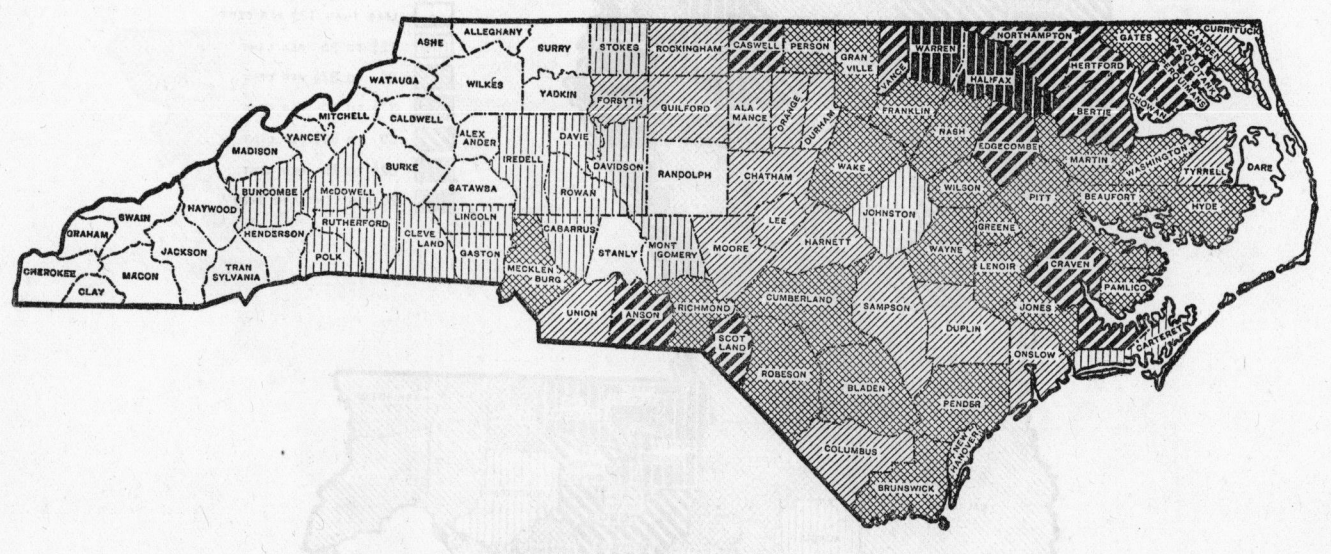

Map XV.—SOUTH CAROLINA.

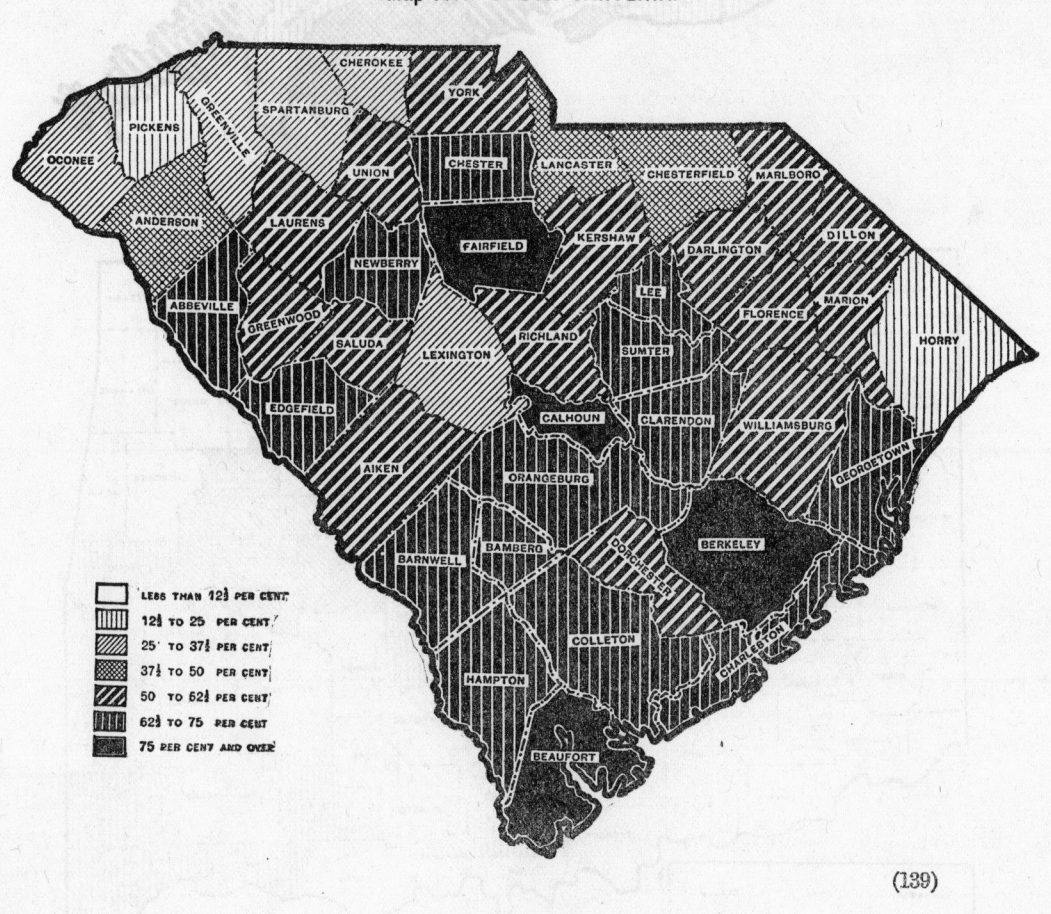

LESS THAN 12½ PER CENT.
12½ TO 25 PER CENT.
25 TO 37½ PER CENT.
37½ TO 50 PER CENT.
50 TO 62½ PER CENT.
62½ TO 75 PER CENT.
75 PER CENT AND OVER.

(139)

PERCENTAGE NEGRO IN THE POPULATION OF LOUISIANA, BY PARISHES, AND OKLAHOMA, BY COUNTIES: 1910.

Map XVI.—LOUISIANA.

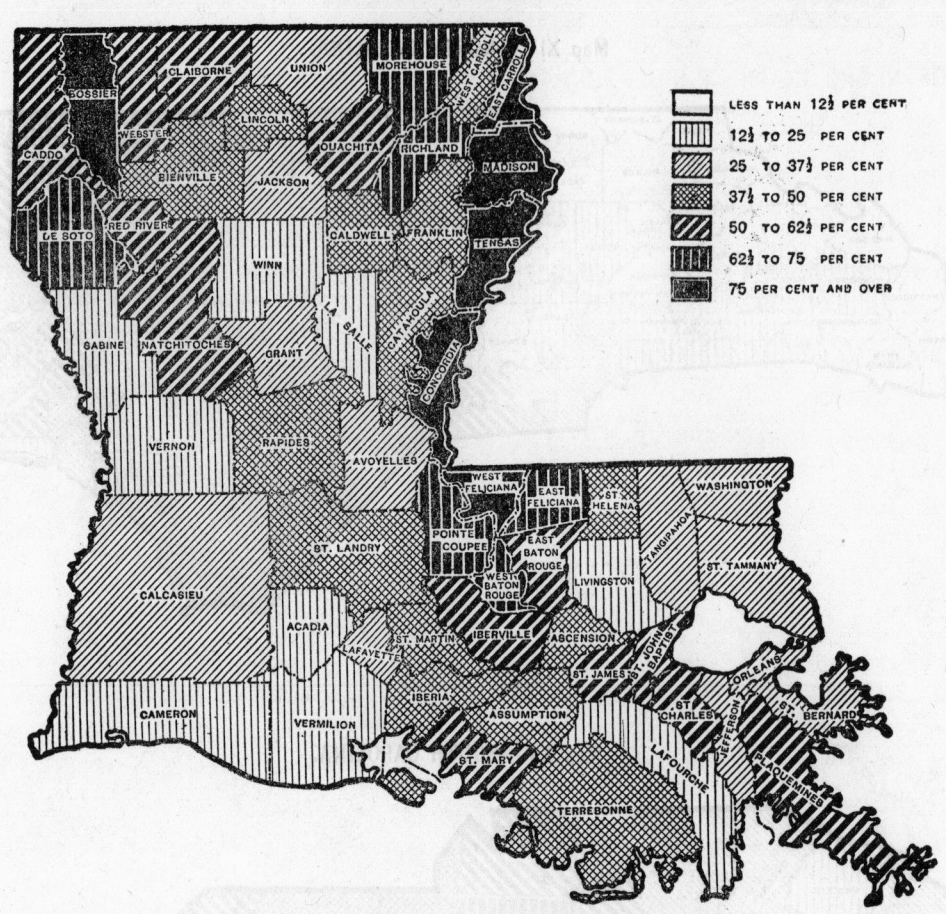

LESS THAN 12½ PER CENT
12½ TO 25 PER CENT
25 TO 37½ PER CENT
37½ TO 50 PER CENT
50 TO 62½ PER CENT
62½ TO 75 PER CENT
75 PER CENT AND OVER

Map XVII.—OKLAHOMA.

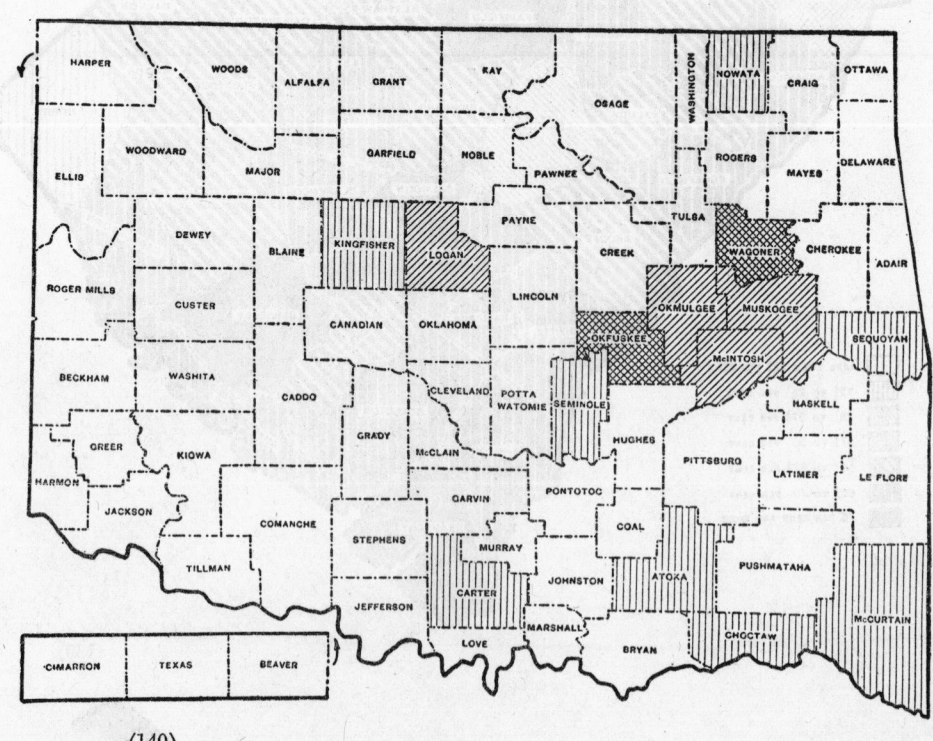

PERCENTAGE NEGRO IN THE POPULATION OF WEST VIRGINIA AND VIRGINIA, BY COUNTIES: 1910.

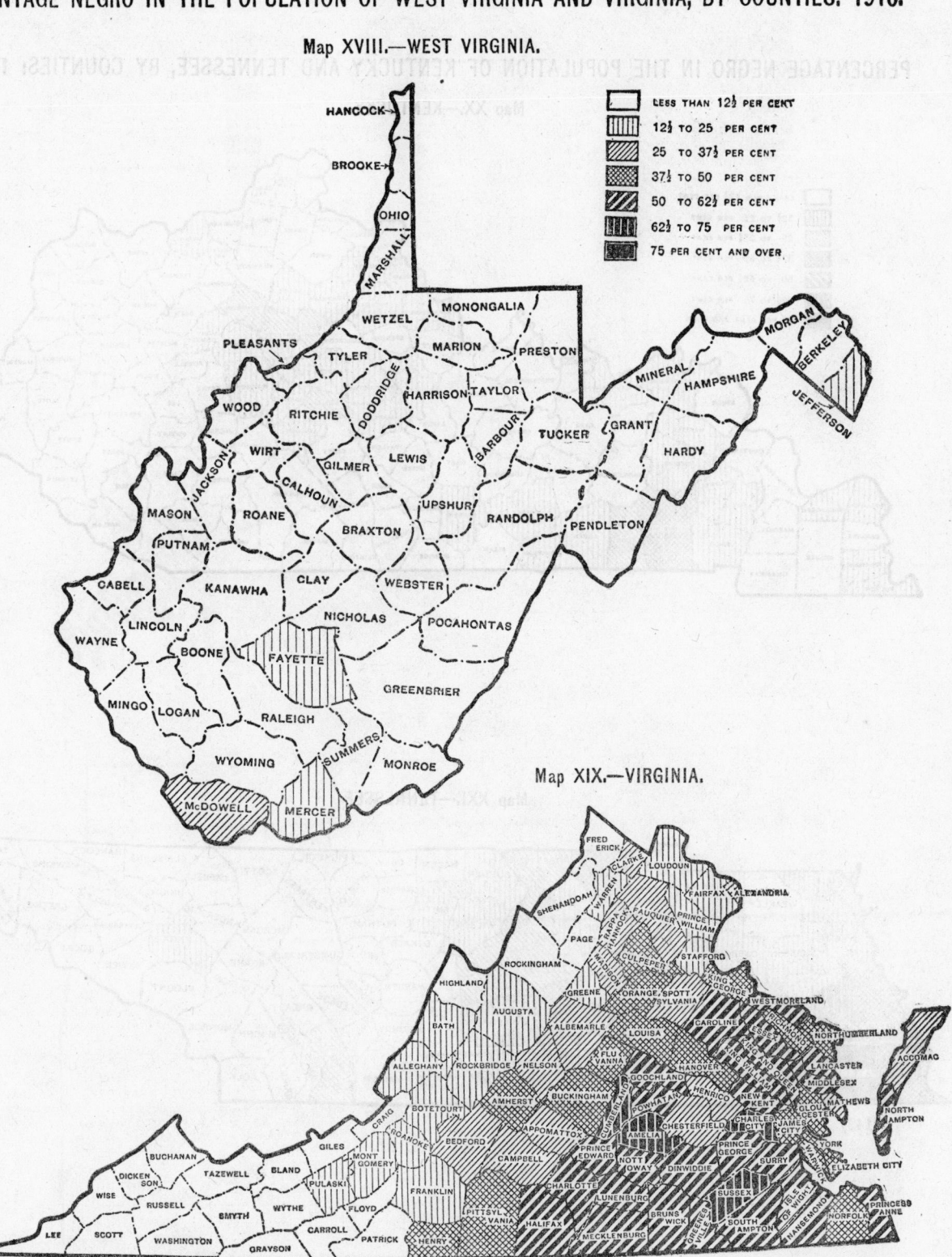

Map XVIII.—WEST VIRGINIA.

Map XIX.—VIRGINIA.

LESS THAN 12½ PER CENT
12½ TO 25 PER CENT
25 TO 37½ PER CENT
37½ TO 50 PER CENT
50 TO 62½ PER CENT
62½ TO 75 PER CENT
75 PER CENT AND OVER

PERCENTAGE NEGRO IN THE POPULATION OF WEST VIRGINIA AND VIRGINIA, BY COUNTIES: 1910.

MAP XVIII.—WEST VIRGINIA.

PERCENTAGE NEGRO IN THE POPULATION OF KENTUCKY AND TENNESSEE, BY COUNTIES: 1910.

Map XX.—KENTUCKY.

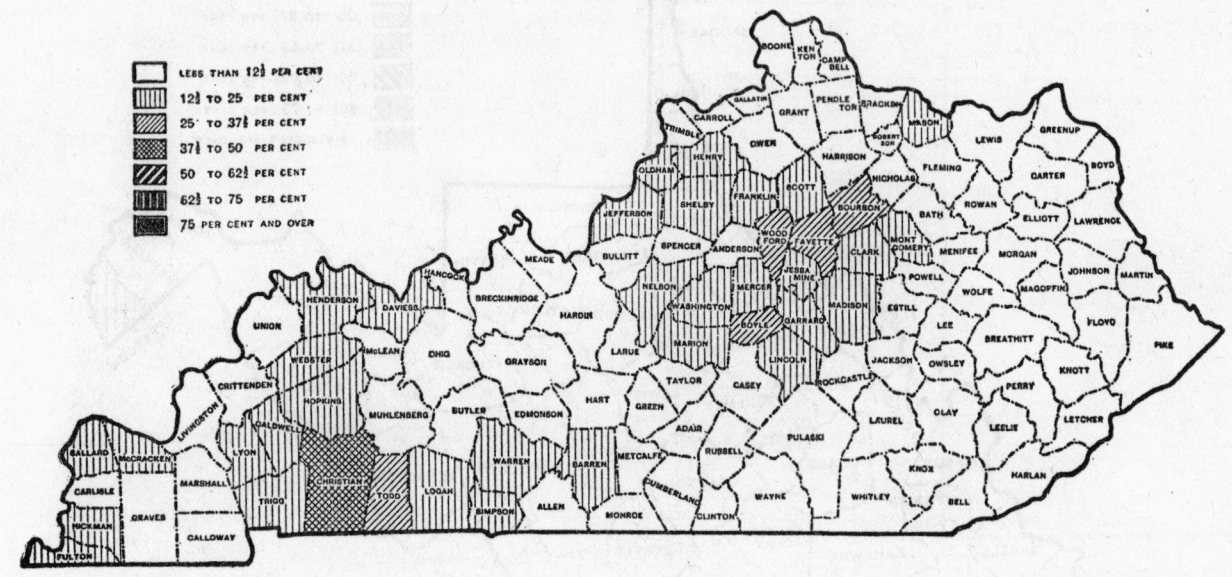

Map XXI.—TENNESSEE

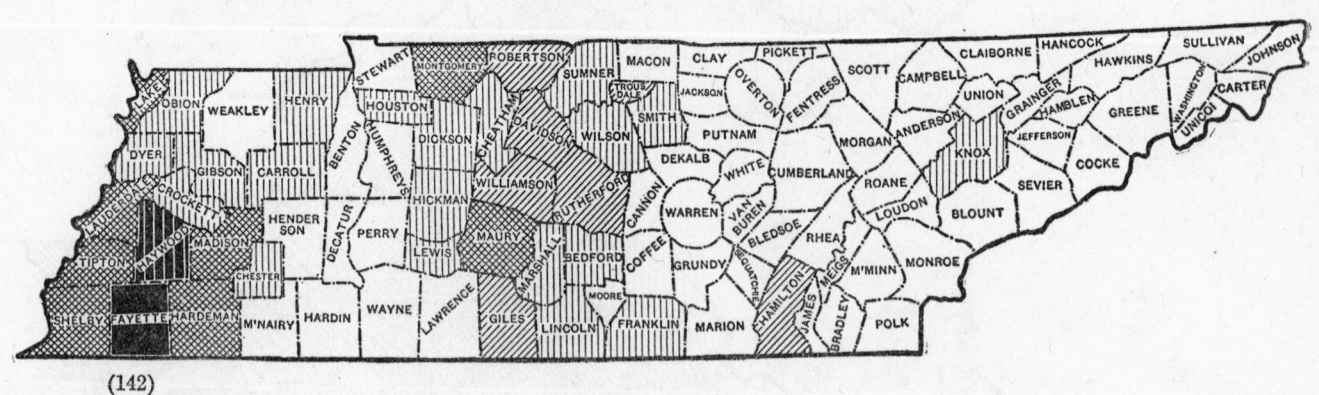

PERCENTAGE NEGRO IN THE POPULATION OF TEXAS, BY COUNTIES: 1910.

Map XXII.—TEXAS.

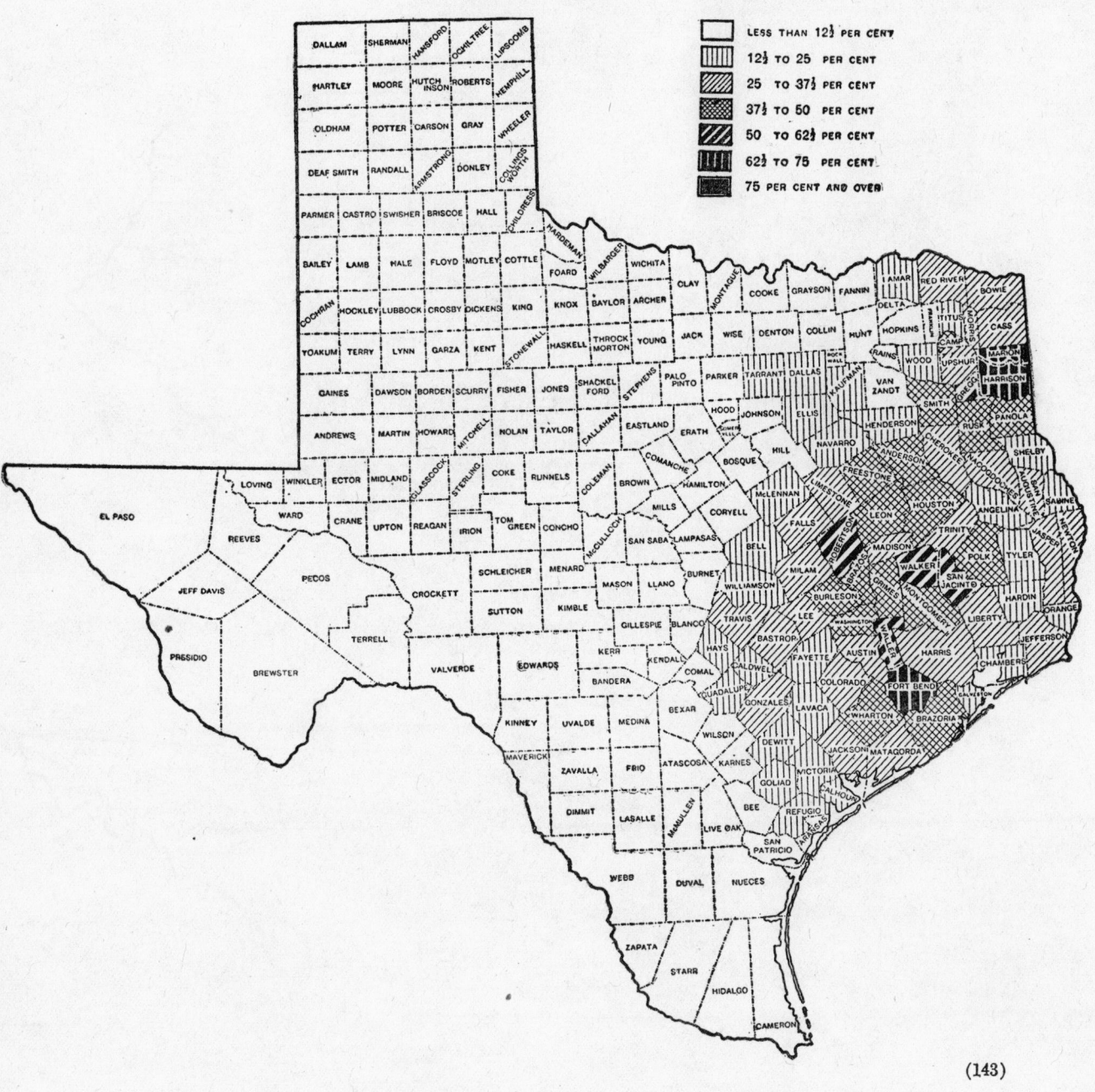

LESS THAN 12½ PER CENT

12½ TO 25 PER CENT

25 TO 37½ PER CENT

37½ TO 50 PER CENT

50 TO 62½ PER CENT

62½ TO 75 PER CENT

75 PER CENT AND OVER

(143)

PERCENTAGE NEGRO IN THE POPULATION OF TEXAS, BY COUNTIES: 1910.

Map XXII.—TEXAS.

PART III.—PHYSICAL CHARACTERISTICS.

Chapter IX.—Sex Composition.

NEGRO MALES AND FEMALES AT EACH CENSUS: 1820–1910.

The Negro population was returned by sex for the first time at the census of 1820. At this and the succeeding census the number of males exceeded the number of females, but at each of the eight censuses, 1840–1910, the number of females has exceeded the number of males.

In 1910 the number of males was 4,885,881, the number of females, 4,941,882, and the excess of females, 56,001. The sex ratio—i. e., number of males per 1,000 females in the population—in 1910 was 989. This ratio indicates that on the average per 1,000 Negro population the number of males was 497 (or 49.7 per cent), of females 503 (or 50.3 per cent), and the average excess of females 6 (or 0.6 per cent of the Negro population). In terms of population, the sex ratio of 989 signifies that on the average, in a population in which there were 1,000 females, there would be 989 males, giving an excess of females over males of 11 in a population of 1,989. These are equivalent statements of the proportion of males to females in the Negro population in 1910.

The number of males and of females in the Negro population, the excess of males or of females, and the number of males per 1,000 females, at each census, 1820 to 1910, is given in Table 1.

Table 1	NEGRO POPULATION.					
YEAR.	Both sexes.	Male.	Female.	Excess of—		Males to 1,000 females.
				Males.	Females.	
1910.........	9,827,763	4,885,881	4,941,882	....	56,001	989
1900.........	8,833,994	4,386,547	4,447,447	....	60,900	986
1890.........	7,488,676	3,735,603	3,753,073	....	17,470	995
1880.........	6,580,793	3,253,115	3,327,678	....	74,563	978
1870.........	4,880,009	2,393,263	2,486,746	....	93,483	962
1860.........	4,441,830	2,216,744	2,225,086	....	8,342	996
1850.........	3,638,808	1,811,258	1,827,550	....	16,292	991
1840.........	2,873,648	1,432,988	1,440,660	....	7,672	995
1830.........	2,328,642	1,166,276	1,162,366	3,910	....	1,003
1820.........	1,771,656	900,796	870,860	29,936	....	1,034

The sex ratio in the Negro population is little affected by emigration or immigration. In a sense it is a natural ratio for this class of the population, since it is practically determined by the ratio at birth, and the mortality rate of males and of females. There are, however, no statistics available for the Negro population, or for any class of population, in the United States as a whole, which determine accurately the sex ratio at birth. The age returns show the sex distribution of the population under 1 year of age, and within the area of registration for deaths, the mortality of children under 1 year by weeks and months is shown. But only a comparatively small proportion of the Negro population is resident within the registration area, and neither the age returns nor the mortality returns are sufficiently accurate and detailed to determine the sex ratio at birth. In countries with accurate birth statistics it seems to be generally true that the number of males exceeds the number of females at birth. In France, for example, among living births in 1910 the number of males was 395,669 and of females 378,721, the number of males to 1,000 females being 1,046.

As appears in the analysis of the age returns (see diagram on page 163), there is a slight excess of females in the Negro population under 1 year of age; a marked excess in the age period 15 to 29 years; and a deficiency at each year of age, with exception of a few years, in the age period 30 to 85 years. The sex ratio is an average covering all ages. It shows that the excess of females in the younger ages overbalances the excess of males in the more advanced ages.

The excess of females over males in the Negro population has appeared persistently in the census returns covering a period of 70 years. The excess was greatest absolutely and relatively, at the census of 1870, which gave a ratio of 962 males to 1,000 females, covering an excess of females numbering 93,493. The proportion of males for this class of the population, as for other classes, may have been reduced by the war, but it is not improbable that the ratio was affected by the undercounting at the census of 1870. If the returns at the census of 1890—also, as regards the Negro population, a defective enumeration—be disregarded, it would appear that the proportion of males in the Negro population has increased somewhat in recent decades—from 978 males per 1,000 females in 1880, to 986 in 1900, and to 989 in 1910. The proportion in 1910 was only slightly different from the proportion in 1850.

It may be noted that outside of Europe an excess of males is more common in the population of different countries than an excess of females. A compilation made in the Thirteenth Census, covering countries which embraced approximately one-half of the population of the world in 1900 gave a sex ratio of 1,009 males to 1,000 females for this population aggregate. Europe was the only continental area showing an excess of females, the number of males to 1,000 females in the population of Europe being 967. The sex ratio for European countries generally has been lowered by emigration, since more males emigrate than females. In France, however, whose population is not greatly affected by emigration, the number of males to 1,000 females in 1910 was 967. In France the proportion of males in the population had decreased very slightly at each quinquennial census since 1880.

SEX RATIO BY CLASSES.

Figures corresponding to those given in Table 1 for the Negro population as returned at each census, 1820 to 1910, are given in Table 2 for each class of the population as returned in 1910.

Table 2	POPULATION: 1910.				
RACIAL CLASS.	Male.	Female.	Excess of—		Males to 1,000 females.
			Males.	Females.	
All classes.........	47,332,277	44,639,989	2,692,288	....	1,060
Negro..................	4,885,881	4,941,882	....	56,001	989
White................	42,178,245	39,553,712	2,624,533	....	1,066
Native.............	34,654,457	33,731,955	922,502	....	1,027
Native parentage....	25,229,218	24,259,357	969,861	....	1,040
Mixed parentage....	2,968,446	3,013,080	....	44,634	985
Foreign parentage...	6,456,793	6,459,518	....	2,725	1,000
Foreign born.........	7,523,788	5,821,757	1,702,031	....	1,292
Indian.................	135,133	130,550	4,583	....	1,035
Chinese...............	66,856	4,675	62,181	....	14,301
Japanese..............	63,070	9,087	53,983	....	6,941
All other.............	3,092	83	3,009	....	(1)

[1] Number of females less than 100.

In those classes of the population which are entirely or largely immigrant—the foreign-born white, the Chinese and the Japanese—the proportion of males to females greatly exceeds any natural proportion determined by the sex ratio at birth and mortality. In these classes the ratio ranged in 1910 from 1,292 males to 1,000 females among foreign-born whites to 14,301 males to 1,000 females among the Chinese. Since, however, the Negro population is almost entirely native, comparison with the immigrant classes has little significance. In the native white population, and in the Indian population, which like the Negro is a native element, the number of males exceeded the number of females, the ratio for the native white population being 1,027, and for the Indian 1,035 males to 1,000 females. In the native white population of native parentage the number of males exceeded the number of females by 969,861, giving an average for this class of 1,040 males to 1,000 females. Among native whites of mixed parentage (one parent native and one foreign born) and of foreign parentage (both parents foreign born), on the other hand, the number of females exceeded the number of males.

Probably the sex ratio in these three classes of native whites is somewhat affected by errors in classification by nativity and parentage. Persons of unknown nativity were classified as native and persons of unknown parentage as of native parentage. Moreover, some foreign-born persons may have returned themselves or may have been returned by the enumerator in the absence of specific information, as natives, and some as natives of foreign or mixed parentage may have returned themselves or may have been returned as of native parentage. As males predominate in the foreign-born population, the classification of foreign-born persons as natives would tend to raise the proportion of males in the native population. It is probably true also that specific information was lacking more frequently in the case of males than of females, since males are more apt to be absent from home when the enumerator calls. It is believed, however, that these errors are not sufficient to account for the entire excess of males in the native white population. This class has shown an excess of males at each census at which the population has been returned by nativity.

In Table 3 the sex ratio is shown for the Negro population and for nativity and parentage classes of the white population at each census for which data are available.

Table 3	MALES TO 1,000 FEMALES.					
		White population.				
YEAR.	Negro population.	Total.	Native.			Foreign born.
			Total.	Native parentage.	Foreign or mixed parentage.	
1910	989	1,066	1,027	1,040	995	1,292
1900	986	1,049	1,028	1,037	1,003	1,174
1890	995	1,054	1,029	1,035	1,010	1,187
1880	978	1,040	1,021	(1)	(1)	1,159
1870	962	1,028	1,006	(1)	(1)	1,153
1860	996	1,053	1,037	(1)	(1)	1,151
1850	991	1,052	1,031	(1)	(1)	1,238
1840	995	1,045	(1)	(1)	(1)	(1)
1830	1,003	1,038	(1)	(1)	(1)	(1)
1820	1,034	1,032	(1)	(1)	(1)	(1)

[1] No data available.

With exception of a decrease for 1870, the proportion of males to females in the native white population has remained fairly constant, an excess of males being revealed at each census beginning with that of 1850, which was the first census to distinguish the native and the foreign-born elements in the white population. At each of these censuses, as has been noted, the Negro population revealed an excess of females.

SEX RATIO OF NEGRO AND WHITE POPULATION, BY SECTIONS AND DIVISIONS.

The sex composition of the Negro population in 1910 is shown, by sections and southern divisions, in Table 4, together with the sex ratio for the Negro population at four censuses, and of the native and foreign-born white population at the census of 1910.

There was a deficiency of males in the Negro population of the South as a whole, and an excess of males in the Negro population of the North and West in 1910. During the decade 1900–1910, however, the number of males per 1,000 females decreased markedly in the West—from 1,306 in 1900 to 1,207 in 1910—and the decrease in the preceding decade, from 1,575 in 1890, was equally marked.

NEGRO POPULATION CLASSIFIED BY SEX, 1910; NEGRO SEX RATIO, 1880–1910; AND SEX RATIO FOR WHITE CLASSES, 1910: BY SECTIONS AND SOUTHERN DIVISIONS.

Table 4	NEGRO POPULATION: 1910.					MALES TO 1,000 FEMALES.						
SECTION AND DIVISION.	Both sexes.	Male.	Female.	Excess of—		Negro population.				White population: 1910		
				Males.	Females.	1910	1900	1890	1880	Total.	Native.	Foreign born.
United States....................	9,827,763	4,885,881	4,941,882	....	56,001	989	986	995	978	1,066	1,027	1,292
The South....................	8,749,427	4,339,625	4,409,802	....	70,177	984	982	990	975	1,052	1,041	1,420
South Atlantic...........	4,112,488	2,029,808	2,082,680	....	52,872	975	969	979	968	1,032	1,018	1,469
East South Central...............	2,652,513	1,315,792	1,336,721	....	20,929	984	989	993	973	1,036	1,031	1,392
West South Central.............	1,984,426	994,025	990,401	3,624	....	1,004	999	1,012	997	1,093	1,079	1,388
The North....................	1,027,674	518,544	509,130	9,414	....	1,018	1,017	1,030	997	1,050	1,007	1,235
The West....................	50,662	27,712	22,950	4,762	....	1,207	1,306	1,575	1,414	1,262	1,153	1,845

Within the South itself the West South Central division showed in 1910 a slight excess of males over females. The proportion of males was lowest in the South Atlantic division, in which the number of males to 1,000 females was 975. In the East South Central division it was 984, and in the West South Central 1,004. During the decade the proportion of males increased in the South Atlantic and in the West South Central divisions, and decreased in the East South Central division.

In each division of the South the native white population returned an excess of males, the relative excess being least in the South Atlantic division—with a ratio of 1,018 males to 1,000 females, and greatest in the West South Central division, 1,079 to 1,000.

SEX COMPOSITION OF NEGRO POPULATION, BY STATES: 1910, 1900, 1890, AND 1880.

In Table 5 (p. 150) the number of Negro males and females and the sex ratio are given, by states, for four census years, and for 1910 the excess of males or of females.[1]

In 10 Southern states and in the District of Columbia females were in excess in the Negro population in 1910, and in 6 Southern states males were in excess. Among these states the proportion of males was highest in West Virginia, in which state the number of males per 1,000 females in the Negro population was 1,328. The other states showing an excess of males in the Negro population were Delaware, Florida, Kentucky, Arkansas, and Oklahoma. In all of the Northern and Western states except in a group of contiguous states in New England and the Middle Atlantic divisions—i. e., Massachusetts, Rhode Island, Connecticut, New York, New Jersey, and Pennsylvania—males were in excess in the Negro population. As is shown in a subsequent table (Table 14) the excess of females in these six states is confined to the urban population, which is sufficiently large to more than offset by its sex distribution the excess of males in the rural population.

In 9 Southern states and in the District of Columbia the proportion of males increased during the decade 1900–1910; in 6 states it decreased, and in 1 state it remained unchanged. As compared with 1880, the proportion of males was higher in 1910 in 10 Southern states and the District of Columbia, and lower in 5 states.

In Table 6 (p. 151) the states are arranged in order according to the sex ratio in the Negro population in 1910, 1900, and 1890, and the Negro population is cumulated by states.

The proportion of males in 1910 was lowest in the District of Columbia and highest in Vermont, the number of males per 1,000 females being 822 in the District and 2,618 in Vermont. In 1900 and in 1890 also the proportion was lower in the District than in any state. In both of these years the proportion was highest in Arizona—in 1900 2,810 and in 1890 6,375 males to 1,000 females. The median ratio (i. e., the ratio of the median population in the cumulated populations of Table 6) was lower in 1910 than in 1900, although the average ratio for the population as a whole was higher. The very high ratios in each of the three years covered by Table 6, however, relate generally to small Negro populations. In 1910, for example, 99 per cent of the Negro population lived in states in which the number of males did not exceed 1,185 per 1,000 females; 90 per cent lived in states in which the ratio did not exceed 1,046 to 1,000. In 1900, 99.3 per cent lived in states with ratios lower than 1,185, and in 1890, 99 per cent.

[1] The black and mulatto Negro population of states is classified by sex for the year 1860 in Table 24 of Chapter XI, and for 1910 in Table 26 of that chapter.

NUMBER OF MALES AND FEMALES AND RATIO OF MALES TO FEMALES IN THE NEGRO POPULATION, BY DIVISIONS AND STATES: 1910, 1900, 1890, AND 1880.

Table 5

MALES AND FEMALES IN THE NEGRO POPULATION.

DIVISION AND STATE.	1910 Male.	1910 Female.	Excess of— Males.	Excess of— Females.	1900 Male.	1900 Female.	1890 Male.	1890 Female.	1880 Male.	1880 Female.	Males to 1,000 females. 1910	1900	1890	1880
UNITED STATES.....	4,885,881	4,941,882	....	56,001	4,386,547	4,447,447	3,735,603	3,753,073	3,253,115	3,327,678	989	986	995	978
GEOGRAPHIC DIVISIONS:														
New England.........	32,783	33,523	....	740	28,579	30,520	21,633	22,947	19,223	20,702	978	936	943	929
Middle Atlantic........	203,466	214,404	....	10,938	159,711	166,210	111,644	113,682	90,891	98,601	949	961	982	922
East North Central ...	156,431	144,405	12,026	....	134,445	123,397	108,096	98,927	95,093	88,205	1,083	1,090	1,093	1,078
West North Central ...	125,864	116,798	9,066	....	121,272	116,637	114,288	109,801	101,922	100,401	1,078	1,040	1,041	1,015
South Atlantic........	2,029,808	2,082,680	....	52,872	1,835,525	1,893,492	1,613,769	1,648,921	1,446,862	1,494,340	975	969	979	968
East South Central......	1,315,792	1,336,721	....	20,929	1,243,082	1,256,804	1,056,343	1,063,454	949,225	975,771	984	989	993	973
West South Central ...	994,025	990,401	3,624	....	846,797	847,269	693,264	684,826	542,956	544,749	1,004	999	1,012	997
Mountain............	11,766	9,701	2,065	....	9,104	6,486	8,372	4,599	2,997	2,025	1,213	1,404	1,820	1,480
Pacific...............	15,946	13,249	2,697	....	8,032	6,632	8,194	5,916	3,946	2,884	1,204	1,211	1,385	1,368
NEW ENGLAND:														
Maine...............	700	663	37	....	670	649	614	576	765	686	1,056	1,032	1,066	1,115
New Hampshire.......	298	276	12	....	327	335	323	291	341	344	1,043	976	1,110	991
Vermont.............	1,173	448	725	....	454	372	493	444	566	491	2,618	1,220	1,110	1,153
Massachusetts.........	18,748	19,307	....	559	15,591	16,383	10,879	11,265	9,049	9,648	971	952	966	938
Rhode Island.........	4,645	4,884	....	239	4,290	4,802	3,394	3,999	2,952	3,536	951	893	849	835
Connecticut..........	7,229	7,945	....	716	7,247	7,979	5,930	6,372	5,550	5,997	910	908	931	925
MIDDLE ATLANTIC:														
New York........	64,034	70,157	....	6,123	46,618	52,614	33,503	36,589	30,852	34,252	913	886	916	901
New Jersey...........	43,602	46,158	....	2,556	33,745	36,099	23,410	24,228	18,846	20,007	945	935	966	942
Pennsylvania..........	95,830	98,089	....	2,259	79,348	77,497	54,731	52,865	41,193	44,342	977	1,024	1,035	929
EAST NORTH CENTRAL:														
Ohio................	57,995	53,457	4,538	....	49,985	46,916	45,076	42,037	40,962	38,938	1,085	1,065	1,072	1,052
Indiana.............	31,044	29,276	1,768	....	29,701	27,804	23,523	21,692	20,267	18,961	1,060	1,068	1,084	1,069
Illinois.............	56,909	52,140	4,769	....	45,121	39,957	30,148	26,880	24,507	21,861	1,091	1,129	1,122	1,121
Michigan.............	9,007	8,108	899	....	8,220	7,596	7,986	7,237	7,836	7,264	1,111	1,082	1,103	1,079
Wisconsin............	1,476	1,424	52	....	1,418	1,124	1,363	1,081	1,521	1,181	1,037	1,262	1,261	1,288
WEST NORTH CENTRAL:														
Minnesota...........	4,183	2,901	1,282	....	2,836	2,123	2,167	1,516	905	659	1,442	1,336	1,429	1,373
Iowa................	8,120	6,853	1,267	....	6,875	5,818	5,712	4,973	5,191	4,325	1,185	1,182	1,149	1,200
Missouri.............	80,489	76,963	3,526	....	81,206	80,028	75,336	74,848	72,153	73,197	1,046	1,015	1,007	986
North Dakota.........	381	236	145	....	173	113	219	154 }	225	176 {	1,614	1,531	1,422	....
South Dakota........	468	349	119	....	272	193	363	178			1,341	1,409	2,039	....
Nebraska............	4,259	3,430	829	....	3,368	2,901	5,243	3,670	1,296	1,089	1,242	1,161	1,429	1,190
Kansas..............	27,964	26,066	1,898	....	26,542	25,461	25,248	24,462	22,152	20,955	1,073	1,042	1,032	1,057
SOUTH ATLANTIC:														
Delaware.............	16,011	15,170	841	....	15,616	15,081	14,455	13,931	13,327	13,115	1,055	1,035	1,038	1,016
Maryland............	114,749	117,501	....	2,752	115,617	119,447	105,684	109,973	102,505	107,725	977	968	961	952
District of Columbia...	42,615	51,831	....	9,216	38,348	48,354	33,721	41,851	26,238	33,358	822	793	806	787
Virginia.............	330,542	340,554	....	10,012	323,459	337,263	310,828	324,610	308,935	322,681	971	959	958	957
West Virginia........	36,607	27,566	9,041	....	25,167	18,332	17,991	14,699	13,482	12,404	1,328	1,373	1,224	1,087
North Carolina.......	339,581	358,262	....	18,681	303,624	320,845	275,230	285,788	262,363	268,914	948	946	963	976
South Carolina.......	408,078	427,765	....	19,687	383,626	398,695	341,821	347,113	297,787	306,545	954	962	985	971
Georgia.............	580,263	596,724	....	16,461	509,869	524,944	430,072	428,743	359,157	365,976	972	971	1,003	981
Florida..............	161,362	147,307	14,055	....	120,199	110,531	83,967	82,213	63,068	63,622	1,095	1,087	1,021	991
EAST SOUTH CENTRAL:														
Kentucky............	131,492	130,164	1,328	....	142,073	142,633	133,547	134,524	133,798	137,653	1,010	996	993	972
Tennessee...........	233,710	239,378	....	5,668	238,388	241,855	213,521	217,157	197,467	205,684	976	986	983	960
Alabama............	447,794	460,488	....	12,694	409,237	418,070	336,997	341,492	295,001	305,102	972	979	987	967
Mississippi..........	502,796	506,691	....	3,895	453,384	454,246	372,278	370,281	322,959	327,332	992	998	1,005	987
WEST SOUTH CENTRAL:														
Arkansas............	223,323	219,568	3,755	....	185,342	181,514	159,014	150,103	107,331	103,335	1,017	1,021	1,059	1,039
Louisiana...........	353,824	360,050	....	6,226	322,664	328,140	277,134	282,059	238,879	244,776	983	983	983	976
Oklahoma [1]........	71,937	65,675	6,262	....	28,656	27,028	11,655	9,954	......	......	1,095	1,060	1,171	....
Texas...............	344,941	345,108	....	167	310,135	310,587	245,461	242,710	196,746	196,638	1,000	999	1,011	1,001
MOUNTAIN:														
Montana............	1,058	776	282	....	912	611	1,053	437	191	155	1,363	1,493	2,410	1,232
Idaho...............	398	253	145	....	166	127	118	83	39	14	1,573	1,307	(²)	(²)
Wyoming............	1,544	691	853	....	631	309	652	270	160	138	2,234	2,042	2,415	1,159
Colorado............	5,867	5,586	281	....	4,473	4,097	3,602	2,613	1,433	1,002	1,050	1,092	1,378	1,430
New Mexico..........	891	737	154	....	1,023	587	1,220	736	638	377	1,209	1,743	1,658	1,692
Arizona.............	1,054	955	99	....	1,363	485	1,173	184	104	51	1,104	2,810	6,375	(²)
Utah................	691	453	238	....	454	218	392	196	124	108	1,525	2,083	2,000	1,148
Nevada.............	263	250	13	....	82	52	162	80	308	180	1,052	(²)	(²)	1,711
PACIFIC:														
Washington..........	3,736	2,322	1,414	....	1,589	925	1,104	498	209	116	1,609	1,718	2,217	1,802
Oregon..............	907	585	322	....	677	428	743	443	270	217	1,550	1,582	1,677	1,244
California...........	11,303	10,342	961	....	5,766	5,279	6,347	4,975	3,467	2,551	1,093	1,092	1,276	1,359

[1] Includes population of Indian Territory for 1900 and 1890.   [²] Ratio not shown where the number of females is less than 100.

NEGRO POPULATION CUMULATED BY STATES, RANGED IN ORDER BY SEX RATIO: 1910, 1900, AND 1890.

NEGRO POPULATION, CUMULATED BY STATES, BY SEX RATIOS.

Table 6 — STATES RANGED IN ORDER BY SEX RATIO.	1910 Males to 1,000 females.	Popula-tion.	Cumulated population. Number.	Per cent.	STATES RANGED IN ORDER BY SEX RATIO.	1900 Males to 1,000 females.	Popula-tion.	Cumulated population. Number.	Per cent.	STATES RANGED IN ORDER BY SEX RATIO.	1890 Males to 1,000 females.	Popula-tion.	Cumulated population. Number.	Per cent.
United States..	989	9,827,763	....	......	United States..	986	8,833,994	....	......	United States..	995	7,488,676	....	......
1 Dist. of Columbia.	822	94,446	94,446	1.0	1 Dist. of Columbia	793	86,702	86,702	1.0	1 Dist. of Columbia	806	75,572	75,572	1.0
2 Connecticut....	910	15,174	109,620	1.1	2 New York.....	886	99,232	185,934	2.1	2 Rhode Island....	849	7,393	82,965	1.1
3 New York.......	913	134,191	243,811	2.5	3 Rhode Island....	893	9,092	195,026	2.2	3 New York......	916	70,092	153,057	2.0
4 New Jersey.....	945	89,760	333,571	3.4	4 Connecticut.....	908	15,226	210,252	2.4	4 Connecticut....	931	12,302	165,359	2.2
5 North Carolina..	948	697,843	1,031,414	10.5	5 New Jersey.....	935	69,844	280,096	3.2	5 Virginia.........	958	635,438	800,797	10.7
6 Rhode Island.....	951	9,529	1,040,943	10.6	6 North Carolina..	946	624,469	904,565	10.2	6 Maryland.......	961	215,657	1,016,454	13.6
7 South Carolina....	954	835,843	1,876,786	19.1	7 Massachusetts...	952	31,974	936,539	10.6	7 North Carolina..	963	561,018	1,577,472	21.1
8 Massachusetts...	971	38,055	1,914,841	19.5	8 Virginia........	959	660,722	1,597,261	18.1	8 Massachusetts...	966	22,144	1,599,616	21.4
9 Virginia.........	971	671,096	2,585,937	26.3	9 South Carolina..	962	782,321	2,379,582	26.9	9 New Jersey.....	966	47,638	1,647,254	22.0
10 Alabama.........	972	908,282	3,494,219	35.6	10 Maryland.......	968	235,064	2,614,646	29.6	10 Louisiana.......	983	559,193	2,206,447	29.5
11 Georgia.........	972	1,176,987	4,671,206	47.5	11 Georgia........	971	1,034,813	3,649,459	41.3	11 Tennessee.......	983	430,678	2,637,125	35.2
12 Tennessee.......	976	473,088	5,144,294	52.3	12 New Hampshire	976	662	3,650,121	41.3	12 South Carolina..	985	688,934	3,326,059	44.4
13 Maryland........	977	232,250	5,376,544	54.7	13 Alabama........	979	827,307	4,477,428	50.7	13 Alabama........	987	678,489	4,004,548	53.5
14 Pennsylvania....	977	193,919	5,570,463	56.7	14 Louisiana.......	983	650,804	5,128,232	58.1	14 Kentucky.......	993	268,071	4,272,619	57.1
15 Louisiana........	983	713,874	6,284,337	63.9	15 Tennessee......	986	480,243	5,608,475	63.5	15 Georgia........	1,003	858,815	5,131,434	68.5
16 Mississippi.......	992	1,009,487	7,293,824	74.2	16 Kentucky.......	996	284,706	5,893,181	66.7	16 Mississippi.......	1,005	742,559	5,873,993	78.4
17 Texas...........	1,000	690,049	7,983,873	81.2	17 Mississippi......	998	907,811	6,800,811	77.0	17 Missouri........	1,007	150,184	6,024,177	80.4
18 Kentucky........	1,010	261,656	8,245,529	83.9	18 Texas..........	999	620,722	7,421,533	84.0	18 Texas..........	1,011	488,171	6,512,348	87.0
19 Arkansas........	1,017	442,891	8,688,420	88.4	19 Missouri........	1,015	161,234	7,582,767	85.8	19 Florida.........	1,021	166,180	6,678,528	89.2
20 Wisconsin........	1,037	2,900	8,691,320	88.4	20 Arkansas.......	1,021	366,856	7,949,623	90.0	20 Kansas.........	1,032	49,710	6,728,238	89.8
21 New Hampshire..	1,043	564	8,691,884	88.4	21 Pennsylvania...	1,024	156,845	8,106,468	91.8	21 Pennsylvania...	1,035	107,596	6,835,834	91.3
22 Missouri.........	1,046	157,452	8,849,336	90.0	22 Maine..........	1,032	1,319	8,107,787	91.8	22 Delaware.......	1,038	28,386	6,864,220	91.7
23 Colorado........	1,050	11,453	8,860,789	90.2	23 Delaware.......	1,035	30,697	8,138,484	92.1	23 Arkansas.......	1,059	309,117	7,173,337	95.8
24 Nevada.........	1,052	513	8,861,302	90.2	24 Kansas.........	1,042	52,003	8,190,487	92.7	24 Maine..........	1,066	1,190	7,174,527	95.8
25 Delaware.........	1,055	31,181	8,892,483	90.5	25 Oklahoma [1]....	1,060	55,684	8,246,171	93.3	25 Ohio...........	1,072	87,113	7,261,640	97.0
26 Maine...........	1,056	1,363	8,893,846	90.5	26 Ohio...........	1,065	96,901	8,343,072	94.4	26 Indiana........	1,084	45,215	7,306,855	97.6
27 Indiana.........	1,060	60,320	8,954,166	91.1	27 Indiana........	1,068	57,505	8,400,577	95.1	27 Michigan.......	1,103	15,223	7,322,078	97.8
28 Kansas..........	1,073	54,030	9,008,196	91.7	28 Michigan.......	1,082	15,816	8,416,393	95.3	28 New Hampshire	1,110	614	7,322,692	97.8
29 Ohio............	1,085	111,452	9,119,648	92.8	29 Florida.........	1,087	230,730	8,647,123	97.9	29 Vermont.......	1,110	937	7,323,629	97.8
30 Illinois..........	1,091	109,049	9,228,697	93.9	30 California.......	1,092	11,045	8,658,168	98.0	30 Illinois........	1,122	57,028	7,380,657	98.6
31 California........	1,093	21,645	9,250,342	94.1	31 Colorado.......	1,092	8,570	8,666,738	98.1	31 Iowa..........	1,149	10,685	7,391,342	98.7
32 Florida..........	1,095	308,669	9,559,011	97.3	32 Illinois.........	1,129	85,078	8,751,816	99.1	32 Oklahoma [1].....	1,171	21,609	7,412,951	99.0
33 Oklahoma........	1,095	137,612	9,696,623	98.7	33 Nebraska.......	1,161	6,269	8,758,085	99.1	33 West Virginia...	1,224	32,690	7,445,641	99.4
34 Arizona.........	1,104	2,009	9,698,632	98.7	34 Iowa..........	1,182	12,693	8,770,778	99.3	34 Wisconsin......	1,261	2,444	7,448,085	99.5
35 Michigan........	1,111	17,115	9,715,747	98.9	35 Vermont.......	1,220	826	8,771,604	99.3	35 California......	1,276	11,322	7,459,407	99.6
36 Iowa............	1,185	14,973	9,730,720	99.0	36 Wisconsin......	1,262	2,542	8,774,146	99.3	36 Colorado.......	1,378	6,215	7,465,622	99.7
37 New Mexico......	1,209	1,628	9,732,348	99.0	37 Idaho.........	1,307	293	8,774,439	99.3	37 Idaho [2]........	1,422	201	7,465,823	99.7
38 Nebraska........	1,242	7,689	9,740,037	99.1	38 Minnesota......	1,336	4,959	8,779,398	99.4	38 North Dakota...	1,422	373	7,466,196	99.7
39 West Virginia...	1,328	64,173	9,804,210	99.8	39 West Virginia...	1,373	43,499	8,822,897	99.9	39 Minnesota......	1,429	3,683	7,469,879	99.7
40 South Dakota...	1,341	817	9,805,027	99.8	40 South Dakota...	1,409	465	8,823,362	99.9	40 Nebraska.......	1,429	8,913	7,478,792	99.9
41 Montana........	1,363	1,834	9,806,861	99.8	41 Montana.......	1,493	1,523	8,824,885	99.9	41 New Mexico.....	1,658	1,956	7,480,748	99.9
42 Minnesota.......	1,442	7,084	9,813,945	99.9	42 North Dakota...	1,531	286	8,825,171	99.9	42 Oregon........	1,677	1,186	7,481,934	99.9
43 Utah...........	1,525	1,144	9,815,089	99.9	43 Nevada [2]........	1,577	134	8,825,305	99.9	43 Utah..........	2,000	588	7,482,522	99.9
44 Oregon.........	1,550	1,492	9,816,581	99.9	44 Oregon........	1,582	1,105	8,826,410	99.9	44 Nevada [2].......	2,025	242	7,482,764	99.9
45 Idaho..........	1,573	651	9,817,232	99.9	45 Washington.....	1,718	2,514	8,828,924	99.9	45 South Dakota...	2,039	541	7,483,305	99.9
46 Washington......	1,609	6,058	9,823,290	100.0	46 New Mexico.....	1,743	1,610	8,830,534	100.0	46 Washington.....	2,217	1,602	7,484,907	99.9
47 North Dakota...	1,614	617	9,823,907	100.0	47 Wyoming.......	2,042	940	8,831,474	100.0	47 Montana.......	2,410	1,490	7,486,397	100.0
48 Wyoming........	2,234	2,235	9,826,142	100.0	48 Utah..........	2,083	672	8,832,146	100.0	48 Wyoming.......	2,415	922	7,487,319	100.0
49 Vermont.........	2,618	1,621	9,827,763	100.0	49 Arizona........	2,810	1,848	8,833,994	100.0	49 Arizona........	6,375	1,357	7,488,676	100.0

[1] Includes population of Indian Territory. [2] Number of females less than 100 in Nevada for 1900 and 1890, and in Idaho for 1890.

In 1910, 81.2 per cent, or more than four-fifths, of the Negro population lived in states in which the number of females equaled or exceeded the number of males; in 1900, 84 per cent, and in 1890, 57.1 per cent.

The range of variation in the sex ratios was less in 1910 than it was in 1900 or in 1890.[1]

[1] The quartile deviation in 1910 (i. e., one-half of the difference between the ratios of the quartile states by the cumulated populations of Table 6) was less than in 1900 but greater than in 1890, the deviations for these years being, respectively, 14.5, 18, and 11 in the number of males per 1,000 females. These figures indicate that the distribution of the Negro population by sex was somewhat more even from state to state in 1910 than it was in 1900 but was somewhat less even than in 1890, although the range of extreme variation was greater in 1890.

SEX RATIO IN THE "BLACK BELT."

The sex distribution of the Negro population of counties is given in General Table III.

In Table 7 aggregates and sex ratios are shown for southern counties in which Negroes constituted 50 per cent or more of the population in 1910, and for counties having a smaller proportion Negro.

In the aggregate for counties in which the population was 50 per cent or more Negro in 1910, the proportion of males was smaller than it was in the aggregate for other counties, in the country as a whole and in each of the three southern divisions, although in several

Southern states the proportion of males was higher in the majority Negro counties than in other counties. The differences between the sex ratios of these two aggregates may be associated in certain Southern states with the tendency which has been noted, of Negroes to move out of the black belt. While this movement is not simple in character, as regards the two sexes, it would appear that the tendency is stronger among males than among females. In Alabama, for example, the number of males to 1,000 females was 936 in the black belt counties and 1,017 in other counties. In Florida the number of males per 1,000 females in the majority Negro counties was 1,058, and in other counties 1,116. It would appear that the migration of Negro males into this state has been sufficient to raise the proportion of males in the population considerably above the average proportion in the Negro population as a whole, but to a much less degree in the majority Negro counties as compared with other counties.

The sex composition of the Negro population of any county may, however, be variously affected by the migratory shiftings of the population, which in some cases tend to increase and in other cases to diminish the proportion of males to females. Throughout the country the rural Negro population is predominantly male, and the urban Negro population is predominantly female.

Table 7

| SECTION, DIVISION, AND STATE. | Counties 50 per cent or more Negro. | | Counties less than 50 per cent Negro. | | MALES TO 1,000 FEMALES IN NEGRO POPULATION: 1910. | |
	Male.	Female.	Male.	Female.	Counties 50 per cent or more Negro	Counties less than 50 per cent Negro.
United States......	1,941,060	1,991,064	2,944,821	2,950,818	975	998
The South.............	1,941,060	1,991,064	2,398,565	2,418,738	975	992
South Atlantic......	979,430	1,008,298	1,050,378	1,074,382	971	978
East South Central..	627,768	649,312	688,024	687,409	967	1,001
West South Central..	333,862	333,454	660,163	656,947	1,001	1,005
The North.............			518,544	509,130		1,018
The West.............			27,712	22,950		1,207
THE SOUTH.						
South Atlantic:						
Delaware...........			16,011	15,170		1,055
Maryland...........	4,485	4,087	110,264	113,414	1,097	972
District of Columbia..			42,615	51,831		822
Virginia...........	136,257	134,480	194,285	206,074	1,013	943
West Virginia.......			36,607	27,566		1,328
North Carolina......	81,303	85,217	258,278	273,045	954	946
South Carolina......	340,719	358,752	67,359	69,013	950	976
Georgia.............	361,943	374,029	218,320	222,695	968	980
Florida.............	54,723	51,733	106,639	95,574	1,058	1,116
East South Central:						
Kentucky...........			131,492	130,164		1,010
Tennessee..........	20,110	20,302	213,600	219,076	991	975
Alabama............	235,620	251,779	212,174	208,709	936	1,017
Mississippi.........	372,038	377,231	130,758	129,460	986	1,010
West South Central:						
Arkansas............	114,644	111,501	108,679	108,067	1,028	1,006
Louisiana...........	176,981	179,726	176,863	180,324	985	981
Oklahoma...........			71,937	65,675		1,095
Texas..............	42,237	42,227	302,704	302,881	1,000	1,000

Table title row: NEGRO POPULATION: 1910.

The migration into northern and western communities is partly rural and partly urban in direction, and within the South also these two sorts of migrations are continuously modifying the sex composition of the

Negro population locally. Obviously a county will be variously affected by these migratory shiftings according as it is receiving or is sending forth migrants, according as it is urban or rural in character, and, if rural, according as it is fully or only incompletely exploited agriculturally, and finally according as it is proximate to or remote from large urban centers. Local variations in sex ratios reflect the influences of migratory shiftings of population, and would not develop to any appreciable extent in the absence of such shiftings.

URBAN AND RURAL POPULATION.

In Table 8 the sex ratio in 1910 and in 1900 is given for the urban and rural Negro population and white population classes.

Table 8

| RACIAL CLASS. | MALES TO 1,000 FEMALES. | | | |
| | Urban population. | | Rural population. | |
	1910	1900	1910	1900
Negro.............	908	878	1,021	1,021
White.............	1,022	991	1,111	1,095
Native............	973	970	1,072	1,066
Native parentage......	993	984	1,067	1,061
Mixed parentage........	933	[1]	1,068	[1]
Foreign parentage........	951	[1]	1,111	[1]
Foreign-born........	1,189	1,063	1,611	1,438

[1] Data not available.

Among Negroes in 1910 the number of males per 1,000 females was 908 in the urban population and 1,021 in the rural. During the decade the proportion of males increased in the urban Negro population, but remained unchanged in the rural population. Among native whites of native, mixed, and foreign parentage, as among Negroes, there was a deficiency of males in the urban population and an excess of males in the rural, and among foreign-born whites the excess of males was much greater in the rural than it was in the urban population.

In Table 9 the sex ratio is given for the urban Negro population by classes of urban communities.

Table 9

| | NEGRO POPULATION: 1910. | | | | | | |
| | Urban communities. | | | | | | Rural communities. |
	Total.	Places of 500,000 or more.	Places of 100,000 to 500,000.	Places of 25,000 to 100,000.	Places of 10,000 to 25,000.	Places of 2,500 to 10,000.	
Both sexes........	2,689,229	396,615	626,946	602,040	408,362	655,266	7,138,534
Male...........	1,279,484	189,837	297,674	286,286	193,721	311,966	3,606,397
Female.......	1,409,745	206,778	329,272	315,754	214,641	343,300	3,532,137
Excess—							
Of males.....							74,260
Of females.....	130,261	16,941	31,598	29,468	20,920	31,334	
Males to 1,000 females...........	908	918	904	907	903	909	1,021

The ratio does not appear to vary in any fixed relationship with reference to size of community, the deficiency of males being most marked in places of 10,000 to 25,000 inhabitants, in which the number of males per 1,000 females was 903, and least marked in places of 500,000 or more, in which it was 918. The predominance of females in the urban population seems to be determined by conditions which obtain generally in small as well as in large urban communities. Males may enter more largely into the long-distance migration to the large cities of the North, than they do into the relatively short-distance migration to the smaller cities in the country as a whole.

Table 10 gives the sex ratio by classes of urban communities for the Negro and white classes. In this table, also, the variations in the sex ratios seem to be determined by factors other than size of urban community.

Table 10	MALES TO 1,000 FEMALES: 1910.						
		Urban population.					
RACIAL CLASS.	Total.	Places of 500,000 to more.	Places of 100,000 to 500,000.	Places of 25,000 to 100,000.	Places of 10,000 to 25,000.	Places of 2,500 to 10,000.	Rural population.
Negro	908	918	904	907	903	909	1,021
White	1,022	1,008	1,032	1,020	1,027	1,027	1,111
Native	973	964	980	975	971	977	1,072
Native parentage	993	981	1,016	996	987	985	1,067
Mixed parentage	933	941	931	925	923	936	1,068
Foreign parentage	951	957	939	947	947	963	1,111
Foreign born	1,189	1,096	1,222	1,201	1,305	1,363	1,611

The sex ratio in the urban and rural population, Negro and white, is given in Table 11, by sections and southern divisions.

Table 11	MALES TO 1,000 FEMALES: 1910.					
		White population.				
			Native.			
SECTION AND DIVISION.	Negro population.	Total.	Total.	Native parentage.	Foreign or mixed parentage.	Foreign born.
	URBAN COMMUNITIES.					
United States	908	1,022	973	993	946	1,189
The South	876	997	979	989	928	1,227
South Atlantic	860	976	956	960	931	1,211
East South Central	879	977	964	979	885	1,232
West South Central	906	1,044	1,026	1,042	951	1,249
The North	977	1,013	963	980	943	1,165
The West	1,083	1,150	1,065	1,109	993	1,520
	RURAL COMMUNITIES.					
United States	1,021	1,111	1,072	1,067	1,095	1,611
The South	1,015	1,070	1,059	1,057	1,114	1,686
South Atlantic	1,010	1,053	1,041	1,039	1,098	2,193
East South Central	1,011	1,050	1,046	1,045	1,101	1,792
West South Central	1,033	1,108	1,094	1,092	1,121	1,488
The North	1,175	1,105	1,061	1,056	1,076	1,484
The West	1,827	1,382	1,240	1,249	1,217	2,353

The excess of females in the urban Negro population was most marked in the South, and among southern divisions, in the South Atlantic division, in which the number of males per 1,000 females was 860. In the rural population of this division there were 1,010 males to 1,000 females. Similar, but somewhat less considerable differences in the proportions for the urban and rural populations obtain in the East and West South Central divisions. In the North the number of males per 1,000 females was 977 in the urban population, and 1,175 in the rural; in the West, 1,083 in the urban, and 1,827 in the rural. The proportion of males is higher among native whites than among Negroes, in both the urban and the rural population of the South, and lower among native whites than among Negroes in the urban and rural population of the North and West. Inasmuch as the urban population is increasing by net migration from country districts, the ratios shown in Table 11 indicate that this migration cityward in the Negro population is predominantly female as regards urban communities in the South.

Table 12 (p. 154) gives for each of the nine geographic divisions the number of Negro and white males and females in the urban and rural population, covering the two years, 1910 and 1900.

Table 13 (p. 154) gives similar data by divisions for classes of urban communities in 1910.

Table 14 (p. 155) classifies the urban and rural Negro population of the states in 1910, by sex, giving the sex ratio for each class of population. In every state except Vermont, North Dakota, Oklahoma, Nevada, and Minnesota the proportion of males in the rural Negro population exceeded that in the urban. Among the Southern states in the urban population the proportion was lowest in Mississippi, 823 males to 1,000 females, and highest in Oklahoma, 1,115 males to 1,000 females; in the rural population the proportion was lowest in North Carolina, 972 males to 1,000 females, and highest in West Virginia, 1,424 males to 1,000 females. West Virginia and Oklahoma were the only Southern states showing an excess of males in the urban population, and North Carolina, South Carolina, and Alabama, the only Southern states showing an excess of females in the rural population. In the North Central states, except Wisconsin and Kansas, males are in excess in both the urban and rural populations, and this condition obtains in some other states with small Negro populations, in which males largely predominate.

PRINCIPAL CITIES.

Tables 15 and 16 (pp. 156 and 157) present data for cities. In Table 15 the number of Negro males and females and the sex ratio are shown for cities of 100,000 or more population, covering the years 1910, 1900, and 1890, together with the sex ratio in 1910 for classes of the white population. Table 16 gives the Negro population by sex, and the sex ratio in 1910, for cities of 25,000 to 100,000 population. In both these tables the cities are grouped by sections, totals being given for each section.

In 1910 there were 9 southern cities having a population of 100,000 or more, and in the Negro population of each of these cities the females outnumbered the males, the lowest proportion of males being that of Nashville, Tenn., in which the number of males to 1,000 females was 800. The lowest proportion for any northern or western city was that of Worcester, Mass., 849 males to 1,000 females. The highest proportion was that of San Francisco, 1,661 males to 1,000

NEGRO AND WHITE MALES AND FEMALES AND SEX RATIO, IN THE URBAN AND RURAL POPULATION, BY DIVISIONS: 1910, 1900.

Table 12 DIVISION AND RACIAL CLASS.	RURAL POPULATION.						URBAN POPULATION.					
	1910			1900			1910			1900		
	Male.	Female.	Males to 1,000 females.	Male.	Female.	Males to 1,000 females.	Male.	Female.	Males to 1,000 females.	Male.	Female.	Males to 1,000 females.
United States:												
Negro	3,606,397	3,532,137	1,021	3,448,850	3,379,172	1,021	1,279,484	1,409,745	908	937,697	1,068,275	878
White	22,048,566	19,851,478	1,111	19,907,997	18,183,209	1,095	20,129,679	19,702,234	1,022	14,293,738	14,424,252	991
New England:												
Negro	3,087	2,342	1,318	2,925	2,644	1,106	29,696	31,181	952	25,654	27,876	920
White	564,484	526,063	1,073	573,786	541,125	1,060	2,663,122	2,726,845	977	2,156,335	2,255,780	956
Middle Atlantic:												
Negro	42,013	36,611	1,148	42,128	36,024	1,169	161,453	177,793	908	117,583	130,186	903
White	2,884,541	2,621,990	1,100	2,728,626	2,564,936	1,064	6,711,807	6,662,114	1,007	4,858,337	4,958,963	980
East North Central:												
Negro	38,548	31,746	1,214	42,460	35,261	1,204	117,883	112,659	1,046	91,985	88,136	1,044
White	4,460,277	4,085,693	1,092	4,522,733	4,150,732	1,090	4,762,884	4,618,768	1,031	3,509,714	3,526,874	995
West North Central:												
Negro	42,055	36,306	1,158	51,867	46,679	1,111	83,809	80,492	1,041	69,405	69,958	992
White	4,051,171	3,594,358	1,127	3,845,352	3,414,541	1,126	1,892,713	1,813,379	1,044	1,423,018	1,382,906	1,029
South Atlantic:												
Negro	1,609,189	1,593,779	1,010	1,522,403	1,510,242	1,008	420,619	488,901	860	313,122	383,250	817
White	3,021,412	2,869,201	1,053	2,629,429	2,542,080	1,034	1,077,166	1,103,824	976	752,540	782,009	962
East South Central:												
Negro	1,077,589	1,065,827	1,011	1,064,191	1,049,427	1,014	238,203	270,894	879	178,891	207,377	863
White	2,401,427	2,288,159	1,050	2,195,957	2,104,385	1,044	526,175	538,565	977	368,881	375,624	982
West South Central:												
Negro	786,901	761,687	1,033	716,301	695,609	1,030	207,124	228,714	906	130,496	151,660	860
White	2,735,979	2,469,779	1,108	2,104,427	1,893,776	1,111	774,108	741,625	1,044	386,881	385,981	1,002
Mountain:												
Negro	3,848	2,173	1,771	4,052	1,704	2,378	7,918	7,528	1,052	5,052	4,782	1,056
White	923,474	672,690	1,373	607,874	445,105	1,366	488,674	435,617	1,122	276,568	250,308	1,105
Pacific:												
Negro	3,167	1,666	1,901	2,523	1,582	1,595	12,779	11,583	1,103	5,509	5,050	1,091
White	1,005,801	723,545	1,390	699,813	526,529	1,329	1,233,030	1,061,497	1,162	561,464	505,807	1,110

NEGRO AND WHITE MALES AND FEMALES AND SEX RATIO FOR CLASSES OF CITIES, BY DIVISIONS: 1910.

Table 13 DIVISION AND RACIAL CLASS.	POPULATION OF PLACES HAVING IN 1910 A POPULATION OF—														
	2,500 to 10,000.			10,000 to 25,000.			25,000 to 100,000.			100,000 to 500,000.			500,000 and over.		
	Male.	Female.	Males to 1,000 females.	Male.	Female.	Males to 1,000 females.	Male.	Female.	Males to 1,000 females.	Male.	Female.	Males to 1,000 females.	Male.	Female.	Males to 1,000 females.
United States:															
Negro	311,966	343,300	909	193,721	214,641	903	286,286	315,754	907	297,674	329,272	904	189,837	206,778	918
White	3,951,056	3,847,145	1,027	2,627,246	2,559,332	1,027	3,851,950	3,774,973	1,020	4,124,897	3,992,220	1,033	5,574,530	5,528,564	1,008
New England:															
Negro	4,831	4,091	1,181	2,789	3,180	877	7,434	8,343	891	7,978	8,667	921	6,664	6,900	966
White	631,865	632,325	999	459,609	470,533	977	796,308	824,774	965	453,538	465,319	975	321,802	333,894	964
Middle Atlantic:															
Negro	13,795	14,988	920	16,095	17,067	943	25,693	27,463	936	10,945	11,409	959	94,925	106,866	888
White	832,038	801,454	1,038	668,834	647,326	1,033	1,031,004	1,025,780	1,005	865,181	861,763	1,004	3,314,750	3,325,791	997
East North Central:															
Negro	19,063	18,796	1,014	15,454	15,017	1,029	21,626	19,736	1,096	34,714	33,585	1,034	27,026	25,525	1,059
White	933,369	933,345	1,000	691,618	673,308	1,027	773,249	738,485	1,047	978,878	968,418	1,011	1,385,770	1,305,212	1,062
West North Central:															
Negro	17,265	17,260	1,000	11,225	10,789	1,041	15,484	14,591	1,061	17,667	16,061	1,100	22,168	21,792	1,017
White	509,523	495,847	1,028	219,755	212,717	1,033	397,727	373,590	1,065	442,316	412,129	1,073	323,392	319,096	1,013
South Atlantic:															
Negro	119,739	135,832	882	62,968	72,238	872	111,552	129,361	862	87,306	105,775	825	39,054	45,695	855
White	252,653	254,585	992	152,409	156,973	971	237,657	233,458	1,018	205,631	214,237	960	228,816	244,571	936
East South Central:															
Negro	73,518	84,760	867	40,113	46,771	858	37,820	44,324	853	86,752	95,039	913	......	......	......
White	151,099	156,948	963	66,231	67,203	986	101,432	105,647	960	207,413	208,767	994	......	......	......
West South Central:															
Negro	60,765	64,902	936	42,247	46,868	901	63,166	68,628	920	40,946	48,316	847	......	......	......
White	254,432	243,250	1,046	135,966	128,751	1,056	261,794	242,137	1,081	121,916	127,487	956	......	......	......
Mountain:															
Negro	1,832	1,624	1,128	1,451	1,328	1,093	1,983	1,802	1,100	2,652	2,774	956	......	......	......
White	190,388	162,176	1,174	75,608	63,395	1,193	118,719	106,934	1,110	103,959	103,112	1,008	......	......	......
Pacific:															
Negro	1,158	1,047	1,106	1,379	1,384	996	1,528	1,506	1,015	8,714	7,646	1,140	......	......	......
White	195,689	167,215	1,170	157,216	139,126	1,130	134,060	124,168	1,080	746,065	630,988	1,182	......	......	......

females. In New York City there were 850 males to 1,000 females. In this group of cities the proportion of males increased in each section of the country during the decade 1900–1910, although there were 14 northern and western cities and 1 southern city, Memphis, in which the proportion decreased.

The Negro populations of northern and western cities of 25,000 to 100,000 population, are generally small, and in a number of these cities males outnumbered females in 1910. In only 5 of the 35 southern cities of this group, however, was there an excess of males over females.

TABLE **14.**—URBAN AND RURAL NEGRO POPULATION CLASSIFIED BY SEX, WITH SEX RATIO AND PERCENTAGE URBAN, BY DIVISIONS AND STATES: 1910.

DIVISION AND STATE.	NEGRO POPULATION: 1910.										
	Urban communities.			Rural communities.			Males to 1,000 females.		Percentage urban.		
	Both sexes.	Male.	Female.	Both sexes.	Male.	Female.	Urban communities.	Rural communities.	Both sexes.	Male.	Female.
UNITED STATES	2,689,229	1,279,484	1,409,745	7,138,534	3,606,397	3,532,137	908	1,021	27.4	26.2	28.5
GEOGRAPHIC DIVISIONS:											
New England	60,877	29,696	31,181	5,429	3,087	2,342	952	1,318	91.8	90.6	93.0
Middle Atlantic	339,246	161,453	177,793	78,624	42,013	36,611	908	1,148	81.2	79.4	82.9
East North Central	230,542	117,883	112,659	70,294	38,548	31,746	1,046	1,214	76.6	75.4	78.0
West North Central	164,301	83,809	80,492	78,361	42,055	36,306	1,041	1,158	67.7	66.6	68.9
South Atlantic	909,520	420,619	488,901	3,202,968	1,609,189	1,593,779	860	1,010	22.1	20.7	23.5
East South Central	509,097	238,203	270,894	2,143,416	1,077,589	1,065,827	879	1,011	19.2	18.1	20.3
West South Central	435,838	207,124	228,714	1,548,588	786,901	761,687	906	1,033	22.0	20.8	23.1
Mountain	15,446	7,918	7,528	6,021	3,848	2,173	1,052	1,771	72.0	67.3	77.6
Pacific	24,362	12,779	11,583	4,833	3,167	1,666	1,103	1,901	83.4	80.1	87.4
NEW ENGLAND:											
Maine	924	451	473	439	249	190	953	1,311	67.8	64.4	71.3
New Hampshire	356	159	197	208	129	79	807	(1)	63.1	55.2	71.4
Vermont	1,341	1,004	337	280	169	111	2,979	1,523	82.7	85.6	75.2
Massachusetts	35,243	17,101	18,142	2,812	1,647	1,165	943	1,414	92.6	91.2	94.0
Rhode Island	9,055	4,379	4,676	474	266	208	936	1,279	95.0	94.3	95.7
Connecticut	13,958	6,602	7,356	1,216	627	589	897	1,065	92.0	91.3	92.6
MIDDLE ATLANTIC:											
New York	117,486	54,643	62,843	16,705	9,391	7,314	870	1,284	87.6	85.3	89.6
New Jersey	65,427	30,782	34,645	24,333	12,820	11,513	888	1,114	72.9	70.6	75.1
Pennsylvania	156,333	76,028	80,305	37,586	19,802	17,784	947	1,113	80.6	79.3	81.9
EAST NORTH CENTRAL:											
Ohio	82,282	42,074	40,208	29,170	15,921	13,249	1,046	1,202	73.8	72.5	75.2
Indiana	48,425	24,485	23,940	11,895	6,559	5,336	1,023	1,229	80.3	78.9	81.8
Illinois	85,538	44,015	41,523	23,511	12,894	10,617	1,060	1,214	78.4	77.3	79.6
Michigan	12,156	6,255	5,901	4,959	2,752	2,207	1,060	1,247	71.0	69.4	72.8
Wisconsin	2,141	1,054	1,087	759	422	337	970	1,252	73.8	71.4	76.3
WEST NORTH CENTRAL:											
Minnesota	6,518	3,864	2,654	566	319	247	1,456	1,291	92.0	92.4	91.5
Iowa	9,786	5,215	4,571	5,187	2,905	2,282	1,141	1,273	65.4	64.2	66.7
Missouri	104,462	52,618	51,844	52,990	27,871	25,119	1,015	1,110	66.3	65.4	67.4
North Dakota	306	197	109	311	184	127	1,807	1,449	49.6	51.7	46.2
South Dakota	412	228	184	405	240	165	1,239	1,455	50.4	48.7	52.7
Nebraska	6,621	3,626	2,995	1,068	633	435	1,211	1,455	86.1	85.1	87.3
Kansas	36,196	18,061	18,135	17,834	9,903	7,931	996	1,249	67.0	64.6	69.6
SOUTH ATLANTIC:											
Delaware	11,157	5,392	5,765	20,024	10,619	9,405	935	1,129	35.8	33.7	38.0
Maryland	99,230	45,946	53,284	133,020	68,803	64,217	862	1,071	42.7	40.0	45.3
District of Columbia	94,446	42,615	51,831				822		100.0	100.0	100.0
Virginia	158,218	72,804	85,414	512,878	257,738	255,140	852	1,010	23.6	22.0	25.1
West Virginia	15,380	7,945	7,435	48,793	28,662	20,131	1,069	1,424	24.0	21.7	27.0
North Carolina	115,975	52,796	63,179	581,868	286,785	295,083	836	972	16.6	15.5	17.6
South Carolina	101,702	45,979	55,723	734,141	362,099	372,042	825	973	12.2	11.3	13.0
Georgia	224,826	103,231	121,595	952,161	477,032	475,129	849	1,004	19.1	17.8	20.4
Florida	88,586	43,911	44,675	220,083	117,451	102,632	983	1,144	28.7	27.2	30.3
EAST SOUTH CENTRAL:											
Kentucky	106,631	51,186	55,445	155,025	80,306	74,719	923	1,075	40.8	38.9	42.6
Tennessee	150,506	70,375	80,131	322,582	163,335	159,247	878	1,026	31.8	30.1	33.5
Alabama	156,603	73,579	83,024	751,679	374,215	377,464	886	991	17.2	16.4	18.0
Mississippi	95,357	43,063	52,294	914,130	459,733	454,397	823	1,012	9.4	8.6	10.3
WEST SOUTH CENTRAL:											
Arkansas	59,147	28,712	30,435	383,744	194,611	189,133	943	1,029	13.4	12.9	13.9
Louisiana	160,845	73,842	87,003	553,029	279,982	273,047	849	1,025	22.5	20.9	24.2
Oklahoma	36,982	19,497	17,485	100,630	52,440	48,190	1,115	1,088	26.9	27.1	26.6
Texas	178,864	85,073	93,791	511,185	259,868	251,317	907	1,034	25.9	24.7	27.2
MOUNTAIN:											
Montana	1,455	830	625	379	228	151	1,328	1,510	79.3	78.4	80.5
Idaho	426	252	174	225	146	79	1,448	(1)	65.4	63.3	68.8
Wyoming	1,041	539	502	1,194	1,005	189	1,074	5,317	46.6	34.9	72.6
Colorado	9,359	4,646	4,713	2,094	1,221	873	986	1,399	81.7	79.2	84.4
New Mexico	795	393	402	833	498	335	978	1,487	48.8	44.1	54.5
Arizona	1,310	626	684	699	428	271	915	1,579	65.2	59.4	71.6
Utah	959	573	386	185	118	67	1,484	(1)	83.8	82.9	85.2
Nevada	101	59	42	412	204	208		981	19.7	22.4	16.8
PACIFIC:											
Washington	4,699	2,738	1,961	1,359	998	361	1,396	2,765	77.6	73.3	84.5
Oregon	1,264	756	508	228	151	77	1,488	(1)	84.7	83.4	86.8
California	18,399	9,285	9,114	3,246	2,018	1,228	1,019	1,643	85.0	82.1	88.1

[1] Ratio not shown where the number of females is less than 100.

TABLE 15.—NEGRO MALES AND FEMALES, AND MALES TO 1,000 FEMALES, FOR CITIES OF 100,000 INHABITANTS AND OVER: 1910, 1900, AND 1890; AND MALES TO 1,000 FEMALES IN CLASSES OF THE WHITE POPULATION: 1910.

CITY.	NEGRO POPULATION. 1910 Male.	1910 Female.	1900 Male.	1900 Female.	1890 [1] Male.	1890 [1] Female.	MALES TO 1,000 FEMALES. Negro population. 1910	1900	1890 [1]	White population: 1910. Total.	Native. Total.	Native parentage.	Foreign or mixed parentage.	Foreign born.
Total, all cities having a population of 100,000 or more	487,511	536,050	369,158	420,337			909	878		1,019	972	1,000	947	1,137
Cities of the South	254,058	294,825	202,100	245,199			862	824		961	946	961	900	1,091
Cities of the North	222,087	230,805	161,874	170,031			962	952		1,012	965	991	947	1,115
Cities of the West	11,366	10,420	5,184	5,107			1,091	1,015		1,158	1,063	1,121	983	1,506
CITIES OF THE SOUTH.														
Atlanta, Ga	23,219	28,683	14,806	20,921			810	708		992	973	978	910	1,504
Baltimore, Md	39,054	45,695	35,063	44,195	28,979	38,125	855	793	760	936	922	926	916	1,006
Birmingham, Ala	25,662	26,643	7,738	8,837			963	876		1,073	1,048	1,053	1,013	1,458
Louisville, Ky	19,602	20,920	18,842	20,297	13,330	15,321	937	928	870	942	932	962	870	1,035
Memphis, Tenn	25,259	27,182	24,551	25,359			929	968		1,089	1,060	1,085	947	1,474
Nashville, Tenn	16,229	20,294	13,269	16,775			800	791		947	941	952	851	1,114
New Orleans, La	40,946	48,316	35,129	42,585	28,780	35,711	847	825	806	956	937	976	864	1,121
Richmond, Va	21,472	25,261	14,354	17,876			850	803		951	936	936	935	1,272
Washington, D. C	42,615	51,831	38,348	48,354	33,721	41,851	822	793	806	949	931	934	919	1,130
CITIES OF THE NORTH.														
Albany, N. Y	497	540	642	536			920	1,198		928	915	933	894	989
Boston, Mass	6,664	6,900	5,904	5,687	4,168	3,957	966	1,038	1,053	964	967	961	971	958
Bridgeport, Conn	657	675	516	633			973	815		1,062	981	1,022	952	1,223
Buffalo, N. Y	933	840	899	799	569	549	1,111	1,125	1,036	1,005	961	1,002	935	1,128
Cambridge, Mass	2,227	2,480	1,845	2,043			898	903		916	924	888	948	902
Chicago, Ill	22,685	21,418	16,073	14,077	7,938	6,333	1,059	1,142	1,253	1,061	983	1,038	958	1,211
Cincinnati, Ohio	9,905	9,734	7,156	7,326	5,733	5,922	1,018	977	968	950	930	979	875	1,059
Cleveland, Ohio	4,341	4,107	3,177	2,811	1,587	1,402	1,057	1,130		1,065	978	1,016	956	1,246
Columbus, Ohio	6,784	5,955	4,311	3,890			1,139	1,108	1,181	1,006	975	997	905	1,356
Dayton, Ohio	2,475	2,367	1,718	1,669			1,046	1,029		1,018	970	999	891	1,440
Detroit, Mich	2,985	2,756	2,014	2,097	1,692	1,739	1,083	960	973	1,066	991	1,054	954	1,229
Fall River, Mass	174	181	118	206			961	573		933	942	929	946	921
Grand Rapids, Mich	347	318	298	306			1,091	974		973	915	959	876	1,164
Indianapolis, Ind	10,803	11,013	7,902	8,029	4,585	4,548	981	984	1,008	987	957	972	905	1,344
Jersey City, N. J	3,020	2,940	1,846	1,858	1,017	1,082	1,027	994	940	1,054	997	1,027	976	1,205
Kansas City, Mo	11,885	11,681	8,560	9,007	6,864	6,836	1,017	950	1,004	1,038	1,006	1,026	942	1,323
Lowell, Mass	62	71	67	69			[2]	[2]		940	918	893	930	973
Milwaukee, Wis	478	502	471	391	261	188	952	1,205	1,388	1,028	936	980	918	1,280
Minneapolis, Minn	1,499	1,093	830	718	797	523	1,371	1,156	1,524	1,089	1,006	1,114	926	1,328
New Haven, Conn	1,711	1,850	1,355	1,532			925	884		997	945	948	943	1,114
New York, N. Y	42,143	49,566	27,132	33,534	15,168	18,720	850	809	810	1,000	966	980	958	1,051
Manhattan Borough	28,024	32,510	16,239	20,007			862	812		1,002	971	991	963	1,036
Bronx Borough	1,911	2,206	1,161	1,209			866	960		1,016	974	1,006	959	1,098
Brooklyn Borough	10,245	12,463	8,127	10,240			822	794		983	949	954	946	1,050
Queens Borough	1,440	1,758	1,119	1,492			819	750		1,033	990	1,006	979	1,151
Richmond Borough	523	629	486	586			831	829		1,086	1,035	1,053	1,018	1,226
Newark, N. J	4,477	4,998	3,034	3,660	1,879	2,262	896	829	831	998	949	961	941	1,106
Omaha, Nebr	2,379	2,047	1,755	1,688	2,693	1,873	1,162	1,040	1,438	1,089	1,044	1,088	988	1,258
Paterson, N. J	710	829	542	640			856	847		989	945	942	947	1,070
Philadelphia, Pa	39,431	45,028	28,940	33,673	18,099	21,272	876	859	851	968	948	951	944	1,029
Pittsburgh, Pa.[3]	13,351	12,272	11,222	9,133	5,879	4,478	1,088	1,229	1,313	1,048	970	990	951	1,287
Providence, R. I	2,577	2,739	2,283	2,534	1,849	2,114	941	901	875	966	932	932	932	1,033
Rochester, N. Y	424	455	291	310	253	306	932	939	827	937	940	974	910	1,126
St. Louis, Mo	22,168	21,792	17,496	18,020	13,064	13,801	1,017	971	947	1,013	960	999	919	1,269
St. Paul, Minn	1,904	1,240	1,327	936	850	626	1,535	1,418	1,358	1,080	1,021	1,119	961	1,262
Scranton, Pa	305	262	294	227			1,164	1,295		1,020	939	967	920	1,272
Syracuse, N. Y	579	545	497	537			1,062	926		1,005	947	983	903	1,232
Toledo, Ohio	937	940	852	858			997	993		1,010	969	990	943	1,202
Worcester, Mass	570	671	507	597			849	849		1,012	949	952	947	1,151
CITIES OF THE WEST.														
Denver, Colo	2,652	2,774	1,881	2,042	1,702	1,343	956	921	1,267	1,008	976	1,002	933	1,158
Los Angeles, Cal	3,682	3,917	1,015	1,116			940	909		1,013	967	998	902	1,218
Oakland, Cal	1,614	1,441	524	502			1,120	1,044		1,039	960	999	918	1,306
Portland, Oreg	608	437	458	317			1,391	1,445		1,274	1,172	1,237	1,050	1,727
San Francisco, Cal	1,025	617	872	782	1,022	825	1,661	1,115	1,239	1,258	1,114	1,269	1,011	1,624
Seattle, Wash	1,394	902	212	194			1,545	1,093		1,312	1,175	1,261	1,041	1,796
Spokane, Wash	391	332	222	154			1,178	1,442		1,216	1,116	1,153	1,045	1,715

[1] Data available for those cities only which had in 1890 a population of 100,000 or more.
[2] Ratio not shown where the number of females is less than 100.
[3] Includes population of Allegheny for 1900 and 1890.

Table 16.—NEGRO MALES AND FEMALES, AND MALES TO 1,000 FEMALES, FOR CITIES OF 25,000 TO 100,000 INHABITANTS: 1910.

CITY.	Male.	Female.	Males[1] to 1,000 females.
Total, all cities having a population of 25,000 to 100,000	286,286	315,754	907
Cities of the South	212,538	242,313	877
Cities of the North	70,237	70,133	1,001
Cities of the West	3,511	3,308	1,061
CITIES OF THE SOUTH.			
Augusta, Ga	8,160	10,184	801
Austin, Tex	3,388	4,090	828
Charleston, S.C	13,714	17,342	791
Charlotte, N.C	5,201	6,551	794
Chattanooga, Tenn	8,848	9,094	973
Columbia, S.C	5,226	6,320	827
Covington, Ky	1,398	1,501	931
Dallas, Tex	8,680	9,344	929
El Paso, Tex	710	742	957
Fort Worth, Tex	6,781	6,499	1,043
Galveston, Tex	3,881	4,155	934
Houston, Tex	11,218	12,711	883
Huntington, W. Va	1,152	988	1,166
Jacksonville, Fla	14,556	14,737	988
Knoxville, Tenn	3,600	4,038	892
Lexington, Ky	5,075	5,936	855
Little Rock, Ark	7,060	7,479	944
Lynchburg, Va	4,029	5,437	741
Macon, Ga	8,305	9,845	844
Mobile, Ala	10,344	12,419	833
Montgomery, Ala	8,293	11,029	752
Muskogee, Okla	3,996	3,835	1,042
Newport, Ky	262	307	853
Norfolk, Va	11,887	13,152	904
Oklahoma City, Okla	3,534	3,012	1,173
Portsmouth, Va	5,542	6,075	912
Roanoke, Va	3,650	4,274	854
San Antonio, Tex	4,909	5,807	845
Savannah, Ga	15,218	18,028	844
Shreveport, La	6,226	7,670	812
Tampa, Fla	4,431	4,520	980
Waco, Tex	2,783	3,284	847
Wheeling, W. Va	609	592	1,029
Wilmington, Del	4,390	4,691	936
Wilmington, N.C	5,482	6,625	827
CITIES OF THE NORTH.			
Akron, Ohio	357	300	1,190
Allentown, Pa	62	72	....
Altoona, Pa	232	221	1,050
Amsterdam, N.Y	54	64	....
Atlantic City, N.J	4,851	4,983	974
Auburn, N.Y	276	251	1,100
Aurora, Ill	140	153	915
Battle Creek, Mich	283	292	969
Bay City, Mich	80	80	....
Bayonne, N.J	266	295	902
Binghamton, N.Y	312	323	966
Bloomington, Ill	409	400	1,023
Brockton, Mass	257	274	938
Brookline town, Mass	61	160	381
Camden, N.J	2,949	3,127	943
Canton, Ohio	174	117	1,487
Cedar Rapids, Iowa	120	93	....
Chelsea, Mass	105	137	766
Chester, Pa	2,363	2,432	972
Chicopee, Mass	6	1	....

CITY.	Male.	Female.	Males[1] to 1,000 females.
CITIES OF THE NORTH—con.			
Clinton, Iowa	253	179	1,413
Council Bluffs, Iowa	201	119	1,689
Danville, Ill	753	712	1,058
Davenport, Iowa	315	254	1,240
Decatur, Ill	392	384	1,021
Des Moines, Iowa	1,490	1,440	1,035
Dubuque, Iowa	60	36	....
Duluth, Minn	236	174	1,356
Easton, Pa	155	129	1,202
East Orange, N.J	715	1,192	600
East St. Louis, Ill	3,233	2,649	1,220
Elgin, Ill	87	84	....
Elizabeth, N.J	654	727	900
Elmira, N.Y	279	234	1,192
Erie, Pa	177	163	1,086
Evansville, Ind	3,220	3,046	1,057
Everett, Mass	373	422	884
Fitchburg, Mass	22	20	....
Flint, Mich	217	180	1,206
Fort Wayne, Ind	297	275	1,080
Green Bay, Wis	22	23	....
Hamilton, Ohio	396	329	1,204
Harrisburg, Pa	2,232	2,303	969
Hartford, Conn	797	948	841
Haverhill, Mass	185	212	873
Hazleton, Pa	13	6	....
Hoboken, N.J	60	60	....
Holyoke, Mass	19	26	....
Jackson, Mich	188	166	1,133
Jamestown, N.Y	57	51	....
Johnstown, Pa	238	204	1,167
Joliet, Ill	261	236	1,106
Joplin, Mo	397	404	983
Kalamazoo, Mich	360	325	1,108
Kansas City, Kans	4,622	4,664	991
Kingston, N.Y	316	314	1,006
La Crosse, Wis	26	33	....
Lancaster, Pa	392	411	954
Lansing, Mich	174	180	967
Lawrence, Mass	163	102	1,598
Lewiston, Me	25	22	....
Lima, Ohio	528	450	1,173
Lincoln, Nebr	414	319	1,298
Lorain, Ohio	193	182	1,060
Lynn, Mass	352	348	1,011
McKeesport, Pa	406	393	1,033
Madison, Wis	69	74	....
Malden, Mass	218	268	813
Manchester, N.H	20	16	....
Meriden town, Conn.[2]	69	64	....
Mount Vernon, N.Y	363	533	681
Nashua, N.H	7	8	....
New Bedford, Mass	1,485	1,400	1,061
New Britain, Conn	39	55	....
New Rochelle, N.Y	718	1,036	693
Newark, Ohio	174	172	1,012
Newburgh, N.Y	282	322	876
Newcastle, Pa	276	253	1,091
Newport, R.I	718	882	814
Newton, Mass	182	285	639
Niagara Falls, N.Y	151	115	1,313
Norristown borough, Pa	490	525	933
Norwichtown, Conn	277	350	791
Orange, N.J	1,143	1,336	856
Oshkosh, Wis	45	53	....

CITY.	Male.	Female.	Males[1] to 1,000 females.
CITIES OF THE NORTH—con.			
Passaic, N.J	239	296	807
Pawtucket, R.I	107	127	843
Peoria, Ill	867	702	1,235
Perth Amboy, N.J	74	91	....
Pittsfield, Mass	166	154	1,078
Portland, Me	116	157	739
Poughkeepsie, N.Y	307	392	783
Quincy, Ill	804	792	1,015
Quincy, Mass	22	23	....
Racine, Wis	54	58	....
Reading, Pa	409	378	1,082
Rockford, Ill	93	104	894
Saginaw, Mich	164	149	1,101
St. Joseph, Mo	2,241	2,008	1,116
Salem, Mass	77	86	....
Schenectady, N.Y	123	151	815
Sheboygan, Wis	3	6	....
Shenandoah borough, Pa	4	4	....
Sioux City, Iowa	166	139	1,194
Somerville, Mass	93	124	750
South Bend, Ind	313	291	1,076
South Omaha, Nebr	432	285	1,516
Springfield, Ill	1,500	1,461	1,027
Springfield, Mass	670	805	832
Springfield, Mo	1,003	992	1,011
Springfield, Ohio	2,594	2,339	1,109
Stamford town, Conn.[3]	143	200	715
Superior, Wis	79	103	767
Taunton, Mass	159	138	1,152
Terre Haute, Ind	1,336	1,257	1,063
Topeka, Kans	2,185	2,353	929
Trenton, N.J	1,424	1,157	1,231
Troy, N.Y	289	362	798
Utica, N.Y	182	175	1,040
Waltham, Mass	25	37	....
Warwick town, R.I	82	91	....
Waterbury, Conn	384	391	982
Waterloo, Iowa	15	9	....
Watertown, N.Y	40	36	....
West Hoboken town, N.J	24	32	....
Wichita, Kans	1,334	1,123	1,188
Wilkes-Barre, Pa	357	316	1,130
Williamsport, Pa	438	519	844
Woonsocket, R.I	10	10	....
Yonkers, N.Y	732	817	896
York, Pa	569	662	860
Youngstown, Ohio	1,072	864	1,241
Zanesville, Ohio	669	715	936
CITIES OF THE WEST.			
Berkeley, Cal	102	145	703
Butte, Mont	142	98	....
Colorado Springs, Colo	505	602	839
Ogden, Utah	125	78	....
Pasadena, Cal	342	402	851
Pueblo, Colo	777	721	1,078
Sacramento, Cal	270	216	1,250
Salt Lake City, Utah	434	303	1,432
San Diego, Cal	300	207	1,010
San Jose, Cal	83	99	....
Tacoma, Wash	431	347	1,242

[1] Ratio not shown where the number of females is less than 100.　　[2] Meriden town includes Meriden city.　　[3] Stamford town includes Stamford city.

CHAPTER X.—AGE COMPOSITION.

THE AGE INQUIRY.

Returns of age for the Negro population have been made at each census, beginning with that of 1820, which distinguished four age classes in the returns of free colored persons and of slaves. The age classes distinguished at the several censuses, 1820–1910, for the colored and white population elements, are given in Table 1.

Table 1 AGE CLASSES SHOWN, BY SEX, AT SEVERAL CENSUSES: 1820–1910.

1820		1830 and 1840		1850 and 1860	1870	1880–1910
Colored.[1]	White.	Colored.[1]	White.	Colored[1] and white classes.		
Under 14 yrs. 14 to 25 yrs. 26 to 44 yrs. 45 yrs. and over.	Under 10 yrs. 10 to 15 yrs. 16 to 25 yrs. 26 to 44 yrs. 45 yrs. and over. Males between 16 and 18 yrs.	Under 10 yrs. 10 to 23 yrs. 24 to 35 yrs. 36 to 54 yrs. 55 to 99 yrs. 100 yrs. and over.	Under 5 yrs. 5 to 9 yrs. 10 to 14 yrs. 15 to 19 yrs. 20 to 29 yrs. 30 to 39 yrs. 40 to 49 yrs. 50 to 59 yrs. 60 to 69 yrs. 70 to 79 yrs. 80 to 89 yrs. 90 to 99 yrs. 100 yrs. and over.	Under 1 yr. 1 to 4 yrs. 5 to 9 yrs. 10 to 14 yrs. 15 to 19 yrs. 20 to 29 yrs. 30 to 39 yrs. 40 to 49 yrs. 50 to 59 yrs. 60 to 69 yrs. 70 to 79 yrs. 80 to 89 yrs. 90 to 99 yrs. 100 yrs. and over. Unknown.	Under 1 yr. 1 yr. 2 yrs. 3 yrs. 4 yrs. 5 to 9 yrs. 10 to 14 yrs. 15 to 17 yrs. 18 to 19 yrs. 20 yrs. 21 to 24 yrs. 25 to 79 yrs. by 5-yr. periods. 80 to 89 yrs. 90 to 99 yrs. 100 yrs. and over. Unknown.	By single years of age.

[1] The free colored population and the slave population are shown separately at each of the five censuses, 1820 to 1860. In the reports of these censuses and at the census of 1870 the term "colored" is used to designate the Negro population; in subsequent censuses the aggregate colored embraces Indians, Chinese, and Japanese, with Negroes. In 1880 and 1890 the age tabulation is given for the aggregate colored only, although for some age periods data are available in the 1890 census for Negroes separately from other colored. In 1900 and 1910 single years of age are shown for Negroes, separately from other colored.

At the censuses of 1830 and 1840, the age classification for the colored population was somewhat more detailed than it was in 1820, but at each of the three censuses—1820, 1830, and 1840—less detail by age was shown for the colored than for the white population. Beginning with 1850, the same detail by age is shown at each census for the colored as for other classes.

The classification in the censuses of 1850 and 1860 is by five and ten year periods, the number under 1 being shown separately. The 1870 classification is by five-year periods to the age of 79 and by ten-year periods for the ages 80 to 99, with detail by single years for the population under 5, and by special groupings for the population 15 to 24. At each of the last four censuses, 1880–1910, the age returns have been tabulated for race and nativity classes, by single years of age.

The 1910 population schedule called for a return of age at last birthday by full years, and in the case of children under 2 years of age, for a return of age by months.

In the tabulations based upon these returns the population is classified by completed years of age, a child being classified as five years of age, for example, during and until he has completed his sixth year. The average age of the population classified as five years of age is accordingly nearly five and one-half years.

VALUE OF AGE STATISTICS.

In many lines of statistical inquiry compilations have comparatively little significance except as they are developed under an age classification of the population. This is true generally of those compilations embraced under the designation of vital statistics and relating to mortality, duration of life, morbidity, and fecundity.

Deaths, for example, are reported by age of decedent, and to determine specific mortality rates, deaths classified by age must be related to the population similarly classified. Specific birth rates, marriage rates, fecundity rates, and morbidity rates, also as well as mortality rates, imply an age classification of the population.

While the age classification is fundamental in all vital statistics, its value is by no means restricted to this field of statistical compilation. In many lines of statistical inquiry relating to social conditions and progress, accurate age data are essential. This is obviously true of the inquiry relating to school attendance, where the number of children of school age attending school in any community is in itself a comparatively barren fact, which can acquire significance only through relation to the total population of that age, and to the number not in school. It is equally true of marital condition statistics that they are barren of significance except under an age classification, since age is one prime factor determining marital condition. Occupations statistics, also, derive significance in a large degree from the age classification, and it may be noted that, as regards the Negro element in the population, the age classification is extremely important in any analysis of the data relating to illiteracy, since the degree of illiteracy varies consistently with age. In other lines of inquiry, local and general, such, for example, as those relating to the dependent, the defective, and the delinquent classes, age groupings of the population are essential for the determination of significant indexes and proportions.

The Negro population is a native population, unaffected by immigration or emigration. Its age composition is, therefore, a natural composition determined by its rates of natality and of mortality. Changes in the relative size of the age classes composing the population necessarily reflect changes in one or both of these rates, and are significant of changes in social or economic conditions involving the welfare of the class. Since accurate and complete statistics of births and deaths are not available for the Negro population of the South, except in very restricted areas, the vital characteristics of this class, as regards fecundity and longevity, must be determined chiefly through an analysis of the age data.

The detail shown in the following age tables is presented for the value it may have in special lines of inquiry. The tables require comparatively little explanatory comment, and some of the discussion which might have been introduced in connection with them has been reserved for a separate chapter in which the number of children is related to the number of women of childbearing age.

RETURNS BY SINGLE YEARS OF AGE: 1910 AND 1900.

Although the population schedule called for a return of ages under 2 years by months, the unit of compilation in the following tables is a full year, the first 2 years of age being designated "under 1 year" and "1 year," respectively. Table 2, classifying the Negro population by sex and single years of age is, therefore, the basic age table, from which other tables are in large part derived by the combination of ages and the computation of percentages and ratios.

In the Negro population, which is increasing naturally by excess of births over deaths and is practically unaffected by immigration or emigration, the number of children under 1 year of age must generally under normal conditions exceed the number 1 year of age; the number 1 year of age must exceed the number 2 years, and similarly, throughout the life period, to the most advanced age reported, the number in any given year of age must generally exceed the number in the next succeeding year.

The decrease by single years of age represents principally the depletion of the population by mortality. Of the children under 1 year of age who survive to the end of their first year a certain number die in the age of 1 year; and of the survivors, a varying proportion die in each succeeding year of age. In the census tabulation by age, however, the decrease in population from age to age is not entirely due to mortality. The age classification shows the number of survivors among children born each year during a period preceding the census enumeration equivalent approximately to 100 years. A portion of the decrease by age represents, therefore, natural growth of population, which constantly brings forward into successive ages in annual waves of population increase a larger number of individuals. Stated differently, it represents the decrease in number of children born each year, as one recedes into the past from the year of census enumeration. The number of children returned at the census as under 1 year of age, for example, are the survivors of children born during the 12 months preceding the enumeration, while the number returned as 1 year of age are the survivors of children born in the year ending 12 months prior to the enumeration; and if the number of births is increasing from year to year, the number of children returned as under 1 year will tend constantly to exceed the number sufficient under the prevailing infant mortality rate to maintain without increase the population 1 year of age. Under these conditions the difference between the population under 1 and the population 1 year of age, at any given time, will represent in part annual increase in the number of children born and surviving, and in part the effects of mortality during the first two years of life. Similarly the decrease shown at other ages is in part an effect of population growth and in part an effect of mortality.

Under stable specific mortality rates natural increase of population advances through the successive years of age, creating a proportion in the younger ages which is constantly somewhat in excess of that required by the specific mortalities to maintain without increase the population in the older ages. Improvement in the specific mortality rates will affect the age composition of the population variously according to the specific mortality reduced—a reduction of infant mortality tending to increase the number and temporarily the proportion of children in the population, while a decrease of mortality in the older ages tends to increase the proportion surviving in these ages, thereby diminishing permanently the proportion in the younger ages.

In a classification of the population by single years of age the regular diminution of the age groups from age to age is modified by variations in the birth rate, and in specific mortality rates, during an extended period in the past—a period equal in duration to the life period of persons enumerated. An excessive infant mortality in some year may, for example, create a deficiency in the age group comprising the survivors of children born in that year. The age composition of the Negro population at the present time undoubtedly reflects in some slight variations from the normal or life table distribution in advanced ages the abnormal conditions prevailing during the decade of the Civil War.

Very slight variations from the normal or life-table age distribution may be accounted for as occasioned by accidental conditions in the past affecting birth and death rates, but any excessive variation shown in the tabulation of the census age returns is conclusive evidence of error in those returns.

In the case of the Negro population these errors have been very considerable at each census. They result in part from the fact that a large number of individuals enumerated are ignorant of their exact age; in part, from the fact that the person enumerated is not in every instance interviewed directly by the enumerator, the statement of age being in many such cases an estimate; and, in part, from the fact that age is in some cases intentionally misrepresented. A child, for example, may be erroneously returned as above the age limit of compulsory school attendance, or above the limit fixed in child-labor legislation. Males nearly 21 years of age may erroneously report themselves as of voting age, and in other cases age is intentionally understated.

Enumerators were instructed to report an estimate of age in any case where the exact age could not be ascertained, and in estimating ages of adults there is a marked tendency to report ages ending in 0 or in 5. To report, for example, a person approximately 50 years of age as exactly 50. An examination of Table 2, and of Diagram I, will reveal clearly the marked concentration upon these ages in the adult population, male and female. The number of males reported at the ages 29, 30, and 31 years, for example, is respectively, 65,666, 114,699, and 45,572; of females, 67,645, 118,858, and 44,171. The number reported for the age 30, in the case of both males and females, exceeded the number reported as 1 year of age. In the more advanced ages the concentration is relatively more marked, the numbers reported for the ages 59, 60, and 61, for example, being, in the case of males, 14,962, 49,275, and 10,565; and in the case of females, 12,475, 47,300, and 8,120. This sort of concentration is undoubtedly accounted for almost entirely by ignorance as to exact age, although in some cases, as has been noted, this ignorance pertains to the age not of oneself but of another person for whom one is filling out a schedule.

Tabulation of the age returns for the Negro population under 20 years of age develops in the age grouping irregularities quite different in character from those noted in the older population. In these younger ages there is a general concentration upon the even years of age, among both males and females. For the entire age period under 20 years, the number reported for each even year exceeds the number reported for the preceding odd year, with exception of the age 4 as compared with 3 among females and the age 8 as compared with 7 among males. The concentration upon even ages is especially remarkable in the age period 10 to 20 years, and for this period is more considerable among females than males. Some of this concentration may arise as an indirect consequence of compulsory school attendance and child-labor laws, in which even rather than odd years—12, 14, and 16 rather than 11, 13, and 15—are commonly specified as age limits. It would appear, however, that there is a natural tendency in estimating the ages of young persons—whose ages can be more nearly approximated by estimate than can the ages of older persons—to fix upon even rather than odd years.

The deficiency in the number of children 1 year of age as compared with the number 2 years of age is probably to be accounted for largely by the return of some children in their second year of age as 2 years old. The relatively small number of children in the ages 1 year and under 1 year, as compared with the number 2, 3, and 4 years of age, would seem to indicate, however, a considerable number of omissions in the enumeration of infants.

The life-table age distribution of the Negro population is shown in comparison with that of the white population in the diagram included in the chapter on "Mortality in the registration area." While this life-table distribution undoubtedly approximates the actual distribution of the Negro population, it is to be noted that the life table is constructed upon data relating to certain of the registration states—all of them Northern states with a relatively small Negro population. The eccentric divergencies, however, of the age distribution of the Negro population, as enumerated, from the life-table distribution are occasioned principally by errors in the returns due to ignorance of exact age, and it may be remarked that a high degree of inaccuracy in age returns, such as characterizes the returns for Negroes, is commonly, as it is in the case of the Negroes, associated with a high degree of illiteracy.

Since it is based upon specific mortality rates calculated from data pertaining to deaths during the three years, 1909, 1910, and 1911, and to the population of restricted areas, the life-table distribution by age of Negro males and females may not represent accurately the natural age distribution in the country as a whole. A discussion of the life tables will be found in the chapter on mortality, but the essential differences in the two age distributions—the one based upon schedule returns of the total population and the other upon specific mortality data relating to certain years and areas—should be borne in mind in comparing the diagram given on page 163 with the life table diagram. The life-table distribution by age is that of a stationary population showing the mortality rates indicated by the data for the three years covered, while the distribution by age shown in the schedule returns for the year 1910 is that of a population which has been increasing in the past at varying rates, under varying birth and death rates. In its age and sex composition the enumerated population reflects conditions which have obtained throughout a past period of considerable duration. Its composition in 1910 was undoubtedly more or less affected by conditions obtaining in the Civil War and reconstruction periods, and even under the regime of slavery. Considerable discrepancies in one as compared with the other age distribu-

NEGRO POPULATION CLASSIFIED BY SEX AND SINGLE YEARS OF AGE, AND NUMBER IN EACH YEAR OF AGE PER 100,000 UNDER 1 YEAR: 1910 AND 1900.

Table 2

	NEGRO POPULATION.											
AGE.	1910			1900			Per 100,000 under 1 year of age.					
							1910			1900		
	Both sexes.	Male.	Female.	Both sexes.	Male.	Female.	Both sexes.	Male.	Female.	Both sexes.	Male.	Female.
All ages	9,827,763	4,885,881	4,941,882	8,833,994	4,386,547	4,447,447	3,893,943	3,893,956	3,893,480	3,612,937	3,615,416	3,610,494
Under 1 year	252,386	125,459	126,927	244,510	121,329	123,181	100,000	100,000	100,000	100,000	100,000	100,000
1 year	219,240	109,357	109,883	231,940	115,102	116,838	86,867	87,166	86,572	94,859	94,868	94,851
2 years	260,037	130,192	129,845	248,922	124,334	124,585	103,031	103,773	102,299	101,804	102,477	101,142
3 years	264,547	130,526	134,021	244,083	120,671	123,412	104,818	104,039	105,589	99,825	99,458	100,188
4 years	267,078	133,786	133,292	246,200	123,051	123,149	105,821	106,637	105,015	100,691	101,419	99,974
5 years	255,703	126,709	128,994	245,385	122,168	123,217	101,314	100,996	101,628	100,358	100,692	100,029
6 years	262,815	129,804	133,011	251,875	124,929	126,946	104,132	103,463	104,793	103,012	102,967	103,056
7 years	251,742	125,950	125,792	241,767	120,747	121,020	99,745	100,391	99,106	98,878	99,520	98,246
8 years	252,473	124,937	127,536	245,996	122,726	123,270	100,034	99,584	100,480	100,608	101,151	100,072
9 years	223,820	111,775	112,045	217,735	109,840	107,895	88,682	89,093	88,275	89,050	90,531	87,591
10 years	242,509	122,880	119,629	241,487	122,701	118,786	96,087	97,944	94,250	98,764	101,131	96,432
11 years	195,048	97,062	97,986	193,865	97,293	96,572	77,282	77,366	77,199	79,287	80,189	78,398
12 years	261,300	131,267	130,033	237,494	119,589	117,905	103,532	104,629	102,447	97,131	98,566	95,717
13 years	221,861	110,226	111,635	207,501	103,776	103,725	87,905	87,858	87,952	84,864	85,533	84,205
14 years	234,548	116,639	117,909	211,643	105,283	106,360	92,932	92,970	92,895	86,558	86,775	86,344
15 years	207,555	101,921	105,634	198,494	97,899	100,595	82,237	81,238	83,224	81,180	80,689	81,664
16 years	224,403	106,679	117,724	205,537	98,771	106,766	88,913	85,031	92,749	84,061	81,408	86,674
17 years	203,847	100,185	103,662	186,663	91,137	95,526	80,768	79,855	81,671	76,342	75,116	77,549
18 years	231,307	108,316	122,991	211,345	100,703	110,642	91,648	86,336	96,899	86,436	83,000	89,821
19 years	193,304	90,844	102,460	179,983	85,240	94,743	76,591	72,409	80,724	73,610	70,255	76,914
20 years	215,625	92,494	123,131	222,417	98,956	123,461	85,435	73,724	97,009	90,964	81,560	100,227
21 years	196,600	100,178	96,422	179,596	92,449	87,147	77,897	79,849	75,967	73,451	76,197	70,747
22 years	216,269	101,974	114,295	200,961	95,076	105,885	85,690	81,281	90,048	82,189	78,362	85,959
23 years	200,705	92,960	107,745	182,805	85,731	97,074	79,523	74,096	84,887	74,764	70,660	78,806
24 years	201,596	94,551	107,045	183,393	86,709	96,684	79,876	75,364	84,336	75,004	71,466	78,489
25 years	218,093	101,523	116,570	209,908	99,446	110,462	86,412	80,921	91,840	85,848	81,964	89,675
26 years	177,605	83,100	94,505	148,041	71,458	76,583	70,370	66,237	74,456	60,546	58,896	62,171
27 years	159,423	77,595	81,828	133,358	66,528	66,830	63,166	61,849	64,469	54,541	54,333	54,253
28 years	192,795	93,921	98,874	141,024	70,528	70,496	76,389	74,862	77,898	57,676	58,130	57,230
29 years	133,311	65,666	67,645	105,148	52,637	52,511	52,820	52,341	53,294	43,003	43,384	42,629
30 years	233,557	114,699	118,858	192,436	95,910	96,526	92,540	91,423	93,643	78,703	79,050	78,361
31 years	89,743	45,572	44,171	66,996	34,518	32,478	35,558	36,324	34,800	27,400	28,450	26,366
32 years	128,545	63,470	65,075	90,999	45,186	45,813	50,932	50,590	51,270	37,217	37,243	37,192
33 years	106,042	52,894	53,148	84,141	41,818	42,323	42,016	42,160	41,873	34,412	34,467	34,358
34 years	110,202	55,528	54,674	90,035	44,698	45,337	43,664	44,260	43,075	36,823	36,840	36,805
35 years	184,182	94,561	89,621	150,710	74,496	76,214	72,976	75,372	70,608	61,638	61,400	61,872
36 years	115,720	57,054	58,666	79,976	38,629	41,347	45,850	45,476	46,220	32,709	31,838	33,566
37 years	96,694	48,830	47,864	71,489	35,245	36,244	38,312	38,921	37,710	29,238	29,049	29,423
38 years	136,025	68,778	67,247	91,648	44,834	46,814	53,896	54,821	52,981	37,482	36,952	38,004
39 years	100,828	51,227	49,601	80,864	40,167	40,697	39,950	40,832	39,078	33,072	33,106	33,038
40 years	186,178	93,149	93,029	167,046	79,300	87,746	73,767	74,247	73,293	68,319	65,359	71,233
41 years	56,545	29,794	26,751	42,358	21,901	20,457	22,404	23,748	21,076	17,324	18,051	16,607
42 years	84,809	43,041	41,768	59,604	29,431	30,173	33,603	34,307	32,907	24,377	24,257	24,495
43 years	63,616	31,532	32,084	46,191	22,723	23,468	25,206	25,133	25,278	18,891	18,728	19,052
44 years	64,265	32,164	32,101	52,017	25,735	26,282	25,463	25,637	25,291	21,274	21,211	21,336
45 years	129,838	66,921	62,917	112,275	55,595	56,680	51,444	53,341	49,569	45,918	45,822	46,014
46 years	58,210	30,580	27,630	49,743	27,110	22,633	23,064	24,374	21,768	20,344	22,344	18,374
47 years	53,808	28,528	25,280	48,463	26,305	22,158	21,320	22,739	19,917	19,820	21,681	17,988
48 years	80,337	40,258	40,079	61,383	31,232	30,151	31,831	32,089	31,576	25,104	25,742	24,477
49 years	63,716	33,641	30,075	54,520	28,253	26,267	25,245	26,814	23,695	22,298	23,286	21,324
50 years	142,123	73,147	68,976	138,280	67,914	70,366	56,312	58,304	54,343	56,554	55,975	57,124
51 years	39,305	22,906	16,399	33,203	19,247	13,956	15,573	18,258	12,920	13,579	15,863	11,330
52 years	57,560	33,491	24,069	46,661	26,922	19,739	22,806	26,695	18,963	19,083	22,189	16,024
53 years	40,728	23,753	16,975	34,409	19,899	14,510	16,137	18,933	13,374	14,073	16,401	11,779
54 years	46,354	26,090	20,264	38,434	21,206	17,228	18,366	20,796	15,965	15,719	17,478	13,986
55 years	68,408	36,621	31,787	64,973	34,013	30,960	27,105	29,190	25,044	26,573	28,034	25,134
56 years	45,350	25,854	19,496	35,086	20,281	14,805	17,969	20,608	15,360	14,350	16,716	12,019
57 years	30,205	17,360	12,845	24,392	13,935	10,457	11,968	13,387	10,120	9,976	11,485	8,489
58 years	38,222	20,293	17,929	28,065	14,806	13,259	15,144	16,175	14,125	11,478	12,203	10,764
59 years	27,437	14,962	12,475	26,660	14,288	12,372	10,871	11,926	9,828	10,903	11,776	10,044
60 years	96,575	49,275	47,300	92,756	46,011	46,745	38,265	39,276	37,266	37,935	37,923	37,948
61 years	18,685	10,565	8,120	13,696	8,006	5,690	7,403	8,421	6,397	5,601	6,599	4,619
62 years	25,927	14,893	11,034	19,367	11,204	8,163	10,273	11,871	8,693	7,921	9,234	6,627
63 years	23,976	14,115	9,861	17,987	10,676	7,311	9,500	11,251	7,769	7,356	8,799	5,935
64 years	21,339	12,301	9,038	17,881	10,064	7,817	8,455	9,805	7,121	7,313	8,295	6,346
65 years	56,886	29,683	27,203	47,437	24,452	22,985	22,539	23,660	21,432	19,401	20,153	18,660
66 years	16,871	10,132	6,739	14,181	8,549	5,632	6,685	8,076	5,309	5,800	7,046	4,572
67 years	15,837	9,322	6,515	13,388	8,022	5,366	6,275	7,430	5,133	5,475	6,612	4,356
68 years	19,695	10,663	9,032	14,612	7,924	6,688	7,804	8,499	7,116	5,976	6,531	5,429
69 years	14,261	8,156	6,105	13,053	7,071	5,982	5,650	6,501	4,810	5,338	5,823	4,856
70 years	42,899	20,594	22,305	43,132	20,224	22,908	16,997	16,415	17,573	17,640	16,669	18,597
71 years	7,805	4,314	3,491	5,916	3,271	2,645	3,092	3,439	2,750	2,420	2,696	2,147
72 years	11,592	6,397	5,195	9,140	4,994	4,146	4,593	5,099	4,093	3,738	4,116	3,366
73 years	8,358	4,706	3,652	6,725	3,750	2,975	3,312	3,751	2,877	2,750	3,091	2,415
74 years	8,185	4,573	3,612	7,469	3,996	3,473	3,243	3,645	2,846	3,055	3,294	2,819

NEGRO POPULATION CLASSIFIED BY SEX AND SINGLE YEARS OF AGE, AND NUMBER IN EACH YEAR OF AGE PER 100,000 UNDER 1 YEAR: 1910 AND 1900—Continued.

Table 2—Continued.	NEGRO POPULATION.											
	1910			1900			Per 100,000 under 1 year of age.					
AGE.							1910			1900		
	Both sexes.	Male.	Female.	Both sexes.	Male.	Female.	Both sexes.	Male.	Female.	Both sexes.	Male.	Female.
75 years	21,005	10,139	10,866	20,433	9,737	10,696	8,323	8,082	8,561	8,357	8,025	8,683
76 years	7,529	4,137	3,392	5,847	3,204	2,643	2,983	3,297	2,672	2,391	2,641	2,146
77 years	4,721	2,799	1,922	4,080	2,268	1,812	1,871	2,231	1,514	1,669	1,869	1,471
78 years	6,754	3,485	3,269	5,430	2,879	2,551	2,676	2,778	2,575	2,221	2,373	2,071
79 years	4,009	2,107	1,902	4,630	2,387	2,243	1,588	1,679	1,498	1,894	1,967	1,821
80 years	15,054	6,434	8,620	16,431	6,977	9,454	5,965	5,128	6,791	6,720	5,750	7,675
81 years	2,537	1,264	1,273	2,091	1,128	963	1,005	1,008	1,003	855	930	782
82 years	2,989	1,487	1,502	2,802	1,461	1,341	1,184	1,185	1,183	1,146	1,204	1,089
83 years	2,393	1,195	1,198	1,974	1,007	967	948	953	944	807	830	785
84 years	2,606	1,316	1,290	2,229	1,082	1,147	1,033	1,049	1,016	912	892	931
85 years	4,961	2,142	2,819	4,633	1,976	2,657	1,966	1,707	2,221	1,895	1,629	2,157
86 years	1,907	948	959	1,592	841	751	756	756	756	651	693	610
87 years	1,757	890	867	1,448	743	705	696	709	683	592	612	572
88 years	1,335	643	692	1,288	637	651	529	513	545	527	525	528
89 years	1,206	541	665	1,122	516	606	478	431	524	459	425	492
90 years	3,718	1,393	2,325	3,648	1,342	2,306	1,473	1,110	1,832	1,492	1,106	1,872
91 years	563	276	287	395	189	206	223	220	226	162	156	167
92 years	622	300	322	496	222	274	246	239	254	203	183	222
93 years	514	216	298	382	163	219	204	172	235	156	134	178
94 years	433	209	224	372	169	203	172	167	176	152	139	165
95 years	1,092	420	672	923	346	577	433	335	529	377	285	468
96 years	379	176	203	388	168	220	150	140	160	159	138	179
97 years	267	118	149	295	124	171	106	94	117	121	102	139
98 years	480	210	270	475	167	308	190	167	213	194	138	250
99 years	229	93	136	353	153	200	91	74	107	144	126	162
100 years and over	2,675	1,004	1,671	2,553	886	1,667	1,060	800	1,317	1,044	730	1,353
Age unknown	31,040	17,076	13,964	48,811	25,157	23,654	12,299	13,611	11,002	19,963	20,735	19,203

tion are, therefore, entirely consistent with accuracy of data. Conclusive evidence of inaccuracy in the schedule age returns is found not in a comparison with the life tables for Negro males and females, but in the fact that these returns themselves develop in tabulation an age composition which in detail is inconsistent with any reasonable assumption regarding mortality and birth rates in the past.

Irregularities in the distribution of the population by single years of age, similar to those which have been noted in the returns for 1910, characterized also the returns for 1900, as may be seen by reference to Table 2.

NUMBER IN EACH AGE PER 100,000 UNDER 1 YEAR.

In addition to the population figures for the two years, 1910 and 1900, Table 2 gives the number of Negro males and females in each year of age per 100,000 under 1 year.

At nearly every year of age the number living per 100,000 under 1 in 1910, exceeded the corresponding figure for 1900. The total Negro population per 100,000 under 1 was 3,893,941 in 1910, and 3,612,937 in 1900, the excess of the 1910 over the 1900 figure being 281,006. There is no reason to believe that any considerable proportion of this difference, if any whatever, is due to a greater proportion of omissions, in 1910 as compared with 1900, in the enumeration of infants. Assuming that the two censuses covered were equally accurate and complete in their returns of age, it seems probable that the increase noted has resulted in part from a decrease in the birth rate, tending to reduce the proportion of children in the population, and in part from a general improvement in mortality, tending to increase the proportion of survivors for each age, and the total population relatively to the number under 1 year of age.

CENTENARIANS.

Of the 3,555 centenarians reported in the total population of all classes at the census of 1910, 2,675, or more than three-fourths, were Negroes, the number of centenarians per 100,000 of all ages being for Negroes 27.2, and for whites 0.9. The proportion of centenarians, which is exceedingly small for all classes, probably is not, in fact, appreciably if in any degree greater among Negroes than it is among whites. The proportion shown in the returns is inconsistent with the age distribution of the Negro population itself as indicated in the census life tables for Negroes, in which the proportion of centenarians indicated for a stationary population is 5 per 100,000. The proportion in the enumerated population, which is increasing, would be somewhat lower.

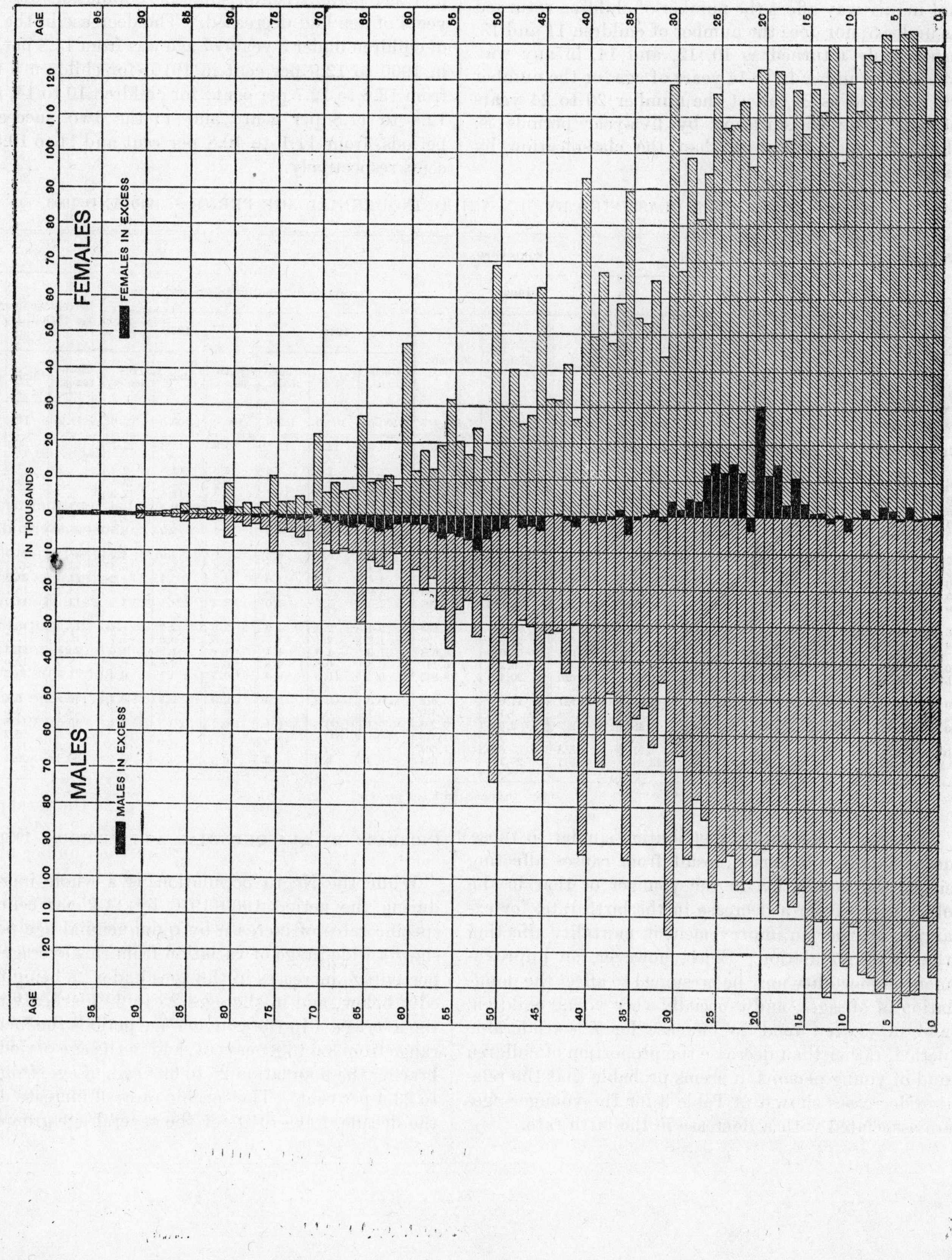

Diagram I.—NEGRO POPULATION CLASSIFIED BY SEX AND SINGLE YEARS OF AGE, WITH EXCESS OF MALES OR FEMALES AT EACH AGE: 1910.

DISTRIBUTION BY QUINQUENNIAL AGE PERIODS: 1910 AND 1900.

Some of the error in the return of ages is avoided by classifications which group the population by age periods. The number of children 1 year of age, erroneously returned as 2 years of age, for example, does not in any way affect the number of children returned as under 5; nor does the number of children 11 and 13, erroneously returned as 10, 12, and 14, in any way affect the number 10 to 14 years of age; or the number 20, returned as 21, affect the number 20 to 24 years of age. The classification by five-year periods is, therefore, more accurate than the classification by single years.

Table 3 summarizes by quinquennial age periods the data shown in Table 2 by single years, and gives the percentage distribution by age periods, and the percentage increases for the population in each age period.

In 1910, as compared with 1900, the proportion of Negro males and females in each of the five quinquennial age periods comprising the population under 25 years of age had decreased. The decrease in the case of children under 5 years of age was from 13.8 per cent in 1900 to 12.9 per cent in 1910; for children 5 to 9, from 13.6 to 12.7 per cent; for children 10 to 14, from 12.4 to 11.8 per cent; and in the two succeeding periods, from 11.1 to 10.8 per cent and 11 to 10.5 per cent, respectively.

NEGRO POPULATION CLASSIFIED BY SEX AND QUINQUENNIAL AGE PERIODS: 1910 AND 1900.

Table 3	NEGRO POPULATION.						Percentage distribution by age period.						Percentage increase by age period: 1900–1910.		
AGE PERIOD.	1910			1900			1910			1900					
	Both sexes.	Male.	Female.	Both sexes.	Male.	Female.	Both sexes.	Male.	Female.	Both sexes.	Male.	Female.	Both sexes.	Male.	Female.
All ages.........	9,827,763	4,885,881	4,941,882	8,833,994	4,386,547	4,447,447	100.0	100.0	100.0	100.0	100.0	100.0	11.2	11.4	11.1
Under 5 years........	1,263,288	629,320	633,968	1,215,655	604,487	611,168	12.9	12.9	12.8	13.8	13.8	13.7	3.9	4.1	3.7
Under 1 year.....	252,386	125,459	126,927	244,510	121,329	123,181	2.6	2.6	2.6	2.8	2.8	2.8	3.2	3.4	3.0
5 to 9 years..........	1,246,553	619,175	627,378	1,202,758	600,410	602,348	12.7	12.7	12.7	13.6	13.7	13.5	3.6	3.1	4.2
10 to 14 years........	1,155,266	578,074	577,192	1,091,990	548,642	543,348	11.8	11.8	11.7	12.4	12.5	12.2	5.8	5.4	6.2
15 to 19 years........	1,060,416	507,945	552,471	982,022	473,750	508,272	10.8	10.4	11.2	11.1	10.8	11.4	8.0	7.2	8.7
20 to 24 years........	1,030,795	482,157	548,638	969,172	458,921	510,251	10.5	9.9	11.1	11.0	10.5	11.5	6.4	5.1	7.5
25 to 29 years........	881,227	421,805	459,422	737,479	360,597	376,882	9.0	8.6	9.3	8.3	8.2	8.5	19.5	17.0	21.9
30 to 34 years........	668,089	332,163	335,926	524,607	262,130	262,477	6.8	6.8	6.8	5.9	6.0	5.9	27.4	26.7	28.0
35 to 39 years........	633,449	320,450	312,999	474,687	233,371	241,316	6.4	6.6	6.3	5.4	5.3	5.4	33.4	37.3	29.7
40 to 44 years........	455,413	229,680	225,733	367,216	179,090	188,126	4.6	4.7	4.6	4.2	4.1	4.2	24.0	28.2	20.0
45 to 49 years........	335,909	199,928	185,981	326,384	168,495	157,889	3.9	4.1	3.8	3.7	3.8	3.6	18.2	18.7	17.8
50 to 54 years........	326,070	179,387	146,683	290,987	155,188	135,799	3.3	3.7	3.0	3.3	3.5	3.1	12.1	15.6	8.0
55 to 59 years........	209,622	115,090	94,532	179,176	97,323	81,853	2.1	2.4	1.9	2.0	2.2	1.8	17.0	18.3	15.5
60 to 64 years........	186,502	101,149	85,353	161,687	85,961	75,726	1.9	2.1	1.7	1.8	2.0	1.7	15.3	17.7	12.7
65 to 69 years........	123,550	67,956	55,594	102,671	56,018	46,653	1.3	1.4	1.1	1.2	1.3	1.0	20.3	21.3	19.2
70 to 74 years........	78,839	40,584	38,255	72,382	36,235	36,147	0.8	0.8	0.8	0.8	0.8	0.8	8.9	12.0	5.8
75 to 79 years........	44,018	22,667	21,351	40,420	20,475	19,945	0.4	0.5	0.4	0.5	0.5	0.4	8.9	10.7	7.0
80 to 84 years........	25,579	11,696	13,883	25,527	11,655	13,872	0.3	0.2	0.3	0.3	0.3	0.3	0.2	0.4	0.1
85 to 89 years........	11,166	5,164	6,002	10,083	4,713	5,370	0.1	0.1	0.1	0.1	0.1	0.1	10.7	9.6	11.8
90 to 94 years........	5,850	2,394	3,456	5,293	2,085	3,208	0.1	(1)	0.1	0.1	(1)	0.1	10.5	14.8	7.7
95 to 99 years........	2,447	1,017	1,430	2,434	958	1,476	(1)	(1)	(1)	(1)	(1)	(1)	0.5	6.2	– 3.1
100 years and over....	2,675	1,004	1,671	2,553	886	1,667	(1)	(1)	(1)	(1)	(1)	(1)	4.8	13.3	0.2
Age unknown........	31,040	17,076	13,964	48,811	25,157	23,654	0.3	0.3	0.3	0.6	0.6	0.5	–36.4	–32.1	–41.0

1 Less than one-tenth of 1 per cent.

Changes in percentage distribution similar to those noted might, obviously, result from causes affecting either the population in the younger or that in the older ages—from a decrease in the birth rate, for example, or from an improvement in mortality affecting the adult population. Since, however, an improvement in mortality may be presumed to affect the population of all ages, and especially very young children, and may even tend to increase for a considerable period, rather than decrease the proportion of children and of young persons, it seems probable that the relative decreases shown in Table 3 for the younger ages are associated with a decrease in the birth rate.

INCREASE BY QUINQUENNIAL AGE PERIODS: 1900–1910.

While the Negro population as a whole increased during the period 1900–1910 by 11.2 per cent, the specific rates of increase by quinquennial age periods show a wide range of variation from this average—the percentage increases in the ages under 25 being markedly below, and in the ages 25 to 69 markedly above the average. In the younger age periods the increases range from 3.6 to 8 per cent, and in the age periods embracing the population 25 to 69 years of age, from 12.1 to 33.4 per cent. The specific rates of increase during the decade, 1900–1910, for the several age groups are of course, implied in the relative percentage distributions by age of the population in 1900 and in 1910.

Making due allowance for improvement in mortality, the rates of increase maintained in the younger ages tend eventually to develop in the older ages. This tendency may be simply illustrated. In Table 3 the population under 5 in 1910 compared with the population under 5 in 1900 develops a percentage increase of 3.9. If as these two population groups advance in age they are subjected to the same rates of mortality at each age, the surviving populations will maintain a constant numerical relationship to one another, one being constantly 3.9 per cent in excess of the other. Under this assumption 3.9 per cent will develop as the decennial increase for the age group 10 to 14 years, in 1920; for the age group 20 to 24 years,

in 1930, and for corresponding older groups at successive censuses. Similarly, the percentage increase of 33.4 shown in Table 3 for the age groups 35 to 39 years, since it is a comparison of survivors to the age 35 to 39 years, among children born in the period 1860–1865, with survivors to the same age among children born in the period 1870–1875, represents the high birth rates of these periods and possibly a relative deficiency of births during the Civil War period, or of survivors among children born in that period, as compared with survivors for the later period.

It will be apparent that the different rates shown for the several age groups indicate a retardation in the rate of growth, and that the rate of decennial growth indicated for the total Negro population by the increases of the lower age groups does not exceed 4 per cent.

NEGRO POPULATION IN YEARS SPECIFIED, CLASSIFIED BY SEX AND AGE PERIODS: 1830 TO 1910.[1]

Table 4

AGE PERIOD.	NEGRO POPULATION.															
	Number.								Percentage distribution by age period.							
	1910	1900	1890	1870	1860	1850	1840	1830	1910	1900	1890	1870	1860	1850	1840	1830
BOTH SEXES.																
All ages	9,827,763	8,833,994	7,488,676	4,880,009	4,441,830	3,638,808	2,873,648	2,328,642								
Age unknown	31,040	48,811	[2] 54,449	28	26,258	3,978	190									
Known age	9,796,723	8,785,183	7,434,227	4,879,981	4,415,572	3,634,830	2,873,458	2,328,642	100.0	100.0	100.0	100.0	100.0	100.0	100.0	100.0
Under 5 years	1,263,288	1,215,655	....	791,421	719,084	601,315			12.9	13.8	......	16.2	16.3	16.5		
Under 1 year	252,386	244,510	....	152,622	126,280	91,785			2.6	2.8	......	3.1	2.9	2.5		
5 to 9 years	1,246,553	1,202,758	....	659,831	637,806	537,140			12.7	13.7	......	13.5	14.4	14.8		
10 to 14 years	1,155,266	1,091,990	1,033,701	645,311	601,647	488,500			11.8	12.4	13.9	13.2	13.6	13.4		
15 to 19 years	1,060,416	982,022	871,118	520,550	501,593	401,076			10.8	11.2	11.7	10.7	11.4	11.0		
20 years and over	5,071,200	4,292,758	3,388,340	2,262,868	1,955,442	1,606,799			51.8	48.9	45.6	46.4	44.3	44.2		
Under 10 years	2,509,841	2,418,413	1,451,252	1,356,890	1,138,455	955,461	797,167		25.6	27.5	28.8	29.7	30.7	31.3	33.3	34.2
10 to 19 years	2,215,682	2,074,012	1,904,819	1,165,861	1,103,240	889,576			22.6	23.6	25.6	23.9	25.0	24.5		
20 to 29 years	1,912,022	1,706,651	1,291,099	877,902	783,603	649,757			19.5	19.4	17.4	18.0	17.7	17.9		
30 to 39 years	1,301,538	999,294	....	543,587	500,598	408,880			13.3	11.4	......	11.1	11.3	11.2		
40 to 49 years	841,322	693,600	....	385,788	324,519	257,872			8.6	7.9	......	7.9	7.3	7.1		
50 to 59 years	535,692	470,163	....	242,219	183,693	151,369			5.5	5.4	......	5.0	4.2	4.2		
60 to 69 years	310,052	264,358	....	135,978	106,475	88,704			3.2	3.0	......	2.8	2.4	2.4		
70 to 79 years	122,857	112,802	....	53,006	38,193	33,170			1.3	1.3	......	1.1	0.9	0.9		
80 to 89 years	36,745	35,610	....	16,951	12,536	11,736			0.4	0.4	......	0.3	0.3	0.3		
90 to 99 years	8,297	7,727	....	4,900	3,885	3,543			0.1	0.1	......	0.1	0.1	0.1		
10 to 23 years	3,044,881	2,859,791	....	....	....	....	890,567	712,554	31.1	32.6	......	......	......	......	31.0	30.6
24 to 35 years	1,935,094	1,596,189	....	....	....	....	552,141	431,562	19.8	18.2	......	......	......	......	19.2	18.5
36 to 54 years	1,616,659	1,308,564	....	....	....	....	343,108	277,365	16.5	14.9	......	......	......	......	11.9	11.9
55 to 99 years	687,573	599,673	....	291,692	....	....	130,201	107,915	7.0	6.8	......	6.0	......	......	4.5	4.6
100 years and over	2,675	2,553	....	2,537	1,940	1,768	1,980	2,079	(3)	(3)	......	0.1	(3)	(3)	0.1	0.1
MALE.																
All ages	4,885,881	4,386,547	3,735,603	2,393,263	2,216,744	1,811,258	1,432,988	1,166,276								
Age unknown	17,076	25,157	[2] 28,477	11	13,764	2,020	113									
Known age	4,868,805	4,361,390	3,707,126	2,393,252	2,202,980	1,809,238	1,432,875	1,166,276	100.0	100.0	100.0	100.0	100.0	100.0	100.0	100.0
Under 5 years	629,320	604,487	....	396,812	354,999	297,407			12.9	13.9	......	16.6	16.1	16.4		
Under 1 year	125,459	121,329	....	75,985	61,462	44,919			2.6	2.8	......	3.2	2.8	2.5		
5 to 9 years	619,175	600,410	....	331,795	317,999	267,969			12.7	13.8	......	13.9	14.4	14.8		
10 to 14 years	578,074	548,642	526,450	329,339	307,374	247,541			11.9	12.6	14.2	13.8	14.0	13.7		
15 to 19 years	507,945	473,750	422,258	251,822	245,104	196,564			10.4	10.9	11.4	10.5	11.1	10.9		
20 years and over	2,534,291	2,134,101	1,679,028	1,083,484	977,504	799,757			52.1	48.9	45.3	45.3	44.4	44.2		
Under 10 years	1,248,495	1,204,897	1,079,390	728,607	672,998	565,376	478,922	402,173	25.6	27.6	29.1	30.4	30.5	31.2	33.4	34.5
10 to 19 years	1,086,019	1,022,392	948,708	581,161	552,478	444,105			22.3	23.4	25.6	24.3	25.1	24.5		
20 to 29 years	903,962	819,518	622,436	407,558	394,185	325,377			18.6	18.8	16.8	17.0	17.9	18.0		
30 to 39 years	652,613	495,501	....	253,646	247,378	201,453			13.4	11.4	......	10.6	11.2	11.1		
40 to 49 years	429,608	347,585	....	186,590	162,220	127,351			8.8	8.0	......	7.8	7.4	7.0		
50 to 59 years	294,477	252,511	....	128,178	93,106	77,025			6.0	5.8	......	5.4	4.2	4.3		
60 to 69 years	169,105	141,979	....	71,460	53,909	44,773			3.5	3.3	......	3.0	2.4	2.5		
70 to 79 years	63,251	56,710	....	25,714	18,631	16,044			1.3	1.3	......	1.1	0.8	0.9		
80 to 89 years	16,860	16,368	....	7,553	5,632	5,484			0.3	0.4	......	0.3	0.3	0.3		
90 to 99 years	3,411	3,043	....	1,900	1,644	1,530			0.1	0.1	......	0.1	0.1	0.1		
10 to 23 years	1,473,625	1,394,604	....	....	....	....	443,930	355,646	30.3	32.0	......	......	......	......	31.0	30.5
24 to 35 years	943,080	783,932	....	....	....	....	270,681	213,235	19.4	18.0	......	......	......	......	18.9	18.3
36 to 54 years	834,884	661,648	....	....	....	....	173,522	141,151	17.1	15.2	......	......	......	......	12.1	12.1
55 to 99 years	367,717	315,423	....	150,864	....	....	64,781	53,054	7.6	7.2	......	6.3	......	......	4.5	4.5
100 years and over	1,004	886	....	885	799	720	1,039	1,017	(3)	(3)	......	(3)	(3)	(3)	0.1	0.1
FEMALE.																
All ages	4,941,882	4,447,447	3,753,073	2,486,746	2,225,086	1,827,550	1,440,660	1,162,366								
Age unknown	13,964	23,654	[2] 25,972	17	12,494	1,958	77									
Known age	4,927,918	4,423,793	3,727,101	2,486,729	2,212,592	1,825,592	1,440,583	1,162,366	100.0	100.0	100.0	100.0	100.0	100.0	100.0	100.0
Under 5 years	633,968	611,168	....	394,609	364,085	303,908			12.9	13.8	......	15.9	16.5	16.6		
Under 1 year	126,927	123,181	....	76,637	64,818	46,866			2.6	2.8	......	3.1	2.9	2.6		
5 to 9 years	627,378	602,348	....	328,036	319,807	269,171			12.7	13.6	......	13.2	14.5	14.7		
10 to 14 years	577,192	543,348	507,251	315,972	294,273	240,959			11.7	12.3	13.6	12.7	13.3	13.2		
15 to 19 years	552,471	508,272	448,860	268,728	256,489	204,512			11.2	11.5	12.0	10.8	11.6	11.2		
20 years and over	2,536,909	2,158,657	1,709,312	1,179,384	977,938	807,042			51.5	48.8	45.9	47.4	44.2	44.2		
Under 10 years	1,261,346	1,213,516	1,061,678	722,645	683,892	573,079	476,539	394,994	25.6	27.4	28.5	29.1	30.9	31.4	33.1	34.0
10 to 19 years	1,129,663	1,051,620	956,111	584,700	550,762	445,471			22.9	23.8	25.7	23.5	24.9	24.4		
20 to 29 years	1,008,060	887,133	668,663	470,344	389,418	324,380			20.5	20.1	17.9	18.9	17.6	17.8		
30 to 39 years	648,925	503,793	....	289,941	253,220	207,427			13.2	11.4	......	11.7	11.4	11.4		
40 to 49 years	411,714	346,015	....	199,198	162,299	130,521			8.4	7.8	......	8.0	7.3	7.1		
50 to 59 years	241,215	217,652	....	114,041	90,587	74,344			4.9	4.9	......	4.6	4.1	4.1		
60 to 69 years	140,947	122,379	....	64,518	52,566	43,931			2.9	2.8	......	2.6	2.4	2.4		
70 to 79 years	59,606	56,092	....	27,292	19,562	17,126			1.2	1.3	......	1.1	0.9	0.9		
80 to 89 years	19,885	19,242	....	9,398	6,904	6,252			0.4	0.4	......	0.4	0.3	0.3		
90 to 99 years	4,886	4,684	....	3,000	2,241	2,013			0.1	0.1	......	0.1	0.1	0.1		
10 to 23 years	1,571,256	1,465,187	....	....	....	....	446,637	356,908	31.9	33.1	......	......	......	......	31.0	30.7
24 to 35 years	992,014	812,257	....	....	....	....	281,460	218,327	20.1	18.4	......	......	......	......	19.5	18.8
36 to 54 years	781,775	646,916	....	....	....	....	169,586	136,214	15.9	14.6	......	......	......	......	11.8	11.7
55 to 99 years	319,856	284,250	....	140,828	....	....	65,420	54,861	6.5	6.4	......	5.7	......	......	4.5	4.7
100 years and over	1,671	1,667	....	1,652	1,141	1,048	941	1,062	(3)	(3)	......	0.1	0.1	0.1	0.1	0.1

[1] No data available for 1880.
[2] Includes Negroes enumerated in Indian Territory and on Indian reservations, males 10,042, females 8,594, total 18,636, for whom statistics of age are not available.
[3] Less than one-tenth of 1 per cent.

AGE DISTRIBUTION AT EACH CENSUS: 1820–1910.

Table 4 gives the distribution of the Negro population by sex and age periods at each census, 1830 to 1910, except that of 1880—and Table 5, the distribution in 1820 in comparison with 1900 and 1910. No tabulation by age for Negroes separate from other colored population was made in the 1880 census, and only a partial classification in the 1890 census.

In Table 4 the various age groupings of the earlier censuses have been introduced, and so far as possible data available in later censuses have been compiled under the earlier age classifications. For 1910 and for 1900 the single-year age groups can be compiled under any of the earlier classifications—under those of 1830 and 1840, for example, showing under 10 years of age, 10 to 23, 24 to 35, 36 to 54, 55 to 99, and 100 years and over. Only the first and last of these classes, however, can be shown for succeeding censuses prior to 1900. The quinquennial age classes for the population under 20 years of age, distinguished in the 1850 classification and generally in the classifications of later censuses, can not be shown for 1840 or 1830.

Since the age classes of the several censuses overlap, the population shown in Table 4 for those classes in combination necessarily overlap also where data are available in full detail. Three complete distributions of the Negro population by age are in fact given in Table 4 for the years 1910 and 1900, the first showing quinquennial age periods for the population under 20 years of age, with the total 20 years and over; the second, ten-year age periods covering all ages; and the third showing the age classes of 1830 and 1840. The detail by five-year periods for the population under 20 years of age and by ten-year periods for the older population is available for 1850, 1860, 1870, 1900, and 1910. For the age period "under 10 years" data are available in each census 1830 to 1910—always excepting 1880. No other of the classes shown in Table 4, however, can be carried back through the several years in an unbroken series. The percentage distributions for each year are based upon the population of known age.

The proportion of the population under 10 years of age has declined in each decade from 34.2 per cent, or a little over one-third, in 1830 to 25.6 per cent, or a little over one-fourth, in 1910. In both years the proportion under 10 was practically the same for males as for females. In this period the proportion of the population 10 to 23 years of age increased slightly—from 30.6 per cent in 1830 to 31.1 per cent in 1910; the proportion 24 to 35 years of age increased from 18.5 to 19.8 per cent; the proportion 36 to 54 years, from 11.9 to 16.5 per cent; and the proportion 55 to 99 years, from 4.6 to 7 per cent.

Comparing 1850 with 1910, the proportion of the Negro population 20 years of age and over increased from 44.2 per cent in 1850 to 51.8 per cent in 1910. In this period the proportion in each of the quinquen-

nial classes comprising the population under 20 years of age decreased—for the age group under 5 years from 16.5 per cent in 1850 to 12.9 per cent in 1910; for the age 5 to 9 years, from 14.8 to 12.7 per cent; for the age 10 to 14 years, from 13.4 to 11.8 per cent; and for the age 15 to 19 years, from 11 to 10.8 per cent.

According to Table 5, which presents the classification of 1820, the proportion of the Negro population under 14 years of age decreased from 43 per cent in 1820 to 35 per cent in 1910; the proportion 14 to 26 years increased from 25.9 to 26 per cent; the proportion 26 to 45 years, from 20.7 to 24.7 per cent; and the proportion 45 and over, from 10.4 to 14.3 per cent.

Table 5	NEGRO POPULATION.					
AGE PERIOD.	Number.			Percentage distribution by age periods.		
	1910	1900	1820	1910	1900	1820
BOTH SEXES.						
All ages...............	9,827,763	8,833,994	1,771,658	....	....	....
Age unknown..............	31,040	48,811				
Known age...............	9,796,723	8,785,183	1,771,658	100.0	100.0	100.0
Under 14 years..........	3,430,559	3,298,760	761,753	35.0	37.5	43.0
14 to 26 years..........	2,543,852	2,372,745	458,372	26.0	27.0	25.9
26 to 45 years..........	2,420,085	1,894,081	367,047	24.7	21.6	20.7
45 years and over......	1,402,227	1,219,597	184,486	14.3	13.9	10.4
MALE.						
All ages...............	4,885,881	4,386,547	900,798	....	....	....
Age unknown..............	17,076	25,157				
Known age...............	4,868,805	4,361,390	900,798	100.0	100.0	100.0
Under 14 years..........	1,709,930	1,648,256	391,511	35.1	27.8	43.5
14 to 26 years..........	1,208,264	1,137,400	227,136	24.8	26.1	25.2
26 to 45 years..........	1,202,575	935,742	187,173	24.7	21.5	20.8
45 years and over......	748,036	639,992	94,978	15.4	14.7	10.5
FEMALE.						
All ages...............	4,941,882	4,447,447	870,860	....	....	....
Age unknown..............	13,964	23,654				
Known age...............	4,927,918	4,423,793	870,860	100.0	100.0	100.0
Under 14 years..........	1,720,629	1,650,504	370,242	34.9	37.3	42.5
14 to 26 years..........	1,335,588	1,235,345	231,236	27.1	27.9	26.6
26 to 45 years..........	1,217,510	958,339	179,874	24.7	21.7	20.7
45 years and over......	654,191	579,605	89,508	13.3	13.1	10.3

From the figures given in Tables 4 and 5 it would appear that the decrease noted for the decade, 1900–1910, of the proportion in the younger ages, has been fairly continuous throughout a considerable period. Incidentally it may be noted that the changes in age composition, during the entire period for which data are available, indicate for the Negro population a material increase in economic power, in so far as economic power is dependent upon age, since relatively to the total Negro population the proportion in the economically productive ages has constantly increased, while the proportion in the dependent ages of childhood and youth has declined.

SEX DISTRIBUTION BY AGE.

The sex distribution by single years of age of the Negro population as enumerated is extremely irregular and divergent, as compared with the life table distribution. The discrepancies between the two distributions will be apparent upon reference to the age pyramid diagrams.

According to the enumerated returns, females are in excess in each of the single year ages 13 to 30 years, excepting the age 21, and are generally in the minority in the older ages up to the age of 80. In the life-table population females are in excess at all ages, the excess being greater in the older than it is in the younger ages. The excess of males shown in the enumerated population for the more advanced ages seems, therefore, quite inconsistent with the specific mortality rates of the life table. Some of the enumerated excess of females in the younger ages is probably accounted for by understatement of age by females.

In Table 6 the excess of males or of females in the Negro population, and the number of males per 1,000 females is shown by quinquennial age periods for the years 1910 and 1900, the sex ratio of the native white population in 1910 being introduced for comparison. The 1910 data as regard Negroes are illustrated by Diagram II.

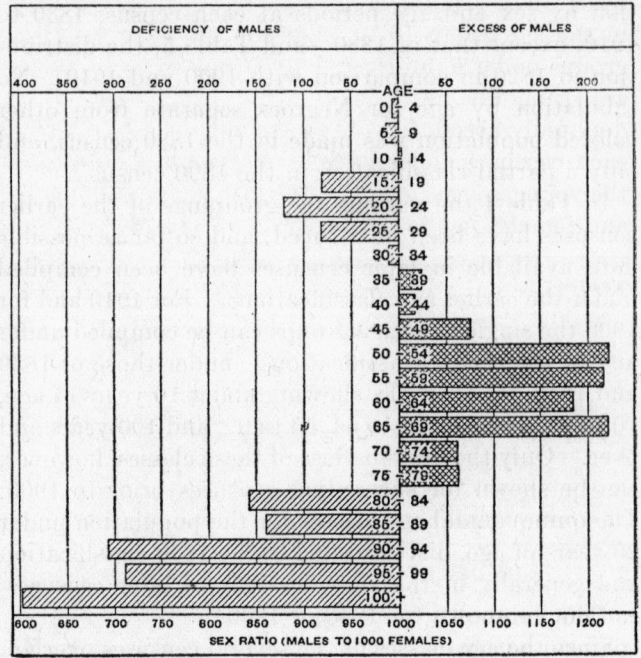

DIAGRAM II.—DEFICIENCY OR EXCESS OF MALES PER 1,000 FEMALES BY AGE PERIODS, IN THE NEGRO POPULATION: 1910.

The sex ratios for the native white population indicate an excess of males at each age except 20 to 24 years in the population under 70 years of age and an excess of females in the more advanced ages. The highest ratio for the native white population is that of 1,120 males to 1,000 females in the age 50–54 years, which age group shows the highest ratio also for the Negro population—1,223 males to 1,000 females. Although the native white population shows an excess of males throughout the younger ages, while the Negro population shows for these ages an excess of females, in the middle age periods the excess of males is relatively less in the native white than it is in the Negro population.

Table 6

| AGE PERIOD. | NEGRO POPULATION. | | | | MALES TO 1,000 FEMALES. | | |
| | 1910 | | 1900 | | Negro population. | | Native white population, |
	Excess of males.	Excess of females.	Excess of males.	Excess of females.	1910	1900	1910
All ages............	......	56,001	......	60,900	989	986	1,027
Under 5 years...........	......	4,648	......	6,681	993	989	1,029
Under 1 year........	......	1,468	......	1,852	988	985	1,032
5 to 9 years...........	......	8,203	......	1,938	987	997	1,023
10 to 14 years...........	882	......	5,294	......	1,002	1,010	1,024
15 to 19 years...........	......	44,526	......	34,522	919	932	1,000
20 to 24 years...........	......	66,481	......	51,330	879	899	981
25 to 29 years...........	......	37,617	......	16,285	918	957	1,003
30 to 34 years...........	......	3,763	......	347	989	999	1,024
35 to 39 years...........	7,451	......	......	7,945	1,024	967	1,047
40 to 44 years...........	3,947	......	......	9,036	1,017	952	1,056
45 to 49 years...........	13,947	......	10,606	......	1,075	1,067	1,068
50 to 54 years...........	32,704	......	19,389	......	1,223	1,143	1,120
55 to 59 years...........	20,558	......	15,470	......	1,217	1,189	1,109
60 to 64 years...........	15,796	......	10,235	......	1,185	1,135	1,069
65 to 69 years...........	12,362	......	9,365	......	1,222	1,201	1,023
70 to 74 years...........	2,329	......	......	88	1,061	1,002	995
75 to 79 years...........	1,316	......	530	......	1,062	1,027	959
80 to 84 years...........	......	2,187	......	2,217	842	840	891
85 to 89 years...........	......	838	......	657	860	878	804
90 to 94 year	......	1,062	......	1,123	693	650	751
95 to 99 years...........	......	413	......	518	711	649	626
100 years and over........	......	667	......	781	601	531	738
Age unknown............	3,112	......	1,503	......	1,223	1,064	2,214

It will be apparent from Table 6 that the sex ratio showed a wider range of variation from age group to age group in 1910 than it did in 1900. In both years, however, an excess of females over males is shown for each of the age groups comprising, in the aggregate, the population under 35 years, except for the age 10 to 14, an excess of males for each of the age groups comprising the population 45 to 79 years, and an excess of females in the more advanced ages. In view of the irregularity of the sex distribution of the Negro population by age, this degree of correspondence between 1910 and 1900 is remarkable.

Table 7

| AGE PERIOD. | MALES TO 1,000 FEMALES IN THE NEGRO POPULATION. | | | | | | | |
	1910	1900	1890	1870	1860	1850	1840	1830
All ages............	988	986	995	962	996	991	995	1,003
Age unknown..	1,223	1,064	1,096	(1)	1,102	1,032	(1)	......
Known age.....	988	986	995	962	956	991	995	1,003
Under 5 years...........	993	989	......	1,006	975	979	......	......
Under 1 year.......	988	985	......	991	948	958	......	......
5 to 9 years...........	987	997	......	1,011	994	996	......	......
10 to 14 years...........	1,002	1,010	1,038	1,042	1,045	1,027	......	......
15 to 19 years...........	919	932	941	937	956	961	......	......
20 years and over.......	999	989	982	919	1,000	991	......	......
Under 10 years.......	990	993	1,017	1,008	984	987	1,005	1,018
10 to 19 years.......	961	972	992	994	1,003	997	......	......
20 to 29 years.......	897	924	931	867	1,012	1,003	......	......
30 to 39 years.......	1,006	984	......	875	977	971	......	......
40 to 49 years.......	1,043	1,005	......	937	1,000	976	......	......
50 to 59 years.......	1,221	1,160	......	1,124	1,028	1,036	......	......
60 to 69 years.......	1,200	1,160	......	1,108	1,026	1,019	......	......
70 to 79 years.......	1,061	1,011	......	942	952	937	......	......
80 to 89 years.......	848	851	......	804	816	877	......	......
90 to 99 years.......	698	650	......	633	734	760	......	......
10 to 23 years...........	938	952	......	......	......	......	994	996
24 to 35 years...........	951	965	......	......	......	......	962	977
36 to 54 years...........	1,068	1,023	......	......	......	......	1,023	1,036
55 to 99 years...........	1,150	1,110	......	1,071	......	......	990	967
100 years and over.......	601	531	......	536	700	687	1,104	958

[1] Ratio not shown, the number of females being less than 100.

Tables 7 and 8 present the sex ratio for the age classes shown in Tables 4 and 5. At each census for which data are available an excess of males is shown in the age group 10 to 14 years, although in the age groups under 5, under 1, 5 to 9, and 15 to 19, females are generally in excess. This irregularity is undoubtedly accounted for by errors in the returns. At each census females have been generally in excess in the younger ages, males in the late middle life periods, and females in the more advanced ages.

Table 8 AGE PERIOD.	MALES TO 1,000 FEMALES IN THE NEGRO POPULATION.		
	1910	1900	1820
All ages............................	989	986	1,034
Age unknown........................	1,223	1,064	....
Known age..........................	988	986	1,034
Under 14 years.....................	994	999	1,057
14 to 26 years.....................	905	921	982
26 to 45 years.....................	988	976	1,041
45 years and over..................	1,143	1,104	1,061

AGE DISTRIBUTION BY RACIAL CLASSES.

The composition of the Negro population in comparison with other racial elements in 1910 is given in Table 9 by sex and by reduced detail of age.

The proportion under 1 year of age, and under 5 years is somewhat smaller in the Negro than it is in the aggregate native white population; the proportion 5 to 14, 15 to 24, and 25 to 44, somewhat larger; and the proportion 45 to 64 and 65 and over, somewhat smaller.

It should be borne in mind that parents of native children are in many cases foreign-born, and that in such cases the classification by nativity separates the children from the parents. Similarly within the native population the children of natives of foreign or of mixed parentage are natives of native parentage, the classification by parentage in these cases, also separating children from parents. The proportion of children in the aggregate native white population, and in the native white population of native parentage, therefore, exceeds the proportion representing natural increase for these classes. The foreign-born white population in 1910 exceeded 13,000,000 and children born of this population during the 5 years preceding the census enumeration are classified as native whites of foreign or mixed parentage. The native white population of foreign or mixed parentage exceeded 18,000,000, and children born of this population in the five years preceding the enumeration, together with the children of native whites of native parentage are classed as natives of native parentage under 5 years of age.

These factors invalidate comparisons by age of the Negro population with the several nativity and parentage white classes. To the extent that Negroes intermarry with whites, however, an effect upon the age distribution of Negroes results similar to that resulting from the white nativity and parentage classification, since the children of mixed Negro and white parentage are generally classified as Negroes, thus increasing the proportion of children among Negroes.

The Indian population shows a larger proportion under 5 years, under 1, and 5 to 14, than the Negro; a smaller proportion 15 to 44; and a somewhat larger proportion 45 and over.

In each class except the Negroes, males are in excess in the ages under 5, under 1, and 5 to 14 years of age. Among native whites of native parentage males are in excess at all ages shown except in the population 65 and over.

Table 10 gives in comparison the distribution by age of the Negroes, native whites, and foreign-born whites, for the years 1910, 1900, and 1890, and Table 11, the distribution for these classes and years, by cumulative age periods.

In Table 11 it is shown for the age 45 years, for example—similar data being shown for other ages—that the Negro population under 45 years of age increased from 6,454,544 in 1890 to 8,394,496 in 1910; that the Negro population 45 years and older increased from 979,683 in 1890 to 1,402,227 in 1910; that the proportion under 45 in the Negro population of known age decreased slightly during this period—from 86.8 per cent in 1890, to 85.7 per cent in 1910; that the corresponding proportion decreased slightly in the native white population of native parentage—from 82.8 to 81.9 per cent—decreased markedly in the native white population of foreign or mixed parentage—from 95.4 to 87.4 per cent—and increased slightly in the foreign-born white population—from 65 to 65.6 per cent; that in the Negro population, as in each class of the native white population, the proportion under 45 among females exceeded the corresponding proportion among males.

The growth during the last two decades of the Negro population broadly classified by age, as over or under specified ages, is given in Table 12 (p. 172), which shows, for example, that the Negro population under 15 years of age increased in the decade 1900–1910 by 4.4 per cent, as compared with an increase for the population 15 years of age and over of 16.2 per cent. The population under 25 years of age increased 5.4 per cent and the population 25 and over 21.6 per cent. The corresponding percentages for the population under and over the precise age 45 years were 11 and 15. Comparison with the preceding decade is somewhat invalidated by the defective character of the 1890 enumeration, the increases for this decade being generally affected by the under count of Negroes in 1890. The fact that the increase in the younger ages is at a lower rate than it is in the more advanced ages has been commented upon.

NEGRO AND OTHER CLASSES OF POPULATION, CLASSIFIED BY SEX AND AGE PERIODS: 1910.

Table 9

AGE PERIOD AND SEX.	Total.	Negro.	White. Total.	Native. Total.	Native parentage.	Mixed parentage.	Foreign parentage.	Foreign born.	Indian.	Chinese, Japanese, and all other.

POPULATION: 1910.

White. — Native.

NUMBER.

BOTH SEXES.

AGE PERIOD AND SEX.	Total.	Negro.	White Total.	Native Total.	Native parentage.	Mixed parentage.	Foreign parentage.	Foreign born.	Indian.	Chinese, Japanese, and all other.
All ages	91,972,266	9,827,763	81,731,957	68,386,412	49,488,575	5,981,526	12,916,311	13,345,545	265,683	146,863
Under 5 years	10,631,364	1,263,288	9,322,914	9,220,407	6,546,282	854,278	1,819,847	102,507	40,384	4,778
Under 1 year	2,217,342	252,386	1,955,605	1,948,870	1,369,140	172,974	406,756	6,735	8,216	1,135
5 to 14 years	18,867,772	2,401,819	16,393,581	15,736,742	11,185,298	1,607,330	2,944,114	656,839	67,934	4,438
15 to 24 years	18,120,587	2,091,211	15,954,802	13,850,660	9,771,977	1,387,574	2,691,109	2,104,142	50,330	24,244
25 to 44 years	26,809,875	2,638,178	24,036,529	18,156,550	12,946,441	1,547,087	3,663,022	5,879,979	60,175	74,993
45 to 64 years	13,424,089	1,108,103	12,249,904	8,857,386	6,740,000	486,351	1,631,035	3,392,518	32,925	33,157
65 years and over	3,949,524	294,124	3,640,003	2,456,654	2,201,068	95,987	159,599	1,183,349	12,986	2,411
Age unknown	169,055	31,040	134,224	108,013	97,509	2,919	7,585	26,211	949	2,842

MALE.

AGE PERIOD AND SEX.	Total.	Negro.	White Total.	Native Total.	Native parentage.	Mixed parentage.	Foreign parentage.	Foreign born.	Indian.	Chinese, etc.
All ages	47,332,277	4,885,881	42,178,245	34,654,457	25,229,218	2,968,446	6,456,793	7,523,788	135,133	133,018
Under 5 years	5,380,596	629,320	4,728,650	4,676,710	3,326,237	432,860	917,613	51,940	20,202	2,424
Under 1 year	1,123,409	125,459	993,242	989,715	696,200	87,793	205,722	3,527	4,127	581
5 to 14 years	9,525,876	1,197,249	8,291,470	7,959,515	5,669,886	810,227	1,479,402	331,955	34,548	2,609
15 to 24 years	9,107,572	990,102	8,070,098	6,894,424	4,885,442	682,402	1,326,580	1,175,674	25,877	21,495
25 to 44 years	14,054,482	1,304,098	12,650,614	9,207,844	6,642,210	747,242	1,818,392	3,442,770	30,840	68,930
45 to 64 years	7,163,332	595,554	6,518,282	4,623,547	3,547,325	246,736	829,486	1,894,735	17,055	32,441
65 years and over	1,985,976	152,482	1,825,019	1,218,011	1,089,349	47,438	81,224	607,008	6,130	2,345
Age unknown	114,443	17,076	94,112	74,406	68,769	1,541	4,096	19,706	481	2,774

FEMALE.

AGE PERIOD AND SEX.	Total.	Negro.	White Total.	Native Total.	Native parentage.	Mixed parentage.	Foreign parentage.	Foreign born.	Indian.	Chinese, etc.
All ages	44,639,989	4,941,882	39,553,712	33,731,955	24,259,357	3,013,080	6,459,518	5,821,757	130,550	13,845
Under 5 years	5,250,768	633,968	4,594,264	4,543,697	3,220,045	421,418	902,234	50,567	20,182	2,354
Under 1 year	1,093,933	126,927	962,363	959,155	672,940	85,181	201,034	3,208	4,089	554
5 to 14 years	9,341,896	1,204,570	8,102,111	7,777,227	5,515,412	797,103	1,464,712	324,884	33,386	1,829
15 to 24 years	9,013,015	1,101,109	7,884,704	6,956,236	4,886,535	705,172	1,364,529	928,468	24,453	2,749
25 to 44 years	12,755,393	1,334,080	11,385,915	8,948,706	6,304,231	799,845	1,844,630	2,437,209	29,335	6,063
45 to 64 years	6,260,757	512,549	5,731,622	4,233,839	3,192,675	239,615	801,549	1,497,783	15,870	716
65 years and over	1,963,548	141,642	1,814,984	1,238,643	1,111,719	48,549	78,375	576,341	6,856	66
Age unknown	54,612	13,964	40,112	33,607	28,740	1,378	3,489	6,505	468	68

PERCENTAGE DISTRIBUTION BY AGE PERIODS.

BOTH SEXES.

AGE PERIOD AND SEX.	Total.	Negro.	White Total.	Native Total.	Native parentage.	Mixed parentage.	Foreign parentage.	Foreign born.	Indian.	Chinese, etc.
All ages	100.0	100.0	100.0	100.0	100.0	100.0	100.0	100.0	100.0	100.0
Under 5 years	11.6	12.9	11.4	13.5	13.2	14.3	14.1	0.8	15.2	3.3
Under 1 year	2.4	2.6	2.4	2.8	2.8	2.9	3.1	0.1	3.1	0.8
5 to 14 years	20.5	24.4	20.1	23.0	22.6	26.9	22.8	4.9	25.6	3.0
15 to 24 years	19.7	21.3	19.5	20.3	19.7	23.2	20.8	15.8	18.9	16.5
25 to 44 years	29.1	26.8	29.4	26.5	26.2	25.9	28.4	44.1	22.6	51.1
45 to 64 years	14.6	11.3	15.0	13.0	13.6	8.1	12.6	25.4	12.4	22.6
65 years and over	4.3	3.0	4.5	3.6	4.4	1.6	1.2	8.9	4.9	1.6
Age unknown	0.2	0.3	0.2	0.2	0.2	(1)	0.1	0.2	0.4	1.9

MALE.

AGE PERIOD AND SEX.	Total.	Negro.	White Total.	Native Total.	Native parentage.	Mixed parentage.	Foreign parentage.	Foreign born.	Indian.	Chinese, etc.
All ages	100.0	100.0	100.0	100.0	100.0	100.0	100.0	100.0	100.0	100.0
Under 5 years	11.4	12.9	11.2	13.5	13.2	14.6	14.2	0.7	14.9	1.8
Under 1 year	2.4	2.6	2.4	2.9	2.8	3.0	3.2	(1)	3.1	0.4
5 to 14 years	20.1	24.5	19.7	23.0	22.5	27.3	22.9	4.4	25.6	2.0
15 to 24 years	19.2	20.3	19.1	19.9	19.4	23.0	20.5	15.6	19.1	16.2
25 to 44 years	29.7	26.7	30.0	26.6	26.3	25.2	28.2	45.8	22.8	51.8
45 to 64 years	15.1	12.2	15.5	13.3	14.1	8.3	12.8	25.2	12.6	24.4
65 years and over	4.2	3.1	4.3	3.5	4.3	1.6	1.3	8.1	4.5	1.8
Age unknown	0.2	0.3	0.2	0.2	0.3	0.1	0.1	0.3	0.4	2.1

FEMALE.

AGE PERIOD AND SEX.	Total.	Negro.	White Total.	Native Total.	Native parentage.	Mixed parentage.	Foreign parentage.	Foreign born.	Indian.	Chinese, etc.
All ages	100.0	100.0	100.0	100.0	100.0	100.0	100.0	100.0	100.0	100.0
Under 5 years	11.8	12.8	11.6	13.5	13.3	14.0	14.0	0.9	15.5	17.0
Under 1 year	2.5	2.6	2.4	2.8	2.8	2.8	3.1	0.1	3.1	4.0
5 to 14 years	20.9	24.4	20.5	23.1	22.7	26.5	22.7	5.6	25.6	13.2
15 to 24 years	20.2	22.3	19.9	20.6	20.1	23.4	21.1	15.9	18.7	19.9
25 to 44 years	28.6	27.0	28.8	26.5	26.0	26.5	28.6	41.9	22.5	43.8
45 to 64 years	14.0	10.4	14.5	12.6	13.2	8.0	12.4	25.7	12.2	5.2
65 years and over	4.4	2.9	4.6	3.7	4.6	1.6	1.2	9.9	5.3	0.5
Age unknown	0.1	0.3	0.1	0.1	0.1	(1)	0.1	0.1	0.4	0.5

MALES TO 1,000 FEMALES.

AGE PERIOD.	Total.	Negro.	White Total.	Native Total.	Native parentage.	Mixed parentage.	Foreign parentage.	Foreign born.	Indian.	Chinese, etc.
All ages	1,060	989	1,066	1,027	1,040	985	1,000	1,292	1,035	9,608
Under 5 years	1,025	993	1,029	1,029	1,033	1,027	1,017	1,027	1,001	1,030
Under 1 year	1,026	988	1,032	1,032	1,034	1,030	1,023	1,100	1,009	1,048
5 to 14 years	1,020	994	1,023	1,023	1,028	1,016	1,010	1,022	1,035	1,426
15 to 24 years	1,010	899	1,024	991	1,000	968	972	1,266	1,058	7,819
25 to 44 years	1,102	978	1,111	1,029	1,054	934	986	1,413	1,051	11,369
45 to 64 years	1,144	1,162	1,137	1,092	1,111	1,030	1,035	1,265	1,075	45,309
65 years and over	1,011	1,077	1,006	983	980	977	1,036	1,053	894	(2)
Age unknown	2,096	1,223	2,346	2,214	2,393	1,118	1,174	3,029	1,028	(2)

[1] Less than one-tenth of 1 per cent.   [2] Ratio not shown, the number of females being less than 100.

NEGRO, NATIVE WHITE, AND FOREIGN-BORN WHITE POPULATION, CLASSIFIED BY BROAD AGE PERIODS: 1910, 1900, AND 1890.

Table 10

AGE PERIOD.	POPULATION.											
	All classes.			Negro.			Native white.			Foreign-born white.		
	1910	1900	1890	1910	1900	1890	1910	1900	1890	1910	1900	1890
	NUMBER.											
All ages.........	91,972,266	75,994,575	62,622,250	9,827,763	8,833,994	7,470,040	68,386,412	56,595,379	45,862,023	13,345,545	10,213,817	9,121,867
Under 5 years........	10,631,364	9,170,628	7,634,693	1,263,288	1,215,655	[1] 1,047,574	9,220,407	7,867,583	6,493,019	102,507	52,369	86,629
5 to 14 years........	18,867,772	16,954,357	14,607,507	2,401,819	2,294,748	[1] 2,127,195	15,736,742	14,138,807	11,820,410	656,839	458,757	644,730
15 to 24 years.......	18,120,587	14,891,105	12,754,239	2,091,211	1,951,194	1,602,666	13,850,660	11,397,005	9,685,145	2,104,142	1,481,228	1,438,669
25 to 44 years.......	26,809,875	21,297,427	16,858,086	2,638,178	2,103,989	1,677,109	18,156,550	14,665,552	11,351,992	5,879,979	4,414,590	3,745,105
45 to 64 years.......	13,424,089	10,399,976	8,188,272	1,108,103	958,234	767,999	8,857,386	6,549,888	4,895,125	3,392,518	2,831,646	2,499,813
65 years and over......	3,949,524	3,080,498	2,417,288	294,124	261,363	211,684	2,456,654	1,856,372	1,519,808	1,183,349	950,347	682,304
Age unknown.......	169,055	200,584	162,165	31,040	48,811	35,813	108,013	120,172	96,524	26,211	24,880	24,617
	PERCENTAGE DISTRIBUTION BY AGE PERIODS.											
All ages.........	100.0	100.0	100.0	100.0	100.0	100.0	100.0	100.0	100.0	100.0	100.0	100.0
Under 5 years........	11.6	12.1	12.2	12.9	13.8	[1] 14.0	13.5	13.9	14.2	0.8	0.5	0.9
5 to 14 years........	20.5	22.3	23.3	24.4	26.0	[1] 28.5	23.0	25.0	25.8	4.9	4.5	7.1
15 to 24 years.......	19.7	19.6	20.4	21.3	22.1	21.5	20.3	20.1	21.1	15.8	14.5	15.8
25 to 44 years.......	29.1	28.0	26.9	26.8	23.8	22.5	26.5	25.9	24.8	44.1	43.2	41.1
45 to 64 years.......	14.6	13.7	13.1	11.3	10.8	10.3	13.0	11.6	10.7	25.4	27.7	27.4
65 years and over......	4.3	4.1	3.9	3.0	3.0	2.8	3.6	3.3	3.3	8.9	9.3	7.5
Age unknown........	0.2	0.3	0.3	0.3	0.6	0.5	0.2	0.2	0.2	0.2	0.2	0.3

[1] These figures are estimates. The Negro population under 15 years of age was shown by the 1890 census and was 3,174,769, but the number under 5 and the number from 5 to 14 were not distinguished. This distinction was, however, made for the total colored population, the figures being 1,055,045 and 2,142,367, respectively. Applying to the figure for the Negroes under 15 the same proportions for the two age groups as were found for the total colored, the figures and percentages given in the table have been calculated. There is no appreciable error, since the Negroes constitute the great bulk of the colored and since there is no very material difference between the Negroes and the other colored with respect to the distribution of the persons under 15 between the two age groups.

DISTRIBUTION BY CUMULATIVE AGE PERIODS, OF THE NEGRO POPULATION OF KNOWN AGE, AND OF CLASSES OF THE WHITE POPULATION, BY SEX: 1910, 1900, AND 1890.

Table 11

AGE AND CENSUS YEAR.	NEGRO POPULATION OF KNOWN AGE.						PERCENTAGE UNDER AGE SPECIFIED.											
	Under age specified.			Of age specified or older.			Negro population.			Native white population of native parentage.			Native white population of foreign or mixed parentage.			Foreign-born white population.		
	Both sexes.	Male.	Female.	Both sexes.	Male.	Female.	Both sexes.	Male.	Female.	Both sexes.	Male.	Female.	Both sexes.	Male.	Female.	Both sexes.	Male.	Female.
0 years of age:																		
1910...........	....	....	....	9,796,723	4,868,805	4,927,918	......											
1900...........	....	....	....	8,785,183	4,361,390	4,423,793												
1890...........	....	....	....	7,434,227	3,707,126	3,727,101												
5 years:																		
1910...........	1,263,288	629,320	633,968	8,533,435	4,239,485	4,293,950	12.9	12.9	12.9	13.3	13.2	13.3	14.2	14.3	14.0	0.8	0.7	0.9
1900...........	1,215,655	604,487	611,168	7,569,528	3,756,903	3,812,625	13.8	13.9	13.8	13.4	13.4	13.4	15.4	15.5	15.3	0.5	0.5	0.6
1890...........	[1] 1,047,574	[2]	[2]	[1] 6,386,653	[2]	[2]	[1] 14.0	[2]	[2]	13.3	13.3	13.2	16.9	17.0	16.8	1.0	0.9	1.0
10 years:																		
1910...........	2,509,841	1,248,495	1,261,346	7,286,882	3,620,310	3,666,572	25.6	25.6	25.6	25.1	25.0	25.2	26.4	26.7	26.1	3.0	2.7	3.4
1900...........	2,418,413	1,204,897	1,213,516	6,366,770	3,156,493	3,210,277	27.5	27.6	27.4	26.1	26.0	26.1	30.2	30.3	30.0	2.0	1.8	2.1
1890...........	2,141,068	1,079,390	1,061,678	5,293,159	2,627,736	2,665,423	28.8	29.1	28.5	26.2	26.3	26.2	32.5	32.7	32.3	3.7	3.4	4.0
15 years:																		
1910...........	3,665,107	1,826,569	1,838,538	6,131,616	3,042,236	3,089,380	37.4	37.5	37.3	35.9	35.8	36.1	38.3	38.6	37.9	5.7	5.1	6.5
1900...........	3,510,403	1,753,539	1,756,864	5,274,780	2,607,851	2,666,929	40.0	40.2	39.7	37.5	37.4	37.6	42.9	43.1	42.7	5.0	4.7	5.4
1890...........	3,174,769	1,605,840	1,568,929	4,259,458	2,101,286	2,158,172	42.7	43.3	42.1	37.8	37.9	37.7	46.7	46.9	46.5	8.0	7.5	8.7
20 years:																		
1910...........	4,725,523	2,334,514	2,391,009	5,071,200	2,534,291	2,536,909	48.2	47.9	48.5	46.2	45.9	46.5	49.9	50.3	49.6	10.8	9.8	12.0
1900...........	4,492,425	2,227,289	2,265,136	4,292,758	2,134,101	2,158,657	51.1	51.1	51.2	47.8	47.6	48.1	54.1	54.1	54.0	10.5	9.6	11.6
1890...........	4,045,887	2,028,098	2,017,789	3,388,340	1,679,028	1,709,312	54.4	54.7	54.1	48.1	48.0	48.3	60.6	60.6	60.7	13.8	12.7	15.0
25 years:																		
1910...........	5,756,318	2,816,671	2,939,647	4,040,405	2,052,134	1,988,271	58.8	57.9	59.7	55.7	55.2	56.2	59.9	60.0	59.7	21.5	20.8	22.4
1900...........	5,461,597	2,686,210	2,775,387	3,323,586	1,675,180	1,648,406	62.2	61.6	62.7	57.2	56.7	57.6	64.4	64.1	64.6	19.6	17.9	21.5
1890...........	4,777,435	2,378,490	2,398,945	2,656,792	1,328,636	1,328,156	64.3	64.2	64.4	57.4	57.2	57.6	72.3	72.0	72.7	23.9	22.4	25.6
30 years:																		
1910...........	6,637,545	3,238,476	3,399,069	3,159,178	1,630,329	1,528,849	67.8	66.5	69.0	63.9	63.3	64.5	68.0	68.0	68.1	34.0	34.0	34.0
1900...........	6,199,076	3,046,807	3,152,269	2,586,107	1,314,583	1,271,524	70.6	69.9	71.3	65.0	64.6	65.4	73.7	73.3	74.0	30.3	28.6	32.3
1890...........	5,336,986	2,650,534	2,686,452	2,097,241	1,056,592	1,040,649	71.8	71.5	72.1	64.9	64.7	65.1	81.3	80.8	81.7	35.6	34.6	36.9
35 years:																		
1910...........	7,305,634	3,570,639	3,734,995	2,491,089	1,298,166	1,192,923	74.6	73.3	75.8	70.8	70.2	71.3	75.2	75.1	75.4	45.3	45.8	44.6
1900...........	6,723,683	3,308,937	3,414,746	2,061,500	1,052,453	1,009,047	76.5	75.9	77.2	71.5	71.2	71.8	81.2	80.8	81.5	41.8	40.7	43.2
1890...........	5,746,963	2,853,895	2,893,068	1,687,264	853,231	834,033	77.3	77.0	77.6	71.8	71.7	71.9	88.1	88.1	88.8	46.0	45.7	46.3
45 years:																		
1910...........	8,394,496	4,120,769	4,273,727	1,402,227	748,036	654,191	85.4	84.6	86.7	81.9	81.6	82.2	87.4	87.2	87.7	65.6	66.7	64.3
1900...........	7,565,586	3,721,398	3,844,188	1,219,597	639,992	579,605	86.1	85.3	86.9	82.3	82.2	82.4	92.4	92.2	92.7	62.9	63.0	62.7
1890...........	6,454,544	3,197,753	3,256,791	979,683	509,373	470,310	86.8	86.3	87.4	82.8	82.9	82.7	95.4	95.3	95.6	65.0	65.4	64.6
55 years:																		
1910...........	9,106,475	4,500,084	4,606,391	690,248	368,721	321,527	93.0	92.4	93.5	90.0	90.0	90.1	95.5	95.4	95.6	81.2	82.4	79.6
1900...........	8,182,957	4,045,081	4,137,876	602,226	316,309	285,917	93.1	92.7	93.5	90.5	90.7	90.3	97.2	97.2	97.3	79.0	79.5	78.4
1890...........	6,954,223	3,455,054	3,499,169	480,004	252,072	227,932	93.5	93.2	93.9	90.8	90.8	90.7	98.2	98.1	98.2	81.5	81.9	81.0
65 years:																		
1910...........	9,502,599	4,716,323	4,786,276	294,124	152,482	141,642	97.0	96.9	97.1	95.5	95.7	95.4	98.6	98.6	98.7	91.1	91.9	90.1
1900...........	8,523,820	4,228,365	4,295,455	261,363	133,025	128,338	97.0	96.9	97.1	95.8	95.9	95.7	99.1	99.1	99.1	90.7	91.0	90.3
1890...........	7,222,543	3,599,815	3,622,728	211,684	107,311	104,373	97.2	97.1	97.2	95.8	95.9	95.8	99.2	99.2	99.3	92.5	92.7	92.3

[1] Estimate. See note, table 10.   [2] Data not available.

Table 12 AGE.	PERCENTAGE INCREASE OF NEGRO POPULATION.		AGE.	PERCENTAGE INCREASE OF NEGRO POPULATION.	
	Under age specified.	Of age specified or older.		Under age specified.	Of age specified or older.
10 years:			25 years:		
1900–1910......	....	11.2	1900–1910......	5.4	21.6
1890–1900......	....	18.0	1890–1900......	14.3	25.1
15 years:			45 years:		
1900–1910......	4.4	16.2	1900–1910......	11.0	15.0
1890–1900......	10.6	23.8	1890–1900......	17.2	24.5

PERCENTAGE NEGRO BY AGE PERIODS: 1910 AND 1900.

Excepting the very advanced ages, at each of the last two censuses, the proportion Negro in the total population of all classes, was higher in the younger ages than it was in the older. This proportion is shown by quinquennial age periods in Table 13. The relatively low proportions in the adult ages generally, are accounted for principally by immigration of whites in these ages.

Table 13 AGE PERIOD.	POPULATION.					
	Total.		Negro.			
			Number.		Per cent.	
	1910	1900	1910	1900	1910	1900
All ages.........	91,972,266	75,994,575	9,827,763	8,833,994	10.7	11.6
Under 5 years.......	10,631,364	9,170,628	1,263,288	1,215,655	11.9	13.3
Under 1 year...	2,217,342	1,916,892	252,386	244,510	11.4	12.8
5 to 9 years........	9,760,632	8,874,123	1,246,553	1,202,758	12.8	13.6
10 to 14 years.......	9,107,140	8,080,234	1,155,266	1,091,990	12.7	13.5
15 to 19 years.......	9,063,603	7,556,089	1,060,416	982,022	11.7	13.0
20 to 24 years.......	9,056,984	7,335,016	1,030,795	969,172	11.4	13.2
25 to 29 years.......	8,180,003	6,529,441	881,227	737,479	10.8	11.3
30 to 34 years.......	6,972,185	5,556,039	668,089	524,607	9.6	9.4
35 to 39 years.......	6,396,100	4,964,781	633,449	474,687	9.9	9.6
40 to 44 years.......	5,261,587	4,247,166	455,413	367,216	8.7	8.6
45 to 49 years.......	4,469,197	3,454,612	385,909	326,384	8.6	9.4
50 to 54 years.......	3,900,791	2,942,829	326,070	290,987	8.4	9.9
55 to 59 years.......	2,786,951	2,211,172	209,622	179,176	7.5	8.1
60 to 64 years.......	2,267,150	1,791,363	186,502	161,687	8.2	9.0
65 to 69 years.......	1,679,503	1,302,926	123,550	102,671	7.4	7.9
70 to 74 years.......	1,113,728	883,841	78,839	72,382	7.1	8.2
75 to 79 years.......	667,302	519,857	44,018	40,420	6.6	7.8
80 to 84 years.......	321,754	251,512	25,579	25,527	7.9	10.1
85 to 89 years.......	122,818	88,600	11,166	10,083	9.1	11.4
90 to 94 years.......	33,473	23,992	5,850	5,293	17.5	22.1
95 to 99 years.......	7,391	6,266	2,447	2,434	33.1	38.8
100 years and over..	3,555	3,504	2,675	2,553	75.2	72.9
Age unknown......	169,055	200,584	31,040	48,811	18.4	24.3

The lowest proportion Negro in 1910 was that of 6.6 per cent for the age period 75 to 79 years. This age period shows the lowest proportion, 7.8 per cent. also in 1900. The highest proportion at each census, except at very advanced ages, was that for the age 5 to 9 years—12.8 per cent in 1910, and 13.6 per cent in 1900. The high proportions in the population 90 years of age and over—17.5 per cent in the population 90 to 94 years, 33.1 per cent in the population 95 to 99 years, and 75.2 per cent in the population 100 years and over are undoubtedly accounted for by errors in the age returns to which attention has already been directed, the tendency to overstate age among very elderly persons being stronger among Negroes than among other classes. This overstatement of age also diminishes slightly the proportion for certain less advanced age periods.

MEDIAN AGE: 1820–1910.

Table 14 gives the median age of the Negro and of the white populations at each census, 1820 to 1910—except that for the years 1880 and 1890, the data are for the aggregate colored population—with details for white classes in 1910. Table 22 (p. 179) gives the median age of the Negro population in 1910 and in 1900, and of the colored population in 1890 and 1880, by states.

Table 14 YEAR AND RACIAL CLASS.	MEDIAN AGE IN YEARS.		
	Both sexes.	Male.	Female.
1910.			
All classes....................	24.0	24.6	23.5
Negro..............................	20.8	21.1	20.6
White..............................	24.4	24.9	23.9
Native white........................	21.4	21.5	21.3
Native parentage.................	21.9	22.1	21.7
Foreign or mixed parentage...........	20.0	19.9	20.2
Foreign-born white.................	37.1	36.7	37.6
Indian..............................	19.1	19.2	19.0
1900.			
Negro..............................	19.4	19.5	19.4
White..............................	23.4	23.8	22.9
1890.			
Colored.............................	17.8	17.9	17.8
White..............................	21.9	21.3	21.6
1880.			
Colored.............................	18.0	18.0	18.0
White..............................	21.3	21.6	21.0
1870.			
Negro..............................	18.5	18.2	18.8
White..............................	20.4	20.5	20.3
1860.			
Negro..............................	17.7	17.8	17.5
White..............................	19.7	20.1	19.3
1850.			
Negro..............................	17.3	17.3	17.4
White..............................	19.1	19.5	18.8
1840.			
Negro..............................	17.3	17.0	17.5
White..............................	17.9	17.9	17.8
1830.			
Negro..............................	16.9	16.7	17.1
White..............................	17.2	17.2	17.3
1820.			
Negro..............................	17.2	16.9	17.4
White..............................	16.5	16.5	16.6

Since in the earlier censuses age is not shown by single years, the median age, i. e., that age which divides a population or class into two equal groups, the number older being exactly equal to the number younger, can not be so exactly determined, as it can for the last four censuses. In the case of the Negro population at the several censuses 1830 to 1870, inclusive, the determination of the median age involves an estimated distribution of the population 15 to 19 years of age by single years. The margin of error in this distribution, which is based upon the enumerated distribution in 1900, probably does not exceed in its effect upon the median age a variation of a few months. In the estimate for Negroes in 1820, which involves a distribution of the population 14 to 26 years of age, by single years, the margin of error is somewhat greater.

During the decade, 1900–1910, the median age of the Negro population increased from 19.4 to 20.8 years, and in 1910 was exceeded slightly by the median age of the native white population, 21.4 years. In both classes it was slightly higher in 1910 among males than among females—21.1 as compared with 20.6 years among Negroes, and 21.5 as compared with 21.3 years among native whites. In 1820 the median age of the Negro population, 17.2 years, exceeded that of the aggregate white population, 16.5 years, but at each succeeding census the figure for whites has exceeded that for Negroes. The median age for the aggregate white population, it should be noted, is materially affected by the age distribution of the foreign-born whites, a relatively small proportion of whom are in the younger ages. The effect of the inclusion of the foreign born upon the median age of the whites is apparent in the 1910 figures, the difference between the median age of the native whites, 21.4 years, and of the aggregate whites, 24.4 years, being attributable to the foreign born.

It should perhaps be noted that although median age is determined by the age distribution of the population living at the time of the census enumeration, it is not necessarily affected by changes in age distribution from census to census which would affect the average age of the living. So long, for example, as exactly 50 per cent of the Negro population are under 20.8 years of age, the median age will be 20.8 years, whatever changes take place in the age distribution of the population above or below that age. While the advance in the median age from census to census, in the case of Negroes as of whites, is probably occasioned in part by improvement in mortality which has increased the duration of life, it undoubtedly represents in part decline in the birth rate. Improvement in mortality and decline in the birth rate, obviously both tend to raise median age—the one by increasing the number surviving to ages above the median, and the other by reducing the number in the younger ages.

POPULATION OF SECTIONS AND DIVISIONS CLASSIFIED BY AGE.

Tables 15 to 18 summarize the age data for the three sections—the North, the South, and the West—and for the three southern geographic divisions—the South Atlantic, the East South Central, and the West South Central. In Table 39 (pp. 194–196) is given detail by age and sex for each of the nine divisions, and for each state, including northern as well as southern divisions and states.

While some differences as regards age composition might, in the case of the Negroes as of other population classes, develop in these several areas in consequence of conditions affecting birth rates and specific mortality rates, it will be clear that the differences actually shown in the tabulations of the census returns are to be explained as occasioned principally by migration.

The effect of migration upon age composition in any section or division is more or less apparent in proportion as migrants—representing net gain or loss by migration—are numerous relatively to the population of the given area. The net migration of Negroes into the North and West from the South has accordingly affected age composition more in the North and West than it has in the South, since the great mass of the Negro population is resident in the South, and relatively to population the proportion of migrants among Negroes is much larger for the North and West than it is for the South. The migration, for example, of 5,000 Negroes aged 20 to 24 years, from the South into the West, while it would not materially affect the age composition of the Negro population living in the South, would very materially affect the age composition of the Negro population living in the West, where the proportion for the age group 20 to 24 years would be nearly doubled.

As will appear upon examination of Table 15, some slight depletion of the adult age groups by net migration northward and westward is perceptible in the Negro population of the South, but the effect of this net migration is much more apparent in the age compositions of the North and West. The proportion of children under 5 years of age, for example, was 13.4 per cent in the South, 8.1 per cent in the North, and 6.4 per cent in the West. Similar proportions obtain for the age groups 5 to 9, 10 to 14, and 15 to 19 years. In the South 50.1 per cent, in the North 31.8 per cent, and in the West 25.7 per cent of the Negro population were under 20 years of age. In the case of each of these age groups the proportion shown in the population of the South is slightly above, and the proportion shown in the population of the North and West is markedly below that shown in the Negro population as a whole. In the older ages the proportions for the South are below, and those for the North and West above the average for the country as a whole. The proportion in the age group 35 to 44 years, for example, was 11.1 per cent in the country as a whole, 10.4 per cent in the South, 16.4 per cent in the North, and 19.3 per cent in the West.

Generally in the North and the West, as well as in the South, the proportion of children decreased, and the proportion of adults increased during the decade 1900–1910. Migration during the decade has, therefore, been sufficient to prevent any approach to a normal age distribution in the North and West.

As between the three southern divisions for which data are given in Table 15 the differences in age composition of the Negro population are inconsiderable.

Of the two tables following on page 174, Table 16 gives, for the age periods and areas shown in Table 15, the percentage distribution of Negro males and females in 1910.

NEGRO POPULATION CLASSIFIED BY AGE PERIODS, BY SECTIONS AND SOUTHERN DIVISIONS: 1910 AND 1900.

Table 15

AGE PERIOD.	United States.		The South. Total.		South Atlantic division.		East South Central division.		West South Central division.		The North.		The West.	
	1910	1900	1910	1900	1910	1900	1910	1900	1910	1900	1910	1900	1910	1900
NUMBER.														
All ages	9,827,763	8,833,994	8,749,427	7,922,969	4,112,488	3,729,017	2,652,513	2,499,886	1,984,426	1,694,066	1,027,674	880,771	50,662	30,254
Under 5 years	1,263,288	1,215,655	1,176,331	1,135,793	570,516	545,284	347,803	348,061	258,012	242,448	83,729	77,794	3,228	2,068
5 to 9 years	1,246,553	1,202,758	1,164,557	1,122,201	555,036	527,900	343,812	348,997	265,709	245,304	78,892	78,233	3,104	2,324
10 to 14 years	1,155,266	1,091,990	1,073,980	1,012,214	513,239	476,108	320,476	316,984	240,265	219,122	78,205	77,597	3,081	2,179
15 to 19 years	1,060,416	982,022	970,716	893,199	457,053	423,855	294,183	283,363	219,480	185,981	86,126	86,506	3,574	2,317
20 to 24 years	1,030,795	969,172	911,603	856,655	426,876	400,667	274,935	273,069	209,792	182,919	113,923	108,993	5,269	3,524
25 to 29 years	881,227	737,479	749,782	633,384	341,665	286,748	230,624	204,948	177,493	141,688	124,832	100,587	6,613	3,508
30 to 34 years	668,089	524,607	557,466	444,709	253,860	205,472	171,477	141,938	132,129	97,299	104,600	76,637	6,023	3,261
35 to 44 years	1,088,862	841,903	910,025	713,990	421,374	342,794	278,306	222,312	210,345	148,884	169,052	122,427	9,785	5,486
45 to 54 years	711,979	617,371	607,895	537,826	279,676	248,740	191,801	174,614	136,418	114,472	98,341	76,529	5,743	3,016
55 to 64 years	396,124	340,863	343,958	299,315	162,623	144,525	108,199	95,882	73,136	58,908	49,737	40,236	2,429	1,312
65 years and over	294,124	261,363	256,694	232,217	119,140	111,321	82,481	75,917	55,073	44,979	35,973	28,311	1,457	835
Age unknown	31,040	48,811	26,420	41,466	11,430	15,603	8,416	13,801	6,574	12,062	4,264	6,921	356	424
PERCENTAGE DISTRIBUTION BY AGE PERIODS.														
All ages	100.0	100.0	100.0	100.0	100.0	100.0	100.0	100.0	100.0	100.0	100.0	100.0	100.0	100.0
Under 5 years	12.9	13.8	13.4	14.3	13.9	14.6	13.1	13.9	13.0	14.3	8.1	8.8	6.4	6.8
5 to 9 years	12.7	13.6	13.3	14.2	13.5	14.2	13.0	14.0	13.4	14.5	7.7	8.9	6.1	7.7
10 to 14 years	11.8	12.4	12.3	12.8	12.5	12.8	12.1	12.7	12.1	12.9	7.6	8.8	6.1	7.2
15 to 19 years	10.8	11.1	11.1	11.3	11.1	11.4	11.1	11.3	11.1	11.0	8.4	9.8	7.1	7.7
20 to 24 years	10.5	11.0	10.4	10.8	10.4	10.7	10.4	10.9	10.6	10.8	11.1	12.4	10.4	11.6
25 to 29 years	9.0	8.3	8.6	8.0	8.3	7.7	8.7	8.2	8.9	8.4	12.1	11.4	13.1	11.6
30 to 34 years	6.8	5.9	6.4	5.6	6.2	5.5	6.5	5.7	6.7	5.7	10.2	8.7	11.9	10.8
35 to 44 years	11.1	9.5	10.4	9.0	10.2	9.2	10.5	8.9	10.6	8.8	16.4	13.9	19.3	18.1
45 to 54 years	7.2	7.0	6.9	6.8	6.8	6.7	7.2	7.0	6.9	6.8	9.6	8.7	11.3	10.0
55 to 64 years	4.0	3.9	3.9	3.8	4.0	3.9	4.1	3.8	3.7	3.5	4.8	4.6	4.8	4.3
65 years and over	3.0	3.0	2.9	2.9	2.9	3.0	3.1	3.0	2.8	2.7	3.5	3.2	2.9	2.8
Age unknown	0.3	0.6	0.3	0.5	0.3	0.4	0.3	0.6	0.3	0.7	0.4	0.8	0.7	1.4

PERCENTAGE DISTRIBUTION, BY AGE PERIODS, OF NEGRO MALES AND FEMALES, BY SECTIONS AND SOUTHERN DIVISIONS: 1910.

Table 16   PERCENTAGE DISTRIBUTION BY AGE PERIODS OF NEGRO MALES AND FEMALES: 1910.

AGE PERIOD.	United States.		The South. Total.		South Atlantic division.		East South Central division.		West South Central division.		The North.		The West.	
	Males.	Females.	Males.	Females.	Males.	Females.	Males.	Females.	Males.	Females.	Males.	Females.	Males.	Females.
All ages	100.0	100.0	100.0	100.0	100.0	100.0	100.0	100.0	100.0	100.0	100.0	100.0	100.0	100.0
Under 5 years	12.9	12.8	13.5	13.4	14.0	13.8	13.2	13.0	12.9	13.1	8.0	8.3	5.6	7.3
5 to 9 years	12.7	12.7	13.3	13.3	13.6	13.4	13.0	12.9	13.3	13.4	7.5	7.9	5.5	6.9
10 to 14 years	11.8	11.7	12.4	12.1	12.7	12.3	12.3	11.9	12.0	12.2	7.3	7.9	5.4	6.9
15 to 19 years	10.4	11.2	10.7	11.5	10.7	11.5	10.8	11.4	10.6	11.5	7.8	9.0	6.1	8.2
20 to 24 years	9.9	11.1	9.8	11.0	9.8	11.0	9.7	11.0	10.0	11.2	10.4	11.8	10.2	10.7
25 to 29 years	8.6	9.3	8.2	8.9	7.9	8.7	8.3	9.1	8.7	9.2	12.0	12.3	13.0	13.1
30 to 34 years	6.8	6.8	6.3	6.4	6.1	6.2	6.3	6.6	6.7	6.6	10.5	9.9	12.6	11.0
35 to 44 years	11.3	10.9	10.5	10.3	10.3	10.2	10.4	10.6	10.8	10.4	17.5	15.4	20.6	17.8
45 to 54 years	7.8	6.7	7.5	6.4	7.1	6.5	7.8	6.6	7.7	6.1	10.1	9.0	12.2	10.2
55 to 64 years	4.4	3.6	4.3	3.5	4.4	3.5	4.5	3.7	4.1	3.3	5.0	4.6	5.2	4.3
65 years and over	3.1	2.9	3.1	2.8	3.1	2.7	3.3	3.0	2.9	2.7	3.5	3.5	2.9	2.8
Age unknown	0.3	0.3	0.3	0.3	0.3	0.2	0.3	0.3	0.4	0.3	0.5	0.3	0.8	0.6

In the North and West a larger proportion of females than of males are in each of the age periods under 30 years, but the differences in distribution by age between males and females in the several areas are not marked.

A comparison of the percentage distribution, by age, of Negroes and whites in the several sections and southern divisions is presented in Table 17, the 1910 populations represented by these percentages being given in Table 18 in somewhat greater detail of age.

PERCENTAGE DISTRIBUTION BY BROAD AGE PERIODS OF THE NEGRO POPULATION AND OF CLASSES OF THE WHITE POPULATION, BY SECTIONS AND SOUTHERN DIVISIONS: 1910 AND 1900.

Table 17 — PERCENTAGE DISTRIBUTION BY AGE PERIODS.

SECTION, DIVISION, AND RACIAL CLASS.	All ages.		Under 5 years.		5 to 14 years.		15 to 24 years.		25 to 44 years.		45 to 64 years.		65 years and over.		Age unknown.	
	1910	1900	1910	1900	1910	1900	1910	1900	1910	1900	1910	1900	1910	1900	1910	1900
UNITED STATES.																
Negro	100.0	100.0	12.9	13.8	24.4	26.0	21.3	22.1	26.8	23.8	11.3	10.8	3.0	3.0	0.3	0.6
Native white:																
Native parentage	100.0	100.0	13.2	13.3	22.6	24.0	19.7	19.6	26.2	25.1	13.6	13.5	4.4	4.2	0.2	0.3
Foreign or mixed parentage	100.0	100.0	14.2	15.4	24.1	27.5	21.6	21.5	27.6	28.1	11.2	6.6	1.4	0.9	0.1	0.1
Foreign-born white	100.0	100.0	0.8	0.5	4.9	4.5	15.8	14.5	44.1	43.2	25.4	27.7	8.9	9.3	0.2	0.2
THE SOUTH.																
Negro	100.0	100.0	13.4	14.3	25.6	26.9	21.5	22.1	25.3	22.6	10.9	10.6	2.9	2.9	0.3	0.5
Native white:																
Native parentage	100.0	100.0	14.6	14.6	24.5	26.0	20.3	20.8	25.1	23.6	12.1	11.8	3.3	3.0	0.1	0.2
Foreign or mixed parentage	100.0	100.0	11.9	12.3	21.3	23.9	19.6	21.2	30.2	31.7	14.8	9.4	2.1	1.6	0.1	0.1
Foreign-born white	100.0	100.0	1.2	0.7	6.4	5.2	14.6	12.4	39.9	37.5	26.7	32.1	10.9	11.7	0.3	0.4
SOUTH ATLANTIC DIVISION.																
Negro	100.0	100.0	13.9	14.6	26.0	26.9	21.5	22.1	24.7	22.4	10.8	10.5	2.9	3.0	0.3	0.4
Native white:																
Native parentage	100.0	100.0	14.0	14.0	23.8	25.0	20.0	20.6	25.4	24.0	12.9	12.6	3.8	3.5	0.1	0.2
Foreign or mixed parentage	100.0	100.0	12.4	11.4	20.1	21.8	18.3	20.0	30.0	33.6	16.4	11.2	2.7	2.0	0.1	0.1
Foreign-born white	100.0	100.0	0.9	0.4	5.5	4.3	16.1	12.4	43.4	38.5	23.8	31.1	10.0	13.0	0.3	0.3
EAST SOUTH CENTRAL DIVISION.																
Negro	100.0	100.0	13.1	13.9	25.0	26.6	21.5	22.3	25.7	22.8	11.3	10.8	3.1	3.0	0.3	0.6
Native white:																
Native parentage	100.0	100.0	14.6	14.6	24.6	25.9	20.2	20.9	24.6	23.4	12.3	11.9	3.5	3.1	0.1	0.2
Foreign or mixed parentage	100.0	100.0	7.0	8.2	15.0	19.4	18.1	22.2	37.2	37.9	20.0	10.5	2.6	1.8	0.1	0.1
Foreign-born white	100.0	100.0	0.5	0.2	3.9	2.6	9.7	8.6	34.5	32.5	33.3	39.0	17.9	16.7	0.2	0.3
WEST SOUTH CENTRAL DIVISION.																
Negro	100.0	100.0	13.0	14.3	25.5	27.4	21.6	21.8	26.2	22.9	10.6	10.2	2.8	2.7	0.3	0.7
Native white:																
Native parentage	100.0	100.0	15.2	15.7	25.5	27.4	20.6	20.8	25.0	23.1	11.0	10.6	2.5	2.1	0.2	0.2
Foreign or mixed parentage	100.0	100.0	13.2	15.0	24.5	27.7	21.1	21.6	28.0	27.1	11.7	7.4	1.5	1.1	0.1	0.1
Foreign-born white	100.0	100.0	1.7	1.1	7.9	6.8	14.5	13.6	38.3	38.5	27.5	30.5	9.8	9.0	0.4	0.5
THE NORTH.																
Negro	100.0	100.0	8.1	8.8	15.3	17.7	19.5	22.2	38.8	34.0	14.4	13.3	3.5	3.2	0.4	0.8
Native white:																
Native parentage	100.0	100.0	12.5	12.6	21.6	22.9	19.4	19.0	26.4	25.7	14.6	14.5	5.3	4.9	0.2	0.3
Foreign or mixed parentage	100.0	100.0	14.5	15.7	24.5	27.8	21.7	21.4	27.0	27.8	11.0	6.5	1.3	0.8	0.1	0.1
Foreign-born white	100.0	100.0	0.7	0.5	4.9	4.6	16.1	14.9	44.0	43.2	25.2	27.3	8.9	9.3	0.2	0.2
THE WEST.																
Negro	100.0	100.0	6.4	6.8	12.2	14.9	17.5	19.3	44.3	40.5	16.1	14.3	2.9	2.8	0.7	1.4
Native white:																
Native parentage	100.0	100.0	12.1	12.3	20.0	22.5	19.4	18.5	30.3	28.9	14.0	13.2	3.8	3.7	0.4	0.9
Foreign or mixed parentage	100.0	100.0	12.2	14.3	21.9	27.9	22.2	22.0	31.4	28.5	10.9	6.3	1.3	0.9	0.1	0.1
Foreign-born white	100.0	100.0	0.8	0.4	3.9	3.1	13.6	11.0	46.8	47.5	26.8	29.6	7.7	7.9	0.4	0.5

In the South the proportion of children under 5 years of age in the native white population of native parentage exceeded that in the Negro population, the percentages under 5 being 14.6 for native whites of native parentage and 13.4 for Negroes in 1910 and 14.6 and 14.2, respectively, in 1900. At each census the proportion 5 to 14 and 15 to 24 years of age was higher among Negroes than among native whites of native parentage; the proportion 25 to 44 years of age was slightly higher among Negroes in 1910 and among native whites of native parentage in 1900; and at each census the proportion 45 to 64 and 65 and over was smaller among Negroes. The decline during the decade 1900–1910 in the proportion of children under 5, noted in the case of Negroes does not appear in the case of native whites of native parentage in the totals for the South, although it appears in the total for the West South Central division, and in those for the North and the West. This may be explained in part by the migration of adults in this class of population northward and westward. The age distributions of Negroes and of native whites of native parentage in each of the three southern divisions are, on the whole, remarkable rather for their similarities than for their differences.

It may be noted that the proportions under 5, 5 to 14, and 15 to 24 in the Negro population of the South at each of the last two censuses exceeded the corresponding proportions for the native white population of native parentage in the North and West. This is remarkable because of the large number of native whites of foreign or mixed parentage in the North and West, whose children are natives of native parentage.

The percentage Negro in the population classified by age periods is given for sections and Southern divisions in Table 19 for 1910 and 1900.

Single years of age for ages under 25 years are shown by sex in Table 20, for the Negro population of the several sections and southern divisions in 1910.

The irregularities in distribution by single years of age, which have been noted in the totals for the Negro population as a whole, appear in the figures for each section and division shown in Table 20. In each Southern division the number under 1 year of age is, relatively to the numbers 2, 3, and 4 years of age, so small as to indicate omissions in the enumeration of infants; in each area for both males and females fewer children were reported 1 year of age than were reported for each of the ages 2 years, 3 years, and 4 years—with the inconsiderable exception in the West, that fewer females were reported for the age 2 years than for the age 1 year; and in each area concentrations are in evidence upon even years of age.

NEGRO POPULATION AND CLASSES OF THE WHITE POPULATION, CLASSIFIED BY AGE PERIODS, BY SECTIONS AND SOUTHERN DIVISIONS: 1910.

Table 18 SECTION, DIVISION, AND RACIAL CLASS.	POPULATION: 1910.												
	All ages.	Under 5 years.	5 to 9 years.	10 to 14 years.	15 to 19 years.	20 to 24 years.	25 to 29 years.	30 to 34 years.	35 to 44 years.	45 to 54 years.	55 to 64 years.	65 years and over.	Age unknown.
UNITED STATES.													
All classes.............	91,972,266	10,631,364	9,760,632	9,107,140	9,063,603	9,056,984	8,180,003	6,972,185	11,657,687	8,369,988	5,054,101	3,949,524	169,055
Negro.....................	9,827,763	1,263,288	1,246,553	1,155,266	1,060,416	1,030,795	881,227	668,089	1,088,862	711,979	396,124	294,124	31,040
Native white:													
Native parentage.............	49,488,575	6,546,282	5,861,015	5,324,283	5,089,055	4,682,922	4,049,074	3,401,601	5,495,766	4,022,103	2,717,897	2,201,068	97,509
Foreign or mixed parentage..	18,897,837	2,674,125	2,315,649	2,235,795	2,205,575	1,873,108	1,545,366	1,359,960	2,304,783	1,522,857	594,529	255,586	10,504
Foreign-born white.............	13,345,545	102,507	298,509	358,330	673,761	1,430,381	1,662,696	1,505,715	2,711,568	2,071,415	1,321,103	1,183,349	26,211
THE SOUTH.													
All classes.............	29,389,330	4,053,348	3,750,535	3,381,932	3,141,631	2,873,464	2,426,387	1,974,660	3,158,691	2,208,197	1,382,388	983,394	54,703
Negro.....................	8,749,427	1,176,331	1,164,557	1,073,980	970,716	911,603	749,782	557,466	910,025	607,895	343,958	256,694	26,420
Native white:													
Native parentage.............	18,561,146	2,702,147	2,413,795	2,139,915	1,992,684	1,768,938	1,488,071	1,240,902	1,922,185	1,352,355	896,745	618,974	24,435
Foreign or mixed parentage..	1,260,103	149,410	136,803	131,669	130,289	117,061	103,909	98,288	178,884	129,647	56,445	26,573	1,125
Foreign-born white.............	726,171	8,910	21,550	25,087	38,081	67,654	77,929	72,754	138,926	112,362	81,608	78,902	2,408
SOUTH ATLANTIC.													
All classes.............	12,194,895	1,657,219	1,524,850	1,396,058	1,289,792	1,193,525	1,000,453	815,946	1,325,796	932,819	597,751	439,628	21,058
Negro.....................	4,112,488	570,516	555,036	513,239	457,053	426,876	341,665	253,860	421,374	279,676	162,623	119,140	11,430
Native white:													
Native parentage.............	7,341,205	1,027,812	915,529	830,589	773,565	696,449	587,969	495,892	780,597	562,293	383,224	278,967	8,319
Foreign or mixed parentage..	439,843	54,686	45,386	42,842	42,599	37,848	33,944	33,294	64,634	49,143	23,029	12,072	366
Foreign-born white.............	290,555	2,575	7,593	8,259	15,526	31,373	36,047	32,259	57,896	40,630	28,377	29,089	931
EAST SOUTH CENTRAL.													
All classes.............	8,409,901	1,160,471	1,070,852	969,343	905,052	814,177	685,911	555,365	893,208	640,396	402,681	297,289	15,156
Negro.....................	2,652,513	347,803	343,812	320,476	294,183	274,935	230,624	171,477	278,306	191,801	108,199	82,481	8,416
Native white:													
Native parentage.............	5,452,492	796,697	709,965	629,684	588,058	514,065	428,451	355,933	559,019	402,393	268,356	193,484	6,387
Foreign or mixed parentage..	214,977	15,048	15,158	17,025	19,622	19,353	19,306	20,476	40,152	30,572	12,431	5,654	180
Foreign-born white.............	86,857	426	1,538	1,812	2,882	5,548	7,290	7,290	15,393	15,391	13,550	15,567	170
WEST SOUTH CENTRAL.													
All classes.............	8,784,534	1,235,658	1,154,833	1,016,531	946,787	865,762	740,023	603,349	939,687	634,982	381,956	246,477	18,489
Negro.....................	1,984,426	258,012	265,709	240,265	219,480	209,792	177,493	132,129	210,345	136,418	73,136	55,073	6,574
Native white:													
Native parentage.............	5,767,449	877,638	788,301	679,642	631,061	558,424	471,651	389,077	582,569	387,669	245,165	146,523	9,729
Foreign or mixed parentage..	605,283	79,676	76,259	71,802	68,068	59,860	50,659	44,518	74,098	49,932	20,985	8,847	579
Foreign-born white.............	348,759	5,909	12,419	15,016	19,673	30,733	34,592	33,205	65,637	56,341	39,681	34,246	1,307
THE NORTH.													
All classes.............	55,757,115	5,909,586	5,403,840	5,163,075	5,330,302	5,486,602	5,044,380	4,379,440	7,499,249	5,463,289	3,291,788	2,697,624	87,940
Negro.....................	1,027,674	83,729	78,892	78,205	86,126	113,923	124,832	104,600	169,052	98,341	49,737	35,973	4,264
Native white:													
Native parentage.............	27,352,035	3,412,551	3,069,248	2,847,255	2,762,466	2,555,907	2,219,762	1,871,954	3,118,453	2,352,734	1,638,504	1,445,947	57,254
Foreign or mixed parentage..	15,967,158	2,320,380	1,994,384	1,922,670	1,884,564	1,576,243	1,279,302	1,120,325	1,904,513	1,260,412	489,416	206,889	8,060
Foreign-born white.............	11,321,016	83,593	252,672	306,632	588,705	1,232,783	1,412,985	1,275,677	2,294,388	1,742,027	1,108,770	1,004,699	18,085
THE WEST.													
All classes.............	6,825,821	668,430	606,257	562,133	591,670	696,918	709,236	618,085	999,747	698,502	379,925	268,506	26,412
Negro.....................	50,662	3,228	3,104	3,081	3,574	5,269	6,613	6,023	9,785	5,743	2,429	1,457	356
Native white:													
Native parentage.............	3,575,394	431,584	377,972	337,113	333,905	358,077	341,241	288,745	455,128	317,014	182,648	136,147	15,820
Foreign or mixed parentage..	1,670,576	204,335	184,462	181,456	190,722	179,804	162,155	141,347	221,386	132,798	48,668	22,124	1,319
Foreign-born white.............	1,298,358	10,004	24,287	26,611	46,975	129,944	171,782	157,284	278,254	217,026	130,725	99,748	5,718

PERCENTAGE NEGRO IN THE POPULATION, CLASSIFIED BY AGE PERIODS, BY SECTIONS AND SOUTHERN DIVISIONS: 1910 AND 1900.

Table 19

PERCENTAGE NEGRO IN THE POPULATION OF AGE SPECIFIED.

AGE PERIOD.	United States.		The South.										The North.		The West.	
			Total.		South Atlantic division.		East South Central division.		West South Central division.							
	1910	1900	1910	1900	1910	1900	1910	1900	1910	1900			1910	1900	1910	1900
All ages	10.7	11.6	29.8	32.3	33.7	35.7	31.5	33.1	22.6	25.9			1.8	1.9	0.7	0.7
Under 5 years	11.9	13.3	29.0	32.8	34.4	37.7	30.0	33.0	20.9	25.3			1.4	1.5	0.5	0.5
5 to 9 years	12.8	13.6	31.1	33.8	36.4	38.3	32.1	34.3	23.0	26.6			1.5	1.5	0.5	0.5
10 to 14 years	12.7	13.5	31.8	33.9	36.8	38.2	33.1	34.4	23.6	26.8			1.5	1.6	0.5	0.6
15 to 19 years	11.7	13.0	30.9	33.3	35.4	37.3	32.5	33.9	23.2	26.2			1.6	1.9	0.6	0.6
20 to 24 years	11.4	13.2	31.7	34.7	35.8	38.0	33.8	35.6	24.2	28.2			2.1	2.4	0.8	0.9
25 to 29 years	10.8	11.3	30.9	32.4	34.2	35.1	33.6	34.0	24.0	26.7			2.5	2.4	0.9	0.9
30 to 34 years	9.6	9.4	28.2	29.9	33.1	32.4	30.9	31.1	21.9	24.4			2.4	2.1	1.0	0.9
35 to 44 years	9.3	9.1	28.8	29.4	31.8	32.3	31.2	30.3	22.4	23.5			2.3	2.0	1.0	0.9
45 to 54 years	8.5	9.7	27.5	29.3	30.0	31.3	30.0	30.9	21.5	24.1			1.8	1.8	0.8	0.8
55 to 64 years	7.8	8.5	24.9	28.4	27.2	30.2	26.9	29.4	19.1	23.7			1.5	1.8	0.6	0.6
65 years and over	7.4	8.5	26.1	30.3	27.1	30.8	27.7	31.3	22.3	27.9			1.3	1.3	0.5	0.5
Age unknown	18.4	24.3	48.3	53.5	54.3	55.1	55.5	56.3	35.6	48.7			4.8	7.2	1.3	1.6

NEGRO MALES AND FEMALES UNDER 25 YEARS OF AGE, CLASSIFIED BY SINGLE YEARS OF AGE, BY SECTIONS AND SOUTHERN DIVISIONS: 1910.

Table 20

NEGRO POPULATION: 1910.

AGE.	United States.		The South.								The North.		The West.	
			Total.		South Atlantic division.		East South Central division.		West South Central division.					
	Male.	Female.	Male.	Female.	Male.	Female.	Male.	Female.	Male.	Female.	Male.	Female.	Male.	Female.
All ages	4,885,881	4,941,882	4,339,625	4,409,802	2,029,808	2,082,680	1,315,792	1,336,721	994,025	990,401	518,544	509,130	27,712	22,950
Under 25 years	2,816,671	2,939,647	2,595,339	2,701,848	1,233,210	1,289,510	776,930	804,279	585,199	608,059	212,263	228,612	9,069	9,187
Under 1 year	125,459	126,927	116,230	117,862	57,676	58,230	34,036	34,419	24,518	25,213	8,906	8,732	323	333
1 year	109,357	109,883	101,799	101,918	49,837	50,097	29,685	29,558	22,277	22,263	7,278	7,634	280	331
2 years	130,192	129,845	121,443	120,807	58,335	58,396	35,983	35,624	27,125	26,787	8,441	8,718	308	320
3 years	130,526	134,021	121,838	124,815	57,762	59,567	36,866	37,357	27,210	27,891	8,345	8,874	343	332
4 years	133,786	133,292	125,190	124,429	60,491	60,125	37,332	36,943	27,367	27,361	8,303	8,498	293	365
5 years	126,709	128,994	118,470	120,424	55,818	57,196	35,454	36,219	27,198	27,009	7,926	8,238	313	332
6 years	129,804	133,011	121,402	124,337	58,704	60,416	35,356	36,040	27,342	27,881	8,090	8,328	312	346
7 years	125,950	125,792	117,914	117,493	55,907	55,839	34,425	34,726	27,582	26,928	7,726	8,009	310	290
8 years	124,937	127,536	117,247	119,316	55,294	56,696	34,727	34,996	27,226	27,624	7,400	7,928	290	292
9 years	111,775	112,045	103,929	104,025	49,687	49,479	31,007	30,862	23,235	23,684	7,551	7,696	295	324
10 years	122,880	119,629	114,884	111,249	55,289	53,642	33,936	32,731	25,659	24,876	7,687	8,054	309	326
11 years	97,062	97,986	90,019	90,419	42,899	43,357	26,859	26,691	20,261	20,371	6,786	7,290	257	277
12 years	131,267	130,033	123,037	121,199	59,048	58,858	36,917	35,524	27,072	26,817	7,922	8,498	308	336
13 years	110,226	111,635	102,392	103,341	48,491	48,841	31,042	30,830	22,859	23,670	7,537	7,983	297	311
14 years	116,639	117,909	108,382	109,058	51,500	51,314	32,988	32,958	23,894	24,786	7,936	8,512	321	339
15 years	101,921	105,634	94,418	97,365	44,489	46,136	28,913	29,271	21,016	21,958	7,218	7,970	285	299
16 years	106,679	117,724	98,437	108,732	46,097	51,893	30,839	32,551	21,501	24,288	7,919	8,622	323	370
17 years	100,185	103,662	91,985	94,690	41,574	44,974	29,429	28,337	20,982	21,379	7,864	8,617	336	355
18 years	108,316	122,991	99,401	112,306	46,927	52,938	30,011	34,164	22,463	25,204	8,572	10,228	343	457
19 years	90,844	102,460	81,506	91,876	39,028	42,997	23,171	27,497	19,307	21,382	8,928	10,188	410	396
20 years	92,494	123,131	83,063	111,074	39,591	52,114	24,356	33,726	19,116	25,234	8,996	11,600	435	457
21 years	100,178	96,422	89,285	85,636	41,815	40,225	26,537	25,839	20,933	19,572	10,422	10,380	471	406
22 years	101,974	114,295	90,244	101,718	41,926	48,242	27,301	30,484	21,017	22,992	11,153	12,121	577	456
23 years	92,960	107,745	81,097	94,602	37,555	44,360	24,743	28,663	18,799	21,579	11,203	12,603	660	540
24 years	94,551	107,045	81,727	93,157	37,470	43,578	25,017	28,269	19,240	21,310	12,154	13,291	670	597
25 years and over	2,052,134	1,988,271	1,729,905	1,695,915	790,191	788,147	534,501	528,387	405,213	379,381	303,794	278,741	18,435	13,615
Age unknown	17,076	13,964	14,381	12,039	6,407	5,023	4,361	4,055	3,613	2,961	2,487	1,777	208	148

Variations in age composition from state to state, as is true of variations from one section or division to another, are principally effects of migration. The age compositions of the relatively small Negro populations of the several Northern and Western states are fairly represented in the totals for the North and the West, and need not be further considered in detail. In each of these states the proportion in the adult ages is increased and the proportion of children diminished by the accession of immigrants.

The percentage distribution by age, of the Negro population and of classes of the white population in 1910 and in 1900 is shown for Southern states in Table 21. In these states—exclusive of the District of Columbia—the proportion under 5 years of age ranged in 1910 from 9.8 per cent in Kentucky to 15.4 per cent in the Carolinas, North and South. The proportion in this age group was low in the border states of Delaware, Maryland, West Virginia, and Kentucky; and high in the contiguous black-belt states of North Carolina,

South Carolina, Georgia, Alabama, and Mississippi. In each of the Southern states the proportion of children under 5, and 5 to 14 years of age, declined during the decade, 1900–1910; in each of these states except Louisiana and Texas, the proportion of the population 15 to 24 declined in the same period; in each state, the proportion 25 to 44 increased; and in each state except North Carolina, South Carolina, and Louisiana the proportion 45 to 64 increased. In 6 states the proportion 65 and over increased, in 4 states and in the District of Columbia it remained unchanged, and in 6 it decreased. The changes are in many instances slight, but are in the case of the population of each state generally consistent with those changes which have been noted in the age composition of the Negro population as a whole, since in each state, as in the country as a whole, the proportion in the younger ages has declined, and the proportion in the middle life ages has increased. This general tendency is of course variously affected in the several states by interstate migration.

PERCENTAGE DISTRIBUTION, BY BROAD AGE PERIODS, OF THE NEGRO POPULATION AND OF CLASSES OF THE WHITE POPULATION, BY SOUTHERN STATES: 1910 AND 1900.

Table 21	PERCENTAGE DISTRIBUTION BY AGE PERIODS.															
SOUTHERN STATE AND RACIAL CLASS.	All ages.		Under 5 years.		5 to 14 years.		15 to 24 years.		25 to 44 years.		45 to 64 years.		65 years and over.		Age unknown.	
	1910	1900	1910	1900	1910	1900	1910	1900	1910	1900	1910	1900	1910	1900	1910	1900
SOUTH ATLANTIC DIVISION.																
DELAWARE.																
Negro	100.0	100.0	9.9	11.8	22.0	22.6	20.4	21.2	28.8	27.3	14.6	13.0	4.0	3.5	0.4	0.6
Native white:																
Native parentage	100.0	100.0	10.2	11.0	19.6	21.5	19.1	19.2	27.9	27.1	17.5	16.0	5.6	4.9	0.1	0.2
Foreign or mixed parentage	100.0	100.0	14.7	13.8	22.6	24.0	19.6	19.5	26.8	31.8	14.2	9.1	2.0	1.6	0.1	0.1
Foreign-born white	100.0	100.0	0.7	0.5	4.4	3.8	16.8	14.1	45.1	43.9	24.1	27.9	8.7	9.4	0.3	0.4
MARYLAND.																
Negro	100.0	100.0	11.2	12.0	21.7	23.0	20.2	21.5	29.1	26.7	13.8	12.7	3.7	3.2	0.2	0.9
Native white:																
Native parentage	100.0	100.0	11.7	12.6	22.0	23.6	20.0	20.1	27.3	25.8	14.4	13.7	4.5	4.0	0.1	0.2
Foreign or mixed parentage	100.0	100.0	11.0	11.6	20.2	22.3	18.9	20.0	30.1	34.0	17.5	10.5	2.3	1.4	0.1	0.1
Foreign-born white	100.0	100.0	0.6	0.3	5.4	4.5	13.8	12.7	40.1	36.7	27.6	31.6	12.4	13.8	0.1	0.3
DISTRICT OF COLUMBIA.																
Negro	100.0	100.0	7.7	8.4	15.2	17.0	21.1	23.8	37.9	33.2	14.4	14.3	3.1	3.1	0.5	0.1
Native white:																
Native parentage	100.0	100.0	9.3	9.4	16.7	18.5	19.2	19.4	33.4	32.0	15.6	16.5	5.5	4.0	0.4	0.2
Foreign or mixed parentage	100.0	100.0	8.3	8.4	15.0	16.9	16.7	20.6	38.2	39.8	18.3	12.4	3.3	1.9	0.2	(1)
Foreign-born white	100.0	100.0	0.6	0.3	4.0	2.5	11.9	9.4	43.0	36.9	26.0	36.2	14.1	14.8	0.4	(1)
VIRGINIA.																
Negro	100.0	100.0	12.9	13.7	25.6	26.8	21.1	21.6	24.6	22.5	12.2	11.6	3.5	3.5	0.2	0.4
Native white:																
Native parentage	100.0	100.0	13.4	13.6	23.6	24.2	19.6	20.5	25.6	24.3	13.5	13.2	4.3	4.0	0.1	0.1
Foreign or mixed parentage	100.0	100.0	13.1	11.7	21.8	22.0	18.9	19.9	27.6	31.3	14.7	12.1	3.7	3.0	0.1	0.1
Foreign-born white	100.0	100.0	0.9	0.5	5.8	3.6	14.3	10.8	43.4	38.1	24.2	31.2	11.1	15.4	0.3	0.3
WEST VIRGINIA.																
Negro	100.0	100.0	10.9	11.0	18.2	19.5	24.1	26.7	35.1	29.5	9.5	9.3	2.0	2.2	0.3	1.8
Native white:																
Native parentage	100.0	100.0	14.5	14.9	24.4	25.4	20.1	20.9	25.6	24.0	11.7	11.2	3.5	3.2	0.1	0.3
Foreign or mixed parentage	100.0	100.0	17.0	9.4	18.3	18.1	15.0	20.4	29.9	36.9	16.8	12.5	3.0	2.6	0.1	0.1
Foreign-born white	100.0	100.0	1.3	0.4	5.6	3.6	22.5	13.3	49.8	39.8	14.8	29.2	5.3	13.0	0.7	0.8
NORTH CAROLINA.																
Negro	100.0	100.0	15.4	15.5	27.2	27.4	21.5	22.5	21.8	19.9	10.8	11.1	3.1	3.1	0.3	0.5
Native white:																
Native parentage	100.0	100.0	15.0	14.8	24.7	25.9	20.1	20.5	23.7	22.5	12.8	12.5	3.7	3.6	0.1	0.1
Foreign or mixed parentage	100.0	100.0	13.1	12.7	22.9	23.5	18.6	19.0	26.9	26.8	14.1	12.7	4.3	5.3	0.1	.....
Foreign-born white	100.0	100.0	1.0	0.3	5.9	4.7	14.3	11.5	43.2	39.4	25.7	31.7	9.7	12.1	0.3	0.3

[1] Less than one-tenth of 1 per cent.

PERCENTAGE DISTRIBUTION, BY BROAD AGE PERIODS, OF THE NEGRO POPULATION AND OF CLASSES OF THE WHITE POPULATION, BY SOUTHERN STATES: 1910 AND 1900.—Continued.

Table 21

SOUTHERN STATE AND RACIAL CLASS.	All ages.		Under 5 years.		5 to 14 years.		15 to 24 years.		25 to 44 years.		45 to 64 years.		65 years and over.		Age unknown.	
	1910	1900	1910	1900	1910	1900	1910	1900	1910	1900	1910	1900	1910	1900	1910	1900
SOUTH CAROLINA.																
Negro	100.0	100.0	15.4	16.0	28.4	29.0	22.1	22.4	22.2	20.2	9.2	9.4	2.6	2.8	0.2	0.1
Native white:																
Native parentage	100.0	100.0	14.9	14.3	24.4	25.8	20.7	21.8	24.7	22.9	12.0	12.1	3.2	3.0	0.1	0.1
Foreign or mixed parentage	100.0	100.0	9.1	9.3	17.4	20.0	18.1	20.7	32.1	33.1	19.1	13.2	3.9	3.7	0.2	0.1
Foreign-born white	100.0	100.0	0.8	0.1	4.0	2.6	12.2	8.6	40.7	35.6	28.0	35.5	14.2	17.5	0.2	0.1
GEORGIA.																
Negro	100.0	100.0	14.2	15.2	26.8	27.8	21.5	21.7	24.2	22.3	10.3	9.8	2.7	2.8	0.2	0.4
Native white:																
Native parentage	100.0	100.0	14.8	14.5	24.6	26.0	20.1	21.0	24.8	23.2	12.2	12.1	3.3	3.1	0.1	0.2
Foreign or mixed parentage	100.0	100.0	10.2	10.5	18.5	21.9	19.3	20.0	31.9	32.1	16.7	12.3	3.4	3.1	0.1	0.1
Foreign-born white	100.0	100.0	0.6	0.3	4.8	4.3	14.5	10.1	43.4	40.5	26.4	31.7	10.2	12.8	0.2	0.3
FLORIDA.																
Negro	100.0	100.0	12.0	13.8	23.0	24.6	21.5	22.7	30.6	26.3	10.1	9.5	2.1	2.4	0.7	0.7
Native white:																
Native parentage	100.0	100.0	14.1	14.4	23.6	25.9	20.1	20.2	26.1	24.2	12.6	12.3	3.3	2.7	0.3	0.4
Foreign or mixed parentage	100.0	100.0	18.1	17.6	26.2	30.5	20.0	18.7	22.5	22.7	10.7	8.9	2.4	1.5	0.1	0.1
Foreign-born white	100.0	100.0	1.6	1.0	7.3	7.2	18.5	15.8	43.2	43.2	22.5	26.2	6.7	6.3	0.3	0.2
EAST SOUTH CENTRAL DIVISION.																
KENTUCKY.																
Negro	100.0	100.0	9.8	11.1	20.3	23.3	21.4	21.9	29.6	26.9	14.5	12.3	4.0	3.4	0.4	1.0
Native white:																
Native parentage	100.0	100.0	14.1	14.5	24.5	25.9	20.2	20.4	24.8	24.0	12.5	11.7	3.8	3.3	0.1	0.2
Foreign or mixed parentage	100.0	100.0	4.7	7.0	12.3	18.0	17.8	22.6	40.7	41.1	22.2	9.9	2.2	1.3	0.1	0.1
Foreign-born white	100.0	100.0	0.3	0.1	1.9	1.7	6.9	7.3	29.8	29.4	37.1	41.1	23.7	20.0	0.2	0.4
TENNESSEE.																
Negro	100.0	100.0	12.0	13.0	23.1	25.5	22.3	22.7	26.4	23.3	12.5	11.7	3.4	3.1	0.3	0.7
Native white:																
Native parentage	100.0	100.0	14.2	14.1	23.9	25.4	20.2	21.0	24.9	23.7	12.8	12.2	3.8	3.3	0.1	0.3
Foreign or mixed parentage	100.0	100.0	8.0	9.1	16.4	20.9	18.7	22.3	35.5	34.3	18.0	10.8	3.2	2.5	0.1	0.1
Foreign-born white	100.0	100.0	0.5	0.4	4.5	3.5	10.9	9.5	36.1	35.4	31.6	37.7	16.2	13.3	0.1	0.3
ALABAMA.																
Negro	100.0	100.0	13.7	14.4	25.8	27.1	21.2	22.2	24.7	21.4	11.4	11.2	2.9	3.0	0.3	0.6
Native white:																
Native parentage	100.0	100.0	15.6	15.1	25.1	26.5	20.3	21.2	24.0	22.3	11.9	11.9	3.0	2.8	0.1	0.2
Foreign or mixed parentage	100.0	100.0	12.7	11.7	22.2	23.2	19.2	20.1	28.2	30.9	14.8	11.3	2.8	2.6	0.1	0.1
Foreign-born white	100.0	100.0	0.8	0.5	5.8	4.1	12.8	12.6	41.2	38.6	29.8	33.6	9.5	10.3	0.2	0.3
MISSISSIPPI.																
Negro	100.0	100.0	14.0	14.8	26.5	27.9	21.3	22.2	25.1	22.4	9.9	9.5	2.9	2.9	0.3	0.3
Native white:																
Native parentage	100.0	100.0	15.3	15.1	25.3	26.6	20.2	21.2	24.5	22.7	11.4	11.5	3.1	2.7	0.1	0.1
Foreign or mixed parentage	100.0	100.0	10.0	8.6	17.2	20.4	17.5	21.9	32.9	32.8	18.6	13.4	3.5	2.9	0.2	0.1
Foreign-born white	100.0	100.0	0.7	0.3	6.9	3.2	12.8	8.1	37.8	34.6	27.9	38.4	13.7	15.1	0.3	0.3
WEST SOUTH CENTRAL DIVISION.																
ARKANSAS.																
Negro	100.0	100.0	12.9	14.0	25.1	26.9	21.8	22.4	26.0	22.6	11.4	11.0	2.4	2.3	0.2	0.8
Native white:																
Native parentage	100.0	100.0	15.7	15.0	25.0	27.5	20.4	21.0	24.3	22.7	11.5	11.3	2.9	2.3	0.1	0.2
Foreign or mixed parentage	100.0	100.0	10.4	11.2	20.6	25.5	20.6	20.2	30.0	28.9	15.4	11.7	2.9	2.3	(1)	0.1
Foreign-born white	100.0	100.0	0.6	0.3	4.4	3.4	9.5	10.4	38.0	38.5	34.4	37.9	12.9	9.1	0.2	0.4
LOUISIANA.																
Negro	100.0	100.0	12.9	14.3	25.5	27.1	21.2	21.2	26.7	23.7	10.3	10.4	3.1	3.1	0.3	0.4
Native white:																
Native parentage	100.0	100.0	15.4	16.8	26.8	28.4	21.1	20.9	24.4	22.1	9.6	9.6	2.3	2.1	0.3	0.1
Foreign or mixed parentage	100.0	100.0	10.1	9.4	17.3	18.1	16.1	20.9	35.3	39.1	18.9	11.1	2.3	1.3	0.1	(1)
Foreign-born white	100.0	100.0	0.6	1.0	5.3	6.1	12.8	10.6	37.8	33.7	29.0	34.6	14.3	13.7	0.2	0.2
OKLAHOMA.																
Negro	100.0	100.0	13.2	14.2	25.1	26.0	21.3	21.6	26.9	23.0	10.7	11.3	2.4	2.8	0.4	1.1
Native white:																
Native parentage	100.0	100.0	15.2	15.4	24.8	26.7	20.3	20.0	26.1	25.2	11.1	10.6	2.3	1.7	0.2	0.3
Foreign or mixed parentage	100.0	100.0	10.8	14.4	22.4	26.7	20.6	19.3	30.4	28.4	13.7	9.6	2.1	1.5	0.1	0.1
Foreign-born white	100.0	100.0	0.7	0.4	4.0	4.3	11.0	11.9	42.6	44.3	31.6	31.4	9.7	7.4	0.4	0.3
TEXAS.																
Negro	100.0	100.0	13.1	14.6	25.8	28.2	22.1	22.1	25.7	22.2	10.2	9.5	2.8	2.4	0.4	1.0
Native white:																
Native parentage	100.0	100.0	15.0	15.8	25.5	27.3	20.7	20.9	25.0	23.0	11.1	10.6	2.6	2.2	0.1	0.2
Foreign or mixed parentage	100.0	100.0	15.0	17.5	27.6	31.7	22.9	22.5	24.9	22.2	8.6	5.2	0.9	0.8	0.1	0.1
Foreign-born white	100.0	100.0	2.2	1.2	9.3	7.6	15.7	14.9	37.6	39.2	26.1	28.7	8.7	7.8	0.4	0.6

1 Less than one-tenth of 1 per cent.

In Table 22 the states have been listed in order according to the median age of the Negro population, at the censuses of 1910 and 1900, and according to median age of the colored population at the censuses of 1890 and 1880, states having a Negro or colored population of less than 1,000 being omitted.

For the Southern states generally, with the exception of Oklahoma, the data for the aggregate colored population in 1890 and in 1880 may be accepted as fairly comparable with the data for Negroes in 1900 and in 1910, since in these states the colored population other than Negro is relatively too small materially to affect the state figures. In some of the Northern and Western states, however, the colored other than Negro are relatively to the Negro so numerous as to impair the comparability of the figures.

It will be noted that the states in which the median age is low are those in which the proportion of children is large. The five states showing the lowest median age in 1910, for example—South Carolina, North Carolina, Georgia, Mississippi, and Alabama—are the five contiguous black-belt states in which, as has been remarked, the proportion of children under 5 exceeded the corresponding proportion in any other of the Southern states.

In each of the 16 Southern states in 1910 the median age of the Negro population was lower and the proportion of children higher than it was in any of the Northern or Western states. The range of median age for the Southern states was from 17.5 years in South Carolina to 24.2 years in Kentucky; and for the Northern states, from 26.1 years in Kansas to 33.1 years in Oregon. The states showing a high median age are those in which the proportion of migrants is high.

MEDIAN AGE, BY STATES, OF THE NEGRO POPULATION: 1910 AND 1900—AND OF THE NEGRO, INDIAN, AND MONGOLIAN POPULATION: 1890 AND 1880.

Table 22 STATES HAVING AT LEAST 1,000 NEGROES IN 1910.	Median age of Negro population: 1910.	STATE OR TERRITORY HAVING AT LEAST 1,000 NEGROES IN 1900.	Median age of Negro population: 1900.	STATE OR TERRITORY HAVING AT LEAST 1,000 NEGROES IN 1890.[2]	Median age of Negro, Indian, and Mongolian population: 1890.	STATE OR TERRITORY HAVING AT LEAST 1,000 NEGROES IN 1880.[3]	Median age of Negro, Indian, and Mongolian population: 1880.
United States	20.8	United States	19.4	United States	18.3	United States	18.0
South Carolina	17.5	South Carolina	17.0	South Carolina	16.1	Texas	15.8
North Carolina	18.1	North Carolina	17.8	Texas	16.6	Mississippi	16.1
Georgia	18.9	Texas	18.0	Mississippi	16.8	South Carolina	16.2
Mississippi	19.0	Georgia	18.1	North Carolina	16.8	Georgia	16.4
Alabama	19.7	Mississippi	18.1	Georgia	17.1	North Carolina	16.4
Texas	19.9						
		Alabama	18.5	Alabama	17.4	Alabama	16.7
Virginia	20.1	Arkansas	18.8	Arkansas	17.4	Arkansas	16.7
Arkansas	20.2	Louisiana	18.9	Virginia	17.7	Tennessee	16.9
Louisiana	20.3	Virginia	18.9	Louisiana	17.9	Virginia	17.2
Oklahoma	20.3	Oklahoma[1]	19.0	Tennessee	18.1	Florida	17.3
Tennessee	21.5						
		Tennessee	19.8	Florida	18.4	Louisiana	18.4
Florida	22.1	Florida	20.3	Kentucky	19.5	Kentucky	18.5
Maryland	23.4	Maryland	21.7	Kansas	19.8	Kansas	19.1
Delaware	23.8	Kentucky	21.8	West Virginia	20.3	Missouri	19.2
West Virginia	23.9	Delaware	22.3	Maryland	20.5	West Virginia	19.3
Kentucky	24.2						
		West Virginia	22.3	Missouri	20.7	Maryland	20.0
Kansas	26.1	Kansas	22.8	Wisconsin	20.8	Delaware	20.1
Missouri	27.1	Missouri	23.5	Delaware	21.3	Wisconsin	20.4
Vermont	27.1	Indiana	24.8	Indiana	22.4	Minnesota	21.0
District of Columbia	27.2	District of Columbia	25.3	Iowa	22.9	Indiana	21.1
New Jersey	27.4						
		New Jersey	25.3	District of Columbia	23.2	Vermont	21.3
Pennsylvania	27.5	Pennsylvania	25.5	New Mexico	23.3	Michigan	21.5
Indiana	27.6	Ohio	25.6	Ohio	23.4	Ohio	21.6
Iowa	27.7	Iowa	25.7	Nebraska	23.5	Illinois	22.0
Maine	27.9	Arizona	25.9	Oklahoma	23.5	Iowa	22.0
Massachusetts	28.2						
		Connecticut	26.1	Illinois	23.8	New Mexico	22.2
New York	28.2	Illinois	26.3	Michigan	24.0	Nebraska	22.6
Connecticut	28.3	Nebraska	26.3	Minnesota	24.4	District of Columbia	23.3
Wyoming	28.3	New York	26.4	Pennsylvania	24.5	New Jersey	23.9
New Mexico	28.4						
Illinois	28.6	Michigan	26.8	New Jersey	24.6	Pennsylvania	24.0
		New Mexico	26.8	Connecticut	26.2	Maine	25.2
Ohio	28.6	Massachusetts	26.9	New York	26.8	Colorado	25.8
Rhode Island	28.6	Maine	27.1	Maine	26.9	Connecticut	25.8
Nebraska	29.2						
Wisconsin	29.3	Rhode Island	27.3	Massachusetts	27.0	New York	25.9
Michigan	29.4	California	28.1	Colorado	28.1	Massachusetts	26.3
		Wisconsin	28.2	Arizona	28.3	Rhode Island	27.3
Arizona	29.6	Colorado	29.1	Rhode Island	28.3	California	30.1
California	29.7						
Colorado	30.2	Minnesota	29.1	Washington	28.4		
Minnesota	30.7	Washington	30.1	Montana	30.9		
		Montana	30.5	California	32.8		
Washington	30.9	Oregon	30.7	Oregon	32.9		
Utah	31.1						
Montana	32.0						
Oregon	33.1						

[1] Includes population of Indian Territory for 1900.
[2] Except Indian Territory, the population of which was not returned by age.
[3] Except Indian Territory, the population of which was not enumerated.

Table 37 gives for sections, southern divisions, and Southern states, the Negro population classified by age periods, in 1910 and in 1900; Table 38, for Southern states the Negro population under 25 years classified by sex and single years of age; and Table 39, for the nine geographic divisions, and for all states, including the Northern and Western, the Negro population classified by sex and by quinquennial age periods. These tables present actual numbers only, and no analysis of them is undertaken, beyond that which is found in the preceding summary and derivative tables of this chapter.

URBAN AND RURAL POPULATION CLASSIFIED BY AGE.

The age distribution of the urban population and of the rural population in 1910 is given in Table 23 for the Negro population and for the nativity and parentage classes of the white population.

As has been explained elsewhere the urban aggregate embraces the population of all towns and cities of 2,500 inhabitants or more; the rural, the population of smaller cities and towns, together with that of country districts. One of these aggregates is constantly receiving accessions from the other in consequence of the constant drift of population into the cities. This drift cityward, in response to the gravity pull of the urban community, naturally affects principally the population in the middle ages, since the population in the younger ages is dependent and incapable of moving freely, while the population in the older ages is more settled, less venturous, and less capable of fulfilling the requirements of urban conditions.

In the age distributions of Table 23 it is apparent that a much larger proportion of the urban than of the rural Negro population are in the economically productive ages of middle life. The Negro population of urban communities in 1910 numbered 2,689,229, and of rural communities 7,138,534. Of the urban 36.6 per cent were in the ages 25 to 44 years, and of the rural 23.2 per cent. For this age group the proportion had been raised in the urban population above, and depressed in the rural population below, the average of 26.8 per cent in the Negro population as a whole.

Upon comparison of the percentages given in Table 16 (p. 174) for the Negro population as a whole, with those given in Table 23 for the urban and rural aggregates, it will be seen that the age distribution of the urban population is more abnormal than that of the rural. This is accounted for by the fact that, since the aggregate urban population is smaller than the aggregate rural, migrants moving into urban communities constitute a larger proportion of the urban than of the rural population, and consequently affect the age composition more in the urban than in the rural aggregate.

Of the urban Negro population 8.5 per cent were under 5 years of age, and of the rural 14.5 per cent, the proportion for the Negro population as a whole, urban and rural combined, being 12.9 per cent. It is probable that a higher rate of natural increase and a lower rate of infant mortality obtains in rural than in urban communities, and that the lower proportion of children in the urban population is in part the effect of a relatively low birth rate combined with a relatively high rate of infant mortality. Undoubtedly, however, as regards age composition, the differences between urban and rural populations, as between different sections of the country, originate principally in migration. By depleting the adult ages of the rural population migration cityward raises the proportion of children in the rural aggregate, and by adding to the adult ages of the urban population depresses the proportion of children in the urban aggregate.

URBAN AND RURAL NEGRO AND WHITE POPULATION, CLASSIFIED BY BROAD AGE PERIODS: 1910.

Table 23 AGE PERIOD.	URBAN POPULATION: 1910.					RURAL POPULATION: 1910.				
	All classes.	Negro.	Native white.		Foreign-born white.	All classes.	Negro.	Native white.		Foreign-born white.
			Native parentage.	Foreign or mixed parentage.				Native parentage.	Foreign or mixed parentage.	
	NUMBER.									
All ages [1]	42,623,383	2,689,229	17,849,644	12,346,900	9,635,369	49,348,883	7,138,534	31,638,931	6,550,937	3,710,176
Under 5 years	4,200,291	229,080	2,044,886	1,846,699	75,372	6,431,073	1,034,208	4,501,396	827,426	27,135
5 to 14 years	7,401,325	454,219	3,486,880	2,950,392	503,771	11,466,447	1,947,600	7,698,418	1,601,052	153,068
15 to 24 years	8,573,829	578,299	3,659,032	2,673,889	1,644,462	9,546,758	1,512,912	6,112,945	1,404,794	459,680
25 to 44 years	14,168,853	985,374	5,330,953	3,415,057	4,390,378	12,641,022	1,652,804	7,615,488	1,795,052	1,489,601
45 to 64 years	6,487,864	351,259	2,495,622	1,318,912	2,299,020	6,936,225	756,844	4,244,378	798,474	1,093,498
65 years and over	1,693,010	77,435	771,790	135,454	706,918	2,256,514	216,689	1,429,278	120,132	476,431
	PERCENTAGE DISTRIBUTION BY AGE PERIODS.									
All ages	100.0	100.0	100.0	100.0	100.0	100.0	100.0	100.0	100.0	100.0
Under 5 years	9.9	8.5	11.5	15.0	0.8	13.0	14.5	14.2	12.6	0.7
5 to 14 years	17.4	16.9	19.5	23.9	5.2	23.2	27.3	24.3	24.4	4.1
15 to 24 years	20.1	21.5	20.5	21.7	17.1	19.3	21.2	19.3	21.4	12.4
25 to 44 years	33.2	36.6	29.9	27.7	45.6	25.6	23.2	24.1	27.4	40.1
45 to 64 years	15.2	13.1	14.0	10.7	23.9	14.1	10.6	13.4	12.2	29.5
65 years and over	4.0	2.9	4.3	1.1	7.3	4.6	3.0	4.5	1.8	12.8

[1] Includes persons of unknown age.

URBAN AND RURAL NEGRO POPULATION, CLASSIFIED BY SEX AND AGE PERIODS, BY SECTIONS AND SOUTHERN DIVISIONS: 1910.

Table 24

SEX AND AGE PERIOD.	United States.		The South.										The North.		The West.	
			Total.		South Atlantic division.		East South Central division.		West South Central division.							
	Urban.	Rural.	Urban.	Rural.	Urban.	Rural.	Urban.	Rural.	Urban.	Rural.			Urban.	Rural.	Urban.	Rural.
BOTH SEXES.	NUMBER.															
All ages	2,689,229	7,138,534	1,854,455	6,894,972	909,520	3,202,968	509,097	2,143,416	435,838	1,548,588	794,966	232,708	39,808	10,854		
Under 5 years	229,080	1,034,208	166,646	1,009,690	83,710	486,806	43,105	304,698	39,826	218,186	59,872	23,857	2,567	661		
5 to 14 years	454,219	1,947,600	339,746	1,898,791	167,954	900,321	89,109	575,179	82,683	423,291	109,720	47,377	4,753	1,432		
15 to 24 years	578,299	1,512,912	418,046	1,464,273	206,667	677,262	113,114	456,004	98,265	331,007	153,434	46,615	6,819	2,024		
25 to 44 years	985,374	1,652,804	636,026	1,581,247	307,169	709,730	177,844	502,563	151,013	368,954	331,435	67,049	17,913	4,508		
45 to 64 years	351,259	756,844	231,511	720,342	114,604	327,695	67,249	232,751	49,658	159,896	113,348	34,730	6,400	1,772		
65 years and over	77,435	216,689	52,745	203,949	24,599	94,541	16,016	66,465	12,130	42,943	23,642	12,331	1,048	409		
Age unknown	13,563	17,477	9,740	16,680	4,817	6,613	2,660	5,756	2,263	4,311	3,515	749	308	48		
MALE.																
All ages	1,279,484	3,606,397	865,946	3,473,679	420,619	1,609,189	238,203	1,077,589	207,124	786,901	392,841	125,703	20,697	7,015		
Under 5 years	113,158	516,162	82,557	503,943	41,510	242,591	21,355	152,547	19,692	108,805	29,380	11,893	1,221	326		
5 to 14 years	218,721	978,528	163,791	953,885	80,705	451,932	42,937	289,774	40,149	212,179	52,642	23,919	2,288	724		
15 to 24 years	253,239	736,863	180,588	710,575	88,229	328,243	49,511	220,806	42,848	161,526	69,493	24,936	3,158	1,352		
25 to 44 years	477,609	826,489	298,366	786,031	142,510	352,263	83,019	246,437	72,837	187,331	169,546	37,360	9,697	3,098		
45 to 64 years	174,362	421,192	112,102	400,021	54,287	179,116	32,914	129,332	24,901	91,573	58,641	19,953	3,619	1,218		
65 years and over	34,973	117,509	23,332	110,053	10,741	51,274	7,125	35,674	5,466	23,105	11,104	7,190	537	266		
Age unknown	7,422	9,654	5,210	9,171	2,637	3,770	1,342	3,019	1,231	2,382	2,035	452	177	31		
FEMALE.																
All ages	1,409,745	3,532,137	988,509	3,421,293	488,901	1,593,779	270,894	1,065,827	228,714	761,687	402,125	107,005	19,111	3,839		
Under 5 years	115,922	518,046	84,084	505,747	42,200	244,215	21,750	152,151	20,134	109,381	30,492	11,964	1,346	335		
5 to 14 years	235,498	969,072	175,955	944,906	87,249	448,389	46,172	285,405	42,534	211,112	57,078	23,458	2,465	708		
15 to 24 years	325,060	776,049	237,458	753,698	118,438	349,019	63,603	235,198	55,417	169,481	83,941	21,679	3,661	672		
25 to 44 years	507,765	826,315	337,660	795,216	164,659	357,467	94,825	256,126	78,176	181,623	161,889	29,689	8,216	1,410		
45 to 64 years	176,897	335,652	119,409	320,321	60,317	148,579	34,335	103,419	24,757	68,323	54,707	14,777	2,781	554		
65 years and over	42,462	99,180	29,413	93,896	13,858	43,267	8,891	30,791	6,664	19,838	12,538	5,141	511	143		
Age unknown	6,141	7,823	4,530	7,509	2,180	2,843	1,318	2,737	1,032	1,929	1,480	297	131	17		
BOTH SEXES.	PERCENTAGE DISTRIBUTION BY AGE PERIODS.															
All ages	100.0	100.0	100.0	100.0	100.0	100.0	100.0	100.0	100.0	100.0	100.0	100.0	100.0	100.0		
Under 5 years	8.5	14.5	9.0	14.6	9.2	15.2	8.5	14.2	9.1	14.1	7.5	10.3	6.4	6.1		
5 to 14 years	16.9	27.3	18.3	27.5	18.5	28.1	17.5	26.8	19.0	27.3	13.8	20.4	11.9	13.2		
15 to 24 years	21.5	21.2	22.5	21.2	22.7	21.1	22.2	21.3	22.5	21.4	19.3	20.0	17.1	18.6		
25 to 44 years	36.6	23.2	34.3	22.9	33.8	22.2	34.9	23.4	34.6	23.8	41.7	28.8	45.0	41.5		
45 to 64 years	13.1	10.6	12.5	10.4	12.6	10.2	13.2	10.9	11.4	10.3	14.3	14.9	16.1	16.3		
65 years and over	2.9	3.0	2.8	3.0	2.7	3.0	3.1	3.1	2.8	2.8	3.0	5.3	2.6	3.8		
Age unknown	0.5	0.2	0.5	0.2	0.5	0.2	0.5	0.3	0.5	0.3	0.4	0.3	0.8	0.4		
MALE.																
All ages	100.0	100.0	100.0	100.0	100.0	100.0	100.0	100.0	100.0	100.0	100.0	100.0	100.0	100.0		
Under 5 years	8.8	14.3	9.5	14.5	9.9	15.1	9.0	14.2	9.5	13.8	7.5	9.5	5.9	4.6		
5 to 14 years	17.1	27.1	18.9	27.5	19.2	28.1	18.0	26.9	19.4	27.0	13.4	19.0	11.1	10.3		
15 to 24 years	19.8	20.4	20.9	20.5	21.0	20.4	20.8	20.5	20.7	20.5	17.7	19.8	15.3	19.3		
25 to 44 years	37.3	22.9	34.5	22.6	33.9	21.9	34.9	22.9	35.2	23.8	43.2	29.7	46.9	44.2		
45 to 64 years	13.6	11.7	12.9	11.5	12.9	11.1	13.8	12.0	12.0	11.6	14.9	15.9	17.5	17.4		
65 years and over	2.7	3.3	2.7	3.2	2.6	3.2	3.0	3.3	2.6	2.9	2.8	5.7	2.6	3.8		
Age unknown	0.6	0.3	0.6	0.3	0.6	0.2	0.6	0.3	0.6	0.3	0.5	0.4	0.9	0.4		
FEMALE.																
All ages	100.0	100.0	100.0	100.0	100.0	100.0	100.0	100.0	100.0	100.0	100.0	100.0	100.0	100.0		
Under 5 years	8.2	14.7	8.5	14.8	8.6	15.3	8.0	14.3	8.8	14.4	7.6	11.2	7.0	8.7		
5 to 14 years	16.7	27.4	17.8	27.6	17.8	28.1	17.0	26.8	18.6	27.7	14.2	21.9	12.9	18.4		
15 to 24 years	23.1	22.0	24.0	22.0	24.2	21.9	23.5	22.1	24.2	22.3	20.9	20.3	19.2	17.5		
25 to 44 years	36.0	23.4	34.2	23.2	33.7	22.4	35.0	24.0	34.2	23.8	40.3	27.7	43.0	36.7		
45 to 64 years	12.5	9.5	12.1	9.4	12.3	9.3	12.7	9.7	10.8	9.0	13.6	13.8	14.6	14.4		
65 years and over	3.0	2.8	3.0	2.7	2.8	2.7	3.3	2.9	2.9	2.6	3.1	4.8	2.7	3.7		
Age unknown	0.4	0.2	0.5	0.2	0.4	0.2	0.5	0.3	0.5	0.3	0.4	0.3	0.7	0.4		

Among native whites of native parentage, as among Negroes, the proportion of children under 5, and 5 to 14 years of age was smaller in the urban than in the rural population. Among native whites of foreign or mixed parentage the proportion of children under 5 was larger, and the proportion 5 to 14 slightly smaller in the urban population; and among the foreign-born whites the proportion in each age group was slightly larger in the urban population. It should perhaps be remarked that these figures do not indicate any tendency on the part of the foreign white stock to have more children in urban than in rural communities. The high proportion of children in the urban white population of foreign or mixed parentage, is accounted for by the presence in urban communities of a relatively large foreign-born population, whose children born in this country are natives of foreign or mixed parentage. In the case of the foreign born, the proportion of children relates to children born in foreign countries, and has, therefore, no significance whatever as regards natural increase of urban and rural populations. In the case of the native whites of native parentage also, comparisons with Negroes, embracing the country as a whole, are similarly invalidated by the parentage classification. Approximately two-thirds—65.3 per cent—of the native whites of foreign or mixed parentage and only a little over one-third—36.1 per cent—of the native whites of native parentage were in urban communities in 1910. Since children of native whites of foreign or mixed parentage are natives of native parentage, the proportion of children among natives of native parentage is raised in both the urban and the rural population above the proportion representing natural increase, and is raised more for the urban than for the rural population, because native whites of foreign or mixed parentage are relatively to native whites of native parentage much more numerous in urban than in rural communities.

Table 24 shows, for sections and southern divisions, the distribution by age and sex of the Negro urban and rural population in 1910. In the urban population the deficiency of children, and the concentration in the ages 25 to 44 years is more marked in the North and West than it is in the South. Of the males living in urban communities in the South 9.5 per cent were under 5 years of age, in the North 7.5 per cent, and in the West 5.9 per cent, the corresponding figures for females being 8.5, 7.6, and 7 per cent. The proportions for the age group 25 to 44 years in the urban Negro population, were for males 34.5 per cent in the South, 43.2 per cent in the North, and 46.9 per cent in the West; for females, 34.2, 40.3, and 43 per cent, respectively.

The rural Negro population of the North and West, as well as the urban has been largely recruited by migrants from the South. It presents, therefore, an age composition similar to that of the urban population, although the deficiency of children, and the concentration in the adult middle ages in the rural population of the North and West is generally less marked than in the urban population.

PERCENTAGE DISTRIBUTION BY AGE PERIODS OF THE URBAN AND RURAL NEGRO AND WHITE POPULATION, BY SECTIONS AND SOUTHERN DIVISIONS: 1910.

Table 25	PERCENTAGE DISTRIBUTION BY AGE PERIODS: 1910.													
	Urban population.							Rural population.						
SECTION, DIVISION, AND RACIAL CLASS.	All ages.[1]	Under 5 years.	5 to 14 years.	15 to 24 years.	25 to 44 years.	45 to 64 years.	65 years and over.	All ages.[1]	Under 5 years.	5 to 14 years.	15 to 24 years.	25 to 44 years.	45 to 64 years.	65 years and over.
UNITED STATES.														
Negro	100.0	8.5	16.9	21.5	36.6	13.1	2.9	100.0	14.5	27.3	21.2	23.2	10.6	3.0
Native white:														
Native parentage	100.0	11.5	19.5	20.5	29.9	14.0	4.3	100.0	14.2	24.3	19.3	24.1	13.4	4.5
Foreign or mixed parentage	100.0	15.0	23.9	21.7	27.7	10.7	1.1	100.0	12.6	24.4	21.4	27.4	12.2	1.8
Foreign-born white	100.0	0.8	5.2	17.1	45.6	23.9	7.3	100.0	0.7	4.1	12.4	40.1	29.5	12.8
THE SOUTH.														
Negro	100.0	9.0	18.3	22.5	34.3	12.5	2.8	100.0	14.6	27.5	21.2	22.9	10.4	3.0
Native white:														
Native parentage	100.0	11.4	20.0	21.5	30.8	12.8	3.2	100.0	15.3	25.6	20.0	23.6	12.0	3.4
Foreign or mixed parentage	100.0	10.1	18.1	19.0	33.9	16.8	2.0	100.0	14.1	25.3	20.4	25.6	12.3	2.2
Foreign-born white	100.0	1.0	5.8	14.2	40.4	26.9	11.5	100.0	1.5	7.2	14.9	39.3	26.5	10.1
SOUTH ATLANTIC DIVISION.														
Negro	100.0	9.2	18.5	22.7	33.8	12.6	2.7	100.0	15.2	28.1	21.1	22.2	10.2	3.0
Native white:														
Native parentage	100.0	11.2	19.4	21.2	30.8	13.5	3.6	100.0	14.8	25.1	19.7	23.8	12.7	3.8
Foreign or mixed parentage	100.0	11.9	19.8	18.8	30.8	16.3	2.3	100.0	13.7	20.6	17.1	27.9	16.7	3.9
Foreign-born white	100.0	0.8	5.6	15.6	42.6	24.7	10.3	100.0	1.0	5.1	17.1	45.0	21.9	9.4
EAST SOUTH CENTRAL DIVISION.														
Negro	100.0	8.5	17.5	22.2	34.9	13.2	3.1	100.0	14.2	26.8	21.3	23.4	10.9	3.1
Native white:														
Native parentage	100.0	11.4	20.1	21.8	30.5	12.8	3.2	100.0	15.2	25.4	19.9	23.6	12.2	3.6
Foreign or mixed parentage	100.0	6.3	13.8	18.4	39.5	19.9	2.0	100.0	8.7	17.6	17.5	31.8	20.1	4.2
Foreign-born white	100.0	0.4	3.5	9.8	35.1	33.5	17.5	100.0	0.7	4.5	9.6	33.2	33.0	18.7
WEST SOUTH CENTRAL DIVISION.														
Negro	100.0	9.1	19.0	22.5	34.6	11.4	2.8	100.0	14.1	27.3	21.4	23.8	10.3	2.8
Native white:														
Native parentage	100.0	11.7	20.9	21.6	31.0	11.7	2.6	100.0	16.1	26.6	20.4	23.6	10.8	2.5
Foreign or mixed parentage	100.0	10.0	18.6	19.7	34.5	15.4	1.7	100.0	15.2	28.2	22.0	23.8	9.4	1.3
Foreign-born white	100.0	1.4	6.8	14.2	39.6	27.1	10.6	100.0	1.9	8.5	14.6	37.4	27.8	9.3
THE NORTH.														
Negro	100.0	7.5	13.8	19.3	41.7	14.3	3.0	100.0	10.3	20.4	20.0	28.8	14.9	5.3
Native white:														
Native parentage	100.0	11.6	19.7	20.3	29.1	14.2	4.7	100.0	13.2	23.3	18.7	24.1	14.9	5.8
Foreign or mixed parentage	100.0	15.6	24.6	21.7	26.7	10.2	1.0	100.0	12.3	24.3	21.6	27.4	12.4	1.9
Foreign-born white	100.0	0.8	5.3	17.5	45.6	23.5	7.1	100.0	0.6	3.8	11.6	39.0	30.5	14.3
THE WEST.														
Negro	100.0	6.4	11.9	17.1	45.0	16.1	2.6	100.0	6.1	13.2	18.6	41.5	16.3	3.8
Native white:														
Native parentage	100.0	10.1	17.0	19.8	34.0	14.7	3.9	100.0	13.7	22.5	19.0	27.4	13.4	3.7
Foreign or mixed parentage	100.0	11.1	19.7	22.8	33.8	11.2	1.3	100.0	13.6	24.5	21.4	28.6	10.4	1.4
Foreign-born white	100.0	0.7	3.8	12.9	47.4	27.0	7.7	100.0	0.8	4.0	14.5	46.0	26.6	7.6

[1] Includes persons of unknown age.

Comparison of age composition in the urban and rural population is made in Table 25 by racial classes, for the several sections and southern divisions.

In connection with Table 25 it is to be remarked that the native white population of foreign or mixed parentage is, relatively to the native white population of native parentage, much smaller in the South than it is in the North and West, and that consequently the proportion of children among native whites of native parentage is much less affected in the South than it is in the North and West, by the inclusion of children of foreign origin. Obviously the high proportion of children in the urban native white population of foreign or mixed parentage in the North—i. e., 15.6 per cent, which exceeds the rural percentage of 12.3 for the same class—is explained by the fact that the foreign-born population is largely resident in urban communities of the North.

In the urban population the proportion under 5 years of age in 1910 was higher, and the proportion 25 to 44 years of age lower, among native whites of native parentage, than among Negroes, in each section and southern division. These and other differences between the several classes, as regards age composition of the urban and rural elements, arise from differences in the rates of natality and mortality, differences in the proportion of migrants, and differences in the distribution of the white population by nativity and parentage.

Statistics for Southern states are given in Table 40 similar to those given in Table 25 for sections and southern divisions. The urban and rural Negro population classified by age periods is given for all states in Table 41.

Since the drift from country to city affects principally the adult ages—and probably also, in part because the birth rate is generally higher, and the infant mortality lower, in rural than in urban communities—the percentage urban is generally higher for the adult population than it is in the population under 5, and 5 to 14 years of age.

In the Negro population the percentage urban increases from 18.1 for the age under 5 years to 37.4 for the age 25 to 44 years, and decreases to 26.3 for the age 65 years and over. In the native white population, also, the maximum percentage urban, 48.2, is for the age 25 to 44 years, and in this class, as among Negroes, the percentage falls off for the more advanced ages.

The percentage urban is given by age periods and sex, for Negroes and native whites, in Table 26.

PERCENTAGE URBAN IN THE NEGRO AND NATIVE WHITE POPULATION, CLASSIFIED BY SEX AND AGE PERIODS, BY SECTIONS AND SOUTHERN DIVISIONS: 1910.

Table 26															
	PERCENTAGE URBAN: 1910.														
	The United States.		The South.										The North.		The West.	
AGE.			Total		South Atlantic.		East South Central.		West South Central.							
	Negro.	Native White.	Negro.	Native White.	Negro.	Native White.	Negro.	Native White.	Negro.	Native White.	Negro.	Native White.	Negro.	Native White.
BOTH SEXES.														
All ages	27.4	44.2	21.2	22.1	22.1	25.6	19.2	17.8	22.0	21.6	77.4	53.8	78.6	48.0
Under 5 years	18.1	42.2	14.2	17.2	14.7	20.8	12.4	13.2	15.4	16.5	71.5	54.7	79.5	41.3
5 to 14 years	18.9	40.9	15.2	17.9	15.7	21.1	13.4	14.1	16.3	17.5	69.8	52.1	76.8	41.8
15 to 24 years	27.7	45.7	22.2	23.0	23.4	26.7	19.9	18.8	22.9	22.3	76.7	55.6	77.2	49.4
25 to 44 years	37.4	48.2	28.7	27.2	30.2	30.7	26.1	22.5	29.0	27.0	83.2	56.7	79.9	53.0
45 to 64 years	31.7	43.1	24.3	24.1	25.9	27.3	22.4	19.6	23.7	24.1	76.5	50.3	78.3	49.6
65 years and over	26.3	36.9	20.5	20.5	20.6	23.4	19.4	15.1	22.0	22.1	65.7	42.3	71.9	47.4
Age unknown	43.7	62.0	36.9	42.6	42.1	43.2	31.6	33.1	34.4	48.2	82.4	69.2	86.5	63.7
MALE.														
All ages	26.2	43.0	20.0	21.4	20.7	24.8	18.1	17.2	20.8	21.1	75.8	52.6	74.7	46.2
Under 5 years	18.0	42.0	14.1	17.1	14.6	20.3	12.3	13.1	15.3	16.4	71.2	54.6	78.9	41.3
5 to 14 years	18.3	40.4	14.7	17.5	15.2	20.7	12.9	13.7	15.9	17.2	68.8	51.6	76.0	41.2
15 to 24 years	25.6	44.2	20.3	22.1	21.2	25.8	18.3	18.0	21.0	21.2	73.6	54.0	70.0	46.9
25 to 44 years	36.6	47.0	27.5	26.7	28.8	30.0	25.2	22.1	28.0	26.7	81.9	55.4	75.8	51.0
45 to 64 years	29.3	40.8	21.9	22.5	23.3	25.5	20.3	18.3	21.4	22.6	74.6	48.2	74.8	46.0
65 years and over	22.9	33.6	17.5	18.3	17.3	21.1	16.6	13.2	19.1	20.0	60.7	38.7	66.9	41.8
Age unknown	43.5	63.0	36.2	44.9	41.2	41.7	30.8	36.4	34.1	51.9	81.8	69.8	85.1	62.2
FEMALE.														
All ages	28.5	45.4	22.4	22.8	23.5	26.4	20.3	18.4	23.1	22.2	79.0	55.0	83.3	50.0
Under 5 years	18.3	42.4	14.3	17.3	14.7	20.9	12.5	13.3	15.5	16.6	71.8	54.9	80.1	41.3
5 to 14 years	19.6	41.4	15.7	18.3	16.3	21.5	13.9	14.4	16.8	17.8	70.9	52.6	77.7	42.4
15 to 24 years	29.5	47.3	24.0	23.9	25.3	27.6	21.3	19.5	24.6	23.4	79.5	57.3	84.5	52.2
25 to 44 years	38.1	49.4	29.8	27.7	31.5	31.4	27.0	22.9	30.1	27.4	84.5	57.9	85.4	55.5
45 to 64 years	34.5	45.5	27.2	25.9	28.9	29.2	24.9	21.1	26.6	26.0	78.7	52.5	83.4	54.5
65 years and over	30.0	40.2	23.9	22.7	24.3	25.6	22.4	17.1	25.1	24.4	70.9	45.8	78.1	54.8
Age unknown	44.0	59.9	37.6	38.4	43.0	45.4	32.5	28.4	34.9	39.3	83.3	67.9	88.5	68.5

In the South the percentage urban among Negroes ranges from 14.2 in the population under 5 years of age to 28.7 in the population 25 to 44 years, the corresponding figures for the native whites being in the population under 5 years, 17.2 per cent, and in the population 25 to 44 years, 27.2 per cent. In the North and West the percentage urban is exceedingly high at all ages among Negroes, ranging in the North from 65.7 per cent in the population 65 years and over to 83.2 per cent, or approximately five-sixths in the population 25 to 44 years; and in the West, from 71.9 per cent in the population 65 years and over to 79.9 in the population 25 to 44 years. At every age the Negro population is predominantly rural in the South and predominantly urban in the North and West. This is true of both males and females.

The excess of males or females in the urban and rural Negro population, classified by age, is shown in Table 27 for the South, the North, and the West.

Table 27 — NEGRO POPULATION: 1910.

AGE.	Excess of males or females.				Males to 1,000 females.	
	Urban population.		Rural population.		Urban population.	Rural population.
	Males.	Females.	Males.	Females.		
UNITED STATES.						
All ages		130,261	74,260		908	1,021
Under 5 years		2,764		1,884	976	996
5 to 14 years		16,777	9,456		929	1,010
15 to 24 years		71,821		39,186	779	949
25 to 44 years		30,156	174		941	1,000
45 to 64 years		2,535	85,540		986	1,255
65 years and over		7,489	18,329		824	1,185
Age unknown	1,281		1,831		1,209	1,234
THE SOUTH.						
All ages		122,563	52,386		876	1,015
Under 5 years		1,527		1,804	982	996
5 to 14 years		12,164	8,979		931	1,009
15 to 24 years		56,870		43,123	760	943
25 to 44 years		39,294		9,185	884	988
45 to 64 years		7,307	79,700		939	1,249
65 years and over		6,081	16,157		793	1,172
Age unknown	680		1,662		1,150	1,221
THE NORTH.						
All ages		9,284	18,698		977	1,175
Under 5 years		1,112		71	964	994
5 to 14 years		4,436	461		922	1,020
15 to 24 years		14,448	3,257		828	1,150
25 to 44 years	7,657		7,671		1,047	1,258
45 to 64 years	3,934		5,176		1,072	1,350
65 years and over		1,434	2,049		886	1,399
Age unknown	555		155		1,375	1,522
THE WEST.						
All ages	1,586		3,176		1,083	1,827
Under 5 years		125		9	907	973
5 to 14 years		177	16		928	1,023
15 to 24 years		503	680		863	2,012
25 to 44 years	1,481		1,688		1,180	2,197
45 to 64 years	838		664		1,301	2,199
65 years and over	26		123		1,051	1,860
Age unknown	46		14		1,351	1,824

At each age in each geographic section the proportion of males was higher in the rural than it was in the urban population. In the adult rural Negro population of the West males outnumbered females by more than 2 to 1—the number of males per 1,000 females being 2,012 for the age 15 to 24 years, 2,197 for the age 25 to 44 years, and 2,199 for the age 45 to 64. For the southern rural Negro population the highest ratio is that of 1,249 males to 1,000 females in the age 45 to 64 years.

In the adult Negro population, both urban and rural, the proportion of males was generally higher in the North and West than it was in the South.

Females outnumbered males in 1910 in all ages in the urban Negro population of the South, the greatest disparity between the sexes being for the age period 15 to 24 years. In this age period the excess of females over males amounted to 56,870, the sex ratio being 760 males to 1,000 females. In the urban Negro population of the North and West females were in excess in the ages under 25 years and males in the ages 25 to 65 years.

The sex ratios of Table 27, for the Negro urban and rural population as a whole, indicate that the migration cityward of females generally exceeds that of males, since at all ages the proportion of males is relatively lower in the urban than in the rural population. Differences between the mortality rates of males and females living in urban and in rural communities may, however, affect the ratios for certain ages.

As regards any given section of the country, obviously the sex ratios of the urban and rural population in the adult ages may be entirely independent of one another. The high proportion of males in the rural population of the West, for example, does not imply a low proportion in urban communities of this or of any other section, since the ratios may be largely determined by migration from urban or rural communities of other sections. In the country as a whole, however, differences in the sex ratios between urban and rural communities must originate principally in the net drift of the population into urban communities.

The percentage Negro in the urban and rural population, classified by age, is shown by sections in Table 28.

At each age Negroes constituted in 1910 a larger proportion of the aggregate rural population of the country than they did of the aggregate urban, the percentage Negro ranging in the rural population from 9.6 to 17, and in the urban from 4.6 to 7. This higher proportion in the rural is explained by the fact that since the Negro population is largely resident in the South, which is predominantly rural, the proportion rural in the Negro population as a whole exceeds the proportion rural in the white population as a whole.

No such marked difference between the urban and the rural percentage Negro is observable in the figures for the several sections as appears in the aggregate for the country as a whole. In the North and West the percentage Negro is, in fact, higher in the urban population, and in the South it is not very materially higher in the rural than it is in the urban population

Table 28	POPULATION: 1910.					
AGE PERIOD.	All classes.		Negro.		Percentage Negro.	
	Urban.	Rural.	Urban.	Rural.	Urban.	Rural.
UNITED STATES.						
All ages........	42,623,383	49,348,883	2,689,229	7,138,534	6.3	14.5
Under 5 years........	4,200,291	6,431,073	229,080	1,034,208	5.5	16.1
5 to 14 years..........	7,401,325	11,466,447	454,219	1,947,600	6.1	17.0
15 to 24 years..........	8,573,829	9,546,758	578,299	1,512,912	6.7	15.8
25 to 44 years..........	14,168,853	12,641,022	985,374	1,652,804	7.0	13.1
45 to 64 years..........	6,487,864	6,936,225	351,259	756,844	5.4	10.9
65 years and over.....	1,693,010	2,256,514	77,435	216,689	4.6	9.6
Age unknown........	98,211	70,844	13,563	17,477	13.8	24.7
THE SOUTH.						
All ages........	6,623,838	22,765,492	1,854,455	6,894,972	28.0	30.3
Under 5 years........	661,338	3,392,010	166,646	1,009,690	25.2	29.8
5 to 14 years..........	1,225,980	5,906,487	339,746	1,898,791	27.7	32.1
15 to 24 years..........	1,397,110	4,617,985	418,046	1,464,273	29.9	31.7
25 to 44 years..........	2,163,672	5,396,066	636,026	1,581,247	29.4	29.3
45 to 64 years..........	924,033	2,666,552	231,511	720,342	25.1	27.0
65 years and over.....	229,992	753,402	52,745	203,949	22.9	27.1
Age unknown........	21,713	32,990	9,740	16,680	44.9	50.2
THE NORTH.						
All ages........	32,669,705	23,087,410	794,966	232,708	2.4	1.0
Under 5 years........	3,266,003	2,643,583	59,872	23,857	1.8	0.9
5 to 14 years..........	5,688,427	4,878,488	109,720	47,377	1.9	1.0
15 to 24 years..........	6,540,902	4,276,002	153,434	46,615	2.3	1.1
25 to 44 years..........	10,768,387	6,154,682	331,435	67,049	3.1	1.1
45 to 64 years..........	5,014,060	3,741,017	113,348	34,730	2.3	0.9
65 years and over.....	1,331,670	1,365,954	23,642	12,331	1.8	0.9
Age unknown........	60,256	27,684	3,515	749	5.8	2.7
THE WEST.						
All ages........	3,329,840	3,495,981	39,808	10,854	1.2	0.3
Under 5 years........	272,950	395,480	2,567	661	0.9	0.2
5 to 14 years..........	486,918	681,472	4,753	1,432	1.0	0.2
15 to 24 years..........	635,817	652,771	6,819	2,024	1.1	0.3
25 to 44 years..........	1,236,794	1,090,274	17,913	4,508	1.4	0.4
45 to 64 years..........	549,771	528,656	6,400	1,772	1.2	0.3
65 years and over.....	131,348	137,158	1,048	409	0.8	0.3
Age unknown........	16,242	10,170	308	48	1.9	0.5

Obviously the percentage Negro in the population at different ages in urban and rural communities is affected by migratory shiftings of the white, as well as of the Negro population.

In the South the proportion Negro in the population 25 to 44 years of age was practically the same in the urban as in the rural population—29.4 per cent in the urban and 29.3 per cent in the rural. In the younger, and in the more advanced ages the proportion Negro was higher in the rural population than it was in the urban. The highest proportion Negro is that of 32.1 per cent, for the rural population 5 to 14 years of age in the South. The highest proportions in the urban population are for the age 15 to 24 years 29.9 per cent, and 25 to 44 years, 29.4 per cent.

In the North and West at all ages the proportion Negro was higher in the urban than in the rural population, the maximum percentage being that of 3.1 for the age period 25 to 44 years in the North.

POPULATION OF CLASSES OF CITIES CLASSIFIED BY AGE.

In Table 29 the age distribution of the urban Negro population is shown for classes of cities. The proportions under 5, 5 to 14, and 15 to 24 years of age in 1910 were smallest in the aggregate for the 8 cities of 500,000 inhabitants or more, increased from class to class in the aggregates for the 42 cities of 100,000 to 500,000, for the 179 cities of 25,000 to 100,000 and for the 2,173 cities of 2,500 to 25,000 inhabitants. The proportion in the age group 25 to 44 years was largest in the aggregate for cities of 500,000 or more and decreased from class to class. For cities of 500,000 or more the proportion under 5 years of age was 7.3 per cent, and the proportion 25 to 44 years, 45 per cent, the corresponding proportions for cities of 2,500 to 25,000 being 9.7 and 31.6 per cent.

Similar variations in age composition from one urban class to another are observable in the statistics for the South separately, and for the North, the variations shown for the relatively small urban Negro population of the West being less regular.

Conditions obtaining in small urban communities undoubtedly approach nearly to conditions obtaining in rural towns and villages, but the aggregate rural, including the scattered population of country districts, develops considerable differences in comparison with the class of small cities.

In Table 30 statistics of age composition are given for the Negro population living in cities of less than 25,000 inhabitants and in rural districts, in cities of 25,000 to 100,000, and in cities of 100,000 and over. For these three classes data are available for 1900, and a comparison of 1910 with 1900 is made in Table 30. For each of these classes in the country as a whole, and in the South and the North, the proportion under 5, 5 to 14, and 15 to 24 years of age was smaller in 1910 than in 1900, and for each class the proportion 25 to 44 years was larger.

CLASSIFICATION BY AGE PERIODS OF THE NEGRO POPULATION LIVING IN URBAN AND RURAL COMMUNITIES, AND IN CLASSES OF CITIES, BY SECTIONS: 1910.

Table 29	NEGRO POPULATION: 1910.												
	Number.							Percentage distribution by age periods.					
			Urban.							Urban.			
AGE PERIOD.	Total.	Rural.	Total.	Cities of 2,500 to 25,000.	Cities of 25,000 to 100,000.	Cities of 100,000 to 500,000.	Cities of 500,000 and over.	Total.	Rural.	Total.	Cities of 2,500 to 25,000.	Cities of 25,000 to 100,000.	Cities of 100,000 to 500,000.	Cities of 500,000 and over.
UNITED STATES.													
All ages............	9,827,763	7,138,534	2,689,229	1,063,628	602,040	626,946	396,615	100.0	100.0	100.0	100.0	100.0	100.0	100.0
Under 5 years.........	1,263,288	1,034,208	229,080	103,345	48,799	47,911	29,025	12.9	14.5	8.5	9.7	8.1	7.6	7.3
5 to 14 years.........	2,401,819	1,947,600	454,219	211,911	98,821	94,262	49,225	24.4	27.3	16.9	19.9	16.4	15.0	12.4
15 to 24 years........	2,091,211	1,512,912	578,299	234,989	132,615	134,308	76,387	21.3	21.2	21.5	22.1	22.0	21.4	19.3
25 to 44 years........	2,638,178	1,652,804	985,374	336,336	226,249	244,432	178,357	26.8	23.2	36.6	31.6	37.6	39.0	45.0
45 to 64 years........	1,108,103	756,844	351,259	135,595	76,425	85,984	53,255	11.3	10.6	13.1	12.7	12.7	13.7	13.4
65 years and over.....	294,124	216,689	77,435	35,272	15,705	17,478	8,980	3.0	3.0	2.9	3.3	2.6	2.8	2.3
Age unknown...........	31,040	17,477	13,563	6,180	3,426	2,571	1,386	0.3	0.2	0.5	0.6	0.6	0.4	0.3
THE SOUTH.													
All ages............	8,749,427	6,894,972	1,854,455	850,721	454,851	464,134	84,749	100.0	100.0	100.0	100.0	100.0	100.0	100.0
Under 5 years.........	1,176,331	1,009,690	166,641	85,701	37,251	37,061	6,628	13.4	14.6	9.0	10.1	8.2	8.0	7.8
5 to 14 years.........	2,238,537	1,898,791	339,746	176,001	76,954	74,224	12,567	25.6	27.5	18.3	20.7	16.9	16.0	14.8
15 to 24 years........	1,882,319	1,464,273	418,046	192,328	104,239	103,659	17,820	21.5	21.2	22.5	22.6	22.9	22.3	21.0
25 to 44 years........	2,217,273	1,581,247	636,026	262,907	168,028	172,861	32,230	25.3	22.9	34.3	30.9	36.9	37.2	38.0
45 to 64 years........	951,853	720,342	231,511	102,727	54,499	61,447	12,838	10.9	10.4	12.5	12.1	12.0	13.2	15.1
65 years and over.....	256,694	203,949	52,745	26,071	10,968	13,254	2,452	2.9	3.0	2.8	3.1	2.4	2.9	2.9
Age unknown...........	26,420	16,680	9,740	4,986	2,912	1,628	214	0.3	0.2	0.5	0.6	0.6	0.4	0.3
THE NORTH.													
All ages............	1,027,674	232,708	794,966	201,704	140,370	141,026	311,866	100.0	100.0	100.0	100.0	100.0	100.0	100.0
Under 5 years.........	83,729	23,857	59,872	16,853	11,139	9,483	22,397	8.1	10.3	7.5	8.4	7.9	6.7	7.2
5 to 14 years.........	157,097	47,377	109,720	34,447	21,004	17,611	36,658	15.3	20.4	13.8	17.1	15.0	12.5	11.8
15 to 24 years........	200,049	46,615	153,434	40,722	27,292	26,853	58,567	19.5	20.0	19.3	20.2	19.4	19.0	18.8
25 to 44 years........	398,484	67,049	331,435	85,169	55,169	61,530	146,127	38.8	28.8	41.7	34.0	39.3	43.6	46.9
45 to 64 years........	148,078	34,730	113,348	31,092	20,774	21,065	40,417	14.4	14.9	14.3	15.4	14.8	14.9	13.0
65 years and over.....	35,973	12,331	23,642	8,871	4,568	3,675	6,528	3.5	5.3	3.0	4.4	3.3	2.6	2.1
Age unknown...........	4,264	749	3,515	1,110	424	809	1,172	0.4	0.3	0.4	0.6	0.3	0.6	0.4
THE WEST.													
All ages............	50,662	10,854	39,808	11,203	6,819	21,786	....	100.0	100.0	100.0	100.0	100.0	100.0	....
Under 5 years.........	3,228	661	2,567	791	409	1,367	....	6.4	6.1	6.4	7.1	6.0	6.3	....
5 to 14 years.........	6,185	1,432	4,753	1,463	863	2,427	....	12.2	13.2	11.9	13.1	12.7	11.1	....
15 to 24 years........	8,843	2,024	6,819	1,939	1,084	3,796	....	17.5	18.6	17.1	17.3	15.9	17.4	....
25 to 44 years........	22,421	4,508	17,913	4,820	3,052	10,041	....	44.3	41.5	45.0	43.0	44.8	46.1	....
45 to 64 years........	8,172	1,772	6,400	1,776	1,152	3,472	....	16.1	16.3	16.1	15.9	16.9	15.9	....
65 years and over.....	1,457	409	1,048	330	169	549	....	2.9	3.8	2.6	2.9	2.5	2.5	....
Age unknown...........	356	48	308	84	90	134	....	0.7	0.4	0.8	0.7	1.3	0.6	....

NEGRO POPULATION LIVING IN CLASSES OF COMMUNITIES, CLASSIFIED BY BROAD AGE PERIODS, BYSECTIONS: 1910 AND 1900.

Table 30	NEGRO POPULATION.															
	Number.								Percentage distribution by age.							
AGE.	Total.		In cities under 25,000 and rural districts.		In cities of 25,000–100,000.		In cities of 100,000 and over.		Total.		In cities under 25,000 and rural districts.		In cities of 25,000–100,000.		In cities of 100,000 and over.	
	1910	1900	1910	1900	1910	1900	1910	1900	1910	1900	1910	1900	1910	1900	1910	1900
UNITED STATES.																
All ages	9,827,763	8,833,994	8,202,162	7,697,295	602,040	468,445	1,023,561	668,254	100.0	100.0	100.0	100.0	100.0	100.0	100.0	100.0
Under 5 years	1,263,288	1,215,655	1,137,553	1,121,763	48,799	40,461	76,936	53,431	12.9	13.8	13.9	14.6	8.1	8.6	7.5	8.0
5 to 14 years	2,401,819	2,294,748	2,159,511	2,102,476	98,821	86,929	143,487	105,343	24.4	26.0	26.3	27.3	16.4	18.6	14.0	15.8
15 to 24 years	2,091,211	1,951,194	1,747,901	1,693,417	132,615	108,376	210,695	149,401	21.3	22.1	21.3	22.0	22.0	23.1	20.6	22.4
25 to 44 years	2,638,178	2,103,989	1,989,140	1,691,967	226,249	158,681	422,789	253,341	26.8	23.8	24.3	22.0	37.6	33.9	41.3	37.9
45 to 64 years	1,108,103	958,234	892,439	812,926	76,425	58,363	139,239	86,945	11.3	10.8	10.9	10.6	12.7	12.5	13.6	13.0
65 years and over	294,124	261,363	251,961	233,137	15,705	11,471	26,458	16,755	3.0	3.0	3.1	3.0	2.6	2.4	2.6	2.5
Age unknown	31,040	48,811	23,657	41,609	3,426	4,164	3,957	3,038	0.3	0.6	0.3	0.5	0.6	0.9	0.4	0.5
THE SOUTH.																
All ages	8,749,427	7,922,969	7,745,693	7,224,092	454,851	366,154	548,883	332,723	100.0	100.0	100.0	100.0	100.0	100.0	100.0	100.0
Under 5 years	1,176,331	1,135,793	1,095,391	1,075,286	37,251	32,025	43,689	28,482	13.4	14.3	14.1	14.9	8.2	8.7	8.0	8.6
5 to 14 years	2,238,537	2,134,415	2,074,792	2,004,337	76,954	70,234	86,791	59,844	25.6	26.9	26.8	27.7	16.9	19.2	15.8	18.0
15 to 24 years	1,882,319	1,749,854	1,656,601	1,588,118	104,239	86,333	121,479	75,403	21.5	22.1	21.4	22.0	22.9	23.6	22.1	22.7
25 to 44 years	2,217,273	1,792,083	1,844,154	1,557,501	168,028	121,519	205,091	113,063	25.3	22.6	23.8	21.6	36.9	33.2	37.4	34.0
45 to 64 years	951,853	837,141	823,069	747,659	54,499	44,256	74,285	45,226	10.9	10.6	10.6	10.3	12.0	12.1	13.5	13.6
65 years and over	256,694	232,217	230,020	213,939	10,968	8,711	15,706	9,567	2.9	2.9	3.0	3.0	2.4	2.4	2.9	2.9
Age unknown	26,420	41,466	21,666	37,252	2,912	3,076	1,842	1,138	0.3	0.5	0.3	0.5	0.6	0.8	0.3	0.3
THE NORTH.																
All ages	1,027,674	880,771	434,412	455,688	140,370	97,260	452,892	327,823	100.0	100.0	100.0	100.0	100.0	100.0	100.0	100.0
Under 5 years	83,729	77,794	40,710	45,244	11,139	8,141	31,880	24,409	8.1	8.8	9.4	9.9	7.9	8.4	7.0	7.4
5 to 14 years	157,097	155,830	81,824	95,529	21,004	16,008	54,269	44,293	15.3	17.7	18.8	21.0	15.0	16.5	12.0	13.5
15 to 24 years	200,049	195,499	87,337	101,671	27,292	21,172	85,420	72,656	19.5	22.2	20.1	22.3	19.4	21.8	18.9	22.2
25 to 44 years	398,484	299,651	135,658	127,632	55,169	34,849	207,657	137,170	38.8	34.0	31.2	28.0	39.3	35.8	45.9	41.8
45 to 64 years	148,078	116,765	65,822	62,797	20,774	13,427	61,482	40,541	14.4	13.3	15.2	13.8	14.8	13.8	13.6	12.4
65 years and over	35,973	28,311	21,202	18,679	4,568	2,650	10,203	6,982	3.5	3.2	4.9	4.1	3.3	2.7	2.3	2.1
Age unknown	4,264	6,921	1,859	4,136	424	1,013	1,981	1,772	0.4	0.8	0.4	0.9	0.3	1.0	0.4	0.5
THE WEST.																
All ages	50,662	30,254	22,057	17,515	6,819	5,031	21,786	7,708	100.0	100.0	100.0	100.0	100.0	100.0	100.0	100.0
Under 5 years	3,228	2,068	1,452	1,233	409	295	1,367	540	6.4	6.8	6.6	7.1	6.0	5.9	6.3	7.0
5 to 14 years	6,185	4,503	2,895	2,610	863	687	2,427	1,206	12.2	14.9	13.1	14.9	12.7	13.7	11.1	15.6
15 to 24 years	8,843	5,841	3,963	3,628	1,084	871	3,796	1,342	17.5	19.3	18.0	20.7	15.9	17.3	17.4	17.4
25 to 44 years	22,421	12,255	9,328	6,834	3,052	2,313	10,041	3,108	44.3	40.5	42.3	39.0	44.8	46.0	46.1	40.3
45 to 64 years	8,172	4,328	3,548	2,470	1,152	680	3,472	1,178	16.1	14.3	16.1	14.1	16.9	13.5	15.9	15.3
65 years and over	1,457	835	739	519	169	110	549	206	2.9	2.8	3.4	3.0	2.5	2.2	2.5	2.7
Age unknown	356	424	132	221	90	75	134	128	0.7	1.4	0.6	1.3	1.3	1.5	0.6	1.7

POPULATION OF INDIVIDUAL CITIES CLASSIFIED BY AGE.

Statistics for individual cities are given in Tables 43, 44, and 45 (pp. 201 to 206). Table 43 gives the number of Negro males and females classified by quinquennial age periods for the 50 cities having a total population—white and colored—of 100,000 or more in 1910; Table 44, in less detail by age, statistics for the 68 cities of 25,000 to 100,000, having in 1910 a Negro population of 1,000 or more; and Table 45 by still broader age periods, statistics for the 88 cities of 10,000 to 25,000, having in 1910 a Negro population of 1,000 or more.

Among these cities Washington, D. C., reported in 1910 the largest Negro population (94,446), New York City the second largest (91,709), and New Orleans the third largest (89,262). The Negro populations of New York City and New Orleans were approximately equal, and a comparison of the age distributions of the Negro populations of these two cities, one a typical northern and one a typical southern city, is made in Table 31.

While the age distributions of the Negro population in these two cities are similar, the deficiency of children under 5, and the concentration in the ages 25 to 44 years are more considerable in New York City, among both males and females. The percentage increases of the several age groups during the decade, 1900–1910, show a wide range of variation. In New Orleans although the number of children under 5 increased 6.1 per cent, the number 5 to 14 decreased 2 per cent. For the age group 15 to 24, the increase was 16.7 per cent; for the age group 25 to 44, 30 per cent, and in the succeeding age groups 7.6 and 9.6 per cent. For each age period the percentage increase was much higher in New York City, in which the Negro population under 5 years increased 46.2 per cent; 5 to

14 years, 34.1 per cent; 15 to 24 years, 28.2 per cent; 25 to 44 years, 72.3 per cent, and in succeeding age groups 42.9 and 47.9 per cent. In view of the low rate of increase of children under 5 in New Orleans (6.1 per cent) the relatively high rate (20 per cent) shown for children under 1 seems improbable, and may indicate inaccuracies or omissions in the returns of infants at the census of 1900.

In general the individual cities for which age statistics are given in Tables 43, 44, and 45, show the characteristics as regards age composition that have been noted in the urban population, and in classes of urban communities.

Table 31 — NEGRO POPULATION.

AGE.	Both sexes.		Male.		Female.	
	New Orleans.	New York City.	New Orleans.	New York City.	New Orleans.	New York City.
NUMBER: 1910.						
All ages............	89,262	91,709	40,946	42,143	48,316	49,566
Under 5 years............	7,624	6,676	3,736	3,227	3,888	3,449
Under 1 year..........	1,612	1,594	802	814	810	780
5 to 14 years............	15,554	9,972	7,518	4,647	8,036	5,325
15 to 24 years............	18,949	18,644	7,947	7,770	11,002	10,874
25 to 44 years............	32,396	44,014	15,043	20,993	17,353	23,021
45 to 64 years............	11,445	10,441	5,336	4,732	6,109	5,709
65 years and over..........	3,036	1,690	1,207	643	1,829	1,047
Age unknown............	258	272	159	131	99	141
PERCENTAGE DISTRIBUTION: 1910.						
All ages............	100.0	100.0	100.0	100.0	100.0	100.0
Under 5 years............	8.5	7.3	9.1	7.7	8.0	7.0
Under 1 year..........	1.8	1.7	2.0	1.9	1.7	1.6
5 to 14 years............	17.4	10.8	18.4	11.0	16.6	10.7
15 to 24 years............	21.2	20.3	19.4	18.4	22.8	21.9
25 to 44 years............	36.3	48.0	36.7	49.8	35.9	46.4
45 to 64 years............	12.8	11.4	13.0	11.2	12.6	11.5
65 years and over..........	3.4	1.8	2.9	1.5	3.8	2.1
Age unknown............	0.3	0.3	0.4	0.3	0.3	0.3
INCREASE: 1900-1910.						
All ages............	11,548	31,043	5,817	15,011	5,731	16,032
Under 5 years............	440	2,110	127	1,060	313	1,050
Under 1 year..........	269	482	126	287	143	195
5 to 14 years............	−315	2,536	−207	1,083	−108	1,453
15 to 24 years............	2,708	4,105	1,184	2,003	1,524	2,102
25 to 44 years............	7,472	18,462	3,817	9,131	3,655	9,331
45 to 64 years............	807	3,135	642	1,413	165	1,722
65 years and over..........	266	547	136	231	130	316
Age unknown............	170	148	118	90	52	58
INCREASE, PER CENT: 1900-1910.						
All ages............	14.9	51.2	16.6	55.3	13.5	47.8
Under 5 years............	6.1	46.2	3.5	48.9	8.8	43.8
Under 1 year..........	20.0	43.3	18.6	54.5	21.4	33.3
5 to 14 years............	−2.0	34.1	−2.7	30.4	−1.3	37.5
15 to 24 years............	16.7	28.2	17.5	34.7	16.1	24.0
25 to 44 years............	30.0	72.3	34.0	77.0	26.7	68.2
45 to 64 years............	7.6	42.9	13.7	42.6	2.8	43.2
65 years and over..........	9.6	47.9	12.7	56.1	7.7	43.2
Age unknown............	193.2	119.4	287.8	219.5	110.6	69.9

POPULATION 21 YEARS OF AGE AND OVER.

The number and the percentage 21 years of age and over in 1910 are given in Table 32 for the Negro population and for classes of the white population. Details for divisions and states, and for urban and rural communities are given in Table 42 (p. 200).

Table 32 — POPULATION 21 YEARS OF AGE AND OVER: 1910.

SECTION AND DIVISION.	All classes.	Negro.	White.		
			Total.	Native.	Foreign born.
BOTH SEXES.					
Number.					
United States........	51,554,905	4,886,615	46,416,750	34,762,825	11,653,925
The South.............	14,460,922	4,169,706	10,252,168	9,632,384	619,784
South Atlantic........	6,078,546	1,924,939	4,148,137	3,897,115	251,022
East South Central.....	4,133,250	1,288,157	2,843,624	2,764,389	79,235
West South Central.....	4,249,126	956,610	3,260,407	2,970,880	289,527
The North.............	32,829,374	680,126	32,096,512	22,231,809	9,864,703
The West.............	4,264,609	36,783	4,068,070	2,898,632	1,169,438
Percentage of all ages.					
United States........	56.1	49.7	56.8	50.8	87.3
The South.............	49.2	47.7	49.9	48.6	85.3
South Atlantic........	49.8	46.8	51.4	50.1	86.4
East South Central.....	49.1	48.6	49.4	48.8	91.2
West South Central.....	48.4	48.2	48.5	46.6	83.0
The North.............	58.9	66.2	58.7	51.3	87.1
The West.............	62.5	72.6	62.2	55.3	90.1
MALE.					
Number.					
United States........	26,999,151	2,458,873	24,357,514	17,710,697	6,646,817
The South.............	7,428,980	2,086,639	5,320,964	4,952,051	368,913
South Atlantic........	3,071,428	955,364	2,112,547	1,961,882	150,665
East South Central.....	2,096,186	642,460	1,452,776	1,406,468	46,308
West South Central.....	2,261,366	488,815	1,755,641	1,583,701	171,940
The North.............	17,037,734	351,213	16,650,920	11,139,051	5,511,869
The West.............	2,532,437	21,021	2,385,630	1,619,595	766,035
Percentage of all ages.					
United States........	57.0	50.3	57.7	51.1	88.3
The South.............	49.8	48.1	50.5	49.0	86.6
South Atlantic........	50.1	47.1	51.5	50.0	87.2
East South Central.....	49.4	48.8	49.6	48.9	91.6
West South Central.....	49.8	49.2	50.0	47.9	84.8
The North.............	59.6	67.7	59.5	51.2	88.1
The West.............	65.9	75.9	65.3	57.7	91.0
FEMALE.					
Number.					
United States........	24,555,754	2,427,742	22,059,236	17,052,128	5,007,108
The South.............	7,031,942	2,083,067	4,931,204	4,680,333	250,871
South Atlantic........	3,007,118	969,575	2,035,590	1,935,233	100,357
East South Central.....	2,037,064	645,697	1,390,848	1,357,921	32,927
West South Central.....	1,987,760	467,795	1,504,766	1,387,179	117,587
The North.............	15,791,640	328,913	15,445,592	11,092,758	4,352,834
The West.............	1,732,172	15,762	1,682,440	1,279,037	403,403
Percentage of all ages.					
United States........	55.0	49.1	55.8	50.6	86.0
The South.............	48.6	47.2	49.3	48.2	83.6
South Atlantic........	49.6	46.6	51.2	50.2	85.3
East South Central.....	48.9	48.3	49.2	48.7	90.7
West South Central.....	46.9	47.2	46.9	45.3	80.5
The North.............	58.1	64.6	58.0	51.4	85.9
The West.............	58.1	68.7	58.1	52.5	88.4

The Negro population 21 years of age and over in 1910 numbered 4,886,615, or 49.7 per cent of the total Negro population. For this class of the population, as for native whites, the age 21 years is very close to the median age, which divides the class into two equal groups—the median age being for the Negroes 20.8 years, and for the native whites 21.4 years. The proportion 21 and over in the aggregate white population—56.8 per cent in 1910—is raised above the proportion for the native whites by the high proportion (87.3 per cent) among the foreign-born whites.

In the North and West, the proportion 21 and over in the Negro population is very much higher than it is in the South, the proportion being, in 1910, 47.7 per cent in the South, 66.2 per cent in the North, and 72.6 per cent in the West. In each section and southern division the proportion is higher for males than for females.

The number of males per 1,000 females in the Negro and white population 21 years of age and over is shown in Table 33 for sections and southern divisions.

Table 33	MALES TO 1,000 FEMALES IN THE POPULATION 21 YEARS AND OVER: 1910.				
SECTION AND DIVISION.	All classes.	Negro.	Whites.		
			Total.	Native.	Foreign born.
United States...........	1,100	1,013	1,104	1,039	1,327
The South..................	1,056	1,002	1,079	1,058	1,471
South Atlantic.............	1,021	985	1,038	1,014	1,501
East South Central......	1,029	995	1,045	1,036	1,406
West South Central.......	1,138	1,045	1,167	1,142	1,462
The North..................	1,079	1,068	1,078	1,004	1,266
The West..................	1,462	1,334	1,418	1,266	1,899

In the population 21 and over, the number of males exceeds the number of females among Negroes and among native and foreign-born whites, but the excess is greater among native whites than it is among Negroes and very much greater among foreign-born whites than it is among native whites or Negroes.

In the South as a whole, however, the excess of males in the Negro population 21 and over is very slight, the number of males to 1,000 females in 1910 being for this section 1,002. In two southern divisions there was, in fact, excess of females, the number of males to 1,000 females being in the South At-

lantic division 985, and in the East South Central, 995. The corresponding figure for the West South Central division was 1,045; for the North as a whole, 1,068, and for the West 1,334.

The percentage Negro in the total population 21 years of age and over classified by sex is given in Table 34 for sections and southern divisions, covering the two years 1910 and 1900. Corresponding data for males is shown in Table 35 for all divisions and states.

Table 34	PERCENTAGE NEGRO IN THE POPULATION 21 YEARS OF AGE AND OVER.					
DIVISION.	Both sexes.		Male.		Female.	
	1910	1900	1910	1900	1910	1900
United States.............	9.5	10.1	9.1	9.7	9.9	10.5
The South.................	28.8	30.9	28.1	30.1	29.6	31.7
South Atlantic..........	31.7	33.2	31.1	32.7	32.2	33.7
East South Central........	31.2	32.1	30.6	31.6	31.7	32.6
West South Central.......	22.5	25.5	21.6	24.3	23.5	26.8
The North.................	2.1	2.0	2.1	2.0	2.1	2.0
The West..................	0.9	0.9	0.8	0.9	0.9	0.9

In 1910 the proportion Negro in the total population 21 and over was 9.5 per cent, or somewhat less than one-tenth. The proportion among males was 9.1 per cent, and among females 9.9 per cent. In each of the three southern divisions, it was much higher, being 22.5 per cent in the West South Central division, 31.2 per cent in the East South Central, and 31.7 per cent in the South Atlantic. While nearly one-third of the population 21 and over in the South Atlantic and East South Central divisions was Negro, the corresponding proportion for the North was only 2.9 per cent, and for the West 0.9 per cent.

PERCENTAGE NEGRO IN THE POPULATION 21 YEARS OF AGE AND OVER, BY DIVISIONS AND STATES: 1910 AND 1900.

Table 35 DIVISION AND STATE.	PERCENTAGE NEGRO AMONG MALES 21 YEARS OF AGE AND OVER.		DIVISION AND STATE.	PERCENTAGE NEGRO AMONG MALES 21 YEARS OF AGE AND OVER.		DIVISION AND STATE.	PERCENTAGE NEGRO AMONG MALES 21 YEARS OF AGE AND OVER.	
	1910	1900		1910	1900		1910	1900
UNITED STATES...............	9.1	9.7	EAST NORTH CENTRAL:			EAST SOUTH CENTRAL:		
			Ohio......................	2.6	2.6	Kentucky.....................	12.5	13.7
GEOGRAPHIC DIVISIONS:			Indiana....................	2.5	2.5	Tennessee....................	21.6	23.0
New England..............	1.1	1.1	Illinois....................	2.3	2.1	Alabama.....................	41.7	43.8
Middle Atlantic..........	2.3	2.3	Michigan...................	0.7	0.7	Mississippi..................	54.7	56.7
East North Central........	1.9	1.8	Wisconsin..................	0.2	0.2	WEST SOUTH CENTRAL:		
West North Central........	2.4	2.4	WEST NORTH CENTRAL:			Arkansas....................	28.1	27.8
South Atlantic.............	31.1	32.7	Minnesota..................	0.5	0.4	Louisiana...................	42.0	45.2
East South Central.........	30.6	31.6	Iowa.......................	0.8	0.7	Oklahoma....................	8.2	6.8
West South Central........	21.6	24.3	Missouri...................	5.4	5.4	Texas......................	16.6	18.6
Mountain..................	1.0	1.2	North Dakota...............	0.2	0.1	MOUNTAIN:		
Pacific....................	0.7	0.6	South Dakota...............	0.2	0.2	Montana....................	0.5	0.7
NEW ENGLAND:			Nebraska...................	0.9	0.8	Idaho......................	0.3	0.2
Maine.....................	0.2	0.2	Kansas.....................	3.5	3.6	Wyoming....................	2.1	1.3
New Hampshire.............	0.1	0.2	SOUTH ATLANTIC:			Colorado....................	1.6	1.7
Vermont...................	0.9	0.3	Delaware...................	14.6	15.5	New Mexico.................	0.7	1.4
Massachusetts.............	1.2	1.2	Maryland...................	17.4	18.8	Arizona....................	1.0	2.5
Rhode Island..............	1.9	2.2	District of Columbia.......	26.6	27.5	Utah.......................	0.5	0.5
Connecticut...............	1.4	1.6	Virginia...................	30.5	32.6	Nevada.....................	0.6	0.4
MIDDLE ATLANTIC:			West Virginia..............	6.7	6.0	PACIFIC:		
New York..................	1.6	1.4	North Carolina.............	29.0	30.4	Washington..................	0.7	0.6
New Jersey................	3.7	3.9	South Carolina.............	50.5	54.0	Oregon.....................	0.3	0.4
Pennsylvania..............	2.8	2.8	Georgia....................	43.0	44.5	California..................	0.9	0.7
			Florida....................	41.9	44.0			

During the decade, 1900-1910, the proportion Negro in the total population 21 and over declined from 10.1 per cent to 9.5 per cent. The decline in the

South as a whole was from 30.9 per cent in 1900 to 28.8 per cent in 1910. In each southern division and in the North, also, the proportion fell off during this decade. Among males, as shown in Table 35, the proportion declined in each Southern state, excepting West Virginia, Arkansas, and Oklahoma.

Negroes constitute a larger proportion of the rural than of the urban male population 21 and over in the country as a whole, and in each southern division, the percentage Negro in the male population of this age being 12.1 per cent in the aggregate rural, and 6.1 per cent in the aggregate urban population. (See Table 42). In the northern and western divisions the percentage Negro for this age class was higher in urban than in rural communities. In 8 Southern states it was higher in the rural than it was in the urban, and in 8 states it was higher in the urban. For the rural population in the Southern states the percentage ranged from 6.5 per cent in West Virginia to 56.5 per cent in Mississippi; and in the urban population from 7.4 in West Virginia to 43.3 per cent in Mississippi. The maximum percentage for the urban populations of states—that of 43.3 for Mississippi—is exceeded by the percentage for the rural population in South Carolina, Georgia, Mississippi, and Louisiana.

MALES OF MILITIA AGE.

Table 36 shows by sections and southern divisions the number of males 18 to 44 years of age, in the Negro and white population. Statitsics for states are given in Table 42.

Of the Negro males in 1910, 1,985,415, or 40.6 per cent of all Negro males were 18 to 44 years of age, the proportion being somewhat lower in the South and higher in the North and West. These Negro males constituted 9.7 per cent of the total male population 18 to 44 years of age. In the South the proportion Negro in the male population of militia age was 28.9 per cent, in the North 2.2 per cent, and in the West 0.9.

NEGRO AND WHITE MALES OF MILITIA AGE, BY SECTIONS AND SOUTHERN DIVISIONS: 1910.

Table 36	MALE POPULATION OF MILITIA AGE: 1910.						
RACIAL CLASS.	United States.	The South.				The North.	The West.
		Total.	South Atlantic division.	East South Central division.	West South Central division		
	NUMBER 18 TO 44 YEARS OF AGE.						
All classes...............	20,473,684	5,846,414	2,405,895	1,627,471	1,813,048	12,716,180	1,911,090
Negro....................	1,985,415	1,690,720	779,085	510,592	401,043	278,334	16,361
White...................	18,351,870	4,138,331	1,624,216	1,116,158	1,397,957	12,411,473	1,802,066
Native................	13,880,182	3,910,504	1,520,380	1,093,776	1,296,348	8,684,498	1,285,180
Foreign born..........	4,471,688	227,827	103,836	22,382	101,609	3,726,975	516,886
	PERCENTAGE 18 TO 44 YEARS OF AGE.						
All classes...............	43.3	39.2	39.2	38.3	39.9	44.5	49.7
Negro....................	40.6	39.0	38.4	38.8	40.3	53.7	59.0
White...................	43.5	39.3	39.6	38.1	39.8	44.3	49.4
Native................	40.1	38.7	38.7	38.0	39.2	40.0	45.8
Foreign born..........	59.4	53.5	60.1	44.3	50.1	59.6	61.4
	PERCENTAGE DISTRIBUTION BY RACIAL CLASS.						
All classes...............	100.0	100.0	100.0	100.0	100.0	100.0	100.0
Negro....................	9.7	28.9	32.4	31.4	22.1	2.2	0.9
White...................	89.6	70.8	67.5	68.6	77.1	97.6	94.3
Native................	67.8	66.9	63.2	67.2	71.5	68.3	67.2
Foreign born..........	21.8	3.9	4.3	1.4	5.6	29.3	27.0

TABLE **37.**—NEGRO POPULATION, CLASSIFIED BY AGE PERIODS, BY SECTIONS, SOUTHERN DIVISIONS, AND SOUTHERN STATES: 1910 AND 1900.

SECTION, DIVISION, AND STATE.	NEGRO POPULATION.												
	All ages.	Under 5 years.	5 to 9 years.	10 to 14 years.	15 to 19 years.	20 to 24 years.	25 to 29 years.	30 to 34 years.	35 to 44 years.	45 to 54 years.	55 to 64 years.	65 years and over.	Age unknown.
1910													
UNITED STATES	9,827,763	1,263,288	1,246,553	1,155,266	1,060,416	1,030,795	881,227	668,089	1,088,862	711,979	396,124	294,124	31,040
THE SOUTH	8,749,427	1,176,331	1,164,557	1,073,980	970,716	911,603	749,782	557,466	910,025	607,895	343,958	256,694	26,420
South Atlantic division	4,112,488	570,516	555,036	513,239	457,053	426,876	341,665	253,860	421,374	279,676	162,623	119,140	11,430
East South Central division	2,652,513	347,803	343,812	320,476	294,183	274,935	230,624	171,477	278,306	191,801	108,199	82,481	8,416
West South Central division	1,984,426	258,012	265,709	240,265	219,480	209,792	177,493	132,129	210,345	136,418	73,136	55,073	6,574
THE NORTH	1,027,674	83,729	78,892	78,205	86,126	113,923	124,832	104,600	169,052	98,341	49,737	35,973	4,264
THE WEST	50,662	3,228	3,104	3,081	3,574	5,269	6,613	6,023	9,785	5,743	2,429	1,457	356
South Atlantic division:													
Delaware	31,181	3,089	3,315	3,540	3,228	3,142	2,583	2,233	4,154	2,903	1,635	1,240	119
Maryland	232,250	25,987	25,809	24,595	23,398	23,591	21,023	16,570	30,097	20,822	11,264	8,575	519
District of Columbia	94,446	7,290	7,192	7,211	8,620	11,333	11,572	8,963	15,255	9,088	4,492	2,957	473
Virginia	671,096	86,555	88,123	83,395	75,047	66,503	52,324	40,358	72,406	51,730	29,863	23,521	1,271
West Virginia	64,173	6,974	6,274	5,424	6,575	8,891	8,265	5,754	8,484	4,187	1,886	1,257	202
North Carolina	697,843	107,297	100,151	89,416	80,253	69,485	52,293	38,240	61,526	46,260	29,083	21,428	2,411
South Carolina	835,843	128,712	123,067	114,341	99,118	85,305	63,247	46,194	75,811	46,216	30,280	21,817	1,735
Georgia	1,176,987	167,498	163,294	152,029	129,923	123,295	98,274	71,459	115,255	77,110	44,235	31,959	2,656
Florida	308,669	37,114	37,811	33,288	30,891	35,331	32,084	24,089	38,386	21,360	9,885	6,386	2,044
East South Central division:													
Kentucky	261,656	25,541	26,087	26,984	28,163	27,856	24,148	19,294	34,000	24,494	13,441	10,503	1,145
Tennessee	473,088	56,580	55,845	53,344	54,363	51,187	42,188	31,848	50,969	37,930	21,357	16,155	1,322
Alabama	908,282	123,991	121,935	112,129	99,130	93,670	78,334	55,845	90,450	68,415	34,834	26,770	2,779
Mississippi	1,009,487	141,691	139,945	128,019	112,527	102,222	85,954	64,490	102,887	60,962	38,567	29,053	3,170
West South Central division:													
Arkansas	442,891	57,330	58,552	52,679	50,309	46,220	39,488	29,729	46,066	34,411	16,188	10,827	1,092
Louisiana	713,874	92,439	95,985	85,917	76,868	74,119	63,677	47,489	79,455	46,232	27,581	21,886	2,226
Oklahoma	137,612	18,186	18,269	16,208	14,974	14,344	12,601	9,662	14,744	9,688	5,042	3,303	591
Texas	690,049	90,057	92,903	85,461	77,329	75,109	61,727	45,249	70,080	46,087	24,325	19,057	2,665
1900													
UNITED STATES	8,833,994	1,215,655	1,202,758	1,091,990	982,022	969,172	737,479	524,607	841,903	617,371	340,863	261,363	48,811
THE SOUTH	7,922,969	1,135,793	1,122,201	1,012,214	893,199	856,655	633,384	444,709	713,990	537,826	299,315	232,217	41,466
South Atlantic division	3,729,017	545,284	527,900	476,108	423,855	400,667	286,748	205,472	342,794	248,740	144,525	111,321	15,603
East South Central division	2,499,886	348,061	348,997	316,984	283,363	273,069	204,948	141,938	222,312	174,614	95,882	75,917	13,801
West South Central division	1,694,066	242,448	245,304	219,122	185,981	182,919	141,688	97,299	148,884	114,472	58,908	44,979	12,062
THE NORTH	880,771	77,794	78,233	77,597	86,506	108,993	100,587	76,637	122,427	76,529	40,236	28,311	6,921
THE WEST	30,254	2,068	2,324	2,179	2,317	3,524	3,508	3,261	5,486	3,016	1,312	835	424
South Atlantic division:													
Delaware	30,697	3,622	3,548	3,401	3,243	3,253	2,628	2,015	3,724	2,521	1,467	1,079	196
Maryland	235,064	28,116	27,586	26,539	25,312	25,247	20,303	14,754	27,751	18,936	10,883	7,565	2,072
District of Columbia	86,702	7,278	7,475	7,301	8,970	11,650	9,682	6,883	12,232	8,462	3,977	2,712	80
Virginia	660,722	90,332	91,469	85,609	76,424	66,278	46,714	35,730	65,997	48,530	28,158	23,126	2,355
West Virginia	43,499	4,793	4,403	4,079	5,033	6,585	5,032	3,264	4,537	2,709	1,338	961	765
North Carolina	624,469	96,945	89,833	81,296	74,751	65,656	43,776	30,364	50,150	43,661	25,476	19,576	2,985
South Carolina	782,321	125,254	119,669	106,982	93,535	82,082	54,399	39,040	64,808	44,886	28,727	21,778	1,161
Georgia	1,034,813	157,201	153,516	134,540	112,431	111,663	82,143	57,912	90,469	64,408	37,104	29,056	4,370
Florida	230,730	31,743	30,401	26,361	24,156	28,253	22,071	15,510	23,126	14,627	7,395	5,468	1,619
East South Central division:													
Kentucky	284,706	31,706	33,280	33,155	31,333	30,946	25,586	18,181	32,745	22,527	12,600	9,660	2,987
Tennessee	480,243	62,388	63,022	59,343	55,989	53,110	39,900	28,087	43,829	36,078	20,173	14,760	3,564
Alabama	827,307	119,275	118,403	105,926	93,246	90,314	66,023	45,044	66,363	62,540	30,137	25,093	4,943
Mississippi	907,630	134,692	134,292	118,560	102,795	98,699	73,439	50,626	79,375	53,469	32,972	26,404	2,307
West South Central division:													
Arkansas	366,856	51,255	51,793	46,714	41,231	40,853	30,861	20,957	31,211	27,912	12,612	8,446	3,011
Louisiana	650,804	92,759	93,447	82,803	69,091	68,705	55,719	38,039	60,427	42,971	24,600	19,898	2,345
Oklahoma	55,684	7,916	7,570	6,908	6,285	5,726	4,438	3,110	5,236	4,052	2,264	1,542	637
Texas	620,722	90,518	92,494	82,697	69,374	67,635	50,670	35,193	52,010	39,537	19,432	15,093	6,069

TABLE 38.—NEGRO MALES AND FEMALES UNDER 25 YEARS OF AGE, CLASSIFIED BY SINGLE YEARS OF AGE, BY SOUTHERN STATES: 1910.

NEGRO POPULATION: 1910.

AGE	The South. Male.	Female.	Delaware. Male.	Female.	Maryland. Male.	Female.	District of Columbia. Male.	Female.	Virginia. Male.	Female.	West Virginia. Male.	Female.	North Carolina. Male.	Female.	South Carolina. Male.	Female.	Georgia. Male.	Female.
All ages	4,339,625	4,409,802	16,011	15,170	114,749	117,501	42,615	51,831	330,542	340,554	36,607	27,566	339,581	358,262	408,078	427,765	580,263	596,724
Under 25 years	2,595,339	2,701,848	8,246	8,068	60,173	63,207	18,942	22,704	196,260	203,363	18,310	15,828	217,394	229,208	268,505	282,038	359,135	376,904
Under 1 year	116,230	117,862	325	321	2,660	2,650	732	726	8,888	9,013	740	731	11,316	11,536	12,977	12,957	16,449	16,543
1 year	101,799	101,918	255	252	2,195	2,200	638	683	7,218	7,444	636	617	9,600	9,726	11,399	11,305	14,704	14,730
2 years	121,443	120,807	318	314	2,545	2,729	730	747	8,830	8,895	699	712	10,753	10,843	13,228	13,159	17,367	17,186
3 years	121,838	124,815	296	321	2,565	2,760	758	776	8,784	9,099	764	688	10,561	10,907	12,926	13,343	17,328	17,682
4 years	125,190	124,429	324	363	2,790	2,893	723	777	9,207	9,177	695	692	11,049	11,006	13,940	13,478	17,777	17,732
5 years	118,470	120,424	336	347	2,525	2,646	735	758	8,768	8,923	621	673	10,173	10,360	12,525	12,758	16,317	16,936
6 years	121,402	124,337	322	354	2,627	2,712	723	761	8,768	8,836	625	715	10,906	11,428	13,225	13,531	17,457	17,965
7 years	117,914	117,493	313	347	2,609	2,625	734	756	9,289	9,319	617	622	9,942	9,858	12,192	12,363	16,415	16,281
8 years	117,247	119,316	323	343	2,486	2,656	658	763	8,637	9,073	610	659	9,889	10,078	12,488	12,471	16,326	16,745
9 years	103,929	104,025	313	317	2,412	2,511	644	660	8,196	8,314	542	590	8,752	8,765	10,873	10,641	14,571	14,281
10 years	114,884	111,249	363	341	2,517	2,558	713	769	8,754	8,600	564	561	9,506	9,289	12,747	12,145	16,419	15,768
11 years	90,019	90,419	321	286	2,203	2,249	629	675	7,132	7,044	503	511	7,558	7,879	9,119	8,106	12,656	12,638
12 years	123,037	121,199	394	363	2,631	2,643	711	863	9,636	9,493	577	562	10,203	10,172	13,574	13,561	17,386	17,500
13 years	102,392	103,341	364	337	2,381	2,516	646	743	7,918	7,905	519	512	8,708	8,616	10,437	10,648	14,548	14,355
14 years	108,382	109,058	429	342	2,412	2,485	685	777	8,462	8,451	578	537	8,679	8,806	11,408	11,476	15,601	15,158
15 years	94,418	97,365	344	328	2,134	2,298	658	819	7,358	7,767	523	514	7,870	8,106	9,412	9,993	13,453	13,387
16 years	98,437	108,732	337	309	2,288	2,440	712	915	7,553	8,369	603	570	8,087	8,842	10,477	11,727	13,072	15,251
17 years	91,985	94,690	311	328	2,240	2,356	735	877	7,237	7,418	659	541	7,916	7,867	8,961	9,451	10,823	13,058
18 years	99,401	112,306	344	338	2,315	2,660	791	1,162	7,636	8,209	951	636	8,263	9,187	10,624	11,646	12,647	15,436
19 years	81,506	91,876	312	277	2,183	2,484	821	1,130	6,584	6,916	985	593	6,616	7,499	7,968	8,859	10,728	12,068
20 years	83,063	111,074	317	361	2,068	2,531	818	1,245	6,094	7,445	839	663	6,482	8,256	8,423	11,763	11,405	16,087
21 years	89,285	85,636	319	237	2,272	2,028	913	1,087	6,629	6,515	1,084	633	6,806	7,221	8,341	8,106	11,990	11,301
22 years	90,244	101,718	337	324	2,443	2,626	1,006	1,326	6,836	7,537	1,102	786	6,349	8,306	7,635	9,715	12,423	13,885
23 years	81,097	94,692	296	293	2,351	2,448	997	1,478	5,969	6,887	1,141	745	5,685	7,541	6,823	8,889	10,762	12,596
24 years	81,727	93,157	333	325	2,321	2,503	1,032	1,431	5,877	6,714	1,133	765	5,725	7,114	6,783	8,827	10,511	12,335
25 years and over	1,729,905	1,695,915	7,699	7,049	54,328	54,023	23,490	28,837	133,542	136,660	18,165	11,668	120,908	127,922	138,608	144,957	219,677	218,615
Age unknown	14,381	12,039	66	53	248	271	183	290	740	531	132	70	1,279	1,132	965	770	1,451	1,205

AGE	SOUTH ATLANTIC DIVISION—continued. Florida. Male.	Female.	Kentucky. Male.	Female.	Tennessee. Male.	Female.	Alabama. Male.	Female.	Mississippi. Male.	Female.	Arkansas. Male.	Female.	Louisiana. Male.	Female.	Oklahoma. Male.	Female.	Texas. Male.	Female.
All ages	161,362	147,307	131,492	130,164	233,710	239,378	447,794	460,488	502,796	506,691	223,323	219,568	353,824	360,050	71,937	65,675	344,941	345,108
Under 25 years	86,245	88,190	66,716	67,915	133,232	138,087	269,230	281,625	307,752	316,652	129,689	135,401	207,571	217,757	40,851	41,130	207,088	213,771
Under 1 year	3,589	3,753	2,568	2,608	5,800	5,906	12,017	12,227	13,651	13,678	5,289	5,515	8,695	8,740	1,718	1,826	8,816	9,132
1 year	3,192	3,140	2,235	2,229	4,880	4,846	10,343	10,561	12,227	11,922	4,959	5,116	7,709	7,888	1,660	1,601	7,949	7,658
2 years	3,865	3,811	2,497	2,579	5,772	5,772	13,002	12,763	14,712	14,510	6,029	6,140	9,646	9,655	1,854	1,849	9,485	9,254
3 years	3,780	3,991	2,616	2,655	5,915	5,892	13,067	13,484	15,268	15,326	5,995	6,187	9,870	10,183	1,886	1,978	9,459	9,543
4 years	3,986	4,007	2,784	2,770	5,878	5,919	13,379	13,148	15,291	15,106	6,073	6,027	9,947	10,106	1,910	1,904	9,437	9,324
5 years	3,818	3,795	2,554	2,478	5,501	5,761	12,538	12,978	14,861	15,002	5,881	5,967	10,014	9,919	1,882	1,777	9,421	9,346
6 years	4,051	4,114	2,675	2,803	5,945	5,856	12,220	12,510	14,516	14,871	6,141	6,504	10,048	10,347	1,971	1,907	9,182	9,123
7 years	3,796	3,668	2,646	2,550	5,525	5,477	12,465	12,800	13,789	13,899	5,749	5,852	9,732	9,511	1,823	1,842	10,278	9,723
8 years	3,877	3,908	2,597	2,701	5,656	5,720	12,306	12,480	14,168	14,095	6,108	5,972	9,691	9,797	1,900	1,891	7,809	9,828
9 years	3,384	3,400	2,550	2,533	5,140	5,264	10,802	10,836	12,515	12,229	5,244	5,134	8,535	8,391	1,647	1,629	7,809	8,530
10 years	3,706	3,611	2,704	2,654	5,435	5,293	12,029	11,663	13,768	13,121	5,487	5,393	9,215	8,870	1,721	1,763	9,236	8,850
11 years	2,778	2,849	2,337	2,405	4,569	4,645	9,212	9,133	10,741	10,508	4,475	4,498	6,992	7,117	1,387	1,455	7,407	7,301
12 years	3,936	3,701	2,889	2,747	5,967	5,771	13,154	12,668	14,907	14,338	5,728	5,847	10,109	9,955	1,748	1,777	9,487	9,238
13 years	2,970	3,209	2,720	2,797	5,204	5,188	10,809	10,591	12,309	12,254	5,140	5,289	8,066	8,313	1,518	1,589	8,135	8,479
14 years	3,246	3,282	2,890	2,841	5,663	5,609	11,426	11,444	13,009	13,064	5,252	5,570	8,549	8,731	1,641	1,641	8,452	8,876
15 years	2,737	2,924	2,603	2,814	5,038	5,088	9,965	9,968	11,307	11,401	4,742	4,887	7,348	7,955	1,430	1,445	7,496	7,671
16 years	2,968	3,470	2,852	2,971	5,363	5,829	10,588	11,259	12,036	12,492	5,082	5,387	7,448	8,814	1,534	1,550	7,409	7,504
17 years	2,692	3,078	2,714	2,744	5,494	5,361	9,793	9,528	11,428	10,704	4,970	4,876	7,069	7,595	1,637	1,404	7,830	8,832
18 years	3,356	3,664	3,026	3,013	5,656	6,109	9,734	11,860	11,404	13,182	5,236	6,016	7,760	8,689	1,417	1,460	7,077	7,432
19 years	2,831	3,171	2,651	2,775	4,963	5,271	7,263	9,172	8,294	10,279	4,266	4,847	6,547	7,643				
20 years	3,145	3,763	2,690	3,084	5,013	6,094	7,759	11,739	8,894	12,809	4,137	5,602	6,623	9,120	1,382	1,544	6,974	8,968
21 years	3,461	3,097	2,648	2,625	4,980	5,054	8,936	8,686	9,973	9,054	4,794	4,307	7,074	6,889	1,485	1,343	7,580	7,033
22 years	3,795	3,737	2,984	2,894	4,745	5,622	9,451	10,498	10,121	11,470	4,583	4,961	7,579	8,404	1,430	1,410	6,784	7,754
23 years	3,531	3,483	2,719	2,833	4,455	5,484	8,457	9,922	9,112	10,424	4,127	4,673	6,558	7,705	1,330	1,447	6,756	7,618
24 years	3,755	3,564	2,567	2,812	4,484	5,256	8,515	9,707	9,451	10,494	4,227	4,809	6,747	7,420	1,510	1,463	6,756	7,618
25 years and over	73,774	58,416	64,185	61,695	99,795	100,652	177,131	177,517	193,390	188,523	93,049	83,660	144,996	141,324	30,743	24,297	136,425	130,100
Age unknown	1,343	701	591	554	683	639	1,433	1,346	1,654	1,516	585	507	1,257	969	343	248	1,428	1,237

TABLE 39.—NEGRO MALES AND FEMALES, CLASSIFIED BY QUINQUENNIAL AGE PERIODS, BY DIVISIONS AND STATES: 1910.

AGE PERIOD.	UNITED STATES.		NEW ENGLAND DIVISION.		MIDDLE ATLANTIC DIVISION.		EAST NORTH CENTRAL DIVISION.		WEST NORTH CENTRAL DIVISION.		SOUTH ATLANTIC DIVISION.	
	Male.	Female.	Male.	Female.	Male.	Female.	Male.	Female.	Male.	Female.	Male.	Female.
All ages	4,885,881	4,941,882	32,783	33,523	203,466	214,404	156,431	144,405	125,864	116,798	2,029,808	2,082,680
Under 5 years	629,320	633,968	2,876	3,000	17,384	17,914	11,566	11,862	9,447	9,680	284,101	286,415
Under 1 year	125,459	126,927	654	657	4,027	3,743	2,419	2,432	1,806	1,900	57,676	58,230
5 to 9 years	619,175	627,378	2,518	2,591	15,074	15,952	11,251	11,612	9,850	10,044	275,410	279,626
10 to 14 years	578,074	577,192	2,434	2,658	14,136	15,512	11,377	11,807	9,921	10,360	257,227	256,012
15 to 19 years	507,945	552,471	2,345	2,805	14,704	17,948	12,374	13,265	11,078	11,607	218,115	238,938
20 to 24 years	482,157	548,638	3,243	3,424	21,539	27,179	15,897	16,149	13,249	13,243	198,357	228,519
25 to 29 years	421,805	459,422	3,946	3,885	26,375	29,557	17,659	16,579	14,076	12,755	160,852	180,813
30 to 34 years	332,163	335,926	3,410	3,267	23,188	22,916	15,723	13,774	11,960	10,362	124,299	129,561
35 to 39 years	320,450	312,999	3,348	3,156	21,885	20,279	15,502	12,861	11,576	9,563	120,899	122,015
40 to 44 years	229,680	225,733	2,372	2,296	15,543	13,726	11,643	9,366	8,700	7,236	88,723	89,737
45 to 49 years	199,928	185,981	1,898	1,806	11,092	10,394	9,058	7,630	7,161	5,959	70,156	74,792
50 to 54 years	179,387	146,683	1,460	1,508	8,124	7,779	7,716	6,070	5,933	4,753	74,308	60,420
55 to 59 years	115,090	94,532	1,009	1,007	4,816	4,899	5,160	4,173	4,021	3,217	45,881	38,300
60 to 64 years	101,149	85,353	741	790	3,609	3,745	3,849	3,149	2,947	2,605	43,058	35,384
65 to 69 years	67,956	55,594	515	503	2,524	2,480	3,084	2,273	2,237	1,823	28,154	23,044
70 to 74 years	40,584	38,255	305	334	1,543	1,621	1,814	1,453	1,372	1,290	16,668	15,590
75 to 79 years	22,667	21,351	155	209	734	976	1,046	895	845	751	8,873	8,396
80 to 84 years	11,696	13,883	78	124	296	531	482	486	287	484	4,720	5,439
85 to 89 years	5,164	6,002	27	51	143	220	214	255	241	236	1,975	2,235
90 to 94 years	2,394	3,456	14	22	38	99	70	103	75	115	898	1,303
95 to 99 years	1,017	1,430	6	10	22	54	26	56	28	71	374	513
100 years and over	1,004	1,671	1	2	10	39	30	46	32	67	353	605
Age unknown	17,076	13,964	82	75	687	584	890	541	828	577	6,407	5,023

AGE PERIOD.	EAST SOUTH CENTRAL DIVISION.		WEST SOUTH CENTRAL DIVISION.		MOUNTAIN DIVISION.		PACIFIC DIVISION.		ALABAMA.		ARIZONA.	
	Male.	Female.	Male.	Female.	Male.	Female.	Male.	Female.	Male.	Female.	Male.	Female.
All ages	1,315,792	1,336,721	994,025	990,401	11,766	9,701	15,946	13,249	447,794	460,488	1,054	955
Under 5 years	173,902	173,901	128,497	129,515	642	708	905	973	61,808	62,183	80	76
Under 1 year	34,036	34,419	24,518	25,213	135	142	188	191	12,017	12,227	17	16
5 to 9 years	170,969	172,843	132,583	133,126	663	699	857	885	60,331	61,604	82	80
10 to 14 years	161,742	158,734	119,745	120,520	642	644	850	945	56,630	55,499	65	65
15 to 19 years	142,363	151,820	105,269	114,211	657	773	1,040	1,104	47,343	51,787	53	83
20 to 24 years	127,954	146,981	99,105	110,687	1,192	1,096	1,621	1,360	43,118	50,552	75	117
25 to 29 years	109,142	121,482	86,157	91,336	1,539	1,346	2,059	1,669	36,831	41,503	118	133
30 to 34 years	83,462	88,015	66,621	65,508	1,532	1,097	1,968	1,426	26,660	29,185	106	103
35 to 39 years	80,749	82,394	63,262	60,372	1,396	998	1,833	1,361	25,679	28,132	150	100
40 to 44 years	56,103	59,060	44,128	42,583	1,082	728	1,386	1,001	16,814	19,825	100	70
45 to 49 years	54,438	49,860	44,151	34,131	803	574	1,171	835	23,433	17,203	69	66
50 to 54 years	48,496	39,007	31,931	26,205	589	375	830	566	15,036	12,743	56	20
55 to 59 years	31,928	25,366	21,448	17,010	363	229	464	331	10,184	8,021	37	12
60 to 64 years	27,384	23,521	18,944	15,734	262	155	355	270	8,784	7,845	23	18
65 to 69 years	18,613	15,121	12,437	10,086	168	106	224	158	5,767	4,917	19	5
70 to 74 years	11,214	10,729	7,464	7,088	81	45	123	105	3,572	3,527	8	2
75 to 79 years	6,647	6,018	4,255	3,986	40	42	72	78	2,127	1,897	4	
80 to 84 years	3,399	4,050	2,372	2,698	18	29	44	42	1,206	1,408	2	1
85 to 89 years	1,561	1,761	983	1,224	6	4	14	16	531	608	1	1
90 to 94 years	722	1,051	570	741	1	5	6	17	258	372		
95 to 99 years	322	433	234	291	1		4	2	120	148		
100 years and over	321	519	256	388		2	1	3	129	183		1
Age unknown	4,361	4,055	3,613	2,961	89	46	119	102	1,433	1,346	6	2

AGE PERIOD.	ARKANSAS.		CALIFORNIA.		COLORADO.		CONNECTICUT.		DELAWARE.		DISTRICT OF COLUMBIA.	
	Male.	Female.	Male.	Female.	Male.	Female.	Male.	Female.	Male.	Female.	Male.	Female.
All ages	223,323	219,568	11,303	10,342	5,867	5,586	7,229	7,945	16,011	15,170	42,615	51,831
Under 5 years	28,456	28,874	732	787	335	373	636	671	1,518	1,571	3,581	3,709
Under 1 year	5,289	5,515	150	149	80	69	145	148	325	321	732	726
5 to 9 years	28,987	29,565	698	729	378	377	618	651	1,607	1,708	3,494	3,698
10 to 14 years	26,082	26,597	690	777	393	414	604	640	1,871	1,669	3,384	3,827
15 to 19 years	24,296	26,013	848	904	401	451	513	700	1,648	1,580	3,717	4,903
20 to 24 years	21,868	24,352	1,114	1,069	507	594	621	829	1,602	1,540	4,766	6,567
25 to 29 years	19,174	20,314	1,343	1,230	658	726	715	889	1,332	1,251	5,045	6,527
30 to 34 years	14,942	14,787	1,256	1,040	652	611	723	773	1,123	1,110	4,013	4,950
35 to 39 years	13,957	13,651	1,159	1,005	667	591	733	716	1,178	1,072	4,072	4,856
40 to 44 years	9,184	9,274	935	781	587	434	551	548	1,020	884	2,964	3,363
45 to 49 years	12,620	7,851	816	650	451	345	427	393	824	766	2,255	2,772
50 to 54 years	7,998	5,942	612	468	334	250	340	348	713	600	1,833	2,228
55 to 59 years	5,377	3,642	356	277	172	151	236	249	456	385	1,129	1,354
60 to 64 years	3,956	3,213	281	224	135	95	191	202	419	375	902	1,107
65 to 69 years	2,590	1,957	188	132	90	72	145	129	306	259	612	706
70 to 74 years	1,480	1,325	97	88	37	26	81	87	186	164	340	472
75 to 79 years	868	704	65	65	19	23	45	55	80	90	170	218
80 to 84 years	476	509	36	37	7	22	20	23	40	58	90	149
85 to 89 years	203	221	11	12	3	2	7	14	10	21	36	69
90 to 94 years	119	137	6	16		4	3	4	10	8	18	37
95 to 99 years	46	48	4	2	1		2	3		5	5	15
100 years and over	59	85	1	1			1	1	2	1	6	14
Age unknown	585	507	55	48	40	25	17	20	66	53	183	290

TABLE 39.—NEGRO MALES AND FEMALES, CLASSIFIED BY QUINQUENNIAL AGE PERIODS, BY DIVISIONS AND STATES: 1910—Continued.

AGE PERIOD.	FLORIDA.		GEORGIA.		IDAHO.		ILLINOIS.		INDIANA.		IOWA.	
	Male.	Female.	Male.	Female.	Male.	Female.	Male.	Female.	Male.	Female.	Male.	Female.
All ages	161,362	147,307	580,263	596,724	398	253	56,909	52,140	31,044	29,276	8,120	6,853
Under 5 years	18,412	18,702	83,625	83,873	19	21	3,997	4,251	2,351	2,412	621	624
Under 1 year	3,589	3,753	16,449	16,543	5	5	869	819	490	497	123	128
5 to 9 years	18,926	18,885	81,086	82,208	15	18	3,881	3,992	2,435	2,472	686	662
10 to 14 years	16,636	16,652	76,610	75,419	14	5	3,832	3,936	2,410	2,574	591	624
15 to 19 years	14,584	16,307	60,723	69,200	13	20	4,256	4,475	2,624	2,828	646	670
20 to 24 years	17,687	17,644	57,091	66,204	49	29	5,878	5,914	3,224	3,220	792	714
25 to 29 years	16,696	15,388	46,011	52,263	63	36	6,917	6,475	3,364	3,246	799	702
30 to 34 years	13,347	10,742	34,764	36,695	49	29	6,424	5,481	2,857	2,660	733	580
35 to 39 years	12,782	9,723	33,410	34,129	55	23	6,172	4,972	2,789	2,540	785	616
40 to 44 years	9,255	6,626	23,319	24,397	34	21	4,423	3,506	2,185	1,848	607	426
45 to 49 years	7,812	5,254	16,162	20,326	30	18	3,240	2,750	1,666	1,509	576	360
50 to 54 years	4,779	3,515	24,255	16,367	18	12	2,602	2,064	1,657	1,304	398	268
55 to 59 years	3,359	2,262	12,248	9,982	18	8	1,669	1,318	1,129	860	283	154
60 to 64 years	2,324	1,940	12,693	9,312	7	3	1,183	1,005	809	626	204	163
65 to 69 years	1,571	1,156	7,543	5,897	6	....	914	710	657	434	140	108
70 to 74 years	825	801	4,317	4,030	4	4	518	458	360	295	97	69
75 to 79 years	523	403	2,450	2,292	2	4	291	262	216	177	53	43
80 to 84 years	257	302	1,371	1,538	1	1	131	158	112	81	29	15
85 to 89 years	123	143	573	639	....	....	67	79	45	52	12	9
90 to 94 years	62	79	285	372	....	....	24	41	17	20	4	4
95 to 99 years	26	34	139	170	....	....	12	24	5	13	1	4
100 years and over	33	48	137	206	....	....	13	20	4	10	....	3
Age unknown	1,343	701	1,451	1,205	1	1	465	249	128	95	63	35

AGE PERIOD.	KANSAS.		KENTUCKY.		LOUISIANA.		MAINE.		MARYLAND.		MASSACHUSETTS.		MICHIGAN	
	Male.	Female.	Male.	Female.	Male.	Female.	Male.	Female.	Male.	Female.	Male.	Female.	Male.	Female.
All ages	27,964	26,066	131,492	130,164	353,824	360,050	700	663	114,749	117,501	18,748	19,307	9,007	8,108
Under 5 years	2,261	2,366	12,700	12,841	45,867	46,572	56	61	12,755	13,232	1,665	1,783	650	635
Under 1 year	448	436	2,568	2,608	8,695	8,740	17	11	2,660	2,650	378	391	140	132
5 to 9 years	2,400	2,461	13,022	13,065	48,020	47,965	34	46	12,659	13,150	1,454	1,435	630	643
10 to 14 years	2,426	2,545	13,540	13,444	42,931	42,986	56	61	12,144	12,451	1,392	1,513	640	636
15 to 19 years	2,734	2,784	13,846	14,317	36,172	40,696	65	80	11,160	12,238	1,331	1,539	684	694
20 to 24 years	2,894	2,784	13,608	14,248	34,581	39,538	76	58	11,455	12,136	1,801	2,030	846	866
25 to 29 years	2,805	2,461	11,850	12,298	30,854	32,823	74	61	9,988	11,035	2,338	2,286	953	868
30 to 34 years	2,233	2,030	9,661	9,633	23,717	23,772	50	52	8,217	8,353	1,968	1,945	833	717
35 to 39 years	2,244	1,896	9,655	9,289	23,494	22,631	57	47	8,375	8,232	1,987	1,912	868	665
40 to 44 years	1,632	1,482	7,855	7,201	17,477	15,853	45	34	6,853	6,637	1,383	1,341	661	537
45 to 49 years	1,464	1,326	6,763	6,347	13,064	12,471	36	41	5,813	5,627	1,115	1,043	563	495
50 to 54 years	1,342	1,116	6,210	5,174	10,873	9,824	33	35	4,927	4,455	817	818	474	396
55 to 59 years	946	782	3,905	3,481	8,074	6,656	38	25	3,272	2,832	536	531	357	292
60 to 64 years	763	635	3,028	3,027	6,552	6,299	33	21	2,620	2,540	377	431	283	236
65 to 69 years	696	470	2,281	2,035	4,510	4,143	20	14	1,973	1,789	245	263	231	168
70 to 74 years	458	346	1,509	1,453	2,992	3,003	9	8	1,296	1,226	144	176	156	112
75 to 79 years	276	196	832	868	1,657	1,685	12	5	566	647	79	115	77	74
80 to 84 years	115	137	357	485	966	1,104	3	5	256	365	40	66	45	28
85 to 89 years	63	66	172	199	393	512	2	4	103	154	14	29	10	20
90 to 94 years	29	37	64	108	205	301	....	1	36	67	8	10	3	7
95 to 99 years	8	21	23	50	92	116	....	....	25	37	3	7	2	2
100 years and over	14	20	20	47	76	131	....	....	8	27	....	....	2	1
Age unknown	161	105	591	554	1,257	969	1	4	248	271	51	34	39	16

AGE PERIOD.	MINNESOTA.		MISSISSIPPI.		MISSOURI.		MONTANA.		NEBRASKA.		NEVADA.		NEW HAMPSHIRE.	
	Male.	Female.	Male.	Female.	Male.	Female.	Male.	Female.	Male.	Female.	Male.	Female.	Male.	Female.
All ages	4,183	2,901	502,796	506,691	80,489	76,963	1,058	776	4,259	3,430	263	250	288	276
Under 5 years	186	196	71,149	70,542	6,088	6,211	46	59	244	233	10	16	19	21
Under 1 year	37	38	13,651	13,678	1,139	1,241	6	15	47	49	3	3	4	5
5 to 9 years	162	174	69,849	70,096	6,288	6,480	49	47	264	223	7	11	22	22
10 to 14 years	178	197	64,734	63,285	6,468	6,722	52	43	210	228	8	10	23	22
15 to 19 years	221	215	54,469	58,058	7,187	7,578	46	58	250	303	6	9	23	30
20 to 24 years	373	336	47,551	54,671	8,631	8,896	93	86	452	440	17	24	22	23
25 to 29 years	678	377	40,873	45,081	9,023	8,629	135	103	641	502	30	33	23	43
30 to 34 years	608	401	31,833	32,657	7,752	6,895	134	84	537	396	42	38	22	23
35 to 39 years	579	355	30,706	29,464	7,372	6,299	146	93	501	338	42	38	32	19
40 to 44 years	404	205	21,817	20,900	5,618	4,859	89	61	366	234	32	23	24	11
45 to 49 years	309	149	15,017	16,641	4,498	3,901	67	56	262	198	19	17	17	15
50 to 54 years	179	101	16,014	13,290	3,763	3,121	61	32	210	130	15	13	24	22
55 to 59 years	109	58	10,820	8,860	2,534	2,131	54	15	130	75	11	7	12	5
60 to 64 years	54	37	10,729	8,158	1,836	1,711	42	14	73	48	6	4	9	2
65 to 69 years	45	38	6,886	5,092	1,298	1,173	12	8	49	30	6	2	10	8
70 to 74 years	28	19	3,988	3,624	755	834	9	5	28	17	3	1	4	2
75 to 79 years	16	16	2,390	2,031	479	479	3	5	6	8	3	1	3	4
80 to 84 years	5	4	1,247	1,392	132	320	4	....	6	8	2	....	1	2
85 to 89 years	4	3	558	612	157	157	1	....	5	....	....	....	2	....
90 to 94 years	....	2	275	372	39	69	....	....	2	3	1	1	....	....
95 to 99 years	....	1	117	148	18	43	....	....	1	1	....	....	....	....
100 years and over	....	....	120	201	18	43	....	....	....	1	....	....	....	....
Age unknown	45	17	1,654	1,516	535	412	15	7	11	7	3	2	1	2

TABLE 39.—NEGRO MALES AND FEMALES, CLASSIFIED BY QUINQUENNIAL AGE PERIODS, BY DIVISIONS AND STATES: 1910—Continued.

AGE PERIOD.	NEW JERSEY.		NEW MEXICO.		NEW YORK.		NORTH CAROLINA.		NORTH DAKOTA.		OHIO.		OKLAHOMA.	
	Male.	Female.	Male.	Female.	Male.	Female.	Male.	Female.	Male.	Female.	Male.	Female.	Male.	Female.
All ages	43,602	46,158	891	737	64,034	70,157	339,581	358,262	381	236	57,995	53,457	71,937	65,675
Under 5 years	3,897	4,025	69	81	4,920	5,141	53,279	54,018	17	20	4,477	4,444	9,028	9,158
Under 1 year	886	843	14	17	1,177	1,123	11,316	11,536	4	5	898	959	1,718	1,826
5 to 9 years	3,514	3,747	56	78	3,944	4,343	49,662	50,489	16	18	4,221	4,400	9,223	9,046
10 to 14 years	3,360	3,518	48	58	3,742	4,188	44,654	44,762	17	13	4,403	4,561	8,015	8,193
15 to 19 years	3,475	3,953	64	59	4,363	5,455	38,752	41,501	15	21	4,705	5,150	7,448	7,526
20 to 24 years	4,513	5,611	74	78	7,771	9,710	31,047	38,438	53	29	5,830	5,971	7,137	7,207
25 to 29 years	4,952	5,623	98	108	9,666	11,007	23,438	28,855	69	35	6,254	5,779	6,481	6,120
30 to 34 years	4,423	4,635	118	78	8,092	8,109	17,808	20,432	45	28	5,439	4,793	5,244	4,418
35 to 39 years	4,413	4,282	94	61	7,133	6,855	16,890	19,211	44	25	5,502	4,561	4,965	3,810
40 to 44 years	3,319	3,020	72	45	4,729	4,493	11,485	13,940	31	9	4,260	3,378	3,267	2,702
45 to 49 years	2,407	2,333	58	25	3,197	3,476	10,893	12,101	19	9	3,485	2,801	2,626	2,146
50 to 54 years	1,916	1,776	45	18	2,258	2,537	12,778	10,488	19	7	2,906	2,250	3,215	1,701
55 to 59 years	1,064	1,194	29	16	1,434	1,537	9,335	6,845	12	12	1,956	1,675	1,859	1,151
60 to 64 years	851	890	26	9	1,064	1,193	6,904	5,999	7	5	1,528	1,257	1,229	803
65 to 69 years	634	595	21	11	732	814	4,928	3,993	2	2	1,238	933	840	543
70 to 74 years	400	390	11	4	441	507	3,114	2,736			769	573	461	399
75 to 79 years	194	240	4	4	219	283	1,766	1,521	2		451	371	275	200
80 to 84 years	81	115		2	95	179	894	961		1	186	216	143	137
85 to 89 years	42	47	1		39	79	372	399			91	104	67	73
90 to 94 years	9	28			10	34	177	243			25	34	39	46
95 to 99 years	7	12			4	21	67	90		1	7	15	9	16
100 years and over	3	11			4	12	59	108			10	14	23	32
Age unknown	128	113	3	2	177	184	1,279	1,132	13	1	252	177	343	248

AGE PERIOD.	OREGON.		PENNSYLVANIA.		RHODE ISLAND.		SOUTH CAROLINA.		SOUTH DAKOTA.		TENNESSEE.		TEXAS.	
	Male.	Female.	Male.	Female.	Male.	Female.	Male.	Female.	Male.	Female.	Male.	Female.	Male.	Female.
All ages	907	585	95,830	98,089	4,645	4,884	408,078	427,765	468	349	233,710	239,378	344,941	345,108
Under 5 years	34	36	8,567	8,748	450	412	64,470	64,242	30	30	28,245	28,335	45,146	44,911
Under 1 year	7	9	1,964	1,777	101	87	12,977	12,957	8	3	5,800	5,906	8,816	9,132
5 to 9 years	35	28	7,616	7,862	356	398	61,303	61,764	34	26	27,767	28,078	46,353	46,550
10 to 14 years	23	31	7,034	7,806	329	385	57,285	57,056	31	31	26,838	26,506	42,717	42,744
15 to 19 years	34	33	6,866	8,540	351	421	47,442	51,676	25	36	26,705	27,658	37,353	39,976
20 to 24 years	90	66	9,255	11,858	464	423	38,005	47,300	54	44	23,677	27,510	35,519	39,590
25 to 29 years	126	76	11,757	12,927	513	548	28,739	34,508	61	49	19,588	22,600	29,648	32,079
30 to 34 years	134	78	10,673	10,172	464	433	21,790	24,404	52	32	15,308	16,540	22,718	22,531
35 to 39 years	137	72	10,339	9,142	459	426	21,206	22,663	51	34	14,709	15,509	20,846	20,280
40 to 44 years	112	50	7,495	6,213	315	341	15,687	16,255	42	21	9,617	11,134	14,200	14,754
45 to 49 years	67	44	5,488	4,585	264	297	11,030	13,090	33	16	9,225	9,669	15,841	11,663
50 to 54 years	49	21	3,950	3,466	219	269	11,560	10,536	22	10	11,236	7,800	9,845	8,738
55 to 59 years	21	12	2,318	2,168	165	183	7,341	6,769	7	5	7,019	5,004	6,138	5,561
60 to 64 years	23	15	1,694	1,662	111	128	9,501	6,669	10	6	4,843	4,491	7,207	5,419
65 to 69 years	3	4	1,158	1,071	85	83	5,727	4,175	7	2	3,679	3,077	4,497	3,443
70 to 74 years	4	5	702	724	57	58	3,123	2,854	6	5	2,145	2,125	2,531	2,361
75 to 79 years	3	9	321	453	14	29	1,504	1,367	2	2	1,298	1,222	1,455	1,397
80 to 84 years	4	1	120	237	13	23	791	903			589	765	787	948
85 to 89 years	1	2	62	94	3	4	350	340			300	342	320	418
90 to 94 years		1	19	37	1	7	141	237	1		125	199	207	257
95 to 99 years			11	21	1		59	79			62	87	87	111
100 years and over			3	16		1	59	108			52	88	98	140
Age unknown	7	1	382	287	11	15	965	770			683	639	1,428	1,237

AGE PERIOD.	UTAH.		VERMONT.		VIRGINIA.		WASHINGTON.		WEST VIRGINIA.		WISCONSIN.		WYOMING.	
	Male.	Female.	Male.	Female.	Male.	Female.	Male.	Female.	Male.	Female.	Male.	Female.	Male.	Female.
All ages	691	453	1,173	448	330,542	340,554	3,736	2,322	36,607	27,566	1,476	1,424	1,544	691
Under 5 years	28	28	50	52	42,927	43,628	139	150	3,534	3,440	91	120	55	54
Under 1 year	6	8	9	15	8,888	9,013	31	33	740	731	22	25	4	9
5 to 9 years	29	33	34	39	43,658	44,465	124	128	3,015	3,259	84	105	47	55
10 to 14 years	28	27	35	37	41,902	41,493	137	137	2,741	2,683	92	100	34	22
15 to 19 years	28	42	62	35	36,368	38,679	158	167	3,721	2,854	105	118	46	51
20 to 24 years	64	53	259	61	31,405	35,098	417	225	5,299	3,592	119	178	313	115
25 to 29 years	81	75	283	58	24,558	27,766	590	363	5,045	3,220	171	211	356	132
30 to 34 years	125	59	183	41	19,680	20,678	578	308	3,557	2,197	170	123	306	95
35 to 39 years	92	39	80	36	19,814	20,251	537	284	3,172	1,878	171	123	150	53
40 to 44 years	73	41	54	21	16,015	16,326	339	170	2,125	1,309	114	97	95	33
45 to 49 years	45	22	39	17	13,949	13,870	288	141	1,418	986	104	75	64	25
50 to 54 years	31	11	27	16	12,346	11,565	169	77	1,117	666	77	56	29	19
55 to 59 years	26	11	22	14	8,099	7,451	87	42	642	420	49	28	16	9
60 to 64 years	11	3	20	6	7,267	7,046	51	31	428	396	46	25	12	9
65 to 69 years	9	3	10	6	5,168	4,816	33	22	326	253	44	28	5	5
70 to 74 years	4	1	10	3	3,312	3,150	22	12	155	157	11	15	5	2
75 to 79 years	3	2	2	1	1,721	1,763	4	4	93	95	11	11	2	3
80 to 84 years	2		1	5	966	1,114	4	4	55	49	8	3		3
85 to 89 years		1	1		390	452	2	2	18	18	1			
90 to 94 years					161	252			8	8	1	1		
95 to 99 years					51	76			2	7		2		
100 years and over					45	84		2	4	9	1	1		1
Age unknown	12	2	1		740	531	57	53	132	70	6	4	9	5

TABLE **40.**—PERCENTAGE DISTRIBUTION, BY AGE PERIODS, OF URBAN AND RURAL NEGRO AND WHITE POPULATION CLASSES, BY SOUTHERN STATES: 1910.

STATE AND RACIAL CLASS.	PERCENTAGE DISTRIBUTION BY AGE PERIODS: 1910.													
	Urban population.							Rural population.						
	All ages.[1]	Under 5 years.	5 to 14 years.	15 to 24 years.	25 to 44 years.	45 to 64 years.	65 years and over.	All ages.[1]	Under 5 years.	5 to 14 years.	15 to 24 years.	25 to 44 years.	45 to 64 years.	65 years and over.
SOUTH ATLANTIC DIVISION.														
DELAWARE.														
Negro	100.0	6.8	17.0	19.4	35.5	17.1	3.9	100.0	11.7	24.8	21.0	25.0	13.2	4.0
Native white:														
Native parentage	100.0	10.4	17.8	20.0	30.6	16.2	4.9	100.0	10.1	20.8	18.4	26.1	18.3	6.2
Foreign or mixed parentage	100.0	15.7	23.1	20.0	26.1	13.3	1.7	100.0	10.8	20.7	17.9	29.3	17.9	3.2
Foreign-born white	100.0	0.7	4.2	17.8	46.3	22.9	7.8	100.0	0.6	5.2	12.5	40.0	29.2	12.4
MARYLAND.														
Negro	100.0	8.1	15.5	21.0	36.9	15.2	3.1	100.0	13.5	26.3	19.7	23.4	12.8	4.1
Native white:														
Native parentage	100.0	11.1	20.3	21.6	29.3	13.7	3.9	100.0	12.2	23.3	18.8	25.7	14.9	5.1
Foreign or mixed parentage	100.0	11.4	20.3	19.2	29.8	17.1	2.1	100.0	9.6	19.9	18.0	31.1	18.5	2.9
Foreign-born white	100.0	0.6	5.9	14.7	40.5	26.6	11.6	100.0	0.5	3.5	10.9	38.6	31.0	15.4
DISTRICT OF COLUMBIA.														
Negro	100.0	7.7	15.2	21.1	37.9	14.4	3.1	....						......
Native white:														
Native parentage	100.0	9.3	16.7	19.2	33.4	15.6	5.5	....						......
Foreign or mixed parentage	100.0	8.3	15.0	16.7	38.2	18.3	3.3	....						......
Foreign-born white	100.0	0.6	4.0	11.9	43.0	26.0	14.1	....						......
VIRGINIA.														
Negro	100.0	9.0	18.1	23.6	33.6	12.8	2.7	100.0	14.1	27.9	20.3	21.8	12.0	3.8
Native white:														
Native parentage	100.0	10.7	18.8	21.3	31.3	14.0	3.7	100.0	14.1	24.9	19.1	24.0	13.3	4.5
Foreign or mixed parentage	100.0	12.0	20.3	20.1	29.8	15.2	2.5	100.0	14.6	23.6	17.4	24.9	14.1	5.4
Foreign-born white	100.0	0.9	5.5	15.1	45.2	24.0	9.0	100.0	0.8	6.1	13.4	41.6	24.5	13.2
WEST VIRGINIA.														
Negro	100.0	8.4	15.9	23.5	37.4	11.9	2.5	100.0	11.6	19.0	24.3	34.3	8.7	1.8
Native white:														
Native parentage	100.0	11.7	19.7	22.0	31.4	12.2	2.8	100.0	15.1	25.3	19.8	24.5	11.7	3.6
Foreign or mixed parentage	100.0	11.2	16.3	16.7	35.1	18.5	2.2	100.0	22.0	19.9	13.7	25.4	15.3	3.6
Foreign-born white	100.0	0.8	4.2	18.6	45.5	21.3	9.4	100.0	1.5	6.1	24.0	51.4	12.4	3.7
NORTH CAROLINA.														
Negro	100.0	11.2	21.1	23.7	28.2	12.1	2.8	100.0	16.2	28.4	21.0	20.5	10.5	3.1
Native white:														
Native parentage	100.0	12.4	20.4	21.7	29.3	12.9	3.1	100.0	15.4	25.3	19.8	22.8	12.8	3.8
Foreign parentage	100.0	13.5	23.5	19.0	28.5	13.1	2.2	100.0	12.7	22.2	18.2	25.2	15.1	6.6
Foreign-born white	100.0	0.8	5.8	14.2	45.3	25.0	8.8	100.0	1.2	6.0	14.4	41.0	26.4	10.6
SOUTH CAROLINA.														
Negro	100.0	10.6	20.8	23.8	30.6	11.0	2.5	100.0	16.1	29.5	21.8	21.0	8.9	2.6
Native white:														
Native parentage	100.0	12.1	20.4	22.0	29.7	12.6	3.0	100.0	15.5	25.2	20.4	23.7	11.9	3.2
Foreign parentage	100.0	8.9	16.5	18.0	33.7	19.6	3.1	100.0	9.6	19.2	18.3	28.8	18.3	5.7
Foreign-born white	100.0	0.6	4.0	12.0	40.9	27.6	14.8	100.0	1.1	4.0	12.5	40.3	28.9	12.9
GEORGIA.														
Negro	100.0	9.2	19.2	22.9	33.4	12.1	2.7	100.0	15.4	28.6	21.2	22.0	9.9	2.7
Native white:														
Native parentage	100.0	11.6	19.6	21.2	31.3	12.9	3.2	100.0	15.7	25.8	19.9	23.2	12.0	3.4
Foreign parentage	100.0	10.3	18.9	19.2	33.0	16.0	2.5	100.0	9.6	17.3	19.9	28.5	18.5	6.1
Foreign-born white	100.0	0.6	5.2	14.7	44.0	25.8	9.5	100.0	0.5	3.2	13.9	41.2	28.5	12.5
FLORIDA.														
Negro	100.0	8.6	18.6	22.1	37.3	10.7	1.8	100.0	13.4	24.8	21.2	28.0	9.9	2.2
Native white:														
Native parentage	100.0	11.1	19.0	20.5	32.4	13.1	3.2	100.0	14.9	24.9	19.9	24.3	12.5	3.3
Foreign or mixed parentage	100.0	20.9	27.8	20.2	21.0	8.5	1.4	100.0	12.1	22.9	19.6	25.7	15.4	4.3
Foreign-born white	100.0	1.9	8.7	21.0	43.1	19.9	5.2	100.0	0.8	3.7	12.0	43.3	29.3	10.6
EAST SOUTH CENTRAL DIVISION.														
KENTUCKY.														
Negro	100.0	6.9	15.6	21.3	36.0	15.9	3.7	100.0	11.7	23.5	21.5	25.2	13.5	4.2
Native white:														
Native parentage	100.0	11.4	20.8	22.3	29.1	12.9	3.4	100.0	14.7	25.3	19.7	24.0	12.4	3.9
Foreign or mixed parentage	100.0	4.5	12.0	18.2	41.8	21.6	1.8	100.0	5.4	13.2	16.5	37.2	24.1	3.6
Foreign-born white	100.0	0.3	2.1	6.8	30.2	37.5	22.9	100.0	0.3	1.5	7.4	28.6	35.9	26.2
TENNESSEE.														
Negro	100.0	7.9	16.3	23.5	35.6	13.2	3.1	100.0	13.8	26.2	21.8	22.2	12.2	3.6
Native white:														
Native parentage	100.0	10.7	18.8	21.8	31.8	13.4	3.2	100.0	14.8	24.9	19.9	23.7	12.7	3.9
Foreign or mixed parentage	100.0	7.5	15.2	18.9	38.6	17.7	2.0	100.0	9.1	19.0	18.4	29.3	18.4	5.7
Foreign-born white	100.0	0.5	4.9	12.4	38.5	30.6	13.0	100.0	0.7	3.6	7.8	31.1	33.6	23.1

[1] Includes persons of unknown age.

TABLE **40.**—PERCENTAGE DISTRIBUTION, BY AGE PERIODS, OF URBAN AND RURAL NEGRO AND WHITE POPULATION CLASSES, BY SOUTHERN STATES: 1910—Continued.

| | PERCENTAGE DISTRIBUTION BY AGE PERIODS: 1910. | | | | | | | | | | | | |
| | Urban population. | | | | | | | Rural population. | | | | | |
STATE AND RACIAL CLASS.	All ages.[1]	Under 5 years.	5 to 14 years.	15 to 24 years.	25 to 44 years.	45 to 64 years.	65 years and over.	All ages.[1]	Under 5 years.	5 to 14 years	15 to 24 years.	25 to 44 years.	45 to 64 years.	65 years and over.
SOUTH ATLANTIC DIVISION.														
ALABAMA.														
Negro	100.0	9.3	18.7	21.9	34.5	12.5	2.6	100.0	14.6	27.2	21.1	22.7	11.1	3.0
Native white:														
Native parentage	100.0	12.4	20.2	21.2	31.0	12.3	2.7	100.0	16.2	26.0	20.2	22.7	11.8	3.1
Foreign or mixed parentage	100.0	11.7	19.8	19.3	31.6	15.4	2.2	100.0	14.2	25.5	19.1	23.5	13.9	3.7
Foreign-born white	100.0	0.6	5.6	14.0	42.7	27.9	9.1	100.0	1.0	6.0	11.3	39.3	32.1	9.9
MISSISSIPPI.														
Negro	100.0	9.7	19.5	21.7	33.5	11.4	3.4	100.0	14.5	27.3	21.2	24.2	9.7	2.8
Native white:														
Native parentage	100.0	11.8	20.8	20.9	30.5	12.3	3.1	100.0	15.8	26.0	20.1	23.6	11.3	3.1
Foreign or mixed parentage	100.0	9.4	16.3	17.7	35.4	18.4	2.7	100.0	10.7	18.3	17.3	30.1	18.9	4.6
Foreign-born white	100.0	0.6	4.5	11.9	40.5	27.9	14.2	100.0	0.7	9.1	13.6	25.1	27.8	13.3
WEST SOUTH CENTRAL DIVISION.														
ARKANSAS.														
Negro	100.0	8.9	17.9	23.2	34.8	12.1	2.6	100.0	13.6	26.2	21.6	24.7	11.3	2.4
Native white:														
Native parentage	100.0	11.5	19.6	21.0	31.6	13.0	3.0	100.0	16.3	25.8	20.3	23.4	11.3	2.8
Foreign or mixed parentage	100.0	7.5	16.5	21.4	36.9	15.5	2.1	100.0	12.0	23.0	20.2	26.0	15.4	3.4
Foreign-born white	100.0	0.5	2.3	9.4	42.0	32.2	13.3	100.0	0.7	5.5	9.5	35.8	35.7	12.7
LOUISIANA.														
Negro	100.0	9.3	19.3	21.9	34.0	11.8	3.2	100.0	14.0	27.3	20.9	24.6	9.9	3.0
Native white:														
Native parentage	100.0	12.9	24.6	23.2	27.2	9.1	2.1	100.0	16.4	27.6	20.3	23.3	9.8	2.4
Foreign or mixed parentage	100.0	7.1	14.0	16.3	39.4	20.9	2.3	100.0	19.1	27.4	15.3	22.9	12.9	2.4
Foreign-born white	100.0	0.6	4.0	11.1	35.4	30.8	17.9	100.0	0.7	7.5	16.0	42.1	25.7	7.8
OKLAHOMA.														
Negro	100.0	9.5	18.6	23.5	35.4	10.2	2.0	100.0	14.6	27.4	20.5	23.8	10.9	2.5
Native white:														
Native parentage	100.0	11.5	19.1	21.2	33.1	12.2	2.5	100.0	16.0	26.1	20.0	24.5	10.9	2.3
Foreign or mixed parentage	100.0	8.1	15.6	19.9	38.3	16.0	2.1	100.0	11.8	24.7	20.8	27.7	12.8	2.0
Foreign-born white	100.0	0.7	3.1	12.9	47.0	27.3	8.1	100.0	0.7	4.4	10.3	40.9	33.2	10.4
TEXAS.														
Negro	100.0	9.0	19.1	22.7	35.0	11.0	2.6	100.0	14.5	28.2	21.9	22.4	9.9	2.8
Native white:														
Native parentage	100.0	11.5	20.5	21.4	31.4	12.1	2.8	100.0	15.9	26.9	20.6	23.2	10.8	2.5
Foreign or mixed parentage	100.0	12.8	22.9	22.0	29.8	11.2	1.2	100.0	16.0	29.8	23.3	22.6	7.4	0.8
Foreign-born white	100.0	1.8	8.8	15.9	40.0	25.2	8.0	100.0	2.3	9.6	15.6	36.3	26.5	9.0

[1] Includes persons of unknown age.

TABLE 41.—URBAN AND RURAL NEGRO POPULATION, CLASSIFIED BY AGE PERIODS, BY STATES: 1910.

NEGRO POPULATION: 1910.

NEW ENGLAND DIVISION. / MIDDLE ATLANTIC DIVISION.

AGE PERIOD.	Maine (Urban)	Maine (Rural)	New Hampshire (Urban)	New Hampshire (Rural)	Vermont (Urban)	Vermont (Rural)	Massachusetts (Urban)	Massachusetts (Rural)	Rhode Island (Urban)	Rhode Island (Rural)	Connecticut (Urban)	Connecticut (Rural)	New York (Urban)	New York (Rural)
All ages	924	439	356	208	1,341	280	35,243	2,812	9,055	474	13,958	1,216	117,486	16,705
Under 5 years	77	40	22	18	68	34	3,101	347	814	48	1,179	128	8,571	1,490
5 to 14 years	141	56	47	37	84	61	5,250	544	1,396	72	2,272	241	13,664	2,553
15 to 24 years	186	93	63	35	360	57	6,162	539	1,541	118	2,463	200	23,656	3,643
25 to 44 years	295	125	123	74	700	56	14,259	901	3,360	139	5,307	341	54,325	5,759
45 to 64 years	170	92	74	32	103	58	5,339	329	1,562	74	2,164	222	14,348	2,348
65 years and over	50	33	25	11	26	13	1,056	143	356	23	537	83	2,596	877
Age unknown	5	......	2	1	......	1	76	9	26	......	36	1	326	35

MIDDLE ATLANTIC DIVISION—con. / EAST NORTH CENTRAL DIVISION.

AGE PERIOD.	New Jersey (Urban)	New Jersey (Rural)	Pennsylvania (Urban)	Pennsylvania (Rural)	Ohio (Urban)	Ohio (Rural)	Indiana (Urban)	Indiana (Rural)	Illinois (Urban)	Illinois (Rural)	Michigan (Urban)	Michigan (Rural)	Wisconsin (Urban)	Wisconsin (Rural)
All ages	65,427	24,333	156,333	37,586	82,282	29,170	48,425	11,895	85,538	23,511	12,156	4,959	2,141	759
Under 5 years	5,474	2,448	13,319	3,996	5,869	3,052	3,565	1,198	5,861	2,387	803	482	132	79
5 to 14 years	9,563	4,576	22,575	7,743	11,391	6,194	7,348	2,543	10,910	4,731	1,612	937	232	149
15 to 24 years	12,519	5,033	28,967	7,552	16,166	5,490	9,652	2,244	15,950	4,573	2,253	837	378	142
25 to 44 years	26,916	7,751	66,721	11,997	32,477	7,489	18,273	3,216	37,482	6,888	4,819	1,283	968	212
45 to 64 years	9,076	3,355	20,474	4,857	13,003	4,855	7,649	1,911	12,304	3,527	2,103	993	347	113
65 years and over	1,678	1,130	3,722	1,327	3,029	2,008	1,739	759	2,421	1,301	518	420	78	60
Age unknown	201	40	555	114	347	82	199	24	610	104	48	7	6	4

WEST NORTH CENTRAL DIVISION.

AGE PERIOD.	Minnesota (Urban)	Minnesota (Rural)	Iowa (Urban)	Iowa (Rural)	Missouri (Urban)	Missouri (Rural)	North Dakota (Urban)	North Dakota (Rural)	South Dakota (Urban)	South Dakota (Rural)	Nebraska (Urban)	Nebraska (Rural)	Kansas (Urban)	Kansas (Rural)
All ages	6,518	566	9,786	5,187	104,462	52,990	306	311	412	405	6,621	1,068	36,196	17,834
Under 5 years	314	68	713	532	6,596	5,703	9	28	31	29	396	81	2,958	1,669
5 to 14 years	633	78	1,542	1,021	13,972	11,986	20	44	52	70	768	157	6,248	3,584
15 to 24 years	1,045	100	1,817	1,005	21,351	10,941	58	60	77	82	1,236	209	7,534	3,662
25 to 44 years	3,411	196	3,644	1,604	43,026	13,421	162	124	200	142	3,110	405	11,857	4,926
45 to 64 years	906	90	1,587	819	15,458	8,037	43	47	44	65	958	168	5,636	2,738
65 years and over	148	33	413	178	3,323	2,691	3	5	8	17	139	44	1,777	1,175
Age unknown	61	1	70	28	736	211	11	3	......	......	14	4	186	80

SOUTH ATLANTIC DIVISION.

AGE PERIOD.	Delaware (Urban)	Delaware (Rural)	Maryland (Urban)	Maryland (Rural)	District of Columbia (Urban)	District of Columbia (Rural)	Virginia (Urban)	Virginia (Rural)	West Virginia (Urban)	West Virginia (Rural)	North Carolina (Urban)	North Carolina (Rural)	South Carolina (Urban)	South Carolina (Rural)
All ages	11,157	20,024	99,230	133,020	94,446	......	158,218	512,878	15,380	48,793	115,975	581,868	101,702	734,141
Under 5 years	756	2,333	8,015	17,972	7,290	......	14,224	72,331	1,293	5,681	13,024	94,273	10,741	117,971
5 to 14 years	1,898	4,957	15,389	35,015	14,403	......	28,612	142,906	2,450	9,248	24,459	165,108	21,151	216,257
15 to 24 years	2,159	4,211	20,849	26,140	19,953	......	37,382	104,168	3,609	11,857	27,502	122,236	24,219	160,204
25 to 44 years	3,962	5,008	36,576	31,114	35,790	......	53,121	111,967	5,746	16,757	32,717	119,342	31,099	154,153
45 to 64 years	1,904	2,634	15,046	17,040	13,580	......	20,237	61,356	1,837	4,236	14,079	61,264	11,155	65,341
65 years and over	435	805	3,113	5,462	2,957	......	4,235	19,286	392	865	3,212	18,216	2,557	19,260
Age unknown	43	76	242	277	473	......	407	864	53	149	982	1,429	780	955

SOUTH ATLANTIC DIVISION—con. / EAST SOUTH CENTRAL DIVISION. / WEST SOUTH CENTRAL DIVISION.

AGE PERIOD.	Georgia (Urban)	Georgia (Rural)	Florida (Urban)	Florida (Rural)	Kentucky (Urban)	Kentucky (Rural)	Tennessee (Urban)	Tennessee (Rural)	Alabama (Urban)	Alabama (Rural)	Mississippi (Urban)	Mississippi (Rural)	Arkansas (Urban)	Arkansas (Rural)
All ages	224,826	952,161	88,586	220,083	106,631	155,025	150,506	322,582	156,603	751,679	95,357	914,130	59,147	383,744
Under 5 years	20,747	146,751	7,620	29,494	7,400	18,141	11,953	44,627	14,531	109,460	9,221	132,470	5,237	52,093
5 to 14 years	43,153	272,170	16,439	54,660	16,619	36,542	24,576	84,613	29,335	204,729	18,579	249,385	10,593	100,638
15 to 24 years	51,431	201,787	19,563	46,659	22,741	33,278	35,324	70,226	34,348	158,452	20,701	194,048	13,743	82,786
25 to 44 years	75,119	209,869	33,039	61,520	38,369	39,073	53,524	71,481	53,963	170,666	31,988	221,343	20,610	94,673
45 to 64 years	27,268	94,077	9,498	21,747	16,978	20,957	19,826	39,461	19,587	83,662	10,858	88,671	7,179	43,420
65 years and over	6,101	25,858	1,597	4,789	3,959	6,544	4,673	11,482	4,137	22,633	3,247	25,806	1,517	9,310
Age unknown	1,007	1,649	830	1,214	565	580	630	692	702	2,077	763	2,407	268	824

WEST SOUTH CENTRAL DIVISION—continued. / MOUNTAIN DIVISION.

AGE PERIOD.	Louisiana (Urban)	Louisiana (Rural)	Oklahoma (Urban)	Oklahoma (Rural)	Texas (Urban)	Texas (Rural)	Montana (Urban)	Montana (Rural)	Idaho (Urban)	Idaho (Rural)	Wyoming (Urban)	Wyoming (Rural)	Colorado (Urban)	Colorado (Rural)
All ages	160,845	553,029	36,982	100,630	178,864	511,185	1,455	379	426	225	1,041	1,194	9,359	2,094
Under 5 years	15,005	77,434	3,505	14,681	16,079	73,978	84	21	19	21	86	23	574	134
5 to 14 years	30,998	150,904	6,891	27,586	34,201	144,163	147	44	23	29	110	48	1,232	330
15 to 24 years	35,204	115,783	8,693	20,625	40,625	111,813	233	50	75	36	220	305	1,558	395
25 to 44 years	54,757	135,864	13,080	23,927	62,566	114,490	689	156	226	84	494	726	4,105	821
45 to 64 years	18,959	54,854	3,758	10,972	19,762	50,650	253	88	69	45	107	76	1,591	342
65 years and over	5,214	16,672	756	2,547	4,643	14,414	30	17	12	10	18	8	243	63
Age unknown	708	1,518	299	292	988	1,677	19	3	2	......	6	8	56	9

MOUNTAIN DIVISION—continued. / PACIFIC DIVISION.

AGE PERIOD.	New Mexico (Urban)	New Mexico (Rural)	Arizona (Urban)	Arizona (Rural)	Utah (Urban)	Utah (Rural)	Nevada (Urban)	Nevada (Rural)	Washington (Urban)	Washington (Rural)	Oregon (Urban)	Oregon (Rural)	California (Urban)	California (Rural)
All ages	795	833	1,310	699	959	185	101	412	4,699	1,359	1,264	228	18,399	3,246
Under 5 years	75	75	96	60	40	16	4	22	218	71	59	11	1,312	207
5 to 14 years	106	134	171	121	78	39	6	30	389	137	89	28	2,402	492
15 to 24 years	124	151	225	103	148	39	13	43	719	248	176	47	3,328	607
25 to 44 years	345	329	605	275	536	49	57	221	2,530	639	710	75	7,616	1,133
45 to 64 years	111	115	183	118	130	30	16	76	663	223	197	55	3,080	604
65 years and over	30	28	23	21	13	12	5	15	77	34	27	10	570	191
Age unknown	4	1	7	1	14	......	......	5	103	7	6	2	91	12

TABLE 42.—NEGRO MALES AND FEMALES 21 YEARS OF AGE AND OVER, NEGRO MALES 21 YEARS AND OVER IN URBAN AND RURAL COMMUNITIES, AND NEGRO MALES (OF MILITIA AGE, 18 TO 44 YEARS), BY DIVISIONS AND STATES: 1910.

DIVISION AND STATE.	NEGROES 21 YEARS OF AGE AND OVER: 1910.					PERCENTAGE NEGRO IN TOTAL MALE POPULATION 21 YEARS OF AGE AND OVER: 1910.			NEGRO MALES OF MILITIA AGE, 18 TO 44 YEARS: 1910.	
	Total.	Male.			Female.	Total.	In urban communities.	In rural communities.	Number.	Per cent of total males of militia age.
		Total.	In urban communities.	In rural communities.						
UNITED STATES	4,886,615	2,458,873	811,945	1,646,928	2,427,742	9.1	6.1	12.1	1,985,415	9.7
GEOGRAPHIC DIVISIONS:										
New England	43,896	22,074	20,170	1,904	21,822	1.1	1.2	0.5	17,325	1.2
Middle Atlantic	280,865	138,750	113,137	25,613	142,115	2.3	2.7	1.5	115,040	2.5
East North Central	199,868	107,170	83,991	23,179	92,698	1.9	2.8	0.9	81,757	2.0
West North Central	155,497	83,219	58,938	24,281	72,278	2.4	4.6	1.1	64,212	2.5
South Atlantic	1,924,939	955,364	250,083	705,281	969,575	31.1	28.0	32.4	779,085	32.4
East South Central	1,288,157	642,460	146,339	496,121	645,697	30.6	31.8	30.3	510,592	31.4
West South Central	956,610	488,815	123,640	365,175	467,795	21.6	21.0	21.8	401,043	22.1
Mountain	15,678	8,992	6,010	2,982	6,686	1.0	1.8	0.5	7,011	1.0
Pacific	21,105	12,029	9,637	2,392	9,076	0.7	1.0	0.3	9,350	0.8
NEW ENGLAND:										
Maine	877	476	296	180	401	0.2	0.3	0.2	330	0.2
New Hampshire	376	200	116	84	176	0.1	0.2	0.1	137	0.2
Vermont	1,252	975	879	96	277	0.9	1.7	0.2	895	1.2
Massachusetts	25,239	12,591	11,610	981	12,648	1.2	1.2	1.2	10,054	1.3
Rhode Island	6,245	3,067	2,899	168	3,178	1.9	1.8	2.7	2,357	1.9
Connecticut	9,907	4,765	4,370	395	5,142	1.4	1.4	1.0	3,552	1.4
MIDDLE ATLANTIC:										
New York	95,177	45,877	39,600	6,277	49,300	1.6	1.8	1.0	39,488	1.8
New Jersey	58,467	28,601	20,832	7,769	29,866	3.7	3.6	3.9	23,099	3.9
Pennsylvania	127,221	64,272	52,705	11,567	62,949	2.8	3.7	1.3	52,453	2.9
EAST NORTH CENTRAL:										
Ohio	72,871	39,188	29,787	9,401	33,683	2.6	3.5	1.5	29,269	2.7
Indiana	39,037	20,651	16,769	3,882	18,386	2.5	4.6	0.9	15,530	2.7
Illinois	74,355	39,983	32,103	7,880	34,372	2.3	2.9	1.2	31,702	2.4
Michigan	11,584	6,266	4,509	1,757	5,318	0.7	1.1	0.4	4,459	0.7
Wisconsin	2,021	1,082	823	259	939	0.2	0.3	0.1	797	0.2
WEST NORTH CENTRAL:										
Minnesota	5,451	3,390	3,163	227	2,061	0.5	1.1	0.1	2,743	0.6
Iowa	9,567	5,443	3,665	1,778	4,124	0.8	1.7	0.4	4,011	0.8
Missouri	100,978	52,921	37,468	15,453	48,057	5.4	8.3	3.0	41,441	5.7
North Dakota	469	311	168	143	158	0.2	0.8	0.1	250	0.2
South Dakota	561	341	171	170	220	0.2	0.6	0.1	271	0.2
Nebraska	5,594	3,225	2,763	462	2,369	0.9	2.7	0.2	2,600	1.0
Kansas	32,877	17,588	11,540	6,048	15,289	3.5	7.4	1.7	12,896	3.5
SOUTH ATLANTIC:										
Delaware	17,331	9,050	3,574	5,476	8,281	14.6	11.7	17.5	6,911	15.5
Maryland	127,862	63,963	30,294	33,669	63,899	17.4	15.8	19.1	49,386	18.2
District of Columbia	62,070	27,621	27,621		34,449	26.6	26.6		22,472	28.7
Virginia	324,437	159,593	43,548	116,045	164,844	30.5	31.6	30.1	125,692	31.5
West Virginia	37,424	22,757	5,223	17,534	14,667	6.7	7.4	6.5	21,134	7.7
North Carolina	305,988	146,752	27,600	119,152	159,236	29.0	33.8	28.1	115,547	29.5
South Carolina	350,419	169,155	24,728	144,427	181,264	50.5	42.1	52.3	144,019	52.0
Georgia	536,751	266,814	60,115	206,699	269,937	43.0	39.9	44.0	217,970	43.8
Florida	162,657	89,659	27,380	62,279	72,998	41.9	40.6	42.4	75,954	44.2
EAST SOUTH CENTRAL:										
Kentucky	149,107	75,694	33,556	42,138	73,413	12.5	20.3	9.6	58,306	12.7
Tennessee	241,849	119,142	43,903	75,239	122,707	21.6	33.3	17.9	93,709	22.1
Alabama	431,599	213,923	44,146	169,777	217,676	41.7	41.6	41.7	166,099	41.4
Mississippi	465,602	233,701	24,734	208,967	231,901	54.7	43.3	56.5	192,478	55.7
WEST SOUTH CENTRAL:										
Arkansas	214,282	111,365	17,438	93,927	102,917	28.1	28.3	28.1	88,627	28.4
Louisiana	346,922	174,211	43,293	130,918	172,711	42.0	31.1	47.5	144,430	42.7
Oklahoma	67,049	36,841	12,252	24,589	30,208	8.2	11.5	7.2	30,148	8.4
Texas	328,357	166,398	50,657	115,741	161,959	16.6	18.0	16.0	137,838	17.1
MOUNTAIN:										
Montana	1,404	851	665	186	553	0.5	1.3	0.2	613	0.5
Idaho	515	328	217	111	187	0.3	0.8	0.1	253	0.3
Wyoming	1,819	1,325	400	925	494	2.1	2.2	2.1	1,253	2.3
Colorado	8,144	4,283	3,441	842	3,861	1.6	2.5	0.6	3,241	1.6
New Mexico	1,085	644	288	356	441	0.7	2.1	0.4	474	0.6
Arizona	1,399	764	458	306	635	1.0	2.0	0.6	568	1.0
Utah	881	568	489	79	313	0.5	1.0	0.1	445	0.5
Nevada	431	229	52	177	202	0.6	0.9	0.5	164	0.6
PACIFIC:										
Washington	4,817	3,120	2,288	832	1,697	0.7	0.9	0.4	2,538	0.7
Oregon	1,209	766	648	118	443	0.3	0.5	0.1	613	0.3
California	15,079	8,143	6,701	1,442	6,936	0.9	1.2	0.4	6,199	0.9

TABLE 43.—NEGRO MALES AND FEMALES, CLASSIFIED BY AGE PERIODS, BY CITIES HAVING 100,000 INHABITANTS OR MORE: 1910.

AGE PERIOD.	ALBANY, N.Y.		ATLANTA, GA.		BALTIMORE, MD.		BIRMINGHAM, ALA.		BOSTON, MASS.		BRIDGEPORT, CONN.		BUFFALO, N.Y.	
	Male.	Female.	Male.	Female.	Male.	Female.	Male.	Female.	Male.	Female.	Male.	Female.	Male.	Female.
All ages	497	540	23,219	28,683	39,054	45,695	25,662	26,643	6,664	6,900	657	675	933	840
Under 5 years	19	16	2,273	2,349	3,253	3,375	2,276	2,322	445	497	56	58	45	43
Under 1 year	4	6	514	490	684	662	476	466	89	126	14	13	5	11
5 to 9 years	33	45	2,116	2,168	3,060	3,356	2,198	2,315	366	376	58	52	43	46
10 to 14 years	30	34	2,230	2,377	2,759	3,392	2,096	2,300	371	455	29	46	54	55
15 to 19 years	29	47	2,250	3,017	3,084	4,523	2,172	2,706	336	469	35	48	42	61
20 to 24 years	61	76	2,941	4,243	4,358	5,855	3,210	3,779	660	738	71	87	102	105
25 to 29 years	48	65	2,917	3,910	4,632	5,712	3,557	3,806	909	935	95	75	143	132
30 to 34 years	59	71	1,981	2,481	3,853	4,084	2,477	2,541	839	833	78	75	127	94
35 to 39 years	67	43	1,821	2,288	3,718	4,071	2,442	2,338	871	828	86	79	105	98
40 to 44 years	34	31	1,221	1,585	3,020	3,140	1,541	1,367	619	573	49	45	84	66
45 to 49 years	33	34	914	1,380	2,517	2,597	1,493	1,101	456	388	32	30	57	50
50 to 54 years	31	25	962	1,001	1,843	1,976	875	708	345	273	23	29	47	40
55 to 59 years	16	17	522	647	1,064	1,126	499	425	188	191	15	23	40	12
60 to 64 years	11	14	454	484	769	946	297	303	126	137	15	12	21	20
65 to 69 years	9	9	254	315	538	622	171	202	67	82	4	9	11	6
70 to 74 years	5	5	169	167	275	385	92	133	33	54	7	4	8	4
75 to 79 years	6	5	81	119	128	208	43	78	17	26	4	1	3	3
80 to 84 years	1	1	30	58	54	109	22	46	5	19	.....	.....	.....	.....
85 to 89 years	.....	.....	16	29	28	50	20	29	4	10	.....	1	.....	2
90 to 94 years	.....	1	5	16	6	24	5	8	1	2	.....	.....	.....	.....
95 to 99 years	.....	1	9	3	5	14	5	5	.....	4	.....	.....	.....	.....
100 years and over	.....	.....	1	9	.....	6	2	7	.....	.....	.....	1	.....	.....
Age unknown	5	1	52	37	90	124	169	124	6	10	.....	.....	.....	.....

AGE PERIOD.	CAMBRIDGE, MASS.		CHICAGO, ILL.		CINCINNATI, OHIO.		CLEVELAND, OHIO.		COLUMBUS, OHIO.		DAYTON, OHIO.		DENVER, COLO.	
	Male.	Female.	Male.	Female.	Male.	Female.	Male.	Female.	Male.	Female.	Male.	Female.	Male.	Female.
All ages	2,227	2,480	22,685	21,418	9,905	9,734	4,341	4,107	6,784	5,955	2,475	2,367	2,652	2,774
Under 5 years	237	243	1,218	1,254	586	562	246	273	408	428	202	172	147	166
Under 1 year	54	52	279	265	121	137	50	68	76	93	36	39	37	33
5 to 9 years	202	203	1,033	1,114	482	547	218	235	365	419	159	166	138	161
10 to 14 years	203	220	1,062	1,088	591	623	247	238	382	412	138	153	164	169
15 to 19 years	171	231	1,203	1,415	696	810	258	311	475	581	152	203	167	210
20 to 24 years	185	244	2,330	2,541	1,090	1,329	506	537	820	768	252	312	241	315
25 to 29 years	235	272	3,359	3,207	1,370	1,385	589	613	974	780	312	287	330	390
30 to 34 years	193	220	3,282	2,839	1,063	1,076	568	480	857	605	276	274	317	295
35 to 39 years	233	252	3,076	2,577	1,128	1,002	577	457	718	582	287	240	325	316
40 to 44 years	146	161	2,165	1,717	911	741	393	293	551	382	195	149	268	225
45 to 49 years	134	125	1,508	1,261	687	506	262	222	449	311	166	135	196	186
50 to 54 years	97	95	968	890	511	379	223	173	307	237	130	82	161	116
55 to 59 years	78	71	541	507	301	248	93	91	169	157	64	73	71	87
60 to 64 years	48	63	346	360	189	168	66	55	114	117	52	44	56	47
65 to 69 years	37	33	195	231	99	130	35	41	83	63	23	37	42	33
70 to 74 years	13	26	84	135	59	71	23	30	52	43	23	15	8	14
75 to 79 years	8	12	53	85	26	28	9	23	28	23	9	10	9	17
80 to 84 years	2	4	14	40	14	25	13	18	7	16	7	7	.....	14
85 to 89 years	3	2	12	31	4	12	2	5	1	10	.....	5	2	2
90 to 94 years	.....	1	1	9	.....	5	1	2	1	2	1	.....	.....	.....
95 to 99 years	.....	.....	1	4	.....	1	.....	.....	1	2	.....	.....	.....	.....
100 years and over	.....	2	.....	2	2	3	.....	2	1	2	.....	.....	.....	1
Age unknown	2	2	234	111	96	83	12	8	21	16	8	3	10	10

AGE PERIOD.	DETROIT, MICH.		FALL RIVER, MASS.		GRAND RAPIDS, MICH.		INDIANAPOLIS, IND.		JERSEY CITY, N.J.		KANSAS CITY, MO.		LOS ANGELES, CAL.	
	Male.	Female.	Male.	Female.	Male.	Female.	Male.	Female.	Male.	Female.	Male.	Female.	Male.	Female.
All ages	2,985	2,756	174	181	347	318	10,803	11,013	3,020	2,940	11,885	11,681	3,682	3,917
Under 5 years	176	154	12	13	19	17	787	770	270	287	623	588	265	291
Under 1 year	40	33	3	3	6	2	179	167	69	60	123	112	59	55
5 to 9 years	166	177	13	9	21	24	761	762	216	239	565	624	253	284
10 to 14 years	178	164	6	13	16	13	734	789	199	208	590	687	280	364
15 to 19 years	191	194	5	14	20	23	765	955	172	219	784	958	363	426
20 to 24 years	338	358	31	12	30	36	1,191	1,348	311	342	1,337	1,621	419	500
25 to 29 years	421	388	25	23	42	43	1,300	1,415	360	372	1,838	1,808	425	390
30 to 34 years	357	321	29	21	42	28	1,126	1,155	380	342	1,530	1,435	373	401
35 to 39 years	344	276	21	20	31	28	1,113	1,060	277	216	1,422	1,246	304	291
40 to 44 years	253	190	12	14	24	20	802	764	192	153	1,043	828	272	245
45 to 49 years	189	169	6	15	28	24	575	614	130	99	761	591	196	179
50 to 54 years	137	128	8	12	17	20	597	504	50	71	504	435	104	98
55 to 59 years	84	78	2	6	16	15	389	319	50	.....	312	268	83	67
60 to 64 years	52	62	3	6	17	5	278	218	40	44	182	161	50	40
65 to 69 years	41	43	.....	1	11	6	171	141	17	24	98	112	26	21
70 to 74 years	22	24	1	1	3	7	84	78	7	14	46	83	7	13
75 to 79 years	12	18	.....	1	1	2	54	50	4	6	27	51	7	10
80 to 84 years	5	2	.....	.....	2	.....	20	19	1	4	10	28	2	3
85 to 89 years	1	3	.....	.....	.....	4	13	11	3	.....	6	6	2	3
90 to 94 years	.....	1	.....	.....	.....	1	1	6	.....	.....	1	6	1	1
95 to 99 years	.....	1	.....	.....	.....	1	2	5	.....	.....	.....	4	.....	.....
100 years and over	.....	.....	.....	.....	.....	2	.....	.....	.....	.....	.....	.....	.....	.....
Age unknown	17	5	.....	.....	5	3	39	30	6	5	203	132	9	18

TABLE 43.—NEGRO MALES AND FEMALES, CLASSIFIED BY AGE PERIODS, BY CITIES HAVING 100,000 INHABITANTS OR MORE: 1910—Continued.

AGE PERIOD.	LOUISVILLE, KY.		LOWELL, MASS.		MEMPHIS, TENN.		MILWAUKEE, WIS.		MINNEAPOLIS, MINN.		NASHVILLE, TENN.		NEW HAVEN, CONN.	
	Male.	Female.	Male.	Female.	Male.	Female.	Male.	Female.	Male.	Female.	Male.	Female.	Male.	Female.
All ages	19,602	20,920	62	71	25,259	27,182	478	502	1,499	1,093	16,229	20,294	1,711	1,850
Under 5 years	1,190	1,268	3	8	1,834	1,895	24	22	58	55	1,356	1,365	134	137
Under 1 year	255	255		1	374	394	6	8	11	11	313	257	27	30
5 to 9 years	1,266	1,254	4	5	1,787	1,949	11	33	61	54	1,417	1,467	128	118
10 to 14 years	1,374	1,545	3	1	1,626	1,828	21	16	59	77	1,523	1,705	128	122
15 to 19 years	1,716	1,888	7	8	2,240	2,641	19	29	77	73	1,815	2,201	114	122
20 to 24 years	2,223	2,605	3	7	3,313	4,055	52	84	132	128	1,833	2,688	128	142
25 to 29 years	2,507	2,648	5	10	3,629	4,054	65	102	242	149	1,622	2,383	164	192
30 to 34 years	2,056	2,217	8	5	2,834	2,894	70	48	211	168	1,265	1,774	179	255
35 to 39 years	1,994	1,925	8	4	2,477	2,350	72	56	200	146	1,246	1,758	180	197
40 to 44 years	1,550	1,444	3	6	1,668	1,502	46	37	155	82	923	1,262	193	173
45 to 49 years	1,223	1,249	7	3	1,161	1,250	39	24	125	51	805	1,067	165	156
50 to 54 years	931	925	1	3	1,011	903	26	17	61	38	949	905	95	101
55 to 59 years	556	608	2	5	578	540	12	13	29	22	515	522	74	73
60 to 64 years	381	506	3	2	363	463	10	8	16	13	353	440	59	57
65 to 69 years	252	306	2		290	296	7	5	10	10	265	328	33	50
70 to 74 years	157	202	1	1	170	230		3	11	5	159	182	31	32
75 to 79 years	76	103	1	1	107	129	2	1	8	4	99	106	12	25
80 to 84 years	40	62			39	83			3	1	34	55	9	13
85 to 89 years	15	34		1	28	30			1	1	22	33	6	2
90 to 94 years	4	19			11	12		1		1	10	24	1	2
95 to 99 years	2	12			4	5		1		1	4	7		
100 years and over	1	1			3	5					7	11	2	1
Age unknown	88	99	1		86	68	2	2	40	14	7	11	4	2

AGE PERIOD.	NEW ORLEANS, LA.		NEW YORK CITY, N. Y.		NEW YORK CITY, BY BOROUGHS.									
					Manhattan Borough.		Bronx Borough.		Brooklyn Borough.		Queens Borough.		Richmond Borough.	
	Male.	Female.	Male.	Female.	Male.	Female.	Male.	Female.	Male.	Female.	Male.	Female.	Male.	Female.
All ages	40,946	48,316	42,143	49,566	28,024	32,510	1,911	2,206	10,245	12,463	1,440	1,758	523	629
Under 5 years	3,736	3,888	3,227	3,449	1,943	2,111	190	203	898	926	150	148	46	61
Under 1 year	802	810	814	780	497	495	51	41	221	196	33	34	12	14
5 to 9 years	3,806	4,018	2,401	2,713	1,349	1,560	149	160	749	800	111	134	43	59
10 to 14 years	3,712	4,018	2,246	2,612	1,237	1,491	136	143	729	787	100	140	44	51
15 to 19 years	3,698	5,057	2,660	3,620	1,685	2,250	140	152	687	985	104	164	44	69
20 to 24 years	4,249	5,945	5,110	7,254	3,700	4,972	164	280	1,044	1,680	155	242	47	80
25 to 29 years	4,618	5,730	6,904	8,479	5,056	6,060	216	303	1,418	1,834	165	205	49	77
30 to 34 years	3,763	4,419	5,756	6,154	4,088	4,295	227	228	1,218	1,411	167	160	56	60
35 to 39 years	3,770	4,184	5,051	5,115	3,475	3,493	204	219	1,174	1,218	137	150	61	35
40 to 44 years	2,892	3,020	3,282	3,273	2,185	2,169	150	137	811	820	106	114	30	33
45 to 49 years	2,162	2,254	2,111	2,423	1,360	1,583	106	100	544	626	80	87	21	27
50 to 54 years	1,542	1,726	1,334	1,635	824	987	74	68	363	478	54	70	19	32
55 to 59 years	944	1,117	787	963	432	553	57	49	241	312	40	38	17	11
60 to 64 years	688	1,012	500	688	259	383	25	41	166	221	29	29	21	14
65 to 69 years	525	738	335	461	174	227	30	36	102	154	22	36	7	8
70 to 74 years	331	487	166	280	82	129	13	43	54	84	6	18	11	6
75 to 79 years	191	280	77	146	37	73	13	14	19	52	7	4	1	3
80 to 84 years	101	174	41	80	14	31	8	14	14	28	3	6	2	1
85 to 89 years	35	74	17	48	7	27	4	4	2	11	3	5	1	1
90 to 94 years	14	45	3	11		1	1	2	1	6		1	2	1
95 to 99 years	4	15	3	14	1	5	1	2	1	4		3		
100 years and over	6	16	1	7	1	2		2		2		1		
Age unknown	159	99	131	141	115	108	4	6	10	24	1	3	1	

AGE PERIOD.	NEWARK, N. J.		OAKLAND, CAL.		OMAHA, NEB.		PATERSON, N. J.		PHILADELPHIA, PA.		PITTSBURGH, PA.		PORTLAND, OREG.	
	Male.	Female.	Male.	Female.	Male.	Female.	Male.	Female.	Male.	Female.	Male.	Female.	Male.	Female.
All ages	4,477	4,998	1,614	1,441	2,379	2,047	710	829	39,431	45,028	13,351	12,272	608	437
Under 5 years	428	447	107	109	122	121	56	76	3,391	3,472	1,128	1,112	21	24
Under 1 year	98	102	25	25	18	23	16	9	825	770	239	220	4	6
5 to 9 years	363	349	97	86	121	118	66	54	2,716	2,907	978	964	22	20
10 to 14 years	272	354	53	78	92	110	76	47	2,348	2,859	871	972	15	17
15 to 19 years	334	416	94	107	123	152	50	68	2,268	3,475	849	973	16	21
20 to 24 years	407	597	173	147	248	273	62	116	3,935	5,989	1,207	1,369	48	50
25 to 29 years	528	657	214	181	361	340	77	107	5,486	6,702	1,816	1,784	81	65
30 to 34 years	523	574	206	174	346	266	71	84	4,981	5,298	1,673	1,424	100	66
35 to 39 years	502	498	185	150	319	221	68	103	4,757	4,645	1,591	1,294	110	62
40 to 44 years	379	320	141	121	223	136	62	62	3,287	3,041	1,198	822	83	42
45 to 49 years	264	260	135	87	165	126	39	21	2,396	2,205	772	536	43	31
50 to 54 years	207	175	83	67	115	72	32	32	1,596	1,629	560	359	32	12
55 to 59 years	92	129	37	45	70	46	20	19	857	907	260	235	14	8
60 to 64 years	78	80	39	36	25	21	12	12	563	701	187	167	14	9
65 to 69 years	47	46	23	17	20	19	6	11	362	419	109	92		1
70 to 74 years	22	43	12	9	12	7	8	8	191	299	55	53	2	3
75 to 79 years	12	23	11	14	8	8	3	7	81	188	25	29	1	5
80 to 84 years	5	10	1	6	2	6	1		32	91	8	17	2	1
85 to 89 years	1	3	2	1	3			1	14	36	4	10	1	
90 to 94 years		2		4	2	1			2	15	2	2		
95 to 99 years		1							3	13				
100 years and over	1		1	1			1			6		3		
Age unknown	12	14	1	1	2	4		2	165	131	58	55	3	

TABLE **43.**—NEGRO MALES AND FEMALES, CLASSIFIED BY AGE PERIODS, BY CITIES HAVING 100,000 INHABITANTS OR MORE: 1910—Concluded.

AGE PERIOD.	PROVIDENCE, R. I.		RICHMOND, VA.		ROCHESTER, N. Y.		ST. LOUIS, MO.		ST. PAUL, MINN.		SAN FRANCISCO, CAL.		SCRANTON, PA.	
	Male.	Female.	Male.	Female.	Male.	Female.	Male.	Female.	Male.	Female.	Male.	Female.	Male.	Female.
All ages	2,577	2,739	21,472	25,261	424	455	22,168	21,792	1,904	1,240	1,025	617	305	262
Under 5 years	257	201	1,975	2,044	24	34	1,314	1,371	81	83	52	49	17	20
Under 1 year	58	40	492	504	7	4	248	290	18	11	11	11	2	8
5 to 9 years	167	205	1,825	2,013	29	23	1,243	1,345	68	72	34	27	23	25
10 to 14 years	175	208	1,894	1,994	25	32	1,293	1,387	74	75	28	37	23	17
15 to 19 years	169	229	2,054	2,753	34	26	1,567	1,752	86	91	63	44	23	29
20 to 24 years	255	255	2,788	3,626	49	70	2,479	2,756	179	153	120	75	27	34
25 to 29 years	317	330	2,668	3,008	61	69	3,082	3,005	347	174	185	86	36	39
30 to 34 years	278	254	1,914	2,113	53	56	2,850	2,506	301	175	146	71	41	21
35 to 39 years	276	242	1,827	2,026	40	39	2,655	2,207	271	143	115	71	41	26
40 to 44 years	178	209	1,303	1,818	28	24	1,818	1,592	182	88	80	43	22	19
45 to 49 years	154	164	1,153	1,345	24	28	1,397	1,212	129	67	63	44	21	18
50 to 54 years	106	158	791	952	32	23	911	875	79	42	46	21	14	4
55 to 59 years	100	102	453	598	12	14	532	586	46	25	27	11	10	5
60 to 64 years	63	73	338	523	10	8	388	475	28	14	20	12	3	2
65 to 69 years	39	34	224	321	3	5	284	267	15	17	20	7	2	1
70 to 74 years	27	36	103	146	....	....	160	178	6	9	9	7	1	....
75 to 79 years	5	13	42	81	....	1	84	91	8	6	8	5	1	1
80 to 84 years	4	13	24	45	....	2	39	62	1	2	2	3	....	1
85 to 89 years	2	....	8	17	....	1	13	30	3	2	2	1	....	....
90 to 94 years	1	4	4	13	....	....	4	10	....	1	....	....	....	....
95 to 99 years	....	....	1	5	....	....	6	11	....	....	....	....	....	....
100 years and over	....	1	1	3	....	....	3	10	....	....	....	....	....	....
Age unknown	4	8	82	74	....	....	46	64	....	1	5	3	....	....

AGE PERIOD.	SEATTLE, WASH.		SPOKANE, WASH.		SYRACUSE, N. Y.		TOLEDO, OHIO.		WASHINGTON, D. C.		WORCESTER, MASS.	
	Male.	Female.	Male.	Female.	Male.	Female.	Male.	Female.	Male.	Female.	Male.	Female.
All ages	1,394	902	391	332	579	545	937	940	42,615	51,831	570	671
Under 5 years	53	46	17	20	35	31	54	60	3,581	3,709	54	50
Under 1 year	9	12	7	3	8	5	16	10	732	726	13	12
5 to 9 years	38	34	15	12	42	44	55	59	3,494	3,698	47	59
10 to 14 years	47	46	20	17	24	36	38	65	3,384	3,827	34	54
15 to 19 years	34	54	29	23	35	39	54	62	3,717	4,903	43	49
20 to 24 years	160	106	32	34	42	63	90	136	4,766	6,567	32	70
25 to 29 years	254	173	45	50	57	69	124	131	5,045	6,527	60	56
30 to 34 years	250	137	49	49	72	66	108	103	4,013	4,950	57	62
35 to 39 years	202	102	62	49	74	53	106	94	4,072	4,856	61	58
40 to 44 years	131	57	50	34	57	30	94	54	2,964	3,363	40	52
45 to 49 years	87	48	32	14	53	38	68	56	2,255	2,772	41	39
50 to 54 years	48	26	19	9	30	26	52	43	1,833	2,228	27	41
55 to 59 years	24	16	10	5	23	16	33	24	1,129	1,354	26	21
60 to 64 years	15	7	4	8	12	11	22	21	902	1,107	22	18
65 to 69 years	9	5	4	4	10	7	20	17	612	706	9	20
70 to 74 years	8	3	2	1	5	3	11	5	340	472	8	11
75 to 79 years	1	2	....	....	5	3	5	5	170	218	5	6
80 to 84 years	....	2	....	....	1	4	....	....	90	149	1	2
85 to 89 years	....	....	....	....	....	....	1	3	36	69	....	....
90 to 94 years	....	....	....	....	....	....	1	....	18	37	1	2
95 to 99 years	....	....	....	....	....	....	....	....	5	15	....	1
100 years and over	....	1	....	....	....	....	....	....	6	14	....	....
Age unknown	33	37	1	3	2	6	1	2	183	290	2	....

TABLE 44.—NEGRO MALES AND FEMALES, CLASSIFIED BY AGE PERIODS, BY CITIES OF 25,000 TO 100,000 INHABITANTS HAVING A NEGRO POPULATION OF 1,000 OR MORE: 1910.

NEGRO POPULATION: 1910.

AGE PERIOD.	ALABAMA.				ARKANSAS.		COLORADO.				CONNECTICUT.		DELAWARE.		FLORIDA.			
	Mobile.		Montgomery.		Little Rock.		Colorado Springs.		Pueblo.		Hartford.		Wilmington.		Jacksonville.		Tampa.	
	Male.	Female.	Male.	Female.	Male.	Female.	Male.	Female.	Male.	Female.	Male.	Female.	Male.	Female.	Male.	Female.	Male.	Female.
All ages	10,344	12,419	8,293	11,029	7,060	7,479	505	602	777	721	797	948	4,390	4,691	14,556	14,737	4,431	4,520
Under 5 years	873	990	712	817	523	672	33	42	42	55	69	81	286	291	1,120	1,114	379	392
Under 1 year	151	183	148	158	100	118	4	11	11	5	19	20	73	59	244	230	91	87
5 to 9 years	962	995	777	866	559	568	47	42	51	60	74	72	328	378	1,131	1,142	377	407
10 to 14 years	883	1,001	816	944	498	546	51	53	47	55	80	72	386	399	1,133	1,183	312	351
15 to 19 years	858	1,199	864	1,120	702	882	33	35	45	66	62	72	337	439	1,197	1,538	351	464
20 to 24 years	1,118	1,670	751	1,321	975	1,004	42	67	69	66	55	103	443	642	1,776	2,157	572	668
25 to 34 years	2,207	2,682	1,454	2,228	1,604	1,715	98	149	168	161	142	205	857	926	3,664	3,737	1,168	1,101
35 to 44 years	1,791	1,826	1,228	1,703	1,064	1,066	100	97	184	131	168	166	772	766	2,702	2,155	770	644
45 to 64 years	1,291	1,545	1,401	1,579	928	896	82	92	146	112	120	146	809	759	1,568	1,413	435	426
65 years and over	264	398	259	417	183	184	11	20	15	9	23	25	150	173	215	263	49	51
Age unknown	97	113	31	34	24	46	8	5	10	6	4	6	22	18	50	35	18	16

AGE PERIOD.	GEORGIA.						ILLINOIS.										INDIANA.	
	Augusta.		Macon.		Savannah.		Danville.		East St. Louis.		Peoria.		Quincy.		Springfield.		Evansville.	
	Male.	Female.	Male.	Female.	Male.	Female.	Male.	Female.	Male.	Female.	Male.	Female.	Male.	Female.	Male.	Female.	Male.	Female.
All ages	8,160	10,184	8,305	9,845	15,218	18,028	753	712	3,233	2,649	867	702	804	792	1,500	1,461	3,220	3,046
Under 5 years	657	669	765	747	1,294	1,329	61	66	238	273	45	48	43	62	111	110	208	220
Under 1 year	126	148	131	136	284	280	8	16	56	49	10	13	7	13	17	18	37	38
5 to 9 years	694	690	793	836	1,264	1,517	56	49	220	258	60	44	54	42	96	123	220	229
10 to 14 years	740	866	789	931	1,191	1,473	46	55	179	195	47	56	71	63	122	122	236	278
15 to 19 years	829	1,139	794	1,025	1,257	1,802	59	72	246	243	54	61	67	70	130	123	255	310
20 to 24 years	956	1,399	940	1,348	1,744	2,688	78	88	408	366	103	81	75	100	149	158	360	363
25 to 34 years	1,665	2,200	1,679	1,998	3,603	4,238	165	154	949	686	246	176	145	138	315	312	730	630
35 to 44 years	1,338	1,538	1,048	1,282	2,733	2,621	147	118	549	366	154	125	133	113	261	220	556	485
45 to 64 years	1,048	1,332	1,097	1,223	1,886	1,951	109	98	368	227	134	86	154	149	261	210	544	421
65 years and over	213	330	240	284	206	374	27	11	66	28	23	22	57	47	48	79	107	105
Age unknown	20	21	160	171	40	35	5	1	10	7	1	3	5	8	7	4	4	5

AGE PERIOD.	INDIANA—continued.		IOWA.		KANSAS.						KENTUCKY.				LOUISIANA.		MASSACHUSETTS.	
	Terre Haute.		Des Moines.		Kansas City.		Topeka.		Wichita.		Covington.		Lexington.		Shreveport.		New Bedford.	
	Male.	Female.	Male.	Female.	Male.	Female.	Male.	Female.	Male.	Female.	Male.	Female.	Male.	Female.	Male.	Female.	Male.	Female.
All ages	1,336	1,257	1,490	1,440	4,622	4,664	2,185	2,353	1,334	1,123	1,398	1,501	5,075	5,936	6,226	7,670	1,485	1,400
Under 5 years	90	96	109	120	351	394	166	174	110	94	114	107	341	340	570	611	185	195
Under 1 year	16	29	30	27	74	65	31	29	16	22	18	22	64	68	106	112	56	53
5 to 9 years	111	103	108	124	381	388	183	206	96	114	86	81	385	355	712	689	129	129
10 to 14 years	82	111	95	105	341	387	186	197	96	88	100	95	419	431	593	640	78	104
15 to 19 years	125	118	109	129	372	469	245	249	117	117	110	126	470	555	532	871	122	95
20 to 24 years	153	181	156	186	464	510	223	256	173	136	141	184	486	713	673	1,067	181	139
25 to 34 years	317	267	326	330	948	964	356	420	309	260	316	339	963	1,183	1,362	1,727	378	274
35 to 44 years	220	186	291	234	795	721	295	322	220	157	248	255	880	947	907	1,004	215	188
45 to 64 years	196	161	245	167	772	645	400	400	168	112	246	260	940	1,095	710	832	157	209
65 years and over	39	32	38	34	173	178	127	123	39	40	37	54	187	309	148	21	40	67
Age unknown	3	2	15	11	25	8	4	6	6	5	......	2	4	8	19	10	......	......

AGE PERIOD.	MASSACHUSETTS—con.		MISSOURI.				NEW JERSEY.											
	Springfield.		St. Joseph.		Springfield.		Atlantic City.		Camden.		East Orange.		Elizabeth.		Orange.		Trenton.	
	Male.	Female.	Male.	Female.	Male.	Female.	Male.	Female.	Male.	Female.	Male.	Female.	Male.	Female.	Male.	Female.	Male.	Female.
All ages	670	805	2,241	2,008	1,003	992	4,851	4,983	2,949	3,127	715	1,192	654	727	1,143	1,336	1,424	1,157
Under 5 years	60	58	128	127	82	68	268	268	279	290	81	91	63	79	127	102	91	92
Under 1 year	12	10	27	25	11	16	56	58	63	61	12	14	19	15	20	24	18	18
5 to 9 years	44	60	144	130	94	83	239	266	262	247	82	77	67	70	102	104	53	73
10 to 14 years	52	70	136	140	96	94	231	272	216	248	67	67	52	64	103	111	68	74
15 to 19 years	59	75	188	211	123	103	277	290	212	285	42	118	62	69	79	96	71	122
20 to 24 years	58	83	274	244	109	121	555	637	273	361	84	225	61	74	107	164	169	144
25 to 34 years	144	189	569	483	149	174	1,427	1,500	550	611	146	287	134	155	249	325	405	249
35 to 44 years	114	105	400	322	131	146	1,119	1,023	518	481	113	175	114	105	196	215	291	177
45 to 64 years	120	134	344	278	177	153	625	620	524	483	82	133	87	91	152	189	235	179
65 years and over	19	26	57	71	36	44	82	85	108	116	18	19	12	16	22	24	41	47
Age unknown	......	5	1	2	6	6	28	22	7	5	......	......	2	4	22	6	......	......

TABLE 44.—NEGRO MALES AND FEMALES, CLASSIFIED BY AGE PERIODS, BY CITIES OF 25,000 TO 100,000 INHABITANTS HAVING A NEGRO POPULATION OF 1,000 OR MORE: 1910—Continued.

NEGRO POPULATION: 1910.

AGE PERIOD.	New Rochelle.		Yonkers.		Charlotte.		Wilmington.		Springfield.		Youngstown.		Zanesville.		Muskogee.	
	Male.	Female.	Male.	Female.	Male.	Female.	Male.	Female.	Male.	Female.	Male.	Female.	Male.	Female.	Male.	Female.
	NEW YORK.				NORTH CAROLINA.				OHIO.						OKLAHOMA.	
All ages	718	1,036	732	817	5,201	6,551	5,482	6,625	2,594	2,339	1,072	864	669	715	3,996	3,835
Under 5 years	96	92	70	66	597	628	666	614	201	179	78	81	68	62	319	377
Under 1 year	22	22	19	11	128	125	145	144	47	39	17	19	10	11	64	78
5 to 9 years	60	68	62	57	591	627	604	595	209	200	78	76	57	71	409	406
10 to 14 years	59	59	44	43	537	585	539	585	183	205	54	66	50	49	349	357
15 to 19 years	46	93	46	76	538	773	498	661	218	219	60	78	61	76	386	439
20 to 24 years	86	171	81	126	579	1,003	597	852	244	257	113	101	66	87	472	497
25 to 34 years	176	271	189	213	876	1,255	873	1,153	521	468	295	231	119	122	824	836
35 to 44 years	116	177	135	120	635	753	615	859	397	315	227	130	108	101	590	472
45 to 64 years	69	91	95	105	674	764	689	885	465	400	142	77	113	106	494	320
65 years and over	9	13	10	11	149	145	159	215	126	91	17	13	24	40	65	50
Age unknown	1	1			25	18	242	206	30	5	8	2	3	1	88	81

AGE PERIOD.	Oklahoma City.		Chester.		Harrisburg.		Norristown Borough.		York.		Newport.		Charleston.		Columbia.	
	Male.	Female.	Male.	Female.	Male.	Female.	Male.	Female.	Male.	Female.	Male.	Female.	Male.	Female.	Male.	Female.
	OKLA.—con.		PENNSYLVANIA.								RHODE ISLAND.		SOUTH CAROLINA.			
All ages	3,534	3,012	2,363	2,432	2,232	2,303	490	525	569	662	718	882	13,714	17,342	5,226	6,320
Under 5 years	246	309	196	217	167	188	47	46	51	78	63	62	1,471	1,514	527	514
Under 1 year	42	63	58	28	48	28	11	10	11	16	16	13	278	293	98	117
5 to 9 years	291	267	177	212	151	157	52	58	49	62	62	74	1,385	1,604	476	548
10 to 14 years	229	228	171	231	161	173	36	49	41	62	45	58	1,376	1,536	509	550
15 to 19 years	262	312	168	204	161	214	34	37	45	54	52	59	1,314	1,884	513	698
20 to 24 years	587	537	234	278	223	284	46	45	57	83	79	69	1,472	2,365	702	1,003
25 to 34 years	966	726	537	510	503	501	101	110	118	140	146	170	2,469	3,419	1,049	1,252
35 to 44 years	566	359	439	363	403	336	87	71	98	77	116	157	2,146	2,583	707	817
45 to 64 years	321	223	387	329	379	373	68	82	91	82	124	180	1,688	1,928	515	688
65 years and over	56	44	59	85	82	74	18	25	19	24	26	52	296	435	112	167
Age unknown	10	7	5	3	2	3	1	2			5	1	97	74	116	83

AGE PERIOD.	Chattanooga.		Knoxville.		Austin.		Dallas.		El Paso.		Fort Worth.		Galveston.		Houston.	
	Male.	Female.	Male.	Female.	Male.	Female.	Male.	Female.	Male.	Female.	Male.	Female.	Male.	Female.	Male.	Female.
	TENNESSEE.				TEXAS.											
All ages	8,848	9,094	3,600	4,038	3,388	4,090	8,680	9,344	710	742	6,781	6,499	3,881	4,155	11,218	12,711
Under 5 years	772	716	283	263	315	344	613	658	57	57	532	531	276	269	909	881
Under 1 year	160	153	60	58	54	59	114	125	13	6	89	97	68	51	179	179
5 to 9 years	707	739	242	297	388	408	683	657	63	49	562	620	290	296	962	997
10 to 14 years	632	711	303	301	333	408	640	689	42	60	483	527	280	314	947	1,035
15 to 19 years	826	967	388	484	371	465	729	964	51	63	537	636	304	398	935	1,324
20 to 24 years	1,210	1,327	437	563	321	494	1,106	1,434	54	90	967	1,010	448	549	1,350	1,913
25 to 34 years	2,059	2,194	775	883	607	773	2,268	2,510	185	234	1,908	1,725	938	1,047	2,587	3,095
35 to 44 years	1,358	1,299	595	590	428	529	1,475	1,315	143	111	1,036	829	726	663	1,866	1,789
45 to 64 years	1,050	887	462	520	450	498	1,003	920	83	62	616	509	517	505	1,351	1,293
65 years and over	159	202	63	81	120	145	146	185	8	10	73	79	95	101	258	307
Age unknown	75	52	52	56	55	26	17	12	24	6	67	33	7	13	53	77

AGE PERIOD.	San Antonio.		Waco.		Lynchburg.		Norfolk.		Portsmouth.		Roanoke.		Huntington.		Wheeling.	
	Male.	Female.	Male.	Female.	Male.	Female.	Male.	Female.	Male.	Female.	Male.	Female.	Male.	Female.	Male.	Female.
	TEXAS—con.				VIRGINIA.								WEST VIRGINIA.			
All ages	4,909	5,807	2,783	3,284	4,029	5,437	11,887	13,152	5,542	6,075	3,650	4,274	1,152	988	609	592
Under 5 years	452	443	263	228	451	431	992	1,016	514	550	384	382	79	71	44	35
Under 1 year	85	95	50	32	99	89	189	217	103	120	100	90	12	10	10	7
5 to 9 years	468	460	273	280	442	389	945	1,027	541	567	358	398	84	97	33	36
10 to 14 years	463	513	276	326	404	482	856	983	477	500	375	415	103	83	22	27
15 to 19 years	492	612	267	341	409	705	1,003	1,301	508	580	391	545	108	116	42	47
20 to 24 years	624	871	304	474	461	826	1,628	2,017	695	826	420	633	138	138	57	83
25 to 34 years	1,049	1,329	510	659	619	922	2,794	3,002	1,166	1,306	706	809	268	197	146	159
35 to 44 years	644	788	432	474	525	696	2,028	1,982	844	861	544	540	198	142	131	99
45 to 64 years	518	563	347	396	562	793	1,411	1,521	686	733	398	434	146	123	118	85
65 years and over	138	173	79	92	135	184	209	295	106	148	71	110	25	21	15	20
Age unknown	61	55	32	14	21	9	21	8	5	4	3	8	3		1	1

TABLE **45.**—NEGRO MALES AND FEMALES, CLASSIFIED BY BROAD AGE PERIODS, BY CITIES HAVING 10,000 TO 25,000 INHABITANTS AND A NEGRO POPULATION OF 1,000 OR MORE: 1910.

CITY.	NEGRO POPULATION: 1910.															
	Male.								Female.							
	All ages.	Under 5 years.		5 to 9 years.	10 to 19 years.	20 to 44 years.	45 years and over.	Age un-known.	All ages.	Under 5 years.		5 to 9 years.	10 to 19 years.	20 to 44 years.	45 years and over.	Age un-known.
		Total.	Under 1 year.							Total.	Under 1 year.					
Alexandria, La	2,700	304	46	329	599	1,113	332	23	3,154	309	40	378	755	1,341	363	8
Alexandria, Va	1,970	158	31	171	359	905	374	3	2,218	197	35	181	388	969	479	4
Alton, Ill	623	53	13	57	113	290	109	1	537	55	4	41	111	238	89	3
Anniston, Ala	2,180	245	57	237	440	820	416	22	2,390	246	49	273	509	1,048	294	20
Argenta, Ark	2,186	214	45	181	330	1,168	292	1	2,024	205	45	181	359	1,000	278	1
Asbury Park, N. J	837	49	10	57	116	423	191	1	1,097	65	18	67	130	613	221	1
Asheville, N. C	2,363	271	53	261	494	990	331	16	2,996	290	59	270	620	1,433	379	1
Atchison, Kans	1,335	98	10	111	257	563	303	3	1,283	94	11	104	256	542	285	4
Athens, Ga	2,847	314	68	338	636	1,087	472	.....	3,469	344	74	358	782	1,457	528	2
Baton Rouge, La	3,430	323	58	352	684	1,481	516	74	4,469	390	73	378	1,019	1,936	684	62
Beaumont, Tex	3,276	345	61	314	558	1,720	338	1	3,620	278	49	333	683	2,020	305	1
Bessemer, Ala	3,176	270	46	282	533	1,606	480	5	3,034	282	70	296	572	1,574	306	4
Bluefield, W. Va	1,113	127	22	83	170	618	115	.....	1,125	108	27	123	219	580	95	.....
Bristol, Tenn.[1]	1,030	108	23	106	223	435	152	6	1,187	126	32	121	242	538	156	4
Brunswick, Ga	2,695	250	46	286	448	1,268	411	32	2,872	245	41	276	618	1,367	342	24
Cairo, Ill	2,692	182	35	187	452	1,356	511	4	2,742	179	34	202	483	1,453	421	4
Carlisle, Pa	517	45	10	68	108	184	112	.....	602	57	8	60	114	215	155	1
Charleston, W. Va	1,484	137	22	125	258	740	221	3	1,602	144	31	131	298	790	235	4
Chickasha, Okla	675	54	10	78	113	345	85	.....	590	72	12	65	109	305	38	1
Coatesville, Pa	839	96	28	74	103	454	102	10	681	75	13	62	130	333	76	5
Coffeyville, Kans	620	52	11	57	101	306	96	8	689	82	17	72	135	303	92	5
Columbus, Ga	3,287	354	78	362	716	1,355	484	16	4,357	351	74	393	874	2,033	692	14
Cumberland, Md	516	50	11	54	93	213	105	1	551	57	11	62	114	218	100	.....
Danville, Va	2,683	308	66	300	641	990	426	18	3,524	266	52	318	787	1,579	566	8
Denison, Tex	1,345	137	23	144	260	566	232	6	1,454	147	33	139	329	650	188	1
Durham, N. C	3,106	311	37	321	742	1,249	449	34	3,763	370	53	370	854	1,679	457	33
Evanston, Ill	568	47	13	58	82	301	78	2	592	68	13	46	79	303	93	3
Frankfort, Ky	1,659	64	13	75	204	1,049	265	2	1,192	67	16	70	212	553	288	2
Frederick, Md	692	74	9	68	140	216	192	2	776	77	17	80	153	292	169	5
Fort Scott, Kans	506	45	13	45	108	182	122	4	541	55	12	48	94	212	127	5
Fort Smith, Ark	2,135	176	31	178	400	1,019	348	14	2,321	209	46	226	468	1,083	324	11
Gadsden, Ala	1,896	186	43	195	352	868	291	4	1,539	183	40	164	329	704	157	2
Greensboro, N. C	2,566	339	75	295	554	1,053	320	5	3,144	351	74	310	672	1,439	370	2
Greenville, S. C	2,829	319	52	329	638	1,128	415	.....	3,490	369	97	337	765	1,538	480	1
Guthrie, Okla	1,434	171	30	181	254	508	316	4	1,542	170	28	183	326	594	265	4
Hagerstown, Md	538	37	5	47	90	229	125	10	587	44	11	44	94	264	136	5
Hannibal, Mo	878	53	9	51	125	418	230	1	968	63	13	67	172	417	249	.....
Hattiesburg, Miss	2,055	226	50	236	411	1,001	178	3	2,302	261	50	244	464	1,130	201	2
Henderson, Ky	1,421	116	23	136	269	572	307	21	1,595	121	25	119	333	703	308	11
Hot Springs, Ark	1,795	117	20	144	286	902	325	21	2,032	96	24	149	335	1,093	331	28
Ironton, Ohio	546	50	10	47	78	271	97	3	500	43	11	62	108	192	95	.....
Jackson, Miss	4,752	513	109	463	869	2,207	653	47	5,802	506	92	555	1,072	2,866	760	43
Jackson, Tenn	2,623	262	58	275	522	1,153	407	4	3,096	257	54	264	638	1,461	473	3
Jacksonville, Ill	610	50	10	47	99	261	145	8	635	53	14	56	113	265	140	8
Jefferson City, Mo	1,312	40	8	63	143	909	157	.....	612	45	9	43	143	257	120	4
Jeffersonville, Ind	729	68	13	73	130	299	157	2	806	73	18	66	162	337	165	3
Keokuk, Iowa	484	24	3	37	74	208	136	5	532	41	8	36	96	215	137	7
Key West, Fla	2,605	343	84	329	519	964	449	1	2,910	324	62	367	622	1,128	469	.....
Lake Charles, La	2,157	264	47	285	458	925	203	22	2,280	255	40	264	541	988	206	26
Lawrence, Kans	822	59	14	59	154	324	212	14	942	71	16	72	180	359	253	7
Leavenworth, Kans	1,166	72	10	97	212	489	290	6	1,311	84	21	112	241	522	339	13
Long Branch, N. J	574	49	10	49	93	289	94	.....	674	65	18	75	127	307	100	.....
McAlester, Okla	1,870	158	19	145	298	1,045	220	4	1,127	116	26	141	220	536	111	3
Marshall, Tex	2,267	265	43	281	489	836	396	.....	2,730	266	52	286	635	1,136	406	1
Meridian, Miss	4,273	462	100	462	866	1,806	574	103	5,048	503	84	509	1,016	2,303	596	121
Monroe, La	2,331	254	39	251	435	1,046	342	3	2,989	284	50	294	561	1,433	416	1
Montclair, N. J	1,009	106	28	89	164	510	130	10	1,476	101	17	99	232	875	152	17
Muncie, Ind	511	34	9	34	81	252	108	2	494	41	9	37	88	234	92	2
Natchez, Miss	2,705	293	60	334	564	995	470	49	3,995	283	56	331	788	1,734	788	71
New Albany, Ind	801	64	11	70	133	344	190	.....	782	56	13	72	146	338	167	3
Newport News, Va	3,714	306	53	319	532	2,192	347	18	3,545	338	59	374	658	1,856	311	8
Owensboro, Ky	1,470	100	25	120	315	635	284	16	1,645	109	14	132	329	757	309	9
Paducah, Ky	2,879	205	47	233	503	1,450	453	35	3,168	230	50	230	606	1,584	479	39
Palestine, Tex	1,632	186	42	152	335	700	256	3	1,922	189	48	179	385	879	288	2
Paris, Tex	1,467	161	40	193	336	555	219	3	1,664	142	16	200	389	702	223	8
Pensacola, Fla	4,923	472	87	504	934	2,348	661	4	5,291	466	83	574	1,068	2,534	644	5
Petersburg, Va	4,831	508	110	567	1,066	1,805	827	58	6,183	557	113	585	1,330	2,514	1,181	16
Pine Bluff, Ark	2,836	261	60	272	513	1,290	479	21	3,288	269	58	264	612	1,627	496	20
Plainfield, N. J	788	77	14	58	136	380	136	1	1,045	72	15	73	182	554	163	1
Raleigh, N. C	3,275	322	72	381	713	1,206	643	10	4,097	356	71	393	868	1,727	739	14
Richmond, Ind	601	51	11	55	85	245	140	25	590	51	12	40	129	237	118	15
Rome, Ga	1,709	194	37	178	336	691	306	4	2,049	203	39	208	422	859	351	6
Sedalia, Mo	903	54	8	56	174	418	201	.....	968	60	7	57	215	425	210	1
Selma, Ala	3,300	312	67	307	693	1,300	672	16	4,563	342	71	366	898	2,053	884	20
Sherman, Tex	1,061	87	11	118	205	434	187	30	1,159	96	22	101	234	517	187	24
Spartansburg, S. C	3,152	400	90	377	729	1,249	393	4	3,721	393	77	392	843	1,647	441	5
Staunton, Va	1,053	96	20	97	198	444	217	1	1,423	99	20	117	310	615	280	2
Steelton, Pa	674	53	17	50	120	362	88	1	560	68	13	45	134	247	66	.....
Temple, Tex	1,404	145	30	173	284	644	151	7	1,410	134	25	161	283	691	134	7
Texarkana, Ark.[2]	2,406	261	54	270	431	1,092	330	22	2,913	229	38	319	646	1,400	300	19
Tulsa, Okla	990	83	14	83	161	571	91	1	969	106	22	75	197	512	78	1
Tyler, Tex	1,331	142	24	181	273	497	218	20	1,623	180	37	184	341	698	199	21
Uniontown, Pa	655	60	15	63	100	335	97	.....	625	72	14	61	117	284	91	.....
Vicksburg, Miss	5,231	463	70	537	962	2,250	1,008	11	6,822	439	70	560	1,220	3,296	1,298	9
Washington, Pa	746	90	22	77	121	327	126	5	725	72	19	74	143	322	110	4
Waycross, Ga	3,769	380	34	441	631	1,929	383	5	2,960	333	44	367	635	1,328	295	2
West Chester, Pa	852	60	7	73	142	388	187	2	1,016	76	22	94	196	437	210	3
Winston, N. C	3,809	331	90	374	924	1,720	457	3	4,019	361	76	403	817	1,985	445	8

[1] Joint population of Bristol, Tenn., and Bristol, Va.　　　　[2] Joint population of Texarkana, Ark., and Texarkana, Tex.

CHAPTER XI.—COLOR—BLACK AND MULATTO ELEMENTS.

SIGNIFICANCE OF THE TERMS "BLACK" AND "MULATTO."

The classification of the Negro population as "black" and "mulatto" does not correspond accurately to any physiological characteristic, although it is a classification which measures with some uncertain degree of accuracy the admixture of white blood in the population classified as Negro. Increase in the proportion mulatto in the Negro population may, however, obviously result, and undoubtedly has in the past largely resulted, from the marriage of mulattoes to blacks, as well as from mixed marriages of Negroes and whites.

Of the Negro race one-fifth were returned as mulattoes at the 1910 census; that is, as not being "evidently full-blooded Negroes," as the instructions to the enumerators read, but having, in the judgment of the enumerator, "some proportion or perceptible trace of Negro blood."

Under a condition of complete segregation of the races this proportion not "evidently full-blooded Negro" must inevitably increase, unless the fact that the children of mixed black and mulatto marriages are not "full-blooded Negroes" becomes imperceptible in the case of at least one-half of such children, assuming a uniform natural increase for the black and mulatto elements of the Negro population.

The perceptibility of a trace of Negro or of white blood probably does not correspond uniformly to the physiological proportion of Negro and white blood in the individuals enumerated. Moreover, perceptibility is dependent upon the ability of the enumerator to perceive, and this ability varies from enumerator to enumerator.

There are undoubtedly many individuals in the United States in whom the trace of white blood has become absolutely imperceptible, and many other individuals in whom the trace, although perceptible, is not in fact perceived by the enumerator. Similarly the trace of Negro blood may have become imperceptible, or be unperceived in individual cases.

The census classification is necessarily based upon perceptibility, qualified by the ability of the enumerator to perceive.

At the census of 1910 enumerators were instructed to indicate the color or race of each person enumerated, distinguishing blacks and mulattoes in the Negro population in accordance with the definition following:

> For census purposes the term "black" includes all persons who are evidently full-blooded Negroes, while the term "mulatto" includes all other persons having some proportion or perceptible trace of Negro blood.

Substantially similar instructions were given to enumerators in 1870, the term mulatto being defined in 1870 to include "quadroons, octoroons, and all persons having any perceptible trace of African blood." Instructions at the census of 1890, however, differed materially from those of 1910 and 1870. In 1890 the term "black" was defined to include all persons "having three-fourths or more 'black blood,'" other persons with any proportion of "black" blood being classified as "mulattoes," "quadroons," or "octoroons." This classification was made under the following instructions to enumerators:

> Be particularly careful to distinguish between blacks, mulattoes, quadroons, and octoroons. The word "black" should be used to describe those persons who have three-fourths or more black blood; "mulatto," those persons who have three-eighths to five-eighths black blood; "quadroon," those persons who have one-fourth black blood; and "octoroon," those persons who have one-eighth or any trace of black blood.[1]

At the censuses of 1850 and 1860 the terms "black" and "mulatto" appear not to have been defined. In 1850 enumerators were instructed simply in enumerating colored persons to write "B" or "M" in the space on the schedule, to indicate black or mulatto, leaving the space blank in the case of whites. In 1860 no instructions are known to have been given to enumerators. No data are available in published reports for the census years 1880 and 1900.

It will be noted that the classification of 1890 provides by implication for a finer distinction in the case of individuals with a comparatively small proportion than it does in the case of individuals with a large proportion of Negro blood. The enumerator was instructed to distinguish persons having one-eighth from persons having one-fourth or two-eighths Negro blood; persons having one-fourth from persons having three to five eighths; and these persons from those having three-fourths or more.

If the exact proportion of Negro and white blood could be accurately determined by the enumerator in each individual case these fractions—one-eighth, one-fourth, three to five eighths, and three-fourths or more would obviously not provide for the classification of the Negro population, since there is no reason to suppose that the number of persons having two, or

---

[1] Regarding the classification of the Negro population of mixed blood in 1890, as mulattoes, quadroons, and octoroons, the following statement is made in the report of the Eleventh Census: "These figures are of little value. Indeed, as an indication of the extent to which the races have mingled, they are misleading." (Census of 1890, Population, Part I, p. xciii.) The aggregate number in the several classes as returned in 1890 was as follows: Blacks, 6,337,980; mulattoes, 956,989; quadroons, 105,135; octoroons, 69,936.

four sixteenths—that is, octoroons or quadroons in the literal sense of these terms—are more numerous than persons having three or five sixteenths. Under the 1890 definitions the class mulatto included persons having from three to five eighths Negro blood, and by implication persons having more than five-eighths—rather than more than three-fourths—were to be classified as blacks. Persons having between one-fourth and one-half Negro blood were divided between mulattoes and quadroons. Consistently with this principle of classification persons having between one-eighth and two-eighths of Negro blood must, it would seem, have been divided by the enumerators—although without specific instructions—between quadroons and octoroons. The extensions indicated in instructions to enumerators make the 1890 classes represent the following proportions: Black, ten-sixteenths or more; mulatto, six to ten sixteenths; quadroons, three to six sixteenths; and octoroons, less than three-sixteenths.

The fractions noted indicate class limits, within which every gradation of intermixture is comprehended, the exact proportion of intermixture in the great majority of cases being in all probability a proportion which can not be accurately stated by any fraction with a small denominator, and ranging by minute gradation, in the aggregate, from an imperceptible trace of white to an imperceptible trace of Negro blood. The provision in the 1890 census law, that "the population schedule shall include an inquiry as to the number of Negroes, mulattoes, quadroons, and octoroons," implies that these classes as distinct classes compose in the aggregate the Negro population, which obviously is not the case, if by octoroon, for example, one means a person in whom the proportion of Negro blood is precisely one-eighth.[1]

---

[1] The fine gradations of admixture of white blood in the Negro population may be simply illustrated. If, for example, six individuals, in which the proportions of Negro blood are respectively precisely one-sixteenth, one-eighth, two-eighths, four-eighths, six-eighths, and eight-eighths, be presumed to intermarry, the number of possible different proportions in their children are 14; and if the group be presumed to be segregated for several generations, the possible different proportions in their great-grandchildren would be represented by approximately 70 fractions having 128 as a denominator and numbers ranging between 17 to 100 as numerators. If the proportions of Negro blood in the original parents were not precisely represented by the fractions given above—as would almost certainly be the case in any group of individuals selected from the Negro population of mixed blood—the number of possible different proportions in the children of third generation would be much greater. Under the assumption made, of complete segregation, the extreme range of differences in the proportion of Negro blood would tend to become less from generation to generation, but the number of different proportions, owing to the finer gradation, would tend to increase indefinitely. The tendency would be for the group collectively to approach a uniform proportion, from which individual proportions would vary by gradations becoming increasingly minute and various. In the hypothetical group supposed above, this limiting uniform proportion would slightly exceed seven-sixteenths Negro. In the mulatto population of the United States as a whole the number of proportions of intermixture is exceedingly great, and there is no reason to suppose that these proportions are concentrated in any considerable degree upon such simple fractions as one-eighth, or one-quarter, or one-half. In the Negro population at the present time, it is not mathematically improbable that any given union of a mulatto with either a black or a mulatto, will in its offspring represent a unique proportion of admixture of white blood.

No attempt has been made at any census, except that of 1890, to secure a return classifying the Negro population of mixed blood according to the proportions of Negro blood. At other censuses the general principle of classification has been to return Negroes showing perceptible traces of white blood as mulattoes, and all others as black. To the extent that the white strain is perceptible in individuals three-fourths (or more than five-eighths) black, they would under the 1910 instructions to enumerators be classified as mulattoes, while under the 1890 instructions they would be classified as black. Some of the increase in the proportion mulatto shown by the census returns—from 15.2 per cent in 1890 to 20.9 per cent in 1910—may, therefore, be a consequence of differences in the instructions to enumerators.

PROPORTION MULATTO: 1850–1910.

In the period of 60 years, 1850 to 1910, the proportion mulatto in the Negro population increased, as is shown in Table 1, from 11.2 to 20.9 per cent, the number of mulattoes per 1,000 blacks being 126 in 1850, and 264 in 1910.

Table 1	NEGRO POPULATION.				
YEAR.	Total.	Black.[1]	Mulatto.[1]		Mulattoes to 1,000 blacks.
			Number.	Per cent.	
1910	9,827,763	7,777,077	2,050,686	20.9	264
1900	8,833,994				
1890	[2] 7,488,676	6,337,980	1,132,060	15.2	179
1880	6,580,793				
1870	4,880,009	4,295,960	584,049	12.0	136
1860	4,441,830	3,853,467	588,363	13.2	153
1850	3,638,808	3,233,057	405,751	11.2	126

[1] No data for 1880 or 1900.
[2] Includes 18,636 Negroes enumerated in Indian Territory, not distinguished as black or mulatto.

In comparing the proportion mulatto at the several censuses for which data are available, allowance must be made for the differences noted above in instructions to enumerators, and also for inaccuracy in the returns. The very considerable increase in the proportion mulatto shown for the entire period, 1850–1910, makes a decrease for any decade in this period, such as is shown for the decade, 1860–1870, highly improbable, and it is to be noted that this decrease developed in the returns of a census—that of 1870—which was admittedly very defective as regards the Negro population. It may be fairly assumed that the change in the proportion mulatto has not been interrupted or reversed in any decade.

In the 20 years, 1850–1870, the percentage mulatto increased from 11.2 to 12, or by 0.8; in the succeeding period of 20 years, 1870–1890, it increased from 12 to 15.2, or by 3.2; and in the 20 years 1890–1910, from 15.2 to 20.9, or by 5.7.

It is not improbable that the increase in the proportion mulatto has, in fact, become as is indicated by the census returns, more rapid from period to period. This might naturally result—even without any continuous infusion of white blood—from the intermarriage of mulattoes with blacks, since the children of such marriages will be mulattoes, under the 1910 definition of the term, provided they show perceptible traces of white blood. The mulatto element increases naturally by the union of mulattoes with mulattoes, of mulattoes with blacks, and of Negroes with whites, while the black increase is largely restricted to the union of blacks with blacks.

In the dissemination of white blood it is conceivable that a stage will be reached at some period in the future where the absorption of the mulatto by the black element in consequence of the white strain becoming imperceptible will equal or even exceed the absorption of the black by the mulatto element—a stage, that is to say, where the trace of white blood will become imperceptible to the census enumerator in the case of at least one-half of the children of mixed mulatto and black parentage. But whatever proportion mulatto future censuses may show for the Negro population, it is inevitable that the dissemination of white blood within the Negro population shall continue to embrace from period to period a larger proportion of that population, until in fact the entire Negro population is affected.

As this gradual modification of the racial character progresses the black element in the population must decrease, and tend to disappear. Under these conditions the standard of classification as black and mulatto may change, the term mulatto being defined with reference not to a pure-blooded Negro, but with reference to a Negro somewhat affected by the general diffusion of white blood.

It is probably true that a much greater proportion than 20.9 per cent of the Negro population in 1910 were of mixed parentage. The proportion more or less affected by the dissemination has been estimated as high as three-fourths, and although no adequate data are available to substantiate such an estimate, the estimate is not in itself improbable. This would mean that in the gradual modification of the Negro population, traces of white blood have already become imperceptible to the census enumerator in approximately one-half of that population, the imperceptibility being probably due in part to a modification of the standard of discrimination, by accepting as the racial type of unmixed descent that type which represents, not the one-quarter of the population which is in fact pure blooded, but the one-half which is slightly modified by the general dissemination of white blood. A progressive modification of the standard of discrimination might obviously prevent the proportion mulatto from increasing, or even occasion it to decline under a condition of complete segregation of the races as the race develops uniformity of type.

In 1850 the proportion mulatto in the free colored population greatly exceeded the proportion in the slave population, the number of mulattoes to 1,000

blacks being 581 in the free colored population of 434,495, and 83 in the slave population of 3,204,313.

A table in the compendium of the Seventh Census gives the ratio of mulattoes to blacks in the Negro population, free and slave, of the several states and territories as shown in Table 2, the ratios representing populations shown in Table 25 (p. 221).

Table 2 STATE AND TERRITORY.	MULATTOES TO 100 BLACKS IN THE NEGRO POPULATION: 1850.		
	Total.	Free.	Slave.
United States	12.55	58.13	8.34
STATES.			
Alabama	7.24	299.47	6.73
Arkansas	16.53	202.49	15.61
California	9.94	9.94	
Connecticut	30.51	30.51	
Delaware	9.29	10.03	3.76
District of Columbia	42.18	48.30	27.80
Florida	10.20	306.99	8.33
Georgia	6.71	108.91	6.31
Illinois	85.53	85.53	
Indiana	89.56	89.56	
Iowa	87.08	87.08	
Kentucky	17.15	35.63	16.40
Louisiana	14.85	416.78	8.82
Maine	51.51	51.51	
Maryland	14.98	22.28	9.56
Massachusetts	34.80	34.80	
Michigan	76.31	76.31	
Mississippi	7.01	215.25	6.80
Missouri	18.69	55.19	78.40
New Hampshire	54.76	54.76	
New Jersey	18.19	18.38	1.72
New York	19.89	19.89	
North Carolina	12.06	167.72	6.19
Ohio	129.52	129.52	
Pennsylvania	40.07	40.07	
Rhode Island	24.87	24.87	
South Carolina	4.48	95.29	3.36
Tennessee	10.88	142.71	9.29
Texas	15.73	183.57	15.27
Vermont	40.23	40.23	
Virginia	17.84	188.13	10.34
Wisconsin	87.87	87.87	
TERRITORIES.[1]			
Minnesota	143.75	143.75	
New Mexico	266.67	266.67	
Oregon	360.00	360.00	
Utah	108.33	60.00	188.89

[1] The Negro population of the territories was as follows: Free, Minnesota, black 16, mulatto 23; New Mexico, black 6, mulatto 16; Oregon, black 45, mulatto 162; Utah, black 15, mulatto 9; 26 slaves, 9 black and 17 mulatto, were reported from Utah, "on their way to California."

At each of the four censuses—1850, 1870, 1890, and 1910—the proportion mulatto in the Negro population has been lowest in the South, and at each of these censuses except that of 1850 it has been highest in the West. In 1910 the percentage mulatto was 20.1 in the South, 26.6 in the North, and 32.1 in the West. In the South the proportion mulatto increased from 10 in 1850, to 11.1 in 1870, to 13.7 in 1890, and to 20.1 in 1910. In the North the percentage decreased from 24.8 in 1850 to 20.3 in 1870, increased to 28 in 1890, and decreased to 26.6 in 1910. In the West the percentage increased from 23.4 in 1850 to 35.6 in 1870, and to 39.2 in 1890, and decreased to 32.1 in 1910. These proportions and the populations which they represent are given in Table 3.

The decrease in the proportion mulatto in the Negro population of the North and West during the 20 years 1890–1910 is probably accounted for by the migration of Negroes into these sections from the South. While the proportion mulatto among migrants out of the South may be higher than it is in the Negro population of the South as a whole, it may very well have been considerably below the proportion in the Negro population resident in the North and West.

The number of mulattoes to 1,000 blacks in 1910 was 252 in the South, 363 in the North, and 473 in the West.

Table 3 SECTION.	NEGRO POPULATION.				
	Total.	Black.	Mulatto. Number.	Mulatto. Per cent.	Mulattoes to 1,000 blacks.
1910					
United States.........	9,827,763	7,777,077	2,050,686	20.9	264
The South...............	8,749,427	6,988,567	1,760,860	20.1	252
The North...............	1,027,674	754,115	273,559	26.6	363
The West...............	50,662	34,395	16,267	32.1	473
1890					
United States.........	¹7,488,676	6,337,980	1,132,060	15.2	179
The South...............	¹6,760,577	5,816,997	924,944	13.7	159
The North...............	701,018	504,506	196,512	28.0	390
The West...............	27,081	16,477	10,604	39.2	644
1870					
United States.........	4,880,009	4,295,960	584,049	12.0	136
The South...............	4,420,811	3,931,107	489,704	11.1	125
The North...............	452,818	360,744	92,074	20.3	255
The West...............	6,380	4,109	2,271	35.6	553
1850					
United States.........	3,638,808	3,233,057	405,751	11.2	126
The South...............	3,352,198	3,017,490	334,708	10.0	111
The North...............	285,369	214,617	70,752	24.8	329
The West...............	1,241	950	291	23.4	306

¹ Includes 18,636 Negroes enumerated in Indian Territory, not distinguished as black or mulatto.

INCREASE OF THE BLACK AND MULATTO ELEMENTS: 1850–1910.

The increases shown in Table 4 relate to the populations of Table 3. Omissions in the enumeration of Negroes in the South at the census of 1870 (see p. 26) affect the increases shown in Table 3 for the South and for the country as a whole, in the two 20-year periods 1850–1870 and 1870–1890, these increases as developed from the census returns being for the earlier period below, and for the later period above the true increases. Omissions at the census of 1870 do not, of course, affect the increases for the entire period of 60 years from 1850 to 1910 in any section of the country. Nor do they affect the increases shown for the North and the West in the periods 1850–1870 and 1870–1890, since the omissions were in the Southern states. The high percentage increases of the West in the earlier periods represent small absolute increases, chiefly by migration of Negroes into this section. As shown in Table 3, the total Negro population of the West in 1850 was only 1,241, the number of blacks being 950 and the number of mulattoes 291. Little specific

significance attaches to percentage increases based upon these small populations, and in Table 4 they have been combined with the populations of the North in computing increases for the period 1850–1910.

Table 4 SECTION.	Number. Total.	Number. Black.	Number. Mulatto.	Per cent. Total.	Per cent. Black.	Per cent. Mulatto.	Mulattoes to 1,000 blacks.
1850–1910							
United States....	6,188,955	4,544,020	1,644,935	170.1	140.5	405.4	362
The South..........	5,397,229	3,971,077	1,426,152	161.0	131.6	426.1	359
The North and West.	791,726	572,943	218,783	276.2	265.8	308.0	382
1890–1910							
United States....	2,357,723	1,439,097	918,626	31.2	22.7	81.1	638
The South..........	2,007,486	1,171,570	835,916	29.7	20.1	90.4	714
The North..........	326,656	249,609	77,047	46.6	49.5	39.2	309
The West..........	23,581	17,918	5,663	87.1	108.7	53.4	316
1870–1890							
United States¹...	2,590,031	2,042,020	548,011	53.5	47.5	93.8	268
The South¹........	2,321,130	1,885,890	435,240	52.5	48.0	88.9	231
The North..........	248,200	143,762	104,438	54.8	39.9	113.4	726
The West..........	20,701	12,368	8,333	324.5	301.0	366.9	674
1850–1870							
United States....	1,241,201	1,062,903	178,298	34.1	32.9	43.9	168
The South..........	1,068,613	913,617	154,996	31.8	30.3	46.3	170
The North..........	167,449	146,127	21,322	58.7	68.1	30.2	146
The West..........	5,139	3,159	1,980	414.1	331.7	680.4	627

¹ Does not include 18,636 Negroes enumerated in Indian Territory, not distinguished as black and mulatto.

In the period of 60 years, 1850–1910, the increase of the black element in the Negro population amounted to 4,544,020, or 140.5 per cent, and the increase of the mulatto element to 1,644,935, or 405.4 per cent. The black population in 1910 was less than two and one-half times as great as in 1850, while the mulatto population in 1910 was more than five times as great as in 1850.

These relative increases obtained approximately in the South. In the North and West the relative increase of the blacks was greater, and of the mulattoes less than in the South, the percentage increase for the period of 60 years being for the black element, in the Negro population of the North and West combined 265.8 per cent, and in the mulatto element 308. Since the black element has during the period constituted more than two-thirds of the combined Negro population of these sections, and has constituted from nine-tenths to four-fifths of the Negro population of the South, the rate of growth of the Negro population as a whole approximates more nearly to that of the black, than to that of the mulatto element. In the South although the mulatto element increased from 1850 to 1910 by 426.1 per cent, the total Negro population of the South increased only 161 per cent, a rate not greatly in excess of that shown by the black element, of 131.6 per cent. The corresponding increases per cent in the North and West were 308 for the mulatto element, 276.2 for the total Negro population, and 265.8 for the black element.

In the 20 years 1890–1910, the black element in the South increased 20.1 per cent and the mulatto element 90.4 per cent, and in each preceding 20-year period the relative increase of the mulattoes greatly exceeded that of the blacks. In the North and in the West the black element increased in the period 1890–1910 more rapidly than the mulatto, the percentage being 49.5 in the North and 108.7 in the West for blacks, as compared with 39.2 and 53.4 for mulattoes. In the preceding period of 20 years the mulatto element increased more rapidly than the black in both of these sections, and in the period 1850–1870 the black element increased more rapidly than the mulatto in the North, the reverse being the case in the small Negro population of the West.

Migration of Negroes from the South into the North and West undoubtedly accounts for the relatively more rapid increase of the black element as compared with the mulatto increase in these sections in the period 1890–1910. The proportion mulatto in the Negro population of the South in 1890 (13.7 per cent) was less than one-half as great as the proportion in the North (28 per cent), and if approximately the same proportion obtained among the Negro emigrants out of the South as obtained in the Negro population resident in the South, the effect of migration would be to add relatively larger numbers to the black than to the mulatto elements of the North and West.

The relatively low rate of increase (39.9 per cent) of the black element in the North in the period 1870–1890, as compared with the rate for the mulatto element in this section in the same period (113.4 per cent) is more difficult to explain, as is also the relatively low rate of increase of the mulatto element of the North in the period 1890–1910 (39.2 per cent) as compared with the rate for this element in the preceding 20-year period (113.4 per cent). These differences can not, it would seem, be accounted for by the differences noted above, in instructions to enumerators at the several censuses, as regards definition of the term "mulatto," since these differences, in so far as they affected the returns, would tend to an understatement of the mulatto increase in the earlier period and to an overstatement of that increase in the later period. The figures would seem to indicate that the proportion mulatto among migrants out of the South was greater in the period 1870–1890 than it was in the period 1890–1910. The absolute increase of the black element in the North was 143,762 in the period 1870–1890, and 249,609 in the period 1890–1910, the absolute increases for the mulatto element in these periods being 104,438 and 77,047—the absolute increase of the black element being much greater, and of the mulatto element considerably smaller in the period 1890–1910 than in the 20 years preceding.

The Negro population is classified as black and mulatto, by divisions and states, and the percentage black and mulatto given in Table 22 (p. 218) for the three census years 1910, 1890, and 1870. The increases based upon this table are given in Table 23 (p. 219). Table 24 (p. 220) for divisions and states relates to the year 1860, and classifies the free and slave, black and mulatto population by sex. Similar data, without distinction of sex, are given, by states, in Table 25 for the year 1850.

PROPORTION MULATTO, BY SEX: 1910, 1870, AND 1860.

Data are available for the black and mulatto population by sex for the years 1910, 1870, and 1860, and in Table 5 the distribution by sex in the three years specified is shown for these elements of the Negro population, together with the excess of males or of females in each element, the number of males per 1,000 females, and the percentage black and mulatto for males and for females.

Table 5	NEGRO POPULATION.[1]							
YEAR AND CLASS OF POPULATION.	Both sexes.	Male.	Female.	Excess—		Males to 1,000 females.	Percentage distribution by color.	
				Of males.	Of females.		Males.	Females.
1910. Total....	9,827,763	4,885,881	4,941,882	....	56,001	989	100.0	100.0
Black........	7,777,077	3,922,332	3,854,745	67,587	....	1,018	80.3	78.0
Mulatto......	2,050,686	963,549	1,087,137	....	123,588	886	19.7	22.0
1870. Total....	4,880,009	2,393,263	2,486,746	....	93,483	962	100.0	100.0
Black........	4,295,960	2,115,367	2,180,593	....	65,226	970	88.4	87.7
Mulatto......	584,049	277,896	306,153	....	28,257	908	11.6	12.3
1860. Total....	4,441,830	2,216,744	2,225,086	....	8,342	996	100.0	100.0
Black........	3,853,467	1,936,536	1,916,931	19,605	....	1,010	87.4	86.2
Mulatto......	588,363	280,208	308,155	....	27,947	909	12.6	13.8

[1] The classification by sex of the black and mulatto population was not made in the report for 1890; nor in the report for 1850, except for the free colored in Connecticut, Louisiana, New York City, and New Orleans. (See Table 8 of Chapter VI.)

At each of these censuses the number of females in the mulatto population exceeded the number of males, the number of males to 1,000 females being markedly lower in 1910 (886) than at either of the two earlier censuses (908 in 1870 and 909 in 1860).

In the black population the number of males exceeded the number of females in 1910 and in 1860, the returns for 1870 showing an excess of females in the black as in the mulatto population. This excess of females shown for 1870 in the census returns of the black population may have developed in consequence of the extensive omissions in the enumeration of Negroes at the Ninth Census, since it is not improbable that a larger proportion of males—who would be generally away from the home at the time the enumerator called—than of females failed of enumeration.

The excess of females in the Negro population as a whole has been commented upon (see Chapter IX, and also section on "Sex distribution by age" of Chapter X), and it appears from Table 5 that this excess is specifically characteristic of the mulatto element.

The percentage mulatto among males increased from 12.6 in 1860 to 19.7 in 1910, and among females from 13.8 in 1860 to 22 in 1910.

In Table 6 the sex distribution of the black and mulatto population is shown by sections.

Table 6

SECTION.	NEGRO POPULATION: 1910.			
	Total.	Black.	Mulatto.	Percentage mulatto.
	MALE.			
United States	4,885,881	3,922,332	963,549	19.7
The South	4,339,625	3,516,671	822,954	19.0
The North	518,544	386,244	132,300	25.5
The West	27,712	19,417	8,295	29.9
	FEMALE.			
United States	4,941,882	3,854,745	1,087,137	22.0
The South	4,409,802	3,471,896	937,906	21.3
The North	509,130	367,871	141,259	27.7
The West	22,950	14,978	7,972	34.7
	MALES TO 1,000 FEMALES.			
United States	989	1,018	886	
The South	984	1,013	877	
The North	1,018	1,050	937	
The West	1,207	1,296	1,041	

In each section, as in the country as a whole, the proportion mulatto among females in 1910 exceeded the proportion among males, the percentage mulatto being in the South 19 for males and 21.3 for females, in the North 25.5 for males and 27.7 for females, and in the West 29.9 for males and 34.7 for females.

The excess of males and of females, and the number of males per 1,000 females, in the black and mulatto elements, are shown in Table 7 by sections for 1910.

Table 7

SECTION.	BLACKS AND MULATTOES: 1910.					
	Excess of males.		Excess of females.		Males to 1,000 females.	
	Black population.	Mulatto population.	Black population.	Mulatto population.	Black population.	Mulatto population.
United States	65,587			123,588	1,018	886
The South	44,775			114,952	1,013	877
The North	18,373			8,959	1,050	937
The West	4,439		323		1,296	1,041

Table 26 (p. 222) classifies the black and mulatto population of divisions and states in 1910 by sex, giving the excess of males and of females in each element, and the sex ratio. The sex distinction in the classification of the black and mulatto population is shown also for 1860, in Table 24 (p. 220).

The sex ratios of the Negro population, black and mulatto, are given in Table 8 in comparison with corresponding ratios for the other racial classes in the population for the three years for which data are available for the black and mulatto elements.

Table 8

RACIAL CLASS.	MALES TO 1,000 FEMALES.		
	1910	1870	1860
Total population	1,060	1,022	1,047
Negro	989	962	996
Black	1,018	970	1,010
Mulatto	886	908	909
White	1,066	1,028	1,053
Native	1,027	1,006	1,037
Native parentage	1,040		
Foreign or mixed parentage	995		
Foreign-born	1,292	1,153	1,151
Indian	1,035	950	1,190
Chinese	14,301	12,841	18,581
Japanese	6,941	(1)	

[1] Number of females less than 100.

In each of the racial classes distinguished in Table 8, except among Negroes, and specifically among mulattoes, and among native whites of foreign or mixed parentage, the number of males exceeded the number of females, in 1910. In 1870 and in 1860, also, excess of males over females characterizes all classes shown, other than Negro, except that females exceeded males in the Indian population in 1870.

PROPORTION MULATTO, BY AGE: 1910.

Table 9 gives the percentage mulatto in the Negro population classified by age periods, for the United States as a whole, and for each of the three geographic sections in 1910. The populations which these percentages represent are given in Table 27 (p. 223), which gives corresponding data for each of the three southern divisions. Similar data are given for Southern states in Table 28.

Table 9

AGE.	PERCENTAGE MULATTO IN THE NEGRO POPULATION: 1910.							
	United States.		The South.		The North.		The West.	
	Male.	Female.	Male.	Female.	Male.	Female.	Male.	Female.
All ages	19.7	22.0	19.0	21.3	25.5	27.7	29.9	34.7
Under 5 years	22.0	22.5	21.3	21.8	31.0	31.2	40.7	38.8
Under 1 year	24.0	24.2	23.3	23.5	32.0	32.2	43.0	39.6
5 to 9 years	20.9	21.5	20.2	20.8	30.4	30.1	37.4	38.8
10 to 14 years	20.5	21.5	19.9	20.8	29.2	29.3	36.8	37.1
15 to 19 years	20.4	22.6	19.7	22.0	27.9	29.0	36.7	38.6
20 to 44 years	19.0	22.6	18.1	21.8	24.1	27.1	27.6	34.0
45 years and over	17.4	20.3	16.5	19.5	22.9	25.5	27.8	31.6
Age unknown	17.0	18.7	16.6	18.5	18.6	19.7	21.2	18.2

In the Negro population as a whole, and in the Negro population of each geographic section, among both males and females, the percentage mulatto is highest in the population under 1 year of age, and lowest in the population 45 years of age and over, except that in the West the proportion among males 45 and over slightly exceeds the proportion among males 20 to 44 years of age.

While the change in the proportion mulatto by age is more or less irregular in the several sections, the proportion in the younger ages generally exceeds the proportion in the older ages among both males and females. This would necessarily be the case in a population in which the proportion mulatto was increasing by the gradual dissemination of white blood through the intermarriage of mulattoes with blacks, each generation showing a larger proportion affected with a strain of white blood.

PROPORTION OF CHILDREN IN THE BLACK AND MULATTO POPULATION.

Table 10 gives the percentage under 5 years of age in the black and mulatto elements of the Negro population, male and female.

Table 10 SEX.	PERCENTAGE UNDER 5 YEARS OF AGE IN THE NEGRO POPULATION: 1910.		
	Total.	Black.	Mulatto.
Both sexes	12.9	12.6	13.7
Male	12.9	12.5	14.4
Female	12.8	12.7	13.1

Of the mulatto population 13.7 per cent were under 5 years of age in 1910, and of the black population 12.6 per cent. In the black population the proportion under 5 among females (12.7 per cent) slightly exceeded the proportion among males (12.5 per cent) and in the mulatto population the proportion among males (14.4 per cent) considerably exceeded the proportion among females (13.1 per cent).

While the higher proportion of children in the mulatto population might result from a higher birth rate in this element, as compared with the black element, or from a higher mortality in the adult population among mulattoes, as compared with blacks, the more probable explanation is to be found in the mixed marriages of mulattoes with blacks. The children of such marriages will in a majority of cases be classified as mulattoes, although only one-half of the parents are in this class. In other words, to the extent that blacks marry mulattoes they are in a majority of cases estopped from any natural increase whatever since their children are credited to the mulatto element.

PROPORTION MULATTO IN THE URBAN AND RURAL POPULATION.

The aggregate urban and rural Negro population, male and female, is classified as black and mulatto in Table 11, for the country as a whole and for each geographic section, the percentage mulatto in the urban and in the rural aggregates being given.

In each section in 1910 the proportion mulatto in the urban population exceeded the proportion in the rural, the percentage mulatto in the aggregate urban for the country as a whole being 27.2, and in the

aggregate rural 18.5. These were practically the proportions obtaining in the South.

Table 11 SECTION.	NEGRO POPULATION: 1910.					
	Urban.		Rural.		Percentage mulatto.	
	Black.	Mulatto.	Black.	Mulatto.	Urban.	Rural.
BOTH SEXES.						
United States	1,957,709	731,520	5,819,368	1,319,166	27.2	18.5
The South	1,350,050	504,405	5,638,517	1,256,455	27.2	18.2
The North	581,167	213,799	172,948	59,760	26.9	25.7
The West	26,492	13,316	7,903	2,951	33.4	23.7
MALE.						
United States	952,085	327,399	2,970,247	636,150	25.6	17.6
The South	646,439	219,507	2,870,232	603,447	25.3	17.4
The North	281,494	101,347	94,750	30,953	26.5	24.6
The West	14,152	6,545	5,265	1,750	31.6	24.9
FEMALE.						
United States	1,005,624	404,121	2,849,121	683,016	28.7	19.3
The South	703,611	284,898	2,768,285	653,008	28.8	19.1
The North	289,673	112,452	78,198	28,807	28.0	26.9
The West	12,340	6,771	2,638	1,201	35.4	31.3

In the North the proportion mulatto in the urban (26.9 per cent) is slightly lower than the corresponding proportion in the South. In the West 33.4 per cent, or one-third, of the urban Negro population is mulatto.

The proportion mulatto in the rural population of the North (25.7 per cent) and West (23.7 per cent) exceeds the corresponding proportion in the South, the rural proportion in the North approaching nearly to the urban proportion in the North and in the South.

The proportion mulatto among males is lower than among females in both the urban and the rural population.

Table 12 gives the number of males to 1,000 females in the black and mulatto population classified as urban and rural.

Table 12 RACIAL CLASS.	MALES TO 1,000 FEMALES: 1910.	
	Urban population.	Rural population.
Negro population	908	1,021
Black	947	1,043
Mulatto	810	931

In the urban population black and mulatto the number of females exceeds the number of males. In the rural black population males are in excess, and in the rural mulatto population females.

CLASSES OF URBAN COMMUNITIES.

Table 13 gives, by sex, the black and mulatto aggregate population for classes of urban communities, the percentage mulatto and the sex ratio being given for these urban classes.

Table 13

COLOR AND SEX.	NEGRO POPULATION: 1910.						
		Urban communities.					Rural communities.
	Total.	Places of 500,000 or more.	Places of 100,000 to 500,000.	Places of 25,000 to 100,000.	Places of 10,000 to 25,000.	Places of 2,500 to 10,000.	
	NUMBER.						
Negro:							
Both sexes....	2,689,229	396,615	626,946	602,040	408,362	655,266	7,138,534
Male........	1,279,484	189,837	297,674	286,286	193,721	311,966	3,606,397
Female.....	1,409,745	206,778	329,272	315,754	214,641	343,300	3,532,137
Black:							
Both sexes......	1,957,709	295,134	429,709	449,907	301,026	481,933	5,819,368
Male........	952,085	143,000	210,064	218,215	146,240	234,566	2,970,247
Female.......	1,005,624	152,134	219,645	231,692	154,786	247,367	2,849,121
Mulatto:							
Both sexes......	731,520	101,481	197,237	152,133	107,336	173,333	1,319,166
Male........	327,399	46,837	87,610	68,071	47,481	77,400	636,150
Female.......	404,121	54,644	109,627	84,062	59,855	95,933	683,016
	PERCENTAGE MULATTO.						
Both sexes........	27.2	25.6	31.5	25.3	26.3	26.5	18.5
Male...........	25.6	24.7	29.4	23.8	24.5	24.8	17.6
Female.........	28.7	26.4	33.3	26.6	27.9	27.9	19.3
	MALES TO 1,000 FEMALES.						
Negro...........	908	918	904	907	903	909	1,021
Black...........	947	940	956	942	945	948	1,043
Mulatto.........	810	857	799	810	793	807	931

In the aggregate for each class of cities shown in Table 13 the percentage mulatto among both males and females exceeds the percentage mulatto in the rural aggregate, and in each urban aggregate, black and mulatto, the number of females exceeds the number of males.

The excess of males over females in the black and mulatto aggregates shown in Table 13 is given in Table 14, which distributes the excess of females in each of these elements by urban communities.

Table 14

CLASS OF COMMUNITY.	NEGRO POPULATION: 1910.					
	Total.		Black.		Mulatto.	
	Excess of males.	Excess of females.	Excess of males.	Excess of females.	Excess of males.	Excess of females.
Total...............	....	56,001	67,587	....	....	123,588
Urban population.........	....	130,261	....	53,539	....	76,722
Places of 500,000 or more.	....	16,941	....	9,134	....	7,807
Places of 100,000 to 500,000.	....	31,598	....	9,581	....	22,017
Places of 25,000 to 100,000.	....	29,468	....	13,477	....	15,991
Places of 10,000 to 25,000.	....	20,920	....	8,546	....	12,374
Places of 2,500 to 10,000..	....	31,334	....	12,801	....	18,533
Rural population........	74,260	....	121,126	....	....	46,866

Table 29 (p. 227) classifies the black and mulatto urban and rural population, male and female, by divisions and states. The percentage mulatto in the urban and rural aggregates, the percentage urban in the male and female black and mulatto population, and the sex ratio in the urban and rural black and mulatto population are given, by states, in Table 30 (p. 228).

BLACK AND MULATTO POPULATION OF INDIVIDUAL CITIES.

Table 15 shows the percentage mulatto in the population of each of the 96 cities having in 1910 a Negro population of 5,000 or more. In 28 of these cities—20 in the South, 7 in the North, and 1 in the West—mulattoes constituted one-third or more of the Negro population. Greenville, S. C., with a Negro population 53.7 per cent mulatto, was the only one of the cities listed in Table 14 in which mulattoes constituted one-half or more of the Negro population. The seven other cities in which mulattoes constituted 40 per cent or more of the Negro population were the following: Portsmouth, Va. (49.5 per cent); Norfolk, Va. (48.7 per cent); Petersburg, Va. (48.2 per cent); Paducah, Ky. (47.3 per cent); Chicago, Ill. (41.6 per cent); Galveston, Tex. (41.2 per cent); and Detroit, Mich. (40 per cent). In 20 other of these cities the percentage mulatto ranged between 33.3 and 39.9.

The black and mulatto populations of the cities listed in Table 15 are given in Table 31 (p. 229).

Table 15

CITY.	Percentage mulatto: 1910.	CITY.	Percentage mulatto: 1910.
Greenville, S. C...............	53.7	Memphis, Tenn................	26.4
Portsmouth, Va................	49.5	Winston, N. C.................	25.7
Norfolk, Va....................	48.7	San Antonio, Tex.............	25.4
Petersburg, Va................	48.2	Savannah, Ga.................	25.2
Paducah, Ky..................	47.3	New York, N. Y..............	24.9
Chicago, Ill...................	41.6	Spartanburg, S. C............	24.5
Galveston, Tex................	41.2	Little Rock, Ark.............	23.8
Detroit, Mich.................	40.0	Charleston, S. C.............	23.6
Richmond, Va.................	39.9	Texarkana, Ark [1]...........	23.5
Muskogee, Okla...............	39.6	Pittsburgh, Pa...............	23.4
Denver, Colo..................	39.2	Athens, Ga..................	23.1
Chattanooga, Tenn............	38.4	Oklahoma City, Okla........	22.8
Lynchburg, Va................	37.9	Brunswick, Ga..............	22.6
Louisville, Ky................	36.6	Charlotte, N. C.............	21.9
Danville, Va.................	36.0	Evansville, Ind.............	21.9
Washington, D. C.............	34.9	Baltimore, Md...............	21.5
Waycross, Ga.................	34.9	Birmingham, Ala............	21.4
Providence, R. I..............	34.8	New Bern, N. C.............	21.4
Columbus, Ga.................	34.5	Greensboro, N. C............	20.6
Kansas City, Kans............	34.5	Knoxville, Tenn.............	20.2
Boston, Mass.................	34.3	Newark, N. J................	18.3
New Orleans, La..............	34.1	Lexington, Ky..............	18.0
Asheville, N. C...............	34.0	Pensacola, Fla..............	17.2
St. Louis, Mo.................	34.0	Indianapolis, Ind...........	17.1
Tampa, Fla..................	33.9	Dallas, Tex.................	17.0
Roanoke, Va..................	33.6	Augusta, Ga................	16.8
Durham, N. C.................	33.4	Bessemer, Ala..............	16.7
Columbus, Ohio...............	33.3	Philadelphia, Pa...........	16.6
Los Angeles, Cal..............	32.9	Camden, N. J...............	16.2
Nashville, Tenn..............	32.8	Alexandria, La.............	16.0
Kansas City, Mo..............	32.5	Fort Worth, Tex............	16.0
Atlanta, Ga..................	32.4	Houston, Tex...............	15.9
Cairo, Ill....................	32.2	Texarkana, Tex [1]..........	14.6
Baton Rouge, La..............	31.6	Atlantic City, N. J.........	14.2
Columbia, S. C...............	31.6	Newport News, Va...........	14.2
Helena, Ark..................	31.3	Shreveport, La..............	14.0
East St. Louis, Ill............	30.8	Austin, Tex.................	13.8
Pine Bluff, Ark..............	30.1	Greenville, Miss............	13.8
Jackson, Tenn................	29.8	Waco, Tex..................	13.7
Cincinnati, Ohio.............	29.6	Jacksonville, Fla...........	13.6
Cleveland, Ohio..............	29.6	Beaumont, Tex..............	13.2
Key West, Fla................	28.9	Monroe, La.................	12.5
Montgomery, Ala.............	27.7	Meridian, Miss.............	12.4
Vicksburg, Miss..............	27.6	Macon, Ga.................	12.3
Jackson, Miss................	27.3	Jersey City, N. J...........	12.2
Natchez, Miss................	26.8	Wilmington, Del............	10.9
Mobile, Ala..................	26.5	Selma, Ala.................	9.2
Wilmington, N. C.............	26.5	Raleigh, N. C...............	9.0

[1] Joint population of Texarkana, Miller County, Ark., and Texarkana, Bowie County, Tex., 15,445; Negro population, 5,319; black, 4,357; mulatto, 962, or 18.1 per cent.

SCHOOL ATTENDANCE OF BLACK AND MULATTO CHILDREN.[1]

The number of school age attending school and not attending school, of any kind, at any time between September 1, 1909, and April 15, 1910, is given, for the black and mulatto populations by sections, divisions and Southern states, in Table 32 (p. 230). Table 16 assembles the aggregates for sections, and gives the percentage in school by age periods.

Table 16

AGE.	NEGRO POPULATION: 1910.					
	Black.		Mulatto.		Percentage in school.	
	In school.	Not in school.	In school.	Not in school.	Black.	Mulatto.
	UNITED STATES.					
6 to 20 years	1,230,843	1,465,328	388,856	337,130	45.7	53.6
6 to 9 years	369,352	411,993	119,602	89,903	47.3	57.1
10 to 14 years	607,401	305,247	184,594	58,024	66.6	76.1
15 to 20 years	254,090	748,088	84,660	189,203	25.4	30.9
	THE SOUTH.					
6 to 20 years	1,125,347	1,388,786	341,593	308,770	44.8	52.5
6 to 9 years	334,665	401,270	103,879	85,849	45.5	54.8
10 to 14 years	556,481	298,902	162,621	55,976	65.1	74.4
15 to 20 years	234,201	688,614	75,093	166,945	25.4	31.0
	THE NORTH.					
6 to 20 years	101,758	73,975	44,914	27,008	57.9	62.4
6 to 9 years	33,509	10,363	15,003	3,853	76.4	79.6
10 to 14 years	49,153	6,170	20,906	1,976	88.8	91.4
15 to 20 years	19,096	57,442	9,005	21,179	24.9	30.9
	THE WEST.					
6 to 20 years	3,738	2,567	2,349	1,352	59.3	63.5
6 to 9 years	1,178	360	720	201	76.6	78.2
10 to 14 years	1,767	175	1,067	72	91.0	93.7
15 to 20 years	793	2,032	562	1,079	28.1	34.2

The black population 6 to 20 years of age, returned as attending school in 1910 numbered 1,230,843, and the number returned as not in school 1,465,328. Of the total not in school, 411,993 were 6 to 9 years of age, 305,247 were 10 to 14 years of age, and 748,088 were 15 to 20 years of age. Of the 305,247 black children 10 to 14 years of age not in school, 298,902 were in the South, 6,170 in the North, and 175 in the West. For black children of this age the percentage attending school was 65.1 in the South, 88.8 in the North, and 91 in the West.

The number of mulattoes 6 to 20 years of age returned as attending school in 1910 was 388,856, and the number not attending school 337,130. Of the mulatto children 10 to 14 not attending school, 55,976 were in the South, 1,976 in the North, and 72 in the West, the percentage in school for these children

[1] For data relating to school attendance of the Negro population, see Chapter XV.

being 74.4 in the South, 91.4 in the North, and 93.7 in the West.

The proportion attending school in the population of school age among mulattoes exceeds the proportion among blacks in each section of the country.

Table 17 gives the percentage attending school by sex for the black and mulatto population of school age.

Table 17

AGE.	PERCENTAGE IN SCHOOL: 1910.			
	Male population.		Female population.	
	Black.	Mulatto.	Black.	Mulatto.
6 to 20 years	43.7	52.3	47.5	54.7
6 to 9 years	46.1	56.1	48.5	58.0
10 to 14 years	63.6	69.6	73.6	78.5
15 to 20 years	22.7	27.8	28.3	33.0

At each age period a larger proportion of females than of males were attending school in both the black and the mulatto population; and at each age period for both males and females the proportion in school was higher for mulattoes than for blacks.

The black and mulatto population 6 to 20 years of age, and the percentage in school for each class of Negro population is given in Table 18 by divisions and Southern states. Tables 19 and 20, also, present data for the black and mulatto element in the Negro population.

Table 18

SECTION, DIVISION, AND STATE.	NEGRO POPULATION 6 TO 20 YEARS OF AGE.				PERCENTAGE IN SCHOOL.	
	Total.	Black.	Mulatto.		Black.	Mulatto.
			Number.	Per cent.		
United States	3,422,157	2,696.171	725,986	21.2	45.6	53.6
The South	3,164,496	2,514,133	650,363	20.6	44.8	52.5
The North	247,655	175,733	71,922	29.0	57.9	62.4
The West	10,006	6,305	3,701	37.0	59.3	63.5
The South:						
South Atlantic	1,504,019	1,186,665	317,354	21.1	45.3	53.2
East South Central	944,880	759,535	185,345	19.6	45.6	54.2
West South Central	715,597	567,933	147,664	20.6	42.4	48.9
The North:						
New England	15,539	9,860	5,679	36.5	65.4	66.1
Middle Atlantic	95,194	74,808	20,386	21.4	56.6	61.2
East North Central	72,837	46,717	26,120	35.9	59.7	63.5
West North Central	64,085	44,348	19,737	30.8	56.7	61.3
The West:						
Mountain	4,170	2,758	1,412	33.9	59.8	62.5
Pacific	5,836	3,547	2,289	39.2	58.9	64.0
THE SOUTH.						
South Atlantic:						
Delaware	10,078	8,785	1,293	12.8	56.5	66.0
Maryland	73,230	59,194	14,036	19.2	51.5	56.6
District of Columbia	23,593	15,245	8,348	35.4	57.7	62.4
Virginia	242,413	160,037	82,376	34.0	44.9	51.5
West Virginia	18,481	11,818	6,663	36.1	51.3	56.2
North Carolina	264,025	208,314	55,711	21.1	52.9	58.8
South Carolina	331,429	277,698	53,731	16.2	44.3	53.6
Georgia	439,485	361,255	78,230	17.8	40.5	49.5
Florida	101,285	84,319	16,966	16.8	43.0	49.5
East South Central:						
Kentucky	81,976	60,436	21,540	26.3	52.6	56.9
Tennessee	163,397	121,084	42,313	25.9	45.2	53.1
Alabama	327,176	270,891	56,285	17.2	39.0	48.7
Mississippi	372,331	307,124	65,207	17.5	50.3	58.8
West South Central:						
Arkansas	159,431	129,485	29,946	18.8	47.6	52.7
Louisiana	254,580	198,809	55,771	21.9	27.2	34.9
Oklahoma	48,718	34,004	14,714	30.2	62.0	67.9
Texas	252,868	205,635	47,233	18.7	50.5	57.0

SECTION, DIVISION, STATE, AND SEX.	Table 19 — PERCENTAGE IN SCHOOL OF NEGRO POPULATION 6 TO 20 YEARS OF AGE: 1910.							
	Total.		6 to 9 years of age.		10 to 14 years of age.		15 to 20 years of age.	
	Black.	Mulatto.	Black.	Mulatto.	Black.	Mulatto.	Black.	Mulatto.
BOTH SEXES.								
United States.......	45.6	53.6	47.3	57.1	66.6	76.1	25.4	30.9
The South......	44.8	52.5	45.5	54.8	65.1	74.4	25.4	31.0
The North......	57.9	62.4	76.4	79.6	88.8	91.4	24.9	29.8
The West......	59.3	63.5	76.6	78.2	91.0	93.7	28.1	34.2
MALE.								
United States.......	43.7	52.3	46.1	56.1	63.6	73.6	22.7	28.3
The South.........	42.7	51.1	44.3	53.6	62.0	71.7	22.6	28.3
South Atlantic......	43.0	51.5	45.8	55.3	62.6	72.4	21.3	27.1
East South Central...	43.6	52.9	45.0	55.7	62.1	72.9	24.5	31.1
West South Central...	40.9	47.8	40.2	47.5	60.6	68.5	22.6	27.3
The North..........	57.9	63.0	75.8	79.8	88.6	91.3	24.3	28.6
New England..........	66.0	64.7	87.3	87.4	93.7	94.6	27.2	26.4
Middle Atlantic......	58.2	62.8	77.3	79.6	90.0	92.7	21.5	25.7
East North Central...	58.7	64.0	77.5	82.0	89.9	92.7	25.3	29.2
West North Central...	55.1	61.2	68.9	75.5	83.8	86.9	26.8	31.3
The West.............	57.7	63.2	76.5	78.0	90.8	93.3	24.7	32.8
Mountain.............	59.7	63.5	73.4	72.5	90.4	92.9	26.9	34.3
Pacific..............	56.2	63.1	79.5	81.3	91.0	93.5	23.2	31.9
The South.								
South Atlantic........	43.0	51.5	45.8	55.3	62.6	72.4	21.3	27.1
Delaware.............	57.4	70.0	63.2	76.5	82.2	91.7	30.5	41.4
Maryland............	51.0	57.3	58.6	65.7	76.3	82.8	22.1	26.4
Dist. Columbia.......	58.6	61.4	73.3	75.3	89.1	89.5	26.8	32.2
Virginia.............	42.5	49.8	40.1	48.9	65.6	73.7	21.8	26.7
West Virginia........	46.3	52.5	68.5	69.1	80.5	81.3	16.7	21.8
North Carolina.......	50.8	57.5	51.7	59.1	69.1	75.1	32.2	38.0
South Carolina.......	42.0	51.9	41.2	52.9	61.4	72.4	23.1	29.2
Georgia..............	37.7	47.1	44.3	56.0	55.1	66.0	13.2	18.9
Florida..............	40.7	47.5	46.1	56.2	59.6	67.0	18.3	21.4
East South Central.......	43.6	52.9	45.0	55.7	62.1	72.9	24.5	31.1
Kentucky.............	50.0	56.0	56.2	64.3	75.8	81.4	25.4	28.9
Tennessee............	42.7	51.5	44.5	55.5	64.7	73.8	23.1	29.1
Alabama.............	36.8	46.8	34.4	44.6	53.7	65.8	21.7	29.0
Mississippi..........	48.5	58.1	52.6	62.8	65.9	75.7	27.4	35.2
West South Central.......	40.9	47.8	40.2	47.5	60.6	68.5	22.6	27.3
Arkansas.............	46.3	51.1	47.7	52.8	62.7	67.6	30.4	33.6
Louisiana............	25.7	33.7	26.5	34.5	39.8	51.7	11.0	14.5
Oklahoma............	60.5	68.0	62.6	70.0	83.3	88.0	38.8	46.5
Texas................	48.7	55.7	45.2	52.6	75.7	82.8	25.6	31.9
FEMALE.								
United States.......	47.5	54.7	48.5	58.0	69.6	78.5	27.8	33.0
The South............	46.8	53.8	46.7	55.8	68.2	77.0	28.0	33.2
South Atlantic......	47.6	54.7	48.3	57.0	69.5	78.5	27.5	33.2
East South Central...	47.7	55.4	47.6	58.2	68.4	78.3	29.8	35.0
West South Central...	43.8	49.9	42.0	50.4	65.1	72.2	26.5	31.0
The North............	57.9	62.0	76.9	79.3	89.1	91.5	25.5	30.9
New England..........	64.9	67.4	87.5	86.0	94.9	93.9	29.7	32.9
Middle Atlantic......	55.1	59.8	77.6	79.8	89.4	92.1	20.2	25.1
East North Central...	60.6	63.0	79.5	81.2	90.4	92.5	28.6	31.8
West North Central...	58.2	61.4	70.6	74.2	85.8	88.8	31.2	35.0
The West.............	60.8	63.7	76.7	78.4	91.2	94.1	31.3	35.5
Mountain.............	59.8	61.7	75.9	76.6	89.7	90.8	30.8	33.6
Pacific..............	61.5	64.9	77.3	79.6	92.3	96.0	31.7	36.6
The South.								
South Atlantic........	47.6	54.7	48.3	57.0	69.5	78.5	27.5	33.2
Delaware.............	55.5	62.3	64.4	72.8	83.8	88.5	25.4	29.8
Maryland............	51.9	56.0	60.8	66.4	79.2	84.0	22.1	27.3
Dist. Columbia.......	56.9	63.2	74.5	79.1	91.1	92.9	26.7	37.9
Virginia.............	47.4	53.0	43.5	50.6	70.7	78.0	28.9	33.2
West Virginia........	57.1	60.0	69.1	70.2	84.8	86.8	27.4	33.2
North Carolina.......	55.0	60.0	53.6	59.9	74.1	80.2	38.9	42.5
South Carolina.......	46.4	55.2	43.7	54.7	67.6	77.7	29.4	35.8
Georgia..............	43.3	51.7	46.8	58.0	65.4	75.9	20.8	26.8
Florida..............	45.3	51.1	49.3	58.5	66.4	74.5	24.3	28.1
East South Central.......	47.7	55.4	47.6	58.2	68.4	78.3	29.8	35.0
Kentucky.............	55.2	57.7	58.7	63.3	79.3	84.7	34.1	34.6
Tennessee............	47.7	54.5	47.5	57.9	70.0	78.8	30.0	34.0
Alabama.............	41.2	50.5	36.9	48.7	61.2	72.9	26.8	33.2
Mississippi..........	52.1	59.5	55.3	65.0	72.1	80.5	31.4	37.6
West South Central.......	43.8	49.9	42.0	50.4	65.1	72.2	26.5	31.0
Arkansas.............	48.9	54.2	48.6	54.2	67.7	73.8	33.1	38.4
Louisiana............	28.6	36.0	28.4	38.3	44.5	55.0	14.8	18.7
Oklahoma............	63.6	67.7	65.8	71.5	85.5	89.8	41.7	45.3
Texas................	52.2	58.2	47.3	55.4	80.1	86.1	31.3	36.8

As a class the mulattoes include 20.9 per cent, or a little over one-fifth, of the entire Negro population, and a slightly larger proportion, 21.2 per cent, of the population 6 to 20 years of age. They are proportionally more numerous in the North and West than in the South, constituting 29 and 37 per cent, respectively, of the Negro population 6 to 20 years of age in those sections. The proportion is nearly uniform in the three southern divisions, but in the northern divisions varies from 21.4 per cent in the Middle Atlantic to 36.5 per cent in the New England division. In the Southern states the lowest percentages are found in Delaware, South Carolina, Florida, Alabama, and Mississippi; the highest in West Virginia, the District of Columbia, and Virginia. The percentage in North Carolina is considerably higher than in South Carolina.

For each section and each division, except the West South Central, the percentage in school of mulattoes 6 to 20 years of age represents the majority of that age period; and in the southern divisions the only states showing less than 50 per cent are Georgia, Florida, Alabama, and Louisiana. The highest percentages are those for Oklahoma, 67.9; Delaware, 66; the District of Columbia, 62.4, and North Carolina and Mississippi, each 58.8. Compared with the percentages for the blacks, those for the mulattoes are higher in each section, division, and Southern state, the excess in favor of the mulattoes being greater in the South than in the North.

Similarly, as may be noted in Table 19, the different age periods show higher percentages for the mulattoes than for the blacks, among both males and females. This is true for each age period and for both sexes in every Southern state, and is true in the North and West except in New England and in the Mountain division, although the difference in the percentages for mulattoes as compared with blacks is in some cases slight. The situation in the Southern states as well as in the several sections, and for the two sexes, is set forth by age periods in the percentages of Table 19.

In general, it seems to be the fact that in those sections where opportunities are equal for all classes of population the difference between the blacks and mulattoes diminishes. This will be apparent from Table 20 which shows the excess of the percentage in school of mulattoes over blacks, by sections and age periods.

Table 20 — SECTION.	EXCESS OF PERCENTAGE IN SCHOOL: MULATTOES OVER BLACKS.			
	Total, 6 to 20 years of age.	6 to 9 years of age.	10 to 14 years of age.	15 to 20 years of age.
United States..................	8.0	9.8	9.5	5.5
The South......................	7.7	9.3	9.3	5.6
The North......................	4.5	3.2	2.6	4.9
The West.......................	4.2	1.6	2.7	6.1

ILLITERACY OF BLACKS AND MULATTOES.[1]

The number and percentage illiterate in the black and mulatto, male and female, population 10 years of age and over, and in the male population 21 years of age and over, are given, by divisions and states, in Table 33 (p. 231). Table 21 summarizes the data relating to illiteracy for these elements of the Negro population, by sections and southern divisions.

In 1910 illiterates constituted 32.3 per cent of the male and 33.4 per cent of the female black population 10 years of age and over, the corresponding proportions in the mulatto population being 20.8 per cent for males and 21.2 per cent for females. These propor-

[1] For data relating to illiteracy in the Negro population, see Chapter XVI.

tions are equivalent approximately to one-third of the black population and to one-fifth of the mulatto population, male and female.

In the Negro population, male and female, the proportion illiterate was higher among blacks than among mulattoes in each section and southern division.

In both the black and the mulatto population, as a whole, the proportion illiterate is higher for females than for males.

The proportion illiterate among adult males 21 years of age and over was 35.5 per cent for blacks and 23.6 per cent for mulattoes. This proportion was highest in the Negro population of the East South Central division (41.4 for blacks, and 28.6 for mulattoes) and was lowest in the West (7.1 for blacks, and 5.6 for mulattoes).

ILLITERACY IN THE BLACK AND MULATTO POPULATION 10 YEARS OF AGE AND OVER, CLASSIFIED BY SEX, BY SECTIONS AND SOUTHERN DIVISIONS: 1910.

Table 21

SECTION AND SOUTHERN DIVISION.	Male. Black.	Male. Mulatto.	Female. Black.	Female. Mulatto.	Illiterate. Number. Male. Black.	Illiterate. Number. Male. Mulatto.	Illiterate. Number. Female. Black.	Illiterate. Number. Female. Mulatto.	Illiterate. Per cent. Male. Black.	Illiterate. Per cent. Male. Mulatto.	Illiterate. Per cent. Female. Black.	Illiterate. Per cent. Female. Mulatto.	Illiterate Males 21 yrs. Black. Number.	Illiterate Males 21 yrs. Black. Per cent.	Illiterate Males 21 yrs. Mulatto. Number.	Illiterate Males 21 yrs. Mulatto. Per cent.
United States	2,941,656	695,730	2,870,657	809,879	951,074	144,926	959,746	171,985	32.3	20.8	33.4	21.2	711,865	35.5	107,270	23.6
The South	2,593,275	580,888	2,547,131	687,245	914,427	136,812	920,811	161,911	35.3	23.6	36.2	23.6	677,376	39.4	99,805	27.2
South Atlantic	1,189,572	280,725	1,184,051	332,588	412,962	64,145	416,925	75,400	34.7	22.8	35.2	22.7	304,332	39.0	46,888	26.6
East South Central	803,975	166,946	788,310	201,667	297,375	40,518	295,172	48,442	37.0	24.3	37.4	24.0	222,522	41.4	30,155	28.6
West South Central	599,728	133,217	574,770	152,990	204,090	32,149	208,714	38,069	34.0	24.1	36.3	24.9	150,522	37.3	22,762	26.8
The North	330,833	107,745	310,547	115,928	35,500	7,755	37,722	9,682	10.7	7.2	12.1	8.4	33,405	12.5	7,141	8.6
The West	17,548	7,097	12,979	6,706	1,147	359	1,213	392	6.5	5.1	9.3	5.8	1,084	7.1	324	5.6

TABLE **22.**—NEGRO POPULATION, CLASSIFIED AS BLACK AND MULATTO, BY DIVISIONS AND STATES: 1910, 1890, AND 1870.

[Classification as black and mulatto not available for 1900 or 1880.]

DIVISION AND STATE.	NEGRO POPULATION.									PER CENT OF TOTAL NEGRO POPULATION.					
	1910			1890			1870			1910		1890		1870	
	Total.	Black.	Mulatto.	Total.	Black.	Mulatto.	Total.	Black.	Mulatto.	Black.	Mulatto.	Black.	Mulatto.	Black.	Mulatto.
UNITED STATES	9,827,763	7,777,077	2,050,686	7,488,676	6,337,980	1,132,060	4,880,009	4,295,960	584,049	79.1	20.9	84.8	15.2	88.0	12.0
GEOGRAPHIC DIVISIONS:															
New England	66,306	44,156	22,150	44,580	30,001	14,579	31,705	22,625	9,080	66.6	33.4	67.3	32.7	71.4	28.6
Middle Atlantic	417,870	335,901	81,969	225,326	177,174	48,152	148,033	126,044	21,989	80.4	19.6	78.6	21.4	85.1	14.9
East North Central	300,836	201,027	99,809	207,023	130,024	76,999	130,497	92,372	38,125	66.8	33.2	62.8	37.2	70.8	29.2
West North Central	242,662	173,031	69,631	224,089	167,307	56,782	142,583	119,703	22,880	71.3	28.7	74.7	25.3	84.0	16.0
South Atlantic	4,112,488	3,256,669	855,819	3,262,690	2,823,905	438,785	2,216,705	1,985,984	230,721	79.2	20.8	86.6	13.4	89.6	10.4
East South Central	2,652,513	2,145,458	507,055	2,119,797	1,830,762	289,035	1,464,252	1,302,024	162,228	80.9	19.1	86.4	13.6	88.9	11.1
West South Central	1,984,426	1,586,440	397,986	1,378,090	1,162,330	197,124	739,854	643,099	96,755	79.9	20.1	85.5	14.5	86.9	13.1
Mountain	21,467	15,332	6,135	12,971	8,334	4,637	1,555	1,082	473	71.4	28.6	64.3	35.7	69.6	30.4
Pacific	29,195	19,063	10,132	14,110	8,143	5,967	4,825	3,027	1,798	65.3	34.7	57.7	42.3	62.7	37.3
NEW ENGLAND:															
Maine	1,363	737	626	1,190	507	683	1,606	1,014	592	54.1	45.9	42.6	57.4	63.1	36.9
New Hampshire	564	356	208	614	248	366	580	436	144	63.1	36.9	40.4	59.6	75.2	24.8
Vermont	1,621	1,185	436	937	521	416	924	677	247	73.1	26.9	55.6	44.4	73.3	26.7
Massachusetts	38,055	24,100	13,955	22,144	14,108	8,036	13,947	9,686	4,261	63.3	36.7	63.7	36.3	69.4	30.6
Rhode Island	9,529	6,350	3,179	7,393	5,396	1,997	4,980	3,820	1,160	66.6	33.4	73.0	27.0	76.7	23.3
Connecticut	15,174	11,428	3,746	12,302	9,221	3,081	9,668	6,992	2,676	75.3	24.7	75.0	25.0	72.3	27.7
MIDDLE ATLANTIC:															
New York	134,191	103,583	30,608	70,092	54,852	15,240	52,081	46,498	5,583	77.2	22.8	78.3	21.7	89.3	10.7
New Jersey	89,760	75,553	14,207	47,638	40,436	7,202	30,658	27,105	3,553	84.2	15.8	84.9	15.1	88.4	11.6
Pennsylvania	193,919	156,765	37,154	107,596	81,886	25,710	65,294	52,441	12,853	80.8	19.2	76.1	23.9	80.3	19.7
EAST NORTH CENTRAL:															
Ohio	111,452	72,203	39,249	87,113	50,078	37,035	63,213	45,374	17,839	64.8	35.2	57.5	42.5	71.8	28.2
Indiana	60,320	45,767	14,553	45,215	31,557	13,658	24,560	17,548	7,012	75.9	24.1	69.8	30.2	71.4	28.6
Illinois	109,049	72,221	36,828	57,028	40,346	16,682	28,762	21,419	7,343	66.2	33.8	70.7	29.3	74.5	25.5
Michigan	17,115	9,079	8,036	15,223	7,036	8,187	11,849	6,434	5,415	53.0	47.0	46.2	53.8	54.3	45.7
Wisconsin	2,900	1,757	1,143	2,444	1,007	1,437	2,113	1,597	516	60.6	39.4	41.2	58.8	75.6	24.4
WEST NORTH CENTRAL:															
Minnesota	7,084	4,468	2,616	3,683	1,981	1,702	759	514	245	63.1	36.9	53.8	46.2	67.7	32.3
Iowa	14,973	11,329	3,644	10,685	7,503	3,182	5,762	4,669	1,093	75.7	24.3	70.2	29.8	81.0	19.0
Missouri	157,452	112,762	44,690	150,184	114,739	35,445	118,071	100,412	17,659	71.6	28.4	76.4	23.6	85.0	15.0
North Dakota	617	460	157	373	153	220	94	71	23	74.6	25.4	41.0	59.0	(1)	(1)
South Dakota	817	521	296	541	310	231				63.8	36.2	57.3	42.7		
Nebraska	7,689	5,602	2,087	8,913	6,091	2,822	789	738	51	72.9	27.1	68.3	31.7	93.5	6.5
Kansas	54,030	37,889	16,141	49,710	36,530	13,180	17,108	13,299	3,809	70.1	29.9	73.5	26.5	77.7	22.3
SOUTH ATLANTIC:															
Delaware	31,181	27,475	3,706	28,386	24,837	3,549	22,794	20,570	2,224	88.1	11.9	87.5	12.5	90.2	9.8
Maryland	232,250	189,098	43,152	215,657	181,296	34,361	175,391	151,463	23,928	81.4	18.6	84.1	15.9	86.4	13.6
District of Columbia	94,446	61,494	32,952	75,572	55,736	19,836	43,404	35,372	8,032	65.1	34.9	73.8	26.2	81.5	18.5
Virginia	671,096	448,186	222,910	635,438	512,997	122,441	512,841	440,593	72,248	66.8	33.2	80.7	19.3	85.9	14.1
West Virginia	64,173	43,294	20,879	32,690	23,336	9,354	17,980	13,640	4,340	67.5	32.5	71.4	28.6	75.9	24.1
North Carolina	697,843	553,720	144,123	561,018	483,817	77,201	391,650	354,209	37,441	79.3	20.7	86.2	13.8	90.4	9.6
South Carolina	835,843	701,462	134,381	688,934	621,781	67,153	415,814	387,985	27,829	83.9	16.1	90.3	9.7	93.3	6.7
Georgia	1,176,987	972,782	204,205	858,815	773,682	85,133	545,142	501,814	43,328	82.7	17.3	90.1	9.9	92.1	7.9
Florida	308,669	259,158	49,511	166,180	146,423	19,757	91,689	80,338	11,351	84.0	16.0	88.1	11.9	87.6	12.4
EAST SOUTH CENTRAL:															
Kentucky	261,656	195,713	65,943	268,071	216,085	51,986	222,210	177,499	44,711	74.8	25.2	80.6	19.4	79.9	20.1
Tennessee	473,088	354,391	118,697	430,678	356,215	74,463	322,331	292,029	30,302	74.9	25.1	82.7	17.3	90.6	9.4
Alabama	908,282	756,872	151,410	678,489	601,069	77,420	475,510	433,698	41,812	83.3	16.7	88.6	11.4	91.2	8.8
Mississippi	1,009,487	838,482	171,005	742,559	657,393	85,166	444,201	398,798	45,403	83.1	16.9	88.5	11.5	89.8	10.2
WEST SOUTH CENTRAL:															
Arkansas	442,891	361,520	81,371	309,117	269,487	39,630	122,169	109,831	12,338	81.6	18.4	87.2	12.8	89.9	10.1
Louisiana	713,874	561,297	152,577	559,193	468,240	90,953	364,210	307,610	56,600	78.6	21.4	83.7	16.3	84.5	15.5
Oklahoma	137,612	98,269	39,343	²21,609	2,156	817				71.4	28.6	72.5	27.5		
Texas	690,049	565,354	124,695	488,171	422,447	65,724	253,475	225,658	27,817	81.9	18.1	86.5	13.5	89.0	11.0
MOUNTAIN:															
Montana	1,834	1,223	611	1,490	1,086	404	183	137	46	66.7	33.3	72.9	27.1	74.9	25.1
Idaho	651	425	226	201	100	101	60	60		65.3	34.7	49.8	50.2	(1)	
Wyoming	2,235	1,942	293	922	671	251	183	96	87	86.9	13.1	72.8	27.2	52.5	47.5
Colorado	11,453	7,815	3,638	6,215	4,056	2,159	456	272	184	68.2	31.8	65.3	34.7	59.6	40.4
New Mexico	1,628	1,189	439	1,956	970	986	172	116	56	73.0	27.0	49.6	50.4	67.4	32.6
Arizona	2,009	1,561	448	1,357	932	425	26	26		77.7	22.3	68.7	31.3	(1)	
Utah	1,144	854	290	588	379	209	118	85	33	74.7	25.3	64.5	35.5	72.0	28.0
Nevada	513	323	190	242	140	102	357	290	67	63.0	37.0	57.9	42.1	81.2	18.8
PACIFIC:															
Washington	6,058	4,218	1,840	1,602	1,044	558	207	56	151	69.6	30.4	65.2	34.8	27.1	72.9
Oregon	1,492	1,058	434	1,186	557	629	346	259	87	70.9	29.1	47.0	53.0	74.9	25.1
California	21,645	13,787	7,858	11,322	6,542	4,780	4,272	2,712	1,560	63.7	36.3	57.8	42.2	63.5	36.5

¹ Per cent not shown where base is less than 100.   ² Includes 18,636 Negroes enumerated in Indian Territory, not distinguished as black or mulatto.

TABLE **23.**—INCREASE IN BLACK AND MULATTO POPULATION, BY DIVISIONS AND STATES: 1870–1890, 1890–1910, AND 1870–1910.

[A minus sign (−) denotes decrease.   Per cent not shown where base is less than 100.]

INCREASE OF BLACK AND MULATTO POPULATION.

DIVISION AND STATE.	Number 1890–1910 Black	Number 1890–1910 Mulatto	Number 1870–1890 Black	Number 1870–1890 Mulatto	Number 1870–1910 Black	Number 1870–1910 Mulatto	Per cent 1890–1910 Total Negro population	Per cent 1890–1910 Black	Per cent 1890–1910 Mulatto	Per cent 1870–1890 Total Negro population	Per cent 1870–1890 Black	Per cent 1870–1890 Mulatto	Per cent 1870–1910 Total Negro population	Per cent 1870–1910 Black	Per cent 1870–1910 Mulatto
UNITED STATES	1,439,097	918,626	2,042,020	548,011	3,481,117	1,466,637	31.2	22.7	81.1	53.5	47.5	93.8	101.4	81.0	251.1
GEOGRAPHIC DIVISIONS:															
New England	14,155	7,571	7,376	5,499	21,531	13,070	48.7	47.2	51.9	40.6	32.6	60.6	109.1	95.2	143.9
Middle Atlantic	158,727	33,817	51,130	26,163	209,857	59,980	85.5	89.6	70.2	52.2	40.6	119.0	182.3	166.5	272.8
East North Central	71,003	22,810	37,652	38,874	108,655	61,684	45.3	54.6	29.6	58.6	40.8	102.0	130.5	117.6	161.8
West North Central	5,724	12,849	47,604	33,902	53,328	46,751	8.3	3.4	22.6	57.2	39.8	148.2	70.2	44.6	204.3
South Atlantic	432,764	417,034	837,921	208,064	1,270,685	625,098	26.0	15.3	95.0	47.2	42.2	90.2	85.5	64.0	270.9
East South Central	314,696	218,020	528,738	126,807	843,434	344,827	25.1	17.2	75.4	44.8	40.6	78.2	81.2	64.8	212.6
West South Central	[1]424,110	[1]200,862	[1]519,231	[1]100,369	943,341	301,231	44.0	36.5	101.9	86.3	80.7	103.7	168.2	146.7	311.3
Mountain	6,998	1,498	7,252	4,164	14,250	5,662	65.5	84.0	32.3	734.1	670.2	880.3	1,280.5	1,317.0	1,197.0
Pacific	10,920	4,165	5,116	4,169	16,036	8,334	106.9	134.1	69.8	192.4	169.0	231.9	505.1	529.8	463.5
NEW ENGLAND:															
Maine	230	−57	−507	91	−277	34	14.5	45.4	−8.3	−25.9	−50.0	15.4	−15.1	−27.3	5.7
New Hampshire	108	−158	−188	222	−80	64	−8.1	43.5	−43.2	5.9	−43.1	154.2	−2.8	−18.3	44.4
Vermont	664	20	−156	169	508	189	73.0	127.4	4.8	1.4	−23.0	68.4	75.4	75.0	76.5
Massachusetts	9,992	5,919	4,422	3,775	14,414	9,694	71.9	70.8	73.7	58.8	45.7	88.6	172.9	148.8	227.5
Rhode Island	954	1,182	1,576	837	2,530	2,019	28.9	17.7	59.2	48.5	41.3	72.2	91.3	66.2	174.1
Connecticut	2,207	665	2,229	405	4,436	1,070	23.3	22.2	21.6	27.2	31.9	15.1	57.0	63.4	40.0
MIDDLE ATLANTIC:															
New York	48,731	15,368	8,354	9,657	57,085	25,025	91.4	88.8	100.8	34.6	18.0	173.0	157.7	122.8	448.2
New Jersey	35,117	7,005	13,331	3,649	48,448	10,654	88.4	86.8	97.3	55.4	49.2	102.7	192.8	178.7	299.9
Pennsylvania	74,879	11,444	29,445	12,857	104,324	24,301	80.2	91.4	44.5	64.8	56.1	100.0	197.0	198.9	189.1
EAST NORTH CENTRAL:															
Ohio	22,125	2,214	4,704	19,196	26,829	21,410	27.9	44.2	6.0	37.8	10.4	107.6	76.3	59.1	120.0
Indiana	14,210	895	14,009	6,646	28,219	7,541	33.4	45.0	6.6	84.1	79.8	94.8	145.6	160.8	107.5
Illinois	31,875	20,146	18,927	9,339	50,802	29,485	91.2	79.0	120.8	98.3	88.4	127.2	279.1	237.2	401.5
Michigan	2,043	−151	602	2,772	2,645	2,621	12.4	29.0	−1.8	28.5	9.4	51.2	44.4	41.1	48.4
Wisconsin	750	−294	−590	921	160	627	18.7	74.5	−20.5	15.7	−36.9	178.5	37.2	10.0	121.5
WEST NORTH CENTRAL:															
Minnesota	2,487	914	1,467	1,457	3,954	2,371	92.3	125.5	53.7	385.2	285.4	594.7	833.3	769.3	967.8
Iowa	3,826	462	2,834	2,089	6,660	2,551	40.1	51.0	14.5	85.4	60.7	191.1	159.9	142.6	233.4
Missouri	−1,977	9,245	14,327	17,786	12,350	27,031	4.8	−1.7	26.1	27.2	14.3	100.7	33.4	12.3	153.1
North Dakota	307	−63	392	428	910	430	65.4	200.7	−28.6	......	......	......	......	......	......
South Dakota	211	65					51.0	68.1	28.1						
Nebraska	−489	−735	5,353	2,771	4,864	2,036	−13.7	−8.0	−26.0	1,029.7	725.3	......	874.5	659.1	......
Kansas	1,359	2,961	23,231	9,371	24,590	12,332	8.7	3.7	22.5	190.6	174.7	246.0	215.8	184.9	323.8
SOUTH ATLANTIC:															
Delaware	2,638	157	4,267	1,325	6,905	1,482	9.8	10.6	4.4	24.5	20.7	59.6	36.8	33.6	66.6
Maryland	7,802	8,791	29,833	10,433	37,635	19,224	7.7	4.3	25.6	23.0	19.7	43.6	32.4	24.8	80.3
District of Columbia	5,758	13,116	20,364	11,804	26,122	24,920	25.0	10.3	66.1	74.1	57.6	147.0	117.6	73.8	310.3
Virginia	−64,811	100,469	72,404	50,193	7,593	150,662	5.6	−12.6	82.1	23.9	16.4	69.5	30.9	1.7	208.5
West Virginia	19,958	11,525	9,696	5,014	29,654	16,539	96.3	85.5	123.2	81.8	71.1	115.5	256.9	217.4	381.1
North Carolina	69,903	66,922	129,608	39,760	199,511	106,682	24.4	14.4	86.7	43.2	36.6	106.2	78.2	56.3	284.9
South Carolina	79,681	67,228	233,796	39,324	313,477	106,552	21.3	12.8	100.1	65.7	60.3	141.3	101.0	80.8	382.9
Georgia	199,100	119,072	271,868	41,805	470,968	160,877	37.0	25.7	139.9	57.5	54.2	96.5	115.9	93.9	371.3
Florida	112,735	29,754	66,085	8,406	178,820	38,160	85.7	77.0	150.6	81.2	82.3	74.1	236.6	222.6	336.2
EAST SOUTH CENTRAL:															
Kentucky	−20,372	13,957	38,586	7,275	18,214	21,232	−2.4	−9.4	26.8	20.6	21.7	16.3	17.8	10.3	47.5
Tennessee	−1,824	44,234	64,186	44,161	62,362	88,395	9.8	−0.5	59.4	33.6	22.0	145.7	46.8	21.4	291.7
Alabama	155,803	73,990	167,371	35,608	323,174	109,598	33.9	25.9	95.6	42.7	38.6	85.2	91.0	74.5	262.1
Mississippi	181,089	85,839	258,595	39,763	439,684	125,602	35.9	27.5	100.8	67.2	64.8	87.6	127.3	110.3	276.6
WEST SOUTH CENTRAL:															
Arkansas	92,033	41,741	159,656	27,292	251,689	69,033	43.3	34.2	105.3	153.0	145.4	221.2	262.5	229.2	559.5
Louisiana	93,057	61,624	160,630	34,353	253,687	95,977	27.7	19.9	67.8	53.5	52.2	60.7	96.0	82.5	169.6
Oklahoma	[1]96,113	[1]38,526	......	......	98,269	39,343	536.8								
Texas	142,907	58,971	196,789	37,907	339,696	96,878	41.4	33.8	89.7	92.6	87.2	136.3	172.2	150.5	348.3
MOUNTAIN:															
Montana	137	207	949	358	1,086	565	23.1	12.6	51.2	714.2	692.7	......	902.2	792.7	......
Idaho	325	125	40	101	365	226	223.9	325.0	123.8						
Wyoming	1,271	42	575	164	1,846	206	142.4	189.4	16.7	403.8			1,121.3		
Colorado	3,759	1,479	3,784	1,975	7,543	3,454	84.3	92.7	68.5	1,262.9	1,391.2	1,073.4	2,411.6	2,773.2	1,877.2
New Mexico	219	−547	854	930	1,073	383	−16.8	22.6	−55.5	1,037.2	736.2		846.5	925.0	
Arizona	629	23	906	425	1,535	448	48.0	67.5	5.4						
Utah	475	81	294	176	769	257	94.6	125.3	38.8	398.3			869.5		
Nevada	183	88	−150	35	33	123	112.0	130.7	86.3	−32.2	−51.7		43.7	11.4	
PACIFIC:															
Washington	3,174	1,282	988	407	4,162	1,689	278.2	304.0	229.7	673.9	......	269.5	2,826.6	......	1,118.5
Oregon	501	−195	298	542	799	347	25.8	89.9	−31.0	242.8	115.1	......	331.2	308.5	......
California	7,245	3,078	3,830	3,220	11,075	6,298	91.2	110.7	64.4	165.0	141.2	206.4	406.7	408.4	403.7

[1] Includes 2,156 blacks and 817 mulattoes enumerated in Oklahoma Territory in 1890, but does not include 18,636 Negroes enumerated in Indian Territory who were not classified as black and mulatto.

TABLE 24.—BLACK AND MULATTO POPULATION, FREE AND SLAVE, CLASSIFIED BY SEX, BY DIVISIONS AND STATES: 1860.

DIVISION AND STATE.	Both sexes Black	Both sexes Mulatto	Male Black	Male Mulatto	Female Black	Female Mulatto	Free Both sexes Black	Free Both sexes Mulatto	Free Male Black	Free Male Mulatto	Free Female Black	Free Female Mulatto	Slave Both sexes Black	Slave Both sexes Mulatto	Slave Male Black	Slave Male Mulatto	Slave Female Black	Slave Female Mulatto
UNITED STATES	3,853,478	588,352	1,936,315	280,430	1,917,163	307,922	311,331	176,739	150,599	83,521	160,732	93,218	3,542,147	411,613	1,785,716	196,909	1,756,431	214,704
GEOGRAPHIC DIVISIONS:																		
New England	17,663	7,048	8,416	3,303	9,247	3,745	17,663	7,048	8,416	3,303	9,247	3,745						
Middle Atlantic	100,905	30,385	48,053	13,917	52,852	16,468	100,896	30,376	48,050	13,914	52,846	16,462	9	9	3	3	6	6
East North Central	33,862	29,837	17,501	14,761	16,361	15,076	33,862	29,837	17,501	14,761	16,361	15,076						
West North Central	95,900	24,640	48,549	11,527	47,351	13,113	2,876	2,716	1,419	1,291	1,457	1,425	93,024	21,924	47,130	10,236	45,894	11,688
South Atlantic	1,813,497	244,701	906,127	116,931	907,370	127,770	139,243	78,510	66,618	36,991	72,625	41,519	1,674,254	166,191	839,509	79,940	834,745	86,251
East South Central	1,231,477	162,883	619,241	77,470	612,236	85,413	10,379	11,068	5,111	5,154	5,268	5,914	1,221,098	151,815	614,130	72,316	606,968	79,499
West South Central	557,376	87,177	286,439	41,433	270,937	45,744	3,628	15,518	1,504	7,028	2,124	8,490	553,748	71,659	284,935	34,405	268,813	37,254
Mountain	148	87	90	58	58	29	134	72	81	49	53	23	14	15	9	9	5	6
Pacific	2,650	1,594	1,899	1,030	751	564	2,650	1,594	1,899	1,030	751	564						
NEW ENGLAND:																		
Maine	693	634	351	308	342	326	693	634	351	308	342	326						
New Hampshire	241	253	123	130	118	123	241	253	123	130	118	123						
Vermont	517	192	276	95	241	97	517	192	276	95	241	97						
Massachusetts	6,531	3,071	3,055	1,414	3,476	1,657	6,531	3,071	3,055	1,414	3,476	1,657						
Rhode Island	2,955	997	1,369	462	1,586	535	2,955	997	1,369	462	1,586	535						
Connecticut	6,726	1,901	3,242	894	3,484	1,007	6,726	1,901	3,242	894	3,484	1,007						
MIDDLE ATLANTIC:																		
New York	41,224	7,781	19,491	3,687	21,733	4,094	41,224	7,781	19,491	3,687	21,733	4,094						
New Jersey	21,874	3,462	10,721	1,598	11,153	1,864	21,865	3,453	10,718	1,595	11,147	1,858	9	9	3	3	6	6
Pennsylvania	37,807	19,142	17,841	8,632	19,966	10,510	37,807	19,142	17,841	8,632	19,966	10,510						
EAST NORTH CENTRAL:																		
Ohio	19,982	16,691	10,271	8,171	9,711	8,520	19,982	16,691	10,271	8,171	9,711	8,520						
Indiana	5,981	5,447	3,102	2,689	2,879	2,758	5,981	5,447	3,102	2,689	2,879	2,758						
Illinois	4,041	3,587	2,031	1,778	2,010	1,809	4,041	3,587	2,031	1,778	2,010	1,809						
Michigan	3,424	3,375	1,842	1,725	1,582	1,650	3,424	3,375	1,842	1,725	1,582	1,650						
Wisconsin	434	737	255	398	179	339	434	737	255	398	179	339						
WEST NORTH CENTRAL:																		
Minnesota	90	169	39	87	51	82	90	169	39	87	51	82						
Iowa	501	568	275	291	226	277	501	568	275	291	226	277						
Missouri	94,915	23,588	48,052	11,005	46,863	12,583	1,898	1,674	925	772	973	902	93,017	21,914	47,127	10,233	45,890	11,681
Nebraska	35	47	17	24	18	23	28	39	14	21	14	18	7	8	3	3	4	5
Kansas	359	268	166	120	193	148	359	266	166	120	193	146		2				2
SOUTH ATLANTIC:																		
Delaware	18,648	2,979	9,261	1,488	9,387	1,491	16,933	2,896	8,439	1,450	8,494	1,446	1,715	83	822	38	893	45
Maryland	146,218	24,913	72,633	11,426	73,585	13,487	67,902	16,040	32,507	7,239	35,395	8,801	78,316	8,873	40,126	4,187	38,190	4,686
District of Columbia	8,883	5,433	3,708	2,206	5,175	3,227	6,631	4,500	2,847	1,855	3,784	2,645	2,252	933	861	351	1,391	582
Virginia	455,443	93,464	232,657	44,547	222,786	48,917	34,557	23,485	16,648	11,073	17,909	12,412	420,886	69,979	216,009	33,474	204,877	36,505
North Carolina	316,724	44,798	159,241	22,108	157,483	22,690	8,655	21,808	4,046	10,834	4,609	10,974	308,069	22,990	155,195	11,274	152,874	11,716
South Carolina	384,006	28,314	187,566	13,553	196,440	14,761	2,780	7,134	1,263	3,285	1,517	3,849	381,226	21,180	186,303	10,268	194,923	10,912
Georgia	426,794	38,904	212,164	18,698	214,630	20,206	1,496	2,004	732	937	764	1,067	425,298	36,900	211,432	17,761	213,866	19,139
Florida	56,781	5,896	28,897	2,905	27,884	2,991	289	643	136	318	153	325	56,492	5,253	28,761	2,587	27,731	2,666
EAST SOUTH CENTRAL:																		
Kentucky	188,809	47,358	95,954	22,156	92,855	25,202	6,607	4,077	3,223	1,878	3,384	2,199	182,202	43,281	92,731	20,278	89,471	23,003
Tennessee	241,141	41,878	120,199	19,709	120,942	22,169	3,008	4,292	1,516	2,022	1,492	2,270	238,133	37,586	118,683	17,687	119,450	19,899
Alabama	401,342	36,428	201,550	17,470	199,792	18,958	592	2,098	292	962	300	1,136	400,750	34,330	201,258	16,508	199,492	17,822
Mississippi	400,185	37,219	201,538	18,135	198,647	19,084	172	601	80	292	92	309	400,013	36,618	201,458	17,843	198,555	18,775
WEST SOUTH CENTRAL:																		
Arkansas	97,123	14,136	49,266	6,980	47,857	7,156	57	87	30	42	27	45	97,066	14,049	49,236	6,938	47,830	7,111
Louisiana	302,592	47,781	157,725	22,531	144,867	25,250	3,489	15,158	1,438	6,841	2,051	8,317	299,103	32,623	156,287	15,690	142,816	16,933
Texas	157,661	25,260	79,448	11,922	78,213	13,338	82	273	36	145	46	128	157,579	24,987	79,412	11,777	78,167	13,210
MOUNTAIN:																		
Colorado	33	13	28	9	5	4	33	13	28	9	5	4						
New Mexico	46	39	22	23	24	16	46	39	22	23	24	16						
Utah	42	17	21	10	21	7	28	2	12	1	16	1	14	15	9	9	5	6
Nevada	27	18	19	16	8	2	27	18	19	16	8	2						
PACIFIC:																		
Washington	27	3	24	2	3	1	27	3	24	2	3	1						
Oregon	66	62	44	32	22	30	66	62	44	32	22	30						
California	2,557	1,529	1,831	996	726	533	2,557	1,529	1,831	996	726	533						

TABLE 25.—BLACK AND MULATTO POPULATION, FREE AND SLAVE, BY DIVISIONS AND STATES: 1850.

DIVISION AND STATE.	NEGRO POPULATION: 1850.								
	Total.	Black.	Mulatto.	Free.			Slave.		
				Total.	Black.	Mulatto.	Total.	Black.	Mulatto.
UNITED STATES	3,638,808	3,233,057	405,751	434,495	275,400	159,095	3,204,313	2,957,657	246,656
GEOGRAPHIC DIVISIONS:									
New England	23,021	17,301	5,720	23,021	17,301	5,720			
Middle Atlantic	126,741	99,560	27,181	126,505	99,328	27,177	236	232	4
East North Central	45,195	21,688	23,507	45,195	21,688	23,507			
West North Central	90,412	76,068	14,344	2,990	1,881	1,109	87,422	74,187	13,235
South Atlantic	1,860,871	1,674,968	185,903	197,474	119,652	77,822	1,663,397	1,555,316	108,081
East South Central	1,122,790	1,022,631	100,159	19,628	10,889	8,739	1,103,162	1,011,742	91,420
West South Central	368,537	319,891	48,646	18,467	3,720	14,747	350,070	316,171	33,899
Mountain	72	30	42	46	21	25	26	9	17
Pacific	1,169	920	249	1,169	920	249			
NEW ENGLAND:									
Maine	1,356	895	461	1,356	895	461			
New Hampshire	520	336	184	520	336	184			
Vermont	718	512	206	718	512	206			
Massachusetts	9,064	6,724	2,340	9,064	6,724	2,340			
Rhode Island	3,670	2,939	731	3,670	2,939	731			
Connecticut	7,693	5,895	1,798	7,693	5,895	1,798			
MIDDLE ATLANTIC:									
New York	49,069	40,930	8,139	49,069	40,930	8,139			
New Jersey	24,046	20,345	3,701	23,810	20,113	3,697	236	232	4
Pennsylvania	53,626	38,285	15,341	53,626	38,285	15,341			
EAST NORTH CENTRAL:									
Ohio	25,279	11,014	14,265	25,279	11,014	14,265			
Indiana	11,262	5,941	5,321	11,262	5,941	5,321			
Illinois	5,436	2,930	2,506	5,436	2,930	2,506			
Michigan	2,583	1,465	1,118	2,583	1,465	1,118			
Wisconsin	635	338	297	635	338	297			
WEST NORTH CENTRAL:									
Minnesota	39	16	23	39	16	23			
Iowa	333	178	155	333	178	155			
Missouri	90,040	75,874	14,166	2,618	1,687	931	87,422	74,187	13,235
SOUTH ATLANTIC:									
Delaware	20,363	18,632	1,731	18,073	16,425	1,648	2,290	2,207	83
Maryland	165,091	143,588	21,503	74,723	61,109	13,614	90,368	82,479	7,889
District of Columbia	13,746	9,668	4,078	10,059	6,783	3,276	3,687	2,885	802
Virginia	526,861	447,086	79,775	54,333	18,857	35,476	472,528	428,229	44,299
North Carolina	316,011	281,991	34,020	27,463	10,258	17,205	288,548	271,733	16,815
South Carolina	393,944	377,070	16,874	8,960	4,588	4,372	384,984	372,482	12,502
Georgia	384,613	360,416	24,197	2,931	1,403	1,528	381,682	359,013	22,669
Florida	40,242	36,517	3,725	932	229	703	39,310	36,288	3,022
EAST SOUTH CENTRAL:									
Kentucky	220,992	188,633	32,359	10,011	7,381	2,630	210,981	181,252	29,729
Tennessee	245,881	221,749	24,132	6,422	2,646	3,776	239,459	219,103	20,356
Alabama	345,109	321,806	23,303	2,265	567	1,698	342,844	321,239	21,605
Mississippi	310,808	290,443	20,365	930	295	635	309,878	290,148	19,730
WEST SOUTH CENTRAL:									
Arkansas	47,708	40,940	6,768	608	201	407	47,100	40,739	6,361
Louisiana	262,271	228,353	33,918	17,462	3,379	14,083	244,809	224,974	19,835
Texas	58,558	50,598	7,960	397	140	257	58,161	50,458	7,703
MOUNTAIN:									
New Mexico	22	6	16	22	6	16			
Utah	50	24	26	24	15	9	26	9	17
PACIFIC:									
Oregon	207	45	162	207	45	162			
California	962	875	87	962	875	87			

TABLE 26.—BLACK AND MULATTO POPULATION, CLASSIFIED BY SEX, WITH EXCESS OF MALES OR FEMALES, AND SEX RATIO, BY DIVISIONS AND STATES: 1910.

DIVISION AND STATE.	BLACK AND MULATTO POPULATION: 1910.											
	Black.						Mulatto.					
	Total.	Male.	Female.	Excess of—		Males to 1,000 females.	Total.	Male.	Female.	Excess of—		Males to 1,000 females.
				Males.	Females.					Males.	Females.	
UNITED STATES	7,777,077	3,922,332	3,854,745	67,587		1,018	2,050,686	963,549	1,087,137		123,588	886
GEOGRAPHIC DIVISIONS:												
New England	44,156	21,737	22,419		682	970	22,150	11,046	11,104		58	995
Middle Atlantic	335,901	165,079	170,822		5,743	966	81,969	38,387	43,582		5,195	881
East North Central	201,027	107,294	93,733	13,561		1,145	99,809	49,137	50,672		1,535	970
West North Central	173,031	92,134	80,897	11,237		1,139	69,631	33,730	35,901		2,171	940
South Atlantic	3,256,669	1,629,697	1,626,972	2,725		1,002	855,819	400,111	455,708		55,597	878
East South Central	2,145,458	1,081,064	1,064,394	16,670		1,016	507,055	234,728	272,327		37,599	862
West South Central	1,586,440	805,910	780,530	25,380		1,033	397,986	188,115	209,871		21,756	896
Mountain	15,332	8,697	6,635	2,062		1,311	6,135	3,069	3,066	3		1,001
Pacific	19,063	10,720	8,343	2,377		1,285	10,132	5,226	4,906	320		1,065
NEW ENGLAND:												
Maine	737	385	352	33		1,094	626	315	311	4		1,013
New Hampshire	356	167	189		22	884	208	121	87	34		(1)
Vermont	1,185	916	269	647		3,405	436	257	179	78		1,436
Massachusetts	24,100	11,652	12,448		796	936	13,955	7,096	6,859	237		1,035
Rhode Island	6,350	3,124	3,226		102	968	3,179	1,521	1,658		137	917
Connecticut	11,428	5,493	5,935		442	926	3,746	1,736	2,010		274	864
MIDDLE ATLANTIC:												
New York	103,583	50,009	53,574		3,565	933	30,608	14,025	16,583		2,558	846
New Jersey	75,553	36,914	38,639		1,725	955	14,207	6,688	7,519		831	889
Pennsylvania	156,765	78,156	78,609		453	994	37,154	17,674	19,480		1,806	907
EAST NORTH CENTRAL:												
Ohio	72,203	38,664	33,539	5,125		1,153	39,249	19,331	19,918		587	971
Indiana	45,767	23,935	21,832	2,103		1,096	14,553	7,109	7,444		335	955
Illinois	72,221	38,851	33,370	5,481		1,164	36,828	18,058	18,770		712	962
Michigan	9,079	4,941	4,138	803		1,194	8,036	4,066	3,970	96		1,024
Wisconsin	1,757	903	854	49		1,057	1,143	573	570	3		1,005
WEST NORTH CENTRAL:												
Minnesota	4,468	2,689	1,779	910		1,512	2,616	1,494	1,122	372		1,332
Iowa	11,329	6,282	5,047	1,235		1,245	3,644	1,838	1,806	32		1,018
Missouri	112,762	59,277	53,485	5,792		1,108	44,690	21,212	23,478		2,266	903
North Dakota	460	286	174	112		1,644	157	95	62	33		(1)
South Dakota	521	304	217	87		1,401	296	164	132	32		1,242
Nebraska	5,602	3,175	2,427	748		1,308	2,087	1,084	1,003	81		1,081
Kansas	37,889	20,121	17,768	2,353		1,132	16,141	7,843	8,298		455	945
SOUTH ATLANTIC:												
Delaware	27,475	14,235	13,240	995		1,075	3,706	1,776	1,930		154	920
Maryland	189,098	94,910	94,188	722		1,008	43,152	19,839	23,313		3,474	851
District of Columbia	61,494	28,254	33,240		4,986	850	32,952	14,361	18,591		4,230	772
Virginia	448,186	225,365	222,821	2,544		1,011	222,910	105,177	117,733		12,556	893
West Virginia	43,294	25,630	17,664	7,966		1,451	20,879	10,977	9,902	1,075		1,109
North Carolina	553,720	272,299	281,421		9,122	968	144,123	67,282	76,841		9,559	876
South Carolina	701,462	345,142	356,320		11,178	969	134,381	62,936	71,445		8,509	881
Georgia	972,782	486,012	486,770		758	998	204,205	94,251	109,954		15,703	857
Florida	259,158	137,850	121,308	16,542		1,136	49,511	23,512	25,999		2,487	904
EAST SOUTH CENTRAL:												
Kentucky	195,713	101,071	94,642	6,429		1,068	65,943	30,421	35,522		5,101	856
Tennessee	354,391	179,678	174,713	4,965		1,028	118,697	54,032	64,665		10,633	836
Alabama	756,872	377,869	379,003		1,134	997	151,410	69,925	81,485		11,560	858
Mississippi	838,482	422,446	416,036	6,410		1,015	171,005	80,350	90,655		10,305	886
WEST SOUTH CENTRAL:												
Arkansas	361,520	184,637	176,883	7,754		1,044	81,371	38,686	42,685		3,999	906
Louisiana	561,297	282,094	279,203	2,891		1,010	152,577	71,730	80,847		9,117	887
Oklahoma	98,269	52,360	45,909	6,451		1,141	39,343	19,577	19,766		189	990
Texas	565,354	286,819	278,535	8,284		1,030	124,695	58,122	66,573		8,451	873
MOUNTAIN:												
Montana	1,223	726	497	229		1,461	611	332	279	53		1,190
Idaho	425	269	156	113		1,724	226	129	97	32		(1)
Wyoming	1,942	1,374	568	806		2,419	293	170	123	47		1,382
Colorado	7,815	4,117	3,698	419		1,113	3,638	1,750	1,888		138	927
New Mexico	1,189	673	516	157		1,304	439	218	221		3	986
Arizona	1,561	820	741	79		1,107	448	234	214	20		1,093
Utah	854	536	318	218		1,686	290	155	135	20		1,148
Nevada	323	182	141	41		1,291	190	81	109		28	743
PACIFIC:												
Washington	4,218	2,680	1,538	1,142		1,742	1,840	1,056	784	272		1,347
Oregon	1,058	662	396	266		1,672	434	245	189	56		1,296
California	13,787	7,378	6,409	969		1,151	7,858	3,925	3,933		8	998

1 Ratio not shown where the number of females is less than 100.

TABLE **27.**—NEGRO POPULATION, BLACK AND MULATTO, CLASSIFIED BY SEX AND AGE PERIODS, WITH PERCENTAGE MULATTO, BY SECTIONS AND SOUTHERN DIVISIONS: 1910.

SECTION, DIVISION, AND AGE PERIOD.	NEGRO POPULATION: 1910.											
	Both sexes.			Male.			Female.			Percentage mulatto.		
	Total.	Black.	Mulatto.	Total.	Black.	Mulatto.	Total.	Black.	Mulatto.	Both sexes.	Male.	Female.
UNITED STATES.												
All ages	9,827,763	7,777,077	2,050,686	4,885,881	3,922,332	963,549	4,941,882	3,854,745	1,087,137	20.9	19.7	22.0
Under 5 years	1,263,288	982,172	281,116	629,320	490,746	138,574	633,968	491,426	142,542	22.3	22.0	22.5
Under 1 year	252,386	191,582	60,804	125,459	95,337	30,122	126,927	96,245	30,682	24.1	24.0	24.2
5 to 9 years	1,246,553	982,592	263,961	619,175	489,930	129,245	627,378	492,662	134,716	21.2	20.9	21.5
10 to 14 years	1,155,266	912,648	242,618	578,074	459,433	118,641	577,192	453,215	123,977	21.0	20.5	21.5
15 to 19 years	1,060,416	831,539	228,877	507,945	404,094	103,851	552,471	427,445	125,026	21.6	20.4	22.6
20 to 44 years	3,668,973	2,903,882	765,091	1,786,255	1,446,365	339,890	1,882,718	1,457,517	425,201	20.9	19.0	22.6
45 years and over	1,402,227	1,138,712	263,515	748,036	617,587	130,449	654,191	521,125	133,066	18.8	17.4	20.3
Age unknown	31,040	25,532	5,508	17,076	14,177	2,899	13,964	11,355	2,609	17.7	17.0	18.7
THE SOUTH.												
All ages	8,749,427	6,988,567	1,760,860	4,339,625	3,516,671	822,954	4,409,802	3,471,896	937,906	20.1	19.0	21.3
Under 5 years	1,176,331	922,542	253,789	586,500	461,356	125,144	589,831	461,186	128,645	21.6	21.3	21.8
Under 1 year	234,092	179,220	54,872	116,230	89,096	27,134	117,862	90,124	27,738	23.4	23.3	23.5
5 to 9 years	1,164,557	925,619	238,938	578,962	462,040	116,922	585,595	463,579	122,016	20.5	20.2	20.8
10 to 14 years	1,073,980	855,383	218,597	538,714	431,667	107,047	535,266	423,716	111,550	20.4	19.9	20.8
15 to 19 years	970,716	767,716	203,000	465,747	373,806	91,941	504,969	393,910	111,059	20.9	19.7	22.0
20 to 44 years	3,128,876	2,503,197	625,679	1,509,813	1,236,991	272,822	1,619,063	1,266,206	352,857	20.0	18.1	21.8
45 years and over	1,208,547	992,314	216,233	645,508	538,822	106,686	563,039	453,492	109,547	17.9	16.5	19.5
Age unknown	26,420	21,796	4,624	14,381	11,989	2,392	12,039	9,807	2,232	17.5	16.6	18.5
SOUTH ATLANTIC DIVISION.												
All ages	4,112,488	3,256,669	855,819	2,029,808	1,629,697	400,111	2,082,680	1,626,972	455,708	20.8	19.7	21.9
Under 5 years	570,516	444,617	125,899	284,101	221,961	62,140	286,415	222,656	63,759	22.1	21.9	22.3
Under 1 year	115,906	88,249	27,657	57,676	43,998	13,678	58,230	44,251	13,979	23.9	23.7	24.0
5 to 9 years	555,036	438,429	116,607	275,410	218,164	57,246	279,626	220,265	59,361	21.0	20.8	21.2
10 to 14 years	513,239	405,905	107,334	257,227	204,614	52,613	256,012	201,291	54,721	20.9	20.5	21.4
15 to 19 years	457,053	358,698	98,355	218,475	173,897	44,578	238,938	185,161	53,777	21.5	20.4	22.5
20 to 44 years	1,443,775	1,144,156	299,619	693,130	562,172	130,958	750,645	581,984	168,661	20.8	18.9	22.5
45 years and over	561,439	455,698	105,741	295,418	244,055	51,363	266,021	211,643	54,378	18.8	17.4	20.4
Age unknown	11,430	9,166	2,264	6,407	5,194	1,213	5,023	3,972	1,051	19.8	18.9	20.9
EAST SOUTH CENTRAL DIVISION.												
All ages	2,652,513	2,145,458	507,055	1,315,792	1,081,064	234,728	1,336,721	1,064,394	272,327	19.1	17.8	20.4
Under 5 years	347,803	276,411	71,392	173,902	138,726	35,176	173,901	137,685	36,216	20.5	20.2	20.8
Under 1 year	68,455	53,099	15,356	34,036	26,466	7,570	34,419	26,633	7,786	22.4	22.2	22.6
5 to 9 years	343,812	276,762	67,050	170,969	138,363	32,606	172,843	138,399	34,444	19.5	19.1	19.9
10 to 14 years	320,476	258,429	62,047	161,742	131,325	30,417	158,734	127,104	31,630	19.4	18.8	19.9
15 to 19 years	294,183	235,119	59,064	142,363	115,552	26,811	151,820	119,567	32,253	20.1	18.8	21.2
20 to 44 years	955,342	773,152	182,190	457,410	379,796	77,614	497,932	393,356	104,576	19.1	17.0	21.0
45 years and over	382,481	318,561	63,920	205,045	173,603	31,442	177,436	144,958	32,478	16.7	15.3	18.3
Age unknown	8,416	7,024	1,392	4,361	3,699	662	4,055	3,325	730	16.5	15.2	18.0
WEST SOUTH CENTRAL DIVISION.												
All ages	1,984,426	1,586,440	397,986	994,025	805,910	188,115	990,401	780,530	209,871	20.1	18.9	21.2
Under 5 years	258,012	201,514	56,498	128,497	100,669	27,828	129,515	100,845	28,670	21.9	21.7	22.1
Under 1 year	49,731	37,872	11,859	24,518	18,632	5,886	25,213	19,240	5,973	23.8	24.0	23.7
5 to 9 years	265,709	210,428	55,281	132,583	105,513	27,070	133,126	104,915	28,211	20.8	20.4	21.2
10 to 14 years	240,265	191,049	49,216	119,745	95,728	24,017	120,520	95,321	25,199	20.5	20.1	20.9
15 to 19 years	219,480	173,899	45,581	105,269	84,717	20,552	114,211	89,182	25,029	20.8	19.5	21.9
20 to 44 years	729,759	585,889	143,870	359,273	295,023	64,250	370,486	290,866	79,620	19.7	17.9	21.5
45 years and over	264,627	218,055	46,572	145,045	121,164	23,881	119,582	96,891	22,691	17.6	16.5	19.0
Age unknown	6,574	5,606	968	3,613	3,096	517	2,961	2,510	451	14.7	14.3	15.2
THE NORTH.												
All ages	1,027,674	754,115	273,559	518,544	386,244	132,300	509,130	367,871	141,259	26.6	25.5	27.7
Under 5 years	83,729	57,684	26,045	41,273	28,473	12,800	42,456	29,211	13,245	31.1	31.0	31.2
Under 1 year	17,638	11,977	5,661	8,906	6,057	2,849	8,732	5,920	2,812	32.1	32.0	32.2
5 to 9 years	78,892	55,051	23,841	38,693	26,938	11,755	40,199	28,113	12,086	30.2	30.4	30.1
10 to 14 years	78,205	55,323	22,882	37,868	26,823	11,045	40,337	28,500	11,837	29.3	29.2	29.3
15 to 19 years	86,126	61,596	24,530	40,501	29,214	11,287	45,625	32,382	13,243	28.5	27.9	29.0
20 to 44 years	512,407	381,409	130,998	260,834	198,077	62,757	251,573	183,332	68,241	25.6	24.1	27.1
45 years and over	184,051	139,601	44,450	96,888	74,695	22,193	87,163	64,906	22,257	24.2	22.9	25.5
Age unknown	4,264	3,451	813	2,487	2,024	463	1,777	1,427	350	19.1	18.6	19.7
THE WEST.												
All ages	50,662	34,395	16,267	27,712	19,417	8,295	22,950	14,978	7,972	32.1	29.9	34.7
Under 5 years	3,228	1,946	1,282	1,547	917	630	1,681	1,029	652	39.7	40.7	38.8
Under 1 year	656	385	271	323	184	139	333	201	132	41.3	43.0	39.6
5 to 9 years	3,104	1,922	1,182	1,520	952	568	1,584	970	614	38.1	37.4	38.8
10 to 14 years	3,081	1,942	1,139	1,492	943	549	1,589	999	590	37.0	36.8	37.1
15 to 19 years	3,574	2,227	1,347	1,697	1,074	623	1,877	1,153	724	37.7	36.7	38.6
20 to 44 years	27,690	19,276	8,414	15,608	11,297	4,311	12,082	7,979	4,103	30.4	27.6	34.0
45 years and over	9,629	6,797	2,832	5,640	4,070	1,570	3,989	2,727	1,262	29.4	27.8	31.6
Age unknown	356	285	71	208	164	44	148	121	27	19.9	21.2	18.2

TABLE 28.—NEGRO POPULATION, BLACK AND MULATTO, CLASSIFIED BY SEX AND AGE PERIODS, WITH PERCENTAGE MULATTO, BY SOUTHERN STATES: 1910.

STATE AND AGE PERIOD.	NEGRO POPULATION: 1910.											
	Both sexes.			Male.			Female.			Percentage mulatto.		
	Total.	Black.	Mulatto.	Total.	Black.	Mulatto.	Total.	Black.	Mulatto.	Both sexes.	Male.	Female.
SOUTH ATLANTIC DIVISION.												
DELAWARE.												
All ages	31,181	27,475	3,706	16,011	14,235	1,776	15,170	13,240	1,930	11.9	11.1	12.7
Under 5 years	3,089	2,617	472	1,518	1,278	240	1,571	1,339	232	15.3	15.8	14.8
Under 1 year	646	529	117	325	263	62	321	266	55	18.1	19.1	17.1
5 to 9 years	3,315	2,842	473	1,607	1,380	227	1,708	1,462	246	14.3	14.1	14.4
10 to 14 years	3,540	3,085	455	1,871	1,643	228	1,669	1,442	227	12.9	12.2	13.6
15 to 19 years	3,228	2,849	379	1,648	1,471	177	1,580	1,378	202	11.7	10.7	12.8
20 to 44 years	12,112	10,743	1,369	6,255	5,623	632	5,857	5,120	737	11.3	10.1	12.6
45 years and over	5,778	5,223	555	3,046	2,777	269	2,732	2,446	286	9.6	8.8	10.5
Age unknown	119	116	3	66	63	3	53	53	....	2.5	4.5	....
MARYLAND.												
All ages	232,250	189,098	43,152	114,749	94,910	19,839	117,501	94,188	23,313	18.6	17.3	19.8
Under 5 years	25,987	20,649	5,338	12,755	10,151	2,604	13,232	10,498	2,734	20.5	20.4	20.7
Under 1 year	5,310	4,165	1,145	2,660	2,079	581	2,650	2,086	564	21.6	21.8	21.3
5 to 9 years	25,809	20,834	4,975	12,659	10,233	2,426	13,150	10,601	2,549	19.3	19.2	19.4
10 to 14 years	24,595	19,959	4,636	12,144	9,885	2,259	12,451	10,074	2,377	18.8	18.6	19.1
15 to 19 years	23,398	18,806	4,592	11,160	9,108	2,052	12,238	9,698	2,540	19.6	18.4	20.8
20 to 44 years	91,281	74,437	16,844	44,888	37,517	7,371	46,393	36,920	9,473	18.5	16.4	20.4
45 years and over	40,661	33,976	6,685	20,895	17,803	3,092	19,766	16,173	3,593	16.4	14.8	18.2
Age unknown	519	437	82	248	213	35	271	224	47	15.8	14.1	17.3
DISTRICT OF COLUMBIA.												
All ages	94,446	61,494	32,952	42,615	28,254	14,361	51,831	33,240	18,591	34.9	33.7	35.9
Under 5 years	7,290	4,596	2,694	3,581	2,249	1,332	3,709	2,347	1,362	37.0	37.2	36.7
Under 1 year	1,458	893	565	732	442	290	726	451	275	38.8	39.6	37.9
5 to 9 years	7,192	4,714	2,478	3,494	2,319	1,175	3,698	2,395	1,303	34.5	33.6	35.2
10 to 14 years	7,211	4,660	2,551	3,384	2,199	1,185	3,827	2,461	1,366	35.4	35.0	35.7
15 to 19 years	8,620	5,530	3,090	3,717	2,413	1,304	4,903	3,117	1,786	35.8	35.1	36.4
20 to 44 years	47,123	30,586	16,537	20,860	13,885	6,975	26,263	16,701	9,562	35.1	33.4	36.4
45 years and over	16,537	11,098	5,439	7,396	5,074	2,322	9,141	6,024	3,117	32.9	31.4	34.1
Age unknown	473	310	163	183	115	68	290	195	95	34.5	37.2	32.8
VIRGINIA.												
All ages	671,096	448,186	222,910	330,542	225,365	105,177	340,554	222,821	117,733	33.2	31.8	34.6
Under 5 years	86,555	55,159	31,396	42,927	27,411	15,516	43,628	27,748	15,880	36.3	36.1	36.4
Under 1 year	17,901	11,051	6,850	8,888	5,479	3,409	9,013	5,572	3,441	38.3	38.4	38.2
5 to 9 years	88,123	57,878	30,245	43,658	28,774	14,884	44,465	29,104	15,361	34.3	34.1	34.5
10 to 14 years	83,395	55,397	27,998	41,902	28,073	13,829	41,493	27,324	14,169	33.6	33.0	34.1
15 to 19 years	75,047	49,360	25,687	36,368	24,490	11,878	38,679	24,870	13,809	34.2	32.7	35.7
20 to 44 years	231,591	154,791	76,800	111,472	77,083	34,389	120,119	77,708	42,411	33.2	30.8	35.3
45 years and over	105,114	74,792	30,322	53,475	39,068	14,407	51,639	35,724	15,915	28.8	26.9	30.8
Age unknown	1,271	809	462	740	466	274	531	343	188	36.3	37.0	35.4
WEST VIRGINIA.												
All ages	64,173	43,294	20,879	36,607	25,630	10,977	27,566	17,664	9,902	32.5	30.0	35.9
Under 5 years	6,974	4,246	2,728	3,534	2,187	1,347	3,440	2,059	1,381	39.1	38.1	40.1
Under 1 year	1,471	850	621	740	429	311	731	421	310	42.2	42.0	42.4
5 to 9 years	6,274	3,938	2,336	3,015	1,896	1,119	3,259	2,042	1,217	37.2	37.1	37.3
10 to 14 years	5,424	3,415	2,009	2,741	1,717	1,024	2,683	1,698	985	37.0	37.4	36.7
15 to 19 years	6,575	4,239	2,336	3,721	2,508	1,213	2,854	1,731	1,123	35.5	32.6	39.3
20 to 44 years	31,394	22,098	9,296	19,198	14,119	5,079	12,196	7,979	4,217	29.6	26.5	34.6
45 years and over	7,330	5,236	2,094	4,266	3,130	1,136	3,064	2,106	958	28.6	26.6	31.3
Age unknown	202	122	80	132	73	59	70	49	21	39.6	44.7	30.0
NORTH CAROLINA.												
All ages	697,843	553,720	144,123	339,581	272,299	67,282	358,262	281,421	76,841	20.7	19.8	21.4
Under 5 years	107,297	83,150	24,147	53,279	41,305	11,974	54,018	41,845	12,173	22.5	22.5	22.5
Under 1 year	22,852	17,343	5,509	11,316	8,609	2,707	11,536	8,734	2,802	24.1	23.9	24.3
5 to 9 years	100,151	78,790	21,361	49,662	39,143	10,519	50,489	39,647	10,842	21.3	21.2	21.5
10 to 14 years	89,416	70,577	18,839	44,654	35,361	9,293	44,762	35,216	9,546	21.1	20.8	21.3
15 to 19 years	80,253	63,386	16,867	38,752	30,921	7,831	41,501	32,465	9,036	21.0	20.2	21.8
20 to 44 years	221,544	176,871	44,673	100,668	82,035	18,633	120,876	94,836	26,040	20.2	18.5	21.5
45 years and over	96,771	78,965	17,806	51,287	42,467	8,820	45,484	36,498	8,986	18.4	17.2	19.8
Age unknown	2,411	1,981	430	1,279	1,067	212	1,132	914	218	17.8	16.6	19.3
SOUTH CAROLINA.												
All ages	835,843	701,462	134,381	408,078	345,142	62,936	427,765	356,320	71,445	16.1	15.4	16.7
Under 5 years	128,712	106,660	22,052	64,470	53,583	10,887	64,242	53,077	11,165	17.1	16.9	17.4
Under 1 year	25,934	21,142	4,792	12,977	10,634	2,343	12,957	10,508	2,449	18.5	18.1	18.9
5 to 9 years	123,067	103,246	19,821	61,303	51,539	9,764	61,764	51,707	10,057	16.1	15.9	16.3
10 to 14 years	114,341	95,742	18,599	57,285	48,100	9,185	57,056	47,642	9,414	16.3	16.0	16.5
15 to 19 years	99,118	82,858	16,260	47,442	40,031	7,411	51,676	42,827	8,849	16.4	15.6	17.1
20 to 44 years	270,557	227,355	43,202	125,427	106,876	18,551	145,130	120,479	24,651	16.0	14.8	17.0
45 years and over	98,313	84,225	14,088	51,186	44,245	6,941	47,127	39,980	7,147	14.3	13.6	15.2
Age unknown	1,735	1,376	359	965	768	197	770	608	162	20.7	20.4	21.0

TABLE 28.—NEGRO POPULATION, BLACK AND MULATTO, CLASSIFED BY SEX AND AGE PERIODS, WITH PERCENTAGE MULATTO, BY SOUTHERN STATES: 1910—Continued.

STATE AND AGE PERIOD.	NEGRO POPULATION: 1910.											
	Both sexes.			Male.			Female.			Percentage mulatto.		
	Total.	Black.	Mulatto.	Total.	Black.	Mulatto.	Total.	Black.	Mulatto.	Both sexes.	Male.	Female.
GEORGIA.												
All ages	1,176,987	972,782	204,205	580,263	486,012	94,251	596,724	486,770	109,954	17.3	16.2	18.4
Under 5 years	167,498	136,696	30,802	83,625	68,422	15,203	83,873	68,274	15,599	18.4	18.2	18.6
Under 1 year	32,992	26,299	6,693	16,449	13,121	3,328	16,543	13,178	3,365	20.3	20.2	20.3
5 to 9 years	163,294	134,570	28,724	81,086	66,998	14,088	82,208	67,572	14,636	17.6	17.4	17.8
10 to 14 years	152,029	125,288	26,741	76,610	63,609	13,001	75,419	61,679	13,740	17.6	17.0	18.2
15 to 19 years	129,923	106,140	23,783	60,723	50,304	10,419	69,200	55,836	13,364	18.3	17.2	19.3
20 to 44 years	408,283	337,792	70,491	194,595	164,731	29,864	213,688	173,061	40,627	17.3	15.3	19.0
45 years and over	153,304	130,052	23,252	82,173	70,717	11,456	71,131	59,335	11,796	15.2	13.9	16.6
Age unknown	2,656	2,244	412	1,451	1,231	220	1,205	1,013	192	15.5	15.2	15.9
FLORIDA.												
All ages	308,669	259,158	49,511	161,362	137,850	23,512	147,307	121,308	25,999	16.0	14.6	17.6
Under 5 years	37,114	30,844	6,270	18,412	15,375	3,037	18,702	15,469	3,233	16.9	16.5	17.3
Under 1 year	7,342	5,977	1,365	3,589	2,942	647	3,753	3,035	718	18.6	18.0	19.1
5 to 9 years	37,811	31,617	6,194	18,926	15,882	3,044	18,885	15,735	3,150	16.4	16.1	16.7
10 to 14 years	33,288	27,782	5,506	16,636	14,027	2,609	16,652	13,755	2,897	16.5	15.7	17.4
15 to 19 years	30,891	25,530	5,361	14,584	12,291	2,293	16,307	13,239	3,068	17.4	15.7	18.8
20 to 44 years	129,890	109,483	20,407	69,767	60,303	9,464	60,123	49,180	10,943	15.7	13.6	18.2
45 years and over	37,631	32,131	5,500	21,694	18,774	2,920	15,937	13,357	2,580	14.6	13.5	16.2
Age unknown	2,044	1,771	273	1,343	1,198	145	701	573	128	13.4	10.8	18.3
EAST SOUTH CENTRAL DIVISION.												
KENTUCKY.												
All ages	261,656	195,713	65,943	131,492	101,071	30,421	130,164	94,642	35,522	25.2	23.1	27.3
Under 5 years	25,541	18,406	7,135	12,700	9,207	3,493	12,841	9,199	3,642	27.9	27.5	28.4
Under 1 year	5,176	3,645	1,531	2,568	1,817	751	2,608	1,828	780	29.6	29.2	29.9
5 to 9 years	26,087	19,169	6,918	13,022	9,667	3,355	13,065	9,502	3,563	26.5	25.8	27.3
10 to 14 years	26,984	19,941	7,043	13,540	10,071	3,469	13,444	9,870	3,574	26.1	25.6	26.6
15 to 19 years	28,163	20,756	7,407	13,846	10,413	3,433	14,317	10,343	3,974	26.3	24.8	27.8
20 to 44 years	105,298	78,069	27,229	52,629	40,663	11,966	52,669	37,406	15,263	25.9	22.7	29.0
45 years and over	48,438	38,413	10,025	25,164	20,553	4,611	23,274	17,860	5,414	20.7	18.3	23.3
Age unknown	1,145	959	186	591	497	94	554	462	92	16.2	15.9	16.6
TENNESSEE.												
All ages	473,088	354,391	118,697	233,710	179,678	54,032	239,378	174,713	64,665	25.1	23.1	27.0
Under 5 years	56,580	40,849	15,731	28,245	20,486	7,759	28,335	20,363	7,972	27.8	27.5	28.1
Under 1 year	11,706	8,317	3,389	5,800	4,135	1,665	5,906	4,182	1,724	29.0	28.7	29.2
5 to 9 years	55,845	41,152	14,693	27,767	20,654	7,113	28,078	20,498	7,580	26.3	25.6	27.0
10 to 14 years	53,344	39,638	13,706	26,838	20,189	6,649	26,506	19,449	7,057	25.7	24.8	26.6
15 to 19 years	54,363	40,227	14,136	26,705	20,216	6,489	27,658	20,011	7,647	26.0	24.3	27.6
20 to 44 years	176,192	131,952	44,240	82,899	64,688	18,211	93,293	67,264	26,029	25.1	22.0	27.9
45 years and over	75,442	59,493	15,949	40,573	32,872	7,701	34,869	26,621	8,248	21.1	19.0	23.7
Age unknown	1,322	1,080	242	683	573	110	639	507	132	18.3	16.1	20.7
ALABAMA.												
All ages	908,282	756,872	151,410	447,794	377,869	69,925	460,488	379,003	81,485	16.7	15.6	17.7
Under 5 years	123,991	101,897	22,094	61,808	51,026	10,782	62,183	50,871	11,312	17.8	17.4	18.2
Under 1 year	24,244	19,468	4,776	12,017	9,699	2,318	12,227	9,769	2,458	19.7	19.3	20.1
5 to 9 years	121,935	101,155	20,780	60,331	50,226	10,105	61,604	50,929	10,675	17.0	16.7	17.3
10 to 14 years	112,129	93,028	19,101	56,630	47,230	9,400	55,499	45,798	9,701	17.0	16.6	17.5
15 to 19 years	99,130	81,697	17,433	47,343	39,500	7,843	51,787	42,197	9,590	17.6	16.6	18.5
20 to 44 years	318,299	265,421	52,878	149,102	127,040	22,062	169,197	138,381	30,816	16.6	14.8	18.2
45 years and over	130,019	111,265	18,754	71,147	61,591	9,556	58,872	49,674	9,198	14.4	13.4	15.6
Age unknown	2,779	2,409	370	1,433	1,256	177	1,346	1,153	193	13.3	12.4	14.3
MISSISSIPPI.												
All ages	1,009,487	838,482	171,005	502,796	422,446	80,350	506,691	416,036	90,655	16.9	16.0	17.9
Under 5 years	141,691	115,259	26,432	71,149	58,007	13,142	70,542	57,252	13,290	18.7	18.5	18.8
Under 1 year	27,329	21,669	5,660	13,651	10,815	2,836	13,678	10,854	2,824	20.7	20.8	20.6
5 to 9 years	139,945	115,286	24,659	69,849	57,816	12,033	70,096	57,470	12,626	17.6	17.2	18.0
10 to 14 years	128,019	105,822	22,197	64,734	53,835	10,899	63,285	51,987	11,298	17.3	16.8	17.9
15 to 19 years	112,527	92,439	20,088	54,469	45,423	9,046	58,058	47,016	11,042	17.9	16.6	19.0
20 to 44 years	355,553	297,710	57,843	172,780	147,405	25,375	182,773	150,305	32,468	16.3	14.7	17.8
45 years and over	128,582	109,390	19,192	68,161	58,587	9,574	60,421	50,803	9,618	14.9	14.0	15.9
Age unknown	3,170	2,576	594	1,654	1,373	281	1,516	1,203	313	18.7	17.0	20.6

NEGRO POPULATION.

TABLE 28.—NEGRO POPULATION, BLACK AND MULATTO, CLASSIFIED BY SEX AND AGE PERIODS, WITH PERCENTAGE MULATTO, BY SOUTHERN STATES: 1910—Continued.

STATE AND AGE PERIOD.	NEGRO POPULATION: 1910.											
	Both sexes.			Male.			F5male.			Percentage mulatto.		
	Total.	Black.	Mulatto.	Total.	Black.	Mulatto.	Total.	Black.	Mulatto.	Both sexes.	Male.	Female.
WEST SOUTH CENTRAL DIVISION.												
ARKANSAS.												
All ages	442,891	361,520	81,371	223,323	184,637	38,686	219,568	176,883	42,685	18.4	17.3	19.4
Under 5 years	57,330	45,776	11,554	28,456	22,750	5,706	28,874	23,026	5,848	20.2	20.1	20.3
Under 1 year	10,804	8,402	2,402	5,289	4,086	1,203	5,515	4,316	1,199	22.2	22.7	21.7
5 to 9 years	58,552	47,470	11,082	28,987	23,601	5,386	29,565	23,869	5,696	18.9	18.6	19.3
10 to 14 years	52,679	42,838	9,841	26,082	21,301	4,781	26,597	21,537	5,060	18.7	18.3	19.0
15 to 19 years	50,309	40,895	9,414	24,296	20,083	4,213	26,013	20,812	5,201	18.7	17.3	20.0
20 to 44 years	161,503	132,041	29,462	79,125	65,957	13,168	82,378	66,084	16,294	18.2	16.6	19.8
45 years and over	61,426	51,622	9,804	35,792	30,476	5,316	25,634	21,146	4,488	16.0	14.9	17.5
Age unknown	1,092	878	214	585	469	116	507	409	98	19.6	19.8	19.3
LOUISIANA.												
All ages	713,874	561,297	152,577	353,824	282,094	71,730	360,050	279,203	80,847	21.4	20.3	22.5
Under 5 years	92,439	71,074	21,365	45,867	35,322	10,545	46,572	35,752	10,820	23.1	23.0	23.2
Under 1 year	17,435	13,051	4,384	8,695	6,468	2,227	8,740	6,583	2,157	25.1	25.6	24.7
5 to 9 years	95,985	75,029	20,956	48,020	37,714	10,306	47,965	37,315	10,650	21.8	21.5	22.2
10 to 14 years	85,917	67,244	18,673	42,931	33,796	9,135	42,986	33,448	9,538	21.7	21.3	22.2
15 to 19 years	76,868	59,695	17,173	36,172	28,563	7,609	40,696	31,132	9,564	22.3	21.0	23.5
20 to 44 years	264,740	209,310	55,430	130,123	105,150	24,973	134,617	104,160	30,457	20.9	19.2	22.6
45 years and over	95,699	77,061	18,638	49,454	40,462	8,992	46,245	36,599	9,646	19.5	18.2	20.9
Age unknown	2,226	1,884	342	1,257	1,087	170	969	797	172	15.4	13.5	17.8
OKLAHOMA.												
All ages	137,612	98,269	39,343	71,937	52,360	19,577	65,675	45,909	19,766	28.6	27.2	30.1
Under 5 years	18,186	12,396	5,790	9,028	6,172	2,856	9,158	6,224	2,934	31.8	31.6	32.0
Under 1 year	3,544	2,379	1,165	1,718	1,177	541	1,826	1,203	624	32.9	31.5	34.2
5 to 9 years	18,269	12,619	5,650	9,223	6,397	2,826	9,046	6,222	2,824	30.9	30.6	31.2
10 to 14 years	16,208	11,305	4,903	8,015	5,555	2,460	8,193	5,750	2,443	30.3	30.7	29.8
15 to 19 years	14,974	10,513	4,461	7,448	5,315	2,133	7,526	5,198	2,328	29.8	28.6	30.9
20 to 44 years	51,351	37,375	13,976	27,094	20,435	6,659	24,257	16,940	7,317	27.2	24.6	30.2
45 years and over	18,033	13,578	4,455	10,786	8,201	2,585	7,247	5,377	1,870	24.7	24.0	25.8
Age unknown	591	483	108	343	285	58	248	198	50	18.3	16.9	20.2
TEXAS.												
All ages	690,049	565,354	124,695	344,941	286,819	58,122	345,108	278,535	66,573	18.1	16.8	19.3
Under 5 years	90,057	72,268	17,789	45,146	36,425	8,721	44,911	35,843	9,068	19.8	19.3	20.2
Under 1 year	17,948	14,040	3,908	8,816	6,901	1,915	9,132	7,139	1,993	21.8	21.7	21.8
5 to 9 years	92,903	75,310	17,593	46,353	37,801	8,552	46,550	37,509	9,041	18.9	18.4	19.4
10 to 14 years	85,461	69,662	15,799	42,717	35,076	7,641	42,744	34,586	8,158	18.5	17.9	19.1
15 to 19 years	77,329	62,796	14,533	37,353	30,756	6,597	39,976	32,040	7,936	18.8	17.7	19.9
20 to 44 years	252,165	207,163	45,002	122,931	103,481	19,450	129,234	103,682	25,552	17.8	15.8	19.8
45 years and under	89,469	75,794	13,675	49,013	42,025	6,988	40,456	33,769	6,687	15.3	14.3	16.5
Age unknown	2,665	2,361	304	1,428	1,255	173	1,237	1,106	131	11.4	12.1	10.6

TABLE 29.—URBAN AND RURAL BLACK AND MULATTO POPULATION CLASSIFIED BY SEX, BY DIVISIONS AND STATES: 1910.

DIVISION AND STATE.	NEGRO POPULATION: 1910.											
	Urban.						Rural.					
	Both sexes.		Male.		Female.		Both sexes.		Male.		Female.	
	Black.	Mulatto.	Black.	Mulatto.	Black.	Mulatto.	Black.	Mulatto.	Black	Mulatto.	Black.	Mulatto.
UNITED STATES	1,957,709	731,520	952,085	327,399	1,005,624	404,121	5,819,368	1,319,166	2,970,247	636,150	2,849,121	683,016
GEOGRAPHIC DIVISIONS:												
New England	41,342	19,535	20,228	9,468	21,114	10,067	2,814	2,615	1,509	1,578	1,305	1,037
Middle Atlantic	270,946	68,300	130,050	31,403	140,896	36,897	64,955	13,669	35,029	6,984	29,926	6,685
East North Central	155,398	75,144	81,765	36,118	73,633	39,026	45,629	24,665	25,529	13,019	20,100	11,646
West North Central	113,481	50,820	59,451	24,358	54,030	26,462	59,550	18,811	32,683	9,372	26,867	9,439
South Atlantic	652,247	257,273	308,584	112,035	343,663	145,238	2,604,422	598,546	1,321,113	288,076	1,283,309	310,470
East South Central	373,417	135,680	180,024	58,179	193,393	77,501	1,772,041	371,375	901,040	176,549	871,001	194,826
West South Central	324,386	111,452	157,831	49,293	166,555	62,159	1,262,054	286,534	648,079	138,822	613,975	147,712
Mountain	10,867	4,579	5,729	2,189	5,138	2,390	4,465	1,556	2,968	880	1,497	676
Pacific	15,625	8,737	8,423	4,356	7,202	4,381	3,438	1,395	2,297	870	1,141	525
NEW ENGLAND:												
Maine	528	396	277	174	251	222	209	230	108	141	101	89
New Hampshire	270	86	110	49	160	37	86	122	57	72	29	50
Vermont	1,059	282	841	163	218	119	126	154	75	94	51	60
Massachusetts	22,952	12,291	11,044	6,057	11,908	6,234	1,148	1,664	608	1,039	540	625
Rhode Island	6,009	3,046	2,932	1,447	3,077	1,599	341	133	192	74	149	59
Connecticut	10,524	3,434	5,024	1,578	5,500	1,856	904	312	469	158	435	154
MIDDLE ATLANTIC:												
New York	89,488	27,998	42,028	12,615	47,460	15,383	14,095	2,610	7,981	1,410	6,114	1,200
New Jersey	54,962	10,465	25,932	4,850	29,030	5,615	20,591	3,742	10,982	1,838	9,609	1,904
Pennsylvania	126,496	29,837	62,090	13,938	64,406	15,899	30,269	7,317	16,066	3,736	14,203	3,581
EAST NORTH CENTRAL:												
Ohio	54,565	27,717	28,866	13,208	25,699	14,509	17,638	11,532	9,798	6,123	7,840	5,409
Indiana	36,746	11,679	18,895	5,590	17,851	6,089	9,021	2,874	5,040	1,519	3,981	1,355
Illinois	55,472	30,066	29,438	14,577	26,034	15,489	16,749	6,762	9,413	3,481	7,336	3,281
Michigan	7,276	4,880	3,893	2,362	3,383	2,518	1,803	3,156	1,048	1,704	755	1,452
Wisconsin	1,339	802	673	381	666	421	418	341	230	192	188	149
WEST NORTH CENTRAL:												
Minnesota	4,117	2,401	2,502	1,362	1,615	1,039	351	215	187	132	164	83
Iowa	7,066	2,720	3,881	1,334	3,185	1,386	4,263	924	2,401	504	1,862	420
Missouri	72,042	32,420	37,343	15,275	34,699	17,145	40,720	12,270	21,934	5,937	18,786	6,333
North Dakota	230	76	147	50	83	26	230	81	139	45	91	36
South Dakota	277	135	161	67	116	68	244	161	143	97	101	64
Nebraska	4,844	1,777	2,712	914	2,132	863	758	310	463	170	295	140
Kansas	24,905	11,291	12,705	5,356	12,200	5,935	12,984	4,850	7,416	2,487	5,568	2,363
SOUTH ATLANTIC:												
Delaware	10,064	1,093	4,913	479	5,151	614	17,411	2,613	9,322	1,297	8,089	1,316
Maryland	77,148	22,082	36,292	9,654	40,856	12,428	111,950	21,070	58,618	10,185	53,332	10,885
District of Columbia	61,494	32,952	28,254	14,361	33,240	18,591	....	....	....	....	....	....
Virginia	95,447	62,771	44,950	27,854	50,497	34,917	352,739	160,139	180,415	77,323	172,324	82,816
West Virginia	10,163	5,217	5,463	2,482	4,700	2,735	33,131	15,662	20,167	8,495	12,964	7,167
North Carolina	90,404	25,571	41,896	10,900	48,508	14,671	463,316	118,552	230,403	56,382	232,913	62,170
South Carolina	71,945	29,757	33,095	12,884	38,850	16,873	629,517	104,624	312,047	50,052	317,470	54,572
Georgia	167,375	57,451	78,931	24,300	88,444	33,151	805,407	146,754	407,081	69,951	398,326	76,803
Florida	68,207	20,379	34,790	9,121	33,417	11,258	190,951	29,132	103,060	14,391	87,891	14,741
EAST SOUTH CENTRAL:												
Kentucky	74,010	32,621	36,734	14,452	37,276	18,169	121,703	33,322	64,337	15,969	57,366	17,353
Tennessee	106,142	44,364	51,301	19,074	54,841	25,290	248,249	74,333	128,377	34,958	119,872	39,375
Alabama	119,920	36,683	58,000	15,579	61,920	21,104	636,952	114,727	319,869	54,346	317,083	60,381
Mississippi	73,345	22,012	33,989	9,074	39,356	12,938	765,137	148,993	388,457	71,276	376,680	77,717
WEST SOUTH CENTRAL:												
Arkansas	43,528	15,619	21,535	7,177	21,993	8,442	317,992	65,752	163,102	31,509	154,890	34,243
Louisiana	113,134	47,711	53,267	20,575	59,867	27,136	448,163	104,866	228,827	51,155	219,336	53,711
Oklahoma	25,906	11,076	14,063	5,434	11,843	5,642	72,363	28,267	38,297	14,143	34,066	14,124
Texas	141,818	37,046	68,966	16,107	72,852	20,939	423,536	87,649	217,853	42,015	205,683	45,634
MOUNTAIN:												
Montana	930	525	543	287	387	238	293	86	183	45	110	41
Idaho	262	164	163	89	99	75	163	62	106	40	57	22
Wyoming	869	172	458	81	411	91	1,073	121	916	89	157	32
Colorado	6,380	2,979	3,274	1,372	3,106	1,607	1,435	659	843	378	592	281
New Mexico	650	145	335	58	315	87	539	294	338	160	201	134
Arizona	1,034	276	489	137	545	139	527	172	331	97	196	75
Utah	678	281	426	147	252	134	176	9	110	8	66	1
Nevada	64	37	41	18	23	19	259	153	141	63	118	90
PACIFIC:												
Washington	3,214	1,485	1,909	829	1,305	656	1,004	355	771	227	233	128
Oregon	933	331	580	176	353	155	125	103	82	69	43	34
California	11,478	6,921	5,934	3,351	5,544	3,570	2,309	937	1,444	574	865	363

TABLE **30.**—PERCENTAGE MULATTO IN THE URBAN AND RURAL NEGRO POPULATION, AND PERCENTAGE URBAN, AND MALES TO 1,000 FEMALES IN THE URBAN AND RURAL BLACK AND MULATTO POPULATION, BY DIVISIONS AND STATES: 1910.

DIVISION AND STATE.	NEGRO POPULATION: 1910.															
	Percentage mulatto.						Percentage urban.						Males to 1,000 females.			
	Urban communities.			Rural communities.			Both sexes.		Male.		Female.		Urban communities.		Rural communities.	
	Both sexes.	Male.	Female.	Both sexes.	Male.	Female.	Black.	Mulatto.	Black.	Mulatto.	Black.	Mulatto.	Black.	Mulatto.	Black.	Mulatto.
UNITED STATES	27.2	25.6	28.7	18.5	17.6	19.3	25.2	35.7	24.3	34.0	26.1	37.2	947	810	1,043	931
GEOGRAPHIC DIVISIONS:																
New England	32.1	31.9	32.3	48.2	51.1	44.3	93.6	88.2	93.1	85.7	94.2	90.7	958	940	1,156	1,522
Middle Atlantic	20.1	19.5	20.8	17.4	16.6	18.3	80.7	83.3	78.8	81.8	82.5	84.7	923	851	1,171	1,045
East North Central	32.6	30.6	34.6	35.1	33.8	36.7	77.3	75.3	76.2	73.5	78.6	77.0	1,110	925	1,270	1,118
West North Central	30.9	29.1	32.9	24.0	22.3	26.0	65.6	73.0	64.5	72.2	66.8	73.7	1,100	920	1,216	993
South Atlantic	28.3	26.6	29.7	18.7	17.9	19.5	20.0	30.1	18.9	28.0	21.1	31.9	898	771	1,029	928
East South Central	26.7	24.4	28.6	17.3	16.4	18.3	17.4	26.8	16.7	24.8	18.2	28.5	932	751	1,034	906
West South Central	25.6	23.8	27.2	18.5	17.6	19.4	20.4	28.0	19.6	26.2	21.3	29.6	948	793	1,056	940
Mountain	29.6	27.6	31.7	25.8	22.9	31.1	70.9	74.6	65.9	71.3	77.4	78.0	1,115	916	1,983	1,302
Pacific	35.9	34.1	37.8	28.9	27.5	31.5	82.0	86.2	78.6	83.4	86.3	89.3	1,170	994	2,013	1,657
NEW ENGLAND:																
Maine	42.9	38.6	46.9	52.4	56.6	46.8	71.6	63.3	71.9	55.2	71.3	71.4	1,104	784	1,069	(2)
New Hampshire	24.2	30.8	18.8	58.7	55.8	(1)	75.8	41.3	65.9	40.5	84.7	(1)	688	(2)	(2)	(2)
Vermont	21.0	16.2	35.3	55.0	55.6	54.1	89.4	64.7	91.8	63.4	81.0	66.5	3,858	1,370	(2)	(2)
Massachusetts	34.9	35.4	34.4	59.2	63.1	53.6	95.2	88.1	94.8	85.4	95.7	90.9	927	972	1,126	1,662
Rhode Island	33.6	33.0	34.2	28.1	27.8	28.4	94.6	95.8	93.9	95.1	95.4	96.4	953	905	1,289	(2)
Connecticut	24.6	23.9	25.2	25.7	25.2	26.1	92.1	91.7	91.5	90.9	92.7	92.3	913	850	1,078	1,026
MIDDLE ATLANTIC:																
New York	23.8	23.1	24.5	15.6	15.0	16.4	86.4	91.5	84.0	89.9	88.6	92.8	886	820	1,305	1,175
New Jersey	16.0	15.8	16.2	15.4	14.3	16.5	72.7	73.7	70.2	72.5	75.1	74.7	893	864	1,143	965
Pennsylvania	19.1	18.3	19.8	19.5	18.9	20.1	80.7	80.3	79.4	78.9	81.9	81.6	964	877	1,131	1,043
EAST NORTH CENTRAL:																
Ohio	33.7	31.4	36.1	39.5	38.5	40.8	75.6	70.6	74.7	68.3	76.6	72.8	1,123	910	1,250	1,132
Indiana	24.1	22.8	25.4	24.2	23.2	25.4	80.3	80.3	78.9	78.6	81.8	81.8	1,058	918	1,266	1,121
Illinois	35.1	33.1	37.3	28.8	27.0	30.9	76.8	81.6	75.8	80.7	78.0	82.5	1,131	941	1,283	1,061
Michigan	40.1	37.8	42.7	63.6	61.9	65.8	80.1	60.7	78.8	58.1	81.8	63.4	1,151	938	1,388	1,174
Wisconsin	37.5	36.1	38.7	44.9	45.5	44.2	76.2	70.2	74.5	66.5	78.0	73.9	1,011	905	1,223	1,289
WEST NORTH CENTRAL:																
Minnesota	36.8	35.2	39.1	38.0	41.4	33.6	92.1	91.8	93.0	91.2	90.8	92.6	1,549	1,311	1,140	(2)
Iowa	27.8	25.6	30.3	17.8	17.3	18.4	62.4	74.6	61.8	72.6	63.1	76.7	1,219	962	1,289	1,200
Missouri	31.0	29.0	33.1	23.2	21.3	25.2	63.9	72.5	63.0	72.0	64.9	73.0	1,076	891	1,168	937
North Dakota	24.8	25.4	23.9	26.0	24.5	28.3	50.0	48.4	51.4	(1)	47.7	(1)	(2)	(2)	(2)	(2)
South Dakota	32.8	29.4	37.0	29.8	40.4	38.8	53.2	45.6	53.0	40.9	53.5	51.5	1,388	(2)	1,416	(2)
Nebraska	26.8	25.2	28.8	29.0	26.9	32.2	86.5	85.1	85.4	84.3	87.8	86.0	1,272	1,059	1,569	1,214
Kansas	31.2	29.7	32.7	27.2	25.1	29.8	65.7	70.0	63.1	68.3	68.7	71.5	1,041	902	1,332	1,052
SOUTH ATLANTIC:																
Delaware	9.8	8.9	10.7	13.0	12.2	14.0	36.6	29.5	34.5	27.0	38.9	31.8	954	780	1,152	986
Maryland	22.3	21.0	23.3	15.8	14.8	17.0	40.8	51.2	38.2	48.7	43.4	53.3	888	777	1,099	936
District of Columbia	34.9	33.7	35.9				100.0	100.0	100.0	100.0	100.0	100.0	850	772	(2)	(2)
Virginia	39.7	38.3	40.9	31.2	30.0	32.5	21.3	28.2	19.9	26.5	22.7	29.7	890	798	1,047	934
West Virginia	33.9	31.2	36.8	32.1	29.6	35.6	23.5	25.0	21.3	22.6	26.6	27.6	1,162	907	1,556	1,185
North Carolina	22.0	20.6	23.2	20.4	19.7	21.1	16.3	17.7	15.4	16.2	17.2	19.1	864	743	989	907
South Carolina	29.3	28.0	30.3	14.3	13.8	14.7	10.3	22.1	9.6	20.5	10.9	23.6	852	764	983	917
Georgia	25.6	23.5	27.3	15.4	14.7	16.2	17.2	28.1	16.2	25.8	18.2	30.1	892	733	1,022	911
Florida	23.0	20.8	25.2	13.2	12.3	14.4	26.3	41.2	25.2	38.8	27.5	43.3	1,041	810	1,173	976
EAST SOUTH CENTRAL:																
Kentucky	30.6	28.2	32.8	21.5	19.9	23.2	37.8	49.5	36.3	47.5	39.4	51.1	985	795	1,122	920
Tennessee	29.5	27.1	31.6	23.0	21.4	24.7	30.0	37.4	28.6	35.3	31.4	39.1	935	754	1,071	888
Alabama	23.4	21.2	25.4	15.3	14.5	16.0	15.8	24.2	15.3	22.3	16.3	25.9	937	738	1,009	900
Mississippi	23.1	21.1	24.7	16.3	15.5	17.1	8.7	12.9	8.0	11.3	9.5	14.3	864	701	1,031	917
WEST SOUTH CENTRAL:																
Arkansas	26.4	25.0	27.7	17.1	16.2	18.1	12.0	19.2	11.7	18.6	12.4	19.8	979	850	1,053	920
Louisiana	29.7	27.9	31.2	19.0	18.3	19.7	20.2	31.3	18.9	28.7	21.3	33.6	890	758	1,043	952
Oklahoma	29.9	27.9	32.3	28.1	27.0	29.3	26.4	28.2	26.9	27.8	25.8	28.5	1,187	963	1,124	1,001
Texas	20.7	18.9	22.3	17.1	16.2	18.2	25.1	29.7	24.0	27.7	26.2	31.5	947	769	1,059	921
MOUNTAIN:																
Montana	36.1	34.6	38.1	22.7	19.7	27.2	76.0	85.9	74.8	86.4	77.9	85.3	1,403	1,206	1,664	(2)
Idaho	38.5	35.3	43.1	27.6	27.4	(1)	61.6	72.6	60.6	69.0	63.5	(1)	(2)	(2)	(2)	(2)
Wyoming	16.5	15.0	18.1	10.1	8.9	16.9	44.7	58.7	33.3	47.6	72.4	74.0	1,114	(2)	5,834	(2)
Colorado	31.8	29.5	34.1	31.5	31.0	32.2	81.6	81.9	79.5	78.4	84.0	85.1	1,054	854	1,424	1,345
New Mexico	18.2	14.8	21.6	35.3	32.1	40.0	54.7	33.0	49.8	26.6	61.0	39.4	1,063	(2)	1,682	1,194
Arizona	21.1	21.9	20.3	24.6	22.7	27.7	66.2	61.6	59.6	58.5	73.5	65.0	897	986	1,689	(2)
Utah	29.3	25.7	34.7	4.9	6.8	(1)	79.4	96.9	79.5	94.8	79.2	99.3	1,690	1,097	(2)	(2)
Nevada	36.6	(1)	(1)	37.1	30.9	43.3	19.8	19.5	22.5	(1)	16.3	17.4	(2)	(2)	1,195	(2)
PACIFIC:																
Washington	31.6	30.3	33.5	26.1	22.7	35.5	76.2	80.7	71.2	78.5	84.9	83.7	1,463	1,264	3,309	1,773
Oregon	26.2	23.3	30.5	45.2	45.7	(1)	88.2	76.3	87.6	71.8	89.1	82.0	1,643	1,135	(2)	(2)
California	37.6	36.1	39.2	28.9	28.4	29.6	83.3	88.1	80.4	85.4	86.5	90.8	1,070	939	1,669	1,581

[1] Per cent not shown where base is less than 100. [2] Ratio not shown, the number of females being less than 100.

TABLE 31.—NEGRO POPULATION, DISTINGUISHED AS BLACK AND MULATTO, IN CITIES HAVING 5,000 NEGROES OR MORE: 1910.

CITY.	Total population: 1910	NEGRO POPULATION. Total.	Black.	Mu-latto.	PER CENT OF TOTAL NEGRO POPULATION. Black.	Mu-latto.
ALABAMA.						
Bessemer	10,864	6,210	5,171	1,039	83.3	16.7
Birmingham	132,685	52,305	41,102	11,203	78.6	21.4
Mobile	51,521	22,763	16,728	6,035	73.5	26.5
Montgomery	38,136	19,322	13,965	5,357	72.3	27.7
Selma	13,649	7,863	7,143	720	90.8	9.2
ARKANSAS.						
Helena	8,772	5,596	3,845	1,751	68.7	31.3
Little Rock	45,941	14,539	11,074	3,465	76.2	23.8
Pine Bluff	15,102	6,124	4,280	1,844	69.9	30.1
Texarkana[1]	5,655	2,101	1,608	493	76.5	23.5
CALIFORNIA.						
Los Angeles	319,198	7,599	5,101	2,498	67.1	32.9
COLORADO.						
Denver	213,381	5,426	3,297	2,129	60.8	39.2
DELAWARE.						
Wilmington	87,411	9,081	8,090	991	89.1	10.9
DISTRICT OF COLUMBIA.						
Washington	331,069	94,446	61,494	32,952	65.1	34.9
FLORIDA.						
Jacksonville	57,699	29,293	25,314	3,979	86.4	13.6
Key West	19,945	5,515	3,923	1,592	71.1	28.9
Pensacola	22,982	10,214	8,453	1,761	82.8	17.2
Tampa	37,782	8,951	5,913	3,038	66.1	33.9
GEORGIA.						
Athens	14,913	6,316	4,859	1,457	76.9	23.1
Atlanta	154,839	51,902	35,071	16,831	67.6	32.4
Augusta	41,040	18,344	15,260	3,084	83.2	16.8
Brunswick	10,182	5,567	4,307	1,260	77.4	22.6
Columbus	20,554	7,644	5,010	2,634	65.5	34.5
Macon	40,665	18,150	15,921	2,229	87.7	12.3
Savannah	65,064	33,246	24,881	8,365	74.8	25.2
Waycross	14,485	6,729	4,378	2,351	65.1	34.9
ILLINOIS.						
Cairo	14,548	5,434	3,686	1,748	67.8	32.2
Chicago	2,185,283	44,103	25,760	18,343	58.4	41.6
East St. Louis	58,547	5,882	4,070	1,812	69.2	30.8
INDIANA.						
Evansville	69,647	6,266	4,891	1,375	78.1	21.9
Indianapolis	233,650	21,816	18,088	3,728	82.9	17.1
KANSAS.						
Kansas City	82,331	9,286	6,080	3,206	65.5	34.5
KENTUCKY.						
Lexington	35,099	11,011	9,026	1,985	82.0	18.0
Louisville	223,928	40,522	25,708	14,814	63.4	36.6
Paducah	22,760	6,047	3,186	2,861	52.7	47.3
LOUISIANA.						
Alexandria	11,213	5,854	4,917	937	84.0	16.0
Baton Rouge	14,897	7,899	5,402	2,497	68.4	31.6
Monroe	10,209	5,320	4,656	664	87.5	12.5
New Orleans	339,075	89,262	58,782	30,480	65.9	34.1
Shreveport	28,015	13,896	11,953	1,943	86.0	14.0
MARYLAND.						
Baltimore	558,485	84,749	66,508	18,241	78.5	21.5
MASSACHUSETTS.						
Boston	670,585	13,564	8,905	4,659	65.7	34.3
MICHIGAN.						
Detroit	465,766	5,741	3,444	2,297	60.0	40.0
MISSISSIPPI.						
Greenville	9,610	6,010	5,179	831	86.2	13.8
Jackson	21,262	10,554	7,668	2,886	72.7	27.3
Meridian	23,285	9,321	8,166	1,155	87.6	12.4
Natchez	11,791	6,700	4,907	1,793	73.2	26.8
Vicksburg	20,814	12,053	8,722	3,331	72.4	27.6
MISSOURI.						
Kansas City	248,381	23,566	15,906	7,660	67.5	32.5
St. Louis	687,029	43,960	29,004	14,956	66.0	34.0
NEW JERSEY.						
Atlantic City	46,150	9,834	8,441	1,393	85.8	14.2
Camden	94,538	6,076	5,093	983	83.8	16.2
Jersey City	267,779	5,960	5,233	727	87.8	12.2
Newark	347,469	9,475	7,741	1,734	81.7	18.3
NEW YORK.						
New York	4,766,883	91,709	68,914	22,795	75.1	24.9
Manhattan Borough	*2,331,542*	*60,534*	*44,697*	*15,837*	*73.8*	*26.2*
Bronx Borough	*430,980*	*4,117*	*3,030*	*1,087*	*73.6*	*26.4*
Brooklyn Borough	*1,634,351*	*22,708*	*17,682*	*5,026*	*77.9*	*22.1*
Queens Borough	*284,041*	*3,198*	*2,445*	*753*	*76.5*	*23.5*
Richmond Borough	*85,969*	*1,152*	*1,060*	*92*	*92.0*	*8.0*
NORTH CAROLINA.						
Asheville	18,762	5,359	3,535	1,824	66.0	34.0
Charlotte	34,014	11,752	9,181	2,571	78.1	21.9
Durham	18,241	6,869	4,572	2,297	66.6	33.4
Greensboro	15,895	5,710	4,536	1,174	79.4	20.6
Newbern	9,961	5,649	4,439	1,210	78.6	21.4
Raleigh	19,218	7,372	6,705	667	91.0	9.0
Wilmington	25,748	12,107	8,897	3,210	73.5	26.5
Winston	17,167	7,828	5,814	2,014	74.3	25.7
OHIO.						
Cincinnati	363,591	19,639	13,834	5,805	70.4	29.6
Cleveland	560,663	8,448	5,944	2,504	70.4	29.6
Columbus	181,511	12,739	8,503	4,236	66.7	33.3
OKLAHOMA.						
Muskogee	25,278	7,831	4,728	3,103	60.4	39.6
Oklahoma City	64,205	6,546	5,054	1,492	77.2	22.8
PENNSYLVANIA.						
Philadelphia	1,549,008	84,459	70,479	13,980	83.4	16.6
Pittsburgh	533,905	25,623	19,620	6,003	76.6	23.4
RHODE ISLAND.						
Providence	224,326	5,316	3,468	1,848	65.2	34.8
SOUTH CAROLINA.						
Charleston	58,833	31,056	23,733	7,323	76.4	23.6
Columbia	26,319	11,546	7,903	3,643	68.4	31.6
Greenville	15,741	6,319	2,924	3,395	46.3	53.7
Spartanburg	17,517	6,873	5,192	1,681	75.5	24.5
TENNESSEE.						
Chattanooga	44,604	17,942	11,056	6,886	61.6	38.4
Jackson	15,779	5,719	4,015	1,704	70.2	29.8
Knoxville	36,346	7,638	6,097	1,541	79.8	20.2
Memphis	131,105	52,441	38,592	13,849	73.6	26.4
Nashville	110,364	36,523	24,536	11,987	67.2	32.8
TEXAS.						
Austin	29,860	7,478	6,445	1,033	86.2	13.8
Beaumont	20,640	6,896	5,987	909	86.8	13.2
Dallas	92,104	18,024	14,968	3,056	83.0	17.0
Fort Worth	73,312	13,280	11,149	2,131	84.0	16.0
Galveston	36,981	8,036	4,725	3,311	58.8	41.2
Houston	78,800	23,929	20,125	3,804	84.1	15.9
San Antonio	96,614	10,716	7,992	2,724	74.6	25.4
Texarkana[1]	9,790	3,218	2,749	469	85.4	14.6
Waco	26,425	6,067	5,233	834	86.3	13.7
VIRGINIA.						
Danville	19,020	6,207	3,971	2,236	64.0	36.0
Lynchburg	29,494	9,466	5,875	3,591	62.1	37.9
Newport News	20,205	7,259	6,226	1,033	85.8	14.2
Norfolk	67,452	25,039	12,839	12,200	51.3	48.7
Petersburg	24,127	11,014	5,704	5,310	51.8	48.2
Portsmouth	33,190	11,617	5,865	5,752	50.5	49.5
Richmond	127,628	46,733	28,088	18,645	60.1	39.9
Roanoke	34,874	7,924	5,265	2,659	66.4	33.6

[1] Joint population of Texarkana, Miller County, Ark., and Texarkana, Bowie County, Tex., 15,445; Negro population, 5,319; black, 4,357, or 81.9 per cent; mulatto, 962, or 18.1 per cent.

TABLE **32.**—SCHOOL ATTENDANCE OF THE BLACK AND MULATTO POPULATION—NUMBER IN SCHOOL AND NOT IN SCHOOL, BY AGE PERIODS, BY SECTIONS, SOUTHERN DIVISIONS, AND STATES: 1910.

NEGRO POPULATION 6 TO 20 YEARS OF AGE: 1910.

SECTION, DIVISION, STATE, AND SEX.	Total Black in school	Total Black not in school	Total Mulatto in school	Total Mulatto not in school	6 to 9 Black in school	6 to 9 Black not in school	6 to 9 Mulatto in school	6 to 9 Mulatto not in school	10 to 14 Black in school	10 to 14 Black not in school	10 to 14 Mulatto in school	10 to 14 Mulatto not in school	15 to 20 Black in school	15 to 20 Black not in school	15 to 20 Mulatto in school	15 to 20 Mulatto not in school
BOTH SEXES.																
United States	1,230,843	1,465,328	388,856	337,130	369,352	411,993	119,602	89,903	607,401	305,247	184,594	58,024	254,090	748,088	84,660	189,203
The North	101,758	73,975	44,914	27,008	33,509	10,363	15,003	3,853	49,153	6,170	20,906	1,976	19,096	57,442	9,005	21,179
The South	1,125,347	1,388,786	341,593	308,770	334,665	401,270	103,879	85,849	556,481	298,902	162,621	55,976	234,201	688,614	75,093	166,945
The West	3,738	2,567	2,349	1,352	1,178	360	720	201	1,767	175	1,067	72	793	2,032	562	1,079
MALE.																
United States	580,473	747,618	179,340	163,548	179,656	210,332	57,506	44,972	292,167	167,266	87,319	31,322	108,650	370,020	34,515	87,254
The North	48,743	35,386	21,407	12,596	16,273	5,196	7,421	1,877	23,768	3,055	10,079	966	8,702	27,135	3,907	9,753
New England	3,008	1,551	1,791	977	1,053	153	683	123	1,469	99	819	47	486	1,299	289	807
Middle Atlantic	20,185	14,510	5,963	3,533	7,114	2,087	2,174	558	9,967	1,108	2,839	222	3,104	11,315	950	2,753
East North Central	13,441	9,467	7,975	4,486	4,351	1,263	2,714	597	6,566	736	3,778	297	2,524	7,468	1,483	3,592
West North Central	12,109	9,858	5,678	3,600	3,755	1,693	1,850	599	5,766	1,112	2,643	400	2,588	7,053	1,185	2,601
The South	529,952	710,930	156,826	150,308	162,800	204,957	49,738	42,997	267,543	164,124	76,728	30,319	99,609	341,849	30,360	76,992
South Atlantic	251,406	332,833	77,425	72,861	79,644	94,376	25,212	20,360	128,046	76,568	38,116	14,497	43,716	161,889	14,097	38,004
East South Central	164,142	212,630	46,144	41,060	49,445	60,406	14,304	11,360	81,494	49,831	22,163	8,254	33,203	102,393	9,677	21,446
West South Central	114,404	165,467	33,257	36,387	33,711	50,175	10,222	11,277	58,003	37,725	16,449	7,568	22,690	77,567	6,586	17,542
The West	1,778	1,302	1,107	644	583	179	347	98	856	87	512	37	339	1,036	248	509
Mountain	802	542	424	244	276	100	121	46	378	40	208	16	148	402	95	182
Pacific	976	760	683	400	307	79	226	52	478	47	304	21	191	634	153	327
South Atlantic	251,406	332,833	77,425	72,861	79,644	94,376	25,212	20,360	128,046	76,568	38,116	14,497	43,716	161,889	14,097	38,004
Delaware	2,568	1,909	441	189	685	399	143	44	1,350	293	209	19	533	1,217	89	126
Maryland	14,766	14,189	3,755	2,796	4,821	3,403	1,255	655	7,545	2,340	1,871	388	2,400	8,446	629	1,753
District of Columbia	4,092	2,888	2,269	1,429	1,342	489	699	229	1,959	240	1,000	125	791	2,159	510	1,075
Virginia	33,885	45,857	19,700	19,812	9,219	13,749	5,834	6,088	18,416	9,657	10,186	3,643	6,250	22,451	3,680	10,081
West Virginia	2,930	3,402	1,765	1,598	1,027	473	618	276	1,382	335	832	192	521	2,594	315	1,130
North Carolina	52,206	50,502	15,325	11,344	16,117	15,065	4,907	3,400	24,430	10,931	6,975	2,318	11,659	24,506	3,443	5,626
South Carolina	57,316	79,003	13,287	12,322	16,882	24,118	4,114	3,664	29,535	18,565	6,648	2,537	10,899	36,320	2,525	6,121
Georgia	66,698	110,353	17,177	19,279	23,712	29,849	6,273	4,935	35,070	28,539	8,586	4,415	7,916	51,965	2,318	9,929
Florida	16,945	24,730	3,706	4,092	5,839	6,831	1,369	1,069	8,359	5,668	1,749	860	2,747	12,231	588	2,163
East South Central	164,142	212,630	46,144	41,060	49,445	60,406	14,304	11,360	81,494	49,831	22,163	8,254	33,203	102,393	9,677	21,446
Kentucky	15,183	15,155	5,719	4,487	4,376	3,410	1,724	958	7,636	2,435	2,825	644	3,171	9,310	1,170	2,885
Tennessee	26,037	34,920	10,231	9,634	7,417	9,242	3,114	2,493	13,058	7,131	4,905	1,744	5,562	18,547	2,212	5,397
Alabama	49,016	84,082	12,368	14,059	13,693	26,132	3,555	4,413	25,339	21,891	6,183	3,217	9,984	36,059	2,630	6,429
Mississippi	73,906	78,473	17,826	12,880	23,959	21,622	5,911	3,496	35,461	18,374	8,250	2,649	14,486	38,477	3,665	6,735
West South Central	114,404	165,467	33,257	36,387	33,711	50,175	10,222	11,277	58,003	37,725	16,449	7,568	22,690	77,567	6,586	17,542
Arkansas	29,476	34,134	7,158	6,853	8,969	9,135	2,270	2,030	13,357	7,944	3,233	1,548	7,150	16,353	1,655	3,275
Louisiana	25,075	72,406	8,845	17,406	7,906	21,906	2,826	5,368	13,448	20,348	4,726	4,409	3,721	30,152	1,293	7,629
Oklahoma	10,283	6,708	4,893	2,302	3,191	1,905	1,572	673	4,630	925	2,164	296	2,462	3,878	1,157	1,333
Texas	49,570	52,219	12,361	9,826	13,645	16,527	3,544	3,206	26,568	8,508	6,326	1,315	9,357	27,184	2,481	5,305
FEMALE.																
United States	650,370	717,710	209,516	173,582	189,696	201,661	62,096	44,931	315,234	137,981	97,275	26,702	145,440	378,068	50,145	101,949
The North	53,015	38,589	23,507	14,412	17,236	5,167	7,582	1,976	25,385	3,115	10,827	1,010	10,394	30,307	5,098	11,426
New England	3,440	1,861	1,962	949	1,138	162	690	112	1,622	88	890	58	680	1,611	382	779
Middle Atlantic	22,119	17,994	6,513	4,377	7,613	2,202	2,206	559	10,839	1,291	3,115	267	3,667	14,501	1,192	3,551
East North Central	14,436	9,373	8,610	5,049	4,608	1,191	2,791	645	6,839	729	3,919	320	2,989	7,453	1,900	4,084
West North Central	13,020	9,361	6,422	4,037	3,877	1,612	1,895	660	6,085	1,007	2,903	365	3,058	6,742	1,624	3,012
The South	595,395	677,856	184,767	158,462	171,865	196,313	54,141	42,852	288,938	134,778	85,893	25,657	134,592	346,765	44,733	89,953
South Atlantic	286,681	315,745	91,462	75,606	84,666	90,527	26,943	20,294	139,914	61,377	42,934	11,787	62,101	163,841	21,585	43,525
East South Central	182,568	200,195	54,376	43,765	52,062	57,250	15,890	11,422	86,937	40,167	24,755	6,875	43,569	102,778	13,731	25,468
West South Central	126,146	161,916	38,929	39,091	35,137	48,536	11,308	11,136	62,087	33,234	18,204	6,995	28,922	80,146	9,417	20,960
The West	1,960	1,265	1,242	708	595	181	373	103	911	88	555	35	454	996	314	570
Mountain	846	568	459	285	268	85	151	46	383	44	197	20	195	439	111	219
Pacific	1,114	697	783	423	327	96	222	57	528	44	358	15	259	557	203	351
South Atlantic	286,681	315,745	91,462	75,606	84,666	90,527	26,943	20,294	139,914	61,377	42,934	11,787	62,101	163,841	21,585	43,525
Delaware	2,393	1,915	413	250	754	410	139	52	1,208	234	201	26	431	1,265	73	172
Maryland	15,705	14,534	4,191	3,294	5,142	3,313	1,360	689	7,977	2,097	1,997	380	2,586	9,124	834	2,225
District of Columbia	4,699	3,566	2,940	1,710	1,417	486	820	217	2,241	220	1,269	97	1,041	2,860	851	1,396
Virginia	38,040	42,255	22,721	20,143	10,118	13,168	6,207	6,049	19,330	7,994	11,057	3,112	8,592	21,093	5,457	10,982
West Virginia	3,130	2,356	1,981	1,319	1,119	501	678	288	1,416	282	855	130	595	1,573	448	901
North Carolina	58,072	47,534	17,436	11,606	16,885	14,642	5,151	3,451	26,082	9,133	7,653	1,893	15,105	23,758	4,632	6,262
South Carolina	65,610	75,769	15,513	12,609	17,919	23,123	4,353	3,611	32,213	15,429	7,317	2,097	15,478	37,217	3,843	6,901
Georgia	79,735	104,469	21,581	20,193	25,112	28,514	6,757	4,889	40,320	21,359	10,428	3,312	14,303	54,596	4,396	11,992
Florida	19,297	23,347	4,686	4,482	6,200	6,364	1,478	1,048	9,127	4,628	2,157	740	3,970	12,355	1,051	2,694
East South Central	182,568	200,195	54,376	43,765	52,062	57,250	15,890	11,422	86,937	40,167	24,755	6,875	43,569	102,778	13,731	25,468
Kentucky	16,617	13,481	6,541	4,793	4,521	3,185	1,824	1,057	7,827	2,043	3,028	546	4,269	8,253	1,689	3,190
Tennessee	28,652	31,475	12,233	10,215	7,735	8,542	3,495	2,545	13,608	5,841	5,563	1,494	7,309	17,092	3,175	6,176
Alabama	56,743	81,050	15,064	14,794	14,827	25,343	4,116	4,340	28,032	17,766	7,068	2,633	13,884	37,941	3,880	7,821
Mississippi	80,556	74,189	20,538	13,963	24,979	20,180	6,455	3,480	37,470	14,517	9,096	2,202	18,107	39,492	4,987	8,281
West South Central	126,146	161,916	38,929	39,091	35,137	48,536	11,308	11,136	62,087	33,234	18,204	6,995	28,922	80,146	9,417	20,960
Arkansas	32,203	33,672	8,630	7,305	9,246	9,781	2,478	2,093	14,586	6,951	3,733	1,327	8,371	16,940	2,419	3,885
Louisiana	28,931	72,397	10,627	18,893	8,418	21,239	3,209	5,180	14,873	18,575	5,248	4,290	5,640	32,583	2,170	9,423
Oklahoma	10,815	6,198	5,092	2,427	3,281	1,703	1,634	651	4,914	836	2,195	248	2,620	3,659	1,263	1,528
Texas	54,197	49,649	14,580	10,466	14,192	15,813	3,987	3,212	27,714	6,872	7,028	1,130	12,291	26,964	3,565	6,124

TABLE 33.—ILLITERACY IN THE BLACK AND MULATTO POPULATION 10 YEARS OF AGE AND OVER, CLASSIFIED BY SEX, AND FOR MALES 21 YEARS OF AGE AND OVER: 1910.

[Per cent not shown where base is less than 100.]

DIVISION AND STATE.	Black Male	Black Female	Mulatto Male	Mulatto Female	Illit. Black Male	Illit. Black Female	Illit. Mulatto Male	Illit. Mulatto Female	Pct Black Male	Pct Black Female	Pct Mulatto Male	Pct Mulatto Female	Black Total	Black Illit.	Mulatto Total	Mulatto Illit.
UNITED STATES	2,941,656	2,870,657	695,730	809,879	951,074	959,746	144,926	171,985	32.3	33.4	20.8	21.2	2,003,553	711,865	455,320	107,270
GEOGRAPHIC DIVISIONS:																
New England	18,609	19,126	8,780	8,806	1,186	1,392	921	842	6.4	7.3	10.5	9.6	15,256	1,140	6,818	827
Middle Atlantic	140,149	144,734	30,859	35,804	11,001	13,135	1,572	2,103	7.8	9.1	5.1	5.9	114,655	10,384	24,095	1,442
East North Central	93,050	79,098	40,564	41,833	11,036	10,749	2,861	3,425	11.9	13.6	7.1	8.2	75,756	10,594	31,414	2,691
West North Central	79,025	67,589	27,542	29,485	12,277	12,446	2,401	3,312	15.5	18.4	8.7	11.2	62,506	11,287	20,713	2,181
South Atlantic	1,189,572	1,184,051	280,725	332,588	412,962	416,925	64,145	75,400	34.7	35.2	22.8	22.7	779,353	304,332	176,011	46,888
East South Central	803,975	788,310	166,946	201,667	297,375	295,172	40,518	48,442	37.0	37.4	24.3	24.0	537,054	222,522	105,406	30,155
West South Central	599,728	574,770	133,217	152,990	204,090	208,714	32,149	38,069	34.0	36.3	24.1	24.9	403,743	150,522	85,072	22,762
Mountian	7,826	5,738	2,635	2,556	568	570	186	173	7.3	9.9	7.1	6.8	6,858	542	2,134	165
Pacific	9,722	7,241	4,462	4,150	579	643	173	219	6.0	8.9	3.9	5.3	8,372	542	3,657	159
NEW ENGLAND:																
Maine	349	307	261	249	33	19	23	18	9.5	6.2	8.8	7.2	282	33	194	22
New Hampshire	148	163	99	70	21	21	9		14.2	12.9			133	21	67	8
Vermont	874	223	215	134	20	19	21	9	2.3	8.5	9.8	6.7	820	20	155	18
Massachusetts	9,992	10,683	5,637	5,406	584	682	702	616	5.8	6.4	12.5	11.4	8,150	555	4,441	631
Rhode Island	2,628	2,730	1,211	1,344	263	262	107	120	10.0	9.6	8.8	8.9	2,141	251	926	94
Connecticut	4,618	5,020	1,357	1,603	265	389	59	79	5.7	7.7	4.3	4.9	3,730	260	1,035	54
MIDDLE ATLANTIC:																
New York	43,678	46,673	11,492	14,000	2,181	2,880	252	455	5.0	6.2	2.2	3.2	36,612	2,063	9,265	232
New Jersey	30,893	32,279	5,298	6,107	2,954	3,658	342	451	9.6	11.3	6.5	7.4	24,606	2,753	3,995	299
Pennsylvania	65,578	65,782	14,069	15,697	5,866	6,597	978	1,197	8.9	10.0	7.0	7.6	53,437	5,568	10,835	911
EAST NORTH CENTRAL:																
Ohio	33,528	28,301	15,769	16,312	4,102	3,729	1,268	1,361	12.2	13.2	8.0	8.3	27,239	3,970	11,949	1,199
Indiana	20,465	18,304	5,793	6,088	2,862	2,896	541	660	14.0	15.8	9.3	10.8	16,259	2,794	4,392	518
Illinois	33,853	28,165	15,178	15,732	3,767	3,833	885	1,228	11.1	13.6	5.8	7.8	27,875	3,535	12,108	814
Michigan	4,361	3,584	3,366	3,246	263	252	148	163	6.0	7.0	4.4	5.0	3,650	255	2,616	142
Wisconsin	843	744	458	455	42	39	19	13	5.0	5.2	4.1	2.9	733	40	249	18
WEST NORTH CENTRAL:																
Minnesota	2,487	1,561	1,348	970	79	63	47	26	3.2	4.0	3.5	2.7	2,233	76	1,157	47
Iowa	5,324	4,115	1,489	1,452	556	485	106	125	10.4	11.8	7.1	8.6	4,325	525	1,118	101
Missouri	50,761	44,834	17,352	19,438	9,366	9,440	1,795	2,461	18.5	21.1	10.3	12.7	39,860	8,479	13,061	1,589
North Dakota	265	150	83	48	14	9	2	1	5.3	6.0			244	14	67	2
South Dakota	259	181	145	112	15	10	9	4	5.8	5.5	6.2	3.6	216	15	125	9
Nebraska	2,852	2,137	899	837	197	195	36	54	6.9	9.1	4.0	6.5	2,507	195	718	36
Kansas	17,077	14,611	6,226	6,628	2,050	2,244	406	641	12.0	15.4	6.5	9.7	13,121	1,983	4,467	397
SOUTH ATLANTIC:																
Delaware	11,577	10,439	1,309	1,452	2,988	2,832	232	293	25.8	27.1	17.7	20.2	8,184	2,615	866	214
Maryland	74,526	73,089	14,809	18,030	18,518	18,518	2,334	2,919	24.8	25.3	15.8	16.2	53,795	15,568	10,168	1,916
District of Columbia	23,686	28,498	11,854	15,926	3,200	5,233	815	1,566	13.5	18.4	6.9	9.8	18,537	3,044	9,084	757
Virginia	169,180	165,969	74,777	86,492	57,937	54,597	17,225	19,191	34.2	32.9	23.0	22.2	112,406	44,823	47,187	13,044
West Virginia	21,547	13,563	8,511	7,304	4,919	2,808	1,486	1,134	22.8	20.7	17.5	15.5	16,715	4,248	6,042	1,209
North Carolina	191,851	199,929	44,789	53,826	64,185	66,989	11,489	13,640	33.5	33.5	25.7	25.3	120,325	48,229	26,427	8,440
South Carolina	240,020	251,536	42,285	50,223	95,993	105,845	11,001	13,403	40.0	42.1	26.0	26.7	144,701	65,481	24,454	7,376
Georgia	350,592	350,924	64,960	79,719	137,865	134,434	16,601	19,739	39.3	38.3	25.6	24.8	227,102	99,329	39,712	11,708
Florida	106,593	90,104	17,431	19,616	27,357	25,669	2,962	3,515	25.7	28.5	17.0	17.9	77,588	20,995	12,071	2,224
EAST SOUTH CENTRAL:																
Kentucky	82,197	75,941	23,573	28,317	25,100	22,252	4,806	5,742	30.5	29.3	20.4	20.3	59,645	21,841	16,049	4,117
Tennessee	138,538	133,852	39,160	49,113	41,396	39,267	7,981	9,892	29.9	29.3	20.4	20.1	94,240	32,183	24,902	6,090
Alabama	276,617	277,203	49,038	59,498	115,730	119,588	13,655	16,655	41.8	43.1	27.8	28.0	183,344	83,201	30,579	9,543
Mississippi	306,623	301,314	55,175	64,739	115,149	114,065	14,071	16,153	37.6	37.9	25.5	25.0	199,825	85,297	33,876	10,405
WEST SOUTH CENTRAL:																
Arkansas	138,286	129,988	27,594	31,141	37,006	37,854	5,227	6,311	26.8	29.1	18.9	20.3	93,482	28,206	17,883	3,807
Louisiana	209,058	206,136	50,879	59,377	104,682	110,208	17,943	21,315	50.1	53.5	35.3	35.9	141,389	72,349	32,822	11,827
Oklahoma	39,791	33,463	13,895	14,008	7,069	7,117	1,733	1,939	17.8	21.3	12.5	13.8	27,896	5,946	8,945	1,450
Texas	212,593	205,183	40,849	48,464	55,333	53,535	7,246	8,504	26.0	26.1	17.7	17.5	140,976	44,021	25,422	5,678
MOUNTAIN:																
Montana	668	432	295	238	54	28	21	11	8.1	6.5	7.1	4.6	607	54	244	21
Idaho	254	131	110	83	15	14	3	5	5.9	10.7	2.7		230	13	98	3
Wyoming	1,286	483	156	99	45	47	8	2	3.5	9.7	5.1		1,190	42	135	8
Colorado	3,658	3,243	1,496	1,593	292	351	104	109	8.0	10.8	7.0	6.8	3,107	285	1,176	88
New Mexico	595	417	171	161	74	63	27	27	12.4	15.1	15.8	16.8	518	66	126	22
Arizona	699	619	193	180	51	47	17	7	7.3	7.6	8.8	3.9	596	47	168	17
Utah	494	282	140	110	25	12	3	9	5.1	4.3	2.1	8.2	448	23	120	3
Nevada	172	131	74	92	12	8	3	3	7.0	6.1			162	12	67	3
PACIFIC:																
Washington	2,526	1,372	947	672	95	90	31	23	3.8	6.6	3.3	3.4	2,299	91	821	30
Oregon	623	355	215	166	18	12	7	9	2.9	3.4	3.3	5.4	585	17	181	7
California	6,573	5,514	3,300	3,312	466	541	135	187	7.1	9.8	4.1	5.6	5,488	434	2,655	122

PART IV.—VITAL STATISTICS.

Chapter XII.—MARITAL CONDITION.

MARITAL CONDITION CLASSES.

In the census tabulations relating to marital condition four classes of persons are distinguished—the single, the married, the widowed, and the divorced. Generally in the tables this distinction is confined to the population 15 years of age and over, since only an inconsiderable portion of the population under 15 are married, widowed, or divorced.

ACCURACY OF DATA.

It is recognized that the error attaching to the return of marital condition may be considerable. In some cases males who are or have been married, but are living apart from their families, may return themselves as single; females who have never been married, especially mothers with young children dependent upon them, may return themselves as either married, widowed, or divorced; married females deserted by their husbands may return themselves as widowed, the deserting husbands returning themselves as single; widowed males may return themselves as single; divorced males may return themselves as either single or widowed; and divorced females may return themselves as widowed. Where the return of marital condition is made by a third person, who does not know the facts, it is probably commonly presumed, and in some cases erroneously, that persons living apart from their families, especially males, are single. The result of these errors in combination would be, as regards the classification of males overstatement of the number single and understatement of the number married, widowed, or divorced, and as regards the classification of females overstatement of the number married and widowed, and understatement of the number single or divorced.

MARITAL CONDITION: 1910, 1900, AND 1890.

In Table 1 (p. 236) the classification by marital condition of the Negro population of all ages combined, and separately of the population under 15 years of age and 15 years and over, is given for 1910, 1900, and 1890, together with the excess of males or of females in each marital class. In 1910 cases of unknown marital condition in the population under 15 were classified as single.

In the total Negro population of all ages 59.6 per cent of the males and 53.9 per cent of the females were returned as single in 1910, and 40.1 per cent of the males and 45.9 per cent of the females as married, widowed, or divorced. The aggregate single embraced all persons who had not been married at any time previous to the census enumeration, and the aggregate married, widowed, or divorced all other individuals of known marital condition, all of whom must have been married at some time previous to the date of enumeration, and some of whom had been either widowed or divorced.

Practically all of the population under 15 years of age was single, the number married, widowed, or divorced among the 1,826,569 males under 15 years of age in 1910 being only 139, and among the 1,838,538 females only 756. If it be assumed that all of those under 15 that were returned as having been married were in the age 14 years, as undoubtedly practically all of them were, approximately 1 male per 1,000 males aged 14, and 6 females per 1,000 females aged 14, were or had been married.

In the Negro population 15 years of age and over 35.4 per cent of the males and 26.6 per cent of the females in 1910 were single, and 64 per cent of the males and 73.1 per cent of the females were married, widowed, or divorced.

The number of females exceeded the number of males in the Negro population 15 years of age and over at each of the three censuses, but the distribution of males differed materially from the distribution of females to the several marital condition classes, giving at each census a large excess of males in the class of single persons, and of females in the class of married, widowed, and divorced persons.

The number of married males is necessarily at all times approximately equal to the number of married females, and would be exactly equal, as returned by the census, if the husband and wife were in every case both living within the area of census enumeration, and were correctly returned on the schedule as married. The small excess of females among married Negroes 15 years of age and over as returned at the several censuses (26,721 in a married population of 3,525,177 in 1910, 20,931 in 2,866,683 in 1900, and 11,921 in 2,362,947 in 1890) is probably accounted for in part by married males returning themselves or being returned as single; and in part by single females returning themselves as married. In some instances, however, married males may have emigrated to outlying possessions or to foreign countries, leaving their wives in the states, and it is probable that more males than females are omitted in the enumeration of the population. Among married whites, on the other hand, there is an excess of males over females, which probably represents immigrant husbands whose wives are still in foreign countries.

MARITAL CONDITION OF THE NEGRO POPULATION: 1910, 1900, AND 1890.

Table 1

NEGRO POPULATION.

AGE PERIOD AND MARITAL CLASS.	Male. 1910	Male. 1900	Male. 1890[1]	Female. 1910	Female. 1900	Female. 1890[1]	Pct. Male 1910	Pct. Male 1900	Pct. Male 1890	Pct. Female 1910	Pct. Female 1900	Pct. Female 1890	Excess 1910 Of male.	Excess 1910 Of female.	Excess 1900 Of male.	Excess 1900 Of female.	Excess 1890 Of male.	Excess 1890 Of female.
All ages	4,885,881	4,386,547	3,725,561	4,941,882	4,447,447	3,744,479	100.0	100.0	100.0	100.0	100.0	100.0	......	56,001	......	60,900	......	18,918
Single	2,909,902	2,786,580	2,448,567	2,661,778	2,559,682	2,220,946	59.6	63.5	65.7	53.9	57.6	59.3	248,124	......	226,898	......	227,621	......
Married, widowed, or divorced	1,959,483	1,585,312	1,272,421	2,269,822	1,880,727	1,518,605	40.1	36.1	34.2	45.9	42.3	40.5	......	310,339	......	295,415	......	246,184
Married	1,749,359	1,423,039	1,175,525	1,776,643	1,444,533	1,187,706	35.8	32.4	31.6	36.0	32.5	31.7	......	27,284	......	21,494	......	12,181
Widowed	189,976	151,245	91,683	459,889	414,151	320,205	3.9	3.4	2.5	9.3	9.3	8.6	......	269,913	......	262,906	......	228,522
Divorced	20,148	11,028	5,213	33,290	22,043	10,694	0.4	0.3	0.1	0.7	0.5	0.3	......	13,142	......	11,015	......	5,481
Unknown	16,496	14,655	4,573	10,282	7,038	4,928	0.3	0.3	0.1	0.2	0.2	0.1	6,214	......	7,617	......	......	355
Under 15 years	1,826,569	1,753,539	1,605,840	1,838,538	1,756,864	1,568,929	100.0	100.0	100.0	100.0	100.0	100.0	......	11,969	......	3,325	36,911	......
Single	1,826,430	1,753,295	1,605,803	1,837,782	1,755,999	1,568,632	100.0	100.0	100.0	100.0	100.0	100.0	......	11,352	......	2,704	37,171	......
Married, widowed, or divorced	139	167	13	756	770	289	(2)	(2)	(2)	(2)	(2)	(2)	......	617	......	603	......	276
Married	131	153	12	694	716	272	(2)	(2)	(2)	(2)	(2)	(2)	......	563	......	563	......	260
Widowed	6	12	......	58	44	11	(2)	(2)	(2)	(2)	(2)	(2)	......	52	......	32	......	11
Divorced	2	2	1	4	10	6	(2)	(2)	(2)	(2)	(2)	(2)	......	2	......	8	......	5
Unknown	......	77	24	......	95	8	......	(2)	(2)	......	(2)	(2)	......	......	......	18	16	......
15 years and over	3,059,312	2,633,008	2,119,721	3,103,344	2,690,583	2,175,550	100.0	100.0	100.0	100.0	100.0	100.0	......	44,032	......	57,575	......	55,829
Single	1,083,472	1,033,285	842,764	823,996	803,683	652,314	35.4	39.2	39.8	26.6	29.9	30.0	259,476	......	229,602	......	190,450	......
Married, widowed, or divorced	1,959,344	1,585,145	1,272,408	2,269,066	1,879,957	1,518,316	64.0	60.2	60.0	73.1	69.9	69.8	......	309,722	......	294,812	......	245,908
Married	1,749,228	1,422,886	1,175,513	1,775,949	1,443,817	1,187,434	57.2	54.0	55.5	57.2	53.7	54.6	......	26,721	......	20,931	......	11,921
Widowed	189,970	151,233	91,683	459,831	414,107	320,194	6.2	5.7	4.3	14.8	15.4	14.7	......	269,861	......	262,874	......	228,511
Divorced	20,146	11,026	5,212	33,286	22,033	10,688	0.7	0.4	0.2	1.1	0.8	0.5	......	13,140	......	11,007	......	5,476
Unknown	16,496	14,578	4,549	10,282	6,943	4,920	0.5	0.6	0.2	0.3	0.3	0.2	6,214	......	7,635	......	......	371

[1] Exclusive of 10,042 males and 8,594 females specially enumerated in 1890 in Indian Territory and on Indian reservations, for whom statistics of marital conditions are not available.
[2] Less than one-tenth of 1 per cent.

In the widowed and divorced population there was at each census an excess of females (among the widowed an excess of 269,861 in 1910, of 262,874 in 1900, and of 228,511 in 1890; and among the divorced of 13,140 in 1910, of 11,007 in 1900, and of 5,476 in 1890). The sex distribution of these classes is explained by the fact that females as compared with males generally marry at younger ages. The marriage relationship is, therefore, naturally, since the husband is generally older, more often broken by death of the husband than by death of the wife, and consequently the number of widows in the population always exceeds the number of widowers. It is probably true also, that remarriages are more common among widowed males than among widowed females. Since the number married among females is approximately equal to the number married among males, the excess of females among widowed and divorced persons, to the extent that it exceeds the excess of females in the population 15 years of age and over, involves a corresponding deficiency of females—or excess of males— in the single population.

In the case both of males and of females the proportion single in the Negro population 15 years of age and over decreased in each of the two decades covered by Table 1, the decrease being very slight in the decade 1890–1900, but more marked in the decade 1900–1910. The proportion married increased during the decade 1900–1910 from 54 per cent to 57.2 per cent among males, and from 53.7 to 57.2 per cent among females. In the preceding decade the proportion married decreased among both males and females.

Table 2 gives the increase of each marital class in the population 15 years of age and over for each of the two decades 1890–1900 and 1900–1910.

Table 2

INCREASE IN NEGRO POPULATION.

AGE PERIOD AND MARITAL CLASS.	Number. 1900–1910[1] Male	Number. 1900–1910[1] Female	Number. 1890–1900[2] Male	Number. 1890–1900[2] Female	Per cent. 1900–1910[1] Male	Per cent. 1900–1910[1] Female	Per cent. 1890–1900[2] Male	Per cent. 1890–1900[2] Female
All ages	499,334	494,435	660,986	702,968	11.4	11.1	17.7	18.8
Under 15 years of age	73,030	81,674	147,699	187,935	4.2	4.6	9.2	12.0
Single	73,135	81,783	147,492	187,367	4.2	4.7	9.2	11.9
Married, widowed, or divorced	−28	−14	154	481	−16.8	−1.8	(2)	166.4
Unknown	−77	−95	53	87	(3)	(3)	(3)	(3)
15 years of age and over	426,304	412,761	513,287	515,033	16.2	15.3	24.2	23.7
Single	50,187	20,313	190,521	151,369	4.9	2.5	22.6	23.2
Married, widowed, or divorced	374,199	389,109	312,737	361,641	23.6	20.7	24.6	23.8
Married	326,342	332,132	247,373	256,383	22.9	23.0	21.0	21.6
Widowed	38,737	45,724	59,550	93,913	25.6	11.0	65.0	29.3
Divorced	9,120	11,253	5,814	11,345	82.7	51.1	111.6	106.1
Unknown	1,918	3,339	10,029	2,023	13.2	48.1	220.5	41.1

[1] A minus sign (−) denotes decrease.
[2] The increase for the decade 1890–1900 is figured on the population in 1890 exclusive of the population specially enumerated in 1890 in Indian Territory and upon Indian reservations. These areas, which returned a Negro population of 18,636 in 1890, are included in the 1900 area of census enumeration.
[3] Per cent not shown where base is less than 100.

The increase for the population 15 years of age and over amounted in the decade 1900–1910 to 16.2 per cent for males and to 15.3 per cent for females, these rates being considerably above the rates for males and for females returned as single, and considerably below the rates for other marital classes. The increase in the aggregate of married, widowed, or divorced males during the decade 1900–1910 was 23.6 per cent, and for single males 4.9 per cent, the corresponding increases for females being 20.7 and 2.5 per cent. No such marked difference in the percentages obtained in the decade 1890–1900, in which decade the number of single males increased 22.6 per cent, and the number of married, widowed, and divorced males 24.6 per cent, the corresponding percentages for females being 23.2 and 23.8 per cent.

The highest percentage increases in each decade for both males and females are for the class of divorced persons, the increase of 9,120 in the number of divorced males in the decade 1900–1910 amounting to 82.7 per cent, and the increase of 11,253 in the number of divorced females to 51.1 per cent. These increases, however, relate to numerically small groups, and constitute comparatively small proportions of the total increase.

COMPARISON WITH OTHER RACIAL CLASSES.

The marital condition of Negroes in comparison with that of other classes of population in 1910 is given in Table 3 for the total of all ages, and separately for the population under 15 years of age, and 15 years of age and over, together with the percentage distribution by marital condition for each racial class.

MARITAL CONDITION OF THE NEGRO AND OF OTHER CLASSES OF THE POPULATION: 1910.

Table 3

AGE PERIOD AND RACIAL CLASS.	Male. Total.	Single.	Married, widowed, or divorced. Total.	Married.	Widowed.	Divorced.	Marital condition unknown.	Female. Total.	Single.	Married, widowed, or divorced. Total.	Married.	Widowed.	Divorced.	Marital condition unknown.
							NUMBER.							
All ages...............	47,332,277	27,455,607	19,721,146	18,093,498	1,471,472	156,176	155,524	44,639,989	23,522,121	21,049,696	17,688,169	3,176,426	185,101	68,172
Negro...............	4,885,881	2,909,902	1,959,483	1,749,359	189,976	20,148	16,496	4,941,882	2,661,778	2,269,822	1,776,643	459,889	33,290	10,282
White...............	42,178,245	24,379,558	17,664,375	16,254,696	1,274,464	135,215	134,312	39,553,712	20,784,712	18,711,714	15,854,757	2,706,127	150,830	57,286
Other...............	268,151	166,147	97,288	89,443	7,032	813	4,716	144,395	75,631	68,160	56,769	10,410	981	604
Under 15 years of age....	14,906,472	14,905,478	994	898	82	14	....	14,592,664	14,588,951	3,713	3,482	198	33	....
Negro...............	1,826,569	1,826,430	139	131	6	2	....	1,838,538	1,837,782	756	694	58	4	....
White...............	13,020,120	13,019,276	844	756	76	12	....	12,696,375	12,693,463	2,912	2,746	137	29	....
Other...............	59,783	59,772	11	11	....	....	....	57,751	57,706	45	42	3	....	....
15 years of age and over..	32,425,805	12,550,129	19,720,152	18,092,600	1,471,390	156,162	155,524	30,047,325	8,933,170	21,045,983	17,684,687	3,176,228	185,068	68,172
Negro...............	3,059,312	1,083,472	1,959,344	1,749,228	189,970	20,146	16,496	3,103,344	823,996	2,269,066	1,775,949	459,831	33,286	10,282
White...............	29,158,125	11,360,282	17,663,531	16,253,940	1,274,388	135,203	134,312	26,857,337	8,091,249	18,708,802	15,852,011	2,705,990	150,801	57,286
Native.............	22,018,232	9,091,366	12,823,611	11,821,805	889,662	112,144	103,255	21,411,031	7,097,139	14,264,145	12,228,008	1,905,878	130,259	49,747
Native parentage.....	16,233,095	6,185,324	9,960,438	9,144,099	728,883	87,456	87,333	15,523,900	4,644,122	10,842,998	9,219,385	1,523,560	100,053	35,780
Mixed parentage.....	1,725,359	916,915	803,581	751,631	43,733	8,217	4,863	1,794,559	792,897	997,647	880,458	105,970	11,219	4,015
Foreign parentage.....	4,059,778	1,989,127	2,059,592	1,926,075	117,046	16,471	11,059	4,092,572	1,660,120	2,423,500	2,128,165	276,348	18,987	8,952
Foreign born..........	7,139,893	2,268,916	4,839,920	4,432,135	384,726	23,059	31,057	5,446,306	994,110	4,444,657	3,624,003	800,112	20,542	7,539
Indian................	80,383	27,391	52,152	46,154	5,319	679	840	76,982	16,324	60,125	49,095	10,071	959	533
Chinese...............	64,394	34,330	27,633	26,449	1,139	45	2,431	2,955	680	2,250	2,016	229	5	25
Japanese..............	60,536	42,688	16,499	15,918	495	86	1,349	6,648	908	5,694	5,581	96	17	46
Other.................	3,055	1,966	993	911	79	3	96	59	13	46	35	11	....	....
							PERCENTAGE DISTRIBUTION BY MARITAL CLASS.							
All ages...............	100.0	58.0	41.7	38.2	3.1	0.3	0.3	100.0	52.7	47.2	39.6	7.1	0.4	0.2
Negro...............	100.0	59.6	40.1	35.8	3.9	0.4	0.3	100.0	53.9	45.9	36.0	9.3	0.7	0.2
White...............	100.0	57.8	41.9	38.5	3.0	0.3	0.3	100.0	52.5	47.3	40.1	6.8	0.4	0.1
Other...............	100.0	62.0	36.3	33.4	2.6	0.3	1.8	100.0	52.4	47.2	39.3	7.2	0.7	0.4
Under 15 years of age....	100.0	100.0	(1)	(1)	(1)	(1)	....	100.0	100.0	(1)	(1)	(1)	(1)	....
Negro...............	100.0	100.0	(1)	(1)	(1)	(1)	....	100.0	100.0	(1)	(1)	(1)	(1)	....
White...............	100.0	100.0	(1)	(1)	(1)	(1)	....	100.0	100.0	(1)	(1)	(1)	(1)	....
Other...............	100.0	100.0	(1)	(1)	....	....	....	100.0	100.0	0.1	0.1	(1)	....	....
15 years of age and over..	100.0	38.7	60.8	55.8	4.5	0.5	0.5	100.0	29.7	70.0	58.9	10.6	0.6	0.2
Negro...............	100.0	35.4	64.0	57.2	6.2	0.7	0.5	100.0	26.6	73.1	57.2	14.8	1.1	0.3
White...............	100.0	39.0	60.6	55.7	4.4	0.5	0.5	100.0	30.1	69.7	59.0	10.1	0.6	0.2
Native.............	100.0	41.3	58.2	53.7	4.0	0.5	0.5	100.0	33.1	66.6	57.1	8.9	0.6	0.2
Native parentage.....	100.0	38.1	61.4	56.3	4.5	0.5	0.5	100.0	29.9	69.8	59.4	9.8	0.6	0.2
Mixed parentage......	100.0	53.1	46.6	43.6	2.5	0.5	0.3	100.0	44.2	55.6	49.1	5.9	0.6	0.2
Foreign parentage.....	100.0	49.0	50.7	47.4	2.9	0.4	0.3	100.0	40.6	59.2	52.0	6.8	0.5	0.2
Foreign born..........	100.0	31.8	67.8	62.1	5.4	0.3	0.4	100.0	18.3	81.6	66.5	14.7	0.4	0.1
Indian................	100.0	34.1	64.9	57.4	6.6	0.8	1.0	100.0	21.2	78.1	63.8	13.1	1.2	0.7
Chinese...............	100.0	53.3	42.9	41.1	1.8	0.1	3.8	100.0	23.0	76.1	68.2	7.7	0.2	0.8
Japanese..............	100.0	70.5	27.3	26.3	0.8	0.1	2.2	100.0	13.7	85.6	84.0	1.4	0.3	0.7
Other.................	100.0	64.4	32.5	29.8	2.6	0.1	3.1	100.0	(2)	(2)	(2)	(2)	....	....

1 Less than one-tenth of 1 per cent.   2 Per cent not shown where base is less than 100.

The proportion single among Negro males and females 15 years of age and over in 1910 was lower than it was for any class of the native whites. This lower proportion may be explained in part by the fact that on the average Negroes marry at a younger age than whites, which accounts, also, in part for the somewhat higher proportion widowed among Negroes as compared with whites. The low proportion single among foreign-born whites is accounted for by the comparatively small proportion of this class in the ages of 15 to 19 years, in which age group the proportion single is large for all classes.

The proportion married is lower among Negro than among white females, and higher among Negro than among white males. The proportion widowed and the proportion divorced is higher among Negroes than among whites for both males and females.

The percentage single, married, widowed, and divorced, in each of the three years, 1910, 1900, and 1890, is given in Table 4 for Negro and for white males and females.

Table 4	PERCENTAGE.							
	Single.		Married.		Widowed.		Divorced.	
AGE PERIOD AND YEAR.	Negro popu-lation.	White popu-lation.	Negro popu-lation.	White popu-lation.	Negro popu-lation.	White popu-lation.	Negro popu-lation.	White popu-lation.
MALE.								
All ages:								
1910.........	59.6	57.8	35.8	38.5	3.9	3.0	0.4	0.3
1900.........	63.5	60.1	32.4	36.4	3.5	3.0	0.3	0.2
1890.........	65.7	61.7	31.6	35.4	2.5	2.6	0.1	0.2
Under 15 years of age:								
1910.............	100.0	100.0	(1)	(1)	(1)	(1)	(1)	(1)
1900.............	100.0	100.0	(1)	(1)	(1)	(1)	(1)	(1)
1890.............	100.0	100.0	(1)	(1)	(1)	(1)	(1)	(1)
15 years of age and over:								
1910.............	35.4	39.0	57.2	55.7	6.2	4.4	0.7	0.5
1900.............	39.2	40.2	54.0	54.6	5.8	4.5	0.4	0.3
1890.............	39.8	41.7	55.5	53.9	4.3	3.9	0.2	0.3
FEMALE.								
All ages:								
1910.........	53.9	52.5	36.0	40.1	9.3	6.8	0.7	0.4
1900.........	57.5	54.8	32.5	37.8	9.3	7.0	0.5	0.3
1890.........	59.3	55.8	31.7	37.1	8.6	6.8	0.3	0.2
Under 15 years of age:								
1910.............	100.0	100.0	(1)	(1)	(1)	(1)	(1)	(1)
1900.............	100.0	100.0	(1)	(1)	(1)	(1)	(1)	(1)
1890.............	100.0	100.0	(1)	(1)	(1)	(1)	(1)	(1)
15 years of age and over:								
1910.............	26.6	30.1	57.2	59.0	14.8	10.1	1.1	0.6
1900.............	29.9	31.4	53.7	57.3	15.4	10.7	0.8	0.4
1890.............	30.0	32.0	54.6	57.0	14.7	10.5	0.5	0.4

[1] Less than one-tenth of 1 per cent.

Among whites as among Negroes of both sexes the proportion single decreased in each decade. The proportion married among Negro and white males and females 15 and over increased during the decade 1900–1910, although in the preceding decade this proportion among Negroes fell off slightly. The proportion widowed increased slightly in each decade among Negro males. Among Negro females 15 and over it increased somewhat in the decade 1890–1900, but

decreased in the decade 1900–1910, being practically the same in 1910 as in 1890. The proportion divorced among both males and females, Negro and white, increased during the period covered by the table.

Single, widowed, and divorced persons, making up in the aggregate the unmarried portion of the population, constituted in 1910, 63.9 per cent of Negro males, and 63.9 per cent of Negro females of all ages. For the population 15 years of age and over the corresponding percentages were 42.3 and 42.4. In the case both of males and of females these proportions had decreased in 1910 as compared with 1900. In the preceding decade the proportion single, widowed, or divorced increased in the adult Negro population. In each year it was slightly higher for females than for males in the Negro population, and higher for males than for females in each class of the white population.

SEX RATIO BY MARITAL CONDITION.

The sex ratio, or number of males per 1,000 females, is shown in Table 5 for the Negro and for the white population, classified by marital condition.

Table 5	MALES TO 1,000 FEMALES.					
AGE PERIOD AND MARITAL CLASS.	Negro population.			White population.		
	1910	1900	1890	1910	1900	1890
Total.................	989	986	995	1,066	1,049	1,053
Under 15 years of age...........	993	998	1,024	1,025	1,024	1,032
Single........................	994	998	1,024	1,026	1,024	1,032
Married, widowed, or divorced.	184	217	45	290	170	10
15 years of age and over.........	986	979	974	1,086	1,062	1,065
Single........................	1,315	1,286	1,292	1,404	1,360	1,387
Married, widowed, or divorced.	864	843	838	944	921	910
Married....................	985	986	990	1,025	1,011	1,007
Widowed....................	413	365	286	471	445	394
Divorced...................	605	500	488	897	793	717
Unknown....................	1,604	2,100	925	2,345	2,663	3,527

In the total Negro population 15 years of age and over the number of males to 1,000 females in 1910 was 986. This was approximately the proportion in the married population (985), the proportion being much higher in the population classified as single (1,315), and much lower among widowed persons (413), and among divorced persons (605).

The proportion of males among widowed and among divorced persons increased in each decade—the number of males per 1,000 females among widowed persons from 286 in 1890 to 413 in 1910, and among divorced persons from 488 in 1890 to 605 in 1910.

As compared with the corresponding ratio in the white population, the proportion of males was lower in the total population 15 years of age and over, and in each of the marital classes, among Negroes.

MARITAL CONDITION BY AGE PERIODS.

The marital condition of the Negro population 15 years of age and over classified by age periods is given in Table 6.

The figures represented in this table are partially illustrated by Diagram I (p. 240) showing for the Negro population in 1910, classified by sex and age periods, the percentages single, married, and widowed. Diagram II (p. 242), shows for this year in less detail of age the number single, and the number married, widowed, or divorced.

The percentage single decreases from age period to age period among both males and females (from 96.9 per cent among males and 81.2 per cent among females 15 to 19 years of age, to 4.1 and 3.7 per cent, respectively, among males and females 65 and over), the decrease being very rapid in the age periods 15 to 19, 20 to 24, and 25 to 29 years.

MARITAL CONDITION BY AGE PERIODS FOR THE NEGRO POPULATION: 1910.

Table 6	NEGRO POPULATION: 1910.													
	Male.							Female.						
AGE PERIOD.	Total.	Single.	Married, widowed, or divorced.				Marital condition unknown.	Total.	Single.	Married, widowed, or divorced.				Marital condition unknown.
			Total.	Married.	Widowed.	Divorced.				Total.	Married.	Widowed.	Divorced.	
	NUMBER.													
15 years of age and over....	3,059,312	1,083,472	1,959,344	1,749,228	189,970	20,146	16,496	3,103,344	823,996	2,269,066	1,775,949	459,831	33,286	10,282
15 to 19 years............	507,945	492,153	11,584	11,064	416	104	4,208	552,471	448,515	100,221	94,087	4,929	1,205	3,735
20 to 24 years............	482,157	287,994	191,079	182,110	7,160	1,809	3,084	548,638	191,396	355,425	323,773	25,776	5,876	1,817
25 to 29 years............	421,805	125,439	294,565	277,822	13,458	3,285	1,801	459,422	78,708	379,858	336,360	36,379	7,119	856
30 to 34 years............	332,163	63,757	267,253	249,327	14,803	3,123	1,153	335,926	36,974	298,490	256,187	36,974	5,329	462
35 to 44 years............	550,130	67,203	481,503	439,901	36,144	5,458	1,424	538,732	38,105	499,956	401,069	90,839	8,048	671
45 to 54 years............	379,315	25,869	352,753	308,831	40,384	3,538	693	332,664	15,537	316,653	220,800	92,175	3,678	474
55 to 64 years............	216,239	10,792	205,022	168,881	34,425	1,716	425	179,885	6,946	172,570	95,023	76,271	1,276	369
65 years and over........	152,482	6,285	145,560	102,670	41,891	999	637	141,642	5,243	135,825	42,404	92,856	565	574
Age unknown.............	17,076	3,980	10,025	8,622	1,289	114	3,071	13,964	2,572	10,068	6,246	3,632	190	1,324
	PERCENTAGE DISTRIBUTION BY MARITAL CLASS.													
15 years of age and over.....	100.0	35.4	64.0	57.2	6.2	0.7	0.5	100.0	26.6	73.1	57.2	14.8	1.1	0.3
15 to 19 years............	100.0	96.9	2.3	2.2	0.1	(1)	0.8	100.0	81.2	18.1	17.0	0.9	0.2	0.7
20 to 24 years............	100.0	59.7	39.6	37.8	1.5	0.4	0.6	100.0	34.9	64.8	59.0	4.7	1.1	0.3
25 to 29 years............	100.0	29.7	69.8	65.9	3.2	0.8	0.4	100.0	17.1	82.7	73.2	7.9	1.5	0.2
30 to 34 years............	100.0	19.2	80.5	75.1	4.5	0.9	0.3	100.0	11.0	88.9	76.3	11.0	1.6	0.1
35 to 44 years............	100.0	12.2	87.5	80.0	6.6	1.0	0.3	100.0	7.1	92.8	74.4	16.9	1.5	0.1
45 to 54 years............	100.0	6.8	93.0	81.4	10.6	0.9	0.2	100.0	4.7	95.2	66.4	27.7	1.1	0.1
55 to 64 years............	100.0	5.0	94.8	78.1	15.9	0.8	0.2	100.0	3.9	95.9	52.8	42.4	0.7	0.2
65 years and over........	100.0	4.1	95.5	67.3	27.5	0.7	0.4	100.0	3.7	95.9	29.9	65.6	0.4	0.4
Age unknown.............	100.0	23.3	58.7	50.5	7.5	0.7	18.0	100.0	18.4	72.1	44.7	26.0	1.4	9.5

1 Less than one-tenth of 1 per cent.

In these younger ages the percentage married necessarily increases very nearly in proportion as the percentage single decreases. In the more advanced ages, however, the increase in the percentage widowed covers a very considerable decrease in the proportion married. Among females the proportion married decreases rapidly after middle life (from a maximum of 76.3 per cent in the age period 30 to 34 years, to 29.9 per cent among females 65 and over), the decrease among males (from a maximum of 81.4 per cent in the age period 45 to 54 years, to 67.3 per cent among males 65 and over), beginning later in life and being much less considerable. At all ages the proportion widowed is higher for females than for males, and in advanced ages very much higher. Among females this proportion increases from 0.9 per cent in the population 15 to 19 years of age, to 65.6 per cent in the population 65 years of age and over, the corresponding increase among males being from 0.1 to 27.5 per cent. It thus appears that in 1910 nearly two-thirds of the females and over one-fourth of the males 65 years of age and over were widowed. The rela-

tively large proportion widowed among Negro females arises naturally in consequence of the fact that wives are generally younger than their husbands. It is probably true, also, that the rate of mortality is lower among females than among males in the advanced ages and that, as has been noted, a larger proportion of widowed males than of widowed females remarry.

Table 7 is a comparative table covering the last three censuses and showing for Negro males and females, classified by age, the percentage in each marital class and in the aggregate of the three classes embracing married, widowed, and divorced persons.

During the decade 1900-1910 the percentage single declined among both males and females in each of the age groups shown in Table 7, and the percentage married increased in each group except in the case of males 45 to 64 years of age and 65 years of age and over. In the preceding decade the percentage single declined slightly among Negro males and females 15 to 19 years of age, and among males declined also for the age group 20 to 24 years, females showing a slight increase for the age 20 to 24 years. Among both males and females, however, in this decade the percentage single increased for each of the periods embracing the ages 25 to 64 years.

DIAGRAM I.—PERCENTAGE SINGLE, MARRIED, AND WIDOWED, FOR NEGRO MALES AND FEMALES, BY AGE PERIODS: 1910.

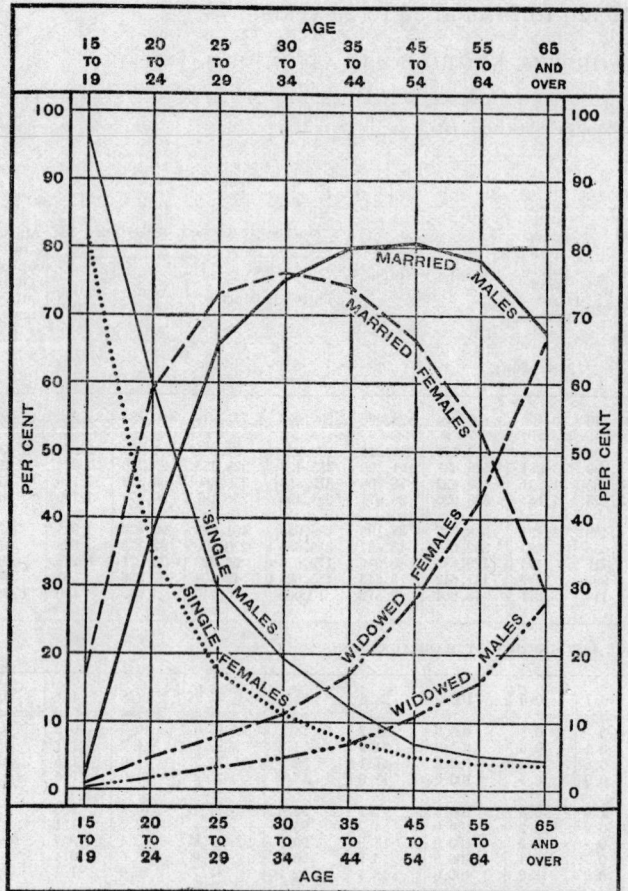

The percentage widowed has generally increased among males in the several age groups. Among females this proportion has not changed materially, the percentage among Negro females 65 years of age and over being 66.1 in 1890 and 65.6 in 1910; among females aged 45 to 64 years, 33.4 in 1890 and 32.9 in 1910; among those aged 35 to 44 years 17 in 1890 and 16.9 in 1910; and among those aged 25 to 34 years 9.1 in 1890 and 9.2 in 1910.

The percentage divorced has tended to increase for each age group among both males and females. It is slightly higher in the ages of middle life than it is in the younger or in the more advanced ages.

The percentage representing the proportion in the aggregate of the three classes embracing all persons who were at the time of the census, or had been at some time previous married, naturally increases from age to age, the increase for Negro males being in 1910 from 2.3 per cent in the population 15 to 19, to 95.5 per cent in the population 65 years of age and over, and for Negro females from 18.1 to 95.9 per cent in these age groups, respectively.

Table 7	NEGRO POPULATION 15 YEARS OF AGE AND OVER.						
SEX AND YEAR.	Total.	15 to 19 years.	20 to 24 years.	25 to 34 years.	35 to 44 years.	45 to 64 years.	65 years and over.
PERCENTAGE SINGLE.							
Male:							
1910	35.4	96.9	59.7	25.1	12.2	6.2	4.1
1900	39.2	97.9	64.3	27.9	13.2	6.5	4.6
1890	39.8	99.0	65.7	25.1	11.3	6.2	5.4
Female:							
1910	26.6	81.2	34.9	14.5	7.1	4.4	3.7
1900	29.9	83.2	39.8	17.4	8.0	4.7	4.3
1890	30.0	84.9	38.0	15.0	7.3	4.5	4.3
PERCENTAGE MARRIED.							
Male:							
1910	57.2	2.2	37.8	69.9	80.0	80.2	67.3
1900	54.0	1.7	33.8	67.7	79.1	80.4	69.6
1890	55.5	0.9	33.4	71.8	82.9	84.4	74.4
Female:							
1910	57.2	17.0	59.0	74.5	74.4	61.6	29.9
1900	53.7	15.6	54.6	71.0	72.3	60.7	28.9
1890	54.6	14.4	57.3	74.8	74.6	61.3	29.0
PERCENTAGE WIDOWED.							
Male:							
1910	6.2	0.1	1.5	3.7	6.6	12.6	27.5
1900	5.8	0.1	1.1	3.4	6.7	12.2	25.0
1890	4.3	(1)	0.7	2.6	5.2	9.2	19.6
Female:							
1910	14.8	0.9	4.7	9.2	16.9	32.9	65.6
1900	15.4	0.9	4.7	10.1	18.3	33.7	66.0
1890	14.7	0.5	4.0	9.1	17.0	33.4	66.1
PERCENTAGE DIVORCED.							
Male:							
1910	0.7	(1)	0.4	0.8	1.0	0.9	0.7
1900	0.4	(1)	0.2	0.5	0.7	0.7	0.4
1890	0.2	(1)	0.1	0.3	0.4	0.4	0.3
Female:							
1910	1.1	0.2	1.1	1.6	1.5	1.0	0.4
1900	0.8	0.1	0.8	1.3	1.2	0.7	0.3
1890	0.5	0.1	0.4	0.8	0.8	0.5	0.2
PERCENTAGE MARRIED, WIDOWED, OR DIVORCED.							
Male:							
1910	64.0	2.3	39.6	74.5	87.5	93.7	95.5
1900	60.2	1.8	35.1	71.6	86.5	93.3	95.0
1890	60.0	0.9	34.2	74.7	88.5	93.9	94.3
Female:							
1910	73.1	18.1	64.8	85.3	92.8	95.4	95.9
1900	69.9	16.6	60.0	82.4	91.9	95.1	95.2
1890	69.8	15.0	61.7	84.8	92.4	95.2	95.3

[1] Less than one-tenth of 1 per cent.

The percentages of Table 7 are illustrated by Diagram III on page 242, showing the percentage married, widowed, or divorced by sex and age periods for the Negro population in 1910, 1900, and 1890. In the diagram it is apparent that while the percentages for females exceed those for males in the younger ages, the percentages for the two sexes tend to become equal in the more advanced ages. In the population 65 and over, for example, in 1910 the percentage married among males (67.3) slightly exceeded the percentage widowed among females (65.6), and the percentage widowed among males (27.5) was slightly exceeded by the percentage married among females (29.9), the sums of the percentages for these two marital classes (94.8 for males, and 95.5 for females) being approximately equal, although the percentage married was very much higher and the percentage widowed very much lower among males than among females. The number of divorced persons in this age period was too small to materially affect the percentages for the several marital classes combined.

Comparison of Negroes with whites, as regards distribution by marital classes in 1910, is shown in Table 8, with detail by age.

Table 8 — POPULATION 15 YEARS OF AGE AND OVER.

AGE PERIOD.	Male.				Female.			
	Negro.	White			Negro.	White		
		Total.	Native.	Foreign born.		Total.	Native.	Foreign born.
PERCENTAGE SINGLE.								
Total	35.4	39.0	41.3	31.8	26.6	30.1	33.1	18.3
15 to 19 years	96.9	98.4	98.4	98.6	81.2	88.8	89.1	86.3
20 to 24 years	59.7	76.7	75.8	80.3	34.9	50.3	51.3	44.9
25 to 29 years	29.7	44.1	42.3	49.1	17.1	26.0	26.9	22.3
30 to 34 years	19.2	26.5	25.8	28.5	11.0	16.8	17.7	13.2
35 to 44 years	12.2	17.0	16.9	17.3	7.1	11.9	12.9	8.6
45 to 54 years	6.8	11.4	11.3	11.6	4.7	8.9	9.9	6.1
55 to 64 years	5.0	8.5	8.2	9.1	3.9	7.3	8.2	5.2
65 years and over	4.1	6.3	6.0	7.1	3.7	6.5	7.5	4.5
PERCENTAGE MARRIED.								
Total	57.2	55.7	53.7	62.1	57.2	59.0	57.1	66.5
15 to 19 years	2.2	1.0	1.0	0.8	17.0	10.5	10.3	13.1
20 to 24 years	37.8	22.4	23.3	19.0	59.0	48.4	47.3	54.3
25 to 29 years	65.9	54.5	56.1	49.9	73.2	71.5	70.5	75.9
30 to 34 years	75.1	71.2	71.7	69.9	76.3	79.3	78.2	83.5
35 to 44 years	80.0	79.3	79.1	79.7	74.4	80.7	79.7	84.1
45 to 54 years	81.4	81.7	81.5	82.1	66.4	75.6	75.0	77.4
55 to 64 years	78.1	79.2	79.6	78.2	52.8	62.9	63.6	61.1
65 years and over	67.3	65.5	67.1	62.5	29.9	35.4	35.7	34.7
PERCENTAGE WIDOWED.								
Total	6.2	4.4	4.0	5.4	14.8	10.1	8.9	14.7
15 to 19 years	0.1	(1)	(1)	(1)	0.9	0.1	0.1	0.1
20 to 24 years	1.5	0.3	0.3	0.2	4.7	0.7	0.8	0.5
25 to 29 years	3.2	0.8	0.9	0.5	7.9	1.7	1.8	1.4
30 to 34 years	4.5	1.5	1.7	1.1	11.0	3.1	3.2	2.8
35 to 44 years	6.6	2.9	3.1	2.4	16.9	6.5	6.4	6.8
45 to 54 years	10.6	6.0	6.2	5.6	27.7	14.6	14.2	15.9
55 to 64 years	15.9	11.3	11.1	11.9	42.4	29.0	27.4	33.1
65 years and over	27.5	27.1	25.9	29.6	65.6	57.5	56.2	60.4
PERCENTAGE DIVORCED.								
Total	0.7	0.5	0.5	0.3	1.1	0.6	0.6	0.4
15 to 19 years	(1)	(1)	(1)	(1)	0.2	0.1	0.1	(1)
20 to 24 years	0.4	0.1	0.1	(1)	1.1	0.4	0.4	0.1
25 to 29 years	0.8	0.3	0.4	0.1	1.5	0.6	0.7	0.3
30 to 34 years	0.9	0.5	0.6	0.2	1.6	0.8	0.8	0.4
35 to 44 years	1.0	0.7	0.8	0.4	1.5	0.8	0.9	0.5
45 to 54 years	0.9	0.8	0.9	0.5	1.1	0.8	0.9	0.5
55 to 64 years	0.8	0.8	0.9	0.6	0.7	0.6	0.7	0.5
65 years and over	0.7	0.7	0.7	0.5	0.4	0.3	0.4	0.3
PERCENTAGE MARRIED, WIDOWED, OR DIVORCED.								
Total	64.0	60.6	58.2	67.8	73.1	69.7	66.6	81.6
15 to 19 years	2.3	1.0	1.0	0.8	18.1	10.7	10.5	13.2
20 to 24 years	39.6	22.8	23.8	19.2	64.8	49.5	48.5	54.9
25 to 29 years	69.8	55.6	57.4	50.5	82.7	73.8	72.9	77.6
30 to 34 years	80.5	73.2	74.0	71.2	88.9	83.2	82.2	86.7
35 to 44 years	87.5	82.8	83.0	82.5	92.8	88.0	87.0	91.4
45 to 54 years	93.0	88.5	88.6	88.2	95.2	91.0	90.1	93.8
55 to 64 years	94.8	91.4	91.6	90.7	95.9	92.6	91.7	94.7
65 years and over	95.5	93.3	93.7	92.6	95.9	93.2	92.2	95.3

1 Less than one-tenth of 1 per cent.

21857°—18——16

In 1910 the percentage single for each age group shown in Table 8 was lower for Negroes than for native or for foreign-born whites, among both males and females, although in the total population 15 years of age and over, all ages combined, the proportion single was lower for foreign-born whites than for Negroes. The difference was most marked in the age group 20 to 24 years, in which the proportion single among males was 59.7 per cent for Negroes, 75.8 per cent for native whites, and 80.3 per cent for foreign-born whites; and among females 34.9 per cent for Negroes, 51.3 per cent for native whites, and 44.9 per cent among foreign-born whites.

For males the age of maximum percentage married in each class of whites, as among Negroes, was the age 45 to 54 years, and for females 35 to 44 years in each class of whites, and 30 to 34 years among Negroes.

The proportion married increases in the younger ages more rapidly among the Negroes than among whites in both sexes.

In the several classes the proportion widowed, which is at all ages lower for males than for females, becomes considerable in the population 45 years of age and over. Among Negro males 45 to 54 years of age in 1910 the percentage widowed was 10.6; among native white males 6.2, and among foreign-born white males 5.6. The corresponding percentages for the age group 55 to 64 years were 15.9 for Negroes, 11.1 for native whites, and 11.9 for foreign-born whites. In the population 65 years of age and over the proportion widowed was practically the same among Negro as among white males (27.5 per cent for Negroes and 27.1 for whites), the percentage for Negroes being somewhat above that for native whites (25.9), and somewhat below that for foreign-born whites (29.6).

Among females in 1910 the percentage widowed for Negroes exceeded the corresponding percentage for native whites at all ages. For the age group 30 to 34 years, the percentage widowed among females was 11 for Negroes and 3.2 for native whites; for the age 35 to 44 years the corresponding percentages were 16.9 and 6.4; for the age 45 to 54 years, 27.7 and 14.2; for the age 55 to 64 years, 42.4 and 27.4; and for the age 65 years and over, 65.6 and 56.2.

As regards the percentage divorced in the several classes, it is generally so small and probable inaccuracies in the returns for all classes are so considerable that little significance attaches to differences which may be noted in the table.

In Table 9 the distribution of the Negro population by marital condition is shown in comparison with that of native whites of native parentage in 1910, and in Diagrams IV and V (p. 242) and VI (p. 243) these distributions are illustrated.

DIAGRAM **II.**—NUMBER SINGLE AND NUMBER MARRIED, WIDOWED, OR DIVORCED, FOR NEGRO MALES AND
FEMALES, BY AGE PERIODS: 1910.

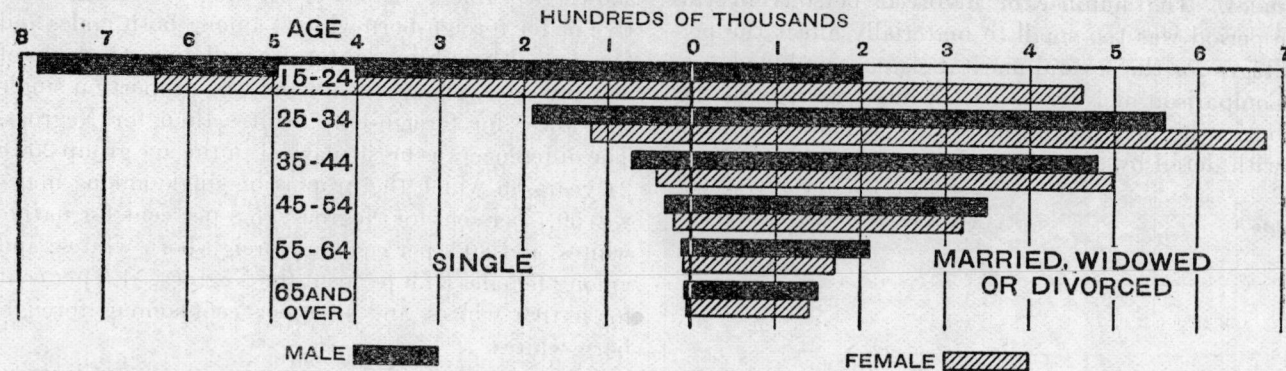

DIAGRAM **III.**—PERCENTAGE MARRIED, WIDOWED, OR DIVORCED,
FOR NEGRO MALES AND FEMALES, BY AGE PERIODS: 1910, 1900,
AND 1890.

DIAGRAM **IV.**—PERCENTAGE WIDOWED, FOR NEGROES AND FOR
NATIVE WHITES OF NATIVE PARENTAGE, BY SEX AND AGE
PERIODS: 1910.

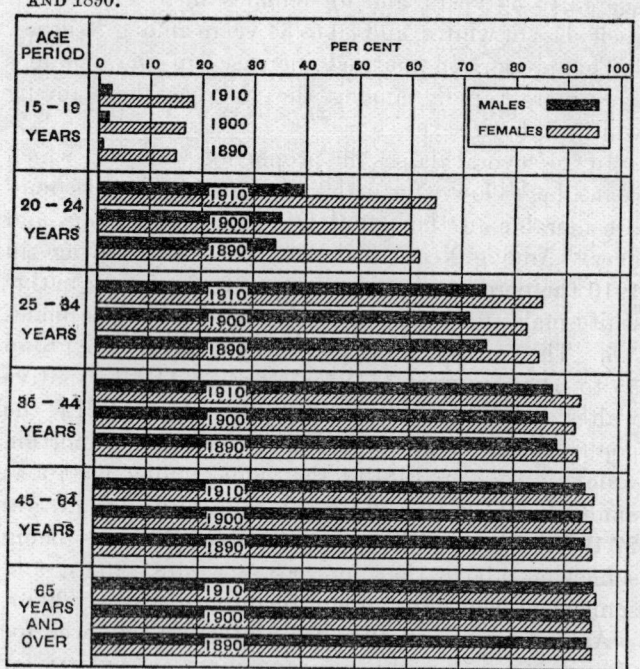

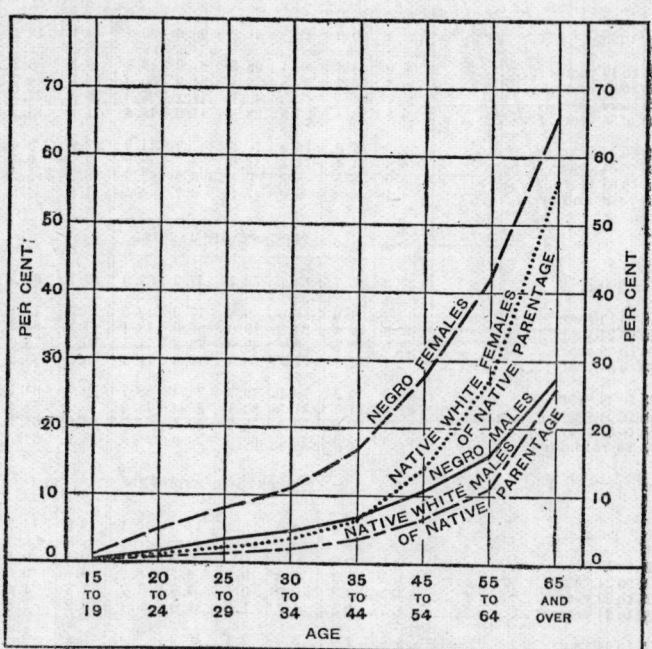

DIAGRAM **V.**—PERCENTAGE SINGLE, AND PERCENTAGE MARRIED, WIDOWED, OR DIVORCED, FOR NEGROES
AND FOR NATIVE WHITES OF NATIVE PARENTAGE, BY SEX AND AGE PERIODS: 1910.

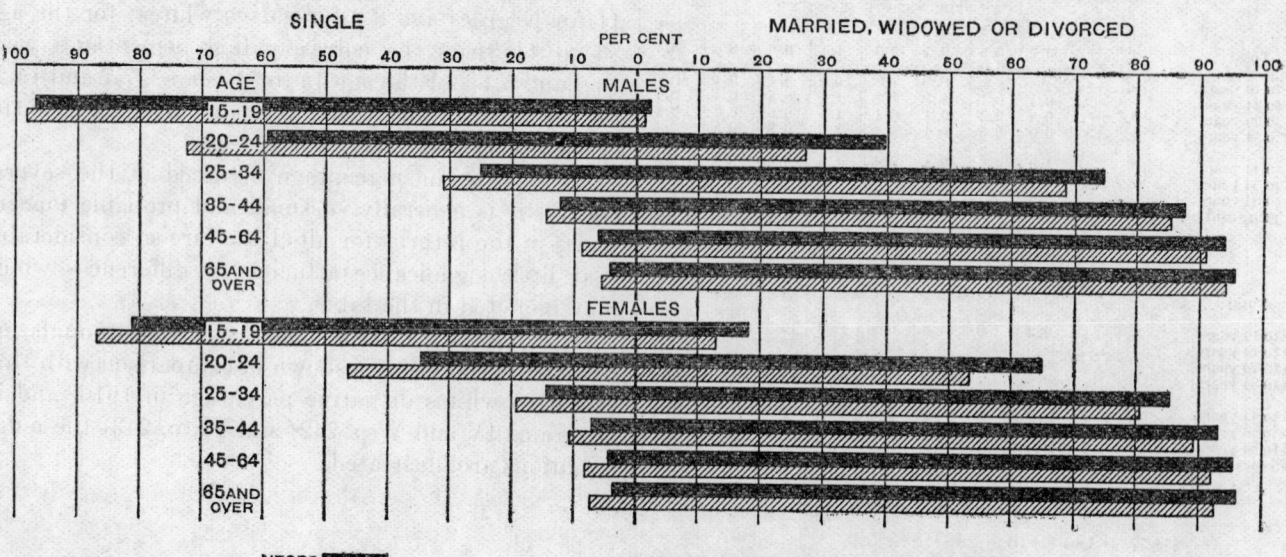

DIAGRAM **VI.**—PERCENTAGE MARRIED, FOR NEGROES AND FOR NATIVE WHITES OF NATIVE PARENTAGE, BY SEX AND AGE PERIODS: 1910.

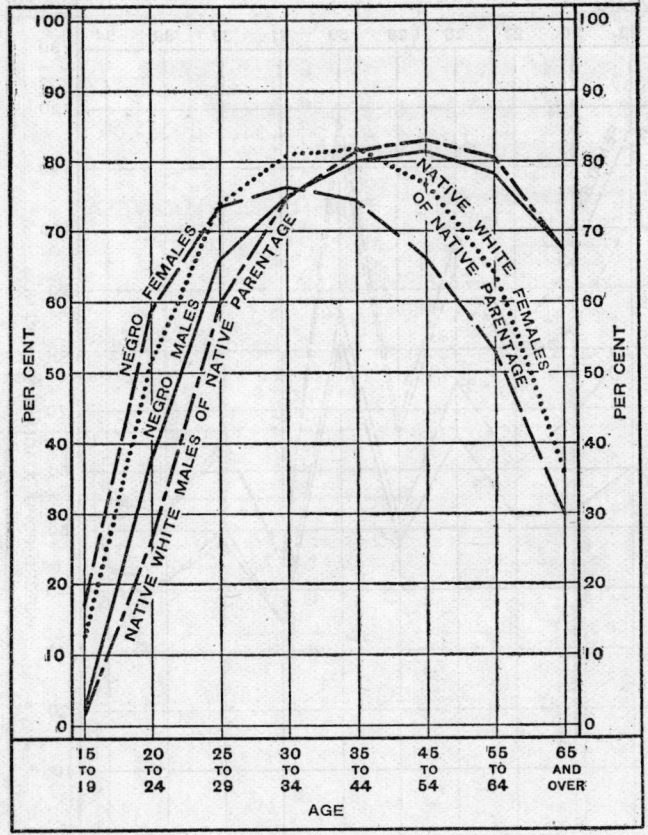

The percentage married is somewhat higher among Negro males than among native white males of native parentage in the ages under 35 years, and somewhat lower in the ages 35 to 64 years, there being no difference between the classes in the percentage for the population 65 years of age and over. Among females the percentage married is higher among Negroes than among native whites of native parentage in the ages under 25 years, and is higher among native whites of native parentage for all older ages. The percentage widowed among native whites of native parentage, which is at all ages below that for Negroes, does not vary materially from the percentage shown in Table 8 for the aggregate native white population. At each age, among males and females, the percentage single is lower, and the percentage married, widowed, and divorced higher among Negroes than it is among native whites of native parentage. These differences in marital conditions between Negroes and native whites of native parentage are apparent in the diagrams.

MARITAL CONDITION BY SINGLE YEARS OF AGE FOR THE AGES 15 TO 34 YEARS.

Marital condition in 1910 of the Negro population, classified by single years of age for the ages 15 to 34 years, is shown in Table 10. In Diagram VII (p. 244) the number of married males and females in each single year of age shown in Table 10, is compared with the total male and female population in that age.

By reference to Diagram VII, it will be seen that the curves for married males and females move generally with the curves for total males and females. The irregularities in the reports of age have been considered in the chapter on age composition, and need not be further commented upon in this connection. These irregularities do not very materially affect the proportion in the several marital condition classes, although the numbers in these classes, as in the total population, fluctuate irregularly. It will be noted, for example, that the very marked concentration of males and females in the age 30 is registered by an almost equally marked concentration of married males and females in this age. The number of married males aged 29 years was 47,770, the number aged 30 years 81,822, and the number aged 31 years, 34,137. For these ages the percentage married was 72.7 for the age 29 years, 71.3 for the age 30 years, and 74.9 for the age 31 years. Among females the fluctuation in numbers is equally marked, the percentage married showing in the case of females as in the case of males, a slight depression for the age 30 years, which probably does not in fact characterize this year of age.

The percentage single decreases from year to year for each of the single years of age shown in Table 10, in the case both of males and of females, except that the percentage single for the age 30 is slightly higher

Table 9

PRECENTAGE OF POPULATION 15 YEARS OF AGE AND OVER: 1910.

AGE PERIOD.	Single.		Married.		Widowed.		Divorced.	
	Negro.	Native white of native parentage.	Negro.	Native white of native parentage.	Negro.	Native white of native parentage.	Negro.	Native white of native parentage.
MALE.								
Total..........	35.4	38.1	57.2	56.3	6.2	4.5	0.7	0.5
15 to 19 years........	96.9	98.1	2.2	1.3	0.1	(1)	(1)	(1)
20 to 24 years........	59.7	72.5	37.8	26.5	1.5	0.4	0.4	0.2
25 to 29 years........	29.7	38.5	65.9	59.8	3.2	1.1	0.8	0.4
30 to 34 years........	19.2	22.7	75.1	74.7	4.5	1.8	0.9	0.6
35 to 44 years........	12.2	14.5	80.0	81.3	6.6	3.2	1.0	0.8
45 to 54 years........	6.8	9.8	81.4	82.8	10.6	6.2	0.9	0.9
55 to 64 years........	5.0	7.5	78.1	80.4	15.9	11.1	0.8	0.9
65 years and over	4.1	5.6	67.3	67.3	27.5	26.0	0.7	0.7
FEMALE.								
Total..........	26.6	29.9	57.2	59.4	14.8	9.8	1.1	0.6
15 to 19 years........	81.2	86.7	17.0	12.5	0.9	0.2	0.2	0.1
20 to 24 years........	34.9	46.6	59.0	51.8	4.7	0.9	1.1	0.5
25 to 29 years........	17.1	23.3	73.2	73.9	7.9	1.9	1.5	0.8
30 to 34 years........	11.0	14.9	76.3	80.9	11.0	3.2	1.6	0.9
35 to 44 years........	7.1	10.8	74.4	81.9	16.9	6.3	1.5	1.0
45 to 54 years........	4.7	8.5	66.4	76.7	27.7	13.8	1.1	0.9
55 to 64 years........	3.9	7.7	52.8	64.5	42.4	27.0	0.7	0.7
65 years and over....	3.7	7.4	29.9	35.8	65.6	56.2	0.4	0.4

1 Less than one-tenth of 1 per cent.

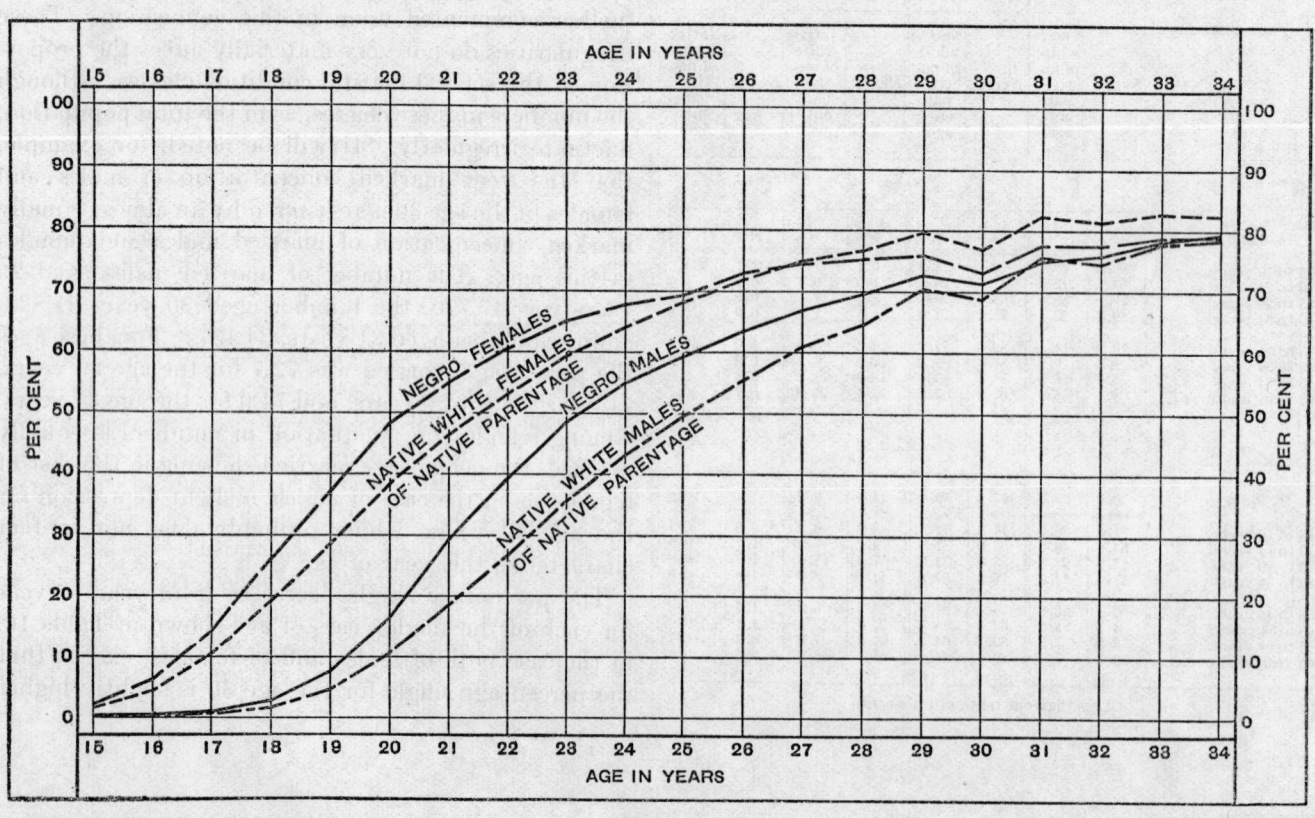

DIAGRAM **VII.**—TOTAL AND MARRIED MALES AND FEMALES IN THE NEGRO POPULATION, BY SINGLE
YEARS OF AGE, FOR THE AGES 15 TO 34: 1910.

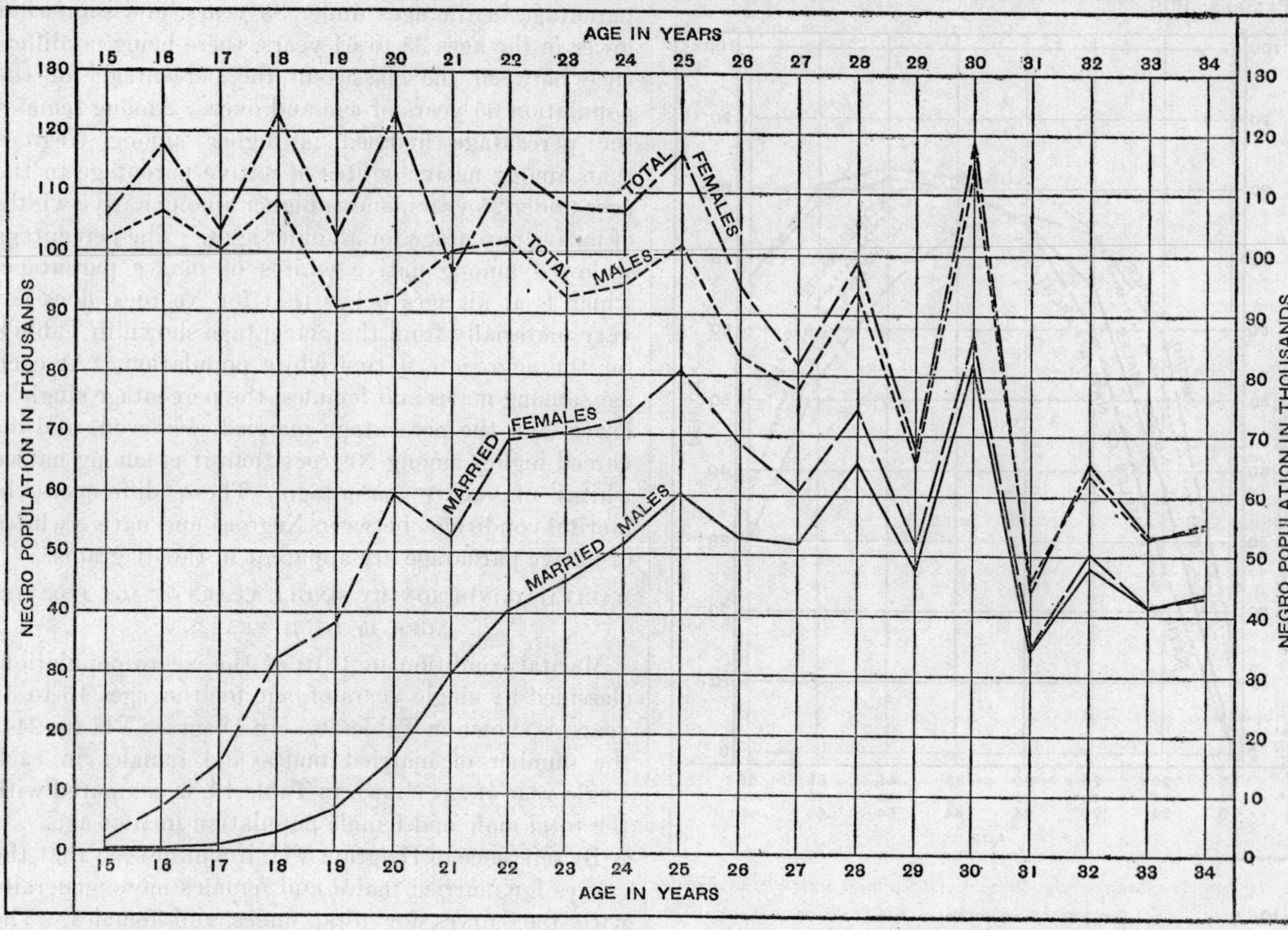

DIAGRAM **VIII.**—PERCENTAGE MARRIED, BY SINGLE YEARS OF AGE FOR THE AGES 15 TO 34, FOR NEGRO
MALES AND FEMALES AND FOR NATIVE WHITE MALES AND FEMALES OF NATIVE PARENTAGE: 1910.

than for the age 29 years. The percentage married increases from year to year with the single exception already noted that the percentage for the age 30 is lower than for the age 29 years. The percentage widowed or divorced tends to increase, although the changes by single years are inconsiderable.

MARITAL CONDITION BY SINGLE YEARS OF AGE FOR THE NEGRO POPULATION 15 TO 34 YEARS OF AGE: 1910.

Table 10

NEGRO POPULATION: 1910.

AGE.	Number.										Percentage.					
	Total.		Single.		Married.		Widowed or divorced.		Marital condition unknown.		Single.		Married.		Widowed or divorced.	
	Male.	Female.	Male.	Female.	Male.	Female.	Male.	Female.	Male.	Female.	Male.	Female.	Male.	Female.	Male.	Female.
15 to 34 years	3,042,236	3,089,380	1,079,492	821,424	1,740,606	1,769,703	208,713	489,295	13,425	8,958	35.5	26.6	57.2	57.3	6.9	15.8
15 years	101,921	105,634	101,133	102,791	119	1,998	11	165	658	680	99.2	97.3	0.1	1.9	(1)	0.2
16 years	106,679	117,724	105,427	109,016	219	7,256	29	447	1,004	1,005	98.8	92.6	0.2	6.2	(1)	0.4
17 years	100,185	103,662	98,436	87,399	806	14,582	57	913	886	768	98.3	84.3	0.8	14.1	0.1	0.9
18 years	108,316	122,991	104,136	88,072	3,068	32,137	151	1,980	961	802	96.1	71.6	2.8	26.1	0.1	1.6
19 years	90,844	102,460	83,021	61,237	6,852	38,114	272	2,629	699	480	91.4	59.8	7.5	37.2	0.3	2.6
20 years	92,494	123,131	75,738	58,234	15,265	59,512	739	4,777	752	608	81.9	47.3	16.5	48.3	0.8	3.9
21 years	100,178	96,422	68,576	38,769	29,684	52,721	1,213	4,606	705	326	68.5	40.2	29.6	54.7	1.2	4.8
22 years	101,974	114,295	59,215	38,161	40,155	69,004	1,958	6,755	646	375	58.1	33.4	39.4	60.4	1.9	5.9
23 years	92,960	107,745	44,994	30,070	45,186	70,048	2,289	7,374	491	253	48.4	27.9	48.6	65.0	2.5	6.8
24 years	94,551	107,045	39,471	26,162	51,820	72,488	2,770	8,140	490	255	41.7	24.4	54.8	67.7	2.9	7.6
25 years	101,523	116,570	37,236	25,290	60,052	80,814	3,718	10,190	517	276	36.7	21.7	59.2	69.3	3.7	8.7
26 years	83,100	94,505	26,809	17,253	52,793	68,966	3,113	8,120	385	166	32.3	18.3	63.5	73.0	3.7	8.6
27 years	77,595	81,828	22,170	13,107	51,961	60,923	3,142	7,653	322	145	28.6	16.0	67.0	74.5	4.0	9.4
28 years	93,921	98,874	24,389	14,387	65,246	74,343	3,941	9,977	345	167	26.0	14.6	69.5	75.2	4.2	10.1
29 years	65,666	67,645	14,835	8,671	47,770	51,314	2,829	7,558	232	102	22.6	12.8	72.7	75.9	4.3	11.2
30 years	114,699	118,858	26,225	16,631	81,822	86,671	6,178	15,341	474	215	22.9	14.0	71.3	72.9	5.4	12.9
31 years	45,572	44,171	8,948	4,668	34,137	34,240	2,311	5,215	176	48	19.6	10.6	74.9	77.5	5.1	11.8
32 years	63,470	65,075	11,859	6,687	48,064	50,456	3,341	7,846	206	86	18.7	10.3	75.7	77.5	5.3	12.1
33 years	52,894	53,148	8,457	4,550	41,348	41,709	2,939	6,829	150	60	16.0	8.6	78.2	78.5	5.6	12.8
34 years	55,528	54,674	8,268	4,438	43,956	43,111	3,157	7,072	147	53	14.9	8.1	79.2	78.9	5.7	12.9
35 to 44 years	550,130	538,732	67,203	38,105	439,901	401,069	41,602	98,887	1,424	671	12.2	7.1	80.0	74.4	7.6	18.4
45 to 54 years	379,315	332,664	25,869	15,537	308,831	220,800	43,922	95,853	693	474	6.8	4.7	81.4	66.4	11.6	28.8
55 to 64 years	216,239	179,885	10,792	6,946	168,881	95,023	36,141	77,547	425	369	5.0	3.9	78.1	52.8	16.7	43.1
65 years and over	152,482	141,642	6,285	5,243	102,670	42,404	42,890	93,421	637	574	4.1	3.7	67.3	29.9	28.1	66.0

¹ Less than one-tenth of 1 per cent.

Table 11

AGE.	PERCENTAGE MARRIED IN THE POPULATION: 1910.			
	Male.		Female.	
	Negro.	Native white of native parentage.	Negro.	Native white of native parentage.
15 years	0.1	(1)	1.9	1.5
16 years	0.2	0.1	6.2	4.4
17 years	0.8	0.4	14.1	10.1
18 years	2.8	1.6	26.1	19.0
19 years	7.5	4.6	37.2	28.4
20 years	16.5	10.2	48.3	38.3
21 years	29.6	18.3	54.7	46.0
22 years	39.4	26.6	60.4	52.9
23 years	48.6	35.6	65.0	59.3
24 years	54.8	43.1	67.7	63.9
25 years	59.2	49.8	69.3	68.0
26 years	63.5	55.4	73.0	71.9
27 years	67.0	60.9	74.5	74.9
28 years	69.5	64.2	75.2	76.7
29 years	72.7	70.3	75.9	79.7
30 years	71.3	68.8	72.9	76.8
31 years	74.9	75.5	77.5	82.4
32 years	75.7	74.5	77.5	81.4
33 years	78.2	78.0	78.5	83.0
34 years	79.2	78.7	78.9	82.5
35 to 44 years	80.0	81.3	74.4	81.9
45 to 54 years	81.4	82.8	66.4	76.7
55 to 64 years	78.1	80.4	52.8	64.5
65 years and over	67.3	67.3	29.9	35.8

¹ Less than one-tenth of 1 per cent.

Table 11 gives data for Negroes in comparison with native whites of native parentage, showing for 1910 the percentage married by single years of age. This table is illustrated by Diagram VIII (p. 244), in which the two upper curves represent the percentage married for females and the two lower curves the percentage married for males among Negroes and native whites of native parentage, respectively. The tendency of Negroes to marry younger is indicated by the more rapid ascent of the curves for Negroes.

SECTIONS AND DIVISIONS.

The marital condition of the Negro population is shown by sections and divisions for 1910 in Table 12.

In no one of the areas covered by Table 12 does the number married, widowed, or divorced in the population under 15 years of age amount to any appreciable proportion of the population of that age. When related not to the total under 15, but to the total in the age 14—on the assumption that all under 15 returned as having been married were in the age 14—the proportion married, widowed, or divorced amounted in the South to 0.1 per cent, or 1 in 1,000, for males, and to 0.6 per cent, or 6 in 1,000 for females.

MARITAL CONDITION OF THE NEGRO POPULATION, BY SECTIONS AND SOUTHERN DIVISIONS: 1910.

Table 12

SEX AND SECTION AND DIVISION.	Under 15 years of age.			15 years of age and over.					
	Total.	Single.	Married, widowed, or divorced.	Total.[1]	Single.	Married, widowed, or divorced.			
						Total.[1]	Married.	Widowed.	Divorced.
MALE.					NUMBER.				
United States	1,826,569	1,826,430	139	3,059,312	1,083,472	1,959,344	1,749,228	189,970	20,146
The South	1,704,176	1,704,047	129	2,635,449	915,961	1,705,432	1,527,069	162,326	16,037
South Atlantic	816,738	816,680	58	1,213,070	431,943	773,945	701,837	67,831	4,277
East South Central	506,613	506,571	42	809,179	272,322	533,393	473,135	53,596	6,662
West South Central	380,825	380,796	29	613,200	211,696	398,094	352,097	40,899	5,098
The North	117,834	117,824	10	400,710	156,984	241,471	211,363	26,364	3,744
The West	4,559	4,559	....	23,153	10,527	12,441	10,796	1,280	365
				PERCENTAGE DISTRIBUTION BY MARITAL CLASS.					
United States	100.0	100.0	(2)	100.0	35.4	64.0	57.2	6.2	0.7
The South	100.0	100.0	(2)	100.0	34.8	64.7	57.9	6.2	0.6
South Atlantic	100.0	100.0	(2)	100.0	35.6	63.8	57.9	5.6	0.4
East South Central	100.0	100.0	(2)	100.0	33.7	65.9	58.5	6.6	0.8
West South Central	100.0	100.0	(2)	100.0	34.5	64.9	57.4	6.7	0.8
The North	100.0	100.0	(2)	100.0	39.2	50.3	52.7	6.6	0.9
The West	100.0	100.0	....	100.0	45.5	53.7	46.6	5.5	1.6
				EXCESS OF MALES OVER FEMALES.					
United States					259,476				
The South					202,878				
South Atlantic					76,631				
East South Central	1,135	1,326			64,531				
West South Central				5,960	61,716				
The North				14,572	50,234		16		
The West				5,057	6,364		551		
FEMALE.					NUMBER.				
United States	1,838,538	1,837,782	756	3,103,344	823,996	2,269,066	1,775,949	459,831	33,286
The South	1,710,692	1,709,978	714	2,699,110	713,083	1,976,998	1,554,357	394,169	28,472
South Atlantic	822,053	821,725	328	1,260,627	355,312	901,033	716,955	176,715	7,363
East South Central	505,478	505,245	233	831,243	207,791	620,879	480,406	128,500	11,973
West South Central	383,161	383,008	153	607,240	149,980	455,086	356,996	88,954	9,136
The North	122,992	122,955	37	386,138	106,750	278,228	211,347	62,536	4,345
The West	4,854	4,849	5	18,096	4,163	13,840	10,245	3,126	469
				PERCENTAGE DISTRIBUTION BY MARITAL CLASS.					
United States	100.0	100.0	(2)	100.0	26.6	73.1	57.2	14.8	1.1
The South	100.0	100.0	(2)	100.0	26.4	73.2	57.6	14.6	1.1
South Atlantic	100.0	100.0	(2)	100.0	28.2	71.5	56.9	14.0	0.6
East South Central	100.0	100.0	(2)	100.0	25.0	74.7	57.8	15.5	1.4
West South Central	100.0	100.0	(2)	100.0	24.7	74.9	58.8	14.6	1.5
The North	100.0	100.0	(2)	100.0	27.6	72.1	54.7	16.2	1.1
The West	100.0	100.0	(2)	100.0	23.0	76.5	56.6	17.3	2.6
				EXCESS OF FEMALES OVER MALES.					
United States	11,969	11,352	617	44,032		309,722	26,721	269,861	13,140
The South	6,516	5,931	585	63,661		271,566	27,288	231,843	12,435
South Atlantic	5,315	5,045	270	47,557		127,088	15,118	108,884	3,086
East South Central			191	22,064		87,486	7,271	74,904	5,311
West South Central	2,336	2,212	124			56,992	4,899	48,055	4,038
The North	5,158	5,131	27			36,757		36,172	601
The West	295	290	5			1,399		1,846	104

[1] Includes those of unknown marital condition.   [2] Less than one-tenth of 1 per cent.

Among Negro males 15 years of age and over the proportion single was highest in the West (45.5 per cent) and higher in the North (39.2 per cent) than it was in the South (34.8 per cent), no marked differences appearing in the proportion single as between the several southern divisions. The excess of males which is a consequence of the selection effected by migration, in the population resident in the North, is obviously a condition tending to retard or prevent marriage for males. The proportion single among Negro females was not materially higher in the North than it was in the South (27.6 as compared with 26.4

per cent), and this percentage was lowest in the West (23 per cent), where the deficiency of females in the population was relatively greatest. In the southern divisions the percentage single among females was highest in the South Atlantic division (28.2), and lowest in the West South Central division (24.7).

The percentage married, widowed, and divorced is complementary to the percentage single, being relatively high or low in those sections in which the percentage single is low or high.

The table shows that there were resident in the South, in 1910, 162,326 widowed males in the Negro population 15 years of age and over; in the North, 26,364, and in the West, 1,280. The number of widowed females in the South was 394,169, in the North 62,536, and in the West 3,126. The proportion widowed among both males and females does not vary markedly from section to section or from division to division. Among males the lowest proportion widowed is that of 5.5 per cent, in the West; and the highest proportion that of 6.7 per cent in the West South Central division. Among females the lowest proportion widowed is that of 14 per cent in the

South Atlantic division, the highest that of 17.3 per cent in the West.

The number of divorced males in the South was 16,037, in the North, 3,744, and in the West, 365; the corresponding numbers for females being 28,472, 4,345, and 469. The proportion divorced for males ranged from 0.4 per cent in the South Atlantic division to 1.6 in the West, and for females, from 0.6 per cent in the South Atlantic to 2.6 in the West.

In each geographic section and division of the country there was in 1910, a considerable excess of males in the Negro population returned as single (amounting to 202,878 in the South, 50,234 in the North, and 6,364 in the West). Among married, widowed or divorced persons in each of these areas, there was an excess of females (amounting to 271,566 in the South, 36,757 in the North, and 1,399 in the West), except that a small excess of males for married persons was reported from the North and from the West.

Table 13 gives for the three years 1910, 1900, and 1890, data corresponding to that given in Table 15, except that the three southern divisions are not shown separately in Table 13.

MARITAL CONDITION OF THE NEGRO POPULATION, BY SECTIONS: 1910, 1900, AND 1890.

Table 13	NEGRO POPULATION.											
SECTION, AGE PERIOD, AND MARITAL CLASS.	Male.			Female.			Male.			Female.		
	1910	1900	1890[1]	1910	1900	1890[1]	1910	1900	1890	1910	1900	1890
	NUMBER.						PERCENTAGE DISTRIBUTION BY MARITAL CLASS.					
THE SOUTH.												
All ages	4,339,625	3,925,404	3,353,334	4,409,802	3,997,565	3,388,607	....	....	....	....	....	....
Under 15 years of age [2]	1,704,176	1,635,805	1,492,532	1,710,692	1,634,403	1,455,846	100.0	100.0	100.0	100.0	100.0	100.0
Single	1,704,047	1,635,589	1,192,501	1,709,978	1,633,579	1,455,563	100.0	100.0	100.0	100.0	100.0	100.0
Married, widowed, or divorced	129	152	12	714	734	276	([3])	([3])	([3])	([3])	([3])	([3])
15 years of age and over	2,635,449	2,289,599	1,860,802	2,699,110	2,363,162	1,932,761	100.0	100.0	100.0	100.0	100.0	100.0
Single	915,961	879,668	726,383	713,083	698,010	575,815	34.8	38.4	39.0	26.4	29.5	29.8
Married, widowed, or divorced	1,705,432	1,397,906	1,130,614	1,976,998	1,659,385	1,352,447	64.7	61.1	60.8	73.2	70.2	70.0
Married	1,527,069	1,258,611	1,047,668	1,554,357	1,278,965	1,062,932	57.9	55.0	56.3	57.6	54.1	55.0
Widowed	162,326	130,333	78,811	394,169	361,256	280,398	6.2	5.7	4.2	14.6	15.3	14.5
Divorced	16,037	8,962	4,135	28,472	19,164	9,117	0.6	0.4	0.2	1.1	0.8	0.5
Unknown	14,056	12,025	3,805	9,029	5,767	4,499	0.5	0.5	0.2	0.3	0.2	0.2
THE NORTH.												
All ages	518,544	444,007	355,661	509,130	436,764	345,357	....	....	....	....	....	....
Under 15 years of age [2]	117,834	114,470	110,047	122,992	119,154	110,086	100.0	100.0	100.0	100.0	100.0	100.0
Single	117,824	114,442	110,041	122,955	119,117	110,074	100.0	100.0	100.0	100.0	100.0	100.0
Married, widowed, or divorced	10	15	1	37	32	11	([3])	([3])	([3])	([3])	([3])	([3])
15 years of age and over	400,710	329,537	245,614	386,138	317,610	235,271	100.0	100.0	100.0	100.0	100.0	100.0
Single	156,984	146,297	108,068	106,750	103,074	74,323	39.2	44.4	44.0	27.6	32.5	31.6
Married, widowed, or divorced	241,471	180,948	136,859	278,228	213,419	160,558	60.3	54.9	55.7	72.1	67.2	68.2
Married	211,363	158,918	123,500	211,347	159,650	120,487	52.7	48.2	50.3	54.7	50.3	51.2
Widowed	26,364	20,101	12,380	62,536	51,088	38,607	6.6	6.1	5.0	16.2	16.1	16.4
Divorced	3,744	1,929	979	4,345	2,681	1,464	0.9	0.6	0.4	1.1	0.8	0.6
Unknown	2,255	2,292	687	1,160	1,117	390	0.6	0.7	0.3	0.3	0.4	0.2
THE WEST.												
All ages	27,712	17,136	16,566	22,950	13,118	10,515	....	....	....	....	....	....
Under 15 years of age [2]	4,559	3,264	3,261	4,854	3,307	2,997	100.0	100.0	100.0	100.0	100.0	100.0
Single	4,559	3,264	3,261	4,849	3,303	2,995	100.0	100.0	100.0	99.9	99.9	99.9
Married, widowed, or divorced	....	....	....	5	4	2	([3])	([3])	([3])	0.1	0.1	0.1
15 years of age and over	23,153	13,872	13,305	18,096	9,811	7,518	100.0	100.0	100.0	100.0	100.0	100.0
Single	10,527	7,320	8,313	4,163	2,599	2,176	45.5	52.8	62.5	23.0	26.5	28.9
Married, widowed, or divorced	12,441	6,291	4,935	13,840	7,153	5,311	53.7	45.4	37.1	76.5	72.9	70.6
Married	10,796	5,357	4,345	10,245	5,202	4,015	46.6	38.6	32.7	56.6	53.0	53.4
Widowed	1,280	799	492	3,126	1,763	1,189	5.5	5.8	3.7	17.3	18.0	15.8
Divorced	365	135	98	469	188	107	1.6	1.0	0.7	2.6	1.9	1.4
Unknown	185	261	57	93	59	31	0.8	1.9	0.4	0.5	0.6	0.4

[1] Exclusive of persons specially enumerated in Indian Territory and on Indian reservations for whom statistics of marital condition are not available.
[2] Totals include persons of unknown marital condition in 1900 and 1890.
[3] Less than one-tenth of 1 per cent.

Among Negro males the percentage single in the South declined in the two decades covered by Table 13 (from 39 per cent in 1890 to 38.4 per cent in 1900, and to 34.8 per cent in 1910). The percentage married, in the South, declined slightly in the first decade (from 56.3 to 55 per cent), and increased during the last decade (to 57.9). Among Negro females, also, the percentage single declined in each of the two decades (from 29.8 per cent in 1890 to 29.5 per cent in 1900, and to 26.4 in 1910), and as in the case of males, the percentage married declined slightly in the decade from 1890 to 1900 (from 55 to 54.1 per cent), and increased in the decade from 1900 to 1910 (to 57.6 per cent).

In the North and West the percentage single among both males and females declined during the last decade, the percentage married increasing.

The percentage in each marital class is shown in Table 14, for the Negro and white population 15 years of age and over, in 1910, in each of the three geographic sections.

among males in the North it was slightly lower for native whites than for Negroes.

The percentage widowed in the South was slightly higher for the foreign-born white than for Negro males, but was higher among Negroes than among native whites in every section and among both males and females.

In each section the percentage divorced, although this percentage is very small in all classes, was slightly higher among Negroes than for the white classes.

In each section the percentage married, widowed, or divorced was higher among Negroes than among native whites for both males and females.

The number of males per 1,000 females in each marital class of Negro and white population is shown in Table 15, by sections. In the Negro population 15 years of age and over, in the South, the number of males per 1,000 females was 1,285 among those returned as single, and 863 among those returned as married, widowed, or divorced. The number of males per 1,000 females in the single population was higher in the North (1,471) than it was in the South (1,285), and was much higher in the West than it was in any other section of the country (2,529). In the married population the number of males per 1,000 females was 982 in the South, 1,000 in the North, and 1,054 in the West. In the population returned as widowed it was 412 in the South, 422 in the North, and 409 in the West. The corresponding figures for whites were, among married persons, 1,005 in the South, 1,028 in the North, and 1,061 in the West, and among the widowed, 466 in the South, 463 in the North, and 565 in the West.

Table 14

POPULATION 15 YEARS OF AGE AND OVER: 1910.

RACIAL CLASS.	Male.			Female.		
	The South.	The North.	The West.	The South.	The North.	The West.
PERCENTAGE SINGLE.						
Negro	34.8	39.2	45.5	26.4	27.6	23.0
White	36.8	38.7	45.8	28.1	31.2	26.9
Native born	37.2	42.4	46.5	28.7	35.4	30.1
Foreign born	30.1	30.2	44.0	15.1	18.8	14.6
PERCENTAGE MARRIED.						
Negro	57.9	52.7	46.6	57.6	54.7	56.6
White	58.2	56.0	48.2	61.5	57.9	61.9
Native	58.0	52.6	47.7	61.3	55.0	59.9
Foreign born	62.2	63.8	49.4	65.7	66.4	69.1
PERCENTAGE WIDOWED.						
Negro	6.2	6.6	5.5	14.6	16.2	17.3
White	4.3	4.4	4.1	9.8	10.2	9.9
Native	4.1	4.0	3.8	9.4	8.7	8.5
Foreign born	6.8	5.4	4.7	18.6	14.4	15.2
PERCENTAGE DIVORCED.						
Negro	0.6	0.9	1.6	1.1	1.1	2.6
White	0.3	0.4	1.0	0.4	0.5	1.1
Native	0.3	0.5	1.0	0.4	0.6	1.2
Foreign born	0.4	0.3	0.7	0.4	0.3	0.9
PERCENTAGE MARRIED, WIDOWED, OR DIVORCED.						
Negro	64.7	60.3	53.7	73.2	72.1	76.5
White	62.8	60.9	53.2	71.7	68.6	72.9
Native	62.4	57.2	52.5	71.1	64.4	69.6
Foreign born	69.4	69.5	54.8	84.7	81.1	85.2

Table 15

MALES TO 1,000 FEMALES: 1910.

AGE PERIOD AND MARITAL CLASS.	Negro population.			White population.		
	The South.	The North.	The West.	The South.	The North.	The West.
Total	984	1,018	1,207	1,052	1,050	1,262
Under 15 years of age	996	958	939	1,038	1,019	1,029
Single	997	958	940	1,038	1,020	1,029
Married, widowed, or divorced	181	(1)	(1)	125	558	524
15 years of age and over	976	1,038	1,279	1,062	1,064	1,363
Single	1,285	1,471	2,529	1,391	1,322	2,324
Married, widowed, or divorced	863	868	899	930	943	995
Married	982	1,000	1,054	1,005	1,028	1,061
Widowed	412	422	409	466	463	565
Divorced	563	862	778	776	874	1,137
Unknown	1,557	1,944	(1)	1,775	2,134	5,792

[1] Ratio not shown, the number of females being less than 100.

The percentage in each marital class is given in Table 16, for the Negro population of each section, classified by age periods, in 1910, 1900, and 1890.

The percentage single decreased among Negro males and females, and the percentage married increased in each geographic section of the country during the decade 1900–1910, for the age groups 15 to 19 years, 20 to 24 years, 25 to 34 years, and 35 to 44 years.

In each of the sections among males and females the percentage single for Negroes was lower than that for native whites, and higher than that for foreign-born whites. In each section the percentage married was lower for Negroes than for native whites, except that

PERCENTAGE IN EACH MARITAL CLASS, BY AGE PERIODS, FOR THE NEGRO POPULATION 15 YEARS OF AGE AND OVER, BY SECTIONS: 1910, 1900, AND 1890.

Table 16

SECTION AND YEAR.	Total.		15 to 19 years.		20 to 24 years.		25 to 34 years.		35 to 44 years.		45 to 64 years.		65 years and over.	
	Male.	Female.	Male.	Female.	Male.	Female.	Male.	Female.	Male.	Female.	Male.	Female.	Male.	Female.
PERCENTAGE SINGLE.														
The South:														
1910	34.8	26.4	96.8	80.7	57.9	33.4	22.2	13.3	10.0	6.4	4.9	4.0	3.5	3.5
1900	38.4	29.5	97.8	82.7	62.3	38.0	25.0	16.3	11.2	7.4	5.5	4.5	4.1	4.1
1890	39.0	29.8	99.0	84.5	63.6	36.6	22.3	14.2	9.7	7.0	5.2	4.3	5.0	4.1
The North:														
1910	39.2	27.6	98.1	86.7	73.2	46.9	39.1	21.8	22.1	10.8	13.1	6.7	7.7	5.2
1900	44.4	32.5	98.8	88.5	78.7	53.5	43.5	24.5	22.9	11.2	12.5	6.7	7.8	6.0
1890	44.0	31.6	99.5	89.6	80.4	50.0	39.9	20.9	19.5	10.1	10.3	6.4	8.0	5.8
The West:														
1910	45.5	23.0	98.4	83.9	79.4	40.1	50.9	18.4	30.9	8.3	21.8	5.8	17.7	4.6
1900	52.8	26.5	98.5	85.7	87.3	46.4	58.5	22.1	35.7	8.4	26.7	5.7	24.1	3.9
1890	62.5	28.9	99.7	82.6	89.4	46.3	68.4	20.1	43.2	10.8	31.0	6.1	28.5	6.6
PERCENTAGE MARRIED.														
The South:														
1910	57.9	57.6	2.3	17.5	39.5	60.3	72.6	75.5	82.2	75.3	81.7	62.6	68.7	30.6
1900	55.0	54.1	1.8	16.1	35.7	56.0	70.5	71.8	81.2	73.0	81.7	61.5	70.7	29.5
1890	56.3	55.0	1.0	14.9	35.4	58.6	74.5	75.6	84.6	75.2	85.4	62.1	75.5	29.6
The North:														
1910	52.7	54.7	1.2	12.2	25.2	49.2	57.0	68.6	70.0	69.9	71.3	55.5	58.2	25.6
1900	48.2	50.3	0.9	10.8	20.2	43.0	53.1	65.6	69.1	68.5	72.2	55.1	60.8	24.5
1890	50.3	51.2	0.4	9.9	18.9	46.6	57.2	69.5	74.0	70.5	77.7	55.6	66.3	24.9
The West:														
1910	46.6	56.6	1.2	15.1	19.1	53.1	45.4	69.2	61.1	69.1	63.6	54.4	51.1	21.9
1900	38.6	53.0	0.9	13.2	10.6	47.6	37.4	64.3	56.3	68.1	58.2	53.1	42.1	22.4
1890	32.7	53.4	0.3	16.6	10.0	49.5	29.3	68.4	50.5	67.2	56.7	50.5	46.7	27.5
PERCENTAGE WIDOWED.														
The South:														
1910	6.2	14.6	0.1	0.9	1.6	4.9	4.0	9.4	6.6	16.7	12.3	32.3	26.8	65.1
1900	5.7	15.3	0.1	0.9	1.2	4.9	3.6	10.4	6.8	18.3	12.0	33.2	24.5	65.7
1890	4.2	14.5	(1)	0.5	0.7	4.1	2.7	9.2	5.2	16.9	8.9	32.9	19.0	65.7
The North:														
1910	6.6	16.2	0.1	0.4	0.8	2.8	2.7	7.9	6.3	17.6	14.0	36.5	32.1	68.4
1900	6.1	16.1	(1)	0.4	0.6	2.7	2.5	8.5	6.8	18.8	14.0	37.2	30.0	68.8
1890	5.0	16.4	(1)	0.4	0.4	2.8	2.3	8.5	5.6	18.4	11.1	37.2	25.0	68.9
The West:														
1910	5.5	17.3	....	0.4	0.6	3.8	2.0	9.2	5.5	19.0	11.8	37.4	28.9	72.3
1900	5.8	18.0	....	0.7	0.5	4.6	2.2	10.7	6.2	20.3	12.7	39.1	31.8	71.7
1890	3.7	15.8	....	0.6	0.1	3.1	1.4	9.2	4.6	19.6	10.4	42.3	23.7	65.1
PERCENTAGE DIVORCED.														
The South:														
1910	0.6	1.1	(1)	0.2	0.4	1.1	0.8	1.6	0.9	1.5	0.8	0.9	0.6	0.4
1900	0.4	0.8	(1)	0.1	0.2	0.8	0.5	1.3	0.6	1.2	0.6	0.7	0.4	0.3
1890	0.2	0.5	(1)	0.1	0.1	0.4	0.3	0.8	0.4	0.7	0.3	0.4	0.3	0.2
The North:														
1910	0.9	1.1	(1)	0.2	0.3	0.9	0.9	1.5	1.4	1.5	1.4	1.1	1.1	0.4
1900	0.6	0.8	(1)	0.1	0.1	0.7	0.5	1.2	0.9	1.3	1.0	0.8	0.8	0.3
1890	0.4	0.6	(1)	0.1	0.1	0.5	0.3	0.9	0.6	1.0	0.7	0.6	0.5	0.2
The West:														
1910	1.6	2.6	0.1	0.4	0.5	2.7	1.3	3.1	2.1	3.3	2.4	2.3	1.5	1.2
1900	1.0	1.9	....	0.3	0.4	0.9	0.9	2.4	1.2	2.8	1.6	1.7	1.5	0.8
1890	0.7	1.4	....	0.3	(1)	0.9	0.5	2.1	1.3	2.2	1.6	1.0	1.1	0.8
PERCENTAGE MARRIED, WIDOWED, OR DIVORCED.														
The South:														
1910	64.7	73.2	2.4	18.6	41.5	66.3	77.4	86.5	89.7	93.5	94.9	95.9	96.1	96.1
1900	61.1	70.2	1.9	17.2	37.0	61.8	74.6	83.5	88.6	92.4	94.3	95.3	95.5	95.4
1890	60.8	70.0	1.0	15.4	36.2	63.1	77.5	85.6	90.2	92.8	94.6	95.5	94.7	95.5
The North:														
1910	60.3	72.1	1.2	12.8	26.3	52.8	60.6	78.0	77.7	89.1	86.7	93.1	91.3	94.4
1900	54.9	67.2	1.0	11.3	20.9	46.3	56.1	75.3	76.8	88.6	87.2	93.1	91.5	93.5
1890	55.7	68.2	0.4	10.3	19.4	49.8	59.8	78.9	80.3	89.8	89.5	93.4	91.8	93.9
The West:														
1910	53.7	76.5	1.3	15.9	20.2	59.6	48.7	81.5	68.7	91.4	77.8	94.1	81.4	95.4
1900	45.4	72.9	0.9	14.2	11.5	53.1	40.5	77.3	63.7	91.3	72.6	94.0	75.3	95.0
1890	37.1	70.6	0.3	17.4	10.2	53.4	31.2	79.7	56.4	89.0	68.7	93.7	71.5	93.4

1 Less than one-tenth of 1 per cent.

In the South the percentage married in the Negro population 15 to 19 years of age increased among males from 1 in 1890 to 1.8 in 1900, and to 2.3 in 1910, and among females from 14.9 in 1890 to 16.1 in 1900, and to 17.5 in 1910. In the population 20 to 24 years of age the percentage married among Negro males increased from 35.4 in 1890 to 35.7 in 1900, and to 39.5 in 1910; among females the percentage decreased in the decade 1890 to 1900, from 58.6 to 56 per cent, and increased in the decade 1900–1910 to 60.3 per cent. In the more advanced ages the percentage married decreased among both males and females during the decade 1890–1900, and increased during the decade 1900–1910, except that it remained unchanged in the latter decade among males 45 to 64, and decreased among males 65 and over.

In the North, as in the South, the percentage married increased during the decade 1900–1910 in each age group among both males and females, except among males 45 to 64, and 65 and over, and in the West this percentage increased in each age and sex group without exception. In the North and West the percentage married at each age, in 1910 as at preceding censuses, was below that obtaining in the South.

The percentage widowed among females 45 to 64, and 65 and over in the South and in the North remained practically unchanged during the two decades. In the South at each census approximately one-third (from 32.3 to 33.2 per cent) of the females 45 to 64, and approximately two-thirds (from 65.1 to 65.7 per cent) of the females 65 and over were widowed, the corresponding proportions being somewhat higher in the North and in the West.

The percentage in each marital class among Negroes, classified by age in 1910, is given in comparison with corresponding percentage for whites in Table 17.

In each of the three geographic sections the proportion married in the population 15 to 19 and 20 to 24 years, both male and female, was higher among Negroes than among whites, and in the more advanced ages was lower among Negroes than among whites, except among Negro males in the South aged 25 to 29 years, and 65 years and over.

In each section, at each age, among both males and females, the proportion widowed among Negroes exceeded that among whites.

Table 28 (p. 261) shows the marital condition of the Negro population in detail by age for each of the nine geographic divisions in 1910, the age classification in this table being somewhat more detailed than that of other tables showing marital condition by sections and divisions. The table shows, for example, that of the total number of Negro males living in New England in 1910 (32,783), 18,172, or 55.4 per cent, were single; 12,894, or 39.3 per cent, were married; 1,454, or 4.4 per cent, were widowed; and 177 were divorced. Of the total, 7,828 were under 15 years of age, all of these

males being single except 1, who was returned as married. The number of males 15 years of age and over was 24,955, of whom 10,345, or 41.5 per cent, were single; 12,893, or 51.7 per cent, were married; 1,454, or 5.8 per cent, were widowed, and 177 were divorced. Each marital condition class is distributed by 12 age periods—under 15 years, 15 and over, 15 to 19, 20 to 24, 25 to 34, 25 to 29, 30 to 34, 35 to 44, 45 to 64, 45 to 54, 55 to 64, 65 and over, and age unknown. The number of males is thus distributed by marital condition and age in detail, and similar data are given for the 33,523 Negro females resident in this division.

THE STATES.

Statistics of marital condition in the several states are given in Tables 29 and 30 (pp. 263 to 266). Table 29 gives the marital condition of the Negro population by divisions and states, in each of the three years 1910, 1900, and 1890, showing for each state the number of Negro males and females 15 years of age and over returned at each of these censuses as single, married, widowed, divorced, or of unknown marital condition. Table 30 shows marital condition, by age periods, for the Negro population, by sections, southern divisions, and Southern states in 1910, the number and the percentage in each marital class being given by age periods. The percentages of Table 18 (p. 252) represent the populations of Table 29.

In the Southern states the percentage single in 1910 among Negro males ranged from 32.2 in Mississippi to 48.1 in West Virginia; the percentage married, from 45.7 in West Virginia to 61.1 in South Carolina; and the percentage widowed, from 4.8 in South Carolina to 7.8 in Arkansas. Among Negro females the percentage single in the Southern states ranged from 21.6 in Florida to 32 in North Carolina, the percentage in the District of Columbia being 33.1; the percentage married, from 53.3 in Virginia to 64 in Oklahoma, the percentage for the District of Columbia being 47; and the percentage widowed, from 11.1 in West Virginia to 16.8 in Kentucky and in Tennessee.

URBAN AND RURAL COMMUNITIES.

Statistics of marital condition for the population, classified as urban and rural, and for the urban population, classified according to size of urban communities, are given in Tables 19 to 26.

In Table 19 the Negro population 15 years of age and over, in 1910, living in urban communities—i. e., in communities of 2,500 or more inhabitants—and in rural communities, is classified by sex, age, and marital condition. The table shows that 947,605 of the 3,059,312 Negro males 15 years of age and over in 1910 were living in urban, and 2,111,707 in rural communities; that of those living in urban communities 350,598, or 37 per cent, and of those living in rural communities 732,874, or 34.7 per cent, were single; that of the urban male population 590,757, or 62.3 per cent, and of the rural, 1,368,587, or 64.8 per cent, were married, widowed, or divorced—the number and proportion in each of the several marital condition classes being separately shown. Similar data are given for females 15 years of age and over, and for males and females in each age group.

PERCENTAGE IN EACH MARITAL CLASS FOR THE NEGRO AND WHITE POPULATION, CLASSIFIED BY SEX AND AGE PERIODS, BY SECTIONS: 1910.

Table 17

AGE PERIOD.	POPULATION: 1910.											
	Male.						Female.					
	The South.		The North.		The West.		The South.		The North.		The West.	
	Negro.	White.	Negro.	White.	Negro.	White.	Negro.	White.	Negro.	White.	Negro.	White.
PERCENTAGE SINGLE.												
15 years of age and over	34.8	36.8	39.2	38.7	45.5	45.8	26.4	28.1	27.6	31.2	23.0	26.9
15 to 19 years	96.8	97.4	98.1	98.8	98.4	98.8	80.7	82.0	86.7	91.7	83.9	88.5
20 to 24 years	57.9	68.3	73.2	78.8	79.4	82.8	33.4	39.9	46.9	54.5	40.1	46.4
25 to 29 years	26.7	34.5	45.5	45.2	56.5	57.1	15.7	19.6	26.0	28.6	22.6	23.2
30 to 34 years	16.4	19.7	31.8	26.8	45.1	39.5	10.0	12.7	16.6	18.4	13.3	14.1
35 to 44 years	10.0	12.2	22.1	16.9	30.9	27.4	6.4	9.3	10.8	13.0	8.3	9.2
45 to 54 years	5.5	8.1	14.1	11.1	22.0	19.9	4.3	7.7	7.2	9.6	5.7	6.0
55 to 64 years	4.0	6.3	11.0	8.2	21.3	16.6	3.5	7.5	5.9	7.6	6.2	4.3
65 years and over	3.5	5.2	7.7	5.8	17.7	13.5	3.5	7.8	5.2	6.5	4.6	3.4
PERCENTAGE MARRIED.												
15 years of age and over	57.9	58.2	52.7	56.0	46.6	48.2	57.6	61.5	54.7	57.9	56.6	61.9
15 to 19 years	2.3	2.0	1.2	0.7	1.2	0.6	17.5	17.1	12.2	7.7	15.1	10.8
20 to 24 years	39.5	30.5	25.2	20.4	19.1	16.1	60.3	58.1	49.2	44.4	53.1	51.9
25 to 29 years	68.6	63.6	51.5	53.6	40.6	41.0	74.4	77.2	66.3	69.3	67.4	73.5
30 to 34 years	77.7	77.8	63.3	71.2	50.3	57.6	77.2	82.8	71.5	77.9	71.5	81.0
35 to 44 years	82.2	83.9	70.0	79.5	61.1	67.7	75.3	82.7	69.9	80.0	69.1	82.0
45 to 54 years	83.0	84.8	72.6	82.1	65.2	71.8	67.5	75.7	60.1	75.5	58.8	76.5
55 to 64 years	79.5	81.7	68.8	79.6	59.6	69.7	53.8	62.1	46.7	63.2	43.9	62.6
65 years and over	68.7	68.6	58.2	65.5	51.1	58.4	30.6	33.9	25.6	35.7	21.9	36.0
PERCENTAGE WIDOWED.												
15 years of age and over	6.2	4.3	6.6	4.4	5.5	4.1	14.6	9.8	16.2	10.2	17.3	9.9
15 to 19 years	0.1	(1)	0.1	(1)	....	(1)	0.9	0.3	0.4	0.1	0.4	0.1
20 to 24 years	1.6	0.5	0.8	0.2	0.6	0.2	4.9	1.3	2.8	0.5	3.8	0.8
25 to 29 years	3.4	1.3	2.0	0.7	1.3	0.7	8.2	2.4	6.1	1.4	7.0	1.8
30 to 34 years	4.7	2.0	3.5	1.4	2.7	1.4	11.1	3.8	10.2	2.8	11.8	3.3
35 to 44 years	6.6	3.4	6.3	2.7	5.5	3.0	16.7	7.3	17.6	6.1	19.0	7.0
45 to 54 years	10.5	6.5	11.7	5.8	9.9	6.2	27.1	15.9	31.4	14.1	32.8	15.8
55 to 64 years	15.6	11.4	18.6	11.3	16.3	11.6	41.7	29.8	46.4	28.5	48.4	31.8
65 years and over	26.8	25.5	32.1	27.8	28.9	25.7	65.1	57.7	68.4	57.2	72.3	59.8
PERCENTAGE DIVORCED.												
15 years of age and over	0.6	0.3	0.9	0.4	1.6	1.0	1.1	0.4	1.1	0.5	2.6	1.1
15 to 19 years	(1)	(1)	(1)	(1)	0.1	(1)	0.2	0.1	0.2	(1)	0.4	0.1
20 to 24 years	0.4	0.2	0.3	0.1	0.5	0.2	1.1	0.4	0.9	0.3	2.7	0.7
25 to 29 years	0.8	0.3	0.7	0.3	1.3	0.5	1.6	0.6	1.4	0.6	2.8	1.3
30 to 34 years	0.9	0.4	1.1	0.5	1.4	0.9	1.6	0.6	1.6	0.7	3.4	1.4
35 to 44 years	0.9	0.4	1.4	0.6	2.1	1.3	1.5	0.6	1.5	0.8	3.3	1.7
45 to 54 years	0.8	0.5	1.4	0.8	2.4	1.7	1.1	0.5	1.2	0.8	2.7	1.6
55 to 64 years	0.7	0.5	1.3	0.8	2.6	1.8	0.7	0.4	0.8	0.6	1.4	1.2
65 years and over	0.6	0.4	1.1	0.6	1.5	1.5	0.4	0.3	0.4	0.3	1.2	0.6
PERCENTAGE MARRIED, WIDOWED OR DIVORCED.												
15 years of age and over	64.7	62.8	60.3	60.9	53.7	53.2	73.2	71.7	72.1	68.6	76.5	72.9
15 to 19 years	2.4	2.0	1.2	0.7	1.3	0.6	18.6	17.5	12.8	7.8	15.9	11.0
20 to 24 years	41.5	31.2	26.3	20.7	20.2	16.5	66.3	59.8	52.8	45.2	59.6	53.4
25 to 29 years	72.8	65.2	54.2	54.5	43.1	42.1	84.1	80.2	73.8	71.3	77.1	76.6
30 to 34 years	83.3	80.1	67.9	73.1	54.4	59.8	89.9	87.2	83.3	81.5	86.7	85.8
35 to 44 years	89.7	87.7	77.7	82.9	68.7	72.0	93.5	90.6	89.1	86.9	91.4	90.8
45 to 54 years	94.3	91.7	85.7	88.7	77.5	79.7	95.6	92.2	92.7	90.4	94.3	93.9
55 to 64 years	95.8	93.6	88.7	91.7	78.5	83.0	96.2	92.3	94.0	92.3	93.7	95.6
65 years and over	96.1	94.5	91.3	93.9	81.4	85.6	96.1	91.9	94.4	93.3	95.4	96.4

1 Less than one-tenth of 1 per cent.

PERCENTAGE SINGLE, MARRIED, AND WIDOWED IN THE NEGRO POPULATION, BY DIVISIONS AND STATES: 1910, 1900, AND 1890.

Table 18

NEGRO POPULATION 15 YEARS OF AGE AND OVER.

DIVISION AND STATE.	Male. Percentage single.			Male. Percentage married.			Male. Percentage widowed.			Female. Percentage single.			Female. Percentage married.			Female. Percentage widowed.		
	1910	1900	1890	1910	1900	1890	1910	1900	1890	1910	1900	1890	1910	1900	1890	1910	1900	1890
UNITED STATES	35.4	39.2	39.8	57.2	54.0	55.5	6.2	5.7	4.3	26.6	29.9	30.0	57.2	53.7	54.6	14.8	15.4	14.7
GEOGRAPHIC DIVISIONS:																		
New England	41.5	43.3	42.5	51.7	49.8	51.9	5.8	5.8	4.9	32.1	35.7	34.4	50.0	46.8	47.8	16.8	16.3	17.1
Middle Atlantic	39.2	45.5	45.2	54.5	48.7	49.8	5.5	5.0	4.6	30.7	36.2	34.5	53.3	48.1	48.3	15.2	15.0	17.0
East North Central	38.8	43.8	43.4	51.7	47.6	50.2	7.3	7.0	5.6	24.3	28.7	29.3	56.8	53.1	53.9	16.8	16.6	15.8
West North Central	39.0	43.8	43.5	51.4	48.0	50.6	7.5	6.8	5.0	24.6	29.8	29.6	56.2	51.6	53.0	17.2	17.1	16.4
South Atlantic	35.6	39.0	39.9	57.9	54.9	56.0	5.6	5.2	3.9	28.2	31.3	31.7	56.9	53.5	54.1	14.0	14.4	13.6
East South Central	33.7	38.2	38.7	58.5	54.8	56.3	6.6	6.1	4.6	25.0	28.6	28.9	57.8	54.0	54.9	15.5	16.2	15.5
West South Central	34.5	37.4	37.6	57.4	55.2	57.1	6.7	6.2	4.6	24.7	26.9	26.6	58.8	55.7	57.3	14.6	15.9	15.2
Mountain	43.9	54.8	67.6	47.6	36.5	28.3	5.8	5.7	2.9	22.5	25.7	32.4	56.6	53.7	50.3	17.5	17.6	14.9
Pacific	46.6	50.3	56.7	45.9	41.2	37.7	5.3	5.9	4.6	23.4	27.3	26.0	56.6	52.3	56.0	17.1	18.3	16.6
NEW ENGLAND:																		
Maine	45.1	44.5	46.2	44.9	46.6	47.1	8.3	5.6	5.6	38.8	35.9	36.0	43.8	46.0	45.6	14.9	17.1	17.7
New Hampshire	41.5	48.5	51.3	48.5	40.9	42.0	7.9	8.0	5.5	39.8	46.4	42.3	46.0	37.2	41.3	12.3	13.9	15.9
Vermont	72.6	47.4	42.0	23.5	43.4	49.4	2.6	5.5	7.4	26.3	37.6	31.2	62.2	46.5	51.2	9.1	14.7	17.3
Massachusetts	41.7	44.3	43.6	51.9	49.5	51.4	5.3	5.0	4.6	32.8	35.1	34.3	49.6	47.3	48.0	16.8	16.4	17.2
Rhode Island	40.0	41.6	39.1	53.0	51.7	54.6	5.9	5.8	5.7	30.0	35.2	34.3	49.9	46.0	46.0	18.2	17.5	18.4
Connecticut	35.2	41.2	41.7	56.5	50.7	52.6	7.5	7.2	4.5	31.3	36.8	34.3	51.1	46.8	48.8	16.5	15.3	16.1
MIDDLE ATLANTIC:																		
New York	41.1	45.5	43.8	53.3	49.1	51.1	4.9	4.8	4.7	32.3	38.1	35.0	50.6	44.7	45.8	16.3	16.6	18.9
New Jersey	37.2	41.9	43.4	56.8	51.5	51.9	5.4	4.9	4.2	29.5	34.7	33.7	55.2	49.8	50.9	14.7	14.4	15.1
Pennsylvania	38.8	47.0	46.9	54.3	47.2	48.1	6.0	5.1	4.6	30.1	35.6	34.6	54.5	49.7	48.8	14.6	14.1	16.1
EAST NORTH CENTRAL:																		
Ohio	39.6	42.9	43.6	51.7	48.8	50.4	7.0	6.9	5.4	26.5	30.5	30.6	56.5	52.9	53.0	15.3	15.3	15.6
Indiana	37.9	42.0	43.5	51.7	48.0	49.7	8.3	7.7	5.9	24.0	28.1	29.1	55.9	52.5	53.5	17.7	17.1	15.8
Illinois	38.6	46.0	43.7	51.7	45.8	49.8	7.2	6.6	5.6	22.2	26.8	27.4	57.7	53.6	55.4	17.9	18.0	16.4
Michigan	36.8	41.7	40.9	53.5	49.5	52.5	7.0	7.4	5.7	24.5	28.7	28.7	57.7	53.9	55.0	15.6	15.9	15.2
Wisconsin	43.9	50.7	45.3	45.6	41.1	47.1	7.4	6.5	6.6	32.5	33.6	33.2	50.0	49.9	51.1	15.0	14.6	13.9
WEST NORTH CENTRAL:																		
Minnesota	48.5	51.3	53.6	44.2	41.5	41.9	5.1	4.8	3.4	27.5	29.3	26.1	56.9	53.7	59.0	13.8	14.6	14.1
Iowa	37.8	43.3	44.1	51.8	47.7	50.1	7.4	6.5	5.0	22.5	27.6	28.0	60.9	56.6	57.3	13.7	14.0	13.7
Missouri	38.9	44.5	43.3	51.4	47.6	50.8	7.8	6.7	5.2	24.7	30.4	30.3	54.9	50.3	51.3	18.3	18.0	17.4
North Dakota	57.4	59.8	62.3	32.3	28.0	32.7	4.5	10.6	4.3	30.3	(1)	(1)	57.3	(1)	(1)	8.6	(1)	(1)
South Dakota	45.6	58.1	58.8	47.2	35.3	34.7	5.6	4.2	6.1	30.2	25.6	23.8	58.0	58.9	59.8	10.3	14.0	13.9
Nebraska	43.5	53.7	57.2	48.1	39.9	37.9	6.7	5.2	3.2	23.4	33.9	33.5	59.2	48.2	53.5	16.3	16.3	11.8
Kansas	36.9	39.0	39.1	53.5	51.8	54.7	7.4	7.5	5.4	24.3	28.0	27.6	58.1	54.9	56.9	15.6	15.4	14.6
SOUTH ATLANTIC:																		
Delaware	41.0	43.2	43.8	51.0	49.3	51.4	7.2	6.3	4.6	30.8	32.3	31.4	54.6	53.2	56.0	13.9	13.9	12.5
Maryland	39.0	42.3	42.1	53.8	51.1	53.2	6.6	5.5	4.4	31.1	34.4	34.5	54.2	50.4	50.9	14.1	14.3	14.3
District of Columbia	37.7	41.0	41.2	55.6	52.5	54.1	5.8	6.1	4.3	33.1	38.8	38.0	47.0	42.0	42.6	18.9	18.6	18.1
Virginia	39.3	42.6	43.1	54.3	51.3	52.2	5.8	5.4	4.5	31.7	35.4	36.4	53.3	49.4	48.8	14.3	14.7	14.2
West Virginia	48.1	53.9	54.0	45.7	39.1	41.5	4.9	4.3	3.5	25.4	31.8	34.8	62.2	54.7	52.8	11.1	12.4	11.7
North Carolina	36.2	39.3	40.9	58.2	54.8	55.0	5.0	5.0	3.9	32.0	35.5	34.5	54.9	51.3	52.2	12.3	12.7	12.8
South Carolina	33.5	35.9	35.8	61.1	59.0	60.6	4.8	4.6	3.5	27.9	29.5	28.6	57.8	56.6	58.4	13.8	13.4	12.6
Georgia	32.3	35.8	38.4	60.9	57.7	57.7	5.9	5.3	3.6	24.6	27.0	27.5	59.3	56.3	57.7	15.0	15.6	14.0
Florida	35.6	41.7	39.5	54.9	51.5	56.0	6.1	5.5	3.9	21.6	25.1	27.5	63.7	59.0	58.5	12.5	14.6	12.9
EAST SOUTH CENTRAL:																		
Kentucky	38.2	42.3	42.4	52.6	49.5	51.5	7.6	6.9	5.3	27.4	30.8	31.2	53.9	50.1	50.8	16.8	17.6	16.9
Tennessee	35.0	40.2	39.8	56.4	52.2	54.7	7.3	6.5	4.9	25.9	29.9	29.7	55.5	51.4	52.7	16.8	17.3	16.6
Alabama	32.9	37.2	37.7	59.7	56.3	57.8	6.4	5.8	4.1	25.1	28.6	28.8	57.7	54.3	55.8	15.5	16.1	14.9
Mississippi	32.2	36.6	37.4	60.3	56.9	57.7	6.2	5.8	4.5	23.8	27.3	27.5	60.2	56.5	57.0	14.3	15.2	14.7
WEST SOUTH CENTRAL:																		
Arkansas	32.6	36.7	37.9	58.1	55.0	56.0	7.8	7.2	5.5	22.9	25.5	24.7	60.9	57.5	60.3	14.4	15.7	14.1
Louisiana	35.4	36.8	36.2	57.8	56.8	59.0	5.8	5.8	4.2	25.9	26.9	26.7	57.5	55.8	56.9	15.3	16.3	15.7
Oklahoma	35.4	37.0	31.5	55.5	54.8	62.3	7.5	6.9	5.2	21.8	24.3	22.7	64.0	60.9	66.7	12.4	13.0	9.5
Texas	34.7	38.6	39.0	57.0	53.7	55.7	6.6	6.0	4.4	25.1	27.9	27.5	57.8	54.1	55.9	14.5	15.8	15.3
MOUNTAIN:																		
Montana	49.8	63.4	78.5	43.1	28.9	19.3	4.5	5.6	1.2	26.0	27.0	35.3	57.4	49.3	47.9	13.1	20.8	14.4
Idaho	51.1	61.8	(1)	40.6	34.7	(1)	4.9	3.5	(1)	29.2	(1)	(1)	54.1	(1)	(1)	14.4	(1)	(1)
Wyoming	70.2	65.1	78.5	25.9	27.6	16.8	2.1	5.9	3.6	27.1	43.6	35.9	54.6	49.6	47.1	13.6	4.7	13.6
Colorado	36.2	42.2	56.2	54.8	47.4	38.5	6.7	6.5	3.8	21.2	24.8	31.7	57.2	53.4	50.0	18.7	18.7	16.1
New Mexico	39.4	57.9	63.9	49.7	32.9	32.5	8.5	4.4	2.9	20.6	22.0	33.9	58.7	58.8	52.7	17.3	17.1	12.1
Arizona	37.8	73.0	85.0	52.5	20.8	12.6	6.5	4.6	1.5	22.8	22.4	25.2	54.8	60.2	60.0	19.2	15.1	11.9
Utah	43.4	70.7	66.3	44.4	23.1	29.5	5.6	3.7	1.9	22.2	22.2	28.0	60.5	58.2	55.3	11.5	15.0	11.4
Nevada	44.5	(1)	73.8	44.5	(1)	19.3	8.8	(1)	5.5	23.9	(1)	(1)	45.5	(1)	(1)	24.4	(1)	(1)
PACIFIC:																		
Washington	54.5	64.9	65.3	38.8	28.9	28.5	3.8	4.5	4.9	22.9	26.2	27.3	59.4	57.9	59.3	12.7	14.2	11.6
Oregon	52.1	58.4	66.9	40.9	33.9	29.0	5.2	5.3	2.8	20.2	40.0	23.9	59.2	41.2	57.1	18.0	16.5	16.6
California	43.3	45.7	53.5	48.9	45.3	40.7	5.9	6.3	4.7	23.7	26.4	26.1	55.8	52.3	55.5	18.1	19.3	17.1

¹ Per cent not shown where base is less than 100.

MARITAL CONDITION BY AGE PERIODS OF URBAN AND RURAL NEGRO POPULATION: 1910.

Table 19

NEGRO POPULATION: 1910.

AGE PERIOD AND CLASS OF POPULATION.	Total.		Single.		Married, widowed, or divorced.								Marital condition unknown.	
					Total.		Married.		Widowed.		Divorced.			
	Male.	Female.	Male.	Female.	Male.	Female.	Male.	Female.	Male.	Female.	Male.	Female.	Male.	Female.
NUMBER.														
15 years and over	3,059,312	3,103,344	1,083,472	823,996	1,959,344	2,269,066	1,749,228	1,775,949	189,970	459,831	20,146	33,286	16,496	10,282
Urban	947,605	1,058,325	350,598	292,992	590,757	761,658	519,740	544,179	63,075	202,182	7,942	15,297	6,250	3,675
Rural	2,111,707	2,045,019	732,874	531,004	1,368,587	1,507,408	1,229,488	1,231,770	126,895	257,649	12,204	17,989	10,246	6,607
15 to 19 years:														
Urban	111,172	142,255	108,150	119,824	2,164	21,566	2,056	19,869	86	1,303	22	394	858	865
Rural	396,773	410,216	384,003	328,691	9,420	78,655	9,008	74,218	330	3,626	82	811	3,350	2,870
20 to 24 years														
Urban	142,067	182,805	93,923	78,189	47,131	103,980	44,847	92,407	1,727	9,156	557	2,417	1,013	636
Rural	340,090	365,833	194,071	113,207	143,948	251,445	137,263	231,366	5,433	16,620	1,252	3,459	2,071	1,181
25 to 34 years:														
Urban	273,678	304,303	90,244	61,019	182,065	242,705	170,098	201,987	9,372	34,636	2,595	6,082	1,369	579
Rural	480,290	491,045	98,952	54,663	379,753	435,643	357,051	390,560	18,889	38,717	3,813	6,366	1,585	739
35 to 44 years:														
Urban	203,931	203,462	36,765	20,414	166,444	182,746	149,729	132,356	14,222	46,362	2,493	4,028	722	302
Rural	346,199	335,270	30,438	17,691	315,059	317,210	290,172	268,713	21,922	44,477	2,965	4,020	702	369
45 to 64 years:														
Urban	174,362	176,897	17,707	10,647	156,222	165,907	128,504	86,310	25,737	77,480	1,981	2,117	433	343
Rural	421,192	335,652	18,954	11,836	401,553	323,316	349,208	229,513	49,072	90,966	3,273	2,837	685	500
65 years and over:														
Urban	34,973	42,462	2,046	1,790	32,796	40,501	21,174	8,872	11,392	31,460	230	169	131	171
Rural	117,509	99,180	4,239	3,453	112,764	95,324	81,496	33,532	30,499	61,396	769	396	506	403
Age unknown:														
Urban	7,422	6,141	1,763	1,109	3,935	4,253	3,332	2,378	539	1,785	64	90	1,724	779
Rural	9,654	7,823	2,217	1,463	6,090	5,815	5,290	3,868	750	1,847	50	100	1,347	545
PERCENTAGE DISTRIBUTION BY MARITAL CLASS.														
15 years and over	100.0	100.0	35.4	26.6	64.0	73.1	57.2	57.2	6.2	14.8	0.7	1.1	0.5	0.3
Urban	100.0	100.0	37.0	27.7	62.3	72.0	54.8	51.4	6.7	19.1	0.8	1.4	0.7	0.3
Rural	100.0	100.0	34.7	26.0	64.8	73.7	58.2	60.2	6.0	12.6	0.6	0.9	0.5	0.3
15 to 19 years:														
Urban	100.0	100.0	97.3	84.2	1.9	15.2	1.8	14.0	0.1	0.9	(1)	0.3	0.7	0.6
Rural	100.0	100.0	96.8	80.1	2.4	19.2	2.3	18.1	0.1	0.9	(1)	0.2	0.8	0.7
20 to 24 years:														
Urban	100.0	100.0	66.1	42.8	33.2	56.9	31.6	50.5	1.2	5.0	0.4	1.3	0.7	0.3
Rural	100.0	100.0	57.1	30.9	42.3	68.7	40.4	63.2	1.6	4.5	0.4	0.9	0.6	0.3
25 to 34 years:														
Urban	100.0	100.0	33.0	20.1	66.5	79.8	62.2	66.4	3.4	11.4	0.9	2.0	0.5	0.2
Rural	100.0	100.0	20.6	11.1	79.1	88.7	74.3	79.5	3.9	7.9	0.8	1.3	0.3	0.2
35 to 44 years:														
Urban	100.0	100.0	18.0	10.0	81.6	89.8	73.4	65.1	7.0	22.8	1.2	2.0	0.4	0.1
Rural	100.0	100.0	8.8	5.3	91.0	94.6	83.8	80.1	6.3	13.3	0.9	1.2	0.2	0.1
45 to 64 years:														
Urban	100.0	100.0	10.2	6.0	89.6	93.8	73.7	48.8	14.8	43.8	1.1	1.2	0.2	0.2
Rural	100.0	100.0	4.5	3.5	95.3	96.3	82.9	68.4	11.7	27.1	0.8	0.8	0.2	0.1
65 years and over:														
Urban	100.0	100.0	5.9	4.2	93.8	95.4	60.5	20.9	32.6	74.1	0.7	0.4	0.4	0.4
Rural	100.0	100.0	3.6	3.5	96.0	96.1	69.4	33.8	26.0	61.9	0.7	0.4	0.4	0.4
Age unknown:														
Urban	100.0	100.0	23.8	18.1	53.0	69.3	44.9	38.7	7.3	29.1	0.9	1.5	23.2	12.7
Rural	100.0	100.0	23.0	18.7	63.1	74.3	54.8	49.4	7.8	23.6	0.5	1.3	14.0	7.0

[1] Less than one-tenth of 1 per cent.

The percentage single was somewhat higher, and the percentage married, widowed, or divorced somewhat lower in the urban than in the rural Negro population 15 years of age and over, both male and female.

In the age groups 15 to 19 years, 20 to 24 years, and 25 to 34 years, the percentage married was lower for males than for females in both the urban and the rural population, and in the older age groups higher for males than for females.

In the urban male Negro population, the percentage married increases from 1.8 in the age group 15 to 19 years to a maximum of 73.7 in the age group 45 to 64 years, and decreases to 60.5 in the population 65 years and over. The maximum percentage married is reached somewhat earlier, and is somewhat higher in the rural population, in which the percentage increases from 2.3 in the age 15 to 19 to 83.8 in the age 35 to 44, and decreases to 69.4 in the age 65

and over. Among females in urban communities the percentage married increases from 14 in the age 15 to 19, to a maximum of 66.4 in the age 25 to 34, and decreases to 20.9 in the age 65 and over; and in rural communities it increases from 18.1 in the age group 15 to 19 years to 80.1 in the age 35 to 44, and decreases to 33.8 in the population 65 and over.

In each age period the differences of marital condition as between males and females are very considerable in both the urban and the rural population. Of the urban population 65 years of age and over, for example, 60.5 per cent of the males, and 20.9 per cent of the females were married; and 32.6 per cent of the males, and 74.1 per cent of the females were widowed. In the rural population of this age the percentage married was 69.4 for males and 33.8 for females; and the percentage widowed, 26 for males and 61.9 for females.

Table 20	MALES TO 1,000 FEMALES IN THE NEGRO POPULATION: 1910.						
AGE PERIOD AND CLASS OF COMMUNITY.	Total.	Single.	Married, widowed, or divorced.				Marital condition unknown.
			Total.	Married.	Widowed.	Divorced.	
15 years of age and over—							
Urban communities.	895	1,197	776	955	312	519	1,701
Rural communities.	1,033	1,380	908	998	493	678	1,551
15 to 19 years:							
Urban communities.....	781	903	100	103	66	56	992
Rural communities.....	967	1,168	120	121	91	101	1,167
20 to 24 years:							
Urban communities.....	777	1,201	453	485	189	230	1,593
Rural communities.....	930	1,714	572	593	327	362	1,754
25 to 34 years:							
Urban communities.....	899	1,479	750	842	271	427	2,364
Rural communities.....	978	1,810	872	914	488	599	2,145
35 to 44 years:							
Urban communities.....	1,002	1,801	911	1,131	307	619	2,391
Rural communities.....	1,033	1,721	993	1,080	493	738	1,902
45 to 64 years:							
Urban communities.....	986	1,663	942	1,489	332	936	1,262
Rural communities.....	1,255	1,601	1,242	1,522	539	1,154	1,370
65 years and over:							
Urban communities.....	824	1,143	810	2,387	362	1,361	766
Rural communities.....	1,185	1,228	1,183	2,430	497	1,942	1,256
Age unknown:							
Urban communities.....	1,209	1,590	925	1,401	302	(¹)	2,213
Rural communities.....	1,234	1,515	1,047	1,368	406	500	2,472

¹ Ratio not shown, the number of females, being less than 100.

The differences in marital condition by age are apparent in the sex ratios shown in Table 20. In the single population the number of males per 1,000 females in urban communities increases from 903 in the age 15 to 19 years, to 1,801 in the age 35 to 44 years, and decreases to 1,143 in the age 65 years and over; in rural communities, it increases from 1,168 in the age 15 to 19, to 1,810 in the age 25 to 34, and decreases to 1,228 in the age 65 and over. In the married population of urban communities the number of males per 1,000 females increases from 103 in the age 15 to 19 to 2,387 in the age 65 and over and in the married population of rural communities from 121 to 2,430. In the widowed population of urban communities, the proportion of males increases from 66 males per 1,000 females in the age 15 to 19, to 362 per 1,000 in the age 65 and over, and in the widowed population of rural communities from 91 per 1,000 in the age 15 to 19 to 539 per 1,000 in the age 45 to 64, decreasing to 497 per 1,000 in the population 65 years of age and over. In the class of divorced persons, the increase in the number of males per 1,000 females from the oldest to the youngest age period is in urban communities from 56 to 1,361, and in rural communities from 101 to 1,942.

The large excess of females in the married population 15 to 19, and of males in the married population 65 years of age and over, is of course accounted for by the fact already noted that husbands are generally older than their wives.

In Table 21 the percentage in each marital class is shown, by age periods, for the urban and rural Negro and white population, and for native and foreign-born whites.

At all ages in the urban and rural population, male and female, the proportion single is lower among Negroes than among native whites. In the urban and the rural female population, and in the urban male population, the proportion married is higher for Negroes than for native whites in the younger ages, and higher for native whites than for Negroes in the older ages, the proportion married in the rural male population being higher for Negroes at all ages than for native whites. At all ages, in the urban and rural population, male and female, the proportion widowed is higher for Negroes than for native whites.

The tendency of Negroes to marry at younger ages than whites, which has been noted in connection with preceding tables, is clearly in evidence in the statistics for urban and rural communities. In the urban population 31.6 per cent of Negro males aged 20 to 24 years, as compared with 19.8 per cent of native white males of this age, were married, the corresponding percentages for rural communities being 40.4 for Negroes and 26.3 for native whites. Among females 20 to 24 years of age in urban communities, the percentage married was 50.5 for Negroes and 38.7 for native whites; the corresponding percentages in the rural communities being 63.2 and 55.6.

The percentage married, widowed, or divorced in urban and rural communities is given in Table 22 by combined age periods for the Negro population, and in detail of nativity and parentage for the white population.

The differentiation of native whites by parentage, made in Table 22, develops the fact that the proportion married, widowed, or divorced is higher among native whites of native parentage—male and female, at each age shown, in urban and in rural communities—than it is among natives of foreign or mixed parentage, and that the percentage among native whites of native parentage approaches, more nearly than that among native whites of foreign or mixed parentage, to the proportion in the Negro population. In the urban population 15 to 24 years of age, for example, among males the percentage married, widowed, or divorced in 1910 was 7.3 for native whites of foreign or mixed parentage, 12.4 for native whites of native parentage, and 19.5 for Negroes; among females the percentage was 18.1 for native whites of foreign or mixed parentage, 26.9 for native whites of native parentage, and 38.6 for Negroes. In the rural population the corresponding percentages were for males 7, 14.3, and 20.8, and for females, 23.5, 35.6, and 42.5.

PERCENTAGE SINGLE, MARRIED, WIDOWED, AND DIVORCED, BY AGE PERIODS, IN THE NEGRO POPULATION AND IN CLASSES OF THE WHITE POPULATION, IN URBAN AND RURAL COMMUNITIES: 1910.

Table 21

POPULATION 15 YEARS OF AGE AND OVER.

CLASS OF POPULATION.	Male.							Female.						
	Total.	15 to 19 years.	20 to 24 years.	25 to 34 years.	35 to 44 years.	45 to 64 years.	65 years and over.	Total.	15 to 19 years.	20 to 24 years.	25 to 34 years.	35 to 44 years.	45 to 64 years.	65 years and over.
PERCENTAGE SINGLE.														
URBAN.														
Negro	37.0	97.3	66.1	33.0	18.0	10.2	5.9	27.7	84.2	42.8	20.1	10.0	6.0	4.2
White	40.1	98.8	79.3	38.7	18.2	10.6	6.2	33.2	92.1	57.0	26.6	14.9	10.1	7.3
Native	44.4	98.8	79.4	39.5	19.7	11.4	6.2	38.1	92.8	59.9	29.3	17.4	12.0	8.8
Foreign-born	31.7	98.6	79.1	37.4	15.7	9.3	6.2	20.9	87.9	47.7	19.9	9.6	6.6	5.3
RURAL.														
Negro	34.7	96.8	57.1	20.6	8.8	4.5	3.6	26.0	80.1	30.9	11.1	5.3	3.5	3.5
White	37.8	98.1	73.9	32.5	15.6	10.0	6.4	26.7	85.8	42.3	15.7	8.2	6.4	5.8
Native	38.9	98.1	72.7	30.3	14.5	9.2	5.8	28.7	86.0	43.0	16.2	8.6	6.9	6.6
Foreign-born	32.0	98.3	83.4	44.6	21.0	13.4	8.3	10.0	77.6	30.2	10.6	5.2	3.6	3.0
PERCENTAGE MARRIED.														
URBAN.														
Negro	54.8	1.8	31.6	62.2	73.4	73.7	60.5	51.4	14.0	50.5	66.4	65.1	48.8	20.9
White	54.8	0.7	19.9	59.5	78.0	80.3	64.4	54.9	7.3	41.7	69.8	76.2	65.0	30.0
Native	50.8	0.7	19.8	58.5	76.0	79.2	66.2	51.2	6.6	38.7	66.8	73.3	63.8	29.9
Foreign-born	62.7	0.8	20.2	61.3	81.2	81.9	62.1	63.9	11.5	51.4	77.4	82.2	67.1	30.2
RURAL.														
Negro	58.2	2.3	40.4	74.3	83.8	82.9	69.4	60.2	18.1	63.2	79.5	80.1	68.4	33.8
White	56.7	1.3	25.1	65.6	80.7	81.2	66.3	63.7	13.5	56.3	81.7	86.4	77.0	40.3
Native	56.0	1.3	26.3	67.7	81.7	81.9	67.5	62.5	13.3	55.6	81.1	85.9	76.5	39.7
Foreign-born	60.7	0.9	15.7	54.0	76.0	78.2	62.9	74.6	21.6	68.8	87.5	90.1	79.7	42.7
PERCENTAGE WIDOWED.														
URBAN.														
Negro	6.7	0.1	1.2	3.4	7.0	14.8	32.6	19.1	0.9	5.0	11.4	22.8	43.8	74.1
White	4.1	(1)	0.2	1.0	2.9	8.2	28.7	11.1	0.1	0.7	2.6	7.8	24.0	62.2
Native	3.7	(1)	0.2	1.2	3.1	8.2	26.7	9.7	0.1	0.7	2.8	8.0	23.0	60.7
Foreign-born	5.0	(1)	0.1	0.8	2.5	8.2	31.1	14.6	0.1	0.5	2.2	7.5	25.7	64.1
RURAL.														
Negro	6.0	0.1	1.6	3.9	6.3	11.7	26.0	12.6	0.9	4.5	7.9	13.3	27.1	61.9
White	4.6	(1)	0.4	1.3	2.9	7.8	26.1	8.9	0.2	0.8	2.0	4.8	15.9	53.2
Native	4.3	(1)	0.4	1.4	3.0	7.9	25.5	8.2	0.2	0.9	2.0	4.8	15.9	53.1
Foreign-born	6.4	(1)	0.2	0.8	2.3	7.5	27.9	14.9	0.2	0.6	1.6	4.3	16.1	53.8
PERCENTAGE DIVORCED.														
URBAN.														
Negro	0.8	(1)	0.4	0.9	1.2	1.1	0.7	1.4	0.3	1.3	2.0	2.0	1.2	0.4
White	0.5	(1)	0.1	0.4	0.7	0.8	0.6	0.7	0.1	0.4	0.8	1.0	0.8	0.3
Native	0.6	(1)	0.1	0.6	1.0	1.0	0.7	0.8	0.1	0.5	1.0	1.3	1.0	0.4
Foreign-born	0.3	(1)	(1)	0.2	0.4	0.5	0.4	0.4	(1)	0.1	0.4	0.5	0.5	0.3
RURAL.														
Negro	0.6	(1)	0.4	0.8	0.9	0.8	0.7	0.9	0.2	0.9	1.3	1.2	0.8	0.4
White	0.4	(1)	0.1	0.4	0.6	0.8	0.7	0.4	0.1	0.3	0.5	0.6	0.6	0.4
Native	0.5	(1)	0.1	0.4	0.6	0.8	0.7	0.4	0.1	0.3	0.5	0.6	0.6	0.4
Foreign-born	0.4	(1)	(1)	0.1	0.4	0.7	0.7	0.1	0.1	0.3	0.4	0.5		0.3
PERCENTAGE MARRIED, WIDOWED, OR DIVORCED.														
URBAN.														
Negro	62.3	1.9	33.2	66.5	81.6	89.6	93.8	72.0	15.2	56.9	79.8	89.8	93.8	95.4
White	59.4	0.7	20.2	61.0	81.6	89.3	93.6	66.6	7.4	42.8	73.3	85.0	89.8	92.5
Native	55.0	0.7	20.1	60.3	80.1	88.4	93.6	61.6	6.7	39.9	70.5	82.6	87.9	91.0
Foreign-born	67.9	0.8	20.3	62.2	84.0	90.6	93.6	78.9	11.6	52.1	80.0	90.3	93.3	94.5
RURAL.														
Negro	64.8	2.4	42.3	79.1	91.0	95.3	96.0	73.7	19.2	68.7	88.7	94.6	96.3	96.1
White	61.8	1.3	25.6	67.2	84.2	89.8	93.1	73.1	13.8	57.5	84.2	91.7	93.5	93.9
Native	60.8	1.3	26.8	69.5	85.4	90.6	93.7	71.1	13.6	56.8	83.7	91.3	93.0	93.1
Foreign-born	67.4	0.9	15.9	54.9	78.7	86.4	91.4	89.8	21.9	69.6	89.3	94.8	96.3	96.8

[1] Less than one-tenth of 1 per cent.

Table 22	PERCENTAGE MARRIED, WIDOWED, OR DIVORCED IN THE POPULATION 15 YEARS OF AGE AND OVER: 1910.							
CLASS OF POPULATION.	Total.		15 to 24 years of age.		25 to 44 years of age.		45 years and over.	
	Male.	Female.	Male.	Female.	Male.	Female.	Male.	Female.
URBAN.								
Negro............................	62.3	72.0	19.5	38.6	73.0	83.8	90.3	94.1
White............................	59.4	66.6	11.2	26.0	69.9	78.4	90.1	90.4
Native.........................	55.0	61.6	10.2	23.1	68.8	75.6	89.4	88.5
Native parentage..........	59.0	65.7	12.4	26.9	71.4	78.6	90.8	89.7
Foreign or mixed parentage.....................	48.3	55.2	7.3	18.1	64.3	71.2	86.1	85.9
Foreign born................	67.9	78.9	14.5	38.0	71.9	84.8	91.2	93.6
RURAL.								
Negro............................	64.8	73.7	20.8	42.5	84.1	91.1	95.5	96.3
White............................	61.8	73.1	12.8	34.2	74.8	87.5	90.6	93.6
Native.........................	60.8	71.1	12.9	33.4	76.5	86.9	91.3	93.0
Native parentage..........	62.8	72.6	14.3	35.6	78.7	87.9	92.1	93.2
Foreign or mixed parentage.....................	51.5	64.0	7.0	23.5	67.1	82.6	86.5	91.8
Foreign born................	67.4	89.8	11.5	53.3	66.2	92.1	87.9	96.4

Tables 23, 24, 25, and 26 are summary tables presenting statistics of marital condition in the urban and rural population of the North, the South, and the West. In the first two of these tables (23 and 24) the aggregate urban population in these sections and in the country as a whole is shown by classes of cities, distinguishing urban communities of 2,500 to 25,000 population, 25,000 to 100,000, and 100,000 and over. Table 25 without distinguishing classes of cities, introduces data for the white urban and rural population, classified by nativity, in comparison with data for Negroes, and Table 26 distinguishes age groups in the Negro urban and rural population of the several geographic sections.

Table 31 (p. 269) gives statistics for each of the nine geographic divisions, showing marital condition of the urban and rural Negro population, classified by broad age periods, and Table 32 (p. 271) gives statistics for states, showing marital condition of the urban and rural Negro population without distinction of age.

In the rural Negro population among males and females the percentage single is lowest in the South and highest in the West. The percentage married in the rural Negro population, male and female, is highest in the South. Among males this percentage is lowest in the West, the percentage in the West being 36.1, as compared with 58.7 in the South and 49.6 in the North. Among females the differences in the percentage married, from section to section, are inconsiderable, the percentage in the South being 60.3, in the North 58.8, and in the West 60.2.

In the urban population the percentage married among males is highest in the South and among females it is lowest in the South. The differences in the percentage widowed, from section to section, and in the percentage divorced are not marked, although the percentage divorced among males and females, in urban as in rural communities, is somewhat higher in the West than it is in either the South or the North.

In the South, among both males and females, the percentage single is highest in the population living in cities of 100,000 and over, and lowest in the rural population. In the North and West the percentage single in cities of this class, among both males and females, is lower than it is in the rural population. In the South the percentage married, among both males and females, is lowest in the cities of 100,000 or more population, and highest in the rural population. In the North and West, the percentage married, among males, is lowest in the rural population and highest in cities of 100,000 or more; and among females is lowest for the class of small cities of 2,500 to 25,000 and highest in the rural population.

As regards the statistics for classes of cities shown in Tables 23 and 24, it is probably true that the marital condition of the population is affected much more by geographic location of the city, than it is by the size of the urban community.

The number of males per 1,000 females in the Negro population, classified by marital condition, is shown, by geographic sections, in Table 24 for the urban and rural population and for classes of cities.

In the single population there was in 1910 an excess of males over females in the urban and in the rural population, and in each class of cities in each of three sections, the excess being much more marked in the rural population in all sections of the country than it was in the urban aggregate or in any of the classes of cities distinguished. In the class of married persons there was an excess of females in the rural population of the South and an excess of males in the rural population of the North and West. In the urban population and in each class of cities there was an excess of females in this marital class in the South and in the North, and an excess of males in the West, except for cities of 25,000 to 100,000 in the West. In the widowed population the excess of females was very marked in each rural and urban class of population in each section, but was very much greater in each class of the urban population than it was in the rural in each of the three sections. Among divorced persons in urban and rural communities in each section, females largely outnumbered males, except in the rural population of the North, in which the number of males per 1,000 females was 1,553.

MARITAL CONDITION OF THE NEGRO POPULATION 15 YEARS OF AGE AND OVER, IN URBAN AND RURAL COMMUNITIES AND IN CLASSES OF CITIES: 1910.

Table 23

NEGRO POPULATION 15 YEARS OF AGE AND OVER: 1910.

SECTION AND CLASS OF COMMUNITY.	Total.		Single.		Married, widowed, or divorced.								Marital condition unknown.	
					Total.		Married.		Widowed.		Divorced.			
	Male.	Female.	Male.	Female.	Male.	Female.	Male.	Female.	Male.	Female.	Male.	Female.	Male.	Female.
NUMBER.														
UNITED STATES.														
Rural communities	2,111,707	2,045,019	732,874	531,004	1,368,587	1,507,408	1,229,488	1,231,770	126,895	257,649	12,204	17,989	10,246	6,607
Urban communities	947,605	1,058,325	350,598	292,992	590,757	761,658	519,740	544,179	63,075	202,182	7,942	15,297	6,250	3,675
Cities of 2,500 to 25,000	351,825	396,547	126,922	110,146	221,404	284,740	194,605	203,764	23,672	74,289	3,127	6,687	3,499	1,661
Cities of 25,000 to 100,000	214,737	239,683	78,619	63,924	134,900	174,880	118,150	124,800	14,899	46,413	1,851	3,667	1,218	879
Cities of 100,000 and over	381,043	422,095	145,057	118,922	234,453	302,038	206,985	215,615	24,504	81,480	2,964	4,943	1,533	1,135
THE SOUTH.														
Rural communities	2,015,851	1,970,640	692,530	510,627	1,313,831	1,453,662	1,182,780	1,187,985	119,789	248,298	11,262	17,379	9,490	6,351
Urban communities	619,598	728,470	223,431	202,456	391,601	523,336	344,289	366,372	42,537	145,871	4,775	11,093	4,566	2,678
Cities of 2,500 to 25,000	271,402	317,617	95,469	87,702	172,958	228,549	152,527	161,633	18,240	61,390	2,191	5,526	2,975	1,366
Cities of 25,000 to 100,000	157,179	183,467	56,722	48,774	99,562	133,992	87,239	93,654	11,125	37,436	1,198	2,902	895	701
Cities of 100,000 and over	191,017	227,386	71,240	65,980	119,081	160,795	104,523	111,085	13,172	47,045	1,386	2,665	696	611
THE NORTH.														
Rural communities	89,891	71,583	37,004	19,731	52,168	51,602	44,557	42,102	6,760	8,952	851	548	719	250
Urban communities	310,819	314,555	119,980	87,019	189,303	226,626	166,806	169,245	19,604	53,584	2,893	3,797	1,536	910
Cities of 2,500 to 25,000	75,678	74,726	29,411	21,391	45,772	53,050	39,783	39,879	5,146	12,154	843	1,017	495	285
Cities of 25,000 to 100,000	54,652	53,575	20,746	14,537	33,652	38,887	29,446	29,662	3,601	8,517	605	708	254	151
Cities of 100,000 and over	180,489	186,254	69,823	51,091	109,879	134,689	97,577	99,704	10,857	32,913	1,445	2,072	787	474
THE WEST.														
Rural communities	5,965	2,796	3,340	646	2,588	2,144	2,151	1,683	346	399	91	62	37	6
Urban communities	17,188	15,300	7,187	3,517	9,853	11,696	8,645	8,562	934	2,727	274	407	148	87
Cities of 2,500 to 25,000	4,745	4,204	2,042	1,053	2,674	3,141	2,295	2,252	286	745	93	144	29	10
Cities of 25,000 to 100,000	2,906	2,641	1,151	613	1,686	2,001	1,465	1,484	173	460	48	57	69	27
Cities of 100,000 and over	9,537	8,455	3,994	1,851	5,493	6,554	4,885	4,826	475	1,522	133	206	50	50
PERCENTAGE DISTRIBUTION BY MARITAL CLASS.														
UNITED STATES.														
Rural communities	100.0	100.0	34.7	26.0	64.8	73.7	58.2	60.2	6.0	12.6	0.6	0.9	0.5	0.3
Urban communities	100.0	100.0	37.0	27.7	62.3	72.0	54.8	51.4	6.7	19.1	0.8	1.4	0.7	0.3
Cities of 2,500 to 25,000	100.0	100.0	36.1	27.8	62.9	71.8	55.3	51.4	6.7	18.7	0.9	1.7	1.0	0.4
Cities of 25,000 to 100,000	100.0	100.0	36.6	26.7	62.8	73.0	55.0	52.1	6.9	19.4	0.9	1.5	0.6	0.4
Cities of 100,000 and over	100.0	100.0	38.1	28.2	61.5	71.6	54.3	51.1	6.4	19.3	0.8	1.2	0.4	0.3
THE SOUTH.														
Rural communities	100.0	100.0	34.4	25.9	65.2	73.8	58.7	60.3	5.9	12.6	0.6	0.9	0.5	0.3
Urban communities	100.0	100.0	36.1	27.8	63.2	71.8	55.6	50.3	6.9	20.0	0.8	1.5	0.7	0.4
Cities of 2,500 to 25,000	100.0	100.0	35.2	27.6	63.7	72.0	56.2	50.9	6.7	19.3	0.8	1.7	1.1	0.4
Cities of 25,000 to 100,000	100.0	100.0	36.1	26.6	63.3	73.0	55.5	51.0	7.1	20.4	0.8	1.6	0.6	0.4
Cities of 100,000 and over	100.0	100.0	37.3	29.0	62.3	70.7	54.7	48.9	6.9	20.7	0.7	1.2	0.4	0.3
THE NORTH.														
Rural communities	100.0	100.0	41.2	27.6	58.0	72.1	49.6	58.8	7.5	12.5	0.9	0.8	0.8	0.3
Urban communities	100.0	100.0	38.6	27.7	60.9	72.0	53.7	53.8	6.3	17.0	0.9	1.2	0.5	0.3
Cities of 2,500 to 25,000	100.0	100.0	38.9	28.6	60.5	71.0	52.6	53.4	6.8	16.3	1.1	1.4	0.7	0.4
Cities of 25,000 to 100,000	100.0	100.0	38.0	27.1	61.6	72.6	53.9	55.4	6.6	15.9	1.1	1.3	0.5	0.3
Cities of 100,000 and over	100.0	100.0	38.7	27.4	60.9	72.3	54.1	53.5	6.0	17.7	0.8	1.1	0.4	0.3
THE WEST.														
Rural communities	100.0	100.0	56.0	23.1	43.4	76.7	36.1	60.2	5.8	14.3	1.5	2.2	0.6	0.2
Urban communities	100.0	100.0	41.8	23.0	57.3	76.4	50.3	56.0	5.4	17.8	1.6	2.7	0.9	0.6
Cities of 2,500 to 25,000	100.0	100.0	43.0	25.0	56.4	74.7	48.4	53.6	6.0	17.7	2.0	3.4	0.6	0.2
Cities of 25,000 to 100,000	100.0	100.0	39.6	23.2	58.0	75.8	50.4	56.2	6.0	17.4	1.7	2.2	2.4	1.0
Cities of 100,000 and over	100.0	100.0	41.9	21.9	57.6	77.5	51.2	57.1	5.0	18.0	1.4	2.4	0.5	0.6

Table 24

MALES TO 1,000 FEMALES IN THE NEGRO POPULATION 15 YEARS OF AGE AND OVER: 1910.

SECTION AND CLASS OF COMMUNITY.	Total.	Single.	Married, widowed, or divorced.				Marital condition unknown.
			Total.	Married.	Widowed.	Divorced.	
UNITED STATES.							
Rural communities..........	1,033	1,380	908	998	493	678	1,551
Urban communities..........	895	1,197	776	955	312	519	1,701
Cities of 2,500 to 25,000......	887	1,152	778	955	319	468	2,107
Cities of 25,000 to 100,000.....	896	1,230	771	947	321	505	1,386
Cities of 100,000 and over.....	903	1,220	776	960	301	600	1,351
THE SOUTH.							
Rural communities..........	1,023	1,356	904	996	482	648	1,494
Urban communities..........	851	1,104	748	940	292	430	1,705
Cities of 2,500 to 25,000......	854	1,089	757	944	297	396	2,178
Cities of 25,000 to 100,000.....	857	1,163	743	932	297	413	1,277
Cities of 100,000 and over.....	840	1,080	741	941	280	521	1,139
THE NORTH.							
Rural communities..........	1,256	1,875	1,011	1,059	755	1,553	2,876
Urban communities..........	988	1,379	835	986	366	762	1.688
Cities of 2,500 to 25,000......	1,013	1,375	863	998	423	829	1,737
Cities of 25,000 to 100,000.....	1,020	1,427	865	993	423	855	1,682
Cities of 100,000 and over.....	969	1,367	816	979	330	697	1,660
THE WEST.							
Rural communities..........	2,133	5,170	1,207	1,278	867	(1)	(1)
Urban communities..........	1,123	2,044	842	1,010	343	673	(1)
Cities of 2,500 to 25,000......	1,129	1,939	851	1,019	384	646	(1)
Cities of 25,000 to 100,000.....	1,100	1,878	843	987	376	(1)	(1)
Cities of 100,000 and over.....	1,128	2,158	838	1,012	312	646	(1)

[1] Ratio not shown, the number of females being less than 100.

In each section of the country, as may be seen by reference to Table 25, the percentage single in the urban and in the rural population of both sexes was lower among Negroes than among native whites in 1910, except in the rural male population of the North and West. In each section the percentage married in the urban population of both sexes was higher for Negroes than for native whites, except that the proportion married among native white females in the South exceeded that among Negro females; in the rural population of both sexes in each section the percentage married was higher among native whites than among Negroes. In each section of the country in the urban and in the rural population of both sexes the percentage widowed was higher among Negroes than among native whites.

In the urban Negro population 15 to 24 years of age, 25 to 44 years of age, and 45 years and over the percentage single among males was lowest in the South and highest in the West. (See Table 26.) Among females in these age groups it was lowest in the West and highest in the North, although the differences in the percentages for females were not very marked. In the rural population of both sexes in these age groups the percentage single was lower in the South than it was in the North or West.

In the urban population the percentage married among males in each age group was highest in the South and lowest in the West; among females in each age group it was highest in the West and lowest in the South, except that in the age group 15 to 24 years it was slightly higher in the South than it was in the North.

In the rural population in each age group the percentage married among males was highest in the South and lowest in the West, the differences from section to section being very marked. For the Negro male population 25 to 44 years of age in rural communities, for example, the percentage married was 79.2 in the South, 62 in the North, and 40.1 in the West. The differences from section to section in the percentage married among females were much less considerable than among males, the percentages for females corresponding to those just given for males being 79.9 in the South, 77.8 in the North, and 72.4 in the West.

Table 25

POPULATION 15 YEARS OF AGE AND OVER: 1910

SECTION, CLASS OF COMMUNITY, AND RACIAL CLASS.	Percentage single.		Percentage married.		Percentage widowed.		Percentage married, widowed, or divorced.	
	Male.	Female.	Male.	Female.	Male.	Female.	Male.	Female.
UNITED STATES.								
Urban communities:								
Negro...............	37.0	27.7	54.8	51.4	6.7	19.1	62.3	72.0
White...............	40.1	33.2	54.8	54.9	4.1	11.1	59.4	66.6
Native.............	44.4	38.1	50.8	51.2	3.7	9.7	55.0	61.6
Foreign born......	31.7	20.9	62.7	63.9	5.0	14.6	67.9	78.9
Rural communities:								
Negro...............	34.7	26.0	58.2	60.2	6.0	12.6	64.8	73.7
White...............	37.8	26.7	56.7	63.7	4.6	8.9	61.8	73.1
Native.............	38.9	28.7	56.0	62.5	4.3	8.2	60.8	71.1
Foreign born......	32.0	10.0	60.7	74.6	6.4	14.9	67.4	89.8
THE SOUTH.								
Urban communities:								
Negro...............	36.1	27.8	55.6	50.3	6.9	20.0	63.2	71.8
White...............	39.6	31.8	55.1	54.6	4.3	12.7	59.8	68.0
Native.............	41.0	33.2	54.0	54.1	3.9	11.7	58.4	66.5
Foreign born......	29.2	17.4	63.1	60.1	6.9	21.8	70.4	82.3
Rural communities:								
Negro...............	34.4	25.9	58.7	60.3	5.9	12.6	65.2	73.8
White...............	35.8	26.7	59.3	64.0	4.3	8.7	63.9	73.1
Native.............	36.0	27.1	59.2	63.8	4.2	8.6	63.7	72.7
Foreign born......	31.1	11.7	61.3	73.6	6.7	14.1	68.3	88.1
THE NORTH.								
Urban communities:								
Negro...............	38.6	27.7	53.7	53.8	6.3	17.0	60.9	72.0
White...............	39.7	33.7	55.4	54.6	4.1	10.8	59.9	66.1
Native.............	44.8	39.6	50.5	50.2	3.6	9.2	54.6	60.1
Foreign born......	30.9	21.3	63.7	64.1	4.9	14.2	68.8	78.6
Rural communities:								
Negro...............	41.2	27.6	49.6	58.8	7.5	12.5	58.0	72.1
White...............	37.4	27.1	56.8	63.1	4.9	9.2	62.2	72.7
Native.............	39.6	30.0	55.0	61.2	4.4	8.1	60.0	69.7
Foreign born......	28.3	9.9	64.1	74.4	6.8	15.3	71.2	90.0
THE WEST.								
Urban communities:								
Negro...............	41.8	23.0	50.3	56.0	5.4	17.8	57.3	76.4
White...............	44.5	29.3	49.3	57.4	3.9	11.5	54.3	70.4
Native.............	46.1	32.9	48.2	55.4	3.5	9.9	52.8	66.8
Foreign born......	40.8	17.7	51.9	64.3	4.9	16.7	57.6	82.1
Rural communities:								
Negro...............	56.0	23.1	36.1	60.2	5.8	14.3	43.4	76.7
White...............	47.1	23.7	47.1	67.5	4.3	7.9	52.2	76.1
Native.............	47.0	26.9	47.2	65.4	4.2	6.8	52.3	72.9
Foreign born......	47.2	9.7	46.8	76.9	4.6	12.7	52.1	90.2

In the single Negro population, urban and rural, in each age group, and in each of the three geographic sections, there was an excess of males over females, except that there was a slight excess of females in the urban population of 15 to 24 years in the South. The excess was greater in the North than it was in the South in each age group, and was most marked in the West. In the age group 25 to 44 years, for example, the number of males to 1,000 females in the urban population was 1,362 in the South, 1,845 in the North, and 3,153 in the West; in the rural population the corresponding numbers are 1,702 in the South, 2,881 in the North, and 8,916 in the West.

MARITAL CONDITION IN URBAN AND RURAL COMMUNITIES, OF NEGRO MALES AND FEMALES 15 YEARS OF AGE AND OVER CLASSIFIED BY AGE PERIODS, BY SECTIONS: 1910.

Table 26 — NEGRO POPULATION: 1910.

AGE PERIOD AND SECTION.	Number.										Percentage.						Males to 1,000 females.		
	Total.		Single.		Married.		Widowed.		Divorced.		Single.		Married.		Widowed.		Single.	Married.	Widowed.
	Male.	Female.	Male.	Female.	Male.	Female.	Male.	Female.	Male.	Female.	Male.	Female.	Male.	Female.	Male.	Female.			
URBAN COMMUNITIES.																			
15 years and over:																			
United States	947,605	1,058,325	350,598	292,992	519,740	544,179	63,075	202,182	7,942	15,297	37.0	27.7	54.8	51.4	6.7	19.1	1,197	955	312
The South	619,598	728,470	223,431	202,456	344,289	366,372	42,537	145,871	4,775	11,093	36.1	27.8	55.6	50.3	6.9	20.0	1,104	940	292
The North	310,819	314,555	119,980	87,019	166,806	169,245	19,604	53,584	2,893	3,797	38.6	27.7	53.7	53.8	6.3	17.0	1,379	986	366
The West	17,188	15,300	7,187	3,517	8,645	8,562	934	2,727	274	407	41.8	23.0	50.3	56.0	5.4	17.8	2,044	1,010	343
15 to 24 years—																			
United States	253,239	325,060	202,073	198,013	46,903	112,276	1,813	10,459	579	2,811	79.8	60.9	18.5	34.5	0.7	3.2	1,021	418	173
The South	180,588	237,458	141,987	142,473	35,194	82,838	1,470	8,772	422	2,231	78.6	60.0	19.5	34.9	0.8	3.7	997	425	168
The North	69,493	83,941	57,400	53,377	11,274	28,112	329	1,595	143	512	82.6	63.6	16.2	33.5	0.5	1.9	1,075	401	206
The West	3,158	3,661	2,686	2,163	435	1,326	14	92	14	68	85.1	59.1	13.8	36.2	0.4	2.5	1,242	328	(1)
25 to 44 years—																			
United States	477,609	507,765	127,009	81,433	319,827	334,343	23,594	80,998	5,088	10,110	26.6	16.0	67.0	65.8	4.9	16.0	1,560	957	291
The South	298,366	337,660	69,812	51,251	207,850	219,371	15,998	59,103	3,053	7,270	23.4	15.2	69.7	65.0	5.4	17.5	1,362	947	271
The North	169,546	161,889	53,527	29,018	106,518	109,335	7,251	20,767	1,852	2,575	31.6	17.9	62.8	67.5	4.3	12.8	1,845	974	349
The West	9,697	8,216	3,670	1,164	5,459	5,637	345	1,128	183	265	37.8	14.2	56.3	68.6	3.6	13.7	3,153	968	306
45 years and over—																			
United States	209,335	219,359	19,753	12,437	149,678	95,182	37,129	108,940	2,211	2,286	9.4	5.7	71.5	43.4	17.7	49.7	1,588	1,573	341
The South	135,434	148,822	10,412	7,885	98,672	62,408	24,674	76,613	1,257	1,525	7.7	5.3	72.9	41.9	18.2	51.5	1,320	1,581	322
The North	69,745	67,245	8,553	4,380	48,298	31,214	11,886	30,840	880	690	12.3	6.5	69.2	46.4	17.0	45.9	1,953	1,547	385
The West	4,156	3,292	788	172	2,708	1,560	569	1,487	74	71	19.0	5.2	65.2	47.4	13.7	45.2	4,581	1,736	383
RURAL COMMUNITIES.																			
15 years and over:																			
United States	2,111,707	2,045,019	732,874	531,004	1,229,488	1,231,770	126,895	257,649	12,204	17,989	34.7	26.0	58.2	60.2	6.0	12.6	1,380	998	493
The South	2,015,851	1,970,640	692,530	510,627	1,182,780	1,187,985	119,789	248,298	11,262	17,379	34.4	25.9	58.7	60.3	5.9	12.6	1,356	996	482
The North	89,891	71,583	37,004	19,731	44,557	42,102	6,760	8,952	851	548	41.2	27.6	49.6	58.8	7.5	12.5	1,875	1,058	755
The West	5,965	2,796	3,340	646	2,151	1,683	346	399	91	62	56.0	23.1	36.1	60.2	5.8	14.3	5,170	1,278	867
15 to 24 years—																			
United States	736,863	776,049	578,074	441,898	146,271	305,584	5,763	20,246	1,334	4,270	78.5	56.9	19.9	39.4	0.8	2.6	1,308	479	285
The South	710,575	753,698	555,057	427,187	143,355	298,373	5,660	19,984	1,298	4,185	78.1	56.7	20.2	39.6	0.8	2.7	1,299	480	283
The North	24,936	21,679	21,799	14,314	2,794	6,951	99	253	35	79	87.4	66.0	11.2	32.1	0.4	1.2	1,523	402	391
The West	1,352	672	1,218	397	122	260	4	9	1	6	90.1	59.1	9.0	38.7	0.3	1.3	3,068	469	(1)
25 to 44 years—																			
United States	826,489	826,315	129,390	72,354	647,223	659,273	40,811	83,194	6,778	10,386	15.7	8.8	78.3	79.8	4.9	10.1	1,788	982	491
The South	786,031	795,216	115,724	68,010	622,820	635,140	39,066	81,012	6,327	10,021	14.7	8.6	79.2	79.9	5.0	10.2	1,702	981	482
The North	37,360	29,689	11,963	4,153	23,161	23,112	1,638	2,027	417	323	32.0	14.0	62.0	77.8	4.4	6.8	2,881	1,002	808
The West	3,098	1,410	1,703	191	1,242	1,021	107	155	34	42	55.0	13.5	40.1	72.4	3.5	11.0	8,916	1,216	690
45 years and over—																			
United States	538,701	434,832	23,193	15,289	430,704	263,045	79,571	152,362	4,042	3,233	4.3	3.5	80.0	60.5	14.8	35.0	1,517	1,637	522
The South	510,074	414,217	19,652	14,021	411,518	250,748	74,365	145,534	3,591	3,074	3.9	3.4	80.7	60.5	14.6	35.1	1,402	1,641	511
The North	27,143	19,918	3,132	1,216	18,410	11,901	4,973	6,594	395	145	11.5	6.1	67.8	59.7	18.3	33.1	2,576	1,547	754
The West	1,484	697	409	52	776	396	233	234	56	14	27.6	7.5	52.3	56.8	15.7	33.6	(1)	1,960	996

1 Ratio not shown, the number of females being less than 100.

PRINCIPAL CITIES.

Statistics of marital condition for individual cities are given in Tables 33, 34, and 35 (pp. 273 to 282).

Table 33 gives the number in each marital class in 1910, by sex, for cities having in 1910 a total population, white and colored, of 100,000 or more, and corresponding data, so far as data are available, for these same cities in 1900 and in 1890. The data are available for the earlier years only in cases where the city reported in these years a population of 100,000 or more.

Table 34 gives for cities having in 1910 a total population of 100,000 or more, and a Negro population 15 years of age and over of 10,000 or more, statistics of marital condition of the Negro population, classified by sex and age periods, showing the number and percentage single, married, and widowed, and the number divorced by six age classes.

Table 35 gives statistics of marital condition in 1910 for the Negro population in cities having in 1910 a population of 25,000 inhabitants or more, the cities being grouped by states in which they are located. This table shows for the Negro population 15 years of age and over, classified by sex, the number and percentage single, the number and percentage married, the number widowed, and the number divorced.

Table 27, following, assembles certain percentages given in Table 34, showing the percentage married, by age classes, for 19 cities of 100,000 or more population in 1910. Of these cities, 9 are southern and 10 are northern.

Table 27	PERCENTAGE MARRIED IN THE NEGRO POPULATION 15 YEARS OF AGE AND OVER: 1910.						
CITY.	Total.	15 to 19 years.	20 to 24 years.	25 to 34 years.	35 to 44 years.	45 to 64 years.	65 years and over.
				MALE.			
SOUTHERN CITIES.							
Atlanta, Ga	58.7	3.2	41.5	69.9	80.3	76.9	62.5
Baltimore, Md	53.5	1.1	30.3	57.8	70.4	70.6	60.8
Birmingham, Ala	56.7	1.7	33.5	66.3	74.8	76.8	55.8
Louisville, Ky	49.3	1.7	31.9	52.8	64.1	65.8	57.6
Memphis, Tenn	52.9	2.8	32.3	60.7	71.1	69.1	61.3
Nashville, Tenn	55.2	4.1	37.6	64.0	74.4	75.9	61.0
New Orleans, La	56.8	2.0	35.0	67.7	75.7	72.6	57.8
Richmond, Va	52.2	1.2	27.2	60.8	75.3	73.5	59.2
Washington, D. C	55.6	1.5	29.6	63.2	75.5	73.6	59.1
NORTHERN CITIES.							
Boston, Mass	50.7	1.2	18.9	49.3	66.1	66.5	48.0
Chicago, Ill	52.0	1.8	24.5	53.4	66.0	66.3	55.0
Cincinnati, Ohio	52.0	1.4	29.4	56.4	66.1	65.0	51.5
Columbus, Ohio	49.3	1.5	25.0	51.0	64.9	67.4	54.0
Indianapolis, Ind	53.7	2.9	27.0	58.1	68.8	70.1	58.4
Kansas City, Mo	52.0	1.7	28.0	55.7	66.5	67.3	57.6
New York, N. Y	56.0	1.1	28.3	60.6	74.3	72.7	58.2
Philadelphia, Pa	57.2	1.0	29.9	61.6	71.6	70.9	57.1
Pittsburgh, Pa	53.9	1.2	22.0	58.2	69.1	69.1	56.7
St. Louis, Mo	51.4	1.7	25.3	56.1	65.7	66.4	55.8
				FEMALE.			
SOUTHERN CITIES.							
Atlanta, Ga	49.7	18.1	55.6	62.5	59.6	42.2	18.2
Baltimore, Md	48.1	8.4	42.2	61.8	63.9	49.1	20.2
Birmingham, Ala	56.3	21.1	59.9	70.0	67.2	46.9	18.1
Louisville, Ky	48.5	15.9	48.7	60.6	59.7	45.4	18.8
Memphis, Tenn	52.2	20.1	54.1	65.6	60.9	45.4	18.7
Nashville, Tenn	44.6	16.3	47.0	56.3	55.8	42.4	17.6
New Orleans, La	49.7	15.7	52.2	67.5	62.7	41.3	15.6
Richmond, Va	44.0	9.1	41.0	60.7	59.5	39.8	15.2
Washington, D. C	47.0	9.3	43.9	61.7	61.2	42.7	19.2
NORTHERN CITIES.							
Boston, Mass	48.6	7.9	43.4	60.5	59.5	42.3	15.7
Chicago, Ill	55.6	15.2	54.0	68.3	65.0	44.9	15.1
Cincinnati, Ohio	53.8	17.5	50.0	66.1	67.4	46.8	20.0
Columbus, Ohio	57.2	16.7	51.8	72.8	73.0	53.2	22.5
Indianapolis, Ind	54.3	15.1	52.2	66.3	65.7	53.4	23.5
Kansas City, Mo	54.1	18.1	52.3	64.9	64.1	50.1	21.7
New York, N. Y	50.2	10.1	44.5	62.6	60.6	42.2	15.5
Philadelphia, Pa	52.2	9.9	46.0	65.6	64.8	45.2	19.2
Pittsburgh, Pa	60.1	11.4	52.0	73.8	74.6	55.5	18.0
St. Louis, Mo	54.3	18.9	54.3	68.7	63.7	45.1	19.4

Among males the percentage married was highest in Atlanta (58.7), and lowest in Louisville (49.3) and Columbus (49.3). Among females the percentage married was highest in Pittsburgh (60.1), and lowest in Richmond (44). In only two of the 9 southern cities (Birmingham and Memphis) did the percentage married among Negro females 15 years of age and over amount to 50 per cent or more, and in only 1 of the 10 northern cities (Boston) did this percentage fall below 50. In the case of males, the percentage married fell below 50 in only two cities—one southern (Louisville) and one northern (Columbus)—there being no marked differences in the percentage for males as between the northern and the southern group of cities.

Among males 15 to 19 years of age the percentage married in the southern cities ranged from 1.1 in Baltimore to 4.1 in Nashville, and in northern cities from 1 in Philadelphia to 2.9 in Indianapolis. Among females of this age in southern cities the percentage married ranged from 8.4 in Baltimore to 21.1 in Birmingham, and in northern cities from 7.9 in Boston to 18.9 in St. Louis. In all cities, southern and northern, among males and females, the percentage married is much higher for the age 20 to 24 years than it is in the age 15 to 19, and much higher for the age 25 to 34 than it is in the age 20 to 24. Among males in each city it is higher for the age 35 to 44 than for the age 25 to 34, but among females in 15 of the 19 cities, the percentage married for the age 35 to 44 is lower than for the age 25 to 34. Among males the percentage married in the population 45 to 64 years of age does not vary markedly from the percentage in the population 35 to 44 years, although in each city the percentage among males falls in the population 65 and over. Among females there is in each city a marked decline in the percentage married in the age 45 to 64, as compared with the age 35 to 44, and a still more marked decline in the population 65 and over.

TABLE 28.—MARITAL CONDITION OF THE NEGRO POPULATION, BY AGE PERIODS AND SEX, BY DIVISIONS: 1910.

| DIVISION AND AGE PERIOD. | MALES. | | | | | | | | FEMALES. | | | | | | | |
| | Total.[1] | Single. | | Married. | | Widowed. | | Divorced. | Total.[1] | Single. | | Married. | | Widowed. | | Divorced. |
		Number.	Per cent.	Number.	Per cent.	Number.	Per cent.			Number.	Per cent.	Number.	Per cent.	Number.	Per cent.	
NEW ENGLAND.																
Total	32,783	18,172	55.4	12,894	39.3	1,454	4.4	177	33,523	16,368	48.8	12,643	37.7	4,235	12.6	236
Under 15 years of age	7,828	7,827	100.0	1	(2)	....	....	....	8,249	8,247	100.0	2	(2)	....	....	....
15 years and over	24,955	10,345	41.5	12,893	51.7	1,454	5.8	177	25,274	8,121	32.1	12,641	50.0	4,235	16.8	236
15 to 19 years	2,345	2,309	98.5	31	1.3	....	....	....	2,805	2,546	90.8	245	8.7	4	0.1	1
20 to 24 years	8,243	2,530	78.0	685	21.1	14	0.4	6	3,424	1,949	56.9	1,420	41.5	40	1.2	10
25 to 34 years	7,356	3,283	44.6	3,880	52.7	136	1.8	35	7,152	1,986	27.8	4,629	64.7	449	6.3	82
25 to 29 years	3,946	2,093	53.0	1,772	44.9	51	1.3	17	3,885	1,248	32.1	2,412	62.1	180	4.6	41
30 to 34 years	3,410	1,190	34.9	2,108	61.8	85	2.5	18	3,267	738	22.6	2,217	67.9	269	8.2	41
35 to 44 years	5,720	1,375	24.0	3,982	69.6	287	5.0	.70	5,452	911	16.7	3,547	65.1	927	17.0	65
45 to 64 years	5,108	736	14.4	3,666	71.8	646	12.6	58	5,111	576	11.3	2,529	49.5	1,933	37.8	68
45 to 54 years	3,358	492	14.7	2,445	72.8	379	11.3	41	3,314	398	12.0	1,809	54.6	1,056	31.9	48
55 to 64 years	1,750	244	13.9	1,221	69.8	267	15.3	17	1,797	178	9.9	720	40.1	877	48.8	20
65 years and over	1,101	95	8.6	631	57.3	366	33.2	8	1,255	134	10.7	250	19.9	863	68.8	5
Age unknown	82	17	(3)	18	(3)	5	(3)	....	75	19	(3)	21	(3)	19	(3)	5
MIDDLE ATLANTIC.																
Total	203,466	108,127	53.1	85,527	42.0	8,673	4.3	500	214,404	100,105	46.7	87,996	41.0	25,089	11.7	787
Under 15 years of age	46,594	46,599	100.0	4	(2)	....	....	....	49,378	49,369	100.0	7	(2)	2	(2)	....
15 years and over	156,872	61,537	39.2	85,523	54.5	8,673	5.5	500	165,026	50,736	30.7	87,989	53.3	25,087	15.2	787
15 to 19 years	14,704	14,462	98.4	143	1.0	6	(2)	....	17,948	16,021	89.3	1,780	9.9	46	0.3	11
20 to 24 years	24,539	15,619	72.5	5,675	26.3	113	0.5	20	27,179	13,810	50.8	12,707	46.8	521	1.9	72
25 to 34 years	49,563	18,718	37.8	29,514	59.5	1,079	2.2	115	52,473	13,323	25.4	34,995	66.7	3,747	7.1	334
25 to 29 years	26,375	11,604	44.0	14,234	54.0	416	1.6	39	29,557	8,850	29.9	18,890	63.9	1,591	5.4	177
30 to 34 years	23,188	7,114	30.7	15,280	65.9	663	2.9	76	22,916	4,473	19.5	16,105	70.3	2,156	9.4	157
35 to 44 years	37,428	8,157	21.8	26,917	71.9	2,093	5.6	190	34,005	4,498	13.2	23,030	67.7	6,200	18.2	233
45 to 64 years	27,641	3,889	14.1	19,884	71.9	3,646	13.2	158	26,817	2,514	9.4	13,802	51.5	10,327	38.5	122
45 to 54 years	19,216	2,855	14.9	14,108	73.4	2,100	10.9	112	18,173	1,810	10.0	10,080	55.5	6,144	33.8	104
55 to 64 years	8,425	1,034	12.3	5,776	68.6	1,546	18.4	46	8,644	704	8.1	3,722	43.1	4,183	48.4	18
65 years and over	5,310	500	9.4	3,093	58.2	1,689	31.8	16	6,020	436	7.2	1,427	23.7	4,129	68.6	12
Age unknown	687	192	27.9	297	43.2	47	6.8	1	584	134	22.9	248	42.5	117	20.0	3
EAST NORTH CENTRAL.																
Total	156,431	81,591	52.2	63,247	40.4	8,950	5.7	1,767	144,405	61,845	42.8	62,026	43.0	18,295	12.7	1,881
Under 15 years of age	34,194	34,190	100.0	4	(2)	....	....	....	35,281	35,274	100.0	6	(2)	1	(2)	....
15 years and over	122,237	47,401	38.8	63,243	51.7	8,950	7.3	1,767	109,124	26,571	24.3	62,020	56.8	18,294	16.8	1,881
15 to 19 years	12,374	12,123	98.0	168	1.4	9	0.1	1	13,265	11,254	84.8	1,859	14.0	59	0.4	28
20 to 24 years	15,897	11,689	73.5	3,911	24.6	140	0.9	74	16,149	6,866	42.5	8,423	52.2	565	3.5	243
25 to 34 years	33,382	13,236	39.7	18,455	55.3	1,038	3.1	511	30,353	5,432	17.9	21,524	70.9	2,640	8.7	702
25 to 29 years	17,659	8,156	46.2	8,809	49.9	402	2.3	214	16,579	3,622	21.3	11,418	68.9	1,147	6.9	353
30 to 34 years	15,723	5,080	32.3	9,646	61.3	636	4.0	297	13,774	1,810	13.1	10,106	73.4	1,493	10.8	349
35 to 44 years	27,145	6,165	22.7	18,508	68.2	1,816	6.7	587	22,227	1,818	8.2	16,130	72.6	3,731	16.8	523
45 to 64 years	25,783	3,462	13.4	18,110	70.2	3,674	14.2	468	21,022	948	4.5	12,340	58.7	7,350	35.0	349
45 to 54 years	16,774	2,483	14.8	11,959	71.3	1,979	11.8	320	13,700	658	4.8	8,701	63.5	4,072	29.7	245
55 to 64 years	9,009	979	10.9	6,151	68.3	1,695	18.8	148	7,322	290	4.0	3,639	49.7	3,278	44.8	104
65 years and over	6,766	504	7.4	3,787	56.0	2,217	32.8	112	5,567	188	3.4	1,511	27.1	3,815	68.5	32
Age unknown	890	222	24.9	304	34.2	56	6.3	14	541	65	12.0	233	43.1	134	24.8	4
WEST NORTH CENTRAL.																
Total	125,864	66,918	53.2	49,705	39.5	7,287	5.8	1,300	116,798	51,387	44.0	48,716	41.7	14,920	12.8	1,441
Under 15 years of age	29,218	29,217	100.0	1	(2)	....	....	....	30,084	30,065	99.9	19	0.1	....	....	....
15 years and over	96,646	37,701	39.0	49,704	51.4	7,287	7.5	1,300	86,714	21,322	24.6	48,697	56.2	14,920	17.2	1,441
15 to 19 years	11,078	10,827	97.7	133	1.2	7	0.1	3	11,607	9,718	83.7	1,688	14.5	73	0.6	37
20 to 24 years	13,249	9,640	72.8	3,322	25.1	139	1.0	74	13,243	5,527	41.7	6,941	52.4	540	4.1	189
25 to 34 years	26,036	10,246	39.4	14,433	55.4	910	3.5	368	23,117	3,937	17.0	16,431	71.1	2,141	9.3	568
25 to 29 years	14,076	6,356	45.2	7,118	50.6	393	2.8	160	12,755	2,611	20.5	8,893	69.7	937	7.3	291
30 to 34 years	11,960	3,890	32.5	7,315	61.2	517	4.3	208	10,362	1,326	12.8	7,538	72.7	1,204	11.6	277
35 to 44 years	20,276	4,310	21.3	13,990	69.0	1,530	7.5	393	16,799	1,266	7.5	12,161	72.4	2,959	17.6	391
45 to 64 years	20,062	2,189	10.9	14,410	71.8	3,029	15.1	393	16,534	634	3.8	9,913	60.0	5,738	34.7	222
45 to 54 years	13,094	1,560	11.9	9,561	73.0	1,681	12.8	269	10,712	424	4.0	6,983	65.2	3,124	29.2	166
55 to 64 years	6,968	629	9.0	4,849	69.6	1,348	19.3	124	5,822	210	3.6	2,930	50.3	2,614	44.9	56
65 years and over	5,117	310	6.1	3,127	61.1	1,592	31.1	62	4,837	166	3.4	1,343	27.8	3,279	67.8	25
Age unknown	828	179	21.6	289	34.9	80	9.7	7	577	74	12.8	220	38.1	190	32.9	9
SOUTH ATLANTIC.																
Total	2,029,808	1,248,623	61.5	701,891	34.6	67,834	3.3	4,278	2,082,680	1,177,037	56.5	717,261	34.4	176,734	8.5	7,366
Under 15 years of age	816,738	816,680	100.0	54	(2)	3	(2)	1	822,053	821,725	100.0	306	(2)	19	(2)	3
15 years and over	1,213,070	431,943	35.6	701,837	57.9	67,831	5.6	4,277	1,260,627	355,312	28.2	716,955	56.9	176,715	14.0	7,363
15 to 19 years	218,115	210,899	96.7	5,115	2.3	155	0.1	31	238,938	196,586	82.3	38,756	16.2	1,568	0.7	275
20 to 24 years	198,357	117,148	59.1	77,068	38.9	2,270	1.1	346	228,519	82,295	36.0	135,215	59.2	8,908	3.9	1,266
25 to 34 years	285,151	65,473	23.0	207,969	72.9	9,007	3.2	1,255	310,374	46,649	15.0	234,555	75.6	26,019	8.4	2,594
25 to 29 years	160,852	44,288	27.5	110,841	68.9	4,165	2.6	639	180,813	31,821	17.6	134,404	74.3	12,778	7.1	1,444
30 to 34 years	124,299	21,185	17.0	97,128	78.1	4,842	3.9	616	129,561	14,828	11.4	100,151	77.3	13,241	10.2	1,150
35 to 44 years	209,622	21,926	10.5	173,389	82.7	12,420	5.9	1,185	211,752	15,975	7.5	158,984	75.1	34,612	16.3	1,923
45 to 64 years	233,403	12,575	5.4	191,733	82.1	27,434	11.8	1,216	208,896	10,303	4.9	129,635	62.1	67,525	32.3	1,138
45 to 54 years	144,464	8,724	6.0	120,234	83.2	14,410	10.0	813	135,212	7,087	5.2	90,271	66.8	36,843	27.2	843
55 to 64 years	88,939	3,851	4.3	71,499	80.4	13,024	14.6	403	73,684	3,216	4.4	39,364	53.4	30,682	41.6	295
65 years and over	62,015	2,374	3.8	43,106	69.5	16,101	26.0	222	57,125	2,400	4.2	17,547	30.7	36,833	64.5	129
Age unknown	6,407	1,548	24.2	3,457	54.0	444	6.9	22	5,023	1,104	22.0	2,263	45.1	1,250	24.9	38

[1] Total includes persons whose marital condition was not reported. [2] Less than one-tenth of 1 per cent. [3] Per cent not shown where base is less than 100.

TABLE 28.—MARITAL CONDITION OF THE NEGRO POPULATION, BY AGE PERIODS AND SEX, BY DIVISIONS: 1910—Continued.

DIVISION AND AGE PERIOD.	MALES.								FEMALES.							
	Total.[1]	Single.		Married.		Widowed.		Divorced.	Total.[1]	Single.		Married.		Widowed.		Divorced.
		Number.	Per cent.	Number.	Per cent.	Number.	Per cent.			Number.	Per cent.	Number.	Per cent.	Number.	Per cent.	
EAST SOUTH CENTRAL.																
Total	1,315,792	788,893	59.2	473,175	36.0	53,597	4.1	6,663	1,336,721	713,036	53.3	480,621	36.0	128,517	9.6	11,974
Under 15 years of age	506,613	506,571	100.0	40	(²)	1	(²)	1	505,478	505,245	100.0	215	(²)	17	(²)	1
15 years and over	809,179	272,322	33.7	473,135	58.5	53,596	6.6	6,662	831,243	207,791	25.0	480,406	57.8	128,500	15.5	11,973
15 to 19 years	142,363	137,737	96.8	3,383	2.4	131	0.1	44	151,820	120,568	79.4	28,095	18.5	1,739	1.1	469
20 to 24 years	127,954	71,541	55.9	52,483	41.0	2,530	2.0	755	146,981	45,977	31.3	89,780	61.1	8,547	5.8	2,236
25 to 34 years	192,604	40,604	21.1	140,337	72.9	8,899	4.6	2,226	209,497	25,957	12.4	156,934	74.9	21,720	10.4	4,586
25 to 29 years	109,142	27,673	25.4	75,522	69.2	5,445	4.1	1,194	121,482	17,674	14.5	89,767	73.9	11,106	9.1	2,743
30 to 34 years	83,462	12,931	15.5	64,815	77.7	4,454	5.3	1,032	88,015	8,283	9.4	67,167	76.3	10,614	12.1	1,843
35 to 44 years	136,852	12,821	9.4	112,256	82.0	9,825	7.2	1,702	141,454	8,486	6.0	105,707	74.7	24,369	17.2	2,723
45 to 64 years	162,246	7,267	4.5	132,857	81.9	20,277	12.5	1,575	137,754	4,892	3.6	86,212	62.6	44,740	32.5	1,676
45 to 54 years	102,934	5,141	5.0	85,730	83.3	10,865	10.6	1,039	88,867	3,380	3.8	60,005	67.5	24,128	27.2	1,232
55 to 64 years	59,312	2,126	3.6	47,127	79.5	9,412	15.9	536	48,887	1,512	3.1	26,207	53.6	20,612	42.2	444
65 years and over	42,799	1,367	3.2	29,406	68.7	11,579	27.1	319	39,682	1,227	3.1	11,831	29.8	26,276	66.2	206
Age unknown	4,361	985	22.6	2,413	55.3	355	8.1	41	4,055	684	16.9	1,847	45.5	1,109	27.3	77
WEST SOUTH CENTRAL.																
Total	994,025	592,492	59.6	352,124	35.4	40,901	4.1	5,098	990,401	532,988	53.8	357,131	36.1	88,972	9.0	9,136
Under 15 years of age	380,825	380,796	100.0	27	(²)	2	(²)	......	383,161	383,008	100.0	135	(²)	18	(²)	......
15 years and over	613,200	211,696	34.5	352,097	57.4	40,899	6.7	5,098	607,240	149,980	24.7	356,996	58.8	88,954	14.6	9,136
15 to 19 years	105,269	102,126	97.0	2,070	2.0	108	0.1	24	114,211	90,247	79.0	21,381	18.7	1,433	1.3	376
20 to 24 years	99,105	57,593	58.1	38,436	38.8	1,936	2.0	520	110,687	33,987	30.7	67,984	61.4	6,561	5.9	1,794
25 to 34 years	152,778	34,025	22.3	109,340	71.6	7,052	4.6	1,803	156,844	17,381	11.1	119,645	76.3	16,130	10.3	3,411
25 to 29 years	86,157	23,237	27.0	58,067	67.4	3,539	4.1	976	91,336	12,200	13.4	68,545	75.0	8,430	9.2	1,986
30 to 34 years	66,621	10,788	16.2	51,273	77.0	3,513	5.3	827	65,508	5,181	7.9	51,100	78.0	7,700	11.8	1,425
35 to 44 years	107,390	10,687	10.0	87,379	81.4	7,861	7.3	1,209	102,955	4,813	4.7	78,686	76.4	17,265	16.8	2,054
45 to 64 years	116,474	5,488	4.7	93,978	80.7	15,533	13.3	1,268	93,080	2,422	2.6	59,579	64.0	29,585	31.8	1,302
45 to 54 years	76,082	3,866	5.1	62,581	82.3	8,635	11.3	863	60,336	1,647	2.7	41,570	68.9	16,037	26.6	977
55 to 64 years	40,392	1,622	4.0	31,397	77.7	6,898	17.1	405	32,744	775	2.4	18,009	55.0	13,548	41.4	32
65 years and over	28,571	993	3.5	19,110	66.9	8,115	28.4	248	26,502	662	2.5	8,352	31.5	17,188	64.9	148
Age unknown	3,613	784	21.7	1,790	49.5	294	8.1	26	2,961	468	15.8	1,369	46.2	792	26.7	51
MOUNTAIN.																
Total	11,766	6,255	53.2	4,673	39.7	574	4.9	179	9,701	3,766	38.8	4,335	44.7	1,342	13.8	224
Under 15 years of age	1,947	1,947	100.0	......	......	......	......	......	2,051	2,048	99.9	2	0.1	1	(²)	......
15 years and over	9,819	4,308	43.9	4,673	47.6	574	5.8	179	7,650	1,718	22.5	4,333	56.6	1,341	17.5	224
15 to 19 years	657	645	98.3	10	1.5	......	......	1	773	615	79.6	145	18.8	4	0.5	6
20 to 24 years	1,192	925	77.5	245	20.6	7	0.6	7	1,096	406	37.0	607	55.4	46	4.2	33
25 to 34 years	3,071	1,485	48.4	1,457	47.4	61	2.0	45	2,443	461	18.9	1,651	67.6	238	9.7	86
25 to 29 years	1,539	838	54.5	651	42.3	23	1.5	17	1,346	303	22.5	886	65.8	107	7.9	44
30 to 34 years	1,532	647	42.2	806	52.6	38	2.5	28	1,097	158	14.4	765	69.7	131	11.9	42
35 to 44 years	2,478	729	29.4	1,513	61.1	154	6.2	67	1,726	132	7.6	1,160	67.2	364	21.1	60
45 to 64 years	2,017	438	21.7	1,265	62.7	252	12.5	53	1,333	78	5.9	708	53.1	512	38.4	33
45 to 54 years	1,392	284	20.4	914	65.7	153	11.0	34	949	50	5.3	543	57.2	324	34.1	31
55 to 64 years	625	154	24.6	351	56.2	99	15.8	19	384	28	7.3	165	43.0	188	49.0	2
65 years and over	315	59	18.7	154	48.9	97	30.8	4	233	14	6.0	43	18.5	170	73.0	6
Age unknown	89	26	(³)	29	(³)	3	(³)	2	46	12	(³)	19	(³)	7	(³)	......
PACIFIC.																
Total	15,946	8,831	55.4	6,123	38.4	706	4.4	186	13,249	5,246	39.6	5,914	44.6	1,785	13.5	245
Under 15 years of age	2,612	2,612	100.0	......	......	......	......	......	2,803	2,801	99.9	2	0.1	......	......	......
15 years and over	13,334	6,219	46.6	6,123	45.9	706	5.3	186	10,446	2,445	23.4	5,912	56.6	1,785	17.1	245
15 to 19 years	1,040	1,024	98.5	11	1.1	......	......	......	1,104	960	87.0	138	12.5	3	0.3	2
20 to 24 years	1,621	1,309	80.8	291	18.0	11	0.7	7	1,360	579	42.6	696	51.2	48	3.5	33
25 to 34 years	4,027	2,126	52.8	1,764	43.8	79	2.0	50	3,095	556	18.0	2,183	70.5	269	8.7	85
25 to 29 years	2,059	1,194	58.0	808	39.2	24	1.2	29	1,669	379	22.7	1,145	68.6	103	6.2	40
30 to 34 years	1,968	932	47.4	956	48.6	55	2.8	21	1,426	177	12.4	1,038	72.8	166	11.6	45
35 to 44 years	3,219	1,033	32.1	1,967	61.1	158	4.9	55	2,362	206	8.7	1,664	70.4	412	17.4	76
45 to 64 years	2,820	617	21.9	1,809	64.1	318	11.3	65	2,002	116	5.8	1,105	55.2	736	36.8	44
45 to 54 years	2,001	464	23.2	1,299	64.9	182	9.1	47	1,401	83	5.9	838	59.8	447	31.9	32
55 to 64 years	819	153	18.7	510	62.3	136	16.6	18	601	33	5.5	267	44.4	289	48.1	12
65 years and over	488	83	17.0	256	52.5	135	27.7	8	421	16	3.8	100	23.8	303	72.0	2
Age unknown	119	27	22.7	25	21.0	5	4.2	1	102	12	11.8	26	25.5	14	13.7	3

[1] Total includes persons whose marital condition was not reported. [2] Less than one-tenth of 1 per cent. [3] Per cent not shown where base is less than 100.

TABLE 29.—MARITAL CONDITION OF THE NEGRO POPULATION, BY DIVISIONS AND STATES: 1910, 1900, AND 1890.

DIVISION AND STATE.	NEGRO POPULATION 15 YEARS OF AGE AND OVER: 1910.											
	Male.						Female.					
	Total.	Single.	Married.	Widowed.	Divorced.	Unknown.	Total.	Single.	Married.	Widowed.	Divorced.	Unknown.
UNITED STATES	3,059,312	1,083,472	1,749,228	189,970	20,146	16,496	3,103,344	823,996	1,775,949	459,831	33,286	10,282
GEOGRAPHIC DIVISIONS:												
New England	24,955	10,345	12,893	1,454	177	86	25,274	8,121	12,641	4,235	236	41
Middle Atlantic	156,872	61,537	85,523	8,673	500	639	165,026	50,736	87,989	25,087	787	427
East North Central	122,237	47,401	63,243	8,950	1,767	876	109,124	26,571	62,020	18,294	1,881	358
West North Central	96,646	37,701	49,704	7,287	1,300	654	86,714	21,322	48,697	14,920	1,441	334
South Atlantic	1,213,070	431,943	701,837	67,831	4,277	7,182	1,260,627	355,312	716,955	176,715	7,363	4,282
East South Central	809,179	272,322	473,135	53,596	6,662	3,464	831,243	207,791	480,406	128,500	11,973	2,573
West South Central	613,200	211,696	352,097	40,899	5,098	3,410	607,240	149,980	356,996	88,954	9,136	2,174
Mountain	9,819	4,308	4,673	574	179	85	7,650	1,718	4,333	1,341	224	34
Pacific	13,334	6,219	6,123	706	186	100	10,446	2,445	5,912	1,785	245	59
NEW ENGLAND:												
Maine	554	250	249	46	9	....	495	192	217	74	11	1
New Hampshire	229	95	111	18	4	1	211	84	97	26	1	3
Vermont	1,054	765	248	27	14	....	320	84	199	29	8	....
Massachusetts	14,237	5,941	7,391	753	87	65	14,576	4,783	7,232	2,447	100	14
Rhode Island	3,510	1,404	1,860	208	32	6	3,689	1,108	1,841	673	53	14
Connecticut	5,371	1,890	3,034	402	31	14	5,983	1,870	3,055	986	63	9
MIDDLE ATLANTIC:												
New York	51,428	21,151	27,435	2,533	164	145	56,485	18,268	28,577	9,206	292	142
New Jersey	32,831	12,228	18,649	1,775	88	91	34,868	10,302	19,256	5,112	109	89
Pennsylvania	72,613	28,158	39,439	4,365	248	403	73,673	22,166	40,156	10,769	386	196
EAST NORTH CENTRAL:												
Ohio	44,894	17,774	23,210	3,162	558	190	40,052	10,596	22,641	6,138	564	113
Indiana	23,848	9,045	12,327	1,969	418	89	21,818	5,238	12,204	3,851	487	38
Illinois	45,199	17,441	23,361	3,232	635	530	39,961	8,860	23,051	7,172	690	188
Michigan	7,087	2,610	3,794	498	130	55	6,194	1,520	3,575	968	114	17
Wisconsin	1,209	531	551	89	26	12	1,099	357	549	165	26	2
WEST NORTH CENTRAL:												
Minnesota	3,657	1,772	1,618	187	38	42	2,334	641	1,328	322	31	12
Iowa	6,222	2,350	3,221	462	143	46	4,943	1,112	3,008	677	128	18
Missouri	61,645	23,967	31,714	4,811	742	411	57,550	14,240	31,613	10,553	926	218
North Dakota	331	190	107	15	5	14	185	56	106	16	7	....
South Dakota	373	170	176	21	6	....	262	79	152	27	4	....
Nebraska	3,541	1,541	1,702	237	54	7	2,746	643	1,627	417	55	4
Kansas	20,877	7,711	11,166	1,554	312	134	18,694	4,551	10,863	2,908	290	82
SOUTH ATLANTIC:												
Delaware	11,015	4,518	5,621	791	34	51	10,222	3,145	5,579	1,423	35	40
Maryland	77,191	30,141	41,495	5,090	264	201	78,668	24,469	42,607	11,103	337	152
District of Columbia	32,156	12,132	17,863	1,880	183	98	40,597	13,443	19,065	7,665	284	140
Virginia	202,055	79,328	109,723	11,782	682	540	210,968	66,902	112,351	30,200	1,123	392
West Virginia	27,317	13,144	12,487	1,330	182	174	18,184	4,615	11,304	2,011	204	50
North Carolina	191,986	69,483	111,770	9,514	427	792	208,993	66,965	114,810	25,765	803	650
South Carolina	225,020	75,462	137,488	10,880	271	919	244,703	68,178	141,327	33,694	659	845
Georgia	338,942	109,458	206,386	20,017	1,281	1,800	355,224	87,461	210,607	53,229	2,726	1,201
Florida	107,388	38,277	59,004	6,547	953	2,607	93,068	20,134	59,305	11,625	1,192	812
EAST SOUTH CENTRAL:												
Kentucky	92,230	35,239	48,538	7,019	1,050	384	90,814	24,849	48,951	15,245	1,476	293
Tennessee	150,860	52,874	85,020	11,029	1,282	655	156,459	40,455	86,908	26,243	2,344	509
Alabama	269,025	88,577	160,594	17,101	2,011	742	281,202	70,466	162,347	43,684	4,222	483
Mississippi	297,064	95,632	178,983	18,447	2,319	1,683	302,768	72,021	182,200	43,328	3,931	1,288
WEST SOUTH CENTRAL:												
Arkansas	139,798	45,591	81,279	10,857	1,190	881	134,532	30,748	81,917	19,385	1,889	593
Louisiana	217,006	76,748	125,446	12,684	967	1,161	222,527	57,639	127,984	34,101	2,069	734
Oklahoma	45,671	16,170	25,345	3,428	460	268	39,278	8,566	25,136	4,871	555	150
Texas	210,725	73,187	120,027	13,930	2,481	1,100	210,903	53,027	121,959	30,597	4,623	697
MOUNTAIN:												
Montana	911	454	393	41	15	8	627	163	360	82	22	....
Idaho	350	179	142	17	10	2	209	61	113	30	3	2
Wyoming	1,408	988	364	29	16	11	560	152	306	76	26	....
Colorado	4,761	1,722	2,608	317	95	19	4,422	936	2,529	828	111	18
New Mexico	718	283	357	61	14	3	520	107	305	90	17	1
Arizona	827	313	434	54	16	10	734	167	402	141	22	2
Utah	606	263	269	34	8	32	365	81	221	42	10	11
Nevada	238	106	106	21	5	....	213	51	97	52	13	....
PACIFIC:												
Washington	3,336	1,819	1,296	126	50	45	1,907	437	1,133	242	48	47
Oregon	815	425	333	42	13	2	490	99	290	83	13	....
California	9,183	3,975	4,494	538	123	53	8,049	1,909	4,489	1,455	184	12

TABLE 29.—MARITAL CONDITION OF THE NEGRO POPULATION, BY DIVISIONS AND STATES: 1910, 1900, AND 1890—Continued.

DIVISION AND STATE.	NEGRO POPULATION 15 YEARS OF AGE AND OVER: 1910.											
	Male.						Female.					
	Total.	Single.	Married.	Widowed.	Divorced.	Unknown.	Total.	Single.	Married.	Widowed.	Divorced.	Unknown.
UNITED STATES	2,633,008	1,033,285	1,422,886	151,233	11,026	14,578	2,690,583	803,683	1,443,817	414,107	22,033	6,943
GEOGRAPHIC DIVISIONS:												
New England	21,671	9,373	10,799	1,247	92	160	23,063	8,245	10,795	3,759	166	98
Middle Atlantic	121,613	55,329	59,166	6,037	267	814	125,612	45,502	60,370	18,859	417	464
East North Central	100,537	44,036	47,806	7,026	927	742	88,333	25,310	46,879	14,683	1,189	272
West North Central	85,716	37,559	41,147	5,791	643	576	80,602	24,017	41,606	13,787	909	283
South Atlantic	1,063,554	414,861	584,372	55,150	2,542	6,629	1,116,171	349,621	597,272	160,817	5,637	2,824
East South Central	733,058	280,308	401,997	44,558	3,316	2,879	752,786	215,626	406,331	121,931	7,176	1,722
West South Central	492,987	184,499	272,242	30,625	3,104	2,517	494,205	132,763	275,362	78,508	6,351	1,221
Mountain	7,626	4,176	2,781	431	71	167	4,973	1,277	2,671	876	104	45
Pacific	6,246	3,144	2,576	368	64	94	4,838	1,322	2,531	887	84	14
NEW ENGLAND:												
Maine	521	232	243	29	7	10	457	164	210	78	3	2
New Hampshire	264	128	108	21	3	4	274	127	102	38	6	1
Vermont	348	165	151	19	3	10	258	97	120	38	3	
Massachusetts	12,001	5,317	5,936	606	36	106	12,371	4,343	5,851	2,035	60	82
Rhode Island	3,198	1,329	1,653	187	17	12	3,689	1,298	1,696	647	43	5
Connecticut	5,339	2,202	2,708	385	26	18	6,014	2,216	2,816	923	51	8
MIDDLE ATLANTIC:												
New York	36,600	16,651	17,971	1,760	85	133	41,595	15,831	18,603	6,905	160	96
New Jersey	25,086	10,509	12,921	1,222	47	387	27,046	9,378	13,456	3,908	78	226
Pennsylvania	59,927	28,169	28,274	3,055	135	294	56,971	20,293	28,311	8,046	179	142
EAST NORTH CENTRAL:												
Ohio	36,781	15,785	17,967	2,549	274	206	33,251	10,139	17,597	5,091	346	78
Indiana	21,708	9,113	10,414	1,668	323	190	19,582	5,511	10,280	3,350	380	61
Illinois	34,748	15,992	15,909	2,280	268	299	29,183	7,807	15,631	5,248	376	121
Michigan	6,153	2,565	3,045	455	55	33	5,472	1,569	2,949	871	72	11
Wisconsin	1,147	581	471	74	7	14	845	284	422	123	15	1
WEST NORTH CENTRAL:												
Minnesota	2,376	1,218	985	113	24	36	1,619	475	869	237	31	7
Iowa	5,209	2,258	2,487	338	76	50	4,148	1,146	2,346	581	48	27
Missouri	56,932	25,347	27,079	3,812	375	319	55,340	16,804	27,825	9,955	582	174
North Dakota	132	79	37	14	1	1	75	28	36	11		
South Dakota	215	125	76	9	3	2	129	33	76	18	2	
Nebraska	2,710	1,455	1,082	141	20	12	2,171	736	1,047	354	25	9
Kansas	18,142	7,077	9,401	1,364	144	156	17,120	4,795	9,407	2,631	221	66
SOUTH ATLANTIC:												
Delaware	10,360	4,479	5,108	657	22	94	9,766	3,154	5,197	1,353	21	41
Maryland	74,958	31,674	38,287	4,147	137	713	77,865	26,768	39,252	11,129	248	468
District of Columbia	27,726	11,354	14,570	1,683	90	29	36,922	14,321	15,501	6,854	212	34
Virginia	190,739	81,296	97,886	10,250	426	881	202,573	71,612	100,042	29,680	688	551
West Virginia	18,484	9,967	7,232	786	83	416	11,740	3,735	6,419	1,459	71	56
North Carolina	169,613	66,719	93,001	8,512	311	1,070	186,782	66,244	95,908	23,642	641	347
South Carolina	207,960	74,754	122,688	9,615	195	708	222,456	65,676	125,905	29,912	673	290
Georgia	287,619	102,919	166,418	15,319	908	2,055	301,937	81,524	170,025	47,117	2,389	882
Florida	76,095	31,699	39,182	4,181	370	663	66,130	16,587	39,023	9,671	694	155
EAST SOUTH CENTRAL:												
Kentucky	93,156	39,400	46,140	6,397	608	611	93,409	28,756	46,805	16,400	1,109	339
Tennessee	145,671	58,572	76,069	9,520	654	856	149,819	44,854	77,070	25,923	1,444	528
Alabama	236,223	87,863	133,009	13,622	1,078	651	247,480	70,805	134,299	39,735	2,338	303
Mississippi	258,008	94,473	146,779	15,019	976	761	262,078	71,211	148,157	39,873	2,285	552
WEST SOUTH CENTRAL:												
Arkansas	110,886	40,700	61,002	8,000	630	554	106,208	27,036	61,110	16,631	1,203	228
Louisiana	187,585	69,053	106,535	10,830	752	415	194,210	52,281	108,306	31,689	1,667	267
Oklahoma	17,598	6,512	9,647	1,211	120	108	15,692	3,821	9,553	2,036	214	68
Texas	176,918	68,234	95,058	10,584	1,602	1,440	178,095	49,625	96,393	28,152	3,267	658
MOUNTAIN:												
Montana	771	489	223	43	6	10	477	129	235	99	13	1
Idaho	144	89	50	5			93	26	49	14	3	1
Wyoming	539	351	149	32	4	3	234	102	116	11	3	2
Colorado	3,602	1,520	1,706	235	35	106	3,185	789	1,700	595	64	37
New Mexico	878	508	289	39	13	29	427	94	251	73	9	
Arizona	1,216	888	253	56	9	10	357	80	215	54	7	1
Utah	403	285	93	15	4	6	153	34	89	23	4	3
Nevada	73	46	18	6		3	47	23	16	7	1	
PACIFIC:												
Washington	598	388	173	27	9	1	710	186	411	101	9	3
Oregon	1,362	796	462	72	13	19	345	138	142	57	8	
California	4,286	1,960	1,941	269	42	74	3,783	998	1,978	729	67	11

TABLE 29.—MARITAL CONDITION OF THE NEGRO POPULATION, BY DIVISIONS AND STATES: 1910, 1900, AND 1890—Continued.

| DIVISION AND STATE. | NEGRO POPULATION 15 YEARS OF AGE AND OVER: 1890.[1] | | | | | | | | | | | |
| | Male. | | | | | | Female. | | | | | |
	Total.	Single.	Married.	Widowed.	Divorced.	Unknown.	Total.	Single.	Married.	Widowed.	Divorced.	Unknown.
UNITED STATES	2,119,721	842,764	1,175,513	91,683	5,212	4,549	2,175,550	652,314	1,187,434	320,194	10,688	4,920
GEOGRAPHIC DIVISIONS:												
New England	15,924	6,774	8,263	778	65	44	16,807	5,779	8,028	2,880	93	27
Middle Atlantic	81,552	36,883	40,599	3,713	103	254	82,557	28,523	39,836	13,856	174	168
East North Central	74,601	32,395	37,437	4,179	435	155	66,130	19,357	35,620	10,446	627	80
West North Central	73,537	32,016	37,201	3,710	376	234	69,777	20,664	37,003	11,425	570	115
South Atlantic	892,567	355,956	499,573	34,594	1,153	1,291	942,587	298,713	510,127	128,239	2,714	2,794
East South Central	590,870	228,566	332,455	26,945	1,663	1,241	611,087	176,434	335,542	94,431	3,718	962
West South Central	377,365	141,861	215,640	17,272	1,319	1,273	379,087	100,668	217,263	57,728	2,685	743
Mountain	7,089	4,789	2,003	209	48	40	3,444	1,116	1,734	514	58	22
Pacific	6,216	3,524	2,342	283	50	17	4,074	1,060	2,281	675	49	9
NEW ENGLAND:												
Maine	448	207	211	25	2	3	417	150	190	74	1	2
New Hampshire	238	122	100	13	2	1	201	85	83	32	1	
Vermont	350	147	173	26	3	1	295	92	151	51	1	
Massachusetts	8,103	3,533	4,162	376	17	15	8,333	2,858	3,998	1,435	31	11
Rhode Island	2,492	975	1,360	143	12	2	2,986	1,024	1,375	550	33	4
Connecticut	4,293	1,790	2,257	195	29	22	4,575	1,570	2,231	738	26	10
MIDDLE ATLANTIC:												
New York	24,913	10,912	12,723	1,175	26	77	27,647	9,687	12,665	5,213	45	37
New Jersey	16,906	7,334	8,769	708	17	78	17,420	5,878	8,864	2,624	32	22
Pennsylvania	39,733	18,637	19,107	1,830	60	99	37,490	12,958	18,307	6,019	97	109
EAST NORTH CENTRAL:												
Ohio	31,071	13,535	15,659	1,675	151	51	28,242	8,639	14,959	4,393	218	33
Indiana	15,894	6,919	7,896	933	113	33	14,256	4,142	7,626	2,258	204	26
Illinois	21,087	9,221	10,497	1,190	140	39	17,997	4,928	9,962	2,950	150	7
Michigan	5,604	2,292	2,940	319	27	26	4,936	1,416	2,716	748	45	11
Wisconsin	945	428	445	62	4	6	699	232	357	97	10	3
WEST NORTH CENTRAL:												
Minnesota	1,802	965	755	61	12	9	1,144	299	675	161	7	2
Iowa	3,952	1,741	1,980	197	28	6	3,229	904	1,849	441	30	5
Missouri	47,595	20,613	24,175	2,452	199	156	47,585	14,404	24,429	8,291	372	89
North Dakota	162	101	53	7		1	93	29	49	15		
South Dakota	294	173	102	18	1		122	29	73	17	1	2
Nebraska	3,921	2,242	1,485	125	21	48	2,461	824	1,316	291	27	3
Kansas	15,811	6,181	8,651	850	115	14	15,143	4,175	8,612	2,209	133	14
SOUTH ATLANTIC:												
Delaware	9,355	4,097	4,806	434	9	9	8,764	2,749	4,905	1,096	7	7
Maryland	64,958	27,329	34,585	2,841	71	132	69,460	23,934	35,377	9,921	133	95
District of Columbia	22,628	9,330	12,240	980	33	45	30,075	11,689	12,805	5,444	99	38
Virginia	173,118	74,676	90,303	7,727	228	184	189,142	68,942	92,290	26,941	432	537
West Virginia	12,009	6,484	4,980	416	30	99	8,826	3,070	4,656	1,035	45	20
North Carolina	147,594	60,355	81,209	5,684	164	182	160,687	55,490	83,905	20,518	369	405
South Carolina	178,161	63,747	107,966	6,186	161	101	187,688	53,611	109,596	23,580	372	529
Georgia	236,036	90,689	136,228	8,436	289	394	240,498	66,170	138,833	33,575	901	1,019
Florida	48,708	19,249	27,256	1,890	168	145	47,447	13,058	27,760	6,129	356	144
EAST SOUTH CENTRAL:												
Kentucky	80,843	34,248	41,620	4,320	310	345	82,412	25,684	41,868	13,910	690	260
Tennessee	121,910	48,472	66,709	5,990	423	316	128,003	38,017	67,521	21,237	1,049	179
Alabama	187,150	70,605	108,085	7,690	486	284	194,996	56,115	108,850	28,977	979	75
Mississippi	200,967	75,241	116,041	8,945	444	296	205,676	56,618	117,303	30,307	1,000	448
WEST SOUTH CENTRAL:												
Arkansas	90,371	34,262	50,592	4,928	330	259	83,400	20,588	50,284	11,788	591	149
Louisiana	153,992	55,804	90,874	6,463	375	476	162,620	43,467	92,468	25,566	787	332
Oklahoma	1,048	330	653	55	6	4	872	198	582	83	3	6
Texas	131,954	51,465	73,521	5,826	608	534	132,195	36,415	73,929	20,291	1,304	256
MOUNTAIN:												
Montana	977	767	189	12		9	334	118	160	48	1	7
Idaho	93	60	23	7	3		57	22	23	10	2	
Wyoming	582	457	98	21	3	3	206	74	97	28	4	3
Colorado	2,941	1,653	1,132	111	23	22	1,983	628	992	319	39	5
New Mexico	923	590	300	27	6		531	180	280	64	7	
Arizona	1,113	946	140	17	10		135	34	81	16	4	
Utah	315	209	93	6	1	6	132	37	73	15	1	6
Nevada	145	107	28	8	2		66	23	28	14		1
PACIFIC:												
Washington	980	640	279	48	8	5	396	108	235	46	7	
Oregon	599	401	174	17	4	3	301	72	172	50	4	3
California	4,637	2,483	1,889	218	38	9	3,377	880	1,874	579	38	6

[1] Exclusive of persons specially enumerated in Indian Territory and on Indian reservations for whom statistics of marital conditions are not available.

TABLE **30.**—MARITAL CONDITION BY AGE PERIODS OF NEGRO POPULATION, BY SECTIONS, SOUTHERN DIVISIONS, AND SOUTHERN STATES: 1910.

SECTION, DIVISION, STATE, AND AGE PERIOD.	Male.								Female.							
	Number.					Percentage.			Number.					Percentage.		
	Total.	Single.	Married.	Widowed.	Divorced.	Single.	Married.	Widowed.	Total.	Single.	Married.	Widowed.	Divorced.	Single.	Married.	Widowed.
UNITED STATES.																
15 years and over [1]	3,059,312	1,083,472	1,749,228	189,970	20,146	35.4	57.2	6.2	3,103,344	823,996	1,775,949	459,831	33,286	26.6	57.2	14.8
15 to 19 years	507,945	492,153	11,064	416	104	96.9	2.2	0.1	552,471	448,515	94,087	4,929	1,205	81.2	17.0	0.9
20 to 24 years	482,157	287,994	182,110	7,160	1,809	59.7	37.8	1.5	548,638	191,396	323,773	25,776	5,876	34.9	59.0	4.7
25 to 34 years	753,968	189,196	527,149	28,261	6,408	25.1	69.9	3.7	795,348	115,682	592,547	73,353	12,448	14.5	74.5	9.2
35 to 44 years	550,130	67,203	439,901	36,144	5,458	12.2	80.0	6.6	538,732	38,105	401,069	90,839	8,048	7.1	74.4	16.9
45 to 64 years	595,554	36,661	477,712	74,809	5,254	6.2	80.2	12.6	512,549	22,483	315,823	168,446	4,954	4.4	61.6	32.9
65 years and over	152,482	6,285	102,670	41,891	999	4.1	67.3	27.5	141,642	5,243	42,404	92,856	565	3.7	29.9	65.6
Age unknown	17,076	3,980	8,622	1,289	114	23.3	50.5	7.5	13,964	2,572	6,246	3,632	190	18.4	44.7	26.0
THE NORTH.																
15 years and over [1]	400,710	156,984	211,363	26,364	3,744	39.2	52.7	6.6	386,138	106,750	211,347	62,536	4,345	27.6	54.7	16.2
15 to 19 years	40,501	39,721	475	22	4	98.1	1.2	0.1	45,625	39,539	5,572	182	77	86.7	12.2	0.4
20 to 24 years	53,928	39,478	13,593	406	174	73.2	25.2	0.8	59,995	28,152	29,491	1,666	514	46.9	49.2	2.8
25 to 34 years	116,337	45,483	66,282	3,163	1,029	39.1	57.0	2.7	113,095	24,678	77,579	8,977	1,686	21.8	68.6	7.9
35 to 44 years	90,569	20,007	63,397	5,726	1,240	22.1	70.0	6.3	78,483	8,493	54,868	13,817	1,212	10.8	69.9	17.6
45 to 64 years	78,594	10,276	56,070	10,995	1,077	13.1	71.3	14.0	69,484	4,672	38,584	25,348	761	6.7	55.5	36.5
65 years and over	18,294	1,409	10,638	5,864	198	7.7	58.2	32.1	17,679	924	4,531	12,086	74	5.2	25.6	68.4
Age unknown	2,487	610	908	188	22	24.5	36.5	7.6	1,777	292	722	460	21	16.4	40.6	25.9
THE SOUTH.																
15 years and over [1]	2,635,449	915,961	1,527,069	162,326	16,037	34.8	57.9	6.2	2,699,110	713,083	1,554,357	394,169	28,472	26.4	57.6	14.6
15 to 19 years	465,747	450,762	10,568	394	99	96.8	2.3	0.1	504,969	407,401	88,232	4,740	1,120	80.7	17.5	0.9
20 to 24 years	425,416	246,282	167,981	6,736	1,621	57.9	39.5	1.6	486,187	162,259	292,979	24,016	5,296	33.4	60.3	4.9
25 to 34 years	630,533	140,102	457,646	24,958	5,284	22.2	72.6	4.0	676,715	89,987	511,134	63,869	10,591	13.3	75.5	9.4
35 to 44 years	453,864	45,434	373,024	30,106	4,096	10.0	82.2	6.6	456,161	29,274	343,377	76,246	6,700	6.4	75.3	16.7
45 to 64 years	512,123	25,330	418,568	63,244	4,059	4.9	81.7	12.3	439,730	17,617	275,426	141,850	4,116	4.0	62.6	32.3
65 years and over	133,385	4,734	91,622	35,795	789	3.5	68.7	26.8	123,309	4,289	37,730	80,297	483	3.5	30.6	65.1
Age unknown	14,381	3,317	7,660	1,093	89	23.1	53.3	7.6	12,039	2,256	5,479	3,151	166	18.7	45.5	26.2
THE WEST.																
15 years and over [1]	23,153	10,527	10,796	1,280	365	45.5	46.6	5.5	18,096	4,163	10,245	3,126	469	23.0	56.6	17.3
15 to 19 years	1,697	1,670	21	......	1	98.4	1.2	......	1,877	1,575	283	7	8	83.9	15.1	0.4
20 to 24 years	2,813	2,234	536	18	14	79.4	19.1	0.6	2,456	985	1,303	94	66	40.1	53.1	3.8
25 to 34 years	7,098	3,611	3,221	140	95	50.9	45.4	2.0	5,538	1,017	3,834	507	171	18.4	69.2	9.2
35 to 44 years	5,697	1,762	3,480	312	122	30.9	61.1	5.5	4,088	338	2,824	776	136	8.3	69.1	19.0
45 to 64 years	4,837	1,055	3,074	570	118	21.8	63.6	11.8	3,335	194	1,813	1,248	77	5.8	54.4	37.4
65 years and over	803	142	410	232	12	17.7	51.1	28.9	654	30	143	473	8	4.6	21.9	72.3
Age unknown	208	53	54	8	3	25.5	26.0	3.8	148	24	45	21	3	16.2	30.4	14.2
SOUTHERN DIVISIONS.																
SOUTH ATLANTIC.																
15 years and over [1]	1,213,070	431,943	701,837	67,831	4,277	35.6	57.9	5.6	1,260,627	355,312	716,955	176,715	7,363	28.2	56.9	14.0
15 to 19 years	218,115	210,899	5,115	155	31	96.7	2.3	0.1	238,938	196,586	38,756	1,568	275	82.3	16.2	0.7
20 to 24 years	198,357	117,148	77,068	2,270	346	59.1	38.9	1.1	228,519	82,295	135,215	8,908	1,266	36.0	59.2	3.9
25 to 34 years	285,151	65,473	207,969	9,007	1,255	23.0	72.9	3.2	310,374	46,649	234,555	26,019	2,594	15.0	75.6	8.4
35 to 44 years	209,622	21,926	173,389	12,420	1,185	10.5	82.7	5.9	211,752	15,975	158,984	34,612	1,923	7.5	75.1	16.3
45 to 64 years	233,403	12,575	191,733	27,434	1,216	5.4	82.1	11.8	208,896	10,303	129,635	67,525	1,138	4.9	62.1	32.3
65 years and over	62,015	2,374	43,106	16,101	222	3.8	69.5	26.0	57,125	2,400	17,547	36,833	129	4.2	30.7	64.5
Age unknown	6,407	1,548	3,457	444	22	24.2	54.0	6.9	5,023	1,104	2,263	1,250	38	22.0	45.1	24.9
EAST SOUTH CENTRAL.																
15 years and over [1]	809,179	272,322	473,135	53,596	6,662	33.7	58.5	6.6	831,243	207,791	480,406	128,500	11,973	25.0	57.8	15.5
15 to 19 years	142,363	137,737	3,383	131	44	96.8	2.4	0.1	151,820	120,568	28,095	1,739	469	79.4	18.5	1.1
20 to 24 years	127,954	71,541	52,483	2,530	755	55.9	41.0	2.0	146,981	45,977	89,780	8,547	2,236	31.3	61.1	5.8
25 to 34 years	192,604	40,604	140,337	8,899	2,226	21.1	72.9	4.6	209,497	25,957	156,934	21,720	4,586	12.4	74.9	10.4
35 to 44 years	136,852	12,821	112,256	9,825	1,702	9.4	82.0	7.2	141,454	8,486	105,707	24,369	2,723	6.0	74.7	17.2
45 to 64 years	162,246	7,267	132,857	20,277	1,575	4.5	81.9	12.5	137,754	4,892	86,212	44,740	1,676	3.6	62.6	32.5
65 years and over	42,799	1,367	29,406	11,579	319	3.2	68.7	27.1	39,682	1,227	11,831	26,276	206	3.1	29.8	66.2
Age unknown	4,361	985	2,413	355	41	22.6	55.3	8.1	4,055	684	1,847	1,109	77	16.9	45.5	27.3
WEST SOUTH CENTRAL.																
15 years and over [1]	613,200	211,696	352,097	40,899	5,098	34.5	57.4	6.7	607,240	149,980	356,996	88,954	9,136	24.7	58.8	14.6
15 to 19 years	105,269	102,126	2,070	108	24	97.0	2.0	0.1	114,211	90,247	21,381	1,433	376	79.0	18.7	1.3
20 to 24 years	99,105	57,593	38,430	1,936	520	58.1	38.8	2.0	110,687	33,987	67,984	6,561	1,794	30.7	61.4	5.9
25 to 34 years	152,778	34,025	109,340	7,052	1,803	22.3	71.6	4.6	156,844	17,381	119,645	16,130	3,411	11.1	76.3	10.3
35 to 44 years	107,390	10,687	87,379	7,861	1,209	10.0	81.4	7.3	102,955	4,813	78,686	17,265	2,054	4.7	76.4	16.8
45 to 64 years	116,474	5,488	93,978	15,533	1,268	4.7	80.7	13.3	93,080	2,422	59,579	29,585	1,302	2.6	64.0	31.8
65 years and over	28,571	993	19,110	8,115	248	3.5	66.9	28.4	26,502	662	8,352	17,188	148	2.5	31.5	64.9
Age unknown	3,613	784	1,790	294	26	21.7	49.5	8.1	2,961	468	1,369	792	51	15.8	46.2	26.7
SOUTHERN STATES.																
SOUTH ATLANTIC.																
DELAWARE.																
15 years and over [1]	11,015	4,518	5,621	791	34	41.0	51.0	7.2	10,222	3,145	5,579	1,423	35	30.8	54.6	13.9
15 to 19 years	1,648	1,633	12	......	......	99.1	0.7	......	1,580	1,398	162	3	......	88.5	10.3	0.2
20 to 24 years	1,602	1,172	413	9	......	73.2	25.8	0.6	1,540	765	744	23	3	49.7	48.3	1.5
25 to 34 years	2,455	904	1,452	76	7	36.8	59.1	3.1	2,361	577	1,646	117	16	24.4	69.7	5.0
35 to 44 years	2,198	453	1,584	143	14	20.6	72.1	6.5	1,956	206	1,493	249	4	10.5	76.3	12.7
45 to 64 years	2,412	287	1,756	353	11	11.9	72.8	14.6	2,126	147	1,314	653	11	6.9	61.8	30.7
65 years and over	634	52	368	207	1	8.2	58.0	32.6	606	40	197	368	......	6.6	32.5	60.7
Age unknown	66	17	36	3	1	(2)	(2)	(2)	53	12	23	10	1	(2)	(2)	(2)

[1] Includes persons whose marital condition was not reported. [2] Per cent not shown where base is less than 100.

TABLE 30.—MARITAL CONDITION BY AGE PERIODS OF NEGRO POPULATION, BY SECTIONS, SOUTHERN DIVISIONS, AND SOUTHERN STATES: 1910—Continued.

SECTION, DIVISION, STATE, AND AGE PERIOD.	NEGRO POPULATION: 1910.															
	Male.								Female.							
	Number.					Percentage.			Number.					Percentage.		
	Total.	Single.	Married.	Widowed.	Divorced.	Single.	Married.	Widowed.	Total.	Single.	Married.	Widowed.	Divorced.	Single.	Married.	Widowed.
SOUTHERN STATES—Con.																
SOUTH ATLANTIC—Con.																
MARYLAND.																
15 years and over[1]......	77,191	30,141	41,495	5,090	264	39.0	53.8	6.6	78,668	24,469	42,607	11,103	337	31.1	54.2	14.1
15 to 19 years........	11,160	11,035	74	2	....	98.9	0.7	(2)	12,238	10,952	1,212	31	1	89.5	9.9	0.3
20 to 24 years........	11,455	8,137	3,215	64	7	71.0	28.1	0.6	12,136	5,789	6,060	236	21	47.7	49.9	1.9
25 to 34 years........	18,205	6,165	11,434	494	76	33.9	62.8	2.7	19,388	4,420	13,697	1,157	92	22.8	70.6	6.0
35 to 44 years........	15,228	2,666	11,479	976	75	17.5	75.4	6.4	14,869	1,763	10,865	2,093	132	11.9	73.1	14.1
45 to 64 years........	16,632	1,789	12,451	2,281	87	10.8	74.9	13.7	15,454	1,187	9,339	4,838	78	7.7	60.4	31.3
65 years and over....	4,263	283	2,701	1,253	18	6.6	63.4	29.4	4,312	291	1,319	2,684	10	6.7	30.6	62.2
Age unknown......	248	66	141	20	1	26.6	56.9	8.1	271	67	115	64	3	24.7	42.4	23.6
DISTRICT OF COLUMBIA.																
15 years and over[1]......	32,156	12,132	17,863	1,880	183	37.7	55.6	5.8	40,597	13,443	19,065	7,665	284	33.1	47.0	18.9
15 to 19 years........	3,717	3,636	55	1	....	97.8	1.5	(2)	4,903	4,404	457	5	3	89.8	9.3	0.1
20 to 24 years........	4,766	3,286	1,411	32	10	68.9	29.6	0.7	6,567	3,492	2,883	143	24	53.2	43.9	2.2
25 to 34 years........	9,058	3,077	5,723	190	51	34.0	63.2	2.1	11,477	3,316	7,081	953	102	28.9	61.7	8.3
35 to 44 years........	7,036	1,269	5,313	382	61	18.0	75.5	5.4	8,219	1,286	5,028	1,782	109	15.6	61.2	21.7
45 to 64 years........	6,119	720	4,506	838	51	11.8	73.6	13.7	7,461	749	3,185	3,463	42	10.0	42.7	46.4
65 years and over....	1,277	86	755	423	9	6.7	59.1	33.1	1,680	117	322	1,234	4	7.0	19.2	73.5
Age unknown......	183	58	100	14	1	31.7	54.6	7.7	290	79	109	85	....	27.2	37.6	29.3
VIRGINIA.																
15 years and over[1]......	202,055	79,328	109,723	11,782	682	39.3	54.3	5.8	210,968	66,902	112,351	30,200	1,123	31.7	53.3	14.3
15 to 19 years........	36,368	35,966	257	7	1	98.9	0.7	(2)	38,679	34,656	3,763	105	26	89.6	9.7	0.3
20 to 24 years........	31,405	22,494	8,569	203	35	71.6	27.3	0.6	35,098	16,276	17,795	796	156	46.4	50.7	2.3
25 to 34 years........	44,238	13,051	29,748	1,154	195	29.5	67.2	2.6	48,444	9,333	35,574	3,113	365	19.3	73.4	6.4
35 to 44 years........	35,829	4,494	29,067	2,037	177	12.5	81.1	5.7	36,577	3,464	27,352	5,398	330	9.5	74.8	14.8
45 to 64 years........	41,661	2,602	33,728	5,075	223	6.2	81.0	12.2	39,932	2,504	24,208	12,964	212	6.3	60.6	32.5
65 years and over....	11,814	517	7,974	3,232	50	4.4	67.5	27.4	11,707	553	3,433	7,667	30	4.7	29.3	65.5
Age unknown......	740	204	380	74	1	27.6	51.4	10.0	531	116	226	157	4	21.8	42.6	29.6
WEST VIRGINIA.																
15 years and over[1]......	27,317	13,144	12,487	1,330	182	48.1	45.7	4.9	18,184	4,615	11,304	2,011	204	25.4	62.2	11.1
15 to 19 years........	3,721	3,677	38	1	....	98.8	1.0	(2)	2,854	2,230	596	15	3	78.1	20.9	0.5
20 to 24 years........	5,299	4,071	1,164	30	13	76.8	22.0	0.6	3,592	1,174	2,283	97	25	32.7	63.6	2.7
25 to 34 years........	8,602	3,690	4,591	233	46	42.9	53.4	2.7	5,417	752	4,238	326	93	13.9	78.2	6.0
35 to 44 years........	5,297	1,176	3,685	348	68	22.2	69.6	6.6	3,187	246	2,454	426	55	7.7	77.0	13.4
45 to 64 years........	3,605	433	2,594	506	53	12.0	72.0	14.0	2,468	157	1,533	745	26	6.4	62.1	30.2
65 years and over....	661	71	371	207	2	10.7	56.1	31.3	596	38	169	385	2	6.4	28.4	64.6
Age unknown......	132	26	44	5	....	19.7	33.3	3.8	70	18	31	17	....	(3)	(3)	(3)
NORTH CAROLINA.																
15 years and over[1]......	191,986	69,483	111,770	9,514	427	36.2	58.2	5.0	208,993	66,965	114,810	25,765	803	32.0	54.9	12.3
15 to 19 years........	38,752	37,849	625	14	....	97.7	1.6	(2)	41,501	35,766	5,370	117	14	86.2	12.9	0.3
20 to 24 years........	31,047	18,701	11,901	264	28	60.2	38.3	0.9	38,438	16,072	21,138	985	117	41.8	55.0	2.6
25 to 34 years........	41,246	8,292	31,626	1,127	100	20.1	76.7	2.7	49,287	8,905	36,793	3,240	277	18.1	74.7	6.6
35 to 44 years........	28,375	2,233	24,600	1,393	95	7.9	86.7	4.9	33,151	3,129	25,337	4,444	206	9.4	76.4	13.4
45 to 64 years........	39,910	1,666	34,157	3,870	166	4.2	85.6	9.7	35,433	2,247	22,516	10,458	159	6.3	63.5	29.5
65 years and over....	11,377	411	8,155	2,741	38	3.6	71.7	24.1	10,051	543	3,174	6,262	24	5.4	31.6	62.3
Age unknown......	1,279	331	706	105	....	25.9	55.2	8.2	1,132	303	482	259	6	26.8	42.6	22.9
SOUTH CAROLINA.																
15 years and over[1]......	225,020	75,462	137,488	10,880	271	33.5	61.1	4.8	244,703	68,178	141,327	33,694	659	27.9	57.8	13.8
15 to 18 years........	47,442	45,453	1,663	29	4	95.8	3.5	0.1	51,676	41,946	9,100	291	21	81.2	17.6	0.6
20 to 24 years........	38,005	18,686	18,692	411	29	49.2	49.2	1.1	47,300	15,107	30,059	1,859	118	31.9	63.5	3.9
25 to 34 years........	50,529	7,346	41,539	1,414	84	14.5	82.2	2.8	58,912	7,198	45,865	5,493	240	12.2	77.9	9.3
35 to 44 years........	36,893	2,110	32,677	1,973	64	5.7	88.6	5.3	38,918	2,218	29,405	7,078	168	5.7	75.6	18.2
45 to 64 years........	39,432	1,289	33,662	4,332	73	3.3	85.4	11.0	37,064	1,209	23,404	12,281	102	3.3	63.1	33.1
65 years and over....	11,754	321	8,714	2,663	15	2.7	74.1	22.7	10,063	329	3,162	6,501	8	3.3	31.4	64.6
Age unknown......	965	257	541	58	2	26.6	56.1	6.0	770	171	332	191	2	22.2	43.1	24.8
GEORGIA.																
15 years and over[1]......	338,942	109,458	206,386	20,017	1,281	32.3	60.9	5.9	355,224	87,461	210,607	53,229	2,726	24.6	59.3	15.0
15 to 19 years........	60,723	57,799	2,119	88	23	95.2	3.5	0.1	69,200	53,388	14,217	836	152	77.2	20.5	1.2
20 to 24 years........	57,091	29,639	25,850	1,002	158	51.9	45.3	1.8	66,204	19,058	42,411	3,939	562	28.8	64.1	5.9
25 to 34 years........	80,775	14,369	62,520	3,212	404	17.8	77.4	4.0	88,958	9,657	68,776	9,424	966	10.9	77.3	10.6
35 to 44 years........	56,729	4,329	48,473	3,507	295	7.6	85.4	6.2	58,526	2,967	44,186	10,685	629	5.1	75.5	18.3
45 to 64 years........	65,358	2,514	54,710	7,708	331	3.8	83.7	11.8	55,987	1,738	35,656	18,172	368	3.1	63.7	32.5
65 years and over....	16,815	499	11,824	4,379	63	3.0	70.3	26.0	15,144	420	4,784	9,859	39	2.8	31.6	65.1
Age unknown......	1,451	309	890	121	7	21.3	61.3	8.3	1,205	233	577	314	10	19.3	47.9	26.1
FLORIDA.																
15 years and over[1]......	107,388	38,277	59,004	6,547	953	35.6	54.9	6.1	93,068	20,134	59,305	11,625	1,192	21.6	63.7	12.5
15 to 19 years........	14,584	13,851	272	13	3	95.0	1.9	0.1	16,307	11,846	3,879	165	55	72.6	23.8	1.0
20 to 24 years........	17,687	10,962	5,853	255	66	62.0	33.1	1.4	17,644	4,562	11,842	830	240	25.9	67.1	4.7
25 to 34 years........	30,043	8,579	19,336	1,107	292	28.6	64.4	3.7	26,130	2,491	20,885	2,196	443	9.5	79.9	8.4
35 to 44 years........	22,037	3,196	16,511	1,661	336	14.5	74.9	7.5	16,349	696	12,861	2,457	290	4.3	78.7	15.0
45 to 64 years........	18,274	1,275	14,169	2,471	221	7.0	77.5	13.5	12,971	365	8,480	3,951	140	2.8	65.4	30.5
65 years and over....	3,420	134	2,244	996	26	3.9	65.6	29.1	2,966	69	987	1,873	12	2.3	33.3	63.1
Age unknown......	1,343	280	619	44	9	20.8	46.1	3.3	701	105	368	153	12	15.0	52.5	21.8

[1] Includes persons whose marital condition was not reported. [2] Less than one-tenth of 1 per cent. [3] Per cent not shown where base is less than 100.

TABLE **30.**—MARITAL CONDITION BY AGE PERIODS OF NEGRO POPULATION, BY SECTIONS, SOUTHERN DIVISIONS, AND SOUTHERN STATES: 1910—Continued.

SECTION, DIVISION, STATE, AND AGE PERIOD.	NEGRO POPULATION: 1910.																
	Male.								Female.								
	Number.					Percentage.			Number.					Percentage.			
	Total.	Single.	Married.	Wid- owed.	Di- vorced.	Sin- gle.	Mar- ried.	Wid- owed.	Total.	Single.	Married.	Wid- owed.	Di- vorced.	Sin- gle.	Mar- ried.	Wid- owed.	
EAST SOUTH CENTRAL.																	
KENTUCKY.																	
15 years and over [1]	92,230	35,239	48,538	7,019	1,050	38.2	52.6	7.6	90,814	24,849	48,951	15,245	1,476	27.4	53.9	16.8	
15 to 19 years	13,846	13,497	280	12	4	97.5	2.0	0.1	14,317	12,025	2,092	99	35	84.0	14.6	0.7	
20 to 24 years	13,608	9,190	4,108	163	81	67.5	30.2	1.2	14,248	5,929	7,467	586	218	41.6	52.4	4.1	
25 to 34 years	21,511	7,161	13,072	890	327	33.3	60.8	4.1	21,931	4,112	15,262	1,968	558	18.7	69.6	9.0	
35 to 44 years	17,510	3,072	12,774	1,319	309	17.5	73.0	7.5	16,490	1,462	11,844	2,773	389	8.9	71.8	16.8	
45 to 64 years	19,906	1,913	14,737	2,934	280	9.6	74.0	14.7	18,029	1,011	10,661	6,091	231	5.6	59.1	33.8	
65 years and over	5,258	302	3,259	1,636	43	5.7	62.0	31.1	5,245	228	1,425	3,543	37	4.3	27.2	67.6	
Age unknown	591	104	308	65	6	17.6	52.1	11.0	554	82	200	185	8	14.8	36.1	33.4	
TENNESSEE.																	
15 years and over [1]	150,860	52,874	85,020	11,029	1,282	35.0	56.4	7.3	156,459	40,455	86,908	26,243	2,344	25.9	55.5	16.8	
15 to 19 years	56,705	25,541	929	35	6	95.6	3.5	0.1	27,658	22,158	4,995	303	76	80.1	18.1	1.1	
20 to 24 years	23,677	13,711	9,221	496	141	57.9	38.9	2.1	27,510	9,644	15,750	1,578	449	35.1	57.3	5.7	
25 to 34 years	34,896	8,713	23,921	1,703	423	25.0	68.5	4.9	39,140	5,494	28,312	4,327	919	14.0	72.3	11.1	
35 to 44 years	24,326	2,734	19,247	1,952	345	11.2	79.1	8.0	26,643	1,775	19,310	4,978	541	6.7	72.5	18.7	
45 to 64 years	32,323	1,684	25,905	4,366	312	5.2	80.1	13.5	26,964	992	16,216	9,387	314	3.7	60.1	34.8	
65 years and over	8,250	330	5,445	2,411	43	4.0	66.0	29.2	7,905	269	2,081	5,480	26	3.4	26.3	69.3	
Age unknown	683	161	352	66	12	23.6	51.5	9.7	639	123	244	190	9	19.2	38.2	29.7	
ALABAMA.																	
15 years and over [1]	269,025	88,577	160,594	17,101	2,011	32.9	59.7	6.4	281,202	70,466	162,347	43,684	4,222	25.1	57.7	15.5	
15 to 19 years	47,343	46,269	841	35	14	97.7	1.8	0.1	51,787	41,787	9,095	574	170	80.7	17.6	1.1	
20 to 24 years	43,118	23,854	18,094	818	214	55.3	42.0	1.9	50,552	15,322	31,354	3,038	768	30.3	62.0	6.0	
25 to 34 years	63,491	12,154	47,656	2,894	681	19.1	75.1	4.6	70,688	8,397	52,921	7,652	1,663	11.9	74.9	10.8	
35 to 44 years	42,493	3,574	35,399	3,008	470	8.4	83.3	7.1	47,957	2,782	35,729	8,479	918	5.8	74.5	17.7	
45 to 64 years	57,437	2,020	48,244	6,599	510	3.5	84.0	11.5	45,812	1,553	28,536	15,072	601	3.4	62.3	32.9	
65 years and over	13,710	357	9,546	3,661	109	2.6	69.6	26.7	13,060	360	4,038	8,573	62	2.8	30.9	65.6	
Age unknown	1,433	349	814	86	13	24.4	56.8	6.0	1,346	265	674	296	40	19.7	50.1	22.0	
MISSISSIPPI.																	
15 years and over [1]	297,064	95,632	178,983	18,447	2,319	32.2	60.3	6.2	302,768	72,021	182,200	43,328	3,931	23.8	60.2	14.3	
15 to 19 years	54,469	52,430	1,333	49	20	96.3	2.4	0.1	58,058	44,598	11,913	763	188	76.8	20.5	1.3	
20 to 24 years	47,551	24,786	21,060	1,053	319	52.1	44.3	2.2	54,671	15,082	35,209	3,345	801	27.6	64.4	6.1	
25 to 34 years	72,706	12,576	55,688	3,412	795	17.3	76.6	4.7	77,738	7,954	60,439	7,773	1,446	10.2	77.7	10.0	
35 to 44 years	52,523	3,441	44,836	3,546	578	6.6	85.4	6.8	50,364	2,467	38,824	8,139	875	4.9	77.1	16.2	
45 to 64 years	52,580	1,650	43,971	6,378	473	3.1	83.6	12.1	46,949	1,336	30,799	14,190	530	2.8	65.6	30.2	
65 years and over	15,581	378	11,156	3,871	124	2.4	71.6	24.8	13,472	370	4,287	8,680	71	2.7	31.8	64.4	
Age unknown	1,654	371	939	138	10	22.4	56.8	8.3	1,516	214	729	438	20	14.1	48.1	28.9	
WEST SOUTH CENTRAL.																	
ARKANSAS.																	
15 years and over [1]	139,798	45,591	81,279	10,857	1,190	32.6	58.1	7.8	134,532	30,748	81,917	19,385	1,889	22.9	60.9	14.4	
15 to 19 years	24,296	23,460	383	31	5	96.6	1.6	0.1	26,013	20,159	5,122	377	71	77.5	19.7	1.4	
20 to 24 years	21,868	12,385	8,630	570	116	56.6	39.5	2.6	24,352	6,709	15,446	1,707	420	27.6	63.4	7.0	
25 to 34 years	34,116	6,777	24,636	2,184	444	19.9	72.2	6.4	35,101	2,810	27,700	3,819	706	8.0	78.9	10.9	
35 to 44 years	23,141	1,772	18,936	2,098	289	7.7	81.8	9.1	22,925	593	18,208	3,706	389	2.6	79.4	16.2	
45 to 64 years	29,951	934	24,471	4,203	291	3.1	81.7	14.0	20,648	312	13,648	6,382	263	1.5	66.1	30.9	
65 years and over	5,841	144	3,897	1,728	41	2.5	66.7	29.6	4,986	95	1,593	3,237	29	1.9	31.9	64.9	
Age unknown	585	119	326	43	4	20.3	55.7	7.4	507	70	200	157	11	13.8	39.4	31.0	
LOUISIANA.																	
15 years and over [1]	217,006	76,748	125,446	12,684	967	35.4	57.8	5.8	222,527	57,639	127,984	34,101	2,069	25.9	57.5	15.3	
15 to 19 years	36,172	35,246	683	23	7	97.4	1.9	0.1	40,696	32,889	7,057	399	101	80.8	17.3	1.0	
20 to 24 years	34,581	20,811	13,036	435	94	60.2	37.7	1.3	39,538	13,063	23,872	2,051	416	33.0	60.4	5.2	
25 to 34 years	54,571	13,082	39,195	1,756	319	24.0	71.8	3.2	56,595	7,528	42,623	5,619	720	13.3	75.3	9.9	
35 to 44 years	40,971	4,525	33,706	2,399	240	11.0	82.3	5.9	38,484	2,410	28,775	6,739	521	6.3	74.8	17.5	
45 to 64 years	38,563	2,357	30,998	4,900	247	6.1	80.4	12.7	35,250	1,213	21,874	11,817	279	3.4	62.1	33.5	
65 years and over	10,891	456	7,248	3,094	56	4.2	66.6	28.4	10,995	361	3,316	7,231	21	3.3	30.2	65.8	
Age unknown	1,257	271	580	77	4	21.6	46.1	6.1	969	175	467	245	11	18.1	48.2	25.3	
OKLAHOMA.																	
15 years and over [1]	45,671	16,170	25,345	3,428	460	35.4	55.5	7.5	39,278	8,566	25,136	4,871	555	21.8	64.0	12.4	
15 to 19 years	7,448	7,240	134	4	2	97.2	1.8	0.1	7,526	5,748	1,590	117	23	76.4	21.1	1.6	
20 to 24 years	7,137	4,425	2,469	172	37	62.0	34.6	2.4	7,207	1,819	4,833	405	124	25.2	67.1	5.6	
25 to 34 years	11,725	2,966	7,944	624	146	25.3	67.8	5.3	10,538	725	8,596	987	213	6.9	81.6	9.4	
35 to 44 years	8,232	936	6,386	765	121	11.4	77.6	9.3	6,512	151	5,324	934	97	2.3	81.8	14.3	
45 to 64 years	8,929	445	6,999	1,336	132	5.0	78.4	15.0	5,801	66	4,173	1,465	82	1.1	71.9	25.3	
65 years and over	1,857	67	1,264	499	20	3.6	68.1	26.9	1,446	19	509	898	8	1.3	35.2	62.1	
Age unknown	343	91	149	28	2	26.5	43.4	8.2	248	38	111	65	8	15.3	44.8	26.2	
TEXAS.																	
15 years and over [1]	210,725	73,187	120,027	13,930	2,481	34.7	57.0	6.6	210,903	53,027	121,959	30,597	4,623	25.1	57.8	14.5	
15 to 19 years	37,353	36,180	870	50	10	96.9	2.3	0.1	39,976	31,451	7,612	540	181	78.7	19.0	1.4	
20 to 24 years	35,519	19,972	14,295	759	273	56.2	40.2	2.1	39,590	12,396	23,833	2,398	834	31.3	60.2	6.1	
25 to 34 years	52,366	11,200	37,565	2,488	894	21.4	71.7	4.8	54,610	6,318	40,726	5,705	1,772	11.6	74.6	10.4	
35 to 44 years	35,046	3,454	28,351	2,599	559	9.9	80.9	7.4	35,034	1,659	26,379	5,886	1,047	4.7	75.3	16.8	
45 to 64 years	39,031	1,752	31,510	5,094	598	4.5	80.7	13.1	31,381	831	19,884	9,921	678	2.6	63.4	31.6	
65 years and over	9,982	326	6,701	2,794	131	3.3	67.1	28.0	9,075	187	2,934	5,822	90	2.1	32.3	64.2	
Age unknown	1,428	303	735	146	16	21.2	51.5	10.2	1,237	185	591	325	21	15.0	47.8	26.3	

[1] Includes persons whose marital condition was not reported.   [2] Less than one-tenth of 1 per cent.   [3] Per cent not shown where base is less than 100.

TABLE **31.**—MARITAL CONDITION OF THE URBAN AND RURAL NEGRO POPULATION, BY SEX AND AGE PERIODS, BY DIVISIONS: 1910.

DIVISION, CLASS OF COMMUNITY, AND AGE PERIOD.	MALES 15 YEARS OF AGE AND OVER.								FEMALES 15 YEARS OF AGE AND OVER.								
	Total.[1]	Single.		Married.		Widowed.		Divorced	Per cent married, widowed, or divorced.	Total.[1]	Single.		Married.		Widowed.		Divorced	Per cent married, widowed, or divorced.
		Number.	Per cent.	Number.	Per cent.	Number.	Per ct.				Number.	Per cent.	Number.	Per cent.	Number.	Per cent.		
UNITED STATES.																		
Urban communities	947,605	350,598	37.0	519,740	54.8	63,075	6.7	7,942	62.3	1,058,325	292,992	27.7	544,179	51.4	202,182	19.1	15,297	72.0
15 to 24 years	253,239	202,073	79.8	46,903	18.5	1,813	0.7	579	19.5	325,060	198,013	60.9	112,276	34.5	10,459	3.2	2,811	38.6
25 to 44 years	477,609	127,009	26.6	319,827	67.0	23,594	4.9	5,088	73.0	507,765	81,433	16.0	334,343	65.8	80,998	16.0	10,110	83,8
45 years and over	209,335	19,753	9.4	149,678	71.5	37,129	17.7	2,211	90.3	219,359	12,437	5.7	95,182	43.4	108,940	49.7	2,286	94.1
Age unknown	7,422	1,763	23.8	3,332	44.9	539	7.3	64	53.0	6,141	1,109	18.1	2,378	38.7	1,785	29.1	90	69.3
Rural communities	2,111,707	732,874	34.7	1,229,488	58.2	126,895	6.0	12,204	64.8	2,045,019	531,004	26.0	1,231,770	60.2	257,649	12.6	17,989	73.7
15 to 24 years	736,863	578,074	78.5	146,271	19.9	5,763	0.8	1,334	20.8	776,049	441,898	56.9	305,584	39.4	20,246	2.6	4,270	42.5
25 to 44 years	826,489	129,390	15.7	647,223	78.3	40,811	4.9	6,778	84.1	826,315	72,354	8.8	659,273	79.8	83,194	10.1	10,386	91.1
45 years and over	538,701	23,193	4.3	430,704	80.0	79,571	14.8	4,042	95.5	434,832	15,289	3.5	263,045	60.5	152,362	35.0	3,233	96.3
Age unknown	9,654	2,217	23.0	5,290	54.8	750	7.8	50	63.1	7,823	1,463	18.7	3,868	49.4	1,847	23.6	100	74.3
GEOGRAPHIC DIVISIONS.																		
NEW ENGLAND.																		
Urban communities	22,724	9,312	41.0	11,873	52.2	1,308	5.8	156	58.7	23,702	7,620	32.1	11,800	49.8	4,020	17.0	228	67.7
15 to 24 years	4,996	4,320	86.5	648	13.0	14	0.3	6	13.4	5,779	4,175	72.2	1,536	26.6	44	0.8	11	27.5
25 to 44 years	12,071	4,238	35.1	7,316	60.6	396	3.3	99	64.7	11,973	2,772	23.2	7,713	64.4	1,338	11.2	142	76.8
45 years and over	5,578	739	13.2	3,892	69.8	893	16.0	51	86.7	5,884	655	11.1	2,534	43.1	2,621	44.5	70	88.8
Age unknown	79	15	(2)	17	(2)	5	(2)			66	18	(2)	17	(2)	17	(2)	5	(2)
Rural communities	2,231	1,033	46.3	1,020	45.7	146	6.5	21	53.2	1,572	501	31.9	841	53.5	215	13.7	8	67.7
15 to 24 years	592	519	87.7	68	11.5				11.5	450	320	71.1	129	28.7				28.7
25 to 44 years	1,005	420	41.8	546	54.3	27	2.7	6	57.6	631	125	19.8	463	73.4	38	6.0	5	80.2
45 years and over	631	92	14.6	405	64.2	119	18.9	15	85.4	482	55	11.4	245	50.8	175	36.3	3	87.8
Age unknown	3	2	(2)	1	(2)					9	1	(2)	4	(2)	2	(2)		
MIDDLE ATLANTIC.																		
Urban communities	126,298	48,097	38.1	70,568	55.9	6,809	5.4	422	61.6	139,782	43,114	30.8	73,576	52.6	22,051	15.8	701	68.9
15 to 24 years	27,522	22,498	81.7	4,812	17.5	97	0.4	18	17.9	37,620	24,835	66.0	12,067	32.1	512	1.4	78	33.6
25 to 44 years	72,936	22,181	30.4	47,689	65.4	2,672	3.7	267	69.4	75,026	15,778	21.0	49,569	66.1	9,083	12.1	506	78.8
45 years and over	25,269	3,259	12.9	17,820	70.5	4,007	15.9	136	86.9	26,625	2,378	8.9	11,730	44.1	12,354	46.4	114	90.9
Age unknown	571	159	27.8	247	43.3	33	5.8	1	49.2	511	123	24.1	210	41.1	102	20.0	3	61.6
Rural communities	30,574	13,440	44.0	14,955	48.9	1,864	6.1	78	55.3	25,244	7,622	30.2	14,413	57.1	3,036	12.0	86	69.5
15 to 24 years	8,721	7,583	87.0	1,006	11.5	22	0.3	2	11.8	7,507	4,996	66.6	2,420	32.2	55	0.7	5	33.0
25 to 44 years	14,055	4,694	33.4	8,742	62.2	500	3.6	38	66.0	11,452	2,043	17.8	8,456	73.8	864	7.5	61	81.9
45 years and over	7,682	1,130	14.7	5,157	67.1	1,328	17.3	38	84.9	6,212	572	9.2	3,499	56.3	2,102	33.8	20	90.5
Age unknown	116	33	28.4	50	43.1	14	12.1		55.2	73	11	(2)	38	(2)	15	(2)		
EAST NORTH CENTRAL.																		
Urban communities	94,649	36,495	38.6	49,725	52.5	6,516	6.9	1,371	60.9	88,170	21,212	24.1	49,393	56.0	15,610	17.7	1,673	75.6
15 to 24 years	21,115	17,445	82.6	3,371	16.0	118	0.6	61	16.8	23,284	14,050	60.3	8,344	35.8	546	2.3	246	39.2
25 to 44 years	49,786	15,951	32.0	30,446	61.2	2,343	4.7	911	67.7	44,233	6,262	14.2	30,922	69.9	5,885	13.3	1,107	85.7
45 years and over	22,999	2,905	12.6	15,658	68.1	4,010	17.4	387	87.2	20,192	845	4.2	9,931	49.2	9,069	44.9	316	95.7
Age unknown	749	194	25.9	250	33.4	45	6.0	12	41.0	461	55	11.9	196	42.5	110	23.9	4	67.2
Rural communities	27,588	10,906	39.5	13,518	49.0	2,434	8.8	396	59.3	20,954	5,359	25.6	12,627	60.3	2,684	12.8	208	74.1
15 to 24 years	7,156	6,367	89.0	708	9.9	31	0.4	14	10.5	6,130	4,070	66.4	1,938	31.6	78	1.3	25	33.3
25 to 44 years	10,741	3,450	32.1	6,517	60.7	511	4.8	187	67.2	8,347	988	11.8	6,732	80.7	486	5.8	118	87.9
45 years and over	9,550	1,061	11.1	6,239	65.3	1,881	19.7	193	87.0	6,397	291	4.5	3,920	61.3	2,096	32.8	65	95.1
Age unknown	141	28	19.9	54	38.3	11	7.8	2	47.5	80	10	(2)	37	(2)	24	(2)		
WEST NORTH CENTRAL.																		
Urban communities	67,148	26,076	38.8	34,640	51.6	4,971	7.4	944	60.4	62,901	15,073	24.0	34,476	54.8	11,903	18.9	1,195	75.6
15 to 24 years	15,860	13,137	82.8	2,443	15.4	100	0.6	58	16.4	17,258	10,317	59.8	6,165	35.7	493	2.9	177	39.6
25 to 44 years	34,753	11,157	32.1	21,067	60.6	1,840	5.3	575	67.6	30,657	4,206	13.7	21,131	68.9	4,461	14.6	820	86.2
45 years and over	15,899	1,650	10.4	10,928	68.7	2,976	18.7	306	89.4	14,544	502	3.5	7,009	48.3	6,796	46.7	190	96.3
Age unknown	636	132	20.8	202	31.8	55	8.6	5	41.2	442	48	10.9	161	36.4	153	34.6	8	72.9
Rural communities	29,498	11,625	39.4	15,064	51.1	2,316	7.9	356	60.1	23,813	6,249	26.2	14,221	59.7	3,017	12.7	246	73.4
15 to 24 years	8,467	7,330	86.6	1,012	12.0	46	0.5	19	12.7	7,592	4,928	64.9	2,464	32.5	120	1.6	49	34.7
25 to 44 years	11,559	3,399	29.4	7,356	63.6	600	5.2	186	70.4	9,259	997	10.8	7,461	80.6	639	6.9	139	89.0
45 years and over	9,280	849	9.1	6,609	71.2	1,645	17.7	149	90.5	6,827	298	4.4	4,237	62.1	2,221	32.5	57	95.4
Age unknown	192	47	24.5	87	45.3	25	13.0	2	59.4	135	26	19.3	59	43.7	37	27.4	1	71.9

[1] Total includes persons whose marital condition was not reported.   [2] Per cent not shown where base is less than 100.

TABLE **31.**—MARITAL CONDITION OF THE URBAN AND RURAL NEGRO POPULATION, BY SEX AND AGE PERIODS, BY DIVISIONS: 1910—Continued.

DIVISION, CLASS OF COMMUNITY, AND AGE PERIOD.	MALES 15 YEARS OF AGE AND OVER.									FEMALES 15 YEARS OF AGE AND OVER.								
	Total.[1]	Single. Number.	Per cent.	Married. Number.	Per cent.	Widowed. Number.	Per ct.	Divorced.	Per cent married, widowed, or divorced.	Total.[1]	Single. Number.	Per cent.	Married. Number.	Per cent.	Widowed. Number.	Per cent.	Divorced.	Per cent married, widowed, or divorced.
SOUTH ATLANTIC.																		
Urban communities	298,404	109,568	36.7	166,024	55.6	18,692	6.3	1,279	62.3	359,452	108,442	30.2	177,747	49.4	69,189	19.2	2,795	69.5
15 to 24 years	88,229	69,536	78.8	17,098	19.4	529	0.6	76	20.1	118,438	75,574	63.0	39,300	33.2	3,457	2.9	471	36.5
25 to 44 years	142,510	34,037	23.9	99,786	70.0	6,665	4.7	814	75.3	164,659	28,613	17.4	106,499	64.7	27,338	16.6	1,887	82.4
45 years and over	65,028	5,294	8.1	47,794	73.5	11,317	17.4	380	91.5	74,175	4,779	6.4	31,078	41.9	37,742	50.9	425	93.4
Age unknown	2,637	701	26.6	1,346	51.0	181	6.9	9	58.2	2,180	476	21.8	870	39.9	652	29.9	12	70.4
Rural communities	914,666	322,375	35.2	535,813	58.6	49,139	5.4	2,998	64.3	901,175	246,870	27.4	539,208	59.8	107,526	11.9	4,568	72.3
15 to 24 years	328,243	258,511	78.8	65,085	19.8	1,896	0.6	301	20.5	349,019	204,307	58.5	134,671	38.6	7,019	2.0	1,070	40.9
25 to 44 years	352,263	53,362	15.1	281,572	79.9	14,762	4.2	1,626	84.6	357,467	34,011	9.5	287,040	80.3	33,293	9.3	2,630	90.3
45 years and over	230,390	9,655	4.2	187,045	81.2	32,218	14.0	1,058	95.6	191,846	7,924	4.1	116,104	60.5	66,616	34.7	842	95.7
Age unknown	3,770	847	22.5	2,111	56.0	263	7.0	13	63.3	2,843	628	22.1	1,393	49.0	598	21.0	26	70.9
EAST SOUTH CENTRAL.																		
Urban communities	173,911	61,509	35.4	96,188	55.3	13,656	7.9	1,918	64.3	202,972	51,956	25.6	101,722	50.1	44,477	21.9	4,279	74.1
15 to 24 years	49,511	39,015	78.8	9,605	19.4	531	1.1	177	20.8	63,603	36,680	57.7	22,858	35.9	3,015	4.7	893	42.1
25 to 44 years	83,019	19,360	23.3	56,917	68.6	5,377	6.5	1,207	76.5	94,825	13,129	13.8	60,637	63.9	18,144	19.1	2,793	86.0
45 years and over	40,039	2,831	7.1	29,000	72.4	7,622	19.0	518	92.8	43,226	1,921	4.4	17,749	41.1	22,912	53.0	565	95.4
Age unknown	1,342	303	22.6	666	49.6	126	9.4	16	60.2	1,318	226	17.1	478	36.3	406	30.8	28	69.2
Rural communities	635,268	210,813	33.2	376,947	59.3	39,940	6.3	4,744	66.4	628,271	155,835	24.8	378,684	60.3	84,023	13.4	7,694	74.9
15 to 24 years	220,806	170,263	77.1	46,261	21.0	2,130	1.0	622	22.2	235,198	129,865	55.2	95,017	40.4	7,271	3.1	1,812	44.3
25 to 44 years	246,437	34,065	13.8	195,676	79.4	13,347	5.4	2,721	85.9	256,126	21,314	8.3	202,004	78.9	27,945	10.9	4,516	91.5
45 years and over	165,006	5,803	3.5	133,263	80.8	24,234	14.7	1,376	96.3	134,210	4,198	3.1	80,294	59.8	48,104	35.8	1,317	96.7
Age unknown	3,019	682	22.6	1,747	57.9	229	7.6	25	66.3	2,737	458	16.7	1,369	50.0	703	25.7	49	77.5
WEST SOUTH CENTRAL.																		
Urban communities	147,283	52,354	35.5	82,077	55.7	10,189	6.9	1,578	63.7	166,046	42,058	25.3	86,903	52.3	32,205	19.4	4,019	74.2
15 to 24 years	42,848	33,436	78.0	8,491	19.8	410	1.0	169	21.2	55,417	31,219	56.3	20,680	37.3	2,300	4.2	867	43.0
25 to 44 years	72,837	16,415	22.5	51,147	70.2	3,956	5.4	1,032	77.1	78,176	9,509	12.2	52,235	66.8	13,621	17.4	2,590	87.6
45 years and over	30,367	2,287	7.5	21,878	72.0	5,735	18.9	359	92.1	31,421	1,185	3.8	13,581	43.2	15,959	50.8	535	95.7
Age unknown	1,231	216	17.5	561	45.6	88	7.1	18	54.2	1,032	145	14.1	407	39.4	325	31.5	27	73.5
Rural communities	465,917	159,342	34.2	270,020	58.0	30,710	6.6	3,520	65.3	441,194	107,922	24.5	270,093	61.2	56,749	12.9	5,117	75.2
15 to 24 years	161,526	126,283	78.2	32,009	19.8	1,634	1.0	375	21.1	169,481	93,015	54.9	68,685	40.5	5,694	3.4	1,303	44.7
25 to 44 years	187,331	28,297	15.1	145,572	77.7	10,957	5.8	1,980	84.6	181,623	12,685	7.0	146,096	80.4	19,774	10.9	2,875	92.9
45 years and over	114,678	4,194	3.7	91,210	79.5	17,913	15.6	1,157	96.2	88,161	1,899	2.2	54,350	61.6	30,814	35.0	915	97.6
Age unknown	2,382	568	23.8	1,229	51.6	206	8.6	8	60.6	1,929	323	16.7	962	49.9	467	24.2	24	75.3
MOUNTAIN.																		
Urban communities	6,546	2,520	38.5	3,439	52.5	388	5.9	133	60.5	6,049	1,357	22.4	3,361	55.6	1,115	18.4	185	77.1
15 to 24 years	1,131	928	82.1	186	16.4	5	0.4	7	17.5	1,465	806	55.0	573	39.1	45	3.1	34	44.5
25 to 44 years	3,752	1,279	34.1	2,204	58.7	149	4.0	91	65.1	3,305	482	14.6	2,193	66.4	494	14.9	120	84.9
45 years and over	1,592	293	18.4	1,027	64.5	232	14.6	33	81.2	1,242	61	4.9	580	46.7	569	45.8	31	95.0
Age unknown	71	20	(2)	22	(2)	2	(2)	2	(2)	37	8	(2)	15	(2)	7	(2)		
Rural communities	3,273	1,788	54.6	1,234	37.7	186	5.7	46	44.8	1,601	361	22.5	972	60.7	226	14.1	39	77.3
15 to 24 years	718	643	89.6	69	9.6	2	0.3	1	10.0	404	215	53.2	179	44.3	5	1.2	5	46.8
25 to 44 years	1,797	935	52.0	766	42.6	66	3.7	21	47.5	864	111	12.8	618	71.5	108	12.5	26	87.0
45 years and over	740	204	27.6	392	53.0	117	15.8	24	72.0	324	31	9.6	171	52.8	113	34.9	8	90.1
Age unknown	18	6	(2)	7	(2)	1	(2)			9	4	(2)	4	(2)				
PACIFIC.																		
Urban communities	10,642	4,667	43.9	5,206	48.9	546	5.1	141	55.4	9,251	2,160	23.3	5,201	56.2	1,612	17.4	222	76.0
15 to 24 years	2,027	1,758	86.7	249	12.3	9	0.4	7	13.1	2,196	1,357	61.8	753	34.3	47	2.1	34	38.0
25 to 44 years	5,945	2,391	40.2	3,255	54.8	196	3.3	92	59.6	4,911	682	13.9	3,444	70.1	634	12.9	145	86.0
45 years and over	2,564	495	19.3	1,681	65.6	337	13.1	41	80.3	2,050	111	5.4	980	47.8	918	44.8	40	94.5
Age unknown	106	23	21.7	21	19.8	4	3.8	1	24.5	94	10	(2)	24	(2)	13	(2)	3	
Rural communities	2,692	1,552	57.7	917	34.1	160	5.9	45	41.7	1,195	285	23.8	711	59.5	173	14.5	23	75.9
15 to 24 years	634	575	90.7	53	8.4	2	0.3		8.7	268	182	67.9	81	30.2	4	1.5	1	32.1
25 to 44 years	1,301	768	59.0	476	36.6	41	3.2	13	40.7	546	80	14.7	403	73.8	47	8.6	16	85.3
45 years and over	744	205	27.6	384	51.6	116	15.6	32	71.5	373	21	5.6	225	60.3	121	32.4	6	94.4
Age unknown	13	4	(2)	4	(2)	1	(2)			8	2	(2)	2	(2)	1	(2)		

[1] Total includes persons whose marital condition was not reported.   [2] Per cent not shown where base is less than 100.

TABLE **32.**—MARITAL CONDITION OF THE URBAN AND RURAL NEGRO POPULATION, BY DIVISIONS AND STATES: 1910.

[Per cent not shown where base is less than 100.]

DIVISION, STATE, AND CLASS OF POPULATION.	NEGRO POPULATION 15 YEARS OF AGE AND OVER: 1910.													
	Male.							Female.						
	Number.					Percentage.		Number.					Percentage.	
	Total.[1]	Single.	Married.	Widowed.	Divorced.	Single.	Married.	Total.[1]	Single.	Married.	Widowed.	Divorced.	Single.	Married.
UNITED STATES:														
Urban	947,605	350,598	519,740	63,075	7,942	37.0	54.8	1,058,325	292,992	544,179	202,182	15,297	27.7	51.4
Rural	2,111,707	732,874	1,229,488	126,895	12,204	34.7	58.2	2,045,019	531,004	1,231,770	257,649	17,989	26.0	60.2
New England:														
Urban	22,724	9,312	11,873	1,308	156	41.0	52.2	23,702	7,620	11,800	4,020	228	32.1	49.8
Rural	2,231	1,033	1,020	146	21	46.3	45.1	1,572	501	841	215	8	31.9	53.5
Middle Atlantic:														
Urban	126,298	48,097	70,568	6,809	422	38.1	55.9	139,782	43,114	73,576	22,051	701	30.8	52.6
Rural	30,574	13,440	14,955	1,864	78	44.0	48.9	25,244	7,622	14,413	3,036	86	30.2	57.1
East North Central:														
Urban	94,649	36,495	49,725	6,516	1,371	38.6	52.5	88,170	21,212	49,393	15,610	1,673	24.1	56.0
Rural	27,588	10,906	13,518	2,434	396	39.5	49.0	20,954	5,359	12,627	2,684	208	25.6	60.3
West North Central:														
Urban	67,148	26,076	34,640	4,971	944	38.8	51.6	62,901	15,073	34,476	11,903	1,195	24.0	54.8
Rural	29,498	11,625	15,064	2,316	356	39.4	51.1	23,813	6,249	14,221	3,017	246	26.2	59.7
South Atlantic:														
Urban	298,404	109,568	166,024	18,692	1,279	36.7	55.6	359,452	108,442	177,747	69,189	2,795	30.2	49.4
Rural	914,666	322,375	535,813	49,139	2,998	35.2	58.6	901,175	246,870	539,208	107,526	4,568	27.4	59.8
East South Central:														
Urban	173,911	61,509	96,188	13,656	1,918	35.4	55.3	202,972	51,956	101,722	44,477	4,279	25.6	50.1
Rural	635,268	210,813	376,947	39,940	4,744	33.2	59.3	628,271	155,835	378,684	84,023	7,694	24.8	60.3
West South Central:														
Urban	147,283	52,354	82,077	10,189	1,578	35.5	55.7	166,046	42,058	86,903	32,205	4,019	25.3	52.3
Rural	465,917	159,342	270,020	30,710	3,520	34.2	58.0	441,194	107,922	270,093	56,749	5,117	24.5	61.2
Mountain:														
Urban	6,546	2,520	3,439	388	133	38.5	52.5	6,049	1,357	3,361	1,115	185	22.4	55.6
Rural	3,273	1,788	1,234	186	46	54.6	37.7	1,601	361	972	226	39	22.5	60.7
Pacific:														
Urban	10,642	4,667	5,206	546	141	43.9	48.9	9,251	2,160	5,201	1,612	222	23.3	56.2
Rural	2,692	1,552	917	160	45	57.7	34.1	1,195	285	711	173	23	23.8	59.5
NEW ENGLAND.														
Maine:														
Urban	356	163	159	28	6	45.8	44.7	350	134	155	52	9	38.3	44.3
Rural	198	87	90	18	3	43.9	45.5	145	58	62	22	2	40.0	42.8
New Hampshire:														
Urban	129	51	64	11	3	39.5	49.6	158	70	64	21	1	44.3	40.5
Rural	100	44	47	7	1	44.0	47.0	53	14	33	5		....	....
Vermont:														
Urban	935	706	197	20	12	75.5	21.1	254	60	164	22	8	23.6	64.6
Rural	119	59	51	7	2	49.6	42.9	66	24	35	7		....	....
Massachusetts:														
Urban	13,078	5,384	6,871	688	79	41.2	52.5	13,814	4,564	6,796	2,346	98	33.0	49.2
Rural	1,159	557	520	65	8	48.1	44.9	762	219	436	101	2	28.7	57.2
Rhode Island:														
Urban	3,301	1,295	1,774	196	30	39.2	53.7	3,544	1,057	1,765	655	53	29.8	49.8
Rural	209	109	86	12	2	52.2	41.1	145	51	76	18		35.2	52.4
Connecticut:														
Urban	4,925	1,713	2,808	365	26	34.8	57.0	5,582	1,735	2,856	924	59	31.1	51.2
Rural	446	177	226	37	5	39.7	50.7	401	135	199	62	4	33.7	49.6
MIDDLE ATLANTIC.														
New York:														
Urban	44,067	17,396	24,285	2,103	155	39.5	55.1	51,184	16,570	25,685	8,520	278	32.4	50.2
Rural	7,361	3,755	3,150	430	9	51.0	42.8	5,301	1,698	2,892	686	14	32.0	54.6
New Jersey:														
Urban	23,490	8,372	13,755	1,224	68	35.6	58.6	26,900	8,155	14,510	4,083	92	30.3	53.9
Rural	9,341	3,856	4,894	551	20	41.3	52.4	7,968	2,147	4,746	1,029	17	26.9	59.6
Pennsylvania:														
Urban	58,741	22,329	32,528	3,482	199	38.0	55.4	61,698	18,389	33,381	9,448	331	29.8	54.1
Rural	13,872	5,829	6,911	883	49	42.0	49.8	11,975	3,777	6,775	1,321	55	31.5	56.6
EAST NORTH CENTRAL.														
Ohio:														
Urban	33,635	13,192	17,701	2,176	417	39.2	52.6	31,387	8,282	17,495	5,033	484	26.4	55.7
Rural	11,259	4,582	5,509	986	141	40.7	48.9	8,665	2,314	5,146	1,105	80	26.7	59.4
Indiana:														
Urban	19,179	7,235	9,997	1,525	355	37.7	52.1	18,333	4,385	10,020	3,449	449	23.9	54.7
Rural	4,669	1,810	2,330	444	63	38.8	49.9	3,485	853	2,184	402	38	24.5	62.7
Illinois:														
Urban	35,871	13,813	18,857	2,431	495	38.5	52.6	32,896	7,103	18,807	6,219	624	21.6	57.2
Rural	9,328	3,628	4,504	801	140	38.9	48.3	7,065	1,757	4,244	953	66	24.9	60.1
Michigan:														
Urban	5,069	1,864	2,753	322	86	36.8	54.3	4,672	1,167	2,630	769	91	25.0	56.3
Rural	2,018	746	1,041	176	44	37.0	51.6	1,522	353	945	199	23	23.2	62.1
Wisconsin:														
Urban	895	391	417	62	18	43.7	46.6	882	275	441	140	25	31.2	50.0
Rural	314	140	134	27	8	44.6	42.7	217	82	108	25	1	37.8	49.8
WEST NORTH CENTRAL.														
Minnesota:														
Urban	3,402	1,629	1,523	173	36	47.9	44.8	2,169	579	1,245	303	31	26.7	57.4
Rural	255	143	95	14	2	56.1	37.3	165	62	83	19		37.6	50.3
Iowa:														
Urban	4,100	1,554	2,101	318	94	37.9	51.2	3,431	784	1,996	547	95	22.9	58.2
Rural	2,122	796	1,120	144	49	37.5	52.8	1,512	328	1,012	130	33	21.7	66.9
Missouri:														
Urban	42,614	16,675	21,789	3,262	556	39.1	51.1	41,280	9,963	21,973	8,391	780	24.1	53.2
Rural	19,031	7,292	9,925	1,549	186	38.3	52.2	16,270	4,277	9,640	2,162	146	26.3	59.3
North Dakota:														
Urban	178	98	59	7	3	55.1	33.1	99	24	58	11	6	....	....
Rural	153	92	48	8	2	60.1	31.4	86	32	48	5	1	....	....
South Dakota:														
Urban	183	72	98	10	3	39.3	53.6	146	43	84	16	3	29.5	57.5
Rural	190	98	78	11	3	51.6	41.1	116	36	68	11	1	31.0	58.6

[1] Includes persons whose marital condition was not reported.

TABLE **32.**—MARITAL CONDITION OF THE URBAN AND RURAL NEGRO POPULATION, BY DIVISIONS AND STATES: 1910—Continued.

[Per cent not shown where base is less than 100.]

DIVISION, STATE, AND CLASS OF POPULATION.	NEGRO POPULATION 15 YEARS OF AGE AND OVER: 1910.													
	Male.							Female.						
	Number.					Percentage.		Number.					Percentage.	
	Total.[1]	Single.	Married.	Widowed.	Divorced.	Single.	Married.	Total.[1]	Single.	Married.	Widowed.	Divorced.	Single.	Married.
WEST NORTH CENTRAL—contd.														
Nebraska:														
Urban	3,027	1,292	1,477	205	47	42.7	48.8	2,430	548	1,455	377	47	22.6	59.9
Rural	514	249	225	32	7	48.4	43.8	316	95	172	40	8	30.1	54.4
Kansas:														
Urban	13,644	4,756	7,593	996	205	34.9	55.7	13,346	3,132	7,665	2,258	233	23.5	57.4
Rural	7,233	2,955	3,573	558	107	40.9	49.4	5,348	1,419	3,198	650	57	26.5	59.8
SOUTH ATLANTIC.														
Delaware:														
Urban	4,093	1,639	2,043	374	13	40.0	49.9	4,410	1,457	2,097	806	25	33.0	47.6
Rural	6,922	2,879	3,578	417	21	41.6	51.7	5,812	1,688	3,482	617	10	29.0	59.9
Maryland:														
Urban	34,853	13,471	18,681	2,453	162	38.7	53.6	40,973	13,891	19,892	6,891	231	33.9	48.5
Rural	42,338	16,670	22,814	2,637	102	39.4	53.9	37,695	10,578	22,715	4,212	106	28.1	60.3
District of Columbia:														
Urban	32,156	12,132	17,863	1,880	183	37.7	55.6	40,597	13,443	19,065	7,665	284	33.1	47.0
Rural														
Virginia:														
Urban	52,109	21,556	27,080	3,090	223	41.4	52.0	63,273	21,879	28,729	12,080	479	34.6	45.4
Rural	149,946	57,772	82,643	8,692	459	38.5	55.1	147,695	45,023	83,622	18,120	644	30.5	56.6
West Virginia:														
Urban	6,110	2,822	2,910	303	44	46.2	47.6	5,527	1,792	2,842	813	67	32.4	51.4
Rural	21,207	10,322	9,577	1,027	138	48.7	45.2	12,657	2,823	8,462	1,198	137	22.3	66.9
North Carolina:														
Urban	34,574	12,475	19,841	1,948	73	36.1	57.4	43,918	14,222	21,353	7,937	200	32.4	48.6
Rural	157,412	57,008	91,929	7,566	354	36.2	58.4	165,075	52,743	93,457	17,828	603	32.0	56.6
South Carolina:														
Urban	30,474	10,130	18,157	1,867	43	33.2	59.6	39,336	11,114	19,548	8,331	123	28.3	49.7
Rural	194,546	65,332	119,331	9,013	228	33.6	61.3	205,367	57,064	121,779	25,363	536	27.8	59.3
Georgia:														
Urban	71,907	24,287	42,166	4,896	245	33.8	58.6	89,019	22,888	45,613	19,494	829	25.7	51.2
Rural	267,035	85,171	164,220	15,121	1,036	31.9	61.5	266,205	64,573	164,994	33,735	1,897	24.3	62.0
Florida:														
Urban	32,128	11,056	17,283	1,881	293	34.4	53.8	32,399	7,756	18,608	5,172	557	23.9	57.4
Rural	75,260	27,221	41,721	4,666	660	36.2	55.4	60,669	12,378	40,697	6,453	635	20.4	67.1
EAST SOUTH CENTRAL.														
Kentucky:														
Urban	39,421	15,585	20,111	3,034	520	39.5	51.0	43,191	12,242	20,939	9,002	867	28.3	48.5
Rural	52,809	19,654	28,427	3,985	530	37.2	53.8	47,623	12,607	28,012	6,243	609	26.5	58.8
Tennessee:														
Urban	52,602	18,859	28,503	4,381	706	35.9	54.2	61,375	15,650	30,376	13,763	1,481	25.5	49.5
Rural	98,258	34,015	56,517	6,648	576	34.6	57.5	95,084	24,805	56,532	12,480	863	26.1	59.5
Alabama:														
Urban	52,223	17,300	30,121	4,181	456	33.1	57.7	60,514	14,316	31,544	13,354	1,163	23.7	52.1
Rural	216,802	71,277	130,473	12,920	1,555	32.9	60.2	220,688	56,150	130,803	30,330	3,059	25.4	59.3
Mississippi:														
Urban	29,665	9,765	17,453	2,060	236	32.9	58.8	37,892	9,748	18,863	8,358	768	25.7	49.8
Rural	267,399	85,867	161,530	16,387	2,083	32.1	60.4	264,876	62,273	163,337	34,970	3,163	23.5	61.7
WEST SOUTH CENTRAL.														
Arkansas:														
Urban	20,973	7,753	11,164	1,662	280	37.0	53.2	22,344	5,369	11,669	4,540	665	24.0	52.2
Rural	118,825	37,838	70,115	9,195	910	31.8	59.0	112,188	25,379	70,248	14,845	1,224	22.6	62.6
Louisiana:														
Urban	51,565	18,421	29,495	2,972	246	35.7	57.2	63,277	17,654	31,561	12,984	730	27.9	49.9
Rural	165,441	58,327	95,951	9,712	721	35.3	58.0	159,250	39,985	96,423	21,117	1,339	25.1	60.5
Oklahoma:														
Urban	14,389	5,410	7,606	1,086	150	37.6	52.9	12,197	2,573	7,502	1,783	260	21.1	61.5
Rural	31,282	10,760	17,739	2,342	310	34.4	56.7	27,081	5,993	17,634	3,088	295	22.1	65.1
Texas:														
Urban	60,356	20,770	33,812	4,469	902	34.4	56.0	68,228	16,462	36,171	12,898	2,364	24.1	53.0
Rural	150,369	52,417	86,215	9,461	1,579	34.9	57.3	142,675	36,565	85,788	17,699	2,259	25.6	60.1
MOUNTAIN.														
Montana:														
Urban	710	345	318	26	13	48.6	44.8	514	134	293	68	19	26.1	57.0
Rural	201	109	75	15	2	54.2	37.3	113	29	67	14	3	25.7	59.3
Idaho:														
Urban	232	121	95	11	5	52.2	40.9	152	40	85	23	3	26.3	55.9
Rural	118	58	47	6	5	49.2	39.8	57	21	28	7			
Wyoming:														
Urban	437	212	197	12	11	48.5	45.1	408	123	203	56	26	30.1	49.8
Rural	971	776	167	17	5	79.9	17.2	152	29	103	20		19.1	67.8
Colorado:														
Urban	3,785	1,340	2,100	252	75	35.4	55.5	3,768	810	2,095	748	99	21.5	55.6
Rural	976	382	508	65	20	39.1	52.0	654	126	434	80	12	19.3	66.4
New Mexico:														
Urban	320	102	181	26	10	31.9	56.6	294	52	170	62	9	17.7	57.8
Rural	398	181	176	35	4	45.5	44.2	226	55	135	28	8	24.3	59.7
Arizona:														
Urban	494	162	291	28	11	32.8	58.9	549	124	296	111	16	22.6	53.9
Rural	333	151	143	26	5	45.3	42.9	185	43	106	30	6	23.2	57.3
Utah:														
Urban	513	213	232	29	7	41.5	45.2	328	68	199	40	10	20.7	60.7
Rural	93	50	37	5	1			37	13	22	2			
Nevada:														
Urban	55	25	25	4	1			36	6	20	7	3		
Rural	183	81	81	17	4	44.3	44.3	177	45	77	45	10	25.4	43.5
PACIFIC.														
Washington:														
Urban	2,445	1,231	1,036	98	37	50.3	42.4	1,647	393	951	214	44	23.9	57.7
Rural	891	588	260	28	13	66.0	29.2	260	44	182	28	4	16.9	70.0
Oregon:														
Urban	682	349	287	36	9	51.2	42.1	434	79	265	77	13	18.2	61.1
Rural	133	76	46	6	4	57.1	34.6	56	20	25	11			
California:														
Urban	7,515	3,087	3,883	412	95	41.1	51.7	7,170	1,688	3,985	1,321	165	23.5	55.6
Rural	1,668	888	611	126	28	53.2	36.6	879	221	504	134	19	25.1	57.3

[1] Includes persons whose marital condition was not reported.

TABLE **33.**—MARITAL CONDITION OF THE NEGRO POPULATION, BY CITIES OF 100,000 OR MORE INHABITANTS: 1910, 1900, AND 1890.

| CITY. | NEGRO POPULATION 15 YEARS OF AGE AND OVER: 1910. | | | | | | | | | | | |
| | Male. | | | | | | Female. | | | | | |
	Total	Single.	Married.	Widowed.	Divorced.	Marital condition unknown.	Total.	Single.	Married.	Widowed.	Divorced.	Marital condition unknown.
Albany, N.Y.	415	171	208	32	4	....	445	146	214	82	3	....
Atlanta, Ga.	16,600	5,776	9,736	1,024	46	18	21,789	5,597	10,834	5,221	121	16
Baltimore, Md.	29,982	11,651	16,045	2,060	146	80	35,572	12,170	17,095	6,044	197	66
Birmingham, Ala.	19,092	6,436	10,821	1,679	109	47	19,706	3,964	11,103	4,387	234	18
Boston, Mass.	5,482	2,359	2,778	303	37	5	5,572	1,744	2,710	1,069	47	2
Bridgeport, Conn.	514	206	272	33	2	1	519	140	282	89	5	3
Buffalo, N.Y.	791	362	366	53	8	2	696	223	363	107	1	2
Cambrdge, Mass.	1,585	520	964	91	7	3	1,814	539	1,000	266	9	....
Chicago, Ill.	19,372	7,631	10,076	1,232	279	154	17,962	3,800	9,978	3,746	355	83
Cincinnati, Ohio	8,246	3,268	4,284	550	81	63	8,002	2,054	4,305	1,482	126	35
Cleveland, Ohio	3,630	1,350	2,017	194	53	16	3,361	819	1,965	513	61	3
Columbus, Ohio	5,629	2,429	2,774	347	66	13	4,696	1,215	2,687	699	82	13
Dayton, Ohio	1,976	713	1,085	138	26	4	1,876	468	1,096	280	30	2
Denver, Colo.	2,203	787	1,233	128	48	7	2,278	504	1,249	447	72	6
Detroit, Mich.	2,465	938	1,343	130	27	27	2,261	545	1,286	388	34	8
Fall River, Mass.	143	59	77	7	....	6	146	43	69	33	1	2
Grand Rapids, Mich.	291	96	164	23	2	6	264	59	158	40	5	2
Indianapolis, Ind.	8,521	3,093	4,576	690	142	20	8,692	1,963	4,723	1,809	189	8
Jersey City, N.J.	2,335	861	1,353	111	7	3	2,206	500	1,344	352	7	3
Kansas City, Mo.	10,107	3,818	5,251	727	168	143	9,782	2,275	5,295	1,920	246	46
Los Angeles, Cal.	2,921	1,002	1,747	144	25	3	3,070	668	1,783	568	47	4
Louisville, Ky.	15,772	6,399	7,780	1,288	224	81	16,853	4,612	8,170	3,638	361	72
Lowell, Mass.	52	22	24	5	1	....	57	24	19	12	1	1
Memphis, Tenn.	20,012	7,371	10,586	1,633	366	56	21,510	4,951	11,234	4,587	706	32
Milwaukee, Wis.	422	175	203	29	9	6	431	144	198	76	13	....
Minneapolis, Minn.	1,321	588	601	83	14	35	907	235	516	130	16	10
Nashville, Tenn.	11,933	4,140	6,584	1,067	137	5	15,757	4,222	7,025	4,154	348	8
New Haven, Conn.	1,335	461	767	98	6	3	1,473	400	775	284	13	1
New Orleans, La.	29,692	10,783	16,879	1,634	113	283	36,392	10,179	18,100	7,597	293	223
New York, N.Y.	34,269	13,335	19,196	1,540	101	97	40,792	13,174	20,466	6,844	206	102
Manhattan Borough	23,495	9,472	12,885	979	74	85	27,348	8,800	13,688	4,612	159	89
Bronx Borough	1,436	460	883	87	2	4	1,700	493	927	273	5	2
Brooklyn Borough	7,869	2,869	4,573	398	21	8	9,950	3,251	4,985	1,665	39	10
Queens Borough	1,079	395	633	48	3	....	1,336	459	643	232	2	....
Richmond Borough	390	139	222	28	1	....	458	171	223	62	1	1
Newark, N.J.	3,414	1,115	2,117	163	10	9	3,848	1,045	2,196	591	11	5
Oakland, Cal.	1,357	617	650	72	17	1	1,168	241	665	231	29	2
Omaha, Nebr.	2,044	871	999	136	36	2	1,698	404	986	270	35	3
Paterson, N.J.	512	169	313	27	....	3	652	193	367	84	4	4
Philadelphia, Pa.	30,976	11,360	17,727	1,713	86	90	35,790	11,156	18,678	5,726	145	85
Pittsburgh, Pa.	10,374	4,070	5,594	645	32	33	9,224	2,313	5,547	1,269	80	15
Portland, Oreg.	550	263	253	26	8	....	376	65	236	63	12	....
Providence, R.I.	1,978	768	1,068	121	20	1	2,125	600	1,062	418	43	2
Richmond, Va.	15,778	6,552	8,229	907	62	28	19,210	6,842	8,459	3,752	121	36
Rochester, N.Y.	346	138	187	19	2	....	366	124	198	40	2	2
St. Louis, Mo.	18,318	7,271	9,415	1,421	169	42	17,689	3,916	9,607	3,860	276	30
St. Paul, Minn.	1,681	838	749	75	16	3	1,010	270	587	141	11	1
San Francisco, Cal.	911	526	308	55	13	9	504	152	254	76	22	....
Scranton, Pa.	242	114	117	11	....	....	200	64	107	28	....	1
Seattle, Wash.	1,256	677	498	35	17	29	776	175	446	102	17	36
Spokane, Wash.	339	122	196	15	5	1	283	46	193	35	7	2
Syracuse, N.Y.	478	192	250	28	7	1	434	124	239	68	2	1
Toledo, Ohio	790	306	412	56	15	1	756	212	432	100	11	1
Washington, D.C.	32,156	12,132	17,863	1,880	183	98	40,597	13,443	19,065	7,665	284	140
Worcester, Mass.	435	156	250	26	2	1	508	160	249	97	2	....

TABLE **33.**—MARITAL CONDITION OF THE NEGRO POPULATION, BY CITIES OF 100,000 OR MORE INHABITANTS 1910, 1900, AND 1890—Continued.

| CITY. | NEGRO POPULATION 15 YEARS OF AGE AND OVER: 1900. | | | | | | | | | | | |
| | Male. | | | | | | Female. | | | | | |
	Total.	Single.	Married.	Widowed.	Divorced.	Marital condition unknown.	Total.	Single.	Married.	Widowed.	Divorced.	Marital condition unknown.
Albany, N. Y.[1]												
Atlanta, Ga.												
Baltimore, Md.	25,510	10,334	13,510	1,510	57	99	33,438	12,791	14,461	5,929	142	115
Birmingham, Ala.												
Boston, Mass.	4,885	2,305	2,286	225	10	59	4,467	1,417	2,178	817	23	32
Bridgeport, Conn.[1]												
Buffalo, N. Y.	741	347	352	39	1	2	643	194	342	99	8	......
Cambridge, Mass.[1]												
Chicago, Ill.	13,783	6,757	6,072	801	79	74	11,622	2,995	5,996	2,461	142	28
Cincinnati, Ohio	5,661	2,460	2,830	333	28	10	5,752	1,698	2,913	1,079	56	6
Cleveland, Ohio	2,626	1,232	1,236	132	16	10	2,193	637	1,214	311	30	1
Columbus, Ohio	3,416	1,672	1,508	188	19	29	2,926	990	1,410	482	32	12
Dayton, Ohio[1]												
Denver, Colo.	1,488	611	726	110	17	24	1,621	447	797	338	29	10
Detroit, Mich.	1,563	646	811	95	9	2	1,630	506	801	308	13	2
Fall River, Mass.	90	42	47	1	......	......	172	78	66	26	......	2
Grand Rapids, Mich.[1]												
Indianapolis, Ind.	6,041	2,322	3,048	449	112	110	6,092	1,604	3,112	1,163	186	27
Jersey City, N. J.	1,408	557	781	64	1	5	1,394	381	784	220	8	1
Kansas City, Mo.	6,764	2,910	3,315	456	78	5	7,097	2,051	3,450	1,451	139	6
Los Angeles, Cal.	731	262	415	35	10	9	804	198	429	160	14	3
Louisville, Ky.	14,557	6,685	6,595	1,066	113	98	15,797	5,013	6,896	3,581	260	47
Lowell, Mass.[1]												
Memphis, Tenn.	17,420	8,106	7,638	1,435	82	159	18,366	5,711	7,936	4,378	212	129
Milwaukee, Wis.	398	205	171	10	1	11	313	99	156	47	10	1
Minneapolis, Minn.	690	319	324	37	9	1	550	146	292	97	15	......
Nashville, Tenn.[1]												
New Haven, Conn.	1,011	359	562	83	5	2	1,165	341	587	226	11	......
New Orleans, La.	23,795	8,919	13,279	1,489	84	24	30,866	8,978	14,225	7,386	248	29
New York, N. Y.	21,401	9,380	11,067	865	45	44	27,263	10,376	11,968	4,771	96	52
Manhattan Borough	14,094	6,211	7,277	534	31	41	17,524	6,508	7,823	3,080	64	49
Bronx Borough												
Brooklyn Borough	6,134	2,674	3,175	273	9	3	8,162	3,206	3,476	1,452	25	3
Queens Borough[2]												
Richmond Borough[2]												
Newark, N. J.	2,254	822	1,330	91	5	6	2,799	893	1,426	470	8	2
Oakland, Cal.[1]												
Omaha, Nebr.	1,449	732	632	70	12	3	1,305	417	623	252	12	1
Paterson, N. J.	400	142	234	20	1	3	514	180	269	59	5	1
Philadelphia, Pa.	22,636	10,245	11,223	1,034	29	105	26,717	10,543	11,980	4,058	59	77
Pittsburgh, Pa.[3]	8,845	4,387	3,992	412	14	40	6,689	1,939	3,806	900	35	9
Portland, Oreg.												
Providence R. I.	1,720	651	944	112	9	4	1,942	617	936	360	28	1
Richmond, Va.[1]												
Rochester, N. Y.	228	107	106	13	2	......	233	82	106	43	2	......
St. Louis, Mo.	13,603	5,972	6,619	862	65	85	14,089	4,040	6,899	2,996	105	49
St. Paul, Minn.	1,146	596	466	44	9	31	727	195	404	109	12	7
San Francisco, Cal.	690	325	279	49	6	31	628	183	295	131	17	2
Scranton, Pa.	227	94	115	12	4	2	171	35	113	21	1	1
Seattle, Wash.[1]												
Spokane, Wash.[1]												
Syracuse, N. Y.	390	138	234	17	1	......	421	134	220	61	6	......
Toledo, Ohio	669	255	359	45	4	6	700	223	352	115	7	3
Washington, D. C.	27,726	11,354	14,570	1,683	90	29	36,922	14,321	15,501	6,854	212	34
Worcester, Mass.	401	167	215	17	2	......	436	140	221	70	5	......

[1] Population less than 100,000 in 1900. [2] Data not available for 1900. [3] Includes population of Allegheny.

TABLE **33.**—MARITAL CONDITION OF THE NEGRO POPULATION, BY CITIES OF 100,000 OR MORE INHABITANTS: 1910, 1900, AND 1890—Continued.

| CITY. | NEGRO POPULATION 15 YEARS OF AGE AND OVER: 1890. | | | | | | | | | | | |
| | Male. | | | | | | Female. | | | | | |
	Total.	Single.	Married.	Widowed.	Divorced.	Marital condition unknown.	Total.	Single.	Married.	Widowed.	Divorced.	Marital condition unknown.
Albany, N. Y.[1]												
Atlanta, Ga.[1]							28,174	10,606	12,396	5,055	87	30
Baltimore, Md	20,159	7,720	11,430	974	27	8						
Birmingham, Ala.[1]												
Boston, Mass	3,362	1,643	1,581	128	2	8	3,101	1,045	1,466	572	11	7
Bridgeport, Conn.[1]												
Buffalo, N. Y	438	165	247	24		2	422	147	214	58		
Cambridge, Mass.[1]							5,084	1,418	2,723	883	56	4
Chicago, Ill	6,772	3,449	3,024	241	30	28	4,559	1,292	2,274	963	25	5
Cincinnati, Ohio	4,438	1,998	2,234	192	7	7	1,070	313	565	178	11	3
Cleveland, Ohio	1,278	584	624	57	7	6						
Columbus, Ohio[1]												
Dayton, Ohio[1]							1,041	337	527	162	14	1
Denver, Colo	1,403	789	548	53	6	7	1,318	398	662	247	4	7
Detroit, Mich	1,305	534	694	72	3	2						
Fall River, Mass.[1]												
Grand Rapids, Mich.[1]							3,282	930	1,671	619	57	5
Indianapolis, Ind	3,285	1,380	1,688	191	22	4	816	257	437	118	4	
Jersey City, N. J	763	290	444	25	3	1	5,174	1,627	2,636	844	62	5
Kansas City, Mo	5,173	2,455	2,477	219	12	10						
Los Angeles, Cal.[1]							11,349	3,639	5,008	2,545	149	8
Louisville, Ky	9,619	4,193	4,779	573	59	15						
Lowell, Mass.[1]												
Memphis, Tenn.[1]							140	40	76	21	3	
Milwaukee, Wis	202	97	94	7		4						
Minneapolis, Minn	669	377	253	26	6	7	407	95	243	67	2	
Nashville, Tenn.[1]												
New Haven, Conn.[1]							25,186	7,334	11,740	5,955	139	18
New Orleans, La	18,577	6,683	10,959	890	29	16	14,912	5,337	6,432	3,108	15	20
New York, N. Y.[2]	11,466	4,904	6,043	504	6	9						
Manhattan Borough												
Bronx Borough							4,402	1,551	1,929	906	3	13
Brooklyn Borough	3,240	1,271	1,815	148	2	4						
Queens Borough												
Richmond Borough												
Newark, N. J	1,357	485	814	57	1		1,685	561	828	283	9	4
Oakland, Cal.[1]							1,351	489	678	170	12	2
Omaha, Nebr	2,101	1,226	759	61	13	42						
Paterson, N. J.[1]							16,606	6,267	7,154	3,078	35	72
Philadelphia, Pa	13,768	6,041	7,042	603	15	67						
Pittsburgh, Pa.[3]	4,561	2,398	1,977	174	6	6	3,155	909	1,737	492	16	1
Portland, Oreg.[1]							1,570	483	775	291	19	2
Providence, R. I	1,343	477	780	80	5	1						
Richmond, Va.[1]							239	82	98	57		2
Rochester, N. Y	183	84	91	7		1						
St. Louis, Mo	9,488	4,009	4,901	491	35	52	10,071	2,777	5,002	2,201	72	19
St. Paul, Minn	735	365	341	24	4	1	502	127	300	71	3	1
San Francisco, Cal	807	448	313	38	6	2	624	160	307	149	7	1
Scranton, Pa.[1]												
Seattle, Wash.[1]												
Spokane, Wash.[1]												
Syracuse, N. Y.[1]												
Toledo, Ohio[1]							30,075	11,689	12,805	5,444	99	38
Washington, D. C	22,628	9,330	12,240	980	33	45						
Worcester, Mass.[1]												

[1] Population less than 100,000 in 1890.
[2] Figures for 1890 are for the combined population of New York and Brooklyn cities as constituted at that census; statistics of marital condition of the population of the present area of New York city are not available.
[3] Includes population of Allegheny.

NEGRO POPULATION.

TABLE **34.**—MARITAL CONDITION OF THE NEGRO POPULATION CLASSIFIED BY SEX AND AGE PERIODS, FOR CITIES HAVING IN 1910 A POPULATION OF 100,000 OR MORE AND A NEGRO POPULATION 15 YEARS OF AGE AND OVER OF 10,000 OR MORE: 1910.

[Percentage not shown where base is less than 100.]

CITY AND AGE PERIOD.	NEGRO POPULATION: 1910.															
	Male.								Female.							
	Number.					Percentage.			Number.					Percentage.		
	Total.[1]	Single.	Married.	Widowed.	Divorced.	Single.	Married.	Widowed.	Total.[1]	Single.	Married.	Widowed.	Divorced.	Single.	Married.	Widowed.
ATLANTA, GA.																
15 years and over	16,600	5,776	9,736	1,024	46	34.8	58.7	6.2	21,789	5,597	10,834	5,221	121	25.7	49.7	24.0
15 to 19 years	2,250	2,171	73	3	2	96.5	3.2	0.1	3,017	2,422	545	41	5	80.3	18.1	1.4
20 to 24 years	2,941	1,683	1,220	26	8	57.2	41.5	0.9	4,243	1,522	2,360	335	25	35.9	55.6	7.9
25 to 34 years	4,898	1,294	3,422	170	10	26.4	69.9	3.5	6,391	1,149	3,995	1,193	50	18.0	62.5	18.7
35 to 44 years	3,042	387	2,443	200	9	12.7	80.3	6.6	3,873	295	2,310	1,239	27	7.6	59.6	32.0
45 to 64 years	2,852	206	2,192	436	17	7.2	76.9	15.3	3,512	163	1,481	1,854	12	4.6	42.2	52.8
65 years and over	565	27	353	182		4.8	62.5	32.2	716	38	130	546	2	5.3	18.2	76.3
Age unknown	52	8	33	7					37	8	13	13				
BALTIMORE, MD.																
15 years and over	29,982	11,651	16,045	2,060	146	38.9	53.5	6.9	35,572	12,170	17,095	6,044	197	34.2	48.1	17.0
15 to 19 years	3,084	3,040	34	2		98.6	1.1	0.1	4,523	4,121	379	13	1	91.1	8.4	0.3
20 to 24 years	4,358	2,997	1,321	25	4	68.8	30.3	0.6	5,855	3,215	2,473	140	10	54.9	42.2	2.4
25 to 34 years	8,485	3,253	4,901	271	43	38.3	57.8	3.2	9,796	2,899	6,054	780	49	29.6	61.8	8.0
35 to 44 years	6,738	1,451	4,742	478	47	21.5	70.4	7.1	7,211	1,116	4,605	1,402	83	15.5	63.9	19.4
45 to 64 years	6,193	818	4,374	947	45	13.2	70.6	15.3	6,645	667	3,261	2,662	48	10.0	49.1	40.1
65 years and over	1,034	62	629	333	7	6.0	60.8	32.2	1,418	113	287	1,012	4	8.0	20.2	71.4
Age unknown	90	30	44	4					124	39	36	35	2	31.5	29.0	28.2
BIRMINGHAM, ALA.																
15 years and over	19,092	6,436	10,821	1,679	109	33.7	56.7	8.8	19,706	3,964	11,103	4,387	234	20.1	56.3	22.3
15 to 19 years	2,172	2,127	37	3		97.9	1.7	0.1	2,706	2,045	572	73	14	75.6	21.1	2.7
20 to 24 years	3,210	2,039	1,075	83	9	63.5	33.5	2.6	3,779	1,065	2,262	399	50	28.2	59.9	10.6
25 to 34 years	6,034	1,566	4,003	414	42	26.0	66.3	6.9	6,347	612	4,443	1,196	94	9.6	70.0	18.8
35 to 44 years	3,983	505	2,981	459	35	12.7	74.8	11.5	3,705	161	2,489	1,005	48	4.3	67.2	27.1
45 to 64 years	3,164	143	2,431	564	21	4.5	76.8	17.8	2,537	50	1,191	1,277	18	2.0	46.9	50.3
65 years and over	360	8	201	148	1	2.2	55.8	41.1	508	10	92	404	2	2.0	18.1	79.5
Age unknown	169	48	93	8	1	28.4	55.0	4.7	124	21	54	33	8	16.9	43.5	26.6
BOSTON, MASS.																
15 years and over	5,482	2,359	2,778	303	37	43.0	50.7	5.5	5,572	1,744	2,710	1,069	47	31.3	48.6	19.2
15 to 19 years	336	332	4			98.8	1.2		469	430	37	1	1	91.7	7.9	0.2
20 to 24 years	660	527	125	4	4	79.8	18.9	0.6	738	402	320	12	4	54.5	43.4	1.6
25 to 34 years	1,748	846	861	29	10	48.4	49.3	1.7	1,768	537	1,070	140	20	30.4	60.5	7.9
35 to 44 years	1,490	421	985	70	14	28.3	66.1	4.7	1,401	230	833	323	15	16.4	59.5	23.1
45 to 64 years	1,115	215	742	150	8	19.3	66.5	13.5	989	121	418	444	6	12.2	42.3	44.9
65 years and over	127	15	61	50	1	11.8	48.0	39.4	197	19	31	146	1	9.6	15.7	74.1
Age unknown	6	3							10	5	1	3				
CHICAGO, ILL.																
15 years and over	19,372	7,631	10,076	1,232	279	39.4	52.0	6.4	17,962	3,800	9,978	3,746	355	21.2	55.6	20.9
15 to 19 years	1,203	1,171	22	1		97.3	1.8	0.1	1,415	1,166	215	15	4	82.4	15.2	1.1
20 to 24 years	2,330	1,718	571	20	9	73.7	24.5	0.9	2,541	1,025	1,373	103	36	40.3	54.0	4.1
25 to 34 years	6,641	2,770	3,547	211	100	41.7	53.4	3.2	6,046	1,076	4,132	690	137	17.8	68.3	11.4
35 to 44 years	5,241	1,301	3,459	367	103	24.8	66.0	7.0	4,294	375	2,791	1,003	120	8.7	65.0	23.4
45 to 64 years	3,363	579	2,231	490	60	17.2	66.3	14.0	3,018	136	1,354	1,468	56	4.5	44.9	48.6
65 years and over	360	24	198	133	5	6.7	55.0	36.9	537	8	81	445	1	1.5	15.1	82.9
Age unknown	234	68	48	10	2	29.1	20.5	4.3	111	14	32	22	1	12.6	28.8	19.8
CINCINNATI, OHIO.																
15 years and over	8,246	3,268	4,284	550	81	39.6	52.0	6.7	8,002	2,054	4,305	1,482	126	25.7	53.8	18.5
15 to 19 years	696	685	10			98.4	1.4		810	662	142	4	2	81.7	17.5	0.5
20 to 24 years	1,090	753	321	12	4	69.1	29.4	1.1	1,329	592	664	53	20	44.5	50.0	4.0
25 to 34 years	2,433	961	1,373	75	16	39.5	56.4	3.1	2,461	528	1,626	254	49	21.5	66.1	10.3
35 to 44 years	2,039	519	1,347	127	43	25.5	66.1	6.2	1,743	174	1,175	365	29	10.0	67.4	20.9
45 to 64 years	1,688	313	1,097	261	16	18.5	65.0	15.5	1,301	80	609	591	21	6.1	46.8	45.4
65 years and over	204	27	105	71	1	13.2	51.5	34.8	275	9	55	209	2	3.3	20.0	76.0
Age unknown	96	10	31	4	1				83	9	34	6	3			
COLUMBUS, OHIO.																
15 years and over	5,629	2,429	2,774	347	66	43.2	49.3	6.2	4,696	1,215	2,687	699	82	25.9	57.2	14.9
15 to 19 years	475	466	7			98.1	1.5		581	477	97	4		82.1	16.7	0.7
20 to 24 years	820	606	205	4	2	73.9	25.0	0.5	768	340	398	17	11	44.3	51.8	2.2
25 to 34 years	1,831	827	933	45	23	45.2	51.0	2.5	1,385	252	1,008	92	32	18.2	72.8	6.6
35 to 44 years	1,269	344	824	77	21	27.1	64.9	6.1	964	91	704	141	25	9.4	73.0	14.6
45 to 64 years	1,039	164	700	155	20	15.8	67.4	14.9	822	46	437	325	13	5.6	53.2	39.5
65 years and over	174	15	94	65		8.6	54.0	37.4	160	8	36	114	1	5.0	22.5	71.3
Age unknown	21	7	11	1					16	1	7	6				
INDIANAPOLIS, IND.																
15 years and over	8,521	3,093	4,576	690	142	36.3	53.7	8.1	8,692	1,963	4,723	1,809	189	22.6	54.3	20.8
15 to 19 years	765	739	22	3		96.6	2.9	0.4	955	798	149	5	3	83.6	15.6	0.5
20 to 24 years	1,191	814	321	15	11	70.9	27.0	1.3	1,348	548	703	64	33	40.7	52.2	4.7
25 to 34 years	2,426	859	1,410	102	49	35.4	58.1	4.2	2,570	438	1,705	356	69	17.0	66.3	13.9
35 to 44 years	1,915	382	1,319	168	46	19.9	68.8	8.8	1,824	124	1,199	439	62	6.8	65.7	24.1
45 to 64 years	1,839	228	1,290	288	31	12.4	70.1	15.7	1,655	44	883	705	21	2.7	53.4	42.6
65 years and over	346	28	202	112	3	8.1	58.4	32.4	310	8	73	228	1	2.6	23.5	73.5
Age unknown	39	13	12	2	2				30	3	11	12				

[1] Includes persons whose marital condition was not reported.

TABLE **34.**—MARITAL CONDITION OF THE NEGRO POPULATION CLASSIFIED BY SEX AND AGE PERIODS, FOR CITIES HAVING IN 1910 A POPULATION OF 100,000 OR MORE AND A NEGRO POPULATION 15 YEARS OF AGE AND OVER OF 10,000 OR MORE: 1910—Continued.

[Pecrentage not shown where base is less than 100.]

CITY AND AGE PERIOD.	NEGRO POPULATION: 1910.															
	Male.								Female.							
	Number.					Percentage.			Number.					Percentage.		
	Total.[1]	Single.	Married.	Widowed.	Divorced.	Single.	Married.	Widowed.	Total.[1]	Single.	Married.	Widowed.	Divorced.	Single.	Married.	Widowed.
KANSAS CITY, MO.																
15 years and over	10,107	3,818	5,251	727	168	37.8	52.0	7.2	9,782	2,275	5,295	1,920	246	23.3	54.1	19.6
15 to 19 years	784	762	13	1		97.2	1.7	0.1	958	774	173	7	3	80.8	18.1	0.7
20 to 24 years	1,337	939	375	10	7	70.2	28.0	0.7	1,621	653	847	86	32	40.3	52.3	5.3
25 to 34 years	3,368	1,293	1,877	128	54	38.4	55.7	3.8	3,243	608	2,105	418	107	18.7	64.9	12.9
35 to 44 years	2,465	538	1,640	215	58	21.8	66.5	8.7	2,074	165	1,330	507	71	8.0	64.1	24.4
45 to 64 years	1,759	224	1,184	302	46	12.7	67.3	17.2	1,455	51	729	645	29	3.5	50.1	44.3
65 years and over	191	13	110	64	2	6.8	57.6	33.5	299	10	65	221	3	3.3	21.7	73.9
Age unknown	203	49	52	7	1	24.1	25.6	3.4	132	14	46	36	1	10.6	34.8	27.3
LOUISVILLE, KY.																
15 years and over	15,772	6,399	7,780	1,288	224	40.6	49.3	8.2	16,853	4,612	8,170	3,638	361	27.4	48.5	21.6
15 to 19 years	1,716	1,682	30	1		98.0	1.7	0.1	1,888	1,559	301	19	5	82.6	15.9	1.0
20 to 24 years	2,223	1,480	709	21	11	66.6	31.9	0.9	2,605	1,188	1,269	109	35	45.6	48.7	4.2
25 to 34 years	4,563	1,876	2,409	199	72	41.1	52.8	4.4	4,865	1,168	2,947	614	133	24.0	60.6	12.6
35 to 44 years	3,544	868	2,273	318	80	24.5	64.1	9.0	3,369	408	2,011	824	124	12.1	59.7	24.5
45 to 64 years	3,091	440	2,034	553	59	14.2	65.8	17.9	3,288	241	1,493	1,492	60	7.3	45.4	45.4
65 years and over	547	38	315	191	2	6.9	57.6	34.9	739	44	139	552	4	6.0	18.8	74.7
Age unknown	88	15	10	5					99	4	10	28				
MEMPHIS, TENN.																
15 years and over	20,012	7,371	10,586	1,633	366	36.8	52.9	8.2	21,510	4,951	11,234	4,587	706	23.0	52.2	21.3
15 to 19 years	2,240	2,167	63	2	1	96.7	2.8	0.1	2,641	2,031	530	60	19	76.9	20.1	2.3
20 to 24 years	3,313	2,129	1,070	69	36	64.3	32.3	2.1	4,055	1,419	2,193	306	123	35.0	54.1	7.5
25 to 34 years	6,463	2,060	3,923	337	135	31.9	60.7	5.2	6,948	1,064	4,560	1,004	317	15.3	65.6	14.5
35 to 44 years	4,145	675	2,949	405	114	16.3	71.1	9.8	3,852	307	2,347	1,023	174	8.0	60.9	26.6
45 to 64 years	3,113	296	2,151	590	72	9.5	69.1	19.0	3,156	98	1,433	1,565	58	3.1	45.4	49.6
65 years and over	652	27	400	217	7	4.1	61.3	33.3	790	27	148	611	4	3.4	18.7	77.3
Age unknown	86	17	30	13	1				68	5	23	18	11			
NASHVILLE, TENN.																
15 years and over	11,933	4,140	6,584	1,067	137	34.7	55.2	8.9	15,757	4,222	7,025	4,154	348	26.8	44.6	26.4
15 to 19 years	1,815	1,734	75	6		95.5	4.1	0.3	2,201	1,799	359	28	13	81.7	16.3	1.3
20 to 24 years	1,833	1,089	689	35	19	59.4	37.6	1.9	2,688	1,138	1,264	217	69	42.3	47.0	8.1
25 to 34 years	2,887	825	1,849	167	43	28.6	64.0	5.8	4,157	844	2,342	812	157	20.3	56.3	19.5
35 to 44 years	2,169	297	1,613	226	33	13.7	74.4	10.4	3,020	281	1,684	984	69	9.3	55.8	32.6
45 to 64 years	2,622	166	1,990	426	39	6.3	75.9	16.2	2,934	144	1,243	1,508	38	4.9	42.4	51.4
65 years and over	600	24	366	207	3	4.0	61.0	34.5	746	11	131	601	2	1.5	17.6	80.6
Age unknown	7	5	2						11	5	2	4				
NEW ORLEANS, LA.																
15 years and over	29,692	10,783	16,879	1,634	113	36.3	56.8	5.5	36,392	10,179	18,100	7,597	293	28.0	49.7	20.9
15 to 19 years	3,698	3,597	75	1		97.3	2.0	(1)	5,057	4,168	793	31	7	82.4	15.7	0.6
20 to 24 years	4,249	2,684	1,487	30	11	63.2	35.0	0.7	5,945	2,529	3,106	213	55	42.5	52.2	3.6
25 to 34 years	8,381	2,455	5,674	163	38	29.3	67.7	1.9	10,149	2,095	6,846	1,061	110	20.6	67.5	10.5
35 to 44 years	6,662	1,231	5,041	326	35	18.5	75.7	4.9	7,204	837	4,519	1,742	95	11.6	62.7	24.2
45 to 64 years	5,336	696	3,873	714	28	13.0	72.6	13.4	6,109	439	2,522	3,099	23	7.2	41.3	50.7
65 years and over	1,207	100	698	395	1	8.3	57.8	32.7	1,829	99	285	1,409	1	5.4	15.6	77.0
Age unknown	159	20	31	5		12.6	19.5	3.1	99	12	29	42	2			
NEW YORK, N. Y.																
15 years and over	34,269	13,335	19,196	1,540	101	38.9	56.0	4.5	40,792	13,174	20,466	6,844	206	32.3	50.2	16.8
15 to 19 years	2,660	2,623	30	2		98.6	1.1	0.1	3,620	3,231	367	10	3	89.3	10.1	0.3
20 to 24 years	5,110	3,628	1,446	24	4	71.0	28.3	0.5	7,254	3,805	3,228	177	27	52.5	44.5	2.4
25 to 34 years	12,660	4,686	7,672	262	24	37.0	60.6	2.1	14,633	4,088	9,167	1,246	106	27.9	62.6	8.5
35 to 44 years	8,333	1,652	6,192	432	48	19.8	74.3	5.2	8,388	1,302	5,084	1,953	41	15.5	60.6	23.3
45 to 64 years	4,732	654	3,442	602	23	13.8	72.7	12.7	5,709	645	2,412	2,618	25	11.3	42.2	45.9
65 years and over	643	55	374	211	2	8.6	58.2	32.8	1,047	69	162	809	3	6.6	15.5	77.3
Age unknown	131	37	40	7		28.2	30.5	5.3	141	34	46	31	1	24.1	32.6	22.0
PHILADELPHIA, PA.																
15 years and over	30,976	11,360	17,727	1,713	86	36.7	57.2	5.5	35,790	11,156	18,678	5,726	145	31.2	52.2	16.0
15 to 19 years	2,268	2,233	22	2		98.5	1.0	0.1	3,475	3,094	344	10	3	89.0	9.9	0.3
20 to 24 years	3,935	2,720	1,177	23	5	69.1	29.9	0.6	5,989	3,085	2,755	121	13	51.5	46.0	2.0
25 to 34 years	10,467	3,742	6,446	241	16	35.8	61.6	2.3	12,000	3,156	7,877	897	59	26.3	65.6	7.5
35 to 44 years	8,044	1,790	5,761	451	32	22.3	71.6	5.6	7,686	1,112	4,978	1,536	51	14.5	64.8	20.0
45 to 64 years	5,412	768	3,838	763	33	14.2	70.9	14.1	5,442	588	2,461	2,366	18	10.8	45.2	43.5
65 years and over	685	65	391	225		9.5	57.1	32.8	1,067	91	205	768		8.5	19.2	72.0
Age unknown	165	42	92	8		25.5	55.8	4.8	131	30	58	28	1	22.9	44.3	21.4

[1] Includes persons whose marital condition was not reported.

TABLE **34.**—MARITAL CONDITION OF THE NEGRO POPULATION CLASSIFIED BY SEX AND AGE PERIODS, FOR CITIES HAVING IN 1910 A POPULATION OF 100,000 OR MORE AND A NEGRO POPULATION 15 YEARS OF AGE AND OVER OF 10,000 OR MORE: 1910—Continued.

[Percentage not shown where base is less than 100.]

CITY AND AGE PERIOD.	NEGRO POPULATION: 1910.																
	Male.								Female.							
	Number.					Percentage.			Number.					Percentage.		
	Total.[1]	Single.	Married.	Wid-owed.	Di-vorced.	Single.	Mar-ried.	Wid-owed.	Total.[1]	Single.	Married.	Wid-owed.	Di-vorced.	Single.	Mar-ried.	Wid-owed.
PITTSBURGH, PA.																
15 years and over	10,374	4,070	5,594	645	32	39.2	53.9	6.2	9,224	2,313	5,547	1,269	80	25.1	60.1	13.8
15 to 19 years	849	837	10	1		98.6	1.2	0.1	973	858	111			88.2	11.4	
20 to 24 years	1,207	922	266	11	1	76.4	22.0	0.9	1,369	617	712	33	6	45.1	52.0	2.4
25 to 34 years	3,489	1,338	2,030	101	11	38.3	58.2	2.9	3,208	571	2,368	241	28	17.8	73.8	7.5
35 to 44 years	2,789	642	1,928	203	12	23.0	69.1	7.3	2,116	176	1,579	328	30	8.3	74.6	15.5
45 to 64 years	1,779	280	1,229	260	8	15.7	69.1	14.6	1,297	56	720	506	14	4.3	55.5	39.0
65 years and over	203	21	115	67		10.3	56.7	33.0	206	10	37	157	2	4.9	18.0	76.2
Age unknown	58	30	16	2					55	25	20	4				
RICHMOND, VA.																
15 years and over	15,778	6,552	8,229	907	62	41.5	52.2	5.7	19,210	6,842	8,459	3,752	121	35.6	44.0	19.5
15 to 19 years	2,054	2,026	24	1		98.6	1.2	(1)	2,753	2,492	251	4		90.5	9.1	0.1
20 to 24 years	2,788	1,993	759	24	6	71.5	27.2	0.9	3,626	2,039	1,485	82	10	56.2	41.0	2.3
25 to 34 years	4,582	1,633	2,785	139	19	35.6	60.8	3.0	5,121	1,433	3,106	517	59	28.0	60.7	10.1
35 to 44 years	3,130	574	2,357	177	18	18.3	75.3	5.7	3,587	528	2,135	886	33	14.7	59.5	24.7
45 to 64 years	2,735	285	2,010	415	18	10.4	73.5	15.2	3,418	300	1,361	1,735	15	8.8	39.8	50.8
65 years and over	407	20	241	144	1	4.9	59.2	35.4	631	31	96	501	2	4.9	15.2	79.4
Age unknown	82	21	53	7					74	19	25	27	2			
ST. LOUIS, MO.																
15 years and over	18,318	7,271	9,415	1,421	169	39.7	51.4	7.8	17,689	3,916	9,607	3,860	276	22.1	54.3	21.8
15 to 19 years	1,567	1,534	27			97.9	1.7		1,752	1,392	332	17	4	79.5	18.9	1.0
20 to 24 years	2,479	1,816	628	24	7	73.3	25.3	1.0	2,756	1,080	1,496	142	33	39.2	54.3	5.2
25 to 34 years	5,932	2,342	3,325	210	44	39.5	56.1	3.5	5,511	972	3,788	630	118	17.6	68.7	11.4
35 to 44 years	4,473	1,090	2,940	373	67	24.4	65.7	8.3	3,799	336	2,420	958	80	8.8	63.7	25.2
45 to 64 years	3,228	430	2,145	603	46	13.3	66.4	18.7	3,148	118	1,419	1,568	38	3.7	45.1	49.8
65 years and over	593	53	331	204	5	8.9	55.8	34.4	659	16	128	510	2	2.4	19.4	77.4
Age unknown	46	6	19	7					64	2	24	35	1			
WASHINGTON, D. C.																
15 years and over	32,156	12,132	17,863	1,880	183	37.7	55.6	5.8	40,597	13,443	19,065	7,665	284	33.1	47.0	18.9
15 to 19 years	3,717	3,636	55	1		97.8	1.5	(1)	4,903	4,404	457	5	3	89.8	9.3	0.1
20 to 24 years	4,766	3,286	1,411	32	10	68.9	29.6	0.7	6,567	3,492	2,883	143	24	53.2	43.9	2.2
25 to 34 years	9,058	3,077	5,723	190	51	34.0	63.2	2.1	11,477	3,316	7,081	953	102	28.9	61.7	8.3
35 to 44 years	7,036	1,269	5,313	382	61	18.0	75.5	5.4	8,219	1,286	5,028	1,782	109	15.6	61.2	21.7
45 to 64 years	6,119	720	4,506	838	51	11.8	73.6	13.7	7,461	749	3,185	3,463	42	10.0	42.7	46.4
65 years and over	1,277	86	755	423	9	6.7	59.1	33.1	1,680	117	322	1,234	4	10.0	42.7	46.4
Age unknown	183	58	100	14	1	31.7	54.6	7.7	290	79	109	85		27.2	37.6	29.3

[1] Includes persons whose marital condition was not reported.

TABLE 35.—MARITAL CONDITION OF THE NEGRO POPULATION CLASSIFIED BY SEX, IN CITIES HAVING 25,000 INHABITANTS OR MORE: 1910.

CITY.	MALES 15 YEARS OF AGE AND OVER.							FEMALES 15 YEARS OF AGE AND OVER.						
	Total.[1]	Single.		Married.		Widowed.	Divorced.	Total.[1]	Single.		Married.		Widowed.	Divorced.
		Number.	Per cent.	Number.	Per cent.				Number.	Per cent.	Number.	Per cent.		
ALABAMA.														
Birmingham	19,092	6,436	33.7	10,821	56.7	1,679	109	19,706	3,964	20.1	11,103	56.3	4,387	234
Mobile	7,626	2,588	33.9	4,330	56.8	613	51	9,433	2,455	26.0	4,605	48.8	2,193	141
Montgomery	5,988	1,845	30.8	3,601	60.1	505	21	8,402	2,104	25.0	4,130	49.2	2,060	84
ARKANSAS.														
Little Rock	5,480	1,997	36.4	2,965	54.1	447	66	5,793	1,347	23.3	3,018	52.1	1,246	178
CALIFORNIA.														
Berkeley	71	27	(2)	40	(2)	2	1	115	41	35.7	52	45.2	17	5
Los Angeles	2,921	1,002	34.3	1,747	59.8	144	25	3,070	668	21.8	1,783	58.1	568	47
Oakland	1,357	617	45.5	650	47.9	72	17	1,168	241	20.6	665	56.9	231	29
Pasadena	257	69	26.8	170	66.1	14	1	319	65	20.4	183	57.4	63	6
Sacramento	232	117	50.4	101	43.5	9	3	174	49	28.2	95	54.6	28	2
San Diego	258	103	39.9	111	43.0	20	12	249	59	23.7	133	53.4	51	6
San Francisco	911	526	57.7	308	33.8	55	13	504	152	30.2	254	50.4	76	22
San Jose	69	21	(2)	42	(2)	5	1	82	16	(2)	49	(2)	14	3
COLORADO.														
Colorado Springs	374	109	29.1	224	59.9	31	6	465	94	20.2	245	52.7	113	8
Denver	2,203	787	35.7	1,233	56.0	128	48	2,278	504	22.1	1,249	54.8	447	72
Pueblo	637	238	37.4	331	52.0	51	12	551	118	21.4	330	59.9	94	7
CONNECTICUT.														
Bridgeport	514	206	40.1	272	52.9	33	2	519	140	27.0	282	54.3	89	5
Hartford	574	187	32.6	338	58.9	46	1	723	235	32.5	354	49.0	125	8
Meriden town	49	29	(2)	13	(2)	5	1	44	22	(2)	12	(2)	9	1
Meriden city	*49*	*29*	*(2)*	*13*	*(2)*	*5*	*1*	*44*	*22*	*(2)*	*12*	*(2)*	*9*	*1*
New Britain	30	11	(2)	16	(2)	3	....	38	15	(2)	21	(2)	2	....
New Haven	1,335	461	34.5	767	57.5	98	6	1,473	400	27.2	775	52.6	284	13
Norwich town	222	94	42.3	113	50.9	15	....	276	98	35.5	118	42.8	59	1
Stamford town	106	40	37.7	60	56.6	6	....	164	72	43.9	70	42.7	17	5
Stamford city	*103*	*38*	*36.9*	*59*	*57.3*	*6*	....	*156*	*65*	*41.7*	*69*	*44.2*	*17*	*4*
Waterbury	278	92	33.1	171	61.5	13	2	277	76	27.4	163	58.8	34	....
DELAWARE.														
Wilmington	3,390	1,343	39.6	1,700	50.1	314	13	3,623	1,184	32.7	1,747	48.2	647	25
DISTRICT OF COLUMBIA.														
Washington	32,156	12,132	37.7	17,863	55.6	1,880	183	40,597	13,443	33.1	19,065	47.0	7,665	284
FLORIDA.														
Jacksonville	11,172	4,166	37.3	6,131	54.9	706	99	11,298	2,665	23.6	6,598	58.4	1,840	152
Tampa	3,363	1,414	42.0	1,703	50.6	196	34	3,370	739	21.9	1,885	55.9	656	77
GEORGIA.														
Atlanta	16,600	5,776	34.8	9,736	58.7	1,024	46	21,789	5,597	25.7	10,834	49.7	5,221	121
Augusta	6,069	2,146	35.4	3,443	56.7	443	15	7,959	2,338	29.4	3,706	46.6	1,824	60
Macon	5,958	1,859	31.2	3,551	59.6	494	13	7,331	1,730	23.6	3,801	51.8	1,718	68
Savannah	11,469	3,694	32.2	6,970	60.8	727	52	13,709	3,389	24.7	7,593	55.4	2,564	140
ILLINOIS.														
Aurora	116	45	38.8	57	49.1	6	2	106	23	21.7	63	59.4	19	1
Bloomington	316	128	40.5	156	49.4	25	7	290	79	27.2	147	50.7	59	5
Chicago	19,372	7,631	39.4	10,076	52.0	1,232	279	17,962	3,800	21.2	9,978	55.6	3,746	355
Danville	590	194	32.9	335	56.8	42	18	542	101	18.6	342	63.1	85	14
Decatur	303	118	38.9	146	48.2	30	9	302	72	23.8	164	54.3	61	5
East St. Louis	2,596	1,004	38.7	1,386	53.4	164	33	1,923	335	17.4	1,337	69.5	222	26
Elgin	65	21	(2)	38	(2)	4	1	71	13	(2)	38	(2)	16	4
Joliet	214	92	43.0	108	50.5	11	3	181	36	19.9	119	65.7	20	6
Peoria	715	328	45.9	318	44.5	50	13	554	137	24.7	323	58.3	70	18
Quincy	636	229	36.0	345	54.2	51	9	625	149	23.8	363	58.1	101	9
Rockford	79	31	(2)	41	(2)	6	....	88	32	(2)	46	(2)	9	1
Springfield	1,171	439	37.5	623	53.2	99	9	1,106	252	22.8	609	55.1	221	22
INDIANA.														
Evansville	2,556	1,014	39.7	1,270	49.7	228	40	2,319	572	24.7	1,271	54.8	429	45
Fort Wayne	235	98	41.7	122	51.9	8	7	225	57	25.3	122	54.2	35	10
Indianapolis	8,521	3,093	36.3	4,576	53.7	690	142	8,692	1,963	22.6	4,723	54.3	1,809	189
South Bend	249	74	29.7	149	59.8	22	3	219	33	15.1	147	67.1	33	6
Terre Haute	1,053	431	40.9	509	48.3	71	31	947	228	24.1	520	54.9	154	40
IOWA.														
Cedar Rapids	96	41	(2)	47	(2)	8	....	73	13	(2)	47	(2)	9	4
Clinton	162	68	42.0	78	48.1	11	5	114	20	17.5	68	59.6	18	8
Council Bluffs	177	88	49.7	75	42.4	10	4	96	17	(2)	59	(2)	17	3
Davenport	243	111	45.7	110	45.3	15	5	198	48	24.2	112	56.6	37	1
Des Moines	1,178	383	32.5	679	57.6	69	29	1,091	240	22.0	657	60.2	155	34
Dubuque	50	26	(2)	20	(2)	4	....	25	3	(2)	18	(2)	4	....
Sioux City	137	62	45.3	64	46.7	10	....	102	26	25.5	62	60.8	10	3
Waterloo	15	6	(2)	7	(2)	2	....	9	3	(2)	6	(2)	....	....
KANSAS.														
Kansas City	3,549	1,062	29.9	2,106	59.3	305	63	3,495	699	20.0	2,106	60.2	630	52
Topeka	1,650	575	34.8	934	56.6	119	19	1,776	461	26.0	947	53.3	329	37
Wichita	1,032	410	39.7	531	51.5	60	28	827	186	22.5	525	63.5	99	13

[1] Total includes persons whose marital condition was not reported.　　[2] Per cent not shown where base is less than 100.

TABLE 35.—MARITAL CONDITION OF THE NEGRO POPULATION CLASSIFIED BY SEX, IN CITIES HAVING 25,000 INHABITANTS OR MORE: 1910—Continued.

CITY.	MALES 15 YEARS OF AGE AND OVER.							FEMALES 15 YEARS OF AGE AND OVER.						
	Total.[1]	Single.		Married.		Widowed.	Divorced.	Total.[1]	Single.		Married.		Widowed.	Divorced.
		Number.	Per cent.	Number.	Per cent.				Number.	Per cent.	Number.	Per cent.		
KENTUCKY.														
Covington	1,098	403	36.7	598	54.5	76	21	1,220	324	26.6	617	50.6	256	23
Lexington	3,930	1,591	40.5	2,036	51.8	254	43	4,810	1,411	29.3	2,251	46.8	1,057	76
Louisville	15,772	6,399	40.6	7,780	49.3	1,288	224	16,853	4,612	27.4	8,170	48.5	3,638	361
Newport	199	67	33.7	114	57.3	15	3	232	53	22.8	127	54.7	46	6
LOUISIANA.														
New Orleans	29,692	10,783	36.3	16,879	56.8	1,634	113	36,392	10,179	28.0	18,100	49.7	7,597	293
Shreveport	4,351	1,525	35.0	2,496	57.4	303	20	5,730	1,561	27.2	2,567	44.8	1,498	97
MAINE.														
Lewiston	22	14	(2)	6	(2)	2		18	9	(2)	5	(2)	4	
Portland	94	42	(2)	46	(2)	6		126	45	35.7	60	47.6	20	1
MARYLAND.														
Baltimore	29,982	11,651	38.9	16,045	53.5	2,060	146	35,572	12,170	34.2	17,095	48.1	6,044	197
MASSACHUSETTS.														
Boston	5,482	2,359	43.0	2,778	50.7	303	37	5,572	1,744	31.3	2,710	48.6	1,069	47
Brockton	177	57	32.2	110	62.1	5	4	191	76	39.8	93	48.7	20	2
Brookline town	54	29	(2)	20	(2)	4	1	153	92	60.1	41	26.8	20	
Cambridge	1,585	520	32.8	964	60.8	91	7	1,814	539	29.7	1,000	55.1	266	9
Chelsea	77	21	(2)	42	(2)	12		98	39	(2)	41	(2)	18	
Chicopee	6	6	(2)					1	1	(2)				
Everett	243	79	32.5	156	64.2	7		296	90	30.4	157	53.0	45	2
Fall River	143	59	41.3	77	53.8	7		146	43	29.5	69	47.3	33	1
Fitchburg	20	5	(2)	15	(2)			17	4	(2)	11	(2)	2	
Haverhill	140	52	37.1	74	52.9	10	4	162	49	30.2	85	52.5	26	2
Holyoke	13	8	(2)	5	(2)			19	10	(2)	9	(2)		
Lawrence	144	92	63.9	51	35.4		1	66	18	(2)	44	(2)	4	
Lowell	52	22	(2)	24	(2)	5	1	57	24	(2)	19	(2)	12	1
Lynn	260	104	40.0	141	54.2	13	2	257	63	24.5	151	58.8	42	1
Malden	142	44	31.0	84	59.2	13	1	184	55	29.9	98	53.3	29	2
New Bedford	1,093	489	44.7	549	50.2	51	1	972	253	26.0	519	53.4	193	7
Newton	124	36	29.0	83	66.9	5		233	114	48.9	86	36.9	31	1
Pittsfield	116	38	32.8	64	55.2	12	2	115	37	32.2	56	48.7	22	
Quincy	18	12	(2)	6	(2)			17	10	(2)	5	(2)	2	
Salem	59	21	(2)	32	(2)	6		75	35	(2)	27	(2)	12	1
Somerville	64	25	(2)	39	(2)			94	32	(2)	53	(2)	8	1
Springfield	514	179	34.8	300	58.4	24	11	617	222	36.0	307	49.8	80	5
Taunton	108	43	39.8	63	58.3	1	1	85	20	(2)	53	(2)	12	
Waltham	12	6	(2)	6	(2)			31	18	(2)	9	(2)	3	1
Worcester	435	156	35.9	250	57.5	26	2	508	160	31.5	249	49.0	97	2
MICHIGAN.														
Battle Creek	223	73	32.7	127	57.0	19	3	227	64	28.2	127	55.9	32	4
Bay City	69	26	(2)	33	(2)	6	4	58	12	(2)	34	(2)	12	
Detroit	2,465	938	38.1	1,343	54.5	130	27	2,261	545	24.1	1,286	56.9	388	34
Flint	171	79	46.2	83	48.5	5	4	138	44	31.9	76	55.1	15	3
Grand Rapids	291	96	33.0	164	56.4	23	2	264	59	22.3	158	59.8	40	5
Jackson	169	56	33.1	83	49.1	16	13	132	36	27.3	68	51.5	22	6
Kalamazoo	283	95	33.6	156	55.1	21	7	260	66	25.4	152	58.5	35	7
Lansing	124	34	27.4	75	60.5	12	2	142	32	22.5	75	52.8	31	4
Saginaw	137	60	43.8	65	47.4	9	3	127	35	27.6	64	50.4	19	5
MINNESOTA.														
Duluth	212	102	48.1	99	46.7	6	2	140	30	21.4	90	64.3	17	3
Minneapolis	1,321	588	44.5	601	45.5	83	14	907	235	25.9	516	56.9	130	16
St. Paul	1,681	838	49.9	749	44.6	75	16	1,010	270	26.7	587	58.1	141	11
MISSOURI.														
Joplin	322	132	41.0	159	49.4	25	4	321	86	26.8	164	51.1	58	13
Kansas City	10,107	3,818	37.8	5,251	52.0	727	168	9,782	2,275	23.3	5,295	54.1	1,920	246
St. Joseph	1,833	779	42.5	880	48.0	130	37	1,611	401	24.9	877	54.4	282	43
St. Louis	18,318	7,271	39.7	9,415	51.4	1,421	169	17,689	3,916	22.1	9,607	54.3	3,860	276
Springfield	731	267	36.5	400	54.7	50	4	747	189	25.3	408	54.6	132	13
MONTANA.														
Butte	124	67	54.0	54	43.5	3		83	22	(2)	45	(2)	12	4
NEBRASKA.														
Lincoln	338	135	39.9	171	50.6	25	5	264	43	16.3	177	67.0	40	4
Omaha	2,044	871	42.6	999	48.9	136	36	1,698	404	23.8	986	58.1	270	35
South Omaha	348	165	47.4	154	44.3	23	4	212	42	19.8	138	65.1	29	3
NEW HAMPSHIRE.														
Manchester	15	5	(2)	7	(2)	3		11	7	(2)	2	(2)	2	
Nashua	5	2	(2)	3	(2)			7	2	(2)	5	(2)		

[1] Total includes persons whose marital condition was not reported. [2] Per cent not shown where base is less than 100.

TABLE 35.—MARITAL CONDITION OF THE NEGRO POPULATION CLASSIFIED BY SEX, IN CITIES HAVING 25,000 INHABITANTS OR MORE: 1910—Continued.

CITY.	MALES 15 YEARS OF AGE AND OVER.							FEMALES 15 YEARS OF AGE AND OVER.						
	Total.[1]	Single.		Married.		Wid-owed.	Divorced.	Total.[1]	Single.		Married.		Wid-owed.	Divorced.
		Number.	Per cent.	Number.	Per cent.				Number.	Per cent.	Number.	Per cent.		
NEW JERSEY.														
Atlantic City	4,113	1,764	42.9	2,060	50.1	251	12	4,177	1,256	30.1	2,157	51.6	720	24
Bayonne	182	51	28.0	120	65.9	10	1	202	45	22.3	121	59.9	36	....
Camden	2,192	727	33.2	1,312	59.9	137	6	2,342	597	25.5	1,363	58.2	375	2
East Orange	485	144	29.7	319	65.8	20	....	957	429	44.8	417	43.6	110	1
Elizabeth	472	161	34.1	289	61.2	22	....	514	150	29.2	292	56.8	70	2
Hoboken	43	21	(2)	22	(2)	....	....	48	15	(2)	24	(2)	9	....
Jersey City	2,335	861	36.9	1,353	57.9	111	7	2,206	500	22.7	1,344	60.9	352	7
Newark	3,414	1,115	32.7	2,117	62.0	163	10	3,848	1,045	27.2	2,196	57.1	591	11
Orange	811	231	28.5	548	67.6	29	2	1,019	272	26.7	598	58.7	143	5
Passaic	179	64	35.8	105	58.7	9	1	233	70	30.0	120	51.5	42	1
Paterson	512	169	33.0	313	61.1	27	....	652	193	29.6	367	56.3	84	4
Perth Amboy	54	18	(2)	33	(2)	3	....	62	21	(2)	37	(2)	4	....
Trenton	1,212	464	38.3	662	54.6	73	10	918	271	29.5	513	55.9	129	4
West Hoboken town	20	5	(2)	15	(2)	....	....	20	5	(2)	14	(2)	1	....
NEW YORK.														
Albany	415	171	41.2	208	50.1	32	4	445	146	32.8	214	48.1	82	3
Amsterdam	38	7	(2)	29	(2)	2	....	51	7	(2)	33	(2)	11	....
Auburn	229	112	48.9	107	46.7	10	....	195	65	33.3	101	51.8	27	2
Binghamton	264	105	39.8	133	50.4	18	1	271	76	28.0	133	49.1	58	2
Buffalo	791	362	45.8	366	46.3	53	8	696	223	32.0	363	52.2	107	1
Elmira	239	130	54.4	89	37.2	19	1	199	55	27.6	98	49.2	41	5
Jamestown	42	14	(2)	24	(2)	3	1	42	14	(2)	23	(2)	4	1
Kingston	229	103	45.0	113	49.3	12	....	218	66	30.3	117	53.7	30	4
Mount Vernon	274	102	37.2	156	56.9	15	1	436	192	44.0	176	40.4	66	2
New Rochelle	503	160	31.8	322	64.0	16	5	817	298	36.5	389	47.6	118	10
New York	34,269	13,335	38.9	19,196	56.0	1,540	101	40,792	13,174	32.3	20,466	50.2	6,844	206
Manhattan Borough	*23,495*	*9,472*	*40.3*	*12,885*	*54.8*	*979*	*74*	*27,348*	*8,800*	*32.2*	*13,688*	*50.1*	*4,612*	*159*
Bronx Borough	*1,436*	*460*	*32.0*	*883*	*61.5*	*87*	*2*	*1,700*	*493*	*29.0*	*927*	*54.5*	*273*	*5*
Brooklyn Borough	*7,869*	*2,869*	*36.5*	*4,573*	*58.1*	*398*	*21*	*9,950*	*3,251*	*32.7*	*4,985*	*50.1*	*1,665*	*39*
Queens Borough	*1,079*	*395*	*36.6*	*633*	*58.7*	*48*	*3*	*1,336*	*459*	*34.4*	*643*	*48.1*	*232*	*2*
Richmond Borough	*390*	*139*	*35.6*	*222*	*56.9*	*28*	*1*	*458*	*171*	*37.3*	*223*	*48.7*	*62*	*1*
Newburgh	211	80	37.9	109	51.7	15	2	270	101	37.4	115	42.6	49	1
Niagara Falls	130	53	40.8	64	49.2	10	3	98	14	(2)	59	(2)	23	2
Poughkeepsie	244	84	34.4	145	59.4	13	1	314	98	31.2	158	50.3	57	1
Rochester	346	138	39.9	187	54.0	19	2	366	124	33.9	198	54.1	40	2
Schenectady	95	27	(2)	64	(2)	4	....	127	38	29.9	66	52.0	21	2
Syracuse	478	192	40.2	250	52.3	28	7	434	124	28.6	239	55.1	68	2
Troy	243	88	36.2	129	53.1	22	4	296	94	31.8	146	49.3	55	1
Utica	141	58	41.1	72	51.1	11	....	135	36	26.7	76	56.3	22	....
Watertown	33	11	(2)	18	(2)	3	....	29	5	(2)	17	(2)	7	....
Yonkers	556	192	34.5	339	61.0	25	....	651	214	32.9	338	51.9	92	6
NORTH CAROLINA.														
Charlotte	3,476	1,143	32.9	2,103	60.5	218	5	4,711	1,454	30.9	2,291	48.6	929	25
Wilmington	3,673	1,333	36.3	2,136	58.2	181	5	4,831	1,526	31.6	2,393	49.5	875	13
OHIO.														
Akron	277	118	42.6	131	47.3	16	9	217	52	24.0	127	58.5	34	3
Canton	140	65	46.4	65	46.4	7	2	92	31	(2)	49	(2)	11	1
Cincinnati	8,246	3,268	39.6	4,284	52.0	550	81	8,002	2,054	25.7	4,305	53.8	1,482	126
Cleveland	3,630	1,350	37.2	2,017	55.6	194	53	3,351	819	24.4	1,965	58.5	513	61
Columbus	5,629	2,429	43.2	2,774	49.3	347	66	4,696	1,215	25.9	2,687	57.2	699	82
Dayton	1,976	713	36.1	1,085	54.9	138	36	1,876	468	24.9	1,096	58.4	280	30
Hamilton	322	123	38.2	169	52.5	20	8	237	44	18.6	154	65.0	29	9
Lima	390	138	35.4	221	56.7	26	....	342	78	22.8	212	62.0	48	4
Lorain	147	63	42.9	76	51.7	7	1	124	35	28.2	76	61.3	12	1
Newark	141	62	44.0	67	47.5	9	2	132	48	36.4	61	46.2	18	5
Springfield	2,001	713	35.6	1,127	56.3	133	18	1,755	398	22.7	1,109	63.2	221	19
Toledo	790	306	38.7	412	52.2	56	15	756	212	28.0	432	57.1	100	11
Youngstown	862	362	42.0	445	51.6	44	4	641	140	21.8	415	64.7	77	7
Zanesville	494	195	39.5	277	56.1	18	4	533	160	30.0	284	53.3	84	5
OKLAHOMA.														
Muskogee	2,919	1,038	35.6	1,584	54.3	228	29	2,695	582	21.6	1,661	61.6	371	65
Oklahoma City	2,768	1,061	38.3	1,489	53.8	183	19	2,208	422	19.1	1,430	64.8	303	45
OREGON.														
Portland	550	263	47.8	253	46.0	26	8	376	65	17.3	236	62.8	63	12
PENNSYLVANIA.														
Allentown	52	15	(2)	34	(2)	2	1	54	11	(2)	35	(2)	8	....
Altoona	187	77	41.2	101	54.0	9	....	165	42	25.5	98	59.4	23	1
Chester	1,819	686	37.7	975	53.6	131	4	1,772	496	28.0	973	54.9	274	7
Easton	115	52	45.2	53	46.1	10	....	99	27	(2)	51	(2)	19	2
Erie	149	54	36.2	66	44.3	21	4	130	38	29.2	63	48.5	24	5
Harrisburg	1,753	746	42.6	881	50.3	115	11	1,785	546	30.6	922	51.7	306	11
Hazleton	11	7	(2)	4	(2)	....	....	3	1	(2)	2	(2)	....	....
Johnstown	196	87	44.4	98	50.0	8	....	163	44	27.0	99	60.7	19	1
Lancaster	308	111	36.0	166	53.9	27	2	313	93	29.7	159	50.8	56	4
McKeesport	283	90	31.8	173	61.1	19	1	280	77	27.5	168	60.0	35	....
New Castle	215	93	43.3	103	47.9	18	1	197	58	29.4	105	53.3	32	....
Norristown borough	355	149	42.0	180	50.7	19	2	372	126	33.9	181	48.7	60	1
Philadelphia	30,976	11,360	36.7	17,727	57.2	1,713	86	35,790	11,156	31.2	18,678	52.2	5,726	145
Pittsburgh	10,374	4,070	39.2	5,594	53.9	645	32	9,224	2,313	25.1	5,547	60.1	1,269	80
Reading	326	103	31.6	191	58.6	31	1	287	88	30.7	162	56.4	33	2
Scranton	242	114	47.1	117	48.3	11	....	200	64	32.0	107	53.5	28	....
Shenandoah borough	2	1	(2)	1	(2)	....	....							
Wilkes-Barre	274	112	40.9	146	53.3	12	3	230	53	23.0	142	61.7	34	1
Williamsport	307	89	29.0	181	59.0	35	2	387	129	33.3	177	45.7	80	1
York	428	150	35.0	252	58.9	24	2	460	141	30.7	256	55.7	57	2

[1] Total includes persons whose marital condition was not reported. [2] Per cent not shown where base is less than 100.

TABLE 35.—MARITAL CONDITION OF THE NEGRO POPULATION CLASSIFIED BY SEX, IN CITIES HAVING 25,000 INHABITANTS OR MORE: 1910—Continued.

CITY.	MALES 15 YEARS OF AGE AND OVER.							FEMALES 15 YEARS OF AGE AND OVER.						
	Total.[1]	Single.		Married.		Wid-owed.	Divorced.	Total.[1]	Single.		Married.		Wid-owed.	Divorced.
		Number.	Per cent.	Number.	Per cent.				Number.	Per cent.	Number.	Per cent.		
RHODE ISLAND.														
Newport	548	210	38.3	306	55.8	27	3	688	218	31.7	327	47.5	137	6
Pawtucket	79	29	(2)	48	(2)	2		86	29	(2)	47	(2)	9	1
Providence	1,978	768	38.8	1,068	54.0	121	20	2,125	600	28.2	1,062	50.0	418	43
Warwick town	65	21	(2)	32	(2)	7	3	66	21	(2)	36	(2)	9	
Woonsocket	9	4	(2)	5	(2)			6	3	(2)	2	(2)	1	
SOUTH CAROLINA.														
Charleston	9,482	3,103	32.7	5,570	58.7	649	20	12,688	3,483	27.5	6,001	47.3	3,030	58
Columbia	3,714	1,308	35.2	2,171	58.5	200	4	4,708	1,362	28.9	2,309	49.0	1,015	5
TENNESSEE.														
Chattanooga	6,737	2,415	35.8	3,597	53.4	624	73	6,928	1,524	22.0	3,798	54.8	1,463	126
Knoxville	2,772	1,163	42.0	1,386	50.0	177	22	3,177	999	31.4	1,498	47.2	621	42
Memphis	20,012	7,371	36.8	10,586	52.9	1,633	366	21,510	4,951	23.0	11,234	52.2	4,587	706
Nashville	11,933	4,140	34.7	6,584	55.2	1,067	137	15,757	4,222	26.8	7,025	44.6	4,154	348
TEXAS.														
Austin	2,352	795	33.8	1,284	54.6	149	41	2,930	830	28.3	1,380	47.1	524	103
Dallas	6,744	2,480	36.8	3,581	53.1	559	115	7,340	1,634	22.3	3,790	51.6	1,648	255
El Paso	548	195	35.6	309	56.4	10	9	576	129	22.4	358	62.2	78	7
Fort Worth	5,204	1,847	35.5	2,853	54.8	333	83	4,821	879	18.2	2,976	61.7	784	146
Galveston	3,035	1,142	37.6	1,597	52.6	240	54	3,276	861	26.3	1,632	49.8	646	133
Houston	8,400	2,784	33.1	4,790	57.0	724	80	9,798	2,422	24.7	5,196	53.0	1,854	305
San Antonio	3,526	1,180	33.5	2,006	56.9	236	75	4,391	1,123	25.6	2,260	51.5	796	191
Waco	1,971	685	34.8	1,081	54.8	154	26	2,450	647	26.4	1,183	48.3	523	68
UTAH.														
Ogden	113	36	31.9	47	41.6	3	1	66	12	(2)	36	(2)	8	1
Salt Lake City	389	168	43.2	183	47.0	26	6	258	52	20.2	163	63.2	22	9
VIRGINIA.														
Lynchburg	2,732	1,011	37.0	1,541	56.4	163	15	4,135	1,570	38.0	1,714	41.5	800	50
Norfolk	9,094	4,028	44.3	4,488	49.4	529	33	10,126	3,177	31.4	4,876	48.2	1,982	81
Portsmouth	4,010	1,737	43.3	2,001	49.9	248	14	4,458	1,339	30.0	2,165	48.6	933	20
Richmond	15,778	6,552	41.5	8,229	52.2	907	62	19,210	6,842	35.6	8,459	44.0	3,752	121
Roanoke	2,533	1,021	40.3	1,359	53.7	139	12	3,079	1,124	36.5	1,447	47.0	475	28
WASHINGTON.														
Seattle	1,256	677	53.9	498	39.6	35	17	776	175	22.6	446	57.5	102	17
Spokane	339	122	36.0	196	57.8	15	5	283	46	16.3	193	68.2	35	7
Tacoma	382	196	51.3	162	42.4	9	5	279	85	30.5	153	54.8	28	6
WEST VIRGINIA.														
Huntington	886	426	48.1	402	45.4	36	13	737	244	33.1	388	52.6	100	5
Wheeling	510	189	37.1	273	53.5	43		494	143	28.9	263	53.2	81	4
WISCONSIN.														
Green Bay	17	6	(2)	10	(2)		1	17	5	(2)	11	(2)	1	
La Crosse	21	8	(2)	9	(2)	4		22	6	(2)	10	(2)	5	1
Madison	52	21	(2)	26	(2)	5		53	9	(2)	35	(2)	7	2
Milwaukee	422	175	41.5	203	48.1	29	9	431	144	33.4	198	45.9	76	13
Oshkosh	31	11	(2)	18	(2)		2	39	9	(2)	24	(2)	3	3
Racine	48	22	(2)	25	(2)	1		45	11	(2)	27	(2)	7	
Sheboygan	1	1	(2)					4	1	(2)	2	(2)	1	
Superior	71	33	(2)	34	(2)	3	1	88	31	(2)	40	(2)	16	1

[1] Total includes persons whose marital condition was not reported.　　　　[2] Per cent not shown where base is less than 100.

Chapter XIII.—FERTILITY—PROPORTION OF CHILDREN TO WOMEN OF CHILD-BEARING AGE.

CHILDREN UNDER 14 YEARS OF AGE IN 1820.

The age composition of the Negro as of the white population at the several censuses indicates a continuous decline in the proportion of children, practically uninterrupted over a long period. The change in the proportion of children during a period of 90 years is summarized in Table 1, which compares 1820, the first year in which the age of the Negro population was returned at the decennial census, with 1900 and 1910, giving the number and the proportion of children under 14 in the population, and the number of children of this age per 1,000 women in the ages 14 to 44 years.

Because of the peculiar age classification of 1820, comparison of that year with the census years immediately succeeding can not be made, and because of differences between the age classification for Negroes and that for whites in 1820, some factors of estimate, as regards the number of white children and women in 1820, enter into the comparisons made in Table 1. These factors, as is explained in the note to the table, involve a distribution of the aggregate number of white children in the six-year age period 10 to 15 years inclusive, at the census of 1820, into two age groups as being under or over the precise age of 14 years, and this distribution is made upon the simple assumption that two-thirds of the children 10 to 15 were in the ages 10 to 13 years. The assumption somewhat underestimates the number of children, but is approximately correct owing to the low mortality in the ages 10 to 15 years. At each of the last four censuses, those, namely, of 1880, 1890, 1900, and 1910, for which data are available by single years of age, the number of white children returned for the ages 10 to 13 years slightly exceeded two-thirds of the number returned as 10 to 15. The margin of error in the assumption made can not, however, be considerable in its effect upon the proportion of children. The method of estimating employed for 1820 when applied to the 1910 data gives, in fact, for the proportion of children under 14 exactly the percentage, worked to one place of decimals (29.5), that is obtained for that year from the enumerated totals, by single years of age, and gives approximately the true ratio of children to women (see note to Table 1). No factors of estimate enter into any of the figures for the Negro population, estimates being employed with reference to the white population in order to produce figures for whites comparable with those available for Negroes.

In 1820, although the proportion of children under 14 in the Negro population (43 per cent) was approximately the same as the proportion in these ages in the white population (estimated to be 43.7 per cent), the number of such children per 1,000 women 14 to 44 years of age in the Negro population (1,853) was very considerably below the number in the white population (estimated to be 1,999). In 1910 both the proportion of children in the Negro population (34.9 per cent) and the proportion of children to women (1,344 per 1,000) very considerably exceeded the corresponding proportions among whites (29.5 per cent and 1,202 per 1,000).

| Table 1 | | Total. | Women 14 to 44 years of age. | CHILDREN UNDER 14 YEARS OF AGE. | | |
YEAR.				Number.	Per cent of total.	Per 1,000 women 14 to 44.
		NEGRO POPULATION.				
1910		9,827,763	2,553,098	3,430,559	34.9	1,344
1900		8,833,994	2,193,684	3,298,760	37.3	1,504
1820		1,771,656	411,110	761,753	43.0	1,853
		WHITE POPULATION.				
1910		81,731,957	20,061,647	24,109,893	29.5	1,202
1900		66,809,196	16,243,198	21,166,188	31.7	1,303
1820		7,866,797	[1]1,718,570	[1]3,435,228	[1]43.7	[1]1,999

[1] Estimate. The age classification for 1820 gives for white males and females, the number under 10, 10 to 15, 16 to 25, 26 to 44, and 45 and over. In estimating the number of white females 14 to 44 years of age, and the number of white children under 14, it is assumed that one-third of the children 10 to 15 years of age were in the ages 14 and 15. Tested by the returns of 1910, 1900, 1890, and 1880, the method of estimating employed gives, as would be expected, a slight excess of females in the ages 14 and 15 years, and deficiency of children 10 to 13. If one-third of the number of white females returned at the census of 1910 as 10 to 15 years of age be added to the number returned as 16 to 44, the result (20,090,745) exceeds the enumerated number of females 14 to 44 years of age (20,061,647) by 12,922, or by less than one-tenth of 1 per cent. This is the deficiency of female children under 14, by estimate as compared with the enumerated number, the corresponding deficiency for males being 15,084. If the number of white children under 14 per thousand white women 14 to 44 in 1910 had been estimated as in 1820, it would have been 1,200 or 2 less than the enumerated number of 1,202. The relatively more rapid increase of population in the earlier period would tend to create an age distribution in which the proportion 10 to 13 in the total 10 to 15 would exceed the proportion found in later years. It seems probable, therefore, that the number of white children under 14 per 1,000 white women 14 to 44 in 1820 exceeded 2,000.

In each class of population the decline in the proportion of children under 14 for the period of 90 years, 1820 to 1910, is very marked. Among Negroes it is somewhat less than it is among whites, although it is to be noted that in the later decades of this period, for which data are available in greater detail, the decrease in the number of children under 5 years of age per 1,000 women 15 to 44 is in the aggregate somewhat greater among Negroes than among whites, the result being a closer approximation of the ratio for Negroes to that for whites. (See Table 3, p. 286.)

PROPORTION OF WOMEN AND OF CHILDREN AT EACH CENSUS: 1830–1910.

Detail regarding the number and the proportion of women 15 to 44 years of age and of children under 10, under 5, and under 1, as returned at each census,

1830 to 1910, is given in Table 2 for Negroes and whites.

As returned on the schedules the number of Negro children under 1 year of age decreased 9.5 per cent in the decade 1880–1890, and increased 18.9 per cent in the decade 1890–1900; and the number of children under 5 decreased 5.3 per cent in the decade 1880–1890, and increased 16.1 per cent in the decade 1890–1900. The decreases for the earlier decade were undoubtedly in part a direct consequence of omissions in the enumeration of the Negro population at the census of 1890. (See p. 27.)

These omissions and those at the census of 1870 (see p. 26) would not necessarily affect the proportion of children in the Negro population, since the proportion of omissions might be the same among children as in the older population, but the returns for these years obviously can not be accepted with any high degree of confidence in their accuracy as regards age composition.

It is to be noted, further, that the age returns for 1890 are essentially defective, not only on account of omissions, but also in consequence of a change in the form of the age inquiry at that census. In 1890 enumerators were instructed to return "age at nearest birthday," the age returned at other censuses being "age at last birthday." This change in the form of the inquiry would reduce the proportion of children in the population enumerated, especially the proportion of children under 1 year of age, below the proportion which would be returned where the inquiry called for age at last birthday.[1]

Data are available showing the proportion of children under 10 years of age in the Negro and in the white population at each census beginning with that of 1830. It will be seen by reference to Table 2 that, excepting the decade 1870–1880, the proportion of children under 10 years of age in the Negro population tended to fall off with a fair degree of regularity in the decades covered by the table, from approximately one-third, or 342 per 1,000 population (34.2 per cent) in 1830, nearly to one-fourth, or 255 per 1,000 population (25.5 per cent) in 1910. For the white population each census has shown a decrease in the proportion of children under 10—from 325 per 1,000 population (32.5 per cent) in 1830 to 218 per 1,000 population (21.8 per cent) in 1910. At each census the number of children under 10 per 1,000 Negro population has exceeded the corresponding number for the white population, the excess amounting to 16 in 1830, in which year the number for whites most nearly approximates that for Negroes—to 66 in 1880—which is the year of greatest difference, and to 36 in 1910.

No data are available for the Negro population under 5 and under 1 in the years 1830 and 1840. In the period from 1850 to 1910 the proportion under 5, as well as the proportion under 10, tended to decline from census to census, the aggregate decrease for children under 5 being from 16.5 per cent in 1850 to 12.9 per cent in 1910. A similar decline is shown for the white population from 14.8 per cent to 11.4 per cent.

The proportion under 1 in the Negro population was highest in 1880 and was nearly the same in 1910 as in 1850, the percentages being 2.5 in 1850, 3.5 in 1880, and 2.6 in 1910. In the white population the proportion under 1 declined from a maximum of 3 per cent in 1860 to 2.4 per cent in 1910, the percentage in 1850 (2.7) being slightly lower than that of 1860.

The decline in the proportion of children in the Negro and in the white population is undoubtedly in large part a direct consequence of a decline in the birth rate, but a decline in the proportion of children may indicate also improvement in specific mortality rates. It is probably true of the Negro population that its general mortality rate affecting all ages in some degree has decreased in recent decades, and as regards the white population evidence of a general decrease is conclusive. The natural consequence of such a decrease in a sufficiently long period would be a decrease in the proportion of children, although the first effect of a reduction in mortality, if confined principally to mortality of infants and very young children, would be to increase temporarily the proportion of children. Improvement in mortality from period to period, and differences in mortality between the classes, must be taken into account in considering the proportion of children in the Negro and in the white population in different years.

The change in the proportion of women 15 to 44 years of age in the Negro and in the white population has been much less considerable in the period covered by Table 2 than the change in the proportion of children. In 1850 women 15 to 44 constituted 22.3

---

[1] Classified according to age at nearest birthday children 6 to 18 months old would be returned as 1 year of age, leaving for the age under 1 year only children less than 6 months old, while classified according to age at last birthday all children under 12 months old would be returned as under 1 year of age. As regards the age group under 5 years, the classification by age at nearest birthday includes in this group children up to the age of 54 months (4½ years), while the classification according to age at last birthday includes children up to the age of 60 months (5 years). If enumerators had followed instructions in 1890 a very great decrease must have developed from the schedule returns in the number of children under 1 year of age for the decade 1880–1890, and a marked increase for the succeeding decade. As shown in Table 2, according to the returns, the percentage under 1 year of age in the Negro population declined during the decade 1880–1890 from 3.5 to 2.8, and was the same in 1900 as in 1890. In the white population also a small decrease in the proportion under 1 year of age is shown for the decade 1880–1890, and no change for the decade 1890–1900, while among both Negroes and whites the decrease in the proportion of children under 5 and under 10 was more considerable in the earlier of these two decades. These changes were undoubtedly in some degree effects of the change noted in the age inquiry, but it is evident that enumerators can not generally have followed instructions at the census of 1890, as regards children under 1 year of age, restricting that class to children under 6 months old, since such a restriction would have developed much greater differences in the proportion for this age than are shown in the returns.

per cent of the Negro and 22.5 per cent of the white population. The proportion tended to increase slightly from decade to decade to 24.8 per cent for Negroes and to 23.6 per cent for whites in 1910, the differences between the percentages for Negroes and those for whites being generally small.

NUMBER, INCREASE, AND PROPORTION OF NEGRO AND WHITE WOMEN 15 TO 44 YEARS OF AGE, AND OF CHILDREN UNDER 10, UNDER 5, AND UNDER 1, AT EACH CENSUS: 1830–1910.

Table 2

YEAR AND DECADE.	Total.		Women 15 to 44 years of age.		POPULATION.[1] Children. Under 10 years of age.		Under 5 years of age.		Under 1 year of age.	
	Negro.	White.	Negro.	White.	Negro.	White.	Negro.	White.	Negro.	White.
NUMBER.										
1910	9,827,763	81,731,957	2,435,189	19,270,619	2,509,841	17,798,087	1,263,288	9,322,914	252,386	1,955,605
1900	8,833,994	66,809,196	2,087,324	15,576,952	2,418,413	15,558,278	1,215,655	7,919,952	244,510	1,667,060
1890[2]	7,470,040	54,983,890	1,687,862	12,725,641	2,141,068	13,052,816	1,047,419	6,579,648	205,566	1,359,120
1880	6,580,793	43,402,970	1,456,750	9,893,804	2,136,473	11,242,570	1,106,479	5,800,151	227,078	1,218,787
1870	4,880,009	33,589,377	1,144,253	7,742,221	1,451,252	8,871,507	791,421	4,719,792	152,622	947,309
1860	4,441,830	26,922,537	993,017	6,101,015	1,356,890	7,645,543	719,084	4,117,445	126,280	807,435
1850	3,638,808	19,553,068	811,825	4,393,523	1,138,455	5,600,586	601,315	2,896,458	91,785	537,661
1840	2,873,648	14,195,805	....	3,106,055	955,461	4,485,052	....	2,474,062	....	....
1830	2,328,642	10,537,378	....	2,269,582	797,167	3,427,730	....	1,894,914	....	....
PERCENTAGE IN EACH AGE GROUP.										
1910	100.0	100.0	24.8	23.6	25.5	21.8	12.9	11.4	2.6	2.4
1900	100.0	100.0	23.6	23.3	27.4	23.3	13.8	11.9	2.8	2.5
1890	100.0	100.0	22.6	23.2	28.7	23.7	14.0	12.0	2.8	2.5
1880	100.0	100.0	22.1	22.8	32.5	25.9	16.8	13.4	3.5	2.8
1870	100.0	100.0	23.4	23.0	29.7	26.4	16.2	14.1	3.1	2.8
1860	100.0	100.0	22.4	22.7	30.5	28.4	16.2	15.3	2.8	3.0
1850	100.0	100.0	22.3	22.5	31.3	28.6	16.5	14.8	2.5	2.7
1840	100.0	100.0	....	21.9	33.2	31.6	....	17.4	....	....
1830	100.0	100.0	....	21.5	34.2	32.5	....	18.0	....	....
INCREASE.[3]										
1900–1910	993,769	14,922,761	347,865	3,693,667	91,428	2,239,809	47,633	1,402,962	7,876	288,545
1890–1900[4]	1,345,318	11,707,938	399,462	2,851,311	277,345	2,505,462	168,236	1,340,304	38,944	307,940
1880–1890	889,247	11,580,920	231,112	2,731,837	4,595	1,810,246	−59,060	779,497	−21,512	140,333
1870–1880	1,700,784	9,813,593	312,497	2,151,583	685,221	2,371,063	315,058	1,080,359	74,456	271,478
1860–1870	438,179	6,666,840	151,236	1,641,206	94,362	1,225,964	72,337	602,347	26,342	139,874
1850–1860	803,022	7,369,469	181,192	1,707,492	218,435	2,044,957	117,769	1,220,987	34,495	269,774
1840–1850	765,160	5,357,263	....	1,287,468	182,994	1,115,534	....	422,396	....	....
1830–1840	545,006	3,658,427	....	836,473	158,294	1,057,322	....	579,148	....	....
INCREASE PER CENT.[3]										
1900–1910	11.2	22.3	16.7	23.7	3.8	14.4	3.9	17.7	3.2	17.3
1890–1900	18.0	21.3	23.7	22.1	13.0	19.2	16.1	20.4	18.9	22.7
1880–1890	13.5	26.7	15.9	27.6	0.2	16.1	−5.3	13.4	−9.5	11.5
1870–1880	34.9	29.2	27.3	27.8	47.2	26.7	39.8	22.9	48.8	28.7
1860–1870	9.9	24.8	15.2	26.9	7.0	16.0	10.1	14.6	20.6	17.3
1850–1860	22.1	37.7	22.3	38.9	19.2	36.5	19.6	42.2	37.6	50.2
1840–1850	26.6	37.7	....	41.5	19.2	24.9	....	17.1	....	....
1830–1840	23.4	34.7	....	56.9	19.9	30.8	....	30.6	....	....

[1] Figures in italics are estimates. The number of Negro children under 5 in 1890 is estimated by assuming that the proportion under 5 in the colored other than Negro under 10 was the same in 1890 as in 1900 (51.5 per cent), data being available for Negro and for colored under 10 and under 5 in 1900, for colored in these age groups in 1890, and for Negro under 10 in 1890. The margin of error is measured by the probability of change during the decade 1890–1900, in the proportion under 5 of the colored population other than Negro under 10. As the total colored population other than Negro under 10 in 1890 amounted to only 14,807, in a total colored under 10 of 2,151,606, any change in the proportion under 5 of the colored other than Negro under 10 would be immaterial in its effect upon the estimate for Negroes under 5. Similarly the number of Negroes under 1 in 1890 is estimated by assuming that the proportion under 1 in the colored population other than Negro under 5 was the same in 1890 as in 1900 (26.9 per cent), the estimated number of colored other than Negro under 5 in 1890 being 7,626, and the estimated number under 1 year, 2,048, in a total colored under 5 of 1,055,045, and under 1 of 207,614. In this case also, the number of colored other than Negro under 1 is too small for any error in the estimate materially to affect the figures for Negroes.

In estimating the number of Negro females 15 to 44 years of age in 1880, it is assumed that of colored females other than Negro the proportion 15 to 44 years of age was the same in 1880 as in 1890 (31.4 per cent). The total number of colored females, other than Negro in 1880 was 37,215, of whom 32,422 were Indians, 4,779 were Chinese, and 14 were Japanese. The racial character of the colored population other than Negro—exclusive of the specially enumerated in 1890—did not change materially during the decade 1880–1890, and it is improbable that there was any material change in the age distribution of females in this population element. In this case, as in the case of children under 5, and under 1 in 1890, the number of colored other than Negro in the aggregate of colored females (37,125 in a total of 1,468,424), is too small for any change in the age of distribution during the decade to be of material consequence in estimating the number of Negro females 15 to 44. In estimating the number of Negro children under 10 in 1880, it is assumed that the proportion under 10 in the colored other than Negro was the same in 1880 as in 1890 (8.8 per cent). In this case the margin of error in the estimate is measured by the probability of change in the proportion under 10 among the colored other than Negro, numbering 172,020 in 1880, in an aggregate colored of 2,151,606. The number of Negro children under 5 in 1880 is estimated by assuming that the proportion under 5 in the total under 10 was the same among Negroes as in the aggregate colored under 10 (51.8 per cent). This percentage can not have been materially affected by the colored other than Negro under 10, estimated to number in 1880 only 15,132 in an aggregate colored under 5 of 2,151,606. The number of Negro children under 1 in 1880 is estimated by assuming that the proportion under 1 among colored other than Negro under 5 was the same in 1880 as in 1900 (26.9 per cent). The total colored other than Negro under 5 in 1880, as estimated, was 7,886, in an aggregate colored under 5 of 1,114,365, and the colored other than Negro under 1 in 1880, as estimated was 2,118 in an aggregate colored of 229,196.

In estimating the number of Negro females 15 to 44 years of age in 1850 and in 1860, it is assumed that of Negro females 40 to 49 years of age in each of these years, the proportion 40 to 44 was the same as among Negro females 40 to 49 in 1870 (57.9 per cent). The error in the estimates is determined by the variation from census to census in the proportion 40 to 44 among females 40 to 49 years of age. The changing age distribution of the Negro population during the period for which data are available would indicate as probable that the percentage 40 to 44 among females 40 to 49 was somewhat higher in 1860 and in 1850 than it was in 1870, since in the 30 years 1870 to 1900 this proportion declined from 57.9 to 54.4 per cent, being only slightly higher, 54.8 per cent, in 1910 than in 1900. But no probable variation in the proportion would be of material consequence in the estimates.

In the case of each of these estimates it may be stated that the margin of error is probably no greater than the margin of error in the enumeration of the Negro population, and that the estimates are probably as close to the true population in each case as would have been figures obtained by a tabulation of scheduled returns.

The number of white females 15 to 44 in the years 1830, 1840, 1850, and 1860 is estimated by assuming that among white females 40 to 49 years of age the proportion 40 to 44 was the same in these years as in 1870.

[2] Exclusive of the specially enumerated in 1890.

[3] A minus sign (−) denotes decrease.

[4] The increase, 1890–1900, is figured on the population in 1890, including in the population for that year the specially enumerated.

CHILDREN UNDER 5 PER 1,000 WOMEN 15 TO 44 YEARS OF AGE AT EACH CENSUS: 1850 TO 1910.

In the succeeding tables of this chapter the number of children under 5 is related to the number of women 15 to 44 years of age, and the number of children per 1,000 women in these ages is given.

Table 3 gives these numbers for the Negro population at each census for which data are available for the Negroes, and introduces similar figures for whites. It shows, for example, that the number of children under 5 per 1,000 women 15 to 44 decreased among Negroes from 741 in 1850 to 519 in 1910, and among whites from 659 in 1850 to 484 in 1910. In each decade among Negroes, as among whites, the number of children per 1,000 women decreased, except that the number increased for Negroes, in the decade ending in 1880 (according to the schedule returns), and for whites in the decade ending 1860.

At each census the number of children relatively to the number of women was greater among Negroes than among whites, although in consequence of the somewhat more rapid decrease for Negroes, the difference in the ratios of children to women between Negroes and whites was less in 1910 than in any earlier year.

As compared with the ratio in 1910, the number of children per 1,000 women 15 to 44 in 1850 was greater by 222 in the case of Negroes, and by 175 in the case of whites, these numbers being the excess of the number of children per 1,000 women in 1850 over the number in 1910.

Table 3	Negro women 15 to 44 years of age.[1]	Negro children under 5 years of age.[1]	CHILDREN UNDER 5 PER 1,000 WOMEN 15 TO 44 YEARS OF AGE.[1]							
			Number.		Excess of Negro over white.	Decrease.[2]		Excess over 1910.	
YEAR.			Negro.	White.		Negro.	White.	Negro.	White.
1910....	2,435,189	1,263,288	519	484	35	63	24		
1900....	2,087,324	1,215,655	582	508	74	39	9	63	24
1890[3]..	1,687,862	1,047,419	621	517	104	139	69	102	33
1880....	1,456,750	1,106,479	760	586	174	+68	24	241	102
1870....	1,144,253	791,421	692	610	82	32	65	173	126
1860....	993,017	719,084	724	675	49	17	+16	205	191
1850....	811,825	601,315	741	659	82			222	175

[1] Figures in italics are estimates. See Note 1, Table 2, p. 285.
[2] A plus sign (+) denotes increase.
[3] Exclusive of specially enumerated.

COMPARISON OF NEGRO WITH OTHER RACE AND NATIVITY ELEMENTS.

In the census returns children of foreign-born parents are classified as native of foreign parentage, and children having one parent native and one parent foreign born as natives of mixed parentage. For the aggregate population of all ages a further differentiation is made in the tabulations from the schedules, distinguishing natives born of native mothers and foreign-born fathers from natives born of foreign mothers and native fathers. The age classification, however, is not extended to these latter classes, and it

is therefore necessary in any attempt to arrive at a figure which will represent the proportion of children to women for native white women and their children, as distinguished from foreign-born white women and their children, to estimate the number of children under 5 years of age born of native mothers and the number born in this country of foreign-born mothers. Such estimates have been made in Table 4, as explained in the note attached to the table, and ratios of children to women figured for native and for foreign-born white women. The table includes, also, data for Negroes, for the aggregate white population, for Indians, and for the "other colored" population.

Table 4	POPULATION: 1910.			
		Children under 5 years of age.		
			Having mother of class specified.	
RACIAL CLASS.	Women 15 to 44 years of age.	Of class specified.	Number.	Per 1,000 women 15 to 44.
All classes..............	21,768,408	10,631,364	10,631,364	488
Negro..................	2,435,189	1,263,288	1,263,288	519
White..................	19,270,619	9,322,914	9,322,914	484
Native white..............	15,904,942	....	7,106,686	447
Both parents native...........	....	6,546,282	....	
Native mother and foreign father....	....	[1] 560,404	....	
Foreign-born white..........	3,365,677	102,507	2,216,228	658
Both parents foreign born.......	....	1,819,847	....	
Foreign mother and native father...	....	[1] 293,874	....	
Indian................	53,788	40,384	40,384	751
Chinese, Japanese, and other colored.	8,812	4,778	4,778	542

[1] Estimate. It is assumed that in the native white population of mixed parentage (i. e., reporting one parent native and one foreign born), the proportion under 5 years of age (14.3 per cent) obtained equally among those reporting native mothers and foreign fathers (3,923,845), and those reporting foreign mothers and native fathers (2,057,681), being the same for each of these classes as in the aggregate for the two classes combined (the aggregate of mixed parentage), for which age data are available.

Accepting the estimates of Table 4 as being approximately correct, it will be apparent that the proportion of children under 5 to women 15 to 44 was higher in 1910 for Negro women than it was for native white women, and lower for Negro women than it was for foreign-born white women. In 1910 the number of children per 1,000 women was 519 in the case of Negro women, 447 in the case of native white women, and 658 in the case of foreign-born white women.

The corresponding ratio for the Indian population was 751 per 1,000, and for the Chinese, Japanese, and other colored combined 542.

Ratios similar to those presented in Table 4 are given in Table 5 for Negro and for native and foreign-born white women covering the three years 1910, 1900, and 1890.

As has been noted already, the ratio of children to women has tended to decline from census to census in the case both of Negroes and of whites, and it appears from Table 5 that this decline is in evidence in the case both of native white women and their children and of foreign-born white women and their children, although the proportion for foreign-born white women and their children was somewhat higher in 1900 than in 1890. In the case of native white women and their children, the ratio declined from 476 in 1890 to 464 in 1900, and to 447 in 1910. The corresponding figures for foreign-born white women and their children were 699 in 1890, 722 in 1900, and 658 in 1910.

Table 5 CLASS OF POPULATION.	1910	1900	1890
	CHILDREN UNDER 5 PER 1,000 WOMEN 15 TO 44.[1]		
Negro women and their children........	519	582	*621*
White women and their children........	484	508	517
Native white women and their children..............................	*447*	*464*	*476*
Foreign-born white women and their children...........................	*658*	*722*	*699*
	WOMEN 15 TO 44 YEARS OF AGE.		
Negro...............................	2,435,189	2,087,324	1,687,862
White...............................	19,270,619	15,576,952	12,725,641
Native.............................	15,904,942	12,889,028	10,395,970
Foreign born.......................	3,365,677	2,687,924	2,329,671
	CHILDREN UNDER 5 YEARS OF AGE.[1]		
Negro...............................	1,263,288	1,215,655	*1,047,419*
White...............................	9,322,914	7,919,952	6,579,648
Mother native.....................	*7,106,686*	*5,978,814*	*4,952,318*
Native—Both parents native...	6,546,282	5,464,881	4,550,682
Native—Mother native, father foreign born..................	*560,404*	*513,933*	*401,636*
Mother foreign born..............	*2,216,228*	*1,941,138*	*1,627,330*
Foreign born......................	102,507	52,369	86,629
Native—Both parents foreign born............................	1,819,847	1,632,761	1,365,115
Native—Mother foreign born, father native..................	*293,874*	*256,008*	*175,586*

[1] Figures in italics are estimates. For method of estimating the number of Negro children under 5 and of Negro women 15 to 44 in 1890, and of white children of native and of foreign-born mothers in 1910, see footnotes to Tables 2 and 4.

In estimating for 1900 the number of native white children having native and having foreign mothers, it is assumed that among the 3,346,652 native whites reporting native mothers and foreign fathers in 1900 the proportion under 5 was the same as among the total of native whites having one or both parents foreign born (15.4 per cent). In 1910 the proportion under 5 (14.1 per cent) among native whites of foreign parentage (both parents foreign born), was practically the same as the corresponding proportion (14.3 per cent) among native whites of mixed parentage (one parent, either father or mother, native and the other foreign born), and it is improbable that the proportion under 5 among native whites reporting native mothers and foreign fathers differed materially from that among those reporting foreign mothers and native fathers. As regards the derived number of children under 5 per 1,000 white women 15 to 44, the margin of error is inconsiderable in the case of native white women, of whose children 5,464,881 were classified as native, both parents native. To this number is added 513,933 as the estimated number of native white children of foreign fathers and native mothers. The number of children born of native mothers is, therefore, more than nine-tenths a compiled and tabulated figure, the estimate applying to less than one-tenth. The number of children per 1,000 native white women would not be materially affected by any probable error in this estimate. An error of 10 per cent, or of 51,000, in the estimate of 513,933, would mean that the number of children per 1,000 native white women as estimated was 4 too large or too small—that it should have been either 443 or 451 instead of 447. As regards the foreign white women, an error in the estimate would have a more considerable effect upon the proportion of children, an error of 51,000, for example, being equivalent to an error of approximately 19 in the number of children per 1,000 foreign white women. Such an error would, however, involve a difference in the proportion of children under 5 between the total of native whites having one or both parents foreign born and the component class of those having native mothers and foreign fathers greater by about twenty times than the difference which actually obtained in 1910 in this proportion between native whites one or both parents foreign born as a whole and the component class, native whites one parent foreign and one native.

Similarly in Table 5 in estimating for 1890, it is assumed that among the 2,378,729 native whites reporting native mothers the proportion under 5 was the same as among the total of native whites reporting one or both parents foreign born (16.9 per cent).

SECTIONS AND DIVISIONS.

Table 6 gives the number of children per 1,000 women 15 to 44 in the several geographic sections and southern divisions, covering the four census years 1880 to 1910. For the years 1880 and 1890 requisite data are not available by sections and divisions for the Negro population separately, the classification of these years being for the aggregate colored. In Table 6 data are given for the colored population in these years and in 1900, and for Negroes in 1900 and in 1910. The variation of the figures for the aggregate colored from those for Negroes in the several sections and divisions may be noted in the figures for 1900, for which year ratios are given for Negroes, together with corresponding figures for the aggregate colored. In the South as a whole the number of children per 1,000 women in 1900 was 621 in the aggregate colored, and 619 in the Negro population. In the South Atlantic and in the East South Central division the ratios are the same for Negroes as for the aggregate colored, being 630 to 1,000 in the South Atlantic and 598 per 1,000 in the East South Central division. In the West South Central division a slight difference develops between the ratio for Negroes and that for the aggregate colored, the number of children per 1,000 women being 627 for Negroes and 633 for the total colored. In the North the difference is more considerable—the corresponding numbers being 317 for Negroes and 336 for the colored—and in the West it is very marked—the numbers being 269 and 516, respectively. It is apparent from these figures for 1900 that no particular significance attaches to the ratios for the aggregate colored in the West in 1880 and in 1890 as indexes of conditions obtaining in these years in the Negro population of this section, and that considerable allowance must be made for incomparability of data in the North. In the South, however, the number of colored other than Negro was too small to affect materially the ratios for the aggregate colored, which may therefore be accepted as ratios for the Negro population.

In the South among Negroes the number of children per 1,000 women 15 to 44 declined from 793 in 1880 (colored population) to 554 in 1910, the corresponding decline for the white population being from 711 in 1880 to 617 in 1910. In this section the ratio of children to women was higher among Negroes than among whites in 1880, and higher among whites than among Negroes in 1910.

In each of the southern divisions the ratio in 1910 was higher for whites than for Negroes.

Among Negroes in the South and in each of the three southern divisions, in each decade covered by Table 6 the proportion of children fell off. In the white population also in each of these areas the proportion of children declined during each decade, with the exception of slight increases in the decade 1890–1900 in the South as a whole, and specifically in the South Atlantic division.

Table 6 — CHILDREN UNDER 5 PER 1,000 WOMEN, 15-44.

SECTION, DIVISION, AND RACIAL CLASS.	1910	1900	1890	1880	Increase (+) or decrease (−).		
					1900-1910	1890-1900	1880-1890
United States:							
Negro	519	582	¹621	¹760	−63	¹−39	¹−139
Colored		585	619	759		−34	−140
White	484	508	517	586	−24	−9	−69
The South:							
Negro	554	619			−65		
Colored		621	648	793		−27	−145
White	617	633	631	711	−16	+2	−80
South Atlantic—							
Negro	577	630			−53		
Colored		630	638	787		−8	−149
White	589	595	587	666	−6	+8	−79
East South Central—							
Negro	535	598			−63		
Colored		598	639	785		−41	−146
White	626	630	631	712	−4	−1	−81
West South Central—							
Negro	532	627			−95		
Colored		633	690	824		−57	−134
White	644	692	713	813	−48	−21	−100
The North:							
Negro	282	317			−35		
Colored		336	402	514		−66	−112
White	442	470	482	544	−28	−12	−62
The West:							
Negro	231	269			−38		
Colored		516	379	419		+137	−40
White	434	477	516	634	−43	−39	−118

¹ Estimated. See Note 1, Table 2, p. 285.

The proportion of children to women in the Negro population of the North and West is, relatively to the proportion in the South, much lower, the number of children under 5 per 1,000 women 15 to 44 in 1910 being in the North 282 and in the West 231, as compared with 554 in the South.

CHILDREN UNDER 5 YEARS OF AGE PER 1,000 MARRIED WOMEN.

The number of children under 5 in the several divisions in 1910 and in 1900 is related in Table 7 to the number of married women 15 years of age and over.

Table 7 — POPULATION: 1910.

SECTION, DIVISION, AND YEAR.	Married females 15 years of age and over.		Children under 5 years of age.		Children under 5 per 1,000 married females 15 and over.	
	Negro.	White.	Negro.	White.	Negro.	White.
United States:						
1910	1,775,949	15,852,011	1,263,288	9,322,914	711	588
1900	1,443,817	12,319,767	1,215,655	7,919,952	842	643
The South:						
1910	1,554,357	3,821,383	1,176,331	2,860,467	757	749
1900	1,278,965	2,849,481	1,135,793	2,315,571	888	813
The North:						
1910	211,347	10,782,530	83,729	5,816,524	396	539
1900	159,650	8,782,772	77,794	5,195,996	487	592
The West:						
1910	10,245	1,248,098	3,228	645,923	315	518
1900	5,202	687,514	2,068	408,385	398	594

While the proportion married among Negro females 15 years of age and over was somewhat higher in the South than it was in the North and West in 1910—57.6 in the South, 54.7 in the North, and 56.6 in the West—the differences in the proportion married between the several sections do not seem sufficient to account for the differences in the proportion of children.

Per 1,000 married Negro women in the country as a whole the number of children under 5 was 711 in 1910 and 842 in 1900, the corresponding figures for whites being 588 and 643. In the several sections in 1910 the number of Negro children per 1,000 married women was 757 for the South, 396 for the North, and 315 for the West. In each section the number of children under 5 per 1,000 married women declined during the decade among Negroes and among whites. In both classes of population the proportion of children to married women was much higher in the South than it was in the North. In the South the proportion of 757 per 1,000 among Negroes slightly exceeded the proportion of 749 per 1,000 among whites, while in other sections, although the proportion for whites was much lower than the proportion for whites in the South, the proportion for Negroes was much lower than that for whites.

THE STATES.

Data corresponding to the data given in Table 6 for sections and southern divisions are given in Table 8 for Southern states. For the Negro and for the white population the number of women 15 to 44 years of age, of children under 5, and of children under 5 per 1,000 women 15 to 44, is given for 1910 and for 1900 in Table 11 (p. 294) for all states and for each of the nine geographic divisions.

In each Southern state in the decade 1900–1910 the proportion of children under 5 to women 15 to 44 in the Negro population decreased, and except for small increases in South Carolina, Georgia, Alabama, Mississippi, and Arkansas, the corresponding proportion for whites also decreased. By reference to Table 11 it may be seen that decreases were general in the Northern and Western states, as well as in the Southern—only five Northern states—four of them in New England—and four Western showed increases in the proportion of children for Negroes, and four Northern states—three of them in New England—and no Western state, increases for whites.

In the Southern states, among Negroes in 1910 the number of children under 5 per 1,000 women 15 to 44 ranged from 381 in Kentucky to 661 in North Carolina (the number for the District of Columbia being 234), and among whites from 422 in Delaware to 700 in Arkansas (the number for the District being 299); in the North (see Table 11) the range for Negroes is from 158 in Nevada to 405 in Vermont, and for whites from 347 in California to 670 in North Dakota.

The number of Negro women 15 to 44 years of age living in the Middle Atlantic division in 1910 was 131,605, the number of children under 5 years of age 35,298, giving a ratio of 268 children per 1,000 women, which is less than one-half the corresponding ratio of 577 for the South Atlantic division and almost precisely one-half the ratio of 535 for the East South Central division, and of 532 for the West South Central division.

DIVISION, STATE, AND RACIAL CLASS.	CHILDREN UNDER 5 PER 1,000 WOMEN, 15 TO 44 YEARS OF AGE.				Increase (+) or decrease (−).		
	1910	1900	1890	1880	1900–1910	1890–1900	1880–1890
SOUTH ATLANTIC.							
Delaware:							
Negro	415	500	......	......	−85		
Colored	......	499	522	632	......	−23	−110
White	422	446	441	516	−24	+5	−75
Maryland:							
Negro	443	483	......	......	−40		
Colored	......	483	515	614	......	−32	−99
White	431	461	471	539	−30	−10	−68
District of Columbia:							
Negro	234	254	......	......	−20		
Colored	......	254	299	428	......	−45	−129
White	299	302	320	420	−3	−18	−100
Virginia:							
Negro	545	594	......	......	−49		
Colored	......	594	594	762	......	......	−168
White	577	591	569	657	−14	+22	−88
West Virginia:							
Negro	463	514	......	......	−51		
Colored	......	514	570	699	......	−56	−129
White	638	649	644	757	−11	+5	−113
North Carolina:							
Negro	661	674	......	......	−13		
Colored	......	674	661	838	......	+13	−177
White	675	677	659	703	−2	+18	−44
South Carolina:							
Negro	654	712	......	......	−58		
Colored	......	712	720	867	......	−8	−147
White	647	630	627	714	+17	+3	−87
Georgia:							
Negro	592	663	......	......	−71		
Colored	......	663	676	818	......	−13	−142
White	647	642	642	721	+5	......	−79
Florida:							
Negro	486	599	......	......	−113		
Colored	......	599	621	752	......	−22	−131
White	600	639	630	718	−39	+9	−88
EAST SOUTH CENTRAL.							
Kentucky:							
Negro	381	454	......	......	−73		
Colored	......	454	549	664	......	−95	−115
White	583	601	603	681	−18	−2	−78
Tennessee:							
Negro	468	544	......	......	−76		
Colored	......	544	609	770	......	−65	−161
White	609	615	624	721	−6	−9	−97
Alabama:							
Negro	561	624	......	......	−63		
Colored	......	624	644	792	......	−20	−148
White	691	680	672	734	+11	+8	−62
Mississippi:							
Negro	588	652	......	......	−64		
Colored	......	652	689	843	......	−37	−154
White	677	675	675	747	+2	......	−72
WEST SOUTH CENTRAL.							
Arkansas:							
Negro	529	611	......	......	−82		
Colored	......	611	684	863	......	−73	−179
White	700	689	744	845	+11	−55	−101
Louisiana:							
Negro	527	620	......	......	−93		
Colored	......	620	680	773	......	−60	−93
White	612	652	631	680	−40	+21	−49
Oklahoma:							
Negro	572	658	......	......	−86		
Colored	......	631	533	......	......	+98	......
White	664	722	701	......	−58	+21	......
Texas:							
Negro	532	642	......	......	−110		
Colored	......	642	707	869	......	−65	−162
White	625	698	727	853	−73	−29	−126

Although the ratio of children under 5 to women 15 to 44 was higher in the Negro population as a whole in 1910 than it was in the white population—being 519 per 1,000 for Negroes, as compared with 484 for whites—it was lower for Negroes than for whites in each of the nine geographic divisions, and with exception of two states—Maryland and North Carolina— lower for Negroes than for whites in each state. The explanation of this apparent inconsistency of the ratios for the divisions and states with the ratios for

the country as a whole is that approximately nine-tenths of the Negro population was resident in the South, where the ratios for both Negroes and whites are high relatively to ratios in the North and West, while nearly three-fourths of the white population were resident in the North and West. The high ratios of the South are heavily weighted in the average for the Negro population as a whole, and the relatively low ratios of the North and West in the average for the white population.

Proportion of children under 5 to women of child-bearing age in the Negro and in the white population is shown by states for the years 1910 and 1900 on Maps I to IV (pp. 291, 292). An extremely significant feature of these maps—in the case of each population class, but specially in the case of Negroes—is the remarkable decrease, in 1910 as compared with 1900, in the aggregate black area, i. e., in the area representing states in which the proportion of children to women exceeded 600 children under 5 to 1,000 women 15 to 44. In the case of Negroes in 1900, this area included all of the "black belt" states, constituting a solid band of states from North Carolina to Texas; and in 1910 only 2 states, North and South Carolina. For whites the area representing a ratio of 600 children to 1,000 women included 20 states—14 Southern and 6 Northern and Western—in 1900, and 15 states— 13 Southern and 2 Northern and Western—in 1910. Comparison of the hachures on the maps for the two years makes apparent the general decrease in the proportion of children in areas of low as well as of high proportion. In the case of Negroes this is strikingly apparent in the extension of the white area, in 1910 as compared with 1900.

URBAN AND RURAL POPULATION.

A tabulation relating to the proportion of children in the population living in urban communities of 25,000 or more inhabitants in 1910, and in the population living in smaller urban communities and rural districts, is summarized in Table 9 by geographic sections. Similar data are given, by states and geographic divisions, in Table 12 (p. 295).

The classification of Table 9 does not, it will be noted, distinguish the urban from the rural population, since in this table all of the urban population which in 1910 lived in communities of less than 25,000 inhabitants is classified with the rural population, giving an aggregate population living outside cities of 25,000 inhabitants which is partly urban and partly rural. Since, however, the population living in cities of 25,000 or more inhabitants is entirely urban, and the population living outside such cities is predominantly rural, the differences in the proportion of children between the two aggregates distinguished in Table 9 may be accepted as generally characteristic of differences obtaining between the urban and rural aggregates. It is perhaps fair to assume that the ratio of children shown for the population living outside cities of 25,000 or more inhabitants is somewhat below the ratio obtaining in the purely rural population, and that the ratio shown for cities of 25,000 and over is somewhat below the ratio obtaining in the urban population as a whole.

Table 9

SECTION.	POPULATION: 1910.					
	Women 15 to 44 years of age.		Children under 5 years of age.		Children under 5 per 1,000 women 15 to 44.	
	Negro.	White.	Negro.	White.	Negro.	White.
IN CITIES OF 25,000 OR MORE INHABITANTS.						
United States..	525,748	7,179,064	125,735	2,644,464	239	368
The South..........	326,184	736,250	80,940	265,349	248	360
The North..........	190,985	5,869,010	43,019	2,217,303	225	378
The West	8,579	573,804	1,776	161,812	207	282
OUTSIDE CITIES OF 25,000 OR MORE INHABITANTS.						
United States..	1,909,441	12,091,555	1,137,553	6,678,450	596	552
The South..........	1,797,848	3,899,976	1,095,391	2,595,118	609	665
The North..........	106,213	7,278,815	40,710	3,599,221	383	494
The West..........	5,380	912,764	1,452	484,111	270	530

The general significance of the differences developed in Table 9 is not materially affected by the exclusion of small cities from the urban group. The table indicates clearly that the proportion of children is much lower in cities than it is in rural communities. The number of children under 5 per 1,000 women 15 to 44 in the Negro population of cities of 25,000 or more inhabitants in 1910 was 239 in the country as a whole, 248 in the South, 225 in the North, and 207 in the West; in the Negro population living outside such cities the corresponding number was 596 in the country as a whole, 609 in the South, 383 in the North, and 270 in the West.

The most marked difference developed in the table is that between the proportion of children in the Negro population of southern cities of 25,000 and over and the Negro population in the South outside such cities, the number of children per 1,000 women being for the population of the cities 248 and for the balance of the population, urban and rural, 609. In the North and in the West the corresponding differ-

ence is much less marked, the proportion for the population living outside of cities of 25,000 and over being very much lower in the North and West than it is in the South. In the case of the white population, also, the most marked difference in proportions as developed in Table 9 is that obtaining in the South, where the number of children per 1,000 women was 360 for the white population living in cities of 25,000 and over and 665 for the population living in the South outside such cities.

In each section of the country, in the population living in and living outside cities of 25,000 or more inhabitants, the proportion of children in 1910 was higher for whites than for Negroes. In the aggregate for the United States of population living outside cities of 25,000 or more, however, the ratio was higher for Negroes, the explanation of the seeming inconsistency of the ratios for sections with ratio for the total of this aggregate being—as in the case noted above of state and divisional ratios—that the high ratio of the South is heavily weighted in the aggregate for Negroes

URBAN COMMUNITIES.

Data relating to the proportion of children in the Negro and white population in 1910 and in 1900 are given in Table 10 for the 39 cities of 25,000 or more inhabitants in 1910, which reported in that year a Negro population of 10,000 or more. In this group of selected cities the number of Negro children under 5 per 1,000 Negro women, 15 to 44 ranged in 1910 from 153 in Kansas City, Mo., to 363 in Wilmington, N. C.

In 30 of the 39 cities shown in Table 10 the ratio of children to women in the Negro population decreased in the decade 1900–1910, and in 3 it increased, comparable data covering the two years 1910 and 1900 not being available for the 6 remaining cities.

In each of the 39 cities, without exception, the proportion of children was lower in the Negro than it was in the white population.

In Table 13 (p. 296) statistics are given for each city of 25,000 or more inhabitants in 1910, showing the number of Negro women 15 to 44, of Negro children under 5, and for those cities in which the number of women 15 to 44 was 1,000 or more, the number of children per 1,000 women.

MAP I.—NEGRO CHILDREN UNDER 5 YEARS OF AGE TO 1,000 NEGRO WOMEN 15 TO 44, BY STATES: 1910.

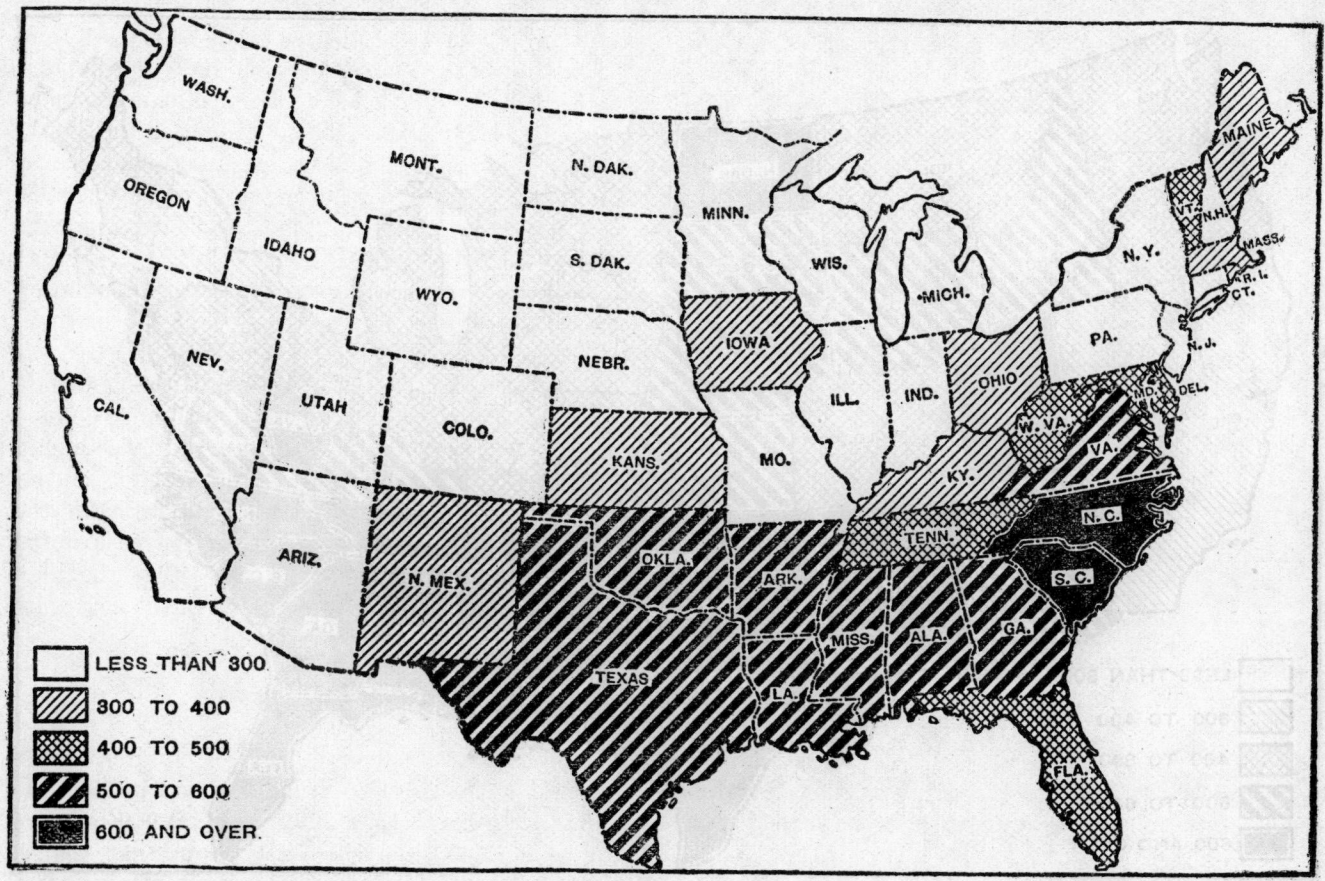

MAP II.—NEGRO CHILDREN UNDER 5 YEARS OF AGE TO 1,000 NEGRO WOMEN 15 TO 44, BY STATES: 1900.

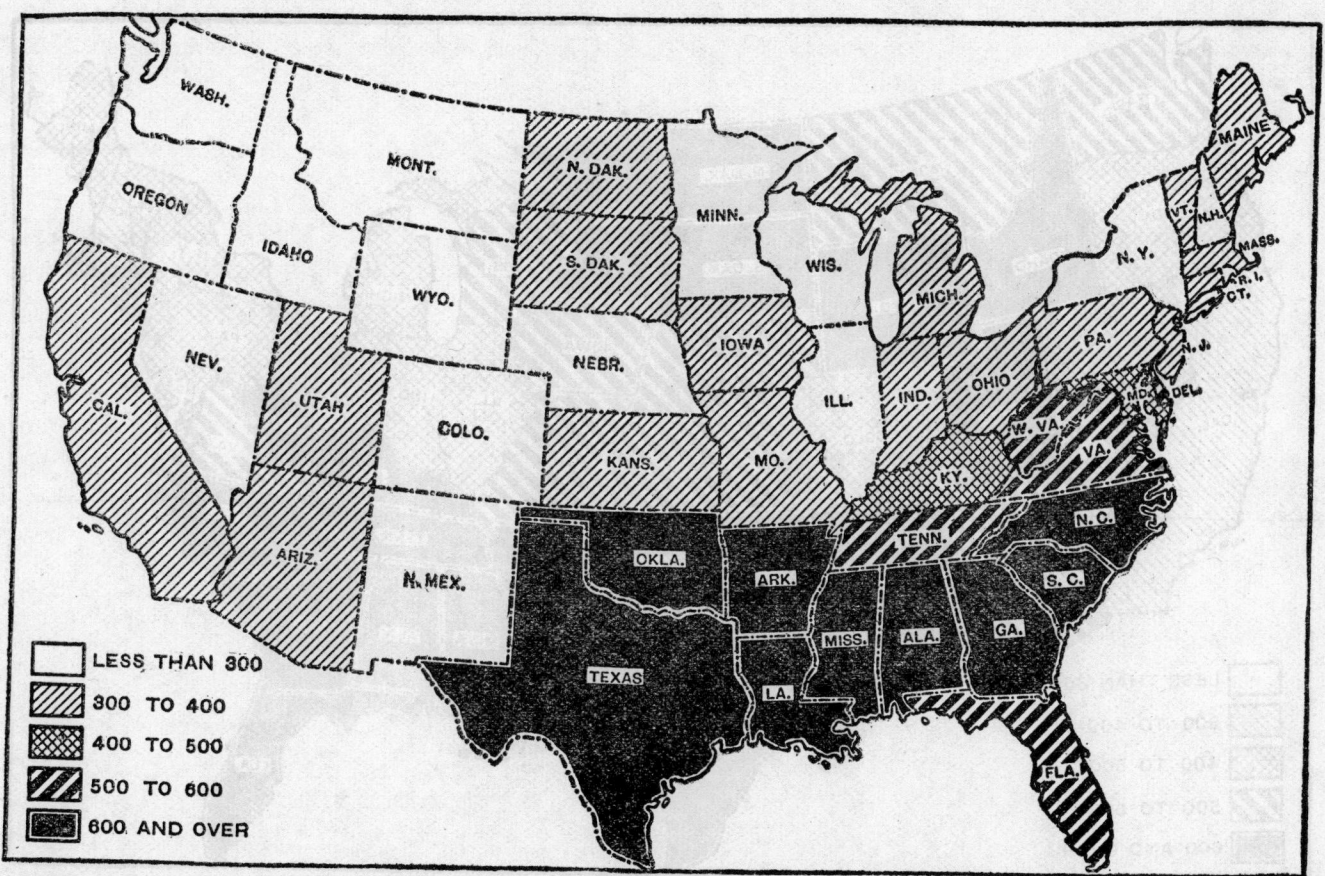

MAP III.—WHITE CHILDREN UNDER 5 YEARS OF AGE TO 1,000 WHITE WOMEN 15 TO 44, BY STATES: 1910.

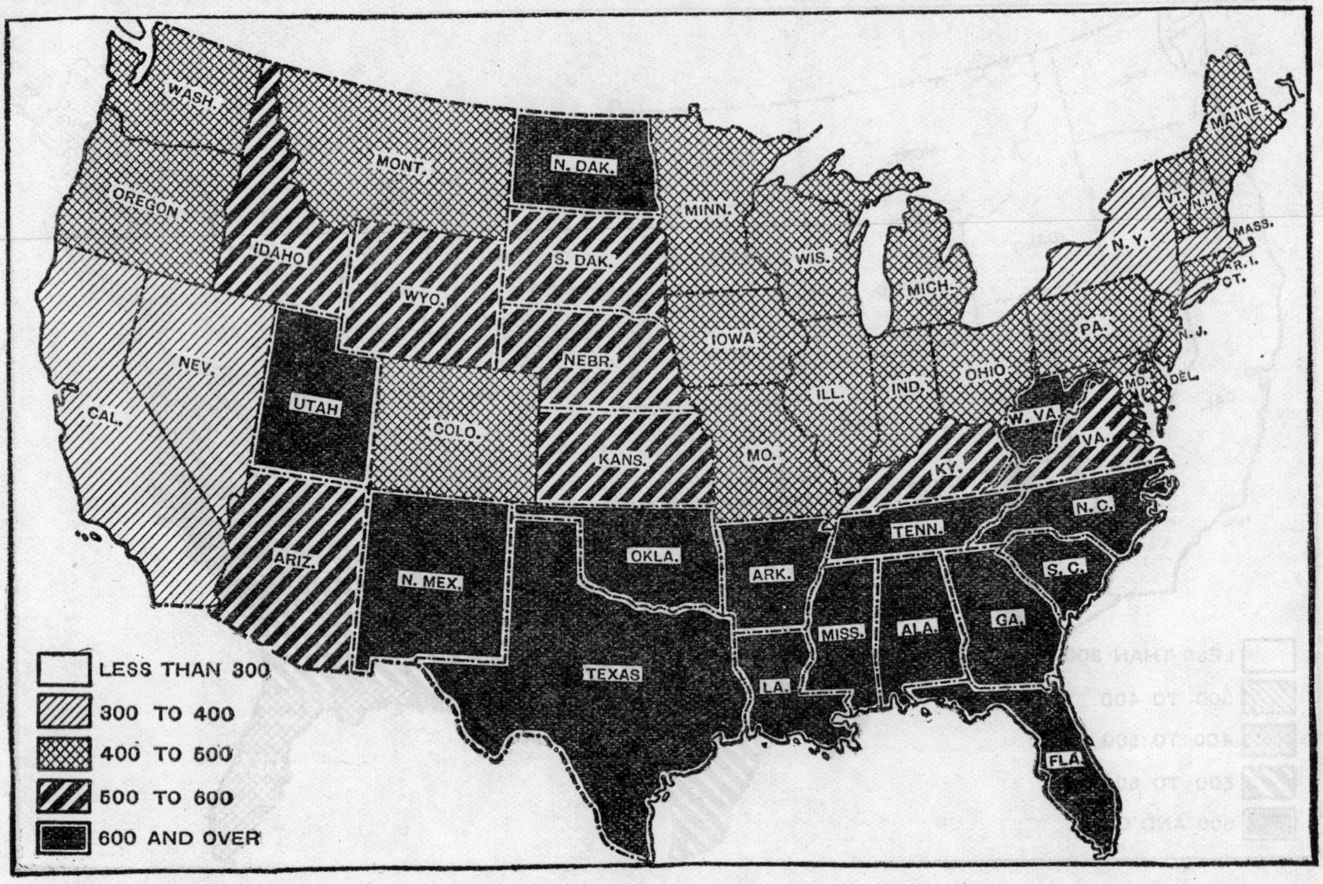

MAP IV.—WHITE CHILDREN UNDER 5 YEARS OF AGE TO 1,000 WHITE WOMEN 15 TO 44, BY STATES: 1900.

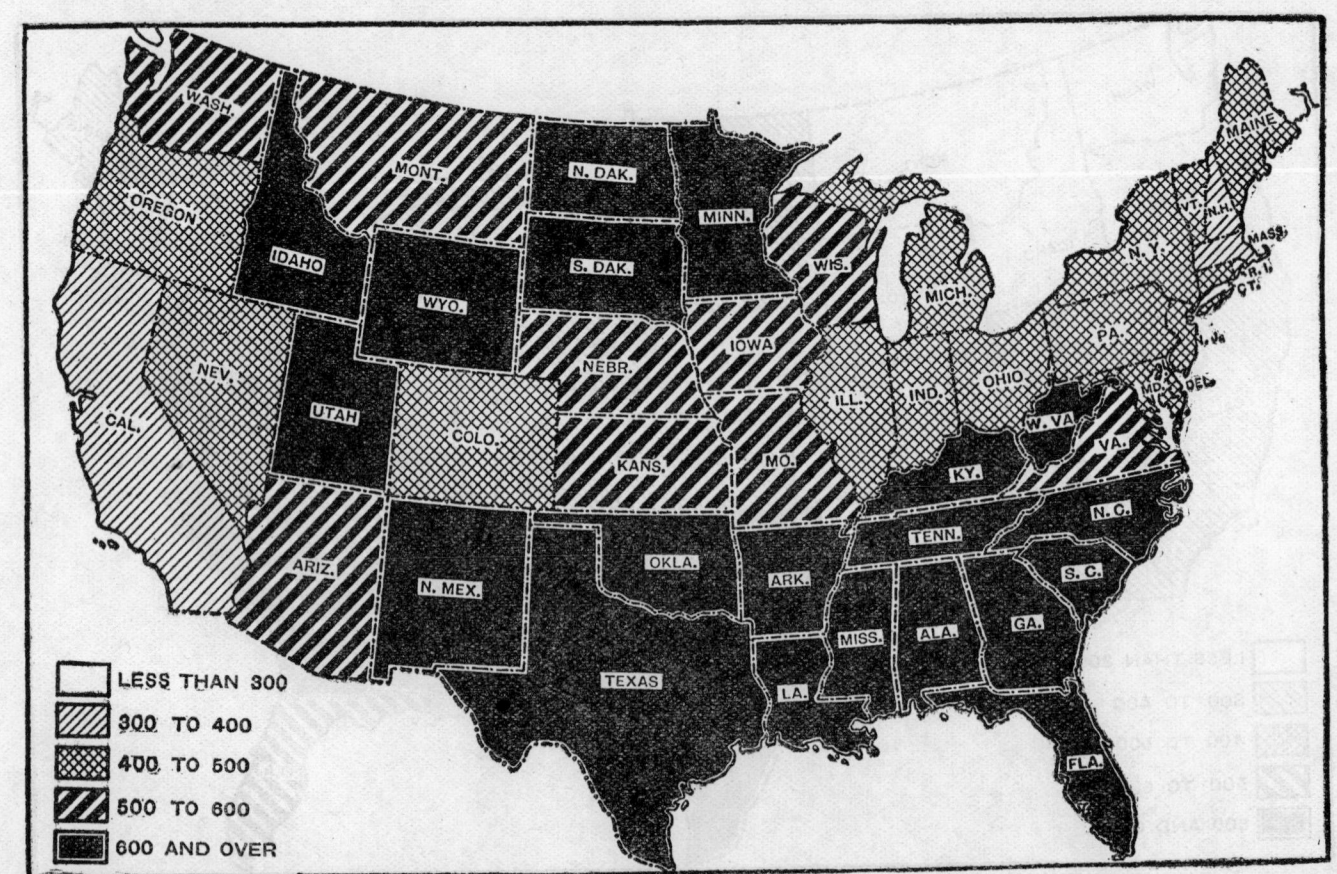

TABLE 10.—WOMEN 15 TO 44 YEARS OF AGE, CHILDREN UNDER 5 YEARS, AND NUMBER AND INCREASE OR DECREASE OF CHILDREN PER 1,000 WOMEN, BY CITIES OF 25,000 OR MORE INHABITANTS HAVING IN 1910 A NEGRO POPULATION OF 10,000 OR MORE: 1910 AND 1900.

CITY.	WOMEN 15 TO 44 YEARS OF AGE.				CHILDREN UNDER 5 YEARS OF AGE.				CHILDREN UNDER 5 PER 1,000 WOMEN 15 TO 44 YEARS OF AGE.					
	Negro.		White.		Negro.		White.		Negro.		White.		Increase (+) or decrease (−): 1900–1910.	
	1910	1900	1910	1900	1910	1900	1910	1900	1910	1900	1910	1900	Negro.	White.
Atlanta, Ga	17,524	12,348	28,425	14,670	4,622	3,316	10,964	5,312	264	269	386	362	−5	+24
Augusta, Ga	6,276	5,874	6,235	5,639	1,326	1,708	2,182	2,099	211	291	350	372	−80	−22
Baltimore, Md	27,385	26,158	125,906	112,773	6,628	6,705	45,356	43,807	242	256	360	388	−14	−28
Birmingham, Ala	16,537	5,675	20,929	5,564	4,598	1,421	9,604	2,203	278	250	459	396	+28	+63
Boston, Mass	4,376	3,556	177,409	152,339	942	936	62,746	56,415	215	263	354	370	−48	−16
Charleston, S. C	10,251	9,802	7,282	6,423	2,985	3,062	2,681	2,224	291	312	368	346	−21	+22
Charlotte, N. C	3,784	(1)	5,967	(1)	1,225	(1)	2,756	(1)	324	......	462			
Chattanooga, Tenn	5,787	4,026	7,423	4,605	1,488	1,097	2,449	1,610	257	272	330	350	−15	−20
Chicago, Ill	14,296	9,548	567,465	434,047	2,472	1,611	221,270	188,730	173	169	390	435	+4	−45
Cincinnati, Ohio	6,343	4,609	95,230	85,714	1,148	996	28,023	28,825	181	216	294	336	−35	−42
Columbia, S. C	3,770	(1)	4,031	(1)	1,041	(1)	1,529	(1)	276	......	379			
Columbus, Ohio	3,698	2,290	46,464	32,223	836	574	13,497	9,556	226	251	290	297	−25	−7
Dallas, Tex	6,223	3,013	20,581	8,964	1,271	718	6,775	3,344	204	238	329	373	−34	−44
Fort Worth, Tex	4,200	1,366	15,566	5,813	1,063	361	5,887	2,410	253	264	378	415	−11	−37
Houston, Tex	8,121	4,802	14,639	7,410	1,790	1,144	4,986	2,975	220	238	341	401	−18	−60
Indianapolis, Ind	6,697	4,702	58,623	42,709	1,557	1,167	17,139	13,396	232	248	292	314	−16	−22
Jacksonville, Fla	9,587	4,990	7,838	3,218	2,234	1,543	2,608	1,196	233	309	333	372	−76	−39
Kansas City, Mo	7,896	5,914	64,274	41,453	1,211	1,076	17,376	12,357	153	182	270	298	−29	−28
Lexington, Ky	3,398	3,171	6,734	4,603	681	753	1,821	1,151	200	237	270	250	−37	+20
Little Rock, Ark	4,667	4,355	8,785	6,217	1,095	1,166	3,010	2,316	235	268	343	373	−33	−30
Louisville, Ky	12,727	12,099	49,983	45,063	2,458	2,747	16,390	16,152	193	227	328	358	−34	−30
Macon, Ga	5,653	(1)	6,025	(1)	1,512	(1)	2,363	(1)	267	......	392			
Memphis, Tenn	17,496	14,822	21,300	13,418	3,729	4,568	7,024	5,087	213	308	330	379	−95	−49
Mobile, Ala	7,377	5,320	7,804	5,714	1,863	1,429	2,772	1,992	253	269	355	349	−16	+6
Montgomery, Ala	6,372	5,532	5,008	3,511	1,529	1,639	1,844	1,281	240	296	368	365	−56	+3
Nashville, Tenn	12,066	9,654	20,334	13,790	2,721	2,480	7,451	4,882	226	257	366	371	−31	−51
New Orleans, La	28,355	23,176	65,833	54,234	7,624	7,184	24,413	22,878	269	310	371	422	−41	−51
New York, N. Y	33,895	22,462	1,270,461	903,485	6,676	4,566	500,248	392,651	197	203	394	435	−6	−41
Norfolk, Va	8,302	6,571	11,824	6,902	2,008	1,918	4,185	2,675	242	292	354	388	−50	−34
Philadelphia, Pa	29,150	22,038	386,611	326,065	6,863	5,328	146,045	125,790	235	242	378	386	−7	−8
Pittsburgh, Pa	7,666	5,640	132,321	110,563	2,240	1,830	55,546	49,090	292	324	420	444	−32	−24
Portsmouth, Va	3,573	(1)	4,877	(1)	1,064	(1)	2,279	(1)	298	......	467			
Richmond, Va	15,087	10,450	22,228	14,133	4,019	2,747	7,583	4,988	266	263	341	353	+3	−12
St. Louis, Mo	13,818	11,060	176,800	143,101	2,685	2,403	57,399	54,620	194	217	325	382	−23	−57
San Antonio, Tex	3,600	2,247	23,040	11,869	895	718	9,080	4,943	249	320	394	416	−71	−22
Savannah, Ga	11,349	9,570	8,445	6,811	2,623	2,399	3,382	2,570	231	251	400	377	−20	+23
Shreveport, La	4,669	(1)	3,698	(1)	1,181	(1)	1,365	(1)	253	......	369			
Washington, D. C	31,166	28,634	64,794	52,537	7,290	7,278	19,361	15,862	234	254	299	302	−20	−3
Wilmington, N. C	3,525	(1)	3,530	(1)	1,280	(1)	1,547	(1)	363	......	438			

1 Data for 1900 not available.

TABLE 11.—NEGRO AND WHITE WOMEN 15 TO 44 YEARS OF AGE, CHILDREN UNDER 5 YEARS, AND NUMBER AND INCREASE OR DECREASE OF CHILDREN PER 1,000 WOMEN, BY DIVISIONS AND STATES: 1910 AND 1900.

DIVISION AND STATE.	WOMEN 15 TO 44 YEARS OF AGE.				CHILDREN UNDER 5 YEARS OF AGE.				CHILDREN UNDER 5 PER 1,000 WOMEN 15 TO 44 YEARS OF AGE.					
	Negro.		White.		Negro.		White.		Negro.		White.		Increase (+) or decrease (−); 1900–1910.	
	1910	1900	1910	1900	1910	1900	1910	1900	1910	1900	1910	1900	Negro.	White.
UNITED STATES	2,435,189	2,087,324	19,270,619	15,576,952	1,263,288	1,215,655	9,322,914	7,919,952	519	582	484	508	−63	−24
GEOGRAPHIC DIVISIONS:														
New England	18,833	17,526	1,608,443	1,389,119	5,876	5,382	634,679	548,678	312	307	395	395	+5	......
Middle Atlantic	131,605	100,004	4,673,693	3,727,053	35,298	29,075	2,013,901	1,660,162	268	291	431	445	−23	−14
East North Central	81,994	66,806	4,254,070	3,692,487	23,428	21,827	1,881,855	1,750,302	286	327	442	474	−41	−32
West North Central	64,766	60,851	2,611,619	2,253,085	19,127	21,510	1,286,089	1,236,854	295	353	492	549	−58	−57
South Atlantic	989,583	865,498	1,842,406	1,514,406	570,516	545,284	1,085,073	901,325	577	630	589	595	−53	−6
East South Central	649,752	582,279	1,297,554	1,123,231	347,803	348,061	812,171	707,449	535	598	626	630	−63	−4
West South Central	484,697	386,666	1,496,266	1,021,310	258,012	242,448	963,223	706,797	532	627	644	692	−95	−48
Mountain	6,038	4,042	553,000	336,603	1,350	981	293,222	193,876	224	243	530	576	−19	−46
Pacific	7,921	3,652	933,568	519,658	1,878	1,087	352,701	214,509	237	298	378	413	−61	−35
NEW ENGLAND:														
Maine	332	316	165,072	157,723	117	118	71,637	65,480	352	373	434	415	−21	+19
New Hampshire	149	220	98,665	96,986	40	37	39,538	38,190	268	168	401	394	+100	+7
Vermont	252	189	77,676	75,914	102	75	34,065	32,776	405	397	439	432	+7	+7
Massachusetts	11,053	9,520	860,006	729,499	3,448	2,954	325,327	279,203	312	310	378	383	+8	−5
Rhode Island	2,592	2,672	135,988	108,598	862	793	53,191	42,657	333	297	391	393	+2	−2
Connecticut	4,455	4,609	271,036	220,399	1,307	1,405	110,921	90,372	293	305	409	410	+36	−1
													−12	
MIDDLE ATLANTIC:														
New York	45,629	33,210	2,301,760	1,819,786	10,061	7,762	887,997	744,939	220	234	386	409	−14	−23
New Jersey	27,124	21,012	610,292	449,664	7,922	6,453	258,995	199,987	292	307	424	445	−15	−21
Pennsylvania	58,852	45,782	1,761,641	1,457,603	17,315	14,860	866,909	715,236	294	325	492	491	−31	+1
EAST NORTH CENTRAL:														
Ohio	29,632	24,703	1,116,496	974,221	8,921	8,566	470,533	423,236	301	347	421	434	−46	−13
Indiana	16,342	14,862	617,469	576,136	4,763	5,054	270,732	269,711	291	340	438	468	−49	−30
Illinois	30,823	22,680	1,350,430	1,135,080	8,248	6,744	589,677	543,273	268	297	437	479	−29	−42
Michigan	4,347	3,919	641,765	551,288	1,285	1,287	296,338	258,597	296	328	462	469	−32	−7
Wisconsin	850	642	527,910	455,762	211	176	254,575	255,485	248	274	482	561	−26	−79
WEST NORTH CENTRAL:														
Minnesota	1,889	1,330	466,546	376,833	382	323	225,165	226,418	202	243	483	601	−41	−118
Iowa	3,708	3,119	509,502	503,555	1,245	983	234,755	262,404	336	315	461	521	+21	−60
Missouri	43,156	42,012	750,965	686,947	12,299	14,797	348,159	349,224	285	352	464	508	−67	−44
North Dakota	147	59	121,503	61,961	37	18	81,414	46,725	252	305	670	754	−53	−84
South Dakota	216	93	123,104	78,074	60	37	70,860	52,212	278	398	576	669	−120	−93
Nebraska	2,213	1,770	269,703	231,608	477	422	139,142	132,940	216	238	516	574	−22	−58
Kansas	13,437	12,468	370,296	314,107	4,627	4,930	186,594	166,931	344	395	504	531	−51	−27
SOUTH ATLANTIC:														
Delaware	7,437	7,253	40,136	36,231	3,089	3,622	16,956	16,173	415	500	422	446	−85	−24
Maryland	58,631	58,267	259,462	230,869	25,987	28,116	111,724	106,463	443	483	431	461	−40	−30
District of Columbia	31,166	28,634	64,794	52,537	7,290	7,278	19,361	15,862	234	254	299	302	−20	−3
Virginia	158,798	152,045	315,526	268,651	86,555	90,332	182,181	158,692	545	594	577	591	−49	−14
West Virginia	15,050	9,325	254,080	201,247	6,974	4,793	162,140	130,672	463	514	638	649	−51	−11
North Carolina	162,377	143,744	331,856	274,530	107,297	96,945	224,088	185,901	661	674	675	677	−13	−2
South Carolina	196,806	176,021	153,969	124,336	128,712	125,254	99,685	78,373	654	712	647	630	−58	+17
Georgia	282,888	237,245	322,963	261,933	167,498	157,201	209,117	168,264	592	663	647	642	−71	+5
Florida	76,430	52,964	99,620	64,072	37,114	31,743	59,821	40,925	486	599	600	639	−113	−39
EAST SOUTH CENTRAL:														
Kentucky	66,986	69,889	461,544	419,961	25,541	31,706	268,918	252,507	381	454	583	601	−73	−18
Tennessee	120,951	114,644	390,451	345,711	56,580	62,388	237,978	212,515	468	544	609	615	−76	−6
Alabama	220,984	191,017	271,560	217,749	123,991	119,275	187,531	148,007	561	624	691	680	−63	+11
Mississippi	240,831	206,729	173,999	139,810	141,691	134,692	117,744	94,420	588	652	677	675	−64	+2
WEST SOUTH CENTRAL:														
Arkansas	108,391	83,932	247,596	200,996	57,330	51,255	173,298	138,549	529	611	700	689	−82	+11
Louisiana	175,313	149,619	214,828	163,446	92,439	92,759	131,491	106,531	527	620	612	652	−93	−40
Oklahoma	31,783	12,026	315,490	138,251	18,186	7,916	209,623	99,858	572	658	664	722	−86	−58
Texas	169,210	141,089	718,352	518,617	90,057	90,518	448,811	361,859	532	642	625	698	−110	−73
MOUNTAIN:														
Montana	485	398	75,329	44,959	105	95	36,754	25,292	216	239	488	563	−23	−75
Idaho	158	75	66,713	30,151	40	14	39,963	21,030	253	187	599	697	+66	−98
Wyoming	479	206	27,328	16,183	109	59	15,009	10,179	228	286	549	629	−58	−80
Colorado	3,407	2,541	186,200	123,005	708	575	81,601	56,287	208	226	438	458	−18	−20
New Mexico	429	360	65,952	37,737	150	95	41,754	25,329	350	264	633	671	+86	−38
Arizona	606	310	36,337	18,510	156	93	20,172	11,090	257	300	555	599	−43	−44
Utah	309	122	80,400	59,177	56	46	52,150	41,503	181	377	649	701	−196	−52
Nevada	165	30	14,741	6,881	26	4	5,819	3,166	158	133	395	460	+25	−65
PACIFIC:														
Washington	1,517	582	246,962	101,973	289	139	106,325	51,775	190	239	431	508	−49	−77
Oregon	375	289	147,375	87,377	70	39	59,327	40,339	187	135	403	462	+52	−59
California	6,029	2,781	539,231	330,308	1,519	909	187,049	122,395	252	327	347	371	−75	−24

TABLE **12.**—WOMEN 15 TO 44 YEARS OF AGE, AND CHILDREN UNDER 5 YEARS, IN THE TOTAL POPULATION, AND IN THE POPULATION LIVING IN AND LIVING OUTSIDE OF CITIES OF 25,000 OR MORE INHABITANTS, BY DIVISIONS AND STATES: 1910.

DIVISION AND STATE.	NEGRO POPULATION: 1910.						CHILDREN UNDER 5 PER 1,000 WOMEN 15 TO 44 YEARS OF AGE: 1910.					
	Women 15 to 44 years of age.			Children under 5 years of age.			Negro population.			White population.		
	Total.	In cities of 25,000 or more.	Outside of cities of 25,000 or more.	Total.	In cities of 25,000 or more.	Outside of cities of 25,000 or more.	Total.	In cities of 25,000 or more.	Outside of cities of 25,000 or more.	Total.	In cities of 25,000 or more.	Outside of cities of 25,000 or more.
UNITED STATES	2,435,189	525,748	1,909,441	-1,263,288	125,735	1,137,553	519	239	596	484	368	552
GEOGRAPHIC DIVISIONS:												
New England	18,833	13,908	4,925	5,876	3,915	1,961	312	281	398	395	375	416
Middle Atlantic	131,605	94,374	37,231	35,298	21,854	13,444	268	232	361	431	392	488
East North Central	81,994	49,521	32,473	23,428	10,599	12,829	286	214	395	442	375	484
West North Central	64,766	33,182	31,584	19,127	6,651	12,476	295	200	395	492	325	544
South Atlantic	989,583	169,439	820,144	570,516	43,082	527,434	577	254	643	589	363	645
East South Central	649,752	85,368	564,384	347,803	19,879	327,924	535	233	581	626	350	667
West South Central	484,697	71,377	413,320	258,012	17,979	240,033	532	252	581	644	365	687
Mountain	6,038	2,867	3,171	1,350	531	819	224	185	258	530	344	579
Pacific	7,921	5,712	2,209	1,878	1,245	633	237	218	287	378	266	485
NEW ENGLAND:												
Maine	332	103	229	117	21	96	352	204	419	434	326	451
New Hampshire	149	11	138	40	6	34	268	545	246	401	373	410
Vermont	252		252	102		102	405		405	439		439
Massachusetts	11,053	9,020	2,033	3,448	2,566	882	312	284	434	378	371	393
Rhode Island	2,592	2,093	499	862	618	244	333	295	489	391	374	431
Connecticut	4,455	2,681	1,774	1,307	704	603	293	263	340	409	405	414
MIDDLE ATLANTIC:												
New York	45,629	38,594	7,035	10,061	7,684	2,377	220	200	338	386	382	396
New Jersey	27,124	13,726	13,398	7,922	3,556	4,366	292	259	326	424	427	421
Pennsylvania	58,852	42,054	16,798	17,315	10,614	6,701	294	252	399	492	398	562
EAST NORTH CENTRAL:												
Ohio	29,632	17,822	11,810	8,921	3,943	4,978	301	221	422	421	368	458
Indiana	16,342	9,601	6,741	4,763	2,256	2,507	291	235	372	438	323	467
Illinois	30,823	18,847	11,976	8,248	3,731	4,517	268	198	377	437	382	492
Michigan	4,347	2,681	1,666	1,285	569	716	296	212	430	462	383	502
Wisconsin	850	570	280	211	100	111	248	175	396	482	393	518
WEST NORTH CENTRAL:												
Minnesota	1,889	1,686	203	382	300	82	202	178	404	483	323	565
Iowa	3,708	1,353	2,355	1,245	370	875	336	273	372	461	332	487
Missouri	43,156	23,790	19,366	12,299	4,356	7,943	285	183	410	464	315	551
North Dakota	147		147	37		37	252		252	670		670
South Dakota	216		216	60		60	278		278	576		576
Nebraska	2,213	1,772	441	477	336	141	216	190	320	516	349	554
Kansas	13,437	4,581	8,856	4,627	1,289	3,338	344	281	377	504	359	523
SOUTH ATLANTIC:												
Delaware	7,437	2,673	4,764	3,089	577	2,512	415	216	527	422	404	440
Maryland	58,631	27,385	31,246	25,987	6,628	19,359	443	242	620	431	360	497
District of Columbia	31,166	31,166		7,290	7,290		234	234		299	299	
Virginia	158,798	32,638	126,160	86,555	8,739	77,816	545	268	617	577	375	617
West Virginia	15,050	981	14,069	6,974	229	6,745	463	233	479	638	374	659
North Carolina	162,377	7,309	155,068	107,297	2,505	104,792	661	343	676	675	453	682
South Carolina	196,806	14,021	182,785	128,712	4,026	124,686	654	287	682	647	372	669
Georgia	282,888	40,802	242,086	167,498	10,083	157,415	592	247	650	647	385	695
Florida	76,430	12,464	63,966	37,114	3,005	34,109	486	241	533	600	420	633
EAST SOUTH CENTRAL:												
Kentucky	66,986	17,213	49,773	25,541	3,405	22,136	381	198	445	583	325	636
Tennessee	120,951	37,869	83,082	56,580	8,484	48,096	468	224	579	609	341	656
Alabama	220,984	30,286	190,698	123,991	7,990	116,001	561	264	608	691	421	729
Mississippi	240,831		240,831	141,691		141,691	588		588	677		677
WEST SOUTH CENTRAL:												
Arkansas	108,391	4,667	103,724	57,330	1,095	56,235	529	235	542	700	343	713
Louisiana	175,313	33,024	142,289	92,439	8,805	83,634	527	267	588	612	371	728
Oklahoma	31,783	4,178	27,605	18,186	1,251	16,935	572	299	613	664	338	686
Texas	169,210	29,508	139,702	90,057	6,828	83,229	532	231	596	625	368	668
MOUNTAIN:												
Montana	485	65	420	105	7	98	216	108	233	488	345	510
Idaho	158		158	40		40	253		253	599		599
Wyoming	479		479	109		109	228		228	549		549
Colorado	3,407	2,523	884	708	485	223	208	192	252	438	301	532
New Mexico	429		429	150		150	350		350	633		633
Arizona	606		606	156		156	257		257	555		555
Utah	309	279	30	56	39	17	181	140	567	649	454	762
Nevada	165		165	26		26	158		158	395		395
PACIFIC:												
Washington	1,517	1,087	430	289	180	109	191	166	253	431	244	653
Oregon	375	306	69	70	45	25	187	147	362	403	267	477
California	6,029	4,319	1,710	1,519	1,020	499	252	236	292	347	277	418

TABLE 13.—NEGRO WOMEN 15 TO 44 YEARS OF AGE, CHILDREN UNDER 5 YEARS, AND NUMBER OF CHILDREN PER 1,000 WOMEN, BY CITIES OF 25,000 OR MORE INHABITANTS: 1910.

CITY.	Women 15 to 44 years of age.	Children under 5 years. Number.	Children under 5 years. Per 1,000 women 15 to 44.
ALABAMA.			
Birmingham	16,537	4,598	278
Mobile	7,377	1,863	253
Montgomery	6,372	1,529	240
ARKANSAS.			
Little Rock	4,667	1,095	235
CALIFORNIA.			
Berkeley	87	15	(1)
Los Angeles	2,372	556	234
Oakland	880	216	(1)
Pasadena	217	59	(1)
Sacramento	133	29	(1)
San Diego	185	29	(1)
San Francisco	390	101	(1)
San Jose	55	15	(1)
COLORADO.			
Colorado Springs	348	75	(1)
Denver	1,751	313	179
Pueblo	424	97	(1)
CONNECTICUT.			
Bridgeport [2]	409	114	(1)
Hartford [2]	546	150	(1)
Meriden town	30	11	(1)
Meriden city	30	11	(1)
New Britain [2]	31	5	(1)
New Haven [2]	1,115	271	243
Norwich town	180	35	(1)
Stamford town	146	33	(1)
Stamford city	139	33	(1)
Waterbury [2]	224	85	(1)
DELAWARE.			
Wilmington	2,673	577	216
DISTRICT OF COLUMBIA.			
Washington	31,166	7,290	234
FLORIDA.			
Jacksonville	9,587	2,234	233
Tampa	2,877	771	268
GEORGIA.			
Atlanta	12,524	4,622	264
Augusta	6,276	1,326	211
Macon	5,653	1,512	267
Savannah	11,349	2,623	231
ILLINOIS.			
Aurora	75	16	(1)
Bloomington	223	72	(1)
Chicago	14,296	2,472	173
Danville	432	127	(1)
Decatur	222	53	(1)
East St. Louis	1,661	511	308
Elgin	42	15	(1)
Joliet	151	35	(1)
Peoria	443	93	(1)
Quincy	421	105	(1)
Rockford	68	11	(1)
Springfield	813	221	(1)
INDIANA.			
Evansville	1,788	428	239
Fort Wayne	191	32	(1)
Indianapolis	6,697	1,557	232
South Bend	173	53	(1)
Terre Haute	752	186	(1)
IOWA.			
Cedar Rapids	55	14	(1)
Clinton	87	59	(1)
Council Bluffs	72	8	(1)
Davenport	149	33	(1)
Des Moines	879	229	(1)
Dubuque	18	6	(1)
Sioux City	85	21	(1)
Waterloo	8		(1)

CITY.	Women 15 to 44 years of age.	Children under 5 years. Number.	Children under 5 years. Per 1,000 women 15 to 44.
KANSAS.			
Kansas City	2,664	745	280
Topeka	1,247	340	273
Wichita	670	204	(1)
KENTUCKY.			
Covington	904	219	(1)
Lexington	3,398	681	200
Louisville	12,727	2,458	193
Newport	184	47	(1)
LOUISIANA.			
New Orleans	28,355	7,624	269
Shreveport	4,669	1,181	253
MAINE.			
Lewiston	12	3	(1)
Portland	91	18	(1)
MARYLAND.			
Baltimore	27,385	6,628	224
MASSACHUSETTS.			
Boston	4,376	942	215
Brockton	165	58	(1)
Brookline town	130	6	(1)
Cambridge	1,380	480	348
Chelsea	73	22	(1)
Chicopee	1		(1)
Everett	223	75	(1)
Fall River	104	25	(1)
Fitchburg	9	2	(1)
Haverhill	120	35	(1)
Holyoke	18	7	(1)
Lawrence	57	27	(1)
Lowell	40	11	(1)
Lynn	177	64	(1)
Malden	138	55	(1)
New Bedford	696	380	(1)
Newton	192	43	(1)
Pittsfield	93	32	(1)
Quincy	13	5	(1)
Salem	50	10	(1)
Somerville	75	12	(1)
Springfield	452	118	(1)
Taunton	66	50	(1)
Waltham	25	3	(1)
Worcester	347	104	(1)
MICHIGAN.			
Battle Creek	165	57	(1)
Bay City	38	16	(1)
Detroit	1,727	330	191
Flint	106	30	(1)
Grand Rapids	178	36	(1)
Jackson	97	12	(1)
Kalamazoo	189	51	(1)
Lansing	88	24	(1)
Saginaw	93	13	(1)
MINNESOTA.			
Duluth	116	23	(1)
Minneapolis	746	113	(1)
St. Paul	824	164	(1)
MISSOURI.			
Joplin	272	55	(1)
Kansas City	7,896	1,211	153
St. Joseph	1,260	255	202
St. Louis	13,818	2,685	194
Springfield	544	150	(1)
MONTANA.			
Butte	65	7	(1)
NEBRASKA.			
Lincoln	206	41	(1)
Omaha	1,388	243	175
South Omaha	178	52	(1)
NEW HAMPSHIRE.			
Manchester	8	4	(1)
Nashua	3	2	(1)

CITY.	Women 15 to 44 years of age.	Children under 5 years. Number.	Children under 5 years. Per 1,000 women 15 to 44.
NEW JERSEY.			
Atlantic City	3,450	536	155
Bayonne	160	79	(1)
Camden	1,738	569	327
East Orange	805	172	(1)
Elizabeth	403	142	(1)
Hoboken	40	6	(1)
Jersey City	1,784	557	312
Newark	3,062	875	286
Orange	800	229	(1)
Passaic	180	47	(1)
Paterson	540	132	(1)
Perth Amboy	52	22	(1)
Trenton	692	183	(1)
West Hoboken town	20	7	(1)
NEW YORK.			
Albany	333	35	(1)
Amsterdam	39	14	(1)
Auburn	143	45	(1)
Binghamton	181	34	(1)
Buffalo	556	88	(1)
Elmira	125	24	(1)
Jamestown	27	6	(1)
Kingston	165	62	(1)
Mount Vernon	381	67	(1)
New Rochelle	712	188	(1)
New York	33,895	6,676	197
Manhattan Borough	23,239	4,054	174
Bronx Borough	1,319	393	298
Brooklyn Borough	7,948	1,824	229
Queens Borough	1,035	298	288
Richmond Borough	354	107	(1)
Newburgh	187	37	(1)
Niagara Falls	76	15	(1)
Poughkeepsie	214	55	(1)
Rochester	284	58	(1)
Schenectady	101	16	(1)
Syracuse	320	66	(1)
Troy	203	36	(1)
Utica	99	22	(1)
Watertown	18	4	(1)
Yonkers	535	136	(1)
NORTH CAROLINA.			
Charlotte	3,784	1,225	324
Wilmington	3,525	1,280	363
OHIO.			
Akron	150	54	(1)
Canton	72	16	(1)
Cincinnati	6,343	1,148	181
Cleveland	2,691	519	193
Columbus	3,698	836	226
Dayton	1,465	374	255
Hamilton	194	62	(1)
Lima	258	83	(1)
Lorain	90	42	(1)
Newark	87	26	(1)
Springfield	1,259	380	302
Toledo	580	114	(1)
Youngstown	549	159	(1)
Zanesville	386	130	(1)
OKLAHOMA.			
Muskogee	2,244	696	310
Oklahoma City	1,934	555	287
OREGON.			
Portland	306	45	(1)
PENNSYLVANIA.			
Allentown	44	13	(1)
Altoona	120	31	(1)
Chester	1,355	413	305
Easton	70	23	(1)
Erie	92	14	(1)
Harrisburg	1,335	355	266
Hazleton	2	3	(1)
Johnstown	13	30	(1)
Lancaster	226	50	(1)
McKeesport	236	80	(1)
New Castle	156	43	(1)
Norristown borough	263	93	(1)
Philadelphia	29,150	6,863	235
Pittsburgh	7,666	2,240	292
Reading	245	60	(1)
Scranton	168	37	(1)
Shenandoah borough		4	(1)
Wilkes-Barre	168	49	(1)
Williamsport	272	84	(1)
York	354	129	(1)

[1] Ratios not shown for cities having less than 1,000 Negro women 15 to 44 years of age.   [2] Town and city coextensive.

TABLE **13.**—NEGRO WOMEN 15 TO 44 YEARS OF AGE, CHILDREN UNDER 5 YEARS, AND NUMBER OF CHILDREN PER 1,000 WOMEN, BY CITIES OF 25,000 OR MORE INHABITANTS, 1910—Continued.

CITY.	NEGRO POPULATION: 1910.			CITY.	NEGRO POPULATION: 1910.			CITY.	NEGRO POPULATION: 1910.		
	Women 15 to 44 years of age.	Children under 5 years.			Women 15 to 44 years of age.	Children under 5 years.			Women 15 to 44 years of age.	Children under 5 years.	
		Number.	Per 1,000 women 15 to 44.			Number.	Per 1,000 women 15 to 44.			Number.	Per 1,000 women 15 to 44.
RHODE ISLAND.				TEXAS.				WASHINGTON.			
Newport	455	125	(1)	Austin	2,261	659	291	Seattle	629	99	(1)
Pawtucket	70	21	(1)	Dallas	6,223	1,271	204	Spokane	239	37	(1)
Providence	1,519	458	302	El Paso	498	114	(1)	Tacoma	219	44	(1)
Warwick town	46	11	(1)	Fort Worth	4,200	1,063	253				
Woonsocket	3	3	(1)	Galveston	2,657	545	205	WEST VIRGINIA.			
				Houston	8,121	1,790	220				
SOUTH CAROLINA.				San Antonio	3,600	895	249	Huntington	593	150	(1)
				Waco	1,948	491	252	Wheeling	388	79	(1)
Charleston	10,251	2,985	291								
Columbia	3,770	1,041	276	UTAH.				WISCONSIN.			
				Ogden	55	6	(1)	Green Bay	14	6	(1)
TENNESSEE.				Salt Lake City	224	33	(1)	La Crosse	17	1	(1)
								Madison	43	15	(1)
Chattanooga	5,787	1,488	257	VIRGINIA.				Milwaukee	356	46	(1)
Knoxville	2,520	546	217	Lynchburg	3,149	882	280	Oshkosh	29	14	(1)
Memphis	17,496	3,729	213	Norfolk	8,302	2,008	242	Racine	36	5	(1)
Nashville	12,066	2,721	226	Portsmouth	3,573	1,064	298	Sheboygan	3	3	(1)
				Richmond	15,087	4,019	266	Superior	72	10	(1)
				Roanoke	2,527	766	303				

[1] Ratios not shown for cities having less than 1,000 Negro women 15 to 44 years of age.

DECENNIAL CENSUS MORTALITY STATISTICS: 1850–1900.

At each decennial census, 1850 to 1900, mortality data were collected upon a separate mortality schedule, calling for a return in the case of each person who had died during the twelve months preceding the date of enumeration. On this schedule were specified to be returned for each decedent, detail of color, sex, age, marital condition, nativity, parentage (1870–1900), occupation, month in which death occurred, cause of death, number of days ill (1850, 1860), length of residence in county (1880–1900), name of place where disease was contracted (1880, 1890), name of attending physician (1880–1900), whether insane or idiot (1880, 1890), and whether a Union or Confederate veteran (1890).

The census of 1850 secured returns of 52,566 deaths in the slave population, giving a rate 16.4 per 1,000 population enumerated. Deaths in the free population, including the free colored, which were not distinguished from the white deaths, numbered 270,706 giving a rate of 13.5 per 1,000. In the compendium of the 1850 census (p. 105) the opinion is expressed that "the true number of deaths in the Union for 1850, considering it a sickly year, could not have fallen short of one in every fifty persons for all classes, which would swell the total deaths of the census from 323,272 to 463,839." It is thus assumed that omissions of deaths amounted to 140,000, and the statement is made that "in regard to the number of deaths, the returns of the census are not likely to deceive any one, since an attempt to reason from them would exhibit a degree of vitality and healthfulness in the United States unparalleled in the annals of any nation." (p. 58.) [1]

At each subsequent census the incompleteness of the mortality data was obvious in the returns, and freely admitted in the reports. Some value attached to the data as indicating the principal causes of death, but practically no value attached to the returns as providing data for determining mortality rates.

At the censuses of 1880, 1890, and 1900, the mortality schedule was withdrawn from enumerators in certain areas—comprising in 1880 the states of New Jersey and Massachusetts, and restricted areas in other states, and in succeeding census years a somewhat more extended area, (see maps on page 301)—and for

[1] It is interesting to find expressed in the Compendium of 1850, which published the results of the first effort to gather mortality data at the decennial census, the opinion that "nothing short of a registration system in the states can give the required data (relative to births, marriages, and deaths) satisfactorily," since "people will not, or can not, remember and report to the census taker the number of the facts, and the particulars of them which occur in the period of a whole year to 18 months prior to the time of his calling."

these areas the return of mortality was made up from records in registration offices.

The return of deaths from these designated areas within which local registration records were accepted, and no direct enumeration of deaths undertaken, were much more complete than the returns in the areas secured by enumerators on the mortality schedule.

This will be apparent from the summary of mortality returns for the year 1900, as given in Table 1. In the area of death registration the number of Negro deaths per 1,000 population was 30.2, and in the area of death enumeration 13.7, the corresponding figures for the white population being 17.3 and 10.6.

Table 1		CENSUS OF 1900.		
		Deaths in year ending May 31, 1910.		
AREA.	Negro population June 1, 1900.	Negro.		White per 1,000 population.
		Number.	Per 1,000 population.	
United States	8,833,994	140,934	16.0	13.4
Area of death registration	1,180,546	35,710	30.2	17.3
Area of death enumeration	7,653,448	105,224	13.7	10.6

There is no reason to believe that the true death rate in 1900 was higher in the area of death registration than in other sections of the country. The excess of the rate within the area of registration, over the rate outside of this area, represents with approximate accuracy omissions in the returns made by enumerators.

It will be obvious that the mortality returns of the decennial censuses, 1850–1900, are incomparable with the data collected annually for the registration area beginning with the calendar year 1900, and in the following tables no attempt is made to relate this earlier data to the data of the annual reports of mortality statistics.

DECENNIAL MORTALITY OF THE NEGRO AND NATIVE WHITE POPULATION CLASSIFIED BY AGE: 1900–1910.

The age classification of the population as returned at the several censuses provides a rough measure of mortality in the country as a whole, and is in fact the only index of mortality embracing the entire Negro population.

Since the Negro population is almost entirely native, and little affected by immigration, some inferences may be drawn from a comparison of the age groups as determined at successive censuses. This comparison is made in Table 2, for the two censuses 1900 and 1910. The assumption underlying the table is that survivors in 1910, of the population enumerated in 1900, would be in specific age groups—that, for example, the Negro population returned in 1910 as being 10 to 19 years of age, embraced all survivors of the Negro population returned in 1900 as being under 10 years of age, that the population 20 to 29 in 1910 embraced survivors of those returned in 1900 as 10 to 19, and similarly of each other age group shown in Table 2. The further assumption is made—which seems warranted in the case of the Negro population, although a similar assumption would not be warranted as regards the aggregate white population—that the decrease during the decade 1900–1910, in the number enumerated as, for example, under 10 in 1900, and 10 to 19 in 1910, is due to mortality, and is not affected materially by net immigration or emigration. Similar assumptions may be made regarding the native white population for which class data are given in Table 2 in comparison with data for Negroes.

DECENNIAL MORTALITY OF NEGRO AND WHITE POPULATION, BY AGE PERIODS: 1900–1910.

Table 2	1900			1910			1900–1910				
AGE.	Population.		Age.	Population.		Age in 1900.	Decennial mortality.				
							Number.		Per cent.		
	Negro.	Native white.		Negro.	Native white.		Negro.	Native white.	Negro.	Native white.
MALE.										
All known ages	4,361,390	28,604,760	10 years and over	3,620,310	25,768,627	All known ages.	741,080	2,836,133	17.0	9.9
Under 10 years	1,204,897	7,773,510	10 to 19 years	1,086,019	7,472,190	Under 10 years	118,878	301,320	9.9	3.9
10 to 19 years	1,022,392	6,348,380	20 to 29 years	903,962	6,048,683	10 to 19 years	118,430	299,697	11.6	4.7
20 to 44 years	1,494,109	10,186,820	30 to 54 years	1,261,608	9,301,193	20 to 44 years	232,501	885,627	15.6	8.7
45 to 64 years	506,967	3,373,886	55 to 74 years	324,779	2,611,581	45 to 64 years	182,188	762,305	35.9	22.6
65 years and over	133,025	922,164	75 years and over	43,942	334,980	65 years and over	89,083	587,184	67.0	63.7
FEMALE.										
All known ages	4,423,793	27,870,447	10 years and over	3,666,572	25,112,701	All known ages.	757,221	2,757,746	17.1	9.9
Under 10 years	1,213,516	7,585,207	10 to 19 years	1,129,663	7,382,518	Under 10 years	83,853	202,689	6.9	2.7
10 to 19 years	1,051,620	6,280,736	20 to 29 years	1,008,060	6,101,787	10 to 19 years	43,560	178,949	4.1	2.8
20 to 44 years	1,579,052	9,894,294	30 to 54 years	1,207,322	8,805,877	20 to 44 years	371,730	1,088,417	23.5	11.0
45 to 64 years	451,267	3,176,002	55 to 74 years	273,734	2,456,319	45 to 64 years	177,533	719,683	39.3	22.7
65 years and over	128,338	934,208	75 years and over	47,793	366,200	65 years and over	80,545	568,008	62.8	60.8

It appears in Table 2 that the aggregate decrease by mortality during the decade 1900–1910 in the population enumerated in 1900 amounted in the case of the Negro population to 741,080, or 17 per cent, and in the case of the native white population to 2,836,133, or 9.9 per cent. Comparing the population enumerated in 1900 as under 10 years of age, with the population enumerated in 1910 as 10 to 19 years of age, the decrease amounted in the Negro population to 118,878, or 9.9 per cent, and in the case of the native white population to 301,320, or 3.9 per cent. Comparing the age groups 10 to 19 and 20 to 29, the percentage decreases amounted for Negroes to 11.6 and for native whites to 4.7. The corresponding rates for the age groups 20 to 44 and 30 to 54 are 15.6 for Negroes and 8.7 for native whites; for the age groups 45 to 64 and 55 to 74 they are 35.9 for Negroes and 22.6 for native whites, and for the age groups 65 and over and 75 and over they are 67 for Negroes and 63.9 for native whites.

These rates should be carefully distinguished from the mortality rates shown in other tables for the Negro population. The decennial mortality rate given in Table 2 does not relate the number of deaths during the decade 1900–1910 to the mean population of the decade or to the population at the beginning of the decade. The total number of deaths occurring in the Negro population during the decade can not be determined from any data available, since these deaths include the deaths of children born subsequently to the census of 1900 and dying prior to the census of 1910. For any age group the decrease by mortality in a period of 10 years is a specific and peculiar rate, which, although it is capable of reduction to an average annual rate of mortality, is not even when so reduced comparable with an annual death rate per 1,000 population.

Very considerable significance does, however, attach to the comparison made in Table 2 of the decennial mortality of Negroes with the decennial mortality of native whites. It is apparent that the entire Negro population during the decade 1900–1910 suffered a mortality greatly in excess of that shown by the native white population.

The causes of the excessive mortality of the Negro population could not be determined from the mortality data except by inferences based upon a much more detailed analysis of these data by small areas and specific causes of death than can be undertaken in a general report. Even such an analysis, however detailed and searching, would leave room for speculation regarding the precise influence upon mortality of varying factors of environment, economic status, and racial character. It may be pointed out, however, that the inference certainly is not in any degree warranted by the data that the differences in mortality between Negroes and other classes are racial or natural differences in the sense that they would persist under different environmental and economic conditions for these classes. Until the contrary fact is established, the probability is rather, on the contrary, that the differences in mortality represent environmental factors, which may be remedied by gradual improvement in the social, economic, and hygienic status of the Negro population.

That such improvement shall be achieved is unquestionably of vital importance to the Negro race, and there is no obvious reason why it should not be rapid and complete, provided a concerted and persistent social effort on the part of the Negro race is made for its achievement. Substantial improvement in mortality may be designated as a social obligation resting upon the Negro population, although responsibility for the excessive mortality in this class undoubtedly rests in some degree upon the community as a whole.

THE REGISTRATION AREA FOR DEATHS: 1900–1915.

Beginning with the year 1900, data relating to mortality have been compiled from records of deaths annually for those states and cities which provide by state law or municipal ordinances for the proper registration of deaths and furnish the Census Bureau with transcripts of death records covering in the estimation of the bureau (based upon such evidence as is available) at least 90 per cent of all deaths occurring. These states and cities in the aggregate constitute the registration area for deaths.

In 1915 the area included 25 states, the District of Columbia, and 41 cities in nonregistration states, and embraced two-thirds (67.1 per cent) of the total population of the country. In 1900 the registration area, as determined by an examination of mortality returns at the Twelfth Census, embraced 10 states, and 153 cities in other states. The extension of the area during the period 1900–1915, as will be apparent from the maps on page 301, has been largely confined to the northern and western sections of the country, although three Southern states—Kentucky, Maryland, and Virginia, and municipalities of 1,000 or more population in North Carolina, together with 30 cities in nonregistration Southern states, were included in the area as defined in 1915. Kentucky and Virginia have been admitted to the area since 1910. The maps on

the following page for 1880 and 1890 indicate registration states at the decennial censuses for these years.

During the entire period 1900–1915, the great mass of the Negro population has been resident in the nonregistration area. The proportion living in the registration area was only 13.5 per cent in 1900, 19.7 per cent in 1910, and 30.4 per cent in 1915. It will be obvious that statistics of deaths for the census years 1900 and 1910—for which years only are population figures available—are as regards the Negro population, very incomplete.

It may be noted further that the Negro population of the registration area is largely an urban population. This results from the fact that the Negro population of the Northern registration states is largely urban, while generally throughout the South only cities are included in the registration area. A small rural population in the North and West is included in the area, but the large rural population in the South is almost entirely excluded.

In Table 3 the Negro population in the registration area and in the nonregistration area is given, by sections and southern divisions, for the three years 1900, 1910, and 1915, with percentage distributions of these populations, by geographic areas.

Table 3	NEGRO POPULATION.				PERCENTAGE DISTRIBUTION BY GEOGRAPHIC SECTIONS.[1]		
		Registration area.					
SECTION, DIVISION, AND YEAR.	Total.	Number.	Per cent of total.[1]	Nonregistration area.	Total Negro population.	Negro population of registration area.	Negro population of nonregistration area.
United States:							
1915........	[2]9,827,763	[2]2,987,817	30.4	[2]6,839,946	100.0	100.0	100.0
1910........	9,827,763	1,935,976	19.7	7,891,787	100.0	100.0	100.0
1900........	8,833,994	1,189,023	13.5	7,644,971	100.0	100.0	100.0
The South:							
1915..........	[2]8,749,427	[2]1,992,600	22.8	[2]6,756,827	89.0	66.7	98.8
1910..........	8,749,427	1,066,246	12.2	7,683,181	89.0	55.1	97.4
1900..........	7,922,969	620,677	7.8	7,302,292	89.7	52.2	95.5
South Atlantic:							
1915..........	[2]4,112,488	[2]1,363,840	33.2	[2]2,748,648	41.8	45.6	40.2
1910..........	4,112,488	717,203	17.4	3,395,285	41.8	37.0	43.0
1900..........	3,729,017	390,562	10.5	3,338,455	42.2	32.8	43.7
East South Central:							
1915..........	[2]2,652,513	[2]519,294	19.6	[2]2,133,219	27.0	17.4	31.2
1910..........	2,652,513	241,029	9.1	2,411,484	27.0	12.5	30.6
1900..........	2,499,886	144,863	5.8	2,355,023	28.3	12.2	30.8
West South Central:							
1915..........	[2]1,984,426	[2]109,466	5.5	[2]1,874,960	20.2	3.7	27.4
1910..........	1,984,426	108,014	5.4	1,876,412	20.2	5.6	23.8
1900..........	1,694,066	85,252	5.0	1,608,814	19.2	7.2	21.0
The North:							
1915..........	[2]1,027,674	[2]952,038	92.6	[2]75,636	10.5	31.9	1.1
1910..........	1,027,674	826,551	80.4	201,123	10.5	42.7	2.5
1900..........	880,771	554,851	63.0	325,920	10.0	46.7	4.3
The West:							
1915..........	[2]50,662	[2]43,179	85.2	[2]7,483	0.5	1.4	0.1
1910..........	50,662	43,179	85.2	7,483	0.5	2.2	0.1
1900..........	30,254	13,495	44.6	16,759	0.3	1.1	0.2

[1] The percentages for 1915 are figured upon the 1910 populations of the registration and nonregistration areas as defined in 1915. These percentages indicate the effect of the extension of the registration area between 1910 and 1915, on the assumption that the Negro increase in this period was at the same rate in the registration as in the nonregistration areas.

[2] Population in 1910 of areas as defined in 1915.

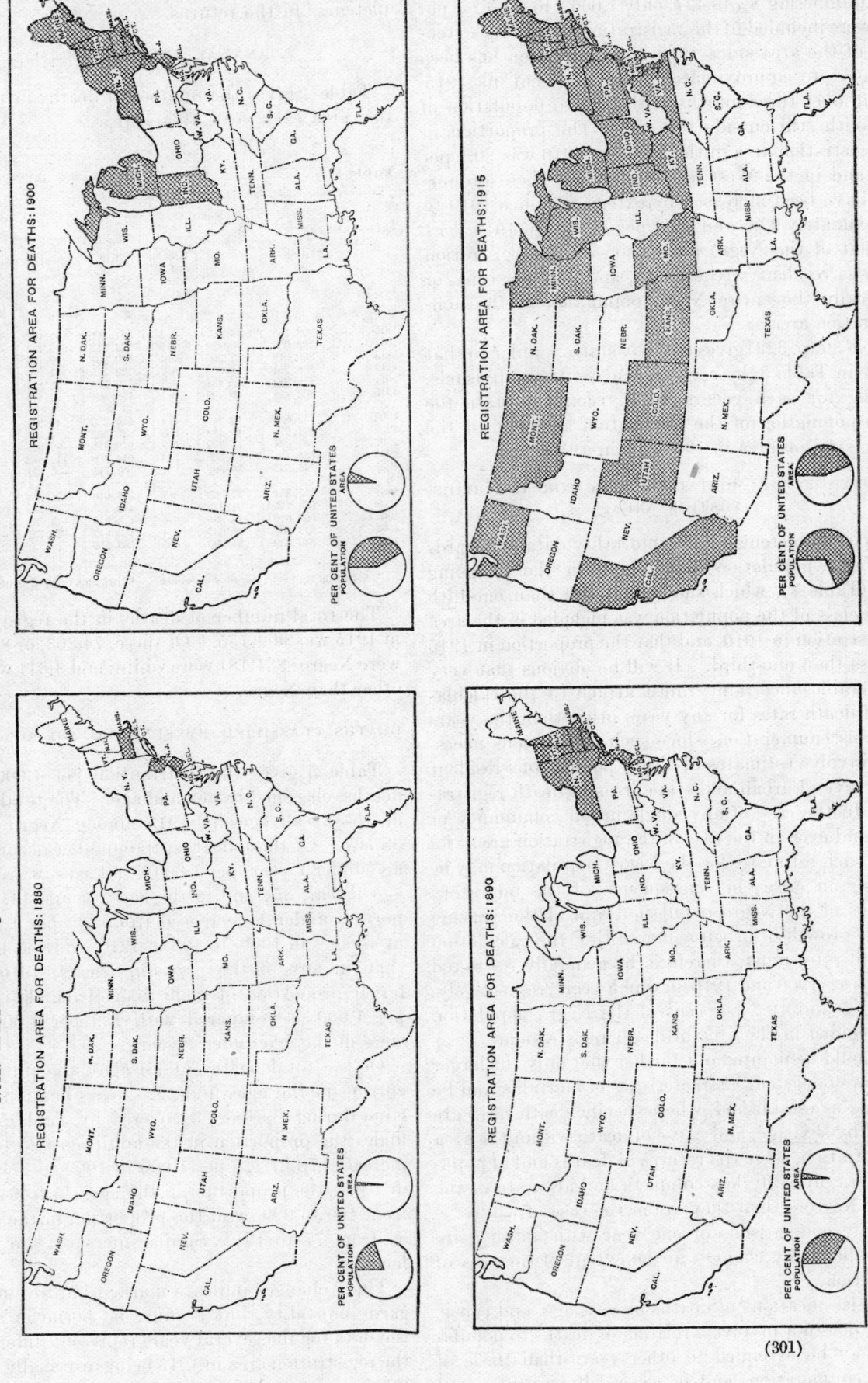

GROWTH OF THE REGISTRATION AREA FOR DEATHS: 1880–1915.

NOTE.—In addition to the registration states (shaded in the cartograms) the registration area included certain cities in nonregistration states.

REGISTRATION AREA FOR DEATHS: 1900

REGISTRATION AREA FOR DEATHS: 1915

REGISTRATION AREA FOR DEATHS: 1880

REGISTRATION AREA FOR DEATHS: 1890

PER CENT OF UNITED STATES AREA
POPULATION

(301)

Of the Negro population resident in the South in 1910, numbering 8,749,427, only 1,066,246, or 12.2 per cent were included in the registration area. By extensions of the area since 1910, this proportion has been increased to approximately 22.8 per cent in 1915, leaving over three-fourths of the Negro population of the South still outside the area. The proportion in the registration area in the North in 1910 was 80.4 per cent, and in the West 85.2 per cent. These proportions have been increased by extensions since 1910 to approximately 92.6 and 85.2 per cent. In 1910, 55.1 per cent of the Negro population of the registration area was resident in the South, and 97.4 per cent, or practically the entire Negro population of the nonregistration area.

Table 30 (p. 322) gives data, by states, similar to that shown in Table 3, by sections and southern divisions, showing for each geographic division and state the Negro population of the registration area and of the nonregistration area in 1900 and in 1910.

VALIDITY OF THE MORTALITY DATA FOR THE REGISTRATION AREA.

The incompleteness of the mortality data as regards the Negro population is apparent in the foregoing table (Table 3), which shows that less than one-fifth of this class of the population was included in the area of registration in 1910, and that the proportion in 1915 was less than one-third. It will be obvious that very considerable uncertainty must attach to the calculation of death rates for any years other than the years of census enumeration, since such calculations necessarily involve estimates of Negro populations resident in the several urban and state areas of death registration. In the case of any single urban community or state, and even in the case of the registration area as a whole, such estimates for the Negro population may be seriously in error, in consequence of the migratory shiftings of the Negro population and of the varying rates of growth of urban communities, the calculation of death rates must, therefore, be generally restricted to the years 1900 and 1910, in which years, respectively, only 13.5 and 19.7 per cent of the Negro population was included in the area of death registration.

It should be pointed out further that only the larger and more persistent characteristics of mortality can be accepted as established, where specific death rates are figured by sex, age, and cause of death within the area of registration, since the returns of deaths and of population are probably less complete and accurate in the case of Negroes than they are in the case of whites.

Finally comparisons of one year with another are made difficult by changes in the extent of the area of registration.

The classifications of deaths by sex, age, and cause, since it does not involve a relation of deaths to population, may be extended to other years than those of census enumeration, and in general it may be noted that the value of such classifications may not be seriously impaired by a considerable degree of incompleteness in the returns.

ANNUAL DEATHS: 1900–1915.

Table 4 gives the number of deaths in the registration area each year, 1900–1915.

Table 4	DEATHS IN REGISTRATION AREA.						
CALENDAR YEAR.	Total.[2]	Negro.		White.	Increase.[1]		
		Number.	Per cent of total deaths.		Total.[2]	Negro.	White.
1915......	909,155	74,363	8.2	831,181	11,096	3,934	6,862
1914......	898,059	70,429	7.8	824,319	7,211	3,163	4,115
1913......	890,848	67,266	7.6	820,204	52,597	11,216	41,069
1912......	838,251	56,050	6.7	779,135	−1,033	−381	−635
1911......	839,284	56,431	6.7	779,770	33,872	6,932	26,462
1910......	805,412	49,499	6.1	753,308	72,874	6,259	67,078
1909......	732,538	43,240	5.9	686,230	40,964	127	40,668
1908......	691,574	43,113	6.2	645,562	4,540	−189	4,591
1907......	687,034	43,302	6.3	640,971	28,929	1,794	26,902
1906......	658,105	41,508	6.3	614,069	112,572	5,007	106,354
1905......	545,533	36,501	6.7	507,715	−5,821	−564	−5,301
1904......	551,354	37,065	6.7	513,016	26,939	2,149	24,779
1903......	524,415	34,916	6.7	488,237	15,775	1,221	14,592
1902......	508,640	33,695	6.6	473,645	−9,567	660	−10,197
1901......	518,207	33,035	6.4	483,842	−21,732	−1,960	−19,727
1900......	539,939	34,995	6.5	503,569	....	....	....

[1] A minus sign (−) denotes decrease.   [2] Includes colored other than Negro.

The total number of deaths in the registration area in 1915 was 909,155. Of these, 74,363, or 8.2 per cent, were Negro; 831,181 were white; and 3,611 were colored other than Negro.

DEATHS CLASSIFIED BY SEX AND AGE OF DECEDENT.

Table 5 gives the distribution per 1,000 of Negro deaths, classified by sex and age. The total number of deaths at all ages in 1915 among Negro males was 38,567. Of these deaths, the number occurring in the age under 1 year, per 1,000 at all ages, was 157; in the age 1 year, 35; and in the age 2 years, 14. The proportion under 1 decreased from 239 per 1,000 deaths at all ages in 1900, to 196 in 1910, and was less in 1915 than in any of the preceding years, 1910–1914. A larger proportion of male than of female deaths, 157 per 1,000 as compared with 139 per 1,000 in 1915, were in the age under 1 year.

Of the total deaths at all ages, the proportion occurring in the ages under 25 years has tended to decline during the period covered by Table 5. Among males the proportion in the adult ages 25 to 44 years increased from 227 per 1,000 in 1900 to 277 per 1,000 in 1915; the proportion in the ages 45 to 64 increased from 169 to 229; and the proportion in the ages 65 to 84 from 77 to 121. Similar increases are shown for females.

These changes indicate marked improvement as regards mortality, but it must be borne in mind that the data for the several years represent different areas, the registration area in 1915 being, especially as regards the Negro population, much more extensive than the area in 1900, or even in 1910.

NEGRO DEATHS AT ALL AGES, AND NUMBER AT AGE SPECIFIED PER 1,000 AT ALL AGES, IN THE REGISTRATION AREA, BY SEX: FOR EACH YEAR, 1910–1915, AND IN 1900.

Table 5 — NEGRO DEATHS IN THE REGISTRATION AREA.

SEX AND YEAR.	Total at all ages.	Number at age specified, per 1,000 at all ages.[1]														
		All ages.	Under 1 year.	1 year.	2 years.	3 years.	4 years.	5 to 9 years.	10 to 14 years.	15 to 19 years.	20 to 24 years.	25 to 44 years.	45 to 64 years.	65 to 84 years.	85 years and over.	Age unknown.
MALE.																
1915	38,567	1,000	157	35	14	8	5	18	17	36	61	277	229	121	18	5
1914	36,846	1,000	171	36	16	9	7	19	17	36	63	270	218	114	17	5
1913	35,267	1,000	174	38	17	10	7	21	16	38	63	269	214	111	15	7
1912	29,600	1,000	164	36	16	10	6	19	16	37	64	282	222	110	15	5
1911	29,386	1,000	173	45	20	11	8	22	18	37	63	272	210	103	14	5
1910	25,840	1,000	196	46	20	10	7	19	17	35	62	274	204	95	12	2
1900	17,772	1,000	239	61	26	16	10	28	21	40	69	227	169	77	12	5
FEMALE.																
1915	35,796	1,000	139	36	15	9	6	20	22	50	72	264	216	123	25	3
1914	33,583	1,000	156	38	18	11	7	24	21	50	69	258	206	112	26	4
1913	31,999	1,000	163	39	18	11	7	24	22	52	69	252	203	110	24	6
1912	26,450	1,000	159	39	18	10	7	21	21	51	69	259	207	112	23	4
1911	27,045	1,000	162	46	21	12	8	23	23	51	72	252	200	102	26	3
1910	23,659	1,000	181	48	22	12	8	22	22	47	69	256	193	99	21	1
1900	17,223	1,000	213	58	28	16	10	32	31	52	72	213	162	88	20	3

[1] For number of deaths in each age for the years specified (except 1915), see Table 39, p. 356.

In Table 6 the age distribution of Negro deaths is given in comparison with a similar distribution of white deaths, for the years 1915 and 1900 the age classification being more detailed than that of Table 5.

Table 6

AGE.	DEATHS IN REGISTRATION AREA.						AGE	DEATHS IN REGISTRATION AREA.					
	1915				1900			1915				1900	
	Negro.			White.	Negro.	White.		Negro.			White.	Negro.	White.
	Total.	Male.	Female.					Total.	Male.	Female.			
	NUMBER.							NUMBER PER 1,000 DEATHS AT ALL AGES.					
All ages	74,363	38,567	35,796	831,181	34,995	503,569	All ages	1,000	1,000	1,000	1,000	1,000	1,000
Under 1 year	11,034	6,052	4,982	136,866	7,914	103,662	Under 1 year	148	157	139	165	226	206
1 year	2,637	1,354	1,283	26,131	2,082	24,616	1 year	35	35	36	31	59	49
2 years	1,097	559	538	11,257	950	11,166	2 years	15	14	15	14	27	22
3 years	635	296	339	7,018	555	7,249	3 years	9	8	9	8	16	14
4 years	432	210	222	5,201	339	5,435	4 years	6	5	6	6	10	11
5 to 9 years	1,435	711	724	16,203	1,062	14,587	5 to 9 years	19	18	20	19	30	29
10 to 14 years	1,412	640	772	11,106	909	8,218	10 to 14 years	19	17	22	13	26	16
15 to 19 years	3,155	1,373	1,782	17,918	1,608	12,851	15 to 19 years	42	36	50	22	46	26
20 to 24 years	4,935	2,371	2,564	27,473	2,461	19,710	20 to 24 years	66	61	72	33	70	39
25 to 29 years	5,022	2,512	2,510	30,387	2,221	22,237	25 to 29 years	68	65	70	37	63	44
30 to 34 years	4,712	2,466	2,246	31,411	1,826	21,780	30 to 34 years	63	64	63	38	52	43
35 to 39 years	5,477	3,023	2,454	35,083	1,891	22,567	35 to 39 years	74	78	69	42	54	45
40 to 44 years	4,895	2,664	2,231	36,423	1,764	21,448	40 to 44 years	66	69	62	44	50	43
45 to 49 years	4,555	2,487	2,068	40,036	1,626	20,758	45 to 49 years	61	64	58	48	46	41
50 to 54 years	4,712	2,519	2,193	44,992	1,653	22,501	50 to 54 years	63	65	61	54	47	45
55 to 59 years	3,702	1,947	1,755	49,302	1,289	23,662	55 to 59 years	50	50	49	59	37	47
60 to 64 years	3,591	1,869	1,722	53,974	1,237	26,343	60 to 64 years	48	48	48	65	35	52
65 to 69 years	3,032	1,557	1,475	59,238	1,037	28,041	65 to 69 years	41	40	41	71	30	56
70 to 74 years	2,772	1,498	1,274	62,979	820	28,190	70 to 74 years	37	39	36	76	23	56
75 to 79 years	1,890	960	930	55,794	579	24,857	75 to 79 years	25	25	26	67	17	49
80 to 84 years	1,359	646	713	40,727	459	18,380	80 to 84 years	18	17	20	49	13	36
85 to 89 years	728	353	375	21,537	251	9,385	85 to 89 years	10	9	10	26	7	19
90 to 94 years	414	162	252	7,332	148	3,216	90 to 94 years	6	4	7	9	4	6
95 to 99 years	197	75	122	1,666	167	940	95 to 99 years	3	2	3	2	5	2
100 years and over	239	86	153	291	....	1,770	100 years and over	3	2	4	(1)	....	4
Age unknown	294	177	117	836	147	1,770	Age unknown	4	5	3	1	....	4

[1] Less than 1.

From Table 6 it appears that the proportion of white deaths under 1 year of age in 1915 exceeded the corresponding proportion in the Negro population, the number of deaths under 1 per 1,000 deaths at all ages being 165 for whites and 148 for Negroes. In 1900 the proportion for Negroes of 226 per 1,000 exceeded that for whites of 206 per 1,000. A larger proportion of Negro than of white deaths was in each of the age periods 10 to 54 years, and a larger proportion of white than of Negro deaths in the more advanced age periods.

Table 6 is partially illustrated by Diagrams I and II, on the following page, which show for combinations of the age periods of Table 6, the distribution of Negro deaths in 1915 in comparison with 1900 (Diagram I), and in comparison with the distribution of white deaths in 1915 (Diagram II).

DIAGRAM I.—NEGRO DEATHS AT AGE SPECIFIED, PER 1,000 DEATHS AT ALL AGES, IN THE REGISTRATION AREA: 1915 AND 1900.

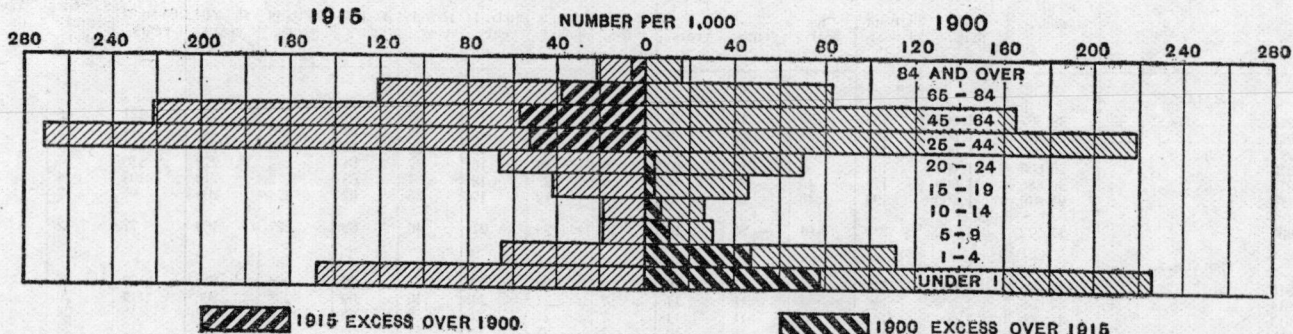

In Diagram I the barred area indicates the shifting in the proportion of deaths, which has reduced the proportion of deaths in the ages under 25 and increased the proportion in the ages 25 and over. The barred area in Diagram II indicates the relatively high proportion of Negro, as compared with white deaths in the middle ages of life, especially in the years 25 to 44.

GENERAL DEATH RATE: 1910 AND 1900.

The general death rate of the Negro population of the registration area for the calendar year 1910 was 25.5, this being the number of Negro deaths during the calendar year 1910 per 1,000 Negro population on July 1, as estimated upon the basis of the census enumeration of April 15, 1910.

In 1900 the general death rate for the Negro population of the registration area as defined in that year was 29.4 per 1,000 population. The number of deaths occurring was, therefore, 3.9 less per 1,000 population in 1910 than in 1900.

DIAGRAM II.—NEGRO AND WHITE DEATHS AT AGE SPECIFIED, PER 1,000 DEATHS AT ALL AGES, IN THE REGISTRATION AREA: 1915.

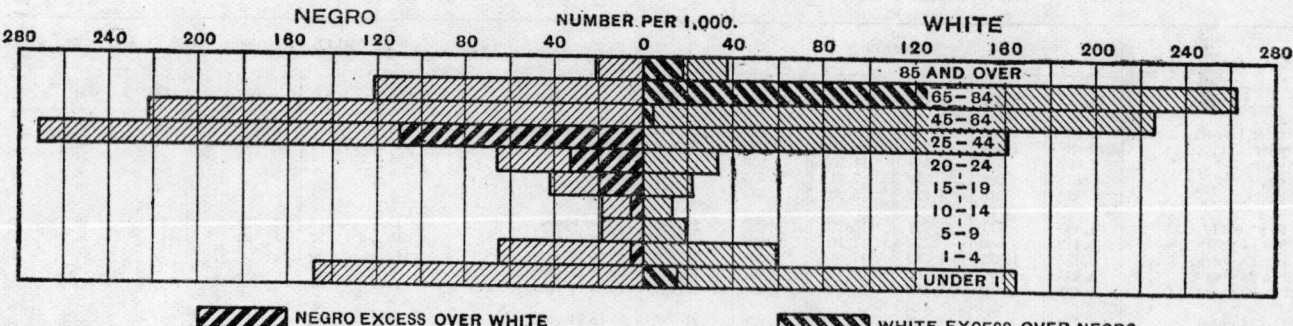

The 1910 death rate of 25.5 represented 49,499 Negro deaths, and a Negro population of 1,943,969; the 1900 rate of 29.4 represented 34,995 deaths and a Negro population of 1,189,023. While the decline of 3.9 in the death rate can not be taken as an accurate index of improvement in mortality, since the areas compared are not identical, it will be noted that the 1910 rate represents, as compared with the 1900 rate, a larger proportion of the total Negro population. The improvement in mortality during the decade within and without the area of registration may have been greater or less than the improvement indicated by the decline in the death rate as calculated for the different registration areas of the two years. Since the rate in each year represents a population that is largely urban, it probably exceeds the true death rate in the Negro population as a whole.

Table 7 gives the population and mortality figures for the Negro and white population of the registration area in the two census years 1910 and 1900. In both these years the rate for Negroes greatly exceeded the rate for whites, the excess of the Negro over the white rate amounting in 1910 to 10.9 (the difference between the rate for whites of 14.6 and the rate for Negroes of 25.5), and in 1900, to 12.3 (the difference between 17.1 and 29.4). The excess of the Negro over the white rate was thus somewhat less in 1910 than the excess in 1900.

Table 7	REGISTRATION AREA.							
	Population.			Deaths in calendar year—		Deaths per 1,000 population.		
RACIAL CLASS.	Enumeration of April 15, 1910.	July 1, 1910 (estimate).	June 1, 1900.	1910	1900	1910	1900	Decrease, 1900–1910.
All classes..	53,620,262	53,843,896	30,765,618	805,412	539,939	15.0	17.6	2.6
Negro........	1,935,976	1,943,969	1,189,023	49,499	34,995	25.5	29.4	3.9
White........	51,472,967	51,680,821	29,505,687	753,308	503,569	14.6	17.1	2.5
Other........	211,319	219,106	70,908	2,605	1,375	11.9	19.4	7.5

COMPARISON OF NEGRO DEATH RATE WITH RATE FOR OTHER CLASSES: 1910.

In Table 8 the number of deaths per 1,000 population in each race, nativity, and parentage class is given for 1910. The rates in this table are figured upon the populations in each class as enumerated on April 15, 1910, no estimates for July 1 being undertaken in detail by classes. The rates for Negroes and whites and for all classes combined are not materially affected by this slight change in the population base, as may be seen by comparison of Table 8 with Table 7, the rate for Negroes in 1910, for example, being 25.5 in Table 7 and 25.7 in Table 8.

Table 8	REGISTRATION AREA: 1910.[1]		
CLASS OF POPULATION.	Population April 15, 1910.	Deaths: Calendar year 1910.	
		Number.	Per 1,000 population.
All classes...................	53,409,475	801,735	15.0
Negro........................	1,866,407	47,989	25.7
White........................	51,331,794	751,121	14.6
Native [2]	39,908,911	554,417	13.9
Native parentage [3]	24,654,457	353,082	14.3
Foreign parentage........	10,667,210	148,456	13.9
Mixed parentage.........	4,587,244	52,879	11.5
Foreign born...............	11,422,883	196,704	17.2
Indian, Chinese, Japanese, and all other.......	211,274	2,625	12.4
Indian.....................	80,266	886	11.0
Chinese....................	63,960	1,055	16.5
Japanese...................	64,419	664	10.3
Other......................	2,629	20	7.6

[1] Except cities in North Carolina of less than 10,000, for which population data in detail by classes shown are not available.
[2] Includes unknown nativity.
[3] Includes unknown parentage.

Considerable allowance must be made for the possibility of error in the data for the several parentage classes—error in the return of parentage for population and for deaths, and error resulting from the distribution of population and deaths of unknown parentage. Comparisons of Negroes and white classes with the Chinese and Japanese are of little significance, owing to the abnormal age distribution of the Chinese and Japanese, and comparison of natives with the foreign-born whites also in a lesser degree

are invalidated by differences in the age composition of the several classes. Finally, it is not improbable that a larger proportion of Indian than of other deaths escape registration, with the result that the Indian death rate is depressed relatively to rates for other classes.

The most significant comparison in Table 8 is that between Negroes and native whites, which show death rates, respectively, of 25.7 and 14.6. A further analysis of the data is, however, required to separate so far as possible the urban from the rural elements in these classes. [See sections on urban and rural mortality (p. 315), and mortality by registration cities (p. 320).]

COMPARISON WITH RATES FOR FOREIGN COUNTRIES: 1800–1910.

The general death rate of the Negro population in the registration area is given in Table 9 in comparison with the annual average death rate for the aggregate populations of foreign countries, the annual averages for foreign countries being figured by decades covering in so far as data are available the period from 1800 to 1910.

In this table the countries are listed in order according to their death rate in the year 1910. The rates for this year range from 9.7 in New Zealand, to 33.3 in Mexico. Only 4 of the countries listed (Ceylon, Russia in Europe, Chile, and Mexico) show for this year (1909 in the case of Russia), rates higher than that for the Negroes of the registration area.

In comparatively recent decades, however, the rates for these foreign populations have, in a number of cases, approximated closely or exceeded the 1910 Negro rate of 25.5. The Netherlands, with a 1910 rate of 13.6, shows for the decade 1861–1870 an average rate of 25.4, and for the two preceding decades 25.6 and 26.2, respectively. Belgium, with a 1910 rate of 15.2, shows for the decade 1861–1870 an average of 24.4 and for the three preceding decades averages of 22.5, 24.3, and 25.9, respectively. Germany, with a 1910 rate of 16.2, shows for the decade 1881–1890 an average of 25.1 and for preceding decades averages of 27.2, 26.9, 26.4, 26.8, 28.8, and 26.7. Finland, with a 1910 rate of 16.5, shows for the decade 1861–1870 an average of 32.2, the rates for preceding decades being 28.7, 23.5, 28.2, 24.9, 26.4, and 31.9. France, with a 1910 rate of 17.8, shows for the decade 1881–1890 an average of 22.1 and for preceding decades rates ranging from 23.7 to 26.1. Italy, with a 1910 rate of 19.9, shows for the decade 1891–1900 an average 24.2 and for preceding decades averages of 27.3 and 29.9. Austria, with a 1910 rate of 21.3, shows averages ranging from 23.3 in the decade 1901–1910 to 33.2 in the decade 1841–1850. Serbia's decennial averages range from 23.3 to 34.3; Spain's from 25.2 to 31.7; the two decades shown for Bulgaria give averages of 23.2 and 26; the three decades shown for Hungary give averages of 25.7, 29.9, and 32.5; and in Roumania the averages range from 25.8 to 31.3. Very generally in these countries the death rate has been materially reduced in recent decades from averages exceeding the Negro rate, and the assumption may fairly be made that the present high mortality of the Negro population may be similarly reduced.

DEATH RATES IN FOREIGN COUNTRIES—ANNUAL AVERAGE NUMBER OF DEATHS PER 1,000 POPULATION, BY DECADES.

Table 9 — DEATHS EXCLUSIVE OF STILLBIRTHS, PER 1,000 POPULATION.[1]

COUNTRY.	1910	Decrease 1910 from average 1891–1900.	Annual average by decades.										
			1901–1910	1891–1900	1881–1890	1871–1880	1861–1870	1851–1860	1841–1850	1831–1840	1821–1830	1811–1820	1801–1810
New Zealand	9.7	0.1	9.8	9.8	10.4	12.2	12.9						
Australia	10.4	2.6	11.2	13.0	15.2	15.7	16.5						
Denmark	12.9	4.6	14.2	17.5	18.6	19.4	19.9	20.6	20.4	23.1	21.9	21.4	23.7
England and Wales	13.5	4.7	15.4	18.2	19.1	21.4	22.5	22.2	22.4				
Norway	13.5	2.8	14.2	16.3	17.0	17.0	18.0	17.1	18.1	20.2	18.9	21.0	25.2
Netherlands	13.6	4.8	15.1	18.4	21.0	24.3	25.4	25.6	26.2				
Ontario, Province of	14.0	2.9 [2]	13.5	11.1	11.2								
Sweden	14.0	2.4	14.9	16.4	16.9	18.3	20.2	21.7	20.6	22.8	23.6	25.8	27.9
United States, registration area	15.0	2.6 [3]		17.6 [4]									
Negro population	25.5	3.9 [3]		29.4 [4]									
White population	14.6	2.5 [3]		17.1 [4]									
Switzerland	15.1	3.9	16.7	19.0	20.8	23.4							
Belgium	15.2	4.0	16.4	19.2	20.5	22.6	24.4	22.5	24.3	25.9			
Scotland	15.3	3.4	16.6	18.7	19.2	21.6	22.1						
Uruguay	15.3	0.1	14.1	15.4	17.8								
Germany	16.2	6.0	18.7	22.2	25.1	27.2	26.9	26.4	26.8	28.8 [5]	26.7 [5]		
Finland	16.5	3.2	18.0	19.7	21.1	22.2	32.2	28.7	23.5	28.2	24.9	26.4	31.9
Luxembourg	16.7		18.8										
Ireland	17.1	1.1	17.4	18.2	17.9	18.3	16.6 [6]						
France	17.8	3.7	19.4	21.5	22.1	23.7	23.6	23.9	23.3	24.8	25.2	26.1	
Portugal	19.6	1.7	20.2	21.3	22.6 [7]								
Italy	19.9	4.3	21.6	24.2	27.3	29.9 [8]							
Venezuela	20.4												
Japan	20.9	0.0	20.7	20.9	19.9								
Austria	21.3	5.3	23.3	26.6	29.5	31.5	30.7	31.4	33.2	32.5	28.6		
Argentina	21.7												
Serbia	22.1	4.9	23.3	27.0	25.2	34.3	30.7 [9]						
Jamaica	23.1	1.0 [2]	23.5	22.1	23.1								
Spain	23.3	6.2	25.2	29.5	31.7		30.8						
Bulgaria	23.5	2.5	23.2	26.0									
Hungary	23.6	6.3	25.7	29.9	32.5								
Roumania	24.8	4.4	25.8	29.2	27.5	31.3	26.1						
Ceylon	27.3	0.3	28.8	27.6	24.4								
Russia, in Europe	28.9 [10]			34.1									
Chile	31.1	0.4 [2]	31.0	30.7	31.5								
Mexico	33.3												

[1] Foreign rates taken from Statistique internationale du mouvement de la population, Vol. II, pp. 3–28, Statistique générale de la France.
[2] Increase.
[3] Decrease for 1910 compared with 1900.
[4] For the year 1900.
[5] Prussia.
[6] For the period 1864–1870.
[7] For the period 1886–1890.
[8] For the period 1872–1880.
[9] For the period 1862–1870.
[10] For 1909.

SPECIFIC MORTALITY BY SEX AND AGE PERIODS: 1910 AND 1900.

Table 13 gives for the aggregate population of the registration states the specific mortality rates in the Negro and white population classified by sex and age for the two years 1910 and 1900. The tabulation does not cover the registration areas in the non-registration states, the age classification by sex and racial class being available for only a portion of these areas. Tables 10, 11, and 12 are derived from Table 13, and are partially illustrated by Diagrams III, IV, and V (p. 309)—Diagram III relating to Negro deaths in the year 1910 only; Diagram IV, to Negro deaths in 1910 and 1900, both sexes combined; and Diagram V, to Negro and white deaths, both sexes combined, in 1910. The tables thus carry figures for whites and for 1900 not shown in the diagrams, and show figures for males and females separately, which are shown on the diagrams only for the two sexes combined.

In Table 10 a comparison is made of the specific mortality rates for males with the corresponding rates for females. In the Negro population under 1 year of age in 1910 the number of deaths per 1,000 among males (280.3) exceeded the number for females (243.2) by 37.1, the corresponding excess for 1900 being 70.3. In 1910 white male deaths per 1,000 population under 1 exceeded female by 27.8.

In the Negro population at each age, except the age 10 to 14, 15 to 19, and 85 and over, the number of male deaths per 1,000 exceeded the number of female deaths. In the white population the mortality rate for males exceeded that for females at each age shown in Table 10.

Table 10

AGE.	Negro.						White.
	1910				1900		1910
	Number.		Excess of male over female.	Excess of female over male.	Excess of male over female.	Excess of female over male.	Excess of male over female.
	Male.	Female.					
All ages	25.3	22.1	3.2	....	2.3	....	1.8
Under 1 year	280.3	243.2	37.1	....	70.3	....	27.8
1 to 4 years	32.6	29.4	3.2	0.0	0.9	....	1.2
5 to 9 years	6.0	6.0	0.0	0.0	0.0	0.0	0.3
10 to 14 years	5.2	6.1	....	0.9	....	5.2	0.2
15 to 19 years	9.5	10.7	....	1.2	....	0.2	0.5
20 to 24 years	12.9	10.9	2.0	....	1.3	....	0.7
25 to 44 years	17.2	14.2	3.0	....	0.5	....	1.4
45 to 64 years	33.5	31.1	2.4	....	1.6	....	3.8
65 to 84 years	86.6	78.5	8.1	....	6.2	....	6.3
85 years and over	213.2	214.9	....	1.7	....	55.6	10.0
Age unknown	13.5	7.2	6.3	....	6.6	....	3.4

DEATHS IN THE REGISTRATION STATES PER 1,000 POPULATION AT AGE SPECIFIED.

In the male and female Negro population under 1 year of age, 1 to 4 years, 5 to 9 years, 10 to 14 years, 15 to 19 years, and 65 to 84 years, the number of deaths per 1,000 living in these ages in 1910 was less than the number in 1900. In other words, these several age groups showed improvement as regards mortality for the decade 1900–1910. Among both males and females the mortality rate for the ages 25 to 44 and 45 to 64 was slightly higher in 1910 than in 1900. In the population 85 and over the rate for males decreased and the rate for females increased. The white population, both male and female, shows improvement in mortality at each age. Changes in the specific mortality rates are given in Table 11 and are illustrated for Negro deaths without distinction of sex in Diagram IV (p. 309).

The excess of Negro over white deaths per 1,000 living at each age in the registration states is shown in Table 12. In 1910 and in 1900, among both males and females, at each age, excepting the age 85 years and over, Negro mortality exceeded white mortality. In the younger ages generally the excess was less in 1910 than in 1900, but in the ages 25 to 44, and 45 to 64, it was greater in 1910 than in 1900. By reference to Table 13 it will be seen that in these ages mortality decreased slightly in the white population and increased in the Negro population.

Table 11

AGE.	Negro.				White.	
	Male.		Female.		Male.	Female.
	Excess 1900 over 1910.	Excess 1910 over 1900.	Excess 1900 over 1910.	Excess 1910 over 1900.	Excess 1900 over 1910.	
All ages	1.5	....	2.4	....	2.4	2.7
Under 1 year	99.7	....	66.5	....	32.4	27.0
1 to 4 years	12.4	....	14.7	....	5.9	5.6
5 to 9 years	2.9	....	2.9	....	1.0	1.2
10 to 14 years	1.2	....	5.5	....	0.4	0.7
15 to 19 years	1.7	....	0.7	....	0.9	1.4
20 to 24 years	....	0.7	0.0	0.0	1.4	1.7
25 to 44 years	....	3.3	....	0.8	1.2	2.1
45 to 64 years	....	1.4	....	0.6	0.6	2.4
65 to 84 years	2.6	....	4.5	....	1.0	0.9
85 years and over	40.0	....	....	17.3	10.0	6.8
Age unknown	5.5	....	5.7	....	19.3	28.3

DEATHS IN THE REGISTRATION STATES PER 1,000 POPULATION AT AGE SPECIFIED.

In the case of Negro males 25 to 44 years of age the increase in mortality was not inconsiderable, the change being from 13.9 in 1900 to 17.2 in 1910. The rate for white males of this age decreased from 9.3 in 1900 to 8.1 in 1910. These changes are given in Table 12, the 1910 figures for both sexes combined being illustrated in Diagram V.

Table 12

AGE.	1910		1900	
	Male.	Female.	Male.	Female.
All ages	9.9	8.5	9.0	8.2
Under 1 year	136.9	127.6	204.2	167.1
1 to 4 years	18.3	16.3	24.8	25.4
5 to 9 years	2.4	2.7	4.3	4.4
10 to 14 years	2.8	3.9	3.6	8.7
15 to 19 years	5.7	7.4	6.5	6.7
20 to 24 years	7.4	6.1	5.3	4.4
25 to 44 years	9.1	7.5	4.6	4.6
45 to 64 years	13.4	14.8	11.4	11.8
65 to 84 years	9.6	7.8	11.2	11.4
85 years and over	[1]47.0	[1]35.3	[1]17.0	[1]59.4
Age unknown	3.4	0.5	[1]10.4	[1]22.6

EXCESS OF NEGRO OVER WHITE DEATHS IN THE REGISTRATION STATES, PER 1,000 POPULATION OF EACH CLASS AT AGE SPECIFIED.

[1] Excess of white over Negro.

NEGRO POPULATION AND DEATHS IN THE REGISTRATION STATES, AND NEGRO AND WHITE DEATH RATES, BY SEX AND AGE PERIODS, WITH PERCENTAGE DISTRIBUTION BY AGE PERIODS OF NEGRO AND WHITE POPULATION AND DEATHS: 1910 AND 1900.

Table 13

AGE PERIOD.	Negro population.[2]		Deaths at age specified during calendar year.		Deaths[3] per 1,000 population of age specified.				Percentage distribution by age.							
					Negro population.		White population.		Population.				Deaths.			
									Negro.		White.		Negro.		White.	
	1910	1900	1910	1900	1910	1900	1910	1900	1910	1900	1910	1900	1910	1900	1910	1900
BOTH SEXES.																
All ages	1,051,877	388,198	24,908	9,954	23.7	25.6	14.6	17.0	100.0	100.0	100.0	100.0	100.0	100.0	100.0	100.0
Under 5 years	92,690	33,216	7,398	3,637	79.8	109.5	38.0	49.0	8.8	8.6	10.3	10.4	29.7	36.5	27.1	30.0
Under 1 year	19,634	7,196	5,143	2,479	261.9	344.5	129.7	159.4	1.9	1.9	2.2	2.2	20.6	24.9	19.3	20.6
5 to 9 years	87,054	31,681	520	282	6.0	8.9	3.4	4.6	8.3	8.2	9.4	10.0	2.1	2.8	2.2	2.7
10 to 14 years	85,035	30,677	482	280	5.7	9.1	2.3	2.9	8.1	7.9	9.0	9.1	1.9	2.8	1.4	1.5
15 to 19 years	90,267	37,513	916	424	10.1	11.3	3.6	4.7	8.6	9.7	9.4	9.0	3.7	4.3	2.3	2.5
20 to 24 years	115,494	51,509	1,365	590	11.8	11.5	5.2	6.7	11.0	13.3	9.8	9.4	5.5	5.9	3.5	3.7
25 to 44 years	393,247	135,301	6,183	1,849	15.7	13.7	7.5	9.0	37.4	34.9	31.0	30.9	24.8	18.6	15.9	16.4
45 to 64 years	149,317	53,853	4,829	1,686	32.3	31.3	18.3	19.7	14.2	13.9	16.1	15.7	19.4	16.9	20.2	18.2
65 to 84 years	33,244	11,376	2,746	977	82.6	85.9	73.8	74.7	3.2	2.9	4.7	4.9	11.0	9.8	23.8	21.4
85 years and over	2,016	893	432	194	214.2	217.2	254.6	262.6	0.2	0.2	0.2	0.2	1.7	2.0	3.5	3.2
Age unknown	3,513	2,179	37	35	10.5	16.1	9.0	31.2	0.3	0.6	0.2	0.2	0.1	0.4	0.1	0.3
MALE.																
All ages	519,973	185,211	13,151	4,972	25.3	26.8	15.4	17.8	100.0	100.0	100.0	100.0	100.0	100.0	100.0	100.0
Under 5 years	45,631	16,239	3,949	1,924	86.5	118.5	41.4	53.1	8.8	8.8	10.2	10.5	30.0	38.7	27.3	31.4
Under 1 year	9,933	3,563	2,784	1,354	280.3	380.0	143.4	175.8	1.9	1.9	2.1	2.2	21.2	27.2	19.9	22.0
5 to 9 years	42,555	15,424	254	138	6.0	8.9	3.6	4.6	8.2	8.3	9.3	10.0	1.9	2.8	2.1	2.6
10 to 14 years	41,121	14,604	213	94	5.2	6.4	2.4	2.8	7.9	7.9	8.8	9.1	1.6	1.9	1.4	1.5
15 to 19 years	41,746	16,721	396	187	9.5	11.2	3.8	4.7	8.0	9.0	9.1	8.8	3.0	3.8	2.3	2.4
20 to 24 years	53,590	22,815	692	278	12.9	12.2	5.5	6.9	10.3	12.3	9.7	9.1	5.3	5.6	3.5	3.5
25 to 44 years	198,630	65,624	3,415	912	17.2	13.9	8.1	9.3	38.2	35.4	31.7	31.4	26.0	18.3	16.6	16.4
45 to 64 years	77,329	26,994	2,593	866	33.5	32.1	20.1	20.7	14.9	14.6	16.3	15.8	19.7	17.4	21.3	18.4
65 to 84 years	16,767	5,266	1,453	470	86.6	89.2	77.0	78.0	3.2	2.8	4.5	4.7	11.0	9.5	22.5	20.7
85 years and over	755	316	161	80	213.2	253.2	260.2	270.2	0.1	0.2	0.2	0.2	1.2	1.6	2.9	2.6
Age unknown	1,849	1,208	25	23	13.5	19.0	10.1	29.4	0.4	0.7	0.2	0.3	0.2	0.5	0.1	0.4
FEMALE.																
All ages	531,904	202,987	11,757	4,982	22.1	24.5	13.6	16.3	100.0	100.0	100.0	100.0	100.0	100.0	100.0	100.0
Under 5 years	47,059	16,977	3,449	1,713	73.0	100.9	34.6	44.8	8.8	8.4	10.5	10.3	29.3	34.4	26.7	28.5
Under 1 year	9,701	3,633	2,359	1,125	243.2	309.7	115.6	142.6	1.8	1.8	2.2	2.2	20.1	22.6	18.7	19.1
5 to 9 years	44,499	16,257	266	144	6.0	8.9	3.3	4.5	8.4	8.0	9.6	9.9	2.3	2.9	2.3	2.8
10 to 14 years	43,914	16,073	269	186	6.1	11.6	2.2	2.9	8.3	7.9	9.2	9.1	2.3	3.7	1.5	1.6
15 to 19 years	48,521	20,792	520	237	10.7	11.4	3.3	4.7	9.1	10.3	9.6	9.2	4.4	4.8	2.4	2.6
20 to 24 years	61,904	28,694	673	312	10.9	10.9	4.8	6.5	11.6	14.1	9.9	9.8	5.7	6.3	3.5	3.9
25 to 44 years	194,617	69,677	2,768	937	14.2	13.4	6.7	8.8	36.6	34.3	30.2	30.5	23.5	18.8	15.0	16.4
45 to 64 years	71,988	26,859	2,236	820	31.1	30.5	16.3	18.7	13.5	13.2	15.8	15.6	19.0	16.5	18.9	18.0
65 to 84 years	16,477	6,110	1,293	507	78.5	83.0	70.7	71.6	3.1	3.0	4.9	5.0	11.0	10.2	25.4	22.2
85 years and over	1,261	577	271	114	214.9	197.6	250.2	257.0	0.2	0.3	0.2	0.2	2.3	2.3	4.2	3.8
Age unknown	1,664	971	12	12	7.2	12.4	6.7	35.0	0.3	0.5	0.1	0.1	0.1	0.2	(⁴)	0.3

[1] Includes the District of Columbia, but does not include North Carolina, 1910.
[2] Population as of Apr. 15, 1910, and June 1, 1900.
[3] Exclusive of stillbirths.
[4] Less than one-tenth of 1 per cent.

DIAGRAM III.—NEGRO DEATHS AT AGE SPECIFIED, PER 1,000 LIVING AT THAT AGE IN THE REGISTRATION STATES, BY SEX: 1910.

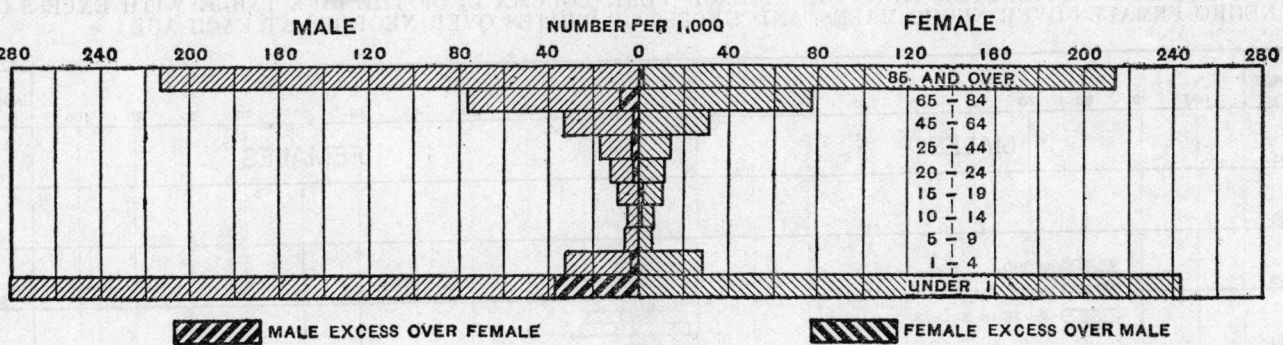

DIAGRAM IV.—NEGRO DEATHS AT AGE SPECIFIED, PER 1,000 LIVING AT THAT AGE IN THE REGISTRATION STATES: 1910 AND 1900.

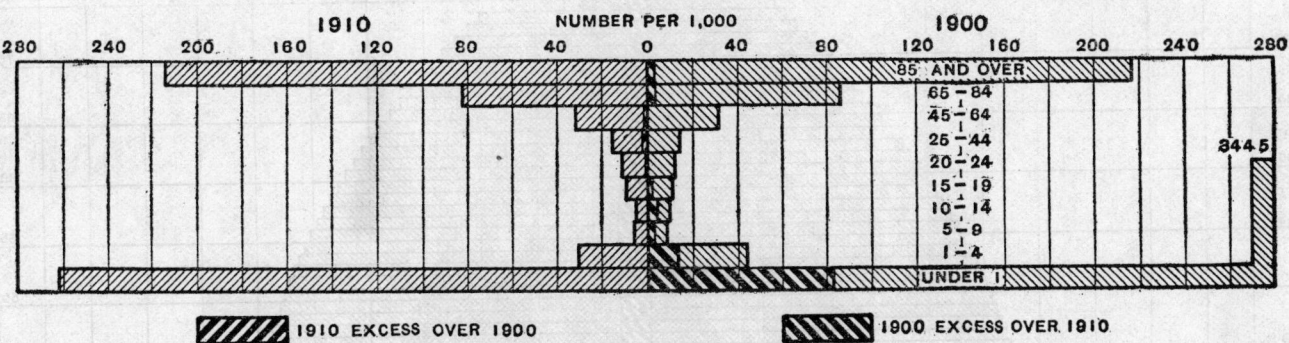

DIAGRAM V.—NEGRO AND WHITE DEATHS AT AGE SPECIFIED, PER 1,000 LIVING AT THAT AGE IN THE REGISTRATION STATES: 1910.

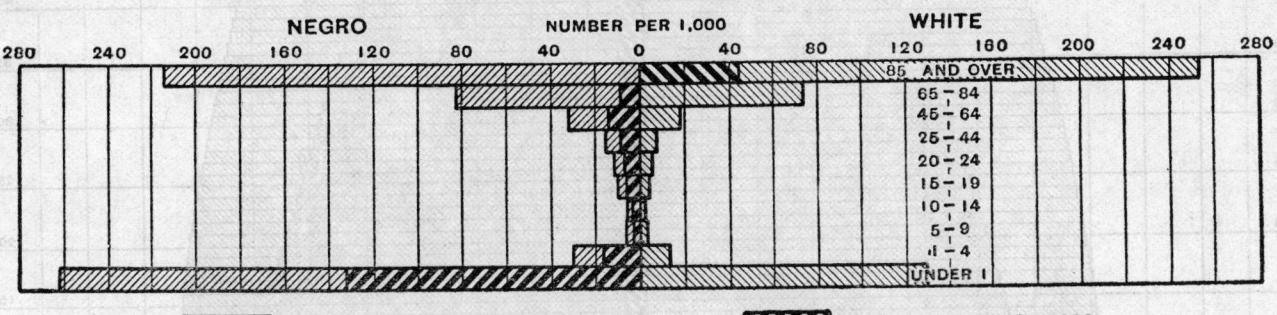

NEGRO LIFE TABLE.

Life tables have been compiled for the Negro population, one for Negro males and one for Negro females, and are reproduced as Tables 31a and 31b, (pp. 323 to 326) of this report. Selected years and columns from these tables are given in Table 14, which embraces also comparable data for white males and females.

Where adequate data are available, the life table constitutes an accurate measure of mortality for any population class, the data required for the calculation of a life table being accurate statistics of deaths and of population, by sex and age.

In the case of the Negro population as a whole these data are not available. The Negro life tables are, therefore, necessarily based upon data relating to selected areas, namely, those areas for which approximately accurate and complete mortality and population statistics are available.

Specifically the areas represented by the Negro life tables are the 10 original registration states,[1] and the District of Columbia. These states are all Northern states, the only southern area included being the District of Columbia.

The estimated Negro population of this area on July 1, 1910, was 463,698, the number of males being 223,884, and the number of females 239,814. The number of deaths reported for this population in the three years 1909, 1910, and 1911 was 17,471 for males and 15,853 for females.

The calculation of the Negro life tables involved a relation of male and female deaths, classified by single years of age—and in the case of deaths under 1 year, by months of age—to the number of males and females living in each age. By this relationship a refined

[1] Maine, New Hampshire, Vermont, Massachusetts, Rhode Island, Connecticut, New York, New Jersey, Indiana, and Michigan.

DIAGRAM **VI.**—LIFE TABLE DISTRIBUTION, BY AGE AND SEX, OF THE NEGRO AND WHITE POPULATION—
NUMBER LIVING AT AGE SPECIFIED IN A STATIONARY POPULATION SUSTAINED BY 100,000 BIRTHS OF EACH
SEX EQUALLY DISTRIBUTED THROUGHOUT EACH YEAR (COLUMN L_x OF THE LIFE TABLE) WITH EXCESS OF
NEGRO FEMALES OVER NEGRO MALES, AND EXCESS OF WHITES OVER NEGROES AT EACH AGE.

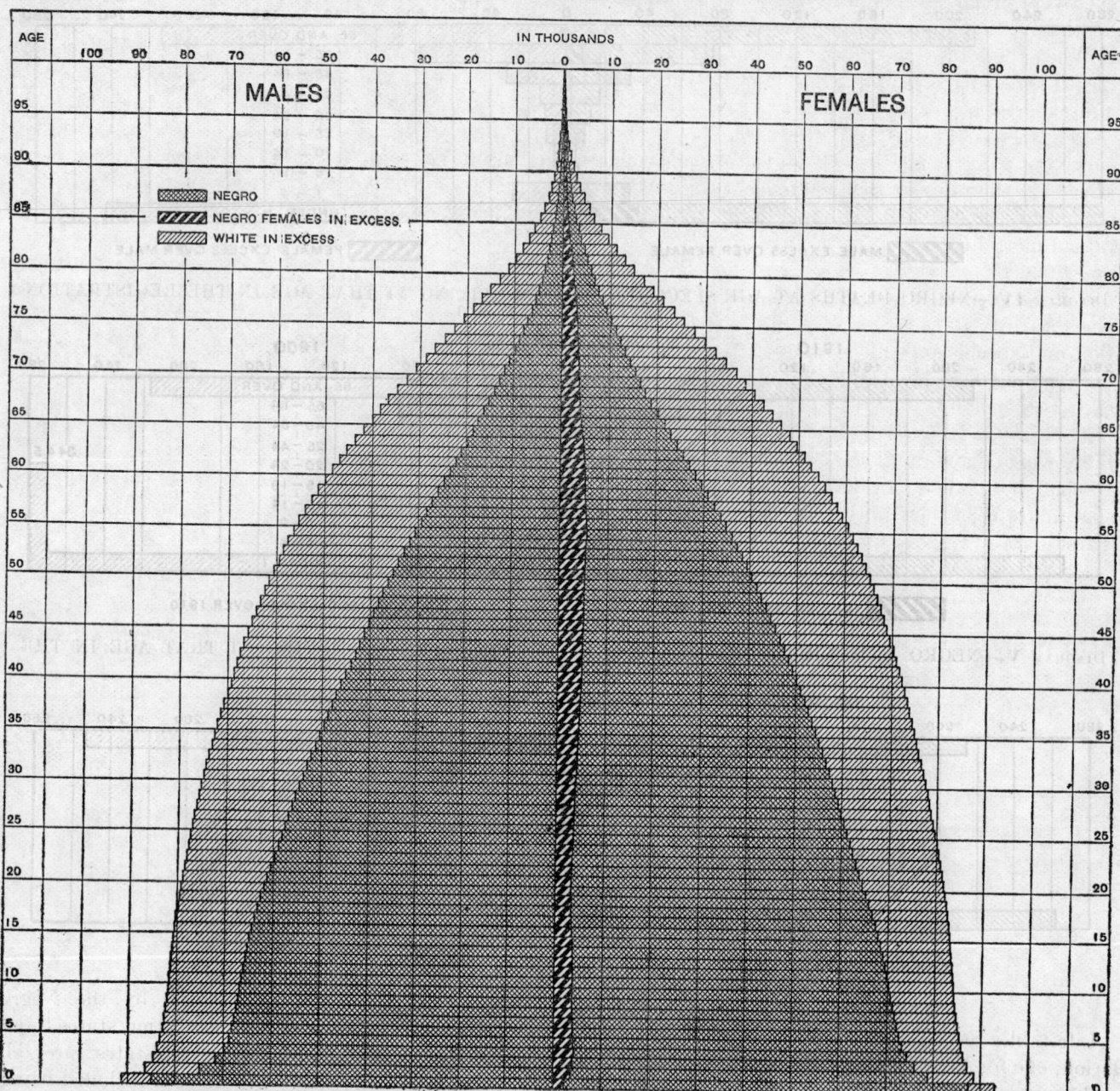

mortality rate is determined for each year (or month) of age. Prior to the calculation of these rates, however, inaccuracies in the age returns are eliminated by correcting the age distribution of the population to make it conform to a normal distribution. The mathematical processes employed in correcting the age distribution need not be considered here in detail. The effect produced upon the age distribution of the population may be easily comprehended by comparing the age diagram on page — with that above. One of those diagrams represents the distribution of the total Negro population according to returns of sex and age, and the other the sex and age distribution of the Negro life table population in comparison with that of the white life table population. The effect resulting from correction of the age distribution is elimination of the concentrations in the adult population upon ages ending in 0 and in 5, and of other irregularities of distribution, especially in the younger ages. By the application of formulas, which have been scientifically determined, an age distribution of the population is produced which undoubtedly conforms closely to the actual age distribution of the population represented by the age returns.

When for any given year or series of years the mean number living in each age and the number of deaths occurring annually in each age has been accurately determined, the specific mortality rates for each year of age are found by dividing the number of deaths by the population living in that age.

When these rates have been determined, it is possible to construct the life tables showing survivorship and expectation of life for each age.

The Negro life table for males shows (1) the number surviving to each age in 100,000 male children born alive; (2) the number dying in each year (or month) of age in 100,000 male children born alive; (3) the rate of mortality, or number dying in each age interval per 1,000 alive at the beginning of the age interval; (4) the expectation of life, or average number of years to live at each age; and (5) the age composition and specific mortality indicated for a stationary male population maintained by 100,000 male births each year (columns 6, 7, 8, and 9 of Table 31a).

Table 14 is restricted to those columns of the life table which show number of survivors to each age in 100,000 born alive, number of deaths in each age, specific rate of mortality, and expectation of life. These data are given for selected years of age. The table shows, for example, that in 100,000 Negro male children born alive, 78,065 survive the first year of age, the corresponding number for females being 81,493, and for white males and females 87,674 and 89,774, respectively. In 100,000 Negro male children born alive, 21,935 die under 1 year of age—that is to say, before completing 1 year of age; the corresponding number for Negro females being 18,507, and for white males and females, 12,326 and 10,226, respectively. These numbers indicate a mortality rate, or number of deaths in the first year of age per 1,000 children born alive, of 219.35 for Negro males, 185.07 for Negro females, 123.26 for white males, and 102.26 for white females. The expectation of life at birth indicated in the life table is 34.05 years for Negro males, 37.67 years for Negro females; 50.23 years for white males and 53.62 for white females.

The expectation of life in the case of children who survive to the exact age of 1 year is increased in the case of Negro males from 34.05 years, the expectation at birth, to 42.53 years, and in the case of Negro females from 37.67 to 45.15 years.

LIFE TABLE DATA COVERING SELECTED YEARS OF AGE FOR NEGRO AND WHITE MALES AND FEMALES.

Table 14	OF 100,000 BORN ALIVE.								RATE OF MORTALITY—NUMBER DYING IN AGE INTERVAL AMONG 1,000 ALIVE AT BEGINNING OF AGE INTERVAL.				COMPLETE EXPECTATION OF LIFE—AVERAGE LENGTH OF LIFE REMAINING TO EACH ONE ALIVE AT BEGINNING OF AGE INTERVAL.			
	Number alive at beginning of age interval.				Number dying in age interval.											
	Negro.		White.		Negro.		White.		Negro.		White.		Negro.		White.	
AGE INTERVAL.	Male.	Female.	Male.	Female.	Male.	Female.	Male.	Female.	Male.	Female.	Male.	Female.	Male.	Female.	Male.	Female.
Months:																
0-1	100,000	100,000	100,000	100,000	7,370	6,380	4,844	3,787	73.70	63.80	48.44	37.87	34.05	37.67	50.23	53.62
1-2	92,630	93,620	95,156	96,213	1,977	1,746	1,242	991	21.35	18.66	13.05	10.29	36.68	40.15	52.71	55.64
2-3	90,653	91,874	93,914	95,222	1,831	1,555	1,012	850	20.19	16.93	10.78	8.93	37.39	40.83	53.32	56.14
3-4	88,822	90,319	92,902	94,372	1,695	1,394	863	740	19.09	15.44	9.28	7.84	38.08	41.45	53.82	56.56
4-5	87,127	88,925	92,039	93,632	1,561	1,252	750	648	17.91	14.08	8.15	6.92	38.74	42.01	54.24	56.92
5-6	85,566	87,673	91,289	92,984	1,425	1,134	673	578	16.66	12.94	7.37	6.21	39.36	42.53	54.60	57.24
6-7	84,141	86,539	90,616	92,406	1,290	1,036	610	526	15.33	11.96	6.73	5.70	39.94	43.00	54.92	57.51
7-8	82,851	85,503	90,006	91,880	1,153	948	553	486	13.93	11.09	6.15	5.28	40.48	43.44	55.21	57.76
8-9	81,698	84,555	89,453	91,394	1,037	874	503	450	12.69	10.34	5.62	4.93	40.97	43.84	55.47	57.98
9-10	80,661	83,681	88,950	90,944	937	800	457	421	11.62	9.56	5.14	4.62	41.41	44.22	55.70	58.18
10-11	79,724	82,881	88,493	90,523	857	725	420	390	10.75	8.75	4.74	4.31	41.81	44.56	55.90	58.37
11-12	78,867	82,156	88,073	90,133	802	663	399	359	10.16	8.07	4.53	3.98	42.18	44.87	56.08	58.54
Years:																
0-1	100,000	100,000	100,000	100,000	21,935	18,507	12,326	10,226	219.35	185.07	123.26	102.26	34.05	37.67	50.23	53.62
1-2	78,065	81,493	87,674	89,774	5,216	4,796	2,473	2,319	66.82	58.84	28.21	25.83	42.53	45.15	56.26	58.69
2-3	72,849	76,697	85,201	87,455	2,341	1,878	1,084	999	32.14	24.50	12.73	11.43	44.55	46.95	58.88	59.24
3-4	70,508	74,819	84,117	86,456	1,197	1,187	668	644	16.97	15.85	7.93	7.45	45.01	47.12	56.60	58.92
4-5	69,311	73,632	83,449	85,812	722	864	477	463	10.42	11.74	5.72	5.39	44.78	46.87	56.05	58.35
5-6	68,589	72,768	82,972	85,349	587	617	391	382	8.56	8.47	4.71	4.47	44.25	46.42	55.37	57.67
10-11	66,377	70,508	81,519	83,979	334	365	194	173	5.02	5.18	2.38	2.06	40.65	42.84	51.32	53.57
15-16	64,478	68,218	80,549	83,093	508	647	228	220	7.87	9.49	2.83	2.65	36.77	39.18	46.91	49.12
20-21	61,426	64,764	79,116	81,750	735	696	387	343	11.96	10.74	4.89	4.20	33.46	36.14	42.71	44.88
25-26	57,736	61,430	77,047	79,865	709	614	426	417	12.28	9.99	5.54	5.22	30.44	32.97	38.79	40.88
30-31	54,073	58,281	74,810	77,676	809	700	494	469	14.96	12.02	6.60	6.03	27.33	29.61	34.87	36.96
35-36	49,865	54,595	72,108	75,200	862	767	614	536	17.28	14.05	8.52	7.13	24.42	26.44	31.08	33.09
40-41	45,414	50,568	68,848	72,425	955	885	704	582	21.03	17.50	10.22	8.03	21.57	23.34	27.43	29.26
45-46	40,563	45,947	65,115	69,341	973	976	823	687	23.99	21.25	12.64	9.91	18.85	20.43	23.86	25.45
50-51	35,427	40,886	60,741	65,629	1,113	1,044	943	827	31.42	25.52	15.53	12.59	16.21	17.65	20.39	21.74
55-56	29,754	35,415	55,622	61,053	1,175	1,234	1,196	1,094	39.50	34.85	21.50	17.93	13.82	14.98	17.03	18.18
60-61	23,750	28,908	48,987	54,900	1,206	1,318	1,506	1,418	50.79	45.58	30.75	25.83	11.67	12.78	13.98	14.92
65-66	17,806	22,302	40,862	47,086	1,145	1,346	1,789	1,783	64.33	60.37	43.79	37.86	9.74	10.82	11.25	11.97
70-71	12,295	15,871	31,527	37,482	1,032	1,131	1,959	2,123	83.98	71.27	62.14	56.63	8.00	9.22	8.83	9.38
75-76	7,494	10,657	21,585	26,569	846	932	1,997	2,192	112.77	87.47	92.53	82.52	6.58	7.55	6.75	7.20
80-81	3,894	6,324	12,160	15,929	511	757	1,651	2,004	131.27	119.68	135.75	125.79	5.53	6.05	5.09	5.35
85-86	1,747	3,029	5,145	7,152	314	488	983	1,275	179.82	161.05	191.11	178.32	4.48	5.09	3.88	4.06
90-91	595	1,206	1,523	2,291	119	208	389	567	201.01	172.34	255.17	247.59	4.01	4.50	2.99	3.00
95-96	189	448	289	434	43	93	94	145	227.76	205.91	324.86	334.23	3.15	3.45	2.31	2.27
100-101	40	112	51	44	13	34	13	19	336.29	303.35	427.46	420.99	2.14	2.39	1.68	1.74

Among Negro children, male and female, expectation of life increases during the first 3 years of life to 45.01 years at the exact age of 3 years for Negro males, and 47.12 years for Negro females. Among white children expectation of life increases during the first 2 years of life to 58.88 years for white males arrived at the exact age of 2 years, and to 59.24 years for white females. This increase in the expectation of life over expectation at birth develops in proportion as the initial period of excessive mortality is passed. Children who have survived the excessive mortality of the first 2 or 3 years of life obviously have a greater chance of surviving to maturity and old age than they had at birth. In subsequent ages expectation of life necessarily decreases with advancing age, although expectation of life does not decrease in any fixed proportion to advancing age.

SURVIVAL OF INFANCY AND ADOLESCENCE.

As regards Negro and white males and females, the figures given in Table 15, showing the number of survivors to the age 1 year and to the age 20 years in 1,000 children born alive, are taken from the life tables prepared by the Bureau of the Census. The figures for the male population of foreign countries are reproduced from the official publication of the French Government to which reference is made in the table. In this table the foreign countries are arranged in order according to the number of survivors to the age 1 year in 1,000 male children born.

Table 15 COUNTRY AND SEX.	IN 1,000 BORN, NUMBER SURVIVING TO THE AGE OF—	
	1 year.	20 years.
UNITED STATES: 1910.[1]		
Males:		
Negro	781	614
White	877	791
Females:		
Negro	815	648
White	898	817
MALES IN FOREIGN COUNTRIES.[2]		
Sweden (1891–1910)	898	793
Norway (1891–1900)	895	777
Australia (1891–1910)	894	824
Denmark (1895–1905)	862	784
Japan (1899–1903)	843	713
Netherlands (1890–1909)	843	742
France (1898–1903)	837	729
Switzerland (1889–1900)	835	743
Belgium (1891–1900)	831	722
England (1891–1900)	828	712
Italy (1899–1902)	825	665
Germany (1891–1910)	782	679
Austria-Hungary (1900–1901)	758	615
India (1901)	715	452

[1] The 10 original registration states and the District of Columbia.
[2] Statistique internationale du mouvement de la population, Vol. II, pp. xix–xx.

It will be noted that survivorship to full maturity is very largely determined in the first year of age. In the Negro population the number of survivors to the age 1 year in 1,000 males born alive, is 781, giving a mortality for the first year of age of 219 per 1,000 born. In the age period of 19 years, from the exact age 1

year to the exact age 20 years, the number of survivors is reduced to 614 or by 133. The mortality spread over these 19 years is, therefore, less in the aggregate than the specific mortality in the first year of age, i. e. the age "under 1 year," and this is true of white males and of females, Negro and white. It is true, also, of males in foreign countries, excepting Sweden and Norway, that the mortality in the first year of age exceeds the mortality in the 19 succeeding years of childhood and adolescence. In Germany, for example, in the period of 20 years 1891–1910, the average mortality per 1,000 male children born was 218 in the first year of age, and 103 in the age period 1 to 19 years inclusive; and in Austria-Hungary, in the two years 1900–1901, the mortality for the first year of age was 242, and for the succeeding period of 19 years, 143.

DURATION OF MATURITY AND OF OLD AGE.

The average number of years lived in the productive ages 20 to 60 years, for all children born, and for survivors to the age 20 years, is shown in Table 16, and the average duration of old age or average expectation of life at the age of 60 years, in Table 17, data for foreign male populations being taken from the source cited above.

In 1,000 children born a certain number on the average—among Negro males the number is 237—survive to the age 60 years, and for these children the duration of maturity, defining maturity as the life period between the exact ages 20 and 60 years, is 40 years; a certain number in 1,000 children born—among Negro males, 386—do not survive to the age 20 years; and a certain number—among Negro males, 377—surviving to the age of 20 years, die in the ages of maturity. Among 1,000 children born therefore, the duration of maturity varies from zero to 40 years, and the average duration per child born, and per child surviving to the age 20 years is a vital characteristic of considerable interest.

In the Negro population the average number of years lived in the ages 20 to 60 years is 18 for males and 19.9 for females. In the white population the corresponding averages are 27.1 years for males and 28.6 years for females. It thus appears that the average duration of maturity among Negro males is shorter than it is among Negro females, and that the average for the Negro population is materially shorter than it is for the white population. The average duration of maturity for Negro males is in fact less than the corresponding average for males in any of the foreign countries listed in Table 16, with exception of India.

If the number of years lived in the ages 20 to 60 years be related to the number, not of children born, but of survivors to the age 20 years, an average duration of maturity is found for Negro males of 29.3 years, for Negro females of 30.7 years, for white males of 34.2 years, and for white females of 35 years. Among survivors to the age 20 years, the difference between Negroes and whites, as regards average duration of maturity, is less marked than it is as regards the average calculated for all children born. In these figures the effect of the relatively high infant mortality of the Negro population is apparent.

Table 16 COUNTRY AND SEX.	DURATION OF MATURITY—AVERAGE NUMBER OF YEARS LIVED IN THE AGES 20 TO 60 YEARS.	
	Per child born.	Among survivors to the age of 20 years.
UNITED STATES: 1910.[1]		
Males:		
Negro	18.0	29.3
White	27.1	34.2
Females:		
Negro	19.9	30.7
White	28.6	35.0
MALES IN FOREIGN COUNTRIES.[2]		
Australia	28.6	34.9
Sweden	27.6	34.7
Denmark	27.5	35.1
Netherlands	26.0	35.0
Norway	25.8	33.2
Switzerland	25.0	33.6
Belgium	24.5	33.9
France	24.3	33.4
England	24.0	33.8
Japan	23.7	33.2
Germany	23.2	34.2
Italy	22.9	34.4
Austria-Hungary	19.9	33.2
India	11.9	26.4

[1] The 10 original registration states and the District of Columbia.
[2] Statistique internationale du mouvement de la population. Vol. II, pp. xix and xxi. For periods to which data relate, see Table 15.

Table 17 COUNTRY AND SEX.	Duration of old age—Average years to live for survivors to age 60 years.	COUNTRY AND SEX.	Duration of old age—Average years to live for survivors to age 60 years.
UNITED STATES: 1910.[1]		MALES IN FOREIGN COUNTRIES [2]—contd.	
Males:			
Negro	11.7	Netherlands	14.4
White	14.0	France	13.8
Females:		Italy	13.6
Negro	12.8	Belgium	13.4
White	14.9		
		Germany	13.0
MALES IN FOREIGN COUNTRIES.[2]		England	12.9
		Japan	12.8
Norway	16.4	Switzerland	12.5
Sweden	15.8	Austria-Hungary	[3] 12.3
Denmark	14.8	India	9.5
Australia	14.2		

[1] The 10 original registration states and the District of Columbia.
[2] Statistique internationale du mouvement de la population, Vol. II, p. xviii. For periods to which data relate, see Table 15.
[3] Probable duration of life.

For Negroes arrived at the age of 60 years, also, the expectation of life (11.7 years for males and 12.8 years for females) is somewhat less than it is for the white population (14 years and 14.9 years), although the expectation for Negro males is not very materially less than the expectation for males at this age in several European countries—the figure for Germany,

for example, being 13 years; for England, 12.9 years; and for Switzerland, 12.5 years.

CAUSE OF DEATH.

Table 18 classifies deaths in 1913 and in 1910 by principal causes of death, giving for Negroes and whites the number of deaths from each specified cause per 1,000 deaths from all causes, and per 100,000 population. The causes of death are arranged in order according to the number occurring in the Negro population in 1913.

The three principal causes of death in the Negro population—namely, tuberculosis, pneumonia, and organic diseases of the heart—are the principal causes of death also for the white population. Per 1,000 deaths from all causes in 1913, in the Negro population, 366, or more than one-third, and in the white population, 291, are classified under one or other of these three causes.

Relatively to other causes tuberculosis is, however, much more prevalent in the Negro population than in the white. Per 1,000 deaths in the Negro population 176, and in the white population 98, result from some form of tuberculosis. In the white population pneumonia and organic diseases of the heart are nearly of equal importance with tuberculosis as causes of death, the number of deaths from these two causes per 1,000 deaths from all causes being 94 and 99, respectively. In the Negro population these causes are relatively to other causes much less prevalent than tuberculosis, the number per 1,000 deaths from all causes in the Negro population being for pneumonia 100, and for organic diseases of the heart 90.

Violent deaths, excepting suicide, were of the same frequency relatively to other causes, although not relatively to population, among Negroes as among whites, the number of such deaths—which include deaths from all accidental injuries and from homicide—per 1,000 deaths from all causes being 66 in each class of the population.

In general the principal causes of death among Negro males are the principal causes also among Negro females. In 1913 the number of deaths from tuberculosis, for example, per 1,000 deaths from all causes was 177 for males and 175 for females; from pneumonia 107 for males, and 91 for females; and from organic diseases of the heart, 88 for males and 91 for females.

As has been shown in preceding tables, the general death rate from all causes in 1910 was much higher for the Negro element of the population in the registration area than for the white element. In this year per 100,000 population the number of deaths from all causes was 2,546 among Negroes and 1,457 among whites. This higher general rate involves necessarily higher specific mortality rates for the several causes specified in Table 18, and with few exceptions the number of deaths from each specified cause per 100,000 population was higher in 1910 among Negroes than among whites. The exceptions are cancer—with a rate per 100,000 population of 57 among Negroes and of 77 among whites, cirrhosis of the liver, diphtheria, and croup, measles, diabetes, suicide, erysipelas, and scarlet fever. These are, however, minor causes of death among both Negroes and whites.

Tuberculosis developed a rate per 100,000 population in 1910 of 463 among Negroes, which was more than three times the tuberculosis rate of 148 per 100,000 white population. The rate for pneumonia among Negroes was 298, or more than twice the pneumonia rate of 142 among whites. The rate for organic diseases of the heart was 212 among Negroes and 139 among whites.

Comparison with the white rates of mortality from specific causes provides a rough measure of the possibility of improvement in Negro mortality. In the white population the prevalence of tuberculosis has been diminished in recent years, and there is no reason to believe that this reduction will not continue in the future. The high tuberculosis rate of the Negro population resident in the registration area undoubtedly reflects unfavorable environmental conditions, which can be largely if not wholly remedied through concerted and intelligent social effort on the part of Negroes and of whites.

It is not improbable that among certain classes in urban communities, and in certain sections of the country, the mortality from specific causes is as high among whites as among Negroes, but no adequate data are available for determining mortality rates for the different social or economic classes of either Negroes or whites. It should be borne in mind, however, that the great mass of the Negro population, including nearly the entire rural Negro population of the South, is outside the area of death registration, and it is highly probable that mortality is much lower in this rural element than it is in the population of the registration area, which is, as has been noted, largely urban and largely a migrant population. In the North, the urban Negro population, at least to the extent that it is a migrant population native of the South, is subjected to conditions similar in some respects to those encountered by the foreign immigrant, and the difficulties of adjustment to these conditions may be reflected in the higher mortalities from such causes as tuberculosis and pneumonia.

NEGRO AND WHITE DEATHS FROM SPECIFIED CAUSES: 1913 AND 1910.

Table 18	NEGRO DEATHS IN THE REGISTRATION AREA FROM SPECIFIED CAUSES.				DEATHS FROM SPECIFIED CAUSES PER 1,000 DEATHS FROM ALL CAUSES.						DEATHS FROM SPECIFIED CAUSES PER 100,000 POPULATION: 1910.	
	1913			1910	1913				1910			
CAUSE OF DEATH.					Negro.			White.				
	Both sexes.	Male.	Female.		Both sexes.	Male.	Female.		Negro.	White.	Negro.	White.
All causes	67,266	35,267	31,999	49,499	1,000	1,000	1,000	1,000	1,000	1,000	2,546	1,457
Tuberculosis	11,851	6,241	5,610	8,998	176	177	175	98	182	102	463	148
Pneumonia	6,702	3,783	2,919	5,796	100	107	91	94	117	98	298	142
Organic diseases of the heart	6,030	3,120	2,910	4,120	90	88	91	99	83	95	212	139
Nephritis, Bright's disease	5,239	2,873	2,366	3,533	78	81	74	73	71	66	182	96
Violent deaths, except suicide	4,413	3,403	1,010	2,609	66	96	32	66	53	61	134	88
Congenital debility and malformations	3,059	1,621	1,438	2,140	45	46	45	60	43	51	110	74
Diarrhea and enteritis (under 2 years)	2,750	1,465	1,285	2,792	41	42	40	54	56	68	144	99
Cerebral hemorrhage and softening	2,567	1,161	1,406	1,705	38	33	45	56	34	52	88	76
Cancer	1,767	510	1,257	1,100	26	14	39	59	22	53	57	77
Typhoid	1,190	637	553	798	18	18	17	12	16	16	41	23
Bronchitis	878	442	436	793	13	13	14	13	16	16	41	23
Puerperal fever and affections	796		796	532	12		25	11	11	10	27	15
Whooping cough	691	319	372	588	10	9	12	7	12	7	30	11
Influenza	587	270	317	511	9	8	10	9	10	10	26	14
Meningitis	532	319	213	369	8	9	7	7	7	10	19	14
Malaria	501	235	266	413	7	7	8	1	8	1	21	1
Hernia, intestinal obstruction	449	256	193	316	7	7	6	8	6	8	16	12
Cirrhosis of the liver	417	260	157	265	6	7	5	10	5	10	14	14
Diphtheria and croup	342	161	181	231	5	5	6	14	5	15	12	22
Measles	334	163	171	181	5	5	5	9	4	8	9	12
Appendicitis	318	177	141	225	5	5	4	9	5	8	12	11
Rheumatism	299	113	186	208	4	3	6	5	4	5	11	7
Diabetes	258	129	129	142	4	4	4	11	3	10	7	15
Suicide	207	144	63	162	3	4	2	12	3	11	8	16
Erysipelas	63	38	25	83	1	1	1	3	2	3	4	5
Scarlet fever	55	28	27	71	1	1	1	7	1	8	4	12
Smallpox	16	9	7	12	(1)	(1)	(1)	(1)	(1)	(1)	1	(1)
All other and unknown causes	14,955	7,390	7,565	10,806	222	210	236	192	218	198	556	289

[1] Less than 1 per 1,000.

INFANT MORTALITY.

Infant mortality by months of age is shown in Table 14—the partial life table for Negroes and whites—and in the complete life tables for Negro males and females—Tables 31a and 31b.

In the Negro population the number dying in the age interval 0–1 month—that is to say, in the age under 1 month—in the course of a year is very nearly equal to the population living in that age, the population living in the age under 1 month, as figured for the stationary life table population, to one annual death in the same age interval, being 1.07 for Negro males and 1.24 for Negro females. The corresponding number for white males is 1.66 and for white females, 2.14. For this age interval the death rate per month per 1,000 is 73.70 for Negro males and 63.80 for Negro females; the corresponding rates for white males and females being 48.44 and 37.87.

The mortality rate for this first month of age among both Negroes and whites is more than three times the rate for the second month. After the first month of age the decrease in the mortality rate in succeeding months of age is gradual—from 21.35 in the second month to 10.16 in the twelfth month for Negro males; from 18.66 to 8.07 for Negro females; from 13.05 to 4.53 for white males; and from 10.29 to 3.98 for white females. The rapid decline in mortality during the first month of age and the gradual decline in succeeding months is illustrated in Diagram VII, on page 321.

Table 19 gives, for convenience in comparison, the mortality rate under 1 year of age for Negroes and whites, male and female, in 1910 and in 1900, together with the excess of the Negro over the white rate, the excess of the male over the female rate, and the excess of the 1900 over the 1910 rate.

Table 19	DEATHS PER 1,000 POPULATION UNDER 1 YEAR OF AGE.		
SEX AND YEAR.	Negro.	White.	Excess of Negro over white.
Both sexes:			
1910	261.9	129.7	132.2
1900	344.5	159.4	185.1
Male:			
1910	280.3	143.4	136.9
1900	380.0	175.8	204.2
Female:			
1910	243.2	115.6	127.6
1900	309.7	142.6	167.1
Excess, male over female:			
1910	37.1	27.8	
1900	70.3	33.2	
Excess, 1900 over 1910:			
Both sexes	82.6	29.7	
Male	99.7	32.4	
Female	66.5	27.0	

Although Negro infant mortality in 1910 was greatly in excess of white infant mortality—the excess of the Negro over the white rate being 136.9 for males, and 127.6 for females—the figures for 1910 indicate marked improvement during the decade 1900–1910. In this period infant mortality among Negro males declined from 380 in 1900 to 280.3 in 1910, the decrease in the rate amounting to 99.7, and the rate for Negro females declined from 309.7 in 1900 to 243.2 in 1910, the decrease amounting to 66.5.

URBAN AND RURAL MORTALITY.

The general death rate of the Negro, white, native white, and foreign-born white population, classified as urban and rural, is given in Table 20 for the country as a whole, for the South, and for the North and West. In this table the term "urban" relates to cities in the registration area having a population of 10,000 or more, and the term "rural" to smaller cities and to rural communities. The population classified as rural, therefore, embraces a considerable small-city population in the registration states, which under the definitions of the terms urban and rural in other sections of this report would be classified as urban. Outside of the registration states, cities of less than 10,000 population are not included in the registration area. The urban population of Table 20 is purely urban, although it does not of course embrace the entire Negro or white population living in cities of 10,000 or more, but only the population of such cities which are included in the registration area.

Table 20	REGISTRATION AREA: 1910.					
	Population, April 15.[1]		Deaths during calendar year.			
SECTION AND RACIAL CLASS.					Per 1,000 population.	
	Urban.	Rural.	Urban.	Rural.	Urban.	Rural.
United States:						
Negro	1,517,099	349,308	41,176	6,813	27.1	19.5
White	29,460,643	21,871,151	459,648	291,493	15.6	13.3
Native	21,317,297	18,591,614	320,455	233,965	15.0	12.6
Foreign born	8,143,346	3,279,537	139,193	57,528	17.1	17.5
The South:						
Negro	852,836	143,841	24,951	2,626	29.3	18.3
White	2,304,159	544,164	38,654	6,489	16.8	11.9
Native	2,058,455	518,672	31,800	5,917	15.4	11.4
Foreign born	245,704	25,492	6,854	572	27.9	22.4
The North and West:						
Negro	664,263	205,467	16,225	4,187	24.4	20.4
White	27,156,484	21,326,987	420,994	285,004	15.5	13.4
Native	19,258,842	18,072,942	288,655	228,048	15.0	12.6
Foreign born	7,897,642	3,254,045	132,339	56,956	16.8	17.5

[1] In this table "Urban" includes cities of 10,000 and over; "Rural" includes smaller communities and country districts. Rural population and deaths for North Carolina are not included.

For this urban population the general death rate in 1910 was 27.1 among Negroes and 15.6 among whites, and in the rural population, (as defined above), the general death rate was 19.5 for Negroes and 13.3 for whites. The excess of the urban over the rural rate was, therefore, 7.6 for Negroes and 2.3 for whites. In the urban population the Negro mortality exceeded the white by 11.5, and in the rural population by only 6.2. Urbanization appears to be in the case of the Negro population, to a somewhat greater degree than is true of the white population, a condition of high mortality.

In the urban Negro population of the South, the general death rate in 1910 was 29.3, and in the rural Negro population of the South, so far as that population was included in the registration area, the general death rate was 18.3, or less than two-thirds of the urban rate.

Mortality in the foreign-born white population of the southern cities nearly equaled that of the Negroes— the rate being 27.9 for foreign-born whites, as compared with 29.3 for Negroes—and in the rural population the mortality of the foreign-born white exceeded that of the Negroes—the rate being 22.4, as compared with 18.3 for Negroes.

Negro mortality was lower in northern and western, than in southern cities (24.4 as compared with 29.3), and higher in the rural population of the North and West than in the rural population of the South (20.4 as compared with 18.3). This relatively high mortality in the rural population of the North and West may be in part accounted for by the fact that of the population classified as rural a larger proportion in the North and West than in the South is small-city population, the rural mortality in the North and West tending therefore to approximate the urban mortality.

URBAN MORTALITY IN THE SOUTH AND IN THE NORTH AND WEST.

The specific mortality by sex and age of the aggregate Negro and white population living in selected registration cities of 25,000 or more population in 1910 is shown in Table 21, which tabulates the data separately for southern cities as a group and for northern and western cities.

NEGRO DEATHS AND DEATHS PER 1,000 POPULATION, BY SEX AND AGE PERIODS, FOR SELECTED REGISTRATION CITIES: 1910.

Table 21 — REGISTRATION CITIES OF 25,000 OR MORE POPULATION AND OF 2,500 NEGROES: 1910.

SECTION AND AGE PERIOD.	Negro population.			Negro deaths of age specified during calendar year: 1910.			Deaths per 1,000 population of age specified.					
							Both sexes.		Male.		Female.	
	Both sexes.	Male.	Female.	Both sexes.	Male.	Female.	Negro.	White.	Negro.	White.	Negro.	White.
UNITED STATES.												
All ages	1,297,761	615,139	682,622	35,811	18,810	17,001	27.6	15.8	30.6	17.3	24.9	14.4
Under 5 years	99,850	49,193	50,657	9,501	5,071	4,430	95.2	45.2	103.1	49.0	87.5	41.3
Under 1 year	21,292	10,722	10,570	6,561	3,597	2,964	308.1	146.1	335.5	159.8	280.4	132.1
1 to 4 years	78,558	38,471	40,087	2,940	1,474	1,466	37.4	17.7	38.3	18.6	36.5	16.7
5 to 9 years	94,908	45,913	48,995	713	344	369	7.5	4.1	7.5	4.2	7.5	4.0
10 to 14 years	94,668	44,599	50,069	635	298	337	6.7	2.5	6.7	2.6	6.7	2.4
15 to 19 years	111,960	48,619	63,341	1,395	652	743	12.5	3.9	13.4	4.3	11.7	3.5
20 to 24 years	159,611	69,092	90,519	2,447	1,228	1,219	15.3	5.4	17.8	5.8	13.5	4.9
25 to 34 years	306,498	145,455	161,043	5,257	2,807	2,450	17.2	7.3	19.3	8.0	15.2	6.6
35 to 44 years	217,059	109,228	107,831	5,025	2,793	2,232	23.2	11.2	25.6	13.2	20.7	9.1
45 to 64 years	174,165	85,723	88,442	7,408	3,984	3,424	42.5	24.2	46.5	27.9	38.7	20.4
65 years and over	33,593	14,397	19,196	3,403	1,618	1,785	101.3	90.9	112.4	97.4	93.0	85.6
Age unknown	5,449	2,920	2,529	27	15	12	5.0	2.0	5.1	2.4	4.7	1.0
THE SOUTH.												
All ages	781,297	360,960	420,337	22,906	11,879	11,027	29.3	16.7	32.9	18.2	26.2	15.2
Under 5 years	63,100	31,061	32,039	5,953	3,168	2,785	94.3	40.5	102.0	43.4	86.9	37.5
Under 1 year	13,180	6,612	6,568	4,199	2,313	1,886	318.6	136.1	349.8	145.3	287.1	126.8
1 to 4 years	49,920	24,449	25,471	1,754	855	899	35.1	15.5	35.0	16.8	35.3	14.2
5 to 9 years	62,996	30,484	32,512	435	210	225	6.9	3.6	6.9	3.6	6.9	3.6
10 to 14 years	63,245	29,865	33,380	433	211	222	6.8	2.7	7.1	2.9	6.7	2.6
15 to 19 years	75,046	32,315	42,731	978	464	514	13.0	4.4	14.4	4.6	12.0	4.2
20 to 24 years	98,871	41,900	56,971	1,683	839	844	17.0	6.4	20.0	6.6	14.8	6.1
25 to 34 years	170,256	77,845	92,411	3,320	1,715	1,605	19.5	8.2	22.0	9.0	17.4	7.4
35 to 44 years	120,117	57,837	62,280	3,063	1,644	1,419	25.5	11.5	28.4	13.6	22.8	9.5
45 to 64 years	102,993	48,945	54,046	4,777	2,538	2,239	46.4	25.3	51.9	29.9	41.4	20.8
65 years and over	21,389	9,024	12,365	2,246	1,081	1,165	105.0	98.4	119.8	109.5	94.2	89.8
Age unknown	3,284	1,682	1,602	18	9	9	5.5	2.5	5.4	2.6	5.6	2.4
THE NORTH AND WEST.												
All ages	516,464	254,179	262,285	12,905	6,931	5,974	25.0	15.7	27.3	17.2	22.8	14.3
Under 5 years	36,750	18,132	18,618	3,548	1,903	1,645	96.5	45.8	105.0	49.7	88.4	41.8
Under 1 year	8,112	4,110	4,002	2,362	1,284	1,078	291.2	147.4	312.4	161.6	269.4	132.8
1 to 4 years	28,638	14,022	14,616	1,186	619	567	41.4	17.9	44.1	18.9	38.8	17.0
5 to 9 years	31,912	15,429	16,483	278	134	144	8.7	4.2	8.7	4.3	8.7	4.0
10 to 14 years	31,423	14,734	16,689	202	87	117	6.4	2.5	5.9	2.6	6.9	2.3
15 to 19 years	36,914	16,304	20,610	417	188	229	11.3	3.8	11.5	4.2	11.1	3.4
20 to 24 years	60,740	27,192	33,548	764	389	375	12.6	5.2	14.3	5.7	11.2	4.7
25 to 34 years	136,242	67,610	68,632	1,937	1,092	845	14.2	7.2	16.1	7.9	12.3	6.5
35 to 44 years	96,942	51,391	45,551	1,962	1,149	813	20.2	11.2	22.4	13.1	17.8	9.1
45 to 64 years	71,172	36,776	34,396	2,631	1,446	1,185	37.0	24.0	39.3	27.6	34.5	20.3
65 years and over	12,204	5,373	6,831	1,157	537	620	94.8	89.7	99.9	95.5	90.8	84.8
Age unknown	2,165	1,238	927	9	6	3	4.2	1.9	4.8	2.4	3.2	0.8

With reference to these aggregates of urban population, it appears: (1) That mortality among Negroes, male and female, in 1910 exceeded that among whites at each age period shown in southern and in northern and western cities; (2) that mortality among Negro males at all ages, with inconsiderable exceptions, exceeded mortality among Negro females in the South and in the North and West; (3) that among Negroes, male and female, infant mortality in the South exceeded infant mortality in the North and West, although mortality among Negro children 1 to 4 and 5 to 9 was slightly higher in the North and West; and (4) that in the adult Negro population male and female, mortality in the South exceeded mortality in the North and West.

The principal causes of death for the aggregate of Negro population in selected registration cities are shown in Table 22—the cities selected for this analysis being registration cities of 100,000 or more population in 1910, and of 2,500 or more Negro population.

Table 22

NEGRO DEATHS FROM SPECIFIED CAUSE: 1910.

CAUSE OF DEATH.	Number.		Distribution per 1,000.		Per 100,000 population.	
	Southern cities.[1]	Northern and western cities.[1]	Southern cities.[1]	Northern and western cities.[1]	Southern cities.[1]	Northern and western cities.[1]
All causes	15,955	11,393	1,000	1,000	2,893	2,514
Tuberculosis	2,602	2,507	163	220	472	553
Pneumonia	1,410	1,022	88	90	256	226
Violent deaths, except suicide	927	569	58	50	168	126
Diarrhea and enteritis (under 2 years)	851	656	53	58	154	145
Bronchopneumonia	558	557	35	49	101	123
Congenital debility	309	169	19	15	56	37
Bronchitis	263	226	16	20	48	50
Typhoid	237	111	15	10	43	25
Diarrhea and enteritis (2 years and over)	206	74	13	6	37	16
Influenza	206	59	13	5	37	13
Malaria	131	9	8	1	24	2
Meningitis	131	61	8	5	24	14
Whooping cough	129	123	8	11	23	27
Measles	41	58	3	5	7	13
Diphtheria	40	80	3	7	7	18
Suicide	33	52	2	5	6	12
Scarlet fever	16	24	1	2	3	5
Other causes	7,865	5,036	493	442	1,426	1,111

[1] Includes all registration cities of 100,000 or more population and having a Negro population of 2,500 or more in 1910.

On the average in northern and western cities in 1910 tuberculosis was the cause of death in 220 out of 1,000 cases of mortality, that is to say, in 4 or 5 cases of death in the population of all ages 1 death on the average resulted from tuberculosis and 3 or 4 deaths from all other causes combined. Tuberculosis was less predominant in southern cities, where the proportion was 163 deaths from this cause to 1,000 deaths from all causes, or approximately 1 death from tuberculosis to 5 deaths from all other causes combined. Per 100,000 population the death rate from tuberculosis in northern and western cities was 553 and in southern cities, 472.

Other causes of death showing a higher rate in northern and western than in southern cities included bronchopneumonia, bronchitis, whooping cough, measles, and diphtheria. The mortality for pneumonia was higher in southern than in northern and western cities, the number of deaths from this cause per 100,000 population being 256 in the South and 226 in the North and West. Other diseases showing higher rates for the southern cities included diarrhea and enteritis, congenital debility, typhoid, influenza, malaria, and meningitis.

Negro deaths under 1 year in the selected cities are classified in Table 23 by age in days, weeks, or months, for the years 1914 and 1910.

Table 23

NEGRO DEATHS UNDER 1 YEAR IN SELECTED REGISTRATION CITIES.[1]

AGE.	Number.		Distribution per 1,000.	
	Southern cities.	Northern and western cities.	Southern cities.	Northern and western cities.
1914				
Total under 1 year	2,286	2,355	1,000	1,000
Under 1 day	252	275	110	117
1 day, under 1 week	318	309	139	131
1 week, under 1 month	295	279	129	118
1 month, under 6 months	869	860	380	365
6 months and over	552	632	241	268
1910				
Total under 1 year	2,833	2,735	1,000	1,000
Under 1 day	214	213	76	78
1 day, under 1 week	364	343	128	125
1 week, under 1 month	368	317	130	116
1 month, under 6 months	1,197	1,023	423	374
6 months and over	690	839	244	307

[1] Includes all registration cities of 100,000 or more population having a Negro population of 2,500 or more in 1910.

In 1914 approximately one-fourth of the deaths under 1 year of age in southern and in northern and western cities were infants under 1 week old. Approximately three-fourths of the deaths under 1 year were of infants under 6 months old.

The distribution of infant deaths by the ages shown in Table 23 does not develop any very marked differences between southern and northern and western cities, but the proportion occurring at age under 1 day, in the total of infant deaths returned for 1914, very considerably exceeded the corresponding proportion for 1910. This may be due to stricter enforcement of death registration for infants in the registration area as defined in 1914 than obtained in the area as defined in 1910.

The principal causes of infant mortality in the aggregate population of the larger registration cities are shown in Table 24, deaths from each cause being classified by age in days, weeks, and months.

The most frequent cause of infant mortality shown in Table 24 is diarrhea and enteritis, the proportion of deaths from this cause being 252 in 1,000 deaths from all causes, or approximately 1 in 4. Other principal causes of infant mortality are premature birth, congenital debility, bronchopneumonia, and pneumonia.

Premature birth is given as the cause of death in 247 out of 397 cases of infant mortality under 1 day, the other chief causes of deaths under 1 day being congenital debility, injuries at birth, and malformations. Premature birth is the most frequent cause of death in the age period "1 day, under 1 week," congenital debility becoming an important cause in this period and the most frequent cause in the period "1 week, under 1 month." Diarrhea and enteritis become the predominant causes of death among infants more than 1 month old, other important causes after the first month being bronchopneumonia, pneumonia, and in the earlier months congenital debility.

Table 24

NEGRO DEATHS UNDER 1 YEAR IN SELECTED REGISTRATION CITIES[1]: 1910.

CAUSE OF DEATH	Total.		Under 1 day.	1 day, under 1 week.	1 week, under 1 mo.	1 mo., under 6 mos.	6 mos. and over.
	Number.	Distribution per 1,000.					
All causes	5,038	1,000	397	636	609	2,033	1,363
Diarrhea and enteritis	1,272	252	2	13	88	706	463
Premature birth	646	128	247	269	102	28	
Congenital debility	556	110	36	144	159	212	5
Bronchopneumonia	467	93		9	27	211	220
Pneumonia	392	78	1	12	32	175	172
Acute bronchitis	174	35	1	7	20	85	61
Convulsions	163	32	3	33	30	59	38
Syphilis	150	30	19	22	27	67	15
Whooping cough	109	22			2	45	62
Malformations	99	20	24	45	11	12	7
Tuberculosis	86	17		1	2	40	43
Diseases of the stomach	69	14		4	9	39	17
External causes	69	14	9	7	6	30	17
Injuries at birth	58	12	36	16	4	2	
Tetanus	51	10	2	21	27		1
Meningitis	44	9		2	5	18	19
Dysentery	22	4			1	11	10
Influenza	22	4		1	2	9	10
Diphtheria and croup	21	4			4	12	5
Measles	19	4			2	5	12
Organic diseases of the heart	12	2		1	1	6	4
Erysipelas	6	1			3	1	2
Scarlet fever	2	(2)				2	
Other and unknown	529	105	17	29	45	258	180

[1] Includes all registration cities of 100,000 or more population and having a Negro population of 2,500 or more in 1910.
[2] Less than 1 per 1,000.

MONTH OF INCIDENCE OF URBAN MORTALITY.

In Table 25 the 15,955 Negro deaths occurring in 1910 in the selected southern cities of the registration area, and the 11,393 Negro deaths in the selected northern and western cities, are classified according to months of incidence, the distribution per 1,000 by months being shown, and the rate of mortality per 100,000 population in each month, and per day. The monthly mortality rate tends to vary with the number of days in the month. This accidental fluctuation is eliminated in the average per day for each month.

In the southern cities January, February, and June were the months of maximum mortality rate,

and September the month of lowest mortality. In the northern and western cities, March and April were the months of highest, and September and October the months of lowest mortality.

Table 25

NEGRO DEATHS: 1910.[1]

MONTH.	Number.		Distribution per 1,000 by months.		Per 100,000 population.			
							Average per day.	
	Southern cities.	Northern and western cities.	Southern cities.	Northern and western cities.	Southern cities.	Northern and western cities.	Southern cities.	Northern and western cities.
Total, 1910.	15,955	11,393	1,000	1,000	2,893	2,514	7.9	6.9
January	1,478	1,041	92	91	268	230	8.6	7.4
February	1,295	942	81	83	235	208	8.4	7.4
March	1,377	1,101	86	97	250	243	8.1	7.8
April	1,306	1,032	82	91	237	228	7.9	7.6
May	1,341	963	84	85	243	213	7.8	6.9
June	1,399	954	88	84	254	211	8.5	7.0
July	1,384	1,002	87	88	251	221	8.1	7.1
August	1,313	894	82	78	238	197	7.7	6.4
September	1,126	808	71	71	204	178	6.8	5.9
October	1,249	831	78	73	227	183	7.3	5.9
November	1,336	860	84	75	242	190	8.1	6.3
December	1,351	965	85	85	245	213	7.9	6.9

[1] Includes all registration cities of 100,000 or more population and having a Negro population of 2,500 or more in 1910.

MORTALITY BY REGISTRATION STATES.

The Negro and white death rate in the several states of the registration area in 1910 and in 1900 is given in Table 26. None of the Southern states was included in the area in 1900, and only two Southern states, Maryland and North Carolina (municipalities of 1,000 or more population), were included in the area in 1910.

In Maryland, with a Negro population of 232,657, the death rate in 1910 was 23 for Negroes and 14.5 for whites. In Pennsylvania, with a Negro population of 194,646, the death rate was 24 for Negroes, and 15.4 for whites. In each of the other states reporting a considerable Negro population a similar difference in mortality obtained between Negroes and whites.

In New York state, whose Negro population in 1900 exceeded that of any other registration state, the rate of Negro mortality per 1,000 population declined from 27.6 in 1900 to 24.9 in 1910. In New Jersey, also, which reported the second largest Negro population in 1900, the rate declined slightly from 23.9 to 23, while in Indiana, which reported the third largest population in 1900, the rate increased from 21.7 to 23.7.

In a majority of the Northern states, however, the Negro populations are too small to establish rates as generally characteristic of conditions obtaining within the states severally. Variations from state to state, and changes within any state during the decade, may represent in the main differences in age composition of the population groups compared.

Table 26

STATE.	NEGRO POPULATION.		NEGRO DEATHS IN CALENDAR YEAR.		DEATHS PER 1,000 POPULATION.			
					Negro.		White.	
	July 1, 1910 (estimate).	June 1, 1900.	1910	1900	1910	1900	1910	1900
Total...........	1,182,654	388,198	27,932	9,954	23.6	24.1	14.6	17.1
California.............	21,816	......	442	......	20.3	.....	13.5	.....
Colorado.............	11,531	......	289	......	25.1	.....	13.6	.....
Connecticut..........	15,233	15,226	373	352	24.5	23.1	15.5	17.9
District of Columbia..	94,763	86,702	2,759	2,685	29.1	31.0	15.8	18.3
Indiana..............	60,408	57,505	1,433	1,250	23.7	21.7	13.2	14.0
Maine................	1,365	1,319	19	24	13.9	18.2	17.1	17.1
Maryland............	232,657	......	5,343	......	23.0	.....	14.5	.....
Massachusetts........	38,189	31,974	809	681	21.2	21.3	16.0	18.2
Michigan............	17,165	15,816	426	290	24.8	18.3	14.1	14.0
Minnesota...........	7,107	......	135	......	19.0	.....	10.9	.....
Montana.............	1,848	......	43	......	23.3	.....	10.8	.....
New Hampshire.......	565	662	14	8	24.8	12.1	17.3	18.6
New Jersey...........	90,248	69,844	2,073	1,666	23.0	23.9	15.2	17.5
New York............	134,764	99,232	3,350	2,743	24.9	27.6	16.0	18.1
North Carolina [1].....	127,216	......	3,024	......	23.8	.....	15.9	.....
Ohio.................	111,755	......	2,260	......	20.2	.....	13.5	.....
Pennsylvania........	194,646	......	4,669	......	24.0	.....	15.4	.....
Rhode Island..........	9,571	9,092	248	238	25.9	26.2	16.9	20.3
Utah.................	1,150	......	32	......	27.8	.....	10.8	.....
Vermont.............	1,622	826	29	17	17.9	20.6	16.0	16.6
Washington..........	6,128	......	97	......	15.8	.....	9.8	.....
Wisconsin...........	2,907	......	65	......	22.4	.....	12.0	.....

[1] Includes only municipalities having 1,000 population and over in 1900.

Table 27 shows the death rate in 1910 for Negroes and for the nativity and parentage classes of the whites, by states.

Table 27

REGISTRATION STATES AND DISTRICT OF COLUMBIA: 1910.

STATE.	Negro population, Apr. 15, 1910.	Negro deaths, calendar year 1910.	Deaths per 1,000 population of specified class.				
			Negro.	Native white.			For-eign-born white.
				Native parentage.	Foreign parentage.	Mixed parentage.	
Total..........	1,075,736	25,532	23.7	14.2	14.0	11.6	17.0
California.............	21,645	442	20.4	13.4	9.9	10.1	18.4
Colorado.............	11,453	289	25.2	12.9	12.0	11.2	19.6
Connecticut..........	15,174	373	24.6	17.1	15.2	12.7	14.8
District of Columbia...	94,446	2,759	29.2	15.3	12.4	10.4	27.5
Indiana..............	60,320	1,433	23.8	12.6	12.2	11.7	24.6
Maine...............	1,363	19	13.9	17.3	18.0	16.9	16.1
Maryland............	232,250	5,343	23.0	13.5	12.8	13.7	24.0
Massachusetts.......	38,055	809	21.3	17.5	15.7	13.7	15.6
Michigan............	17,115	426	24.9	14.9	10.5	10.9	18.1
Minnesota...........	7,084	135	19.1	11.6	7.3	8.3	16.0
Montana.............	1,834	43	23.4	11.0	9.3	9.2	12.4
New Hampshire.....	564	14	24.8	19.4	16.8	13.2	14.1
New Jersey..........	89,760	2,073	23.1	15.3	15.7	12.2	16.0
New York...........	134,191	3,350	25.0	16.1	16.4	13.0	16.6
North Carolina......	126,566	3,024	23.9	[1]16.7	[1]20.9	[1]18.8	[1]25.1
Ohio................	111,452	2,260	20.3	12.8	13.8	9.2	19.7
Pennsylvania........	193,919	4,669	24.1	14.0	19.3	14.7	16.3
Rhode Island........	9,529	248	26.0	19.0	17.1	15.1	15.6
Utah................	1,144	32	28.0	10.4	7.5	7.5	19.2
Vermont.............	1,621	29	17.9	16.7	13.3	11.6	18.1
Washington.........	6,058	97	16.0	10.3	7.6	8.2	11.6
Wisconsin...........	2,900	65	22.4	12.0	7.8	8.2	20.3

[1] Does not include cities of less than 10,000 inhabitants or rural districts in North Carolina.

The rates in this table are figured upon the population as enumerated on April 15, 1910, no estimate being undertaken of the population on July 1, for the several parentage and nativity classes. This change of population base accounts for the slight difference between the rates shown in Table 27 and those shown in Table 26 for the Negro population.

In 6 of the registration states in 1910—namely, Indiana, Maine, Maryland, Montana, North Carolina, and Vermont—the death rate of the foreign-born white population exceeded that of the Negro population, and in several other states the foreign-born white rate approximated the Negro rate. In 1 state—Maine, which reported a Negro population in 1910 of only 1,363—the death rate for Negroes (13.9) was lower than that for any other class of the population. In 2 states, native whites of native parentage showed the lowest rate; in 6 states, native whites of foreign parentage, and in 11 states and the District of Columbia, native whites of mixed parentage; in Utah the lowest rate, 7.5, being that for native whites of foreign parentage and also for native whites of mixed parentage.

In Table 28 infant mortality in the Negro and white population is shown for registration states reporting 100 or more Negro deaths under 1 year of age in 1910.

Table 28

STATE.	POPULATION UNDER 1 YEAR OF AGE APRIL 15, 1910.		DEATHS UNDER 1 YEAR OF AGE IN CALENDAR YEAR 1910.		Per 1,000 population under 1 year.		
	Negro.	White.	Negro.	White.	Negro.	White.	Excess Negro over white.
Dist. Columbia..	1,458	4,025	581	489	398.5	121.0	277.5
Indiana.........	987	55,107	218	5,777	220.8	104.8	116.0
Maryland.......	5,310	22,552	1,264	2,975	238.0	131.9	106.1
Massachusetts...	769	69,934	139	11,235	180.7	160.7	20.0
New Jersey......	1,729	54,465	504	7,858	291.5	144.3	147.2
New York.......	2,300	189,072	709	26,784	308.3	141.7	166.6
Ohio...........	1,857	96,912	356	11,089	191.7	114.4	77.3
Pennsylvania...	3,741	185,751	1,063	27,313	284.1	147.0	137.1

In the Negro population of the District of Columbia under 1 year of age in 1910 the number of deaths per 1,000 population was 398.5. The Negro infant mortality rate of the District in this year exceeded that of any of the registration states shown in Table 28. The infant mortality rate for New York state was 308.3 among Negroes and 141.7 among whites; in New Jersey 291.5 among Negroes and 144.3 among whites; in Pennsylvania 284.1 among Negroes and 147 among whites; in Maryland 238 among Negroes and 131.9 among whites; in Indiana 220.8 among Negroes and 104.8 among whites; in Ohio 191.7 among Negroes and 114.4 among whites; and in Massachusetts 180.7 among Negroes and 160.7 among whites.

In Massachusetts the Negro rate most nearly approximates that for the white population, the excess of the Negro over the white rate being only 20 in Massachusetts as compared with 277.5 in the District of Columbia, 166.6 in New York, 147.2 in New Jersey, and large differences in other states.

MORTALITY BY REGISTRATION CITIES.

Table 29 gives the number of Negro and white deaths, and the death rate per 1,000 population for 57 registration cities in 1910 and 1900. The table embraces all registration cities having a Negro population of at least 2,500 in 1910, for which comparable data were available covering the two years.

NEGRO AND WHITE DEATHS, AND DEATH RATES, BY CITIES: 1910 AND 1900.

Table 29 CITY.	NUMBER OF DEATHS.				DEATH RATE PER 1,000 POPULATION.				INCREASE (+) OR DECREASE (−) PER 1,000 POPULATION: 1900–1910.	
	1910		1900		1910		1900			
	Negro.	White.	Negro.	White.	Negro.	White.	Negro.	White.	Negro.	White.
Total for 57 cities [1]	33,803	270,546	30,658	236,516	27.8	15.9	31.2	18.4	−3.4	−2.5
NORTHERN AND WESTERN CITIES.										
Total for 33 cities	12,483	237,421	9,891	205,868	25.1	15.7	27.1	18.2	−2.0	−2.5
Atlantic City, N. J	172	627	106	375	17.3	17.1	16.3	17.6	+1.0	−0.5
Boston, Mass	317	11,224	312	11,100	23.3	17.1	26.9	20.3	−3.6	−3.2
Cambridge, Mass	75	1,501	105	1,466	15.9	15.0	27.0	16.7	−11.1	−1.7
Camden, N. J	192	1,437	186	1,182	31.5	16.2	33.4	16.8	−1.9	−0.6
Chicago, Ill	1,075	32,130	712	25,337	24.3	15.0	23.6	15.2	+0.7	−0.2
Cincinnati, Ohio	569	5,750	430	5,496	28.9	16.7	29.7	17.6	−0.8	−0.9
Cleveland, Ohio	167	7,880	99	6,627	19.6	14.2	16.5	17.6	+3.1	−3.4
Columbus, Ohio	262	2,548	187	1,801	20.4	15.0	22.8	15.3	−2.4	−0.3
Dayton, Ohio	99	1,625	68	1,267	20.4	14.5	20.1	15.5	+0.3	−1.0
Denver, Colo	132	3,389	89	2,444	24.1	16.2	22.7	18.9	+1.4	−2.7
Detroit, Mich	146	7,305	103	4,552	25.2	15.8	25.1	16.2	+0.1	−0.4
Evansville, Ind	117	831	150	781	18.9	13.5	20.0	15.2	−1.1	−1.7
Harrisburg, Pa	98	842	104	800	21.5	14.1	25.3	17.4	−3.8	−3.3
Indianapolis, Ind	548	3,275	383	2,503	25.0	15.4	24.0	16.3	+1.0	−0.9
Jersey City, N. J	123	4,278	83	4,191	20.5	16.3	22.4	20.7	−1.9	−4.4
Kansas City, Mo	644	3,317	438	2,236	27.1	14.7	24.9	15.3	+2.2	−0.6
Los Angeles, Cal	136	4,299	62	1,809	17.6	13.9	29.1	18.4	−11.5	−4.5
Minneapolis, Minn	56	3,681	22	2,286	21.5	12.2	14.2	11.4	+7.3	+0.8
Newark, N. J	296	5,484	202	4,755	31.1	16.1	30.2	19.9	+0.9	−3.8
New Bedford, Mass	85	1,727	32	1,293	29.2	18.3	19.0	21.3	+10.2	−3.0
New Haven, Conn	91	2,126	82	1,886	25.5	16.3	28.4	18.0	−2.9	−1.7
New York, N. Y	2,391	74,274	1,950	68,799	25.9	15.8	32.1	20.4	−6.2	−4.6
Manhattan Borough	1,473	37,129	1,242	38,146	24.2	16.3	34.3	21.1	−10.1	−4.8
Bronx Borough	208	6,755	75	3,674	50.0	15.7	31.6	18.6	+18.4	−2.9
Brooklyn Borough	598	25,070	533	22,932	26.2	15.5	29.0	20.0	−2.8	−4.5
Queens Borough	82	3,882	66	2,702	25.4	13.7	25.3	18.0	+0.1	−4.3
Richmond Borough	30	1,438	34	1,345	25.9	16.9	31.7	20.4	−5.8	−3.5
Oakland, Cal	52	1,791	19	1,031	16.8	12.5	18.5	15.9	+1.7	−3.4
Omaha, Nebr	105	1,769	67	1,141	23.6	14.7	19.5	11.5	−4.1	+3.2
Philadelphia, Pa	2,276	24,740	1,894	25,055	26.9	16.8	30.2	20.4	−3.3	−3.6
Pittsburgh, Pa.[2]	601	8,993	526	8,290	23.4	17.7	25.8	19.2	−2.4	−1.5
Providence, R. I	139	3,837	140	3,513	26.0	17.5	29.1	20.6	−3.1	−3.1
St. Joseph, Mo	98	957	68	701	23.0	13.0	10.9	7.2	+12.1	+5.8
St. Louis, Mo	1,149	9,733	1,096	9,223	26.0	15.1	30.9	17.1	−4.9	−2.0
St. Paul, Minn	49	2,508	30	1,601	15.5	11.8	13.3	10.0	+2.2	+1.8
Springfield, Ill	67	793	57	548	22.5	16.2	25.6	17.1	−3.1	−0.9
Terre Haute, Ind	67	864	40	557	25.7	15.5	26.3	15.8	−0.6	−0.3
Trenton, N. J	89	1,886	49	1,222	34.3	19.9	23.4	17.2	+10.9	+2.7
SOUTHERN CITIES.										
Total for 24 cities	21,320	33,125	20,767	30,648	29.6	16.9	33.6	19.8	−4.0	−2.9
Alexandria, Va	138	189	160	205	32.9	17.0	35.3	20.5	−2.4	−3.5
Annapolis, Md	97	83	126	110	30.5	15.3	42.0	20.0	−11.5	−4.7
Atlanta, Ga	1,328	1,609	977	1,006	25.4	15.5	27.3	18.6	−1.9	−3.1
Baltimore, Md	2,597	8,152	2,653	8,242	30.6	17.2	33.5	19.2	−2.9	−2.0
Charleston, S. C	1,221	526	1,399	554	39.3	18.9	44.4	22.9	−5.1	−4.0
Covington, Ky	59	802	81	743	20.3	15.9	32.6	18.4	−12.3	−2.5
Jacksonville, Fla	710	482	532	324	24.0	16.8	32.8	26.6	−8.8	−9.8
Key West, Fla	147	301	147	271	26.6	20.8	26.4	23.5	+0.2	−2.7
Louisville, Ky	1,089	2,667	1,070	2,802	26.7	14.4	27.3	16.9	−0.6	−2.5
Lynchburg, Va	231	242	298	218	24.3	12.0	36.1	20.5	−11.8	−8.5
Memphis, Tenn	1,492	1,326	1,218	1,084	28.3	16.8	24.4	20.7	+3.9	−3.9
Mobile, Ala	673	512	564	481	29.4	17.7	33.1	22.5	−3.7	−4.8
Nashville, Tenn	950	1,113	965	956	26.0	15.0	32.1	18.8	−6.1	−3.8
Norfolk, Va	775	700	770	496	30.8	16.5	38.1	18.8	−7.3	−2.3
New Orleans, La	2,933	4,311	3,184	4,420	32.8	17.2	41.0	21.2	−8.2	−4.0
Paducah, Ky	164	274	224	323	27.0	16.3	38.5	23.7	−11.5	−7.4
Petersburg, Va	377	264	379	279	34.2	20.1	35.3	25.2	−1.1	−5.1
Raleigh, N. C	247	290	227	183	33.4	24.4	39.7	23.1	−6.3	+1.3
Richmond, Va	1,416	1,470	1,214	1,251	30.2	18.1	37.7	23.7	−7.5	−5.6
San Antonio, Tex	233	1,917	171	1,038	21.5	22.1	22.7	22.7	−1.2	−0.6
Savannah, Ga	1,134	616	1,070	612	34.1	19.4	38.1	23.4	−4.0	−4.0
Washington, D. C	2,759	3,744	2,685	3,511	29.1	15.8	31.0	18.3	−1.9	−2.5
Wilmington, Del	225	1,322	269	1,277	24.7	16.8	27.6	19.1	−2.9	−2.3
Wilmington, N. C	325	213	384	262	26.7	15.6	36.9	24.8	−10.2	−9.2

[1] Includes all cities for which data were available for 1900 and for 1910 which reported in 1910 a Negro population of 2,500 or more.   [2] Includes Allegheny, 1900.

In 15 of the 33 northern and western cities, the Negro death rate was higher and in 18 cities it was lower in 1910 than it was in 1900. In each of the 24 southern cities with exception of two the Negro death rate was lower in 1910 than in 1900.

In each of the 57 cities the Negro death rate exceeded the white in 1910, and also, with two exceptions, in 1900, the difference in the case of most cities being very considerable. In the group of southern cities the Negro death rate in 1910 ranged from 20.3 in Covington, Ky., to 39.3 in Charleston, S. C.; and in the group of northern cities from 15.5 in St. Paul, Minn., to 34.3 in Trenton, N. J.

In 10 southern and in 3 northern cities the Negro death rate in 1910 exceeded 30, the maximum rate for any city being that of 39.3 for Charleston, S. C. In 1900 the Negro rate exceeded 30 in 18 of the southern cities and in 5 of the northern cities, and in 3 southern cities exceeded 40. The lowest rate shown for any southern city in 1900 was that of 22.7 for San Antonio, Tex. The average Negro death rate for the southern cities as a group declined from 33.6 in 1900 to 29.6 in 1910; and for the northern cities from 27.1 to 25.1.

GENERAL TABLES.

The general tables, numbered 30 to 39, present statistics of mortality in detail for areas of death registration.

Reference has been made to Table 30, which gives, by states, the Negro population of the registration area, and of the nonregistration area in 1915, 1910, and 1900; and to the Negro life tables (Tables 31a and 31b).

Table 32 gives, for the registration states and for selected registration cities, the Negro and white population, and deaths, and deaths per 1,000 population, for the two years 1910 and 1900.

Table 33 gives, for Negroes, native whites of native parentage, native whites of foreign parentage, and foreign-born whites, the population, number of deaths, and deaths per 1,000 population in 1910, for registration cities having a total population of 10,000 or more and a Negro population of 2,500 or more.

Table 34 gives data, by age periods, for these same cities.

Table 35 gives, for selected registration cities, the number of Negro deaths in each year 1910–1914, and in 1900, and the number and percentage of deaths under 1 year and under 5 years.

Table 36 classifies Negro deaths in 1910, by month of incidence, for selected cities.

Table 37 classifies Negro deaths in 1913, by sex and cause of death, for registration states and for selected registration cities.

Table 38 classifies Negro and white deaths in 1910, both sexes combined, by cause of death, for the registration states and for selected registration cities.

Table 39 classifies Negro deaths in each year 1910–1914, and 1900, by sex and age, for registration states and selected registration cities.

DIAGRAM **VII.**—MONTHLY RATE OF MORTALITY PER 1,000, FOR NEGRO AND WHITE MALES AND FEMALES ($1000q_x$), FOR FIRST YEAR OF LIFE, BY AGE INTERVALS OF ONE MONTH.

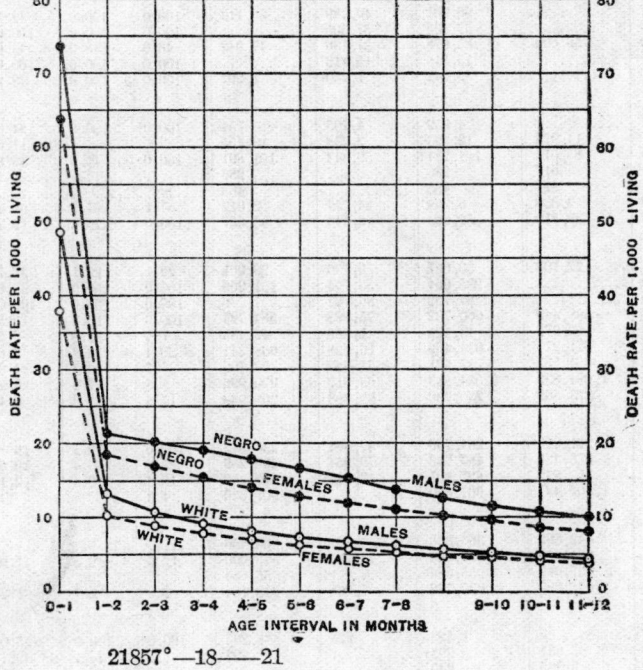

21857°—18——21

Table 30.—NEGRO POPULATION OF THE REGISTRATION AREA AND OF THE NONREGISTRATION AREA, AND PERCENTAGE IN THE AREA, BY DIVISIONS AND STATES: 1915, 1910, AND 1900.

DIVISION AND STATE.	NEGRO POPULATION.								Percentage in registration area.		
	1910					1900					
	Total.	Registration area: 1915.	Nonregistration area: 1915.	Registration area: 1910.	Nonregistration area: 1910.	Total.	Registration area: 1900.	Nonregistration area: 1900.	1915[1]	1910	1900
UNITED STATES	9,827,763	2,987,817	6,839,946	1,935,976	7,891,787	8,833,994	1,189,023	7,644,971	30.4	19.7	13.5
GEOGRAPHIC DIVISIONS:											
New England	66,306	66,306		66,306		59,099	59,099		100.0	100.0	100.0
Middle Atlantic	417,870	417,870		417,870		325,921	266,867	59,054	100.0	100.0	81.9
East North Central	300,836	244,137	56,699	244,137	56,699	257,842	152,496	105,346	81.2	81.2	59.1
West North Central	242,662	223,725	18,937	98,238	144,424	237,909	76,389	161,520	92.2	40.5	32.1
South Atlantic	4,112,488	1,363,840	2,748,648	717,203	3,395,285	3,729,017	390,562	3,338,455	33.2	17.4	10.5
East South Central	2,652,513	519,294	2,133,219	241,029	2,411,484	2,499,886	144,863	2,355,023	19.6	9.1	5.8
West South Central	1,984,426	109,466	1,874,960	108,014	1,876,412	1,694,066	85,252	1,608,814	5.5	5.4	5.0
Mountain	21,467	14,431	7,036	14,431	7,036	15,590	5,837	9,753	67.2	67.2	37.4
Pacific	29,195	28,748	447	28,748	447	14,664	7,658	7,006	98.5	98.5	52.2
NEW ENGLAND:											
Maine	1,363	1,363		1,363		1,319	1,319		100.0	100.0	100.0
New Hampshire	564	564		564		662	662		100.0	100.0	100.0
Vermont	1,621	1,621		1,621		826	826		100.0	100.0	100.0
Massachusetts	38,055	38,055		38,055		31,974	31,974		100.0	100.0	100.0
Rhode Island	9,529	9,529		9,529		9,092	9,092		100.0	100.0	100.0
Connecticut	15,174	15,174		15,174		15,226	15,226		100.0	100.0	100.0
MIDDLE ATLANTIC:											
New York	134,191	134,191		134,191		99,232	99,232		100.0	100.0	100.0
New Jersey	89,760	89,760		89,760		69,844	69,844		100.0	100.0	100.0
Pennsylvania	193,919	193,919		193,919		156,845	97,791	59,054	100.0	100.0	62.3
EAST NORTH CENTRAL:											
Ohio	111,452	111,452		111,452		96,901	40,789	56,112	100.0	100.0	42.1
Indiana	60,320	60,320		60,320		57,505	57,505		100.0	100.0	100.0
Illinois	109,049	52,350	56,699	52,350	56,699	85,078	37,136	47,942	48.0	48.0	43.6
Michigan	17,115	17,115		17,115		15,816	15,816		100.0	100.0	100.0
Wisconsin	2,900	2,900		2,900		2,542	1,250	1,292	100.0	100.0	49.2
WEST NORTH CENTRAL:											
Minnesota	7,084	7,084		7,084		4,959	4,205	754	100.0	100.0	84.8
Iowa	14,973		14,973		14,973	12,693	2,238	10,455			17.6
Missouri	157,452	157,452		71,775	85,677	161,234	59,343	101,891	100.0	45.6	36.8
North Dakota	617		617		617	286		286			
South Dakota	817		817		817	465		465			
Nebraska	7,689	5,159	2,530	5,159	2,530	6,269	4,257	2,012	67.1	67.1	67.9
Kansas	54,030	54,030		14,220	39,810	52,003	6,346	45,657	100.0	26.3	12.2
SOUTH ATLANTIC:											
Delaware	31,181	9,081	22,100	9,081	22,100	30,697	9,736	20,961	29.1	29.1	31.7
Maryland	232,250	232,250		232,250		235,064	83,795	151,269	100.0	100.0	35.6
District of Columbia	94,446	94,446		94,446		86,702	86,702		100.0	100.0	100.0
Virginia	671,096	671,096		102,647	568,449	660,722	75,998	584,724	100.0	15.3	11.5
West Virginia	64,173	1,201	62,972	1,201	62,972	43,499	1,066	42,433	1.9	1.9	2.5
North Carolina	697,843	142,507	555,336	126,566	571,277	624,469	16,128	608,341	20.4	18.3	2.6
South Carolina	835,843	55,794	780,049	31,056	804,787	782,321	31,522	750,799	6.7	3.7	4.0
Georgia	1,176,987	103,492	1,073,495	85,148	1,091,839	1,034,813	63,817	970,996	8.8	7.2	6.2
Florida	308,669	53,973	254,696	34,808	273,861	230,730	21,798	208,932	17.5	11.3	9.4
EAST SOUTH CENTRAL:											
Kentucky	261,656	261,656		50,037	211,619	284,706	47,864	236,842	100.0	19.1	16.8
Tennessee	473,088	120,263	352,825	96,602	376,486	480,243	79,954	400,289	25.4	20.4	16.6
Alabama	908,282	94,390	813,892	94,390	813,892	827,307	17,045	810,262	10.4	10.4	2.1
Mississippi	1,009,487	42,985	966,502		1,009,487	907,630		907,630	4.3		
WEST SOUTH CENTRAL:											
Arkansas	442,891		442,891		442,891	366,856		366,856			
Louisiana	713,874	89,262	624,612	89,262	624,612	650,804	77,714	573,090	12.5	12.5	11.9
Oklahoma	137,612		137,612		137,612	55,684		55,684			
Texas	690,049	20,204	669,845	18,752	671,297	620,722	7,538	613,184	2.9	2.7	1.2
MOUNTAIN:											
Montana	1,834	1,834		1,834		1,523	228	1,295	100.0	100.0	15.0
Idaho	651		651		651	293		293			
Wyoming	2,235		2,235		2,235	940		940			
Colorado	11,453	11,453		11,453		8,570	5,331	3,239	100.0	100.0	62.2
New Mexico	1,628		1,628		1,628	1,610		1,610			
Arizona	2,009		2,009		2,009	1,848		1,848			
Utah	1,144	1,144		1,144		672	278	394	100.0	100.0	41.4
Nevada	513		513		513	134		134			
PACIFIC:											
Washington	6,058	6,058		6,058		2,514	713	1,801	100.0	100.0	28.4
Oregon	1,492	1,045	447	1,045	447	1,105	775	330	70.0	70.0	70.1
California	21,645	21,645		21,645		11,045	6,170	4,875	100.0	100.0	56.0

[1] Percentage based on 1910 population.

TABLE 31a.—LIFE TABLE FOR NEGRO MALES IN THE ORIGINAL REGISTRATION STATES: 1910.

[Based on the estimated population July 1, 1910 (223,884), and on the reported deaths in 1909 (5,531), in 1910 (6,052), and in 1911 (5,888). The original registration states include Maine, New Hampshire, Vermont, Massachusetts, Rhode Island, Connecticut, New York, New Jersey, Indiana, and Michigan, and the District of Columbia.]

AGE INTERVAL.	OF 100,000 MALES BORN ALIVE:		RATE OF MORTALITY PER THOUSAND.	COMPLETE EXPECTATION OF LIFE.	STATIONARY MALE POPULATION, UNAFFECTED BY EMIGRATION AND IMMIGRATION, WHICH, ASSUMING THE MORTALITY RATES IN COLUMN 4, WOULD RESULT IF 100,000 MALES WERE BORN ALIVE UNIFORMLY THROUGHOUT EACH YEAR.			
Period of lifetime between two exact ages.	Number alive at beginning of age interval.	Number dying in age interval.	Number dying in age interval among 1,000 alive at beginning of age interval.	Average length of life remaining to each one alive at beginning of age interval.	Population living in age interval.	Population living in age interval to one annual death in same age interval.	Total population living in current and all higher age intervals.	Average death rate per thousand of the total population living in current and all higher age intervals.
x to $x+1$	l_x	d_x	$1000q_x$	$\overset{\circ}{e}_x$	L_x	L_x/d_x	T_x	$1000/\overset{\circ}{e}_x$
1	2	3	4	5	6	7	8	9

INFANT MORTALITY—FIRST YEAR OF LIFE BY AGE INTERVALS OF ONE MONTH.

Months.			Monthly rate.	In years.				Annual rate.
0-1	100 000	7 370	73.70	34.05	7 873	1.07	3 405 206	29.37
1-2	92 630	1 977	21.35	36.68	7 637	3.86	3 397 333	27.26
2-3	90 653	1 831	20.19	37.39	7 478	4.08	3 389 696	26.75
3-4	88 822	1 695	19.09	38.08	7 331	4.33	3 382 218	26.26
4-5	87 127	1 561	17.91	38.74	7 196	4.61	3 374 887	25.81
5-6	85 566	1 425	16.66	39.36	7 071	4.96	3 367 691	25.41
6-7	84 141	1 290	15.33	39.94	6 958	5.39	3 360 620	25.04
7-8	82 851	1 153	13.93	40.48	6 856	5.95	3 353 662	24.70
8-9	81 698	1 037	12.69	40.97	6 765	6.52	3 346 806	24.41
9-10	80 661	937	11.62	41.41	6 683	7.13	3 340 041	24.15
10-11	79 724	857	10.75	41.81	6 608	7.71	3 333 358	23.92
11-12	78 867	802	10.16	42.18	6 539	8.15	3 326 750	23.71

LIFE TABLE FOR WHOLE RANGE OF LIFE BY AGE INTERVALS OF ONE YEAR.

Years.			Annual rate.	In years.				Annual rate.
0-1	100 000	21 935	219.35	34.05	84 995	3.87	3 405 206	29.37
1-2	78 065	5 216	66.82	42.53	74 988	14.38	3 320 211	23.51
2-3	72 849	2 341	32.14	44.55	71 608	30.59	3 245 223	22.45
3-4	70 508	1 197	16.97	45.01	69 885	58.38	3 173 615	22.22
4-5	69 311	722	10.42	44.78	68 936	95.48	3 103 730	22.33
5-6	68 589	587	8.56	44.25	68 295	116.35	3 034 794	22.60
6-7	68 002	492	7.22	43.62	67 756	137.72	2 966 499	22.93
7-8	67 510	420	6.22	42.94	67 300	160.24	2 898 743	23.29
8-9	67 090	371	5.53	42.20	66 905	180.34	2 831 443	23.70
9-10	66 719	342	5.14	41.44	66 548	194.58	2 764 538	24.13
10-11	66 377	334	5.02	40.65	66 210	198.23	2 697 990	24.60
11-12	66 043	342	5.18	39.85	65 872	192.61	2 631 780	25.09
12-13	65 701	366	5.58	39.05	65 518	179.01	2 565 908	25.61
13-14	65 335	405	6.19	38.27	65 133	160.82	2 500 390	26.13
14-15	64 930	452	6.97	37.51	64 704	143.15	2 435 257	26.66
15-16	64 478	508	7.87	36.77	64 224	126.43	2 370 553	27.20
16-17	63 970	565	8.84	36.05	63 687	112.72	2 306 329	27.74
17-18	63 405	619	9.75	35.37	63 095	101.93	2 242 642	28.27
18-19	62 786	661	10.53	34.71	62 456	94.49	2 179 547	28.81
19-20	62 125	699	11.26	34.08	61 775	88.38	2 117 091	29.34
20-21	61 426	735	11.96	33.46	61 059	83.07	2 055 316	29.89
21-22	60 691	751	12.39	32.86	60 315	80.31	1 994 257	30.43
22-23	59 940	748	12.47	32.26	59 566	79.63	1 933 942	31.00
23-24	59 192	734	12.39	31.67	58 825	80.14	1 874 376	31.58
24-25	58 458	722	12.35	31.06	58 097	80.47	1 815 551	32.20
25-26	57 736	709	12.28	30.44	57 382	80.93	1 757 454	32.85
26-27	57 027	706	12.40	29.81	56 674	80.27	1 700 072	33.55
27-28	56 321	722	12.82	29.18	55 960	77.51	1 643 398	34.27
28-29	55 599	750	13.48	28.55	55 224	73.63	1 587 438	35.03
29-30	54 849	776	14.16	27.94	54 461	70.18	1 532 214	35.79
30-31	54 073	809	14.96	27.33	53 668	66.34	1 477 753	36.59
31-32	53 264	837	15.71	26.74	52 845	63.14	1 424 085	37.40
32-33	52 427	850	16.22	26.16	52 002	61.18	1 371 240	38.23
33-34	51 577	854	16.55	25.58	51 150	59.89	1 319 238	39.09
34-35	50 723	858	16.92	25.00	50 294	58.62	1 268 088	40.00
35-36	49 865	862	17.28	24.42	49 434	57.35	1 217 794	40.95
36-37	49 003	868	17.73	23.84	48 569	55.96	1 168 360	41.95
37-38	48 135	885	18.38	23.26	47 692	53.89	1 119 791	42.99
38-39	47 250	907	19.19	22.69	46 797	51.60	1 072 099	44.07
39-40	46 343	929	20.05	22.12	45 878	49.38	1 025 302	45.21
40-41	45 414	955	21.03	21.57	44 936	47.05	979 424	46.36
41-42	44 459	973	21.89	21.02	43 972	45.19	934 488	47.57
42-43	43 486	977	22.47	20.48	42 997	44.01	890 516	48.83
43-44	42 509	973	22.89	19.94	42 022	43.19	847 519	50.15
44-45	41 536	973	23.42	19.39	41 049	42.19	805 497	51.57

TABLE 31a.—LIFE TABLE FOR NEGRO MALES IN THE ORIGINAL REGISTRATION STATES: 1910.

[Based on the estimated population July 1, 1910 (223,884), and on the reported deaths in 1909 (5,531), in 1910 (6,052), and in 1911 (5,888). The original registration states include Maine, New Hampshire, Vermont, Massachusetts, Rhode Island, Connecticut, New York, New Jersey, Indiana, and Michigan, and the District of Columbia.]

AGE INTERVAL.	OF 100,000 MALES BORN ALIVE:		RATE OF MORTALITY PER THOUSAND.	COMPLETE EXPECTATION OF LIFE.	STATIONARY MALE POPULATION, Unaffected by Emigration and Immigration, which, Assuming the Mortality Rates in Column 4, would result if 100,000 Males were Born Alive Uniformly Throughout Each Year.			
Period of lifetime between two exact ages.	Number alive at beginning of age interval.	Number dying in age interval.	Number dying in age interval among 1,000 alive at beginning of age interval.	Average length of life remaining to each one alive at beginning of age interval.	Population living in age interval.	Population living in age interval to one annual death in same age interval.	Total population living in current and all higher age intervals.	Average death rate per thousand of the total population living in current and all higher age intervals.
x to $x+1$	l_x	d_x	$1000q_x$	$\overset{\circ}{e}_x$	L_x	L_x/d_x	T_x	$1000/\overset{\circ}{e}_x$
1	2	3	4	5	6	7	8	9

LIFE TABLE FOR WHOLE RANGE OF LIFE BY AGE INTERVALS OF ONE YEAR—Continued.

Years.			Annual rate.	In years.				Annual rate.
45-46	40 563	973	23.99	18.85	40 076	41.19	764 448	53.05
46-47	39 590	988	24.96	18.30	39 096	39.57	724 372	54.64
47-48	38 602	1 023	26.49	17.75	38 090	37.23	685 276	56.34
48-49	37 579	1 061	28.24	17.22	37 048	34.92	647 186	58.07
49-50	36 518	1 091	29.86	16.71	35 972	32.97	610 138	59.84
50-51	35 427	1 113	31.42	16.21	34 871	31.33	574 166	61.69
51-52	34 314	1 126	32.81	15.72	33 751	29.97	539 295	63.61
52-53	33 188	1 133	34.16	15.23	32 622	28.79	505 544	65.66
53-54	32 055	1 144	35.68	14.75	31 483	27.52	472 922	67.80
54-55	30 911	1 157	37.43	14.28	30 333	26.22	441 439	70.03
55-56	29 754	1 175	39.50	13.82	29 167	24.82	411 106	72.36
56-57	28 579	1 196	41.85	13.36	27 981	23.40	381 939	74.85
57-58	27 383	1 210	44.17	12.93	26 778	22.13	353 958	77.34
58-59	26 173	1 211	46.30	12.50	25 567	21.11	327 180	80.00
59-60	24 962	1 212	48.53	12.08	24 356	20.10	301 613	82.78
60-61	23 750	1 206	50.79	11.67	23 147	19.19	277 257	85.69
61-62	22 544	1 198	53.14	11.27	21 945	18.32	254 110	88.73
62-63	21 346	1 190	55.76	10.88	20 751	17.44	232 165	91.91
63-64	20 156	1 182	58.65	10.49	19 565	16.55	211 414	95.33
64-65	18 974	1 168	61.52	10.11	18 390	15.74	191 849	98.91
65-66	17 806	1 145	64.33	9.74	17 234	15.05	173 459	102.67
66-67	16 661	1 123	67.40	9.38	16 099	14.34	156 225	106.61
67-68	15 538	1 102	70.93	9.02	14 987	13.60	140 126	110.86
68-69	14 436	1 082	74.96	8.67	13 895	12.84	125 139	115.34
69-70	13 354	1 059	79.27	8.33	12 824	12.11	111 244	120.05
70-71	12 295	1 032	83.98	8.00	11 779	11.41	98 420	125.00
71-72	11 263	1 002	88.92	7.69	10 762	10.74	86 641	130.04
72-73	10 261	964	93.94	7.39	9 779	10.14	75 879	135.32
73-74	9 297	922	99.17	7.11	8 836	9.58	66 100	140.65
74-75	8 375	881	105.27	6.84	7 934	9.01	57 264	146.20
75-76	7 494	846	112.77	6.58	7 071	8.36	49 330	151.98
76-77	6 648	797	119.97	6.36	6 250	7.84	42 259	157.23
77-78	5 851	730	124.82	6.15	5 486	7.52	36 009	162.60
78-79	5 121	651	127.14	5.96	4 795	7.37	30 523	167.79
79-80	4 470	576	128.82	5.76	4 182	7.26	25 728	173.61
80-81	3 894	511	131.27	5.53	3 638	7.12	21 546	180.83
81-82	3 383	466	137.57	5.29	3 150	6.77	17 908	189.04
82-83	2 917	426	146.08	5.06	2 704	6.35	14 758	197.63
83-84	2 491	390	156.61	4.84	2 296	5.89	12 054	206.61
84-85	2 101	354	168.31	4.64	1 924	5.44	9 758	215.52
85-86	1 747	314	179.82	4.48	1 590	5.06	7 834	223.21
86-87	1 433	272	189.67	4.36	1 297	4.77	6 244	229.36
87-88	1 161	228	196.74	4.26	1 047	4.58	4 947	234.74
88-89	933	187	200.57	4.18	839	4.49	3 900	239.23
89-90	746	151	201.59	4.10	671	4.46	3 061	243.90
90-91	595	119	201.01	4.01	536	4.47	2 390	249.38
91-92	476	96	200.52	3.89	428	4.49	1 854	257.07
92-93	380	76	201.86	3.75	342	4.45	1 426	266.67
93-94	304	63	206.44	3.57	272	4.34	1 084	280.11
94-95	241	52	215.03	3.37	215	4.15	812	296.74
95-96	189	43	227.76	3.15	168	3.89	597	317.46
96-97	146	36	244.29	2.93	128	3.59	429	341.30
97-98	110	29	263.98	2.72	96	3.29	301	367.65
98-99	81	23	286.16	2.51	70	2.99	205	398.41
99-100	58	18	310.34	2.32	49	2.72	135	431.03
100-101	40	13	336.29	2.14	33	2.47	86	467.29
101-102	27	10	363.98	1.97	22	2.25	53	507.61
102-103	17	7	393.51	1.81	14	2.04	31	552.49
103-104	10	4	425.09	1.66	8	1.85	17	602.41
104-105	6	3	458.83	1.53	5	1.68	9	653.59
105-106	3	1	495.02	1.40	2	1.52	4	714.29
106-107	2	1	533.75	1.27	1	1.37	2	787.40
107-108	1	1	575.15	1.16	1	1.24	1	862.07

TABLE **31b.**—LIFE TABLE FOR NEGRO FEMALES IN THE ORIGINAL REGISTRATION STATES: 1910.

[Based on the estimated population July 1, 1910 (239,814), and on the reported deaths in 1909 (5,025), in 1910 (5,481), and in 1911 (5,347). The original registration states include Maine, New Hampshire, Vermont, Massachusetts, Rhode Island, Connecticut, New York, New Jersey, Indiana, and Michigan, and the District of Columbia.]

AGE INTERVAL.	OF 100,000 FEMALES BORN ALIVE:		RATE OF MORTALITY PER THOUSAND.	COMPLETE EXPECTATION OF LIFE.	STATIONARY FEMALE POPULATION, UNAFFECTED BY EMIGRATION AND IMMIGRATION, WHICH, ASSUMING THE MORTALITY RATES IN COLUMN 4, WOULD RESULT IF 100,000 FEMALES WERE BORN ALIVE UNIFORMLY THROUGHOUT EACH YEAR.			
Period of lifetime between two exact ages.	Number alive at beginning of age interval.	Number dying in age interval.	Number dying in age interval among 1,000 alive at beginning of age interval.	Average length of life remaining to each one alive at beginning of age interval.	Population living in age interval.	Population living in age interval to one annual death in same age interval.	Total population living in current and all higher age intervals.	Average death rate per thousand of the total population living in current and all higher age intervals.
x to $x+1$	l_x	d_x	$1000q_x$	$\overset{\circ}{e}_x$	L_x	L_x/d_x	T_x	$1000/\overset{\circ}{e}_x$
1	2	3	4	5	6	7	8	9

INFANT MORTALITY—FIRST YEAR OF LIFE BY AGE INTERVALS OF ONE MONTH.

Months.			Monthly rate.	In years.				Annual rate.
0-1	100 000	6 380	63.80	37.67	7 935	1.24	3 766 879	26.55
1-2	93 620	1 746	18.66	40.15	7 729	4.43	3 758 944	24.91
2-3	91 874	1 555	16.93	40.83	7 591	4.88	3 751 215	24.49
3-4	90 319	1 394	15.44	41.45	7 468	5.36	3 743 624	24.13
4-5	88 925	1 252	14.08	42.01	7 358	5.88	3 736 156	23.80
5-6	87 673	1 134	12.94	42.53	7 259	6.40	3 728 798	23.51
6-7	86 539	1 036	11.96	43.00	7 168	6.92	3 721 539	23.26
7-8	85 503	948	11.09	43.44	7 086	7.47	3 714 371	23.02
8-9	84 555	874	10.34	43.84	7 010	8.02	3 707 285	22.81
9-10	83 681	800	9.56	44.22	6 940	8.68	3 700 275	22.61
10-11	82 881	725	8.75	44.56	6 877	9.49	3 693 335	22.44
11-12	82 156	663	8.07	44.87	6 819	10.29	3 686 458	22.29

LIFE TABLE FOR WHOLE RANGE OF LIFE BY AGE INTERVALS OF ONE YEAR.

Years.			Annual rate.	In years.				Annual rate.
0-1	100 000	18 507	185.07	37.67	87 240	4.71	3 766 879	26.55
1-2	81 493	4 796	58.84	45.15	78 664	16.40	3 679 639	22.15
2-3	76 697	1 878	24.50	46.95	75 702	40.31	3 600 975	21.30
3-4	74 819	1 187	15.85	47.12	74 202	62.51	3 525 273	21.22
4-5	73 632	864	11.74	46.87	73 183	84.70	3 451 071	21.34
5-6	72 768	617	8.47	46.42	72 459	117.44	3 377 888	21.54
6-7	72 151	499	6.92	45.81	71 902	144.09	3 305 429	21.83
7-8	71 652	418	5.84	45.13	71 443	170.92	3 233 527	22.16
8-9	71 234	371	5.21	44.39	71 048	191.50	3 162 084	22.53
9-10	70 863	355	5.01	43.62	70 685	199.11	3 091 036	22.93
10-11	70 508	365	5.18	42.84	70 325	192.67	3 020 351	23.34
11-12	70 143	398	5.67	42.06	69 944	175.74	2 950 026	23.78
12-13	69 745	447	6.41	41.29	69 521	155.53	2 880 082	24.22
13-14	69 298	506	7.31	40.56	69 045	136.45	2 810 561	24.65
14-15	68 792	574	8.34	39.85	68 505	119.35	2 741 516	25.09
15-16	68 218	647	9.49	39.18	67 894	104.94	2 673 011	25.52
16-17	67 571	698	10.32	38.55	67 222	96.31	2 605 117	25.94
17-18	66 873	710	10.62	37.95	66 518	93.69	2 537 895	26.35
18-19	66 163	702	10.61	37.35	65 812	93.75	2 471 377	26.77
19-20	65 461	697	10.66	36.75	65 112	93.42	2 405 565	27.21
20-21	64 764	696	10.74	36.14	64 416	92.55	2 340 453	27.67
21-22	64 068	687	10.71	35.53	63 725	92.76	2 276 037	28.15
22-23	63 381	669	10.56	34.90	63 047	94.24	2 212 312	28.65
23-24	62 712	650	10.36	34.27	62 387	95.98	2 149 265	29.18
24-25	62 062	632	10.19	33.63	61 746	97.70	2 086 878	29.74
25-26	61 430	614	9.99	32.97	61 123	99.55	2 025 132	30.33
26-27	60 816	607	9.98	32.29	60 513	99.69	1 964 009	30.97
27-28	60 209	618	10.26	31.61	59 900	96.93	1 903 496	31.64
28-29	59 591	642	10.77	30.94	59 270	92.32	1 843 596	32.32
29-30	58 949	668	11.33	30.27	58 615	87.75	1 784 326	33.04
30-31	58 281	700	12.02	29.61	57 931	82.76	1 725 711	33.77
31-32	57 581	730	12.68	28.96	57 216	78.38	1 667 780	34.53
32-33	56 851	746	13.12	28.33	56 478	75.71	1 610 564	35.30
33-34	56 105	751	13.39	27.70	55 729	74.21	1 554 086	36.10
34-35	55 354	759	13.72	27.07	54 974	72.43	1 498 357	36.94
35-36	54 595	767	14.05	26.44	54 211	70.68	1 443 383	37.82
36-37	53 828	779	14.47	25.81	53 439	68.60	1 389 172	38.74
37-38	53 049	799	15.07	25.18	52 649	65.89	1 335 733	39.71
38-39	52 250	827	15.83	24.56	51 836	62.68	1 283 084	40.72
39-40	51 423	855	16.62	23.94	50 995	59.64	1 231 248	41.77
40-41	50 568	885	17.50	23.34	50 126	56.64	1 180 253	42.84
41-42	49 683	911	18.33	22.75	49 228	54.04	1 130 127	43.96
42-43	48 772	928	19.03	22.16	48 308	52.06	1 080 899	45.13
43-44	47 844	940	19.65	21.58	47 374	50.40	1 032 591	46.34
44-45	46 904	957	20.39	21.00	46 426	48.51	985 217	47.62

TABLE **31b.**—LIFE TABLE FOR NEGRO FEMALES IN THE ORIGINAL REGISTRATION STATES: 1910.

[Based on the estimated population July 1, 1910 (239,814), and on the reported deaths in 1909 (5,025), in 1910 (5,481), and in 1911 (5,347). The original registration states include Maine, New Hampshire, Vermont, Massachusetts, Rhode Island, Connecticut, New York, New Jersey, Indiana, and Michigan, and the District of Columbia.]

AGE INTERVAL.	Of 100,000 Females Born Alive:		RATE OF MORTALITY PER THOUSAND.	COMPLETE EXPECTATION OF LIFE.	STATIONARY FEMALE POPULATION, Unaffected by Emigration and Immigration, which, Assuming the Mortality Rates in Column 4, would result if 100,000 Females were Born Alive Uniformly Throughout Each Year.			
Period of lifetime between two exact ages.	Number alive at beginning of age interval.	Number dying in age interval.	Number dying in age interval among 1,000 alive at beginning of age interval.	Average length of life remaining to each one alive at beginning of age interval.	Population living in age interval.	Population living in age interval to one annual death in same age interval.	Total population living in current and all higher age intervals.	Average death rate per thousand of the total population living in current and all higher age intervals.
x to $x+1$	l_x	d_x	$1000q_x$	$\overset{\circ}{e}_x$	L_x	L_x/d_x	T_x	$1000/\overset{\circ}{e}_x$
1	2	3	4	5	6	7	8	9

LIFE TABLE FOR WHOLE RANGE OF LIFE BY AGE INTERVALS OF ONE YEAR—Continued.

Years.			Annual rate.	In years.				Annual rate.
45–46	45 947	976	21.25	20.43	45 459	46.58	938 791	48.95
46–47	44 971	998	22.19	19.86	44 472	44.56	893 332	50.35
47–48	43 973	1 017	23.13	19.30	43 465	42.74	848 860	51.81
48–49	42 956	1 030	23.99	18.75	42 441	41.20	805 395	53.33
49–50	41 926	1 040	24.80	18.20	41 406	39.81	762 954	54.95
50–51	40 886	1 044	25.52	17.65	40 364	38.66	721 548	56.66
51–52	39 842	1 053	26.43	17.10	39 316	37.34	681 184	58.48
52–53	38 789	1 079	27.82	16.55	38 250	35.45	641 868	60.42
53–54	37 710	1 123	29.78	16.01	37 149	33.08	603 618	62.46
54–55	36 587	1 172	32.04	15.48	36 001	30.72	566 469	64.60
55–56	35 415	1 234	34.85	14.98	34 798	28.20	530 468	66.76
56–57	34 181	1 294	37.87	14.50	33 534	25.91	495 670	68.97
57–58	32 887	1 326	40.30	14.05	32 224	24.30	462 136	71.17
58–59	31 561	1 326	42.04	13.62	30 898	23.30	429 912	73.42
59–60	30 235	1 327	43.88	13.20	29 571	22.28	399 014	75.76
60–61	28 908	1 318	45.58	12.78	28 249	21.43	369 443	78.25
61–62	27 590	1 309	47.46	12.37	26 936	20.58	341 194	80.84
62–63	26 281	1 313	49.98	11.96	25 624	19.52	314 258	83.61
63–64	24 968	1 329	53.19	11.56	24 303	18.29	288 634	86.51
64–65	23 639	1 337	56.57	11.18	22 971	17.18	264 331	89.45
65–66	22 302	1 346	60.37	10.82	21 629	16.07	241 360	92.42
66–67	20 956	1 340	63.96	10.49	20 286	15.14	219 731	95.33
67–68	19 616	1 306	66.54	10.17	18 963	14.52	199 445	98.33
68–69	18 310	1 248	68.16	9.86	17 686	14.17	180 482	101.42
69–70	17 062	1 191	69.83	9.54	16 467	13.83	162 796	104.82
70–71	15 871	1 131	71.27	9.22	15 305	13.53	146 329	108.46
71–72	14 740	1 077	73.03	8.89	14 202	13.19	131 024	112.49
72–73	13 663	1 034	75.74	8.55	13 146	12.71	116 822	116.96
73–74	12 629	1 004	79.45	8.21	12 127	12.08	103 676	121.80
74–75	11 625	968	83.30	7.88	11 141	11.51	91 549	126.90
75–76	10 657	932	87.47	7.55	10 191	10.93	80 408	132.45
76–77	9 725	900	92.52	7.22	9 275	10.31	70 217	138.50
77–78	8 825	869	98.44	6.91	8 391	9.66	60 942	144.72
78–79	7 956	834	104.91	6.61	7 539	9.04	52 551	151.29
79–80	7 122	798	111.96	6.32	6 723	8.42	45 012	158.23
80–81	6 324	757	119.68	6.05	5 946	7.86	38 289	165.29
81–82	5 567	712	128.03	5.81	5 211	7.31	32 343	172.12
82–83	4 855	665	136.81	5.59	4 522	6.81	27 132	178.89
83–84	4 190	610	145.64	5.40	3 885	6.37	22 610	185.19
84–85	3 580	551	153.94	5.23	3 305	6.00	18 725	191.20
85–86	3 029	488	161.05	5.09	2 785	5.71	15 420	196.46
86–87	2 541	423	166.48	4.97	2 330	5.51	12 635	201.21
87–88	2 118	360	169.98	4.86	1 938	5.38	10 305	205.76
88–89	1 758	302	171.67	4.76	1 607	5.33	8 367	210.08
89–90	1 456	250	172.13	4.64	1 331	5.31	6 760	215.52
90–91	1 206	208	172.34	4.50	1 102	5.30	5 429	222.22
91–92	998	173	173.52	4.34	911	5.26	4 327	230.41
92–93	825	146	176.82	4.14	752	5.16	3 416	241.55
93–94	679	124	183.14	3.92	617	4.96	2 664	255.10
94–95	555	107	192.85	3.69	501	4.69	2 047	271.00
95–96	448	93	205.91	3.45	402	4.36	1 546	289.86
96–97	355	78	221.84	3.22	316	4.01	1 144	310.56
97–98	277	67	240.02	2.99	243	3.67	828	334.45
98–99	210	54	259.87	2.78	183	3.35	585	359.71
99–100	156	44	281.03	2.58	134	3.06	402	387.60
100–101	112	34	303.35	2.39	95	2.80	268	418.41
101–102	78	26	326.96	2.21	65	2.56	173	452.49
102–103	52	18	352.15	2.05	43	2.34	108	487.80
103–104	34	13	379.35	1.89	28	2.14	65	529.10
104–105	21	9	409.20	1.73	17	1.94	37	578.03
105–106	12	5	441.90	1.59	10	1.76	20	628.93
106–107	7	3	477.43	1.45	5	1.59	10	689.66
107–108	4	2	516.06	1.32	3	1.44	5	757.58
108–109	2	1	558.12	1.20	1	1.29	2	833.33
109–110	1	1	604.00	1.08	1	1.16	1	925.93

TABLE **32.**—NEGRO AND WHITE POPULATION, DEATHS, AND DEATH RATES, BY REGISTRATION STATES AND SELECTED CITIES: 1910 AND 1900.

[Only cities having at least 2,500 Negro population in 1910 are shown separately.]

STATE AND CITY.	1910				1900		
	Population.		Number of deaths.	Death rate per 1,000 population.	Population, census June 1.	Number of deaths.	Death rate per 1,000 population.
	Census, Apr. 15.	Estimated as of July 1.					
REGISTRATION STATES.							
CALIFORNIA:[1]							
Negro	21,645	21,816	442	20.3			
White	2,259,672	2,277,568	30,685	13.5			
Los Angeles—							
Negro	7,599	7,715	136	17.6	2,131	62	29.1
White	305,307	309,982	4,299	13.9	98,082	1,809	18.4
Oakland—							
Negro	3,055	3,088	52	16.8	1,026	19	18.5
White	141,956	143,494	1,791	12.5	64,788	1,031	15.9
Balance of state[1]—							
Negro	10,991	11,013	254	23.1			
White	1,812,409	1,824,092	24,595	13.5			
COLORADO:[1]							
Negro	11,453	11,531	289	25.1			
White	783,415	788,780	10,730	13.6			
Denver—							
Negro	5,426	5,466	132	24.1	3,923	89	22.7
White	207,071	208,616	3,389	16.2	129,609	2,444	18.9
Balance of state[1]—							
Negro	6,027	6,065	157	25.9			
White	576,344	580,164	7,341	12.7			
CONNECTICUT:							
Negro	15,174	15,233	373	24.5	15,226	352	23.1
White	1,098,897	1,103,189	17,120	15.5	892,424	16,002	17.9
New Haven—							
Negro	3,561	3,575	91	25.5	2,887	82	28.4
White	129,944	130,469	2,126	16.3	105,038	1,886	18.0
Balance of state—							
Negro	11,613	11,658	282	24.2	12,339	270	21.9
White	968,953	972,720	14,994	15.4	787,386	14,116	17.9
DIST. OF COLUMBIA:							
Negro	94,446	94,763	2,759	29.1	86,702	2,685	31.0
White	236,128	236,917	3,744	15.8	191,532	3,511	18.3
INDIANA:							
Negro	60,320	60,408	1,433	23.7	57,505	1,250	21.7
White	2,639,961	2,643,764	35,011	13.2	2,458,502	34,457	14.0
Evansville—							
Negro	6,266	[2]6,185	117	18.9	7,518	150	20.0
White	63,377	[2]61,731	831	13.5	51,486	781	15.2
Indianapolis—							
Negro	21,816	21,927	548	25.0	15,931	383	24.0
White	211,780	212,856	3,275	15.4	153,201	2,503	16.3
Terre Haute—							
Negro	2,593	2,605	67	25.7	1,520	40	26.3
White	55,546	55,800	864	15.5	35,146	557	15.8
Balance of state—							
Negro	29,645	29,691	701	23.6	32,536	677	21.1
White	2,309,258	2,313,377	30,041	13.0	2,218,669	30,616	13.8
MAINE:							
Negro	1,363	1,365	19	13.9	1,319	24	18.2
White	739,995	741,003	12,703	17.1	692,226	11,843	17.1
MARYLAND:[1]							
Negro	232,250	232,657	5,343	23.0			
White	1,062,639	1,064,496	15,458	14.5			
Annapolis—							
Negro	3,184	3,185	97	30.5	3,002	126	42.0
White	5,408	5,409	83	15.3	5,512	110	20.0
Baltimore—							
Negro	84,749	84,908	2,597	30.6	79,258	2,653	33.5
White	473,387	474,273	8,152	17.2	429,218	8,242	19.2
Balance of state[1]—							
Negro	144,317	144,564	2,649	18.3			
White	583,844	584,814	7,223	12.4			
MASSACHUSETTS:							
Negro	38,055	38,189	809	21.2	31,974	681	21.3
White	3,324,926	3,336,616	53,455	16.0	2,769,764	50,467	18.2
Boston—							
Negro	13,564	13,611	317	23.3	11,591	312	26.9
White	655,696	657,959	11,224	17.1	548,083	11,100	20.3
Cambridge—							
Negro	4,707	4,719	75	15.9	3,888	105	27.0
White	100,017	100,277	1,501	15.0	87,875	1,466	16.7
New Bedford—							
Negro	2,885	2,907	85	29.2	1,685	32	19.0
White	93,699	94,399	1,727	18.3	60,633	1,293	21.3
Balance of state—							
Negro	16,899	16,952	332	19.6	14,810	232	16.0
White	2,475,514	2,483,981	39,003	15.7	2,073,173	36,608	17.8
MICHIGAN:							
Negro	17,115	17,165	426	24.8	15,816	290	18.3
White	2,785,247	2,793,384	39,262	14.1	2,398,563	33,525	14.0
Detroit—							
Negro	5,741	5,785	146	25.2	4,111	103	25.1
White	459,926	463,435	7,305	15.8	281,575	4,552	16.2
Balance of state—							
Negro	11,374	11,380	280	24.6	11,705	187	16.0
White	2,325,321	2,329,949	31,957	13.7	2,116,988	28,973	13.7
MINNESOTA:[1]							
Negro	7,084	7,107	135	19.0			
White	2,059,227	2,066,015	22,470	10.9			
Minneapolis—							
Negro	2,592	2,610	56	21.5	1,548	22	14.2
White	298,672	300,735	3,681	12.2	201,113	2,286	11.4
REGISTRATION STATES—Contd.							
MINNESOTA—Contd.							
St. Paul—							
Negro	3,144	3,160	49	15.5	2,263	30	13.3
White	211,516	212,590	2,508	11.8	160,764	1,601	10.0
Balance of state[1]—							
Negro	1,348	1,337	30	22.4			
White	1,549,039	1,552,690	16,281	10.5			
MONTANA:[1]							
Negro	1,834	1,848	43	23.3			
White	360,580	363,265	3,909	10.8			
NEW HAMPSHIRE:							
Negro	564	565	14	24.8	662	8	12.1
White	429,906	430,305	7,438	17.3	410,791	7,626	18.6
NEW JERSEY:							
Negro	89,760	90,248	2,073	23.0	69,844	1,666	23.9
White	2,445,894	2,459,185	37,422	15.2	1,812,317	31,771	17.5
Atlantic City—							
Negro	9,834	9,917	172	17.3	6,513	106	16.3
White	36,231	36,584	627	17.1	21,267	375	17.6
Camden—							
Negro	6,076	6,101	192	31.5	5,576	186	33.4
White	88,391	88,758	1,437	16.2	70,288	1,182	16.8
Jersey City—							
Negro	5,960	5,989	123	20.5	3,704	83	22.4
White	261,659	262,923	4,278	16.3	202,510	4,191	20.7
Newark—							
Negro	9,475	9,531	296	31.1	6,694	202	30.2
White	337,742	339,745	5,484	16.1	239,108	4,755	19.9
Trenton—							
Negro	2,581	2,594	89	34.3	2,096	49	23.4
White	94,198	94,681	1,886	19.9	71,149	1,222	17.2
Balance of state—							
Negro	55,834	56,116	1,201	21.4	45,261	1,040	23.0
White	1,627,673	1,636,494	23,710	14.5	1,207,995	20,046	16.6
NEW YORK:							
Negro	134,191	134,764	3,350	24.9	99,232	2,743	27.6
White	8,966,845	9,005,136	144,144	16.0	7,156,881	129,408	18.1
New York City—							
Negro	91,709	92,192	2,391	25.9	60,666	1,950	32.1
White	4,669,162	4,696,639	74,274	15.8	3,369,898	68,799	20.4
Bronx Borough—							
Negro	4,117	4,163	208	50.0	2,370	75	31.6
White	426,650	431,458	6,755	15.7	197,923	3,674	18.6
Brooklyn Borough—							
Negro	22,708	22,845	598	26.2	18,367	533	29.0
White	1,610,487	1,620,191	25,070	15.5	1,146,909	22,932	20.0
Manhattan Borough—							
Negro	60,534	60,798	1,473	24.2	36,246	1,242	34.3
White	2,266,578	2,276,422	37,129	16.3	1,808,968	38,146	21.1
Queens Borough—							
Negro	3,198	3,229	82	25.4	2,611	66	25.3
White	280,691	283,419	3,882	13.7	150,235	2,702	18.0
Richmond Borough—							
Negro	1,152	1,157	30	25.9	1,072	34	31.7
White	84,756	85,149	1,438	16.9	65,863	1,345	20.4
Balance of state—							
Negro	42,482	42,572	959	22.5	38,566	793	20.6
White	4,297,683	4,308,497	69,870	16.2	3,786,983	60,609	16.0
NORTH CAROLINA:[1]							
Negro	126,566	127,216	3,024	23.8			
White	233,198	234,721	3,728	15.9			
Asheville[1]—							
Negro	5,359	5,379	135	25.1			
White	13,401	13,451	235	17.5			
Charlotte[1]—							
Negro	11,752	11,819	299	25.3			
White	22,259	22,387	306	13.7			
Durham[1]—							
Negro	6,869	6,955	179	25.7			
White	11,372	11,515	189	16.4			
Greensboro[1]—							
Negro	5,710	5,755	143	24.8			
White	10,184	10,263	162	15.8			
Raleigh—							
Negro	7,372	7,384	247	33.5	5,721	227	39.7
White	11,846	11,865	290	24.4	7,921	183	23.1
Wilmington—							
Negro	12,107	12,155	325	26.7	10,407	384	36.9
White	13,627	13,680	213	15.6	10,556	262	24.8
Winston[1]—							
Negro	7,828	7,897	186	23.6			
White	9,336	9,418	166	17.6			
Balance of state[1]—							
Negro	69,569	69,872	1,510	21.6			
White	141,173	142,142	2,167	15.2			
OHIO:[1]							
Negro	111,452	111,755	2,260	20.2			
White	4,654,897	4,667,454	63,194	13.5			

[1] Not included in the registration area in 1900.   [2] Exclusive of population of Howell town; annexation declared illegal.

TABLE 32.—NEGRO AND WHITE POPULATION, DEATHS, AND DEATH RATES, BY REGISTRATION STATES AND SELECTED CITIES: 1910 AND 1900—Continued.

[Only cities having at least 2,500 Negro population in 1910 are shown separately.]

STATE AND CITY.	1910 Population Census, Apr. 15.	1910 Population Estimated as of July 1.	1910 Number of deaths.	1910 Death rate per 1,000 population.	1900 Population, census June 1.	1900 Number of deaths.	1900 Death rate per 1,000 population.
REGISTRATION STATES—Contd.							
OHIO—Continued.							
Cincinnati—							
Negro	19,639	19,673	569	28.9	14,482	430	29.7
White	343,919	344,505	5,750	16.7	311,404	5,496	17.6
Cleveland—							
Negro	8,448	8,499	167	19.6	5,988	99	16.5
White	551,925	555,275	7,880	14.2	375,664	6,627	17.6
Columbus—							
Negro	12,739	12,814	262	20.4	8,201	187	22.8
White	168,709	169,697	2,548	15.0	117,335	1,801	15.3
Dayton—							
Negro	4,842	4,857	99	20.4	3,387	68	20.1
White	111,707	112,049	1,625	14.5	81,923	1,267	15.5
Springfield[1]—							
Negro	4,933	4,949	78	15.8			
White	41,976	42,115	543	12.9			
Balance of state[1]—							
Negro	60,851	60,963	1,085	17.8			
White	3,436,661	3,443,813	44,848	13.0			
PENNSYLVANIA:[1]							
Negro	193,919	194,646	4,669	24.0			
White	7,467,713	7,495,727	115,094	15.4			
Chester[1]—							
Negro	4,795	4,807	107	22.3			
White	33,724	33,808	542	16.0			
Harrisburg—							
Negro	4,535	4,554	98	21.5	4,107	104	25.3
White	59,636	59,880	842	14.1	46,044	800	17.4
Philadelphia—							
Negro	84,459	84,753	2,276	26.9	62,613	1,894	30.2
White	1,463,371	1,468,459	24,740	16.8	1,229,673	25,055	20.4
Pittsburgh[2]—							
Negro	25,623	25,694	601	23.4	20,355	526	25.8
White	508,008	509,413	8,993	17.7	430,973	8,290	19.2
Balance of state[1]—							
Negro	74,507	74,838	1,587	21.2			
White	5,402,974	5,421,167	79,977	14.7			
RHODE ISLAND:							
Negro	9,529	9,571	248	25.9	9,092	238	26.2
White	532,492	534,853	9,051	16.9	419,050	8,525	20.3
Providence—							
Negro	5,316	5,340	139	26.0	4,817	140	29.1
White	218,623	219,625	3,837	17.5	170,508	3,513	20.6
Balance of state—							
Negro	4,213	4,231	109	25.8	4,275	98	22.9
White	313,869	315,228	5,214	16.5	248,542	5,012	20.2
UTAH:[1]							
Negro	1,144	1,150	32	27.8			
White	366,583	368,584	3,998	10.8			
VERMONT:							
Negro	1,621	1,622	29	17.9	826	17	20.6
White	354,298	354,557	5,674	16.0	342,771	5,675	16.6
WASHINGTON:[1]							
Negro	6,058	6,128	97	15.8			
White	1,109,111	1,121,894	11,017	9.8			
WISCONSIN:							
Negro	2,900	2,907	65	22.4			
White	2,320,555	2,326,110	27,896	12.0			
CITIES IN NONREGISTRATION STATES.							
ALABAMA:							
Birmingham[1]—							
Negro	52,305	52,958	1,391	26.3			
White	80,369	81,373	1,206	14.8			
Mobile—							
Negro	22,763	22,851	673	29.5	17,045	564	33.1
White	28,737	28,849	512	17.7	21,402	481	22.5
Montgomery[1]—							
Negro	19,322	19,401	680	35.1			
White	18,802	18,878	328	17.4			
DELAWARE:							
Wilmington—							
Negro	9,081	9,105	225	24.7	9,736	269	27.6
White	78,309	78,515	1,322	16.8	66,738	1,277	19.1
FLORIDA:							
Jacksonville—							
Negro	29,293	29,608	710	24.0	16,236	532	32.8
White	28,329	28,632	482	16.8	12,158	324	26.6
Key West—							
Negro	5,515	5,532	147	26.6	5,562	147	26.4
White	14,409	14,452	301	20.8	11,526	271	23.5
GEORGIA:							
Atlanta—							
Negro	51,902	52,288	1,328	25.4	35,727	977	27.3
White	102,861	103,626	1,609	15.5	54,090	1,006	18.6
Savannah—							
Negro	33,246	33,203	1,134	34.1	28,090	1,070	38.1
White	31,784	31,829	616	19.4	26,109	612	23.4
ILLINOIS:							
Chicago—							
Negro	44,103	44,310	1,075	24.3	30,150	712	23.6
White	2,139,057	2,149,108	32,130	15.0	1,667,140	25,337	15.2
Springfield—							
Negro	2,961	2,979	67	22.5	2,227	57	25.6
White	48,699	48,992	793	16.2	31,925	548	17.1

STATE AND CITY.	1910 Population Census, Apr. 15.	1910 Population Estimated as of July 1.	1910 Number of deaths.	1910 Death rate per 1,000 population.	1900 Population, census June 1.	1900 Number of deaths.	1900 Death rate per 1,000 population.
CITIES IN NONREGISTRATION STATES—Continued.							
ILLINOIS—Continued.							
Other cities—							
Negro	5,286	5,311	98	18.5	4,759	102	21.4
White	153,601	154,320	2,266	14.7	135,864	2,180	16.0
KANSAS:							
Kansas City[1]—							
Negro	9,286	9,403	237	25.2			
White	72,996	73,907	1,152	15.6			
Other cities—							
Negro	4,934	4,961	104	21.0	3,421	75	21.9
White	66,857	67,416	908	13.5	32,108	490	15.3
KENTUCKY:							
Covington—							
Negro	2,899	2,906	59	20.3	2,487	81	32.6
White	50,358	50,481	802	15.9	40,434	743	18.4
Louisville—							
Negro	40,522	40,819	1,089	26.7	39,139	1,070	27.3
White	183,390	184,732	2,667	14.4	165,590	2,802	16.9
Newport—							
Negro	569	570	11	19.3	424	14	33.0
White	29,740	29,781	433	14.5	27,877	601	21.5
Paducah—							
Negro	6,047	6,066	164	27.0	5,814	224	38.5
White	16,710	16,761	274	16.3	13,621	323	23.7
LOUISIANA:							
New Orleans—							
Negro	89,262	89,552	2,933	32.8	77,714	3,184	41.0
White	249,403	250,209	4,311	17.2	208,946	4,420	21.2
MISSOURI:							
Kansas City—							
Negro	23,566	23,724	644	27.1	17,567	438	24.9
White	224,677	226,179	3,317	14.7	146,090	2,236	15.3
St. Joseph—							
Negro	4,249	4,263	98	23.0	6,260	68	10.9
White	73,128	73,376	957	13.0	96,712	701	7.2
St. Louis—							
Negro	43,960	44,111	1,149	26.0	35,516	1,096	30.9
White	642,488	644,693	9,733	15.1	539,385	9,223	17.1
NEBRASKA:							
Lincoln—							
Negro	733	735	10	13.6	814	17	20.9
White	43,222	43,350	475	11.0	39,324	433	11.0
Omaha—							
Negro	4,426	4,442	105	23.6	3,443	67	19.5
White	119,580	120,017	1,769	14.7	99,009	1,141	11.5
OREGON:							
Portland—							
Negro	1,045	1,058	19	18.0	775	5	6.5
White	198,952	201,357	2,225	11.1	80,614	846	10.5
SOUTH CAROLINA:							
Charleston—							
Negro	31,056	31,090	1,221	39.3	31,522	1,399	44.4
White	27,764	27,794	526	18.9	24,238	554	22.9
TENNESEE:							
Knoxville[1]—							
Negro	7,638	7,654	203	26.5			
White	28,706	28,768	432	15.0			
Memphis—							
Negro	52,441	52,681	1,492	28.3	49,910	1,218	14.4
White	78,590	78,950	1,326	16.8	52,380	1,084	20.7
Nashville—							
Negro	36,523	36,597	950	26.0	30,044	965	32.1
White	73,831	73,981	1,113	15.0	50,796	956	18.8
TEXAS:							
Galveston[1]—							
Negro	8,036	8,072	183	22.7			
White	28,895	29,022	417	14.4			
San Antonio—							
Negro	10,716	10,818	233	21.5	7,538	171	22.7
White	85,801	86,612	1,917	22.1	45,722	1,038	22.7
VIRGINIA:							
Alexandria—							
Negro	4,188	4,193	138	32.9	4,533	160	35.3
White	11,132	11,144	189	17.0	9,986	205	20.5
Danville[1]—							
Negro	6,207	6,218	167	26.9			
White	12,811	12,834	221	17.2			
Lynchburg—							
Negro	9,466	9,503	231	24.3	8,254	298	36.1
White	20,023	20,102	242	12.0	10,637	218	20.5
Norfolk—							
Negro	25,039	25,139	775	30.8	20,230	770	38.1
White	42,353	42,522	700	16.5	26,317	496	18.8
Petersburg—							
Negro	11,014	11,036	377	34.2	10,751	379	35.3
White	13,112	13,139	264	20.1	11,057	279	25.2
Richmond—							
Negro	46,733	46,865	1,416	30.2	32,230	1,214	37.7
White	80,879	81,108	1,470	18.1	52,798	1,251	23.7
WEST VIRGINIA:							
Wheeling—							
Negro	1,201	1,203	31	25.8	1,066	24	22.5
White	40,433	40,489	700	17.3	37,804	573	15.2

[1] Not included in the registration area in 1900.   [2] Includes Allegheny in 1900.

TABLE **33.**—DEATHS AND DEATH RATES, BY CLASS OF POPULATION, FOR SELECTED REGISTRATION CITIES: 1910.

REGISTRATION CITIES HAVING IN 1910 A POPULATION OF 10,000 OR MORE AND A NEGRO POPULATION OF 2,500 OR MORE.

CITY.	Population: April 15, 1910.				Deaths: Calendar year 1910.				Deaths per 1,000 population.			
	Negro.	Native white— Of native parentage.	Native white— Of foreign or mixed parentage.	Foreign-born white.	Negro.	Native white— Of native parentage.	Native white— Of foreign or mixed parentage.	Foreign-born white.	Negro.	Native white— Of native parentage.	Native white— Of foreign or mixed parentage.	Foreign-born white.
All cities	1,367,054	6,224,355	6,109,198	5,104,866	37,791	100,431	88,353	87,661	27.6	16.1	14.5	17.2
Southern cities	850,590	1,500,403	458,204	235,699	24,886	24,431	5,843	6,513	29.3	16.3	12.8	27.6
Northern and Western cities	516,464	4,723,952	5,650,994	4,869,167	12,905	76,000	82,510	81,148	25.0	16.1	14.6	16.7
SOUTHERN CITIES.												
ALABAMA.												
Birmingham	52,305	66,312	8,357	5,700	1,391	993	102	111	26.6	15.0	12.2	19.5
Mobile	22,763	20,944	5,585	2,208	673	396	30	86	29.6	18.9	5.4	38.9
Montgomery	19,322	16,708	1,390	704	680	307	5	16	35.2	18.4	3.6	22.7
DELAWARE.												
Wilmington	9,081	44,937	19,694	13,678	225	791	284	247	24.8	17.6	14.4	18.1
DISTRICT OF COLUMBIA.												
Washington	94,446	166,711	45,066	24,351	2,759	2,553	521	670	29.2	15.3	11.6	27.5
FLORIDA.												
Jacksonville	29,293	22,628	3,213	2,488	710	398	20	64	24.2	17.6	6.2	25.7
Key West	5,515	3,212	6,509	4,688	147	199	....	102	26.7	62.0	....	21.8
GEORGIA.												
Atlanta	51,902	91,987	6,464	4,410	1,328	1,458	87	64	25.6	15.9	13.5	14.5
Savannah	33,246	22,634	5,818	3,332	1,134	493	....	123	34.1	21.8	....	36.9
KENTUCKY.												
Covington	2,899	31,079	15,346	3,933	59	446	151	205	20.4	14.4	9.8	52.1
Louisville	40,522	113,543	52,411	17,436	1,089	1,755	384	528	26.9	15.5	7.3	30.3
Paducah	6,047	15,022	1,341	347	164	248	3	23	27.1	16.5	2.2	66.3
LOUISIANA.												
New Orleans	89,262	147,473	74,244	27,686	2,933	2,023	1,165	1,123	32.9	13.7	15.7	40.6
MARYLAND.												
Annapolis	3,184	4,160	791	457	97	56	19	8	30.5	13.5	24.0	17.5
Baltimore	84,749	261,474	134,870	77,043	2,597	4,421	1,868	1,863	30.6	16.9	13.9	24.2
NORTH CAROLINA.												
Asheville	5,359	12,436	579	386	135	193	24	18	25.2	15.5	41.5	46.6
Charlotte	11,752	21,208	579	472	299	292	7	7	25.4	13.8	12.1	14.8
Durham	6,869	10,875	269	228	179	184	2	3	26.1	16.9	7.4	13.2
Greensboro	5,710	9,590	369	225	143	155	2	5	25.0	16.2	5.4	22.2
Raleigh	7,372	11,461	234	151	247	275	9	6	33.5	24.0	38.5	39.7
Wilmington	12,107	12,417	766	444	325	189	12	12	26.8	15.2	15.7	27.0
Winston	7,828	9,040	172	124	186	163	3	....	23.8	18.0	17.4	....
SOUTH CAROLINA.												
Charleston	31,056	20,458	4,902	2,404	1,221	360	67	99	39.3	17.6	13.7	41.2
TENNESSEE.												
Knoxville	7,638	26,300	1,623	783	203	384	22	26	26.6	14.6	13.6	33.2
Memphis	52,441	59,985	12,138	6,467	1,492	1,049	118	159	28.5	17.5	9.7	24.6
Nashville	36,523	63,687	7,151	2,993	950	945	90	78	26.0	14.8	12.6	26.1
TEXAS.												
Galveston	8,036	12,643	10,088	6,164	183	170	91	156	22.8	13.4	9.0	25.3
San Antonio	10,716	44,629	23,765	17,407	233	851	563	503	21.7	19.1	23.7	28.9
VIRGINIA.												
Alexandria	4,188	9,923	889	320	138	182	....	7	33.0	18.3	....	21.9
Danville	6,207	12,387	241	183	167	213	4	4	26.9	17.2	16.6	21.9
Lynchburg	9,466	18,743	830	450	231	226	6	10	24.4	12.1	7.2	22.2
Norfolk	25,039	34,471	4,318	3,564	775	579	60	61	31.0	16.8	13.9	17.1
Petersburg	11,014	12,196	528	388	377	248	8	8	34.2	20.3	15.2	20.6
Richmond	46,733	69,130	7,664	4,085	1,416	1,236	116	118	30.3	17.9	15.1	28.9
NORTHERN AND WESTERN CITIES.												
CALIFORNIA.												
Los Angeles	7,599	169,967	74,756	60,584	136	2,303	892	1,104	17.9	13.5	11.9	18.2
Oakland	3,055	55,198	49,936	36,822	52	689	449	653	17.0	12.5	9.0	17.7
COLORADO.												
Denver	5,426	106,945	61,185	38,941	132	1,757	755	877	24.3	16.4	12.3	22.5
CONNECTICUT.												
New Haven	3,561	37,726	49,434	42,784	91	655	722	749	25.6	17.4	14.6	17.5

TABLE 33.—DEATHS AND DEATH RATES, BY CLASS OF POPULATION, FOR SELECTED REGISTRATION CITIES: 1910—Continued.

	REGISTRATION CITIES HAVING IN 1910 A POPULATION OF 10,000 OR MORE AND A NEGRO POPULATION OF 2,500 OR MORE.											
	Population: April 15, 1910.				Deaths: Calendar year 1910.				Deaths per 1,000 population.			
		Native white—				Native white—				Native white—		
CITY.	Negro.	Of native parentage.	Of foreign or mixed parentage.	Foreign-born white.	Negro.	Of native parentage.	Of foreign or mixed parentage.	Foreign-born white.	Negro.	Of native parentage.	Of foreign or mixed parentage.	Foreign-born white.
NORTHERN AND WESTERN CITIES—Con.												
INDIANA.												
Evansville	6,266	41,945	16,970	4,462	117	485	190	156	18.7	11.6	11.2	35.0
Indianapolis	21,816	150,593	41,420	19,767	548	2,249	519	507	25.1	14.9	12.5	25.6
Terre Haute	2,593	42,586	9,164	3,796	67	640	95	129	25.8	15.0	10.4	34.0
MASSACHUSETTS.												
Boston	13,564	157,870	257,104	240,722	317	3,106	3,963	4,155	23.4	19.7	15.4	17.3
Cambridge	4,707	25,615	39,794	34,608	75	412	522	567	15.9	16.1	13.1	16.4
New Bedford	2,885	18,738	32,336	42,625	85	377	880	470	29.5	20.1	27.2	11.0
MICHIGAN.												
Detroit	5,741	115,106	188,255	156,565	146	2,175	2,751	2,379	25.4	18.9	14.6	15.2
MINNESOTA.												
Minneapolis	2,592	96,186	116,548	85,938	56	1,300	1,163	1,218	21.6	13.5	10.0	14.2
St. Paul	3,144	61,594	93,398	56,524	49	825	813	870	15.6	13.4	8.7	15.4
NEW JERSEY.												
Atlantic City	9,834	22,410	7,421	6,400	172	358	149	120	17.5	16.0	20.1	18.8
Camden	6,076	49,581	23,128	15,682	192	840	375	222	31.6	16.9	16.2	14.2
Jersey City	5,960	74,861	109,101	77,697	123	1,182	1,621	1,475	20.6	15.8	14.9	19.0
Newark	9,475	94,737	132,350	110,655	296	1,670	1,961	1,853	31.2	17.6	14.8	16.7
Trenton	2,581	38,679	29,209	26,310	89	800	613	473	34.5	20.7	21.0	18.0
NEW YORK.												
New York City	91,709	921,318	1,820,141	1,927,703	2,391	15,990	29,344	28,940	26.1	17.4	16.1	15.0
Bronx Borough	4,117	92,569	185,146	148,935	208	1,251	2,689	2,815	50.5	13.5	14.5	18.9
Brooklyn Borough	22,708	375,548	663,583	571,356	598	5,720	10,208	9,142	26.3	15.2	15.4	16.0
Manhattan Borough	60,534	344,351	818,208	1,104,019	1,473	7,556	14,506	15,067	24.3	21.9	17.7	13.6
Queens Borough	3,198	80,607	120,969	79,115	82	994	1,485	1,403	25.6	12.3	12.3	17.7
Richmond Borough	1,152	28,243	32,235	24,278	30	469	456	513	26.0	16.6	14.1	21.1
OHIO.												
Cincinnati	19,639	154,937	132,190	56,792	569	2,287	1,687	1,776	29.0	14.8	12.8	31.3
Cleveland	8,448	132,314	223,908	195,703	167	2,088	3,001	2,791	19.8	15.8	13.4	14.3
Columbus	12,739	116,846	35,578	16,285	262	1,742	401	405	20.6	14.9	11.3	24.9
Dayton	4,842	72,301	25,559	13,847	99	992	345	288	20.4	13.7	13.5	20.8
Springfield	4,933	30,577	8,243	3,156	78	418	57	68	15.8	13.7	6.9	21.5
PENNSYLVANIA.												
Chester	4,795	17,793	9,258	6,673	107	241	169	132	22.3	13.5	18.3	19.8
Harrisburg	4,535	49,576	5,926	4,134	98	654	109	79	21.6	13.2	18.4	19.1
Philadelphia	84,459	584,008	496,785	382,578	2,276	9,977	7,663	7,100	26.9	17.1	15.4	18.6
Pittsburgh	25,623	176,089	191,483	140,436	601	2,900	3,451	2,642	23.5	16.5	18.0	18.8
RHODE ISLAND.												
Providence	5,316	59,966	82,354	76,303	139	1,173	1,400	1,264	26.1	19.6	17.0	16.6
ILLINOIS.												
Chicago	44,103	445,139	912,701	781,217	1,075	7,073	12,240	12,817	24.4	15.9	13.4	16.4
Springfield	2,961	27,944	13,855	6,900	67	531	92	170	22.6	19.0	6.6	24.6
KANSAS.												
Kansas City	9,286	48,021	14,631	10,344	237	720	221	211	25.5	15.0	15.1	20.4
MISSOURI.												
Kansas City	23,566	153,717	45,633	25,327	644	2,213	552	552	27.3	14.4	12.1	21.8
St. Joseph	4,249	50,316	14,699	8,113	98	651	146	160	23.1	12.9	9.9	19.7
St. Louis	43,960	269,836	246,946	125,706	1,149	3,689	2,803	3,241	26.1	13.7	11.4	25.8
NEBRASKA.												
Omaha	4,426	52,917	39,595	27,068	105	838	396	535	23.7	15.8	10.0	19.8

TABLE **34.**—NEGRO POPULATION AND DEATHS AND NEGRO AND WHITE DEATH RATES, BY AGE PERIODS, BY REGISTRATION CITIES:[1] 1910 AND 1900.

CITY AND AGE PERIOD.	NEGRO POPULATION. Number.		Deaths. Number.		Deaths. Per 1,000 population.		WHITE DEATHS PER 1,000 POPULATION.	
	1910	1900	1910	1900	1910	1900	1910	1900
SOUTHERN CITIES.								
ALEXANDRIA, VA.								
All ages	4,188	4,533	138	160	33.0	35.3	17.0	20.5
Under 5 years	355	416	34	54	95.8	129.8	36.4	65.5
Under 1 year	66	87	19	38	287.9	436.8	167.5	216.0
5 to 9 years	352	(2)	1	7	2.8	(2)	0.9	(2)
10 to 19 years	747	(2)	9	13	12.0	(2)	5.6	(2)
20 to 44 years	1,874	(2)	52	32	27.7	(2)	8.3	(2)
45 years and over	853	(2)	42	53	49.2	(2)	43.3	(2)
ASHEVILLE, N.C.[3]								
All ages	5,359		135		25.2		17.5	
Under 5 years	561		39		69.5		23.4	
Under 1 year	112		24		214.3		72.0	
5 to 9 years	531		7		13.2		0.7	
10 to 19 years	1,114		10		9.0		6.2	
20 to 44 years	2,423		45		18.6		19.0	
45 years and over	710		34		47.9		33.0	
ATLANTA, GA.								
All ages	51,902	35,727	1,328	977	25.6	27.3	15.6	18.6
Under 5 years	4,622	3,316	340	361	73.6	108.9	38.4	62.3
Under 1 year	1,004	621	235	244	234.1	392.9	121.7	208.6
5 to 9 years	4,284	3,665	17	14	4.0	3.8	3.1	4.8
10 to 19 years	9,874	7,594	98	75	9.9	9.9	3.8	4.6
20 to 44 years	25,388	15,810	527	292	20.8	18.5	8.8	10.2
45 years and over	7,645	5,165	342	233	44.7	45.1	39.7	40.8
BALTIMORE, MD.								
All ages	84,749	79,258	2,597	2,653	30.6	33.5	17.2	19.2
Under 5 years	6,628	6,705	776	1,107	117.1	165.1	46.5	61.0
Under 1 year	1,346	1,462	579	766	430.2	523.9	176.3	203.7
5 to 9 years	6,416	6,923	43	106	6.7	15.3	3.5	5.3
10 to 19 years	13,758	14,502	150	182	10.9	12.5	3.3	3.7
20 to 44 years	42,443	37,826	809	647	19.1	17.1	8.2	9.9
45 years and over	15,290	12,810	818	611	53.5	47.7	40.1	40.6
BIRMINGHAM, ALA.[3]								
All ages	52,305		1,391		26.6		15.0	
Under 5 years	4,598		325		70.7		34.9	
Under 1 year	942		198		210.2		96.6	
5 to 9 years	4,513		36		8.0		4.8	
10 to 19 years	9,274		109		11.8		3.3	
20 to 44 years	27,058		606		22.4		10.0	
45 years and over	6,569		315		48.0		36.2	
CHARLESTON, S.C.								
All ages	31,056	31,522	1,221	1,399	39.3	44.4	18.9	22.9
Under 5 years	2,985	3,062	453	504	151.8	164.6	44.8	56.7
Under 1 year	571	659	307	350	537.6	531.1	159.8	214.8
5 to 9 years	2,989	3,395	26	38	8.7	11.2	5.3	3.3
10 to 19 years	6,110	6,565	67	95	11.0	14.5	3.3	6.1
20 to 44 years	14,454	13,749	367	422	25.4	30.7	7.8	12.3
45 years and over	4,347	4,743	308	340	70.8	71.7	50.0	55.5
CHARLOTTE, N.C.[3]								
All ages	11,752		299		25.4		13.7	
Under 5 years	1,225		86		70.2		33.0	
Under 1 year	253		46		181.8		74.6	
5 to 9 years	1,218		11		9.0		3.1	
10 to 19 years	2,433		19		7.8		3.2	
20 to 44 years	5,101		99		19.4		6.4	
45 years and over	1,732		84		48.5		40.5	
COVINGTON, KY.[3]								
All ages	2,899		59		20.4		15.9	
Under 5 years	219		14		63.9		40.2	
Under 1 year	40		8		200.0		136.7	
5 to 9 years	167						3.2	
10 to 19 years	431		2		4.6		3.2	
20 to 44 years	1,483		23		15.5		7.9	
45 years and over	597		20		33.5		38.7	

CITY AND AGE PERIOD.	NEGRO POPULATION. Number.		Deaths. Number.		Deaths. Per 1,000 population.		WHITE DEATHS PER 1,000 POPULATION.	
	1910	1900	1910	1900	1910	1900	1910	1900
SOUTHERN CITIES—Continued.								
DANVILLE, VA.[3]								
All ages	6,207		167		26.9		17.3	
Under 5 years	574		42		73.2		57.9	
Under 1 year	118		24		203.4		151.1	
5 to 9 years	618		4		6.5		6.5	
10 to 19 years	1,428		13		9.1		5.3	
20 to 44 years	2,569		49		19.1		10.0	
45 years and over	992		58		58.5		29.8	
DURHAM, N.C.[3]								
All ages	6,869		179		26.0		16.6	
Under 5 years	681		58		85.2		55.5	
Under 1 year	90		37		411.1		137.5	
5 to 9 years	691		7		101.3		3.7	
10 to 19 years	1,596		21		13.2		3.1	
20 to 44 years	2,928		58		19.8		8.8	
45 years and over	906		35		38.6		37.3	
GALVESTON, TEX.[3]								
All ages	8,036		183		22.8		14.4	
Under 5 years	545		29		53.2		28.3	
Under 1 year	119		23		193.3		99.8	
5 to 9 years	586		2		3.4		1.9	
10 to 19 years	1,296		13		10.0		2.2	
20 to 44 years	4,371		77		17.6		9.3	
45 years and over	1,218		61		50.1		38.1	
GREENSBORO, N.C.[3]								
All ages	5,710		143		25.0		15.9	
Under 5 years	690		48		69.6		38.2	
Under 1 year	149		34		228.2		113.3	
5 to 9 years	605						3.1	
10 to 19 years	1,226		6		4.9		3.7	
20 to 44 years	2,492		52		20.9		7.5	
45 years and over	690		37		53.6		44.8	
JACKSONVILLE, FLA.								
All ages	29,293	16,236	710	532	24.2	32.8	17.0	26.6
Under 5 years	2,234	1,543	142	172	63.6	111.5	33.7	66.9
Under 1 year	474	311	102	122	215.2	392.3	129.5	177.7
5 to 9 years	2,273	1,689	12	25	5.3	14.8	4.1	4.9
10 to 19 years	5,051	3,119	48	31	9.5	9.9	5.1	7.9
20 to 44 years	16,191	7,442	305	163	18.8	21.9	10.7	16.4
45 years and over	3,459	1,921	198	140	57.2	72.9	44.8	62.8
KEY WEST, FLA.								
All ages	5,515	5,562	147	147	26.6	26.4	20.9	23.5
Under 5 years	667	739	65	67	97.4	90.7	74.2	99.1
Under 1 year	146	177	48	56	328.8	316.4	263.8	318.3
5 to 9 years	696	(2)	1	3	1.4	(2)	2.8	(2)
10 to 19 years	1,141	(2)	7	7	6.1	(2)	3.7	(2)
20 to 44 years	2,092	(2)	34	45	16.2	(2)	9.2	(2)
45 years and over	918	(2)	40	24	43.6	(2)	42.7	(2)
KNOXVILLE, TENN.[3]								
All ages	7,638		203		26.6		15.0	
Under 5 years	546		56		102.6		33.7	
Under 1 year	118		36		305.1		119.4	
5 to 9 years	539		2		3.7		1.2	
10 to 19 years	1,476		18		12.2		5.0	
20 to 44 years	3,843		76		19.8		10.6	
45 years and over	1,126		51		45.3		35.9	
LOUISVILLE, KY.								
All ages	40,522	39,139	1,089	1,070	26.9	27.3	14.5	16.9
Under 5 years	2,458	2,747	226	288	91.9	104.8	32.9	43.3
Under 1 year	510	577	131	171	256.9	296.4	114.7	137.9
5 to 9 years	2,520	2,940	20	27	7.9	9.2	3.9	4.4
10 to 19 years	6,523	6,797	69	73	10.6	10.7	3.7	4.7
20 to 44 years	21,169	19,718	393	358	18.6	18.2	7.8	9.4
45 years and over	7,665	6,568	380	308	49.6	46.9	34.9	39.3

[1] Includes cities of 10,000 or more population, with 2,500 Negro inhabitants in 1910. [2] Data not available. [3] Not included in registration area in 1900.

TABLE 34.—NEGRO POPULATION AND DEATHS AND NEGRO AND WHITE DEATH RATES, BY AGE PERIODS, BY REGISTRATION CITIES:[1] 1910 AND 1900—Continued.

SOUTHERN CITIES—Continued.

CITY AND AGE PERIOD.	Number. 1910	Number. 1900	Deaths. Number 1910	Deaths. Number 1900	Deaths. Per 1,000 pop. 1910	Deaths. Per 1,000 pop. 1900	White deaths per 1,000 pop. 1910	White deaths per 1,000 pop. 1900
LYNCHBURG, VA.								
All ages	9,466	8,254	231	298	24.4	36.1	12.1	20.5
Under 5 years	882	874	76	119	86.2	136.2	33.5	57.8
Under 1 year	188	186	58	73	308.5	392.5	101.0	178.7
5 to 9 years	831	(2)	7	12	8.4	(2)	3.2	(2)
10 to 19 years	2,000	(2)	8	19	4.0	(2)	3.1	(2)
20 to 44 years	4,049	(2)	61	76	15.1	(2)	5.0	(2)
45 years and over	1,674	(2)	79	67	47.2	(2)	32.3	(2)
MEMPHIS, TENN.								
All ages	52,441	49,910	1,492	1,218	28.4	24.4	16.9	20.7
Under 5 years	3,729	4,568	266	326	71.3	71.4	37.4	44.6
Under 1 year	768	672	169	176	220.1	261.9	120.1	149.2
5 to 9 years	3,736	5,169	27	48	7.2	9.3	4.6	7.5
10 to 19 years	8,335	9,436	132	116	15.8	12.3	4.7	5.8
20 to 44 years	28,776	23,772	628	456	21.8	19.2	10.7	14.8
45 years and over	7,711	6,856	438	272	56.8	39.7	41.4	48.4
MOBILE, ALA.								
All ages	22,763	17,045	673	564	29.6	33.1	17.8	22.5
Under 5 years	1,863	1,429	145	180	77.8	126.0	24.9	61.7
Under 1 year	334	281	102	133	305.4	473.3	79.4	235.4
5 to 9 years	1,957	1,603	10	26	5.1	16.2	3.0	4.9
10 to 19 years	3,941	3,228	35	30	8.9	9.3	4.8	3.8
20 to 44 years	11,294	7,728	253	163	22.4	21.1	11.7	15.0
45 years and over	3,498	2,757	229	164	65.5	59.5	48.2	48.8
MONTGOMERY, ALA.[3]								
All ages	19,322	....	680	......	35.2	......	17.4	......
Under 5 years	1,529	......	156	......	102.0	......	40.1	......
Under 1 year	306	......	104	......	339.9	......	117.3	......
5 to 9 years	1,643	......	11	......	6.7	......	3.5	......
10 to 19 years	3,744	......	54	......	14.4	......	2.8	......
20 to 44 years	8,685	......	221	......	25.4	......	8.9	......
45 years and over	3,656	......	238	......	65.1	......	47.3	......
NASHVILLE, TENN.								
All ages	36,523	30,044	950	965	26.0	32.1	15.1	18.8
Under 5 years	2,721	2,480	219	309	80.5	124.6	31.7	57.4
Under 1 year	570	511	147	186	257.9	364.0	90.5	161.3
5 to 9 years	2,884	2,695	25	33	8.7	12.2	2.8	3.8
10 to 19 years	7,244	6,385	67	98	9.2	15.3	4.2	5.3
20 to 44 years	16,754	13,216	297	259	17.7	19.6	9.1	10.5
45 years and over	6,902	5,244	342	265	49.6	50.5	36.9	41.9
NORFOLK, VA.								
All ages	25,039	20,230	775	770	31.0	38.1	16.5	18.8
Under 5 years	2,008	1,918	223	330	111.0	172.1	36.3	60.9
Under 1 year	406	419	163	226	401.5	539.4	122.3	214.7
5 to 9 years	1,972	1,711	26	15	13.2	8.8	3.4	3.8
10 to 19 years	4,143	3,601	47	37	11.3	10.3	3.4	3.6
20 to 44 years	13,451	10,315	298	222	22.2	21.5	8.5	9.6
45 years and over	3,436	2,627	181	164	52.7	62.4	45.9	41.8
NEW ORLEANS, LA.								
All ages	89,262	77,714	2,933	3,184	32.8	41.0	17.3	21.2
Under 5 years	7,624	7,184	616	779	80.8	108.4	37.2	53.5
Under 1 year	1,612	1,343	443	514	274.8	382.7	118.1	168.7
5 to 9 years	7,824	7,960	63	96	8.0	12.1	3.2	4.6
10 to 19 years	16,485	15,534	159	275	9.6	17.7	3.3	4.0
20 to 44 years	42,590	33,540	1,079	1,116	25.3	33.3	10.3	13.6
45 years and over	14,481	13,408	1,016	917	70.2	68.4	45.4	48.4
PADUCAH, KY.								
All ages	6,047	5,814	164	224	27.1	38.5	16.4	23.7
Under 5 years	435	446	32	62	73.6	139.0	38.5	88.8
Under 1 year	97	97	20	31	206.2	319.6	117.8	220.2
5 to 9 years	463	(2)	6	8	13.0	(2)	2.6	(2)
10 to 19 years	1,109	(2)	10	22	9.0	(2)	5.7	(2)
20 to 44 years	3,034	(2)	61	70	20.1	(2)	9.8	(2)
45 years and over	932	(2)	50	57	53.6	(2)	37.0	(2)
PETERSBURG, VA.								
All ages	11,014	10,751	377	379	34.2	35.3	20.1	25.2
Under 5 years	1,065	1,155	136	141	127.7	122.1	54.6	68.3
Under 1 year	223	259	107	103	479.8	397.7	182.8	217.6
5 to 9 years	1,152	(2)	12	13	10.4	(2)	7.5	(2)
10 to 19 years	2,396	(2)	19	27	7.9	(2)	6.6	(2)
20 to 44 years	4,319	(2)	95	89	22.0	(2)	10.2	(2)
45 years and over	2,008	(2)	115	103	57.3	(2)	41.9	(2)
RALEIGH, N. C.								
All ages	7,372	5,721	247	227	33.5	39.7	24.5	23.1
Under 5 years	678	612	70	96	103.2	156.9	50.1	65.0
Under 1 year	143	124	54	49	377.6	395.2	186.0	133.7
5 to 9 years	774	(2)	2	6	2.6	(2)	1.0	(2)
10 to 19 years	1,581	(2)	25	13	15.8	(2)	3.3	(2)
20 to 44 years	2,933	(2)	59	42	20.1	(2)	13.4	(3)
45 years and over	1,382	(2)	91	67	65.8	(2)	63.6	(2)
RICHMOND, VA.								
All ages	46,733	32,230	1,416	1,214	30.3	37.7	18.2	23.7
Under 5 years	4,019	2,747	479	444	119.2	161.6	47.6	65.2
Under 1 year	996	629	350	330	351.4	524.6	157.3	213.4
5 to 9 years	3,838	2,840	19	30	5.0	10.6	4.3	4.1
10 to 19 years	8,695	6,467	74	78	8.5	12.1	3.4	5.2
20 to 44 years	22,834	14,868	433	355	19.0	23.9	9.0	13.3
45 years and over	7,191	5,174	410	300	57.0	58.0	45.2	54.0
SAN ANTONIO, TEX.								
All ages	10,716	7,538	233	171	21.7	22.7	22.3	22.7
Under 5 years	895	718	61	50	68.2	69.6	65.4	63.1
Under 1 year	180	141	48	31	266.7	219.9	217.8	200.6
5 to 9 years	928	776	1	3	1.1	3.9	5.0	5.4
10 to 19 years	2,080	1,537	12	17	5.8	11.1	5.6	5.1
20 to 44 years	5,305	3,415	90	61	17.0	17.9	14.3	17.9
45 years and over	1,392	953	68	38	48.8	39.9	45.1	43.1
SAVANNAH, GA.								
All ages	33,246	28,090	1,134	1,070	34.1	38.1	19.4	23.4
Under 5 years	2,623	2,399	333	335	127.0	139.6	39.6	62.3
Under 1 year	564	484	242	227	429.1	469.0	120.4	193.4
5 to 9 years	2,781	2,610	23	30	8.3	11.5	3.8	7.9
10 to 19 years	5,723	5,028	65	80	11.4	15.9	4.2	6.7
20 to 44 years	17,627	14,546	400	350	22.7	24.1	11.0	14.1
45 years and over	4,417	3,309	313	260	70.9	78.6	52.8	52.6
WASHINGTON, D. C.								
All ages	94,446	86,702	2,759	2,685	29.2	31.0	15.9	18.3
Under 5 years	7,290	7,278	749	1,039	102.7	142.8	33.7	52.4
Under 1 year	1,458	1,514	581	740	398.5	488.8	121.0	189.9
5 to 9 years	7,192	7,475	43	78	6.0	10.4	3.1	4.7
10 to 19 years	15,831	16,271	125	198	7.9	12.2	2.8	3.9
20 to 44 years	47,123	40,447	873	622	18.5	15.4	6.6	9.1
45 years and over	16,537	15,151	969	748	58.6	49.4	40.8	39.8
WILMINGTON, DEL.								
All ages	9,081	9,736	225	269	24.8	27.6	16.9	19.1
Under 5 years	577	849	73	108	126.5	127.2	52.7	61.4
Under 1 year	132	187	48	72	363.6	385.0	176.2	183.0
5 to 9 years	706	838	6	8	8.5	9.5	5.1	7.6
10 to 19 years	1,561	1,787	23	24	14.7	13.4	4.7	5.0
20 to 44 years	4,306	4,619	50	58	11.6	12.6	7.5	9.3
45 years and over	1,891	1,565	72	70	38.1	44.7	34.4	38.0
WILMINGTON, N. C.								
All ages	12,107	10,407	325	384	26.8	36.9	15.6	24.8
Under 5 years	1,280	1,076	110	151	85.9	140.3	45.9	80.0
Under 1 year	289	217	79	103	273.4	474.7	144.1	189.8
5 to 9 years	1,199	(2)	5	12	4.2	(2)	1.6	(2)
10 to 19 years	2,283	(2)	17	18	7.4	(2)	2.9	(2)
20 to 44 years	4,949	(2)	101	96	20.4	(2)	7.1	(2)
45 years and over	1,948	(2)	91	98	46.7	(2)	37.6	(2)

[1] Includes cities of 10,000 or more population, with 2,500 Negro inhabitants in 1910.   [2] Data not available.   [3] Not included in registration area in 1900.

TABLE **34.**—NEGRO POPULATION AND DEATHS AND NEGRO AND WHITE DEATH RATES, BY AGE PERIODS, BY REGISTRATION CITIES:[1] 1910 AND 1900—Continued.

CITY AND AGE PERIOD.	NEGRO POPULATION. Number.		Deaths. Number.		Deaths. Per 1,000 population.		WHITE DEATHS PER 1,000 POPULATION.	
	1910	1900	1910	1900	1910	1900	1910	1900
SOUTHERN CITIES—Continued.								
WINSTON, N. C.[2]								
All ages	7,828	......	186	......	23.8	......	17.8	......
Under 5 years	692		53		76.6		60.7	
Under 1 year	166		30		180.7		194.0	
5 to 9 years	777		4		5.1		1.0	
10 to 19 years	1,741		15		8.6		4.0	
20 to 44 years	3,705		60		16.2		9.5	
45 years and over	902		53		58.8		38.6	
NORTHERN AND WESTERN CITIES.								
ATLANTIC CITY, N. J.								
All ages	9,834	6,513	172	106	17.5	16.3	17.3	17.6
Under 5 years	536	375	55	45	102.6	120.0	50.5	65.0
Under 1 year	114	83	43	33	377.2	397.6	192.8	204.1
5 to 9 years	505	311	5	2	9.9	6.4	3.0	6.3
10 to 19 years	1,070	702	7	6	6.5	8.5	3.0	3.3
20 to 44 years	6,261	3,911	61	31	9.7	7.9	7.5	7.7
45 years and over	1,412	696	44	22	31.1	31.6	43.5	37.7
BOSTON, MASS.								
All ages	13,564	11,591	317	312	23.4	26.9	17.1	20.3
Under 5 years	942	936	75	112	79.6	119.7	48.4	63.8
Under 1 year	215	211	44	68	204.7	322.3	165.0	189.0
5 to 9 years	742	709	2	7	2.7	9.9	4.4	6.8
10 to 19 years	1,631	1,331	16	15	9.8	11.3	3.3	4.3
20 to 44 years	7,805	6,703	99	100	12.7	14.9	8.2	10.3
45 years and over	2,428	1,778	125	78	51.5	43.9	38.7	41.1
CAMBRIDGE, MASS.								
All ages	4,707	3,888	75	105	15.9	27.0	15.0	16.7
Under 5 years	480	448	24	41	50.0	91.5	36.6	51.9
Under 1 year	106	103	15	30	141.5	291.3	125.4	167.8
5 to 9 years	405	372	......	2	......	5.4	2.8	6.3
10 to 19 years	825	625	6	8	7.3	12.8	3.2	3.9
20 to 44 years	2,141	1,809	18	29	8.4	16.0	7.4	7.7
45 years and over	852	614	27	24	31.7	39.1	35.2	34.7
CAMDEN, N. J.								
All ages	6,076	5,576	192	186	31.6	33.4	16.3	16.8
Under 5 years	569	521	65	89	114.2	170.8	50.3	63.6
Under 1 year	124	113	46	54	371.0	477.9	167.2	189.3
5 to 9 years	509	492	5	14	9.8	28.5	6.4	10.3
10 to 19 years	961	960	8	17	8.3	17.7	4.2	4.3
20 to 44 years	2,794	2,497	49	29	17.5	11.6	7.0	7.0
45 years and over	1,231	1,009	65	37	52.0	36.7	32.9	28.0
CHESTER, PA.[2]								
All ages	4,795	......	107	......	22.3	......	16.1	......
Under 5 years	413		42		101.7		54.0	
Under 1 year	86		20		232.6		206.7	
5 to 9 years	389		2		5.1		5.7	
10 to 19 years	774		2		2.6		5.0	
20 to 44 years	2,351		32		13.6		6.9	
45 years and over	860		29		33.7		32.7	
CHICAGO, ILL.								
All ages	44,103	30,150	1,075	712	24.4	23.6	15.0	15.2
Under 5 years	2,472	1,611	184	161	74.4	99.9	44.9	44.3
Under 1 year	544	323	113	101	207.7	312.7	138.7	136.8
5 to 9 years	2,147	1,536	21	18	9.8	11.7	4.2	5.5
10 to 19 years	4,768	3,645	47	40	9.9	11.0	3.1	3.7
20 to 44 years	27,093	18,997	465	299	17.2	15.7	7.7	8.4
45 years and over	7,278	4,211	358	194	49.2	46.1	35.4	35.3
CINCINNATI, OHIO.								
All ages	19,639	14,482	569	430	29.0	29.7	16.7	17.6
Under 5 years	1,148	996	121	105	105.4	105.4	41.9	47.5
Under 1 year	258	236	83	64	321.7	271.2	142.3	154.6
5 to 9 years	1,029	1,018	10	13	9.7	12.8	3.4	3.7
10 to 19 years	2,720	2,205	25	27	9.2	12.2	3.0	3.7
20 to 44 years	11,095	7,909	236	180	21.3	22.8	9.5	10.7
45 years and over	3,468	2,314	176	105	50.7	45.4	37.7	40.6

CITY AND AGE PERIOD.	NEGRO POPULATION. Number.		Deaths. Number.		Deaths. Per 1,000 population.		WHITE DEATHS PER 1,000 POPULATION.	
	1910	1900	1910	1900	1910	1900	1910	1900
NORTHERN AND WESTERN CITIES—Contd.								
CLEVELAND, OHIO.								
All ages	8,448	5,988	167	99	19.8	16.5	14.3	17.6
Under 5 years	519	371	38	34	73.2	91.6	44.5	57.6
Under 1 year	118	77	25	25	211.9	324.7	146.6	199.0
5 to 9 years	453	429	4	2	8.8	4.7	3.1	5.4
10 to 19 years	1,054	803	8	4	7.6	5.0	2.9	4.1
20 to 44 years	5,013	3,523	62	30	12.4	8.5	6.6	9.6
45 years and over	1,389	840	55	29	39.6	34.5	33.4	35.8
COLUMBUS, OHIO.								
All ages	12,739	8,201	262	187	20.6	22.8	15.1	15.3
Under 5 years	836	574	51	34	61.0	59.2	36.8	39.1
Under 1 year	169	108	43	14	254.4	129.6	187.1	135.0
5 to 9 years	784	644	2	4	2.6	6.2	3.5	6.2
10 to 19 years	1,850	1,425	17	17	9.2	11.9	4.2	4.8
20 to 44 years	7,037	4,195	104	65	14.8	15.5	8.3	9.9
45 years and over	2,195	1,296	88	62	40.1	47.8	34.7	33.1
DAYTON, OHIO.								
All ages	4,842	3,387	99	68	20.4	20.1	14.5	15.5
Under 5 years	374	248	26	21	69.5	84.7	39.4	41.3
Under 1 year	75	59	19	18	253.3	305.1	143.1	147.2
5 to 9 years	325	274	4	3	12.3	10.9	3.8	6.4
10 to 19 years	646	612	7	8	10.8	13.1	2.9	3.9
20 to 44 years	2,584	1,720	31	19	12.0	11.0	7.3	7.7
45 years and over	902	521	31	17	34.4	32.6	31.9	36.3
DENVER, COLO.								
All ages	5,426	3,923	132	89	24.3	22.7	16.4	18.9
Under 5 years	313	241	25	20	79.9	83.0	34.7	46.8
Under 1 year	70	50	20	13	285.7	260.0	131.1	165.5
5 to 9 years	299	297	......	2	......	6.7	4.0	4.7
10 to 19 years	710	579	2	4	2.8	6.9	4.0	5.9
20 to 44 years	3,022	2,076	59	35	19.5	16.9	12.1	15.6
45 years and over	1,062	650	46	28	43.3	42.7	33.2	34.3
DETROIT, MICH.								
All ages	5,741	4,111	146	103	25.4	25.1	15.9	16.2
Under 5 years	330	300	36	21	109.1	70.0	56.2	55.2
Under 1 year	73	66	26	10	356.2	151.5	203.6	202.0
5 to 9 years	343	317	2	2	5.8	6.3	5.3	3.9
10 to 19 years	727	650	8	8	11.0	12.3	3.7	3.8
20 to 44 years	3,246	2,047	44	25	13.6	12.2	6.9	8.0
45 years and over	1,073	793	56	46	52.2	58.0	33.0	33.1
EVANSVILLE, IND.								
All ages	6,266	7,518	117	150	18.7	20.0	13.1	15.2
Under 5 years	428	639	34	42	79.4	65.7	34.8	46.5
Under 1 year	75	114	22	26	293.3	228.1	129.4	166.0
5 to 9 years	449	725	3	2	6.7	2.8	2.1	5.9
10 to 19 years	1,079	1,480	7	12	6.5	8.1	3.4	3.7
20 to 44 years	3,124	3,573	37	42	11.8	11.8	8.2	8.3
45 years and over	1,177	1,088	35	52	29.7	47.8	27.2	34.3
HARRISBURG, PA.								
All ages	4,535	4,107	98	104	21.6	25.3	14.1	17.4
Under 5 years	355	344	27	33	76.1	95.9	38.7	57.8
Under 1 year	76	68	17	17	223.7	250.0	148.3	187.6
5 to 9 years	308	359	3	5	9.7	13.9	6.8	5.2
10 to 19 years	709	814	6	15	8.5	18.4	2.8	3.5
20 to 44 years	2,250	1,817	31	16	13.8	8.8	7.0	7.8
45 years and over	908	769	31	33	34.1	42.9	30.8	38.1
INDIANAPOLIS, IND.								
All ages	21,816	15,931	548	383	25.1	24.0	15.5	16.3
Under 5 years	1,557	1,167	121	123	77.7	105.4	39.6	48.7
Under 1 year	346	252	79	74	228.3	293.7	136.6	167.0
5 to 9 years	1,523	1,273	14	8	9.2	6.3	3.4	5.1
10 to 19 years	3,243	2,838	33	32	10.2	11.3	3.2	3.8
20 to 44 years	11,274	7,673	181	104	16.1	13.6	8.0	9.0
45 years and over	4,150	2,739	199	116	48.0	42.4	36.2	36.0

[1] Includes cities of 10,000 or more population, with 2,500 Negro inhabitants in 1910.　　[2] Not included in registration area in 1900.

TABLE **34.**—NEGRO POPULATION AND DEATHS AND NEGRO AND WHITE DEATH RATES, BY AGE PERIODS, BY REGISTRATION CITIES:[1] 1910 AND 1900—Continued.

CITY AND AGE PERIOD.	NEGRO POPULATION.						WHITE DEATHS PER 1,000 POPULATION.	
	Number.		Deaths.					
			Number.		Per 1,000 population.			
	1910	1900	1910	1900	1910	1900	1910	1900
NORTHREN AND WESTERN CITIES—Contd.								
JERSEY CITY, N. J.								
All ages	5,960	3,704	123	83	20.6	22.4	16.3	20.7
Under 5 years	557	317	37	24	66.4	75.7	44.9	59.6
Under 1 year	129	64	22	13	170.5	203.1	152.8	190.0
5 to 9 years	455	299	3	3	6.6	10.0	3.5	5.1
10 to 19 years	798	564	5	3	6.3	5.3	3.2	4.8
20 to 44 years	3,278	2,007	40	29	12.2	14.4	9.3	12.2
45 years and over	861	516	38	24	44.1	46.5	38.8	42.5
KANSAS CITY, KANS.[2]								
All ages	9,286	......	237	......	24.1	......	15.8	......
Under 5 years	745	......	45	......	60.4	......	40.9	......
Under 1 year	139	......	29	......	208.6	......	140.8	......
5 to 9 years	769	......	5	......	6.5	......	4.3	......
10 to 19 years	1,569	......	18	......	11.5	......	4.0	......
20 to 44 years	4,402	......	84	......	19.1	......	8.4	......
45 years and over	1,768	......	84	......	47.5	......	38.1	......
KANSAS CITY, MO.								
All ages	23,566	17,567	644	438	27.3	24.9	14.8	15.3
Under 5 years	1,211	1,076	128	130	105.7	120.8	42.0	51.0
Under 1 year	235	223	94	78	400.0	349.8	155.3	164.2
5 to 9 years	1,189	1,289	19	15	16.0	11.6	6.0	5.5
10 to 19 years	3,019	2,992	45	40	14.9	13.4	4.3	4.7
20 to 44 years	14,108	9,860	259	169	18.4	17.1	8.0	8.9
45 years and over	3,704	2,303	192	81	51.8	35.2	32.8	31.2
LOS ANGELES, CAL.								
All ages	7,599	2,131	136	62	17.9	29.1	14.1	18.4
Under 5 years	556	198	21	22	37.8	111.1	32.8	44.2
Under 1 year	114	41	16	18	140.4	439.0	109.7	170.7
5 to 9 years	515	217	2	2	3.9	9.2	2.5	5.6
10 to 19 years	1,181	368	7	4	5.9	4.7	3.0	4.7
20 to 44 years	3,892	940	62	23	15.9	24.5	8.3	13.0
45 years and over	1,428	385	44	11	30.8	28.6	30.1	36.3
MINNEAPOLIS, MINN.								
All ages	2,592	1,548	56	22	21.6	14.2	12.3	11.4
Under 5 years	113	101	9	3	79.6	29.7	35.0	31.6
Under 1 year	22	23	4	2	181.8	87.0	114.0	107.3
5 to 9 years	115	115	......	1	......	8.7	4.9	5.2
10 to 19 years	286	192	2	5	7.0	26.0	3.5	3.9
20 to 44 years	1,613	898	16	10	9.9	11.1	6.6	6.6
45 years and over	411	233	29	3	70.6	12.9	28.3	25.2
NEWARK, N. J.								
All ages	9,475	6,694	296	202	31.2	30.2	16.2	19.9
Under 5 years	875	605	108	92	123.4	152.1	44.3	60.9
Under 1 year	200	146	70	67	350.0	458.9	140.9	177.5
5 to 9 years	712	554	9	11	12.6	19.9	4.2	4.9
10 to 19 years	1,376	1,063	10	9	7.3	8.5	3.2	3.9
20 to 44 years	4,985	3,385	89	44	17.9	13.0	8.7	10.9
45 years and over	1,501	1,061	80	45	53.3	42.4	37.6	40.9
NEW BEDFORD, MASS.								
All ages	2,885	1,685	85	32	29.5	19.0	18.4	21.3
Under 5 years	380	139	36	10	94.7	71.9	82.4	84.0
Under 1 year	109	39	25	5	229.4	128.2	269.9	284.2
5 to 9 years	258	123	......	......	......	......	5.2	4.7
10 to 19 years	399	279	......	1	(3)	3.6	3.2	5.2
20 to 44 years	1,375	767	33	8	24.0	10.4	5.8	7.9
45 years and over	473	375	16	11	33.8	29.3	31.5	38.0
NEW HAVEN, CONN.								
All ages	3,561	2,887	91	82	25.6	28.4	16.4	18.0
Under 5 years	271	244	20	27	73.8	110.7	40.0	52.0
Under 1 year	57	50	14	22	245.6	440.0	132.8	179.8
5 to 9 years	246	242	3	2	12.2	8.3	3.5	3.7
10 to 19 years	506	481	4	6	7.9	12.5	2.8	3.5
20 to 44 years	1,854	1,304	25	15	13.5	11.5	7.9	8.8
45 years and over	678	613	39	32	57.5	52.2	40.0	39.6

CITY AND AGE PERIOD.	NEGRO POPULATION.						WHITE DEATHS PER 1,000 POPULATION.	
	Number.		Deaths.					
			Number.		Per 1,000 population.			
	1910	1900	1910	1900	1910	1900	1910	1900
NORTHERN AND WESTERN CITIES—Contd.								
NEW YORK, N. Y.								
All ages	91,709	60,666	2,391	1,950	26.1	32.1	15.9	20.4
Under 5 years	6,676	4,566	809	802	121.2	175.6	46.8	63.7
Under 1 year	1,594	1,112	530	550	332.5	494.6	143.5	188.1
5 to 9 years	5,114	3,846	50	55	9.8	14.3	4.2	5.8
10 to 19 years	11,138	8,899	105	101	9.4	11.3	3.0	3.6
20 to 44 years	56,378	34,782	877	543	15.6	15.6	8.3	11.5
45 years and over	12,131	8,449	550	449	45.3	53.1	37.7	41.9
Manhattan Borough.[2]								
All ages	60,534	......	1,473	1,242	24.3	......	16.4	......
Under 5 years	4,054	......	522	519	128.8	......	53.9	......
Under 1 year	992	......	354	353	356.9	......	143.5	......
5 to 9 years	2,909	......	27	23	9.3	......	4.3	......
10 to 19 years	6,663	......	62	56	9.3	......	2.9	......
20 to 44 years	39,493	......	561	369	14.2	......	8.1	......
45 years and over	7,192	......	301	275	41.9	......	38.3	......
Bronx Borough.[2]								
All ages	4,117	......	208	75	50.5	......	15.8	......
Under 5 years	393	......	39	19	99.2	......	34.2	......
Under 1 year	92	......	20	17	217.4	......	107.5	......
5 to 9 years	309	......	4	4	12.9	......	3.8	......
10 to 19 years	571	......	8	......	14.0	......	3.6	......
20 to 44 years	2,128	......	85	19	39.9	......	11.0	......
45 years and over	706	......	72	27	102.0	......	38.5	......
Brooklyn Borough.								
All ages	22,708	18,367	598	553	26.3	30.1	15.6	20.0
Under 5 years	1,824	1,491	214	223	117.3	149.6	42.4	63.5
Under 1 year	417	366	135	153	323.7	418.0	128.1	192.5
5 to 9 years	1,549	1,322	16	24	10.3	18.2	4.3	6.1
10 to 19 years	3,188	2,965	28	35	8.8	11.8	2.9	3.7
20 to 44 years	12,628	9,808	192	128	15.2	13.1	8.0	10.9
45 years and over	3,485	2,775	148	123	42.5	44.3	37.2	39.3
Queens Borough.								
All ages	3,198	2,611	82	66	25.6	25.3	13.8	18.0
Under 5 years	298	236	26	30	87.2	127.1	39.1	50.1
Under 1 year	67	51	16	19	238.8	372.5	129.3	159.8
5 to 9 years	245	198	3	3	12.2	15.2	3.6	5.3
10 to 19 years	508	496	5	2	9.8	4.0	2.4	3.4
20 to 44 years	1,601	1,224	29	16	18.1	13.1	7.1	10.1
45 years and over	542	456	19	15	35.1	32.9	33.4	39.1
Richmond Borough.								
All ages	1,152	1,072	30	34	26.0	31.7	17.0	20.4
Under 5 years	107	111	8	11	74.8	99.1	42.8	57.7
Under 1 year	26	28	5	8	192.3	285.7	159.4	188.5
5 to 9 years	102	92	......	1	......	10.9	3.2	6.6
10 to 19 years	208	211	2	2	9.6	9.5	3.0	3.9
20 to 44 years	528	444	10	11	18.9	24.8	8.6	10.0
45 years and over	206	213	10	9	48.5	42.3	41.5	44.5
OAKLAND, CAL.								
All ages	3,055	1,026	52	19	17.0	18.5	12.6	15.9
Under 5 years	216	46	11	2	50.9	43.5	27.5	31.4
Under 1 year	50	12	4	......	80.0	......	93.3	100.0
5 to 9 years	183	80	1	2	5.5	25.0	3.3	3.4
10 to 19 years	332	165	2	2	6.0	12.1	2.7	3.9
20 to 44 years	1,692	484	17	6	10.0	12.4	5.6	9.6
45 years and over	630	232	21	7	33.3	30.2	31.4	36.5
OMAHA, NEBR.								
All ages	4,426	3,443	105	67	23.7	19.5	14.8	11.5
Under 5 years	243	219	12	14	49.4	63.9	36.3	39.6
Under 1 year	41	45	11	10	268.3	222.2	137.5	139.2
5 to 9 years	239	239	1	3	4.2	12.6	4.7	3.9
10 to 19 years	477	553	8	4	16.8	7.2	5.0	3.5
20 to 44 years	2,733	1,955	53	22	19.4	11.3	8.5	6.4
45 years and over	728	463	31	24	42.6	51.8	34.3	24.8

[1] Includes cities of 10,000 or more population, with 2,500 Negro inhabitants in 1910.   [2] Not included in registration area in 1900.   [3] Less than one-tenth of 1 per cent.

TABLE 34.—NEGRO POPULATION AND DEATHS AND NEGRO AND WHITE DEATH RATES, BY AGE PERIODS, BY REGISTRATION CITIES:[1] 1910 AND 1900—Continued.

CITY AND AGE PERIOD.	NEGRO POPULATION.						WHITE DEATHS PER 1,000 POPULATION.	
	Number.		Deaths.					
			Number.		Per 1,000 population.			
	1910	1900	1910	1900	1910	1900	1910	1900
NORTHERN AND WESTERN CITIES—Contd.								
PHILADELPHIA, PA.								
All ages	84,459	62,613	2,276	1,894	26.9	30.2	16.9	20.4
Under 5 years	6,863	5,328	793	796	115.5	149.4	47.9	65.0
Under 1 year	1,595	1,232	544	532	341.1	431.8	153.0	197.5
5 to 9 years	5,623	4,199	56	57	10.0	13.6	4.1	7.0
10 to 19 years	10,950	9,001	105	114	9.6	12.7	2.9	4.0
20 to 44 years	48,121	35,296	756	530	15.7	15.1	8.1	9.9
45 years and over	12,606	8,511	566	397	44.9	46.6	38.1	42.3
PITTSBURGH, PA.								
All ages	25,623	17,040	601	526	23.5	30.9	17.7	19.7
Under 5 years	2,240	1,535	225	180	100.4	117.3	58.8	65.2
Under 1 year	459	334	140	117	305.0	350.3	174.8	186.6
5 to 9 years	1,942	1,290	15	19	7.7	14.7	4.9	5.9
10 to 19 years	3,665	2,551	28	34	7.6	13.3	3.6	5.5
20 to 44 years	14,178	9,790	177	185	12.5	18.9	9.0	11.4
45 years and over	3,485	1,830	156	107	44.8	58.5	36.9	36.4
PROVIDENCE, R. I.								
All ages	5,316	4,817	139	140	26.1	29.1	17.6	20.6
Under 5 years	458	442	43	52	93.9	117.6	53.0	71.2
Under 1 year	98	103	32	29	326.5	281.6	170.8	217.3
5 to 9 years	372	378	5	2	13.4	5.3	3.8	5.7
10 to 19 years	781	727	7	9	9.0	12.4	3.7	4.3
20 to 44 years	2,594	2,301	31	26	12.0	11.3	8.0	10.5
45 years and over	1,099	960	53	51	48.2	53.1	38.8	38.8
ST. JOSEPH, MO.								
All ages	4,249	6,260	98	68	23.1	10.9	13.1	7.2
Under 5 years	255	481	15	13	58.8	27.0	29.2	15.5
Under 1 year	52	81	10	6	192.3	74.1	101.4	70.0
5 to 9 years	274	539	2	4	7.3	7.4	3.5	2.4
10 to 19 years	675	1,337	6	7	8.9	5.2	3.4	2.5
20 to 44 years	2,292	3,154	41	22	17.9	7.0	7.5	4.0
45 years and over	750	706	32	21	42.7	29.7	31.6	22.7
ST. LOUIS, MO.								
All ages	43,960	35,516	1,149	1,096	26.1	30.9	15.1	17.1
Under 5 years	2,685	2,403	236	264	87.9	109.9	37.9	45.3
Under 1 year	538	459	147	166	273.2	361.7	129.6	147.2
5 to 9 years	2,588	2,542	20	34	7.7	13.4	4.2	6.0
10 to 19 years	5,999	6,184	47	72	7.8	11.6	2.9	4.0
20 to 44 years	24,950	18,376	466	387	18.7	21.1	8.0	9.9
45 years and over	7,628	5,610	377	333	49.4	59.4	38.2	41.3

CITY AND AGE PERIOD.	NEGRO POPULATION.						WHITE DEATHS PER 1,000 POPULATION.	
	Number.		Deaths.					
			Number.		Per 1,000 population.			
	1910	1900	1910	1900	1910	1900	1910	1900
NORTHERN AND WESTERN CITIES—Contd.								
ST. PAUL, MINN.								
All ages	3,144	2,263	49	30	15.6	13.3	11.9	10.0
Under 5 years	164	134	5	5	30.5	37.3	38.7	29.4
Under 1 year	29	23	3	4	103.4	173.9	131.0	106.8
5 to 9 years	140	149	1	2	7.1	13.4	6.7	3.3
10 to 19 years	326	233	2	1	6.1	4.3	3.7	3.2
20 to 44 years	2,013	1,373	18	15	8.9	10.9	5.1	5.4
45 years and over	500	309	23	7	46.0	22.7	28.0	24.9
SPRINGFIELD, ILL.								
All ages	2,961	2,227	67	57	22.6	25.6	16.3	17.2
Under 5 years	221	212	16	16	72.4	75.5	40.1	45.8
Under 1 year	35	31	12	13	342.9	419.4	157.2	141.3
5 to 9 years	219	193	2	....	9.1	....	4.1	4.8
10 to 19 years	497	425	5	3	10.1	7.1	4.3	5.5
20 to 44 years	1,415	977	23	16	16.3	16.4	9.5	10.6
45 years and over	598	410	21	22	35.1	53.7	35.1	35.4
SPRINGFIELD, OHIO.[2]								
All ages	4,933	....	78	....	15.8	....	12.9	....
Under 5 years	380	....	15	....	39.5	....	30.6	....
Under 1 year	86	....	11	....	127.9	....	118.3	....
5 to 9 years	409	....	6	....	14.7	....	3.0	....
10 to 19 years	825	....	1	....	1.2	....	2.7	....
20 to 44 years	2,202	....	26	....	11.8	....	6.1	....
45 years and over	1,082	....	30	....	27.7	....	29.8	....
TERRE HAUTE, IND.								
All ages	2,593	1,520	67	40	25.8	26.3	15.6	15.8
Under 5 years	186	147	23	19	123.7	129.3	42.3	52.1
Under 1 year	45	36	16	13	355.6	361.1	142.5	172.9
5 to 9 years	214	136	....	1	....	7.4	3.8	6.8
10 to 19 years	436	269	5	1	11.5	3.7	3.8	4.9
20 to 44 years	1,324	732	26	8	19.6	10.9	8.2	8.5
45 years and over	428	225	13	11	30.4	48.9	35.5	29.9
TRENTON, N. J.								
All ages	2,581	2,096	89	49	34.5	23.4	20.0	17.2
Under 5 years	183	120	17	13	92.9	108.3	65.2	54.2
Under 1 year	36	31	14	10	388.9	322.6	215.6	186.9
5 to 9 years	126	117	1	1	7.9	8.5	3.2	3.2
10 to 19 years	335	331	8	5	23.9	15.1	3.9	3.8
20 to 44 years	1,435	1,138	35	16	24.4	14.1	9.5	8.1
45 years and over	502	365	28	12	55.8	32.9	43.2	37.4

[1] Includes cities of 10,000 or more population, with 2,500 Negro inhabitants in 1910.   [2] Not included in registration area in 1900.

NEGRO POPULATION.

TABLE 35.—NUMBER AND PERCENTAGE OF NEGRO DEATHS UNDER

CITY.	NUMBER OF DEATHS.[1]													
	All ages.							Children under 1 year.						
	1910–1914						1900	1910–1914						1900
	Total.	1914	1913	1912	1911	1910		Total.	1914	1913	1912	1911	1910	
The registration area:														
1 Negro	299,675	70,429	67,266	56,050	56,431	49,499	34,995	50,753	11,543	11,348	9,042	9,470	9,350	7,914
2 White	3,956,736	824,319	820,204	779,135	779,770	753,308	503,569	712,351	142,946	147,414	137,912	139,429	144,650	103,662
CITIES IN THE REGISTRATION AREA.														
3 Alexandria, Va.	643	125	118	131	131	138	160	123	32	25	25	22	19	38
4 Annapolis, Md.	(²)	(²)	(²)	(²)	(²)	97	126	22	(²)	(²)	(²)	(²)	22	50
5 Atlanta, Ga.	7,056	1,384	1,469	1,381	1,494	1,328	977	1,062	190	223	202	212	235	244
6 Atlantic City, N. J.	854	182	165	170	165	172	106	173	35	36	31	28	43	33
7 Baltimore, Md.	13,083	2,600	2,709	2,533	2,644	2,597	2,653	2,595	491	522	476	527	579	766
8 Boston, Mass.	1,732	369	357	334	355	317	312	261	47	61	51	58	44	68
9 Cambridge, Mass.	417	88	81	74	99	75	105	73	18	12	11	17	15	30
10 Camden, N. J.	854	183	169	149	161	192	186	189	34	34	40	35	46	54
11 Charleston, S. C.	6,121	1,175	1,174	1,299	1,252	1,221	1,399	1,342	240	255	281	259	307	350
12 Chicago, Ill.	5,672	1,164	1,184	1,230	1,019	1,075	712	548	110	106	123	96	113	101
13 Cincinnati, Ohio	3,098	642	665	626	596	569	430	339	75	52	73	56	83	64
14 Cleveland, Ohio	967	207	193	190	210	167	99	127	22	27	25	28	25	25
15 Columbus, Ohio	1,426	316	299	294	255	262	187	201	53	35	31	39	43	14
16 Covington, Ky.	456	113	91	100	93	59	81	48	11	12	8	9	8	14
17 Dayton, Ohio	586	115	138	134	100	99	68	85	13	15	18	20	19	18
18 Denver, Colo	621	133	125	103	128	132	89	55	11	6	3	15	20	13
19 Detroit, Mich	749	158	166	142	137	146	103	107	19	23	18	21	26	10
20 Evansville, Ind	733	147	164	150	155	117	150	108	19	23	14	30	22	26
21 Harrisburg, Pa.	501	93	118	104	88	98	104	79	8	20	17	17	17	17
22 Indianapolis, Ind.	2,735	571	582	534	500	548	383	380	82	88	71	60	79	74
23 Jacksonville, Fla.	3,882	783	773	775	841	710	532	574	113	119	123	117	102	122
24 Jersey City, N. J.	598	114	114	115	132	123	83	114	23	18	29	22	22	13
25 Kansas City, Mo.	3,195	631	625	678	617	644	438	343	58	50	68	73	94	78
26 Key West, Fla.	632	101	98	114	172	147	147	167	18	25	24	52	48	56
27 Los Angeles, Cal.	888	190	218	196	148	136	62	86	19	27	12	12	16	18
28 Louisville, Ky.	5,298	1,015	1,047	1,083	1,064	1,089	1,070	573	108	120	116	98	131	171
29 Lynchburg, Va.	1,315	275	286	263	260	231	298	309	62	78	56	55	58	73
30 Memphis, Tenn.	7,883	1,695	1,586	1,604	1,506	1,492	1,218	848	157	167	189	166	169	176
31 Minneapolis, Minn.	288	62	59	50	61	56	22	26	6	5	3	8	4	2
32 Mobile, Ala.	3,271	648	619	617	714	673	564	476	81	94	105	94	102	133
33 Nashville, Tenn.	4,992	994	903	1,053	1,092	950	965	674	134	103	152	138	147	186
34 Newark, N. J.	1,476	318	273	279	310	296	202	333	69	61	56	77	70	67
35 New Bedford, Mass.	330	67	58	65	55	85	32	73	13	15	10	10	25	5
36 New Haven, Conn.	510	106	119	86	108	91	82	91	20	18	16	23	14	22
37 New Orleans, La.	14,673	3,011	2,994	2,901	2,834	2,933	3,184	1,936	366	396	323	408	443	514
38 New York, N. Y.	12,205	2,546	2,344	2,492	2,432	2,391	1,950	2,429	453	435	502	509	530	550
39 Manhattan Borough	7,926	1,680	1,568	1,644	1,561	1,473	1,242	1,627	303	302	326	342	354	353
40 Bronx Borough	583	91	98	89	97	208	75	76	14	12	17	13	20	17
41 Brooklyn Borough	3,059	637	566	620	638	598	533	587	109	100	124	119	135	153
42 Queens Borough	485	105	82	110	106	82	66	111	24	12	29	30	16	19
43 Richmond Borough	152	33	30	29	30	30	34	28	3	9	6	5	5	8
44 Norfolk, Va.	4,680	975	945	953	1,032	775	770	946	185	180	198	220	163	226
45 Oakland, Cal.	296	59	67	66	52	52	19	33	4	11	11	3	4	......
46 Omaha, Nebr.	545	111	118	98	113	105	67	42	6	7	9	9	11	10
47 Paducah, Ky.	950	181	205	203	197	164	224	126	24	27	24	31	20	31
48 Petersburg, Va.	1,828	380	368	349	354	377	379	434	90	85	79	73	107	103
49 Philadelphia, Pa.	10,424	2,261	2,192	1,690	2,005	2,276	1,894	2,250	449	468	333	456	544	532
50 Pittsburgh, Pa.	2,699	585	585	496	432	601	526	513	104	110	77	82	140	117
51 Providence, R. I.	780	181	147	171	142	139	140	150	30	26	35	27	32	29
52 Raleigh, N. C.	1,301	301	224	251	278	247	227	251	64	41	38	54	54	49
53 Richmond, Va.	6,768	1,360	1,306	1,340	1,346	1,416	1,214	1,506	285	274	300	297	350	330
54 St. Joseph, Mo.	436	82	99	88	69	98	68	44	7	13	7	7	10	6
55 St. Louis, Mo.	6,040	1,257	1,247	1,217	1,170	1,149	1,096	676	136	134	118	141	147	166
56 St. Paul, Minn.	282	54	71	58	50	49	30	22	1	6	6	6	3	4
57 San Antonio, Tex.	1,312	265	268	298	248	233	171	184	34	23	45	34	48	31
58 Springfield, Ill.	362	81	78	74	62	67	57	51	11	18	8	3	11	13
59 Savannah, Ga.	5,854	1,147	1,111	1,162	1,300	1,134	1,070	1,102	219	216	194	231	242	227
60 Terre Haute, Ind.	321	69	67	61	57	67	40	66	13	11	17	9	16	13
61 Trenton, N. J.	411	89	88	80	65	89	49	46	12	10	6	4	14	10
62 Washington, D. C.	12,753	2,360	2,431	2,644	2,559	2,759	2,685	2,313	369	428	471	464	581	740
63 Wilmington, Del.	1,208	246	253	255	229	225	269	255	53	51	55	48	48	72
64 Wilmington, N. C.	1,976	405	374	400	472	325	384	497	102	100	100	116	79	103

[1] Exclusive of stillbirths.

1 YEAR AND UNDER 5 YEARS, BY CITIES: 1910–1914 AND 1900.

NUMBER OF DEATHS [1]—continued.							PER 100 DEATHS: ALL AGES.														
Children under 5 years.							Deaths of children under 1 year.							Deaths of children under 5 years.							
	1910–1914					1900		1910–1914					1900		1910–1914					1900	
Total.	1914	1913	1912	1911	1910		Total.	1914	1913	1912	1911	1910		Total.	1914	1913	1912	1911	1910		
73,751	16,537	16,317	13,015	14,251	13,631	11,840	17	16	17	16	17	19	23	25	23	24	23	25	28	34	1
993,179	196,721	207,843	190,889	194,570	203,156	152,128	18	17	18	18	18	19	21	25	24	25	24	25	27	30	2
167	35	33	36	29	34	54	19	26	21	19	17	14	24	26	28	28	27	22	25	34	3
(²)	(²)	(²)	(²)	(²)	38	70	(²)	(²)	(²)	(²)	(²)	23	40	(²)	(²)	(²)	(²)	(²)	39	56	4
1,681	296	342	334	369	340	361	15	14	15	15	14	18	25	24	21	23	24	25	26	37	5
218	43	45	41	34	55	45	20	19	22	18	17	25	31	26	24	27	24	21	32	42	6
3,642	708	735	676	747	776	1,107	20	19	19	19	19	22	29	28	27	27	27	28	30	42	7
397	64	89	74	95	75	112	15	13	17	15	16	14	22	23	17	25	22	27	24	36	8
114	26	22	13	29	24	41	18	20	15	15	17	20	29	27	30	27	18	29	32	39	9
269	47	54	50	53	65	89	22	19	20	27	22	24	29	31	26	32	34	33	34	48	10
1,944	343	377	405	366	453	504	22	29	22	21	21	25	25	32	29	32	31	29	37	36	11
906	186	170	200	166	184	161	9	9	9	10	9	11	14	16	16	14	16	16	17	23	12
525	103	87	114	100	121	105	11	12	8	12	9	15	15	17	16	13	18	17	21	24	13
185	30	35	34	48	38	34	13	11	14	13	13	15	25	19	14	18	18	23	23	34	14
279	71	54	48	55	51	34	14	17	12	11	15	16	7	20	22	18	16	22	19	18	15
80	18	16	15	17	14	22	11	10	13	8	10	14	17	18	16	18	15	18	24	27	16
115	20	20	24	25	26	21	15	11	11	13	20	19	26	20	17	14	18	25	26	31	17
82	19	11	8	19	25	20	9	8	5	3	12	15	15	13	14	9	8	15	19	22	18
152	28	31	28	29	36	21	14	12	14	13	15	18	10	20	18	19	20	21	25	20	19
155	30	28	23	40	34	42	15	13	14	9	19	19	17	21	20	17	15	26	29	28	20
113	11	24	26	25	27	33	16	9	17	16	19	17	16	23	12	20	25	28	28	32	21
561	120	111	114	95	121	123	14	14	15	13	12	14	19	21	21	19	21	19	22	32	22
800	152	165	153	188	142	172	15	14	15	16	14	14	23	21	19	21	20	22	20	32	23
184	38	32	37	40	37	24	19	20	16	25	17	18	16	31	33	28	32	30	30	29	24
495	90	83	97	97	128	130	11	9	8	10	12	15	13	15	14	13	14	16	20	30	25
234	25	32	35	77	65	67	26	18	26	21	30	33	38	37	25	33	29	45	44	46	26
129	28	36	21	23	21	22	10	10	12	6	8	12	29	15	15	17	11	16	15	35	27
922	148	187	166	195	226	288	11	11	11	11	9	12	16	17	15	18	15	18	21	27	28
403	73	96	84	74	76	119	23	23	27	21	21	25	24	31	27	34	15	28	33	40	29
1,301	235	254	285	261	266	326	11	9	11	12	11	11	14	16	14	16	18	17	18	27	30
38	7	6	6	10	9	3	9	10	8	6	13	7	9	13	11	10	12	16	16	14	31
630	110	118	133	124	145	180	15	12	15	17	13	13	24	19	17	19	22	17	22	32	32
1,060	192	164	240	245	219	309	14	13	11	14	13	15	19	21	19	18	23	22	23	32	33
497	111	85	84	109	108	92	22	22	22	20	25	24	33	34	35	31	30	35	36	46	34
122	19	27	16	24	36	10	22	19	26	15	18	29	16	37	28	47	25	44	42	31	35
128	27	26	22	33	20	27	18	19	15	19	21	15	27	25	25	22	26	31	22	33	36
2,756	524	579	452	585	616	779	13	12	13	11	14	15	16	19	17	19	16	21	21	24	37
3,694	706	685	757	737	809	802	20	18	19	20	21	22	28	30	28	29	30	30	34	41	38
2,448	472	469	490	495	522	519	21	18	19	20	22	24	28	31	28	30	30	32	35	42	39
128	24	18	26	21	39	19	13	15	12	19	13	10	23	22	26	18	29	22	19	25	40
919	171	167	192	175	214	223	19	17	18	20	19	23	26	30	27	30	31	27	36	37	41
156	33	19	39	39	26	30	23	23	15	26	28	20	29	32	31	23	35	37	32	45	42
43	6	12	10	7	8	11	18	9	30	21	17	17	24	28	18	40	34	23	27	32	43
1,303	266	242	259	313	223	330	20	19	19	21	21	21	29	28	27	26	27	30	29	43	44
55	8	15	14	7	11	2	11	7	16	17	6	7	......	19	14	22	21	13	21	11	45
54	10	9	10	13	12	14	8	5	6	9	8	10	15	10	9	8	10	12	11	21	46
203	40	39	46	46	32	62	13	13	13	12	16	12	14	21	22	19	23	23	20	28	47
602	120	115	108	123	136	141	24	24	23	23	21	28	27	33	32	31	31	35	36	37	48
3,146	628	620	455	650	793	796	22	20	21	20	23	24	28	30	28	28	27	32	35	42	49
810	147	178	124	136	225	180	19	18	19	16	19	23	22	30	25	30	25	31	37	34	50
228	51	38	57	39	43	52	19	17	18	20	19	23	21	29	28	26	33	27	31	37	51
350	80	65	57	78	70	96	19	21	18	15	19	22	22	27	27	29	22	28	28	42	52
1,998	388	358	375	398	479	444	22	21	21	22	22	25	27	30	29	27	28	30	34	37	53
60	8	13	14	10	15	13	10	9	13	8	10	10	9	14	10	13	16	14	15	19	54
1,091	214	223	199	219	236	264	11	11	11	10	12	13	15	18	17	18	16	19	21	24	55
30	2	7	7	9	5	5	8	2	8	10	12	6	13	11	4	10	12	18	10	17	56
255	42	36	68	48	61	50	14	13	9	15	14	21	18	19	16	13	23	19	26	29	57
78	15	21	16	10	16	16	14	14	23	11	5	16	23	22	19	27	22	16	24	28	58
1,531	303	282	266	347	333	335	19	19	19	17	18	21	21	26	26	25	23	27	29	31	59
80	14	13	20	10	23	19	21	19	16	28	16	24	33	25	20	19	33	18	34	48	60
66	18	16	9	6	17	13	11	13	11	8	6	16	20	16	20	18	11	9	19	27	61
3,116	488	580	642	657	749	1,039	18	16	18	18	18	21	28	24	21	24	24	26	27	39	62
362	72	74	79	64	73	108	21	22	20	22	21	21	27	30	29	29	31	28	32	40	63
715	141	131	130	203	110	151	25	25	27	25	25	24	27	36	35	35	33	43	34	39	64

21857°—18——22

² Data not available.

TABLE **36.**—NEGRO DEATHS, BY SEX AND CAUSE OF DEATH, FOR REGIS

REGISTRATION AREA AND SEX.	All causes.	Ty-phoid fever.	Mala-ria.	Small-pox.	Measles.	Scarlet fever.	Whoop-ing cough.	Diph-theria and croup.	Influ-enza.	Ery-sipelas.	Tuber-culosis of the lungs.	Tuber-culous menin-gitis.	Other forms of tu-berculosis.	Rheu-ma-tism.
SUMMARY.														
The registration area:														
1 Male	35,267	637	235	9	163	28	319	161	270	38	5,583	219	439	113
2 Female	31,999	553	266	7	171	27	372	181	317	25	5,012	177	421	186
Registration states[1]—														
3 Male	26,473	527	111	8	147	21	271	119	193	27	4,344	187	342	97
4 Female	24,090	465	136	6	149	20	326	146	217	18	3,987	159	334	145
Registration cities in nonregistra- tion states—														
5 Male	8,794	110	124	1	16	7	48	42	77	11	1,239	32	97	16
6 Female	7,909	88	130	*1	22	7	46	35	100	7	1,025	18	87	41
Selected cities in registration area[2]—														
7 Male	20,272	260	133	2	74	20	134	91	136	30	3,247	139	247	44
8 Female	18,352	224	167	4	77	19	145	95	179	14	2,617	116	220	100
REGISTRATION STATES.														
California:														
9 Male	348	3							1	1	82	4	12	1
10 Female	245	2			1		2		2		56	5	1	1
Colorado:														
11 Male	127	1				1				1	34	1	2	
12 Female	105	1				1		1			19			1
Connecticut:														
13 Male	192	5						1			27	5		1
14 Female	169						1	1	3		25	1	1	
Indiana:														
15 Male	828	21	3		3	1	9	4	6		152	6	12	2
16 Female	653	11	3		3	1	7	4	1	3	120	6	23	6
Kentucky:														
17 Male	2,885	84	22		6		47	9	47	4	474	21	46	14
18 Female	2,720	83	32		10		47	20	41	3	533	15	46	23
Maine:														
19 Male	19										4			
20 Female	4													
Maryland:														
21 Male	2,958	71	2	1	26	*1	43	10	26	3	447	13	32	3
22 Female	2,774	81	7		20	2	52	19	27	1	429	16	29	10
Massachusetts:														
23 Male	468	1			3		5	7			88	4	13	1
24 Female	373	3			1	1	6	1	2		51	9	4	1
Michigan:														
25 Male	248	4							1		34	2	3	2
26 Female	167	1			1			3			20	1	4	
Minnesota:														
27 Male	104	1							2		30		3	
28 Female	55				1	1		1			7			
Missouri:														
29 Male	2,082	35	14		7	2	18	6	18	3	462	14	33	8
30 Female	1,681	22	12	1	10		24	8	13	4	349	6	22	12
Montana:														
31 Male	32	1									6			
32 Female	18							1						
New Hampshire														
33 Male	2													
34 Female	3						1				1			
New Jersey:														
35 Male	1,003	3	2		3	1	16	5	4		186	10	8	5
36 Female	1,014	13			2	2	16	5	6		143	12	18	7
New York:														
37 Male	1,703	7			7	4	18	15	8	3	364	23	21	4
38 Female	1,533	8	2		4	3	12	15	5	1	294	33	14	5
North Carolina:[3]														
39 Male	1,537	53	22	1	8	1	25	5	12	1	171	7	16	3
40 Female	1,602	45	24	1	16	1	29	15	20		253	5	20	11
Ohio:														
41 Male	1,650	31	3	1	5	2	13	8	10	2	327	13	14	8
42 Female	1,170	22	3	1	3	1	25	8	13	1	203	4	21	5
Pennsylvania:														
43 Male	2,449	43	1	1	22	4	21	13	9	5	431	28	31	11
44 Female	2,128	25	2		14	5	37	11	7	1	353	17	39	24
Rhode Island:														
45 Male	147	1				1	3	1			28	4	6	
46 Female	114					1	1		2		17		1	
Utah:														
47 Male	15										5			
48 Female	8										1		1	
Vermont:														
49 Male	9								1		1			
50 Female	2													
Virginia:														
51 Male	6,324	148	41	4	52	2	45	32	46	3	770	21	62	32
52 Female	6,312	140	49	3	58	1	57	30	59	4	928	19	74	35
Washington:														
53 Male	63				1		1			1	11		2	
54 Female	37				1						4	1	1	
Wisconsin:														
55 Male	32										6			
56 Female	20						2		1					

[1] Includes the District of Columbia. [2] Registration cities having in 1910 a Negro population of 2,500 or more, including the District of Columbia.

TRATION STATES AND SELECTED CITIES [1] IN THE REGISTRATION AREA: 1913.

NEGRO DEATHS IN 1913 FROM—

Cancer.	Diabetes.	Meningitis.	Cerebral hemorrhage and softening.	Organic diseases of the heart.	Bronchitis.	Pneumonia (all forms).	Other respiratory diseases.	Diarrhea and enteritis (under 2 years).	Appendicitis.	Hernia, intestinal obstruction.	Cirrhosis of the liver.	Nephritis, Bright's disease.	Puerperal fever.	Other puerperal affections.	Congenital debility and malformations.	Violent deaths (excluding suicide).	Suicide.	All other defined causes.	Ill-defined and unknown causes.	
510	129	319	1,161	3,120	442	3,783	393	1,465	177	256	260	2,873	.....	.....	1,621	3,403	144	5,720	1,277	1
1,257	129	213	1,406	2,910	436	2,919	346	1,285	141	193	157	2,366	347	449	1,438	1,010	63	6,030	1,189	2
409	101	196	888	2,393	363	2,834	294	1,143	121	194	187	2,011	.....	.....	1,267	2,394	112	4,131	1,041	3
980	109	149	1,076	2,232	356	2,199	252	975	99	132	104	1,681	258	344	1,104	762	50	4,140	980	4
101	28	123	273	727	79	949	99	322	56	62	73	862	.....	.....	354	1,009	32	1,589	236	5
277	20	64	330	678	80	720	94	310	42	61	53	685	89	105	334	248	13	1,890	209	6
297	62	218	648	1,830	283	2,482	240	848	130	170	153	1,831	.....	.....	953	1,910	78	3,272	310	7
738	77	140	809	1,799	264	1,940	214	768	103	129	104	1,538	208	230	883	557	40	3,536	298	8
9	2	5	6	44	.....	30	5	6	2	5	3	25	.....	.....	18	35	6	43	.....	9
20	.....	3	25	23	.....	15	1	5	2	1	4	8	2	2	6	6	.....	52	.....	10
2	.....	1	2	17	2	13	.....	.....	1	1	1	10	.....	.....	2	12	2	21	.....	11
4	1	1	3	15	.....	9	1	.....	2	.....	2	5	2	2	3	1	2	27	2	12
11	1	1	7	12	3	20	3	5	2	2	2	20	.....	.....	13	18	2	28	3	13
12	4	3	13	23	1	10	3	3	.....	3	1	14	2	2	10	6	1	26	.....	14
10	8	1	31	96	10	82	9	26	6	9	10	55	.....	.....	36	94	9	117	.....	15
38	5	1	32	75	13	45	9	15	4	8	7	40	9	9	23	23	4	105	.....	16
35	5	29	89	242	37	250	39	77	13	13	22	221	.....	.....	141	334	8	488	68	17
94	6	19	99	178	50	204	35	72	8	15	11	178	31	24	126	113	3	541	60	18
1	.....	.....	2	1	.....	.....	.....	.....	.....	.....	.....	2	.....	.....	2	2	1	4	.....	19
1	.....	.....	.....	.....	.....	.....	.....	.....	.....	.....	.....	.....	.....	.....	1	.....	.....	2	.....	20
54	8	26	108	243	50	352	23	177	17	13	19	241	.....	.....	211	202	8	460	68	21
100	16	21	128	237	54	293	24	162	9	19	10	211	34	40	175	61	2	424	61	22
6	3	1	12	56	7	59	6	17	3	3	1	32	.....	.....	23	45	4	66	2	23
21	4	2	25	53	12	39	1	13	1	2	1	23	5	4	18	10	1	57	2	24
5	.....	5	9	28	1	19	2	11	2	3	2	27	.....	.....	7	18	4	58	1	25
7	1	1	13	20	1	12	1	7	1	1	1	14	2	2	6	7	.....	37	3	26
2	3	.....	1	9	1	10	1	2	.....	.....	1	11	.....	.....	1	8	1	17	.....	27
3	.....	.....	2	15	1	3	.....	.....	.....	.....	.....	6	1	.....	3	2	.....	9	.....	28
41	14	12	51	167	35	242	18	57	13	27	23	158	.....	.....	56	215	11	296	26	29
72	8	15	58	183	17	170	12	49	11	10	9	132	18	14	57	48	8	279	28	30
.....	.....	.....	1	2	.....	3	.....	.....	.....	.....	1	1	.....	.....	1	6	.....	10	.....	31
1	1	.....	3	1	.....	1	.....	.....	.....	.....	1	3	.....	.....	1	1	.....	3	1	32
.....	.....	.....	.....	.....	.....	.....	.....	.....	.....	.....	.....	.....	.....	.....	1	.....	1	.....	.....	33
.....	.....	.....	.....	.....	.....	.....	.....	.....	.....	.....	.....	.....	.....	.....	.....	.....	.....	.....	.....	34
24	4	4	32	84	21	144	12	49	3	9	5	81	.....	.....	74	66	2	142	4	35
44	11	4	57	112	20	104	10	53	6	6	3	88	11	14	63	24	5	148	7	36
22	6	10	43	158	25	269	5	72	7	15	11	142	.....	.....	91	127	10	212	4	37
71	7	7	63	169	18	200	4	61	12	8	6	162	17	13	71	33	6	200	9	38
15	1	26	47	120	13	156	10	111	9	12	11	106	.....	.....	62	154	5	258	96	39
55	3	27	54	132	22	131	16	92	7	5	2	86	17	31	52	51	.....	294	85	40
28	12	18	70	213	7	171	19	52	9	11	14	108	.....	.....	49	204	6	209	13	41
63	8	8	64	154	9	121	7	35	7	7	4	62	11	14	33	69	3	173	8	42
43	10	5	59	200	35	353	38	129	10	18	12	193	.....	.....	132	195	10	366	21	43
110	8	5	56	197	28	269	22	105	11	13	10	171	23	23	110	72	6	341	13	44
1	2	1	2	23	1	16	1	5	2	2	1	9	.....	.....	10	8	.....	15	4	45
3	2	1	5	17	1	10	.....	5	2	.....	2	7	.....	1	4	5	.....	24	3	46
.....	.....	.....	1	.....	.....	2	.....	.....	.....	.....	.....	2	.....	.....	.....	.....	2	3	.....	47
1	.....	.....	.....	.....	.....	1	1	.....	.....	.....	.....	.....	.....	.....	.....	2	.....	1	.....	48
.....	.....	1	.....	.....	1	.....	.....	.....	.....	.....	.....	1	.....	.....	.....	2	1	1	.....	49
.....	.....	.....	.....	.....	.....	.....	.....	.....	.....	.....	.....	1	.....	.....	.....	.....	.....	.....	.....	50
75	17	47	257	517	87	502	76	273	16	41	37	441	.....	.....	268	576	13	1,095	728	51
203	13	29	298	494	95	426	82	246	13	25	28	385	61	129	271	194	5	1,167	691	52
.....	.....	.....	4	11	.....	6	1	1	.....	.....	2	6	.....	.....	4	6	2	4	.....	53
5	2	.....	3	4	.....	.....	.....	.....	.....	1	.....	.....	1	.....	.....	2	.....	11	1	54
1	.....	.....	2	6	.....	2	.....	1	.....	.....	2	2	.....	.....	1	3	.....	5	1	55
1	1	.....	2	.....	.....	3	.....	1	.....	.....	.....	.....	.....	.....	2	1	.....	4	1	56

[2] Includes only municipalities having a population of 1,000 or over in 1900.

TABLE **36.**—NEGRO DEATHS, BY SEX AND CAUSE OF DEATH, FOR REGISTRATION

	REGISTRATION AREA AND SEX.	All causes.	Typhoid fever.	Malaria.	Smallpox.	Measles.	Scarlet fever.	Whooping cough.	Diphtheria and croup.	Influenza.	Erysipelas.	Tuberculosis of the lungs.	Tuberculous meningitis.	Other forms of tuberculosis.	Rheumatism.
	SELECTED CITIES IN REGISTRATION AREA.[1]														
	Alexandria, Va.:														
1	Male	56	2					1			1	7		1	1
2	Female	62	2					1		1		3		1	
	Annapolis, Md.:[2]														
3	Male														
4	Female														
	Asheville, N. C.:														
5	Male	71	1					2	1			12	2		1
6	Female	64		1				2	4	4		8	1	3	
	Atlanta, Ga.:														
7	Male	741	9	3		1		10	3	7	1	69	4	2	
8	Female	728	8	2	1	1		9	2	13	1	61	2	8	4
	Atlantic City, N. J.:														
9	Male	68						1				8	1		
10	Female	97	1									7		1	
	Baltimore, Md.:														
11	Male	1,410	15			16	1	9	3	11	2	256	9	14	
12	Female	1,299	29	4		9	1	6	2	9	1	196	12	12	7
	Birmingham, Ala.:														
13	Male	880	17	10		1		4	1	3		122	3	18	3
14	Female	692	13	13		3		4		8		113	2	12	4
	Boston, Mass.:														
15	Male	197						4	2			31	2	2	1
16	Female	160	1					3				20	4	1	
	Cambridge, Mass.:														
17	Male	41							3			7		2	
18	Female	40	1						1	1		7		1	
	Camden, N. J.:														
19	Male	78						1				12			
20	Female	91	3			1		2		1		12	1		1
	Charleston, S. C.:														
21	Male	594	17	4			1	2	1	3		46	1	2	
22	Female	580	4	6		3	1	6	1	1		61		3	
	Charlotte, N. C.:														
23	Male	115	5	1						3		13		1	
24	Female	143	5	5				2	2	5		20		1	
	Chester, Pa.:														
25	Male	69			1	3			1	1		14		1	
26	Female	63				1						9	2	4	1
	Chicago, Ill.:														
27	Male	672	3	1		2	4	1	9		2	148	4	13	1
28	Female	512	2			1	4	2	7	1	2	95	4	8	3
	Cincinnati, Ohio:														
29	Male	387	2	1		1		1		2	2	115	4	2	2
30	Female	278	1	1		1		3		1	1	62	1	2	2
	Cleveland, Ohio:														
31	Male	112	3			1						20	1	1	1
32	Female	81				1						6		1	
	Columbus, Ohio:														
33	Male	186	2					3	2			30			
34	Female	113	1				1	1		3		14		4	
	Covington, Ky.:														
35	Male	55										10	1		
36	Female	36				2		1		1		6	1		
	Danville, Va.:														
37	Male	82	3			1						7	2		
38	Female	74	2	1								5	1		
	Dayton, Ohio:														
39	Male	84								3	1	17			
40	Female	54	3							1	1	10		1	
	Denver, Colo.:														
41	Male	55					1					10		2	
42	Female	70	1				1			1	1	13			1
	Detroit, Mich.:														
43	Male	104	4									14	2	1	2
44	Female	62	1			1				2		8	1		
	Durham, N. C.:														
45	Male	82	3	2		2		2	1			9		1	
46	Female	88	4	1		3				1		12		1	
	Evansville, Ind.:														
47	Male	87	4						1			15		1	
48	Female	77	1	1					1		1	12		1	
	Galveston, Tex.:														
49	Male	122	2					1		1		19	1		1
50	Female	106								2		11	1		1
	Greensboro, N. C.:														
51	Male	69	1			1	1	2	1	2		8		2	
52	Female	70	2			2		2		1		8			
	Harrisburg, Pa.:														
53	Male	67	1							2	1	5	1	1	
54	Female	51								1		2			
	Indianapolis, Ind.:														
55	Male	311	6					2				66	1	4	1
56	Female	271	4	1			1	2	2		1	48		15	3
	Jacksonville, Fla.:														
57	Male	425	4	3				5		2		68		2	
58	Female	348	7	1				3	1			52			
	Jersey City, N. J.:														
59	Male	53		1						1		9	1		
60	Female	61	1									10	1		
	Kansas City, Kans.:														
61	Male	126	1			1		3	1	1		12		1	1
62	Female	143	1	1				3	2	1		29		3	3

[1] Registration cities having in 1910 a Negro population of 2,500 or more, including the District of Columbia.

STATES AND SELECTED CITIES [1] IN THE REGISTRATION AREA: 1913—Continued.

NEGRO DEATHS IN 1913 FROM—

No.	Cancer	Diabetes	Meningitis	Cerebral hemorrhage and softening	Organic diseases of the heart	Bronchitis	Pneumonia (all forms)	Other respiratory diseases	Diarrhea and enteritis (under 2 years)	Appendicitis	Hernia, intestinal obstruction	Cirrhosis of the liver	Nephritis, Bright's disease	Puerperal fever	Other puerperal affections	Congenital debility and malformations	Violent deaths (excluding suicide)	Suicide	All other defined causes	Ill-defined and unknown causes
1	1			3	1	3	6	3	6			2	8			1	5		3	1
2	4	1		3	3	2	4	2	2				4	1			1		23	4
3																				
4																				
5				6	4	4	7		1				3			2	6		18	1
6			2	2	4	1	3	1	2				6	1	1	3	3		10	2
7	5	5	32	32	41	5	110	7	29	7	5	3	73			37	73	6	148	14
8	22	2	12	33	46	8	80	12	28	3	5	5	60	14	12	30	31	1	197	15
9	1				4	13	15		3	1	1	1	10			5	5		11	1
10	7		2		4		11	1	6	1	2	2	7	2	2	5	3	1	19	
11	33	4	14	43	128	28	212	14	62	11	5	12	118			89	78	4	212	7
12	58	8	10	59	140	24	181	11	52	7	15	8	115	14	13	82	27	2	181	4
13	5	3	20	29	64	1	110	9	34	1	6	6	57			35	168	3	124	23
14	14	1	10	30	61	4	69	6	27	6	7	4	34	6	12	29	32	1	158	9
15	5		1	7	22	2	31	2	8		2		14			10	21	3	27	
16	11	2	1	9	31	1	11		4	1	1	1	12	4	1	8	7		26	
17					4		8	1					2			4	3		7	
18	1			1	5	1	10						1			3	1	1	5	
19	3		2	5	5	1	14	1	4		1	1	7			4	5		12	
20	3			6	9	1	12	4	8	1	1		7	1		4	2	1	9	1
21	6		5	37	47	3	66	4	42	2	11	1	67			58	39		115	14
22	11		1	32	52	4	49	9	38	2	7		49	4	7	52	11		152	14
23	1		1	1	12		10	2	2	1	1		6			17			26	12
24	7		3	2	11	3	18	1	3			1	1		1	5	6		31	10
25		1		1	6	2	10	1	4		1		4			3	6		9	
26	3			4	5	3	9	2		1		1	3		1	4	2		8	
27	17	6	4	21	80	1	89	1	21	7	4	10	59			13	62	7	81	1
28	45	5	2	27	67	3	42	4	14	2	5	6	50	3	3	11	16	1	77	
29	4	3	5	6	48	3	46	1	9	3	2	3	26			9	45		42	
30	18	3	4	14	35	2	41	2	4	4	2	1	18	1	2	9	7		43	
31	1	1	2	1	9		16	1	5	3		1	12			6	9	1	17	
32	4	3	1	1	21	1	6	1	1		1		8		2	3	4		16	
33	2	2	4	15	28		23	5	7				10			5	19		27	1
34	4		2	10	17		19	1	3		1		2	3	1	9	2		14	1
35				2	5		5	1	2				11			2	6		9	
36	3	1		2	1		3					1	6	1		1	2		3	2
37			1	1	17	1	11	1	4	2		1	6			2	8		12	2
38	4		2		8	2	13		3	1	1		5		3	3	4		17	2
39	1		1	2	8		9	1	1		4	2	5			5	17		7	
40	2			4	7		4				1		3		2	3	3		9	
41	1		1	1	9	1	7				1	1	5			1	3	1	9	
42	4	1	1	2	10		5	1		1		1	4	2	1	2		2	15	1
43	1		4	5	10		14	1	3	1	3	2	8			4	5	1	19	
44	1			4	6		5		3			1	5	1	2	3	6		11	1
45			4	3	3		7	1	4		2	1	2				9		25	1
46	1		6	1	2	1	7	2	2	2	1		3	1	5	3	1		20	8
47			4		11	2	9	1	3	1			3			4	13	1	14	
48	3		6		15	3	4	1	2		1	2	5		1	3	3		11	
49	1	1	1	3	10		16	2	1		2	1	15			4	12	1	21	3
50	6			2	13	1	7	2			1		19			2	4		31	3
51	1		4	1	7		2		7		2	1	5			3	5		13	
52	5		1	2	4		3	1	5		1		5		1	7	4		14	2
53	1		1	1	8	2	11		1				13			3	6	2	7	
54	1		2	2	5	1	11	1				1	5	1		4	2	1	13	
55	5	3		13	36	3	37	3	6	3	3	3	20			21	32	2	38	
56	14	3	1	13	32	3	19	6	6	2	5	2	17	5	3	8	8	2	45	
57	3	2		13	13	1	31	3	8	3	2	3	41			11	58		101	46
58	9		1	19	20		21	5	8	1	1	2	24	6	3	19	5		104	35
59	2		1	1	4		5		3				7			6	3		8	1
60	2			2	7	4	6		4	2			5	1	1	1	2		12	
61	1		3	3	12	1	11	5	6	2			20			3	17	1	17	3
62	7	1	1	3	9	1	17	2	6	1	1		11	2	3	7	4	1	22	

[1] Data not available.

TABLE **36.**—NEGRO DEATHS, BY SEX AND CAUSE OF DEATH, FOR REGISTRATION

	REGISTRATION AREA AND SEX.	All causes.	Typhoid fever.	Malaria.	Small-pox.	Measles.	Scarlet fever.	Whooping cough.	Diphtheria and croup.	Influenza.	Erysipelas.	Tuberculosis of the lungs.	Tuberculous meningitis.	Other forms of tuberculosis.	Rheumatism.
	SELECTED CITIES IN REGISTRATION AREA[1]—continued.														
	Kansas City, Mo.:														
1	Male	335	5	1			1	1		3	1	78	1	8	2
2	Female	290	4	1	1	2		4	1	2	1	48	1	2	1
	Key West, Fla.:														
3	Male	53	1									7	1	1	
4	Female	45	1							1		10	1		
	Knoxville, Tenn.:[2]														
5	Male														
6	Female														
	Los Angeles, Cal.:														
7	Males	114									1	26	3	3	
8	Females	104	2					1		2		34	3		
	Louisville, Ky.:														
9	Male	565	11	1				13	1	9	2	72	3	8	
10	Female	482	6	7		3		8	2	10		57	1	10	3
	Lynchburg, Va.:														
11	Male	129	1					1	1			17		1	
12	Female	157		1		1		4	1			17	1	4	1
	Memphis, Tenn.:														
13	Male	869	12	39		2	1	4	1	12	1	123	4	3	2
14	Female	717	8	42		5	1	3	6	15	2	103	1	6	4
	Minneapolis, Minn.:														
15	Male	34							1			14		1	
16	Female	25				1			1			2			
	Mobile, Ala.:														
17	Male	328	7	13				2		2	1	56		3	
18	Female	291	4	9				1		6		46		1	1
	Montgomery, Ala.														
19	Male	269	3			1		5		5		21		2	1
20	Female	304	3	3				2	2	4		26		2	1
	Nashville, Tenn.:														
21	Male	438	8	4		2		1		4		45	1	14	1
22	Female	465	4	7		2		3	1	9		63	2	10	
	Newark, N. J.:														
23	Male	134						2				20	1		
24	Female	139						4	2	2		15	3	5	1
	New Bedford, Mass.:														
25	Male	32				1		1				5	2	1	
26	Female	26										2	2	1	
	New Haven, Conn.:														
27	Male	64							1			13	1		1
28	Female	55									1	7	1		
	New Orleans, La.:														
29	Male	1,596	10	7		2	1	3	20	16	3	285	5	14	1
30	Female	1,398	12	7		6		3	11	15	1	168	4	9	9
	New York, N. Y.:														
31	Male	1,184	2			5	2	11	13	5	3	267	18	15	2
32	Female	1,160	3	2		3	3	7	14	3	1	232	27	8	4
	Manhattan Borough—														
33	Male	809				4		5	10	2	3	202	12	7	1
34	Female	759	1			3	3	2	8	1	1	164	17	6	1
	Bronx Borough—														
35	Male	48						1	1			13	1		
36	Female	50									2	13	1		1
	Brooklyn Borough—														
37	Male	275	2			1	2	3	2		3	42	5	7	1
38	Female	291	1	2				3	6			45	9	1	2
	Queens Borough—														
39	Male	31										6			
40	Female	51	1					2				10		1	
	Richmond Borough—														
41	Male	21						2				4		1	
42	Female	9													
	Norfolk, Va.:														
43	Male	474	6	2		1		3		3		56	3	5	3
44	Female	471	6	8				5	1	2		59	3	6	3
	Oakland, Cal.:														
45	Male	35										7		2	1
46	Female	32										5			
	Omaha, Nebr.:														
47	Male	76										12			
48	Female	42	1									7			
	Paducah, Ky.:														
49	Male	105	3	8						1		9		1	1
50	Female	100	1	5					2	2		16		2	1
	Petersburg, Va.:														
51	Male	195	1	1				1		2	1	19	1	4	1
52	Female	173	4	2		1				5		14	1	1	
	Philadelphia, Pa.:														
53	Male	1,131	19			10	2	5	7	2	2	227	12	16	5
54	Female	1,061	9	1		6	2	15	8	5	1	187	8	17	9
	Pittsburgh, Pa.:														
55	Male	314	4			2	2	3	2	1		38	8	4	
56	Female	271	4	1		3	1	6				36	3	6	3
	Providence, R. I.:														
57	Male	86	1			1	1					18	3	5	
58	Female	61					1			1		10			
	Raleigh, N. C.:														
59	Male	110	3	1		2				1		8			
60	Female	114	3	1		1			1			12		2	1
	Richmond, Va.:														
61	Male	658	3			5		4		6	1	72	2	5	1
62	Female	648	6			5	1	4		3	1	76	5	3	7

[1] Registration cities having in 1910 a Negro population of 2,500 or more including the District of Columbia.

STATES AND SELECTED CITIES [1] IN THE REGISTRATION AREA: 1913—Continued.

NEGRO DEATHS IN 1913 FROM—

Cancer.	Diabetes.	Meningitis.	Cerebral hemorrhage and softening.	Organic diseases of the heart.	Bronchitis.	Pneumonia (all forms).	Other respiratory diseases.	Diarrhea and enteritis (under 2 years).	Appendicitis.	Hernia, intestinal obstruction.	Cirrhosis of the liver.	Nephritis, Bright's disease.	Puerperal fever.	Other puerperal affections.	Congenital debility and malformations.	Violent deaths (excluding suicide).	Suicide.	All other defined causes.	Ill-defined and unknown causes.	
4	1	3	10	29	4	26	1	6	2	5	1	29	.....	.....	12	43	6	51	1	1
9	1	7	7	44	6	26	3	7	5	1	1	29	3	1	6	12	1	52	1	2
1	.....	.....	3	1	2	.....	.....	9	.....	.....	1	11	.....	.....	4	5	.....	6	.....	3
.....	.....	.....	3	1	.....	2	.....	6	.....	.....	.....	5	1	.....	2	1	.....	11	.....	4
																				5
																				6
2	1	3	2	11	.....	8	2	3	1	2	1	10	.....	.....	7	11	.....	17	.....	7
4	.....	3	5	12	.....	8	.....	3	.....	.....	2	2	1	1	3	2	.....	16	.....	8
6	.....	4	14	59	12	69	14	10	6	1	6	61	.....	.....	27	51	1	104	.....	9
19	1	2	23	43	18	59	7	14	2	3	.....	36	3	6	25	22	1	90	1	10
.....	.....	1	9	9	4	10	.....	16	.....	3	.....	9	3	2	14	8	.....	22	3	11
6	.....	.....	12	11	7	8	6	13	2	.....	2	15	.....	.....	11	3	.....	26	.....	12
5	1	21	15	59	14	90	18	17	8	4	2	74	.....	.....	22	127	5	126	57	13
25	3	13	21	46	10	53	7	17	7	3	2	40	3	10	16	29	1	164	51	14
.....	.....	.....	.....	4	1	4	1	.....	.....	.....	.....	3	.....	.....	.....	1	.....	4	.....	15
1	.....	.....	2	8	.....	1	.....	.....	.....	.....	.....	2	.....	.....	1	.....	.....	6	.....	16
3	.....	2	10	26	5	24	6	6	3	1	2	42	.....	.....	18	36	.....	56	4	17
11	.....	.....	11	11	5	25	4	12	1	.....	.....	43	7	2	18	7	.....	62	4	18
1	.....	1	14	13	2	13	4	10	5	7	1	27	.....	.....	18	29	1	62	23	19
5	.....	2	10	16	.....	17	3	16	1	1	.....	27	2	1	15	6	1	104	34	20
2	1	3	12	70	3	46	8	7	7	6	5	24	.....	.....	20	59	2	79	4	21
11	1	.....	27	59	7	45	8	11	5	7	4	24	5	3	17	19	1	105	4	22
1	1	.....	6	15	4	19	2	11	1	3	1	13	.....	.....	11	4	.....	19	.....	23
7	1	.....	2	15	7	14	.....	2	1	1	1	18	5	4	10	5	.....	14	.....	24
.....	.....	.....	1	3	.....	4	.....	1	1	.....	.....	1	.....	.....	3	1	.....	6	1	25
1	.....	.....	2	2	2	3	.....	3	.....	.....	1	.....	.....	.....	1	.....	.....	5	1	26
4	.....	.....	5	5	2	7	1	.....	.....	1	.....	8	.....	.....	6	3	2	6	3	27
3	2	.....	7	7	.....	4	.....	1	.....	1	.....	3	2	1	3	2	.....	10	.....	28
30	2	20	29	180	22	177	8	65	4	7	20	189	.....	.....	32	149	3	292	.....	29
56	5	15	58	167	19	145	5	63	5	7	20	191	17	19	51	32	2	276	.....	30
17	2	8	30	102	19	214	4	54	6	11	4	97	.....	.....	64	75	5	128	1	31
55	6	6	28	134	13	166	2	48	10	6	6	114	14	11	57	22	4	146	5	32
11	2	5	19	69	10	147	2	29	4	7	2	63	.....	.....	48	54	5	85	1	33
38	5	4	20	82	8	114	1	32	5	5	4	84	10	4	36	12	3	82	3	34
.....	.....	.....	3	4	.....	5	.....	1	.....	1	.....	2	.....	.....	2	7	.....	7	.....	35
2	.....	.....	.....	8	.....	4	.....	1	.....	.....	.....	7	.....	1	2	1	.....	7	.....	36
5	.....	3	7	26	7	55	2	21	2	3	2	26	.....	.....	9	13	.....	26	.....	37
11	.....	2	8	40	4	44	1	12	5	1	2	13	2	4	14	8	1	48	2	38
1	.....	.....	.....	.....	1	5	.....	3	.....	.....	.....	5	.....	.....	1	1	.....	8	.....	39
4	1	.....	4	.....	.....	2	.....	2	.....	.....	.....	9	2	2	3	1	.....	7	.....	40
.....	.....	.....	1	3	1	2	.....	1	.....	.....	.....	1	.....	.....	4	.....	.....	2	.....	41
.....	.....	.....	.....	1	.....	2	.....	1	.....	.....	.....	1	.....	.....	2	.....	.....	2	.....	42
12	1	1	30	41	15	63	12	21	1	4	1	38	.....	.....	32	49	.....	68	3	43
14	3	2	33	38	15	41	5	28	2	5	3	35	9	9	34	14	1	82	5	44
.....	.....	1	3	2	.....	5	.....	.....	1	1	.....	1	.....	.....	5	2	2	2	.....	45
6	.....	.....	7	3	.....	2	.....	1	.....	1	.....	1	.....	.....	1	.....	.....	5	.....	46
1	.....	.....	2	5	1	8	.....	1	1	1	3	6	.....	.....	3	21	1	10	.....	47
4	.....	1	2	5	.....	4	1	.....	.....	1	2	2	1	1	.....	3	1	6	.....	48
.....	.....	2	3	4	8	6	2	2	.....	.....	1	7	.....	.....	3	26	.....	19	3	49
1	.....	.....	3	8	5	4	.....	2	.....	.....	1	12	1	.....	5	4	.....	18	3	50
2	1	.....	10	14	.....	20	1	16	1	.....	4	30	.....	.....	17	11	.....	33	4	51
5	.....	1	9	13	.....	15	7	16	.....	.....	2	21	1	3	19	4	.....	29	.....	52
27	3	1	16	85	19	156	19	73	5	13	9	111	.....	.....	67	49	1	166	4	53
56	7	1	19	111	13	115	13	67	5	6	5	98	12	11	52	40	2	156	4	54
6	.....	.....	3	32	5	79	7	17	2	1	.....	12	.....	.....	14	25	.....	45	2	55
12	.....	1	6	18	4	55	2	14	2	2	1	21	2	3	13	11	.....	41	.....	56
1	2	.....	.....	12	.....	12	.....	4	1	1	.....	5	.....	.....	6	4	.....	6	3	57
1	.....	.....	2	10	.....	5	.....	5	2	.....	1	2	.....	1	3	3	.....	12	2	58
2	.....	1	6	15	.....	12	.....	5	3	1	2	9	.....	.....	8	11	.....	17	3	59
6	.....	1	2	12	1	12	.....	8	.....	.....	.....	4	.....	7	6	5	.....	26	3	60
6	3	8	41	59	21	70	15	30	3	6	5	58	.....	.....	39	70	2	113	10	61
27	1	2	57	55	18	69	19	24	2	6	5	55	12	4	50	16	2	102	15	62

[2] Data not available.

TABLE 36.—NEGRO DEATHS, BY SEX AND CAUSE OF DEATH, FOR REGISTRATION

REGISTRATION AREA AND SEX.	All causes.	Typhoid fever.	Malaria.	Smallpox.	Measles.	Scarlet fever.	Whooping cough.	Diphtheria and croup.	Influenza.	Erysipelas.	Tuberculosis of the lungs.	Tuberculous meningitis.	Other forms of tuberculosis.	Rheumatism.
SELECTED CITIES IN REGISTRATION AREA [1]—continued.														
St. Joseph, Mo.:														
1 Male	56	1							1		6			
2 Female	43	2									5		1	
St. Louis, Mo.:														
3 Male	712	9	2		4		3	5	1	2	135	10	10	
4 Female	535	6	2		3		2	4	3		86	2	6	4
St. Paul, Minn.:														
5 Male	46	1					1				12		2	
6 Female	25				1						4			
San Antonio, Tex.:														
7 Male	144	2							5		33	1	3	
8 Female	124		1						1		24		4	
Savannah, Ga.:														
9 Male	548	5	23		1		1		7	1	70	1	6	
10 Female	563	8	25				1		10		51	1	7	2
Springfield, Ill.:														
11 Male	40	1						1			4			1
12 Female	38		1		1						7			
Springfield, Ohio:														
13 Male	59	2					1	1			6		1	1
14 Female	47	1		1				2	2		4			1
Terre Haute, Ind.:														
15 Male	41								1		4		1	1
16 Female	26				1						3		1	1
Trenton, N. J.:														
17 Male	47	1									14	1		
18 Female	41	2									4		2	
Washington, D. C.:														
19 Male	1,248	14	1		4	1	7	1	4		204	11	26	2
20 Female	1,183	8	2		4		7	3	15		181	9	15	4
Wilmington, Del.:														
21 Male	133				1		1	1	1		14	4	2	
22 Female	120	3					2		1		10			1
Wilmington, N. C.:														
23 Male	188	6	2				1		2		16	1	4	
24 Female	186	5	1				2		2		18	1	2	3
Winston, N. C.:														
25 Male	183	11		1			5		1	1	26	1	1	1
26 Female	175	7		1			6	3			30	1	2	3

[1] Registration cities having in 1910 a Negro population of 2,500 or more, including the District of Columbia.

STATES AND SELECTED CITIES [1] IN THE REGISTRATION AREA: 1913—Continued.

								NEGRO DEATHS IN 1913 FROM—												
Cancer.	Diabetes.	Meningitis.	Cerebral hemorrhage and softening.	Organic diseases of the heart.	Bronchitis.	Pneumonia (all forms).	Other respiratory diseases.	Diarrhea and enteritis (under 2 years).	Appendicitis.	Hernia, intestinal obstruction.	Cirrhosis of the liver.	Nephritis, Bright's disease.	Puerperal fever.	Other puerperal affections.	Congenital debility and malformations.	Violent deaths (excluding suicide).	Suicide.	All other defined causes.	Ill-defined and unknown causes.	
3			4	1	4	9		1		2		5			3	8		8		1
1		1	3	5	2	3		1		1		1	2	1	2	2		10		2
20	4	6	14	64	11	86	12	15	8	12	13	66			13	71	4	112		3
27	3	3	21	50	5	75	5	14	2	4	4	68	3	1	16	12	4	99	1	4
	1			4		3		2			1	5			1	5	1	7		5
2				6	1	1						2	1		2	2		3		6
		3	2	7	5	4		5	1		2	21			7	12		29	2	7
7			6	8	1	9	2	4	2	2	2	9	1	3	2	4		30	2	8
6	1	4	13	25	4	47	6	25	2		2	45			33	47		149	24	9
12	1	2	12	29	6	51	8	36	2	2	1	37	7	7	27	22		177	19	10
				4		5	1	3	1	1	1	6			3	2	1	5		11
2				2		7		2				1	1		3	1		10		12
		1	9	4		5	1	1				6			1	8	1	10		13
3			3	5		7		2			1		1			2		11		14
			1	6	2	4		4		2		1			1	5	1	7		15
2			2	1	1	2			1			3		1	2	1		4		16
2			1	3		6		1		1		2				6		9		17
3	1		3	4	1	8		2				3		1			1	5	1	18
24	5	3	55	142	26	133	26	72	6	10	7	117			64	64	4	213	2	19
51	8	2	76	128	13	132	23	51	3	8	2	83	11	20	69	31	4	215	5	20
5	1	1	7	11		24		5		1		11			7	19		17		21
		2	7	9	3	16	2	6		1		10	1	3	8	4		28	3	22
		1	8	23	1	26		18		2		16			11	10	1	38	1	23
4			10	23	2	15	1	17				16	1	6	4	5		46	2	24
2		9	4	12		25		12	1	1		9			4	19	1	15	21	25
5		10	7	14		15	2	12	1	1		7	1	6	3	6		16	16	26

TABLE 37.—NEGRO AND WHITE DEATHS, BY CAUSE OF DEATH, FOR REGIS

REGISTRATION AREA AND RACIAL CLASS.	All causes.	Typhoid fever.	Malaria.	Small-pox.	Measles.	Scarlet fever.	Whooping cough.	Diphtheria and croup.	Influenza.	Erysipelas.	Tuberculosis of the lungs.	Tuberculous meningitis.	Other forms of tuberculosis.	Rheumatism.
SUMMARY.														
The registration area:														
1 Negro	49,499	798	413	12	181	71	588	233	509	83	8,111	230	657	208
2 White	753,308	11,791	741	190	6,394	6,182	5,524	11,275	7,251	2,356	66,498	4,394	5,741	3,782
Registration states[2]—														
3 Negro	27,932	426	96	6	118	49	448	153	247	45	4,869	179	443	116
4 White	673,203	10,399	538	183	5,849	5,379	5,098	9,925	6,565	2,136	58,726	3,976	5,173	3,421
Registration cities in nonregistration states—														
5 Negro	21,567	372	317	6	63	22	140	80	262	38	3,242	51	214	92
6 White	80,105	1,392	203	7	545	803	426	1,350	686	220	7,772	418	568	361
Selected cities in registration area[1]—														
7 Negro	37,724	565	362	8	126	44	341	164	382	66	6,075	169	445	152
8 White	275,652	3,507	303	20	2,307	2,621	1,620	4,945	1,779	963	28,382	2,108	1,830	1,322
REGISTRATION STATES.														
California:														
9 Negro	442	3	2		3			1	1		98	1	9	2
10 White	30,685	429	72	1	168	70	270	210	148	75	3,927	221	321	118
Colorado:														
11 Negro	289	2			2	2		1		2	58	2	3	
12 White	10,730	326	9	7	62	102	35	129	77	43	1,607	55	76	56
Connecticut:														
13 Negro	373	3					4	4	3		54	3	11	2
14 White	17,120	162	28		92	129	142	277	240	55	1,411	90	108	93
Indiana:														
15 Negro	1,433	15	5		10	5	12	8	17	7	284	7	65	4
16 White	35,011	901	108	1	438	198	385	384	520	125	3,635	248	474	174
Maine:														
17 Negro	19								1		3			
18 White	12,703	151	3		97	41	97	99	122	24	894	87	126	49
Maryland:														
19 Negro	5,343	109	4		7	3	149	24	52	8	853	13	53	22
20 White	15,458	419	18		46	65	142	147	149	55	1,457	72	112	70
Massachusetts:														
21 Negro	809	6			5	1	5	7	1	1	167	4	15	5
22 White	53,455	415	23		387	271	281	698	446	176	4,477	461	369	219
Michigan:														
23 Negro	426	11		1	4	1	4	3		2	66		8	4
24 White	39,262	656	21	119	250	302	298	492	430	127	2,209	107	309	227
Minnesota:														
25 Negro	135	3			3		1		3		21	2	2	
26 White	22,470	664	2	10	241	300	154	540	98	78	1,855	157	224	133
Montana:														
27 Negro	43	4									11	1	1	
28 White	3,909	142		2	16	61	40	61	24	14	277	12	28	28
New Hampshire:														
29 Negro	14							1			1			
30 White	7,438	46	1		29	8	42	76	93	21	491	30	63	23
New Jersey:														
31 Negro	2,073	21	3		6	6	67	9	4		356	30	37	10
32 White	37,422	350	23		247	275	358	738	308	129	3,702	255	258	201
New York:														
33 Negro	3,350	24	5	2	15	10	28	20	22	8	628	40	44	14
34 White	144,144	1,373	77	6	1,254	1,643	715	2,414	1,194	470	13,793	1,084	858	707
North Carolina:[3]														
35 Negro	3,024	81	68	2	23	1	28	19	49	2	478	6	37	13
36 White	3,728	128	52	4	75	7	34	48	53	11	419	17	26	10
Ohio:														
37 Negro	2,260	38	4	1	18	4	27	9	19	4	462	16	44	12
38 White	63,194	1,275	36	12	769	284	564	576	887	216	5,761	312	613	372
Pennsylvania:														
39 Negro	4,669	68			19	12	91	38	37	8	818	40	88	13
40 White	115,094	1,824	50	8	1,218	1,082	1,022	2,197	1,160	330	8,167	440	710	587
Rhode Island:														
41 Negro	248	3					4	2	1		29	3		
42 White	9,051	71	5		177	22	47	132	98	18	826	83	52	31
Utah:														
43 Negro	32	1									6			1
44 White	3,998	128		2	5	108	64	73	31	21	126	10	21	40
Vermont:														
45 Negro	29						1				3			
46 White	5,674	50	3		24	11	51	32	147	15	325	32	44	15
Washington:														
47 Negro	97	1							3		19	1	4	
48 White	11,017	301	1	8	68	81	167	144	50	40	909	80	132	52
Wisconsin:														
49 Negro	65	1				1	1	1			10	1	2	
50 White	27,896	543	2	3	185	308	181	430	248	83	2,128	105	233	192
SELECTED CITIES IN REGISTRATION AREA.[1]														
Alexandria, Va.:														
51 Negro	138	9							1		16		1	1
52 White	189	11		1					2		11		3	1
Annapolis, Md.:														
53 Negro	97	2					4		1		7		1	
54 White	83	4					1		2		8	1		
Asheville, N.C.:														
55 Negro	135	4						1	1		27	2	1	
56 White	235	3					1	2	6	1	97	5	5	1

[1] Registration cities having in 1910 a Negro population of 2,500 or more, including the District of Columbia.   [2] Includes the District of Columbia.

TRATION STATES AND SELECTED CITIES [1] IN THE REGISTRATION AREA: 1910.

NEGRO AND WHITE DEATHS IN 1910 FROM—

Cancer.	Diabetes.	Meningitis.	Cerebral hemorrhage and softening.	Organic diseases of the heart.	Bronchitis.	Pneumonia (all forms).	Other respiratory diseases.	Diarrhea and enteritis (under 2 years).	Appendicitis.	Hernia, intestinal obstruction.	Cirrhosis of the liver.	Nephritis, Bright's disease.	Puerperal fever.	Other puerperal affections.	Congenital debility and malformations.	Violent deaths (excluding suicide).	Suicide.	All other defined causes.	Ill-defined and unknown causes.	
1,100	142	369	1,705	4,120	793	5,796	619	2,792	225	316	265	3,533	274	258	2,140	2,609	162	8,565	1,622	1
39,875	7,888	7,208	39,008	71,902	11,806	73,490	8,043	51,379	5,884	6,346	7,187	49,693	3,609	4,293	38,135	45,720	8,378	130,572	10,773	2
665	90	202	1,024	2,368	484	3,314	297	1,730	129	181	118	1,891	146	154	1,330	1,322	107	4,340	845	3
35,638	7,183	6,419	36,135	65,262	10,924	64,335	7,249	45,376	5,008	5,578	6,204	46,365	3,181	3,894	34,647	40,958	7,158	117,397	9,924	4
435	52	167	681	1,752	309	2,482	322	1,062	96	135	147	1,642	128	104	810	1,287	55	4,225	777	5
4,237	705	789	2,873	6,640	882	9,155	794	6,003	876	768	983	6,328	428	399	3,488	4,762	1,220	13,175	849	6
810	108	268	1,251	3,195	626	4,596	499	2,142	165	241	212	2,826	224	186	1,649	2,013	112	6,589	1,143	7
14,332	2,827	2,482	11,222	24,346	4,400	32,005	2,798	20,762	2,534	2,372	3,236	21,757	1,421	1,468	13,581	15,039	3,570	40,882	2,911	8
26	1	7	8	38	3	44	3	8	1	3	2	35	1	4	10	35	5	86	2	9
1,948	370	320	1,569	3,711	352	2,157	302	881	254	288	425	2,001	103	172	1,114	2,381	663	5,456	188	10
9	1	3	9	23	1	28	3	10	5	2	2	14	3	3	8	43	5	44	1	11
458	66	116	384	668	90	968	150	517	119	85	74	622	82	65	593	1,143	161	1,722	63	12
5	1	5	20	45	9	33	4	12	2	3	3	42	3	2	20	23	3	47	7	13
888	220	218	1,115	1,752	304	1,653	168	1,150	95	133	158	1,181	62	81	943	863	197	2,856	256	14
35	6	7	52	126	19	143	9	71	9	9	8	111	7	5	56	75	11	229	6	15
1,863	371	252	1,970	3,586	441	2,706	265	2,045	250	292	298	2,103	230	207	1,637	2,064	370	6,376	94	16
1			2									3				3		5	1	17
753	128	167	907	1,368	211	1,237	166	650	92	105	62	793	46	64	542	522	85	2,641	374	18
115	11	43	196	430	75	562	42	366	25	29	18	376	22	34	293	229	8	874	298	19
827	153	181	782	1,278	264	1,373	182	975	75	117	107	1,288	50	85	869	745	126	2,705	524	20
29	5	7	32	95	19	105	4	29	3	4	2	55	1		39	24	6	120	13	21
3,127	646	581	3,283	5,905	997	5,773	458	4,081	368	411	338	2,924	165	246	2,993	2,482	420	9,381	653	22
21	3	1	14	48	8	44	11	9	8	3	4	27	1	1	13	24	6	67	9	23
2,089	415	404	2,097	4,248	737	2,607	523	2,328	351	387	341	1,903	194	275	2,429	2,183	380	8,923	901	24
7		2	4	16	2	16	2	2	2	1	2	14		1	5	5	3	16		25
1,393	243	203	895	1,680	270	1,778	234	1,338	318	230	136	1,169	114	132	1,147	1,553	239	4,470	472	26
	1		2	4		3	1	2				2	1			3	1	5	1	27
156	36	47	116	252	37	277	54	222	64	44	36	218	26	35	207	539	80	682	76	28
1			2	1		1									1		1	4		29
423	80	127	520	864	148	641	104	403	35	55	29	480	18	34	417	293	53	1,658	133	30
42	13	23	90	159	42	251	18	151	9	14	10	136	7	5	111	81	6	309	47	31
1,848	420	404	2,224	3,344	565	3,906	384	2,853	233	252	429	2,806	184	201	1,946	2,143	429	5,456	551	32
89	9	21	113	243	71	513	25	210	23	25	17	257	24	12	187	163	12	436	40	33
7,634	1,685	1,129	7,372	14,828	2,443	16,574	1,345	9,527	1,052	1,182	1,635	11,466	591	757	6,754	7,774	1,519	22,053	1,236	34
46	8	28	83	218	44	297	37	196	7	13	9	134	19	35	95	136	2	569	241	35
125	22	54	132	217	44	313	33	303	35	21	27	208	8	49	171	135	24	772	151	36
70	6	18	89	235	24	250	17	102	9	22	14	143	11	6	82	130	11	341	22	78
3,529	646	727	3,550	6,526	1,012	5,131	622	3,935	442	533	653	3,585	371	339	3,069	4,125	668	11,517	537	33
101	16	23	151	361	105	650	69	355	14	30	19	297	22	32	214	207	17	652	102	39
4,999	970	861	5,938	9,539	1,974	12,185	1,618	10,725	627	863	975	6,944	634	753	6,450	8,028	958	18,665	2,593	40
10	2	3	10	37	7	29	2	20	1			17	1	1	8	8		42	8	41
463	103	71	512	840	174	1,003	78	816	55	67	76	658	26	54	424	437	80	1,439	113	42
			1			6		2				2	1	1	1	2	1	8		43
134	52	46	136	298	66	425	59	182	61	55	18	236	30	38	290	334	38	734	137	44
1			1	3		5	1		1			3				7	1	2		45
392	76	43	455	787	106	511	38	206	59	46	32	379	22	39	250	255	46	1,155	28	46
	2	2	6	6		10		3	1		1	11			1	11		15		47
586	122	71	528	839	73	802	98	420	140	104	71	617	95	96	604	1,344	220	1,978	176	48
3			1	6		8		3			1	4			7	2		12	1	49
1,757	309	363	1,365	2,298	550	2,054	321	1,691	256	272	256	1,456	113	154	1,622	1,466	330	6,006	616	50
1		2	4	10	5	16	6	6	1		1	7			2	5	2	30	12	51
8	2	2	3	19	1	14		8		3	3	20			12	6	2	47	10	52
		4	6	3	5	9		8	1	1		11			3	6		17	6	53
9	2		6	5	1	7	3		1		2	5		1	2	7	1	12	2	54
3			3	4		21	4	6	1		1	8		2	4	5		28	8	55
5	1	3	9	8	4	9	3	6	4	1	2	8		1	10	9	1	29	5	56

[1] Includes only municipalities having a population of 1,000 or over in 1900.

Table 37.—NEGRO AND WHITE DEATHS, BY CAUSE OF DEATH, FOR REGISTRATION

NEGRO AND WHITE DEATHS IN 1910 FROM—

	REGISTRATION AREA AND RACIAL CLASS.	All causes.	Typhoid fever.	Malaria.	Small-pox.	Measles.	Scarlet fever.	Whooping cough.	Diphtheria and croup.	Influenza.	Erysipelas.	Tuberculosis of the lungs.	Tuberculous meningitis.	Other forms of tuberculosis.	Rheumatism.
	SELECTED CITIES IN REGISTRATION AREA[1]—continued.														
	Atlanta, Ga.:														
1	Negro	1,328	20	3	1	2	......	9	9	7	2	155	2	8	8
2	White	1,609	58	1	......	12	8	7	20	6	1	127	8	7	6
	Baltimore, Md.:														
3	Negro	2,597	42	2	......	1	2	38	4	13	4	458	12	25	8
4	White	8,152	193	9	......	19	46	47	60	51	37	816	45	46	31
	Birmingham, Ala.:														
5	Negro	1,391	26	25	......	13	......	4	4	9	1	250	......	5	2
6	White	1,206	40	10	......	11	4	9	12	8	5	119	1	1	6
	Boston, Mass.:														
7	Negro	317	1	......	......	1	1	1	5	1	1	61	......	6	5
8	White	11,224	75	1	......	95	61	50	156	50	55	1,092	144	71	38
	Cambridge, Mass.:														
9	Negro	75	......	......	......	1	......	......	......	......	......	11	1	......	......
10	White	1,501	10	......	......	3	3	4	24	8	1	247	14	10	4
	Camden, N. J.:														
11	Negro	192	1	......	......	1	......	6	2	......	......	14	3	3	......
12	White	1,437	15	......	......	11	9	19	61	9	4	104	8	12	8
	Charleston, S. C.:														
13	Negro	1,221	20	11	......	9	......	22	4	8	2	122	1	7	1
14	White	526	13	7	......	4	1	10	4	3	2	31	1	4	3
	Charlotte, N. C.:														
15	Negro	299	6	14	......	1	......	......	......	8	......	25	......	5	......
16	White	306	11	1	1	6	......	......	3	4	......	18	1	1	1
	Chester, Pa.:														
17	Negro	107	4	......	......	......	......	1	......	2	......	9	......	3	......
18	White	542	12	1	......	1	1	6	6	8	2	56	4	4	2
	Chicago, Ill.:														
19	Negro	1,075	10	......	......	5	1	4	5	5	......	223	8	17	3
20	White	32,130	289	11	1	186	403	169	817	141	89	3,241	214	194	159
	Cincinnati, Ohio:														
21	Negro	569	2	1	......	6	1	2	2	1	1	161	4	9	2
22	White	5,750	30	......	......	53	15	28	34	76	23	792	46	45	22
	Cleveland, Ohio:														
23	Negro	167	3	......	......	2	......	1	1	3	2	33	3	2	3
24	White	7,880	98	1	2	94	71	36	119	48	29	684	58	46	54
	Columbus, Ohio:														
25	Negro	262	3	......	......	2	......	3	......	1	......	46	3	6	......
26	White	2,548	30	......	......	41	6	16	21	14	11	278	10	46	14
	Covington, Ky.:														
27	Negro	59	......	1	......	......	......	......	......	1	......	14	......	1	1
28	White	802	8	......	......	3	......	4	6	13	4	110	6	6	4
	Danville, Va.:														
29	Negro	167	4	6	......	......	1	2	1	2	......	14	......	1	1
30	White	221	9	3	......	......	1	......	6	4	1	30	......	1	......
	Dayton, Ohio:														
31	Negro	99	2	......	......	......	......	1	......	1	......	21	1	4	......
32	White	1,625	23	1	......	2	11	22	13	10	4	168	12	15	8
	Denver, Colo.:														
33	Negro	132	......	......	......	......	......	......	......	......	2	28	......	1	......
34	White	3,389	57	2	......	7	37	5	40	20	22	619	25	35	23
	Detroit, Mich.:														
35	Negro	146	1	......	......	......	1	2	2	......	......	16	......	4	2
36	White	7,305	107	3	......	31	75	106	157	25	25	449	23	52	27
	Durham, N. C.:														
37	Negro	179	5	1	......	7	......	......	......	4	......	36	......	3	......
38	White	189	4	3	......	11	2	1	2	6	......	24	......	1	......
	Evansville, Ind.:														
39	Negro	117	4	2	......	......	......	......	......	3	1	21	......	2	......
40	White	831	19	6	......	9	......	6	6	7	2	104	2	10	5
	Galveston, Tex.:														
41	Negro	183	4	1	......	......	......	......	......	......	......	28	......	1	......
42	White	417	8	1	1	......	......	......	3	4	1	41	......	2	1
	Greensboro, N. C.:														
43	Negro	143	1	2	......	......	......	1	......	5	......	26	......	3	......
44	White	162	6	2	......	1	......	......	2	......	......	11	2	2	......
	Harrisburg, Pa.:														
45	Negro	98	3	......	......	......	......	1	2	1	......	16	......	1	1
46	White	842	18	1	......	3	5	5	42	8	2	64	2	5	8
	Indianapolis, Ind.:														
47	Negro	548	4	......	......	7	2	1	2	8	4	97	3	21	2
48	White	3,275	62	4	......	35	8	40	14	46	24	323	36	45	26
	Jacksonville, Fla.:														
49	Negro	710	20	29	......	......	1	5	1	7	......	107	......	3	3
50	White	482	40	13	......	1	2	1	1	1	4	28	2	3	1
	Jersey City, N. J.:														
51	Negro	123	......	......	......	......	......	......	......	......	......	21	1	4	......
52	White	4,278	31	3	......	23	46	13	83	19	20	453	19	21	37
	Kansas City, Kans.:														
53	Negro	237	13	2	......	1	......	......	4	1	1	45	......	1	2
54	White	1,152	66	1	1	21	9	......	25	4	5	82	......	16	5
	Kansas City, Mo.:														
55	Negro	644	19	......	......	6	2	3	7	3	......	149	2	8	2
56	White	3,317	117	10	2	65	56	5	47	25	7	225	8	28	14
	Key West, Fla.:														
57	Negro	147	3	2	......	......	......	......	......	1	......	24	......	1	......
58	White	301	11	......	......	2	1	2	2	1	1	26	......	1	......
	Knoxville, Tenn.:														
59	Negro	203	4	......	......	2	......	......	......	2	......	33	2	13	......
60	White	432	8	1	......	5	2	......	6	7	1	51	3	13	4
	Los Angeles, Cal.:														
61	Negro	136	......	1	......	......	......	......	......	......	......	38	......	4	1
62	White	4,299	44	2	......	50	14	19	24	20	12	683	30	50	21

[1] Registration cities having in 1910 a Negro population of 2,500 or more, including the District of Columbia.

STATES AND SELECTED CITIES [1] IN THE REGISTRATION AREA: 1910—Continued.

NEGRO AND WHITE DEATHS IN 1910 FROM—																				
Cancer.	Diabetes.	Meningitis.	Cerebral hemorrhage and softening.	Organic diseases of the heart.	Bronchitis.	Pneumonia (all forms).	Other respiratory diseases.	Diarrhea and enteritis (under 2 years).	Appendicitis.	Hernia, intestinal obstruction.	Cirrhosis of the liver.	Nephritis, Bright's disease.	Puerperal fever.	Other puerperal affections.	Congenital debility and malformations.	Violent deaths (excluding suicide).	Suicide.	All other defined causes.	Ill-defined and unknown causes.	No.
26	3	10	46	77	19	233	9	62	9	12	5	87	18	6	51	95	5	278	51	1
72	14	10	60	91	9	141	16	92	22	11	5	166	18	14	88	80	17	384	38	2
56	9	21	96	272	30	289	21	169	15	14	8	216	10	14	169	97	2	396	84	3
482	92	103	414	700	143	780	99	470	54	74	65	783	24	44	524	344	79	1,270	208	4
31	3	19	45	96	1	180	5	83	6	10	14	54	13	8	30	137	3	228	86	5
52	3	15	49	72		124	7	110	19	8	12	56	3	8	57	114	24	199	48	6
14	3	1	10	50	3	49	1	7	1		1	19			12	11	2	45	3	7
688	137	104	607	1,302	163	1,383	79	671	109	91	96	582	38	56	591	634	100	1,792	113	8
1	1		6	7	2	12	2	3			1	6		1	4	2	1	13	1	9
84	15	10	86	154	27	180	14	96	12	16	7	76	2	3	85	59	8	231	8	10
4		2	11	17	3	42	4	7		1		15			7	14	2	27	6	11
62	14	26	62	136	5	168	24	91	11	13	11	114	13	4	89	100	13	190	31	12
15		3	67	102	5	88	15	110		5	3	143	6	10	97	35	3	241	66	13
25	4	1	36	42	5	31	5	32	2	6	4	63	1	3	22	23	6	121	11	14
2		2	6	18	10	38	2	11	1	1	1	16		1	7	10	1	82	32	15
15	4	4	10	17	5	31	1	24	3	2	2	15		4	17	15	2	82	6	16
1			3	9		26	2	7	1	1	1	2	1	1	5	7		18	3	17
17	7	6	32	40	6	62	8	49	6	5	2	35	1	8	32	46	1	65	11	18
44	7	4	26	132	2	165	6	40	4	13	6	94	8	3	28	58	7	146	1	19
1,760	340	210	832	2,809	169	5,113	195	3,471	320	248	379	2,403	170	154	1,138	2,030	449	3,992	34	20
6	2	2	18	56	10	75	4	29	2	3	4	38	1	1	18	36		68	4	21
304	67	81	268	609	161	506	51	299	48	61	106	462	28	25	240	315	63	871	21	22
4	2	1	3	19	1	14	2	9	1	1		10			7	10		29	1	23
408	73	58	348	560	219	704	84	949	81	64	92	520	51	49	404	461	103	1,290	22	24
10		2	8	33	2	32	3	10		6		13	3		10	23	2	38	3	25
156	27	34	137	269	23	216	19	105	31	23	23	132	19	14	109	183	42	477	22	26
1			1	3		7	1	1			1	6		1	2	3		12	2	27
28	5	14	39	64	5	72	11	27	7	5	10	90	2	3	55	44	9	125	23	28
1		3	7	18	2	23	2	4		2	1	17	1	1	3	10		34	6	29
2		11	3	7	3	7	3	15	2	3	1	13	2		11	10		66	7	30
2		3	1	10	3	16	1	6	1	1	1	6	3		2	3	3	7		31
104	15	34	97	180	7	171	12	101	15	15	19	101	13	5	93	98	24	227	5	32
7		3	5	16	1	11	1	5	1	2		9	1	2	5	9	2	20	1	33
193	25	47	144	258	22	281	40	110	49	30	32	229	25	18	177	167	66	577	7	34
4	1	1	4	18	3	26	3	3	1	1	1	7	1		5	12	4	19	4	35
326	67	126	251	497	139	752	106	578	74	96	77	308	47	49	657	388	118	1,349	226	36
2		2	2	11	3	21	4	7	2	2	2	2	1		5	7	2	40	12	37
12		4	7	7	5	15	1	14	2	1	2	6	1		9	4	2	34	9	38
3	1		4	13	2	14	1	8			1	12	2		4	4		21		39
57	7	8	23	76	15	79	9	56	9	4	12	45	9	5	42	54	14	131		40
6	1	1	6	14	1	8	3	2		3	4	22	2		7	9	2	53	5	41
24	3	3	11	35	3	37	4	11	5	3	6	55		2	29	19	6	90	10	42
4	1	1	3	6		12	2	6		2		4	2		4	6		21	29	43
8	1	2	5	6	3	21	2	10		1	3	18		2	7	8	1	29	9	44
3	1		4	14	1	10	1	6				4			2	5		16	6	45
35	9	3	77	82	9	64	5	32	4	8	6	56	3	5	49	65	9	140	18	46
13	3	3	16	51	7	66	2	21	3	4	4	51	4		26	36	5	82		47
169	41	18	175	324	38	269	23	156	30	38	46	204	22	13	156	169	51	662	8	48
4	1	3	19	32	4	67	13	18	1	3	1	49	3	7	30	54	3	159	63	49
17	1	3	23	36	4	36	10	9	5	3	2	42	7		29	32	6	100	20	50
		3	6	16	3	21		11			3	7			4	7		14	2	51
184	37	54	206	346	59	463	50	383	27	32	76	336	26	20	229	274	61	571	76	52
10	1	2	13	23	3	24	2	4		1	2	13			7	11	2	50	1	53
55	17	17	40	91	17	127	16	52	9	12	11	69	11	5	69	67	13	201	18	54
14		4	10	58	6	78	2	23	3	4	5	35	7	3	24	49	2	100	16	55
188	28	44	130	285	27	288	37	99	52	34	31	203	21	14	214	259	83	637	34	56
3		2	5	4	3	8		31			1	10		1	3	2		37	6	57
15	1	8	14	25	2	12		37		2	1	14		3	29	3	4	58	27	58
1		3	8	17	3	26	8	3	3		2	6	2	1	10	13	1	37	5	59
15		6	27	36	5	29	3	19	8	6	4	28	2	2	15	29	5	88	4	60
6	1	2	3	12	1	12		3		2		10	1	3	1	10	1	23	1	61
329	45	54	195	424	44	256	41	75	47	47	50	294	9	24	210	264	92	808	22	62

NEGRO POPULATION.

TABLE **37.**—NEGRO AND WHITE DEATHS, BY CAUSE OF DEATH, FOR REGISTRATION

	REGISTRATION AREA AND RACIAL CLASS.	All causes.	Typhoid fever.	Malaria.	Small-pox.	Measles.	Scarlet fever.	Whooping cough.	Diphtheria and croup.	Influenza.	Erysipelas.	Tuberculosis of the lungs.	Tuberculous meningitis.	Other forms of tuberculosis.	Rheumatism.
	SELECTED CITIES IN REGISTRATION AREA[1]—continued.														
	Louisville, Ky.:														
1	Negro	1,089	27	7		1	6	15		10	5	183	4	5	4
2	White	2,667	44	1		2	15	26	24	20	6	316	12	22	6
	Lynchburg, Va.:														
3	Negro	231	3		1	1		2	4	3		16		13	1
4	White	242	6			1	4		6	5	1	12	5	9	
	Memphis, Tenn.:														
5	Negro	1,492	21	63		3	1	4	8	27	19	214	1	8	8
6	White	1,326	15	34		5	6	1	14	13	18	115	7	5	5
	Minneapolis, Minn.:														
7	Negro	56	2						1			11		1	
8	White	3,681	176		1	48	50	7	129	4	14	356	28	30	21
	Mobile, Ala.:														
9	Negro	673	26	22				6	1	7		134		6	5
10	White	512	13	7			2		1	5	7	68	4	10	3
	Montgomery, Ala.:														
11	Negro	680	6	32	1			2	1	8		87	1	5	
12	White	328	8	2			1		1	2	3	22		4	1
	Nashville, Tenn.:														
13	Negro	950	17	7		2		3	2	25	1	119	8	22	7
14	White	1,113	37	4		3	2	3	5	17	2	115	5	15	3
	Newark, N. J.:														
15	Negro	296		1		1		10	2			56	1	5	2
16	White	5,484	46	2		55	42	55	105	40	31	691	71	34	26
	New Bedford, Mass.:														
17	Negro	85	1					1				19		1	
18	White	1,727	20	1		40	5	7	25	3	4	91	15	10	5
	New Haven, Conn.:														
19	Negro	91						2				14	1	3	
20	White	2,126	24	6		6	11	11	17	19	11	183	20	14	8
	New Orleans, La.:														
21	Negro	2,933	40	15	2	7	4	6	7	65	3	449	4	24	21
22	White	4,311	67	18		59	24	8	30	107	10	454	17	20	16
	New York, N. Y.:														
23	Negro	2,391	15	3	2	11	4	15	19	16	4	465	33	27	9
24	White	74,274	541	29	3	682	955	267	1,690	279	293	8,368	780	405	379
	Manhattan Borough—														
25	Negro	1,473	8	1	1	6	2	9	12	3	2	294	19	14	4
26	White	37,129	259	7	3	250	451	141	883	123	191	3,751	470	212	140
	Bronx Borough—														
27	Negro	208	2			1	1	3	1			68	7	3	1
28	White	6,755	39	4		53	76	23	132	23	15	1,724	79	24	26
	Brooklyn Borough—														
29	Negro	598	4	1	1	4	1	3	6	12	1	89	5	7	3
30	White	25,070	192	13		345	383	79	554	104	80	2,397	198	144	182
	Queens Borough—														
31	Negro	82		1						1	1	12		3	1
32	White	3,882	41	5		28	32	20	101	19	6	346	25	17	23
	Richmond Borough—														
33	Negro	30	1									2	2		
34	White	1,438	10			6	13	4	20	10	1	150	8	8	8
	Norfolk, Va.:														
35	Negro	775	12	16	1			6	1	5		112		11	3
36	White	700	11	3		1	1	5	5	10		52	7	5	
	Oakland, Cal.:														
37	Negro	52										9		1	
38	White	1,791	23	2		6	5	29	10	6	5	154	13	9	7
	Omaha, Nebr.:														
39	Negro	105	8						1	1	1	31		3	
40	White	1,769	100	1		7	19	19	16	9	8	121	11	13	8
	Paducah, Ky.:														
41	Negro	164	7	14						2		27	1	3	
42	White	274	8	5		2			1		3	2	35	2	2	1
	Petersburg, Va.:														
43	Negro	377	3	9				1		10	15		43	1	2	2
44	White	264	13				1			4	2		32	5	5	1
	Philadelphia, Pa.:														
45	Negro	2,276	31			6	6	46	27	9	5	448	26	41	5
46	White	24,740	241	7	5	158	146	271	452	150	75	2,548	158	138	117
	Pittsburgh, Pa.:														
47	Negro	601	7			9	1	15	2	2	1	67	6	12	2
48	White	8,993	142	2		168	118	62	134	74	21	488	61	58	39
	Providence, R. I.:														
49	Negro	139	2					3	2			16	3		
50	White	3,837	38	1		71	15	22	47	37	5	330	39	30	9
	Raleigh, N. C.:														
51	Negro	247	6	3		2		3	2	1		29		3	4
52	White	290	9	2		4		4		3	2	20	1	1	
	Richmond, Va.:														
53	Negro	1,416	12	4		9		24	3	13	1	155	8	10	2
54	White	1,470	15	2		18		23	10	19	1	131	5	16	5
	St. Joseph, Mo.:														
55	Negro	98	5				1			1		26		2	1
56	White	957	25	4		27		14	18	7	2	82		12	9
	St. Louis, Mo.:														
57	Negro	1,149	8	4		1	5	14	1	9		211	7	22	8
58	White	9,733	94	30		63	182	43	110	120	18	937	38	59	48
	St. Paul, Minn.:														
59	Negro	49							2			10	1		
60	White	2,508	42		1	32	65	11	136	2	9	228	21	34	14

[1] Registration cities having in 1910 a Negro population of 2,500 or more, including the District of Columbia.

STATES AND SELECTED CITIES [1] IN THE REGISTRATION AREA: 1910—Continued.

NEGRO AND WHITE DEATHS IN 1910 FROM—

Cancer.	Diabetes.	Meningitis.	Cerebral hemorrhage and softening.	Organic diseases of the heart.	Bronchitis.	Pneumonia (all forms).	Other respiratory diseases.	Diarrhea and enteritis (under 2 years).	Appendicitis.	Hernia, intestinal obstruction.	Cirrhosis of the liver.	Nephritis, Bright's disease.	Puerperal fever.	Other puerperal affections.	Congenital debility and malformations.	Violent deaths (excluding suicide).	Suicide.	All other defined causes.	Ill-defined and unknown causes.	
15	3	15	27	127	37	138	24	13	3	5	4	64	3	1	49	45	2	229	18	1
120	19	52	114	227	46	204	74	51	24	29	23	208	7	5	170	111	34	590	65	2
2		2	6	19	8	29	3	13		3		14	3	4	10	6		41	24	3
6	2	4	13	28	6	19	4	17	2	5	1	9		6	11	8	4	40	8	4
24	5	24	20	99	32	155	23	46	14	10	6	86	15	9	15	159	3	268	102	5
60	6	25	40	77	8	103	17	84	22	23	19	105	9	4	43	98	27	268	50	6
1			2	9	1	11			1		2	6					1	7		7
207	32	41	125	281	30	347	33	240	55	41	23	218	25	14	148	221	52	672	12	8
18	2	3	23	54	5	26	4	35	6	4	4	67	3	4	19	35	1	134	19	9
33	6	5	19	44	4	12	2	13	8	7	4	67	4	4	22	24	2	104	4	10
10	1	5	21	37	5	43	11	34	3	6	4	55	2	4	36	32		199	29	11
18	3	3	19	19		19	6	22		4	6	29		2	13	20	6	85	10	12
16	1	8	28	109	10	146	17	42	9	9	2	38	7	6	38	40	1	193	17	13
58	10	15	45	92	13	96	13	60	20	23	8	53	6	2	47	70	19	241	11	14
5	2	4	20	19	12	29	1	28		1	1	23	1	2	22	9	2	34	3	15
286	74	54	328	452	118	599	58	369	46	38	79	428	32	28	300	292	72	596	37	16
		2	3	5	7	13	1	7				5			4	3		9	4	17
57	14	38	68	145	38	169	22	310	10	13	7	55	4	7	123	65	8	304	44	18
1			4	12	3	5	1	1	1	1	2	17	1	1	6	4		7	4	19
127	25	21	109	226	41	274	22	115	17	20	14	153	9	8	95	115	16	343	46	20
70	5	15	76	278	49	355	24	150	12	15	44	341	10	12	95	167	7	549	12	21
220	24	33	179	426	64	303	46	298	31	33	93	469	23	28	122	220	67	780	22	22
66	5	13	64	160	59	385	18	162	17	17	13	200	20	10	150	96	7	276	30	23
3,678	890	535	2,570	6,426	1,324	10,304	660	5,744	609	560	957	6,633	356	416	3,739	3,646	802	9,059	695	24
38	4	8	35	93	22	248	12	99	10	11	6	123	14	6	106	96	4	177	27	25
1,890	489	312	1,081	2,800	508	5,318	347	2,850	318	290	438	3,394	189	194	2,199	1,985	435	4,702	509	26
6		1	10	20	2	24	2	5	2		1	18		1	3	5	1	19	1	27
325	80	47	284	535	71	707	46	319	42	43	82	562	34	31	249	279	66	683	52	28
18	1	3	15	40	34	98	4	50	4	5	6	49	5	2	36	25	2	64		29
1,200	261	142	953	2,612	664	3,609	218	2,134	214	196	359	2,186	114	162	1,024	1,069	244	2,996	42	30
2		1	2	5		11		6		1		8	1	1	5	7		12	1	31
190	38	28	198	363	66	497	35	337	23	23	55	338	16	15	209	233	41	460	54	32
2			2	2	1	4		2	1			2				4		4	1	33
73	22	6	54	116	15	173	14	104	12	8	23	153	3	14	58	80	16	218	38	34
21		5	12	68	11	93	15	62	2	3	4	51	9	1	34	56	3	145	13	35
32	6	10	35	71	10	53	15	35	8	7	5	54	3	9	38	40	16	143	10	36
2				3	1	6	1		1		1	8			2	6	2	9		37
126	22	22	96	292	23	138	24	58	18	7	23	136	3	16	77	126	46	267	2	38
3			2	15		7	1	4			1	6			3	6	2	10		39
111	10	13	68	135	14	191	17	74	52	30	19	85	11	5	76	121	29	374	2	40
2	1	3	7	6	4	20	3	3		2	1	5			3	7		34	11	41
9	1	7	9	13		37	3	8	3	2		20			13	18	1	56	13	42
6		2	21	26	5	34	5	38	2	1	1	36	3	1	15	21	1	54	19	43
7		6	16	17		19	1	17	3		1	38		2	17	10	4	38	5	44
44	9	5	59	168	53	289	34	194	7	15	8	172	15	13	100	97	7	301	36	45
1,278	241	114	1,106	2,522	468	2,307	325	2,142	178	205	273	2,498	127	135	1,058	1,195	300	3,566	236	46
16	1	3	25	47	21	128	6	56	1	4	2	29	2	3	27	23	2	73	8	47
335	45	70	323	626	261	1,604	133	893	59	69	94	371	69	46	478	696	120	1,237	97	48
8	1	2	5	18	2	16	1	15	1			14		1	5	5		15	4	49
219	42	28	217	386	63	422	32	264	45	38	41	309	18	27	181	207	38	566	50	50
10	1	5	3	22	3	25	4	22		1	1	11		3	10	19	1	48	6	51
6	3	1	8	22	4	15	9	18		1	5	32		4	9	8	4	91	4	52
26	5	10	95	90	30	155	57	107	6	5	5	104	7	4	79	76	2	249	63	53
84	10	13	103	135	18	97	26	64	26	14	21	139	4	12	82	84	10	237	46	54
1			2	8	3	10	2	3		1	1	7	1		1	2	1	18	1	55
48	9	6	50	81	8	66	9	29	26	12	12	70	5	8	31	55	19	211	2	56
36	7	4	33	116	30	128	10	30	7	7	17	112	5	2	40	62	1	210	2	57
550	82	71	367	789	277	978	104	566	67	108	193	1,028	62	44	423	542	198	1,498	44	58
5		1	1	5		5	2		1		1	8		1	1	2	1	4		59
177	23	24	100	196	37	206	18	151	41	25	17	137	11	13	152	114	29	406	36	60

TABLE **37.**—NEGRO AND WHITE DEATHS, BY CAUSE OF DEATH, FOR REGISTRATION

| | | NEGRO AND WHITE DEATHS IN 1910 FROM— | | | | | | | | | | | | |
REGISTRATION AREA AND RACIAL CLASS.	All causes.	Ty-phoid fever.	Mala-ria.	Small-pox.	Measles.	Scarlet fever.	Whoop-ing cough.	Diph-theria and croup.	Influ-enza.	Ery-sipelas.	Tuber-culosis of the lungs.	Tuber-culous menin-gitis.	Other forms of tu-bercu-losis.	Rheu-ma-tism.
SELECTED CITIES IN REGISTRATION AREA [1]—continued.														
San Antonio, Tex.:														
1 Negro	233	4	1	.....	.....	.....	.....	.....	4	.....	46	.....	4	.....
2 White	1,917	45	12	1	3	.....	8	8	58	.....	362	4	8	5
Savannah, Ga.:														
3 Negro	1,134	5	43	.....	.....	.....	6	2	12	2	125	.....	4	.....
4 White	616	11	15	.....	1	5	.....	3	12	.....	39	6	4	3
Springfield, Ill.: [2]														
5 Negro	.....	.....	.....	.....	.....	.....	.....	.....	.....	.....	.....	.....	.....	.....
6 White	.....	.....	.....	.....	.....	.....	.....	.....	.....	.....	.....	.....	.....	.....
Springfield, Ohio:														
7 Negro	78	1	.....	.....	1	.....	1	1	.....	.....	13	1	2	.....
8 White	543	4	.....	.....	.....	1	17	7	11	5	46	.....	1	3
Terre Haute, Ind.:														
9 Negro	67	.....	1	.....	.....	.....	3	.....	2	.....	7	.....	2	.....
10 White	864	17	5	.....	13	12	8	16	7	2	82	1	11	6
Trenton, N. J.:														
11 Negro	89	4	.....	.....	.....	.....	4	.....	.....	.....	22	.....	3	1
12 White	1,886	45	1	.....	17	10	30	30	14	6	183	7	17	11
Washington, D. C.:														
13 Negro	2,759	32	5	.....	3	3	26	3	37	3	444	9	20	14
14 White	3,744	45	4	.....	1	11	9	28	42	10	330	18	16	24
Wilmington, Del.:														
15 Negro	225	2	.....	.....	1	.....	.....	1	3	.....	29	1	1	2
16 White	1,322	31	.....	.....	.....	11	14	25	10	5	113	10	6	4
Wilmington, N. C.:														
17 Negro	325	10	9	.....	.....	.....	.....	1	4	.....	27	2	4	2
18 White	213	9	5	.....	.....	1	.....	.....	4	2	1	18	.....	.....
Winston, N. C.:														
19 Negro	186	6	.....	.....	1	1	5	1	1	.....	35	.....	2	.....
20 White	166	4	.....	.....	3	1	3	2	4	.....	17	1	3	.....

[1] Registration cities having in 1910 a Negro population of 2,500 or more, including the District of Columbia.

STATES AND SELECTED CITIES [1] IN THE REGISTRATION AREA: 1910—Continued.

NEGRO AND WHITE DEATHS IN 1910 FROM—

Cancer.	Diabetes.	Meningitis.	Cerebral hemorrhage and softening.	Organic diseases of the heart.	Bronchitis.	Pneumonia (all forms).	Other respiratory diseases.	Diarrhea and enteritis (under 2 years).	Appendicitis.	Hernia, intestinal obstruction.	Cirrhosis of the liver.	Nephritis, Bright's disease.	Puerperal fever.	Other puerperal affections.	Congenital debility and malformations.	Violent deaths (excluding suicide).	Suicide.	All other defined causes.	Ill-defined and unknown causes.	
6		1	3	8	4	21	5	21	2	2	3	12		1	12	8		55	10	1
65	15	23	47	72	43	103	22	270	13	8	21	99	9	11	102	52	19	345	64	2
6	5	6	35	54	14	126	32	48	1	4	4	62		8	49	58	2	324	97	3
16	5	7	31	54	5	57	15	26		8	2	49		2	25	29	8	151	20	4
																				5
																				6
4		1	3	10		6		3		2	2	4		2	2	3		16		7
28	10	12	31	67	6	31	8	17	3	5	7	24	6	4	23	40	2	120	4	8
3			1	5		6	1	10				4			2	1	2	16	1	9
52	10	11	45	80	13	74	5	55	13	6	9	50	9	5	33	63	27	119	5	10
4	1	1	3	5	2	11	1	3	1	1	1	3	1	1	3	4		9		11
73	18	17	99	117	23	211	18	183	15	19	12	125	20	13	127	108	19	275	23	12
54	5	9	140	271	55	317	48	179	9	22	7	208	23	12	179	111	8	457	46	13
246	50	34	285	434	66	261	47	128	27	36	28	328	17	18	176	149	72	752	52	14
6		4	7	12	7	40	8	9	1	1		11		2	8	14		43	12	15
47	4	36	76	86	15	156	23	93	9	9	8	96	3	6	75	64	7	224	56	16
7	2	2	16	32	1	28	4	28		2		18	4	3	21	22	1	63	12	17
9		2	8	22	3	14	2	25	2		1	8		4	11	13		40	9	18
3	2	4	8	22	1	23		8	1	2		5	1	2	7	9		28	10	19
7		3	6	5		20	1	16	2	2		8			12	4	3	33	6	20

[1] Data not available.

21857°—18——23

TABLE 38.—NEGRO DEATHS BY MONTH OF MORTALITY IN TWO SOUTHERN STATES AND IN REGISTRATION CITIES: 1910.

AREA.	NUMBER OF DEATHS REPORTED FOR THE NEGRO POPULATION: 1910.												
	Total.	January.	February.	March.	April.	May.	June.	July.	August.	September.	October.	November.	December.
SOUTHERN STATES.													
Maryland	5,343	507	473	427	426	379	440	535	453	414	447	426	416
North Carolina	3,024	246	256	257	227	261	240	267	247	229	289	243	262
REGISTRATION CITIES OF 100,000 OR MORE POPULATION AND OF 2,500 NEGROES IN 1910.													
Total	27,348	2,519	2,237	2,478	2,338	2,304	2,353	2,386	2,207	1,934	2,080	2,196	2,316
Southern cities	15,955	1,478	1,295	1,337	1,306	1,341	1,399	1,384	1,313	1,126	1,249	1,336	1,351
Northern and western cities	11,393	1,041	942	1,101	1,032	963	954	1,002	894	808	831	860	965
Southern cities:													
Atlanta, Ga	1,328	104	108	121	135	126	113	98	107	76	112	114	114
Baltimore, Md	2,597	272	237	200	199	192	223	238	217	178	218	210	213
Birmingham, Ala	1,391	117	113	115	99	149	111	123	107	109	109	109	130
Louisville, Ky	1,089	104	94	89	94	101	99	90	94	71	85	86	82
Memphis, Tenn	1,492	134	118	153	122	124	134	124	119	100	110	120	134
Nashville, Tenn	950	98	72	63	68	74	79	93	89	71	72	75	96
New Orleans, La	2,933	265	231	232	272	255	258	236	231	213	219	263	258
Richmond, Va	1,416	131	108	105	110	128	146	129	124	98	113	115	109
Washington, D. C	2,759	253	214	299	207	192	236	253	225	210	211	244	215
Northern and western cities:													
Boston, Mass	317	34	29	30	28	20	31	19	23	32	19	31	21
Cambridge, Mass	75	4	2	7	15	8	9	8	3	2	5	8	4
Chicago, Ill	1,075	102	86	105	80	105	85	78	111	68	62	98	95
Cincinnati, Ohio	569	59	66	53	59	40	46	45	35	30	41	42	53
Cleveland, Ohio	167	14	19	18	17	12	13	9	13	18	9	10	15
Columbus, Ohio	262	17	17	32	20	23	14	25	25	20	20	27	22
Dayton, Ohio	99	9	5	6	13	11	9	11	3	5	9	7	11
Denver, Colo	132	10	11	15	10	11	9	10	14	6	8	9	19
Detroit, Mich	146	15	19	21	14	12	12	14	7	5	5	15	7
Indianapolis, Ind	548	45	37	54	46	46	53	43	41	48	46	43	46
Jersey City, N. J	123	14	10	5	10	12	13	11	9	10	9	11	9
Kansas City, Mo	644	51	58	65	63	59	66	55	46	37	49	43	52
Los Angeles, Cal	136	17	9	15	14	6	13	16	11	5	8	12	10
Minneapolis, Minn	56	5	8	1	5	4	4	8	4	1	6	5	5
Newark, N. J	296	24	16	26	21	22	21	37	24	27	26	20	32
New Haven, Conn	91	6	8	6	7	17	10	7	7	5	10	5	3
New York City	2,391	215	188	213	190	186	205	228	191	209	182	174	210
Bronx Borough	208	17	24	16	13	34	18	8	16	10	20	17	15
Brooklyn Borough	598	62	41	58	58	42	58	53	50	44	36	38	58
Manhattan Borough	1,473	125	116	130	115	102	123	151	111	137	123	112	128
Queens Borough	82	8	4	6	3	5	5	13	10	14	3	7	4
Richmond Borough	30	3	3	3	1	3	1	3	4	4			5
Oakland, Cal	52	4	5	3	6	2	3	5	5		2	8	4
Philadelphia, Pa	2,276	215	199	213	231	188	187	233	172	137	161	147	193
Pittsburgh, Pa	601	61	47	70	72	44	30	50	49	36	53	48	41
Providence, R. I	139	17	10	18	9	8	8	6	21	9	10	9	13
St. Louis, Mo	1,149	99	90	120	97	120	109	79	75	93	86	83	98
St. Paul, Minn	49	4	3	5	5	6	4	5	5		5	5	2

TABLE 39.—DEATHS OF NEGROES IN THE REGISTRATION AREA, BY SEX AND AGE, FOR STATES AND SELECTED CITIES: 1914, 1913, 1912, 1911, 1910, AND 1900.

REGISTRATION AREA, SEX, AND YEAR.	All ages.	DEATHS AT AGE OF—													Deaths at unknown age.
		Under 1 year.	1 year.	2 years.	3 years.	4 years.	5 to 9 years.	10 to 14 years.	15 to 19 years.	20 to 24 years.	25 to 44 years.	45 to 64 years.	65 to 84 years.	85 years and over.	
SUMMARY.															
THE REGISTRATION AREA.															
Males:															
1914	36,846	6,304	1,338	607	327	242	716	633	1,334	2,339	9,965	8,046	4,197	609	189
1913	35,267	6,140	1,356	606	351	234	735	565	1,323	2,217	9,482	7,552	3,927	520	259
1912	29,600	4,840	1,060	476	300	179	551	465	1,105	1,905	8,336	6,559	3,251	432	141
1911	29,386	5,096	1,309	584	315	236	636	515	1,074	1,848	7,991	6,178	3,035	420	149
1910	25,840	5,063	1,194	516	255	188	500	439	916	1,609	7,081	5,281	2,452	303	43
1900	17,772	4,243	1,078	464	279	170	505	373	707	1,226	4,033	3,009	1,373	216	96
Females:															
1914	33,583	5,239	1,275	589	366	250	793	718	1,695	2,306	8,677	6,927	3,746	866	136
1913	31,999	5,208	1,249	591	351	231	774	716	1,653	2,192	8,076	6,480	3,520	776	182
1912	26,450	4,202	1,021	485	257	195	560	543	1,355	1,833	6,855	5,476	2,950	612	106
1911	27,045	4,374	1,242	555	321	219	612	629	1,385	1,939	6,816	5,408	2,756	696	93
1910	23,659	4,287	1,127	519	293	189	524	513	1,102	1,631	6,046	4,565	2,344	487	32
1900	17,223	3,671	1,004	486	276	169	557	536	901	1,235	3,669	2,796	1,522	350	51
REGISTRATION STATES.[1]															
Males:															
1914	28,014	5,064	1,088	448	251	180	565	505	1,019	1,659	7,000	6,018	3,543	517	157
1913	26,473	4,869	1,086	472	266	177	568	436	982	1,526	6,535	5,588	3,264	451	253
1912	19,268	3,250	749	292	200	121	365	304	695	1,110	5,135	4,210	2,384	331	122
1911	19,431	3,497	924	383	195	149	424	326	700	1,108	4,982	3,985	2,294	329	135
1910	14,576	3,097	784	304	152	105	284	243	462	788	3,716	2,825	1,603	186	27
1900	4,972	1,354	340	120	63	47	138	94	187	278	912	866	470	80	23
Female:															
1914	25,319	4,217	1,023	432	294	195	618	572	1,279	1,615	6,066	5,151	3,040	707	110
1913	24,090	4,120	971	462	273	182	592	566	1,256	1,551	5,638	4,793	2,881	624	181
1912	17,102	2,776	706	302	172	129	384	362	890	1,088	4,125	3,525	2,093	452	98
1911	17,630	2,929	852	357	199	160	427	428	885	1,185	4,146	3,439	2,028	511	84
1910	13,356	2,672	718	294	160	116	305	305	609	811	3,113	2,484	1,437	313	19
1900	4,982	1,125	313	151	72	52	144	186	237	312	937	820	507	114	12
REGISTRATION CITIES IN NONREGISTRATION STATES.															
Males:															
1914	8,832	1,240	250	159	76	62	151	128	315	680	2,965	2,028	654	92	32
1913	8,794	1,272	270	134	85	57	166	129	341	691	2,947	1,964	663	69	6
1912	9,956	1,536	300	177	99	58	179	153	396	777	3,095	2,263	814	94	15
1911	9,775	1,577	383	199	120	85	208	186	365	730	2,954	2,152	717	87	12
1910	11,264	1,966	410	212	103	83	216	196	454	821	3,365	2,456	849	117	16
1900	12,800	2,889	738	344	216	123	367	279	520	948	3,121	2,143	903	136	73
Females:															
1914	8,264	1,022	252	157	72	55	175	146	416	691	2,611	1,776	706	159	26
1913	7,909	1,089	278	129	78	49	182	149	397	641	2,438	1,687	639	152	1
1912	9,038	1,380	311	178	82	63	172	175	446	730	2,650	1,883	811	151	6
1911	9,233	1,423	388	196	120	58	181	195	494	743	2,626	1,933	696	172	8
1910	10,303	1,615	409	225	133	73	219	208	493	820	2,933	2,081	907	174	13
1900	12,241	2,546	691	335	204	117	413	350	664	923	2,732	1,976	1,015	236	39
SELECTED CITIES IN REGISTRATION AREA.[1]															
Males:															
1914	20,642	3,351	720	325	193	126	347	305	652	1,388	6,546	4,825	1,657	169	38
1913	20,172	3,329	726	332	204	137	394	296	710	1,317	6,331	4,623	1,607	145	21
1912	20,083	3,227	713	327	203	126	376	298	720	1,381	6,239	4,593	1,685	169	26
1911	19,850	3,409	882	385	224	152	400	346	682	1,319	5,939	4,342	1,578	171	21
1910	19,708	3,809	846	381	200	141	360	315	694	1,288	5,795	4,148	1,541	171	19
1900	15,531	3,721	940	419	250	155	443	322	615	1,122	3,619	2,612	1,086	159	68
Females:															
1914	18,767	2,744	651	324	182	138	424	337	882	1,359	5,482	4,160	1,760	297	27
1913	18,251	2,838	693	317	194	134	437	343	854	1,311	5,245	3,987	1,599	289	10
1912	18,118	2,831	694	336	178	126	366	322	877	1,300	5,127	3,917	1,714	313	17
1911	18,400	2,966	824	376	227	145	381	361	891	1,383	5,046	3,890	1,558	332	20
1910	18,083	3,171	807	394	231	136	399	366	798	1,290	4,941	3,626	1,596	313	15
1900	15,046	3,272	874	420	252	154	498	444	790	1,082	3,267	2,427	1,242	285	39
REGISTRATION STATES.															
CALIFORNIA.															
Males:															
1914	354	35	4	1	2	......	6	3	12	23	124	99	40	5	......
1913	348	41	2	3	......	1	9	5	14	21	121	85	41	5	......
1912	309	19	4	4	2	......	5	1	10	15	123	80	37	9	......
1911	275	17	6	2	1	3	1	3	6	15	107	71	36	7	......
1910	257	27	4	2	2	3	4	3	5	11	96	67	28	5	......
1900[2]															
Females:															
1914	216	14	7	......	......	1	1	......	11	13	96	48	21	4	......
1913	245	22	7	1	1	1	6	5	8	19	80	68	20	7	......
1912	247	30	6	4	2	2	2	5	7	21	81	48	31	8	......
1911	182	18	5	6	......	1	1	4	8	9	58	42	22	8	......
1910	185	21	4	2	4	......	1	3	11	10	56	49	18	6	......
1900[2]															

[1] Includes the District of Columbia. [2] Not in registration area.

TABLE 39.—DEATHS OF NEGROES IN THE REGISTRATION AREA, BY SEX AND AGE, FOR STATES AND SELECTED CITIES: 1914, 1913, 1912, 1911, 1910, AND 1900—Continued.

REGISTRATION AREA, SEX, AND YEAR.	All ages.	DEATHS AT AGE OF—													Deaths at unknown age.
		Under 1 year.	1 year.	2 years.	3 years.	4 years.	5 to 9 years.	10 to 14 years.	15 to 19 years.	20 to 24 years.	25 to 44 years.	45 to 64 years.	65 to 84 years.	85 years and over.	
REGISTRATION STATES—Con.															
COLORADO.															
Males:															
1914	134	12	1		1	1	2	1	3	4	56	42	10	2	
1913	127	10	2		1		1		4	5	53	35	15		
1912	141	10	1			1	1	1	3	10	51	46	14	4	
1911	176	21	2		1	1	1	3	3	7	70	50	15	1	1
1910	167	19	3				2	6	4	15	69	32	14	2	1
1900 [1]															
Females:															
1914	122	9	2	3	3	1			7	7	42	30	12	6	
1913	105	4	2		1		1	2	5	7	38	27	13	5	
1912	79	4	3	3					1	5	22	25	12	1	
1911	112	14	2	3	1		1	4	4	4	35	25	16	2	
1910	122	15	5				1	1	3	4	8	44	25	14	2
1900 [1]															
CONNECTICUT.															
Males:															
1914	211	43	4	4				1	4	7	5	48	46	43	4
1913	192	26	9	2	2	2	1	4	7	5	46	52	31	3	2
1912	178	42	9	4	1	1	2		6	7	36	42	25	2	1
1911	207	43	9	1	4		3	5	2	9	51	55	21	2	2
1910	188	27	12	6	1	2	5	5	5	3	43	53	22	3	1
1900	168	55	8		2	2	4	1	5	4	19	34	25	5	4
Females:															
1914	204	32	12	2	3		6	3	12	9	45	45	29	6	
1913	169	26	5		1	1	4	3	5	3	41	42	31	5	2
1912	157	23	10	3	1		2	1	7	8	31	33	30	5	3
1911	185	32	8	5	7		5	5	7	8	39	35	29	4	1
1910	185	33	9	5	1	3	4		12	6	31	43	32	6	
1900	184	35	11	10		1	6	6	12	10	26	34	26	4	3
INDIANA.															
Males:															
1914	823	105	20	9	8	1	17	17	30	53	214	215	114	16	4
1913	828	108	18	13	12	3	18	14	36	54	204	204	120	20	4
1912	755	86	24	10	5	3	12	9	23	47	193	199	119	23	2
1911	716	92	22	16	6	4	15	15	19	48	179	156	124	18	2
1910	783	110	36	14	7	3	15	8	32	61	182	182	121	10	2
1900	640	123	34	12	8	6	22	19	38	44	104	130	84	10	6
Females:															
1914	634	90	18	13	4	5	11	17	32	33	181	139	71	18	2
1913	653	86	13	6	8		19	21	41	43	161	158	82	15	
1912	621	87	25	10	5	4	20	13	38	43	144	153	62	16	1
1911	610	89	19	8	3	3	9	9	34	35	167	128	85	20	1
1910	650	108	31	10	5	9	14	18	40	41	154	134	65	20	1
1900	610	97	37	19	9	2	13	24	40	52	130	102	62	20	3
KENTUCKY.															
Males:															
1914	3,025	375	104	40	26	18	70	64	129	194	802	679	405	58	61
1913	2,885	448	95	46	35	15	66	44	124	195	711	608	382	56	60
1912	2,844	410	100	50	34	14	47	52	118	215	661	596	405	67	75
1911	3,019	455	140	64	35	24	83	56	153	209	716	567	376	71	70
1910 [1]															
1900 [1]															
Females:															
1914	2,667	362	94	47	26	18	55	73	180	184	638	542	320	97	31
1913	2,720	358	103	64	26	20	65	73	175	202	616	544	353	83	38
1912	2,732	343	86	39	20	20	64	71	162	205	645	567	366	91	53
1911	2,808	364	126	52	27	35	79	83	222	203	588	527	347	113	42
1910 [1]															
1900 [1]															
MAINE.															
Males:															
1914	22		1			1				1	6	5	7		1
1913	19	3							1		5	7	3		
1912	10							2			2	5	1		
1911	8	2									1	1	3	1	
1910	14						1	1		1	6	3	2		1
1900	12	1	1				1				4	1	2	1	1
Females:															
1914	8							1		2	3	2			
1913	4	2									1		1		
1912	1										1				
1911	5	1									1	1	1	1	
1910	5									1	1	2	1		
1900	12	3	1								1		3		
MARYLAND.															
Males:															
1914	2,861	661	135	48	31	15	60	44	105	141	576	586	385	45	29
1913	2,958	740	143	60	30	27	69	34	102	138	617	570	373	34	21
1912	2,794	612	123	57	39	19	62	55	80	137	622	555	366	46	21
1911	2,814	647	153	58	28	29	70	53	109	144	567	523	368	44	21
1910	2,692	707	152	65	30	17	57	56	96	150	529	462	321	39	11
1900 [1]															
Females:															
1914	2,686	587	106	48	30	20	62	57	144	165	534	535	316	66	16
1913	2,774	608	150	57	22	24	73	78	160	148	539	504	320	73	18
1912	2,521	500	106	40	27	24	67	59	141	141	545	491	298	63	19
1911	2,727	559	135	70	36	21	77	71	136	170	553	514	305	66	14
1910	2,651	557	126	69	32	25	64	73	141	149	549	469	321	68	8
1900 [1]															

[1] Not in registration area.

TABLE 39.—DEATHS OF NEGROES IN THE REGISTRATION AREA, BY SEX AND AGE, FOR STATES AND SELECTED CITIES: 1914, 1913, 1912, 1911, 1910, AND 1900—Continued.

REGISTRATION AREA, SEX, AND YEAR.	All ages.	DEATHS AT AGE OF—													Deaths at unknown age.
		Under 1 year.	1 year.	2 years.	3 years.	4 years.	5 to 9 years.	10 to 14 years.	15 to 19 years.	20 to 24 years.	25 to 44 years.	45 to 64 years.	65 to 84 years.	85 years and over.	
REGISTRATION STATES—Con.															
MASSACHUSETTS.															
Males:															
1914	507	83	12	5	6		8	9	21	34	135	140	49	5	
1913	468	73	23	8	3	5	10	10	20	18	133	108	54	3	
1912	461	73	18	5	7	2	12	11	14	29	120	97	69	2	2
1911	452	70	27	12	5	7	9	8	12	20	117	101	56	7	1
1910	432	70	23	8	6	3	10	9	10	20	134	96	39	2	2
1900	344	76	25	9	4	2	7	6	10	20	75	71	31	5	3
Females:															
1914	390	52	20	10	3		6	8	11	10	101	103	52	14	
1913	373	57	20	8	3	4	8	9	10	21	84	85	57	7	
1912	377	58	10	8	2	1	9	4	9	22	95	95	57	7	
1911	389	64	21	4	6	4	8	8	13	17	93	96	48	7	
1910	377	69	18	2	3	8	5	9	13	19	83	84	53	11	
1900	337	73	16	12	7	6	12	9	14	20	74	52	32	9	1
MICHIGAN.															
Males:															
1914	228	17	6	3		1	3	5	9	11	61	44	57	8	3
1913	248	28	5	3	3		5	5	6	13	58	63	48	8	3
1912	214	24	4	3	1		2	4	4	16	56	55	40	5	
1911	240	35	8	2	1		3	3	9	13	52	65	41	6	2
1910	239	32	2	3	1	1	8	4	8	11	50	61	51	7	
1900	150	15	5	1	3	2	3	2	7	7	35	35	26	8	1
Females:															
1914	164	26	5	3	1	1	2	2	6	7	44	36	24	7	
1913	167	24		2	2		2	5	3	7	37	50	27	8	
1912	165	19	5		3	3	1	3	3	8	30	45	37	6	2
1911	159	18	3	1	2	1	7	1	7	4	42	40	24	9	
1910	187	24	10	2	2	1		5	8	10	48	39	33	5	
1900	140	13	10	3	1		2	9	7	8	31	34	17	5	
MINNESOTA.															
Males:															
1914	90	6	1			1		2	1	4	35	30	10		
1913	104	6	2				1	·2	1	9	40	31	11	1	
1912	74	7	2			1		1	2	1	25	32	3		
1911	73	8		1	2		1		1	5	28	18	8	1	
1910	84	9	1	2	1		1		2	6	21	29	12		
1900 [1]															
Females:															
1914	61	5	1				1	1		2	24	19	7	1	
1913	55	6					2		2	2	14	21	8		
1912	52	3	1					1	3	5	20	7	11	1	
1911	57	7	1	1			1	1	1	4	23	12	6		
1910	51	6	1	2		1	1	2		3	17	10	5	3	
1900 [1]															
MISSOURI.															
Males:															
1914	2,052	241	46	31	10	19	33	43	76	141	673	454	233	36	16
1913	2,082	245	73	28	13	10	35	33	81	139	655	477	250	28	15
1912	2,121	230	46	22	17	15	40	25	98	140	685	491	252	46	14
1911	1,948	276	55	23	16	17	29	34	76	122	563	443	224	52	18
1910 [1]															
1900 [1]															
Females:															
1914	1,653	191	50	30	17	14	39	35	79	116	422	365	216	63	16
1913	1,681	226	67	24	20	16	37	30	89	112	466	333	209	40	12
1912	1,700	207	58	26	11	19	41	28	106	117	445	349	209	58	16
1911	1,677	204	60	32	13	10	36	46	89	117	444	324	226	61	15
1910 [1]															
1900 [1]															
MONTANA.															
Males:															
1914	24	1								1	12	8	2		
1913	32	2						1			16	10		2	1
1912	34	3								1	18	9	3		
1911	32	3	1	1					1		12	8	5		1
1910	25	1	1							1	12	7	2	1	
1900 [1]															
Females:															
1914	14		1								5	4	4		
1913	18	1	1							1	5	6	3	1	
1912	17	1									8	7	1		
1911	17	1					1		2		7	4	1		1
1910	18	2			1				2		9	3	1		
1900 [1]															
NEW HAMPSHIRE.															
Males:															
1914	6											1	3		2
1913	2	1									1				
1912	8	2									1	1	4		
1911	7	1					1			2	1	1		1	
1910	7	1	1	1							1	1	1	1	
1900	4	1	1									1	1		
Females:															
1914	5										3	1	1		
1913	3		2										1		
1912	5	1					1	1			1	1			
1911	4	2									1	1			
1910	7			1							2	1	1	1	
1900	4	1							1			1	1		1

[1] Not in registration area.

TABLE 39.—DEATHS OF NEGROES IN THE REGISTRATION AREA, BY SEX AND AGE, FOR STATES AND SELECTED CITIES: 1914, 1913, 1912, 1911, 1910, AND 1900—Continued.

REGISTRATION AREA, SEX, AND YEAR.	All ages.	DEATHS AT AGE OF—													Deaths at unknown age.
		Under 1 year.	1 year.	2 years.	3 years.	4 years.	5 to 9 years.	10 to 14 years.	15 to 19 years.	20 to 24 years.	25 to 44 years.	45 to 64 years.	65 to 84 years.	85 years and over.	
REGISTRATION STATES—Con.															
NEW JERSEY.															
Males:															
1914	1,047	215	49	20	9	10	28	16	37	57	236	228	129	13	
1913	1,003	231	50	22	5	8	27	15	25	45	211	233	122	9	
1912	1,013	224	39	15	9	8	23	19	36	37	237	236	114	16	
1911	1,043	212	53	28	12	8	31	17	39	44	243	236	108	12	
1910	1,042	273	69	27	16	11	21	21	28	38	253	166	110	9	
1900	828	282	67	26	13	8	23	14	27	42	131	105	71	15	4
Females:															
1914	980	172	50	13	6	7	28	23	42	41	228	214	134	21	1
1913	1,014	188	47	31	6	11	25	18	42	52	230	220	119	25	
1912	954	193	43	16	10	12	29	16	41	47	218	181	128	20	
1911	929	180	38	15	12	10	19	23	31	55	208	198	117	23	
1910	1,031	231	61	22	15	7	24	27	41	61	230	190	108	14	
1900	838	188	58	30	9	11	31	43	34	44	154	143	71	18	4
NEW YORK.															
Males:															
1914	1,826	344	101	32	21	19	42	29	46	101	565	355	152	18	1
1913	1,703	318	100	40	21	13	40	25	55	91	523	314	150	13	
1912	1,791	346	92	41	17	19	43	19	64	106	563	312	157	10	2
1911	1,742	355	92	35	22	9	24	14	54	90	538	331	163	15	
1910	1,780	394	107	37	24	18	29	28	54	89	542	305	140	13	
1900	1,418	383	106	39	15	12	38	24	40	87	308	243	108	12	3
Females:															
1914	1,723	260	77	25	28	17	39	39	68	112	512	352	168	24	2
1913	1,533	242	83	30	25	12	43	31	63	103	407	310	163	21	
1912	1,595	305	92	39	23	7	39	34	48	101	418	308	156	25	
1911	1,705	309	71	28	16	14	33	30	58	121	498	320	168	39	
1910	1,570	315	106	31	22	13	39	31	56	106	403	274	142	32	
1900	1,325	344	96	40	15	13	37	45	47	74	262	198	134	20	
NORTH CAROLINA.[1]															
Males:															
1914	2,064	502	117	44	22	13	53	45	83	163	407	357	207	42	9
1913	1,537	361	92	36	15	15	39	40	83	119	288	277	148	15	9
1912	1,507	333	93	26	19	11	41	35	74	108	337	247	157	24	2
1911	1,581	345	131	57	16	16	42	31	66	116	291	257	178	24	11
1910	1,425	313	110	39	18	13	30	30	66	96	301	232	150	25	2
1900 [2]															
Females:															
1914	2,134	443	124	33	25	16	69	53	118	168	503	343	191	31	17
1913	1,602	327	70	31	29	20	48	41	108	131	366	261	138	22	10
1912	1,559	290	79	42	22	11	32	24	90	128	357	272	167	43	2
1911	1,758	312	131	56	29	20	48	41	98	135	358	302	167	52	9
1910	1,599	313	114	51	19	14	39	36	89	138	345	248	144	42	7
1900 [2]															
OHIO.															
Males:															
1914	1,535	186	33	15	14	3	22	24	46	87	439	385	241	40	
1913	1,650	169	54	20	14	7	29	19	55	92	470	415	265	40	1
1912	1,461	178	45	10	11	7	19	19	50	73	403	369	238	38	1
1911	1,353	164	54	23	13	8	25	20	39	84	391	319	184	27	2
1910	1,250	184	41	17	11	8	19	12	36	69	364	297	162	27	3
1900 [2]															
Females:															
1914	1,066	146	30	12	13	7	17	27	44	67	267	221	169	46	
1913	1,170	126	35	19	14	4	29	31	54	72	300	257	191	38	
1912	1,101	137	38	14	10	8	16	26	62	70	286	232	160	41	1
1911	1,012	133	38	15	8	9	26	37	47	81	255	207	126	29	1
1910	1,010	172	41	12	9	4	29	31	52	61	229	215	124	30	1
1900 [2]															
PENNSYLVANIA.															
Males:															
1914	2,565	484	100	42	18	12	50	38	74	124	738	615	243	23	4
1913	2,449	474	106	48	23	21	54	35	73	124	666	567	233	25	
1912	1,952	381	84	26	27	13	31	35	59	91	545	442	199	18	1
1911	2,165	473	108	32	27	18	58	39	66	97	595	431	199	22	
1910	2,497	576	170	49	27	22	53	41	74	121	673	456	213	21	1
1900 [2]															
Females:															
1914	2,130	399	100	42	22	22	50	57	93	97	520	450	238	40	
1913	2,128	399	92	50	15	24	62	49	100	128	553	407	214	35	
1912	1,721	323	88	36	20	6	34	41	97	90	384	366	195	40	1
1911	1,868	378	122	40	26	21	47	42	72	129	445	334	169	43	
1910	2,172	487	141	59	30	22	59	40	84	116	513	380	198	43	
1900 [2]															
RHODE ISLAND.															
Males:															
1914	145	22	7	3	2	2	2		3	13	39	28	20	3	1
1913	147	22	7	2	2	1	6	2	8	7	34	35	20	1	
1912	127	21	11	2	1	2			3	7	35	27	17	1	
1911	137	26	4	5	2	1	3	1	1	8	34	33	17	2	
1910	120	30	2	4	3	1	3	2	2	1	26	25	20	1	
1900	122	31	10	2	3	1	4	3	5	4	19	23	15	2	
Females:															
1914	142	26	10	1		2	3	1	5	12	31	27	22	2	
1913	114	16	6	2	1	1	2	4	1	3	29	28	15	6	
1912	128	23	6	2	1	2	1	7	1	3	31	35	12	4	
1911	109	15	4	1	2	1	4	2	6	7	16	34	14	3	
1910	128	28	5	3		1	4	2	3	2	28	23	24	4	1
1900	116	18	5	1	3	3	2	2	8	4	19	20	23	8	

[1] Includes only municipalities having a population of 1,000 or over in 1900.　　　[2] Not in registration area.

TABLE 39.—DEATHS OF NEGROES IN THE REGISTRATION AREA, BY SEX AND AGE, FOR STATES AND SELECTED CITIES: 1914, 1913, 1912, 1911, 1910, AND 1900—Continued.

REGISTRATION AREA, SEX, AND YEAR.	All ages.	Under 1 year.	1 year.	2 years.	3 years.	4 years.	5 to 9 years.	10 to 14 years.	15 to 19 years.	20 to 24 years.	25 to 44 years.	45 to 64 years.	65 to 84 years.	85 years and over.	Deaths at unknown age.
REGISTRATION STATES—Con.															
UTAH.															
Males:															
1914	16	2								1	6	4	3		
1913	15	1								1	8	4	1		
1912	14									2	8	3	1		
1911	17	1								1	8	5	1	1	
1910	20	4						1		3	10	1	1		
1900 [1]															
Females:															
1914	4	1									3				
1913	8	1									5	2			
1912	5								1		4				
1911	8	3						1			4				
1910	12	1	1								7	2		1	
1900 [1]															
VERMONT.															
Males:															
1914	4											2	2		
1913	9			1					1	1	3	1	2		
1912	15	2		1						3	6	1	2		
1911	18		1		1		2		1	2	7	3	1		
1910	18	2		1	1					2	5	3	2	2	1
1900	10		1							2	1	2	3		1
Females:															
1914															
1913	2										1	1			
1912	4									1		1	1	1	
1911	11	1							1	1	3	1	3	1	
1910	11	2								2	4		2	1	
1900	7		1			1			1			3			1
VIRGINIA.															
Males:															
1914	6,618	1,432	298	129	64	51	142	139	292	409	1,314	1,230	943	154	21
1913	6,324	1,322	265	119	70	42	139	132	258	378	1,298	1,168	830	167	136
1912 [1]															
1911 [1]															
1910 [1]															
1900 [1]															
Females:															
1914	6,566	1,182	277	130	100	52	184	146	335	454	1,400	1,261	803	219	23
1913	6,312	1,199	233	120	84	39	140	149	338	427	1,334	1,176	771	201	101
1912 [1]															
1911 [1]															
1910 [1]															
1900 [1]															
WASHINGTON.															
Males:															
1914	55	1	2						1		30	16	4		1
1913	63	5	2					1	2	3	29	13	6	2	
1912	63	3	1		1	1			1	4	28	20	3	1	1
1911	61	2		1			1		1	1	28	22	3	1	1
1910	65	6	2	1			2	1	1	4	25	13	8		2
1900 [1]															
Females:															
1914	36	4		1	1			1	1	2	14	9	3		
1913	37	2			1		1	1	1	1	15	11	3	1	
1912	36	2		1					1	2	18	6	5	1	
1911	33	1	1						1	1	12	10	6	1	
1910	32	4	2				2		1	1	9	6	6	1	
1900 [1]															
WISCONSIN.															
Males:															
1914	35	4	1	1		1	2				14	8	2	1	1
1913	32	3							1	3	10	7	6	1	1
1912	37		1					1	2	1	11	9	10	1	1
1911	29	4	1						2	4	5	5	6		2
1910	42	9	3				2	2	2	2	9	6	4	1	2
1900 [1]															
Females:															
1914	26	2			1			1	1	2	6	5	7		1
1913	20	4	1					1	1		3	3	3	4	
1912	26	1	2			2	1		1	2	8	5	4		
1911	24	5							1	2	3	6	4	3	
1910	23	6							1	1	4	4	3	3	
1900 [1]															
SELECTED CITIES IN REGISTRATION AREA.															
ALEXANDRIA, VA.															
Males:															
1914	63	15	2			1	3		1	3	19	9	10		
1913	56	10	1		1	2		1		1	19	12	7	2	
1912	79	16	2	1	1		3	2	3	4	12	24	11		
1911	63	14	1	2	1			1	3	6	12	15	7	1	
1910	64	10	5	3	1	1		1	3	2	22	8	8		1
1900	78	22	3	1	2	1	4	4	2	6	11	11	9	1	1
Females:															
1914	62	17						1	3	4	11	16	9	1	
1913	62	15	1	1	1			1	3	3	13	13	6	4	1
1912	52	9	3	3			1		2	2	5	9	10	7	1
1911	68	8	1		2		3		1	2	17	22	10	1	
1910	74	9	1	3	1		1		4	1	7	21	19	5	2
1900	82	16	4	3	2		3	4	3	6	9	22	8	2	

[1] Not in registration area.

NEGRO POPULATION.

TABLE **39.**—DEATHS OF NEGROES IN THE REGISTRATION AREA, BY SEX AND AGE, FOR STATES AND SELECTED CITIES: 1914, 1913, 1912, 1911, 1910, AND 1900—Continued.

REGISTRATION AREA, SEX, AND YEAR.	All ages.	DEATHS AT AGE OF—													Deaths at unknown age.
		Under 1 year.	1 year.	2 years.	3 years.	4 years.	5 to 9 years.	10 to 14 years.	15 to 19 years.	20 to 24 years.	25 to 44 years.	45 to 64 years.	65 to 84 years.	85 years and over.	
SELECTED CITIES IN REGISTRATION AREA—Contd.															
ANNAPOLIS, MD.															
Males:															
1914[1]															
1913[1]															
1912[1]															
1911[1]															
1910	45	12	3	4			2	2		1	2	11	4	7	1
1900	65	25	5	5		2	2			2	4	7	8	5	
Females:															
1914[1]															
1913[1]															
1912[1]															
1911[1]															
1910	52	10	5	2	1	1	2	1	6	1	6	7	8	2	
1900	61	25	6	1	1		3	3	4	1	6		6	3	2
ASHEVILLE, N. C.															
Males:															
1914	92	22	3	1	2		3	2	6	2	24	19	5	2	1
1913	71	14	7			1	2	3	3	2	18	17	4		
1912	72	11	6	2	1		6	2	2	7	20	10	5		
1911	48	8	4				1	1	3	5	14	8	2	2	
1910	55	14	3	2	2	1	2		1	2	16	7	4	1	
1900[2]															
Females:															
1914	69	12	4	2	1		6	1	7	8	11	8	8	1	
1913	64	11	1		3		5	2	9	2	20	4	6	1	
1912	60	10	3	1	2		2	2	2	6	15	6	10	1	
1911	56	6	3	2		2			4	7	18	8	4	2	
1910	80	10	1	4	1	1	5	1	8	6	21	15	7		
1900[2]															
ATLANTA, GA.															
Males:															
1914	666	113	25	22	6	7	10	11	19	52	214	134	47	6	
1913	741	124	30	19	11	9	13	13	37	61	215	167	36	6	
1912	715	112	38	18	8	10	11	11	45	56	199	161	36	8	2
1911	698	94	45	25	13	4	17	13	29	56	202	152	43	5	
1910	647	124	35	13	4	4	10	10	35	53	187	129	38	4	1
1900	493	122	40	12	12	4	6	6	27	45	111	68	32	6	2
Females:															
1914	718	77	15	15	8	8	18	17	26	86	223	172	38	15	
1913	728	99	26	13	7	4	17	18	42	54	230	167	38	13	
1912	666	90	29	19	7	3	11	12	49	66	199	134	40	7	
1911	796	118	31	22	15	2	17	19	56	84	221	155	43	13	
1910	681	111	25	12	7	5	7	21	32	63	224	127	34	10	3
1900	484	122	30	8	7	4	8	11	31	40	96	83	33	11	
ATLANTIC CITY, N. J.															
Males:															
1914	98	23	4				1	2	3	2	32	25	6		
1913	68	16	1	2		1	2	5	1	5	12	17	6		
1912	97	19	1	1	1		2	2	4	8	29	27	3		
1911	83	13	3				4	2	4	4	23	23	6	1	
1910	83	22	3		2		2		4	2	31	14	2	1	
1900	54	16	4	2		1	2	1	4	3	14	5	2		
Females:															
1914	84	12	2	2			3	2	3	4	24	20	9	3	
1913	97	20	3	1		1	4	1	2	4	26	28	5	2	
1912	73	12	4	2	1		3	3	1	7	19	13	7	1	
1911	82	15	2	1			2	5	2	1	30	18	6		
1910	89	21	5		1	1	3	2	1	5	23	21	5	1	
1900	52	17	4	1			2		1	3	11	12	3		
BALTIMORE, MD.															
Males:															
1914	1,348	262	74	18	21	7	19	16	38	78	362	330	120	3	
1913	1,410	290	59	25	7	16	29	12	38	77	409	329	113	6	
1912	1,346	265	58	29	19	7	20	17	31	73	398	313	108	7	1
1911	1,353	283	70	16	12	13	29	22	39	78	364	296	118	13	
1910	1,346	358	52	23	17	9	16	27	36	68	349	279	105	7	
1900	1,266	407	71	51	22	10	51	30	43	70	233	192	78	8	
Females:															
1914	1,252	229	51	20	15	11	37	11	53	76	305	298	134	12	
1913	1,299	232	62	26	8	10	34	21	56	64	326	307	133	20	
1912	1,187	211	49	15	11	12	25	14	57	73	321	268	110	21	
1911	1,291	244	53	29	15	12	28	24	60	75	331	281	120	19	
1910	1,251	221	44	28	16	8	27	36	51	66	326	268	125	34	1
1900	1,387	359	85	51	32	19	55	37	72	83	261	211	97	25	
BIRMINGHAM, ALA.															
Males:															
1914	831	92	20	16	7	2	14	17	34	83	307	175	50	5	9
1913	880	127	25	15	6	6	18	14	43	94	306	174	44	8	
1912	727	92	27	12	9	5	11	7	38	77	240	155	41	13	
1911	689	105	36	17	8	11	13	13	25	61	216	132	45	7	
1910	767	118	34	14	4	12	16	15	44	90	247	127	37	9	
1900[2]															
Females:															
1914	753	94	30	24	9	4	19	18	46	88	240	118	50	10	3
1913	692	92	29	17	11	5	14	19	34	75	229	110	46	11	
1912	672	96	31	20	10	5	13	10	34	59	217	120	50	7	
1911	619	91	29	18	5	6	13	11	36	58	200	105	36	11	
1910	624	80	40	15	7	1	20	12	38	53	216	102	32	8	
1900[2]															

[1] Data not available.   [2] Not in registration area.

TABLE 39.—DEATHS OF NEGROES IN THE REGISTRATION AREA, BY SEX AND AGE, FOR STATES AND SELECTED CITIES: 1914, 1913, 1912, 1911, 1910, AND 1900—Continued.

REGISTRATION AREA, SEX, AND YEAR.	All ages.	Under 1 year.	1 year.	2 years.	3 years.	4 years.	5 to 9 years.	10 to 14 years.	15 to 19 years.	20 to 24 years.	25 to 44 years.	45 to 64 years.	65 to 84 years.	85 years and over.	Deaths at unknown age.
SELECTED CITIES IN REGISTRATION AREA—Contd.															
BOSTON, MASS.															
Males:															
1914	196	25	3	1	3	....	4	3	5	14	52	75	11	....	....
1913	197	39	10	1	....	2	3	5	6	5	58	52	16	....	....
1912	180	34	9	2	2	....	3	4	4	8	49	48	16	....	1
1911	178	31	13	6	2	3	4	4	3	7	50	37	17	1	....
1910	156	22	10	....	5	2	1	4	5	....	48	46	11	2	....
1900	161	35	14	5	3	2	3	1	3	8	42	38	7	....	....
Females:															
1914	173	22	7	3	....	....	5	4	5	4	50	50	18	5	....
1913	160	22	9	3	1	2	3	5	4	10	37	41	22	1	....
1912	154	17	8	2	....	1	3	....	6	10	47	40	18	3	....
1911	177	27	10	2	1	....	4	4	8	8	46	47	19	1	....
1910	161	22	9	....	2	3	1	4	3	9	42	43	20	3	....
1900	151	33	9	4	3	4	4	5	6	8	42	18	13	2	....
CAMBRIDGE, MASS.															
Males:															
1914	48	11	3	1	2	....	1	2	1	....	10	11	4	2	....
1913	41	5	1	1	1	3	4	....	2	2	9	8	4	1	....
1912	39	5	2	....	....	....	3	2	....	3	10	8	6	....	....
1911	54	12	2	4	1	....	1	1	2	1	9	17	3	1	....
1910	44	11	4	2	....	....	....	1	1	2	10	7	6	....	....
1900	44	11	3	1	....	....	1	3	3	5	8	6	2	....	1
Females:															
1914	40	7	2	....	....	....	....	1	2	2	10	9	5	2	....
1913	40	7	4	....	....	....	....	....	2	1	12	7	6	1	....
1912	35	6	....	....	....	....	1	....	....	1	13	9	4	1	....
1911	45	5	2	....	3	....	....	....	1	2	10	17	5	....	....
1910	31	4	2	....	....	1	....	1	3	2	4	8	5	1	....
1900	61	19	2	2	1	2	1	....	2	5	11	7	7	2	....
CAMDEN, N. J.															
Males:															
1914	105	25	7	2	....	....	4	1	4	8	19	24	11	....	....
1913	78	14	5	5	....	....	3	3	2	7	15	20	4	....	....
1912	76	25	1	1	1	....	1	2	2	1	17	15	10	....	....
1911	91	20	7	2	....	....	2	1	6	5	18	18	10	2	....
1910	100	21	10	3	1	....	1	2	2	4	24	16	16	....	....
1900	101	34	15	1	1	2	6	2	2	6	13	8	9	2	....
Females:															
1914	78	9	4	....	....	....	3	3	5	5	17	19	11	2	....
1913	91	20	5	4	1	....	....	3	8	4	24	13	7	2	....
1912	73	15	6	....	1	....	2	....	2	4	15	14	13	1	....
1911	70	15	6	1	2	....	2	2	2	4	14	10	10	2	....
1910	92	25	3	2	....	....	4	2	2	3	18	19	14	....	....
1900	85	20	5	4	5	2	8	12	1	....	10	15	1	2	....
CHARLESTON, S. C.															
Males:															
1914	615	143	21	17	7	3	11	6	15	44	173	141	32	2	....
1913	594	139	33	10	5	3	11	6	19	39	191	107	29	2	....
1912	655	148	36	15	8	4	10	8	22	43	181	144	34	2	....
1911	626	133	24	13	12	3	12	12	22	41	181	140	32	1	....
1910	597	164	30	17	10	4	12	12	18	25	156	113	34	2	....
1900	695	192	39	20	15	4	18	11	30	45	163	104	49	5	....
Females:															
1914	560	97	29	11	9	6	7	6	26	39	175	117	34	4	....
1913	580	116	38	21	5	7	12	14	23	35	147	125	30	7	....
1912	644	133	39	12	7	3	9	15	30	58	166	119	47	5	1
1911	626	126	33	13	6	3	10	17	23	42	189	116	42	6	....
1910	624	143	43	29	10	3	14	10	27	44	142	127	32	....	....
1900	704	158	37	22	11	6	20	17	37	48	166	121	49	12	....
CHARLOTTE, N. C.															
Males:															
1914	186	34	9	3	4	1	1	3	5	12	50	40	21	2	1
1913	115	18	3	....	3	1	2	6	13	10	28	22	9	....	....
1912	109	15	6	2	3	3	5	1	8	7	27	23	8	1	....
1911	114	12	8	5	....	....	3	1	4	15	30	21	12	2	1
1910	147	19	15	4	2	2	4	2	9	14	31	27	15	3	....
1900[1]	....														
Females:															
1914	236	35	7	1	5	3	9	7	18	18	69	49	14	1	....
1913	143	21	7	3	1	5	5	4	7	13	41	19	12	4	1
1912	101	14	4	....	2	....	....	1	7	11	30	21	10	1	....
1911	130	12	4	1	2	2	5	5	9	14	32	28	12	3	1
1910	152	27	8	3	4	2	7	....	....	8	38	31	7	1	....
1900[1]	....														
CHESTER, PA.															
Males:															
1914	73	22	2	....	1	1	1	2	2	4	15	17	7	1	....
1913	69	14	3	1	1	2	4	3	1	5	14	15	6	....	....
1912	65	14	4	1	1	1	1	2	2	2	11	16	10	....	....
1911	50	13	3	....	1	....	1	1	3	2	9	13	4	1	....
1910	58	12	9	3	....	1	1	1	1	2	14	10	4	....	....
1900[1]	....														
Females:															
1914	54	10	5	2	....	....	....	....	2	4	20	9	2	....	....
1913	63	10	7	4	....	1	1	1	1	4	16	13	5	....	....
1912	59	17	4	3	1	....	2	....	....	3	14	8	4	....	....
1911	42	7	5	1	2	....	....	....	....	3	10	9	4	....	....
1910	49	8	5	3	....	1	1	....	....	3	13	9	6	....	....
1900[1]	....														

[1] Not in registration area.

TABLE **39.**—DEATHS OF NEGROES IN THE REGISTRATION AREA, BY SEX AND AGE, FOR STATES AND SELECTED CITIES: 1914, 1913, 1912, 1911, 1910, AND 1900—Continued.

REGISTRATION AREA, SEX, AND YEAR.	All ages.	DEATHS AT AGE OF—													Deaths at unknown age.
		Under 1 year.	1 year.	2 years.	3 years.	4 years.	5 to 9 years.	10 to 14 years.	15 to 19 years.	20 to 24 years.	25 to 44 years.	45 to 64 years.	65 to 84 years.	85 years and over.	
SELECTED CITIES IN REGISTRATION AREA—Contd.															
CHICAGO, ILL.															
Males:															
1914	655	68	22	9	4	5	6	5	16	35	254	188	41	2	......
1913	672	63	15	11	4	5	8	8	16	33	295	154	54	6	......
1912	685	66	21	11	5	1	10	7	19	43	273	184	43	2	......
1911	569	56	24	3	1	1	13	8	22	36	218	158	24	5	......
1910	606	71	15	10	7	1	12	4	15	33	234	154	48	2	......
1900	409	58	14	12	6	5	10	8	12	25	150	79	27	3	......
Females:															
1914	509	42	19	11	1	5	12	4	17	22	175	141	51	9	......
1913	512	43	15	5	7	2	14	8	18	22	167	151	53	7	......
1912	545	57	19	12	5	3	4	10	20	29	174	153	56	3	......
1911	450	40	19	5	11	6	11	7	19	34	152	104	33	9	......
1910	469	42	18	9	8	3	9	11	17	33	165	107	38	9	......
1900	303	43	12	6	3	2	8	7	13	29	95	61	22	2	......
CINCINNATI, OHIO.															
Males:															
1914	396	41	5	3	6	1	6	4	10	33	137	117	28	5	......
1913	387	30	8	6	5	......	4	6	11	22	143	115	34	3	......
1912	376	44	17	3	......	2	3	3	11	23	148	86	31	5	......
1911	370	34	14	10	5	......	3	6	11	41	128	95	20	3	......
1910	343	47	12	8	5	2	3	3	6	16	135	90	15	......	1
1900	212	28	10	7	1	2	6	6	5	18	82	30	15	2	......
Females:															
1914	246	34	6	2	4	1	2	3	7	16	87	55	22	7	......
1913	278	22	5	6	3	2	4	2	10	22	103	62	31	6	......
1912	250	29	7	6	5	1	2	1	20	18	84	49	25	3	......
1911	226	22	9	4	1	1	6	5	11	26	60	56	23	1	1
1910	226	36	9	1	1	......	7	5	11	15	70	49	19	3	......
1900	218	36	10	9	1	1	7	9	7	7	73	42	16	......	......
CLEVELAND, OHIO.															
Males:															
1914	112	9	4	......	......	1	2	1	4	8	38	33	12	......	......
1913	112	19	2	1	......	2	1	2	2	4	37	35	7	......	......
1912	110	14	2	1	2	1	......	......	1	8	34	40	6	1	......
1911	115	16	5	3	1	......	......	1	2	3	52	20	12	......	......
1910	89	6	3	......	4	......	2	2	2	2	33	28	6	1	......
1900	61	14	5	1	......	2	1	......	2	4	10	11	9	2	......
Females:															
1914	95	13	1	......	......	2	3	3	7	7	29	13	13	4	......
1913	81	8	1	1	1	......	3	1	2	7	20	25	9	3	......
1912	80	11	1	2	......	......	1	......	4	5	25	20	9	1	1
1911	95	12	6	4	......	1	5	1	2	10	25	15	11	3	......
1910	78	19	3	3	......	......	2	1	3	6	21	13	6	1	......
1900	38	11	......	1	......	......	1	......	2	3	13	5	2	......	......
COLUMBUS, OHIO.															
Males:															
1914	180	33	3	2	3	......	1	1	3	7	65	38	21	3	......
1913	186	20	5	2	2	......	4	3	8	9	60	47	26	......	......
1912	182	15	4	......	2	1	2	4	4	8	63	40	17	2	......
1911	144	23	9	2	1	......	6	2	2	7	44	32	15	......	1
1910	143	20	1	2	......	1	1	......	6	17	51	32	12	......	......
1900	107	7	4	2	......	1	2	3	5	13	34	24	9	......	3
Females:															
1914	136	20	4	1	4	1	3	4	6	9	27	28	27	2	......
1913	113	15	6	......	3	1	3	3	7	5	29	32	8	1	......
1912	132	16	6	1	1	2	1	1	8	11	46	22	14	3	......
1911	111	16	1	1	......	2	2	5	8	5	28	29	12	2	......
1910	119	23	3	1	......	......	1	1	10	9	27	28	13	3	......
1900	80	7	7	2	3	1	2	2	7	2	16	19	10	......	2
COVINGTON, KY.															
Males:															
1914	68	3	1	2	......	......	2	1	......	12	25	11	10	1	......
1913	55	6	1	1	1	......	1	1	1	8	18	11	3	2	1
1912	59	3	3	......	1	1	1	......	1	7	23	16	3	......	......
1911	52	6	2	1	......	......	2	1	......	3	19	13	3	1	1
1910	30	2	1	......	1	......	......	......	......	1	14	9	2	......	......
1900[1]	......	......	......	......	......	......	......	......	......	......	......	......	......	......	......
Females:															
1914	45	8	1	1	1	1	2	......	......	2	14	10	4	1	......
1913	36	6	1	......	......	......	......	......	......	2	13	11	3	......	......
1912	41	5	2	......	......	......	1	......	1	11	13	5	1	2	
1911	41	3	3	1	......	1	1	1	1	6	5	13	4	2	......
1910	29	6	1	......	2	1	......	......	2	2	6	5	4	......	......
1900[1]	......	......	......	......	......	......	......	......	......	......	......	......	......	......	......
DANVILLE, VA.															
Males:															
1914	80	17	3	1	......	2	3	2	3	5	23	13	6	2	1
1913	82	13	1	2	1	1	4	2	4	6	18	22	6	1	1
1912	63	6	......	......	1	......	1	2	5	3	14	23	7	......	1
1911	76	13	4	8	3	1	1	2	4	4	20	13	3	......	......
1910	70	9	2	6	3	......	2	2	2	4	11	18	9	1	1
1900[1]	......	......	......	......	......	......	......	......	......	......	......	......	......	......	......
Females:															
1914	81	7	2	1	6	......	......	4	6	7	18	25	5	......	......
1913	74	14	2	2	2	......	......	2	4	3	14	23	8	......	......
1912	86	14	3	7	1	......	2	2	8	7	15	17	7	2	1
1911	81	16	5	4	4	1	2	1	5	2	9	26	4	1	1
1910	97	15	......	4	3	......	2	3	6	6	28	21	9	......	......
1900[1]	......	......	......	......	......	......	......	......	......	......	......	......	......	......	......

[1] Not in registration area.

TABLE 39.—DEATHS OF NEGROES IN THE REGISTRATION AREA, BY SEX AND AGE, FOR STATES AND SELECTED CITIES: 1914, 1913, 1912, 1911, 1910, AND 1900—Continued.

REGISTRATION AREA, SEX, AND YEAR.	All ages.	DEATHS AT AGE OF—													Deaths at unknown age.
		Under 1 year.	1 year.	2 years.	3 years.	4 years.	5 to 9 years.	10 to 14 years.	15 to 19 years.	20 to 24 years.	25 to 44 years.	45 to 64 years.	65 to 84 years.	85 years and over.	
SELECTED CITIES IN REGISTRATION AREA—Contd.															
DAYTON, OHIO.															
Males:															
1914	64	9	2	1			1	2	3	2	20	17	7		
1913	84	10	2	1	1		3	1	3	5	29	18	10	1	
1912	71	9			1		3	2	4	2	15	24	10	1	
1911	62	11			1	1	1	1	5	2	17	17	6		
1910	46	11	2				2	1	2	2	9	13	4		
1900	37	13			1			2	1	1	8	7	4		
Females:															
1914	51	4	2	1	1		1	2	2	5	16	12	4	1	
1913	54	5			1		4	1	1	3	15	15	8	1	1
1912	63	9	4	1			3	3	3	4	20	10	5	1	1
1911	38	9	1	1	1		2	1	1	4	10	5	2	1	1
1910	53	8	2	1	2		2	1	3	6	14	7	4	3	
1900	31	5	1	1			3	1	4	3	7	4	2		
DENVER, COLO.															
Males:															
1914	64	6	1			1	1	1	1	3	23	20	5	2	
1913	55	4	2			1	1			4	20	17	6		
1912	58	2	1						2	5	19	21	7	1	
1911	74	9		1			1	1		4	32	19	7		
1910	66	12							1	6	27	13	7		
1900	47	6		2	1		1	3	1	4	14	12	3		
Females:															
1914	69	5	1	3	2				3	4	26	17	6	2	
1913	70	2	2					1	4	5	26	18	9	3	
1912	45	1	2	2			2		1	2	10	17	7	1	
1911	54	6	1	1		1		1	3	3	18	9	10	1	
1910	66	8	5					1		2	24	17	8	1	
1900	42	7	2		1	1	1			4	13	5	6	2	
DETROIT, MICH.															
Males:															
1914	87	9	4				2	1	5	4	27	23	12		
1913	104	14		3	3		3	2	3	6	32	28	10		
1912	80	9	2	2	1		1	1	1	9	28	19	6	1	
1911	83	15	3		1				3	5	22	28	6		
1910	81	13	2	2		1	2	1	2	3	23	20	10	2	
1900	56	5	3		2	1	2	1	3	3	13	16	5	1	1
Females:															
1914	71	10	3	1	1		1	1	4	4	23	15	6	2	
1913	62	9		2			1	1	3	6	14	18	7	1	
1912	62	9	2		1	2	1	1		4	14	20	5	3	
1911	54	6	1	1	1	1	3		2	2	14	16	6	1	
1910	65	13	5					3	2	3	15	15	8	1	
1900	47	5	4	1				2	2	3	6	14	6	4	
DURHAM, N. C.															
Males:															
1914	89	14	4			1	4	2	4	12	14	24	10		
1913	82	16	5	4	3	3	2	3	9	10	10	10	6		1
1912	71	12	3	1	1			1	6	11	22	10	3	1	
1911	82	20	4	4	1	1		1	7	7	12	16	8		1
1910	78	14	2	4	1	1	3	1	8	12	16	11	4	1	
1900 ¹															
Females:															
1914	112	21	5	1	1	1	2	2	10	8	36	14	8	2	1
1913	88	18	3	1	1		2	3	15	4	23	15	3		
1912	91	13	4		4	1	1	1	3	11	22	21	8	2	
1911	114	14	7	1	3	1	4	1	10	17	29	17	8		2
1910	101	23	7	5	1		4	2	10	9	21	14	4	1	
1900 ¹															
EVANSVILLE, IND.															
Males:															
1914	78	11	1		1		2	2	5	4	16	25	8	2	1
1913	87	13			2		1	2	4	6	19	27	12		1
1912	76	4	1		1		2		5	6	26	24	7		
1911	65	11	2					2	2	9	24	9	4		
1910	63	15	1			1	1		5	5	16	12	4	2	1
1900	84	13	6	1	2	1		2	4	6	16	23	9	1	
Females:															
1914	69	8	4	5			2	1	3	7	14	19	5		1
1913	77	10		1	2			4	3	1	23	22	9	2	
1912	74	10	3	2	1	1	1	3	3	3	19	21	5	2	
1911	90	19	2	5		1		1	4	8	21	21	7	1	
1910	54	7	4	2		3	2		4	3	13	16	2		
1900	66	13	5		1		2	3	3	1	19	14	5		
GALVESTON, TEX.															
Males:															
1914	137	11	2				1	2	1	6	59	42	11	2	
1913	122	11	2	2	1		1	1	5	7	47	34	9	1	1
1912	152	13	2				2	4	6	15	50	43	12	1	1
1911	100	11	2		2	1			6	4	35	26	10	1	2
1910	98	13	1	1			1	2	2	9	32	26	8	2	1
1900 ¹															
Females:															
1914	110	11	2		2		4	1	2	11	39	23	10	5	
1913	106	3	2	1		1	1	1	3	7	50	29	4	4	
1912	127	18	3	1	1	1	1	1	4	11	45	30	6	2	3
1911	94	10	3	2			1	3	3	2	33	26	8	2	2
1910	85	10	3			1	1	1	8	4	32	15	8	2	
1900 ¹															

¹ Not in registration area.

NEGRO POPULATION.

TABLE **39.**—DEATHS OF NEGROES IN THE REGISTRATION AREA, BY SEX AND AGE, FOR STATES AND SELECTED CITIES: 1914, 1913, 1912, 1911, 1910, AND 1900—Continued.

REGISTRATION AREA, SEX, AND YEAR.	All ages.	DEATHS AT AGE OF—													Deaths at unknown age.
		Under 1 year.	1 year.	2 years.	3 years.	4 years.	5 to 9 years.	10 to 14 years.	15 to 19 years.	20 to 24 years.	25 to 44 years.	45 to 64 years.	65 to 84 years.	85 years and over.	
SELECTED CITIES IN REGISTRATION AREA—Contd.															
GREENSBORO, N. C.															
Males:															
1914	100	32	5	1	1	...	2	4	6	7	17	16	8	1	...
1913	69	19	7	5	1	1	...	2	2	4	13	12	3		...
1912	69	18	4	1	...	1	1	1	6	4	10	10	11	2	...
1911	60	22	2	2	...	2	...	2	3	3	8	11	5		...
1910	70	21	4	...	2	...	...	2	3	6	20	10	2		...
1900¹															
Females:															
1914	109	23	9	3	...	2	4	2	3	17	20	18	6	2	...
1913	70	14	6	5	2	...	3	2	1	8	9	13	4	2	1
1912	84	24	5	4	...	1	2	4	3	19	15	5	2		...
1911	80	14	4	1	...	4	...	7	6	16	18	8	2		...
1910	73	13	6	2	...	1	...	7	19	13	10	2			...
1900¹															
HARRISBURG, PA.															
Males:															
1914	44	4	1	...		1	1		1	3	13	14	5	1	...
1913	67	11	2	1	...		1	2	2	4	14	19	11		...
1912	48	11	2	...		1		3	3	1	16	6	5		...
1911	43	9	...	1	1		1	2	...	3	12	10	3	1	...
1910	54	8	5	...			2	...	3	5	13	10	7	1	...
1900	59	12	5	...		1	3		3	6	4	4	9	10	...	2
Females:															
1914	49	4	...	1			1		1	6	14	16	5	1	...
1913	51	9	1	...		2	1	3	1	16	8	10		...
1912	56	6	5	1	...		3	2	3	6	12	13	4	1	...
1911	45	8	4	1	1	...	2	1	3	4	7	9	4	1	...
1910	44	9	3	...	1	1	1	2	2	11	11	2		...
1900	45	5	5	3	...	2	2	5	1	4	4	8	6		...
INDIANAPOLIS, IND.															
Males:															
1914	309	43	9	4	3	...	9	8	10	22	85	85	28	3	...
1913	311	47	5	6	4	...	7	5	16	13	90	84	29	5	...
1912	271	32	13	6	3	3	4	3	7	22	72	75	27	4	...
1911	269	29	7	12	4	2	8	6	6	15	70	62	47	1	...
1910	301	38	16	6	1	2	8	3	14	25	75	80	30	3	...
1900	192	46	12	5	3	2	5	5	11	14	30	44	15		...
Females:															
1914	262	39	11	5	3	3	6	8	14	9	84	56	20	4	...
1913	271	41	5	...	3	...	8	6	14	22	77	64	27	4	...
1912	263	39	13	2	2	1	5	4	18	16	59	73	26	5	...
1911	231	31	6	2	2	...	3	4	15	14	67	54	27	5	1
1910	247	41	9	7	...	1	6	5	11	18	63	54	24	8	...
1900	191	28	16	7	3	1	3	4	12	18	42	33	19	5	...
JACKSONVILLE, FLA.															
Males:															
1914	420	60	9	5	...	4	6	4	12	40	158	93	24	5	...
1913	425	59	14	4	5	2	7	4	7	35	171	92	23	2	...
1912	429	62	10	...	3	3	10	5	11	36	140	96	47	6	...
1911	477	60	21	12	4	3	6	12	15	38	166	99	31	3	7
1910	378	55	11	4	2	2	6	8	13	17	145	77	30	3	5
1900	288	74	19	3	4	5	11	4	9	22	58	44	31	3	1
Females:															
1914	363	53	13	6	1	1	3	4	22	30	137	56	25	12	...
1913	348	60	10	5	2	4	10	5	13	22	133	55	26	3	...
1912	346	61	7	1	5	1	6	5	16	32	109	64	31	8	...
1911	364	57	20	7	2	2	7	7	15	29	116	72	18	11	1
1910	332	47	8	5	6	2	6	8	19	33	110	53	26	9	...
1900	244	48	9	5	3	2	14	8	10	24	59	42	16	4	...
JERSEY CITY, N. J.															
Males:															
1914	55	13	3	2	1	1	2	...	1	2	19	8	3		...
1913	53	8	3	2	1	1	3	1	3	...	14	14	3		...
1912	61	16	2	1	1	...		2	...	2	17	16	4		...
1911	73	11	7	4	...	2	2	1	2	2	20	18	4		...
1910	61	12	8	...	1	...	2	1	...	3	19	13	2		...
1900	41	7	3	2	...					5	13	8	3		...
Females:															
1914	59	10	4	2	1	1	3	...	1	...	16	12	9		...
1913	61	10	4	2	...	1	6	...	...	3	19	12	2	2	
1912	54	13	3	...		1	4	1	2	2	12	11	4	1	
1911	59	11	4	1	...		2	2	...	2	16	14	7		...
1910	62	10	5	...	1	...	1	1	3	3	15	15	7	1	
1900	42	6	3	1	...	2	3	...	...	2	9	10	3		...
KANSAS CITY, KANS.															
Males:															
1914	132	18	...	3	1	...	1	2	4	8	39	38	16	2	...
1913	126	18	5	2	3	...	4	3	4	7	33	31	15	1	...
1912	138	16	6	6	...	2	4	1	14	9	42	22	13	2	1
1911	131	19	3	3	1	1	2	1	4	8	36	30	22	1	...
1910	131	20	3	2	...	1	3	1	7	6	41	29	14	3	1
1900¹															
Females:															
1914	123	14	2	2	...	3	4	4	5	11	34	26	15	3	...
1913	143	20	5	3	1	...	4	6	14	9	39	25	12	5	...
1912	149	17	4	3	2	2	6	5	7	9	50	30	11	3	...
1911	127	19	2	2	1	...	2	6	6	11	32	28	13	5	...
1910	106	9	3	1	3	3	2	3	7	4	33	21	14	3	...
1900¹															

¹ Not in registration area.

TABLE **39.**—DEATHS OF NEGROES IN THE REGISTRATION AREA, BY SEX AND AGE, FOR STATES AND SELECTED CITIES: 1914, 1913, 1912, 1911, 1910, AND 1900—Continued.

REGISTRATION AREA, SEX, AND YEAR.	All ages.	DEATHS AT AGE OF—													Deaths at unknown age.
		Under 1 year.	1 year.	2 years.	3 years.	4 years.	5 to 9 years.	10 to 14 years.	15 to 19 years.	20 to 24 years.	25 to 44 years.	45 to 64 years.	65 to 84 years.	85 years and over.	
SELECTED CITIES IN REGISTRATION AREA—Contd.															
KANSAS CITY, MO.															
Males:															
1914	367	31	9	4	1	4	4	4	9	24	162	91	21	3	
1913	335	23	6	4	2	3	4	7	11	22	134	89	26	4	
1912	409	38	4	3	5	7	14	3	21	33	166	92	22	1	
1911	348	35	5	1	3	1	5	3	14	32	137	86	23	3	
1910	347	54	9	6	2	3	10	5	14	33	109	79	17	5	1
1900	211	42	16	8	8	1	6	5	7	18	60	23	9	5	3
Females:															
1914	264	27	6	2	4	2	6	2	10	21	91	56	32	5	
1913	290	27	10	2	3	3	9	4	17	20	105	55	28	7	
1912	269	30	4	2	3	1	7	2	17	29	96	51	23	4	
1911	269	38	10	3	1		4	2	15	29	86	49	29	3	
1910	297	40	8	2	3	1	9	6	20	31	86	60	28	3	
1900	227	36	14	3		2	9	8	20	16	75	32	9	3	
KEY WEST, FLA.															
Males:															
1914	48	10	3	1		1	1	1		4	9	9	9		
1913	53	15	3			1	1	2	1	1	12	9	7	1	
1912	64	17	1		1		2	1	1	2	16	15	8		
1911	87	26	6	4	1	1	4	1	3	3	16	14	8		
1910	64	26	4		2	2		2	1	3	8	12	4		
1900	69	29	4	1			2		2	2	18	8	2		1
Females:															
1914	53	8	1		1		1		2	1	15	15	8	1	
1913	45	10	1	1	1		3	1	2	3	12	7	2		2
1912	50	7	5	3	1			1	2	1	13	5	8	4	
1911	85	26	8	3	1	1		1	2	4	15	16	5	3	
1910	83	22	6	2	1		1		4	4	19	11	10	3	
1900	78	27	4	1	1		1	1	4	5	20	10	2	2	
KNOXVILLE, TENN.															
Males:															
1914	121	14		3	2	1	2	6	4	13	28	34	11	1	2
1913 [1]															
1912	104	17	4	2	1	1	2		4	12	26	19	13	3	
1911	97	18	3				7	5	6	6	28	15	9		
1910	91	19	2	1	3	2		3	6	7	27	16	5		
1900 [1]															
Females:															
1914	123	14	2	2		3	4	4	5	11	34	26	15	3	
1913 [1]															
1912	97	16	2	1			2		10	8	24	24	8	2	
1911	129	17	5	3			4		4	8	51	27	8	2	
1910	112	17	4	6	2		2	2	7	7	35	23	6	1	
1900 [1]															
LOS ANGELES, CAL.															
Males:															
1914	106	13	1	1	1		2	1	1	8	36	32	10		
1913	114	16	2	1			2	1	7	8	35	32	9	1	
1912	105	6	2	2	1		3	1	3	4	49	28	6		
1911	79	6	5	2		1			4	6	29	20	5	1	
1910	77	9	2			1	1	1	2	2	38	12	8	1	
1900	29	10					1			2	2	7	5	2	
Females:															
1914	84	6	5			1	1		4	7	37	17	6		
1913	104	11	3		1	1	3	3	2	12	38	23	5	1	
1912	91	6	2	1		1	2	1	3	13	33	19	8	2	
1911	69	6	1	2			1	3	2	3	26	18	4	3	
1910	59	7	1		1		1	1	3	6	16	16	7		
1900	33	8	1	2	1		1			2	3	11	2	2	
LOUISVILLE, KY.															
Males:															
1914	577	54	14	5	4	1	12	5	9	29	211	178	51	4	
1913	565	71	14	9	8	2	10	6	20	32	176	158	54		5
1912	540	64	8	9	4	2	12	9	18	37	182	133	52	5	5
1911	549	57	27	10	10	2	10	10	23	32	178	146	38	3	3
1910	566	77	24	15	3	7	11	8	24	32	165	154	43	3	
1900	508	94	32	12	6	1	12	10	22	32	136	107	33	4	7
Females:															
1914	438	54	7	7	1	1	4	9	24	26	137	118	42	8	
1913	482	49	14	12	4	4	10	6	23	36	146	123	44	7	4
1912	543	52	11	6	4	6	15	12	21	37	149	157	49	18	6
1911	515	41	21	9	8	10	9	9	39	34	128	132	61	10	4
1910	523	54	13	19	7	7	9	10	27	42	154	121	54	5	1
1900	562	77	28	19	8	11	15	16	25	44	146	97	50	17	9
LYNCHBURG, VA.															
Males:															
1914	136	33	3	3			1	3	6	6	27	39	14	1	
1913	129	43	4		1		1	2	3	6	22	30	13	4	
1912	137	28	12	7	2	1	2		6	7	27	30	12	3	
1911	130	32	5		1		3	1	5	8	29	33	11	2	
1910	116	34	4		1	1	5	2	4	7	19	27	8	4	
1900	148	33	12	7	7	1	9	2	6	9	26	20	14		2
Females:															
1914	139	29	5				5	5	9	12	29	22	19	4	
1913	157	35	9	3		1	2	3	1	14	30	37	21	1	
1912	126	28	5	1			2	5	5	6	34	26	11	3	
1911	130	23	7	4	2			11	13	27	21	18	4		
1910	115	24	7	2	2	1	2		2	13	22	24	11	5	
1900	150	40	13	2	2	2	3	4	7	12	29	17	12	4	3

[1] Not in registration area.

NEGRO POPULATION.

TABLE **39.**—DEATHS OF NEGROES IN THE REGISTRATION AREA, BY SEX AND AGE, FOR STATES AND SELECTED CITIES: 1914, 1913, 1912, 1911, 1910, AND 1900—Continued.

REGISTRATION AREA, SEX, AND YEAR.	All ages.	DEATHS AT AGE OF—													Deaths at unknown age.
		Under 1 year.	1 year.	2 years.	3 years.	4 years.	5 to 9 years.	10 to 14 years.	15 to 19 years.	20 to 24 years.	25 to 44 years.	45 to 64 years.	65 to 84 years.	85 years and over.	
SELECTED CITIES IN REGISTRATION AREA—Contd.															
MEMPHIS, TENN.															
Males:															
1914	882	90	19	12	9	6	12	14	47	90	355	154	43	14	17
1913	869	98	22	11	8	5	15	9	44	87	328	178	58	5	1
1912	841	94	23	14	8	......	12	16	35	81	309	166	72	6	5
1911	801	90	18	15	11	7	18	10	33	76	285	162	67	8	1
1910	761	87	21	11	6	10	14	22	42	73	257	167	41	9	1
1900	632	90	41	14	10	8	21	18	34	69	188	102	33	4	......
Females:															
1914	813	67	13	11	5	3	18	19	53	85	300	156	56	9	18
1913	717	69	20	11	9	1	25	14	45	93	243	130	48	9	......
1912	763	95	20	15	8	8	23	12	40	62	272	140	60	8	......
1911	705	76	20	10	7	7	17	14	42	82	223	147	53	5	2
1910	731	82	25	15	7	2	13	17	51	74	224	160	53	8	......
1900	586	86	33	15	21	8	27	17	47	55	144	91	34	8	......
MINNEAPOLIS, MINN.															
Males:															
1914	35	4	1	......	......	......	......	1	......	1	9	14	5	......	......
1913	34	1	1	......	......	......	1	......	......	3	13	10	4	1	......
1912	33	3	2	......	......	1	......	......	1	......	11	15	......	......	......
1911	32	4	......	......	......	......	......	......	......	1	14	7	5	1	......
1910	37	2	......	1	1	......	1	......	1	1	10	14	7	......	......
1900	9	1	......	......	......	1	......	......	......	......	7	......	......	......	......
Females:															
1914	27	2	......	......	......	......	......	1	......	1	12	7	3	1	......
1913	25	4	......	......	......	......	......	......	......	......	5	13	3	......	......
1912	17	......	......	......	......	......	......	......	......	1	11	2	3	......	......
1911	29	4	1	1	......	......	1	1	......	2	12	5	2	......	......
1910	19	2	1	2	......	......	......	1	......	......	5	5	2	1	......
1900	13	1	......	......	......	......	1	2	3	1	2	3	......	......	......
MOBILE, ALA.															
Males:															
1914	313	39	10	4	......	1	3	4	15	25	110	74	23	5	......
1913	328	48	8	3	......	2	3	11	20	23	107	67	30	6	......
1912	329	60	9	5	4	1	8	2	10	25	98	68	35	4	......
1911	384	47	6	3	4	2	12	8	18	32	119	88	42	3	......
1910	345	52	12	3	3	2	3	6	11	27	104	81	35	6	......
1900	276	73	12	5	6	1	10	2	8	20	58	49	31	1	......
Females:															
1914	335	42	5	5	2	2	5	5	20	19	109	73	39	9	......
1913	291	46	6	3	2	......	2	6	20	25	82	62	32	5	......
1912	288	45	4	1	1	3	10	6	13	23	85	50	41	6	......
1911	330	47	9	3	1	2	6	11	19	17	92	74	32	16	1
1910	328	50	12	4	3	4	7	4	14	32	90	58	40	9	1
1900	288	60	8	6	5	4	16	9	11	16	69	53	24	6	1
MONTGOMERY, ALA.															
Males:															
1914	281	39	11	5	3	5	8	8	12	19	61	70	32	8	......
1913	269	44	12	2	4	......	6	2	4	20	68	68	37	1	1
1912	307	46	6	4	3	1	2	2	14	29	84	64	41	11	......
1911	300	52	16	7	5	5	2	8	12	19	75	67	26	6	......
1910	320	56	16	1	2	2	4	7	19	24	76	65	38	10	......
1900	......	......	......	......	......	......	......	......	......	......	......	......	......	......	......
Females:															
1914	278	27	9	9	3	2	5	5	11	24	85	66	28	4	......
1913	304	49	18	4	3	1	9	3	6	25	89	71	18	8	......
1912	289	26	5	3	3	1	6	2	17	25	86	77	28	10	......
1911	344	45	19	5	8	1	6	6	18	26	92	78	27	13	......
1910	360	48	16	4	7	4	7	6	22	33	88	74	37	14	......
1900	......	......	......	......	......	......	......	......	......	......	......	......	......	......	......
NASHVILLE, TENN.															
Males:															
1914	485	74	13	2	7	5	10	3	14	42	150	113	46	5	1
1913	438	53	18	9	6	3	9	13	18	32	133	107	35	2	......
1912	502	85	20	10	7	3	13	8	23	40	116	111	63	3	......
1911	525	69	33	11	7	9	15	10	19	37	129	130	45	11	......
1910	479	89	25	11	2	5	14	17	18	33	107	103	46	9	......
1900	439	87	45	12	5	7	14	11	23	35	75	69	49	6	1
Females:															
1914	509	60	13	9	6	3	12	15	23	36	154	133	36	9	......
1913	465	50	11	6	4	4	9	13	28	34	140	108	44	14	......
1912	551	67	20	14	7	7	11	15	37	40	140	120	58	15	......
1911	567	69	23	15	8	1	9	18	31	47	163	113	58	12	......
1910	471	58	17	6	4	2	11	7	25	44	113	105	63	16	......
1900	526	99	30	12	8	4	19	26	38	40	109	86	44	11	......
NEWARK, N. J.															
Males:															
1914	152	32	19	4	3	......	4	2	6	2	40	27	12	1	......
1913	134	38	6	2	......	......	1	2	2	3	30	36	13	1	......
1912	142	31	11	4	1	4	5	......	5	5	29	32	13	2	......
1911	165	47	9	1	3	1	5	1	4	6	45	35	8	......	......
1910	159	42	10	9	5	......	4	3	1	6	41	25	12	1	......
1900	112	46	7	2	2	2	5	......	3	5	16	18	4	1	1
Females:															
1914	166	37	9	4	2	1	6	4	3	8	42	35	13	2	......
1913	139	23	7	5	2	2	3	3	6	6	33	30	18	1	......
1912	137	25	6	1	......	1	4	1	8	10	34	27	19	1	......
1911	145	30	7	5	3	3	3	......	5	14	30	30	13	2	......
1910	137	28	9	2	3	......	5	2	4	10	32	32	10	......	......
1900	90	21	6	4	1	......	6	3	3	3	20	13	8	1	......

TABLE **39.**—DEATHS OF NEGROES IN THE REGISTRATION AREA, BY SEX AND AGE, FOR STATES AND SELECTED CITIES: 1914, 1913, 1912, 1911, 1910, AND 1900—Continued.

REGISTRATION AREA, SEX, AND YEAR.	All ages.	DEATHS AT AGE OF—													Deaths at unknown age.
		Under 1 year.	1 year.	2 years.	3 years.	4 years.	5 to 9 years.	10 to 14 years.	15 to 19 years.	20 to 24 years.	25 to 44 years.	45 to 64 years.	65 to 84 years.	85 years and over.	
SELECTED CITIES IN REGISTRATION AREA—Contd.															
NEW BEDFORD, MASS.															
Males:															
1914	45	10	2	1	1				3	3	12	8	5		
1913	32	8	2	4						3	7	7	1		
1912	36	4	2	1	2		1	1	1	4	9	3	8		
1911	31	2	7		1	1	2	1	1	2	4	7	3		
1910	40	11	3	1						4	17	2	2		
1900	16	3	1	1						1	4	2	3		1
Females:															
1914	22	3		2			1		1	1	4	4	6		
1913	26	7	2	1	2	1	1				3	3	5	1	
1912	29	6		1			2	1		1	6	6	6		
1911	24	8	2	2	1					2	5	4			
1910	45	14	2	2		3				1	11	6	4	2	
1900	16	2	1	2				1			3	2	3	1	1
NEW HAVEN, CONN.															
Males:															
1914	57	13	1	1				2	2	1	10	15	11	1	
1913	64	9	3		2	1			2	1	16	20	9	1	
1912	45	8	3				1		1	1	12	11	8		
1911	56	14	2	1	2			3	1	5	14	10	3	1	
1910	40	4	1	1	1		2	1	1	1	13	13	2		
1900	42	14	2		1		1		2	2	3	8	9		
Females:															
1914	49	7	3	1	1		1		1	2	10	17	5	1	
1913	55	9	2				1	2	4		11	14	10	2	
1912	41	8	1	1	1			1	1	2	6	11	7	1	
1911	52	9	3	1	1		2	1		2	12	15	4	2	
1910	51	10	2	1			1		2	1	10	18	6		
1900	40	8	1	1			1	1	3	3	7	10	5		
NEW ORLEANS, LA.															
Males:															
1914	1,556	182	41	19	13	9	35	27	62	105	506	384	156	17	
1913	1,596	199	33	25	14	13	37	20	72	127	513	404	124	15	
1912	1,583	175	19	19	18	9	31	27	55	116	532	399	171	12	
1911	1,511	218	44	22	12	14	32	32	49	117	474	336	143	17	1
1910	1,606	239	39	24	12	7	34	27	58	135	496	369	151	15	
1900	1,664	264	52	39	24	19	40	57	89	146	490	299	120	24	1
Females:															
1914	1,455	184	31	23	13	9	30	21	62	113	412	345	178	32	2
1913	1,398	197	47	24	17	10	34	17	67	108	402	301	151	23	
1912	1,318	148	35	14	6	9	19	21	55	115	401	290	167	38	
1911	1,323	190	44	22	12	7	26	26	75	109	368	279	140	25	
1910	1,327	204	46	16	16	13	29	25	49	107	341	284	168	29	
1900	1,520	250	63	35	22	11	56	36	93	149	331	260	175	39	
NEW YORK, N. Y.															
Males:															
1914	1,296	248	83	25	16	15	33	21	29	78	433	238	72	5	
1913	1,184	244	77	26	15	8	30	17	39	68	380	192	82	6	
1912	1,289	264	74	33	14	14	34	14	42	81	432	210	71	5	1
1911	1,236	267	76	29	18	8	15	12	38	61	400	222	84	6	
1910	1,236	284	84	28	17	14	21	16	33	68	409	193	65	4	
1900	1,006	282	80	31	11	9	27	16	21	73	224	164	63	5	
Females:															
1914	1,250	205	58	24	20	12	31	20	45	80	387	250	108	10	
1913	1,160	191	72	24	18	10	35	23	52	80	319	231	95	10	
1912	1,203	238	66	31	18	5	31	22	35	78	334	221	110	14	
1911	1,196	242	51	21	14	11	22	19	40	85	364	222	91	14	
1910	1,155	246	84	25	16	11	29	19	37	81	319	184	86	18	
1900	944	268	71	29	10	11	28	31	33	45	201	136	71	10	
Manhattan Borough.															
Males:															
1914	841	155	58	14	11	7	25	11	14	65	301	145	32	3	
1913	809	168	52	16	11	3	21	11	30	48	273	126	47	3	
1912	875	180	51	23	9	6	20	5	24	61	313	135	45	2	1
1911	817	176	52	20	9	5	7	10	25	40	281	136	53	3	
1910	762	194	54	19	9	7	12	6	20	41	257	120	22	1	
1900	643	173	57	21	8	4	11	10	11	44	160	113	30	1	
Females:															
1914	839	148	39	17	15	8	19	12	37	50	270	151	67	6	
1913	759	134	47	16	13	9	20	14	37	59	193	157	54	6	
1912	769	146	46	17	11	1	21	12	23	61	213	149	58	11	
1911	744	166	34	15	10	8	12	10	24	61	226	132	41	5	
1910	711	160	49	15	8	7	15	9	27	55	208	115	40	3	
1900	599	180	45	19	6	6	12	15	20	26	139	85	42	4	
Bronx Borough.															
Males:															
1914	49	10	3		2	2					10	17	5		
1913	48	9	1	2		1	1	1	1	4	14	10	3	1	
1912	44	6		1	1	2	5		4	2	11	9	3		
1911	53	9	2	2	2		2	1	1	1	11	17	5		
1910	118	10	6	3		1	2	1	3	7	48	26	10	1	
1900	36	8					3			1	9	5	8	1	
Females:															
1914	42	4	1	1		1	3		2	2	13	6	5	1	
1913	50	3	1	1			3		6	3	2	14	8	9	
1912	45	11	2	1	2			2		1	1	14	6	5	
1911	44	4			1	1	1			3	2	17	9	4	2
1910	90	10	4	2	3		2	1	3	4	26	16	14	5	
1900	39	9	2				1	2	3	2	7	5	7	1	

Table 39.—DEATHS OF NEGROES IN THE REGISTRATION AREA, BY SEX AND AGE, FOR STATES AND SELECTED CITIES: 1914, 1913, 1912, 1911, 1910, AND 1900—Continued.

REGISTRATION AREA, SEX, AND YEAR.	All ages.	Under 1 year.	1 year.	2 years.	3 years.	4 years.	5 to 9 years.	10 to 14 years.	15 to 19 years.	20 to 24 years.	25 to 44 years.	45 to 64 years.	65 to 84 years.	85 years and over.	Deaths at unknown age.
SELECTED CITIES IN REGISTRATION AREA—Contd.															
NEW YORK, N. Y.—contd.															
Brooklyn Borough.															
Males:															
1914	325	63	17	10	3	5	6	6	11	11	102	64	27		
1913	275	54	20	8	3	4	6	4	6	14	83	47	25	1	
1912	294	63	17	9	3	2	5	8	11	15	89	52	19	1	
1911	299	63	17	6	6	2	5	1	10	17	98	55	17	2	
1910	291	69	22	4	8	4	6	6	7	14	81	44	24	2	
1900	267	85	20	6	2	5	11	6	8	21	43	40	19	1	
Females:															
1914	312	46	15	6	4	2	7	8	5	21	84	83	30	1	
1913	291	46	20	6	5	1	12	3	9	14	94	57	23	1	
1912	326	61	17	12	5	3	7	7	10	15	92	52	42	3	
1911	339	56	14	6	3	2	8	9	8	19	105	67	37	5	
1910	307	66	28	6	4	3	10	8	7	20	77	46	25	7	
1900	266	68	19	9	4	5	13	12	9	16	48	40	18	5	
Queens Borough.															
Males:															
1914	58	18	3	1		1	1	4	4	1	14	6	4	1	
1913	31	7	2		1		2		2	1	5	7	4		
1912	58	13	5		1	2	4	1	2	2	14	11	2	1	
1911	51	17	4	1	1	1	1		1	2	7	10	5	1	
1910	46	9	2	2		2	1	3	1	5	16	3	2		
1900	40	10	2	4	1		2		1	3	8	4	2	5	
Females:															
1914	47	6	3		1		2		1	6	14	9	3	2	
1913	51	5	3	1					3	4	17	9	7	2	
1912	52	16	1			1	3	1	1	1	10	14	4		
1911	55	13	2				1		4	2	13	11	7	2	
1910	36	7	1	2	1		2	1		1	7	5	6	3	
1900	26	9	4				1	1			5	5	1		
Richmond Borough.															
Males:															
1914	23	2	2				1			1	6	6	4	1	
1913	21	6	2					1		1	5	2	3	1	
1912	18	2	1			2			1	1	6	2	3		
1911	16	2	1						1	1	3	4	4		
1910	19	2						2		1	7		7		
1900	20	6	1							4	4	2	1	2	
Females:															
1914	10	1				1				1	3	1	3		
1913	9	3	1							1	1		2	1	
1912	11	4		1							5		1		
1911	14	3	1					1		1	3	3	2		
1910	11	3	2			1				1	1	2	1		
1900	14	2	1	1			1	1	1	1	2	1	3		
NORFOLK, VA.															
Males:															
1914	538	110	23	10	3	5	3	9	24	38	162	107	38	3	3
1913	474	87	21	4	7		7	5	16	20	177	94	32	2	2
1912	494	103	13	9	5	3	12	7	17	40	158	99	25	3	
1911	525	119	16	9	8	9	10	16	16	40	147	103	28	4	
1910	420	78	15	5	7	4	10	5	19	31	141	86	18	1	
1900	410	129	16	16	12	5	6	4	11	33	92	63	19	2	2
Females:															
1914	437	79	19	7	4	6	6	5	18	33	149	83	25	3	
1913	471	93	15	6	5	4	11	6	26	35	146	92	26	6	
1912	459	95	9	13	5	4	11	16	19	34	130	91	30	2	
1911	507	101	25	10	11	5	8	12	27	39	145	93	25	6	
1910	355	85	15	6	6	2	16	7	16	25	101	55	19	4	
1900	360	97	24	15	9	7	9	9	13	29	68	55	18	7	
OAKLAND, CAL.															
Males:															
1914	34	3	2		1		2		2	3	7	10	4		
1913	35	7		2			4		2	2	7	6	4	1	
1912	30	7			1		2			2	11	5	2		
1911	30	3			1		1			1	13	6	5		
1910	25	2				1	1			1	6	10	3	1	
1900	6						2		1		2		1		
Females:															
1914	25	1	1						1	3	9	6	3	1	
1913	32	4	2						1	2	4	16	2	1	
1912	36	4	1		1					2	12	6	6	4	
1911	22		1	2					2		5	7	4	1	
1910	27	2	3	1	2				2		10	6		1	
1900	13		2							1	4	3	3		
OMAHA, NEBR.															
Males:															
1914	67	3	3				1		1	5	32	15	5	2	
1913	76	5		1					1	2	41	21	3	1	1
1912	61	6	1						2	3	25	18	5	1	
1911	67	6		1	1		1	1	3	3	25	20	6		
1910	64	8					1	2	2	7	28	14	2		
1900	38	8	3				1		4	1	7	10	3	1	
Females:															
1914	44	3				1			6	3	17	12	2		
1913	42	2	1					1		6	14	14	3		
1912	37	3						2		3	14	6	9		
1911	46	3		1	1		1		1	2	20	12	4	1	
1910	41	3						2		3	15	12	3		
1900	29	2	1				2			1	13	5	3	2	

Table 39.—DEATHS OF NEGROES IN THE REGISTRATION AREA, BY SEX AND AGE, FOR STATES AND SELECTED CITIES: 1914, 1913, 1912, 1911, 1910, AND 1900—Continued.

REGISTRATION AREA, SEX, AND YEAR.	All ages.	DEATHS AT AGE OF—													Deaths at unknown age.
		Under 1 year.	1 year.	2 years.	3 years.	4 years.	5 to 9 years.	10 to 14 years.	15 to 19 years.	20 to 24 years.	25 to 44 years.	45 to 64 years.	65 to 84 years.	85 years and over.	
SELECTED CITIES IN REGISTRATION AREA—Contd.															
PADUCAH, KY.															
Males:															
1914	104	13	2	....	3	1	3	3	5	11	33	26	10	....	2
1913	105	15	....	4	1	1	2	2	4	8	38	21	7	....	2
1912	93	12	4	....	3	1	3	....	1	14	....	13	18	24	
1911	101	19	4	1	1	....	5	....	6	10	28	18	5	3	1
1910	87	14	1	2	2	1	2	3	3	11	18	19	9	....	2
1900	121	19	7	4	2	....	3	4	8	13	35	14	8	1	3
Females:															
1914	77	11	9	1	....	....	2	1	5	5	19	16	6	2	....
1913	100	12	1	1	3	1	4	2	4	10	26	24	11	1	....
1912	110	12	8	3	2	1	3	1	7	10	1	8	19	35	....
1911	96	12	4	....	2	3	3	2	10	5	27	15	10	3	....
1910	77	6	2	2	1	1	4	1	3	5	27	15	7	....	3
1900	103	12	12	4	1	1	5	5	5	7	15	19	13	2	2
PETERSBURG, VA.															
Males:															
1914	178	47	7	6	4	....	3	4	6	10	48	36	7	....	....
1913	195	42	14	2	2	1	4	1	6	10	47	51	13	2	....
1912	178	46	4	6	....	3	3	3	9	15	44	28	17	....	....
1911	178	33	16	10	1	3	5	....	3	11	39	41	13	2	1
1910	171	56	4	7	4	1	5	2	6	6	31	34	14	1	....
1900	189	58	13	7	2	....	6	6	5	7	29	34	15	1	6
Females:															
1914	202	43	11	1	1	....	7	3	10	17	45	49	13	1	1
1913	173	43	5	4	1	1	3	6	8	8	31	39	22	2	....
1912	171	33	10	5	....	1	4	5	10	11	36	38	15	3	....
1911	176	40	14	5	1	....	4	1	4	8	33	51	12	3	....
1910	206	51	6	2	3	2	7	5	6	10	48	41	22	3	....
1900	190	45	10	5	....	1	7	4	12	14	39	36	15	2	....
PHILADELPHIA, PA.															
Males:															
1914	1,227	246	52	25	12	7	19	13	29	52	399	283	83	6	1
1913	1,131	261	44	13	14	12	21	11	32	56	328	254	79	6	....
1912	866	179	38	10	12	6	9	13	21	46	265	187	73	7	....
1911	1,049	252	52	17	10	10	21	20	24	49	312	205	74	3	....
1910	1,196	298	73	24	13	12	28	17	30	59	354	214	67	7	....
1900	974	282	76	31	14	15	30	20	27	53	234	136	49	7	....
Females:															
1914	1,034	203	46	16	11	10	20	21	38	52	268	221	107	21	....
1913	1,061	207	29	19	7	14	27	25	52	76	303	199	92	11	....
1912	824	154	36	10	7	3	16	15	54	41	202	191	82	13	....
1911	956	204	61	20	14	10	24	16	25	64	262	165	73	18	....
1910	1,080	246	66	32	15	14	28	20	38	69	274	174	83	21	....
1900	920	250	72	29	15	12	27	22	45	55	188	117	75	13	....
PITTSBURGH, PA.															
Males:															
1914	311	56	8	4	2	2	8	7	13	18	91	82	19	1	....
1913	314	50	28	8	3	1	13	5	12	17	86	72	16	3	....
1912	266	42	17	3	3	1	8	4	5	13	80	73	16	1	....
1911	241	50	18	4	4	2	11	4	12	8	59	47	21	1	....
1910	332	80	31	4	8	3	6	7	5	13	91	61	23	....	....
1900 [1]	286	58	22	10	7	2	11	5	10	37	63	45	12	4	....
Females:															
1914	274	48	14	6	3	4	17	12	9	10	66	60	22	3	....
1913	271	60	17	7	1	3	11	8	12	11	70	55	11	5	....
1912	230	35	12	5	5	1	3	6	6	10	67	52	22	6	....
1911	191	32	13	6	4	3	7	4	5	18	36	49	10	4	....
1910	269	60	20	9	9	1	9	5	11	8	65	59	12	1	....
1900 [1]	240	59	13	3	5	1	8	9	10	22	63	28	14	4	1
PROVIDENCE, R. I.															
Males:															
1914	97	16	5	3	2	2	2	....	2	12	25	18	10	....	....
1913	86	16	4	2	....	1	6	1	5	2	23	17	9	....	....
1912	90	17	9	2	1	1	....	....	2	5	25	20	8	....	....
1911	77	15	3	4	1	1	2	1	....	5	20	19	5	1	....
1910	74	17	1	1	2	1	3	2	....	1	14	17	15	....	....
1900	77	17	7	2	3	1	2	1	3	3	12	15	9	2	....
Females:															
1914	84	14	7	1	....	1	2	....	4	9	16	18	11	1	....
1913	61	10	3	1	....	1	2	3	1	1	16	14	7	2	....
1912	81	18	5	2	....	2	....	3	1	1	21	20	6	2	....
1911	65	12	1	1	1	....	2	....	2	5	12	19	8	2	....
1910	65	15	4	2	....	2	2	2	3	1	15	16	3	2	....
1900	63	12	5	1	2	2	....	....	5	1	10	11	9	5	....
RALEIGH, N. C.															
Males:															
1914	153	34	7	....	....	1	3	3	5	17	36	27	18	2	....
1913	110	23	7	4	1	....	1	2	5	11	12	26	12	6	....
1912	134	23	6	1	1	....	4	3	7	7	38	26	17	1	....
1911	133	22	6	1	2	....	1	2	7	13	28	28	21	2	....
1910	109	18	7	....	....	....	1	2	10	8	17	24	19	3	....
1900	114	29	16	5	2	....	3	2	3	6	9	20	15	3	1
Females:															
1914	148	30	4	2	2	....	3	2	11	9	39	33	12	1	....
1913	114	18	4	4	3	1	2	2	4	7	34	21	12	1	1
1912	117	15	4	5	1	....	1	1	5	11	33	21	15	4	1
1911	145	32	7	4	3	1	1	3	6	10	37	21	18	2	....
1910	138	36	6	2	....	1	1	7	6	9	25	23	17	5	....
1900	113	20	15	4	1	....	3	....	8	9	18	14	13	2	2

[1] Includes Allegheny.

TABLE 39.—DEATHS OF NEGROES IN THE REGISTRATION AREA, BY SEX AND AGE, FOR STATES AND SELECTED CITIES: 1914, 1913, 1912, 1911, 1910, AND 1900—Continued.

REGISTRATION AREA, SEX, AND YEAR.	All ages.	DEATHS AT AGE OF—													Deaths at unknown age.
		Under 1 year.	1 year.	2 years.	3 years.	4 years.	5 to 9 years.	10 to 14 years.	15 to 19 years.	20 to 24 years.	25 to 44 years.	45 to 64 years.	65 to 84 years.	85 years and over.	
SELECTED CITIES IN REGISTRATION AREA—Contd.															
RICHMOND, VA.															
Males:															
1914	697	158	29	15	3	2	12	8	24	52	199	149	45	1	
1913	658	146	25	8	8	3	5	12	21	40	203	147	39	1	
1912	660	137	14	11	5	3	11	11	18	40	185	168	41	1	
1911	666	154	25	14	9	2	7	7	24	34	200	152	36	2	
1910	727	193	29	18	11	3	7	6	28	44	175	166	44	3	
1900	619	182	35	14	7	3	11	13	22	50	122	120	33	3	4
Females:															
1914	663	127	31	9	8	6	12	6	33	44	174	166	43	4	
1913	648	128	21	9	8	2	13	6	27	42	170	187	29	6	
1912	680	163	27	7	3	5	9	15	21	49	170	165	44	2	
1911	680	143	23	14	9	5	9	9	34	49	176	166	39	4	
1910	689	157	33	22	7	6	12	13	27	43	171	149	43	5	1
1900	595	148	27	17	8	3	19	16	27	45	138	102	34	8	3
ST. JOSEPH, MO.															
Males:															
1914	48	2							3	3	5	14	17	4	
1913	56	8						2	3	3	17	18	3	1	1
1912	44	4				1		2		3	14	10	10		
1911	38	5	1	2			1	1	1	1	7	13	6		
1910	54	8	2	2			1		1	5	18	14	3		
1900	28	1	1	1	1		1	1	1	4	10	4	2		1
Females:															
1914	34	5		1					1	2	12	8	5		
1913	43	5							1	1	17	13	4	1	1
1912	44	3	2	3		1		3	2	2	7	12	7	1	1
1911	31	2					1	1	4	2	7	6	5		3
1910	44	2				1	1	1	4	1	17	8	7		2
1900	40	5	1	1	2		3	2	3	2	6	9	6		
ST. LOUIS, MO.															
Males:															
1914	700	78	14	14	4	6	13	13	17	47	269	159	63	3	
1913	712	70	24	12	5	3	12	9	18	38	261	180	77	3	
1912	682	65	17	8	4	2	11	12	26	32	261	175	63	6	
1911	631	73	21	6	8	3	14	13	20	40	223	160	39	11	
1910	641	76	24	15	3	5	8	5	17	40	238	155	47	6	2
1900	588	82	21	10	15	6	19	6	21	38	182	135	42	6	5
Females:															
1914	557	58	17	12	6	5	13	12	20	34	160	145	61	14	
1913	535	64	23	7	6	9	8	9	18	33	163	124	64	7	
1912	535	53	26	15	2	7	12	12	26	25	161	146	44	6	
1911	539	68	19	11	4	6	12	13	18	30	174	129	46	9	
1910	508	71	16	15	9	2	12	9	16	29	159	103	58	8	1
1900	508	84	27	10	7	2	15	12	33	38	129	91	48	11	1
ST. PAUL, MINN.															
Males:															
1914	29							1		2	14	10	2		
1913	46	4	1					1		4	20	12	4		
1912	30	3						1			10	13	3		
1911	25	3		1	2					2	8	6	3		
1910	27	2	1	1					1	3	6	9	4		
1900	18	2							1	2	10		3		
Females:															
1914	25	1	1				1				10	10	2		
1913	25	2					1		1	1	7	8	5		
1912	28	3	1					1	2	1	8	3	8	1	
1911	25	3								2	9	7	4		
1910	22	1					1		1	1	8	5	3		2
1900	12	2	1				1	1		1	2	2	2		
SAN ANTONIO, TEX.															
Males:															
1914	127	14	1			1	2	2	5	7	47	35	12	1	
1913	144	13	5	4	1	1	2	3	9	16	44	31	15		
1912	172	23	3	3	3	2	2	2	5	14	71	26	13	4	1
1911	132	17	8	1			1	5	4	9	48	30	9		
1910	127	26	4						4	9	37	26	18	2	1
1900	100	21	5	2	2	1	1	3	3	10	33	13	3	2	1
Females:															
1914	138	20	5			1	2	1	9	11	45	23	17	4	
1913	124	10		1	1		2	1	5	19	51	22	11	1	
1912	126	22	7	1	3		1	3	11	12	32	13	13		
1911	116	17	3		2			1	3	10	31	24	9	8	
1910	106	22	7	1		1	1	2	6	12	32	16	3	3	
1900	71	10	4	2	3		2	3	8	5	13		8	3	1
SAVANNAH, GA.															
Males:															
1914	575	121	17	14	8	3	4	6	18	29	199	123	31	2	
1913	548	113	14	6	7	3	13	5	15	41	187	115	28	1	
1912	607	99	16	13	6	5	12	18	24	37	196	141	35	4	1
1911	675	126	21	13	11	6	19	14	25	65	202	127	41	5	
1910	593	135	24	11	7	2	16	11	25	41	163	113	39	6	
1900	551	114	31	10	6	8	16	10	33	41	148	85	34	7	8
Females:															
1914	572	98	20	17	3	2	10	11	27	55	169	119	33	8	
1913	563	103	22	8	2	4	11	9	32	51	169	117	29	6	
1912	555	95	12	14	4	4	10	7	26	50	180	111	37	7	
1911	625	105	31	22	8	4	21	15	29	50	163	139	31	6	1
1910	541	107	22	16	6	3	7	7	22	42	154	109	38	8	
1900	519	113	27	16	8	2	14	13	24	39	122	82	41	11	7

TABLE 39.—DEATHS OF NEGROES IN THE REGISTRATION AREA, BY SEX AND AGE, FOR STATES AND SELECTED CITIES: 1914, 1913, 1912, 1911, 1910, AND 1900—Continued.

REGISTRATION AREA, SEX, AND YEAR.	All ages.	DEATHS AT AGE OF—													Deaths at unknown age.
		Under 1 year.	1 year.	2 years.	3 years.	4 years.	5 to 9 years.	10 to 14 years.	15 to 19 years.	20 to 24 years.	25 to 44 years.	45 to 64 years.	65 to 84 years.	85 years and over.	
SELECTED CITIES IN REGISTRATION AREA—Contd.															
SPRINGFIELD, ILL.															
Males:															
1914	47	9	3							1	4	14	9	7	
1913	40	8	1				1			2	2	10	8	7	1
1912	40	4	4	1						1	2	15	7	7	
1911	34	2	1	2	1	2				1	2	10	7	5	1
1910	38	5	1	1			2	2		1	2	11	10	3	
1900	27	6	2							1	1	5	8	2	2
Females:															
1914	34	2	1							1		11	11	7	1
1913	38	10	1	1						2	1	7	9	4	3
1912	34	4	1				2	1	1	1	4	13	4	4	2
1911	28	1		1						3	2	7	6	5	1
1910	29	6	1	1	1					2	2	8	6	2	
1900	30	7					1		1	1		10	5	5	
SPRINGFIELD, OHIO.															
Males:															
1914	66	11	2				2			1	2	12	24	12	
1913	59	6	2			1	2			1	4	17	17	9	
1912	47	10	1				1	1		1	1	7	12	11	3
1911	38	4	4			1		1	2		1	6	11	8	
1910	38	8	1	1	1		2				2	9	8	5	1
1900 [1]															
Females:															
1914	48	7		1			1	4			4	12	9	7	3
1913	47	7	1								6	11	8	13	1
1912	39	6	4					1			3	6	14	3	2
1911	41	5		2			1	2	5		4	6	12	2	2
1910	40	3			1		4	1			2	13	10	5	1
1900 [1]															
TERRE HAUTE, IND.															
Males:															
1914	43	8					1				4	18	7	3	2
1913	41	8		1			1			1	4	10	11	5	1
1912	31	10	1				1			1	2	5	10	1	
1911	29	5									1	12	6	4	1
1910	31	7	3	1	1					1	3	8	1	5	1
1900	20	7		1			1				2	1		3	
Females:															
1914	26	5		1					2	3	1	11	3	1	
1913	26	3		1					2	3	3	5	5	5	1
1912	30	7		1		1	2	1		3	3	8	4		
1911	28	4	1						1	3	3	11	4	2	2
1910	36	9	1	1					1	3	1	14	3	3	
1900	20	6	2	2	1					1	1	4	2	1	
TRENTON, N. J.															
Males:															
1914	48	7							1	1	6	10	16	7	
1913	47	6	3							1	3	19	13	2	
1912	43	4								1	7	14	12	3	2
1911	44	1	1			1				1	4	21	12	3	
1910	50	6	1	1		1		1		2	5	18	8	6	
1900	34	8	1				1			2	3	10	5		3	1
Females:															
1914	41	5	4	1		1				1	1	7	12	7	2
1913	41	4	1	1	1		2	1		1	2	13	8	5	2
1912	37	2		1	1			2	1	3	1	9	9	5	
1911	21	3							1		1	2	6	5	3
1910	39	8					1		2	2	2	10	9	5	
1900	15	2	1					1	1			3	2	2	1
WASHINGTON, D. C.															
Males:															
1914	1,213	213	36	14	13	9	12	12	29	62	353	302	139	19	
1913	1,248	232	38	20	18	6	19	15	25	65	335	304	153	18	
1912	1,345	244	52	16	9	5	25	17	48	58	369	336	148	18	
1911	1,318	245	57	21	3	5	22	24	40	67	378	284	157	14	1
1910	1,429	303	45	28	4	3	23	13	36	85	365	328	180	16	
1900	1,276	387	82	31	15	14	37	24	53	70	216	221	104	22	
Females:															
1914	1,147	156	21	11	8	7	28	19	63	76	305	288	154	11	
1913	1,183	196	34	17	14	5	24	16	50	69	313	279	139	27	
1912	1,299	227	48	19	13	9	24	18	69	70	332	298	151	21	
1911	1,241	219	67	20	11	9	23	20	47	81	290	280	145	29	
1910	1,330	278	43	23	15	7	20	25	51	76	347	283	142	20	
1900	1,409	353	78	36	28	15	41	47	74	99	237	233	138	30	
WILMINGTON, DEL.															
Males:															
1914	118	27	4	4	2	1	1	1	5	8	20	23	18	2	2
1913	133	24	6	3	2	1	7	4	1	7	31	27	16	2	1
1912	139	34	7	6	1				5	5	19	34	6	1	3
1911	121	32	3	1	2	1	5	2	7	8	19	25	11	3	
1910	122	26	8	5	1		1	4	9	6	23	25	11	2	1
1900	138	38	7	6	4	2	3	4	2	7	26	27	9		1
Females:															
1914	128	26	4	4				1	2	15	27	23	20	3	1
1913	120	27	7	1	2	1			3	3	7	29	28	11	
1912	116	21	4	6				3	2	10	5	27	21	15	
1911	108	16	8	1				3	2	10	5	27	21	6	1	1
1910	103	22	4	5	1		1	5	3	3	18	26	6	1	1
1900	131	34	10	5	1	1	5	12	6	10	15	17	12	3	

[1] Not in registration area.

TABLE 39.—DEATHS OF NEGROES IN THE REGISTRATION AREA, BY SEX AND AGE, FOR STATES AND SELECTED CITIES: 1914, 1913, 1912, 1911, 1910, AND 1900—Continued.

REGISTRATION AREA, SEX, AND YEAR.	All ages.	DEATHS AT AGE OF—													Deaths at unknown age.
		Under 1 year.	1 year.	2 years.	3 years.	4 years.	5 to 9 years.	10 to 14 years.	15 to 19 years.	20 to 24 years.	25 to 44 years.	45 to 64 years.	65 to 84 years.	85 years and over.	
SELECTED CITIES IN REGISTRATION AREA—Contd.															
WILMINGTON, N. C.															
Males:															
1914	204	57	13	5	2	....	7	3	10	12	38	37	16	4	....
1913	188	52	9	5	....	1	2	2	4	13	41	38	19	1	1
1912	213	60	17	2	....	2	2	5	6	17	47	38	16	1	....
1911	261	73	31	9	2	4	5	3	6	10	51	42	23	2	....
1910	167	46	11	4	....	1	3	4	4	8	43	25	15	3	....
1900	206	58	16	3	4	1	7	3	11	16	27	32	15	7	6
Females:															
1914	201	45	14	3	1	1	5	3	10	12	41	37	27	2	....
1913	186	48	11	3	1	1	2	3	10	11	48	31	13	3	1
1912	187	40	5	2	....	2	5	2	11	8	45	44	21	2	....
1911	211	43	26	7	4	4	7	2	4	10	39	47	14	4	....
1910	158	33	10	3	2	....	2	2	7	10	40	26	18	4	1
1900	178	45	13	7	2	2	5	3	1	18	35	27	14	3	3
WINSTON, N. C.															
Males:															
1914	170	44	10	7	1	1	1	6	8	17	38	31	4	2	....
1913	183	32	12	4	2	3	7	6	18	22	46	23	8	....	....
1912	118	16	4	3	2	....	3	7	10	15	30	24	4	....	....
1911	101	22	5	3	2	2	3	3	5	11	21	17	7	....	....
1910	85	18	2	4	1	....	1	2	4	4	25	17	6	....	1
1900 [1]	....	....	....	....	....	....	....	....	....	....	....	....	....	....	....
Females:															
1914	185	38	10	5	2	1	6	8	15	16	48	27	8	1	....
1913	175	31	13	2	7	3	7	7	15	32	29	21	8	....	....
1912	116	20	5	5	6	....	2	3	9	10	35	17	2	2	....
1911	125	24	6	3	3	....	1	5	12	12	29	22	5	3	....
1910	101	12	10	1	3	2	3	4	5	7	24	23	6	1	....
1900 [1]	....	....	....	....	....	....	....	....	....	....	....	....	....	....	....

[1] Not in registration area.

Part V.—EDUCATIONAL AND SOCIAL STATISTICS.

Chapter XV.—SCHOOL ATTENDANCE.[1]

CHARACTER OF THE DATA.

The statistics of Negro school attendance in this chapter are derived from the Thirteenth and earlier census reports.

As regards 1910, the data are based upon the answers to an inquiry addressed by the census enumerators to each person enumerated, asking whether that person had attended school at any time during the period between September 1, 1909, and April 15, 1910, the date of enumeration. If the persons enumerated had, at any time during that period, attended any kind of a school, the question was to be answered in the affirmative. The inquiry relating to school attendance was a general inquiry, to be answered by persons of both sexes, and all ages from infancy upward, and the term "school" covered public and private day schools and night schools, kindergartens, colleges, universities, and professional schools. Since, however, the period covered by the 1910 census returns does not embrace a full year of 12 months, nor even a full school year, but only a portion of the school year of 1909–1910, persons who had in 1909 attended summer schools only were not returned as attending school at all, nor were persons who graduated from school in June, 1909, or who entered school subsequently to April 15, 1910. Comparatively few children, however, enter school during the closing months of the school year, and the census returns may be accepted as practically covering school attendance during the school year 1909–1910.

In interpreting these statistics, comparisons between different sections of the country and different classes of population are both interesting and essential. They are, however, apt to be misleading unless varying conditions are kept in mind.

Among these may be mentioned such disparities as the following: The varying length of the term covered by the school year; the varying grade of the teachers employed; the varying character of the curriculum. A school year of 40 weeks is more productive of results than one of 10 or 12 weeks; a graduate of a high-grade normal school is a better teacher than a graduate of a local grammar or high school, who has never been beyond the local surroundings; a system of graded schools is of far greater educational value

[1] For data relating to school attendance of the black and mulatto population, see section on "School attendance of black and mulatto children" in Chapter XI, p. 215, and Table 16 of that chapter, p. 215.

to a community than the ordinary ungraded school of remote country districts. Into the consideration of these conditions this report of course can not enter, except occasionally, and to a limited extent, but they are referred to as indicating that records of school attendance do not enable one to determine precisely the relative educational status of any given community or class of population.

Generally, where comparisons with other classes seem significant, figures for the white population as a whole are given, rather than for any class of whites, such as the native whites of native or mixed parentage, or the foreign-born whites. In the case of children 6 to 14 years of age, however, subclassifications of whites are introduced.

POPULATION OF ALL AGES IN SCHOOL: 1910.

A summary of the school attendance returns for the total population classified by race, nativity, and parentage, is given in Table 1.

Table	POPULATION: 1910.			PERCENTAGE DISTRIBUTION.	
		In school.			
RACIAL CLASS.	Total.	Number.	Per cent.	Total population.	Population in school.
All classes	91,972,266	18,009,891	19.6	100.0	100.0
Negro	9,827,763	1,670,650	17.0	10.7	9.3
White	81,731,957	16,279,292	19.9	88.9	90.4
Native white	68,386,412	15,627,786	22.9	74.4	86.8
Native parentage	49,488,575	11,110,583	22.5	53.8	61.7
Foreign or mixed parentage	18,897,837	4,517,203	23.9	20.5	25.1
Foreign born	13,345,545	651,506	4.9	14.5	3.6
Indian	265,683	53,458	20.1	0.3	0.3
Chinese	71,531	3,887	5.4	0.1	(1)
Japanese	72,157	2,512	3.5	0.1	(1)
All other	3,175	92	2.9	(1)	(1)

[1] Less than one-tenth of 1 per cent.

In a total population of 91,972,266, there were 18,009,891 persons, constituting 19.6 per cent, or nearly one-fifth of the total population, who had attended school at some time during the period from September 1, 1909, to April 15, 1910. Comparing the different classes of population it will be noted that, with the exception of the foreign-born whites, the Chinese, and the Japanese, the proportion in school, for the several classes, does not vary greatly from the average for all classes combined; of the Negroes 17 per cent, of the native white 22.9 per cent, and of the Indians 20.1 per cent, reported school attendance, the corresponding percentages for the foreign-born whites being 4.9, and for the Chinese and Japanese 5.4 and 3.5, respectively. In considering these comparisons it is to be remembered that the figures given in Table 1 include, for the population of each class, infants and adults as well as children of school age; and for the population in school, every person, young or old, who was reported as attending school. In the following tables, however, the figures both for population and for school attendance are in general restricted to the school-age period or periods.

POPULATION OF SCHOOL AGE IN SCHOOL: 1910.

In presenting a classification by age periods the difficulty is encountered at the outset that while there is a general consensus, there is no absolute agreement as to the period to be included in the term "school age." The classification in the census of 1900 was based on a school-age period of 5 to 20 years, inclusive, while the census of 1910 defined it as including the years 6 to 20. The reports of the Bureau of Education adopt the period 5 to 18 years of age, while the statutes of the individual states designate various age limits for the period of free or compulsory attendance. Table 2 shows the number of persons attending school 6 to 20 years of age—that is to say, the number of school age according to the 1910 census definition—and also the number under 6, and 21 years and over, for both Negroes and whites.

Table 2	POPULATION IN SCHOOL: 1910.			
AGE.	Number.		Percentage distribution.	
	Negro.	White.	Negro.	White.
All ages.............................	1,670,650	16,279,292	100.0	100.0
Under 6 years..........................	28,560	366,800	1.7	2.3
5 years.............................	25,060	320,696	1.5	2.0
Under 5 years.......................	3,500	46,104	0.2	0.3
6 to 20 years..........................	1,619,699	15,624,716	97.0	96.0
6 to 9 years.......................	488,954	5,174,347	29.3	31.8
10 to 14 years.....................	791,995	7,212,607	47.4	44.3
15 to 20 years.....................	338,750	3,237,762	20.3	19.9
15 to 17 years..................	264,005	2,473,283	15.8	15.2
18 to 20 years..................	74,745	764,479	4.5	4.7
21 years and over....................	21,559	284,674	1.3	1.7
Age unknown.........................	832	3,102	(1)	(1)

[1] Less than one-tenth of 1 per cent.

Classified by age, of the total number of Negroes reported in 1910 as having attended school, 1,619,699, or 97 per cent, were of school age, i. e., 6 to 20 years of age; 28,560, or 1.7 per cent, were under 6 years of age; and 22,391, or 1.3 per cent, were 21 years and over. With regard to those under 6, it is to be noted that 25,060 were reported as 5 years of age, leaving 3,500 for the ages under 5.

Nearly one-half (47.4 per cent) of the entire number attending school are in the 10 to 14 year period. If these proportions be compared with the corresponding proportions for whites, it appears that the proportion in the 10 to 14 year period is somewhat larger for Negroes than for whites, although in general the differences in the age distribution of the two classes are not marked.

INCREASE IN SCHOOL ATTENDANCE BY SEX AND AGE: 1900–1910.

Satisfactory comparisons between the statistics of school attendance for the two censuses, 1910 and 1900, are rendered difficult by the change from the 5 to 20 to the 6 to 20 age period as the basis of tabulation, and by a change in the questions presented by the enumerators. In 1900 the question covered the number of months spent in school, while in 1910 the only item recorded was actual presence of the individual in school at some time during the school period. To meet the first difficulty a special tabulation of persons 5 years of age was made in the census of 1910, as a result of which it is possible to show, in Table 3, comparative figures covering the age period 5 to 20. The table shows the number in school and the number not in school.

Among those classified in these tables as "not in school" are, of course, included many who have in past years attended school. A child 14 years of age not in school in 1909–1910, may nevertheless have attended school previously during six or seven years; a young man or woman 20 years of age not in school may have graduated with honor from a high school or college. Making all due allowance, however, for such cases, it remains true that, especially in the earlier age periods, the number "not in school" is significant in relation to one phase of the educational problem of the community.

During the decade 1900–1910 the number of Negroes 5 to 20 years of age attending school increased from 1,083,516 to 1,644,759, the increase amounting to 561,243, or more than 50 per cent. Only 31 per cent of the Negro population of that age were in school in 1900, the proportion in 1910 being 44.7 per cent. Although the population was increasing, the number not in school decreased from 2,415,671 to 2,033,101, the decrease amounting to 382,570, and the percentage not in school falling from 69 to 55.3. In the same decade and covering the same age period, for whites the percentage in school rose from 53.6 to 61.3, and the percentage not in school decreased from 46.4 to 38.7. Thus, for whites the percentage in school increased and the percentage not in school decreased by 7.7; while for Negroes the corresponding change in the percentages amounted to 13.7.

Turning to the component age periods, the number of Negroes in school, 5 to 9 years of age, increased during the decade 229,230; the number 10 to 14 years of age, 204,435; and the number 15 to 20 years of age, 127,578. The increase in the percentage attending school for these several age periods amounted to 17.5, 14.8, and 9, respectively, while the corresponding increases in the percentages for the whites were 12.8, 7.1, and 5.4. It is noteworthy that the increase in the percentage in school for the Negroes was, in each case, greater than that for the whites, indicating a more or less rapid approximation among Negroes to the condition obtaining among whites in regard to school attendance. Especially marked is the increase of school attendance among Negro children 5 to 9 years of age. The number of such children in school increased from 284,784 in 1900 to 514,014 in 1910. In 1900, 76.3 per cent, or more than three-fourths of the children in this age period, were not in school, while in 1910 the proportion not in school had fallen to 58.8 per cent.

NEGRO AND WHITE POPULATION 5 TO 20 YEARS OF AGE IN SCHOOL AND NOT IN SCHOOL, BY SEX AND AGE PERIODS: 1910 AND 1900.

Table 3 — POPULATION 5 TO 20 YEARS OF AGE.

AGE AND CENSUS YEAR.	Negro.						Percentage in school.						Percentage not in school.					
	In school.			Not in school.			Negro.			White.			Negro.			White.		
	Both sexes.	Male.	Female.	Both sexes.	Male.	Female.	Both sexes.	Male.	Female.	Both sexes.	Male.	Female.	Both sexes.	Male.	Female.	Both sexes.	Male.	Female.
5 to 20 years:																		
1910	1,644,759	771,587	873,172	2,033,101	1,026,101	1,007,000	44.7	42.9	46.4	61.3	61.3	61.3	55.3	57.1	53.6	38.7	38.7	38.7
1900	1,083,516	503,099	580,417	2,415,671	1,218,659	1,197,012	31.0	29.2	32.7	53.6	53.4	53.9	69.0	70.8	67.3	46.4	46.6	46.1
Increase, 1900–1910	561,243	268,488	292,755				13.7	13.7	13.7	7.7	7.9	7.4						
Decrease, 1900–1910				382,570	192,558	190,012							13.7	13.7	13.7	7.7	7.9	7.4
5 to 9 years:																		
1910	514,014	248,936	265,078	732,539	370,239	362,300	41.2	40.2	42.3	64.8	64.7	65.0	58.8	59.8	57.7	35.2	35.3	35.0
1900	284,784	139,201	145,583	917,974	461,209	456,765	23.7	23.2	24.2	52.0	52.0	51.9	76.3	76.8	75.8	48.0	48.0	48.1
Increase, 1900–1910	229,230	109,735	119,495				17.5	17.0	18.1	12.8	12.7	13.1						
Decrease, 1900–1910				185,435	90,970	94,465							17.5	17.0	18.1	12.8	12.7	13.1
10 to 14 years:																		
1910	791,995	379,486	412,509	363,271	198,588	164,683	68.6	65.6	71.5	91.1	91.0	91.2	31.4	34.4	28.5	8.9	9.0	8.8
1900	587,560	277,832	309,728	504,430	270,810	233,620	53.8	50.6	57.0	84.0	83.2	84.8	46.2	49.4	43.0	16.0	16.8	15.2
Increase, 1900–1910	204,435	101,654	102,781				14.8	15.0	14.5	7.1	7.8	6.4						
Decrease, 1900–1910				141,159	72,222	68,937							14.8	15.0	14.5	7.1	7.8	6.4
15 to 20 years:																		
1910	338,750	143,165	195,585	937,291	457,274	480,017	26.5	23.8	28.9	33.7	33.7	33.8	73.5	76.2	71.1	66.3	66.3	66.2
1900	211,172	86,066	125,106	993,267	486,640	506,627	17.5	15.0	19.8	28.3	27.8	28.8	82.5	85.0	80.2	71.7	72.2	71.2
Increase, 1900–1910	127,578	57,099	70,479				9.0	8.8	9.1	5.4	5.9	5.0						
Decrease, 1900–1910				55,976	29,366	26,610							9.0	8.8	9.1	5.4	5.9	5.0

Noting the sex distribution of the population in school, it appears that among the Negroes in each age period the females outranked the males as regards the number and percentage attending school at each census, and that the two sexes have made approximately equal advances during the decade, while among the whites the differences in the percentages by sex at each census are inconsiderable.

Table 4 shows the increase per cent for Negroes attending school during the decade 1900–1910, by sex and age periods, and the corresponding increase for the total Negro population of the same sex and age groups.

Table 4 — PERCENTAGE INCREASE OF NEGRO POPULATION: 1900–1910.

AGE PERIOD.	Both sexes.		Male.		Female.	
	Total.	In school.	Total.	In school.	Total.	In school.
5 to 20 years	5.1	51.8	4.4	53.4	5.8	50.4
5 to 9 years	3.6	80.5	3.1	78.8	4.2	82.1
10 to 14 years	5.8	34.8	5.4	36.6	6.2	33.2
15 to 20 years	5.9	60.4	4.8	66.3	6.9	56.3

While the Negro population of the United States as a whole increased by 11.2 per cent during the decade 1900–1910, the increases for the school-age periods were at much lower rates, varying, as shown in Table 4, from 3.6 to 5.9 per cent. The fact that the percentages for those ages are below the average for the entire population is noted and discussed in the chapter on age distribution. It is necessary here to call attention only to the notable difference between them and the percentage increases for the population attending school. The percentage increase of the population 5 to 20 years of age in school was ten times the increase of the total population of that age, the percentages being 51.8 and 5.1, respectively. In the component age periods the corresponding increases are 80.5 and 3.6 per cent for children 5 to 9 years of age, 34.8 and 5.8 per cent for children 10 to 14, and 60.4 and 5.9 per cent for those 15 to 20 years of age.

Comparing the sexes, it may be noted that while for each of the age periods under review the percentage increase in the total population is higher for females than for males, in the school attendance population the percentage increase is higher for males than for females, except in the age period 5 to 9 years.

Some of this apparent improvement may be attributed to a change in the form of the schedule inquiry, which, it is believed, was more favorable to securing correct answers in 1910 than in 1900. Making, however, all due allowance for this change, the actual improvement is very marked.

In Table 5 the increase or decrease of the Negro population 5 to 20 years of age, in school and not in school, is given in comparison with corresponding data for the white population.

Table 5	POPULATION 5 TO 20 YEARS OF AGE.					
AGE PERIOD AND SCHOOL ATTEND-ANCE CLASS.	Number.		Increase: 1900–1910.		Decrease: 1900–1910.	
	1910	1900	Number.	Per cent.	Number.	Per cent.
	NEGRO.					
Total..............	3,677,860	3,499,187	178,673	5.1	....	......
In school........	1,644,759	1,083,516	561,243	51.8	....	......
Not in school....	2,033,101	2,415,671	....	......	382,570	15.8
5 to 9 years of age....	1,246,553	1,202,758	43,795	3.6		
In school........	514,014	284,784	229,230	80.5		
Not in school....	732,539	917,974	....	......	185,435	20.2
10 to 14 years of age..	1,155,266	1,091,990	63,276	5.8		
In school........	791,995	587,560	204,435	34.8		
Not in school....	363,271	504,430	....	......	141,159	28.0
15 to 20 years of age..	1,276,041	1,204,439	71,602	5.9		
In school........	338,750	211,172	127,578	60.4		
Not in school....	937,291	993,267	....	......	55,976	5.6
	WHITE.					
Total..............	25,992,293	22,441,947	3,550,346	15.8	....	......
In school........	15,945,412	12,039,594	3,905,818	32.4	....	......
Not in school....	10,046,881	10,402,353	....	......	355,472	3.4
5 to 9 years of age....	8,475,173	7,638,326	836,847	11.0		
In school........	5,495,043	3,971,175	1,523,868	38.4		
Not in school....	2,980,130	3,667,151	....	......	687,021	18.7
10 to 14 years of age..	7,918,408	6,959,238	959,170	13.8		
In school........	7,212,607	5,846,411	1,366,196	23.4		
Not in school....	705,801	1,112,827	....	......	407,026	36.6
15 to 20 years of age....	9,598,712	7,844,383	1,754,329	22.4		
In school........	3,237,762	2,222,008	1,015,754	45.7		
Not in school....	6,360,950	5,622,375	738,575	13.1		

It will be noted that while the Negro population 5 to 9 years of age increased 43,795, or 3.6 per cent, in the decade 1900–1910, the number of that age in school increased 229,230, or 80.5 per cent, and the number not in school decreased 185,435, or 20.2 per cent. For each age period, although the percentage increase for the white population exceeded that for the Negro population, the percentage increase for the Negro population in school exceeded that for the white population in school, being, in the age period 5 to 9 years, 80.5 for Negroes, as compared with 38.4 for whites; in the age period 10 to 14 years, 34.8 for Negroes, as compared with 23.4 for whites; and in the age period 15 to 20 years, 60.4 for Negroes, as compared with 45.7 for whites.

INCREASE REPRESENTING IMPROVEMENT.

A significant indication of the nature of the increase in school attendance in the Negro population is found in Table 6, showing the proportion of that increase which may be regarded as the natural result of the growth in population, and the proportion due to improved conditions and greater interest in education.

Table 6	NEGRO POPULATION.			
ITEM.	5 to 20 years of age.	5 to 9 years of age.	10 to 14 years of age.	15 to 20 years of age.
Total, 1910......................	3,677,860	1,246,553	1,155,266	1,276,041
Percentage in school, 1900..............	31.0	23.7	53.8	17.5
Corresponding proportion of 1910 population.....................	1,140,273	295,433	621,533	223,307
Number in school:				
1910.................................	1,644,759	514,014	791,995	338,750
1900.................................	1,083,516	284,784	587,560	211,172
Increase of number in school, 1900–1910.	561,243	229,230	204,435	127,578
Due to growth of population......	56,757	10,649	33,973	12,135
Due to increased proportion in school....	504,486	218,581	170,462	115,443

The total number of children 5 to 20 years of age in school was 1,083,516, or 31 per cent of the Negro population of that age in 1900, and 1,644,759, or 44.7 per cent in 1910. If the same general conditions had obtained in 1910 as in 1900 and the same percentage of the population—31 per cent—had been in school, the total number in school would have been 1,140,273, an increase over 1900 of 56,757. In fact the total increase during the decade was 561,243. If the increase of 56,757 be deducted as representing growth of population, there remains 504,486, which may be regarded as the increase resulting from improved conditions and greater interest in education.

Applying the same method to the component age periods, it appears that in the age period 5 to 9 years, only 10,649, or less than 5 per cent of the total increase for that age period may be accounted for by growth in population, the remaining 218,581, or 95 per cent of the total increase, representing improvement in conditions; in the 10 to 14 year period the increase representing growth of population is 33,973, about 16 per cent of the total increase, and that representing improvement, 170,462, or 84 per cent; in the 15 to 20 year period, the figures are 12,135, representing growth of population, and 115,443, representing the general advance in school attendance.

AVERAGE INCREASE IN AMOUNT OF SCHOOLING: 1900–1910.

As has been noted, the census returns include no statement of the number of months or of years of schooling, but only a return in the case of the 1910 census of the fact of attendance or nonattendance at some time during the period September 1, 1909, to April 15, 1910. It is, however, possible to estimate approximately from these returns the number of years in which on an average a child who attains the age of 5 or 6 attends school during the school age period. In the case of the Negro population, for example, the total number 6 to 20 years of age, in 1910 was 3,422,157; of this total, 1,619,699, or 47.3 per cent, were in school, which on the assumption that each child in school attended a full year is equivalent to an average attendance per child during 1909–10, of 47.3 per cent of one year. If this be regarded as representing a permanent condition, children attaining the age of 6 years would, during the school age period of 15 years, attend school on the average approximately 7 years. The corresponding average for Negro males is 6.8 years and for Negro females 7.4 years; for whites, 9.7 years, which is the average also for white males and for white females; for native white males 10 years, and for native white females 9.9 years. By a similar calculation it will be found that Negro children, during the period of 9 years, extending from the age of 6 to the age of 14, inclusive, attend school on the average 5.4 years; native white children of native parentage 7.5 years, and native white children of foreign or mixed parentage 7.9 years. Comparing 1910 with 1900, with reference to school attendance for children during the age period of 16 years, i. e., from the age 5 to and including the age 20, the 1900 returns indicate for Negro children an average attendance at school of 5 years during the age period 5 to 20 years; the 1910 returns for this age period indicate an average attendance of 7.1 years.

It would appear from these figures that Negro children 5 to 20 years of age were receiving on the average two years more of schooling in 1910 than they were receiving in 1900. For the Negro males the advance was from 4.7 to 6.9 years; and for Negro females, from 5.2 to 7.4 years; for white children, from 8.6 to 9.8 years. While these averages may be somewhat affected by changes in the age composition of the population 5 to 20 years of age for the several classes during the decade 1900–1910, they indicate, nevertheless, with a fair degree of accuracy the actual increase in the average amount of schooling received by children during the school-age period. Statistics of school attendance are not available by single years of age for 1900, a correction of the averages by single years of age, therefore, can not be made, but that the changes in age composition are immaterial may be inferred from the fact that a calculation based upon the age periods 5 to 9, 10 to 14, and 15 to 20, for Negroes, gives practically the same results as are obtained by the above calculation based upon the total population 5 to 20 years of age.

SCHOOL ATTENDANCE BY SINGLE YEARS OF AGE: 1910.

Statistics of school attendance by single years, are shown in Table 7. In this table evidence will be found of concentration of population upon even as compared with odd years of age. When the exact age of a child is unknown it appears that it is more commonly reported as 6, 8, 10, or 12 years of age, rather than as 7, 9, 11, or 13. The concentration upon the age of 10 is very marked. The result is a fluctuation in the enumerated population totals from year to year, which certainly does not in fact characterize the actual age distribution of the population. Since, however, the error in the age returns affects the total population and not simply those in school, the percentage in school does not reflect the fluctuations in the population as returned. This percentage indicates, therefore, fairly correctly, the proportion in school for the different years.

NEGRO AND WHITE SCHOOL ATTENDANCE, BY SEX AND SINGLE YEARS OF AGE: 1910.

Table 7	POPULATION 6 TO 20 YEARS OF AGE: 1910.											
	Negro.						Percentage in school.					
							Negro.			White.		
AGE.	Both sexes.		Male.		Female.							
	In school.	Not in school.	In school.	Not in school.	In school.	Not in school.	Both sexes.	Male.	Female.	Both sexes.	Male.	Female.
6 to 20 years	1,619,699	1,802,458	759,813	911,166	859,886	891,292	47.3	45.5	49.1	64.5	64.6	64.5
6 to 9 years	488,954	501,896	237,162	255,304	251,792	246,592	49.3	48.2	50.5	77.2	77.1	77.3
10 to 14 years	791,995	363,271	379,486	198,588	412,509	164,683	68.6	65.6	71.5	91.1	91.0	91.2
15 to 20 years	338,750	937,291	143,165	457,274	195,585	480,017	26.5	23.8	28.9	33.7	33.7	33.8
6 to 9 years:												
6 years	78,124	184,691	37,051	92,753	41,073	91,938	29.7	28.5	30.9	55.5	55.2	55.8
7 years	120,104	131,638	58,270	67,680	61,834	63,958	47.7	46.3	49.2	79.1	79.0	79.2
8 years	146,186	106,287	70,609	54,328	75,577	51,959	57.9	56.5	59.3	86.6	86.5	86.6
9 years	144,540	79,280	71,232	40,543	73,308	38,737	64.6	63.7	65.4	89.4	89.4	89.4
10 to 14 years:												
10 years	169,155	73,354	83,575	39,305	85,580	34,049	69.8	68.0	71.5	93.1	92.9	93.3
11 years	141,723	53,325	68,730	28,332	72,993	24,993	72.7	70.8	74.5	93.7	93.6	93.8
12 years	183,267	78,033	88,619	42,648	94,648	35,385	70.1	67.5	72.8	93.0	92.7	93.2
13 years	151,816	70,045	71,574	38,652	80,242	31,393	68.4	64.9	71.9	91.8	91.7	91.8
14 years	146,034	88,514	66,988	49,651	79,046	38,863	62.3	57.4	67.0	84.1	84.1	84.0
15 to 20 years:												
15 years	111,860	95,695	49,221	52,700	62,639	42,995	53.9	48.3	59.3	70.3	70.1	70.4
16 years	93,055	131,348	38,600	68,079	54,455	63,269	41.5	36.2	46.3	51.8	51.0	52.7
17 years	59,090	144,757	24,727	75,458	34,363	69,299	29.0	24.7	33.1	36.0	35.1	37.0
18 years	41,507	189,800	16,613	91,703	24,894	98,097	17.9	15.3	20.2	23.1	22.9	23.4
19 years	21,110	172,194	8,964	81,880	12,146	90,314	10.9	9.9	11.9	14.8	15.3	14.3
20 years	12,128	203,497	5,040	87,454	7,088	116,043	5.6	5.4	5.8	8.7	9.7	7.8

DIAGRAM I.—PERCENTAGE ATTENDING SCHOOL BY SINGLE YEARS OF AGE, FOR NEGROES, NATIVE WHITES, AND FOREIGN-BORN WHITES: 1910.

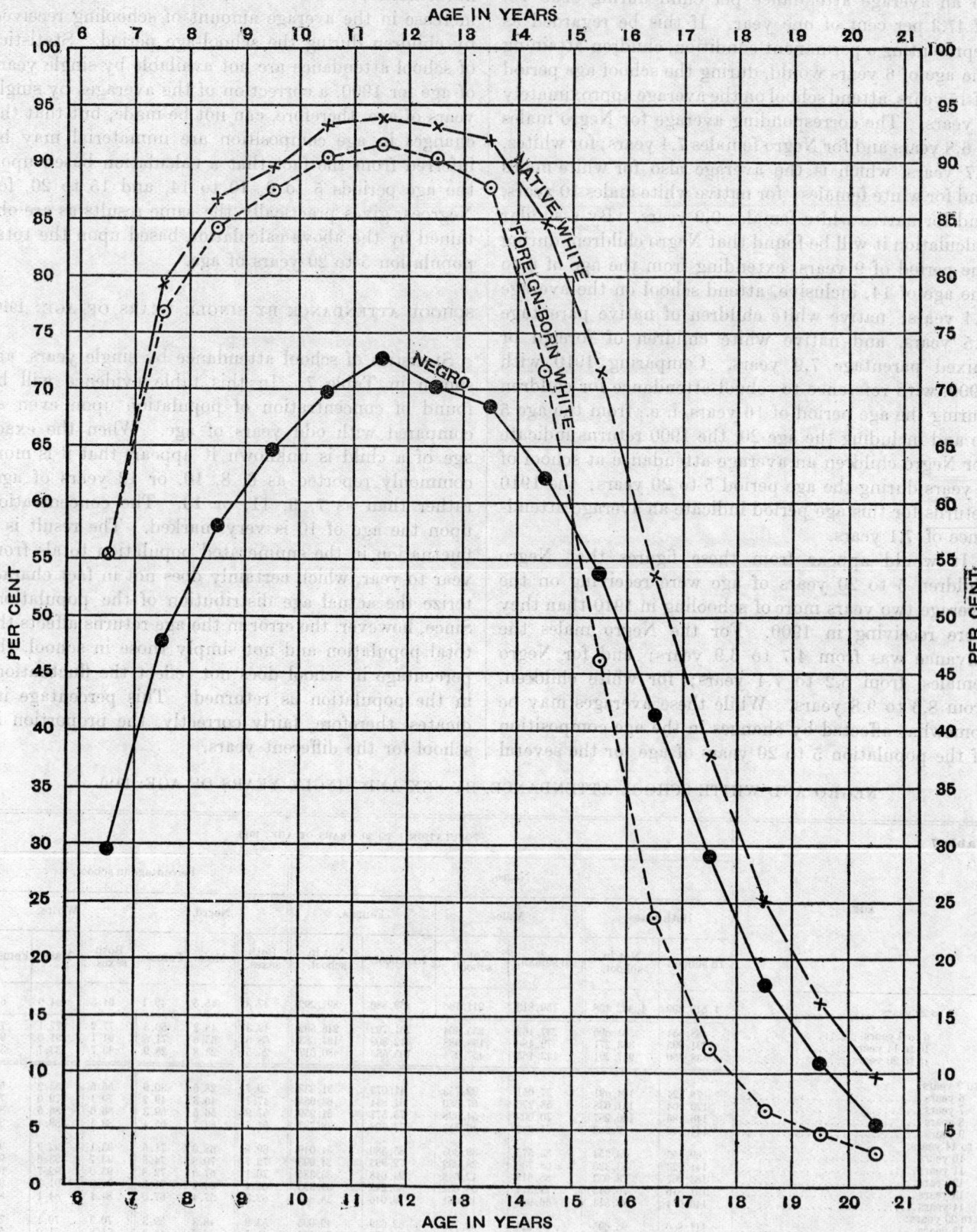

As given in Table 7, the largest numbers reported as attending school were those for 12 years of age, while the highest percentages were those for 11 years. The ages 10, 11, and 12 years are the years of maximum school attendance. The drop in the percentage for those 14 years of age for both Negroes and whites reflects the fact that attendance at school is seldom compulsory for those 14 years of age or older. In each year of age, the whites exceed the Negroes in percentage of attendance, the difference being greatest in the youngest years of the school period.

The data relating to school attendance by single years of age are presented graphically in Diagram I for Negroes, native whites, and foreign-born whites, and in Diagram II for Negroes and whites. The tendency to drop out of school on attaining the age 14 is very apparent in these diagrams.

DIAGRAM II.—PERCENTAGE IN SCHOOL AND NOT IN SCHOOL BY SINGLE YEARS OF AGE, FOR THE NEGRO AND WHITE POPULATION: 1910.

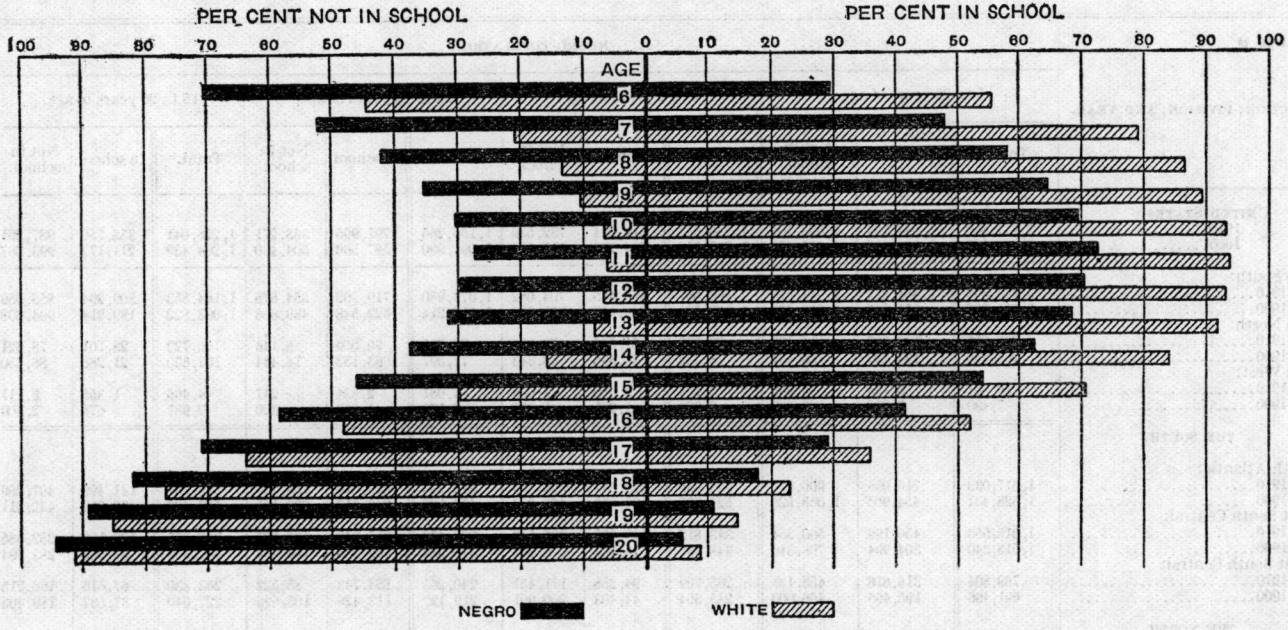

SECTIONS AND DIVISIONS.

Table 8 shows the number and the percentage in school for Negroes and whites, by geographic sections and divisions.

Table 8	POPULATION 6 TO 20 YEARS OF AGE: 1910.						
SECTION AND DIVISION.	Negro.			White, in school.		Percentage distribution of population in school.	
	Total.	In school.		Number.	Per cent.	Negro.	White.
		Number.	Per cent.				
United States.....	3,422,157	1,619,699	47.3	15,624,716	64.5	100.0	100.0
The South.............	3,164,496	1,466,940	46.4	4,279,812	62.1	90.6	27.4
South Atlantic........	1,504,019	706,974	47.0	1,638,589	62.2	43.6	10.5
East South Central....	944,880	447,230	47.3	1,225,752	63.1	27.6	7.8
West South Central...	715,597	312,736	43.7	1,415,471	61.2	19.3	9.1
The North.............	247,655	146,672	59.2	10,208,409	65.3	9.1	65.3
New England.........	15,539	10,201	65.6	1,132,538	66.1	0.6	7.2
Middle Atlantic.......	95,194	54,780	57.5	3,313,591	63.0	3.4	21.2
East North Central....	72,837	44,462	61.0	3,383,070	65.6	2.7	21.7
West North Central...	64,085	37,229	58.1	2,379,210	68.1	2.3	15.2
The West.............	10,006	6,087	60.8	1,136,495	66.5	0.4	7.3
Mountain.............	4,170	2,531	60.7	476,502	67.1	0.2	3.0
Pacific...............	5,836	3,556	60.9	659,993	66.2	0.2	4.2

Approximately nine-tenths of the Negroes reported in 1910 as attending school were in the South, the percentage in that section being 90.6, as against 9.1 per cent in the North and 0.4 per cent in the West. Comparing these figures with those for the whites, it will be noted that the great majority of whites attending school are in the North, the proportion being 65.3 per cent, as against 9.1 for the Negro school population, and the proportion in the South being 27.4 per cent for the whites, as against 90.6 per cent for the Negroes.

Of the total Negro population 6 to 20 years of age in the South, 46.4 per cent had attended school during the school year 1909–1910; in the North, 59.2 per cent; and in the West, 60.8 per cent. For the whites the corresponding percentages were 62.1 in the South, 65.3 in the North, and 66.5 in the West. It thus appears that in the North and West the proportion of Negroes attending school is nearly on a par with that of the whites; while in the South the proportion for Negroes is markedly lower than for whites. The probable explanation is that in the North and West the Negro communities are closely identified with the white communities, have the same facilities for school attendance, and share in the general influences of the community life; while in the South they are to a greater degree isolated in rural and agricultural communities in which the school facilities are relatively inadequate. For both classes the proportion in school is lower in the South than it is in the North, although the difference is inconsiderable in the case of the whites.

The conditions prevailing in the three sections are in general reflected in the several geographic divisions of the North, the South, and the West. In New England where the population is largely centralized and located in urban communities, school attendance of Negroes and of whites is represented by nearly identical proportions, 65.6 and 66.1 per cent, respectively. In the three southern divisions the percentages for both races are below the corresponding percentages for northern and western divisions—being markedly lower in the case of Negroes.

Table 9 shows the Negro population in school and not in school, by age periods, sections, and divisions, in 1910 and in 1900, the comparison being based upon the population 5 to 20 years of age.

NEGRO SCHOOL ATTENDANCE BY AGE PERIODS, BY SECTIONS: 1910 AND 1900.

Table 9 SECTION, DIVISION, AND YEAR.	NEGRO POPULATION.											
	5 to 20 years of age.			5 to 9 years of age.			10 to 14 years of age.			15 to 20 years of age.		
	Total.	In school.	Not in school.	Total.	In school.	Not in school.	Total.	In school.	Not in school.	Total.	In school.	Not in school.
UNITED STATES:												
1910	3,677,860	1,644,759	2,033,101	1,246,553	514,014	732,539	1,155,266	791,995	363,271	1,276,041	338,750	937,291
1900	3,499,187	1,083,516	2,415,671	1,202,758	284,784	917,974	1,091,990	587,560	504,430	1,204,439	211,172	993,267
The South:												
1910	3,403,390	1,488,871	1,914,519	1,164,557	460,475	704,082	1,073,980	719,102	354,878	1,164,853	309,294	855,559
1900	3,228,237	955,365	2,272,872	1,122,201	243,603	878,598	1,012,214	522,548	489,666	1,093,822	189,214	904,608
The North:												
1910	263,819	149,693	114,126	78,892	51,533	27,359	78,205	70,059	8,146	106,722	28,101	78,621
1900	263,460	124,323	139,137	78,233	39,890	38,343	77,597	63,153	14,444	107,630	21,280	86,350
The West:												
1910	10,651	6,195	4,456	3,104	2,006	1,098	3,081	2,834	247	4,466	1,355	3,111
1900	7,490	3,828	3,662	2,324	1,291	1,033	2,179	1,859	320	2,987	678	2,309
THE SOUTH.												
South Atlantic:												
1910	1,617,033	716,056	900,977	555,036	225,547	329,489	513,239	349,010	164,229	548,758	141,499	407,259
1900	1,523,431	454,905	1,068,526	527,900	120,976	406,924	476,108	246,917	229,191	519,423	87,012	432,411
East South Central:												
1910	1,016,553	456,199	560,354	343,812	140,670	203,142	320,476	215,349	105,127	352,265	100,180	252,085
1900	1,013,340	304,994	708,346	348,997	78,224	270,773	316,984	162,205	154,779	347,359	64,565	282,794
West South Central:												
1910	769,804	316,616	453,188	265,709	94,258	171,451	240,265	154,743	85,522	263,830	67,615	196,215
1900	691,466	195,466	496,000	245,304	44,403	200,901	219,122	113,426	105,696	227,040	37,637	189,403
THE NORTH.												
New England:												
1910	16,534	10,587	5,947	5,109	3,950	1,159	5,092	4,800	292	6,333	1,837	4,496
1900	15,467	7,791	7,676	4,698	2,832	1,866	4,285	3,785	500	6,484	1,174	5,310
Middle Atlantic:												
1910	101,707	56,286	45,421	31,026	20,613	10,413	29,648	26,760	2,888	41,033	8,913	32,120
1900	88,455	37,804	50,651	25,689	13,498	12,191	23,932	19,224	4,708	38,834	5,082	33,752
East North Central:												
1910	77,540	45,025	32,515	22,863	15,027	7,836	23,184	21,102	2,082	31,493	8,896	22,597
1900	77,906	40,204	37,702	23,294	12,521	10,773	23,851	20,445	3,406	30,761	7,238	23,523
West North Central:												
1910	68,038	37,795	30,243	19,894	11,943	7,951	20,281	17,397	2,884	27,863	8,455	19,408
1900	81,632	38,524	43,108	24,552	11,039	13,513	25,529	19,699	5,830	31,551	7,786	23,765
THE WEST.												
Mountain:												
1910	4,439	2,572	1,867	1,362	857	505	1,286	1,166	120	1,791	549	1,242
1900	3,536	1,709	1,827	1,026	541	485	984	832	152	1,526	336	1,190
Pacific:												
1910	6,212	3,623	2,589	1,742	1,149	593	1,795	1,668	127	2,675	806	1,869
1900	3,954	2,119	1,835	1,298	750	548	1,195	1,027	168	1,461	342	1,119

In the South the number of children 5 to 20 years of age in school increased from 955,365 in 1900 to 1,488,871 in 1910, an increase of 533,506. This aggregate increase represents an increase of 216,872 in the number of children 5 to 9 years of age in school; an increase of 196,554 for the age group 10 to 14; and of 120,080 for the age group 15 to 20. Although population increased in each age group, the number not in school in each age group decreased.

Table 10 presents, by sections and divisions, the percentage in school for Negroes and for whites, in 1910 and in 1900, by age periods, and the increase in this percentage.

The percentage of school attendance for Negroes 5 to 20 years of age in the South as a whole increased from 29.6 in 1900 to 43.7 in 1910, a gain of 14.1 in the percentage, the corresponding gain for the whites being 12.4. The percentage in school for Negro children 5 to 9 years of age increased from 21.7 to 39.5; for those 10 to 14 from 51.6 to 67, and for those 15 to 20 from 17.3 to 26.6. The gains in the percentages for these age periods were 17.8, 15.4, and 9.3, respectively, for Negroes, and 18.5, 11.1, and 8.1, respectively, for whites. In the several sections and divisions the Negroes show relatively larger gains than the whites, indicating a general approximation to the status of the white population. In each southern division in 1910 approximately two-thirds of the Negro population 10 to 14 years of age were in school; and in three northern divisions more than nine-tenths. For the total 5 to 20 years of age, and in the age groups 5 to 9 and 10 to 14, the highest Negro records are those for the New England division, in which 94.3 per cent of the children 10 to 14 years of age were in school in 1910. The highest white record is for the same division, the percentage of 94.1 per cent being practically identical with that for Negroes in this age group.

PERCENTAGE OF NEGROES AND WHITES IN SCHOOL, BY SECTIONS, DIVISIONS, AND AGE PERIODS: 1910 AND 1900.

Table 10 SECTION, DIVISION, AND AGE PERIOD.	PERCENTAGE IN SCHOOL.				INCREASE IN PERCENTAGE IN SCHOOL 1900–1910.		SECTION, DIVISION, AND AGE PERIOD.	PERCENTAGE IN SCHOOL.				INCREASE IN PERCENTAGE IN SCHOOL 1900–1910.	
	1910		1900					1910		1900			
	Negro.	White.	Negro.	White.	Negro.	White.		Negro.	White.	Negro.	White.	Negro.	White.
UNITED STATES:							THE NORTH.						
5 to 20 years	44.7	61.3	31.0	53.6	13.7	7.7	New England:						
5 to 9 years	41.2	64.8	23.7	52.0	17.5	12.8	5 to 20 years	64.0	64.6	50.4	57.6	13.6	7.0
10 to 14 years	68.6	91.1	53.8	84.0	14.8	7.1	5 to 9 years	77.3	79.5	60.3	66.5	17.0	13.0
15 to 20 years	26.5	33.7	17.5	28.3	9.0	5.4	10 to 14 years	94.3	94.1	88.3	90.0	6.0	4.1
THE SOUTH:							15 to 20 years	29.0	29.0	18.1	24.1	10.9	4.9
5 to 20 years	43.7	58.3	29.6	45.9	14.1	12.4	Middle Atlantic:						
5 to 9 years	39.5	53.1	21.7	34.6	17.8	18.5	5 to 20 years	55.3	60.3	42.7	53.5	12.6	6.8
10 to 14 years	67.0	85.1	51.6	74.0	15.4	11.1	5 to 9 years	66.4	70.4	52.5	59.5	13.9	10.9
15 to 20 years	26.6	39.5	17.3	31.4	9.3	8.1	10 to 14 years	90.3	92.9	80.3	85.8	10.0	7.1
THE NORTH:							15 to 20 years	21.7	26.2	13.1	20.4	8.6	5.8
5 to 20 years	56.7	62.5	47.2	56.5	9.5	6.0	East North Central:						
5 to 9 years	65.3	70.8	51.0	59.3	14.3	11.5	5 to 20 years	58.1	62.6	51.6	56.9	6.5	5.7
10 to 14 years	89.6	93.6	81.4	87.8	8.2	5.8	5 to 9 years	65.7	70.2	53.8	58.4	11.9	11.8
15 to 20 years	26.3	30.8	19.8	26.5	6.5	3.3	10 to 14 years	91.0	93.9	85.7	88.2	5.3	5.7
THE WEST:							15 to 20 years	28.2	31.0	23.5	27.8	4.7	3.2
5 to 20 years	58.2	62.9	51.1	59.2	7.1	3.7	West North Central:						
5 to 9 years	64.6	62.4	55.6	55.2	9.0	7.2	5 to 20 years	55.5	64.9	47.2	59.2	8.3	5.7
10 to 14 years	92.0	93.3	85.3	90.1	6.7	3.2	5 to 9 years	60.0	67.9	45.0	57.3	15.0	10.6
15 to 20 years	30.3	39.5	22.7	35.7	7.6	3.8	10 to 14 years	85.8	93.7	77.2	88.6	8.6	5.1
THE SOUTH.							15 to 20 years	30.3	38.4	24.7	34.1	5.6	4.3
South Atlantic:							THE WEST.						
5 to 20 years	44.3	58.5	29.9	46.9	14.4	11.6	Mountain:						
5 to 9 years	40.6	55.2	22.9	38.6	17.7	16.6	5 to 20 years	57.9	63.0	48.3	56.8	9.6	6.2
10 to 14 years	68.0	85.0	51.9	74.1	16.1	10.9	5 to 9 years	62.9	60.7	52.7	50.3	10.2	10.4
15 to 20 years	25.8	38.0	16.8	30.7	9.0	7.3	10 to 14 years	90.7	91.9	84.6	87.1	6.1	4.8
East South Central:							15 to 20 years	30.7	41.0	22.0	35.7	8.7	5.3
5 to 20 years	44.9	59.3	30.1	46.9	14.8	12.4	Pacific:						
5 to 9 years	40.9	54.3	22.4	36.0	18.5	18.3	5 to 20 years	58.3	62.7	53.6	60.9	4.7	1.8
10 to 14 years	67.2	84.8	51.2	73.4	16.0	11.4	5 to 9 years	66.0	63.7	57.8	59.1	8.2	4.6
15 to 20 years	28.4	41.4	18.6	33.5	9.8	7.9	10 to 14 years	92.9	94.6	85.9	92.2	7.0	2.4
West South Central:							15 to 20 years	30.1	38.4	23.4	35.6	6.7	2.8
5 to 20 years	41.1	57.2	28.3	43.4	12.8	13.8							
5 to 9 years	35.5	49.8	18.1	28.0	17.4	21.8							
10 to 14 years	64.4	85.5	51.8	74.6	12.6	10.9							
15 to 20 years	25.6	39.5	16.6	30.4	9.0	9.1							

A comparison of the number in school with the number not in school is made for Negroes 10 to 14 years of age in 1910 for sections and Southern divisions in Diagram III.

In general, it is evident from the comparisons between the two censuses that school attendance among the Negroes advanced rapidly during the decade in all sections of the country, and especially in the South.

Tables 11, 12, and 13 show statistics of school attendance, by single years of age, by sections and southern divisions.

DIAGRAM III.—NEGROES 10 TO 14 YEARS OF AGE IN SCHOOL AND NOT IN SCHOOL, FOR SOUTHERN DIVISIONS, THE NORTH, AND THE WEST.

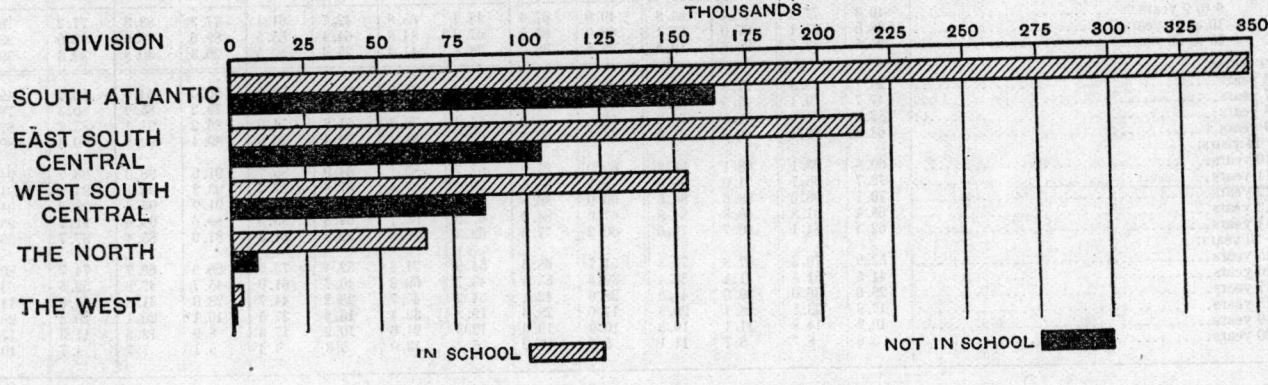

In number and percentage of Negroes in school in different sections of the country by single years of age, the South shows for each single year, as for each age period, the largest numbers and the smallest percentages. The record for the three southern divisions does not vary greatly from the average for the South as a whole. Throughout the South, for the ages 8 to 15 years, inclusive, each year shows a majority of the Negro population of that age in attendance at school.

Table 12 carries out the comparison as regards school attendance, by single years of age, between Negroes and whites in the different sections and southern divisions, and Table 13 gives the converse, showing the percentage not in school.

NEGRO SCHOOL ATTENDANCE BY SINGLE YEARS OF AGE, BY SECTIONS AND SOUTHERN DIVISIONS: 1910.

Table 11

NEGRO POPULATION 6 TO 20 YEARS OF AGE: 1910.

	The South.			South Atlantic division.		East South Central division.		West South Central division.		The North.		The West.	
AGE.	Number.		Percentage in school.	Number in school.	Percentage in school.	Number in school.	Percentage in school.	Number in school.	Percentage in school.	Number in school.	Percentage in school.	Number in school.	Percentage in school.
	In school.	Not in school.											
6 to 20 years...............	1,466,940	1,697,556	46.4	706,974	47.0	447,230	47.3	312,736	43.7	146,672	59.2	6,087	60.8
6 to 9 years...............	438,544	487,119	47.4	216,465	49.0	131,701	48.4	90,378	42.7	48,512	77.3	1,898	77.2
10 to 14 years.............	719,102	354,878	67.0	349,010	68.0	215,349	67.2	154,743	64.4	70,059	89.6	2,834	92.0
15 to 20 years.............	309,294	855,559	26.6	141,499	25.8	100,180	28.4	67,615	25.6	28,101	26.3	1,355	30.3
6 to 9 years:													
6 years................	68,561	177,178	27.9	34,425	28.9	21,543	30.2	12,593	22.8	9,193	56.0	370	56.2
7 years................	107,154	128,253	45.5	53,327	47.7	32,333	46.8	21,494	39.4	12,468	79.2	482	80.3
8 years................	132,485	104,078	56.0	64,782	57.8	39,305	56.4	28,398	51.8	13,214	86.2	487	83.7
9 years................	130,344	77,610	62.7	63,931	64.5	38,520	62.3	27,893	59.4	13,637	89.4	559	90.3
10 to 14 years:													
10 years...............	154,093	72,040	68.1	76,173	69.9	45,120	67.7	32,800	64.9	14,467	91.9	595	93.7
11 years...............	128,098	52,340	71.0	62,738	72.7	37,810	70.6	27,550	67.8	13,123	93.2	502	94.0
12 years...............	167,581	76,655	68.6	82,408	69.9	49,876	68.9	35,297	65.5	15,082	91.9	604	93.8
13 years...............	137,353	68,380	66.8	65,755	67.6	41,431	67.0	30,167	64.8	13,909	89.6	554	91.1
14 years...............	131,977	85,463	60.7	61,936	60.2	41,112	62.3	28,929	59.4	13,478	81.9	579	87.7
15 to 20 years:													
15 years...............	101,274	90,509	52.8	46,816	51.7	31,919	54.9	22,539	52.4	10,150	66.8	436	74.7
16 years...............	85,135	122,034	41.1	38,806	39.6	27,693	43.7	18,636	40.7	7,556	45.7	364	52.5
17 years...............	54,220	132,455	29.0	24,259	28.0	17,998	31.2	11,963	28.2	4,614	28.0	256	37.0
18 years...............	38,317	173,390	18.1	17,560	17.6	12,766	19.9	7,991	16.8	3,024	16.1	166	20.8
19 years...............	19,315	154,067	11.1	8,955	10.9	6,221	12.3	4,139	10.2	1,704	8.9	91	11.3
20 years...............	11,033	183,104	5.7	5,103	5.6	3,583	6.2	2,347	5.3	1,053	5.1	42	4.7

NEGRO AND WHITE PERCENTAGE IN SCHOOL BY SINGLE YEARS OF AGE, BY SECTIONS AND SOUTHERN DIVISIONS: 1910.

Table 12

PERCENTAGE IN SCHOOL: 1910.

	United States.		The South.		South Atlantic division.		East South Central division.		West South Central division.		The North.		The West.	
AGE.	Negro.	White.	Negro.	White.	Negro.	White.	Negro.	White.	Negro.	White.	Negro.	White.	Negro.	White.
6 to 20 years.....................	47.3	64.5	46.4	62.1	47.0	62.2	47.3	63.1	43.7	61.2	59.2	65.3	60.8	66.5
6 to 9 years......................	49.3	77.2	47.4	64.8	49.0	67.4	48.4	65.8	42.7	61.1	77.3	83.3	77.2	75.8
10 to 14 years....................	68.6	91.1	67.0	85.1	68.0	85.0	67.2	84.8	64.4	85.5	89.6	93.6	92.0	93.3
15 to 20 years....................	26.5	33.7	26.6	39.5	25.8	38.0	28.4	41.4	25.6	39.5	26.3	30.8	30.3	39.5
6 to 9 years:														
6 years........................	29.7	55.5	27.9	38.5	28.9	42.0	30.2	40.7	22.8	32.6	56.0	64.5	56.2	49.9
7 years........................	47.7	79.1	45.5	65.1	47.7	68.6	46.8	67.2	39.4	59.6	79.2	85.9	80.3	78.8
8 years........................	57.9	86.6	56.0	76.9	57.8	78.9	56.4	76.8	51.8	74.9	86.2	91.1	83.7	87.0
9 years........................	64.6	89.4	62.7	81.9	64.5	83.2	62.3	81.4	59.4	80.8	89.4	92.8	90.3	89.7
10 to 14 years:														
10 years.......................	69.8	93.1	68.1	86.6	69.9	87.9	67.7	86.1	64.9	85.7	91.9	96.0	93.7	94.0
11 years.......................	72.7	93.7	71.0	88.0	72.7	88.6	70.6	87.4	67.8	87.7	93.2	96.1	94.0	94.7
12 years.......................	70.1	93.0	68.6	86.6	69.9	86.8	68.9	86.3	65.5	86.6	91.9	95.8	93.8	94.3
13 years.......................	68.4	91.8	66.8	84.8	67.6	84.0	67.0	84.7	64.8	85.8	89.6	94.6	91.1	93.6
14 years.......................	62.3	84.1	60.7	79.6	60.2	77.6	62.3	79.9	59.4	81.5	81.9	85.4	87.7	90.1
15 to 20 years:														
15 years.......................	53.9	70.3	52.8	71.3	51.7	68.6	54.9	71.8	52.4	73.9	66.8	68.7	74.7	80.2
16 years.......................	41.5	51.8	41.1	58.4	39.6	55.5	43.7	59.2	40.7	61.0	45.7	47.8	52.5	63.2
17 years.......................	29.0	36.0	29.0	44.0	28.0	42.1	31.2	45.7	28.2	44.7	28.0	31.8	37.0	44.8
18 years.......................	17.9	23.1	18.1	29.3	17.6	28.6	19.9	32.4	16.8	27.5	16.1	20.1	20.8	28.1
19 years.......................	10.9	14.8	11.1	19.2	10.9	19.0	12.3	21.6	10.2	17.3	8.9	12.8	11.3	17.8
20 years.......................	5.6	8.7	5.7	11.1	5.6	11.2	6.2	13.0	5.3	9.4	5.1	7.7	4.7	10.3

NEGRO AND WHITE PERCENTAGE NOT IN SCHOOL BY SINGLE YEARS OF AGE, BY SECTIONS AND SOUTHERN DIVISIONS: 1910.

Table 13

AGE.	PERCENTAGE NOT IN SCHOOL: 1910.													
	United States.		The South.		South Atlantic division.		East South Central division.		West South Central division.		The North.		The West.	
	Negro.	White.	Negro.	White.	Negro.	White.	Negro.	White.	Negro.	White.	Negro.	White.	Negro.	White.
6 to 20 years	52.7	35.5	53.6	37.9	53.0	37.8	52.7	36.9	56.3	38.8	40.8	34.7	39.2	33.5
6 to 9 years	50.7	22.8	52.6	35.2	51.0	32.6	51.6	34.2	57.3	38.9	22.7	16.7	22.8	24.2
10 to 14 years	31.4	8.9	33.0	14.9	32.0	15.0	32.8	15.2	35.6	14.5	10.4	6.4	8.0	6.7
15 to 20 years	73.5	66.3	73.4	60.5	74.2	62.0	71.6	58.6	74.4	60.5	73.7	69.2	69.7	60.5
6 to 9 years:														
6 years	70.3	44.5	72.1	61.5	71.1	58.0	69.8	59.3	77.2	67.4	44.0	35.5	43.8	50.1
7 years	52.3	20.9	54.5	34.9	52.3	31.4	53.2	32.8	60.6	40.4	20.8	14.1	19.7	21.2
8 years	42.1	13.4	44.0	23.1	42.2	21.1	43.6	23.2	48.2	25.1	13.8	8.9	16.3	13.0
9 years	35.4	10.6	37.3	18.1	35.5	16.8	37.7	18.6	40.6	19.2	10.6	7.2	9.7	10.3
10 to 14 years:														
10 years	30.2	6.9	31.9	13.4	30.1	12.1	32.3	13.9	35.1	14.3	8.1	4.0	6.3	6.0
11 years	27.3	6.3	29.0	12.0	27.3	11.4	29.4	12.6	32.2	12.3	6.8	3.9	6.0	5.3
12 years	29.9	7.0	31.4	13.4	30.1	13.2	31.1	13.7	34.5	13.4	8.1	4.2	6.2	5.7
13 years	31.6	8.2	33.2	15.2	32.4	16.0	33.0	15.3	35.2	14.2	10.4	5.4	8.9	6.4
14 years	37.7	15.9	39.3	20.4	39.8	22.4	37.7	20.1	40.6	18.5	18.1	14.6	12.3	9.9
15 to 20 years:														
15 years	46.1	29.7	47.2	28.7	48.3	31.4	45.1	28.2	47.6	26.1	33.2	31.3	25.3	19.8
16 years	58.5	48.2	58.9	41.6	60.4	44.5	56.3	40.8	59.3	39.0	54.3	52.2	47.5	36.8
17 years	71.0	64.0	71.0	56.0	72.0	57.9	68.8	54.3	71.8	55.3	72.0	68.2	63.0	55.2
18 years	82.1	76.9	81.9	70.7	82.4	71.4	80.1	67.6	83.2	72.5	83.9	79.9	79.2	71.9
19 years	89.1	85.2	88.9	80.8	89.1	81.0	87.7	78.4	89.8	82.7	91.1	87.2	88.7	82.2
20 years	94.4	91.3	94.3	88.9	94.4	88.8	93.8	87.0	94.7	90.6	94.9	92.3	95.3	89.7

AGE GROUP 6 TO 14 YEARS.

Perhaps the best index of school attendance of a community is furnished by data for the 6 to 14 year age period. This is the period when there is the least demand or opportunity for wage-earning employment, and the least hindrance to school attendance. With exception of the age 14 years, this period is included, practically, in the period covered by the state laws for compulsory school attendance, where such exist; and as a result, wherever there are any adequate school facilities the presumption is that each child from 6 to 14 years of age is in school unless prevented by sickness or some other abnormal condition. Table 14 presents data for this age group, by racial classes.

Of Negro children 6 to 14 years of age 865,167, or 40.3 per cent, had not attended school at any time during the school year 1909–10. Of this number 841,997 were in the South. The percentage of white children of this age not in school was in the country as a whole 15.3; in the South, 24.4; and in the North, 11.1. Even for the foreign-born white 6 to 14 years of age, the percentage not in school in the country as a whole was only 17.7, although it was much higher in the South, 45.7, where the number of the foreign born is relatively insignificant. In the North the percentage not in school for Negro children 6 to 14 was 15.9, being only slightly larger than the corresponding percentage for white children in the country as a whole. By divisions the highest percentage for Negroes not in school is that of 45.7 in the West South Central division, which happens to be exactly the same

as the percentage for foreign-born whites in the South as a whole, but is markedly above that for foreign-born whites in the South Atlantic and East South Central divisions. In the North and West Negroes rank close with other racial classes in school attendance.

Table 14

SECTION, DIVISION, AND RACIAL CLASS.	CHILDREN 6 TO 14 YEARS OF AGE: 1910.			Percentage.	
	Total.	In school.	Not in school.	In school.	Not in school.
United States	16,832,374	13,706,982	3,125,392	81.4	18.6
Negro	2,146,116	1,280,949	865,167	59.7	40.3
White	14,622,156	12,386,954	2,235,202	84.7	15.3
Native	14,012,387	11,885,146	2,127,241	84.8	15.2
Native parentage	9,946,610	8,305,428	1,641,182	83.5	16.5
Foreign or mixed parentage	4,065,777	3,579,718	486,059	88.0	12.0
Foreign born	609,769	501,808	107,961	82.3	17.7
The South	6,344,089	4,440,259	1,903,830	70.0	30.0
Negro	1,999,643	1,157,646	841,997	57.9	42.1
White	4,322,270	3,267,065	1,055,205	75.6	24.4
Native	4,279,310	3,243,722	1,035,588	75.8	24.2
Native parentage	4,039,263	3,067,810	971,453	75.9	24.1
Foreign or mixed parentage	240,047	175,912	64,135	73.3	26.7
Foreign born	42,960	23,343	19,617	54.3	45.7
The North	9,446,505	8,388,478	1,058,027	88.8	11.2
Negro	140,933	118,571	22,362	84.1	15.9
White	9,290,384	8,258,985	1,031,399	88.9	11.1
Native	8,770,555	7,817,856	952,699	89.1	10.9
Native parentage	5,272,542	4,698,379	574,163	89.1	10.9
Foreign or mixed parentage	3,498,013	3,119,477	378,536	89.2	10.8
Foreign born	519,829	441,129	78,700	84.9	15.1
The West	1,041,780	878,245	163,535	84.3	15.7
Negro	5,540	4,732	808	85.4	14.6
White	1,009,502	860,904	148,598	85.3	14.7
Native	962,522	823,568	138,954	85.6	14.4
Native parentage	634,805	539,239	95,566	84.9	15.1
Foreign or mixed parentage	327,717	284,329	43,388	86.8	13.2
Foreign born	46,980	37,336	9,644	79.5	20.5

DIAGRAM **IV.**—PERCENTAGE IN SCHOOL AND NOT IN SCHOOL OF THE NEGRO AND WHITE POPULATION 10 TO 14 YEARS OF AGE, BY SECTIONS AND SOUTHERN STATES: 1910.

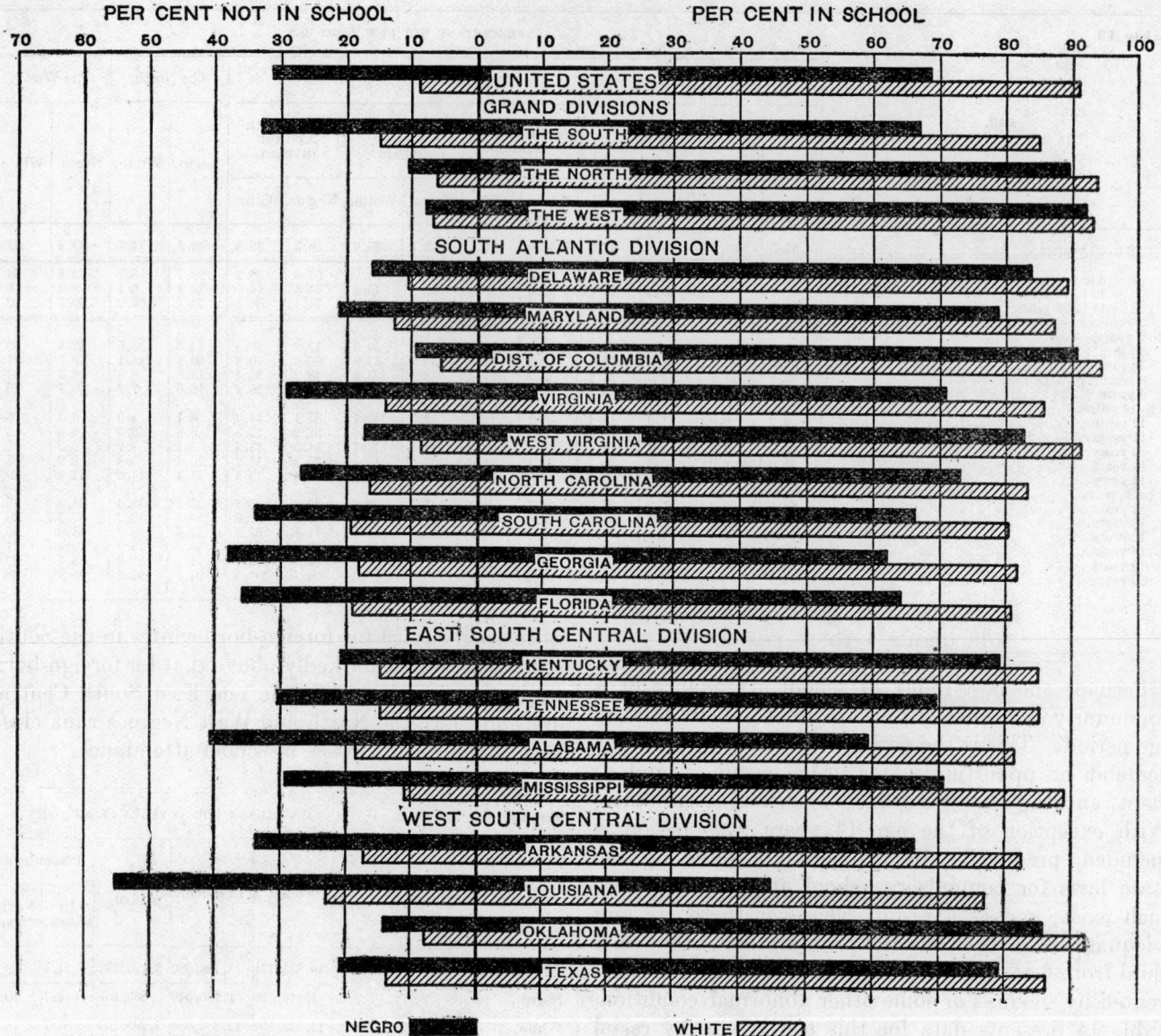

SCHOOL ATTENDANCE BY STATES.

Statistics of school attendance for states are given in Tables 22 to 27 (pp. 391–398), Table 27 covering, for the age 10 to 14, the years 1910, 1900, and 1890. Percentages in school, by sex and age, are given for Southern states in Table 15, which shows also the number of males per 1,000 females in school.

As has been already noted the number of Negro females in school is in excess, sometimes largely in excess, of the number of Negro males. This is true of the country as a whole and of each Southern state for each age period, with the exception of the age periods 10 to 14 and 15 to 20 in the state of Delaware. Likewise the percentage in school for females is higher than the percentage for males, although this higher percentage in school for females does not entirely account for the excess of females in the school population, as becomes evident when the number of each sex not in school is noted. Thus in the 6 to 9 year age period in the country as a whole, the number of girls in school exceeds the number of boys by 14,630, but the number of boys not in school exceeds the number of girls not in school by only 8,712, indicating that a portion of the excess of females in the school population is attributable to the excess of females in the total population of school age. In the 10 to 14 year period the relative excess of females is greater than in the 6 to 9 year period, and in the 15 to 20 year period the number of females in school exceeds the number of males by 52,420, the ratio of males to females in the school population of this age being only 732 to 1,000. Among those not in school of this age, also, the females exceed the males by 22,743. The marked excess of females in this age period is noted in the chapter on age distribution.

Table 15 — NEGRO POPULATION: 1910.

SECTION, DIVISION, AND STATE.	Percentage in school.						Males per 1,000 females in school.		
	6 to 9 years of age.		10 to 14 years of age.		15 to 20 years of age.		6 to 9 years of age.	10 to 14 years of age.	15 to 20 years of age.
	Male.	Female.	Male.	Female.	Male.	Female.			
United States..	48.2	50.5	65.6	71.5	23.8	28.9	942	920	732
The South	46.2	48.6	63.9	70.0	23.7	29.1	940	918	725
South Atlantic	47.8	50.2	64.6	71.4	22.4	28.8	939	909	691
East South Central	47.0	49.7	64.1	70.4	25.7	30.9	938	928	748
West South Central	41.7	43.8	62.2	66.6	23.5	27.5	946	927	764
The North	77.0	77.7	89.4	89.8	25.5	27.1	955	935	814
The West	77.1	77.3	91.7	92.3	27.5	32.9	961	933	764
THE SOUTH.									
South Atlantic:									
Delaware	65.1	65.6	83.3	84.4	31.7	26.0	927	1,106	1,234
Maryland	60.0	61.9	77.5	80.1	22.9	23.2	934	944	886
Dist. of Columbia	74.0	76.1	89.2	91.7	28.7	30.8	912	860	688
Virginia	43.1	45.9	68.3	73.2	23.4	30.5	922	941	707
West Virginia	68.7	69.5	80.8	84.6	18.3	29.7	915	975	802
North Carolina	53.2	54.9	70.3	75.4	33.4	39.7	954	931	765
South Carolina	43.0	45.4	63.2	69.3	24.0	30.5	943	915	695
Georgia	46.3	48.8	57.0	67.3	14.2	21.9	941	860	547
Florida	47.7	50.9	60.8	67.8	18.8	25.0	939	896	664
East South Central:									
Kentucky	58.3	59.9	77.3	80.7	26.3	34.2	961	964	729
Tennessee	47.3	50.3	66.9	72.3	24.5	31.1	938	937	742
Alabama	36.1	39.0	55.7	63.2	22.9	28.0	911	898	710
Mississippi	54.3	57.1	67.5	73.6	28.6	32.6	950	939	786
West South Central:									
Arkansas	48.6	49.7	63.6	68.9	31.0	34.1	959	906	816
Louisiana	28.2	30.6	42.3	46.8	11.7	15.7	923	903	642
Oklahoma	64.9	67.6	84.8	86.8	41.0	42.8	969	956	932
Texas	46.6	48.9	77.0	81.3	26.7	32.4	946	947	747

An excess of females over males in the school population is found in nearly all of the states. The only exceptions are in some of the Northern states and in the state of Delaware, representing in each case a relatively small Negro population.

Among the Southern states West Virginia takes the lead in Negro school attendance for children 6 to 9 years of age, and Oklahoma, for those 10 to 14 years, while Louisiana reports the lowest percentage in each period and for each sex.

Diagram IV represents the percentage in school and not in school of the Negro and white population of sections, and southern divisions and states, for the age 10 to 14 years, in 1910.

URBAN AND RURAL COMMUNITIES.

In Table 28 (p. 399) the statistics of school attendance are given for the population classified as urban and rural. These statistics are summarized by sections in Table 16. It will be recalled that under the census definition the term "urban" covers all cities and incorporated towns with 2,500 or more inhabitants, all other areas, including incorporated places with less than 2,500 inhabitants, all unincorporated towns and villages, and the open country, whether closely or sparsely settled, being regarded as rural.

URBAN AND RURAL SCHOOL ATTENDANCE OF NEGROES AND WHITES, BY SECTIONS: 1910.

Table 16 — POPULATION 6 TO 20 YEARS OF AGE: 1910

SECTION.	Urban.					Rural.				
	Total.	In school.		Percentage distribution.		Total.	In school.		Percentage distribution.	
		Number.	Per cent.	Total.	In school.		Number.	Per cent.	Total.	In school.
NEGRO.										
United States	722,664	373,891	51.7	100.0	100.0	2,699,493	1,245,808	46.1	100.0	100.0
The South	538,291	265,099	49.2	74.5	70.9	2,626,205	1,201,841	45.8	97.3	96.5
The North	176,625	104,043	58.9	24.4	27.8	71,030	42,629	60.0	2.6	3.4
The West	7,748	4,749	61.3	1.1	1.2	2,258	1,338	59.3	0.1	0.1
WHITE.										
United States	10,784,077	6,717,854	62.3	100.0	100.0	13,436,791	8,906,862	66.3	100.0	100.0
The South	1,354,249	804,420	59.4	12.5	12.0	5,533,987	3,475,392	62.8	41.2	39.0
The North	8,665,012	5,410,669	62.4	80.4	80.5	6,959,684	4,797,740	68.9	51.8	53.9
The West	764,816	502,765	65.7	7.1	7.5	943,120	633,730	67.2	7.0	7.1

The total Negro population 6 to 20 years of age, in 1910, was 3,422,157. Of this number, 2,699,493, or 78.9 per cent, were in rural communities and 722,664, or 21.1 per cent, in urban communities. Of the rural population, 1,245,808, or 46.1 per cent, and of the urban population, 373,891, or 51.7 per cent, were in school. The corresponding figures for the whites show that of the total population of school age 55.5 per cent were in rural and 44.5 per cent in urban communities; and that 66.3 per cent of the rural and 62.3 per cent of the urban population were in school.

Taking the country as a whole, therefore, in school attendance the rural Negroes rank lower and the rural whites rank higher, than those in the urban class. Comparing the sections, the percentage in school in both urban and rural communities, for both Negroes and whites, in the South is below the corresponding percentage in the North and West.

In both urban and rural communities the percentages for Negroes correspond more closely to those for whites in the North and West than they do in the South. It is noticeable also that the difference between the percentages for Negroes and whites in the South is far greater in the rural than in the urban districts. Thus the percentage in school in the rural South is 45.8 for Negroes and 62.8 for whites, the difference in the percentages being 17; while in the urban districts the Negro percentage is 49.2 and the white percentage 59.4, the difference being 10.2. In the North where the facilities for the races are more nearly equal, the attendance for Negroes in urban communities is 58.9 per cent and for whites 62.4, the difference being 3.5; and the attendance for Negroes in rural communities is 60 per cent and for whites 68.9, the difference being 8.9.

Table 17 presents data for Negro school attendance in urban and rural communities of the South, North, and West, by age periods.

Table 17

NEGRO POPULATION 6 TO 20 YEARS OF AGE: 1910.

SECTION, DIVISION, AND AGE PERIOD.	Number.				Percentage in school.	
	Urban.		Rural.			
	In school.	Not in school.	In school.	Not in school.	Urban.	Rural.
United States:						
6 to 20 years	373,891	348,773	1,245,808	1,453,685	51.7	46.1
6 to 9 years	120,910	61,832	368,044	440,064	66.2	45.5
10 to 14 years	182,054	43,369	609,941	319,902	80.8	65.6
15 to 20 years	70,927	243,572	267,823	693,719	22.6	27.9
The South:						
6 to 20 years	265,099	273,192	1,201,841	1,424,364	49.2	45.8
6 to 9 years	84,175	52,900	354,369	434,219	61.4	44.9
10 to 14 years	130,186	38,315	588,916	316,563	77.3	65.0
15 to 20 years	50,738	181,977	258,556	673,582	21.8	27.7
South Atlantic—						
6 to 20 years	130,070	135,672	576,904	661,373	48.9	46.6
6 to 9 years	42,188	25,510	174,277	200,047	62.3	46.6
10 to 14 years	63,716	19,857	285,294	144,372	76.2	66.4
15 to 20 years	24,166	90,305	117,333	316,954	21.1	27.0
East South Central—						
6 to 20 years	71,519	71,714	375,711	425,936	49.9	46.9
6 to 9 years	22,136	13,297	109,565	127,141	62.5	46.3
10 to 14 years	34,804	9,842	180,545	95,285	78.0	65.5
15 to 20 years	14,579	48,575	85,601	203,510	23.1	29.6
West South Central—						
6 to 20 years	63,510	65,806	249,226	337,055	49.1	42.5
6 to 9 years	19,851	14,093	70,527	107,031	58.5	39.7
10 to 14 years	31,666	8,616	123,077	76,906	78.6	61.5
15 to 20 years	11,993	43,097	55,622	153,118	21.8	26.6
The North:						
6 to 20 years	104,043	72,582	42,629	28,401	58.9	60.0
6 to 9 years	35,227	8,543	13,285	5,673	80.5	70.1
10 to 14 years	49,661	4,896	20,398	3,250	91.0	86.3
15 to 20 years	19,155	59,143	8,946	19,478	24.5	31.5
The West:						
6 to 20 years	4,749	2,999	1,338	920	61.3	59.3
6 to 9 years	1,508	389	390	172	79.5	69.4
10 to 14 years	2,207	158	627	89	93.3	87.6
15 to 20 years	1,034	2,452	321	659	29.7	32.8

In the country as a whole, and in each section, the percentage attending school in the Negro population is higher for the urban than for the rural communities, in the first two age periods—6 to 9 and 10 to 14 years—and lower in the third—15 to 20 years. For the age period 6 to 9 years the urban school attendance represents a majority of the population of that age in every section of the country, while in the rural districts in every section of the country a majority of the children of this age are still not in school. In the age group 10 to 14 years a majority are in school in both urban and rural districts in each section, the per-

centage in the North rising to 91 for urban and to 86.3 for rural attendance. In the age group 15 to 20 years a great majority in each section are not in school. The explanation of the higher percentage of attendance in rural communities for this last age period is probably to be found in the tendency in the rural districts to commence school later and to continue later than in the urban districts. The higher percentages for urban over rural attendance for children 6 to 9 is probably due in some measure to the difficulty, especially in the remoter rural sections, of getting the younger children to school.

SCHOOL ATTENDANCE IN CITIES.

The statistics for Negro and white school attendance for cities are given in Tables 29 and 30 (pp. 400 and 401).

Table 18

NEGRO POPULATION 6 TO 14 YEARS OF AGE: 1910.

CITY.[1]	Total.	In school.		Number not in school.
		Number.	Per cent.	
New Orleans, La	13,990	9,446	67.5	4,544
Washington, D. C	12,910	10,807	83.7	2,103
Baltimore, Md	11,265	8,509	75.5	2,756
Philadelphia, Pa	9,604	8,051	83.8	1,553
New York, N. Y	8,864	7,783	87.8	1,081
Atlanta, Ga	8,011	5,685	71.0	2,326
Birmingham, Ala	7,982	5,807	72.8	2,175
Richmond, Va	6,927	4,514	65.2	2,413
Memphis, Tenn	6,440	4,317	67.0	2,123
Nashville, Tenn	5,538	4,098	74.0	1,440
Charleston, S. C	5,329	3,470	65.1	1,859
Savannah, Ga	4,917	3,262	66.3	1,655
Louisville, Ky	4,902	4,240	86.5	662
St. Louis, Mo	4,725	3,941	83.4	784
Jacksonville, Fla	4,125	2,996	72.6	1,129
Chicago, Ill	3,840	3,424	89.2	416
Houston, Tex	3,569	2,656	74.4	913
Mobile, Ala	3,451	2,361	68.4	1,090
Norfolk, Va	3,423	2,401	70.1	1,022
Pittsburgh, Pa	3,371	2,833	84.0	538
Montgomery, Ala	3,105	2,064	66.5	1,041
Macon, Ga	3,036	1,963	64.7	1,073
Indianapolis, Ind	2,759	2,496	90.5	263
Augusta, Ga	2,740	1,867	68.1	873
Chattanooga, Tenn	2,486	1,856	74.7	630
Dallas, Tex	2,393	1,738	72.6	655
Shreveport, La	2,353	1,502	63.8	851
Kansas City, Mo	2,251	1,910	84.9	341
Charlotte, N. C	2,135	1,354	63.4	781
Wilmington, N. C	2,067	1,480	71.6	587
Cincinnati, Ohio	2,024	1,807	89.3	21
Fort Worth, Tex	1,956	1,289	65.9	667
Little Rock, Ark	1,941	1,504	77.5	437
Columbia, S. C	1,884	1,247	66.2	637
Portsmouth, Va	1,849	1,225	66.3	624
San Antonio, Tex	1,717	1,238	72.1	479
Lynchburg, Va	1,519	1,059	69.7	460
Lexington, Ky	1,445	1,168	80.8	277
Boston, Mass	1,430	1,337	93.5	93
Roanoke, Va	1,403	1,025	73.1	378
Columbus, Ohio	1,396	1,210	86.7	186
Austin, Tex	1,389	1,093	78.7	296
Muskogee, Okla	1,370	1,007	73.5	363
Wilmington, Del	1,362	1,134	83.3	228
Kansas City, Kans	1,334	1,134	85.0	200
Tampa, Fla	1,289	984	76.3	305
Newark, N. J	1,184	1,076	90.9	108
Galveston, Tex	1,064	816	76.7	248
Waco, Tex	1,056	711	67.3	345
Knoxville, Tenn	1,032	703	68.1	329

[1] Includes cities of 25,000 or more inhabitants having a Negro population 6 to 14 years of age of at least 1,000.

The preceding table (18) gives the total number of Negro children 6 to 14 years of age, the number in school and not in school, and the percentage in school, for each city of 25,000 or more inhabitants which reports 1,000 or more Negro children of the specified age, and Table 20 gives, for these same cities, the percentage of school attendance for both Negroes and whites. In the first table cities are arranged in order of Negro population of specified age, and in the second in order of percentage of attendance.

Of the 50 cities included in the list all but 12 are in the Southern states. In Negro population 6 to 14 years of age, New Orleans leads and Washington, D. C., comes next, while Philadelphia, New York, and St. Louis stand high in the list. In numbers in school, Washington stands first, New Orleans comes next, then Baltimore, Philadelphia, and New York. The 10 cities having tne largest Negro population 6 to 14 years of age, in school and not in school, arranged in the order of the number, are listed in Table 19.

Order.	Table 19 CITY.	Number in school.	Order.	CITY.	Number not in school.
1	Washington, D. C	10,807	1	New Orleans, La	4,544
2	New Orleans, La	9,446	2	Baltimore, Md	2,756
3	Baltimore, Md	8,509	3	Richmond, Va	2,413
4	Philadelphia, Pa	8,051	4	Atlanta, Ga	2,326
5	New York, N. Y	7,783	5	Birmingham, Ala	2,175
6	Birmingham, Ala	5,807	6	Memphis, Tenn	2,123
7	Atlanta, Ga	5,685	7	Washington, D. C	2,103
8	Richmond, Va	4,514	8	Charleston, S. C	1,859
9	Memphis, Tenn	4,317	9	Savannah, Ga	1,655
10	Nashville, Tenn	4,098	10	Philadelphia, Pa	1,553

More significant of the situation, however, are the percentages given in Table 20 for Negroes and whites 6 to 14 years of age.

In northern cities generally the percentage of Negroes attending school is high, and the excess of the percentage for whites over that for Negroes is small. In the case of three cities the percentage for Negroes exceeds that for whites—namely, Chicago, Tampa, and Houston. The greatest excess of the percentage for whites over that for Negroes is 18.8, that shown for Mobile, while in the same state Montgomery shows an excess of only 1.7 and Birmingham of only 2.5. The great divergencies shown by the several cities make it evident that a variety of factors enter into the question of school attendance, and that these factors can not be summed up in any general statement covering the cities as a group, since the statistics for each city represent conditions prevailing locally in that community and, perhaps, nowhere else.

Table 20 CITY.	PERCENTAGE IN SCHOOL FOR CHILDREN 6 TO 14 YEARS OF AGE: 1910.		
	Negro.	White.	Excess of percentage for whites over that for Negroes.
Boston, Mass	93.5	93.7	0.2
Newark, N. J	90.9	92.0	1.1
Indianapolis, Ind	90.5	90.7	0.2
Cincinnati, Ohio	89.3	90.7	1.4
Chicago, Ill	89.2	88.1	[1] 1.1
New York, N. Y	87.8	90.7	2.9
Columbus, Ohio	86.7	89.6	2.9
Louisville, Ky	86.5	88.4	1.9
Kansas City, Kans	85.0	85.7	0.7
Kansas City, Mo	84.9	87.1	2.2
Pittsburgh, Pa	84.0	85.3	1.3
Philadelphia, Pa	83.8	86.3	2.5
Washington, D. C	83.7	87.9	4.2
St. Louis, Mo	83.4	85.6	2.2
Wilmington, Del	83.3	83.6	0.3
Lexington, Ky	80.8	90.3	9.5
Austin, Tex	78.7	78.9	0.2
Little Rock, Ark	77.5	85.7	8.2
Galveston, Tex	76.7	80.4	3.7
Tampa, Fla	76.3	76.1	[1] 0.2
Baltimore, Md	75.5	78.1	2.6
Chattanooga, Tenn	74.7	86.0	12.7
Houston, Tex	74.4	72.0	[1] 2.4
Nashville, Tenn	74.0	79.5	5.5
Muskogee, Okla	73.5	81.5	8.0
Roanoke, Va	73.1	78.5	5.4
Birmingham, Ala	72.8	75.3	2.5
Dallas, Tex	72.6	75.1	2.5
Jacksonville, Fla	72.6	75.5	2.9
San Antonio, Tex	72.1	72.7	0.6
Wilmington, N. C	71.6	81.8	10.2
Atlanta, Ga	71.0	79.6	8.6
Norfolk, Va	70.1	82.4	12.3
Lynchburg, Va	69.7	77.4	7.7
Mobile, Ala	68.4	87.2	18.8
Augusta, Ga	68.1	84.2	16.1
Knoxville, Tenn	68.1	77.0	8.9
New Orleans, La	67.5	80.0	12.5
Waco, Tex	67.3	76.8	9.5
Memphis, Tenn	67.0	82.3	15.3
Montgomery, Ala	66.5	68.2	1.7
Portsmouth, Va	66.3	78.3	12.0
Savannah, Ga	66.3	83.3	17.0
Columbia, S. C	66.2	80.7	14.5
Fort Worth, Tex	65.9	74.0	8.1
Richmond, Va	65.2	79.5	14.3
Charleston, S. C	65.1	81.7	16.6
Macon, Ga	64.7	76.6	11.9
Shreveport, La	63.8	81.2	17.4
Charlotte, N. C	63.4	76.4	13.0

[1] Excess Negro over white.

Table 21 — POPULATION IN CITIES OF 25,000 OR MORE INHABITANTS.

SECTION AND DIVISION.	Negro.			White.		
	In school.		Not in school.	In school.		Not in school.
	Number.	Per cent.		Number.	Per cent.	
6 TO 20 YEARS OF AGE.						
United States	205,478	51.9	190,553	4,404,173	61.0	2,810,181
The South	131,373	49.0	136,894	433,143	57.5	320,516
South Atlantic	68,282	49.1	70,809	210,912	57.1	158,685
East South Central	33,802	49.4	34,606	102,123	59.1	70,620
West South Central	29,289	48.2	31,479	120,108	56.8	91,211
The North	70,768	57.9	51,541	3,669,863	61.2	2,322,474
New England	6,780	67.0	3,340	553,932	65.1	297,374
Middle Atlantic	31,899	56.5	24,543	1,763,163	61.0	1,127,670
East North Central	19,224	58.1	13,853	988,638	59.8	665,923
West North Central	12,865	56.7	9,805	364,130	61.1	232,107
The West	3,337	61.2	2,118	301,167	64.3	167,191
Mountain	1,140	62.9	673	74,363	67.3	36,086
Pacific	2,197	60.3	1,445	226,804	63.4	131,105
6 TO 9 YEARS OF AGE.						
United States	66,782	68.9	30,195	1,543,766	83.4	307,936
The South	41,426	63.2	24,134	139,664	71.5	55,578
South Atlantic	21,673	63.6	12,387	69,842	73.0	25,814
East South Central	10,596	65.7	5,523	32,690	75.0	10,905
West South Central	9,157	59.5	6,224	37,132	66.3	18,859
The North	24,324	80.7	5,810	1,311,419	85.0	230,559
New England	2,367	88.7	302	203,129	90.4	21,501
Middle Atlantic	11,312	79.2	2,968	637,156	84.5	116,787
East North Central	6,555	83.0	1,339	351,005	83.9	67,410
West North Central	4,090	77.3	1,201	120,129	82.9	24,861
The West	1,032	80.4	251	92,683	81.0	21,799
Mountain	360	78.9	96	23,963	82.8	4,961
Pacific	672	81.3	155	68,720	80.3	16,838
10 TO 14 YEARS OF AGE.						
United States	100,277	83.2	20,314	2,091,139	92.4	171,482
The South	64,758	79.2	16,982	207,611	87.8	28,870
South Atlantic	33,669	79.1	8,886	100,837	87.0	15,076
East South Central	16,364	79.1	4,315	48,632	90.2	5,305
West South Central	14,725	79.6	3,781	58,142	87.3	8,489
The North	33,946	91.3	3,231	1,750,114	92.9	133,823
New England	3,133	95.0	164	255,047	94.0	16,183
Middle Atlantic	15,547	90.7	1,588	850,334	92.8	66,282
East North Central	9,196	91.6	841	476,357	92.5	38,390
West North Central	6,070	90.5	638	168,376	92.8	12,968
The West	1,573	94.0	101	133,414	93.8	8,789
Mountain	549	93.1	41	32,924	94.4	1,937
Pacific	1,024	94.5	60	100,490	93.6	6,852
15 TO 20 YEARS OF AGE.						
United States	38,419	21.5	140,044	769,268	24.8	2,330,763
The South	25,189	20.8	95,778	85,868	26.7	236,068
South Atlantic	12,940	20.7	49,536	40,233	25.5	117,795
East South Central	6,842	21.6	24,768	20,801	27.7	54,410
West South Central	5,407	20.1	21,474	24,834	28.0	63,863
The North	12,498	22.7	42,500	608,330	23.7	1,958,092
New England	1,280	30.8	2,874	95,756	26.9	259,690
Middle Atlantic	5,040	20.1	19,987	275,673	22.6	944,001
East North Central	3,473	22.9	11,673	161,276	22.4	560,123
West North Central	2,705	25.3	7,966	75,625	28.0	194,278
The West	732	29.3	1,766	75,070	35.5	136,603
Mountain	231	30.1	536	17,476	37.5	29,188
Pacific	501	28.9	1,230	57,594	34.9	107,415

In Table 21 the statistics of Negro and white school attendance in the aggregate population of cities of 25,000 or more inhabitants, for the entire age period 6 to 20 years, and for the included periods, are presented by sections and divisions. The detail shown in this table for the aggregate population living in cities of 25,000 or more inhabitants is shown, for the individual cities, in Table 30 (p. 401).

Comparison of the percentages in Table 21 with those in Table 16, preceding, shows that the ratios of school attendance for this class of cities do not differ materially from those for the urban population as a whole. The percentage of attendance in the North is higher than that in the South for both Negroes and whites, in each period, except that in the 15 to 20 year period the reverse is true for the whites—due probably to the greater number of foreigners and to the greater opportunities for industrial employment in the North.

In cities of 25,000 or more inhabitants in the South, there were among Negro children 6 to 9 years of age, 24,134 not in school, forming 36.8 per cent of the Negro population of that age; of those 10 to 14 years of age, 16,982, or 20.8 per cent were not attending school; and of those 15 to 20 years of age, 95,778, or 79.2 per cent; making a total not in school of 136,894, or 49 per cent for the population 6 to 20 years of age. The corresponding percentages not in school for the North were 19.3 (as compared with 36.8 in the South), 8.7 (as compared with 20.8 in the South), and 77.3 (as compared with 79.2 in the South), or for the entire period, 57.9 (as compared with 49 in the South).

GENERAL CONCLUSION.

Reviewing the situation as a whole, while it is true that the proportion of Negro children not in school is large, not only in rural communities, but even in large cities; and although in the South, the proportion of Negroes not in school greatly exceeds the corresponding proportion of whites, still the data for school attendance presented in this chapter establishes the fact of rapid improvement in the condition of Negroes in the South. That there should have been an increase of 561,243 in the number of Negroes in school in the United States in 1910 as compared with 1900, while the increase in population of corresponding age was very slight, is important; that of this number 533,506 should be in the South, including 216,872 children 5 to 9 years of age, is most significant. Should the next census show a similar advance, the Negro race in its school attendance will not stand far behind the white.

Table 22.—NEGROES IN SCHOOL AND NOT IN SCHOOL, BY AGE PERIODS, BY DIVISIONS AND STATES: 1910.

[Percentage not shown where base is less than 100.]

DIVISION AND STATE.	Total all ages.	NEGRO POPULATION: 1910.												Number under 6 years of age in school.	Number 21 years of age and over in school.
		6 to 20 years of age.			6 to 9 years of age.			10 to 14 years of age.			15 to 20 years of age.				
		In school.		Not in school.	In school.		Not in school.	In school.		Not in school.	In school.		Not in school.		
		Number.	Per cent.		Number.	Per cent.		Number.	Per cent.		Number.	Per cent.			
UNITED STATES...	9,827,763	1,619,699	47.3	1,802,458	488,954	49.3	501,896	791,995	68.6	363,271	338,750	26.5	937,291	28,560	22,391
GEOGRAPHIC DIVISIONS:															
New England......	66,306	10,201	65.6	5,338	3,564	86.6	550	4,800	94.3	292	1,837	29.0	4,496	453	201
Middle Atlantic.....	417,870	54,780	57.5	40,414	19,107	77.9	5,406	26,760	90.3	2,888	8,913	21.7	32,120	1,795	1,039
East North Central..	300,836	44,462	61.0	28,375	14,464	79.6	3,696	21,102	91.0	2,082	8,896	28.2	22,597	623	1,050
West North Central.	242,662	37,229	58.1	26,856	11,377	71.4	4,564	17,397	85.8	2,884	8,455	30.3	19,408	648	716
South Atlantic......	4,112,488	706,974	47.0	797,045	216,465	49.0	225,557	349,010	68.0	164,229	141,499	25.8	407,259	10,551	9,152
East South Central..	2,652,513	447,230	47.3	497,650	131,701	48.4	140,438	215,349	67.2	105,127	100,180	28.4	252,085	9,893	5,665
West South Central.	1,984,426	312,736	43.7	402,861	90,378	42.7	121,124	154,743	64.4	85,522	67,615	25.6	196,215	4,466	4,491
Mountain...........	21,467	2,531	60.7	1,639	816	74.7	277	1,166	90.7	120	549	30.7	1,242	51	37
Pacific.............	29,195	3,556	60.9	2,280	1,082	79.2	284	1,668	92.9	127	806	30.1	1,869	80	40
NEW ENGLAND:															
Maine...............	1,363	224	63.1	131	58	....	8	108	92.3	9	58	33.7	114	10	2
New Hampshire....	564	77	55.8	61	27	....	7	35	....	5	15	....	49	2	1
Vermont...........	1,621	131	52.2	120	48	....	9	65	95.1	7	18	14.8	104	8	1
Massachusetts.....	38,055	5,850	66.5	2,947	2,043	88.1	275	2,763	95.1	142	1,044	29.2	2,530	273	144
Rhode Island.......	9,529	1,424	62.5	853	503	82.6	106	657	92.0	57	264	27.7	690	56	26
Connecticut........	15,174	2,495	67.1	1,226	885	85.9	145	1,172	94.2	72	438	30.3	1,009	104	27
MIDDLE ATLANTIC:															
New York..........	134,191	15,192	55.9	12,000	5,252	80.5	1,274	7,344	92.6	586	2,596	20.4	10,140	556	421
New Jersey........	89,760	12,892	59.1	8,940	4,626	80.8	1,096	6,170	89.7	708	2,096	22.7	7,136	586	170
Pennsylvania.......	193,919	26,696	57.8	19,474	9,229	75.2	3,036	13,246	89.3	1,594	4,221	22.1	14,844	653	448
EAST NORTH CENTRAL:															
Ohio..............	111,452	17,233	61.9	10,597	5,458	80.4	1,333	8,284	92.4	680	3,491	28.9	8,584	214	273
Indiana...........	60,320	9,699	62.3	5,861	3,277	83.0	670	4,555	91.4	429	1,867	28.2	4,762	91	321
Illinois...........	109,049	14,572	58.7	10,253	4,734	75.7	1,518	6,902	88.9	866	2,936	27.2	7,869	228	378
Michigan..........	17,115	2,561	64.1	1,433	869	85.1	152	1,184	92.8	92	508	29.9	1,189	80	69
Wisconsin.........	2,900	397	63.2	231	126	84.6	23	177	92.2	15	94	32.8	193	10	9
WEST NORTH CENTRAL:															
Minnesota.........	7,084	781	65.7	408	230	83.9	44	354	94.4	21	197	36.5	343	21	36
Iowa..............	14,973	2,495	64.5	1,371	921	87.5	132	1,105	90.9	110	469	29.3	1,129	117	76
Missouri..........	157,452	22,794	54.7	18,888	6,907	67.2	3,368	10,904	82.7	2,286	4,983	27.4	13,234	293	351
North Dakota......	617	60	58.3	43	18	....	8	25	....	5	17	....	30	2	5
South Dakota......	817	122	66.3	62	41	....	7	54	....	8	27	....	47	1	2
Nebraska..........	7,689	930	61.5	582	316	82.9	65	404	92.2	34	210	30.3	483	53	30
Kansas............	54,030	10,047	64.6	5,502	2,944	75.8	940	4,551	91.6	420	2,552	38.1	4,142	161	216
SOUTH ATLANTIC:															
Delaware..........	31,181	5,815	57.7	4,263	1,721	65.4	911	2,968	83.8	572	1,126	28.8	2,780	88	73
Maryland..........	232,250	38,417	52.5	34,813	12,578	60.9	8,060	19,390	78.8	5,205	6,449	23.0	21,548	544	409
District of Columbia	94,446	14,000	59.3	9,593	4,278	75.1	1,421	6,529	90.5	682	3,193	29.9	7,490	535	541
Virginia...........	671,096	114,346	47.2	128,067	31,378	44.6	39,054	58,989	70.7	24,406	23,979	27.1	64,607	1,026	1,286
West Virginia......	64,173	9,806	53.1	8,675	3,442	69.1	1,538	4,485	82.7	939	1,879	23.3	6,198	181	190
North Carolina.....	697,843	143,039	54.2	120,986	43,060	54.1	36,558	65,140	72.9	24,276	34,839	36.7	60,152	1,704	2,024
South Carolina.....	835,843	151,726	45.8	179,703	43,268	44.2	54,516	75,713	66.2	38,628	32,745	27.4	86,559	2,452	1,832
Georgia...........	1,176,987	185,191	42.1	254,294	61,854	47.6	68,187	94,404	62.1	57,625	28,933	18.4	128,482	2,959	2,002
Florida............	308,669	44,634	44.1	56,651	14,886	49.3	15,312	21,392	64.3	11,896	8,356	22.1	29,443	1,062	795
EAST SOUTH CENTRAL:															
Kentucky..........	261,656	44,060	53.7	37,916	12,445	59.1	8,610	21,316	79.0	5,668	10,299	30.3	23,638	483	698
Tennessee.........	473,088	77,153	47.2	86,244	21,761	48.8	22,822	37,134	69.6	16,210	18,258	27.9	47,212	863	1,099
Alabama...........	908,282	133,191	40.7	193,985	36,191	37.5	60,228	66,622	59.4	45,507	30,378	25.6	88,250	1,714	1,731
Mississippi........	1,009,487	192,826	51.8	179,505	61,304	55.7	48,778	90,277	70.5	37,742	41,245	30.7	92,985	6,833	2,137
WEST SOUTH CENTRAL:															
Arkansas..........	442,891	77,467	48.6	81,964	22,963	49.2	23,741	34,909	66.3	17,770	19,595	32.6	40,453	1,231	1,401
Louisiana.........	713,874	73,478	28.9	181,102	22,359	29.4	53,693	38,295	44.6	47,622	12,824	13.8	79,787	1,327	920
Oklahoma.........	137,612	31,083	63.8	17,635	9,678	66.2	4,932	13,903	85.8	2,305	7,502	41.9	10,398	664	427
Texas.............	690,049	130,708	51.7	122,160	35,378	47.7	38,758	67,636	79.1	17,825	27,694	29.7	65,577	1,244	1,743
MOUNTAIN:															
Montana...........	1,834	184	61.3	116	52	....	19	86	....	9	46	34.3	88	2	6
Idaho.............	651	50	....	39	16	....	10	17	....	2	17	....	27	1	1
Wyoming..........	2,235	142	49.7	144	64	....	17	52	....	4	26	17.4	123	3	2
Colorado..........	11,453	1,548	62.7	920	470	75.6	152	750	92.9	57	328	31.6	711	31	22
New Mexico.......	1,628	214	59.0	149	68	65.4	36	87	82.1	19	59	38.6	94	8	3
Arizona...........	2,009	251	60.3	165	93	75.0	31	114	87.7	16	44	27.2	118	4	....
Utah..............	1,144	112	57.1	84	41	....	10	45	....	10	26	....	64	1	2
Nevada...........	513	30	....	22	12	....	2	15	....	3	3	....	17	1	1
PACIFIC:															
Washington........	6,058	515	56.8	391	146	70.9	60	244	89.1	30	125	29.3	301	1	4
Oregon............	1,492	105	53.0	93	34	....	14	45	....	9	26	....	70	....	4
California..........	21,645	2,936	62.0	1,796	902	81.1	210	1,379	94.0	88	655	30.4	1,498	79	32

TABLE **23.**—NEGRO MALES AND FEMALES IN SCHOOL AND NOT IN SCHOOL, BY AGE PERIODS, BY DIVISIONS AND STATES: 1910.

DIVISION AND STATE.	NEGRO POPULATION: 1910.															
	6 to 9 years of age.				10 to 14 years of age.				15 to 20 years of age.				Number under 6 years of age in school.		Number 21 years of age and over in school.	
	Number in school.		Number not in school.		Number in school.		Number not in school.		Number in school.		Number not in school.					
	Male.	Female.	Male.	Female.	Male.	Female.	Male.	Female.	Male.	Female.	Male.	Female.	Male.	Female.	Male.	Female.
UNITED STATES	237,162	251,792	255,304	246,592	379,486	412,509	198,588	164,683	143,165	195,585	457,274	480,017	13,452	15,108	10,604	11,787
GEOGRAPHIC DIVISIONS:																
New England	1,736	1,828	276	274	2,288	2,512	146	146	775	1,062	2,106	2,390	218	235	110	91
Middle Atlantic	9,288	9,819	2,645	2,761	12,806	13,954	1,330	1,558	4,054	4,859	14,068	18,052	856	939	566	473
East North Central	7,065	7,399	1,860	1,836	10,344	10,758	1,033	1,049	4,007	4,889	11,060	11,537	306	317	685	365
West North Central	5,605	5,772	2,292	2,272	8,409	8,988	1,512	1,372	3,773	4,682	9,654	9,754	303	345	402	314
South Atlantic	104,856	111,609	114,736	110,821	166,162	182,848	91,065	73,164	57,813	83,686	199,893	207,366	4,936	5,615	4,067	5,085
East South Central	63,749	67,952	71,766	68,672	103,657	111,692	58,085	47,042	42,880	57,300	123,839	128,246	4,690	5,203	2,619	3,046
West South Central	43,933	46,445	61,452	59,672	74,452	80,291	45,293	40,229	29,276	38,339	95,109	101,106	2,084	2,382	2,111	2,380
Mountain	397	419	146	131	586	580	56	64	243	306	584	658	20	31	23	14
Pacific	533	549	131	153	782	886	68	59	344	462	961	908	39	41	21	19
NEW ENGLAND:																
Maine	24	34	5	3	53	55	3	6	18	40	60	54	3	7	2	....
New Hampshire	15	12	2	5	16	19	2	3	6	9	23	26	1	1	1	....
Vermont	22	26	4	5	32	33	3	4	9	9	70	34	4	4	1	....
Massachusetts	1,008	1,035	144	131	1,318	1,445	74	68	454	590	1,192	1,338	145	128	77	67
Rhode Island	244	259	50	56	307	350	22	35	118	146	325	365	16	40	14	12
Connecticut	423	462	71	74	562	610	42	30	170	268	436	573	49	55	15	12
MIDDLE ATLANTIC:																
New York	2,531	2,721	596	678	3,481	3,863	261	325	1,134	1,462	4,417	5,723	263	293	241	180
New Jersey	2,246	2,380	532	564	3,033	3,137	327	381	1,005	1,091	3,225	3,911	269	317	73	97
Pennsylvania	4,511	4,718	1,517	1,519	6,292	6,954	742	852	1,915	2,306	6,426	8,418	324	329	252	196
EAST NORTH CENTRAL:																
Ohio	2,650	2,808	667	666	4,078	4,206	325	355	1,606	1,885	4,100	4,484	106	108	160	113
Indiana	1,626	1,651	358	312	2,185	2,370	225	204	832	1,035	2,365	2,397	46	45	233	88
Illinois	2,306	2,428	751	767	3,401	3,501	431	435	1,301	1,635	3,915	3,954	110	118	235	143
Michigan	424	445	77	75	595	589	45	47	222	286	599	590	40	40	50	19
Wisconsin	59	67	7	16	85	92	7	8	46	48	81	112	4	6	7	2
WEST NORTH CENTRAL:																
Minnesota	111	119	20	24	170	184	8	13	92	105	175	168	8	13	30	6
Iowa	459	462	75	57	527	578	64	46	201	268	578	551	52	65	55	21
Missouri	3,384	3,523	1,679	1,689	5,262	5,642	1,206	1,080	2,238	2,745	6,486	6,748	153	140	188	163
North Dakota	11	7	4	4	14	11	3	2	7	10	13	17	....	2	3	2
South Dakota	24	17	4	3	27	27	4	4	10	17	22	25	1	....	2	....
Nebraska	173	143	37	28	195	209	15	19	82	128	234	249	27	26	19	11
Kansas	1,443	1,501	473	467	2,214	2,337	212	208	1,143	1,409	2,146	1,996	62	99	105	111
SOUTH ATLANTIC:																
Delaware	828	893	443	468	1,559	1,409	312	260	622	504	1,343	1,437	42	46	37	36
Maryland	6,076	6,502	4,058	4,002	9,416	9,974	2,728	2,477	3,029	3,420	10,199	11,349	245	299	209	200
District of Columbia	2,041	2,237	718	703	3,019	3,510	365	317	1,301	1,892	3,234	4,256	239	296	277	264
Virginia	15,053	16,325	19,837	19,217	28,602	30,387	13,300	11,106	9,930	14,049	32,532	32,075	476	550	607	679
West Virginia	1,645	1,797	749	789	2,214	2,271	527	412	836	1,043	3,724	2,474	89	92	97	93
North Carolina	21,024	22,036	18,465	18,093	31,405	33,735	13,249	11,027	15,102	19,737	30,132	30,020	817	887	846	1,178
South Carolina	20,996	22,272	27,782	26,734	36,183	39,530	21,102	17,526	13,424	19,321	42,441	44,118	1,201	1,251	789	1,043
Georgia	29,985	31,869	34,784	33,403	43,656	50,748	32,954	24,671	10,234	18,699	61,894	66,588	1,344	1,615	854	1,148
Florida	7,208	7,678	7,900	7,412	10,108	11,284	6,528	5,368	3,335	5,021	14,394	15,049	483	579	351	444
EAST SOUTH CENTRAL:																
Kentucky	6,100	6,345	4,368	4,242	10,461	10,855	3,079	2,589	4,341	5,958	12,195	11,443	231	252	309	389
Tennessee	10,531	11,230	11,735	11,087	17,963	19,171	8,875	7,335	7,774	10,484	23,944	23,268	399	464	550	549
Alabama	17,248	18,943	30,545	29,683	31,522	35,100	25,108	20,399	12,614	17,764	42,488	45,762	790	924	805	926
Mississippi	29,870	31,434	25,118	23,660	43,711	46,566	21,023	16,719	18,151	23,094	45,212	47,773	3,270	3,563	955	1,182
WEST SOUTH CENTRAL:																
Arkansas	11,239	11,724	11,867	11,874	16,590	18,319	9,492	8,278	8,805	10,790	19,628	20,825	584	647	730	671
Louisiana	10,732	11,627	27,274	26,419	18,174	20,121	24,757	22,865	5,014	7,810	37,781	42,006	639	688	407	513
Oklahoma	4,763	4,915	2,578	2,354	6,794	7,109	1,221	1,084	3,619	3,883	5,211	5,187	306	358	195	232
Texas	17,199	18,179	19,733	19,025	32,894	34,742	9,823	8,002	11,838	15,856	32,489	33,088	555	689	779	964
MOUNTAIN:																
Montana	27	25	11	8	46	40	6	3	21	25	39	49	2	....	2	4
Idaho	7	9	6	4	13	4	1	1	7	10	15	12	....	1	1	....
Wyoming	33	31	6	11	33	19	1	3	10	16	73	50	1	2	2	....
Colorado	234	236	77	75	364	386	29	28	148	180	330	381	13	18	14	8
New Mexico	31	37	17	19	39	48	9	10	28	31	46	48	1	7	2	1
Arizona	44	49	21	10	59	55	6	10	19	25	44	74	3	....	....	....
Utah	17	24	7	3	25	20	3	7	9	17	29	35	....	1	2	....
Nevada	4	8	1	1	7	8	1	2	1	2	8	9	....	1	....	1
PACIFIC:																
Washington	77	69	22	38	125	119	12	18	51	74	165	136	....	1	1	3
Oregon	17	17	7	7	18	27	5	4	12	14	37	33	....	....	4	....
California	439	463	102	108	639	740	51	37	281	374	759	739	39	40	16	16

TABLE 24.—CHILDREN 6 TO 14 YEARS OF AGE IN SCHOOL AND NOT IN SCHOOL, BY CLASS OF POPULATION, BY DIVISIONS AND STATES: 1910.

[Percentage not shown where base is less than 100.]

DIVISION AND STATE.	CHILDREN 6 TO 14 YEARS OF AGE: 1910.											
	Negro.			Total white.			Native white.			Foreign-born white.		
	In school.		Number not in school.	In school.		Number not in school.	In school.		Number not in school.	In school.		Number not in school.
	Number.	Per cent.		Number.	Per cent.		Number.	Per cent.		Number.	Per cent.	
UNITED STATES	1,280,949	59.7	865,167	12,386,954	84.7	2,235,202	11,885,146	84.8	2,127,241	501,808	82.3	107,961
GEOGRAPHIC DIVISIONS:												
New England	8,364	90.9	842	929,437	91.9	81,773	852,489	92.4	70,266	76,948	87.0	11,507
Middle Atlantic	45,867	84.7	8,294	2,750,359	88.4	359,369	2,524,486	88.7	320,591	225,873	85.3	38,778
East North Central	35,566	86.0	5,778	2,735,634	89.2	331,851	2,637,538	89.4	313,603	98,096	84.3	18,248
West North Central	28,774	79.4	7,448	1,843,555	87.7	258,406	1,803,343	87.9	248,239	40,212	79.8	10,167
South Atlantic	565,475	59.2	389,786	1,263,149	76.8	380,971	1,252,675	76.9	376,864	10,474	71.8	4,107
East South Central	347,050	58.6	245,565	926,257	75.9	293,843	924,069	75.9	292,924	2,188	70.4	919
West South Central	245,121	54.3	206,646	1,077,659	73.9	380,391	1,066,978	74.5	365,800	10,681	42.3	14,591
Mountain	1,982	83.3	397	363,877	83.4	72,232	350,533	83.8	67,553	13,344	74.0	4,679
Pacific	2,750	87.0	411	497,027	86.7	76,366	473,035	86.9	71,401	23,992	82.9	4,965
NEW ENGLAND:												
Maine	166	90.7	17	104,379	89.2	12,635	98,801	89.7	11,328	5,578	81.0	1,307
New Hampshire	62	......	12	59,976	91.2	5,770	55,418	91.7	4,996	4,558	85.5	774
Vermont	113	87.6	16	53,225	92.9	4,054	50,612	93.1	3,741	2,613	89.3	313
Massachusetts	4,806	92.0	417	477,465	92.9	36,592	435,524	93.4	30,937	41,941	88.1	5,655
Rhode Island	1,160	87.7	163	74,551	88.9	9,344	66,195	89.7	7,564	8,356	82.4	1,780
Connecticut	2,057	90.5	217	159,841	92.3	13,378	145,939	92.6	11,700	13,902	89.2	1,678
MIDDLE ATLANTIC:												
New York	12,596	87.1	1,860	1,268,084	90.1	139,805	1,127,787	90.3	121,175	140,297	88.3	18,630
New Jersey	10,796	85.7	1,804	361,927	88.7	46,052	333,955	89.2	40,637	27,972	83.8	5,415
Pennsylvania	22,475	82.9	4,630	1,120,348	86.6	173,512	1,062,744	87.0	158,779	57,604	79.6	14,733
EAST NORTH CENTRAL:												
Ohio	13,742	87.2	2,013	680,858	89.9	76,611	659,179	90.1	72,491	21,679	84.0	4,120
Indiana	7,832	87.7	1,099	403,365	88.2	53,769	399,388	88.3	52,814	3,977	80.6	955
Illinois	11,636	83.0	2,384	826,010	87.9	113,698	785,562	88.1	105,871	40,448	83.8	7,827
Michigan	2,053	89.4	244	428,497	90.7	43,702	409,064	90.9	40,735	19,433	86.8	2,967
Wisconsin	303	88.9	38	396,904	90.0	44,071	384,345	90.2	41,692	12,559	84.1	2,379
WEST NORTH CENTRAL:												
Minnesota	584	90.0	65	343,921	88.9	42,909	331,581	89.0	40,905	12,340	86.0	2,004
Iowa	2,026	89.3	242	364,939	90.7	37,560	360,075	90.8	36,494	4,864	82.0	1,066
Missouri	17,811	75.9	5,654	486,968	85.5	82,291	480,754	85.6	80,808	6,214	80.7	1,483
North Dakota	43	......	13	91,161	80.9	21,522	84,283	81.9	18,577	6,878	70.0	2,945
South Dakota	95	86.4	15	91,581	84.0	17,425	89,072	84.4	16,491	2,509	72.9	934
Nebraska	720	87.9	99	200,104	90.3	21,572	196,130	90.4	20,878	3,974	85.1	694
Kansas	7,495	84.6	1,360	264,881	88.3	35,127	261,448	88.5	34,086	3,433	76.7	1,041
SOUTH ATLANTIC:												
Delaware	4,689	76.0	1,483	23,565	83.2	4,749	23,033	83.4	4,580	532	75.9	169
Maryland	31,968	70.7	13,265	157,261	82.5	33,356	153,325	82.7	32,082	3,936	75.5	1,274
District of Columbia	10,807	83.7	2,103	27,941	87.9	3,840	27,159	88.0	3,717	782	86.4	123
Virginia	90,367	58.7	63,460	210,591	73.4	76,382	209,585	73.4	75,978	1,006	71.3	404
West Virginia	7,927	76.2	2,477	196,139	82.8	40,787	194,261	83.0	39,824	1,878	66.1	963
North Carolina	108,200	64.0	60,834	248,022	75.7	79,665	247,808	75.7	79,549	214	64.8	116
South Carolina	118,981	56.1	93,144	104,937	72.2	40,363	104,773	72.2	40,300	164	72.2	63
Georgia	156,258	55.4	125,812	230,473	74.9	77,164	229,960	74.9	77,002	513	76.0	162
Florida	36,278	57.1	27,208	64,220	72.3	24,665	62,771	72.5	23,832	1,449	63.5	833
EAST SOUTH CENTRAL:												
Kentucky	33,761	70.3	14,278	322,830	76.7	98,244	322,227	76.7	98,127	603	83.8	117
Tennessee	58,895	60.1	39,032	269,551	75.4	88,172	268,934	75.3	88,007	617	78.9	165
Alabama	102,813	49.3	105,735	188,438	70.2	79,845	187,737	70.2	79,548	701	70.2	297
Mississippi	151,581	63.7	86,520	145,438	84.1	27,582	145,171	84.2	27,242	267	44.0	340
WEST SOUTH CENTRAL:												
Arkansas	57,872	58.2	41,511	183,982	74.9	61,808	183,600	74.9	61,506	382	55.8	302
Louisiana	60,654	37.4	101,315	139,433	68.3	64,698	138,134	68.5	63,434	1,299	50.7	1,264
Oklahoma	23,581	76.5	7,237	254,173	82.3	54,542	253,053	82.4	54,184	1,120	75.8	358
Texas	103,014	64.5	56,583	500,071	71.5	199,343	492,191	72.5	186,676	7,880	38.4	12,667
MOUNTAIN:												
Montana	138	83.1	28	45,634	84.2	8,535	43,636	84.7	7,906	1,998	76.1	629
Idaho	33	......	12	49,264	82.5	10,473	48,466	82.6	10,224	798	76.2	249
Wyoming	116	84.7	21	17,458	84.8	3,126	16,785	85.2	2,918	673	76.4	208
Colorado	1,220	85.4	209	111,081	86.8	16,951	106,490	87.0	15,923	4,591	81.7	1,028
New Mexico	155	73.8	55	46,982	76.2	14,661	46,081	76.7	13,969	901	56.6	692
Arizona	207	81.5	47	21,115	75.1	7,001	18,797	77.2	5,557	2,318	61.6	1,444
Utah	86	81.1	20	65,038	86.2	10,386	63,164	86.3	10,015	1,874	83.5	371
Nevada	27	......	5	7,305	86.9	1,099	7,114	87.2	1,041	191	76.7	58
PACIFIC:												
Washington	390	81.3	90	145,330	86.1	23,411	138,052	86.2	22,015	7,278	83.9	1,396
Oregon	79	77.5	23	85,283	85.6	14,340	82,814	85.7	13,825	2,469	82.7	515
California	2,281	88.4	298	266,414	87.3	38,615	252,169	87.6	35,561	14,245	82.3	3,054

TABLE **25.**—NEGROES IN SCHOOL AND NOT IN SCHOOL, BY SINGLE YEARS OF AGE, BY DIVISIONS AND STATES: 1910.

[Percentage not shown where base is less than 100.]

DIVISION AND STATE.	6 years of age. In school. Number.	Per cent.	Number not in school.	7 years of age. In school. Number.	Per cent.	Number not in school.	8 years of age. In school. Number.	Per cent.	Number not in school.	9 years of age. In school. Number.	Per cent.	Number not in school.	10 years of age. In school. Number.	Per cent.	Number not in school.
UNITED STATES	78,124	29.7	184,691	120,104	47.7	131,638	146,186	57.9	106,287	144,540	64.6	79,280	169,155	69.8	73,354
GEOGRAPHIC DIVISIONS:															
New England	740	69.7	321	946	88.7	120	926	93.4	65	952	95.6	44	973	96.5	35
Middle Atlantic	3,656	56.3	2,837	4,939	79.9	1,245	5,159	87.4	744	5,353	90.2	580	5,656	93.4	400
East North Central	2,720	57.9	1,981	3,690	82.0	812	4,065	88.8	515	3,989	91.1	388	4,350	93.3	314
West North Central	2,077	49.9	2,086	2,893	72.6	1,090	3,064	79.5	790	3,343	84.8	598	3,488	86.9	525
South Atlantic	34,425	28.9	84,695	53,327	47.7	58,419	64,782	57.8	47,208	63,931	64.5	35,235	76,173	69.9	32,758
East South Central	21,543	30.2	49,853	32,333	46.8	36,818	39,305	56.4	30,418	38,520	62.3	23,349	45,120	67.7	21,547
West South Central	12,593	22.8	42,630	21,494	39.4	33,016	28,398	51.8	26,452	27,893	59.4	19,026	32,800	64.9	17,735
Mountain	158	52.5	143	206	80.5	50	208	77.9	59	244	90.7	25	256	92.4	21
Pacific	212	59.4	145	276	80.2	68	279	88.6	36	315	90.0	35	339	94.7	19
NEW ENGLAND:															
Maine	11		3	11		3	20		2	16			13		
New Hampshire	3		2	9		2	11		2	4		1	7		1
Vermont	11		5	14		2	14		1	9		1	12		2
Massachusetts	440	71.9	172	541	90.5	57	518	94.7	29	544	97.0	17	573	97.4	15
Rhode Island	104	61.5	65	128	85.3	22	136	92.5	11	135	94.4	8	131	94.9	7
Connecticut	171	69.8	74	243	87.7	34	227	91.9	20	244	93.5	17	237	96.0	10
MIDDLE ATLANTIC:															
New York	1,033	60.3	679	1,359	82.5	288	1,427	89.2	173	1,433	91.4	134	1,538	93.5	107
New Jersey	954	64.0	537	1,178	81.4	269	1,241	89.6	144	1,253	89.6	146	1,325	93.1	98
Pennsylvania	1,669	50.7	1,621	2,402	77.7	688	2,491	85.4	427	2,667	89.9	300	2,793	93.5	195
EAST NORTH CENTRAL:															
Ohio	991	57.3	740	1,398	82.5	297	1,581	90.8	161	1,488	91.7	135	1,695	93.9	110
Indiana	563	59.0	391	849	85.6	143	908	91.7	82	957	94.7	54	917	95.3	45
Illinois	955	56.2	745	1,195	77.8	341	1,289	83.8	250	1,295	87.7	182	1,478	91.0	147
Michigan	186	66.4	94	211	88.3	28	249	93.3	18	223	94.9	12	227	95.8	10
Wisconsin	25		11	37		3	38		4	26		5	33		2
WEST NORTH CENTRAL:															
Minnesota	40		22	60		10	61		4	69		8	51		3
Iowa	226	78.7	61	227	86.6	35	247	92.5	20	221	93.2	16	256	95.5	12
Missouri	1,263	45.8	1,495	1,735	68.3	804	1,818	74.9	608	2,091	81.9	461	2,194	83.7	426
North Dakota	4		1	5		1	7		2	2		4	7		1
South Dakota	5		5	9		2	16			11			11		2
Nebraska	56		26	86	85.1	15	79		13	95	89.6	11	92	92.0	8
Kansas	483	50.4	476	771	77.6	223	836	85.4	143	854	89.7	98	877	92.3	73
SOUTH ATLANTIC:															
Delaware	271	40.1	405	433	65.6	227	502	75.4	164	515	81.7	115	598	84.9	106
Maryland	1,914	35.8	3,425	3,154	60.3	2,080	3,657	71.1	1,485	3,853	78.3	1,070	4,160	82.0	915
District of Columbia	853	57.5	631	1,090	73.2	400	1,199	84.4	222	1,136	87.1	168	1,365	92.1	117
Virginia	3,009	17.1	14,595	7,776	41.8	10,832	9,971	56.3	7,739	10,622	64.3	5,888	12,480	71.9	4,874
West Virginia	637	47.5	703	866	69.9	373	994	78.3	275	945	83.5	187	980	87.1	145
North Carolina	7,742	34.7	14,592	10,605	53.6	9,195	12,610	63.2	7,357	12,103	69.1	5,414	13,761	73.2	5,034
South Carolina	6,923	25.9	19,833	10,465	42.6	14,090	13,027	52.2	11,932	12,853	59.7	8,661	16,472	66.2	8,420
Georgia	10,320	29.1	25,102	15,297	46.8	17,399	18,448	55.8	14,623	17,789	61.7	11,063	21,553	67.0	10,634
Florida	2,756	33.8	5,409	3,641	48.8	3,823	4,374	56.2	3,411	4,115	60.7	2,669	4,804	65.7	2,513
EAST SOUTH CENTRAL:															
Kentucky	1,979	36.1	3,499	3,076	59.2	2,120	3,657	69.0	1,641	3,733	73.4	1,350	4,327	80.8	1,031
Tennessee	3,173	26.9	8,628	5,208	47.3	5,794	6,630	58.3	4,746	6,750	64.9	3,654	7,567	70.5	3,161
Alabama	4,341	17.6	20,389	8,872	35.1	16,393	11,459	46.2	13,327	11,519	53.2	10,119	14,098	59.5	9,594
Mississippi	12,050	41.0	17,337	15,177	54.8	12,511	17,559	62.1	10,704	16,518	66.8	8,226	19,128	71.1	7,761
WEST SOUTH CENTRAL:															
Arkansas	4,180	33.1	8,465	5,683	49.0	5,918	6,806	56.3	5,274	6,294	60.6	4,084	7,263	66.8	3,617
Louisiana	3,486	17.1	16,909	5,266	27.4	13,977	6,740	34.6	12,748	6,867	40.6	10,059	8,226	45.5	9,859
Oklahoma	1,875	48.3	2,003	2,411	65.8	1,254	2,820	74.4	971	2,572	78.5	704	2,980	85.5	504
Texas	3,052	16.7	15,253	8,134	40.7	11,867	12,032	61.7	7,459	12,160	74.4	4,179	14,331	79.2	3,755
MOUNTAIN:															
Montana	8		9	10		4	19		4	15		2	17		2
Idaho	3		5	5		1	2		2	6		2	2		
Wyoming	10		10	16		3	14			24		4	14		
Colorado	96	55.5	77	120	82.2	26	116	75.8	37	138	92.0	12	161	94.7	9
New Mexico	14		17	16		9	16		7	22		3	21		4
Arizona	17		16	23		7	27		6	26		2	29		4
Utah	7		7	13			11		3	10			10		1
Nevada	3		2	3			3			3			2		
PACIFIC:															
Washington	17		26	43		14	35		8	51		12	49		5
Oregon	10		8	9		2	6		1	9		3	17		
California	185	62.5	111	224	81.2	52	238	89.8	27	255	92.7	20	273	95.1	14

TABLE 25.—NEGROES IN SCHOOL AND NOT IN SCHOOL, BY SINGLE YEARS OF AGE, BY DIVISIONS AND STATES: 1910—Continued.

[Percentage not shown where base is less than 100.]

DIVISION AND STATE.	NEGRO POPULATION: 1910.														
	11 years of age.			12 years of age.			13 years of age.			14 years of age.			15 years of age.		
	In school.		Number not in school.	In school.		Number not in school.	In school.		Number not in school.	In school.		Number not in school.	In school.		Number not in school.
	Number.	Per cent.		Number.	Per cent.		Number.	Per cent.		Number.	Per cent.		Number.	Per cent.	
UNITED STATES	141,723	72.7	53,325	183,267	70.1	78,033	151,816	68.4	70,045	146,034	62.3	88,514	111,860	53.9	95,695
GEOGRAPHIC DIVISIONS:															
New England	872	97.8	20	1,013	96.4	38	990	95.0	52	952	86.6	147	670	71.7	265
Middle Atlantic	5,000	94.1	316	5,799	93.1	427	5,311	90.2	574	4,994	81.0	1,171	3,443	62.8	2,039
East North Central	4,041	94.2	249	4,473	93.1	329	4,224	91.5	394	4,014	83.5	796	3,182	68.6	1,459
West North Central	3,210	89.7	368	3,797	87.5	544	3,384	85.1	591	3,518	80.4	856	2,855	69.1	1,275
South Atlantic	62,738	72.7	23,518	82,408	69.9	35,498	65,755	67.6	31,577	61,936	60.2	40,878	46,816	51.7	43,809
East South Central	37,810	70.6	15,740	49,876	68.9	22,565	41,431	67.0	20,441	41,112	62.3	24,834	31,919	54.9	26,265
West South Central	27,550	67.8	13,082	35,297	65.5	18,592	30,167	64.8	16,362	28,929	59.4	19,751	22,539	52.4	20,435
Mountain	195	92.0	17	239	91.6	22	228	89.8	26	248	87.9	34	190	75.7	61
Pacific	307	95.3	15	365	95.3	18	326	92.1	28	331	87.6	47	246	73.9	87
NEW ENGLAND:															
Maine	20	....	2	30	....	3	23	....	1	22	....	3	19	....	10
New Hampshire	4	....	1	7	....		9	....		8	....	3	4	....	6
Vermont	15	....		14	....		13	....	1	11	....	4	7	....	8
Massachusetts	508	98.8	6	585	97.0	18	563	95.9	24	534	87.1	79	376	73.6	135
Rhode Island	107	98.2	2	150	93.2	11	144	91.1	14	125	84.5	23	101	68.7	46
Connecticut	218	96.0	9	227	97.4	6	238	95.2	12	252	87.8	35	163	73.1	60
MIDDLE ATLANTIC:															
New York	1,342	95.3	66	1,577	95.2	79	1,455	92.7	115	1,432	86.7	219	998	67.8	473
New Jersey	1,177	93.3	85	1,286	91.9	113	1,174	88.9	146	1,208	82.0	266	791	63.3	459
Pennsylvania	2,481	93.8	165	2,936	92.6	235	2,682	89.5	313	2,354	77.4	686	1,654	59.9	1,107
EAST NORTH CENTRAL:															
Ohio	1,586	95.4	77	1,770	95.0	94	1,690	92.9	129	1,543	85.1	270	1,293	71.0	529
Indiana	881	95.7	40	959	94.4	57	942	91.7	85	856	80.9	202	616	63.1	361
Illinois	1,316	92.0	115	1,448	90.2	158	1,330	88.8	167	1,330	82.7	279	1,060	68.4	489
Michigan	229	93.9	15	264	94.3	16	217	95.6	10	247	85.8	41	175	69.4	77
Wisconsin	29	....	2	32	....	4	45	....	3	38	....	4	38	....	3
WEST NORTH CENTRAL:															
Minnesota	65	....	3	89	....	5	61	....	3	88	....	7	65	....	10
Iowa	217	93.9	14	231	95.1	12	213	89.9	24	188	79.7	48	169	70.4	71
Missouri	1,981	87.3	289	2,395	84.7	434	2,149	81.9	474	2,185	76.7	663	1,771	65.4	936
North Dakota	4	....	1	6	....	1	2	....		6	....	2	4	....	
South Dakota	10	....	1	10	....	1	7	....	2	16	....	2	11	....	4
Nebraska	81	....	7	97	97.0	3	74	....	4	60	....	12	69	....	29
Kansas	852	94.1	53	969	91.7	88	878	91.3	84	975	88.9	122	766	77.3	225
SOUTH ATLANTIC:															
Delaware	539	88.8	68	642	84.8	115	601	85.7	100	588	76.3	183	433	64.4	239
Maryland	3,767	84.6	685	4,319	81.9	955	3,823	78.1	1,074	3,321	67.8	1,576	2,417	54.5	2,015
District of Columbia	1,228	94.2	76	1,458	92.6	116	1,267	91.2	122	1,211	82.8	251	1,061	71.8	416
Virginia	10,651	75.1	3,525	13,924	72.8	5,205	11,184	70.7	4,639	10,750	63.6	6,163	8,119	53.7	7,006
West Virginia	877	86.5	137	963	84.5	176	831	80.6	200	834	74.8	281	626	60.4	411
North Carolina	11,784	76.3	3,653	15,163	74.4	5,212	12,592	72.7	4,732	11,849	67.7	5,645	10,001	62.6	5,975
South Carolina	12,793	69.7	5,552	18,477	68.1	8,658	14,129	67.0	6,956	13,842	60.5	9,042	10,340	53.3	9,065
Georgia	17,199	68.0	8,095	22,482	64.4	12,404	17,389	60.2	11,514	15,781	51.3	14,978	11,026	41.1	15,814
Florida	3,900	69.3	1,727	4,980	65.2	2,657	3,939	63.7	2,240	3,769	57.7	2,759	2,793	49.3	2,868
EAST SOUTH CENTRAL:															
Kentucky	3,880	81.8	862	4,559	80.9	1,077	4,367	79.2	1,150	4,183	73.0	1,548	3,443	63.6	1,974
Tennessee	6,724	73.0	2,490	8,426	71.8	3,312	7,118	68.5	3,274	7,299	64.8	3,973	5,604	55.3	4,522
Alabama	11,605	63.3	6,740	15,776	61.1	10,046	12,675	59.2	8,725	12,468	54.5	10,402	9,487	47.6	10,446
Mississippi	15,601	73.4	5,648	21,115	72.2	8,130	17,271	70.3	7,292	17,162	65.8	8,911	13,385	58.9	9,323
WEST SOUTH CENTRAL:															
Arkansas	6,132	68.3	2,841	7,875	68.0	3,700	6,893	66.1	3,536	6,746	62.3	4,076	5,683	59.0	3,946
Louisiana	6,865	48.7	7,244	9,215	45.9	10,849	7,398	45.2	8,981	6,591	38.1	10,689	4,776	31.2	10,527
Oklahoma	2,483	87.4	359	3,053	86.6	472	2,673	86.0	434	2,714	83.5	536	2,256	78.5	619
Texas	12,070	82.1	2,638	15,154	80.9	3,571	13,203	79.5	3,411	12,878	74.3	4,450	9,824	64.8	5,343
MOUNTAIN:															
Montana	8	....	2	20	....	4	13	....	1	28	....		15	....	4
Idaho	3	....		3	....		4	....	2	5	....		6	....	
Wyoming	5	....	1	11	....	1	7	....	1	15	....	1	8	....	4
Colorado	134	94.4	8	153	94.4	9	152	92.7	12	150	88.8	19	115	75.2	38
New Mexico	11	....	1	19	....	3	21	....	6	15	....	5	19	....	3
Arizona	27	....	2	19	....	2	15	....	2	24	....	6	17	....	10
Utah	5	....	3	6	....	2	15	....	1	9	....	3	8	....	1
Nevada	2	....		8	....	1	1	....	1	2	....		2	....	1
PACIFIC:															
Washington	43	....	7	62	....	5	45	....	7	45	....	6	41	....	6
Oregon	4	....	1	12	....	2	9	....	3	3	....	3	8	....	5
California	260	97.4	7	291	96.4	11	272	93.8	18	283	88.2	38	197	72.2	76

TABLE 25.—NEGROES IN SCHOOL AND NOT IN SCHOOL, BY SINGLE YEARS OF AGE, BY DIVISIONS AND STATES: 1910—Continued.

[Percentage not shown where base is less than 100.

DIVISION AND STATE.	16 years of age.			17 years of age.			18 years of age.			19 years of age.			20 years of age.			Number under 6 years of age in school.	Number 21 years of age and over in school.
	In school.		Number not in school.	In school.		Number not in school.	In school.		Number not in school.	In school.		Number not in school.	In school.		Number not in school.		
	Number.	Per cent.		Number.	Per cent.		Number.	Per cent.		Number.	Per cent.		Number.	Per cent.			
UNITED STATES....	93,055	41.5	131,348	59,090	29.0	144,757	41,507	17.9	189,800	21,110	10.9	172,194	12,128	5.6	203,497	28,560	22,391
GEOGRAPHIC DIVISIONS:																	
New England.........	462	46.3	536	311	30.5	708	193	17.6	905	122	11.1	978	79	6.7	1,104	453	201
Middle Atlantic....	2,443	39.9	3,685	1,327	21.7	4,792	890	12.2	6,390	492	6.4	7,151	318	3.8	8,063	1,795	1,039
East North Central....	2,375	47.6	2,614	1,494	30.4	3,428	960	17.2	4,636	514	9.4	4,977	371	6.3	5,483	623	1,050
West North Central....	2,276	51.4	2,150	1,482	33.5	2,939	981	20.3	3,845	576	11.8	4,306	285	5.5	4,893	648	716
South Atlantic.......	38,806	39.6	59,184	24,259	28.0	62,289	17,560	17.6	82,305	8,955	10.9	73,070	5,103	5.6	86,602	10,551	9,152
East South Central...	27,693	43.7	35,697	17,998	31.2	39,768	12,766	19.9	51,409	6,221	12.3	44,447	3,583	6.2	54,499	9,893	5,665
West South Central...	18,636	40.7	27,153	11,963	28.2	30,398	7,991	16.8	39,676	4,139	10.2	36,550	2,347	5.3	42,003	4,466	4,491
Mountain.............	155	54.0	132	89	33.3	178	60	19.4	250	38	12.1	277	17	4.7	344	51	37
Pacific...............	209	51.5	197	167	39.4	257	106	21.6	384	53	10.8	438	25	4.7	506	80	40
NEW ENGLAND:																	
Maine...............	15	....	15	13	....	21	5	....	19	4	....	24	2	....	25	10	2
New Hampshire......	4	....	2	3	....	6	2	....	13	2	....	11	....	....	11	2	1
Vermont.............	6	....	12	2	....	10	2	....	19	....	....	31	1	....	24	8	1
Massachusetts........	257	47.5	284	187	32.5	389	113	18.5	498	72	11.4	559	39	5.5	665	273	144
Rhode Island........	72	47.7	79	37	24.0	117	27	16.8	134	14	8.8	145	13	7.1	169	56	26
Connecticut.........	108	42.9	144	69	29.5	165	44	16.5	222	30	12.6	208	24	10.3	210	104	27
MIDDLE ATLANTIC:																	
New York...........	719	41.0	1,035	369	20.6	1,419	249	10.8	2,052	161	6.4	2,343	100	3.4	2,818	556	421
New Jersey..........	615	43.5	800	338	23.7	1,088	199	12.0	1,460	97	5.8	1,581	56	3.1	1,748	586	170
Pennsylvania........	1,109	37.5	1,850	620	21.3	2,285	442	13.3	2,878	234	6.8	3,227	162	4.4	3,497	653	448
EAST NORTH CENTRAL:																	
Ohio.................	900	48.6	953	588	30.6	1,335	387	18.0	1,764	195	9.3	1,911	128	5.8	2,092	214	273
Indiana..............	479	43.7	616	343	32.0	730	207	18.3	926	131	11.2	1,043	91	7.7	1,086	91	321
Illinois.............	833	48.1	898	459	28.3	1,161	300	15.3	1,655	160	8.5	1,716	124	6.0	1,950	228	378
Michigan............	139	52.5	126	93	34.3	178	54	17.8	250	25	8.7	261	22	6.9	297	80	69
Wisconsin...........	24	....	21	11	....	24	12	....	41	3	....	46	6	....	58	10	9
WEST NORTH CENTRAL:																	
Minnesota...........	57	....	29	35	....	47	18	....	76	16	....	83	6	5.8	98	21	36
Iowa................	112	47.7	123	74	29.2	179	68	23.3	224	30	10.1	266	16	5.7	266	117	76
Missouri............	1,314	46.4	1,516	859	30.4	1,971	566	17.9	2,593	321	9.9	2,918	152	4.4	3,300	293	351
North Dakota........	4	....	3	4	....	1	3	....	7	2	....	8	....	....	11	2	5
South Dakota........	9	....	8	5	....	4	2	....	10	....	....	8	....	....	13	1	2
Nebraska............	65	57.5	48	37	34.9	69	21	17.5	99	13	11.2	103	5	3.6	135	53	30
Kansas..............	715	62.8	423	468	41.2	668	303	26.6	836	194	17.4	920	106	9.0	1,070	161	216
SOUTH ATLANTIC:																	
Delaware............	298	46.1	348	203	31.8	436	106	15.5	576	62	10.5	527	24	3.5	654	88	73
Maryland............	1,846	39.0	2,882	1,069	23.3	3,527	627	12.6	4,348	342	7.3	4,325	148	3.2	4,451	544	409
District of Columbia..	812	49.9	815	542	33.6	1,070	403	20.6	1,550	233	11.9	1,718	142	6.9	1,921	535	541
Virginia.............	6,583	41.3	9,339	4,246	29.0	10,409	2,787	17.6	13,058	1,515	11.2	11,985	729	5.4	12,810	1,026	1,286
West Virginia........	485	41.3	688	318	26.5	882	229	14.4	1,358	145	9.2	1,433	76	5.1	1,426	181	190
North Carolina.......	8,834	52.2	8,095	6,380	40.4	9,403	5,124	29.4	12,326	2,779	19.7	11,336	1,721	11.7	13,017	1,704	2,024
South Carolina.......	9,473	42.7	12,731	5,566	30.2	12,846	4,212	18.9	18,058	1,997	11.9	14,830	1,157	5.7	19,029	2,452	1,832
Georgia.............	8,215	29.0	20,108	4,555	19.1	19,326	2,969	10.6	25,114	1,354	5.9	21,442	814	3.0	26,678	2,959	2,002
Florida.............	2,260	35.1	4,178	1,380	23.9	4,390	1,103	15.7	5,917	528	8.8	5,474	292	4.2	6,616	1,062	795
EAST SOUTH CENTRAL:																	
Kentucky............	2,820	48.4	3,003	1,819	33.3	3,639	1,213	20.1	4,826	680	12.5	4,746	324	5.6	5,450	483	698
Tennessee...........	4,941	44.1	6,251	3,307	30.5	7,548	2,451	20.5	9,505	1,223	12.0	9,011	732	6.6	10,375	863	1,099
Alabama.............	8,412	38.5	13,435	5,382	27.9	13,939	3,942	18.3	17,652	1,961	11.9	14,474	1,194	6.1	18,304	1,714	1,731
Mississippi..........	11,520	47.0	13,008	7,490	33.8	14,642	5,160	21.0	19,426	2,357	12.7	16,216	1,333	6.1	20,370	6,833	2,137
WEST SOUTH CENTRAL:																	
Arkansas............	5,079	48.5	5,390	3,702	37.6	6,144	2,768	24.6	8,484	1,512	16.6	7,601	851	8.7	8,888	1,231	1,401
Louisiana...........	3,522	21.7	12,740	2,057	14.0	12,607	1,337	8.1	15,112	712	5.0	13,478	420	2.7	15,323	1,327	920
Oklahoma............	1,960	65.8	1,020	1,399	47.6	1,539	1,055	31.9	2,249	526	18.3	2,351	306	10.5	2,620	664	427
Texas...............	8,075	50.2	8,003	4,805	32.2	10,108	2,831	17.0	13,831	1,389	9.6	13,120	770	4.8	15,172	1,244	1,743
MOUNTAIN:																	
Montana.............	14	....	10	7	....	7	7	....	18	2	....	20	1	....	29	2	6
Idaho...............	6	....	4	2	....	5	1	....	4	1	....	4	1	....	10	1	1
Wyoming............	7	....	4	3	....	7	4	....	23	4	....	33	....	....	52	3	2
Colorado............	92	55.8	73	54	33.1	109	32	17.3	153	25	13.4	161	10	5.3	177	31	22
New Mexico..........	14	....	14	9	....	16	11	....	15	4	....	18	2	....	28	8	3
Arizona.............	11	....	18	10	....	18	4	....	22	1	....	25	1	....	25	4	....
Utah................	10	....	7	4	....	13	1	....	12	1	....	13	2	....	18	1	2
Nevada.............	1	....	2	....	....	3	....	....	3	....	....	3	....	....	5	1	1
PACIFIC:																	
Washington..........	38	....	22	21	....	42	10	....	46	11	....	88	4	4.0	97	1	4
Oregon.............	3	....	4	5	....	11	5	....	5	2	....	19	3	....	26	....	4
California...........	168	49.6	171	141	40.9	204	91	21.5	333	40	10.8	331	18	4.5	383	79	32

TABLE 26.—PERCENTAGE OF NEGRO AND WHITE POPULATION 6 TO 20 YEARS OF AGE, IN SCHOOL, BY SINGLE YEARS OF AGE, BY SECTIONS, DIVISIONS, AND SOUTHERN STATES: 1910.

SECTION, DIVISION, STATE, AND RACIAL CLASS.	PERCENTAGE IN SCHOOL AT EACH YEAR OF AGE: 1910.														
	6 years.	7 years.	8 years.	9 years.	10 years.	11 years.	12 years.	13 years.	14 years.	15 years.	16 years.	17 years.	18 years.	19 years.	20 years.
UNITED STATES:															
Negro	29.7	47.7	57.9	64.6	69.8	72.7	70.1	68.4	62.3	53.9	41.5	29.0	17.9	10.9	5.6
White	55.5	79.1	86.6	89.4	93.1	93.7	93.0	91.8	84.1	70.3	51.8	36.0	23.1	14.8	8.7
THE NORTH:															
Negro	56.0	79.2	86.2	89.4	91.9	93.2	91.9	89.6	81.9	66.8	45.7	28.0	16.1	8.9	5.1
White	64.5	85.9	91.1	92.8	96.0	96.1	95.8	94.6	85.4	68.7	47.8	31.8	20.1	12.8	7.7
New England:															
Negro	69.7	88.7	93.4	95.6	96.5	97.8	96.4	95.0	86.6	71.7	46.3	30.5	17.6	11.1	6.7
White	77.5	90.9	94.2	95.1	97.1	97.0	96.8	95.9	83.8	62.9	43.3	30.3	20.2	13.4	8.1
Middle Atlantic:															
Negro	56.3	79.9	87.4	90.2	93.4	94.1	93.1	90.2	81.0	62.8	39.9	21.7	12.2	6.4	3.8
White	63.6	85.6	91.4	93.1	96.0	96.0	95.6	94.2	83.0	63.5	40.9	25.8	15.8	10.7	6.4
East North Central:															
Negro	57.9	82.0	88.8	91.1	93.3	94.2	93.1	91.5	83.5	68.6	47.6	30.4	17.2	9.4	6.3
White	64.0	86.7	91.5	93.1	96.2	96.4	96.0	94.8	86.0	69.4	48.0	31.7	20.0	12.5	7.4
West North Central:															
Negro	61.5	72.6	79.5	84.8	86.9	89.7	87.5	85.1	80.4	69.1	51.4	33.5	20.3	11.8	5.5
White	60.6	82.8	88.7	90.9	95.2	95.5	95.2	94.2	89.0	78.1	60.2	41.9	26.7	16.5	9.9
THE SOUTH:															
Negro	27.9	45.5	56.0	62.7	68.1	71.0	68.6	66.8	60.7	52.8	41.1	29.0	18.1	11.1	5.7
White	38.5	65.1	76.9	81.9	86.6	88.0	86.6	84.8	79.6	71.3	58.4	44.0	29.3	19.2	11.1
South Atlantic:															
Negro	28.9	47.7	57.8	64.5	69.9	72.7	69.9	67.6	60.2	51.7	39.6	28.0	17.6	10.9	5.6
White	42.0	68.6	78.9	83.2	87.9	88.6	86.8	84.0	77.6	68.6	55.5	42.1	28.6	19.0	11.2
Delaware:															
Negro	40.1	65.6	75.4	81.7	84.9	88.8	84.8	85.7	76.3	64.4	46.1	31.8	15.5	10.5	3.5
White	51.2	78.8	86.1	87.0	92.3	92.2	91.8	89.6	81.9	66.6	47.1	32.4	19.1	11.9	6.7
Maryland:															
Negro	35.8	60.3	71.1	78.3	82.0	84.6	81.9	78.1	67.8	54.5	39.0	23.3	12.6	7.3	3.2
White	51.6	79.1	87.5	90.0	93.7	94.0	91.7	85.7	71.7	56.1	39.0	25.0	15.2	9.5	5.3
District of Columbia:															
Negro	57.5	73.2	84.4	87.1	92.1	94.2	92.6	91.2	82.8	71.8	49.9	33.6	20.6	11.9	6.9
White	61.5	81.8	88.8	90.0	95.2	94.9	95.0	94.8	91.7	81.8	59.2	40.6	24.1	17.8	11.2
Virginia:															
Negro	17.1	41.8	56.3	64.3	71.9	75.1	72.8	70.7	63.6	53.7	41.3	29.0	17.6	11.2	5.4
White	23.4	58.9	75.2	81.3	87.0	88.3	87.5	85.8	80.2	71.7	59.2	45.1	30.0	19.4	11.0
West Virginia:															
Negro	47.5	69.9	78.3	83.5	87.1	86.5	84.5	80.6	74.8	60.4	41.3	26.5	14.4	9.2	5.1
White	48.1	74.5	84.6	88.7	92.5	93.8	92.7	91.5	85.5	74.4	56.9	41.0	27.5	17.9	10.8
North Carolina:															
Negro	34.7	53.6	63.2	69.1	73.2	76.3	74.4	72.7	67.7	62.6	52.2	40.4	29.4	19.7	11.7
White	44.2	68.2	77.0	81.3	86.0	86.8	84.9	81.7	77.7	71.9	63.0	52.3	39.3	28.5	18.4
South Carolina:															
Negro	25.9	42.6	52.2	59.7	66.2	69.7	68.1	67.0	60.5	53.3	42.7	30.2	18.9	11.9	5.7
White	38.4	64.1	74.3	79.1	85.8	85.4	81.8	77.4	71.5	65.2	55.8	44.9	32.5	22.6	12.9
Georgia:															
Negro	29.1	46.8	55.8	61.7	67.0	68.0	64.4	60.2	51.3	41.1	29.0	19.1	10.6	5.9	3.0
White	45.4	68.9	76.9	81.0	84.9	85.2	83.0	80.4	75.0	66.6	54.6	41.2	25.8	16.0	8.3
Florida:															
Negro	33.8	48.8	56.2	60.7	65.7	69.3	65.2	63.7	57.7	49.3	35.1	23.9	15.7	8.8	4.2
White	40.8	64.0	73.0	77.7	82.2	83.7	82.2	80.5	74.5	67.3	55.3	40.9	28.0	18.0	9.8
East South Central:															
Negro	30.2	46.8	56.4	62.3	67.7	70.6	68.9	67.0	62.3	54.9	43.7	31.2	19.9	12.3	6.2
White	40.7	67.2	76.8	81.4	86.1	87.4	86.3	84.7	79.9	71.8	59.2	45.7	32.4	21.6	13.0
Kentucky:															
Negro	36.1	59.2	69.0	73.4	80.8	81.8	80.9	79.2	73.0	63.6	48.4	33.3	20.1	12.5	5.6
White	41.2	69.3	77.6	82.2	86.3	87.8	86.8	85.4	79.2	69.1	54.5	40.3	27.6	18.0	9.7
Tennessee:															
Negro	26.9	47.3	58.3	64.9	70.5	73.0	71.8	68.5	64.8	55.3	44.1	30.5	20.5	12.0	6.6
White	38.8	65.6	75.7	80.6	86.4	87.4	86.4	84.8	80.5	73.0	60.7	46.6	33.2	22.1	13.8
Alabama:															
Negro	17.6	35.1	46.2	53.2	59.5	63.3	61.1	59.2	54.5	47.6	38.5	27.9	18.3	11.9	6.1
White	27.4	58.5	71.8	77.4	82.6	84.2	82.8	80.9	76.6	69.3	57.9	45.6	32.6	22.7	14.7
Mississippi:															
Negro	41.0	54.8	62.1	66.8	71.1	73.4	72.2	70.3	65.8	58.9	47.0	33.8	21.0	12.7	6.1
White	64.0	79.0	85.0	87.9	90.0	91.0	89.9	88.8	85.5	80.1	69.6	57.5	42.1	28.4	17.0
West South Central:															
Negro	22.8	39.4	51.8	59.4	64.9	67.8	65.5	64.8	59.4	52.4	40.7	28.2	16.8	10.2	5.3
White	32.6	59.6	74.9	80.8	85.7	87.7	86.6	85.8	81.5	73.9	61.0	44.7	27.5	17.3	9.4
Arkansas:															
Negro	33.1	49.0	56.3	60.6	66.8	68.3	68.0	66.1	62.3	59.0	48.5	37.6	24.6	16.6	8.7
White	46.0	68.4	75.7	79.6	83.6	84.3	83.4	82.5	79.0	72.9	61.8	48.3	33.1	22.9	13.5
Louisiana:															
Negro	17.1	27.4	34.6	40.6	45.5	48.7	45.9	45.2	38.1	31.2	21.7	14.0	8.1	5.0	2.7
White	37.3	58.8	68.1	74.0	77.7	80.5	78.8	77.6	69.9	59.5	45.6	32.6	21.0	12.9	7.0
Oklahoma:															
Negro	48.3	65.8	74.4	78.5	85.5	87.4	86.6	86.0	83.5	78.5	65.8	47.6	31.9	18.3	10.5
White	48.2	73.9	82.3	86.2	92.3	93.3	92.8	92.4	89.8	84.2	69.6	50.1	31.4	19.1	9.8
Texas:															
Negro	16.7	40.7	61.7	74.4	79.2	82.1	80.9	79.5	74.3	64.8	50.2	32.2	17.0	9.6	4.8
White	18.6	50.6	73.4	80.7	86.0	88.6	87.3	86.5	82.1	74.1	61.3	44.4	25.6	15.8	8.4
THE WEST:															
Negro	56.2	80.3	83.7	90.3	93.7	94.0	93.8	91.1	87.7	74.7	52.5	37.0	20.8	11.3	4.7
White	49.9	78.8	87.0	89.7	94.0	94.7	94.3	93.6	90.1	80.2	63.2	44.8	28.1	17.8	10.3
Mountain:															
Negro	52.5	80.5	77.9	90.7	92.4	92.0	91.6	89.8	87.9	75.7	54.0	33.3	19.4	12.1	4.7
White	49.5	76.7	84.7	87.8	92.3	93.2	92.9	92.2	88.8	80.4	65.4	47.2	29.7	18.5	10.3
Pacific:															
Negro	59.4	80.2	88.6	90.0	94.7	95.3	95.3	92.1	87.6	73.9	51.5	39.4	21.6	10.8	4.7
White	50.1	80.6	88.8	91.1	95.3	95.8	95.4	94.6	91.0	80.1	61.7	43.3	27.0	17.4	10.3

TABLE 27.—NEGROES 10 TO 14 YEARS OF AGE, IN SCHOOL AND NOT IN SCHOOL, BY DIVISIONS AND STATES: 1910, 1900, AND 1890.

[Percentage not shown where base is less than 100.]

DIVISION AND STATE.	NEGRO POPULATION 10 TO 14 YEARS OF AGE.									PERCENTAGE IN SCHOOL OF CHILDREN 10 TO 14 YEARS OF AGE.					
				Number in school.			Number not in school.			Negro.			Whites.		
	1910	1900	1890	1910	1900	1890	1910	1900	1890	1910	1900	1890	1910	1900	1890
UNITED STATES........	1,155,266	1,091,990	1,033,701	791,995	587,560	534,864	363,271	504,430	498,837	68.6	53.8	51.7	91.1	84.0	84.6
GEOGRAPHIC DIVISIONS:															
New England.........	5,092	4,285	3,844	4,800	3,785	3,264	292	500	580	94.3	88.3	84.9	94.1	90.0	90.1
Middle Atlantic........	29,648	23,932	19,943	26,760	19,224	15,000	2,888	4,708	4,943	90.3	80.3	75.2	92.9	85.8	85.3
East North Central....	23,184	23,851	22,052	21,102	20,445	19,113	2,082	3,406	3,539	91.0	85.7	84.4	93.8	88.2	90.6
West North Central....	20,281	25,529	27,063	17,397	19,699	20,099	2,884	5,830	6,964	85.8	77.2	74.3	93.8	88.6	90.6
South Atlantic........	513,239	476,108	469,021	349,010	246,917	226,177	164,229	229,191	242,844	68.0	51.9	48.2	85.0	74.1	73.1
East South Central....	320,476	316,984	299,473	215,349	162,205	155,861	105,127	154,779	143,612	67.2	51.2	52.0	84.8	73.4	74.8
West South Central....	240,265	219,122	189,706	154,743	113,426	93,861	85,522	105,696	95,845	64.4	51.8	49.5	85.5	74.6	72.7
Mountain.............	1,286	984	768	1,166	832	546	120	152	222	90.7	84.6	71.1	91.9	87.1	81.9
Pacific...............	1,795	1,195	1,231	1,668	1,027	943	127	168	288	92.9	85.9	76.6	94.4	92.4	90.4
NEW ENGLAND:															
Maine................	117	113	111	108	88	102	9	25	9	92.3	77.9	91.9	92.4	89.5	92.5
New Hampshire........	40	48	72	35	39	53	5	9	19		94.5	86.9	88.7
Vermont..............	72	72	84	65	62	64	7	10	20			96.6	92.1	89.6
Massachusetts........	2,905	2,201	1,819	2,763	1,966	1,576	142	235	243	95.1	89.3	86.6	94.5	91.2	91.2
Rhode Island.........	714	675	624	657	611	532	57	64	92	92.0	90.5	85.3	91.6	83.9	81.7
Connecticut..........	1,244	1,176	1,134	1,172	1,019	937	72	157	197	94.2	86.6	82.6	94.3	89.9	89.4
MIDDLE ATLANTIC:															
New York.............	7,930	6,493	5,865	7,344	5,356	4,416	586	1,137	1,449	92.6	82.5	75.3	94.4	88.2	86.0
New Jersey...........	6,878	5,402	4,304	6,170	4,141	3,176	708	1,261	1,128	89.7	76.6	73.8	91.8	84.5	85.0
Pennsylvania.........	14,840	12,037	9,774	13,246	9,727	7,408	1,594	2,310	2,366	89.3	80.8	75.8	91.7	83.8	84.6
EAST NORTH CENTRAL:															
Ohio.................	8,964	9,204	9,498	8,284	8,145	8,281	680	1,059	1,217	92.4	88.9	87.2	94.3	91.5	91.7
Indiana..............	4,984	5,682	5,168	4,555	5,025	4,191	429	657	977	91.4	88.4	81.1	93.5	90.5	91.0
Illinois.............	7,768	7,253	6,090	6,902	5,759	5,025	866	1,494	1,065	88.9	79.4	82.5	92.9	83.3	89.7
Michigan.............	1,276	1,514	1,643	1,184	1,355	1,396	92	159	247	92.8	89.5	85.0	95.5	89.9	90.1
Wisconsin............	192	198	253	177	161	220	15	37	33	92.2	81.3	87.0	93.9	88.5	90.9
WEST NORTH CENTRAL:															
Minnesota............	375	288	234	354	241	192	21	47	42	94.4	83.7	82.1	95.7	89.7	90.8
Iowa.................	1,215	1,232	1,165	1,105	991	954	110	241	211	90.9	80.4	81.9	94.0	91.1	93.6
Missouri.............	13,190	17,328	18,450	10,904	12,697	12,834	2,286	4,631	5,616	82.7	73.3	69.6	92.0	83.9	86.5
North Dakota.........	30	36	23	25	30	17	5	6	6				90.2	85.2	84.2
South Dakota.........	62	40	38	54	33	33	8	7	5				92.5	90.8	90.7
Nebraska.............	438	482	775	404	412	615	34	70	160	92.2	85.5	79.4	94.9	91.8	91.3
Kansas...............	4,971	6,123	6,378	4,551	5,295	5,454	420	828	924	91.6	85.6	85.5	95.4	91.2	93.9
SOUTH ATLANTIC:															
Delaware.............	3,540	3,401	3,448	2,968	2,121	1,502	572	1,280	1,946	83.8	62.4	43.6	89.4	82.4	84.8
Maryland.............	24,595	26,539	26,449	19,390	16,857	15,355	5,205	9,682	11,094	78.8	63.5	58.1	87.3	80.1	82.3
District of Columbia....	7,211	7,301	8,216	6,529	5,878	6,211	682	1,423	2,005	90.5	80.5	75.6	94.3	90.9	89.1
Virginia.............	83,395	85,609	93,068	58,989	48,938	50,584	24,406	36,671	42,484	70.7	57.2	54.4	85.7	75.6	75.1
West Virginia........	5,424	4,079	3,878	4,485	2,758	2,409	939	1,321	1,469	82.7	67.6	62.1	91.2	82.7	81.1
North Carolina.......	89,416	81,296	83,184	65,140	44,783	38,302	24,276	36,513	44,882	72.9	55.1	46.0	83.4	67.8	66.0
South Carolina.......	114,341	106,982	104,216	75,713	47,853	45,288	38,628	59,129	58,928	66.2	44.7	43.5	80.3	63.8	63.8
Georgia..............	152,029	134,540	123,920	94,404	61,290	52,107	57,625	73,250	71,813	62.1	45.6	42.0	81.7	70.0	67.0
Florida..............	33,288	26,361	22,642	21,392	16,439	14,419	11,896	9,922	8,223	64.3	62.4	63.7	80.8	77.9	78.5
EAST SOUTH CENTRAL:															
Kentucky.............	26,984	33,155	34,355	21,316	22,594	19,567	5,668	10,561	14,788	79.0	68.1	57.0	85.1	78.1	78.7
Tennessee............	53,344	59,343	59,716	37,134	33,522	33,722	16,210	25,821	25,994	69.6	56.5	56.5	88.8	72.2	75.9
Alabama..............	112,129	105,926	96,694	66,622	43,810	39,893	45,507	62,116	56,801	59.4	41.4	41.3	81.4	65.9	64.4
Mississippi..........	128,019	118,560	108,708	90,277	62,279	62,679	37,742	56,281	46,029	70.5	52.5	57.7	89.0	75.0	77.9
WEST SOUTH CENTRAL:															
Arkansas.............	52,679	46,714	43,398	34,909	25,419	23,715	17,770	21,295	19,683	66.3	54.4	54.6	82.6	70.9	71.9
Louisiana............	85,917	82,803	75,219	38,295	28,751	24,037	47,622	54,052	51,182	44.6	34.7	32.0	76.9	65.5	59.0
Oklahoma.............	16,208	6,908	337	13,903	3,389	142	2,305	3,519	195	85.8	49.1	42.1	92.1	68.6	52.9
Texas................	85,461	82,697	70,752	67,636	55,867	45,967	17,825	26,830	24,785	79.1	67.6	65.0	86.1	80.3	78.0
MOUNTAIN:															
Montana..............	95	91	86	86	77	52	9	14	34				91.6	91.6	83.9
Idaho................	19	18	25	17	17	14	2	1	11				93.5	91.2	84.3
Wyoming..............	56	45	38	52	39	21	4	6	17				91.5	87.1	80.2
Colorado.............	807	593	420	750	513	341	57	80	79	92.9	86.5	81.2	93.5	89.2	86.2
New Mexico...........	106	111	121	87	87	77	19	24	44	82.1	78.4	63.6	85.1	67.3	66.3
Arizona..............	130	87	25	114	7	23	16	13	2	87.7			86.0	80.7	73.2
Utah.................	55	33	50	45	22	16	10	11	34				95.6	92.6	84.1
Nevada...............	18	6	3	15	3	2	3	3	1				93.8	94.2	94.8
PACIFIC:															
Washington...........	274	154	66	244	130	49	30	24	17	89.1	84.5		94.8	93.6	87.3
Oregon...............	54	70	98	45	60	73	9	10	25				94.3	92.9	89.7
California...........	1,467	971	1,067	1,379	837	821	88	134	246	94.0	86.2	76.9	94.7	91.7	91.5

Table 28.—URBAN AND RURAL POPULATION—NEGROES AND WHITES IN SCHOOL AND NOT IN SCHOOL, BY AGE PERIODS, BY SECTIONS, DIVISIONS, AND SOUTHERN STATES: 1910.

[Percentage not shown where base is less than 100.]

SECTION, DIVISION, STATE, AND RACIAL CLASS.	POPULATION 6 TO 9 YEARS OF AGE.						POPULATION 10 TO 14 YEARS OF AGE.						POPULATION 15 TO 20 YEARS OF AGE.					
	Urban.		Rural.		Percentage in school.		Urban.		Rural.		Percentage in school.		Urban.		Rural.		Percentage in school.	
	Number in school.	Number not in school.	Number in school.	Number not in school.	Urban.	Rural.	Number in school.	Number not in school.	Number in school.	Number not in school.	Urban.	Rural.	Number in school.	Number not in school.	Number in school.	Number not in school.	Urban.	Rural.
UNITED STATES:																		
Negro	120,910	61,832	368,044	440,064	66.2	45.5	182,054	43,369	609,941	319,902	80.8	65.6	70,927	243,572	267,823	693,719	22.6	27.5
White	2,319,899	484,575	2,854,448	1,044,826	82.7	73.2	3,141,617	257,208	4,070,990	448,593	92.4	90.1	1,256,338	3,324,440	1,981,424	3,036,510	27.4	39.9
THE NORTH:																		
Negro	35,227	8,543	13,285	5,673	80.5	70.1	49,661	4,896	20,398	3,250	91.0	86.3	19,155	59,143	8,946	19,478	24.5	31.5
White	1,913,499	338,465	1,596,097	365,766	85.0	81.4	2,541,733	190,981	2,207,656	136,187	93.0	94.2	955,437	2,724,897	993,987	1,659,991	26.0	37.5
New England:																		
Negro	3,236	461	328	89	87.5	78.7	4,348	251	452	41	94.5	91.7	1,696	4,036	141	460	29.6	23.5
White	341,176	38,442	66,858	10,525	89.9	86.4	431,942	27,683	89,461	5,123	94.0	94.6	165,026	429,282	38,075	69,104	27.8	35.5
Middle Atlantic:																		
Negro	14,696	3,809	4,411	1,597	79.4	73.4	20,285	2,049	6,475	839	90.8	88.5	6,674	25,073	2,239	7,047	21.0	24.1
White	818,753	154,240	355,826	85,366	84.1	80.7	1,086,548	86,077	489,232	33,686	92.7	93.6	366,759	1,186,073	196,473	399,475	23.6	33.0
East North Central:																		
Negro	10,304	2,151	4,160	1,545	82.7	72.9	14,482	1,368	6,620	714	91.4	90.3	5,845	17,278	3,051	5,319	25.3	36.5
White	549,296	103,387	608,589	124,939	84.2	83.0	738,059	56,283	839,690	47,242	92.9	94.7	279,801	811,119	367,635	631,588	25.6	36.8
West North Central:																		
Negro	6,991	2,122	4,386	2,442	76.7	64.2	10,546	1,228	6,851	1,656	89.6	80.5	4,940	12,756	3,515	6,652	27.9	34.6
White	204,274	42,396	564,824	144,936	82.8	79.6	285,184	20,938	789,273	50,136	93.2	94.0	143,851	298,423	391,804	559,824	32.5	41.2
THE SOUTH:																		
Negro	84,175	52,900	354,369	434,219	61.4	44.9	130,186	38,315	588,916	316,563	77.3	65.0	50,738	181,977	258,556	673,582	21.8	27.7
White	253,172	106,992	1,059,482	605,953	70.3	63.6	377,954	51,884	1,576,457	290,376	87.9	84.4	173,294	390,953	839,453	1,162,266	30.7	41.9
South Atlantic—																		
Negro	42,188	25,510	174,277	200,047	62.3	46.6	63,716	19,857	285,294	144,372	76.2	66.4	24,166	90,305	117,333	316,954	21.1	27.0
White	115,656	45,495	398,242	203,037	71.8	66.2	167,608	25,966	581,643	106,473	86.6	84.5	73,246	183,691	302,194	429,064	28.5	41.3
Delaware:																		
Negro	537	200	1,184	711	72.9	62.5	901	101	2,067	471	89.9	81.4	292	927	834	1,853	24.0	31.0
White	4,367	1,468	5,096	1,617	74.8	75.9	6,430	618	7,672	1,046	91.2	88.0	2,427	7,405	3,492	6,211	24.7	36.0
Maryland:																		
Negro	4,106	2,126	8,472	5,934	65.9	58.8	6,277	1,326	13,113	3,879	82.6	77.2	2,106	9,159	4,343	12,389	18.7	26.0
White	29,765	11,021	35,849	8,985	73.0	80.0	41,952	8,394	49,695	4,956	83.3	90.9	12,491	53,525	18,824	39,752	18.9	32.1
District of Columbia:																		
Negro	4,278	1,421	....	....	75.1	....	6,529	682	....	....	90.5	....	3,193	7,490	....	....	29.9	....
White	11,511	2,852	....	....	80.1	....	16,430	988	....	....	94.3	....	8,880	14,933	....	....	37.3	....
Virginia:																		
Negro	6,388	5,097	24,990	33,957	55.6	42.4	10,878	3,413	48,111	20,993	76.1	69.6	3,998	16,418	19,981	48,189	19.6	29.3
White	15,297	8,321	63,175	46,072	64.8	57.8	25,384	3,056	106,735	18,933	89.3	84.9	12,119	25,932	55,381	74,618	31.8	42.6
West Virginia:																		
Negro	732	263	2,710	1,275	73.6	68.0	1,054	143	3,431	796	88.1	81.2	505	1,393	1,374	4,805	26.6	22.2
White	12,515	3,315	69,057	26,441	79.1	72.3	16,796	1,739	97,771	9,292	90.6	91.3	7,155	18,081	46,854	69,294	28.4	40.3
North Carolina:																		
Negro	6,467	3,666	36,593	32,892	63.8	52.7	8,529	3,308	56,611	20,968	72.1	73.0	3,456	12,494	31,383	47,658	21.7	39.7
White	11,656	4,852	89,851	45,741	70.6	66.3	16,581	3,377	129,934	25,695	83.1	83.5	8,623	17,245	80,127	85,021	33.3	48.5
South Carolina:																		
Negro	4,897	3,530	38,371	50,986	58.1	42.9	7,698	2,990	68,015	35,638	72.0	65.6	2,917	10,939	29,828	75,620	21.1	28.3
White	6,593	3,055	35,692	21,936	68.3	61.9	9,830	2,046	52,822	13,326	82.8	79.9	5,423	10,087	29,153	42,739	35.0	40.6
Georgia:																		
Negro	10,460	6,825	51,394	61,362	60.5	45.6	15,688	5,950	78,716	51,675	72.5	60.4	5,281	23,247	23,652	105,235	18.5	18.4
White	17,175	7,179	79,978	40,133	70.5	66.6	24,778	3,782	108,542	26,070	86.8	80.6	11,764	25,661	52,934	88,339	31.4	37.5
Florida:																		
Negro	4,323	2,382	10,563	12,930	64.5	45.0	6,162	1,944	15,230	9,952	76.0	60.5	2,418	8,238	5,938	21,205	22.7	21.9
White	6,777	3,432	19,544	12,112	66.4	61.7	9,427	1,966	28,472	7,155	82.7	79.9	4,364	10,822	15,429	23,090	28.7	40.1
East South Central—																		
Negro	22,136	13,297	109,565	127,141	62.5	46.3	34,804	9,842	180,545	95,285	78.0	65.5	14,579	48,575	85,601	203,510	23.1	29.6
White	57,721	20,935	318,323	174,600	73.4	64.6	85,638	9,991	464,575	88,317	89.6	84.0	39,586	88,536	259,909	335,318	30.9	43.7
Kentucky:																		
Negro	4,371	1,962	8,074	6,648	69.0	54.8	7,681	1,070	13,635	4,598	87.8	74.8	3,430	9,350	6,869	14,288	26.8	32.5
White	25,039	6,357	105,592	58,202	79.8	64.5	36,438	3,524	155,761	30,161	91.2	83.8	14,493	39,927	79,790	118,344	26.6	40.3
Tennessee:																		
Negro	6,004	3,728	15,757	19,094	61.7	45.2	9,603	2,738	27,531	13,472	77.8	67.1	4,307	15,249	13,951	31,963	22.0	30.4
White	14,681	6,341	93,281	53,467	69.8	63.6	22,910	2,630	138,679	25,734	89.7	84.3	11,928	23,237	79,880	102,229	33.9	43.9
Alabama:																		
Negro	6,698	5,191	29,493	55,037	56.3	34.9	10,463	3,974	56,159	41,533	72.5	57.5	4,228	14,717	26,150	73,533	22.3	26.2
White	10,910	6,395	62,767	47,255	63.0	57.0	16,566	2,895	98,195	23,300	85.1	80.8	8,075	17,399	55,632	73,449	31.7	43.1
Mississippi:																		
Negro	5,063	2,416	56,241	46,362	67.7	54.8	7,057	2,060	83,220	35,682	77.4	70.0	2,614	9,259	38,631	83,726	22.0	31.6
White	7,091	1,842	56,683	15,676	79.4	78.3	9,724	942	71,940	9,122	91.2	88.7	5,090	7,973	44,607	41,296	39.0	51.9
West South Central—																		
Negro	19,851	14,093	70,527	107,031	58.5	39.7	31,666	8,616	123,077	76,906	78.6	61.5	11,993	43,097	55,622	153,118	21.8	26.6
White	79,795	40,562	342,917	228,316	66.3	60.0	124,708	15,927	530,239	95,586	88.7	84.7	60,462	118,726	277,350	397,884	33.7	41.1
Arkansas:																		
Negro	3,075	1,349	19,888	22,392	69.5	47.0	4,179	902	30,730	16,868	82.2	64.6	2,177	5,603	17,418	34,850	28.0	33.3
White	8,601	2,539	70,420	37,087	77.2	65.5	11,461	1,097	93,500	21,085	91.3	81.6	6,574	10,382	55,907	73,412	38.8	43.2
Louisiana:																		
Negro	6,522	6,034	15,837	47,659	51.9	24.9	10,570	4,655	27,725	42,967	69.4	39.2	3,217	17,016	9,607	62,771	15.9	13.3
White	19,226	7,630	37,410	32,130	71.6	53.8	28,616	4,378	54,181	20,560	86.7	72.5	10,770	29,622	24,662	51,716	26.7	32.3
Oklahoma:																		
Negro	2,144	815	7,534	4,117	72.5	64.7	2,810	382	11,093	1,923	88.0	85.2	1,257	3,322	6,245	7,076	27.5	46.9
White	15,810	5,438	90,671	36,453	74.4	71.3	21,739	1,958	125,953	10,693	91.7	92.2	11,771	19,947	68,259	80,291	37.1	46.0
Texas:																		
Negro	8,110	5,895	27,268	32,863	57.9	45.3	14,107	2,677	53,529	15,148	84.1	77.9	5,342	17,156	22,352	48,421	23.7	31.6
White	36,158	24,955	144,416	122,646	59.2	54.1	62,892	8,494	256,605	43,248	88.1	85.6	31,347	58,775	128,522	192,465	34.8	40.0
THE WEST:																		
Negro	1,508	389	390	172	79.5	69.4	2,207	158	627	89	93.3	87.6	1,034	2,452	321	659	29.7	32.8
White	153,228	39,118	198,869	73,107	79.7	73.1	221,930	14,343	286,877	22,030	93.9	92.9	127,607	208,590	147,984	214,253	38.0	40.9
Mountain—																		
Negro	601	181	215	96	76.9	69.1	839	71	327	49	92.2	87.0	380	894	169	348	29.8	32.7
White	51,605	13,802	101,173	39,812	78.9	71.8	72,052	4,922	139,047	13,696	93.6	91.0	40,051	60,135	72,574	101,662	40.0	41.7
Pacific—																		
Negro	907	208	175	76	81.3	69.7	1,368	87	300	40	94.0	88.2	654	1,558	152	311	29.6	32.8
White	101,623	25,316	97,696	33,295	80.1	74.6	149,878	9,421	147,830	8,334	94.1	94.7	87,556	148,455	75,410	112,591	37.1	40.1

TABLE 29.—CHILDREN 6 TO 14 YEARS OF AGE IN SCHOOL AND NOT IN SCHOOL, BY CLASS OF POPULATION, IN CITIES OF 100,000 INHABITANTS OR MORE: 1910.

[Percentage not shown where base is less than 100.]

CITY.	CHILDREN 6 TO 14 YEARS OF AGE: 1910.											
	Negro.			White.			Native white.			Foreign-born white.		
	In school.		Number not in school.	In school.		Number not in school.	In school.		Number not in school.	In school.		Number not in school.
	Number.	Per cent.		Number.	Per cent.		Number.	Per cent.		Number.	Per cent.	
Total, all cities of 100,000 inhabitants or more	109,362	79.5	28,139	3,297,961	89.0	409,139	2,924,440	89.2	354,909	373,521	87.3	54,230
Albany, N. Y	113	90.4	12	11,711	88.5	1,543	11,187	88.4	1,450	524	84.9	93
Atlanta, Ga	5,685	71.0	2,326	12,800	79.6	3,286	12,594	79.6	3,227	206	77.7	59
Baltimore, Md	8,509	75.5	2,756	59,702	78.1	16,916	56,435	77.9	15,844	3,267	75.3	1,072
Birmingham, Ala	5,807	72.8	2,175	10,212	75.3	3,345	9,958	75.3	3,270	254	77.2	75
Boston, Mass	1,337	93.5	93	92,868	93.7	6,231	82,995	94.2	5,139	9,873	90.0	1,092
Bridgeport, Conn	141	87.0	21	13,982	92.4	1,155	12,506	92.8	971	1,476	88.9	184
Buffalo, N. Y	157	89.2	19	60,651	87.6	8,572	56,685	87.9	7,808	3,966	83.8	764
Cambridge, Mass	715	95.1	37	15,001	95.3	747	13,736	95.7	621	1,265	90.9	126
Chicago, Ill	3,424	89.2	416	293,294	88.1	39,622	264,534	88.5	34,304	28,760	84.4	5,318
Cincinnati, Ohio	1,807	89.3	217	43,876	90.7	4,522	42,311	90.9	4,261	1,565	85.7	261
Cleveland, Ohio	775	92.5	63	77,811	90.8	7,852	68,445	91.3	6,543	9,366	87.7	1,309
Columbus, Ohio	1,210	86.7	186	20,315	89.6	2,368	19,826	89.8	2,260	489	81.9	108
Dayton, Ohio	486	87.4	70	13,891	90.2	1,511	13,429	90.4	1,422	462	83.8	89
Denver, Colo	513	88.6	66	25,922	90.3	2,780	24,639	90.3	2,646	1,283	90.5	134
Detroit, Mich	536	87.2	79	59,031	86.5	9,193	52,869	86.9	7,950	6,162	83.2	1,243
Fall River, Mass	36	....	1	19,878	91.8	1,783	17,165	92.3	1,425	2,713	88.3	358
Grand Rapids, Mich	58	....	7	15,326	90.0	1,708	14,244	90.1	1,568	1,082	88.5	140
Indianapolis, Ind	2,496	90.5	263	26,509	90.7	2,715	26,087	90.8	2,631	422	83.4	84
Jersey City, N. J	674	87.1	100	39,881	86.2	6,368	37,345	86.6	5,797	2,536	81.6	571
Kansas City, Mo	1,910	84.9	341	24,658	87.1	3,655	23,774	87.2	3,495	884	84.7	160
Los Angeles, Cal	868	93.0	65	32,697	90.6	3,378	30,242	90.9	3,013	2,455	87.1	365
Louisville, Ky	4,240	86.5	662	25,461	88.4	3,326	25,156	88.5	3,269	305	84.3	57
Lowell, Mass	10	....	2	14,710	91.3	1,397	13,078	92.1	1,123	1,632	85.6	274
Memphis, Tenn	4,317	67.0	2,123	9,050	82.3	1,948	8,825	82.5	1,877	225	76.0	71
Milwaukee, Wis	58	....	14	54,106	87.2	7,932	50,382	87.6	7,139	3,724	82.4	793
Minneapolis, Minn	197	87.6	28	35,712	89.5	4,072	33,307	89.9	3,755	2,405	88.4	317
Nashville, Tenn	4,098	74.0	1,440	9,632	79.5	2,486	9,523	79.5	2,459	109	80.1	27
New Haven, Conn	400	91.7	36	20,065	94.3	1,221	17,826	94.6	1,014	2,239	91.5	207
New Orleans, La	9,446	67.5	4,544	34,919	80.0	8,737	34,173	80.1	8,474	746	73.9	263
New York, N. Y	7,783	87.8	1,081	690,086	90.7	70,914	577,554	91.0	56,916	112,532	88.9	13,998
Manhattan Borough	4,345	87.0	648	304,148	89.8	34,531	234,923	90.1	25,695	69,225	88.7	8,836
Bronx Borough	457	89.3	55	67,751	91.1	6,608	61,598	91.3	5,864	6,153	89.2	744
Brooklyn Borough	2,441	88.3	323	254,751	91.0	25,044	220,937	91.3	21,016	33,814	89.4	4,028
Queens Borough	382	91.4	36	48,802	93.0	3,696	46,344	93.1	3,415	2,458	89.7	281
Richmond Borough	158	89.3	19	14,634	93.4	1,035	13,752	93.7	926	882	89.0	109
Newark, N. J	1,076	90.9	108	51,800	92.0	4,534	45,662	92.3	3,835	6,138	89.8	699
Oakland, Cal	247	88.2	33	16,316	89.0	2,019	15,309	89.1	1,881	1,007	87.9	138
Omaha, Nebr	343	89.8	39	15,279	93.0	1,153	14,396	93.2	1,050	883	89.6	103
Paterson, N. J	192	88.5	25	19,101	90.1	2,094	16,884	90.4	1,785	2,217	87.8	309
Philadelphia, Pa	8,051	83.8	1,553	196,930	86.3	31,332	178,203	86.6	27,646	18,727	83.6	3,686
Pittsburgh, Pa	2,833	84.0	538	69,479	85.3	11,962	64,538	85.6	10,849	4,941	81.6	1,113
Portland, Oreg	48	....	15	18,941	85.9	3,110	17,613	86.2	2,827	1,328	82.4	283
Providence, R. I	603	88.8	76	28,919	89.3	3,483	25,600	90.0	2,834	3,319	83.6	649
Richmond, Va	4,514	65.2	2,413	10,048	79.5	2,585	9,875	79.4	2,556	173	85.6	29
Rochester, N. Y	90	....	6	27,768	91.9	2,446	25,177	92.2	2,142	2,591	89.5	304
St. Louis, Mo	3,941	83.4	784	81,453	85.6	13,695	77,181	85.9	12,716	4,272	81.4	979
St. Paul, Minn	243	93.1	18	28,627	91.6	2,609	27,003	91.8	2,427	1,624	89.9	182
San Francisco, Cal	87	80.6	21	38,082	87.0	5,666	35,269	87.2	5,155	2,813	84.6	511
Scranton, Pa	73	....	7	19,452	83.4	3,866	18,295	84.1	3,470	1,157	74.5	396
Seattle, Wash	127	83.0	26	22,353	85.5	3,779	20,747	85.8	3,427	1,606	82.0	352
Spokane, Wash	54	....	7	11,303	84.1	2,140	10,750	84.3	1,997	553	79.5	143
Syracuse, N. Y	112	88.9	14	16,744	87.9	2,315	15,698	88.2	2,106	1,046	83.3	209
Toledo, Ohio	173	90.6	18	23,322	90.5	2,434	22,237	90.9	2,233	1,085	84.4	201
Washington, D. C	10,807	83.7	2,103	27,941	87.9	3,840	27,159	88.0	3,717	782	86.4	123
Worcester, Mass	159	93.5	11	20,260	91.5	1,880	18,460	91.7	1,669	1,800	89.5	211

TABLE 30.—NEGROES AND WHITES IN SCHOOL AND NOT IN SCHOOL, BY AGE PERIODS, BY CITIES OF 25,000 INHABITANTS OR MORE HAVING A NEGRO POPULATION OF 1,000 OR MORE: 1910.

CITY.	6 to 9 years of age. Negro. In school. Number.	Per cent.	Number not in school.	White. In school. Number.	Per cent.	Number not in school.	10 to 14 years of age. Negro. In school. Number.	Per cent.	Number not in school.	White. In school. Number.	Per cent.	Number not in school.	15 to 20 years of age. Negro. In school. Number.	Per cent.	Number not in school.	White. In school. Number.	Per cent.	Number not in school.
CITIES OF THE SOUTH.																		
Atlanta, Ga.	2,257	66.3	1,147	5,255	70.7	2,173	3,428	74.4	1,179	7,545	87.1	1,113	1,278	19.3	5,341	3,573	29.1	8,689
Augusta, Ga.	714	63.0	420	1,317	81.7	295	1,153	71.8	453	1,581	86.3	250	491	20.1	1,948	668	24.8	2,022
Austin, Tex.	438	67.6	210	961	63.2	559	655	88.4	86	1,905	90.2	207	353	35.3	647	1,375	48.3	1,471
Baltimore, Md.	3,361	65.7	1,753	24,837	72.5	9,431	5,148	83.7	1,003	34,865	82.3	7,485	1,775	18.8	7,675	9,935	17.7	46,301
Birmingham, Ala.	2,365	66.0	1,221	3,970	61.2	2,512	3,442	78.3	954	6,242	88.2	833	1,171	19.4	4,872	2,945	31.5	6,411
Charleston, S. C.	1,365	56.5	1,052	1,479	75.4	483	2,105	72.3	807	2,100	86.9	317	634	15.8	3,373	971	29.4	2,336
Charlotte, N. C.	611	60.3	402	1,220	69.4	539	743	66.2	379	1,727	82.3	372	273	16.4	1,393	805	29.3	1,939
Chattanooga, Tenn.	804	70.3	339	1,315	77.9	374	1,052	78.3	291	2,036	92.2	172	475	21.1	1,773	1,151	36.4	2,008
Columbia, S. C.	506	61.3	319	723	71.4	289	741	70.0	318	1,070	88.4	140	284	18.7	1,237	545	33.1	1,100
Covington, Ky.	103	72.5	39	2,962	85.8	492	171	87.7	24	4,016	89.9	451	74	25.0	222	1,122	18.1	5,087
Dallas, Tex.	648	60.9	416	3,176	59.7	2,142	1,090	82.0	239	5,341	88.7	679	446	20.7	1,707	2,738	31.1	6,071
El Paso, Tex.	58	......	32	1,894	59.3	1,300	78	76.5	24	2,770	79.9	696	41	29.3	99	1,059	25.3	3,125
Fort Worth, Tex.	490	51.8	456	2,655	59.3	1,825	799	79.1	211	4,294	87.4	620	279	18.5	1,232	1,915	28.0	4,935
Galveston, Tex.	296	63.0	174	1,465	68.9	661	520	87.5	74	2,241	90.3	240	200	22.9	675	838	26.9	2,275
Houston, Tex.	995	62.7	592	2,035	53.5	1,769	1,661	83.8	321	3,931	87.8	548	530	18.4	2,343	1,787	28.0	4,606
Huntington, W. Va.	98	69.5	43	1,817	77.7	522	171	91.9	15	2,410	88.1	325	96	34.8	180	1,067	28.5	2,673
Jacksonville, Fla.	1,125	62.2	684	1,096	63.5	630	1,871	80.8	445	1,741	85.7	290	868	25.2	2,578	932	29.5	2,226
Knoxville, Tenn.	263	61.4	165	1,357	66.9	671	440	72.8	164	2,199	84.8	394	205	19.2	862	1,283	32.0	2,722
Lexington, Ky.	423	71.1	172	1,238	84.8	222	745	87.6	105	1,766	94.6	101	378	30.2	873	1,057	40.3	1,564
Little Rock, Ark.	651	72.6	246	1,712	80.1	425	853	81.7	191	2,176	90.7	223	581	29.5	1,390	1,161	32.6	2,404
Louisville, Ky.	1,578	79.6	405	10,499	83.6	2,059	2,662	91.2	257	14,962	92.2	1,267	1,056	23.6	3,416	5,005	22.2	17,521
Lynchburg, Va.	358	56.6	275	914	62.5	548	701	79.1	185	1,576	89.7	181	277	19.8	1,124	854	32.1	1,807
Macon, Ga.	743	56.5	573	1,110	67.9	524	1,220	70.9	500	1,733	83.4	345	431	18.7	1,879	860	30.8	1,936
Memphis, Tenn.	1,784	59.7	1,202	3,670	73.5	1,326	2,533	73.3	921	5,380	89.6	622	1,026	16.6	5,151	2,770	31.3	6,067
Mobile, Ala.	1,017	64.9	550	1,773	83.0	363	1,344	71.3	540	2,347	90.7	242	492	19.1	2,084	1,110	33.2	2,233
Montgomery, Ala.	799	59.4	546	794	59.0	552	1,265	71.9	495	1,231	75.9	391	560	23.2	1,853	638	28.1	1,633
Muskogee, Okla.	409	61.6	255	770	71.1	313	598	84.7	108	1,117	90.6	116	302	30.2	698	635	34.4	1,211
Nashville, Tenn.	1,431	61.9	879	3,497	64.2	1,954	2,667	82.6	561	6,135	92.0	532	1,393	27.9	3,600	3,068	33.5	6,085
New Orleans, La.	3,560	56.9	2,700	14,048	72.6	5,302	5,886	76.1	1,844	20,871	85.3	3,435	1,683	15.7	9,012	6,737	22.4	23,353
Norfolk, Va.	1,036	65.4	548	2,169	70.2	921	1,365	74.2	474	3,318	93.1	247	524	18.0	2,394	1,626	34.5	3,091
Oklahoma City, Okla.	345	78.4	95	2,802	80.5	680	401	81.7	56	3,633	93.8	239	161	20.5	624	2,040	32.0	4,327
Portsmouth, Va.	484	55.5	388	980	62.6	585	741	75.8	236	1,661	91.9	146	249	18.8	1,077	677	24.0	2,147
Richmond, Va.	1,532	50.4	1,507	3,833	68.6	1,755	2,982	76.7	906	6,215	88.2	830	951	16.0	4,995	2,473	25.3	7,291
Roanoke, Va.	371	60.5	242	1,267	61.0	811	654	82.8	136	2,356	92.9	180	275	23.9	874	1,206	36.0	2,144
San Antonio, Tex.	420	56.7	321	3,897	56.7	2,971	818	83.8	158	7,030	86.0	1,141	220	16.0	1,159	2,958	28.2	7,543
Savannah, Ga.	1,301	57.7	952	1,752	76.1	549	1,961	73.6	703	2,502	89.1	306	609	16.1	3,166	959	26.7	2,639
Shreveport, La.	617	55.1	503	656	68.9	296	885	71.8	348	1,014	91.8	91	424	24.6	1,297	590	39.5	904
Tampa, Fla.	436	69.6	190	1,693	70.4	711	548	82.7	115	2,033	81.5	460	187	18.3	837	701	20.2	2,765
Waco, Tex.	230	50.7	224	1,061	63.3	616	481	79.9	121	1,819	87.7	254	187	24.0	591	1,001	37.9	1,638
Washington, D. C.	4,278	75.1	1,421	11,511	80.1	2,852	6,529	90.5	682	16,430	94.3	988	3,193	29.9	7,490	8,880	37.3	14,933
Wheeling, W. Va.	44	......	4	2,203	79.8	558	47	......	2	3,033	88.0	412	12	11.3	94	800	17.4	3,809
Wilmington, Del.	419	72.6	158	3,980	74.5	1,364	715	91.1	70	5,874	91.1	573	241	25.0	723	2,174	23.9	6,910
Wilmington, N. C.	634	67.2	309	686	71.5	274	846	75.3	278	1,067	90.2	116	292	20.1	1,158	527	33.7	1,037
CITIES OF THE NORTH.																		
Albany, N. Y.	54	......	7	4,847	83.3	973	59	......	5	6,864	92.3	570	15	......	80	2,977	28.9	7,341
Atlantic City, N. J.	280	70.2	119	1,862	78.3	517	424	84.3	79	2,325	85.5	393	128	16.9	631	926	26.2	2,606
Boston, Mass.	552	91.4	52	41,130	92.2	3,498	785	95.0	41	51,738	95.0	2,733	313	30.5	712	20,654	30.6	46,816
Bridgeport, Conn.	73	......	14	6,366	91.6	586	68	......	7	7,616	93.0	569	26	25.5	76	2,113	18.3	9,423
Buffalo, N. Y.	57	......	10	24,448	81.0	5,750	100	91.7	9	36,203	92.8	2,822	34	27.0	92	12,564	24.7	38,263
Cambridge, Mass.	303	92.1	26	6,879	94.5	401	412	97.4	11	8,122	95.9	346	171	36.0	304	3,263	31.2	7,183
Camden, N. J.	300	72.6	113	4,990	76.0	1,579	415	89.4	49	6,873	90.0	765	150	25.4	440	1,800	18.1	8,153
Chester, Pa.	230	72.6	87	1,882	78.6	513	355	88.3	47	2,487	87.9	341	85	18.4	376	783	19.4	3,253
Chicago, Ill.	1,426	84.4	264	123,664	82.8	25,634	1,998	92.9	152	169,630	92.4	13,988	819	24.2	2,567	51,407	20.3	202,281
Cincinnati, Ohio	677	83.6	133	17,634	87.3	2,563	1,130	93.1	84	26,242	93.1	1,959	454	23.5	1,474	9,335	22.6	31,930
Cleveland, Ohio	319	90.4	34	34,518	88.3	4,575	456	94.0	29	43,293	93.0	3,277	187	24.8	566	13,309	20.9	50,298
Columbus, Ohio	487	80.9	115	8,536	84.9	1,518	723	91.1	71	11,779	93.3	850	296	22.4	1,025	5,803	30.6	13,138
Danville, Ill.	72	......	10	1,739	89.3	209	95	94.1	6	2,157	94.2	132	33	22.9	111	887	29.9	2,078
Dayton, Ohio	222	83.8	43	6,006	85.6	1,010	264	90.7	27	7,885	94.0	501	94	20.2	372	3,153	25.6	9,146
Des Moines, Iowa	154	88.5	20	4,902	87.6	694	177	88.5	23	6,096	91.7	555	67	22.6	229	3,237	34.5	6,146
Detroit, Mich.	226	82.8	47	25,188	80.2	6,213	310	90.6	32	33,843	91.9	2,980	111	21.9	395	10,121	18.9	43,496
East Orange, N. J.	107	82.9	22	1,767	89.0	219	123	91.8	11	2,184	92.1	188	46	20.7	176	1,340	40.0	2,013
East St. Louis, Ill.	280	74.1	98	2,939	79.3	767	323	86.4	51	3,816	90.6	395	121	19.2	509	1,040	17.2	5,010
Elizabeth, N. J.	73	67.6	35	4,454	80.0	1,114	103	88.8	13	5,967	93.4	423	30	19.5	124	1,760	21.6	6,403
Evansville, Ind.	313	83.0	64	3,622	85.8	598	463	90.1	51	4,769	89.0	587	127	18.0	580	1,334	17.1	6,477
Harrisburg, Pa.	203	82.5	43	3,348	89.8	382	310	92.8	24	4,474	95.5	213	111	23.1	370	1,991	30.7	4,504
Hartford, Conn.	105	84.7	19	6,142	93.1	452	146	96.1	6	7,564	96.9	239	66	40.0	99	3,108	30.5	7,089
Indianapolis, Ind.	1,085	87.8	151	11,535	87.5	1,645	1,411	92.6	112	14,974	93.3	1,070	474	22.1	1,669	5,531	24.2	17,335
Jersey City, N. J.	300	81.7	67	16,791	79.5	4,332	374	91.9	33	23,090	91.9	2,036	137	27.0	371	6,505	21.1	24,257
Kansas City, Kans.	463	76.4	143	4,158	77.4	1,212	671	92.2	57	5,962	92.6	473	363	35.0	674	2,303	26.4	6,434

TABLE 30.—NEGROES AND WHITES IN SCHOOL AND NOT IN SCHOOL, BY AGE PERIODS, BY CITIES OF 25,000 INHABITANTS OR MORE HAVING A NEGRO POPULATION OF 1,000 OR MORE: 1910—Continued.

CITY.	6 to 9 years of age. Negro. In school. Number.	Per cent.	Number not in school.	White. In school. Number.	Per cent.	Number not in school.	10 to 14 years of age. Negro. In school. Number.	Per cent.	Number not in school.	White. In school. Number.	Per cent.	Number not in school.	15 to 20 years of age. Negro. In school. Number.	Per cent.	Number not in school.	White. In school. Number.	Per cent.	Number not in school.
CITIES OF THE NORTH—con.																		
Kansas City, Mo	744	76.4	230	10,086	80.0	2,527	1,166	91.3	111	14,572	92.8	1,128	460	20.0	1,837	7,186	29.2	17,399
Minneapolis, Minn	72	.....	17	14,420	82.7	3,026	125	91.9	11	21,292	95.3	1,046	73	40.3	108	12,666	35.8	22,742
New Bedford, Mass	151	81.6	34	5,870	85.8	975	176	96.7	6	7,302	90.9	811	63	22.3	220	1,735	15.5	9,436
New Haven Conn	180	90.0	20	9,124	93.9	596	220	93.2	16	10,941	94.6	625	101	33.2	203	3,681	25.9	10,549
New Rochelle, N. Y	90	90.0	10	1,800	92.2	152	108	91.5	10	2,339	96.6	82	25	13.0	168	977	33.0	1,986
New York, N. Y	3,261	81.4	745	296,512	86.3	46,998	4,522	93.1	336	393,574	94.3	23,916	1,634	19.6	6,686	129,006	23.2	426,763
Manhattan Borough	1,829	80.8	436	129,195	85.1	22,589	2,516	92.2	212	174,953	93.6	11,942	937	17.5	4,404	59,345	21.4	218,031
Bronx Borough	192	82.4	41	28,870	86.4	4,535	265	95.0	14	38,881	94.9	2,073	87	23.6	282	12,688	25.6	36,871
Brooklyn Borough	1,020	81.7	228	110,846	86.9	16,759	1,421	93.7	95	143,905	94.6	8,285	491	23.0	1,648	45,849	24.5	141,114
Queens Borough	150	84.3	28	21,293	89.9	2,404	232	96.7	8	27,509	95.5	1,292	83	24.6	255	8,344	25.5	24,420
Richmond Borough	70	.....	12	6,308	89.9	711	88	.....	7	8,326	96.3	324	36	27.1	97	2,780	30.5	6,327
Newark, N. J	488	87.5	70	23,144	90.3	2,500	588	93.9	38	28,656	93.4	2,034	242	26.8	661	8,789	22.5	30,317
Newport, R. I	93	85.3	16	1,410	93.3	102	94	91.3	9	1,827	97.0	56	51	35.9	91	2,404	58.2	1,728
Norristown borough, Pa	56	.....	35	1,258	79.9	317	76	.....	9	1,731	87.9	238	15	.....	72	615	20.9	2,323
Omaha, Nebr	158	87.8	22	6,628	90.4	706	185	91.6	17	8,651	95.1	447	91	25.3	268	4,364	31.0	9,732
Orange, N. J	134	89.3	16	1,876	88.7	240	197	92.1	17	2,249	93.9	145	47	22.0	167	800	25.9	2,283
Paterson, N. J	79	.....	15	8,610	89.7	988	113	91.9	10	10,491	90.5	1,106	18	12.1	131	2,465	16.6	12,420
Peoria, Ill	64	.....	20	3,309	84.7	598	88	85.4	15	4,763	92.6	380	28	18.8	121	1,872	25.8	5,392
Philadelphia, Pa	3,416	77.7	981	83,291	81.3	19,112	4,635	89.0	572	113,639	90.3	12,220	1,272	17.2	6,123	31,037	18.8	133,865
Pittsburgh, Pa	1,166	76.3	362	29,069	78.8	7,828	1,667	90.5	176	40,410	90.7	4,134	535	23.9	1,699	12,919	21.7	46,624
Providence, R. I	248	83.8	48	12,346	85.1	2,157	355	92.7	28	16,573	92.6	1,326	140	28.1	358	5,614	23.5	18,317
Quincy, Ill	60	.....	16	1,800	82.6	378	119	88.8	15	2,630	91.2	254	28	16.2	145	1,092	25.5	3,188
St. Joseph, Mo	177	81.6	40	4,053	86.0	661	248	89.9	28	5,445	94.4	320	136	27.1	366	2,313	26.2	6,508
St. Louis, Mo	1,545	75.6	500	33,179	79.7	8,452	2,396	89.4	284	48,274	90.2	5,243	956	22.9	3,226	14,935	19.3	62,356
St. Paul, Minn	99	88.4	13	11,996	87.0	1,790	144	96.6	5	16,631	95.3	819	76	32.3	159	8,238	30.3	18,964
Springfield, Ill	161	83.4	32	2,751	78.6	750	219	89.8	25	3,630	90.3	392	72	23.5	234	1,229	23.1	4,081
Springfield, Mass	76	.....	6	5,164	93.0	390	121	99.2	1	6,555	95.8	285	61	40.9	88	3,198	34.0	6,204
Springfield, Mo	104	70.7	43	1,807	77.5	526	160	84.2	30	2,694	92.6	216	84	29.9	197	1,509	35.4	2,751
Springfield, Ohio	250	79.2	68	2,266	84.1	427	357	92.0	31	3,125	93.9	204	145	26.7	398	1,326	27.3	3,535
Syracuse, N. Y	60	.....	6	7,068	84.2	1,328	52	.....	8	9,676	90.7	987	19	.....	69	4,255	28.6	10,639
Terre Haute, Ind	132	77.6	38	3,176	83.8	616	169	87.6	24	4,258	89.9	477	63	21.5	230	1,702	26.8	4,654
Toledo, Ohio	75	73.9	13	10,253	87.7	1,439	98	95.1	5	13,069	92.9	995	42	26.4	117	4,655	24.2	14,544
Topeka, Kans	221	73.9	78	1,732	72.2	668	351	91.6	32	2,701	92.7	214	219	37.8	361	1,604	34.7	3,014
Trenton, N. J	83	83.0	17	5,944	89.6	693	130	91.5	12	7,425	91.0	737	80	32.8	164	2,747	24.5	8,460
Wichita, Kans	126	74.1	44	2,315	74.4	797	165	89.7	19	3,555	91.8	319	67	22.3	234	2,260	28.3	3,687
Worcester, Mass	74	.....	8	9,014	88.4	1,179	85	.....	3	11,246	94.1	701	26	23.2	86	4,479	28.3	11,372
Yonkers, N. Y	82	.....	10	5,607	92.1	482	82	.....	5	6,878	96.5	249	30	19.5	124	2,629	27.9	6,804
Youngstown, Ohio	71	62.8	42	3,954	72.8	1,475	103	85.8	17	5,220	88.7	666	20	12.0	147	1,723	20.2	6,803
York, Pa	54	.....	26	2,672	86.2	426	85	82.5	18	3,436	91.2	330	21	17.4	100	1,095	21.5	3,997
Zanesville, Ohio	73	72.3	28	1,267	76.1	399	93	.....	6	1,849	94.3	112	43	26.7	118	831	27.7	2,165
CITIES OF THE WEST.																		
Colorado Springs, Colo	65	.....	13	1,480	83.3	296	101	97.1	3	2,126	95.7	96	28	.....	56	1,414	47.3	1,573
Denver, Colo	201	81.7	45	10,844	85.2	1,878	312	93.7	21	15,078	94.4	902	132	28.4	333	7,933	35.8	14,218
Los Angeles, Cal	351	88.6	45	13,658	87.0	2,046	517	96.3	20	19,039	93.5	1,332	232	28.8	573	10,946	35.8	19,606
Oakland, Cal	123	82.6	26	6,576	80.3	1,618	124	94.7	7	9,740	96.0	401	78	30.8	175	5,200	35.8	9,319
Portland, Oreg	20	.....	11	7,450	76.7	2,265	28	.....	4	11,491	93.2	845	16	.....	43	6,986	33.7	13,758
Pueblo, Colo	58	.....	32	2,389	79.7	608	92	90.2	10	2,985	92.5	241	46	33.1	93	1,480	34.2	2,845
San Francisco, Cal	25	.....	18	15,634	80.3	3,837	62	.....	3	22,448	92.5	1,829	25	18.4	111	10,984	28.1	28,159
Seattle, Wash	44	.....	16	8,909	75.5	2,898	83	.....	10	13,444	93.8	881	30	23.4	98	8,333	37.5	13,886

CHAPTER XVI.—ILLITERACY.[1]

ACHIEVEMENT OF LITERACY BY THE NEGRO POPULATION.

A rapid decrease of Negro illiteracy during recent decades is the outstanding fact in the statistics for this class of population. This decrease is an index of improvement throughout the South in facilities available for the common-school education of Negroes and of a general appreciation of the value of literacy as a means of social advancement and efficiency in even the commoner wage-earning occupations.

In considering the data of illiteracy, it should be borne in mind that the percentage of illiteracy for the Negro population as a whole, as for any other class, can respond but slowly to improvement in educational conditions. If, for example, present school facilities throughout the country were to be so improved as to insure ultimate equality of condition as regards literacy between the several classes of whites and the Negroes, a period of half a century or longer would be required to establish that condition of equality in the adult population. Such an extended period would be required because obviously an improvement in school facilities could not materially affect the condition of the adult population except in proportion as that population, naturally reduced in the course of years by mortality, was gradually succeeded by generations of equal literacy.

The manifest improvement in literacy of the adult Negro population indicates, therefore, that improvement of common-school educational facilities has been in progress for a period sufficient materially to affect the entire population of all ages; and an analysis of the returns by age indicates further that the improvement already achieved generally throughout the South, if it is maintained, even without further advance, is certain materially to reduce below its present rate the illiteracy of the Negro population. The process of becoming literate is only partially completed. Present conditions and the improvement which has taken place in recent decades give adequate assurance that excessive illiteracy will in the near future cease to be a characteristic of the Negro population. At the close of the Civil War this class of the population was almost entirely illiterate and

the achievement of general literacy in a period of four or five decades is a fact of immense social importance not only for the Negro race, but as well for the whole community. It is an achievement in part national and in part local of the Negro race, and in a larger sense of the American democracy embracing all racial elements in the population.

DEFINITION OF ILLITERACY.

The basis for the classification of persons as literate or illiterate adopted at the last census, as at previous censuses, was ability to write in some language, irrespective of ability to read, and the inquiry was confined to persons 10 years of age or over. Persons of that age who, as reported by the enumerators, were able to write, whether in English or in some foreign language, were classed as literate, while those who could not write, even though they could read, were classed as illiterate.

ACCURACY OF DATA.

It will be obvious that in securing replies to this inquiry there is opportunity for error. Illiterates may naturally in some instances be unwilling to admit that they can not write and in certain cases the enumerator may be unable to determine the fact of literacy or illiteracy. In general, moreover, enumerators are under some temptation to assume literacy or illiteracy and to make an entry on the schedule without taking the trouble to ask the question covering the entry, with the result that in some cases illiterates are returned as literates or literates as illiterates. It is not improbable that in certain sections of the South white enumerators have been inclined to assume, where specific answers were not obtained to the inquiry, and especially where the person enumerated was not directly interrogated, that whites were able and that Negroes were unable to write, and thus to class the former as literate and the latter as illiterate. In the nature of the case there is no way of determining the margin of error in the returns, but examination and analysis of the returns at different censuses and of those for different sections of the country lead to the conclusion that the figures as given represent fairly the degree of illiteracy characterizing the Negro population of the United States at the present time, as well as the increasing literacy of that class in recent decades.

---

[1] For data relating to illiteracy in the black and mulatto population, see section "Illiteracy of blacks and mulattoes" in Chapter XI, p. 217, and Table 21 of that chapter.

ILLITERACY BY CLASSES.

The whole number of persons 10 years of age and over enumerated at the census of 1910 and the number in this adult population who were reported as unable to write are given in Table 27, page 428, by divisions and states, for the Negro population and for classes of the white population and are given in greater detail as regards race, nativity, and parentage in the following table for the United States as a whole.

Table 1 RACIAL CLASS.	POPULATION 10 YEARS OF AGE AND OVER: 1910.				
	Total.	Illiterate.		Percentage distribution by racial class.	
		Number.	Per cent.	Total.	Illiterate.
All classes...............	71,580,270	5,516,163	7.7	100.0	100.0
Negro.....................	7,317,922	2,227,731	30.4	10.2	40.4
White....................	63,933,870	3,184,633	5.0	89.3	57.7
Native white.............	50,989,341	1,534,272	3.0	71.2	27.8
Foreign-born white........	12,944,529	1,650,361	12.7	18.1	29.9
Indian...................	188,758	85,445	45.3	0.3	1.5
Chinese..................	68,924	10,891	15.8	0.1	0.2
Japanese.................	67,661	6,213	9.2	0.1	0.1
All other................	3,135	1,250	39.9	(1)	(1)

[1] Less than one-tenth of 1 per cent.

The total number of persons in the United States 10 years of age and over reported in 1910 as illiterate was 5,516,163, or 7.7 per cent of the entire population of that age. Of this number 2,227,731 were Negroes, constituting 30.4 per cent, or nearly one-third, of the Negro population of that age. In 1910 Negro illiterates constituted 40.4 per cent of the illiterate population of the country, while the entire Negro population 10 years of age and over constituted only 10.2 per cent of the total population of that age.

Comparing the figures for Negroes with those for other classes, it appears that but 5 per cent of the whites were classed as illiterates; and that of these the foreign-born whites furnished the majority in numbers, and a much larger proportion relatively to the total number foreign born, than did the native whites relatively to the total native white population, the proportion illiterate among foreign-born whites being 12.7 per cent and among native whites 3 per cent. Excepting the Indians, the percentage illiterate for the Negro population exceeded that for any other of the principal population classes.

The excess of Negro illiteracy over the illiteracy of the white population was, however, markedly less in 1910 than it was at either of the two preceding censuses. While the total Negro population 10 years of age and over increased from 5,328,972 in 1890 to 6,415,581 in 1900 and to 7,317,922 in 1910, the number of illiterates in this adult Negro population, as shown in Table 2, decreased from 3,042,668 in 1890 to

2,853,194 in 1900, and to 2,227,731 in 1910, or in terms of percentage from 57.1 per cent in 1890 to 44.5 per cent in 1900, and to 30.4 per cent in 1910. In the same period the percentages for the white population decreased from 7.7 in 1890 to 6.2 in 1900, and to 5 in 1910; the excess of the percentage for Negroes over that for whites being thus reduced from 49.4 in 1890 to 25.4 in 1910.

Table 2 RACIAL CLASS.	ILLITERATES IN THE POPULATION 10 YEARS OF AGE AND OVER.					
	Number.			Per cent.		
	1910	1900	1890 [1]	1910	1900	1890 [1]
All classes............	5,516,163	6,180,069	6,324,702	7.7	10.7	13.3
Negro..................	2,227,731	2,853,194	3,042,668	30.4	44.5	57.1
White..................	3,184,633	3,200,746	3,212,574	5.0	6.2	7.7
Native white..........	1,534,272	1,913,611	2,065,003	3.0	4.6	6.2
Foreign-born white......	1,650,361	1,287,135	1,147,571	12.7	15.9	13.1
Other classes.............	103,799	126,129	69,460	31.6	44.5	45.2

[1] Exclusive of population specially enumerated.

The figures given in Tables 1 and 2 indicate clearly, first, that the illiteracy problem of the United States is very largely a Negro problem, since approximately two-fifths of the illiterates in the country as a whole in 1910 were Negroes; and, second, that as regards this element of the population, the problem is in a fair way of solution, since the increase in literacy among Negroes has been exceedingly rapid in recent years.

SEX AND AGE.

The illiteracy of the Negro population 10 years of age and over, classified by sex and age periods, is given for states in Table 24, page 420, and in somewhat greater detail as regards age in Table 3, following, for the United States as a whole.

The percentage illiterate among Negro males is practically identical with that for females, being 30.1 for males, as compared with 30.7 for females. The difference in these percentages represents an excess of females over males of 35,731 in the illiterate population. The differences between the percentages for males and those for females in the several age periods are, however, much more considerable than the difference shown for the total population 10 years of age and over.

Since the literacy of any community is determined by its educational facilities, where such facilities are deficient, or are of recent establishment, there is a corresponding degree of illiteracy. As is set forth in the chapter on school attendance, there has been a marked increase since 1890 in the number of Negroes attending school. Prior to that date, except in the North and in some limited districts of the South, there were comparatively few educational facilities within reach of the Negro population; and even yet, these facilities are in some sections of the South comparatively meager, whether reference be had to the number of schools, the grade of instruction, or the duration of the school term. The percentage of illiteracy is correspondingly high among this class of the population, and higher among those whose youth antedates the development of educational facilities in recent decades, than it is in the younger generations. This is illustrated in Table 3, which shows that the lowest percentage of illiteracy—18.9—is for the age period 10 to 14 years, and that the percentage increases, with advancing age, the increase becoming especially marked for the age periods including those whose youth coincided in general with the era of reconstruction in the South.

It will be noted that the advance in the percentage illiterate from age period to age period is especially marked in the case of females; the percentage for females in the younger ages—10 to 24 years—being lower, and in the more advanced ages—25 years and over—higher, than for males. For the age period 10 to 14 years, for example, the percentage illiterate was 21.7 among males and 16.1 among females, while for the age period 55 to 64 years the percentage was 55.5 for males and 72 for females. In general, it is true that Negro women past middle age are more illiterate than Negro men, but it would appear that Negro girls and younger women have received at least such elementary school training as is represented by the ability to write, more generally than have Negro boys and young men.

NEGRO AND WHITE ILLITERACY BY SEX AND AGE PERIODS: 1910.

Table 3

AGE PERIOD.	NEGRO POPULATION: 1910.										PERCENTAGE ILLITERATE IN THE WHITE POPULATION: 1910.		
	Both sexes.			Male.			Female.						
	Total.	Illiterate.		Total.	Illiterate.		Total.	Illiterate.		Both sexes.	Male.	Female.
		Number.	Per cent.		Number.	Per cent.		Number.	Per cent.			
10 years and over	7,317,922	2,227,731	30.4	3,637,386	1,096,000	30.1	3,680,536	1,131,731	30.7	5.0	5.0	4.9
10 to 14 years	1,155,266	218,555	18.9	578,074	125,616	21.7	577,192	92,939	16.1	1.8	2.1	1.6
15 to 19 years	1,060,416	214,860	20.3	507,945	126,459	24.9	552,471	88,401	16.0	2.8	3.3	2.4
20 to 24 years	1,030,795	245,860	23.9	482,157	126,970	26.3	548,638	118,890	21.7	4.6	5.2	4.0
25 to 34 years	1,549,316	380,742	24.6	753,968	183,993	24.4	795,348	196,749	24.7	5.2	5.7	4.7
35 to 44 years	1,088,862	351,858	32.3	550,130	152,132	27.7	538,732	199,726	37.1	5.4	5.5	5.4
45 to 54 years	711,979	334,930	47.0	379,315	147,542	38.9	332,664	187,388	56.3	6.3	5.7	6.9
55 to 64 years	396,124	249,584	63.0	216,239	120,046	55.5	179,885	129,538	72.0	7.4	6.4	8.6
65 years and over	294,124	219,255	74.5	152,482	107,877	70.7	141,642	111,378	78.6	9.4	7.4	11.4
Age unknown	31,040	12,087	38.9	17,076	5,365	31.4	13,964	6,722	48.1	6.8	6.1	8.5

DECREASE: 1890-1910.

The collection of statistics of illiteracy was begun by the Bureau of the Census in 1840 and has been continued at each succeeding census. The returns for the censuses for 1840, 1850, and 1860 were, however, so inaccurate, and those for 1870 were so differently classified, as to make satisfactory comparisons with recent censuses impracticable. In the census of 1880, the Negroes were combined with Indians, Chinese, Japanese, and other colored, in the compilations regarding illiteracy, thus impairing the comparability of the statistics for 1880 with those for succeeding census years. In the present report, therefore, compilations comparing 1910 with earlier years are limited to the statistics of the last three censuses.

Attention may, however, be called to one or two facts of interest that appear from the earlier censuses. In them returns were made for the free Negroes on essentially the same basis as for the whites. In 1850 there was a total free Negro population 20 years of age or over of 219,520, and of these, 90,522, or 41.2 per cent, were reported as unable to read and write, leaving nearly 60 per cent in the literate class. There

were 113,629 free Negroes in the South, and of these, 49 per cent, or approximately one-half, were literate.

The censuses of 1890 and 1900 were on the same basis as that of 1910, and Table 4 gives for these three censuses the number and percentage illiterate for the Negro population, by sex and age periods. Diagram I (p. 406) represents the percentages of Table 4 for both sexes combined.

In 1890, 39.8 per cent of the Negro population 10 to 14 years of age were illiterate; in 1900, 30.1 per cent, and in 1910, 18.9 per cent. Thus, for the Negroes of this age, the proportion illiterate decreased in the 20 years from nearly two-fifths to less than one-fifth. In the case of males 10 to 14 years of age the percentage illiterate was 41.9 in 1890, 33.5 in 1900, and 21.7 in 1910; and in the case of females, 37.7 in 1890, 26.8 in 1900, and 16.1 in 1910. A similar decrease from census to census is shown for the older ages.

At each of the earlier censuses as well as at the census of 1910 the percentage illiterate advanced with age. Comparing the ages 10 to 14 years and 65 years and over, for example, the advance for males was in 1910, as has been noted, from 21.7 to 70.7; in 1900 it was from 33.5 to 83.6, and in 1890, from 41.9 to 88.3; for females the corresponding advances were for 1910, from 16.1 to 78.6; for 1900, from 26.8 to 87.2; and for 1890, from 37.7 to 92.1.

Table 4 — NEGRO ILLITERATES.

AGE PERIOD AND CENSUS YEAR.	Number.			Per cent.		
	Both sexes.	Male.	Female.	Both sexes.	Male.	Female.
10 years and over:						
1910	2,227,731	1,096,000	1,131,731	30.4	30.1	30.7
1900	2,853,194	1,371,432	1,481,762	44.5	43.1	45.8
1890 [1]	3,042,668	1,438,923	1,603,745	57.1	54.4	59.8
10 to 14 years:						
1910	218,555	125,616	92,939	18.9	21.7	16.1
1900	328,992	183,540	145,452	30.1	33.5	26.8
1890 [1]	411,726	220,414	191,312	39.8	41.9	37.7
15 to 19 years:						
1910	214,860	126,459	88,401	20.3	24.9	16.0
1900	312,094	173,891	138,203	31.8	36.7	27.2
1890 [1]	371,076	192,853	178,223	42.6	45.7	39.7
20 to 24 years:						
1910	245,860	126,970	118,890	23.9	26.3	21.7
1900	340,516	165,085	175,431	35.1	36.0	34.4
1890 [1]	360,887	163,107	197,780	49.3	46.5	51.9
25 to 34 years:						
1910	380,742	183,993	196,749	24.6	24.4	24.7
1900	496,180	222,516	273,664	39.3	35.7	42.8
1890 [1]	550,551	235,420	315,131	56.8	49.5	63.8
35 to 44 years:						
1910	351,858	152,132	199,726	32.3	27.7	37.1
1900	437,503	177,199	260,304	52.0	43.0	60.6
1890 [1]	498,667	208,451	290,216	70.5	60.6	79.8
45 to 54 years:						
1910	334,930	147,542	187,388	47.0	38.9	56.3
1900	420,438	191,883	228,555	68.1	59.3	77.8
1890 [1]	403,634	192,520	211,114	80.8	74.8	87.1
55 to 64 years:						
1910	249,584	120,046	129,538	63.0	55.5	72.0
1900	267,312	134,535	132,777	78.4	73.4	84.3
1890 [1]	231,490	120,399	111,091	86.3	83.2	89.9
65 years and over:						
1910	219,255	107,877	111,378	74.5	70.7	78.6
1900	223,124	111,158	111,966	85.4	83.6	87.2
1890 [1]	190,899	94,806	96,093	90.2	88.3	92.1
Age unknown:						
1910	12,087	5,365	6,722	38.9	31.4	48.1
1900	27,035	11,625	15,410	55.4	46.2	65.1
1890 [1]	23,738	10,953	12,785	66.3	59.4	73.6

[1] Figures for 1890 are exclusive of illiterate persons in Indian Territory and on Indian reservations specially enumerated but for which illiteracy statistics are not available.

In the Negro population 10 years of age and over as a whole, the percentage of illiteracy among females exceeded that among males by 5.4 in 1890, by 2.7 in 1900, and by only 0.6 in 1910. This approach to a condition of equality as regards illiteracy among males and females was, however, more apparent than real. In the Negro population 10 to 14 years of age, for example, the percentage of illiteracy for males exceeded that for females in 1910 by 5.6; in the population 15 to 19, by 8.9; and in the population 20 to 24, by 4.6. In the older age groups the percentage for females exceeded that for males, the differences in the percentages being, in the population 25 to 34 years of age, 0.3; in the population 35 to 44, 9.4; and in succeeding age groups 17.4, 16.5, 7.9, and 16.7, respectively. In five of the eight age groups shown the differences were less in 1910 than in 1900, but in the case of three age groups the differences were greater in 1900.

Changes in the proportion illiterate from census to census, and differences in the proportion from age to age, with the excess of males or females among illiterates of each age, are shown in Diagram II.

DIAGRAM I.—PERCENTAGE ILLITERATE, BY AGE PERIODS, FOR THE NEGRO POPULATION: 1910, 1900, AND 1890.

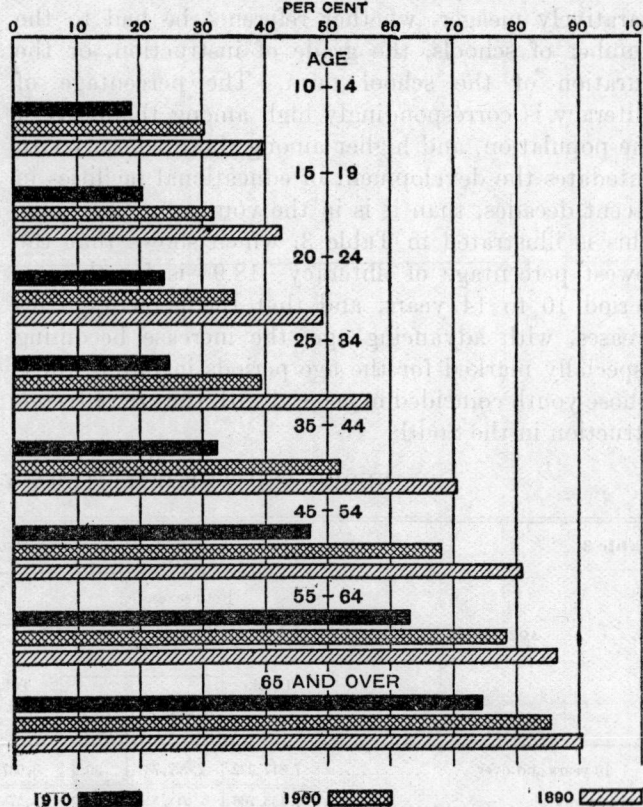

Although the Negro population 10 years of age and over increased during the decade 1900–1910 by 902,341, the number of illiterates decreased by 625,463. The population increase for the preceding decade amounted to 1,086,609 and the decrease in number of illiterates to 189,474. Classified by age, the Negro population in each age group increased and the number of illiterates decreased during the decade ending in 1910. In the decade preceding, also, population increased, and the number of illiterates decreased in each of the age periods comprising the population under 45 years of age—both population and the number of illiterates showing increases for the more advanced age periods. These absolute increases and decreases are shown in Table 5.

Table 5 — NEGRO POPULATION.

AGE PERIOD.	1900–1910		1890–1900	
	Increase of population.	Decrease in number of illiterates.	Increase of population.	Decrease in number of illiterates.
10 years and over	902,341	625,463	1,086,609	189,474
10 to 14 years	63,276	110,437	58,289	82,734
15 to 19 years	78,394	97,234	110,904	58,982
20 to 24 years	61,623	94,656	287,624	20,371
25 to 34 years	287,230	115,438	292,558	54,371
35 to 44 years	246,959	85,645	134,322	61,164
45 to 54 years	94,608	85,508	117,692	[2] 16,804
55 to 64 years	55,261	17,728	72,543	[2] 35,822
65 years and over	32,761	3,869	49,679	[2] 32,225
Age unknown	[1] 17,771	14,948	12,998	[2] 3,297

[1] Decrease.　　　　　[2] Increase.

DIAGRAM II.—PERCENTAGE ILLITERATE BY AGE PERIODS, FOR NEGRO MALES AND FEMALES, WITH EXCESS OF MALES OR FEMALES AT EACH AGE: 1910, 1900, AND 1890.

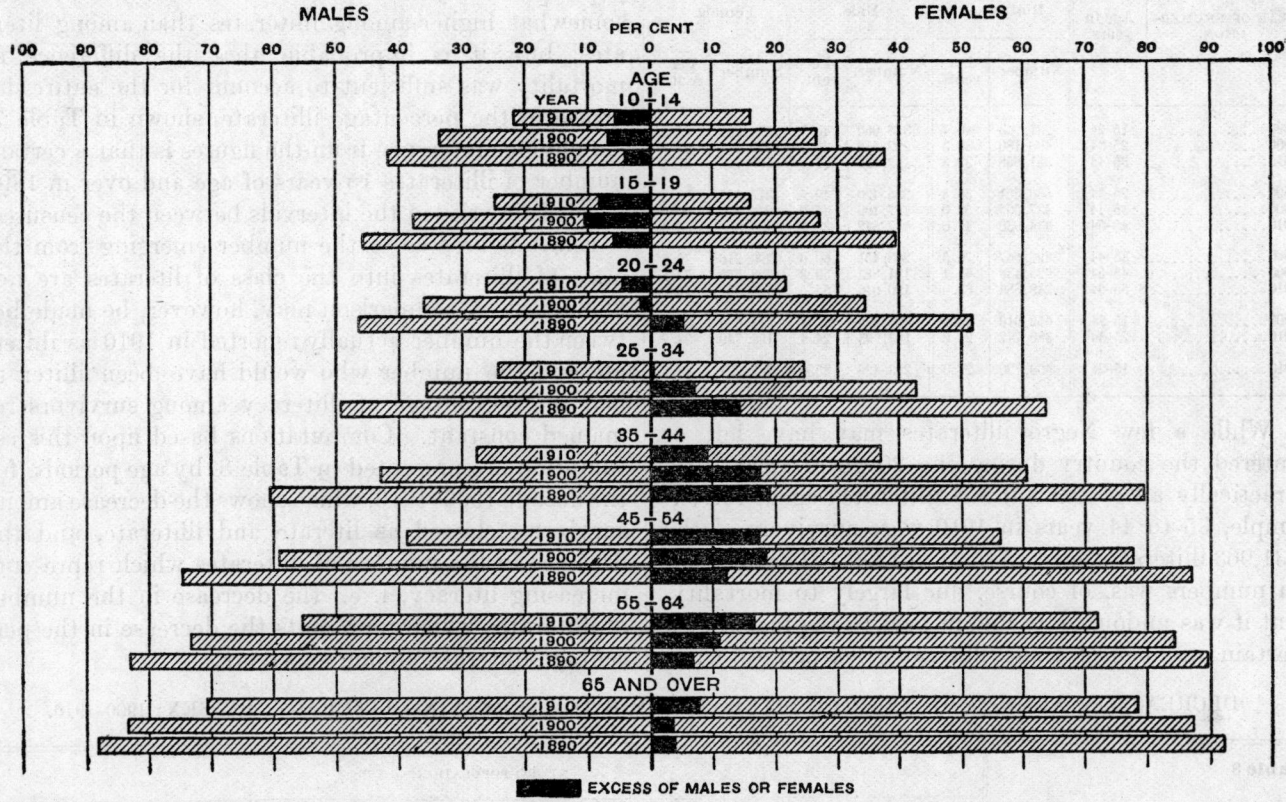

ILLITERATES PER 1,000 POPULATION.

The decreases from census to census in the percentage illiterate for the total Negro population 10 years of age and over, and for each of the several age groups shown in Tables 4 and 5, may be stated as decreases in the number of illiterates per 1,000 population, as in Table 6.

Table 6

CENSUS YEAR.	NEGRO POPULATION.								
	10 years of age and over.	10 to 14 years.	15 to 19 years.	20 to 24 years.	25 to 34 years.	35 to 44 years.	45 to 54 years.	55 to 64 years.	65 years and over.
	NUMBER OF ILLITERATES PER 1,000 POPULATION OF AGE SPECIFIED.								
1910............	304	189	203	239	246	323	470	630	745
1900............	445	301	218	351	393	520	681	784	854
1890............	571	398	426	493	568	705	808	863	902
	DECREASE IN NUMBER OF ILLITERATES PER 1,000 POPULATION.								
1890–1910.......	267	209	223	254	322	382	338	233	157
1900–1910.......	141	112	115	112	147	197	211	154	109
1890–1900.......	126	97	108	142	175	185	127	79	48

In 1890 the number of illiterates per 1,000 Negro population 10 years of age and over was 571; in 1900 it was 445; and in 1910, 304. The decrease in the number of illiterates per 1,000 population amounted to 126 in the decade 1890–1900 and to 141 in the following decade—the total decrease for the 20 years 1890–1910

amounting to 267 per 1,000 population. In 1890, 398 per 1,000 Negro population 10 to 14 years of age were illiterate; in 1910, 189 per 1,000, the decrease in the number of illiterates per 1,000 population of this age amounting to 209 for the 20 years. In 1890, 902 per 1,000 population 65 years of age and over were illiterate, the proportion for this age group in 1910 being 745, and the decrease for the period, 157. Corresponding decreases are shown in Table 6 for each of the other age periods.

RELATIVE DECREASE OF LITERATES AND ILLITERATES IN SPECIFIC AGE GROUPS.

It is of interest to note that, as regards the individuals composing, respectively, the several age groups in 1890, the proportion illiterate among the survivors has decreased from census to census. The persons who were 15 to 24 years of age in 1890, for example, so far as they were still living at succeeding censuses, were 25 to 34 years of age in 1900 and 35 to 44 in 1910. The percentage illiterate for this group of individuals decreased from 45.7 in 1890 to 39.3 in 1900, and to 32.3 in 1910. In Table 7 the number and percentage illiterate among this group of individuals, classified by sex, is given as returned at each of the last three censuses, and corresponding data are given for other age groups. The proportion illiterate decreased in each decade among survivors, both male and female, for each age group.

Table 7

YEAR OF ENUMERATION.	Age in years.	NEGRO ILLITERATES.					
		Both sexes.		Male.		Female.	
		Number.	Per cent.	Number.	Per cent.	Number.	Per cent.
1890	15–24	731,963	45.7	355,960	46.1	376,003	45.3
1900	25–34	496,180	39.3	222,516	35.7	273,664	42.8
1910	35–44	351,858	32.3	152,132	27.7	199,726	37.1
1890	25–34	550,551	56.8	235,420	49.5	315,131	63.8
1900	35–44	437,503	52.0	177,199	43.0	260,304	60.6
1910	45–54	334,930	47.0	147,542	38.9	187,388	56.3
1890	35–44	498,667	70.5	208,451	60.6	290,216	79.8
1900	45–54	420,438	68.1	191,883	59.3	228,555	77.8
1910	55–64	249,584	63.0	120,046	55.5	129,538	72.0
1900	15–24	652,610	33.4	338,976	36.3	313,634	30.8
1910	25–34	380,742	24.6	183,993	24.4	196,749	24.7
1910	15–24	460,720	22.0	253,429	25.6	207,291	18.8

While a few Negro illiterates may have left or entered the country during the 20 years 1890–1910, practically all of the 351,858 illiterates aged, for example, 35 to 44 years in 1910 were survivors of the 731,963 illiterates aged 15 to 24 in 1890. The decrease in numbers was, of course, due largely to mortality, but it was undoubtedly due in part to the fact that a certain number of these illiterates learned to write

during the period. The rate of mortality in the population 15 years of age and over may have been somewhat higher among illiterates than among literates, but it is improbable that the difference in mortality was sufficient to account for the entire decrease in the percentage illiterate, shown in Table 7. An obvious inference from the figures is that a certain number of illiterates 15 years of age and over in 1890 learned to write in the intervals between the censuses.

Exact figures as to the number emerging from the class of illiterates into the class of literates are not available. A comparison may, however, be made between the number actually reported in 1910 as illiterate and the number who would have been illiterate had the percentage of illiteracy among survivors remained constant. Computations based upon this assumption are presented in Table 8, by age periods, for the decade 1900–1910, which shows the decrease among survivors, classed as literate and illiterate, and the decrease in the number of illiterates which represents increasing literacy, i. e., the decrease in the number of illiterates which represents the decrease in the percentage illiterate among survivors.

DECREASE IN NUMBER OF NEGRO ILLITERATES DUE TO INCREASING LITERACY, BY SEX: 1900–1910.

Table 8

AGE PERIOD.		Total.		Literate.				Illiterate.				Decrease,[1] 1900–1910.				Decrease in number of illiterates due to increase in literacy
				Number.		Per cent.		Number.		Per cent.		Number.		Per cent.		
1900	1910	1900	1910	1900	1910	1900	1910	1900	1910	1900	1910	Literate.	Illiterate.	Literate.	Illiterate.	
								BOTH SEXES.								
10 to 14 years	20 to 24 years	1,091,990	1,030,795	762,998	784,935	69.9	76.1	328,992	245,860	30.1	23.9	+21,937	83,132	+2.9	25.3	62,698
15 to 24 years	25 to 34 years	1,951,194	1,549,316	1,298,584	1,168,574	66.6	75.4	652,610	380,742	33.4	24.6	130,010	271,868	10.0	41.7	137,915
25 to 34 years	35 to 44 years	1,262,086	1,088,862	765,906	737,004	60.7	67.7	496,180	351,858	39.3	32.3	28,902	144,322	3.8	29.1	75,115
35 to 44 years	45 to 54 years	841,903	711,979	404,400	377,049	48.0	53.0	437,503	334,930	52.0	47.0	27,351	102,573	6.8	23.4	29,769
45 to 54 years	55 to 64 years	617,371	396,124	196,933	146,540	31.9	37.0	420,438	249,584	68.1	63.0	50,393	170,854	25.6	40.6	18,597
55 years and over	65 years and over	602,226	294,124	111,790	74,869	18.6	25.5	490,436	219,255	81.4	74.5	36,921	271,181	33.0	55.3	20,470
								MALE.								
10 to 14 years	20 to 24 years	548,642	482,157	365,102	355,187	66.5	73.7	183,540	126,970	33.5	26.3	9,915	56,570	2.7	30.8	34,553
15 to 24 years	25 to 34 years	932,671	753,968	593,695	569,975	63.7	75.6	338,976	183,993	36.3	24.4	23,720	154,983	4.0	45.7	89,697
25 to 34 years	35 to 44 years	622,727	550,130	400,211	397,998	64.3	72.3	222,516	152,132	35.7	27.7	2,213	70,384	0.6	31.6	44,264
35 to 44 years	45 to 54 years	412,461	379,315	235,262	231,773	57.0	61.1	177,199	147,542	43.0	38.9	3,489	29,657	1.5	16.7	15,563
45 to 54 years	55 to 64 years	323,683	216,239	131,800	96,193	40.7	44.5	191,883	120,046	59.3	55.5	35,607	71,837	27.0	37.4	8,184
55 years and over	65 years and over	316,309	152,482	70,616	44,605	22.3	29.3	245,693	107,877	77.7	70.7	26,011	137,816	36.8	56.1	10,662
								FEMALE.								
10 to 14 years	20 to 24 years	543,348	548,638	397,896	429,748	73.2	78.3	145,452	118,890	26.8	21.7	+31,852	26,562	+8.0	18.3	28,145
15 to 24 years	25 to 34 years	1,018,523	795,348	704,889	598,599	69.2	75.3	313,634	196,749	30.8	24.7	106,290	116,885	15.1	37.3	48,218
25 to 34 years	35 to 44 years	639,359	538,732	365,695	339,006	57.2	62.9	273,664	199,726	42.8	37.1	26,689	73,938	7.3	27.0	30,851
35 to 44 years	45 to 54 years	429,442	332,664	169,138	145,276	39.4	43.7	260,304	187,388	60.6	56.3	23,862	72,916	14.1	28.0	14,206
45 to 54 years	55 to 64 years	293,688	179,885	65,133	50,347	22.2	28.0	228,555	129,538	77.8	72.0	14,786	99,017	22.7	43.3	10,413
55 years and over	65 years and over	285,917	141,642	41,174	30,264	14.4	21.4	244,743	111,378	85.6	78.6	10,910	133,365	26.5	54.5	9,868

[1] A plus sign (+) denotes increase.

The total Negro population 10 to 14 years of age in 1900 was 1,091,990. The survivors of this group ten years later were included in the group 20 to 24 years of age and numbered 1,030,795. Of the total number reported in 1900, 762,998, or 69.9 per cent, were classed as literate, and 328,992, or 30.1 per cent, as illiterate;

of the survivors in 1910, 784,935, or 76.1 per cent, were classed as literate, and 245,860, or 23.9 per cent, as illiterate. Thus in ten years the number of persons in this group, classed as literate increased—notwithstanding the losses by mortality—by 21,937, while the number of illiterates decreased by 83,132. In this group of individuals the number of literates increased 2.9 per cent during the decade 1900–1910 while the number of illiterates decreased 25.3 per cent. In the succeeding age group the number both of the literates and of the illiterates decreased, but the relative decrease was much greater in the case of the illiterates, being 41.7 for illiterates as compared with 10 per cent for literates. Similarly, as regards the more advanced ages, the percentage decreases were much higher for illiterates than for literates, the differences being so marked as to indicate, even for the more advanced ages, that a considerable number in these age groups learned to write in the interval between the censuses. This statement is true of both males and females.

Had the proportion of illiteracy among survivors of the group of individuals aged 10 to 14 years in 1900 remained unchanged during the decade 1900–1910, the proportion of illiterates in the population 20 to 24 years of age in 1910 would have been 30.1 instead of 23.9 per cent, and the number of illiterates would have been 308,558, instead of only 245,860, as reported in 1910. If it be assumed that the rate of mortality among literates was the same as among illiterates, the difference of 62,698 between these numbers represents approximately the number among survivors in 1910 who had been transferred from the illiterate to the literate class by reason of their having learned to write during the intervening decade. Similar calculations in regard to the other age groups show that the number who had, on the assumption made of equal mortality, passed from the illiterate to the literate class included 137,915 who were 15 to 24 years of age in 1900; 75,115 who were 25 to 34; 29,769 who were 35 to 44; and 20,470 who were 55 years of age and over; giving for the population 10 years of age and over in 1900 a total of 344,564.

ILLITERACY BY GEOGRAPHIC SECTIONS AND DIVISIONS.

In illiteracy, as in every other phase of Negro life in the United States, chief interest centers about conditions in the South. Of the 2,227,731 Negro illiterates in the United States in 1910, 2,133,961, or 95.8 per cent, were in that section of the country. The number and percentage illiterate in the Negro population at each of the last three censuses is shown by sections and southern divisions in Table 9.

The percentage illiterate for Negroes in 1910 was 33.3 in the South, against 10.5 in the North, and 7 in the West. Comparing the three southern divisions, the South Atlantic had the largest number of

illiterates but the lowest percentage, the percentage for the East South Central division being somewhat higher than that in the West South Central. In general, however, as regards the proportion illiterate, the situation is about the same in the three southern divisions.

Table 9	NEGRO POPULATION 10 YEARS OF AGE AND OVER.				
SECTION, DIVISION, AND YEAR.	Total.	Illiterate.		Decennial increase in population.	Decennial decrease[1] in number illiterate.
		Number.	Per cent.		
United States:					
1910	7,317,922	2,227,731	30.4	902,341	625,463
1900	6,415,581	2,853,194	44.5	1,086,609	189,474
1890	5,328,972	3,042,668	57.1		
The South:					
1910	6,408,539	2,133,961	33.3	743,564	583,645
1900	5,664,975	2,717,606	48.0	913,212	165,610
1890	4,751,763	2,883,216	60.7		
South Atlantic division:					
1910	2,986,936	969,432	32.5	331,103	280,847
1900	2,655,833	1,250,279	47.1	351,658	134,353
1890	2,304,175	1,384,632	60.1		
East South Central division:					
1910	1,960,898	681,507	34.8	158,070	206,331
1900	1,802,828	887,838	49.2	301,398	34,826
1890	1,501,430	922,664	61.5		
West South Central division:					
1910	1,460,705	483,022	33.1	254,391	96,467
1900	1,206,314	579,489	48.0	260,156	+3,569
1890	946,158	575,920	60.9		
The North:					
1910	865,053	90,659	10.5	140,309	41,530
1900	724,744	132,189	18.2	170,357	21,962
1890	554,387	154,151	27.8		
The West:					
1910	44,330	3,111	7.0	18,468	288
1900	25,862	3,399	13.1	3,040	1,902
1890	22,822	5,301	23.2		

[1] A plus sign (+) denotes increase.

In the South the percentage illiterate in the Negro population 10 years of age and over decreased from 60.7 in 1890, to 48 in 1900, and to 33.3 in 1910. During the 20 years under review, the Negro population of this age in the South increased 1,656,776, or 34.9 per cent, while the number of illiterates in the South decreased 749,255, or 26 per cent; in the North, population increased 310,666, or 56 per cent, the number of illiterates decreasing by 63,492, or 41.2 per cent; in the West, the population increase was 21,508, or nearly 100 per cent, the decrease in the number of illiterates being 2,190, or 41.3 per cent. In this 20-year period the South Atlantic division showed an increase of 682,761, or 29.6 per cent, in the Negro population 10 years of age and over, and a decrease of 415,200, or 30 per cent, in the number of illiterates included in that population; the East South Central showed a population increase of 459,468, or 30.6 per cent, and a decrease in the number illiterate of 241,157, or 26.1 per cent; the West South Central, a population increase of 514,547, or 54.4 per cent, and a decrease of 92,898, or 16.1 per cent, in the number of illiterates. In the North and in each of the southern divisions the decade 1890–1900 showed greater increases in population and smaller decreases in the number of illiterates than the decade 1900–1910, probably due in part to an undercount of population and of illiterates in 1890. It is, however, clear that progress as regards literacy was uninterrupted during this entire period, and it is certainly a fact significant of educational progress in the South that during the single decade 1900–1910 in this section of the country the number of illiterates in the Negro population 10 years of age and over should have decreased by 583,645, while the total population of that age increased by 743,564.

The decrease in the proportion illiterate, expressed as the number of illiterates per 1,000 population 10 years of age and over, is given in Table 10, by sections and southern divisions, for the period 1890–1910.

Table 10	ILLITERATES PER 1,000 NEGRO POPULATION 10 YEARS OF AGE AND OVER.						
YEAR AND PERIOD.	United States.	The South.				The North.	The West.
		Total.	South Atlantic division.	East South Central division.	West South Central division.		
1910......	304	333	325	348	331	105	70
1900......	445	480	471	492	480	182	131
1890......	571	607	601	615	609	278	232
Decrease: 1890–1910....	267	274	276	267	278	173	162

In the 20-year period 1890–1910 the number of illiterates per 1,000 Negro population 10 years of age and over decreased in the South from 607 to 333, the decrease amounting to 274; the decrease in the North, from 278 to 105, amounted to 173; and the decrease in the West, from 232 to 131, amounted to 162 per 1,000 population.

In Table 11 the number and percentage of illiteracy is shown for Negro males and females for the nine divisions.

Table 11	NEGRO POPULATION 10 YEARS OF AGE AND OVER: 1910.					
SECTION AND DIVISION.	Male.	Female.	Illiterates.			
			Number.		Per cent.	
			Male.	Female.	Male.	Female.
United States.......	3,637,386	3,680,536	1,096,000	1,131,731	30.1	30.7
The North...........	438,578	426,475	43,255	47,404	9.9	11.1
New England........	27,389	27,932	2,107	2,234	7.7	8.0
Middle Atlantic......	171,008	180,538	12,573	15,238	7.4	8.4
East North Central...	133,614	120,931	13,897	14,174	10.4	11.7
West North Central...	106,567	97,074	14,678	15,758	13.8	16.2
The South...........	3,174,163	3,234,376	1,051,239	1,082,722	33.1	33.5
South Atlantic.......	1,470,297	1,516,639	477,107	492,325	32.4	32.5
East South Central...	970,921	989,977	337,893	343,614	34.8	34.7
West South Central...	732,945	727,760	236,239	246,783	32.2	33.9
The West............	24,645	19,685	1,506	1,605	6.1	8.2
Mountain............	10,461	8,294	754	743	7.2	9.0
Pacific.............	14,184	11,391	752	862	5.3	7.6

It has been noted that in the country as a whole in 1910 the percentage illiterate among Negro females was slightly higher than among Negro males—30.7, as compared with 30.1. A corresponding excess in the percentage illiterate for females over the per-

centage for males, though slight, nevertheless obtains in each of the nine geographic divisions, except in the East South Central division. In the three southern divisions, however, and in the South as a whole the percentages for males and for females are practically identical.

The number and percentage illiterate at each of the last three censuses and the decrease in the number of illiterates during the two decades—1890–1900, 1900–1910—are shown for the Negro population, classified by sex, in Table 12, for sections and southern divisions.

The most prominent fact shown in Table 12 is that in each section of the country the absolute decrease in illiteracy during the decade 1900–1910 greatly exceeded that during the decade preceding. This is undoubtedly due in part to the undercounting in 1890, but it seems clear from the data that, as compared with the decreases of the earlier decade, the decreases of the decade 1900–1910 were in fact much more considerable. It should be borne in mind that the sectional and divisional decreases shown in Table 12 were undoubtedly somewhat affected by migratory shiftings of the population during the two decades.

For the South as a whole the total decrease in number of illiterates during the 20 years 1890–1910 amounted to 749,255; of this total, 165,610 is credited to the decade 1890–1900 and 583,645 to the decade following. The decrease in the decade 1890–1900 thus amounted to only a little over one-fifth of the total decrease in the 20 years. Of the decrease in the number of illiterate males in the South, less than one-fifth was in the earlier period, and of the decrease in the number of illiterate females, less than one-third. In the North the decrease during the earlier decade amounted in the case of both males and females to one-third of the total decrease. Only in the West—where the numbers are inconsiderable—was the decrease greater in the earlier decade. In each of the three southern divisions, also, both for males and for females, the larger decreases are those for the later decade. In the South Atlantic division only one-third, approximately, of the decrease in number of illiterate males and of illiterate females during the 20 years was in the earlier decade. In the East South Central division only approximately one-twelfth of the decrease in the number of illiterate males was in the first decade and less than one-fifth of the decrease in the number of illiterate females. In the West South Central division there was a small increase of 4,779 in the number of illiterate males in the decade 1890–1900, and a small decrease of 1,210 in the number of illiterate females; in the decade following the number of illiterate males decreased by 40,926 and of illiterate females by 55,541.

The decreases in the number of Negro illiterates during the decade 1900–1910 and the increases in the Negro population 10 years of age and over are shown in Table 13.

ILLITERATES IN THE NEGRO POPULATION 10 YEARS OF AGE AND OVER, BY SEX, BY SECTIONS AND SOUTHERN DIVISIONS: 1910, 1900, AND 1890.

Table 12

YEAR AND PERIOD.	ILLITERATES IN THE NEGRO POPULATION 10 YEARS OF AGE AND OVER.																		
	The South.												The North.			The West.		
	Both sexes.	Male.	Female.	South Atlantic division.			East South Central division.			West South Central division.			Both sexes.	Male.	Female.	Both sexes.	Male.	Female.
				Both sexes.	Male.	Female.	Both sexes.	Male.	Female.	Both sexes.	Male.	Female.						
NUMBER ILLITERATE.																		
1910	2,133,961	1,051,239	1,082,722	969,432	477,107	492,325	681,507	337,893	343,614	483,022	236,239	246,783	90,659	43,255	47,404	3,111	1,506	1,605
1900	2,717,606	1,306,309	1,411,297	1,250,279	599,160	651,119	887,838	429,984	457,854	579,489	277,165	302,324	132,189	63,379	68,810	3,399	1,744	1,655
1890 [1]	2,883,216	1,362,219	1,520,997	1,384,632	651,436	733,196	922,664	438,397	484,267	575,920	272,386	303,534	154,151	73,613	80,538	5,301	3,091	2,210
PERCENTAGE ILLITERATE.																		
1910	33.3	33.1	33.5	32.5	32.4	32.5	34.8	34.8	34.7	33.1	32.2	33.9	10.5	9.9	11.1	7.0	6.1	8.2
1900	48.0	46.7	49.3	47.1	46.0	48.1	49.2	48.1	50.4	48.0	46.0	50.1	18.2	17.3	19.2	13.1	11.7	15.1
1890 [1]	60.7	58.0	63.3	60.1	57.6	62.5	61.5	58.9	63.9	60.9	57.4	64.3	27.8	26.0	29.6	23.2	21.5	26.2
DECREASE IN NUMBER ILLITERATE.																		
1900–1910	583,645	255,070	328,575	280,847	122,053	158,794	206,331	92,091	114,240	96,467	40,926	55,541	41,530	20,124	21,406	288	238	50
1890–1900	165,610	55,910	109,700	134,353	52,276	82,077	34,826	8,413	26,413	[2] 3,569	[2] 4,779	1,210	21,962	10,234	11,728	1,902	1,347	555
1890–1910	749,255	310,980	438,275	415,200	174,329	240,871	241,157	100,504	140,653	92,898	36,147	56,751	63,492	30,358	33,134	2,190	1,585	605

[1] Figures for 1890 are exclusive of illiterate persons in Indian Territory and on Indian reservations specially enumerated but for which illiterate statistics are not available.
[2] Increase.

Table 13

SECTION AND DIVISION.	INCREASE IN NEGRO POPULATION 10 YEARS OF AGE AND OVER, 1900–1910.		DECREASE IN NUMBER OF NEGRO ILLITERATES, 1900–1910.	
	Male.	Female.	Male.	Female.
United States	455,736	446,605	275,432	350,031
The South	374,729	368,835	255,070	328,575
South Atlantic	167,568	163,535	122,053	158,794
East South Central	77,369	80,701	92,091	114,240
West South Central	129,792	124,599	40,926	55,541
The North	71,289	69,020	20,124	21,406
The West	9,718	8,750	238	50

In each section and division shown in Table 13 the number of Negro males and of Negro females 10 years of age and over increased during the decade 1900–1910, while the number of illiterate males and females decreased. The decrease in the number of illiterates was greater in the case of females than of males, both in the South and in the North, the numbers in the West being inconsiderable. In the South, while the number of males increased by 374,729, the decrease in the number of illiterate males amounted to 255,070; for females, the population increase amounted to 368,835 and the decrease in the number of illiterates to 328,575. In each of the three southern divisions corresponding increases and decreases are shown, the decrease in illiteracy being in each division greater for females than for males. These figures seem to indicate either a greater effort to overcome illiteracy on the part of females than of males, or better opportunities for females to acquire an elementary school training.

The number and percentage illiterate in the Negro population, classified by age, is shown in Table 14.

ILLITERATES IN THE NEGRO POPULATION, CLASSIFIED BY AGE PERIODS, BY SECTIONS AND SOUTHERN DIVISIONS: 1910.

Table 14

AGE PERIOD.	NEGRO POPULATION: 1910.																		
	The South.												The North.			The West.		
	Total.	Illiterate.		South Atlantic division.			East South Central division.			West South Central division.			Total.	Illiterate.		Total.	Illiterate.	
		Number.	Per cent.	Total.	Illiterate.		Total.	Illiterate.		Total.	Illiterate.			Number.	Per cent.		Number.	Per cent.
					Number.	Per cent.		Number.	Per cent.		Number.	Per cent.						
10 years and over.	6,408,539	2,133,961	33.3	2,986,936	969,432	32.5	1,960,898	681,507	34.8	1,460,705	483,022	33.1	865,053	90,659	10.5	44,330	3,111	7.0
10 to 14 years	1,073,980	217,208	20.2	513,239	97,196	18.9	320,476	66,209	20.7	240,265	53,803	22.4	78,205	1,317	1.7	3,081	30	1.0
15 to 24 years	1,882,319	453,097	24.1	883,929	206,434	23.4	569,118	141,986	24.9	429,272	104,677	24.4	200,049	7,347	3.7	8,843	276	3.1
25 to 34 years	1,307,248	367,864	28.1	595,525	166,058	27.9	402,101	116,989	29.1	309,622	84,817	27.4	229,432	12,415	5.4	12,636	463	3.7
35 to 44 years	910,025	335,136	36.8	421,374	152,982	36.3	278,306	106,120	38.1	210,345	76,034	36.1	169,052	16,156	9.6	9,785	566	5.8
45 to 54 years	607,895	315,393	51.9	279,676	142,627	51.0	191,801	103,766	54.1	136,418	69,000	50.6	98,341	18,903	19.2	5,743	634	11.0
55 to 64 years	343,958	232,672	67.6	162,623	108,023	66.4	108,199	75,778	70.0	73,136	48,871	66.8	49,737	16,363	32.9	2,429	549	22.6
65 years and over	256,694	201,448	78.5	119,140	91,829	77.1	82,481	66,616	80.8	55,073	43,003	78.1	35,973	17,246	47.9	1,457	561	38.5
Age unknown	26,420	11,143	42.2	11,430	4,283	37.5	8,416	4,043	48.0	6,574	2,817	42.9	4,264	912	21.4	356	32	9.0

Approximately one-fifth (20.2 per cent) of the Negro children 10 to 14 years of age in the South were illiterate in 1910, the proportion illiterate among Negro children of this age in the North being only 1.7 per cent and in the West, 1 per cent. Comparing age periods, the percentage of illiteracy increases with age, in each of the several sections and divisions, advancing rapidly after the 25 to 34 age period. The percentages for the several age periods do not show any marked divergencies from division to division in the South, those for the South Atlantic and West South Central being generally somewhat lower than those for the East South Central division.

In Table 15 the percentage illiterate in 1910 in the Negro population, classified by age, is given for sections and for each of the nine divisions, the percentages for the sections and for the three southern divisions being repeated from the preceding table.

In each of the nine divisions the percentage of illiteracy increases with age; in New England, for example, the increase was from 0.4 per cent for those aged 10 to 14, to 25 per cent for those aged 65 years and over, and corresponding increases may be noted for other divisions. The adult Negro population of the North and West is to a greater or less degree composed of migrants from the South, and to the extent that it is so tends to reflect the high rates of illiteracy which are and have been in the recent past prevalent in the South. It is, however, probably true that the proportion illiterate among adult Negroes who migrate from the South to the North and West is lower than it is in the nonmigrant population of the South, and this may account in part for the fact that the percentages shown for the Negro population of advanced age in the North and West are lower than those for the population of the same age in the South.

Table 15 — PERCENTAGE ILLITERATE IN THE NEGRO POPULATION OF AGE SPECIFIED: 1910.

SECTION AND DIVISION.	10 years of age and over.	10–14 years of age.	15–24 years of age.	25–34 years of age.	35–44 years of age.	45–54 years of age.	55–64 years of age.	65 years and over.
United States	30.4	18.9	22.0	24.6	32.3	47.0	63.0	74.5
The South	33.3	20.2	24.1	28.1	36.8	51.9	67.6	78.5
South Atlantic	32.5	18.9	23.4	27.9	36.3	51.0	66.4	77.1
East South Central	34.8	20.7	24.9	29.1	38.1	54.1	70.0	80.8
West South Central	33.1	22.4	24.4	27.4	36.1	50.6	66.8	78.1
The North	10.5	1.7	3.7	5.4	9.6	19.2	32.9	47.9
New England	7.8	0.4	4.6	7.1	7.5	10.6	16.5	25.0
Middle Atlantic	7.9	1.0	3.2	4.6	8.1	15.5	25.1	36.4
East North Central	11.0	1.2	3.1	5.1	9.7	19.4	34.0	50.2
West North Central	14.9	3.6	4.9	6.9	12.8	27.3	46.3	63.6
The West	7.0	1.0	3.1	3.7	5.8	11.0	22.6	38.5
Mountain	8.0	1.6	3.9	4.3	7.2	12.4	25.8	41.4
Pacific	6.3	0.6	2.5	3.2	4.7	10.1	20.4	36.7

In Table 16 the percentage of illiteracy is shown for the Negro population, classified by sex and age, for the two census years 1910 and 1900.

Taking the Negro population 10 years of age and over, as a whole, the difference between the sexes, as regards the percentage illiterate, was less in 1910 than in 1900 in each section of the country.

PERCENTAGE ILLITERATE IN THE NEGRO POPULATION, CLASSIFIED BY SEX AND AGE PERIODS, BY SECTIONS AND SOUTHERN DIVISIONS: 1910 AND 1900.

Table 16 — PERCENTAGE ILLITERATE IN THE NEGRO POPULATION OF AGE SPECIFIED.

AGE PERIOD AND YEAR.	United States Both sexes	Male	Female	The South Both sexes	Male	Female	South Atlantic division Both sexes	Male	Female	East South Central division Both sexes	Male	Female	West South Central division Both sexes	Male	Female	The North Both sexes	Male	Female	The West Both sexes	Male	Female
10 years of age and over:																					
1910	30.4	30.1	30.7	33.3	33.1	33.5	32.5	32.4	32.5	34.8	34.8	34.7	33.1	32.2	33.9	10.5	9.9	11.1	7.0	6.1	8.2
1900	44.5	43.1	45.8	48.0	46.7	49.3	47.1	46.0	48.1	49.2	48.1	50.4	48.0	46.0	50.1	18.2	17.3	19.2	13.1	11.7	15.1
10 to 14 years:																					
1910	18.9	21.7	16.1	20.2	23.2	17.3	18.9	22.1	15.8	20.7	23.8	17.5	22.4	24.7	20.1	1.7	2.0	1.4	1.0	1.3	0.7
1900	30.1	33.5	26.8	32.2	35.6	28.7	31.3	35.0	27.5	33.1	36.8	29.4	32.7	35.2	30.1	4.2	4.9	3.5	1.7	2.0	1.3
15 to 24 years:																					
1910	22.0	25.6	18.8	24.1	27.9	20.6	23.4	27.4	19.8	24.9	29.2	21.1	24.4	27.3	21.7	3.7	4.6	2.9	3.1	4.3	1.9
1900	33.4	36.3	30.8	36.5	39.5	33.6	35.9	39.3	32.8	37.1	40.4	34.0	36.7	38.7	34.9	7.3	8.9	5.9	5.2	5.1	5.3
25 to 34 years:																					
1910	24.6	24.4	24.7	28.1	28.1	28.2	27.9	27.9	27.9	29.1	29.5	28.7	27.4	26.7	28.1	5.4	5.8	5.0	3.7	3.6	3.7
1900	39.3	35.7	42.8	44.1	40.2	47.8	43.1	39.3	46.6	45.3	41.7	48.7	44.4	39.8	49.1	11.5	11.5	11.5	7.9	7.4	8.6
35 to 44 years:																					
1910	32.3	27.7	37.1	36.8	31.7	41.9	36.3	31.5	41.1	38.1	33.1	43.0	36.1	30.5	42.1	9.6	8.7	10.6	5.8	4.8	7.2
1900	52.0	43.0	60.6	57.6	47.9	66.6	56.1	46.8	64.8	59.5	49.8	68.3	58.0	47.6	68.1	21.1	18.2	24.4	13.6	11.5	16.6
45 to 54 years:																					
1910	47.0	38.9	56.3	51.9	43.0	62.0	51.0	42.3	60.3	54.1	45.3	64.3	50.6	41.1	62.5	19.2	15.8	23.1	11.0	8.0	15.4
1900	68.1	59.3	77.8	72.8	63.7	82.8	71.6	62.5	81.0	74.5	65.6	84.5	72.7	63.2	84.1	36.9	30.7	43.9	25.8	20.0	35.4
55 to 64 years:																					
1910	63.0	55.5	72.0	67.6	59.8	77.2	66.4	58.8	75.6	70.0	62.1	79.7	66.8	58.5	77.1	32.9	27.1	39.3	22.6	15.7	32.7
1900	78.4	73.4	84.3	82.6	77.6	88.4	81.2	76.3	87.0	84.2	79.4	89.7	78.0	72.7	88.5	48.6	43.4	54.6	38.9	33.6	47.9
65 years and over:																					
1910	74.5	70.7	78.6	78.5	74.9	82.4	77.1	73.5	81.0	80.8	77.4	84.4	78.1	74.1	82.4	47.9	42.4	53.7	38.5	31.3	47.4
1900	85.4	83.6	87.2	88.3	86.7	90.0	87.4	85.6	89.2	89.4	87.9	90.9	89.0	87.3	90.7	62.3	57.8	66.5	46.9	42.3	53.2

The percentage illiterate for females exceeded that for males in the South by 2.6 in 1900 and by only 0.4 in 1910; in the North, by 1.9 in 1900 and by 1.2 in 1910; in the West, by 3.4 in 1900 and by 2.1 in 1910 As has been noted with reference to the country as a whole, however, the differences between the percentages for males and those for females are generally more considerable in the several age groups than they are for the total population 10 years of age and over. In the South, as a whole, the percentage illiterate in 1910 was greater for males than for females in the ages 10 to 14 and 15 to 24 years, nearly the same for males as for females in the ages 25 to 34 years, and greater for females than for males in the more advanced ages. In 1900, also, a smaller proportion of females than of males in the younger ages—10 to 14 and 15 to 24 years—were illiterate, but the percentage illiterate among females aged 25 to 34, as well as in the more advanced ages, was markedly in excess of the percentage for males.

The number of illiterates of each race at the censuses of 1890, 1900, and 1910, and the percentage illiterate in each section of the country, are given in Table 17. The table embraces two arrangements of the percentages, in order to facilitate a comparison, first of one class with another class at the several censuses, and, secondly, as regards each class, a comparison of one year with another.

For each of the three classes in 1910 the percentage illiterate in the South exceeded the corresponding percentage in both the North and the West, being for the Negroes 33.3 in the South, as compared with 10.5 in the North and 7 in the West; for the native whites, 7.5, 1.2, and 1.4, respectively; and for the foreign-born whites, 18.8, 12.7, and 9.5, respectively.

DIAGRAM III.—PERCENTAGE ILLITERATE, BY AGE PERIODS, FOR THE NEGRO, NATIVE WHITE, AND FOREIGN-BORN WHITE POPULATION OF THE SOUTH: 1910.

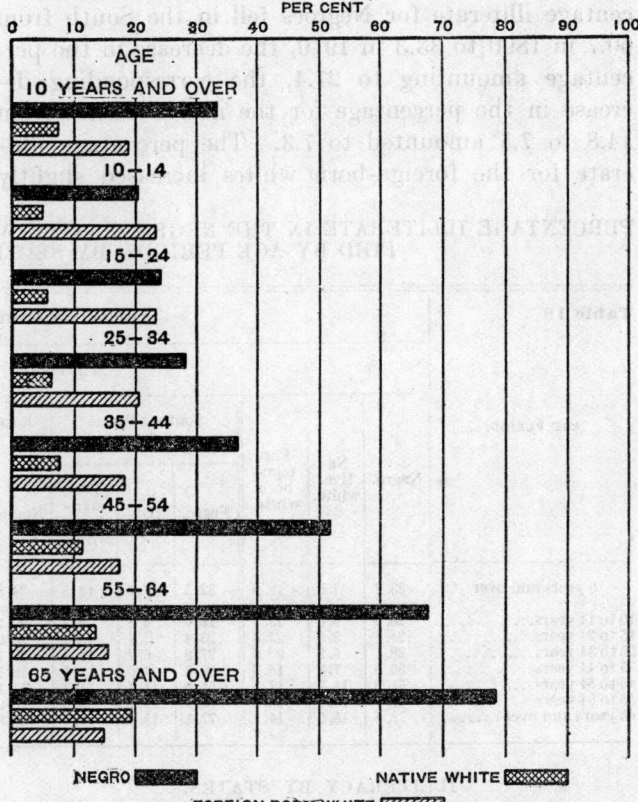

Throughout the South at each census the number of Negro illiterates exceeded the number of white illiterates, although at each census the total number of white illiterates in the country, as a whole, exceeded the number of Negro illiterates, the excess of whites over Negroes being much greater in 1910 than in 1890. In the North and West Negroes constituted a small minority of the total number of illiterates in those sections. It is evident thus that the problem of Negro illiteracy is distinctively a southern problem.

The native whites everywhere show a diminishing number of illiterates from census to census, and this is true, also, of the Negroes, except in the West South Central division. The foreign-born whites, on

Table 17	POPULATION 10 YEARS OF AGE AND OVER.						
		The South.					
RACIAL CLASS AND YEAR.	United States.	Total.	South Atlantic division.	East South Central division.	West South Central division.	The North.	The West.
NUMBER ILLITERATE.							
1910							
Negro	2,227,731	2,133,961	969,432	681,507	483,022	90,659	3,111
White:							
Native	1,534,272	1,079,583	433,809	381,230	264,544	398,496	56,193
Foreign born	1,650,361	130,823	37,934	8,215	84,674	1,398,943	120,595
1900							
Negro	2,853,194	2,717,606	1,250,279	887,838	579,489	132,189	3,399
White:							
Native	1,913,611	1,296,497	541,530	466,328	288,639	555,724	61,390
Foreign born	1,287,135	104,776	26,437	9,253	69,086	1,118,400	63,959
1890							
Negro	3,042,668	2,883,216	1,384,632	922,664	575,920	154,151	5,301
White:							
Native	2,065,003	1,326,834	571,899	499,699	255,236	666,225	71,944
Foreign born	1,147,571	86,149	24,053	9,411	52,685	993,709	67,713
PERCENTAGE ILLITERATE.							
1910							
Negro	30.4	33.3	32.5	34.8	33.1	10.5	7.0
White:							
Native	3.0	7.5	7.6	9.2	5.8	1.2	1.4
Foreign born	12.7	18.8	13.5	9.7	25.6	12.7	9.5
1900							
Negro	44.5	48.0	47.1	49.2	48.0	18.2	13.1
White:							
Native	4.6	11.3	11.4	13.0	9.2	2.0	2.7
Foreign-born	12.9	19.1	12.9	10.4	27.2	12.8	8.5
1890							
Negro	57.1	60.7	60.1	61.5	60.9	27.8	23.2
White:							
Native	6.2	14.8	14.6	16.6	12.5	2.9	4.5
Foreign born	13.1	17.1	12.2	9.5	25.3	13.0	10.4
Negro:							
1910	30.4	33.3	32.5	34.8	33.1	10.5	7.0
1900	44.5	48.0	47.1	49.2	48.0	18.2	13.1
1890	57.1	60.7	60.1	61.5	60.9	27.8	23.2
White:							
Native—							
1910	3.0	7.5	7.6	9.2	5.8	1.2	1.4
1900	4.6	11.3	11.4	13.0	9.2	2.0	2.7
1890	6.2	14.8	14.6	16.6	12.5	2.9	4.5
Foreign born—							
1910	12.7	18.8	13.5	9.7	25.6	12.7	9.5
1900	12.9	19.1	12.9	10.4	27.2	12.8	8.5
1890	13.1	17.1	12.2	9.5	25.3	13.0	10.4

the contrary, show an increase from census to census in each section and division except in the East South Central division, in which this element of the population is numerically insignificant.

The extent of the absolute changes in the South may be briefly indicated. During the 20 years the total number of Negro illiterates in this section fell from 2,883,216 in 1890 to 2,133,961 in 1910, a decrease of 749,255, and the number of native white illiterates from 1,326,834 in 1890 to 1,079,583 in 1910, a decrease of 247,251; while the foreign-born white illiterates increased from 86,149 to 130,823, an increase of 44,674.

In 1890 the illiterate Negroes constituted 67.1 per cent of the total number of illiterates in the South, against 30.8 per cent for the native whites, while in 1910 the percentages were, for the Negroes, 63.8 and for the native whites 32.3 In this period the percentage illiterate for Negroes fell in the South from 60.7 in 1890 to 33.3 in 1910, the decrease in the percentage amounting to 27.4, the corresponding decrease in the percentage for the native whites from 14.8 to 7.5 amounted to 7.3. The percentage illiterate for the foreign-born whites increased slightly but did not change materially during this period, being 17.1 in 1890 and 18.8 in 1910.

The percentage illiterate in 1910 among Negroes, native whites, and foreign-born whites is given in Table 18, by age periods, and represented graphically for the South on Diagram III (p. 413).

In the South as a whole, while the percentage illiterate increases with advancing age for both Negroes and native whites, that for the foreign-born whites remains unchanged for the first two periods and thereafter diminishes with advancing age, seeming to indicate that the older and earlier immigrants were—as compared with the younger and later comers—of a somewhat higher grade of intelligence. In the North the percentages for all three classes at each age are smaller than in the South, except that for the age 65 years and over the percentages for the foreign-born whites are nearly the same in the two sections. In each of the southern divisions the percentages for both Negroes and native whites are in general accord with those for the South as a whole, showing no marked divergencies, although those for the East South Central are somewhat higher than those for the other two divisions.

PERCENTAGE ILLITERATE IN THE NEGRO, NATIVE WHITE, AND FOREIGN-BORN WHITE POPULATION, CLASSIFIED BY AGE PERIODS, BY SECTIONS AND SOUTHERN DIVISIONS: 1910.

Table 18	PERCENTAGE ILLITERATE IN THE POPULATION OF AGE SPECIFIED: 1910.																	
	The South.												The North.			The West.		
AGE PERIOD.	Negro.	Native white.	Foreign-born white.	South Atlantic division.			East South Central division.			West South Central division.			Negro.	Native white.	Foreign-born white.	Negro.	Native white.	Foreign-born white.
				Negro.	Native white.	Foreign-born white.	Negro.	Native white.	Foreign-born white.	Negro.	Native white.	Foreign-born white.						
10 years and over.....	33.3	7.5	18.8	32.5	7.6	13.5	34.8	9.2	9.7	33.1	5.8	25.6	10.5	1.2	12.7	7.0	1.4	9.5
10 to 14 years.............	20.2	5.0	23.3	18.9	4.8	5.3	20.7	5.7	11.4	22.4	4.8	34.6	1.7	0.3	1.8	1.0	0.7	4.7
15 to 24 years.............	24.1	5.6	23.3	23.4	5.4	16.7	24.9	6.6	14.4	24.4	4.8	30.9	3.7	0.6	14.1	3.1	1.0	13.6
25 to 34 years.............	28.1	6.2	20.4	27.9	6.2	16.4	29.1	7.5	11.1	27.4	5.1	26.3	5.4	0.9	14.4	3.7	1.0	11.2
35 to 44 years.............	36.8	7.8	18.2	36.3	7.6	13.5	38.1	9.9	9.1	36.1	6.0	24.4	9.6	1.2	12.4	5.8	1.4	8.8
45 to 54 years.............	51.9	11.2	17.3	51.0	11.4	11.4	54.1	14.4	7.9	50.6	7.9	24.1	19.2	2.0	11.1	11.0	2.0	7.0
55 to 64 years.............	67.6	13.4	15.5	66.4	13.7	9.6	70.0	16.5	7.8	66.8	9.5	22.3	32.9	3.0	11.3	22.6	2.9	7.2
65 years and over.........	78.5	15.5	14.7	77.1	15.7	10.7	80.8	18.9	9.5	78.1	11.0	20.4	47.9	4.4	14.2	38.5	3.6	8.5

ILLITERACY BY STATES.

Statistics of Negro illiteracy in the several states are set forth in Tables 23, 24, 25, 26, 27, and 28 (pp. 419 to 429). In each of the states the percentage of illiteracy in the Negro population decreased during the decade 1900–1910, and in each of the states except Montana—in which the Negro population 10 years of age and over was numerically insignificant—the percentage decreased in the preceding decade also. Thus in practically every state the percentage of illiteracy among Negroes declined during the 20 years covered by the data. In each of the Southern states, except Oklahoma, and in each of the Northern states, with inconsiderable exceptions, the number of Negro illiterates, as well as the percentage illiterate, decreased during the last decade. In Oklahoma, although the number of Negro illiterates increased from 881 in 1890 to 14,870 in 1900 and to 17,858 in 1910, the percentage illiterate in the Negro population 10 years of age and over decreased from 39 in 1890 to 37 in 1900 and to 17.7 in 1910, the increase in the number of illiterates in this state being attributable to migration of illiterates into the state.

In 1910 the illiterate Negro population of Georgia exceeded that of any other state, the number of Negro illiterates reported from this state being 308,639. Other states reporting more than 100,000 illiterates were: Alabama, 265,628; Mississippi, 259,438; Louisiana, 254,148; South Carolina, 226,242; North Carolina, 156,303; Virginia, 148,950; and Texas, 124,618.

The percentage of illiteracy is given, by states, in Table 19 for the Negro population at each of the last three censuses and for the native and foreign-born white population in 1910. In this table the states are ranged in order according to the percentage of Negro illiteracy in 1910.

Table 19 STATE.	PERCENTAGE ILLITERATE.				
	Negro population.			White population, 1910.	
	1910	1900	1890 [1]	Native.	Foreign born.
Louisiana	48.4	61.1	72.1	13.4	24.0
Alabama	40.1	57.4	69.1	9.9	11.3
South Carolina	38.7	52.8	64.1	10.3	6.8
Georgia	36.5	52.4	67.3	7.8	6.0
Mississippi	35.6	49.1	60.8	5.2	15.1
North Carolina	31.9	47.6	60.1	12.3	8.3
United States	30.4	44.5	57.1	3.0	12.7
Virginia	30.0	44.6	57.2	8.0	9.2
Kentucky	27.6	40.1	55.9	10.0	8.3
Tennessee	27.3	41.6	54.2	9.7	8.3
Arkansas	26.4	43.0	53.6	7.0	8.9
Delaware	25.6	38.1	49.5	2.9	19.8
Florida	25.5	38.4	50.5	5.0	10.5
Texas	24.6	38.2	52.5	4.3	30.0
Maryland	23.4	35.1	50.1	2.6	11.9
West Virginia	20.3	32.3	44.5	6.4	23.9
Oklahoma [2]	17.7	37.0	39.0	3.3	9.8
Missouri	17.4	28.1	41.7	2.9	10.1
New Mexico	14.2	19.1	45.8	14.9	31.0
Indiana	13.7	22.6	32.3	2.1	11.7
District of Columbia	13.5	24.3	35.0	0.5	8.2
Kansas	12.0	22.3	32.8	0.8	10.5
Ohio	11.1	17.8	25.4	1.5	11.5
New Hampshire	10.6	11.9	22.5	1.1	14.5
Illinois	10.5	18.1	26.8	1.3	10.1
Iowa	10.3	18.5	26.1	0.8	6.3
New Jersey	9.9	17.2	28.1	0.9	14.7
Rhode Island	9.5	14.1	18.1	1.3	17.3
Pennsylvania	9.1	15.1	23.2	1.3	20.1
Colorado	8.6	13.0	17.6	1.6	11.3
Massachusetts	8.1	10.7	14.3	0.5	12.7
Maine	8.0	14.2	15.9	2.0	13.7
Arizona	7.2	12.7	19.2	4.2	31.5
Nebraska	7.2	11.8	19.1	0.6	7.1
California	7.1	13.4	26.5	0.5	10.0
Montana	7.0	11.4	11.0	0.4	9.4
Idaho	6.4	14.5	24.0	0.3	6.9
Connecticut	6.3	11.5	15.3	0.6	15.4
Michigan	5.7	10.9	18.9	1.1	9.3
Nevada	5.5	23.0	40.2	0.4	7.6
South Dakota	5.5	13.3	20.0	0.4	5.0
New York	5.0	10.8	17.1	0.8	13.7
Wyoming	5.0	17.2	17.8	0.3	9.7
North Dakota	4.8	12.8	29.9	0.5	6.3
Utah	4.8	6.3	26.6	0.4	5.9
Vermont	4.8	14.6	20.4	1.9	13.1
Wisconsin	4.5	11.4	20.0	0.9	8.7
Washington	4.3	11.6	17.7	0.3	4.8
Minnesota	3.4	7.9	12.1	0.5	7.6
Oregon	3.4	8.8	17.1	0.4	6.1

[1] Percentages for 1890 do not include illiterate persons in Indian Territory and on Indian reservations, area specially enumerated, but for which illiteracy statistics are not available.
[2] Includes population of Indian Territory for 1900.

Nearly one-half of Louisiana's Negro population 10 years of age and over in 1910 was illiterate, the percentage of illiteracy being 48.4. In Alabama, the state showing the next largest proportion, 40.1 per cent, or two-fifths, were illiterate. The lowest per-

centage shown by any Southern state in 1910—i. e., Oklahoma's percentage of 17.7—exceeds slightly the highest of the percentages shown for Northern and Western states, in several of which Negro illiteracy in 1910 amounted to less than 5 per cent.

In 13 of the 16 Southern states half or more of the Negro population 10 years of age and over was illiterate in 1890; the percentage illiterate in Delaware, one of the three remaining states, being 49.5. The percentage of Negro illiteracy in Louisiana in 1890 was 72.1; and in Alabama, 69.1. In 1900, 4 states showed a percentage of 50 or more, the highest percentage for any state in this year being again that for Louisiana, 61.1. In 1910 no state reported a Negro illiteracy amounting to 50 per cent, the highest proportion illiterate for any state being 48.4 per cent.

The percentage of illiteracy among foreign-born whites in 1910 exceeded that among Negroes in 27 states.

Statistics for the several states, showing illiteracy among the Negro population by age periods, are given in Table 24, page 420. In the Southern states the only exception to the general rule that illiteracy advances continuously from age period to age period is found in Arkansas, where the percentage of illiteracy for Negroes 15 to 24 years of age is practically identical with the percentage for those aged 10 to 14 years. In several Southern states four-fifths or more of the Negro population 65 years of age and over were illiterate, the lowest percentage illiterate in the population of this age for any Southern state being 65.2 for West Virginia.

The higher percentages for the older ages, as has been pointed out, reflect educational conditions which do not generally obtain in the South at the present time. As indicative of present conditions, statistics for the younger ages are of special interest, and in Table 20 statistics are given, by states, for children 10 to 14 years of age, showing the number and percentage illiterate in 1910 and in 1900 for Negro children, and the percentage illiterate in 1910 for native and foreign-born white children of this age. The states have been arranged in order according to the percentage illiterate for Negro children in 1910.

More than two-fifths of the Negro children 10 to 14 years of age in Louisiana were illiterate in 1910. The percentage illiterate for these children had decreased during the decade from 49.7 to 41, but in 1910 was still greatly in excess of the percentages shown for Negro children in other Southern states, and more than twice the percentage for such children in the South as a whole.

Marked decreases in the proportion illiterate among Negro children in the Southern states generally are shown for the decade 1900–1910. In Alabama, for example, the proportion decreased from 44.6 per cent in 1900 to 27.5 in 1910; in South Carolina, from 38.8 to 23.1; in Georgia, from 36 to 22.1; in North Carolina from 31.3 to 16.6. The lowest percentages in 1910 for Southern states were those for West Virginia, 6.4; Delaware, 6.3; and Oklahoma, 6.2.

In the Northern and Western states generally illiteracy among Negro children 10 to 14 years of age in 1910 amounted to less than 2 per cent, and in a number of these states it was only a fraction of 1 per cent.

ILLITERACY AMONG NEGRO AND WHITE CHILDREN 10 TO 14 YEARS OF AGE, BY STATES.

Table 20	CHILDREN 10 TO 14 YEARS OF AGE.							STATE.	CHILDREN 10 TO 14 YEARS OF AGE						
	Negro: 1910.		Percentage illiterate.[1]						Negro: 1910.		Percentage illiterate.[1]				
			Negro children.		White children: 1910.						Negro children.		White children: 1910.		
STATE.	Total.	Illiterate.	1910	1900	Native of native parentage.	Native of foreign or mixed parentage.	Foreign born.		Total.	Illiterate.	1910	1900	Native of native parentage.	Native of foreign or mixed parentage.	Foreign born.
Louisiana	85,917	35,200	41.0	49.7	11.5	8.6	31.9	District of Columbia	7,211	67	0.9	4.9	0.1	0.3	1.0
Alabama	112,129	30,839	27.5	44.6	7.7	1.5	9.7	Maine	117	1	0.9	3.5	0.6	0.8	2.5
South Carolina	114,341	26,455	23.1	38.8	8.3	1.7	6.9	Ohio	8,964	83	0.9	1.5	0.3	0.1	1.2
Georgia	152,029	33,602	22.1	36.0	5.7	0.8	4.3	Indiana	4,984	38	0.8	1.5	0.3	0.2	1.6
Mississippi	128,019	24,811	19.4	32.0	3.5	2.0	33.6	California	1,467	9	0.6	1.0	0.2	0.3	3.7
United States	1,155,266	218,555	18.9	30.1	2.2	0.6	3.5	Rhode Island	714	4	0.6	0.4	0.2	0.4	2.5
Florida	33,288	5,924	17.8	22.2	5.0	3.4	11.9	Kansas	4,971	26	0.5	2.3	0.2	0.2	4.1
Arkansas	52,679	8,844	16.8	29.4	4.7	2.0	23.7	Michigan	1,276	7	0.5	1.3	0.2	0.2	1.0
North Carolina	89,416	14,861	16.6	31.3	6.8	0.4	1.5	Nebraska	438	2	0.5	1.5	0.2	0.2	1.6
Virginia	83,395	13,370	16.0	26.1	5.7	0.6	4.2	Wisconsin	192	1	0.5	1.5	0.2	0.3	1.2
Tennessee	53,344	8,203	15.4	25.1	5.4	1.0	3.9	New York	7,930	32	0.4	1.3	0.2	0.2	1.5
Texas	85,461	8,748	10.2	17.7	2.7	14.7	37.3	Washington	274	1	0.4		0.1	0.2	0.7
Maryland	24,595	2,345	9.5	15.3	0.9	0.5	2.0	Massachusetts	2,905	9	0.3	1.4	0.1	0.1	1.2
Kentucky	26,984	2,356	8.7	14.9	5.9	0.5	2.2	Minnesota	375	1	0.3	0.7	0.1	0.2	1.1
New Mexico	106	8	7.5	7.2	6.9	8.5	24.0	Connecticut	1,244	1	0.1	0.8	0.1	0.2	1.4
West Virginia	5,424	348	6.4	12.0	2.5	0.7	9.6	Idaho	19				0.2	0.1	1.7
Delaware	3,540	224	6.3	16.2	0.4	0.4	2.3	Montana	95				0.1	0.1	2.5
Oklahoma	16,208	1,011	6.2	30.7	1.7	0.7	5.7	Nevada	18				0.5	0.2	1.6
Missouri	13,190	690	5.2	10.3	1.1	0.2	2.1	New Hampshire	40				0.1	0.3	1.7
Illinois	7,768	141	1.8	4.6	0.4	0.2	1.2	North Dakota	30				0.1	0.6	5.6
Arizona	130	2	1.5		1.5	7.0	20.6	Oregon	54				0.1	0.1	0.8
New Jersey	6,878	90	1.3	4.6	0.2	0.3	2.4	South Dakota	62				0.2	0.2	2.4
Pennsylvania	14,840	175	1.2	2.5	0.3	0.4	3.2	Utah	55	1			0.1	0.2	1.2
Colorado	807	9	1.1	0.5	0.8	0.3	3.9	Vermont	72	3			0.2	0.3	1.5
Iowa	1,215	13	1.1	2.5	0.2	0.2	1.5	Wyoming	56				0.2	0.4	2.7

[1] Per cent not shown where base is less than 100.

URBAN AND RURAL ILLITERACY.

Statistics of illiteracy for the Negro population, classified as urban and rural, are given in Tables 28 and 29 (pp. 429 and 430), and for individual urban communities in Tables 30, 31, and 32 (pp. 432 to 435).

Among Negroes, as among whites, the proportion illiterate in the rural population exceeds that in the urban population. In 1910, of the 2,227,731 Negro illiterates, 1,834,458 were in rural communities and 393,273 in urban communities, the percentage illiterate being 36.1 in the rural and 17.6 in the urban Negro population 10 years of age and over. Approximately one-fifth of the urban Negro population in the South were illiterate in 1910, the percentage illiterate in the three southern divisions being in the South Atlantic division, 21.4; in the East South Central, 23.8; and in the West South Central, 20.3. The corresponding proportions for the rural Negro population in these divisions exceeded one-third, being 36.1, 37.8, and 37.2 per cent, respectively. In the northern and western divisions the proportion illiterate for the urban Negro population ranged from 5.3 per cent in the Pacific division to 12.3 per cent in the West North Central, and in the rural Negro population, from 10.6 in the Mountain to 21 in the West North Central division. The number and percentage illiterate in the urban and rural population are shown in Table 21, for the several sections and divisions.

At the last census the percentage illiterate in the rural Negro population of each state, with exception of New Hampshire and Wyoming, exceeded the corresponding percentage for the urban population. In Louisiana 55.8 per cent of the rural Negro population was illiterate, the percentage for the urban population of this state being 25.8. In Alabama the percentages were 43.5 for the rural population and 26 for the urban; in South Carolina, 40.2 and 29.6, respectively; in Georgia, 39.7 and 24.9. Oklahoma's percentages— 19.9 in the rural and 12.4 in the urban population— were lower than those of any other Southern state. In the Northern and Western states the percentages ranged in the rural Negro population from 1.5 in Wyoming to 25.2 in Missouri; and in the urban population, from 2.7 in Minnesota to 13.9 in Missouri.

URBAN AND RURAL ILLITERACY FOR NEGROES AND WHITE POPULATION CLASSES, BY DIVISIONS: 1910.

Table 21	POPULATION 10 YEARS OF AGE AND OVER: 1910.												
	Negro.						Percentage illiterate.						
				Illiterate.			Negro population.		White population.				
SECTION AND DIVISION.	Total.	Urban.	Rural.						Native of native parentage.		Native of foreign or mixed parentage.		Foreign born.	
				Total.	Urban.	Rural.	Urban.	Rural.	Urban.	Rural.	Urban.	Rural.	Urban.	Rural.
UNITED STATES	7,317,922	2,231,353	5,086,569	2,227,731	393,273	1,834,458	17.6	36.1	0.9	5.4	0.7	1.9	12.6	13.2
The South	6,408,539	1,516,569	4,891,970	2,133,961	330,815	1,803,146	21.8	36.9	2.0	9.3	1.5	8.3	13.4	25.0
The North	865,053	679,931	185,122	90,659	60,386	30,273	8.9	16.4	0.7	2.1	0.6	1.4	13.0	11.9
The West	44,330	34,853	9,477	3,111	2,072	1,039	5.9	11.0	0.5	2.8	0.4	1.2	6.9	12.7
THE SOUTH.														
South Atlantic	2,986,936	741,429	2,245,507	969,432	158,906	810,526	21.4	36.1	2.2	9.8	0.8	2.4	11.6	17.2
East South Central	1,960,898	421,529	1,539,369	681,507	100,257	581,250	23.8	37.8	2.4	11.1	0.8	3.9	9.1	10.9
West South Central	1,460,705	353,611	1,107,094	483,022	71,652	411,370	20.3	37.2	1.4	6.8	2.8	11.4	17.9	30.7
THE NORTH.														
New England	55,321	51,025	4,296	4,341	3,614	727	7.1	16.9	0.5	1.2	1.0	3.6	13.7	15.3
Middle Atlantic	351,546	288,414	63,132	27,811	20,089	7,722	7.0	12.2	0.6	1.9	0.6	1.9	14.9	20.3
East North Central	254,545	198,669	55,876	28,071	19,229	8,842	9.7	15.8	0.9	2.2	0.5	1.5	10.2	9.6
West North Central	203,641	141,823	61,818	30,436	17,454	12,982	12.3	21.0	0.8	2.1	0.5	0.8	8.5	7.0
THE WEST.														
Mountain	18,755	13,505	5,250	1,497	939	558	7.0	10.6	0.9	5.1	0.7	1.7	9.7	14.4
Pacific	25,575	21,348	4,227	1,614	1,133	481	5.3	11.4	0.3	0.6	0.3	0.8	6.0	11.3

ILLITERACY IN CITIES.

In general, it is true of the principal urban communities that the proportion illiterate in their Negro population tends to be relatively high or low, according as the percentage for the Negro population of the state or section in which the city is located is high or low, the percentages being relatively high for southern cities and low for northern and western cities. There is, however, no uniform close correspondence of the percentages for individual cities to that for the urban population as a whole of the state or section in which the city is located. In the case of the larger cities with considerable Negro populations, the percentage of illiteracy is generally, but not in every instance, below the percentage for the urban population of the state in which the city is located. Probably the explanation of this is that conditions in the smaller urban communities approximate those in distinctly rural communities where illiteracy is in general high. Of the Negro population of New Orleans, for example, 18.3 per cent were illiterate in 1910, while the percentage for the urban Negro population of Louisiana as a whole was 25.8; the percentage for Atlanta was 20.9, and for the urban population of Georgia 24.9; for Birmingham, 22.1, and for the urban population of Alabama, 26; for Baltimore, 13.2, for the urban population of Maryland, 14.9; for New York City, 3.6, and for New York state urban, 4.2. In the case of Nashville, Tenn., on the other hand, the percentage of illit-

eracy for the Negro population (22) exceeded that for the urban Negro population of Tennessee (20.7), and it is true in the case of a few other large cities that the percentage of illiteracy among Negroes is somewhat above that for the urban Negro population as a whole.

The relatively low illiteracy of the urban population as a whole and of the larger urban communities in particular, in comparison with the illiteracy of rural districts, may be accounted for in part by the fact that the school facilities provided in urban communities have been superior to those provided in rural districts, and in part to the fact that the percentage of illiteracy among Negroes who migrate from country to city is probably lower than it is among those who remain permanently in the country.

In the cities as in the states, the percentage illiterate advances with age. Of the Negro population 10 to 14 years of age in New Orleans, for example, only 6.5 per cent were illiterate, the percentage for those 65 and over being 57.8; the corresponding percentages for the Negro population of Atlanta were 6.2 and 76.8; for Baltimore, 2 and 46.5; for Birmingham, 6.7 and 72.8; for Louisville, 1.1 and 70; for Memphis, 6 and 65.7; for Nashville, 4.7 and 77.9; for Richmond, 6 and 65.9; for Washington, D. C., 0.9 and 59.7.

In all of the principal cities the proportion illiterate in the Negro population decreased rapidly during the two decades 1890–1910. The decrease in Birmingham, for example, was from 51.5 in 1890 to 22.1 in 1910; in Atlanta, from 48.9 in 1890 to 20.9 in 1910; in Richmond, from 45.7 to 19.6; in Nashville, from 45.4 to 22; in Memphis, from 44.2 to 17.6; in New Orleans, from 43.1 to 18.3; in Louisville, from 41.8 to 18.7; and was equally marked in other urban communities.

ILLITERACY AMONG MALES 21 YEARS OF AGE AND OVER.

Statistics of illiteracy for Negro males 21 years of age and over are given, by states, in Table 24 (p. 420); and for urban communities in General Table I (p. 767); and for counties in General Table III (p. 798).

In 1910 Negro males of this age numbered 2,458,873, and of this total, one-third—819,135, or 33.3 per cent— were illiterate. In 1900 illiterate Negro males 21 and over numbered 976,610, giving a percentage of illiteracy of 47.4. During the decade 1900–1910 the number of Negro males 21 and over increased by 398,571, the number of Negro illiterates of this age decreasing in the same period by 157,475.

For this class of the population, a summary of the statistics of illiteracy is given in Table 22, by sections and southern divisions.

Table 22	MALE POPULATION 21 YEARS OF AGE AND OVER						
	Negro, 1910.		Percentage illiterate.				
SECTION AND DIVISION.			Negro population.		White population, 1910.		
	Total.	Illiterate.	1910	1900	Total.	Native.	Foreign born.
United States......	2,458,873	819,135	33.3	47.4	5.8	3.5	11.9
The South..............	2,086,639	777,181	37.2	51.9	8.9	8.4	16.1
South Atlantic........	955,364	351,220	36.8	51.1	8.9	8.6	13.0
East South Central...	642,460	252,677	39.3	53.6	10.6	10.7	7.8
West South Central..	488,815	173,284	35.4	51.0	7.5	6.0	21.1
The North..............	351,213	40,546	11.5	20.6	5.1	1.7	11.9
The West..............	21,021	1,408	6.7	13.4	3.8	1.2	9.3

Of Negro males of voting age in 1910, illiterates constituted in the South as a whole 37.2 per cent; in the the North, 11.5 per cent; and in the West, 6.7 per cent. The corresponding percentages in 1900 were 51.9, 20.6, and 13.4. In the South Atlantic division the percentage decreased from 51.1 in 1900 to 36.8 in 1910; in the East South Central division, from 53.6 to 39.3; and in the West South Central, from 51 to 35.4.

In Louisiana illiterate Negro males 21 and over numbered, in 1910, 84,176 and constituted 48.3 per cent, or nearly one-half of the Negro males of that age; in Alabama the number of Negro illiterates of this class was 92,744, giving a percentage of illiteracy of 43.4; in Georgia the number was 111,039, giving a percentage of 41.6; in Mississippi, 95,702, giving a percentage of 41. The lowest percentage shown for any Southern state was 20.1, the percentage for Oklahoma. Among Northern and Western states the percentage ranged from 3.1 in Oregon to 19 in Missouri.

Referring to the statistics for cities, it will be found that the percentage illiterate among Negro males 21 and over decreased in Atlanta from 38.3 in 1900 to 21.7 in 1910; in Baltimore, from 26.5 to 13.4; in Birmingham, from 40.2 to 23; in Louisville, from 35 to 20.3; in Memphis, from 37.8 to 16.4; in Nashville, from 36.5 to 25.3; in New Orleans, from 36 to 17.1; in Richmond, from 35.4 to 20.8; in Washington, D. C., from 26.1 to 13.8.

Among Negro males of voting age, the decrease in illiteracy in recent years has been rapid throughout all sections of the South, in both the urban and the rural population. This decrease has undoubtedly continued since the taking of the last census, and it is practically certain to continue in the future until the proportion illiterate among adult males approximates that among males in the younger ages.

TABLE 23.—ILLITERATES IN THE NEGRO POPULATION, BY SEX, BY DIVISIONS AND STATES: 1910, 1900, AND 1890.

[Per cent not shown where base is less than 100.]

DIVISION AND STATE.	NUMBER OF NEGRO ILLITERATES. Both sexes.			Male.			Female.			PERCENTAGE ILLITERATE IN NEGRO POPULATION. Both sexes.			Male.			Female.		
	1910	1900	1890[1]	1910	1900	1890[1]	1910	1900	1890[1]	1910	1900	1890[1]	1910	1900	1890[1]	1910	1900	1890[1]
UNITED STATES	2,227,731	2,853,194	3,042,668	1,096,000	1,371,432	1,438,923	1,131,731	1,481,762	1,603,745	30.4	44.5	57.1	30.1	43.1	54.4	30.7	45.8	59.8
GEOGRAPHIC DIVISIONS:																		
New England	4,341	5,681	5,664	2,107	2,469	2,497	2,234	3,212	3,167	7.8	11.6	15.5	7.7	10.4	14.1	8.0	12.7	16.8
Middle Atlantic	27,811	38,594	41,092	12,573	18,141	19,182	15,238	20,453	21,910	7.9	14.2	22.3	7.4	13.6	21.0	8.4	14.8	23.6
East North Central	28,071	39,280	43,699	13,897	19,498	21,579	14,174	19,782	22,120	11.0	18.5	26.7	10.4	17.4	25.1	11.7	19.7	28.6
West North Central	30,436	48,634	63,696	14,678	23,271	30,355	15,758	25,363	33,341	14.9	25.4	37.4	13.8	23.6	34.7	16.2	27.1	40.2
South Atlantic	969,432	1,250,279	1,384,632	477,107	599,160	651,436	492,325	651,119	733,196	32.5	47.1	60.1	32.4	46.0	57.6	32.5	48.1	62.5
East South Central	681,507	887,838	922,664	337,893	429,984	438,397	343,614	457,854	484,267	34.8	49.2	61.5	34.8	48.1	58.9	34.7	50.4	63.9
West South Central	483,022	579,489	575,920	236,239	277,165	272,386	246,783	302,324	303,534	33.1	48.0	60.9	32.2	46.0	57.4	33.9	50.1	64.3
Mountain	1,497	1,840	2,467	754	967	1,444	743	873	1,023	8.0	13.5	21.8	7.2	11.9	19.2	9.0	15.9	27.1
Pacific	1,614	1,559	2,834	752	777	1,647	862	782	1,187	6.3	12.7	24.6	5.3	11.4	24.0	7.6	14.4	25.5
NEW ENGLAND:																		
Maine	93	155	155	56	83	84	37	72	71	8.0	14.2	15.9	9.2	14.6	16.7	6.7	13.8	15.0
New Hampshire	51	70	115	30	41	55	21	29	60	10.6	11.9	22.5	12.1	14.2	19.9	9.0	9.8	25.6
Vermont	69	99	149	41	61	92	28	38	57	4.8	14.6	20.4	3.8	15.7	23.9	7.8	13.1	16.6
Massachusetts	2,584	2,853	2,607	1,286	1,207	1,106	1,298	1,646	1,501	8.1	10.7	14.3	8.2	9.3	12.3	8.1	12.1	16.2
Rhode Island	752	1,063	1,106	370	452	446	382	611	660	9.5	14.1	18.1	9.6	12.9	16.0	9.4	15.1	19.9
Connecticut	792	1,441	1,532	324	625	714	468	816	818	6.3	11.5	15.3	5.4	10.6	14.8	7.1	12.3	15.8
MIDDLE ATLANTIC:																		
New York	5,768	9,180	10,017	2,433	3,903	4,334	3,335	5,277	5,683	5.0	10.8	17.1	4.4	9.8	15.6	5.5	11.7	18.6
New Jersey	7,405	9,882	10,860	3,296	4,404	5,021	4,109	5,478	5,839	9.9	17.2	28.1	9.1	15.9	26.4	10.7	18.3	29.8
Pennsylvania	14,638	19,532	20,215	6,844	9,834	9,827	7,794	9,698	10,388	9.1	15.1	23.2	8.6	15.0	22.1	9.6	15.3	24.5
EAST NORTH CENTRAL:																		
Ohio	10,460	14,107	17,496	5,370	7,124	8,704	5,090	6,983	8,792	11.1	17.8	25.4	10.9	17.3	24.2	11.4	18.4	26.7
Indiana	6,959	10,594	11,407	3,403	5,330	5,637	3,556	5,264	5,770	13.7	22.6	32.3	13.0	21.7	30.5	14.6	23.4	34.3
Illinois	9,713	12,903	12,111	4,652	6,138	5,792	5,061	6,765	6,319	10.5	18.1	26.8	9.5	16.0	24.0	11.5	20.6	30.0
Michigan	826	1,426	2,306	411	768	1,241	415	658	1,065	5.7	10.9	18.9	5.3	11.1	19.3	6.1	10.6	18.6
Wisconsin	113	250	379	61	138	205	52	112	174	4.5	11.4	20.0	4.7	11.1	19.0	4.3	11.8	21.3
WEST NORTH CENTRAL:																		
Minnesota	215	337	386	126	154	202	89	183	184	3.4	7.9	12.1	3.3	6.1	10.6	3.5	10.4	14.5
Iowa	1,272	1,962	2,177	662	1,058	1,118	610	904	1,059	10.3	18.5	26.1	9.7	18.1	24.5	11.0	19.0	28.0
Missouri	23,062	36,390	47,333	11,161	17,336	22,471	11,901	19,054	24,862	17.4	28.1	41.7	16.4	26.5	39.4	18.5	29.7	44.0
North Dakota	26	31	83	16	19	49	10	12	34	4.8	12.8	29.9	4.6	12.7	27.5	5.1	......	34.0
South Dakota	38	51	91	24	30	75	14	21	16	5.5	13.3	20.0	5.9	13.0	23.6	4.8	13.6	11.8
Nebraska	482	633	1,367	233	281	711	249	352	656	7.2	11.8	19.1	6.2	9.6	16.5	8.4	14.5	23.1
Kansas	5,341	9,230	12,259	2,456	4,393	5,729	2,885	4,837	6,530	12.0	22.3	32.8	10.5	20.7	30.1	13.6	24.0	35.7
SOUTH ATLANTIC:																		
Delaware	6,345	8,967	10,675	3,220	4,367	5,230	3,125	4,600	5,445	25.6	38.1	49.5	25.0	36.1	47.1	26.3	40.2	52.1
Maryland	42,289	63,033	80,644	20,852	30,340	38,022	21,437	32,693	42,622	23.4	35.1	50.1	23.3	34.4	48.5	23.5	35.8	51.6
District of Columbia	10,814	17,462	21,346	4,015	6,716	8,545	6,799	10,746	12,801	13.5	24.3	35.0	11.3	21.6	32.2	15.3	26.3	37.3
Virginia	148,950	213,836	260,599	75,162	105,921	125,041	73,788	107,915	135,558	30.0	44.6	57.2	30.8	45.4	56.8	29.2	44.0	57.7
West Virginia	10,347	11,083	10,985	6,405	6,901	6,233	3,942	4,182	4,752	20.3	32.3	44.5	21.3	33.6	44.6	18.9	30.3	44.2
North Carolina	156,303	208,132	235,238	75,674	97,688	108,452	80,629	110,444	126,786	31.9	47.6	60.1	32.0	46.4	57.2	31.8	48.6	62.8
South Carolina	226,242	283,883	301,169	106,994	132,481	139,428	119,248	151,402	161,741	38.7	52.8	64.1	37.9	50.5	60.2	39.5	55.0	67.8
Georgia	308,639	379,067	403,925	154,466	182,719	192,952	154,173	196,348	210,973	36.5	52.4	67.3	37.2	51.4	64.4	35.8	53.3	70.2
Florida	59,503	64,816	60,051	30,319	32,027	27,533	29,184	32,789	32,518	25.5	38.4	50.5	24.4	35.9	45.8	26.6	41.4	55.4
EAST SOUTH CENTRAL:																		
Kentucky	57,900	88,137	110,507	29,906	44,417	54,623	27,994	43,720	55,884	27.6	40.1	55.9	28.3	40.5	55.6	26.9	39.7	56.2
Tennessee	98,541	147,784	167,881	49,382	72,728	79,186	49,159	75,056	88,695	27.3	41.6	54.2	27.8	41.4	52.0	26.9	41.9	56.4
Alabama	265,628	338,605	330,703	129,385	161,708	156,585	136,243	176,897	174,118	40.1	57.4	69.1	39.7	55.8	66.2	40.5	59.0	71.9
Mississippi	259,438	313,312	313,573	129,220	151,131	148,003	130,218	162,181	165,570	35.6	49.1	60.8	35.7	47.5	57.7	35.6	50.6	64.0
WEST SOUTH CENTRAL:																		
Arkansas	86,398	113,453	116,487	42,233	54,015	54,882	44,165	59,438	61,605	26.4	43.0	53.6	25.5	40.3	48.7	27.4	45.9	59.0
Louisiana	254,148	284,028	282,670	122,625	134,642	133,222	131,523	149,386	149,448	48.4	61.1	72.1	47.2	58.7	69.3	49.5	63.5	74.9
Oklahoma[2]	17,858	14,870	881	8,802	7,589	447	9,056	7,281	434	17.7	37.0	39.0	16.4	35.9	36.3	19.1	38.2	42.3
Texas	124,618	167,138	175,882	62,579	80,919	83,835	62,039	86,219	92,047	24.6	38.2	52.5	24.7	37.0	50.0	24.5	39.3	55.1
MOUNTAIN:																		
Montana	114	152	153	75	80	93	39	72	60	7.0	11.4	11.0	7.8	9.8	9.1	5.8	13.7	16.2
Idaho	37	37	42	18	20	19	19	17	23	6.4	14.5	24.0	4.9	13.2	18.3	8.9	16.3	......
Wyoming	102	141	147	53	106	103	49	35	44	5.0	17.2	17.8	3.7	18.9	17.0	8.4	13.6	19.9
Colorado	856	962	940	396	458	498	460	504	442	8.6	13.0	17.6	7.7	11.8	15.7	9.5	14.4	20.3
New Mexico	191	271	722	101	140	412	90	131	310	14.2	19.1	45.8	13.2	15.1	40.0	15.6	27.0	56.8
Arizona	122	211	245	68	129	192	54	82	53	7.2	12.7	19.2	7.6	10.2	17.1	6.8	20.4	34.9
Utah	49	37	132	28	17	86	21	20	46	4.8	6.3	26.6	4.4	4.1	25.3	5.4	11.7	29.3
Nevada	26	29	86	15	17	41	11	12	45	5.5	23.0	40.2	6.1	......	30.6	4.9	......	......
PACIFIC:																		
Washington	239	259	255	126	146	165	113	113	90	4.3	11.6	17.7	3.6	10.1	16.3	5.5	14.6	21.0
Oregon	46	89	171	25	57	112	21	32	59	3.4	8.8	17.1	3.0	9.0	17.3	4.0	8.4	16.8
California	1,329	1,211	2,408	601	574	1,370	728	637	1,038	7.1	13.4	26.5	6.1	12.1	26.3	8.2	14.8	26.8

[1] Figures for 1890 are exclusive of illiterate persons in Indian Territory and on Indian reservations, areas specially enumerated, but for which illiteracy statistics are not available.

[2] Includes population of Indian Territory for 1900.

TABLE 24.—ILLITERATES IN THE NEGRO POPULATION BY SEX, AND BY AGE PERIODS.

[Per cent not shown where base is less than 100.]

	NEGRO POPULATION: 1910.														
	10 years of age and over.[1]									10 to 14 years of age.			15 to 24 years of age.		
DIVISION AND STATE.	Both sexes.			Male.			Female.				Illiterate.			Illiterate.	
	Total.	Illiterate. Number.	Per cent.	Total.	Illiterate. Number.	Per cent.	Total.	Illiterate. Number.	Per cent.	Total.	Number.	Per cent.	Total.	Number.	Per cent.
1 UNITED STATES	7,317,922	2,227,731	30.4	3,637,386	1,096,000	30.1	3,680,536	1,131,731	30.7	1,155,266	218,555	18.9	2,091,211	460,720	22.0
GEOGRAPHIC DIVISIONS:															
2 New England	55,321	4,341	7.8	27,389	2,107	7.7	27,932	2,234	8.0	5,092	18	0.4	11,817	547	4.6
3 Middle Atlantic	351,546	27,811	7.9	171,008	12,573	7.4	180,538	15,238	8.4	29,648	297	1.0	81,370	2,585	3.2
4 East North Central	254,545	28,071	11.0	133,614	13,897	10.4	120,931	14,174	11.7	23,184	270	1.2	57,685	1,788	3.1
5 West North Central	203,641	30,436	14.9	106,567	14,678	13.8	97,074	15,758	16.2	20,281	732	3.6	49,177	2,427	4.9
6 South Atlantic	2,986,936	969,432	32.5	1,470,297	477,107	32.4	1,516,639	492,325	32.5	513,239	97,196	18.9	883,929	206,434	23.4
7 East South Central	1,960,898	681,507	34.8	970,921	337,893	34.8	989,977	343,614	34.7	320,476	66,209	20.7	569,118	141,986	24.9
8 West South Central	1,460,705	483,022	33.1	732,945	236,239	32.2	727,760	246,783	33.9	240,265	53,803	22.4	429,272	104,677	24.4
9 Mountain	18,755	1,497	8.0	10,461	754	7.2	8,294	743	9.0	1,286	20	1.6	3,718	146	3.9
10 Pacific	25,575	1,614	6.3	14,184	752	5.3	11,391	862	7.6	1,795	10	0.6	5,125	130	2.5
NEW ENGLAND:															
11 Maine	1,166	93	8.0	610	56	9.2	556	37	6.7	117	1	0.9	279	12	4.3
12 New Hampshire	480	51	10.6	247	30	12.1	233	21	9.0	40.	......	......	98	3	......
13 Vermont	1,446	69	4.8	1,089	41	3.8	357	28	7.8	72	3	......	417	7	1.7
14 Massachusetts	31,718	2,584	8.1	15,629	1,286	8.2	16,089	1,298	8.1	2,905	9	0.3	6,701	381	5.7
15 Rhode Island	7,913	752	9.5	3,839	370	9.6	4,074	382	9.4	714	4	0.6	1,659	87	5.2
16 Connecticut	12,598	792	6.3	5,975	324	5.4	6,623	468	7.1	1,244	1	0.1	2,663	57	2.1
MIDDLE ATLANTIC:															
17 New York	115,843	5,768	5.0	55,170	2,433	4.4	60,673	3,335	5.5	7,930	32	0.4	27,299	593	2.2
18 New Jersey	74,577	7,405	9.9	36,191	3,296	9.1	38,386	4,109	10.7	6,878	90	1.3	17,552	798	4.5
19 Pennsylvania	161,126	14,638	9.1	79,647	6,844	8.6	81,479	7,794	9.6	14,840	175	1.2	36,519	1,194	3.3
EAST NORTH CENTRAL:															
20 Ohio	93,910	10,460	11.1	49,297	5,370	10.9	44,613	5,090	11.4	8,964	83	0.9	21,656	685	3.2
21 Indiana	50,650	6,959	13.7	26,258	3,403	13.0	24,392	3,556	14.6	4,984	38	0.8	11,896	313	2.6
22 Illinois	92,928	9,713	10.5	49,031	4,652	9.5	43,897	5,061	11.5	7,768	141	1.8	20,523	746	3.6
23 Michigan	14,557	826	5.7	7,727	411	5.3	6,830	415	6.1	1,276	7	0.5	3,090	38	1.2
24 Wisconsin	2,500	113	4.5	1,301	61	4.7	1,199	52	4.3	192	1	0.5	520	6	1.2
WEST NORTH CENTRAL:															
25 Minnesota	6,366	215	3.4	3,835	126	3.3	2,531	89	3.5	375	1	0.3	1,145	15	1.3
26 Iowa	12,380	1,272	10.3	6,813	662	9.7	5,567	610	11.0	1,215	13	1.1	2,822	73	2.6
27 Missouri	132,385	23,062	17.4	68,113	11,161	16.4	64,292	11,901	18.5	13,190	690	5.2	32,292	2,092	6.5
28 North Dakota	546	26	4.8	348	16	4.6	198	10	5.1	30	......	......	118	3	2.5
29 South Dakota	697	38	5.5	404	24	5.9	293	14	4.8	62	......	......	159	1	0.6
30 Nebraska	6,725	482	7.2	3,751	233	6.2	2,974	249	8.4	438	2	0.5	1,445	23	1.6
31 Kansas	44,542	5,341	12.0	23,303	2,456	10.5	21,239	2,885	13.6	4,971	26	0.5	11,196	220	2.0
SOUTH ATLANTIC:															
32 Delaware	24,777	6,345	25.6	12,886	3,220	25.0	11,891	3,125	26.3	3,540	224	6.3	6,370	799	12.5
33 Maryland	180,454	42,289	23.4	89,335	20,852	23.3	91,119	21,437	23.5	24,595	2,345	9.5	46,989	6,146	13.1
34 District of Columbia	79,964	10,814	13.5	35,540	4,015	11.3	44,424	6,799	15.3	7,211	67	0.9	19,953	872	4.4
35 Virginia	496,418	148,950	30.0	243,957	75,162	30.8	252,461	73,788	29.2	83,395	13,370	16.0	141,550	26,229	18.5
36 West Virginia	50,925	10,347	20.3	30,058	6,405	21.3	20,867	3,942	18.9	5,424	348	6.4	15,466	2,204	14.3
37 North Carolina	490,395	156,303	31.9	236,640	75,674	32.0	253,755	80,629	31.8	89,416	14,861	16.6	149,738	31,049	20.7
38 South Carolina	584,064	226,242	38.7	282,305	106,994	37.9	301,759	119,248	39.5	114,341	26,455	23.1	184,423	58,424	31.7
39 Georgia	846,195	308,639	36.5	415,552	154,466	37.2	430,643	154,173	35.8	152,029	33,602	22.1	253,218	68,135	26.9
40 Florida	233,744	59,503	25.5	124,024	30,319	24.4	109,720	29,184	26.6	33,288	5,924	17.8	66,222	12,576	19.0
EAST SOUTH CENTRAL:															
41 Kentucky	210,028	57,900	27.6	105,770	29,906	28.3	104,258	27,994	26.9	26,984	2,356	8.7	56,019	7,192	12.8
42 Tennessee	360,663	98,541	27.3	177,698	49,382	27.8	182,965	49,159	26.9	53,344	8,203	15.4	105,550	16,894	16.0
43 Alabama	662,356	265,628	40.1	325,655	129,385	39.7	336,701	136,243	40.5	112,129	30,839	27.5	192,800	59,533	30.9
44 Mississippi	727,851	259,438	35.6	361,798	129,220	35.7	366,053	130,218	35.6	128,019	24,811	19.4	214,749	58,367	27.2
WEST SOUTH CENTRAL:															
45 Arkansas	327,009	86,398	26.4	165,880	42,233	25.5	161,129	44,165	27.4	52,679	8,844	16.8	96,529	16,041	16.6
46 Louisiana	525,450	254,148	48.4	259,937	122,625	47.2	265,513	131,523	49.5	85,917	35,200	41.0	150,987	62,624	41.5
47 Oklahoma	101,157	17,858	17.7	53,686	8,802	16.4	47,471	9,056	19.1	16,208	1,011	6.2	29,318	2,977	10.2
48 Texas	507,089	124,618	24.6	253,442	62,579	24.7	253,647	62,039	24.5	85,461	8,748	10.2	152,438	23,035	15.1
MOUNTAIN:															
49 Montana	1,633	114	7.0	963	75	7.8	670	39	5.8	95	......	......	283	8	2.8
50 Idaho	578	37	6.4	364	18	4.9	214	19	8.9	19	......	......	111	5	4.5
51 Wyoming	2,024	102	5.0	1,442	53	3.7	582	49	8.4	56	......	......	525	27	5.1
52 Colorado	9,990	856	8.6	5,154	396	7.7	4,836	460	9.5	807	9	1.1	1,953	71	3.6
53 New Mexico	1,344	191	14.2	766	101	13.2	578	90	15.6	106	8	7.5	275	20	7.3
54 Arizona	1,691	122	7.2	892	68	7.6	799	54	6.8	130	2	1.5	328	11	3.4
55 Utah	1,026	49	4.8	634	28	4.4	392	21	5.4	55	1	......	187	4	2.1
56 Nevada	469	26	5.5	246	15	6.1	223	11	4.9	18	......	......	56	......	......
PACIFIC:															
57 Washington	5,517	239	4.3	3,473	126	3.6	2,044	113	5.5	274	1	0.4	967	14	1.4
58 Oregon	1,359	46	3.4	838	25	3.0	521	21	4.0	54	......	......	223	2	0.9
59 California	18,699	1,329	7.1	9,873	601	6.1	8,826	728	8.2	1,467	9	0.6	3,935	114	2.9

[1] Includes persons of unknown age.

AND FOR MALES 21 YEARS OF AGE AND OVER, BY DIVISIONS AND STATES: 1910.

[Per cent not shown where base is less than 100.]

	NEGRO POPULATION: 1910—continued.																					
25 to 34 years of age.			**35 to 44 years of age.**			**45 to 54 years of age.**			**55 to 64 years of age.**			**65 years and over.**			**Males, 21 year and over.**							
Total.	Illiterate.		Total.	Illiterate.		Total.	Illiterate.		Total.	Illiterate.		Total.	Illiterate.		Total.	Illiterate.						
	Number.	Per cent.		Number.	Per cent.		Number.	Per cent.		Number.	Per cent.		Number.	Per cent.		Number.	Per cent.					
1,549,316	380,742	24.6	1,088,862	351,858	32.3	711,979	334,930	47.0	396,124	249,584	63.0	294,124	219,255	74.5	2,458,873	819,135	33.3	1
14,508	1,029	7.1	11,172	835	7.5	6,672	708	10.6	3,547	585	16.5	2,356	590	25.0	22,074	1,967	8.9	2
102,036	4,737	4.6	71,433	5,756	8.1	37,389	5,787	15.5	17,069	4,290	25.1	11,330	4,129	36.4	138,750	11,826	8.5	3
63,735	3,282	5.1	49,372	4,801	9.7	30,474	5,918	19.4	16,331	5,560	34.0	12,333	6,193	50.2	107,170	13,285	12.4	4
49,153	3,367	6.9	37,075	4,764	12.8	23,806	6,490	27.3	12,790	5,928	46.3	9,954	6,334	63.6	83,219	13,468	16.2	5
595,525	166,058	27.9	421,374	152,982	36.3	279,676	142,627	51.0	162,623	108,023	66.4	119,140	91,829	77.1	955,364	351,220	36.8	6
402,101	116,989	29.1	278,306	106,120	38.1	131,801	103,766	54.1	108,199	75,778	70.0	82,481	66,616	80.8	642,460	252,677	39.3	7
309,622	84,817	27.4	210,345	76,034	36.1	136,418	69,000	50.6	73,136	48,871	66.8	55,073	43,003	78.1	488,815	173,284	35.4	8
5,514	237	4.3	4,204	303	7.2	2,341	291	12.4	1,009	260	25.8	548	227	41.4	8,992	707	7.9	9
7,122	226	3.2	5,581	263	4.7	3,402	343	10.1	1,420	289	20.4	909	334	36.7	12,029	701	5.8	10
237	10	4.2	183	13	7.1	145	13	9.0	117	17	14.5	83	26	......	476	55	11.6	11
111	7	6.3	86	5	......	78	12	......	28	10	......	36	12	......	200	29	14.5	12
565	10	1.8	191	11	5.8	99	14	......	62	9	......	39	14	......	975	38	3.9	13
8,537	710	8.3	6,623	512	7.7	3,793	377	9.9	1,875	291	15.5	1,199	292	24.4	12,591	1,186	9.4	14
1,958	194	9.9	1,541	131	8.5	1,049	126	12.0	587	106	18.1	379	97	25.6	3,067	345	11.2	15
3,100	98	3.2	2,548	163	6.4	1,508	166	11.0	878	152	17.3	620	149	24.0	4,765	314	6.6	16
36,874	1,039	2.8	23,210	1,122	4.8	11,468	1,111	9.7	5,228	873	16.7	3,473	954	27.5	45,877	2,295	5.0	17
19,633	1,195	6.1	15,034	1,392	9.3	8,432	1,509	17.9	3,999	1,177	29.4	2,808	1,187	42.3	28,601	3,052	10.7	18
45,529	2,503	5.5	33,189	3,242	9.8	17,489	3,167	18.1	7,842	2,240	28.6	5,049	1,988	39.4	64,272	6,479	10.1	19
22,265	1,250	5.6	17,701	1,823	10.3	11,442	2,122	18.5	6,416	2,010	31.3	5,037	2,400	47.6	39,188	5,169	13.2	20
12,127	732	6.0	9,362	1,218	13.0	6,136	1,614	26.3	3,424	1,499	43.8	2,498	1,491	59.7	20,651	3,312	16.0	21
25,297	1,223	4.8	19,073	1,630	8.5	10,656	2,013	18.9	5,175	1,866	36.1	3,722	1,982	53.3	39,983	4,349	10.9	22
3,371	64	1.9	2,731	111	4.1	1,928	154	8.0	1,168	168	14.4	938	279	29.7	6,266	397	6.3	23
675	13	1.9	505	19	3.8	312	15	4.8	148	17	11.5	138	41	29.7	1,082	58	5.4	24
2,064	40	1.9	1,543	39	2.5	738	41	5.6	258	24	9.3	181	50	27.6	3,390	123	3.6	25
2,814	145	5.2	2,434	175	7.2	1,602	291	18.2	804	256	31.8	591	297	50.3	5,443	626	11.5	26
32,299	2,754	8.5	24,148	3,835	15.9	15,283	4,936	32.3	8,212	4,294	52.3	6,014	4,170	69.3	52,921	10,068	19.0	27
177	5	2.8	109	6	5.5	54	2	......	36	8	......	8	2	......	311	16	5.1	28
194	6	3.1	148	8	5.4	81	12	......	28	4	......	25	7	......	341	24	7.0	29
2,076	75	3.6	1,439	97	6.7	800	107	13.4	326	88	27.0	183	87	47.5	3,225	231	7.2	30
9,529	342	3.6	7,254	604	8.3	5,248	1,101	21.0	3,126	1,254	40.1	2,952	1,721	58.3	17,588	2,380	13.5	31
4,816	935	19.4	4,154	1,248	30.0	2,903	1,287	44.3	1,635	947	57.9	1,240	846	68.2	9,050	2,829	31.3	32
37,593	6,101	16.2	30,097	7,340	24.4	20,822	8,003	38.4	11,264	6,273	55.7	8,575	5,867	68.4	63,963	17,484	27.3	33
20,535	1,631	7.9	15,255	1,998	13.1	9,088	2,405	26.5	4,492	1,943	43.3	2,957	1,765	59.7	27,621	3,801	13.8	34
92,682	21,100	22.8	72,406	23,496	32.5	51,730	25,490	49.3	29,863	20,272	67.9	23,521	18,466	78.5	159,593	57,867	36.3	35
14,019	2,460	17.5	8,484	1,983	23.4	4,187	1,457	34.8	1,886	1,020	54.1	1,257	819	65.2	22,757	5,457	24.0	36
90,533	25,196	27.8	61,526	22,693	36.9	46,260	24,605	53.2	29,083	19,910	68.5	21,428	16,969	79.2	146,752	56,669	38.6	37
109,441	41,701	38.1	75,811	34,281	45.2	46,216	26,381	57.1	30,280	21,035	69.5	21,817	17,298	79.3	169,155	72,857	43.1	38
169,733	55,476	32.7	115,255	49,588	43.0	77,110	44,422	57.6	44,235	31,088	70.3	31,959	25,309	79.2	266,814	111,037	41.6	39
56,173	11,458	20.4	38,386	10,355	27.0	21,360	8,577	40.2	9,885	5,535	56.0	6,386	4,490	70.3	89,659	23,219	25.9	40
43,442	7,977	18.4	34,000	10,500	30.9	24,494	12,242	50.0	13,441	8,861	65.9	10,503	8,234	78.4	75,694	25,958	34.3	41
74,036	14,398	19.4	50,969	14,303	28.1	37,930	17,806	46.9	21,357	13,826	64.7	16,155	12,553	77.7.	119,142	38,273	32.1	42
134,179	47,011	35.0	90,450	40,087	44.3	68,415	39,418	57.6	34,834	25,464	73.1	26,770	21,955	82.0	213,923	92,744	43.4	43
150,444	47,603	31.6	102,887	41,230	40.1	60,962	34,300	56.3	38,567	27,627	71.6	29,053	23,874	82.2	233,701	95,702	41.0	44
69,217	14,081	20.3	46,066	13,355	29.0	34,411	15,563	45.2	16,188	10,034	62.0	10,827	8,130	75.1	111,365	32,013	28.7	45
111,166	48,815	43.9	79,455	40,524	51.0	46,232	27,972	60.5	27,581	19,981	72.4	21,886	17,823	81.4	174,211	84,176	48.3	46
22,263	2,650	11.9	14,744	2,693	18.3	9,688	3,402	35.1	5,042	2,679	53.1	3,303	2,279	69.0	36,841	7,396	20.1	47
106,976	19,271	18.0	70,080	19,462	27.8	46,087	22,063	47.9	24,325	16,177	66.5	19,057	14,771	77.5	166,398	49,699	29.9	48
456	24	5.3	389	23	5.9	216	14	6.5	125	32	25.6	47	13	......	851	75	8.8	49
177	4	2.3	133	6	4.5	78	5	......	36	8	......	22	9	......	328	16	4.9	50
889	28	3.1	331	21	6.3	137	10	7.3	46	5	......	26	10	......	1,325	50	3.8	51
2,647	109	4.1	2,279	175	7.7	1,380	191	13.8	553	157	28.4	306	139	45.4	4,283	373	8.7	52
402	43	10.7	272	32	11.8	146	33	22.6	80	27	......	58	27	......	644	88	13.7	53
460	22	4.8	420	29	6.9	211	22	10.4	90	18	......	44	17	......	764	64	8.4	54
340	6	1.8	245	10	4.1	109	11	10.1	51	8	......	25	5	......	568	26	4.6	55
143	1	0.7	135	7	5.2	64	5	......	28	5	......	20	7	......	229	15	6.6	56
1,839	49	2.7	1,330	55	4.1	675	52	7.7	211	42	19.9	111	23	20.7	3,120	121	3.9	57
414	4	1.0	371	7	1.9	181	9	5.0	71	11	......	37	12	......	766	24	3.1	58
4,869	173	3.6	3,880	201	5.2	2,546	282	11.1	1,138	236	20.7	761	299	39.3	8,143	556	6.8	59

TABLE 25.—ILLITERATES IN THE NEGRO POPULATION, BY SEX AND AGE PERIODS, BY DIVISIONS: 1910 AND 1900.

DIVISION, SEX, AND CENSUS YEAR.	NUMBER OF NEGRO ILLITERATES.								PERCENTAGE ILLITERATE IN NEGRO POPULATION.							
	Total 10 years of age and over.	10 to 14 years of age.	15 to 24 years of age.	25 to 34 years of age.	35 to 44 years of age.	45 to 54 years of age.	55 to 64 years of age.	65 years and over.	10 years of age and over.	10 to 14 years of age.	15 to 24 years of age.	25 to 34 years of age.	35 to 44 years of age.	45 to 54 years of age.	55 to 64 years of age.	65 years and over.
UNITED STATES:																
Both sexes—																
1910	2,227,731	218,555	460,720	380,742	351,858	334,930	249,584	219,255	30.4	18.9	22.0	24.6	32.3	47.0	63.0	74.5
1900	2,853,194	328,992	652,610	496,180	437,503	420,438	267,312	223,124	44.5	30.1	33.4	39.3	52.0	68.1	78.4	85.4
Male—																
1910	1,096,000	125,616	253,429	183,993	152,132	147,542	120,046	107,877	30.1	21.7	25.6	24.4	27.7	38.9	55.5	70.7
1900	1,371,432	183,540	338,976	222,516	177,199	191,883	134,535	111,158	43.1	33.5	36.3	35.7	43.0	59.3	73.4	83.6
Female—																
1910	1,131,731	92,939	207,291	196,749	199,726	187,388	129,538	111,378	30.7	16.1	18.8	24.7	37.1	56.3	72.0	78.6
1900	1,481,762	145,452	313,634	273,664	260,304	228,555	132,777	111,966	45.8	26.8	30.8	42.8	60.6	77.8	84.3	87.2
NEW ENGLAND:																
Both sexes—																
1910	4,341	18	547	1,029	835	708	585	590	7.8	0.4	4.6	7.1	7.5	10.6	16.5	25.0
1900	5,681	49	683	1,005	1,077	1,255	820	698	11.6	1.1	5.5	8.0	12.3	21.4	28.0	35.4
Male—																
1910	2,107	14	337	637	380	270	220	238	7.7	0.6	6.0	8.7	6.6	8.0	12.6	21.6
1900	2,469	22	346	518	459	492	340	262	10.4	1.1	4.6	8.2	10.7	16.2	22.8	30.5
Female—																
1910	2,234	4	210	392	455	438	365	352	8.0	0.2	3.4	5.5	8.3	13.2	20.3	28.0
1900	3,212	27	337	487	618	763	480	436	12.7	1.2	4.9	7.8	13.9	26.9	33.3	39.3
MIDDLE ATLANTIC:																
Both sexes—																
1910	27,811	297	2,585	4,737	5,756	5,787	4,290	4,129	7.9	1.0	3.2	4.6	8.1	15.5	25.1	36.4
1900	38,594	633	5,338	7,493	8.054	7.575	4.714	4.254	14.2	2.6	7.0	10.3	17.1	28.0	35.4	48.5
Male—																
1910	12,573	152	1,394	2,395	2.746	2,398	1,727	1,661	7.4	1.1	3.8	4.8	7.3	12.5	20.5	31.3
1900	18,141	313	3,026	3,930	3,623	3,243	2,112	1,671	13.6	2.8	8.8	10.6	14.9	23.5	31.2	43.0
Female—																
1910	15,238	145	1,191	2,342	3,010	3,389	2,563	2,468	8.4	0.9	2.6	4.5	8.9	18.6	29.7	41.0
1900	20,453	320	2,312	3,563	4,431	4,332	2,602	2,583	14.8	2.5	5.6	10.0	19.5	32.6	39.7	52.8
EAST NORTH CENTRAL:																
Both sexes—																
1910	28,071	270	1,788	3,282	4,801	5,918	5,560	6,193	11.0	1.2	3.1	5.1	9.7	19.4	34.0	50.2
1900	39,280	576	3,214	5,370	7,654	8,801	6,634	6,052	18.5	2.4	5.9	10.7	20.9	37.3	50.9	66.2
Male—																
1910	13,897	144	1,082	1,870	2,402	2,741	2,546	3,002	10.4	1.3	3.8	5.6	8.8	16.3	28.3	44.4
1900	19,498	351	1,892	2,888	3,667	4,070	3,366	2,876	17.4	3.0	6.9	10.7	18.4	31.2	45.7	60.5
Female—																
1910	14,174	126	706	1,412	2,399	3,177	3,014	3,191	11.7	1.1	2.4	4.7	10.8	23.2	41.2	57.3
1900	19,782	225	1,322	2,482	3,987	4,731	3,268	3,176	19.7	1.8	4.9	10.7	24.0	44.7	57.6	72.4
WEST NORTH CENTRAL:																
Both sexes—																
1910	30,436	732	2,427	3,367	4,764	6,490	5,928	6,334	14.9	3.6	4.9	6.9	12.8	27.3	46.3	63.6
1900	48,634	1,966	5,131	6,546	9,059	10,513	7,378	6,627	25.4	7.7	9.7	15.8	30.2	53.2	67.5	78.6
Male—																
1910	14,678	448	1,501	1,898	2,313	2,890	2,596	2,859	13.8	4.5	6.2	7.3	11.4	22.1	37.3	55.9
1900	23,271	1,157	3,095	3,259	3,955	4,621	3,529	3,112	23.6	9.1	11.8	15.1	24.9	43.4	59.7	74.1
Female—																
1910	15,758	284	926	1,469	2,451	3,600	3,332	3,475	16.2	2.7	3.7	6.4	14.6	33.6	57.2	71.8
1900	25,363	809	2,036	3,287	5,104	5,992	3,849	3,515	27.1	6.3	7.6	16.4	36.1	64.4	76.7	83.2
SOUTH ATLANTIC:																
Both sexes—																
1910	969,432	97,196	206,434	166,058	152,982	142,627	108,023	91,829	32.5	18.9	23.4	27.9	36.3	51.0	66.4	77.1
1900	1,250,279	149,060	296,152	211,990	192,317	178,111	117,355	97,242	47.1	31.3	35.9	43.1	56.1	71.6	81.2	87.4
Male—																
1910	477,107	56,728	114,022	79,421	65,981	61,119	52,285	45,568	32.4	22.1	27.4	27.9	31.5	42.3	58.8	73.5
1900	599,160	83,825	154,067	93,081	77,325	78,812	59,499	48,958	46.0	35.0	39.3	39.3	46.8	62.5	76.3	85.6
Female—																
1910	492,325	40,468	92,412	86,637	87,001	81,508	55,738	46,261	32.5	15.8	19.8	27.9	41.1	60.3	75.6	81.0
1900	651,119	65,235	142,085	118,909	114,992	99,299	57,856	48,284	48.1	27.5	32.8	46.6	64.8	81.0	87.0	89.2
EAST SOUTH CENTRAL:																
Both sexes—																
1910	681,507	66,209	141,986	116,989	106,120	103,766	75,778	66,616	34.8	20.7	24.9	29.1	38.1	54.1	70.0	80.8
1900	887,838	105,061	206,332	157,044	132,309	130,110	80,740	67,846	49.2	33.1	37.1	45.3	59.5	74.5	84.2	89.4
Male—																
1910	337,893	38,486	79,045	56,791	45,315	46,589	36,813	33,122	34.8	23.8	29.2	29.5	33.1	45.3	62.1	77.4
1900	429,984	59,050	108,085	70,907	52,636	60,694	40,916	34,166	48.1	36.8	40.4	41.7	49.8	65.6	79.4	87.9
Female—																
1910	343,614	27,723	62,941	60,198	60,805	57,177	38,965	33,494	34.7	17.5	21.1	28.7	43.0	64.3	79.7	84.4
1900	457,854	46,011	98,247	86,137	79,673	69,416	39,824	33,680	50.4	29.4	34.0	48.7	68.3	84.5	89.7	90.9
WEST SOUTH CENTRAL:																
Both sexes—																
1910	483,022	53,803	104,677	84,817	76,034	69,000	48,871	43,003	33.1	22.4	24.4	27.4	36.1	50.6	66.8	78.1
1900	579,489	71,611	135,457	106,197	86,288	83,196	49,160	40,013	48.0	32.7	36.7	44.4	58.0	72.7	83.5	89.0
Male—																
1910	236,239	29,625	55,854	40,723	32,724	31,264	23,632	21,176	32.2	24.7	27.3	26.7	30.5	41.1	58.5	74.1
1900	277,165	38,801	68,298	47,648	35,159	39,574	24,497	19,911	46.0	35.2	38.7	39.8	47.6	63.2	78.0	87.3
Female—																
1910	246,783	24,178	48,823	44,094	43,310	37,736	25,239	21,827	33.9	20.1	21.7	28.1	42.1	62.5	77.1	82.4
1900	302,324	32,810	67,159	58,549	51,129	43,622	24,663	20,102	50.1	30.1	34.9	49.1	68.1	84.1	89.7	90.7
MOUNTAIN:																
Both sexes—																
1910	1,497	20	146	237	303	291	260	227	8.0	1.6	3.9	4.3	7.2	12.4	25.8	41.4
1900	1,840	24	189	329	416	416	259	147	13.5	2.4	5.8	8.4	14.7	28.5	41.7	52.1
Male—																
1910	754	14	96	113	151	136	130	108	7.2	2.2	5.2	3.7	6.1	9.8	20.8	34.3
1900	967	13	110	179	211	206	151	69	11.9	2.8	5.7	7.7	12.4	22.0	36.8	44.8
Female—																
1910	743	6	50	124	152	155	13 0	119	9.0	0.9	2.7	5.1	8.8	16.3	33.9	51.1
1900	873	11	79	150	205	210	108	78	15.9	2.1	5.9	9.5	18.2	40.1	51.2	60.9
PACIFIC:																
Both sexes—																
1910	1,614	10	130	226	263	343	289	334	6.3	0.6	2.5	3.2	4.7	10.1	20.4	36.7
1900	1,559	12	114	206	329	361	252	245	12.7	1.0	4.4	7.2	12.4	23.2	36.	44.3
Male—																
1910	752	5	98	145	120	135	97	143	5.3	0.6	3.7	3.6	3.7	6.7	11.8	29.3
1900	777	8	57	106	164	171	125	133	11.4	1.4	4.2	6.9	10.5	18.0	30.4	41.0
Female—																
1910	862	5	32	81	143	208	192	191	7.6	0.5	1.3	2.6	6.1	14.8	31.9	45.4
1900	782	4	57	100	165	190	127	112	14.4	0.7	4.6	7.6	14.9	31.4	45.4	48.9

TABLE 26.—ILLITERATES, BY CLASS OF POPULATION AND AGE PERIODS, BY DIVISIONS AND STATES: 1910.

[Per cent not shown where base is less than 100.]

DIVISION, STATE, AND RACIAL CLASS.	ILLITERATES IN POPULATION 10 YEARS OF AGE AND OVER.															
	10 years of age and over.[1]		10 to 14 years of age.		15 to 24 years of age.		25 to 34 years of age.		35 to 44 years of age.		45 to 54 years of age.		55 to 64 years of age.		65 years and over.	
	Number.	Per cent.	Number.	Per cent.	Number.	Per cent.	Number.	Per cent.	Number.	Per cent.	Number.	Per cent.	Number.	Per cent.	Number.	Per cent.
UNITED STATES.																
All classes[2]	5,516,163	7.7	370,136	4.1	1,070,487	5.9	1,102,384	7.3	940,510	8.1	829,153	9.9	607,754	12.0	573,799	14.5
Negro	2,227,731	30.4	218,555	18.9	460,720	22.0	380,742	24.6	351,858	32.3	334,930	47.0	249,584	63.0	219,255	74.5
Native white	1,534,272	3.0	131,991	1.7	288,864	2.1	247,774	2.4	235,489	3.0	248,900	4.5	197,955	6.0	179,219	7.3
Foreign-born white	1,650,361	12.7	12,684	3.5	305,237	14.5	455,188	14.4	333,914	12.3	228,180	11.0	146,922	11.1	163,201	13.8
GEOGRAPHIC DIVISIONS.																
NEW ENGLAND.																
All classes	280,806	5.3	1,970	0.4	51,615	4.3	70,299	6.3	55,982	5.9	42,280	6.1	29,153	6.7	28,645	7.5
Negro	4,341	7.8	18	0.4	547	4.6	1,029	7.1	835	7.5	708	10.6	585	16.5	590	25.0
Native white	33,157	0.9	1,115	0.2	6,350	0.7	6,190	1.0	6,189	1.1	5,552	1.3	4,042	1.4	3,574	1.4
Foreign-born white	242,513	13.8	830	1.5	44,650	13.6	62,913	14.0	48,738	12.5	35,838	13.7	24,440	16.3	24,423	20.4
MIDDLE ATLANTIC.																
All classes	873,812	5.7	7,313	0.4	168,806	4.5	244,305	7.2	183,065	6.8	123,384	6.5	74,112	6.8	70,667	8.3
Negro	27,811	7.9	297	1.0	2,585	3.2	4,737	4.6	5,756	8.1	5,787	15.5	4,290	25.1	4,129	36.4
Native white	108,251	1.0	3,756	0.2	15,601	0.6	15,282	0.7	16,713	1.0	18,719	1.6	16,920	2.4	20,867	3.9
Foreign-born white	735,244	15.8	3,226	2.0	150,367	16.5	223,732	17.9	159,981	16.2	98,318	14.9	52,658	13.8	45,442	14.7
EAST NORTH CENTRAL																
All classes	491,850	3.4	5,327	0.3	65,159	1.8	100,111	3.3	86,664	3.6	80,601	4.4	66,672	6.0	85,807	9.2
Negro	28,071	11.0	270	1.2	1,788	3.1	3,282	5.1	4,801	9.7	5,918	19.4	5,560	34.0	6,193	50.2
Native white	158,065	1.4	4,105	0.3	18,126	0.6	19,851	0.9	24,185	1.4	30,864	2.4	27,889	3.8	32,523	5.8
Foreign-born white	300,613	10.1	773	1.2	44,739	11.1	76,275	11.3	56,670	9.4	42,745	8.3	32,489	9.1	46,224	12.9
WEST NORTH CENTRAL.																
All classes	263,138	2.9	6,697	0.6	34,647	1.5	44,818	2.4	41,437	2.9	43,851	4.1	38,785	6.0	51,738	9.7
Negro	30,436	14.9	732	3.6	2,427	4.9	3,367	6.9	4,764	12.8	6,490	27.3	5,928	46.3	6,334	63.6
Native white	99,023	1.4	4,640	0.4	14,285	0.7	14,999	1.0	15,478	1.4	17,963	2.4	15,101	3.7	16,189	7.9
Foreign-born white	120,573	7.6	772	2.6	16,778	9.5	24,733	7.9	18,803	6.0	16,792	5.5	15,326	7.0	27,010	12.5
SOUTH ATLANTIC.																
All classes	1,444,294	16.0	140,007	10.0	298,874	12.0	248,993	13.7	226,013	17.0	217,415	23.3	166,900	27.9	140,938	32.1
Negro	969,432	32.5	97,196	18.9	206,434	23.4	166,058	27.9	152,982	36.3	142,627	51.0	108,023	66.4	91,829	77.1
Native white	433,809	7.6	42,117	0.5	83,945	0.5	71,156	6.2	64,657	7.6	69,666	11.4	55,827	13.7	45,708	15.7
Foreign-born white	37,934	13.5	437	5.3	7,830	16.7	11,225	16.4	7,838	13.5	4,622	11.4	2,729	9.6	3,120	10.7
EAST SOUTH CENTRAL.																
All classes	1,072,100	17.4	103,293	10.7	219,228	12.8	181,031	14.6	166,964	18.7	167,645	26.2	123,241	30.6	105,760	35.6
Negro	681,507	34.8	66,209	20.7	141,986	24.9	116,989	29.1	106,120	38.1	103,766	54.1	75,778	70.0	66,616	80.8
Native white	381,230	9.2	36,718	5.7	75,721	6.6	62,204	7.5	59,283	9.9	62,541	14.4	46,314	16.5	37,585	18.9
Foreign-born white	8,215	9.7	206	11.4	1,217	14.4	1,615	11.1	1,396	9.1	1,214	7.9	1,056	7.8	1,480	9.5
WEST SOUTH CENTRAL.																
All classes	845,604	13.2	95,759	9.4	186,488	10.3	153,512	11.4	133,568	14.2	119,112	18.8	84,672	22.2	68,251	27.7
Negro	483,022	33.1	53,803	22.4	104,677	24.4	84,817	27.4	76,034	36.1	69,000	50.6	48,871	66.8	43,003	78.1
Native white	264,544	5.8	35,719	4.8	63,747	4.8	48,530	5.1	39,201	6.0	34,439	7.9	25,197	9.5	17,051	11.0
Foreign-born white	84,674	25.6	5,190	34.6	15,588	30.9	17,855	26.3	16,008	24.4	13,554	24.1	8,866	22.3	6,989	20.4
MOUNTAIN.																
All classes	140,737	6.9	8,228	3.4	27,742	5.5	23,144	6.5	26,730	7.4	19,956	8.2	13,534	10.8	11,286	14.4
Negro	1,497	8.0	20	1.6	146	3.9	237	4.3	303	7.2	291	12.4	260	25.8	227	41.4
Native White	45,007	2.9	3,269	1.5	8,955	2.1	7,588	2.1	8,025	3.2	7,499	4.6	5,470	6.9	3,968	8.8
Foreign-born white	52,950	12.5	832	8.3	11,174	17.4	16,589	14.5	10,680	11.4	6,497	9.2	3,615	9.1	2,999	10.6
PACIFIC.																
All classes	103,822	3.0	1,542	0.5	17,928	2.3	27,171	3.3	20,087	3.1	14,909	3.3	10,685	4.2	10,707	5.6
Negro	1,614	6.3	10	0.6	130	2.5	226	3.2	263	4.7	343	10.1	289	20.4	334	36.7
Native white	11,186	0.4	552	0.2	2,134	0.3	1,974	0.3	1,758	0.4	1,657	0.6	1,195	0.8	1,754	1.6
Foreign-born white	67,645	8.0	418	2.5	12,894	11.5	20,251	9.4	13,800	7.5	8,600	5.9	5,743	6.3	5,514	7.7
NEW ENGLAND DIVISION.																
MAINE.																
All classes	24,554	4.1	493	0.8	4,445	3.5	4,852	4.4	4,591	4.6	4,121	5.0	2,969	5.0	3,007	4.9
Negro	93	8.0	1	0.9	12	4.3	10	4.2	13	7.1	13	9.0	17	14.5	26	......
Native white	9,824	2.0	381	0.6	2,280	2.1	1,919	2.2	1,677	2.2	1,430	2.2	1,114	2.3	989	1.9
Foreign-born white	14,394	13.7	106	2.5	2,137	11.0	2,891	11.6	2,850	12.9	2,628	16.5	1,793	19.0	1,950	21.4
NEW HAMPSHIRE.																
All classes	16,386	4.6	123	0.3	2,781	3.7	3,525	5.4	3,178	5.3	2,733	5.6	2,051	6.0	1,923	5.6
Negro	51	10.6	......	......	3	......	7	6.3	5	......	12	......	10	......	12	......
Native white	2,839	1.1	66	0.2	494	0.9	537	1.2	535	1.3	469	1.4	364	1.4	359	1.3
Foreign-born white	13,485	14.5	57	1.7	2,284	12.0	2,978	13.2	2,636	13.2	2,251	16.1	1,674	21.3	1,550	25.3

[1] Includes persons of unknown age. [2] Includes Indians, Chinese, Japanese, and all other.

TABLE 26.—ILLITERATES, BY CLASS OF POPULATION AND AGE PERIODS, BY DIVISIONS AND STATES: 1910—Contd.

[Per cent not shown where base is less than 100.]

DIVISION, STATE, AND RACIAL CLASS.	ILLITERATES IN POPULATION 10 YEARS OF AGE AND OVER.															
	10 years of age and over.[1]		10 to 14 years of age.		15 to 24 years of age.		25 to 34 years of age.		35 to 44 years of age.		45 to 54 years of age.		55 to 64 years of age.		65 years and over.	
	Number.	Per cent.	Number.	Per cent.	Number.	Per cent.	Number.	Per cent.	Number.	Per cent.	Number.	Per cent.	Number.	Per cent.	Number.	Per cent.
NEW ENGLAND DIVISION—Con.																
VERMONT.																
All classes............	10,896	3.7	105	0.3	1,189	2.0	1,817	3.4	1,901	3.9	1,892	4.9	1,658	5.8	2,206	7.5
Negro..................	69	4.8	3	......	7	1.7	10	1.8	11	5.8	14	......	9	......	14	......
Native white...........	4,495	1.9	77	0.3	537	1.0	737	1.8	908	2.4	892	2.9	743	3.2	591	2.5
Foreign-born white......	6,239	13.1	25	1.5	645	8.5	1,069	10.0	981	10.3	986	13.9	906	17.7	1,600	27.3
MASSACHUSETTS.																
All classes............	141,541	5.2	697	0.2	26,364	4.2	36,995	6.2	28,122	5.6	20,616	5.8	14,249	6.8	14,192	8.1
Negro..................	2,584	8.1	9	0.3	381	5.7	710	8.3	512	7.7	377	9.9	291	15.5	292	24.4
Native white...........	9,163	0.5	338	0.1	1,724	0.4	1,751	0.6	1,733	0.7	1,597	0.8	1,095	0.9	900	0.8
Foreign-born white......	129,412	12.7	348	1.2	24,217	12.9	34,430	12.9	25,763	11.2	18,551	12.1	12,842	14.9	12,995	19.2
RHODE ISLAND.																
All classes............	33,854	7.7	290	0.6	6,281	5.9	8,094	8.5	6,968	8.9	5,588	10.1	3,553	10.8	2,961	11.8
Negro..................	752	9.5	4	0.6	87	5.2	194	9.9	131	8.5	126	12.0	106	18.1	97	25.6
Native white...........	3,253	1.3	127	0.3	698	1.0	612	1.2	665	1.7	509	1.9	319	1.8	282	2.0
Foreign-born white......	29,781	17.3	159	2.5	5,492	16.5	7,276	17.1	6,144	16.2	4,939	18.6	3,121	21.3	2,579	24.9
CONNECTICUT.																
All classes............	53,665	6.0	262	0.3	10,555	5.0	15,016	7.8	11,222	7.0	7,330	6.5	4,673	6.8	4,356	7.3
Negro..................	792	6.3	1	0.1	57	2.1	98	3.2	163	6.4	166	11.0	152	17.3	149	24.0
Native white...........	3,583	0.6	126	0.1	617	0.4	634	0.6	671	0.8	655	0.1	407	0.1	453	1.2
Foreign-born white......	49,202	15.4	135	1.4	9,875	15.9	14,269	17.0	10,364	14.9	6,483	14.1	4,104	15.5	3,749	18.2
MIDDLE ATLANTIC DIVISION.																
NEW YORK.																
All classes............	406,020	5.5	2,619	0.3	78,845	4.4	109,836	6.7	83,578	6.4	60,305	6.5	37,220	7.0	33,019	7.9
Negro..................	5,768	5.0	32	0.4	593	2.2	1,039	2.8	1,122	4.8	1,111	9.7	873	16.7	954	27.5
Native white...........	36,318	0.8	1,137	0.2	5,422	0.4	5,649	0.6	6,272	0.8	6,697	1.3	5,431	1.8	5,602	2.4
Foreign-born white......	362,025	13.7	1,424	1.5	72,625	13.8	102,740	15.0	75,769	13.9	52,085	13.8	30,708	13.8	26,241	14.7
NEW JERSEY.																
All classes............	113,502	5.6	1,163	0.5	24,318	5.0	31,863	7.1	23,329	6.4	15,204	6.1	9,134	6.6	8,307	7.8
Negro..................	7,405	9.9	90	1.3	798	4.5	1,195	6.1	1,392	9.3	1,509	17.9	1,177	29.4	1,187	42.3
Native white...........	12,253	0.9	584	0.3	2,324	0.7	1,813	0.7	1,874	0.9	1,970	6.2	1,693	2.1	1,959	3.1
Foreign-born white......	93,551	14.7	485	2.4	21,173	17.8	28,788	17.1	19,954	14.2	11,654	12.4	6,248	11.7	5,159	12.6
PENNSYLVANIA.																
All classes............	354,290	5.9	3,531	0.5	65,643	4.5	102,606	7.8	76,158	7.4	47,875	6.7	27,758	6.6	29,341	9.0
Negro..................	14,638	9.1	175	1.2	1,194	3.3	2,503	5.5	3,242	9.8	3,169	18.1	2,240	28.6	1,988	39.4
Native white...........	59,680	1.3	2,035	0.3	7,855	0.7	7,820	0.9	8,567	1.2	10,052	2.0	9,796	3.2	13,306	5.7
Foreign-born white......	279,668	20.1	1,31	3.2	56,569	21.2	92,204	23.3	64,258	21.5	34,579	18.2	15,702	14.9	14,042	15.7
EAST NORTH CENTRAL DIVISION.																
OHIO.																
All classes............	124,774	3.2	1,304	0.3	16,597	1.8	25,637	3.2	22,608	3.5	19,931	4.1	16,724	5.3	21,442	8.2
Negro..................	10,460	11.1	83	0.9	685	3.2	1,250	5.6	1,823	10.3	2,122	18.5	2,010	31.3	2,400	47.6
Native white...........	47,310	1.5	1,046	0.3	4,465	0.6	5,199	0.8	7,222	1.4	9,280	2.4	8,943	3.7	10,941	5.9
Foreign-born white......	66,887	11.5	173	1.2	11,436	13.1	19,167	13.8	13,526	11.9	8,498	1.6	5,762	8.9	8,096	11.5
INDIANA.																
All classes............	66,213	3.1	714	0.3	6,237	1.2	9,999	2.3	10,214	2.9	12,193	4.4	11,489	6.3	15,151	10.1
Negro..................	6,959	13.7	38	0.8	313	2.6	732	6.0	1,218	13.0	1,614	26.3	1,499	43.8	1,491	59.1
Native white...........	40,955	2.1	633	0.3	3,191	0.7	4,347	1.1	5,683	1.8	8,472	3.4	8,219	5.2	10,312	8.6
Foreign-born white......	18,200	11.7	41	1.6	2,721	14.5	4,904	14.9	3,286	11.5	2,082	8.7	1,762	8.3	3,340	12.2
ILLINOIS.																
All classes............	168,294	3.7	1,805	0.3	26,284	2.3	40,359	4.1	31,457	4.1	25,834	4.8	19,141	6.4	22,881	9.4
Negro..................	9,713	10.5	141	1.8	746	3.6	1,223	4.8	1,630	8.5	2,013	18.9	1,866	36.1	1,982	53.3
Native white...........	40,486	1.3	1,336	0.3	5,159	0.6	5,080	0.8	6,122	1.2	8,047	2.4	7,091	4.0	7,527	5.8
Foreign-born white......	117,751	10.1	327	1.2	20,333	11.4	33,963	11.7	23,597	9.5	15,704	8.1	10,165	8.6	13,366	12.2
MICHIGAN.																
All classes............	74,800	3.8	758	0.3	9,254	1.7	14,462	3.2	13,094	3.6	12,974	4.5	10,829	5.8	13,310	8.5
Negro..................	826	5.7	7	0.5	38	1.2	64	1.9	111	4.1	154	8.0	168	14.4	279	29.7
Native white...........	17,846	1.1	565	0.2	2,838	0.6	2,937	0.9	2,938	1.2	3,068	1.7	2,567	2.3	2,871	3.3
Foreign-born white......	54,113	9.3	130	1.0	6,170	8.6	11,178	9.0	9,676	8.3	9,316	8.6	7,805	10.3	9,792	14.5
WISCONSIN.																
All classes............	57,769	3.2	746	0.3	6,787	1.5	9,654	2.7	9,291	3.3	9,669	4.3	8,489	6.3	13,023	11.0
Negro..................	113	4.5	1	0.5	6	1.2	13	1.9	19	3.8	15	4.8	17	11.5	41	29.7
Native white...........	11,468	0.9	525	0.2	2,473	0.6	2,288	0.9	2,220	1.2	1,997	1.6	1,069	1.9	872	2.6
Foreign-born white......	43,662	8.7	102	1.2	4,079	8.7	7,063	7.9	6,585	6.9	7,145	7.2	6,995	9.0	11,630	13.8

[1] Includes persons of unknown age.

TABLE 26.—ILLITERATES, BY CLASS OF POPULATION AND AGE PERIODS, BY DIVISIONS AND STATES: 1910—Contd.

[Per cent not shown where base is less than 100.]

| DIVISION, STATE, AND RACIAL CLASS. | ILLITERATES IN POPULATION 10 YEARS OF AGE AND OVER. | | | | | | | | | | | | | | | |
| | 10 years of age and over.[1] | | 10 to 14 years of age. | | 15 to 24 years of age. | | 25 to 34 years of age. | | 35 to 44 years of age. | | 45 to 54 years of age. | | 55 to 64 years of age. | | 65 years and over. | |
	Number.	Per cent.	Number.	Per cent.	Number.	Per cent.	Number.	Per cent.	Number.	Per cent.	Number.	Per cent.	Number.	Per cent.	Number.	Per cent.
WEST NORTH CENTRAL DIVISION.																
MINNESOTA.																
All classes	49,336	3.0	565	0.3	6,706	1.6	9,559	2.8	7,970	3.2	7,245	3.7	6,311	6.0	10,830	12.6
Negro	215	3.4	1	0.3	15	1.3	40	1.9	39	2.5	41	5.6	24	9.3	50	27.6
Native white	5,838	0.5	350	0.2	1,361	0.4	1,253	0.6	1,041	0.8	879	1.0	526	1.5	407	1.8
Foreign-born white	40,627	7.6	92	1.1	5,026	8.3	7,863	7.0	6,322	5.7	5,856	5.5	5,376	7.8	9,969	15.8
IOWA.																
All classes	29,889	1.7	536	0.2	3,369	0.8	4,262	1.2	3,700	1.3	4,592	2.1	4,653	3.4	8,649	6.9
Negro	1,272	10.3	13	1.1	73	2.6	145	5.2	175	7.2	291	18.2	256	31.8	297	50.3
Native white	11,541	0.8	465	0.2	1,547	0.4	1,568	0.5	1,537	0.7	2,010	1.2	1,760	1.9	2,591	3.5
Foreign-born white	16,894	6.3	51	1.5	1,704	7.0	2,485	5.6	1,959	4.0	2,277	4.4	2,629	5.9	5,747	11.2
MISSOURI.																
All classes	111,116	4.3	3,744	1.2	14,164	2.2	18,140	3.4	18,426	4.3	20,378	6.6	17,371	9.2	18,372	12.3
Negro	23,062	17.4	690	5.2	2,092	6.5	2,754	8.5	3,835	15.9	4,936	32.3	4,294	52.3	4,170	69.3
Native white	65,242	2.9	2,960	1.0	8,719	1.5	9,737	2.1	10,651	0.3	12,473	4.9	10,403	7.0	10,119	9.4
Foreign-born white	22,631	10.1	91	2.1	3,341	13.7	5,618	13.2	3,886	9.2	2,919	7.4	2,647	8.0	4,079	11.0
NORTH DAKOTA.																
All classes	13,070	3.1	705	1.2	2,579	2.2	2,521	2.5	2,174	3.3	1,994	4.6	1,407	6.5	1,597	12.4
Negro	26	4.8	......		3	2.5	5	2.8	6	5.5	2		8		2	
Native white	1,413	0.5	239	0.5	507	0.5	237	0.4	174	0.5	102	0.6	57	0.8	50	1.5
Foreign-born white	9,474	6.3	345	5.6	1,844	7.5	2,001	5.3	1,635	5.0	1,419	5.5	955	6.7	1,236	13.4
SOUTH DAKOTA.																
All classes	12,750	2.9	394	0.7	1,359	1.1	1,853	1.9	2,052	3.1	2,277	4.6	2,211	7.9	2,558	13.3
Negro	38	5.5	......		1	0.6	6	3.1	8	5.4	12		4		7	
Native white	1,239	0.4	105	0.2	303	0.3	227	0.3	194	0.5	157	0.6	136	1.0	109	1.5
Foreign-born white	4,896	5.0	50	2.4	674	5.7	907	4.4	693	3.4	702	3.6	647	4.9	1,211	11.5
NEBRASKA.																
All classes	18,009	1.9	310	0.3	2,662	1.1	3,562	1.9	2,928	2.1	2,722	2.6	2,353	3.6	3,402	6.7
Negro	482	7.2	2	0.5	23	1.6	75	3.6	97	6.7	107	13.4	88	27.0	87	47.5
Native white	4,278	0.6	215	0.2	702	0.3	740	0.5	622	0.6	658	0.9	576	1.5	749	2.8
Foreign-born white	12,264	7.1	43	1.6	1,795	10.3	2,572	8.0	2,054	5.8	1,820	5.1	1,551	6.1	2,383	10.3
KANSAS.																
All classes	28,968	2.2	443	0.3	3,808	1.1	4,921	1.8	4,187	2.1	4,643	3.0	4,479	4.4	6,330	7.2
Negro	5,341	12.0	26	0.5	220	2.0	342	3.6	604	8.3	1,101	21.0	1,254	40.1	1,721	58.3
Native white	9,472	0.8	306	0.2	1,146	0.4	1,237	0.5	1,259	0.7	1,684	1.4	1,643	2.1	2,164	3.4
Foreign-born white	13,787	10.5	100	4.1	2,394	17.2	3,287	14.2	2,254	9.2	1,799	7.3	1,521	7.5	2,385	10.8
SOUTH ATLANTIC DIVISION.																
DELAWARE.																
All classes	13,240	8.1	293	1.5	1,846	4.8	2,424	7.5	2,510	9.3	2,490	11.6	1,848	13.8	1,755	16.8
Negro	6,345	25.6	224	6.3	799	12.5	935	19.4	1,248	30.0	1,287	44.3	947	57.9	846	68.2
Native white	3,525	2.9	60	0.4	307	0.1	475	0.9	594	3.1	749	4.7	681	6.7	652	8.5
Foreign-born white	3,359	19.8	9	2.3	740	25.3	1,011	23.3	663	18.9	451	17.3	220	13.8	257	17.0
MARYLAND.																
All classes	73,397	7.2	3,257	2.5	10,782	4.3	11,615	5.6	12,702	7.4	13,227	10.4	10,729	13.8	10,802	17.8
Negro	42,289	23.4	2,345	9.5	6,146	13.1	6,101	16.2	7,340	24.4	8,003	38.4	6,273	55.7	5,867	68.4
Native white	18,952	2.6	852	0.8	2,773	1.5	2,606	1.8	2,792	2.3	3,365	3.8	3,150	5.8	3,371	8.6
Foreign-born white	12,047	11.9	59	2.0	1,850	12.9	2,885	13.6	2,540	12.4	1,828	11.2	1,297	10.4	1,562	12.1
DISTRICT OF COLUMBIA.																
All classes	13,812	4.9	93	0.4	1,305	2.1	2,338	3.5	2,561	4.8	2,830	8.3	2,275	11.3	2,248	13.2
Negro	10,814	13.5	67	0.9	872	4.4	1,631	7.9	1,998	13.1	2,405	26.5	1,943	43.3	1,765	59.7
Native white	960	0.5	20	0.1	126	0.3	163	0.4	148	0.5	162	0.8	143	1.1	194	1.8
Foreign-born white	1,944	8.2	5	1.0	297	10.3	531	9.9	387	7.6	239	6.9	175	6.1	286	8.3
VIRGINIA.																
All classes	232,911	15.2	21,917	9.2	42,757	10.4	35,381	11.9	36,383	15.8	38,599	23.3	29,948	28.0	27,225	32.0
Negro	148,950	30.0	13,370	16.0	26,229	18.5	21,100	22.8	23,496	32.5	25,490	49.3	20,272	67.9	18,466	78.5
Native white	81,457	8.0	8,492	5.5	16,070	6.0	13,579	6.9	12,368	8.2	12,794	11.7	9,471	12.7	8,519	14.6
Foreign-born white	2,368	9.2	33	4.2	429	11.3	680	11.2	496	9.0	297	7.7	188	7.2	235	8.0
WEST VIRGINIA.																
All classes	74,866	8.3	3,491	2.7	15,105	6.1	16,129	8.2	13,229	9.5	10,866	12.0	8,328	14.9	7,522	17.8
Negro	10,347	20.3	348	6.4	2,204	14.3	2,460	17.5	1,983	23.4	1,457	34.8	1,020	54.1	819	65.2
Native white	51,407	6.4	3,000	2.4	9,369	4.3	8,780	5.4	8,599	7.1	8,334	10.3	6,915	13.6	6,308	16.6
Foreign-born white	13,075	23.9	143	9.6	3,529	27.5	4,877	27.6	2,633	24.6	1,069	19.8	391	12.7	395	13.1

[1] Includes persons of unknown age.

TABLE 26.—ILLITERATES, BY CLASS OF POPULATION AND AGE PERIODS, BY DIVISIONS AND STATES: 1910—Contd.

[Per cent not shown where base is less than 100.]

| DIVISION, STATE, AND RACIAL CLASS. | ILLITERATES IN POPULATION 10 YEARS OF AGE AND OVER. | | | | | | | | | | | | | | | |
| | 10 years of age and over.[1] | | 10 to 14 years of age. | | 15 to 24 years of age. | | 25 to 34 years of age. | | 35 to 44 years of age. | | 45 to 54 years of age. | | 55 to 64 years of age. | | 65 years and over. | |
	Number.	Per cent.	Number.	Per cent.	Number.	Per cent.	Number.	Per cent.	Number.	Per cent.	Number.	Per cent.	Number.	Per cent.	Number.	Per cent.
SOUTH ATLANTIC DIVISION—Continued.																
NORTH CAROLINA.																
All classes	291,497	18.5	26,955	10.1	56,566	12.5	47,735	15.9	42,396	20.3	47,357	29.5	38,133	35.1	31,127	40.1
Negro	156,303	31.9	14,861	16.6	31,049	20.7	25,196	27.8	22,693	36.9	24,605	53.2	19,910	68.5	16,969	79.2
Native white	132,189	12.3	11,870	6.8	24,831	8.3	21,966	10.5	19,208	13.2	22,310	19.8	17,932	22.8	13,875	25.1
Foreign-born white	477	8.3	3	1.5	111	13.1	132	10.2	103	8.1	62	6.6	32	5.5	27	4.7
SOUTH CAROLINA.																
All classes	276,980	25.7	32,858	17.1	71,271	22.0	50,572	24.1	41,534	28.6	33,185	34.8	26,065	40.2	20,755	47.1
Negro	226,242	38.7	26,455	23.1	58,424	31.7	41,701	38.1	34,281	45.2	26,381	57.1	21,035	69.5	17,298	79.3
Native white	50,245	10.3	6,386	8.2	12,760	9.2	8,736	8.8	7,145	10.5	6,743	14.0	4,995	14.8	3,410	15.9
Foreign-born white	399	6.8	10	6.9	70	9.5	115	9.3	94	7.7	43	4.6	29	3.8	35	4.1
GEORGIA.																
All classes	389,775	20.7	42,861	13.6	83,312	15.4	68,555	17.9	61,643	23.5	57,270	31.5	41,613	35.6	33,384	41.4
Negro	308,639	36.5	33,602	22.1	68,135	26.9	55,490	32.7	49,588	43.0	44,422	57.6	31,088	70.3	25,309	79.2
Native white	80,203	7.8	9,237	5.7	15,007	5.3	12,846	6.1	11,834	8.3	12,732	12.4	10,435	14.7	7,996	16.9
Foreign-born white	875	6.0	17	4.3	162	7.4	225	6.6	206	6.6	105	4.4	81	5.0	77	5.0
FLORIDA.																
All classes	77,816	13.8	8,282	10.3	15,930	10.3	14,244	11.4	13,055	14.6	11,591	20.4	7,961	24.0	6,120	28.1
Negro	59,503	25.5	5,924	17.8	12,576	19.0	11,458	20.4	10,355	27.0	8,577	40.2	5,535	56.0	4,490	70.3
Native white	14,871	5.0	2,200	4.8	2,702	3.3	2,005	3.3	1,969	4.4	2,477	8.1	2,105	10.3	1,383	10.5
Foreign-born white	3,390	10.5	158	11.9	642	10.2	769	10.0	716	10.4	528	11.1	316	11.1	246	10.9
EAST SOUTH CENTRAL DIVISION.																
KENTUCKY.																
All classes	208,084	12.1	15,233	6.0	36,454	8.0	32,603	9.7	36,024	13.5	36,216	18.8	26,748	22.3	23,934	25.4
Negro	57,900	27.6	2,356	8.7	7,192	12.8	7,977	18.4	10,500	30.9	12,242	50.0	8,861	65.9	8,234	78.4
Native white	146,797	10.0	12,851	5.7	28,889	7.3	24,158	8.4	25,037	11.1	23,511	14.6	17,301	17.4	14,740	19.9
Foreign-born white	3,300	8.3	9	2.2	351	12.6	455	8.5	475	7.2	451	6.1	579	7.7	956	10.1
TENNESSEE.																
All classes	221,071	13.6	18,285	7.5	41,070	9.2	33,994	10.5	32,833	14.0	38,725	22.4	29,469	26.6	25,756	30.9
Negro	98,541	27.3	8,203	15.4	16,894	16.0	14,398	19.4	14,303	28.1	17,806	46.9	13,826	64.7	12,553	77.7
Native white	120,966	9.7	10,059	5.3	23,920	7.0	19,260	7.8	18,288	10.1	20,676	15.7	15,459	17.8	12,924	20.1
Foreign-born white	1,488	8.3	18	3.9	240	11.9	323	9.7	231	6.9	227	7.0	174	6.7	274	9.2
ALABAMA.																
All classes	352,710	22.9	41,537	16.4	77,281	17.5	61,402	19.5	52,252	24.9	53,790	33.7	35,617	37.7	29,358	44.9
Negro	265,628	40.1	30,839	27.5	59,533	30.9	47,011	35.0	40,087	44.3	39,418	57.6	25,464	73.1	21,955	82.0
Native white	84,768	9.9	10,606	7.6	17,304	7.0	13,779	7.8	11,727	10.2	13,995	16.0	9,958	17.4	7,249	19.7
Foreign-born white	2,063	11.3	56	9.7	371	15.3	564	13.5	404	11.1	348	10.2	176	7.9	142	7.9
MISSISSIPPI.																
All classes	290,235	22.4	28,238	12.8	64,423	17.3	53,032	19.9	45,855	25.1	38,914	33.8	31,407	40.6	26,712	49.2
Negro	259,438	35.6	24,811	19.4	58,367	27.2	47,603	31.6	41,230	40.1	34,300	56.3	27,627	71.6	23,874	82.2
Native white	28,699	5.2	3,202	3.5	5,608	3.6	5,007	4.4	4,231	5.4	4,359	8.3	3,596	9.6	2,672	11.2
Foreign-born white	1,364	15.1	123	33.6	255	21.3	273	15.7	286	15.9	188	13.4	127	10.5	108	8.4
WEST SOUTH CENTRAL DIVISION.																
ARKANSAS.																
All classes	142,954	12.6	14,820	8.2	26,441	8.1	23,321	10.0	21,950	13.6	25,206	21.6	17,403	25.0	13,368	29.8
Negro	86,398	26.4	8,844	16.8	16,041	16.6	14,081	20.3	13,355	29.0	15,563	45.2	10,034	62.0	8,130	75.1
Native white	55,025	7.0	5,881	4.6	10,184	4.5	8,966	5.6	8,314	7.5	9,334	11.8	7,194	14.1	5,063	15.9
Foreign-born white	1,466	8.9	92	23.7	203	12.7	274	8.9	270	8.0	291	8.5	165	6.9	169	7.7
LOUISIANA.																
All classes	352,179	29.0	47,734	24.6	86,808	25.5	68,780	26.9	56,580	30.7	40,223	34.9	27,762	39.8	22,909	46.1
Negro	254,148	48.4	35,200	41.0	62,624	41.5	48,815	43.9	40,524	51.0	27,972	60.5	19,981	72.4	17,823	81.4
Native white	85,359	13.4	11,935	11.2	22,160	12.2	17,268	12.9	13,390	14.1	10,029	16.6	6,406	18.2	4,028	19.7
Foreign-born white	12,085	24.0	510	31.9	1,906	28.7	2,617	26.6	2,559	26.3	2,127	25.9	1,310	19.3	1,026	13.9
OKLAHOMA.																
All classes	67,567	5.6	4,531	2.4	13,237	4.0	12,080	4.7	10,923	5.9	11,196	9.1	8,766	12.4	6,483	15.8
Negro	17,858	17.7	1,011	6.2	2,977	10.2	2,650	11.9	2,693	18.3	3,402	35.1	2,679	53.1	2,279	69.0
Native white	33,569	3.3	2,536	1.6	7,378	2.6	6,244	2.9	5,313	3.4	5,280	5.2	4,086	7.1	2,683	8.3
Foreign-born white	3,828	9.8	49	5.7	613	13.9	1,017	12.3	783	8.8	589	7.6	389	7.9	382	9.8
TEXAS.																
All classes	282,904	9.9	28,674	6.3	60,002	7.4	49,331	8.2	44,115	10.8	42,487	15.2	30,741	17.9	25,491	23.0
Negro	124,618	24.6	8,748	10.2	23,035	15.1	19,271	18.0	19,462	27.8	22,063	47.9	16,177	66.5	14,771	77.5
Native white	90,591	4.3	15,367	4.3	24,025	3.9	16,052	3.6	12,184	4.1	9,796	5.0	7,511	6.2	5,277	7.4
Foreign-born white	67,295	30.0	4,539	37.3	12,866	34.1	13,947	29.9	12,396	28.4	10,547	28.5	7,002	27.4	5,412	26.1

[1] Includes persons of unknown age.

TABLE 26.—ILLITERATES, BY CLASS OF POPULATION AND AGE PERIODS, BY DIVISIONS AND STATES: 1910—Contd.

[Per cent not shown where base is less than 100.]

DIVISION, STATE, AND RACIAL CLASS.	ILLITERATES IN POPULATION 10 YEARS OF AGE AND OVER.															
	10 years of age and over.[1]		10 to 14 years of age.		15 to 24 years of age.		25 to 34 years of age.		35 to 44 years of age.		45 to 54 years of age.		55 to 64 years of age.		65 years and over.	
	Number.	Per cent.	Number.	Per cent.	Number.	Per cent.	Number.	Per cent.	Number.	Per cent.	Number.	Per cent.	Number.	Per cent.	Number.	Per cent.
MOUNTAIN DIVISION.																
MONTANA.																
All classes	14,457	4.8	398	1.3	2,613	3.6	3,791	4.7	2,831	5.0	2,015	5.6	1,367	8.7	1,040	11.4
Negro	114	7.0			8	2.8	24	5.3	23	5.9	14	6.5	32	25.6	13	
Native white	736	0.4	31	0.1	141	0.3	152	0.3	116	0.4	112	0.6	93	1.1	87	1.8
Foreign-born white	8,445	9.4	36	2.5	1,932	13.3	2,829	10.3	1,621	7.7	888	6.3	421	7.1	343	9.7
IDAHO.																
All classes	5,453	2.2	112	0.4	936	1.5	1,317	2.3	936	2.2	852	2.9	604	4.1	618	6.9
Negro	37	6.4			5	4.5	4	2.3	6	4.5	5		8		9	
Native white	707	0.3	53	0.2	110	0.2	104	0.2	96	0.3	122	0.6	113	0.4	108	2.0
Foreign-born white	2,742	6.9	10	1.7	661	12.6	910	9.2	459	5.0	313	4.2	180	4.2	165	5.5
WYOMING.																
All classes	3,874	3.3	57	0.5	870	2.8	1,388	4.0	767	3.7	425	3.5	213	3.8	148	5.3
Negro	102	5.0			27	5.1	28	3.1	21	6.3	10	7.3	5		10	
Native white	298	0.3	31	0.3	65	0.3	58	0.2	46	0.3	56	0.7	19	0.5	23	1.3
Foreign-born white	2,548	9.7	12	2.7	682	13.6	1,033	11.5	465	8.3	221	6.1	75	4.4	58	6.1
COLORADO.																
All classes	23,780	3.7	605	0.9	4,352	2.9	6,179	4.2	5,009	4.3	3,605	4.3	2,177	4.9	1,649	6.2
Negro	856	8.6	9	1.1	71	3.6	109	4.1	175	7.7	191	13.8	157	28.4	139	45.4
Native white	8,133	1.6	428	0.7	1,584	1.2	1,453	1.3	1,449	1.7	1,379	0.1	928	3.0	780	4.2
Foreign-born white	13,897	11.3	127	3.9	2,566	15.5	4,345	14.0	3,179	11.1	1,925	8.4	1,020	8.1	672	8.5
NEW MEXICO.																
All classes	48,697	20.2	3,824	11.1	9,549	15.1	8,974	17.6	9,068	23.2	7,548	28.0	5,515	34.3	4,095	42.3
Negro	191	14.2	8	7.5	20	7.3	43	10.7	32	11.8	33	22.6	27		27	
Native white	30,338	14.9	2,207	7.1	5,598	10.1	4,809	11.5	5,645	17.6	5,282	23.9	4,002	30.5	2,722	37.0
Foreign-born white	6,580	31.0	201	24.0	1,270	32.7	1,808	31.8	1,345	30.4	912	28.9	579	30.7	438	33.0
ARIZONA.																
All classes	32,953	20.9	2,750	15.2	7,384	19.4	7,810	19.3	6,154	21.7	3,950	23.0	2,493	27.6	2,251	38.9
Negro	122	7.2	2	1.5	11	3.4	22	4.8	29	6.9	22	10.4	18		17	
Native white	3,776	4.2	448	3.6	1,285	5.5	826	3.6	515	3.4	351	3.9	198	4.5	140	5.7
Foreign-born white	13,758	31.5	428	20.6	3,066	35.0	4,275	32.4	2,856	30.3	1,657	30.3	851	29.2	593	33.6
UTAH.																
All classes	6,821	2.5	269	0.7	1,159	1.6	1,604	2.6	1,086	2.6	918	3.2	713	4.6	1,009	8.2
Negro	49	4.8	1		4	2.1	6	1.8	10	4.1	11	10.1	8		5	
Native white	832	0.4	56	0.1	136	0.2	135	0.3	135	0.5	159	0.9	107	1.7	94	2.7
Foreign-born white	3,636	5.9	16	1.2	604	8.0	935	7.2	534	4.7	463	4.2	405	4.6	663	7.8
NEVADA.																
All classes	4,702	6.7	213	4.3	879	6.6	1,081	5.7	879	5.9	643	7.0	452	9.1	476	15.3
Negro	26	5.5					1	0.7	7	5.2	5		5		7	
Native white	187	0.4	15	0.4	36	0.4	51	0.4	23	0.2	38	0.7	10	0.3	14	0.1
Foreign-born white	1,344	7.6	2	1.6	393	14.2	454	8.9	221	5.5	118	4.4	84	4.8	67	5.8
PACIFIC DIVISION.																
WASHINGTON.																
All classes	18,416	2.0	332	0.4	3,214	1.4	4,912	2.1	3,606	2.2	2,627	2.2	1,711	3.0	1,861	5.1
Negro	239	4.3	1	0.4	14	1.4	49	2.7	55	4.1	52	7.7	42	19.9	23	20.7
Native white	1,836	0.3	110	0.1	343	0.2	301	0.2	287	0.3	286	0.3	222	0.6	256	1.2
Foreign-born white	11,233	4.8	37	0.7	2,223	6.6	3,613	5.5	2,414	4.5	1,387	3.3	768	3.7	727	5.4
OREGON.																
All classes	10,504	1.9	112	0.2	1,763	1.3	2,503	1.9	1,922	2.0	1,584	2.2	1,119	2.8	1,372	4.9
Negro	46	3.4			2	0.9	4	1.0	7	1.9	9	5.0	11		12	
Native white	1,841	0.4	62	0.1	265	0.2	279	0.3	235	0.3	279	0.6	245	0.9	441	0.9
Foreign-born white	6,120	6.1	13	0.8	1,276	9.1	1,857	7.3	1,244	5.7	728	4.0	463	4.2	455	5.7
CALIFORNIA.																
All classes	74,902	3.7	1,098	0.6	12,951	3.0	19,756	4.2	14,559	3.9	10,698	4.0	7,855	5.0	7,474	6.0
Negro	1,329	7.1	9	0.6	114	2.9	173	3.6	201	5.2	282	11.1	236	20.7	299	39.3
Native white	7,509	0.5	380	0.2	1,526	0.4	1,394	0.4	1,236	0.5	1,092	0.7	728	0.8	1,057	1.5
Foreign-born white	50,292	10.0	368	3.7	9,395	14.5	14,781	12.0	10,142	9.3	6,485	7.5	4,512	7.7	4,332	8.6

[1] Includes persons of unknown age.

TABLE 27.—ILLITERATES BY CLASS OF POPULATION, 1910, WITH PERCENTAGE ILLITERATE, 1910, 1900 AND 1890, BY DIVISIONS AND STATES.

[Per cent not shown where base is less than 100.]

DIVISION AND STATE.	POPULATION 10 YEARS OF AGE AND OVER.																			
	All classes.					Negro.					Native white.					Foreign-born white.				
	Total, 1910	Illiterate.				Total, 1910	Illiterate.				Total, 1910	Illiterate.				Total, 1910	Illiterate.			
		Number, 1910	Per cent.				Number, 1910	Per cent.				Number, 1910	Per cent.				Number, 1910	Per cent.		
			1910	1900	1890[1]			1910	1900	1890[1]			1910	1900	1890[1]			1910	1900	1890[1]
UNITED STATES	71,580,270	5,516,163	7.7	10.7	13.3	7,317,922	2,227,731	30.4	44.5	57.1	50,989,341	1,534,272	3.0	4.6	6.2	12,944,529	1,650,361	12.7	12.9	13.1
GEOGRAPHIC DIVISIONS:																				
New England	5,330,914	280,806	5.3	6.0	6.3	55,321	4,341	7.8	11.6	15.5	3,512,988	33,157	0.9	1.3	1.5	1,757,244	242,513	13.8	16.2	18.1
Middle Atlantic	15,446,515	873,812	5.7	5.8	6.1	351,546	27,811	7.9	14.2	22.3	10,417,267	108,251	1.0	1.8	2.6	4,661,990	735,244	15.8	15.8	14.6
East North Central	14,568,949	491,850	3.4	4.3	5.7	254,545	28,071	11.0	18.5	26.7	11,311,231	158,065	1.4	2.3	3.5	2,985,823	300,613	10.1	10.2	11.3
West North Central	9,097,311	263,138	2.9	4.1	5.7	203,641	30,436	14.9	25.4	37.4	7,281,144	99,023	1.4	2.3	3.4	1,579,694	120,573	7.6	8.0	9.4
South Atlantic	9,012,826	1,444,294	16.0	23.9	30.9	2,986,936	969,432	32.5	47.1	60.1	5,737,635	433,809	7.6	11.4	14.6	280,387	37,934	13.5	12.9	12.2
East South Central	6,178,578	1,072,100	17.4	24.9	31.1	1,960,898	681,507	34.8	49.2	61.5	4,130,601	381,230	9.2	13.0	16.6	84,893	8,215	9.7	10.4	9.5
West South Central	6,394,043	845,604	13.2	20.5	27.7	1,460,705	483,022	33.1	48.0	60.9	4,550,858	264,544	5.8	9.2	12.5	330,431	84,674	25.6	27.2	25.3
Mountain	2,054,249	140,737	6.9	9.6	11.4	18,755	1,497	8.0	13.5	21.8	1,542,588	45,007	2.9	5.4	9.1	423,068	52,950	12.5	10.6	11.9
Pacific	3,496,885	103,822	3.0	4.2	6.5	25,575	1,614	6.3	12.7	24.6	2,505,029	11,186	0.4	0.9	1.6	840,999	67,645	8.0	7.3	9.5
NEW ENGLAND:																				
Maine	603,893	24,554	4.1	5.1	5.5	1,166	93	8.0	14.2	15.9	496,554	9,824	2.0	2.4	2.5	105,336	14,394	13.7	19.4	24.1
New Hampshire	354,118	16,386	4.6	6.2	6.8	480	51	10.6	11.9	22.5	260,567	2,839	1.1	1.5	1.5	92,976	13,485	14.5	20.5	26.3
Vermont	289,128	10,806	3.7	5.8	6.7	1,446	69	4.8	14.6	20.4	239,999	4,495	1.9	2.9	3.2	47,654	6,239	13.1	21.4	25.8
Massachusetts	2,742,684	141,541	5.2	5.9	6.2	31,718	2,584	8.1	10.7	14.3	1,687,135	9,163	0.5	0.8	0.8	1,020,594	129,412	12.7	14.6	16.2
Rhode Island	440,065	33,854	7.7	8.4	9.8	7,913	752	9.5	14.1	18.1	259,728	3,253	1.3	1.8	2.3	171,904	29,781	17.3	18.7	22.1
Connecticut	901,026	53,665	6.0	5.9	5.3	12,598	792	6.3	11.5	15.3	569,005	3,583	0.6	0.8	1.0	318,780	49,202	15.4	16.3	14.9
MIDDLE ATLANTIC:																				
New York	7,410,819	406,020	5.5	5.5	5.5	115,843	5,768	5.0	10.8	17.1	4,649,532	36,318	0.8	1.2	1.8	2,634,578	362,025	13.7	14.0	13.1
New Jersey	2,027,946	113,502	5.6	5.9	6.5	74,577	7,405	9.9	17.2	28.1	1,315,063	12,253	0.9	1.7	2.7	636,848	93,551	14.7	14.1	13.3
Pennsylvania	6,007,750	354,290	5.9	6.1	6.8	161,126	14,638	9.1	15.1	23.2	4,452,672	59,680	1.3	2.3	3.5	1,390,564	279,668	20.1	19.9	17.8
EAST NORTH CENTRAL:																				
Ohio	3,848,747	124,774	3.2	4.0	5.2	93,910	10,460	11.1	17.8	25.4	3,174,830	47,310	1.5	2.4	3.5	579,274	66,887	11.5	11.1	11.1
Indiana	2,160,405	66,213	3.1	4.6	6.3	50,650	6,959	13.7	22.6	32.3	1,953,626	40,955	2.1	3.6	5.3	155,596	18,200	11.7	11.4	11.0
Illinois	4,493,734	168,294	3.7	4.2	5.2	92,928	9,713	10.5	18.1	26.8	3,229,772	40,486	1.3	2.1	3.1	1,168,559	117,751	10.1	9.1	9.4
Michigan	2,236,252	74,800	3.3	4.2	5.9	14,557	826	5.7	10.9	18.9	1,635,903	17,846	1.1	1.7	2.5	579,803	54,113	9.3	10.3	12.4
Wisconsin	1,829,811	57,769	3.2	4.7	6.7	2,500	113	4.5	11.4	20.0	1,317,100	11,468	0.9	1.3	2.1	502,591	43,662	8.7	11.1	13.4
WEST NORTH CENTRAL:																				
Minnesota	1,628,635	49,336	3.0	4.1	6.0	6,366	215	3.4	7.9	12.1	1,081,512	5,838	0.5	0.8	1.4	533,915	40,627	7.6	8.4	11.1
Iowa	1,760,286	29,889	1.7	2.3	3.6	12,380	1,272	10.3	18.5	26.1	1,478,157	11,541	0.8	1.2	1.8	269,246	16,894	6.3	7.1	9.3
Missouri	2,594,600	111,116	4.3	6.4	9.1	132,385	23,062	17.4	28.1	41.7	2,237,775	65,242	2.9	4.8	6.8	223,578	22,631	10.1	9.3	9.1
North Dakota	424,730	13,070	3.1	5.6	6.0	546	26	4.8	12.8	29.9	268,981	1,413	0.5	0.9	1.8	150,451	9,474	6.3	7.8	8.7
South Dakota	443,466	12,750	2.9	5.0	4.2	697	38	5.5	13.3	20.0	329,931	1,239	0.4	0.6	1.2	98,334	4,896	5.0	6.7	9.0
Nebraska	924,032	18,009	1.9	2.3	3.1	6,725	482	7.2	11.8	19.1	741,487	4,278	0.6	0.8	1.3	172,497	12,264	7.1	6.8	7.3
Kansas	1,321,562	28,968	2.2	2.9	4.0	44,542	5,341	12.0	22.3	32.8	1,143,301	9,472	0.8	1.3	2.0	131,673	13,787	10.5	8.5	8.8
SOUTH ATLANTIC:																				
Delaware	163,080	13,240	8.1	12.0	14.3	24,777	6,345	25.6	38.1	49.5	121,325	3,525	2.9	5.6	6.2	16,940	3,359	19.8	18.3	16.8
Maryland	1,023,950	73,397	7.2	11.1	15.7	180,454	42,289	23.4	35.1	50.1	742,096	18,952	2.6	4.1	5.9	100,951	12,047	11.9	13.4	13.8
District of Columbia	279,088	13,812	4.9	8.6	13.2	79,964	10,814	13.5	24.3	35.0	174,903	960	0.5	0.8	1.7	23,755	1,944	8.2	7.0	9.3
Virginia	1,536,297	232,911	15.2	22.9	30.2	496,418	148,950	30.0	44.6	57.2	1,013,694	81,457	8.0	11.1	14.0	25,639	2,368	9.2	10.9	10.1
West Virginia	903,822	74,866	8.3	11.4	14.4	50,925	10,347	20.3	32.3	44.5	798,132	51,407	6.4	10.0	12.9	54,646	13,075	23.9	21.5	15.1
North Carolina	1,578,595	291,497	18.5	28.7	35.7	490,395	156,303	31.9	47.6	60.1	1,077,063	132,189	12.3	19.5	23.1	5,734	477	8.3	6.1	5.0
South Carolina	1,078,161	276,980	25.7	35.9	45.0	584,064	226,242	38.7	52.8	64.1	487,909	50,245	10.3	13.6	18.1	5,911	399	6.8	6.5	6.3
Georgia	1,885,111	389,775	20.7	30.5	39.8	846,195	308,639	36.5	52.4	67.3	1,023,970	80,203	7.8	11.9	16.5	14,656	875	6.0	7.0	6.4
Florida	564,722	77,816	13.8	21.9	27.8	233,744	59,503	25.5	38.4	50.5	298,543	14,871	5.0	8.6	11.3	32,155	3,390	10.5	11.6	10.8
EAST SOUTH CENTRAL:																				
Kentucky	1,722,644	208,084	12.1	16.5	21.6	210,028	57,900	27.6	40.1	55.9	1,472,827	146,797	10.0	12.8	16.1	39,571	3,300	8.3	10.9	9.8
Tennessee	1,621,179	221,071	13.6	20.7	26.6	360,663	98,541	27.3	41.6	54.2	1,242,319	120,966	9.7	14.2	18.0	17,985	1,488	8.3	9.7	9.5
Alabama	1,541,575	352,710	22.9	34.0	41.0	662,356	265,628	40.1	57.4	69.1	860,279	84,768	9.9	14.8	18.4	18,291	2,063	11.3	9.3	7.9
Mississippi	1,293,180	290,235	22.4	32.0	40.0	727,851	259,438	35.6	49.1	60.8	555,176	28,699	5.2	8.0	11.9	9,046	1,364	15.1	10.7	10.1
WEST SOUTH CENTRAL:																				
Arkansas	1,134,087	142,954	12.6	20.4	26.6	327,009	86,398	26.4	43.0	53.6	790,229	55,025	7.0	11.6	16.6	16,454	1,466	8.9	8.0	7.5
Louisiana	1,213,576	352,179	29.0	38.5	45.8	525,450	254,148	48.4	61.1	72.1	636,646	85,359	13.4	17.3	20.3	50,333	12,085	24.0	28.6	18.7
Oklahoma[2]	1,197,476	67,567	5.6	12.1	5.4	101,157	17,858	17.7	37.0	39.0	1,008,190	33,569	3.3	7.7	3.4	39,064	3,828	9.8	10.8	6.1
Texas	2,848,904	282,904	9.9	14.5	19.7	507,089	124,618	24.6	38.2	52.5	2,115,793	90,591	4.3	6.1	8.3	224,580	67,295	30.0	30.3	29.6
MOUNTAIN:																				
Montana	303,551	14,457	4.8	6.1	5.5	1,633	114	7.0	11.4	11.0	201,669	736	0.4	0.6	1.6	89,456	8,445	9.4	7.0	8.2
Idaho	249,018	5,453	2.2	4.6	5.1	578	37	6.4	14.5	24.0	203,925	707	0.3	0.9	1.9	39,619	2,742	6.9	6.0	8.3
Wyoming	117,585	3,874	3.3	4.0	3.4	2,024	102	5.0	17.2	17.8	86,186	298	0.3	0.7	1.3	26,381	2,548	9.7	8.2	7.1
Colorado	640,846	23,780	3.7	4.2	5.2	9,990	856	8.6	13.0	17.6	504,141	8,133	1.6	2.7	3.8	123,026	13,897	11.3	8.1	7.8
New Mexico	240,990	48,697	20.2	33.2	44.5	1,344	191	14.2	19.1	45.8	203,813	30,338	14.9	29.4	42.8	21,235	6,580	31.0	34.8	30.5
Arizona	157,659	32,953	20.9	29.0	23.4	1,691	122	7.2	12.7	19.2	90,119	3,776	4.2	6.2	7.9	43,724	13,758	31.5	35.3	42.2
Utah	274,778	6,821	2.5	3.1	5.6	1,026	49	4.8	6.3	26.6	207,176	832	0.4	0.8	2.3	61,840	3,636	5.9	6.1	10.3
Nevada	69,822	4,702	6.7	13.3	12.8	469	26	5.5	23.0	40.2	45,559	187	0.4	0.6	0.8	17,787	1,344	7.6	7.5	10.0
PACIFIC:																				
Washington	933,556	18,416	2.0	3.1	4.3	5,517	239	4.3	11.6	17.7	670,029	1,836	0.3	0.5	1.3	234,928	11,233	4.8	4.5	7.0
Oregon	555,631	10,504	1.9	3.3	4.1	1,359	46	3.4	8.8	17.1	438,854	1,841	0.4	0.8	1.8	100,759	6,120	6.1	4.1	7.9
California	2,007,698	74,902	3.7	4.8	7.7	18,699	1,329	7.1	13.4	26.5	1,396,146	7,509	0.5	1.0	1.7	505,312	50,292	10.0	8.7	10.5

[1] Figures for 1890 are exclusive of illiterate persons in Indian Territory and on Indian reservations, areas specially enumerated but for which illiteracy statistics are not available.
[2] Includes population of Indian Territory for 1900.

TABLE 28.—ILLITERATES IN THE NEGRO POPULATION IN URBAN AND RURAL COMMUNITIES, 1910, AND IN CITIES OF 25,000 OR MORE AND OUTSIDE SUCH CITIES, 1910 AND 1900, BY DIVISIONS AND STATES.

	NEGROES 10 YEARS OF AGE AND OVER.																			
DIVISION AND STATE	Urban: 1910.			Rural: 1910.			Cities of 25,000 or more population.						Smaller cities and country districts.						
							1910			1900			1910			1900				
	Total.	Illiterate.		Total.	Illiterate.		Total.	Illiterate.		Total.	Illiterate.		Total.	Illiterate.		Total.	Illiterate.		
		Number.	Per cent.		Number.	Per cent.		Number.	Per cent.		Number.	Per cent.		Number.	Per cent.		Number.	Per cent.	
UNITED STATES....	2,231,353	393,273	17.6	5,086,569	1,834,458	36.1	1,378,149	201,010	14.6	945,909	230,711	24.6	5,939,773	2,026,721	34.1	5,469,672	2,622,483	47.9	
GEOGRAPHIC DIVISIONS:																			
New England.......	51,025	3,614	7.1	4,296	727	16.9	38,728	2,548	6.6	29,860	3,122	10.5	16,593	1,793	10.8	19,159	2,559	13.4	
Middle Atlantic.....	288,414	20,089	7.0	63,132	7,722	12.2	237,292	15,268	6.4	165,538	18,795	11.4	114,254	12,543	11.0	105,619	19,799	18.7	
East North Central..	198,669	19,229	9.7	55,876	8,842	15.8	141,688	12,204	8.6	95,281	13,882	14.6	112,857	15,867	14.1	117,440	25,398	21.6	
West North Central..	141,823	17,454	12.3	61,818	12,982	21.0	94,439	9,790	10.4	71,376	13,460	18.9	109,202	20,646	18.9	120,471	35,174	29.2	
South Atlantic......	741,429	158,906	21.4	2,245,507	810,526	36.1	433,027	81,507	18.8	294,569	86,070	29.2	2,553,909	887,925	34.8	2,361,264	1,164,209	49.3	
East South Central..	421,529	100,257	23.8	1,539,369	581,250	37.8	223,866	47,261	21.1	167,741	59,149	35.3	1,737,032	634,246	36.5	1,635,087	828,689	50.7	
West South Central..	353,611	71,652	20.3	1,107,094	411,370	37.2	183,896	31,099	16.9	110,614	35,138	31.8	1,276,809	451,923	35.4	1,095,700	544,351	49.7	
Mountain...........	13,505	939	7.0	5,250	558	10.6	8,131	539	6.6	4,858	571	11.8	10,624	958	9.0	8,725	1,269	14.5	
Pacific.............	21,348	1,133	5.3	4,227	481	11.4	17,082	794	4.6	6,072	524	8.6	8,493	820	9.7	6,207	1,035	16.7	
NEW ENGLAND:																			
Maine.............	792	53	6.7	374	40	10.7	284	13	4.6	238	21	8.8	882	80	9.1	853	134	15.7	
New Hampshire.....	312	42	13.5	168	9	5.4	43	1	(1)	26	1	(1)	437	50	11.4	560	69	12.3	
Vermont...........	1,229	39	3.2	217	30	13.8							1,446	69	4.8	678	99	14.6	
Massachusetts......	29,528	2,086	7.1	2,190	498	22.7	24,990	1,613	6.5	19,759	1,910	9.7	6,728	971	14.4	6,814	943	13.8	
Rhode Island.......	7,525	706	9.4	388	46	11.9	6,175	538	8.7	4,139	646	15.6	1,738	214	12.3	3,423	417	12.2	
Connecticut........	11,639	688	5.9	959	104	10.8	7,236	383	5.3	5,698	544	9.5	5,362	409	7.6	6,831	897	13.1	
MIDDLE ATLANTIC:																			
New York..........	101,964	4,264	4.2	13,879	1,504	10.8	92,404	3,580	3.9	59,263	4,946	8.3	23,439	2,188	9.3	25,425	4,234	16.7	
New Jersey.........	55,027	4,823	8.8	19,550	2,582	13.2	36,075	3,056	8.5	23,464	3,288	14.0	38,502	4,349	11.3	34,070	6,594	19.4	
Pennsylvania.......	131,423	11,002	8.4	29,703	3,636	12.2	108,813	8,632	7.9	82,811	10,561	12.8	52,313	6,006	11.5	46,124	8,971	19.4	
EAST NORTH CENTRAL:																			
Ohio..............	70,836	7,053	10.0	23,074	3,407	14.8	51,562	4,968	9.6	33,762	5,238	15.5	42,348	5,492	13.0	45,474	8,869	19.5	
Indiana...........	41,226	5,417	13.1	9,424	1,542	16.4	27,335	3,531	12.9	21,577	4,659	21.6	23,315	3,428	14.7	25,395	5,935	23.4	
Illinois...........	74,154	6,224	8.4	18,774	3,489	18.6	53,251	3,334	6.3	33,951	3,498	10.3	39,677	6,379	16.1	37,233	9,405	25.3	
Michigan..........	10,562	460	4.4	3,995	366	9.2	8,098	326	4.0	4,890	407	8.3	6,459	500	7.7	8,249	1,019	12.4	
Wisconsin..........	1,891	75	4.0	609	38	6.2	1,442	45	3.1	1,101	80	7.3	1,058	68	6.4	1,089	170	15.6	
WEST NORTH CENTRAL:																			
Minnesota..........	5,911	158	2.7	455	57	12.5	5,580	138	2.5	3,626	245	6.8	786	77	9.8	657	92	14.0	
Iowa..............	8,258	876	10.6	4,122	396	9.6	4,103	353	8.6	2,587	322	12.4	8,277	919	11.1	8,002	1,640	20.5	
Missouri...........	91,057	12,645	13.9	41,328	10,417	25.2	65,940	7,649	11.6	51,670	10,386	20.1	66,445	15,413	23.2	77,930	26,004	33.4	
North Dakota.......	288	12	4.2	258	14	5.4							546	26	4.8	243	31	12.8	
South Dakota.......	352	15	4.3	345	23	6.7							697	38	5.5	384	51	13.3	
Nebraska..........	5,823	387	6.6	902	95	10.5	5,192	331	6.4	4,196	425	10.1	1,533	151	9.8	1,167	208	17.8	
Kansas............	30,134	3,361	11.2	14,408	1,980	13.7	13,624	1,319	9.7	9,297	2,082	22.4	30,918	4,022	13.0	32,088	7,148	22.3	
SOUTH ATLANTIC:																			
Delaware..........	9,505	1,787	18.8	15,272	4,558	29.8	7,798	1,457	18.7	8,049	2,384	29.6	16,979	4,888	28.8	15,478	6,583	42.5	
Maryland..........	83,429	12,441	14.9	97,025	29,848	30.8	71,705	9,438	13.2	65,630	16,846	25.7	108,749	32,851	30.2	113,732	46,187	40.6	
District of Columbia..	79,964	10,814	13.5				79,964	10,814	13.5	71,949	17,462	24.3							
Virginia...........	129,673	28,635	22.1	366,745	120,315	32.8	83,535	17,495	20.9	43,244	14,961	34.6	412,883	131,455	31.8	435,677	198,875	45.6	
West Virginia.......	12,884	1,778	13.9	38,091	8,569	22.5	2,862	335	11.7	937	192	20.5	48,063	10,012	20.8	33,366	10,891	32.6	
North Carolina......	90,329	23,032	25.5	400,066	133,271	33.3	18,937	4,986	26.3				471,458	151,317	32.1	437,691	208,132	47.6	
South Carolina......	80,498	23,797	29.6	503,566	202,445	40.2	34,563	10,038	29.0	25,065	7,454	29.7	549,501	216,204	39.3	512,333	276,429	54.0	
Georgia............	182,564	45,441	24.9	663,631	263,198	39.7	101,481	22,440	22.1	66,691	23,724	35.6	744,714	286,199	38.4	657,405	355,343	54.1	
Florida............	72,633	11,181	15.4	161,111	48,322	30.0	32,182	4,504	14.0	13,004	3,047	23.4	201,562	54,999	27.3	155,582	61,769	39.7	
EAST SOUTH CENTRAL:																			
Kentucky..........	91,363	21,288	23.3	118,665	36,612	30.9	48,124	9,983	20.7	44,406	14,084	31.7	161,904	47,917	29.6	175,314	74,053	42.2	
Tennessee.........	126,318	26,167	20.7	234,345	72,374	30.9	97,455	18,778	19.3	81,861	27,042	33.0	263,208	79,763	30.3	272,972	120,742	44.2	
Alabama..........	127,174	33,065	26.0	535,182	232,563	43.5	78,287	18,500	23.6	41,474	18,023	43.5	584,069	247,128	42.3	548,155	320,582	58.5	
Mississippi.........	76,674	19,737	25.7	651,177	239,701	36.8							727,851	259,438	35.6	638,646	313,312	49.1	
WEST SOUTH CENTRAL:																			
Arkansas..........	48,398	8,466	17.5	278,611	77,932	28.0	12,317	1,943	15.8	12,065	3,304	27.4	314,692	84,455	26.8	251,743	110,149	43.8	
Louisiana..........	130,067	33,509	25.8	395,383	220,639	55.8	85,128	16,903	19.9	62,570	22,586	36.1	440,322	237,245	53.9	402,028	261,442	65.0	
Oklahoma.........	29,778	3,688	12.4	71,379	14,170	19.9	11,753	1,126	9.6				89,404	16,732	18.7	40,198	14,870	37.0	
Texas.............	145,368	25,989	17.9	361,721	98,629	27.3	74,698	11,127	14.9	35,979	9,248	25.7	432,391	113,491	26.2	401,731	157,890	39.3	
MOUNTAIN:																			
Montana...........	1,298	85	6.5	335	29	8.7	224	10	4.5	222	21	9.5	1,409	104	7.4	1,117	131	11.7	
Idaho.............	390	21	5.4	188	16	8.5							578	37	6.4	255	37	14.5	
Wyoming..........	887	85	9.6	1,137	17	1.5							2,024	102	5.0	818	141	17.2	
Colorado..........	8,187	578	7.1	1,803	278	15.4	7,047	493	7.0	4,401	527	12.0	2,943	363	12.3	2,979	435	14.6	
New Mexico........	655	64	9.8	689	127	18.4							1,344	191	14.2	1,416	271	19.1	
Arizona...........	1,119	64	5.7	572	58	10.1							1,691	122	7.2	1,660	211	12.7	
Utah.............	876	38	4.3	150	11	7.3	860	36	4.2	235	23	9.8	166	13	7.8	354	14	4.0	
Nevada...........	93	4	(1)	376	22	5.9							469	26	5.5	126	29	23.0	
PACIFIC:																			
Washington........	4,304	162	3.8	1,213	77	6.3	3,486	98	2.8	974	57	5.9	2,031	141	6.9	1,252	202	16.1	
Oregon............	1,156	35	3.0	203	11	5.4	958	18	1.9	720	33	4.6	401	28	7.0	293	56	19.1	
California..........	15,888	936	5.9	2,811	393	14.0	12,638	678	5.4	4,378	434	9.9	6,061	651	10.7	4,662	777	16.7	

[1] Per cent not shown where base is less than 100.

TABLE **29.**—ILLITERATES IN URBAN AND RURAL COMMUNITIES, 1910, AND IN CITIES OF 25,000

	DIVISION AND RACIAL CLASS.	POPULATION 10 YEARS OF AGE AND OVER.					
		Urban: 1910.			Rural: 1910.		
		Total.	Illiterate.		Total.	Illiterate.	
			Number.	Per cent.		Number.	Per cent.
	UNITED STATES.						
1	All classes............	34,649,175	1,768,132	5.1	36,931,095	3,748,031	10.1
2	Negro..........	2,231,353	393,273	17.6	5,086,569	1,834,458	36.1
3	Native white......	22,990,744	191,900	0.8	27,998,597	1,342,372	4.8
4	Foreign-born white......	9,331,994	1,172,491	12.6	3,612,535	477,870	13.2
	NEW ENGLAND.						
5	All classes........	4,434,412	247,143	5.6	896,502	33,663	3.8
6	Negro........	51,025	3,614	7.1	4,296	727	16.9
7	Native white......	2,755,513	20,920	0.8	757,475	12,237	1.6
8	Foreign-born white......	1,623,609	222,030	13.7	133,635	20,483	15.3
	MIDDLE ATLANTIC.						
9	All classes........	11,033,550	644,618	5.8	4,412,965	229,194	5.2
10	Negro..........	288,414	20,089	7.0	63,132	7,722	12.2
11	Native white......	6,825,333	40,590	0.6	3,591,934	67,661	1.9
12	Foreign-born white......	3,910,013	582,756	14.9	751,977	152,488	20.3
	EAST NORTH CENTRAL.						
13	All classes........	7,831,590	277,444	3.5	6,737,359	214,406	3.2
14	Negro........	198,669	19,229	9.7	55,876	8,842	15.8
15	Native white......	5,503,297	39,723	0.7	5,807,934	118,342	2.0
16	Foreign-born white......	2,124,920	217,771	10.2	860,903	82,842	9.6
	WEST NORTH CENTRAL.						
17	All classes........	3,203,714	86,958	2.7	5,893,597	176,180	3.0
18	Negro........	141,823	17,454	12.3	61,818	12,982	21.0
19	Native white......	2,442,128	16,358	0.7	4,839,016	82,665	1.7
20	Foreign-born white......	616,718	52,693	8.5	962,976	67,880	7.0
	SOUTH ATLANTIC.						
21	All classes........	2,493,359	211,760	8.5	6,519,467	1,232,534	18.9
22	Negro........	741,429	158,906	21.4	2,245,507	810,526	36.1
23	Native white......	1,565,216	31,008	2.0	4,172,419	402,801	9.7
24	Foreign-born white......	185,142	21,511	11.6	95,245	16,423	17.2
	EAST SOUTH CENTRAL.						
25	All classes........	1,279,677	122,477	9.6	4,898,901	949,623	19.4
26	Negro........	421,529	100,257	23.8	1,539,369	581,250	37.8
27	Native white......	801,015	16,967	2.1	3,329,586	364,263	10.9
28	Foreign-born white......	56,769	5,163	9.1	28,124	3,052	10.9
	WEST SOUTH CENTRAL.						
29	All classes........	1,562,545	112,889	7.2	4,831,498	732,715	15.2
30	Negro........	353,611	71,652	20.3	1,107,094	411,370	37.2
31	Native white......	1,073,754	17,403	1.6	3,477,104	247,141	7.1
32	Foreign-born white......	130,677	23,415	17.9	199,754	61,259	30.7
	MOUNTAIN.						
33	All classes........	772,572	23,962	3.1	1,281,677	116,775	9.1
34	Negro........	13,505	939	7.0	5,250	558	10.6
35	Native white......	583,316	4,947	0.8	959,272	40,060	4.2
36	Foreign-born white......	168,430	16,274	9.7	254,638	36,676	14.4
	PACIFIC.						
37	All classes........	2,037,756	40,881	2.0	1,459,129	62,941	4.3
38	Negro........	21,348	1,133	5.3	4,227	481	11.4
39	Native white......	1,441,172	3,984	0.3	1,063,857	7,202	0.7
40	Foreign-born white......	515,716	30,878	6.0	325,283	36,767	11.3

OR MORE AND OUTSIDE SUCH CITIES, 1910 AND 1900, BY CLASS OF POPULATION, BY DIVISIONS.

POPULATION 10 YEARS OF AGE AND OVER—continued.												
Cities of 25,000 or more population.						Smaller cities and country districts.						
1910			1900			1910			1900			
Total.	Illiterate.		Total.	Illiterate.		Total.	Illiterate.		Total.	Illiterate.		
	Number.	Per cent.		Number.	Per cent.		Number.	Per cent.		Number.	Per cent.	
23,309,875	1,160,808	5.0	15,702,741	895,565	5.7	48,270,395	4,355,355	9.0	42,247,083	5,284,504	12.5	1
1,378,149	201,010	14.6	945,909	230,711	24.4	5,939,773	2,026,721	34.1	5,469,672	2,622,483	47.9	2
14,626,672	81,620	0.6	9,725,450	72,490	0.7	36,362,669	1,452,652	4.0	31,511,212	1,841,121	5.8	3
7,238,010	872,095	12.0	4,980,378	579,870	11.6	5,706,519	778,266	13.6	5,033,878	707,265	14.1	4
2,635,643	153,264	5.8	1,891,680	118,769	6.3	2,695,271	127,542	4.7	2,632,922	153,633	5.8	5
38,728	2,548	6.6	29,860	3,122	10.5	16,593	1,793	10.8	19,159	2,559	13.4	6
1,510,819	7,264	0.5	1,092,233	6,365	0.6	2,002,169	25,893	1.3	1,984,880	33,934	1.7	7
1,082,882	143,023	13.2	766,523	108,496	14.2	674,362	99,490	14.8	626,446	116,492	18.6	8
8,628,976	503,070	5.8	6,125,953	346,723	5.7	6,817,539	370,742	5.4	6,041,606	357,411	5.9	9
237,292	15,268	6.4	165,538	18,795	11.4	114,254	12,543	11.0	105,619	19,799	18.7	10
5,066,485	24,169	0.5	3,722,378	24,147	0.6	5,350,782	84,082	1.6	4,930,045	127,606	2.6	11
3,316,485	462,621	13.9	2,228,606	301,309	13.5	1,345,505	272,623	20.3	999,081	208,127	20.8	12
5,156,478	195,394	3.8	3,415,363	131,880	3.9	9,412,471	296,456	3.1	9,027,939	402,419	4.5	13
141,688	12,204	8.6	95,281	13,882	14.6	112,857	15,867	14.1	117,440	25,398	21.6	14
3,375,885	16,579	0.5	2,143,268	12,877	0.6	7,935,346	141,486	1.8	7,489,916	212,381	2.8	15
1,635,557	166,106	10.2	1,175,075	104,716	8.9	1,350,266	134,507	10.0	1,408,519	158,961	11.3	16
1,981,159	54,146	2.7	1,405,447	45,658	3.2	7,116,152	208,992	2.9	6,433,117	278,365	4.3	17
94,439	9,790	10.4	71,376	13,460	18.9	109,202	20,646	18.9	120,471	35,174	29.2	18
1,450,621	6,505	0.4	987,826	6,537	0.7	5,830,523	92,518	1.6	5,115,463	131,877	2.6	19
434,613	37,541	8.6	345,485	25,503	7.4	1,145,081	83,032	7.3	1,166,042	94,796	8.1	20
1,544,935	110,063	7.1	1,053,990	109,447	10.4	7,467,891	1,334,231	17.9	6,562,169	1,711,899	26.1	21
433,027	81,507	18.8	294,569	86,070	29.2	2,553,909	887,925	34.8	2,361,264	1,164,209	49.3	22
959,392	10,704	1.1	641,934	9,355	1.5	4,778,243	423,105	8.9	4,106,688	532,175	13.0	23
151,283	17,599	11.6	116,196	13,636	11.7	129,104	20,335	15.8	89,013	12,801	14.4	24
732,968	58,034	7.9	530,630	70,124	13.2	5,445,610	1,014,066	18.6	4,943,597	1,294,811	26.2	25
223,866	47,261	21.1	167,741	59,149	35.3	1,737,032	634,246	36.5	1,635,087	828,689	50.7	26
463,973	6,679	1.4	317,066	6,378	2.0	3,666,628	374,551	10.2	3,263,320	459,950	14.1	27
44,964	4,054	9.0	45,707	4,567	10.0	39,929	4,161	10.4	43,067	4,686	10.9	28
795,015	52,546	6.6	419,943	48,904	11.6	5,599,028	793,058	14.2	4,230,045	904,740	21.4	29
183,896	31,099	16.9	110,614	35,138	31.8	1,276,809	451,923	35.4	1,095,700	544,351	49.7	30
522,115	6,901	1.3	253,012	5,248	2.1	4,028,743	257,643	6.4	2,890,368	283,391	9.8	31
87,639	14,313	16.3	55,631	8,298	14.9	242,792	70,361	29.0	198,537	60,788	30.6	32
367,173	8,079	2.2	197,508	4,429	2.2	1,687,076	132,658	7.9	1,078,568	118,472	11.0	33
8,131	539	6.6	4,858	571	11.8	10,624	958	9.0	8,725	1,269	14.5	34
272,092	828	0.3	140,390	435	0.3	1,270,496	44,179	3.5	777,169	49,081	6.3	35
84,609	6,302	7.4	51,364	3,179	6.2	338,459	46,648	13.8	231,803	26,760	11.5	36
1,467,528	26,212	1.8	662,227	19,631	3.0	2,029,357	77,610	3.8	1,297,120	62,754	4.8	37
17,082	794	4.6	6,072	524	8.6	8,493	820	9.7	6,207	1,035	16.7	38
1,005,290	1,991	0.2	427,343	1,148	0.3	1,499,739	9,195	0.6	953,363	10,726	1.1	39
399,978	20,536	5.1	195,791	10,166	5.2	441,021	47,109	10.7	271,370	23,854	8.8	40

TABLE **30.**—ILLITERATES IN THE NEGRO POPULATION, BY SEX AND

		NEGRO POPULATION: 1910.													
		Total, **10** years of age and over.[1]								10 to 14 years.			15 to 24 years.		
		Both sexes.			Male.			Female.								
	CITIES.	Total.	Illiterate.		Total.	Illiterate.		Total.	Illiterate.		Total.	Illiterate.		Total.	Illiterate.	
			Number.	Per cent.		Number.	Per cent.		Number.	Per cent.		Number.	Per cent.		Number.	Per cent.
1	All cities	874,810	110,254	12.6	414,839	44,501	10.7	459,971	65,753	14.3	71,672	2,019	2.8	210,695	12,023	5.7
2	Albany, N. Y	924	39	4.2	445	19	4.3	479	20	4.2	64	......	......	213	6	2.8
3	Atlanta, Ga	42,996	9,005	20.9	18,830	3,502	18.6	24,166	5,503	22.8	4,607	287	6.2	12,451	1,228	9.9
4	Baltimore, Md	71,705	9,438	13.2	32,741	3,766	11.5	38,964	5,672	14.6	6,151	123	2.0	17,820	1,026	5.8
5	Birmingham, Ala	43,194	9,528	22.1	21,188	4,357	20.6	22,006	5,171	23.5	4,396	295	6.7	11,867	1,518	12.8
6	Boston, Mass	11,880	420	3.5	5,853	135	2.3	6,027	285	4.7	826	1	0.1	2,203	16	0.7
7	Bridgeport, Conn	1,108	58	5.2	543	23	4.2	565	35	6.2	75	......	......	241	3	1.2
8	Buffalo, N. Y	1,596	65	4.1	845	40	4.7	751	25	3.3	109	......	......	310	2	0.6
9	Cambridge, Mass	3,822	213	5.6	1,788	74	4.1	2,034	139	6.8	423	1	0.2	831	5	0.6
10	Chicago, Ill	39,484	1,595	4.0	20,434	568	2.8	19,050	1,027	5.4	2,150	4	0.2	7,489	69	0.9
11	Cincinnati, Ohio	17,462	2,503	14.3	8,837	1,220	13.8	8,625	1,283	14.9	1,214	7	0.6	3,925	194	4.9
12	Cleveland, Ohio	7,476	306	4.1	3,877	127	3.3	3,599	179	5.0	485	3	0.6	1,612	15	0.9
13	Columbus, Ohio	11,119	962	8.7	6,011	472	7.9	5,108	490	9.6	794	4	0.5	2,644	91	3.4
14	Dayton, Ohio	4,143	392	9.5	2,114	198	9.4	2,029	194	9.6	291	1	0.3	919	14	1.5
15	Denver, Colo	4,814	291	6.0	2,367	103	4.4	2,447	198	7.7	333	1	0.3	933	8	0.9
16	Detroit, Mich	5,068	176	3.5	2,643	76	2.9	2,425	100	4.1	342	1	0.3	1,081	11	1.0
17	Fall River, Mass	308	25	8.1	149	7	4.7	159	18	11.3	19	......	......	62	1	......
18	Grand Rapids, Mich	584	28	4.8	307	9	2.9	277	19	6.9	29	2	......	109	......	......
19	Indianapolis, Ind	18,736	2,316	12.4	9,255	1,008	10.9	9,481	1,308	13.8	1,523	3	0.2	4,259	74	1.7
20	Jersey City, N. J	4,948	240	4.9	2,534	81	3.2	2,414	159	6.6	407	4	1.0	1,044	19	1.8
21	Kansas City, Mo	21,166	2,038	9.6	10,697	807	7.5	10,469	1,231	11.8	1,277	6	0.5	4,700	88	1.0
22	Los Angeles, Cal	6,528	389	6.0	3,174	121	3.8	3,354	268	8.0	537	3	0.6	1,433	15	1.0
23	Louisville, Ky	35,544	6,662	18.7	17,146	2,923	17.0	18,398	3,739	20.3	2,919	31	1.1	8,432	523	6.2
24	Lowell, Mass	113	3	2.7	55	1	(2)	58	2	(2)	4	......	......	25	......	......
25	Memphis, Tenn	44,976	7,932	17.6	21,638	3,213	14.8	23,338	4,719	20.2	3,454	207	6.0	12,249	1,140	9.3
26	Milwaukee, Wis	890	26	2.9	443	10	2.3	447	16	3.6	37	1	......	184	......	......
27	Minneapolis, Minn	2,364	69	2.9	1,380	39	2.8	984	30	3.0	136	......	......	410	1	0.2
28	Nashville, Tenn	30,918	6,810	22.0	13,456	2,758	20.5	17,462	4,052	23.2	3,228	153	4.7	8,537	707	8.3
29	New Haven, Conn	3,044	137	4.5	1,449	48	3.3	1,595	89	5.6	236	......	......	626	6	1.0
30	New Orleans, La	73,814	13,541	18.3	33,404	5,030	15.1	40,410	8,511	21.1	7,730	503	6.5	18,949	2,010	10.6
31	New York, N. Y	79,919	2,893	3.6	36,515	929	2.5	43,404	1,964	4.5	4,858	15	0.3	18,644	230	1.2
32	Manhattan Borough	53,571	1,711	3.2	24,732	532	2.2	28,839	1,179	4.1	2,728	8	0.3	12,607	140	1.1
33	Bronx Borough	3,415	181	5.3	1,572	66	4.2	1,843	115	6.2	279	2	0.7	736	5	0.7
34	Brooklyn Borough	19,335	806	4.2	8,598	251	2.9	10,737	555	5.2	1,516	5	0.3	4,396	66	1.5
35	Queens Borough	2,655	135	5.1	1,179	55	4.7	1,476	80	5.4	240	......	......	665	17	2.6
36	Richmond Borough	943	60	6.4	434	25	5.8	509	35	6.9	95	......	......	240	2	0.8
37	Newark, N. J	7,888	589	7.5	3,686	225	6.1	4,202	364	8.7	626	2	0.3	1,754	48	2.7
38	Oakland, Cal	2,656	87	3.3	1,410	34	2.4	1,246	53	4.3	131	......	......	521	3	0.6
39	Omaha, Nebr	3,944	249	6.3	2,136	111	5.2	1,808	138	7.6	202	2	1.0	796	12	1.5
40	Paterson, N. J	1,287	146	11.3	588	53	9.0	699	93	13.3	123	1	0.8	296	19	6.4
41	Philadelphia, Pa	71,973	5,595	7.8	33,324	2,190	6.6	38,649	3,405	8.8	5,207	34	0.7	15,667	416	2.7
42	Pittsburgh, Pa	21,441	1,409	6.6	11,245	682	6.1	10,196	727	7.1	1,843	2	0.1	4,398	71	1.6
43	Portland, Oreg	958	18	1.9	565	7	1.2	393	11	2.8	32	......	......	135	......	......
44	Providence, R. I	4,486	434	9.7	2,153	199	9.2	2,333	235	10.1	383	2	0.5	908	48	5.3
45	Richmond, Va	38,876	7,615	19.6	17,672	3,180	18.0	21,204	4,435	20.9	3,888	233	6.0	11,221	1,174	10.5
46	Rochester, N. Y	769	11	1.4	371	6	1.6	398	5	1.3	57	......	......	179	......	......
47	St. Louis, Mo	38,687	4,799	12.4	19,611	1,961	10.0	19,076	2,838	14.9	2,680	18	0.7	8,554	315	3.7
48	St. Paul, Minn	2,840	66	2.3	1,755	26	1.5	1,085	40	3.7	149	......	......	509	1	0.2
49	San Francisco, Cal	1,480	76	5.1	939	44	4.7	541	32	5.9	65	......	......	302	12	4.0
50	Scranton, Pa	482	16	3.3	265	6	2.3	217	10	4.6	40	......	......	113	1	0.9
51	Seattle, Wash	2,125	57	2.7	1,303	26	2.0	822	31	3.8	93	1	......	354	1	0.3
52	Spokane, Wash	659	16	2.4	359	4	1.1	300	12	4.0	37	......	......	118	1	0.8
53	Syracuse, N. Y	972	50	5.1	502	29	5.8	470	21	4.5	60	1	......	179	4	2.2
54	Toledo, Ohio	1,649	71	4.3	828	30	3.6	821	41	5.0	103	......	......	342	4	1.2
55	Washington, D. C	79,964	10,814	13.5	35,540	4,015	11.3	44,424	6,799	15.3	7,211	67	0.9	19,953	872	4.4
56	Worcester, Mass	1,031	36	3.5	469	9	1.9	562	27	4.8	88	......	......	194	1	0.5

[1] Includes persons of unknown age.

AGE PERIODS, BY CITIES OF 100,000 POPULATION AND OVER: 1910.

NEGRO POPULATION: 1910.

25 to 34 years.			35 to 44 years.			45 to 54 years.			55 to 64 years.			65 years and over.			Males 21 years of age and over.			
Total.	Illiterate.		Total.	Illiterate.		Total.	Illiterate.		Total.	Illiterate.		Total.	Illiterate.		Total.	Illiterate.		
	Number.	Per cent.		Number.	Per cent.		Number.	Per cent.		Number.	Per cent.		Number.	Per cent.		Number.	Per cent.	
247,990	18,812	7.6	174,799	22,416	12.8	96,690	23,474	24.3	42,549	16,566	38.9	26,458	14,226	53.8	335,093	40,622	12.1	1
243	3	1.2	175	9	5.1	123	8	6.5	58	5	......	42	6	......	379	19	5.0	2
11,289	1,592	14.1	6,915	1,704	24.6	4,257	1,848	43.4	2,107	1,328	63.0	1,281	984	76.8	13,865	3,012	21.7	3
18,281	1,595	8.7	13,949	2,058	14.8	8,933	2,105	23.6	3,905	1,349	34.5	2,452	1,139	46.5	26,214	3,509	13.4	4
12,381	2,087	16.9	7,688	2,055	26.7	4,177	1,885	45.1	1,524	977	64.1	868	632	72.8	16,441	3,780	23.0	5
3,516	61	1.7	2,891	70	2.4	1,462	105	7.2	642	87	13.6	324	79	24.4	5,070	132	2.6	6
323	9	2.8	259	16	6.2	114	12	10.5	65	10	......	30	8	......	471	23	4.9	7
496	22	4.4	353	8	2.3	194	14	7.2	93	10	......	41	9	......	740	40	5.4	8
920	27	2.9	792	47	5.9	451	29	6.4	260	54	20.8	141	50	35.5	1,384	73	5.3	9
12,687	166	1.3	9,535	288	3.0	4,627	394	8.5	1,754	347	19.8	897	308	34.3	17,845	546	3.1	10
4,894	440	9.0	3,782	636	16.8	2,083	575	27.6	906	354	39.1	479	271	56.6	7,387	1,183	16.0	11
2,250	34	1.5	1,720	59	3.4	880	74	8.4	305	49	16.1	204	71	34.8	3,298	125	3.8	12
3,216	148	4.6	2,233	194	8.7	1,304	185	14.2	557	179	32.1	334	149	44.6	5,028	459	9.1	13
1,149	61	5.3	871	70	8.0	513	89	17.3	233	72	30.9	156	82	52.6	1,781	194	10.9	14
1,332	25	1.9	1,134	49	4.3	659	65	9.9	261	72	27.6	142	69	48.6	1,999	100	5.0	15
1,487	16	1.1	1,063	26	2.4	623	48	7.7	276	33	12.0	174	40	23.0	2,224	72	3.2	16
98	3	......	67	7	......	41	3	......	17	9	......	4	2	......	133	6	4.5	17
155		1.9	103	6	5.8	89	4	......	53	3	......	38	10	......	264	9	3.4	18
4,996	224	4.5	3,739	441	11.8	2,290	597	26.1	1,204	541	44.9	656	426	64.9	7,556	991	13.1	19
1,454	53	3.6	1,171	50	4.3	574	58	10.1	205	31	15.1	82	23	......	2,104	76	3.6	20
6,611	246	3.7	4,539	403	8.9	2,291	558	24.4	923	405	43.9	490	300	61.2	9,101	787	8.6	21
1,734	25	1.4	1,369	73	5.3	892	110	12.3	352	81	23.0	184	80	43.5	2,571	115	4.5	22
9,428	997	10.6	6,913	1,427	20.6	4,328	1,638	37.8	2,051	1,103	53.8	1,286	900	70.0	13,687	2,782	20.3	23
28		......	21		......	14		......	12	2	......	7	1	......	44	1	(2)	24
13,411	1,622	12.1	7,997	1,444	18.1	4,325	1,535	35.5	1,944	1,004	51.6	1,442	948	65.7	17,238	2,825	16.4	25
285	4	1.4	211	5	2.4	106	6	5.7	43	3	......	20	7	......	396	9	2.3	26
770	9	1.2	583	19	3.3	275	19	6.9	80	5	......	56	13	......	1,227	39	3.2	27
7,044	973	13.8	5,189	1,242	23.9	3,726	1,556	41.8	1,830	1,125	61.5	1,346	1,048	77.9	9,713	2,456	25.3	28
811	16	2.0	687	33	4.8	343	30	8.7	199	28	14.1	136	24	17.6	1,191	48	4.0	29
18,530	2,644	14.3	13,866	2,769	20.0	7,684	2,119	28.4	3,761	1,621	43.1	3,036	1,754	57.8	25,269	4,330	17.1	30
27,293	553	2.0	16,721	623	3.7	7,503	599	8.0	2,938	426	14.5	1,690	430	25.4	30,855	891	2.9	31
19,499	332	1.7	11,322	395	3.5	4,754	384	8.1	1,627	237	14.6	811	205	25.3	21,279	508	2.4	32
974	25	2.6	710	32	4.5	348	29	8.3	172	29	16.9	186	59	31.7	1,269	63	5.0	33
5,881	167	2.8	4,023	165	4.1	2,011	153	7.6	940	124	13.2	534	122	22.8	7,011	241	3.4	34
697	23	3.3	507	23	4.5	291	21	7.2	136	23	16.9	115	26	22.6	959	54	5.6	35
242	6	2.5	159	8	5.0	99	12	......	63	13	......	44	18	......	337	25	7.4	36
2,282	118	5.2	1,699	119	7.0	906	127	14.0	379	88	23.2	216	80	37.0	3,015	216	7.2	37
775	6	0.8	597	12	2.0	372	23	6.2	157	18	11.5	101	25	24.8	1,238	34	2.7	38
1,313	43	3.3	899	54	6.0	478	63	13.2	162	36	22.2	88	39	......	1,885	110	5.8	39
339	20	5.9	295	40	13.6	124	18	14.5	63	24	......	45	24	......	453	50	11.0	40
22,467	1,023	4.6	15,730	1,344	8.5	7,826	1,266	16.2	3,028	783	25.9	1,752	685	39.1	28,120	2,108	7.5	41
6,697	238	3.6	4,905	363	7.4	2,227	340	15.3	849	229	27.0	409	158	38.6	9,362	663	7.1	42
312	1	0.3	297	3	1.0	118	3	2.5	45	5	......	16	6	......	525	7	1.3	43
1,179	112	9.5	905	82	9.1	582	68	11.7	338	64	18.9	179	55	30.7	1,765	187	10.6	44
9,703	1,275	13.1	6,717	1,523	22.7	4,241	1,594	37.6	1,912	1,085	56.7	1,038	684	65.9	13,279	2,765	20.8	45
239	2	0.8	131	2	1.5	107	4	3.7	44	3	......	12		......	305	6	2.0	46
11,443	625	5.5	8,272	968	11.7	4,395	1,157	26.3	1,981	902	45.5	1,252	771	61.6	16,381	1,875	11.4	47
997	10	1.0	684	14	2.0	317	9	2.8	113	14	12.4	70	18	......	1,573	26	1.7	48
488	22	4.5	309	17	5.5	174	9	5.2	70	7	......	64	9	......	831	43	5.2	49
137	3	2.2	108	4	3.7	57	7	......	20		......	7	1	......	216	5	2.3	50
814	12	1.5	492	15	3.0	209	14	6.7	62	9	......	31	5	......	1,204	24	2.0	51
193	1	0.5	195	3	1.5	74	4	......	27	6	......	11	1	......	305	4	1.3	52
264	6	2.3	214	7	3.3	147	13	8.8	62	11	......	38	7	......	437	27	6.2	53
466	2	0.4	348	14	4.0	219	17	7.8	100	17	17.0	68	16	......	719	30	4.2	54
20,535	1,631	7.9	15,255	1,998	13.1	9,088	2,405	26.5	4,492	1,943	43.3	2,957	1,765	59.7	27,621	3,801	13.8	55
235	4	1.7	211	3	1.4	148	5	3.4	87	9	......	66	11	......	384	9	2.3	56

2 Per cent not shown where base is less than 100.

TABLE 31.—ILLITERATES BY CLASS OF POPULATION, BY CITIES OF 100,000 POPULATION AND OVER, 1910, WITH PERCENTAGE ILLITERATE: 1910, 1900, AND 1890.

POPULATION 10 YEARS OF AGE AND OVER.

CITY.	All classes.[1]					Negro.					Native white.					Foreign-born white.				
	Total, 1910	Number, 1910	Per cent 1910	1900	1890	Total, 1910	Number, 1910	Per cent 1910	1900	1890	Total, 1910	Number, 1910	Per cent 1910	1900	1890	Total, 1910	Number, 1910	Per cent 1910	1900	1890
Albany, N. Y.	85,244	2,762	3.2	2.8	4.1	924	39	4.2	6.5	16.8	66,553	274	0.4	0.6	1.0	17,726	2,440	13.8	10.0	11.3
Atlanta, Ga.	125,529	10,813	8.6	15.8	23.3	42,996	9,005	20.9	35.1	48.9	78,219	1,545	2.0	2.6	4.4	4,244	250	5.9	8.6	4.5
Baltimore, Md.	456,882	20,325	4.4	7.2	9.8	71,705	9,438	13.2	25.7	37.3	310,427	1,855	0.6	1.3	2.2	74,405	8,952	12.0	12.9	12.4
Birmingham, Ala.	105,630	11,026	10.4	19.1	23.7	43,194	9,528	22.1	40.3	51.5	56,948	666	1.2	1.3	1.8	5,477	829	15.1	13.9	6.6
Boston, Mass.	550,081	24,468	4.4	5.1	5.7	11,880	420	3.5	7.9	13.6	302,689	518	0.2	0.2	0.4	234,240	23,371	10.0	11.3	12.8
Bridgeport, Conn.	82,548	4,440	5.4	5.3	3.1	1,108	58	5.2	12.6	13.6	46,292	141	0.3	0.4	0.4	35,083	4,235	12.1	12.6	7.5
Buffalo, N. Y.	343,146	12,745	3.7	4.8	5.4	1,596	65	4.1	5.4	13.6	226,267	825	0.4	0.5	0.7	115,159	11,838	10.3	12.0	11.4
Cambridge, Mass.	84,566	2,540	3.0	1.6	6.3	3,822	213	5.6	11.0	15.7	46,888	74	0.2	0.3	0.4	33,744	2,241	6.6	9.9	14.2
Chicago, Ill.	1,770,222	79,911	4.5	3.9	4.6	39,484	1,595	4.0	7.5	12.5	971,130	2,260	0.2	0.2	0.4	757,569	75,802	10.0	8.2	8.3
Cincinnati, Ohio.	308,011	9,576	3.1	3.4	4.3	17,462	2,503	14.3	19.8	29.4	235,097	1,773	0.8	0.7	1.0	55,421	5,296	9.6	8.9	8.1
Cleveland, Ohio.	447,731	20,676	4.6	4.7	6.5	7,476	306	4.1	9.4	10.7	251,358	593	0.2	0.3	1.0	188,619	19,721	10.5	10.7	12.7
Columbus, Ohio.	153,667	4,442	2.9	3.2	3.9	11,119	962	8.7	15.9	22.5	126,636	1,476	1.2	1.3	1.7	15,856	1,994	12.6	9.1	7.1
Dayton, Ohio.	96,665	2,224	2.3	2.6	2.9	4,143	392	9.5	12.4	20.6	79,077	400	0.5	0.9	1.2	13,418	1,423	10.6	9.3	6.3
Denver, Colo.	180,326	3,841	2.1	1.8	2.8	4,814	291	6.0	10.0	26.8	136,619	342	0.3	0.2	0.4	38,048	3,076	8.1	5.7	5.5
Detroit, Mich.	376,563	18,731	5.0	4.1	6.7	5,068	176	3.5	8.0	15.7	220,512	911	0.4	0.5	1.1	150,890	17,633	11.7	8.6	12.1
Fall River, Mass.	92,806	12,276	13.2	14.9	15.2	308	25	8.1	11.1	15.0	43,339	733	1.7	2.0	2.1	49,076	11,510	23.5	24.1	23.8
Grand Rapids, Mich.	91,390	2,271	2.5	3.1	4.0	584	28	4.8	8.5	13.9	63,331	145	0.2	0.5	0.6	27,451	2,088	7.6	8.0	9.0
Indianapolis, Ind.	196,875	5,874	3.0	4.3	6.1	18,736	2,316	12.4	20.3	31.4	158,657	1,357	0.9	1.3	1.9	19,431	2,191	11.3	11.1	11.8
Jersey City, N. J.	211,457	11,797	5.6	4.5	5.9	4,948	240	4.9	7.9	18.2	130,677	567	0.4	0.3	0.8	75,677	10,952	14.5	11.4	12.9
Kansas City, Mo.	212,624	4,937	2.3	3.9	5.8	21,166	2,038	9.6	19.5	30.5	166,733	687	0.4	0.7	1.1	24,605	2,192	8.9	8.8	9.2
Los Angeles, Cal.	275,863	5,258	1.9	2.3	5.1	6,528	389	6.0	15.9	26.0	204,820	506	0.2	0.6	1.5	58,666	4,101	7.0	5.3	8.9
Louisville, Ky.	186,810	9,886	5.3	8.8	10.7	35,544	6,662	18.7	31.1	41.8	134,042	1,593	1.2	1.7	2.2	17,208	1,627	9.5	10.8	9.5
Lowell, Mass.	86,486	5,172	6.0	8.8	9.3	113	3	2.7	7.6	31.1	44,146	240	0.5	1.1	0.8	42,170	4,928	11.7	16.3	17.2
Memphis, Tenn.	110,305	8,855	8.0	18.3	21.2	44,976	7,932	17.6	35.1	44.2	58,954	282	0.5	0.8	1.7	6,306	622	9.9	11.3	7.7
Milwaukee, Wis.	302,302	10,765	3.6	3.8	5.3	890	26	2.9	6.1	11.8	193,146	454	0.2	0.4	0.6	108,203	10,274	9.5	8.8	9.9
Minneapolis, Minn.	253,526	6,139	2.4	1.8	2.4	2,364	69	2.9	6.2	9.0	166,902	298	0.2	0.2	0.4	84,124	5,760	6.8	4.4	4.6
Nashville, Tenn.	90,461	7,947	8.8	14.4	20.8	30,918	6,810	22.0	32.4	45.4	56,615	931	1.6	2.9	4.6	2,918	205	7.0	9.9	11.0
New Haven, Conn.	107,465	7,502	7.0	5.6	4.4	3,044	137	4.5	10.3	13.3	62,963	173	0.3	0.3	0.3	41,360	7,179	17.4	14.9	11.6
New Orleans, La.	274,998	18,987	6.9	13.6	15.7	73,814	13,541	18.3	36.1	43.1	173,733	1,838	1.1	2.0	2.5	27,058	3,504	12.9	18.3	15.6
New York, N. Y.	3,821,540	254,208	6.7	6.8	[2] 6.2	79,919	2,893	3.6	8.3	15.0	1,880,581	5,713	0.3	0.4	0.5	1,855,307	245,095	13.2	13.9	12.0
Manhattan Borough	1,900,911	151,218	8.0	} 8.2	......	53,571	1,711	3.2	} 6.6	......	782,411	2,352	0.3	} 0.4	......	1,060,681	146,871	13.8	} 15.5	......
Bronx Borough	341,814	13,783	4.0		......	3,415	181	5.3		......	193,374	415	0.2		......	144,819	13,158	9.1		......
Brooklyn Borough	1,288,347	78,143	6.1	4.6	......	19,335	806	4.2	11.1	......	719,112	2,378	0.3	0.4	......	548,823	74,799	13.6	10.9	......
Queens Borough	222,177	8,374	3.8	4.5	......	2,655	135	5.1	13.2	......	142,020	399	0.3	0.4	......	77,359	7,819	10.1	10.3	......
Richmond Borough	68,291	2,690	3.9	3.5	......	943	60	6.4	13.3	......	43,664	169	0.4	0.5	......	23,625	2,448	10.4	8.4	......
Newark, N. J.	275,974	16,553	6.0	6.1	4.8	7,888	589	7.5	12.8	20.2	161,527	775	0.5	0.6	0.9	106,316	15,131	14.2	14.7	10.1
Oakland, Cal.	126,914	3,863	3.0	2.9	6.0	2,656	87	3.3	5.6	51.2	83,508	335	0.4	0.2	0.4	36,042	3,000	8.3	7.9	11.0
Omaha, Nebr.	104,102	2,798	2.7	2.0	2.9	3,944	249	6.3	10.6	17.7	73,736	184	0.2	0.2	0.5	26,338	2,352	8.9	5.1	6.2
Paterson, N. J.	100,817	6,927	6.9	6.3	7.0	1,287	146	11.3	21.7	33.8	55,635	427	0.8	1.3	2.2	43,805	6,333	14.5	11.6	11.4
Philadelphia, Pa.	1,261,132	57,700	4.6	4.4	5.0	71,973	5,595	7.8	11.1	18.0	818,887	4,476	0.5	0.6	1.2	369,128	47,467	12.9	12.1	11.3
Pittsburgh, Pa.[3]	427,314	26,627	6.2	5.8	6.0	21,441	1,409	6.6	14.4	21.7	268,822	1,209	0.4	0.7	1.1	136,784	23,984	17.5	14.6	12.8
Portland, Oreg.	180,653	2,145	1.2	5.1	2.6	958	18	1.9	4.6	6.1	130,155	180	0.1	0.2	0.3	42,535	1,674	3.9	4.2	5.3
Providence, R. I.	183,805	14,236	7.7	7.0	7.7	4,486	434	9.7	15.9	18.9	104,910	707	0.7	0.9	1.3	74,061	13,039	17.6	16.0	18.0
Richmond, Va.	105,141	8,641	8.2	13.7	20.2	38,876	7,615	19.6	32.2	45.7	62,290	739	1.2	1.7	2.4	3,959	283	7.1	8.9	9.5
Rochester, N. Y.	182,280	6,916	3.8	2.7	3.6	769	11	1.4	5.7	13.4	124,573	344	0.3	0.3	0.5	56,873	6,557	11.5	7.9	8.9
St. Louis, Mo.	572,262	21,123	3.7	4.4	5.9	38,687	4,799	12.4	21.3	34.7	410,931	2,308	0.6	0.9	1.3	122,095	13,899	11.4	9.8	9.1
St. Paul, Minn.	178,833	3,751	2.1	3.1	4.5	2,840	66	2.3	7.3	12.8	120,644	211	0.2	0.3	0.8	55,270	3,459	6.3	7.7	8.1
San Francisco, Cal.	362,826	7,697	2.1	3.1	5.3	1,480	76	5.1	6.4	24.0	218,383	437	0.2	0.2	0.3	128,672	5,987	4.7	5.6	6.6
Scranton, Pa.	100,861	8,933	8.9	8.8	13.0	482	16	3.3	9.5	15.3	66,301	626	0.9	1.7	3.5	34,070	8,289	24.3	20.9	25.7
Seattle, Wash.	205,028	2,217	1.1	1.3	3.0	2,125	57	2.7	5.5	44.5	136,830	113	0.1	0.2	0.4	59,345	1,820	3.1	2.2	5.1
Spokane, Wash.[4]	87,529	1,123	1.3	1.8	......	659	16	2.4	5.7	......	65,650	64	0.1	0.1	......	20,625	898	4.4	5.4	......
Syracuse, N. Y.	114,693	5,629	4.9	3.2	3.9	972	50	5.1	8.8	11.5	83,802	394	0.5	0.7	0.9	29,897	5,179	17.3	9.7	10.6
Toledo, Ohio.	137,762	3,809	2.8	3.7	4.5	1,649	71	4.3	10.5	15.5	104,860	743	0.7	1.1	1.4	31,203	2,990	9.6	10.6	10.1
Washington, D. C.	279,088	13,812	4.9	8.6	13.2	79,964	10,814	13.5	24.3	35.0	174,903	960	0.5	0.8	1.7	23,755	1,914	8.2	7.0	9.3
Worcester, Mass.	118,555	5,977	5.0	4.9	6.4	1,031	36	3.5	8.2	15.7	70,265	291	0.4	0.8	0.9	47,181	5,641	12.0	11.0	15.0

[1] Includes Indians, Chinese, Japanese, and all other.

[2] Combined population of New York and Brooklyn cities as constituted in 1890; statistics of illiteracy of the population of the present area of New York City (2,507,414 in 1890) not available.

[3] Includes the population of Allegheny for 1900 and 1890.

[4] Figures for 1890 not available.

TABLE 32.—ILLITERATES IN THE NEGRO POPULATION, BY SEX, BY CITIES HAVING IN 1910, 100,000 INHABITANTS OR MORE: 1910, 1900, AND 1890.

[Per cent not shown where base is less than 100.]

CITY.	NUMBER OF NEGRO ILLITERATES.									PERCENTAGE ILLITERATE IN NEGRO POPULATION.								
	Both sexes.			Male.			Female.			Both sexes.			Male.			Female.		
	1910	1900	1890[1]	1910	1900	1890[1]	1910	1900	1890[1]	1910	1900	1890[1]	1910	1900	1890[1]	1910	1900	1890[1]
Albany, N. Y.	39	68	167	19	41	108	20	27	59	4.2	6.5	16.8	4.3	7.2	18.5	4.2	5.6	14.4
Atlanta, Ga.	9,005	10,099	10,766	3,502	3,638	4,100	5,503	6,461	6,666	20.9	35.1	48.9	18.6	32.0	43.6	22.8	37.2	52.8
Baltimore, Md.	9,438	16,846	20,364	3,766	6,321	7,374	5,672	10,325	12,990	13.2	25.7	37.3	11.5	22.2	31.9	14.6	28.3	41.3
Birmingham, Ala.	9,528	5,532	4,756	4,357	2,371	2,098	5,171	3,161	2,658	22.1	40.3	51.5	20.6	37.3	46.4	23.5	42.9	56.4
Boston, Mass.	420	786	1,007	135	266	503	285	520	504	3.5	7.9	13.6	2.3	5.2	12.3	4.7	10.9	15.0
Bridgeport, Conn.	58	123	100	23	50	42	35	73	58	5.2	12.6	13.6	4.2	11.5	12.3	6.2	13.6	14.6
Buffalo, N. Y.	65	81	134	40	32	71	25	49	63	4.1	5.4	13.6	4.7	4.1	13.6	3.3	7.0	13.7
Cambridge, Mass.	213	337	255	74	117	109	139	220	146	5.6	11.0	15.7	4.1	8.1	14.4	6.8	13.5	16.9
Chicago, Ill.	1,595	2,014	1,657	568	717	779	1,027	1,297	878	4.0	7.5	12.5	2.8	4.9	10.1	5.4	10.4	15.9
Cincinnati, Ohio	2,503	2,468	2,918	1,220	1,132	1,252	1,283	1,336	1,666	14.3	19.8	29.4	13.8	18.3	25.6	14.9	21.2	33.1
Cleveland, Ohio	306	487	280	127	239	125	179	248	155	4.1	9.4	10.7	3.3	8.6	8.8	5.0	10.4	13.1
Columbus, Ohio	962	1,109	1,047	472	562	585	490	547	462	8.7	15.9	22.5	7.9	15.1	22.6	9.6	16.8	22.2
Dayton, Ohio	392	354	356	198	165	182	194	189	174	9.5	12.4	20.6	9.4	11.4	21.0	9.6	13.4	20.3
Denver, Colo.	291	339	980	103	117	781	188	222	199	6.0	10.0	26.8	4.4	7.2	31.6	7.7	12.6	16.7
Detroit, Mich.	176	278	458	76	121	207	100	157	251	3.5	8.0	15.7	2.9	7.1	14.4	4.1	8.8	17.0
Fall River, Mass.	25	32	25	7	7	14	18	25	11	8.1	11.1	15.0	4.7	6.9		11.3	13.5	
Grand Rapids, Mich.	28	45	68	9	14	35	19	31	33	4.8	8.5	13.9	2.9	5.4	13.9	6.9	11.4	13.9
Indianapolis, Ind.	2,316	2,745	2,348	1,008	1,251	1,088	1,308	1,494	1,260	12.4	20.3	31.4	10.9	18.7	29.2	13.8	22.0	33.6
Jersey City, N. J.	240	244	340	81	92	163	159	152	177	4.9	7.9	18.2	3.2	6.0	16.7	6.6	9.8	19.8
Kansas City, Mo.	2,038	2,958	3,542	807	1,246	1,546	1,231	1,712	1,996	9.6	19.5	30.5	7.5	16.8	26.3	11.8	22.0	34.9
Los Angeles, Cal.	389	273	758	121	103	557	268	170	201	6.0	15.9	26.0	3.8	12.8	23.9	8.0	18.7	34.4
Louisville, Ky.	6,662	10,397	9,886	2,923	4,672	4,243	3,739	5,725	5,643	18.7	31.1	41.8	17.0	29.1	39.0	20.3	32.9	44.2
Lowell, Mass.	3	9	78	1	4	46	2	5	32	2.7	7.6	31.1			33.3			28.3
Memphis, Tenn.	7,932	14,106	10,407	3,213	6,390	4,117	4,719	7,716	6,290	17.6	35.1	44.2	14.8	32.7	38.1	20.2	37.4	49.3
Milwaukee, Wis.	26	47	47	10	22	21	16	25	26	2.9	6.1	11.8	2.3	5.2	8.5	3.6	7.2	17.1
Minneapolis, Minn.	69	83	106	39	35	46	30	48	60	2.9	6.2	9.0	2.8	4.8	6.3	3.0	8.0	13.2
Nashville, Tenn.	6,810	8,059	10,755	2,758	3,153	4,443	4,052	4,906	6,312	22.0	32.4	45.4	20.5	29.4	42.6	23.2	34.7	47.7
New Haven, Conn.	137	248	267	48	87	120	89	161	147	4.5	10.3	13.3	3.3	7.8	12.2	5.6	12.5	14.3
New Orleans, La.	13,541	22,586	21,882	5,030	8,651	8,260	8,511	13,935	13,622	18.3	36.1	43.1	15.1	31.4	37.6	21.1	39.8	47.4
New York, N. Y.[2]	2,893	4,362	4,735	929	1,424	2,156	1,964	2,938	2,579	3.6	8.3	15.0	2.5	6.2	14.1	4.5	10.1	15.9
Manhattan and Bronx Boroughs	1,892	2,224	....	598	624	....	1,294	1,600	....	3.3	6.6	......	2.3	4.2	......	4.2	8.6	.....
Brooklyn Borough	806	1,734	....	251	653	....	555	1,081	....	4.2	11.1	......	2.9	9.7	......	5.2	12.3	.....
Queens Borough	135	288	....	55	94	....	80	194	....	5.1	13.2	......	4.7	10.3	......	5.4	15.4	.....
Richmond Borough	60	116	....	25	53	....	35	63	....	6.4	13.3	......	5.8	13.5	......	6.9	13.2	.....
Newark, N. J.	589	708	711	225	259	303	364	449	408	7.5	12.8	20.2	6.1	10.4	18.5	8.7	14.7	21.7
Oakland, Cal.	87	50	885	34	15	835	53	35	50	3.3	5.6	51.2	2.4	3.3	57.5	4.3	7.8	18.1
Omaha, Nebr.	249	315	686	111	113	350	138	202	336	6.3	10.6	17.7	5.2	7.3	14.8	7.6	14.1	22.3
Paterson, N. J.	146	213	203	53	89	101	93	124	102	11.3	21.7	33.8	9.0	20.3	32.0	13.3	22.8	35.8
Philadelphia, Pa.	5,595	5,883	6,169	2,190	2,342	2,450	3,405	3,541	3,719	7.8	11.1	18.0	6.6	9.6	15.3	8.8	12.3	20.4
Pittsburgh, Pa.[3]	1,409	2,437	1,886	682	1,368	1,133	727	1,069	753	6.6	14.4	21.7	6.1	14.3	22.3	7.1	14.4	21.0
Portland, Oreg.	18	33	302	7	18	167	11	15	135	1.9	4.6	6.1	1.2	4.2	3.6	2.8	5.1	41.4
Providence, R. I.	434	634	629	199	273	254	235	361	375	9.7	15.9	18.9	9.2	14.6	16.1	10.1	16.9	21.5
Richmond, Va.	7,615	8,572	12,127	3,180	3,506	4,977	4,435	5,066	7,150	19.6	32.2	45.7	18.0	30.0	43.6	20.9	33.9	47.3
Rochester, N. Y.	11	29	66	6	18	26	5	11	40	1.4	5.7	13.4	1.6	7.0	11.7	1.3	4.3	14.9
St. Louis, Mo.	4,799	6,516	7,683	1,961	2,539	3,258	2,838	3,977	4,425	12.4	21.3	34.7	10.0	17.0	30.1	14.9	25.5	39.0
St. Paul, Minn.	66	145	175	26	52	90	40	93	85	2.3	7.3	12.8	1.5	4.3	11.0	3.7	11.9	15.5
San Francisco, Cal.	76	92	6,551	44	50	5,509	32	42	1,042	5.1	6.4	24.0	4.7	6.6	22.1	5.9	6.1	44.7
Scranton, Pa.	16	41	34	6	20	21	10	21	13	3.3	9.5	15.3	2.3	8.3	16.7	4.6	11.0	
Seattle, Wash.	57	20	336	26	5	287	31	15	49	2.7	5.5	44.5	2.0	2.5	46.7	3.8	9.0	35.0
Spokane, Wash.[4]	16	19	....	4	7	....	12	12	....	2.4	5.7		1.1	3.5		4.0	9.0	
Syracuse, N. Y.	50	77	83	29	35	43	21	42	40	5.1	8.8	11.5	5.8	8.4	11.8	4.5	9.2	11.3
Toledo, Ohio	71	155	139	30	76	69	41	79	70	4.3	10.5	15.5	3.6	10.5	15.0	5.0	10.5	16.1
Washington, D. C.	10,814	17,462	21,389	4,015	6,716	8,584	6,799	10,746	12,805	13.5	24.3	35.0	11.3	21.6	32.2	15.3	26.3	37.3
Worcester, Mass.	36	75	127	9	27	60	27	48	67	3.5	8.2	15.7	1.9	6.4	14.7	4.8	9.8	16.6

[1] Figures for 1890 are for the entire colored population, separate figures for Negroes not being available.
[2] Statistics of illiteracy of the population of the present area of New York City not available for 1890.
[3] Includes the population of Allegheny for 1900 and 1890.
[4] Figures for 1890 not available.

Chapter XVII.—THE DELINQUENT, DEFECTIVE, AND DEPENDENT CLASSES.

CLASSES FOR WHICH DATA ARE AVAILABLE.

In special reports issued by the Bureau of the Census data are available relating to prisoners and juvenile delinquents, the insane in institutions, the feeble-minded in institutions, the blind, deaf-mutes, and paupers in almshouses. The scope of the detailed statistical analysis and textual treatment of these reports is partially indicated in the following sections, as regards the Negro element in the population; more fully as regards Negro prisoners and juvenile delinquents than as regards Negro defectives and dependents, this fuller treatment being justified by the broader interest attaching to the subject of criminality and by the less

technical character of the census data of criminality, as well as by the fact that the class of prisoners and juvenile delinquents is numerically much larger than any other of the special classes designated. For a complete statistical account of any of the several delinquent, defective, and dependent classes reference must be made to the full reports from which the following data are selected and in which the significance of the data for Negroes is made more clearly apparent by extended analyses and by constant relation of data for Negroes to data for other racial classes, in detail by state areas.

Section I.—PRISONERS AND JUVENILE DELINQUENTS. [1]

The 1910 census of prisoners and juvenile delinquents secured data relating to persons serving sentences in penal or reformatory institutions on January 1, 1910, and also data relating to persons committed under sentence to such institutions during the calendar year 1910. The 3,271 institutions canvassed included 3 Federal penitentiaries, 58 state prisons or penitentiaries, 20 reformatories for adults or adults and juveniles, 100 reformatories for juveniles exclusively, 2,502 county jails or workhouses or similar institutions, and 588 municipal jails or workhouses. In accordance with the usage established at prior censuses the term "juvenile delinquents" distinguishes inmates of reformatories exclusively for juveniles, the term "prison-

ers" including without regard to age the inmates of all other penal or reformatory institutions. The data collected by the census comprised sex, age, race, nativity, marital condition (of prisoners), illiteracy, occupation before commitment, offense of which convicted, and sentence.

RATIO OF COMMITMENTS.

As shown in Table 1, 30.6 per cent of the total number of prisoners and juvenile delinquents enumerated on January 1, 1910, and 21.9 per cent of the total number committed during the year 1910 were Negroes, whereas the percentage Negro in the total population was only 10.7. Per 100,000 Negro population the number of Negro prisoners and juvenile delinquents enumerated on January 1 was 424.6, and the number committed during the year 1,101.7, the ratios for Negroes being markedly in excess of the corresponding ratios shown for whites (114.8 and 467.4 per 100,000 respectively).

[1] Practically all of the text relating to prisoners and juvenile delinquents is taken with immaterial changes from one section—the section on Race—of the census report on Prisoners and Juvenile Delinquents: 1910. This section is not, however, reproduced in full either as regards text or tabular matter, some text and data relating especially to other racial classes than Negroes or presenting detail for Negroes by states being omitted.

NUMBER, RATIO, AND PERCENTAGE DISTRIBUTION OF PRISONERS AND JUVENILE DELINQUENTS, BY RACIAL CLASSES: 1910.

Table 1		PRISONERS AND JUVENILE DELINQUENTS: 1910.							Percentage distribution of population: 1910.
RACIAL CLASS.	Population: 1910.	Number.		Ratio per 100,000 population.		Percentage distribution.			
		Enumerated January 1.	Committed during year.	Enumerated January 1.	Committed during year.	Enumerated January 1.	Committed during year.		
Total	91,972,266	136,472	493,934	148.4	537.0	100.0	100.0		100.0
Negro	9,827,763	41,729	108,268	424.6	1,101.7	30.6	21.9		10.7
White	81,731,957	93,841	382,052	114.8	467.4	68.8	77.3		88.9
Other colored	412,546	902	3,614	218.6	876.0	0.7	0.7		0.4
Indian	265,683	(1)	2,963	(1)	1,115.2	(1)	0.6		0.3
Chinese, Japanese, and other	146,863	(1)	651	(1)	443.3	(1)	0.1		0.2

[1] Separate figures not available.

In every division, as appears in Table 2, the percentage Negro was much higher among prisoners and juvenile delinquents than in the general population, and in every division, also, it was higher for the prison population on January 1 than for the commitments during the year—a fact which indicates that the term of imprisonment for Negroes was above the average for all prisoners.

Table 2	PERCENTAGE NEGRO: 1910.		
		Among prisoners and juvenile delinquents.	
SECTION AND DIVISION.	In total population.	Enumerated Jan. 1.	Committed during year.
United States	10.7	30.6	21.9
The South	29.8	70.1	58.9
South Atlantic	33.7	72.0	61.6
East South Central	31.5	73.1	63.6
West South Central	22.6	62.4	46.0
The North	1.8	13.1	9.6
New England	1.0	4.6	2.6
Middle Atlantic	2.2	12.8	9.4
East North Central	1.6	14.7	11.0
West North Central	2.1	20.8	14.4
The West	0.7	5.9	3.2
Mountain	0.8	7.8	4.4
Pacific	0.7	4.6	2.5
United States penitentiaries		31.3	24.6

Table 3 gives, for Negroes and whites, by sections and southern divisions, and for states having a Negro population of 10,000 or more in 1910, the ratio of commitments per 100,000 population, and a coefficient of difference obtained by dividing the ratio for Negroes by that for whites.

In general, prison and jail commitments are less frequent relatively to the population in the South than in the North for whites as well as for Negroes. It is obvious, however, that the relatively low ratio of commitments in the South, where nine-tenths of the Negroes are located, will have more influence in lowering the ratio for the United States in the case of Negroes than in the case of whites. For this reason figures shown for the United States do not fully reveal the contrast between the two races as regards the frequency of jail and prison commitments, the ratio of commitments for Negroes in the entire United States being about two and one-half times that for the whites, while in the divisions and states, with few exceptions, the difference is more marked. In the South the ratio for Negroes is 3.4, in the North 5.6, and in the West 4.5 times that for whites. In some of the states the contrast is still more striking.

The ratio of commitments for all classes of the population is greater in cities than in rural districts; and that may explain to some extent the fact that the contrast between the two races is more pronounced in the North than in the South. For the North is more urban than the South; and in the North the proportion of

Negroes living in cities, defined as incorporated places of over 2,500 inhabitants, greatly exceeds the proportion of whites living in such places, 77.4 per cent of the northern Negroes being residents of urban territory in 1910, as compared with 58.3 per cent of the northern whites. In the South, on the other hand, the difference between the two races in this respect is not very great; in fact, in the two south central divisions there is practically no difference between the Negroes and whites as regards the percentage living in cities, while in the South Atlantic division the higher percentage is that for whites.

Table 3	PRISONERS AND JUVENILE DELINQUENTS COMMITTED IN 1910.				
	Number.		Ratio of commitments.[1]		
SECTION, DIVISION, AND STATE.	Negro.	White.	Negro.	White.	Coefficient of difference.
			A	B	A÷B
United States	108,268	382,052	1,101.7	467.4	2.4
The South	77,022	53,023	880.3	258.1	3.4
South Atlantic	41,226	25,620	1,002.5	317.4	3.2
Delaware	606	1,432	1,943.5	836.9	2.3
Maryland	5,243	4,298	2,257.5	404.5	5.6
District of Columbia	4,072	1,844	4,311.5	780.9	5.5
Virginia	8,069	4,624	1,202.4	332.7	3.6
West Virginia	1,255	4,974	1,955.7	430.0	4.5
North Carolina	2,050	657	293.8	43.8	6.7
South Carolina	4,397	1,090	526.1	160.5	3.3
Georgia	9,717	2,684	825.6	187.5	4.4
Florida	5,817	4,017	1,884.5	905.5	2.1
East South Central	23,347	13,357	880.2	232.1	3.8
Kentucky	7,228	7,157	2,762.4	352.9	7.8
Tennessee	6,525	3,443	1,379.2	201.2	6.9
Alabama	6,531	2,189	719.0	178.1	4.0
Mississippi	3,063	568	303.4	72.3	4.2
West South Central	12,449	14,046	627.3	209.0	3.0
Arkansas	2,938	2,052	663.4	181.4	3.7
Louisiana	3,376	1,642	472.9	174.5	2.7
Oklahoma	1,627	3,987	1,182.3	276.0	4.3
Texas	4,508	6,365	653.3	198.6	3.3
The North	29,145	274,941	2,836.0	503.2	5.6
Massachusetts	747	31,225	1,962.9	938.1	2.1
Connecticut	386	8,255	2,543.8	751.2	3.4
New York	2,922	45,258	2,177.5	504.7	4.3
New Jersey	1,590	10,550	1,771.4	431.3	4.1
Pennsylvania	6,295	48,297	3,246.2	646.7	5.0
Ohio	2,935	16,921	2,633.4	363.5	7.2
Indiana	2,335	11,363	3,871.0	430.4	9.0
Illinois	3,605	25,513	3,305.9	461.6	7.2
Michigan	415	12,222	2,424.8	438.8	5.5
Iowa	650	12,575	4,341.1	569.2	7.6
Missouri	4,742	11,870	3,011.7	378.6	8.0
Kansas	942	2,587	1,743.5	158.3	11.0
Other Northern states	1,581	38,305	4,912.4	437.8	11.2
The West	1,858	53,379	3,667.4	815.7	4.5
Colorado	404	4,667	3,527.5	595.7	5.9
California	336	15,961	1,552.3	706.3	2.2
Other Western states	1,118	32,751	6,365.3	935.4	6.8
United States penitentiaries	243	709			

[1] Number committed per 100,000 population of the same race.

OFFENSE.

Prisoners and juvenile delinquents, total and Negro, in the country as a whole and in each geographic section, are classified in Table 4 by offense for which committed, the percentage Negro being given for each class of offenders.

OFFENSES FOR WHICH PRISONERS AND JUVENILE DELINQUENTS WERE COMMITTED IN 1910, BY SECTIONS.

Table 4

OFFENSE.	PRISONERS AND JUVENILE DELINQUENTS COMMITTED IN 1910.											
	United States.[1]			The South.			The North.			The West.		
	Total.	Negro.		Total.	Negro.		Total.	Negro.		Total.	Negro.	
		Number.	Per cent.		Number.	Per cent.		Number.	Per cent.		Number.	Per cent.
All offenses	493,934	108,268	21.9	130,684	77,022	58.9	305,008	29,145	9.6	57,255	1,858	3.2
Grave homicide	967	542	56.0	637	474	74.4	222	58	26.1	94	8	[2]
Lesser homicide	1,935	949	49.0	1,195	808	67.6	576	129	22.4	152	10	6.6
Assault	22,670	9,324	41.1	8,907	6,784	76.2	12,010	2,381	19.8	1,717	130	7.6
Robbery	1,728	575	33.3	443	318	71.8	1,008	225	22.3	241	16	6.6
Burglary	8,922	2,725	30.5	2,839	1,954	68.8	4,791	655	13.7	1,145	59	5.2
Larceny	42,716	13,591	31.8	13,615	9,865	72.5	24,302	3,527	14.5	4,704	169	3.6
Fraud	8,936	1,484	16.6	2,316	1,076	46.5	5,662	380	6.7	889	23	2.6
Forgery	2,156	315	14.6	639	244	38.2	1,028	53	5.2	447	7	1.6
Rape	1,480	380	25.7	372	247	66.4	955	122	12.8	144	6	4.2
Prostitution and fornication	6,450	2,166	33.6	1,539	982	63.8	4,620	1,132	24.5	291	52	17.9
Drunkenness and disorderly conduct	262,905	41,760	15.9	57,763	29,424	50.9	176,417	11,735	6.7	28,725	601	2.1
Vagrancy	50,302	8,256	16.4	8,399	4,794	57.1	30,429	2,970	9.8	11,474	492	4.3
Violating liquor laws	7,713	2,458	31.9	3,980	2,053	51.6	2,921	376	12.9	755	22	2.9
Malicious mischief and trespass	10,145	2,186	21.5	3,247	1,657	51.0	6,534	500	7.7	354	19	5.4
Offenses peculiar to children	7,803	839	10.8	1,105	230	20.8	6,084	574	9.4	614	35	5.7
Offense ill-defined or not reported	7,909	2,229	28.2	3,278	1,864	56.9	2,576	328	12.7	1,999	27	1.4
All others	49,197	18,489	37.6	20,410	14,248	69.8	24,873	4,000	16.1	3,510	182	5.2

[1] Includes figures for the United States penitentiaries, which are not shown separately in this table.　　[2] Per cent not shown where base is less than 100.

Negroes, as already noted, constituted a little more than one-fifth (21.9 per cent) of the total number of prisoners and juvenile delinquents committed in the year 1910 for all offenses. They represented 56 per cent of the total number committed for grave homicide, 49 per cent of the total for lesser homicide, and 41.1 per cent of the total for assault. They contributed 33.6 per cent, or one-third, of the commitments for prostitution and fornication, and almost as large a proportion of the commitments for robbery, burglary, and larceny, and for violating liquor laws. On the other hand, they comprised only about 16 per cent of those committed for drunkenness and disorderly conduct and for vagrancy.

While these figures and those given in tables following will probably be generally accepted as indicating that there is more criminality and law breaking among Negroes than among whites and while that conclusion is probably justified by the facts, it should be borne in mind that the difference between the two races in this respect may very well be less than the ratios based on the number of commitments to prison or jail would indicate. It is a question whether the difference shown by the ratios may not be to some extent the result of discrimination in the treatment of white and Negro offenders on the part of the community and the courts. An offense committed by a Negro is perhaps more likely to be punished than the same offense committed by a white man, especially if the victim of the offense committed by the Negro is white, while in the other case the victim is Negro. It is probable that as compared with the white man the Negro when brought to trial on a criminal charge is in fewer instances able to employ expert counsel to defend his case and assist him in taking advantage of any technicalities in the law which may be in his favor. Moreover, in the case of those offenses for which the penalty may be a fine with imprisonment as the alternative if the fine is not paid, it is probable that the Negro is more often unable to pay the fine than the white man and is therefore more likely to be sent to jail; but of course this consideration has little weight in connection with the more serious offenses which are seldom penalized by fines only. On the other hand, it is not improbable that many of the minor offenses committed by Negroes and not directly affecting white people are more likely to be disregarded by the officers of the law than are the same offenses committed by the whites. Although these are questions on which no statistical data can be presented and in regard to which opinions may differ, it seems proper to call attention to them as representing possibilities which ought to be considered before accepting the record of prison commitments as an accurate measure of the difference between the two races in respect to criminality. It must always be borne in mind that the amount of crime punished in different classes or communities may not bear a fixed or unvarying ratio to the amount of crime committed.

The percentage of Negroes in the total number of commitments for any given offense is naturally much larger in the South than in either the North or the West. Thus the percentage of Negroes in the total number of commitments for grave homicide was 26.1 in the North, 74.4 in the South, and 8.5 in the West. But if the several offense groups are ranked with respect to the percentage of Negroes in the commitments it will be found that the order for the North does not differ radically from that for the South, that is to say, an offense for which the rank as respects the percentage of Negroes is relatively high in the North will show a relatively high rank in the South also. Thus in the North the five offenses for which the percentage of Negroes was largest were in the order of the size of the percentage (shown in parentheses) as follows: Grave homicide (26.1), prostitution and fornication (24.5), lesser homicide (22.4), robbery (22.3), and assault (19.8). In the South the corresponding list comprised assault (76.2), grave homicide (74.4), larceny (72.5), robbery (71.8), and burglary (68.8). Three of the specified offenses appear in each list. The list for the North, however, includes prostitution and fornication, ranking second, and lesser homicide, ranking third, offenses which in the South ranked respectively eighth and sixth, while the list for the South includes larceny, ranking third, and burglary, ranking fifth, offenses which in the North ranked sixth and seventh, respectively.

The five offenses for which the percentage of Negroes was smallest were in the North forgery (5.2), fraud (6.7), drunkenness and disorderly conduct (6.7), malicious mischief and trespass (7.7), and offenses peculiar to children (9.4); in the South they were offenses peculiar to children (20.8), forgery (38.2), fraud (46.5), drunkenness and disorderly conduct (50.9), and malicious mischief and trespass (51). The lists are identical, the only difference being one of order caused by the difference in the relative importance of offenses peculiar to children.

In the West the percentage of Negroes was conspicuously high (17.9) in the commitments for prostitution and fornication.

The ratio of commitments per 100,000 population and the coefficient of difference, presented in the preceding table, show that for every offense the contrast between the whites and Negroes is greater in the North than in the South. In this connection reference may be made to the probable influence of the fact already mentioned that in the North the Negroes are concentrated in cities to a much greater degree than the white population.

In Table 6, which presents figures by geographic divisions, the whites and Negroes committed in 1910 are divided into two broad classes as regards offense, one class comprising those committed for drunkenness and disorderly conduct and the other those committed for all other offenses.

Table 6	RATIO OF COMMITMENTS.[1]					
	For all offenses except drunkenness and disorderly conduct.			For drunkenness and disorderly conduct.		
SECTION AND DIVISION.	Negro.	White.	Coefficient of difference.	Negro.	White.	Coefficient of difference.
	A	B	A÷B	A	B	A÷B
United States	676.7	199.6	3.4	424.9	267.8	1.6
The South	544.0	122.2	4.5	336.3	135.9	2.5
South Atlantic	578.5	128.0	4.5	423.9	189.4	2.2
East South Central	523.6	110.7	4.7	356.6	121.4	2.9
West South Central	499.7	124.9	4.0	127.6	84.0	1.5
The North	1,694.1	202.7	8.4	1,141.9	300.5	3.8
New England	1,307.6	242.6	5.4	723.9	536.8	1.3
Middle Atlantic	1,241.5	229.2	5.4	1,344.7	322.2	4.2
East North Central	1,841.9	177.9	10.4	1,287.4	243.6	5.3
West North Central	2,395.9	175.0	13.7	726.5	219.0	3.3
The West	2,481.1	406.5	6.1	1,186.3	409.2	2.9
Mountain	3,498.4	429.7	8.1	1,197.2	388.4	3.1
Pacific	1,733.2	391.9	4.4	1,178.3	422.2	2.8

[1] Number of prisoners and juvenile delinquents committed in 1910 per 100,000 population of the same race.

In the United States as a whole, and in every division, the ratio of commitments for each class of offenses is larger for Negroes than for whites, but the difference between the two races in this respect is always less marked in the case of drunkenness and disorderly conduct than it is for other offenses. Thus for the United States as a whole the ratio of commitments per 100,000 population for drunkenness and disorderly conduct among Negroes (424.9) was one and six-tenths times the corresponding ratio among whites (267.8), but as regards the total for all other offenses the ratio in the case of Negroes (676.7) was three and four-tenths times that in the case of whites (199.6). A similar relationship is indicated by the figures for each section and geographic division, the coefficient of difference between the races being always less for drunkenness and disorderly conduct than for other offenses. In the South as a whole the coefficients were, respectively, two and one-half and four and one-half, which means that in proportion to their

Table 5	RATIO OF COMMITMENTS.[1]					
	The South.			The North.		
OFFENSE.	Negro.	White.	Coefficient of difference.	Negro.	White.	Coefficient of difference.
	A	B	A÷B	A	B	A÷B
All offenses	880.3	258.1	3.4	2,836.0	503.2	5.6
Grave homicide	5.4	0.8	6.8	5.6	0.3	18.7
Lesser homicide	9.2	1.9	4.8	12.6	0.8	15.8
Assault	77.5	10.2	7.6	231.7	17.5	13.2
Robbery	3.6	0.6	6.0	21.9	1.4	15.6
Burglary	22.3	4.3	5.2	63.7	7.6	8.4
Larceny	112.8	18.1	6.2	343.2	37.9	9.1
Fraud	12.3	6.0	2.1	37.0	9.6	3.9
Forgery	2.8	1.9	1.5	5.2	1.8	2.9
Rape	2.8	0.6	4.7	11.9	1.5	7.9
Prostitution and fornication	11.2	2.7	4.1	110.2	6.4	17.2
Drunkenness and disorderly conduct	336.3	135.9	2.5	1,141.9	300.5	3.8
Vagrancy	54.8	17.5	3.1	289.0	50.2	5.8
Violating liquor laws	23.5	9.2	2.6	36.6	4.5	8.1
Malicious mischief and trespass	18.9	7.7	2.5	48.7	11.0	4.4
Offenses peculiar to children	2.6	4.3	0.6	55.9	10.1	5.5
Offense ill-defined or not reported	21.3	6.8	3.1	31.9	4.1	7.8
All others	162.8	29.7	5.5	389.2	37.9	10.3

[1] Number of prisoners and juvenile delinquents committed in 1910 per 100,000 population of the same race.

numbers Negroes in the South are committed for drunkenness and disorderly conduct two and one-half times as often as white men, but are committed for other offenses four and one-half times as often.

As between the North and the South it is very evident that the ratios are to a large degree determined by local conditions affecting both races alike, because for Negroes as well as whites the ratios for each class of offenses distinguished in Table 6 are much lower in the South than in either the North or the West. In respect to either class of offenses it will be found that the difference between the Negroes and the whites in the ratio of commitments is greater in the North than in the South. In this connection it should be remembered that the Negroes are very unevenly distributed over the Northern states, that they are concentrated largely in a few cities or in districts bordering the Southern states, and that many Northern states with a large white population have only a negligible number of Negroes. Accordingly, in any aggregates such as those presented in Table 6 covering groups of states, the difference in the geographic distribution of the two races must have a considerable effect upon the figures, but an effect which can not be easily measured or determined. For instance, in the West North Central division 65 per cent of the Negroes in 1910 were in the one state of Missouri, as compared with 28 per cent of the whites; and consequently conditions in that state have a much greater influence upon the division totals for Negroes than upon those for whites. Moreover, the marked differences in distribution obtain not only as between states but within the same state. In the state of New York, for instance, 78 per cent of the Negroes in 1910 were in the city of New York and only 52 per cent of the whites. It is evident, therefore, that in the Northern states the figures for the two races are affected by local influences which are widely divergent.

SENTENCE.

In Table 7 Negro and white prisoners and juvenile delinquents committed in 1910 are classified with respect to the general character of the sentence imposed, and those committed under sentence of imprisonment without fine are further classified by length of sentence.

Of the 130 offenders sentenced to death, 49, or 37.7 per cent, were Negroes; among those sentenced to imprisonment and fine the proportion of Negroes was 28.3 per cent; and among those imprisoned for nonpayment of fine it was 24.3 per cent. Of the prisoners and juvenile delinquents sentenced to imprisonment without fine, 16.4 per cent were Negroes.

Of those sentenced to imprisonment without fine for a definite term of one year or longer, 40.9 per cent were Negroes; of those sentenced for a term of less

than one year, 13.4 per cent. This difference is partly explained by conditions in the South, where for both races the proportion of commitments for long terms is greater than in the North. In other words, it is in part a sectional difference rather than a racial one. Nevertheless, more detailed tabulations show that even within the same geographic division or the same state the percentage Negro is as a rule greater among those committed for long terms than among those committed for short terms, and that the percentage Negro tends to increase with each extension in the length of the imprisonment sentence, starting with 10.5 for prisoners and juvenile delinquents sentenced for less than one month and reaching 49.3 for those sentenced for five years or over.

Table 7	PRISONERS AND JUVENILE DELINQUENTS COMMITTED IN 1910.					
			Negro.			Percentage distribution by sentence.
SENTENCE.	All classes.	Number.	Per cent of all classes.	White.	Negro.	White.
Total......................	493,934	108,268	21.9	382,052	100.0	100.0
Death.........................	130	49	37.7	80	(1)	(1)
Imprisonment only..............	171,383	28,093	16.4	142,411	25.9	37.3
One year or more [2]...........	20,616	8,440	40.9	12,000	7.8	3.1
Less than one year.............	123,004	16,508	13.4	105,851	15.2	27.7
During minority................	9,229	1,272	13.8	7,946	1.2	2.1
Indeterminate sentence........	17,681	1,663	9.4	15,975	1.5	4.2
Length of sentence not reported	853	210	24.6	639	0.2	0.2
Imprisonment and fine..........	42,006	11,877	28.3	29,742	11.0	7.8
Imprisoned for nonpayment of fine	278,914	67,860	24.3	208,737	62.7	54.6
Nature of sentence not reported...	1,501	389	25.9	1,082	0.4	0.3

[1] Less than one-tenth of 1 per cent.　　　[2] Includes life sentence.

The last columns of Table 7 show the percentage distribution of the white and the Negro prisoners and juvenile delinquents by nature and length of sentence. The death sentence was reported for less than one-tenth of 1 per cent of any class of prisoners, but was relatively more frequent for Negroes committed than for whites. The sentence to imprisonment without fine was imposed upon 37.3 per cent of the white offenders and 25.9 per cent of the Negro. The sentence to imprisonment and fine, on the other hand, was relatively more frequent among the Negro offenders than among the white, 11 per cent of the former as against 7.8 per cent of the latter receiving this form of sentence.

Persons imprisoned for nonpayment of fine comprised 62.7 per cent of the total number of Negroes committed, as compared with 54.6 per cent of the total number of whites. This difference might be regarded as being indicative of the wider prevalence of poverty among Negroes as compared with whites, but from an inspection of Table 8, giving figures by geographic divisions, it appears to be due mainly to the difference in the geographic distribution of the two races.

Table 8

DIVISION.	PRISONERS AND JUVENILE DELINQUENTS COMMITTED IN 1910.					
	Total.		Imprisoned for nonpayment of fine.			
			Number.		Per cent.	
	Negro.	White.	Negro.	White.	Negro.	White.
UNITED STATES.........	108,268	382,052	67,860	208,737	62.7	54.6
THE SOUTH.						
South Atlantic.................	41,226	25,620	27,949	17,466	67.8	68.2
East South Central............	23,347	13,357	15,659	8,496	67.1	63.6
West South Central............	12,449	14,646	7,841	9,524	63.0	67.8
THE NORTH.						
New England.................	1,347	50,511	532	20,226	39.5	40.0
Middle Atlantic..............	10,807	104,105	5,257	47,433	48.6	45.6
East North Central............	9,414	75,550	5,412	47,758	57.5	63.2
West North Central............	7,577	44,775	4,359	27,125	57.5	60.6
THE WEST.						
Mountain.....................	1,008	20,621	472	12,562	46.8	60.9
Pacific.......................	850	32,758	379	18,147	44.6	55.4
United States penitentiaries ...	243	709	....	....	....	....

As regards the percentage imprisoned for nonpayment of fine, shown in the above table, it may be noted that the difference between the two races, although rather marked for the United States as a whole, is much less so in most of the divisions, and furthermore that while for the United States as a whole the percentage for Negroes (62.7) was considerably higher than that for whites (54.6), there are only two divisions, the Middle Atlantic and the East South Central, in which that was likewise the case. In two of the other divisions, New England and the South Atlantic, the two percentages were nearly identical, and in the remaining divisions the percentage for whites was somewhat higher than that for Negroes. It is evident, then, that the comparatively high percentage of commitments for nonpayment of fine shown for Negroes in the total for the United States reflects conditions in the South, where such commitments are more common for both races than in other sections of the United States.

The percentage of prisoners imprisoned for nonpayment of fine, it may be noted, is determined by two independent factors—first the percentage of convicted offenders receiving a sentence of fine only, and second the percentage of those receiving such a sentence who fail or refuse to pay the fine. It is quite probable that within the same state or community a smaller percentage of the Negro offenders than of the white are merely fined, because the figures already presented indicate that a smaller proportion of the Negroes than of the whites are convicted of minor offenses. On the other hand, it is probable that among Negroes who are merely fined the percentage unable to pay is larger than in the same class of white offenders. Thus the one factor would tend to make the percentage imprisoned for nonpayment of fine smaller in the total number of Negro

prisoners committed than in the total number of white, while the other factor would have the opposite tendency; and it may very well be that the fact that in most geographic divisions the percentages for the two races are not far apart indicates that these opposing tendencies nearly equalize or offset each other.

In Table 9 the Negro and white prisoners and juvenile delinquents sentenced to imprisonment only are classified with respect to the term of sentence.

Table 9

LENGTH OF SENTENCE.	PRISONERS AND JUVENILE DELINQUENTS COMMITTED IN 1910 UNDER SENTENCE OF IMPRISONMENT ONLY.			
	Number.		Percentage distribution.	
	Negro.	White.	Negro.	White.
Total.....................	28,093	142,411	100.0	100.0
Life.........................	490	281	1.7	0.2
Definite term................	24,458	117,570	87.1	82.6
1 year or over............	7,950	11,719	28.3	8.2
Less than 1 year..........	16,508	105,851	58.8	74.3
Minority....................	1,272	7,946	4.5	5.6
Indeterminate...............	1,663	15,975	5.9	11.2
Not reported................	210	639	0.7	0.4

Of the white prisoners and juvenile delinquents committed in 1910 under sentence of imprisonment without fine, 74.3 per cent, or nearly three-fourths, were sentenced for a definite term of less than one year; in the case of the Negroes the proportion was much smaller, the percentage being 58.8. On the other hand, the percentage committed for a definite term of one year or over was 28.3 for Negroes, as against 8.2 for whites.

Table 10

DIVISION.	PRISONERS AND JUVENILE DELINQUENTS COMMITTED IN 1910 UNDER SENTENCE OF IMPRISONMENT ONLY.					
	Total.		Receiving indeterminate sentence.			
			Number.		Per cent.	
	Negro.	White.	Negro.	White.	Negro.	White.
UNITED STATES [1]...	28,093	142,411	1,663	15,975	5.9	11.2
THE SOUTH.						
South Atlantic...........	10,638	6,418	126	268	1.2	4.2
East South Central.......	3,904	2,942	90	80	2.3	2.7
West South Central.......	2,953	2,822	138	176	4.7	6.2
THE NORTH.						
New England.............	620	25,370	120	5,956	19.4	22.5
Middle Atlantic...........	4,382	51,145	402	3,750	9.2	7.3
East North Central.......	1,637	17,622	509	3,313	31.1	18.8
West North Central.......	2,880	15,875	190	926	6.6	5.8
THE WEST.						
Mountain.................	494	7,054	64	901	13.0	12.8
Pacific...................	395	12,802	24	605	6.1	4.7

[1] Includes figures for the United States penitentiaries which are not shown separately in this table.

As is shown in the preceding table, the indeterminate sentence was imposed on a considerably larger proportion of the white than of the Negro prisoners and juvenile delinquents (11.2 per cent as compared with 5.9 per cent) partly because it is a form of sentence more common in the North than in the South.

In the South, as in the country as a whole, it was more usual for white prisoners than for Negro. Outside the South, on the other hand, a larger proportion of the Negro prisoners than of the white received this form of sentence in every division except New England.

The following table, presenting a classification by length of sentence, is restricted to prisoners committed for life or for a definite term of imprisonment without fine. It does not, therefore, include those sentenced to death or for their minority or for an indeterminate period, those sentenced to imprisonment and fine, or those imprisoned for nonpayment of fine.

Table 11

PRISONERS AND JUVENILE DELINQUENTS IN 1910 COMMITTED FOR LIFE OR FOR A DEFINITE TERM OF IMPRISONMENT WITHOUT FINE.

LENGTH OF SENTENCE.	Negro.		White.	Percentage distribution by length of sentence.	
	Number.	Per cent of total.		Negro.	White.
Total	24,948	17.4	117,851	100.0	100.0
1 year or over	8,440	40.9	12,000	33.8	10.2
Life	490	62.6	281	2.0	0.2
10 years or over	913	54.8	734	3.7	0.6
5 to 9 years	1,260	46.0	1,465	5.1	1.2
2 to 4 years	3,001	40.4	4,377	12.0	3.7
1 year	2,776	34.7	5,143	11.1	4.4
Less than year	16,508	13.4	105,851	66.2	89.8
7 to 11 months	640	36.8	1,094	2.6	0.9
6 months	2,165	18.9	9,232	8.7	7.8
4 to 5 months	863	22.7	2,919	3.5	2.5
3 months	2,282	14.1	13,871	9.1	11.8
2 months	1,703	15.4	9,318	6.8	7.9
1 month	3,517	12.7	24,009	14.1	20.4
Less than 1 month	5,338	10.5	45,408	21.4	38.5

The table brings out the very marked contrast between the two races as regards the length of sentence. Of the Negroes sentenced to a definite term of imprisonment without fine or for life, 33.8 per cent, or one-third, received a sentence of one year or more, while the corresponding percentage for whites was only 10.2. On the other hand, only 21.4 per cent of the Negroes, as against 38.5 per cent of the whites, received a sentence of less than one month, and 35.5 per cent of the former, as against 58.9 per cent of the latter, received a sentence of less than two months.

That there may be some discrimination between whites and Negroes as regards the penalty imposed for the same offense is not improbable, but it is reasonably certain that this is not the principal explanation of the difference in the length of sentence shown for the two races. Two other factors influence the figures. One is the difference in the practice of the courts and in the laws of different states as regards the penalties prescribed or imposed for crimes and misdemeanors, conditions in the South, where a relatively large proportion of the prison commitments are for long terms, having, of course, more influence upon the totals for Negroes than upon those for whites. The other factor referred to is the difference in the relative number of minor offenses committed by each race. As shown by figures previously presented, 68.3 per cent of the white offenders were committed for drunkenness, disorderly conduct, or vagrancy, while for Negroes the corresponding percentage was but 46.2. A difference such as this would naturally have a marked effect upon the relative length of sentence for the two classes.

Table 12, which gives by geographic divisions the distribution by length of sentence of the prisoners and juvenile delinquents sentenced to imprisonment for life or a definite term without fine, shows that in every geographic division except one, the Mountain division, a larger percentage of the Negro offenders of this class than of the whites were committed for a term of one year or longer. The difference is quite as pronounced in the northern divisions as in the southern, but it is again evident that the difference in the United States as a whole is partly a result of the difference in the geographic distribution of the two races.

Table 12

PRISONERS AND JUVENILE DELINQUENTS COMMITTED IN 1910 FOR LIFE OR FOR A DEFINITE TERM OF IMPRISONMENT WITHOUT FINE.

SECTION, DIVISION, AND RACE.	Total.	Number sentenced for—			Per cent sentenced for—		
		1 year or over.	Less than 1 year.		1 year [1] or over.	Less than 1 year.	
			1 month or over.	Less than 1 month.		1 month or over.	Less than 1 month.
United States:							
Negro	24,948	8,440	11,170	5,338	33.8	44.8	21.4
White	117,851	12,000	60,443	45,408	10.2	51.3	38.5
The South:							
Negro	16,460	6,955	6,645	2,860	42.3	40.4	17.4
White	10,397	3,517	3,928	2,952	33.8	37.8	28.4
South Atlantic—							
Negro	10,061	3,271	5,105	1,685	32.5	50.7	16.7
White	5,471	1,138	2,903	1,430	20.8	53.1	26.1
East South Central—							
Negro	3,627	1,911	732	984	52.7	20.2	27.1
White	2,461	839	440	1,182	34.1	17.9	48.0
West South Central—							
Negro	2,772	1,773	808	191	64.0	29.1	6.9
White	2,465	1,540	585	340	62.5	23.7	13.8
The North:							
Negro	7,546	1,207	4,035	2,304	16.0	53.5	30.5
White	89,580	6,196	48,264	35,120	6.9	53.9	39.2
New England—							
Negro	458	47	333	78	10.3	72.7	17.0
White	18,556	990	13,508	4,058	5.3	72.8	21.9
Middle Atlantic—							
Negro	3,656	359	2,212	1,085	9.8	60.5	29.7
White	44,549	2,281	25,498	16,770	5.1	57.2	37.6
East North Central—							
Negro	906	252	411	243	27.8	45.4	26.8
White	12,698	1,452	5,134	6,112	11.4	40.4	48.1
West North Central—							
Negro	2,526	549	1,079	898	21.7	42.7	35.6
White	13,777	1,473	4,124	8,180	10.7	29.9	59.4
The West:							
Negro	752	88	490	174	11.7	65.2	23.1
White	17,513	1,927	8,250	7,336	11.0	47.1	41.9
Mountain—							
Negro	403	36	300	67	8.9	74.4	16.6
White	5,778	755	2,953	2,070	13.1	51.1	35.8
Pacific—							
Negro	349	52	190	107	14.9	54.4	30.7
White	11,735	1,172	5,297	5,266	10.0	45.1	44.9
United States penitentiaries:							
Negro	190	190			100.0		
White	361	360	1		99.7	0.3	

[1] Includes life sentence.

In most divisions the percentage sentenced for less than one year but not less than one month is larger for the Negroes than for the whites. The difference between the races, however, is most striking as regards the percentage sentenced for less than one month, this percentage being invariably much smaller for the Negroes than for the whites.

Table 13 shows the approximate average length of sentence in months for white and Negro prisoners and juvenile delinquents sentenced to definite terms of imprisonment in each geographic division.

In the United States as a whole the average length of sentence for Negroes is more than three times that for whites, but in none of the geographic divisions except the East North Central is the relative difference as great as this, although in every division except one (the Mountain division), the sentence for Negro offenders is considerably longer than that for white.

| Table 13 | AVERAGE LENGTH OF SENTENCE OF PRISONERS AND JUVENILE DELINQUENTS COMMITTED IN 1910 FOR A DEFINITE TERM OF IMPRISONMENT WITHOUT FINE (MONTHS). | |
DIVISION.	Negro.	White.
United States	17.4	5.2
The South:		
South Atlantic	15.4	9.6
East South Central	31.7	16.2
West South Central	29.7	25.3
The North:		
New England	4.7	3.5
Middle Atlantic	4.9	3.3
East North Central	17.7	4.8
West North Central	9.1	4.5
The West:		
Mountain	5.1	6.2
Pacific	11.8	6.5

AGE.

As shown by Table 14, Negroes constituted about one-third of all prisoners and juvenile delinquents committed who were between the ages of 15 and 25, about one-fourth (24.1 per cent) of those between 25 and 35, hardly more than one-eighth (13.8 per cent) of those between 35 and 45, and less than one-twelfth of those 45 or over. This decrease in the percentage in the older age groups is consistent with the fact that the percentage of Negroes, as shown by figures already presented, is much below the average in the commitments for drunkenness and disorderly conduct and for vagrancy, taken in connection with the further fact that these are offenses which account for a large proportion of the total number of commitments in the older age groups.

Of the prisoners committed when under the age of 15, about one-fifth were Negroes. The proportion is thus considerably smaller than it is in the age groups from 15 to 34, a circumstance which may be due in part to the fact that a larger proportion of the Negroes than of the whites live in states or communities where there are no juvenile reformatories. The establishment of

these institutions doubtless has a tendency to increase the number of commitments of juvenile offenders, since they receive for purposes of reformation children who are guilty of juvenile offenses or misconduct not serious enough to justify commitment to a prison or jail. Therefore, where such institutions are lacking, youthful offenders guilty of those juvenile offenses are apt to be allowed to remain at large in the community. But there is still another important factor to be considered in this connection, namely, that one of the offenses for which large numbers of juveniles are committed—truancy—does not come into existence in any community until laws for compulsory school attendance are adopted and enforced. In short it is an offense which is created by the enactment of such laws; and a larger proportion of the Negroes than of the whites live in sections where there are no such laws, and where there is, therefore, no such offense.

| Table 14 | PRISONERS AND JUVENILE DELINQUENTS COMMITTED IN 1910. | | | | Percentage Negro in the population, 1910. |
| AGE. | Number. | | | Percentage Negro. | |
	Total.	Negro.	White.		
All ages	493,934	108,268	382,052	21.9	10.7
Under 10 years	568	112	456	19.7	12.3
10 to 14 years	9,061	1,992	7,059	22.0	12.7
15 to 17 years	15,793	5,289	10,457	33.5	11.8
18 to 20 years	35,697	12,375	23,080	34.7	11.5
21 to 24 years	64,221	20,834	42,885	32.4	11.3
25 to 34 years	129,974	31,380	97,424	24.1	10.2
35 to 44 years	99,023	13,685	84,630	13.8	9.3
45 to 54 years	56,230	4,411	51,457	7.8	8.5
55 to 64 years	22,408	1,310	20,949	5.8	7.8
65 years and over	7,718	506	7,152	6.6	7.4
Age not reported	53,241	16,374	36,503	30.8	18.4

The number and ratio of commitments, by single years of age and age periods, for Negroes and for whites are shown in Table 15.

Table 15	PRISONERS AND JUVENILE DELINQUENTS COMMITTED IN 1910.				
	Number.		Ratio of commitments.[1]		
AGE.			Negro.	White.	Coefficient of difference.
	Negro.	White.	A	B	A÷B
All ages	108,268	382,052	1,101.7	467.4	2.4
Under 10 years	112	456	4.5	2.6	1.7
10 years	114	596	47.0	36.8	1.3
11 years	176	838	90.2	55.7	1.6
12 years	364	1,400	139.3	85.2	1.6
13 years	513	1,887	231.2	122.1	1.9
14 years	825	2,338	351.7	145.5	2.4
15 years	1,128	2,642	543.5	175.3	3.1
16 years	1,813	3,088	807.9	189.1	4.3
17 years	2,348	4,727	1,151.8	299.9	3.8
18 years	3,831	7,148	1,656.2	423.2	3.9
19 years	4,098	8,175	2,120.0	523.3	4.1
20 years	4,446	7,757	2,061.9	475.8	4.3
21 to 24 years	20,834	42,885	2,555.8	674.7	3.8
25 to 34 years	31,380	97,424	2,025.4	720.4	2.8
35 to 44 years	13,685	84,630	1,256.8	805.1	1.6
45 to 54 years	4,411	51,457	619.5	675.6	0.9
55 to 64 years	1,310	20,949	330.7	452.1	0.7
65 years and over	506	7,152	172.0	196.5	0.9
Age not reported	16,374	36,503			

[1] Number committed per 100,000 population of the same race and age.

As indicated by the coefficient in the above table, the difference between the whites and the Negroes as regards the ratio of commitments is relatively small in the period of childhood but shows a tendency to increase in each older year of life, up to the age of 16. For each age group shown within the age period 16 to 24 years, the ratio of commitments for Negroes is about four times as great as that for whites. In the age group 25 to 34 years, however, the ratio for Negroes is less than three times that for whites, and in the age group 35 to 44 years it is only about one and one-half times as great, while after the age of 44 it is below that for whites.

In the case of the Negroes the ratio of commitments reaches its maximum in the age group 21 to 24 years, while in the case of the whites the maximum falls in the age group 35 to 44 years.

Table 16 shows separately for the whites and the Negroes the number and ratio of commitments, by age groups, in the South and in the North. Although totals are given for the West also, the figures are not given by age because of the small number of Negroes in that section.

The table shows that in every age group, both in the North and in the South, the ratio of commitments is higher for Negroes than for whites, the contrast between the two races in this respect being greater in the North than in the South.

In both sections the contrast between the whites and the Negroes as regards the ratio of commitments is most pronounced between the ages of 15 and 25, and becomes less marked in each older group up to the age of 65. This results from the fact that the ratio for Negroes declines rapidly after the age of 25, while that for whites in the South declines more slowly and in the North increases up to the age of 45.

Both in the North and in the South the ratio for Negroes reaches its maximum in the age group "21 to 24 years." The ratio for whites in the South also reaches its maximum in this age group, but is almost as high in the next two older groups ("25 to 34 years" and "35 to 44 years"); in the North, as already noted, it increases up to the age of 45, the maximum falling in the group "35 to 44 years."

Although for the United States as a whole (see Table 15), the ratio of commitments in each age group above 45 is smaller for Negroes than for whites, Table 16 shows that this is not the case in either the South or the North. This is another instance of the effect which the difference in the geographic distribution of the two races has upon the totals for the United States. Since 89 per cent of the Negroes live in the South as compared with 25 per cent of the whites, the influence which the low ratios generally prevailing in the South have upon the United States totals is greater for Negroes than for whites, and this explains why the ratio of commitments above the age of 45 is lower for Negroes than that for whites in the United States as a

whole, although it is not so in either the North or the South.

Table 16	PRISONERS AND JUVENILE DELINQUENTS COMMITTED IN 1910.				
	Number.		Ratio of commitments.[1]		
AGE.	Negro.	White.	Negro.	White.	Coefficient of difference.
			A	B	A÷B
UNITED STATES.					
All ages	108,268	382,052	1,101.7	467.4	2.4
Under 15 years	2,104	7,515	57.4	29.2	2.0
15 to 17 years	5,289	10,457	831.9	221.7	3.8
18 to 20 years	12,375	23,080	1,932.9	472.8	4.1
21 to 24 years	20,834	42,885	2,555.8	674.7	3.8
25 to 34 years	31,380	97,424	2,025.4	720.4	2.8
35 to 44 years	13,685	84,630	1,256.8	805.1	1.6
45 to 54 years	4,411	51,457	619.5	675.6	0.9
55 to 64 years	1,310	20,949	330.7	452.1	0.7
65 years and over	506	7,152	172.0	196.5	0.9
Age not reported	16,374	36,503	....	....	....
THE SOUTH.					
All ages	77,022	53,023	880.3	258.1	3.4
Under 15 years	1,382	975	40.5	12.6	3.2
15 to 17 years	3,999	1,823	682.9	139.1	4.9
18 to 20 years	9,381	3,613	1,619.6	287.9	5.6
21 to 24 years	14,636	6,192	2,040.0	399.8	5.1
25 to 34 years	20,356	12,191	1,557.2	395.6	3.9
35 to 44 years	8,342	8,599	916.7	383.9	2.4
45 to 54 years	2,632	4,408	433.0	276.5	1.6
55 to 64 years	799	1,767	232.3	170.8	1.4
65 years and over	272	541	106.0	74.7	1.4
Age not reported	15,223	12,914	....	....	....
THE NORTH.					
All ages	29,145	274,941	2,836.0	503.2	5.6
Under 15 years	693	6,059	287.8	37.4	7.7
15 to 17 years	1,233	7,794	2,557.6	253.5	10.1
18 to 20 years	2,816	16,778	4,812.7	514.6	9.4
21 to 24 years	5,810	30,528	6,225.4	715.6	8.7
25 to 34 years	10,262	71,108	4,472.8	774.6	5.8
35 to 44 years	4,987	66,146	2,950.0	904.0	3.3
45 to 54 years	1,653	41,809	1,680.9	780.7	2.2
55 to 64 years	477	17,169	959.0	530.4	1.8
65 years and over	213	5,947	592.1	223.8	2.6
Age not reported	1,001	11,603	....	....	....
THE WEST.					
All ages	1,858	53,379	3,667.4	815.7	4.5
UNITED STATES PENITENTIARIES.					
All ages	243	709	....	....	....

[1] Number committed per 100,000 population of the same race and age.

The coefficient of difference between the North and South as regards the ratio of commitments per 100,000 of whites and Negroes, respectively, is shown by age groups in Table 17.

This table further emphasizes the fact, brought out by the preceding table, that the excess of the ratio of commitments for the North over that for the South is in every age group greater in the case of the Negroes than in that of the whites. This is probably because the Negroes in the North, as already stated, are concentrated in the cities to a much greater extent than the whites, while there is little difference in the distribution of the two races in the South. In the case of both whites and Negroes the difference between the two sections is greatest in the age groups under 15 and over 45. The coefficient of difference for Negroes is fairly uniform between the ages of 18 and 45; while that for the whites is uniform between the ages of 15 and 25, after which it increases regularly up to the age group "55 to 64 years," remaining practically stationary in the final group.

Table 17

AGE.	RATIO OF COMMITMENTS.[1]					
	Negro.			White.		
	In the South.	In the North.	Coefficient of difference.	In the South.	In the North.	Coefficient of difference.
	A	B	B÷A	A	B	B÷A
All ages.	880.3	2,836.0	3.2	258.1	503.2	1.9
Under 15 years.	40.5	287.8	7.1	12.6	37.4	3.0
15 to 17 years.	682.9	2,557.6	3.7	139.1	253.5	1.8
18 to 20 years.	1,619.6	4,812.7	3.0	287.9	514.6	1.8
21 to 24 years.	2,040.0	6,225.4	3.1	399.8	715.6	1.8
25 to 34 years.	1,557.2	4,472.8	2.9	395.6	774.6	2.0
35 to 44 years.	916.7	2,950.0	3.2	383.9	904.0	2.4
45 to 54 years.	433.0	1,680.9	3.9	276.5	780.7	2.8
55 to 64 years.	232.3	959.0	4.1	170.8	530.4	3.1
65 years and over.	106.0	592.1	5.6	74.7	223.8	3.0

[1] Number of prisoners and juvenile delinquents committed in 1910 per 100,000 population of the same race and age.

SEX.

The following table shows the number of Negro and of white prisoners and juvenile delinquents of each sex enumerated on January 1, 1910, and also the number committed during the year:

Table 18

SEX.	PRISONERS AND JUVENILE DELINQUENTS: 1910.					
	Enumerated January 1.			Committed during the year.		
	Total.	Negro.	White.	Total.	Negro.	White.
	NUMBER.					
Both sexes.	136,472	41,729	93,841	493,934	108,268	382,052
Male.	124,424	38,346	85,218	445,368	87,598	354,367
Female.	12,048	3,383	8,623	48,566	20,670	27,685
	PER CENT DISTRIBUTION BY SEX.					
Both sexes.	100.0	100.0	100.0	100.0	100.0	100.0
Male.	91.2	91.1	90.8	90.2	80.9	92.8
Female.	8.8	8.1	9.2	9.8	19.1	7.2
	PER CENT DISTRIBUTION BY RACE.					
Both sexes.	100.0	30.6	68.8	100.0	21.9	77.3
Male.	100.0	30.8	68.5	100.0	19.7	79.6
Female.	100.0	28.1	71.6	100.0	42.6	57.0

In the case of Negroes 19.1 per cent, and in the case of whites 7.2 per cent, of the prisoners and juvenile delinquents committed in the year 1910 were females. Among Negroes, therefore, the ratio of male to female offenders was approximately 4 to 1, the corresponding

ratio for whites being 13 to 1. In this respect the sex contrast is accordingly much greater for the whites than for the Negroes. It follows as a corollary that the proportion of Negroes is greater among females committed than among males; in fact, 42,6 per cent of the total number of female prisoners and juvenile delinquents committed in 1910 were Negroes, as compared with 19.7 per cent of the total number of male offenders.

In the prison and jail population (prisoners and juvenile delinquents enumerated on January 1), as compared with the commitments, the contrasts are not as great as regards either the percentages of females in the totals for each race or the percentage of Negroes in the totals for each sex. Moreover, the percentage of females was larger for whites (9.2) than for Negroes (8.1) and the percentage of Negroes was larger among males (30.8) than among females (28.1). These differences between the prison population and the prison commitments as regards race and sex distribution are probably the outcome of variations in the average term of imprisonment, the figures indicating that the average is greater for Negro males than for white, and at the same time greater for white females than for Negro. The differences in this average are in turn presumably determined largely by differences in the nature and gravity of the offenses for which the different sex and race classes were committed, the figures indicating the probability that in the case of males the proportion of major offenders was greater among Negroes than among whites, and that in the case of the females the difference was the other way, the proportion being probably smaller for Negroes than for whites.

It may be noted, however, that while the classification by offense bears out this inference as regards males it does not make the situation altogether certain as regards females. Other factors, however, may influence the duration of imprisonment, as for instance, the relative number committed to reformatories, which is considerably larger for white females than for Negro.

Table 19 shows the ratio of commitments per 100,000 population for males and females of the white and the Negro race separately.

Table 19

SEX.	PRISONERS AND JUVENILE DELINQUENTS COMMITTED IN 1910.				
	Number.		Ratio of commitments.[1]		
	Negro.	White.	Negro.	White.	Coefficient of difference.
			A	B	A÷B
Both sexes.	108,268	382,052	1,101.7	467.4	2.4
Male.	87,598	354,367	1,792.9	840.2	2.1
Female.	20,670	27,685	418.3	70.0	6.0

[1] Number committed per 100,000 population of the same race and sex.

The contrast between the races as regards the ratio of commitments per 100,000 population was much greater for the female sex than for the male, the ratio for females of the Negro race (418.3 per 100,000) being almost six times the corresponding ratio (70 per 100,000) for females of the white race, while in the case of males the one ratio was hardly more than twice as great as the other (1,792.9 per 100,000 for Negro males, as against 840.2 for white males).

It may be noted that a tabulation by geographic divisions shows that in every division the percentage of Negroes was much larger among the female offenders committed than among the male. In the North 21.9 per cent, or more than one-fifth, of the female offenders were Negroes, as compared with 8.3 per cent of the male offenders; in the South the percentage Negro was 82.1 among female offenders and 55.5 among male offenders. For every geographic division also as well as for the United States as a whole, the difference between the races as regards the ratio of commitments to penal or reformatory institutions was much greater for the female than for the male sex. Thus in the North the coefficient of difference between Negroes and whites was 4.9 for males and 14.7 for females, which means that while Negro males in proportion to their numbers are committed about five times as often as white males, Negro females are committed about fifteen times as often as white females. In the South these coefficients were respectively 3.1 and 10.5. In some of the geographic divisions the contrast is still more striking.

SEX AND OFFENSE.

In Table 20 the prisoners and juvenile delinquents, total and Negro, committed in 1910 are classified by sex and offense.

Table 20 — PRISONERS AND JUVENILE DELINQUENTS COMMITTED IN 1910.

OFFENSE.	Total.		Negro.			
			Number.		Percentage.	
	Male.	Female.	Male.	Female.	Among males.	Among females.
All offenses........	445,368	48,566	87,598	20,670	19.7	42.6
Grave homicide.........	944	23	526	16	55.7	(1)
Lesser homicide.........	1,825	110	869	80	47.6	72.7
Assault.................	21,201	1,469	8,145	1,179	38.4	80.3
Robbery................	1,691	37	544	31	32.2	(1)
Burglary...............	8,847	75	2,673	52	30.2	(1)
Larceny................	40,246	2,470	12,146	1,445	30.2	58.5
Fraud..................	8,858	78	1,461	23	16.5	(1)
Forgery................	2,121	35	302	13	14.2	(1)
Rape...................	1,480	......	380	......	25.7	......
Prostitution and fornication.	1,976	4,474	477	1,689	24.1	37.8
Drunkenness and disorderly conduct.........	234,343	28,562	30,713	11,047	13.1	38.7
Vagrancy..............	46,560	3,742	6,651	1,605	14.3	42.9
Violating liquor laws....	7,219	494	2,197	261	30.4	52.8
Malicious mischief and trespass................	9,962	183	2,034	102	20.9	55.7
Offenses peculiar to children..................	6,260	1,543	606	233	9.7	15.1
Offense ill-defined or not reported...............	7,363	546	1,899	330	25.8	60.4
All others..............	44,472	4,725	15,925	2,564	35.8	54.3

[1] Per cent not shown where base is less than 100.

Among the male offenders as classified by offense the percentage of Negroes reaches its maximum in the group convicted of grave homicide, 526, or 55.7 per cent, of the 944 males committed for this offense being of the Negro race. The next highest percentage of Negroes was that for lesser homicide (47.6), followed by that for assault (38.4). Relatively low percentages are shown for drunkenness and disorderly conduct (13.1), vagrancy (14.3), and forgery (14.2). The lowest percentage is that for offenses peculiar to children (9.7).

Of the 110 females committed for lesser homicide, 80, or 72.7 per cent, were Negroes, and the proportion was about the same in the case of grave homicide, although the percentage is not given in the above table. The percentage of Negroes was still higher among females committed for assault, being 80.3. For larceny it was 58.5. For prostitution and fornication the percentage of Negroes among female offenders was 37.8, which is the lowest percentage shown in the above table, with the exception of that for the group of offenses peculiar to children.

Table 21 gives the ratio of commitments by offense for white and Negro males and females.

Table 21 — RATIO OF COMMITMENT.[1]

OFFENSE.	Male.		Female.		Coefficient of difference.	
	Negro.	White.	Negro.	White.	Male.	Female.
	A.	B.	C.	D.	A÷B.	C÷D.
All offenses.................	1,792.9	840.2	418.3	70.0	2.1	6.0
Grave homicide..............	10.8	1.0	0.3	(2)	11.3	18.3
Lesser homicide.............	17.8	2.2	1.6	0.1	8.1	21.3
Assault.....................	166.7	30.5	23.9	0.7	5.5	32.9
Robbery....................	11.1	2.7	0.6	(2)	4.1	41.4
Burglary...................	54.7	14.6	1.1	0.1	3.7	18.1
Larceny....................	248.6	66.2	29.2	2.6	3.8	11.4
Fraud......................	29.9	17.5	0.5	0.1	1.7	3.3
Forgery....................	6.2	4.3	0.3	0.1	1.4	4.7
Rape.......................	7.8	2.6	......	......	2.2	......
Prostitution and fornication.	9.8	3.5	34.2	7.0	3.2	4.6
Drunkenness and disorderly conduct....................	628.6	477.7	223.5	44.0	1.3	5.1
Vagrancy..................	136.1	94.4	32.5	5.4	1.4	6.0
Violating liquor laws........	45.0	11.4	5.3	0.6	3.9	9.2
Malicious mischief and trespass.	42.7	18.7	2.1	0.2	2.3	10.3
Offenses peculiar to children.	12.4	13.4	4.7	3.3	0.9	1.4
Offense ill-defined or not reported.	38.9	12.8	6.7	0.5	3.0	12.4
All others..................	325.9	66.9	51.9	5.3	4.9	10.0

[1] Number of prisoners and juvenile delinquents committed in 1910 per 100,000 population of the same race and sex.
[2] Less than one-tenth of 1 per 100,000.

For every class of offenses distinguished in the above table, except that of offenses peculiar to children, the ratio of commitments is higher for Negroes than for whites of the same sex, the difference being always greater for females than for males. For some offenses, however, the number of females committed is so small (see Table 20) that one may hesitate to attach much significance to the exact difference in the relative numbers committed as indicated by the ratios. But it is probably significant that in proportion to their numbers 11 times as many Negro women as white were committed for larceny and about 33 times as many for assault. In the case of prostitution and fornication, and of drunkenness and disorderly conduct the difference is not as great, the commitments for these offenses being proportionately about 5 times as frequent among Negro females as among white.

SEX AND AGE.

Table 22 gives the ratio of commitments per 100,000 Negro and per 100,000 white population, by sex and age.

Table 22	RATIO OF COMMITMENTS.					
	Males.		Females.		Coefficient of difference.	
AGE.	Negro.	White.	Negro.	White.	Among males.	Among females.
	A	B	C	D	A÷B	C÷D
All ages..............	1,792.9	840.2	418.3	70.0	2.1	6.0
Under 10 years..............	8.4	4.6	0.6	0.4	1.8	1.3
10 years....................	86.3	68.4	6.7	4.4	1.3	1.5
11 years....................	165.9	104.6	15.3	6.2	1.6	2.5
12 years....................	256.0	155.4	21.5	12.8	1.6	1.7
13 years....................	390.1	219.5	74.3	23.1	1.8	3.2
14 years....................	584.7	240.7	121.3	47.4	2.4	2.6
15 years....................	889.9	288.1	209.2	61.4	3.1	3.4
16 years....................	1,360.2	325.1	307.5	53.6	4.2	5.7
17 years....................	1,865.5	540.9	462.1	53.4	3.4	8.7
18 years....................	2,747.5	806.4	695.2	46.8	3.4	14.9
19 years....................	3,474.1	970.3	919.4	62.0	3.6	14.8
20 years....................	3,493.2	904.0	986.8	61.8	3.9	16.0
21 to 24 years.............	4,121.8	1,218.9	1,121.7	98.2	3.4	11.4
25 to 34 years.............	3,369.4	1,268.7	751.4	116.3	2.7	6.5
35 to 44 years.............	2,139.9	1,392.0	355.1	145.8	1.5	2.4
45 to 54 years.............	1,040.0	1,179.3	140.1	95.2	0.9	1.5
55 to 64 years.............	555.9	815.0	60.0	48.2	0.7	1.2
65 years and over..........	310.2	365.7	23.3	26.3	0.8	0.9

For the Negroes of each sex the ratio of commitments reached its maximum in the age group "21 to 24 years," while for whites of each sex the maximum falls in the age group "35 to 44 years."

In practically every age group the difference between the races as regards the ratio of commitments is more pronounced for females than for males; but the contrast is greatest in the ages from 18 to 24, inclusive, when the ratio for Negro males is between 3 and 4 times as great as that for white males, while the ratio for Negro females is from 11 to 16 times that for white females.

Tabulations by geographic sections show that in every age group the ratio of commitments for either sex of either race is considerably higher in the North than it is for the same sex and race in the South. In the North as well as in the South the ratio of commitments for the Negroes of either sex reaches its maximum in the age group "21 to 24 years" and diminishes steadily in each older age group. This statement is true also of the ratio for the whites in the South; but in the North the ratio for the whites reaches the maximum in the age group "35 to 44 years." In every age group, both in the North and in the South, the ratio of commitments is higher for the Negroes of either sex than for the whites of the same sex, and the radical difference in this respect is always greater for the female sex than for the male. Generally, moreover, the racial difference is greater in the North than in the South, exceptions occurring only in the case of females within the age groups "45 to 54 years" and "55 to 64 years." The totals for the entire United States, presented in Table 22, show that above the age of 45, the ratio of commitments was smaller for Negro males than for white males; but this is not the case in either the North or the South considered separately.

SECTION II.—INSANE AND FEEBLE-MINDED.[1]

NUMBER AND RATIO OF INSANE.

Statistics relative to the insane in institutions for 1910 were obtained by means of a special census covering insane inmates present in institutions for the insane on January 1, 1910 and insane persons admitted to such institutions during the calendar year 1910. The canvass was made through the agency of officials or other persons connected with the institutions who were commissioned as special agents of the Bureau of the Census.

The number of institutions canvassed was 366, and the number of insane for whom data were obtained, 248,560, of whom 187,791 were present in institutions on January 1 and 60,769 were admitted during the year.

[1] For a full presentation of statistics relating to the insane and the feeble-minded, see report of the Bureau of the Census (217 pages) on the Insane and Feeble-minded in Institutions: 1910.

Table 23 classifies the insane enumerated on January 1 and the number admitted during the year, by race in comparison with the total population.

Table 23	INSANE IN HOSPITALS: 1910.				PERCENTAGE DISTRIBUTION: 1910.		
	Number.		Per 100,000 population of specified racial class.		Insane in hospitals.		Total population.
RACIAL CLASS.	Enumerated on January 1.	Admitted during the year.	Enumerated on January 1.	Admitted during the year.	Enumerated on January 1.	Admitted during the year.	
All classes.......	187,791	60,769	204.2	66.1	100.0	100.0	100.0
Negro..............	12,910	4,384	131.4	44.6	6.9	7.2	10.7
White..............	174,224	56,182	213.2	68.7	92.8	92.5	88.9
Indian.............	166	51	62.5	19.2	0.1	0.1	0.3
Other..............	491	152	334.3	103.5	0.3	0.3	0.2

The 187,791 insane in hospitals enumerated on January 1 included 12,910 Negroes, and the 60,769 insane admitted to hospitals during the year included 4,384 Negroes. Negroes thus constituted 6.9 per cent of the insane enumerated at the beginning of the year and 7.2 per cent of the insane admitted during the year. The percentage Negro among the insane was accordingly very considerably below the percentage Negro (10.7) in the general population.

For Negroes the ratio of inmates present on January 1 per 100,000 Negro population was 131.4, the corresponding figure for whites being 213.2. The ratio of admissions per 100,000 population was 44.6 for Negroes and 68.7 for whites.

These ratios did not, however, obtain with any degree of uniformity in the several geographic divisions and states. Outside the South, as is shown in Table 24, the ratios for Negroes were in fact higher than those for whites in each division. In New England, for instance, the ratio per 100,000 population for inmates enumerated on January 1 was 473.6 among Negroes and 296.9 among whites, the corresponding figures for admissions being 153.8 for Negroes and 105.9 for whites.

Central division, 95.6 for Negroes and 125.5 for whites; and in the West South Central, 77.2 for Negroes and 101.4 for whites.

In several Southern states, however, as in the North, higher ratios are shown for Negroes than for whites.

Definite conclusions as to the relative prevalence of insanity among Negroes and whites in the several sections of the country are not warranted by these data. It is quite improbable that there is any variation in the prevalence of insanity among the adult population from state to state, or from division to division, such as seems indicated by the figures given in Table 25. The difference in the relative numbers admitted to asylums for the insane may be influenced by the geographic distribution of the two races, by differences, sectional or racial, in practice as regards taking steps to have the insane placed under institutional care or restraint, and by relative sufficiency of the provisions made for caring for the insane of each race. What the effect of such factors may be it is impossible to determine, but they certainly account largely for the differences which have been noted.

SEX.

Table 25 classifies the insane of each racial class, by sex, and gives for each class the sex ratios among the insane and in the general population.

Table 24

DIVISION AND STATE.	INSANE IN HOSPITALS PER 100,000 POPULATION OF SPECIFIED RACIAL CLASS: 1910.			
	Enumerated on January 1.		Admitted during year.	
	Negro.	White.	Negro.	White.
UNITED STATES	131.4	213.2	44.6	68.7
THE SOUTH.				
South Atlantic	129.1	181.3	46.2	59.7
Delaware	282.2	206.3	73.8	60.8
Maryland	177.8	264.2	55.5	107.6
District of Columbia	686.1	946.5	158.8	188.0
Virginia	199.7	165.1	67.5	56.2
West Virginia	169.9	139.3	49.9	40.0
North Carolina	99.4	121.8	33.8	45.3
South Carolina	77.6	131.3	39.5	46.5
Georgia	83.2	150.4	33.5	50.1
Florida	125.7	103.7	49.6	38.8
East South Central	95.6	125.5	35.8	47.5
Kentucky	217.8	146.4	66.1	52.0
Tennessee	99.8	101.1	54.1	39.5
Alabama	74.1	111.2	27.2	47.5
Mississippi	81.4	146.9	27.1	53.2
West South Central	77.2	101.4	17.3	38.8
Arkansas	34.1	83.2	7.5	19.6
Louisiana	98.8	154.3	17.5	38.9
Oklahoma	93.0	65.6	34.9	47.2
Texas	79.3	108.4	19.9	41.8
THE NORTH.				
New England	473.6	296.9	153.8	105.9
Middle Atlantic	363.7	269.1	105.1	75.3
East North Central	322.4	224.5	101.1	71.8
West North Central	238.6	194.1	107.1	63.3
THE WEST.				
Mountain	265.5	137.6	135.1	62.6
Pacific	322.0	242.4	195.2	82.7

In each southern division, as in the United States as a whole, lower ratios are shown for Negroes than for whites. In the South Atlantic division the ratio for inmates enumerated on January 1 was 129.1 among Negroes and 181.3 among whites; in the East South

Table 25

RACIAL CLASS.	INSANE IN HOSPITALS: 1910.				MALES TO 1,000 FEMALES: 1910.		
	Enumerated on January 1.		Admitted during the year.		Insane in hospitals.		Total population.
	Male.	Female.	Male.	Female.	Enumerated on January 1.	Admitted during the year.	
All classes	98,695	89,096	34,116	26,653	1,108	1,280	1,060
Negro	6,536	6,374	2,304	2,080	1,025	1,108	989
White	91,617	82,607	31,646	24,536	1,109	1,290	1,066
Indian	90	76	32	19	(1)	(1)	1,035
Other	452	39	134	18	(1)	(1)	9,608

[1] Ratio not shown, the number of females being less than 100.

For each racial class the proportion of males was higher among the insane than it was in the general population, and among the insane, as in the general population, the proportion was lower for Negroes than for whites.

Table 26 gives, by geographic divisions, the ratio of insane in hospitals per 100,000 population among Negroes, native whites, and foreign-born whites, classified by sex. In each of the nine divisions, with exception of the East South Central, the ratio of Negro insane admitted to hospitals during the year per 100,000 population was higher for males than for females. In each southern division the ratios among both males and females were lower for Negroes than for whites, and in each northern and western division were higher for Negroes than for whites.

Table 26

DIVISION AND SEX.	INSANE IN HOSPITALS PER 100,000 POPULATION OF SPECIFIED RACIAL CLASS AND SEX: 1910.					
	Enumerated on January 1.			Admitted during the year.		
	Negro.	Native white.	Foreign-born white.	Negro.	Native white.	Foreign-born white.
UNITED STATES.						
Male	133.8	175.0	377.7	47.2	64.0	117.5
Female	129.0	162.3	441.1	42.1	51.7	114.8
THE SOUTH.						
South Atlantic:						
Male	128.9	166.4	579.0	49.0	63.1	131.3
Female	129.2	162.7	402.8	43.5	50.3	106.2
East South Central:						
Male	93.4	122.5	334.4	35.6	53.3	108.8
Female	97.9	120.8	311.2	36.1	39.5	82.6
West South Central:						
Male	74.6	90.6	216.5	18.0	38.1	69.1
Female	79.7	92.4	192.4	16.6	34.6	61.6
THE NORTH.						
New England:						
Male	485.0	280.3	313.6	161.7	100.7	132.0
Female	462.4	251.0	420.7	146.2	86.8	136.9
Middle Atlantic:						
Male	384.3	222.7	343.2	111.6	68.4	106.3
Female	344.2	207.1	494.7	98.9	55.3	120.1
East North Central:						
Male	364.4	183.4	387.7	118.9	68.3	116.9
Female	277.0	166.3	407.3	81.7	55.4	100.3
West North Central:						
Male	274.9	.155.7	436.6	112.8	56.6	108.6
Female	199.5	137.6	450.0	101.0	47.3	114.3
THE WEST.						
Mountain:						
Male	272.0	102.9	347.2	136.0	60.9	135.7
Female	257.7	77.9	284.3	134.0	33.4	84.2
Pacific:						
Male	370.0	178.0	532.8	238.3	72.4	167.8
Female	264.2	142.0	471.3	143.4	47.4	125.0

AGE.

Table 27 gives, by age periods, the number of Negroes and of whites admitted to hospitals for the insane in the country as a whole, in the South, and in the North, with ratios per 100,000 population.

Table 27

AGE.	INSANE ADMITTED TO HOSPITALS: 1910.					
	United States.		The South.		The North.	
	Negro.	White.	Negro.	White.	Negro.	White.
	NUMBER.					
All ages	4,384	56,182	3,193	10,161	1,105	41,118
Under 15 years	54	272	41	114	12	140
15 to 19 years	320	2,215	263	507	56	1,552
20 to 24 years	579	5,101	439	1,079	130	3,619
25 to 29 years	601	6,394	422	1,246	167	4,561
30 to 34 years	568	6,696	425	1,275	133	4,776
35 to 39 years	529	6,945	376	1,258	143	5,059
40 to 44 years	388	6,046	271	962	105	4,504
45 to 49 years	316	5,349	221	837	87	4,050
50 to 54 years	253	4,609	180	769	67	3,449
55 to 59 years	150	3,208	108	528	39	2,450
60 to 64 years	163	2,706	111	473	49	1,983
65 years and over	348	5,807	252	932	90	4,423
Age unknown	115	834	84	181	27	552
	PER 100,000 POPULATION OF SPECIFIED AGE AND RACIAL CLASS.					
All ages	44.6	68.7	36.5	49.5	107.5	75.3
Under 15 years	1.5	1.1	1.2	1.5	5.0	0.9
15 to 19 years	30.2	27.8	27.1	23.5	65.0	29.6
20 to 24 years	56.2	63.9	48.2	55.2	114.1	67.5
25 to 29 years	68.2	88.1	56.3	74.6	133.8	92.9
30 to 34 years	85.0	106.8	76.2	90.3	127.2	111.9
35 to 39 years	79.7	121.2	71.0	99.2	145.7	128.2
40 to 44 years	85.2	126.5	71.3	99.0	148.1	133.6
45 to 49 years	81.9	131.7	67.5	102.6	158.2	140.6
50 to 54 years	77.6	129.6	64.2	98.7	154.6	139.3
55 to 59 years	71.6	125.1	60.0	92.3	137.8	136.7
60 to 64 years	87.4	130.8	67.7	102.2	228.6	137.2
65 years and over	118.3	159.5	98.2	128.6	250.2	166.4

The effect of age upon the ratios for Negroes and for whites in the South and in the North is illustrated in the accompanying diagram.

DIAGRAM I.—RATIO OF NEGRO AND WHITE INSANE ADMITTED TO HOSPITALS IN THE NORTH AND IN THE SOUTH PER 100,000 POPULATION OF THE SAME AGE AND RACE.

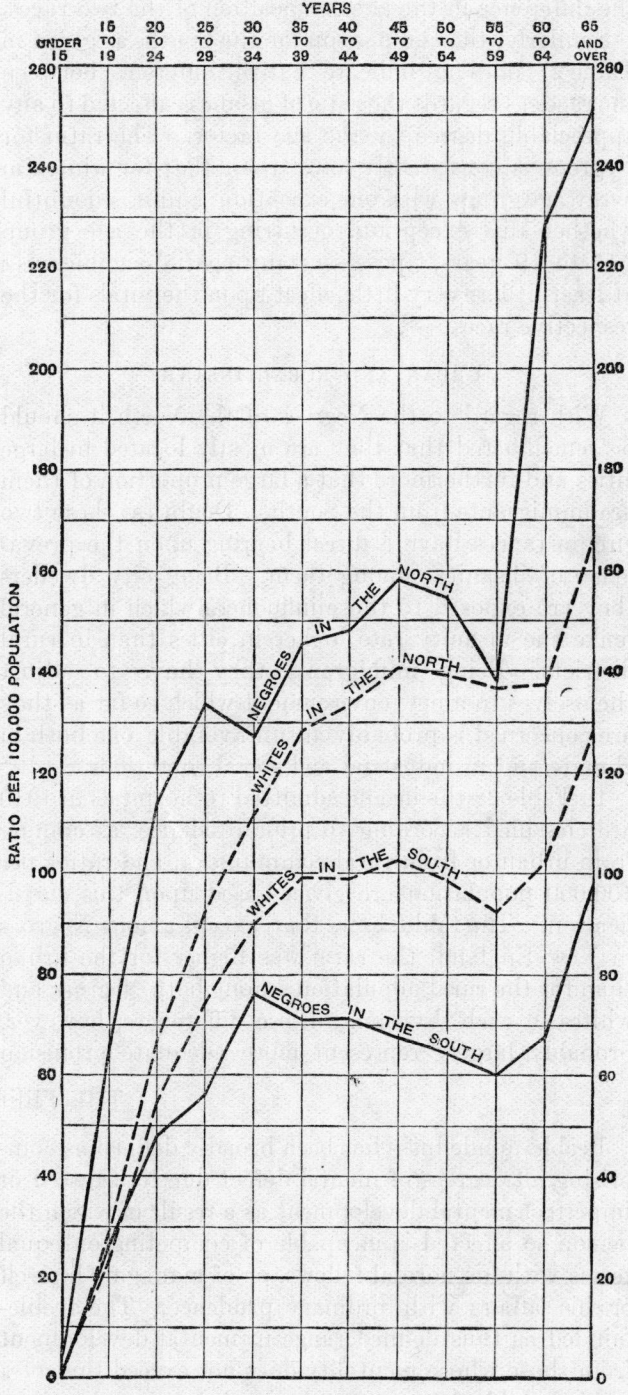

In the North the ratio of admissions was higher for Negroes than for whites in every age group, although in one group, "55 to 59 years," the ratio was practically identical. Too much significance, however, should not be attached to minor variations between the different groups, for the reason that in the North the number of Negroes in the older groups is so small that a small change in the number committed from any one group would have a considerable effect upon the ratio. The comparison is of value mainly as indicating that in the North the higher ratio of admissions for Negroes as compared with whites is not explainable by the difference in the age composition of the two races.

Similarly, the comparison for the South, as given in Table 27, does not indicate that the difference between the races as regards the ratio of insane is affected to any appreciable degree by the age factor. The ratio for Negroes is consistently lower than that for whites in every age group, with one exception, and it is doubtful whether this exception, occurring in the age group "15 to 19 years," possesses any special significance; at least, it has very little effect upon the totals for the respective races.

URBAN AND RURAL INSANE.

With regard to the Negroes of the North it should be remembered that they are mostly located in large cities and furthermore that a large proportion of them are immigrants from the South. Doubtless these two circumstances have a direct bearing upon the prevalence of insanity among them. Being city dwellers they are exposed to those influences which in general make the insanity rate higher in cities than in rural districts. Being immigrants they have to adjust themselves to a new environment which so far as they are concerned is probably an unfavorable one both in climate and in industrial and social conditions.

In Table 28 the insane admitted to hospitals in 1910 are classified according to prior residence, as coming from urban or from rural communities, and ratios per 100,000 population are given based upon this classification. The table shows that, except among Negroes in New England, the ratio was higher for the urban than for the rural population among both Negroes and whites in each division. These differences, however, probably largely represent more adequate provision for the insane in urban communities as compared with rural, and can not be taken as indicating accurately the effect of urban conditions as factors conducing to insanity.

Table 28	INSANE ADMITTED TO HOSPITALS: 1910.				
	Number.			Per 100,000 population of specified racial class.	
DIVISION AND RACIAL CLASS.	From urban communities.	From rural communities.	Prior residence unknown.	From urban communities.	From rural communities.
UNITED STATES	36,654	20,442	3,673	86.0	41.4
Negro	2,098	1,923	363	78.0	26.9
White	34,450	18,454	3,278	86.5	44.0
THE SOUTH.					
South Atlantic	2,968	3,040	717	96.0	33.4
Negro	784	1,017	99	86.2	31.8
White	2,183	2,023	614	100.1	34.3
East South Central	1,058	2,264	363	67.2	33.1
Negro	242	537	171	47.5	25.1
White	816	1,725	191	76.6	36.8
West South Central	1,096	1,758	114	56.0	25.8
Negro	117	197	29	26.8	12.7
White	975	1,549	85	64.3	29.8
THE NORTH.					
New England	5,804	1,009	173	106.4	91.9
Negro	90	10	2	147.8	184.2
White	5,692	999	171	105.6	91.6
Middle Atlantic	11,857	2,548	264	86.4	45.6
Negro	392	36	11	115.6	45.8
White	11,448	2,508	253	85.6	45.5
East North Central	8,132	4,608	451	84.6	53.4
Negro	246	49	9	106.7	69.7
White	7,874	4,553	440	83.9	53.3
West North Central	2,898	3,856	705	74.8	49.7
Negro	165	68	27	100.4	86.8
White	2,724	3,779	677	73.5	49.4
THE WEST.					
Mountain	924	549	150	97.5	32.6
Negro	25	3	1	161.9	49.8
White	897	531	149	97.0	33.3
Pacific	1,917	810	736	80.5	44.8
Negro	37	6	14	151.9	124.1
White	1,841	787	698	80.2	45.5

THE FEEBLE-MINDED.

Feeble-mindedness has been broadly defined as comprising all degrees of mental defect due to arrested or imperfect mental development as a result of which the person so affected is incapable of competing on equal terms with his normal fellows, or of managing himself or his affairs with ordinary prudence. The feeble-minded as thus defined range in mental development from those whose mentality does not exceed that of a normal child of 2 years to those whose mentality is as high as that of a child of 12. The great majority of the feeble-minded are not confined in institutions but live at large; many are inmates of prisons and reformatories; many others are in almshouses, and some are confined in hospitals for the insane. Only a small fraction of the feeble-minded are taken care of in special institutions designed for that class.

Table 29 classifies the feeble-minded in institutions in 1910, and gives ratios per 100,000 population.

Table 29	FEEBLE-MINDED IN INSTITUTIONS: 1910.				PERCENTAGE DISTRIBUTION: 1910.		
	Number.		Per 100,000 of specified racial class.		Feeble-minded.		
RACIAL CLASS.	Enumerated on January 1.	Admitted during the year.	Enumerated on January 1.	Admitted during the year.	Enumerated on January 1.	Admitted during the year.	Total population.
All classes	20,731	3,825	22.5	4.2	100.0	100.0	100.0
Negro	280	85	2.8	0.9	1.4	2.2	10.7
White	20,441	3,737	25.0	4.6	98.6	97.7	88.9
Other	10	3	2.4	0.7	(1)	0.1	0.4

[1] Less than one-tenth of 1 per cent.

Of the 20,731 persons enumerated in institutions for the feeble-minded on January 1, 280 were Negroes; and of the 3,825 feeble-minded persons admitted to such institutions during the year 85 were Negroes. It will be apparent that the ratios shown in Table 29 are largely fictitious so far as regards the relative prevalence of feeble-mindedness among Negroes and whites—the relatively low ratio for Negroes being explained by the fact that approximately nine-tenths of that population were in the South, in which section there were few institutions established for the feeble-minded.

SECTION III.—THE BLIND.[1]

NUMBER AND RATIO.

Census data for the blind in 1910 were secured in part on the general population schedule which carried a column for reporting blindness, and in part on special schedules mailed to each person reported on the general schedule as blind.

Table 30 gives, by racial classes, the number returned as blind on the general schedule, with exception of persons erroneously so classified in the original returns, by the enumerators, and ascertained subsequently, upon return of the special schedule, to be not blind under the census definition of the term.

Table 30	POPULATION: 1910.				
RACIAL CLASS.	Number.		Distribution, per cent.		Blind per 100,000 of class specified.
	Total.	Blind.	Total.	Blind.	
All classes	91,972,266	57,272	100.0	100.0	62.3
Negro	9,827,763	8,849	10.7	15.5	90.0
White	81,731,957	47,585	88.9	83.1	58.2
Indian	265,683	804	0.3	1.4	302.6
Chinese, Japanese, and other	146,863	34	0.2	0.1	23.2

Of the 57,272 persons enumerated on the population schedule as blind in 1910, 8,849, or 15.5 per cent, were Negroes, the proportion Negro in the blind population exceeding the proportion Negro, of 10.7 per cent, in the general population. The number returned as blind per 100,000 Negro population was 90, the corresponding proportion for whites being 58.2 per 100,000. The ratio of blindness for Negroes was higher than that for whites, but lower than that for Indians. The relatively high ratio for Negroes is explained partially by the fact that the Negro population is largely resident in rural districts, where medical facilities are poor. In such communities diseases having blindness as a more or less frequent consequence may be left to run their course unchecked, and generally the country over; these diseases are probably less effectively combated among Negroes than among whites. As a natural consequence the ratio of blindness is higher for Negroes than for whites in each geographic division.

SEX.

Table 31 classifies the blind population in 1910, by racial class and sex.

Table 31	BLIND POPULATION: 1910.					
RACIAL CLASS.	Number.				Per 100,000.	
	Both sexes.	Male.	Female.	Males to 1,000 females.	Male.	Female.
All classes	57,272	32,443	24,829	1,307	68.5	55.6
Negro	8,849	4,971	3,878	1,282	101.7	78.5
White	47,585	26,994	20,591	1,311	64.0	52.1
Indian	804	451	353	1,278	333.7	270.4
Chinese, Japanese, and other	34	27	7	(1)	20.3	50.6

[1] Ratio not shown where number of females is less than 100.

In each racial class the proportion of males in the blind population exceeds the proportion in the general population of that class, the ratio per 100,000 population being higher for males than for females in each class. In the case both of males and of females the ratio for Negroes exceeds the ratio for whites, but is much lower than the ratio for Indians.

AGE.

The diagram on page 452 illustrates the difference between Negroes, native whites, and foreign-born whites in the ratio of blindness at each age, the ratio for Negroes exceeding the ratio for each of the white classes at each age.

Table 32 gives the age distribution of the blind population, classified by sex, race, and nativity.

---

[1] For a full presentation of statistics relating to the blind, see report (342 pages) on the Blind population of the United States: 1910, Bureau of the Census: 1917.

AGE DISTRIBUTION OF THE BLIND POPULATION, CLASSIFIED BY SEX, RACE, AND NATIVITY: 1910.

Table 32

AGE.	BLIND POPULATION: 1910. Number. All classes.	Negro.	Per 100,000 of age and class specified. Negro.	White. Total.	Native.	Foreign born.	AGE.	BLIND POPULATION: 1910. Number. All classes.	Negro.	Per 100,000 of age and class specified. Negro.	White. Total.	Native.	Foreign born.
	MALE.							FEMALE.					
Total............	32,443	4,971	101.7	64.0	61.1	77.3	Total............	24,829	3,878	78.5	52.1	48.8	70.8
Under 5 years........	298	34	5.4	5.5	5.5	3.9	Under 5 years........	253	23	3.6	4.9	4.9	5.9
Under 1 year.....	32	2	1.6	3.0	3.0	....	Under 1 year.....	38	4	3.2	3.4	3.4	....
1 to 4 years........	266	32	6.4	6.1	6.2	4.1	1 to 4 years........	215	19	3.7	5.3	5.3	6.3
5 to 9 years........	672	80	12.9	13.7	13.6	13.9	5 to 9 years........	576	85	13.5	11.6	11.8	6.8
10 to 14 years........	1,108	175	30.3	23.0	23.7	8.3	10 to 14 years........	889	121	21.0	19.4	19.7	13.6
15 to 19 years........	1,218	206	40.6	25.1	26.6	9.1	15 to 19 years........	982	158	28.6	20.4	21.7	5.6
20 to 24 years........	1,268	253	52.5	24.6	28.5	9.3	20 to 24 years........	985	192	35.0	20.0	22.2	7.9
25 to 29 years........	1,355	284	67.3	28.0	34.1	10.7	25 to 29 years........	892	181	39.4	20.2	23.7	5.8
30 to 34 years........	1,416	267	80.4	34.4	41.4	15.3	30 to 34 years........	875	153	45.5	23.8	27.2	10.9
35 to 39 years........	1,604	320	99.9	41.9	49.0	22.8	35 to 39 years........	926	176	56.2	27.3	31.8	11.2
40 to 44 years........	1,787	315	137.1	57.0	65.2	37.4	40 to 44 years........	1,010	149	66.0	37.7	43.1	21.0
45 to 49 years........	2,128	348	174.1	80.9	90.9	57.9	45 to 49 years........	1,197	206	110.8	51.3	58.5	30.6
50 to 54 years........	2,298	403	224.7	97.3	104.9	77.3	50 to 54 years........	1,450	230	156.8	73.5	80.5	51.7
55 to 59 years........	2,243	333	289.3	137.8	145.5	117.9	55 to 59 years........	1,452	205	216.9	102.6	111.8	76.6
60 to 64 years........	2,557	350	346.0	201.0	216.4	166.3	60 to 64 years........	1,926	283	331.6	162.2	176.9	127.5
65 to 69 years........	2,949	380	559.2	316.9	338.6	271.3	65 to 69 years........	2,162	260	467.7	246.6	266.1	202.6
70 to 74 years........	2,758	364	896.9	453.5	481.0	398.3	70 to 74 years........	2,353	304	794.7	393.4	404.0	370.9
75 to 79 years........	2,765	286	1,261.7	795.3	828.6	731.4	75 to 79 years........	2,343	280	1,311.4	648.7	665.7	613.8
80 to 84 years........	2,036	248	2,120.4	1,235.7	1,323.6	1,076.4	80 to 84 years........	2,093	293	2,110.5	1,152.3	1,232.6	991.6
85 years and over.....	1,917	305	3,184.0	2,385.0	2,589.1	2,015.8	85 years and over.....	2,389	554	4,411.2	2,267.5	2,357.8	2,077.7
Age not reported......	75	20	....	....	....	....	Age not reported......	76	25	....	....	....	....

DIAGRAM **II.**—NEGRO, NATIVE WHITE, AND FOREIGN-BORN WHITE BLIND POPULATION PER 100,000 GENERAL POPULATION OF THE SAME RACE, NATIVITY, AND AGE, BY 5-YEAR AGE GROUPS: 1910.

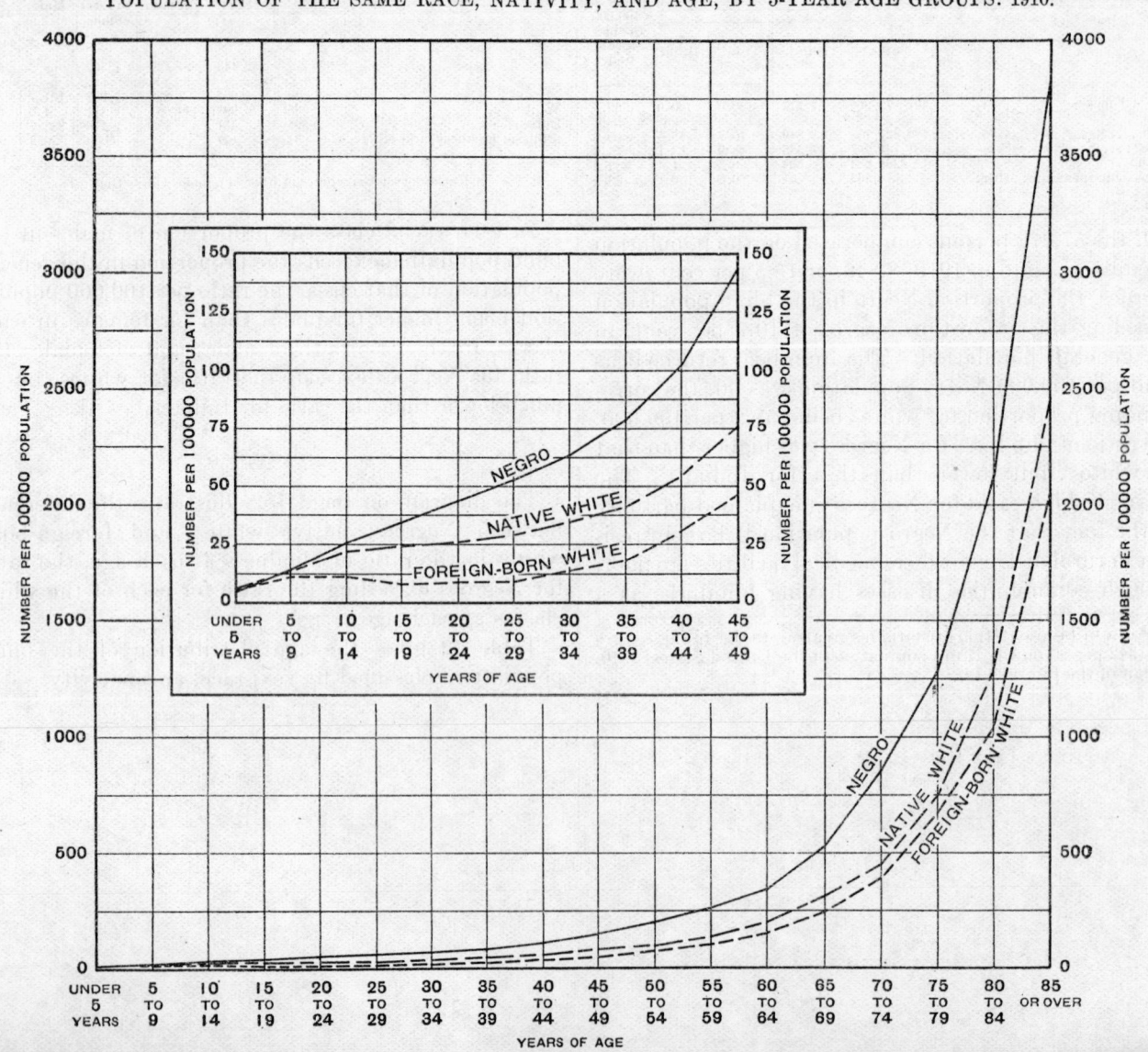

ABILITY TO READ RAISED TYPE.

Table 33 classifies the Negro and the white blind population 5 years of age and over, for whom special schedules were returned in 1910, with reference to ability to read raised type. Of the Negroes, 85 were able to read raised type per 1,000 reporting; and of the whites, 234, the difference being mainly due to a difference in the relative number who had attended a special school for the blind. Among Negro males the number able to read raised type, per 1,000 reporting, was 85 and among Negro females 86, the corresponding numbers for whites being 222 for males and 252 for females.

Table 33	BLIND POPULATION 5 YEARS OF AGE AND OVER FOR WHOM SPECIAL SCHEDULES WERE RETURNED: 1910.[1]				
RACIAL CLASS AND SEX.	Total.	Able to read raised type.	Unable to read raised type.	No report.	Number able to read raised type per 1,000 reporting.
Negro—Both sexes..........	3,604	300	3,224	80	85
Male..........	2,220	184	1,990	46	85
Female..........	1,384	116	1,234	34	86
White—Both sexes..........	25,184	5,735	18,722	727	234
Male..........	14,663	3,175	11,109	379	222
Female..........	10,521	2,560	7,613	348	252

[1] Includes the small number whose age was not reported.

Section IV.—DEAF-MUTES.[1]

NUMBER.

In connection with the Thirteenth Decennial Census a special schedule of inquiry was sent out to every person reported on the general population schedule as deaf and dumb. Upon these schedules data were secured relating to 19,153 deaf-mutes. In Table 34 these deaf-mutes are classified by race.

Table 34	DEAF-MUTES: 1910.		Percentage distribution of total population: 1910.
RACIAL CLASS.	Number.	Percentage distribution.	
All classes..........	19,153	100.0	100.0
Negro..........	1,069	5.6	10.7
White..........	18,016	94.1	88.9
Indian..........	66	0.3	0.3
Chinese and Japanese..........	2	(1)	0.2

[1] Less than one-tenth of 1 per cent.

The 1,069 Negro deaf-mutes constituted 5.6 per cent of the total number of deaf-mutes of all classes, the proportion Negro among deaf-mutes being approximately one-half the percentage Negro in the general population. This is probably to be accounted for in part at least by failure more frequently among Negroes than among whites to return the special schedules mailed out from the Census Office. It may be noted, however, that mortality returns tabulated by the Bureau of the Census indicate that the colored are less susceptible than whites to certain of the diseases which are important causes of adventitious deafness—such, for example, as measles, scarlet fever, and diphtheria. While the death rate from measles in 1914 was only slightly higher for whites than for Negroes, the death rate from diphtheria was nearly twice as great and that for scarlet fever was practi-

cally four times as great for whites as for Negroes. On the other hand, Negroes appear to be somewhat more susceptible to meningitis, another leading cause of deaf-mutism, than are whites.

Although in the South Atlantic and East South Central divisions Negroes formed in 1910 about one-third (33.7 and 31.5 per cent, respectively) of the total population, and in the West South Central division more than one-fifth (22.6 per cent), they contributed less than one-fifth (19.5 per cent) of the deaf and dumb population returning schedules in the South Atlantic division, less than one-sixth (15.2 per cent) of that in the East South Central, and less than one-tenth (9.8 per cent) of that in the West South Central. Since these differences seem entirely too large to be accounted for by the difference in the proportion of the respective races returning the special schedules, the figures rather confirm the supposition that deaf-mutism is less common among Negroes than among whites.

SEX DISTRIBUTION.

Table 35 classifies the deaf-mutes returning special schedules in 1910, by sex and race. Negroes as well as whites show an excess of males among deaf-mutes, although females are in excess in the Negro population as a whole.

Table 35	DEAF-MUTES: 1910.			MALES TO 1,000 FEMALES OF SPECIFIED RACIAL CLASS: 1910.	
RACIAL CLASS.	Both sexes.	Male.	Female.	Deaf-mutes.	Total population.
All classes..........	19,153	10,507	8,646	1,215	1,060
Negro..........	1,069	584	485	1,204	989
White..........	18,016	9,888	8,128	1,217	1 066
Other..........	68	35	33	(1)	1,857

[1] Ratio not shown, number of females being less than 100.

[1] For a full presentation of statistics relating to deaf-mutes, see report on Deaf-mutes in the United States: 1910, Bureau of the Census: 1918.

SCHOOL ATTENDANCE.

Table 36 classifies Negro and native white deaf-mutes with reference to school attendance and instruction.

Table 36 EDUCATION.	DEAF-MUTES 5 YEARS OF AGE AND OVER: 1910.			
	Number.		Percentage distribution.	
	Negro.	Native white.	Negro.	Native white.
Total.........................	1,061	15,889	....	....
No report as to education..........	16	186		
Number reporting.................	1,045	15,703	100.0	100.0
Had attended school...............	548	13,743	52.4	87.5
Special school for the deaf..........	528	13,459	50.5	85.7
Other school only................	20	284	1.9	1.8
Had not attended school...........	497	1,960	47.6	12.5
Private instruction at home...........	9	86	0.9	0.5
No instruction.....................	488	1,874	46.7	11.9

Of the 1,045 Negro deaf-mutes reporting as to school attendance, 548, or 52.4 per cent, reported that they had attended school, and of these 528, or 50.5 per cent of the total reporting, had attended a special school for the deaf; 497 had not attended school, and of these, 9 reported private instruction at home, and 448, or 46.7 per cent of the total, reported that they had received no instruction of any sort either in school or at home. Of the native white deaf-mutes, 87.5 per cent had attended school, and only 11.9 per cent reported that they had received no instruction of any kind.

MEANS OF COMMUNICATION.

In Table 37 the Negro and white deaf-mutes are classified with reference to their ability to use speech, writing, finger spelling, sign language, or miscellaneous methods of communication.

Table 37 MEANS OF COMMUNICATION.	DEAF-MUTES 10 YEARS OF AGE AND OVER: 1910.			
	Number.		Percentage distribution.	
	Negro.	White.	Negro.	White.
Total.....................	983	15,957	100.0	100.0
Able to use speech..................	119	4,056	12.1	25.4
Other means also..................	93	3,796	9.5	23.8
No other means...................	16	147	1.6	0.9
No report as to other means..........	10	113	1.0	0.7
Unable to use speech...............	850	11,850	86.5	74.3
Report other means...............	783	11,381	79.7	71.3
Report no means.................	11	87	1.1	0.5
No report as to other means.......	56	382	5.7	2.4
No report as to means.............	14	51	1.4	0.3
Number reporting:				
Speech.........................	109	3,943	11.1	24.7
Writing........................	400	12,489	40.7	78.3
Finger spelling.................	415	12,284	42.2	77.0
Sign language.................	388	12,281	39.5	77.0
Miscellaneous methods..........	387	1,470	39.4	9.2

Section V.—PAUPERS IN ALMSHOUSES.[1]

NUMBER AND PROPORTION OF ALMSHOUSE PAUPERS.

Recent census statistics relating to paupers are confined to inmates of almshouses. Recipients of outdoor relief are not enumerated, nor are any inmates of institutions other than almshouses. Such statistics are not, of course, presented as measuring the extent of poverty in different communities, since factors other than poverty largely determine the number of paupers in almshouses, such as, for example, the adequacy of the supply of almshouses, the prevailing policy in regard to outdoor relief, climatic conditions, the combination of free hospitals for the poor with almshouses, and the development of special institutions for children and for the physically and mentally defective.

Paupers enumerated in almshouses on January 1, 1910, numbered 84,198, of whom 6,281 were Negroes, and the number admitted to almshouses during the calendar year 1910 was 88,313, of whom 6,807 were Negroes.

For all classes combined and for each class shown separately in Table 38, the number of admissions during the year exceeded the number enumerated on January 1. It is apparent from the figures given that the almshouse population is characteristically transient.

Table 38 RACIAL CLASS.	PAUPERS IN ALMSHOUSES: 1910.				DISTRIBUTION PER CENT: 1910.		
	Number.		Per 100,000 population of specified racial class.		Paupers in almshouses.		Total population.
	Enumerated on Jan. 1.	Admitted during the year.	Enumerated on Jan. 1.	Admitted during the year.	Enumerated on Jan. 1.	Admitted during the year.	
All classes..........	84,198	88,313	91.5	96.0	100.0	100.0	100.0
Negro..................	6,281	6,807	63.9	69.3	7.5	7.7	10.7
White..................	77,734	81,135	95.1	99.3	92.3	91.8	88.9
Indian.................	74	130	27.9	48.9	0.1	0.1	0.3
Other..................	109	241	74.2	164.1	0.1	0.3	0.2

Table 39 classifies Negro and white paupers by sections and divisions. Negroes constituted a large proportion of the almshouse population as of the general population in the three southern divisions, but only an inconsiderable proportion of the almshouse population in the North and West.

The ratio of almshouse pauperism in the country as a whole was about the same in 1910 among Negroes as among native whites. Tabulations by sections and divisions, however, give a ratio much higher for Negroes than for native whites in the North and West, the difference between these classes being less considerable in the South.

Table 39

| SECTION AND DIVISION. | PAUPERS IN ALMSHOUSES: 1910. | | | |
| | Enumerated on January 1. | | Admitted during the year. | |
	Negro.	White.	Negro.	White.
United States	6,281	77,734	6,807	81,135
The South	4,286	9,281	4,338	8,737
South Atlantic	2,578	5,122	2,971	4,969
East South Central	1,356	2,908	967	2,118
West South Central	352	1,251	400	1,650
The North	1,914	61,425	2,180	58,107
New England	178	11,703	246	14,459
Middle Atlantic	678	23,081	848	23,057
East North Central	716	20,626	822	16,277
West North Central	342	6,015	264	4,314
The West	81	7,028	289	14,291
Mountain	19	1,620	83	3,375
Pacific	62	5,408	206	10,916

The ratio of Negro, native white, and foreign-born white paupers in almshouses per 100,000 population in each class is shown, by sections and divisions, in Table 40.

SEX.

Table 41 classifies paupers in almshouses in 1910, by sex, race, and nativity, and gives the sex ratio for paupers in comparison with the corresponding ratio for the total population of each class. For each racial class the proportion of males to females is much higher among paupers than it is in the general population.

Table 40

SECTION AND DIVISION.	PAUPERS IN ALMSHOUSES PER 100,000 POPULATION OF SAME RACE AND NATIVITY: 1910.					
	Enumerated on January 1.			Admitted during the year.		
	Negro.	White.		Negro.	White.	
		Native.	Foreign born.		Native.	Foreign born.
United States	63.9	64.7	248.2	69.3	67.9	249.9
The South	49.0	40.5	160.3	49.6	35.6	185.5
South Atlantic	62.7	56.8	228.5	72.2	52.0	263.3
East South Central	51.1	46.5	267.1	36.5	33.4	124.3
West South Central	17.7	15.2	76.8	20.2	17.4	135.9
The North	186.3	76.2	248.9	212.1	72.4	229.6
New England	268.5	127.7	314.5	371.0	159.7	380.4
Middle Atlantic	162.3	80.6	242.7	202.9	84.6	227.9
East North Central	238.0	81.6	273.5	273.2	64.1	209.3
West North Central	140.9	37.0	147.0	108.8	25.4	104.0
The West	159.9	61.3	291.4	570.4	153.3	462.7
Mountain	88.5	39.0	181.0	386.6	92.4	306.7
Pacific	212.4	76.0	347.4	705.6	193.5	541.9

Table 41

| RACIAL CLASS. | PAUPERS IN ALMSHOUSES: 1910. | | | | MALES TO 1,000 FEMALES: 1910. | | |
| | Enumerated on January 1. | | Admitted during the year. | | Paupers in almshouses. | | Total population. |
	Male.	Female.	Male.	Female.	Enumerated on January 1.	Admitted during the year.	
All classes	57,049	27,149	67,195	21,118	2,101	3,182	1,060
Negro	3,763	2,518	4,612	2,195	1,494	2,101	989
White	53,149	24,585	62,262	18,873	2,162	3,299	1,066
Indian	41	33	95	35	(1)	(1)	1,035
Other	96	13	226	15	(1)	(1)	9,608

[1] Ratio not shown, the number of females being less than 100.

PART VI.—ECONOMIC STATISTICS.

Chapter XVIII.—HOME OWNERSHIP AND SIZE OF FAMILIES.

FARM HOMES AND OTHER HOMES.

For each family returned on the census schedule some information is returned regarding the home occupied by the family, the number of homes being precisely equal to the number of families.

Homes of Negro families are classified in Table 1 as farm homes and other homes, for the three years 1910, 1900, and 1890. A farm home is defined in the instructions to enumerators as "a home located on a farm, for which a farm schedule should be secured."

Table 1 — HOMES OF NEGRO FAMILIES.

CLASS OF HOME.	Number.			Percentage distribution.		
	1910	1900	1890	1910	1900	1890
All homes........	2,173,018	1,833,759	1,410,769	100.0	100.0	100.0
Farm homes........	877,648	758,463	549,632	40.4	41.4	39.0
Other homes........	1,295,370	1,075,296	861,137	59.6	58.6	61.0

At each of the last three censuses approximately two out of five Negro homes on the average have been classified as farm homes. Such homes constituted 40.4 per cent of all Negro homes in 1910, the corresponding percentage for 1900 (41.4) being slightly above, and that for 1890 (39) slightly below the percentage for 1910. Relatively to the total number of Negro homes the proportion of farm homes thus remained fairly constant during this period, although the number of farm homes increased from 549,632 in 1890 to 877,648 in 1910. Homes other than farm homes increased in the same period from 861,137 to 1,295,370.

The number of Negro farm homes (877,648) in 1910 corresponded closely to the number of Negro farms, as given in the chapter on agriculture (893,370), there being a few instances of Negro farms upon which no Negro farm homes were located.

HOME OWNERSHIP INQUIRY.

For the return of information regarding ownership of homes in 1910 two columns were provided on the population schedule, in the first of which each home occupied by a family was described as owned or as rented, and in the second, each owned home as owned free or mortgaged.

The essential instructions given to census enumerators to guide them in making these returns were as follows:

Home owned or rented.—If a dwelling is occupied by more than one family it is the home of each of them, and the question should be answered with reference to each family in the dwelling.

Owned homes.—A home is to be classed as *owned* if it is owned wholly or in part, by the head of the family living in the home, or by the wife of the head or by a son, or a daughter, or other *relative* living in the same house with the head of the family. It is not necessary that full payment for the property should have been made or that the family should be the sole owner.

Rented homes.—Every home not owned, either wholly or in part, by the family living in it should be classed as *rented*, whether rent is actually paid or not.

Home owned free or mortgaged.—This question applies only to those homes classed as owned homes and not to rented homes. All owned homes which are not fully paid for, or upon which there is any encumbrance in the form either of a mortgage or of a lien upon which judgment has been had in a court, are to be reported as mortgaged.

The first investigation as to ownership of homes was made in 1890, in compliance with a special act of Congress, and covered such items as value of mortgaged homes, amount of mortgage debt, and rate of interest. In 1900 the scope of the home-ownership inquiry was restricted, as in 1910, to a classification of homes as owned or rented, and of owned homes as owned free or mortgaged.

HOMES OWNED AND RENTED.

Negro homes are classified as owned or rented in Table 2, for the years 1910, 1900, and 1890. In this table, in order to produce figures comparable with those for 1890, homes for which no report of ownership was made in 1910 and in 1900 have been distributed as owned or rented in proportion to the distribution of homes for which ownership reports were made. In 1890 the apportionment of the no-report cases was by counties, while the apportionment for 1900 and for 1910 is made by geographic divisions. The degree of comparability for divisional and sectional areas would not, however, be materially increased by making the apportionment for 1910 and for 1900 on the basis of returns for counties.

Table 2 — HOMES OF NEGRO FAMILIES.

CLASS OF HOME AND PROPRIETORSHIP.	Number.			Percentage distribution.		
	1910	1900	1890	1910	1900	1890
All homes.........	2,173,018	1,833,759	1,410,769	100.0	100.0	100.0
Owned..............	506,590	397,420	264,288	23.3	21.7	18.7
Rented..............	1,666,428	1,436,339	1,146,481	76.7	78.3	81.3
Farm homes......	877,648	758,463	549,632	100.0	100.0	100.0
Owned..............	221,535	192,993	120,738	25.2	25.4	22.0
Rented..............	656,113	565,470	428,894	74.8	74.6	78.0
Other homes......	1,295,370	1,075,296	861,137	100.0	100.0	100.0
Owned..............	285,055	204,427	143,550	22.0	19.0	16.7
Rented..............	1,010,315	870,869	717,587	78.0	81.0	83.3

The number of homes owned by Negro families occupying them at the time of census enumeration increased from 264,288, or 18.7 per cent of all Negro homes, in 1890, to 397,420, or 21.7 per cent, in 1900, and to 506,590, or 23.3 per cent, in 1910. Of farm homes the proportion owned increased from 22 per cent in 1890 to 25.4 per cent in 1900, the proportion in 1910, 25.2 per cent, being practically the same as in 1900. Of homes other than farm homes, the proportion owned increased from 16.7 per cent in 1890, to 19 per cent in 1900, and to 22 per cent in 1910.

HOMES OWNED FREE AND ENCUMBERED.

Table 3 classifies Negro owned homes in 1910, 1900, and 1890 as owned free and encumbered. In this table, as in Table 2, in order to produce figures comparable with those for 1890, the no-report cases in 1910 and in 1900 have been apportioned in proportion to the known cases, on the basis of divisional totals.

Table 3	OWNED NEGRO HOMES.					
CLASS OF HOME AND PROPRIETORSHIP.	Number.			Percentage distribution.		
	1910	1900	1890	1910	1900	1890
All owned homes....	506,590	397,420	264,288	100.0	100.0	100.0
Free..................	374,853	295,474	234,747	74.0	74.3	88.8
Encumbered..........	131,737	101,946	29,541	26.0	25.7	11.2
Owned farm homes...	221,535	192,993	120,738	100.0	100.0	100.0
Free..................	159,969	138,976	108,483	72.2	72.0	89.8
Encumbered..........	61,566	54,017	12,255	27.8	28.0	10.2
Owned other homes..	285,055	204,427	143,550	100.0	100.0	100.0
Free..................	214,884	156,498	126,264	75.4	76.6	88.0
Encumbered..........	70,171	47,929	17,286	24.6	23.4	12.0

The proportion owned free of owned Negro homes did not change materially during the decade 1900–1910, the percentage owned free for farm homes being 72 in 1900 and 72.2 in 1910, and for other than farm homes 76.6 in 1900 and 75.4 in 1910. These proportions were markedly below those shown for 1890, in which year 89.8 per cent of the owned farm homes, and 88 per cent of the owned other homes, were owned free of mortgage encumbrance.

Although the proportion owned free thus declined in the decade 1890–1900, this decline was not due to any decrease in the number of homes owned free— the number owned free, both of farm homes and of other homes, increasing in this decade as in the decade following—but to a relatively more rapid increase in the number of homes owned under a mortgage or other lien. Such ownership is undoubtedly in many cases a first step out of tenancy.

The increases during the two decades for farm and other homes owned free, owned encumbered, and rented are shown in Table 4.

Owned Negro homes increased during the decade 1900–1910 by 109,170, and during the decade preceding by 133,132, the increase of 242,302 for the entire twenty-year period amounting to an increase of 91.7 per cent, and being sufficient nearly to double the number of owned homes.

Table 4	INCREASE IN HOMES OF NEGRO FAMILIES.					
PROPRIETORSHIP.	All homes.		Farm homes.		Other homes.	
	1900–1910	1890–1900	1900–1910	1890–1900	1900–1910	1890–1900
Total.........	339,259	422,990	119,185	208,831	220,074	214,159
Owned.............	109,170	133,132	28,542	72,255	80,628	60,877
Free.............	79,379	60,727	20,993	30,493	58,386	30,234
Encumbered....	29,791	72,405	7,549	41,762	22,242	30,643
Rented.............	230,089	289,858	90,643	136,576	139,446	153,282

While the absolute increase in the number of rented homes in each decade was more than twice as great as of owned homes, the proportional increase was much smaller for rented than for owned homes, the proportional increase for the twenty-year period amounting to 45.4 per cent for rented as compared with 91.7 per cent for owned homes.

HOMES IN THE SOUTH, THE NORTH, AND THE WEST.

The number of Negro farm homes and other homes is given by geographic sections in Table 5 for the years 1910, 1900, and 1890.

Table 5	HOMES OF NEGRO FAMILIES.					
SECTION AND CENSUS YEAR.	Number.			Percentage distribution.		
	All homes.	Farm homes.	Other homes.	All homes.	Farm homes.	Other homes.
United States:						
1910...........	2,173,018	877,648	1,295,370	100.0	100.0	100.0
1900...........	1,833,759	758,463	1,075,296	100.0	100.0	100.0
1890...........	1,410,769	549,632	861,137	100.0	100.0	100.0
The South:						
1910...........	1,917,391	864,688	1,052,703	88.2	98.5	81.3
1900...........	1,637,024	743,521	893,503	89.3	98.0	83.1
1890...........	1,262,707	533,681	729,026	89.5	97.1	84.7
The North:						
1910...........	242,920	12,431	230,483	11.2	1.4	17.8
1900...........	189,770	14,580	175,190	10.3	1.9	16.3
1890...........	142,937	15,578	127,359	10.1	2.8	14.8
The West:						
1910...........	12,707	523	12,184	0.6	0.1	0.9
1900...........	6,965	362	6,603	0.4	0.0	0.6
1890...........	5,125	373	4,752	0.4	0.1	0.6

Of Negro farm homes, 98.5 per cent were in the South in 1910, 1.4 per cent in the North, and 0.1 per cent in the West. Of homes other than farm homes, 81.3 per cent were in the South, 17.8 per cent in the North, and 0.9 per cent in the West, the proportion in the North being much larger (17.8 per cent as compared with 1.4 per cent) for homes other than farm homes than for farm homes.

The percentage owned is shown for Negro farm and other homes by sections in Table 6, the percentages being based upon the figures given in Table 7 in which the no-report cases for each year have been distributed in proportion to the known cases.

Table 6	PERCENTAGE OWNED OF HOMES OF NEGRO FAMILIES.								
SECTION.	All homes.			Farm homes.			Other homes.		
	1910	1900	1890	1910	1900	1890	1910	1900	1890
United States.	23.3	21.7	18.7	10.2	10.5	8.6	13.1	11.1	10.2
The South......	23.3	21.3	17.7	11.1	11.2	8.9	12.2	10.1	8.8
The North.....	23.0	24.3	27.6	3.2	4.7	6.0	19.8	19.6	21.6
The West......	33.7	29.0	29.1	3.3	3.9	5.6	30.5	25.1	23.5

In the South the percentage owned increased for Negro farm homes from 8.9 per cent in 1890 to 11.2 per cent in 1900, the percentage of 11.1 for 1910 being practically the same as that for 1900. Of homes other than farm homes the percentage owned in the South increased in each decade from 8.8 per cent in 1890 to 10.1 per cent in 1900 and to 12.2 per cent in 1910.

A larger proportion of Negro farm homes in the South were owned in each year than were owned of farm homes in the North and West, while of homes other than farm homes the proportion owned was much higher in the North and West than in the South. In 1910, for example, the percentage owned for Negro farm homes, which was 11.1 in the South, was 3.2 in the North and 3.3 in the West, and the percentage owned of homes other than farm homes, which was 12.2 in the South, was 19.8 in the North and 30.5 in the West.

Table 7 classifies Negro homes in 1910, 1900, and 1890 as owned and rented, and owned homes as free and encumbered, by sections and southern divisions, the no-report cases in each year being distributed in proportion to the known.

NEGRO HOMES, FARM AND OTHER, CLASSIFIED AS OWNED FREE, OWNED ENCUMBERED, AND RENTED, BY SECTIONS AND SOUTHERN DIVISIONS: 1910, 1900, AND 1890.

Table 7	HOMES OF NEGRO FAMILIES.														
	All homes.					Farm homes.					Other homes.				
		Owned.					Owned.					Owned.			
SECTION, DIVISION, AND CENSUS YEAR.	Total.	Total.	Free.	En-cumbered.	Rented.	Total.	Total.	Free.	En-cumbered.	Rented.	Total.	Total.	Free.	En-cumbered.	Rented.
United States:															
1910	2,173,018	506,590	374,853	131,737	1,666,428	877,648	221,535	159,969	61,566	656,113	1,295,370	285,055	214,884	70,171	1,010,315
1900	1,833,759	397,420	295,474	101,946	1,436,339	758,463	192,993	138,976	54,017	565,470	1,075,296	204,427	156,498	47,929	870,869
1890	1,410,769	264,288	234,747	29,541	1,146,481	549,632	120,738	108,483	12,255	428,894	861,137	143,550	126,264	17,286	717,587
The South:															
1910	1,917,391	446,379	340,202	106,177	1,471,012	864,688	213,283	155,472	57,811	651,405	1,052,703	233,096	184,730	48,366	819,607
1900	1,637,024	349,296	267,160	82,136	1,287,728	743,521	183,817	133,731	50,086	559,704	893,503	165,479	133,429	32,050	728,024
1890	1,262,707	223,315	207,675	15,640	1,039,392	533,681	111,831	103,087	8,744	421,850	729,026	111,484	104,588	6,896	617,542
South Atlantic:															
1910	882,647	215,384	169,996	45,388	667,263	351,868	102,438	80,552	21,886	249,430	530,779	112,946	89,444	23,502	417,833
1900	761,105	169,910	133,147	36,763	591,195	293,512	86,794	67,582	19,212	206,718	467,593	83,116	65,565	17,551	384,477
1890	613,236	115,116	107,084	8,032	498,120	218,003	53,261	49,601	3,660	164,742	395,233	61,855	57,483	4,372	333,378
East South Central:															
1910	603,322	123,928	88,334	35,594	479,394	315,353	59,210	37,323	21,887	256,143	287,969	64,718	51,011	13,707	223,251
1900	527,908	97,779	71,495	26,284	430,129	273,753	51,136	33,481	17,655	222,617	254,155	46,643	38,014	8,629	207,512
1890	399,065	60,232	55,643	4,589	338,833	195,702	30,861	27,898	2,963	164,841	203,363	29,371	27,745	1,626	173,992
West South Central:															
1910	431,422	107,067	81,872	25,195	324,355	197,467	51,635	37,597	14,038	145,832	233,955	55,432	44,275	11,157	178,523
1900	348,011	81,607	62,518	19,089	266,404	176,256	45,887	32,668	13,219	130,369	171,755	35,720	29,850	5,870	136,035
1890	250,406	47,967	44,948	3,019	202,439	119,976	27,709	25,588	2,121	92,267	130,430	20,258	19,360	898	110,172
The North:															
1910	242,920	55,926	32,061	23,865	186,994	12,437	7,839	4,201	3,638	4,598	230,483	48,087	27,860	20,227	182,396
1900	189,770	46,105	26,890	19,215	143,665	14,580	8,904	5,028	3,876	5,676	175,190	37,201	21,862	15,339	137,989
1890	142,937	39,480	25,868	13,612	103,457	15,578	8,620	5,165	3,455	6,958	127,359	30,860	20,703	10,157	96,499
The West:															
1910	12,707	4,285	2,590	1,695	8,422	523	413	296	117	110	12,184	3,872	2,294	1,578	8,312
1900	6,965	2,019	1,424	595	4,946	362	272	217	55	90	6,603	1,747	1,207	540	4,856
1890	5,125	1,493	1,204	289	3,632	373	287	231	56	86	4,752	1,206	973	233	3,546

DIVISIONS AND STATES.

Data relating to Negro homes are given for divisions and states in Table 13 (pp. 466 to 469) for the years 1910 and 1900, and in Table 14 (p. 470) for the year 1890. Table 12 (p. 465) gives by divisions and states the number of owned Negro homes in 1910 and in 1900, with the increase for the decade 1900–1910, and the percentage owned, of all Negro homes in each year.

The number of owned Negro homes increased during the decade 1900–1910 in Georgia by 12,099, or 45.4 per cent; in North Carolina by 11,099, or 38.2 per cent; in Virginia by 10,665, or 23.1 per cent; in Alabama by 10,405, or 44.2 per cent. Very considerable increases are shown in Table 12 for other Southern states, and for a number of Northern and Western states.

The percentage owned increased in all the Southern states except West Virginia, Florida, and Oklahoma. It increased in 19 and remained unchanged or decreased in 13 Northern and Western states. Decrease in the percentage owned does not of course necessarily imply in the case of any state a decrease in the number of owned homes. Although the percentage owned decreased in Oklahoma, for example, from 52.4 in 1900 to 35.3 in 1910, the number of homes owned by Negro families occupying them increased in this period from 6,039 to 10,018.

The percentage owned in 1910 ranged in the Southern states from 14.7 in Georgia to 41.3 in Virginia, and in the Northern and Western states from 7.8 in New York to 49.6 in Kansas.

Virginia showed the largest absolute increase in owned farm homes (5,078), Georgia the second largest (4,455), and North Carolina the third largest (3,539). Owned farm homes increased in every Southern state, except West Virginia. The number of such homes decreased in 11 Northern states, the decrease amounting to 692 in Missouri, to 227 in Indiana, and to 177 in Kansas.

Owned other homes increased in every state except New Hampshire and Vermont, the increases for this class of homes being generally much larger than for farm homes. In New Jersey, for example, owned farm homes decreased by 25 and owned other homes increased by 1,119; in Indiana, although owned farm homes decreased by 227, owned other homes increased by 748; in Illinois owned farm homes decreased by 25, and owned other homes increased by 1,558. In each of three northern divisions as a whole (Middle Atlantic, East North Central, and West North Central), owned farm homes decreased, and owned other homes increased. In the South Atlantic division as a whole, owned farm homes increased by 16,027, and owned other homes by 32,625; in the East South Central division owned farm homes increased by 8,399 and owned other homes by 19,572; in the West South Central division owned farm homes increased by 6,023 and owned other homes by 20,266.

NEGRO POPULATION PER OWNED HOME.

Negro population per owned Negro home in the South, the North, and the West is shown in Table 8. In the South the Negro population per owned home decreased from 30 in 1890 to 23 in 1900 and to 20 in 1910. In the North, on the average, one owned Negro home was returned in 1910 per 18 Negroes enumerated in the population, and in the West one owned home per 12 Negroes enumerated.

Table 8	NEGRO POPULATION PER OWNED HOME.		
SECTION.	1910	1900	1890
United States	19	22	28
The South	20	23	30
The North	18	19	18
The West	12	15	18

The number of Negro inhabitants per owned home, and the percentage owned of all Negro homes, are given in Table 9, by divisions and states for the three years 1910, 1900, and 1890. In this table and in Table 12 the figures for 1910 and for 1900 are based upon the number of homes reported owned, no appor-

tionment having been made of the no-report cases. The derived figures for these years as given in Table 9 are, therefore, not entirely comparable with those given for 1890, which are based upon a number of owned homes obtained by apportioning no-report cases in proportion to known cases. The population per owned home as given in Table 9 for 1910 and for 1900 is somewhat in excess of the true figure and the percentage owned somewhat below the true percentage owned.

Table 9	NEGRO INHABITANTS PER OWNED HOME AND PERCENTAGE OWNED OF ALL HOMES: 1910, 1900, 1890.					
DIVISION AND STATE.	Negro inhabitants per owned home.[1]			Percentage owned of Negro homes.[1]		
	1910	1900	1890	1910	1900	1890
UNITED STATES	20	24	28	22.5	20.4	18.7
GEOGRAPHIC DIVISIONS:						
New England	25	27	25	17.2	17.2	18.6
Middle Atlantic	36	37	28	12.6	13.3	17.9
East North Central	15	15	14	27.6	28.4	32.1
West North Central	13	15	15	32.1	31.4	34.7
South Atlantic	20	23	28	23.6	21.0	18.8
East South Central	22	27	35	19.8	17.3	15.1
West South Central	19	22	29	23.9	22.0	19.2
Mountain	14	19	20	28.1	22.6	28.2
Pacific	11	14	16	36.2	31.3	29.9
NEW ENGLAND:						
Maine	11	11	12	42.9	41.4	39.0
New Hampshire	15	20	26	30.6	26.6	21.1
Vermont	35	17	22	20.4	31.8	23.9
Massachusetts	27	29	26	16.2	15.9	17.7
Rhode Island	27	28	29	15.2	15.0	14.4
Connecticut	24	25	22	18.1	18.1	20.6
MIDDLE ATLANTIC:						
New York	55	45	33	7.8	10.5	14.5
New Jersey	24	27	21	18.6	18.6	23.4
Pennsylvania	35	39	30	13.3	12.8	17.8
EAST NORTH CENTRAL:						
Ohio	13	14	14	30.1	30.9	33.3
Indiana	15	16	17	26.4	27.6	28.0
Illinois	18	19	16	23.0	23.3	30.1
Michigan	9	10	10	44.0	42.4	42.1
Wisconsin	17	15	11	25.6	27.1	41.9
WEST NORTH CENTRAL:						
Minnesota	17	35	22	24.7	12.9	19.7
Iowa	13	14	14	29.9	30.9	35.3
Missouri	16	17	17	26.6	27.4	30.1
North Dakota	12	11	10	35.6	38.8	51.4
South Dakota	8	10	9	45.1	43.0	54.2
Nebraska	17	25	30	24.1	19.8	22.5
Kansas	8	9	10	49.6	45.8	50.7
SOUTH ATLANTIC:						
Delaware	21	24	22	23.2	21.6	24.3
Maryland	19	23	25	25.6	23.0	22.1
District of Columbia	46	44	35	10.8	11.4	14.9
Virginia	12	14	21	41.3	36.0	26.6
West Virginia	23	22	22	19.3	24.0	26.0
North Carolina	17	22	28	28.7	23.7	19.4
South Carolina	25	29	33	18.5	16.7	15.6
Georgia	30	39	43	14.7	12.0	12.1
Florida	15	15	16	27.7	29.3	32.0
EAST SOUTH CENTRAL:						
Kentucky	13	16	21	31.8	29.7	26.1
Tennessee	18	23	29	25.3	21.8	18.8
Alabama	27	35	43	16.4	13.2	11.9
Mississippi	26	31	44	16.9	15.0	12.2
WEST SOUTH CENTRAL:						
Arkansas	18	22	26	24.6	21.9	21.0
Louisiana	26	32	38	17.1	14.6	13.6
Oklahoma	14	9	34	35.3	52.4	85.6
Texas	17	17	23	28.5	27.9	24.3
MOUNTAIN:						
Montana	10	20	28	32.8	19.1	23.9
Idaho	14	8	13	28.7	44.4	39.0
Wyoming	32	29	33	18.4	20.0	25.2
Colorado	13	18	21	27.6	22.8	24.3
New Mexico	12	23	12	30.3	18.1	42.6
Arizona	11	22	59	30.7	27.5	20.2
Utah	22	35	31	21.2	16.0	24.4
Nevada	7	7	8	35.7	34.6	40.5
PACIFIC:						
Washington	14	16	24	32.1	28.4	23.3
Oregon	15	23	16	28.2	25.7	43.3
California	10	13	16	37.8	32.4	29.7

[1] In 1890 homes for which no report of ownership was received were apportioned as owned or rented in proportion to homes for which reports of ownership were secured. No corresponding apportionment has been made for Negro homes, by states, for the years 1910 and 1900. Such an apportionment, if it had been made, would have reduced somewhat the population per owned home in 1910 and in 1900, and increased somewhat the percentage owned of Negro homes for these years.

The discrepancies between Table 9 and Tables 6 and 8, in the figures for the country as a whole, showing population per owned home, and percentage owned of Negro homes represent the no-report cases, which are apportioned in Tables 6 and 8. The Negro population per owned home in the United States in 1910, for example, is given in Table 8 as 19 and in Table 9 as 20, and the percentage owned of Negro homes is given in Table 6 as 23.3 and in Table 9 as 22.5.

In the Southern states the Negro population per owned home ranged in 1910 from 13 in Kentucky to 30 in Georgia, the figure for the District of Columbia being 46. In the Northern and Western states the population per owned home ranged from 7 in Nevada to 55 in New York.

URBAN COMMUNITIES.

No complete compilation of data relating to ownership of homes has been made for the aggregate urban and rural Negro population. In Table 10 the number of Negro inhabitants per owned home is shown by divisions and states for the aggregate Negro population of cities having in 1910 a Negro population of 2,500 or more, and this aggregate may be taken as representing with approximate accuracy the condition obtaining in the urban population as a whole.

Generally in the several states of the North the population per owned home is larger in the cities than it is in the population of the state as a whole. More marked differences would develop if comparisons were possible between the aggregate urban and the aggregate rural population of these states. In New York state, for example, it is obvious that the Negro population per owned home, which was 168 for cities reporting in 1910 a Negro population of 2,500 or more, and 55 for the state as a whole including these cities, must have been considerably less than 55 in the rural population of the state. In several Southern states, however, the Negro population per owned Negro home is smaller for aggregate population of the cities than it is for the aggregate population of the state urban and rural combined. In Mississippi, for example, the Negro population per owned home was 15 in the cities and 26 in the state as a whole; in Alabama, 20 in the cities and 27 in the state; and in Georgia, 23 in the cities and 30 in the state.

The number of homes owned free, owned encumbered, and rented by Negro families is given in Table 15 (pp. 471 to 472) for urban communities having a Negro population of 2,500 or more in 1910. Table 16 (p. 473) gives for each of these communities the percentage owned of Negro homes, and Table 17 (p. 474) the Negro inhabitants per owned home.

The lowest percentage owned is that of 2.4 for New York City; the highest that of 67.6 for Marianna, Ark. In 34 of the cities more than one-third of the Negro homes were owned.

Table 10 — NEGRO INHABITANTS PER OWNED HOME FOR THE TOTAL POPULATION AND FOR THE AGGREGATE POPULATION OF SELECTED URBAN COMMUNITIES, BY DIVISIONS AND STATES: 1910.

DIVISION AND STATE.	Negro population: 1910.		Owned homes: 1910.		Negro inhabitants per owned home.		
	Total.	Cities having 2,500 Negro inhabitants or more.	Total.	Cities having 2,500 Negro inhabitants or more.	Total. 1910	Total. 1900	Cities having 2,500 Negro inhabitants or more: 1910.
UNITED STATES....	9,827,763	2,031,691	488,699	77,005	20	26	26
GEOGRAPHIC DIVISIONS:							
New England	66,306	30,033	2,615	612	25	27	49
Middle Atlantic	417,870	245,047	11,736	3,014	36	37	81
East North Central	300,836	145,397	20,620	4,612	15	15	32
West North Central	242,662	101,309	19,138	3,967	13	15	26
South Atlantic	4,112,488	734,207	208,247	28,286	20	23	26
East South Central	2,652,513	405,566	119,291	19,330	22	27	21
West South Central	1,984,426	354,052	102,911	15,963	19	22	22
Mountain	21,467	5,426	1,589	279	14	19	19
Pacific	29,195	10,654	2,552	942	11	14	11
NEW ENGLAND:							
Maine	1,363	....	126	....	11	11	......
New Hampshire	564	....	37	....	15	20	......
Vermont	1,621	....	46	....	35	17	......
Massachusetts	38,055	21,156	1,412	418	27	27	51
Rhode Island	9,529	5,316	358	109	27	29	49
Connecticut	15,174	3,561	636	85	24	25	42
MIDDLE ATLANTIC:							
New York	134,191	91,709	2,437	545	55	45	168
New Jersey	89,760	33,926	3,682	630	24	27	54
Pennsylvania	193,919	119,412	5,617	1,839	35	39	65
EAST NORTH CENTRAL:							
Ohio	111,452	50,601	8,467	1,787	13	14	28
Indiana	60,320	30,675	4,036	1,222	15	16	25
Illinois	109,049	58,380	6,012	1,365	18	19	43
Michigan	17,115	5,741	1,932	238	9	10	24
Wisconsin	2,900	....	173	....	17	15	......
WEST NORTH CENTRAL:							
Minnesota	7,084	5,736	416	300	17	35	19
Iowa	14,973	2,930	1,138	225	13	14	13
Missouri	157,452	71,775	10,130	1,349	16	17	53
North Dakota	617	....	52	....	12	11	......
South Dakota	817	....	97	....	8	10	......
Nebraska	7,689	4,426	454	166	17	25	27
Kansas	54,030	16,442	6,851	1,927	8	9	9
SOUTH ATLANTIC:							
Delaware	31,181	9,081	1,501	231	21	24	39
Maryland	232,250	87,933	12,068	1,017	19	23	86
District of Columbia	94,446	94,446	2,072	2,072	46	44	46
Virginia	671,096	134,777	56,933	5,565	12	14	24
West Virginia	64,173	3,086	2,743	123	23	22	25
North Carolina	697,843	84,603	40,118	5,009	17	22	17
South Carolina	835,843	76,435	33,161	3,217	25	29	24
Georgia	1,176,987	183,557	38,735	7,998	30	39	23
Florida	308,669	60,289	20,916	3,054	15	15	20
EAST SOUTH CENTRAL:							
Kentucky	261,656	76,336	19,774	3,021	13	16	25
Tennessee	473,088	124,548	27,012	4,973	18	23	25
Alabama	908,282	135,463	33,941	6,860	27	35	20
Mississippi	1,009,487	69,219	38,564	4,473	26	31	15
WEST SOUTH CENTRAL:							
Arkansas	442,891	43,844	24,018	3,021	18	22	15
Louisiana	713,874	135,613	27,237	4,952	26	32	27
Oklahoma	137,612	20,350	10,018	1,366	14	9	15
Texas	690,049	154,245	41,638	6,624	17	17	23
MOUNTAIN:							
Montana	1,834	....	182	....	10	20	......
Idaho	651	....	48	....	14	8	......
Wyoming	2,235	....	69	....	32	29	......
Colorado	11,453	5,426	849	279	13	18	19
New Mexico	1,628	....	136	....	12	23	......
Arizona	2,009	....	179	....	11	22	......
Utah	1,144	....	51	....	22	35	......
Nevada	513	....	75	....	7	7	......
PACIFIC:							
Washington	6,058	....	435	....	14	16	......
Oregon	1,492	....	98	....	15	23	......
California	21,645	10,654	2,019	942	10	13	11

The Negro population per owned home in these cities ranged from 7 in Winchester, Ky., to 168 in New York City. In 13 of the cities listed—10 of them southern cities—the Negro population per owned home was less than 10. Birmingham, with a total Negro population of 52,305 and a total of 14,229 Negro families, reported in 1910 one owned Negro home on the average per 22 Negro inhabitants. Baltimore, with a total Negro population of 84,749 and a total of 18,106 Negro families, reported one owned home per 91 Negro inhabitants. The 4 other southern cities reporting a Negro population in excess of 50,000 in 1910 reported a Negro population per owned home as follows: Washington, 46; New Orleans, 37; Memphis, 31; and Atlanta, 29.

Richmond, Va., Louisville, Ky., Nashville, Tenn., Savannah, Ga., Charleston, S. C., Jacksonville, Fla., and Norfolk, Va., the 7 cities with Negro populations between 25,000 and 50,000, show an equally wide range in the ratio of owned homes to population. Among these cities Nashville, Tenn., leads, with one owned home for every 18 Negro inhabitants, while Norfolk, Va., shows only one owned home to every 92 of its Negro population—the lowest ratio of owned homes to population shown for any of the southern municipalities presented in this tabulation. The corresponding figures for the remaining cities of this group were as follows: Jacksonville, Fla., 22; Richmond, Va., 28; Charleston, S. C., 37; Savannah, Ga., 53; and Louisville, Ky., 57.

Among southern cities with a Negro population of 10,000 and less than 25,000, Petersburg, Va., leads with one owned home on the average for 13 Negro inhabitants. The corresponding figure for Wilmington, N. C., is 15; for Little Rock, Ark., and Pensacola, Fla., 16; for Lexington, Ky., and San Antonio, Tex., 17; the other cities in this group ranging from 18 in Jackson, Miss., to 52 in Chattanooga, Tenn.

COUNTIES.

Statistics for counties are given in Table 18 (pp. 475 to 501) which gives for each county having in 1910 a Negro population of 100 or more, the Negro population of the county in 1910, the number of Negro homes, and the number of farm homes and of other homes owned free, owned encumbered, and rented. The table represents a special compilation from the census schedules.

AVERAGE SIZE OF FAMILY.

The term "family" as defined for census enumeration means a "group of persons, whether related by blood or not, who live together as one household, usually sharing the same table."

Such a group is not necessarily a natural family, since on the one hand it is not restricted to persons related to one another by blood or marriage, and, on the other hand, does not in any given case necessarily include all such mutually related persons. It may include persons in any degree of blood or marital relationship, together with persons of no natural relationship whatever, such as boarders, or servants. Older sons and daughters living apart from their parents are returned as members of the households or families with which they are living. One person living alone is counted as a family, and, on the other hand, occupants of a hotel or institution, however numerous, are counted each group as forming collectively a single family.

At the census of 1900 the "private family," most of whose members were related to one another by blood or marriage, was distinguished from the "economic family," such as a construction gang or a group of persons occupying a boarding house, hotel, institution, or lumber camp. The average size of all families in 1900 for the United States was 4.7 persons, and of private families 4.6 persons. It appears that economic families were not, in 1900, sufficiently numerous to affect materially the average size of families in the country as a whole or in the states severally. The distinction between private and economic families was not made in the tabulation for 1910.

Table 11 gives the number of families returned at each of the last three censuses, in the total population and in the Negro population.

| Table 11 | FAMILIES. | | | PERSONS TO A FAMILY. | |
| SECTION AND CENSUS YEAR. | Total number. | Negro. | | Total population. | Negro population. |
		Number.	Per cent.		
United States:					
1910	20,255,555	2,173,018	10.7	4.5	4.5
1900	16,187,715	1,833,759	11.3	4.7	4.8
1890	12,690,152	1,410,769	11.1	4.9	5.3
The South:					
1910	6,163,207	1,917,391	31.1	4.7	4.6
1900	4,938,073	1,637,024	33.2	5.0	4.8
1890	3,758,887	1,262,707	33.6	5.3	5.4
The North:					
1910	12,507,506	242,920	1.9	4.5	4.2
1900	10,318,990	189,770	1.8	4.6	4.6
1890	8,310,847	142,937	1.7	4.8	4.9
The West:					
1910	1,584,842	12,707	0.8	4.3	4.0
1900	939,652	6,965	0.7	4.4	4.4
1890	620,418	5,125	0.8	4.9	5.3

Negro families increased from 1,410,769 in 1890 to 2,173,018 in 1910. They constituted, in 1910, 10.7 per cent of the total number of families in the country, the proportion Negro for families being the same as for population. In 1900 the proportion Negro for families was 11.3, and for population 11.6; and in 1890, 11.1 for families, and 11.9 for population.

In the South Negro families constituted at each census approximately one-third of the total number of families, the proportion having decreased somewhat in each decade—from 33.6 per cent in 1890 to 33.2 per cent in 1900, to 31.1 per cent in 1910. The proportions for the North were 1.7, 1.8, and 1.9 per cent, and for the West 0.8, 0.7, and 0.8 per cent.

The average number of persons per Negro family decreased from 5.3 in 1890 to 4.8 in 1900, and to 4.5 in 1910. In 1900 and in 1890 the average size of Negro families somewhat exceeded, and in 1910 precisely equaled the average for families of all classes combined. In each of the three geographic sections considered separately, however, in 1910, the average size of families among Negroes was somewhat below the average for the section as a whole.

In the Negro population, as in the total population, at each of the last three censuses, the average size of families in the South exceeded the average for families in the North and in the West.

TABLE 12.—OWNED HOMES OF NEGRO FAMILIES—NUMBER, 1910 AND 1900, AND INCREASE, 1900–1910, BY DIVISIONS AND STATES.

DIVISION AND STATE.	OWNED HOMES OF NEGRO FAMILIES.[1]													
	1910			1900			Increase: 1900–1910.						Per cent of all Negro homes.	
							Number.			Per cent.				
	Total.	Farm homes.	Other homes.	Total.	Farm homes.	Other homes.	Total.	Farm homes.	Other homes.	Total.	Farm homes.	Other homes.	1910	1900
UNITED STATES	488,699	220,698	268,001	373,450	191,143	182,307	115,249	29,555	85,694	30.9	15.5	47.0	22.5	20.4
GEOGRAPHIC DIVISIONS:														
New England	2,615	257	2,358	2,215	225	1,990	400	32	368	18.1	14.2	18.5	17.2	17.2
Middle Atlantic	11,736	865	10,871	8,779	903	7,876	2,957	−38	2,995	33.7	−4.2	38.0	12.6	13.3
East North Central	20,620	3,192	17,428	16,661	3,463	13,198	3,959	−271	4,230	23.8	−7.8	32.1	27.6	28.4
West North Central	19,138	3,472	15,666	16,386	4,227	12,159	2,752	−755	3,507	16.8	−17.9	28.8	32.1	31.4
South Atlantic	208,247	102,036	106,211	159,595	86,009	73,586	48,652	16,027	32,625	30.5	18.6	44.3	23.6	21.0
East South Central	119,291	59,027	60,264	91,320	50,628	40,692	27,971	8,399	19,572	30.6	16.6	48.1	19.8	17.3
West South Central	102,911	51,444	51,467	76,622	45,421	31,201	26,289	6,023	20,266	34.3	13.3	65.0	23.9	22.0
Mountain	1,589	178	1,411	801	110	691	788	68	720	98.4	61.8	104.2	28.1	22.6
Pacific	2,552	227	2,325	1,071	157	914	1,481	70	1,411	138.3	44.6	154.4	36.2	31.3
NEW ENGLAND:														
Maine	126	26	100	121	32	89	5	−6	11	4.1	−18.8	12.4	42.9	41.4
New Hampshire	37	15	22	33	8	25	4	7	−3	12.1	87.5	−12.0	30.6	26.6
Vermont	46	17	29	49	10	39	−3	7	−10	−6.1	70.0	−25.6	20.4	31.8
Massachusetts	1,412	101	1,311	1,094	72	1,022	318	29	289	29.1	40.3	28.3	16.2	15.9
Rhode Island	358	26	332	319	19	300	39	7	32	12.2	36.8	10.7	15.2	15.0
Connecticut	636	72	564	599	84	515	37	−12	49	6.2	−14.3	9.5	18.1	18.1
MIDDLE ATLANTIC:														
New York	2,437	210	2,227	2,213	214	1,999	224	−4	228	10.1	−1.9	11.4	7.8	10.5
New Jersey	3,682	289	3,393	2,588	314	2,274	1,094	−25	1,119	42.3	−8.0	49.2	18.6	18.6
Pennsylvania	5,617	366	5,251	3,978	375	3,603	1,639	−9	1,648	41.2	−2.4	45.7	13.3	12.8
EAST NORTH CENTRAL:														
Ohio	8,467	1,358	7,109	6,927	1,379	5,548	1,540	−21	1,561	22.2	−1.5	28.1	30.1	30.9
Indiana	4,036	478	3,558	3,515	705	2,810	521	−227	748	14.8	−32.2	26.6	26.4	27.6
Illinois	6,012	809	5,203	4,479	834	3,645	1,533	−25	1,558	34.2	−3.0	42.7	23.0	23.3
Michigan	1,932	505	1,427	1,573	500	1,073	359	5	354	22.8	1.0	33.0	44.0	42.4
Wisconsin	173	42	131	167	45	122	6	−3	9	3.6	−6.7	7.4	25.6	27.1
WEST NORTH CENTRAL:														
Minnesota	416	24	392	140	22	118	276	2	274	197.1	9.1	232.2	24.7	12.9
Iowa	1,138	136	1,002	900	116	784	238	20	218	26.4	17.2	27.8	29.9	30.9
Missouri	10,130	2,156	7,974	9,535	2,848	6,687	595	−692	1,287	6.2	−24.3	19.2	26.6	27.4
North Dakota	52	23	29	26	12	14	26	11	15	100.0	91.7	107.1	35.6	38.8
South Dakota	97	59	38	46	14	32	51	45	6	110.9	321.4	18.8	45.1	43.0
Nebraska	454	82	372	250	46	204	204	36	168	81.6	78.3	82.4	24.1	19.8
Kansas	6,851	992	5,859	5,489	1,169	4,320	1,362	−177	1,539	24.8	15.1	35.6	49.6	45.8
SOUTH ATLANTIC:														
Delaware	1,501	436	1,065	1,297	336	961	204	100	104	15.7	29.8	10.8	23.2	21.6
Maryland	12,068	4,091	7,977	10,401	3,480	6,921	1,667	611	1,056	16.0	17.6	15.3	25.6	23.0
District of Columbia	2,072	10	2,062	1,964	9	1,955	108	1	107	5.5		5.4	10.8	11.4
Virginia	56,933	32,528	24,405	46,268	27,450	18,818	10,665	5,078	5,587	23.1	18.5	29.7	41.3	36.0
West Virginia	2,743	523	2,220	1,983	573	1,410	760	−50	810	38.3	−8.7	57.4	19.3	24.0
North Carolina	40,118	20,491	19,627	29,019	16,952	12,067	11,099	3,539	7,560	38.2	20.9	62.7	28.7	23.7
South Carolina	33,161	20,431	12,730	26,870	18,874	7,996	6,291	1,557	4,734	23.4	8.2	59.2	18.5	16.7
Georgia	38,735	16,191	22,544	26,636	11,736	14,900	12,099	4,455	7,644	45.4	38.0	51.3	14.7	12.0
Florida	20,916	7,335	13,581	15,157	6,599	8,558	5,759	736	5,023	38.0	11.2	58.7	27.7	29.3
EAST SOUTH CENTRAL:														
Kentucky	19,774	6,077	13,697	17,906	5,915	11,991	1,868	162	1,706	10.4	27.4	14.2	31.8	29.7
Tennessee	27,012	10,942	16,070	21,023	9,819	11,204	5,989	1,123	4,866	28.5	11.4	43.4	25.3	21.8
Alabama	33,941	17,227	16,714	23,536	13,955	9,581	10,405	3,272	7,133	44.2	23.4	74.4	16.4	13.2
Mississippi	38,564	24,781	13,783	28,855	20,939	7,916	9,709	3,842	5,867	33.6	18.4	74.1	16.9	15.0
WEST SOUTH CENTRAL:														
Arkansas	24,018	14,216	9,802	16,838	11,713	5,125	7,180	2,503	4,677	42.6	21.4	91.3	24.6	21.9
Louisiana	27,237	11,077	16,160	20,453	9,577	10,876	6,784	1,500	5,284	33.2	15.7	48.9	17.1	14.6
Oklahoma[2]	10,018	4,956	5,062	6,039	4,005	2,034	3,979	951	3,028	65.9	23.7	148.9	35.3	52.4
Texas	41,638	21,195	20,443	33,292	20126	13,166	8,346	1,069	7,277	25.1	5.3	55.3	28.5	27.9
MOUNTAIN:														
Montana	182	22	160	75	16	59	107	6	101	142.7	37.5	171.2	32.8	19.1
Idaho	48	15	33	36	9	27	12	6	6	33.3	66.7	22.2	28.7	44.4
Wyoming	69	16	53	32	8	24	37	8	29	115.6	100.0	120.8	18.4	20.0
Colorado	849	57	792	467	49	418	382	8	374	81.8	16.3	89.5	27.6	22.8
New Mexico	136	42	94	69	9	60	67	33	34	97.1	366.7	56.7	30.3	18.1
Arizona	179	12	167	85	9	76	94	3	91	110.6	33.3	119.7	30.7	27.5
Utah	51	9	42	19	7	12	32	2	30	168.4	28.6	250.0	21.2	16.0
Nevada	75	5	70	18	3	15	57	2	55	316.7	66.7	366.7	35.7	34.6
PACIFIC:														
Washington	435	71	364	161	56	105	274	15	259	170.2	26.8	246.7	32.1	28.4
Oregon	98	23	75	49	11	38	49	12	37	100.0	109.1	97.4	28.2	25.7
California	2,019	133	1,886	861	90	771	1,158	43	1,115	134.5	47.8	144.6	37.8	32.4

[1] Figures for 1900 represent private families only.   [2] Includes population of Indian Territory for 1900.

TABLE 13.—HOME OWNERSHIP BY DIVISIONS AND STATES: 1910 AND 1900—NUMBER OF FARM HOMES

	DIVISION, STATE, AND YEAR.	NEGRO POPULATION.			NUMBER OF HOMES OF NEGRO FAMILIES.							
						Owned.						No report of ownership.
		Total.	Rural.	Urban.	Total.	Total.	Free.	Encumbered.	No encumbrance report.	Rented.	
1	UNITED STATES: 1910	9,827,763	7,138,534	2,689,229	2,173,018	488,699	346,867	123,044	18,788	1,603,719	80,600
2	1900	8,833,994	6,828,022	2,005,972	1,833,759	373,450	255,156	89,900	28,394	1,335,276	125,033
	GEOGRAPHIC DIVISIONS: New England—										
3	1910	66,306	5,429	60,877	15,214	2,615	1,201	1,371	43	12,302	297
4	1900	59,099	5,569	53,530	12,873	2,215	981	1,182	52	9,941	717
	Middle Atlantic—										
5	1910	417,870	78,624	339,246	93,370	11,736	5,663	5,759	314	77,263	4,371
6	1900	325,921	78,152	247,769	65,965	8,779	4,183	4,265	331	53,576	3,610
	East North Central—										
7	1910	300,836	70,294	230,542	74,654	20,620	11,196	8,776	648	52,364	1,670
8	1900	257,842	77,721	180,121	58,738	16,661	9,054	7,034	573	39,403	2,674
	West North Central—										
9	1910	242,662	78,361	164,301	59,682	19,138	12,027	6,549	562	38,020	2,524
10	1900	237,909	98,546	139,363	52,194	16,386	10,524	5,231	631	33,263	2,545
	South Atlantic—										
11	1910	4,112,488	3,202,968	909,520	882,647	208,247	157,711	42,147	8,389	641,368	33,032
12	1900	3,729,017	3,032,645	696,372	761,105	159,595	114,556	31,706	13,333	545,240	56,270
	East South Central—										
13	1910	2,652,513	2,143,416	509,097	603,322	119,291	81,584	33,495	4,212	463,236	20,795
14	1900	2,499,886	2,113,618	386,268	527,908	91,320	60,987	23,174	7,159	401,441	35,147
	West South Central—										
15	1910	1,984,426	1,548,588	435,838	431,422	102,911	75,045	23,345	4,521	311,047	17,464
16	1900	1,694,066	1,411,910	282,156	348,011	76,622	53,615	16,787	6,220	247,868	23,521
	Mountain—										
17	1910	21,467	6,021	15,446	5,658	1,589	1,081	459	49	3,831	238
18	1900	15,590	5,756	9,834	3,547	801	539	210	52	2,440	306
	Pacific—										
19	1910	29,195	4,833	24,362	7,049	2,552	1,359	1,143	50	4,288	209
20	1900	14,664	4,105	10,559	3,418	1,071	717	311	43	2,104	243
	NEW ENGLAND: Maine—										
21	1910	1,363	439	924	294	126	94	31	1	156	12
22	1900	1,319	401	918	292	121	80	32	9	156	15
	New Hampshire—										
23	1910	564	208	356	121	37	18	18	1	80	4
24	1900	662	243	419	124	33	22	10	1	85	6
	Vermont—										
25	1910	1,621	280	1,341	226	46	27	18	1	176	4
26	1900	826	382	444	154	49	24	23	2	97	8
	Massachusetts—										
27	1910	38,055	2,812	35,243	8,705	1,412	599	799	14	7,136	157
28	1900	31,974	2,107	29,867	6,880	1,094	468	602	24	5,347	439
	Rhode Island—										
29	1910	9,529	474	9,055	2,353	358	160	191	7	1,946	49
30	1900	9,092	669	8,423	2,120	319	132	178	9	1,684	117
	Connecticut—										
31	1910	15,174	1,216	13,958	3,515	636	303	314	19	2,808	71
32	1900	15,226	1,767	13,459	3,303	599	255	337	7	2,572	132
	MIDDLE ATLANTIC: New York—										
33	1910	134,191	16,705	117,486	31,434	2,437	1,224	1,164	49	28,070	927
34	1900	99,232	17,876	81,356	20,982	2,213	1,127	1,027	59	17,784	985
	New Jersey—										
35	1910	89,760	24,333	65,427	19,825	3,682	1,683	1,917	82	15,406	737
36	1900	69,844	23,716	46,128	13,934	2,588	1,108	1,393	87	10,571	775
	Pennsylvania—										
37	1910	193,919	37,586	156,333	42,111	5,617	2,756	2,678	183	33,787	2,707
38	1900	156,845	36,560	120,285	31,049	3,978	1,948	1,845	185	25,221	1,850
	EAST NORTH CENTRAL: Ohio—										
39	1910	111,452	29,170	82,282	28,135	8,467	4,526	3,754	187	19,051	617
40	1900	96,901	31,915	64,986	22,420	6,927	3,677	3,032	218	14,589	904
	Indiana—										
41	1910	60,320	11,895	48,425	15,302	4,036	2,284	1,656	96	10,990	276
42	1900	57,505	15,231	42,274	12,756	3,515	1,929	1,484	102	8,599	642
	Illinois—										
43	1910	109,049	23,511	85,538	26,149	6,012	3,266	2,402	344	19,455	682
44	1900	85,078	24,085	60,993	19,240	4,479	2,539	1,730	210	13,810	951
	Michigan—										
45	1910	17,115	4,959	12,156	4,391	1,932	1,040	874	18	2,382	77
46	1900	15,816	5,807	10,009	3,706	1,573	813	725	35	1,980	153
	Wisconsin—										
47	1910	2,900	759	2,141	677	173	80	90	3	486	18
48	1900	2,542	683	1,859	616	167	96	63	8	425	24
	WEST NORTH CENTRAL: Minnesota—										
49	1910	7,084	566	6,518	1,685	416	247	163	6	1,169	100
50	1900	4,959	464	4,495	1,084	140	84	52	4	859	85
	Iowa—										
51	1910	14,973	5,187	9,786	3,807	1,138	660	417	61	2,599	70
52	1900	12,693	4,596	8,097	2,915	900	521	353	26	1,892	123
	Missouri—										
53	1910	157,452	52,990	104,462	38,134	10,130	6,148	3,668	314	26,206	1,798
54	1900	161,234	71,987	89,247	34,779	9,535	5,908	3,279	348	23,629	1,615
	North Dakota—										
55	1910	617	311	306	146	52	32	16	4	75	19
56	1900	286	161	125	67	26	22	3	1	36	5
	South Dakota—										
57	1910	817	405	412	215	97	57	39	1	100	18
58	1900	465	270	195	107	46	28	11	7	51	10
	Nebraska—										
59	1910	7,689	1,068	6,621	1,885	454	275	170	9	1,337	94
60	1900	6,269	828	5,441	1,263	250	150	83	17	935	78

AND OTHER HOMES OWNED FREE, OWNED ENCUMBERED, AND RENTED BY NEGRO FAMILIES.

Total.	Owned. Total.	Free.	Encumbered.	No encumbrance report.	Rented.	No report of ownership.	Total.	Owned. Total.	Free.	Encumbered.	No encumbrance report.	Rented.	No report of ownership.	
877,648	220,698	156,450	60,167	4,081	653,768	3,182	1,295,370	268,001	190,417	62,877	14,707	949,951	77,418	1
758,463	191,143	128,851	50,140	12,152	560,005	7,315	1,075,296	182,307	126,305	39,760	16,242	775,271	117,718	2
318	257	133	117	7	61		14,896	2,358	1,068	1,254	36	12,241	297	3
296	225	120	100	5	71		12,577	1,990	861	1,082	47	9,870	717	4
1,392	865	436	407	22	514	13	91,978	10,871	5,227	5,352	292	76,749	4,358	5
1,444	903	379	495	29	524	17	64,521	7,876	3,804	3,770	302	53,052	3,593	6
5,004	3,192	1,697	1,470	25	1,792	20	69,650	17,428	9,499	7,306	623	50,572	1,650	7
5,524	3,463	1,895	1,476	92	2,002	59	53,214	13,198	7,159	5,558	481	37,401	2,615	8
5,723	3,472	1,853	1,571	48	2,199	52	53,959	15,666	10,174	4,978	514	35,821	2,472	9
7,316	4,227	2,443	1,658	126	3,024	65	44,878	12,159	8,081	3,573	505	30,239	2,480	10
351,868	102,036	79,089	21,489	1,458	248,451	1,381	530,779	106,211	78,622	20,658	6,931	392,917	31,651	11
293,512	86,009	62,725	17,831	5,453	204,848	2,655	467,593	73,586	51,831	13,875	7,880	340,392	53,615	12
315,353	59,027	36,424	21,360	1,243	255,349	977	287,969	60,264	45,160	12,135	2,969	207,887	19,818	13
273,753	50,628	31,067	16,382	3,179	220,404	2,721	254,155	40,692	29,920	6,792	3,980	181,037	32,426	14
197,467	51,444	36,534	13,641	1,269	145,293	730	233,955	51,467	38,511	9,704	3,252	165,754	16,734	15
176,256	45,421	30,015	12,146	3,260	129,043	1,792	171,755	31,201	23,600	4,641	2,960	118,825	21,729	16
233	178	134	40	4	53	2	5,425	1,411	947	419	45	3,778	236	17
143	110	85	18	7	31	2	3,404	691	454	192	45	2,409	304	18
290	227	150	72	5	56	7	6,759	2,325	1,209	1,071	45	4,232	202	19
219	157	122	34	1	58	4	3,199	914	595	277	42	2,046	239	20
29	26	19	7		3		265	100	75	24	1	153	12	21
34	32	22	9	1	2		258	89	58	23	8	154	15	22
16	15	7	7	1	1		105	22	11	11		79	4	23
13	8	5	2	1	5		111	25	17	8		80	6	24
22	17	7	10		5		204	29	20	8	1	171	4	25
11	10	6	4		1		143	39	18	19	2	96	8	26
114	101	50	50	1	13		8,591	1,311	549	749	13	7,123	157	27
91	72	37	33	2	19		6,789	1,022	431	569	22	5,328	439	28
38	26	16	10		12		2,315	332	144	181	7	1,934	49	29
28	19	10	8	1	9		2,092	300	122	170	8	1,675	117	30
99	72	34	33	5	27		3,416	564	269	281	14	2,781	71	31
119	84	40	44		35		3,184	515	215	293	7	2,537	132	32
311	210	99	105	6	100	1	31,123	2,227	1,125	1,059	43	27,970	926	33
333	214	99	111	4	111	8	20,649	1,999	1,028	916	55	17,673	977	34
489	289	142	139	8	194	6	19,336	3,393	1,541	1,778	74	15,212	731	35
496	314	124	180	10	173	9	13,438	2,274	984	1,213	77	10,398	766	36
592	366	195	163	8	220	6	41,519	5,251	2,561	2,515	175	33,567	2,701	37
615	375	156	204	15	240		30,434	3,603	1,792	1,641	170	24,981	1,850	38
2,009	1,358	805	539	14	646	5	26,126	7,109	3,721	3,215	173	18,405	612	39
2,174	1,379	785	562	32	770	25	20,246	5,548	2,892	2,470	186	13,819	879	40
824	478	246	231	1	343	3	14,478	3,558	2,038	1,425	95	10,647	273	41
1,064	705	415	268	22	344	15	11,692	2,810	1,514	1,216	80	8,255	627	42
1,477	809	409	393	7	656	12	24,672	5,203	2,857	2,009	337	18,799	670	43
1,569	834	472	332	30	719	16	17,671	3,645	2,067	1,398	180	13,091	935	44
640	505	227	275	3	135		3,751	1,427	813	599	15	2,247	77	45
657	500	202	291	7	155	2	3,049	1,073	611	434	28	1,825	151	46
54	42	10	32		12		623	131	70	58	3	474	18	47
60	45	21	23	1	14	1	556	122	75	40	7	411	23	48
42	24	16	8		16	2	1,643	392	231	155	6	1,153	98	49
34	22	7	14	1	11	1	1,050	118	77	38	3	848	84	50
207	136	64	72		71		3,600	1,002	596	345	61	2,528	70	51
197	116	58	58		78	3	2,718	784	463	295	26	1,814	120	52
3,734	2,156	1,092	1,031	33	1,562	16	34,400	7,974	5,056	2,637	281	24,644	1,782	53
5,183	2,848	1,586	1,175	87	2,301	34	29,596	6,687	4,322	2,104	261	21,328	1,581	54
28	23	12	11		5		118	29	20	5	4	70	19	55
14	12	10	1	1	2		53	14	12	2		34	5	56
71	50	36	23		10	2	144	38	21	16	1	90	16	57
20	14	10	3	1	5	1	87	32	18	8	6	46	9	58
109	82	64	18		26	1	1,776	372	211	152	9	1,311	93	59
77	46	27	19		30	1	1,186	204	123	64	17	905	77	60

TABLE **13.**—HOME OWNERSHIP BY DIVISIONS AND STATES: 1910 AND 1900—NUMBER OF FARM HOMES

	DIVISION, STATE, AND YEAR.	NEGRO POPULATION.			NUMBER OF HOMES OF NEGRO FAMILIES.						
		Total.	Rural.	Urban.	Total.	Owned.				Rented.	No report of ownership.
						Total.	Free.	Encumbered.	No encumbrance report.		
	WEST NORTH CENTRAL—Continued. Kansas—										
1	1910	54,030	17,834	36,196	13,810	6,851	4,608	2,076	167	6,534	425
2	1900	52,003	20,240	31,763	11,979	5,489	3,811	1,450	228	5,861	629
	SOUTH ATLANTIC: Delaware—										
3	1910	31,181	20,024	11,157	6,476	1,501	884	543	74	4,669	306
4	1900	30,697	19,160	11,537	6,014	1,297	671	489	137	4,271	446
	Maryland—										
5	1910	232,250	133,020	99,230	47,177	12,068	8,081	3,492	495	32,774	2,335
6	1900	235,064	141,215	93,849	45,310	10,401	6,784	2,763	854	30,826	4,083
	District of Columbia—										
7	1910	94,446	....	94,446	19,246	2,072	1,294	747	31	16,437	737
8	1900	86,702	....	86,702	17,269	1,964	1,269	640	55	14,721	584
	Virginia—										
9	1910	671,096	512,878	158,218	137,771	56,933	45,267	10,259	1,407	77,048	3,790
10	1900	660,722	535,923	124,799	128,530	46,268	34,234	9,054	2,980	75,895	6,367
	West Virginia—										
11	1910	64,173	48,793	15,380	14,197	2,743	2,016	634	93	10,942	512
12	1900	43,499	34,738	8,761	8,248	1,983	1,383	433	167	5,888	377
	North Carolina—										
13	1910	697,843	581,868	115,975	139,713	40,118	29,265	8,965	1,888	95,148	4,447
14	1900	624,469	548,300	76,169	122,208	29,019	20,247	6,129	2,643	85,681	7,508
	South Carolina—										
15	1910	835,843	734,141	101,702	179,490	33,161	25,241	6,441	1,479	139,240	7,089
16	1900	782,321	697,963	84,358	160,521	26,870	19,696	4,926	2,248	121,178	12,473
	Georgia—										
17	1910	1,176,987	952,161	224,826	263,183	38,735	29,122	7,817	1,796	215,459	8,989
18	1900	1,034,813	873,752	161,061	221,254	26,636	19,123	4,988	2,525	174,251	20,367
	Florida—										
19	1910	308,669	220,083	88,586	75,394	20,916	16,541	3,249	1,126	49,651	4,827
20	1900	230,730	181,594	49,136	51,751	15,157	11,149	2,284	1,724	32,529	4,065
	EAST SOUTH CENTRAL: Kentucky—										
21	1910	261,656	155,025	106,631	62,216	19,774	15,351	3,557	866	40,364	2,078
22	1900	284,706	184,561	100,145	60,311	17,906	13,248	3,374	1,284	39,154	3,251
	Tennessee—										
23	1910	473,088	322,582	150,506	106,558	27,012	20,185	5,811	1,016	76,833	2,713
24	1900	480,243	349,099	131,144	96,427	21,023	15,141	3,679	2,203	69,911	5,493
	Alabama—										
25	1910	908,282	751,679	156,603	206,884	33,941	22,729	10,105	1,107	164,024	8,919
26	1900	827,307	729,153	98,154	178,365	23,536	15,480	6,200	1,856	142,819	12,010
	Mississippi—										
27	1910	1,009,487	914,130	95,357	227,664	38,564	23,319	14,022	1,223	182,015	7,085
28	1900	907,630	850,805	56,825	192,805	28,855	17,118	9,921	1,816	149,557	14,393
	WEST SOUTH CENTRAL: Arkansas—										
29	1910	442,891	383,744	59,147	97,787	24,018	15,908	6,879	1,231	69,202	4,567
30	1900	366,856	329,685	37,171	76,803	16,838	10,958	4,436	1,444	54,324	5,641
	Louisiana—										
31	1910	713,874	553,029	160,845	159,350	27,237	20,795	5,195	1,247	125,926	6,187
32	1900	650,804	533,850	116,954	140,264	20,453	15,042	3,941	1,470	108,702	11,109
	Oklahoma [1]—										
33	1910	137,612	100,630	36,982	28,395	10,018	6,645	2,659	714	17,144	1,233
34	1900	55,684	46,982	8,702	11,256	6,039	4,409	490	1,140	4,939	548
	Texas—										
35	1910	690,049	511,185	178,864	145,890	41,638	31,697	8,612	1,329	98,775	5,477
36	1900	620,722	501,393	119,329	119,418	33,292	23,206	7,920	2,166	79,903	6,223
	MOUNTAIN: Montana—										
37	1910	1,834	379	1,455	555	182	134	37	11	336	37
38	1900	1,523	592	931	393	75	56	17	2	280	38
	Idaho—										
39	1910	651	225	426	167	48	31	15	2	100	19
40	1900	293	222	71	81	36	26	7	3	39	6
	Wyoming—										
41	1910	2,235	1,194	1,041	375	69	48	21	....	288	18
42	1900	940	451	489	160	32	27	4	1	116	12
	Colorado—										
43	1910	11,453	2,094	9,359	3,079	849	533	294	22	2,141	89
44	1900	8,570	1,518	7,052	2,052	467	280	163	24	1,493	92
	New Mexico—										
45	1910	1,628	833	795	449	136	111	20	5	304	9
46	1900	1,610	1,029	581	381	69	51	5	13	265	47
	Arizona—										
47	1910	2,009	699	1,310	583	179	122	50	7	376	28
48	1900	1,848	1,518	330	309	85	69	11	5	137	87
	Utah—										
49	1910	1,144	185	959	240	51	32	18	1	154	35
50	1900	672	329	343	119	19	16	2	1	85	15
	Nevada—										
51	1910	513	412	101	210	75	70	4	1	132	3
52	1900	134	97	37	52	18	14	1	3	25	9
	PACIFIC: Washington—										
53	1910	6,058	1,359	4,699	1,356	435	249	179	7	854	67
54	1900	2,514	908	1,606	566	161	140	19	2	356	49
	Oregon—										
55	1910	1,492	228	1,264	347	98	58	38	2	217	32
56	1900	1,105	227	878	191	49	32	7	10	120	22
	California—										
57	1910	21,645	3,246	18,399	5,346	2,019	1,052	926	41	3,217	110
58	1900	11,045	2,970	8,075	2,661	861	545	285	31	1,628	172

[1] Includes population of Indian Territory for 1900.

AND OTHER HOMES OWNED FREE, OWNED ENCUMBERED, AND RENTED BY NEGRO FAMILIES—Continued.

Total.	FARM HOMES. Owned. Total.	Free.	Encumbered.	No encumbrance report.	Rented.	No report of ownership.	Total.	OTHER HOMES. Owned. Total.	Free.	Encumbered.	No encumbrance report.	Rented.	No report of ownership.	
1,532	992	569	408	15	509	31	12,278	5,859	4,039	1,668	152	6,025	394	1
1,791	1,169	745	388	36	597	25	10,188	4,320	3,066	1,062	192	5,264	604	2
966	436	261	169	6	526	4	5,510	1,065	623	374	68	4,143	302	3
827	336	181	124	31	481	10	5,187	961	490	365	106	3,790	436	4
6,653	4,091	2,710	1,357	24	2,536	26	40,524	7,977	5,371	2,135	471	30,238	2,309	5
6,350	3,480	2,228	981	271	2,725	145	38,960	6,921	4,556	1,782	583	28,101	3,938	6
15	10	7	2	1	5		19,231	2,062	1,287	745	30	16,432	737	7
18	9	6	3		9		17,251	1,955	1,263	637	55	14,712	584	8
48,410	32,528	26,972	5,420	136	15,793	89	89,361	24,405	18,295	4,839	1,271	61,255	3,701	9
46,541	27,450	21,113	5,121	1,216	18,812	279	81,989	18,818	13,121	3,933	1,764	57,083	6,088	10
674	523	456	66	1	150	1	13,523	2,220	1,560	568	92	10,792	511	11
824	573	478	77	18	242	9	7,424	1,410	905	356	149	5,646	368	12
63,814	20,491	14,997	5,239	255	43,112	211	75,899	19,627	14,268	3,726	1,633	52,036	4,236	13
55,356	16,952	11,909	4,108	935	38,099	305	66,852	12,067	8,338	2,021	1,708	47,582	7,203	14
95,737	20,431	15,834	4,149	448	74,875	431	83,753	12,730	9,407	2,292	1,031	64,365	6,658	15
86,014	18,874	13,743	3,671	1,460	66,499	641	74,507	7,996	5,953	1,255	788	54,679	11,832	16
120,822	16,191	11,854	3,883	454	104,053	578	142,361	22,544	17,268	3,934	1,342	111,406	8,411	17
83,695	11,736	8,195	2,709	832	70,855	1,104	137,559	14,900	10,928	2,279	1,693	103,396	19,263	18
14,777	7,335	5,998	1,204	133	7,401	41	60,617	13,581	10,543	2,045	993	42,250	4,786	19
13,887	6,599	4,872	1,037	690	7,126	162	37,864	8,558	6,277	1,247	1,034	25,403	3,903	20
11,356	6,077	4,632	1,374	71	5,243	36	50,860	13,697	10,719	2,183	795	35,121	2,042	21
11,985	5,915	4,451	1,179	285	5,927	143	48,326	11,991	8,797	2,195	999	33,227	3,108	22
37,246	10,942	8,198	2,577	167	26,228	76	69,312	16,070	11,987	3,234	849	50,605	2,637	23
35,325	9,819	7,358	1,827	634	25,046	460	61,102	11,204	7,783	1,852	1,569	44,865	5,033	24
107,696	17,227	10,434	6,379	414	90,218	251	99,188	16,714	12,295	3,726	693	73,806	8,668	25
92,830	13,955	8,172	4,764	1,019	77,970	905	85,535	9,581	7,308	1,436	837	64,849	11,105	26
159,055	24,781	13,160	11,030	591	133,660	614	68,609	13,783	10,159	2,992	632	48,355	6,471	27
133,613	20,939	11,086	8,612	1,241	111,461	1,213	59,192	7,916	6,032	1,309	575	38,096	13,180	28
61,177	14,216	9,208	4,621	387	46,543	418	36,610	9,802	6,700	2,258	844	22,659	4,149	29
47,547	11,713	7,481	3,477	755	34,944	890	29,256	5,125	3,477	959	689	19,380	4,751	30
55,094	11,077	8,145	2,669	263	43,906	111	104,256	16,160	12,650	2,526	984	82,020	6,076	31
57,639	9,577	6,495	2,510	572	47,649	413	82,625	10,876	8,547	1,431	898	61,053	10,696	32
13,518	4,956	3,022	1,620	314	8,478	84	14,877	5,062	3,623	1,039	400	8,666	1,149	33
6,735	4,005	2,870	314	821	2,604	126	4,791	2,034	1,539	176	319	2,335	422	34
67,678	21,195	16,159	4,731	305	46,366	117	78,212	20,443	15,538	3,881	1,024	52,409	5,360	35
64,335	20,126	13,169	5,845	1,112	43,846	363	55,083	13,166	10,037	2,075	1,054	36,057	5,860	36
30	22	18	4		8		525	160	116	33	11	328	37	37
24	16	9	6	1	6	2	369	59	47	11	1	274	36	38
17	15	6	9		2		150	33	25	6	2	98	19	39
9	9	7	1	1			72	27	19	6	2	39	6	40
18	16	10	6		2		357	53	38	15		286	18	41
9	8	7	1		1		151	24	20	3	1	115	12	42
88	57	40	17		29	2	2,991	792	493	277	22	2,112	87	43
61	49	41	7	1	12		1,991	418	239	156	23	1,481	92	44
48	42	38	3	1	6		401	94	73	17	4	298	9	45
16	9	5	2	2	7		365	60	46	3	11	258	47	46
14	12	10	1	1	2		569	167	112	49	6	374	28	47
10	9	7		2	1		299	76	62	11	3	136	87	48
12	9	8		1	3		228	42	24	18		151	35	49
10	7	6	1		3		109	12	10	1	1	82	15	50
6	5	4		1	1		204	70	66	4		131	3	51
4	3	3			1		48	15	11	1	3	24	9	52
87	71	49	19	3	16		1,269	364	200	160	4	838	67	53
61	56	50	6		5		505	105	90	13	2	351	49	54
30	23	19	4		7		317	75	39	34	2	210	32	55
15	11	8	3		3	1	176	38	24	4	10	117	21	56
173	133	82	49	2	33	7	5,173	1,886	970	877	39	3,184	103	57
143	90	64	25	1	50	3	2,518	771	481	260	30	1,578	169	58

TABLE 14.—HOME OWNERSHIP, BY DIVISIONS AND STATES: 1890—NUMBER OF FARM HOMES AND OTHER HOMES OWNED FREE, OWNED ENCUMBERED, AND RENTED BY NEGRO FAMILIES.

DIVISION AND STATE.	NUMBER OF HOMES OF NEGRO FAMILIES: 1890.														
	Total.	Owned.			Rented.	Farm homes.						Other homes.				
		Total.	Free.	Encumbered.		Total.	Owned.			Rented.	Total.	Owned.			Rented.
							Total.	Free.	Encumbered.			Total.	Free.	Encumbered.	
UNITED STATES.....	1,410,769	264,288	234,747	29,541	1,146,481	549,632	120,738	108,483	12,255	428,894	861,137	143,550	126,264	17,286	717,587
GEOGRAPHIC DIVISIONS:															
New England.........	9,754	1,814	1,047	767	7,940	357	220	146	74	137	9,397	1,594	901	693	7,803
Middle Atlantic.......	44,158	7,915	4,761	3,154	36,243	1,431	870	448	422	561	42,727	7,045	4,313	2,732	35,682
East North Central...	44,764	14,379	9,241	5,138	30,385	5,795	3,187	1,873	1,314	2,608	38,969	11,192	7,368	3,824	27,777
West North Central...	44,261	15,372	10,819	4,553	28,889	7,995	4,343	2,698	1,645	3,652	36,266	11,029	8,121	2,908	25,237
South Atlantic.......	613,236	115,116	107,084	8,032	498,120	218,003	53,261	49,601	3,660	164,742	395,233	61,855	57,483	4,372	333,378
East South Central ...	399,065	60,232	55,643	4,589	338,833	195,702	30,861	27,898	2,963	164,841	203,363	29,371	27,745	1,626	173,992
West South Central ...	250,406	47,967	44,948	3,019	202,439	119,976	27,709	25,588	2,121	92,267	130,430	20,258	19,360	898	110,172
Mountain.............	2,255	635	519	116	1,620	119	90	81	9	29	2,136	545	438	107	1,591
Pacific..............	2,870	858	685	173	2,012	254	197	150	47	57	2,616	661	535	126	1,955
NEW ENGLAND:															
Maine..............	254	99	71	28	155	36	29	22	7	7	218	70	49	21	148
New Hampshire.......	114	24	13	11	90	8	6	3	3	2	106	18	10	8	88
Vermont.............	176	42	32	10	134	18	13	7	6	5	158	29	25	4	129
Massachusetts........	4,802	848	479	369	3,954	108	75	50	25	33	4,694	773	429	344	3,921
Rhode Island........	1,759	254	152	102	1,505	32	16	13	3	16	1,727	238	139	99	1,489
Connecticut..........	2,649	547	300	247	2,102	155	81	51	30	74	2,494	466	249	217	2,028
MIDDLE ATLANTIC:															
New York............	14,586	2,119	1,259	860	12,467	382	236	111	125	146	14,204	1,883	1,148	735	12,321
New Jersey..........	9,509	2,222	1,289	933	7,287	456	272	128	144	184	9,053	1,950	1,161	789	7,103
Pennsylvania.........	20,063	3,574	2,213	1,361	16,489	593	362	209	153	231	19,470	3,212	2,004	1,208	16,258
EAST NORTH CENTRAL:															
Ohio................	18,821	6,276	4,097	2,179	12,545	2,290	1,323	840	483	967	16,531	4,953	3,257	1,696	11,578
Indiana.............	9,771	2,731	1,702	1,029	7,040	1,083	528	315	213	555	8,688	2,203	1,387	816	6,485
Illinois............	12,014	3,621	2,471	1,150	8,393	1,670	761	479	282	909	10,344	2,860	1,992	868	7,484
Michigan............	3,616	1,524	830	694	2,092	674	507	211	296	167	2,942	1,017	619	398	1,925
Wisconsin...........	542	227	141	86	315	78	68	28	40	10	464	159	113	46	305
WEST NORTH CENTRAL:															
Minnesota...........	860	169	92	77	691	28	20	9	11	8	832	149	83	66	683
Iowa...............	2,166	765	497	268	1,401	188	115	60	55	73	1,978	650	437	213	1,328
Missouri............	29,571	8,894	6,559	2,335	20,677	5,478	2,745	1,812	933	2,733	24,093	6,149	4,747	1,402	17,944
North Dakota........	72	37	26	11	35	23	20	14	6	3	49	17	12	5	32
South Dakota........	107	58	36	22	49	22	18	10	8	4	85	40	26	14	45
Nebraska...........	1,340	302	197	105	1,038	114	67	40	27	47	1,226	235	157	78	991
Kansas.............	10,145	5,147	3,412	1,735	4,998	2,142	1,358	753	605	784	8,003	3,789	2,659	1,130	4,214
SOUTH ATLANTIC:															
Delaware............	5,193	1,264	794	470	3,929	821	288	199	89	1,533	4,372	976	595	381	3,396
Maryland............	38,887	8,596	6,930	1,666	30,291	4,958	2,150	1,691	459	2,808	33,929	6,446	5,239	1,207	27,483
District of Columbia..	14,299	2,132	1,766	366	12,167	52	16	15	1	36	14,247	2,116	1,751	365	12,131
Virginia............	112,404	29,888	28,621	1,267	82,516	31,839	13,678	13,097	581	18,161	80,565	16,210	15,524	686	64,355
West Virginia.......	5,655	1,471	1,182	289	4,184	846	489	436	53	357	4,809	982	746	236	3,827
North Carolina......	102,885	20,010	18,722	1,288	82,875	40,061	10,494	9,670	824	29,567	62,824	9,516	9,052	464	53,308
South Carolina......	135,551	21,101	19,637	1,464	114,450	63,738	13,075	12,048	1,027	50,663	71,813	8,026	7,589	437	63,787
Georgia............	165,037	20,005	19,203	802	145,032	62,849	8,131	7,705	426	54,718	102,188	11,874	11,498	376	90,314
Florida............	33,325	10,649	10,229	420	22,676	12,839	4,940	4,740	200	7,899	20,486	5,709	5,489	220	14,777
EAST SOUTH CENTRAL:															
Kentucky............	49,318	12,877	12,107	770	36,441	10,153	4,110	3,870	240	6,043	39,165	8,767	8,237	530	30,398
Tennessee...........	78,195	14,663	13,626	1,037	63,532	27,860	6,378	5,951	427	21,482	50,335	8,285	7,675	610	42,050
Alabama............	132,311	15,736	14,701	1,035	116,575	69,870	8,847	8,045	802	61,023	62,441	6,889	6,656	233	55,552
Mississippi.........	139,241	16,956	15,209	1,747	122,285	87,819	11,526	10,032	1,494	76,293	51,422	5,430	5,177	253	45,992
WEST SOUTH CENTRAL:															
Arkansas............	56,446	11,844	10,902	942	44,602	33,486	8,004	7,319	685	25,482	22,960	3,840	3,583	257	19,120
Louisiana...........	107,370	14,602	13,882	720	92,768	38,061	6,685	6,257	428	31,376	69,309	7,917	7,625	292	61,392
Oklahoma............	749	641	641	....	108	531	507	507	....	24	218	134	134	....	84
Texas..............	85,841	20,880	19,523	1,357	64,961	47,898	12,513	11,505	1,008	35,385	37,943	8,367	8,018	349	29,576
MOUNTAIN:															
Montana............	222	53	40	13	169	11	10	10	....	1	211	43	30	13	168
Idaho..............	41	16	11	5	25	6	5	2	3	1	35	11	9	2	24
Wyoming............	111	28	25	3	83	4	2	1	1	2	107	26	24	2	81
Colorado............	1,216	296	211	85	920	44	37	34	3	7	1,172	259	177	82	913
New Mexico..........	394	168	161	7	226	40	27	25	2	13	354	141	136	5	213
Arizona............	114	23	22	1	91	5	4	4	....	1	109	19	18	1	90
Utah...............	78	19	19	....	59	6	4	4	....	2	72	15	15	....	57
Nevada.............	79	32	30	2	47	3	1	1	....	2	76	31	29	2	45
PACIFIC:															
Washington..........	292	68	62	6	224	14	11	11	....	3	278	57	51	6	221
Oregon.............	171	74	56	18	97	31	25	20	5	6	140	49	36	13	91
California..........	2,407	716	567	149	1,691	209	161	119	42	48	2,198	555	448	107	1,643

TABLE 15.—HOME OWNERSHIP IN SELECTED URBAN COMMUNITIES—NUMBER OF HOMES OWNED FREE, OWNED ENCUMBERED, AND RENTED, BY NEGRO FAMILIES IN URBAN COMMUNITIES HAVING A NEGRO POPULATION OF 2,500 OR MORE: 1910.

CITY.	Negro population: 1910.	Total.	Owned.			Rented.	No report of ownership.
			Free.	Encumbered.	No encumbrance report.		
ALABAMA.							
Anniston	4,570	1,141	174	166	4	771	26
Bessemer	6,210	1,738	106	111	5	1,473	43
Birmingham	52,305	14,229	1,522	795	23	11,519	370
Dotham	3,483	675	96	94	......	466	19
Gadsden	3,435	714	119	24	1	533	37
Huntsville	3,309	970	303	58	9	585	15
Mobile	22,763	6,274	792	124	30	5,073	255
Montgomery	19,322	5,672	668	276	16	4,583	129
Selma	7,863	2,226	334	107	9	1,696	80
Talladega	2,793	670	277	28	7	310	48
Troy	2,543	658	122	58	4	467	7
Tuscaloosa	4,148	1,073	228	34	2	778	31
Union Springs	2,719	639	122	11	1	440	65
ARKANSAS.							
Argenta	4,210	1,073	186	142	1	721	23
Fort Smith	4,456	1,034	200	103	4	682	45
Helena	5,596	1,526	105	15	67	1,250	89
Hot Springs	3,827	1,049	241	72	49	624	63
Little Rock	14,539	3,277	439	441	17	2,295	85
Marianna	2,991	546	304	65	......	167	10
Pine Bluff	6,124	1,551	310	54	41	1,093	53
Texarkana [1]	2,101	547	123	41	1	373	9
CALIFORNIA.							
Los Angeles	7,599	2,030	304	420	8	1,290	8
Oakland	3,055	712	89	119	2	501	1
COLORADO.							
Denver	5,426	1,380	159	115	5	1,082	19
CONNECTICUT.							
New Haven	3,561	898	39	46	......	812	1
DELAWARE.							
Wilmington	9,081	2,136	100	117	14	1,780	125
DISTRICT OF COLUMBIA.							
Washington	94,446	19,246	1,294	747	31	16,437	737
FLORIDA.							
Gainesville	3,079	804	297	49	2	439	17
Jacksonville	29,293	7,276	977	281	56	5,552	410
Key West	5,515	1,376	122	25	84	1,087	58
Pensacola	10,214	2,778	383	234	19	2,033	109
Tallahassee	3,237	615	146	50	2	412	5
Tampa	8,951	2,378	212	113	2	2,012	39
GEORGIA.							
Albany	4,812	1,391	160	25	6	1,094	106
Americus	4,574	1,270	444	7	2	810	7
Athens	6,316	1,676	322	109	5	1,200	40
Atlanta	51,902	13,620	1,267	481	18	11,502	352
Augusta	18,344	5,679	542	11	49	4,835	242
Brunswick	5,567	1,457	208	47	7	1,138	57
Columbus	7,644	2,156	211	12	2	1,856	75
Cordele	3,209	884	312	32	11	521	8
Dublin	2,769	690	162	87	7	409	25
Elberton	2,919	528	50	33	......	424	21
Griffin	3,425	867	199	48	4	593	23
Macon	18,150	5,419	678	102	81	4,326	232
Milledgeville	2,560	736	238	9	2	486	1
Rome	3,758	1,002	187	80	7	699	29
Savannah	33,246	9,530	430	152	43	8,459	446
Thomasville	3,789	1,065	338	108	4	587	28
Valdosta	3,844	975	155	104	9	682	25
Waycross	6,729	1,388	316	64	11	955	42
ILLINOIS.							
Cairo	5,434	1,517	163	61	5	1,191	97
Chicago	44,103	10,421	315	329	18	9,520	239
East St. Louis	5,882	1,547	81	117	4	1,292	53
Springfield	2,961	751	98	151	23	467	12
INDIANA.							
Evansville	6,266	1,560	100	68	4	1,388	......
Indianapolis	21,816	5,818	451	375	27	4,865	100
Terre Haute	2,593	703	55	132	10	485	21
IOWA.							
Des Moines	2,930	767	113	78	34	542	......

CITY.	Negro population: 1910.	Total.	Owned.			Rented.	No report of ownership.
			Free.	Encumbered.	No encumbrance report.		
KANSAS.							
Atchison	2,618	621	243	55	35	251	37
Kansas City	9,286	2,676	630	388	18	1,590	50
Topeka	4,538	1,258	374	183	1	661	39
KENTUCKY.							
Covington	2,899	813	36	42	......	719	16
Frankfort	2,851	579	119	25	1	434	......
Henderson	3,016	834	159	41	6	608	20
Hopkinsville	4,187	1,006	283	97	10	550	66
Lexington	11,011	3,157	553	89	2	2,484	29
Louisville	40,522	10,959	499	194	18	9,942	306
Owensboro	3,115	836	131	49	1	626	29
Paducah	6,047	1,722	259	40	10	1,361	52
Winchester	2,688	747	296	45	19	337	50
LOUISIANA.							
Alexandria	5,854	1,288	185	44	5	999	55
Baton Rouge	7,899	1,985	288	54	14	1,566	63
Lafayette	2,792	598	200	38	13	336	11
Lake Charles	4,437	961	246	79	4	611	21
Monroe	5,320	1,533	137	87	10	1,269	30
New Iberia	3,480	789	220	56	......	499	14
New Orleans	89,262	21,880	1,854	490	87	18,313	1,136
Plaquemine	2,673	734	80	35	1	607	11
Shreveport	13,896	3,742	597	113	15	2,809	208
MARYLAND.							
Annapolis	3,184	739	56	28	......	640	15
Baltimore	84,749	18,106	675	203	55	15,842	1,331
MASSACHUSETTS.							
Boston	13,564	3,372	49	80	5	3,170	68
Cambridge	4,707	1,155	43	107	......	1,000	5
New Bedford	2,885	677	65	69	......	537	6
MICHIGAN.							
Detroit	5,741	1,383	127	110	1	1,094	51
MINNESOTA.							
Minneapolis	2,592	646	70	48	2	477	49
St. Paul	3,144	748	106	73	1	534	34
MISSISSIPPI.							
Brookhaven	2,732	606	89	70	......	432	15
Columbus	4,401	1,243	316	42	3	867	15
Greenville	6,010	2,002	413	131	10	1,396	52
Greenwood	3,062	821	94	60	......	635	32
Hattiesburg	4,357	1,080	184	92	6	749	49
Jackson	10,554	2,705	404	152	18	2,039	92
Laurel	3,103	758	112	64	4	550	28
Meridian	9,321	2,571	345	175	43	1,916	92
Natchez	6,700	2,041	236	58	2	1,708	37
Vicksburg	12,053	3,823	625	116	27	2,986	69
West Point	2,772	709	280	37	5	370	17
Yazoo City	4,154	1,115	152	108	......	808	47
MISSOURI.							
Kansas City	23,566	6,204	235	329	10	5,244	386
St. Joseph	4,249	1,003	90	69	1	843	......
St. Louis	43,960	10,891	339	269	7	9,788	488
NEBRASKA.							
Omaha	4,426	1,071	69	91	6	857	48
NEW JERSEY.							
Atlantic City	9,834	1,914	31	53	2	1,643	185
Camden	6,076	1,580	138	86	1	1,294	61
Jersey City	5,960	1,435	54	96	3	1,250	32
Newark	9,475	2,328	39	92	1	2,129	67
Trenton	2,581	483	13	20	1	429	20
NEW YORK.							
New York City	91,709	22,452	218	324	3	21,351	556
Manhattan Borough	60,534	15,341	4	18	1	14,943	375
Bronx Borough	4,117	931	22	39	......	850	20
Brooklyn Borough	22,708	5,199	101	164	......	4,804	130
Queens Borough	3,198	726	65	86	2	550	23
Richmond Borough	1,152	255	26	17	......	204	8

[1] Total number of homes in Texarkana, Miller County, Ark., and Texarkana, Bowie County, Tex., 1,342; owned free, 263; owned mortgaged, 115; no encumbrance report, 2; rented, 935; no report of ownership, 27.

TABLE 15.—HOME OWNERSHIP IN SELECTED URBAN COMMUNITIES—NUMBER OF HOMES OWNED FREE, OWNED ENCUMBERED, AND RENTED BY NEGRO FAMILIES IN URBAN COMMUNITIES HAVING A NEGRO POPULATION OF 2,500 OR MORE: 1910—Continued.

CITY.	Negro population: 1910.	NUMBER OF HOMES OF NEGRO FAMILIES: 1910.					
		Total.	Owned.			Rented.	No report of ownership.
			Free.	Encumbered.	No encumbrance report.		
NORTH CAROLINA.							
Asheville	5,359	1,247	244	79	10	878	36
Charlotte	11,752	3,167	349	187	27	2,483	121
Durham	6,869	1,570	171	92	6	1,259	42
Elizabeth City	3,977	886	146	155	18	513	54
Fayetteville	3,293	950	256	14	4	664	12
Goldsboro	2,521	665	94	5	......	549	17
Greensboro	5,710	1,383	229	98	4	1,019	33
Kinston	3,027	719	202	50	14	440	13
Newbern	5,649	1,395	437	46	1	886	25
Raleigh	7,372	1,777	331	75	17	1,344	10
Rocky Mount	3,069	760	142	53	......	552	13
Washington	3,072	757	196	17	3	526	15
Wilmington	12,107	3,048	508	114	195	2,127	104
Wilson	2,998	753	108	50	1	569	25
Winston	7,828	1,916	157	95	9	1,602	53
OHIO.							
Cincinnati	19,639	5,415	161	127	6	5,009	112
Cleveland	8,448	2,225	100	139	3	1,950	33
Columbus	12,739	3,064	235	270	7	2,469	83
Dayton	4,842	1,324	75	221	6	986	36
Springfield	4,933	1,269	155	278	4	832	......
OKLAHOMA.							
Guthrie	2,976	703	306	76	....	299	22
McAlester	2,997	498	105	35	6	334	18
Muskogee	7,831	1,707	419	115	8	1,072	93
Oklahoma City	6,546	1,235	169	115	12	808	131
PENNSYLVANIA.							
Chester	4,795	1,148	74	62	....	967	45
Harrisburg	4,535	1,025	74	72	1	836	42
Philadelphia	84,459	18,095	372	496	37	15,376	1,814
Pittsburgh	25,623	5,949	284	355	12	5,051	247
RHODE ISLAND.							
Providence	5,316	1,402	46	62	1	1,267	26
SOUTH CAROLINA.							
Anderson	3,370	875	68	137	21	623	26
Charleston	31,056	9,370	694	87	55	7,836	698
Columbia	11,546	2,957	261	90	24	2,498	84
Florence	3,536	940	132	79	14	686	29
Georgetown	3,650	1,063	208	22	....	833	......
Greenville	6,319	1,712	198	87	....	1,387	40
SOUTH CAROLINA—Con.							
Greenwood	2,943	593	161	68	4	353	7
Orangeburg	3,017	763	102	54	3	599	5
Spartanburg	6,873	1,710	262	166	3	1,248	31
Sumter	4,125	1,094	57	68	92	823	54
TENNESSEE.							
Chattanooga	17,942	4,845	268	71	5	4,395	106
Clarksville	4,285	1,154	257	33	6	844	14
Jackson	5,719	1,538	250	30	15	1,206	37
Knoxville	7,638	1,834	248	68	8	1,462	48
Memphis	52,441	14,842	1,039	521	111	12,644	527
Nashville	36,523	9,979	1,461	557	25	7,853	83
TEXAS.							
Austin	7,478	1,660	436	170	7	1,004	43
Beaumont	6,896	1,610	256	53	3	1,282	16
Corsicana	2,842	721	206	82	2	408	23
Dallas	18,024	4,256	435	159	7	3,481	174
Denison	2,799	721	205	118	3	380	15
Fort Worth	13,280	3,152	344	175	44	2,412	177
Galveston	8,036	2,023	131	35	3	1,752	102
Houston	23,929	5,890	809	350	24	4,504	203
Marshall	4,997	1,179	383	56	3	723	14
Palestine	3,554	896	213	127	2	518	36
Paris	3,131	793	204	33	2	539	15
San Antonio	10,716	2,402	404	184	34	1,700	80
Temple	2,814	582	64	76	1	388	53
Texarkana [1]	3,218	795	140	74	1	562	18
Tyler	2,954	714	199	29	14	443	29
Waco	6,067	1,288	232	63	29	887	77
VIRGINIA.							
Alexandria	4,188	1,072	229	26	2	729	86
Charlottesville	2,524	578	96	31	11	435	5
Danville	6,207	1,567	297	162	....	1,088	20
Lynchburg	9,466	2,294	486	126	3	1,641	38
Newport News	7,259	1,769	125	141	1	1,459	43
Norfolk	25,039	6,391	208	50	15	5,977	141
Petersburg	11,014	2,894	740	80	14	2,020	40
Portsmouth	11,617	2,948	256	165	2	2,472	53
Richmond	46,733	10,496	1,209	385	52	8,519	331
Roanoke	7,924	1,733	311	160	2	1,233	27
Suffolk	2,806	624	108	71	1	431	13
WEST VIRGINIA.							
Charleston	3,086	640	93	22	8	498	19

[1] Total number of homes in Texarkana, Miller County, Ark., and Texarkana, Bowie County, Tex., 1,342; owned free, 263; owned mortgaged, 115; no encumbrance report, 2; rented, 935; no report of ownership, 27.

TABLE 16.—PERCENTAGE OWNED OF NEGRO HOMES IN URBAN COMMUNITIES HAVING A NEGRO POPULATION OF 2,500 OR MORE: 1910.

CITY.	Percentage owned of all Negro homes.	CITY.	Percentage owned of all Negro homes.	CITY.	Percentage owned of all Negro homes.	CITY.	Percentage owned of all Negro homes.
Albany, Ga	13.7	Dothan, Ala	28.1	McAlester, Okla	29.3	Rocky Mount, N. C	25.7
Alexandria, La	18.2	Dublin, Ga	37.1	Macon, Ga	15.9	Rome, Ga	27.3
Alexandria, Va	24.0	Durham, N. C	17.1	Marianna, Ark	67.6	St. Joseph, Mo	16.0
Americus, Ga	35.7	East St. Louis, Ill	13.1	Marshall, Tex	37.5	St. Louis, Mo	5.6
Anderson, S. C	25.8	Elberton, Ga	15.7	Memphis, Tenn	11.3	St. Paul, Minn	24.1
Annapolis, Md	11.4	Elizabeth City, N. C	36.0	Meridian, Miss	21.9	San Antonio, Tex	25.9
Anniston, Ala	30.1	Evansville, Ind	11.0	Milledgeville, Ga	33.8	Savannah, Ga	6.6
Argenta, Ark	30.7	Fayetteville, N. C	28.8	Minneapolis, Minn	18.6	Selma, Ala	20.2
Asheville, N. C	26.7	Florence, S. C	23.9	Mobile, Ala	15.1	Shreveport, La	19.4
Atchison, Kans	53.6	Fort Smith, Ark	29.7	Monroe, La	15.3	Spartanburg, S. C	25.2
Athens, Ga	26.0	Fort Worth, Tex	17.9	Montgomery, Ala	16.9	Springfield, Ill	36.2
Atlanta, Ga	13.0	Frankfort, Ky	25.0	Muskogee, Okla	31.8	Springfield, Ohio	34.4
Atlantic City, N. J	4.5	Gadsden, Ala	20.2	Nashville, Tenn	20.5	Suffolk, Va	28.8
Augusta, Ga	10.6	Gainesville, Fla	43.3	Natchez, Miss	14.5	Sumter, S. C	19.8
Austin, Tex	36.9	Galveston, Tex	8.4	Newark, N. J	5.7	Talladega, Ala	46.6
Baltimore, Md	5.2	Georgetown, S. C	21.6	New Bedford, Mass	19.8	Tallahassee, Fla	32.2
Baton Rouge, La	17.9	Goldsboro, N. C	14.9	New Bern, N. C	34.7	Tampa, Fla	13.8
Beaumont, Tex	19.4	Greensboro, N. C	23.9	New Haven, Conn	9.5	Temple, Tex	24.2
Bessemer, Ala	12.8	Greenville, Miss	27.7	New Iberia, La	35.0	Terre Haute, Ind	28.0
Birmingham, Ala	16.4	Greenville, S. C	16.6	New Orleans, La	11.1	Texarkana, Ark	30.2
Boston, Mass	4.0	Greenwood, Miss	18.8	Newport News, Va	15.1	Texarkana, Tex	27.0
Brookhaven, Miss	26.2	Greenwood, S. C	39.3	New York, N. Y	2.4	Thomasville, Ga	42.3
Brunswick, Ga	18.0	Griffin, Ga	29.0	Manhattan Borough	0.1	Topeka, Kans	44.4
Cairo, Ill	15.1	Guthrie, Okla	54.3	Bronx Borough	6.6	Trenton, N. J	7.0
Cambridge, Mass	13.0	Hattiesburg, Miss	26.1	Brooklyn Borough	5.1	Troy, Ala	28.0
Camden, N. J	14.2	Harrisburg, Pa	14.3	Queens Borough	21.1		
Charleston, S. C	8.9	Helena, Ark	12.3	Richmond Borough	16.9	Tuscaloosa, Ala	24.6
Charleston, W. Va	19.2	Henderson, Ky	24.7			Tyler, Tex	33.9
Charlotte, N. C	17.8	Hopkinsville, Ky	38.8	Norfolk, Va	4.3	Union Springs, Ala	21.0
Charlottesville, Va	23.9	Hot Springs, Ark	34.5	Oakland, Cal	29.5	Valdosta, Ga	27.5
Chattanooga, Tenn	7.1	Houston, Tex	20.1	Oklahoma City, Okla	24.0		
Chester, Pa	11.8	Huntsville, Ala	38.1	Omaha, Nebr	15.5	Vicksburg, Miss	20.1
Chicago, Ill	6.4	Indianapolis, Ind	14.7	Orangeburg, S. C	20.8	Waco, Tex	25.2
Cincinnati, Ohio	5.4	Jackson, Miss	21.2			Washington, D. C	10.8
Clarksville, Tenn	25.6	Jackson, Tenn	19.2	Owensboro, Ky	21.7	Washington, N. C	28.5
				Paducah, Ky	17.9		
Cleveland, Ohio	10.9	Jacksonville, Fla	18.1	Palestine, Tex	38.2	Waycross, Ga	28.2
Columbia, S. C	12.7	Jersey City, N. J	10.7	Paris, Tex	30.1	West Point, Miss	45.4
Columbus, Ga	10.4	Kansas City, Kans	38.7	Pensacola, Fla	22.9	Wilmington, Del	10.8
Columbus, Miss	29.0	Kansas City, Mo	9.3	Petersburg, Va	28.8	Wilmington, N. C	26.8
Columbus, Ohio	16.7	Key West, Fla	16.8	Philadelphia, Pa	5.0		
Cordele, Ga	40.2	Kinston, N. C	37.0	Pine Bluff, Ark	26.1	Wilson, N. C	21.1
Corsicana, Tex	40.2	Knoxville, Tenn	17.7	Pittsburgh, Pa	10.9	Winchester, Ky	48.2
Covington, Ky	9.6	Lafayette, La	42.0	Plaquemine, La	15.8	Winston, N. C	13.6
Dallas, Tex	14.1	Lake Charles, La	34.2			Yazoo City, Miss	23.3
Danville, Va	29.3	Laurel, Miss	23.7	Portsmouth, Va	14.3		
				Providence, R. I	7.8		
Dayton, Ohio	22.8	Lexington, Ky	20.4	Raleigh, N. C	23.8		
Denison, Tex	45.2	Little Rock, Ark	27.4	Richmond, Va	15.7		
Denver, Colo	20.2	Los Angeles, Cal	36.1	Roanoke, Va	27.3		
Des Moines, Iowa	39.3	Louisville, Ky	6.5				
Detroit, Mich	17.2	Lynchburg, Va	26.8				

TABLE 17.—NEGRO INHABITANTS PER OWNED HOME IN URBAN COMMUNITIES HAVING A NEGRO POPULATION OF 2,500 OR MORE: 1910.

CITY.	Negro inhabitants per owned home.	CITY.	Negro inhabitants per owned home.	CITY.	Negro inhabitants per owned home.	CITY.	Negro inhabitants per owned home.
Albany, Ga.	25	Dothan, Ala.	18	McAlester, Okla.	21	Rocky Mount, N. C.	16
Alexandria, La.	25	Dublin, Ga.	11	Macon, Ga.	21	Rome, Ga.	14
Alexandria, Va.	16	Durham, N. C.	26	Marianna, Ark.	8	St. Joseph, Mo.	27
Americus, Ga.	10	East St. Louis, Ill.	29	Marshall, Tex.	11	St. Louis, Mo.	71
Anderson, S. C.	15	Elberton, Ga.	35	Memphis, Tenn.	31	St. Paul, Minn.	17
Annapolis, Md.	38	Elizabeth City, N. C.	12	Meridian, Miss.	17	San Antonio, Tex.	17
Anniston, Ala.	13	Evansville, Ind.	36	Milledgeville, Ga.	10	Savannah, Ga.	53
Argenta, Ark.	13	Fayetteville, N. C.	12	Minneapolis, Minn.	22	Selma, Ala.	17
Asheville, N. C.	16	Florence, S. C.	16	Mobile, Ala.	24	Shreveport, La.	19
Atchison, Kans.	8	Fort Smith, Ark.	15	Monroe, La.	23	Spartanburg, S. C.	16
Athens, Ga.	14	Fort Worth, Tex.	24	Montgomery, Ala.	20	Springfield, Ill.	11
Atlanta, Ga.	29	Frankfort, Ky.	20	Muskogee, Okla.	14	Springfield, Ohio.	11
Atlantic City, N. J.	114	Gadsden, Ala.	24	Nashville, Tenn.	18	Suffolk, Va.	16
Augusta, Ga.	30	Gainesville, Fla.	9	Natchez, Miss.	23	Sumter, S. C.	19
Austin, Tex.	12	Galveston, Tex.	48	Newark, N. J.	72	Talladega, Ala.	9
Baltimore, Md.	91	Georgetown, S. C.	16	New Bedford, Mass.	22	Tallahassee, Fla.	16
Baton Rouge, La.	22	Goldsboro, N. C.	25	New Bern, N. C.	12	Tampa, Fla.	27
Beaumont, Tex.	22	Greensboro, N. C.	17	New Haven, Conn.	42	Temple, Tex.	20
Bessemer, Ala.	28	Greenville, Miss.	11	New Iberia, La.	13	Terre Haute, Ind.	13
Birmingham, Ala.	22	Greenville, S. C.	22	New Orleans, La.	37	Texarkana, Ark.	13
Boston, Mass.	101	Greenwood, Miss.	20	Newport News, Va.	27	Texarkana, Tex.	15
Brookhaven, Miss.	17	Greenwood, S. C.	13	New York, N. Y.	168	Thomasville, Ga.	8
Brunswick, Ga.	21	Griffin, Ga.	14	Manhattan Borough.	2,632	Topeka, Kans.	8
Cairo, Ill.	24	Guthrie, Okla.	8	Bronx Borough.	67	Trenton, N. J.	76
Cambridge, Mass.	31	Hattiesburg, Miss.	15	Brooklyn Borough.	86	Troy, Ala.	14
Camden, N. J.	27	Harrisburg, Pa.	31	Queens Borough.	21		
Charleston, S. C.	37	Helena, Ark.	30	Richmond Borough.	27	Tuscaloosa, Ala.	16
Charleston, W. Va.	25	Henderson, Ky.	15			Tyler, Tex.	12
Charlotte, N. C.	21	Hopkinsville, Ky.	11	Norfolk, Va.	92	Union Springs, Ala.	20
Charlottesville, Va.	18	Hot Springs, Ark.	11	Oakland, Cal.	15	Valdosta, Ga.	14
Chattanooga, Tenn.	52	Houston, Tex.	20	Oklahoma City, Okla.	22		
Chester, Pa.	35	Huntsville, Ala.	9	Omaha, Nebr.	27	Vicksburg, Miss.	16
Chicago, Ill.	67	Indianapolis, Ind.	26	Orangeburg, S. C.	19	Waco, Tex.	19
Cincinnati, Ohio.	67	Jackson, Miss.	18			Washington, D. C.	46
Clarksville, Tenn.	14	Jackson, Tenn.	19	Owensboro, Ky.	17	Washington, N. C.	14
Cleveland, Ohio.	35	Jacksonville, Fla.	22	Paducah, Ky.	20		
Columbia, S. C.	31	Jersey City, N. J.	39	Palestine, Tex.	10	Waycross, Ga.	17
Columbus, Ga.	34	Kansas City, Kans.	9	Paris, Tex.	13	West Point, Miss.	9
Columbus, Miss.	12	Kansas City, Mo.	41	Pensacola, Fla.	16	Wilmington, Del.	39
Columbus, Ohio.	25	Key West, Fla.	24	Petersburg, Va.	13	Wilmington, N. C.	15
Cordele, Ga.	9	Kinston, N. C.	11	Philadelphia, Pa.	93	Wilson, N. C.	19
Corsicana, Tex.	10	Knoxville, Tenn.	24	Pine Bluff, Ark.	15	Winchester, Ky.	7
Covington, Ky.	37	Lafayette, La.	11	Pittsburgh, Pa.	39	Winston, N. C.	30
Dallas, Tex.	30	Lake Charles, La.	13	Plaquemine, La.	23	Yazoo City, Miss.	16
Danville, Va.	14	Laurel, Miss.	17	Portsmouth, Va.	27		
Dayton, Ohio.	16	Lexington, Ky.	17	Providence, R. I.	49		
Denison, Tex.	9	Little Rock, Ark.	16	Raleigh, N. C.	17		
Denver, Colo.	19	Los Angeles, Cal.	10	Richmond, Va.	28		
Des Moines, Iowa.	13	Louisville, Ky.	57	Roanoke, Va.	18		
Detroit, Mich.	24	Lynchburg, Va.	15				

TABLE 18.—HOME OWNERSHIP BY COUNTIES: 1910—NUMBER OF FARM HOMES AND OTHER HOMES, OWNED FREE, OWNED ENCUMBERED, AND RENTED BY NEGRO FAMILIES.

STATE AND COUNTY.	Negro population: 1910.	Total farm and other homes: 1910.	NUMBER OF FARM HOMES.							NUMBER OF OTHER HOMES.						
			Total.	Owned.				Rented.	No report of ownership.	Total.	Owned.				Rented.	No report of ownership.
				Total.	Free.	Encumbered.	No encumbrance report.				Total.	Free.	Encumbered.	No encumbrance report.		

ALABAMA.

STATE AND COUNTY.	Negro population: 1910.	Total farm and other homes: 1910.	Total.	Total.	Free.	Encumbered.	No encumbrance report.	Rented.	No report of ownership.	Total.	Total.	Free.	Encumbered.	No encumbrance report.	Rented.	No report of ownership.
Total...............	908,282	206,884	107,696	17,227	10,434	6,379	414	90,218	251	99,188	16,714	12,295	3,726	693	73,806	8,668
Autauga..............	11,717	2,714	1,777	310	187	119	4	1,460	7	937	81	60	14	7	684	172
Baldwin..............	5,110	1,165	335	253	227	26	......	82	......	830	339	295	23	21	435	56
Barbour..............	20,456	4,371	2,811	317	176	132	9	2,493	1	1,560	241	208	22	11	1,169	150
Bibb.................	7,710	1,696	639	169	115	53	1	469	1	1,057	138	109	22	7	844	75
Blount...............	1,181	252	90	40	37	3	......	49	1	162	23	18	3	2	132	7
Bullock..............	25,362	5,533	4,003	159	101	53	5	3,832	12	1,530	174	152	17	5	1,147	209
Butler...............	15,373	3,301	1,980	369	167	194	8	1,606	5	1,321	244	184	54	6	963	114
Calhoun..............	10,757	2,468	659	171	121	48	2	488	......	1,809	544	318	213	13	1,180	85
Chambers.............	18,660	3,754	2,723	179	115	53	11	2,541	3	1,031	192	161	15	16	684	155
Cherokee.............	2,606	499	351	92	78	14	......	259	......	148	14	14			113	21
Chilton..............	4,759	958	500	193	101	92	......	307	......	458	65	53	8	4	379	14
Choctaw..............	11,503	2,230	1,854	559	255	299	5	1,294	1	376	23	14	4	5	279	74
Clarke...............	17,311	3,541	2,537	884	575	305	4	1,644	9	1,004	190	129	21	40	684	130
Clay.................	2,648	503	331	72	46	26	......	259	......	172	6	6			139	27
Cleburne.............	711	156	77	12	9	3	......	65	......	79	20	13	7	......	42	17
Coffee...............	5,782	1,138	649	139	89	43	7	507	3	489	70	49	17	4	367	52
Colbert..............	9,449	1,980	917	192	122	68	2	724	1	1,063	269	192	65	12	727	67
Conecuh..............	10,079	2,151	1,532	702	394	303	5	829	1	619	84	54	20	10	495	40
Coosa................	6,256	1,157	952	224	128	95	1	722	6	205	17	12	1	4	164	24
Covington............	8,001	1,724	412	177	101	74	2	235	......	1,312	111	53	49	9	1,104	97
Crenshaw.............	7,514	1,546	1,007	213	94	118	1	793	1	539	37	24	7	6	416	86
Cullam...............	533	107	51	26	20	6	......	25	......	56					50	6
Dale.................	5,810	1,183	737	123	65	58	......	614	......	446	84	57	25	2	333	29
Dallas...............	43,511	10,943	7,158	432	266	125	41	6,713	13	3,785	490	354	108	28	2,676	619
Dekalb...............	854	160	72	26	18	8	......	46	......	88	31	29	1	1	54	3
Elmore...............	13,246	2,856	1,720	390	181	187	22	1,325	5	1,136	108	84	12	12	848	180
Escambia.............	5,569	1,337	278	203	159	43	1	75	......	1,059	308	250	31	27	652	99
Etowah...............	6,804	1,404	186	58	38	19	1	128	......	1,218	221	185	33	3	913	84
Fayette..............	1,866	363	293	91	60	31	......	201	1	70	17	15	......	2	47	6
Franklin.............	1,842	417	104	15	11	4	......	89	......	313	67	56	8	3	240	6
Geneva...............	4,305	908	382	125	69	55	1	257	......	526	74	59	10	5	425	27
Greene...............	19,705	4,678	3,601	335	194	128	13	3,259	7	1,077	54	43	3	8	642	381
Hale.................	21,987	5,122	3,549	500	273	216	11	3,045	4	1,573	142	91	37	14	1,314	117
Henry................	10,150	1,992	1,566	210	98	109	3	1,346	10	426	43	32	8	3	307	76
Houston..............	9,597	1,973	835	146	81	62	3	684	5	1,138	230	127	101	2	812	96
Jackson..............	3,136	651	364	115	72	43	......	249	......	287	103	96	3	4	170	14
Jefferson............	90,617	24,036	426	255	213	37	5	171	......	23,610	3,788	2,439	1,268	81	19,213	609
Lamar................	3,180	616	504	222	119	102	1	282	......	112	13	11	2	......	89	10
Lauderdale...........	7,096	1,526	845	230	163	65	2	615	......	681	279	215	54	10	378	24
Lawrence.............	6,933	1,455	1,210	225	142	82	1	985	......	245	64	52	3	9	128	53
Lee..................	19,643	4,140	2,488	292	170	116	6	2,195	1	1,652	361	272	82	7	1,223	68
Limestone............	10,255	2,191	1,736	255	136	117	2	1,480	1	455	156	136	13	7	286	13
Lowndes..............	28,125	6,627	5,249	353	217	108	28	4,885	11	1,378	61	49	4	8	1,097	220
Macon................	22,039	5,035	3,692	419	203	199	17	3,241	32	1,343	159	112	41	6	1,018	166
Madison..............	18,894	4,292	2,544	456	241	202	13	2,087	1	1,748	563	460	86	17	1,134	51
Marengo..............	30,846	7,286	5,066	625	334	275	16	4,433	8	2,220	346	218	109	19	1,215	659
Marion...............	520	113	89	40	21	19	......	49	......	24					23	1
Marshall.............	1,365	277	137	40	29	11	......	97	......	140	40	34	6	......	96	4
Mobile...............	34,719	8,817	295	256	246	10	......	39	......	8,522	1,894	1,645	199	50	6,298	330
Monroe...............	15,727	3,241	2,529	602	350	242	10	1,927	......	712	46	35	5	6	532	134
Montgomery...........	56,867	14,372	5,722	330	184	111	35	5,382	10	8,650	1,320	865	419	36	6,524	806
Morgan...............	8,198	1,899	622	192	135	57	......	429	1	1,277	321	221	89	11	911	45
Perry................	24,494	5,579	3,769	436	243	180	13	3,325	8	1,810	402	327	49	26	1,095	313
Pickens..............	12,951	2,835	2,197	281	154	120	7	1,914	2	638	34	25	4	5	462	142
Pike.................	14,437	3,129	1,766	157	72	83	2	1,601	8	1,363	214	136	65	13	1,021	128
Randolph.............	5,717	1,118	896	200	142	52	6	696	......	222	38	35	3	......	154	30
Russell..............	20,198	4,164	2,703	269	205	54	10	2,397	37	1,461	156	121	29	6	952	353
St. Clair............	3,632	711	359	152	114	37	1	207	......	352	62	42	2	18	273	17
Shelby...............	7,641	1,686	602	226	164	60	2	374	2	1,084	202	167	31	4	843	39
Sumter...............	23,322	5,022	3,847	534	373	147	14	3,311	2	1,175	80	65	12	3	941	154
Talladega............	18,265	3,701	2,165	527	342	166	19	1,635	3	1,536	402	338	47	17	1,021	113
Tallapoosa...........	11,457	2,230	1,555	257	120	132	5	1,289	9	675	121	83	36	2	456	98
Tuscaloosa...........	19,026	4,420	1,606	428	230	192	6	1,176	2	2,814	390	322	61	7	2,274	150
Walker...............	6,538	1,788	73	40	39	1	......	33	......	1,715	163	125	33	5	1,505	47
Washington...........	6,064	1,224	600	290	213	75	2	307	3	624	131	117	3	11	434	59
Wilcox...............	27,602	6,412	5,372	417	277	112	28	4,942	13	1,040	54	32	9	13	569	417
Winston..............	54	11	....	....	....	....	....	....	....	11						11

TABLE **18.**—HOME OWNERSHIP BY COUNTIES: 1910—NUMBER OF FARM HOMES AND OTHER HOMES, OWNED FREE, OWNED ENCUMBERED, AND RENTED BY NEGRO FAMILIES—Continued.

STATE AND COUNTY.	Negro population: 1910.	Total farm and other homes: 1910.	NUMBER OF FARM HOMES.							NUMBER OF OTHER HOMES.						
			Total.	Owned.				Rented.	No report of ownership.	Total.	Owned.				Rented.	No report of ownership.
				Total.	Free.	Encumbered.	No encumbrance report.				Total.	Free.	Encumbered.	No encumbrance report.		
ARIZONA.																
Total	2,009	583	14	12	10	1	1	2	......	569	167	112	49	6	374	28
Cochise	478	167	7	6	5	1	......	1	......	160	31	22	8	1	122	7
Gila	226	72	1	1	1	......	......	......	......	71	30	23	7	......	37	4
Graham	112	31	1	1	1	......	......	......	......	30	8	8	......	......	20	2
Maricopa	469	130	4	3	2	......	1	1	......	126	43	19	21	3	77	6
Pima	295	85	......	......	......	......	......	......	......	85	28	19	9	......	51	6
Yavapai	148	39	1	1	1	......	......	......	......	38	9	7	2	......	29	......
Yuma	108	14	......	......	......	......	......	......	......	14	9	7	1	1	2	3
Other counties [1]	173	45	......	......	......	......	......	......	......	45	9	7	1	1	36	......
ARKANSAS.																
Total	442,891	97,787	61,177	14,216	9,208	4,621	387	46,543	418	36,610	9,802	6,700	2,258	844	22,659	4,149
Arkansas	4,269	873	666	220	157	56	7	440	6	207	77	58	17	2	115	15
Ashley	13,276	2,788	1,877	342	239	82	21	1,468	67	911	114	98	11	5	485	312
Benton	110	16	1	1	1	......	......	......	......	15	9	9	......	......	......	......
Bradley	4,641	956	383	253	189	63	1	126	4	573	216	159	50	7	323	34
Calhoun	3,413	626	418	290	197	93	......	126	2	208	58	42	8	8	126	24
Chicot	17,682	4,664	3,063	391	183	166	42	2,630	42	1,601	197	137	35	25	1,138	266
Clark	7,367	1,356	724	382	291	79	12	339	3	632	191	147	30	14	389	52
Cleveland	4,334	822	563	311	205	104	2	252	......	259	60	44	6	10	183	16
Columbia	10,869	1,959	1,408	662	434	228	......	743	3	551	103	70	13	20	360	88
Conway	8,298	1,661	1,351	595	363	225	7	755	1	310	139	102	35	2	155	16
Craighead	1,328	329	21	10	3	7	......	11	......	308	93	71	18	4	214	1
Crawford	2,063	394	170	57	37	20	......	113	......	224	105	67	26	12	113	6
Crittenden	19,000	4,363	3,319	267	200	66	1	2,937	115	1,044	259	133	52	74	516	269
Cross	6,127	1,347	914	111	86	18	7	803	......	433	126	107	14	5	262	45
Dallas	4,657	852	406	268	204	63	1	138	......	446	225	166	30	29	207	14
Desha	12,129	3,040	2,135	256	145	59	52	1,870	9	905	109	36	......	73	676	120
Drew	11,789	2,486	1,835	535	269	260	6	1,299	1	651	108	78	24	6	476	67
Faulkner	4,460	834	660	263	168	94	1	397	......	174	79	45	33	1	74	21
Franklin	382	51	32	13	9	4	......	19	......	19	7	6	1	......	9	3
Garland	4,665	1,271	36	27	21	6	......	7	2	1,235	483	326	107	50	683	69
Grant	994	178	139	107	79	28	......	32	......	39	20	16	1	3	13	6
Hempstead	14,100	2,681	1,946	714	480	229	5	1,229	3	735	224	196	22	6	437	74
Hot Spring	1,960	436	104	71	62	8	1	32	1	332	151	105	40	6	170	11
Howard	3,498	671	529	184	135	49	......	343	2	142	28	18	7	3	106	8
Independence	1,264	267	81	24	16	8	......	57	......	186	84	62	18	4	99	3
Izard	242	42	36	19	19	......	......	17	......	6	2	2	......	......	3	1
Jackson	6,203	1,328	744	111	57	51	3	630	3	584	124	90	33	1	427	33
Jefferson	37,692	9,172	6,133	810	477	285	48	5,303	20	3,039	1,027	763	183	81	1,714	298
Johnson	517	93	30	9	8	1	......	21	......	63	22	18	4	......	41	......
Lafayette	7,181	1,556	743	312	191	117	4	428	3	813	158	86	32	40	420	235
Lawrence	750	166	65	17	12	4	1	48	......	101	32	23	7	2	60	9
Lee	19,003	4,237	3,291	699	392	286	21	2,584	8	946	393	317	68	8	423	130
Lincoln	9,967	2,306	1,788	273	169	96	8	1,515	......	518	76	14	6	56	324	118
Little River	5,698	1,233	920	239	161	73	5	680	1	313	91	71	14	6	192	30
Logan	640	114	83	19	8	9	2	63	1	31	7	4	3	......	19	5
Lonoke	11,268	2,492	2,169	273	153	113	7	1,857	39	323	62	50	10	2	217	44
Miller	7,163	1,688	567	169	121	44	4	398	......	1,121	306	223	82	1	795	20
Mississippi	13,472	3,285	1,825	110	51	54	5	1,715	......	1,460	103	66	26	11	659	698
Monroe	12,526	2,799	2,057	317	206	90	21	1,738	2	742	216	123	36	57	475	51
Montgomery	304	70	62	34	31	3	......	28	......	8	1	......	......	1	7	......
Nevada	6,790	1,259	823	331	199	131	1	491	1	436	138	102	25	11	271	27
Ouachita	12,333	2,346	1,280	778	536	233	9	495	7	1,066	295	263	13	19	682	89
Perry	910	154	90	32	23	9	......	58	......	64	14	13	1	......	48	2
Phillips	26,354	6,465	4,087	542	346	166	30	3,515	30	2,378	349	216	51	82	1,772	257
Pike	918	185	92	57	49	8	......	35	......	93	15	15	......	......	77	1
Poinsett	2,121	478	238	24	18	6	......	214	......	240	18	15	......	3	211	11
Pope	1,867	353	228	76	47	26	3	151	1	125	55	43	10	2	57	13
Prairie	4,481	949	629	128	90	38	......	500	1	320	149	120	28	1	157	14
Pulaski	35,462	8,350	2,997	606	476	118	12	2,373	18	5,353	1,646	888	722	36	3,519	188
Randolph	515	109	65	32	25	7	......	33	......	44	9	9	......	......	31	4
St. Francis	15,508	3,420	2,889	469	281	166	22	2,410	10	531	144	102	39	3	298	89
Saline	1,833	443	273	133	102	30	1	139	1	170	65	52	9	4	88	17
Searcy	104	21	......	......	......	......	......	......	......	21	......	......	......	......	21	......
Sebastian	5,410	1,261	106	39	33	5	1	67	......	1,155	350	228	116	6	751	54
Sevier	2,296	410	297	137	116	21	......	159	1	113	28	19	5	4	72	13
Union	13,747	2,518	1,312	630	338	290	2	676	6	1,206	189	126	51	12	956	61
Van Buren	220	31	24	19	15	4	......	5	......	7	4	1	3	......	2	1
Washington	614	154	33	23	13	10	......	10	......	121	58	46	5	7	60	3
White	2,162	419	148	65	48	17	......	83	......	271	132	100	23	9	134	5
Woodruff	11,705	2,505	2,055	222	145	66	11	1,830	3	450	160	107	44	9	211	79
Yell	1,759	357	164	70	43	27	......	93	1	193	89	77	11	1	100	4
Other counties [1]	481	98	53	38	36	2	......	15	......	45	10	10	......	......	30	5

[1] Includes all counties with less than 100 Negro inhabitants.

Table 18.—HOME OWNERSHIP BY COUNTIES: 1910—NUMBER OF FARM HOMES AND OTHER HOMES, OWNED FREE, OWNED ENCUMBERED, AND RENTED BY NEGRO FAMILIES—Continued.

STATE AND COUNTY.	Negro population: 1910.	Total farm and other homes: 1910.	NUMBER OF FARM HOMES.							NUMBER OF OTHER HOMES.						
			Total.	Owned.				Rented.	No report of ownership.	Total.	Owned.				Rented.	No report of ownership.
				Total.	Free.	Encumbered.	No encumbrance report.				Total.	Free.	Encumbered.	No encumbrance report.		
CALIFORNIA.																
Total	21,645	5,346	173	133	82	49	2	33	7	5,173	1,886	970	877	39	3,184	103
Alameda	3,634	841	2	1		1			1	839	251	106	141	4	587	1
Butte	122	43	3	2	1	1			1	40	18	14	4		17	5
Fresno	474	117	23	22	5	17			1	94	45	39	4	2	49	
Kern	369	95	10	8	6	2			2	85	39	26	11	2	46	
Kings	172	40	5	4	1	3			1	35	17	8	8	1	15	3
Los Angeles	9,424	2,513	20	17	13	4			3	2,493	985	455	519	11	1,487	21
Marin	145	9								9	3	2	1		5	1
Monterey	107	30								30	18	11	7		11	1
Riverside	518	126	14	7	4	3		2	5	112	57	32	24	1	50	5
Sacramento	631	120								120	39	14	24	1	76	5
San Bernardino	642	137	4	4	3	1				133	51	24	24	3	75	7
San Diego	684	174	13	10	9		1	3		161	52	29	22	1	97	12
San Francisco	1,642	300	1						1	299	49	30	19		239	11
San Joaquin	307	77	7	4	4				3	70	21	9	8	4	45	4
Santa Barbara	108	26								26	8	3	5		18	
Santa Clara	262	77								77	31	20	11		44	2
Shasta	159	40	1	1	1					39	23	15	8		16	
Solano	250	76	2					2		74	12	8	3	1	57	5
Tulare	190	45	11	10	6	4			1	34	8	4	4		22	4
Yolo	280	75	9	8	5	3			1	66	24	17	6	1	39	3
Yuba	203	43	1	1			1			42	19	17	2		22	1
Other counties [1]	1,322	342	47	34	24	10		11	2	295	116	87	22	7	167	12
COLORADO.																
Total	11,453	3,079	88	57	40	17		29	2	2,991	792	493	277	22	2,112	87
Arapahoe	131	35	9	4	3	1		4	1	26	15	11	4		10	1
Boulder	186	47	2	2		2				45	20	12	7	1	25	
Denver	5,426	1,380								1,380	279	159	115	5	1,082	19
El Paso	1,330	377	9	6	3	3		3		368	137	76	55	6	220	11
Fremont	339	81	2	1	1			1		79	14	10	4		61	4
Huerfano	323	95	2	1		1		1		93	18	12	1	5	70	5
Jefferson	134	15	3	2		2		1		12	9	6	3		3	
Las Animas	379	114								114	16	12	4		94	4
Mesa	160	37	4	4	4					33	9	6	3		19	5
Otero	247	53	9	4	3	1		5		44	14	9	4	1	29	1
Pueblo	1,689	472	12	5	2	3		7		460	150	95	55		285	25
Teller	139	67	1	1	1					66	27	18	7	2	38	1
Other counties [1]	1,000	306	35	27	23	4		7	1	271	84	67	15	2	176	11
CONNECTICUT.																
Total	15,174	3,515	99	72	34	33	5	27		3,416	564	269	281	14	2,781	71
Fairfield	3,516	714	21	12	5	6	1	9		693	98	53	45		572	23
Hartford	2,934	693	26	21	5	16		5		667	126	52	68	6	524	17
Litchfield	758	168	15	11	6	4	1	4		153	38	17	17	4	110	5
Middlesex	367	60	3	1	1			2		57	20	16	4		35	2
New Haven	5,634	1,390	7	4	2	2		3		1,383	176	78	97	1	1,204	3
New London	1,431	370	16	12	7	3	2	4		354	83	42	39	2	257	14
Tolland	109	21	3	3	2	1				18	4	1	3		12	2
Windham	425	99	8	8	6	1	1			91	19	10	8	1	67	5
DELAWARE.																
Total	31,181	6,476	966	436	261	169	6	526	4	5,510	1,065	623	374	68	4,143	302
Kent	7,561	1,551	350	166	80	83	3	183	1	1,201	321	195	114	12	850	30
New Castle	15,682	3,331	108	65	40	23	2	41	2	3,223	455	240	191	24	2,584	184
Sussex	7,938	1,594	508	205	141	63	1	302	1	1,086	289	188	69	32	709	88
DISTRICT OF COLUMBIA.																
Total	94,446	19,246	15	10	7	2	1	5		19,231	2,062	1,287	745	30	16,432	737

[1] Includes all counties with less than 100 Negro inhabitants.

TABLE 18.—HOME OWNERSHIP BY COUNTIES: 1910—NUMBER OF FARM HOMES AND OTHER HOMES, OWNED FREE, OWNED ENCUMBERED, AND RENTED BY NEGRO FAMILIES—Continued.

STATE AND COUNTY.	Negro population: 1910.	Total farm and other homes: 1910.	NUMBER OF FARM HOMES.							NUMBER OF OTHER HOMES.						
			Total.	Owned.				Rented.	No report of ownership.	Total.	Owned.				Rented.	No report of ownership.
				Total.	Free.	Encumbered.	No encumbrance report.				Total.	Free.	Encumbered.	No encumbrance report.		
FLORIDA.																
Total	308,669	75,394	14,777	7,335	5,998	1,204	133	7,401	41	60,617	13,581	10,543	2,045	993	42,250	4,786
Alachua	19,092	4,550	1,514	1,024	820	202	2	487	3	3,036	792	665	93	34	2,145	99
Baker	1,159	305	9	4	2	2	......	5	......	296	59	52	4	3	226	11
Bradford	3,987	1,025	317	172	129	40	3	143	2	708	125	104	11	10	431	152
Brevard	1,399	352	40	31	24	7	......	9	......	312	126	96	20	10	144	42
Calhoun	2,140	510	92	72	57	15	......	20	......	418	78	61	1	16	315	25
Citrus	3,635	1,178	8	7	7	......	......	1	......	1,170	91	80	8	3	1,027	52
Clay	2,453	656	31	25	23	2	......	6	......	625	179	155	18	6	433	13
Columbia	8,411	1,737	837	452	296	154	2	384	1	900	235	202	24	9	624	41
Dade	4,194	1,253	43	25	18	7	......	18	......	1,210	271	188	79	4	901	38
De Soto	2,351	591	9	7	5	1	1	2	......	582	139	119	16	4	349	94
Duval	37,270	9,196	302	243	223	16	4	59	......	8,894	1,908	1,464	360	84	6,500	486
Escambia	15,111	3,985	81	73	73	......	......	8	......	3,904	904	597	253	54	2,852	148
Franklin	2,487	773	2	1	......	1	......	1	......	771	262	222	36	4	494	15
Gadsden	14,965	3,105	1,056	538	453	83	2	518	......	2,049	468	343	70	55	1,504	77
Hamilton	5,533	1,195	428	133	95	38	......	295	......	767	128	94	31	3	541	98
Hernando	2,781	721	68	60	54	6	......	7	1	653	76	73	3	......	559	18
Hillsborough	16,445	4,236	108	97	90	6	1	11	......	4,128	813	542	255	16	3,042	273
Holmes	1,194	325	36	27	18	9	......	9	......	289	31	21	10	......	207	51
Jackson	14,254	3,171	1,912	669	459	190	20	1,240	3	1,259	128	41	11	76	963	168
Jefferson	13,114	2,722	1,511	301	232	36	33	1,195	15	1,211	273	257	9	7	480	458
Lafayette	1,361	329	21	8	7	1	......	13	......	308	7	3	......	4	232	69
Lake	3,627	1,040	106	91	86	4	1	15	......	934	194	176	12	6	678	62
Lee	937	212	7	4	4	......	......	3	......	205	44	42	1	1	123	38
Leon	14,726	3,296	1,716	300	226	33	41	1,407	9	1,580	360	277	70	13	1,031	189
Levy	4,727	1,243	183	145	134	11	......	38	......	1,060	126	107	2	17	906	28
Liberty	2,111	508	82	80	76	4	......	2	......	426	26	23	1	2	393	7
Madison	9,410	1,975	921	170	121	47	2	748	3	1,054	120	107	10	3	746	188
Manatee	2,346	647	36	14	10	4	......	22	......	611	108	77	29	2	479	24
Marion	16,376	4,018	945	832	783	47	2	112	1	3,073	995	931	27	37	1,919	159
Monroe	5,842	1,446	12	4	3	1	......	8	......	1,434	241	122	24	95	1,109	84
Nassau	5,553	1,489	104	99	98	1	......	5	......	1,385	570	511	49	10	776	39
Orange	7,604	1,890	161	139	126	12	1	21	1	1,729	586	450	80	56	998	145
Osceola	927	220	10	9	9	......	......	1	......	210	77	57	17	3	105	28
Palm Beach	2,220	697	78	66	43	23	......	11	1	619	201	148	35	18	297	121
Pasco	2,456	680	13	11	11	......	......	2	......	667	47	46	1	......	559	61
Polk	7,419	1,976	45	36	32	4	......	9	......	1,931	279	238	22	19	1,508	144
Putnam	6,804	1,740	292	261	251	10	......	31	......	1,448	491	244	70	177	815	142
St. John	5,454	1,582	42	39	25	14	......	3	......	1,540	323	265	42	16	932	285
St. Lucie	865	280	44	37	30	6	1	7	......	236	48	36	5	7	180	8
Santa Rosa	4,234	1,089	64	33	29	4	......	31	......	1,025	162	117	12	33	835	28
Sumter	2,255	590	157	123	116	6	1	34	......	433	89	83	1	5	309	35
Suwannee	7,813	1,642	675	407	296	111	......	268	......	967	339	314	17	8	491	137
Taylor	2,689	664	27	8	6	1	1	19	......	637	37	32	5	......	466	134
Volusia	6,592	1,678	96	86	75	10	1	10	......	1,582	609	414	177	18	842	131
Wakulla	2,384	570	121	66	44	8	14	54	1	449	122	78	4	40	318	9
Walton	4,997	1,124	132	112	100	12	......	20	......	992	161	145	13	3	763	68
Washington	4,965	1,183	283	194	179	15	......	89	......	900	133	124	7	2	703	64
GEORGIA.																
Total	1,176,987	263,183	120,822	16,191	11,854	3,883	454	104,053	578	142,361	22,544	17,268	3,934	1,342	111,406	8,411
Appling	2,863	606	252	162	119	42	1	89	1	354	49	36	8	5	287	18
Baker	5,718	1,343	935	98	73	22	3	833	4	408	15	10	2	3	387	6
Baldwin	11,005	2,181	909	56	43	4	9	853	......	1,272	350	330	12	8	904	18
Banks	2,321	430	394	43	27	15	1	350	1	36	4	3	1	......	32	......
Bartow	6,348	1,348	507	77	53	23	1	429	1	841	244	196	40	8	543	54
Ben Hill	4,901	1,180	373	149	98	51	......	224	......	807	227	117	99	11	552	28
Berrien	6,263	1,406	372	94	73	15	6	277	1	1,034	189	136	38	15	819	26
Bibb	27,481	7,658	690	137	108	26	3	552	1	6,968	1,330	1,004	215	111	5,239	399
Brooks	14,086	2,855	1,341	317	197	115	5	1,021	3	1,514	213	125	73	15	1,212	89
Bryan	3,337	759	290	169	157	9	3	121	......	469	65	24	5	36	375	29
Bulloch	10,591	2,094	1,281	212	166	39	7	1,066	3	813	52	36	10	6	729	32
Burke	22,462	5,537	3,379	168	124	34	10	3,206	5	2,158	91	77	9	5	1,960	107
Butts	7,200	1,484	889	50	36	10	4	775	64	595	74	67	6	1	436	85
Calhoun	8,361	1,900	1,110	65	44	16	5	1,026	19	790	70	60	7	3	672	48
Camden	5,113	1,059	565	482	459	15	8	80	3	494	174	163	8	3	287	33
Campbell	3,616	720	500	41	21	19	1	459	......	220	33	20	10	3	162	25
Carroll	6,383	1,292	872	83	69	13	1	789	......	420	74	55	10	9	310	36
Catoosa	476	88	52	17	11	6	......	35	......	36	10	8	2	......	20	6
Charlton	1,189	358	39	29	25	4	......	10	......	319	41	27	11	3	260	18
Chatham	43,981	12,371	240	112	107	4	1	127	1	12,131	1,309	1,041	252	106	10,200	532
Chattahoochee	3,864	780	487	44	29	14	1	443	......	293	7	5	1	1	271	15
Chattooga	2,454	446	316	51	31	20	......	261	4	130	25	23	2	......	96	9
Cherokee	1,168	223	118	19	18	1	......	99	......	105	32	26	3	3	69	4
Clarke	11,767	2,743	824	186	132	54	......	638	......	1,919	484	367	111	6	1,387	48
Clay	6,569	1,406	827	66	32	28	6	758	3	579	73	57	16	......	444	62

TABLE **18.**—HOME OWNERSHIP BY COUNTIES: 1910—NUMBER OF FARM HOMES AND OTHER HOMES, OWNED FREE, OWNED ENCUMBERED, AND RENTED BY NEGRO FAMILIES—Continued.

STATE AND COUNTY.	Negro population: 1910.	Total farm and other homes: 1910.	NUMBER OF FARM HOMES.							NUMBER OF OTHER HOMES.						
			Total.	Owned.				Rented.	No report of ownership.	Total.	Owned.				Rented.	No report of ownership.
				Total.	Free.	Encumbered.	No encumbrance report.				Total.	Free.	Encumbered.	No encumbrance report.		
								GEORGIA—Continued.								
Clayton	4,632	888	669	26	15	11	......	642	1	219	13	13	......	......	192	14
Clinch	3,378	906	142	66	53	13	......	73	3	764	82	73	6	3	669	13
Cobb	7,418	1,612	645	176	104	72	......	468	1	967	241	186	50	5	682	44
Coffee	7,734	1,710	397	122	92	27	3	273	2	1,313	165	125	32	8	1,101	47
Colquitt	4,617	1,145	261	28	21	7	......	232	1	884	120	98	21	1	612	152
Columbia	9,198	1,900	1,376	157	118	26	13	1,209	10	524	26	18	1	7	447	51
Coweta	16,267	3,422	2,135	94	73	21	......	2,040	1	1,287	305	246	51	8	898	84
Crawford	4,922	965	588	99	64	34	1	486	3	377	14	12	1	1	344	19
Crisp	8,616	2,037	670	42	30	11	1	628	......	1,367	364	320	32	12	969	34
Dade	291	66	15	13	13	......	......	2	......	51	7	7	......	......	44	......
Dawson	152	36	31	3	3	......	......	28	......	5	......	......	......	......	5	......
Decatur	16,738	3,726	1,548	545	374	136	35	1,000	3	2,178	318	225	40	53	1,764	96
Dekalb	8,362	1,772	688	95	76	19	......	592	1	1,084	225	181	41	3	826	33
Dodge	8,460	1,713	1,045	194	120	69	5	846	5	668	82	65	15	2	520	66
Dooly	12,728	2,718	1,699	117	79	35	3	1,579	3	1,019	74	60	10	4	849	96
Dougherty	12,049	3,262	954	50	34	13	3	874	30	2,308	221	178	25	18	1,910	177
Douglas	2,171	417	327	66	44	16	6	261	......	90	8	7	......	1	65	17
Early	11,273	2,372	1,547	196	127	63	6	1,350	1	825	44	38	3	3	705	76
Echols	990	226	35	11	11	......	......	24	......	191	......	......	......	......	191	......
Effingham	4,278	943	301	185	147	38	......	116	......	642	116	104	12	......	503	23
Elbert	12,082	2,232	1,423	136	78	58	......	1,287	......	809	98	59	39	......	669	42
Emanuel	9,990	2,171	1,124	185	141	42	2	931	8	1,047	59	52	5	2	869	119
Fannin	162	35	7	3	3	......	......	4	......	28	5	5	......	......	22	1
Fayette	3,815	782	583	21	16	5	......	561	1	199	9	7	1	1	145	45
Floyd	10,482	2,394	746	191	114	74	3	554	1	1,648	404	273	101	30	1,181	63
Forsyth	1,098	218	171	35	21	14	......	136	......	47	5	4	1	......	40	2
Franklin	3,974	782	584	62	45	17	......	522	......	198	10	7	2	1	176	12
Fulton	57,985	15,164	247	41	33	7	1	206	......	14,917	2,118	1,369	702	47	12,378	421
Glascock	1,507	325	227	7	5	2	......	217	3	98	4	3	1	......	73	21
Glynn	9,774	2,362	92	85	77	5	3	6	1	2,270	677	555	76	46	1,508	85
Gordon	1,356	295	147	39	26	13	......	107	1	148	31	27	3	1	105	12
Grady	7,403	1,542	733	186	134	49	3	544	3	809	62	45	8	9	664	83
Greene	11,636	2,592	1,764	161	109	50	2	1,600	3	828	174	138	34	2	626	28
Gwinnett	4,431	857	473	70	42	26	2	402	1	384	89	70	15	4	277	18
Habersham	711	140	63	40	27	13	......	23	......	77	35	34	1	......	37	5
Hall	4,030	866	348	50	33	17	......	298	......	518	81	43	9	29	412	25
Hancock	14,268	2,818	2,075	214	121	45	48	1,849	12	743	37	25	2	10	596	110
Haralson	2,027	433	243	94	63	30	1	149	......	190	84	63	20	1	102	4
Harris	12,865	2,573	1,923	137	102	33	2	1,785	1	650	27	22	1	4	483	140
Hart	5,080	1,043	791	73	39	34	......	718	......	252	33	29	4	......	217	2
Heard	3,756	743	608	61	41	18	2	546	......	135	8	6	......	2	95	32
Henry	10,184	2,013	1,444	101	65	27	9	1,312	31	569	80	53	10	17	439	50
Houston	17,388	3,796	1,682	136	93	35	8	1,545	1	2,114	267	213	46	8	1,743	104
Irwin	4,916	1,096	412	39	25	12	2	373	......	684	121	62	58	1	534	29
Jackson	8,613	1,737	1,168	122	66	53	3	1,046	......	569	46	25	16	5	453	70
Jasper	11,484	2,466	1,771	119	92	27	......	1,651	1	695	68	53	11	4	611	16
Jeff Davis	1,593	357	131	66	53	13	......	65	......	226	27	17	7	3	191	8
Jefferson	12,979	2,726	1,740	162	114	37	11	1,552	26	986	135	114	15	6	706	145
Jenkins	7,296	1,711	893	43	38	2	3	849	1	818	54	43	6	5	731	33
Johnson	5,557	1,145	662	97	84	11	2	559	6	483	35	29	6	......	382	66
Jones	9,288	1,818	1,270	117	67	44	6	1,140	13	548	17	9	......	8	383	148
Laurens	17,544	3,613	2,159	231	129	87	15	1,921	7	1,454	274	170	92	12	1,053	127
Lee	9,992	2,447	1,455	114	67	28	19	1,340	1	992	44	36	3	5	886	62
Liberty	8,355	1,759	1,318	1,198	1,189	8	1	119	1	441	151	140	1	10	253	37
Lincoln	5,175	1,013	812	39	22	15	2	773	......	201	1	......	......	1	159	41
Lowndes	12,955	2,919	1,107	350	260	88	2	754	3	1,812	382	211	139	32	1,312	118
Lumpkin	320	63	40	19	18	1	......	21	......	23	12	9	1	2	10	1
McDuffie	5,985	1,306	864	27	11	11	5	792	45	442	29	20	7	2	337	76
McIntosh	4,978	1,194	153	142	141	......	1	9	2	1,041	766	751	8	7	241	34
Macon	10,581	2,334	1,306	63	40	20	3	1,243	......	1,028	223	132	11	80	763	42
Madison	5,149	970	813	74	51	23	......	739	......	157	19	17	1	1	127	11
Marion	5,364	1,077	711	73	50	23	......	637	1	366	54	51	2	1	248	64
Meriwether	14,730	3,043	2,075	130	88	40	2	1,943	2	968	148	98	44	6	720	100
Miller	3,257	689	357	50	32	18	......	306	1	332	11	9	......	2	293	28
Milton	718	125	102	10	10	......	......	92	......	23	5	3	2	......	14	4
Mitchell	11,649	2,583	1,564	169	103	59	7	1,373	22	1,019	91	64	25	2	800	128
Monroe	13,656	2,725	1,775	193	97	88	8	1,572	10	950	175	118	53	4	597	178
Montgomery	7,310	1,465	947	255	195	48	12	687	5	518	46	32	3	11	419	53
Morgan	13,414	3,153	1,953	103	66	36	1	1,850	......	1,200	102	89	11	2	1,066	32
Murray	402	54	45	11	11	......	......	34	......	9	2	2	......	......	5	2
Muscogee	16,747	4,275	586	61	44	17	......	525	......	3,689	565	442	116	7	3,014	110
Newton	9,458	1,929	1,285	103	68	32	3	1,180	2	644	161	127	32	2	408	75
Oconee	5,162	963	777	55	30	25	......	722	......	186	8	6	2	......	169	9
Oglethorpe	11,338	2,324	1,768	152	99	53	......	1,616	......	556	25	14	8	3	513	18
Paulding	1,588	296	220	60	36	24	......	160	......	76	13	13	......	......	58	5

TABLE **18.**—HOME OWNERSHIP BY COUNTIES: 1910—NUMBER OF FARM HOMES AND OTHER HOMES, OWNED FREE, OWNED ENCUMBERED, AND RENTED BY NEGRO FAMILIES—Continued.

STATE AND COUNTY.	Negro population: 1910.	Total farm and other homes: 1910.	NUMBER OF FARM HOMES.								NUMBER OF OTHER HOMES.						
			Total.	Owned.				Rented.	No report of ownership.	Total.	Owned.				Rented.	No report of ownership.
				Total.	Free.	Encumbered.	No encumbrance report.				Total.	Free.	Encumbered.	No encumbrance report.		

GEORGIA—Continued.

STATE AND COUNTY.	Negro pop.	Total homes	Total	Owned Total	Free	Encum.	No enc. rep.	Rented	No rep.	Total	Owned Total	Free	Encum.	No enc. rep.	Rented	No rep.
Pickens	440	83	14	5	4	1	....	9	....	69	8	5	3	....	59	2
Pierce	2,742	644	212	126	90	36	....	86	....	432	80	54	21	5	338	14
Pike	10,159	2,102	1,294	80	49	26	5	1,214	....	808	166	137	24	5	531	111
Polk	5,697	1,259	614	179	131	45	3	430	5	645	117	93	14	10	476	52
Pulaski	13,504	2,972	1,549	142	100	39	3	1,407	....	1,423	210	115	31	64	1,117	96
Putnam	10,178	2,201	1,529	66	41	23	2	1,463	....	672	87	67	18	2	546	39
Quitman	3,588	769	541	27	18	8	1	512	2	228	12	8	2	2	193	23
Rabun	156	23	12	10	10	....	....	2	....	11	5	4	1	....	6	....
Randolph	12,986	2,749	1,469	175	97	59	19	1,288	6	1,280	305	214	78	13	884	91
Richmond	28,390	8,166	568	93	75	10	8	475	....	7,598	1,105	982	59	64	6,171	322
Rockdale	3,592	711	462	54	36	17	1	406	2	249	60	40	20	....	161	28
Schley	3,291	643	483	34	23	9	2	449	....	160	25	16	8	1	126	9
Screven	12,165	2,559	1,663	244	178	59	7	1,377	42	896	32	20	4	8	789	75
Spalding	10,060	2,237	908	83	50	31	2	821	4	1,329	287	227	54	6	919	123
Stephens	2,222	439	203	36	23	11	2	165	2	236	64	64	....	....	167	5
Stewart	10,381	2,082	1,154	92	63	25	4	1,061	1	928	126	105	13	8	690	112
Sumter	21,243	4,823	2,235	212	170	35	7	1,986	37	2,588	494	470	21	3	2,031	63
Talbot	8,230	1,665	1,218	120	102	17	1	1,098	....	447	44	36	5	3	371	32
Taliaferro	6,450	1,422	1,135	123	95	28	....	1,011	1	287	47	44	2	1	200	40
Tattnall	5,841	1,128	648	210	182	26	2	438	....	480	72	59	6	7	376	32
Taylor	5,379	1,114	653	88	59	29	....	564	1	461	79	71	7	1	334	48
Telfair	4,761	951	429	177	137	35	5	251	1	522	144	85	17	42	335	43
Terrell	16,607	3,709	2,121	84	57	26	1	2,034	3	1,588	172	123	29	20	1,286	130
Thomas	17,086	3,950	1,395	341	236	98	7	1,050	4	2,555	727	512	178	37	1,694	134
Tift	3,777	988	254	47	34	13	....	207	....	734	80	73	3	4	604	50
Toombs	3,411	704	328	70	46	23	1	258	....	376	68	43	21	4	301	7
Troup	15,399	3,430	1,922	142	99	42	1	1,777	3	1,508	251	200	47	4	1,181	76
Turner	4,018	911	387	30	12	18	....	354	3	524	71	47	13	11	427	26
Twiggs	7,396	1,513	1,038	96	75	19	2	940	2	475	11	7	....	4	396	68
Upson	6,998	1,410	877	70	38	32	....	803	4	533	79	62	4	13	390	64
Walker	2,451	524	228	71	43	27	1	157	....	296	58	46	7	5	225	13
Walton	10,070	2,086	1,310	84	59	14	11	1,222	4	776	126	112	10	4	609	41
Ware	8,914	1,925	106	51	47	4	....	55	....	1,819	416	334	64	18	1,336	67
Warren	8,132	1,698	1,163	34	32	2	....	1,112	17	535	94	89	2	3	420	21
Washington	17,393	3,724	2,314	120	82	35	3	2,164	30	1,410	145	135	7	3	1,180	85
Wayne	3,309	834	147	94	82	11	1	53	....	687	123	96	17	10	545	19
Webster	4,182	859	602	50	23	22	5	552	....	257	9	5	....	4	234	14
White	397	75	53	16	15	1	....	37	....	22	4	3	....	1	16	2
Whitfield	1,719	354	104	46	42	4	....	58	....	250	108	92	14	2	138	4
Wilcox	5,505	1,245	599	152	112	40	....	447	....	646	94	84	7	3	536	16
Wilkes	16,598	3,707	2,504	203	163	40	....	2,301	....	1,203	279	234	40	5	868	56
Wilkinson	5,155	994	606	56	50	6	....	549	1	388	53	48	1	4	288	47
Worth	9,517	2,120	1,382	159	88	70	1	1,216	7	738	47	29	10	8	645	46
Other counties[1]	150	27	17	12	12	....	....	5	....	10	3	1	....	2	5	2

IDAHO.

STATE AND COUNTY.	Negro pop.	Total homes	Total	Owned Total	Free	Encum.	No enc. rep.	Rented	No rep.	Total	Owned Total	Free	Encum.	No enc. rep.	Rented	No rep.
Total	651	167	17	15	6	9	....	2	....	150	33	25	6	2	98	19
Ada	168	37	....	....	....	....	....	....	....	37	5	3	2	....	28	4
Bannock	129	26	....	....	....	....	....	....	....	26	2	2	....	....	16	8
Other counties[1]	354	104	17	15	6	9	....	2	....	87	26	20	4	2	54	7

ILLINOIS.

STATE AND COUNTY.	Negro pop.	Total homes	Total	Owned Total	Free	Encum.	No enc. rep.	Rented	No rep.	Total	Owned Total	Free	Encum.	No enc. rep.	Rented	No rep.
Total	109,070	26,149	1,477	809	409	393	7	656	12	24,672	5,203	2,857	2,009	337	18,799	670
Adams	1,880	486	13	7	1	6	....	6	....	473	117	74	40	3	340	16
Alexander	7,775	2,039	116	55	24	30	1	59	2	1,923	389	215	79	95	1,400	134
Bond	160	35	19	11	6	5	....	8	....	16	10	5	5	....	5	1
Bureau	223	63	1	....	....	....	....	1	....	62	25	3	1	21	35	2
Champaign	950	246	9	3	1	2	....	6	....	237	88	38	47	3	149	....
Christian	181	43	9	1	....	1	....	8	....	34	15	6	9	....	18	1
Clinton	285	45	13	5	2	3	....	8	....	32	17	10	7	....	15	....
Coles	201	56	1	1	....	1	....	....	....	55	24	18	6	....	31	....
Cook	46,627	10,933	10	3	2	1	....	7	....	10,923	827	400	406	21	9,851	245
Dekalb	151	39	4	3	2	1	....	1	....	35	9	3	6	....	26	....
Dupage	171	39	1	....	....	....	....	1	....	38	17	12	5	....	21	....
Edgar	312	84	3	2	2	....	....	1	....	81	47	21	26	....	31	3
Fulton	248	56	1	1	....	1	....	....	....	55	12	7	5	....	43	....
Gallatin	606	139	29	14	7	7	....	15	....	110	57	56	1	....	50	3
Hardin	140	33	9	7	7	....	....	2	....	24	11	9	2	....	11	2
Henry	173	46	....	....	....	....	....	....	....	46	16	3	13	....	28	2
Iroquois	172	41	5	1	1	....	....	4	....	36	23	18	5	....	13	....
Jackson	2,696	648	46	18	8	10	....	28	....	602	216	128	83	5	368	18
Jefferson	398	89	9	8	6	2	....	1	....	80	36	13	22	1	44	....
Johnson	164	38	7	3	2	1	....	4	....	31	12	10	2	....	16	3

[1] Includes all counties with less than 100 Negro inhabitants.

TABLE 18.—HOME OWNERSHIP BY COUNTIES: 1910—NUMBER OF FARM HOMES AND OTHER HOMES, OWNED FREE, OWNED ENCUMBERED, AND RENTED BY NEGRO FAMILIES—Continued.

STATE AND COUNTY.	Negro population: 1910.	Total farm and other homes: 1910.	NUMBER OF FARM HOMES.							NUMBER OF OTHER HOMES.						
			Total.	Owned.				Rented.	No report of ownership.	Total.	Owned.				Rented.	No report of ownership.
				Total.	Free.	Encumbered.	No encumbrance report.				Total.	Free.	Encumbered.	No encumbrance report.		
ILLINOIS—Continued.																
Kane	760	182	1	1			1			181	93	60	33		82	6
Kankakee	315	64	8	5	2	2	1	3		56	12	6	6		43	1
Knox	770	215	3	2	2			1		212	124	70	47	7	84	4
La Salle	311	70	5					5		65	19	16	3		46	
Lake	491	113	2	1	1			1		111	21	8	12	1	81	9
Lawrence	289	62	23	20	12	7	1	3		39	14	10	4		25	
Livingston	397	63	1					1		62	35	24	11		27	
Logan	377	95	5	1	1			4		90	30	20	9	1	60	
McDonough	123	30								30	22	13	9		8	
McLean	1,118	250	8	1		1		7		242	76	38	38		166	
Macon	906	230	6	5	3	2		1		224	79	42	33	4	145	
Macoupin	186	48	20	13	4	9		5	2	28	18	16	2		9	1
Madison	3,146	743	51	26	10	16		23	2	692	294	127	132	35	379	19
Marion	651	143	10	10	7	3				133	59	37	22		74	
Massac	2,584	621	131	73	38	35		57	1	490	215	160	53	2	263	12
Menard	107	32								32	13	3	10		19	
Montgomery	238	55	3	3	2	1				52	24	14	10		25	3
Morgan	1,361	341	7	3	3			4		334	120	74	46		210	4
Peoria	1,737	405	3	2	2			1		402	71	37	33	1	308	23
Perry	814	191	13	6	4	2		6	1	178	79	57	21	1	89	10
Pike	162	44	13	10	7	3		3		31	19	11	5	3	11	1
Pope	523	117	56	36	18	18		20		61	24	16	6	2	34	3
Pulaski	5,911	1,371	450	266	118	148		180	4	921	354	242	102	10	567	
Randolph	1,525	267	39	25	15	10		14		228	120	81	37	2	104	4
Rock Island	822	213								213	51	30	21		154	8
St. Clair	8,110	2,161	51	12	9	3		39		2,110	329	118	135	76	1,698	83
Saline	918	237	70	43	23	20		27		167	71	47	23	1	93	3
Sangamon	3,633	896	38	12	6	3	3	26		858	307	111	172	24	537	14
Union	211	31	3	2	1	1		1		28	16	13	3		11	1
Vermilion	2,038	513	6	1	1			5		507	124	45	79		377	6
Warren	576	142	5					5		137	76	44	32		57	4
White	470	110	19	6	3	3		13		91	50	39	11		39	2
Will	1,134	225	11	7	5	2		4		214	49	30	17	2	160	5
Williamson	866	203	15	12	11	1		3		188	42	25	12	5	142	4
Winnebago	257	57	2	2		2				55	31	16	15		23	1
Other counties[1]	1,720	411	94	60	30	29	1	34		317	154	108	35	11	154	9
INDIANA.																
Total	60,320	15,302	824	478	246	231	1	343	3	14,478	3,558	2,038	1,425	95	10,647	273
Allen	601	135	2	1		1		1		133	20	5	15		113	
Bartholomew	319	76	3	1	1			2		73	17	11	6		56	
Boone	123	31	5	4		4		1		26	13	9	4		12	1
Cass	240	66	4							62	18	9	8	1	39	5
Clark	2,745	628	23	14	12	2		9		605	183	152	31		415	7
Clay	227	63	2	1		1		1		61	32	15	17		29	
Daviess	210	52	13	10	8	2		3		39	19	8	10	1	18	2
Dearborn	180	36	16	1	1			15		20	3	2		1	17	
Delaware	1,460	352	5	2	1	1		3		347	73	41	30	2	266	8
Fayette	440	111	3	3	2	1				108	55	20	35		51	2
Floyd	1,749	472	15	12	9	3		3		457	132	99	33		322	3
Gibson	1,445	338	93	61	16	45		32		245	92	51	38	3	153	
Grant	1,528	364	41	29	11	18		12		323	161	107	51	3	158	4
Hamilton	555	148	33	19	8	11		14		115	65	29	21	15	49	1
Hancock	125	31	1					1		30	13	8	4	1	15	2
Harrison	293	75	24	22	13	9		2		51	31	23	7	1	18	2
Hendricks	301	49	16	12	7	5		4		33	12	8	4		20	1
Henry	415	123	17	5	4	1		12		106	50	39	10	1	43	13
Howard	490	120	11	9	3	6		2		109	62	40	22		43	4
Jackson	136	40	2					1	1	38	24	15	9		14	
Jay	171	40	2	1		1		1		38	16	10	6		22	
Jefferson	604	159	20	15	8	7		5		139	56	29	27		78	5
Jennings	295	68	21	16	8	8		5		47	25	16	9		19	3
Johnson	360	83	2	1	1			1		81	39	23	16		40	2
Knox	572	143	10	3	2	1		7		133	41	17	24		87	5
Lake	493	132	3	1		1		2		129	42	35	7		83	4
Laporte	338	36	4	3	1	2		1		32	9	4	5		17	6
Lawrence	345	80	5	5	3	2				75	44	35	9		29	2
Madison	690	195	5	3	2	1		2		190	72	37	34	1	109	9
Marion	23,256	6,124	37	14	11	3		21	2	6,087	976	510	429	37	4,999	112
Miami	109	28	1					1		27	7	6	1		19	1
Monroe	438	114	7	2		2		5		107	44	16	28		61	2
Montgomery	246	62	2	2		2				60	23	16	7		35	2
Ohio	144	42	10	2	1	1		8		32	19	11	8		12	1
Orange	363	76	2	1	1			1		74	7	6	1		67	
Parke	160	47	6	5	2	2	1	1		41	27	13	13	1	13	1
Perry	193	49	7	5	4	1		2		42	19	14	5		22	1
Pike	133	42	2	2	1	1				40	6	1	5		34	
Posey	963	247	16	5	2	3		11		231	66	54	12		165	
Putnam	221	66	5	4	3	1		1		61	27	20	6	1	32	2

[1] Includes all counties with less than 100 Negro inhabitants.

TABLE 18.—HOME OWNERSHIP BY COUNTIES: 1910—NUMBER OF FARM HOMES AND OTHER HOMES, OWNED FREE, OWNED ENCUMBERED, AND RENTED BY NEGRO FAMILIES—Continued.

STATE AND COUNTY.	Negro population: 1910.	Total farm and other homes: 1910.	NUMBER OF FARM HOMES.							NUMBER OF OTHER HOMES.						
			Total.	Owned.				Rented.	No report of ownership.	Total.	Owned.				Rented.	No report of ownership.
				Total.	Free.	Encumbered.	No encumbrance report.				Total.	Free.	Encumbered.	No encumbrance report.		

INDIANA—Continued.

STATE AND COUNTY.	Negro pop.	Total homes.	Total.	Total.	Free.	Encum.	No enc.	Rented.	No rep.	Total.	Total.	Free.	Encum.	No enc.	Rented.	No rep.
Randolph	235	70	36	26	7	19	....	10	....	34	15	6	9	....	18	1
Rush	418	118	23	17	12	5	....	6	....	95	46	27	19	....	47	2
St. Joseph	722	172	2	2	....	2	....	....	....	170	33	15	18	....	132	5
Shelby	483	105	5	3	2	1	....	2	....	100	46	11	35	....	50	4
Spencer	837	209	70	21	10	11	....	49	....	139	42	24	16	2	97	....
Sullivan	120	35	10	5	1	4	....	5	....	25	12	6	6	....	13	....
Tippecanoe	387	95	1	....	....	....	....	1	....	94	29	23	4	2	60	5
Union	101	26	1	1	1	....	....	....	....	25	10	8	2	....	14	1
Vanderburg	6,548	1,587	24	6	3	3	....	18	....	1,563	169	99	66	4	1,394	....
Vermilion	121	33	1	....	....	....	....	1	....	32	4	4	....	....	28	....
Vigo	3,323	883	66	52	34	18	....	14	....	817	229	72	148	9	565	23
Wabash	167	39	2	1	1	....	....	1	....	37	19	5	13	1	17	1
Warrick	456	132	8	2	....	2	....	6	....	124	51	37	10	4	72	1
Wayne	1,591	405	35	22	13	9	....	13	....	370	121	82	37	2	237	12
Other counties [1]	1,135	250	44	24	16	8	....	20	....	206	92	55	35	2	109	5

IOWA.

STATE AND COUNTY.	Negro pop.	Total homes.	Total.	Total.	Free.	Encum.	No enc.	Rented.	No rep.	Total.	Total.	Free.	Encum.	No enc.	Rented.	No rep.
Total	14,973	3,807	207	136	64	72	....	71	....	3,600	1,002	596	345	61	2,528	70
Appanoose	486	129	6	5	2	3	....	1	....	123	35	13	22	....	86	2
Boone	105	29	1	1	....	1	....	....	....	28	12	9	2	1	14	2
Cerro Gordo	148	27	....	....	....	....	....	....	....	27	7	2	5	....	18	2
Clinton	436	106	....	....	....	....	....	....	....	106	24	15	9	....	77	5
Dallas	131	30	....	....	....	....	....	....	....	30	....	....	....	....	30	....
Des Moines	429	125	1	1	1	....	....	....	....	124	31	18	13	....	93	....
Fayette	107	23	16	11	8	3	....	5	....	7	3	2	1	....	3	1
Henry	264	75	3	2	....	2	....	1	....	72	42	29	13	....	30	....
Jasper	182	54	2	1	....	1	....	1	....	52	20	16	3	1	30	2
Lee	1,471	409	36	26	10	16	....	10	....	373	147	90	56	1	226	....
Linn	258	62	2	1	....	1	....	1	....	60	16	7	9	....	40	4
Mahaska	677	180	9	8	8	....	....	1	....	171	53	34	7	12	116	2
Marshall	148	37	1	....	....	....	....	1	....	36	14	8	5	1	18	4
Monroe	2,371	576	43	34	13	21	....	9	....	533	63	42	19	2	466	4
Muscatine	137	45	4	3	2	1	....	1	....	41	17	13	4	....	22	2
Page	262	61	7	6	4	2	....	1	....	54	31	22	9	....	23	....
Polk	3,591	908	3	3	2	1	....	....	....	905	227	114	79	34	678	....
Pottawattamie	353	82	2	2	....	2	....	....	....	80	15	9	6	....	62	3
Scott	572	137	....	....	....	....	....	....	....	137	22	11	11	....	108	7
Wapello	624	183	9	8	2	6	....	1	....	174	68	43	23	2	100	6
Washington	104	25	2	1	1	....	....	1	....	23	12	5	5	2	11	....
Woodbury	317	86	3	1	....	1	....	2	....	83	15	7	8	....	68	....
Other counties [1]	1,800	418	57	22	11	11	....	35	....	361	128	87	36	5	209	24

KANSAS.

STATE AND COUNTY.	Negro pop.	Total homes.	Total.	Total.	Free.	Encum.	No enc.	Rented.	No rep.	Total.	Total.	Free.	Encum.	No enc.	Rented.	No rep.
Total	54,032	13,810	1,532	992	569	408	15	509	31	12,278	5,859	4,039	1,668	152	6,025	394
Allen	1,047	260	17	10	6	4	....	7	....	243	79	52	17	10	149	15
Anderson	161	38	8	6	2	4	....	2	....	30	19	13	6	....	10	1
Atchison	2,992	715	57	43	17	24	2	14	....	658	357	261	58	38	262	39
Barton	388	90	25	13	7	6	....	12	....	65	33	28	4	1	32	....
Bourbon	1,215	323	37	22	12	9	1	15	....	286	172	123	47	2	99	15
Brown	457	105	15	3	1	2	....	12	....	90	51	32	18	1	37	2
Butler	149	32	4	1	1	....	....	3	....	28	14	11	3	....	13	1
Chase	103	28	6	5	4	1	....	1	....	22	10	8	2	....	7	5
Chautauqua	118	30	13	8	6	2	....	5	....	17	13	13	....	....	4	....
Cherokee	1,181	330	47	34	23	11	....	11	2	283	179	147	29	3	104	....
Clay	111	24	....	....	....	....	....	....	....	24	18	18	....	....	6	....
Cowley	571	131	7	4	3	1	....	3	....	124	71	47	23	1	53	....
Crawford	1,563	423	21	13	9	4	....	8	....	402	116	70	44	2	286	....
Dickinson	162	33	8	5	1	4	....	3	....	25	22	20	2	....	3	....
Doniphan	683	188	36	16	8	8	....	20	....	152	102	85	15	2	44	6
Douglas	2,281	628	88	57	30	24	3	30	1	540	289	207	79	3	241	10
Ellsworth	113	33	6	4	3	1	....	2	....	27	17	12	5	....	4	6
Finney	189	54	10	7	5	2	....	3	....	44	29	20	6	3	15	....
Franklin	490	133	24	13	9	3	1	11	....	109	61	22	25	14	44	4
Geary	587	106	4	3	1	2	....	1	....	102	60	42	17	1	41	1
Graham	595	148	110	82	30	52	....	28	....	38	25	19	3	3	10	3
Harvey	415	112	9	5	4	....	1	4	....	103	57	32	25	....	42	4
Jackson	153	40	13	5	2	3	....	8	....	27	14	10	4	....	12	1
Jefferson	451	106	42	23	8	14	1	19	....	64	35	23	12	....	22	7
Johnson	611	159	36	20	12	8	....	16	....	123	58	49	8	1	60	5

[1] Includes all counties with less than 100 Negro inhabitants.

TABLE 18.—HOME OWNERSHIP BY COUNTIES: 1910—NUMBER OF FARM HOMES AND OTHER HOMES, OWNED FREE, OWNED ENCUMBERED, AND RENTED BY NEGRO FAMILIES—Continued.

STATE AND COUNTY	Negro population: 1910.	Total farm and other homes: 1910.	NUMBER OF FARM HOMES.							NUMBER OF OTHER HOMES.						
			Total.	Owned Total.	Free.	Encumbered.	No encumbrance report.	Rented.	No report of ownership.	Total.	Owned Total.	Free.	Encumbered.	No encumbrance report.	Rented.	No report of ownership.
KANSAS—Continued.																
Labette	1,756	436	17	8	5	3		6	3	419	267	207	59	1	152	
Leavenworth	4,071	886	101	58	27	29	2	29	14	785	303	251	47	5	442	40
Linn	323	103	21	14	7	7		7		82	55	49	6		25	2
Logan	298	81	68	65	63	2		3		13	3	3			9	1
Lyon	786	195	38	32	22	10		5	1	157	105	65	38	2	46	6
Marion	132	29	8					8		21	7	5	2		14	
Marshall	244	49	19	10	2	8		9		30	23	10	13		6	1
Miami	873	210	27	10	6	4		17		183	96	71	20	5	77	10
Montgomery	2,966	686	32	14	8	6		18		654	261	158	98	5	393	2
Morris	317	80	24	20	9	11		4		56	33	26	6	1	21	2
Nemaha	164	34	6	1	1			5		28	18	14	4		8	2
Neosho	376	100	2	2	1	1				98	55	36	16	3	43	
Osage	362	89	20	14	6	8		6		69	50	48	2		18	1
Pottawatomie	132	41	6					6		35	21	18	3		11	3
Pratt	218	68	22	15	7	8		7		46	30	22	7	1	13	3
Reno	904	199	13	7	5	2		6		186	105	62	36	7	63	18
Rice	132	35	4	2		1	1	2		31	17	10	7		12	2
Riley	311	90								90	57	40	14	3	28	5
Saline	509	132	6	6	3	3				126	73	41	30	2	41	12
Sedgwick	2,652	604	15	9	5	4		6		589	224	139	83	2	343	22
Shawnee	5,722	1,487	80	60	25	35		20		1,407	649	424	219	6	709	49
Stafford	127	28	17	9	4	4	1	6	2	11	6	5	1		5	
Sumner	328	68	9	3	3			6		59	26	19	7		28	5
Wabaunsee	708	155	61	41	17	24		20		94	61	46	15		31	2
Wyandotte	11,172	3,186	96	54	32	22		34	8	3,090	1,291	806	464	21	1,729	70
Other counties [1]	1,663	470	177	136	107	27	2	41		293	122	100	19	3	158	13
KENTUCKY.																
Total	261,656	62,216	11,356	6,077	4,632	1,374	71	5,243	36	50,860	13,697	10,719	2,183	795	35,121	2,042
Adair	1,475	303	186	129	107	22		57		117	48	41	6	1	61	8
Allen	910	198	116	53	35	17	1	63		82	39	25	11	3	37	6
Anderson	734	190	34	21	20	1		13		156	60	54	5	1	89	7
Ballard	1,585	348	209	78	57	21		131		139	34	21	10	3	95	10
Barren	3,590	777	472	267	217	50		205		305	103	77	12	14	183	19
Bath	1,336	293	82	44	35	7	2	38		211	91	68	11	12	110	10
Bell	2,920	637	14	8	8			6		623	84	64	9	11	528	11
Boone	478	129	59	35	20	15		24		70	19	15	1	3	50	1
Bourbon	5,642	1,470	104	55	44	11		49		1,366	591	543	40	8	719	56
Boyd	822	188	5	1		1		4		183	64	38	24	2	117	2
Boyle	4,153	965	109	84	66	12	6	25		856	353	223	81	49	453	50
Bracken	339	76	11	3	3			8		65	21	19	2		42	2
Breathitt	260	59	29	12	12			17		30	11	10	1		19	
Breckinridge	1,581	348	94	54	45	9		38	2	254	106	98	5	3	134	14
Bullitt	679	132	36	23	19	2	2	13		96	36	27	5	4	56	4
Butler	561	138	53	35	27	8		18		85	42	34	3	5	40	3
Caldwell	2,520	557	153	57	41	16		96		404	100	75	22	3	291	13
Calloway	1,069	231	69	35	19	16		34		162	43	35	7	1	111	8
Campbell	735	175								175	34	14	20		141	
Carlisle	393	80	10	5	5			5		70	33	25	3	5	32	5
Carroll	530	126	29	5	1	4		24		97	31	27	3	1	59	7
Carter	110	28	4	3	3			1		24	7	7			12	5
Casey	278	63	39	30	21	9		9		24	6	5	1		17	1
Christian	15,956	3,492	859	317	231	84	2	538	4	2,633	809	568	153	88	1,565	259
Clark	4,462	1,121	104	82	61	16	5	22		1,017	484	351	62	71	444	89
Clay	494	100	85	34	31	3		51		15	7	1	1	5	8	
Crittenden	588	147	50	32	25	7		18		97	56	45	10	1	40	1
Cumberland	1,024	193	81	37	29	8		44		112	56	44	11	1	56	
Daviess	5,195	1,312	270	104	78	24	2	166		1,042	244	173	61	10	745	53
Edmonson	439	82	60	50	38	12		10		22	9	9			10	3
Estill	106	23	6	5	5			1		17	9	7		2	8	
Fayette	14,879	4,050	109	64	54	10		45		3,941	936	822	110	4	2,963	42
Fleming	1,027	269	52	30	24	6		22		217	97	77	16	4	111	9
Franklin	3,746	773	31	23	22	1		8		742	214	182	29	3	524	4
Fulton	3,356	742	228	11	6	4	1	217		514	116	60	16	40	352	46
Gallatin	274	78	17	10	9	1		7		61	27	16	6	5	29	5
Garrard	2,284	537	215	138	91	42	5	76	1	322	130	96	16	18	179	13
Grant	292	61	9	3	3			6		52	16	13	2	1	36	
Graves	2,899	638	212	76	53	22	1	136		426	150	108	42		274	2
Grayson	333	74	16	12	7	5		4		58	41	33	8		17	
Green	1,343	272	161	106	68	37	1	55		111	33	18	11	4	60	18
Greenup	257	36	3	3	3					33	16	11	5		14	3
Hancock	566	139	37	13	12	1		24		102	55	46	8	1	47	
Hardin	1,826	443	75	66	55	2	9	8	1	368	149	121	10	18	206	13
Harlan	564	141	29	15	14	1		14		112	2	1	1		96	14

[1] Includes all counties with less than 100 Negro inhabitants.

TABLE **18.**—HOME OWNERSHIP BY COUNTIES: 1910—NUMBER OF FARM HOMES AND OTHER HOMES, OWNED FREE, OWNED ENCUMBERED, AND RENTED BY NEGRO FAMILIES—Continued.

STATE AND COUNTY.	Negro population: 1910.	Total farm and other homes: 1910.	NUMBER OF FARM HOMES.							NUMBER OF OTHER HOMES.						
			Total.	Owned.				Rented.	No report of owner-ship.	Total.	Owned.				Rented.	No report of owner-ship.
				Total.	Free.	Encum-bered.	No en-cum-brance report.				Total.	Free.	Encum-bered.	No en-cum-brance report.		
KENTUCKY—Continued.																
Harrison	1,750	413	91	45	31	13	1	45	1	322	104	94	6	4	203	15
Hart	1,991	403	231	114	85	28	1	117	......	172	65	53	6	6	102	5
Henderson	6,818	1,654	436	149	89	58	2	286	1	1,218	327	246	60	21	851	40
Henry	1,792	419	97	26	24	2	......	71	......	322	105	89	12	4	201	16
Hickman	1,766	405	72	34	20	14	......	38	......	333	158	138	19	1	160	15
Hopkins	6,573	1,507	152	50	36	12	2	100	2	1,355	299	196	89	14	997	59
Jefferson	45,794	12,051	146	97	84	13	......	49	......	11,905	1,089	746	319	24	10,474	342
Jessamine	2,962	667	115	70	48	22	......	44	1	552	286	226	32	28	244	22
Kenton	3,228	879	11	6	5	1	......	5	......	868	101	55	46	......	751	16
Knott	157	26	26	12	10	2	......	14	......	......	......	......	......	......	......	......
Knox	1,059	231	44	33	28	5	......	11	......	187	61	52	4	5	123	3
Larue	785	165	47	40	32	8	......	7	......	118	49	40	9	......	69	......
Laurel	657	140	36	29	23	6	......	7	......	104	48	37	8	3	54	2
Lawrence	163	34	3	2	2	......	......	1	......	31	18	14	4	......	13	......
Lee	234	61	12	9	7	2	......	3	......	49	7	6	......	1	32	10
Leslie	132	21	15	13	13	......	......	2	......	6	1	1	......	......	1	4
Lewis	141	28	19	17	11	6	......	2	......	9	5	4	1	......	4	......
Lincoln	2,955	629	210	158	144	9	5	49	3	419	179	139	8	32	197	43
Livingston	670	151	41	20	15	5	......	21	......	110	48	37	11	......	55	7
Logan	5,349	1,147	508	228	160	66	2	277	3	639	220	200	15	5	384	35
Lyon	1,799	263	108	59	49	10	......	49	......	155	52	38	8	6	101	2
McCracken	7,934	2,133	176	116	81	33	2	60	......	1,957	384	311	61	12	1,512	61
McLean	750	170	43	19	15	4	......	23	1	127	57	48	6	3	63	7
Madison	5,698	1,217	541	374	316	55	3	167	......	676	269	207	39	23	384	23
Marion	2,266	517	97	81	53	28	......	16	......	420	111	96	15	......	298	11
Marshall	135	27	14	8	7	1	......	6	......	13	3	3	......	......	10	......
Mason	2,868	685	86	38	33	4	1	42	6	599	222	139	65	18	358	19
Meade	655	139	80	62	50	12	......	18	......	59	37	32	4	1	21	1
Mercer	2,171	570	76	61	52	9	......	15	......	494	196	174	17	5	284	14
Metcalfe	794	166	132	66	33	33	......	66	......	34	7	4	1	2	25	2
Monroe	705	129	72	37	25	12	......	35	......	57	16	12	3	1	38	3
Montgomery	3,192	770	108	76	64	10	2	32	......	662	258	211	24	23	367	37
Muhlenberg	2,911	629	113	76	67	9	......	37	......	516	185	160	23	2	311	20
Nelson	2,935	647	118	96	79	15	2	22	......	529	246	207	22	17	262	21
Nicholas	896	273	35	29	23	6	......	6	......	238	117	76	17	24	107	14
Ohio	1,288	310	70	46	37	8	1	21	3	240	104	88	11	5	132	4
Oldham	1,078	239	37	22	19	3	......	15	......	202	62	57	4	1	127	13
Owen	943	206	75	39	27	11	1	36	......	131	62	51	8	3	61	8
Pendleton	261	69	18	12	9	3	......	6	......	51	29	24	5	......	21	1
Perry	214	37	28	12	11	1	......	16	......	9	3	3	......	......	6	......
Pike	332	76	18	5	5	......	......	13	......	58	7	5	2	......	49	2
Powell	337	94	60	51	46	5	......	9	......	34	5	1	......	4	27	2
Pulaski	1,187	280	68	57	54	3	......	11	......	212	91	72	11	8	109	12
Rockcastle	125	24	9	7	7	......	......	2	......	15	7	7	......	......	8	......
Russell	207	39	25	18	15	3	......	7	......	14	11	8	3	......	3	......
Scott	4,044	1,140	117	63	49	14	......	54	......	1,023	401	338	60	3	573	49
Shelby	3,991	865	153	61	46	13	2	91	1	712	188	152	25	11	494	30
Simpson	2,165	505	113	57	31	26	......	55	1	392	51	40	10	1	324	17
Spencer	758	155	57	34	26	8	......	23	......	98	32	28	3	1	62	4
Taylor	1,429	307	140	109	71	38	......	30	1	167	76	61	10	5	90	1
Todd	5,343	1,172	387	183	119	64	......	204	......	785	235	184	42	9	495	55
Trigg	3,322	688	355	142	108	33	1	211	2	333	121	104	11	6	192	20
Trimble	142	33	15	7	7	......	......	8	......	18	6	6	......	......	12	......
Union	2,414	573	80	27	22	5	......	53	......	493	157	110	32	15	298	38
Warren	6,113	1,440	288	195	140	52	3	92	1	1,152	379	315	49	15	749	24
Washington	1,779	354	151	98	72	26	......	52	1	203	66	56	6	4	130	7
Wayne	739	149	78	58	50	8	......	20	......	71	22	14	4	4	46	3
Webster	2,643	599	96	44	32	11	1	52	......	503	239	209	30	......	257	7
Whitley	1,111	214	15	10	9	......	1	5	......	199	26	22	4	......	171	2
Woodford	3,724	930	82	50	34	16	......	32	......	848	361	314	38	9	430	57
Other counties [1]	672	118	84	52	48	3	1	32	......	34	14	12	1	1	19	1
LOUISIANA.																
Total	713,874	159,350	55,094	11,077	8,145	2,669	263	43,906	111	104,256	16,160	12,650	2,526	984	82,020	6,076
Acadia	6,546	1,280	396	88	75	10	3	308	......	884	365	280	75	10	475	44
Ascension	11,255	2,741	304	237	215	22	......	67	......	2,437	498	457	39	2	1,844	95
Assumption	10,105	2,456	182	18	13	5	......	164	......	2,274	543	465	67	11	1,691	40
Avoyelles	12,039	2,477	1,256	184	110	60	14	1,070	2	1,221	99	59	36	4	1,091	31
Bienville	9,464	1,690	1,174	456	370	84	2	715	3	516	82	60	7	15	377	57
Bossier	16,735	3,898	2,694	630	486	139	5	2,064	......	1,204	62	45	8	9	1,079	63
Caddo	36,142	8,556	3,780	513	423	81	9	3,258	9	4,776	777	639	114	24	3,652	347
Calcasieu	16,562	3,534	326	223	202	16	5	102	1	3,208	731	577	135	19	2,322	155
Caldwell	3,465	647	327	163	150	12	1	164	......	320	45	36	2	7	237	38
Cameron	538	98	84	23	20	3	......	61	......	14	4	4	......	......	7	3
Catahoula	5,195	1,079	728	65	39	18	8	642	21	351	51	50	......	1	259	41
Claiborne	14,938	2,646	2,201	508	335	158	15	1,692	1	445	32	20	11	1	356	57
Concordia	11,941	3,600	1,046	31	25	6	......	1,014	1	1,954	139	127	9	3	1,744	71
De Soto	17,932	3,762	2,929	807	559	215	33	2,118	4	833	104	77	8	19	544	185
East Baton Rouge	21,342	4,865	1,167	179	134	42	3	987	1	3,698	500	388	90	22	3,026	172

[1] Includes all counties with less than 100 Negro inhabitants.

TABLE 18.—HOME OWNERSHIP BY COUNTIES: 1910—NUMBER OF FARM HOMES AND OTHER HOMES, OWNED FREE, OWNED ENCUMBERED, AND RENTED BY NEGRO FAMILIES—Continued.

STATE AND COUNTY.	Negro population: 1910.	Total farm and other homes: 1910.	NUMBER OF FARM HOMES.							NUMBER OF OTHER HOMES.						
			Total.	Owned. Total.	Free.	Encumbered.	No encumbrance report.	Rented.	No report of ownership.	Total.	Owned. Total.	Free.	Encumbered.	No encumbrance report.	Rented.	No report of ownership.
LOUISIANA—Continued.																
East Carroll	10,390	2,847	1,665	54	38	15	1	1,610	1	1,182	192	127	64	1	958	32
East Feliciana	14,536	2,904	1,819	246	149	96	1	1,573	......	1,085	68	55	8	5	948	69
Franklin	5,264	1,167	866	113	74	37	2	753	......	301	2	......	......	2	176	123
Grant	4,869	1,030	439	36	23	13	......	403	......	591	39	26	6	7	531	21
Iberia	14,474	3,003	632	294	200	89	5	337	1	2,371	551	437	103	11	1,596	224
Iberville	19,145	4,999	258	96	63	28	5	162	......	4,741	813	601	78	134	3,790	138
Jackson	3,996	745	487	252	200	50	2	235	......	258	17	13	......	4	233	8
Jefferson	6,785	1,773	33	10	10	......	......	23	......	1,740	380	343	33	4	1,331	29
La Salle	1,953	323	62	38	36	2	......	24	......	261	12	11	......	1	234	15
Lafayette	10,734	1,977	911	182	128	43	11	728	1	1,066	275	219	41	15	724	67
Lafourche	7,973	2,041	168	57	33	22	2	111	......	1,873	228	162	54	12	1,606	39
Lincoln	7,289	1,374	872	286	225	56	5	586	......	502	78	64	14	......	394	30
Livingston	1,377	270	109	53	48	5	......	56	......	161	32	29	1	2	110	19
Madison	9,455	2,633	1,670	37	23	14	......	1,632	1	963	43	18	24	1	748	172
Morehouse	13,971	3,101	2,378	235	187	35	13	2,142	1	723	42	35	5	2	571	110
Natchitoches	20,334	4,255	2,877	461	383	75	3	2,408	8	1,378	273	214	23	36	996	109
Orleans	89,262	21,880	40	21	17	2	2	18	1	21,840	2,410	1,837	488	85	18,295	1,135
Ouachita	14,153	3,407	1,037	221	158	48	15	808	8	2,370	289	180	93	16	1,959	122
Plaquemines	6,847	1,533	199	130	110	20	......	69	......	1,334	286	248	6	32	1,000	48
Pointe Coupee	17,147	3,688	1,675	143	92	49	2	1,531	1	2,013	49	36	10	3	1,766	198
Rapides	21,445	4,476	1,054	157	118	26	13	893	4	3,422	481	340	59	82	2,769	172
Red River	6,212	1,415	1,027	168	93	75	......	857	2	388	9	8	......	1	343	36
Richland	10,463	2,298	1,597	151	120	29	2	1,446	......	701	97	79	11	7	503	101
Sabine	4,164	810	424	186	139	42	5	235	3	386	40	35	2	3	307	39
St. Bernard	1,933	459	11	5	5	......	......	6	......	448	43	41	2	......	385	20
St. Charles	6,720	1,557	99	63	60	2	1	35	1	1,458	346	308	5	33	1,054	58
St. Helena	4,573	825	660	126	87	37	2	534	......	165	13	10	1	2	122	30
St. James	13,164	3,179	72	53	42	10	1	19	......	3,107	682	503	59	120	2,294	131
St. John the Baptist	8,126	1,987	146	40	30	9	1	106	......	1,841	357	287	15	55	1,370	114
St. Landry	31,234	5,974	3,803	690	463	184	43	3,108	5	2,171	290	224	41	25	1,742	139
St. Martin	9,836	1,780	946	308	203	101	4	627	11	834	204	171	23	10	570	60
St. Mary	21,266	4,769	202	141	109	32	......	59	2	4,567	1,150	912	205	33	3,325	92
St. Tammany	6,731	1,504	71	62	57	5	......	9	......	1,433	557	513	35	9	811	65
Tangipahoa	9,135	1,864	436	222	167	55	......	214	......	1,428	261	207	38	16	1,087	80
Tensas	15,613	4,291	2,706	71	43	27	1	2,632	3	1,585	97	81	12	4	1,312	176
Terrebonne	11,194	2,486	101	59	39	20	......	42	......	2,385	716	441	266	9	1,585	84
Union	7,448	1,313	792	361	208	149	4	430	1	521	55	41	9	5	384	82
Vermilion	4,500	803	329	127	88	33	6	198	4	474	178	154	13	11	208	88
Vernon	3,716	788	51	42	39	2	1	8	1	737	56	45	7	4	653	28
Washington	5,458	1,031	423	191	150	41	......	231	1	608	18	11	5	2	502	88
Webster	9,900	1,934	1,029	376	255	116	5	650	3	905	146	103	20	23	711	48
West Baton Rouge	9,223	2,300	348	67	36	30	1	279	2	1,952	168	131	37	......	1,716	68
West Carroll	2,724	629	423	100	81	19	......	323	......	206	6	4	1	1	128	72
West Feliciana	11,012	2,359	1,293	56	31	20	5	1,235	2	1,066	39	35	4	......	954	73
Winn	3,931	840	260	165	129	35	1	95	......	580	40	27	4	9	515	25
MAINE.																
Total	1,363	294	29	26	19	7	......	3	......	265	100	75	24	1	153	12
Cumberland	428	98	9	7	6	1	......	2	......	89	30	20	10	......	53	6
Kennebec	139	24	4	4	1	3	......	......	......	20	7	6	1	......	12	1
Penobscot	246	49	5	5	4	1	......	......	......	44	14	9	5	......	29	1
Sagadahoc	103	32	2	2	2	......	......	......	......	30	16	15	1	......	12	2
Other counties[1]	447	91	9	8	6	2	......	1	......	82	33	25	7	1	47	2
MARYLAND.																
Total	232,250	47,177	6,653	4,091	2,710	1,357	24	2,536	26	40,524	7,977	5,371	2,135	471	30,238	2,309
Allegany	1,517	308	4	2	1	1	......	2	......	304	69	31	36	2	224	11
Anne Arundel	14,136	2,929	458	267	188	79	......	181	10	2,471	508	358	129	21	1,844	119
Baltimore	12,601	2,322	129	87	41	46	......	41	1	2,193	421	266	138	17	1,691	81
Baltimore City	84,749	18,106	2	2	1	......	1	......	......	18,104	931	674	203	54	15,842	1,331
Calvert	5,046	939	442	257	197	59	1	183	2	497	170	141	15	14	305	22
Caroline	4,787	952	395	261	141	120	......	134	......	557	174	98	65	11	376	7
Carroll	2,006	398	33	28	13	15	......	4	1	365	113	70	38	5	235	17
Cecil	3,315	657	65	44	29	15	......	21	......	592	172	98	58	16	398	22
Charles	8,572	1,526	674	361	299	60	2	312	1	852	278	221	30	27	504	70
Dorchester	9,421	1,987	519	309	205	103	1	208	2	1,468	518	361	121	36	903	47
Frederick	5,399	1,195	95	64	38	26	......	30	1	1,100	385	242	129	14	692	23
Garrett	107	20	5	5	2	3	......	......	......	15	5	4	1	......	8	2
Harford	5,116	1,066	201	157	76	78	3	44	......	865	235	139	90	6	587	43
Howard	3,772	683	149	119	60	56	3	30	......	534	105	52	23	30	400	29
Kent	6,162	1,258	160	116	85	31	......	44	......	1,098	444	304	106	34	620	34

1 Includes all counties with less than 100 Negro inhabitants.

TABLE 18.—HOME OWNERSHIP BY COUNTIES: 1910—NUMBER OF FARM HOMES AND OTHER HOMES, OWNED FREE, OWNED ENCUMBERED, AND RENTED BY NEGRO FAMILIES—Continued.

STATE AND COUNTY.	Negro population: 1910.	Total farm and other homes: 1910.	NUMBER OF FARM HOMES.							NUMBER OF OTHER HOMES.						
			Total.	Owned.				Rented.	No report of ownership.	Total.	Owned.				Rented.	No report of ownership.
				Total.	Free.	Encumbered.	No encumbrance report.				Total.	Free.	Encumbered.	No encumbrance report.		
MARYLAND—Continued.																
Montgomery	9,235	1,690	356	275	177	93	5	81	...	1,334	432	339	69	24	836	66
Prince Georges	11,493	2,162	567	302	252	49	1	260	5	1,595	531	293	168	70	939	125
Queen Annes	5,814	1,110	233	147	92	54	1	85	1	877	329	253	65	11	485	63
St. Marys	7,304	1,335	477	258	183	73	2	217	2	858	296	239	39	18	514	48
Somerset	9,476	1,964	566	420	253	166	1	146	...	1,398	719	505	200	14	639	40
Talbot	6,774	1,487	198	142	90	52	...	56	...	1,289	386	237	115	34	864	39
Washington	2,113	446	20	15	9	6	...	5	...	426	123	72	50	1	291	12
Wicomico	6,316	1,285	415	271	147	122	2	144	...	870	396	226	160	10	449	25
Worcester	7,025	1,352	490	182	131	50	...	308	...	862	237	148	87	2	592	33
MASSACHUSETTS.																
Total	38,055	8,705	114	101	50	50	1	13	...	8,591	1,311	549	749	13	7,123	157
Barnstable	897	190	10	9	4	5	...	1	...	180	96	63	33	...	80	4
Berkshire	1,149	239	20	19	14	4	1	1	...	219	66	38	28	...	146	7
Bristol	4,003	923	11	10	2	8	...	1	...	912	185	87	96	2	712	15
Dukes	193	62	3	3	2	1	...	...	...	59	35	26	9	...	24	...
Essex	2,024	474	3	2	1	1	...	1	...	471	90	45	43	2	374	7
Franklin	119	22	8	8	3	5	...	...	...	14	5	3	2	...	9	...
Hampden	1,757	369	6	4	3	1	...	2	...	363	83	23	60	...	276	4
Hampshire	281	53	4	4	1	3	...	...	...	49	23	6	17	...	26	...
Middlesex	8,583	1,931	16	13	6	7	...	3	...	1,915	358	105	250	3	1,543	14
Nantucket	35	11	...	...	...	...	...	...	...	11	9	6	3	...	1	1
Norfolk	797	107	11	10	4	6	...	1	...	96	29	8	21	...	64	3
Plymouth	2,484	476	9	8	3	5	...	1	...	467	129	66	63	...	310	28
Suffolk	13,886	3,443	...	...	...	...	...	...	...	3,443	145	56	84	5	3,228	70
Worcester	1,847	405	13	11	7	4	...	2	...	392	58	17	40	1	330	4
MICHIGAN.																
Total	17,115	4,391	640	505	227	275	3	135	...	3,751	1,427	813	599	15	2,247	77
Allegan	241	66	46	40	20	20	...	6	...	20	12	4	8	...	5	3
Bay	188	49	3	3	3	...	...	...	...	46	18	15	3	...	28	...
Berrien	713	209	23	18	7	11	...	5	...	186	106	52	53	1	78	2
Calhoun	690	184	12	10	5	5	...	2	...	172	91	51	40	...	81	...
Cass	1,444	403	165	121	57	63	1	44	...	238	127	84	40	3	108	3
Genesee	416	97	2	2	...	2	...	1	...	95	55	27	28	...	40	...
Ingham	404	114	4	3	2	1	...	1	...	110	54	21	32	1	56	...
Isabella	135	33	25	23	9	14	...	2	...	8	3	2	1	...	4	1
Jackson	399	108	5	4	1	3	...	1	...	103	40	21	19	...	63	...
Kalamazoo	790	212	9	8	3	4	1	1	...	203	92	51	41	...	111	...
Kent	729	208	11	9	5	4	...	2	...	197	84	49	34	1	113	...
Lenawee	245	65	5	4	3	1	...	1	...	60	41	25	16	...	19	...
Macomb	102	27	...	...	...	...	...	...	...	27	13	9	4	...	14	...
Mecosta	237	52	35	33	16	17	...	2	...	17	9	9	...	...	6	2
Midland	119	27	19	18	5	13	...	1	...	8	5	5	...	...	3	...
Montcalm	105	32	25	21	9	12	...	4	...	7	5	3	2	...	1	1
Oakland	251	49	3	2	1	1	...	1	...	46	31	17	14	...	15	...
Saginaw	343	87	1	1	1	...	...	...	...	86	38	25	11	2	48	...
Van Buren	535	146	65	47	19	28	...	18	...	81	43	19	21	3	36	2
Washtenaw	1,130	305	23	22	8	13	1	1	...	282	167	101	64	2	109	6
Wayne	6,085	1,465	30	19	10	9	...	11	...	1,435	257	139	117	1	1,123	55
Other counties[1]	1,814	453	129	97	43	54	...	32	...	324	136	84	51	1	186	2
MINNESOTA.																
Total	7,084	1,685	42	24	16	8	...	16	2	1,643	392	231	155	6	1,153	98
Hennepin	2,646	660	7	5	3	2	...	1	1	653	124	71	51	2	479	50
Ramsey	3,154	749	1	...	...	...	...	1	...	748	180	106	73	1	534	34
St. Louis	439	117	1	1	1	...	...	...	...	116	29	18	9	2	77	10
Other counties[1]	845	159	33	18	12	6	...	15	...	126	59	36	22	1	63	4
MISSISSIPPI.																
Total	1,009,487	227,664	159,055	24,781	13,160	11,030	591	133,660	614	68,609	13,783	10,159	2,992	632	48,355	6,471
Adams	18,908	5,029	1,744	193	110	81	2	1,550	1	3,285	417	314	93	10	2,699	169
Alcorn	4,275	927	422	121	64	50	7	300	1	505	144	128	11	5	291	70
Amite	12,590	2,447	1,773	334	218	112	4	1,433	6	674	46	38	6	2	553	75
Attala	13,219	2,615	2,112	567	268	296	3	1,540	5	503	158	91	67	...	293	52
Benton	5,037	998	815	95	64	28	3	717	3	183	3	3	...	...	41	139
Bolivar	42,763	11,731	9,594	785	287	476	22	8,792	17	2,137	327	251	66	10	1,473	337
Calhoun	3,812	747	648	121	79	40	2	527	...	99	8	8	...	...	66	25
Carroll	13,475	2,697	2,401	395	139	253	3	2,001	5	296	33	24	9	...	215	48
Chickasaw	12,714	2,535	1,938	330	176	148	6	1,607	1	597	248	218	29	1	317	32
Choctaw	4,169	807	625	224	105	118	1	397	4	182	49	26	20	3	120	13

[1] Includes all counties with less than 100 Negro inhabitants.

TABLE 18.—HOME OWNERSHIP BY COUNTIES: 1910—NUMBER OF FARM HOMES AND OTHER HOMES, OWNED FREE, OWNED ENCUMBERED, AND RENTED BY NEGRO FAMILIES—Continued.

STATE AND COUNTY.	Negro population: 1910.	Total farm and other homes: 1910.	NUMBER OF FARM HOMES.							NUMBER OF OTHER HOMES.						
			Total.	Owned.				Rented.	No report of ownership.	Total.	Owned.				Rented.	No report of ownership.
				Total.	Free.	Encumbered.	No encumbrance report.				Total.	Free.	Encumbered.	No encumbrance report.		
MISSISSIPPI—Continued.																
Claiborne	13,608	3,175	2,066	221	81	131	9	1,843	2	1,109	145	99	43	3	872	92
Clarke	10,262	2,017	1,499	707	430	268	9	792	......	518	120	88	23	9	366	32
Clay	14,105	3,203	2,109	424	255	157	12	1,653	32	1,094	341	291	42	8	665	88
Coahoma	30,382	7,725	6,094	353	157	187	9	5,713	28	1,631	386	299	69	18	1,062	183
Copiah	19,981	4,101	2,964	623	260	354	9	2,340	1	1,137	179	136	39	4	846	112
Covington	5,224	1,071	493	237	118	119	......	256	......	578	104	76	26	2	459	15
De Soto	17,572	3,845	3,520	403	239	161	3	3,113	4	325	68	44	22	2	218	39
Forrest	7,683	1,841	260	149	116	32	1	111	......	1,581	374	206	105	63	1,124	83
Franklin	6,823	1,376	835	175	98	77	......	660	......	541	13	11	1	1	504	24
George	1,827	418	64	60	58	2	......	4	......	354	97	91	3	3	238	19
Greene	1,347	306	129	113	112	1	......	16	......	177	33	31	2	......	123	21
Grenada	11,161	2,459	1,826	289	204	71	14	1,526	11	633	134	102	28	4	414	85
Hancock	4,339	1,109	68	57	53	4	......	11	......	1,041	385	333	34	18	582	74
Harrison	10,643	2,712	127	103	93	8	2	24	......	2,585	734	633	81	20	1,759	92
Hinds	45,407	9,949	6,064	691	386	289	16	5,356	17	3,885	810	562	214	34	2,774	301
Holmes	31,197	6,873	5,560	774	359	345	70	4,705	81	1,313	270	151	109	10	896	147
Issaquena	9,946	2,628	2,087	157	113	31	13	1,918	12	541	26	26	......	1	398	117
Itawamba	1,198	216	198	69	32	37	......	128	1	18	4	3	......	1	13	1
Jackson	5,467	1,391	49	44	42	2	......	5	......	1,342	507	417	86	4	749	86
Jasper	9,013	1,640	1,419	537	220	310	7	880	2	221	23	17	2	4	181	17
Jefferson	14,287	3,061	2,234	244	138	100	6	1,989	1	827	68	39	9	20	687	72
Jefferson Davis	6,757	1,268	1,061	485	245	216	24	575	1	207	25	14	7	4	118	64
Jones	8,417	1,807	406	204	91	113	......	202	......	1,401	336	218	106	12	1,009	56
Kemper	11,691	2,228	1,856	505	266	224	15	1,348	3	372	44	37	4	3	281	47
Lafayette	9,904	2,110	1,789	415	256	150	9	1,373	1	321	136	116	14	6	161	24
Lamar	3,619	730	93	54	44	10	......	39	......	637	125	92	32	1	492	20
Lauderdale	21,875	5,024	1,764	603	353	247	3	1,160	1	3,260	681	427	201	53	2,433	146
Lawrence	5,147	958	740	325	144	180	1	415	......	218	27	16	4	7	154	37
Leake	6,171	1,155	1,069	453	198	253	2	616	......	86	6	5	......	1	49	31
Lee	10,667	2,332	1,700	240	139	100	1	1,458	2	632	212	121	89	2	389	31
Leflore	30,628	7,144	5,692	169	58	79	32	5,496	27	1,452	241	146	93	2	1,075	136
Lincoln	12,054	2,428	1,213	384	175	207	2	828	1	1,215	266	160	103	3	896	53
Lowndes	21,784	5,360	3,243	352	169	162	21	2,886	5	2,117	445	387	54	4	1,511	161
Madison	27,298	6,019	4,758	618	292	312	14	4,137	3	1,261	162	110	46	6	917	182
Marion	6,063	1,086	666	393	234	157	2	272	1	420	67	40	19	8	331	22
Marshall	19,342	3,962	3,350	520	362	153	5	2,820	10	612	195	171	21	3	378	39
Monroe	19,535	4,344	3,293	519	246	236	37	2,765	9	1,051	256	185	54	17	667	128
Montgomery	8,927	1,774	1,355	267	121	135	11	1,083	5	419	94	53	36	5	269	56
Neshoba	2,949	555	469	183	98	84	1	286	......	86	4	2	2	......	54	28
Newton	8,950	1,751	1,189	437	191	245	1	752	......	562	73	58	11	4	449	40
Noxubee	23,947	5,198	4,275	370	226	136	8	3,893	12	923	226	186	35	5	487	210
Oktibbeha	12,675	2,805	2,214	502	241	245	16	1,707	5	591	142	109	32	1	366	83
Panola	21,224	4,370	3,893	444	243	199	2	3,445	4	477	113	75	33	5	328	36
Pearl River	2,422	558	94	64	60	4	......	30	......	464	79	68	6	5	378	7
Perry	2,581	497	183	154	140	14	......	25	4	314	38	36	1	1	228	48
Pike	17,597	3,478	1,792	775	464	307	4	1,015	2	1,686	436	299	82	55	1,013	237
Pontotoc	4,727	958	782	213	118	93	2	567	2	176	53	36	12	5	112	11
Prentiss	2,875	581	425	67	29	36	2	358	......	156	45	31	12	2	107	4
Quitman	8,864	2,165	1,838	153	56	92	5	1,676	9	327	41	25	8	8	213	73
Rankin	14,249	2,855	2,463	755	359	384	12	1,707	1	392	38	21	14	3	312	42
Scott	6,896	1,262	957	334	176	156	2	623	......	305	118	88	26	4	150	37
Sharkey	13,967	3,523	3,041	87	42	45	......	2,949	5	482	40	30	5	5	324	118
Simpson	5,969	1,092	948	368	177	188	3	579	1	144	5	4	......	1	115	24
Smith	2,899	528	396	154	66	88	......	241	1	132	5	4	......	1	118	9
Sunflower	23,281	5,482	4,738	203	83	102	18	4,437	98	744	99	60	37	2	390	255
Tallahatchie	20,180	4,211	3,623	230	113	108	9	3,380	13	588	74	52	14	8	397	117
Tate	11,535	2,459	2,243	178	114	58	6	2,063	2	216	48	30	14	4	162	6
Tippah	2,801	517	420	97	56	40	1	323	......	97	23	15	6	2	63	11
Tishomingo	1,089	247	122	68	54	14	......	54	......	125	65	51	13	1	57	3
Tunica	16,910	4,387	3,889	240	126	99	15	3,613	36	498	40	35	5	......	290	168
Union	4,216	894	629	95	46	49	......	534	......	265	69	60	9	......	186	10
Warren	26,191	7,407	2,563	274	215	53	6	2,287	2	4,844	892	732	129	31	3,791	161
Washington	41,600	11,994	7,700	289	171	96	22	7,335	76	4,294	757	560	177	20	3,137	400
Wayne	5,843	1,135	680	383	240	129	14	295	2	455	108	69	11	28	270	77
Webster	3,286	659	526	167	92	75	......	359	......	133	30	15	11	4	81	22
Wilkinson	13,904	2,918	2,067	223	146	70	7	1,842	2	851	56	50	4	2	735	60
Winston	6,863	1,275	1,099	456	167	289	......	643	......	176	28	20	7	1	120	28
Yalobusha	11,182	2,240	1,607	267	154	111	2	1,334	6	633	120	78	25	17	456	57
Yazoo	35,502	8,285	6,405	450	230	199	21	5,928	27	1,880	346	206	129	11	1,338	196
MISSOURI.																
Total	157,452	38,134	3,734	2,156	1,092	1,031	33	1,562	16	34,400	7,974	5,056	2,637	281	24,644	1,782
Adair	216	60	3	2	......	2	......	1	......	57	23	13	10	......	27	7
Andrew	130	38	6	4	1	3	......	2	......	32	18	13	5	......	14	......
Audrain	1,617	401	42	25	12	13	......	17	......	359	137	99	36	2	205	17
Bates	238	63	3	2	......	2	......	1	......	60	34	20	14	......	25	1
Benton	136	26	9	9	3	5	1	......	......	17	8	5	......	3	8	1

TABLE 18.—HOME OWNERSHIP BY COUNTIES: 1910—NUMBER OF FARM HOMES AND OTHER HOMES, OWNED FREE, OWNED ENCUMBERED, AND RENTED BY NEGRO FAMILIES—Continued.

STATE AND COUNTY.	Negro population: 1910.	Total farm and other homes: 1910.	NUMBER OF FARM HOMES.							NUMBER OF OTHER HOMES.						
			Total.	Owned.				Rented.	No report of ownership.	Total.	Owned.				Rented.	No report of ownership.
				Total.	Free.	Encumbered.	No encumbrance report.				Total.	Free.	Encumbered.	No encumbrance report.		
MISSOURI—Continued.																
Boone	4,185	975	158	95	44	51	....	62	1	817	289	201	83	5	485	43
Buchanan	4,457	1,039	11	4	4	....	....	7	....	1,028	169	94	71	4	859	....
Butler	1,372	322	53	23	15	8	....	30	....	269	111	61	45	5	139	19
Caldwell	278	63	8	5	3	2	....	3	....	55	36	24	12	....	18	1
Callaway	3,514	784	285	229	125	102	2	56	....	499	148	100	44	4	315	36
Cape Girardeau	1,999	419	75	41	15	26	....	33	1	344	102	65	35	2	217	25
Carroll	1,019	263	42	15	11	4	....	27	....	221	137	104	30	3	74	10
Cass	510	125	9	6	5	1	....	3	....	116	66	41	11	14	49	1
Chariton	2,232	490	136	54	22	32	....	77	5	354	150	106	41	3	178	26
Clay	1,052	254	24	13	5	8	....	10	1	230	90	62	28	....	122	18
Clinton	769	187	30	25	12	13	....	5	....	157	86	61	24	1	65	6
Cole	2,157	314	17	12	8	4	....	5	....	297	113	56	57	....	180	4
Cooper	2,878	645	135	107	25	79	3	28	....	510	193	114	74	5	261	56
Dade	235	53	13	10	7	3	....	3	....	40	32	13	14	5	8	....
Daviess	258	72	5	3	1	2	....	2	....	67	38	25	13	....	28	1
Franklin	1,365	315	83	54	33	21	....	29	....	232	104	79	21	4	121	7
Greene	2,625	662	69	46	26	20	....	23	....	593	200	142	56	2	369	24
Grundy	159	57	2	1	....	1	....	1	....	55	27	18	9	....	27	1
Henry	842	197	48	25	17	8	....	23	....	149	63	47	16	....	68	18
Holt	118	33	6	4	....	4	....	2	....	27	17	14	3	....	10	....
Howard	3,152	711	117	61	17	42	2	56	....	594	226	158	67	1	340	28
Howell	127	28	13	11	6	5	....	2	....	15	11	7	4	....	4	....
Iron	179	47	2	2	2	....	....	....	....	45	26	22	2	2	16	3
Jackson	24,936	6,524	21	8	4	2	2	13	....	6,503	718	321	386	11	5,385	400
Jasper	1,368	372	1	1	....	1	....	....	....	371	99	54	44	1	245	27
Jefferson	1,565	324	22	12	10	2	....	10	....	302	109	70	27	12	188	5
Johnson	1,251	312	87	39	16	22	1	48	....	225	127	98	25	4	93	5
Knox	168	39	10	4	4	....	....	5	1	29	14	10	4	....	11	4
Laclede	216	61	19	15	9	6	....	4	....	42	32	20	12	....	10	....
Lafayette	2,869	715	54	34	17	15	2	20	....	661	290	120	118	52	313	58
Lewis	776	183	24	12	5	6	1	12	....	159	76	56	20	....	79	4
Lincoln	1,362	307	131	96	49	46	1	35	....	176	85	71	14	....	84	7
Linn	668	172	15	15	8	7	....	....	....	157	94	65	23	6	61	2
Livingston	596	171	23	15	8	7	....	8	....	148	94	73	19	2	50	4
Macon	1,004	305	33	29	4	16	9	4	....	272	129	83	44	2	139	4
Madison	280	53	5	3	2	1	....	2	....	48	29	15	13	1	18	1
Marion	2,894	724	57	36	17	18	1	21	....	667	238	164	69	5	403	26
Mississippi	2,006	437	136	15	7	7	1	121	....	301	53	33	19	1	169	79
Moniteau	503	113	21	12	9	3	....	9	....	92	51	37	11	3	36	5
Monroe	1,223	290	91	64	24	39	1	26	1	199	77	72	5	....	107	15
Montgomery	1,176	280	86	57	28	29	....	29	....	194	94	67	25	2	89	11
Morgan	410	103	14	12	11	1	....	2	....	89	67	50	17	....	20	2
New Madrid	2,097	494	201	18	16	....	2	182	1	293	67	49	7	11	205	21
Newton	539	126	41	29	17	12	....	12	....	85	54	38	16	....	25	6
Nodaway	155	35	2	2	....	2	....	....	....	33	21	12	9	....	12	....
Osage	149	39	7	5	3	2	....	2	....	32	14	11	3	....	17	1
Pemiscot	1,533	342	92	12	8	3	1	80	....	250	17	15	2	....	197	36
Perry	228	49	21	8	2	6	....	12	1	28	12	10	2	....	14	2
Pettis	2,715	699	78	57	40	17	....	20	1	621	264	217	44	3	332	25
Phelps	136	35	4	3	3	....	....	1	....	31	18	10	8	....	11	2
Pike	3,350	849	211	143	83	60	....	68	....	638	263	191	58	14	350	25
Platte	719	172	21	6	3	3	....	15	....	151	61	43	14	4	90	....
Polk	138	30	6	4	4	....	....	2	....	24	12	10	2	....	12	....
Ralls	610	133	46	26	20	6	....	20	....	87	38	26	7	5	39	10
Randolph	2,458	589	104	78	44	34	....	26	....	485	193	84	74	35	251	41
Ray	1,215	273	30	23	12	11	....	7	....	243	113	75	32	6	125	5
St Charles	1,718	385	63	37	17	19	1	26	....	322	98	57	40	1	208	16
St. Clair	184	46	11	9	7	1	1	2	....	35	17	14	3	....	18	....
St. Francois	556	121	4	3	3	....	....	1	....	117	56	38	18	....	61	....
St. Louis	4,253	996	83	34	16	17	1	47	2	913	384	198	184	2	507	22
St. Louis City	43,960	10,801	9	1	....	1	....	8	....	10,882	614	339	268	7	9,780	488
Ste. Genevieve	386	74	19	15	10	5	....	4	....	55	35	31	4	....	18	2
Saline	3,784	864	154	97	45	52	....	57	....	710	279	192	71	16	420	11
Scott	545	108	16	3	1	2	....	13	....	92	16	13	3	....	41	35
Shelby	558	129	37	26	13	13	....	11	....	92	41	22	19	....	38	13
Vernon	138	41	7	2	1	1	....	5	....	34	14	12	2	....	19	1
Warren	478	96	32	24	16	8	....	8	....	64	30	23	7	....	33	1
Washington	403	92	36	20	13	7	....	16	....	56	33	27	4	2	23	....
Wright	236	60	49	39	7	32	....	10	....	11	6	5	....	1	5	....
Other counties[1]	1,130	238	96	65	37	28	....	30	1	142	74	51	16	7	61	7

[1] Includes all counties with less than 100 Negro inhabitants.

TABLE 18.—HOME OWNERSHIP BY COUNTIES: 1910—NUMBER OF FARM HOMES AND OTHER HOMES, OWNED FREE, OWNED ENCUMBERED, AND RENTED BY NEGRO FAMILIES—Continued.

| STATE AND COUNTY. | Negro population: 1910. | Total farm and other homes: 1910. | NUMBER OF FARM HOMES. | | | | | | | NUMBER OF OTHER HOMES. | | | | | | |
			Total.	Owned Total.	Owned Free.	Owned Encumbered.	Owned No encumbrance report.	Rented.	No report of ownership.	Total.	Owned Total.	Owned Free.	Owned Encumbered.	Owned No encumbrance report.	Rented.	No report of ownership.
MONTANA.																
Total	1,834	555	30	22	18	4		8		525	160	116	33	11	328	37
Cascade	145	44	9	9	8	1				35	18	15	3		15	2
Deer Lodge	130	37								37	1	1			34	2
Lewis and Clark	430	143	1					1		142	29	20	9		106	7
Missoula	133	47								47	13	9	4		34	
Silver Bow	260	87	1	1	1					86	19	13	6		61	6
Yellowstone	167	47	5	3	1	2		2		42	17	10	3	4	19	6
Other counties [1]	569	150	14	9	8	1		5		136	63	48	8	7	59	14
NEBRASKA.																
Total	7,689	1,885	109	82	64	18		26	1	1,776	372	211	152	9	1,311	93
Dawes	105	36								36	11	11			19	6
Douglas	5,208	1,282	4	1		1		3		1,278	198	87	103	8	1,014	66
Hall	129	27	1	1		1				26	10	7	3		15	1
Lancaster	870	210	3	1		1		2		207	75	45	29	1	130	2
Other counties [1]	1,377	330	101	79	64	15		21	1	229	78	61	17		133	18
NEVADA.																
Total	513	210	6	5	4		1	1		204	70	66	4		131	3
Washoe	115	42								42	7	6	1		35	
Other counties [1]	398	168	6	5	4		1	1		162	63	60	3		96	3
NEW HAMPSHIRE.																
Total	564	121	16	15	7	7	1	1		105	22	11	11		79	4
Merrimack	122	24	2	2	1	1				22	5	1	4		17	
Rockingham	158	35	1	1		1				34	5	2	3		25	4
Other counties [1]	284	62	13	12	6	5	1	1		49	12	8	4		37	
NEW JERSEY.																
Total	89,760	19,825	489	289	142	139	8	194	6	19,336	3,393	1,541	1,778	74	15,212	731
Atlantic	10,782	2,143	12	9	4	5		3		2,131	192	75	114	3	1,749	190
Bergen	3,295	644	7	5	1	4		2		637	136	45	91		464	37
Burlington	3,454	774	43	25	10	11	4	14	4	731	207	88	113	6	1,633	35
Camden	9,402	2,279	20	12	5	7		6	2	2,259	540	328	191	21	1,633	86
Cape May	1,444	380	13	9	7	2		4		367	116	68	47	1	242	9
Cumberland	2,641	630	99	62	26	36		37		531	194	107	82	5	311	26
Essex	18,104	4,146	2	1		1		1		4,144	379	96	280	3	3,625	140
Gloucester	2,375	456	47	29	21	8		18		409	105	39	63	3	280	24
Hudson	7,173	1,717								1,717	182	64	115	3	1,496	39
Hunterdon	438	91	9	6	5	1		3		82	19	11	6	2	62	1
Mercer	5,125	990	18	11	4	7		7		972	138	48	88	2	798	36
Middlesex	1,846	354	11	5	2	3		6		343	49	23	25	1	284	10
Monmouth	8,279	1,911	53	37	22	15		16		1,858	515	243	263	9	1,343	
Morris	1,940	366	4	4		1	3			362	60	25	35		297	5
Ocean	438	113	1	1	1					112	23	13	10		87	2
Passaic	2,401	566	3	2	1	1		1		563	26	10	14	2	514	23
Salem	3,324	734	125	62	28	34		63		609	143	84	49	10	442	24
Somerset	1,414	297	17	6	4	2		11		280	71	45	25	1	194	15
Sussex	168	30	1					1		29	6	6			22	1
Union	5,353	1,128	3	3	1	1	1			1,125	282	115	165	2	820	23
Warren	364	76	1					1		75	10	8	2		60	5
NEW MEXICO.																
Total	1,628	449	48	42	38	3	1	6		401	94	73	17	4	298	9
Bernalillo	311	91	4	4	3		1			87	17	11	6		69	1
Chaves	233	60	12	10	8	2		2		48	13	10	2	1	34	1
Colfax	225	76	2	2	2					74	11	4	7		63	
Grant	164	41	3	3	2	1				38	16	14		2	22	
San Miguel	122	37	3	3	3					34	11	11			22	1
Santa Fe	128	30	2	2	2					28	9	8	1		18	1
Other counties [1]	445	114	22	18	18			4		92	17	15	1	1	70	5

[1] Includes all counties with less than 100 Negro inhabitants.

TABLE **18.**—HOME OWNERSHIP BY COUNTIES: 1910—NUMBER OF FARM HOMES AND OTHER HOMES, OWNED FREE, OWNED ENCUMBERED, AND RENTED BY NEGRO FAMILIES—Continued.

STATE AND COUNTY.	Negro popula- tion: 1910.	Total farm and other homes: 1910.	NUMBER OF FARM HOMES.							NUMBER OF OTHER HOMES.						
			Total.	Owned.				Rented.	No report of owner- ship.	Total.	Owned.				Rented.	No report of owner- ship.
				Total.	Free.	Encum- bered.	No en- cum- brance report.				Total.	Free.	Encum- bered.	No en- cum- brance report.		

NEW YORK.

STATE AND COUNTY.	Negro pop.	Total homes.	Total.	Total.	Free.	Encum.	No enc. rep.	Rented.	No rep.	Total.	Total.	Free.	Encum.	No enc. rep.	Rented.	No rep.
Total...........	134,191	31,434	311	210	99	105	6	100	1	31,123	2,227	1,125	1,059	43	27,970	926
Albany............	1,222	315	6	3	....	3	....	3	....	309	23	19	4	....	276	10
Allegany..........	325	80	14	13	7	6	....	1	....	66	27	21	6	....	38	1
Broome............	725	172	10	6	4	2	....	4	....	162	31	17	14	....	128	3
Cattaraugus........	333	80	5	4	3	1	....	1	....	75	27	16	11	....	43	5
Cayuga............	661	113	5	3	2	1	....	2	....	108	41	20	21	....	63	4
Chautauqua........	169	48	5	4	1	3	....	1	....	43	19	7	12	....	22	2
Chemung..........	593	157	3	3	1	2	....	....	....	154	43	21	19	3	111	....
Chenango..........	196	48	3	3	1	2	....	....	....	45	17	12	5	....	26	2
Clinton...........	251	12	....	....	....	....	....	....	....	12	1	1	....	....	11	....
Columbia..........	1,103	227	9	6	3	3	....	3	....	218	36	25	11	....	179	3
Delaware..........	226	48	9	9	....	9	....	....	....	39	10	5	4	1	26	3
Dutchess..........	2,367	440	22	7	4	3	....	14	1	418	66	27	38	1	328	24
Erie..............	2,059	468	3	3	3	....	....	....	....	465	37	15	22	....	409	19
Fulton............	317	77	4	1	1	....	....	3	....	73	25	9	16	....	42	6
Genesee...........	162	36	5	4	2	2	....	1	....	31	10	7	3	....	19	2
Greene............	513	140	10	6	2	4	....	4	....	130	30	18	11	1	92	8
Herkimer..........	196	47	1	1	1	....	....	....	....	46	15	11	2	2	31	....
Jefferson..........	244	90	....	....	....	....	....	....	....	90	12	4	7	1	74	4
Kings.............	22,708	5,199	....	....	....	....	....	....	....	5,199	265	101	164	....	4,804	130
Livingston........	344	56	10	6	4	2	....	4	....	46	19	9	8	2	25	2
Madison...........	296	64	4	2	2	....	....	2	....	60	18	10	7	1	37	5
Monroe............	1,224	274	9	5	1	4	....	4	....	265	50	14	35	1	203	12
Montgomery........	213	57	2	2	2	....	....	....	....	55	11	4	7	....	40	4
Nassau............	2,317	477	4	3	1	2	....	1	....	473	105	75	28	2	329	39
New York..........	64,651	16,272	....	....	....	....	....	....	....	16,272	84	26	57	1	15,793	395
Niagara...........	435	104	1	....	....	....	....	1	....	103	25	15	7	3	75	3
Oneida............	632	149	11	10	6	4	....	1	....	138	18	11	7	....	116	4
Onondaga..........	1,296	303	9	6	3	3	....	3	....	294	45	16	26	3	232	17
Ontario...........	365	86	6	6	3	3	....	....	....	80	27	15	12	....	53	....
Orange............	3,081	627	15	8	5	3	....	7	....	612	97	55	37	5	486	29
Orleans...........	147	32	2	1	....	1	....	1	....	30	13	7	6	....	17	....
Oswego............	437	58	4	3	....	3	....	1	....	54	8	6	2	....	42	4
Otsego............	104	30	4	4	1	3	....	....	....	26	12	7	5	....	11	3
Putnam............	190	26	2	1	1	....	....	1	....	24	....	....	....	....	22	2
Queens............	3,198	725	....	....	....	....	....	....	....	725	153	65	86	2	549	23
Rensselaer.........	798	222	7	4	3	1	....	3	....	215	20	8	12	....	185	10
Richmond..........	1,152	255	....	....	....	....	....	....	....	255	43	26	17	....	204	8
Rockland..........	1,534	313	7	7	4	1	2	....	....	306	43	27	16	....	233	30
Saratoga..........	697	192	6	5	2	3	....	1	....	186	47	35	12	....	134	5
Schenectady.......	288	69	1	1	1	....	....	....	....	68	7	2	5	....	60	1
Schoharie.........	224	51	2	1	1	....	....	1	....	49	18	17	1	....	31	....
Schuyler..........	184	48	10	8	3	5	....	2	....	38	23	15	8	....	15	....
Seneca............	122	23	3	1	....	1	....	2	....	20	8	3	5	....	12	....
Steuben...........	357	92	8	5	1	4	....	3	....	84	43	18	24	1	41	....
Suffolk...........	2,771	528	9	5	2	3	....	4	....	519	160	103	56	1	337	22
Tioga.............	242	66	7	5	3	2	....	2	....	59	26	16	9	1	31	2
Tompkins..........	533	136	8	7	4	3	....	1	....	128	48	18	30	....	77	3
Ulster............	2,026	397	13	9	6	1	2	4	....	384	53	30	20	3	309	22
Washington........	197	36	5	3	....	3	....	2	....	31	12	6	6	....	18	1
Wayne............	194	51	9	4	1	3	....	5	....	42	15	9	6	....	25	2
Westchester.......	8,986	1,696	8	3	1	....	2	5	....	1,688	190	71	113	6	1,450	48
Yates.............	134	34	3	3	1	2	....	....	....	31	15	6	9	....	15	1
Other counties [1]...	452	88	8	6	2	4	....	2	....	80	36	24	10	2	41	3

NORTH CAROLINA.

STATE AND COUNTY.	Negro pop.	Total homes.	Total.	Total.	Free.	Encum.	No enc. rep.	Rented.	No rep.	Total.	Total.	Free.	Encum.	No enc. rep.	Rented.	No rep.
Total...........	697,843	139,713	63,814	20,491	14,997	5,239	255	43,112	211	75,899	19,627	14,268	3,726	1,633	52,036	4,236
Alamance..........	7,173	1,284	609	292	209	81	2	316	1	675	276	201	67	8	378	21
Alexander.........	910	188	125	71	48	23	....	54	....	63	21	16	4	1	41	1
Alleghany.........	340	69	57	41	39	2	....	16	....	12	1	1	....	....	9	2
Anson............	13,326	2,493	1,648	246	148	97	1	1,401	1	845	137	119	14	4	645	63
Ashe.............	550	101	74	64	57	7	....	10	....	27	3	....	....	3	22	2
Beaufort..........	12,941	2,767	730	447	321	119	7	282	1	2,037	611	472	87	52	1,339	87
Bertie............	13,503	2,635	1,849	668	359	268	41	1,169	12	786	193	127	38	28	483	110
Bladen............	8,392	1,627	984	746	630	108	8	236	2	643	267	182	35	50	341	35
Brunswick.........	5,406	1,101	495	373	328	45	....	122	....	606	294	255	3	36	295	17
Buncombe..........	7,982	1,744	166	111	99	12	....	55	....	1,578	470	346	93	31	1,050	58
Burke............	2,570	492	237	173	153	17	3	64	....	255	130	109	15	6	119	6
Cabarrus..........	6,095	1,206	542	63	42	17	4	479	....	664	211	151	48	12	425	28
Caldwell..........	2,416	493	177	140	129	10	1	36	1	316	153	117	28	8	148	15
Camden...........	2,213	384	262	75	36	38	1	187	....	122	16	10	2	4	98	8
Carteret..........	2,292	511	94	45	33	12	....	49	....	417	217	197	16	4	171	29

[1] Includes all counties with less than 100 Negro inhabitants.

TABLE 18.—HOME OWNERSHIP BY COUNTIES: 1910—NUMBER OF FARM HOMES AND OTHER HOMES, OWNED FREE, OWNED ENCUMBERED, AND RENTED BY NEGRO FAMILIES—Continued.

NORTH CAROLINA—Continued.

STATE AND COUNTY.	Negro population: 1910.	Total farm and other homes: 1910.	NUMBER OF FARM HOMES.							NUMBER OF OTHER HOMES.						
			Total.	Owned.				Rented.	No report of ownership.	Total.	Owned.				Rented.	No report of ownership.
				Total.	Free.	Encumbered.	No encumbrance report.				Total.	Free.	Encumbered.	No encumbrance report.		
Caswell	7,651	1,370	810	168	130	36	2	637	5	560	95	78	3	14	397	68
Catawba	3,471	687	266	133	80	53		133		421	189	127	58	4	214	18
Chatham	7,668	1,421	1,042	396	323	73		646		379	69	48	13	8	301	9
Cherokee	503	91	13	11	11			2		78	33	27	6		45	
Chowan	6,159	1,238	397	206	99	107		191		841	270	56	36	178	541	30
Clay	158	29	28	10	10			18		1					1	
Cleveland	5,779	1,085	689	110	70	39	1	579		396	74	65	4	5	309	13
Columbus	8,955	1,761	831	664	557	107		167		930	275	218	26	31	593	62
Craven	14,310	3,304	991	569	487	80	2	422		2,313	739	666	64	9	1,492	82
Cumberland	15,353	3,000	1,223	563	477	79	7	660		1,777	442	381	31	30	1,234	101
Currituck	2,598	472	268	97	65	32		169	2	204	29	27		2	160	15
Dare	495	107	10	10	8	2				97	77	73	4		18	2
Davidson	3,744	775	214	86	44	41	1	128		561	213	167	43	3	335	13
Davie	2,350	441	251	118	70	48		133		190	71	43	17	11	114	5
Duplin	9,281	1,877	1,043	547	394	152	1	496		834	255	196	41	18	527	52
Durham	12,383	2,639	507	114	84	29	1	393		2,132	430	285	136	9	1,645	57
Edgecombe	19,453	4,162	1,820	97	58	34	5	1,720	3	2,342	344	250	59	35	1,773	225
Forsyth	14,027	3,112	290	171	109	62		118	1	2,822	583	360	196	27	2,143	96
Franklin	11,564	2,122	1,357	246	172	73	1	1,108	3	765	142	118	15	9	575	48
Gaston	8,502	1,685	772	167	117	50		605		913	226	174	50	2	644	43
Gates	4,693	845	482	282	150	112	20	184	16	363	54	30	14	10	279	30
Granville	12,239	2,227	1,334	351	222	125	4	982	1	893	197	146	46	5	644	52
Greene	6,096	1,196	869	94	42	42	10	775		327	54	39	11	4	247	26
Guilford	15,379	3,322	647	340	238	102		304	3	2,675	804	513	281	10	1,809	62
Halifax	24,328	4,893	2,875	677	485	176	16	2,196	2	2,018	321	249	50	22	1,523	174
Harnett	6,442	1,209	686	317	281	33	3	368	1	523	88	62	14	12	404	31
Haywood	567	99	15	9	8	1		6		84	42	34	7	1	40	2
Henderson	1,815	400	114	81	63	18		33		286	85	59	23	3	187	14
Hertford	9,098	1,601	1,041	378	234	132	12	657	6	560	179	120	46	13	331	50
Hyde	3,701	655	436	81	58	22	1	354	1	219	27	20	3	4	154	38
Iredell	7,456	1,520	645	238	156	80	2	404	3	875	335	285	43	7	513	27
Jackson	603	110	62	45	41	2	2	17		48	14	12		2	32	2
Johnston	10,169	2,018	1,109	251	145	103	3	858		909	192	131	56	5	688	29
Jones	4,096	768	556	93	55	38		463		212	26	19	6	1	174	12
Lee	3,526	691	329	127	103	24		202		362	91	79	11	1	260	11
Lenoir	10,225	2,155	916	69	44	17	8	778	69	1,239	373	280	73	20	808	58
Lincoln	2,797	552	320	110	78	32		210		232	108	89	18	1	121	3
McDowell	2,080	441	162	115	105	6	4	46	1	279	110	86	23	1	159	10
Macon	576	118	69	50	45	5		18	1	49	27	10		17	20	2
Madison	432	75	27	4	1	1	2	23		48	11	9	2		32	5
Martin	8,838	1,838	818	312	192	117	3	504	2	1,020	254	187	57	10	614	152
Mecklenburg	25,481	5,792	1,722	159	116	43		1,560	3	4,070	617	386	194	37	3,170	283
Mitchell	343	65	29	21	18	3		8		36	8	6		2	26	2
Montgomery	3,660	671	352	137	113	24		215		319	52	40	8	4	252	15
Moore	5,637	1,091	407	217	191	23	3	190		684	312	214	18	80	353	19
Nash	14,104	2,800	1,460	237	160	76	1	1,223		1,340	216	160	51	5	1,116	8
New Hanover	15,302	3,750	172	124	114	10		48		3,578	1,021	686	129	206	2,433	124
Northampton	13,062	2,464	1,710	428	279	147	2	1,279	3	754	101	81	14	6	637	16
Onslow	4,238	788	422	190	165	25		232		366	101	79	13	9	249	16
Orange	4,926	895	494	199	153	45	1	294	1	401	214	186	18	10	172	15
Pamlico	3,773	739	222	135	81	54		86	1	517	219	161	43	15	273	25
Pasquotank	8,357	1,735	517	216	154	55	7	300	1	1,218	414	177	169	68	717	87
Pender	7,620	1,504	777	616	525	87	4	160	1	727	197	163	21	13	464	66
Perquimans	5,589	1,063	498	203	114	89		295		565	165	67	87	11	366	34
Person	7,474	1,397	890	173	126	46	1	716	1	507	74	51	21	2	382	51
Pitt	18,106	3,531	1,795	253	151	99	3	1,537	5	1,736	332	254	56	22	1,172	232
Polk	1,094	225	146	42	28	13	1	103	1	79	23	19		4	50	6
Randolph	3,421	675	344	235	165	70		109		331	168	122	39	7	148	15
Richmond	9,225	1,834	866	243	218	23	2	621	2	968	279	215	23	41	596	93
Robeson	22,518	4,415	2,498	549	481	58	10	1,943	6	1,917	355	279	44	32	1,376	186
Rockingham	10,474	1,925	784	191	153	35	3	591	2	1,141	399	252	78	69	697	45
Rowan	9,074	1,956	498	180	117	57	6	317	1	1,458	346	206	121	19	1,057	55
Rutherford	4,288	831	503	183	146	37		320		328	94	77	15	2	223	11
Sampson	10,043	1,855	1,146	531	401	128	2	610	5	709	243	197	39	7	392	74
Scotland	8,473	1,719	846	70	58	12		774	2	873	99	82	11	6	746	28
Stanly	2,132	417	223	92	80	12		131		194	53	35	16	2	124	17
Stokes	2,569	466	364	96	59	37		266	2	102	29	25	4		62	11
Surry	2,632	523	261	151	104	44	3	110		262	113	68	35	10	144	5
Swain	185	39	19	8	7	1		10	1	20	3	3			17	
Transylvania	638	121	24	14	11	3		9	1	97	45	40	5		50	2
Tyrrell	1,642	309	124	52	20	32		72		185	41	15	7	19	97	47
Union	9,337	1,808	1,237	174	124	48	2	1,063		571	93	65	26	2	423	55
Vance	10,004	1,857	959	300	215	84	1	659		898	264	218	42	4	626	8
Wake	25,870	5,227	2,065	549	383	164	2	1,516		3,162	829	658	131	40	2,295	38
Warren	13,207	2,485	1,760	636	473	154	9	1,114	10	725	192	133	19	40	469	64
Washington	5,503	1,081	253	118	71	42	5	118	17	828	264	204	29	31	477	87
Watauga	246	41	28	18	17		1	10		13	3	3			9	1
Wayne	15,579	3,124	1,431	266	153	113		1,159	6	1,693	337	279	55	3	1,306	50
Wilkes	2,591	472	298	202	166	36		96		174	71	58	11	2	95	22
Wilson	12,350	2,535	1,093	116	71	38	7	976	1	1,442	254	150	93	11	1,066	81
Yadkin	1,174	235	161	89	61	28		72		74	36	31	5		34	4
Yancey	233	47	33	16	13	3		17		14	3	3			11	

TABLE **18.**—HOME OWNERSHIP BY COUNTIES: 1910—NUMBER OF FARM HOMES AND OTHER HOMES, OWNED FREE, OWNED ENCUMBERED, AND RENTED BY NEGRO FAMILIES—Continued.

STATE AND COUNTY.	Negro population: 1910.	Total farm and other homes: 1910.	NUMBER OF FARM HOMES.							NUMBER OF OTHER HOMES.						
			Total.	Owned.				Rented.	No report of ownership.	Total.	Owned.				Rented.	No report of ownership.
				Total.	Free.	Encumbered.	No encumbrance report.				Total.	Free.	Encumbered.	No encumbrance report.		

NORTH DAKOTA.

STATE AND COUNTY.	Negro pop.	Total homes.	Total.	Total.	Free.	Encum.	No enc. rep.	Rented.	No rep.	Total.	Total.	Free.	Encum.	No enc. rep.	Rented.	No rep.
Total	617	146	28	23	12	11	....	5	....	118	29	20	5	4	70	19
Cass	120	25	2	2	1	1	....	....	....	23	4	3	1	....	14	5
Other counties [1]	497	121	26	21	11	10	....	5	....	95	25	17	4	4	56	14

OHIO.

STATE AND COUNTY.	Negro pop.	Total homes.	Total.	Total.	Free.	Encum.	No enc. rep.	Rented.	No rep.	Total.	Total.	Free.	Encum.	No enc. rep.	Rented.	No rep.
Total	111,452	28,135	2,009	1,358	805	539	14	646	5	26,126	7,109	3,721	3,215	173	18,405	612
Adams	184	48	11	7	6	....	1	4	....	37	20	19	1	....	16	1
Allen	1,030	268	3	2	2	....	....	1	....	265	98	29	68	1	67	....
Ashtabula	217	60	6	4	3	1	....	2	....	54	24	12	9	3	29	1
Athens	1,240	300	40	26	16	9	1	14	....	260	94	57	31	6	166	....
Belmont	1,782	409	24	17	10	7	....	7	....	385	119	57	44	18	254	12
Brown	1,288	341	127	64	52	11	1	63	....	214	119	90	26	3	95	....
Butler	1,781	464	16	4	2	2	....	12	....	448	171	87	79	5	268	9
Champaign	1,410	364	25	15	4	11	....	10	....	339	165	84	79	2	161	13
Clark	5,583	1,415	51	32	18	14	....	19	....	1,364	476	183	288	5	888	....
Clermont	865	245	74	44	25	19	....	30	....	171	103	67	34	2	66	2
Clinton	939	266	42	28	14	12	2	14	....	224	97	57	38	2	117	10
Columbiana	967	258	7	4	2	2	....	3	....	251	88	35	53	....	155	8
Cuyahoga	8,763	2,305	7	2	1	1	....	5	....	2,298	277	113	160	4	1,984	37
Darke	376	102	60	46	17	28	1	14	....	42	19	12	4	3	22	1
Delaware	671	151	12	8	3	5	....	4	....	139	61	42	19	....	76	2
Erie	311	70	6	4	....	4	....	2	....	64	29	13	16	....	34	1
Fairfield	449	60	3	3	1	2	....	....	....	57	23	15	8	....	32	2
Fayette	1,231	316	16	11	7	4	....	4	1	300	139	87	48	4	151	10
Franklin	14,006	3,367	42	20	15	5	....	22	....	3,325	615	287	321	7	2,618	92
Gallia	1,875	417	129	106	71	35	....	23	....	288	136	84	44	8	150	2
Greene	3,970	1,077	107	73	30	42	1	33	1	970	524	305	211	8	423	23
Guernsey	489	108	6	4	3	1	....	2	....	102	42	28	14	....	59	1
Hamilton	24,300	6,424	26	12	8	4	....	14	....	6,398	677	368	302	7	5,590	131
Hancock	249	66	6	4	3	1	....	2	....	60	33	26	7	....	26	1
Hardin	556	121	23	8	4	4	....	15	....	98	55	35	17	3	41	2
Harrison	612	135	23	18	9	9	....	5	....	112	70	27	40	3	39	3
Highland	1,379	375	57	39	26	13	....	18	....	318	188	112	74	2	127	3
Hocking	143	38	5	2	2	....	....	2	1	33	8	8	....	....	25	....
Huron	284	75	5	1	1	....	....	4	....	70	26	17	9	....	42	2
Jackson	708	147	75	70	48	22	....	5	....	72	33	26	7	....	38	1
Jefferson	1,647	362	39	20	7	12	1	18	1	323	92	48	31	13	218	13
Knox	323	83	2	1	1	....	....	1	....	81	45	18	26	1	36	....
Lake	237	58	6	1	1	....	....	5	....	52	19	12	7	....	33	....
Lawrence	1,789	435	73	57	44	13	....	16	....	362	145	57	85	3	208	9
Licking	432	99	4	4	2	2	....	....	....	95	42	10	31	1	53	....
Logan	777	208	46	40	14	26	....	6	....	162	87	37	50	....	71	4
Lorain	1,521	414	20	17	10	6	1	3	....	394	191	113	78	....	191	12
Lucas	1,918	518	3	3	....	3	....	....	....	515	98	42	55	1	398	19
Madison	745	197	39	10	3	7	....	29	....	158	52	32	16	4	97	9
Mahoning	2,083	489	5	3	1	2	....	2	....	484	75	47	27	1	377	32
Marion	232	61	....	....	....	....	....	....	....	61	31	14	17	....	30	....
Medina	114	28	1	....	....	....	....	1	....	27	13	11	2	....	14	....
Meigs	690	198	26	21	15	6	....	5	....	172	91	74	15	2	76	5
Mercer	115	31	17	14	6	7	1	3	....	14	8	4	2	2	5	1
Miami	1,109	297	15	8	5	2	1	7	....	282	116	47	47	22	151	15
Montgomery	5,481	1,408	15	8	5	3	....	7	....	1,393	325	85	234	6	1,029	39
Morgan	147	42	21	18	12	6	....	3	....	21	2	1	1	....	18	1
Muskingum	1,686	417	21	16	14	2	....	5	....	396	119	63	50	6	268	9
Paulding	502	116	58	43	9	33	1	15	....	58	35	15	20	....	22	1
Perry	563	152	8	4	4	....	....	4	....	144	56	46	10	....	88	....
Pickaway	695	163	16	3	2	1	....	13	....	147	52	39	13	....	90	5
Pike	717	156	104	86	71	15	....	18	....	52	11	11	....	....	41	....
Portage	192	50	5	3	2	1	....	2	....	45	23	10	13	....	21	1
Preble	265	71	30	20	9	10	1	10	....	41	23	17	5	1	18	....
Richland	253	27	....	....	....	....	....	....	....	27	12	6	6	....	15	....
Ross	2,382	575	110	78	53	24	1	32	....	465	221	140	81	....	237	7
Sandusky	146	46	3	....	....	....	....	3	....	43	14	4	10	....	28	1
Scioto	1,016	231	11	5	4	1	....	6	....	220	87	50	35	2	122	11
Seneca	157	43	2	1	....	1	....	1	....	41	16	8	8	....	25	....
Shelby	231	50	18	9	5	4	....	9	....	32	16	13	3	....	16	....
Stark	752	159	5	4	2	2	....	1	....	154	59	25	31	3	89	6
Summit	757	165	1	....	....	....	....	1	....	164	46	23	23	....	98	20
Trumbull	208	50	4	3	3	....	....	1	....	46	20	15	5	....	26	....
Tuscarawas	194	42	....	....	....	....	....	....	....	42	10	5	5	....	27	5
Union	264	65	13	11	6	5	....	2	....	52	30	15	13	2	19	3
Van Wert	327	81	22	17	4	13	....	5	....	59	48	27	20	1	11	....
Vinton	213	51	8	6	6	....	....	2	....	43	9	8	....	1	34	....
Warren	729	205	36	15	11	4	....	21	....	169	92	55	36	1	76	1
Washington	1,378	310	136	109	61	48	....	26	1	174	83	52	29	2	81	10
Wood	150	38	2	2	....	2	....	....	....	36	17	12	5	....	18	1
Other counties [1]	657	152	30	20	10	10	....	10	....	122	49	28	19	2	71	2

[1] Includes all counties with less than 100 Negro inhabitants.

TABLE 18.—HOME OWNERSHIP BY COUNTIES: 1910—NUMBER OF FARM HOMES AND OTHER HOMES, OWNED FREE, OWNED ENCUMBERED, AND RENTED BY NEGRO FAMILIES—Continued.

STATE AND COUNTY.	Negro population: 1910.	Total farm and other homes: 1910.	NUMBER OF FARM HOMES.							NUMBER OF OTHER HOMES.						
			Total.	Owned.				Rented.	No report of ownership.	Total.	Owned.				Rented.	No report of ownership.
				Total.	Free.	Encumbered.	No encumbrance report.				Total.	Free.	Encumbered.	No encumbrance report.		

OKLAHOMA.

STATE AND COUNTY.	Negro pop.	Total.	Total.	Total.	Free.	Enc.	No enc.	Rented.	No rep.	Total.	Total.	Free.	Enc.	No enc.	Rented.	No rep.
Total............	137,612	28,395	13,518	4,956	3,022	1,620	314	8,478	84	14,877	5,062	3,623	1,039	400	8,666	1,149
Atoka............	2,109	431	219	76	48	20	8	142	1	212	70	40	18	12	123	19
Blaine...........	1,434	329	222	143	67	72	4	78	1	107	61	41	19	1	44	2
Bryan...........	2,184	489	281	107	64	40	3	174	......	208	53	39	10	4	140	15
Caddo...........	1,178	191	88	37	2	23	12	51	......	103	28	24	4	......	72	3
Canadian........	823	178	9	7	....	7	......	2	......	169	74	51	23	......	87	8
Carter...........	4,315	863	387	209	127	73	9	176	2	476	211	166	25	20	252	13
Cherokee........	995	192	112	77	60	15	2	33	2	80	30	24	5	1	41	9
Choctaw.........	4,303	898	489	224	178	43	3	263	2	409	74	50	20	4	296	39
Cleveland.......	456	62	58	31	11	20	......	27	......	4	1	1	......	......	3	......
Coal............	976	352	142	51	34	7	10	87	4	210	52	22	7	23	137	21
Comanche........	962	236	76	27	23	4	......	48	1	160	55	25	6	24	105	......
Craig...........	1,175	258	129	79	64	12	3	50	......	129	50	43	6	1	73	6
Creek...........	2,778	569	310	50	35	11	4	259	1	259	52	28	21	3	182	25
Custer..........	291	53	15	12	8	4	......	3	......	38	17	13	3	1	17	4
Garfield........	822	181	25	19	6	13	......	6	......	156	32	26	6	......	118	6
Garvin..........	2,318	449	255	140	96	39	5	114	1	194	77	54	18	5	104	13
Grady...........	1,731	410	59	43	22	21	......	16	......	351	127	64	61	2	210	14
Greer...........	146	36	20	8	....	8	......	12	......	16	2	2	......	......	13	1
Haskell.........	385	73	46	19	14	4	1	27	......	27	7	......	......	7	13	7
Hughes..........	1,737	326	246	49	30	18	1	197	......	80	16	8	7	1	50	14
Jackson.........	114	23	....	....	....	....	......	....	......	23	....	....	......	......	18	5
Jefferson.......	397	87	6	3	1	2	......	3	......	81	37	30	4	3	39	5
Johnston........	884	185	103	59	35	23	1	43	1	82	23	17	3	3	56	3
Kay.............	109	4	4	3	....	3	......	1	......	....	....	....	......	......	....	......
Kingfisher......	2,392	567	350	241	106	126	9	92	17	217	117	92	21	4	78	22
Kiowa...........	317	67	30	10	9	1	......	20	......	37	....	....	......	......	29	8
Latimer.........	618	161	12	4	4	....	......	7	1	149	23	20	2	1	121	5
Le Flore........	1,781	373	209	85	62	19	4	124	......	164	34	23	8	3	94	36
Lincoln.........	3,945	786	600	199	73	121	5	397	4	186	57	44	13	......	100	29
Logan...........	8,196	1,775	810	347	154	179	14	461	2	965	492	390	95	7	434	39
Love............	1,021	246	176	83	36	34	13	92	1	70	37	26	8	3	22	11
McClain.........	1,081	194	84	49	27	19	3	34	1	110	64	43	15	6	43	3
McCurtain.......	4,576	923	608	293	179	47	67	313	2	315	51	12	......	39	218	46
McIntosh........	5,283	1,043	571	147	107	25	15	424	......	472	213	138	49	26	223	36
Marshall........	319	64	22	4	....	4	......	18	......	42	5	4	1	......	37	......
Mayes...........	799	170	130	104	78	26	......	25	1	40	19	17	1	1	19	2
Murray..........	423	75	16	4	3	1	......	12	......	59	19	12	7	......	39	1
Muskogee........	16,454	3,457	954	393	274	83	36	549	12	2,503	832	613	144	75	1,475	196
Noble...........	642	162	47	19	5	10	4	28	......	115	69	47	20	2	42	4
Nowata..........	1,954	442	271	177	141	35	1	94	......	171	88	57	26	5	72	11
Okfuskee........	8,073	1,570	1,062	125	68	39	18	928	9	508	295	266	21	8	186	27
Oklahoma........	9,227	1,790	421	159	74	85	......	258	4	1,369	326	183	129	14	894	149
Okmulgee........	5,933	1,184	705	121	81	33	7	584	......	479	177	136	24	17	261	41
Osage...........	391	109	26	3	3	....	......	23	......	83	23	22	1	......	45	15
Pawnee..........	806	162	90	13	8	4	1	77	......	72	11	8	3	......	56	5
Payne...........	1,456	341	180	14	6	8	......	164	2	161	29	24	2	3	108	24
Pittsburg.......	5,244	1,032	119	46	28	16	2	73	......	913	286	235	45	6	597	30
Pontotoc........	1,009	229	115	67	50	17	......	48	......	114	24	17	4	3	76	14
Pottawatomie....	2,017	417	158	49	18	31	......	109	......	259	87	36	10	41	162	10
Pushmataha......	385	80	24	9	4	4	1	15	......	56	21	19	1	1	31	4
Rogers..........	620	116	53	29	22	4	3	24	......	63	26	18	6	2	35	2
Seminole........	4,081	795	599	183	132	34	17	413	3	196	46	34	10	2	133	17
Sequoyah........	3,178	662	391	126	99	21	6	263	2	271	72	52	16	4	169	30
Tillman.........	432	81	14	4	1	3	......	10	......	67	7	6	1	......	57	3
Tulsa...........	2,754	479	100	21	14	7	......	79	......	379	96	55	38	3	259	24
Wagoner.........	8,761	1,779	1,147	252	163	69	20	888	7	632	241	191	42	8	326	65
Washington......	434	76	22	15	12	2	1	7	......	54	24	14	10	......	26	4
Other counties[1]	388	113	101	88	56	31	1	13	......	12	2	1	......	1	6	4

OREGON.

STATE AND COUNTY.	Negro pop.	Total.	Total.	Total.	Free.	Enc.	No enc.	Rented.	No rep.	Total.	Total.	Free.	Enc.	No enc.	Rented.	No rep.
Total............	1,492	347	30	23	19	4	....	7	......	317	75	39	34	2	210	32
Multnomah.......	1,081	248	4	4	4	....	......	....	......	244	51	27	24	......	166	27
Other counties[1]	411	99	26	19	15	4	......	7	......	73	24	12	10	2	44	5

PENNSYLVANIA.

STATE AND COUNTY.	Negro pop.	Total.	Total.	Total.	Free.	Enc.	No enc.	Rented.	No rep.	Total.	Total.	Free.	Enc.	No enc.	Rented.	No rep.
Total............	193,919	42,111	592	366	195	163	8	220	6	41,519	5,251	2,561	2,515	175	33,567	2,701
Adams...........	325	80	2	1	1	....	......	1	......	78	18	11	7	......	59	1
Allegheny.......	34,217	7,869	19	3	3	....	......	16	......	7,850	1,008	427	558	23	6,541	301
Armstrong.......	495	128	3	2	1	....	1	1	......	125	29	19	9	1	91	5
Beaver..........	1,235	277	14	5	2	3	......	9	......	263	71	34	37	......	182	10
Bedford.........	365	88	6	5	3	2	......	1	......	82	35	30	5	......	44	3

[1] Includes all counties with less than 100 Negro inhabitants.

TABLE 18.—HOME OWNERSHIP BY COUNTIES: 1910—NUMBER OF FARM HOMES AND OTHER HOMES, OWNED FREE, OWNED ENCUMBERED, AND RENTED BY NEGRO FAMILIES—Continued.

STATE AND COUNTY.	Negro population: 1910.	Total farm and other homes: 1910.	FARM HOMES Total.	Owned Total.	Owned Free.	Owned Encumbered.	Owned No encumbrance report.	Rented.	No report of ownership.	OTHER HOMES Total.	Owned Total.	Owned Free.	Owned Encumbered.	Owned No encumbrance report.	Rented.	No report of ownership.
PENNSYLVANIA—Continued.																
Berks	1,007	215	4	3	1	2	...	1	...	211	16	6	10	...	180	15
Blair	786	207	...	...	...	...	...	...	...	207	84	36	47	1	115	8
Bradford	234	53	4	3	2	1	...	1	...	49	13	8	5	...	36	...
Bucks	1,832	359	27	16	9	7	...	10	1	332	70	32	34	4	243	19
Butler	217	49	4	2	...	2	...	2	...	45	10	5	5	...	33	2
Cambria	640	133	2	2	2	...	...	...	...	131	25	13	12	...	100	6
Center	265	58	1	1	1	...	...	...	...	57	24	21	3	...	31	2
Chester	10,622	2,158	121	86	28	56	2	33	2	2,037	432	196	214	22	1,500	105
Clearfield	315	63	2	1	...	1	...	1	...	61	15	6	9	...	45	1
Clinton	209	45	7	6	5	1	...	1	...	38	8	5	2	1	27	3
Columbia	119	27	1	1	1	...	...	...	...	26	9	6	3	...	15	2
Crawford	355	96	...	...	...	...	...	...	...	96	45	29	16	...	50	1
Cumberland	1,788	456	4	2	2	...	...	...	...	452	124	91	30	3	321	7
Dauphin	6,536	1,452	8	3	3	...	...	4	1	1,444	237	111	123	3	1,156	51
Delaware	11,897	2,377	23	13	5	8	...	9	1	2,354	434	188	237	9	1,805	115
Erie	392	90	5	3	2	1	...	2	...	85	25	16	9	...	57	3
Fayette	5,852	1,367	34	20	15	5	...	14	...	1,333	234	123	85	26	1,054	45
Franklin	1,716	414	18	12	5	7	...	6	...	396	161	111	50	...	216	19
Greene	389	94	16	5	4	1	...	11	...	78	27	16	4	7	50	1
Huntingdon	305	50	2	2	2	...	...	...	...	48	12	11	1	...	33	2
Indiana	183	45	5	3	1	2	...	2	...	40	12	8	3	1	28	...
Jefferson	105	24	4	4	3	1	...	...	...	20	5	5	...	...	15	...
Juniata	171	32	18	17	14	2	1	1	...	14	4	2	2	...	10	...
Lackawanna	696	156	2	...	...	...	...	2	...	154	13	10	3	...	131	10
Lancaster	2,299	529	48	36	18	18	...	12	...	481	95	51	38	6	377	9
Lawrence	699	167	7	4	...	3	...	3	...	160	23	10	13	...	129	8
Lebanon	215	45	...	...	...	...	...	...	...	45	4	3	1	...	39	2
Lehigh	247	57	...	...	...	...	...	...	...	57	3	...	3	...	54	...
Luzerne	924	211	3	3	1	2	...	...	...	208	37	17	20	...	167	4
Lycoming	1,182	277	4	3	1	2	...	1	...	273	84	63	21	...	185	4
McKean	251	68	3	2	2	...	...	1	...	65	24	14	8	2	41	...
Mercer	621	143	12	8	3	2	3	4	...	131	29	16	11	2	94	8
Mifflin	172	42	...	...	...	...	...	...	...	42	11	8	3	...	30	1
Monroe	185	47	2	1	...	1	...	1	...	45	16	4	12	...	29	...
Montgomery	6,021	911	25	9	3	6	...	16	...	886	208	67	137	4	643	35
Northampton	615	153	1	...	...	...	...	1	...	152	11	6	5	...	137	4
Northumberland	237	50	...	...	...	...	...	...	...	50	9	9	...	...	41	...
Philadelphia	84,459	18,095	9	3	1	2	...	5	1	18,086	902	371	494	37	15,371	1,813
Schuylkill	242	55	2	2	2	...	...	...	...	53	7	5	2	...	42	4
Somerset	246	54	1	...	...	...	...	1	...	53	12	8	1	3	39	2
Susquehanna	114	36	6	3	3	...	...	3	...	30	18	10	8	...	12	...
Venango	541	112	2	2	1	1	...	...	...	110	55	34	20	1	53	2
Washington	5,888	1,376	44	20	12	8	...	24	...	1,332	308	169	126	13	987	37
Westmoreland	2,641	615	8	4	3	1	...	4	...	607	93	53	38	2	491	23
York	2,113	438	39	30	20	10	...	9	...	399	56	35	21	...	341	2
Other counties[1]	739	168	20	15	10	5	...	5	...	148	46	32	10	4	97	5
RHODE ISLAND.																
Total	9,529	2,353	38	26	16	10	...	12	...	2,315	332	144	181	7	1,934	49
Bristol	153	36	7	4	3	1	...	3	...	29	5	1	4	...	23	1
Kent	266	65	1	1	1	...	...	...	...	64	23	13	6	4	37	4
Newport	1,881	442	8	6	3	3	...	2	...	434	87	29	58	...	339	8
Providence	6,391	1,625	5	4	3	1	...	1	...	1,620	175	71	103	1	1,414	31
Washington	838	185	17	11	6	5	...	6	...	168	42	30	10	2	121	5
SOUTH CAROLINA.																
Total	835,843	179,490	95,737	20,431	15,834	4,149	448	74,875	431	83,753	12,730	9,407	2,292	1,031	64,365	6,658
Abbeville	22,522	4,749	3,520	305	189	103	13	3,175	40	1,229	332	239	80	13	793	104
Aiken	22,850	5,297	2,434	572	326	233	13	1,856	6	2,863	422	296	71	55	2,201	240
Anderson	26,335	5,320	3,419	301	136	162	3	3,117	1	1,901	382	170	189	23	1,365	154
Bamberg	12,874	2,512	1,520	187	122	56	9	1,329	4	992	84	68	14	2	784	124
Barnwell	24,647	5,383	2,812	309	198	101	10	2,473	30	2,571	174	145	13	16	1,975	422
Beaufort	26,376	6,463	4,216	2,966	2,877	32	57	1,207	43	2,247	870	775	25	70	1,036	341
Berkeley	18,231	4,038	2,580	1,696	1,618	51	27	843	41	1,458	364	293	2	69	783	311
Calhoun	12,739	2,715	1,879	126	91	27	8	1,745	8	836	85	44	13	28	716	35
Charleston	56,033	15,598	3,137	1,473	1,332	93	48	1,641	23	12,461	1,368	1,030	98	240	10,031	1,062
Cherokee	8,510	1,651	962	100	66	31	3	862	...	689	128	96	24	8	511	50
Chester	19,140	4,163	2,473	265	129	133	3	2,205	3	1,690	239	136	98	5	1.332	119
Chesterfield	10,557	2,110	1,127	297	213	77	7	829	1	983	241	201	31	9	641	101
Clarendon	23,393	4,747	3,647	486	323	146	17	3,154	7	1,100	94	66	20	8	811	195
Colleton	22,296	5,046	2,560	1,269	1,073	140	56	1,289	2	2,486	594	543	17	34	1,761	131
Darlington	21,283	4,512	2,338	228	173	51	4	2,110	...	2,174	252	196	50	6	1,864	58

[1] Includes all counties with less than 100 Negro inhabitants.

TABLE 18.—HOME OWNERSHIP BY COUNTIES: 1910—NUMBER OF FARM HOMES AND OTHER HOMES, OWNED FREE, OWNED ENCUMBERED, AND RENTED BY NEGRO FAMILIES—Continued.

STATE AND COUNTY.	Negro population: 1910.	Total farm and other homes: 1910.	NUMBER OF FARM HOMES.								NUMBER OF OTHER HOMES.						
			Total.	Owned.				Rented.	No report of ownership.	Total.	Owned.				Rented.	No report of ownership.
				Total.	Free.	Encumbered.	No encumbrance report.				Total.	Free.	Encumbered.	No encumbrance report.		
SOUTH CAROLINA—Continued.																
Dillon	11,539	2,290	1,421	89	57	22	10	1,332	......	869	107	76	24	7	696	66
Dorchester	10,982	2,235	1,228	635	551	77	7	591	2	1,007	207	183	10	14	658	142
Edgefield	20,114	4,034	3,088	263	130	125	8	2,819	6	946	66	41	13	12	716	164
Fairfield	22,377	4,503	2,782	352	220	120	12	2,422	8	1,721	128	105	18	5	1,449	144
Florence	20,340	4,339	1,946	296	209	86	1	1,648	2	2,393	310	197	97	16	1,989	94
Georgetown	16,110	3,996	523	403	386	7	10	120	......	3,473	1,112	1,034	48	30	2,282	79
Greenville	20,861	4,507	1,917	288	157	126	5	1,628	1	2,590	417	289	126	2	2,089	84
Greenwood	21,302	4,438	2,735	315	199	106	10	2,394	26	1,703	335	240	86	9	1,215	153
Hampton	16,120	3,371	2,122	827	757	66	4	1,292	3	1,249	60	42	5	13	1,085	104
Horry	6,668	1,267	653	410	340	68	2	243	......	614	221	192	15	14	374	19
Kershaw	16,444	3,350	1,782	410	316	85	9	1,370	2	1,568	233	131	77	25	1,211	124
Lancaster	13,115	2,672	1,802	132	88	42	2	1,667	3	870	84	66	16	2	699	87
Laurens	22,753	4,680	2,861	149	79	67	3	2,704	8	1,819	171	94	71	6	1,522	126
Lee	17,251	3,438	2,183	240	138	94	8	1,937	6	1,255	55	24	15	16	1,138	62
Lexington	11,638	2,255	1,339	256	191	63	2	1,075	8	916	79	55	21	3	778	59
Marion	11,208	2,335	1,032	243	161	81	1	789	......	1,303	290	197	85	8	960	53
Marlboro	18,928	3,859	2,245	172	120	48	4	2,073	......	1,614	107	79	16	12	1,370	137
Newberry	22,040	4,711	2,270	219	131	81	7	1,976	75	2,441	248	195	45	8	2,033	160
Oconee	6,848	1,335	816	154	75	77	2	660	2	519	101	67	28	6	366	52
Orangeburg	36,794	7,591	4,220	909	593	298	18	3,279	32	3,371	378	240	90	48	2,812	181
Pickens	5,430	1,028	652	96	62	33	1	556	......	376	67	47	20	......	285	24
Richland	29,533	6,852	1,867	306	210	76	20	1,558	3	4,985	770	565	150	55	4,070	145
Saluda	11,189	2,217	1,748	247	149	92	6	1,496	5	469	5	5	......	......	279	185
Spartanburg	26,410	5,411	2,484	298	194	96	8	2,179	7	2,927	520	331	179	10	2,278	129
Sumter	28,103	5,948	3,148	639	353	283	3	2,497	12	2,800	412	163	153	96	2,189	199
Union	15,471	2,981	1,782	153	108	43	2	1,621	8	1,199	246	187	44	15	815	138
Williamsburg	23,214	4,521	3,338	1,120	863	252	5	2,215	3	1,183	96	81	11	4	1,018	69
York	25,275	5,022	3,129	230	131	99	......	2,899	......	1,893	276	183	84	9	1,385	232
SOUTH DAKOTA.																
Total	817	215	71	59	36	23	......	10	2	144	38	21	16	1	90	16
Lawrence	177	47	3	3	1	2	......	......	......	44	5	4	1	......	34	5
Other counties [1]	640	168	68	56	35	21	......	10	2	100	33	17	15	1	56	11
TENNESSEE.																
Total	473,088	106,558	37,246	10,942	8,198	2,577	167	26,228	76	69,312	16,070	11,987	3,234	849	50,605	2,637
Anderson	921	172	66	56	43	10	3	10	......	106	35	31	4	......	68	3
Bedford	5,486	1,229	447	246	193	52	1	201	......	782	273	230	41	2	474	35
Benton	340	76	39	27	27	......	......	12	......	37	12	12	......	......	22	3
Bledsoe	391	80	46	23	18	5	......	23	......	34	8	7	1	......	26	......
Blount	1,221	254	75	59	45	14	......	16	......	179	93	74	16	3	82	4
Bradley	1,717	374	82	53	35	18	......	29	......	292	138	116	22	......	149	5
Campbell	1,887	467	20	15	13	2	......	5	......	447	66	38	19	9	367	14
Cannon	580	141	55	21	20	1	......	34	......	86	23	21	1	1	56	7
Carroll	5,051	1,024	680	247	158	88	1	433	......	344	86	70	12	4	240	18
Carter	660	138	55	43	36	7	......	12	......	83	35	31	4	......	46	2
Cheatham	1,593	316	125	83	52	31	......	42	......	191	90	61	5	24	100	1
Chester	1,571	295	208	55	43	10	2	152	1	87	20	16	3	1	62	5
Claiborne	819	178	54	35	32	3	......	19	......	124	10	9	1	......	105	9
Clay	289	61	24	13	11	2	......	11	......	37	19	16	3	......	18	......
Cocke	1,051	220	101	73	59	14	......	28	......	119	57	41	8	8	58	4
Coffee	1,624	319	81	55	47	7	1	26	......	238	103	86	12	5	121	14
Crockett	3,611	711	592	98	62	35	1	494	......	119	20	17	2	1	88	11
Davidson	46,710	11,704	442	250	214	32	4	190	2	11,262	2,430	1,745	632	53	8,665	167
Decatur	1,019	215	131	57	54	3	......	74	......	84	24	19	5	......	46	14
Dekalb	835	185	55	33	33	......	......	22	......	130	69	61	4	4	59	2
Dickson	3,079	630	260	200	160	40	......	60	......	370	175	126	17	32	183	12
Dyer	5,685	1,219	529	77	43	31	3	450	2	690	172	121	44	7	497	21
Fayette	22,702	4,231	3,916	371	233	133	5	3,543	2	315	28	25	2	1	246	41
Franklin	3,126	690	211	142	128	14	......	69	......	479	243	218	13	12	217	19
Gibson	9,547	1,941	1,003	276	148	121	7	720	7	938	303	227	56	20	601	34
Giles	10,867	2,247	1,294	389	277	107	5	903	2	953	195	149	40	6	717	41
Grainger	483	100	62	42	34	8	......	20	......	38	6	5	1	......	30	2
Greene	1,369	300	110	72	59	12	1	38	......	190	90	81	8	1	90	10
Grundy	143	26	......	......	......	......	......	......	......	26	6	5	1	......	20	......
Hamblen	1,610	346	75	61	50	11	......	14	......	271	151	123	21	7	111	9
Hamilton	26,026	6,655	144	105	98	7	......	39	......	6,511	1,117	836	262	19	5,241	153
Hancock	481	101	72	31	29	2	......	41	......	29	7	6	......	1	20	2
Hardeman	10,098	1,916	1,452	303	233	57	13	1,145	4	464	123	107	14	2	281	60
Hardin	2,170	443	281	88	73	15	......	191	2	162	81	70	8	3	75	6
Hawkins	1,805	399	167	119	115	4	......	48	......	232	92	86	5	1	126	14
Haywood	17,710	3,384	2,873	554	292	250	12	2,316	3	511	140	111	22	7	325	46

[1] Includes all counties with less than 100 Negro inhabitants.

TABLE 18.—HOME OWNERSHIP BY COUNTIES: 1910—NUMBER OF FARM HOMES AND OTHER HOMES, OWNED FREE, OWNED ENCUMBERED, AND RENTED BY NEGRO FAMILIES—Continued.

STATE AND COUNTY.	Negro population: 1910.	Total farm and other homes: 1910.	NUMBER OF FARM HOMES.							NUMBER OF OTHER HOMES.						
			Total.	Owned.				Rented.	No report of ownership.	Total.	Owned.				Rented.	No report of ownership.
				Total.	Free.	Encumbered.	No encumbrance report.				Total.	Free.	Encumbered.	No encumbrance report.		

TENNESSEE—Continued.

STATE AND COUNTY.																
Henderson	1,918	384	236	92	64	28	......	143	1	148	66	45	20	1	67	15
Henry	5,921	1,229	619	261	178	82	1	358	......	610	182	136	40	6	410	18
Hickman	2,430	499	162	125	90	25	10	37	......	337	98	69	25	4	218	21
Houston	910	184	67	47	40	4	3	20	......	117	65	60	5	......	48	4
Humphreys	1,201	256	53	25	17	7	1	28	......	203	93	73	7	13	94	16
Jackson	302	1	1	......	......	......	......	1	......	......	......	......	......	......	......	......
James	492	107	27	15	15	......	......	12	......	80	46	37	7	2	34	......
Jefferson	1,639	365	80	64	45	19	......	16	......	285	153	97	19	37	109	23
Johnson	377	75	13	12	10	2	......	1	......	62	37	37	......	......	23	2
Knox	12,709	2,925	188	147	136	11	......	40	1	2,737	668	474	142	52	2,000	69
Lake	3,268	759	256	14	4	......	10	242	......	503	8	......	......	8	456	39
Lauderdale	9,554	1,911	1,538	227	105	112	10	1,301	10	373	91	65	23	3	219	63
Lawrence	969	206	65	56	49	6	1	9	......	141	47	37	10	......	91	3
Lewis	854	184	30	25	21	4	......	5	......	154	10	6	2	2	141	3
Lincoln	5,502	1,113	560	126	84	40	2	434	......	553	123	99	18	6	398	32
Loudon	964	213	60	49	31	15	3	11	......	153	75	30	1	44	71	7
McMinn	1,892	416	132	108	102	6	......	24	......	284	116	105	5	6	152	16
McNairy	1,557	325	186	74	58	16	......	112	......	139	45	39	......	6	88	6
Macon	732	142	110	60	52	8	......	50	......	32	6	1	3	2	25	1
Madison	16,167	3,565	1,760	382	261	110	11	1,372	6	1,805	340	280	43	17	1,399	66
Marion	2,289	546	53	41	41	......	......	12	......	493	89	82	5	2	394	10
Marshall	3,414	735	339	157	122	34	1	180	2	396	79	66	10	3	261	56
Maury	16,169	3,819	823	458	369	86	3	365	......	2,996	710	567	94	49	2,189	97
Meigs	566	115	73	38	29	9	......	35	......	42	13	10	1	2	29	......
Monroe	1,167	237	104	77	71	6	......	27	......	133	51	46	3	2	81	1
Montgomery	13,430	3,065	1,084	478	289	187	2	606	......	1,981	540	443	67	30	1,382	59
Moore	334	89	36	23	17	5	1	13	......	53	16	14	2	......	29	8
Morgan	691	18	1	1	1	......	......	......	......	17	5	3	......	2	11	1
Obion	5,293	1,092	208	48	30	18	......	159	1	884	268	170	93	5	588	28
Overton	299	72	24	15	14	1	......	9	......	48	15	14	1	......	32	1
Perry	633	114	43	19	19	......	......	24	......	71	23	19	3	1	40	8
Polk	284	54	25	10	7	3	......	15	......	29	1	1	......	......	27	1
Putnam	892	195	82	49	46	3	......	33	......	113	48	45	3	......	63	2
Rhea	1,316	286	37	24	20	4	......	13	......	249	110	80	28	2	136	3
Roane	2,366	514	95	70	59	9	2	25	......	419	171	140	26	5	232	16
Robertson	6,492	1,326	768	212	113	98	1	554	2	558	113	90	18	5	403	42
Rutherford	11,357	2,505	1,266	555	503	49	3	706	5	1,239	290	247	27	16	844	105
Sequatchie	139	32	3	1	1	......	......	2	......	29	2	2	......	......	25	2
Sevier	378	77	37	23	21	2	......	14	......	40	10	8	......	2	30	......
Shelby	91,719	23,459	5,303	525	431	68	26	4,769	9	18,156	2,941	1,864	905	172	14,532	683
Smith	2,325	449	180	67	56	11	......	112	1	269	58	42	5	11	184	27
Stewart	1,806	365	160	85	62	21	2	75	......	205	57	42	10	5	139	9
Sullivan	1,535	363	29	14	14	......	......	15	......	334	124	92	27	5	204	6
Sumner	5,386	1,150	380	299	269	27	3	77	4	770	307	264	10	33	432	31
Tipton	13,353	2,804	2,312	372	269	97	6	1,933	7	492	131	90	36	5	309	52
Trousdale	1,781	344	123	85	62	21	2	38	......	221	65	46	9	10	142	14
Unicoi	131	36	1	......	......	......	......	1	......	35	......	......	......	......	33	2
Warren	1,949	437	132	89	82	7	......	43	......	305	86	77	8	1	196	23
Washington	2,267	487	47	36	27	9	......	11	......	440	189	139	48	2	238	13
Wayne	845	174	30	7	5	1	1	23	......	144	48	42	4	2	93	3
Weakley	3,470	735	274	106	75	30	1	168	......	461	193	150	41	2	250	18
White	899	208	83	48	44	3	1	35	......	125	36	24	9	3	87	2
Williamson	7,828	1,626	560	250	197	53	......	309	1	1,066	192	149	23	20	807	67
Wilson	6,303	1,336	541	366	292	73	1	174	1	795	276	228	39	9	464	55
Other counties [1]	347	48	20	13	12	1	......	7	......	28	4	4	......	......	24	......

TEXAS.

STATE AND COUNTY.																
Total	690,049	145,890	67,678	21,195	16,159	4,731	305	46,366	117	78,212	20,443	15,538	3,881	1,024	52,409	5,360
Anderson	11,323	2,493	1,461	581	460	110	11	877	3	1,032	363	229	130	4	606	63
Angelina	2,435	534	56	28	28	......	......	28	......	478	48	33	10	5	427	3
Aransas	136	99	1	......	......	......	......	1	......	98	30	23	3	4	67	1
Atascosa	228	50	36	25	19	6	......	11	......	14	5	5	......	......	7	2
Austin	5,018	1,045	775	194	104	82	8	580	1	270	97	87	7	3	154	19
Bastrop	9,428	1,861	1,194	310	179	120	11	870	14	667	303	237	60	6	290	74
Bee	568	102	22	10	7	3	......	12	......	80	33	32	......	1	40	7
Bell	6,302	1,257	216	52	30	22	......	164	......	1,041	224	137	83	4	720	97
Bexar	11,642	2,572	87	46	37	9	......	41	......	2,485	658	430	189	39	1,738	89
Blanco	350	33	29	15	4	11	......	14	......	4	2	2	......	......	2	......
Bosque	848	169	80	28	20	7	1	52	......	89	38	26	10	2	45	6
Bowie	12,734	2,878	1,656	464	401	63	......	1,191	1	1,222	341	236	92	13	846	35
Brazoria	6,237	1,255	773	311	279	31	1	462	......	482	146	123	12	11	252	84
Brazos	8,827	1,978	1,161	234	203	30	1	925	2	817	250	217	30	3	462	105
Brown	525	98	3	2	2	......	......	1	......	95	60	41	19	......	33	2
Burleson	8,587	1,905	1,277	268	197	63	8	1,007	2	628	134	131	2	1	429	65
Burnet	292	60	14	8	7	1	......	6	......	46	18	13	4	1	26	2
Caldwell	5,378	1,050	587	194	120	69	5	391	2	463	133	105	14	14	281	49
Calhoun	491	101	13	4	4	......	......	9	......	88	63	45	18	......	20	5
Camp	4,415	883	664	256	181	74	3	405	3	219	66	54	10	2	128	25

[1] Includes all counties with less than 100 Negro inhabitants.

TABLE 18.—HOME OWNERSHIP BY COUNTIES: 1910—NUMBER OF FARM HOMES AND OTHER HOMES, OWNED FREE, OWNED ENCUMBERED, AND RENTED BY NEGRO FAMILIES—Continued.

TEXAS—Continued.

STATE AND COUNTY.	Negro population: 1910.	Total farm and other homes: 1910.	NUMBER OF FARM HOMES.							NUMBER OF OTHER HOMES.						
			Total.	Owned.				Rented.	No report of ownership.	Total.	Owned.				Rented.	No report of ownership.
				Total.	Free.	Encumbered.	No encumbrance report.				Total.	Free.	Encumbered.	No encumbrance report.		
Cass	9,952	1,864	1,487	656	483	163	10	826	5	377	101	86	5	10	139	137
Chambers	1,032	219	129	105	102	2	1	24		90	41	34	1	6	43	6
Cherokee	7,641	1,446	973	362	274	81	7	611		473	87	69	12	6	365	21
Clay	101	23	6					6		17	4	4			13	
Coleman	253	33								33	6	4		2	26	1
Collin	2,206	538	132	27	18	8	1	103	2	406	150	91	29	30	238	18
Colorado	7,074	1,537	695	162	123	39		533		842	373	319	45	9	453	16
Comal	232	40	11	2	1	1		9		29	4	4			23	2
Cooke	1,688	423	63	17	12	5		46		360	132	90	27	15	224	4
Coryell	488	85	17	6	5	1		11		68	36	34	2		28	4
Dallas	24,355	5,594	578	92	65	21	6	484	2	5,016	801	535	243	23	3,994	221
De Witt	4,753	977	376	130	101	29		246		601	240	203	37		335	26
Delta	809	175	67	20	18	2		47		108	25	19	2	4	74	9
Denton	2,210	462	220	63	39	24		157		242	94	70	23	1	144	4
El Paso	1,562	389								389	94	66	22	6	272	23
Ellis	9,623	2,089	566	35	23	12		531		1,523	422	320	93	9	984	117
Erath	589	140	19	13	9	4		6		121	15	14	1		105	1
Falls	12,612	2,669	1,462	306	213	75	18	1,147	9	1,207	368	282	55	31	647	192
Fannin	5,366	1,184	455	106	78	26	2	348	1	729	233	189	40	4	447	49
Fayette	7,361	1,501	907	207	140	67		700		594	208	174	33	1	363	23
Fort Bend	11,422	2,534	1,628	459	386	68	5	1,164	5	906	149	139	6	4	617	140
Franklin	735	149	123	26	23	3		96	1	26	1			1	18	7
Freestone	8,772	1,773	1,468	514	357	157		954		305	57	34	22	1	207	41
Frio	151	25	13	5	3	2		8		12	6	5	1		6	
Galveston	8,747	2,194	72	43	35	8		29		2,122	195	148	42	5	1,823	104
Gillespie	116	51	19	3	3			16		32	5	1		4	27	
Goliad	1,501	358	141	59	57	2		82		217	89	79	10		123	5
Gonzales	8,212	1,834	1,179	281	221	58	2	896	2	655	124	79	33	12	459	72
Grayson	7,753	1,802	269	85	64	21		183	1	1,533	642	457	176	9	804	87
Gregg	7,781	1,592	917	402	320	81	1	514	1	675	248	193	35	20	410	17
Grimes	9,858	2,053	1,255	283	208	66	9	972		798	179	143	16	20	571	48
Guadalupe	5,681	1,061	674	228	135	90	3	443	3	387	126	97	11	18	252	9
Hardin	2,550	608	15	12	10	1	1	3		593	103	69	4	30	476	14
Harris	30,950	7,574	314	168	149	19		146		7,260	1,749	1,232	463	54	5,234	277
Harrison	23,698	4,784	3,174	1,312	1,095	211	6	1,862		1,610	482	407	57	18	1,084	44
Hays	2,165	422	119	52	41	9	2	67		303	127	79	38	10	156	20
Henderson	4,177	804	582	210	115	95		371	1	222	66	40	21	5	132	24
Hill	4,856	1,084	246	47	31	14	2	198	1	838	268	193	72	3	510	60
Hood	212	45	25	10	4	6		15		20	10	9	1		10	
Hopkins	3,283	592	320	109	82	25	2	211		272	73	56	11	6	180	19
Houston	12,548	2,481	1,661	563	407	126	30	1,097	1	820	120	85	19	16	603	97
Hunt	4,579	989	274	71	56	15		203		715	211	154	42	15	479	25
Jack	118	23								23	10	9	1		10	3
Jackson	2,114	368	240	91	86	5		149		128	53	43	8	2	74	1
Jasper	4,731	875	255	180	176	4		75		620	95	83	4	8	519	6
Jefferson	10,676	2,327	33	19	19			14		2,294	493	387	100	6	1,762	39
Johnson	1,637	337	58	14	11	3		43	1	279	116	93	21	2	152	11
Jones	259	45	1	1	1					44					34	10
Karnes	793	142	61	28	21	7		33		81	20	16	3	1	54	7
Kaufman	8,374	1,633	714	115	64	50	1	596	3	919	232	171	52	9	559	128
Kendall	253	50	8	6	5	1		2		42	19	18	1		22	1
Kerr	248	39	7	4	3	1		3		32	17	11	6		13	2
Kinney	158	27	3	1	1			1	1	24	7	7			12	5
Lamar	10,993	2,335	1,071	232	186	42	4	838	1	1,264	324	246	44	34	864	76
Lampasas	436	96	10	6	5	1		3	1	86	25	20	5		59	2
Lavaca	4,384	873	539	154	75	79		385		334	96	67	28	1	217	21
Lee	4,039	887	706	240	135	104	1	465	1	181	103	92	10	1	65	13
Leon	6,878	1,413	1,170	347	258	83	6	821	2	243	51	46	2	3	161	31
Liberty	3,401	794	276	118	111	5	2	157	1	518	81	60	2	19	425	12
Limestone	9,247	1,916	993	249	161	86	2	743	1	923	176	147	24	5	686	61
McCulloch	189	40	2					2		38	2	2			19	17
McLennan	17,234	3,494	1,154	323	218	99	6	827	4	2,340	692	502	132	58	1,467	181
Madison	2,757	522	426	165	123	40	2	261		96	14	9	3	2	67	15
Marion	6,725	1,446	975	489	428	53	8	476	10	471	144	132		12	287	40
Matagorda	4,457	852	386	94	89	5		292		466	170	141	24	5	273	23
Medina	449	73	33	21	19	2		12		40	11	11			27	2
Milam	9,485	1,983	1,182	187	147	37	3	995		801	251	198	46	7	474	76
Mitchell	192	35	3	1		1		2		32	22	18	4		10	
Montgomery	7,104	1,473	781	266	212	52	2	515		692	163	139	11	13	488	41
Morris	3,706	707	526	142	91	49	2	384		181	33	19	12	2	139	9
Nacogdoches	7,030	1,452	810	245	183	62		564	1	642	80	57	16	7	558	4
Navarro	10,968	2,350	993	219	151	63	5	773	1	1,357	377	269	93	15	895	85
Newton	3,864	696	328	276	272	4		52		368	39	29		10	313	16
Nolan	111	12	1					1		11	3	2	1		7	1
Nueces	742	137	4	1	1			3		133	50	40	10		77	6
Orange	1,898	405	6	4	4			2		399	102	79	8	15	297	
Palo Pinto	528	109	2	1	1			1		107	20	18	1	1	82	5
Panola	8,842	1,651	1,383	481	363	118		902		268	23	21		2	238	7
Parker	693	149	26	14	5	8	1	12		123	65	61	4		51	7
Polk	6,594	1,385	565	266	228	36	2	298	1	820	133	114	3	16	645	42

TABLE 18.—HOME OWNERSHIP BY COUNTIES: 1910—NUMBER OF FARM HOMES AND OTHER HOMES, OWNED FREE, OWNED ENCUMBERED, AND RENTED BY NEGRO FAMILIES—Continued.

STATE AND COUNTY.	Negro population: 1910.	Total farm and other homes: 1910.	FARM HOMES Total.	Owned Total.	Free.	Encumbered.	No encumbrance report.	Rented.	No report of ownership.	OTHER HOMES Total.	Owned Total.	Free.	Encumbered.	No encumbrance report.	Rented.	No report of ownership.
TEXAS—Continued.																
Potter	149	30								30					30	
Rains	616	127	115	46	39	6	1	69		12	8	2		6	2	2
Red River	8,673	1,828	1,367	280	235	41	4	1,082	5	461	154	123	5	26	274	33
Refugio	481	88	27	13	8	5		14		61	29	26		3	32	
Robertson	14,571	3,476	2,209	311	228	80	3	1,898		1,267	504	485	17	2	440	323
Rockwall	731	189	28	7	6	1		21		161	14	11	3		122	25
Runnels	133	23	6	2	1	1		4		17	4	3	1		11	2
Rusk	11,314	2,133	1,816	741	534	203	4	1,074	1	317	86	67	10	9	196	35
Sabine	1,679	315	242	95	86	9		147		73	4	2		2	69	
San Augustine	3,453	622	477	137	115	22		340		145	20	18		2	120	5
San Jacinto	5,193	1,095	849	357	331	22	4	490	2	246	39	33		6	135	72
San Saba	103	12	2	1		1		1		10	5	4	1		5	
Shackleford	126	24	3	2	1	1		1		21	11	8	1	2	10	
Shelby	5,274	947	573	198	162	35	1	375		374	66	56	8	2	267	41
Smith	17,246	3,463	2,423	859	511	303	45	1,558	6	1,040	279	223	37	19	647	114
Tarrant	15,418	3,573	135	68	63	5		66	1	3,438	679	397	234	48	2,575	184
Taylor	639	103								103	46	35	10	1	55	2
Titus	3,118	589	332	95	66	29		237		257	74	71		3	172	11
Tom Green	716	145	1							144	48	35	11	2	93	3
Travis	15,473	3,233	813	186	134	50	2	625	2	2,420	754	552	178	24	1,508	158
Trinity	3,195	652	242	114	99	13	2	128		410	87	63	19	5	307	16
Tyler	2,207	420	179	106	101	5		73		241	48	41	5	2	191	2
Upshur	5,649	1,109	909	304	244	54	6	604	1	200	34	27	3	4	104	62
Uvalde	262	50	3	1	1			2		47	19	13	6		27	1
Val Verde	153	33								33	14	12		2	19	
Van Zandt	1,534	317	216	101	86	15		115		101	28	22	6		54	19
Victoria	3,600	721	256	130	109	21		126		465	182	166	15	1	264	19
Walker	8,362	1,699	1,172	364	283	64	17	807	1	527	145	123	10	12	291	91
Waller	6,712	1,559	1,108	337	261	70	6	771		451	173	160	10	3	238	40
Washington	12,017	2,639	1,622	385	279	104	2	1,234	3	1,017	396	340	43	13	484	137
Wharton	8,889	2,073	1,164	282	236	43	3	881	1	909	107	80	21	6	761	41
Wichita	612	115	1					1		114	26	22	4		84	4
Williamson	7,370	1,452	269	85	63	21	1	184		1,183	389	267	86	36	664	130
Wilson	956	137	82	40	32	8		42		55	18	14	4		32	5
Wood	3,926	789	476	227	175	50	2	247	2	313	95	86	7	2	205	13
Other counties [1]	1,774	330	73	40	29	11		33		257	69	61	4	4	141	47
UTAH.																
Total	1,144	240	12	9	8	1		3		228	42	24	18		151	35
Salt Lake	827	162	6	6	6					156	28	12	16		102	26
Weber	204	47								47	5	4	1		38	4
Other counties [1]	113	31	6	3	2	1		3		25	9	8	1		11	5
VERMONT.																
Total	1,621	226	22	17	7	10		5		204	29	20	8	1	171	4
Chittenden	1,114	131	6	5	3	2		1		125	12	7	5		109	4
Rutland	108	26	4	4		4				22	3	2		1	19	
Other counties [1]	399	69	12	8	4	4		4		57	14	11	3		43	
VIRGINIA.																
Total	671,096	137,771	48,410	32,528	26,972	5,420	136	15,793	89	89,361	24,405	18,295	4,839	1,271	61,255	3,701
Accomac	13,273	2,472	890	144	63	81		746		1,582	263	160	87	16	1,264	55
Albemarle	9,673	1,815	649	589	564	25		59	1	1,166	588	505	32	51	535	43
Alexandria	2,645	617	9	8	8			1		608	311	245	64	2	281	16
Alleghany	2,945	603	19	18	16	2		1		584	171	93	73	5	407	6
Amelia	5,490	1,056	755	582	486	96		170	3	301	82	33	6	43	209	10
Amherst	7,465	1,373	857	531	459	66	6	318	8	516	150	116	19	15	288	78
Appomattox	3,089	560	352	200	158	38	4	152		208	46	27	7	12	128	34
Augusta	4,541	889	165	146	105	39	2	19		724	378	301	53	24	327	19
Bath	1,176	189	21	19	18	1		2		168	65	52	13		67	36
Bedford	8,455	1,594	869	585	486	99		282	2	725	268	239	24	5	439	18
Bland	133	23	15	14	14			1		8	4	1		3	4	
Botetourt	3,495	660	147	132	124	5	3	15		513	242	221	11	10	243	28
Brunswick	11,366	2,149	1,099	628	474	148	6	463	8	1,050	261	197	50	14	704	85
Buckingham	7,570	1,488	986	784	744	40		199	3	502	168	135	1	32	282	52
Campbell	9,002	1,746	817	546	440	106		271		929	408	337	68	3	505	16

[1] Includes all counties with less than 100 Negro inhabitants.

TABLE 18.—HOME OWNERSHIP BY COUNTIES: 1910—NUMBER OF FARM HOMES AND OTHER HOMES, OWNED FREE, OWNED ENCUMBERED, AND RENTED BY NEGRO FAMILIES—Continued.

VIRGINIA—Continued.

STATE AND COUNTY	Negro population: 1910	Total farm and other homes: 1910	NUMBER OF FARM HOMES							NUMBER OF OTHER HOMES						
			Total	Owned Total	Owned Free	Owned Encumbered	Owned No encumbrance report	Rented	No report of ownership	Total	Owned Total	Owned Free	Owned Encumbered	Owned No encumbrance report	Rented	No report of ownership
Caroline	8,750	1,617	1,187	924	763	158	3	261	2	430	132	103	11	18	264	34
Carroll	268	35	19	16	11	5		3		16	3	3			12	1
Charles City	3,765	800	668	614	587	26	1	54		132	31	28	1	2	86	15
Charlotte	8,335	1,606	1,017	604	496	107	1	413		589	116	108	8		433	40
Chesterfield	7,527	1,494	618	524	481	43		94		876	327	286	32	9	516	33
Clarke	1,900	390	26	17	12	5		9		364	179	153	23	3	183	2
Craig	207	39	9	7	6	1		2		30	2	2			27	1
Culpeper	5,262	1,023	525	482	410	71	1	43		498	181	133	22	26	283	34
Cumberland	6,053	1,140	963	644	535	107	2	314	5	177	28	20	2	6	134	15
Dinwiddie	9,368	1,789	1,249	772	640	111	21	467	10	540	55	37	7	11	419	66
Elizabeth City	7,992	1,827	142	104	84	20		35	3	1,685	895	618	251	26	749	41
Essex	5,315	1,092	805	696	604	61	31	108	1	287	143	117	9	17	134	10
Fairfax	4,864	974	324	276	243	33		48		650	329	268	42	19	279	42
Fauquier	7,486	1,419	536	491	415	70	6	45		883	263	199	29	35	553	67
Floyd	837	153	94	80	68	12		14		59	19	15	1	3	40	
Fluvanna	3,374	662	522	438	409	25	4	82	2	140	43	41	1	1	83	14
Franklin	5,435	941	741	423	343	80		318		200	45	34		11	130	25
Frederick	694	134	29	23	17	6		6		105	47	41	4	2	53	5
Giles	755	145	47	34	32	1	1	12	1	98	33	22	6	5	62	3
Gloucester	5,907	1,242	877	845	600	245		32		365	215	161	46	8	143	7
Goochland	5,230	947	637	563	523	40		72	2	310	128	109	4	15	151	31
Grayson	939	177	100	76	67	9		24		77	10	7	1	2	66	1
Greene	1,339	238	104	85	71	14		19		134	72	65	4	3	60	2
Greensville	7,393	1,381	656	351	218	131	2	304	1	725	163	103	31	29	503	59
Halifax	20,013	3,808	2,286	933	760	171	2	1,353		1,522	447	366	75	6	1,048	27
Hanover	7,040	1,331	853	696	617	78	1	157		478	139	85	9	45	294	45
Henrico	6,837	1,267	383	310	286	24		73		884	391	327	53	11	465	28
Henry	7,462	1,377	759	266	229	36	1	493		618	223	167	49	7	378	17
Highland	260	47	19	18	15	3		1		28	11	8		3	15	2
Isle of Wight	7,512	1,449	550	312	206	106		238		899	127	98	18	11	748	24
James City	3,034	635	217	186	171	14	1	31		418	164	119	24	21	215	39
King and Queen	5,373	1,011	827	733	610	121	2	94		184	71	51	4	16	100	13
King George	2,913	546	358	286	234	52		72		188	73	54	16	3	103	12
King William	4,855	923	566	491	442	47	2	74	1	357	147	109	23	15	202	8
Lancaster	5,139	975	622	570	439	130	1	51	1	353	149	107	26	16	187	17
Lee	952	201	57	33	32	1		24		144	10	9		1	131	3
Loudoun	5,221	977	250	203	168	35		46	1	727	228	171	46	11	478	21
Louisa	7,883	1,579	989	890	822	68		96	3	590	333	301	25	7	207	50
Lunenburg	6,811	1,273	873	565	447	114	4	308		400	80	50	12	18	257	63
Madison	3,264	610	359	345	307	38		14		251	86	78	8		160	5
Mathews	2,513	479	250	240	229	10	1	8	2	229	142	115	7	20	57	30
Mecklenburg	16,394	3,106	1,836	933	750	180	3	900	3	1,270	281	216	42	23	913	76
Middlesex	4,636	946	761	711	467	243	1	50		185	68	56	7	5	106	11
Montgomery	2,323	503	144	139	129	10		5		359	236	214	19	3	118	5
Nansemond	15,536	3,232	941	586	420	166		355		2,291	642	408	206	28	1,584	65
Nelson	5,263	985	631	388	362	26		231	12	354	124	110	8	6	207	23
New Kent	2,791	562	383	303	287	16		80		179	67	49	4	14	92	20
Norfolk	31,791	7,077	553	241	192	49		312		6,524	1,889	1,029	832	28	4,474	161
Northampton	9,314	1,846	578	217	88	129		361		1,268	286	139	143	4	918	64
Northumberland	4,267	810	548	483	408	75		65		262	116	88	18	10	133	13
Nottoway	7,347	1,430	847	602	555	46	1	245		583	253	223	18	12	315	15
Orange	5,526	1,048	388	375	310	65		13		660	399	359	38	2	246	15
Page	1,166	259	38	35	30	5		3		221	124	102	18	4	97	
Patrick	1,618	304	254	118	101	17		136		50	9	9			35	6
Pittsylvania	20,163	3,852	1,872	591	469	119	3	1,278	3	1,980	509	366	82	61	1,271	200
Powhatan	3,633	712	438	342	297	44	1	96		274	122	94	15	13	135	17
Prince Edward	8,458	1,690	986	678	571	102	5	304	4	704	233	193	26	14	384	87
Prince George	4,551	970	504	347	237	109	1	157		466	85	57	13	15	251	130
Prince William	2,825	536	200	179	151	26	2	20	1	336	151	126	19	6	171	14
Princess Anne	5,818	1,196	532	288	191	94	3	244		664	153	112	18	23	484	27
Pulaski	2,930	554	93	83	74	9		10		461	210	173	21	16	240	11
Rappahannock	2,148	389	171	150	129	20	1	21		218	56	48	4	4	153	9
Richmond	3,071	550	331	248	234	14		83		219	76	63	4	9	124	19
Roanoke	3,525	709	103	75	68	7		28		606	296	258	29	9	281	29
Rockbridge	3,528	715	94	70	60	10		24		621	301	236	40	25	301	19
Rockingham	2,335	450	70	60	48	12		10		380	172	135	28	9	208	
Russell	1,025	179	37	20	20			17		142	26	20		6	109	7
Scott	503	105	47	24	20	4		23		58	12	10		2	45	1
Shenandoah	493	103	2	2	1	1				101	53	35	18		47	1
Smyth	981	191	41	34	26	8		7		150	76	68	6	2	69	5
Southampton	16,091	3,020	1,429	404	272	130	2	1,023	2	1,591	172	97	51	24	1,338	81
Spotsylvania	3,593	718	544	481	365	116		63		174	82	48	27	7	89	3
Stafford	1,720	288	162	143	112	31		19		126	55	49	3	3	67	4
Surry	6,005	1,208	548	343	219	123	1	205		660	132	81	41	10	455	73
Sussex	8,962	1,716	913	451	322	127	2	462		803	163	109	33	21	593	47
Tazewell	2,820	625	93	56	51	5		37		532	166	152	10	4	342	24
Warren	1,131	209	20	13	10	3		7		189	68	50	16	2	117	4
Warwick	4,334	1,105	177	159	145	14		18		928	225	179	42	4	693	10
Washington	2,312	465	66	49	49			17		399	240	212	16	12	140	19
Westmoreland	4,668	904	610	443	389	53	1	164	3	294	93	87	4	2	151	50

NEGRO POPULATION.

TABLE 18.—HOME OWNERSHIP BY COUNTIES: 1910—NUMBER OF FARM HOMES AND OTHER HOMES, OWNED FREE, OWNED ENCUMBERED, AND RENTED BY NEGRO FAMILIES—Continued.

STATE AND COUNTY.	Negro popula-tion: 1910.	Total farm and other homes: 1910.	NUMBER OF FARM HOMES.							NUMBER OF OTHER HOMES.						
			Total.	Owned.				Rented.	No report of owner-ship.	Total.	Owned.				Rented.	No report of owner-ship.
				Total.	Free.	Encum-bered.	No en-cum-brance report.				Total.	Free.	Encum-bered.	No en-cum-brance report.		

VIRGINIA—Continued.

STATE AND COUNTY.																
Wise	2,861	688	11	6	5	1	.....	5	......	677	55	43	10	2	606	16
Wythe	2,188	468	56	50	46	4	.....	6	......	412	173	125	29	19	224	15
York	3,764	805	565	491	467	24	.....	73	1	240	100	82	16	2	120	20
Other counties[1]	11	1	.....	.....	.....	.....	.....	.....	.....	1	.....	.....	.....	.....	1	.....
INDEPENDENT CITIES:																
Alexandria	4,188	1,072	.....	.....	.....	.....	.....	.....	.....	1,072	257	229	26	2	729	86
Bristol	1,144	270	.....	.....	.....	.....	.....	.....	.....	270	79	70	9	.....	181	10
Buena Vista	416	90	.....	.....	.....	.....	.....	.....	.....	90	39	22	17	.....	41	10
Charlottesville	2,524	576	1	.....	.....	.....	.....	1	.....	575	138	96	31	11	432	5
Clifton Forge	1,092	183	.....	.....	.....	.....	.....	.....	.....	183	72	54	18	.....	104	7
Danville	6,207	1,567	2	2	.....	2	.....	.....	.....	1,565	457	297	160	.....	1,088	20
Fredericksburg	1,480	317	.....	.....	.....	.....	.....	.....	.....	317	89	73	15	1	222	6
Lynchburg	9,466	2,294	2	2	1	1	.....	.....	.....	2,292	613	485	125	3	1,641	38
Newport News	7,259	1,769	1	1	1	.....	.....	.....	.....	1,768	266	124	141	1	1,459	43
Norfolk	25,039	6,391	.....	.....	.....	.....	.....	.....	.....	6,391	273	208	50	15	5,977	141
Petersburg	11,014	2,894	10	9	9	.....	.....	1	.....	2,884	825	731	80	14	2,019	40
Portsmouth	11,617	2,948	.....	.....	.....	.....	.....	.....	.....	2,948	423	256	165	2	2,472	53
Radford	665	125	11	9	5	4	.....	2	.....	114	42	36	6	.....	71	1
Richmond	46,733	10,496	2	1	.....	1	.....	1	.....	10,494	1,645	1,209	384	52	8,518	331
Roanoke	7,924	1,733	.....	.....	.....	.....	.....	.....	.....	1,733	473	311	160	2	1,233	27
Staunton	2,476	559	.....	.....	.....	.....	.....	.....	.....	559	197	182	13	2	348	14
Winchester	1,038	271	1	1	1	.....	.....	.....	.....	270	83	52	27	4	182	5

WASHINGTON.

STATE AND COUNTY.																
Total	6,058	1,356	87	71	49	19	3	16	......	1,269	364	200	160	4	838	67
King	2,487	544	7	5	5	.....	.....	2	.....	537	145	83	60	2	370	22
Kittitas	247	88	7	4	2	1	1	3	.....	81	12	11	1	.....	68	1
Pierce	889	185	6	6	1	5	.....	.....	.....	179	52	32	20	.....	114	13
Snohomish	219	61	2	2	2	.....	.....	.....	.....	59	24	13	10	1	33	2
Spokane	1,170	226	3	2	2	.....	.....	1	.....	223	80	35	45	.....	131	12
Walla Walla	152	30	.....	.....	.....	.....	.....	.....	.....	30	6	4	2	.....	17	7
Yakima	354	90	17	14	12	2	.....	3	.....	73	24	13	11	.....	43	6
Other counties[1]	540	132	45	38	25	11	2	7	.....	87	21	9	11	1	62	4

WEST VIRGINIA.

STATE AND COUNTY.																
Total	64,173	14,197	674	523	456	66	1	150	1	13,523	2,220	1,560	568	92	10,792	511
Barbour	920	186	87	80	71	9	.....	7	.....	99	18	6	1	11	74	7
Berkeley	1,801	380	27	22	21	1	.....	5	.....	353	124	89	30	5	203	26
Boone	164	37	19	14	14	.....	.....	5	.....	18	3	3	.....	.....	15	.....
Braxton	221	38	18	13	11	2	.....	5	.....	20	7	7	.....	.....	13	.....
Brooke	151	35	.....	.....	.....	.....	.....	.....	.....	35	4	3	1	.....	31	.....
Cabell	2,447	467	4	3	3	.....	.....	1	.....	463	150	93	48	9	283	30
Fayette	9,311	2,099	42	35	26	9	.....	7	.....	2,057	147	89	55	3	1,852	58
Grant	253	41	20	10	8	2	.....	10	.....	21	11	9	.....	2	10	.....
Greenbrier	1,779	379	51	47	46	1	.....	4	.....	328	163	136	25	2	151	14
Hampshire	303	75	7	4	3	1	.....	3	.....	68	39	34	3	2	22	7
Hardy	387	72	10	10	10	.....	.....	.....	.....	62	27	25	1	1	34	1
Harrison	1,359	282	8	7	6	1	.....	1	.....	274	97	72	22	3	164	13
Jefferson	3,499	705	37	31	22	9	.....	6	.....	668	262	180	80	2	383	23
Kanawha	6,476	1,401	58	42	38	4	.....	16	.....	1,343	234	176	43	15	1,050	59
Lewis	239	26	1	1	1	.....	.....	.....	.....	25	8	2	.....	6	17	.....
Logan	532	90	3	.....	.....	.....	.....	3	.....	87	1	1	.....	.....	83	3
McDowell	14,667	3,644	7	3	2	1	.....	4	.....	3,637	76	64	12	.....	3,449	112
Marion	851	171	.....	.....	.....	.....	.....	.....	.....	171	15	9	3	3	146	10
Marshall	575	26	1	1	1	.....	.....	.....	.....	25	5	5	.....	.....	18	2
Mason	349	91	4	3	2	1	.....	1	.....	87	34	16	8	10	26	27
Mercer	5,960	1,433	23	18	16	2	.....	5	.....	1,410	297	194	93	10	1,075	38
Mineral	601	121	8	5	4	1	.....	3	.....	113	32	22	9	1	74	7
Mingo	1,236	240	1	1	1	.....	.....	.....	.....	239	6	6	.....	.....	215	18
Monongalia	294	57	5	4	2	2	.....	1	.....	52	13	8	5	.....	36	3
Monroe	673	139	56	40	38	2	.....	15	1	83	44	42	2	.....	36	3
Morgan	177	33	1	1	1	.....	.....	.....	.....	32	11	7	4	.....	20	1
Ohio	1,389	356	3	2	2	.....	.....	1	.....	353	70	52	18	.....	268	15
Pendleton	132	23	10	9	8	1	.....	1	.....	13	6	4	2	.....	6	1
Pocahontas	445	83	23	17	16	1	.....	6	.....	60	10	9	1	.....	49	1
Preston	151	28	2	2	.....	2	.....	.....	.....	26	8	7	1	.....	16	2

[1] Includes all counties with less than 100 Negro inhabitants.

TABLE 18.—HOME OWNERSHIP BY COUNTIES: 1910—NUMBER OF FARM HOMES AND OTHER HOMES, OWNED FREE, OWNED ENCUMBERED, AND RENTED BY NEGRO FAMILIES—Continued.

STATE AND COUNTY.	Negro population: 1910.	Total farm and other homes: 1910.	NUMBER OF FARM HOMES.							NUMBER OF OTHER HOMES.						
			Total.	Owned.				Rented.	No report of ownership.	Total.	Owned.				Rented.	No report of ownership.
				Total.	Free.	Encumbered.	No encumbrance report.				Total.	Free.	Encumbered.	No encumbrance report.		
WEST VIRGINIA—Continued.																
Putnam	435	93	6	4	4			2		87	4	4			83	
Raleigh	2,052	465	10	8	8			2		455	68	42	26		373	14
Randolph	376	58	5	2	1		1	3		53	12	11	1		40	1
Summers	1,130	249	31	24	20	4		7		218	77	58	15	4	135	6
Taylor	527	99	37	29	22	7		8		62	20	10	8	2	39	3
Tucker	344	66	1	1	1					65	1	1			61	3
Tyler	115	26								26	4	3		1	22	
Upshur	226	44	2	2	2					42	22	16	6		19	1
Wayne	169	23	4	3	3			1		19	6	6			13	
Wood	943	243	6	5	4	1		1		237	75	34	41		162	
Wyoming	105	19	14	1	1			13		5					5	
Other counties[1]	409	54	22	19	17	2		3		32	9	5	4		21	2
WISCONSIN.																
Total	2,900	677	54	42	10	32		12		623	131	70	58	3	474	18
Dane	173	44	2					2		42	9	3	6		32	1
Douglas	184	49	2	1		1		1		47	6	5	1		39	2
Milwaukee	996	254								254	13	7	6		237	4
Racine	115	32								32	9	4	5		21	2
Rock	157	37	2	2	1	1				35	7	5	2		26	2
Vernon	116	20	16	14	3	11		2		4	3		2	1	1	
Winnebago	110	20	1	1	1					19	6	3	3		13	
Other counties[1]	1,049	221	31	24	4	20		7		190	78	43	33	2	105	7
WYOMING.																
Total	2,235	375	18	16	10	6		2		357	53	38	15		286	18
Carbon	146	32	1	1				1		31	6	4	2		25	
Laramie	1,607	228	8	7	3	4		1		220	32	23	9		178	10
Sheridan	183	49	4	3	3			1		45	5	1	4		36	4
Sweetwater	101	21								21	2	2			17	2
Other counties[1]	198	45	5	5	4	1				40	8	8			30	2

[1] Includes all counties with less than 100 Negro inhabitants.

THE CLASSIFICATION BY OCCUPATION AND INDUSTRY.

The compilation of the returns of occupation is restricted to the population 10 years of age and over, although some return was entered in the occupational columns of the population schedule for every person enumerated in 1910, the entry in the case of children under 10 years of age being generally "none," although in some cases specific employments were returned for children of this age.

In the case of each person for whom a return was made of occupation, a return was made, also, of the "industry, business, or establishment" in which the person worked.

This double return of occupation by industry provides the data for the detailed tabulation presented in Table 22 (pp. 529 to 551). In this table, for example, the 128,546 Negro males employed by steam railroads are distributed into groups of diverse occupational character, included under such specific designations as officials, station masters, contractors and builders, agents (claim, freight, purchasing, ticket, and station), bookkeepers, stenographers, blacksmiths, cabinetmakers, carpenters, coppersmiths, electricians, engineers (civil, mechanical, stationary, electrical, and locomotive), painters, plumbers, tinners, cooks, gardeners, janitors, molders, motormen, platers and galvanizers, teamsters, upholsterers, and waiters. The full list of occupations specified under "steam railroads," as given in Table 22, comprises every occupation reported by Negro males or females employed by steam railroads in 1910. The list includes, in fact, 90 of the 94 occupational designations shown in the general report of the census, for all employees of steam railways, white and colored, the only occupations specified in the general report for which no Negroes were returned—namely, "designers," "locksmiths," "finishers," and "pattern makers"—being numerically unimportant.

In Tables 17 and 18 (pp. 517 to 522) the industry classification is eliminated, and homogeneous occupational groups are composed, each group comprising all individuals in all industries reporting a given occupation, such as blacksmiths in all industries, or carpenters or plasterers in all industries. Table 17 shows, for example, that 9,727 Negro males were returned in 1910 as blacksmiths. Referring to Table 22 it will be found that 121 of these blacksmiths were employed in coal mines, 3 in copper mines, 19 in iron mines, 53 in quarries, 14 in agricultural implement factories, and varying numbers in other of the 120 industrial and trade groups of Table 22.

The occupational totals of Tables 17 and 18 can not, however, generally be made up completely from the industrial-occupational groups of Table 22, since the full detail of the 428 occupations distinguished in Table 17 for Negro males is not shown for each of the 120 industrial groups of Table 22. Generally the number in any occupation, as given in Table 17, exceeds the sum of the numbers shown separately by industries for this occupation in Table 22, and in the case of a few occupations slight discrepancies arise between these two tables from differences in the classification of small groups of workers. In general, however, it is true that the industrial distribution of each occupational group, designated in Table 17, is shown in detail in Table 22.

PROPORTION GAINFULLY EMPLOYED IN AGRICULTURAL AND IN OTHER PURSUITS: 1910.

Table 1 classifies the Negro population, male and female, 10 years of age and over, in the country as a whole, the South, and the North and West, as gainfully employed and not gainfully employed, and the gainfully employed as employed in agricultural or in other pursuits.

Of the Negro population 10 years of age and over numbering 7,317,922 in 1910, 5,192,535, or 71 per cent, were gainfully employed, and 2,125,387, or 29 per cent, were not gainfully employed. The proportion living in the South of the total Negro population 10 years of age and over was 87.6 per cent; of the gainfully employed, 88.4 per cent; and of the not gainfully employed 85.5 per cent. The proportion male in the total was 49.7 per cent; in the gainfully employed 61.2 per cent; and in the not gainfully employed 21.6 per cent. The proportion living in the South was nearly the same among males as among females, and among the gainfully employed as among those not gainfully employed.

The proportion male in the gainfully employed of the North and West, 66.2 per cent, exceeded somewhat the corresponding proportion of 60.6 per cent for the South; the proportion among those not gainfully employed was much lower than among those gainfully employed, and was practically the same in the North and West as in the South, the percentages being 21.3 and 21.6.

The proportion gainfully employed among both males and females was higher in the South than in the North and West, although the difference in the case of males was inconsiderable. Of Negro females 10 years of age and over, 56 per cent in the South and 45.5 per cent in the North and West were gainfully employed.

Of the 3,178,554 Negro males gainfully employed, 1,842,238 were employed in agricultural and 1,336,316 in nonagricultural pursuits. Of those employed in agricultural pursuits, 1,795,610 were in the South and 46,628 in the North and West.

Of the 2,013,981 Negro females gainfully employed, 1,051,137 were employed in agricultural and 962,844 in nonagricultural pursuits. Of those employed in agricultural pursuits, 1,049,553 were living in the South and 1,584 in the North and West.

Table 1 — NEGRO POPULATION 10 YEARS OF AGE AND OVER: 1910.

| SEX AND SECTION. | Total. | Gainfully employed. | | | Not gainfully employed. |
		Total.	In agriculture, forestry, and animal husbandry.	In other employment.	
NUMBER.					
Both sexes:					
United States	7,317,922	5,192,535	2,893,375	2,299,160	2,125,387
The South	6,408,539	4,592,353	2,845,163	1,747,190	1,816,186
The North and West	909,383	600,182	48,212	551,970	309,201
Male:					
United States	3,637,386	3,178,554	1,842,238	1,336,316	458,832
The South	3,174,163	2,781,233	1,795,610	985,623	392,930
The North and West	463,223	397,321	46,628	350,693	65,902
Female:					
United States	3,680,536	2,013,981	1,051,137	962,844	1,666,555
The South	3,234,376	1,811,120	1,049,553	761,567	1,423,256
The North and West	446,160	202,861	1,584	201,277	243,299
PERCENTAGE DISTRIBUTION BY SECTION.					
Both sexes:					
United States	100.0	100.0	100.0	100.0	100.0
The South	87.6	88.4	98.3	76.0	85.5
The North and West	12.4	11.6	1.7	24.0	14.5
Male:					
United States	100.0	100.0	100.0	100.0	100.0
The South	87.3	87.5	97.5	73.8	85.6
The North and West	12.7	12.5	2.5	26.2	14.4
Female:					
United States	100.0	100.0	100.0	100.0	100.0
The South	87.9	89.9	99.8	79.1	85.4
The North and West	12.1	10.1	0.2	20.9	14.6
PERCENTAGE DISTRIBUTION BY SEX.					
Both sexes:					
United States	100.0	100.0	100.0	100.0	100.0
The South	100.0	100.0	100.0	100.0	100.0
The North and West	100.0	100.0	100.0	100.0	100.0
Male:					
United States	49.7	61.2	63.7	58.1	21.6
The South	49.5	60.6	63.1	56.4	21.6
The North and West	50.9	66.2	96.7	63.5	21.3
Female:					
United States	50.3	38.8	36.3	41.9	78.4
The South	50.5	39.4	36.9	43.6	78.4
The North and West	49.1	33.8	3.3	36.5	78.7
PERCENTAGE DISTRIBUTION BY OCCUPATIONAL GROUP.					
Both sexes:					
United States	100.0	71.0	39.5	31.4	29.0
The South	100.0	71.7	44.4	27.3	28.3
The North and West	100.0	66.0	5.3	60.7	34.0
Male:					
United States	100.0	87.4	50.6	36.7	12.6
The South	100.0	87.6	56.6	31.1	12.4
The North and West	100.0	85.8	10.1	75.7	14.2
Female:					
United States	100.0	54.7	28.6	26.2	45.3
The South	100.0	56.0	32.4	23.5	44.0
The North and West	100.0	45.5	0.4	45.1	54.5

Of the males employed in agricultural pursuits, 97.5 per cent, and of the females, 99.8 per cent were living in the South. Among those employed in nonagricultural pursuits, 73.8 per cent of the males and 79.1 per cent of the females were living in the South.

Of the male Negro population 10 years of age and over in the South, 56.6 per cent were engaged in agricultural and 31.1 per cent in nonagricultural pursuits, the percentages for females being 32.4 and 23.5.

In the North and West 75.7 per cent of the Negro males and 45.1 per cent of the Negro females were engaged in nonagricultural pursuits; the proportion engaged in agricultural pursuits being 10.1 per cent for males and 0.4 per cent for females, and the proportion not gainfully employed 14.2 per cent for males and 54 5 per cent for females.

COMPARISON OF NEGROES WITH WHITES.

In Table 2 the Negro and white population 10 years of age and over, male and female, in the country as a whole is classified as gainfully employed in agricultural and in nonagricultural pursuits, and as not gainfully employed.

Table 2 — POPULATION 10 YEARS OF AGE AND OVER: 1910.[1]

| SEX AND RACIAL CLASS. | Total. | Gainfully employed. | | | Not gainfully employed. |
		Total.	In agriculture, forestry, and animal husbandry.	In other employment.	
NUMBER.					
Both sexes:					
All classes	71,580,270	38,167,336	12,659,082	25,508,254	33,412,934
Negro	7,317,922	5,192,535	2,893,375	2,299,160	2,125,387
White	63,933,870	32,774,056	9,681,069	23,092,987	31,159,814
Other	328,478	200,745	84,638	116,107	127,733
Male:					
All classes	37,027,558	30,091,564	10,851,581	19,239,983	6,935,994
Negro	3,637,386	3,178,554	1,842,238	1,336,316	458,832
White	33,164,229	26,730,347	8,929,937	17,800,410	6,433,882
Other	225,943	182,663	79,406	103,257	43,280
Female:					
All classes	34,552,712	8,075,772	1,807,501	6,268,271	26,476,940
Negro	3,680,536	2,013,981	1,051,137	962,844	1,666,555
White	30,769,641	6,043,709	751,132	5,292,577	24,725,932
Other	102,535	18,082	5,232	12,850	84,453
PERCENTAGE DISTRIBUTION BY SEX.					
Both sexes:					
All classes	100.0	100.0	100.0	100.0	100.0
Negro	100.0	100.0	100.0	100.0	100.0
White	100.0	100.0	100.0	100.0	100.0
Other	100.0	100.0	100.0	100.0	100.0
Male:					
All classes	51.7	78.8	85.7	75.4	20.8
Negro	49.7	61.2	63.7	58.1	21.6
White	51.9	81.6	92.2	77.1	20.6
Other	68.8	91.0	93.8	88.9	33.9
Female:					
All classes	48.3	21.2	14.3	24.6	79.2
Negro	50.3	38.8	36.3	41.9	78.4
White	48.1	18.4	7.8	22.9	79.4
Other	31.2	9.0	6.2	11.1	66.1
PERCENTAGE DISTRIBUTION BY RACIAL CLASS.					
Both sexes:					
All classes	100.0	100.0	100.0	100.0	100.0
Negro	10.2	13.6	22.9	9.0	6.4
White	89.3	85.9	76.5	90.5	93.3
Other	0.5	0.5	0.7	0.5	0.4
Male:					
All classes	100.0	100.0	100.0	100.0	100.0
Negro	9.8	10.6	17.0	6.9	6.6
White	89.6	88.8	82.3	92.5	92.8
Other	0.6	0.6	0.7	0.5	0.6
Female:					
All classes	100.0	100.0	100.0	100.0	100.0
Negro	10.6	24.9	58.2	15.4	6.3
White	89.1	74.8	41.6	84.4	93.4
Other	0.3	0.2	0.3	0.2	0.3
PERCENTAGE DISTRIBUTION BY OCCUPATIONAL GROUP.					
Both sexes:					
All classes	100.0	53.3	17.7	35.6	46.7
Negro	100.0	71.0	39.5	31.4	29.0
White	100.0	51.3	15.1	36.1	48.7
Other	100.0	61.1	25.8	35.3	38.9
Male:					
All classes	100.0	81.3	29.3	52.0	18.7
Negro	100.0	87.4	50.6	36.7	12.6
White	100.0	80.6	26.9	53.7	19.4
Other	100.0	80.8	35.1	45.7	19.2
Female:					
All classes	100.0	23.4	5.2	18.1	76.6
Negro	100.0	54.7	28.6	26.2	45.3
White	100.0	19.6	2.4	17.2	80.4
Other	100.0	17.6	5.1	12.5	82.4

[1] Includes age unknown.

Of the gainfully employed population, 61.2 per cent of the Negroes and 81.6 per cent of the whites were males. Of those not gainfully employed, 21.6 per cent of the Negroes and 20.6 per cent of the whites were males.

Of the gainfully employed male population, 10.6 per cent were Negroes and 88.8 per cent were whites. Of the male population not gainfully employed, 6.6 per cent were Negroes and 92.8 per cent were whites. Of the gainfully employed females, 24.9 per cent were Negroes and 74.8 per cent were whites, and of the not gainfully employed females, 6.3 per cent were Negroes and 93.4 per cent were whites.

The proportion gainfully employed in the male population 10 years of age and over was 87.4 per cent for Negroes and 80.6 per cent for whites. In the female population the correpsonding proportion was 54.7 per cent for Negroes and 19.6 per cent for whites, the proportion gainfully employed among Negro females being markedly higher than among white females.

COMPARISON OF 1910 WITH 1900 AND 1890.

The occupational classification of the Thirteenth Census differs materially from that of preceding censuses, and in making comparisons of 1910 with earlier years it is necessary to recompile the 1910 data, so as to create comparable occupational groups. This has been done in Table 20 (pp. 526 to 527), which classifies Negroes 10 years of age and over gainfully employed in 1910, 1900, and 1890, by sex and occupation, according to the 1900 scheme of occupational classification.

In the Negro population both male and female the proportion gainfully employed increased in each of the last two decades, among males from 79.4 per cent in 1890 to 84.1 per cent in 1900, and to 87.4 per cent in 1910; and among females from 36.2 per cent in 1890 to 40.7 per cent in 1900, and to 54.7 per cent in 1910.

During this period the proportion engaged in agricultural pursuits, as defined by the 1900 classification, remained practically unchanged among Negro males, the percentage in such pursuits being 49.2 in 1890, 49.1 in 1900, and 50.3 in 1910. Among females the proportion engaged in agricultural pursuits increased from 15.9 per cent in 1890 to 18 per cent in 1900, and to 28.6 per cent in 1910. In the same period the proportion of Negro females engaged in nonagricultural pursuits increased from 20.3 per cent in 1890 to 22.7 per cent in 1900 and to 26.2 in 1910; and the proportion not gainfully employed among Negro females 10 years of age and over declined from 63.8 per cent in 1890 to 59.3 per cent in 1900 and to 45.3 per cent in 1910. Table 3 summarizes the general changes which took place during the two decades 1890–1900 and 1900–1910, as regards the gainful employment of Negro males and females.

GAINFULLY EMPLOYED IN AGRICULTURAL AND IN OTHER PURSUITS, AND NOT GAINFULLY EMPLOYED—NUMBER AND PERCENTAGE OF NEGRO MALES AND FEMALES: 1910, 1900, AND 1890.

Table 3

OCCUPATIONAL GROUP.	NEGRO POPULATION 10 YEARS OF AGE AND OVER.[1]					
	Male.			Female.		
	1910	1900	1890	1910	1900	1890
	NUMBER.					
Total	3,637,386	3,181,650	2,646,171	3,680,536	3,233,931	2,682,801
Gainfully employed						
In agricultural pursuits	3,178,554	2,675,497	2,101,379	2,013,981	1,316,840	971,785
In other pursuits	1,830,424	1,561,153	1,300,658	1,051,030	582,001	427,667
Not gainfully employed	1,348,130	1,114,344	800,721	962,951	734,839	544,118
	458,832	506,153	544,792	1,666,555	1,917,091	1,711,016
	PERCENTAGE DISTRIBUTION BY OCCUPATIONAL GROUP.					
Total	100.0	100.0	100.0	100.0	100.0	100.0
Gainfully employed						
In agricultural pursuits	87.4	84.1	79.4	54.7	40.7	36.2
In other pursuits	50.3	49.1	49.2	28.6	18.0	15.9
Not gainfully employed	37.1	35.0	30.3	26.2	22.7	20.3
	12.6	15.9	20.6	45.3	59.3	63.8

[1] Includes age unknown.

AGRICULTURAL PURSUITS.

It will be obvious from the preceding tables that agricultural pursuits as a group constitute in the case of Negroes as in the case of whites a field of gainful employment of preeminent importance. At each of the three censuses, as shown in Table 3, approximately one-half of the total male Negro population 10 years of age and over were returned on the population schedule as engaged in some form of agricultural employment, the proportion of white males so employed in 1910 being, as is shown in Table 2, 26.9 per cent. More than one-quarter of the Negro females 10 years of age and over in 1910 reported some form of agricultural employment, the corresponding proportion for whites being 2.4 per cent. Of the Negro females gainfully employed more than one-half were returned as engaged in agricultural employment, and nearly one-half—967,837 out of 2,013,981 (see Table 19)—of the total Negro females gainfully employed were returned as "farm laborers."

Table 4 distributes the Negro and white male and female population employed in agriculture in 1910, as engaged in general farming, or in specified lines of agriculture, such as gardening, dairy farming, and fruit growing.

Of the 1,842,238 Negro males reporting agricultural employment in 1910, 1,757,509, or 95.4 per cent, were employed on general farms, the corresponding proportion for white males being 92.5 per cent. Of Negro females employed in agriculture, 99.6 per cent were employed in general farming, the proportion for white females being 96.9 per cent.

Of Negro males in agriculture, 24,345 were engaged in turpentine farming, 15,857 in gardening, 2,490 in dairy farming, and 1,925 in fruit growing. It will be apparent that the several special lines of agricultural employment designated in Table 4 are, as regards numbers employed, relatively insignificant when comparison is made with general farming. None of these lines, except turpentine farming, represents more than a fraction of 1 per cent of Negro males employed in agriculture.

The term "operator" embraces all owners, tenants, renters, and croppers; the term "foreman," all persons managing farms for wages or salaries; and the term "laborer" all other persons working on farms. The number of operators corresponds approximately to the number of farms, for which farm schedules were returned in 1910, and for which data are presented in the succeeding chapter on agriculture. By reference to Table 1 of the chapter on agriculture (p. 553) it will be found that the number of farms operated by Negro farmers in 1910 was 893,370. The number of Negro operators, male and female, as shown in Table 5, is 883,733, or 9,637 less than the number of farms operated by Negroes. The discrepancy is accounted for in part by the fact that some farms are operated by Negro managers, classified in Table 5 as "foremen" and by the further fact that some Negro farmers operate more than one farm.

Table 4

GAINFULLY EMPLOYED IN AGRICULTURE, FORESTRY, AND ANIMAL HUSBANDRY: 1910.

CLASS OF FARM.	Total.	Negro.		White.	Other.	Percentage distribution by class of farm.	
		Number.	Per cent.			Negro.	White.
MALE.							
Total............	10,851,581	1,842,238	17.0	8,929,937	79,406	100.0	100.0
General farm........	10,074,199	1,757,509	17.4	8,261,291	55,399	95.4	92.5
Turpentine farm....	28,647	24,345	85.0	4,289	13	1.3	(1)
Garden.............	152,541	15,857	10.4	129,976	6,708	0.9	1.5
Dairy farm..........	92,478	2,490	2.7	89,784	204	0.1	1.0
Orchard............	61,259	1,925	3.1	53,771	5,563	0.1	(1)
Nursery............	14,486	989	6.8	12,987	510	0.1	0.1
Greenhouse.........	25,109	829	3.3	24,130	150	(1)	0.3
Cranberry bog.......	1,754	446	25.4	1,297	11	(1)	(1)
Vineyard............	2,659	20	0.8	2,315	324	(1)	(1)
Other..............	398,449	37,828	9.5	350,097	10,524	2.1	3.9
FEMALE.							
Total............	1,807,501	1,051,137	58.2	751,132	5,232	100.0	100.0
General farm........	1,779,314	1,047,130	58.9	728,052	4,132	99.6	96.9
Turpentine farm....	320	285	89.1	34	1	(1)	(1)
Garden.............	9,423	2,492	26.4	6,759	172	0.2	0.9
Dairy farm..........	5,438	454	8.3	4,973	11	(1)	0.7
Orchard............	3,347	281	8.4	2,823	243	(1)	0.4
Nursery............	421	125	29.7	292	4	(1)	(1)
Greenhouse.........	2,032	62	3.1	1,965	5	(1)	0.3
Cranberry bog.......	86	13	15.1	73	....	(1)	(1)
Vineyard............	159	....	....	156	3	....	(1)
Other..............	6,961	295	4.2	6,005	661	(1)	0.8

1 Less than one-tenth of 1 per cent.

In Tables 5 and 6 Negro and white males and females employed in agricultural pursuits are classified as operators, foremen, and laborers. The full detail of agricultural pursuits is given in Table 16, by states, for Negro males and females in 1910.

Table 5

GAINFULLY EMPLOYED IN AGRICULTURE, FORESTRY, AND ANIMAL HUSBANDRY: 1910.

CLASS OF FARM AND OF WORKER.	Male.			Female.		
	All classes.	Negro.	White.	All classes.	Negro.	White.
Total..........	10,851,581	1,842,238	8,929,937	1,807,501	1,051,137	751,132
Operator....	5,872,005	803,801	5,042,485	273,149	79,932	192,036
Foreman....	48,338	1,690	46,286	7,776	285	7,466
Laborer.....	4,931,238	1,036,747	3,841,166	1,526,576	970,920	551,630
Farm..........	10,074,199	1,757,509	8,261,291	1,779,314	1,047,130	728,052
Operator......	5,606,789	798,397	4,788,967	257,703	79,308	177,468
Foreman......	34,017	1,277	32,524	7,504	269	7,210
Laborer.......	4,433,393	957,835	3,439,800	1,514,107	967,553	543,374
Turpentine farm..	28,647	24,345	4,289	320	285	34
Operator......	508	112	396	3	1	2
Foreman......	898	146	751	1	....	1
Laborer.......	27,241	24,087	3,142	316	284	31
Garden...........	152,541	15,857	129,976	9,423	2,492	6,759
Operator......	75,481	4,009	69,534	4,413	457	3,918
Foreman......	887	57	794	68	11	57
Laborer.......	76,173	11,791	59,648	4,942	2,024	2,784
Dairy farm.......	92,478	2,490	89,784	5,438	454	4,973
Operator......	59,240	174	59,009	2,576	34	2,540
Foreman......	1,001	14	985	85	1	84
Laborer.......	32,237	2,302	29,790	2,777	419	2,349
Orchard..........	61,259	1,925	53,771	3,347	281	2,823
Operator......	39,702	280	38,272	2,179	26	2,140
Foreman......	1,750	40	1,651	52	1	51
Laborer.......	19,807	1,605	13,848	1,116	254	632
Nursery..........	14,486	989	12,987	421	125	292
Operator......	2,931	20	2,825	79	5	73
Foreman......	682	4	673	33	3	30
Laborer.......	10,873	965	9,489	309	117	189
Greenhouse.......	25,109	829	24,130	2,032	62	1,965
Operator......	7,977	96	7,829	1,051	20	1,029
Foreman......	336	4	329	20	....	20
Laborer.......	16,796	729	15,972	961	42	916
Cranberry bog....	1,754	446	1,297	86	13	73
Operator......	306	2	299	18	1	17
Foreman......	132	1	131	....	....	....
Laborer.......	1,316	443	867	68	12	56
Vineyard.........	2,659	20	2,315	159	....	156
Operator......	1,247	1	1,225	79	....	78
Foreman......	123	....	115	2	....	2
Laborer.......	1,289	19	975	78	....	76
Other............	398,449	37,828	350,097	6,961	295	6,005
Operator [1]...	77,824	710	74,129	5,048	80	4,771
Foreman [2]...	8,512	147	8,333	11	....	11
Laborer [3].....	312,113	36,971	267,635	1,902	215	1,223

1 Includes foresters, forestry owners and managers, apiarists, poultry raisers, stock raisers, and landscape gardeners.
2 Includes forestry foreman and stock farm foremen.
3 Includes corn shellers, grain thrashers, wood sawyers, etc.; ditchers; hay and straw balers; irrigators and ditch tenders; choppers and cutters in lumber camps; inspectors and surveyors; log drivers; sawyers; scalers; teamsters; woodchoppers and tie cutters; fishermen and oystermen; poultry yard laborers; stock herders, drovers, and feeders; gardeners employed by steam railroads; and not specified pursuits.

In Table 5 these classes are shown for each of the special lines of agricultural employment designated in Table 4. Table 5 shows, for example, that of the 1,757,509 Negro males employed in general farming 798,397 were returned as farm operators or farmers, 1,277 as farm foremen or managers, and 957,835 as farm laborers. A similar classification is made for each of the other groups, by sex, and for both Negroes and whites.

In Table 6 the classes of workers for other agricultural employment than general farming have been combined, and are shown in the aggregate in comparison with the numbers for general farming.

Of the total number of Negro males employed in general farming, 45.4 per cent were operators or farmers, 0.1 per cent were foremen or managers, and 54.5 per cent were laborers, the corresponding proportions for whites being 56.5, 0.5, and 43 per cent.

FARM LABORERS ON HOME FARMS AND WORKING OUT: 1910.

Farm laborers are classified in Table 7 as working on "home farms" and "working out." Of the 957,835 Negro male agricultural laborers, 441,203 were employed on home farms in 1910, and 516,632 were working away from the home farm. These two groups constitute in the aggregate 92.4 per cent of the total number of Negro agricultural laborers. Laborers working on home farms constituted 42.6 per cent of all agricultural laborers, and laborers working out 49.8 per cent, the corresponding proportions for white males being 43.9 and 45.6 per cent. Of the Negro female agricultural laborers, 72.5 per cent were working on the home farm, and 27.1 per cent were working out. The proportion working out is much lower in the case of females than in the case of males, and is higher in the case of Negro than of white females.

Table 6	GAINFULLY EMPLOYED IN AGRICULTURE, FORESTRY, AND ANIMAL HUSBANDRY: 1910.					
CLASS OF WORKER.	All classes.		Negro.		White.	
	Male.	Female.	Male.	Female.	Male.	Female.
			NUMBER.			
Total........	10,851,581	1,807,501	1,842,238	1,051,137	8,929,937	751,132
Farm.......	10,074,199	1,779,314	1,757,509	1,047,130	8,261,291	728,052
Other.......	777,382	28,187	84,729	4,007	668,646	23,080
Operator.........	5,872,005	273,149	803,801	79,932	5,042,485	192,036
Farm..........	5,606,789	257,703	798,397	79,308	4,788,967	177,468
Other.........	265,216	15,446	5,404	624	253,518	14,568
Foreman..........	48,338	7,776	1,690	285	46,286	7,466
Farm..........	34,017	7,504	1,277	269	32,524	7,210
Other.........	14,321	272	413	16	13,762	256
Laborer..........	4,931,238	1,526,576	1,036,747	970,920	3,841,166	551,630
Farm..........	4,433,393	1,514,107	957,835	967,553	3,439,800	543,374
Other.........	497,845	12,469	78,912	3,367	401,366	8,256
		PERCENTAGE DISTRIBUTION BY CLASS OF WORKER.				
Total........	1.00.0	100.0	100.0	100.0	100.0	100.0
Farm.......	100.0	100.0	100.0	100.0	100.0	100.0
Other.......	100.0	100.0	100.0	100.0	100.0	100.0
Operator.........	54.1	15.1	43.6	7.6	56.5	25.6
Farm..........	55.7	14.5	45.4	7.6	58.0	24.4
Other.........	34.1	54.8	6.4	15.6	37.9	63.1
Foreman..........	0.4	0.4	0.1	(1)	0.5	1.0
Farm..........	0.3	0.4	0.1	(1)	0.4	1.0
Other.........	1.8	1.0	0.5	0.4	2.1	1.1
Laborer..........	45.4	84.5	56.3	92.4	43.0	73.4
Farm..........	44.0	85.1	54.5	92.4	41.6	74.6
Other.........	64.0	44.2	93.1	84.0	60.0	35.8
		PERCENTAGE DISTRIBUTION BY RACIAL CLASS.				
Total........	100.0	100.0	17.0	58.2	82.3	41.6
Farm.......	100.0	100.0	17.7	58.9	82.0	40.9
Other.......	100.0	100.0	10.9	14.2	86.0	81.9
Operator.........	100.0	100.0	13.7	29.3	85.9	70.3
Farm..........	100.0	100.0	14.2	30.8	85.4	68.9
Other.........	100.0	100.0	2.0	4.0	95.6	94.3
Foreman..........	100.0	100.0	3.5	3.7	95.8	96.0
Farm..........	100.0	100.0	3.8	3.6	95.6	96.1
Other.........	100.0	100.0	2.9	5.9	96.1	94.1
Laborer..........	100.0	100.0	21.0	63.6	77.9	36.1
Farm..........	100.0	100.0	21.6	63.9	77.6	35.9
Other.........	100.0	100.0	15.9	27.0	80.6	66.2

1 Less than one-tenth of 1 per cent.

Table 7	LABORERS EMPLOYED IN AGRICULTURE, FORESTRY, AND ANIMAL HUSBANDRY: 1910.					
CLASS OF LABORER.	Both sexes.		Male.		Female.	
	Negro.	White.	Negro.	White.	Negro.	White.
			NUMBER.			
Total.......	2,007,667	4,392,796	1,036,747	3,841,166	970,920	551,630
Farm............	1,925,388	3,983,174	957,835	3,439,800	967,553	543,374
Home farm..	1,145,353	2,157,872	441,203	1,687,461	704,150	470,411
Working out..	780,035	1,825,302	516,632	1,752,339	263,403	72,963
Other............	82,279	409,622	78,912	401,366	3,367	8,256
		PERCENTAGE DISTRIBUTION BY SEX.				
Total.......	100.0	100.0	51.6	87.4	48.4	12.6
Farm............	100.0	100.0	49.7	86.4	50.3	13.6
Home farm...	100.0	100.0	38.5	78.2	61.5	21.8
Working out..	100.0	100.0	66.2	96.0	33.8	4.0
Other............	100.0	100.0	95.9	98.0	4.1	2.0
		PERCENTAGE DISTRIBUTION BY CLASS OF LABOR.				
Total.......	100.0	100.0	100.0	100.0	100.0	100.0
Farm............	95.9	90.7	92.4	89.6	99.7	98.5
Home farm...	57.0	49.1	42.6	43.9	72.5	85.3
Working out..	38.9	41.6	49.8	45.6	27.1	13.2
Other............	4.1	9.3	7.6	10.4	0.3	1.5

EMPLOYMENT IN AGRICULTURAL PURSUITS: 1910, 1900, AND 1890.

Table 8 is in part reproduced from Table 20, in which the 1910 data relating to occupations have been compiled according to the occupational classification of 1900. In this table the number of Negro males and females engaged in specific agricultural pursuits is shown for the years 1910, 1900, and 1890, with the increases for each of the two decades 1900-1910 and 1890-1900.

The number of "farmers, planters, and overseers" among Negro males increased from 541,300 in 1890 to 799,923 in 1910, the increase in the decade 1890-1900 amounting to 144,857, and in the decade 1900-

1910 to 113,766. Agricultural laborers in the same period among Negro males increased from 729,197 in 1890, to 973,695 in 1910, the decennial increases being 105,241 and 139,257.

Table 8	NEGROES 10 YEARS OF AGE AND OVER GAINFULLY EMPLOYED IN AGRICULTURAL PURSUITS.				
OCCUPATIONAL CLASS.	Number.			Increase.[1]	
	1910	1900	1890	1900–1910	1890–1900
		MALE.			
Total.....................	1,830,424	1,561,153	1,300,658	269,271	260,495
Farmers, planters, and overseers...........	799,923	686,157	541,300	113,766	144,857
Agricultural laborers...........	973,695	834,438	729,197	139,257	105,241
Dairymen....................	2,302	403	485	1,899	−82
Gardeners, florists, nurserymen, etc..	4,663	2,288	5,182	2,375	−2,894
Stock raisers, herders, and drovers...........	2,110	1,289	1,300	821	−11
Lumbermen and raftsmen.....	14,293	6,203	3,738	8,090	2,465
Woodchoppers................	8,707	9,656	7,661	−949	1,995
Turpentine farmers and laborers...................	24,345	20,509	} 11,795	{ 3,836	} 8,924
Other agricultural pursuits.....	386	210		176	
		FEMALE.			
Total.....................	1,051,030	582,001	427,667	469,029	154,334
Farmers, planters, and overseers...........	79,677	71,665	49,366	8,012	22,299
Agricultural laborers...........	970,060	509,687	377,531	460,373	132,156
Dairywomen.................	419	134	181	285	−47
Gardeners, florists, etc.........	508	168	306	340	−138
Other agricultural pursuits.....	366	347	283	19	64

[1] A minus sign (−) denotes decrease.

A striking figure in Table 8 is the increase during the decade 1900–1910 in the number of farm laborers among Negro females. This increase, from 509,687 in 1900 to 970,060 in 1910, amounted to 460,373, and was more than three times the corresponding increase for males. In commenting upon the increase during this decade in the number of women gainfully employed, the 1910 Occupations report recites the following two paragraphs from instructions to enumerators in 1910. It is stated that these instructions "may have resulted in the enumerators returning occupations for women who would not have been considered gainful workers by the Twelfth Census enumerators working under different instructions," and "may have had much to do with the numerous increase between 1900 and 1910 in the number of females returned in agricultural pursuits."

144. Column 18. *Trade or profession.*—An entry should be made in this column for *every* person enumerated. The occupation, if any, followed by a child of any age, or by a woman, is just as important, for census purposes, as the occupation followed by a man. Therefore it must never be taken for granted, without inquiry, that a woman or child has no occupation.

154. *Women doing farm work.*—A woman working regularly at outdoor farm work, even though she works on the home farm for her husband, son, or other relative and does not receive money wages, should be returned in column 18 as a *farm laborer*. Distinguish, however, such women who work on the home farm from those who work away from home, by writing in column 19 either *home farm* or *working out*, as the case may require. Of course,

a woman who herself operates or runs a farm should be reported as a *farmer*, and not as a *farm laborer*.

The corresponding instructions in 1900 were as follows:

154. Column 19. *Occupation.*—This question applies to every person 10 years of age and over who is at work—that is, occupied in gainful labor—and calls for the profession, trade, or branch of work upon which each person depends chiefly for support, or in which he is engaged ordinarily during the larger part of the time. (See par. 223.)

160. If a married woman has a gainful occupation, return the occupation accordingly, whether she does the work at her home or goes regularly to a place of employment, and whether she is regularly or only occasionally so employed. For example, "milliner," "dressmaker," "nurse," etc.

161. In farming sections, where a farm is found that is under the management or supervision of a woman as owner or tenant, return the occupation of such woman as "farmer" in all cases.

It seems probable that a large proportion of the apparent increase in the gainful, and specifically in the agricultural, employment of Negro as of white women in the decade 1900–1910, is to be attributed directly to the fact that instructions to enumerators in 1910 were, as regards women, more specific and comprehensive. While, as is pointed out in the Occupations report, the increase in female farm laborers was general, numerically a large proportion of it was, in fact, "confined to the South, to the Negroes, and to children 10 to 15 years of age." It is remarked further that "the figures indicate that a large proportion of the adult Negro males working on the home farm were returned as 'farmers,' while most of the adult Negro females working on the home farm were returned as 'farm laborers.'" (Thirteenth Census, Vol. IV, p. 27.)

AGRICULTURAL EMPLOYMENT IN THE SOUTH, THE NORTH, AND THE WEST: 1910 AND 1900.

In Table 9 the number of "farmers, planters, and overseers," "farm laborers, home farms," and "farm laborers working out" among Negro males and females is shown by sections and southern divisions for the two years 1910 and 1900. In this table, as in Table 8, the compilation is according to the 1900 occupational scheme.

The number of Negro male farmers, planters, and overseers increased in the South from 672,355 in 1900 to 788,393 in 1910, or 116,038; in the North this class of workers decreased from 13,517 in 1900 to 11,082 in 1910; and in the West increased in the same period from 285 to 448. In this decade the number of Negro male farm laborers working on home farms in the South increased from 358,607 to 437,882, or 79,275, and the number working out from 442,670 to 490,887, or 48,217. It will be apparent from Table 9 that the increase in these several classes of workers during the decade 1900–1910 was practically confined to the South, and that in the South it was widely distributed, each southern division showing increases in the number of farmers and farm laborers, male and female.

Table 9

OCCUPATIONAL CLASS AND YEAR.	United States.	The South.				The North.	The West.
		Total.	South Atlantic division.	East South Central division.	West South Central division.		
NUMBER.				MALE.			
Farmers, planters, and overseers:[1]							
1910................	799,923	788,393	317,039	288,503	182,851	11,082	448
1900................	686,157	672,355	259,087	248,616	164,652	13,517	285
Farm laborers, home farm:							
1910................	441,203	437,882	183,470	158,858	95,554	3,248	73
1900................	363,528	358,607	148,708	130,928	78,971	4,847	74
Farm laborers, working out:							
1910................	516,632	490,887	242,806	124,624	123,457	24,985	760
1900................	465,980	442,670	214,763	130,254	97,653	22,949	361
INCREASE:[2] 1900-1910.							
Farmers, planters, and overseers..............	113,766	116,038	57,952	39,887	18,199	−2,435	163
Farm laborers, home farm................	77,675	79,275	34,762	27,930	16,583	−1,599	−1
Farm laborers, working out................	50,652	48,217	28,043	−5,630	25,804	2,036	399
NUMBER.				FEMALE.			
Farmers, planters, and overseers:[1]							
1910................	79,677	79,134	26,831	34,430	17,873	513	30
1900................	71,665	70,918	25,028	29,397	16,493	722	25
Farm laborers, home farm:							
1910................	704,150	703,915	274,891	282,070	146,954	221	14
1900................	323,295	323,181	126,072	134,873	62,236	113	1
Farm laborers, working out:							
1910................	263,403	262,789	129,744	71,985	61,060	598	16
1900................	185,931	185,745	82,753	63,269	39,723	181	5
INCREASE:[2] 1900-1910.							
Farmers, planters, and overseers..............	8,012	8,216	1,803	5,033	1,380	−209	5
Farm laborers, home farm................	380,855	380,734	148,819	147,197	84,718	108	13
Farm laborers, working out................	77,472	77,044	46,991	8,716	21,337	417	11

[1] Includes farmers, dairy farmers, cranberry growers, dairy farm foremen and managers, farm and plantation foremen and managers, cranberry bog foremen and managers, and poultry raisers.
[2] A minus sign (−) denotes decrease.

In Table 10 the ratio of farmers, planters, and overseers, to farm laborers working out in 1910 and in 1900 is shown by sections.

Table 10

SECTION.	NEGRO FARMERS, PLANTERS, AND OVERSEERS PER 1,000 FARM LABORERS WORKING OUT.			
	Male.		Female.	
	1910	1900	1910	1900
United States..................	1,548	1,473	302	385
The South....................	1,606	1,519	301	382
The North....................	444	589	(1)	(1)
The West.....................	(1)	(1)	(1)	(1)

[1] Number of farm laborers working out, less than 1,000.

Among Negro males in the South in both years the number returned as farmers, planters, and overseers greatly exceeded the number returned as farm laborers working out, the ratio of these classes to one another in 1910 being as 1,606 to 1,000. In the North among males the number of farm laborers working out per 1,000 farmers, planters, and overseers was 444, and

among females in the South it was 301. It is noted in the Occupations report for 1910 that adult Negro male laborers working on farms were returned as farmers in some cases where, if correctly classified, they would have been returned as farm laborers, and that Negro women and girls on farms were more apt to be returned as gainfully employed than were white women and girls similarly occupied, and when so returned were generally classified as farm laborers.

NONAGRICULTURAL EMPLOYMENTS.

The principal nonagricultural occupations of Negro males and females are listed in Table 11, in the order of their numerical importance, the occupations shown being those for which data are given by states for males in Table 17 (pp. 570 to 520), and for females in Table 18 (pp. 521 to 522). In these tables each occupation is listed in which in 1910 at least 2,000 Negro males or females were returned in the United States as a whole. These occupations have been selected from the full list of occupations designated in Table 19, on the basis simply of number of workers.

More than one-third of the total number of Negro women returned as gainfully employed in 1910 were returned in two occupational groups, as either "servants" or "laundresses not in laundries," and for both males and females not employed in agriculture some form of unskilled or semiskilled labor in the various lines of service, trade, and industry was returned in a large majority of cases as the gainful employment. Skilled trades, such as molders, plumbers, machinists, chauffeurs, painters, blacksmiths, masons, barbers, and carpenters, are, however, represented in each case by some thousands of workers, as are also such professional groups as physicians and surgeons, trained nurses, and teachers. In general, employment for males is much more diversified than for females.

Table 11

OCCUPATION AND SEX.	Negroes: 1910.
MALES.	
Total, 10 years of age and over.................................	3,637,386
Gainfully employed...	3,178,554
Agriculture, forestry, and animal husbandry......................	1,842,238
Agriculture...	1,806,767
Forestry..	25,474
Animal husbandry...	9,997
Laborers (general and not specified in building trades, etc.)........	151,494
Servants...	92,277
Laborers (saw and planing mills)................................	91,181
Laborers (steam railroad).......................................	86,380
Porters, not in stores..	51,520
Draymen, teamsters, and expressmen............................	50,689
Operatives (coal mines)...	39,530
Laborers, porters, and helpers in stores..........................	36,906
Waiters..	35,664
Laborers (road and street building and repairing).................	33,914
Deliverymen..	31,168
Carpenters...	30,464
Janitors and sextons...	22,419
Barbers, hairdressers, and manicurists..........................	19,446
Dealers, retail..	17,659
Clergymen...	17,427
Longshoremen and stevedores...................................	16,379
Laborers (brick, tile, and terra-cotta factories)..................	15,792
Firemen (except locomotive and fire department).................	14,927

Table 11—Contd.

OCCUPATION AND SEX.	Negroes: 1910.
MALES—continued.	
Helpers in building and hand trades	14,880
Laborers (blast furnaces and rolling mills)	13,519
Hostlers and stable hands	12,965
Laborers (public service)	12,767
Masons, brick and stone	12,401
Laborers (domestic and professional service)	10,380
Operatives (quarries)	9,938
Blacksmiths	9,727
Semiskilled operatives (saw and planing mills)	9,201
Messenger, bundle, and office boys	8,262
Semiskilled operatives (cigar and tobacco factories)	8,039
Painters, glaziers, and varnishers, building	8,035
Drivers, carriage and hack	7,871
Teachers, school	6,991
Laborers (fertilizer factories)	6,934
Launderers, not in laundry	6,573
Sailors and deck hands	6,503
Elevator tenders	6,276
Laborers (lumberyards)	6,201
Plasterers	6,175
Clerks, clerical service	6,077
Laborers (cigar and tobacco factories)	5,768
Laborers (turpentine distilleries)	5,670
Operatives (iron mines)	5,226
Firemen, locomotive	5,188
Engineers, stationary	4,802
Brakemen	4,719
Chauffeurs	4,674
Tailors	4,652
Laborers (cotton mills)	4,256
Bootblacks	3,842
Laborers (lime, cement, and gypsum factories)	3,828
Soldiers, sailors, and marines	3,734
Laborers (coal yards)	3,705
Shoemakers and cobblers, not in factories	3,695
Laborers (car and railroad shops)	3,645
Restaurant, café, and lunch-room keepers	3,635
Guards, watchmen, and doorkeepers, public service	3,541
Salesmen in stores	3,394
Cleaners and renovators of clothing, etc	3,385
Laborers (street railway)	3,341
Machinists and millwrights	3,296
Builders and building contractors	3,272
Musicians and teachers of music	3,259
Furnacemen, smeltermen, heaters, pourers, etc	3,203
Sawyers	3,151
Laborers (slaughter and packing houses)	2,963
Laborers (charcoal and coke works)	2,895
Mail carriers	2,756
Physicians and surgeons	2,744
Bartenders	2,661
Clerks in stores	2,582
Semiskilled operatives (shoe factories)	2,318
Coopers	2,304
Plumbers and gas and steam fitters	2,285
Switchmen and flagmen, steam railroad	2,125
Molders, founders, and casters of iron	2,156
All other	162,695
FEMALES.	
Total, 10 years of age and over	3,680,536
Gainfully employed	2,013,981
Agriculture, forestry, and animal husbandry	1,051,137
Agriculture	1,050,851
Forestry	34
Animal husbandry	252
Servants	415,416
Laundresses, not in laundries	361,551
Dressmakers and seamstresses, not in factories	38,148
Teachers, school	22,441
Midwives and nurses, not trained	19,508
Operatives in laundries	12,196
Housekeepers and stewardesses	10,021
Keepers of boarding and lodging houses	9,183
Operatives, semiskilled, in cigar and tobacco factories	8,267
Waitresses	7,434
Charwomen and cleaners	7,026
Laborers, general, and not specified, in manufactures	6,163
Barbers, hairdressers, and manicurists	3,782
Dealers, retail	2,994
Keepers of restaurants, cafés, and lunch rooms	2,734
Janitresses and sextons	2,452
Laborers (cigar and tobacco factories)	2,405
Musicians and teachers of music	2,347
Nurses, trained	2,158
All other occupations	26,618

INDUSTRIAL AND TRADE GROUPING OF GAINFUL WORKERS.

In Table 12 males and females returned in 1910 as gainfully employed are classified by industries and trades, without distinction by occupation.

The table shows, for example, that of the 669,921 males working in coal mines in 1910, 40,584 were Negroes, and of the 890 females 39 were Negroes. The specific occupations of these workers are given in Table 22 (p. 529), which shows that the 40,584 Negro males included 28,976 miners, 7,649 laborers, 1,580 drivers, 324 firemen, 290 door tenders, 182 engineers, 157 machinists, 121 blacksmiths, 116 bosses, foremen, or overseers, 107 cutters, and approximately 1,000 workers distributed to other employments, of which 32 are designated.

Workers in coal mines constitute 1 of 120 industrial, trade, or service groups for which totals are given in Table 12, and occupational detail in Table 22.

Table 12

INDUSTRY.	GAINFULLY EMPLOYED.			
	All classes.		Negro.	
	Male.	Female.	Male.	Female.
AGRICULTURE, FORESTRY AND ANIMAL HUSBANDRY	10,857,488	1,808,205	1,842,537	1,051,137
Agriculture	10,484,324	1,801,255	1,806,883	1,050,849
Forestry	178,234	138	25,612	34
Animal husbandry	194,930	6,812	10,042	254
EXTRACTION OF MINERALS, INCLUDING QUARRYING AND PRODUCTION OF SALT, OIL, AND GAS	1,057,408	2,553	62,671	84
Coal mines	669,921	890	40,584	39
Copper mines	45,639	42	282	....
Gold and silver mines	64,268	107	301	2
Iron mines	58,105	83	5,370	9
Lead and zinc mines	23,709	51	278	....
Oil wells and gas wells	55,053	252	264	2
Quarries	93,864	175	10,333	15
Salt mines, wells, and factories	5,733	443	208	2
Mines, other and not specified	41,116	510	5,051	15
MANUFACTURING, INCLUDING HAND TRADES	9,051,683	2,163,714	575,845	81,285
Agricultural implement factories	36,012	1,608	594	2
Automobile factories	101,974	3,784	559	10
Bakeries	126,815	17,967	3,174	274
Blank-book, envelope, tag, paper-bag, etc., factories	10,340	8,891	73	14
Blast furnaces and steel rolling mills	394,275	6,764	18,124	96
Box factories (paper)	8,652	14,324	74	21
Box factories (wood)	15,662	2,325	1,545	66
Brass mills	50,272	3,844	356	5
Breweries	68,229	1,467	877	8
Brick, tile, and terra-cotta factories	112,086	2,039	18,703	111
Broom and brush factories	13,733	2,710	769	15
Building and hand trades	2,796,249	614,570	242,387	45,754
Butter and cheese factories	25,557	1,748	168	8
Button factories	9,530	5,681	39	24
Candy factories	22,036	20,648	665	126
Car and railroad shops	128,588	972	4,402	23
Carpet mills	25,493	14,788	252	27
Charcoal and coke works	25,528	72	5,437	17
Chemical factories (not otherwise specified)	50,748	16,816	2,524	56
Cigar and tobacco factories	115,884	79,486	14,717	10,746
Clock and watch factories	17,319	8,717	49	3
Clothing factories (suits, coats, cloaks, and overalls)	273,172	110,986	8,594	937
Clothing factories (except suits, coats, cloaks, and overalls)	45,319	99,993	304	529
Copper factories	21,694	222	140	1
Corset factories	2,864	13,386	14	23
Cotton mills	210,566	148,268	6,333	833
Distilleries	9,538	1,538	731	8
Electric light and power plants	66,063	2,995	2,604	8
Electrical supply factories	70,660	18,255	383	6
Fertilizer factories	13,754	284	7,648	75
Fish curing and packing	7,715	1,360	291	73
Flour and grain mills	52,682	1,559	2,230	21

Table 12—Continued.

INDUSTRY.	GAINFULLY EMPLOYED.			
	All classes.		Negro.	
	Male.	Female.	Male.	Female.
MANUFACTURING, INCLUDING HAND TRADES—Continued.				
Food factories (not otherwise specified)	26,177	8,774	2,722	1,672
Fruit and vegetable canning	10,627	4,926	238	124
Furniture factories	152,382	7,889	4,090	164
Gas works	51,133	2,117	2,430	9
Glass factories	88,059	6,346	2,377	77
Glove factories	7,648	15,039	15	21
Gold and silver factories	17,076	2,945	79	5
Harness and saddle factories	31,956	1,176	410	11
Hat factories (wool and felt)	29,280	11,514	150	11
Hemp and jute mills	4,223	2,852	212	9
Iron and steel factories (not otherwise specified)	523,909	33,119	5,336	91
Iron foundries	163,989	2,664	6,140	32
Jewelry factories	27,168	9,765	95	12
Knitting mills	36,107	71,907	542	274
Lace and embroidery mills	8,052	17,187	29	136
Laundries	72,421	83,306	3,027	12,332
Lead and zinc factories	16,186	734	381	....
Leather belt, leather case, and pocket-book factories	14,003	3,974	95	2
Lime, cement, and gypsum factories	63,789	948	4,961	25
Linen mills	1,841	1,655	21	18
Liquor and beverage factories (not otherwise specified)	19,804	1,179	1,071	37
Marble and stone yards	64,710	891	1,775	13
Metal industries and factories (not otherwise specified)	253,211	6,954	6,305	68
Oil refineries	28,837	880	1,129	5
Paint factories	11,672	1,946	242	4
Paper and pulp mills	76,834	13,965	1,198	75
Piano and organ factories	35,025	2,769	258	4
Potteries	23,878	5,648	473	4
Powder, cartridge, dynamite, fuse, and fireworks factories	10,260	3,163	121	4
Printing and publishing establishments	278,998	76,676	3,543	515
Rope and cordage factories	8,268	4,463	228	34
Rubber factories	44,203	13,897	236	12
Sail, awning, and tent factories	4,103	1,303	62	5
Saw and planing mills	462,981	3,643	110,453	770
Ship and boat building	66,684	382	4,337	10
Shirt, collar, and cuff factories	19,356	50,767	612	482
Shoe factories	149,118	68,549	2,783	184
Silk mills	42,428	53,844	187	373
Slaughter and packing houses	82,643	5,717	5,105	173
Soap factories	9,560	3,929	188	8
Straw factories	3,002	4,227	21	3
Sugar factories and refineries	16,093	515	821	9
Tanneries	60,604	2,903	2,235	37
Textile dyeing, finishing, and printing mills	34,758	7,981	536	109
Textile mills, not specified	30,504	30,087	420	300
Tin-plate factories	21,848	815	316	1
Tinware and enamel-ware factories	68,481	5,778	1,264	35
Trunk factories	6,882	809	86	2
Turpentine distilleries	9,948	82	7,106	56
Wagon and carriage factories	80,679	2,673	1,962	21
Woodworking factories (not otherwise specified)	106,273	9,045	8,216	452
Woolen and worsted mills	82,585	55,729	277	66
Other and not specified industries	562,418	205,601	34,169	2,419
TRANSPORTATION, INCLUDING POSTAL, EXPRESS, TELEGRAPH AND TELEPHONE SERVICE	3,039,764	159,306	274,565	2,083
Express companies	51,470	1,652	2,073	36
Livery stables	137,337	468	20,963	23
Post	150,742	19,078	5,709	166
Railroads, steam	1,529,842	21,754	128,546	1,243
Railways, electric and street	182,357	2,409	4,278	35
Streets, roads, sewers, and bridges, construction and maintenance of	237,119	509	36,894	11
Telegraph and telephone	159,284	109,623	1,867	155
Truck, transfer, cab, and hack companies	366,530	2,147	41,783	53
Water transportation	219,927	1,626	32,263	358
Transportation (other and not specified)	5,156	40	189	3
TRADE, INCLUDING BANKING, INSURANCE, AND WAREHOUSING	3,466,887	675,680	123,635	8,384
Banking and brokerage	187,553	23,159	3,001	207
Insurance	125,136	27,828	1,947	657
Grain elevators	16,203	460	774	3
Real estate	135,883	16,137	949	146
Stockyards	8,170	206	561	5
Warehouses and cold-storage plants	22,414	1,647	2,365	62
Wholesale and retail trade	2,971,528	606,243	114,038	7,304
SERVICE GROUPS, NOT DISTRIBUTED BY INDUSTRIAL GROUPS	2,618,334	3,266,314	299,301	871,008
Domestic and personal service	1,175,993	2,463,413	234,063	840,480
Professional service	933,165	779,324	39,400	30,071
Public service (not elsewhere specified)	509,176	23,577	25,838	457

PROFESSIONAL SERVICE GROUPS.

The number of Negroes and of whites engaged in specified professional services in 1910 is given in Table 13, together with the population, Negro and white, per person in each specified professional service group.

Relatively to population, the number engaged in professional service in 1910 among whites greatly exceeded the number so engaged among Negroes. Among Negroes the average population per professional person was 146, and among whites 51.

Relatively to population clergymen were more numerous among Negroes than among whites, the population per clergyman being 562 among Negroes, and 815 among whites. Each other profession was relatively to population more numerous among whites than among Negroes, and in a large majority of cases the excess of the ratio of population to professional workers among Negroes over the corresponding ratio among whites was very great.

Table 13

OCCUPATION.	PERSONS IN SPECIFIED PROFESSIONAL SERVICE GROUPS: 1910.			
	Negro.	White.	Population per person in specified professional service group.	
			Negro.	White.
Total, professional service	67,245	1,593,791	146	51
Actors	1,279	26,877	7,684	3,041
Architects	59	16,549	166,572	4,939
Artists, sculptors, and teachers of art	329	33,698	29,872	2,425
Authors, editors, and reporters	247	38,370	39,789	2,130
Authors	27	4,334	363,991	18,858
Editors and reporters	220	34,036	44,672	2,401
Chemists, assayers, and metallurgists	123	16,131	79,901	5,066
Civil and mining engineers and surveyors	237	58,687	41,467	1,393
Civil engineers and surveyors	217	51,786	45,289	1,578
Mining engineers	20	6,901	491,388	11,843
Clergymen	17,495	100,315	562	815
College presidents and professors	242	15,419	40,611	5,301
Dentists	478	39,476	20,560	2,070
Designers, draftsmen, and inventors	96	47,338	102,373	1,727
Designers	30	11,755	327,592	6,953
Draftsmen	47	33,257	209,101	2,458
Inventors	19	2,326	517,251	35,138
Lawyers, judges, and justices	798	113,801	12,315	718
Musicians and teachers of music	5,606	133,605	1,753	612
Photographers	404	31,267	24,326	2,614
Physicians and surgeons	3,077	147,741	3,194	553
Showmen	1,066	18,846	9,219	4,337
Teachers	29,485	569,289	333	144
Teachers (athletics, dancing, etc.)	53	3,875	185,429	21,092
Teachers (school)	29,432	565,414	334	145
Trained nurses	2,433	79,844	4,039	1,024
Veterinary surgeons	122	11,524	80,555	7,092
Other professional pursuits	150	15,306	65,518	5,340
Semiprofessional pursuits	2,144	62,518	4,584	1,307
Abstractors, notaries, and justices of peace	117	7,311	83,998	11,179
Fortune tellers, hypnotists, spiritualists, etc	100	1,482	98,278	55,150
Healers (except physicians and surgeons)	332	6,428	29,602	12,715
Keepers of charitable and penal institutions	124	7,358	79,256	11,108
Officials of lodges, societies, etc	279	7,887	35,225	10,363
Religious and charity workers	501	15,408	19,616	5,305
Theatrical owners, managers, and officials	93	11,209	105,675	7,292
Other occupations	598	5,435	16,434	15,038
Attendants and helpers (professional service)	1,375	17,188	7,147	4,755

The population per physician or surgeon, for example, was 3,194 among Negroes, and 553 among whites; per dentist, 20,560 among Negroes, and 2,070 among whites; per college president or professor, 40,611 among Negroes, and 5,301 among whites; per lawyer, judge, or justice, 12,315 among Negroes and 718 among whites; per musician or teacher of music, 1,753 among Negroes, and 612 among whites; per school teacher 334 among Negroes, and 145 among whites; per trained nurse 4,039 among Negroes and 1,024 among whites.

Judged by standards in the white population, it would appear that each of the professions, with the single exception noted, is undermanned among Negroes

OCCUPATIONS OF FREE COLORED MALES IN 1850.

Table 14, showing for 1850 the occupations of free colored males 15 years of age and over in two states and in two cities, is reproduced from the Compendium of the Seventh Census (pp. 80–81). The table is accompanied by the following comment:

Thus, of the free colored population of New York City, sixty were clerks, doctors, druggists, lawyers, merchants, ministers, printers, students, and teachers, or one in about fifty-five; in New Orleans there were one hundred and sixty-five, or one in eleven, engaged in similar pursuits which may be considered as requiring education. The remainder are mechanics, laborers, and waiters. The "other occupations" include for the most part sweeps, scavengers, etc. Of those engaged in pursuits requiring education, one-third are mulattoes, though the proportion of mulattoes to the whole free colored is between a fourth and a fifth.

In Connecticut there are only twenty individuals engaged in occupations requiring education, or one in one hundred of the whole. In Louisiana the number is one hundred and eighty-five, or one in twelve of the whole free colored. The ratios of black and mulatto may also be studied to advantage in the several occupations.

OCCUPATIONS OF FREE COLORED MALES 15 YEARS OF AGE AND OVER IN TWO STATES AND IN TWO CITIES: 1850.

Table 14

OCCUPATION.	CONNECTICUT. Total.	Blacks.	Mulattoes.	LOUISIANA. Total.	Blacks.	Mulattoes.	NEW YORK CITY. Total.	Blacks.	Mulattoes.	NEW ORLEANS. Total.	Blacks.	Mulattoes.
Total	1,973	1,572	401	2,809	492	2,317	3,337	2,617	720	1,792	329	1,463
Apprentices	1		1	11	1	10	2	2		4		4
Architects				1		1				1		1
Bakers				4		4	4	3	1	1		1
Barbers	39	18	21	46	6	40	122	80	42	41	6	35
Barkeepers	1	1		2		2	3	2	1	2		2
Basket makers	10	8	2									
Blacksmiths	12	8	4	26	6	20	1		1	15	4	11
Boarding-house keepers	5	4	1	18	1	17	21	15	6	18	1	17
Boatmen	5	4	1	39	7	32	28	25	3	37	5	32
Bookbinders				4		4				4		4
Brickmakers	1	1		3		3				2		2
Brokers				9	1	8				9	1	8
Butchers				25	1	24	33	30	3	18	1	17
Cabinetmakers				24	3	21				19	2	17
Capitalists				4		4				4		4
Carriage makers	2	1	1									
Carmen	13	8	5	39	19	20	39	28	11	39	19	20
Carpenters	4	3	1	521	74	447	12	10	2	355	56	299
Cigar makers				169	14	155	8	6	2	156	13	143
Clerks	4	1	3	63		63	7	3	4	61		61
Clothiers	1	1		1	1							
Collectors				2		2				2		2
Colliers	5	3	2									
Coachmen	16	9	7	12	5	7	107	96	11	10	4	6
Confectioners							2	2				
Cooks	34	24	10	37	18	19	95	78	17	25	7	18
Coopers	2	2		55	18	37	7	7		43	17	26
Daguerreotypists	1	1										
Doctors				6	1	5	9	7	2	4		4
Druggists							3	1	2			
Dyers	3	2	1									
Engineers				4		4				1		1
Farmers	146	122	24	158	10	148	24	12	12			
Gardeners	5	4	1	13	6	7	7	5	2	9	4	5
Gunsmiths	2	2		4		4	1	1		4		4
Hatters				3		3	2	2				
Hostlers	10	9	1	3		3	11	10	1	3		3
Hunters				9	5	4				7	4	3
Ink makers				5	5							
Jewelers				5		5	3	2	1	5		5
Laborers	1,108	914	194	411	139	272	1,144	957	187	179	71	108
Lawyers				4		4						
Lithographers				1		1				1		1
Mariners	316	262	54	22	2	20	434	316	118	10	1	9
Market men				32	8	24	15	13	2	25	6	19
Masons	1	1		325	68	257				278	65	213
Mechanics (generally)	4	4		58	7	51	2	1	1	52	6	46
Merchants	2	1	1	77	8	69	3	2	1	64	6	58
Ministers	12	9	3	1		1	21	12	9	1		1
Musicians	5	3	2	4		4	24	17	7	4		4
Music teachers				1		1				1		1
Overseers				25	3	22				11	1	10
Painters	2	1	1	30	4	26	4	3	1	28	4	24
Peddlers	1	1		9	2	7				9	2	7
Pilots				2		2				2		2
Planters				244	23	221				2		2
Powder makers	2	2										
Printers	1	1					4	2	2			
Sailmakers	1	1		6	1	5				2		2
Servants	108	83	25	4	2	2	808	612	196			
Sextons	1	1		1		1	12	9	3	1		1
Ship carpenters	1	1		6	2	4				6	2	4
Shoemakers	41	28	13	99	18	81	23	18	5	92	16	76
Stevedores				7	1	6				7	1	6
Stewards	4	3	1	11	2	9	44	34	10	9		9
Students	1	1		7		7	1	1		7		7
Tailors	9	2	7	86	3	83	23	18	5	82	3	79
Tanners	1	1										
Teachers				15	1	14	8	6	2	12		12
Upholsterers				8	1	7				8	1	7
Other occupations	30	17	13				207	160	47			

GENERAL TABLES.

Table 15, below, gives, by divisions and states, the number of Negro males and females 10 years of age and over, with the number and percentage gainfully employed in 1910.

Table 16 (pp. 513 to 516) shows detail of agricultural employment, by states, for Negro males and females in 1910.

Table 17 (pp. 517 to 520) gives, by states, the number of Negro males in each occupation in which an aggregate in the country as a whole of at least 2,000 Negro males were employed in 1910, and Table 18 (pp. 521 to 522), gives similar data for Negro females.

Table 19 (pp. 523 to 525) classifies Negro males and females 10 years of age and over in 1910, by 428 occupational groups.

Table 20 (pp. 526 to 527) classifies Negro males and females in 1910, 1900, and 1890, according to the occupational scheme of 1900.

Table 21 (p. 528) gives, by states, the number of farmers, planters, and overseers of farm laborers on home farms, and of farm laborers working out, for Negro males and females in 1910 and 1900.

Table 22 (pp. 529 to 551) gives for all classes and for Negroes, by sex, occupational detail for 120 industry, trade, and service groups in 1910. For all occupations except those of agriculture, animal husbandry, and forestry, this is the most detailed tabulation made. Several thousand occupational groups being distinguished by sex, industry, and employment. This detail obviously could not advantageously be extended to classifications for the several states. It provides full detail for any analyses and compilations of Negro employments that may be required in special investigations.

TABLE **15.**—NEGRO MALES AND FEMALES 10 YEARS OF AGE AND OVER ENGAGED IN GAINFUL OCCUPATIONS, BY DIVISIONS AND STATES: 1910.

DIVISION AND STATE.	NEGROES 10 YEARS OF AGE AND OVER: 1910.						DIVISION AND STATE.	NEGROES 10 YEARS OF AGE AND OVER: 1910.					
	Male.			Female.				Male.			Female.		
	Total number.	Engaged in gainful occupations.		Total number.	Engaged in gainful occupations.			Total number.	Engaged in gainful occupations.		Total number.	Engaged in gainful occupations.	
		Number.	Per cent.		Number.	Per cent.			Number.	Per cent.		Number.	Per cent.
UNITED STATES	3,637,386	3,178,554	87.4	3,680,536	2,013,981	54.7	SOUTH ATLANTIC:						
							Delaware	12,886	10,512	81.6	11,891	5,313	44.7
GEOGRAPHIC DIVISIONS:							Maryland	89,335	75,495	84.5	91,119	45,231	49.6
New England	27,389	23,607	86.2	27,932	13,899	49.8	District of Columbia	35,540	28,937	81.4	44,424	26,699	60.1
Middle Atlantic	171,008	148,638	86.9	180,538	94,457	52.3	Virginia	243,957	205,093	84.1	252,461	102,729	40.7
East North Central	133,614	113,526	85.0	120,931	46,813	38.7	West Virginia	30,058	26,527	88.3	20,867	6,360	30.5
West North Central	106,567	89,765	84.2	97,074	39,148	40.3	North Carolina	236,640	209,373	88.5	253,755	141,391	55.7
South Atlantic	1,470,297	1,280,335	87.1	1,516,639	828,451	54.6	South Carolina	282,305	250,443	88.7	301,759	201,623	66.8
East South Central	970,921	866,089	89.2	989,977	604,003	61.0	Georgia	415,552	366,612	88.2	430,643	248,924	57.8
West South Central	732,945	634,809	86.6	727,760	378,666	52.0	Florida	124,024	107,343	86.6	109,720	50,181	45.7
Mountain	10,461	9,125	87.2	8,294	3,735	45.0	EAST SOUTH CENTRAL:						
Pacific	14,184	12,660	89.3	11,391	4,809	42.2	Kentucky	105,770	89,018	84.2	104,258	46,510	44.6
							Tennessee	177,698	154,155	86.8	182,965	92,220	50.4
NEW ENGLAND:							Alabama	325,655	295,019	90.6	336,701	214,533	63.7
Maine	610	591	96.9	556	206	37.1	Mississippi	361,798	327,897	90.6	366,053	250,740	68.5
New Hampshire	247	239	96.8	233	128	54.9	WEST SOUTH CENTRAL:						
Vermont	1,089	1,022	93.8	357	123	34.5	Arkansas	165,880	148,088	89.3	161,129	93,248	57.9
Massachusetts	15,629	13,488	86.3	16,089	8,026	49.9	Louisiana	259,937	222,284	85.5	265,513	128,512	48.4
Rhode Island	3,839	3,347	87.2	4,074	2,059	50.5	Oklahoma	53,686	44,793	83.4	47,471	17,659	37.2
Connecticut	5,975	4,920	82.3	6,623	3,357	50.7	Texas	253,442	219,644	86.7	253,647	139,247	54.9
MIDDLE ATLANTIC:							MOUNTAIN:						
New York	55,170	49,205	89.2	60,673	34,782	57.3	Montana	963	819	85.0	670	312	46.6
New Jersey	36,191	30,918	85.4	38,386	20,004	52.1	Idaho	364	335	92.0	214	106	49.5
Pennsylvania	79,647	68,515	86.0	81,479	39,671	48.7	Wyoming	1,442	1,390	96.4	582	283	48.6
EAST NORTH CENTRAL:							Colorado	5,154	4,385	85.1	4,836	2,132	44.1
Ohio	49,297	41,243	83.7	44,613	17,593	39.4	New Mexico	766	672	87.7	578	247	42.7
Indiana	26,258	21,932	83.5	24,392	9,534	39.1	Arizona	892	743	83.3	799	402	50.3
Illinois	49,031	42,624	86.9	43,897	17,105	39.0	Utah	634	555	87.5	392	135	34.4
Michigan	7,727	6,511	84.3	6,830	2,133	31.2	Nevada	246	226	91.9	223	118	52.9
Wisconsin	1,301	1,216	93.5	1,199	448	37.4	PACIFIC:						
WEST NORTH CENTRAL:							Washington	3,473	3,103	89.3	2,044	776	38.0
Minnesota	3,835	3,479	90.7	2,531	923	36.5	Oregon	838	810	96.7	521	230	44.1
Iowa	6,813	5,843	85.8	5,567	1,781	32.0	California	9,873	8,747	88.6	8,826	3,803	43.1
Missouri	68,113	57,984	85.1	64,272	28,796	44.8							
North Dakota	348	309	88.8	198	86	43.4							
South Dakota	404	337	83.4	293	91	31.1							
Nebraska	3,751	3,366	89.7	2,974	1,175	39.5							
Kansas	23,303	18,447	79.2	21,239	6,296	29.6							

TABLE 16.—NEGRO MALES AND FEMALES 10 YEARS OF AGE AND OVER GAINFULLY EMPLOYED IN AGRICULTURE, FORESTRY, AND ANIMAL HUSBANDRY, BY STATES: 1910.

OCCUPATION.	UNITED STATES. Both sexes.	Male.	Female.	ALABAMA. Male.	Female.	ARIZONA. Male.	Female.	ARKANSAS. Male.	Female.	CALIFORNIA. Male.	Female.	COLORADO. Male.	Female.
Agriculture, forestry, and animal husbandry...	2,893,375	1,842,238	1,051,137	201,852	152,054	65	1	108,709	68,790	768	21	262	8
AGRICULTURE	2,857,618	1,806,767	1,050,851	199,897	152,042	43	1	107,069	68,777	694	19	250	7
Dairy farms:													
Farmers	208	174	34	5				6	3	3		2	
Foremen	15	14	1										
Laborers	2,721	2,302	419	141	63			36	17	15		1	
Farms:[1]													
Farmers	877,818	798,509	79,309	95,500	13,096	5		57,669	5,568	109	6	87	4
Foremen	1,692	1,423	269	86	19			52	26	5	1	1	
Laborers—													
Home farm	1,145,353	441,203	704,150	58,152	102,838	1		28,855	49,511	16	3	11	1
Working out	780,035	516,632	263,403	42,761	35,803	24		19,956	13,570	344	2	128	2
Turpentine farms	24,371	24,087	284	2,034	24								
Gardens and greenhouses:													
Florists	116	96	20	1	2								
Gardeners	4,466	4,009	457	151	46	3		86	19	12		3	
Foremen	72	61	11	1				10	7				
Laborers—													
Gardens	13,825	11,801	2,024	715	96	3		289	49	133	5	11	
Greenhouses	771	729	42	35	1			10	1	2			
Orchards, nurseries, etc.:													
Fruit growers and nurserymen	335	303	32	7			1	5	1	15	1	3	
Foremen	49	45	4	3						1	1		
Laborers	2,960	2,589	371	190	54			40	5	36		1	
Other pursuits:													
Corn shellers, hay balers, thrashers, etc.	96	96		1				3					
Cranberry bog laborers	455	443	12										
Ditchers	1,751	1,751		77				36		1			
Landscape gardeners	230	230		27				1		2		2	
Not specified	279	270	9	10			7	15					
FORESTRY	25,508	25,474	34	1,774		1	1	1,478	4	14			
Foresters	17	17						1					
Log and timber camps and lumbering:													
Owners and managers of camps	195	195		24				8					
Foremen and overseers	111	111		3				1					
Lumbermen and raftsmen	14,021	14,005	16	1,028	1			917	4	3			
Teamsters and haulers	2,465	2,465		288				109		1			
Woodchoppers and tie cutters	8,699	8,681	18	431			1	442		10			
ANIMAL HUSBANDRY	10,249	9,997	252	181	11	21		162	9	60	2	12	1
Apiarists	24	23	1	1	1			2					
Fishermen and oystermen	8,268	8,160	108	126	4			135	3	10			
Poultry raisers and poultry yard laborers	368	261	107	5	4			4	4	3	1	1	1
Stock herders, drovers, and feeders	1,387	1,366	21	47	2	16		21		30		7	
Stock raisers	202	187	15	2		5			2	17	1	4	

OCCUPATION.	CONNECTICUT. Male.	Female.	DELAWARE. Male.	Female.	DISTRICT OF COLUMBIA. Male.	Female.	FLORIDA. Male.	Female.	GEORGIA. Male.	Female.	IDAHO. Male.	Female.	ILLINOIS. Male.	Female.
Agriculture, forestry, and animal husbandry....	704	12	5,092	253	387	16	52,348	18,349	258,573	152,513	51	2	4,117	326
AGRICULTURE	673	11	5,048	253	368	16	47,953	18,330	254,814	152,495	46	2	3,972	323
Dairy farms:														
Farmers	2				2		6	1	3	4			2	
Foremen	1								2					
Laborers	23		17		14		67	40	216	74			16	
Farms:[1]														
Farmers	68		794	18	7	2	12,425	1,258	113,655	[1]8,471	24	1	1,311	65
Foremen	9		9		2		110	5	137	25	1		15	1
Laborers—														
Home farm	22		455	107	3	2	6,212	9,834	62,720	98,404	1	1	436	62
Working out	448	9	3,562	113	162	4	14,300	6,891	68,343	45,243	18		1,965	164
Turpentine farms							12,088	137	7,900	96				
Gardens and greenhouses:														
Florists					6		3		7	2			2	1
Gardeners	8		103	3	9	5	408	35	172	28			90	6
Foremen							2		16					
Laborers—														
Gardens	78	1	70	6	104	2	914	98	1,141	57	2		91	20
Greenhouses	4	1	6	5	48	1	37	1	58	1			16	
Orchards, nurseries, etc.:														
Fruit growers and nurserymen	1		14		1		136	4	4	2			7	
Foremen							24		4				1	
Laborers	4		14	1	4		996	21	284	88			11	4
Other pursuits:														
Corn shellers, hay balers, thrashers, etc.							1						2	
Cranberry bog laborers														
Ditchers			3		1		79		130				3	
Landscape gardeners	4		1		5		2		11				2	
Not specified	1						143	5	11				2	
FORESTRY	14		18		4		3,626	9	2,272	6	3		93	
Foresters							2		2					
Log and timber camps and lumbering:														
Owners and managers of camps							28		20					
Foremen and overseers							14		12					
Lumbermen and raftsmen	7		13				1,468	3	778		2		22	
Teamsters and haulers	5						337		245				6	
Woodchoppers and tie cutters	2		5		4		1,777	6	2,215	6	1		65	
ANIMAL HUSBANDRY	17	1	26		15		769	10	487	12	2		52	3
Apiarists							5						1	
Fishermen and oystermen	14	1	23		13		727	7	455	10			20	2
Poultry raisers and poultry yard laborers	2						15	1	8	2			13	
Stock herders, drovers, and feeders	1		3		2		12		22		1		13	
Stock raisers							10	2	2		1		5	1

[1] Includes turpentine farms.

TABLE 16.—NEGRO MALES AND FEMALES 10 YEARS OF AGE AND OVER GAINFULLY EMPLOYED IN AGRICULTURE, FORESTRY, AND ANIMAL HUSBANDRY, BY STATES: 1910—Continued.

OCCUPATION.	INDIANA.		IOWA.		KANSAS.		KENTUCKY.		LOUISIANA.		MAINE.		MARYLAND.	
	Male.	Female.	Male.	Female.	Male.	Female.	Male.	Female.	Male.	Female.	Male.	Female.	Male.	Female.
Agriculture, forestry, and animal husbandry....	2,595	49	475	35	3,109	123	35,989	1,548	140,015	71,858	119	5	31,444	2,103
AGRICULTURE............	2,550	47	434	30	3,064	114	35,637	1,541	135,162	71,844	84	4	29,072	2,084
Dairy farms:														
Farmers....	1		2		1		4		13	2	1		7	
Foremen....			1							1				
Laborers....	26				8		82	4	194	38	1		218	11
Farms:[1]														
Farmers....	710	23	188	12	1,349	64	11,039	444	48,645	5,333	34	2	5,040	173
Foremen....	9	1	3		8		31	4	157	8			57	2
Laborers—														
Home farm....	246	9	58	5	430	9	4,257	599	23,808	37,327	7		2,531	582
Working out....	1,458	11	135	11	1,001	21	19,654	474	59,916	28,906	38	2	19,658	1,099
Turpentine farms....									713					
Gardens and greenhouses:														
Florists....	1		1				5		12				4	
Gardeners....	35		12	2	118	10	118	7	339	31			470	20
Foremen....					1				1				3	
Laborers—														
Gardens....	36	1	17		69	6	366	5	630	143	3		844	132
Greenhouses....	9	2	1		2		29		63	13			41	1
Orchards, nurseries, etc.:														
Fruit growers and nurserymen....	2		3		9	3	2	2	16				6	2
Foremen....									1	1			1	
Laborers....	5				57	1	15	2	97	41			163	62
Other pursuits:														
Corn shellers, hay balers, thrashers, etc.....	3						6		2				4	
Cranberry bog laborers....														
Ditchers....	9		13		6		24		530				24	
Landscape gardeners....					5		4		5				1	
Not specified....									20					
FORESTRY....	19		2		3		79		4,386	4	9		249	3
Foresters....					1		1							
Log and timber camps and lumbering:														
Owners and managers of camps....							1		13		1			
Foremen and overseers....									37					
Lumbermen and raftsmen....	3		1				28		2,801	3	7		93	1
Teamsters and haulers....	3						21		272				34	
Woodchoppers and tie cutters....	13		1		2		28		1,263	1	1		122	2
ANIMAL HUSBANDRY....	26	2	39	5	42	9	273	7	467	10	26	1	2,123	16
Apiarists....							1		1					
Fishermen and oystermen....	4		5		9		12		409	5	26	1	2,074	13
Poultry raisers and poultry yard laborers....	14	2	31	4	7	8	10	6	4	2			18	3
Stock herders, drovers, and feeders....	7		2		16	1	244	1	46	2			30	
Stock raisers....	1		1	1	10		6		7	1			1	

OCCUPATION.	MASSACHUSETTS.		MICHIGAN.		MINNESOTA.		MISSISSIPPI.		MISSOURI.		MONTANA.		NEBRASKA.		NEVADA.	
	Male.	Female.	Male.	Female.	Male.	Female.	Male.	Female.	Male.	Female.	Male.	Female.	Male.	Female.	Male.	Female.
Agriculture, forestry, and animal husbandry...	1,115	42	1,334	52	151	10	268,570	204,024	11,893	394	96	5	206	5	24	3
AGRICULTURE..............	1,053	42	1,286	50	143	10	265,921	204,014	11,722	389	73	5	187	5	18	3
Dairy farms:																
Farmers....	1	1	1	1			3	5	3	1						
Foremen....							2									
Laborers....	16		2				117	47	28				2			
Farms:[1]																
Farmers....	66	4	580	25	60	1	146,309	18,484	3,487	146	28	1	91	5	5	2
Foremen....	2	1	5	2	1	1	146	22	14	7			1			
Laborers—																
Home farm....	15	7	131	12	12	2	77,524	153,772	1,060	69	5	3	10			
Working out....	346	8	487	8	63	6	39,953	31,518	6,862	150	38	1	67		12	1
Turpentine farms....							784	8								
Gardens and greenhouses:																
Florists....	7	1					5	1	1	1						
Gardeners....	14		28	1	4		171	50	98	7			2			
Foremen....								2								
Laborers—																
Gardens....	133	4	22		2		696	90	107	3	2		6	1		
Greenhouses....	7		1	1			22	2	25	3						
Orchards, nurseries, etc.:																
Fruit growers and nurserymen....	2	1	11		1		3		5	2			2			
Foremen....							1		1							
Laborers....	19	2	8				34	13	9				3			
Other pursuits:																
Corn shellers, hay balers, thrashers, etc....			3						4							
Cranberry bog laborers....	423	12														
Ditchers....			7				147		8				3			
Landscape gardeners....	2								10							
Not specified....		1					4									
FORESTRY....	8		40		7		2,457	2	98		13					
Foresters....	4															
Log and timber camps and lumbering:																
Owners and managers of camps....			2		2		17									
Foremen and overseers....							8		1							
Lumbermen and raftsmen....	3		32		3		1,497	1	27							
Teamsters and haulers....			5		1		438		10							
Woodchoppers and tie cutters....	1		1		1		497	1	60		13					
ANIMAL HUSBANDRY....	54		8	2	1		192	8	73	5	10		19		6	
Apiarists....							3									
Fishermen and oystermen....	49		4				140	3	11				1			
Poultry raisers and poultry-yard laborers....	4		1	2	1		7	3	22	4			6			
Stock herders, drovers, and feeders....	1		2				41	2	38		9		9		6	
Stock raisers....			1				1		2	1	1		3			

[1] Includes turpentine farms.

TABLE 16.—NEGRO MALES AND FEMALES 10 YEARS OF AGE AND OVER GAINFULLY EMPLOYED IN AGRICULTURE, FORESTRY, AND ANIMAL HUSBANDRY, BY STATES: 1910—Continued.

OCCUPATION.	NEW HAMPSHIRE.		NEW JERSEY.		NEW MEXICO.		NEW YORK.		NORTH CAROLINA.		NORTH DAKOTA.		OHIO.	
	Male.	Female.	Male.	Female.	Male.	Female.	Male.	Female.	Male.	Female.	Male.	Female.	Male.	Female.
Agriculture, forestry, and animal husbandry...	76	3	5,414	96	124	8	2,805	65	142,028	84,494	83	12	5,226	142
AGRICULTURE	68	3	5,304	95	93	8	2,711	65	137,902	84,470	83	12	5,162	142
Dairy farms:														
Farmers							24		10				5	
Foremen			1				1		3					
Laborers	2		29				88	4	106	18			22	
Farms:[1]														
Farmers	19	2	378	9	35	4	230	15	58,681	4,264	37	9	1,620	64
Foremen	1		20		2		12	1	80	27			9	8
Laborers—														
Home farm	2		177	8	8	3	69	9	37,479	55,090	6	2	405	18
Working out	43	1	3,901	62	42	1	1,820	25	40,366	24,816	40	1	2,727	43
Turpentine farms									61	2				
Gardens and greenhouses:														
Florists			9				2		3	1			2	
Gardeners			59	8	2		22		142	20			106	4
Foremen			1						6	1				
Laborers—														
Gardens	1		610	8	3		367	9	553	203			128	1
Greenhouses			16				31	2	16				46	
Orchards, nurseries, etc.:														
Fruit growers and nurserymen			3				3		2	1			4	1
Foremen			1				2		1					
Laborers			36				23		90	26			36	3
Other pursuits:														
Corn shellers, hay balers, thrashers, etc.			27				1		1				15	
Cranberry bog laborers			20											
Ditchers			5				1		288				32	
Landscape gardeners			9				14		9				4	
Not specified			2			1	1		6				1	
FORESTRY	6		12		4		16		3,465	1			27	
Foresters			1						1					
Log and timber camps and lumbering:														
Owners and managers of camps							1		36				1	
Foremen and overseers			1						14					
Lumbermen and raftsmen	4		6		1		9		2,815				5	
Teamsters and haulers									266				8	
Woodchoppers and tie cutters	2		4		3		6		333	1			13	
ANIMAL HUSBANDRY	2		98	1	27		78		661	23			37	
Apiarists							1		2					
Fishermen and oystermen			70	1			59		634	18			2	
Poultry raisers and poultry yard laborers	1		9				5		3	5			8	
Stock herders, drovers, and feeders	1		18		21		10		20				24	
Stock raisers			1		6		3		2				3	

OCCUPATION.	OKLAHOMA.		OREGON.		PENNSYLVANIA.		RHODE ISLAND.		SOUTH CAROLINA.		SOUTH DAKOTA.		TENNESSEE.	
	Male.	Female.	Male.	Female.	Male.	Female.	Male.	Female.	Male.	Female.	Male.	Female.	Male.	Female.
Agriculture, forestry, and animal husbandry...	26,191	8,068	97	8	4,606	113	337	2	197,431	154,499	105	7	78,276	31,572
AGRICULTURE	25,927	8,064	79	8	4,502	113	301		196,079	154,480	96	6	77,709	31,554
Dairy farms:														
Farmers	1				4				3	3		1	15	6
Foremen									1				1	
Laborers	7	2	1		58		8		75	29			192	25
Farms:[1]														
Farmers	12,991	723	31	4	425	21	27		86,375	9,055	60	5	35,338	2,332
Foremen	14	15			30		2		159	18			38	7
Laborers—														
Home farm	6,330	6,043	14		131	3	4		55,596	100,029	3		18,925	24,861
Working out	6,399	1,262	23	3	3,219	74	217		52,759	45,115	30		22,256	4,190
Turpentine farms									325	2				
Gardens and greenhouses:														
Florists	2	1			9		2		3	1			2	2
Gardeners	69	13			42	2	2		74	16	1		232	25
Foremen					3				4	1			1	
Laborers—														
Gardens	73	4	5	1	369	8	37	2	553	183			513	94
Greenhouses	4				70		2		12	1			35	3
Orchards, nurseries, etc.:														
Fruitgrowers and nurserymen	5		1		3	1	1					3	10	
Foremen			1			1	1							
Laborers	3	1	2		44	3			30	24			102	9
Other pursuits:														
Corn shellers, hay balers, threshers, etc.	1				9								2	
Cranberry bog laborers														
Ditchers	23				5				108		2		24	
Landscape gardeners					79	1							18	
Not specified	4			1	2				2				5	
FORESTRY	212		7		60		1		920	2	1		453	
Foresters					1				2					
Log and timber camps and lumbering:														
Owners and managers of camps			1						9				5	
Foremen and overseers									7					
Lumbermen and raftsmen	105		4		46				669	2			185	
Teamsters and haulers	3		1		5				76		1		114	
Woodchoppers and tie cutters	104		1		8		1		157				148	
ANIMAL HUSBANDRY	52	4	11		44		35	2	432	17	8	1	114	18
Apiarists													1	
Fishermen and oystermen	5				6		35	1	397	6			35	1
Poultry raisers and poultry-yard laborers	1	4			15			1	6	10			16	14
Stock herders, drovers, and feeders	32		6		20				27	1	3		57	2
Stock raisers	14		4		3				2		5	1	5	1

[1] Includes turpentine farms.

TABLE 16.—NEGRO MALES AND FEMALES 10 YEARS OF AGE AND OVER GAINFULLY EMPLOYED IN AGRICULTURE, FORESTRY, AND ANIMAL HUSBANDRY, BY STATES: 1910—Continued.

OCCUPATION.	TEXAS.		UTAH.	VERMONT.		VIRGINIA.		WASHINGTON.		WEST VIRGINIA.		WISCONSIN.		WYOMING.	
	Male.	Female.	Male.	Male.	Female.	Male.	Female.	Male.	Female.	Male.	Female.	Male.	Female.	Male.	Female.
Agriculture, forestry, and animal husbandry....	140,189	77,743	53	87	2	106,184	21,551	260	17	2,332	118	207	15	64	1
AGRICULTURE	138,292	77,723	35	83	2	102,358	21,499	210	16	2,307	118	198	15	35	......
Dairy farms:															
Farmers....................	12			1		26	5	1		1		3	1		
Foremen...................	1														
Laborers..................	138	23		3		328	21	1		3	2	1	1		
Farms:[1]															
Farmers....................	63,222	6,137	14	22	2	38,953	3,407	75	4	578	39	98	5	15	
Foremen...................	63	41				130	24		1	2	2				
Laborers—															
Home farm..............	36,561	54,073	2	8		18,229	10,816	12	3	245	27	16	6	3	
Working out............	37,186	17,322	17	47		42,266	6,418	97	6	1,390	45	71	2	17	
Turpentine farms.......	182	15													
Gardens and greenhouses:															
Florists...................	4					5	7								
Gardeners.................	231	32				556	65	2		12	2	3			
Foremen...................						11									
Laborers—															
Gardens................	467	62	1	1		1,565	732	12		54	1	4			
Greenhouses............	31	2				49	1			1					
Orchards, nurseries, etc.:															
Fruit growers and nurserymen....	1	4				10	2	2	1	4					
Foremen...................						1		1							
Laborers..................	127	10	1	1		83	1	5		15		1			
Other pursuits:															
Corn shellers, hay balers, thrashers, etc.....	8					3									
Cranberry-bog laborers....															
Ditchers..................	30					130		1		1					
Landscape gardeners.......	3					7		1		1					
Not specified.............	25	2				6			1			1			
FORESTRY.....................	1,368	2		4		1,182		42		20		5		2	
Foresters.....................									1						
Log and timber camps, and lumbering:															
Owners and managers of camps....	17					8				1					
Foremen and overseers.....	5					4		1		1		1			
Lumbermen and raftsmen....	677	1		4		688		36		14		4			
Teamsters and haulers.....	99					114				2				1	
Woodchoppers and tie cutters....	570	1				368		4		2				1	
ANIMAL HUSBANDRY.....................	529	18	18			2,644	52	8	1	5		4		27	1
Apiarist......................	5														
Fishermen and oystermen.....	73	1				2,571	31	2		2		2			
Poultry raisers and poultry-yard laborers....	6	8				11	18	2		1					
Stock herders, drovers, and feeders............	399	7	17			56	2	3		2		2		22	1
Stock raisers.................	46	2	1			6	1	1	1					5	

[1] Includes turpentine farms.

TABLE 17.—NEGRO MALES 10 YEARS OF AGE AND OVER GAINFULLY EMPLOYED, BY STATES: 1910.

OCCUPATION.	United States.	Alabama.	Arizona.	Arkansas.	California.	Colorado.	Connecticut.	Delaware.	District of Columbia.	Florida.	Georgia.	Idaho.
Total, 10 years of age and over	3,637,386	325,655	892	165,880	9,873	5,154	5,975	12,886	35,540	124,024	415,552	364
Gainfully employed	3,178,554	295,019	743	148,088	8,747	4,385	4,920	10,512	28,937	107,343	366,612	335
Agriculture, forestry, and animal husbandry	1,842,238	201,852	65	108,709	768	262	704	5,092	387	52,348	258,573	51
Agriculture	1,806,767	199,897	43	107,069	694	250	673	5,048	368	47,953	254,814	46
Forestry	25,474	1,774	1	1,478	14	....	14	18	4	3,626	3,272	3
Animal husbandry	9,997	181	21	162	60	12	17	26	15	769	487	2
Barbers, hairdressers, and manicurists	19,446	877	52	541	222	97	38	46	531	526	1,343	14
Bartenders	2,661	24	8	121	43	24	9	1	67	313	150	2
Blacksmiths	9,727	807	9	426	42	15	17	15	110	340	1,135	1
Bootblacks	3,842	224	10	70	159	22	1	15	66	72	264	5
Brakemen	4,719	791	1	191	3	4	2	1	2	161	586	......
Builders and building contractors	3,272	117	2	101	49	17	12	11	52	93	269	1
Carpenters	30,464	2,601	9	1,120	137	29	59	37	286	2,191	4,537	7
Chauffeurs	4,674	158	1	19	96	25	72	16	133	45	262	2
Cleaners and renovators of clothing, etc	3,385	283	......	123	17	13	3	4	45	140	494	5
Clergymen	17,427	1,230	10	730	86	31	46	95	159	959	1,795	2
Clerks, clerical service	6,077	215	1	93	86	29	48	9	517	128	259	......
Clerks in stores	2,582	122	1	69	21	3	21	13	104	178	166	1
Coopers	2,304	61	......	28	5	1	2	......	7	273	309	......
Dealers, retail	17,659	1,151	6	509	122	30	49	67	613	828	1,733	6
Deliverymen	31,168	1,811	2	856	72	21	211	206	1,399	868	2,640	......
Draymen, teamsters, and expressmen	50,689	2,673	18	1,218	427	101	413	292	1,622	1,818	4,074	3
Drivers, carriage and hack	7,871	525	1	110	10	2	49	24	236	521	928	......
Elevator tenders	6,276	77	1	22	78	35	25	3	309	27	84	......
Engineers, stationary	4,802	261	4	128	32	18	29	26	174	217	216	......
Firemen (except locomotive and fire department)	14,927	1,599	2	490	17	32	23	44	277	655	1,318	1
Firemen, locomotive	5,188	969	1	73	2	8	2	1	7	403	1,007	......
Furnacemen, smeltermen, heaters, pourers, etc	3,203	1,045	......	4	2	4	1	3	2	3	53	1
Guards, watchmen, and doorkeepers, public service	3,541	183	1	152	28	14	17	18	196	166	229	......
Hostlers and stable hands	12,965	518	2	304	96	11	85	129	340	281	697	......
Janitors and sextons	22,419	467	30	240	538	326	266	104	788	210	824	18
Laborers, porters, and helpers in stores	36,906	2,867	10	903	126	97	96	75	1,525	977	3,916	1
Laborers:												
Blast furnaces and rolling mills	13,519	4,730	......	1	16	130	2	201	66	9	334	......
Brick, tile, and terra-cotta factories	15,792	1,027	1	330	56	12	14	129	281	328	1,752	......
Car and railroad shops	3,645	701	......	246	5	1	......	82	......	133	350	......
Coal yards	3,705	110	......	34	5	8	37	101	159	67	227	......
Cotton mills	4,256	465	......	6	......	......	......	9	......	2	995	......
Charcoal and coke works	2,895	689	......	2	......	......	1	1	3	......	1	......
Cigar and tobacco factories	5,768	3	......	1	......	......	5	1	1	51	4	......
Domestic and professional service	10,380	367	8	243	36	15	54	49	274	209	600	2
Fertilizer factories	6,934	575	......	15	1	......	2	19	6	305	1,500	......
General and not specified in manufactures	151,494	6,108	55	3,703	855	426	466	1,057	2,706	8,471	10,280	35
Helpers in building and hand trades	14,880	469	3	252	197	250	24	137	631	189	604	5
Lime, cement, and gypsum factories	3,828	304	......	33	14	21	......	9	49	47	185	......
Lumberyards	6,201	292	1	163	14	3	14	44	185	240	843	......
Public service	12,767	785	5	407	88	26	15	41	1,018	391	1,283	......
Road and street building and repairing	33,914	1,749	4	407	143	46	39	104	2,542	598	3,729	6
Saw and planing mills	91,181	5,402	......	7,391	9	1	7	102	14	6,567	7,598	3
Slaughter and packing houses	2,963	32	1	24	......	......	3	1	9	9	102	......
Steam railroad	86,380	6,091	22	4,471	182	110	25	189	341	3,606	8,876	3
Street railway	3,341	313	......	80	4	5	......	10	71	60	323	......
Turpentine distilleries	5,670	406	......	3	......	......	......	......	......	2,726	1,410	......
Launderers, not in laundry	6,573	458	10	209	24	13	19	13	94	343	766	2
Longshoremen and stevedores	16,379	715	......	5	38	......	35	25	51	1,530	1,683	......
Machinists and millwrights	3,296	311	2	66	46	11	34	10	67	110	261	......
Mail carriers	2,756	194	......	112	24	9	17	9	90	99	272	......
Masons, brick and stone	12,401	976	2	253	81	16	42	15	138	485	1,827	2
Messenger, bundle, and office boys	8,262	439	1	118	54	24	39	47	833	252	977	......
Molders, founders, and casters of iron	2,156	140	2	5	2	4	12	6	2	2	59	......
Musicians and teachers of music	3,259	66	5	66	62	30	15	14	120	60	59	6
Operatives:												
Coal mines	39,530	11,189	......	171	3	297	......	......	1	......	40	1
Iron mines	5,226	3,957	......	......	......	......	1	......	......	......	343	......
Quarries	9,938	1,000	......	142	7	1	11	30	49	138	1,166	4
Semiskilled—												
Cigar and tobacco factories	8,039	59	......	1	7	3	7	1	6	1,488	12	......
Saw and planing mills	9,201	970	......	787	1	......	2	9	6	534	1,094	1
Shoe factories	2,318	......	......	1	2	......	1	1	2	......	21	......
Painters, glaziers, and varnishers, building	8,035	559	......	196	46	8	28	8	144	438	1,128	1
Physicians and surgeons	2,744	113	......	149	12	15	8	4	97	83	173	3
Plasterers	6,175	358	3	78	75	23	3	5	192	175	640	2
Plumbers and gas and steam fitters	2,285	180	1	58	17	9	6	12	74	84	313	1
Porters, not in stores	51,520	1,490	153	1,218	745	637	88	57	984	745	2,451	38
Restaurant, café, and lunch-room keepers	3,635	186	12	108	35	17	16	12	98	141	223	2
Sailors and deck hands	6,503	379	1	106	43	......	4	22	98	318	532	......
Salesmen in stores	3,394	207	1	115	24	31	22	9	64	164	264	......
Sawyers	3,151	203	......	326	1	......	......	5	1	178	277	......
Servants	92,277	4,385	83	2,361	877	321	467	389	2,494	2,417	6,440	47
Shoemakers and cobblers, not in factories	3,695	317	2	104	25	1	8	6	60	118	558	......
Soldiers, sailors, and marines	3,734	22	1	1	58	4	1	3	71	11	41	......
Switchmen and flagmen, steam railroad	2,125	402	......	48	6	9	......	3	4	163	350	1
Tailors	4,652	353	3	171	43	14	11	7	155	379	459	5
Teachers, school	6,991	508	......	440	7	4	2	25	155	195	516	......
Waiters	35,664	772	14	530	465	189	322	162	1,397	856	1,474	14
All other	162,695	9,985	100	4,681	1,008	370	686	971	3,080	7,088	13,336	30

TABLE 17.—NEGRO MALES 10 YEARS OF AGE AND OVER GAINFULLY EMPLOYED, BY STATES: 1910—Continued.

OCCUPATION.	Illinois.	Indiana.	Iowa.	Kansas.	Kentucky.	Louisiana.	Maine.	Maryland.	Massachusetts.	Michigan.	Minnesota.	Mississippi.
Total, 10 years of age and over	49,031	26,258	6,813	23,303	105,770	259,937	610	89,335	15,629	7,727	3,835	361,798
Gainfully employed	42,624	21,932	5,843	18,447	89,018	222,284	591	75,495	13,488	6,511	3,479	327,897
Agriculture, forestry, and animal husbandry	4,117	2,595	475	3,109	35,989	140,015	119	31,444	1,115	1,334	151	268,570
Agriculture	3,972	2,550	434	3,064	35,637	135,162	84	29,072	1,053	1,286	143	265,921
Forestry	93	19	2	3	79	4,386	9	249	8	40	7	2,457
Animal husbandry	52	26	39	42	273	467	26	2,123	54	8	1	192
Barbers, hairdressers, and manicurists	747	570	156	254	725	708	14	444	188	272	157	645
Bar tenders	194	83	8	1	103	157	......	91	6	21	16	6
Blacksmiths	140	70	31	83	419	702	7	121	31	11	6	669
Bootblacks	114	34	24	34	135	181	6	230	33	16	30	120
Brakemen	20	15	3	5	164	356	......	1	8	6	3	397
Builders and building contractors	117	140	15	79	110	193	1	62	29	28	3	84
Carpenters	259	158	26	145	813	2,811	8	383	140	90	9	2,258
Chauffeurs	309	83	19	30	93	108	3	145	165	44	16	20
Cleaners and renovators of clothing, etc	82	38	13	36	100	207	3	25	29	8	1	301
Clergymen	299	215	56	228	649	987	3	414	81	47	14	1,151
Clerks, clerical service	641	74	21	61	108	199	4	123	244	53	31	109
Clerks in stores	89	45	7	32	55	147	3	107	68	4	11	87
Coopers	36	4	1	6	168	504	1	16	15	4	1	47
Dealers, retail	399	190	45	175	542	777	12	782	164	58	15	823
Deliverymen	559	388	50	185	1,538	1,630	3	1,784	331	114	9	1,014
Draymen, teamsters, and expressmen	1,219	718	144	615	1,920	2,554	12	1,917	395	199	46	1,763
Drivers, carriage and hack	74	39	15	17	215	365	1	290	27	21	4	391
Elevator tenders	327	75	14	30	112	45	2	100	224	47	25	22
Engineers, stationary	139	71	22	41	212	302	3	131	85	31	7	151
Firemen (except locomotive and fire department)	488	201	41	64	593	746	2	328	74	30	13	931
Firemen, locomotive	27	5	4	17	29	297	......	4	12	3	2	523
Furnace men, smelter men, heaters, pourers, etc	17	24	1	5	64	3	......	19	1	2	......	......
Guards, watchmen, and doorkeepers, public service	127	55	9	23	99	229	6	67	52	22	7	261
Hostlers and stable hands	213	201	41	117	835	737	6	661	193	31	9	557
Janitors and sextons	1,909	758	224	453	952	215	8	630	722	225	137	231
Laborers, porters, and helpers in stores	855	485	101	339	1,545	1,712		1,880	358	86	79	1,718
Laborers:												
Blast furnaces and rolling mills	380	222	1	2	160	16		1,181	6	5	3	2
Brick, tile, and terra-cotta factories	269	149	29	263	609	618	......	768	21	5	......	628
Car and railroad shops	209	99	......	25	111	31	1	13	4	4	......	231
Coal yards	61	130	12	25	208	216	1	273	112	23	1	61
Cotton mills	......	1	......	......	12	31	2	9	65			54
Charcoal and coke works	3	......	......	1	26	11	......	32	6	......		10
Cigar and tobacco factories	2	25	......	......	1,080	8	......	8	......	2	......	3
Domestic and professional service	327	236	43	112	448	518	6	594	139	28	11	482
Fertilizer factories	3	13	......	......	42	133		643				191
General, and not specified in manufactures	3,984	3,211	657	2,952	7,322	9,581	68	6,674	1,282	684	169	5,567
Helpers in building and hand trades	719	481	117	402	558	409	1	751	144	44	9	216
Lime, cement, and gypsum factories	80	164	17	373	159	44	......	180	4	9	4	22
Lumberyards	188	94	8	33	382	344	......	295	32	10	......	278
Public service	185	193	37	165	341	469	1	300	96	23	10	705
Road and street building and repairing	827	847	105	612	1,614	1,487	4	1,839	87	100	48	672
Saw and planing mills	517	184	11	10	626	16,509	6	704	7	10	7	12,102
Slaughter and packing houses	287	40	41	590	23	56	......	72	18	......	3	21
Steam railroad	1,545	508	189	925	3,988	8,074	9	967	68	42	45	6,085
Street railway	41	128	1	71	281	167	1	31	37	7	3	63
Turpentine distilleries	......				1	143						841
Launderers, not in laundries	111	65	11	58	268	301	1	331	37	6	4	247
Longshoremen and stevedores	187	5	......	......	20	1,588	4	1,933	154	42	......	587
Machinists and millwrights	131	60	7	37	125	116	4	33	102	56	15	109
Mail carriers	152	26	12	27	98	135	2	59	20	18	6	133
Masons, brick and stone	155	129	31	215	477	834	5	110	103	101	11	504
Messenger, bundle, and office boys	180	35	15	29	146	377	3	431	118	25	17	216
Molders, founders, and casters of iron	76	152	5	25	164	16	1	121	22	23	1	3
Musicians and teachers of music	255	71	27	30	112	188	1	138	66	72	50	55
Operatives:												
Coal mines	1,512	376	1,600	619	3,888	4		50	3	41	......	9
Iron mines	1	2	......	......	5	......		22	......	1	7	......
Quarries	329	61	20	367	665	100	2	568	5	4	1	34
Semiskilled—												
Cigar and tobacco factories	33	28	1	......	1,316	215	......	6	9	7	2	1
Saw and planing mills	11	16	1	1	59	1,634	......	44	9	8	1	891
Shoe factories	10	2	2	......	702	43	5	133	204	2	5	......
Painters, glaziers, and varnishers, building	260	66	16	53	220	524	5	93	87	48	13	394
Physicians and surgeons	162	52	15	43	128	127		65	31	11	11	59
Plasterers	180	117	56	169	328	476	1	105	15	44	6	125
Plumbers and gas and steam fitters	71	24	3	38	76	113	2	25	30	12	4	81
Porters, not in stores	4,835	1,145	356	827	1,887	1,988	14	1,054	836	400	940	1,160
Restaurant, café, and lunch-room keepers	115	39	17	55	118	151	4	104	69	13	18	135
Sailors and deck hands	92	81	......	2	177	792	13	750	202	8	......	333
Salesmen in stores	90	49	15	31	68	217	3	80	97	15	7	169
Sawyers	18	12	2	3	43	400		30	9	12		407
Servants	2,646	1,326	290	747	3,862	4,475	44	3,520	1,177	456	310	3,587
Shoemakers and cobblers, not in factories	51	18	4	31	120	145	......	77	25	8	1	162
Soldiers, sailors, and marines	4	5	......	274	8	18	5	70	25	2	......	27
Switchmen and flagmen, steam railroad	25	11	1	25	57	76	......	12	8	......	2	125
Tailors	142	76	7	36	173	281	......	68	50	21	17	155
Teachers, school	74	75	3	70	321	305	......	214	5	6	2	535
Waiters	1,917	642	125	141	998	613	8	2,858	1,192	460	640	512
All other	5,655	3,107	367	1,749	6,111	10,280	135	4,858	1,860	786	273	6,059

TABLE 17.—NEGRO MALES 10 YEARS OF AGE AND OVER GAINFULLY EMPLOYED, BY STATES: 1910—Continued.

OCCUPATION.	Missouri.	Montana.	Nebraska.	Nevada.	New Hampshire.	New Jersey.	New Mexico.	New York.	North Carolina.	North Dakota.	Ohio.	Oklahoma.	Oregon.
Total, 10 years of age and over	68,113	963	3,751	246	247	36,191	766	55,170	236,640	348	49,297	53,686	838
Gainfully employed	57,984	819	3,366	226	239	30,918	672	49,205	209,373	309	41,243	44,793	810
Agriculture, forestry, and animal husbandry	11,893	96	206	24	76	5,414	124	2,805	142,028	83	5,226	26,191	97
Agriculture	11,722	73	187	18	68	5,304	93	2,711	137,902	83	5,162	25,927	79
Forestry	98	13			6	12	4	16	3,465		27	212	7
Animal husbandry	73	10	19	6	2	98	27	78	661		37	52	11
Barbers, hairdressers, and manicurists	767	18	79	8	6	324	16	573	911	9	1,172	367	21
Bartenders	116	8	13			84	6	161	5		131	2	1
Blacksmiths	147	4	13	2	1	49	2	77	640	2	187	132	3
Bootblacks	110	9	10	6	2	76	5	95	164	10	102	36	21
Brakemen	8				1	6		10	305		22	5	
Builders and concrete contractors	101	3	13	1	1	82		103	111	1	255	30	1
Carpenters	309	5	22	6	1	215	2	402	1,979	3	361	448	8
Chauffeurs	326	3	12	1		324	1	663	33		290	11	3
Cleaners and renovators of clothing, etc.	79	3	8			22	5	35	255	1	59	36	
Clergymen	476	6	14	1	1	265	7	243	1,147		324	440	6
Clerks, clerical service	242	3	9	1		142	4	863	154	2	275	30	6
Clerks in stores	56	1	3	1		93		210	116		60	32	3
Coopers	19		2			4		22	77		23	4	
Dealers, retail	413	5	35	7	4	291	5	386	953	1	420	458	7
Deliverymen	1,230	3	43			1,225	8	876	1,364	1	640	90	2
Draymen, teamsters, and expressmen	2,354	25	72	3	10	1,729	13	2,270	2,509	4	1,600	388	12
Drivers, carriage and hack	99		3			367	1	381	709		76	25	1
Elevator tenders	219		11	2		110		3,110	27		197	11	2
Engineers, stationary	100	12	13		1	103	2	424	224		208	47	1
Firemen (except locomotive and fire department)	560	2	31		3	104	9	309	1,265		364	82	
Firemen, locomotive	24	3	3			3		16	485	2	18	11	3
Furnacemen, smeltermen, heaters, pourers, etc.	17					16		15	9		97	3	
Guards, watchmen and doorkeepers, public service	97	1	7			97		178	137		103	17	3
Hostlers and stable hands	547	4	20	1	6	490	1	730	615	7	420	96	3
Janitors and sextons	1,746	66	159	27	4	472	37	1,642	429	10	1,270	410	51
Laborers, porters, and helpers in stores	1,489	11	74	1	3	405	4	1,819	1,015	2	735	302	
Laborers:													
Blast furnaces and rolling mills	283					63		108	60		774	2	
Brick, tile, and terra cotta factories	766	1	22			438		934	1,170		310	213	5
Car and railroad shops	300					1		4	190		81	21	
Coal yards	105	2	15			212		174	66		105	7	
Cotton mills						1		2	682		43	4	
Charcoal and coke works						55			2		61	9	
Cigar and tobacco factories	268					2		8	1,437		6		
Domestic and professional service	332	4	20	1	6	511	3	487	486	3	376	156	3
Fertilizer factories	12					19		8	737		50		
General and not specified in manufactures	7,488	100	321	13	22	3,491	51	3,768	7,650	23	5,395	4,149	46
Helpers in building and hand trades	1,403	9	98	2		784	1	235	301	1	1,059	256	5
Lime, cement, and gypsum factories	314		3			98	2	71	41		120	129	
Lumberyards	61					165		52	387		64	37	1
Public service	232	2	19	1	1	239	6	456	460	1	313	348	3
Road and street building and repairing	1,323	1	139	1		503	2	540	1,687		2,068	1,178	8
Saw and planing mills	202	1				27	3	42	8,647		53	207	6
Slaughter and packing houses	364		178			6		4	13		21	25	2
Steam railroad	2,701	18	48	2	1	180	21	214	5,179	1	843	1,853	24
Street railway	169		4			37		85	85		117	52	
Turpentine distilleries									29				
Launderers, not in laundry	203	3	7	1		150	2	212	323		75	61	1
Longshoremen and stevedores	12					136		1,119	212		11		
Machinists and millwrights	72	1	8	1	3	68	1	182	113	1	167	23	2
Mail carriers	57		9		1	41	3	75	78	2	111	40	2
Masons, brick and stone	236		26	1		198	2	264	1,076	3	345	107	5
Messenger, bundle, and office boys	156	1	5	1		161	1	623	512	1	137	17	4
Molders, founders, and casters of iron	166		1		2	22		37	29		205	2	
Musicians and teachers of music	159	8	25	2	1	100	4	407	44	3	162	41	8
Operatives:													
Coal mines	1,066	3	4			1	78	3	92	2	1,004	737	2
Iron mines	1					32		2	4		1		
Quarries	723	1	1			49	1	73	489		257	48	
Semiskilled—													
Cigar and tobacco factories	112	1	1			12		197	2,005		12	1	
Saw and planing mills	14		2		3	6		14	1,023		9	19	3
Shoe factories	298				5	34		50	1		10		
Painters, glaziers, and varnishers, building	98	2	7	1	1	152		282	575	3	208	54	3
Physicians and surgeons	91	2	13	1		40	1	73	199	1	75	135	1
Plasterers	275	1	43		1	53	1	72	309	2	413	74	1
Plumbers and gas and steam fitters	68		7		1	28	1	71	89		59	38	1
Porters, not in stores	4,332	148	493	33	6	1,255	67	4,329	617	57	2,023	995	157
Restaurant, café, and lunch-room keepers	121	2	15	2	1	91	3	132	152	2	106	150	5
Sailors and deckhands	245					66	2	180	207	1	64	5	1
Salesmen in stores	61	4	16	2		63	1	169	169		81	106	5
Sawyers	12					7		8	296		15	4	
Servants	2,942	73	254	17	24	3,404	87	5,801	4,040	22	2,381	1,465	74
Shoemakers and cobblers, not in factories	36	4	4			38	1	53	346		43	56	1
Soldiers, sailors, and marines	23	9	4		1	3	8	426	33		9	4	1
Switchmen and flagmen, steam railroad	11	8	2	1	1	24	2	18	75		21	8	1
Tailors	115		12	5		59	5	224	181	3	74	99	4
Teachers, school	262					32	1	35	481		67	288	2
Waiters	1,391	31	350	2	2	2,248	13	2,999	723	8	1,029	355	80
All others	5,389	88	315	44	36	3,001	46	5,465	7,985	31	5,575	1,501	80

TABLE 17.—NEGRO MALES 10 YEARS OF AGE AND OVER GAINFULLY EMPLOYED, BY STATES: 1910—Continued.

OCCUPATION.	Pennsylvania.	Rhode Island.	South Carolina.	South Dakota.	Tennessee.	Texas.	Utah.	Vermont.	Virginia.	Washington.	West Virginia.	Wisconsin.	Wyoming.
Total, 10 years of age and over	79,647	3,839	282,305	404	177,698	253,442	634	1,089	243,957	3,473	30,058	1,301	1,442
Gainfully employed	68,515	3,347	250,443	337	154,155	219,644	555	1,022	205,093	3,103	26,527	1,216	1,390
Agriculture, forestry, and animal husbandry	4,606	337	197,431	105	78,276	140,189	53	87	106,184	260	2,332	207	64
Agriculture	4,502	301	196,079	96	77,709	138,292	35	83	102,358	210	2,307	198	35
Forestry	60	1	920	1	453	1,368		4	1,182	42	20	5	2
Animal husbandry	44	35	432	8	114	529	18		2,644	8	5	4	27
Barbers, hairdressers, and manicurists	1,384	43	724	9	1,006	1,068	8	14	1,260	88	329	61	14
Bartenders	75	7	20	1	99	152	16	1	224	30	41	17	3
Blacksmiths	147	6	746	1	742	495	2		1,005	10	97	7	3
Bootblacks	309	14	115	9	155	407	4	6	224	38	45	4	1
Brakemen	11	1	216		268	296			599	2	248	1	
Builders and building contractors	151	3	158	2	307	131	2		201	7	19	1	3
Carpenters	359	15	3,171	1	1,685	1,255	3	5	1,950	25	110	8	3
Chauffeurs	598	44	72		232	107	1		66	7	9	6	1
Cleaners and renovators of clothing, etc	45	2	167	1	269	94	1		298	1	26	4	4
Clergymen	502	16	1,091	1	976	1,473	2	1	971	16	149	7	5
Clerks, clerical service	523	21	69		192	170	2	1	268	16	24	3	4
Clerks in stores	172	14	61		102	114			163	7	18	1	1
Coopers	34	5	51		66	15			485		7	1	
Dealers, retail	962	28	915	2	955	982	1	4	1,611	16	82	15	5
Delivery men	1,871	149	1,195	1	2,280	1,874	4	2	2,473	5	132	7	2
Draymen, teamsters, and expressmen	3,813	217	1,446	1	3,097	3,223	10	4	3,293	68	341	14	12
Drivers, carriage and hack	360	33	546		450	313	1	1	582	3	54	1	
Elevator tenders	454	34	18		135	108	1		112	9	22	10	
Engineers, stationary	374	23	170	1	236	173	2		255	18	106	9	
Firemen (except locomotive and fire department)	599	15	914		949	480		2	1,100	32	126	10	2
Firemen, locomotive	20		465		373	75			263	1	27		
Furnace men, smelter men, heaters, pourers, etc	662		3		310	9			266	1	541		
Guards, watchmen, and doorkeepers, public service	233	19	166		163	154	2	1	163	8	36	5	
Hostlers and stable hands	745	65	491	4	722	820	3	2	942	18	136	7	4
Janitors and sextons	2,158	174	325	10	754	987	15	5	945	157	243	30	18
Laborers, porters, and helpers in stores	1,610	106	1,230	1	3,165	2,223	2	3	2,746	25	149	21	5
Laborers:													
Blast furnaces and rolling mills	2,822	1	22		606	83			1,207	2	18		1
Brick, tile, and terra-cotta factories	841	5	601	1	941	746			1,468	3	38		
Car and railroad shops	59		83		222	297			111	1	29		
Coal yards	399	54	81		164	162		1	276		5	6	
Cotton mills	9	14	1,516		54	38			242				
Charcoal and coke works	238				154	7	1		460		1,122		
Cigar and tobacco factories	12		9		589	6			2,237				
Domestic and professional service	567	13	381	3	512	1,008	1	2	567	18	111	5	3
Fertilizer factories	86		1,229		433	1			911				
General and not specified in manufactures	8,160	370	5,851	34	6,600	12,115	49	21	7,655	195	1,445	102	*67
Helpers in building and hand trades	1,552	18	195	1	606	649	5		902	23	145	4	14
Lime, cement, and gypsum factories	148		35		307	212	1		525	13	86	1	4
Lumber yards	124	16	232		842	428			319		9	1	
Public service	724	11	484		1,344	819	1		657	21	29	8	4
Road and street building and repairing	1,449	18	1,317	2	2,042	1,737	10		1,785	102	66	23	4
Saw and planing mills	75	2	5,386		2,670	7,216		3	8,731	39	77	7	
Slaughter and packing houses	38	1	13		77	809			75	1	4		
Steam railroad	853	30	3,425	4	6,537	8,478	10		7,965	46	2,184	10	22
Street railway	237		53		299	238			251	1	11	4	1
Turpentine distilleries			70			41							
Launderers, not in laundry	167	5	319	1	423	655			509	4	53	2	6
Longshoremen and stevedores	1,428	193	513		23	843			3,279	4	3	1	
Machinists and millwrights	216	19	129	1	198	134	2	2	192	6	32	10	
Mail carriers	105	4	105	2	157	131	1		292	5	19	2	
Masons, brick and stone	299	40	1,183	3	1,104	312	4	3	575	10	78	16	2
Messenger, bundle, and office boys	772	19	367	1	286	302	1	1	463	6	42	4	3
Molders, founders, and casters of iron	106		11		634	27		1	51		3	16	
Musicians and teachers of music	226	10	38	1	103	152	13	1	100	26	24	20	13
Operatives:													
Coal mines	1,773	10	4		1,609	215	6		1,719	114	11,237		47
Iron mines	10				240	4			593				
Quarries	548	13	396		897	232		2	1,097	2	393	2	
Semiskilled—													
Cigar and tobacco factories	150		17	1	382	14			1,918		3	11	
Saw and planing mills	11		451		270	587		1	695	7	3	4	
Shoe factories	15		3		8			4	751	1	2		
Painters, glaziers, and varnishers, building	170	40	1,060	3	413	246	2	2	336	8	25	7	2
Physicians and surgeons	144	4	66		263	168	1	1	127	7	46	4	
Plasterers	235	2	255	2	406	71	8		691	23	58		3
Plumbers and gas and steam fitters	51	5	91		216	170			144		10	1	
Porters, not in stores	2,719	94	716	56	2,933	3,958	86	4	1,422	328	430	138	76
Restaurant, café, and lunch-room keepers	291	16	133		160	252		4	219	12	70	6	2
Sailors and deck hands	132	65	307		366	36			853	5	12	3	
Salesmen in stores	181	11	153	2	155	148			283	9	28	4	1
Sawyers	16		129		149	155			414	2	8	4	1
Servants	5,357	258	3,382	28	5,203	7,355	60	25	5,933	196	1,029	72	74
Shoemakers and cobblers, not in factories	78	6	325		238	93	2		487	5	36		3
Soldiers, sailors, and marines	54	22	29		17	37	1	758	186	652		1	805
Switchmen and flagmen, steam railroad	17		91		254	100			111		51		1
Tailors	122	15	351		221	277	1	3	194	7	49	1	4
Teachers, school	77	1	327	1	420	961			460	1	112		1
Waiters	3,788	95	722	18	1,181	1,444	112	3	2,187	166	366	30	20
All other	8,087	456	5,811	25	12,263	8,088	42	41	13,829	164	1,477	229	52

TABLE 18.—NEGRO FEMALES 10 YEARS OF AGE AND OVER GAINFULLY EMPLOYED, BY STATES: 1910.

OCCUPATION.	United States.	Alabama.	Arizona.	Arkansas.	California.	Colorado.	Connecticut.	Delaware.	District of Columbia.	Florida.	Georgia.	Idaho.
Total, 10 years of age and over	3,680,536	336,701	799	161,129	8,826	4,836	6,623	11,891	44,424	109,720	430,643	214
Gainfully employed	2,013,981	214,533	402	93,248	3,803	2,132	3,357	5,313	26,699	50,181	248,924	106
Agriculture, forestry, and animal husbandry	1,051,137	152,054	1	68,790	21	8	12	253	16	18,349	152,513	2
Agriculture	1,050,851	152,042	1	68,777	19	7	11	253	16	18,330	152,495	2
Forestry	34	1		4						9	6	
Animal husbandry	252	11		9	2	1	1			10	12	
Barbers, hairdressers, and manicurists	3,782	68	8	68	95	47	6	13	168	45	80	1
Charwomen and cleaners	7,026	280	3	94	54	11	42	45	457	155	570	
Dealers, retail	2,994	223	1	99	19	4	5	12	114	122	600	
Dressmakers and seamstresses, not in factory	38,148	2,316	13	1,073	212	86	164	91	1,805	1,995	3,540	5
Housekeepers and stewardesses	10,021	343	12	323	123	60	115	114	181	228	470	2
Janitresses and sextons	2,452	76	2	30	36	20	6	13	87	17	112	
Keepers of boarding and lodging houses	9,183	587	11	527	101	74	30	27	96	467	437	
Keepers of restaurants, cafes, and lunch rooms	2,734	149	5	88	35	26	6	7	86	139	296	2
Laborers, cigar and tobacco factories	2,405									69	2	
Laborers, general, and not specified, in manufactures	6,163	301	3	203	31	18	14	42	55	224	661	3
Laundresses not in laundries	361,551	27,667	130	9,464	734	589	1,056	1,459	7,754	14,312	43,862	19
Midwives and nurses, not trained	19,508	1,875	4	468	91	27	47	48	391	711	2,893	1
Musicians and teachers of music	2,347	100	1	62	30	19	17	6	77	75	128	
Nurses, trained	2,158	139		37	18	3	12	6	91	118	337	1
Operatives in laundries	12,196	631	16	281	128	20	60	38	494	763	1,503	1
Operatives, semiskilled, in cigar and tobacco factories	8,267	2			2		1		2	690	15	
Servants	415,416	24,823	179	10,080	1,763	1,000	1,564	2,937	13,062	9,795	35,628	59
Teachers, school	22,441	1,616	1	883	16	23	14	91	574	721	2,837	2
Waitresses	7,434	153	3	91	60	19	73	44	382	263	245	2
All other occupations	26,618	1,130	9	587	234	78	113	67	807	923	2,195	6

OCCUPATION.	Illinois.	Indiana.	Iowa.	Kansas.	Kentucky.	Louisiana.	Maine.	Maryland.	Massachusetts.	Michigan.	Minnesota.	Mississippi.
Total, 10 years of age and over	43,897	24,392	5,567	21,239	104,258	265,513	556	91,119	16,089	6,830	2,531	366,053
Gainfully employed	17,105	9,534	1,781	6,296	46,510	128,512	206	45,231	8,026	2,133	923	250,740
Agriculture, forestry, and animal husbandry	326	49	35	123	1,548	71,858	5	2,103	42	52	10	204,024
Agriculture	323	47	30	114	1,541	71,844	4	2,084	42	50	10	204,014
Forestry						4		3				2
Animal husbandry	3	2	5	9	7	10	1	16		2		8
Barbers, hairdressers, and manicurists	423	147	37	53	118	105	2	70	80	83	25	51
Charwomen and cleaners	189	93	32	61	137	208	6	394	205	29	8	333
Dealers, retail	44	23	4	27	60	171		112	17	4	6	183
Dressmakers and seamstresses, not in factory	1,163	388	96	244	1,167	2,740	8	1,208	493	125	79	1,843
Housekeepers and stewardesses	371	274	66	188	275	439	11	415	200	62	44	319
Janitresses and sextons	89	50	20	19	119	50	1	107	46	18	5	33
Keepers of boarding and lodging houses	475	161	55	84	275	566		122	185	65	50	548
Keepers of restaurants, cafes, and lunch rooms	108	54	18	53	102	120	1	85	15	15	2	136
Laborers, cigar and tobacco factories		11			240	4		4				
Laborers, general, and not specified	104	60	42	72	144	358		269	22	22	9	421
Laundresses not in laundry	4,935	3,260	498	2,342	18,964	21,184	25	14,667	1,842	398	85	17,913
Midwives and nurses, not trained	129	72	21	52	653	1,179	7	669	94	22	14	1,126
Musicians and teachers of music	174	40	14	43	68	89	1	59	61	25	14	60
Nurses, trained	49	14	2	12	79	99		40	28	8	2	90
Operatives, in laundries	293	118	13	124	301	528	3	579	159	19	19	532
Operatives, semiskilled, in cigar and tobacco factories	4	97			1,410	89		97	1	3	1	
Servants	6,848	4,105	688	2,341	18,886	26,574	108	21,463	3,653	995	409	20,265
Teachers, school	217	167	29	172	1,006	966	5	566	43	19	13	1,872
Waitresses	186	44	21	46	131	130	3	736	135	42	33	123
All other occupations	978	307	90	240	827	1,055	20	1,466	705	127	95	868

TABLE 18.—NEGRO FEMALES 10 YEARS OF AGE AND OVER GAINFULLY EMPLOYED, BY STATES: 1910—Continued.

OCCUPATION.	Missouri.	Montana.	Nebraska.	Nevada.	New Hampshire.	New Jersey.	New Mexico.	New York.	North Carolina.	North Dakota.	Ohio.	Oklahoma.	Oregon.
Total, 10 years of age and over	64,272	670	2,974	223	233	38,386	578	60,673	253,755	198	44,613	47,471	521
Gainfully employed	28,796	312	1,175	118	128	20,004	247	34,782	141,391	86	17,593	17,659	230
Agriculture, forestry, and animal husbandry	394	5	5	3	3	96	8	65	84,494	12	142	8,068	8
Agriculture	389	5	5	3	3	95	8	65	84,470	12	142	8,064	8
Forestry									1				
Animal husbandry	5					1			23			4	
Barbers, hair dressers, and manicurists	268	4	30	1		89	3	344	36		320	33	9
Charwomen and cleaners	194	5	16	2	1	211	1	418	331		258	44	2
Dealers, retail	54	1	3		1	54	1	115		1	48	45	3
Dressmakers and seamstresses, not in factory	729	21	54	4	6	726	5	2,285	1,635	2	944	381	17
Housekeepers and stewardesses	364	13	40	2	7	366	7	622	306	2	445	236	13
Janitresses and sextons	153	5	7		1	53		456	44	1	113	7	2
Keepers of boarding and lodging houses	493	20	35	2	1	207	6	261	216	7	404	224	11
Keepers of restaurants, cafes, and lunch rooms	90	5	11	2		29		93	88	3	82	49	
Laborers, cigar and tobacco factories	8							94	229		3		
Laborers, general, and not specified	147	14	11	3		70		573			124	95	
Laundresses, not in laundry	12,980	48	253	31	17	5,496	64	7,151	22,070	7	5,623	3,425	16
Midwives and nurses, not trained	174	3	8	2	4	172	5	411	1,395	1	149	47	13
Musicians and teachers of music	96	5	6	2		77		201	65	2	125	36	1
Nurses, trained	26	2	4			23		129	115	1	26	13	2
Operatives, in laundries	425	2	30	7	1	180	1	736	586	1	131	89	8
Operatives, semiskilled, in cigar and tobacco factories	28					1		22	2,045		100		
Servants	10,660	138	572	51	76	10,776	137	18,907	23,279	33	7,486	3,860	93
Teachers, school	612		3	1		137	2	121	1,735	3	217	627	4
Waitresses	243	3	27	3	2	848	2	914	137	2	126	66	6
All other occupations	653	18	60	2	8	393	4	1,503	1,897	8	727	314	22

OCCUPATION.	Pennsylvania.	Rhode Island.	South Carolina.	South Dakota.	Tennessee.	Texas.	Utah.	Vermont.	Virginia.	Washington.	West Virginia.	Wisconsin.	Wyoming.
Total, 10 years of age and over	81,479	4,074	301,759	293	182,965	253,647	392	357	252,461	2,044	20,867	1,199	582
Gainfully employed	39,671	2,059	201,623	91	92,220	139,247	135	123	102,729	776	6,360	448	283
Agriculture, forestry, and animal husbandry	113	2	154,499	7	31,572	77,743		2	21,551	17	118	15	1
Agriculture	113		154,480	6	31,554	77,723		2	21,499	16	118	15	
Forestry			2			2							
Animal husbandry		2	17	1	18	18			52	1			1
Barbers, hairdressers, and manicurists	309	11	21	2	133	178	8		99	27	50	12	2
Charwomen and cleaners	689	30	336	6	192	196	1	1	643	9	29	4	1
Dealers, retail	89	1	189	1	130	103			240	2	10	4	
Dressmakers and seamstresses, not in factory	1,673	157	2,376		2,097	1,933	11	5	1,957	55	182	29	10
Housekeepers and stewardesses	906	52	311	4	387	472	3	7	626	42	126	18	9
Janitresses and sextons	256	5	21	1	103	70	2	1	165	4	23	2	1
Keepers of boarding and lodging houses	448	11	141	6	520	693	12	1	268	45	184	14	8
Keepers of restaurants, cafes, and lunch rooms	91	8	148	4	139	134	3	1	173	3	29	2	1
Laborers, cigar and tobacco factories	1		11		232	13			1,578				
Laborers, general, and not specified, in manufactures	222	14	491		184	426	1		561	7	37	10	
Laundresses, not in laundries	7,189	666	19,523	12	25,950	28,070	4	13	27,723	105	1,857	42	57
Midwives and nurses, not trained	338	30	1,418	4	1,385	878	5	5	2,294	30	133	6	4
Musicians and teachers of music	150	14	40	1	110	150	1	1	77	5	12	3	4
Nurses, trained	65	6	116		151	64			211	1	16	1	1
Operatives, in laundries	356	26	295	1	988	815	2		821	9	52	3	8
Operatives, semiskilled, in cigar and tobacco factories	152		50		222	18			3,215				
Servants	24,289	840	18,997	33	24,940	24,152	74	79	34,931	295	3,114	222	157
Teachers, school	244	8	1,560	3	1,369	1,846		1	1,861	14	209	8	3
Waitresses	987	43	162	3	156	290	2	2	355	26	48	7	9
All other occupations	1,104	135	918	3	1,260	1,003	6	4	3,380	80	131	46	7

TABLE 19.—NEGROES 10 YEARS OF AGE AND OVER ENGAGED IN EACH SPECIFIED OCCUPATION, BY SEX: 1910.

OCCUPATION.	Total.	Male.	Female.
Negro population 10 years of age and over	7,317,922	3,637,386	3,680,536
All occupations	5,192,535	3,178,554	2,013,981
AGRICULTURE, FORESTRY, AND ANIMAL HUSBANDRY	2,893,375	1,842,238	1,051,137
Dairy farmers	208	174	34
Dairy farm laborers	2,721	2,302	419
Farmers [1]	877,818	798,509	79,309
Farm laborers	1,949,759	981,922	967,837
Farm laborers (home farm)	1,145,353	441,203	704,150
Farm laborers (working out)	780,035	516,632	263,403
Turpentine farm laborers	24,371	24,087	284
Farm, dairy farm, garden, orchard, etc., foremen	1,828	1,543	285
Dairy farm foremen	15	14	1
Farm foremen [2]	1,692	1,423	269
Garden and greenhouse foremen	72	61	11
Orchard, nursery, etc., foremen	49	45	4
Fishermen and oystermen	8,268	8,160	108
Foresters	17	17	
Gardeners, florists, fruit growers, and nurserymen	5,147	4,638	509
Florists	116	96	20
Fruit growers and nurserymen	335	303	32
Gardeners	4,466	4,009	457
Landscape gardeners	230	230	
Garden, greenhouse, orchard, and nursery laborers	18,011	15,562	2,449
Cranberry bog laborers	455	443	12
Garden laborers	13,825	11,801	2,024
Greenhouse laborers	771	729	42
Orchard and nursery laborers	2,960	2,589	371
Lumbermen, raftsmen, and woodchoppers	25,296	25,262	34
Foremen and overseers	111	111	
Lumbermen and raftsmen	14,021	14,005	16
Teamsters and haulers	2,465	2,465	
Woodchoppers and tie cutters	8,699	8,681	18
Owners and managers of log and timber camps	195	195	
Stock herders, drovers, and feeders	1,387	1,366	21
Stock raisers	202	187	15
Other agricultural and animal husbandry pursuits	2,518	2,401	117
Apiarists	24	23	1
Corn shellers, hay balers, grain thrashers, etc.	96	96	
Ditchers	1,751	1,751	
Poultry raisers and poultry yard laborers	368	261	107
Other and not specified pursuits	279	270	9
EXTRACTION OF MINERALS	61,129	61,048	81
Foremen, overseers, and inspectors	200	200	
Foremen and overseers	190	190	
Inspectors	10	10	
Operators, officials, and managers	146	146	
Managers	17	17	
Officials	3	3	
Operators	126	126	
Coal mine operatives	39,567	39,530	37
Copper mine operatives	272	272	
Gold and silver mine operatives	286	284	2
Iron mine operatives	5,235	5,226	9
Operatives in other and not specified mines	5,067	5,052	15
Lead and zinc mine operatives	259	259	
All other mine operatives	4,808	4,793	15
Quarry operatives	9,953	9,938	15
Oil, gas, and salt well operatives	403	400	3
Oil and gas well operatives	215	214	1
Salt well and works operatives	188	186	2
MANUFACTURING AND MECHANICAL INDUSTRIES	631,377	563,410	67,967
Apprentices	1,854	1,596	258
Apprentices to building and hand trades	853	852	1
Dressmakers' and milliners' apprentices	225		225
Other apprentices	776	744	32
Bakers	2,125	1,928	197
Blacksmiths, forgemen, and hammermen	9,837	9,834	3
Blacksmiths	9,730	9,727	3
Forgemen, hammermen, and welders	107	107	
Boiler makers	475	475	
Brick and stone masons	12,403	12,401	2
Builders and building contractors	3,293	3,272	21
Butchers and dressers (slaughterhouse)	1,099	1,099	
Cabinetmakers	293	292	1
Carpenters	30,468	30,464	4
Compositors, linotypers, and typesetters	1,141	990	151
Coopers	2,305	2,304	1
Dressmakers and seamstresses (not in factory)	38,216	68	38,148
Dyers	255	236	19
Electricians and electrical engineers	703	703	
Electrotypers, stereotypers, and lithographers	41	40	1
Electrotypers and stereotypers	21	21	
Lithographers	20	19	1
Engineers (mechanical)	55	55	
Engineers (stationary)	4,802	4,802	
Engravers	33	29	4
Filers, grinders, buffers, and polishers (metal)	441	434	7
Buffers and polishers	219	213	6
Filers	111	111	
Grinders	111	110	1
Firemen (except locomotive and fire depatmernt)	14,927	14,927	
Foremen and overseers (manufacturing)	1,596	1,548	48

OCCUPATION.	Total.	Male.	Female.
MANUFACTURING AND MECHANICAL INDUSTRIES—Continued.			
Furnacemen, smeltermen, heaters, pourers, etc.	3,206	3,203	3
Furnacemen and smeltermen	2,675	2,672	3
Heaters	136	136	
Ladlers and pourers	53	53	
Puddlers	342	342	
Glass blowers	42	41	1
Jewelers, watchmakers, goldsmiths, and silversmiths	157	153	4
Goldsmiths and silversmiths	37	36	1
Jewelers and lapidaries (factory)	19	18	1
Jewelers and watchmakers (not in factory)	101	99	2
Laborers (not otherwise specified):			
Building and hand trades	172,548	166,374	6,174
General and not specified laborers	157,657	151,494	6,163
Helpers in building and hand trades	14,891	14,880	11
Chemical industries	9,130	9,044	86
Fertilizer factories	7,002	6,934	68
Paint factories	126	126	
Powder, cartridge, fireworks, etc., factories	71	67	4
Other chemical factories	1,931	1,917	14
Clay, glass, and stone industries	22,523	22,357	166
Brick, tile, and terra-cotta factories	15,891	15,792	99
Glass factories	1,704	1,666	38
Lime, cement, and gypsum factories	3,850	3,828	22
Marble and stone yards	737	731	6
Potteries	341	340	1
Iron and steel industries	31,307	31,112	195
Automobile factories	183	180	3
Blast furnaces and rolling mills [3]	13,601	13,519	82
Car and railroad shops	3,664	3,645	19
Wagon and carriage factories	861	855	6
Other iron and steel works	12,998	12,913	85
Other metal industries	826	814	12
Brass mills	115	114	1
Copper factories	92	91	1
Lead and zinc factories	315	315	
Tinware and enamel-ware factories	236	228	8
Other metal factories	68	66	2
Lumber and furniture industries	98,054	97,115	939
Furniture, piano, and organ factories	1,462	1,449	13
Saw and planing mills [4]	91,887	91,181	706
Other woodworking factories	4,705	4,485	220
Textile industries	5,871	5,284	587
Cotton mills	4,663	4,256	407
Silk mills	125	67	58
Woolen and worsted mills	148	129	19
Other textile mills	935	832	103
Other industries	55,895	51,321	4,574
Charcoal and coke works	2,903	2,895	8
Cigar and tobacco factories	8,173	5,768	2,405
Clothing industries	405	357	48
Electric light and power plants	1,143	1,138	5
Electrical supply factories	145	145	
Food industries—			
Bakeries	400	375	25
Butter and cheese factories	88	87	1
Fish curing and packing	271	228	43
Flour and grain mills	1,098	1,088	10
Fruit and vegetable canning, etc.	178	133	45
Slaughter and packing houses	3,080	2,963	117
Sugar factories and refineries	592	584	8
Other food factories	1,963	1,392	571
Gas works	1,671	1,668	3
Liquor and beverage industries	1,384	1,355	29
Oil refineries	905	901	4
Paper and pulp mills	805	772	33
Printing and publishing	689	663	26
Rubber factories	93	92	1
Shoe factories	178	171	7
Tanneries	1,529	1,498	31
Turpentine distilleries	5,719	5,670	49
Other factories	22,483	21,378	1,105
Loom fixers	8	8	
Machinists, millwrights, and toolmakers	3,323	3,322	1
Machinists and millwrights	3,296	3,296	
Toolmakers and die setters and sinkers	27	26	1
Managers and superintendents (manufacturing)	227	218	9
Manufacturers and officials	1,760	1,708	52
Manufacturers	1,727	1,677	50
Officials	33	31	2
Mechanics (not otherwise specified)	752	752	
Gunsmiths, locksmiths, and bellhangers	38	38	
Wheelwrights	90	90	
Other mechanics	624	624	
Millers (grain, flour, feed, etc.)	383	382	1
Milliners and millinery dealers	991	38	953
Molders, founders, and casters (metal)	2,221	2,221	
Brass molders, founders, and casters	55	55	
Iron molders, founders, and casters	2,156	2,156	
Other molders, founders, and casters	10	10	
Oilers of machinery	416	416	
Painters, glaziers, varnishers, enamelers, etc.	8,927	8,915	12
Enamelers, lacquerers, and japanners	24	24	
Painters, glaziers, and varnishers (building)	8,040	8,035	5
Painters, glaziers, and varnishers (factory)	863	856	7
Paper hangers	968	954	14
Pattern and model makers	53	50	3
Plasterers	6,175	6,175	
Plumbers and gas and steam fitters	2,285	2,285	
Pressmen (printing)	136	132	4

[1] Includes turpentine farmers.   [2] Includes turpentine farm foremen.   [3] Includes tin-plate mills.   [4] Includes wooden-box factories.

TABLE 19.—NEGROES 10 YEARS OF AGE AND OVER ENGAGED IN EACH SPECIFIED OCCUPATION, BY SEX: 1910—Contd.

OCCUPATION.	Total.	Male.	Female.	OCCUPATION.	Total.	Male.	Female.
MANUFACTURING AND MECHANICAL INDUSTRIES—Continued.				**MANUFACTURING AND MECHANICAL INDUSTRIES**—Continued.			
				Semiskilled operatives—Continued.			
Rollers and roll hands (metal)	322	322		Other industries	6,969	6,101	868
Roofers and slaters	613	613		Electrical supply factories	42	39	3
Sawyers	3,152	3,151	1	Paper-box factories	49	30	19
Semiskilled operatives (not otherwise specified):				Rubber factories	85	77	8
Chemical industries	764	722	42	Other factories	6,793	5,955	838
Paint factories	69	68	1	Sewers and sewing-machine operators (factory)[4]	1,924	679	1,245
Powder, cartridge, fireworks, etc., factories	20	20		Shoemakers and cobblers (not in factory)	3,739	3,695	44
Other chemical factories	675	634	41	Skilled occupations (not otherwise specified)	113	113	
Cigar and tobacco factories	16,306	8,039	8,267	Annealers and temperers (metal)	20	20	
Clay, glass, and stone industries	2,544	2,489	55	Piano and organ tuners	50	50	
Brick, tile, and terra-cotta factories	1,057	1,048	9	Wood carvers	14	14	
Glass factories	561	524	37	Other skilled occupations	29	29	
Lime, cement, and gypsum factories	496	494	2	Stonecutters	500	500	
Marble and stone yards	341	336	5	Structural-iron workers (building)	80	80	
Potteries	89	87	2	Tailors and tailoresses	5,043	4,652	391
Clothing industries	2,910	2,389	521	Tinsmiths and coppersmiths	884	883	1
Hat factories (felt)	64	59	5	Coppersmiths	15	15	
Suit, coat, cloak, and overall factories	2,231	1,998	233	Tinsmiths	869	868	1
Other clothing factories	615	332	283	Upholsterers	809	784	25
Food industries	3,803	2,391	1,412				
Bakeries	147	124	23	**TRANSPORTATION** [5]	255,969	254,683	1,286
Butter and cheese factories	29	24	5				
Candy factories	480	387	93	Water transportation (selected occupations):			
Flour and grain mills	240	230	10	Boatmen, canalmen, and lock keepers	260	260	
Fruit and vegetable canning, etc	131	52	79	Captains, masters, mates, and pilots	465	465	
Slaughter and packing houses	391	343	48	Longshoremen and stevedores	16,405	16,379	26
Other food factories	2,385	1,231	1,154	Sailors and deck hands	6,508	6,503	5
Harness and saddle industries	277	270	7	Road and street transportation (selected occupations):			
Iron and steel industries	6,094	5,983	111	Carriage and hack drivers	7,878	7,871	7
Automobile factories	62	58	4	Chauffeurs	4,676	4,674	2
Blast furnaces and rolling mills[1]	1,813	1,804	9	Draymen, teamsters, and expressmen[6]	50,711	50,689	22
Car and railroad shops[2]	663	656	7	Foremen of livery and transfer companies	426	426	
Wagon and carriage factories	202	194	8	Garage keepers and managers	33	33	
Other iron and steel works	3,354	3,271	83	Hostlers and stable hands	12,967	12,965	2
Other metal industries	300	258	42	Livery-stable keepers and managers	403	395	8
Brass mills	83	79	4	Proprietors and managers of transfer companies	651	636	15
Clock and watch factories	10	9	1	Railroad transportation (selected occupations):			
Gold and silver and jewelry factories	37	27	10	Baggagemen and freight agents	242	242	
Lead and zinc factories	11	11		Baggagemen	225	225	
Tinware and enamel-ware factories	133	107	26	Freight agents	17	17	
Other metal factories	26	25	1	Boiler washers and engine hostlers	1,328	1,328	
Liquor and beverage industries	471	453	18	Brakemen	4,719	4,719	
Breweries	67	65	2	Conductors (steam railroad)	120	120	
Distilleries	65	61	4	Conductors (street railroad)	44	44	
Other liquor and beverage factories	339	327	12	Foremen and overseers	987	982	5
Lumber and furniture industries	11,941	11,473	468	Laborers	90,560	89,721	839
Furniture, piano, and organ factories	1,212	1,094	118	Steam railroad	87,188	86,380	808
Saw and planing mills[3]	9,322	9,201	121	Street railroad	3,372	3,341	31
Other woodworking factories	1,407	1,178	229	Locomotive engineers	355	355	
Paper and pulp mills	203	163	40	Locomotive firemen	5,188	5,188	
Printing and publishing	491	313	178	Motormen	108	108	
Shoe factories	2,485	2,318	167	Officials and superintendents	39	39	
Tanneries	596	591	5	Steam railroad	37	37	
Textile industries—				Street railroad	2	2	
Beamers, warpers, and slashers	25	13	12	Switchmen, flagmen, and yardmen	2,471	2,469	2
Cotton mills	13	10	3	Switchmen and flagmen (steam railroad)	2,127	2,125	2
Silk mills	8		8	Switchmen and flagmen (street railroad)	33	33	
Woolen and worsted mills	1	1		Yardmen (steam railroad)	311	311	
Other textile mills	3	2	1	Ticket and station agents	50	44	6
Bobbin boys, doffers, and carriers	62	48	14	Express, post, telegraph, and telephone (selected occupations):			
Cotton mills	48	39	9	Agents (express companies)	12	12	
Silk mills	1	1		Express messengers and railway mail clerks	796	796	
Woolen and worsted mills	4	3	1	Express messengers	94	94	
Other textile mills	9	5	4	Railway mail clerks	702	702	
Carders, combers, and lappers	140	123	17	Mail carriers	2,781	2,756	25
Cotton mills	101	88	13	Telegraph and telephone linemen	488	488	
Silk mills				Telegraph messengers	263	262	1
Woolen and worsted mills	7	7		Telegraph operators	73	57	16
Other textile mills	32	28	4	Telephone operators	289	197	92
Drawers, rovers, and twisters	113	74	39	Other transportation pursuits:			
Cotton mills	81	59	22	Foremen and overseers (not otherwise specified)	246	246	
Silk mills	11	2	9	Road and street building and repairing	97	97	
Woolen and worsted mills	4		4	Telegraph and telephone companies	5	5	
Other textile mills	17	13	4	Water transportation	137	137	
Spinners	169	73	96	Other transportation	7	7	
Cotton mills	110	43	67	Inspectors	190	186	4
Silk mills	9	1	8	Steam railroad	178	175	3
Woolen and worsted mills	15	10	5	Street railroad	6	6	
Other textile mills	35	19	16	Other transportation	6	5	1
Weavers	339	162	177	Laborers (not otherwise specified)	40,626	40,489	137
Cotton mills	83	53	30	Road and street building and repairing	33,914	33,914	
Silk mills	75	2	73	Street cleaning	1,009	1,009	
Woolen and worsted mills	14	4	10	Other transportation	5,703	5,566	137
Other textile mills	167	103	64	Proprietors, officials, and managers (not otherwise specified)	59	59	
Winders, reelers, and spoolers	150	35	115	Telegraph and telephone companies	5	5	
Cotton mills	44	12	32	Other transportation	54	54	
Silk mills	80	6	74	Other occupations (semiskilled)	2,552	2,480	72
Woolen and worsted mills	3		3	Steam railroad	2,007	1,960	47
Other textile mills	23	17	6	Street railroad	123	120	3
Other occupations	2,500	1,566	934	Other transportation	422	400	22
Cotton mills	1,030	744	286				
Silk mills	195	60	135				
Woolen and worsted mills	88	69	19				
Other textile mills	1,187	693	494				

[1] Includes tin-plate mills.
[2] Includes car repairers for street and steam railroads.
[3] Includes wooden-box factories.
[4] Includes sewers and sewing-machine operators in all factories except shoe and harness factories, and sack sewers in cement, sugar, and grain mills.
[5] Does not include the 15,116 porters, the 2,396 waiters, and the 2,943 cooks employed by steam railroads: or the 1,247 porters, the 650 waiters, and the 1,537 cooks employed by other transportation companies. These 23,889 workers are reported on page 525, under "Domestic and personal service."
[6] Teamsters in agriculture, forestry, and the extraction of minerals are classified with the other workers in those industries, respectively, and drivers for bakeries and laundries are classified with deliverymen in trade.

TABLE 19.—NEGROES 10 YEARS OF AGE AND OVER ENGAGED IN EACH SPECIFIED OCCUPATION, BY SEX: 1910.—Contd.

OCCUPATION.	Total.	Male.	Female.
TRADE	119,491	112,464	7,027
Bankers, brokers, and money lenders	336	309	27
Bankers and bank officials	135	122	13
Commercial brokers and commission men	76	71	5
Loan brokers and loan company officials	11	11	.....
Pawnbrokers	19	18	1
Stockbrokers	36	32	4
Brokers not specified and promoters	59	55	4
Clerks in stores[1]	3,497	2,582	915
Commercial travelers	332	286	46
Decorators, drapers, and window dressers	46	42	4
Deliverymen	31,196	31,168	28
Bakeries and laundries	659	657	2
Stores	30,537	30,511	26
Floorwalkers, foremen, and overseers	318	309	9
Floorwalkers and foremen in stores	267	258	9
Foremen in warehouses, stockyards, etc	51	51	.....
Inspectors, gaugers, and samplers	890	874	16
Insurance agents and officials	1,833	1,520	313
Insurance agents	1,728	1,419	309
Officials of insurance companies	105	101	4
Laborers in coal and lumber yards, warehouses, etc	12,772	12,711	61
Coal yards	3,708	3,705	3
Elevators	625	624	1
Lumberyards	6,205	6,201	4
Stockyards	531	531	.....
Warehouses	1,703	1,650	53
Laborers, porters, and helpers in stores	37,576	36,906	670
Newsboys	1,221	1,207	14
Proprietors, officials, and managers (not otherwise specified)	205	119	86
Employment office keepers	148	65	83
Proprietors, etc., elevators	8	8	.....
Proprietors, etc., warehouses	23	23	.....
Other proprietors, officials, and managers	26	23	3
Real-estate agents and officials	762	717	45
Retail dealers	20,653	17,659	2,994
Salesmen and saleswomen	5,178	3,680	1,498
Auctioneers	14	14	.....
Demonstrators	45	21	24
Sales agents	420	251	169
Salesmen and saleswomen (stores)	4,699	3,394	1,305
Undertakers	953	907	46
Wholesale dealers, importers, and exporters	241	229	12
Other pursuits (semiskilled)	1,482	1,239	243
Fruit graders and packers	348	168	180
Meat cutters	225	224	1
Other occupations	909	847	62
PUBLIC SERVICE (not elsewhere classified)	22,382	22,033	349
Firemen (fire department)	321	321	.....
Guards, watchmen, and doorkeepers	3,544	3,541	3
Laborers (public service)	13,005	12,767	238
Garbage men and scavengers	1,100	1,100	.....
Other laborers	11,905	11,667	238
Marshals, sheriffs, detectives, etc	246	235	11
Detectives	72	70	2
Marshals and constables	121	121	.....
Probation and truant officers	16	7	9
Sheriffs	37	37	.....
Officials and inspectors (city and county)	251	227	24
Officials and inspectors (city)	182	172	10
Officials and inspectors (county)	69	55	14
Officials and inspectors (state and United States)	426	369	57
Officials and inspectors (state)	33	30	3
Officials and inspectors (United States)	393	339	54
Policemen	576	576	.....
Soldiers, sailors, and marines[2]	3,734	3,734	.....
Other pursuits	279	263	16
Life-savers	12	12	.....
Lighthouse keepers	36	34	2
Other occupations	231	217	14
PROFESSIONAL SERVICE	67,245	37,600	29,645
Actors	1,279	750	529
Architects	59	56	3
Artists, sculptors, and teachers of art	329	201	128
Authors, editors, and reporters	247	219	28
Authors	27	19	8
Editors and reporters	220	200	20
Chemists, assayers, and metallurgists	123	119	4

OCCUPATION.	Total.	Male.	Female.
PROFESSIONAL SERVICE—Continued.			
Civil and mining engineers and surveyors	237	237	.....
Civil engineers and surveyors	217	217	.....
Mining engineers	20	20	.....
Clergymen	17,495	17,427	68
College presidents and professors	242	169	73
Dentists	478	452	26
Designers, draftsmen, and inventors	96	92	4
Designers	30	29	1
Draftsmen	47	45	2
Inventors	19	18	1
Lawyers, judges, and justices	798	796	2
Musicians and teachers of music	5,606	3,259	2,347
Photographers	404	363	41
Physicians and surgeons	3,077	2,744	333
Showmen	1,066	1,006	60
Teachers	29,485	7,035	22,450
Teachers (athletics, dancing, etc.)	53	44	9
Teachers (school)	29,432	6,991	22,441
Trained nurses	2,433	275	2,158
Veterinary surgeons	122	122	.....
Other professional pursuits	150	94	56
Semiprofessional pursuits	2,144	1,389	755
Abstractors, notaries, and justices of peace	117	96	21
Fortune tellers, hypnotists, spiritualists, etc	100	29	71
Healers (except physicians and surgeons)	332	141	191
Keepers of charitable and penal institutions	124	87	37
Officials of lodges, societies, etc	279	183	96
Religious and charity workers	501	169	332
Theatrical owners, managers, and officials	93	91	2
Other occupations	598	593	5
Attendants and helpers (professional service)	1,375	795	580
DOMESTIC AND PERSONAL SERVICE	1,122,231	268,874	853,357
Barbers, hairdressers, and manicurists	23,228	19,446	3,782
Bartenders	2,666	2,661	5
Billiard room, dance hall, skating rink, etc., keepers	1,011	926	85
Billiard and pool room keepers	875	866	9
Dance hall, skating rink, etc., keepers	136	60	76
Boarding and lodging house keepers	10,601	1,418	9,183
Bootblacks	3,850	3,842	8
Charwomen and cleaners	8,644	1,618	7,026
Elevator tenders	6,278	6,276	2
Hotel keepers and managers	973	620	353
Housekeepers and stewards	11,624	1,603	10,021
Janitors and sextons	24,871	22,419	2,452
Laborers (domestic and personal service)	11,087	10,380	707
Launderers and laundresses (not in laundry)	368,124	6,573	361,551
Laundry operatives[3]	14,146	1,950	12,196
Laundry owners, officials, and managers[3]	210	164	46
Midwives and nurses (not trained)	20,536	1,028	19,508
Midwives	1,634	.....	1,634
Nurses (not trained)[2]	18,902	1,028	17,874
Porters (except in stores)[2]	51,538	51,520	18
Restaurant, café, and lunch-room keepers	6,369	3,635	2,734
Saloon keepers	652	636	16
Servants	507,693	92,277	415,416
Bell boys, chore boys, etc	8,212	7,934	278
Chambermaids	14,082	11	14,071
Coachmen and footmen	7,679	7,679	.....
Cooks[4]	238,392	32,453	205,939
Other servants	239,328	44,200	195,128
Waiters	43,098	35,664	7,434
Other pursuits	5,032	4,218	814
Bathhouse keepers and attendants	798	358	440
Cemetery keepers	216	212	4
Cleaners and renovators (clothing, etc.)	3,744	3,385	359
Umbrella menders and scissors grinders	30	28	2
Other occupations	244	235	9
CLERICAL OCCUPATIONS	19,336	16,204	3,132
Agents, canvassers, and collectors	997	782	215
Agents	264	226	38
Canvassers	284	166	118
Collectors	449	390	59
Bookkeepers, cashiers, and accountants	1,675	766	909
Clerks (except clerks in stores)	7,030	6,077	953
Shipping clerks	1,010	996	14
Other clerks	6,020	5,081	939
Messenger, bundle, and office boys[4]	8,553	8,262	291
Bundle and cash boys and girls	105	88	17
Messenger, errand, and office boys	8,448	8,174	274
Stenographers and typewriters	1,081	317	764

[1] Many of the "clerks" in stores evidently are "salesmen and saleswomen."
[2] Includes only those resident in continental United States at the date of the enumeration.
[3] Some owners of hand laundries are included with "laundry operatives."
[4] Except telegraph and telephone messengers.

TABLE 20.—NEGROES 10 YEARS OF AGE AND OVER GAINFULLY EMPLOYED, BY SEX AND OCCUPATION: 1910, 1900, AND 1890—COMPILATION ACCORDING TO OCCUPATIONAL CLASSIFICATION OF 1900.

OCCUPATIONAL CLASSIFICATION.	BOTH SEXES.			MALE.			FEMALE.		
	1910	1900	1890	1910	1900	1890	1910	1900	1890
All occupations	5,192,535	3,992,337	3,073,164	3,178,554	2,675,497	2,101,379	2,013,981	1,316,840	971,785
AGRICULTURAL PURSUITS.									
Total	2,881,454	2,143,154	1,728,325	1,830,424	1,561,153	1,300,658	1,051,030	582,001	427,667
Agricultural laborers	1,943,755	1,344,125	1,106,728	973,695	834,438	729,197	970,060	509,687	377,531
Dairymen and dairywomen	2,721	537	666	2,302	403	485	419	134	181
Farmers, planters, and overseers	879,600	757,822	590,666	799,923	686,157	541,300	79,677	71,665	49,366
Gardeners, florists, nurserymen, etc	5,171	2,456	5,488	4,663	2,288	5,182	508	168	306
Lumbermen and raftsmen	14,309	6,222	3,742	14,293	6,203	3,738	16	19	4
Stock raisers, herders, and drovers	2,147	1,311	1,325	2,110	1,289	1,300	37	22	25
Woodchoppers	8,725	9,703	7,676	8,707	9,656	7,661	18	47	15
Turpentine farmers and laborers	24,630	20,744	12,034	24,345	20,509	11,795	285	235	239
Other agricultural pursuits	396	234		386	210		10	24	
PROFESSIONAL SERVICE.									
Total	66,246	47,219	33,994	38,077	31,625	25,170	28,169	15,594	8,824
Actors, professional showmen, etc	3,088	2,020	1,490	2,464	1,764	1,422	624	256	68
Architects, designers, draftsmen, etc	154	52	44	147	52	44	7		
Artists and teachers of art	329	236	150	201	150	84	128	86	66
Clergymen	17,996	15,528	12,159	17,596	15,364	12,110	400	164	49
Dentists	478	212	120	452	205	118	26	7	2
Electricians, engineers (civil, etc.), and surveyors	970	305	279	970	303	278		2	1
Journalists	220	210	134	200	199	129	20	11	5
Lawyers	915	728	431	892	718	431	23	10	
Literary and scientific persons	315	99	91	240	74	69	75	25	22
Musicians and teachers of music	5,606	3,915	1,881	3,259	2,730	1,287	2,347	1,185	594
Officials (Government)	1,071	645	1,115	940	595	1,090	131	50	25
Physicians and surgeons	3,409	1,734	909	2,885	1,574	794	524	160	115
Teachers and professors in college, etc	29,772	21,267	15,100	7,225	7,743	7,236	22,547	13,524	7,864
Other professional service	1,923	268	91	606	154	78	1,317	114	13
DOMESTIC AND PERSONAL SERVICE.									
Total	1,357,598	1,317,859	956,754	496,101	635,933	450,765	861,497	681,926	505,989
Barbers and hairdressers	22,534	19,942	17,480	19,441	18,958	16,966	3,093	984	514
Boarding and lodging house keepers	10,401	4,187	2,323	1,418	611	537	9,183	3,576	1,786
Hotel keepers	973	481	420	620	329	294	353	152	126
Janitors and sextons	24,871	11,536	5,945	22,419	10,676	5,500	2,452	860	445
Laborers (not specified)	246,240	545,935	349,002	238,985	463,492	310,733	7,255	82,443	38,269
Launderers and laundresses	382,510	220,104	153,684	8,691	1,877	2,144	373,819	218,227	151,540
Nurses and midwives	22,969	19,431	5,213	1,303	759	323	21,666	18,672	4,890
Restaurant keepers	6,369	3,993	2,157	3,635	2,697	1,606	2,734	1,296	551
Saloon keepers	1,663	890	932	1,562	869	862	101	21	70
Bartenders	2,666	2,472	1,878	2,661	2,450	1,874	5	22	4
Servants and waiters	605,506	465,734	401,215	175,643	120,361	101,742	429,863	345,373	299,473
Housekeepers and stewards	11,624	10,596	9,248	1,603	1,190	1,144	10,021	9,406	8,104
Soldiers, sailors, and marines (United States)	3,734	3,498	2,782	3,734	3,498	2,782			
Watchmen, policemen, firemen, etc	4,648	2,993	2,019	4,634	2,958	2,015	14	35	4
Other domestic and personal service	10,690	6,067	2,456	9,752	5,208	2,243	938	859	312
TRADE AND TRANSPORTATION.									
Total	334,422	208,989	145,717	323,046	204,852	143,371	11,376	4,137	2,346
Agents	4,355	2,105	1,172	3,526	1,834	1,108	829	271	64
Bankers and brokers	241	82	114	224	82	111	17		3
Boatmen and sailors	7,469	6,504	6,545	7,455	6,486	6,543	14	18	2
Bookkeepers and accountants	1,628	475	293	748	281	239	880	194	54
Clerks and copyists	13,578	6,172	4,972	11,711	5,612	4,618	1,867	560	354
Stenographers and typewriters	1,081	395	126	317	218	94	764	177	32
Commercial travelers	332	187	103	286	175	95	46	12	8
Draymen, hackmen, teamsters, etc	96,897	67,585	43,963	96,838	67,396	43,914	59	189	49
Foremen and overseers	1,854	565	471	1,840	555	460	14	10	11
Hostlers	12,976	14,496	10,500	12,974	14,472	10,486	2	24	14
Hucksters and peddlers	3,434	3,270	2,516	2,745	2,762	2,041	689	508	475
Livery stable keepers	403	509	390	395	505	390	8	4	
Merchants and dealers (except wholesale)	13,924	9,095	6,646	11,680	8,235	6,027	2,244	860	619
Merchants and dealers (wholesale)	257	148	535	245	145	529	12	3	6
Messengers and errand and office boys	8,816	5,075	4,119	8,524	4,930	4,046	292	145	73
Officials of banks and companies	1,115	149	213	1,080	143	213	35	6	
Packers and shippers	2,944	1,865	567	2,575	1,619	530	369	246	37
Porters and helpers (in stores, etc.)	45,256	28,977	11,694	44,471	28,779	11,649	785	198	45
Salesmen and saleswomen [s]	4,699	2,799	1,166	3,394	2,396	1,023	1,305	403	143
Steam railroad employees	103,606	55,327	47,548	102,740	55,117	47,316	866	210	232
Street railway employees	3,748	629	589	3,713	625	589	35	4	
Telegraph and telephone linemen	1,058	529	271	1,047	529	271	11		
Telegraph and telephone operators	362	69	156	254	58	93	108	11	63
Undertakers	953	453	231	907	439	227	46	14	4
Other persons in trade and transportation	3,436	1,529	817	3,357	1,459	759	79	70	58
MANUFACTURING AND MECHANICAL PURSUITS.									
Total	552,815	275,116	208,374	490,906	241,934	181,415	61,909	33,182	26,959
Building trades.									
Carpenters and joiners	31,549	21,113	22,581	31,540	21,067	22,573	9	46	8
Masons (brick and stone)	23,650	14,386	9,760	23,646	14,370	9,758	4	16	2
Painters, glaziers, and varnishers	9,063	5,782	4,447	9,051	5,749	4,438	12	33	9
Paper hangers	1,026	586	274	1,011	580	272	15	6	2

TABLE 20.—NEGROES 10 YEARS OF AGE AND OVER GAINFULLY EMPLOYED, BY SEX AND OCCUPATION: 1910, 1900, AND 1890—COMPILATION ACCORDING TO OCCUPATIONAL CLASSIFICATION OF 1900—Continued.

OCCUPATIONAL CLASSIFICATION.	BOTH SEXES.			MALE.			FEMALE.		
	1910	1900	1890	1910	1900	1890	1910	1900	1890
MANUFACTURING AND MECHANICAL PURSUITS—continued.									
Building trades—Continued.									
Plasterers	6,783	3,757	4,006	6,783	3,748	4,003	....	9	3
Plumbers and gas and steam fitters	3,506	1,193	635	3,506	1,192	634	....	1	1
Roofers and slaters	721	368	243	721	367	243	....	1	
Mechanics (not otherwise specified)	612	377	746	612	376	746	....	1	
Chemical and allied products.									
Oil well and oil works employees	1,688	2,378	811	1,664	2,352	806	24	26	5
Other chemical workers	9,836	1,179	414	9,715	1,147	408	121	32	6
Clay, glass, and stone products.									
Brick and tile makers, etc	16,941	9,970	10,521	16,835	9,931	10,495	106	39	26
Glass workers	2,243	427	252	2,174	420	247	69	7	5
Marble and stone cutters [8]	1,513	1,257	1,279	1,502	1,252	1,279	11	5	....
Potters	421	212	193	418	210	189	3	2	4
Fishing and mining.									
Fishermen and oystermen	8,268	10,427	10,071	8,160	10,323	9,950	108	104	121
Miners and quarrymen	60,598	36,561	19,007	60,520	36,439	18,986	78	122	21
Food and kindred products.									
Bakers	2,564	1,521	1,135	2,336	1,422	1,064	228	99	71
Butter and cheese makers [8]	116	322	81	110	276	76	6	46	5
Confectioners [8]	707	541	477	594	474	405	113	67	72
Millers	1,577	895	1,487	1,561	886	1,484	16	9	3
Other food preparers	12,901	4,475	2,746	10,844	4,186	2,702	2,057	289	44
Iron and steel and their products.									
Blacksmiths	10,995	10,100	10,988	10,988	10,083	10,984	7	17	4
Machinists	3,120	1,263	857	3,120	1,258	857	....	5	
Steam-boiler makers	475	335	157	475	335	157	....	....	
Other iron and steel workers	33,101	13,293	7,357	32,884	13,263	7,316	217	30	41
Leather and its finished products.									
Boot and shoe makers and repairers	6,415	4,574	5,087	6,199	4,506	5,004	216	68	8
Harness and saddle makers and repairers [8]	332	270	295	343	266	295	9	4	
Leather curriers and tanners	2,139	1,073	1,103	2,103	1,059	1,100	36	14	3
Trunk and leather-case makers	108	23	68	106	23	67	2	....	1
Liquor and other beverages.									
Bottlers and soda-water makers, etc	914	160	88	878	157	85	36	3	3
Brewers and maltsters	429	155	136	423	154	136	6	1	
Distillers and rectifiers	505	323	472	500	322	472	5	1	
Lumber and its remanufactures.									
Cabinetmakers	469	342	345	463	340	345	6	2	....
Coopers	2,370	2,964	2,648	2,357	2,953	2,648	13	11	....
Saw and planing mill employees	108,811	33,266	17,276	108,045	33,156	17,247	766	110	29
Other woodworkers	10,566	2,803	2,016	9,946	2,641	1,927	620	162	89
Metals and metal products other than iron and steel.									
Brass workers	303	110	89	298	109	89	5	1	....
Clock and watch makers and repairers	121	109	61	118	106	60	3	3	1
Gold and silver workers	127	66	66	107	64	66	20	2	....
Tin plate and tinware makers	1,502	924	764	1,469	901	757	33	23	7
Other metal workers	4,351	353	462	4,294	348	456	57	5	6
Paper and printing.									
Bookbinders	278	86	66	158	52	52	120	34	14
Engravers	32	22	25	28	21	23	4	1	2
Paper and pulp mill operatives	1,093	321	255	989	252	230	104	69	25
Printers, lithographers, and pressmen	2,244	1,220	944	1,996	1,119	872	248	101	72
Textiles.									
Bleachery and dye-works operatives	556	446	225	461	390	187	95	56	38
Carpet factory operatives	246	43	83	221	36	43	25	7	40
Cotton mill operatives	6,178	1,425	1,077	5,299	1,079	820	879	346	257
Hosiery and knitting mill operatives	718	36	64	447	15	39	271	21	25
Silk mill operatives	513	136	24	143	61	11	370	75	13
Woolen mill operatives	262	169	346	205	94	268	57	75	78
Other textile mill operatives	1,231	330	3,736	868	262	3,328	363	68	408
Dressmakers	20,265	12,569	7,586	58	55	7	20,207	12,514	7,579
Milliners	1,015	180	386	38	6	3	977	174	383
Seamstresses	18,642	11,537	11,846	134	86	24	18,508	11,451	11,822
Tailors and tailoresses	7,901	1,845	1,330	7,032	1,531	960	869	314	370
Hat and cap makers	107	22	56	96	20	52	11	2	4
Shirt, collar, and cuff makers	980	181	85	504	46	30	476	135	55
Other textile workers	503	159	83	240	68	35	263	91	48
Miscellaneous industries.									
Broom and brush makers	738	213	174	725	209	172	13	4	2
Charcoal, coke, and lime burners	5,250	3,870	1,595	5,233	3,861	1,593	17	9	2
Engineers and firemen (not locomotive)	20,169	10,224	6,326	20,169	10,215	6,326	....	9	....
Glove makers	30	15	10	9	5	6	21	10	4
Manufacturers and officials, etc	5,418	1,186	1,077	5,336	1,165	1,074	82	21	3
Model and pattern makers	53	24	18	50	24	18	3	....	
Photographers	404	247	190	363	230	184	41	17	6
Rubber-factory operatives	178	44	42	170	42	39	8	2	3
Tobacco and cigar factory operatives	24,014	15,349	15,004	13,363	10,232	10,480	10,651	5,117	4,524
Upholsterers	1,127	1,045	724	1,049	986	695	78	59	29
Other miscellaneous industries	49,214	21,939	13,496	47,103	20,961	13,018	2,111	978	478

TABLE 21.—NEGRO FARMERS, PLANTERS, AND OVERSEERS; FARM LABORERS, HOME FARM; AND FARM LABORERS, WORKING OUT; BY DIVISONS AND STATES: 1910 AND 1900.

DIVISION AND STATE.	NEGRO POPULATION 10 YEARS OF AGE AND OVER GAINFULLY EMPLOYED.											
	Male.						Female.					
	Farmers, planters, and overseers.[1]		Farm laborers, home farm.		Farm laborers, working out.		Farmers, planters, and overseers.[1]		Farm laborers, home farm.		Farm laborers, working out.	
	1910	1900	1910	1900	1910	1900	1910	1900	1910	1900	1910	1900
UNITED STATES	799,923	686,157	441,203	363,528	516,632	465,980	79,677	71,665	704,150	323,295	263,403	185,931
GEOGRAPHIC DIVISIONS:												
New Engand	264	234	58	36	1,139	1,457	14	18	7	....	20	6
Middle Atlantic	1,133	1,289	377	320	8,940	8,177	46	53	20	7	161	53
East North Central	4,375	5,059	1,234	1,883	6,708	5,319	198	265	107	28	228	47
West North Central	5,310	6,935	1,579	2,608	8,198	7,996	255	386	87	78	189	75
South Atlantic	317,039	259,087	183,470	148,708	242,806	214,763	26,831	25,028	274,891	126,072	129,744	82,753
East South Central	288,503	248,616	158,858	130,928	124,624	130,254	34,430	29,397	282,070	134,873	71,985	63,269
West South Central	182,851	164,652	95,554	78,971	123,457	97,653	17,873	16,493	146,954	62,236	61,060	39,723
Mountain	220	116	31	15	296	97	13	10	8	....	5	....
Pacific	228	169	42	59	464	264	17	15	6	1	11	5
NEW ENGLAND:												
Maine	35	21	7	3	38	20	2	4	....	....	2	....
New Hampshire	21	11	2	....	43	29	2	1	....	....	1	....
Vermont	23	12	8	1	47	67	2	1	....	....	....	1
Massachusetts	73	70	15	12	346	479	7	5	7	....	8	....
Rhode Island	30	29	4	2	217	271	1	3	....	....	....	1
Connecticut	82	91	22	18	448	591	....	4	....	....	9	4
MIDDLE ATLANTIC:												
New York	267	320	69	68	1,820	1,842	16	16	9	1	25	13
New Jersey	404	472	177	125	3,901	3,638	9	16	8	2	62	27
Pennsylvania	462	497	131	127	3,219	2,697	21	21	3	4	74	13
EAST NORTH CENTRAL:												
Ohio	1,636	1,945	405	720	2,727	2,082	72	115	18	7	43	11
Indiana	721	950	246	329	1,458	1,232	25	48	9	5	11	7
Illinois	1,330	1,467	436	625	1,965	1,562	66	70	62	15	164	25
Michigan	587	639	131	188	487	404	29	29	12	1	8	2
Wisconsin	101	58	16	21	71	39	6	3	6	....	2	2
WEST NORTH CENTRAL:												
Minnesota	61	33	12	6	63	33	2	2	2	....	6	....
Iowa	195	194	58	54	135	203	12	8	5	2	11	2
Missouri	3,506	4,852	1,060	2,029	6,862	6,493	155	294	69	69	150	67
North Dakota	37	11	6	3	40	15	9	1	2	....	1	2
South Dakota	60	19	3	....	30	15	6	1	....	....	....	....
Nebraska	92	70	10	17	67	47	5	8	....	1	....	....
Kansas	1,359	1,756	430	499	1,001	1,190	66	72	9	6	21	4
SOUTH ATLANTIC:												
Delaware	803	788	455	359	3,562	2,746	18	25	107	14	113	24
Maryland	5,106	5,178	2,531	2,790	19,658	17,848	178	263	582	189	1,099	327
District of Columbia	11	38	3	4	162	217	2	....	2	1	4	....
Virginia	39,113	37,470	18,229	17,228	42,266	35,161	3,450	3,726	10,816	3,467	6,418	4,739
West Virginia	581	694	245	270	1,390	1,061	41	44	27	....	45	6
North Carolina	58,767	49,540	37,479	30,683	40,366	36,382	4,295	4,261	55,090	21,030	24,816	15,674
South Carolina	86,534	75,752	55,596	45,917	52,759	49,274	9,083	9,014	100,029	53,305	45,115	31,682
Georgia	113,687	77,606	62,720	45,707	68,343	64,900	8,499	6,025	98,404	43,029	45,243	27,354
Florida	12,437	12,021	6,212	5,750	14,300	7,174	1,265	1,670	9,834	5,037	6,891	2,047
EAST SOUTH CENTRAL:												
Kentucky	11,074	11,261	4,257	5,376	19,654	19,890	451	598	599	299	474	232
Tennessee	35,394	32,503	18,925	17,338	22,256	23,034	2,348	2,382	24,861	9,600	4,190	4,281
Alabama	95,581	82,878	58,152	49,275	42,761	44,541	13,118	12,077	102,838	56,343	35,803	30,201
Mississippi	146,454	121,974	77,524	58,939	39,953	42,789	18,513	14,340	153,772	68,631	31,518	28,505
WEST SOUTH CENTRAL:												
Arkansas	57,728	44,796	28,855	20,849	19,956	20,602	5,601	4,852	49,511	15,931	13,570	9,551
Louisiana	48,814	53,133	23,808	27,329	59,916	47,738	5,346	5,332	37,327	31,160	28,906	22,069
Oklahoma	13,007	[2]6,236	6,330	2,568	6,399	2,199	742	[2]535	6,043	474	1,262	196
Texas	63,302	60,487	36,561	28,225	37,186	27,114	6,184	5,774	54,073	14,671	17,322	7,907
MOUNTAIN:												
Montana	28	21	5	2	38	19	1	3	3	....	1	....
Idaho	25	9	1	2	18	7	1	....	1	....	....	....
Wyoming	15	5	3	....	17	16	....	1	....	....	....	....
Colorado	91	47	11	5	128	27	5	5	1	....	2	....
New Mexico	37	12	8	2	42	10	4	1	3	....	1	....
Arizona	5	8	1	....	24	5	....	....	....	....	....	....
Utah	14	10	2	4	17	6	....	....	....	....	....	....
Nevada	5	4	....	....	12	7	2	....	....	....	1	....
PACIFIC:												
Washington	77	43	12	19	97	21	5	2	3	....	6	1
Oregon	32	16	14	5	23	15	4	1	....	....	3	1
California	119	110	16	35	344	228	8	12	3	1	2	3

[1] Includes farmers, dairy farmers, cranberry growers, dairy farm foremen and managers, farm and plantation foremen and managers, cranberry bog foremen and managers, and poultry raisers.
[2] Includes Indian Territory.

TABLE 22.—GAINFUL WORKERS 10 YEARS OF AGE AND OVER, ALL CLASSES AND NEGRO, CLASSIFIED BY SEX, INDUSTRY, AND OCCUPATION: 1910.

AGRICULTURE, ANIMAL HUSBANDRY, AND FORESTRY.

INDUSTRY AND OCCUPATION.	ALL CLASSES. Male.	Female.	NEGRO. Male.	Female.
AGRICULTURE [1]	10,484,324	1,801,255	1,806,883	1,050,849
Agricultural pursuits [2]	10,479,743	1,800,638	1,806,527	1,050,851
Bookkeepers	738	303	9	....
Clerks	301	123	2	....
Stenographers and typewriters	62	236	2	....
Blacksmiths	722	....	216	....
Engineers	3,073	....	155	....
Machinists	82	....	12	....
ANIMAL HUSBANDRY [2]	194,533	6,667	9,997	252
FORESTRY	178,234	138	25,612	34
Forestry pursuits [2]	173,450	81	25,474	34
Bookkeepers	524	40	5	....
Clerks	444	12	6	....
Stenographers and typewriters	13	5	2	....
Blacksmiths	724	....	21	....
Engineers	2,519	....	96	....
Saw filers	560	....	8	....

EXTRACTION OF MINERALS, INCLUDING QUARRYING AND PRODUCTION OF SALT, OIL, AND GAS.

INDUSTRY AND OCCUPATION.	ALL CLASSES. Male.	Female.	NEGRO. Male.	Female.
COAL MINES	669,921	890	40,584	39
Owners and operators	2,361	9	12	....
Officials	284	1	2	....
Managers and superintendents	3,479	2	8	....
Bosses, foremen, and overseers	12,526	....	116	....
Bookkeepers, cashiers, and accountants	2,335	193	17	....
Clerks	2,227	80	6	2
Draftsmen	82	....	2	....
Messenger, errand, and office boys	136	....	5	....
Purchasing agents	45	....	1	....
Stenographers and typewriters	177	199	1	....
Weighers	2,125	1	10	....
Blacksmiths	4,373	....	121	....
Boiler makers	377	....	14	....
Carpenters	3,579	....	13	....
Electricians and electrical engineers	1,795	....	15	....
Engineers (civil, mining, and mechanical)	1,306	....	9	....
Engineers (stationary)	9,487	....	182	....
Machinists and millwrights	2,511	....	157	....
Masons	408	....	8	....
Mechanics (not otherwise specified)	196	....	3	....
Painters	66	....	1	....
Plumbers	183	....	2	....
Blasters and powder men	399	....	47	....
Breaker hands	12,191	12	35	....
Cagers and gripmen	797	....	52	....
Car builders and repairs	197	....	5	....
Car runners	3,023	....	93	....
Cutters	1,421	....	107	....
Door tenderers	3,526	3	290	....
Drillers	582	....	48	....
Drivers	19,308	8	1,580	....
Fan runners	93	....	1	....
Firemen	4,730	....	324	....
Inspectors	897	....	3	....
Laborers	137,847	356	7,649	33
Miners	425,798	....	28,976	....
Motormen	2,868	....	90	....
Oilers	395	....	10	....
Screeners and washers	659	....	46	....
Shaft tenders	438	....	6	....
Timbermen	1,667	....	72	....
Other and not specified occupations	3,027	26	445	4
COPPER MINES	45,639	42	282	....
Bosses, foremen, and overseers	856	....	1	....
Blacksmiths	662	....	3	....
Carpenters	562	....	1	....
Engineers (stationary)	1,249	....	3	....
Machinists and millwrights	591	....	1	....
Drivers	354	....	4	....
Firemen	396	....	1	....
Laborers	5,372	15	152	....
Miners	29,091	....	113	....
Timbermen	799	....	3	....
Other and not specified occupations	5,707	27	....	....
GOLD AND SILVER MINES	64,268	107	301	2
Owners and operators	1,486	22	2	....
Officials	96	3	1	....
Bosses, foremen, and overseers	887	....	1	....
GOLD AND SILVER MINES—Contd.				
Blacksmiths	885	....	1	....
Engineers (stationary)	1,551	....	4	....
Machinists and millwrights	545	....	1	....
Mechanics (not otherwise specified)	76	....	1	....
Amalgamators, cyanide men and vannermen	257	....	1	....
Drivers	421	....	7	....
Firemen	157	....	6	....
Laborers	4,109	39	121	2
Machine men	389	....	1	....
Millmen and crushermen	781	....	2	....
Miners	48,048	....	151	....
Timbermen	285	....	1	....
Other and not specified occupations	4,295	43	....	....
IRON MINES	58,105	83	5,370	9
Owners and operators	141	....	14	....
Managers and superintendents	406	....	1	....
Bosses, foremen, and overseers	1,642	....	9	....
Bookkeepers, cashiers, and accountants	360	11	4	....
Messenger, errand, and office boys	53	....	9	....
Other clerical pursuits	39	....	1	....
Blacksmiths	773	....	19	....
Carpenters	689	....	4	....
Engineers (civil, mining, and mechanical)	245	....	1	....
Engineers (stationary)	1,721	....	10	....
Machinists and millwrights	564	....	4	....
Masons	45	....	3	....
Plumbers	140	....	2	....
Carmen and motormen	1,825	....	13	....
Drillers	864	....	6	....
Drivers	823	....	200	....
Firemen	750	....	56	....
Inspectors	45	....	4	....
Laborers	16,315	32	1,477	9
Millmen and crushermen	106	....	4	....
Miners	28,517	....	3,442	....
Screeners and washers	115	....	39	....
Timbermen	392	....	8	....
Other and not specified occupations	1,535	40	40	....
LEAD AND ZINC MINES	23,709	51	278	....
Bosses, foremen, and overseers	538	....	1	....
Engineers (civil, mining, and mechanical)	165	....	3	....
Engineers (stationary)	1,411	....	1	....
Machinists and millwrights	217	....	1	....
Carmen and motormen	116	....	1	....
Drillers	816	....	1	....
Drivers	455	....	7	....
Firemen	213	....	13	....
Laborers	5,056	14	136	....
Machine hands (not specified)	794	....	1	....
Millmen and crushermen	157	....	1	....
Miners	11,059	....	111	....
Screeners and washers	644	....	1	....
Other and not specified occupations	2,068	37	....	....
OIL WELLS AND GAS WELLS	55,053	252	264	2
Owners and operators	5,676	29	6	....
Bosses, foremen, and overseers	1,641	....	2	....

[1] Landscape gardeners are classified under "Professional service," and gardeners employed by steam railroads under "Steam railroads."
[2] For detail by occupation, see Table 16, p. 513.

TABLE 22.—GAINFUL WORKERS 10 YEARS OF AGE AND OVER, ALL CLASSES AND NEGRO, CLASSIFIED BY SEX, INDUSTRY, AND OCCUPATION: 1910—Continued.

EXTRACTION OF MINERALS, INCLUDING QUARRYING AND PRODUCTION OF SALT, OIL, AND GAS—Continued.

INDUSTRY AND OCCUPATION.	ALL CLASSES.		NEGRO.	
	Male.	Female.	Male.	Female.
OIL WELLS AND GAS WELLS—Contd.				
Clerks	402	17	1	....
Stenographers and typewriters	78	126	1	1
Engineers (stationary)	1,286	.....	8	....
Mechanics (not otherwise specified)	127	.....	3	....
Tool dressers	4,759	.....	7	....
Derrick and rig builders	1,142	.....	1	....
Drillers	9,181	.....	8	....
Firemen	609	.....	4	....
Laborers	9,843	4	125	....
Oilers	185	.....	2	....
Pipe pullers	259	.....	3	....
Pumpers	9,543	1	13	....
Teamsters	2,970	1	63	....
Other and not specified occupations	7,352	74	17	1
QUARRIES	93,864	175	10,333	15
Owners and operators	1,423	8	38	....
Managers and superintendents	1,274	5	4	....
Bosses, foremen, and overseers	2,966	.....	39	....
Bookkeepers, cashiers, and accountants	359	43	4	....
Clerks	424	18	1	....
Messenger, errand, and office boys	156	1	41	....
Weighers	104	1	1	....
Blacksmiths	1,425	.....	53	....
Carpenters	240	.....	7	....
Engineers (stationary)	2,543	.....	58	....
Machinists and millwrights	403	.....	14	....
Masons	519	.....	57	....
Mechanics (not otherwise specified)	106	.....	17	....
Apprentices	65	.....	1	....
Bell-ringers	129	.....	5	....
Blasters and powdermen	811	.....	186	....
Block makers and trimmers	2,648	.....	98	....
Carmen	257	.....	144	....
Cranemen	403	.....	12	....
Drillers	2,645	.....	405	....
Drivers	3,214	1	408	....
Firemen	788	.....	55	....
Inspectors	39	.....	2	....
Laborers	50,975	28	7,097	8
Machine hands (not specified)	409	.....	11	....
Quarrymen	17,277	.....	1,297	....
Other and not specified occupations	2,262	70	278	7

INDUSTRY AND OCCUPATION.	ALL CLASSES.		NEGRO.	
	Male.	Female.	Male.	Female.
SALT MINES, WELLS, AND FACTORIES	5,733	443	208	2
Owners and operators	68	1	1	....
Bosses, foremen, and overseers	212	9	2	....
Messenger, errand, and office boys	11	2	1	....
Blacksmiths	66	.....	1	....
Coopers	223	.....	8	....
Engineers (stationary)	223	.....	1	....
Firemen	149	.....	7	....
Laborers	3,258	151	140	2
Miners	237	.....	21	....
Packers	168	64	3	....
Sewers	9	69	2	....
Teamsters	105	.....	12	....
Other and not specified occupations	1,004	147	9	....
MINES, OTHER AND NOT SPECIFIED	41,116	510	5,051	15
Owners and operators	2,339	13	53	....
Managers and superintendents	1,152	2	4	....
Bosses, foremen, and overseers	865	.....	19	....
Bookkeepers, cashiers, and accountants	706	62	5	....
Other clerical pursuits	52	1	1	....
Blacksmiths	458	.....	19	....
Carpenters	447	.....	37	....
Engineers (civil, mining, and mechanical)	4,301	.....	7	....
Engineers (stationary)	1,167	.....	23	....
Machinists	399	.....	6	....
Mechanics (not otherwise specified)	140	.....	5	....
Asphalt miners and laborers	132	.....	23	....
Bauxite miners and laborers	200	1	12	....
Carmen and motormen	59	.....	2	....
Drillers	253	.....	10	....
Drivers	580	.....	142	....
Firemen	238	.....	75	....
Graphite miners and laborers	178	.....	15	....
Laborers	3,920	11	232	2
Mica miners and laborers	277	29	11	....
Miners	14,944	.....	260	....
Phosphate miners and laborers	4,582	11	3,820	10
Quicksilver miners and laborers	126	.....	2	....
Spar miners and laborers	501	1	15	....
Sulphur miners and laborers	485	.....	33	....
Timbermen	108	.....	3	....
Other and not specified occupations	2,507	379	217	3

MANUFACTURING, INCLUDING HAND TRADES.

INDUSTRY AND OCCUPATION.	ALL CLASSES.		NEGRO.	
	Male.	Female.	Male.	Female.
AGRICULTURAL IMPLEMENT FACTORIES	36,012	1,608	594	2
Manufacturers and proprietors	570	2	2	....
Foremen and overseers	1,069	9	4	....
Bookkeepers, cashiers, and accountants	1,013	196	1	....
Clerks (general)	1,321	152	2	1
Clerks (shipping)	581	3	3	....
Blacksmiths	1,552	.....	14	....
Carpenters	680	.....	4	....
Electricians and electrical engineers	93	.....	1	....
Engineers (stationary)	227	.....	2	....
Machinists	4,581	.....	17	....
Mechanics (not otherwise specified)	257	.....	2	....
Painters	971	9	17	....
Wheelwrights	34	.....	1	....
Apprentices	95	.....	1	....
Assemblers and erectors	452	.....	1	....
Core makers	323	168	2	....
Drillers	325	.....	2	....
Firemen	179	.....	19	....
Fitters	468	.....	1	....
Forgemen and hammermen	128	.....	1	....
Grinders (metal)	530	.....	31	....
Helpers	407	12	11	....
Laborers	10,930	113	301	1
Machine hands	778	30	1	....
Molders	2,338	1	55	....
Oilers	57	.....	1	....
Packers	217	3	3	....
Pattern makers	390	1	1	....
Polishers	334	2	11	....
Teamsters	325	.....	11	....
Woodworkers (not specified)	628	2	3	....
Other and not specified occupations	4,159	905	68	....

INDUSTRY AND OCCUPATION.	ALL CLASSES.		NEGRO.	
	Male.	Female.	Male.	Female.
AUTOMOBILE FACTORIES	101,974	3,784	559	10
Manufacturers and proprietors	987	.....	2	....
Managers and superintendents	1,612	1	1	....
Foremen and overseers	2,293	49	6	....
Bookkeepers, cashiers, and accountants	1,782	517	1	....
Clerks (general)	3,948	356	5	1
Clerks (shipping)	712	6	5	....
Designers	154	1	1	....
Draftsmen	1,070	1	1	....
Messenger, errand, and office boys	330	4	5	....
Stenographers and typewriters	331	1,743	.....	2
Blacksmiths	1,341	.....	3	....
Carpenters	1,398	.....	3	....
Electricians and electrical engineers	1,196	.....	7	....
Engineers (stationary)	720	.....	4	....
Machinists	28,569	.....	84	....
Mechanics (not otherwise specified)	1,766	.....	16	....
Millwrights	398	.....	1	....
Painters	4,120	11	9	....
Plumbers	288	.....	6	....
Apprentices	1,096	8	5	....
Assemblers and erectors	3,620	28	3	....
Bench hands	466	3	3	....
Body makers (not specified)	1,329	9	7	1
Braziers	117	.....	2	....
Carriage and wagon builders	203	11	1	....
Chauffeurs	779	1	37	....
Core makers	231	21	3	....
Finishers	931	12	1	....
Firemen	234	.....	5	....
Forgemen and hammermen	209	.....	1	....
Helpers	926	16	12	....
Inspectors	1,233	25	1	....
Laborers	15,555	137	180	3
Lathe hands and turners	337	1	1	....

TABLE 22.—GAINFUL WORKERS 10 YEARS OF AGE AND OVER, ALL CLASSES AND NEGRO, CLASSIFIED BY SEX, INDUSTRY, AND OCCUPATION: 1910—Continued.

MANUFACTURING, INCLUDING HAND TRADES—Continued.

INDUSTRY AND OCCUPATION.	ALL CLASSES.		NEGRO.	
	Male.	Female.	Male.	Female.
AUTOMOBILE FACTORIES—Continued.				
Machine hands (not specified)	1,784	173	1	
Molders	527	2	5	
Oilers	113	2	3	
Packers and wrappers	126	22	1	
Polishers	1,404	25	10	
Press hands	236	9		1
Repairers	678	9	7	1
Rubber workers (not specified)	168	1	2	
Solderers	160	7	1	
Teamsters	260		14	
Testers	1,578		4	
Woodworkers (not specified)	1,579	8	1	
Other and not specified occupations	13,080	565	88	1
BAKERIES	126,815	17,967	3,174	274
Manufacturers and proprietors	12,686	1,169	60	15
Managers and superintendents	1,193	153	3	
Foremen and overseers	1,152	306	7	1
Bookkeepers, cashiers, and accountants	1,157	915	1	3
Clerks (general)	2,068	3,415	7	3
Clerks (shipping)	1,021	22	2	
Messenger, errand, and office boys	440	15	39	2
Stenographers and typewriters	45	388		3
Carpenters	143		2	
Engineers (stationary)	277		9	
Machinists and millwrights	134		2	
Apprentices	2,081	100	59	1
Bakers	84,752	4,779	1,928	197
Carton and paper box makers	72	60	1	
Deliverymen and teamsters	12,020	6	288	
Firemen	170		24	
Frosters and icers	78	274		1
Helpers	1,466	520	87	9
Laborers	3,739	737	372	23
Mixers	155	18	12	
Packers	534	3,938	11	8
Wrappers	59	273		1
Other and not specified occupations	1,373	879	260	7
BLANK BOOK, ENVELOPE, TAG, PAPER BAG, ETC., FACTORIES	10,340	8,891	73	14
Manufacturers and proprietors	774	18	1	
Clerks (general)	688	520	4	
Clerks (shipping)	423	19	4	
Designers	147	38	1	
Messenger, errand, and office boys	165	20	1	1
Stenographers and typewriters	42	422		1
Machinists	441		2	
Box makers	75	298	2	
Cutters	824	345	4	1
Firemen	47		1	
Helpers	135	107	1	
Inspectors	25	188	1	
Laborers	1,089	460	18	2
Machine hands (not specified)	382	1,110	1	
Packers, wrappers, and sealers	288	530	7	
Printers	1,072	210	3	
Sorters	16	390	1	2
Teamsters	124		5	
Other and not specified occupations	3,583	4,216	16	7
BLAST FURNACES AND STEEL ROLLING MILLS	394,275	6,764	18,124	96
Manufacturers and proprietors	1,742	1	5	
Officials	972	9	2	
Managers and superintendents	3,589	2	2	
Foremen and overseers	9,362	63	132	
Bookkeepers, cashiers, and accountants	4,206	480	7	2
Clerks (general)	11,571	544	66	
Clerks (shipping)	2,017	12	6	
Designers	52		1	
Draftsmen	2,187	2	2	
Messenger, errand, and office boys	1,248	8	37	
Purchasing agents	237		1	
Stenographers and typewriters	1,055	2,489	5	3
Weighers	1,102	3	19	
Blacksmiths	3,909		77	
Boiler makers	1,868		16	
Carpenters	2,674		14	
Coopers	80		2	
Electricians and electrical engineers	3,470	1	21	
Engineers (stationary)	5,606		83	
Machinists	17,634		92	
Masons	1,706		24	

INDUSTRY AND OCCUPATION.	ALL CLASSES.		NEGRO.	
	Male.	Female.	Male.	Female.
BLAST FURNACES AND STEEL ROLLING MILLS—Continued.				
Mechanics (not otherwise specified)	881	2	15	
Millwrights	1,461		18	
Painters	662	2	17	
Plumbers	1,674		24	
Tool makers	565	4	4	
Annealers and temperers	411		5	
Apprentices	1,313	5	12	
Bench hands	127	7	2	
Blowers	257		15	
Catchers	1,527		33	
Chippers	968		67	
Core makers	1,632	175	69	
Cranemen	4,912		95	
Cutters	1,151	5	60	
Drawers	5,957	14	163	
Drillers	430		5	
Firemen	3,705		414	
Fitters	499	3	11	
Forgemen and welders	2,214		30	
Furnace tenders and fillers	3,174		417	
Galvanizers and platers	1,062	5	15	
Gas makers	590	4	78	1
Gaugers	243		5	
Grinders	148		7	
Hammermen	1,024		23	
Heaters	5,709	2	89	
Helpers	7,097	28	310	
Inspectors	1,845		22	
Laborers	193,193	1,136	13,337	80
Ladlers and pourers	395		34	
Lathe hands, planers, and turners	558	4	5	
Levermen	296		4	
Machine hands (not specified)	1,532	193	14	
Melters and cupola tenders	890	1	56	1
Molders	10,323		211	
Motormen	143		11	
Oilers	999		24	
Packers	396	29	6	
Pattern makers	1,698	5	1	
Polishers and buffers	588	9	48	
Pot pullers	451	2	57	
Press hands	544	6	7	1
Puddlers	5,441		304	
Riggers	1,051		36	
Riveters	611		8	
Rollers, roughers, and finishers	9,740	8	165	
Roll turners	698		4	
Sawyers	142		4	
Shearers	2,072		86	
Stampers	150	2	3	
Straighteners	683		19	
Teamsters	1,806		222	
Testers	203		12	
Threaders	128	19	3	
Water tenders	508	1	22	
Weavers	805	114	3	
Winders, reelers, and spoolers	373	286	6	1
Other and not specified occupations	30,333	1,048	773	7
BOX FACTORIES (PAPER)	8,652	14,324	74	21
Foremen and overseers	336	233		1
Clerks (general)	161	105	1	
Clerks (shipping)	140	9	3	
Engineers (stationary)	43		1	
Cutters	934	382	1	
Folders	112	840	2	3
Helpers	105	202	1	1
Laborers	789	609	19	1
Machine hands (not specified)	143	420		2
Packers and wrappers	133	178	3	
Pasters, gluers, and turners	277	1,785	4	1
Press hands	351	168	4	
Printers	280	24	2	
Teamsters	282		8	
Other and not specified occupations	4,566	9,369	25	12
BOX FACTORIES (WOOD)	15,662	2,325	1,545	66
Manufacturers and proprietors	634	4	6	
Managers and superintendents	195	2	1	
Foremen and overseers	348	24	3	
Bookkeepers, cashiers, and accountants	122	39	1	
Clerks (general)	70	22	3	
Clerks (shipping)	90		2	
Messenger, errand, and office boys	21	1	1	
Cabinetmakers	82		1	
Carpenters	654		12	
Engineers (stationary)	134		5	
Machinists and millwrights	198	1	8	
Mechanics (not otherwise specified)	66	3	2	

TABLE 22.—GAINFUL WORKERS 10 YEARS OF AGE AND OVER, ALL CLASSES AND NEGRO, CLASSIFIED BY SEX, INDUSTRY, AND OCCUPATION: 1910—Continued.

MANUFACTURING, INCLUDING HAND TRADES—Continued.

INDUSTRY AND OCCUPATION.	ALL CLASSES.		NEGRO.	
	Male.	Female.	Male.	Female.
BOX FACTORIES (WOOD)—Contd.				
Apprentices	43	6	......	2
Cutters	114	1	2	
Firemen	108	......	33	
Helpers	144	26	21	7
Laborers	4,727	291	1,206	30
Liners, pasters, and trimmers	61	636	6	
Machine hands (not specified)	243	50	1	2
Nailers	1,134	46	9	
Planers	275	2	15	
Sawyers	2,515	12	93	
Teamsters	253	......	32	
Other and not specified occupations	3,431	1,159	82	25
BRASS MILLS	50,272	3,844	356	5
Managers and superintendents	604	1	1	
Foremen and overseers	1,460	49	3	
Clerks (general)	1,006	202	2	
Clerks (shipping)	528	10	3	
Messenger, errand, and office boys	196	8	3	
Weighers	52	1	2	
Blacksmiths	149	......	1	
Machinists	2,960	2	9	
Mechanics (not otherwise specified)	206	......	2	
Tool makers	789	......	1	
Annealers and temperers	78	2	2	
Apprentices	466	4	2	
Core makers	863	288	1	
Cutters	100	4	1	
Drillers	104	4	1	
Finishers	4,025	47	6	
Firemen	214	......	3	
Forgemen, hammermen, and welders	25	......	1	
Furnacemen, heaters, and melters	306	......	10	
Grinders	262	3	2	
Helpers	861	33	15	
Inspectors	256	104	2	1
Laborers	10,552	277	114	1
Lathe hands and turners	527	9	7	
Machine hands (not specified)	828	171	3	
Molders and founders	6,509	3	55	
Packers and wrappers	228	311	4	
Polishers and buffers	4,585	126	30	
Press hands and stampers	911	624	6	1
Rollers	536	......	6	
Sawyers	46	......	1	
Teamsters	264	......	17	
Other and not specified occupations	9,776	1,561	40	2
BREWERIES	68,229	1,467	877	8
Officials	602	4	11	
Managers and superintendents	1,342	......	45	
Foremen and overseers	1,610	5	9	
Bookkeepers, cashiers, and accountants	3,331	221	1	
Clerks (general)	1,105	68	2	
Clerks (shipping)	629	6	1	
Messenger, errand, and office boys	113	1	9	
Stenographers and typewriters	195	285	......	1
Blacksmiths	150	......	3	
Coopers	1,376	......	7	
Engineers (stationary)	2,625	......	7	
Machinists and millwrights	585	......	2	
Mechanics (not otherwise specified)	49	......	1	
Painters	214	......	1	
Plumbers	304	......	3	
Bottlers	6,461	170	28	
Brewers	11,088	......	12	
Firemen	1,634	......	30	
Helpers	485	9	7	
Inspectors	85	21	1	
Laborers	12,024	259	395	4
Maltsters	1,152	......	1	
Packers	242	40	2	
Teamsters	15,074	......	285	
Other and not specified occupations	5,754	378	14	3
BRICK, TILE, AND TERRA-COTTA FACTORIES	112,086	2,039	18,703	111
Manufacturers and proprietors	3,514	19	32	
Managers and superintendents	2,066	1	12	
Foremen and overseers	2,690	5	75	
Bookkeepers, cashiers, and accountants	934	189	2	2
Clerks (general)	564	87	3	
Clerks (shipping)	163	2	4	
Messenger, errand, and office boys	122	5	16	1
Stenographers and typewriters	95	310	1	
Other clerical pursuits	25	......	1	

INDUSTRY AND OCCUPATION.	ALL CLASSES.		NEGRO.	
	Male.	Female.	Male.	Female.
BRICK, TILE, AND TERRA-COTTA FACTORIES—Continued.				
Blacksmiths	324	......	10	
Carpenters	366	......	8	
Engineers (stationary)	2,007	......	74	
Machinists and millwrights	770	......	26	
Mechanics (not otherwise specified)	604	......	51	
Painters	41	1	2	
Plumbers	43	......	1	
Apprentices	95	......	9	
Burners	1,593	......	121	
Cutters	210	3	11	
Finishers	131	4	3	
Firemen	2,061	......	473	
Glazers and enamelers	78	32	1	
Kilnmen	197	......	4	
Laborers	75,140	565	15,568	97
Machine hands (not otherwise specified)	211	12	22	
Mixers and temperers	192	7	8	
Molders and pressers	2,806	80	208	
Packers	129	42	11	
Pattern makers	249	4	1	
Setters	1,995	56	220	2
Sorters	151	97	4	
Teamsters	4,721	......	1,056	
Other and not specified occupations	7,799	518	665	9
BROOM AND BRUSH FACTORIES	13,733	2,710	769	15
Manufacturers and proprietors	1,937	23	30	
Messenger, errand, and office boys	52	2	1	
Stenographers and typewriters	12	104	1	
Engineers (stationary)	50	......	2	
Machinists and millwrights	90	......	1	
Mechanics (not otherwise specified)	49	......	1	
Bunchers and tiers	72	9	18	
Cutters and trimmers	72	40	1	
Finishers	144	73	1	
Helpers	107	51	6	1
Laborers	1,336	225	104	3
Machine hands (not specified)	99	83	4	
Packers	37	71	1	1
Sewers and binders	147	28	7	
Sorters	239	134	7	1
Teamsters	75	......	5	
Winders	139	13	1	
Other and not specified occupations	9,076	1,854	578	9
BUILDING AND HAND TRADES	2,796,249	614,570	242,387	45,754
Builders and building contractors	155,073	833	2,852	20
House movers and wreckers	2,881	5	122	
Managers and superintendents	4,720	7	16	
Foremen and overseers	8,658	2	138	
Agents	145	2	3	
Bookkeepers, cashiers, and accountants	4,283	2,014	23	10
Clerks	4,318	509	17	2
Collectors	77	1	2	
Messenger, errand, and office boys	445	7	37	
Stenographers and typewriters	479	1,980	......	2
Blacksmiths	163,074	29	7,862	2
Blacksmiths' apprentices	2,814	2	178	
Blacksmiths' helpers	11,423	14	1,081	4
Boiler makers	93	......	5	
Carpenters and joiners	682,453	37	29,039	4
Carpenters' apprentices	6,061	8	253	1
Carpenters' helpers	7,120	13	823	4
Coopers	1,104	......	63	
Dressmakers (not in factory)	1,238	319,593	54	19,860
Dressmakers' apprentices	7	5,989	......	201
Drillers (excavation)	576	......	96	
Electricians	46,992	32	293	
Electricians' apprentices	2,660	1	8	
Electricians' helpers	870	2	11	
Engineers (stationary)	2,973	......	97	
Fence builders	725	19	45	1
Firemen	711	......	60	
Jewelers (not dealers)	15,701	485	99	2
Laborers (building and not specified)	840,230	15,774	149,167	6,159
Machinists	8,512	1	99	
Masons	160,136	15	12,014	2
Masons' apprentices	2,501	2	171	
Masons' helpers	32,263	6	11,074	2
Mechanics (not otherwise specified)	2,016	......	117	
Milliners and millinery dealers	5,459	122,447	38	953
Milliners' apprentices	24	5,991	......	24
Painters, glaziers, and varnishers	273,060	381	8,035	5
Painters', glaziers', and varnishers' apprentices	2,653	9	68	
Painters', glaziers', and varnishers' helpers	1,659	17	82	

TABLE 22.—GAINFUL WORKERS 10 YEARS OF AGE AND OVER, ALL CLASSES AND NEGRO, CLASSIFIED BY SEX, INDUSTRY, AND OCCUPATION: 1910—Continued.

MANUFACTURING, INCLUDING HAND TRADES—Continued.

INDUSTRY AND OCCUPATION.	ALL CLASSES. Male.	Female.	NEGRO. Male.	Female.
BUILDING AND HAND TRADES—Contd.				
Paper hangers	24,780	797	954	14
Paper hangers' apprentices	440	4	15	
Paper hangers' helpers	341	22	42	1
Piano and organ tuners (not in factory)	4,818	85	41	
Plasterers	47,676	6	6,175	
Plasterers' apprentices	669		82	
Plasterers' helpers	2,180	2	526	
Plumbers	119,596		1,996	
Plumbers' apprentices	9,899	4	71	
Plumbers' helpers	9,638	4	1,150	
Roofers and slaters	14,078		613	
Roofers' and slaters' apprentices	302	2	6	
Roofers' and slaters' helpers	728	1	102	
Seamstresses (not in factory)	110	124,326	14	18,216
Shoemakers (not in factory)	68,788	782	3,695	44
Structural ironworkers (building)	11,427		80	
Weavers (blankets, etc., not in factory)	335	4,950	1	10
Weavers (carpets, not in factory)	1,816	5,831	13	36
Well borers and diggers	10,485	1	1,147	
Whitewashers	1,663	5	1,039	3
Other and not specified occupations	10,293	1,521	483	172
BUTTER AND CHEESE FACTORIES	25,557	1,748	168	8
Manufacturers and proprietors	2,762	25	2	
Bookkeepers, cashiers, and accountants	465	569		1
Clerks (general)	384	169	1	
Clerks (shipping)	143	3	1	
Stenographers and typewriters	32	263		1
Engineers (stationary)	332		2	
Mechanics (not otherwise specified)	77		1	
Firemen	95		4	
Inspectors	195	28	1	
Laborers	4,685	128	87	1
Teamsters	2,329	3	36	
Other and not specified occupations	14,058	560	33	5
BUTTON FACTORIES	9,530	5,681	39	24
Clerks (general)	133	154	1	
Clerks (shipping)	82	20	1	
Messenger, errand, and office boys	82	13	2	
Tool makers	104		1	
Carders and sewers	22	566		4
Cutters and drillers	3,259	281	8	2
Grinders	131	50	1	2
Helpers	64	63		1
Laborers	788	314	14	3
Machine hands (not specified)	289	400	1	3
Polishers and buffers	106	57	2	1
Other and not specified occupations	4,470	3,763	8	10
CANDY FACTORIES	22,036	20,648	665	126
Manufacturers and proprietors	2,641	83	8	1
Managers and superintendents	429	40	2	
Foremen and overseers	402	838	1	
Bookkeepers, cashiers, and accountants	353	348	1	
Clerks (general)	499	426	3	
Clerks (shipping)	621	19	5	
Messenger, errand, and office boys	103	32	5	
Engineers (stationary)	175		3	
Machinists	126		1	
Mechanics (not otherwise specified)	52		3	
Apprentices	278	33	2	
Candy makers (not specified)	11,890	5,480	335	50
Dippers and coaters	233	4,680	1	6
Firemen	81		10	
Helpers	452	296	25	5
Laborers	1,841	1,119	123	29
Packers	493	4,654	11	8
Teamsters	507		37	
Wrappers	58	1,620	3	4
Other and not specified occupations	802	980	86	23
CAR AND RAILROAD SHOPS	128,588	972	4,402	23
Manufacturers and proprietors	141		1	
Officials	133			
Foremen and overseers	3,620	17	19	
Clerks (general)	2,569	113	6	
Clerks (shipping)	149	2	2	
Messenger, errand, and office boys	192	1	6	

INDUSTRY AND OCCUPATION.	ALL CLASSES. Male.	Female.	NEGRO. Male.	Female.
CAR AND RAILROAD SHOPS—Contd.				
Blacksmiths	5,038		90	
Boiler makers	1,292		7	
Cabinetmakers	1,318		2	
Carpenters	16,610		72	
Coopers	28		1	
Electricians and electrical engineers	945		4	
Engineers (stationary)	538		7	
Machinists	9,937		41	
Mechanics (not otherwise specified)	265		3	
Millwrights	137		1	
Painters	5,204	11	35	
Plumbers	1,019		1	
Tinners	818		2	
Wheelwrights	55		1	
Apprentices	395	1	1	
Assemblers	145		1	
Car builders (not specified)	4,764	16	46	
Core makers	258	17	5	
Cranemen	271		1	
Cutters	99	1	1	
Drillers	416		2	
Firemen	591		77	
Heaters	449		1	
Helpers	2,176	23	85	
Inspectors	1,131	6	6	
Laborers	47,979	220	3,639	19
Machine hands (not specified)	790	22	5	
Molders	1,687		30	
Oilers	178		9	
Pattern makers	398	1	1	
Polishers	217		1	
Press hands	370		1	
Repairers	4,799	15	25	
Sawyers	121		2	
Sewers	1	98		3
Teamsters	292		15	
Upholsterers	621	11	2	
Woodworkers (not specified)	545	1	1	
Other and not specified occupations	9,887	396	143	1
CARPET MILLS	25,493	14,788	252	27
Manufacturers and proprietors	672	20	9	
Foremen and overseers	792	78		1
Bookkeepers, cashiers, and accountants	288	156	1	2
Clerks (general)	401	75	2	
Engineers (stationary)	136		1	
Machinists	727		1	
Painters	79		2	
Apprentices	86	8	1	2
Beamers, warpers, and slashers	274	69	2	
Bobbin boys, doffers, and carriers	315	267	1	
Carders	270	48	1	
Cleaners and washers	188	21	3	
Cutters	274	51	8	
Dyers	641	29	2	
Firemen	183		2	
Laborers	3,391	297	30	
Machine hands (not specified)	107	114	2	
Pickers	154	438	3	1
Printers	773	123	3	1
Setters	110	1,527		9
Sewers	298	866	64	
Spinners	567	837	2	
Weavers	8,483	4,460	35	8
Winders, reelers, and spoolers	262	2,418		1
Wool sorters	79	27	1	
Other and not specified occupations	5,943	2,859	73	4
CHARCOAL AND COKE WORKS	25,528	72	5,437	17
Manufacturers and proprietors	173		19	
Managers and superintendents	215		1	
Foremen and overseers	676		21	
Clerks	158		1	
Messenger, errand, and office boys	11		1	
Blacksmiths	147		4	
Boiler makers	24		1	
Carpenters	243		10	
Electricians and electrical engineers	79		1	
Engineers (stationary)	235		16	
Machinists and millwrights	215		2	
Masons	300		21	
Mechanics (not otherwise specified)	30		1	
Plumbers	46		1	
Car shifters	101		10	
Charcoal burners (not specified)	765	8	291	6
Coke burners (not specified)	98		28	
Coke drawers	8,306	3	1,791	2
Coke-oven chargers	248	1	60	

TABLE 22.—GAINFUL WORKERS 10 YEARS OF AGE AND OVER, ALL CLASSES AND NEGRO, CLASSIFIED BY SEX, INDUSTRY, AND OCCUPATION: 1910—Continued.

MANUFACTURING, INCLUDING HAND TRADES—Continued.

INDUSTRY AND OCCUPATION.	ALL CLASSES. Male.	ALL CLASSES. Female.	NEGRO. Male.	NEGRO. Female.
CHARCOAL AND COKE WORKS—Contd.				
Coke-oven levelers	511		39	
Firemen	255		40	
Helpers	100		18	
Laborers	11,331	15	2,877	8
Motormen	43		12	
Teamsters	463		67	
Other and not specified occupations	755	45	104	1
CHEMICAL FACTORIES (NOT OTHERWISE SPECIFIED)	50,748	16,816	2,524	56
Manufacturers and proprietors	4,552	202	35	2
Officials	628	27	2	
Managers and superintendents	2,208	143	3	
Foremen and overseers	1,888	580	25	2
Bookkeepers, cashiers, and accountants	1,635	1,054	1	
Clerks (general)	2,655	2,256	14	6
Clerks (shipping)	1,205	45	23	
Collectors	37	1	2	
Messenger, errand, and office boys	444	42	22	
Stenographers and typewriters	265	2,610		1
Blacksmiths	170		6	
Carpenters and cabinetmakers	493		6	
Coopers	273		3	
Electricians and electrical engineers	247		2	
Engineers (stationary)	1,025		26	
Machinists and millwrights	1,013		10	
Mechanics (not otherwise specified)	110		3	
Plumbers	351		2	
Apprentices	146	8	2	
Firemen	1,103		77	
Helpers	469	257	24	7
Inspectors	138	74	3	
Labelers	86	1,335	3	2
Laborers	19,966	1,227	1,814	14
Oilers	105		4	
Packers	1,052	2,242	31	1
Printers	178	30	1	
Teamsters	1,429		77	
Wrappers	27	598	1	1
Other and not specified occupations	6,850	4,085	302	20
CIGAR AND TOBACCO FACTORIES	115,884	79,486	14,717	10,746
Manufacturers and proprietors	13,159	163	48	2
Managers and superintendents	1,290	10	12	
Foremen and overseers	2,245	463	71	2
Bookkeepers, cashiers, and accountants	1,439	535	2	
Clerks (general)	1,391	528	22	3
Clerks (shipping)	765	72	19	2
Messenger, errand, and office boys	246	16	18	
Purchasing agents	131		2	
Weighers	122	125	61	2
Carpenters	158		8	
Coopers	203		135	
Engineers (stationary)	206		25	
Machinists	536		55	
Mechanics (not otherwise specified)	50		4	
Painters	31		3	
Plumbers	32		3	
Tinners	26		1	
Apprentices	1,072	190	23	2
Bag makers	9	273	3	60
Banders, labelers, and stampers	351	2,236	83	44
Bunch makers	600	3,478	43	22
Casers and dippers	214	7	67	
Cigar makers (not specified)	58,725	28,767	1,804	158
Cigarette makers (not specified)	460	738	2	1
Cutters	274	82	28	4
Dryers	160	20	41	8
Firemen	234		107	
Hangers and shakers-out	121	183	55	162
Helpers	287	254	22	22
Inspectors	195	160	14	13
Laborers	11,347	4,921	5,705	2,391
Machine hands (not specified)	471	368	137	29
Packers (cigar and cigarette)	2,733	3,367	18	8
Packers (tobacco)	1,475	2,218	466	53
Pressers and prizers	879	92	471	12
Rollers (cigar and cigarette)	1,706	6,316	33	42
Rollers (lump or plug)	675	313	486	113
Sorters, classers, and selectors	1,306	1,906	344	695
Stainers	29	34	4	1
Strippers and stemmers	5,251	16,974	2,703	6,077
Sweepers	89	35	63	14
Teamsters	432		139	
Tiers	285	348	210	242
Twisters	438	42	80	16
Wrappers (plug)	503	796	256	199
Other and not specified occupations	3,533	3,306	821	347

INDUSTRY AND OCCUPATION.	ALL CLASSES. Male.	ALL CLASSES. Female.	NEGRO. Male.	NEGRO. Female.
CLOCK AND WATCH FACTORIES	17,319	8,717	49	3
Manufacturers and proprietors	892	4	8	
Clerks (general)	269	409	1	
Clerks (shipping)	107	7	2	
Stenographers and typewriters	11	172	1	
Other clerical pursuits	31		1	
Engineers (stationary)	66		1	
Engravers	706	102		1
Machinists	1,144	2	1	
Tool makers	293	7		1
Bench hands	186	328		1
Firemen	40		2	
Jewelers	408	137	3	
Laborers	1,254	593	10	
Lathe hands and turners	283	139	1	
Repairers	283	24	4	
Teamsters	44		1	
Other and not specified occupations	11,302	6,793	13	
CLOTHING FACTORIES (SUITS, COATS, CLOAKS, AND OVERALLS)	273,172	110,986	8,594	937
Manufacturers and proprietors	17,457	276	304	6
Contractors	339	16	2	
Officials	103	2	1	
Managers and superintendents	1,055	80	13	1
Foremen and overseers	1,659	931	1	2
Bookkeepers, cashiers, and accountants	1,339	1,664	10	9
Clerks (general)	2,075	1,251	26	8
Clerks (shipping)	1,261	32	39	
Messenger, errand, and office boys	1,904	151	294	9
Stenographers and typewriters	109	1,008		6
Engineers (stationary)	71		3	
Machinists and millwrights	256		5	
Apprentices	1,807	716	133	8
Cutters	17,254	487	28	2
Fitters	187	473	1	1
Helpers	543	470	62	7
Inspectors	709	702	3	5
Laborers	1,643	1,261	275	19
Packers, folders, and wrappers	323	174	30	2
Porters	717		603	
Pressers	21,426	1,223	1,447	147
Sewers and sewing machine operators	29,126	52,855	149	233
Spongers	532	25	12	
Tailors and tailoresses	163,795	40,813	4,652	391
Teamsters	272		41	
Trimmers	1,319	410	13	8
Other and not specified occupations	5,891	5,966	447	73
CLOTHING FACTORIES (EXCEPT SUITS, COATS, CLOAKS, AND OVERALLS)	45,319	99,993	304	529
Manufacturers and proprietors	6,529	261	7	
Contractors	72	5		1
Managers and superintendents	829	121	1	
Foremen and overseers	952	2,200	3	3
Bookkeepers, cashiers, and accountants	739	1,343	2	2
Clerks (general)	1,249	1,103	8	2
Clerks (shipping)	1,135	97	15	1
Designers	1,061	898		1
Messenger, errand, and office boys	446	238	7	15
Purchasing agents	47	33		1
Stenographers and typewriters	70	746		2
Engineers (stationary)	78		4	
Machinists and millwrights	246		1	
Cap makers (not otherwise specified)	2,407	663	2	1
Cutters	7,639	742	7	2
Dressmakers (not otherwise specified)	758	17,578	4	146
Fitters	112	1,587		3
Helpers	114	262	2	
Inspectors	311	1,899		4
Laborers	672	973	10	6
Necktie and neckwear makers (not specified)	253	1,754		1
Packers, folders, and wrappers	333	1,111	11	5
Pressers	3,432	1,637	27	42
Sewers and sewing machine operators	12,815	54,344	90	253
Shirt makers (not specified)	420	731	25	
Teamsters	89		5	
Trimmers	268	1,120	3	13
Waist makers (not specified)	415	3,141	1	11
Other and not specified occupations	1,828	5,406	69	14

TABLE 22.—GAINFUL WORKERS 10 YEARS OF AGE AND OVER, ALL CLASSES AND NEGRO, CLASSIFIED BY SEX, INDUSTRY, AND OCCUPATION: 1910—Continued.

MANUFACTURING, INCLUDING HAND TRADES—Continued.

INDUSTRY AND OCCUPATION.	ALL CLASSES.		NEGRO.	
	Male.	Female.	Male.	Female.
COPPER FACTORIES	21,694	222	140	1
Clerks (general)	317	11	1	
Messenger, errand, and office boys	54		3	
Boiler makers	127		1	
Coppersmiths	1,749		10	
Engineers (stationary)	273		6	
Carmen and motormen	193		4	
Dippers and pourers	120		2	
Firemen	329		1	
Furnacemen and smeltermen	1,393		3	
Helpers	249	2	1	
Laborers	11,528	53	91	1
Molders	95		3	
Rollers	155		1	
Teamsters	137		3	
Other and not specified occupations	4,975	156	10	
CORSET FACTORIES	2,864	13,386	14	23
Clerks (general)	216	243	1	1
Messenger, errand, and office boys	35	37		3
Engineers (stationary)	29		1	
Machinists and millwrights	127		1	
Cutters	375	50		1
Fitters	5	132	1	
Laborers	284	543	3	1
Packers, folders, and wrappers	54	192		2
Sewers and sewing machine operators	237	7,285		5
Other and not specified occupations	1,502	4,904	7	10
COTTON MILLS	210,566	148,268	6,333	883
Manufacturers and proprietors	631	3	1	
Officials	588	3	1	
Managers and superintendents	1,713	2	1	
Foremen and overseers	6,848	217	37	1
Bookkeepers, cashiers, and accountants	1,467	614	2	
Clerks (general)	1,412	380	9	
Clerks (shipping)	687	29	2	
Messenger, errand, and office boys	282	24	26	2
Purchasing agents	61	1	1	
Stenographers and typewriters	119	436	1	
Weighers	177	8	11	
Blacksmiths	224		6	
Carpenters	1,471		5	
Electricians and electrical engineers	377		3	
Engineers (stationary)	1,433		18	
Machinists and millwrights	4,186		42	
Mechanics	377		2	
Painters	425	3	11	
Plumbers	329		1	
Apprentices	154	31	1	
Back tenders	1,022	52	2	
Band boys	298	43	1	
Beamers	1,696	243		1
Bleachers	298	19	10	
Bobbin boys, doffers, and carriers	14,100	2,357	38	9
Card grinders	1,065	4	15	
Card strippers	350	18	4	9
Carders, combers, and lappers	11,729	4,210	88	13
Cloth cutters	328	197	1	2
Creelers	202	175	1	5
Doublers and twisters	2,317	1,427	10	1
Drawers	839	899	9	1
Drawers-in	740	3,025	14	
Dyers	1,977	51	88	1
Finishers	701	770	1	1
Firemen	1,903		447	
Folders, rollers, and balers (cloth)	1,561	695	32	1
Harness makers	59	116	1	
Helpers	1,006	296	19	3
Inspectors	968	2,914	26	5
Laborers	28,702	5,305	4,073	268
Loom fixers	7,893			
Machine hands	1,588	1,615	18	32
Nappers	392	8	1	
Oilers	2,051	7	22	
Packers	554	267	33	
Pickers, breakers, and cleaners	2,631	256	186	68
Pressers and calenderers	497	81	19	3
Roll coverers	368	30	4	
Scrubbers	337	134	67	29
Section hands	1,542	21	2	
Sewers and cloth menders	332	1,458	3	26
Slashers and dressers	2,092	157	3	1
Slubbers	1,155	137	2	
Sorters	119	275	8	66
Spare hands	612	179	5	1
Speeders and rovers	5,224	7,474	38	20
Spinners	15,874	32,151	43	67
COTTON MILLS—Continued.				
Stampers	99	85	6	
Sweepers	2,998	328	116	110
Teamsters	1,203		247	
Trimmers	58	636	1	
Warpers	1,067	2,438	7	1
Washers	189	39	15	6
Weavers	48,929	43,911	53	30
Winders, reelers, and spoolers	3,226	24,283	12	32
Other and not specified occupations	14,714	7,731	359	68
DISTILLERIES	9,538	1,538	731	8
Manufacturers and proprietors	476	1	1	
Officials	98	1	1	
Managers and superintendents	310		2	
Foremen and overseers	239	32	5	
Bookkeepers, cashiers, and accountants	486	96	3	
Clerks (general)	481	97	6	
Clerks (shipping)	112	2	1	
Messenger, errand, and office boys	48	2	1	
Stenographers and typewriters	48	374		1
Carpenters	61		1	
Coopers	342		8	
Engineers (stationary)	253		11	
Machinists and millwrights	87		3	
Mechanics (not otherwise specified)	51	1	2	
Bottlers	433	306	10	2
Compounders	750	3	13	
Distillers and rectifiers	937	1	20	
Firemen	367		94	
Gaugers	242		3	
Labelers	42	382	5	
Laborers	2,638	133	436	3
Millers	140		9	
Teamsters	277		52	
Other and not specified occupations	620	107	44	2
ELECTRIC LIGHT AND POWER PLANTS.	66,063	2,995	2,604	8
Managers and superintendents	2,550		1	
Foremen and overseers	1,165	1	24	
Bookkeepers, cashiers, and accountants	1,965	790	1	1
Clerks (general)	2,333	472	7	1
Collectors	412	24	2	
Messenger, errand, and office boys	281	8	8	
Blacksmiths	190		9	
Boiler makers	76		5	
Carpenters	333		6	
Electricians and electrical engineers	20,898	7	120	
Engineers (stationary)	7,332	1	100	
Machinists and millwrights	1,919		17	
Masons	87		2	
Mechanics (not otherwise specified)	235	1	5	
Painters	83		1	
Plumbers	479		5	
Firemen	4,809		807	
Helpers	403		13	
Inspectors	617	94	2	
Laborers	7,999	162	1,137	3
Linemen	6,405		152	
Meter men	312		1	
Oilers	985		22	
Switchboard operators	252	21	1	
Teamsters	480		59	
Water tenders	128		3	
Other and not specified occupations	3,335	1,414	94	3
ELECTRICAL SUPPLY FACTORIES	70,660	18,255	383	6
Manufacturers and proprietors	876	2	2	
Managers and superintendents	1,287	4	1	
Foremen and overseers	1,978	320	5	
Bookkeepers, cashiers, and accountants	1,999	861	2	
Clerks (general)	5,643	1,664	8	
Clerks (shipping)	839	18	4	
Draftsmen	1,354	2	4	
Messenger, errand, and office boys	846	31	3	
Stenographers and typewriters	388	2,643		2
Boiler makers	28		1	
Carpenters	601		1	
Coppersmiths	31		1	
Electricians and electrical engineers	10,978	16	28	
Engineers (stationary)	1,382	1	10	
Machinists	9,997	3	26	
Mechanics (not otherwise specified)	498	1	1	
Painters	352	18	5	
Toolmakers	1,119		4	

TABLE 22.—GAINFUL WORKERS 10 YEARS OF AGE AND OVER, ALL CLASSES AND NEGRO, CLASSIFIED BY SEX, INDUSTRY, AND OCCUPATION: 1910—Continued.

MANUFACTURING, INCLUDING HAND TRADES—Continued.

INDUSTRY AND OCCUPATION.	ALL CLASSES.		NEGRO.	
	Male.	Female.	Male.	Female.
ELECTRICAL SUPPLY FACTORIES—Con.				
Apprentices	1,484	33	2	....
Battery makers (not specified)	121	23	2	....
Drillers	299	5	1	....
Finishers	162	65	1	....
Firemen	345	....	22	....
Fuse makers (not specified)	41	76	1	....
Glass blowers	66	31	2	....
Grinders	105	2	1	....
Helpers	1,152	269	3	....
Inspectors	1,080	752	....	1
Insulators	542	592	2	1
Laborers	10,018	1,373	145	....
Lamp makers (not specified)	124	604	1	....
Machine hands (not specified)	935	775	1	....
Molders	897	1	2	....
Motormen	34	....	2	....
Packers	356	206	6	....
Pasters and cementers	20	198	1	....
Pattern makers	545	7	1	....
Polishers and buffers	526	70	2	1
Repairers	151	30	1	....
Teamsters	303	....	18	....
Testers	409	349	2	....
Winders	1,859	2,232	1	....
Other and not specified occupations	8,890	4,978	57	1
FERTILIZER FACTORIES	13,754	284	7,648	75
Manufacturers and proprietors	337	2	6	....
Managers and superintendents	519	3	5	....
Foremen and overseers	413	2	36	....
Bookkeepers, cashiers, and accountants	396	24	2	....
Clerks	396	15	5	1
Messenger, errand, and office boys	45	....	22	....
Weighers	53	....	7	....
Blacksmiths	43	....	17	....
Carpenters	75	....	3	....
Engineers (stationary)	185	....	29	....
Machinists and millwrights	138	....	11	....
Mechanics (not otherwise specified)	61	....	4	....
Firemen	219	....	138	....
Laborers	9,753	90	6,930	68
Mixers	118	....	93	....
Teamsters	251	....	73	....
Other and not specified occupations	752	148	267	6
FISH CURING AND PACKING	7,715	1,360	291	73
Foremen and overseers	283	7	3	....
Bookkeepers, cashiers, and accountants	156	44	1	....
Clerks	135	23	2	....
Engineers (stationary)	67	....	3	....
Teamsters	61	....	6	....
Canners	264	17	2	1
Cutters and flakers	226	61	6	23
Laborers	4,637	233	228	43
Packers	538	559	22	1
Skinners, dressers, and cleaners	251	147	8	1
Other and not specified occupations	1,097	269	10	4
FLOUR AND GRAIN MILLS	52,682	1,559	2,230	21
Manufacturers and proprietors	4,912	42	29	....
Managers and superintendents	1,485	3	5	....
Foremen and overseers	701	10	9	....
Bookkeepers, cashiers, and accountants	1,452	518	3	....
Clerks (general)	541	61	2	....
Clerks (shipping)	251	1	3	....
Messenger, errand, and office boys	51	2	3	....
Weighers	70	3	1	....
Carpenters	86	....	1	....
Coopers	379	....	12	....
Engineers (stationary)	2,266	....	71	....
Machinists	212	....	2	....
Mechanics (not otherwise specified)	87	....	5	....
Millwrights	751	....	2	....
Apprentices	109	2	4	....
Firemen	641	....	165	....
Helpers	228	7	10	....
Inspectors	94	....	9	....
Laborers	9,040	90	1,086	10
Millers	22,573	59	369	1
Oilers	323	....	5	....
Packers	2,442	120	129	5
Teamsters	2,258	....	246	....
Other and not specified occupations	1,730	641	119	5

INDUSTRY AND OCCUPATION.	ALL CLASSES.		NEGRO.	
	Male.	Female.	Male.	Female.
FOOD FACTORIES (NOT OTHERWISE SPECIFIED)	26,177	8,774	2,722	1,672
Manufacturers and proprietors	3,124	86	35	3
Managers and superintendents	1,133	32	2	1
Foremen and overseers	898	182	21	3
Bookkeepers, cashiers, and accountants	808	360	1	1
Clerks (general)	733	318	6	....
Clerks (shipping)	419	10	3	....
Messenger, errand, and office boys	95	7	5	....
Other clerical pursuits	27	1	1	....
Carpenters	120	....	1	....
Coopers	120	....	13	....
Engineers (stationary)	478	....	13	....
Machinists and millwrights	420	....	11	....
Mechanics (not otherwise specified)	40	....	1	....
Tinners	82	....	1	....
Chocolate and cocoa makers (not otherwise specified)	307	89	1	....
Clam and oyster canners (not otherwise specified)	1,970	1,007	808	602
Coffee roasters (not otherwise specified)	892	168	27	....
Firemen	273	....	37	....
Helpers	237	89	21	3
Ice cream makers (not otherwise specified)	1,544	36	122	7
Inspectors	290	80	3	45
Labelers and stampers	48	403	3	4
Laborers	6,806	1,450	1,269	541
Machine hands (not specified)	113	141	1	4
Milk condensers (not otherwise specified)	506	497	4	1
Millers	359	....	4	....
Packers	626	1,643	46	15
Teamsters	1,409	....	118	....
Wrappers	37	406	....	2
Other and not specified occupations	2,263	1,769	144	440
FRUIT AND VEGETABLE CANNING	10,627	4,926	238	124
Manufacturers and proprietors	915	32	1	....
Managers and superintendents	854	1	1	....
Foremen and overseers	632	179	4	....
Bookkeepers, cashiers, and accountants	390	178	1	....
Clerks (general)	254	93	2	....
Clerks (shipping)	171	5	1	....
Messenger, errand, and office boys	35	5	2	....
Coopers	90	....	1	....
Engineers (stationary)	212	....	3	....
Firemen	89	....	9	....
Labelers	39	511	....	4
Laborers	3,682	982	133	45
Packers	351	759	10	3
Teamsters	445	....	15	....
Other and not specified occupations	2,468	2,171	55	72
FURNITURE FACTORIES	152,382	7,889	4,090	164
Manufacturers and proprietors	4,386	28	48	....
Officials	548	6	1	....
Managers and superintendents	1,717	12	1	....
Foremen and overseers	3,244	141	10	1
Clerks (general)	1,288	351	7	1
Clerks (shipping)	1,582	10	11	....
Messenger, errand, and office boys	252	13	8	1
Stenographers and typewriters	154	1,050	....	1
Blacksmiths	109	....	1	....
Cabinetmakers	32,272	8	269	1
Carpenters	5,132	....	43	....
Electricians and electrical engineers	57	....	1	....
Engineers (stationary)	869	....	8	....
Machinists	2,893	....	25	....
Mechanics (not otherwise specified)	402	....	12	....
Painters	5,337	148	90	1
Wood carvers	2,108	13	7	....
Apprentices	1,406	17	22	....
Assemblers and erectors	588	13	2	....
Bench hands	176	8	1	....
Borers and drill-press hands	208	6	3	....
Caners and seaters	1,712	898	279	91
Cutters	314	79	5	1
Finishers	8,169	101	86	1
Firemen	522	....	71	....
Fitters	216	5	1	....
Glaziers	157	4	3	....
Gluers	901	18	7	....
Helpers	836	59	20	....
Inspectors	278	56	3	....
Laborers	23,055	516	1,365	11
Machine hands (not specified)	3,405	135	23	2

TABLE 22.—GAINFUL WORKERS 10 YEARS OF AGE AND OVER, ALL CLASSES AND NEGRO, CLASSIFIED BY SEX, INDUSTRY, AND OCCUPATION: 1910—Continued.

MANUFACTURING, INCLUDING HAND TRADES—Continued.

INDUSTRY AND OCCUPATION.	ALL CLASSES.		NEGRO.	
	Male.	Female.	Male.	Female.
FURNITURE FACTORIES—Contd.				
Oilers	64		9	
Packers and wrappers	2,566	254	99	2
Planers	565	1	1	
Polishers	2,875	73	32	1
Repairers	1,036	34	171	5
Reedworkers	950	358	12	4
Sanders and buffers	2,026	66	18	
Saw filers	151		2	
Sawyers	2,365		31	
Sewers	32	749		5
Teamsters	2,019		183	
Trimmers	1,040	272		1
Turners, molders, and shapers	1,673	9	6	1
Upholsterers	16,487	1,068	772	25
Veneerers	329	2	1	
Other and not specified occupations	13,911	1,308	320	8
GAS WORKS	51,133	2,117	2,430	9
Manufacturers and proprietors	184	1	1	
Officials	423	2	1	
Managers and superintendents	2,208	4	1	
Foremen and overseers	2,276	1	27	
Bookkeepers, cashiers, and accountants	2,998	889	1	2
Clerks (general)	4,000	472	7	2
Collectors	1,595	9	1	
Messenger, errand, and office boys	260	2	15	
Blacksmiths	195		5	
Carpenters	204		1	
Electricians and electrical engineers	317		1	
Engineers (stationary)	1,520		19	
Machinists and millwrights	753		3	
Masons	101		2	
Mechanics (not otherwise specified)	177		1	
Painters	69		2	
Plumbers	6,199		103	
Tinners	41		1	
Firemen and stokers	2,554		305	
Helpers	393		19	
Inspectors	1,895	6	4	1
Laborers	16,135	12	1,648	3
Light trimmers	248		14	
Oilers	89		3	
Provers and testers	147		4	
Teamsters	1,094		58	
Other and not specified occupations	5,058	719	183	1
GLASS FACTORIES	88,059	6,346	2,377	77
Manufacturers and proprietors	917	3	1	
Managers and superintendents	989	4	2	
Foremen and overseers	1,330	65	10	
Clerks (general)	865	244	4	
Clerks (shipping)	517	16	5	
Designers	149	28	1	
Draftsmen	27		1	
Messenger, errand, and office boys	181	6	11	
Purchasing agents	25		1	
Stenographers and typewriters	91	627	1	
Blacksmiths	328		3	
Carpenters	272		2	
Engineers (stationary)	497		7	
Machinists and millwrights	930		2	
Mechanics (not otherwise specified)	72		1	
Apprentices	1,073	15	5	
Blowers	15,408	59	39	1
Box makers	437	29	7	
Carriers and shove boys	1,459	14	41	2
Casters and rollers (plate glass)	355	3	14	
Cutters	6,103	221	12	
Decorators	368	436	7	
Engravers	207	25	1	
Etchers and markers	55	68	1	
Finishers	979	41	6	
Firemen	473		48	
Gas makers	145	1	62	
Gatherers	3,838	14	1	
Glazers	1,419	29	16	1
Grinders	1,140	121	9	
Helpers	1,031	59	38	2
Inspectors	97	191	1	
Laborers	23,688	937	1,662	37
Ladlers	85		9	
Lehr tenders	280	2	13	
Machine hands (not specified)	430	55	19	
Mixers (batch)	287	2	21	
Mold boys	813	1	44	
Mold makers	331	1		1
Packers and wrappers	2,316	887	23	5
Polishers and buffers	910	116	1	1
Pressers and molders	1,468	35	1	2

INDUSTRY AND OCCUPATION.	ALL CLASSES.		NEGRO.	
	Male.	Female.	Male.	Female.
GLASS FACTORIES—Continued.				
Roughers	72	3	1	
Smoothers	358	20		1
Snappers-up and stickers-up	1,705	9	44	3
Sorters	139	385	2	1
Teamsters	461		31	
Teasers	196	3	8	
Washers	72	88	2	3
Other and not specified occupations	12,671	1,483	136	13
GLOVE FACTORIES	7,648	15,039	15	21
Manufacturers and proprietors	720	23	1	
Stenographers and typewriters	12	137	1	
Engineers (stationary)	40		1	
Machinists	55		1	
Cutters	2,980	128	2	
Inspectors	23	251		2
Laborers	445	421	6	
Packers and wrappers	22	117	1	
Sewers and sewing machine operators	945	7,821	1	8
Teamsters	35		1	
Other and not specified occupations	2,371	6,141		11
GOLD AND SILVER FACTORIES	17,076	2,945	79	5
Manufacturers and proprietors	530	1	1	
Clerks (general)	416	161	2	
Clerks (shipping)	119	11	1	
Electricians and electrical engineers	52		1	
Engineers (stationary)	75		1	
Mechanics (not otherwise specified)	112	6	2	
Apprentices	364	17	1	
Beaters	607	76		1
Cleaners and washers	66	63	2	
Firemen	54		2	
Goldsmiths and silversmiths	3,762	61	27	
Laborers	1,093	175	10	
Melters	121		1	
Molders	196	5	3	
Platers	1,386	86	4	
Polishers and buffers	2,424	314	3	2
Refiners	218	3	2	
Teamsters	34		1	
Other and not specified occupations	5,447	1,966	15	2
HARNESS AND SADDLE FACTORIES	31,956	1,176	410	11
Manufacturers and proprietors	6,545	17	28	
Foremen and overseers	312	13	1	
Clerks (general)	288	47	3	
Clerks (shipping)	159	2	2	
Messenger, errand, and office boys	35		2	
Stenographers and typewriters	38	179		1
Mechanics (not otherwise specified)	58	3	1	
Apprentices	579	3	4	
Collar makers	542	14	83	
Cutters	288	1	1	
Harness makers	19,352	261	160	4
Laborers	1,210	88	81	1
Packers	65	39	6	
Polishers and buffers	89	14	2	
Teamsters	33		4	
Other and not specified occupations	2,363	495	32	2
HAT FACTORIES (WOOL AND FELT)	29,280	11,514	150	11
Foremen and overseers	573	239	1	
Clerks (general)	476	166	3	
Clerks (shipping)	316	9	3	
Messenger, errand, and office boys	197	12	2	
Carpenters	57		1	
Engineers (stationary)	156		3	
Apprentices	571	53	2	
Blockers and pressers	1,229	118	5	
Box makers	100	106	1	
Dyers and colorers	233	58	13	1
Finishers	4,200	214	1	
Firemen	86		4	
Flangers and curlers	504	15	1	

TABLE 22.—GAINFUL WORKERS 10 YEARS OF AGE AND OVER, ALL CLASSES AND NEGRO, CLASSIFIED BY SEX, INDUSTRY, AND OCCUPATION: 1910—Continued.

MANUFACTURING, INCLUDING HAND TRADES—Continued.

INDUSTRY AND OCCUPATION.	ALL CLASSES. Male.	Female.	NEGRO. Male.	Female.
HAT FACTORIES (WOOL AND FELT)—Contd.				
Fur feeders	140	97	......	1
Hatters (not specified)	8,621	825	28	1
Helpers	162	50	2	......
Laborers	1,537	218	31	1
Packers	274	59	8	......
Sizers, hardeners, and stiffeners	1,897	55	3	......
Teamsters	69	......	6	......
Trimmers and sewers	317	6,111	1	3
Wirers	112	86	1	......
Other and not specified occupations	7,453	3,023	30	4
HEMP AND JUTE MILLS	4,223	2,852	212	9
Clerks (general)	115	15	1	......
Messenger, errand, and office boys	16	1	1	......
Engineers (stationary)	49	......	1	......
Breakers	71	1	15	......
Carders and spreaders	145	83	20	......
Doffers	117	211	2	......
Firemen	46	......	1	......
Laborers	1,274	160	105	7
Machine hands (not specified)	148	126	2	......
Oilers	57	......	1	......
Packers	63	10	1	......
Spinners	268	1,064	12	......
Teamsters	34	......	4	......
Weavers	424	227	13	......
Winders, reelers, and spoolers	171	370	6	......
Other and not specified occupations	1,225	584	27	2
IRON AND STEEL FACTORIES (NOT OTHERWISE SPECIFIED)	523,909	33,119	5,336	91
Manufacturers and proprietors	11,265	58	32	......
Officials	2,459	31	1	......
Managers and superintendents	7,828	20	1	......
Foremen and overseers	13,746	458	30	2
Bookkeepers, cashiers, and accountants	7,133	2,910	10	3
Clerks (general)	12,782	2,355	38	2
Clerks (shipping)	4,173	85	27	......
Collectors	224	4	1	......
Draftsmen	6,117	7	11	......
Messenger, errand, and office boys	2,074	49	36	......
Stenographers and typewriters	1,503	6,655	4	4
Weighers	216	13	6	1
Blacksmiths	8,281	......	114	......
Boiler makers	3,659	......	24	......
Carpenters	3,916	......	18	......
Die setters and sinkers	2,744	4	1	......
Electricians and electrical engineers	2,910	2	6	......
Engineers (stationary)	4,187	......	51	......
Engravers	88	18	......	1
Machinists	145,740	4	392	......
Masons	272	......	4	......
Mechanics (not otherwise specified)	4,672	5	43	......
Millwrights	1,371	......	4	......
Painters	3,570	176	26	......
Plumbers	2,154	......	5	......
Tinners	1,068	1	3	......
Adjusters	743	20	2	......
Annealers and temperers	1,010	4	1	......
Apprentices	12,494	26	29	1
Assemblers and erectors	5,236	319	23	......
Bench hands	1,267	375	3	1
Bolt makers and headers	1,048	20	5	......
Box makers	297	322	1	1
Bridge works operatives (not specified)	1,816	......	3	......
Buffers	1,299	86	12	......
Chain makers (not specified)	1,382	41	53	1
Core makers	1,680	170	9	......
Cranemen	1,191	......	26	......
Cutlery makers (not specified)	2,405	206	4	......
Cutlers	2,435	337	27	......
Dippers	118	43	5	......
Drillers	2,742	127	17	......
Elevator tenders	298	......	5	......
Filers	2,418	91	15	......
Finishers	2,081	150	18	......
Firemen	1,770	......	84	......
Fitters	1,208	38	6	......
Forgemen	1,513	......	12	......
Furnace and cupola tenders	126	......	4	......
Grinders	5,673	349	37	1
Gun and pistol makers (not otherwise specified)	1,288	75	5	......
Hammermen	994	......	11	......
Heaters	1,070	1	5	......

INDUSTRY AND OCCUPATION.	ALL CLASSES. Male.	Female.	NEGRO. Male.	Female.
IRON AND STEEL FACTORIES (NOT OTHERWISE SPECIFIED)—Contd.				
Helpers	10,986	400	276	3
Inspectors	4,177	1,346	11	3
Janitors	346	12	63	4
Laborers	92,564	3,473	2,909	33
Lacquerers, japanners, and enamelers	1,225	289	12	......
Lathe hands, planers, and millers	3,432	44	12	......
Lock makers (not otherwise specified)	3,045	158	12	2
Machine hands (not otherwise specified)	11,735	2,986	61	7
Molders	9,937	12	68	......
Oilers	641	6	15	......
Packers and wrappers	2,152	2,109	27	11
Pattern makers	5,353	42	5	......
Platers	1,412	53	6	......
Polishers	8,035	357	24	......
Porters	263	......	79	......
Press hands and stampers	3,080	763	5	......
Repairers	3,591	44	89	3
Riveters	1,128	49	6	......
Rollers	456	8	5	......
Sand blasters	99	2	3	......
Sawyers	383	......	6	......
Scrubbers and sweepers	224	15	10	......
Solderers	174	16	1	......
Sorters	213	811	3	1
Teamsters	2,388	......	117	......
Testers	610	24	1	......
Tool factory operatives (not specified)	12,601	50	26	......
Weavers	905	353	1	......
Wire fence, spring, and screen makers (not specified)	2,855	252	34	1
Other and not specified occupations	30,145	3,790	139	5
IRON FOUNDRIES	163,989	2,664	6,140	32
Manufacturers and proprietors	2,179	10	5	......
Foremen and overseers	3,297	33	34	......
Bookkeepers, cashiers, and accountants	1,477	357	2	......
Clerks (general)	2,009	195	16	......
Clerks (shipping)	981	5	13	......
Messenger, errand, and office boys	239	4	10	......
Weighers	82	......	7	......
Blacksmiths, forgemen, and hammermen	1,291	......	24	......
Boiler makers	16,883	......	190	......
Carpenters	635	......	6	......
Electricians and electrical engineers	290	......	3	......
Engineers (stationary)	944	......	14	......
Machinists	5,788	......	59	......
Masons	100	......	3	......
Mechanics (not otherwise specified)	369	......	9	......
Millwrights	84	......	1	......
Painters	289	5	10	......
Plumbers	787	......	7	......
Tinners	865	......	4	......
Tool makers	147	1	2	......
Annealers and temperers	36	......	3	......
Apprentices	2,619	10	13	......
Assemblers	3,288	24	25	2
Core makers	4,054	342	61	1
Cranemen	626	......	31	......
Cutters	233	2	24	......
Drillers	318	2	4	......
Enamelers	109	63	6	......
Filers	141	1	4	......
Finishers	290	3	8	......
Firemen	926	......	103	......
Fitters	341	1	7	......
Furnace and cupola tenders	917	......	101	......
Grinders	407	......	15	......
Heaters	261	1	1	......
Helpers	5,212	35	398	......
Inspectors	727	6	12	......
Laborers	41,444	274	3,532	23
Ladlers and pourers	65	......	12	......
Lathe hands, turners, and planers	103	1	3	......
Machine hands (not specified)	408	17	3	......
Molders	43,771	6	748	......
Oilers	73	......	3	......
Packers	389	50	11	1
Pattern makers	1,990	9	7	......
Platers	341	3	6	......
Polishers and buffers	1,872	6	33	......
Press hands	233	3	3	......
Puddlers	109	......	18	......
Repairers	910	7	111	1
Riveters	647	4	6	......
Rollers	149	......	31	......
Teamsters	960	......	113	......
Other and not specified occupations	11,284	1,184	265	4

TABLE 22.—GAINFUL WORKERS 10 YEARS OF AGE AND OVER, ALL CLASSES AND NEGRO, CLASSIFIED BY SEX, INDUSTRY, AND OCCUPATION: 1910—Continued.

MANUFACTURING, INCLUDING HAND TRADES—Continued.

INDUSTRY AND OCCUPATION.	ALL CLASSES.		NEGRO.	
	Male.	Female.	Male.	Female.
JEWELRY FACTORIES	27,168	9,765	95	12
Manufacturers and proprietors	1,964	21	3	......
Foremen and overseers	456	106	1	1
Clerks (shipping)	196	100	11	......
Designers	257	39	1	......
Messenger, errand, and office boys	265	13	7	......
Engravers	2,178	89	5	......
Mechanics (not otherwise specified)	47	1	1	......
Apprentices	1,406	52	4	......
Bench hands	1,860	925	1	......
Chain makers (not specified)	256	989	......	3
Colorers	402	23	2	......
Helpers	89	45	1	......
Jewelers	6,249	1,120	16	......
Laborers	528	140	5	1
Lapidaries	2,092	573	2	1
Makers of jewelry articles (not specified)	211	163	1	......
Packers	64	384	4	1
Polishers	1,808	706	2	1
Press hands and stampers	911	268	2	2
Refiners	39	1	1	......
Solderers	246	420	1	......
Teamsters	15	....	2	......
Other and not specified occupations	5,629	3,587	22	2
KNITTING MILLS	36,107	71,907	542	274
Foremen and overseers	1,786	1,151	2	......
Bookkeepers, cashiers, and accountants	474	429	1	1
Clerks (shipping)	647	37	4	......
Messenger, errand, and office boys	126	36	5	......
Electricians	32	....	1	......
Engineers (stationary)	375	....	5	......
Machinists and millwrights	1,477	2	6	......
Boarders	1,895	142	2	8
Bobbin boys and doffers	127	64	......	2
Brushers and nappers	121	34	1	......
Cutters	1,028	1,287	2	1
Dyers	600	19	21	......
Firemen	211	....	22	......
Inspectors	165	2,591	3	19
Knitters	7,703	15,652	99	61
Laborers	4,210	3,520	115	30
Loopers and toppers	890	9,924	161	20
Machine hands (not specified)	700	4,255	2	2
Menders and darners	105	3,198	......	60
Packers and folders	601	2,324	5	5
Pairers and sorters	176	911	3	6
Pressers and balers	1,203	323	8	1
Sewers and sewing machine operators	682	11,903	5	11
Spinners	1,137	499	2	3
Stampers and labelers	91	507	......	1
Tape pullers and ribbon runners	30	400	......	1
Teamsters	162	....	14	......
Turners	650	336	9	1
Winders, reelers, and spoolers	620	2,714	2	1
Other and not specified occupations	8,083	9,649	42	40
LACE AND EMBROIDERY MILLS	8,052	17,187	29	136
Manufacturers and proprietors	785	60	1	......
Foremen and overseers	171	341	1	......
Clerks (general)	527	334	....	1
Machinists and loom fixers	170	....	1	......
Crocheters and knitters	23	102	1	9
Cutters	61	306	......	10
Embroiderers	1,001	3,409	1	7
Fancy workers (not in factory)	234	3,840	....	72
Finishers	23	168	......	2
Helpers	86	131	1	......
Laborers	459	234	4	......
Menders and darners	15	1,075	......	1
Packers, folders, and wrappers	56	320	2	......
Pressers	22	112	......	3
Sewers and sewing machine operators	566	1,338	1	12
Winders, rulers, and spoolers	134	435	3	1
Other and not specified occupations	3,719	4,982	13	18

INDUSTRY AND OCCUPATION.	ALL CLASSES.		NEGRO.	
	Male.	Female.	Male.	Female.
LAUNDRIES	72,421	83,306	3,027	12,332
Owners and proprietors	14,695	746	149	44
Officials	191	7	1	......
Managers and superintendents	2,171	233	14	2
Foremen and overseers	1,674	1,397	20	6
Agents	874	69	9	1
Bookkeepers, cashiers, and accountants	907	3,234	1	19
Clerks (general)	1,147	2,019	11	18
Clerks (shipping)	96	46	......	1
Collectors	454	13	1	......
Messenger, errand, and office boys	745	48	53	3
Stenographers and typewriters	42	453	......	3
Engineers (stationary)	1,635	....	68	......
Machinists	382	....	18	......
Mechanics (not otherwise specified)	78	....	6	......
Apprentices	50	19	....	2
Drivers and deliverymen	11,992	12	369	2
Dyers	61	18	4	3
Finishers and polishers	167	640	2	21
Firemen	596	....	179	......
Folders	38	951	2	37
Helpers	989	810	49	81
Ironers and pressers	4,227	9,985	91	659
Laborers	5,422	3,340	596	694
Laundresses and laundrymen (not specified)	19,183	47,323	991	10,371
Manglers	137	2,154	8	41
Markers	870	2,046	13	15
Porters	186	2	142	......
Seamstresses	10	375	1	30
Shakers	15	222	1	8
Sorters	361	1,403	7	6
Starchers	226	1,966	11	40
Wrappers and packers	117	513	2	6
Wringers	214	38	52	4
Other and not specified occupations	2,469	3,224	156	215
LEAD AND ZINC FACTORIES	16,186	734	381	......
Foremen and overseers	498	12	5	......
Clerks (general)	367	93	1	......
Clerks (shipping)	94	3	1	......
Messenger, errand, and office boys	88	....	2	......
Engineers (stationary)	280	....	1	......
Machinists	438	1	1	......
Finishers	127	9	1	......
Firemen	669	....	7	......
Furnacemen, smeltermen, and burners	1,457	3	7	......
Helpers	116	13	1	......
Jigmen	107	....	1	......
Laborers	7,868	74	315	......
Machine hands (not otherwise specified)	67	40	2	......
Molders and casters	369	2	1	......
Motormen	51	....	4	......
Type founders	512	50	4	......
Teamsters	200	....	7	......
Other and not specified occupations	2,878	434	20	......
LEATHER BELT, LEATHER CASE, AND POCKETBOOK FACTORIES	14,003	3,974	95	2
Manufacturers and proprietors	1,125	14	4	......
Officials	81	1	1	......
Managers and superintendents	313	4	1	......
Bookkeepers, cashiers, and accountants	294	212	1	1
Clerks (general)	398	100	2	......
Clerks (shipping)	270	10	4	......
Messenger, errand, and office boys	112	7	2	......
Machinists	200	....	4	......
Belt makers (not otherwise specified)	1,194	159	6	......
Framers	97	18	1	......
Laborers	1,755	147	48	......
Press hands and stampers	140	31	2	......
Stitchers and finishers	391	376	2	......
Teamsters	76	....	3	......
Other and not specified occupations	7,557	2,895	14	1

TABLE 22.—GAINFUL WORKERS 10 YEARS OF AGE AND OVER, ALL CLASSES AND NEGRO, CLASSIFIED BY SEX, INDUSTRY, AND OCCUPATION: 1910—Continued.

MANUFACTURING, INCLUDING HAND TRADES—Continued.

INDUSTRY AND OCCUPATION.	ALL CLASSES. Male.	ALL CLASSES. Female.	NEGRO. Male.	NEGRO. Female.
LIME, CEMENT, AND GYPSUM FACTORIES	63,789	948	4,961	25
Manufacturers and proprietors	2,598	13	22	......
Officials	297	5	2	......
Managers and superintendents	1,378	3	3	......
Foremen and overseers	2,574	......	32	......
Bookkeepers, cashiers, and accountants	913	154	......	1
Clerks (general)	950	74	10	......
Clerks (shipping)	143	3	1	......
Messenger, errand, and office boys	108	1	4	......
Weighers	98	2	8	......
Blacksmiths	430	......	9	......
Carpenters	794	......	8	......
Coopers	674	......	39	......
Engineers (stationary)	1,501	......	33	......
Machinists and millwrights	1,383	......	7	......
Masons	289	......	17	......
Mechanics (not otherwise specified)	115	......	4	......
Painters	51	......	1	......
Plumbers	117	......	1	......
Apprentices	69	......	1	......
Burners	1,003	......	31	......
Cranemen and riggers	128	......	5	......
Finishers	457	......	33	......
Firemen	1,364	......	122	......
Grinders	584	......	14	......
Inspectors	234	......	4	......
Kilnmen	213	......	2	......
Laborers	35,713	152	3,826	22
Machine hands (not specified)	182	3	6	......
Mixers	449	......	80	......
Molders and pressers	301	......	7	......
Motormen	63	......	3	......
Oilers	430	......	6	......
Packers	1,394	2	110	......
Repairers	468	......	3	......
Teamsters	2,191	......	303	......
Other and not specified occupations	4,133	536	204	2
LINEN MILLS	1,841	1,655	21	18
Carders and spreaders	82	65	3	4
Doffers	28	47	......	2
Drawers and twisters	16	82	......	2
Laborers	475	256	12	2
Spinners	62	275	......	2
Teamsters	22	......	2	......
Weavers	118	169	......	1
Other and not specified occupations	1,038	761	4	5
LIQUOR AND BEVERAGE FACTORIES (NOT OTHERWISE SPECIFIED)	19,804	1,179	1,071	37
Manufacturers and proprietors	4,472	58	21	1
Managers and superintendents	980	19	2	......
Foremen and overseers	506	26	2	......
Bookkeepers, cashiers, and accountants	499	221	2	......
Clerks (general)	334	53	3	2
Clerks (shipping)	130	3	1	......
Messenger, errand, and office boys	40	1	2	......
Engineers (stationary)	130	......	3	......
Machinists and millwrights	80	......	1	......
Mechanics (not otherwise specified)	41	......	1	......
Bottlers	4,395	199	264	7
Helpers	180	5	10	......
Labelers	80	179	2	3
Laborers	3,620	154	524	22
Mineral and soda water makers (not specified)	215	4	7	......
Packers and wrappers	94	25	3	......
Teamsters	2,713	......	135	......
Other and not specified occupations	1,295	232	88	2
MARBLE AND STONE YARDS	64,710	891	1,775	13
Manufacturers and proprietors	4,216	24	15	......
Foremen and overseers	861	1	4	......
Draftsmen	385	3	1	......
Messenger, errand, and office boys	77	3	2	......
Stenographers and typewriters	141	366	......	2
Blacksmiths	482	......	5	......
Engineers (stationary)	542	......	12	......
Machinists and millwrights	397	......	5	......
Masons and monument setters	1,413	......	35	......
Mechanics (not otherwise specified)	84	......	3	......
Tool makers	231	......	4	......

INDUSTRY AND OCCUPATION.	ALL CLASSES. Male.	ALL CLASSES. Female.	NEGRO. Male.	NEGRO. Female.
MARBLE AND STONE YARDS—Contd.				
Apprentices	669	......	4	......
Block makers and cleaners	146	......	13	......
Cranemen	255	......	2	......
Drillers	298	......	33	......
Firemen	121	......	11	......
Grinders	140	......	2	......
Helpers	345	......	15	......
Laborers	6,807	67	731	6
Planers	639	......	2	......
Polishers	3,340	58	210	2
Sawyers	698	......	16	......
Stonecutters	35,732	5	500	......
Teamsters	1,178	......	88	......
Other and not specified occupations	5,513	364	62	3
METAL INDUSTRIES AND FACTORIES (NOT OTHERWISE SPECIFIED)	253,211	6,954	6,305	68
Manufacturers and proprietors	2,756	31	6	1
Managers and superintendents	1,405	22	1	1
Foremen and overseers	3,097	158	27	3
Bookkeepers, cashiers, and accountants	1,318	409	2	......
Clerks (general)	1,796	285	13	......
Clerks (shipping)	1,295	24	8	......
Collectors	24	2	2	......
Messenger, errand, and office boys	253	36	2	......
Stenographers and typewriters	220	838	5	4
Blacksmiths	1,314	1	48	......
Boiler makers	352	......	13	......
Carpenters	481	......	5	......
Coopers	86	......	2	......
Electricians and electrical engineers	374	2	2	......
Engineers (mechanical)	94	......	5	......
Engineers (stationary)	587	......	6	......
Engravers	219	6	6	......
Gunsmiths, locksmiths, and bellhangers	2,980	3	37	......
Machinists	85,722	2	636	......
Mechanics (not otherwise specified)	417	3	7	......
Millwrights	116	......	1	......
Painters	276	18	8	......
Plumbers	243	......	2	......
Tinners	2,020	......	12	......
Tool makers	618	......	1	......
Annealers and temperers	177	......	6	......
Apprentices	10,447	63	39	......
Assemblers and fitters	193	48	3	......
Core makers	7,142	635	87	1
Cranemen	781	......	21	......
Cupola tenders and melters	483	......	39	......
Drillers	199	6	3	......
Enamelers	169	36	6	......
Finishers	147	35	1	......
Firemen	673	......	87	......
Forgemen and hammermen	276	......	9	......
Furnacemen and smeltermen	580	......	22	......
Grinders	445	......	12	......
Heaters	98	......	2	......
Helpers	6,428	153	306	3
Inspectors	285	218	5	......
Laborers	45,075	786	3,281	24
Ladlers and pourers	93	......	5	......
Lathe hands, turners, and planers	187	11	1	......
Machine hands (not otherwise specified)	492	118	9	1
Molders	42,261	37	1,022	......
Packers and wrappers	252	225	2	......
Pattern makers	2,246	22	9	1
Platers	2,135	56	7	......
Polishers and buffers	3,683	148	26	2
Press hands and stampers	602	171	6	......
Puddlers	96	......	15	......
Riveters	96	6	1	1
Rollers and catchers	160	1	7	......
Smeltermen	187	......	2	......
Solderers	553	108	5	......
Spinners	555	207	1	9
Teamsters	671	......	66	......
Woodworkers (not otherwise specified)	204	......	4	......
Other and not specified occupations	17,077	2,024	334	17
OIL REFINERIES	28,837	880	1,129	5
Managers and superintendents	1,204	2	1	......
Foremen and overseers	1,073	......	9	......
Bookkeepers, cashiers, and accountants	1,267	166	1	1
Clerks (general)	1,447	98	8	......
Clerks (shipping)	293	6	2	......
Messenger, errand, and office boys	178	3	2	......
Stenographers and typewriters	193	455	1	......
Boiler makers	898	......	2	......
Carpenters	336	......	2	......

TABLE 22.—GAINFUL WORKERS 10 YEARS OF AGE AND OVER, ALL CLASSES AND NEGRO, CLASSIFIED BY SEX, INDUSTRY, AND OCCUPATION: 1910—Continued.

MANUFACTURING, INCLUDING HAND TRADES—Continued.

INDUSTRY AND OCCUPATION.	ALL CLASSES. Male.	Female.	NEGRO. Male.	Female.
OIL REFINERIES—Continued.				
Coopers	793		11	
Electricians and electrical engineers	123		1	
Engineers (stationary)	946		7	
Machinists and millwrights	747		6	
Masons	103		2	
Painters	109	1	1	
Plumbers	972		4	
Compounders and treaters	245		3	
Distillers and refiners	984		12	
Firemen	1,442		62	
Gaugers and testers	215	2	1	
Helpers	252	7	2	
Inspectors	252		1	
Laborers	11,145	63	901	4
Oilers	64		3	
Press hands	133	7	2	
Teamsters	1,072		43	
Other and not specified occupations	2,351	70	32	
PAINT FACTORIES	11,672	1,946	242	4
Manufacturers and proprietors	899	2	2	
Managers and superintendents	657	12		1
Foremen and overseers	566	60	1	
Bookkeepers, cashiers, and accountants	484	244	1	
Clerks (general)	655	230	4	1
Clerks (shipping)	446	5	2	
Messenger, errand, and office boys	112	4	2	
Stenographers and typewriters	65	637		1
Engineers (stationary)	188		4	
Painters	277		4	
Apprentices	63	1	1	
Firemen	85		2	
Grinders	191		5	
Helpers	130	15	2	
Inspectors	52	10	1	
Labelers	32	328	2	1
Laborers	2,841	117	126	
Mixers	1,274	24	33	
Packers	291	57	3	
Teamsters	347		16	
Other and not specified occupations	2,017	200	31	
PAPER AND PULP MILLS	76,834	13,965	1,198	75
Manufacturers and proprietors	1,029	3	1	
Foremen and overseers	2,290	145	10	
Bookkeepers, cashiers, and accountants	1,122	425	1	
Clerks (general)	1,506	424	7	
Clerks (shipping)	1,014	17	6	
Messenger, errand, and office boys	240	8	6	1
Blacksmiths	225		2	
Boiler makers	34		3	
Electricians and electrical engineers	315		1	
Engineers (stationary)	1,876		11	
Machinists	1,727		7	
Masons	43		5	
Mechanics (not otherwise specified)	191	2	1	
Millwrights	1,383		1	
Acid makers	235	2	2	
Back tenders (paper mill)	948	14	2	
Beatermen	1,872	2	18	
Bleachers	318	3	4	
Calenderers and platers	785	1,341	9	4
Chippers (pulp wood)	84		9	
Colorers and color mixers	363	8	3	
Cookers (pulp)	187		3	
Cutters and trimmers (paper)	1,868	1,597	15	2
Finishers	1,856	895	2	
Firemen	2,448		64	
Folders	42	286		1
Grinders	767	5	3	
Helpers	880	181	11	1
Laborers	28,061	1,418	753	30
Loftsmen and dryers (paper mill)	286	4	3	
Machine hands, not specified (paper mill)	3,166	487	5	
Oilers	328		2	
Packers, wrappers, and sealers	525	347	26	
Paper sorters	157	1,856	4	20
Press hands	506	43	4	
Rag pickers and sorters	143	1,055	4	6
Sawyers (pulp wood)	90		1	
Stackers (paper)	45	99	1	
Teamsters	1,361		83	
Winders, rollers, and reelers	479	165	3	
Other and not specified occupations	16,039	3,133	102	10
PIANO AND ORGAN FACTORIES	35,025	2,769	258	4
Manufacturers and proprietors	815	4	3	
Managers and superintendents	504	2	1	
Foremen and overseers	702	41	2	
Clerks (general)	364	145	3	1
Clerks (shipping)	178	2	3	
Messenger, errand, and office boys	121	5	4	
Stenographers and typewriters	64	430	1	
Cabinetmakers	2,316		3	
Carpenters	826		1	
Engineers (stationary)	191		2	
Machinists and millwrights	808		1	
Painters	1,437	24	2	
Action makers	1,253	356	3	
Apprentices	423	4	2	
Cutters	90	20	1	
Drill-press hands	82	20	2	
Finishers	2,311	32	4	
Firemen	106		3	
Fitters	65	20	1	
Gluers	270	59	2	
Helpers	412	66	5	1
Key makers (not specified)	257	80	1	
Laborers	4,079	358	83	1
Machine hands (not specified)	407	91	1	
Molders	95		1	
Oilers	58		1	
Packers	166	26	6	
Polishers	3,459	45	26	
Repairers	358	5	12	
Sanders and buffers	80	3	1	
Stringers	404	48	1	
Teamsters	303		26	
Tuners	1,710	20	9	
Woodworkers (not specified)	799	22	1	
Other and not specified occupations	9,512	841	40	1
POTTERIES	23,878	5,648	473	4
Manufacturers and proprietors	386	5	1	
Foremen and overseers	473	79	2	
Bookkeepers, cashiers, and accountants	252	99	1	
Clerks (general)	176	53	1	
Clerks (shipping)	128	4	1	
Other clerical pursuits	30		1	
Carpenters	80		1	
Engineers (stationary)	285		3	
Machinists and millwrights	137		1	
Mechanics (not otherwise specified)	89		4	
Dippers	279	159		1
Finishers	304	660	5	1
Firemen	280		9	
Gilders and painters	133	180	1	
Glazers	75	27	1	
Helpers	179	69	1	
Jigger men and jolly men	814	2	3	
Kilnmen	2,170	119	7	
Laborers	6,470	476	333	1
Packers	739	73	9	
Potters (not specified)	3,224	338	27	
Pressers and molders	2,679	42	17	1
Puggers, mixers, and temperers	163	4	2	
Sagger makers	226	6	2	
Teamsters	255		19	
Turners	295	17	2	
Other and not specified occupations	3,557	3,236	19	
POWDER, CARTRIDGE, DYNAMITE, FUSE, AND FIREWORKS FACTORIES	10,260	3,163	121	4
Foremen and overseers	397	32	2	
Clerks (general)	353	71	1	
Clerks (shipping)	91	2	1	
Stenographers and typewriters	64	261	1	
Engineers (stationary)	202		2	
Machinists and millwrights	594		1	
Plumbers	111		1	
Tinners	51		19	
Cartridge factory operatives (not otherwise specified)	969	1,537	2	
Firemen	160		3	
Laborers	3,946	330	67	4
Powder and dynamite factory operatives (not otherwise specified)	1,307	105	18	
Other and not specified occupations	2,015	825	3	

TABLE 22.—GAINFUL WORKERS 10 YEARS OF AGE AND OVER, ALL CLASSES AND NEGRO, CLASSIFIED BY SEX, INDUSTRY, AND OCCUPATION: 1910—Continued.

MANUFACTURING, INCLUDING HAND TRADES—Continued.

INDUSTRY AND OCCUPATION.	ALL CLASSES. Male.	ALL CLASSES. Female.	NEGRO. Male.	NEGRO. Female.
PRINTING AND PUBLISHING ESTABLISHMENTS	278,998	76,676	3,543	515
Manufacturers and proprietors	21,391	426	169	4
Officials	1,376	92	4	2
Managers and superintendents	8,679	233	28	.....
Foremen and overseers	4,370	1,048	16	3
Agents	13,712	974	61	12
Bookkeepers, cashiers, and accountants	5,478	5,703	6	27
Clerks (general)	10,591	8,766	67	33
Clerks (shipping)	1,604	85	40	.....
Collectors	1,304	134	7	.....
Draftsmen	191	5	1	.....
Messenger, errand, and office boys	5,189	204	135	1
Proof readers	2,317	2,658	8	20
Purchasing agents	96	.....	1	.....
Stenographers and typewriters	1,149	10,093	11	43
Boiler makers	85	.....	4	.....
Carpenters	133	.....	1	.....
Electricians and electrical engineers	268	.....	2	.....
Engineers (stationary)	607	2	13	.....
Engravers	6,498	189	9	2
Machinists	2,059	.....	14	.....
Mechanics (not otherwise specified)	109	1	1	.....
Painters	26	.....	1	.....
Apprentices	11,376	935	56	9
Bookbinders (not specified)	13,489	14,137	51	40
Compositors and typesetters	111,489	13,681	984	138
Cutters	1,672	215	18	1
Electrotypers and stereotypers	4,268	100	21	.....
Embossers, gilders, and stampers	722	418	6	1
Finishers	402	84	1	.....
Firemen	258	.....	19	.....
Folders	351	3,514	3	8
Gatherers	38	267	1	3
Helpers	1,508	1,079	93	61
Inspectors	184	558	3	5
Laborers	4,092	1,344	642	20
Lithographers	7,661	477	19	1
Packers and wrappers	553	419	24	1
Pasters	106	406	2	1
Press feeders	6,285	4,019	45	17
Pressmen	19,666	114	132	4
Rulers (paper)	1,114	158	4	.....
Sewers and sewing machine operators	43	1,278	.....	4
Teamsters	1,415	.....	65	.....
Other and not specified occupations	5,074	2,860	755	54
ROPE AND CORDAGE FACTORIES	8,268	4,463	228	34
Manufacturers and proprietors	207	5	1	.....
Foremen and overseers	391	54	1	.....
Clerks (shipping)	92	5	1	.....
Machinists	351	.....	2	.....
Firemen	47	.....	6	.....
Helpers	69	53	1	.....
Laborers	3,126	656	138	1
Machine hands (not specified)	233	517	5	.....
Spinners	247	650	1	4
Teamsters	75	.....	3	.....
Twisters	56	133	1	1
Weavers and knitters	119	301	5	2
Winders, spoolers, and ballers	173	398	1	.....
Other and not specified occupations	3,082	1,691	62	26
RUBBER FACTORIES	44,203	13,897	236	12
Foremen and overseers	1,588	206	3	.....
Bookkeepers, cashiers, and accountants	944	370	.....	1
Clerks (general)	1,719	498	5	.....
Clerks (shipping)	677	22	10	.....
Messenger, errand, and office boys	296	14	.....	1
Blacksmiths	88	.....	1	.....
Carpenters	270	.....	1	.....
Engineers (stationary)	358	.....	4	.....
Machinists and millwrights	1,047	.....	1	.....
Mechanics (not otherwise specified)	106	.....	3	.....
Boot and shoe makers (not specified)	3,155	3,855	5	1
Calender men	339	1	1	.....
Coaters and spreaders	138	8	.....	1
Cutters	1,618	119	4	.....
Firemen	327	.....	2	.....
Helpers	410	158	2	.....
Hose makers (not specified)	754	69	3	.....
Inspectors	484	388	3	.....
Laborers	12,193	1,319	92	1
Machine hands (not specified)	463	390	3	.....
Makers of rubber goods (not specified)	346	495	2	.....

INDUSTRY AND OCCUPATION.	ALL CLASSES. Male.	ALL CLASSES. Female.	NEGRO. Male.	NEGRO. Female.
RUBBER FACTORIES—Continued.				
Mixers	341	13	2	.....
Packers	658	471	2	.....
Polishers and buffers	234	84	1	.....
Press hands	557	37	6	1
Rubber makers (not specified)	129	63	1	.....
Sewers and sewing machine operators	116	641	1	.....
Stamp makers (not specified)	151	18	2	1
Teamsters	252	.....	5	.....
Tire makers (not specified)	2,662	92	2	.....
Varnishers	204	26	2	1
Vulcanizers and curers	520	8	2	.....
Weavers	202	275	1	.....
Winders, reelers, and spoolers	44	81	1	.....
Other and not specified occupations	10,813	4,176	63	4
SAIL, AWNING, AND TENT FACTORIES	4,103	1,303	62	5
Manufacturers and proprietors	831	22	10	.....
Awning hangers	241	.....	2	.....
Awning and tent makers (not specified)	795	258	7	1
Laborers	234	29	12	.....
Sailmakers (not specified)	1,183	33	26	.....
Sewers	58	592	1	1
Teamsters	51	.....	2	.....
Other and not specified occupations	710	369	2	3
SAW AND PLANING MILLS	462,981	3,643	110,453	770
Manufacturers and proprietors	21,331	29	219	.....
Officials	659	3	3	.....
Managers and superintendents	7,064	9	30	.....
Foremen and overseers	10,897	5	281	.....
Bookkeepers, cashiers, and accountants	4,239	662	18	1
Clerks (general)	1,823	89	45	2
Clerks (shipping)	1,309	7	12	1
Designers	21	.....	1	.....
Draftsmen	208	.....	1	.....
Messenger, errand, and office boys	341	2	86	.....
Purchasing agents	204	.....	2	.....
Blacksmiths	1,682	.....	183	.....
Boiler makers	44	.....	4	.....
Cabinetmakers	1,748	.....	3	.....
Carpenters	9,297	.....	203	.....
Coopers	52	.....	8	.....
Electricians	206	.....	3	.....
Engineers (stationary)	10,847	.....	454	.....
Machinists	5,295	.....	157	.....
Mechanics (not otherwise specified)	848	.....	24	.....
Millwrights	4,003	.....	68	.....
Painters	490	1	44	.....
Plumbers	185	.....	11	.....
Apprentices	422	.....	12	.....
Axmen	1,479	.....	573	.....
Bench hands	257	3	8	.....
Block setters	2,541	.....	640	.....
Carriage men	1,233	.....	416	.....
Checkers and tallymen	1,661	5	62	.....
Cutters	556	4	62	1
Finishers	530	2	51	.....
Firemen	10,186	.....	2,991	.....
Glaziers	879	5	53	1
Gluers	136	9	6	.....
Helpers	1,018	14	80	2
Inspectors, graders, and sorters	6,577	41	720	6
Laborers	253,560	1,486	89,954	676
Log turners	856	.....	287	.....
Loggers and log drivers	4,203	.....	982	.....
Machine hands (not specified)	3,980	31	244	3
Markers	446	1	31	1
Measurers, scalers, and surveyors	2,581	.....	39	.....
Oilers	672	.....	70	.....
Packers	1,300	15	101	.....
Planers and jointers	3,295	1	303	.....
Polishers and sanders	129	6	4	.....
Press hands	125	.....	6	.....
Saw filers and setters	6,285	2	90	.....
Sawyers	30,828	2	2,667	1
Shingle weavers	2,488	.....	18	.....
Teamsters	16,463	2	3,574	1
Turners and molders	1,494	5	36	.....
Woodworkers (not specified)	2,813	16	6	.....
Wrappers	168	44	26	.....
Other and not specified occupations	21,027	1,142	4,481	74
SHIP AND BOAT BUILDING	66,684	382	4,337	10
Manufacturers and proprietors	1,443	1	7	.....
Managers and superintendents	325	.....	2	.....
Foremen and overseers	891	3	10	.....

TABLE 22.—GAINFUL WORKERS 10 YEARS OF AGE AND OVER, ALL CLASSES AND NEGRO, CLASSIFIED BY SEX, INDUSTRY, AND OCCUPATION: 1910—Continued.

MANUFACTURING, INCLUDING HAND TRADES—Continued.

INDUSTRY AND OCCUPATION.	ALL CLASSES. Male.	ALL CLASSES. Female.	NEGRO. Male.	NEGRO. Female.
SHIP AND BOAT BUILDING—Contd.				
Bookkeepers, cashiers, and accountants..	518	56	1	....
Clerks (general)	1,479	62	25	....
Draftsmen	913	....	1	....
Messenger, errand, and office boys	223	....	21	....
Stenographers and typewriters	152	180	4	....
Blacksmiths and shipsmiths	1,324	....	55	....
Boiler makers	2,025	....	12	....
Carpenters and shipwrights	16,417	....	318	....
Coopers	45	....	1	....
Electricians and electrical engineers	1,076	....	9	....
Engineers (stationary)	688	....	21	....
Machinists	5,680	....	66	....
Masons	27	....	3	....
Mechanics (not otherwise specified)	214	....	12	....
Millwrights	62	....	1	....
Painters	1,629	2	33	....
Plumbers	1,240	....	7	....
Tinners	170	....	1	....
Tool makers	108	....	1	....
Apprentices	576	....	11	....
Calkers	2,618	....	231	....
Cranemen	95	....	2	....
Drillers	659	....	70	....
Firemen	344	....	63	....
Fitters-up	308	....	2	....
Heaters	353	....	15	....
Helpers	1,345	1	82	....
Ironworkers (not specified)	1,314	1	4	....
Laborers	11,973	7	2,917	5
Molders	370	....	7	....
Pattern makers	481	....	3	....
Riggers	1,633	....	54	....
Riveters and bolters-up	1,695	....	85	....
Ship and boat builders (not specified)	2,980	11	25	....
Teamsters	242	....	50	....
Other and not specified occupations	3,049	58	105	5
SHIRT, COLLAR, AND CUFF FACTORIES.	19,356	50,767	612	482
Managers and superintendents	471	34	1	....
Foremen and overseers	685	1,109	1	....
Clerks (general)	737	424	6	....
Clerks (shipping)	477	18	5	....
Messenger, errand, and office boys	215	55	9	3
Engineers (stationary)	138	....	1	....
Machinists	334	....	1	....
Mechanics (not otherwise specified)	34	....	1	....
Cutters	3,125	222	12	2
Firemen	53	....	3	....
Helpers	90	161	2	1
Inserters and pasters	6	568	....	2
Inspectors	171	1,932	1	10
Laborers	804	1,323	26	10
Laundry workers (not specified)	212	529	2	27
Packers, folders, and wrappers	502	789	9	3
Pressers and ironers	2,592	1,373	35	88
Sewers and sewing machine operators	3,056	30,971	210	264
Stampers and labelers	64	213	2	1
Starchersh	99	837	....	1
Teamsters	121	....	18	....
Trimmers	119	316	5	2
Turners	692	1,401	....	9
Other and not specified occupations	4,559	8,492	262	59
SHOE FACTORIES.	149,118	68,549	2,783	184
Manufacturers and proprietors	2,655	19	5	....
Officials	221	....	1	....
Foremen and overseers	5,236	1,215	24	2
Bookkeepers, cashiers, and accountants	1,146	2,259	2	2
Clerks (general)	1,951	1,734	17	3
Clerks (shipping)	1,263	36	12	....
Messenger, errand, and office boys	550	104	21	....
Stenographers and typewriters	173	1,391	....	1
Electricians and electrical engineers	74	....	1	....
Engineers (stationary)	547	....	4	....
Machinists	1,288	....	6	....
Mechanics (not otherwise specified)	115	....	1	....
Painters	100	15	6	....
Tool makers	25	....	2	....
Apprentices	1,058	101	23	....
Beaters-out	1,164	71	19	....
Blackers and stainers	653	437	21	3
Bow makers and tiers	33	178	2	....
Buffers, sanders, and scourers	1,721	77	41	....
Burnishers	685	18	2	....
Buttoners and buttonhole makers	64	511	....	3
Cementers, gluers, and pasters	590	1,532	39	22

INDUSTRY AND OCCUPATION.	ALL CLASSES. Male.	ALL CLASSES. Female.	NEGRO. Male.	NEGRO. Female.
SHOE FACTORIES—Continued.				
Channelers	434	10	5	....
Cutters	23,348	807	117	7
Dyers	110	42	1	....
Edgers and edge setters	3,836	95	50	....
Elevator tenders	194	....	10	....
Eyeleters	227	356	7	....
Fillers	123	54	3	....
Finishers	4,422	1,131	19	2
Firemen	257	....	12	....
Fitters	2,118	1,570	35	2
Folders and beaders	98	1,410	6	1
Heel makers	4,202	890	66	2
Helpers	1,182	609	8	4
Inspectors	601	375	47	3
Ironers	421	142	19	....
Janitors	123	4	31	2
Laborers	7,851	2,312	149	6
Lacers	127	818	16	2
Lasters	14,530	271	133	....
Machine operators (not specified)	3,719	3,968	34	5
Markers	99	410	4	....
Nailers and peggers	1,540	304	29	2
Packers	1,352	2,489	31	3
Paper box makers	93	158	2	1
Perforators and punchers	83	244	2	....
Polishers, brushers, and cleaners	1,063	592	45	....
Pressers, molders, and counter makers	955	756	12	2
Repairers	291	726	1	3
Rounders and breasters	749	17	5	....
Scrubbers and sweepers	101	13	22	1
Sewers and sewing machine operators	7,717	24,870	175	68
Shankers	147	31	6	....
Shoemakers (not specified)	23,617	3,273	1,157	8
Skivers	791	987	11	2
Sole layers	511	30	7	....
Solers	421	116	1	....
Sorters and matchers	1,512	560	10	1
Stampers	368	496	9	3
Table hands	30	848	....	2
Teamsters	229	....	13	....
Treers	2,304	163	14	....
Trimmers	2,504	1,044	32	9
Turners	550	190	5	....
Wheelers	238	24	8	....
Other and not specified occupations	12,618	5,646	165	7
SILK MILLS	42,428	53,844	187	373
Officials	68	1	1	....
Managers and superintendents	662	5	1	....
Foremen and overseers	1,453	951	4	6
Bookkeepers, cashiers, and accountants	727	451	3	....
Clerks (general)	1,040	387	1	....
Clerks (shipping)	381	50	3	....
Messenger, errand, and office boys	358	26	3	....
Carpenters	144	....	1	....
Engineers (stationary)	329	....	3	....
Machinists and millwrights	675	....	2	....
Mechanics (not otherwise specified)	72	4	1	....
Bobbin boys, doffers, and carriers	320	297	1	....
Braid and ribbon makers (not specified)	92	229	....	1
Card cutters and lacers	107	224	3	....
Cutters	284	114	....	1
Doublers and twisters	1,312	2,207	2	9
Dyers	1,365	24	6	....
Firemen	246	....	4	....
Helpers	834	239	3	3
Inspectors	172	399	....	1
Laborers	2,620	1,099	67	58
Loom fixers	1,496	....	3	....
Machine hands (not specified)	128	296	....	1
Packers	100	204	....	1
Sewers and menders	54	515	....	2
Spinners	1,046	2,397	1	8
Teamsters	165	....	3	....
Warp pickers	181	2,010	....	1
Warpers	1,142	3,190	....	8
Weavers	18,343	17,507	2	72
Winders, reelers, and spoolers	1,222	14,904	6	74
Other and not specified occupations	5,290	6,114	63	127
SLAUGHTER AND PACKING HOUSES	82,643	5,717	5,105	173
Manufacturers and proprietors	1,071	8	4	....
Managers and superintendents	2,090	....	2	....
Foremen and overseers	2,598	74	18	1
Bookkeepers, cashiers, and accountants	3,189	423	1	1
Clerks (general)	4,337	314	15	....
Clerks (shipping)	1,044	15	9	1
Messenger, errand, and office boys	647	14	7	....
Stenographers and typewriters	322	980	....	1
Weighers	526	23	2	....

TABLE 22.—GAINFUL WORKERS 10 YEARS OF AGE AND OVER, ALL CLASSES AND NEGRO, CLASSIFIED BY SEX, INDUSTRY, AND OCCUPATION: 1910—Continued.

MANUFACTURING, INCLUDING HAND TRADES—Continued.

INDUSTRY AND OCCUPATION.	ALL CLASSES. Male.	ALL CLASSES. Female.	NEGRO. Male.	NEGRO. Female.
SLAUGHTER AND PACKING HOUSES—Continued.				
Blacksmiths	193		3	
Boiler makers	81		1	
Carpenters	894		4	
Coopers	702		17	
Electricians and electrical engineers	294		1	
Engineers (stationary)	996		19	
Machinists	605		10	
Masons	28		1	
Mechanics (not otherwise specified)	83		1	
Millwrights and mechanical engineers	298		2	
Painters	144	15	2	
Plumbers	539		11	
Tinners	326		1	
Apprentices	121		6	
Branders and stampers	136	12	4	1
Butchers and dressers	16,349	2	1,099	
Canners	74	209	3	2
Cutters	801	405	35	11
Elevator tenders	203		9	
Firemen	594		82	
Gutters, gut cleaners, etc	142	31	7	2
Helpers	312	65	31	
Inspectors	750	26	13	
Janitors	200	8	78	1
Killers	82		10	
Labelers	33	232	1	1
Laborers	32,325	1,421	2,955	115
Lard renderers	266	8	9	2
Oilers	184		7	
Packers	1,488	588	97	17
Picklers	106	6	3	
Sausage makers	1,180	187	16	2
Smokers and curers	253	1	12	
Stock drivers	103		5	
Teamsters	2,761		264	
Wrappers	47	162	2	3
Other and not specified occupations	3,126	488	226	12
SOAP FACTORIES	9,560	3,929	188	8
Manufacturers and proprietors	624	15	3	1
Foremen and overseers	326	84	1	
Clerks (general)	484	825		2
Clerks (shipping)	232	9	2	
Other clerical pursuits	48	8		1
Engineers (stationary)	147		3	
Machinists and millwrights	171		1	
Mechanics (not otherwise specified)	103		1	
Firemen	136		4	
Helpers	107	29	2	
Labelers	17	83		1
Laborers	3,169	255	102	
Packers	340	372	5	
Pressers and molders	207	15	5	
Teamsters	555		14	
Wrappers	102	1,042	1	1
Other and not specified occupations	2,792	1,192	44	2
STRAW FACTORIES	3,002	4,227	21	3
Clerks (shipping)	47	1	1	
Blockers and pressers	399	16	2	
Dyers	70	2	2	
Hatters (not specified)	565	496	1	1
Laborers	317	94	13	1
Trimmers	22	505		1
Other and not specified occupations	1,582	3,113	2	
SUGAR FACTORIES AND REFINERIES	16,093	515	821	9
Manufacturers and proprietors	96		1	
Officials	58		1	
Foremen and overseers	591	10	5	
Bookkeepers, cashiers, and accountants	451	29	1	
Clerks (general)	653	23	1	
Weighers	181	11	16	
Blacksmiths	91		3	
Boiler makers	32		1	
Carpenters	158		4	
Coopers	354		25	
Electricians and electrical engineers	138		1	
Engineers (stationary)	640		40	
Machinists and millwrights	597		8	
Mechanics (not otherwise specified)	106		8	
Plumbers	169		5	

INDUSTRY AND OCCUPATION.	ALL CLASSES. Male.	ALL CLASSES. Female.	NEGRO. Male.	NEGRO. Female.
SUGAR FACTORIES AND REFINERIES—Continued.				
Boilers	441	3	13	
Firemen	307		26	
Laborers	8,641	108	583	8
Oilers	76	1	3	
Packers	64	105	2	
Refiners	113	2	1	
Samplers	119		7	
Teamsters	362		19	
Other and not specified occupations	1,655	223	47	1
TANNERIES	60,604	2,903	2,235	37
Manufacturers and proprietors	1,154	2	10	
Foremen and overseers	1,562	30	13	
Bookkeepers, cashiers, and accountants	680	244	2	
Clerks (general)	609	83	2	
Clerks (shipping)	438	6	6	
Stenographers and typewriters	74	312	1	1
Carpenters	333		2	
Electricians and electrical engineers	63		1	
Engineers (stationary)	524		11	
Machinists and millwrights	402		13	
Apprentices	158	6	1	
Beamsters	2,038	5	72	
Buffers	341	3	3	
Colorers and blackers	525	10	17	
Curriers	2,028	15	29	
Cutters	697	106	6	
Dressers	1,649	214	8	
Finishers	2,005	55	16	
Firemen	556		36	
Glazers and rollers	2,451	488	25	
Grainers	381	3	31	
Helpers	362	48	5	
Inspectors and graders	155	16	1	
Japanners	351	4	1	
Laborers	20,223	295	1,485	31
Machine hands	408	36	12	
Oilers	151	18	10	
Packers	153	31	7	
Press hands and stampers	283	17	4	
Setters-out	211		2	
Shavers and scrapers	751	8	10	
Sorters	1,004	102	3	
Splitters	484		1	
Stakers	1,153	5	1	
Tackers	1,276	11	2	
Tanners	8,213	43	226	1
Teamsters	572		41	
Trimmers	343	140	3	
Other and not specified occupations	5,843	547	116	4
TEXTILE DYEING, FINISHING, AND PRINTING MILLS	34,758	7,981	536	109
Manufacturers and proprietors	1,607	89	61	1
Managers and superintendents	486	44	3	1
Foremen and overseers	1,118	163	6	1
Agents, canvassers, and collectors	64	1	2	
Bookkeepers, cashiers, and accountants	448	484	1	4
Clerks (general)	692	650	2	5
Designers	78	9	1	
Messenger, errand, and office boys	279	27	7	
Stenographers and typewriters	43	292	1	2
Engineers (stationary)	393		4	
Machinists and millwrights	608		3	
Mechanics (not otherwise specified)	81		3	
Apprentices	148	16	2	
Back tenders	122	15	1	
Bleachers	768	60	6	1
Calenderers	427	84	2	
Cleaners and washers	797	167	33	9
Color grinders and mixers	362	7	4	
Dryers	190	48	2	
Dyers	5,486	331	78	14
Finishers	565	185		2
Firemen	466		10	
Folders and rollers	995	539	2	1
Helpers	1,778	98	4	3
Inspectors	151	185		3
Laborers	9,341	588	193	6
Layers-out and stampers	91	111	1	
Machine hands (not specified)	430	312	2	
Packers and wrappers	268	212	1	
Pressers	476	1,219	36	47
Printers	1,029	30	1	
Sewers	94	725	2	3
Starchers	235	7	2	
Teamsters	818		21	
Other and not specified occupations	3,824	1,283	39	6

TABLE 22.—GAINFUL WORKERS 10 YEARS OF AGE AND OVER, ALL CLASSES AND NEGRO, CLASSIFIED BY SEX, INDUSTRY, AND OCCUPATION: 1910—Continued.

MANUFACTURING, INCLUDING HAND TRADES—Continued.

INDUSTRY AND OCCUPATION.	ALL CLASSES.		NEGRO.		INDUSTRY AND OCCUPATION.	ALL CLASSES.		NEGRO.	
	Male.	Female.	Male.	Female.		Male.	Female.	Male.	Female.
TEXTILE MILLS (NOT SPECIFIED).....	30,504	30,087	420	300	TINWARE AND ENAMELWARE FACTORIES—Continued.				
Manufacturers and proprietors	1,223	21	1	....	Painters	165	53	5	....
Officials	97	2	2	....	Plumbers	311	....	5	....
Managers and superintendents	689	14	1	1	Tinners	44,764	17	801	1
Foremen and overseers	1,395	402	3	2	Tool makers	206	....	2	....
Clerks (general)	714	345	1	....	Apprentices	1,999	7	28	....
Clerks (shipping)	499	37	3	....	Can cappers and headers	103	56	2	1
Messenger, errand, and office boys	178	18	1	....	Cutters	244	61	7	4
Other clerical pursuits	25	....	1	....	Dippers	104	454	1	1
Carpenters	139	....	1	....	Firemen	101	....	4	....
Machinists and millwrights	1,008	....	3	....	Galvanizers and platers	93	5	7	....
Mechanics (not otherwise specified)	79	....	1	....	Helpers	881	102	31	1
Apprentices	115	29	....	1	Inspectors	68	103	1	....
Bag and sack makers (not otherwise specified)	110	278	4	27	Laborers	6,697	869	228	8
Bleachers	75	7	2	....	Machine hands (not specified)	564	568	....	2
Bobbin boys, doffers, and carriers	380	351	2	....	Packers and wrappers	435	560	8	2
Braiders	247	615	2	....	Polishers and buffers	69	45	1	....
Carders, combers, and lappers	724	372	4	....	Press hands and stampers	848	347	2	2
Cutters	577	266	1	4	Solderers	413	232	3	6
Drawers, rovers, and speeders	86	284	10	....	Sorters	41	235	1	....
Dyers	475	7	8	....	Teamsters	297	....	30	....
Finishers	733	894	3	47	Other and not specified occupations	4,240	1,534	52	7
Firemen	182	....	8	....					
Folders, rollers, and wrappers	174	366	2	1	TRUNK FACTORIES	6,882	809	86	2
Fringe and tassel makers	28	334	....	1					
Helpers	321	189	2	1	Clerks (general)	106	26	....	1
Inspectors	513	870	1	1	Clerks (shipping)	99	....	2	....
Laborers	3,406	1,264	214	51	Engineers (stationary)	25	....	1	....
Loom fixers	911	....	1	....	Machinists and millwrights	44	....	1	....
Machine hands (not specified)	493	1,663	2	4	Laborers	904	76	34	....
Oilers	57	....	1	....	Liners and pasters	43	191	1	....
Packers	206	296	5	1	Teamsters	70	....	18	....
Pickers	171	52	2	....	Other and not specified occupations	5,591	516	29	1
Pressers	272	106	10	....					
Quilt makers (not specified)	53	316	1	47	TURPENTINE DISTILLERIES	9,948	82	7,106	56
Sewers and menders	240	2,921	24	46					
Shearers	41	29	1	....	Manufacturers and proprietors	747	2	24	....
Sorters	149	142	....	12	Officials	38	....	1	....
Spinners	1,550	1,924	2	7	Managers and superintendents	227	....	8	....
Teamsters	214	....	13	....	Foremen and overseers	98	....	12	....
Twisters	283	718	1	1	Bookkeepers, cashiers, and accountants	105	3	3	....
Warpers	205	355	....	1	Clerks	98	1	5	....
Weavers	6,270	5,559	33	9	Messenger, errand, and office boys	9	....	3	....
Winders, reelers, and spoolers	416	4,629	5	3	Coopers	387	....	318	....
Other and not specified occupations	4,781	4,412	38	32	Machinists	25	....	1	....
					Mechanics (not otherwise specified)	76	....	11	....
TIN PLATE FACTORIES	21,848	815	316	1	Distillers	949	....	498	....
Foremen and overseers	381	17	1	....	Laborers	6,353	51	5,669	49
					Teamsters	286	1	231	1
Messenger, errand, and office boys	36	1	1	....	Other and not specified occupations	550	24	322	6
Blacksmiths	110	....	2	....					
Engineers (stationary)	149	....	1	....	WAGON AND CARRIAGE FACTORIES	80,679	2,673	1,962	21
Machinists and millwrights	402	....	2	....					
Mechanics	67	....	2	....	Manufacturers and proprietors	5,250	19	9	....
Tinners	928	....	7	....	Managers and superintendents	1,010	3	3	....
Annealers	37	....	1	....	Foremen and overseers	1,578	56	5	....
Catchers	1,190	2	29	....	Bookkeepers, cashiers, and accountants	910	316	....	1
Cranemen	117	....	6	....	Clerks (general)	801	136	2	1
Doublers	1,132	....	7	....	Clerks (shipping)	494	5	5	....
Firemen	163	....	10	....	Messenger, errand, and office boys	106	4	5	....
Heaters	1,723	....	19	....	Purchasing agents	68	....	1	....
Helpers	454	7	9	....	Stenographers and typewriters	114	649	....	1
Laborers	7,610	213	145	1	Blacksmiths	8,804	1	296	1
Picklers and dippers	374	3	9	....	Carpenters	1,660	....	26	....
Platers	110	....	1	....	Electricians and electrical engineers	47	....	1	....
Press hands	121	1	1	....	Engineers (stationary)	360	....	9	....
Rollers and roughers	2,392	4	12	....	Machinists	2,081	....	16	....
Shearers	499	5	10	....	Mechanics (not otherwise specified)	371	....	14	....
Teamsters	44	....	3	....	Millwrights	161	....	3	....
Other and not specified occupations	3,809	562	38	....	Painters	16,415	70	237	2
					Wheelwrights	2,777	....	58	....
TINWARE AND ENAMELWARE FACTORIES	68,481	5,778	1,264	35	Wood carvers	44	....	1	....
Manufacturers and proprietors	2,573	9	23	....	Apprentices	627	3	10	....
Foremen and overseers	893	65	3	....	Assemblers and erectors	311	15	3	....
Clerks (general)	678	174	1	....	Body makers (not specified)	534	4	2	....
Clerks (shipping)	281	5	4	....	Coach, carriage, and wagon makers (not specified)	5,614	42	33	1
Designers	23	3	1	....	Cutters	201	24	1	....
Messenger, errand, and office boys	98	4	1	....	Drillers	151	4	4	....
Stenographers and typewriters	45	270	1	....	Finishers	624	14	9	....
Blacksmiths and hammermen	60	....	1	....	Firemen	294	....	51	....
Engineers (stationary)	121	....	5	....					
Machinists	910	....	2	....					
Mechanics (not otherwise specified)	156	....	3	....					

TABLE 22.—GAINFUL WORKERS 10 YEARS OF AGE AND OVER, ALL CLASSES AND NEGRO, CLASSIFIED BY SEX, INDUSTRY, AND OCCUPATION: 1910—Continued.

MANUFACTURING, INCLUDING HAND TRADES—Continued.

INDUSTRY AND OCCUPATION.	ALL CLASSES.		NEGRO.	
	Male.	Female.	Male.	Female.
WAGON AND CARRIAGE FACTORIES—Continued.				
Grinders	75		1	
Hammermen and welders	181		3	
Helpers	561	23	12	1
Inspectors	413	14	4	
Ironers and tire setters	272		3	
Laborers	12,216	159	854	6
Lathe hands and turners	614	7	19	
Machine hands (not specified)	578	131	7	
Molders	226		4	
Packers	441	25	23	2
Planers	72		1	
Polishers and buffers	450	3	6	
Press hands	116	7	1	
Repairers	235	4	2	
Sawyers	340		29	
Teamsters	539		57	
Top builders (not specified)	116	131		1
Trimmers	4,258	291	9	
Upholsterers	345	160	1	
Woodworkers (not specified)	3,308	16	10	
Other and not specified occupations	3,916	337	112	4
WOODWORKING FACTORIES (NOT OTHERWISE SPECIFIED)	106,273	9,045	8,216	452
Manufacturers and proprietors	5,015	38	43	1
Managers and superintendents	1,684	6	6	
Foremen and overseers	2,773	91	34	
Bookkeepers, cashiers, and accountants	922	350	4	
Clerks (general)	675	160	10	
Clerks (shipping)	507	12	6	
Designers	128	4	10	
Messenger, errand, and office boys	179	10	6	
Blacksmiths	171		9	
Cabinetmakers	648		6	
Carpenters	1,396		45	
Coopers	16,462	7	1,514	1
Engineers (stationary)	916		23	
Machinists	2,129		34	
Mechanics (not otherwise specified)	454		13	
Millwrights	188		2	
Painters and gilders	1,752	124	25	
Wood carvers	2,401	38	6	
Apprentices	711	7	82	1
Basket makers (not specified)	3,584	2,546	350	159
Cutters	1,150	211	57	
Finishers	2,504	52	15	
Firemen	892		197	
Fitters and matchers	259	19	11	
Gluers	135	22	1	
Helpers	770	103	42	12
Hoop makers (not otherwise specified)	423	7	11	
Inspectors	449	56	12	
Laborers	27,650	1,334	4,483	220
Machine hands (not specified)	1,636	413	22	1
Packers	443	651	35	2
Picture-frame makers	2,229	165	27	
Planers	406	1	22	
Polishers	522	26	4	
Rattan and reed workers	576	89	45	2
Sanders and buffers	302	11	1	
Saw filers	190		3	
Sawyers	3,122	4	250	
Sorters	208	663	3	
Stave makers	1,328	6	135	
Teamsters	1,882		193	
Turners and molders	5,146	79	31	4
Veneerers	257	22	8	
Wrappers	70	84	4	4
Other and not specified occupations	11,029	1,634	376	45
WOOLEN AND WORSTED MILLS	82,585	55,729	277	66
Foremen and overseers	3,205	206	2	
Clerks (general)	1,231	293	1	1
Clerks (shipping)	769	21	6	
Messenger, errand, and office boys	242	20	1	
Engineers (stationary)	622		3	
Machinists and millwrights	1,554		2	
Back boys	76	6	1	
Bobbin boys, doffers, and carriers	1,750	1,069	3	1
Brushers, jiggers, and nappers	182	154	2	1
Burlers	98	2,869		1
Card strippers and cleaners	276	51	1	
Carders	3,369	427	7	
Dressers and slashers	1,597	58	1	
WOOLEN AND WORSTED MILLS—Con.				
Driers	472	69	5	
Dyers	2,224	42	11	
Finishers	2,549	'949	3	
Firemen	803		7	
Folders, rollers, and wrappers	182	168	2	1
Fullers	254		1	
Helpers	686	323	4	
Inspectors	846	881	1	1
Laborers	10,093	1,967	129	9
Loom fixers	2,279		1	
Machine hands (not specified)	565	752		1
Packers	257	170	8	
Pickers	774	266	6	9
Pressers	528	41	2	
Scrubbers and sweepers	78	63		4
Sewers and menders	207	6,009	1	4
Spare hands	77	12	1	
Speckers	33	726		1
Spinners	6,997	6,390	10	5
Teamsters	625		11	
Twisters	431	2,389		4
Weavers	17,197	14,660	4	10
Winders, reelers, and spoolers	932	6,611		3
Wool pullers	74	15		6
Wool sorters	3,023	447	10	1
Wool washers and scourers	1,185	199	5	
Other and not specified occupations	14,243	7,403	25	3
OTHER AND NOT SPECIFIED INDUSTRIES	562,418	205,601	34,169	2,419
Manufacturers and proprietors	20,389	449	237	11
Officials	3,240	66	4	
Managers and superintendents	12,438	211	33	3
Foremen and overseers	14,435	2,824	232	10
Agents and solicitors	100	17	1	
Bookkeepers, cashiers, accountants, and auditors	42,256	23,625	96	114
Clerks (general)	53,427	24,773	350	227
Clerks (shipping)	9,719	330	126	2
Collectors	243	10	1	
Designers	476	215	4	
Draftsmen	1,127	2	1	
Messenger, errand, and office boys	7,379	542	337	23
Purchasing agents	522	11	2	
Stenographers and typewriters	11,100	67,742	84	270
Weighers	333	26	26	
Blacksmiths	2,830		67	
Cabinetmakers	688		4	
Carpenters	9,407		104	
Coopers	409		58	
Electricians and electrical engineers	3,352	3	22	
Engineers (mechanical)	438		3	
Engineers (stationary)	72,600	3	1,562	
Engravers	2,024	54	7	
Machinists and millwrights	7,312	3	159	
Masons	589		39	
Mechanics (not otherwise specified)	5,936		196	
Painters	4,342	281	55	2
Plumbers	2,268		23	
Tinners	207		1	
Tool makers	49		1	
Wheelwrights	501		25	
Apprentices	3,992	286	61	5
Artificial flower makers	1,238	8,616	4	30
Asbestos workers	1,197	129	4	
Bone and ivory makers	520	121	5	
Box makers (not otherwise specified)	9,313	9,491	158	13
Camera and kodak makers	1,081	686	2	1
Celluloid workers	538	249	1	
Cotton ginners	1,342	39	497	28
Cottonseed and linseed oil workers	881	34	551	19
Drillers	913	2	46	
Elevator tenders	799		65	
Firemen	24,990		3,830	
Fur workers	7,715	2,720	17	8
Hair workers	1,636	1,894	11	64
Helpers	4,777	1,608	172	9
Inspectors	1,545	1,416	27	1
Janitors	686	59	209	18
Labelers	107	917	8	4
Laborers	129,148	11,968	21,039	1,054
Looking-glass makers	687	33	5	
Machine hands (not otherwise specified)	6,372	5,430	65	42
Mattress makers	3,202	924	250	53
Mica workers	82	263	1	1
Musical instrument makers	1,065	108	6	1
Oilers	1,355	1	91	
Optical workers	2,691	776	7	4
Packers and wrappers	3,231	3,752	141	22
Pattern makers	6,691	319	17	2
Pencil makers	539	793	10	

TABLE 22.—GAINFUL WORKERS 10 YEARS OF AGE AND OVER, ALL CLASSES AND NEGRO, CLASSIFIED BY SEX, INDUSTRY, AND OCCUPATION: 1910—Continued.

MANUFACTURING, INCLUDING HAND TRADES—Continued.

INDUSTRY AND OCCUPATION.	ALL CLASSES.		NEGRO.	
	Male.	Female.	Male.	Female.
OTHER AND NOT SPECIFIED INDUSTRIES—Continued.				
Planers	280		7	
Polishers and buffers	3,938	421	26	1
Porters	1,144		468	
Press hands, drillers, and stampers	3,520	1,042	135	32
Sawyers	1,479		39	
Scrubbers and sweepers	375	138	24	41
Sewers and sewing machine operators	244	918	13	18
Teamsters	7,829	1	1,137	
OTHER AND NOT SPECIFIED INDUSTRIES—Continued.				
Toy and novelty makers	1,795	1,628	9	4
Turners	839	23	9	
Umbrella and parasol makers	1,197	1,795	9	2
Upholsterers	236	5	3	
Whip makers	665	288	34	1
Window shade makers	668	213	4	2
Other and not specified occupations	29,740	25,308	1,092	277

TRANSPORTATION, INCLUDING POSTAL, EXPRESS, TELEGRAPH AND TELEPHONE SERVICE.

INDUSTRY AND OCCUPATION.	ALL CLASSES.		NEGRO.	
	Male.	Female.	Male.	Female.
EXPRESS COMPANIES	51,470	1,652	2,073	36
Managers and superintendents	823		2	
Foremen and overseers	526	1	6	
Accountants and auditors	494	20		1
Agents	5,804	71	12	
Bookkeepers and cashiers	2,395	357		7
Clerks (general)	11,004	634	39	10
Clerks (shipping)	358	5	2	1
Collectors	339	2	1	
Messenger, errand, and office boys	1,193	20	18	1
Stenographers and typewriters	466	493	1	1
Blacksmiths	71		2	
Carpenters	50		1	
Drivers	16,584	2	1,116	1
Express messengers	6,778	3	94	
Helpers	726	16	22	6
Laborers	2,212	14	441	7
Porters	765		266	
Other and not specified occupations	852	14	50	1
LIVERY STABLES	137,337	468	20,963	23
Livery-stable keepers	31,258	169	315	8
Managers and superintendents	3,321	14	80	
Foremen and overseers	4,970		390	
Bookkeepers, cashiers, and accountants	700	196	5	4
Clerks	428	21	10	1
Messenger, errand, and office boys	132		40	
Blacksmiths	111		9	
Mechanics (not otherwise specified)	63		1	
Carriage and hack drivers	32,673	36	7,044	7
Hostlers and stable hands	63,382	6	12,965	2
Porters	160	1	99	1
Other and not specified occupations	139	25	5	
POST	150,742	19,078	5,709	166
Postmasters	19,127	8,722	104	49
Bookkeepers, cashiers, and accountants	327	151		1
Clerks (general)	33,754	8,906	1,478	44
Clerks (railway mail)	15,240		702	
Mail carriers	79,667	1,011	2,756	25
Messenger, errand, and office boys	722	11	67	2
Stenographers and typewriters	125	109	4	1
Engineers (stationary)	36		3	
Janitors	653	76	273	15
Laborers	536	70	150	28
Porters	244		136	
Other and not specified occupations	311	22	36	1
RAILROADS, STEAM	1,529,842	21,754	128,546	1,243
Officials	1,741	1	5	
General agents, paymasters, and road-masters	4,604		6	
Station masters	487		6	
Train masters	1,169		3	
Contractors and builders	4,222		37	
Managers and superintendents	5,749	1	12	
Foremen and overseers	65,038	222	946	5
Accountants and auditors	7,237	328	13	
Agents (claim)	1,621	1	3	
Agents (freight)	4,755	5	17	
Agents (purchasing)	198		2	
Agents (ticket and station)	21,894	901	41	5
Agents (miscellaneous and not specified)	13,201	267	25	3
RAILROADS, STEAM—Continued.				
Baggagemen	12,250		225	
Bookkeepers	11,195	1,145	19	3
Cashiers	3,539	235	4	1
Clerks (general)	115,095	5,713	448	24
Clerks (shipping)	2,090	25	34	
Collectors	767	6	2	
Draftsmen	1,826	2	1	
Messenger, errand, and office boys	4,530	48	321	6
Stenographers and typewriters	8,858	8,195	16	6
Train dispatchers	6,053		5	
Weighers	839		11	
Blacksmiths	10,371		276	
Boiler makers	15,127		161	
Cabinetmakers	894		2	
Carpenters	31,341		274	
Coopers	239		19	
Coppersmiths	867		3	
Electricians and electrical engineers	6,714	1	21	
Engineers (civil) and surveyors	7,879		18	
Engineers (mechanical)	345		1	
Engineers (stationary)	5,248		73	
Machinists	48,655		332	
Masons	1,178		27	
Mechanics (not otherwise specified)	1,743		49	
Millwrights	123		1	
Painters	6,888		103	
Plumbers	4,937		27	
Tinners	2,145		13	
Tool makers	192		1	
Wheelwrights	26		2	
Apprentices	2,475		6	
Boiler washers and engine hostlers	10,409		1,328	
Brakemen	92,111		4,714	
Bridge workers (not specified)	1,050		65	
Car repairers (not specified)	22,208	80	336	6
Conductors	65,604		120	
Cooks	4,900	508	2,711	232
Core makers	109		2	
Cranemen	528		11	
Cutters	161		7	
Drillers	563		62	
Elevator tenders	193		31	
Engineers (locomotive)	96,229		355	
Filers and grinders	65		1	
Firemen (locomotive)	76,381		5,188	
Firemen (except locomotive)	4,424		326	
Gardeners	199		10	
Hammermen	172		8	
Heaters	164		1	
Inspectors (car and signal)	27,239	136	166	3
Inspectors (freight)	286		9	
Janitors	1,634	185	579	36
Laborers	451,915	2,010	70,109	626
Lamplighters	993	2	63	1
Locomotive repairers (not specified)	185		10	
Machine hands (not specified)	658	5	8	
Molders	840	2	5	
Motormen	2,487		20	
Oilers and greasers	1,585		152	
Planers	71		2	
Platers and galvanizers	106	1	11	
Polishers and buffers	133	1	4	
Porters	17,297	1	15,115	1
Press hands	147		14	
Pumpers	1,963		70	
Riveters	105		5	
Sawyers	71		5	
Section hands	81,395		14,778	
Starters	263		1	
Stewards	289	28	30	9
Sweepers	6,610	1,238	1,493	182
Switchmen, flagmen, and gatemen	73,367	52	2,125	2
Teamsters	5,378		599	
Train callers	3,561	2	125	1
Upholsterers	580	3	5	
Waiters	2,675	106	2,350	46
Yardmen (not otherwise specified)	7,990		159	
Other and not specified occupations	18,201	298	1,651	45

TABLE 22.—GAINFUL WORKERS 10 YEARS OF AGE AND OVER, ALL CLASSES AND NEGRO, CLASSIFIED BY SEX, INDUSTRY, AND OCCUPATION: 1910—Continued.

TRANSPORTATION, INCLUDING POSTAL, EXPRESS, TELEGRAPH AND TELEPHONE SERVICE—Continued.

INDUSTRY AND OCCUPATION.	ALL CLASSES. Male.	ALL CLASSES. Female.	NEGRO. Male.	NEGRO. Female.	INDUSTRY AND OCCUPATION.	ALL CLASSES. Male.	ALL CLASSES. Female.	NEGRO. Male.	NEGRO. Female.
RAILWAYS, ELECTRIC AND STREET ...	182,357	2,409	4,278	35	TELEGRAPH AND TELEPHONE—Con.				
Managers and superintendents	1,946	....	2	....	Apprentices	583	50	1	1
Foremen and overseers	3,677	18	36	....	Firemen	49	....	2	....
Accountants and auditors	396	68	1	....	Helpers	241	33	11	1
Agents (except ticket)	804	31	3	....	Inspectors	2,485	135	3	1
Agents (ticket)	1,036	307	3	1	Janitors	360	51	90	14
Bookkeepers and cashiers	1,224	479	1	....	Laborers	5,239	33	537	9
Clerks (general)	3,273	615	9	....	Porters	140	....	83	....
Collectors	126	23	1	....	Teamsters	826	....	25	....
Messenger, errand, and office boys	240	8	10	....	Telegraph linemen	4,477	....	95	....
Stenographers and typewriters	276	599	2	....	Telegraph operators	61,734	8,219	57	16
Blacksmiths	629	....	11	....	Telephone linemen	23,870	3	393	....
Boiler makers	73	....	2	....	Telephone operators	9,631	88,262	197	92
Carpenters	1,443	....	8	....	Other and not specified occupations	1,467	216	20	8
Electricians and electrical engineers	5,823	1	20	....					
Engineers (stationary)	836	....	6	....	TRUCK, TRANSFER, CAB, AND HACK COMPANIES	366,530	2,147	41,783	53
Machinists	1,782	1	7	....	Proprietors of transfer companies	13,587	206	617	15
Masons	84	....	2	....	Managers of transfer companies	1,676	24	19	....
Mechanics (not otherwise specified)	395	....	2	....	Foremen of transfer companies	1,636	....	36	....
Painters	793	....	6	....	Proprietors of garages	3,719	18	10	....
Plumbers	305	....	1	....	Managers of garages	1,537	5	23	....
Tinners	64	....	1	....	Agents	439	2	1	....
Brakemen	461	....	5	....	Bookkeepers, cashiers, and accountants	1,647	881	22	14
Car repairers (not specified)	1,550	8	19	....	Clerks (general)	2,448	240	12	1
Conductors	56,932	....	44	....	Clerks (shipping)	152	1	3	....
Firemen	503	....	58	....	Messenger, errand, and office boys	333	....	26	....
Guards	1,526	1	1	....	Stenographers and typewriters	143	619	1	1
Helpers	261	3	14	....	Blacksmiths	143	....	3	....
Inspectors	2,265	3	6	....	Carpenters	65	....	1	....
Laborers	27,118	176	3,303	28	Electricians and electrical engineers	271	....	3	....
Linemen	2,159	....	58	....	Machinists	16,626	....	277	....
Motormen	56,218	....	58	....	Painters	132	....	1	....
Oilers	340	....	19	....	Chauffeurs	44,973	32	4,637	2
Porters	365	....	289	....	Draymen, teamsters, and expressmen	271,999	61	35,451	18
Sweepers	223	26	24	3	Garage laborers	4,462	6	627	....
Switchmen and flagmen	2,153	....	33	....	Other and not specified occupations	542	52	13	2
Teamsters and drivers	1,278	....	104	....					
Other and not specified occupations	3,780	42	109	3	WATER TRANSPORTATION	219,927	1,626	32,263	358
STREETS, ROADS, SEWERS, AND BRIDGES, CONSTRUCTION AND MAINTENANCE OF	237,119	509	36,894	11	Owners of water craft	933	14	33	....
Contractors and builders	10,720	10	234	1	Construction contractors	596	1	27	....
Managers and superintendents	931	2	7	....	Officials of companies	346	1	2	....
Foremen and overseers	7,064	....	97	....	Managers and superintendents	1,214	....	7	....
Bookkeepers, cashiers, and accountants	297	52	3	1	Foremen and overseers (construction)	1,392	....	57	....
Clerks	619	24	2	2	Agents	1,740	10	7	....
Messenger, errand, and office boys	95	....	23	....	Bookkeepers, cashiers, and accountants	1,499	140	4	1
Blacksmiths	161	....	12	....	Clerks (general)	5,715	165	41	4
Carpenters	6,997	....	69	....	Clerks (shipping)	462	3	9	....
Engineers (steam)	3,529	....	81	....	Messenger, errand, and office boys	276	....	25	....
Machinists	295	....	15	....	Stenographers and typewriters	280	437	2	....
Masons	716	....	68	....	Weighers	204	....	10	....
Mechanics (not otherwise specified)	126	....	12	....	Blacksmiths	314	....	13	....
Painters	255	....	5	....	Carpenters	2,225	....	34	....
Plumbers	98	....	16	....	Coopers	107	....	10	....
Bridge and toll-gate tenders	2,201	331	25	2	Electricians	317	....	5	....
Firemen	915	....	46	....	Engineers (ship or boat)	20,212	1	328	....
Inspectors	303	....	1	....	Machinists	991	....	12	....
Laborers (construction)	180,468	....	33,914	....	Masons	36	....	2	....
Lamplighters	1,934	1	51	....	Mechanics	146	....	5	....
Street cleaners	9,946	....	1,009	....	Painters	171	....	6	....
Teamsters	8,538	....	1,097	......	Plumbers	154	....	2	....
Other and not specified occupations	911	89	107	5	Baggagemen	84	....	4	....
					Boathouse keepers and boatmen	2,366	11	142	....
TELEGRAPH AND TELEPHONE	159,284	109,623	1,867	155	Canal and lock tenders	1,406	3	92	....
Officials	731	17	1	....	Canal boat operators	1,517	1	26	....
Managers and superintendents	7,949	1,392	4	....	Captains and masters	15,866	....	329	....
Foremen and overseers	3,439	404	5	....	Cooks (ship or boat)	4,688	382	1,414	123
Agents	1,649	29	2	....	Deck hands	17,996	12	4,328	5
Bookkeepers, cashiers, and accountants	3,092	3,351	4	5	Divers	386	....	7	....
Clerks (general)	7,325	4,310	20	4	Drillers (excavation)	113	....	6	....
Clerks (shipping)	95	8	3	....	Firemen (ship or boat)	10,530	....	1,173	....
Collectors	1,671	403	2	....	Gatemen (ferries)	370	7	4	....
Messenger, errand, and office boys	9,074	78	262	1	Harbor and dock masters	1,624	....	80	....
Stenographers and typewriters	364	2,625	....	3	Inspectors	255	....	1	....
Blacksmiths	57	....	2	....	Laborers (construction)	14,177	90	3,609	78
Carpenters and cabinetmakers	296	....	6	....	Longshoremen	51,800	41	11,604	25
Electricians and electrical engineers	11,148	4	37	....	Mates (ship or boat)	3,281	....	44	....
Engineers (stationary)	779	....	1	....	Oilers (ship or boat)	1,789	1	16	....
Machinists	344	....	1	....	Pilots	5,095	....	92	....
Painters	116	....	2	....	Porters (ship or boat)	662	1	373	....
Plumbers	53	....	1	....	Pursers (ship or boat)	622	....	1	....
					Sailors	28,502	....	2,175	....
					Stevedores	11,013	3	4,775	1
					Stewards	3,418	249	368	101
					Teamsters	719	....	188	....
					Waiters	1,255	19	638	11
					Other and not specified occupations	1,063	34	133	9

TABLE 22.—GAINFUL WORKERS 10 YEARS OF AGE AND OVER, ALL CLASSES AND NEGRO, CLASSIFIED BY SEX, INDUSTRY, AND OCCUPATION: 1910—Continued.

TRANSPORTATION, INCLUDING POSTAL, EXPRESS, TELEGRAPH AND TELEPHONE SERVICE—Continued.

INDUSTRY AND OCCUPATION.	ALL CLASSES. Male.	ALL CLASSES. Female.	NEGRO. Male.	NEGRO. Female.
TRANSPORTATION (OTHER AND NOT SPECIFIED)	5,156	40	189	3
Owners and proprietors	48		2	
Officials	67	2	1	
Foremen (pipe line)	288		1	
Agents (not specified transportation)	87	1	1	
Clerks	402	14	1	
Plumbers (pipe line)	57		1	
TRANSPORTATION (OTHER AND NOT SPECIFIED)—Continued.				
Laborers (pipe line)	2,105		58	
Laborers (not specified transportation)	414	3	24	2
Linemen (pipe line)	500		1	
Not specified ditch diggers in cities	338		95	
Teamsters (pipe line)	86	1	3	1
Other and not specified occupations	764	19	1	

TRADE, INCLUDING BANKING, INSURANCE, AND WAREHOUSING.

INDUSTRY AND OCCUPATION.	ALL CLASSES. Male.	ALL CLASSES. Female.	NEGRO. Male.	NEGRO. Female.
BANKING AND BROKERAGE	187,553	23,159	3,001	207
Bank cashiers	32,034	1,347	67	9
Bankers and bank officials	22,353	325	55	4
Commercial brokers and commission men	23,690	319	71	5
Loan brokers and loan company officials	1,989	122	11	
Pawnbrokers	1,191	41	18	1
Promoters	2,389	21	12	
Stockbrokers	13,522	207	32	4
Not specified brokers	6,002	252	43	4
Accountants and auditors	1,967	115	1	
Bookkeepers	24,096	4,933	48	27
Clerks	45,977	3,748	143	27
Collectors	1,332	39	15	
Inspectors	234	6	2	
Messenger, errand, and office boys	4,396		301	1
Stenographers and typewriters	2,001	11,287	9	26
Elevator tenders	333		72	
Janitors	2,706	279	1,140	83
Porters	1,311	1	958	
Scrubwomen	13	102	3	16
Other and not specified occupations	17			
INSURANCE	125,136	27,828	1,947	657
Officials	2,234	54	19	1
Managers and superintendents	7,142	71	82	3
Foremen and overseers	124	14	2	
Accountants and auditors	1,215	123	3	
Actuaries	286	10	7	
Adjusters	1,484	4	3	
Agents	82,743	2,521	1,387	309
Bookkeepers	5,034	3,642	24	108
Cashiers	1,351	580	3	5
Clerks	15,678	6,219	69	132
Collectors	3,423	115	169	33
Inspectors	1,699	12	29	
Messenger, errand, and office boys	978	9	38	1
Stenographers and typewriters	1,334	14,418	4	58
Janitors	109	18	45	2
Porters	141		60	
Other and not specified occupations	161	18	3	5
GRAIN ELEVATORS	16,203	460	774	3
Proprietors	1,580	3	4	
Officials	536	3	2	
Managers and superintendents	2,989	7	2	
Foremen and overseers	701	2	6	
Bookkeepers and accountants	627	194	2	
Clerks	746	23	5	
Stenographers and typewriters	47	169		1
Carpenters	138		1	
Electricians and electrical engineers	111		2	
Engineers (stationary)	1,011		16	
Machinists	153		4	
Mechanics (not otherwise specified)	33		1	
Firemen	165		16	
Laborers	6,335	11	624	1
Oilers	89		5	
Teamsters	385		47	
Other and not specified occupations	557	48	37	1
REAL ESTATE	135,883	16,137	949	146
Agents and officials	122,935	2,927	717	45
Bookkeepers, cashiers, and accountants	3,578	2,525	7	32
Clerks	5,675	1,290	44	13
Collectors	1,434	63	37	1
REAL ESTATE—Continued.				
Messenger, errand, and office boys	740	10	24	3
Stenographers and typewriters	1,292	9,295	9	45
Elevator tenders	32		6	
Porters	188		103	
Scrubwomen	9	27	2	7
STOCK YARDS	8,170	206	561	5
Managers and superintendents	267		3	
Foremen and overseers	337		6	
Bookkeepers, cashiers, and accountants	334	36	2	
Clerks	566	39	4	3
Weighers	185		3	
Drivers and yardmen	1,173		44	
Inspectors	162		6	
Laborers and feeders	4,818	7	487	
Other and not specified occupations	328	124	6	2
WAREHOUSES AND COLD STORAGE PLANTS	22,414	1,647	2,365	62
Proprietors	2,070	12	13	
Managers	1,939	3	10	
Foremen and overseers	1,430	13	35	
Bookkeepers, cashiers, and accountants	1,069	263	4	3
Clerks (general)	1,669	114	25	
Clerks (shipping)	601	12	5	1
Collectors	43	3	1	1
Weighers	154		10	
Blacksmiths	60		1	
Carpenters	67		2	
Coopers	28		12	
Engineers (stationary)	653		13	
Machinists	83		2	
Millwrights	50		15	
Firemen	200		25	
Inspectors	152	6	13	
Laborers	8,080	638	1,650	53
Packers	789	56	47	
Porters	381	1	118	1
Teamsters	1,704	1	320	
Other and not specified occupations	1,192	525	44	3
WHOLESALE AND RETAIL TRADE	2,971,528	606,243	114,038	7,304
Merchants and dealers (wholesale).[1]				
Importers and exporters	4,722	183	4	2
Jobbers	3,033	148	77	3
Other wholesale dealers	42,368	594	148	7
Merchants and dealers (retail).[1]				
Agricultural implements and wagons	8,410	108	12	5
Art stores and artists' materials	1,955	415	8	19
Automobiles	4,545	52	9	
Bicycles	1,486	46	22	1
Books	2,796	322	8	1
Boots and shoes	18,470	876	59	10
Butchers and meat dealers	122,757	1,291	2,905	52
Buyers and shippers of grain	11,454	81	12	
Buyers and shippers of live stock	32,346	170	286	6
Buyers and shippers of other farm produce	6,806	58	42	3
Buyers and shippers (not specified)	883	13	7	1
Candy and confectionery	21,601	7,937	253	131
Cigars and tobacco	16,375	1,353	104	9
Carpets and rugs	1,152	86	7	1
Clothing and men's furnishings	34,229	1,044	132	39
Coal and wood	23,942	524	1,078	82

[1] Includes managers and superintendents.

TABLE 22.—GAINFUL WORKERS 10 YEARS OF AGE AND OVER, ALL CLASSES AND NEGRO, CLASSIFIED BY SEX, INDUSTRY, AND OCCUPATION: 1910—Continued.

TRADE, INCLUDING BANKING, INSURANCE, AND WAREHOUSING—Continued.

INDUSTRY AND OCCUPATION.	ALL CLASSES. Male.	ALL CLASSES. Female.	NEGRO. Male.	NEGRO. Female.
WHOLESALE AND RETAIL TRADE—Con.				
Merchants and dealers (retail)[1]—Contd.				
Coffee and tea	5,112	239	20	3
Crockery, glassware, and queensware	2,298	210	8	1
Curios, antiques, and novelties	2,377	358	6	
Delicatessen stores	2,313	718	5	4
Department stores	8,564	406	16	2
Drugs and medicines	65,414	2,161	530	165
Dry goods, fancy goods, and notions	57,321	7,962	215	65
Five and ten cent and variety stores	3,294	1,037	8	6
Florists (dealers)[2]	2,527	407	28	7
Flour and feed	9,363	106	40	3
Fruit	18,228	772	135	23
Furniture	21,739	470	129	5
Furs	2,043	237	5	2
Gas fixtures and electrical supplies	1,497	29	1	1
General stores	84,734	3,325	649	87
Groceries	176,993	18,439	4,564	986
Hardware, stoves, and cutlery	38,980	683	60	16
Harness and saddlery	7,484	57	30	
Hucksters and peddlers	76,630	3,785	2,745	689
Ice	7,220	141	188	20
Jewelry	29,403	559	199	7
Junk	15,079	140	776	18
Leather and hides	2,436	39	8	1
Liquors and wines	17,404	332	117	6
Lumber	26,245	240	118	11
Milk	13,851	843	75	34
Music and musical instruments	4,963	259	8	2
Newsdealers	6,534	541	89	12
Oil, paint, and wall paper	6,596	222	16	1
Opticians	5,954	330	18	2
Produce and provisions	28,358	1,281	658	98
Rags	1,805	170	115	15
Rubber goods	489	4	5	
Stationery	5,136	687	43	3
Timber	752	13	9	
Other specified retail dealers	18,973	1,410	148	59
Not specified retail dealers	40,610	4,115	936	280
Other persons in trade.				
Employment office keepers	1,540	720	65	83
Undertakers	19,921	813	907	46
Proprietors of other trade companies	1,146	20	4	1
Officials of other trade companies	4,038	104	9	1

INDUSTRY AND OCCUPATION.	ALL CLASSES. Male.	ALL CLASSES. Female.	NEGRO. Male.	NEGRO. Female.
WHOLESALE AND RETAIL TRADE—Con.				
Other persons in trade—Continued.				
Managers of other trade companies	3,821	109	3	1
Floorwalkers, foremen, and overseers	14,900	3,046	258	9
Accountants	4,208	1,188	21	
Agents (not specified)	7,109	774	84	20
Bookkeepers	69,832	62,185	138	211
Cashiers in stores	5,291	23,209	8	35
Clerks in stores	275,589	111,594	2,582	915
Clerks (shipping)	25,019	469	421	4
Collectors	17,616	985	139	24
Messenger, errand, and office boys	40,482	2,120	4,397	124
Stenographers and typewriters	6,363	44,921	18	75
Weighers	1,721	78	72	2
Engineers (stationary)	1,668		56	
Machinists	1,263		32	
Apprentices	3,569	98	52	
Auctioneers	3,985	5	14	
Bundle and cash boys and girls	4,274	6,592	88	17
Canvassers and solicitors	13,054	4,586	166	117
Commercial travelers	161,027	2,593	286	46
Decorators, drapers, and window dressers	4,902	439	42	4
Deliverymen	205,457	132	30,511	26
Demonstrators	1,250	3,130	21	24
Elevator tenders	3,072	3	884	1
Firemen	262		39	
Fruit graders and packers	2,677	2,038	168	180
Gaugers, measurers, and samplers	1,573	129	604	8
Inspectors	8,168	1,619	240	8
Janitors	2,781	207	1,184	61
Labelers	44	376	2	4
Laborers (coal yards)	16,655	8	3,705	3
Laborers (lumber yards)	43,389	9	6,201	4
Laborers (stores)	64,264	3,829	11,011	444
Meat cutters	15,378	27	224	1
Newsboys	29,435	273	1,207	14
Packers	9,960	2,953	524	23
Porters	33,905	335	25,895	226
Rag sorters	951	727	28	26
Sales agents	31,424	4,098	251	169
Salesmen and saleswomen	624,742	250,438	3,394	1,305
Scrubbers and sweepers	121	155	14	32
Other and not specified occupations	6,033	1,081	181	4

SERVICE GROUPS NOT DISTRIBUTED BY INDUSTRIAL GROUPS.

INDUSTRY AND OCCUPATION.	ALL CLASSES. Male.	ALL CLASSES. Female.	NEGRO. Male.	NEGRO. Female.
DOMESTIC AND PERSONAL SERVICE[3]	1,175,993	2,463,413	234,063	840,480
Barbers and hairdressers	172,946	17,064	19,441	3,093
Bartenders	100,984	250	2,661	5
Bathhouse keepers and attendants	3,125	1,470	358	440
Bell boys, chore boys, door boys, etc.	17,667	662	7,934	278
Billiard and pool room keepers	13,700	159	866	9
Boarding and lodging house keepers	23,052	142,400	1,418	9,183
Bootblacks	14,000	20	3,842	8
Bowling alley, dance hall, shooting gallery, skating rink, etc., keepers	2,243	659	60	76
Butlers	13,168		8,428	
Cemetery keepers	4,811	31	212	4
Chambermaids	187	39,602	11	14,071
Charwomen and cleaners (not otherwise specified)	7,031	26,531	1,597	6,962
Cleaners and renovators (clothing, etc.)	12,215	2,645	3,385	359
Coachmen	25,171		7,628	
Cooks	107,416	332,546	28,328	205,584
Elevator tenders	16,974	20	4,998	1
Firemen	5,924		810	
Footmen	496		51	
Hotel keepers and managers	50,269	14,235	620	353
Housekeepers and stewards	12,233	173,056	1,205	9,911
Hunters, trappers, and guides	3,840	47	206	3
Janitors	75,188	20,127	17,243	2,124
Laborers	48,106	3,065	10,047	668
Laundresses and laundrymen (not in laundry)	13,693	520,004	6,573	361,551
Manicurists	31	5,234	5	689
Midwives		6,205		1,634
Nursemaids, ladies' maids, valets, etc.	2,436	21,786	880	10,239
Nurses (not trained)	15,926	110,912	1,028	17,874
Porters	54,560	52	30,178	12
Restaurant, café, and lunch-room keepers	50,316	10,516	3,635	2,734
Saloon keepers	66,724	1,491	636	16
Servants (not otherwise specified)	86,547	914,063	34,892	184,889
Sextons	3,891	235	662	60
Umbrella menders and scissors grinders	1,016	37	28	2
Waiters	98,565	85,673	32,676	7,377
Other specified occupations	89	144	14	4
Not specified occupations	127	73	15	2

INDUSTRY AND OCCUPATION.	ALL CLASSES. Male.	ALL CLASSES. Female.	NEGRO. Male.	NEGRO. Female.
DOMESTIC AND PERSONAL SERVICE—Continued.				
Occupations connected with domestic and personal service.				
Bookkeepers, cashiers, and accountants	6,027	6,729	68	102
Clerks	33,016	3,841	548	106
Messenger, errand, and office boys	1,600	149	429	47
Purchasing agents	17	9		1
Stenographers and typewriters	246	1,671	4	9
Drivers and teamsters	680		60	
Engineers (stationary)	9,552		376	
Machinists	188		7	
PROFESSIONAL SERVICE	933,165	779,324	39,400	30,071
Actors	16,305	11,992	750	529
Architects and architects' apprentices:				
Architects	16,311	302	56	3
Apprentices	404	20	3	
Artists and teachers of art:				
Artists	16,878	13,387	191	116
Teachers	318	2,042	2	10
Authors	2,310	2,058	19	8
Chemists, assayers, and metallurgists	15,547	579	112	4
Clergymen	117,333	685	17,427	68
Designers (not otherwise specified)	1,033	534	7	
Draftsmen (not otherwise specified) and draftsmen's apprentices:				
Draftsmen	13,392	352	17	2
Apprentices	667	15	1	
Editors	15,876	1,461	134	12
Engineers (not elsewhere specified):				
Civil	31,625	5	69	
Electrical	10,136	1	60	
Mechanical	9,797		46	
Fortune tellers, hypnotists, spiritualists, etc.	380	1,220	29	71
Gamekeepers	138	16	2	1
Inventors	2,303	44	18	1

[1] Includes managers and superintendents. [2] Growers of flowers are shown under "Agriculture," p. 513. [3] For laundries, see under "Manufacturing," p. 539.

TABLE 22.—GAINFUL WORKERS 10 YEARS OF AGE AND OVER, ALL CLASSES AND NEGRO, CLASSIFIED BY SEX, INDUSTRY, AND OCCUPATION: 1910—Continued.

SERVICE GROUPS NOT DISTRIBUTED BY INDUSTRIAL GROUPS—Continued.

INDUSTRY AND OCCUPATION.	ALL CLASSES. Male.	ALL CLASSES. Female.	NEGRO. Male.	NEGRO. Female.
PROFESSIONAL SERVICE—Contd.				
Journalists	3,060	508	24	1
Keepers of charitable and penal institutions	1,127	1,548	23	31
Keepers of pleasure resorts, race tracks, etc	2,706	223	50	4
Landscape gardeners	3,777	15	230	....
Legal profession:				
Abstractors, notaries, and justices of the peace	6,660	785	96	21
Judges, justices, and magistrates	6,816	....	19	....
Lawyers	107,330	558	777	2
Librarians and librarians' assistants:				
Librarians	1,594	5,829	15	15
Assistants	507	2,792	8	7
Literary persons (not otherwise specified)	2,329	1,263	39	31
Medical profession:				
Dentists	38,743	1,254	452	26
Dentists' assistants and apprentices	544	1,504	46	58
Healers, except physicians and surgeons	2,162	4,672	141	191
Nurses, trained	5,819	76,508	275	2,158
Physicians and surgeons	142,117	9,015	2,744	333
Veterinary surgeons	11,652	....	122	....
Musicians and teachers of music:				
Musicians	39,163	15,595	2,769	605
Teachers	15,669	68,783	490	1,742
Officials of lodges, etc	6,245	1,970	183	96
Photographers	26,811	4,964	363	41
Professors and presidents of colleges	12,710	2,958	169	73
Religious and charity workers	7,081	8,889	169	332
Reporters	11,265	2,212	42	7
School-teachers	118,442	476,864	6,991	22,441
Scientific persons (not otherwise specified)	2,781	346	18	5
Sculptors	1,479	100	8	2
Secretaries of schools	595	644	15	5
Showmen	18,988	1,108	1,006	60
Surveyors (not otherwise specified)	8,403	....	105	....
Teachers of athletics, dancing, etc	2,768	1,163	44	9
Theatrical agents	1,057	21	9	....
Theatrical owners, managers, and officials	11,027	295	91	2
Turfmen and sportsmen	2,743	1	541	....
Other and not specified professional pursuits	461	105	....	....
Nonprofessional workers in professional service.				
Bookkeepers, cashiers, and accountants	3,061	4,568	40	94
Clerks	10,330	6,727	115	100
Messenger, errand, and office boys	2,866	135	273	13
Physicians' and surgeons' attendants	689	3,451	180	471
Stenographers and typewriters	4,337	34,392	61	158
Ticket sellers in theaters, etc	1,108	2,156	17	29
Drivers for professional people	1,986	1	767	....
Engineers (stationary)	691	....	11	....
Firemen	141	....	13	....
Laborers	2,159	150	333	39
Stage carpenters	1,838	....	12	....
Stage hands and circus helpers	6,444	392	477	44
Ushers in theaters	2,131	147	84	....
PUBLIC SERVICE (NOT ELSEWHERE CLASSIFIED)	509,176	23,577	25,838	457
Federal officials and employees.				
Appraisers, examiners, and inspectors	5,873	202	83	4
Customs and revenue officials	1,961	47	34	....
Other United States officials	1,492	8	10	....
Officials of foreign governments	295	....	1	....
Bookkeepers and cashiers	1,125	238	9	2
Clerks (foreign governments)	132	16	5	....
Clerks (United States)	19,024	5,158	572	88
Messenger, errand, and office boys	1,858	31	720	10
Stenographers and typewriters	1,571	1,758	29	14
Doorkeepers	140	....	11	....
Engineers (stationary)	498	....	26	....
Firemen	168	....	43	....
PUBLIC SERVICE (NOT ELSEWHERE CLASSIFIED)—Continued.				
State officials and employees.				
Inspectors of food and food products	508	15	2	....
Other state officials	6,154	525	28	3
Bookkeepers and accountants	628	292	5	9
Clerks	2,202	708	40	3
Stenographers and typewriters	444	1,236	4	1
Engineers (stationary)	324	....	6	....
Firemen	214	....	17	....
Laborers	1,273	20	95	1
Teamsters	311	....	15	....
Other and not specified occupations	363	17	52	1
County officials and employees.				
Keepers of charitable and penal institutions	2,917	246	33	4
Surveyors	1,420	....	5	....
Other county officials	17,469	1,575	55	14
Bookkeepers	1,125	432	6	2
Clerks	5,232	1,653	38	4
Stenographers and typewriters	1,102	1,768	13	2
Laborers	616	1	148	....
Other and not specified occupations	319	15	18	2
City and town officials and employees.				
Inspectors of food and food products	1,464	24	11	2
Keepers of charitable and penal institutions	1,202	451	31	2
Surveyors	2,701	....	20	....
Other city officials	30,735	987	161	8
Bookkeepers	2,461	774	7	....
Clerks	11,400	1,888	90	14
Stenographers and typewriters	865	2,093	9	2
Weighers	649	4	3	....
Foremen (city works)	3,684	2	52	....
Engineers (stationary)	7,393	....	100	....
Firemen (city fire department)	35,606	....	321	....
Firemen (city works)	3,138	....	221	....
Garbage men and scavengers	4,227	....	1,100	....
Laborers	56,123	504	10,085	150
Machinists	796	....	10	....
Meter readers	391	....	6	....
Oilers	540	....	13	....
Teamsters	10,688	1	1,671	....
Other and not specified occupations	775	41	51	2
Army and Navy.				
Officers (Army)	4,434	....	21	....
Officers (Navy)	1,687	....	8	....
Officers (Army or Navy not specified)	91	....	1	....
Soldiers	60,187	....	3,168	....
Sailors	13,798	....	517	....
Enlisted men (Army or Navy not specified)	89	....	8	....
Marines	3,079	....	41	....
Police.				
United States marshals	573	1	6	....
County sheriffs	7,131	3	37	....
City marshals	4,704	....	36	....
Constables	3,794	1	79	....
Detectives	6,162	187	70	2
Guards in public institutions, etc	6,839	79	166	2
Policemen	61,980	....	576	....
Probation and truant officers	855	188	7	9
Watchmen	71,189	24	3,364	1
Miscellaneous occupations.				
Foremen and overseers	223	19	6	1
Gaugers, samplers, and weighers	1,422	12	75	....
Laborers	4,266	204	1,339	87
Life-savers	2,158	....	12	....
Lighthouse keepers	1,552	41	34	2
Porters	221	....	113	....
Teamsters	175	....	31	....
Other and not specified occupations	971	88	38	9

SCHEME OF PRESENTATION.

As compiled for farms and for tenure classes of farms in this chapter, statistics of agriculture relate to the following topics: Number of farms; farm acreage, improved and unimproved; value of farm property, including land, buildings, implements and machinery, and live stock; farm animals; crops; size of farms; term of occupancy; and mortgage indebtedness.

Summary tables relating to each of these topics, with two exceptions, are presented in Section I for farms without distinction by tenure, and in Section II for tenure classes of farms. Size of farms is shown without distinction by tenure in Section I, but is not shown by tenure in Section II; and mortgage indebtedness is shown for owned farms only. Tables 45 to 73 are general tables for states and counties, from which the summary tables of Sections I and II are, with few exceptions, derived.

Under this arrangement statistics in greater or less detail relating to any of the topics noted above will generally be found in each section and in the General Tables. Term of occupancy, for example, is shown in Section I for colored and white farmers of the South, the North, and the West (Table 27); in Section II for colored and white owners free, owners mortgaged, part owners, cash tenants, share tenants, and managers, in the South (Tables 42 and 43); and in Table 70 for these tenure classes of colored farmers, by states.

The general tables give statistics in various combinations for state and county areas. Table 73, for example, gives for southern counties detail for size of farm and for tenure classes, and gives for each tenure class detail of acreage; value of land, buildings, and implements and machinery; number of dairy cows, work horses, and work mules; and acreage and yield of cotton and corn, on colored farms. The table thus assembles data by counties. The diverse and composite character of the general tables precludes an arrangement of them strictly in accordance with the order in which topics are taken up in Sections I and II, although this order is followed in so far as the character of the tables permit.

The more detailed tabulations are for farms of colored operators, data for Negroes separately from other colored operators not being available in compilations made from the schedules. The value of these statistics relating to the aggregate colored, as statistical statements of conditions and tendencies obtaining among Negro farm operators, varies from state to state, as the proportion colored other than Negro varies in the aggregate of colored farm operators. Two state tables have been introduced (Tables 45 and 55), classifying the colored farm operators and colored owners, managers, and tenants, as Negro and "other colored." These tables show that in all Southern states, excepting Oklahoma, and in some of the Northern states, Negroes constitute so large a majority of the colored farm operators that statistics for colored operators may be accepted as fairly representing the Negro element. Among such Northern states are New Jersey (Negro farmers 472, other colored 4), Pennsylvania (Negro 543, other colored 3), Ohio (Negro 1,948, other colored 2), Indiana (Negro 785, other colored 20), Illinois (Negro 1,422, other colored 3), Iowa (Negro 187, other colored 14), Missouri (Negro 3,656, other colored 10), Kansas (Negro 1,532, other colored 159), and the New England states (Negro 310, other colored 32).

In certain states, however, the Indian, Chinese, and Japanese elements combined, i. e., the "other colored" element, outnumber Negroes among colored farm operators, and in other states these elements constitute so large a proportion of the colored operators that statistics for the colored can not be accepted as being necessarily indicative of conditions and tendencies obtaining among Negroes. Such states include all of the states of the Mountain and Pacific divisions, and among Northern states the following: New York (Negro farm operators 295, other colored 644), Wisconsin (Negro 48, other colored 543), Minnesota (Negro 29, other colored 264), North Dakota (Negro 22, other colored 721), South Dakota (Negro 67, other colored 2,741), and Nebraska (Negro 96, other colored 366).

In the West as a whole, which comprises the states of the Mountain and Pacific divisions, comparatively few of the colored farmers—only 482 out of 12,858—are Negroes. Statistics for colored farmers in this section obviously have no specific value for Negroes. In the states of the North combined, Negroes constitute approximately two-thirds—12,052 in a total of 17,884—of the colored farm operators, the proportion non-Negro in the aggregate colored of this section also being sufficiently large to invalidate the data, although, as has been noted, Negroes largely predominate among the colored farmers of individual Northern states.

In the South as a whole, and in each Southern state, with the exception of Oklahoma, the colored other than Negro constitute a negligible proportion among colored operators. Of the colored operators in the South, numbering 890,141 in 1910, 880,836 were Negroes and 9,305 were Indian, Chinese, and Japanese.

Of this non-Negro element in the aggregate colored, 7,462 were in Oklahoma, constituting approximately one-third of the colored farmers in this state; 1,200 were in North Carolina, in a total colored for the state of 65,656; and only 643 were in the 14 other Southern states.

It will be apparent from these figures that statistics for colored farm operators in the South and in the several Southern states, with exception of Oklahoma, are practically equivalent to statistics for Negroes.

Generally, in the tables following, therefore, where statistics are not available in published reports for Negroes separately from other colored and have not been specially compiled for Negroes in this report, the tables are restricted to the South. In some cases, however, statistics are given for colored operators in Northern and Western states, in order to cover those individual states in which Negroes largely predominate among colored operators. In other tables summary totals are given for colored operators in the North and West in order to distribute the aggregate shown for the United States as a whole, and by way of formally completing tables which give statistics for white farmers of the South, North, and West in comparison with statistics for colored operators in those sections. Such tables include, therefore, some totals for colored farm operators to which little specific significance attaches—totals which develop as statistical remainders in the compilation of data for the South separately, and for whites in comparison with Negroes by geographic sections. Generally, however, as noted above, such totals have been eliminated by restricting the tabulation to the South.

Of Negro farm operators, 98.6 per cent in 1910 were in the South, and for nearly this proportion of Negro operators statistics in detail are practically available, Oklahoma being the only extensive southern area within which the colored other than Negro are sufficiently numerous to invalidate the data. Interest naturally attaches, however, specially to the condition of Negro farmers in the North and West, although they constitute only 1.4 per cent of the total number of Negro farmers in the country as a whole, and some compilations for Negroes have, therefore, been made for the Northern states.

Three general tables for counties have been compiled, one (Table 71) giving statistics of acreage and value of farm property on farms operated by Negroes, for all counties reporting Negro farmers; one (Table 72) giving statistics of acreage, and of acreage and yield of cotton and corn, for colored and white farmers in southern counties; and one (Table 73) giving, as has been noted, statistics of size of farms, and detail for tenure classes of farms operated by colored farmers in southern counties.

SECTION I.—STATISTICS OF NEGRO FARMS.

NUMBER OF FARMERS.

Negro farmers in 1910 numbered 893,370, constituting 14 per cent of the total number of farmers of all classes in the country as a whole.

Table 1 distributes population and farm operators in 1910 and in 1900 by racial classes.

During the decade the proportion Negro declined slightly in the population (from 11.6 per cent in 1900 to 10.7 per cent in 1910) and increased slightly among farm operators (from 13 per cent in 1900 to 14 per cent in 1910).

Table 2 shows the increase in population and in the number of farm operators during the decade 1900–1910 and the number of farm operators per 1,000 population at the beginning and end of the decade, by racial classes.

Table 1 RACIAL CLASS.	POPULATION.		FARM OPERATORS.	
	1910	1900	1910	1900
	NUMBER.			
All classes	91,972,266	75,994,575	6,361,502	5,737,372
Negro	9,827,763	8,833,994	893,370	746,715
White	81,731,957	66,809,196	5,440,619	4,969,608
Indian	265,683	237,196	24,251	19,910
Chinese	71,531	89,863	760	1,100
Japanese	72,157	24,326	2,502	39
Other	3,175			
	PERCENTAGE DISTRIBUTION BY RACIAL CLASS.			
All classes	100.0	100.0	100.0	100.0
Negro	10.7	11.6	14.0	13.0
White	88.9	87.6	85.5	86.6
Indian	0.3	0.3	0.4	0.3
Chinese	0.1	0.1	(1)	(1)
Japanese	0.1	(1)	(1)	(1)
Other	(1)			

[1] Less than one-tenth of 1 per cent.

Table 2 RACIAL CLASS.	INCREASE:[1] 1900–1910.				FARM OPERATORS PER 1,000 POPULATION OF EACH CLASS.	
	Number.		Per cent.			
	Population.	Farm operators.	Population.	Farm operators.	1910	1900
All classes	15,977,691	624,130	21.0	10.9	69	76
Negro	993,769	146,655	11.2	19.6	91	85
White	14,922,761	471,011	22.3	9.5	67	74
Indian	28,487	4,341	12.0	21.8	91	84
Chinese	−18,332	−340	−20.4	−30.9	11	12
Japanese	47,831	2,463	196.6	6,315.4	35	2
Other	3,175					

[1] A minus sign (−) denotes decrease.

Negro farm operators increased during the decade 1900–1910 by 146,655, or 19.6 per cent, the increase in the number of farm operators being at a much more rapid rate than the increase of the Negro population (11.2 per cent). In the same period white farm operators increased 9.5 per cent, the white increase per cent for farm operators being less than one-half the corresponding rate for Negroes, and less than one-half the rate of increase of the white population (22.3 per cent). In this period, therefore, agriculture became, relatively to other fields of employment, more important among Negroes, in so far as numbers engaged may be accepted as an index of importance, and less important, relatively to other fields of employment, among whites.

The number of farm operators per 1,000 population increased among Negroes from 85 in 1900 to 91 in 1910, and declined among whites from 74 to 67.

Only a very small proportion of the Negro farm operators were in the North and West in either 1910 or 1900 and this small proportion declined during the decade (from 1.9 per cent in 1900 to 1.4 per cent in 1910). In 1910, 39.7 per cent, or nearly two-fifths of the Negro operators were in the South Atlantic division, 36.4 per cent were in the East South Central division, and 22.5 per cent were in the West South Central division. The geographic distribution of Negro farm operators, by sections and divisions, in 1910 was not materially different from their distribution in 1900.

In each of these years more than one-half of the white farm operators were in the North, the percent-age in the North in 1910 being 52.8, in the South, 40.6, and in the West, 6.6.

The distribution of farm operators, Negro and white, by sections and southern divisions, in 1910 and in 1900 is shown in Table 3.

Table 3	FARM OPERATORS.			
	Negro.		White.	
SECTION AND DIVISION.	1910	1900	1910	1900
	NUMBER.			
United States...............	893,370	746,715	5,440,619	4,969,608
The South......................	880,836	732,362	2,207,406	1,879,721
South Atlantic...............	354,530	287,933	756,019	673,354
East South Central...........	324,884	267,530	717,262	635,418
West South Central...........	201,422	176,899	734,125	570,949
The North......................	12,052	14,016	2,872,734	2,855,033
The West......................	482	337	360,479	234,854
	PERCENTAGE DISTRIBUTION BY SECTIONS AND DIVISIONS.			
United States...............	100.0	100.0	100.0	100.0
The South......................	98.6	98.1	40.6	37.8
South Atlantic...............	39.7	38.6	13.9	13.5
East South Central...........	36.4	35.8	13.2	12.8
West South Central...........	22.5	23.7	13.5	11.5
The North......................	1.3	1.9	52.8	57.4
The West......................	0.1	(1)	6.6	4.7

1 Less than one-tenth of 1 per cent.

MAP I.—FARMS OF COLORED FARMERS—PERCENTAGE OF ALL FARMS, BY STATES: 1910 (SOUTHERN STATES ONLY).

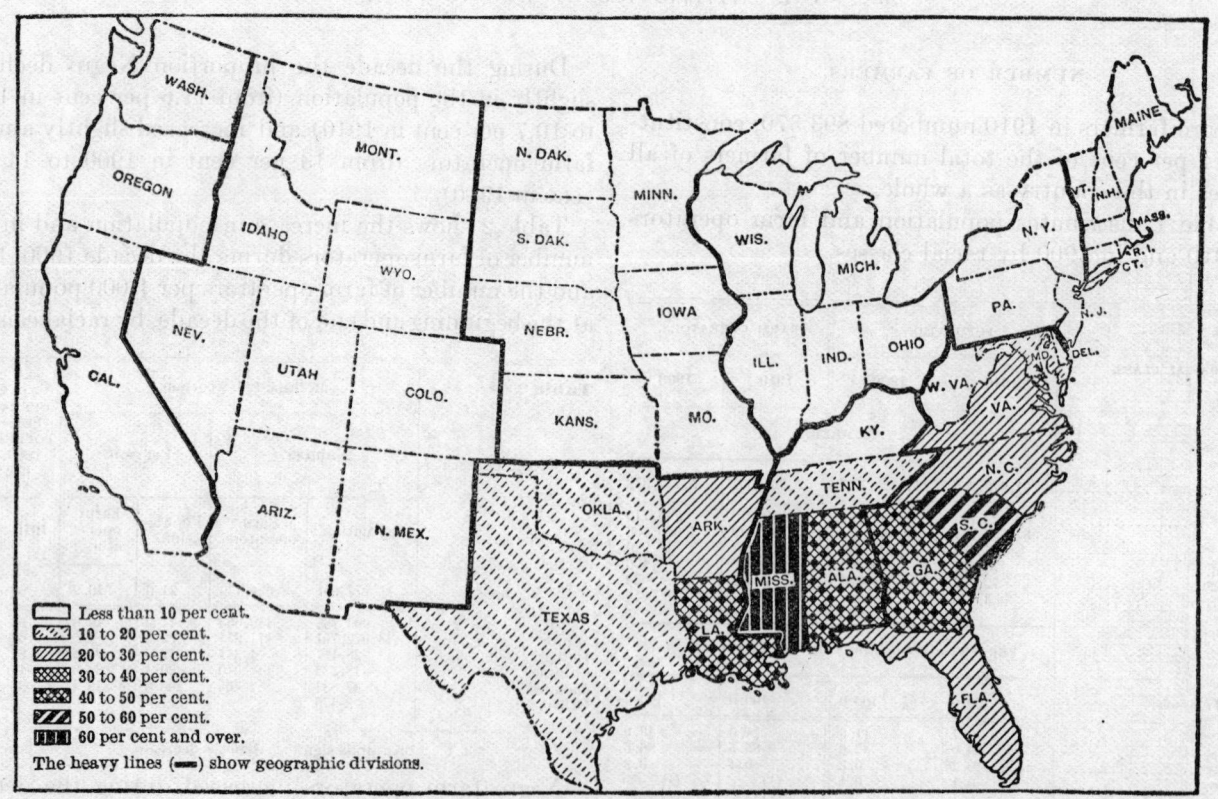

Less than 10 per cent.
10 to 20 per cent.
20 to 30 per cent.
30 to 40 per cent.
40 to 50 per cent.
50 to 60 per cent.
60 per cent and over.

The heavy lines (▬) show geographic divisions.

The number of Negro farm operators increased in the South during the decade by 148,474, or 20.3 per cent, and in the North decreased by 1,964, or 14 per cent. In the South Atlantic and in the East South Central division the increase per cent of Negro farm operators exceeded that of white farm operators, while in the West South Central division, and in the West, the increase per cent for whites exceeded that for Negroes.

Table 4 shows these increases, together with the proportion of farm operators in the Negro and white population in 1910 and in 1900.

Table 4	INCREASE OF FARM OPERATORS:[1] 1900–1910.				FARM OPERATORS PER 1,000 POPULATION OF EACH CLASS.			
SECTION AND DIVISION.	Number.		Per cent.		Negro.		White.	
	Negro.	White.	Negro.	White.	1910	1900	1910	1900
United States......	146,655	471,011	19.6	9.5	91	85	67	74
The South............	148,474	327,685	20.3	17.4	101	92	107	114
South Atlantic.......	66,597	82,665	23.1	12.3	86	77	94	100
East South Central...	57,354	81,844	21.4	12.9	122	107	125	126
West South Central...	24,523	163,176	13.9	28.6	102	104	109	120
The North............	−1,964	17,701	−14.0	0.6	12	16	53	62
The West.............	145	125,625	43.0	53.5	10	11	55	61

[1] A minus sign (−) denotes decrease.

DIAGRAM I.—NUMBER OF FARMS CLASSIFIED BY COLOR AND NATIVITY OF OPERATOR, BY STATES: 1910.

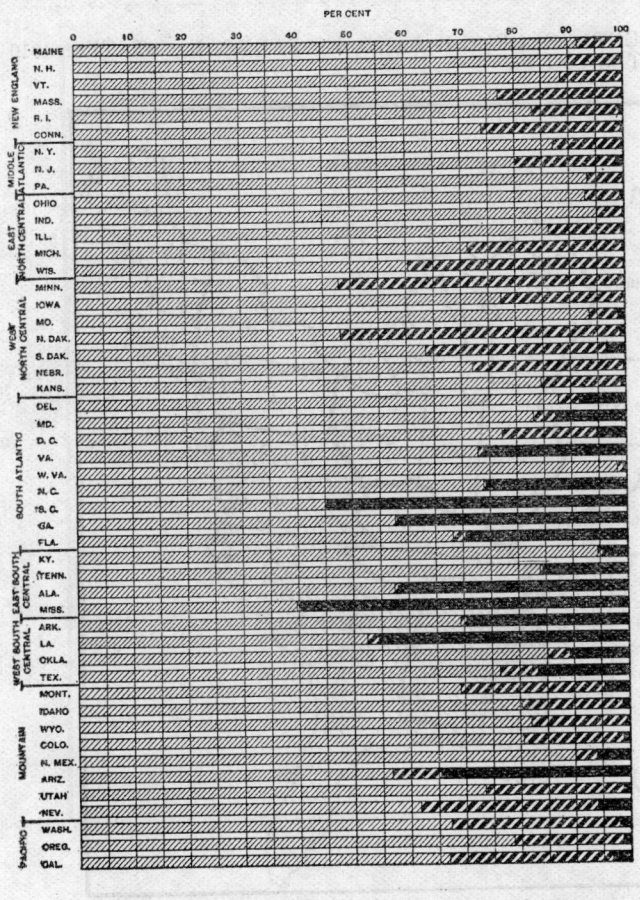

NATIVE WHITE   FOREIGN BORN WHITE   NEGRO AND OTHER NONWHITE

The proportion of farm operators in the Negro population increased during the decade from 77 to 86 per 1,000 population in the South Atlantic division, and from 107 to 122 per 1,000 population in the East South Central division. In the West South Central division the proportion declined slightly—from 104 to 102 per 1,000 population. The small proportion of farmers in the Negro population of the North declined in this period from 16 to 11 per 1,000 population, and in the West from 11 to 10 per 1,000 population. In this period the proportion of farmers in the white population of each section and division declined.

Table 45 (p. 588) gives the number of colored, Negro, and white farm operators, by divisions and states, for the years 1910 and 1900, with the increase during the decade for Negro and white operators, the number of Negro farm operators per 1,000 Negro population in 1910 and in 1900, and the number of Negro farm operators per 1,000 colored operators in 1910.

FARM ACREAGE: TOTAL, IMPROVED, AND UNIMPROVED.

The aggregate acreage, acreage improved, and acreage unimproved, of farms operated by Negroes and by whites in 1910 and in 1900, and the increase in these acreages during the decade 1900–1910, are shown in Tables 46, 47, and 48 (pp. 589, 590, and 591), by divisions and states. Table 5 summarizes the increases of Table 48, by sections.

Table 5	INCREASE:[1] 1900–1910.					
SECTION AND DIVISION.	Acres in farms.		Improved acres in farms.		Unimproved acres in farms.	
	Of Negroes.	Of whites.	Of Negroes.	Of whites.	Of Negroes.	Of whites.
United States	4,045,590	35,340,269	4,482,404	59,216,959	−436,814	−23,876,690
The South.....	3,998,034	−11,580,562	4,449,629	20,061,623	−451,595	−31,642,185
The North.....	−2,848	30,383,959	−2,674	28,509,537	−174	1,874,422
The West......	50,404	16,536,872	35,449	10,645,799	14,955	5,891,073

[1] A minus sign (−) denotes decrease.

The acreage in Negro farms increased during the decade from 38,233,920 acres in 1900 to 42,279,510 acres in 1910, the increase amounting to 4,045,590 acres.

This increase was nearly all in the South, in which section the acreage operated by Negroes increased by 3,998,034 acres, although in the same period the total acreage operated by white farmers decreased in the South by 11,580,562 acres.

In the North Negro farm acreage fell off slightly, by 2,848 acres, and in the West increased by 50,404 acres.

The aggregate acreage of improved land in Negro farms increased from 23,362,786 acres in 1900 to 27,845,190 acres in 1910, the increase amounting to 4,482,404 acres. In the same period unimproved acreage in Negro farms decreased from 14,871,134 to 14,434,320 acres, the decrease amounting to 436,814 acres. Unimproved acreage in Negro farms decreased in the South by 451,595 acres, and in the North by 174 acres, and increased in the West by 14,955 acres.

Improved acreage operated by white farmers in the South increased by 20,061,623 acres, the decrease noted above in total farm acreage of whites in the South developing from the decrease of 31,642,185 acres in unimproved farm land.

Table 6 shows the percentage distribution, by sections and southern divisions, of total, improved, and unimproved land in farms of Negroes and whites in 1910.

Table 6	PERCENTAGE DISTRIBUTION BY SECTION AND DIVISION: 1910.					
SECTION AND DIVISION.	All land in farms.		Improved land in farms.		Unimproved land in farms.	
	Of Negroes.	Of whites.	Of Negroes.	Of whites.	Of Negroes.	Of whites.
United States............	100.0	100.0	100.0	100.0	100.0	100.0
The South..............	97.6	37.5	97.6	27.4	97.8	49.4
South Atlantic........	41.6	10.3	39.3	8.3	46.1	12.7
East South Central........	32.1	8.2	34.3	7.7	27.9	8.8
West South Central........	23.9	19.0	23.9	11.4	23.8	27.9
The North..............	2.1	49.4	2.2	64.3	1.7	31.8
The West..............	0.3	13.2	0.2	8.3	0.5	18.8

Only 2.4 per cent of the farm acreage operated by Negroes in 1910, as compared with 62.5 per cent of white farm acreage, was in the Northern and Western states. The proportion in the South Atlantic division of the total Negro farm acreage was 41.6 per cent, or more than two-fifths, the corresponding proportion for white farm acreage being 10.3 per cent, or approximately one-tenth. For the East South Central division the proportion was 32.1 per cent for Negro farm acreage and 8.2 per cent for white farm acreage, and in the West South Central division, 23.9 and 19 per cent, respectively.

The proportion of Negro farm acreage to total farm acreage in the several sections and divisions—stated as the number of acres, of acres improved, and of acres unimproved, in farms operated by Negroes per 1,000 acres in all farms in the specified areas—is shown in Table 7 for the two census years 1910 and 1900.

Table 7	ACRES IN FARMS OPERATED BY NEGROES PER 1,000 ACRES IN ALL FARMS.					
SECTION AND DIVISION.	All farm land.		Improved farm land.		Unimproved farm land.	
	1910	1900	1910	1900	1910	1900
United States............	48	46	58	56	36	35
The South..............	116	103	180	180	69	62
South Atlantic............	170	149	226	193	120	115
East South Central........	167	155	217	203	107	108
West South Central........	60	52	114	142	31	25
The North..............	2	2	2	2	2	2
The West..............	1	1	1	1	1	1

MAP II.—LAND IN FARMS OF COLORED FARMERS—PERCENTAGE OF ALL LAND IN FARMS, BY STATES: 1910 (SOUTHERN STATES ONLY).

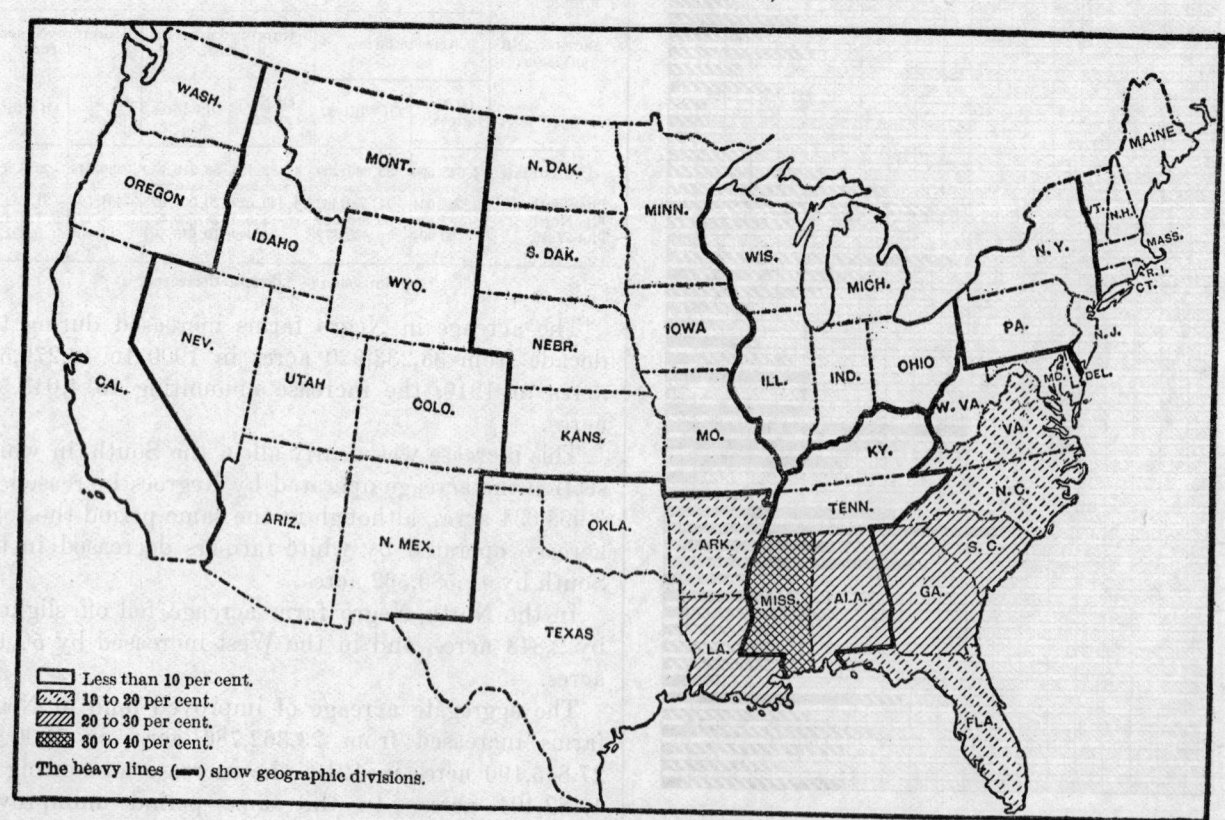

Per 1,000 acres in farms in 1910 in the country as a whole, 48 acres were operated by Negroes, the proportion operated by Negroes having increased slightly during the decade—from 46 per 1,000 in 1900.

In the South the number of acres in Negro farms per 1,000 acres in all farms was 116 in 1910, the proportion having increased during the decade from 103 in 1900. In the North Negro farm acreage per 1,000 total acreage averaged only 2 acres, and in the West, only 1 acre.

In each southern division the proportion of Negro farm acreage to total farm acreage showed a material increase during the decade 1900–1910, the greatest increase and the highest proportion being in the South Atlantic division, in which the number of acres in Negro farms per 1,000 acres in all farms increased from 149 in 1900 to 170 in 1910.

The average number of acres per farm, for Negro and white farms in 1910 and in 1900, is shown in Table 8 for the Southern states, with the decrease in the average size of farms during the decade.

The average acreage per Negro farm decreased from 51.2 acres in 1900 to 47.3 acres in 1910, the decrease amounting in the average to 3.9 acres. In the same period the average acreage of white farms decreased from 160.3 to 153 acres, giving a decrease for the average size of 7.3 acres.

In the South as a whole, and in each southern division the average acreage per farm of Negro farms decreased during the decade. In the North the average acreage for Negro farms increased from 62.2 to 72.1 acres, and in the West from 225.5 to 262.3 acres.

Table 8	AVERAGE NUMBER OF ACRES PER FARM.					
	1910		1900		Decrease:[1] 1900–1910.	
DIVISION AND STATE.	Negro farms.	White farms.	Negro farms.	White farms.	Negro farms.	White farms.
United States...............	47.3	153.0	51.2	160.3	3.9	7.3
The South......................	46.9	141.3	50.9	172.1	4.0	30.8
South Atlantic...............	49.7	113.9	54.1	131.7	4.4	17.8
East South Central.........	41.8	94.7	47.1	108.0	5.3	13.3
West South Central.........	50.2	215.0	51.5	291.0	1.3	76.0
The North....................	72.1	143.0	62.2	133.3	+9.9	+9.7
The West.....................	262.3	303.8	225.5	395.8	+36.8	92.0
THE SOUTH.						
South Atlantic:						
Delaware.................	61.8	99.0	64.3	114.3	2.5	15.3
Maryland................	56.3	110.4	64.1	119.4	7.8	9.0
District of Columbia.........	7.9	29.1	18.1	32.5	10.2	3.4
Virginia..................	46.5	127.0	49.7	143.7	1.2	16.7
West Virginia............	48.8	104.1	56.0	115.2	7.2	11.1
North Carolina..........	48.4	102.4	53.6	116.6	5.2	14.2
South Carolina..........	40.7	120.2	44.4	145.7	3.7	25.5
Georgia.................	57.9	117.9	66.1	147.4	8.2	29.5
Florida..................	52.3	127.1	53.0	133.6	0.7	6.5
East South Central:						
Kentucky................	37.5	87.9	39.8	96.4	2.3	8.5
Tennessee...............	41.9	88.8	45.7	98.5	3.8	9.7
Alabama................	46.1*	102.6	50.2	123.6	4.1	21.0
Mississippi.............	39.2	110.4	45.9	133.9	6.7	23.5
West South Central:						
Arkansas................	41.7	97.7	49.0	108.8	7.3	11.1
Louisiana...............	38.7	126.6	40.3	150.7	1.6	24.1
Oklahoma...............	80.8	156.8	98.9	222.9	18.1	66.1
Texas...................	61.1	310.9	58.6	425.5	+2.5	114.6

[1] A plus sign (+) denotes increase.

MAP III.—IMPROVED LAND IN FARMS OF COLORED FARMERS—PERCENTAGE OF ALL IMPROVED LAND, BY STATES: 1910 (SOUTHERN STATES ONLY).

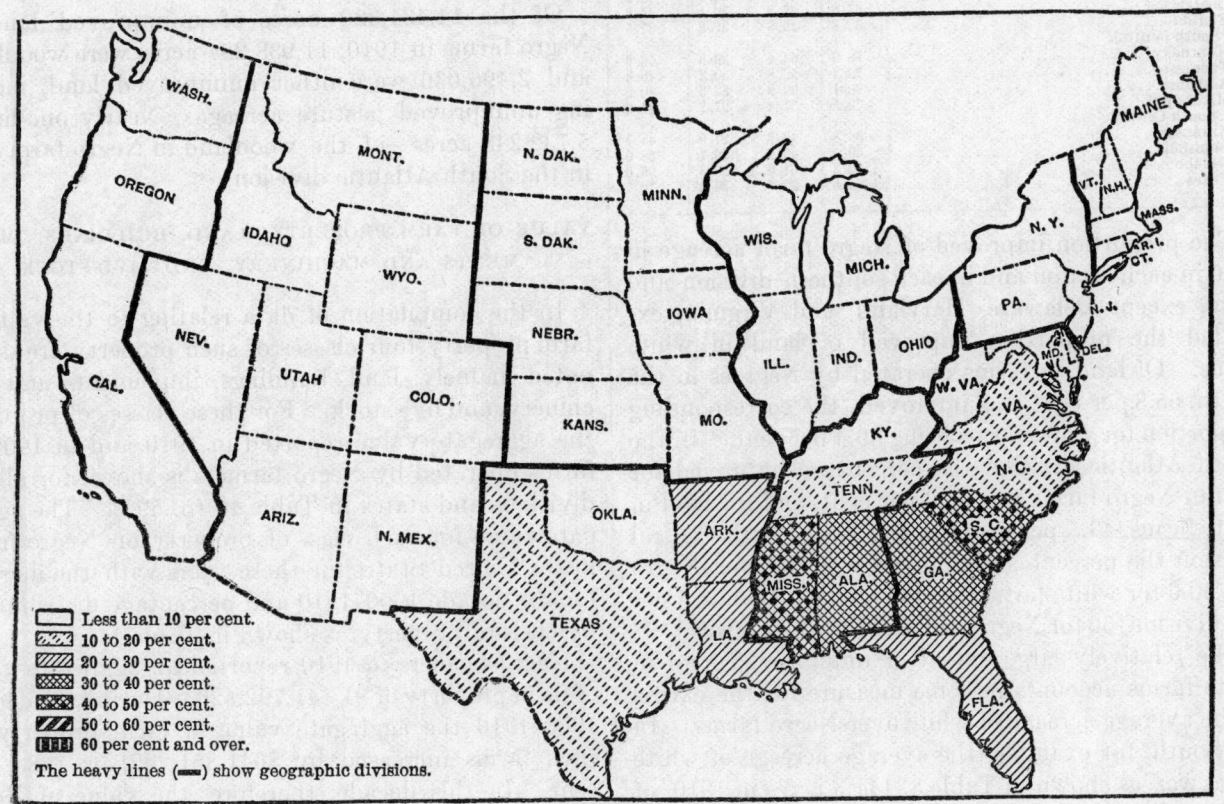

In each Southern state during the decade the average acreage per farm decreased for both Negro and white farms, with the single exception that the average acreage of Negro farms in Texas increased by 2.5 acres.

The range in average acreage per farm in the Southern states in 1910 was from 37.5 acres in Kentucky to 80.8 acres in Oklahoma for Negro farms, and from 87.9 acres in Kentucky to 310.9 acres in Texas for white farms.

The percentage improved of all land in farms and the average number of acres improved per farm in 1910 is shown in Table 9 for sections and southern divisions and states.

Table 9

DIVISION AND STATE.	PERCENTAGE IMPROVED: 1910.		AVERAGE NUMBER OF ACRES IMPROVED PER FARM: 1910.	
	Of land in Negro farms.	Of land in white farms.	Negro farms.	White farms.
United States	65.9	54.0	31.2	82.6
The South	65.8	39.4	30.8	55.7
South Atlantic	62.2	43.5	30.9	49.6
East South Central	70.3	50.6	29.4	47.9
West South Central	66.0	32.4	33.1	69.6
The North	71.2	70.3	72.1	100.6
The West	44.5	34.3	116.8	104.1
THE SOUTH.				
South Atlantic:				
Delaware	65.0	68.9	40.2	68.2
Maryland	61.0	66.7	34.3	73.7
District of Columbia	100.0	84.4	7.9	24.6
Virginia	49.7	50.8	23.1	64.4
West Virginia	58.6	55.1	28.6	57.3
North Carolina	54.5	36.8	26.4	37.7
South Carolina	65.9	36.6	26.8	43.9
Georgia	67.6	37.8	39.1	44.6
Florida	62.8	29.5	32.8	37.5
East South Central:				
Kentucky	78.0	64.4	29.3	56.6
Tennessee	72.4	52.8	30.3	46.8
Alabama	70.1	39.2	32.3	40.2
Mississippi	79.5	37.4	27.2	41.2
West South Central:				
Arkansas	66.8	42.7	27.9	41.7
Louisiana	69.1	45.8	26.7	58.0
Oklahoma	62.3	61.6	50.3	96.6
Texas	64.8	22.7	39.6	70.7

The proportion improved of Negro farm acreage in 1910 in each section and in each southern division and state, except Delaware, Maryland, and Virginia, exceeded the proportion improved of land in white farms. Of land in farms operated by Negroes in the South, 65.8 per cent was improved, the corresponding proportion for white farms being 39.4 per cent. In the South Atlantic division the percentage improved for land in Negro farms was 62.2 per cent, and for land in white farms, 43.5 per cent; in the East South Central division the percentage improved was 70.3 for Negro and 50.6 for white farms; and in the West South Central division, 66 for Negro and 32.4 for white farms.

The relatively large extent of unimproved land in white farms accounts in some measure for the excess of the average acreage of white over Negro farms. In the South, for example, the average acreage of white farms was, as shown in Table 8, 141.3 acres in 1910, of which, as shown in Table 9, 39.3 per cent was improved

land, giving an average of 55.7 acres improved per white farm; the average acreage of Negro farms in the South was 46.9 acres, of which 65.8 per cent was improved, giving an average acreage improved per Negro farm of 30.8 acres. On the basis of total acreage Negro farms in the South averaged less than one-third the size of white farms, while on the basis of improved acreage they averaged nearly three-fifths the size of white farms. On the basis of improved acreage Negro farms in the West averaged larger than white farms, the average number of acres improved per farm in the West being 116.8 for Negro farms and 104.1 for white farms. For no other area shown in Table 9, however, does the average for Negro farms exceed that for white farms.

Table 10 distinguishes acreage in woodland from other unimproved land in farms. This distinction is made in the acreage reported for Negro farms, by counties, with totals for states, in Table 71 (p. 642).

Table 10 — ACRES IN FARMS OPERATED BY NEGROES: 1910.

SECTION AND DIVISION.	Total.	Improved.	Unimproved.		
			Total.	Woodland.	Other.
United States	42,279,510	27,845,190	14,434,320	11,938,284	2,496,036
The South	41,284,471	27,170,413	14,114,058	11,797,439	2,316,619
South Atlantic	17,605,488	10,956,415	6,649,073	5,732,248	916,825
East South Central	13,573,980	9,548,129	4,025,851	3,196,381	829,470
West South Central	10,105,003	6,665,869	3,439,134	2,868,810	570,324
The North	868,630	618,478	250,152	129,660	120,492
The West	126,409	56,299	70,110	11,185	58,925

Of the 14,434,320 acres of unimproved land in Negro farms in 1910, 11,938,284 acres were woodland, and 2,496,036 were other unimproved land, including unimproved pasture acreage. Nearly one-half— 5,732,248 acres—of the woodland in Negro farms was in the South Atlantic division.

VALUE OF FARM PROPERTY: LAND, BUILDINGS, IMPLEMENTS AND MACHINERY, AND LIVE STOCK.

In the compilation of data relating to the value of farm property, four classes of such property are designated, namely, land, buildings, implements and machinery, and live stock. For these classes of property, the aggregate value reported in 1910 and in 1900 on farms operated by Negro farmers is shown for all the divisions and states in Table 49 (p. 592). The aggregate value for each class of property on Negro farms in the United States for these years with the increase for the decade 1900–1910 and percentage distribution, by class of property, is shown in Table 11.

Negro farmers in 1910 reported an aggregate value of farm property of $1,141,792,526. During the decade 1900–1910 the aggregate value of farm property on such farms increased by $641,851,292, or 128.4 per cent. In this decade, therefore, the value of Negro farm property more than doubled.

DIAGRAM II.—AVERAGE VALUE OF FARM PROPERTY PER FARM, FOR COLORED AND WHITE FARMERS, BY STATES: 1910 (SOUTHERN STATES ONLY).

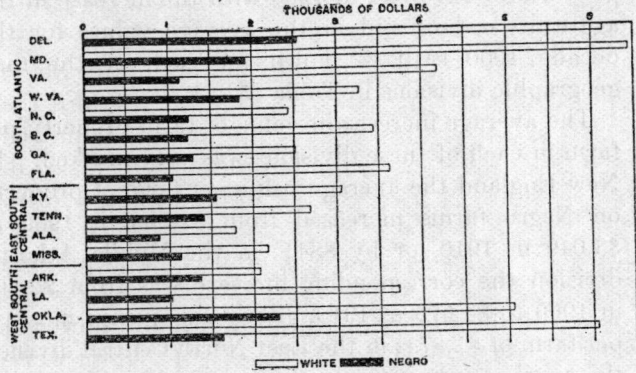

DIAGRAM IV.—AVERAGE VALUE OF FARM PROPERTY PER ACRE, FOR COLORED AND WHITE FARMERS, BY STATES: 1910.

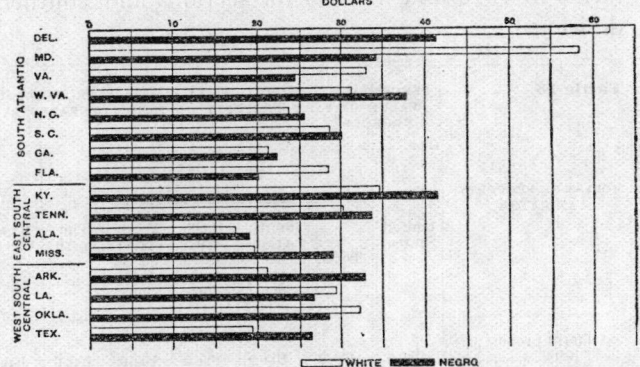

DIAGRAM III.—AVERAGE VALUE OF FARM PROPERTY PER FARM FOR COLORED AND WHITE FARMERS, BY STATES: 1900 (SOUTHERN STATES ONLY).

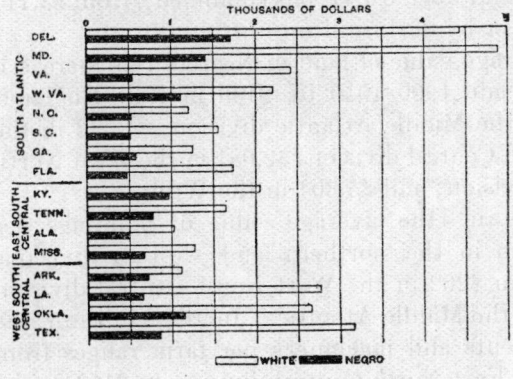

DIAGRAM V.—AVERAGE VALUE OF FARM PROPERTY PER ACRE FOR COLORED AND WHITE FARMERS, BY STATES: 1910.

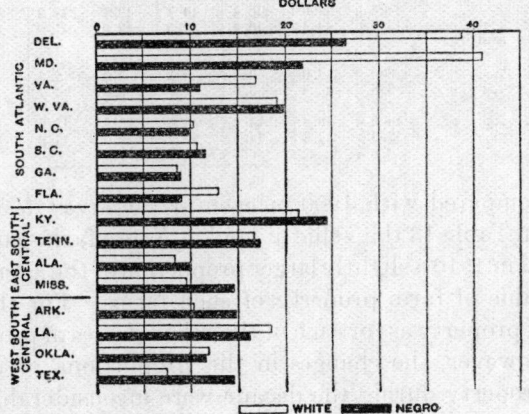

Table 11

VALUE OF FARM PROPERTY ON FARMS OPERATED BY NEGROES.

CLASS OF FARM PROPERTY.	Amount.		Increase: 1900–1910.		Percentage distribution.	
	1910	1900	Amount.	Per cent.	1910	1900
Total.....	$1,141,792,526	$499,941,234	$641,851,292	128.4	100.0	100.0
Land.........	756,158,264	324,242,997	431,915,267	133.2	66.2	64.9
Buildings.....	166,559,439	71,902,265	94,657,174	131.6	14.6	14.4
Implements and machinery.....	34,178,052	18,859,757	15,318,295	81.2	3.0	3.8
Live stock.....	184,896,771	84,936,215	99,960,556	117.7	16.2	17.0

The value of land in Negro farms increased from $324,242,997 in 1900 to $756,158,264 in 1910, the increase amounting to $431,915,267, or 133.2 per cent. In this period the value of buildings on Negro farms increased by $94,657,174, or 131.6 per cent, the value of implements and machinery increased $15,318,295, or 81.2 per cent, and the value of live stock increased $99,960,556, or 117.7 per cent.

In 1910, as in 1900, the value of land constituted approximately two-thirds of the total value of farm property reported for Negroes. The distribution of the aggregate value of farm property, by classes of property in 1910, did not differ materially from that in 1900.

In Table 12 the average value per farm of farm property on Negro farms is shown for 1910 and 1900, with the increase in average value for the decade 1900–1910.

Table 12

CLASS OF FARM PROPERTY.	AVERAGE VALUE PER FARM OF FARM PROPERTY ON FARMS OPERATED BY NEGROES.			
	1910	1900	Increase: 1900–1910.	
			Amount.	Per cent.
Total..............	$1,278	$669	$609	91.0
Land....................	846	434	412	94.9
Buildings....................	187	96	91	94.8
Implements and machinery..........	38	25	13	52.0
Live stock....................	207	114	93	81.6

Negro farms reported a value of farm property in 1910 averaging $1,278 per farm. The corresponding average for 1900 was $669 and the increase in the average for the decade 1900–1910 $609, or 91 per cent. Average value per farm of farm property nearly doubled in the ten years 1900–1910. Similar large proportional increases are shown for the average value per farm of land, which increased from $434 to $846, or by 94.9 per cent; of buildings, which increased from $96 to $187, or 94.8 per cent; and of live stock, which increased from $114 to $207, or by 81.6 per cent. The increase in the average value of implements and machinery per farm on Negro farms is absolutely and relatively much less than for other classes of farm property.

Table 13 shows the proportional distribution, by class of farm property, of the values reported on Negro farms in 1910 and in 1900 for sections and southern divisions.

Table 13

PERCENTAGE DISTRIBUTION, BY CLASS OF PROPERTY, OF VALUE OF FARM PROPERTY ON FARMS OPERATED BY NEGROES.

CLASS OF PROPERTY AND YEAR.	United States.	The South.				The North.	The West.
		Total.	South Atlantic division.	East South Central division.	West South Central division.		
All farm property:							
1910	100.0	100.0	100.0	100.0	100.0	100.0	100.0
1900	100.0	100.0	100.0	100.0	100.0	100.0	100.0
Land:							
1910	66.2	66.0	66.7	63.6	67.8	70.3	76.9
1900	64.9	64.5	65.2	63.3	65.2	70.1	68.4
Buildings:							
1910	14.6	14.6	16.1	14.7	12.4	14.3	6.3
1900	14.4	14.4	16.4	13.5	13.0	15.0	10.6
Implements and machinery:							
1910	3.0	3.0	3.0	3.1	3.0	2.5	2.2
1900	3.8	3.8	3.6	4.0	3.8	3.2	3.4
Live stock:							
1910	16.2	16.4	14.2	18.6	16.9	12.9	14.6
1900	17.0	17.3	14.8	19.2	18.0	11.8	17.6

As compared with 1900 in each of the areas designated in Table 13 the value of land in Negro farms constituted in 1910 a slightly larger proportion of the aggregate value of farm property of such farms. For this class of property as for each of the other classes of property, however, the changes in the proportions of all farm property during the decade were inconsiderable.

The percentage distribution, by sections, of the aggregate of each class of Negro farm property is shown in Table 14 for 1900 and for 1910.

Table 14

PERCENTAGE DISTRIBUTION, BY SECTIONS, OF VALUE OF FARM PROPERTY ON FARMS OPERATED BY NEGROES.

SECTION AND YEAR.	Total.	Land.	Buildings.	Implements and machinery.	Live stock.
United States:					
1910	100.0	100.0	100.0	100.0	100.0
1900	100.0	100.0	100.0	100.0	100.0
The South:					
1910	94.9	94.6	95.2	95.8	95.9
1900	93.9	93.4	93.7	94.9	95.7
The North:					
1910	4.7	5.0	4.6	3.9	3.7
1900	5.9	6.4	6.1	4.9	4.1
The West:					
1910	0.4	0.5	0.2	0.3	0.4
1900	0.2	0.2	0.2	0.2	0.2

For each of the main classes of farm property the proportion reported from Negro farms in the South in 1910 exceeded slightly the corresponding proportion reported in 1900. Of the aggregate value of farm property in 1910, 94.9 per cent was reported from Negro farms in the South; 4.7 from Negro farms in the North, and 0.4 per cent for Negro farms in the West.

The aggregate value of each class of farm property on farms operated by Negroes and the average value per farm in 1910 and in 1900 with the increase in the aggregate values and in the average values for the decade 1900–1910 is shown for each of the nine geographic divisions in Table 15.

The average increase in value of farm property per farm in each of these divisions was very marked. In New England the average value per farm of property on Negro farms increased from $2,208 in 1900 to $3,049 in 1910, or by $841; in the Middle Atlantic division the corresponding increase was from $2,801 in 1900 to $4,675 in 1910, giving an average increase per farm of $1,874; in the East North Central division the average value increased from $2,227 to $4,143, or by $1,916; in the West North Central division, from $1,847 to $4,713, or by $2,866, and in the West (the Mountain and Pacific divisions combined), from $3,117 to $9,670, or by $6,453.

The average value of land in Negro farms increased in the decade 1900–1910 by $165 in New England; $1,054 in the Middle Atlantic division; $1,382 in the East North Central division; $2,081 in the West North Central division; and $5,304 in the West.

Increase in the average value of buildings per Negro farm in the northern and western divisions ranges from $262 in the West North Central division to $577 in the Middle Atlantic. Increase in the value of implements and machinery per farm ranges from $28 in the East North Central division to $106 in the Mountain division, and the increase in the average value of live stock from $149 in New England to $1,219 in the Mountain division.

It will be apparent from the figures given in Table 15 that the increases in the aggregate values of different classes of farm property and in the average values per Negro farm during the decade 1900–1910 were very marked in all sections of the country.

Table 15

VALUE OF PROPERTY ON FARMS OPERATED BY NEGROES.

SECTION AND DIVISION.	Aggregate.			Average per farm.		
	1910	1900	Increase: 1910–1900.	1910	1900	Increase: 1910–1900.
	TOTAL.					
United States	$1,141,792,526	$499,941,234	$641,851,292	$1,278	$669	$608
The South	1,083,658,351	469,506,555	614,151,796	1,230	641	589
South Atlantic	440,876,367	162,841,284	278,035,083	1,244	566	678
East South Central	356,989,149	170,985,641	186,003,508	1,099	639	460
West South Central	285,792,835	135,679,630	150,113,205	1,419	767	652
The North	53,473,329	29,384,290	24,089,039	4,437	2,096	2,341
New England	945,061	582,851	362,210	3,049	2,208	841
Middle Atlantic	6,123,854	4,193,394	1,930,460	4,675	2,801	1,874
East North Central	20,063,311	11,535,146	8,528,165	4,143	2,227	1,916
West North Central	26,341,103	13,072,899	13,268,204	4,713	1,847	2,866
The West	4,660,846	1,050,389	3,610,457	9,670	3,117	6,553
Mountain	1,610,050	382,943	1,227,107	7,352	2,879	4,473
Pacific	3,050,796	667,446	2,383,350	11,600	3,272	8,328

Table 15—Contd. VALUE OF PROPERTY ON FARMS OPERATED BY NEGROES.

SECTION AND DIVISION.	Aggregate.			Average per farm.		
	1910	1900	Increase: 1910–1900.	1910	1900	Increase: 1910–1900.
LAND.						
United States....	$756,158,264	$324,242,997	$431,915,267	$846	$434	$412
The South..........	714,988,872	302,933,342	412,055,530	812	414	398
South Atlantic.....	294,198,215	106,251,076	187,947,139	830	369	461
East South Central.	227,012,113	108,254,534	118,757,579	699	405	294
West South Central.	193,778,544	88,427,732	105,350,812	962	500	462
The North..........	37,584,524	20,590,880	16,993,644	3,119	1,469	1,650
New England......	427,635	320,384	107,251	1,379	1,214	165
Middle Atlantic....	3,432,477	2,344,334	1,088,143	2,620	1,566	1,054
East North Central.	14,669,103	8,527,575	6,141,528	3,029	1,647	1,382
West North Central	19,055,309	9,398,587	9,656,722	3,409	1,328	2,081
The West..........	3,584,868	718,775	2,866,093	7,437	2,133	5,304
Mountain..........	1,033,530	241,285	792,245	4,719	1,814	2,905
Pacific............	2,551,338	477,490	2,073,848	9,701	2,341	7,360
BUILDINGS.						
United States....	$166,559,439	$71,902,265	$94,657,174	$187	$96	$91
The South..........	158,593,538	67,392,514	91,201,024	180	92	88
South Atlantic.....	70,870,030	26,658,379	44,211,651	200	93	107
East South Central.	52,419,081	23,113,572	29,305,509	161	86	75
West South Central.	35,304,427	17,620,563	17,683,864	175	100	75
The North..........	7,671,864	4,398,877	3,272,987	637	314	323
New England......	374,725	195,330	179,395	1,209	740	469
Middle Atlantic....	1,866,870	1,270,170	596,700	1,425	848	577
East North Central.	2,808,546	1,468,470	1,340,076	580	284	296
West North Central	2,621,723	1,464,907	1,156,816	469	207	262
The West..........	294,037	110,874	183,163	610	329	281
Mountain..........	122,465	42,229	80,236	559	318	241
Pacific............	171,572	68,645	102,927	652	336	316
IMPLEMENTS AND MACHINERY.						
United States....	$34,178,052	$18,859,757	$15,318,295	$38	$25	$13
The South..........	32,755,291	17,893,841	14,861,450	37	24	13
South Atlantic.....	13,148,827	5,879,229	7,269,598	37	20	17
East South Central.	11,163,547	6,847,843	4,315,704	34	26	8
West South Central.	8,442,917	5,166,769	3,276,148	42	29	13
The North..........	1,322,473	929,902	392,571	110	66	44
New England......	42,771	21,428	21,343	138	81	57
Middle Atlantic....	250,259	185,349	64,910	191	124	67
East North Central.	440,693	326,208	114,485	91	63	28
West North Central	588,750	396,917	191,833	105	56	49
The West..........	100,288	36,014	64,274	208	107	101
Mountain..........	47,564	14,698	32,866	217	111	106
Pacific............	52,724	21,316	31,408	200	104	96
LIVE STOCK.						
United States....	$184,896,771	$84,936,215	$99,960,556	$207	$114	$93
The South..........	177,320,650	81,286,858	96,033,792	201	111	90
South Atlantic.....	62,659,295	24,052,600	38,606,695	177	84	93
East South Central.	66,394,408	32,769,692	33,624,716	204	122	82
West South Central.	48,266,947	24,464,566	23,802,381	240	138	102
The North..........	6,894,468	3,464,631	3,429,837	572	247	325
New England......	99,930	45,709	54,221	322	173	149
Middle Atlantic....	574,248	393,541	180,707	438	263	175
East North Central.	2,144,969	1,212,893	932,076	443	234	209
West North Central	4,075,321	1,812,488	2,262,833	729	256	473
The West..........	681,653	184,726	496,927	1,414	548	866
Mountain..........	406,491	84,731	321,760	1,856	637	1,219
Pacific............	275,162	99,995	175,167	1,046	490	556

FARM ANIMALS: FARMS REPORTING, AND VALUE AND NUMBER OF ANIMALS.

Statistics for classes of farm animals, by states, are presented in Tables 63, 64, 65 (pp. 620 to 622), and Table 69 (pp. 628 to 637), and for counties in Southern states in Table 73 (pp. 698 to 764).

Each of these tables distinguishes tenure classes of farms. Tables 16 to 22, following, summarize the data for classes of live stock on farms without distinguishing tenure classes. Table 16 gives for 1910 and for 1900 the number and percentage of colored farms reporting and not reporting domestic animals, poultry, and bees, with the increase for 1900–1910. The totals shown in Table 16 for the North and West combined, as has been explained in the introductory section of this chapter, relate to a colored aggregate in which classes other than Negro constitute so large a proportion as to invalidate the significance of the data for Negro farms.

Table 16 COLORED FARMS REPORTING AND NOT REPORTING LIVE STOCK.

SECTION AND YEAR.	Total.	Domestic animals.		Poultry.		Bees.	
		Farms reporting.	Farms not reporting.	Farms reporting.	Farms not reporting.	Farms reporting.	Farms not reporting.
NUMBER OF FARMS.							
United States:							
1910..............	920,883	833,374	87,509	730,055	190,828	20,943	899,940
1900..............	767,764	710,118	57,646	623,649	144,115	29,252	738,512
The South:							
1910.................	890,141	804,994	85,147	714,043	176,098	20,342	869,799
1900.................	740,670	684,571	56,099	606,991	133,679	28,514	712,156
The North and West:							
1910.................	30,742	28,380	2,362	16,012	14,730	601	30,141
1900.................	27,094	25,547	1,547	16,658	10,436	738	26,356
PERCENTAGE OF TOTAL.							
United States:							
1910..............	100.0	90.5	9.5	79.3	20.7	2.3	97.7
1900..............	100.0	92.5	7.5	81.2	18.8	3.8	96.2
The South:							
1910..............	100.0	90.4	9.6	80.2	19.8	2.3	97.7
1900..............	100.0	92.4	7.6	82.0	18.0	3.8	96.2
The North and West:							
1910.................	100.0	92.3	7.7	52.1	47.9	2.0	98.0
1900.................	100.0	94.3	5.7	61.5	38.5	2.7	97.3
INCREASE[1] IN NUMBER OF FARMS: 1900–1910.							
United States.........	153,119	123,256	29,863	106,406	46,713	−8,309	161,428
The South.............	149,471	120,423	29,048	107,052	42,419	−8,172	157,643
The North and West....	3,648	2,833	815	−646	4,294	−137	3,785

[1] A minus sign (−) denotes decrease.

Of the 890,141 colored farms in the South in 1910, 804,994, or 90.4 per cent, reported domestic animals, and 85,147, or 9.6 per cent, did not report domestic animals. The proportion reporting domestic animals on colored farms in the South was somewhat smaller in 1910 than in 1900, although the number of such farms increased by 120,423 during the decade 1900–1910. In this period the proportion of colored farms reporting poultry, and the proportion reporting bees also declined, although the number of farms reporting poultry increased by 107,052.

The principal classes of farm animals are distinguished in Table 17, and the number of colored farms reporting and not reporting each class of animals designated is given for 1910 and for 1900, the corresponding data being given for white farms in 1910.

Table 17

FARMS REPORTING AND NOT REPORTING ANIMALS OF CLASS SPECIFIED.[1]

CLASS OF ANIMAL.	Colored farms.				White farms: 1910.	
	Reporting.		Not reporting.		Reporting.	Not reporting.
	1910	1900	1910	1900		
	UNITED STATES.					
Neat cattle	570,068	412,201	350,815	355,563	4,714,848	725,771
Dairy cows	524,535	348,857	396,348	418,907	4,616,334	824,285
Horses	360,708	360,557	560,175	407,207	4,332,106	1,108,513
Mules	444,877	350,567	476,006	417,197	1,424,128	4,016,491
Sheep	6,743	6,802	914,140	760,962	604,151	4,836,468
Swine	612,069	521,207	308,814	246,557	3,739,682	1,700,937
	THE SOUTH.					
Neat cattle	551,940	397,314	338,201	343,356	1,874,362	333,044
Dairy cows	512,242	337,870	377,899	402,800	1,822,363	385,043
Horses	334,537	337,129	555,604	403,541	1,437,122	770,284
Mules	441,178	346,771	448,963	393,899	1,037,204	1,170,202
Sheep	3,386	5,365	886,755	735,305	180,908	2,026,498
Swine	602,090	509,495	288,051	231,175	1,628,751	578,655
	THE NORTH AND WEST.					
Neat cattle	18,128	14,887	12,614	12,207	2,840,486	392,727
Dairy cows	12,293	10,987	18,449	16,107	2,793,971	439,242
Horses	26,171	23,428	4,571	3,666	2,894,984	338,229
Mules	3,699	3,796	27,043	23,298	386,924	2,846,289
Sheep	3,357	1,437	27,385	25,657	423,243	2,809,970
Swine	9,979	11,712	20,763	15,382	2,110,931	1,122,282

[1] For total number of colored farms in 1910 and in 1900, distributed in this table as reporting and not reporting, see Table 16. The number of white farms in 1910 was as follows: United States, 5,440,619; the South, 2,207,406; the North and West, 3,233,213.

In the South the number of colored farms reporting neat cattle increased from 397,314 in 1900 to 551,940 in 1910, and the number not reporting neat cattle decreased in the same period from 343,356 to 338,201. The number of colored farms reporting dairy cows in the South increased from 337,870 in 1900 to 512,242 in 1910, the number not reporting decreasing from 402,800 in 1900 to 377,899 in 1910. The number of farms reporting horses fell off slightly during this period—from 337,129 to 334,537—this decrease being much more than offset by the large increase in the number of farms reporting mules—from 346,771 in 1900 to 441,178 in 1910. The number of farms reporting swine also showed a very large increase—from 509,495 in 1900 to 602,090 in 1910.

The percentages of Table 18, which are based upon the figures given in Table 17, show the proportion of farms reporting the several classes of farm animals in the South and in the North and West for Negro farms in 1910 and 1900 and for white farms in 1910.

A smaller proportion of colored farms than of white farms in the South reported each of the several classes of animals designated in Table 18, with the exception that the proportion of colored farms reporting mules in the South was slightly greater than the proportion of white farms reporting animals of this kind. The proportion of colored farms in the South reporting neat cattle, dairy cows, and mules increased during the decade and the proportion reporting horses declined, slight declines being shown also for sheep and for swine.

Table 18

PERCENTAGE REPORTING ANIMALS OF CLASS SPECIFIED.

CLASS OF ANIMAL.	The South.			The North and West.		
	Of colored farms.		Of white farms: 1910	Of colored farms.		Of white farms: 1910
	1910	1900		1910	1900	
Neat cattle	62.0	53.6	84.9	59.0	54.9	87.9
Dairy cows	57.5	45.6	82.6	40.0	40.6	86.4
Horses	37.6	45.5	65.1	85.1	86.5	89.5
Mules	49.6	46.8	47.0	12.0	14.0	12.0
Sheep	0.4	0.7	8.2	10.9	5.3	13.1
Swine	67.6	68.8	73.8	32.5	43.2	65.3

Less than two-thirds of the colored farms in the South in 1910 reported dairy cows, and slightly more than two-thirds of the colored farms reported swine.

The aggregate value of domestic animals, poultry, and bees reported by colored and by white farms in 1910 and in 1900 is given, by sections, in Table 19.

Table 19

SECTION AND CLASS OF FARM.	VALUE REPORTED.				
	1910	1900	Increase:[1] 1900–1910.	Percentage distribution.	
				1910	1900
	DOMESTIC ANIMALS.				
United States	$4,760,060,093	$2,979,197,586	$1,780,862,507	100.0	100.0
Colored farms	199,095,103	95,470,177	103,624,926	4.2	3.2
White farms	4,560,964,990	2,883,727,409	1,677,237,581	95.8	96.8
The South	1,284,298,714	782,407,960	501,890,754	100.0	100.0
Colored farms	177,461,964	85,216,337	92,245,627	13.8	10.9
White farms	1,106,836,750	697,191,623	409,645,127	86.2	89.1
The North and West	3,475,761,379	2,196,789,626	1,278,971,753	100.0	100.0
Colored farms	21,633,139	10,253,840	11,379,299	0.6	0.5
White farms	3,454,128,240	2,186,535,786	1,267,592,454	99.4	99.5
	POULTRY.				
United States	$154,663,220	$85,807,818	$68,855,402	100.0	100.0
Colored farms	5,505,445	4,019,577	1,485,868	3.6	4.7
White farms	149,157,775	81,788,241	67,369,534	96.4	95.3
The South	37,415,336	24,222,562	13,192,774	100.0	100.0
Colored farms	5,121,775	3,788,792	1,332,983	13.7	15.6
White farms	32,293,561	20,433,770	11,859,791	86.3	84.4
The North and West	117,247,884	61,585,256	55,662,628	100.0	100.0
Colored farms	383,670	230,785	152,885	0.3	0.4
White farms	116,864,214	61,354,471	55,509,743	99.7	99.6
	BEES.				
United States	$10,373,615	$10,178,087	$195,528	100.0	100.0
Colored farms	158,148	185,086	−26,938	1.5	1.8
White farms	10,215,467	9,993,001	222,466	98.5	98.2
The South	3,689,547	4,178,033	−488,486	100.0	100.0
Colored farms	148,385	176,914	−28,529	4.0	4.2
White farms	3,541,162	4,001,119	−459,957	96.0	95.8
The North and West	6,684,068	6,000,054	684,014	100.0	100.0
Colored farms	9,763	8,172	1,591	0.1	0.1
White farms	6,674,305	5,991,882	682,423	99.9	99.9

[1] A minus sign (−) denotes decrease.

The value of domestic animals on colored farms in the South increased from $85,216,337 in 1900 to $177,461,964 in 1910, the increase amounting to $92,245,627. Of the aggregate value of domestic animals on all farms, white and colored, the proportion on colored farms increased during the decade from 10.9 per cent in 1900 to 13.8 per cent in 1910.

The value of poultry reported on colored farms in the South increased from $3,788,792 in 1900 to $5,121,775 in 1910, the increase amounting to $1,332,983. The proportion reported by colored farms of the aggregate value of poultry on all farms in the South decreased from 15.6 per cent in 1900 to 13.7 per cent in 1910.

Table 20 gives, for each class of domestic animals on colored and on white farms in 1910, the aggregate value reported, the average value per farm, and the percentage reported by colored farms of the aggregate value reported on all farms.

The average value per farm of each class of farm animals was lower on colored than on white farms. The value of neat cattle per farm in the South averaged $37.11 on colored farms and $151.85 on white farms; of horses, $53.40 on colored farms and $169.66 on white farms; of mules, $94.51 on colored farms and $133.25 on white farms; of swine, $13.85 on colored farms and $31.12 on white farms. Colored farms reported only very inconsiderable values per farm of sheep, asses and burros, and goats.

Table 21 gives the number and value of matured animals of specified classes on colored and white farms in the South and in the North and West, together with the average value per head for each class of animals in 1910.

Table 20 — VALUE OF DOMESTIC ANIMALS ON FARMS: 1910.

CLASS OF ANIMAL.	Aggregate. Total.	Colored farms.	White farms.	Average per farm. Colored farms.	White farms.	Of total, percentage on colored farms.
UNITED STATES.						
Total	$4,760,060,093	$199,095,103	$4,560,964,990	$216.20	$838.32	4.2
Neat cattle	1,499,523,607	39,475,839	1,460,047,768	42.87	268.36	2.6
Horses	2,083,588,195	58,190,838	2,025,397,357	63.19	372.27	2.8
Mules	525,391,863	85,128,116	440,263,747	92.44	80.92	16.2
Sheep	232,841,585	2,545,227	230,296,358	2.76	42.33	1.1
Swine	399,338,308	13,152,267	386,186,041	14.28	70.98	3.3
Asses and burros	13,200,112	228,630	12,971,482	0.25	2.38	1.7
Goats	6,176,423	374,186	5,802,237	0.41	1.07	6.1
THE SOUTH.						
Total	$1,284,298,714	$177,461,964	$1,106,836,750	$199.36	$501.42	13.8
Neat cattle	368,180,311	33,028,881	335,151,430	37.11	151.83	9.0
Horses	422,048,624	47,537,525	374,511,099	53.40	169.66	11.3
Mules	378,258,226	84,127,172	294,131,054	94.51	133.25	22.2
Sheep	25,611,834	200,128	25,411,706	0.22	11.51	0.8
Swine	81,017,335	12,331,574	68,685,761	13.85	31.12	15.2
Asses and burros	5,963,005	176,400	5,786,605	0.20	2.62	3.0
Goats	3,219,379	60,284	3,159,095	0.07	1.43	1.9
THE NORTH AND WEST.						
Total	$3,475,761,379	$21,633,139	$3,454,128,240	$703.70	$1,068.33	0.6
Neat cattle	1,131,343,296	6,446,958	1,124,896,338	209.71	347.92	0.6
Horses	1,661,539,571	10,653,313	1,650,886,258	346.54	510.60	0.6
Mules	147,133,637	1,000,944	146,132,693	32.56	45.20	0.7
Sheep	207,229,751	2,345,099	204,884,652	76.28	63.37	1.1
Swine	318,320,973	820,693	317,500,280	26.70	98.20	0.3
Asses and burros	7,237,107	52,230	7,184,877	1.70	2.22	0.7
Goats	2,957,044	313,902	2,643,142	10.21	0.82	10.6

Table 21 — MATURE ANIMALS ON FARMS: 1910.

CLASS OF ANIMAL.	Number of animals. Colored farms.	White farms.	Value of animals. Colored farms.	White farms.	Value per head. Colored farms.	White farms.	White excess.
UNITED STATES.							
Dairy cows	969,685	19,655,747	$22,240,132	$683,996,175	$22.94	$34.80	$11.86
Work horses	649,907	16,780,511	54,942,151	1,903,612,666	84.54	113.44	28.90
Work mules	653,576	3,133,740	84,451,579	413,530,751	129.21	131.96	2.75
Sheep	751,068	38,892,978	2,141,579	201,374,565	2.85	5.18	2.33
Hogs	2,184,943	32,949,154	11,090,162	341,067,796	5.08	10.35	5.27
THE SOUTH.							
Dairy cows	929,893	4,758,485	$20,803,304	$130,043,230	$22.37	$27.33	$4.96
Work horses	509,091	3,564,855	45,880,457	350,100,726	90.12	98.21	8.09
Work mules	645,321	2,188,166	83,514,577	282,108,899	129.42	128.92	¹0.50
Sheep	45,867	4,683,109	146,398	19,131,062	3.19	4.09	0.90
Hogs	2,117,916	10,266,535	10,376,574	59,389,940	4.90	5.78	0.88
THE NORTH AND WEST.							
Dairy cows	39,792	14,897,262	$1,436,828	$553,952,945	$36.11	$37.18	$1.07
Work horses	140,816	13,215,656	9,061,694	1,553,511,940	64.35	117.55	53.20
Work mules	8,255	945,574	937,002	131,421,852	113.51	138.99	25.48
Sheep	705,201	34,209,869	1,995,181	182,243,503	2.83	5.33	2.50
Hogs	67,027	22,682,619	713,588	281,677,856	10.65	12.42	1.77

¹ Colored excess.

The value of neat cattle reported on colored farms in the South in 1910 was $33,028,881, constituting 9 per cent of the aggregate value of neat cattle reported on all farms in the South. The aggregate value of horses on colored farms was $47,537,525, or 11.3 per cent of the aggregate value of horses reported on all farms; the value of mules reported on colored farms was $84,127,172, or 22.2 per cent of the aggregate value for this class of animals in the South; and the value of swine on colored farms was $12,331,574, or 15.2 per cent of the aggregate value of swine on all farms.

The average value per head of dairy cows, work horses, sheep, and hogs on colored farms in the South was in the case of each class of animals below the average for animals on white farms, there being practically no difference between colored and white farms as regards the average value per head of work mules. The value of dairy cows on colored farms of the South averaged $22.37 per head and on white farms, $27.33; of work horses, $90.12 on colored and $98.21 on white farms; of work mules, $129.42 on colored and $128.92 on white farms; of sheep, $3.19 on colored and $4.09 on white farms; and of hogs, $4.90 on colored and $5.78 on white farms.

The number of farms reporting and not reporting dairy cows, work horses, and work mules, and the average number of each class of animals per 100 farms and per 100 farms reporting in 1910, is shown in Table 22 for colored farms in the South and in each southern division.

Table 22 — FARMS OPERATED BY COLORED FARMERS: 1910.

DIVISION AND CLASS OF ANIMAL.	Number of farms.	Reporting specified class of animal.				Number not reporting specified class of animal.
		Number of farms.	Animals reported.		Per 100 farms reporting.	
			Aggregate.	Per 100 farms.		
The South	890,141					
Dairy cows		512,242	929,883	104	182	377,899
Work horses		332,370	509,087	57	153	557,771
Work mules		436,398	645,320	72	148	453,743
South Atlantic	355,862					
Dairy cows		189,758	285,141	80	150	166,104
Work horses		108,252	140,394	39	130	247,610
Work mules		166,050	221,694	62	134	189,812
East South Central	325,218					
Dairy cows		203,679	358,406	110	176	121,539
Work horses		113,134	158,346	49	140	212,084
Work mules		170,094	248,161	76	146	155,124
West South Central	209,061					
Dairy cows		118,805	286,336	137	241	90,256
Work horses		110,984	210,347	101	190	98,077
Work mules		100,254	175,465	84	175	108,807

Of the 890,141 farms operated by colored farmers in the South 512,242 reported dairy cows, and 377,899 did not report this class of animal; 332,370 farms reported, and 557,771 did not report work horses; and 436,398 reported, and 453,743 did not report work mules.

Relatively to the number of farms, dairy cows on colored farms were most numerous in the West South Central division, the average number per 100 farms being 137 in this division, 80 in the South Atlantic division, and 110 in the East South Central division. Work horses, also, relatively to the number of farms, were most numerous in the West South Central division, averaging 101 per 100 farms in this division, 39 per 100 farms in the South Atlantic and 49 per 100 farms in the East South Central division.

CROPS: FARMS REPORTING, ACREAGE, YIELD, AND VALUE.

Statistics of farms reporting acreage, yield, and value for 20 selected crops on colored farms in the South are given, by divisions and states, in Table 50 (pp. 594 to 600). Acreage in selected crops on colored farms of the South in 1909 and in 1899, is given, by divisions and states, in Table 51 (p. 601); and acreage in selected crops on colored and white farms of the South in 1909, by divisions and states, in Table 52 (p. 602). The geographic distribution of the cotton and corn acreage and of the 1909 yield of these crops on colored and white farms is shown in detail for counties in Table 72 (pp. 674 to 697).

Table 23 assembles the totals for the South, of farms reporting acreage, yield and value for the 20 crops covered, by divisions and states, in Table 50.

FARMS REPORTING SPECIFIED CROP, ACREAGE, YIELD, AND VALUE OF CROP: 1910.

Table 23 — FARMS REPORTING SPECIFIED CROP IN THE SOUTH: 1909.

CROP.	Number of farms.			Acres in crop.			Yield of crop.			Value of crop.		
	Total.	Colored farms.		Total.	Colored farms.		Total.	Colored farms.		Total.	Colored farms.	
		Number.	Per cent.		Acres.	Per cent.		Yield.	Per cent.		Value.	Per cent.
Cotton	1,706,767	684,721	40.1	31,946,142	12,096,638	52.7	Bales. 10,594,360	Bales. 4,065,978	38.4	$700,199,244	$269,868,346	32.4
Corn	2,571,566	744,458	28.9	37,627,319	7,377,221	19.6	Bushels. 623,068,626	Bushels. 94,876,350	15.2	443,460,455	76,918,406	17.3
Cotton seed	1,706,767	684,721	40.1	31,946,142	12,096,638	52.7	Tons. 5,297,182	Tons. 2,032,991	38.4	122,521,349	47,068,246	38.4
Tobacco	260,287	42,470	16.3	1,049,617	169,568	16.2	Pounds. 802,618,483	Pounds. 109,433,038	13.6	78,506,324	9,813,199	12.5
Sweet potatoes	1,015,019	295,854	29.1	583,042	166,072	28.5	Bushels. 52,227,661	Bushels. 12,047,068	23.1	31,528,482	7,491,817	23.8
Hay and forage	(1)	(1)	(1)	8,620,243	468,581	5.4	Tons. 8,866,596	Tons. 468,394	5.2	97,264,658	5,003,872	5.1
Peanuts	217,379	77,984	35.9	869,176	236,139	27.2	Bushels. 19,400,338	Bushels. 5,069,004	26.1	18,253,270	4,797,046	26.3
Oats	495,381	81,831	16.5	3,516,128	321,960	9.2	60,126,382	4,358,927	7.2	32,688,105	2,726,848	8.3
Potatoes	847,863	97,875	11.5	477,064	50,680	10.6	39,332,677	3,438,024	8.7	25,472,023	2,410,099	9.5
Wheat	331,069	36,553	11.0	5,112,675	204,387	4.0	59,121,317	1,829,742	3.0	61,854,632	1,939,790	3.1
Dry peas	209,064	72,989	34.9	1,009,836	284,854	28.2	3,803,461	1,038,529	27.3	6,461,667	1,737,609	26.9
Rice	13,706	4,967	36.2	610,163	29,235	4.8	21,838,520	889,103	4.1	16,019,567	677,542	4.2
Alfalfa	32,754	1,172	3.6	340,651	6,611	1.9	Tons. 574,149	Tons. 11,901	2.1	6,654,473	171,836	2.6
Rye	40,769	1,941	4.8	213,563	6,597	3.1	Bushels. 1,772,320	Bushels. 48,279	2.7	1,484,934	44,111	3.0
Dry edible beans	47,549	2,881	6.1	47,808	3,742	7.8	301,927	22,083	7.3	527,201	37,143	7.0
Kafir corn	54,193	593	1.1	1,108,129	3,402	0.3	10,546,626	40,430	0.4	6,338,581	23,343	0.4
Soy beans	2,055	252	12.3	14,029	1,401	9.9	169,379	14,042	8.3	225,512	17,817	7.9
Broom corn	16,172	245	1.5	228,569	691	0.3	Pounds. 46,005,312	Pounds. 164,447	0.4	2,774,354	9,601	0.3
Buckwheat	22,798	268	1.2	89,757	997	1.1	Bushels. 1,269,120	Bushels. 11,089	1.0	829,668	6,915	0.8
Barley	5,291	98	1.9	35,202	193	0.5	710,883	3,960	0.6	463,987	2,890	0.6

1 Data not available.

These crops include the principal crops grown on southern farms, and the extent to which they are grown on farms operated by colored farmers is a fair indication of the importance of the agricultural activities of the Negro population in this section of the country. In Table 23 the crops are listed in order according to the aggregate value of the 1909 yield on colored farms.

The number of southern farms reporting cotton in 1909 was 1,706,767, of which 684,721, or 40.1 per cent, were operated by colored farmers; the acreage in cotton on these farms was 31,946,142 acres, of which 12,096,638 acres, or 52.7 per cent of the total acres in cotton on all farms, were on farms operated by colored farmers; the yield of cotton was 10,594,360 bales, of which 4,065,978, or 38.4 per cent, were grown on colored farms; and the value of the crop was $700,199,244, of which $269,868,346, or 32.4 per cent, represented the product of colored farms. It thus appears that more than one-half of the cotton acreage in the South in 1909, nearly two-fifths of the yield, and approximately one-third of the value of the yield was reported by colored farms.

To the value of this crop must be added $47,068,246, the value of the cotton seed produced in 1909. The value of these two crops combined exceeded the value of all other crops combined on colored farms.

It is apparent in Table 23 that colored farmers to a much greater degree than white farmers, in proportion to their numbers and the acreage in their farms, were occupied in the culture of cotton. Of the aggregate value of corn grown on southern farms, only 17.3 per cent, or approximately one-half the proportion shown for cotton (32.4 per cent), represented the yield of colored farms. The value of tobacco grown on colored farms represented 12.5 per cent of the total value of this crop in the South, and on the basis of value, colored farms produced 23.8 per cent of the sweet potatoes, 26.3 per cent of the peanuts, 26.9 per cent of the dry peas, and less than 10 per cent of other crops designated in Table 23, the proportions for these other crops ranging from 0.6 per cent for barley to 9.5 per cent for potatoes.

The crops grown on colored farms are naturally determined primarily by the geographic distribution of the colored farming population, which is largely concentrated in the cotton belt of the South.

The average yield and value, per colored farm reporting, and per acre planted, is given in Table 24 for each of the 20 crops designated in Table 23.

Per colored farm reporting cotton in 1909, the average yield was 5.9 bales, and the average value of the crop, $394.12. Per acre planted to this crop on colored farms, the average yield was three-tenths of 1 bale, and the average value, $22.31. To these values must be added the average values of cotton seed,

$68.74 per farm, and $3.89 per acre planted to cotton. The average yield of corn per colored farm reporting corn was 127.4 bushels, and the average value of the crop $103.32. Per acre planted to corn, the average yield was 12.9 bushels, and the average value of the crop, $10.43. Tobacco showed the second largest average value per farm reporting ($231.06), and the largest value of any crop per acre planted ($57.87). Average value of crop per farm reporting for other crops than those mentioned ranged from $12.89 for dry edible beans to $146.62 for alfalfa; and average value of crop per acre planted, from $6.10 for dry peas to $47.56 for potatoes.

Table 24	COLORED FARMS IN THE SOUTH: 1909.				
CROP.		Average yield of crop.		Average value of crop.	
	Unit of measure.	Per farm reporting.	Per acre planted.	Per farm reporting.	Per acre planted.
Cotton	Bales	5.9	0.3	$394.13	$22.31
Corn	Bushels	127.4	12.9	103.32	10.43
Cotton seed	Tons	3.0	0.2	68.74	3.89
Tobacco	Pounds	2,576.7	645.4	231.06	57.87
Sweet potatoes	Bushels	40.7	72.5	25.32	45.11
Hay and forage	Tons	(1)	1.0	(1)	10.68
Peanuts	Bushels	65.0	21.5	61.51	20.31
Oats	Bushels	53.3	13.5	33.32	8.47
Potatoes	Bushels	35.1	67.8	24.62	47.56
Wheat	Bushels	50.1	9.0	53.07	9.49
Dry peas	Bushels	14.2	3.6	23.81	6.10
Rice	Bushels	179.0	30.4	136.41	23.18
Alfalfa	Tons	10.2	1.8	146.62	25.99
Rye	Bushels	24.9	7.3	22.73	6.69
Dry edible beans	Bushels	7.7	5.9	12.89	9.93
Kafir corn	Bushels	68.2	11.9	39.36	6.86
Soy beans	Bushels	55.7	10.0	70.70	12.72
Broom corn	Pounds	671.2	238.0	39.19	13.89
Buckwheat	Bushels	41.4	11.1	25.80	6.94
Barley	Bushels	40.4	20.5	29.49	14.97

1 Data not available.

Acreage in nine principal crops on colored and white farms in 1909 and in 1899 is shown for the South and for each of the three southern divisions in Table 25, which gives, also, the percentage in colored farms of the total acreage reported for each crop in these years and the increase for the decade 1900–1910.

The acreage reported by colored farms in 1909 for each of the crops specified in Table 25, excepting rice and wheat, was greater than the acreage reported for these crops in 1899, and excepting oats and wheat, a larger acreage was reported also on white farms in 1909 than in 1899 for each crop.

Of the total southern acreage in corn, cotton, and wheat, a slightly smaller proportion was reported by colored farms in 1909 than in 1899, and of the total acreage in rice a much smaller proportion was on colored farms in 1909 than in 1899. Other crops show a slightly larger proportion on colored farms, of the total acreage in 1909 as compared with 1899.

Acreage in cotton on colored farms in 1909 exceeded the acreage in this crop on colored farms in 1899 by 2,440,376 acres, or by 25.3 per cent, the corresponding increase for white acreage in cotton being 5,276,470 acres and 36.2 per cent. Colored acreage in hay and forage in 1909 exceeded the acreage in this crop in 1899 on colored farms by 152,053 acres, or 48 per cent, and on white farms by 2,423,326 acres, or 42.3 per cent.

The relatively small acreage in rice on colored farms fell off in 1909 as compared with 1899 by 40.3 per cent, white farms showing an increase of 98.1 per cent.

COLORED AND WHITE ACREAGE IN SPECIFIED CROPS, WITH DECENNIAL INCREASE, BY SOUTHERN DIVISIONS: 1910 AND 1900.

Table 25

CROP.	— ACRES IN SPECIFIED CROPS AND OTHER IMPROVED ACRES.											
	1909 Total	1909 Colored farms	1909 White farms	1899 Total	1899 Colored farms	1899 White farms	Pct in colored farms 1909	Pct in colored farms 1899	Increase Acres Colored farms	Increase Acres White farms	Increase Per cent Colored farms	Increase Per cent White farms
THE SOUTH.												
Total improved	140,690,852	27,735,743	122,955,109	126,108,093	23,214,607	102,893,486	19.7	18.4	4,521,136	20,061,623	19.5	19.5
Corn	37,627,319	7,377,221	30,250,098	34,919,379	6,993,999	27,925,380	19.6	20.0	382,518	2,324,718	5.5	8.3
Cotton	31,946,142	12,096,638	19,849,504	24,229,296	9,656,262	14,573,034	37.9	39.9	2,440,376	5,276,470	25.3	36.2
Hay and forage	8,620,243	468,581	8,151,662	6,044,864	316,528	5,728,336	5.4	5.2	152,053	2,423,326	48.0	42.3
Oats	3,516,128	321,960	3,194,168	3,596,372	261,982	3,334,390	9.2	7.3	59,978	−140,222	22.9	−4.2
Potatoes	477,064	50,680	426,384	310,495	30,308	280,187	10.6	9.8	20,372	146,197	67.2	52.2
Rice	610,163	29,235	580,928	342,214	48,980	293,234	4.8	14.3	−19,745	287,694	−40.3	98.1
Sweet potatoes	583,042	166,072	416,970	478,291	132,891	345,400	28.5	27.8	33,181	71,570	25.0	20.7
Tobacco	1,049,617	169,568	880,049	927,609	142,145	785,464	16.2	15.3	27,423	94,585	19.3	12.0
Wheat	5,112,675	204,387	4,908,288	9,291,042	435,036	8,856,006	4.0	4.7	−230,649	−3,947,718	−53.0	−44.6
Other improved	51,148,459	6,851,401	54,297,058	45,968,531	5,196,476	40,772,055	13.4	11.3	1,655,629	13,525,003	31.9	33.2
SOUTH ATLANTIC DIVISION.												
Total improved	48,479,733	10,990,069	37,489,664	42,100,226	8,895,862	33,204,364	22.7	21.1	2,094,207	4,285,300	23.5	12.9
Corn	11,386,984	3,066,496	8,320,488	12,024,742	2,855,482	9,169,260	26.9	23.7	210,310	−848,772	7.4	−9.3
Cotton	9,002,776	4,442,773	4,560,003	6,842,489	3,005,870	3,836,619	49.3	43.9	1,436,903	723,384	47.8	18.9
Hay and forage	2,856,398	189,680	2,666,718	2,161,201	105,189	2,056,012	6.6	4.9	84,491	610,706	80.3	29.7
Oats	1,368,832	213,778	1,155,054	1,268,081	152,717	1,115,364	15.6	12.0	61,061	39,690	40.0	3.6
Potatoes	239,762	29,508	210,254	157,481	15,839	141,642	12.3	10.1	13,669	68,612	86.3	48.4
Rice	27,080	7,836	19,244	127,369	38,246	89,123	28.9	30.0	−30,410	−69,879	−79.5	−78.4
Sweet potatoes	295,879	88,459	207,420	263,925	75,262	188,663	29.9	28.5	13,197	18,757	17.5	9.9
Tobacco	487,411	131,019	356,392	465,754	104,801	360,953	26.9	22.5	26,218	−4,561	25.0	−1.3
Wheat	2,241,345	152,828	2,088,517	3,368,872	253,516	3,115,356	6.8	7.5	−100,688	−1,026,839	−39.7	−33.0
Other improved	20,573,266	2,667,692	17,905,574	15,420,312	2,288,940	13,131,372	13.0	14.8	379,456	4,774,202	16.6	36.4
EAST SOUTH CENTRAL DIVISION.												
Total improved	33,946,846	9,556,529	34,390,317	40,237,337	8,191,628	32,045,709	28.2	20.4	1,364,901	2,344,608	16.7	7.3
Corn	11,328,268	2,309,639	9,018,629	11,713,504	2,387,838	9,325,666	20.4	20.4	−78,199	−307,037	−3.3	−3.3
Cotton	7,926,019	4,614,339	3,311,680	6,725,588	3,870,109	2,855,479	58.2	57.5	744,230	456,201	19.2	16.0
Hay and forage	2,487,554	137,315	2,350,239	1,513,371	68,645	1,444,726	5.5	4.5	68,670	905,513	100.0	62.7
Oats	870,672	69,132	801,630	855,842	53,774	802,068	7.9	6.3	15,358	−438	28.6	−0.1
Potatoes	119,541	9,077	110,464	80,138	7,314	72,824	7.6	9.1	1,763	37,640	24.1	51.7
Rice	560	76	484	4,424	977	3,447	13.6	22.1	−901	−2,963	−92.2	−86.0
Sweet potatoes	160,756	48,086	112,670	126,586	37,918	88,668	29.9	30.0	10,168	24,002	26.8	27.1
Tobacco	560,523	38,425	522,098	457,998	37,052	420,946	6.9	8.1	1,373	101,152	3.7	24.0
Wheat	1,315,243	37,876	1,277,367	2,987,483	99,886	2,887,597	2.9	3.3	−62,010	−1,610,230	−62.1	−55.8
Other improved	9,177,620	2,292,564	16,885,056	15,772,403	1,628,115	14,144,288	25.0	10.3	664,449	2,740,768	40.8	19.4
WEST SOUTH CENTRAL DIVISION.												
Total improved	58,264,273	7,189,145	51,075,128	39,770,530	6,127,117	33,643,413	12.3	15.4	1,062,028	17,431,715	17.3	51.8
Corn	14,912,067	2,001,086	12,910,981	11,181,133	1,750,679	9,430,454	13.4	15.7	250,407	3,480,527	14.3	36.9
Cotton	15,017,347	3,039,526	11,977,821	10,661,219	2,780,283	7,880,936	20.2	26.0	259,243	4,096,885	9.3	52.0
Hay and forage	3,276,291	141,586	3,134,705	2,370,292	142,694	2,227,598	4.3	6.0	−1,108	907,107	−0.8	40.7
Oats	1,276,534	39,050	1,237,484	1,472,449	55,491	1,416,958	3.1	3.8	−16,441	−179,474	−29.6	−12.7
Potatoes	117,761	12,095	105,666	72,876	7,155	65,721	10.3	9.8	4,940	39,945	69.0	60.8
Rice	582,523	21,323	561,200	210,421	9,757	200,664	3.7	4.6	11,566	360,536	118.5	179.7
Sweet potatoes	126,407	29,527	96,880	87,780	19,711	68,069	23.4	22.5	9,816	28,811	49.8	42.3
Tobacco	1,683	124	1,559	3,857	292	3,565	7.4	8.0	−168	−2,006	−57.5	−56.3
Wheat	1,556,087	13,683	1,542,404	2,934,687	81,634	2,853,053	0.9	2.8	−67,951	−1,310,649	−83.2	−45.9
Other improved	21,397,573	1,891,145	19,506,428	10,775,816	1,279,421	9,496,395	8.8	11.9	611,724	10,010,033	47.8	105.4

[1] A minus sign (−) denotes decrease.

Acreage in cotton showed substantial increases on both colored and white farms in each of the three southern divisions. Acreage in corn increased on colored farms, and decreased on white farms in the South Atlantic division, decreased on both colored and white farms in the East South Central division, and increased on both colored and white farms in the West South Central division.

While the acreage in each of the principal crops on colored and white farms was distributed over areas of large extent in the South, it may be noted that for some of these crops, such as cotton, tobacco, and rice, the acreage was largely within certain states, no acreage whatever being reported from certain states, while for other crops the acreage was distributed throughout the entire South. Table 50 (pp. 594 to 600) shows, for example, that no acreage in cotton was reported from Delaware, Maryland, or West Virginia, that only small acreages were reported from Virginia and Kentucky, and that the principal cotton-growing states were North and South Carolina, Georgia, Alabama, Mississippi, Arkansas, Oklahoma, and Texas—nearly one-third of the total cotton acreage in the South being in the state of Texas, which produced nearly one-fourth of the 1909 yield. Only 13.7 per cent of the cotton acreage of Texas, however, was in farms operated by colored farmers, the proportion on colored farms in Mississippi being 66.6 per cent; in Louisiana, 53.7 per cent; in South Carolina, 53.4 per cent; in Alabama, 52.6 per cent; and in Georgia, 50.5 per cent.

Corn acreage was reported from colored farms in every Southern state, the acreage ranging from 4,421 acres in West Virginia to 1,278,627 acres in Georgia.

Although some acreage in tobacco was reported from each Southern state, except Delaware, only a very small aggregate acreage in this crop was reported from the Gulf states. Of the tobacco acreage in Kentucky, which amounted to 469,795 acres—being more than double the acreage reported by any other state—only 26,298 acres, or 5.6 per cent of the total, were on colored farms. Of the tobacco acreage in North Carolina, amounting to 221,890 acres, 56,471 acres, or 25.4 per cent, were on colored farms; and of the acreage in Virginia, amounting to 185,427 acres, 59,051 acres, or 31.8 per cent, were on colored farms.

The acreage in sweet potatoes was widely distributed throughout the South, the proportion on colored farms ranging from 0.1 per cent in West Virginia to 47.9 per cent in South Carolina. The rice acreage was practically confined to South Carolina, Georgia, Arkansas, Louisiana, and Texas, more than five-sixths of the entire acreage being in Louisiana and Texas, in which states only a small proportion of the rice acreage was on colored farms (4.4 per cent in Louisiana and 3.1 per cent in Texas).

SIZE OF FARMS.

Farms operated by colored and by white farmers are classified, by size, in Table 53 (pp. 603 to 606), distinguishing 10 size groups. In this table is given for each southern state in 1910 and in 1900, the number of farms under 3 acres, 3 to 9, 10 to 19, 20 to 49, 50 to 99, 100 to 174, 175 to 259, 260 to 499, 500 to 999, and 1,000 acres and over. For each of these groups there is given also the increase or decrease in number of farms during the decade 1900–1910, and the number of colored farms per 1,000 of all farms in each size group.

Table 26 gives for 1910 totals for the South for the size groups specified above.

Table 26	FARMS IN THE SOUTH: 1910.					
	Number.			Distribution per 1,000.		Colored farms per 1,000 all farms.
SIZE OF FARM.	Total.	Colored farms.	White farms.	Colored farms.	White farms.	
Total............	3,097,547	890,141	2,207,406	1,000	1,000	287
Under 3 acres.........	2,928	402	2,526	(1)	1	137
3 to 9 acres............	157,320	61,953	95,277	70	43	394
10 to 19 acres........	340,456	151,894	188,562	171	85	446
20 to 49 acres.........	955,907	426,540	529,367	479	240	446
50 to 99 acres.........	694,737	152,244	542,493	171	246	219
100 to 174 acres.......	561,724	68,599	492,945	77	223	122
175 to 259 acres.......	187,549	17,394	170,155	20	77	93
260 to 499 acres.......	135,063	8,779	126,284	10	57	65
500 to 999 acres.......	41,183	1,881	39,302	2	18	46
1,000 acres or more....	20,950	455	20,495	1	9	22

1 Less than 1.

Nearly one-half (426,540) of the total number of colored farms in the South in 1910 were in the size group 20 to 49 acres, the average number of such farms per 1,000 colored farms of all sizes being 479. Colored farms of 10 to 19 acres per 1,000 farms of all sizes numbered 171, this being the proportional number also for the size group 50 to 99 acres. Farms of less than 10 acres numbered 70 per 1,000 farms of all sizes; and farms of 100 acres or more, 110.

As compared with white farms in the South, farms operated by colored farmers were more largely concentrated in the size group 20 to 49 acres, the number per 1,000 for this size group being nearly twice as great for colored as for white farms (479 as compared with 240). A larger proportion of white than of colored farms were in each of the size groups including farms of 50 or more acres.

The relatively greater concentration of colored farms in the size groups 3 to 9, 10 to 19, and 20 to 49 acres is apparent in the proportion colored in farms of these sizes, as shown in the last column of Table 26. In the South colored farms numbered 287 per 1,000 farms of all sizes, but in the size groups 10 to 19 and 20 to 49 acres, colored farms numbered 446 per 1,000, and in the size group 3 to 9 acres, 394 per 1,000.

TERM OF OCCUPANCY.

Colored farms in 1910 are classified by term of occupancy in Table 70 (pp. 638 to 641), by tenure classes for all divisions and states. The aggregates of this table without distinction of tenure are given for sections and southern divisions in Table 27, together with corresponding figures for white farms.

Of the 920,883 colored farms in the United States in 1910, 837,227, or 90.9 per cent, reported term of occupancy. Of these farms reporting, 191,808, or 22.9 per cent, reported occupancy of less than one year; 105,781, or 12.6 per cent, occupancy of one year; 242,724, or 29 per cent, occupancy of two to four years; 131,354, or 15.7 per cent, occupancy of five to nine years, and 165,560, or 19.8 per cent, occupancy of ten years and over. For each term of occupancy of less than five years a larger proportion of colored than of white farms was reported, the proportion reporting occupancy of five to nine, and of ten years and over being larger for white than for colored farms (15.7 and 19.8 per cent for colored, as compared with 17.4 and 33 for white farms).

COLORED AND WHITE FARMS CLASSIFIED BY TERMS OF OCCUPANCY, BY SECTIONS AND SOUTHERN DIVISIONS: 1910.

Table 27

CLASS OF FARM, SECTION, AND DIVISION.	Number of farms.	Total.		Less than 1 year.	1 year.	2 to 4 years.	5 to 9 years.	10 years and over.	Distribution per cent by term of occupancy.					
		Number.	Per cent of all farms.						Total.	Less than 1 year.	1 year.	2 to 4 years.	5 to 9 years.	10 years and over.
COLORED FARMS.														
United States........	920,883	837,227	90.9	191,808	105,781	242,724	131,354	165,560	100.0	22.9	12.6	29.0	15.7	19.8
The South...............	890,141	814,284	91.5	189,324	103,714	237,107	127,586	156,553	100.0	23.3	12.7	29.1	15.7	19.2
South Atlantic........	355,862	326,932	91.9	67,259	41,506	95,713	52,222	70,232	100.0	20.6	12.7	29.3	16.0	21.5
East South Central.....	325,218	299,774	92.2	75,463	37,621	88,533	46,949	51,208	100.0	25.2	12.6	29.5	15.7	17.1
West South Central....	209,061	187,578	89.7	46,602	24,587	52,861	28,415	35,113	100.0	24.9	13.1	28.2	15.2	18.7
The North...............	17,884	14,685	82.1	1,642	1,307	3,340	2,568	5,828	100.0	11.2	8.9	22.7	17.5	39.7
The West...............	12,858	8,258	64.2	842	760	2,277	1,200	3,179	100.0	10.2	9.2	27.6	14.5	38.5
WHITE FARMS.														
United States........	5,440,619	4,957,541	91.1	808,485	522,079	1,128,883	861,114	1,636,980	100.0	16.3	10.5	22.8	17.4	33.0
The South...............	2,207,406	1,997,830	90.5	434,268	229,434	474,524	312,140	547,464	100.0	21.7	11.5	23.8	15.6	27.4
South Atlantic........	756,019	679,532	89.9	109,346	68,669	154,283	111,285	235,949	100.0	16.1	10.1	22.7	16.4	34.7
East South Central.....	717,262	651,455	90.8	137,353	71,627	152,703	102,357	187,415	100.0	21.1	11.0	23.4	15.7	28.8
West South Central....	734,125	666,843	90.8	187,569	89,138	167,538	98,498	124,100	100.0	28.1	13.4	25.1	14.8	18.6
The North...............	2,872,734	2,630,982	91.6	324,662	252,097	558,228	486,122	1,009,873	100.0	12.3	9.6	21.2	18.5	38.4
The West...............	360,479	328,729	91.2	49,555	40,548	96,131	62,852	79,643	100.0	15.1	12.3	29.2	19.1	24.2

The distribution by term of occupancy of colored farms does not vary materially from one southern division to another. In the North and West this distribution for colored farms approximates the distribution shown for white farms in these sections.

It may be noted that in the case of farmers reporting occupancy of less than one year the occupancy of the farmer reporting may or may not have covered the crop year 1909; and similarly in the case of farmers reporting occupancy of one year, the occupancy of the farmer may have covered either one or two crop years. The classification by occupancy therefore does not indicate accurately what proportion of the farmers reporting had grown crops on the farms which they were occu-

pying at the date of the census enumeration. In the case of some of the farmers reporting occupancy of less than one year reports of acreage in crops in 1909 would be for occupiers other than the farmer in occupancy at the time of census enumeration, and would on that account probably be somewhat less accurate than the reports made by other occupiers. In some few instances crops reported for colored farms may have been grown by white operators in 1909, and crops reported for white farms may have been grown by colored operators in 1909. It is, however, improbable that such inaccuracies materially affect the crop aggregates reported for all farms.

SECTION II.—STATISTICS FOR TENURE CLASSES.

DEFINITION OF TENURE.

The three main tenure classes distinguished in compilations of data for farms are "owners," "tenants," and "managers." In the more detailed classifications by tenure owners owning entire farm operated are distinguished from "part owners"—that is to say, from owners renting some of the land operated—and three classes of tenants, namely, "share," "cash," and "share-cash," are distinguished.

In instructions to enumerators in 1910, an owner is defined as "a person holding the title to *all* the land operated by him;" and a part owner as an operator

who "in addition to operating a farm owned by him, operates a tract of land that is leased by him from some one else." The several tenant classes are defined as follows:

A tenant is a farm operator who leases all the land operated by him—

If he pays a proportionate share of the products or crops, say one-half or one-third, to the owner for the use of the land, then he is a *share-tenant* and should be so returned. But if (1) he pays a fixed rental in money, say $200 a year, or (2) a stated amount of produce, say 100 bushels of wheat or 5 bales of cotton, or (3) if he agrees to work for the owner of the land a specified number of days, say two days every week, then in either case he is a *cash tenant*, and should be so returned. It should be noted, therefore, that the word

MAP IV.

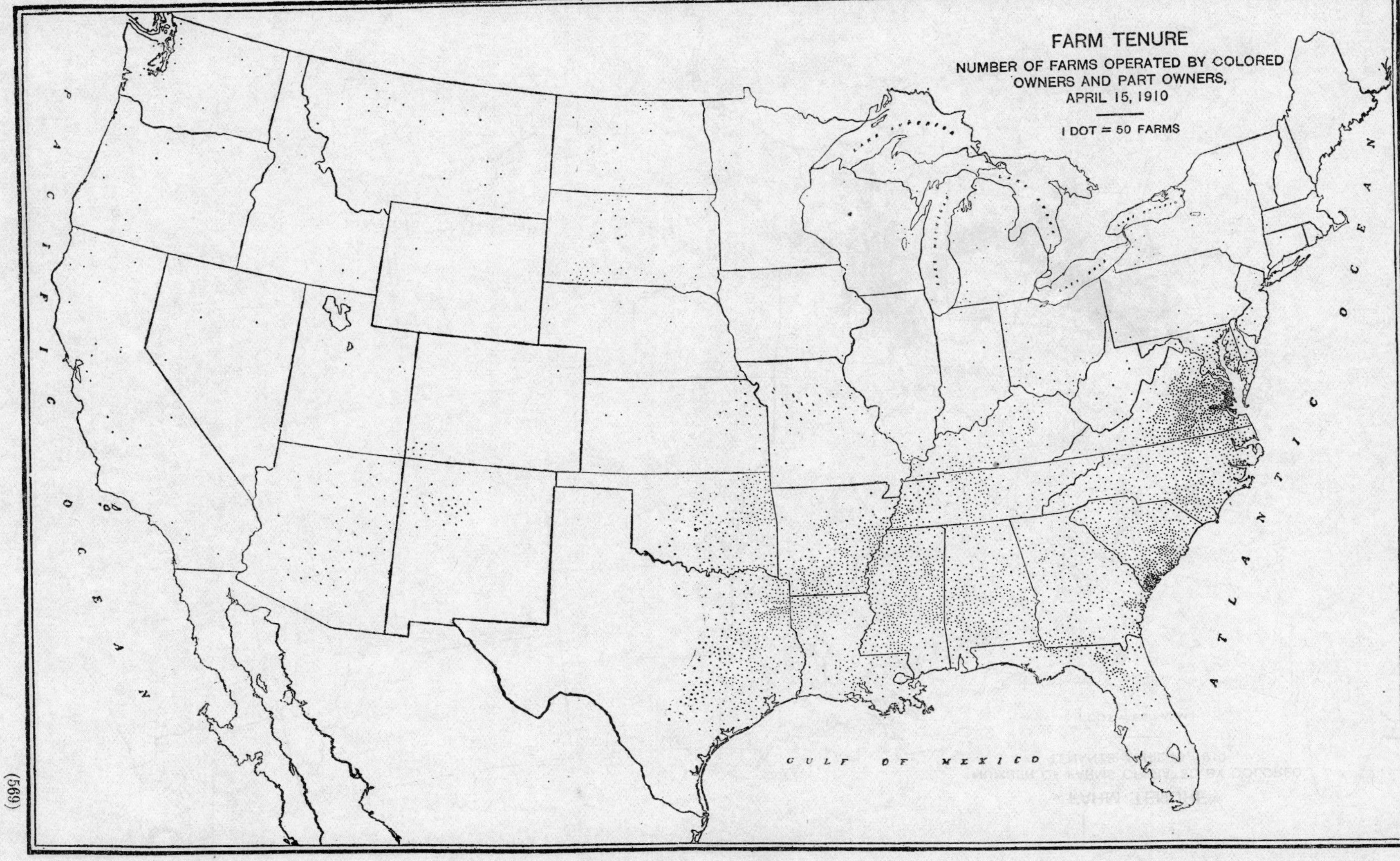

FARM TENURE

NUMBER OF FARMS OPERATED BY COLORED
OWNERS AND PART OWNERS,
APRIL 15, 1910

1 DOT = 50 FARMS

ATLANTIC OCEAN

PACIFIC OCEAN

GULF OF MEXICO

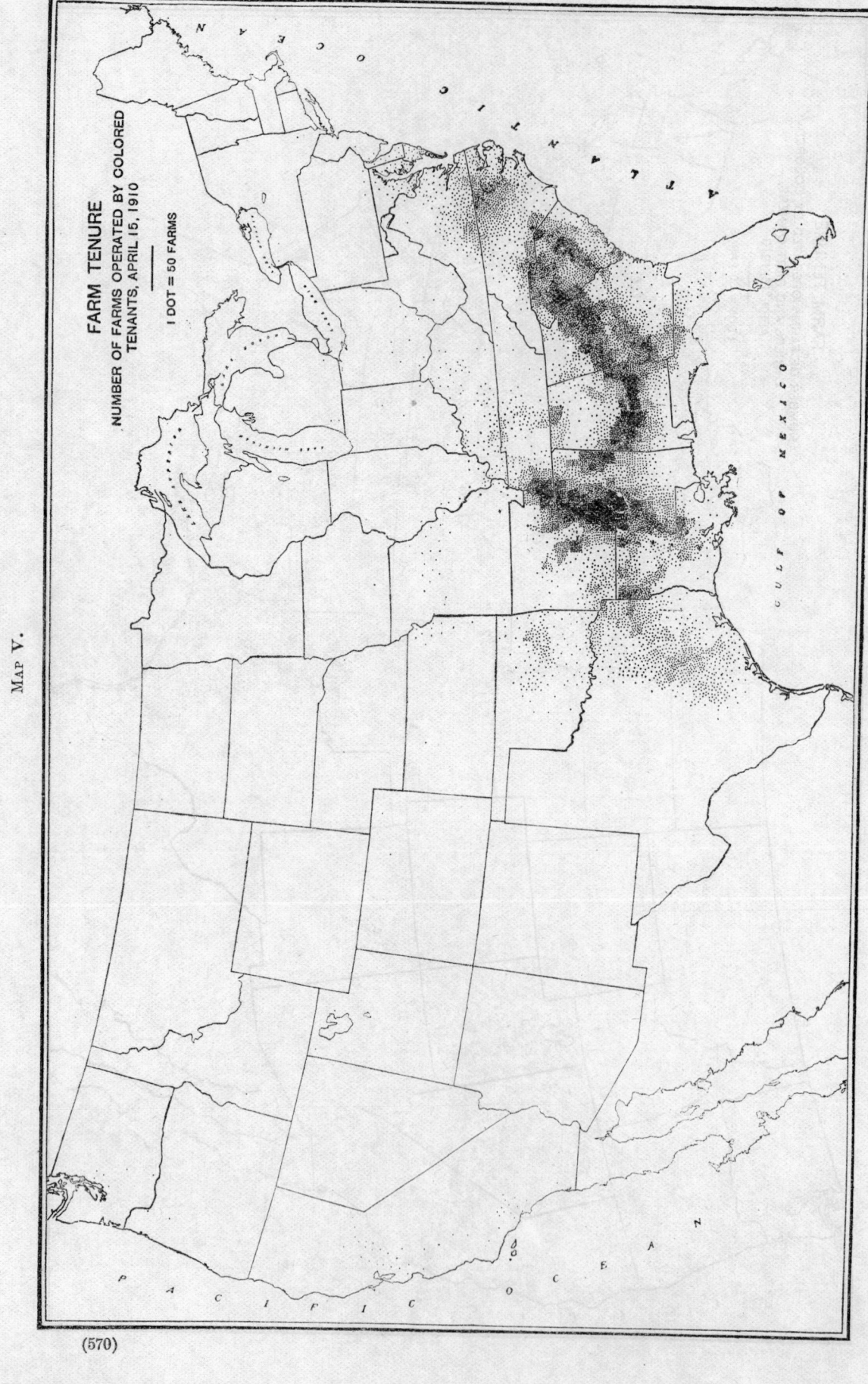

MAP V.

FARM TENURE

NUMBER OF FARMS OPERATED BY COLORED
TENANTS, APRIL 15, 1910

1 DOT = 50 FARMS

(570)

cash, as here used, means not necessarily money, but a definite and fixed amount of either money, produce, or labor, as the case may be, paid as rent.

It may happen that a tenant pays both kinds of rent. He may pay for a single tract of land both a fixed amount of money, produce, or labor, and a proportionate share of the crops, or he may rent one tract of land on one basis and another tract on the other basis. In both such cases he is to be returned as a *share-cash tenant*.

Owners owning entire farms operated are further distinguished according to the return of mortgage indebtedness, as "owners free" and "owners mortgaged."

Enumerators were instructed to report as managers, operators of farms operated for owners or for public institutions "by one who received wages or a salary for his services as manager, superintendent, or overseer."

These distinctions give, for the most detailed tabulations (see, for example, Tables 30 and 57) seven tenure classes—owners free, owners mortgaged, part owners, share tenants, cash tenants, share-cash tenants, and managers. In many of the tables, however, combinations of these classes have been made, where full detail by tenure has seemed relatively insignificant, or data for the minor tenure classes have not been available.

NUMBER OF FARMS IN EACH TENURE CLASS.

Farm operators in 1910, of all classes combined, and of Negroes, native whites, and foreign-born whites separately, are classified in Table 28 as owners, tenants, and managers.

Table 28	FARM OPERATORS: 1910.						
TENURE.	Total.	Negro.	Native white.	Foreign-born white.	Percentage distribution by tenure.		
					Negro.	Native white.	Foreign-born white.
UNITED STATES.							
Total.....	6,361,502	893,370	4,771,063	669,556	100.0	100.0	100.0
Owners.......	3,948,722	218,972	3,162,584	544,917	24.5	66.3	81.4
Tenants......	2,354,676	672,964	1,558,392	118,166	75.3	32.7	17.6
Managers.....	58,104	1,434	50,087	6,473	0.2	1.0	1.0
THE SOUTH.							
Total.....	3,097,547	880,836	2,153,945	53,461	100.0	100.0	100.0
Owners.......	1,544,511	211,087	1,290,070	35,974	24.0	59.9	67.3
Tenants......	1,536,752	668,559	849,295	16,983	75.9	39.4	31.8
Managers.....	16,284	1,190	14,580	504	0.1	0.7	0.9
THE NORTH.							
Total.....	2,890,618	12,052	2,340,612	532,122	100.0	100.0	100.0
Owners.......	2,091,434	7,498	1,640,930	437,542	62.2	70.1	82.2
Tenants......	765,501	4,330	670,792	90,028	35.9	28.7	16.9
Managers.....	33,683	224	28,890	4,552	1.9	1.2	0.9
THE WEST.							
Total.....	373,337	482	276,506	83,973	100.0	100.0	100.0
Owners.......	312,777	387	231,584	71,401	80.3	83.8	85.0
Tenants......	52,423	75	38,305	11,155	15.6	13.8	13.3
Managers.....	8,137	20	6,617	1,417	4.1	2.4	1.7

Of the 893,370 Negro farmers in 1910, 218,972 were returned as owners of the farms they were operating, 672,964 were returned as tenant farmers, and 1,434 as farm managers. Of the farms operated by Negro owners, 211,087 were in the South, 7,498 were in the North, and 387 were in the West.

Owned farms constituted 24.5 per cent of all Negro farms, the proportion owned by the operator being 1 in 4; of farms operated by native whites, 66.3 per cent, or 2 out of 3, were so owned; and of farms operated by foreign-born whites, 81.4 per cent, or 4 out of 5. In the South 24 per cent, in the North, 62.2 per cent, and in the West, 80.3 per cent of the Negro farms were owned, the percentage owned of Negro farms in the North and West being much higher than in the South, and approximating more nearly to the percentage owned of native white farms.

In the South 75.9 per cent, or 3 out of 4 Negro farmers, were tenants, the proportion in the North being 35.9 per cent or approximately 1 in 3 Negro farmers, and in the West 15.6 per cent or approximately 1 in 6 Negro farmers.

Managers constituted only 0.2 per cent of Negro farmers in the country as a whole, the proportion among white farmers, native and foreign-born, being 1 per cent. Per 1,000 Negro farmers in the South, 1 was returned as a manager, the number of managers per 1,000 native white farmers being 7, and per 1,000 foreign-born white farmers, 9. In the North and West there were more managers per 1,000 farmers among Negroes than among either native or foreign-born whites, the number of Negro farmers in these sections (12,052 in the North and 482 in the West) being, however, inconsiderable relatively to the number in the South (880,836), and relatively to the number of white farmers in the North (2,872,734) and West (360,479).

Table 29 introduces data for the year 1900 in comparison with data for 1910, as regards the number of Negro farm owners, managers, and tenants.

During the decade 1900–1910 the number of Negro farm owners increased from 187,797 in 1900 to 218,972 in 1910, the increase amounting to 31,175. Negro tenant farmers increased in the same period from 557,174 to 672,964, the increase amounting to 115,790.

It may fairly be assumed that these increases largely represent, in one case the advance of tenant farmers into the class of farm owners, and in the other the advance of farm laborers into the class of tenant farmers, although precise data are not available regarding the number of such changes. Even without any increase in the number of owners, obviously a considerable number of tenants might become owners during any period, the number of new owners recruited from the tenants merely offsetting in whole or in part the decrease by mortality or by abandonment of farming among owners, and similarly a considerable number of laborers might enter the tenant class without developing any increase in the class of tenants, the new tenants offsetting the decrease of tenants by progression of tenants into the class of owners, by mortality, and by abandonment of farming. Both owners and tenants, as well as farm laborers, are undoubtedly recruited also directly from the nonfarming population, as may be inferred from the increasing proportion of farmers in the Negro population (see Table 2).

Table 29

TENURE.	NEGRO FARM OPERATORS.				
	1910	1900	Increase:[1] 1900-1910.	Percentage distribution by tenure.	
				1910	1900
UNITED STATES.					
Total.................	893,370	746,715	146,655	100.0	100.0
Owners.................	218,972	187,797	31,175	24.5	25.1
Tenants.................	672,964	557,174	115,790	75.3	74.6
Managers.................	1,434	1,744	−310	0.2	0.2
THE SOUTH.					
Total.................	880,836	732,362	148,474	100.0	100.0
Owners.................	211,087	179,418	31,669	24.0	24.5
Tenants.................	668,559	551,383	117,176	75.9	75.3
Managers.................	1,190	1,561	−371	0.1	0.2
THE NORTH.					
Total.................	12,052	14,016	−1,964	100.0	100.0
Owners.................	7,498	8,122	−624	62.2	57.9
Tenants.................	4,330	5,718	−1,388	35.9	40.8
Managers.................	224	176	48	1.9	1.3
THE WEST.					
Total.................	482	337	145	100.0	100.0
Owners.................	387	257	130	80.3	76.3
Tenants.................	75	73	2	15.6	21.7
Managers.................	20	7	13	4.1	2.1

A minus sign (−) denotes decrease.

In the South there was practically no change during the decade in the relative number of owners and of tenants among Negro farm operators, the percentage in these classes being for owners 24.5 in 1900 and 24 in 1910, and for tenants 75.3 in 1900 and 75.9 in 1910. In the North and West the proportion of owners among Negro farmers increased—from 57.9 to 62.2 per cent in the North, and from 76.3 to 80.3 per cent in the West.

Table 30 classifies colored and white farm operators of the South in greater detail of tenure, distinguishing three classes of owners—owners free, owners mortgaged, and part owners—and three classes of tenants—cash tenants, share tenants, and share-cash tenants. While data have not been compiled in this detail of tenure for Negroes, data for the aggregate

colored in the South are, as has been noted, practically equivalent to data for Negroes.

Table 30

TENURE.	FARMS IN THE SOUTH: 1910.			
	Number.		Percentage distribution.	
	Colored.	White.	Colored.	White.
Total.................	890,141	2,207,406	100.0	100.0
Owners.................	218,467	1,326,044	24.5	60.1
Free.................	128,557	908,211	14.4	41.1
Mortgaged.................	46,733	245,889	5.3	11.1
Part.................	43,177	171,944	4.9	7.8
Tenants.................	670,474	866,278	75.3	39.2
Cash.................	260,966	192,094	29.3	8.7
Share.................	370,306	611,370	41.6	27.7
Share-cash.................	14,218	25,447	1.6	1.2
Not specified.................	24,984	37,367	2.8	1.7
Managers.................	1,200	15,084	0.1	0.7

The 43,177 colored farmers classified as part owners, i. e., owners farming some leased land in addition to land owned by them, constituted 4.9 per cent of the colored farmers in the South, the corresponding proportion for white farmers being 7.8 per cent. Cash tenants constituted 29.3 per cent of the colored and 8.7 per cent of the white farm operators. More than two-fifths of the colored farm operators were share tenants, the percentage in this class being 41.6 for colored operators and 27.7 for white operators. Share-cash tenants constituted only 1.6 per cent of colored operators and 1.2 per cent of white operators.

Statistics of the number of farms classified by tenure are given in the general tables, for divisions and states, as follows: Negro farms in 1910 and in 1900 are classified as operated by owners, tenants, and managers, in Table 54 (p. 607), which gives also the increase for each tenure class during the decade 1900–1910. Table 55 (p. 608) classifies farms of colored owners, tenants, and managers, in 1910, as operated by Negro and by other colored farmers. Table 56 (p. 609) classifies colored and white farmers of the South, in 1910 and 1900, as owners, part owners, share tenants, cash tenants, and managers. Table 57 (p. 610) classifies farms of colored and of white operators in the South in 1910, in full detail of tenure, distinguishing seven tenure classes of operators—owners free, owners mortgaged, part owners, cash tenants, share tenants, share-cash tenants, and managers—and giving the percentage distribution of farms in each state by this detail of tenure.

FARM ACREAGE UNDER EACH TENURE.

The number of acres in colored and white farms classified by tenure, distinguishing owners free, owners mortgaged, part owners, cash tenants, share and share-cash tenants, and managers, is given for

MAP **VI.**—FARMS OF COLORED OWNERS—PERCENTAGE OF ALL COLORED FARMS, BY STATES: 1910 (SOUTHERN STATES ONLY).

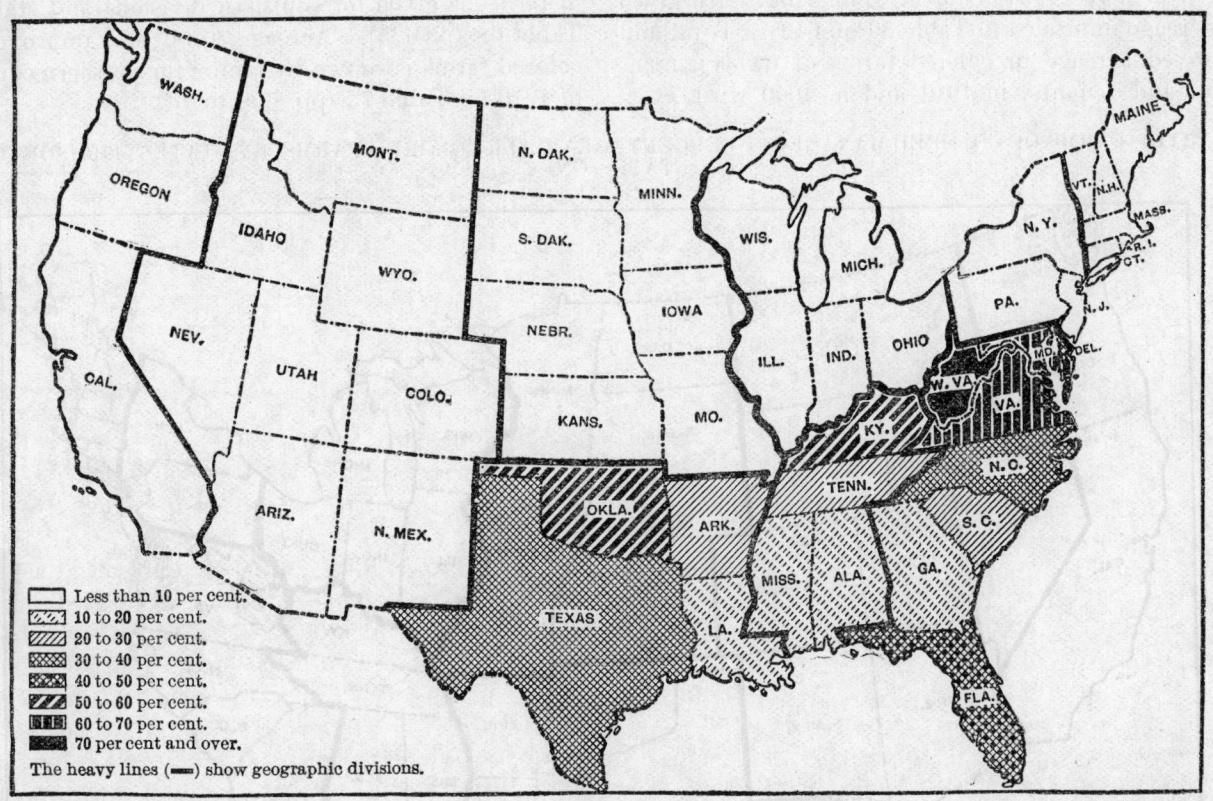

MAP **VII.**—FARMS OF COLORED TENANTS—PERCENTAGE OF ALL COLORED FARMS, BY STATES: 1910 (SOUTHERN STATES ONLY).

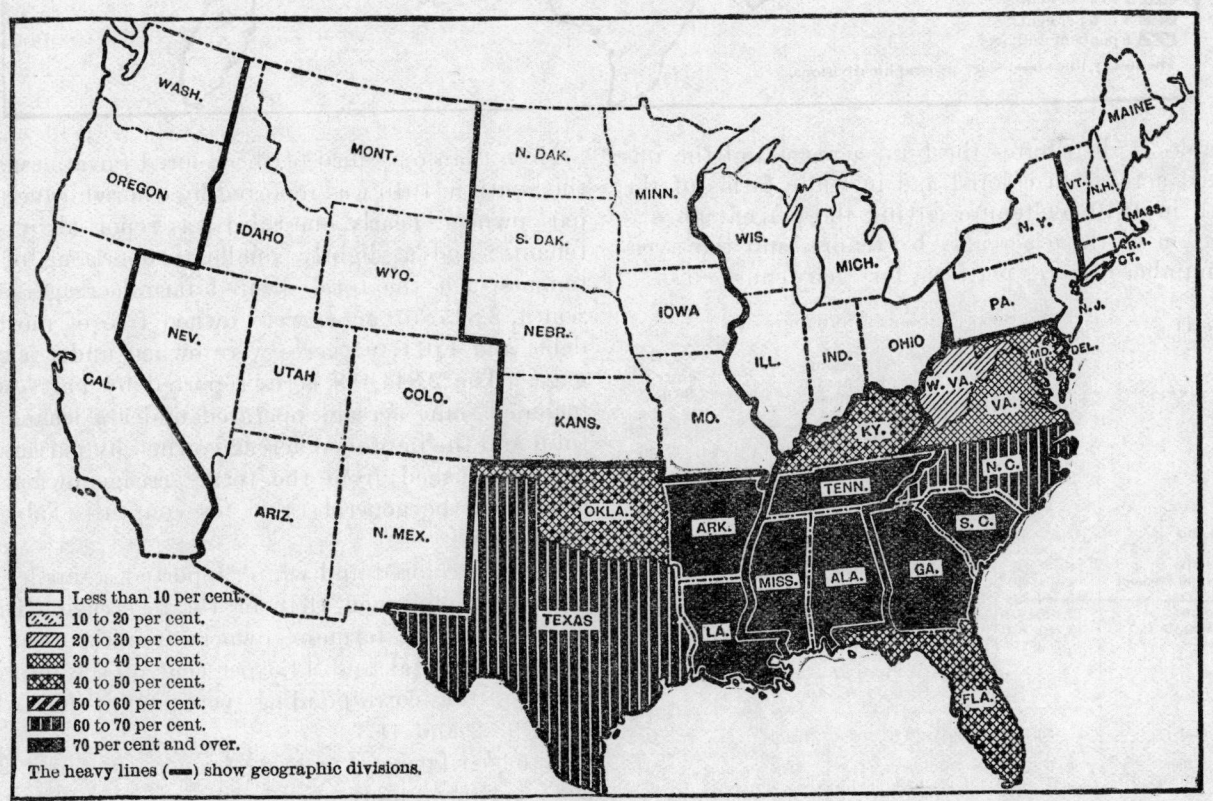

1910 in Table 58 (p. 612), with the percentage distribution of acreage by tenure. Similar data are given for acreage improved in Table 59 (p. 613). Total and improved acreage in colored farms of owners, managers, and tenants, in 1910 and in 1900 with average acres per farm, and percentage improved of land in farms, is given for southern divisions and states in Table 68 (p. 625). Acreage, total and improved, in colored farms is shown by tenure for southern counties in 1910, in Table 73 (pp. 698 to 764).

MAP VIII.—FARMS OF COLORED MANAGERS—PERCENTAGE OF ALL COLORED FARMS, BY STATES: 1910 (SOUTHERN STATES ONLY).

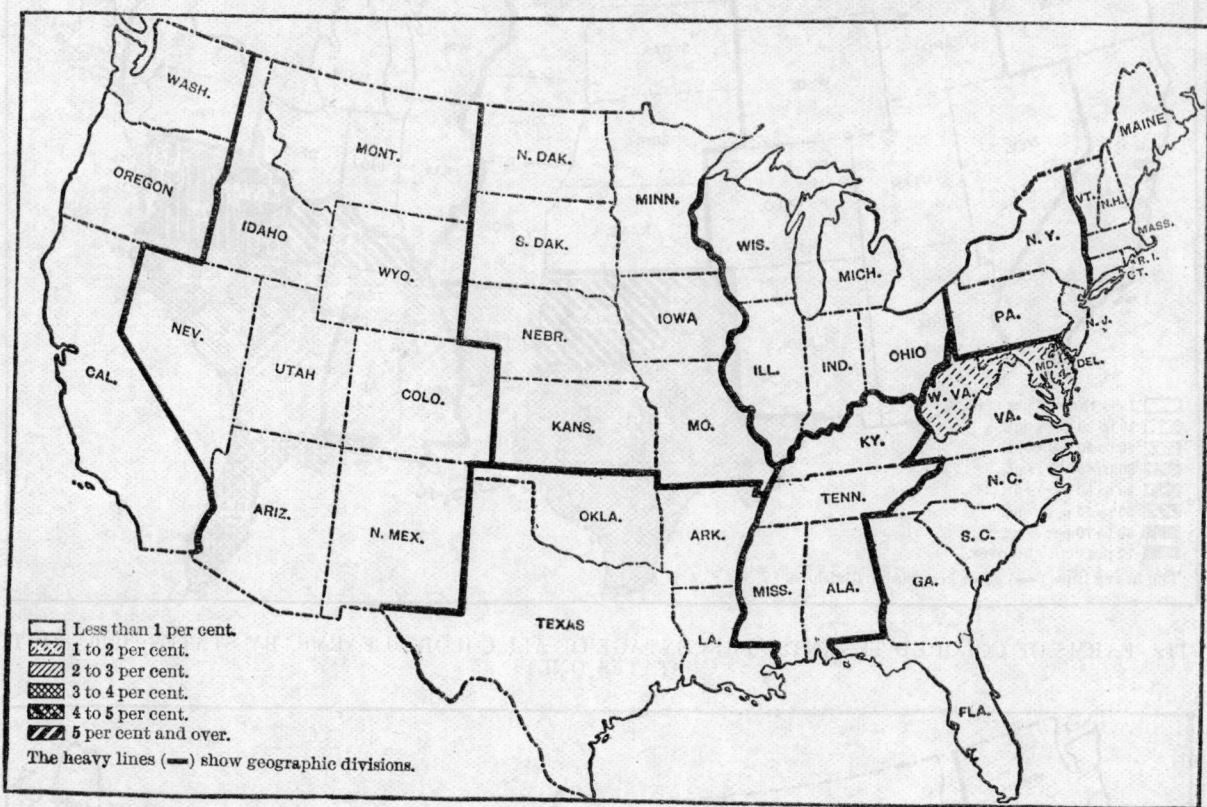

Legend:
- Less than 1 per cent.
- 1 to 2 per cent.
- 2 to 3 per cent.
- 3 to 4 per cent.
- 4 to 5 per cent.
- 5 per cent and over.

The heavy lines (——) show geographic divisions.

Table 31 distributes the total acreage and the improved acreage in colored and in white farms of the South in 1910 by tenure, giving the percentage distribution of these acreages by tenure, and the average number of acres per farm for each tenure class.

Table 31	ACRES IN FARMS IN THE SOUTH: 1910.					
TENURE.	Colored.	White.	Percentage distribution by tenure.		Average per farm.	
			Colored.	White.	Colored.	White.
ALL LAND.						
Total..........	42,609,117	311,843,743	100.0	100.0	47.9	141.3
Owners, free........	8,835,857	134,584,147	20.7	43.2	68.7	148.2
Owners, mortgaged..	4,011,491	46,759,094	9.4	15.0	85.8	190.2
Part owners.........	2,844,188	33,580,452	6.7	10.8	65.9	195.3
Cash tenants [1].......	12,876,308	26,275,674	30.2	8.4	45.0	114.5
Share tenants [2].....	13,691,494	46,328,127	32.1	14.9	35.6	72.4
Managers...........	349,779	24,316,249	0.8	7.8	291.5	1,612.1
IMPROVED LAND.						
Total..........	27,735,743	122,955,109	100.0	100.0	31.2	55.7
Owners, free........	4,005,552	50,780,626	14.5	41.3	31.2	55.9
Owners, mortgaged..	1,893,013	16,588,921	6.8	13.5	40.5	67.5
Part owners........	1,632,554	12,212,994	5.9	9.9	37.8	71.0
Cash tenants [1].......	9,218,158	10,839,130	33.3	9.0	32.2	42.2
Share tenants [2].....	10,878,217	29,407,345	39.3	23.9	28.3	46.2
Managers...........	108,249	3,126,093	0.4	2.5	90.2	207.2

[1] Includes not specified tenure.　　　[2] Includes share-cash tenants.

More than one-third of the colored farm acreage in the South in 1910 was reported by colored owners and part owners; nearly one-third was reported by share tenants; and a slightly smaller proportion, by cash tenants. Of the total colored farm acreage in the South, 8,835,857 acres were owned free of mortgage debt, and 4,011,491 acres were owned under a mortgage. The 2,844,188 acres reported by part owners included some acreage operated under a lease. The total and the improved acreage owned by part owners is distinguished from the total acreage owned and leased, in the general table for counties (Table 73) cited above.

Owners, colored and white, reported a smaller proportion of improved than of total acreage. In the case of colored farmers, owners free reported 20.7 per cent of total and 14.5 per cent of the improved acreage, the corresponding percentages for whites being 43.2 and 41.3.

Managed farms of colored farmers averaged 291.5 acres per farm, mortgaged farms averaged 85.8 acres, farms owned free 68.7 acres, farms partly owned 65.9 acres, cash tenant farms 45 acres, and share tenant farms 35.6 acres.

In improved acreage, as in total acreage, the average acreage per farm of mortgaged farms, colored and white, exceeded that of farms owned free. The average acreage improved of colored farms owned free was slightly less than that of colored farms operated by cash tenants.

Colored operators of each tenure class, as compared with white operators, reported on the average a much smaller acreage per farm, the excess of white over colored acreage being more marked in the averages for total than for improved land in farms.

In Table 32 acreage operated by colored tenants is distributed by tenant tenures, for sections and southern divisions in 1910.

ACREAGE OF COLORED TENANT FARMS, BY TENANT TENURES, BY SECTIONS AND SOUTHERN DIVISIONS: 1910.

Table 32	ACREAGE OPERATED BY COLORED TENANTS: 1910.													
		The South.							The South.					
TENURE.	United States.	Total.	South Atlantic division.	East South Central division.	West South Central division.	The North.	The West.	United States.	Total.	South Atlantic division.	East South Central division.	West South Central division.	The North.	The West.
	NUMBER OF ACRES.							PERCENTAGE DISTRIBUTION BY TENURE.						
All tenants..	27,129,953	26,567,802	11,883,633	8,979,405	5,704,764	339,657	222,494	100.0	100.0	100.0	100.0	100.0	100.0	100.0
Cash..........	11,898,533	11,705,291	5,394,424	5,037,289	1,273,578	81,491	111,751	43.9	44.1	45.4	56.1	22.3	24.0	50.2
Share..........	13,358,580	13,074,769	5,660,907	3,453,809	3,960,053	200,678	83,133	49.2	49.2	47.6	38.5	69.4	59.1	37.4
Share-cash.........	655,093	616,725	240,823	177,296	198,606	29,340	9,028	2.4	2.3	2.0	2.0	3.5	8.6	4.1
Unspecified.......	1,217,747	1,171,017	587,479	311,011	272,527	28,148	18,582	4.5	4.4	4.9	3.5	4.8	8.3	8.4

In the South as a whole, nearly one-half (49.2 per cent) of the acreage on farms of colored tenant farmers was in farms of share tenants—that is, tenants renting under an agreement to pay "a proportionate share of the products or crops" as rent. Acreage operated under this tenure was relatively to the total acreage in tenant farms largest in the West South Central division, in which division more than two-thirds (69.4 per cent) of the colored acreage in tenant farms was rented on shares.

Cash tenants operated 44.1 per cent of the total acreage in colored tenant farms of the South, the proportion under this tenure being highest (56.1 per cent) in the East South Central division.

Table 33 distributes acreage, total and improved, reported by colored and by white farmers of the South as a whole, and of each southern division, in 1910 and in 1900, as in farms of owners, part owners, cash tenants, share tenants, and managers, giving the increase for the decade 1900–1910, the percentage improved at the beginning and at the end of the decade, and average acres per farm of all land and of land improved.

During the decade 1900–1910 the acreage in colored farms of owners in the South increased from 11,512,424 acres in 1900 to 12,847,348 acres in 1910, the increase amounting to 1,334,924 acres. Acreage reported by part owners increased by 997,928 acres, and acreage reported by share tenants by 1,909,024 acres. Cash tenant acreage in the same period decreased by 166,066 acres, and managed acreage by 78,739 acres.

While the increase of improved acreage for colored owners and part owners in the South was less than the increase in total acreage in such farms, the increase of improved acreage for tenant farms was greater than the increase for total acreage in tenant farms. Cash tenant acreage of improved land in fact increased by 677,525 acres, although the total acreage in such farms decreased, as stated above, by 166,066 acres; and in the same period the increase of 2,358,790 acres in improved acreage for share tenant farms exceeded the increase of 1,909,024 acres in total acreage of share tenant farms by 449,766 acres. For each tenure class of colored and white farms, the percentage improved of the total land in farms increased.

In the South Atlantic division the acreage in owned farms for colored owners increased by 826,505 acres, and for white owners decreased in the same period by 2,291,823 acres. In the East South Central division owned acreage increased for colored operators by 394,855 acres, and decreased for white operators by 2,460,832 acres. In the West South Central division owned colored acreage increased by 113,564 acres, and owned white acreage by 15,186,502 acres.

For colored farms of each tenure class, average size of farm and average acres improved per farm did not change materially during the decade. Average size increased slightly for colored owners and part owners, and more considerably for colored managers, and decreased for colored tenants, cash and share. Average acreage improved per farm increased for colored owners, part owners, cash tenants, and managers, and decreased for share tenants.

The average size of colored farms wholly owned by operators in the South Atlantic division was 56 acres, in the East South Central division 80 acres, and in the West South Central division 95.9 acres, the corresponding averages for white farms wholly owned being 131.7, 119.5, and 238.1 acres.

MAP IX.—LAND IN FARMS OF COLORED OWNERS—PERCENTAGE OF ALL LAND IN COLORED FARMS, BY
STATES: 1910 (SOUTHERN STATES ONLY).

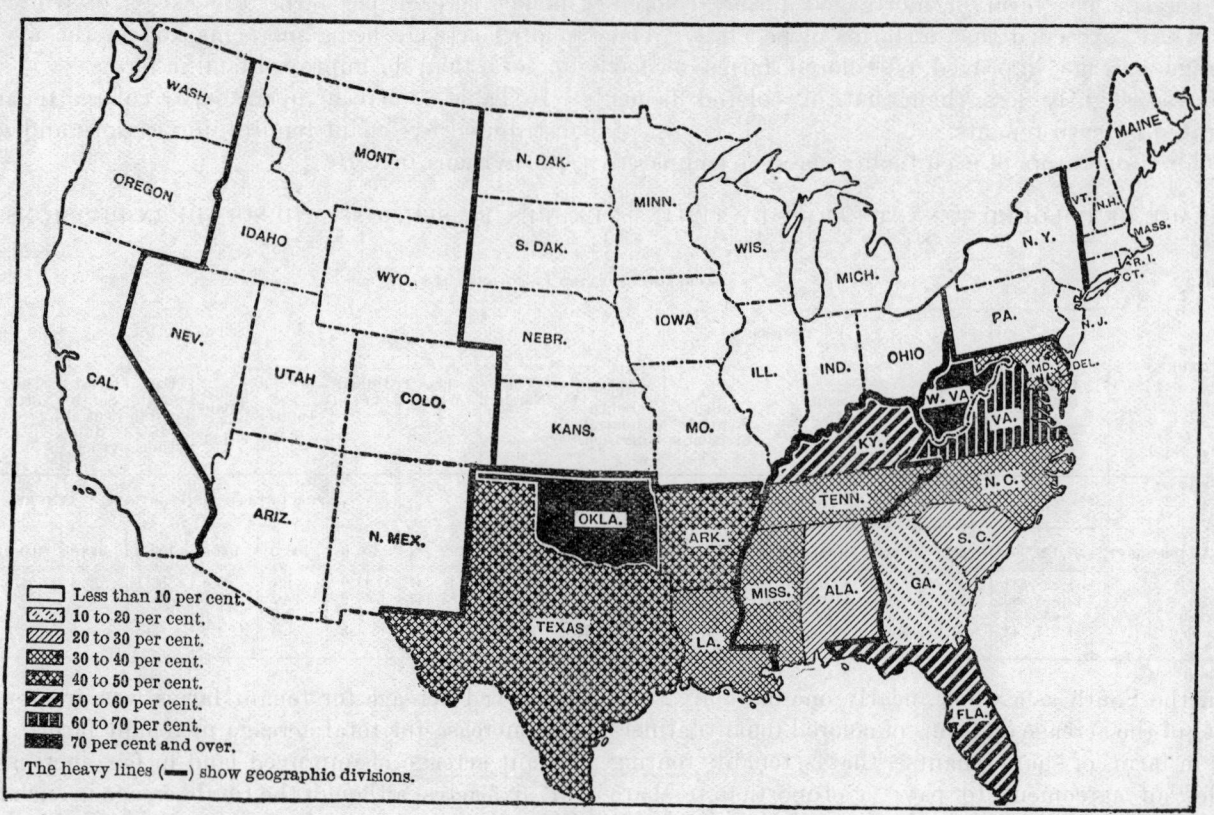

MAP X.—LAND IN FARMS OF COLORED TENANTS—PERCENTAGE OF ALL LAND IN COLORED FARMS, BY
STATES: 1910 (SOUTHERN STATES ONLY).

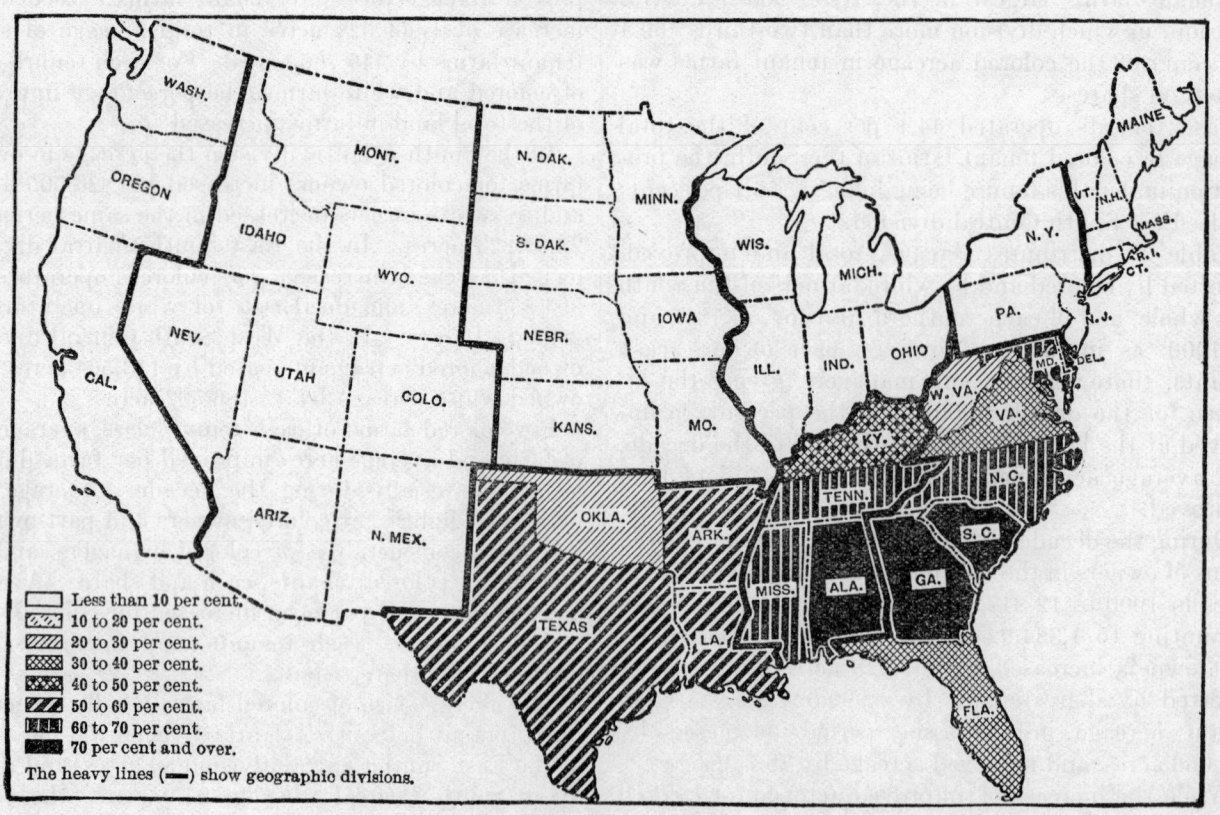

Cash tenant farms of colored operators averaged 52.8 acres in the South Atlantic division, 39.6 acres in the East South Central division, and 41 acres in the West South Central division, the corresponding averages for white cash tenant farms being 87.6, 71.6, and 194.8 acres. In each division share tenant farms of colored and of white farmers averaged smaller in size than cash tenant farms.

Tenant farms, cash and share, colored and white, in each southern division, averaged smaller in 1910 than in 1900, except for white share tenant farms in the West South Central division.

COLORED AND WHITE ACREAGE, TOTAL AND IMPROVED, BY TENURE CLASSES, WITH DECENNIAL INCREASE, AND AVERAGE ACRES PER FARM, BY SOUTHERN DIVISIONS: 1910 AND 1900.

Table 33

| DIVISION AND TENURE. | ACRES IN FARMS. | | | | | | | | AVERAGE ACRES PER FARM. | | | |
| | Total. | | Improved. | | Increase:[1] 1900–1910. | | Percentage improved. | | Total. | | Improved. | |
	1910	1900	1910	1900	Total.	Improved.	1910	1900	1910	1900	1910	1900
THE SOUTH.												
Colored operators.												
Total	42,609,117	38,612,046	27,735,743	23,214,607	3,997,071	4,521,136	65.1	60.1	47.9	52.1	31.2	31.3
Owners	12,847,348	11,512,424	5,898,565	5,030,912	1,334,924	867,653	45.9	43.7	73.3	72.6	33.6	31.7
Part owners	2,844,188	1,846,260	1,632,554	995,893	997,928	636,661	57.4	53.9	65.9	65.5	37.8	35.3
Cash tenants	12,876,308	13,042,374	9,218,158	8,540,633	−166,066	677,525	71.6	65.5	45.0	48.0	32.2	31.4
Share tenants	13,691,494	11,782,470	10,878,217	8,519,427	1,909,024	2,358,790	79.5	72.3	35.6	40.0	28.3	30.4
Managers	349,779	428,518	108,249	127,742	−78,739	−19,493	30.9	29.8	291.5	269.0	90.2	80.2
White operators.												
Total	311,843,743	323,424,305	122,955,109	102,893,486	−11,580,562	20,061,623	39.4	31.8	141.3	172.1	55.7	54.7
Owners	181,343,241	170,909,394	67,369,547	62,442,183	10,433,847	4,927,364	37.2	36.5	157.1	158.4	58.4	5779
Part owners	33,580,452	38,847,090	12,212,994	7,497,960	−5,266,638	4,715,034	36.4	19.3	195.3	369.4	71.0	71.3
Cash tenants	26,275,674	26,245,180	10,839,130	8,827,588	30,494	2,011,542	41.3	33.6	114.5	140.3	42.2	47.2
Share tenants	46,328,127	36,545,215	29,407,345	21,074,171	9,782,912	8,333,174	63.5	57.7	72.4	74.3	46.2	42.9
Managers	24,316,249	50,877,426	3,126,093	3,051,584	−26,561,177	74,509	12.9	6.0	1,612.1	2,962.8	207.2	177.7
SOUTH ATLANTIC.												
Colored operators.												
Total	17,675,382	15,637,265	10,990,069	8,895,862	2,038,117	2,094,207	62.2	56.9	49.7	54.1	30.9	30.8
Owners	4,531,973	3,705,468	2,066,650	1,683,837	826,505	382,813	45.6	45.4	56.0	52.3	25.5	23.8
Part owners	1,114,405	721,971	629,297	415,395	392,434	213,902	56.5	50.5	52.9	50.5	29.9	29.0
Cash tenants	5,981,903	5,622,017	3,900,843	3,276,171	359,886	624,672	65.2	58.3	52.8	55.9	34.5	32.6
Share tenants	5,901,730	5,386,735	4,331,992	3,453,695	514,995	878,297	73.4	64.1	42.2	52.7	30.9	33.8
Managers	145,371	201,074	61,287	66,764	−55,703	−5,477	42.2	33.2	201.9	207.3	85.1	68.8
White operators.												
Total	86,106,873	88,660,241	37,489,664	37,204,364	−2,553,368	285,300	43.5	42.0	113.9	131.7	49.6	55.3
Owners	58,030,441	60,322,264	23,511,797	23,782,838	−2,291,823	−271,041	40.5	39.4	131.7	147.2	53.4	58.0
Part owners	5,452,964	4,176,173	2,636,523	1,918,005	1,276,791	718,518	48.4	45.9	107.9	128.1	52.2	58.8
Cash tenants	7,689,142	7,863,904	3,532,513	3,427,467	−174,762	105,046	45.9	43.6	87.6	109.1	40.3	47.5
Share tenants	11,715,307	13,037,370	6,641,034	6,855,181	−1,322,063	−214,147	56.7	52.6	69.1	86.5	39.2	45.5
Managers	3,219,019	3,260,530	1,167,797	1,220,873	−41,511	−53,076	36.3	37.4	424.8	400.3	154.1	149.9
EAST SOUTH CENTRAL.												
Colored operators.												
Total	13,595,717	12,621,318	9,556,529	8,191,628	974,399	1,364,901	70.3	64.9	41.8	47.1	29.4	30.6
Owners	3,706,211	3,311,356	1,723,981	1,413,387	394,855	310,594	46.5	42.7	80.0	79.2	37.2	33.8
Part owners	833,741	526,497	489,664	300,633	307,244	189,031	58.7	57.1	67.1	65.0	39.4	37.1
Cash tenants	5,348,300	5,544,632	4,170,455	3,944,072	−196,332	226,383	78.0	71.1	39.6	44.3	30.9	31.5
Share tenants	3,631,105	3,178,445	3,146,192	2,507,670	452,660	638,522	86.6	78.9	27.7	34.3	24.0	27.1
Managers	76,360	60,388	26,237	25,866	15,972	371	34.4	42.8	306.7	186.4	105.4	79.8
White operators.												
Total	67,924,912	68,626,325	34,390,317	32,045,709	−701,413	2,344,608	50.6	46.7	94.7	108.0	47.9	50.4
Owners	46,929,634	49,390,466	22,029,780	21,481,882	−2,460,832	547,898	46.9	43.5	119.5	131.2	56.1	57.0
Part owners	5,662,386	4,153,157	3,140,497	2,178,197	1,509,229	962,300	55.5	52.4	95.9	111.6	53.2	58.6
Cash tenants	5,245,221	5,285,477	2,815,572	2,763,049	−40,256	52,523	53.7	52.3	71.6	81.3	38.4	42.5
Share tenants	8,560,564	8,234,163	5,851,914	5,008,184	326,401	843,730	68.4	60.8	45.2	54.1	30.9	32.9
Managers	1,527,107	1,563,062	552,554	614,397	−35,955	−61,843	36.2	39.3	502.2	357.5	181.7	140.5
WEST SOUTH CENTRAL.												
Colored operators.												
Total	11,338,018	10,353,463	7,189,145	6,127,117	984,555	1,062,028	63.4	59.2	54.2	56.3	34.4	33.3
Owners	4,609,164	4,495,600	2,107,934	1,933,688	113,564	174,246	45.7	43.0	95.9	98.0	43.9	42.2
Part owners	896,042	597,792	513,593	279,865	298,250	233,728	57.3	46.8	92.3	103.2	52.9	48.3
Cash tenants	1,546,105	1,875,725	1,146,860	1,320,390	−329,620	−173,530	74.2	70.4	41.0	40.8	30.4	28.7
Share tenants	4,158,659	3,217,290	3,400,033	2,558,062	941,369	841,971	81.8	79.5	36.7	37.4	30.0	29.8
Managers	128,048	167,056	20,725	35,112	−39,008	−14,387	16.2	21.0	554.3	558.7	89.7	117.4
White operators.												
Total	157,811,958	166,137,739	51,075,128	33,643,413	−8,325,781	17,431,715	32.4	20.3	215.0	291.0	69.6	58.9
Owners	76,383,166	61,196,664	21,827,970	17,177,463	15,186,502	4,650,507	28.6	28.1	238.1	209.4	68.0	58.8
Part owners	22,465,102	30,517,760	6,435,974	3,401,758	−8,052,658	3,034,216	28.6	11.1	360.4	862.7	103.2	96.2
Cash tenants	13,341,311	13,095,799	4,491,045	2,637,072	245,512	1,853,973	33.7	20.1	194.8	262.2	65.6	52.8
Share tenants	26,052,256	15,273,682	16,914,397	9,210,806	10,778,574	7,703,591	64.9	60.3	93.7	80.9	60.8	48.8
Managers	19,570,123	46,053,834	1,405,742	1,216,314	−26,483,711	189,428	7.2	2.6	4,383.0	9,893.4	314.8	261.3

[1] A minus sign (−) denotes decrease.

VALUE OF FARM PROPERTY BY TENURE OF FARM.

The following tables give values, by divisions and states, for farms classified by tenure: Table 60 (p. 614), the value of land in colored and white farms of the South in 1910; Table 61 (p. 616), similar data for the value of buildings; Table 62 (p. 618), similar data for the value of implements and machinery; Table 68 (pp. 625 and 626), in less detail by tenure, for colored farms in 1910 and in 1900, the combined value of land and buildings, with average value per farm and per acre in farms; Table 69 (pp. 628 to 637), values of classes of live stock on farms.

Aggregate values for colored and white farms of the South, of all farm property, and of each of the four classes of farm property distinguished—land, buildings, implements and machinery, and live stock—are given in Table 34, for tenure classes, covering the two years 1910 and 1900, with increases for the decade 1900–1910, percentage distribution of values by tenure of farm, and average values per farm in each tenure class.

VALUE OF CLASSES OF FARM PROPERTY ON COLORED AND WHITE FARMS, BY TENURE CLASSES, WITH DECENNIAL INCREASE, PERCENTAGE DISTRIBUTION BY TENURE, AND AVERAGE PER FARM: 1910 AND 1900.

Table 34 — VALUE OF FARM PROPERTY IN THE SOUTH.

TENURE.	Colored farms. 1910	Colored farms. 1900	White farms. 1910	White farms. 1900	Increase:[1] 1900–1910 Colored farms.	Increase:[1] 1900–1910 White farms.	Pct. dist. Colored 1910	Pct. dist. Colored 1900	Pct. dist. White 1910	Pct. dist. White 1900	Avg. Colored 1910	Avg. Colored 1900	Avg. White 1910	Avg. White 1900
ALL FARM PROPERTY.														
Total	$1,116,641,576	$488,049,236	$7,855,485,313	$3,781,805,483	$628,592,340	$4,073,679,830	100.0	100.0	100.0	100.0	$1,254	$659	$3,559	$2,012
Owners	275,323,227	123,754,396	4,436,972,500	2,222,681,923	151,568,831	2,214,290,577	24.7	25.4	56.5	58.8	1,571	781	3,845	2,061
Free	[2]190,691,973	(3)	[2]3,253,836,841	(3)	(3)	(3)	17.1	(3)	41.4	(3)	1,483	(3)	3,583	(3)
Mortgaged	[2]83,013,998	(3)	[2]1,160,691,114	(3)	(3)	(3)	7.4	(3)	14.8	(3)	1,776	(3)	4,720	(3)
Part owners	71,558,043	21,660,387	749,783,780	310,211,532	49,897,656	439,569,248	6.4	4.4	9.5	8.2	1,657	768	4,361	2,950
Cash tenants	342,387,968	166,766,057	701,220,541	330,543,855	175,611,911	370,676,686	30.7	34.2	8.9	8.7	1,197	614	3,056	1,767
Share tenants	415,312,935	168,466,783	1,535,676,035	594,493,283	246,846,152	941,182,752	37.2	34.5	19.5	15.7	1,080	600	2,411	1,209
Managers	12,059,403	7,391,613	431,835,457	323,874,890	4,667,790	107,960,567	1.1	1.5	5.5	8.6	10,050	4,640	28,629	18,861
LAND.														
Total	$737,632,122	$310,718,726	$5,188,642,947	$2,251,041,223	$426,913,396	$2,937,601,724	100.0	100.0	100.0	100.0	$829	$420	$2,351	$1,198
Owners	166,711,526	69,149,276	2,784,198,306	1,288,825,482	97,562,250	1,495,372,824	22.6	22.3	53.7	57.3	951	436	2,412	1,195
Free	114,480,372	(3)	2,018,861,909	(3)	(3)	(3)	15.5	(3)	39.0	(3)	891	(3)	2,223	(3)
Mortgaged	52,231,154	(3)	765,336,397	(3)	(3)	(3)	7.1	(3)	14.8	(3)	1,118	(3)	3,113	(3)
Part owners	45,564,045	12,847,560	506,514,471	179,997,100	32,716,485	326,517,371	6.2	4.1	9.8	8.0	1,055	456	2,946	1,711
Cash tenants	223,447,037	108,587,760	484,059,699	207,206,348	114,859,277	276,853,351	30.3	34.9	9.3	9.2	781	400	2,110	1,108
Share tenants	293,652,660	115,798,440	1,092,399,374	386,046,353	177,854,220	706,353,021	39.8	37.3	21.1	17.1	764	413	1,715	785
Managers	8,256,854	4,335,690	321,471,097	188,965,940	3,921,164	132,505,157	1.1	1.4	6.2	8.4	6,881	2,722	21,312	11,004
BUILDINGS.														
Total	$162,500,212	$69,562,242	$1,264,655,914	$647,699,318	$92,937,970	$616,956,596	100.0	100.0	100.0	100.0	$183	$94	$573	$345
Owners	49,633,158	21,111,122	834,411,202	439,526,766	28,522,036	394,884,436	30.5	30.3	66.0	67.9	283	133	723	407
Free	35,775,640	(3)	643,867,091	(3)	(3)	(3)	22.0	(3)	50.9	(3)	278	(3)	709	(3)
Mortgaged	13,857,518	(3)	190,544,111	(3)	(3)	(3)	8.5	(3)	15.1	(3)	297	(3)	775	(3)
Part owners	11,083,509	3,511,370	98,811,108	39,472,610	7,572,139	69,338,498	6.8	5.0	7.8	6.1	257	125	575	375
Cash tenants	44,585,708	20,894,660	92,421,342	47,395,682	23,691,048	45,025,660	27.4	30.0	7.3	7.3	156	77	403	253
Share tenants	55,082,742	22,836,470	192,535,212	89,696,340	32,246,272	102,838,872	33.9	32.8	15.2	13.8	143	81	302	182
Managers	2,115,095	1,208,620	46,477,050	31,607,920	906,475	14,869,130	1.3	1.7	3.8	4.9	1,763	759	3,081	1,841
IMPLEMENTS AND MACHINERY.														
Total	$33,777,118	$18,586,225	$259,512,739	$161,424,950	$15,190,893	$98,087,789	100.0	100.0	100.0	100.0	$38	$25	$118	$86
Owners	10,798,831	5,795,970	158,755,449	98,161,120	5,002,861	60,594,329	32.0	31.2	61.2	60.8	62	37	138	91
Free	7,514,838	(3)	116,186,391	(3)	(3)	(3)	22.2	(3)	44.8	(3)	58	(3)	128	(3)
Mortgaged	3,283,993	(3)	42,569,058	(3)	(3)	(3)	9.7	(3)	16.4	(3)	70	(3)	173	(3)
Part owners	2,490,431	935,600	23,472,047	10,365,830	1,554,831	13,106,217	27.4	5.0	9.0	6.4	58	33	137	99
Cash tenants	11,337,009	6,405,775	20,110,267	11,303,060	4,931,234	8,807,207	33.6	34.5	7.7	7.0	40	24	88	60
Share tenants	8,841,943	5,247,960	43,911,243	22,957,740	3,593,983	20,953,503	26.2	28.2	16.9	14.2	23	19	69	47
Managers	308,904	200,920	13,263,733	18,637,200	107,984	−5,373,467	0.9	1.1	5.1	11.5	257	126	879	1,085
LIVE STOCK.														
Total	$182,732,124	$89,182,043	$1,142,673,713	$721,639,992	$93,550,081	$421,033,721	100.0	100.0	100.0	100.0	$205	$120	$518	$384
Owners	48,179,712	27,698,028	659,607,543	396,168,555	20,481,684	263,438,988	26.4	31.1	57.7	54.9	275	175	572	367
Free	[2]32,921,123	(3)	[2]474,921,450	(3)	(3)	(3)	[2]18.6	(3)	[2]42.9	(3)	[2]256	(3)	[2]523	(3)
Mortgaged	[2]13,641,333	(3)	[2]162,241,548	(3)	(3)	(3)	[2]7.7	(3)	[2]14.7	(3)	[2]292	(3)	[2]660	(3)
Part owners	12,420,058	4,365,857	129,983,154	80,375,992	8,054,291	40,607,162	6.8	4.9	10.6	11.1	288	155	704	764
Cash tenants	63,018,214	30,887,862	104,629,233	64,638,765	32,130,352	39,990,468	34.5	34.6	9.2	9.0	220	114	456	345
Share tenants	57,735,590	24,583,913	206,830,206	95,792,850	33,151,677	111,037,356	31.6	27.6	18.1	13.3	150	88	325	195
Managers	1,378,550	1,646,383	50,623,577	84,663,830	−267,833	−34,040,253	0.8	1.8	4.4	11.7	1,149	1,034	3,356	4,930

[1] A minus sign (−) denotes decrease.   [2] Does not include value of poultry and bees included in total for owners.   [3] Data not available.

MAP **XI.**—LAND IN FARMS OF COLORED MANAGERS—PERCENTAGE OF ALL LAND IN COLORED FARMS, BY
STATES: 1910 (SOUTHERN STATES ONLY).

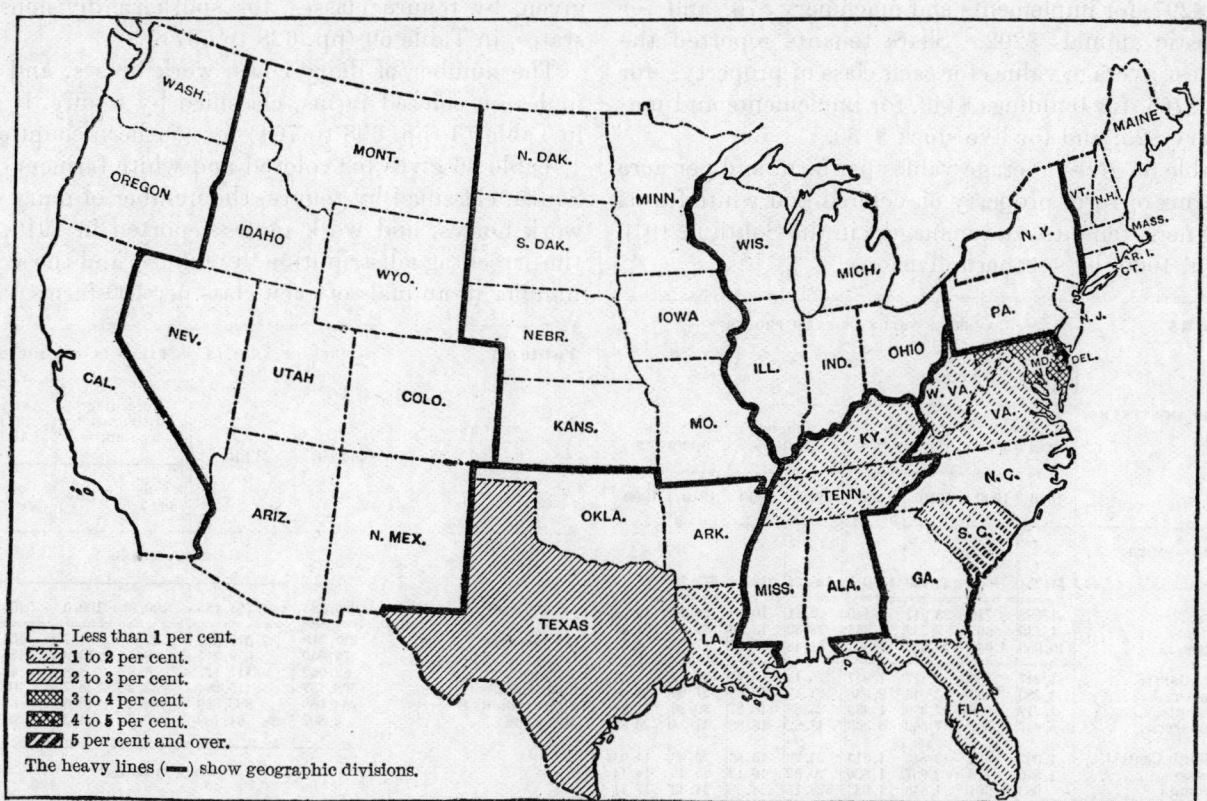

The value of farm property on owned colored farms
of the South increased from $123,754,396 in 1900 to
$275,323,227 in 1910, giving an increase for this class
of farms of $151,568,831. Farm property on partly
owned colored farms increased from $21,660,387 to
$71,558,043, giving an increase of $49,897,656. On
cash tenant farms the property value increased from
$166,766,057 to $342,387,968, or by $175,611,911; on
share tenant farms, from $168,466,783 to $415,312,935,
or by $246,846,152; and on managed farms, from
$7,391,613 to $12,059,403, or by $4,667,790.

For all colored, as for all white farms of the South
combined, and for each tenure class of farms, except
farms operated by managers, the increase in value of
farm property during the decade 1900–1910 exceeded
the aggregate value of farm property on farms in 1900.

Similarly the increase during the decade in the value
of land in colored farms of each tenure class, excepting
manager farms, exceeded the aggregate land values reported for each class in 1900; the increase in the value
of buildings for each tenure class of farms, without exception of managed farms, exceeded the value of buildings on such farms in 1900; and the increase in the
value of live stock, with exception of owned farms and
managed farms, exceeded the value of live stock on
farms in 1900. The increase in the value of implements and machinery was, relatively to the values reported in 1900, generally less than the relative increase
of other classes of farm property, although the value

of this class of property, also, increased rapidly during
the decade—nearly doubling on owned colored farms.

Of the aggregate value of farm property on colored
farms of the South ($1,116,641,576), 24.7 per cent, or
nearly one-fourth, was on owned farms in 1910, 30.7
per cent was on cash tenant farms and 37.2 per cent,
on share tenant farms. The percentage distribution
by tenure of farm property value in 1900 was not
materially different from that of 1910. Owned colored
farms in 1910 reported 22.6 per cent of the total land
value of farms operated by colored farmers, 30.5 per
cent of the value reported for buildings on colored
farms, 32 per cent of the value of implements and
machinery, and 26.4 per cent of the value of live stock.
These proportions are below the corresponding proportions shown for white owners.

The average value per farm of all farm property
on colored farms in 1910 was $1,254; for colored owners,
$1,571; for part owners, $1,657; for cash tenants, $1,197;
and for share tenants, $1,080. As compared with cor-
responding averages for 1900, the averages for 1910
show increases of $790 for owned farms, $889 for
partly owned farms, $583 for cash tenant farms, and
$480 for share tenant farms.

Managers reported the largest average value per
farm of all farm property ($10,050), and of each class
of property.

Excepting managers, mortgaged owners reported the
largest average value for each class of farm property,

the values reported being for land $1,118, for buildings $297, for implements and machinery $70, and for domestic animals $292. Share tenants reported the smallest average values for each class of property—for land $764, for buildings $143, for implements and machinery $23, and for live stock $150.

Table 35 gives average values per farm and per acre in farms of farm property on colored and white farms of owners, tenants, and managers in the South in 1910 and in 1900, by southern divisions.

Table 35	AVERAGE VALUE OF FARM PROPERTY.							
	Per farm.				Per acre.			
DIVISION AND TENURE.	Colored operators.		White operators.		Colored operators.		White operators.	
	1910	1900	1910	1900	1910	1900	1910	1900
THE SOUTH.								
Total...........	$1,254	$659	$3,559	$2,012	$26.21	$12.64	$25.19	$11.69
Owners..............	1,588	779	3,911	2,140	22.11	10.89	24.13	12.08
Tenants............	1,130	607	2,582	1,363	28.52	13.50	30.81	14.73
Managers..........	10,050	4,640	28,629	18,861	34.48	17.25	17.76	6.37
South Atlantic........	1,247	566	3,317	1,917	25.11	10.45	29.12	14.56
Owners...........	1,280	553	3,613	2,038	23.12	10.63	27.96	13.98
Tenants...........	1,212	558	2,330	1,439	25.83	10.27	30.89	15.34
Managers..........	8,847	3,397	17,562	8,363	43.82	16.39	41.34	20.89
East South Central....	1,099	639	2,545	1,613	26.28	13.56	26.88	14.93
Owners...........	1,570	778	2,967	1,830	20.32	10.12	25.49	14.14
Tenants...........	983	601	1,646	1,083	29.15	14.99	31.30	17.41
Managers..........	13,146	4,628	17,421	7,404	42.87	24.83	34.69	20.71
West South Central...	1,509	835	4,798	2,568	27.83	14.83	22.32	8.83
Owners...........	2,148	1,152	5,407	2,668	22.54	11.69	20.96	9.53
Tenants...........	1,251	693	3,478	1,546	33.13	17.95	30.60	13.01
Managers..........	10,460	8,687	55,045	47,988	18.87	15.55	12.56	4.85

Average value of farm property on owned colored farms in the South Atlantic division increased during the decade from $553 in 1900 to $1,280 in 1910; in the East South Central division, from $778 to $1,570; and in the West South Central division, from $1,152 to $2,148. Average value of farm property on colored tenant farms increased in the South Atlantic division from $558 to $1,212; in the East South Central division, from $601 to $983; and in the West South Central division, from $693 to $1,251. The average property value of farms of colored managers more than doubled in the South Atlantic and East South Central divisions.

Per acre in farms, property values of colored owned and tenant farms in the South approximately doubled or more than doubled during the decade 1900–1910.

FARM ANIMALS BY TENURE OF FARM.

The number of dairy cows, work horses, and work mules, on colored and white farms of the South, classified by tenure, is given for southern divisions and states in Tables 63, 64, and 65 (pp. 620 to 622).

The number of colored and white farms reporting and not reporting domestic animals, horses, neat cattle, mules, hogs and pigs, sheep and lambs, asses and burros, goats and kids, poultry and bees, in 1910, with value reported for each class of live stock, is given, by tenure classes, for southern divisions and states, in Table 69 (pp. 628 to 637).

The number of dairy cows, work horses, and work mules on colored farms, classified by tenure, is given in Table 73 (pp. 698 to 764) for southern counties.

Table 36 gives for colored and white farmers of the South, classified by tenure, the number of dairy cows, work horses, and work mules reported in 1910, with the percentage distribution, by tenure, and the average number of animals of each class per 100 farms.

Table 36	NUMBER OF ANIMALS ON FARMS IN THE SOUTH: 1910.					
TENURE.	Colored.	White.	Percentage distribution by tenure.		Average per 100 farms. (All farms.)	
			Colored.	White.	Colored.	White.
DAIRY COWS.						
Total............	929,883	4,758,485	100.0	100.0	104	216
Owners, free.......	211,318	2,315,071	22.7	48.7	164	255
Owners, mortgaged.....	79,950	659,945	8.6	13.9	171	268
Part owners.........	62,962	417,127	6.8	8.8	146	243
Cash tenants [1]......	308,757	416,294	33.2	8.7	108	181
Share tenants [2]......	264,089	885,859	28.4	18.6	69	139
Managers...........	2,807	64,189	0.3	1.3	234	426
WORK HORSES.						
Total............	509,087	3,564,855	100.0	100.0	57	161
Owners, free.......	130,102	1,528,189	25.6	42.9	101	168
Owners, mortgaged.....	46,272	546,570	9.1	15.3	99	222
Part owners.........	41,715	368,390	8.2	10.3	97	214
Cash tenants [1]......	141,798	301,721	27.9	8.5	50	131
Share tenants [2]......	146,815	747,712	28.8	21.0	38	117
Managers...........	2,385	72,273	0.5	2.0	199	479
WORK MULES.						
Total............	645,320	2,188,166	100.0	100.0	72	99
Owners, free.......	82,998	855,973	12.9	39.1	65	94
Owners, mortgaged.....	44,446	296,726	6.9	13.6	95	121
Part owners.........	37,307	205,911	5.8	9.4	86	120
Cash tenants [1]......	246,934	216,728	38.3	9.9	86	94
Share tenants [2]......	231,263	547,085	35.8	25.0	60	86
Managers...........	2,372	65,743	0.4	3.0	198	436

[1] Includes not specified tenure.   [2] Includes share-cash tenants.

Per 100 farms, colored managers reported the largest number of dairy cows, work horses, and work mules in 1910, and share tenants reported the fewest animals of these classes. The number of dairy cows reported by colored owners free per 100 farms was 164, by colored owners mortgaged 171, and by colored part owners 146, the corresponding figures for these classes of white owners being 255, 268, and 243; the number of work horses reported by these classes was 101, 99, and 97 for colored owners, and 168, 222, and 214 for white owners; the number of work mules 65, 95, and 86 for colored owners, and 94, 121, and 120 for white owners.

Number of farms reporting these classes of animals with number of animals reported, and average number per 100 farms, is given in Table 37, by tenure classes for southern divisions.

COLORED FARMS REPORTING DAIRY COWS, WORK HORSES, AND WORK MULES, BY TENURE CLASSES FOR SOUTHERN DIVISIONS: 1910.

Table 37

DIVISION AND CLASS OF ANIMAL.	Total.	Owners, free.	Owners, mortgaged.	Part owners.	Cash[1] tenants.	Share[2] tenants.	Managers.
NUMBER OF FARMS REPORTING.							
The South:							
Dairy cows	512,242	91,048	35,951	31,102	180,459	172,996	686
Work horses	332,370	74,420	27,150	24,975	103,409	101,727	689
Work mules	436,398	48,219	25,100	21,472	168,599	172,411	597
South Atlantic:							
Dairy cows	189,758	39,010	10,911	13,040	64,340	62,067	390
Work horses	108,252	31,077	8,792	10,716	31,916	25,359	392
Work mules	166,050	16,066	6,881	8,110	65,076	69,603	314
East South Central:							
Dairy cows	203,679	23,395	14,905	10,158	93,414	61,640	167
Work horses	113,134	16,698	9,766	7,165	50,772	28,590	143
Work mules	170,094	14,396	11,076	7,380	83,083	54,007	152
West South Central:							
Dairy cows	118,805	28,643	10,135	7,904	22,705	49,289	129
Work horses	110,984	26,645	8,592	7,094	20,721	47,778	154
Work mules	100,254	17,757	7,143	5,982	20,440	48,801	131
NUMBER OF ANIMALS REPORTED.							
The South:							
Dairy cows	929,883	211,318	79,950	62,962	308,757	264,089	2,807
Work horses	509,087	130,102	46,272	41,715	141,798	146,815	2,385
Work mules	645,320	82,998	44,446	37,307	246,934	231,263	2,372
South Atlantic:							
Dairy cows	285,141	69,990	18,488	20,227	93,407	81,645	1,384
Work horses	140,394	41,792	12,177	14,483	38,026	32,891	1,025
Work mules	221,694	23,611	10,900	11,859	89,617	84,708	999
NUMBER OF ANIMALS REPORTED—continued.							
East South Central:							
Dairy cows	358,406	49,925	31,732	19,825	165,573	90,575	776
Work horses	158,346	25,960	14,933	11,213	69,390	36,264	586
Work mules	248,161	24,630	19,125	13,020	122,436	68,209	741
West South Central:							
Dairy cows	286,336	91,403	29,730	22,910	49,777	91,869	647
Work horses	210,347	62,350	19,162	16,019	34,382	77,660	774
Work mules	175,465	34,757	14,421	12,428	34,881	78,346	632
AVERAGE NUMBER OF ANIMALS PER 100 FARMS (ALL FARMS).							
The South:							
Dairy cows	104	164	171	146	108	69	234
Work horses	57	101	99	97	50	38	199
Work mules	72	65	95	86	86	60	198
South Atlantic:							
Dairy cows	80	110	107	96	83	58	192
Work horses	39	66	71	69	34	23	142
Work mules	62	37	63	56	79	61	139
East South Central:							
Dairy cows	110	173	182	160	123	69	312
Work horses	49	90	86	90	51	28	235
Work mules	76	85	110	105	91	52	298
West South Central:							
Dairy cows	137	254	246	236	132	81	280
Work horses	101	173	158	165	91	69	335
Work mules	84	97	119	128	92	69	274

[1] Includes not specified tenure. [2] Includes share-cash tenants.

Relatively to the number of farms in each tenure class, dairy cows, work horses, and work mules in 1910 were most numerous on farms of the West South Central division, the only exception being that more dairy cows per 100 farms were reported by colored managers in the East South Central division than in either of the other southern divisions.

Number of farms reporting and not reporting these classes of animals in 1910 is shown for Southern states, by tenure, in Table 38.

COLORED FARMS REPORTING AND NOT REPORTING DAIRY COWS, WORK HORSES, AND WORK MULES, BY TENURE CLASSES, BY SOUTHERN STATES: 1910.

Table 38 — FARMS OPERATED BY COLORED FARMERS: 1910.

DIVISION AND STATE.	Total. Reporting.	Total. Not reporting.	Owners. Reporting.	Owners. Not reporting.	Part owners. Reporting.	Part owners. Not reporting.	Cash tenants. Reporting.	Cash tenants. Not reporting.	Share tenants. Reporting.	Share tenants. Not reporting.	Managers. Reporting.	Managers. Not reporting.
DAIRY COWS.												
THE SOUTH.												
Total	512,242	377,899	126,999	48,291	31,102	12,075	180,459	105,491	172,996	211,528	686	514
South Atlantic	189,758	166,104	49,921	30,993	13,040	8,007	64,340	48,857	62,067	77,917	390	330
East South Central	203,679	121,539	38,300	8,020	10,158	2,259	93,414	41,599	61,640	69,579	167	82
West South Central	118,805	90,256	38,778	9,278	7,904	1,809	22,705	15,035	49,289	64,032	129	102
SOUTH ATLANTIC.												
Delaware	478	444	174	173	24	35	36	39	232	193	12	4
Maryland	3,218	3,154	1,510	1,791	275	374	276	339	1,089	631	68	19
District of Columbia	4	8	1	5	1	1	2	1	......	......	......	1
Virginia	29,282	18,832	17,274	9,546	3,713	1,695	2,110	2,308	6,076	5,212	109	71
West Virginia	552	156	396	91	60	11	38	25	54	26	4	3
North Carolina	30,674	34,982	8,276	6,546	3,617	3,004	5,805	5,804	12,936	19,594	40	34
South Carolina	50,930	45,868	9,838	6,239	2,740	1,555	21,511	19,119	16,778	18,887	63	68
Georgia	68,114	54,445	9,431	3,428	2,072	767	32,181	18,298	24,357	31,902	73	50
Florida	6,506	8,215	3,021	3,174	538	565	2,381	2,924	545	1,472	21	80
EAST SOUTH CENTRAL.												
Kentucky	7,013	4,717	3,134	1,332	1,007	456	361	241	2,483	2,676	28	12
Tennessee	26,015	12,293	6,083	1,657	2,413	547	9,032	2,769	8,453	7,303	34	17
Alabama	74,465	35,978	10,679	2,330	3,395	678	44,644	19,689	15,713	13,263	34	18
Mississippi	96,186	68,551	18,404	2,701	3,343	578	39,377	18,900	34,991	46,337	71	35
WEST SOUTH CENTRAL.												
Arkansas	35,939	27,654	10,100	1,760	2,347	455	12,495	7,308	10,968	18,114	29	17
Louisiana	28,581	26,298	7,808	1,791	880	246	5,415	4,158	14,439	20,065	39	38
Oklahoma	13,232	7,439	7,297	2,622	980	251	1,212	785	3,731	3,766	12	15
Texas	41,053	28,865	13,573	3,105	3,697	857	3,583	2,784	20,151	22,087	49	32

COLORED FARMS REPORTING AND NOT REPORTING DAIRY COWS, WORK HORSES, AND WORK MULES, BY
TENURE CLASSES, BY SOUTHERN STATES: 1910—Continued.

Table 38—Continued.

FARMS OPERATED BY COLORED FARMERS: 1910.

DIVISION AND STATE.	Total.		Owners.		Part owners.		Cash tenants.		Share tenants.		Managers.	
	Reporting	Not reporting.	Reporting.	Not reporting.	Reporting.	Not reporting.	Reporting.	Not reporting.	Reporting.	Not reporting.	Reporting.	Not reporting.
WORK HORSES.												
THE SOUTH. Total	332,370	557,771	101,570	73,720	24,975	18,202	103,409	182,541	101,727	282,797	689	511
South Atlantic	108,252	247,610	39,869	41,045	10,716	10,331	31,916	81,281	25,359	114,625	392	328
East South Central	113,134	212,084	26,464	19,856	7,165	5,252	50,772	84,241	28,590	102,629	143	106
West South Central	110,984	98,077	35,237	12,819	7,094	2,619	20,721	17,019	47,778	65,543	154	77
SOUTH ATLANTIC.												
Delaware	759	163	303	44	52	7	51	24	338	87	15	1
Maryland	4,715	1,657	2,332	969	562	87	419	196	1,324	396	78	9
District of Columbia	11	1	5	1	2		3				1	
Virginia	27,198	20,916	15,755	11,065	3,732	1,676	2,323	2,095	5,270	6,018	118	62
West Virginia	455	253	322	165	53	18	37	26	40	40	3	4
North Carolina	20,574	45,082	5,858	8,964	2,664	3,957	4,424	7,185	7,591	24,939	37	37
South Carolina	23,438	73,360	6,329	9,748	1,745	2,550	10,744	29,886	4,568	31,097	52	79
Georgia	23,618	98,941	5,190	7,669	1,174	1,665	11,599	38,880	5,605	50,654	50	73
Florida	7,484	7,237	3,775	2,420	732	371	2,316	2,989	623	1,394	38	63
EAST SOUTH CENTRAL.												
Kentucky	6,111	5,619	2,745	1,721	985	478	341	261	2,017	3,142	23	17
Tennessee	19,466	18,842	4,825	2,915	1,970	990	7,356	4,445	5,284	10,472	31	20
Alabama	28,453	81,990	5,506	7,503	1,852	2,221	17,130	47,203	3,942	25,034	23	29
Mississippi	59,104	105,633	13,388	7,717	2,358	1,563	25,945	32,332	17,347	63,981	66	40
WEST SOUTH CENTRAL.												
Arkansas	24,557	39,036	7,133	4,727	1,716	1,086	9,060	10,743	6,624	22,458	24	22
Louisiana	28,832	26,047	6,945	2,654	806	320	5,933	3,640	15,162	19,402	46	31
Oklahoma	16,224	4,447	8,743	1,176	1,092	139	1,526	471	4,843	2,654	20	7
Texas	41,371	28,547	12,416	4,262	3,480	1,074	4,202	2,165	21,209	21,029	64	17
WORK MULES.												
THE SOUTH. Total	436,398	453,743	73,319	101,971	21,472	21,705	168,599	117,351	172,411	212,113	597	603
South Atlantic	166,050	189,812	22,947	57,967	8,110	12,937	65,076	48,121	69,603	70,381	314	406
East South Central	170,094	155,124	25,472	20,848	7,380	5,037	83,083	51,930	54,007	77,212	152	97
West South Central	100,254	108,807	24,900	23,156	5,982	3,731	20,440	17,300	48,801	64,520	131	100
SOUTH ATLANTIC.												
Delaware	180	742	40	307	8	51	10	65	115	310	7	9
Maryland	626	5,746	202	3,099	58	591	60	555	273	1,447	33	54
District of Columbia	1	11		6		2	1	2			1	
Virginia	6,237	41,877	2,961	23,859	886	4,522	644	3,774	1,704	9,584	42	138
West Virginia	58	650	40	447	4	67	6	57	8	72		7
North Carolina	26,830	38,826	5,319	9,503	2,858	3,763	5,097	6,512	13,516	19,014	40	34
South Carolina	47,054	49,744	6,065	10,012	2,168	2,127	19,755	20,875	18,983	16,682	83	48
Georgia	81,213	41,346	7,060	5,799	1,837	1,002	37,837	12,642	34,392	21,867	87	36
Florida	3,851	10,870	1,260	4,935	291	812	1,666	3,639	612	1,405	22	79
EAST SOUTH CENTRAL.												
Kentucky	3,336	8,394	1,554	2,912	547	916	227	375	987	4,172	21	19
Tennessee	17,536	20,772	8,696	4,044	1,684	1,276	7,319	4,482	4,800	10,956	37	14
Alabama	62,443	48.000	7,393	5,616	2,627	1,446	37,580	26,753	14,815	14,161	28	24
Mississippi	86,779	77,958	12,829	8,276	2,522	1,399	37,957	20,320	33,405	47,923	66	40
WEST SOUTH CENTRAL.												
Arkansas	32,695	30,898	7,395	4,465	1,818	984	12,119	7,684	11,351	17,751	32	14
Louisiana	23,930	30,949	4,672	4,927	690	436	4,364	5,209	14,156	20,348	48	29
Oklahoma	7,684	12,987	3,409	6,510	567	664	864	1,133	2,835	4,662	9	18
Texas	35,945	33,973	9,424	7,254	2,907	1,647	3,098	3,274	20,479	21,750	42	39

In the South as a whole, 126,799 colored owners reported dairy cows and 48,291 owners did not report dairy cows, 101,570 owners reported and 73,720 did not report work horses, 73,319 owners reported and 101,971 did not report work mules.

Of colored cash tenants, 180,459 reported and 105,491 did not report dairy cows, and of share tenants 172,996 reported and 211,528 did not report this class of animals, the number of farms not reporting among share tenants exceeding the number reporting.

Among colored owners, part owners, and managers in the South, the number of farms reporting exceeded the number not reporting work horses. Among colored owners, part owners, share tenants, and managers, the number of farms not reporting exceeded the number reporting work mules, and among cash tenants, the number reporting exceeded the number not reporting mules.

Dairy cows were reported by a majority of colored farmers in each southern division and in each Southern state, excepting North Carolina and Florida; work horses were reported by a majority of colored farmers in Delaware, Maryland, Virginia, West Virginia, Florida, Kentucky, Tennessee, Louisiana, Oklahoma, and Texas. In Alabama 28,453 colored farmers reported and 81,990 did not report work horses, and in

Mississippi 59,104 reported and 105,633 did not report. A majority of the colored farms in these two states and in South Carolina, Arkansas, and Texas reported work mules.

CROPS BY TENURE OF FARM.

Acres in corn on colored and white farms of the South, classified by tenure, are given for the crop year 1909, by divisions and states, in Table 66 (p. 623), and acres in cotton, in Table 67 (p. 624), with percentage distribution of these acreages by tenure of farms. Acreage and yield of these two crops on colored farms, classified by tenure, are given, for southern counties, in Table 73 (pp. 698 to 764).

Acreages of corn and cotton in the South in 1909 on colored and white farms are distributed, by tenure, in Table 39, which gives also the percentage on colored farms of the total acreage reported by each tenure class.

Table 39 — ACRES IN CROP SPECIFIED ON FARMS IN THE SOUTH: 1909.

TENURE.	Total.	On colored farms.	On white farms.	Percentage distribution by tenure. Colored.	White.	Percentage on colored farms.
			CORN.			
Total.........	37,627,319	7,377,221	30,250,098	100.0	100.0	19.6
Owners, free........	12,942,116	1,197,845	11,744,271	16.2	38.8	9.3
Owners, mortgaged.	4,276,426	505,239	3,771,187	6.8	12.5	11.8
Part owners........	3,413,758	476,709	2,937,049	6.5	9.7	14.0
Cash tenants [1]......	5,417,421	2,314,540	3,102,881	31.4	10.3	42.7
Share tenants [2]......	11,094,179	2,861,607	8,232,572	38.8	27.2	25.8
Managers..........	483,419	21,281	462,138	0.3	1.5	4.4
			COTTON.			
Total.........	31,946,142	12,096,638	19,849,504	100.0	100.0	37.9
Owners, free........	6,541,507	1,019,469	5,522,038	8.4	27.8	15.6
Owners, mortgaged.	3,335,997	627,287	2,708,710	5.2	13.6	18.8
Part owners........	1,976,747	499,841	1,476,906	4.1	7.4	25.3
Cash tenants [1]......	7,216,231	4,829,018	2,387,213	39.9	12.0	66.9
Share tenants [2]......	12,586,510	5,104,042	7,482,468	42.2	37.7	40.6
Managers..........	289,150	16,981	272,169	0.1	1.4	5.7

[1] Includes not specified tenure.　　[2] Includes share-cash tenants.

Of the 7,377,221 acres in corn on colored farms of the South in 1909, 2,861,607, or 38.8 per cent, were on share tenant farms, and of the 12,096,638 acres in cotton, 5,104,042, or 42.2 per cent, were on share tenant farms. Somewhat smaller proportions of these acreages were on cash tenant farms. Tenants, cash and share combined, reported approximately two-thirds of the corn acreage and four-fifths of the cotton acreage. White tenants reported less than two-fifths of the corn and less than half of the cotton acreage on white farms in the South.

Of the corn acreage reported by each tenure class, the percentage on colored farms ranged from 4.4 for managed farms to 42.7 for cash tenant farms, and of the cotton acreage, from 5.7 for managed farms to 66.9 for cash tenant farms.

The number of farms reporting corn, average acres in corn per farm reporting, and average yield in bushels per acre planted are given, by tenure of farm, for southern divisions and states, in Table 40, and number of farms reporting cotton, with average acreage and yield per farm reporting cotton, in Table 41.

Oklahoma reported in 1909 the largest average acreage in corn (23.6 acres) for colored farms, and South Carolina the smallest (7.7 acres). Texas reported the largest average acreage in cotton (23.1 acres), the average for Georgia being only slightly less (22.8 acres). Of the states from which cotton was reported on colored farms, Virginia reported the smallest average acreage per farm (4.3 acres).

Among colored owners free, average acreages in corn ranged from 5.2 acres in Delaware to 24.5 acres in Oklahoma; among owners mortgaged, from 6.5 for Maryland to 27.9 for Oklahoma; among part owners, from 8.7 in South Carolina to 34 in Oklahoma; among cash tenants, from 7.2 in Arkansas to 19.8 in Oklahoma; among share tenants, from 6.7 in Arkansas to 32.1 in West Virginia; and among managers, from 8.5 in Texas to 44.1 acres in Louisiana.

Average yield per acre planted was generally larger on managed farms than on farms of any other tenure, ranging from 11.6 bushels in Oklahoma to 41.6 bushels in Maryland. On farms owned free, yield of corn per acre ranged from 10.3 bushels in Alabama to 24 bushels in West Virginia; on cash tenant farms, from 9.3 bushels in Georgia to 25.3 bushels in Kentucky; on share tenant farms, from 10.7 bushels in Alabama to 25.8 bushels in Kentucky.

Table 40 — COLORED FARMERS REPORTING CORN: 1909.

DIVISION AND STATE.	Total.	Owners, free.	Owners, mortgaged.	Part owners.	Cash and not specified tenants.	Share and share-cash tenants.	Managers.
THE SOUTH.			NUMBER OF FARMS.				
Total.............	744,458	115,067	43,191	39,658	247,067	298,724	1,017
South Atlantic..........	311,725	57,602	15,852	19,757	101,168	116,775	571
East South Central......	265,078	25,673	16,128	11,169	115,003	96,925	180
West South Central.....	167,655	31,792	11,211	8,732	30,896	84,748	276
SOUTH ATLANTIC.							
Delaware............	836	172	139	55	59	396	15
Maryland............	5,269	1,705	909	580	480	1,530	65
District of Columbia.....	1					1	
Virginia............	43,401	19,800	4,217	5,208	3,940	10,072	164
West Virginia..........	500	306	62	44	53	30	5
North Carolina........	57,911	10,118	3,490	6,139	10,318	27,772	74
South Carolina........	84,744	11,912	3,130	4,107	35,741	29,737	117
Georgia............	106,426	9,049	2,974	2,923	45,940	45,742	105
Florida............	12,637	4,540	931	1,007	4,637	1,496	26
EAST SOUTH CENTRAL.							
Kentucky............	8,184	2,707	793	1,118	428	3,104	34
Tennessee............	32,779	5,026	1,714	2,681	10,743	12,578	37
Alabama............	93,839	7,277	4,681	3,742	54,271	23,833	35
Mississippi............	130,276	10,663	8,940	3,628	49,561	57,410	74
WEST SOUTH CENTRAL.							
Arkansas............	48,120	7,034	3,545	2,503	16,016	18,983	39
Louisiana............	45,790	6,790	2,380	957	8,119	27,493	51
Oklahoma............	15,643	6,050	1,913	1,091	1,488	5,087	14
Texas............	58,102	11,918	3,373	4,181	5,273	33,185	172

Table 40—Contd. — COLORED FARMERS REPORTING CORN: 1909.

AVERAGE ACRES IN CORN PER FARM REPORTING CORN.

DIVISION AND STATE.	Total.	Owners, free.	Owners, mortgaged.	Part owners.	Cash and not specified tenants.	Share and share-cash tenants.	Managers.
THE SOUTH.							
Total	9.9	10.4	11.7	12.0	9.4	9.6	20.9
South Atlantic	9.8	8.2	10.2	10.5	10.6	9.8	20.3
East South Central	8.7	10.0	10.8	11.4	8.3	8.1	27.4
West South Central	11.9	14.6	15.2	16.3	9.3	11.0	17.9
SOUTH ATLANTIC.							
Delaware	15.1	8.9	8.9	13.6	12.8	20.1	28.6
Maryland	9.9	5.2	6.5	9.4	9.6	16.9	20.3
District of Columbia	2.0			2.0			
Virginia	7.8	6.5	7.4	10.3	7.9	9.0	14.9
West Virginia	8.8	6.7	7.8	11.1	7.3	32.1	9.6
North Carolina	9.2	8.1	9.2	9.9	9.1	9.5	19.4
South Carolina	7.7	7.0	9.9	8.7	7.7	7.6	16.5
Georgia	12.0	12.1	14.7	13.0	12.8	11.0	27.3
Florida	15.1	12.8	16.5	15.5	16.7	16.0	43.4
EAST SOUTH CENTRAL.							
Kentucky	12.7	10.1	11.8	14.7	16.1	13.9	23.5
Tennessee	10.8	10.0	11.6	13.1	10.3	10.9	35.9
Alabama	8.7	9.8	10.8	10.6	8.2	8.8	28.6
Mississippi	7.9	10.2	10.5	10.0	8.0	6.9	24.3
WEST SOUTH CENTRAL.							
Arkansas	8.0	10.8	11.1	11.2	7.2	6.7	16.6
Louisiana	11.0	12.1	12.5	17.6	9.8	10.7	44.1
Oklahoma	23.6	24.5	27.9	34.0	19.8	19.9	41.9
Texas	12.7	13.4	14.3	14.5	11.5	12.3	8.5

AVERAGE YIELD IN BUSHELS PER ACRE PLANTED.

DIVISION AND STATE.	Total.	Owners, free.	Owners, mortgaged.	Part owners.	Cash and not specified tenants.	Share and share-cash tenants.	Managers.
THE SOUTH.							
Total	12.9	13.2	12.2	13.5	11.5	13.7	20.2
South Atlantic	11.2	12.5	11.1	11.8	9.9	11.8	20.0
East South Central	13.0	13.1	11.4	15.0	12.0	14.2	19.7
West South Central	15.2	14.0	13.9	14.7	16.5	15.7	21.1
SOUTH ATLANTIC.							
Delaware	20.0	21.1	18.7	19.5	20.6	19.5	28.6
Maryland	18.9	18.2	18.1	18.7	20.0	18.0	41.6
District of Columbia	25.0			25.0			
Virginia	14.7	14.6	13.7	14.1	13.2	15.8	19.3
West Virginia	23.9	24.0	24.8	26.7	23.1	22.2	25.3
North Carolina	11.0	10.7	10.1	10.8	9.6	11.7	21.4
South Carolina	11.2	12.7	10.3	11.2	10.3	11.8	17.3
Georgia	10.1	10.9	9.5	10.1	9.3	10.8	13.0
Florida	10.8	11.7	10.0	10.2	10.3	11.0	13.7
EAST SOUTH CENTRAL.							
Kentucky	23.5	19.4	19.9	24.9	25.3	25.8	31.7
Tennessee	17.8	17.2	16.6	19.4	14.8	20.2	24.7
Alabama	10.5	10.3	9.3	10.6	10.5	10.7	14.3
Mississippi	12.3	11.6	10.6	11.1	12.6	12.7	13.9
WEST SOUTH CENTRAL.							
Arkansas	15.8	13.6	12.3	14.0	18.1	16.5	17.8
Louisiana	14.7	12.7	13.7	14.6	14.6	15.4	15.3
Oklahoma	16.1	16.1	15.9	15.9	17.2	15.9	11.6
Texas	14.8	12.8	13.3	14.3	15.5	15.6	35.1

Table 41 — COLORED FARMERS REPORTING COTTON: 1909.

NUMBER OF FARMS.

DIVISION AND STATE.	Total.	Owners, free.	Owners, mortgaged.	Part owners.	Cash and not specified tenants.	Share and share-cash tenants.	Managers.
THE SOUTH.							
Total	684,721	73,666	34,541	28,786	251,866	295,356	506
South Atlantic	253,286	27,943	9,608	11,841	98,179	105,472	243
East South Central	266,450	19,196	14,813	8,973	122,406	100,919	143
West South Central	164,985	26,527	10,120	7,972	31,281	88,965	120
SOUTH ATLANTIC.							
Delaware							
Maryland							
District of Columbia							
Virginia	3,102	724	359	246	881	940	2
West Virginia							
North Carolina	44,256	5,931	2,478	4,312	9,655	21,849	31
South Carolina	88,904	11,577	3,125	4,104	37,302	32,689	107
Georgia	108,115	7,296	2,919	2,538	46,531	48,741	90
Florida	8,909	2,415	727	641	3,860	1,253	13
EAST SOUTH CENTRAL.							
Kentucky	155	1	1	2	34	117	
Tennessee	24,740	2,061	1,016	1,392	10,667	9,596	8
Alabama	100,506	6,946	4,730	3,840	59,599	25,364	27
Mississippi	141,049	10,188	9,066	3,739	52,106	65,842	108
WEST SOUTH CENTRAL.							
Arkansas	54,296	6,939	3,641	2,435	17,821	23,425	35
Louisiana	40,607	5,515	1,907	744	6,956	25,455	30
Oklahoma	11,270	3,047	1,240	647	1,326	4,999	11
Texas	58,812	11,026	3,332	4,146	5,178	35,086	44

AVERAGE ACRES IN COTTON PER FARM REPORTING COTTON.

DIVISION AND STATE.	Total.	Owners, free.	Owners, mortgaged.	Part owners.	Cash and not specified tenants.	Share and share-cash tenants.	Managers.
THE SOUTH.							
Total	17.7	13.8	18.2	17.4	19.2	17.3	33.6
South Atlantic	17.5	11.3	16.5	13.6	19.3	18.0	26.0
East South Central	17.3	14.9	17.9	18.2	19.2	15.3	46.9
West South Central	18.4	15.8	20.1	22.0	18.6	18.6	32.9
SOUTH ATLANTIC.							
Delaware							
Maryland							
District of Columbia							
Virginia	4.3	4.0	4.3	3.9	4.6	4.4	19.0
West Virginia							
North Carolina	10.7	7.3	8.8	8.6	11.5	12.0	5.6
South Carolina	15.3	9.6	17.7	14.6	15.2	17.4	26.2
Georgia	22.8	18.2	24.0	21.6	24.9	21.5	34.9
Florida	13.7	10.3	14.0	12.7	15.1	16.2	12.9
EAST SOUTH CENTRAL.							
Kentucky	18.9	5.0	18.0	9.0	22.2	18.3	
Tennessee	15.7	12.8	16.5	14.6	17.9	13.8	23.0
Alabama	19.5	15.9	20.1	20.1	20.3	18.5	15.6
Mississippi	16.0	14.7	16.9	17.7	18.2	14.3	56.5
WEST SOUTH CENTRAL.							
Arkansas	17.5	15.3	17.9	19.1	19.7	16.2	27.0
Louisiana	12.7	12.3	14.0	15.0	13.3	12.4	34.9
Oklahoma	19.3	14.2	19.9	21.4	22.5	21.1	15.5
Texas	23.1	18.2	25.9	25.1	20.8	24.4	40.5

AVERAGE YIELD IN BALES PER FARM REPORTING COTTON.

DIVISION AND STATE.	Total.	Owners, free.	Owners, mortgaged.	Part owners.	Cash and not specified tenants.	Share and share-cash tenants.	Managers.
THE SOUTH.							
Total	5.9	4.4	5.3	5.5	6.2	6.2	12.5
South Atlantic	7.1	4.7	6.3	5.6	7.2	7.9	15.1
East South Central	5.1	4.4	4.9	5.1	5.4	4.9	10.0
West South Central	5.5	4.2	5.0	5.7	6.5	5.5	10.5
SOUTH ATLANTIC.							
Delaware							
Maryland							
District of Columbia							
Virginia	1.6	1.6	1.6	1.4	1.6	1.7	4.5
West Virginia							
North Carolina	5.3	3.5	3.7	3.8	5.2	6.2	15.4
South Carolina	6.9	4.5	7.3	6.5	6.2	8.5	15.1
Georgia	8.6	7.1	8.7	8.1	8.8	8.5	17.0
Florida	3.2	2.5	2.8	3.0	3.5	3.8	2.0
EAST SOUTH CENTRAL.							
Kentucky	9.5	1.0	6.0	3.0	10.6	9.5	
Tennessee	4.7	3.8	4.8	4.6	5.3	4.3	4.9
Alabama	5.1	4.5	5.3	5.4	5.0	5.4	26.1
Mississippi	5.2	4.5	4.8	5.1	5.8	4.8	6.3
WEST SOUTH CENTRAL.							
Arkansas	6.4	4.7	5.0	5.9	7.9	6.1	9.5
Louisiana	3.5	2.9	3.1	3.2	3.8	3.6	11.6
Oklahoma	6.3	4.4	5.5	6.5	7.7	7.2	6.3
Texas	5.8	4.4	6.0	5.9	5.1	6.3	11.5

Average acreage in cotton per farm in states reporting cotton on colored farms was lowest in Virginia for each tenure class, except managers. It was highest for owners free in Georgia and Texas (18.2 acres); highest for owners mortgaged, part owners, share tenants, and managers in Texas (the averages being 25.9, 25.1, 24.4, and 40.5 acres, respectively); and highest for cash tenants in Oklahoma (22.5 acres).

Average yield in bales per farm reporting cotton was lowest in Virginia which, as noted above, reported the smallest average acreage in cotton for colored farms reporting cotton. Average yield per farm was highest for colored owners free in Arkansas (4.7 bales); for owners mortgaged and for part owners in Georgia (8.7 and 8.1 bales, respectively); for cash and for share tenants in Kentucky (10.6 and 9.5 bales, respectively); and for managers in Alabama (26.1 bales).

TERM OF OCCUPANCY AND TENURE OF FARMS.

Term of occupancy and tenure of farms is shown for colored farms in all divisions and states in Table 70 (pp. 638 to 641).

Summary totals for colored and white farms in the South are given in Table 42, with the percentage distribution of farms in each tenure class, by term of occupancy.

Table 42 SECTION AND TERM OF OCCUPANCY.	FARM OPERATORS IN THE SOUTH: 1910.						
	Total.	Owners, free.	Owners, mortgaged.	Part owners.	Cash tenants.	Share tenants.	Managers.
	NUMBER.						
COLORED.							
Total..........	890,141	128,557	46,733	43,177	285,950	384,524	1,200
Less than 1 year......	189,324	2,808	1,928	3,510	50,621	130,250	207
1 year...............	103,714	3,424	2,314	3,188	35,049	59,616	123
2 to 4 years..........	237,107	16,821	8,904	9,804	92,767	108,477	334
5 to 9 years..........	127,586	22,770	9,639	8,988	48,560	37,403	226
10 years and over.....	156,553	59,541	16,427	14,653	41,287	24,446	199
Not specified.........	75,857	23,193	7,521	3,034	17,666	24,332	111
WHITE.							
Total..........	2,207,406	908,211	245,889	171,944	229,461	636,817	15,084
Less than 1 year......	434,268	36,844	26,506	21,427	75,208	270,983	3,300
1 year...............	229,434	38,898	22,845	17,323	38,099	110,267	2,002
2 to 4 years..........	474,524	144,203	60,568	44,182	64,783	156,637	4,151
5 to 9 years..........	312,140	160,407	45,782	34,664	23,707	45,382	2,198
10 years and over.....	547,464	404,105	58,792	44,388	14,353	23,767	2,059
Not specified.........	209,576	123,754	31,396	9,960	13,311	29,781	1,374
	PERCENTAGE DISTRIBUTION BY TERM OF OCCUPANCY.						
COLORED.							
Total..........	100.0	100.0	100.0	100.0	100.0	100.0	100.0
Less than 1 year......	21.3	2.2	4.1	8.1	17.7	33.9	17.3
1 year...............	11.7	2.7	5.0	7.4	12.3	15.5	10.3
2 to 4 years..........	26.6	13.1	19.1	22.7	32.4	28.2	27.8
5 to 9 years..........	14.3	17.7	20.6	20.8	17.0	9.7	18.8
10 years and over.....	17.6	46.3	35.2	33.9	14.4	6.4	16.6
Not specified.........	8.5	18.0	16.1	7.0	6.2	6.3	9.3
WHITE.							
Total..........	100.0	100.0	100.0	100.0	100.0	100.0	100.0
Less than 1 year......	19.7	4.1	10.8	12.5	32.8	42.6	21.9
1 year...............	10.4	4.3	9.3	10.1	16.6	17.3	13.3
2 to 4 years..........	21.5	15.9	24.6	25.7	28.2	24.6	27.5
5 to 9 years..........	14.1	17.7	18.6	20.2	10.3	7.1	14.6
10 years and over.....	24.8	44.5	23.9	25.8	6.3	3.7	13.7
Not specified.........	9.5	13.6	12.8	5.8	5.8	4.7	9.1

Of the 128,557 colored owners in the South, only 2,808, or 2.2 per cent, reported occupancy of less than 1 year. The percentage reporting less than 1 year of occupancy among mortgaged owners was 4.1; among part owners, 8.1; among cash tenants, 17.7; among share tenants, 33.9; and among managers, 17.3. Of colored share tenants, 15.5 per cent reported occupancy of 1 year and 28.2, occupancy of 2 to 4 years. Thus less than one-sixth of the colored share tenants were operating farms in 1910, which they had occupied for a period of 5 years or more.

Of colored owners free, 17.7 per cent reported occupancy of 5 to 9 years and 46.3 per cent, occupancy of 10 years and over. The corresponding proportions for owners mortgaged were 20.6 and 35.2 per cent, and for part owners, 20.8 and 33.9 per cent.

Approximately one-third of the cash tenants reported occupancy of 2 to 4 years, the proportion reporting shorter terms of occupancy being greater than the corresponding proportion for owners and less than the corresponding proportion for tenants and managers.

It appears from these figures that occupancy among colored farmers is much less permanent among share tenants than it is among cash tenants or owners, and this is true also of white farm operators in the South. Of white share tenants, 42.6 per cent reported occupancy of less than 1 year, the proportion reporting this short term of occupancy being greater for white than for colored share tenants. Occupancy of 1 year was reported by 17.3 per cent of white share tenants and occupancy of 2 to 4 years, by 24.6 per cent, the proportion reporting occupancy of 5 years or more being approximately one-tenth. Of white owners free, 17.7 per cent reported occupancy of 5 to 9 years and 44.5 per cent, occupancy of 10 years and over. In general occupancy was somewhat less permanent among white operators, of both owner and tenant classes, than among colored operators, the proportion of operators in each tenure class reporting short-term occupancy being greater and the proportion reporting long-term occupancy, smaller among white than among colored operators. Owing to the larger proportion of tenants among colored operators, however, the proportion of colored operators as a whole reporting short-term occupancy was greater and the proportion reporting occupancy of 10 years and over was less than among white operators.

Table 43 gives, for the three southern divisions, the percentage distribution of each tenure class of colored farmers, by term of occupancy, and the percentage distribution, by tenure of operators, reporting each term of occupancy.

Among colored share tenants the proportion reporting occupancy of less than 1 year was 32 per cent in the South Atlantic division, 37.2 per cent in the East South Central division, and 32.3 per cent in the West South Central division. Such tenants constituted 66.7 per cent, or two-thirds, of all colored operators reporting occupancy of less than 1 year in the South Atlantic division, 64.7 per cent of those reporting less than 1 year in the East South Central division, and 78.5 per cent of those reporting less than 1 year in the West South Central division. In each division the proportion of share tenants among colored farm operators, classified by term of occupancy, declines as term of occupancy lengthens. In the South Atlantic division the decline is from 66.7 per cent among operators reporting less than 1 year to 12.4 per cent among operators reporting 10 years and over. The corresponding decline in the East South Central division is from 64.7 to 14.9 per cent, and in the West South Central division, from 78.5 to 23 per cent.

The proportion of owners free, owners mortgaged, and part owners in each southern division increases with term of occupancy, for owners free, for example, in the South Atlantic division from 1.8 among operators reporting less than 1 year to 47.8 among those reporting 10 years and over; in the East South Central division, from 2.1 to 47 per cent; and in the West South Central division, from 2.9 to 43.1 per cent.

PERCENTAGE DISTRIBUTION OF COLORED FARMERS BY TERM OF OCCUPANCY AND TENURE, BY SOUTHERN DIVISIONS: 1910.

Table 43 — COLORED FARMERS: 1910.

DIVISION AND TERM OF OCCUPANCY.	Percentage distribution by term of occupancy.							Percentage distribution by tenure.						
	Total.	Owners, free.	Owners, mortgaged.	Part owners.	Cash tenants.	Share tenants.	Managers.	Total.	Owners, free.	Owners, mortgaged.	Part owners.	Cash tenants.	Share tenants.	Managers.
SOUTH ATLANTIC.														
Total	100.0	100.0	100.0	100.0	100.0	100.0	100.0	100.0	17.9	4.8	5.9	31.8	39.3	0.2
Less than 1 year	18.9	1.8	4.0	7.0	16.8	32.0	14.6	100.0	1.7	1.0	2.2	28.2	66.7	0.2
1 year	11.6	2.4	5.1	6.9	12.8	16.4	9.6	100.0	3.8	2.1	3.5	35.0	55.4	0.2
2 to 4 years	26.9	13.3	19.2	22.2	33.1	29.7	30.4	100.0	8.9	3.4	4.9	39.1	43.5	0.2
5 to 9 years	14.7	17.3	19.2	20.1	17.3	10.0	21.2	100.0	21.1	6.3	8.1	37.6	26.7	0.3
10 years and over	19.7	47.8	36.8	36.8	14.9	6.2	15.7	100.0	43.4	9.0	11.0	24.0	12.4	0.2
Not reported	8.1	17.3	15.8	6.9	5.1	5.6	8.5	100.0	38.1	9.4	5.1	19.9	27.3	0.2
EAST SOUTH CENTRAL.														
Total	100.0	100.0	100.0	100.0	100.0	100.0	100.0	100.0	8.9	5.3	3.8	41.5	40.3	0.1
Less than 1 year	23.2	2.1	4.0	8.8	17.9	37.2	18.1	100.0	0.8	0.9	1.4	32.0	64.7	0.1
1 year	11.6	2.9	4.6	7.2	11.6	14.8	11.2	100.0	2.2	2.1	2.4	41.7	51.6	0.1
2 to 4 years	27.2	13.8	19.4	24.1	32.4	26.2	28.1	100.0	4.5	3.9	3.4	49.3	38.9	0.1
5 to 9 years	14.4	18.5	21.4	21.6	17.2	9.1	12.1	100.0	11.4	7.9	5.7	49.5	25.5	0.1
10 years and over	15.8	47.0	35.7	32.0	14.6	5.8	20.1	100.0	26.5	12.1	7.8	38.5	14.9	0.1
Not reported	7.8	15.7	14.9	6.3	6.3	6.8	10.4	100.0	17.8	10.2	3.1	33.5	35.3	0.1
WEST SOUTH CENTRAL.														
Total	100.0	100.0	100.0	100.0	100.0	100.0	100.0	100.0	17.2	5.8	4.6	18.0	54.2	0.1
Less than 1 year	22.3	2.9	4.5	9.8	19.7	32.3	24.7	100.0	2.2	1.2	2.0	16.0	78.5	0.1
1 year	11.8	2.9	5.4	8.6	12.8	15.2	11.3	100.0	4.2	2.6	3.4	19.7	70.0	0.1
2 to 4 years	25.3	12.1	18.4	21.9	30.9	28.6	19.5	100.0	8.2	4.2	4.0	22.0	61.4	0.1
5 to 9 years	13.6	17.8	21.6	21.5	15.2	10.2	18.6	100.0	22.6	9.2	7.4	20.1	40.6	0.1
10 years and over	16.8	43.1	31.9	30.0	12.5	7.1	15.6	100.0	44.1	11.0	8.3	13.5	23.0	0.1
Not reported	10.3	21.2	18.2	8.1	8.9	6.6	10.4	100.0	35.5	10.3	3.7	15.7	34.8	0.1

In each division the proportion of cash tenants is highest among operators reporting terms of occupancy of 2 to 4 or 5 to 9 years, declining among operators reporting 10 years and over. The decline in the proportion of tenants, cash and share, among long-term occupiers may result from the advance of tenants into the class of owners.

It should be remarked that the term of occupancy reported by an operator does not necessarily apply to his tenure. An owner reporting occupancy of 10 years, for example, may have been during 9 years, or during any portion of his occupancy, a cash or share tenant or a manager of the farm he was operating as an owner at the time of the census enumeration. In such a case the entire period of occupancy, whether as tenant, manager, or owner, is credited to the operator classified as an owner.

MORTGAGE INDEBTEDNESS OF OWNED FARMS.

The mortgage indebtedness of farms wholly owned by colored operators in 1910 is given in Table 44, for southern divisions and states.

Of the 218,467 farms of colored owners in the South, 152,426, or 69.8 per cent, were owned free of mortgage debt, 59,662 were mortgaged, and for 6,379, or 2.9 per cent, no report regarding mortgage indebtedness was made.

Data regarding amount of mortgage debt of partly owned farms have not been compiled. The number of mortgaged colored farms, consisting of owned land only, numbered 41,432 in 1910. The aggregate value of land and buildings upon those farms was $59,865,633 and the aggregate amount of mortgage debt, $16,953,463, or 28.3 per cent of the realty value of the farms.

Of all farms owned by colored operators in 1910, the percentage mortgaged ranged, by states, from 14 in West Virginia to 45.5 in Mississippi. For mortgaged farms wholly owned by colored operators the proportion of mortgage debt to realty value of the farm ranged, by states, from 20.2 per cent in Oklahoma to 33.8 per cent in Alabama.

MORTGAGE INDEBTEDNESS OF COLORED OWNERS, BY SOUTHERN STATES: 1910.

Table 44

FARMS OPERATED BY COLORED OWNERS: 1910.

DIVISION AND STATE.	Number.				Percentage.				Mortgaged farms consisting of owned land only.		Mortgage debt.	
	Total.	Owners, free.	Owners, mortgaged.	No report.	Total.	Owners, free.	Owners, mortgaged.	No report.	Number.	Value of land and buildings.	Amount.	Per cent of value of land and buildings.
THE SOUTH.												
Total..........	218,467	152,426	59,662	6,379	100.0	69.8	27.3	2.9	41,432	$59,865,633	$16,953,463	28.3
South Atlantic..........	101,961	77,064	22,533	2,364	100.0	75.6	22.1	2.3	15,582	20,583,811	5,577,004	27.1
East South Central..........	58,737	35,023	21,942	1,772	100.0	59.6	37.4	3.0	15,268	19,904,163	6,391,842	32.3
West South Central..........	57,769	40,339	15,187	2,243	100.0	69.8	26.3	3.9	10,582	19,477,659	4,984,617	25.6
SOUTH ATLANTIC.												
Delaware..........	406	231	171	4	100.0	56.9	42.1	1.0	137	197,500	62,794	31.8
Maryland..........	3,950	2,582	1,334	34	100.0	65.4	33.8	0.8	1,056	1,202,584	358,490	29.8
District of Columbia..........	8	4	3	1	100.0	50.0	37.5	12.5	3	12,000	4,600	38.3
Virginia..........	32,228	26,200	5,609	419	100.0	81.3	17.4	1.3	4,304	4,386,949	1,037,658	23.7
West Virginia..........	558	479	78	1	100.0	85.8	14.0	0.2	67	126,609	31,210	24.7
North Carolina..........	21,443	15,433	5,609	401	100.0	72.0	26.1	1.9	3,464	4,435,616	1,134,853	25.6
South Carolina..........	20,372	15,268	4,386	718	100.0	75.0	21.5	3.5	2,842	4,870,642	1,333,696	27.4
Georgia..........	15,698	11,025	4,059	614	100.0	70.2	25.9	3.9	2,739	4,298,361	1,376,654	32.0
Florida..........	7,298	5,842	1,284	172	100.0	80.0	17.6	2.4	970	1,053,550	237,049	22.5
EAST SOUTH CENTRAL.												
Kentucky..........	5,929	4,488	1,319	122	100.0	75.7	22.2	2.1	906	1,153,510	320,579	27.8
Tennessee..........	10,700	7,781	2,687	232	100.0	72.7	25.1	2.2	1,742	2,080,982	691,155	33.2
Alabama..........	17,082	9,951	6,551	580	100.0	58.3	38.3	3.4	4,293	4,778,354	1,612,895	33.8
Mississippi..........	25,026	12,803	11,385	838	100.0	51.2	45.5	3.3	8,327	11,791,317	3,767,213	31.9
WEST SOUTH CENTRAL.												
Arkansas..........	14,662	9,111	4,913	638	100.0	62.1	33.5	4.4	3,521	5,308,624	1,408,613	26.5
Louisiana..........	10,725	7,736	2,637	352	100.0	72.1	24.6	3.3	1,971	2,631,991	784,216	29.8
Oklahoma..........	11,150	7,806	2,633	711	100.0	70.0	23.6	6.4	1,900	5,986,167	1,209,079	20.2
Texas..........	21,232	15,686	5,004	542	100.0	73.9	23.6	2.5	3,190	5,550,877	1,582,709	28.5

STATISTICS BY TENURE FOR SOUTHERN COUNTIES.

Table 73 (pp. 698 to 764) gives, for southern counties reporting 100 or more colored farmers in 1910, general statistics for colored farms, classified by tenure. The table includes, also, as has been noted, a classification of colored farms, by size, without distinction of tenure for the size classes.

By a combination of the data shown in this table, averages per farm and per acre, corresponding to those shown for states in the preceding sections of this chapter, may be obtained for counties, in detail of tenure for colored owners free, owners mortgaged, part owners, cash tenants, and share tenants.

For each of these tenure classes is given, by counties, the number of farms; total acreage; acreage improved; value of land, of buildings, and of implements and machinery; number of dairy cows, of work horses, and of work mules; and acreage and yield of cotton, and of corn in 1909. For part owners, owned acreage is shown separately from total acreage, owned improved acreage, separately from total improved acreage, and value of land and buildings owned, separately from total values of land and of buildings. Total and improved farm acreage, and acreage and yield of cotton

and of corn in 1909 are given, with other totals, in Table 72 (pp. 674 to 697) for colored and white farms.

From these figures for any given county the following percentages and averages relating to colored farms may be obtained: The percentage distribution of farms, and of the acreages, values, animals, and crop acreages and yields noted above, by tenure, and for each of the tenure classes specified—average acreage per farm; average acreage improved per farm; percentage of farm land improved; average value of land, of buildings, and of implements and machinery per farm, and per acre, of total and of improved land in farms; average number of dairy cows, of work horses, and of work mules per farm; average acreage in cotton and in corn, per farm; average yield of these crops per farm and per acre planted; percentage of total and of improved farm acreage in these crops. For partly owned farms the percentage owned of total and of improved acreage and of the combined value of land and buildings may be obtained.

Table 73 thus gives, by counties, for colored farms— in addition to the classification of farms by size—70 independent items carrying the distinction of tenure, from which approximately 175 derived averages and percentages, such as have been specified, may be obtained for each southern county shown.

TABLE 45.—NUMBER OF COLORED, NEGRO, AND WHITE FARM OPERATORS, BY DIVISIONS AND STATES: 1910 AND 1900.

DIVISION AND STATE.	FARM OPERATORS.												NEGRO FARM OPERATORS.		
	1910					1900					Increase:[1] 1900–1910.		Per 1,000 Negro population.		Per 1,000 colored operators: 1910.
	Total.	Colored.			White.	Total.	Colored.			White.	Negro.	White.	1910	1900	
		Total.	Negro.	Other.			Total.	Negro.	Other.						
UNITED STATES	6,361,502	920,883	893,370	27,513	5,440,619	5,737,372	767,764	746,715	21,049	4,969,608	146,655	471,011	91	76	970
GEOGRAPHIC DIVISIONS.															
New England	188,802	342	310	32	188,460	191,888	294	264	30	191,594	46	−3,134	5	4	906
Middle Atlantic	468,379	1,961	1,310	651	466,418	485,618	1,846	1,497	349	483,772	−187	−17,354	3	5	668
East North Central	1,123,489	5,717	4,843	874	1,117,772	1,135,823	6,013	5,179	834	1,129,810	−336	−12,038	16	20	847
West North Central	1,109,948	9,864	5,589	4,275	1,100,084	1,060,744	10,887	7,076	3,811	1,049,857	−1,487	50,227	23	30	567
South Atlantic	1,111,881	355,862	354,530	1,332	756,019	962,225	288,871	287,933	938	673,354	66,597	82,665	86	77	996
East South Central	1,042,480	325,218	324,884	334	717,262	903,313	267,895	267,530	365	635,418	57,354	81,844	122	107	996
West South Central	943,186	209,061	201,422	7,639	734,125	754,853	183,904	176,899	7,005	570,949	24,523	163,176	102	104	963
Mountain	183,446	8,028	219	7,809	175,418	101,327	4,806	133	4,673	96,521	86	78,897	10	9	27
Pacific	189,891	4,830	263	4,567	185,061	141,581	3,248	204	3,044	138,333	59	46,728	9	14	54
NEW ENGLAND:															
Maine	60,016	29	28	1	59,987	59,299	29	24	5	59,270	4	717	20	18	966
New Hampshire	27,053	15	14	1	27,038	29,324	10	10	......	29,314	4	−2,276	25	15	933
Vermont	32,709	20	20	......	32,689	33,104	8	8	......	33,096	12	−407	12	10	1,000
Massachusetts	36,917	124	103	21	36,793	37,715	110	87	23	37,605	16	−812	3	3	831
Rhode Island	5,292	41	40	1	5,251	5,498	28	28	......	5,470	12	−219	4	3	976
Connecticut	26,815	113	105	8	26,702	26,948	109	107	2	26,839	−2	−137	7	7	929
MIDDLE ATLANTIC:															
New York	215,597	939	295	644	214,658	226,720	785	443	342	225,935	−148	−11,277	2	4	314
New Jersey	33,487	476	472	4	33,011	34,650	470	469	1	34,180	3	−1,169	5	7	992
Pennsylvania	219,295	546	543	3	218,749	224,248	591	585	6	223,657	−42	−4,908	3	4	995
EAST NORTH CENTRAL:															
Ohio	272,045	1,950	1,948	2	270,095	276,719	1,969	1,966	3	274,750	−18	−4,655	17	20	999
Indiana	215,485	805	785	20	214,680	221,897	1,062	1,043	19	220,835	−258	−6,155	13	18	975
Illinois	251,872	1,425	1,422	3	250,447	264,151	1,489	1,486	3	262,662	−64	−12,215	13	17	998
Michigan	206,960	946	640	306	206,014	203,261	973	626	347	202,288	14	3,726	37	40	677
Wisconsin	177,127	591	48	543	176,536	169,795	520	58	462	169,275	−10	7,261	17	23	81
WEST NORTH CENTRAL:															
Minnesota	156,137	293	29	264	155,844	154,659	372	31	341	154,287	−2	1,557	4	6	99
Iowa	217,044	201	187	14	216,843	228,622	227	200	27	228,395	−13	−11,552	12	16	930
Missouri	277,244	3,666	3,656	10	273,578	284,886	4,953	4,950	3	279,933	−1,294	−6,355	23	31	997
North Dakota	74,360	743	22	721	73,617	45,332	1,334	18	1,316	43,998	4	29,619	36	63	30
South Dakota	77,644	2,808	67	2,741	74,836	52,622	1,806	17	1,789	50,816	50	24,020	82	37	24
Nebraska	129,678	462	96	366	129,216	121,525	329	78	251	121,196	18	8,020	12	12	208
Kansas	177,841	1,691	1,532	159	176,150	173,098	1,866	1,782	84	171,232	−250	4,918	28	34	906
SOUTH ATLANTIC:															
Delaware	10,836	922	922	......	9,914	9,687	818	817	1	8,869	105	1,045	30	27	1,000
Maryland	48,923	6,372	6,370	2	42,551	46,012	5,843	5,842	1	40,169	528	2,382	27	25	1,000
District of Columbia	217	12	12	......	205	269	17	17	......	252	−5	−47	(2)	(2)	1,000
Virginia	184,018	48,114	48,039	75	135,904	167,886	44,834	44,795	39	123,052	3,244	12,852	72	68	998
West Virginia	96,685	708	707	1	95,977	92,874	742	742	......	92,132	−35	3,845	11	17	999
North Carolina	253,725	65,656	64,456	1,200	188,069	224,637	54,864	53,996	868	169,773	10,460	18,296	92	86	982
South Carolina	176,434	96,798	96,772	26	79,636	155,355	85,401	85,381	20	69,954	11,391	9,682	116	109	1,000
Georgia	291,027	122,559	122,554	5	168,468	224,691	82,826	82,822	4	141,865	39,732	26,603	104	80	1,000
Florida	50,016	14,721	14,698	23	35,295	40,814	13,526	13,521	5	27,288	1,177	8,007	48	59	998
EAST SOUTH CENTRAL:															
Kentucky	259,185	11,730	11,709	21	247,455	234,667	11,238	11,227	11	223,429	482	24,026	45	39	998
Tennessee	246,012	38,308	38,300	8	207,704	224,623	33,895	33,883	12	190,728	4,417	16,976	81	71	1,000
Alabama	262,901	110,443	110,387	56	152,458	223,220	94,083	94,069	14	129,137	16,318	23,321	122	114	999
Mississippi	274,382	164,737	164,488	249	109,645	220,803	128,679	128,351	328	92,124	36,137	17,521	163	141	998
WEST SOUTH CENTRAL:															
Arkansas	214,678	63,593	63,578	15	151,085	178,694	46,983	46,978	5	131,711	16,600	19,374	144	128	1,000
Louisiana	120,546	54,879	54,819	60	65,667	115,969	58,160	58,096	64	57,809	−3,277	7,858	77	80	999
Oklahoma	190,192	20,671	[3]13,209	7,462	169,521	[3]108,000	[3]13,225	[3]6,353	[3]6,872	[3]94,775	6,856	74,746	96	114	639
Texas	417,770	69,918	69,816	102	347,852	352,190	65,536	65,472	64	286,654	4,344	61,198	101	105	999
MOUNTAIN:															
Montana	26,214	1,196	29	1,167	25,018	13,370	328	21	307	13,042	8	11,976	16	14	24
Idaho	30,807	405	13	392	30,402	17,471	595	9	586	16,876	4	13,526	20	31	32
Wyoming	10,987	65	19	46	10,922	6,095	173	2	171	5,922	17	5,000	9	2	292
Colorado	46,170	574	81	493	45,596	24,700	73	58	15	24,627	23	20,969	7	7	141
New Mexico	35,676	2,148	48	2,100	33,528	12,311	1,418	14	1,404	10,893	34	22,635	29	9	22
Arizona	9,227	3,203	12	3,191	6,024	5,809	1,803	15	1,788	4,006	−3	2,018	6	8	4
Utah	21,676	276	11	265	21,400	19,387	243	11	232	19,144	......	2,256	9	16	40
Nevada	2,689	161	6	155	2,528	2,184	173	3	170	2,011	3	517	12	22	37
PACIFIC:															
Washington	56,192	1,125	77	1,048	55,067	33,202	1,090	55	1,035	32,112	22	22,955	13	22	68
Oregon	45,502	627	27	600	44,875	35,837	551	14	537	35,286	13	9,589	18	13	43
California	88,197	3,078	159	2,919	85,119	72,542	1,607	135	1,472	70,935	24	14,184	7	12	52

[1] A minus sign (−) denotes decrease.   [2] Less than 1.   [3] Includes Indian Territory.

TABLE **46.**—ACREAGE IN FARMS OPERATED BY NEGROES AND BY WHITES, BY DIVISIONS AND STATES: 1910 AND 1900.

DIVISION AND STATE.	All farms.		Farms operated by Negroes.		Farms operated by whites.		ACRES IN FARMS OPERATED BY NEGROES PER 1,000 ACRES IN ALL FARMS.	
	1910	1900	1910	1900	1910	1900	1910	1900
UNITED STATES	878,798,325	838,591,774	42,279,510	38,233,920	832,166,020	796,825,751	48	46
GEOGRAPHIC DIVISIONS:								
New England	19,714,931	20,548,999	14,759	13,038	19,698,623	20,534,229	1	1
Middle Atlantic	43,191,056	44,860,090	74,849	71,369	43,078,966	44,767,621	2	2
East North Central	117,929,148	116,340,761	287,513	284,606	117,589,897	115,987,374	2	2
West North Central	232,648,121	201,008,713	491,509	502,465	230,456,459	199,150,762	2	2
South Atlantic	103,782,255	104,297,506	17,605,488	15,573,561	86,106,873	88,660,241	170	149
East South Central	81,520,629	81,247,643	13,573,980	12,601,782	67,924,912	68,626,325	167	155
West South Central	169,149,976	176,491,202	10,105,003	9,111,094	157,811,958	166,137,739	60	52
Mountain	59,533,420	46,397,284	62,807	40,023	58,748,762	46,060,329	1	1
Pacific	51,328,789	47,399,576	63,602	35,982	50,749,570	46,901,131	1	1
NEW ENGLAND:								
Maine	6,296,859	6,299,946	1,280	1,043	6,295,369	6,298,591	(1)	(1)
New Hampshire	3,249,458	3,609,864	923	562	3,248,530	3,609,302	(1)	(1)
Vermont	4,663,577	4,724,440	1,917	1,246	4,661,660	4,723,194	(1)	(1)
Massachusetts	2,875,941	3,147,064	3,535	3,967	2,871,377	3,141,734	1	1
Rhode Island	443,308	455,602	1,664	2,084	441,634	453,518	4	5
Connecticut	2,185,788	2,312,083	5,440	4,136	2,180,053	2,307,890	2	2
MIDDLE ATLANTIC:								
New York	22,030,367	22,648,109	22,552	26,735	21,971,024	22,600,592	1	1
New Jersey	2,573,857	2,840,966	22,200	19,205	2,551,497	2,821,755	9	7
Pennsylvania	18,586,832	19,371,015	30,097	25,429	18,556,445	19,345,274	2	1
EAST NORTH CENTRAL:								
Ohio	24,105,708	24,501,985	106,742	105,494	23,998,961	24,396,326	4	4
Indiana	21,299,823	21,619,623	43,627	52,251	21,254,834	21,566,143	2	2
Illinois	32,522,937	32,794,728	87,784	83,107	32,435,051	32,711,516	3	3
Michigan	18,940,614	17,561,698	45,331	38,259	18,880,909	17,508,295	2	2
Wisconsin	21,060,066	19,862,727	4,029	5,495	21,020,142	19,805,094	(1)	(1)
WEST NORTH CENTRAL:								
Minnesota	27,675,823	26,248,498	2,362	4,493	27,652,207	26,182,627	(1)	(1)
Iowa	33,930,688	34,574,337	13,617	15,359	33,916,710	34,558,319	(1)	(1)
Missouri	34,591,248	33,997,873	229,255	271,333	34,361,183	33,726,480	7	8
North Dakota	28,426,650	15,542,640	5,484	18,572	28,231,630	15,384,354	(1)	1
South Dakota	26,016,892	19,070,616	20,753	9,027	24,571,572	17,957,655	1	(1)
Nebraska	38,622,021	29,911,779	36,585	15,067	38,541,471	29,865,004	1	1
Kansas	43,384,799	41,662,970	183,453	173,614	43,181,686	41,476,323	4	4
SOUTH ATLANTIC:								
Delaware	1,038,866	1,066,228	56,973	52,558	981,893	1,013,662	55	49
Maryland	5,057,140	5,170,075	358,509	374,276	4,698,623	4,795,774	71	72
District of Columbia	6,063	8,489	95	308	5,968	8,181	16	36
Virginia	19,495,636	19,907,883	2,233,883	2,227,198	17,257,416	17,678,765	115	112
West Virginia	10,026,442	10,654,513	34,520	41,584	9,991,901	10,612,929	3	4
North Carolina	22,439,129	22,749,356	3,121,827	2,894,210	19,253,325	19,794,218	139	127
South Carolina	13,512,028	13,985,014	3,939,592	3,791,510	9,571,552	10,192,938	292	271
Georgia	26,953,413	26,392,057	7,091,949	5,474,889	19,861,362	20,917,083	263	207
Florida	5,253,538	4,363,891	768,140	717,028	4,484,833	3,646,691	146	164
EAST SOUTH CENTRAL:								
Kentucky	22,189,127	21,979,422	439,657	446,955	21,748,350	21,531,566	20	20
Tennessee	20,041,657	20,342,058	1,605,694	1,549,683	18,435,579	18,791,962	80	76
Alabama	20,732,312	20,685,427	5,083,552	4,719,069	15,640,877	15,965,260	245	228
Mississippi	18,557,533	18,240,736	6,445,077	5,886,075	12,100,106	12,337,537	347	323
WEST SOUTH CENTRAL:								
Arkansas	17,416,075	16,636,719	2,652,684	2,303,336	14,762,752	14,333,097	152	138
Louisiana	10,439,481	11,059,127	2,121,258	2,343,365	8,315,160	8,711,079	203	212
Oklahoma	28,859,353	2 22,988,339	1,066,863	2 628,414	26,582,642	2 21,128,187	37	27
Texas	112,435,067	125,807,017	4,264,198	3,835,979	108,151,404	121,965,376	38	30
MOUNTAIN:								
Montana	13,545,603	11,844,454	7,918	4,410	13,253,237	11,801,728	1	(1)
Idaho	5,283,604	3,204,903	1,043	1,105	5,224,913	3,101,553	(1)	(1)
Wyoming	8,543,010	8,124,536	6,202	800	8,532,201	8,101,350	1	(1)
Colorado	13,532,113	9,474,588	32,003	11,027	13,424,263	9,461,241	2	1
New Mexico	11,270,021	5,130,878	11,633	18,578	11,086,792	5,049,808	1	4
Arizona	1,246,613	1,935,327	1,222	1,850	1,145,737	1,889,376	1	1
Utah	3,397,699	4,116,951	506	648	3,374,792	4,097,153	(1)	(1)
Nevada	2,714,757	2,565,647	2,280	1,605	2,706,827	2,558,120	1	1
PACIFIC:								
Washington	11,712,235	8,499,297	7,651	8,008	11,611,390	8,378,339	1	1
Oregon	11,685,110	10,071,328	3,021	2,510	11,669,729	9,864,481	(1)	(1)
California	27,931,444	28,828,951	52,930	25,464	27,668,451	28,658,311	2	1

1 Less than 1.　　　　2 Includes Indian Territory.

TABLE 47.—ACREAGE IMPROVED AND UNIMPROVED IN FARMS OPERATED BY NEGROES AND BY WHITES, BY DIVISIONS AND STATES: 1910 AND 1900.

DIVISION AND STATE.	ACRES IN FARMS.							
	Improved land.				Unimproved land.			
	Farms operated by Negroes.		Farms operated by whites.		Farms operated by Negroes.		Farms operated by whites.	
	1910	1900	1910	1900	1910	1900	1910	1900
UNITED STATES	27,845,190	23,362,786	449,418,265	390,201,306	14,434,320	14,871,134	382,747,755	406,624.445
GEOGRAPHIC DIVISIONS:								
New England	5,669	5,708	7,248,822	8,128,180	9,090	7,330	12,449,801	12,406,049
Middle Atlantic	49,469	49,371	29,250,638	30,722,666	25,380	21,998	13,828,328	14,044,955
East North Central	222,774	221,550	88,702,567	86,429,877	64,739	63,056	28,887,330	29,557,497
West North Central	340,566	344,523	163,735,756	135,147,523	150,943	157,942	66,720,703	64,003,239
South Atlantic	10,956,415	8,874,506	37,489,664	37,204,364	6,649,073	6,699,055	48,617,209	51,455,877
East South Central	9,548,129	8,183,108	34,390,317	32,045,709	4,025,851	4,418,674	33,534,595	36,580,616
West South Central	6,665,869	5,663,170	51,075,128	33,643,413	3,439,134	3,447,924	106,736,830	132,494,326
Mountain	11,531	5,631	15,773,427	8,281,131	51,276	34,392	42,975,335	37,779,198
Pacific	44,768	15,219	21,751,946	18,598,443	18,834	20,763	28,997,624	28,302,688
NEW ENGLAND:								
Maine	624	387	2,359,993	2,386,428	656	656	3,935,376	3,912,163
New Hampshire	293	181	928,887	1,076,698	630	381	2,319,643	2,532,604
Vermont	634	671	1,633,331	2,125,953	1,283	575	3,028,329	2,597,241
Massachusetts	1,305	1,787	1,162,960	1,289,926	2,230	2,180	1,708,417	1,851,808
Rhode Island	582	834	177,752	186,520	1,082	1,250	263,882	266,998
Connecticut	2,231	1,848	985,899	1,062,655	3,209	2,288	1,194,154	1,245,235
MIDDLE ATLANTIC:								
New York	15,301	17,013	14,808,120	15,568,986	7,251	9,722	7,162,904	7,031,606
New Jersey	15,016	14,181	1,788,211	1,962,855	7,184	5,024	763,286	858,900
Pennsylvania	19,152	18,177	12,654,307	13,190,825	10,945	7,252	5,902,138	6,154,449
EAST NORTH CENTRAL:								
Ohio	83,311	85,792	19,144,653	19,158,541	23,431	19,702	4,854,308	5,237,785
Indiana	36,865	42,448	16,893,488	16,636,963	6,762	9,803	4,361,346	4,929,180
Illinois	68,299	64,154	27,979,926	27,634,970	19,485	18,953	4,455,125	5,076,546
Michigan	32,260	26,694	12,792,283	11,765,500	13,071	11,565	6,088,626	5,742,795
Wisconsin	2,039	2,462	11,892,217	11,233,903	1,990	3,033	9,127,925	8,571.191
WEST NORTH CENTRAL:								
Minnesota	1,631	1,876	19,628,989	18,425,561	731	2,617	8,023,218	7,757,066
Iowa	10,647	12,235	29,480,206	29,884,658	2,970	3,124	4,436,504	4,673,661
Missouri	172,200	195,522	24,408,746	22,704,491	57,055	75,811	9,952,437	11,021,989
North Dakota	4,142	4,019	20,406,121	9,600,293	1,342	9,553	7,825,509	5,784,061
South Dakota	8,817	3,488	15,706,380	11,204,609	11,936	5,539	8,865,192	6,753,046
Nebraska	11,923	8,335	24,341,688	18,414,267	24,662	6,732	14,199,783	11,450,737
Kansas	131,206	119,048	29,763,626	24,913,644	52,247	54,566	13,418,060	16,562,679
SOUTH ATLANTIC:								
Delaware	37,076	34,608	676,462	719,394	19,897	17,950	305,431	294,268
Maryland	218,574	238,644	3,136,185	3,277,684	139,935	135,632	1,562,438	1,518,090
District of Columbia	95	232	5,038	5,702		76	930	2,479
Virginia	1,109,235	1,124,544	8,758,850	8,969,347	1,124,648	1,102,654	8,498,566	8,709,418
West Virginia	20,236	23,066	5,501,500	5,475,915	14,284	18,518	4,490,401	5,137,014
North Carolina	1,700,102	1,437,313	7,082,344	6,869,859	1,421,725	1,456,897	12,170,981	12,924,359
South Carolina	2,597,497	2,273,501	3,499,775	3,501,917	1,342,095	1,518,009	6,071,777	6,691,021
Georgia	4,791,460	3,322,596	7,506,455	7,292,998	2,300,489	2,152,293	12,354,907	13,624,085
Florida	482,140	420,002	1,323,055	1,091,548	286,000	297,026	3,161,778	2,555,143
EAST SOUTH CENTRAL:								
Kentucky	342,895	340,832	14,010,777	13,400,805	96,762	106,123	7,737,573	8,130,761
Tennessee	1,161,985	1,036,640	9,728,208	9,209,149	443,709	513,043	8,707,371	9,582,813
Alabama	3,561,674	3,063,679	6,130,405	5,591,088	1,521,878	1,655,390	9,510,472	10,374,172
Mississippi	4,481,575	3,741,957	4,520,927	3,844,667	1,963,502	2,144,118	7,579,179	8,492,870
WEST SOUTH CENTRAL:								
Arkansas	1,772,702	1,375,051	6,303,048	5,578,549	879,982	928,285	8,459,704	8,754,548
Louisiana	1,465,775	1,572,507	3,809,409	3,092,009	655,483	769,858	4,505,751	5,619,070
Oklahoma	664,434	1 285,969	16,378,518	1 7,827,271	402,429	1 342,445	10,204,124	1 13,300,916
Texas	2,762,958	2,428,643	24,584,153	17,145,584	1,501,240	1,407,336	83,567,251	104,819,792
MOUNTAIN:								
Montana	1,751	780	3,609,567	1,716,407	6,167	3,630	9,643,670	10,085,321
Idaho	346	481	2,751,145	1,377,944	697	624	2,473,768	1,723,609
Wyoming	1,521	50	1,251,126	790,391	4,681	750	7,281,075	7,310,959
Colorado	4,776	2,520	4,287,410	2,271,191	27,227	8,507	9,136,853	7,190,050
New Mexico	1,574	235	1,446,220	303,074	10,059	18,343	9,640,572	4,746,734
Arizona	186	473	323,767	226,809	1,036	1,377	821,970	1,662,567
Utah	262	302	1,356,660	1,625,841	244	346	2,018,132	3,071,312
Nevada	1,115	790	747,532	569,474	1,165	815	1,959,295	1,988,646
PACIFIC:								
Washington	2,828	1,268	6,340,269	3,433,549	4,823	6,740	5,271,121	4,944,790
Oregon	1,104	502	4,203,339	3,285,068	1,917	2,008	7,266,390	6,579,413
California	40,836	13,449	11,208,338	11,879,826	12,094	12,015	16,460,113	16,778,485

1 Includes Indian Territory.

TABLE 48.—INCREASE IN ACREAGE—TOTAL, IMPROVED, AND UNIMPROVED—OF NEGRO AND WHITE FARMS, BY DIVISIONS AND STATES: 1900–1910.

DIVISION AND STATE.	INCREASE:[1] 1900–1910.								
	Acres in farms.			Acres improved.			Acres unimproved.		
	All farms.	Negro farms.	White farms.	All farms.	Negro farms.	White farms.	All farms.	Negro farms.	White farms.
UNITED STATES	40,206,551	4,045,590	35,340,269	63,953,263	4,482,404	59,216,959	−23,746,712	−436,814	−23,876,700
GEOGRAPHIC DIVISIONS:									
New England	−834,068	1,721	−835,606	−879,499	−39	−879,358	45,431	1,760	43,752
Middle Atlantic	−1,669,034	3,480	−1,688,655	−1,465,317	98	−1,472,028	−203,717	3,382	−216,627
East North Central	1,588,387	2,907	1,602,523	2,276,957	1,224	2,272,690	−688,570	1,683	−670,167
West North Central	31,639,408	−10,956	31,305,697	28,641,034	−3,957	28,588,233	2,998,374	−6,999	2,717,464
South Atlantic	−515,251	2,031,927	−2,553,368	2,379,507	2,081,909	285,300	−2,894,758	−49,982	−2,838,668
East South Central	272,986	972,198	−701,413	3,709,509	1,365,021	2,344,608	−3,436,523	−392,823	−3,046,021
West South Central	−7,341,226	993,909	−8,325,781	18,493,743	1,002,699	17,431,715	−25,834,969	−8,790	−25,757,496
Mountain	13,136,136	22,784	12,688,433	7,512,426	5,900	7,492,296	5,623,710	16,884	5,196,137
Pacific	3,929,213	27,620	3,848,439	3,284,903	29,549	3,153,503	644,310	−1,929	694,936
NEW ENGLAND:									
Maine	−3,087	237	−3,222	−26,232	237	−26,435	23,145	....	23,213
New Hampshire	−360,406	361	−360,772	−147,694	112	−147,811	−212,712	249	−212,961
Vermont	−60,863	671	−61,534	−492,659	−37	−492,622	431,796	708	431,088
Massachusetts	−271,123	−432	−270,357	−127,631	−482	−126,966	−143,492	50	−143,391
Rhode Island	−12,294	−420	−11,884	−9,010	−252	−8,768	−3,284	−168	−3,116
Connecticut	−126,295	1,304	−127,837	−76,273	383	−76,756	−50,022	921	−51,081
MIDDLE ATLANTIC:									
New York	−617,742	−4,183	−629,568	−755,947	−1,712	−760,866	138,205	−2,471	131,298
New Jersey	−267,109	2,995	−270,258	−173,706	835	−174,644	−93,403	2,160	−95,614
Pennsylvania	−784,183	4,668	−788,829	−535,664	975	−536,518	−248,519	3,693	−252,311
EAST NORTH CENTRAL:									
Ohio	−396,277	1,248	−397,365	−16,503	−2,481	−13,888	−379,774	3,729	−383,477
Indiana	−319,800	−8,624	−311,309	250,894	−5,583	256,525	−570,694	−3,041	−567,834
Illinois	−271,791	4,677	−276,465	349,104	4,145	344,956	−620,895	532	−621,421
Michigan	1,378,916	7,072	1,372,614	1,032,828	5,566	1,026,783	346,088	1,506	345,831
Wisconsin	1,197,339	−1,466	1,215,048	660,634	−423	658,314	536,705	−1,043	556,734
WEST NORTH CENTRAL:									
Minnesota	1,427,325	−2,131	1,469,580	1,200,948	−245	1,203,428	226,377	−1,886	266,152
Iowa	−643,649	−1,742	−641,609	−406,353	−1,588	−404,452	−237,296	−154	−237,157
Missouri	593,375	−42,078	634,703	1,681,143	−23,322	1,704,255	−1,087,768	−18,756	−1,069,552
North Dakota	12,884,010	−8,088	12,847,276	10,810,572	123	10,805,828	2,073,438	−8,211	2,041,448
South Dakota	6,946,276	11,726	6,613,917	4,541,225	5,329	4,501,771	2,405,051	6,397	2,112,146
Nebraska	8,710,242	21,518	8,676,467	5,949,982	3,588	5,927,421	2,760,260	17,930	2,749,046
Kansas	1,721,829	9,839	1,705,363	4,863,517	12,158	4,849,982	−3,141,688	−2,319	−3,144,619
SOUTH ATLANTIC:									
Delaware	−27,362	4,415	−31,769	−40,472	2,468	−42,932	13,110	1,947	11,163
Maryland	−112,935	−15,767	−97,151	−161,585	−20,070	−141,499	48,650	4,303	44,348
District of Columbia	−2,426	−213	−2,213	−801	−137	−664	−1,625	−76	−1,549
Virginia	−412,247	6,685	−421,349	−224,747	−15,309	−210,497	−187,500	21,994	−210,852
West Virginia	−628,071	−7,064	−621,028	22,776	−2,830	25,585	−650,847	−4,234	−646,613
North Carolina	−310,227	227,617	−540,869	485,950	262,789	212,485	−796,177	−35,172	−753,378
South Carolina	−472,986	148,082	−621,386	322,258	323,996	−2,142	−795,244	−175,914	−619,244
Georgia	561,356	1,617,060	−1,055,721	1,682,373	1,468,864	213,457	−1,121,017	148,196	−1,269,178
Florida	889,647	51,112	838,142	293,755	62,138	231,507	595,892	−11,026	606,635
EAST SOUTH CENTRAL:									
Kentucky	209,705	−7,298	216,784	612,503	2,063	609,972	−402,798	−9,361	−393,188
Tennessee	−300,401	56,011	−356,383	644,534	125,345	519,059	−944,935	−69,334	−875,442
Alabama	46,885	364,483	−324,383	1,038,590	497,995	539,317	−991,705	−133,512	−863,700
Mississippi	316,797	559,002	−237,431	1,413,882	739,618	676,260	−1,097,085	−180,616	−913,691
WEST SOUTH CENTRAL:									
Arkansas	779,356	349,348	429,655	1,122,519	397,651	724,499	−343,163	−48,303	−294,844
Louisiana	−619,646	−222,107	−395,919	609,484	−107,732	717,400	−1,229,130	−114,375	−1,113,319
Oklahoma	5,871,014	438,449	5,454,455	8,977,150	378,465	8,551,247	−3,106,136	59,984	−3,096,792
Texas	−13,371,950	428,219	−13,813,972	7,784,590	334,315	7,438,569	−21,156,540	93,904	−21,252,541
MOUNTAIN:									
Montana	1,701,149	3,508	1,451,509	1,903,608	971	1,893,160	−202,459	2,537	−441,651
Idaho	2,078,701	−62	2,123,360	1,365,622	−135	1,373,201	713,079	73	750,159
Wyoming	418,474	5,402	430,851	463,828	1,471	460,735	−45,354	3,931	−29,884
Colorado	4,057,525	20,976	3,963,022	2,028,133	2,256	2,016,219	2,029,392	18,720	1,946,803
New Mexico	6,139,143	−6,945	6,036,984	1,140,318	1,339	1,143,146	4,998,825	−8,284	4,893,838
Arizona	−688,714	−628	−743,639	95,652	−287	96,958	−784,366	−341	−840,597
Utah	−719,252	−142	−722,361	336,094	−40	330,819	−1,055,346	−102	−1,053,180
Nevada	149,110	675	148,707	179,171	325	178,058	−30,061	350	−29,351
PACIFIC:									
Washington	3,212,938	−357	3,233,051	2,907,351	1,560	2,906,720	305,587	−1,917	326,331
Oregon	1,613,782	511	1,605,248	946,495	602	918,271	667,287	−91	686,977
California	−897,507	27,466	−989,860	−568,943	27,387	−671,488	−328,564	79	−318,372

[1] A minus sign (−) denotes decrease.

TABLE 49.—NUMBER AND VALUE OF FARMS OPERATED BY

[A minus sign (−) denotes decrease.]

	DIVISION AND STATE.	NUMBER OF FARMS.		Increase.		VALUE OF FARM PROPERTY. Total.		Increase.		Land.		Increase.	
		1910	1900	Amount.	Per cent.	1910	1900	Amount.	Per cent.	1910	1900	Amount.	Per cent.
	UNITED STATES....	893,370	746,715	146,655	19.6	$1,141,792,526	$499,941,234	$641,851,292	128.4	$756,158,264	$324,242,997	$431,915,267	133.2
	GEOGRAPHIC DIVISIONS:												
1	New England........	310	264	46	17.4	945,061	582,851	362,210	62.1	427,635	320,384	107,251	33.5
2	Middle Atlantic......	1,310	1,497	−187	−12.5	6,123,854	4,193,394	1,930,460	46.0	3,432,477	2,344,334	1,088,143	46.4
3	East North Central...	4,843	5,179	−336	−6.5	20,063,311	11,535,146	8,528,165	73.9	14,669,103	8,527,575	6,141,528	72.0
4	West North Central..	5,589	7,076	−1,487	−21.0	26,341,103	13,072,899	13,268,204	101.5	19,055,309	9,398,587	9,656,722	102.7
5	South Atlantic.......	354,530	287,933	66,597	23.1	440,876,367	162,841,284	278,035,083	170.7	294,198,215	106,251,076	187,947,139	176.9
6	East South Central..	324,884	267,530	57,354	21.4	356,989,149	170,985,641	186,003,508	108.8	227,012,113	108,254,534	118,757,579	109.7
7	West South Central..	201,422	176,899	24,523	13.9	285,792,835	135,679,630	150,113,205	110.6	193,778,544	88,427,732	105,350,812	119.1
8	Mountain...........	219	133	86	64.7	1,610,050	382,943	1,227,107	320.0	1,033,530	241,285	792,245	328.3
9	Pacific.............	263	204	59	28.9	3,050,796	667,446	2,383,350	357.1	2,551,338	477,490	2,073,848	434.3
	NEW ENGLAND:												
10	Maine.............	28	24	4	(1)	46,182	24,012	22,170	92.3	16,575	11,460	5,115	44.6
11	New Hampshire.....	14	10	4	(1)	71,776	12,620	59,156	468.7	30,750	4,740	26,010	548.7
12	Vermont...........	20	8	12	(1)	53,166	60,350	−7,184	−11.9	20,100	43,000	−22,900	−53.3
13	Massachusetts......	103	87	16	(1)	298,064	195,880	102,184	52.2	129,490	101,784	27,706	27.2
14	Rhode Island........	40	28	12	(1)	78,886	65,450	13,436	20.5	37,950	37,150	800	2.2
15	Connecticut........	105	107	−2	−1.9	396,987	224,539	172,448	76.8	192,770	122,250	70,520	57.7
	MIDDLE ATLANTIC:												
16	New York..........	295	443	−148	−33.4	1,480,541	1,114,787	365,754	32.8	752,365	553,314	199,051	36.0
17	New Jersey.........	472	469	3	0.6	1,962,818	1,047,178	915,640	87.4	1,025,917	526,730	499,187	94.8
18	Pennsylvania.......	543	585	−42	−7.2	2,680,495	2,031,429	649,066	32.0	1,654,195	1,264,290	389,905	30.8
	EAST NORTH CENTRAL:												
19	Ohio...............	1,948	1,966	−18	−0.9	6,901,721	4,297,922	2,603,799	60.6	4,862,138	3,147,105	1,715,033	54.5
20	Indiana............	785	1,043	−258	−24.7	3,724,754	2,336,581	1,388,173	59.4	2,878,997	1,741,460	1,137,537	65.3
21	Illinois............	1,422	1,486	−64	−4.3	6,778,746	3,326,319	3,452,427	103.8	5,299,868	2,584,730	2,715,138	105.0
22	Michigan..........	640	626	14	2.2	2,439,921	1,441,866	998,055	69.2	1,490,450	963,995	526,455	54.6
23	Wisconsin..........	48	58	−10	(1)	218,169	132,458	85,711	64.7	137,650	90,285	47,365	52.5
	WEST NORTH CENTRAL:												
24	Minnesota..........	29	31	−2	(1)	143,827	99,755	44,072	44.2	94,815	71,704	23,111	32.2
25	Iowa..............	187	200	−13	−6.5	1,234,660	783,343	451,317	57.6	869,300	546,410	322,890	59.1
26	Missouri...........	3,656	4,950	−1,294	−26.1	14,095,370	7,969,326	6,126,044	76.9	10,556,515	5,855,470	4,701,045	80.3
27	North Dakota.......	22	18	4	(1)	214,307	94,994	119,313	125.6	139,100	61,925	77,175	124.6
28	South Dakota.......	67	17	50	(1)	1,617,893	89,496	1,528,397	1,707.8	467,935	63,335	404,600	638.8
29	Nebraska..........	96	78	18	(1)	582,071	278,081	303,990	109.3	459,350	174,645	284,705	163.0
30	Kansas............	1,532	1,782	−250	−14.0	8,452,975	3,757,904	4,695,071	124.9	6,468,294	2,625,098	3,843,196	146.4
	SOUTH ATLANTIC:												
31	Delaware..........	922	817	105	12.9	2,350,845	1,393,830	957,015	68.7	1,451,457	870,720	580,737	66.7
32	Maryland..........	6,370	5,842	528	9.0	12,249,019	8,208,572	4,040,447	49.2	7,096,892	4,848,120	2,248,772	46.4
33	District of Columbia..	12	17	−5	(1)	93,671	304,592	−210,921	−69.2	66,600	276,300	−209,700	−75.9
34	Virginia...........	48,039	44,795	3,244	7.2	54,651,043	24,490,106	30,160,937	123.2	32,497,542	14,457,950	18,039,592	124.8
35	West Virginia......	707	742	−35	−4.7	1,304,721	827,711	477,010	57.6	827,749	553,670	274,079	49.5
36	North Carolina.....	64,456	53,996	10,460	19.4	78,675,830	28,458,176	50,217,654	176.5	53,125,563	18,850,775	34,274,788	181.8
37	South Carolina.....	96,772	85,381	11,391	13.3	118,314,985	43,992,879	74,322,106	168.9	84,018,490	30,186,395	53,832,095	178.3
38	Georgia...........	122,554	82,822	39,732	48.0	157,870,357	48,698,931	109,171,426	224.2	105,849,590	32,512,900	73,336,690	225.6
39	Florida............	14,698	13,521	1,177	8.7	15,365,896	6,466,487	8,899,409	137.6	9,264,332	3,694,246	5,570,086	150.8
	EAST SOUTH CENTRAL:												
40	Kentucky..........	11,709	11,227	482	4.3	18,252,353	10,950,268	7,302,085	66.7	12,227,341	7,228,835	4,998,506	69.1
41	Tennessee.........	38,300	33,883	4,417	13.0	54,073,706	26,735,588	27,338,118	102.3	35,237,523	16,950,860	18,286,663	107.9
42	Alabama..........	110,387	94,069	16,318	17.3	97,261,114	46,908,811	50,352,303	107.3	59,258,839	29,072,925	30,185,914	103.8
43	Mississippi........	164,488	128,351	36,137	28.2	187,401,976	86,390,974	101,011,002	116.9	120,288,410	55,001,914	65,286,496	118.7
	WEST SOUTH CENTRAL:												
44	Arkansas..........	63,578	46,978	16,600	35.3	87,119,083	34,191,174	52,927,909	154.8	57,920,360	22,660,525	25,259,835	155.6
45	Louisiana..........	54,819	58,096	−3,277	−5.6	56,472,403	37,995,093	18,477,310	48.6	36,170,690	24,187,645	11,983,045	49.5
46	Oklahoma..........	13,209	6,353	6,856	107.9	30,347,738	7,313,156	23,034,582	315.0	21,788,491	4,165,553	17,622,938	423.1
47	Texas.............	69,816	65,472	4,344	6.6	111,853,611	56,180,207	55,673,404	99.1	77,899,003	37,414,009	40,484,994	108.2
	MOUNTAIN:												
48	Montana...........	29	21	8	(1)	206,533	46,672	159,861	342.5	97,255	29,875	67,380	225.5
49	Idaho.............	13	9	4	(1)	62,706	23,166	39,540	170.7	47,525	16,570	30,955	186.8
50	Wyoming..........	19	2	17	(1)	148,988	3,108	145,880	4,693.7	121,145	1,600	119,545	7,471.6
51	Colorado..........	81	58	23	(1)	565,135	150,359	414,776	275.9	427,930	102,805	325,125	316.3
52	New Mexico........	48	14	34	(1)	344,544	32,275	312,269	967.5	181,175	23,625	157,550	666.9
53	Arizona...........	12	15	−3	(1)	62,630	65,969	−3,339	−5.0	23,500	26,960	−3,460	12.8
54	Utah..............	11	11	....	....	105,963	20,675	85,288	412.5	70,500	15,300	55,200	360.8
55	Nevada...........	6	3	3	(1)	113,551	40,719	72,832	178.9	64,500	24,550	39,950	162.7
	PACIFIC:												
56	Washington........	77	55	22	(1)	572,129	131,227	440,902	336.0	427,170	93,280	333,890	357.9
57	Oregon............	27	14	13	(1)	201,726	38,417	163,309	425.1	129,878	23,290	106,588	457.9
58	California..........	159	135	24	17.8	2,276,941	497,802	1,779,139	357.0	1,994,290	360,920	1,633,370	452.6

[1] Per cent not shown where base is less than 100.

NEGROES, BY DIVISIONS AND STATES: 1910 AND 1900.

[A minus sign (−) denotes decrease.]

	VALUE OF FARM PROPERTY—continued.											
	Buildings.				Implements and machinery.				Live stock.			
	1910	1900	Increase Amount.	Increase Per cent.	1910	1900	Increase Amount.	Increase Per cent.	1910	1900	Increase Amount.	Increase Per cent.
	$166,559,439	$71,902,265	$94,657,174	131.6	$34,178,052	$18,859,757	$15,318,295	81.2	$184,896,771	$84,936,215	$99,960,556	117.7
1	374,725	195,330	179,395	91.8	42,771	21,428	21,343	99.6	99,930	45,709	54,221	118.6
2	1,866,870	1,270,170	596,700	47.0	250,259	185,349	64,910	35.0	574,248	393,541	180,707	45.9
3	2,808,546	1,468,470	1,340,076	91.3	440,693	326,208	114,485	35.1	2,144,969	1,212,893	932,076	76.8
4	2,621,723	1,464,907	1,156,816	79.0	588,750	396,917	191,833	48.3	4,075,321	1,812,488	2,262,833	124.8
5	70,870,030	26,658,379	44,211,651	165.8	13,148,827	5,879,229	7,269,598	123.6	62,659,295	24,052,600	38,606,695	160.5
6	52,419,081	23,113,572	29,305,509	126.8	11,163,547	6,847,843	4,315,704	63.0	66,394,408	32,769,692	33,624,716	102.6
7	35,304,427	17,620,563	17,683,864	100.4	8,442,917	5,166,769	3,276,148	63.4	48,266,947	24,464,566	23,802,381	97.3
8	122,465	42,229	80,236	190.0	47,564	14,698	32,866	223.6	406,491	84,731	321,760	379.7
9	171,572	68,645	102,927	149.9	52,724	21,316	31,408	147.3	275,162	99,995	175,167	175.2
10	20,275	8,490	11,785	138.8	3,230	1,318	1,912	145.1	6,102	2,744	3,358	122.4
11	30,550	5,350	25,200	471.0	2,955	850	2,105	247.6	7,521	1,680	5,841	347.7
12	22,250	10,200	12,050	118.1	2,960	1,430	1,530	107.0	7,856	5,720	2,136	37.3
13	128,575	73,250	55,325	75.5	12,057	7,055	5,002	70.9	27,942	13,791	14,151	102.6
14	24,650	19,950	4,700	23.6	5,320	3,350	1,970	58.8	10,966	5,000	5,966	119.3
15	148,425	78,090	70,335	90.1	16,249	7,425	8,824	118.8	39,543	16,774	22,769	135.7
16	482,165	363,000	119,165	32.8	72,093	65,594	6,499	9.9	173,918	132,879	41,039	30.9
17	663,820	370,190	293,630	79.3	84,146	53,440	30,706	57.5	188,935	96,818	92,117	95.1
18	720,885	536,980	183,905	34.2	94,020	66,315	27,705	41.8	211,395	163,844	47,551	29.0
19	1,126,937	571,525	555,412	97.2	148,278	119,325	28,953	24.3	764,368	459,967	304,401	66.2
20	438,750	284,960	153,790	54.0	63,115	60,135	2,980	5.0	343,892	250,026	93,866	37.5
21	672,724	339,510	333,214	98.1	133,518	86,320	47,198	54.7	672,636	315,759	356,877	113.0
22	534,235	253,110	281,125	111.1	89,257	55,945	33,312	59.5	325,979	168,816	157,163	93.1
23	35,900	19,365	16,535	85.4	6,525	4,483	2,042	45.5	38,094	18,325	19,769	107.9
24	29,100	16,440	12,660	77.0	4,995	2,780	2,215	79.7	14,917	8,831	6,086	68.9
25	185,195	100,470	84,725	84.3	37,948	23,225	14,723	63.4	142,217	113,238	28,979	25.6
26	1,449,928	863,720	586,208	67.9	315,800	220,432	95,368	43.3	1,773,127	1,029,704	743,423	72.2
27	15,000	7,890	7,110	90.1	9,450	11,165	−1,715	−15.4	50,757	14,014	36,743	262.2
28	39,470	8,395	31,075	370.2	18,764	2,735	16,029	586.1	1,091,724	15,031	1,076,693	7,163.1
29	54,010	25,240	28,770	114.0	11,280	9,622	1,658	17.2	57,431	68,574	−11,143	−16.2
30	849,020	442,752	406,268	91.8	190,513	126,958	63,555	50.1	945,148	563,096	382,052	67.8
31	530,259	302,730	227,529	75.2	100,090	73,230	26,860	36.7	269,039	147,150	121,889	82.8
32	3,170,392	2,037,240	1,133,152	55.6	436,940	331,400	105,540	31.8	1,544,795	991,812	552,983	55.8
33	22,800	16,200	6,600	40.7	955	9,790	−8,835	−90.2	3,316	2,302	1,014	44.0
34	12,645,749	5,491,185	7,154,564	130.3	1,849,785	929,885	919,900	98.9	7,657,967	3,611,086	4,046,881	112.1
35	247,455	134,190	113,265	84.4	31,543	21,750	9,793	45.0	197,974	118,101	79,873	67.6
36	13,668,028	4,979,727	8,688,301	174.5	2,202,330	941,010	1,261,320	134.0	9,679,909	3,686,664	5,993,245	162.6
37	14,947,954	5,741,625	9,206,329	160.3	3,367,160	1,592,615	1,774,545	111.4	15,981,381	6,472,244	9,509,137	146.9
38	23,027,442	6,818,890	16,208,552	237.7	4,558,897	1,683,910	2,874,987	170.7	24,434,428	7,683,231	16,751,197	218.0
39	2,609,951	1,136,592	1,473,359	129.6	601,127	295,639	305,488	103.3	2,890,486	1,340,010	1,550,476	115.7
40	2,789,887	1,723,555	1,066,332	61.9	420,535	355,713	64,822	18.2	2,814,590	1,642,165	1,172,425	71.4
41	6,945,703	3,633,900	3,311,803	91.1	1,820,921	1,270,127	550,794	43.4	10,069,559	4,880,701	5,188,858	106.3
42	14,575,233	6,133,565	8,441,668	137.6	3,323,893	1,927,840	1,396,053	72.4	20,103,149	9,774,481	10,328,668	105.7
43	28,108,258	11,622,552	16,485,706	141.8	5,598,198	3,294,163	2,304,035	69.9	33,407,110	16,472,345	16,934,765	102.8
44	11,058,104	4,216,715	6,841,389	162.2	2,788,446	1,241,610	1,546,836	124.6	15,352,173	6,072,324	9,279,849	152.8
45	8,721,228	5,584,345	3,136,883	56.2	1,681,187	1,439,730	241,457	16.8	9,899,298	6,783,373	3,115,925	45.9
46	2,764,024	667,158	2,096,866	314.3	813,125	315,852	497,273	157.4	4,982,098	2,164,593	2,817,505	130.2
47	12,761,071	7,152,345	5,608,726	78.4	3,160,159	2,169,577	990,582	45.7	18,033,378	9,444,276	8,589,102	90.9
48	17,425	5,525	11,900	215.4	14,575	2,725	11,850	434.9	77,278	8,547	68,731	804.2
49	6,725	1,845	4,880	264.5	2,265	1,411	854	60.5	6,191	3,340	2,851	85.4
50	8,055	600	7,455	1,242.5	2,935	400	2,535	633.8	16,853	508	16,345	3,217.5
51	49,590	19,155	30,435	158.9	14,945	5,340	9,605	179.9	72,670	23,059	49,611	215.1
52	18,070	3,450	14,620	423.8	7,983	1,357	6,626	488.3	137,316	3,843	133,473	3,473.1
53	6,600	6,350	250	3.9	1,921	2,340	−419	−17.9	30,609	30,319	290	1.0
54	10,000	2,854	7,146	250.4	1,115	810	305	37.7	24,348	1,711	22,637	1,323.0
55	6,000	2,450	3,550	144.9	1,825	315	1,510	479.4	41,226	13,404	27,822	207.6
56	43,455	16,870	26,585	157.6	11,169	3,984	7,185	180.3	90,335	17,093	73,242	428.5
57	21,472	4,885	16,587	339.5	5,515	1,210	4,305	355.8	44,861	9,032	35,829	396.7
58	106,645	46,890	59,755	127.4	36,040	16,122	19,918	123.5	139,966	73,870	66,096	89.5

TABLE 50.—CROPS IN 1909 ON FARMS IN THE SOUTH—FARMS REPORTING, ACREAGE, YIELD, AND VALUE OF SPECIFIED CROPS ON ALL FARMS AND ON COLORED FARMS, BY DIVISIONS AND STATES.

COTTON.

DIVISION AND STATE.	Number of farms reporting crop. Total.	Colored farms. Number.	Colored farms. Per cent.	Acreage in crop. All farms.	Colored farms. Acres.	Colored farms. Per cent.	Yield of crop. All farms.	Colored farms. Amount.	Colored farms. Per cent.	Value of crop. All farms.	Colored farms. Amount.	Colored farms. Per cent.
THE SOUTH	1,706,767	684,721	40.1	31,946,142	12,096,638	52.7	Bales. 10,594,360	Bales. 4,065,978	38.4	$700,199,244	$269,868,346	32.4
South Atlantic	556,504	253,286	45.5	9,002,776	4,442,773	49.3	4,012,942	1,806,026	45.0	254,636,958	113,311,266	44.5
East South Central	522,735	266,450	51.0	7,926,019	4,614,339	58.2	2,524,714	1,356,813	53.7	175,543,582	95,717,387	54.5
West South Central	627,528	164,985	26.3	15,017,347	3,039,526	20.2	4,056,704	903,139	22.3	270,018,704	60,839,693	22.5
South Atlantic:												
Delaware												
Maryland												
District of Columbia												
Virginia	5,283	3,102	58.7	25,147	13,362	53.1	10,480	5,051	48.2	695,721	334,465	48.0
West Virginia												
North Carolina	129,704	44,256	34.1	1,274,404	474,889	37.3	665,132	232,536	35.0	42,066,099	14,551,099	34.6
South Carolina	158,167	88,904	56.2	2,556,467	1,364,375	53.4	1,279,866	612,953	47.9	80,337,945	38,248,916	47.6
Georgia	242,673	108,115	44.6	4,883,304	2,468,242	50.5	1,992,408	927,162	46.5	126,695,612	58,195,483	45.9
Florida	20,677	8,909	43.1	263,454	121,905	46.3	65,056	28,324	43.5	4,841,581	1,981,303	40.9
East South Central:												
Kentucky	504	155	30.8	7,811	2,937	37.6	3,469	1,478	42.6	223,024	96,247	43.1
Tennessee	67,663	24,740	36.6	787,516	387,527	49.2	264,562	116,874	44.2	17,966,517	8,062,110	44.9
Alabama	224,871	100,506	44.7	3,730,482	1,960,709	52.6	1,129,527	510,465	45.2	74,205,236	33,261,538	44.8
Mississippi	229,697	141,049	61.4	3,400,210	2,263,166	66.6	1,127,156	727,996	64.6	83,148,805	54,297,492	65.3
West South Central:												
Arkansas	148,311	54,296	36.6	2,153,222	949,734	44.1	776,879	348,635	44.9	54,559,503	25,262,870	46.3
Louisiana	74,373	40,607	54.6	957,011	514,352	53.7	268,909	141,882	52.8	17,324,804	9,203,157	53.1
Oklahoma [1]	88,140	11,270	12.8	1,976,935	217,231	11.0	555,742	70,738	12.7	35,399,356	4,314,200	12.2
Texas	316,704	58,812	18.6	9,930,179	1,358,209	13.7	2,455,174	341,884	13.9	162,735,041	22,059,466	13.5

CORN.

DIVISION AND STATE.	Total.	Number.	Per cent.	All farms.	Acres.	Per cent.	All farms.	Amount.	Per cent.	All farms.	Amount.	Per cent.
THE SOUTH	2,571,566	744,458	28.9	37,627,319	7,377,221	19.6	Bushels. 623,068,626	Bushels. 94,876,350	15.2	$443,460,455	$76,918,406	17.3
South Atlantic	974,833	311,725	32.0	11,386,984	3,066,496	26.9	179,511,702	34,442,488	19.2	149,449,304	31,149,841	20.8
East South Central	882,737	265,078	30.0	11,328,268	2,309,639	20.4	210,154,917	30,038,296	14.3	150,975,613	25,377,730	16.8
West South Central	713,996	167,655	23.5	14,912,067	2,001,086	13.4	233,402,007	30,395,566	13.0	143,035,538	20,390,835	14.3
South Atlantic:												
Delaware	9,923	836	8.4	188,755	12,636	6.7	4,839,548	252,478	5.2	2,903,442	146,047	5.0
Maryland	42,084	5,269	12.5	647,012	52,139	8.1	17,911,436	985,310	5.5	11,015,298	601,694	5.5
District of Columbia	68	1	1.5	426	2	0.5	12,667	50	0.4	9,635	40	0.4
Virginia	163,680	43,401	26.5	1,860,359	338,378	18.2	38,295,141	4,966,904	13.0	28,885,944	4,011,144	13.9
West Virginia	83,028	500	0.6	676,311	4,421	0.5	17,119,097	105,814	0.6	11,907,261	62,943	0.5
North Carolina	228,322	57,911	25.4	2,459,457	535,037	21.8	34,063,531	5,876,253	17.3	31,286,102	5,482,779	17.5
South Carolina	156,589	84,744	54.1	1,565,832	653,856	41.8	20,871,946	7,309,064	35.0	20,682,632	7,237,073	35.0
Georgia	253,410	106,426	42.0	3,383,061	1,278,627	37.8	39,374,569	12,881,533	32.7	37,079,981	12,049,851	32.5
Florida	37,729	12,637	33.5	605,771	191,400	31.6	7,023,767	2,065,082	29.4	5,709,009	1,558,270	27.3
East South Central:												
Kentucky	216,224	8,184	3.8	3,436,340	104,055	3.0	83,348,024	2,442,054	2.9	50,449,112	1,445,369	2.9
Tennessee	211,119	32,779	15.5	3,146,348	354,996	11.3	67,682,489	6,331,010	9.4	45,819,093	4,616,979	10.1
Alabama	229,113	93,839	41.0	2,572,968	818,175	31.8	30,695,737	8,557,923	27.9	28,677,032	7,912,376	27.6
Mississippi	226,281	130,276	57.6	2,172,612	1,032,413	47.5	28,428,667	12,707,309	44.7	26,030,376	11,403,006	43.8
West South Central:												
Arkansas	176,106	48,120	27.3	2,277,116	386,913	17.0	37,609,544	6,107,452	16.2	27,910,044	5,103,515	18.3
Louisiana	100,943	45,790	45.4	1,590,830	505,431	31.1	26,010,361	7,432,322	28.6	16,480,322	4,623,633	28.0
Oklahoma	148,590	15,643	10.5	5,914,069	369,918	6.3	94,283,407	5,949,363	6.3	48,080,554	3,019,703	6.3
Texas	288,357	58,102	20.1	5,130,052	738,924	14.4	75,498,695	10,906,429	14.4	50,564,618	7,643,984	15.1

COTTON SEED.[2]

DIVISION AND STATE.	Total.	Number.	Per cent.	All farms.	Acres.	Per cent.	All farms.	Amount.	Per cent.	All farms.	Amount.	Per cent.
THE SOUTH							Tons. 5,297,182	Tons. 2,032,991	38.4	$122,521,349	$47,068,246	38.4
South Atlantic							2,006,471	903,014	45.0	50,501,177	21,781,036	43.1
East South Central							1,262,358	678,407	53.7	28,747,084	15,524,367	54.0
West South Central							2,028,353	451,570	22.3	43,273,088	9,762,843	22.6
South Atlantic:												
Delaware												
Maryland												
District of Columbia												
Virginia							5,240	2,526	48.2	126,546	61,003	48.2
West Virginia												
North Carolina							332,566	116,268	35.0	8,417,246	2,942,743	35.0
South Carolina							639,933	306,477	47.9	16,043,122	7,683,378	47.9
Georgia							996,204	463,581	46.5	23,241,446	10,815,345	46.5
Florida							32,528	14,162	43.5	639,826	278,567	43.5
East South Central:												
Kentucky							1,735	739	42.6	23,590	10,050	42.6
Tennessee							132,281	58,437	44.2	2,715,670	1,199,712	44.2
Alabama							564,764	255,233	45.2	12,803,196	5,786,132	45.2
Mississippi							563,578	363,998	64.6	13,204,628	8,528,473	64.6
West South Central:												
Arkansas							388,440	174,318	44.9	8,596,180	3,857,657	44.9
Louisiana							134,455	70,941	52.8	2,949,943	1,556,464	52.8
Oklahoma							277,871	35,369	12.7	5,788,052	736,736	12.7
Texas							1,227,587	170,942	13.9	25,938,913	3,612,004	13.9

[1] A small percentage of the crop in Oklahoma was produced by Indians, who are included with Negroes in the census classification "colored."
[2] Estimated yield and value based on cotton crop.

Table **50.**—CROPS IN 1909 ON FARMS IN THE SOUTH—FARMS REPORTING, ACREAGE, YIELD, AND VALUE OF SPECIFIED CROPS ON ALL FARMS AND ON COLORED FARMS, BY DIVISIONS AND STATES—Continued.

DIVISION AND STATE.	Number of farms reporting crop.			Acreage in crop.			Yield of crop.			Value of crop.		
	Total.	Colored farms.		All farms.	Colored farms.		All farms.	Colored farms.		All farms.	Colored farms.	
		Number.	Per cent.		Acres.	Per cent.		Amount.	Per cent.		Amount.	Per cent.
TOBACCO.												
							Pounds.	*Pounds.*				
THE SOUTH	260,287	42,470	16.3	1,049,617	169,568	16.2	802,618,483	109,433,038	13.6	$78,506,324	$9,813,199	12.5
South Atlantic	120,731	33,717	27.9	487,411	131,019	26.9	334,569,496	80,767,734	24.1	32,843,156	7,319,700	22.3
East South Central	135,360	8,300	6.1	560,523	38,425	6.8	467,348,072	28,620,776	6.1	45,548,716	2,485,182	14.5
West South Central	4,196	453	10.8	1,683	124	7.4	700,915	44,528	6.4	114,452	8,317	7.3
South Atlantic:												
Delaware												
Maryland	4,392	1,303	29.7	26,072	7,055	27.1	17,845,699	4,010,587	22.5	1,457,112	325,267	22.3
District of Columbia												
Virginia	44,472	16,705	37.6	185,427	59,051	31.8	132,979,390	37,568,274	28.2	12,169,086	3,274,760	26.9
West Virginia	9,299	7	0.1	17,928	15	0.1	14,336,400	8,461	0.1	1,923,180	906	(1)
North Carolina	51,926	12,701	24.5	221,890	56,471	25.4	138,813,163	32,783,801	23.6	13,847,559	3,171,381	22.9
South Carolina	8,166	2,700	33.1	30,082	7,884	26.2	25,583,049	6,005,630	23.5	2,123,576	484,428	22.8
Georgia	1,760	88	5.0	2,025	95	4.7	1,485,994	60,260	4.1	297,167	7,508	2.5
Florida	716	213	29.7	3,987	448	11.2	3,505,801	330,721	9.4	1,025,476	55,450	5.4
East South Central:												
Kentucky	108,050	5,388	5.0	469,795	26,298	5.6	398,482,301	19,670,377	4.9	39,868,753	1,749,790	4.4
Tennessee	25,637	2,608	10.2	90,468	12,087	13.4	68,756,599	8,933,339	13.0	5,661,681	732,721	12.9
Alabama	1,267	117	9.2	211	22	10.4	90,572	8,595	9.5	14,892	1,204	8.1
Mississippi	406	187	46.0	49	18	36.7	18,600	8,465	45.5	3,390	1,467	43.0
West South Central:												
Arkansas	3,329	325	9.8	758	50	6.6	316,418	18,733	5.9	40,489	2,925	7.2
Louisiana	208	37	17.8	519	37	7.1	172,418	12,311	7.1	42,617	3,520	8.3
Oklahoma	207	39	18.8	82	17	20.7	50,546	6,316	12.5	5,312	694	13.1
Texas	452	52	11.5	324	20	6.2	161,533	7,168	4.4	26,034	1,178	4.5
SWEET POTATOES.												
							Bushels.	*Bushels.*				
THE SOUTH	1,015,019	295,854	29.1	583,042	166,072	28.5	52,227,661	12,047,068	23.1	$31,528,482	$7,491,817	23.8
South Atlantic	484,044	156,436	32.3	295,879	88,459	29.9	29,628,153	6,898,014	23.3	16,146,222	3,876,236	24.0
East South Central	368,122	96,052	26.1	160,756	48,086	29.9	13,573,580	3,173,155	23.4	9,116,510	2,308,140	25.3
West South Central	162,853	43,366	27.2	126,407	29,527	23.4	9,025,928	1,975,899	21.9	6,265,750	1,307,441	20.9
South Atlantic:												
Delaware	4,566	388	8.5	5,229	408	7.8	733,746	51,841	7.1	276,679	18,718	6.8
Maryland	11,175	1,610	14.4	7,956	840	10.6	1,065,956	84,232	7.9	483,751	38,168	7.9
District of Columbia	53	3	5.7	126	11	8.7	19,662	185	0.9	13,287	122	0.9
Virginia	67,506	22,480	33.3	40,838	13,094	32.1	5,270,202	1,409,041	26.7	2,681,472	721,405	26.9
West Virginia	15,632	11	0.1	2,079	3	0.1	215,582	262	0.1	170,086	237	0.1
North Carolina	142,238	32,559	22.9	84,740	17,488	20.6	8,493,283	1,375,050	16.2	4,333,297	720,809	16.6
South Carolina	88,340	44,801	50.7	48,878	23,399	47.9	4,319,926	1,610,248	37.3	2,606,606	967,968	37.1
Georgia	131,458	48,035	36.5	84,038	27,327	32.5	7,426,131	1,984,022	26.7	4,349,806	1,184,965	27.2
Florida	23,076	6,549	28.4	21,995	5,889	26.8	2,083,665	383,133	18.4	1,231,238	223,844	18.2
East South Central:												
Kentucky	63,646	1,380	2.2	11,882	222	1.9	1,326,245	22,443	1.7	839,454	14,733	1.8
Tennessee	89,361	8,369	9.4	26,216	2,694	10.3	2,504,490	212,990	8.5	1,625,056	146,599	9.0
Alabama	117,522	41,840	35.6	66,613	23,418	35.2	5,314,857	1,418,179	26.7	3,578,710	1,003,800	28.0
Mississippi	97,593	44,463	45.6	56,045	21,752	38.8	4,427,988	1,519,543	34.3	3,073,290	1,143,008	37.2
West South Central:												
Arkansas	53,297	13,252	24.9	22,388	5,589	25.0	1,685,308	404,891	24.0	1,359,669	339,212	24.9
Louisiana	52,074	18,775	36.1	56,953	16,490	29.0	4,251,086	1,118,549	26.3	2,357,729	605,152	25.7
Oklahoma	9,480	1,596	16.8	5,056	825	16.3	359,451	49,822	13.9	350,553	49,737	14.2
Texas	48,002	9,743	20.3	42,010	6,623	15.8	2,730,083	402,637	14.7	2,197,799	313,340	14.3
HAY AND FORAGE.												
							Tons.	*Tons.*				
THE SOUTH				8,620,243	468,581	5.4	8,866,596	468,394	5.2	$97,264,658	$5,008,872	5.1
South Atlantic				2,856,398	189,680	6.6	2,917,870	174,793	6.0	37,836,676	2,177,009	5.8
East South Central				2,487,554	137,315	5.5	2,565,716	137,957	5.4	29,644,661	1,634,059	5.5
West South Central				3,276,291	141,586	4.3	3,383,010	155,644	4.6	29,783,321	1,192,804	4.0
South Atlantic:												
Delaware				80,669	2,621	3.2	103,575	3,430	3.3	1,174,473	33,448	2.8
Maryland				398,842	8,799	2.2	477,564	9,734	2.0	6,011,749	119,921	2.0
District of Columbia				962			2,148			25,633		
Virginia				773,577	36,027	4.7	823,383	34,609	4.2	10,256,998	469,902	4.6
West Virginia				708,900	1,804	0.3	639,104	1,728	0.3	7,492,747	21,761	0.3
North Carolina				375,795	48,915	13.0	369,362	48,748	13.2	4,781,562	290,232	6.1
South Carolina				209,767	45,055	21.5	186,131	34,173	18.4	3,189,122	585,679	18.4
Georgia				253,157	39,375	15.6	261,333	36,326	13.9	4,056,907	569,275	14.0
Florida				54,729	7,084	12.9	55,300	6,045	10.9	847,485	86,791	10.2
East South Central:												
Kentucky				966,377	11,703	1.2	957,241	10,943	1.1	10,306,344	118,581	1.2
Tennessee				1,052,816	43,900	4.2	1,077,836	40,399	0.4	12,617,538	493,424	3.9
Alabama				238,656	35,593	14.9	251,403	35,738	14.2	3,357,132	439,366	13.1
Mississippi				229,705	46,119	20.1	279,236	50,877	18.2	3,363,647	582,688	17.3
West South Central:												
Arkansas				435,915	16,456	3.8	461,817	19,233	4.2	4,887,139	239,774	4.9
Louisiana				180,811	14,077	7.7	245,815	19,162	7.8	2,433,101	178,054	7.3
Oklahoma				1,347,508	92,610	6.9	1,417,533	93,942	6.6	9,638,648	517,174	5.4
Texas				1,311,967	18,443	1.4	1,257,845	23,307	1.9	12,824,433	257,802	2.0

[1] Less than one-tenth of 1 per cent.

TABLE 50.—CROPS IN 1909 ON FARMS IN THE SOUTH—FARMS REPORTING, ACREAGE, YIELD, AND VALUE OF SPECIFIED CROPS ON ALL FARMS AND ON COLORED FARMS, BY DIVISIONS AND STATES—Continued.

CROPS IN 1909.

DIVISION AND STATE.	Number of farms reporting crop.			Acreage in crop.			Yield of crop.			Value of crop.		
	Total.	Colored farms.		All farms.	Colored farms.		All farms.	Colored farms.		All farms.	Colored farms.	
		Number.	Per cent.		Acres.	Per cent.		Amount.	Per cent.		Amount.	Per cent.
PEANUTS.												
							Bushels.	Bushels.				
THE SOUTH	217,379	77,984	35.9	869,176	236,139	27.2	19,400,338	5,069,004	26.1	$18,253,270	$4,797,046	26.3
South Atlantic	102,128	39,405	38.6	634,436	199,518	31.4	15,305,253	4,470,237	29.2	14,341,058	4,190,919	29.2
East South Central	64,960	25,491	39.2	133,637	22,751	17.0	2,407,562	371,777	15.4	2,196,522	370,621	16.9
West South Central	50,291	13,088	26.0	101,103	13,870	13.7	1,687,523	226,990	13.5	1,715,690	235,506	13.7
South Atlantic:												
Delaware	10	1	10.0	25	7	28.0	202	160	79.2	196	132	67.3
Maryland	12	1	8.3	1			30	2	6.7	37	7	18.9
District of Columbia												
Virginia	12,927	6,227	48.2	145,213	55,134	38.0	4,284,340	1,404,523	32.8	4,239,832	1,390,104	32.8
West Virginia	21						64			168		
North Carolina	31,503	11,972	38.0	195,134	76,264	39.1	5,980,919	2,000,778	33.5	5,368,826	1,813,564	33.8
South Carolina	5,846	2,487	42.5	7,596	2,081	27.4	154,822	36,925	23.8	144,211	34,293	23.8
Georgia	32,590	11,891	36.5	160,317	39,230	24.5	2,569,787	585,432	22.8	2,440,926	540,806	22.2
Florida	19,219	6,826	35.5	126,150	26,802	21.2	2,315,089	442,417	19.1	2,146,862	412,013	19.2
East South Central:												
Kentucky	140	6	4.3	79			1,735	8	0.5	1,867	13	0.7
Tennessee	3,947	213	5.4	18,952	608	3.2	547,240	15,157	2.7	386,765	10,382	2.7
Alabama	37,702	14,547	38.6	100,609	17,818	17.7	1,573,796	272,786	17.3	1,490,654	264,630	17.7
Mississippi	23,171	10,725	46.3	13,997	4,325	30.9	284,791	83,826	29.4	317,236	95,596	30.1
West South Central:												
Arkansas	10,025	2,777	27.7	10,192	2,196	21.5	168,608	35,435	21.0	183,364	40,068	21.8
Louisiana	14,492	4,932	34.0	25,020	4,612	18.4	412,037	77,705	18.9	422,232	77,574	18.4
Oklahoma	1,299	203	15.6	1,564	150	9.6	31,880	2,526	7.9	34,984	3,504	10.0
Texas	24,475	5,176	21.1	64,327	6,912	10.7	1,074,998	111,324	10.4	1,075,110	114,360	10.6
OATS.												
							Bushels.	Bushels.				
THE SOUTH	495,381	81,831	16.5	3,516,128	321,960	9.2	60,126,382	4,358,927	7.2	$32,688,105	$2,726,848	8.3
South Atlantic	251,129	57,463	22.9	1,368,832	213,778	15.6	21,206,000	2,758,384	13.0	13,388,578	1,842,629	13.8
East South Central	144,577	18,105	12.5	870,762	69,132	7.9	11,646,687	840,120	7.2	6,535,286	521,697	8.0
West South Central	99,675	6,263	6.3	1,276,534	39,050	3.1	27,273,695	760,423	2.8	12,764,241	362,522	2.8
South Atlantic:												
Delaware	698	19	2.7	4,226	81	1.9	98,239	794	0.8	51,022	396	0.8
Maryland	8,831	212	2.4	49,210	822	1.7	1,160,663	14,065	1.2	584,395	7,031	1.2
District of Columbia	2			13			375			165		
Virginia	36,306	5,340	14.7	204,455	18,021	8.8	2,884,495	192,882	6.7	1,609,973	118,527	7.4
West Virginia	22,412	81	0.4	103,758	287	0.3	1,728,806	4,192	0.2	912,388	2,437	0.3
North Carolina	48,958	6,619	13.5	228,120	22,761	10.0	2,782,508	246,857	8.9	1,741,561	156,174	9.0
South Carolina	57,398	22,610	39.4	324,180	80,443	24.8	5,745,291	1,150,309	20.0	3,809,345	763,909	20.1
Georgia	70,379	20,728	29.5	411,664	82,401	20.0	6,199,243	1,033,728	16.7	4,236,625	705,315	16.6
Florida	6,145	1,854	30.2	43,206	8,962	20.7	606,380	115,557	19.1	443,104	88,840	20.0
East South Central:												
Kentucky	25,548	489	1.9	174,315	3,024	1.7	2,406,064	44,601	1.9	1,216,187	22,414	1.8
Tennessee	44,432	2,434	5.5	342,086	12,891	3.8	4,720,692	172,714	3.7	2,378,464	87,724	3.7
Alabama	51,857	10,247	19.8	257,276	37,648	14.6	3,251,146	443,387	13.6	2,117,703	293,505	13.9
Mississippi	22,740	4,935	21.7	97,085	15,569	16.0	1,268,785	179,418	14.1	822,932	118,054	14.3
West South Central:												
Arkansas	31,836	2,078	6.5	197,449	6,699	3.4	3,212,891	79,038	2.5	1,641,752	48,244	2.9
Louisiana	4,579	841	18.4	29,711	3,235	10.9	420,033	34,546	8.2	250,588	21,473	8.6
Oklahoma	33,002	1,630	4.9	609,373	20,105	3.3	16,606,154	504,053	3.0	7,172,267	213,779	3.0
Texas	30,258	1,714	5.7	440,001	9,011	2.0	7,034,617	142,786	2.0	3,699,634	79,026	2.1
POTATOES.												
							Bushels.	Bushels.				
THE SOUTH	847,863	97,875	11.5	477,064	50,680	10.6	39,332,677	3,438,024	8.7	$25,472,023	$2,410,099	9.5
South Atlantic	350,428	48,128	13.7	239,762	29,508	12.4	22,102,630	2,179,583	9.9	14,091,735	1,479,417	10.5
East South Central	307,436	28,778	9.4	119,541	9,077	7.6	9,816,160	569,753	5.8	5,940,784	429,879	7.2
West South Central	189,999	20,969	11.0	117,761	12,095	10.3	7,413,887	688,688	9.3	5,439,504	500,803	9.2
South Atlantic:												
Delaware	7,641	565	7.4	9,703	491	5.1	880,360	40,187	4.6	453,400	18,669	4.1
Maryland	34,870	3,054	8.8	39,299	1,865	4.7	3,444,311	133,434	3.9	1,782,954	66,515	3.7
District of Columbia	91	6	6.6	226	4	1.8	32,028	490	1.5	20,231	303	1.5
Virginia	106,499	22,471	21.1	86,927	16,501	19.0	8,770,778	1,318,800	15.0	5,667,557	895,815	15.8
West Virginia	81,297	261	0.3	42,621	98	0.2	4,077,066	9,427	0.2	2,278,638	5,410	2.4
North Carolina	77,421	9,282	12.0	31,990	3,401	10.6	2,372,260	226,454	9.5	1,755,413	167,934	9.6
South Carolina	13,656	4,999	36.6	8,610	2,424	28.2	782,430	146,139	18.7	609,424	102,532	16.8
Georgia	23,861	5,919	24.8	11,877	3,197	26.9	886,430	196,042	22.1	684,427	135,659	19.8
Florida	5,092	1,571	30.9	8,509	1,527	17.9	856,967	108,610	12.7	839,691	86,580	10.3
East South Central:												
Kentucky	130,076	2,860	2.1	55,750	905	1.6	5,120,141	76,871	1.5	2,724,043	42,992	1.6
Tennessee	111,967	8,333	7.4	40,963	2,490	6.1	2,922,713	145,028	5.0	1,790,233	93,276	5.2
Alabama	37,374	6,694	17.9	14,486	2,830	19.5	1,128,564	162,593	14.4	884,497	130,256	14.7
Mississippi	28,019	10,891	38.9	8,342	2,852	34.2	644,742	185,261	28.7	542,011	163,355	30.1
West South Central:												
Arkansas	79,127	9,304	11.8	29,719	2,678	9.0	2,096,893	158,093	7.5	1,439,991	125,367	8.7
Louisiana	18,230	4,159	22.8	19,655	3,586	18.2	1,183,525	196,119	16.1	924,311	143,804	10.6
Oklahoma	45,369	3,320	7.3	32,295	3,267	10.1	1,897,486	189,637	10.0	1,250,052	115,081	9.2
Texas	47,273	4,186	8.9	36,092	2,564	7.1	2,235,983	144,839	6.5	1,825,150	116,551	6.4

TABLE **50.**—CROPS IN 1909 ON FARMS IN THE SOUTH—FARMS REPORTING, ACREAGE, YIELD, AND VALUE OF SPECIFIED CROPS ON ALL FARMS AND ON COLORED FARMS, BY DIVISIONS AND STATES—Continued.

CROPS IN 1909.

Division and State	Farms: Total	Farms: Colored No.	Farms: Colored %	Acreage: All farms	Acreage: Colored Acres	Acreage: %	Yield: All farms	Yield: Colored Amount	Yield: %	Value: All farms	Value: Colored Amount	Value: %
WHEAT.												
THE SOUTH	331,069	36,553	11.0	5,112,675	204,387	4.0	Bushels. 59,121,317	Bushels. 1,829,742	3.0	$61,854,632	$1,939,790	3.1
South Atlantic	212,246	32,717	15.4	2,241,345	152,828	6.8	26,650,768	1,262,466	4.7	28,725,004	1,360,487	4.7
East South Central	83,775	3,290	3.9	1,315,243	37,876	2.9	15,374,422	409,673	2.7	15,851,025	419,715	2.6
West South Central	35,048	546	1.6	1,556,087	13,683	0.9	17,096,127	157,603	0.9	17,278,603	159,588	0.9
South Atlantic:												
Delaware	4,827	215	4.5	111,215	3,679	3.3	1,643,572	45,429	2.8	1,697,539	46,543	2.7
Maryland	23,358	1,305	5.6	589,893	16,479	2.8	9,463,457	189,012	2.0	9,876,480	194,072	2.0
District of Columbia												
Virginia	63,405	13,462	21.2	692,907	58,293	8.4	8,076,989	509,787	6.3	8,776,061	526,592	6.0
West Virginia	22,344	125	0.6	209,315	1,448	0.7	2,575,996	20,693	0.8	2,697,141	21,278	0.8
North Carolina	65,124	8,652	13.3	501,912	45,747	9.1	3,827,145	311,842	8.1	4,420,322	347,806	7.9
South Carolina	11,356	3,946	34.7	43,028	11,586	26.9	310,614	73,416	23.6	385,835	91,782	23.8
Georgia	21,827	5,010	23.0	93,065	15,594	16.8	752,858	112,265	14.9	871,494	132,397	15.2
Florida	5	2	40.0	10	2	20.0	137	22	16.0	132	17	12.9
East South Central:												
Kentucky	37,164	988	2.7	681,323	14,185	2.0	8,739,260	166,781	1.9	8,812,469	166,868	1.9
Tennessee	44,013	1,896	4.3	619,861	22,070	3.6	6,516,539	229,190	3.5	6,913,335	239,025	3.5
Alabama	2,463	355	14.4	13,665	1,518	11.1	113,953	12,625	11.1	120,873	13,000	10.8
Mississippi	135	51	37.8	394	103	26.1	4,670	1,077	23.1	4,348	822	18.9
West South Central:												
Arkansas	5,197	133	2.6	60,426	743	1.2	526,414	3,305	0.6	532,712	3,356	0.6
Louisiana	23			65			488			508		
Oklahoma	23,003	362	1.6	1,169,420	11,777	1.0	14,008,334	143,400	1.0	13,854,322	142,969	1.0
Texas	6,825	51	0.7	326,176	1,163	0.4	2,560,891	10,898	0.4	2,891,061	13,263	0.5
DRY PEAS.												
THE SOUTH	209,064	72,989	34.9	1,009,836	284,854	28.2	Bushels. 3,803,461	Bushels. 1,038,529	27.3	$6,461,667	$1,737,609	26.9
South Atlantic	118,172	45,297	38.3	667,705	216,842	32.6	2,242,244	687,987	30.9	3,805,792	1,165,660	30.6
East South Central	58,833	19,984	34.0	203,229	47,706	23.5	882,471	229,529	26.0	1,560,726	387,563	24.8
West South Central	32,059	7,708	24.0	138,902	20,306	14.6	678,746	121,013	17.8	1,095,149	184,386	16.8
South Atlantic:												
Delaware	523	29	5.5	1,615	50	3.1	12,521	366	2.9	25,278	738	2.9
Maryland	350	32	9.1	742	44	5.9	5,603	660	11.8	11,143	1,284	11.5
District of Columbia												
Virginia	4,462	1,587	35.6	12,091	2,624	21.7	66,488	15,445	23.2	127,211	29,944	23.5
West Virginia	93			232			1,490			3,312		
North Carolina	39,726	8,349	21.0	169,934	33,262	19.6	651,567	102,470	15.7	1,024,228	160,362	15.6
South Carolina	35,660	18,997	53.3	265,632	103,257	38.9	711,853	301,354	43.2	1,311,454	543,123	41.4
Georgia	34,716	15,133	43.6	210,315	75,312	35.8	736,009	248,350	33.7	1,204,783	398,171	33.0
Florida	2,642	1,170	44.3	7,144	2,293	32.1	56,713	19,342	34.1	98,383	32,038	32.6
East South Central:												
Kentucky	1,732	39	2.3	8,465	193	2.3	44,772	764	1.7	84,514	1,286	1.5
Tennessee	10,175	1,402	13.8	36,640	3,515	9.6	133,924	12,084	9.0	245,434	22,819	9.3
Alabama	26,905	10,988	40.8	85,034	24,592	28.9	418,007	138,733	33.2	660,270	209,719	31.8
Mississippi	20,021	7,555	37.7	73,090	19,406	26.6	285,768	77,948	27.3	570,508	153,739	26.9
West South Central:												
Arkansas	13,821	2,995	21.7	52,730	7,325	14.0	229,444	42,640	18.6	376,076	67,271	17.9
Louisiana	6,330	1,974	31.2	33,150	5,240	15.8	161,659	32,421	20.6	252,362	45,067	17.9
Oklahoma	1,612	290	18.0	6,245	489	7.8	33,282	3,836	11.6	63,857	7,605	11.9
Texas	10,296	2,449	23.8	46,777	7,252	15.5	254,361	42,116	16.6	402,854	64,443	16.0
RICE.												
THE SOUTH	13,706	4,967	36.2	610,163	29,235	4.8	Bushels. 21,838,520	Bushels. 889,103	4.1	$16,019,567	$677,542	4.2
South Atlantic	5,527	3,843	69.5	27,080	7,836	28.9	713,966	166,119	23.3	691,372	157,887	22.8
East South Central	596	156	26.2	560	76	13.6	10,006	1,318	13.2	10,547	1,618	15.3
West South Central	7,583	968	12.8	582,523	21,323	3.7	21,114,548	721,666	3.4	15,317,648	518,037	3.4
South Atlantic:												
Delaware												
Maryland												
District of Columbia												
Virginia												
West Virginia												
North Carolina	161	64	39.8	521	195	37.4	11,357	4,042	35.6	10,269	4,056	39.5
South Carolina	3,017	2,379	78.9	19,491	5,401	27.7	541,570	110,188	20.3	520,000	100,977	19.4
Georgia	1,740	1,241	71.3	6,445	2,088	32.4	148,698	49,534	33.3	145,813	50,124	34.4
Florida	609	159	26.2	623	152	24.4	12,341	2,355	19.1	15,290	2,730	17.9
East South Central:												
Kentucky												
Tennessee												
Alabama	238	50	21.0	279	15	5.4	5,170	402	7.8	5,179	564	10.9
Mississippi	358	106	29.6	281	61	21.7	4,836	916	18.9	5,368	1,054	19.6
West South Central:												
Arkansas	290	5	1.7	27,419	68	0.2	1,282,830	4,352	0.3	1,158,103	3,091	0.3
Louisiana	6,138	932	15.2	317,518	13,894	4.4	10,839,973	390,359	3.6	8,053,222	314,096	3.9
Oklahoma												
Texas	1,155	31	2.7	237,586	7,361	3.1	8,991,745	326,955	3.6	6,106,323	200,850	3.3

TABLE **50.**—CROPS IN 1909 ON FARMS IN THE SOUTH—FARMS REPORTING, ACREAGE, YIELD, AND VALUE OF SPECIFIED CROPS ON ALL FARMS AND ON COLORED FARMS, BY DIVISIONS AND STATES—Continued.

DIVISION AND STATE.	CROPS IN 1909.											
	Number of farms reporting crop.			Acreage in crop.			Yield of crop.			Value of crop.		
	Total.	Colored farms.		All farms.	Colored farms.		All farms.	Colored farms.		All farms.	Colored farms.	
		Number.	Per cent.		Acres.	Per cent.		Amount.	Per cent.		Amount.	Per cent.
ALFALFA.												
							Tons.	Tons.				
THE SOUTH	32,754	1,172	3.6	340,651	6,611	1.9	574,149	11,901	2.1	$6,654,473	$171,836	2.6
South Atlantic	2,362	134	5.7	8,710	298	3.4	18,967	453	2.4	291,294	6,361	2.2
East South Central	5,878	357	6.1	41,784	1,541	3.7	74,194	2,304	3.1	973,044	36,898	3.8
West South Central	24,516	681	2.8	290,157	4,772	1.6	480,988	9,144	1.9	5,390,135	108,577	2.0
South Atlantic:												
Delaware	70	4	5.7	205	10	4.9	580	16	2.8	7,927	208	2.6
Maryland	789	14	1.8	3,188	64	2.0	6,806	144	2.1	104,633	1,812	1.7
District of Columbia	1			28			108			1,620		
Virginia	796	69	8.7	3,126	122	3.9	7,203	180	2.5	109,409	2,543	2.3
West Virginia	179			696			1,406			17,932		
North Carolina	272	22	8.1	735	54	7.3	1,394	59	4.2	22,276	770	3.5
South Carolina	65	2	3.1	138	1	0.7	328	1	0.3	6,853	21	0.3
Georgia	182	23	12.6	545	47	8.6	1,079	53	4.9	19,758	1,007	5.1
Florida	8			49			63			886		
East South Central:												
Kentucky	3,676	18	0.5	20,229	57	0.3	37,978	88	0.2	426,879	940	0.2
Tennessee	945	36	3.8	5,323	168	3.2	10,600	206	1.9	138,525	2,720	2.0
Alabama	416	89	21.4	6,987	598	8.6	8,906	799	9.0	137,970	14,165	10.3
Mississippi	841	214	25.4	9,245	718	7.8	16,710	1,211	7.2	269,670	19,073	7.1
West South Central:												
Arkansas	2,363	207	8.8	15,929	853	5.4	33,231	1,600	4.8	443,875	23,138	5.2
Louisiana	685	143	20.9	12,073	939	7.8	28,146	1,999	7.1	376,562	27,062	7.2
Oklahoma	17,467	249	1.4	206,823	2,512	1.2	321,675	4,966	1.5	3,230,384	50,051	1.5
Texas	4,001	82	2.0	55,332	468	0.8	97,936	579	0.6	1,339,314	8,326	0.6
RYE.												
							Bushels.	Bushels.				
THE SOUTH	40,769	1,941	4.8	213,563	6,597	3.1	1,772,320	48,279	2.7	$1,484,934	$44,111	3.0
South Atlantic	32,982	1,773	5.4	157,546	5,469	3.5	1,322,474	39,044	2.9	1,106,617	36,179	3.3
East South Central	6,940	145	2.1	50,091	996	2.0	400,709	7,847	2.0	337,152	6,836	2.0
West South Central	847	23	2.7	5,926	132	2.2	49,137	1,388	2.8	41,165	1,096	2.7
South Atlantic:												
Delaware	210	13	6.2	1,017	39	3.8	11,423	389	3.4	8,169	272	3.3
Maryland	5,181	215	4.1	28,093	929	3.3	357,562	9,174	2.6	252,691	6,581	2.6
District of Columbia	2			13			190			135		
Virginia	8,509	524	6.2	47,890	1,728	3.6	438,345	13,994	3.2	344,241	11,080	3.2
West Virginia	2,774	1	(1)	15,679	7	(1)	148,676	70	(1)	122,258	56	(1)
North Carolina	12,830	706	5.5	48,685	1,957	4.0	280,431	10,033	3.6	269,566	9,981	3.7
South Carolina	1,043	141	13.5	2,958	358	12.1	20,631	2,151	10.4	32,197	3,651	11.3
Georgia	2,340	154	6.6	12,352	307	2.5	59,937	2,182	3.6	69,365	3,102	4.5
Florida	93	19	20.4	859	144	16.8	5,279	1,051	19.9	7,995	1,456	18.2
East South Central:												
Kentucky	3,488	43	1.2	26,813	357	1.3	255,532	3,561	1.4	202,534	3,085	1.5
Tennessee	3,166	86	2.7	22,798	615	2.7	140,925	3,980	2.8	129,845	3,464	2.7
Alabama	267	15	5.6	437	24	5.5	3,736	304	8.1	4,314	286	6.6
Mississippi	19	1	5.3	43			516	2	0.4	459	1	0.2
West South Central:												
Arkansas	303	12	4.0	1,080	27	2.5	7,354	389	5.3	6,834	268	3.1
Louisiana	9			19			193			236		
Oklahoma	396	9	2.3	4,291	88	2.1	37,240	881	2.4	30,364	706	2.3
Texas	139	2	1.4	536	17	3.2	4,350	118	2.7	3,731	122	3.3
DRY EDIBLE BEANS.												
							Bushels.	Bushels.				
THE SOUTH	47,549	2,881	6.1	47,808	3,742	7.8	301,927	22,083	7.3	$527,201	$37,143	7.0
South Atlantic	25,544	2,202	8.6	25,776	2,497	9.7	162,853	16,333	10.0	291,885	28,029	9.6
East South Central	20,558	476	2.3	18,481	628	3.4	114,022	3,270	2.9	189,599	5,680	3.0
West South Central	1,447	203	14.0	3,551	617	17.4	25,052	2,480	9.5	45,717	3,434	7.5
South Atlantic:												
Delaware	102	12	11.8	55	[2]1	1.8	648	32	4.9	1,387	77	5.6
Maryland	312	26	8.3	196	11	5.6	1,833	122	6.7	3,342	247	7.4
District of Columbia												
Virginia	7,660	1,131	14.8	4,777	498	10.4	29,435	3,525	12.0	61,864	7,877	12.7
West Virginia	8,626			8,111			39,794			81,049		
North Carolina	6,574	529	8.0	5,521	623	11.3	35,937	4,704	13.1	57,528	6,839	11.8
South Carolina	517	242	46.8	1,528	628	41.1	6,825	2,937	43.0	12,778	5,324	41.6
Georgia	1,329	197	14.8	2,947	553	18.8	16,546	2,729	16.5	30,018	4,322	14.4
Florida	424	65	15.3	2,641	183	6.9	31,835	2,284	7.2	43,919	3,343	7.6
East South Central:												
Kentucky	14,248	123	0.9	12,434	117	0.9	70,557	530	0.8	105,309	741	0.7
Tennessee	5,312	116	2.2	3,398	114	3.3	19,526	477	2.4	40,966	1,067	2.6
Alabama	647	159	24.6	1,557	240	15.4	15,212	1,615	10.6	19,887	2,534	12.7
Mississippi	351	78	22.2	1,092	157	14.4	8,727	648	7.4	23,647	1,338	5.7
West South Central:												
Arkansas	538	122	22.7	819	401	50.0	4,080	1,639	40.2	6,588	2,197	33.3
Louisiana	78	6	7.7	311	9	2.9	5,557	40	0.7	6,982	55	0.8
Oklahoma	224	20	8.9	575	13	2.3	2,529	85	3.4	5,942	124	2.1
Texas	607	55	9.1	1,846	194	10.5	12,895	716	5.6	26,205	1,058	4.0

1 Less than one-tenth of 1 per cent.   2 Acreage of farms less than 1 acre not included.

TABLE **50.**—CROPS IN 1909 ON FARMS IN THE SOUTH—FARMS REPORTING, ACREAGE, YIELD, AND VALUE OF SPECIFIED CROPS ON ALL FARMS AND ON COLORED FARMS, BY DIVISIONS AND STATES—Continued.

	CROPS IN 1909.											
DIVISION AND STATE.	Number of farms reporting crop.			Acreage in crop.			Yield of crop.			Value of crop.		
	Total.	Colored farms.		All farms.	Colored farms.		All farms.	Colored farms.		All farms.	Colored farms.	
		Number.	Per cent.		Acres.	Per cent.		Amount.	Per cent.		Amount.	Per cent.
KAFIR CORN.												
THE SOUTH.............	54,193	593	1.1	1,108,129	3,402	0.3	*Bushels.* 10,546,626	*Bushels.* 40,430	0.4	$6,338,581	$23,343	0.4
South Atlantic..............	125	13	10.4	230	18	7.8	3,561	214	6.0	2,918	201	6.9
East South Central..........	215	4	1.9	493	5	1.0	6,453	121	1.9	4,998	117	2.3
West South Central..........	53,853	576	1.1	1,107,406	3,379	0.3	10,536,612	40,095	0.4	6,330,665	23,025	0.4
South Atlantic:												
Delaware................	2	......	......	1	......	......	25	......	......	25	......	......
Maryland................	9	1	11.1	19	......	......	238	10	4.2	173	5	2.9
District of Columbia......	......	......	......	......	......	......	......	......	......	......	......	......
Virginia................	33	5	15.1	80	5	6.2	1,438	41	2.9	1,032	38	3.7
West Virginia...........	16	......	......	26	......	......	467	......	......	326	......	......
North Carolina..........	32	1	3.1	65	4	6.1	599	20	3.3	537	20	3.7
South Carolina..........	7	4	57.1	8	7	87.5	135	116	85.9	132	111	84.1
Georgia.................	14	1	7.1	15	1	6.6	237	15	6.3	258	12	4.7
Florida.................	12	1	8.3	16	1	6.2	422	12	2.8	435	15	3.4
East South Central:												
Kentucky................	87	1	1.1	190	1	0.5	2,404	10	0.4	1,588	6	0.4
Tennessee...............	45	......	......	119	......	......	1,539	......	......	1,093	......	......
Alabama.................	51	1	2.0	140	1	0.7	1,716	80	4.7	1,611	80	5.0
Mississippi.............	32	2	6.2	44	3	6.8	794	31	3.9	706	31	4.4
West South Central:												
Arkansas................	530	7	1.3	1,294	10	0.8	15,284	192	1.3	12,074	202	1.7
Louisiana...............	32	2	6.2	213	1	0.5	2,132	27	1.3	2,092	22	1.1
Oklahoma................	29,660	541	1.8	532,515	3,202	0.6	4,658,752	38,468	0.8	2,531,036	21,700	0.9
Texas...................	23,631	26	0.1	573,384	166	(1)	5,860,444	1,408	(1)	3,785,463	1,101	(1)
SOY BEANS.												
THE SOUTH.............	2,055	252	12.3	14,029	1,401	9.9	*Bushels.* 169,379	*Bushels.* 14,042	8.3	$225,512	$17,817	7.9
South Atlantic..............	1,397	203	14.5	10.079	1,166	11.6	132,408	12,339	9.3	175,963	15,361	8.7
East South Central..........	655	48	7.3	3,946	234	5.9	36,833	1,698	4.6	49,211	2,451	5.0
West South Central..........	3	1	33.3	4	1	25.0	138	5	3.6	338	5	1.5
South Atlantic:												
Delaware................	......	......	......	......	......	......	......	......	......	......	......	......
Maryland................	......	......	......	......	......	......	......	......	......	......	......	......
District of Columbia......	......	......	......	......	......	......	......	......	......	......	......	......
Virginia................	6	1	16.7	29	5	17.2	415	100	24.1	695	100	14.4
West Virginia...........	......	......	......	......	......	......	......	......	......	......	......	......
North Carolina..........	264	46	17.4	1,249	188	15.1	13,313	1,953	14.7	14,141	1,980	14.0
South Carolina..........	1	......	......	1	......	......	12	......	......	36	......	......
Georgia.................	[2]66	2	3.0	437	12	2.7	4,264	190	4.5	8,612	420	4.9
Florida.................	1,060	154	14.5	8,363	961	11.5	114,404	10,096	8.8	152,479	12,861	8.4
East South Central:												
Kentucky................	6	......	......	8	......	......	27	......	......	53	......	......
Tennessee...............	41	2	4.9	256	......	......	2,037	4	0.2	3,387	8	0.2
Alabama.................	602	45	7.5	3,667	234	6.4	34,617	1,689	4.9	45,393	2,431	5.4
Mississippi.............	6	1	16.7	15	......	......	152	5	3.3	378	12	3.2
West South Central:												
Arkansas................	......	......	......	......	......	......	......	......	......	......	......	......
Louisiana...............	2	......	......	3	......	......	133	......	......	333	......	......
Oklahoma................	......	......	......	......	......	......	......	......	......	......	......	......
Texas...................	1	1	100.0	1	1	100.0	5	5	100.0	5	5	100.0
BROOM CORN.												
THE SOUTH.............	16,172	245	1.5	228,569	691	0.3	*Pounds.* 46,005,312	*Pounds.* 164,447	0.4	$2,774,354	$9,601	0.3
South Atlantic..............	1,514	41	2.7	223	29	13.0	113,479	10,588	9.3	10,619	911	8.6
East South Central..........	3,419	99	2.9	1,896	102	5.4	582,834	23,879	4.1	48,484	1,654	3.4
West South Central..........	11,239	105	0.9	226,450	560	0.2	45,308,999	129,980	0.3	2,715,251	7,036	0.3
South Atlantic:												
Delaware................	21	2	9.5	13	......	......	4,198	65	1.5	492	10	2.0
Maryland................	291	1	0.3	19	......	......	18,599	60	0.3	2,006	2	(1)
District of Columbia......	......	......	......	......	......	......	......	......	......	......	......	......
Virginia................	666	26	3.9	107	5	4.7	46,016	2,996	6.5	3,586	180	5.2
West Virginia...........	397	......	......	45	......	......	30,456	......	......	3,229	......	......
North Carolina..........	128	8	6.3	15	3	20.0	6,493	1,242	19.1	549	98	17.9
South Carolina..........	3	1	33.3	2	......	......	650	100	15.4	63	10	15.9
Georgia.................	8	3	37.5	22	21	95.5	7,067	6,125	86.7	694	611	88.0
Florida.................	......	......	......	......	......	......	......	......	......	......	......	......
East South Central:												
Kentucky................	1,041	12	1.2	342	5	1.5	157,286	3,193	2.0	13,641	169	1.2
Tennessee...............	2,220	76	3.4	1,348	68	5.0	347,064	15,851	4.6	27,733	1,172	4.2
Alabama.................	115	5	4.3	52	3	5.8	17,910	445	2.5	1,562	30	1.9
Mississippi.............	43	6	14.0	154	26	16.9	60,574	4,390	7.2	5,548	283	5.1
West South Central:												
Arkansas................	294	6	2.0	332	5	1.5	106,576	1,467	1.4	8,198	87	1.1
Louisiana...............	263	57	21.7	320	35	10.9	92,208	10,653	11.6	7,285	949	13.0
Oklahoma................	10,151	38	0.4	216,350	494	0.2	42,741,725	113,310	0.3	2,559,235	5,737	0.2
Texas...................	531	4	0.8	9,448	26	0.3	2,368,490	4,550	0.2	140,533	264	0.2

[1] Less than one-tenth of 1 per cent.   [2] Includes velvet beans.

TABLE 50.—CROPS IN 1909 ON FARMS IN THE SOUTH—FARMS REPORTING, ACREAGE, YIELD, AND VALUE OF SPECIFIED CROPS ON ALL FARMS AND ON COLORED FARMS, BY DIVISIONS AND STATES—Continued.

DIVISION AND STATE.	Number of farms reporting crop.			Acreage in crop.			Yield of crop.			Value of crop.		
	Total.	Colored farms.		All farms.	Colored farms.		All farms.	Colored farms.		All farms.	Colored farms.	
		Number.	Per cent.		Acres.	Per cent.		Amount.	Per cent.		Amount.	Per cent.
BUCKWHEAT.							*Bushels.*	*Bushels.*				
THE SOUTH	22,793	268	1.2	89,757	997	1.1	1,269,120	11,089	1.0	$829,668	$6,915	0.8
South Atlantic	21,466	263	1.2	84,864	975	1.1	1,216,608	10,873	0.9	791,546	6,796	0.9
East South Central	1,296	4	0.3	4,772	20	0.4	51,525	136	0.3	37,268	79	0.2
West South Central	31	1	3.2	121	2	1.7	987	80	8.1	854	40	4.7
South Atlantic:												
Delaware	743	54	7.3	4,002	227	5.6	53,903	2,268	4.2	30,839	1,203	3.9
Maryland	2,411	38	1.6	10,388	205	2.2	152,216	2,961	1.9	99,216	1,651	1.7
District of Columbia												
Virginia	5,954	83	1.4	25,481	317	1.2	332,222	3,200	1.0	196,196	1,920	1.0
West Virginia	9,028	2	(1)	33,323	2	(1)	533,670	58	(1)	351,171	33	(1)
North Carolina	3,304	75	2.3	11,606	202	1.7	144,186	2,167	1.5	113,577	1,708	1.5
South Carolina	6	3	50.0	9	5	55.5	84	53	63.0	101	65	64.4
Georgia	20	8	40.0	55	17	30.9	327	166	50.8	446	216	48.4
Florida												
East South Central:												
Kentucky	452	3	0.7	1,887	19	1.0	18,074	116	0.6	12,028	65	0.5
Tennessee	831	1	0.1	2,867	1	(1)	33,249	20	(1)	25,078	14	(1)
Alabama	13			18		(1)	202		(1)	162		(1)
Mississippi												
West South Central:												
Arkansas	13			20		(1)	123		(1)	133		
Louisiana	1					(1)	16			16		
Oklahoma	12	1	8.3	43	2	4.6	375	80	21.0	370	40	10.8
Texas	5			57		(1)	473			335		
BARLEY.							*Bushels.*	*Bushels.*				
THE SOUTH	5,291	98	1.9	35,202	193	0.5	710,883	3,960	0.6	$463,987	$2,890	0.6
South Atlantic	3,775	83	2.2	15,561	94	0.6	409,615	2,120	0.5	276,981	1,684	0.6
East South Central	442	8	1.8	5,388	69	1.3	119,922	1,220	1.0	79,171	696	0.9
West South Central	1,074	7	0.7	14,253	30	0.2	181,346	620	0.3	107,835	510	0.5
South Atlantic:												
Delaware	8	1	12.5	31			422	10	2.4	288	5	1.7
Maryland	1,215	7	0.6	4,494	20	0.4	135,454	698	0.5	79,231	314	0.4
District of Columbia												
Virginia	2,057	10	0.5	9,890	40	0.4	253,649	872	0.3	179,712	642	0.4
West Virginia	119			408			8,407			5,640		
North Carolina	149	2	1.3	504	3	0.6	7,535	21	0.3	6,863	18	0.3
South Carolina	190	57	30.0	189	26	13.8	3,483	440	12.6	4,297	604	14.1
Georgia	36	6	16.6	44	5	11.4	655	79	12.1	942	101	10.7
Florida	1			1			10			8		
East South Central:												
Kentucky	175	1	0.6	2,738	15	0.5	65,596	300	0.5	42,929	150	0.3
Tennessee	248	7	2.8	2,567	54	2.1	53,201	920	1.7	35,363	546	1.5
Alabama	14			41			372			336		
Mississippi	5			42			753			543		
West South Central:												
Arkansas	41	2	4.9	82	11	13.4	1,267	260	20.5	1,136	265	23.3
Louisiana												
Oklahoma	834	4	0.5	10,283	9	0.1	127,641	160	0.1	75,059	95	0.1
Texas	199	1	0.5	3,888	10	0.3	52,438	200	0.4	31,640	150	0.5

[1] Less than one-tenth of 1 per cent.

TABLE 51.—ACREAGE IN SELECTED CROPS ON COLORED FARMS OF THE SOUTH, BY DIVISIONS AND STATES: 1909 AND 1899.

DIVISION AND STATE.	ACRES IN SPECIFIED CROPS ON FARMS OF COLORED FARMERS.									
	1909	1899	1909	1899	1909	1899	1909	1899	1909	1899
	CORN.		COTTON.		HAY AND FORAGE.		OATS.		POTATOES.	
THE SOUTH	7,377,221	6,993,999	12,096,638	9,656,262	468,581	316,528	321,960	261,982	50,680	30,308
South Atlantic	3,066,496	2,855,482	4,442,773	3,005,870	189,680	105,189	213,778	152,717	29,508	15,839
East South Central	2,309,639	2,387,838	4,614,339	3,870,109	137,315	68,645	69,132	53,774	9,077	7,314
West South Central	2,001,086	1,750,679	3,039,526	2,780,283	141,586	142,694	39,050	55,491	12,095	7,155
South Atlantic:										
Delaware	12,636	11 055			2,621	2,237	81	98	491	264
Maryland	52,139	54,476			8,799	6,675	822	1,093	1,865	1,223
District of Columbia	2	16				20		3	4	9
Virginia	338,378	327,566	13,362	11,937	36,027	28,928	18,021	26,492	16,501	6,535
West Virginia	4,421	5,103			1,804	1,883	287	365	98	150
North Carolina	535,037	537,044	474,889	321,654	48,915	16,170	22,761	25,864	3,401	2,094
South Carolina	653,856	688,000	1,364,375	1,021,700	45,055	29,217	80,443	44,458	2,424	2,669
Georgia	1,278,627	1,051,877	2,468,242	1,544,897	39,375	17,139	82,401	49,545	3,197	1,960
Florida	191,400	180,345	121,905	105,682	7,084	2,920	8,962	4,799	1,527	935
East South Central:										
Kentucky	104,055	108,911	2,937	135	11,703	12,492	3,024	5,818	905	655
Tennessee	354,996	365,264	387,527	308,333	43,900	26,884	12,891	7,351	2,490	1,874
Alabama	818,175	854,877	1,960,709	1,644,079	35,593	12,621	37,648	27,452	2,830	2,501
Mississippi	1,032,413	1,058,786	2,263,166	1,917,562	46,119	16,648	15,569	13,153	2,852	2,284
West South Central:										
Arkansas	386,913	359,981	949,734	700,351	16,456	10,710	6,699	12,135	2,678	2,263
Louisiana	505,431	450,501	514,352	784,216	14,077	6,646	3,235	3,952	3,586	1,600
Oklahoma [1]	369,818	254,095	217,231	90,262	92,610	108,414	20,105	20,418	3,267	1,497
Texas	738,924	686,102	1,358,209	1,205,454	18,443	16,924	9,011	18,986	2,564	1,795

DIVISION AND STATE.	ACRES IN SPECIFIED CROPS ON FARMS OF COLORED FARMERS.							
	1909	1899	1909	1899	1909	1899	1909	1899
	RICE.		SWEET POTATOES.		TOBACCO.		WHEAT.	
THE SOUTH	29,235	48,980	166,072	132,891	169,568	142,145	204,387	435,036
South Atlantic	7,836	38,246	88,459	75,262	131,019	104,801	152,828	253,516
East South Central	76	977	48,086	37,918	38,425	37,052	37,876	99,886
West South Central	21,323	9,757	29,527	19,711	124	292	13,683	81,634
South Atlantic:								
Delaware			408	133			3,679	3,579
Maryland			840	623	7,055	11,208	16,479	20,594
District of Columbia			11	9				
Virginia		17	13,094	10,171	59,051	47,383	58,293	61,876
West Virginia			3	15	15	31	1,448	2,773
North Carolina	195	5,418	17,488	13,146	56,471	41,296	45,747	69,837
South Carolina	5,401	26,243	23,399	24,440	7,884	4,247	11,586	49,300
Georgia	2,088	5,521	27,327	19,724	95	165	15,594	45,542
Florida	152	1,047	5,889	7,001	448	471	2	15
East South Central:								
Kentucky			222	269	26,298	27,122	14,185	32,162
Tennessee			2,694	2,044	12,087	9,823	22,070	54,245
Alabama	15	442	23,418	20,235	22	59	1,518	12,774
Mississippi	61	535	21,752	15,370	18	48	103	705
West South Central:								
Arkansas	68	5	5,589	3,411	50	104	743	8,233
Louisiana	13,894	9,748	16,490	7,937	37	48		24
Oklahoma [1]			825	549	17	57	11,777	61,890
Texas	7,361	4	6,623	7,814	20	83	1,163	11,487

[1] Includes Indian Territory for 1899.

TABLE 52.—ACREAGE IN SELECTED CROPS ON COLORED AND WHITE FARMS OF THE SOUTH, BY DIVISIONS AND STATES: 1909.

ACRES IN SPECIFIED CROPS: 1909.

DIVISION AND STATE.	CORN.		COTTON.		HAY AND FORAGE.		OATS.		PEANUTS.	
	Colored farms.	White farms.	Colored farms.	White farms.	Colored farms.	White farms.	Colored farms.	White farms.	Colored farms.	White farms.
THE SOUTH	7,377,221	30,250,098	12,096,638	19,849,504	468,581	8,151,662	321,960	3,194,168	236,139	633,037
South Atlantic	3,066,496	8,320,488	4,442,773	4,560,003	189,680	2,666,718	213,778	1,155,054	199,518	434,918
East South Central	2,309,639	9,018,629	4,614,339	3,311,680	137,315	2,350,239	69,132	801,630	22,751	110,886
West South Central	2,001,086	12,910,981	3,039,526	11,977,821	141,586	3,134,705	39,050	1,237,484	13,870	87,233
South Atlantic:										
Delaware	12,636	176,119			2,621	78,048	81	4,145	7	18
Maryland	52,139	594,873			8,799	390,043	822	48,388		1
District of Columbia	2	424				962		13		
Virginia	338,378	1,521,981	13,362	11,785	36,027	737,550	18,021	186,434	55,134	90,079
West Virginia	4,421	671,890			1,804	707,096	287	103,471		
North Carolina	535,087	1,924,420	474,889	799,515	48,915	326,880	22,761	205,359	76,264	118,870
South Carolina	653,856	911,976	1,364,375	1,192,092	45,055	164,712	80,443	243,737	2,081	5,515
Georgia	1,278,627	2,104,434	2,468,242	2,415,062	39,375	213,782	82,401	329,263	39,230	121,087
Florida	191,400	414,371	121,905	141,549	7,084	47,645	8,962	34,244	26,802	99,348
East South Central:										
Kentucky	104,055	3,332,285	2,937	4,874	11,703	954,674	3,024	171,291		79
Tennessee	354,996	2,791,352	387,527	399,989	43,900	1,008,916	12,891	329,195	608	18,344
Alabama	818,175	1,754,793	1,960,709	1,769,773	35,593	203,063	37,648	219,628	17,818	82,791
Mississippi	1,032,413	1,140,199	2,263,166	1,137,044	46,119	183,586	15,569	81,516	4,325	9,672
West South Central:										
Arkansas	386,913	1,890,203	949,734	1,203,488	16,456	419,459	6,699	190,750	2,196	7,996
Louisiana	505,431	1,085,399	514,352	442,659	14,077	166,734	3,235	26,476	4,612	20,408
Oklahoma	369,818	5,544,251	217,231	1,759,704	92,610	1,254,988	20,105	589,268	150	1,414
Texas	738,924	4,391,128	1,358,209	8,571,970	18,443	1,293,524	9,011	430,990	6,912	57,415

DIVISION AND STATE.	POTATOES.		RICE.		SWEET POTATOES.		TOBACCO.		WHEAT.	
	Colored farms.	White farms.	Colored farms.	White farms.	Colored farms.	White farms.	Colored farms.	White farms.	Colored farms.	White farms.
THE SOUTH	50,680	426,384	29,235	580,928	166,072	416,970	169,568	880,049	204,387	4,908,288
South Atlantic	29,508	210,254	7,836	19,244	88,459	207,420	131,019	356,392	152,828	2,088,517
East South Central	9,077	110,464	76	484	48,086	112,670	38,425	522,098	37,876	1,277,367
West South Central	12,095	105,666	21,323	561,200	29,527	96,880	124	1,559	13,683	1,542,404
South Atlantic:										
Delaware	491	9,212			408	4,821			3,679	107,536
Maryland	1,865	37,434			840	7,116	7,055	19,017	16,479	573,414
District of Columbia	4	222			11	115				
Virginia	16,501	70,426			13,094	27,744	59,051	126,376	58,293	634,614
West Virginia	98	42,523			3	2,076	15	17,913	1,448	207,867
North Carolina	3,401	28,589	195	326	17,488	67,252	56,471	165,419	45,747	456,165
South Carolina	2,424	6,186	5,401	14,090	23,399	25,479	7,884	22,198	11,586	31,442
Georgia	3,197	8,680	2,088	4,357	27,327	56,711	95	1,930	15,594	77,471
Florida	1,527	6,982	152	471	5,889	16,106	448	3,539	2	8
East South Central:										
Kentucky	905	54,845			222	11,660	26,298	443,497	14,185	667,138
Tennessee	2,490	38,473			2,694	23,522	12,087	78,381	22,070	597,791
Alabama	2,830	11,656	15	264	23,418	43,195	22	189	1,518	12,147
Mississippi	2,852	5,490	61	220	21,752	34,293	18	31	103	291
West South Central:										
Arkansas	2,678	27,041	68	27,351	5,589	16,799	50	708	743	59,683
Louisiana	3,586	16,069	13,894	303,624	16,490	40,463	37	482		65
Oklahoma	3,267	29,028			825	4,231	17	65	11,777	1,157,643
Texas	2,564	33,528	7,361	230,225	6,623	35,387	20	304	1,163	325,013

Table 53.—SIZE OF FARMS—FARMS OPERATED BY COLORED AND BY WHITE FARMERS, CLASSIFIED BY SIZE, FOR SOUTHERN STATES: 1910 AND 1900.

DIVISION, STATE, AND SIZE OF FARM.	FARMS.													
	Total number.		Operated by colored farmers.							Operated by white farmers.				
			Number.		Per 1,000 farms of specified size.		Increase:[1] 1900-1910.	Distribution per 1,000.		Number.		Increase:[1] 1900-1910.	Distribution per 1,000.	
	1910	1900	1910	1900	1910	1900		1910	1900	1910	1900		1910	1900
THE SOUTH.														
Total	3,097,547	2,620,391	890,141	740,670	287	283	149,471	1,000	1,000	2,207,406	1,879,721	327,685	1,000	1,000
Under 3 acres	2,928	12,972	402	4,300	137	331	−3,898	......	6	2,526	8,672	−6,146	1	5
3 to 9 acres	157,320	112,528	61,953	50,004	394	444	11,949	70	68	95,277	62,524	32,753	43	33
10 to 19 acres	340,456	259,922	151,894	118,876	446	457	33,018	171	160	188,562	141,046	47,516	85	75
20 to 49 acres	955,907	764,114	426,540	340,106	446	445	86,434	479	459	529,367	424,008	105,359	240	226
50 to 99 acres	694,737	583,047	152,244	132,350	219	227	19,894	171	179	542,493	450,697	91,796	246	240
100 to 174 acres	561,724	518,836	68,599	66,501	122	128	2,098	77	90	492,945	452,335	40,610	223	241
175 to 259 acres	187,549	176,087	17,394	16,545	93	94	849	20	22	170,155	159,542	10,613	77	85
260 to 499 acres	135,063	127,899	8,779	8,995	65	70	−216	10	12	126,284	118,904	7,380	57	63
500 to 999 acres	41,183	42,015	1,881	2,292	46	55	−411	2	3	39,302	39,723	−421	18	21
1,000 acres and over	20,950	22,971	455	701	22	31	−246	1	1	20,495	22,270	−1,775	9	12
SOUTH ATLANTIC.														
Total	1,111,881	962,225	355,862	288,871	320	300	66,991	1,000	1,000	756,019	673,354	82,665	1,000	1,000
Under 3 acres	1,127	6,196	194	2,855	172	461	−2,661	......	10	933	3,341	−2,408	1	5
3 to 9 acres	72,010	54,270	30,621	27,360	425	504	3,261	86	95	41,389	26,910	14,479	55	40
10 to 19 acres	113,819	86,699	48,229	40,525	424	467	7,704	136	140	65,590	46,174	19,416	87	69
20 to 49 acres	354,207	265,623	167,080	121,282	472	457	45,798	470	420	187,127	144,341	42,786	248	214
50 to 99 acres	251,901	216,522	66,849	54,401	265	251	12,448	188	188	185,052	162,121	22,931	245	241
100 to 174 acres	181,336	181,290	29,858	28,700	165	158	1,158	84	99	151,478	152,590	−1,112	200	227
175 to 259 acres	70,299	75,197	8,246	8,352	117	111	−106	23	29	62,053	66,845	−4,792	82	99
260 to 499 acres	47,600	53,344	3,824	4,106	80	77	−282	11	14	43,776	49,238	−5,462	58	73
500 to 999 acres	14,555	17,191	797	1,062	55	62	−265	2	4	13,758	16,129	−2,371	18	24
1,000 acres and over	5,027	5,893	164	228	33	39	−64	(2)	1	4,863	5,665	−802	6	8
EAST SOUTH CENTRAL.														
Total	1,042,480	903,313	325,218	267,895	312	297	57,323	1,000	1,000	717,262	635,418	81,844	1,000	1,000
Under 3 acres	828	3,565	122	835	147	234	−713	......	3	706	2,730	−2,024	1	4
3 to 9 acres	61,325	41,113	21,769	15,430	355	375	6,339	67	58	39,466	25,683	13,783	55	40
10 to 19 acres	149,551	108,681	64,113	45,527	429	419	18,586	197	170	85,438	63,154	22,284	119	99
20 to 49 acres	350,256	280,010	164,639	132,080	470	472	32,559	506	493	185,617	147,930	37,687	259	233
50 to 99 acres	225,976	204,914	48,061	46,507	213	227	1,554	148	174	177,915	158,407	19,508	248	249
100 to 174 acres	157,414	159,531	19,118	19,884	121	125	−766	59	74	138,296	139,647	−1,351	193	220
175 to 259 acres	53,528	55,480	4,522	4,471	84	81	51	14	17	49,006	51,009	−2,003	68	80
260 to 499 acres	32,769	37,303	2,386	2,601	73	70	−215	7	10	30,383	34,702	−4,319	42	55
500 to 999 acres	8,396	9,777	403	468	48	48	−65	1	2	7,993	9,309	−1,316	11	15
1,000 acres and over	2,527	2,939	85	92	34	31	−7	(2)	(2)	2,442	2,847	−405	3	4
WEST SOUTH CENTRAL.														
Total	943,186	754,853	209,061	183,904	222	244	25,157	1,000	1,000	734,125	570,949	163,176	1,000	1,000
Under 3 acres	973	3,211	86	610	88	190	−524	......	3	887	2,601	−1,714	1	5
3 to 9 acres	23,985	17,145	9,563	7,214	399	421	2,349	46	39	14,422	9,931	4,491	20	17
10 to 19 acres	77,086	64,542	39,552	32,824	513	509	6,728	189	178	37,534	31,718	5,816	51	56
20 to 49 acres	251,444	218,481	94,821	86,744	377	397	8,077	454	472	156,623	131,737	24,886	213	231
50 to 99 acres	216,860	161,611	37,334	31,442	172	195	5,892	179	171	179,526	130,169	49,357	245	228
100 to 174 acres	222,794	178,015	19,623	17,917	88	101	1,706	94	97	203,171	160,098	43,073	277	280
175 to 259 acres	63,722	45,410	4,626	3,722	73	82	904	22	20	59,096	41,688	17,408	80	73
260 to 499 acres	54,694	37,252	2,569	2,288	47	61	281	12	12	52,125	34,964	17,161	71	61
500 to 999 acres	18,232	15,047	681	762	37	51	−81	3	4	17,551	14,285	3,266	24	25
1,000 acres and over	13,396	14,139	206	381	15	27	−175	1	2	13,190	13,758	−568	18	24
SOUTH ATLANTIC.														
DELAWARE.														
Total	10,836	9,687	922	818	85	84	104	1,000	1,000	9,914	8,869	1,045	1,000	1,000
Under 3 acres	32	38	3	6	94	158	−3	3	7	29	32	−3	3	4
3 to 9 acres	672	292	125	89	186	305	36	136	109	547	203	344	55	23
10 to 19 acres	831	547	165	124	199	227	41	179	152	666	423	243	67	48
20 to 49 acres	1,988	1,568	221	221	111	141	......	240	270	1,767	1,347	420	178	152
50 to 99 acres	2,977	2,610	195	203	66	78	−8	211	248	2,782	2,407	375	281	271
100 to 174 acres	2,849	2,923	153	116	54	40	37	166	142	2,696	2,807	−111	272	316
175 to 259 acres	994	1,133	42	42	42	37	......	46	51	952	1,091	−139	96	123
260 to 499 acres	435	500	14	14	32	28	......	15	17	421	486	−65	42	55
500 to 999 acres	52	71	4	3	77	42	1	4	4	48	68	−20	5	8
1,000 acres and over	6	5	......	......	......	......	......	......	......	6	5	1	1	1
MARYLAND.														
Total	48,923	46,012	6,372	5,843	130	127	529	1,000	1,000	42,551	40,169	2,382	1,000	1,000
Under 3 acres	148	442	7	128	47	290	−121	1	22	141	314	−173	3	8
3 to 9 acres	4,977	3,393	1,608	1,124	323	331	484	252	192	3,369	2,269	1,100	79	56
10 to 19 acres	5,107	4,315	1,327	1,170	260	271	157	208	200	3,780	3,145	635	89	78
20 to 49 acres	8,629	7,683	1,386	1,216	161	158	170	218	208	7,243	6,467	776	170	161
50 to 99 acres	9,946	9,307	767	745	77	80	22	120	128	9,179	8,562	617	216	213
100 to 174 acres	11,457	11,543	780	883	68	76	−103	122	151	10,677	10,660	17	251	265
175 to 259 acres	5,043	5,389	311	345	62	64	−34	49	59	4,732	5,044	−312	111	126
260 to 499 acres	3,027	3,270	146	193	48	59	−47	23	33	2,881	3,077	−196	68	77
500 to 999 acres	506	591	35	35	69	59	......	5	6	471	556	−85	11	14
1,000 acres and over	83	79	5	4	60	51	1	1	1	78	75	3	2	2

[1] A minus sign (−) denotes decrease.   [2] Less than 1.

TABLE 53.—SIZE OF FARMS—FARMS OPERATED BY COLORED AND BY WHITE FARMERS, CLASSIFIED BY SIZE, FOR SOUTHERN STATES: 1910 AND 1900—Continued.

DIVISION, STATE, AND SIZE OF FARM.	Total number.		Operated by colored farmers.							Operated by white farmers.				
			Number.		Per 1,000 farms of specified size.		Increase:[1] 1900–1910.	Distribution per 1,000.		Number.		Increase:[1] 1900–1910.	Distribution per 1,000.	
	1910	1900	1910	1900	1910	1900		1910	1900	1910	1900		1910	1900
SOUTH ATLANTIC—Continued.														
DISTRICT OF COLUMBIA.														
Total	217	269	12	17	55	63	−5	1,000	1,000	205	252	−47	1,000	1,000
Under 3 acres	29	16	4	1	138	63	3	333	59	25	15	10	122	60
3 to 9 acres	32	51	4	7	125	137	−3	333	411	28	44	−16	137	175
10 to 19 acres	61	87	2	5	33	57	−3	167	294	59	82	−23	288	325
20 to 49 acres	65	71	2	2	31	28		167	118	63	69	−6	307	274
50 to 99 acres	13	11		2		182	−2		118	17	29	−12	83	115
100 to 174 acres	10	9								10	9	1	49	36
175 to 259 acres		2									2	−2		8
260 to 499 acres	3									3			15	
500 to 999 acres		2									2	−2		8
1,000 acres and over														
VIRGINIA.														
Total	184,018	167,886	48,114	44,834	261	267	3,280	1,000	1,000	135,904	123,052	12,852	1,000	1,000
Under 3 acres	227	1,671	44	832	194	498	−788	1	19	183	839	−656	1	7
3 to 9 acres	17,464	12,898	6,979	6,300	400	488	679	145	141	10,485	6,598	3,887	77	54
10 to 19 acres	22,055	18,334	10,079	9,274	457	506	805	209	207	11,976	9,060	2,916	88	74
20 to 49 acres	42,390	35,644	16,431	14,300	388	401	2,131	342	319	25,959	21,344	4,615	191	173
50 to 99 acres	38,342	33,948	8,685	7,686	227	226	999	181	171	29,657	26,262	3,395	218	213
100 to 174 acres	32,997	32,466	4,166	4,367	126	135	−201	87	97	28,831	28,099	732	212	228
175 to 259 acres	14,963	15,348	1,070	1,158	72	75	−88	22	26	13,893	14,190	−297	102	115
260 to 499 acres	11,138	12,377	530	697	48	56	−167	11	16	10,608	11,680	−1,072	78	95
500 to 999 acres	3,450	4,100	112	193	32	47	−81	2	4	3,338	3,907	−569	25	32
1,000 acres and over	992	1,100	18	27	18	25	−9	(²)	1	974	1,073	−99	7	9
WEST VIRGINIA.														
Total	96,685	92,874	708	742	7	8	−34	1,000	1,000	95,977	92,132	3,845	1,000	1,000
Under 3 acres	117	599	3	26	26	43	−23	4	35	114	573	−459	1	6
3 to 9 acres	7,419	5,342	137	113	18	21	24	194	152	7,282	5,229	2,053	76	57
10 to 19 acres	7,863	7,140	139	123	18	17	16	196	166	7,724	7,017	707	80	76
20 to 49 acres	20,323	19,306	191	206	9	11	−15	270	278	20,132	19,100	1,032	210	207
50 to 99 acres	26,806	25,529	147	152	5	6	−5	208	205	26,659	25,377	1,282	278	275
100 to 174 acres	20,156	20,164	57	82	3	4	−25	81	111	20,099	20,082	17	209	218
175 to 259 acres	7,481	7,542	21	21	3	3		30	28	7,460	7,521	−61	78	82
260 to 499 acres	4,767	5,127	12	14	3	3	−2	17	19	4,755	5,113	−358	50	55
500 to 999 acres	1,316	1,511		4		3	−4		5	1,316	1,507	−191	14	16
1,000 acres and over	437	614	1	1	2	2		1	1	436	613	−177	5	7
NORTH CAROLINA.														
Total	253,725	224,637	65,656	54,864	259	244	10,792	1,000	1,000	188,069	169,773	18,296	1,000	1,000
Under 3 acres	116	1,202	32	531	276	442	−499		10	84	671	−587		4
3 to 9 acres	14,868	11,323	5,296	4,761	356	420	535	81	87	9,572	6,562	3,010	51	39
10 to 19 acres	28,240	20,659	10,920	8,553	387	414	2,367	166	156	17,320	12,106	5,214	92	71
20 to 49 acres	75,629	59,913	29,250	22,273	387	372	6,977	446	406	46,379	37,640	8,739	247	222
50 to 99 acres	62,157	55,028	12,197	10,635	196	193	1,562	186	194	49,960	44,393	5,567	266	261
100 to 174 acres	43,987	44,052	5,668	5,614	129	127	54	86	102	38,319	38,438	−119	204	226
175 to 259 acres	15,629	17,012	1,447	1,471	93	86	−24	22	27	14,182	15,541	−1,359	75	92
260 to 499 acres	9,625	11,224	677	765	70	68	−88	10	14	8,948	10,459	−1,511	48	62
500 to 999 acres	2,669	3,275	139	205	52	63	−66	2	4	2,530	3,070	−540	13	18
1,000 acres and over	805	949	30	56	37	59	−26	(²)	1	775	893	−118	4	5
SOUTH CAROLINA.														
Total	176,434	155,355	96,798	85,401	549	550	11,397	1,000	1,000	79,636	69,954	9,682	1,000	1,000
Under 3 acres	53	1,193	19	963	358	807	−944		11	34	230	−196		3
3 to 9 acres	14,218	13,075	11,368	11,002	800	841	366	117	129	2,850	2,073	777	36	30
10 to 19 acres	23,714	18,828	16,152	14,406	681	765	1,746	167	169	7,562	4,422	3,140	95	63
20 to 49 acres	70,582	54,384	47,050	36,801	667	677	10,249	486	431	23,532	17,583	5,949	295	251
50 to 99 acres	33,147	29,944	14,304	13,439	432	449	865	148	157	18,843	16,505	2,338	237	236
100 to 174 acres	19,427	20,532	5,633	6,154	290	300	−521	58	72	13,794	14,378	−584	173	206
175 to 259 acres	7,164	7,866	1,346	1,554	188	198	−208	14	18	5,818	6,312	−494	73	90
260 to 499 acres	5,375	6,209	708	815	132	131	−107	7	10	4,667	5,394	−727	59	77
500 to 999 acres	1,942	2,314	164	209	84	90	−45	2	2	1,778	2,105	−327	22	30
1,000 acres and over	812	1,010	54	58	67	57	−4	1	1	758	952	−194	10	14
GEORGIA.														
Total	291,027	224,691	122,559	82,826	421	369	39,733	1,000	1,000	168,468	141,865	26,603	1,000	1,000
Under 3 acres	98	451	16	239	163	530	−223		3	82	212	−130		1
3 to 9 acres	8,602	5,604	3,770	2,833	438	506	937	31	34	4,832	2,771	2,061	29	20
10 to 19 acres	20,929	13,301	7,780	5,247	372	394	2,533	63	63	13,149	8,054	5,095	78	57
20 to 49 acres	117,432	73,408	65,410	39,652	557	540	25,758	534	479	52,022	33,756	18,266	309	238
50 to 99 acres	68,510	52,251	27,811	19,076	406	365	8,735	227	230	40,699	33,175	7,524	242	234
100 to 174 acres	42,275	41,661	12,117	10,324	287	248	1,793	99	125	30,158	31,337	−1,179	179	221
175 to 259 acres	16,436	18,646	3,704	3,540	225	190	164	30	43	12,732	15,106	−2,374	76	106
260 to 499 acres	11,274	12,793	1,579	1,475	140	115	104	13	18	9,695	11,318	−1,623	58	80
500 to 999 acres	3,950	4,718	320	368	81	78	−48	3	4	3,630	4,350	−720	22	31
1,000 acres and over	1,521	1,858	52	72	34	39	−20	(²)	1	1,469	1,786	−317	9	13

[1] A minus sign (−) denotes decrease. [2] Less than 1.

TABLE 53.—SIZE OF FARMS—FARMS OPERATED BY COLORED AND BY WHITE FARMERS, CLASSIFIED BY SIZE FOR SOUTHERN STATES: 1910 AND 1900—Continued.

DIVISION, STATE, AND SIZE OF FARM.	Total number.		Operated by colored farmers.							Operated by white farmers.				
			Number.		Per 1,000 farms of specified size.		Increase[1] 1900–1910.	Distribution per 1,000.		Number.		Increase[1] 1900–1910.	Distribution per 1,000.	
	1910	1900	1910	1900	1910	1900		1910	1900	1910	1900		1910	1900
SOUTH ATLANTIC—Continued.														
FLORIDA.														
Total	50,016	40,814	14,721	13,526	294	331	1,195	1,000	1,000	35,295	27,288	8,007	1,000	1,000
Under 3 acres	307	584	66	129	215	221	−63	4	10	241	455	−214	7	17
3 to 9 acres	3,758	2,292	1,334	1,131	355	493	203	91	84	2,424	1,161	1,263	69	43
10 to 19 acres	5,019	3,488	1,665	1,623	332	465	42	113	120	3,354	1,865	1,489	95	68
20 to 49 acres	17,169	13,646	7,139	6,611	416	484	528	485	489	10,030	7,035	2,995	284	258
50 to 99 acres	9,999	7,874	2,743	2,463	274	313	280	186	182	7,256	5,411	1,845	206	198
100 to 174 acres	8,178	7,940	1,284	1,160	157	146	124	87	86	6,894	6,780	114	195	248
175 to 259 acres	2,589	2,259	305	221	118	98	84	21	16	2,284	2,038	246	65	75
260 to 499 acres	1,956	1,844	158	133	81	72	25	11	10	1,798	1,711	87	51	63
500 to 999 acres	670	609	23	45	34	74	−22	2	3	647	564	83	18	21
1,000 acres and over	371	278	4	10	11	36	−6	(2)	1	367	268	99	10	10
EAST SOUTH CENTRAL.														
KENTUCKY.														
Total	259,185	234,667	11,730	11,238	45	48	492	1,000	1,000	247,455	223,429	24,026	1,000	1,000
Under 3 acres	315	1,175	28	162	89	138	−134	2	14	287	1,013	−726	1	5
3 to 9 acres	21,777	14,960	2,202	1,771	101	118	431	188	158	19,575	13,189	6,386	79	59
10 to 19 acres	33,380	26,769	2,945	2,777	88	104	168	251	247	30,435	23,992	6,443	123	107
20 to 49 acres	58,537	51,850	3,970	3,796	68	73	174	338	338	54,567	48,054	6,513	221	215
50 to 99 acres	65,778	60,435	1,565	1,629	24	27	−64	133	145	64,213	58,806	5,407	259	263
100 to 174 acres	50,134	48,564	756	806	15	17	−50	64	72	49,378	47,758	1,620	200	214
175 to 259 acres	17,315	17,480	182	197	11	11	−15	16	18	17,133	17,283	−150	69	77
260 to 499 acres	9,324	10,406	69	81	7	8	−12	6	7	9,255	10,325	−1,070	37	46
500 to 999 acres	2,181	2,470	12	15	6	6	−3	1	1	2,169	2,455	−286	9	11
1,000 acres and over	444	558	1	4	2	7	−3	(2)	(2)	443	554	−111	2	2
TENNESSEE.														
Total	246,012	224,623	38,308	33,895	156	151	4,413	1,000	1,000	207,704	190,728	16,976	1,000	1,000
Under 3 acres	143	1,123	7	158	49	141	−151	......	5	136	965	−829	1	5
3 to 9 acres	14,713	9,902	2,391	1,992	163	201	399	62	59	12,322	7,910	4,412	59	41
10 to 19 acres	32,485	25,517	6,883	5,749	212	225	1,134	180	170	25,602	19,768	5,834	123	104
20 to 49 acres	72,212	61,442	19,063	15,826	264	258	3,237	498	467	53,149	45,616	7,533	256	239
50 to 99 acres	60,105	57,265	6,866	6,569	114	115	297	179	194	53,239	50,696	2,543	256	266
100 to 174 acres	41,545	42,476	2,369	2,731	57	64	−362	62	81	39,176	39,745	−569	189	208
175 to 259 acres	14,149	15,108	490	565	35	37	−75	13	17	13,659	14,543	−884	66	76
260 to 499 acres	8,301	9,166	196	262	24	29	−66	5	8	8,105	8,904	−799	39	47
500 to 999 acres	1,878	2,058	34	35	18	17	−1	1	1	1,844	2,023	−179	9	11
1,000 acres and over	481	566	9	8	19	14	1	(2)	(2)	472	558	−86	2	3
ALABAMA.														
Total	262,901	223,220	110,443	94,083	420	421	16,360	1,000	1,000	152,458	129,137	23,321	1,000	1,000
Under 3 acres	130	768	22	309	169	402	−287	......	3	108	459	−351	1	4
3 to 9 acres	13,613	10,009	9,229	7,240	678	723	1,989	84	77	4,384	2,769	1,615	29	21
10 to 19 acres	28,115	20,866	13,410	10,876	477	521	2,534	121	116	14,705	9,990	4,715	96	77
20 to 49 acres	106,841	80,784	57,766	46,445	541	575	11,321	523	494	49,075	34,339	14,736	322	266
50 to 99 acres	55,448	47,745	19,679	18,572	355	389	1,107	178	197	35,769	29,173	6,596	235	226
100 to 174 acres	35,563	37,111	7,288	7,424	205	200	−136	66	79	28,275	29,687	−1,412	185	230
175 to 259 acres	11,932	12,561	1,755	1,819	147	145	−64	16	19	10,177	10,742	−565	67	83
260 to 499 acres	8,161	9,632	1,086	1,138	133	118	−52	10	12	7,075	8,494	−1,419	46	66
500 to 999 acres	2,276	2,788	173	223	76	80	−50	2	2	2,103	2,565	−462	14	20
1,000 acres and over	822	956	35	37	43	39	−2	(2)	(2)	787	919	−132	5	7
MISSISSIPPI.														
Total	274,382	220,803	164,737	128,679	600	583	36,058	1,000	1,000	109,645	92,124	17,521	1,000	1,000
Under 3 acres	240	499	65	206	271	413	−141	......	2	175	293	−118	2	3
3 to 9 acres	11,132	6,242	7,947	4,427	714	709	3,520	48	34	3,185	1,815	1,370	29	20
10 to 19 acres	55,571	35,529	40,875	26,125	736	735	14,750	248	203	14,696	9,404	5,292	134	102
20 to 49 acres	112,666	85,934	83,840	66,013	744	768	17,827	509	513	28,826	19,921	8,905	263	216
50 to 99 acres	44,645	39,469	19,951	19,737	447	500	214	121	153	24,694	19,732	4,962	225	214
100 to 174 acres	30,172	31,380	8,705	8,923	289	284	−218	53	69	21,467	22,457	−990	196	244
175 to 259 acres	10,132	10,331	2,095	1,890	207	183	205	13	15	8,037	8,441	−404	73	92
260 to 499 acres	6,983	8,099	1,035	1,120	148	138	−85	6	9	5,948	6,979	−1,031	54	76
500 to 999 acres	2,061	2,461	184	195	89	79	−11	1	2	1,877	2,266	−389	17	25
1,000 acres and over	780	859	40	43	51	50	−3	(2)	(2)	740	816	−76	7	9

[1] A minus sign (−) denotes decrease. [2] Less than 1.

TABLE 53.—SIZE OF FARMS—FARMS OPERATED BY COLORED AND BY WHITE FARMERS, CLASSIFIED BY SIZE, FOR SOUTHERN STATES: 1910 AND 1900—Continued.

DIVISION, STATE, AND SIZE OF FARM.	Total number.		Operated by colored farmers.							Operated by white farmers.				
			Number.		Per 1,000 farms of specified size.		Increase:[1] 1900–1910.	Distribution per 1,000.		Number.		Increase:[1] 1900–1910.	Distribution per 1,000.	
	1910	1900	1910	1900	1910	1900		1910	1900	1910	1900		1910	1900
WEST SOUTH CENTRAL.														
ARKANSAS.														
Total	214,678	178,694	63,593	46,983	296	263	16,610	1,000	1,000	151,085	131,711	19,374	1,000	1,000
Under 3 acres	114	529	15	88	132	166	−73	.....	2	99	441	−342	1	3
3 to 9 acres	6,270	3,945	2,716	1,571	433	398	1,145	43	33	3,554	2,374	1,180	24	18
10 to 19 acres	29,875	20,191	16,273	9,562	545	474	6,711	256	204	13,602	10,629	2,973	90	81
20 to 49 acres	74,983	55,332	31,156	23,222	416	420	7,934	490	494	43,827	32,110	11,717	290	244
50 to 99 acres	45,373	38,595	8,191	7,274	181	188	917	129	155	37,182	31,321	5,861	246	238
100 to 174 acres	39,353	42,007	3,798	3,895	97	93	−97	60	83	35,555	38,112	−2,557	235	289
175 to 259 acres	11,135	10,569	909	822	82	78	87	14	17	10,226	9,747	479	68	74
160 to 499 acres	6,014	5,871	450	440	75	75	10	7	9	5,564	5,431	133	37	41
200 to 999 acres	1,163	1,239	72	82	62	66	−10	1	2	1,091	1,157	−66	7	9
5,000 acres and over	398	416	13	27	33	65	−14	(2)	1	385	389	−4	3	3
LOUISIANA.														
Total	120,546	115,969	54,879	58,160	455	502	−3,281	1,000	1,000	65,667	57,809	7,858	1,000	1,000
Under 3 acres	344	992	33	266	96	268	−233	1	5	311	726	−415	5	13
3 to 9 acres	6,671	4,730	4,335	3,068	650	649	1,267	79	53	2,336	1,662	674	36	29
10 to 19 acres	22,241	20,060	15,353	14,716	690	734	637	280	253	6,888	5,344	1,544	105	92
20 to 49 acres	46,389	44,622	25,161	29,156	542	653	−3,995	458	501	21,228	15,466	5,762	323	268
50 to 99 acres	20,248	18,179	6,041	6,451	298	355	−410	110	111	14,207	11,728	2,479	216	203
100 to 174 acres	13,681	15,633	2,753	3,210	201	205	−457	50	55	10,928	12,423	−1,495	166	215
175 to 259 acres	4,645	4,839	694	707	149	146	−13	13	12	3,951	4,132	−181	60	71
260 to 499 acres	3,761	4,176	384	437	102	105	−53	7	8	3,377	3,739	−362	51	65
500 to 999 acres	1,548	1,688	89	120	57	71	−31	2	2	1,459	1,568	−109	22	27
1,000 acres and over	1,018	1,050	36	29	35	28	7	1	(2)	982	1,021	−39	15	18
OKLAHOMA.														
Total	190,192	³108,000	20,671	³13,225	109	122	7,446	1,000	1,000	169,521	³94,775	74,746	1,000	1,000
Under 3 acres	104	388	15	98	144	253	−83	1	7	89	290	−201	1	3
3 to 9 acres	1,975	1,685	430	864	218	513	−434	21	65	1,545	821	724	9	9
10 to 19 acres	5,079	4,658	1,171	1,567	231	336	−396	57	118	3,908	3,091	817	23	33
20 to 49 acres	31,489	19,390	6,328	3,155	201	163	3,173	306	239	25,161	16,235	8,926	148	171
50 to 99 acres	39,002	16,300	5,436	2,145	139	132	3,291	263	162	33,566	14,155	19,411	198	149
100 to 174 acres	75,186	48,983	4,904	3,424	65	70	1,480	237	259	70,282	45,559	24,723	415	481
175 to 259 acres	16,078	6,002	1,096	591	68	98	505	53	45	14,982	5,411	9,571	88	57
260 to 499 acres	17,734	7,204	870	702	49	97	168	42	53	16,864	6,502	10,362	99	69
500 to 999 acres	2,688	1,937	318	409	118	211	−91	15	31	2,370	1,528	842	14	16
1,000 acres and over	857	1,453	103	270	120	186	−167	5	20	754	1,183	−429	4	12
TEXAS.														
Total	417,770	352,190	69,918	65,536	167	186	4,382	1,000	1,000	347,852	286,654	61,198	1,000	1,000
Under 3 acres	411	1,302	23	158	56	121	−135	.....	2	388	1,144	−756	1	4
3 to 9 acres	9,069	6,785	2,082	1,711	230	252	371	30	26	6,987	5,074	1,913	20	18
10 to 19 acres	19,891	19,633	6,755	6,979	340	355	−224	97	106	13,136	12,654	482	38	44
20 to 49 acres	98,583	99,137	32,176	31,211	326	315	965	460	476	66,407	67,926	−1,519	191	237
50 to 99 acres	112,237	88,537	17,666	15,572	157	176	2,094	253	238	94,571	72,965	21,606	272	255
100 to 174 acres	94,574	71,392	8,168	7,388	86	103	780	117	113	86,406	64,004	22,402	248	223
175 to 259 acres	31,864	24,000	1,927	1,602	60	67	325	28	24	29,937	22,398	7,539	86	78
260 to 499 acres	27,185	20,001	865	709	32	35	156	12	11	26,320	19,292	7,028	76	67
500 to 999 acres	12,833	10,183	202	151	16	15	51	3	2	12,631	10,032	2,599	36	35
1,000 acres and over	11,123	11,220	54	55	5	5	−1	1	1	11,069	11,165	−96	32	39

[1] A minus sign (−) denotes decrease.   [2] Less than 1.   [3] Includes Indian Territory.

TABLE 54.—NEGRO FARMERS—OWNERS, TENANTS, AND MANAGERS, BY DIVISIONS AND STATES: 1910 AND 1900.

[A minus sign (−) denotes decrease.]

DIVISION AND STATE.	1910				1900				INCREASE DURING DECADE.							
									Total.		Owners.		Tenants.		Managers.	
	Total.	Owners.	Tenants.	Managers.	Total.	Owners.	Tenants.	Managers.	Number.	Per cent.	Number.	Per cent.	Number.	Per cent.	Number.	Per cent.
UNITED STATES	893,370	218,972	672,964	1,434	746,715	187,797	557,174	1,744	146,655	19.6	31,175	16.6	115,790	20.8	−310	−17.8
GEOGRAPHIC DIVISIONS:																
New England	310	240	51	19	264	197	54	13	46	17.4	43	21.8	−3	(1)	6	(1)
Middle Atlantic	1,310	793	447	70	1,497	953	490	54	−187	−12.5	−160	−16.8	−43	−8.8	16	(1)
East North Central	4,843	3,095	1,677	71	5,179	3,064	2,070	45	−336	−6.5	31	1.0	−393	−19.0	26	(1)
West North Central	5,589	3,370	2,155	64	7,076	3,908	3,104	64	−1,487	−21.0	−538	−13.8	−949	−30.6	......	......
South Atlantic	354,530	101,135	252,676	719	287,933	84,389	202,578	966	66,597	23.1	16,746	19.8	50,098	24.7	−247	−25.6
East South Central	324,884	58,610	266,025	249	267,530	49,888	217,318	324	57,354	21.4	8,722	17.5	48,707	22.4	−75	−23.1
West South Central	201,422	51,342	149,858	222	176,899	45,141	131,487	271	24,523	13.9	6,201	13.7	18,371	14.0	−49	−18.1
Mountain	219	176	34	9	133	104	26	3	86	64.7	72	69.2	8	(1)	6	(1)
Pacific	263	211	41	11	204	153	47	4	59	28.9	58	37.9	−6	(1)	7	(1)
NEW ENGLAND:																
Maine	28	24	3	1	24	22	1	1	4	(1)	2	(1)	2	(1)	......	(1)
New Hampshire	14	11	2	1	10	8	2	......	4	(1)	3	(1)	......	......	1	......
Vermont	20	17	2	1	8	7	1	......	12	(1)	10	(1)	1	(1)	1	......
Massachusetts	103	89	10	4	87	67	16	4	16	(1)	22	(1)	−6	(1)	......	......
Rhode Island	40	28	12	......	28	16	11	1	12	(1)	12	(1)	1	(1)	−1	(1)
Connecticut	105	71	22	12	107	77	23	7	−2	−1.9	−6	(1)	−1	(1)	5	(1)
MIDDLE ATLANTIC:																
New York	295	193	90	12	443	326	105	12	−148	−33.4	−133	−40.8	−15	−14.3	......	......
New Jersey	472	262	183	27	469	280	170	19	3	0.6	−18	−6.4	13	7.6	8	(1)
Pennsylvania	543	338	174	31	585	347	215	23	−42	−7.2	−9	−2.6	−41	−19.1	8	(1)
EAST NORTH CENTRAL:																
Ohio	1,948	1,311	609	28	1,966	1,236	702	28	−18	−0.9	75	6.1	−93	−13.2	......	......
Indiana	785	456	314	15	1,043	587	447	9	−258	−24.7	−131	−22.3	−133	−29.8	6	(1)
Illinois	1,422	787	617	18	1,486	724	757	5	−64	−4.3	63	8.7	−140	−18.5	13	(1)
Michigan	640	502	129	9	626	472	151	3	14	2.2	30	6.4	−22	−14.6	6	(1)
Wisconsin	48	39	8	1	58	45	13	......	−10	(1)	−6	(1)	−5	(1)	1	......
WEST NORTH CENTRAL:																
Minnesota	29	16	12	1	31	18	11	2	−2	(1)	−2	(1)	1	(1)	−1	(1)
Iowa	187	122	63	2	200	107	89	4	−13	−6.5	15	14.0	−26	(1)	−2	(1)
Missouri	3,656	2,104	1,511	41	4,950	2,657	2,256	37	−1,294	−26.1	−553	−20.8	−745	−33.0	4	(1)
North Dakota	22	18	4	......	18	13	5	......	4	(1)	5	(1)	−1	(1)	......	......
South Dakota	67	57	10	......	17	15	2	......	50	(1)	42	(1)	8	(1)	......	......
Nebraska	96	75	21	......	78	45	29	4	18	(1)	30	(1)	−8	(1)	−4	(1)
Kansas	1,532	978	534	20	1,782	1,053	712	17	−250	−14.0	−75	−7.1	−178	−25.0	3	(1)
SOUTH ATLANTIC:																
Delaware	922	406	500	16	817	331	471	15	105	12.9	75	22.7	29	6.2	1	(1)
Maryland	6,370	3,949	2,334	87	5,842	3,262	2,475	105	528	9.0	687	21.1	−141	−5.7	−18	−17.1
District of Columbia	12	8	3	1	17	5	10	2	−5	(1)	3	(1)	−7	(1)	−1	(1)
Virginia	48,039	32,168	15,691	180	44,795	26,527	18,030	238	3,244	7.2	5,641	21.3	−2,339	−13.0	−58	−24.4
West Virginia	707	557	143	7	742	534	200	8	−35	−4.7	23	4.3	−57	−28.5	−1	(1)
North Carolina	64,456	20,707	43,676	73	53,996	16,834	37,043	119	10,460	19.4	3,873	23.0	6,633	17.9	−46	−38.7
South Carolina	96,772	20,356	76,285	131	85,381	18,970	66,231	180	11,391	13.3	1,386	7.3	10,054	15.2	−49	−27.2
Georgia	122,554	15,698	106,733	123	82,822	11,375	71,239	208	39,732	48.0	4,323	38.0	35,494	49.8	−85	−40.9
Florida	14,698	7,286	7,311	101	13,521	6,551	6,879	91	1,177	8.7	735	11.2	432	6.3	10	(1)
EAST SOUTH CENTRAL:																
Kentucky	11,709	5,916	5,753	40	11,227	5,391	5,773	63	482	4.3	525	9.7	−20	−0.3	−23	(1)
Tennessee	38,300	10,698	27,551	51	33,883	9,414	24,387	82	4,417	13.0	1,284	13.6	3,164	13.0	−31	(1)
Alabama	110,387	17,047	93,288	52	94,069	14,110	79,887	72	16,318	17.3	2,937	20.8	13,401	16.8	−20	(1)
Mississippi	164,488	24,949	139,433	106	128,351	20,973	107,271	107	36,137	28.2	3,976	19.0	32,162	30.0	−1	−0.9
WEST SOUTH CENTRAL:																
Arkansas	63,578	14,660	48,872	46	46,978	11,941	34,957	80	16,600	35.3	2,719	22.8	13,915	39.8	−34	(1)
Louisiana	54,819	10,681	44,062	76	58,096	9,378	48,639	79	−3,277	−5.6	1,303	13.9	−4,577	−9.4	−3	(1)
Oklahoma	13,209	4,819	8,370	20	6,353	3,683	2,649	21	6,856	107.9	1,136	30.8	5,721	216.0	−1	(1)
Texas	69,816	21,182	48,554	80	65,472	20,139	45,242	91	4,344	6.6	1,043	5.2	3,312	7.3	−11	(1)
MOUNTAIN:																
Montana	29	22	5	2	21	18	3	......	8	(1)	4	(1)	2	(1)	2	......
Idaho	13	13	......	......	9	8	1	......	4	(1)	5	(1)	−1	(1)	......	......
Wyoming	19	17	1	1	2	2	......	......	17	(1)	15	(1)	1	(1)	1	......
Colorado	81	58	22	1	58	45	13	......	23	(1)	13	(1)	9	(1)	1	......
New Mexico	48	41	3	4	14	10	4	......	34	(1)	31	(1)	−1	(1)	4	......
Arizona	12	10	2	......	15	11	1	3	−3	(1)	−1	(1)	1	(1)	−3	(1)
Utah	11	11	......	......	11	8	3	......	......	......	3	(1)	−3	(1)	......	......
Nevada	6	4	1	1	3	2	1	......	3	(1)	2	(1)	......	......	1	......
PACIFIC:																
Washington	77	64	11	2	55	49	5	1	22	(1)	15	(1)	6	(1)	1	(1)
Oregon	27	22	4	1	14	11	3	......	13	(1)	11	(1)	1	(1)	1	......
California	159	125	26	8	135	93	39	3	24	17.8	32	(1)	−13	(1)	5	(1)

1 Per cent not shown where base is less than 100.

TABLE 55.—COLORED FARMS OF OWNERS, TENANTS, AND MANAGERS CLASSIFIED AS NEGRO AND OTHER COLORED, BY DIVISIONS AND STATES: 1910.

DIVISION AND STATE.	Total.			Owners.			Tenants.			Managers.		
	Colored.	Negro.	Other colored.	Colored.	Negro.	Other colored.	Colored.	Negro.	Other. colored.	Colored.	Negro.	Other colored.
UNITED STATES	920,883	893,370	27,513	241,221	218,972	22,249	678,118	672,964	5,154	1,544	1,434	110
GEOGRAPHIC DIVISIONS:												
New England	342	310	32	271	240	31	52	51	1	19	19	
Middle Atlantic	1,961	1,310	651	1,414	793	621	475	447	28	72	70	2
East North Central	5,717	4,843	874	3,908	3,095	813	1,735	1,677	58	74	71	3
West North Central	9,864	5,589	4,275	7,369	3,370	3,999	2,419	2,155	264	76	64	12
South Atlantic	355,862	354,530	1,332	101,961	101,135	826	253,181	252,676	505	720	719	1
East South Central	325,218	324,884	334	58,737	58,610	127	266,232	266,025	207	249	249	
West South Central	209,061	201,422	7,639	57,769	51,342	6,427	151,061	149,858	1,203	231	222	9
Mountain	8,028	219	7,809	7,675	176	7,499	331	34	297	22	0	13
Pacific	4,830	263	4,567	2,117	211	1,906	2,632	41	2,591	81	11	70
NEW ENGLAND:												
Maine	29	28	1	25	24	1	3	3		1	1	
New Hampshire	15	14	1	12	11	1	2	2		1	1	
Vermont	20	20		17	17		2	2		1	1	
Massachusetts	124	103	21	109	89	20	11	10	1	4	4	
Rhode Island	41	40	1	29	28	1	12	12				
Connecticut	113	105	8	79	71	8	22	22		12	12	
MIDDLE ATLANTIC:												
New York	939	295	644	808	193	615	117	90	27	14	12	2
New Jersey	476	472	4	265	262	3	184	183	1	27	27	
Pennsylvania	546	543	3	341	338	3	174	174		31	31	
EAST NORTH CENTRAL:												
Ohio	1,950	1,948	2	1,313	1,311	2	609	609		28	28	
Indiana	805	785	20	472	456	16	318	314	4	15	15	
Illinois	1,425	1,422	3	789	787	2	618	617	1	18	18	
Michigan	946	640	306	785	502	283	152	129	23	9	9	
Wisconsin	591	48	543	549	39	510	38	8	30	4	1	3
WEST NORTH CENTRAL:												
Minnesota	293	29	264	194	16	178	97	12	85	2	1	1
Iowa	201	187	14	136	122	14	63	63		2	2	
Missouri	3,666	3,656	10	2,109	2,104	5	1,516	1,511	5	41	41	
North Dakota	743	22	721	727	18	709	14	4	10	2		2
South Dakota	2,808	67	2,741	2,736	57	2,679	65	10	55	7		7
Nebraska	462	96	366	369	75	294	92	21	71	1		1
Kansas	1,691	1,532	159	1,098	978	120	572	534	38	21	20	1
SOUTH ATLANTIC:												
Delaware	922	922		406	406		500	500		16	16	
Maryland	6,372	6,370	2	3,950	3,949	1	2,335	2,334	1	87	87	
District of Columbia	12	12		8	8		3	3		1	1	
Virginia	48,114	48,039	75	32,228	32,168	60	15,706	15,691	15	180	180	
West Virginia	708	707	1	558	557	1	143	143		7	7	
North Carolina	65,656	64,456	1,200	21,443	20,707	736	44,139	43,676	463	74	73	1
South Carolina	96,798	96,772	26	20,372	20,356	16	76,295	76,285	10	131	131	
Georgia	122,559	122,554	5	15,698	15,698		106,738	106,733	5	123	123	
Florida	14,721	14,698	23	7,298	7,286	12	7,322	7,311	11	101	101	
EAST SOUTH CENTRAL:												
Kentucky	11,730	11,709	21	5,929	5,916	13	5,761	5,753	8	40	40	
Tennessee	38,308	38,300	8	10,700	10,698	2	27,557	27,551	6	51	51	
Alabama	110,443	110,387	56	17,082	17,047	35	93,309	93,288	21	52	52	
Mississippi	164,737	164,488	249	25,026	24,949	77	139,605	139,433	172	106	106	
WEST SOUTH CENTRAL:												
Arkansas	63,593	63,578	15	14,662	14,660	2	48,885	48,872	13	46	46	
Louisiana	54,879	54,819	60	10,725	10,681	44	44,077	44,062	15	77	76	1
Oklahoma	20,671	13,209	7,462	11,150	4,819	6,331	9,494	8,370	1,124	27	20	7
Texas	69,918	69,816	102	21,232	21,182	50	48,605	48,554	51	81	80	1
MOUNTAIN:												
Montana	1,196	29	1,167	1,167	22	1,145	26	5	21	3	2	1
Idaho	405	13	392	343	13	330	62		62			
Wyoming	65	19	46	61	17	44	3	1	2	1	1	
Colorado	574	81	493	466	58	408	107	22	85	1	1	
New Mexico	2,148	48	2,100	2,121	41	2,080	23	3	20	4	4	
Arizona	3,203	12	3,191	3,149	10	3,139	43	2	41	11		11
Utah	276	11	265	216	11	205	59		59	1		1
Nevada	161	6	155	152	4	148	8	1	7	1	1	
PACIFIC:												
Washington	1,125	77	1,048	701	64	637	413	11	402	11	2	9
Oregon	627	27	600	478	22	456	141	4	137	8	1	7
California	3,078	159	2,919	938	125	813	2,078	8	2,070	62	26	36

TABLE 56.—COLORED AND WHITE FARMERS CLASSIFIED BY TENURE, 1910 AND 1900, WITH INCREASE, 1900–1910, BY SOUTHERN DIVISIONS AND STATES.

DIVISION AND STATE.	Colored 1910	Colored 1900	Colored Increase[1] Number	Colored Increase[1] Per cent	White 1910	White 1900	White Increase[1] Number	White Increase[1] Per cent
THE SOUTH.								
Total	890,141	740,670	149,471	20.2	2,207,406	1,879,721	327,685	17.4
Owners	175,290	158,479	16,811	10.6	1,154,100	1,078,635	75,465	7.0
Part owners	43,177	28,197	14,980	53.1	229,461	187,088	42,373	22.6
Share tenants[2]	384,524	280,699	103,825	37.0	636,817	491,655	145,162	29.5
Cash tenants[3]	285,950	271,702	14,248	5.2	171,944	105,171	66,773	63.5
Managers	1,200	1,593	−393	−24.7	15,084	17,172	−2,088	−12.2
SOUTH ATLANTIC	355,862	288,871	66,991	23.2	756,019	673,354	82,665	12.3
Owners	80,914	70,814	10,100	14.3	440,644	409,799	30,845	7.5
Part owners	21,047	14,302	6,745	47.2	50,549	32,597	17,952	55.1
Share tenants[2]	139,984	102,188	37,796	37.0	169,514	150,711	18,803	12.5
Cash tenants[3]	113,197	100,597	12,600	12.5	87,734	72,102	15,632	21.7
Managers	720	970	−250	−25.8	7,578	8,145	−567	−7.0
E. SOUTH CENTRAL	325,218	267,895	57,323	21.4	717,262	635,418	81,844	12.9
Owners	46,320	41,811	4,509	10.8	392,657	376,576	16,081	4.3
Part owners	12,417	8,100	4,317	53.3	59,058	37,199	21,859	58.8
Share tenants[2]	131,219	92,556	38,663	41.8	189,259	152,222	37,037	24.3
Cash tenants[3]	135,013	125,104	9,909	7.9	73,247	65,049	8,198	12.6
Managers	249	324	−75	−23.1	3,041	4,372	−1,331	−30.4
W. SOUTH CENTRAL	209,061	183,904	25,157	13.7	734,125	570,949	163,176	28.6
Owners	48,056	45,854	2,202	4.8	320,799	292,260	28,539	9.8
Part owners	9,713	5,795	3,918	67.6	62,337	35,375	26,962	76.2
Share tenants[2]	113,321	85,955	27,366	31.8	278,044	188,722	89,322	47.3
Cash tenants[3]	37,740	46,001	−8,261	−18.0	68,480	49,937	18,543	37.1
Managers	231	299	−68	−22.7	4,465	4,655	−190	−4.1
SOUTH ATLANTIC.								
DELAWARE	922	818	104	12.7	9,914	8,869	1,045	11.8
Owners	347	298	49	16.4	5,518	4,068	1,450	35.6
Part owners	59	34	25	73.5	254	280	−26	−9.3
Share tenants[2]	425	396	29	7.3	3,244	3,726	−482	−12.9
Cash tenants[3]	75	75			791	679	112	16.5
Managers	16	15	1	6.7	107	116	−9	−7.8
MARYLAND	6,372	5,843	529	9.1	42,551	40,169	2,382	5.9
Owners	3,301	2,891	410	14.2	27,819	25,127	2,692	10.7
Part owners	649	371	278	74.9	1,750	1,124	626	55.7
Share tenants[2]	1,720	1,913	−193	−10.1	8,602	9,478	−876	−9.2
Cash tenants[3]	615	563	52	9.2	3,479	3,493	−14	−0.4
Managers	87	105	−18	−17.1	901	947	−46	−4.9
DIST. COLUMBIA	12	17	−5	−29.4	205	252	−47	−18.7
Owners	6	4	2	50.0	105	119	−14	−11.8
Part owners	2	1	1	100.0	5	9	−4	−44.4
Share tenants[2]					2	3	−1	−33.3
Cash tenants[3]	3	10	−7	−70.0	79	103	−24	−23.3
Managers	1	2	−1	−50.0	14	18	−4	−22.2
VIRGINIA	48,114	44,834	3,280	7.3	135,904	123,052	12,852	10.4
Owners	26,820	22,943	3,877	16.9	91,144	80,830	10,314	12.8
Part owners	5,408	3,623	1,785	49.3	10,292	6,759	3,533	52.3
Share tenants[2]	11,288	11,139	149	1.3	23,392	23,808	−416	−1.7
Cash tenants[3]	4,418	6,891	−2,473	−35.9	9,631	9,758	−127	−1.3
Managers	180	238	−58	−24.4	1,445	1,897	−452	−23.8
WEST VIRGINIA	708	742	−34	−4.6	95,977	92,132	3,845	4.2
Owners	487	480	7	1.5	67,831	66,429	1,402	2.1
Part owners	71	54	17	31.5	7,589	4,566	3,023	66.2
Share tenants[2]	80	132	−52	−39.4	10,419	12,633	−2,214	−17.5
Cash tenants[3]	63	68	−5	−7.4	9,273	7,458	1,815	24.3
Managers	7	8	−1	−12.5	865	1,046	−181	−17.3
NORTH CAROLINA	65,656	54,864	10,792	19.7	188,069	169,773	18,296	10.8
Owners	14,822	13,290	1,532	11.5	106,560	101,828	4,732	4.6
Part owners	6,621	4,230	2,391	56.5	17,317	11,224	6,093	54.3
Share tenants[2]	32,530	26,892	5,638	21.0	49,718	46,200	3,518	7.6
Cash tenants[3]	11,609	10,331	1,278	12.4	13,430	9,585	3,845	40.1
Managers	74	121	−47	−38.8	1,044	936	108	11.5
SOUTH CAROLINA	96,798	85,401	11,397	13.3	79,636	69,954	9,682	13.8
Owners	16,077	15,594	483	3.1	39,446	37,513	1,933	5.2
Part owners	4,295	3,376	919	27.2	4,532	2,934	1,598	54.5
Share tenants[2]	35,665	23,817	11,848	49.7	19,301	14,021	5,280	37.7
Cash tenants[3]	40,630	42,434	−1,804	−4.3	15,625	14,612	1,013	6.9
Managers	131	180	−49	−27.2	732	874	−142	−16.2

DIVISION AND STATE.	Colored 1910	Colored 1900	Colored Increase[1] Number	Colored Increase[1] Per cent	White 1910	White 1900	White Increase[1] Number	White Increase[1] Per cent
SOUTH ATLANTIC—Continued.								
GEORGIA	122,559	82,826	39,733	48.0	168,468	141,865	26,603	18.8
Owners	12,859	9,613	3,246	33.8	75,909	72,883	3,026	4.2
Part owners	2,839	1,762	1,077	61.1	7,021	4,271	2,750	64.4
Share tenants[2]	56,259	36,515	19,744	54.1	52,334	39,295	13,039	33.2
Cash tenants[3]	50,479	34,728	15,751	45.4	31,908	24,022	7,886	32.8
Managers	123	208	−85	−40.9	1,296	1,394	−98	−7.0
FLORIDA	14,721	13,526	1,195	8.8	35,295	27,288	8,007	29.3
Owners	6,195	5,701	494	8.7	26,312	21,002	5,310	25.3
Part owners	1,103	851	252	29.6	1,789	1,430	359	25.1
Share tenants[2]	2,017	1,384	633	45.7	2,502	1,547	955	61.7
Cash tenants[3]	5,305	5,497	−192	−3.5	3,518	2,392	1,126	47.1
Managers	101	93	8	8.6	1,174	917	257	28.0
E. SOUTH CENTRAL.								
KENTUCKY	11,730	11,238	492	4.4	247,455	223,429	24,026	10.8
Owners	4,466	4,322	144	3.3	144,366	137,015	7,351	5.4
Part owners	1,463	1,080	383	35.5	20,037	13,579	6,458	47.6
Share tenants[2]	5,159	4,984	175	3.5	67,441	55,305	12,136	21.9
Cash tenants[3]	602	789	−187	−23.7	14,658	15,987	−1,329	−8.3
Managers	40	63	−23	−36.5	953	1,543	−590	−38.2
TENNESSEE	38,308	33,895	4,413	13.0	207,704	190,728	16,976	8.9
Owners	7,740	7,736	4	[4]	112,341	110,809	1,532	1.4
Part owners	2,960	1,690	1,270	75.1	21,084	11,962	9,122	76.3
Share tenants[2]	15,756	13,478	2,278	16.9	55,375	49,314	6,061	12.3
Cash tenants[3]	11,801	10,909	892	8.2	18,129	17,439	690	4.0
Managers	51	82	−31	−37.8	775	1,204	−429	−35.6
ALABAMA	110,443	94,083	16,360	17.4	152,458	129,137	23,321	18.1
Owners	13,009	11,239	1,770	15.7	74,580	70,676	3,904	5.5
Part owners	4,073	2,871	1,202	41.9	12,267	8,686	3,581	41.2
Share tenants[2]	28,976	23,689	5,287	22.3	40,804	30,855	9,949	32.2
Cash tenants[3]	64,333	56,212	8,121	14.4	24,213	18,118	6,095	33.6
Managers	52	72	−20	−27.8	594	802	−208	−25.9
MISSISSIPPI	164,737	128,679	36,058	28.0	109,645	92,124	17,521	19.0
Owners	21,105	18,514	2,591	14.0	61,370	58,076	3,294	5.7
Part owners	3,921	2,459	1,462	59.5	5,670	2,972	2,698	90.8
Share tenants[2]	81,328	50,405	30,923	61.3	25,639	16,748	8,891	53.1
Cash tenants[3]	58,277	57,194	1,083	1.9	16,247	13,505	2,742	20.3
Managers	106	107	−1	−0.9	719	823	−104	−12.6
W. SOUTH CENTRAL.								
ARKANSAS	63,593	46,983	16,610	35.4	151,085	131,711	19,374	14.7
Owners	11,860	10,166	1,694	16.7	76,006	75,628	378	0.5
Part owners	2,802	1,775	1,027	57.9	15,981	9,166	6,815	74.4
Share tenants[2]	29,082	19,120	9,962	52.1	42,501	34,717	7,784	22.4
Cash tenants[3]	19,803	15,842	3,961	25.0	15,880	11,461	4,419	38.6
Managers	46	80	−34	−42.5	717	739	−22	−3.0
LOUISIANA	54,879	58,160	−3,281	−5.6	65,667	57,809	7,858	13.6
Owners	9,599	8,503	1,096	12.9	38,991	36,564	2,427	6.6
Part owners	1,126	875	251	28.7	3,273	1,759	1,514	86.1
Share tenants[2]	34,504	27,502	7,002	25.5	15,568	10,810	4,758	44.0
Cash tenants[3]	9,573	21,201	−11,628	−54.8	6,962	7,721	−759	−9.8
Managers	77	79	−2	−2.5	873	955	−82	−8.6
OKLAHOMA	20,671	[5]13,225	7,446	56.3	169,521	[5]94,775	74,746	78.9
Owners	9,919	9,944	−25	−0.3	54,965	43,675	11,290	25.9
Part owners	1,231	247	984	398.4	19,289	6,343	12,946	204.1
Share tenants[2]	7,497	2,467	5,030	203.9	68,821	30,880	37,941	122.9
Cash tenants[3]	1,997	518	1,479	285.5	25,822	13,385	12,437	92.9
Managers	27	49	−22	−44.9	624	492	132	26.8
TEXAS	69,918	65,536	4,382	6.7	347,852	286,654	61,198	21.3
Owners	16,678	17,241	−563	−3.3	150,837	136,393	14,444	10.6
Part owners	4,554	2,898	1,656	57.1	23,794	18,107	5,687	31.4
Share tenants[2]	42,238	36,866	5,372	14.6	151,154	112,315	38,839	34.6
Cash tenants[3]	6,367	8,440	−2,073	−24.6	19,816	17,370	2,446	14.1
Managers	81	91	−10	−11.0	2,251	2,469	−218	−8.8

[1] A minus sign (−) denotes decrease.
[2] Includes not specified tenure.
[3] Includes share-cash tenants.
[4] Less than one-tenth of 1 per cent.
[5] Includes Indian Territory.

TABLE 57.—COLORED AND WHITE FARMS CLASSIFIED BY SEVEN TENURES, WITH PERCENTAGE DISTRIBUTION BY TENURE, BY SOUTHERN DIVISIONS AND STATES: 1910.

DIVISION AND STATE.	FARMS OPERATED BY COLORED FARMERS: 1910.										
		Owners and part owners.				Tenants.					Managers.
	Total.	Total.	Owners.		Part owners.	Total.	Cash tenants.	Share tenants.	Share-cash tenants.	Tenants not specified.	
			Free.	Mortgaged.							
NUMBER OF FARMS.											
THE SOUTH.											
Total................	890,141	218,467	128,557	46,733	43,177	670,474	260,966	370,306	14,218	24,984	1,200
South Atlantic............	355,862	101,961	63,701	17,213	21,047	253,181	101,664	135,203	4,781	11,533	720
East South Central.......	325,218	58,737	28,906	17,414	12,417	266,232	126,968	126,229	4,990	8,045	249
West South Central.......	209,061	57,769	35,950	12,166	9,713	151,061	32,334	108,874	4,447	5,406	231
SOUTH ATLANTIC.											
Delaware.................	922	406	198	149	59	500	55	421	4	20	16
Maryland.................	6,372	3,950	2,191	1,110	649	2,335	405	1,685	35	210	87
District of Columbia......	12	8	3	3	2	3	....	....	....	3	1
Virginia.................	48,114	32,228	22,220	4,600	5,408	15,706	3,661	10,906	382	757	180
West Virginia............	708	558	417	70	71	143	62	78	2	1	7
North Carolina...........	65,656	21,443	11,088	3,734	6,621	44,139	10,110	31,609	921	1,499	74
South Carolina...........	96,798	20,372	12,895	3,272	4,295	76,295	36,658	34,169	1,496	3,972	131
Georgia..................	122,559	15,698	9,649	3,210	2,839	106,738	46,451	54,464	1,795	4,028	123
Florida..................	14,721	7,298	5,130	1,065	1,103	7,322	4,259	1,871	146	1,046	101
EAST SOUTH CENTRAL.											
Kentucky.................	11,730	5,929	3,488	978	1,463	5,761	473	5,013	146	129	40
Tennessee................	38,308	10,700	5,826	1,914	2,960	27,557	11,038	15,257	499	763	51
Alabama..................	110,443	17,082	8,030	4,979	4,073	93,309	61,235	27,687	1,289	3,098	52
Mississippi..............	164,737	25,026	11,562	9,543	3,921	139,605	54,222	78,272	3,056	4,055	106
WEST SOUTH CENTRAL.											
Arkansas.................	63,593	14,662	7,891	3,969	2,802	48,885	17,104	27,582	1,500	2,699	46
Louisiana................	54,879	10,725	7,312	2,287	1,126	44,077	8,723	33,596	908	850	77
Oklahoma.................	20,671	11,150	7,713	2,206	1,231	9,494	1,398	7,249	248	599	27
Texas....................	69,918	21,232	13,034	3,644	4,554	48,605	5,109	40,447	1,791	1,258	81
PERCENTAGE DISTRIBUTION OF FARMS BY TENURE.											
THE SOUTH.											
Total...................	100.0	24.5	14.4	5.3	4.9	75.3	29.3	41.6	1.6	2.8	0.1
South Atlantic...........	100.0	28.7	17.9	4.8	5.9	71.1	28.6	38.0	1.3	3.2	0.2
East South Central......	100.0	18.1	8.9	5.4	3.8	81.9	39.0	38.8	1.5	2.5	0.1
West South Central......	100.0	27.6	17.2	5.8	4.6	72.3	15.5	52.1	2.1	2.6	0.1
SOUTH ATLANTIC.											
Delaware.................	100.0	44.0	21.5	16.2	6.4	54.2	6.0	45.7	0.4	2.2	1.7
Maryland.................	100.0	62.0	34.4	17.4	10.2	36.6	6.4	26.4	0.5	3.3	1.4
District of Columbia.....	100.0	66.7	25.0	25.0	16.7	25.0	25.0	....	....	....	8.3
Virginia.................	100.0	67.0	46.2	9.6	11.2	32.6	7.6	22.7	0.8	1.6	0.4
West Virginia............	100.0	78.8	58.9	9.9	10.0	20.2	8.8	11.0	0.3	0.1	1.0
North Carolina...........	100.0	32.7	16.9	5.7	10.1	67.2	15.4	48.1	1.4	2.3	0.1
South Carolina...........	100.0	21.0	13.2	3.4	4.4	78.8	37.9	35.3	1.5	4.1	0.1
Georgia..................	100.0	12.8	7.9	2.6	2.3	87.1	37.9	44.4	1.5	3.3	0.1
Florida..................	100.0	49.6	34.8	7.2	7.5	49.7	28.9	12.7	1.0	7.1	0.7
EAST SOUTH CENTRAL.											
Kentucky.................	100.0	50.5	29.7	8.3	12.5	49.1	4.0	42.7	1.2	1.1	0.3
Tennessee................	100.0	27.9	15.2	5.0	7.7	71.9	28.8	39.8	1.3	2.0	1.0
Alabama..................	100.0	15.5	7.3	4.5	3.7	84.5	55.4	25.1	1.2	2.8	....
Mississippi..............	100.0	15.2	7.0	5.8	2.4	84.7	32.9	47.5	1.9	2.5	0.1
WEST SOUTH CENTRAL.											
Arkansas.................	100.0	23.1	12.4	6.2	4.4	76.9	26.9	43.4	2.4	4.2	0.1
Louisiana................	100.0	19.5	13.3	4.2	2.1	80.3	15.9	61.2	1.7	1.5	0.1
Oklahoma.................	100.0	53.9	37.3	10.7	6.0	45.9	6.8	35.1	1.2	2.9	0.1
Texas....................	100.0	30.4	18.6	5.2	6.5	69.5	7.3	57.8	2.6	1.8	0.1

TABLE **57.**—COLORED AND WHITE FARMS CLASSIFIED BY SEVEN TENURES, WITH PERCENTAGE DISTRIBUTION BY TENURE, BY SOUTHERN DIVISIONS AND STATES: 1910—Continued.

DIVISION AND STATE.	Total.	Owners and part owners.				Tenants.					Managers.
		Total.	Owners.		Part owners.	Total.	Cash tenants.	Share tenants.	Share-cash tenants.	Tenants not specified.	
			Free.	Mortgaged.							

FARMS OPERATED BY WHITE FARMERS: 1910.

NUMBER OF FARMS.

THE SOUTH.

DIVISION AND STATE.	Total.	Total.	Free.	Mortgaged.	Part owners.	Total.	Cash tenants.	Share tenants.	Share-cash tenants.	Tenants not specified.	Managers.
Total	2,207,406	1,326,044	908,211	245,889	171,944	866,278	192,094	611,370	25,447	37,367	15,084
South Atlantic	756,019	491,193	364,156	76,488	50,549	257,248	74,953	164,178	5,336	12,781	7,578
East South Central	717,262	451,715	316,252	76,405	59,058	262,506	65,284	181,694	7,565	7,963	3,041
West South Central	734,125	383,136	227,803	92,996	62,337	346,524	51,857	265,498	12,546	16,623	4,465
SOUTH ATLANTIC.											
Delaware	9,914	5,772	3,531	1,987	254	4,035	564	3,201	43	227	107
Maryland	42,551	29,569	17,697	10,122	1,750	12,081	2,533	8,433	169	946	901
District of Columbia	205	110	88	17	5	81	79	2	....		14
Virginia	135,904	101,436	77,239	13,905	10,292	33,023	7,752	22,566	826	1,879	1,445
West Virginia	95,977	75,420	59,537	8,294	7,589	19,692	8,498	9,498	921	775	865
North Carolina	188,069	123,877	89,681	16,879	17,317	63,148	10,598	48,606	1,112	2,832	1,044
South Carolina	79,636	43,978	30,286	9,160	4,532	34,926	13,610	18,471	830	2,015	732
Georgia	168,468	82,930	63,310	12,599	7,021	84,242	28,772	51,040	1,294	3,136	1,296
Florida	35,295	28,191	22,787	3,525	1,789	6,020	2,547	2,361	141	971	1,174
EAST SOUTH CENTRAL.											
Kentucky	247,455	164,403	117,774	26,592	20,037	82,099	12,228	64,163	3,278	2,430	953
Tennessee	207,704	133,425	95,477	16,864	21,084	73,504	16,398	52,990	2,385	1,731	775
Alabama	152,458	86,847	57,760	16,820	12,267	65,017	22,125	39,665	1,139	2,088	594
Mississippi	109,645	67,040	45,241	16,129	5,670	41,886	14,533	24,876	763	1,714	719
WEST SOUTH CENTRAL.											
Arkansas	151,085	91,987	61,921	14,085	15,981	58,381	13,301	40,971	1,530	2,579	717
Louisiana	65,667	42,264	32,652	6,339	3,273	22,530	5,763	15,114	454	1,199	873
Oklahoma	169,521	74,254	30,956	24,009	19,289	94,643	20,353	65,107	3,714	5,469	624
Texas	347,852	174,631	102,274	48,563	23,794	170,970	12,440	144,306	6,848	7,376	2,251

PERCENTAGE DISTRIBUTION OF FARMS, BY TENURE.

DIVISION AND STATE.	Total.	Total.	Free.	Mortgaged.	Part owners.	Total.	Cash tenants.	Share tenants.	Share-cash tenants.	Tenants not specified.	Managers.
THE SOUTH.											
Total	100.0	60.1	41.1	11.1	7.8	39.2	8.7	27.7	1.2	1.7	0.7
South Atlantic	100.0	65.0	48.2	10.1	6.7	34.0	9.9	21.7	0.7	1.7	1.0
East South Central	100.0	63.0	44.1	10.7	8.2	36.6	9.1	25.3	1.1	1.1	0.4
West South Central	100.0	52.2	31.0	12.7	8.5	47.2	7.1	36.2	1.7	2.3	0.6
SOUTH ATLANTIC.											
Delaware	100.0	58.2	35.6	20.0	2.6	40.7	5.7	32.3	0.4	2.3	1.1
Maryland	100.0	69.5	41.6	23.8	4.1	28.4	6.0	19.8	0.4	2.2	2.1
District of Columbia	100.0	53.7	42.9	8.3	2.4	39.5	38.5	1.0	....		6.8
Virginia	100.0	74.6	56.8	10.2	7.6	24.3	5.7	16.6	0.6	1.4	1.1
West Virginia	100.0	78.6	62.0	8.6	7.9	20.5	8.9	9.9	1.0	0.8	0.9
North Carolina	100.0	65.9	47.7	9.0	9.2	33.6	5.6	25.8	0.6	1.5	0.6
South Carolina	100.0	55.2	38.0	11.5	5.7	43.9	17.1	23.2	1.0	2.5	0.9
Georgia	100.0	49.2	37.6	7.5	4.2	50.0	17.1	30.3	0.8	1.9	0.8
Florida	100.0	79.6	64.6	10.0	5.1	17.1	7.2	6.7	0.4	2.8	3.3
EAST SOUTH CENTRAL.											
Kentucky	100.0	66.4	47.6	10.7	8.1	33.2	4.9	25.9	1.3	1.0	0.4
Tennessee	100.0	64.2	46.0	8.1	10.2	35.4	7.9	25.5	1.1	0.8	0.4
Alabama	100.0	57.0	37.9	11.0	8.0	42.6	14.5	26.0	0.7	1.4	0.4
Mississippi	100.0	61.1	41.3	14.7	5.2	38.2	13.3	22.7	0.7	1.6	0.7
WEST SOUTH CENTRAL.											
Arkansas	100.0	60.9	41.0	9.3	10.6	38.6	8.8	27.1	1.0	1.7	0.5
Louisiana	100.0	64.4	49.7	9.7	5.0	34.3	8.8	23.0	0.7	1.8	1.3
Oklahoma	100.0	43.8	18.3	14.2	11.4	55.8	12.0	38.4	2.2	3.2	0.4
Texas	100.0	50.2	29.4	14.0	6.8	49.2	3.6	41.5	2.0	2.1	0.6

TABLE 58.—ACRES IN COLORED AND WHITE FARMS, CLASSIFIED BY TENURE, BY SOUTHERN DIVISIONS AND STATES: 1910.

DIVISION AND STATE.	FARMS OPERATED BY COLORED FARMERS: 1910.							FARMS OPERATED BY WHITE FARMERS: 1910.						
	Total.	Owners and part owners.			Tenants.		Managers.	Total.	Owners and part owners.			Tenants.		Managers.
		Owners.		Part owners.	Cash and not specified.	Share and share-cash.			Owners.		Part owners.	Cash and not specified.	Share and share-cash.	
		Free.	Mortgaged.						Free.	Mortgaged.				
	NUMBER OF ACRES.													
THE SOUTH.														
Total............	42,609,117	8,835,857	4,011,491	2,844,188	12,876,308	13,691,494	349,779	311,843,743	134,584,147	46,759,094	33,580,452	26,275,674	46,328,127	24,316,249
South Atlantic.........	17,675,382	3,280,891	1,251,082	1,114,405	5,981,903	5,901,730	145,371	86,106,873	48,158,522	9,871,919	5,452,964	7,689,142	11,715,307	3,219,019
East South Central.....	13,595,717	2,149,433	1,556,778	833,741	5,348,300	3,631,105	76,360	67,924,912	38,000,187	8,929,447	5,662,386	5,245,221	8,560,564	1,527,107
West South Central....	11,338,018	3,405,533	1,203,631	896,042	1,546,105	4,158,659	128,048	157,811,958	48,425,438	27,957,728	22,465,102	13,341,311	26,052,256	19,570,123
SOUTH ATLANTIC.														
Delaware...............	56,973	6,439	4,999	2,177	4,112	36,851	2,395	981,893	286,098	161,003	16,111	67,545	432,367	18,769
Maryland...............	358,517	58,733	39,195	24,111	41,820	181,297	13,361	4,698,623	1,632,616	965,268	185,395	368,132	1,353,282	193,930
District of Columbia....	95	15	3	40	33	....	4	5,968	1,866	336	169	2,069	76	1,452
Virginia...............	2,238,220	889,297	243,224	248,702	244,343	582,669	29,985	17,257,416	10,209,308	1,941,675	1,183,139	1,090,454	2,202,500	630,340
West Virginia..........	34,541	19,894	3,040	3,023	2,190	5,739	655	9,991,901	6,429,302	885,909	843,027	827,918	721,898	283,847
North Carolina.........	3,185,804	604,292	257,037	336,167	601,283	1,368,033	18,992	19,253,325	10,981,223	1,936,085	1,541,519	1,146,502	3,084,611	563,385
South Carolina.........	3,940,476	607,767	271,588	218,689	1,595,244	1,204,734	42,454	9,571,552	4,931,808	1,461,880	559,771	1,191,907	921,228	504,958
Georgia................	7,092,051	785,895	346,221	217,387	3,272,972	2,442,025	27,551	19,861,362	10,614,095	2,050,484	837,210	2,761,942	2,846,060	751,571
Florida................	768,705	308,558	85,775	64,109	219,906	80,382	9,974	4,484,833	3,072,206	469,279	286,623	232,673	153,285	270,767
EAST SOUTH CENTRAL.														
Kentucky...............	440,777	143,507	51,080	60,776	25,139	155,957	4,318	21,748,350	12,708,031	2,744,751	1,754,610	1,180,895	3,049,121	310,942
Tennessee..............	1,606,078	307,399	125,686	157,591	525,125	472,595	17,682	18,435,579	10,347,702	1,785,151	1,949,108	1,204,724	2,831,647	317,247
Alabama................	5,091,435	660,075	498,567	308,077	2,611,447	995,787	17,482	15,640,877	8,268,042	2,236,398	1,308,947	1,764,461	1,713,744	349,285
Mississippi............	6,457,427	1,038,452	881,445	307,297	2,186,589	2,006,766	36,878	12,100,106	6,676,412	2,163,147	649,721	1,095,141	966,052	549,633
WEST SOUTH CENTRAL.														
Arkansas...............	2,653,323	636,899	353,283	213,932	695,584	747,532	6,093	14,762,752	7,759,104	1,700,909	1,725,415	1,133,811	2,121,420	322,093
Louisiana..............	2,124,321	567,301	188,352	79,042	323,641	945,009	20,976	8,315,160	4,272,176	1,191,593	467,659	638,716	779,635	965,381
Oklahoma...............	2,276,711	1,100,167	289,952	209,536	203,293	467,468	6,295	26,582,642	4,974,762	4,037,695	5,384,683	4,288,425	7,474,693	422,384
Texas..................	4,283,663	1,101,166	372,044	393,532	323,587	1,998,650	94,684	108,151,404	31,419,396	21,027,531	14,887,345	7,280,359	15,676,508	17,860,265
	PERCENTAGE DISTRIBUTION OF ACREAGE, BY TENURE.													
THE SOUTH.														
Total............	100.0	20.7	9.4	6.7	30.2	32.1	0.8	100.0	43.2	15.0	10.8	8.4	14.9	7.8
South Atlantic.........	100.0	18.6	7.1	6.3	33.8	33.4	0.8	100.0	55.9	11.5	6.3	8.9	13.6	3.7
East South Central.....	100.0	15.8	11.4	6.1	39.3	26.7	0.6	100.0	55.9	13.1	8.3	7.7	12.6	2.2
West South Central.....	100.0	30.0	10.6	7.9	13.6	36.7	1.1	100.0	30.7	17.7	14.2	8.5	16.5	12.4
SOUTH ATLANTIC.														
Delaware...............	100.0	11.3	8.8	3.8	7.2	64.7	4.2	100.0	29.1	16.4	1.6	6.9	44.0	1.9
Maryland...............	100.0	16.4	10.9	6.7	11.7	50.6	3.7	100.0	34.7	20.5	3.9	7.8	28.8	4.1
District of Columbia....	100.0	15.8	3.2	42.1	34.7	....	4.2	100.0	31.3	5.6	2.8	34.7	1.3	24.3
Virginia...............	100.0	39.7	10.9	11.1	10.9	26.0	1.3	100.0	59.2	11.3	6.9	6.3	12.8	3.7
West Virginia..........	100.0	57.6	8.8	8.8	6.3	16.6	1.9	100.0	64.3	8.9	8.4	8.3	7.2	2.8
North Carolina.........	100.0	19.0	8.1	10.6	18.9	42.9	0.6	100.0	57.0	10.1	8.0	6.0	16.0	2.9
South Carolina.........	100.0	15.4	6.9	5.5	40.5	30.6	1.1	100.0	51.5	15.3	5.8	12.5	9.6	5.3
Georgia................	100.0	11.1	4.9	3.1	46.1	34.4	0.4	100.0	53.4	10.3	4.2	13.9	14.3	3.8
Florida................	100.0	40.1	11.2	8.3	28.6	10.5	1.3	100.0	68.5	10.5	6.4	5.2	3.4	6.0
EAST SOUTH CENTRAL.														
Kentucky...............	100.0	32.6	11.6	13.8	5.7	35.4	1.0	100.0	58.4	12.6	8.1	5.4	14.0	1.4
Tennessee..............	100.0	19.1	7.8	9.8	32.7	29.4	1.1	100.0	56.1	9.7	10.6	6.5	15.4	1.7
Alabama................	100.0	13.0	9.8	6.1	51.3	19.6	0.3	100.0	52.9	14.3	8.4	11.3	11.0	2.2
Mississippi............	100.0	16.1	13.7	4.8	33.9	31.1	0.6	100.0	55.2	17.9	5.4	9.1	8.0	4.5
WEST SOUTH CENTRAL.														
Arkansas...............	100.0	24.0	13.3	8.1	26.2	28.2	0.2	100.0	52.6	11.5	11.7	7.7	14.4	2.2
Louisiana..............	100.0	26.7	8.9	3.7	15.2	44.5	1.0	100.0	51.4	14.3	5.6	7.7	9.4	11.6
Oklahoma...............	100.0	48.3	12.7	9.2	8.9	20.5	0.3	100.0	18.7	15.2	20.3	16.1	28.1	1.6
Texas..................	100.0	25.7	8.7	9.2	7.6	46.6	2.2	100.0	29.1	19.5	13.8	6.7	14.5	16.5

TABLE 59.—ACRES IMPROVED IN COLORED AND WHITE FARMS, CLASSIFIED BY TENURE, BY SOUTHERN DIVISIONS AND STATES: 1910.

NUMBER OF ACRES IMPROVED.

DIVISION AND STATE.	FARMS OPERATED BY COLORED FARMERS: 1910.							FARMS OPERATED BY WHITE FARMERS: 1910.						
	Total.	Owners Free.	Owners Mortgaged.	Part owners.	Tenants Cash and not specified.	Tenants Share and share-cash.	Managers.	Total.	Owners Free.	Owners Mortgaged.	Part owners.	Tenants Cash and not specified.	Tenants Share and share-cash.	Managers.
THE SOUTH. Total	27,735,743	4,005,552	1,893,013	1,632,554	9,218,158	10,878,217	108,249	122,955,109	50,780,626	16,588,921	12,212,994	10,839,130	29,407,345	3,126,093
South Atlantic	10,990,069	1,493,024	573,626	629,297	3,900,843	4,331,992	61,287	37,489,664	19,157,380	4,354,417	2,636,523	3,532,513	6,641,034	1,167,797
East South Central	9,556,529	988,088	735,893	489,664	4,170,455	3,146,192	26,237	34,390,317	17,563,414	4,466,366	3,140,497	2,815,572	5,851,914	552,554
West South Central	7,189,145	1,524,440	583,494	513,593	1,146,860	3,400,033	20,725	51,075,128	14,059,832	7,768,138	6,435,974	4,491,045	16,914,397	1,405,742
SOUTH ATLANTIC.														
Delaware	37,076	4,070	3,458	1,746	2,647	23,121	2,034	676,462	186,182	114,928	11,693	44,802	303,304	15,553
Maryland	218,582	35,176	24,125	17,263	23,463	109,540	9,015	3,136,185	1,029,132	653,241	124,545	228,397	980,616	120,254
District of Columbia	95	15	3	40	33	....	4	5,038	1,640	262	167	1,645	65	1,259
Virginia	1,111,208	421,031	108,228	140,099	104,938	322,866	14,046	8,758,850	5,115,695	1,009,731	677,002	452,183	1,197,757	306,482
West Virginia	20,257	10,521	2,007	1,994	1,166	3,967	602	7,082,344	3,698,312	700,169	628,735	442,156	1,458,234	154,738
North Carolina	1,730,712	236,163	105,115	171,289	326,085	886,816	5,244	3,499,775	1,512,529	517,790	231,112	568,930	542,482	126,932
South Carolina	2,598,224	286,275	123,158	129,914	1,073,124	970,879	14,874	7,506,455	3,197,819	725,350	363,730	1,343,048	1,639,374	237,134
Georgia	4,791,562	352,940	163,893	127,563	2,189,038	1,946,912	11,216	5,501,500	3,591,580	484,568	515,433	332,822	443,865	133,232
Florida	482,353	146,833	43,639	39,389	180,349	67,891	4,252	1,323,055	824,491	148,378	84,106	118,530	75,337	72,213
EAST SOUTH CENTRAL.														
Kentucky	343,694	98,385	36,681	50,723	18,795	135,533	3,577	14,010,777	7,776,139	1,874,722	1,250,094	692,792	2,245,899	171,131
Tennessee	1,162,276	168,597	74,137	106,958	397,328	408,478	6,778	9,728,208	5,032,536	962,808	1,116,463	664,998	1,842,263	109,140
Alabama	3,563,176	283,558	222,641	169,620	2,037,433	844,912	5,012	6,130,405	2,607,153	817,021	520,239	919,774	1,151,131	115,087
Mississippi	4,487,383	437,548	402,434	162,363	1,716,899	1,757,269	10,870	4,520,927	2,147,586	811,815	253,701	538,008	612,621	157,196
WEST SOUTH CENTRAL.														
Arkansas	1,773,206	275,226	152,155	113,884	577,603	651,270	3,068	6,303,048	2,832,442	712,899	728,516	596,598	1,322,962	109,631
Louisiana	1,466,607	259,152	92,766	47,732	243,487	815,423	8,047	3,809,409	1,681,845	543,051	241,216	359,417	577,485	406,395
Oklahoma	1,172,819	459,420	156,867	118,307	102,533	334,208	1,484	16,378,518	2,807,653	2,528,269	3,251,649	2,295,853	5,319,651	175,443
Texas	2,776,513	530,642	181,706	233,670	223,237	1,599,132	8,126	24,584,153	6,737,892	3,983,919	2,214,593	1,239,177	9,694,299	714,273

PERCENTAGE DISTRIBUTION OF IMPROVED ACREAGE, BY TENURE.

DIVISION AND STATE.	FARMS OPERATED BY COLORED FARMERS: 1910.							FARMS OPERATED BY WHITE FARMERS: 1910.						
	Total.	Owners Free.	Owners Mortgaged.	Part owners.	Tenants Cash and not specified.	Tenants Share and share-cash.	Managers.	Total.	Owners Free.	Owners Mortgaged.	Part owners.	Tenants Cash and not specified.	Tenants Share and share-cash.	Managers.
THE SOUTH. Total	100.0	14.5	6.8	5.9	33.3	39.3	0.4	100.0	41.3	13.5	9.9	9.0	23.9	2.5
South Atlantic	100.0	13.7	5.2	5.8	35.7	39.6	0.6	100.0	51.1	11.6	7.0	9.4	17.7	3.1
East South Central	100.0	10.3	7.7	5.1	43.6	32.9	0.3	100.0	51.1	13.0	9.1	8.2	17.0	1.6
West South Central	100.0	21.2	8.1	7.1	15.9	47.3	0.3	100.0	27.5	15.2	12.6	8.8	33.1	2.8
SOUTH ATLANTIC.														
Delaware	100.0	11.0	9.3	4.7	7.1	62.4	5.5	100.0	27.5	17.0	1.7	6.6	44.8	2.3
Maryland	100.0	16.1	11.0	7.9	10.7	50.1	4.1	100.0	32.8	20.8	4.0	7.3	31.3	3.8
District of Columbia	100.0	15.8	3.2	42.1	34.7	....	4.2	100.0	32.6	5.2	3.3	32.7	1.3	25.0
Virginia	100.0	40.1	10.3	13.3	10.0	30.7	1.3	100.0	58.4	11.5	7.7	5.2	13.7	3.5
West Virginia	100.0	51.9	9.9	9.8	5.8	19.6	3.0	100.0	52.2	9.9	8.9	6.2	20.6	2.2
North Carolina	100.0	13.6	6.1	9.9	18.8	51.2	0.3	100.0	43.2	14.8	6.6	16.3	15.5	3.6
South Carolina	100.0	11.0	4.7	5.0	41.2	37.4	0.6	100.0	42.6	9.7	4.8	17.9	21.8	3.2
Georgia	100.0	7.4	3.4	2.7	45.7	40.6	0.2	100.0	65.3	8.8	9.4	6.0	8.1	2.4
Florida	100.0	30.4	9.0	8.2	37.4	14.1	0.9	100.0	62.3	11.2	6.4	9.0	5.7	5.5
EAST SOUTH CENTRAL.														
Kentucky	100.0	28.6	10.7	14.8	5.5	39.4	1.0	100.0	55.5	13.4	8.9	4.9	16.0	1.2
Tennessee	100.0	14.5	6.4	9.2	34.2	35.1	0.6	100.0	51.7	9.9	11.5	6.8	18.9	1.1
Alabama	100.0	8.0	6.2	4.8	57.2	23.7	0.1	100.0	42.5	13.3	8.5	15.0	18.8	1.9
Mississippi	100.0	9.8	9.0	3.6	38.3	39.2	0.2	100.0	47.5	18.0	5.6	11.9	13.6	3.5
WEST SOUTH CENTRAL.														
Arkansas	100.0	15.5	8.6	6.4	32.6	36.7	0.2	100.0	44.9	11.3	11.6	9.5	21.0	1.7
Louisiana	100.0	17.7	6.3	3.3	16.6	55.6	0.5	100.0	44.1	14.3	6.3	9.4	15.2	10.7
Oklahoma	100.0	39.2	13.4	10.1	8.7	28.5	0.1	100.0	17.1	15.4	19.9	14.0	32.5	1.1
Texas	100.0	19.1	6.5	8.4	8.0	57.6	0.3	100.0	27.4	16.2	9.0	5.0	39.4	2.9

TABLE 60.—VALUE OF LAND IN COLORED AND WHITE FARMS, CLASSIFIED BY TENURE, BY SOUTHERN DIVISIONS AND STATES: 1910.

DIVISION AND STATE.	FARMS OPERATED BY COLORED FARMERS: 1910.						
	Total.	Owners and part owners.			Tenants.		Managers.
		Owners.		Part owners.	Cash and not specified.	Share and share-cash.	
		Free.	Mortgaged.				
VALUE OF LAND.							
THE SOUTH.							
Total	$737,632,122	$114,480,372	$52,231,154	$45,564,045	$223,447,037	$293,652,660	$8,256,854
South Atlantic	296,561,108	43,098,439	17,020,641	17,867,341	94,784,203	119,369,413	4,421,071
East South Central	227,201,422	24,695,529	17,310,814	12,816,279	92,763,817	77,633,218	1,981,765
West South Central	213,869,592	46,686,404	17,899,699	14,880,425	35,899,017	96,650,029	1,854,018
SOUTH ATLANTIC.							
Delaware	1,451,457	161,370	137,615	63,606	99,810	889,156	99,900
Maryland	7,098,692	1,132,183	814,566	563,931	1,005,089	2,816,093	766,830
District of Columbia	66,600	11,900	5,900	14,000	28,000	....	6,800
Virginia	32,553,640	11,885,058	3,215,804	3,759,469	4,169,564	8,492,620	1,031,125
West Virginia	828,589	397,117	95,520	68,125	75,960	166,167	25,700
North Carolina	55,362,178	7,944,466	3,586,871	5,532,251	9,892,373	28,038,967	367,250
South Carolina	84,046,645	9,102,777	4,377,557	4,062,509	30,946,365	34,670,128	887,309
Georgia	105,855,590	8,885,677	3,890,860	3,181,540	45,961,551	43,338,970	596,992
Florida	9,297,717	3,577,891	895,948	621,910	2,605,491	957,312	639,165
EAST SOUTH CENTRAL.							
Kentucky	12,238,866	2,567,926	959,173	2,005,785	802,471	5,615,851	287,660
Tennessee	35,244,393	4,557,480	1,828,198	3,145,363	12,836,927	12,189,490	686,935
Alabama	59,324,679	5,924,448	4,165,183	3,217,875	32,106,811	13,655,798	254,564
Mississippi	120,393,484	11,645,675	10,358,260	4,447,256	47,017,608	46,172,079	752,606
WEST SOUTH CENTRAL.							
Arkansas	57,952,855	8,563,203	4,853,616	3,300,608	20,969,618	20,057,895	207,915
Louisiana	36,202,905	6,195,618	2,362,012	1,444,130	5,718,760	19,966,339	516,046
Oklahoma	40,971,750	17,964,631	5,634,485	3,924,485	3,123,160	10,207,267	117,722
Texas	78,742,082	13,962,952	5,049,586	6,211,202	6,087,479	46,418,528	1,012,335
PERCENTAGE DISTRIBUTION OF VALUE OF LAND, BY TENURE.							
THE SOUTH.							
Total	100.0	15.5	7.1	6.2	30.3	39.8	1.1
South Atlantic	100.0	14.5	5.7	6.0	32.0	40.3	1.5
East South Central	100.0	10.9	7.6	5.6	40.8	34.2	0.9
West South Central	100.0	21.8	8.4	7.0	16.8	45.2	0.9
SOUTH ATLANTIC.							
Delaware	100.0	11.1	9.5	4.4	6.9	61.3	6.9
Maryland	100.0	15.9	11.5	7.9	14.2	39.7	10.8
District of Columbia	100.0	17.9	8.9	21.0	42.0	....	10.2
Virginia	100.0	36.5	9.9	11.5	12.8	26.1	3.2
West Virginia	100.0	47.9	11.5	8.2	9.2	20.1	3.1
North Carolina	100.0	14.3	6.5	10.0	17.9	50.6	0.7
South Carolina	100.0	10.8	5.2	4.8	36.8	41.3	1.1
Georgia	100.0	8.4	3.7	3.0	43.4	40.9	0.6
Florida	100.0	38.5	9.6	6.7	28.0	10.3	6.9
EAST SOUTH CENTRAL.							
Kentucky	100.0	21.0	7.8	16.4	6.6	45.9	2.4
Tennessee	100.0	12.9	5.2	8.9	36.4	34.6	1.9
Alabama	100.0	10.0	7.0	5.4	54.1	23.0	0.4
Mississippi	100.0	9.7	8.6	3.7	39.1	38.4	0.6
WEST SOUTH CENTRAL.							
Arkansas	100.0	14.8	8.4	5.7	36.2	34.6	0.4
Louisiana	100.0	17.1	6.5	4.0	15.8	55.2	1.4
Oklahoma	100.0	43.8	13.8	9.6	7.6	24.9	0.3
Texas	100.0	17.7	6.4	7.9	7.7	59.0	1.3

TABLE 60.—VALUE OF LAND IN COLORED AND WHITE FARMS, CLASSIFIED BY TENURE, BY SOUTHERN DIVISIONS AND STATES: 1910—Continued.

DIVISION AND STATE.	FARMS OPERATED BY WHITE FARMERS: 1910.						
	Total.	Owners and part owners.			Tenants.		Managers.
		Owners.		Part owners.	Cash and not specified.	Share and share-cash.	
		Free.	Mortgaged.				
THE SOUTH.	VALUE OF LAND.						
Total	$5,188,642,947	$2,018,861,909	$765,336,397	$506,514,471	$484,059,699	$1,092,399,374	$321,471,097
South Atlantic	1,586,788,567	790,928,349	191,869,715	105,325,180	158,362,655	245,322,642	94,980,026
East South Central	1,099,625,442	536,982,171	144,743,135	101,648,052	108,509,267	171,614,978	36,127,839
West South Central	2,502,228,938	690,951,389	428,723,547	299,541,239	217,187,777	675,461,754	190,363,232
SOUTH ATLANTIC.							
Delaware	33,486,704	9,698,677	5,564,816	554,715	3,217,480	13,439,711	1,011,305
Maryland	156,352,922	46,419,880	28,554,836	5,944,247	16,063,985	42,162,889	17,207,085
District of Columbia	7,127,350	1,506,700	181,400	156,200	2,327,250	33,000	2,922,800
Virginia	362,105,272	200,986,175	44,087,525	28,904,050	24,376,750	43,675,477	20,075,295
West Virginia	206,247,170	123,348,559	17,010,822	18,555,227	21,875,403	17,870,804	7,586,355
North Carolina	287,802,767	151,168,780	29,601,971	23,823,796	18,579,149	53,261,792	11,367,279
South Carolina	184,728,209	86,020,390	29,209,757	11,074,040	25,297,225	24,521,819	8,604,978
Georgia	264,497,825	121,335,772	27,285,599	11,906,010	42,684,412	48,050,979	13,235,053
Florida	84,440,348	50,443,416	10,372,989	4,406,895	3,941,001	2,306,171	12,969,876
EAST SOUTH CENTRAL.							
Kentucky	472,225,751	233,695,480	62,714,489	44,955,802	37,931,013	80,452,945	12,476,022
Tennessee	336,171,390	166,661,784	36,086,459	36,850,392	31,051,661	57,199,079	8,322,015
Alabama	157,619,496	71,999,613	22,241,669	12,699,516	23,616,218	21,747,695	5,314,785
Mississippi	133,608,805	64,625,294	23,700,518	7,142,342	15,910,375	12,215,259	10,015,017
WEST SOUTH CENTRAL.							
Arkansas	188,068,595	77,910,595	24,773,408	19,408,203	22,246,244	34,654,146	9,075,999
Louisiana	151,600,372	59,905,716	22,736,400	10,316,782	16,509,405	18,442,967	23,689,102
Oklahoma	608,094,918	115,679,728	104,147,090	113,570,994	83,077,148	184,141,448	7,478,510
Texas	1,554,465,053	437,455,350	277,066,649	156,245,260	95,354,980	438,223,193	150,119,621
THE SOUTH.	PERCENTAGE DISTRIBUTION OF VALUE OF LAND, BY TENURE.						
Total	100.0	39.0	14.3	9.8	9.3	21.1	6.2
South Atlantic	100.0	49.8	12.1	6.6	10.0	15.5	6.0
East South Central	100.0	48.8	13.2	9.2	9.9	15.6	3.3
West South Central	100.0	27.6	17.1	12.0	8.7	27.0	7.6
SOUTH ATLANTIC.							
Delaware	100.0	29.0	16.6	1.7	9.6	40.1	3.0
Maryland	100.0	29.7	18.3	3.8	10.3	27.0	11.0
District of Columbia	100.0	21.1	2.5	2.2	32.7	0.5	41.0
Virginia	100.0	55.5	12.2	8.0	6.7	12.1	5.5
West Virginia	100.0	59.8	8.2	9.0	10.6	8.7	3.7
North Carolina	100.0	52.5	10.3	8.3	6.5	18.5	3.9
South Carolina	100.0	46.6	15.8	6.0	13.7	13.3	4.7
Georgia	100.0	45.9	10.3	4.5	16.1	18.2	5.0
Florida	100.0	59.7	12.3	5.2	4.7	2.7	15.4
EAST SOUTH CENTRAL.							
Kentucky	100.0	49.5	13.3	9.5	8.0	17.0	2.6
Tennessee	100.0	49.6	10.7	11.0	9.2	17.0	2.5
Alabama	100.0	45.7	14.1	8.1	15.0	13.8	3.4
Mississippi	100.0	48.4	17.7	5.3	11.9	9.1	7.5
WEST SOUTH CENTRAL.							
Arkansas	100.0	41.4	13.2	10.3	11.8	18.4	4.8
Louisiana	100.0	39.5	15.0	6.8	10.9	12.2	15.6
Oklahoma	100.0	19.0	17.1	18.7	13.7	30.3	1.2
Texas	100.0	28.1	17.8	10.1	6.1	28.2	9.7

TABLE 61.—VALUE OF BUILDINGS ON COLORED AND WHITE FARMS, CLASSIFIED BY TENURE, BY SOUTHERN DIVISIONS AND STATES: 1910.

DIVISION AND STATE.	FARMS OPERATED BY COLORED FARMERS: 1910.						
	Total.	Owners and part owners.			Tenants.		Managers.
		Owners.		Part owners.	Cash and not specified.	Share and share-cash.	
		Free.	Mortgaged.				
	VALUE OF BUILDINGS.						
THE SOUTH.							
Total	$162,500,212	$35,775,640	$13,857,518	$11,083,509	$44,585,708	$55,082,742	$2,115,095
South Atlantic	71,145,960	16,929,889	5,334,804	5,317,505	18,954,362	23,302,790	1,306,610
East South Central	52,466,336	8,143,342	4,857,256	3,113,994	19,356,642	16,404,597	590,505
West South Central	38,887,916	10,702,409	3,665,458	2,652,010	6,274,704	15,375,355	217,980
SOUTH ATLANTIC.							
Delaware	530,259	84,625	77,385	22,950	32,690	266,709	45,900
Maryland	3,171,092	724,503	441,188	248,402	309,060	1,042,219	405,720
District of Columbia	22,800	6,500	6,100	4,000	5,000	....	1,200
Virginia	12,670,864	6,290,120	1,403,484	1,505,599	939,244	2,232,727	299,690
West Virginia	247,805	126,715	33,989	16,795	17,405	42,906	9,995
North Carolina	13,904,038	3,007,544	1,122,318	1,616,639	2,140,264	5,827,523	189,750
South Carolina	14,953,109	2,698,142	975,145	896,161	5,358,123	4,931,953	93,585
Georgia	23,028,142	2,750,531	1,038,598	793,704	9,526,559	8,757,705	161,045
Florida	2,617,851	1,241,209	236,597	213,255	626,017	201,048	99,725
EAST SOUTH CENTRAL.							
Kentucky	2,793,042	878,219	293,497	449,568	145,658	936,305	89,795
Tennessee	6,948,173	1,468,333	479,928	700,478	2,138,002	2,043,862	117,570
Alabama	14,594,048	1,948,083	1,184,847	845,066	7,325,794	3,130,093	160,165
Mississippi	28,131,073	3,848,707	2,898,984	1,118,882	9,747,188	10,294,337	222,975
WEST SOUTH CENTRAL.							
Arkansas	11,060,254	2,187,548	1,087,951	701,289	3,557,215	3,495,251	31,000
Louisiana	8,730,753	1,866,784	605,314	305,712	1,440,786	4,424,132	88,025
Oklahoma	6,250,043	3,209,644	1,020,704	571,399	338,403	1,091,153	18,740
Texas	12,846,866	3,438,433	951,489	1,073,610	938,300	6,364,819	80,215
	PERCENTAGE DISTRIBUTION OF VALUE OF BUILDINGS, BY TENURE.						
THE SOUTH.							
Total	100.0	22.0	8.5	6.8	27.4	33.9	1.3
South Atlantic	100.0	23.8	7.5	7.5	26.6	32.8	1.8
East South Central	100.0	15.5	9.3	5.9	36.9	31.3	1.1
West South Central	100.0	27.5	9.4	6.8	16.1	39.5	0.6
SOUTH ATLANTIC.							
Delaware	100.0	16.0	14.6	4.3	6.2	50.3	8.7
Maryland	100.0	22.8	13.9	7.8	9.7	32.9	12.8
District of Columbia	100.0	28.5	26.8	17.5	21.9	....	5.3
Virginia	100.0	49.6	11.1	11.9	7.4	17.6	2.4
West Virginia	100.0	51.1	13.7	6.8	7.0	17.3	4.0
North Carolina	100.0	21.6	8.1	11.6	15.4	41.9	1.4
South Carolina	100.0	18.0	6.5	6.0	35.8	33.0	0.6
Georgia	100.0	11.9	4.5	3.4	41.4	38.0	0.7
Florida	100.0	47.4	9.0	8.1	23.9	7.7	3.8
EAST SOUTH CENTRAL.							
Kentucky	100.0	31.4	10.5	16.1	5.2	33.5	3.2
Tennessee	100.0	21.1	6.9	10.1	30.8	29.4	1.7
Alabama	100.0	13.3	8.1	5.8	50.2	21.4	1.1
Mississippi	100.0	13.7	10.3	4.0	34.6	36.6	0.8
WEST SOUTH CENTRAL.							
Arkansas	100.0	19.8	9.8	6.3	32.2	31.6	0.3
Louisiana	100.0	21.4	6.9	3.5	16.5	50.7	1.0
Oklahoma	100.0	51.4	16.3	9.1	5.4	17.5	0.3
Texas	100.0	26.8	7.4	8.4	7.3	49.5	0.6

TABLE **61.**—VALUE OF BUILDINGS ON COLORED AND WHITE FARMS, CLASSIFIED BY TENURE, BY SOUTHERN DIVISIONS AND STATES: 1910—Continued.

DIVISION AND STATE.	Total.	Owners and part owners.			Tenants.		Managers.
		Owners.		Part owners.	Cash and not specified.	Share and share-cash.	
		Free.	Mortgaged.				

FARMS OPERATED BY WHITE FARMERS: 1910.

VALUE OF BUILDINGS.

THE SOUTH.							
Total	$1,264,655,914	$643,867,091	$190,544,111	$98,811,108	$92,421,342	$192,535,212	$46,477,050
South Atlantic	531,940,839	294,225,200	73,651,850	31,725,368	40,302,372	67,204,466	24,831,583
East South Central	359,104,639	201,864,497	50,462,300	29,115,157	26,517,086	42,248,047	8,897,552
West South Central	373,610,436	147,777,394	66,429,961	37,970,583	25,601,884	83,082,699	12,747,915
SOUTH ATLANTIC.							
Delaware	17,687,563	7,073,198	3,434,360	301,750	1,459,000	4,800,080	619,175
Maryland	75,114,417	28,754,106	16,296,556	2,916,307	5,504,700	15,553,642	6,089,106
District of Columbia	1,014,593	303,300	40,000	43,800	312,450	5,000	310,043
Virginia	124,728,286	75,999,939	16,994,618	7,809,454	6,200,564	11,775,395	5,948,316
West Virginia	57,067,390	38,274,137	5,536,060	4,531,402	3,206,929	4,005,247	1,513,615
North Carolina	99,555,624	58,946,594	11,172,463	7,810,398	5,186,413	14,154,791	2,284,965
South Carolina	49,160,118	25,855,463	8,345,472	3,085,899	5,625,253	4,547,764	1,700,267
Georgia	85,822,775	44,981,974	9,295,085	4,276,426	11,786,565	11,821,894	3,660,831
Florida	21,790,073	14,036,489	2,537,236	949,932	1,020,498	540,653	2,705,265
EAST SOUTH CENTRAL.							
Kentucky	148,201,713	82,898,540	21,702,413	11,717,411	8,179,352	19,720,952	3,983,045
Tennessee	102,158,631	59,186,346	11,416,724	9,986,167	7,156,292	12,546,804	1,866,298
Alabama	56,715,368	29,997,805	8,007,672	4,640,521	6,583,248	6,249,943	1,236,179
Mississippi	52,028,927	29,781,806	9,355,491	2,771,058	4,598,194	3,730,348	1,812,030
WEST SOUTH CENTRAL.							
Arkansas	52,085,109	27,147,282	6,723,667	5,224,640	4,350,675	7,513,096	1,125,749
Louisiana	41,010,420	19,745,360	6,246,617	2,391,091	3,504,865	3,513,366	5,609,121
Oklahoma	83,360,513	20,880,869	17,206,144	14,052,129	9,345,275	20,742,497	1,133,599
Texas	197,154,394	80,003,883	36,253,533	16,302,723	8,401,069	51,313,740	4,879,446

PERCENTAGE DISTRIBUTION OF VALUE OF BUILDINGS, BY TENURE.

THE SOUTH.							
Total	100.0	50.9	15.1	7.8	7.3	15.2	3.8
South Atlantic	100.0	55.3	13.8	6.0	7.6	12.6	4.7
East South Central	100.0	56.2	14.1	8.1	7.4	11.8	2.5
West South Central	100.0	39.6	17.8	10.2	6.9	22.2	3.4
SOUTH ATLANTIC.							
Delaware	100.0	40.0	19.4	1.7	8.2	27.1	3.5
Maryland	100.0	38.3	21.7	3.9	7.3	20.7	8.1
District of Columbia	100.0	29.9	3.9	4.3	30.8	0.5	30.6
Virginia	100.0	60.9	13.6	6.3	5.0	9.4	4.8
West Virginia	100.0	67.1	9.7	7.9	5.6	7.0	2.7
North Carolina	100.0	59.2	11.2	7.8	5.2	14.2	2.3
South Carolina	100.0	52.6	17.0	6.3	11.4	9.3	3.5
Georgia	100.0	52.4	10.8	5.0	13.7	13.8	4.3
Florida	100.0	64.4	11.6	4.4	4.7	2.5	12.4
EAST SOUTH CENTRAL.							
Kentucky	100.0	55.9	14.6	7.9	5.5	13.3	2.7
Tennessee	100.0	57.9	11.2	9.8	7.0	12.3	1.8
Alabama	100.0	52.9	14.1	8.2	11.6	11.0	2.2
Mississippi	100.0	57.2	17.9	5.3	8.8	7.2	3.5
WEST SOUTH CENTRAL.							
Arkansas	100.0	52.1	12.9	10.0	8.4	14.4	2.2
Louisiana	100.0	48.1	15.2	5.8	8.5	8.6	13.7
Oklahoma	100.0	25.0	20.6	16.9	11.2	24.9	1.4
Texas	100.0	40.6	18.4	8.3	4.3	26.0	2.5

TABLE **62.**—VALUE OF IMPLEMENTS AND MACHINERY ON COLORED AND WHITE FARMS, CLASSIFIED BY TENURE, BY SOUTHERN DIVISIONS AND STATES: 1910.

DIVISION AND STATE.	FARMS OPERATED BY COLORED FARMERS: 1910.						
	Total.	Owners and part owners.			Tenants.		Managers.
		Owners.		Part owners.	Cash and not specified.	Share and share-cash.	
		Free.	Mortgaged.				
	VALUE OF IMPLEMENTS AND MACHINERY.						
THE SOUTH.							
Total	$33,777,118	$7,514,838	$3,283,993	$2,490,431	$11,337,009	$8,841,943	$308,904
South Atlantic	13,214,737	3,055,014	1,041,635	979,507	4,435,291	3,539,782	163,508
East South Central	11,176,951	1,793,423	1,226,439	749,423	5,131,034	2,198,354	78,278
West South Central	9,385,430	2,666,401	1,015,919	761,501	1,770,684	3,103,807	67,118
SOUTH ATLANTIC.							
Delaware	100,090	18,673	16,299	6,133	6,413	47,082	5,490
Maryland	437,070	109,946	67,744	39,825	42,793	135,556	41,206
District of Columbia	955	300	375	75	155		50
Virginia	1,852,503	882,939	212,431	232,705	148,392	347,178	28,858
West Virginia	31,693	15,804	3,336	2,755	1,400	7,650	748
North Carolina	2,261,470	511,087	210,657	267,498	425,032	830,301	16,895
South Carolina	3,368,463	635,774	245,422	218,952	1,394,511	845,150	28,654
Georgia	4,559,962	623,825	230,483	165,075	2,232,637	1,281,741	26,201
Florida	602,531	256,666	54,888	46,489	183,958	45,124	15,406
EAST SOUTH CENTRAL.							
Kentucky	420,909	135,096	53,858	75,106	27,222	121,890	7,737
Tennessee	1,821,238	370,173	136,434	193,300	740,943	368,019	12,369
Alabama	3,332,509	436,991	293,036	206,535	1,901,064	479,126	15,757
Mississippi	5,602,295	851,163	743,111	274,482	2,461,805	1,229,319	42,415
WEST SOUTH CENTRAL.							
Arkansas	2,789,157	629,102	319,677	188,104	1,078,927	557,888	15,459
Louisiana	1,684,573	422,801	145,327	73,926	329,616	692,224	20,679
Oklahoma	1,637,769	764,892	244,304	151,003	119,324	355,074	3,172
Texas	3,273,931	849,606	306,611	348,468	242,817	1,498,621	27,808
PERCENTAGE DISTRIBUTION OF VALUE OF IMPLEMENTS AND MACHINERY, BY TENURE							
THE SOUTH.							
Total	100.0	22.2	9.7	7.4	33.6	26.2	0.9
South Atlantic	100.0	23.1	7.9	7.4	33.6	26.8	1.2
East South Central	100.0	16.0	11.0	6.7	45.9	19.7	0.7
West South Central	100.0	28.4	10.8	8.1	18.9	33.1	0.7
SOUTH ATLANTIC.							
Delaware	100.0	18.7	16.3	6.1	6.4	47.0	5.5
Maryland	100.0	25.2	15.5	9.1	9.8	31.0	9.4
District of Columbia	100.0	31.4	39.3	7.9	16.2		5.2
Virginia	100.0	47.7	11.5	12.6	8.0	18.7	1.6
West Virginia	100.0	49.9	10.5	8.7	4.4	24.1	2.4
North Carolina	100.0	22.6	9.3	11.8	18.8	36.7	0.7
South Carolina	100.0	18.9	7.3	6.5	41.4	25.1	0.9
Georgia	100.0	13.7	5.1	3.6	49.0	28.1	0.6
Florida	100.0	42.4	9.1	7.7	30.5	7.5	2.6
EAST SOUTH CENTRAL.							
Kentucky	100.0	32.1	12.8	17.8	6.5	29.0	1.8
Tennessee	100.0	20.3	7.5	10.6	40.7	20.2	0.7
Alabama	100.0	13.1	8.8	6.2	57.0	14.4	0.5
Mississippi	100.0	15.2	13.3	4.9	44.0	21.9	0.8
WEST SOUTH CENTRAL.							
Arkansas	100.0	22.6	11.5	6.7	38.7	20.0	0.6
Louisiana	100.0	25.1	8.6	4.4	19.6	41.0	1.2
Oklahoma	100.0	46.7	14.9	9.2	7.3	21.7	0.2
Texas	100.0	25.9	9.4	10.6	7.4	45.8	0.9

TABLE 62.—VALUE OF IMPLEMENTS AND MACHINERY ON COLORED AND WHITE FARMS, CLASSIFIED BY TENURE, BY SOUTHERN DIVISIONS AND STATES: 1910—Continued.

DIVISION AND STATE.	Total.	FARMS OPERATED BY WHITE FARMERS: 1910.					Managers.
		Owners and part owners.			Tenants.		
		Owners.		Part owners.	Cash and not specified.	Share and share-cash.	
		Free.	Mortgaged.				
		VALUE OF IMPLEMENTS AND MACHINERY.					
THE SOUTH							
Total............	$259,512,739	$116,186,391	$42,569,058	$23,472,047	$20,110,267	$43,911,243	$13,263,733
South Atlantic................	85,015,410	45,804,758	12,841,262	5,387,568	6,679,974	10,524,452	3,777,396
East South Central............	64,162,382	34,277,918	9,536,429	5,905,940	5,165,736	7,415,181	1,861,178
West South Central............	110,334,947	36,103,715	20,191,367	12,178,539	8,264,557	25,971,610	7,625,159
SOUTH ATLANTIC.							
Delaware................	3,106,005	1,095,169	665,315	48,821	242,778	965,033	88,889
Maryland................	11,422,701	4,251,167	2,758,480	457,735	820,039	2,515,342	619,938
District of Columbia........	91,395	11,635	2,500	4,800	11,110	300	61,050
Virginia................	16,263,380	9,554,711	2,382,774	1,129,641	760,561	1,660,810	774,883
West Virginia............	6,979,820	4,671,696	710,824	597,602	341,645	496,597	161,456
North Carolina...........	16,180,149	9,589,740	1,966,347	1,352,417	804,192	1,991,741	475,712
South Carolina...........	10,740,390	5,537,579	1,898,828	731,995	1,262,984	848,656	460,348
Georgia................	16,388,094	8,593,689	1,965,428	867,811	2,249,297	1,933,498	778,371
Florida................	3,843,476	2,499,372	490,766	196,746	187,368	112,475	356,749
EAST SOUTH CENTRAL.							
Kentucky................	20,430,937	11,002,088	3,118,490	1,899,652	1,153,764	2,684,055	572,888
Tennessee................	19,470,933	10,594,368	2,211,019	2,198,835	1,518,370	2,675,011	273,330
Alabama................	12,957,495	6,706,140	1,961,248	1,152,108	1,493,779	1,318,933	325,287
Mississippi..............	11,303,017	5,975,322	2,245,672	655,345	999,823	737,182	689,673
WEST SOUTH CENTRAL.							
Arkansas................	14,075,041	6,785,939	2,023,069	1,516,996	1,197,355	1,998,671	553,011
Louisiana................	17,292,480	6,113,486	2,697,149	940,461	1,288,941	1,001,834	5,250,609
Oklahoma................	25,451,097	5,316,926	4,957,638	4,800,325	3,235,436	6,896,143	244,629
Texas..................	53,516,329	17,887,364	10,513,511	4,920,757	2,542,825	16,074,962	1,576,910
		PERCENTAGE DISTRIBUTION OF VALUE OF IMPLEMENTS AND MACHINERY, BY TENURE.					
THE SOUTH.							
Total............	100.0	44.8	16.4	9.0	7.7	16.9	5.1
South Atlantic..............	100.0	53.9	15.1	6.3	7.9	12.4	4.4
East South Central..........	100.0	53.4	14.9	9.2	8.1	11.6	2.9
West South Central..........	100.0	32.7	18.3	11.0	7.5	23.5	6.9
SOUTH ATLANTIC.							
Delaware................	100.0	35.3	21.4	1.6	7.8	31.1	2.9
Maryland................	100.0	37.2	24.1	4.0	7.2	22.0	5.4
District of Columbia........	100.0	12.7	2.7	5.3	12.2	0.3	66.8
Virginia................	100.0	58.7	14.7	6.9	4.7	10.2	4.8
West Virginia............	100.0	66.9	10.2	8.6	4.9	7.1	2.3
North Carolina...........	100.0	59.3	12.2	8.4	5.0	12.3	2.9
South Carolina...........	100.0	51.6	17.7	6.8	11.8	7.9	4.3
Georgia................	100.0	52.4	12.0	5.3	13.7	11.8	4.7
Florida................	100.0	65.0	12.8	5.1	4.9	2.9	9.3
EAST SOUTH CENTRAL.							
Kentucky................	100.0	53.9	15.3	9.3	5.6	13.1	2.8
Tennessee................	100.0	54.4	11.4	11.3	7.8	13.7	1.4
Alabama................	100.0	51.8	15.1	8.9	11.5	10.2	2.5
Mississippi..............	100.0	52.9	19.9	5.8	8.8	6.5	6.1
WEST SOUTH CENTRAL.							
Arkansas................	100.0	48.2	14.4	10.8	8.5	14.2	3.9
Louisiana................	100.0	35.4	15.6	5.4	7.5	5.8	30.4
Oklahoma................	100.0	20.9	19.5	18.9	12.7	27.1	9.6
Texas..................	100.0	33.4	19.6	9.2	4.8	30.0	29.5

TABLE 63.—NUMBER OF DAIRY COWS ON COLORED AND WHITE FARMS, CLASSIFIED BY TENURE, BY SOUTHERN DIVISIONS AND STATES: 1910.

DIVISION AND STATE.	FARMS OPERATED BY COLORED FARMERS: 1910.							FARMS OPERATED BY WHITE FARMERS: 1910.						
	Total.	Owners and part owners.			Tenants.		Managers.	Total.	Owners and part owners.			Tenants.		Managers.
		Owners.		Part owners.	Cash and not specified.	Share and share-cash.			Owners.		Part owners.	Cash and not specified.	Share and share-cash.	
		Free.	Mortgaged.						Free.	Mortgaged.				
NUMBER OF DAIRY COWS.														
THE SOUTH.														
Total	929,883	211,318	79,950	62,962	308,757	264,089	2,807	4,758,485	2,315,071	659,945	417,127	416,294	885,859	64,189
South Atlantic	285,141	69,990	18,488	20,227	93,407	81,645	1,384	1,525,613	851,121	182,191	100,789	128,025	234,349	29,138
East South Central	358,406	49,925	31,732	19,825	165,573	90,575	776	1,269,655	666,386	161,287	110,589	115,008	202,113	14,272
West South Central	286,336	91,403	29,730	22,910	49,777	91,869	647	1,963,217	797,564	316,467	205,749	173,261	449,397	20,779
SOUTH ATLANTIC.														
Delaware	1,077	148	139	42	69	615	64	34,631	8,763	6,437	442	3,586	14,420	983
Maryland	6,339	1,554	906	492	522	2,611	254	160,520	54,827	36,715	5,705	12,279	45,754	5,240
District of Columbia	11	8	....	1	2	....	....	846	133	8	1	285	1	418
Virginia	42,242	21,264	4,154	5,434	2,900	8,042	448	314,042	191,317	36,795	25,054	16,190	36,881	7,805
West Virginia	1,111	637	125	119	75	135	20	238,428	159,848	21,110	20,625	16,333	17,814	2,698
North Carolina	42,637	9,448	3,289	5,022	7,972	16,740	166	266,277	151,862	26,568	24,777	14,017	45,678	3,375
South Carolina	70,886	13,211	3,659	4,073	29,241	20,531	171	109,956	53,522	15,708	6,546	15,437	16,180	2,563
Georgia	104,966	16,342	4,869	3,791	47,808	31,950	206	300,744	155,049	29,740	13,423	43,531	54,342	4,659
Florida	15,872	7,378	1,347	1,253	4,818	1,021	55	100,169	75,800	9,110	4,216	6,367	3,279	1,397
EAST SOUTH CENTRAL.														
Kentucky	9,882	3,595	1,045	1,451	531	3,155	105	399,952	219,284	50,109	34,842	22,275	69,620	3,822
Tennessee	42,522	8,010	2,868	3,963	16,079	11,454	148	354,582	187,684	33,096	38,717	29,292	62,047	3,746
Alabama	126,570	13,821	8,420	6,922	75,410	21,741	256	264,966	125,626	35,242	23,396	35,992	41,451	3,259
Mississippi	179,432	24,499	19,399	7,489	73,553	54,225	267	250,155	133,792	42,840	13,634	27,449	28,995	3,445
WEST SOUTH CENTRAL.														
Arkansas	81,122	19,793	9,563	6,410	26,655	18,590	111	344,671	180,403	37,690	39,597	28,602	56,540	1,839
Louisiana	64,204	17,928	5,152	2,158	12,117	26,613	236	214,893	131,840	25,404	10,358	18,246	24,349	4,696
Oklahoma	40,874	21,191	5,699	3,550	2,836	7,566	32	489,922	101,263	87,594	79,804	77,547	141,646	2,068
Texas	100,136	32,491	9,316	10,792	8,169	39,100	268	913,731	384,058	165,779	75,990	48,866	226,862	12,176
PERCENTAGE DISTRIBUTION OF DAIRY COWS, BY TENURE.														
THE SOUTH.														
Total	100.0	22.7	8.6	6.8	33.2	28.4	0.3	100.0	48.7	13.9	8.8	8.7	18.6	1.3
South Atlantic	100.0	24.5	6.5	7.1	32.8	28.6	0.5	100.0	55.8	11.9	6.6	8.4	15.4	1.9
East South Central	100.0	13.9	8.9	5.5	46.2	25.3	0.2	100.0	52.5	12.7	8.7	9.1	15.9	1.1
West South Central	100.0	31.9	10.4	8.0	17.4	32.1	0.2	100.0	40.6	16.1	10.5	8.8	22.9	1.1
SOUTH ATLANTIC.														
Delaware	100.0	13.7	12.9	3.9	6.4	57.1	6.0	100.0	25.3	18.6	1.3	10.4	41.6	2.8
Maryland	100.0	24.5	14.3	7.8	8.2	41.2	4.0	100.0	34.2	22.9	3.6	7.6	28.5	3.3
District of Columbia	100.0	72.7	....	9.1	18.2	....	....	100.0	15.7	0.9	(1)	33.7	(1)	49.4
Virginia	100.0	50.3	9.8	12.9	6.9	19.0	1.1	100.0	60.9	11.7	8.0	5.2	11.7	2.5
West Virginia	100.0	57.3	11.3	10.7	6.8	12.2	1.8	100.0	67.0	8.9	8.7	6.9	7.5	1.1
North Carolina	100.0	22.2	7.7	11.8	18.7	39.3	0.4	100.0	57.0	10.0	9.3	5.3	17.2	1.3
South Carolina	100.0	18.6	5.2	5.7	41.3	29.0	0.2	100.0	48.7	14.3	6.0	14.0	14.7	2.3
Georgia	100.0	15.6	4.6	3.6	45.5	30.4	0.2	100.0	51.6	9.9	4.5	14.5	18.1	1.5
Florida	100.0	46.5	8.5	7.9	30.4	6.4	0.3	100.0	75.7	9.1	4.2	6.4	3.3	1.4
EAST SOUTH CENTRAL.														
Kentucky	100.0	36.4	10.6	14.7	5.4	31.9	1.1	100.0	54.8	12.5	8.7	5.6	17.4	1.0
Tennessee	100.0	18.8	6.7	9.3	37.8	26.9	0.3	100.0	52.9	9.3	10.9	8.3	17.5	1.1
Alabama	100.0	10.9	6.7	5.5	59.6	17.2	0.2	100.0	47.4	13.3	8.8	13.6	15.6	1.2
Mississippi	100.0	13.7	10.8	4.2	41.0	30.2	0.1	100.0	53.5	17.1	5.5	11.0	11.6	1.4
WEST SOUTH CENTRAL.														
Arkansas	100.0	24.4	11.8	7.9	32.9	22.9	0.1	100.0	52.3	10.9	11.5	8.3	16.4	0.5
Louisiana	100.0	27.9	8.0	3.4	18.9	41.5	0.4	100.0	61.4	11.8	4.8	8.5	11.3	2.2
Oklahoma	100.0	51.8	13.9	8.7	6.9	18.5	0.1	100.0	20.7	17.9	16.3	15.8	28.9	0.4
Texas	100.0	32.4	9.3	10.8	8.2	39.0	0.3	100.0	42.0	18.1	8.3	5.3	24.8	1.3

[1] Less than one-tenth of 1 per cent.

TABLE 64.—NUMBER OF WORK HORSES ON COLORED AND WHITE FARMS, CLASSIFIED BY TENURE, BY SOUTHERN DIVISIONS AND STATES: 1910.

DIVISION AND STATE.	FARMS OPERATED BY COLORED FARMERS: 1910.							FARMS OPERATED BY WHITE FARMERS: 1910.						
	Total.	Owners and part owners.			Tenants.		Managers.	Total.	Owners and part owners.			Tenants.		Managers.
		Owners.		Part owners.	Cash and not specified.	Share and share-cash.			Owners.		Part owners.	Cash and not specified.	Share and share-cash.	
		Free.	Mortgaged.						Free.	Mortgaged.				
NUMBER OF WORK HORSES.														
THE SOUTH.														
Total	509,087	130,102	46,272	41,715	141,798	146,815	2,385	3,564,855	1,528,189	546,570	368,390	301,721	747,712	72,273
South Atlantic	140,394	41,792	12,177	14,483	38,026	32,891	1,025	866,091	469,365	114,181	62,260	67,705	133,572	19,008
East South Central	158,346	25,960	14,933	11,213	69,390	36,264	586	851,449	449,358	111,556	82,090	67,773	131,282	9,390
West South Central	210,347	62,350	19,162	16,019	34,382	77,660	774	1,847,315	609,466	320,833	224,040	166,243	482,858	43,875
SOUTH ATLANTIC.														
Delaware	1,529	276	238	99	105	750	61	28,103	8,235	5,391	510	2,160	11,279	528
Maryland	9,169	2,387	1,402	941	856	3,297	286	128,109	44,461	28,187	5,212	9,143	36,798	4,308
District of Columbia	18	4	2	8	3	....	1	545	183	29	13	184	6	130
Virginia	38,905	18,290	4,120	5,621	3,123	7,401	350	249,954	148,604	31,260	20,269	12,871	30,528	6,422
West Virginia	888	472	96	90	59	149	22	158,669	103,611	15,138	15,203	8,978	13,405	2,334
North Carolina	24,926	5,073	2,315	3,241	5,249	8,985	63	131,023	72,765	14,523	11,708	8,358	21,781	1,888
South Carolina	27,075	6,135	1,556	2,062	12,106	5,132	84	49,896	24,410	7,607	3,337	8,556	5,070	916
Georgia	28,090	4,864	1,595	1,454	13,617	6,458	102	86,571	43,581	8,785	4,346	14,914	13,318	1,627
Florida	9,794	4,291	853	967	2,908	719	56	33,221	23,515	3,261	1,662	2,541	1,387	855
EAST SOUTH CENTRAL.														
Kentucky	10,362	3,545	1,146	1,736	587	3,120	228	377,433	203,470	52,269	36,127	18,546	63,186	3,835
Tennessee	30,097	6,009	2,165	3,342	11,354	7,117	110	270,230	145,686	27,833	30,839	21,275	42,364	2,233
Alabama	35,816	4,673	2,665	2,503	21,292	4,603	80	89,448	42,615	11,682	8,445	13,126	12,279	1,301
Mississippi	82,071	11,733	8,957	3,632	36,157	21,424	168	114,338	57,587	19,772	6,679	14,826	13,453	2,021
WEST SOUTH CENTRAL.														
Arkansas	36,948	7,920	3,719	2,808	13,987	8,469	45	191,531	91,282	21,979	21,835	17,637	37,011	1,787
Louisiana	47,589	9,923	3,027	1,569	9,113	23,824	133	117,015	61,270	13,502	6,974	10,292	21,329	3,648
Oklahoma	51,953	25,645	6,641	4,535	3,846	11,181	105	591,465	119,711	103,152	100,834	86,955	176,639	4,174
Texas	73,857	18,862	5,775	7,107	7,436	34,186	491	947,304	337,203	182,200	94,397	51,359	247,879	34,266
PERCENTAGE DISTRIBUTION OF WORK HORSES, BY TENURE.														
THE SOUTH.														
Total	100.0	25.6	9.1	8.2	27.9	28.8	0.5	100.0	42.9	15.3	10.3	8.5	21.0	2.0
South Atlantic	100.0	29.8	8.7	10.3	27.1	23.4	0.7	100.0	54.2	13.2	7.2	7.8	15.4	2.2
East South Central	100.0	16.4	9.4	7.1	43.8	22.9	0.4	100.0	52.8	13.1	9.6	8.0	15.4	1.1
West South Central	100.0	29.6	9.1	7.6	16.3	36.9	0.4	100.0	33.0	17.4	12.1	9.0	26.1	2.4
SOUTH ATLANTIC.														
Delaware	100.0	18.1	15.6	6.5	6.9	49.1	4.0	100.0	29.3	19.2	1.8	7.7	40.1	1.9
Maryland	100.0	26.0	15.3	10.3	9.3	36.0	3.1	100.0	34.7	22.0	4.1	7.1	28.7	3.4
District of Columbia	100.0	22.2	11.1	44.4	16.7	....	5.6	100.0	33.6	5.3	2.4	33.8	1.1	23.9
Virginia	100.0	47.0	10.6	14.4	8.0	19.0	0.9	100.0	59.5	12.5	8.1	5.1	12.2	2.6
West Virginia	100.0	53.2	10.8	10.1	6.6	16.8	2.5	100.0	65.3	9.5	9.6	5.7	8.4	1.5
North Carolina	100.0	20.4	9.3	13.0	21.1	36.0	0.3	100.0	55.5	11.1	8.9	6.4	16.6	1.4
South Carolina	100.0	22.7	5.7	7.6	44.7	19.0	0.3	100.0	48.9	15.2	6.7	17.1	10.2	1.8
Georgia	100.0	17.3	5.7	5.2	48.5	23.0	0.4	100.0	50.3	10.1	5.0	17.2	15.4	1.9
Florida	100.0	43.8	8.7	9.9	29.7	7.3	0.6	100.0	70.8	9.8	5.0	7.6	4.2	2.6
EAST SOUTH CENTRAL.														
Kentucky	100.0	34.2	11.1	16.8	5.7	30.1	2.2	100.0	53.9	13.8	9.6	4.9	16.7	1.0
Tennessee	100.0	20.0	7.2	11.1	37.7	23.6	0.4	100.0	53.9	10.3	11.4	7.9	15.7	0.8
Alabama	100.0	13.0	7.4	7.0	59.4	12.9	0.2	100.0	47.6	13.1	9.4	14.7	13.7	1.5
Mississippi	100.0	14.3	10.9	4.4	44.1	26.1	0.2	100.0	50.4	17.3	5.8	13.0	11.8	1.8
WEST SOUTH CENTRAL.														
Arkansas	100.0	21.4	10.1	7.6	37.9	22.9	0.1	100.0	47.7	11.5	11.4	9.2	19.3	0.9
Louisiana	100.0	20.9	6.4	3.3	19.1	50.1	0.3	100.0	52.4	11.5	6.0	8.8	18.2	3.1
Oklahoma	100.0	49.4	12.8	8.7	7.4	21.5	0.2	100.0	20.2	17.4	17.0	14.7	30.0	7.1
Texas	100.0	25.5	7.8	9.6	10.1	46.3	0.7	100.0	35.6	19.2	10.0	5.4	26.2	3.6

TABLE 65.—NUMBER OF WORK MULES ON COLORED AND WHITE FARMS, CLASSIFIED BY TENURE, BY SOUTHERN DIVISIONS AND STATES: 1910.

DIVISION AND STATE.	FARMS OPERATED BY COLORED FARMERS: 1910.							FARMS OPERATED BY WHITE FARMERS: 1910.						
	Total.	Owners and part owners.			Tenants.		Managers.	Total.	Owners and part owners.			Tenants.		Managers.
		Owners.		Part owners.	Cash and not specified.	Share and share-cash.			Owners.		Part owners.	Cash and not specified.	Share and share-cash.	
		Free.	Mortgaged.						Free.	Mortgaged.				
NUMBER OF WORK MULES.														
THE SOUTH.														
Total......	645,320	82,998	44,446	37,307	246,934	231,263	2,372	2,188,166	855,973	296,726	205,911	216,728	547,085	65,743
South Atlantic.............	221,694	23,611	10,900	11,859	89,617	84,708	999	514,649	241,170	60,455	36,638	63,639	95,892	16,855
East South Central.........	248,161	24,630	19,125	13,020	122,436	68,209	741	676,717	320,691	88,427	67,159	67,083	119,538	13,819
West South Central........	175,465	34,757	14,421	12,428	34,881	78,346	632	996,800	294,112	147,844	102,114	86,006	331,655	35,069
SOUTH ATLANTIC.														
Delaware..................	349	53	35	12	16	213	20	5,327	2,067	850	133	193	1,958	126
Maryland.................	1,178	183	131	87	115	521	141	20,320	6,464	4,522	880	1,519	5,661	1,274
District of Columbia......	1				1			52	5		15	8	3	21
Virginia..................	8,783	3,351	938	1,269	835	2,234	156	47,295	26,927	5,590	3,449	3,038	6,042	2,187
West Virginia............	81	45	7	8	9	12		10,719	6,786	792	961	955	930	295
North Carolina...........	34,532	5,058	2,223	3,795	6,577	16,765	114	136,603	69,692	14,420	13,812	8,974	26,902	2,803
South Carolina...........	61,761	5,659	3,265	3,242	26,864	22,539	192	93,045	39,959	14,183	6,762	14,813	13,962	3,366
Georgia..................	109,983	7,947	3,836	3,028	53,151	41,687	334	183,248	78,415	17,959	9,362	32,639	39,402	5,471
Florida..................	5,026	1,315	465	418	2,049	737	42	18,102	10,855	2,139	1,264	1,500	1,032	1,312
EAST SOUTH CENTRAL.														
Kentucky.................	6,157	1,888	781	1,021	516	1,883	68	189,518	99,632	25,722	18,283	10,811	32,052	3,018
Tennessee................	28,526	4,485	2,035	3,026	11,619	7,173	188	211,756	101,139	20,717	27,107	18,833	41,638	2,322
Alabama.................	87,172	6,552	5,236	4,345	52,780	18,073	186	155,113	64,379	20,823	14,550	22,791	29,732	2,838
Mississippi..............	126,306	11,705	11,073	4,628	57,521	41,080	299	120,330	55,541	21,165	7,219	14,648	16,116	5,641
WEST SOUTH CENTRAL.														
Arkansas.................	52,772	8,633	4,917	3,464	20,717	14,920	121	153,680	67,032	15,089	18,443	18,203	30,977	3,936
Louisiana................	35,760	5,992	2,240	1,396	6,548	19,370	214	92,907	35,296	13,357	6,721	9,813	11,565	16,155
Oklahoma................	17,854	6,272	2,205	1,526	1,942	5,887	22	202,136	32,255	27,816	30,748	33,174	76,443	1,700
Texas...................	69,079	13,860	5,059	6,042	5,674	38,169	275	548,077	159,529	91,582	46,202	24,816	212,670	13,278
PERCENTAGE DISTRIBUTION OF WORK MULES, BY TENURE.														
THE SOUTH.														
Total......	100.0	12.9	6.9	5.8	38.3	35.8	0.4	100.0	39.1	13.6	9.4	9.9	25.0	3.0
South Atlantic.............	100.0	10.7	4.9	5.3	40.4	38.2	0.5	100.0	46.9	11.7	7.1	12.4	18.6	3.3
East South Central.........	100.0	9.9	7.7	5.2	49.3	27.5	0.3	100.0	47.4	13.1	9.9	9.9	17.7	2.0
West South Central........	100.0	19.8	8.2	7.1	19.9	44.7	0.4	100.0	29.5	14.8	10.2	8.6	33.3	3.5
SOUTH ATLANTIC.														
Delaware..................	100.0	15.2	10.0	3.4	4.6	61.0	5.7	100.0	38.8	16.0	2.5	3.6	36.8	2.4
Maryland.................	100.0	15.5	11.1	7.4	9.8	44.2	12.0	100.0	31.8	22.3	4.3	7.5	27.9	6.3
District of Columbia......	100.0				100.0			100.0	9.6		28.8	15.4	5.8	40.4
Virginia..................	100.0	38.2	10.7	14.4	9.5	25.4	1.8	100.0	57.0	11.8	7.3	6.4	12.8	4.6
West Virginia............	100.0	55.6	8.6	9.9	11.1	14.8		100.0	63.3	7.4	9.0	8.9	8.7	2.8
North Carolina...........	100.0	14.6	6.4	11.0	19.0	48.5	0.3	100.0	51.0	10.6	10.1	6.6	19.7	2.1
South Carolina...........	100.0	9.2	5.3	5.2	43.5	36.5	0.3	100.0	42.9	15.2	7.3	15.9	15.0	3.6
Georgia..................	100.0	7.2	3.5	2.8	48.3	37.9	0.3	100.0	42.8	9.8	5.1	17.8	21.5	3.0
Florida..................	100.0	26.2	9.3	8.3	40.8	14.7	0.8	100.0	60.0	11.8	7.0	8.3	5.7	7.2
EAST SOUTH CENTRAL.														
Kentucky.................	100.0	30.7	12.7	16.6	8.4	30.6	1.1	100.0	52.6	13.6	9.6	5.7	16.9	1.6
Tennessee................	100.0	15.7	7.2	10.6	40.7	25.1	0.6	100.0	47.8	9.8	12.8	8.9	19.7	1.1
Alabama.................	100.0	7.5	6.0	5.0	60.5	20.7	0.2	100.0	41.5	13.4	9.4	14.7	19.2	1.8
Mississippi..............	100.0	9.3	8.8	3.7	45.6	32.5	0.2	100.0	46.2	17.6	6.0	12.2	13.4	4.7
WEST SOUTH CENTRAL.														
Arkansas.................	100.0	16.4	9.3	6.6	39.3	28.3	0.2	100.0	43.6	9.8	12.0	11.8	20.2	2.6
Louisiana................	100.0	16.8	6.3	3.9	18.3	54.2	0.6	100.0	38.0	14.4	7.2	10.6	12.4	17.4
Oklahoma................	100.0	35.1	12.3	8.5	10.9	33.0	0.1	100.0	16.0	13.8	15.2	16.4	37.8	0.8
Texas...................	100.0	20.1	7.3	8.7	8.2	55.3	0.4	100.0	29.1	16.7	8.4	4.5	38.8	2.4

TABLE **66.**—NUMBER OF ACRES IN CORN ON COLORED AND WHITE FARMS, CLASSIFIED BY TENURE, BY SOUTHERN DIVISIONS AND STATES: 1910.

	FARMS OPERATED BY COLORED FARMERS: 1910.						FARMS OPERATED BY WHITE FARMERS: 1910.						
		Owners and part owners.			Tenants.				Owners and part owners.			Tenants.		
DIVISION AND STATE.	Total.	Owners.		Part owners.	Cash, and not specified.	Share and share-cash.	Managers.	Total.	Owners.		Part owners.	Cash, and not specified.	Share and share-cash.	Managers.
		Free.	Mortgaged.						Free.	Mortgaged.				
						NUMBER OF ACRES IN CORN.								
THE SOUTH.														
Total............	7,377,221	1,197,845	505,239	476,709	2,314,540	2,861,607	21,281	30,250,098	11,744,271	3,771,187	2,937,049	3,102,881	8,232,572	462,138
South Atlantic........	3,066,496	474,580	161,109	206,686	1,068,857	1,143,861	11,403	8,320,488	4,018,322	930,806	589,655	881,696	1,724,573	175,436
East South Central....	2,309,639	257,804	173,461	127,320	959,744	786,379	4,931	9,018,629	4,247,513	1,078,513	862,826	794,199	1,936,710	98,868
West South Central...	2,001,086	465,461	170,669	142,703	285,939	931,367	4,947	12,910,981	3,478,436	1,761,868	1,484,568	1,426,986	4,571,289	187,834
SOUTH ATLANTIC.														
Delaware.............	12,636	1,532	1,232	746	754	7,943	429	176,119	54,114	27,104	4,534	9,434	78,513	2,420
Maryland.............	52,139	8,937	5,901	5,459	4,607	25,915	1,320	594,873	188,052	121,553	24,633	42,555	200,261	17,819
District of Columbia...	2			2				424	128	34	12	173	5	72
Virginia..............	338,378	128,589	31,343	53,650	31,322	91,026	2,448	1,521,981	826,907	179,336	124,101	96,686	255,703	39,248
West Virginia.........	4,421	2,054	482	487	387	963	48	671,890	401,391	60,101	62,671	52,008	88,505	7,214
North Carolina........	535,037	82,350	32,021	60,963	93,554	264,909	1,240	1,924,420	953,537	184,362	188,670	125,902	446,200	25,749
South Carolina........	653,856	83,749	30,930	35,746	275,023	226,480	1,928	911,976	403,807	125,420	62,300	146,564	150,555	23,330
Georgia...............	1,278,627	109,368	43,827	34,028	585,814	502,728	2,862	2,104,434	922,304	189,741	98,378	367,840	478,617	47,554
Florida...............	191,400	58,001	15,373	15,605	77,396	23,897	1,128	414,371	268,082	43,155	24,356	40,534	26,214	12,030
EAST SOUTH CENTRAL.														
Kentucky.............	104,055	27,302	9,349	16,415	6,899	43,291	799	3,332,285	1,681,396	418,692	308,841	195,549	698,730	29,077
Tennessee............	354,996	50,490	19,850	35,148	110,677	137,501	1,330	2,791,352	1,295,368	254,568	337,399	218,205	665,728	20,084
Alabama..............	818,175	71,442	50,565	39,573	444,842	210,752	1,001	1,754,793	740,379	214,430	154,596	248,236	379,715	17,437
Mississippi...........	1,032,413	108,570	93,697	36,184	397,326	394,835	1,801	1,140,199	530,370	190,823	61,990	132,209	192,537	32,270
WEST SOUTH CENTRAL.														
Arkansas.............	386,913	75,729	39,434	28,018	115,962	127,121	649	1,890,203	850,184	182,757	229,554	163,124	446,210	18,374
Louisiana.............	505,431	82,092	29,631	16,865	79,709	294,888	2,248	1,085,399	500,329	141,652	64,800	101,116	181,035	96,467
Oklahoma............	369,818	148,033	53,367	37,132	29,417	101,283	586	5,544,251	780,866	806,444	816,245	974,855	2,137,714	28,127
Texas................	738,924	159,609	48,237	60,688	60,851	408,075	1,464	4,391,128	1,347,057	631,015	373,969	187,891	1,806,330	44,866
						PERCENTAGE DISTRIBUTION OF ACRES IN CORN, BY TENURE.								
THE SOUTH.														
Total............	100.0	16.2	6.8	6.5	31.4	38.8	0.3	100.0	38.8	12.5	9.7	10.3	27.2	1.5
South Atlantic........	100.0	15.5	5.3	6.7	34.9	37.3	0.4	100.0	48.3	11.2	7.1	10.6	20.7	2.1
East South Central....	100.0	11.2	7.5	5.5	41.6	34.0	0.2	100.0	47.1	12.0	9.6	8.8	21.5	1.1
West South Central....	100.0	23.3	8.5	7.1	14.3	46.5	0.2	100.0	26.9	13.6	11.5	11.1	35.4	1.5
SOUTH ATLANTIC.														
Delaware.............	100.0	12.1	9.7	5.9	6.0	62.9	3.4	100.0	30.7	15.4	2.6	5.4	44.6	1.4
Maryland.............	100.0	17.1	11.3	10.5	8.8	49.7	2.5	100.0	31.6	20.4	4.1	7.2	33.7	3.0
District of Columbia...	100.0			100.0				100.0	30.2	8.0	2.8	40.8	1.2	17.0
Virginia..............	100.0	38.0	9.3	15.9	9.3	26.9	0.7	100.0	54.3	11.8	8.2	6.4	16.8	2.6
West Virginia.........	100.0	46.5	10.9	11.0	8.8	21.8	1.1	100.0	59.7	8.9	9.3	7.7	13.2	1.1
North Carolina........	100.0	15.4	6.0	11.4	17.5	49.5	0.2	100.0	49.5	9.6	9.8	6.5	23.2	1.3
South Carolina........	100.0	12.8	4.7	5.5	42.1	34.6	0.3	100.0	44.3	13.8	6.8	16.1	16.5	2.6
Georgia...............	100.0	8.6	3.4	2.7	45.8	39.3	0.2	100.0	43.8	9.0	4.7	17.5	22.7	2.3
Florida...............	100.0	30.3	8.0	8.2	40.4	12.5	0.6	100.0	64.7	10.4	5.9	9.8	6.3	2.9
EAST SOUTH CENTRAL.														
Kentucky.............	100.0	26.2	9.0	15.8	6.6	41.6	0.8	100.0	50.5	12.6	9.3	5.9	21.0	0.9
Tennessee............	100.0	14.2	5.6	9.9	31.2	38.7	0.4	100.0	46.4	9.1	12.1	7.8	23.8	0.7
Alabama..............	100.0	8.7	6.2	4.8	54.4	25.8	0.1	100.0	42.2	12.2	8.8	14.1	21.6	1.0
Mississippi...........	100.0	10.5	9.1	3.5	38.5	38.2	0.2	100.0	46.5	16.7	5.4	11.6	16.9	2.8
WEST SOUTH CENTRAL.														
Arkansas.............	100.0	19.6	10.2	7.2	30.0	32.9	0.2	100.0	45.0	9.7	12.1	8.6	23.6	1.0
Louisiana.............	100.0	16.2	5.9	3.3	15.8	58.3	0.4	100.0	46.1	13.1	6.0	9.3	16.7	8.9
Oklahoma............	100.0	40.0	14.4	10.0	8.0	27.4	0.2	100.0	14.1	14.5	14.7	17.6	38.6	0.5
Texas................	100.0	21.6	6.5	8.2	8.2	55.2	0.2	100.0	30.7	14.4	8.5	4.3	41.1	1.0

TABLE 67.—NUMBER OF ACRES IN COTTON ON COLORED AND WHITE FARMS, CLASSIFIED BY TENURE, BY SOUTHERN DIVISIONS AND STATES: 1910.

DIVISION AND STATE.	FARMS OPERATED BY COLORED FARMERS: 1910.							FARMS OPERATED BY WHITE FARMERS: 1910.						
	Total.	Owners and part owners.			Tenants.		Managers.	Total.	Owners and part owners.			Tenants.		Managers.
		Owners.		Part owners.	Cash, and not specified.	Share and share-cash.			Owners.		Part owners.	Cash, and not specified.	Share and share-cash.	
		Free.	Mortgaged.						Free.	Mortgaged.				
	NUMBER OF ACRES IN COTTON.													
THE SOUTH.														
Total...........	12,096,638	1,019,469	627,287	499,841	4,829,018	5,104,042	16,981	19,849,504	5,522,038	2,708,710	1,476,906	2,387,213	7,482,468	272,169
South Atlantic........	4,442,773	314,907	158,973	160,574	1,898,749	1 903 244	6,326	4,560,003	1,650,125	487,228	265,585	900,317	1,146,469	110,279
East South Central....	4,614,339	286,063	265,133	163,670	2,349,151	1,543,611	6,711	3,311,680	1,144,551	480,138	251,456	619,350	752,018	64,167
West South Central....	3,039,526	418,499	203,181	175,597	581,118	1,657,187	3,944	11,977,821	2,727,362	1,741,344	959,865	867,546	5,583,981	97,723
SOUTH ATLANTIC.														
Delaware.............														
Maryland............														
District of Columbia...														
Virginia.............	13,362	2,888	1,558	948	3,817	4,113	38	11,785	5,484	1,461	702	1,915	2,093	130
West Virginia........														
North Carolina.......	474,889	43,194	21,884	36,905	111,208	261,524	174	799,515	317,348	78,629	64,294	91,060	228,501	19,683
South Carolina.......	1,364,375	111,040	55,378	59,771	568,212	567,166	2,808	1,192,092	430,774	169,551	79,502	234,666	245,417	32,182
Georgia..............	2,468,242	132,891	70,006	54,790	1,157,314	1,050,103	3,138	2,415,062	819,947	216,458	112,307	553,628	656,408	56,314
Florida..............	121,905	24,894	10,147	8,160	58,198	20,338	168	141,549	76,572	21,129	8,780	19,048	14,050	1,970
EAST SOUTH CENTRAL.														
Kentucky.............	2,937	5	18	18	754	2,142	....	4,874	863	168	199	1,492	2,037	115
Tennessee............	387,527	26,316	16,792	20,343	191,006	132,886	184	399,989	113,532	35,146	42,663	102,190	105,232	1,226
Alabama.............	1,960,709	110,385	95,110	77,113	1,208,159	469,520	422	1,769,773	596,091	240,517	145,895	342,768	422,386	22,116
Mississippi..........	2,263,166	149,357	153,213	66,196	949,232	939,063	6,105	1,137,044	434,065	204,307	62,699	172,900	222,363	40,710
WEST SOUTH CENTRAL.														
Arkansas.............	949,734	106,502	65,333	46,474	350,665	379,816	944	1,203,488	399,157	113,337	134,847	193,688	341,711	20,748
Louisiana............	514,352	67,705	26,783	11,147	92,814	314,855	1,048	442,659	205,671	63,679	20,346	39,276	82,121	31,566
Oklahoma............	217,231	43,364	24,739	13,868	29,795	105,294	171	1,759,704	189,730	252,465	174,496	259,769	879,914	3,330
Texas................	1,358,209	200,928	86,326	104,108	107,844	857,222	1,781	8,571,970	1,932,804	1,311,863	630,176	374,813	4,280,235	42,079
	PERCENTAGE DISTRIBUTION OF ACRES IN COTTON, BY TENURE.													
THE SOUTH.														
Total...........	100.0	8.4	5.2	4.1	39.9	42.2	0.1	100.0	27.8	13.6	7.4	12.0	37.7	1.4
South Atlantic........	100.0	7.1	3.6	3.6	42.7	42.8	0.1	100.0	36.2	10.7	5.8	19.7	25.1	2.4
East South Central....	100.0	6.2	5.7	3.5	50.9	33.5	0.1	100.0	34.6	14.5	7.6	18.7	22.7	1.9
West South Central....	100.0	13.8	6.7	5.8	19.1	54.5	0.1	100.0	22.8	14.5	8.0	7.2	46.6	0.8
SOUTH ATLANTIC.														
Delaware.............														
Maryland............														
District of Columbia...														
Virginia.............	100.0	21.6	11.7	7.1	28.6	30.8	0.3	100.0	46.5	12.4	6.0	16.2	17.8	1.1
West Virginia........														
North Carolina.......	100.0	9.1	4.6	7.8	23.4	55.1	(1)	100.0	39.7	9.8	8.0	11.4	28.6	2.5
South Carolina.......	100.0	8.1	4.1	4.4	41.6	41.6	0.2	100.0	36.1	14.2	6.7	19.7	20.6	2.7
Georgia..............	100.0	5.4	2.8	2.2	46.9	42.5	0.1	100.0	34.0	9.0	4.7	22.9	27.2	2.3
Florida..............	100.0	20.4	8.3	6.7	47.7	16.7	0.1	100.0	54.1	14.9	6.2	13.5	9.9	1.4
EAST SOUTH CENTRAL.														
Kentucky.............	100.0	0.2	0.6	0.6	25.7	72.9	....	100.0	17.7	3.4	4.1	30.6	41.8	2.4
Tennessee............	100.0	6.8	4.3	5.2	49.3	34.3	(1)	100.0	28.4	8.8	10.7	25.5	26.3	0.3
Alabama.............	100.0	5.6	4.9	3.9	61.6	23.9	(1)	100.0	33.7	13.6	8.2	19.4	23.9	1.2
Mississippi..........	100.0	6.6	6.8	2.9	41.9	41.5	0.3	100.0	38.2	18.0	5.5	15.2	19.6	3.6
WEST SOUTH CENTRAL.														
Arkansas.............	100.0	11.2	6.9	4.9	36.9	40.0	0.1	100.0	33.2	9.4	11.2	16.1	28.4	1.7
Louisiana............	100.0	13.2	5.2	2.2	18.0	61.2	0.2	100.0	46.5	14.4	4.6	8.9	18.6	7.1
Oklahoma............	100.0	20.0	11.4	6.4	13.7	48.5	0.1	100.0	10.8	14.3	9.9	14.8	50.0	0.2
Texas................	100.0	14.8	6.4	7.7	7.9	63.1	0.1	100.0	22.5	15.3	7.4	4.4	49.9	0.5

1 Less than one-tenth of 1 per cent.

TABLE **68.**—COLORED FARM ACREAGE, TOTAL AND IMPROVED, AND VALUE OF LAND AND BUILDINGS, BY TENURE OF FARM, WITH AVERAGE ACREAGE PER FARM, PERCENTAGE IMPROVED OF FARM ACREAGE, AND AVERAGE VALUE OF LAND AND BUILDINGS PER FARM AND PER ACRE, BY SOUTHERN DIVISIONS AND STATES: 1910 AND 1900.

DIVISION, STATE, AND TENURE CLASS.	FARMS OPERATED BY COLORED FARMERS.															
	Acres in farms.				Value of land and buildings.		Average acres per farm.				Percentage improved of farm acreage.		Average value of land and buildings.			
	Total.		Improved.				Total.		Improved.				Per farm.		Per acre.	
	1910	1900	1910	1900	1910	1900	1910	1900	1910	1900	1910	1900	1910	1900	1910	1900
THE SOUTH.																
Total	42,609,117	38,612,046	27,735,743	23,214,607	$900,132,334	$380,280,968	47.9	52.1	31.2	31.3	65.1	60.1	$1,011	$513	$21.13	$9.85
Owners	15,691,536	13,358,684	7,531,119	6,026,805	272,992,238	106,619,328	71.8	71.6	34.5	32.3	48.0	45.1	125	571	17.40	7.98
Managers	349,779	428,518	108,249	127,742	10,371,949	5,544,310	291.5	269.0	90.2	80.2	30.9	29.8	8,643	3,480	29.65	12.94
Tenants	26,567,802	24,824,844	20,096,375	17,060,060	616,768,147	268,117,330	39.6	44.9	30.0	30.9	75.6	68.7	920	485	23.21	10.80
SOUTH ATLANTIC	17,675,382	15,637,265	10,990,069	8,895,862	367,707,068	133,387,758	49.7	54.1	30.9	30.8	62.2	56.9	1,033	462	20.80	8.53
Owners	5,646,378	4,427,439	2,695,947	2,099,232	105,568,619	36,982,908	55.4	52.0	26.4	24.7	47.7	47.4	7,955	3,028	39.40	14.61
Managers	145,371	201,074	61,287	66,764	5,727,681	2,937,580	201.9	207.3	85.1	68.8	42.2	33.2	1,013	461	21.58	8.49
Tenants	11,883,633	11,008,752	8,232,835	6,729,866	256,410,768	93,467,270	46.9	54.3	32.5	33.2	69.3	61.1				
EAST SOUTH CENTRAL	13,595,717	12,621,318	9,556,529	8,191,628	279,667,758	131,453,610	41.8	47.1	29.4	30.6	70.3	64.9	1,208	572	20.57	10.42
Owners	4,539,952	3,837,853	2,213,645	1,714,020	70,937,214	28,539,910	77.3	76.9	37.7	34.3	48.8	44.7	10,330	3,960	15.63	7.44
Managers	76,360	60,388	26,237	25,866	2,572,270	1,282,910	306.7	186.4	105.4	79.8	34.4	42.8	774	467	33.69	21.24
Tenants	8,979,405	8,723,077	7,316,647	6,451,742	206,158,274	101,630,790	33.7	40.1	27.5	29.6	81.5	74.0			22.96	11.65
WEST SOUTH CENTRAL	11,338,018	10,353,463	7,189,145	6,127,117	252,757,508	115,439,600	54.2	56.3	34.4	34.4	63.4	59.2	1,209	628	22.29	11.15
Owners	5,505,206	5,093,392	2,621,527	2,213,553	96,486,405	41,096,510	95.3	98.6	45.4	42.9	47.6	43.5	1,670	796	17.53	8.07
Managers	128,048	167,056	20,725	35,112	2,071,998	1,323,820	554.3	558.7	89.7	117.4	16.2	21.0	8,970	4,427	16.18	7.92
Tenants	5,704,764	5,093,015	4,546,893	3,878,452	154,199,105	73,019,270	37.8	33.6	30.1	29.4	79.7	76.2	1,021	553	27.03	14.34
SOUTH ATLANTIC.																
Total	17,675,382	15,637,265	10,990,069	8,895,862	367,707,068	133,387,758	49.7	54.1	30.9	30.8	62.2	56.9	1,033	462	20.80	8.53
DELAWARE	56,973	52,566	37,076	34,616	1,981,716	1,174,250	61.8	64.3	40.2	42.3	65.1	65.9	2,149	1,436	34.78	22.34
Owners	13,615	12,373	9,274	8,579	547,551	285,190	33.5	37.3	22.8	25.8	68.1	69.3	1,349	859	40.22	23.05
Managers	2,395	1,525	2,034	1,144	145,800	101,450	149.7	101.7	127.1	76.3	84.9	75.0	9,113	6,763	60.88	66.52
Tenants	40,963	38,668	25,768	24,893	1,288,365	787,610	81.9	82.1	51.5	52.9	62.9	64.4	2,577	1,672	31.45	20.37
MARYLAND	358,517	374,301	218,582	238,668	10,269,784	6,886,360	56.3	64.1	34.3	40.8	61.0	63.8	1,612	1,179	28.65	18.40
Owners	122,039	101,491	76,564	69,826	2,275,640	625,350	30.9	31.1	19.4	21.4	62.7	68.8	994	698	32.16	22.42
Managers	13,361	12,305	9,015	8,342	1,172,550	625,350	153.6	117.2	103.6	79.4	67.5	67.8	13,478	5,956	87.76	50.82
Tenants	223,117	260,505	133,003	160,500	5,172,461	3,985,370	95.6	105.2	57.0	64.8	59.6	61.6	2,215	1,610	23.18	15.30
DISTRICT OF COLUMBIA	95	308	95	232	89,400	292,500	7.9	18.1	7.9	13.6	100.0	75.3	7,450	17,206	941.05	949.68
Owners	58	29	58	25	48,400	27,700	7.2	5.8	7.2	5.0	100.0	86.0	6,050	5,540	834.48	955.17
Managers	4	21	4	21	8,000	141,000	4.0	10.5	4.0	10.5	100.0	100.0	8,000	7,050	2,000.00	6,714.29
Tenants	33	258	33	186	33,000	123,800	11.0	25.8	11.0	18.6	100.0	72.0	11,000	12,380	1,000.00	479.84
VIRGINIA	2,238,220	2,229,118	1,111,208	1,125,458	45,224,504	19,982,450	46.5	49.7	23.1	25.1	49.6	50.5	940	446	20.21	8.96
Owners	1,381,223	1,031,331	669,358	540,719	28,059,534	10,110,600	42.9	38.8	20.8	20.4	48.5	52.4	871	381	20.31	9.80
Managers	29,985	34,960	14,046	15,095	1,330,815	561,340	166.6	146.9	78.0	63.4	46.8	43.2	7,393	2,359	44.38	16.06
Tenants	827,012	1,162,827	427,804	569,644	15,834,155	9,310,510	52.7	64.5	27.2	31.6	51.7	49.0	1,008	516	19.15	8.01
WEST VIRGINIA	34,541	41,584	20,257	23,066	1,076,394	687,860	48.8	56.0	28.6	31.1	58.6	55.5	1,520	927	31.16	16.54
Owners	25,957	25,797	14,522	14,511	738,261	383,380	46.3	27.2	26.0	27.2	55.9	56.3	1,323	718	28.44	14.86
Managers	655	1,529	602	1,148	35,695	61,400	93.6	191.1	86.0	143.5	91.9	75.1	5,099	7,675	54.50	40.16
Tenants	7,929	14,258	5,133	7,407	302,438	243,080	55.4	71.3	35.9	37.0	64.7	51.9	2,115	1,215	38.14	17.05
NORTH CAROLINA	3,185,804	2,955,138	1,730,712	1,457,247	69,266,216	24,253,120	48.5	53.9	26.4	26.6	54.3	49.3	1,055	442	21.74	8.21
Owners	1,197,496	965,462	512,567	395,106	22,810,089	7,123,890	55.8	55.1	23.9	22.6	42.8	40.9	1,064	407	19.05	7.38
Managers	18,992	39,503	5,244	6,585	557,000	267,750	256.6	326.5	70.9	54.4	27.6	16.7	7,527	2,213	29.33	6.78
Tenants	1,969,316	1,950,183	1,212,901	1,055,556	45,899,127	16,861,480	44.6	52.4	27.5	28.4	61.6	54.1	1,040	453	23.31	8.65
SOUTH CAROLINA	3,940,476	3,792,076	2,598,224	2,273,824	98,999,754	35,934,560	40.7	44.4	26.8	26.6	65.9	60.0	1,023	421	25.12	9.48
Owners	1,098,044	962,667	539,347	469,322	22,112,291	8,713,900	53.9	50.7	26.5	24.7	49.1	48.8	1,085	459	20.14	9.05
Managers	42,454	46,170	14,874	13,215	980,894	372,760	324.1	256.5	113.5	73.4	35.0	28.6	7,488	2,071	23.10	8.07
Tenants	2,799,978	2,783,239	2,044,003	1,791,287	75,906,569	26,847,900	36.7	42.0	26.8	27.0	73.0	64.4	995	405	27.11	9.65
GEORGIA	7,092,051	5,474,974	4,791,562	3,322,646	128,883,732	39,341,240	57.9	66.1	39.1	40.1	67.6	60.7	1,052	475	18.17	7.19
Owners	1,349,503	924,262	644,396	408,684	20,540,910	5,669,250	86.0	81.3	41.0	35.9	47.8	44.2	1,309	498	15.22	6.13
Managers	27,551	52,676	11,216	15,622	758,037	443,540	224.0	253.2	91.2	75.1	40.7	29.7	6,163	2,132	27.51	8.42
Tenants	5,714,997	4,498,036	4,135,950	2,898,340	107,584,785	33,228,450	53.5	60.1	38.7	40.7	72.4	64.4	1,008	466	18.82	7.39
FLORIDA	768,705	717,200	482,353	420,105	11,915,568	4,835,418	52.2	53.0	32.8	31.1	62.7	58.6	809	357	15.50	6.74
Owners	458,443	404,037	229,861	192,460	6,786,810	2,393,358	62.8	61.7	31.5	29.4	50.1	47.6	930	365	14.80	5.92
Managers	9,974	12,385	4,252	5,592	738,890	362,990	98.8	133.2	42.1	60.1	42.6	45.2	7,316	3,903	74.08	29.31
Tenants	300,288	300,778	248,240	222,053	4,389,868	2,079,070	41.0	43.7	33.9	32.3	82.7	73.8	600	302	14.62	6.91

TABLE 68.—COLORED FARM ACREAGE, TOTAL AND IMPROVED, AND VALUE OF LAND AND BUILDINGS, BY TENURE OF FARM, WITH AVERAGE ACREAGE PER FARM, PERCENTAGE IMPROVED OF FARM ACREAGE, AND AVERAGE VALUE OF LAND AND BUILDINGS PER FARM AND PER ACRE, BY SOUTHERN DIVISIONS AND STATES: 1910 AND 1900—Continued.

| DIVISION, STATE, AND TENURE CLASS. | Acres in farms. | | | | Value of land and buildings. | | Average acres per farm. | | | | Percentage improved of farm acreage. | | Average value of land and buildings. | | | |
| | Total. | | Improved. | | | | Total. | | Improved. | | | | Per farm. | | Per acre. | |
	1910	1900	1910	1900	1910	1900	1910	1900	1910	1900	1910	1900	1910	1900	1910	1900
EAST SOUTH CENTRAL.																
Total	13,595,717	12,621,318	9,556,529	8,191,628	$279,667,758	$131,453,610	41.8	47.1	29.4	30.6	70.3	64.9	$860	$491	$20.57	$10.42
KENTUCKY	440,777	447,856	343,694	341,163	15,031,908	8,955,540	37.6	39.9	29.3	30.4	78.0	76.2	1,281	797	34.10	20.00
Owners	255,363	236,150	185,789	166,528	7,154,168	3,559,590	43.1	43.7	31.3	30.8	72.8	70.5	1,207	659	28.02	15.07
Managers	4,318	8,907	3,577	6,057	377,455	397,780	108.0	141.4	89.4	96.1	82.8	68.0	9,436	6,314	87.41	44.66
Tenants	181,096	202,799	154,328	168,578	7,500,285	4,998,170	31.4	35.1	26.8	29.2	85.2	83.1	1,302	866	41.42	24.65
TENNESSEE	1,606,078	1,550,096	1,162,276	1,036,801	42,192,566	20,590,150	41.9	45.7	30.3	30.6	72.4	66.9	1,101	607	26.27	13.28
Owners	590,676	493,824	349,692	270,934	12,179,780	5,277,040	55.2	52.4	32.7	28.7	59.2	54.9	1,138	560	20.62	10.69
Managers	17,682	11,966	6,778	6,901	804,505	388,030	346.7	145.9	132.9	84.2	38.3	57.7	15,775	4,732	45.50	32.43
Tenants	997,720	1,044,306	805,806	758,966	29,208,281	14,925,080	36.2	42.8	29.2	31.1	80.8	72.7	1,060	612	29.28	14.29
ALABAMA	5,091,435	4,720,167	3,563,176	3,063,903	73,918,727	35,213,250	46.1	50.2	32.3	32.6	70.0	64.9	669	374	14.52	7.46
Owners	1,466,719	1,216,813	675,819	523,568	17,285,502	6,644,310	85.9	86.2	39.6	37.1	46.1	43.0	1,012	471	11.79	5.46
Managers	17,482	14,212	5,012	5,649	414,729	123,720	336.2	197.4	96.4	78.5	28.7	39.7	7,976	1,718	23.72	8.71
Tenants	3,607,234	3,489,142	2,882,345	2,534,686	56,218,496	28,445,220	38.7	43.7	30.9	31.7	79.9	72.6	602	356	15.58	8.15
MISSISSIPPI	6,457,427	5,903,199	4,487,383	3,749,761	148,524,557	66,694,670	39.2	45.9	27.2	29.1	69.5	63.5	902	518	23.00	11.30
Owners	2,227,194	1,891,066	1,002,345	752,990	34,317,764	13,058,970	89.0	90.2	40.1	35.9	45.0	39.8	1,371	471	15.41	6.91
Managers	36,878	25,303	10,870	7,259	975,581	373,380	347.9	236.5	102.5	67.8	29.5	28.7	9,204	3,490	26.45	14.76
Tenants	4,193,355	3,986,830	3,474,168	2,989,512	113,231,212	53,262,320	30.0	37.1	24.9	27.8	82.8	75.0	811	495	27.00	13.36
WEST SOUTH CENTRAL.																
Total	11,338,018	10,353,463	7,189,145	6,127,117	252,757,508	115,439,600	54.2	56.3	34.4	33.3	63.4	59.2	1,209			
ARKANSAS	2,653,323	2,303,622	1,773,206	1,375,186	69,013,109	26,880,130	41.7	49.0	27.9	29.3	66.8	59.7	1,085	572	26.01	11.67
Owners	1,204,114	1,035,292	541,265	423,732	20,694,215	7,198,450	82.1	86.9	36.9	35.5	45.0	40.9	1,411	603	17.19	6.95
Managers	6,093	14,906	3,068	5,329	238,915	179,200	132.5	186.3	66.7	66.6	50.4	35.8	5,194	2,240	39.21	12.02
Tenants	1,443,116	1,253,424	1,228,873	946,125	48,079,979	19,502,480	29.5	35.9	25.1	27.1	85.2	75.5	984	558	33.32	15.56
LOUISIANA	2,124,321	2,348,048	1,466,607	1,574,523	44,933,658	29,797,970	38.7	40.4	26.7	27.1	69.0	67.1	819	512	21.15	12.69
Owners	834,695	744,250	399,650	323,020	12,779,570	6,006,480	77.8	79.4	37.3	34.4	47.9	43.4	1,192	640	15.31	8.07
Managers	20,976	19,656	8,047	8,251	604,071	273,710	272.4	248.8	104.5	104.4	38.4	42.0	7,845	3,465	28.80	13.93
Tenants	1,268,650	1,584,142	1,058,910	1,243,252	31,550,017	23,517,780	28.8	32.5	24.0	25.5	83.5	78.5	716	483	24.87	14.85
OKLAHOMA	2,276,711	[1]1,860,152	1,172,819	[1]746,916	47,221,793	[1]14,149,980	110.1	[1]140.7	56.7	[1]56.5	51.5	[1]40.2	2,284	[1]1,070	20.74	[1]7.61
Owners	1,599,655	[1]1,553,094	734,594	622,208	32,325,348	11,996,340	143.5	152.4	65.9	61.1	45.9	40.1	2,899	1,177	20.21	7.72
Managers	6,295	[1]95,420	1,484	12,828	136,462	364,370	233.1	[1]1,947.3	55.0	261.8	23.6	13.4	5,054	7,436	21.68	3.82
Tenants	670,761	[1]211,638	436,741	111,880	14,759,983	1,789,270	70.7	70.9	46.0	37.5	65.1	52.9	1,555	599	22.00	8.45
TEXAS	4,283,663	3,841,641	2,776,513	2,430,492	91,588,948	44,611,520	61.3	58.6	39.7	37.1	64.8	63.3	1,310	681	21.38	11.61
Owners	1,866,742	1,760,756	946,018	844,593	30,687,272	15,895,240	87.9	87.4	44.6	41.9	50.7	48.0	1,445	789	16.44	9.03
Managers	94,684	37,074	8,704	8,126	1,092,550	506,540	1,168.9	407.4	100.3	95.6	8.6	23.5	13,488	5,566	11.54	13.66
Tenants	2,322,237	2,043,811	1,822,369	1,577,195	59,809,126	28,209,740	47.8	45.1	37.5	34.8	78.5	77.2	1,231	623	25.75	13.80

[1] Includes Indian Territory.

TABLE **69.**—NUMBER OF FARMS REPORTING AND NOT REPORTING LIVE STOCK, AND VALUE OF EACH FOR SOUTHERN

	DIVISION, STATE, COLOR OF FARMER, AND TENURE CLASS.	Number of farms.	LIVE STOCK ON FARMS.											
			Domestic animals.											
			Total.			Horses.			Neat cattle.			Mules.		
			Farms reporting.	Farms not reporting.	Value.	Farms reporting.	Farms not reporting.	Value.	Farms reporting.	Farms not reporting.	Value.	Farms reporting.	Farms not reporting.	Value.
	THE SOUTH.													
1	Colored farmers........	890,141	[1] 804,994	85,147	$177,461,964	334,537	555,604	$47,537,525	551,940	338,201	$33,028,881	441,178	448,963	$84,127,172
2	Owners, free.............	128,557	121,856	6,701	32,921,123	74,930	53,627	11,664,679	99,180	29,377	8,461,971	49,174	79,383	9,956,968
3	Owners, mortgaged.........	46,733	45,393	1,340	13,641,333	27,310	19,423	4,256,599	38,032	8,701	2,893,798	25,465	21,268	5,424,462
4	Part owners.............	43,177	42,058	1,119	12,038,689	25,098	18,079	3,911,815	33,632	9,545	2,624,308	21,817	21,360	4,620,451
5	Cash tenants.............	285,950	267,869	18,081	61,459,567	104,112	181,838	14,397,570	195,128	90,822	10,160,831	170,569	115,381	32,946,564
6	Share tenants.............	384,524	326,748	57,776	56,043,805	102,389	282,135	12,700,874	185,216	199,308	8,616,588	173,546	210,978	30,788,483
7	Managers.................	1,200	[1] 1,070	130	1,357,447	698	502	605,988	752	448	271,385	607	593	390,244
8	White farmers..........	2,207,406	2,118,896	88,510	[2] 1,106,838,990	1,437,122	770,284	374,511,099	1,874,362	333,044	335,151,430	1,037,204	1,170,202	294,131,054
9	Owners, free.............	908,211	884,823	23,388	474,921,450	639,427	268,784	164,900,373	829,439	78,772	144,399,038	410,409	497,802	115,476,367
10	Owners, mortgaged.........	245,889	241,481	4,408	162,241,548	184,735	61,154	57,519,836	223,767	22,122	48,762,402	127,732	118,157	40,021,654
11	Part owners.............	171,944	169,926	2,018	117,791,944	123,585	48,359	38,540,462	158,115	13,829	39,703,373	92,245	79,699	28,129,531
12	Cash tenants.............	229,461	218,111	11,350	101,745,745	134,501	94,960	31,224,368	178,383	51,078	32,600,988	110,285	119,176	29,784,731
13	Share tenants.............	636,817	591,200	45,617	199,924,868	344,222	292,595	73,943,192	473,169	163,648	40,597,993	288,209	348,608	70,841,951
14	Managers.................	15,084	13,355	1,729	50,211,195	10,652	4,432	8,382,868	11,489	3,595	29,087,636	8,324	6,760	9,876,820
	SOUTH ATLANTIC DIVISION.													
15	Colored farmers........	355,862	[1] 326,019	29,843	60,861,363	108,770	247,092	15,137,274	213,381	142,481	9,792,304	167,613	188,249	31,706,615
16	Owners, free.............	63,701	59,211	4,490	11,220,399	31,264	32,437	4,383,862	45,037	18,664	2,660,935	16,227	47,474	3,185,741
17	Owners, mortgaged.........	17,213	16,403	810	3,685,804	8,823	8,390	1,286,698	12,119	5,094	653,289	6,923	10,290	1,459,312
18	Part owners.............	21,047	20,382	665	4,146,642	10,762	10,285	1,500,242	14,880	6,167	756,745	8,177	12,870	1,580,121
19	Cash tenants.............	113,197	105,892	7,305	20,928,525	32,067	81,130	4,191,058	73,043	40,154	3,039,473	66,177	47,020	12,389,202
20	Share tenants.............	139,984	123,489	16,495	20,412,844	25,459	114,525	3,634,506	67,866	72,118	2,576,917	69,791	70,193	12,915,438
21	Managers.................	720	[1] 642	78	467,149	395	325	140,908	436	284	104,945	318	402	176,801
22	White farmers..........	756,019	722,527	33,492	[2] 290,466,705	426,579	329,440	106,221,851	628,356	127,663	79,747,228	290,813	465,206	76,092,715
23	Owners, free.............	364,156	352,902	11,254	156,610,576	233,749	130,407	57,514,446	323,796	40,360	47,154,862	129,625	234,531	35,572,070
24	Owners, mortgaged.........	76,488	74,459	2,029	35,993,256	50,908	25,580	14,268,717	66,701	9,787	9,146,384	30,455	46,033	9,123,024
25	Part owners.............	50,549	49,669	880	20,573,472	30,575	19,974	7,654,560	44,498	6,051	5,565,110	20,434	30,115	5,366,617
26	Cash tenants.............	87,734	82,749	4,985	25,129,697	41,697	46,037	8,147,391	64,755	22,979	5,489,274	39,963	47,771	9,441,051
27	Share tenants.............	169,514	156,173	13,341	42,900,725	64,667	104,847	15,820,029	123,058	46,456	9,685,060	66,815	102,699	13,697,407
28	Managers.................	7,578	6,575	1,003	9,258,969	4,983	2,595	2,816,708	5,548	2,030	2,706,538	3,521	4,057	2,892,546
	EAST SOUTH CENTRAL DIVISION.													
29	Colored farmers........	325,218	290,576	34,642	64,656,143	114,038	211,180	16,575,542	213,391	111,827	11,561,231	171,593	153,625	32,067,227
30	Owners, free.............	28,906	27,611	1,295	8,044,169	16,832	12,074	2,614,760	24,336	4,570	1,786,685	14,685	14,221	2,998,711
31	Owners, mortgaged.........	17,414	17,064	350	5,222,824	9,829	7,585	1,464,173	15,436	1,978	1,065,606	11,200	6,214	2,324,045
32	Part owners.............	12,417	12,106	311	3,734,132	7,205	5,212	1,159,848	10,552	1,865	677,684	7,507	4,910	1,629,145
33	Cash tenants.............	135,013	126,610	8,403	30,297,514	51,162	83,851	7,280,172	98,153	36,860	5,211,155	83,683	51,330	15,904,363
34	Share tenants.............	131,219	106,969	24,250	16,741,706	28,864	102,355	3,656,346	64,740	66,479	2,768,979	54,366	76,853	9,077,708
35	Managers.................	249	216	33	615,798	146	103	400,243	174	75	51,122	152	97	133,255
36	White farmers..........	717,262	684,546	32,716	[2] 291,388,121	435,903	281,359	101,495,757	624,776	92,486	63,840,048	353,615	363,647	93,041,311
37	Owners, free.............	316,252	308,520	7,732	151,233,692	217,870	98,382	53,667,331	295,472	20,780	34,901,921	161,776	154,476	44,155,638
38	Owners, mortgaged.........	76,405	75,197	1,208	38,064,466	52,762	23,643	13,334,661	71,230	5,175	8,111,905	43,899	32,506	12,015,121
39	Part owners.............	59,058	58,383	675	28,152,101	40,041	19,017	9,822,964	55,192	3,866	5,766,009	34,112	24,946	9,415,715
40	Cash tenants.............	73,247	69,422	3,825	24,608,961	39,997	33,250	7,929,899	59,015	14,232	5,164,483	36,834	36,413	9,264,101
41	Share tenants.............	189,259	170,217	19,042	43,314,503	83,022	106,237	14,718,516	141,330	47,929	8,552,841	75,030	114,229	16,126,060
42	Managers.................	3,041	2,807	234	6,014,098	2,211	830	2,022,386	2,537	504	1,342,889	1,964	1,077	2,064,676
	WEST SOUTH CENTRAL DIVISION.													
43	Colored farmers........	209,061	188,399	20,662	51,944,458	111,729	97,332	15,824,709	125,168	83,893	11,675,346	101,972	107,089	20,353,330
44	Owners, free.............	35,950	35,034	916	13,656,555	26,834	9,116	4,666,057	29,807	6,143	4,014,351	18,262	17,688	3,772,516
45	Owners, mortgaged.........	12,106	11,926	180	4,732,705	8,658	3,448	1,505,728	10,477	1,629	1,174,903	7,342	4,764	1,641,105
46	Part owners.............	9,713	9,570	143	4,157,915	7,131	2,582	1,251,725	8,200	1,513	1,189,879	6,133	3,580	1,411,185
47	Cash tenants.............	37,740	35,367	2,373	10,233,528	20,883	16,857	2,926,340	23,932	13,808	1,910,203	20,709	17,031	4,652,999
48	Share tenants.............	113,321	96,290	17,031	18,889,255	48,066	65,255	5,410,022	52,610	60,711	3,270,692	49,389	63,932	8,795,337
49	Managers.................	231	212	19	274,500	157	74	64,837	142	89	115,318	137	94	80,188
50	White farmers..........	734,125	711,823	22,302	[2] 524,984,164	574,640	159,485	166,793,491	621,230	112,895	191,564,154	392,776	341,349	124,997,028
51	Owners, free.............	227,803	223,401	4,402	167,077,182	187,808	39,995	53,718,596	210,171	17,632	62,342,255	119,008	108,795	35,748,659
52	Owners, mortgaged.........	92,996	91,825	1,171	88,183,826	81,065	11,931	29,916,458	85,836	7,160	31,504,113	53,378	39,618	18,883,509
53	Part owners.............	62,337	61,874	463	69,066,371	52,969	9,368	21,062,938	58,425	3,912	28,372,254	37,699	24,638	13,347,199
54	Cash tenants.............	68,480	65,940	2,540	52,007,087	52,807	15,673	15,147,078	54,613	13,867	21,947,231	33,488	34,992	11,079,579
55	Share tenants.............	278,044	264,810	13,234	113,709,640	196,533	81,511	43,404,647	208,781	69,263	22,360,092	146,364	131,680	41,018,484
56	Managers.................	4,465	3,973	492	34,938,128	3,458	1,007	3,543,774	3,404	1,061	25,038,209	2,839	1,626	4,919,598

[1] Correction of an error in West Virginia has reduced the number of managers by 1, as compared with figures previously published.
[2] The total for the white farmers of the South includes $2,240 not distributed by tenure, which represents value of animals (Belgian hares, ostriches, etc.) not shown separately in this table. Of this total $10 are included in the total for the South Atlantic division, $300 in the total for the East South Central division, and $1,930 in the total for the West South Central division.

CLASS OF LIVE STOCK REPORTED, BY TENURE OF FARMER, FOR COLORED AND FOR WHITE FARMERS, STATES: 1910.

LIVE STOCK ON FARMS.																	
Domestic animals.												**Poultry.**			**Bees.**		
Hogs and pigs.			**Sheep and lambs.**			**Asses and burros.**			**Goats and kids.**								
Farms reporting.	Farms not reporting.	Value.	Farms reporting.	Farms not reporting.	Value.	Farms reporting.	Farms not reporting.	Value.	Farms reporting.	Farms not reporting.	Value.	Farms reporting.	Farms not reporting.	Value.	Farms reporting.	Value.	
602,090	288,051	$12,331,574	3,386	886,755	$200,128	1,353	888,788	$176,400	7,531	882,610	$60,284	714,043	176,098	$5,121,775	20,342	$148,385	1
96,503	32,054	2,665,627	1,676	126,881	81,119	481	128,076	66,129	2,216	126,341	24,630	113,450	15,107	1,133,308	6,223	55,890	2
37,446	9,287	1,009,994	475	46,258	22,194	214	46,519	26,196	922	45,811	8,090	42,903	3,830	408,464	2,451	19,594	3
34,596	8,581	835,855	346	42,831	20,107	154	43,023	20,638	698	42,479	5,515	39,834	3,343	365,686	2,201	15,683	4
206,102	79,848	3,906,120	257	285,693	8,960	201	285,749	27,478	2,280	283,670	12,044	234,661	51,289	1,525,526	5,215	33,121	5
226,737	157,787	3,842,172	561	383,963	51,897	297	384,227	34,674	1,384	383,140	9,117	282,360	102,164	1,668,246	4,215	23,539	6
706	494	71,806	71	1,129	15,851	6	1,194	1,285	31	1,169	888	835	365	20,545	37	558	7
1,628,751	578,655	68,685,761	180,908	2,026,498	25,411,706	21,757	2,185,649	5,786,605	4 44,487	2,162,919	3,159,095	1,963,127	244,279	32,293,561	278,301	3,541,162	8
718,419	189,792	31,927,943	119,380	788,831	14,272,126	10,249	897,962	2,836,373	25,720	882,491	1,109,230	839,767	68,444	15,188,015	167,950	2,268,679	9
193,818	52,071	10,352,014	19,869	226,020	3,733,403	4,086	241,803	1,156,624	6,610	239,279	695,615	229,836	16,053	4,528,058	34,407	458,878	10
140,610	31,334	6,967,678	16,226	155,718	2,930,855	2,671	169,273	762,697	3,979	167,965	757,348	162,397	9,547	2,898,234	26,249	292,976	11
157,812	71,649	6,076,371	6,617	222,844	1,406,927	1,371	228,090	352,262	3,446	226,015	300,098	192,389	37,072	2,695,858	14,930	187,630	12
408,589	228,228	11,940,838	17,148	619,669	1,982,884	2,970	633,847	499,801	4,098	632,719	118,209	527,839	108,978	6,599,556	33,475	305,782	13
9,503	5,581	1,420,917	1,668	13,416	1,085,511	410	14,674	178,848	634	14,450	178,595	10,899	4,185	383,840	1,290	27,217	14
248,163	107,699	4,103,272	1,228	354,634	81,762	157	355,705	21,797	3,053	352,809	18,339	292,583	63,279	1,980,773	8,498	55,735	15
46,518	17,183	952,845	538	63,163	23,800	45	63,656	6,523	928	62,773	6,693	55,209	8,492	511,781	2,554	21,796	16
13,302	3,911	276,500	106	17,107	6,451	15	17,198	1,713	285	16,928	1,841	15,604	1,609	139,791	764	5,430	17
16,625	4,422	298,152	135	20,912	7,865	15	21,032	1,800	315	20,732	1,717	19,246	1,801	157,405	932	6,101	18
81,897	31,300	1,294,038	103	113,094	3,688	43	113,154	6,522	882	112,315	4,544	93,437	19,760	552,980	2,293	12,348	19
89,400	50,584	1,247,641	301	139,683	30,008	38	139,946	5,164	631	139,353	3,170	108,577	31,407	607,571	1,935	9,663	20
421	299	34,096	45	675	9,950	1	719	75	12	708	374	510	210	11,245	20	397	21
571,104	184,915	18,731,086	75,218	680,801	9,003,985	1,920	754,099	452,411	5 13,968	742,051	217,419	679,175	76,844	11,650,734	119,580	1,518,842	22
288,597	75,559	10,327,679	51,045	313,111	5,661,553	1,091	363,065	242,389	8,477	355,679	137,577	337,701	26,455	6,224,837	75,734	1,048,119	23
59,349	17,139	2,328,865	7,277	69,211	1,026,340	266	76,222	67,469	1,841	74,647	32,457	71,500	4,988	1,602,618	12,311	159,174	24
41,314	9,235	1,225,951	5,950	44,599	708,445	159	50,390	40,022	989	49,560	12,767	47,554	2,995	769,629	10,449	116,604	25
61,923	25,811	1,639,867	3,062	84,672	366,684	149	87,585	32,967	1,243	86,491	12,463	73,786	13,948	983,512	7,095	71,307	26
115,098	54,416	2,690,882	6,949	162,565	958,401	196	169,318	35,979	1,193	168,321	12,967	143,017	26,497	1,848,273	13,283	110,230	27
4,823	2,755	517,842	935	6,643	282,562	59	7,519	33,585	225	7,353	9,188	5,617	1,961	221,865	708	13,408	28
217,436	107,782	4,281,432	1,400	323,818	83,030	517	324,701	69,266	2,725	322,493	18,415	256,522	68,696	1,739,543	6,788	49,099	29
22,056	6,850	580,932	684	28,222	35,711	166	28,740	20,933	651	28,255	6,437	26,325	2,581	258,063	1,682	14,828	30
14,108	3,306	343,981	248	17,166	11,781	90	17,324	9,884	409	17,005	3,354	16,183	1,231	141,374	1,023	7,689	31
9,886	2,531	248,815	156	12,261	8,243	66	12,351	8,905	242	12,175	1,492	11,566	851	110,205	681	4,344	32
98,127	36,886	1,881,631	101	134,912	3,622	86	134,927	11,637	1,026	133,987	4,934	110,066	24,947	716,016	2,417	16,329	33
73,103	58,116	1,201,353	190	131,029	18,036	105	131,114	17,197	390	130,829	2,087	92,205	39,014	507,086	973	5,795	34
156	93	24,720	21	228	5,637	4	245	710	7	242	111	177	72	6,799	12	114	35
521,034	196,228	21,269,568	86,639	630,623	9,216,799	7,341	709,921	2,278,188	14,553	702,709	246,150	640,623	76,639	10,133,655	96,460	1,068,046	36
248,483	67,769	11,194,345	56,656	259,596	5,761,067	4,250	312,002	1,403,490	8,494	307,758	149,900	295,074	21,178	5,272,760	60,070	715,575	37
60,809	15,596	2,938,726	9,694	66,711	1,253,093	1,083	75,322	372,583	2,283	74,122	38,377	71,998	4,407	1,246,067	12,056	123,057	38
47,390	11,668	2,049,380	8,149	50,909	852,090	803	58,255	225,059	1,416	57,642	20,884	56,099	2,959	968,976	9,311	89,061	39
49,271	23,976	1,697,447	2,927	70,320	443,915	379	72,868	96,644	985	72,262	12,472	60,777	12,470	755,345	4,958	57,129	40
112,981	76,278	3,063,257	8,734	180,525	702,112	721	188,538	133,472	1,215	188,044	18,245	154,343	34,916	1,818,675	9,736	78,438	41
2,100	941	326,413	479	2,562	204,522	105	2,936	46,940	160	2,881	6,272	2,332	709	71,832	329	4,786	42
136,491	72,570	3,946,870	758	208,303	35,336	679	208,382	85,337	1,753	207,308	23,530	164,938	44,123	1,401,459	5,056	43,551	43
27,929	8,021	1,131,850	454	35,496	21,608	270	35,680	38,673	637	35,313	11,500	31,916	4,034	363,464	1,987	19,266	44
10,036	2,070	389,513	121	11,985	3,962	109	11,997	14,599	228	11,878	2,895	11,116	990	127,299	664	6,475	45
8,085	1,628	288,888	55	9,658	3,999	73	9,640	9,933	141	9,572	2,306	9,022	691	98,076	588	5,238	46
26,078	11,662	730,451	53	37,687	1,650	72	37,668	9,319	372	37,368	2,566	31,158	6,582	256,530	505	4,444	47
64,234	49,087	1,393,178	70	113,251	3,853	154	113,167	12,313	363	112,958	3,860	81,578	31,743	553,589	1,307	8,081	48
129	102	12,990	5	226	264	1	230	500	12	219	403	148	83	2,501	5	47	49
536,613	197,512	28,685,107	19,051	715,074	7,190,922	12,496	721,629	3,056,006	5 15,966	718,159	2,695,526	643,329	90,796	10,509,172	62,261	954,274	50
181,339	46,464	10,405,919	11,679	216,124	2,849,506	4,908	222,895	1,190,494	8,749	219,054	821,753	206,992	20,811	3,690,418	32,146	504,985	51
73,660	19,336	5,084,423	2,898	90,098	1,453,970	2,737	90,259	716,572	2,486	90,510	624,781	86,338	6,658	1,679,373	10,040	176,647	52
51,906	10,431	3,692,347	2,127	60,210	1,370,320	1,709	60,628	497,616	1,574	60,763	723,697	58,744	3,593	1,159,629	6,489	87,311	53
46,618	21,862	2,739,057	628	67,852	596,328	843	67,637	222,651	1,218	67,262	275,163	57,826	10,654	957,001	2,877	59,194	54
180,510	97,534	6,186,699	1,465	276,579	322,371	2,053	275,991	330,350	1,690	276,354	86,997	230,479	47,565	2,932,608	10,456	117,114	55
2,580	1,885	576,662	254	4,211	598,427	246	4,219	98,323	249	4,216	163,135	2,950	1,515	90,143	253	9,023	56

[3] The value of horses of owners, as given in this table for Texas, is $93,770 in excess; and as given for Oklahoma, $1,100 less than figures previously published. The value of tenant's horses, as given in the table for Texas, is $93,770 less than previously published report, while, as given for Oklahoma, it is $1,100 greater. The combined disparities affect the West South Central total and the total for the South; the discrepancy, as compared with figures previously published, being $92,670, excess for owners and deficiency for tenants, and being due to incorrect classification, in the earlier report, of amounts specified by tenure.

[4] By correction of errors the number of farms reporting goats and kids is reduced, as compared with figures previously published for Georgia, by 5 and for Texas by 1, and is increased for Louisiana by 3; giving a net reduction of 3 for the South as a whole.

[5] Footnote 4 is explanatory.

TABLE **69.**—NUMBER OF FARMS REPORTING AND NOT REPORTING LIVE STOCK, AND VALUE OF EACH FOR SOUTHERN

			LIVE STOCK ON FARMS.										
			Domestic animals.										
DIVISION, STATE, COLOR OF FARMER, AND TENURE CLASS.	Number of farms.	Total.			Horses.			Neat cattle.			Mules.		
		Farms reporting.	Farms not reporting.	Value.	Farms reporting.	Farms not reporting.	Value.	Farms reporting.	Farms not reporting.	Value.	Farms reporting.	Farms not reporting.	Value.
SOUTH ATLANTIC DIVISION.													
DELAWARE.													
1 Colored farmers.........	922	860	62	$249,576	762	160	$144,651	515	407	$47,353	183	739	$39,533
2 Owners, free.............	198	184	14	41,455	172	26	24,745	102	96	6,072	24	174	7,250
3 Owners, mortgaged.........	149	143	6	34,292	132	17	23,210	84	65	5,291	16	133	3,495
4 Part owners...............	59	57	2	13,923	53	6	9,980	28	31	1,635	8	51	1,315
5 Cash tenants.............	75	66	9	14,205	51	24	9,175	38	37	2,732	11	64	1,308
6 Share tenants............	425	394	31	131,365	339	86	70,941	250	175	27,706	117	308	23,465
7 Managers.................	16	16	....	14,336	15	1	6,600	13	3	3,917	7	9	2,700
8 White farmers..........	9,914	9,590	324	5,993,792	9,095	819	3,307,140	7,983	1,931	1,600,980	2,539	7,375	724,600
9 Owners, free.............	3,531	3,382	149	1,769,660	3,197	334	994,870	2,820	711	382,502	944	2,587	283,177
10 Owners, mortgaged.........	1,987	1,944	43	1,122,821	1,868	119	628,521	1,658	329	308,269	409	1,578	118,421
11 Part owners...............	254	249	5	104,311	236	18	59,600	176	78	21,092	64	190	17,190
12 Cash tenants.............	791	734	57	481,063	696	95	259,420	582	209	176,215	95	696	25,120
13 Share tenants............	3,244	3,182	62	2,350,281	3,002	242	1,290,281	2,659	585	651,160	987	2,257	262,727
14 Managers.................	107	99	8	165,656	96	11	74,448	88	19	61,742	40	67	17,965
MARYLAND.													
15 Colored farmers.........	6,372	5,782	590	1,448,418	4,724	1,648	880,307	3,491	2,881	307,010	641	5,731	141,218
16 Owners, free.............	2,191	1,936	255	336,838	1,496	695	219,809	1,069	1,122	70,711	120	2,071	19,148
17 Owners, mortgaged.........	1,110	998	112	212,249	840	270	139,476	563	547	41,066	86	1,024	15,030
18 Part owners...............	649	630	19	134,679	564	85	91,971	317	332	23,944	62	587	9,645
19 Cash tenants.............	615	540	75	132,765	420	195	84,227	296	319	24,826	62	553	13,760
20 Share tenants............	1,720	1,594	126	549,634	1,326	394	308,144	1,174	546	132,260	276	1,444	61,110
21 Managers.................	87	84	3	82,253	78	9	36,680	72	15	14,203	35	52	22,525
22 White farmers..........	42,551	40,890	1,661	29,201 543	37,650	4,901	15,907,160	36,162	6,389	7,562,516	8,228	34,323	2,902,363
23 Owners, free.............	17,697	16,835	862	9,894,701	15,251	2,446	5,458,096	14,812	2,885	2,580,109	2,676	15,021	919,927
24 Owners, mortgaged.........	10,122	9,803	319	6,544,225	9,014	1,108	3,578,978	8,745	1,377	1,728,702	1,950	8,172	636,999
25 Part owners...............	1,750	1,702	48	1,161,636	1,608	142	661,005	1,373	377	271,130	371	1,379	130,138
26 Cash tenants.............	3,479	3,246	233	2,092,025	2,928	551	1,121,135	2,658	821	568,401	622	2,857	223,509
27 Share tenants............	8,602	8,444	158	8,205,322	8,046	556	4,474,182	7,809	793	2,044,974	2,304	6,298	792,510
28 Managers.................	901	860	41	1,303,634	803	98	613,764	765	136	369,200	305	596	199,280
DISTRICT OF COLUMBIA.													
29 Colored farmers.........	12	11	1	2,370	11	1	1,550	4	8	655	1	11	150
30 Owners, free.............	3	3	....	800	3	......	300	1	2	500	....	3	....
31 Owners, mortgaged.........	3	2	1	150	2	1	150	....	3	....	....	3	....
32 Part owners...............	2	2	....	925	2	......	850	1	1	60	....	2	....
33 Cash tenants.............	3	3	....	395	3	......	150	2	1	95	1	2	150
34 Share tenants............	......	......	....	....	......	......	....	....	......	....	....	......	....
35 Managers.................	1	1	....	100	1	......	100	....	1	....	....	1	....
36 White farmers..........	205	193	12	143,203	184	21	53,476	105	100	74,650	16	189	5,710
37 Owners, free.............	88	82	6	24,560	77	11	15,915	39	49	8,036	4	84	145
38 Owners, mortgaged.........	17	16	1	3,069	16	1	2,400	7	10	519	....	17	....
39 Part owners...............	5	5	....	2,770	5	......	1,220	1	4	35	2	3	1,500
40 Cash tenants.............	79	74	5	34,514	70	9	15,320	44	35	17,361	6	73	640
41 Share tenants............	2	2	....	623	2	......	340	1	1	25	1	1	225
42 Managers.................	14	14	....	77,667	14	......	18,281	13	1	48,674	3	11	3,200
VIRGINIA.													
43 Colored farmers.........	48,114	44,624	3,490	7,251,533	27,370	20,744	3,955,495	32,459	15,655	1,630,955	6,426	41,688	1,076,193
44 Owners, free.............	22,220	20,559	1,661	3,320,981	13,007	9,213	1,846,895	15,886	6,334	816,969	2,395	19,825	402,640
45 Owners, mortgaged.........	4,600	4,309	291	754,090	2,865	1,735	421,831	3,126	1,474	157,384	682	3,918	114,924
46 Part owners...............	5,408	5,265	143	1,005,463	3,753	1,655	564,502	4,063	1,345	208,696	917	4,491	156,205
47 Cash tenants.............	4,418	4,039	379	559,044	2,330	2,088	296,579	2,472	1,946	114,819	657	3,761	95,186
48 Share tenants............	11,288	10,283	1,005	1,492,832	5,295	5,993	778,338	6,786	4,502	294,377	1,733	9,555	284,442
49 Managers.................	180	169	11	119,123	120	60	47,350	126	54	38,710	42	138	22,796
50 White farmers..........	135,904	131,195	4,709	63,941,310	100,388	35,516	30,902,115	121,313	14,591	19,493,116	24,262	111,642	6,519,323
51 Owners, free.............	77,239	75,135	2,104	38,023,906	59,718	17,521	18,236,802	71,196	6,043	11,807,004	13,918	63,321	3,742,753
52 Owners, mortgaged.........	13,905	13,571	334	7,784,622	11,269	2,636	3,924,346	12,446	1,459	2,220,863	2,707	11,198	777,640
53 Part owners...............	10,292	10,148	144	5,412,212	7,755	2,537	2,570,197	9,664	628	1,765,555	1,759	8,533	468,872
54 Cash tenants.............	9,631	9,042	589	3,044,118	6,430	3,201	1,501,017	7,542	2,089	822,696	1,659	7,972	396,298
55 Share tenants............	23,392	21,942	1,450	7,155,439	14,037	9,355	3,685,433	19,210	4,182	1,937,167	3,706	19,686	802,310
56 Managers.................	1,445	1,357	88	2,521,013	1,179	266	984,320	1,255	190	939,831	513	932	331,450
WEST VIRGINIA.													
57 Colored farmers.........	708	[1] 660	48	189,179	459	249	103,014	567	141	55,256	63	645	8,405
58 Owners, free.............	417	397	20	96,161	280	137	48,904	348	69	32,466	37	380	4,410
59 Owners, mortgaged.........	70	67	3	18,160	45	25	9,175	59	11	4,947	6	64	710
60 Part owners...............	71	67	4	17,854	54	17	10,125	60	11	5,177	5	66	845
61 Cash tenants.............	63	54	9	11,044	37	26	5,995	38	25	2,758	6	57	980
62 Share tenants............	80	68	12	39,164	40	40	23,365	57	23	8,763	9	71	1,660
63 Managers.................	7	[1] 7	......	6,796	3	4	5,450	5	2	1,145	....	7	....

[1] Error of 1 as compared with figures previously published.

CLASS OF LIVE STOCK REPORTED, BY TENURE OF FARMER, FOR COLORED AND FOR WHITE FARMERS, STATES: 1910—Continued.

					LIVE STOCK ON FARMS.												
			Domestic animals.									Poultry.			Bees.		
Hogs and pigs.			Sheep and lambs.			Asses and burros.			Goats and kids.								
Farms reporting.	Farms not reporting.	Value.	Farms reporting.	Farms not reporting.	Value.	Farms reporting.	Farms not reporting.	Value.	Farms reporting.	Farms not reporting.	Value.	Farms reporting.	Farms not reporting.	Value.	Farms reporting.	Value.	
639	283	$17,544	7	915	$481	....	922	....	2	920	$14	816	106	$19,278	30	$185	1
135	63	3,324	1	197	55	....	198	....	1	197	9	181	17	3,946	7	51	2
97	52	2,296	....	149	....	....	149	....	....	149	....	136	13	2,970	3	12	3
43	16	993	....	59	....	....	59	....	....	59	....	52	7	1,004	2	13	4
49	26	954	1	74	36	....	75	....	....	75	....	64	11	1,131	3	45	5
302	123	9,073	4	421	175	....	425	....	1	424	5	369	56	9,482	15	64	6
13	3	904	1	15	215	....	16	....	....	16	....	14	2	745	....	....	7
7,287	2,627	320,366	259	9,655	36,417	17	9,897	$3,975	33	9,881	314	9,279	635	540,868	1,089	13,424	8
2,550	981	100,206	58	3,473	7,720	4	3,527	1,075	4	3,527	110	3,249	282	194,846	520	6,704	9
1,361	626	59,600	51	1,936	6,025	6	1,981	1,915	11	1,976	70	1,899	88	124,318	222	3,161	10
199	55	6,217	6	248	212	....	254	....	....	254	....	229	25	11,698	39	392	11
438	353	18,666	15	776	1,597	....	791	....	4	787	45	720	71	36,320	34	518	12
2,664	580	124,998	124	3,120	20,066	6	3,238	960	14	3,230	89	3,090	154	163,453	269	2,584	13
75	32	10,679	5	102	797	1	106	25	....	107	....	92	15	10,233	5	65	14
4,221	2,151	90,452	228	6,144	28,884	1	6,371	500	5	6,367	47	5,795	577	95,397	137	1,130	15
1,372	819	24,042	31	2,160	2,628	1	2,190	500	....	2,191	....	1,963	228	27,373	47	353	16
686	424	14,794	22	1,088	1,878	....	1,110	....	2	1,108	5	1,023	87	16,465	22	337	17
439	210	7,735	7	642	1,384	....	649	....	....	649	....	614	35	9,066	15	68	18
380	235	7,942	16	599	1,998	....	615	....	1	614	12	534	81	8,475	9	58	19
1,286	434	32,263	132	1,588	15,857	....	1,720	....	....	1,720	....	1,589	131	31,536	42	284	20
58	29	3,676	20	67	5,139	....	87	....	2	85	30	72	15	2,482	2	30	21
30,973	11,578	1,675,405	6,000	36,551	1,114,081	64	42,487	34,950	193	42,358	5,068	40,259	2,292	1,763,173	4,049	60,473	22
12,285	5,412	590,979	2,133	15,564	330,845	19	17,678	12,730	81	17,616	2,015	16,646	1,051	692,623	2,023	32,079	23
7,223	2,899	374,101	1,233	8,889	219,520	16	10,106	4,568	43	10,079	1,357	9,710	412	426,718	989	14,792	24
1,262	488	60,906	178	1,572	37,838	4	1,746	575	5	1,745	44	1,653	97	65,705	213	2,754	25
2,218	1,261	110,047	337	3,142	66,878	4	3,475	1,900	20	3,459	155	3,169	310	123,263	191	2,770	26
7,399	1,203	467,879	1,975	6,627	415,859	13	8,589	9,382	36	8,566	536	8,281	321	401,432	577	6,395	27
586	315	71,493	144	757	43,141	8	893	5,795	8	893	961	800	101	53,432	56	1,683	28
1	11	15	....	12	....	....	12	....	....	12	....	7	5	946	....	....	29
....	3	....	....	3	....	....	3	....	....	3	....	2	1	25	....	....	30
....	3	....	....	3	....	....	3	....	....	3	....	1	2	40	....	....	31
1	1	15	....	2	....	....	2	....	....	2	....	2	....	822	....	....	32
....	3	....	....	3	....	....	3	....	....	3	....	1	2	24	....	....	33
....	....	....	....	....	....	....	....	....	....	....	....	....	....	....	....	....	34
....	1	....	....	1	....	....	1	....	....	1	....	1	....	35	....	....	35
49	156	9,367	....	205	....	....	205	....	....	205	....	152	53	5,531	13	790	36
19	69	464	....	88	....	....	88	....	....	88	....	69	19	2,088	4	50	37
4	13	150	....	17	....	....	17	....	....	17	....	10	7	349	1	50	38
1	4	15	....	5	....	....	5	....	....	5	....	2	3	33	....	....	39
17	62	1,193	....	79	....	....	79	....	....	79	....	59	20	1,817	6	585	40
2	....	33	....	2	....	....	2	....	....	2	....	1	1	27	....	....	41
6	8	7,512	....	14	....	....	14	....	....	14	....	11	3	1,217	2	105	42
35,398	12,716	556,155	342	47,772	27,324	44	48,070	5,023	74	48,040	388	43,307	4,807	413,037	944	7,330	43
16,155	6,065	243,580	177	22,043	9,403	10	22,210	1,385	25	22,195	109	20,208	2,012	202,889	478	4,105	44
3,420	1,180	57,114	31	4,569	2,320	3	4,597	428	12	4,588	89	4,216	384	41,995	102	720	45
4,327	1,081	70,433	46	5,362	4,822	6	5,402	760	9	5,399	45	5,128	280	55,244	153	1,054	46
3,162	1,256	51,678	14	4,404	467	4	4,414	270	16	4,402	45	3,787	631	32,004	42	187	47
8,216	3,072	126,772	59	11,229	6,698	21	11,267	2,180	11	11,277	25	9,825	1,463	77,836	163	1,205	48
118	62	6,578	15	165	3,614	....	180	....	1	179	75	143	37	3,069	6	59	49
104,778	31,126	3,609,525	21,172	114,732	3,272,702	406	135,498	116,631	664	135,240	27,898	126,900	9,004	2,982,925	21,493	295,293	50
60,730	16,509	2,094,918	14,500	62,739	2,058,575	240	76,999	68,090	386	76,853	15,764	73,318	3,921	1,780,144	14,712	212,624	51
10,672	3,233	460,890	2,028	11,877	382,857	48	13,857	12,975	91	13,814	5,051	13,142	763	382,036	1,898	25,943	52
8,477	1,815	280,155	1,935	8,357	317,655	29	10,263	8,405	51	10,241	1,373	9,904	388	233,453	2,063	25,407	53
6,750	2,881	195,192	742	8,889	119,618	22	9,609	8,006	39	9,592	1,291	8,527	1,104	169,435	664	7,609	54
17,097	6,295	454,274	1,621	21,771	264,195	51	23,341	10,550	66	23,326	1,510	20,779	2,613	354,280	1,988	19,871	55
1,052	393	124,096	346	1,099	129,802	16	1,429	8,605	31	1,414	2,909	1,230	215	63,577	168	3,839	56
485	223	15,184	92	616	7,240	1	707	75	1	707	5	642	66	8,019	54	782	57
279	138	7,114	57	360	3,192	1	416	75	....	417	....	378	39	4,297	32	384	58
51	19	2,423	9	61	900	....	70	....	1	69	5	66	4	989	5	98	59
51	20	1,506	11	60	401	....	71	....	....	71	....	67	4	711	8	147	60
41	22	1,185	3	60	126	....	63	....	....	63	....	54	9	599	4	50	61
59	21	2,755	12	68	2,621	....	80	....	....	80	....	73	7	1,299	5	103	62
4	3	201	....	7	....	....	7	....	....	7	....	4	3	124	....	....	63

TABLE **69.**—NUMBER OF FARMS REPORTING AND NOT REPORTING LIVE STOCK, AND VALUE OF EACH FOR SOUTHERN

	DIVISION, STATE, COLOR OF FARMER, AND TENURE CLASS.	Number of farms.	Total.			Horses.			Neat cattle.			Mules.		
			Farms reporting.	Farms not reporting.	Value.	Farms reporting.	Farms not reporting.	Value.	Farms reporting.	Farms not reporting.	Value.	Farms reporting.	Farms not reporting.	Value.
	SOUTH ATLANTIC DIVISION—Continued.													
	WEST VIRGINIA—continued.													
1	White farmers	95,977	91,518	4,459	$41,129,257	70,318	25,659	$18,480,367	88,192	7,785	$15,805,508	6,566	89,411	$1,331,355
2	Owners, free	59,537	57,662	1,875	27,159,349	46,300	13,237	12,081,768	56,235	3,302	10,529,831	4,188	55,349	853,725
3	Owners, mortgaged	8,294	7,951	343	3,695,533	6,318	1,976	1,769,086	7,591	703	1,320,694	469	7,825	101,025
4	Part owners	7,589	7,436	153	3,908,198	6,253	1,336	1,784,426	7,260	329	1,523,632	558	7,031	117,427
5	Cash tenants	9,273	8,393	880	2,360,731	4,869	4,404	967,702	7,809	1,464	985,535	689	8,584	101,155
6	Share tenants	10,419	9,311	1,108	3,046,145	5,967	4,452	1,543,815	8,582	1,837	975,173	578	9,841	112,207
7	Managers	865	765	100	959,301	611	254	333,570	715	150	470,643	84	781	45,816
	NORTH CAROLINA.													
8	Colored farmers	65,656	60,000	5,656	9,540,042	20,661	44,995	2,633,730	35,962	29,694	1,566,208	26,962	38,694	4,529,905
9	Owners, free	11,088	10,291	797	1,725,018	4,101	6,987	543,883	7,452	3,636	383,995	3,769	7,319	631,809
10	Owners, mortgaged	3,734	3,567	167	698,641	1,781	1,953	240,880	2,488	1,246	122,130	1,588	2,146	276,238
11	Part owners	6,621	6,369	252	1,084,898	2,677	3,944	331,635	4,303	2,318	192,479	2,880	3,741	470,036
12	Cash tenants	11,609	11,005	604	1,830,765	4,446	7,163	547,734	7,079	4,530	309,728	5,076	6,533	826,900
13	Share tenants	32,530	28,701	3,829	4,155,538	7,619	24,911	960,348	14,597	17,933	548,465	13,607	18,923	2,307,972
14	Managers	74	67	7	45,182	37	37	9,250	43	31	9,411	42	32	16,950
15	White farmers	188,069	180,103	7,966	50,510,689	88,547	99,522	15,794,404	150,196	37,873	10,983,846	83,785	104,284	19,169,782
16	Owners, free	89,681	87,340	2,341	27,992,599	47,209	42,472	8,962,243	78,091	11,590	6,516,677	41,066	48,615	9,852,267
17	Owners, mortgaged	16,879	16,499	380	5,381,846	9,320	7,559	1,724,604	14,193	2,686	1,121,552	8,256	8,623	2,049,348
18	Part owners	17,317	17,031	286	4,601,743	8,213	9,104	1,366,995	14,659	2,658	955,824	8,811	8,506	1,894,849
19	Cash tenants	13,430	12,650	780	3,023,355	6,185	7,245	979,336	9,214	4,216	535,283	5,825	7,605	1,258,805
20	Share tenants	49,718	45,617	4,101	8,438,942	16,973	32,745	2,486,247	33,275	16,443	1,617,825	19,179	30,539	3,648,028
21	Managers	1,044	966	78	1,072,204	647	397	274,979	764	280	236,685	648	396	466,485
	SOUTH CAROLINA.													
22	Colored farmers	96,798	86,879	9,919	15,536,823	23,511	73,287	3,190,306	59,102	37,696	2,548,991	48,114	48,684	8,951,989
23	Owners, free	12,805	11,836	969	2,241,158	5,109	7,696	722,790	9,379	3,426	523,963	4,041	8,764	827,461
24	Owners, mortgaged	3,272	3,162	110	828,598	1,248	2,024	189,672	2,545	727	134,717	2,034	1,238	460,269
25	Part owners	4,295	4,161	134	925,325	1,747	2,548	239,881	3,266	1,029	163,720	2,172	2,123	468,801
26	Cash tenants	40,630	36,551	4,079	6,475,806	10,775	29,855	1,397,790	25,762	14,868	1,077,105	20,785	19,845	3,655,927
27	Share tenants	35,665	31,051	4,614	5,004,507	4,580	31,085	628,028	18,080	17,585	640,614	18,999	16,666	3,503,736
28	Managers	131	118	13	61,429	52	79	12,145	70	61	8,872	83	48	35,795
29	White farmers	79,636	75,967	3,669	28,253,320	35,122	44,514	6,956,872	60,932	18,704	4,539,268	49,685	29,951	14,878,372
30	Owners, free	30,286	29,583	703	13,114,816	16,436	13,850	3,449,524	25,766	4,520	2,277,011	19,749	10,537	6,427,702
31	Owners, mortgaged	9,160	9,009	151	4,429,568	4,913	4,247	1,099,416	7,945	1,215	710,664	6,500	2,660	2,325,244
32	Part owners	4,532	4,486	46	1,994,329	2,285	2,247	464,210	3,739	793	277,299	3,234	1,298	1,120,715
33	Cash tenants	15,625	14,765	860	4,330,856	6,724	8,901	1,170,909	10,442	5,183	595,418	9,228	6,397	2,308,069
34	Share tenants	19,301	17,422	1,879	3,433,658	4,329	14,972	629,605	12,485	6,816	542,682	10,379	8,922	2,088,825
35	Managers	732	702	30	950,093	435	297	143,208	555	177	136,194	595	137	607,817
	GEORGIA.													
36	Colored farmers	122,559	113,818	8,741	23,872,291	23,745	98,814	3,180,702	73,413	49,146	3,003,939	81,349	41,210	16,215,253
37	Owners, free	9,649	9,291	358	2,368,322	3,936	5,713	532,275	7,691	1,958	521,582	4,892	4,757	1,100,953
38	Owners, mortgaged	3,210	3,159	51	908,290	1,278	1,932	174,429	2,666	544	141,477	2,189	1,021	522,786
39	Part owners	2,839	2,775	64	726,104	1,178	1,661	151,102	2,228	611	113,097	1,841	998	411,729
40	Cash tenants	50,479	48,774	1,705	11,001,304	11,669	38,810	1,528,441	34,470	16,009	1,325,375	37,903	12,576	7,498,235
41	Share tenants	56,259	49,702	6,557	8,762,956	5,633	50,626	779,757	26,278	29,981	886,148	34,437	21,822	6,613,015
42	Managers	123	117	6	105,315	51	72	14,698	80	43	16,260	87	36	68,535
43	White farmers	168,468	161,576	6,892	54,245,807	63,512	104,956	11,013,137	139,790	28,678	11,057,019	105,163	63,305	27,759,358
44	Owners, free	63,310	62,202	1,108	25,934,261	30,518	32,792	5,644,908	58,304	5,006	6,037,359	40,678	22,632	11,840,337
45	Owners, mortgaged	12,599	12,446	153	5,550,503	6,018	6,581	1,152,602	11,640	959	1,130,189	8,883	3,716	2,783,585
46	Part owners	7,021	6,930	91	2,646,605	3,115	3,906	554,331	6,371	650	477,413	4,910	2,111	1,418,265
47	Cash tenants	31,908	30,712	1,196	8,814,882	11,849	20,059	1,851,161	24,559	7,349	1,452,611	20,802	11,106	4,901,340
48	Share tenants	52,334	48,059	4,275	9,692,390	11,240	41,094	1,558,249	37,851	14,483	1,707,816	28,880	23,454	5,837,346
49	Managers	1,296	1,227	69	1,607,166	772	524	251,886	1,065	231	251,631	1,010	286	978,485
	FLORIDA.													
50	Colored farmers	14,721	13,385	1,336	2,771,131	7,527	7,194	1,047,519	7,868	6,853	631,937	3,874	10,847	743,969
51	Owners, free	5,130	4,714	416	1,089,666	3,160	1,970	444,261	3,109	2,021	304,677	949	4,181	192,070
52	Owners, mortgaged	1,065	996	69	231,334	632	433	87,875	588	477	46,277	322	743	65,860
53	Part owners	1,103	1,056	47	237,471	734	369	100,196	614	489	47,937	292	811	61,745
54	Cash tenants	5,305	4,860	445	903,197	2,336	2,969	320,967	2,886	2,419	182,035	1,676	3,629	296,756
55	Share tenants	2,017	1,696	321	276,848	627	1,390	85,585	644	1,373	38,584	613	1,404	120,038
56	Managers	101	63	38	32,615	38	63	8,635	27	74	12,427	22	79	7,500
57	White farmers	35,295	31,495	3,800	17,047,774	21,763	13,532	3,807,180	23,683	11,612	8,630,325	10,569	24,726	2,801,852
58	Owners, free	22,787	20,681	2,106	12,696,724	15,043	7,744	2,670,320	16,533	6,254	7,016,333	6,402	16,385	1,652,037
59	Owners, mortgaged	3,525	3,220	305	1,481,069	2,172	1,353	388,764	2,476	1,049	604,932	1,281	2,244	330,762
60	Part owners	1,789	1,682	107	741,668	1,105	684	192,576	1,255	534	273,130	725	1,064	197,661
61	Cash tenants	3,518	3,133	385	948,153	1,946	1,572	281,391	1,905	1,613	335,754	1,037	2,481	226,115
62	Share tenants	2,502	2,194	308	577,925	1,071	1,431	151,877	1,186	1,316	208,238	801	1,701	153,229
63	Managers	1,174	585	589	602,235	426	748	122,252	328	846	191,938	323	851	242,048

CLASS OF LIVE STOCK REPORTED, BY TENURE OF FARMER, FOR COLORED AND FOR WHITE FARMERS, STATES: 1910—Continued.

LIVE STOCK ON FARMS.

Hogs and pigs.			Sheep and lambs.			Asses and burros.			Goats and kids.			Poultry.			Bees.		
Farms reporting.	Farms not reporting.	Value.	Farms reporting.	Farms not reporting.	Value.	Farms reporting.	Farms not reporting.	Value.	Farms reporting.	Farms not reporting.	Value.	Farms reporting.	Farms not reporting.	Value.	Farms reporting.	Value.	
66,399	29,578	$2,072,208	26,087	69,890	$3,393,661	123	95,854	$25,481	384	95,593	$20,677	88,561	7,416	$1,620,681	23,981	$388,155	1
42,853	16,684	1,321,375	18,866	40,671	2,342,493	74	59,463	18,345	268	59,269	11,812	55,855	3,682	1,044,782	17,259	291,966	2
5,530	2,764	189,607	2,218	6,076	307,392	17	8,277	2,956	39	8,255	4,773	7,697	597	158,753	1,925	28,761	3
5,752	1,837	183,302	2,136	5,453	297,479	10	7,579	965	35	7,554	967	7,256	333	145,340	2,214	31,848	4
5,488	3,785	148,944	1,301	7,972	155,173	11	9,262	1,300	22	9,251	922	7,978	1,295	108,153	1,235	18,834	5
6,278	4,141	202,352	1,300	9,119	209,425	8	10,411	1,380	14	10,405	1,793	9,104	1,315	144,566	1,201	14,188	6
498	367	26,628	266	599	81,699	3	862	535	6	859	410	671	194	19,087	147	2,558	7
48,568	17,088	792,065	355	65,301	8,849	44	65,612	5,583	696	64,960	3,702	55,008	10,648	340,872	2,295	16,200	8
8,566	2,522	156,243	180	10,908	4,696	21	11,067	2,983	201	10,887	1,409	9,562	1,526	66,942	720	6,765	9
2,957	777	57,889	31	3,703	828	5	3,729	335	74	3,660	341	3,386	348	24,754	231	1,628	10
5,328	1,293	88,558	53	6,568	851	7	6,614	640	117	6,504	699	6,010	611	37,845	378	2,588	11
8,872	2,737	144,423	21	11,588	289	8	11,601	1,325	86	11,523	366	9,744	1,865	59,296	327	1,711	12
22,791	9,739	335,650	68	32,462	1,917	3	32,527	300	217	32,313	886	26,251	6,279	151,326	634	3,325	13
54	20	9,302	2	72	268		74		1	73	1	55	19	709	5	183	14
149,559	38,510	3,845,981	14,355	173,714	550,368	731	187,338	126,971	3,551	184,518	39,337	168,800	19,269	1,871,698	33,953	370,483	15
75,080	14,601	2,144,611	10,243	79,438	413,248	426	89,255	77,580	2,083	87,598	25,973	83,039	6,642	1,017,429	21,367	253,128	16
13,822	3,057	419,293	1,104	15,775	46,236	82	16,797	16,115	452	16,427	4,698	15,683	1,196	196,512	3,186	35,567	17
14,667	2,650	331,503	1,292	16,025	39,167	77	17,240	9,805	399	16,918	3,600	16,227	1,090	168,125	3,762	35,728	18
9,910	3,520	225,986	340	13,090	10,509	67	13,363	12,335	170	13,260	1,101	11,266	2,164	109,863	1,223	10,365	19
35,299	14,419	646,187	1,284	48,434	31,115	67	49,651	7,086	390	49,328	2,454	41,766	7,952	353,431	4,309	33,801	20
781	263	78,401	92	952	10,093	12	1,032	4,050	57	987	1,511	819	225	26,338	106	1,894	21
61,988	34,810	833,101	91	96,707	4,113	29	96,769	4,248	941	95,857	4,075	77,196	19,602	436,184	1,904	12,550	22
8,131	4,674	163,469	39	12,766	1,835	4	12,801	445	256	12,549	1,195	9,960	2,845	81,656	405	3,360	23
2,485	787	42,876	6	3,266	477	2	3,270	190	75	3,197	397	2,936	336	21,263	184	1,214	24
3,233	1,062	52,523	11	4,284	110		4,295		84	4,211	290	3,757	538	24,703	153	1,234	25
26,606	14,024	340,523	23	40,607	321	18	40,612	2,685	358	40,272	1,455	32,662	7,968	174,577	684	4,403	26
21,464	14,201	229,804	8	35,657	765	4	35,661	853	164	35,501	707	27,793	7,872	132,699	474	2,315	27
69	62	3,906	4	127	605	1	130	75	4	127	31	88	43	1,286	4	24	28
59,882	19,754	1,719,243	1,640	77,996	77,249	199	79,437	58,663	2,234	77,402	23,653	69,659	9,977	770,431	10,624	122,072	29
25,008	5,278	876,323	1,059	29,227	50,098	88	30,198	20,907	1,240	29,046	13,251	27,777	2,509	366,862	5,515	73,425	30
7,586	1,574	256,326	227	8,933	11,729	48	9,112	21,557	371	8,789	4,632	8,582	578	113,205	1,593	19,116	31
3,821	711	120,113	116	4,416	3,871	21	4,511	6,162	191	4,341	1,959	4,212	320	49,611	717	6,970	32
10,945	4,680	243,579	127	15,498	5,887	18	15,607	5,236	258	15,367	1,758	12,683	2,942	118,259	1,230	10,421	33
11,975	7,326	167,347	68	19,233	1,783	17	19,284	2,651	136	19,165	765	15,839	3,462	108,221	1,497	11,207	34
547	185	55,555	43	689	3,881	7	725	2,150	38	694	1,288	566	166	14,273	72	933	35
85,780	36,779	1,455,524	98	122,461	4,407	28	122,531	5,438	1,058	121,501	7,028	97,681	24,878	551,068	2,635	12,132	36
7,970	1,679	208,929	43	9,606	1,706	4	9,645	750	284	9,365	2,127	8,584	1,065	71,107	619	3,293	37
2,725	485	68,229	6	3,204	43	2	3,208	590	91	3,119	736	2,920	290	22,150	160	918	38
2,314	525	49,054	7	2,832	297	2	2,837	400	79	2,760	425	2,599	240	18,734	168	711	39
38,800	11,679	644,613	21	50,458	277	12	50,467	2,092	377	50,102	2,271	42,341	8,138	244,178	1,108	5,006	40
33,887	22,372	479,022	18	56,241	1,975	8	56,251	1,606	225	56,034	1,433	41,150	15,109	193,542	579	2,198	41
84	39	5,677	3	120	109		123		2	121	36	87	36	1,357	1	6	42
127,667	40,801	3,973,492	5,069	163,399	303,805	300	168,168	75,965	[1] 5,238	163,230	63,031	147,038	21,430	1,537,585	20,532	175,110	43
53,703	9,607	2,093,349	3,663	59,647	239,148	189	63,121	38,342	3,176	60,134	40,818	58,798	4,512	755,365	11,498	108,018	44
10,712	1,887	433,379	371	12,228	37,063	37	12,562	5,478	667	11,932	8,207	11,797	802	143,619	2,066	17,939	45
5,786	1,235	172,302	267	6,754	8,490	13	7,008	13,725	204	6,817	2,079	6,531	490	72,528	1,215	10,048	46
23,761	8,147	596,614	185	31,723	4,246	20	31,888	2,950	648	31,260	5,960	26,662	5,246	238,871	2,337	17,725	47
32,695	19,639	569,620	557	51,777	11,382	31	52,303	3,555	470	51,864	4,422	42,256	10,078	304,655	3,306	20,676	48
1,010	286	108,228	26	1,270	3,476	10	1,286	11,915	73	1,223	1,545	994	302	22,547	110	704	49
11,083	3,638	343,232	15	14,706	464	10	14,711	930	276	14,445	3,080	12,131	2,590	115,972	499	5,426	50
3,910	1,220	146,144	10	5,120	285	4	5,126	385	161	4,969	1,844	4,371	759	53,546	246	3,485	51
881	184	30,879	1	1,064	5	3	1,062	170	30	1,035	268	920	145	9,165	57	503	52
889	214	27,335		1,103			1,103		26	1,077	258	1,017	86	9,276	55	286	53
3,987	1,318	102,720	4	5,301	174	1	5,304	150	44	5,261	395	4,250	1,055	32,696	116	888	54
1,395	622	32,302		2,017		2	2,015	225	13	2,004	114	1,527	490	9,851	23	169	55
21	80	3,852		101			101		2	99	201	46	55	1,438	2	95	56
24,510	10,785	1,505,499	636	34,659	255,702	80	35,215	9,775	1,671	33,624	37,441	28,527	6,768	557,842	3,846	93,042	57
16,369	6,418	1,105,454	523	22,264	219,426	51	22,736	5,320	1,239	21,548	27,834	18,950	3,837	370,698	2,836	70,125	58
2,439	1,086	135,519	45	3,480	15,518	12	3,513	1,905	167	3,358	3,669	2,980	545	57,108	431	13,845	59
1,349	440	71,438	20	1,769	3,733	5	1,784	385	104	1,685	2,745	1,540	249	23,136	226	3,457	61
2,396	1,122	99,646	15	3,503	2,776	7	3,511	1,240	82	3,436	1,231	2,722	796	77,531	175	2,480	62
1,689	813	58,192	20	2,482	4,576	3	2,499	415	67	2,435	1,398	1,901	601	18,208	136	1,508	63
268	906	35,250	13	1,161	9,673	2	1,172	510	12	1,162	564	434	740	11,161	42	1,627	64

[1] Note 4 on page 629 is explanatory.

NEGRO POPULATION.

			LIVE STOCK ON FARMS.										
			Domestic animals.										
	DIVISION, STATE, COLOR OF FARMER, AND TENURE CLASS	Number of farms.	Total.			Horses.			Neat cattle.			Mules.		
			Farms reporting.	Farms not reporting.	Value.	Farms reporting.	Farms not reporting.	Value.	Farms reporting.	Farms not reporting.	Value.	Farms reporting.	Farms not reporting.	Value.
	EAST SOUTH CENTRAL DIVISION.													
	KENTUCKY.													
1	Colored farmers	11,730	9,762	1,968	$2,690,133	6,153	5,577	$1,289,207	7,244	4,486	$442,085	3,475	8,255	$697,409
2	Owners, free	3,488	3,151	337	763,556	2,120	1,368	323,211	2,511	977	157,400	1,184	2,304	200,208
3	Owners, mortgaged	978	903	75	260,104	647	331	104,782	725	253	47,180	443	535	81,465
4	Part owners	1,463	1,360	103	390,999	986	477	165,665	1,036	427	66,564	564	899	120,330
5	Cash tenants	602	505	97	155,174	343	259	53,987	375	227	24,668	232	370	61,180
6	Share tenants	5,159	3,811	1,348	754,306	2,034	3,125	299,614	2,568	2,591	138,616	1,031	4,128	223,506
7	Managers	40	32	8	365,994	23	17	341,948	29	11	7,657	21	19	10,720
8	White farmers	247,455	232,147	15,308	109,915,279	169,792	77,663	43,506,913	213,364	34,091	25,529,486	94,321	153,134	25,704,681
9	Owners, free	117,774	114,015	3,759	59,791,661	88,326	29,448	23,157,440	108,871	8,903	14,405,917	49,595	68,179	13,554,712
10	Owners, mortgaged	26,592	26,013	579	15,183,795	21,320	5,272	6,189,109	24,440	2,152	3,215,055	12,522	14,070	3,521,135
11	Part owners	20,037	19,609	428	10,329,992	15,341	4,696	4,079,144	18,426	1,611	2,348,852	9,049	10,988	2,493,065
12	Cash tenants	14,658	13,383	1,275	5,929,441	8,623	6,035	2,151,656	11,902	2,756	1,457,404	4,914	9,744	1,504,026
13	Share tenants	67,441	58,255	9,186	16,169,229	35,481	31,960	6,690,433	48,919	18,522	3,512,841	17,714	49,727	4,193,566
14	Managers	953	872	81	2,511,161	701	252	1,239,131	806	147	589,417	527	426	438,177
	TENNESSEE.													
15	Colored farmers	38,308	34,867	3,441	9,752,223	19,629	18,679	3,616,278	26,896	11,412	1,587,642	17,987	20,321	3,835,080
16	Owners, free	5,826	5,477	349	1,717,451	3,582	2,244	699,554	4,661	1,165	310,445	2,693	3,133	567,481
17	Owners, mortgaged	1,914	1,856	58	668,639	1,280	634	253,801	1,604	310	108,880	1,141	773	258,051
18	Part owners	2,960	2,883	77	1,020,774	1,982	978	392,245	2,479	481	152,189	1,743	1,217	398,173
19	Cash tenants	11,801	11,450	351	3,807,770	7,410	4,391	1,412,904	9,333	2,468	575,371	7,432	4,369	1,598,855
20	Share tenants	15,756	13,154	2,602	2,450,297	5,341	10,415	838,449	8,782	6,974	425,346	4,941	10,815	968,140
21	Managers	51	47	4	87,292	34	17	19,325	37	14	15,411	37	14	44,380
22	White farmers	207,704	199,193	8,511	96,855,899	134,209	73,495	35,703,766	183,094	24,610	19,103,076	105,900	101,804	31,265,730
23	Owners, free	95,477	93,124	2,353	50,843,080	68,157	27,320	19,400,138	89,269	6,208	10,478,720	49,331	46,146	15,004,530
24	Owners, mortgaged	16,864	16,558	306	9,941,199	12,616	4,248	3,743,285	15,639	1,225	1,913,849	9,782	7,082	3,037,635
25	Part owners	21,084	20,968	116	11,485,983	14,943	6,141	4,100,682	19,899	1,185	2,069,357	13,150	7,934	4,060,076
26	Cash tenants	18,129	17,306	823	7,720,707	11,571	6,558	2,766,616	14,951	3,178	1,476,121	9,492	8,637	2,779,466
27	Share tenants	55,375	50,521	4,854	15,670,793	26,369	29,006	5,364,422	42,674	12,701	2,840,652	23,652	31,723	6,008,583
28	Managers	775	716	59	1,194,137	553	222	328,623	662	113	324,377	493	282	375,440
	ALABAMA.													
29	Colored farmers	110,443	100,897	9,546	19,597,952	28,696	81,747	3,590,898	79,448	30,995	3,864,648	62,760	47,683	10,873,562
30	Owners, free	8,030	7,710	320	1,862,817	3,548	4,482	458,550	6,926	1,104	465,331	4,192	3,838	790,761
31	Owners, mortgaged	4,979	4,873	106	1,241,511	2,008	2,971	262,134	4,428	551	264,924	3,247	1,732	628,317
32	Part owners	4,073	4,011	62	1,055,863	1,861	2,212	243,692	3,592	481	213,583	2,644	1,429	526,086
33	Cash tenants	64,333	58,971	5,362	11,601,967	17,267	47,066	2,119,518	47,770	16,563	2,299,482	37,792	26,541	6,440,748
34	Share tenants	28,976	25,291	3,685	3,756,162	3,989	24,987	486,544	16,698	12,278	606,073	14,857	14,119	2,453,145
35	Managers	52	41	11	79,632	23	29	20,460	34	18	15,255	28	24	34,505
36	White farmers	152,458	147,293	5,165	43,976,722	62,812	89,646	10,060,386	132,783	19,675	9,604,978	92,913	59,545	20,703,655
37	Owners, free	57,760	56,772	988	20,043,981	28,665	29,095	4,861,929	54,414	3,346	4,736,762	36,041	21,719	8,564,086
38	Owners, mortgaged	16,820	16,641	179	5,944,558	7,650	9,170	1,315,798	15,836	984	1,333,662	11,478	5,342	2,781,390
39	Part owners	12,267	12,189	78	3,993,809	5,826	6,441	932,600	11,569	698	825,845	8,425	3,842	1,933,248
40	Cash tenants	24,213	23,213	1,000	6,165,868	9,839	14,374	1,456,712	19,510	4,703	1,239,174	14,388	9,825	3,048,079
41	Share tenants	40,804	37,935	2,869	7,001,856	10,441	30,363	1,318,552	30,974	9,830	1,280,158	22,165	18,639	3,984,833
42	Managers	594	543	51	826,650	391	203	174,795	480	114	189,377	416	178	392,019
	MISSISSIPPI.													
43	Colored farmers	164,737	145,050	19,687	32,615,835	59,560	105,177	8,079,159	99,803	64,934	5,666,856	87,371	77,366	16,661,176
44	Owners, free	11,562	11,273	289	3,700,345	7,582	3,980	1,133,445	10,238	1,324	853,509	6,616	4,946	1,440,261
45	Owners, mortgaged	9,543	9,432	111	3,052,570	5,894	3,649	843,456	8,679	864	644,622	6,369	3,174	1,356,212
46	Part owners	3,921	3,852	69	1,266,496	2,376	1,545	358,246	3,445	476	245,348	2,556	1,365	584,556
47	Cash tenants	58,277	55,684	2,593	14,732,603	26,142	32,135	3,693,763	40,675	17,602	2,311,634	38,227	20,050	7,803,580
48	Share tenants	81,328	64,713	16,615	9,780,941	17,500	63,828	2,031,739	36,692	44,636	1,598,944	33,537	47,791	5,432,917
49	Managers	106	96	10	82,880	66	40	18,510	74	32	12,799	66	40	43,650
50	White farmers	109,645	105,913	3,732	40,639,921	69,090	40,555	12,224,692	95,535	14,110	9,602,508	60,481	49,164	15,367,245
51	Owners, free	45,241	44,609	632	20,554,970	32,722	12,519	6,247,824	42,918	2,323	5,280,522	26,809	18,432	7,032,310
52	Owners, mortgaged	16,129	15,985	144	6,994,914	11,176	4,953	2,086,469	15,315	814	1,649,339	10,117	6,012	2,674,961
53	Part owners	5,670	5,617	53	2,342,317	3,931	1,739	710,538	5,298	372	521,955	3,488	2,182	929,326
54	Cash tenants	16,247	15,520	727	4,792,945	9,964	6,283	1,554,915	12,652	3,595	991,784	8,040	8,207	1,932,530
55	Share tenants	25,639	23,506	2,133	4,472,625	10,731	14,908	1,345,109	18,763	6,876	919,190	11,499	14,140	1,939,078
56	Managers	719	676	43	1,482,150	566	153	279,837	589	130	239,718	528	191	859,040

CLASS OF LIVE STOCK REPORTED, BY TENURE OF FARMER, FOR COLORED AND FOR WHITE FARMERS, STATES: 1910—Continued.

LIVE STOCK ON FARMS.

| Domestic animals. | | | | | | | | | | | | Poultry. | | | Bees. | | |
| Hogs and pigs. | | | Sheep and lambs. | | | Asses and burros. | | | Goats and kids. | | | | | | | | |
Farms reporting.	Farms not reporting.	Value.	Farms reporting.	Farms not reporting.	Value.	Farms reporting.	Farms not reporting.	Value.	Farms reporting.	Farms not reporting.	Value.	Farms reporting.	Farms not reporting.	Value.	Farms reporting.	Value.	
6,625	5,105	$219,061	342	11,388	$29,318	50	11,680	$12,573	45	11,685	$480	9,657	2,073	$125,928	340	$2,612	
2,176	1,312	67,242	183	3,305	12,452	29	3,459	2,846	17	3,471	197	3,105	383	41,438	159	1,410	1
633	345	21,275	55	923	5,023	5	973	255	8	970	124	904	74	13,223	37	220	2
970	493	35,261	35	1,428	2,763	5	1,458	402	4	1,459	14	1,337	126	19,346	72	403	3
359	243	14,474	8	594	771	......	602	....	4	598	94	523	79	6,951	11	94	4
2,464	2,695	76,363	56	5,103	7,086	11	5,148	9,070	12	5,147	51	3,755	1,404	43,984	60	479	5
23	17	4,446	5	35	1,223	......	40	....	......	40	......	33	7	936	1	6	6
																	7
166,221	81,234	8,732,631	45,355	202,100	5,544,680	2,074	245,381	835,703	2,668	244,787	61,185	221,805	25,650	4,335,943	35,263	416,767	8
86,233	31,541	4,683,343	29,841	87,933	3,429,981	1,220	116,554	522,572	1,544	116,230	37,696	109,282	8,492	2,305,678	23,084	295,085	9
19,381	7,211	1,271,871	5,537	21,055	817,098	379	26,213	160,104	438	26,154	9,423	25,022	1,570	574,521	4,102	46,381	10
14,928	5,109	835,607	3,779	16,258	501,499	169	19,868	66,275	260	19,777	5,550	19,005	1,032	400,584	3,169	30,462	11
8,837	5,821	514,103	1,526	13,132	270,988	73	14,585	29,706	99	14,559	1,558	12,522	2,136	219,714	1,152	12,976	12
36,216	31,225	1,306,101	4,464	62,977	412,532	215	67,226	47,646	295	67,146	6,110	55,190	12,251	811,018	3,630	30,176	13
626	327	121,606	208	745	112,582	18	935	9,400	32	921	848	784	169	24,428	126	1,687	14
26,794	11,514	656,119	426	37,882	32,155	201	38,107	21,575	405	37,903	3,374	32,970	5,338	315,072	611	5,131	15
4,254	1,572	121,482	206	5,620	10,634	71	5,755	6,914	92	5,734	941	5,446	380	65,352	219	1,938	16
1,472	442	42,812	44	1,870	2,537	24	1,890	2,122	43	1,871	436	1,800	114	21,434	68	536	17
2,394	566	69,593	70	2,890	3,842	36	2,924	4,408	45	2,915	324	2,837	123	34,552	116	987	18
9,216	2,585	215,748	16	11,785	533	26	11,775	3,407	138	11,663	952	10,449	1,352	92,280	89	698	19
9,422	6,334	203,259	78	15,678	10,347	41	15,715	4,064	84	15,672	692	12,400	3,356	100,752	119	972	20
36	15	3,225	12	39	4,262	3	48	660	3	48	29	38	13	702	....	......	21
155,050	52,654	6,673,503	29,561	178,143	2,977,041	3,584	204,120	1,053,491	4,454	203,250	79,292	189,741	17,963	3,442,265	27,095	335,488	22
75,144	20,333	3,472,508	18,842	76,635	1,783,871	2,124	93,353	656,906	2,446	93,031	46,407	90,188	5,289	1,800,161	16,889	224,030	23
13,242	3,622	720,808	2,608	14,256	371,348	391	16,473	143,879	587	16,277	10,395	16,015	849	327,159	2,450	29,808	24
17,305	3,779	793,140	3,370	17,714	324,820	480	20,604	130,573	541	20,543	7,335	20,297	787	396,767	3,301	35,178	25
12,576	5,553	498,215	1,007	17,122	155,186	176	17,953	41,016	310	17,819	4,087	15,698	2,431	241,407	1,137	14,685	26
36,230	19,145	1,109,943	3,558	51,817	269,548	378	54,997	70,092	518	54,857	8,553	46,927	8,448	656,233	3,228	30,687	27
553	222	78,889	176	599	73,268	35	740	11,025	52	723	2,515	616	159	20,538	90	1,100	28
75,173	35,270	1,240,019	175	110,268	8,520	96	110,347	12,760	1,230	109,213	7,545	87,138	23,305	498,501	3,286	23,059	29
6,150	1,880	137,268	78	7,952	5,350	20	8,010	3,238	248	7,782	2,319	7,153	877	54,564	623	6,422	30
3,983	996	81,891	44	4,935	1,604	13	4,966	1,265	129	4,850	1,376	4,541	438	32,040	403	2,990	31
3,299	774	68,632	18	4,055	534	17	4,056	2,530	130	3,943	806	3,769	304	26,290	292	1,866	32
45,076	19,257	734,140	28	64,305	888	33	64,300	4,635	620	63,713	2,556	50,528	13,805	285,136	1,606	9,965	33
16,635	12,341	208,738	6	28,970	112	13	28,963	1,092	101	28,875	458	21,116	7,860	96,606	357	1,736	34
30	22	9,350	1	51	32	......	52	....	2	50	30	31	21	3,865	5	80	35
115,078	37,380	3,116,501	6,453	146,005	291,399	797	151,661	130,987	4,437	148,021	68,816	134,344	18,114	1,308,738	20,625	189,862	36
48,278	9,482	1,561,534	4,184	53,576	206,906	412	57,348	69,738	2,604	55,156	43,026	53,729	4,031	618,520	11,737	113,704	37
14,145	2,675	445,677	784	16,036	35,187	129	16,691	21,775	697	16,123	11,069	15,807	1,013	167,174	2,895	25,212	38
10,287	1,980	266,556	705	11,562	16,993	99	12,168	13,072	435	11,832	5,495	11,539	728	116,370	2,081	16,885	39
16,872	7,341	398,132	225	23,988	8,324	73	24,140	10,402	394	23,819	5,045	19,895	4,318	171,568	1,855	19,933	40
25,084	15,720	395,607	498	40,306	13,474	60	40,744	6,375	270	40,534	2,857	32,949	7,855	223,509	1,990	13,107	41
412	182	48,995	57	537	10,515	24	570	9,625	37	557	1,324	425	169	11,597	67	1,021	42
108,844	55,893	2,166,233	457	164,280	13,037	170	164,567	22,358	1,045	163,692	7,016	126,757	37,980	800,042	2,551	18,297	43
9,476	2,086	254,940	217	11,345	7,275	46	11,516	7,935	294	11,268	2,980	10,621	941	96,709	681	5,058	44
8,020	1,523	198,003	105	9,438	2,617	48	9,495	6,242	229	9,314	1,418	8,938	605	74,677	515	3,943	45
3,223	698	75,329	33	3,888	1,104	8	3,913	1,565	63	3,858	348	3,623	298	30,017	201	1,088	46
43,476	14,801	917,269	49	58,228	1,430	27	58,250	3,595	264	58,013	1,332	48,566	9,711	331,649	711	5,572	47
44,582	36,746	712,993	50	81,278	491	40	81,288	2,971	193	81,135	886	54,934	26,394	265,744	437	2,608	48
67	39	7,699	3	103	120	1	105	50	2	104	52	75	31	1,246	6	28	49
84,685	24,960	2,746,933	5,270	104,375	403,679	886	108,759	258,007	2,994	106,651	36,857	94,733	14,912	1,046,709	13,477	125,929	50
38,828	6,413	1,476,960	3,789	41,452	340,309	494	44,747	154,274	1,900	43,341	22,771	41,875	3,366	548,401	8,360	82,756	51
14,041	2,088	500,370	765	15,364	29,460	184	15,945	46,825	561	15,568	7,490	15,154	975	177,213	2,609	21,656	52
4,870	800	154,077	295	5,375	8,778	55	5,615	15,139	180	5,490	2,504	5,258	412	55,255	760	6,536	53
10,986	5,261	286,997	169	16,078	9,417	57	16,190	15,520	182	16,065	1,782	12,662	3,585	122,656	814	9,535	54
15,451	10,188	251,606	214	25,425	7,558	68	25,571	9,359	132	25,507	725	19,277	6,362	127,915	888	4,468	55
509	210	76,923	38	681	8,157	28	691	16,890	39	680	1,585	507	212	15,269	46	978	56

TABLE **69.**—NUMBER OF FARMS REPORTING AND NOT REPORTING LIVE STOCK, AND VALUE OF EACH FOR SOUTHERN

	DIVISION, STATE, COLOR OF FARMER, AND TENURE CLASS.	Number of farms.	Total.			Horses.			Neat cattle.			Mules.		
			Farms reporting.	Farms not reporting.	Value.	Farms reporting.	Farms not reporting.	Value.	Farms reporting.	Farms not reporting.	Value.	Farms reporting.	Farms not reporting.	Value.
	WEST SOUTH CENTRAL DIVISION.													
	ARKANSAS.													
1	Colored farmers	63,593	55,062	8,531	$14,970,299	24,803	38,790	$3,692,674	37,608	25,985	$2,738,936	33,070	30,523	$7,443,089
2	Owners, free	7,891	7,681	210	2,767,245	4,910	2,981	753,740	6,958	933	663,417	4,831	3,060	1,118,533
3	Owners, mortgaged	3,969	3,909	60	1,417,728	2,304	1,665	351,896	3,496	473	316,644	2,692	1,277	636,043
4	Part owners	2,802	2,752	50	987,021	1,725	1,077	261,818	2,429	373	200,851	1,841	961	452,540
5	Cash tenants	19,803	18,380	1,423	6,086,568	9,164	10,639	1,547,906	13,064	6,739	970,381	12,262	7,541	3,162,956
6	Share tenants	29,082	22,299	6,783	3,679,980	6,674	22,408	771,909	11,631	17,451	581,250	11,411	17,671	2,055,807
7	Managers	46	41	5	31,757	26	20	5,405	30	16	6,393	33	13	17,210
8	White farmers	151,085	145,726	5,359	56,824,187	99,590	51,495	19,459,535	129,886	21,199	12,721,730	76,944	74,141	19,684,938
9	Owners, free	61,921	60,859	1,062	27,296,269	45,141	16,780	9,386,352	57,903	4,018	6,774,638	33,351	28,570	8,493,467
10	Owners, mortgaged	14,085	13,883	202	6,253,193	10,534	3,551	2,265,290	13,006	1,079	1,459,317	7,271	6,814	1,945,971
11	Part owners	15,981	15,846	135	6,522,082	11,164	4,817	2,213,223	14,979	1,002	1,401,587	9,416	6,565	2,350,298
12	Cash tenants	15,880	15,255	625	5,756,814	9,818	6,062	1,792,653	12,476	3,404	1,060,786	8,327	7,553	2,470,729
13	Share tenants	42,501	39,321	3,180	9,949,925	22,470	20,031	3,589,554	31,045	11,456	1,857,918	18,164	24,337	3,828,458
14	Managers	717	562	155	1,045,904	463	254	212,463	477	240	167,484	415	302	596,015
	LOUISIANA.													
15	Colored farmers	54,879	49,539	5,340	9,560,165	29,006	25,873	2,928,177	29,998	24,881	1,957,704	24,150	30,729	3,751,187
16	Owners, free	7,312	7,154	158	1,971,177	5,389	1,923	617,667	6,192	1,120	571,755	3,473	3,839	589,279
17	Owners, mortgaged	2,287	2,240	47	642,626	1,607	680	192,031	1,928	359	161,197	1,258	1,029	226,914
18	Part owners	1,126	1,103	23	350,522	811	315	97,224	922	204	71,426	702	424	151,270
19	Cash tenants	9,573	9,112	461	1,817,215	5,966	3,607	585,959	5,721	3,852	350,026	4,400	5,173	708,786
20	Share tenants	34,504	29,858	4,646	4,715,015	15,186	19,318	1,421,499	15,192	19,312	786,301	14,268	20,236	2,047,145
21	Managers	77	72	5	63,610	47	30	13,797	43	34	16,999	49	28	27,793
22	White farmers	65,667	63,710	1,957	33,754,518	50,559	15,108	8,861,518	55,357	10,310	9,647,650	27,518	38,149	11,873,775
23	Owners, free	32,652	32,189	463	16,473,886	26,119	6,533	4,513,133	30,230	2,422	5,803,692	14,072	18,580	4,087,603
24	Owners, mortgaged	6,339	6,260	79	4,411,667	5,101	1,238	1,112,154	5,666	673	1,175,229	3,146	3,193	1,722,220
25	Part owners	3,273	3,238	35	2,170,543	2,671	602	540,094	2,985	288	559,484	1,692	1,581	891,634
26	Cash tenants	6,962	6,632	330	3,229,390	5,086	1,876	861,563	5,023	1,939	791,617	2,715	4,247	1,350,744
27	Share tenants	15,568	14,601	967	4,052,958	10,911	4,657	1,402,468	10,810	4,758	931,030	5,242	10,326	1,373,013
28	Managers	873	790	83	3,416,074	671	202	432,106	643	230	386,598	651	222	2,448,561
	OKLAHOMA.													
29	Colored farmers	20,671	19,353	1,318	9,753,448	16,307	4,364	4,020,719	13,715	6,956	2,878,165	8,182	12,489	2,030,294
30	Owners, free	7,713	7,473	240	4,585,520	6,857	856	1,973,182	5,728	1,985	1,469,818	2,726	4,987	722,118
31	Owners, mortgaged	2,206	2,160	46	1,246,429	1,929	277	530,654	1,805	401	322,784	974	1,232	263,328
32	Part owners	1,231	1,210	21	1,106,256	1,098	133	386,718	1,001	230	452,657	618	613	187,935
33	Cash tenants	1,997	1,894	103	840,982	1,531	466	305,102	1,271	726	266,997	901	1,096	214,126
34	Share tenants	7,497	6,594	903	1,930,489	4,872	2,625	815,623	3,895	3,602	335,839	2,954	4,543	639,812
35	Managers	27	22	5	43,772	20	7	9,440	15	12	30,070	9	18	2,975
36	White farmers	169,521	164,467	5,054	138,899,535	146,897	22,624	59,630,942	143,127	26,394	40,309,436	82,306	87,215	26,587,930
37	Owners, free	30,956	29,547	1,409	27,320,460	27,551	3,405	12,441,222	26,316	4,640	7,828,139	13,035	17,921	4,355,868
38	Owners, mortgaged	24,009	23,657	352	23,009,148	22,421	1,588	11,096,638	22,073	1,936	5,423,916	11,539	12,470	3,840,728
39	Part owners	19,289	19,185	104	25,222,879	18,385	904	10,789,983	18,142	1,147	7,672,158	10,828	8,461	4,352,814
40	Cash tenants	25,822	25,129	693	24,588,223	22,462	3,360	8,306,810	21,896	3,926	10,195,623	12,838	12,984	4,294,420
41	Share tenants	68,821	66,367	2,454	35,652,151	55,557	13,264	16,556,163	54,198	14,623	6,912,897	33,726	35,095	9,510,581
42	Managers	624	582	42	3,106,674	521	103	440,126	502	122	2,276,703	340	284	233,519
	TEXAS.													
43	Colored farmers	69,918	64,445	5,473	17,660,546	41,613	28,305	5,183,139	43,847	26,071	4,100,541	36,570	33,348	7,128,760
44	Owners, free	13,034	12,726	308	4,332,613	9,678	3,356	1,321,468	10,929	2,105	1,309,361	7,232	5,802	1,342,586
45	Owners, mortgaged	3,644	3,617	27	1,425,922	2,818	826	431,147	3,248	396	374,278	2,418	1,226	514,820
46	Part owners	4,554	4,505	49	1,714,116	3,497	1,057	505,965	3,848	706	464,945	2,972	1,582	619,440
47	Cash tenants	6,367	5,981	386	1,488,763	4,222	2,145	487,373	3,876	2,491	322,799	3,146	3,221	567,131
48	Share tenants	42,238	37,539	4,699	8,563,771	21,334	20,904	2,400,991	21,892	20,346	1,567,302	20,756	21,482	4,052,573
49	Managers	81	77	4	135,361	64	17	36,195	54	27	61,856	46	35	32,210
50	White farmers	347,852	337,920	9,932	295,503,994	277,594	70,258	78,841,496	292,860	54,992	128,885,338	206,008	141,844	66,850,385
51	Owners, free	102,274	100,806	1,468	95,986,567	88,997	13,277	27,377,889	95,722	6,552	41,935,786	58,550	43,724	18,811,721
52	Owners, mortgaged	48,563	48,025	538	54,509,818	43,009	5,554	15,442,376	45,091	3,472	23,445,651	31,422	17,141	11,374,590
53	Part owners	23,794	23,605	189	35,150,867	20,749	3,045	7,519,638	22,319	1,475	18,739,025	15,763	8,031	5,752,453
54	Cash tenants	19,816	18,924	892	18,432,660	15,441	4,375	4,186,052	15,218	4,598	9,899,205	9,608	10,208	2,963,686
55	Share tenants	151,154	144,521	6,633	64,054,606	107,595	43,559	21,856,462	112,728	38,426	12,658,247	89,232	61,922	26,306,432
56	Managers	2,251	2,039	212	27,369,476	1,803	448	2,459,079	1,782	469	22,207,424	1,433	818	1,641,503

CLASS OF LIVE STOCK REPORTED, BY TENURE OF FARMER, FOR COLORED AND FOR WHITE FARMERS, STATES: 1910—Continued.

LIVE STOCK ON FARMS.

| Domestic animals. | | | | | | | | | | | | Poultry. | | | Bees. | | |
| Hogs and pigs. | | | Sheep and lambs. | | | Asses and burros. | | | Goats and kids. | | | | | | | | |
Farms reporting.	Farms not reporting.	Value.	Farms reporting.	Farms not reporting.	Value.	Farms reporting.	Farms not reporting.	Value.	Farms reporting.	Farms not reporting.	Value.	Farms reporting.	Farms not reporting.	Value.	Farms reporting.	Value.	
40,291	23,302	$1,065,710	241	63,352	$6,514	93	63,500	$17,518	724	62,869	$5,858	49,815	13,778	$373,480	1,309	$11,685	1
6,488	1,403	219,768	127	7,764	3,801	29	7,862	6,220	175	7,716	1,766	7,251	640	70,228	459	3,674	2
3,346	623	109,350	51	3,918	1,131	11	3,958	1,579	114	3,855	1,085	3,693	276	35,841	236	2,070	3
2,335	467	69,376	25	2,777	491	8	2,794	1,385	65	2,737	560	2,638	164	23,033	167	1,951	4
13,686	6,117	397,177	19	19,784	621	28	19,775	5,968	249	19,554	1,559	16,482	3,321	134,485	235	2,360	5
14,408	14,674	267,351	18	29,064	455	17	29,065	2,366	114	28,968	842	19,716	9,366	109,478	210	1,619	6
28	18	2,688	1	45	15	....	46	....	7	39	46	35	11	415	2	11	7
116,918	34,167	4,105,214	8,156	142,929	321,470	1,722	149,363	452,220	4,066	147,019	79,080	134,001	17,084	1,689,952	18,383	188,364	8
52,728	9,193	2,118,110	5,325	56,596	212,876	1,004	60,917	263,059	2,361	59,560	47,767	57,743	4,178	848,972	11,166	117,259	9
11,463	2,622	463,492	817	13,268	39,963	214	13,871	68,875	490	13,595	10,285	13,258	827	191,359	2,124	24,732	10
13,897	2,084	445,925	1,139	14,842	40,813	237	15,744	61,616	495	15,486	8,620	15,162	819	185,979	2,352	18,674	11
11,127	4,753	402,502	168	15,712	7,491	83	15,797	19,071	285	15,595	3,582	13,431	2,449	152,001	866	11,975	12
27,314	15,187	619,954	677	41,824	17,920	168	42,333	30,433	400	42,101	5,688	33,960	8,541	301,320	1,840	15,235	13
389	328	55,231	30	687	2,407	16	701	9,166	35	682	3,138	447	270	10,321	35	489	14
35,935	18,944	902,146	265	54,614	11,716	46	54,833	5,860	436	54,443	3,375	42,203	12,676	340,152	696	5,193	15
5,732	1,580	180,479	162	7,150	8,361	16	7,296	2,090	143	7,169	1,546	6,501	811	70,619	297	2,209	16
1,877	410	59,947	38	2,249	1,004	11	2,276	1,160	46	2,241	373	2,063	224	22,349	74	824	17
937	189	27,946	9	1,117	385	5	1,121	2,130	16	1,110	141	1,050	76	11,941	33	184	18
6,728	2,845	171,186	28	9,545	795	4	9,569	80	89	9,484	383	7,781	1,792	62,694	98	919	19
20,613	13,891	457,816	25	34,479	954	10	34,494	400	141	34,363	900	24,758	9,746	171,512	193	1,027	20
48	29	4,772	3	74	217	....	77	....	1	76	32	50	27	1,037	1	30	21
50,633	15,034	2,921,900	3,391	62,276	331,330	283	65,384	64,366	[1]3,121	62,546	53,979	56,236	9,431	986,462	4,232	52,995	22
27,079	5,573	1,712,276	2,525	30,127	275,122	176	32,476	43,051	2,120	30,532	39,009	29,288	3,364	527,595	3,003	36,905	23
5,229	1,110	365,003	396	5,943	24,276	42	6,297	8,145	307	6,032	4,640	5,659	680	116,086	445	5,081	24
2,789	484	162,460	156	3,117	8,327	24	3,249	4,685	163	3,110	3,859	3,024	249	60,276	263	6,220	25
4,507	2,455	213,597	104	6,858	7,119	11	6,951	2,650	253	6,709	2,100	5,391	1,571	85,864	207	2,044	26
10,481	5,087	336,625	130	15,438	5,414	14	15,554	2,075	233	15,335	2,333	12,332	3,236	171,222	297	2,413	27
548	325	131,939	80	793	11,072	16	857	3,760	45	828	2,038	542	331	25,419	17	332	28
13,791	6,880	774,355	121	20,550	7,801	174	20,497	35,981	220	20,451	6,133	17,320	3,351	239,927	485	5,135	29
5,512	2,201	391,747	92	7,621	4,851	87	7,626	19,989	146	7,567	3,815	6,506	1,207	104,972	307	3,259	30
1,681	525	120,326	17	2,189	952	32	2,174	7,420	35	2,171	965	1,998	208	34,452	68	889	31
986	245	72,660	7	1,224	1,875	19	1,212	3,440	17	1,214	971	1,116	115	22,202	54	504	32
1,311	686	52,377	1	1,996	19	16	1,981	2,172	8	1,989	189	1,660	337	20,115	17	107	33
4,292	3,205	135,990	3	7,494	72	20	7,477	2,960	14	7,483	193	6,026	1,471	58,013	39	376	34
9	18	1,255	1	26	32	....	27	....	....	27	....	14	13	173	....	....	35
121,950	47,571	11,223,286	759	168,762	246,063	2,706	166,815	845,324	1,216	168,305	56,554	151,329	18,192	3,474,016	4,331	59,126	36
21,743	9,213	2,405,258	217	30,739	71,049	611	30,345	197,191	296	30,660	21,733	26,673	4,283	723,820	1,071	17,565	37
18,829	5,180	2,386,044	172	23,837	52,609	553	23,456	195,747	229	23,780	13,466	22,390	1,619	637,616	663	11,981	38
15,870	3,419	2,118,727	167	19,122	82,910	561	18,728	198,734	200	19,089	7,553	18,211	1,078	554,849	619	8,459	39
18,789	7,033	1,653,592	84	25,738	19,468	362	25,460	112,464	193	25,629	5,846	23,205	2,617	505,643	618	7,556	40
46,327	22,494	2,519,429	110	68,711	13,897	595	68,226	132,793	282	68,539	6,391	60,372	8,449	1,038,678	1,328	13,041	41
392	232	140,236	9	615	6,130	24	600	8,395	16	608	1,565	478	146	13,410	32	524	42
46,474	23,444	1,204,659	131	69,787	9,305	366	69,552	25,978	373	69,545	8,164	55,600	14,318	447,900	2,566	21,538	43
10,197	2,837	339,856	73	12,961	4,595	138	12,896	10,374	173	12,861	4,373	11,658	1,376	117,645	924	10,124	44
3,132	512	99,890	15	3,629	875	55	3,589	4,440	33	3,611	472	3,362	282	34,657	286	2,692	45
3,827	727	118,906	14	4,540	1,248	41	4,513	2,978	43	4,511	634	4,218	336	40,900	334	2,599	46
4,353	2,014	109,711	5	6,362	215	24	6,343	1,099	26	6,341	435	5,235	1,132	39,236	155	1,058	47
24,921	17,317	532,021	24	42,214	2,372	107	42,131	6,587	94	42,144	1,925	31,078	11,160	214,586	865	5,059	48
44	37	4,275	....	81	....	1	80	500	4	77	325	49	32	876	2	6	49
247,112	100,740	10,434,707	6,745	341,107	6,292,059	7,785	340,067	1,694,096	[1]7,563	340,289	2,505,913	301,763	46,089	4,358,742	35,315	653,789	50
79,789	22,485	4,170,275	3,612	98,662	2,290,459	3,117	99,157	687,193	3,972	98,302	713,244	93,288	8,986	1,590,031	16,906	333,256	51
38,139	10,424	1,869,884	1,513	47,050	1,337,122	1,928	46,635	443,805	1,460	47,103	596,390	45,031	3,532	734,312	6,808	134,853	52
19,350	4,444	965,235	665	23,129	1,238,270	887	22,907	232,581	716	23,078	703,665	22,347	1,447	358,525	3,255	53,958	53
12,195	7,621	469,366	272	19,544	562,250	387	19,429	88,466	487	19,329	263,635	15,799	4,017	213,493	1,186	37,619	54
96,388	54,766	2,710,691	548	150,606	285,140	1,276	149,878	165,049	775	150,379	72,585	123,815	27,339	1,421,388	6,991	86,425	55
1,251	1,000	249,256	135	2,116	578,818	190	2,061	77,002	153	2,098	156,394	1,483	768	40,993	169	7,678	56

[1] Note 4 on page 629 is explanatory.

TABLE **70.**—COLORED FARMS CLASSIFIED BY TENURE AND TERM OF OCCUPANCY, BY DIVISIONS AND STATES: 1910.

DIVISION, STATE, AND TERM OF OCCUPANCY.	COLORED FARMS: 1910.						
	Total.	Owners, free.	Owners, mortgaged.	Part owners.	Cash tenants.	Share tenants.	Managers.
UNITED STATES.							
Total	920,883	145,924	49,885	45,412	289,944	388,174	1,544
Less than 1 year	191,808	3,198	2,097	3,677	51,385	131,155	296
1 year	105,781	3,904	2,503	3,353	35,669	60,176	176
2 to 4 years	242,724	18,613	9,499	10,229	94,331	109,633	419
5 to 9 years	131,354	24,558	10,202	9,402	49,056	37,861	275
10 years and over	165,560	65,605	17,724	15,561	41,616	24,808	246
Not reported	83,656	30,046	7,860	3,190	17,887	24,541	132
NEW ENGLAND.							
Total	342	152	105	14	47	5	19
Less than 1 year	20	6	3	....	7	1	3
1 year	24	6	10	....	7	....	1
2 to 4 years	80	21	26	4	19	3	7
5 to 9 years	56	21	22	4	7	....	2
10 years and over	148	88	41	5	7	1	6
Not reported	14	10	3	1	....	....	....
MIDDLE ATLANTIC.							
Total	1,961	913	372	129	257	218	72
Less than 1 year	138	9	19	2	50	43	15
1 year	173	32	31	18	28	47	17
2 to 4 years	388	131	76	21	72	71	17
5 to 9 years	302	120	65	25	55	24	13
10 years and over	776	498	159	57	34	21	7
Not reported	184	123	22	6	18	12	3
EAST NORTH CENTRAL.							
Total	5,717	1,785	1,234	889	536	1,199	74
Less than 1 year	578	58	61	75	102	261	21
1 year	507	64	66	71	94	201	11
2 to 4 years	1,148	212	214	172	171	362	17
5 to 9 years	889	261	226	166	67	162	7
10 years and over	2,070	974	506	357	68	151	14
Not reported	525	216	161	48	34	62	4
WEST NORTH CENTRAL.							
Total	9,864	5,151	1,137	1,081	851	1,568	76
Less than 1 year	906	137	54	84	179	428	24
1 year	603	145	49	65	115	216	13
2 to 4 years	1,724	639	162	197	255	454	17
5 to 9 years	1,321	573	195	200	133	209	11
10 years and over	2,834	1,558	549	447	114	161	5
Not reported	2,476	2,099	128	88	55	100	6
SOUTH ATLANTIC.							
Total	355,862	63,701	17,213	21,047	113,197	139,984	720
Less than 1 year	67,259	1,149	689	1,468	18,999	44,849	105
1 year	41,506	1,559	870	1,459	14,543	23,006	69
2 to 4 years	95,713	8,467	3,297	4,680	37,441	41,609	219
5 to 9 years	52,222	11,013	3,297	4,221	19,614	13,924	153
10 years and over	70,232	30,484	6,342	7,756	16,832	8,705	113
Not reported	28,930	11,029	2,718	1,463	5,768	7,891	61
EAST SOUTH CENTRAL.							
Total	325,218	28,906	17,414	12,417	135,013	131,219	249
Less than 1 year	75,463	617	690	1,090	24,181	48,840	45
1 year	37,621	835	792	894	15,671	19,401	28
2 to 4 years	88,533	4,004	3,381	2,994	43,684	34,400	70
5 to 9 years	46,949	5,339	3,731	2,677	23,221	11,951	30
10 years and over	51,208	13,575	6,221	3,979	19,727	7,656	50
Not reported	25,444	4,536	2,599	783	8,529	8,971	26
WEST SOUTH CENTRAL.							
Total	209,061	35,950	12,106	9,713	37,740	113,321	231
Less than 1 year	46,602	1,042	549	952	7,441	36,561	57
1 year	24,587	1,030	652	835	4,835	17,209	26
2 to 4 years	52,861	4,350	2,226	2,130	11,642	32,468	45
5 to 9 years	28,415	6,418	2,611	2,090	5,725	11,528	43
10 years and over	35,113	15,482	3,864	2,918	4,728	8,085	36
Not reported	21,483	7,628	2,204	788	3,369	7,470	24
MOUNTAIN.							
Total	8,028	7,592	49	34	229	102	22
Less than 1 year	233	137	7	1	44	40	4
1 year	257	185	5	4	43	17	3
2 to 4 years	672	542	8	11	79	31	1
5 to 9 years	631	585	11	6	25	2	2
10 years and over	2,256	2,213	9	10	14	3	7
Not reported	3,979	3,930	9	2	24	9	5

DIVISION, STATE, AND TERM OF OCCUPANCY.	COLORED FARMS: 1910.						
	Total.	Owners, free.	Owners, mortgaged.	Part owners.	Cash tenants.	Share tenants.	Managers.
PACIFIC.							
Total	4,830	1,774	255	88	2,074	558	81
Less than 1 year	609	43	25	5	382	132	22
1 year	503	48	28	7	333	79	8
2 to 4 years	1,605	247	109	20	968	235	26
5 to 9 years	569	228	44	13	209	61	14
10 years and over	923	733	33	32	92	25	8
Not reported	621	475	16	11	90	26	3
NEW ENGLAND.							
MAINE.							
Total	29	18	7	....	3	....	1
Less than 1 year	1	....	....	....	1	....	....
1 year	2	....	1	....	....	....	1
2 to 4 years	6	3	2	....	1	....	....
5 to 9 years	4	2	1	....	1	....	....
10 years and over	13	10	3	....	....	....	....
Not reported	3	3	....	....	....	....	....
NEW HAMPSHIRE.							
Total	15	7	5	....	2	....	1
Less than 1 year	2	1	....	....	....	....	1
1 year	1	....	....	....	1	....	....
2 to 4 years	1	....	1	....	....	....	....
5 to 9 years	3	1	2	....	....	....	....
10 years and over	7	4	2	....	1	....	....
Not reported	1	1	....	....	....	....	....
VERMONT.							
Total	20	9	7	1	1	1	1
Less than 1 year	2	1	....	....	....	....	1
1 year	2	1	1	....	....	....	....
2 to 4 years	5	1	2	1	....	1	....
5 to 9 years	3	2	1	....	....	....	....
10 years and over	7	4	2	....	1	....	....
Not reported	1	....	1	....	....	....	....
MASSACHUSETTS.							
Total	124	64	42	3	10	1	4
Less than 1 year	5	1	3	....	1	....	....
1 year	9	1	4	....	4	....	....
2 to 4 years	23	8	8	....	4	1	2
5 to 9 years	22	9	9	3	1	....	....
10 years and over	57	39	16	....	....	....	2
Not reported	8	6	2	....	....	....	....
RHODE ISLAND.							
Total	41	16	9	4	12	....	....
Less than 1 year	5	1	....	....	4	....	....
1 year	2	1	....	....	1	....	....
2 to 4 years	10	3	4	1	2	....	....
5 to 9 years	5	3	....	....	2	....	....
10 years and over	18	8	5	2	3	....	....
Not reported	1	....	....	....	1	....	....
CONNECTICUT.							
Total	113	38	35	6	19	3	12
Less than 1 year	5	2	....	....	1	1	1
1 year	8	3	4	....	1	....	....
2 to 4 years	35	6	9	2	12	1	5
5 to 9 years	19	4	9	1	3	....	2
10 years and over	46	23	13	3	2	1	4
Not reported	....	....	....	....	....	....	....
MIDDLE ATLANTIC.							
NEW YORK.							
Total	939	618	109	81	64	53	14
Less than 1 year	43	5	3	2	15	16	2
1 year	76	27	10	10	11	14	4
2 to 4 years	151	86	24	12	11	14	4
5 to 9 years	131	83	15	17	11	3	2
10 years and over	425	324	48	36	12	4	1
Not reported	113	93	9	4	4	2	1
NEW JERSEY.							
Total	476	118	124	23	73	111	27
Less than 1 year	45	2	8	....	12	15	8
1 year	40	....	10	3	5	18	4
2 to 4 years	115	19	25	3	23	40	5
5 to 9 years	83	17	21	4	19	17	5
10 years and over	162	68	54	12	10	14	4
Not reported	31	12	6	1	4	7	1

TABLE 70.—COLORED FARMS CLASSIFIED BY TENURE AND TERM OF OCCUPANCY, BY DIVISIONS AND STATES: 1910—Continued.

DIVISION, STATE, AND TERM OF OCCUPANCY.	Total.	Owners, free.	Owners, mortgaged.	Part owners.	Cash tenants.	Share tenants.	Managers.
MIDDLE ATLANTIC—Continued.							
PENNSYLVANIA.							
Total	546	177	139	25	120	54	31
Less than 1 year	50	2	8	......	23	12	5
1 year	57	5	11	5	12	15	9
2 to 4 years	122	26	27	6	38	17	8
5 to 9 years	88	20	29	4	25	4	6
10 years and over	189	106	57	9	12	3	2
Not reported	40	18	7	1	10	3	1
EAST NORTH CENTRAL.							
OHIO.							
Total	1,950	584	399	330	180	429	28
Less than 1 year	230	18	24	29	35	115	9
1 year	169	13	27	28	37	58	6
2 to 4 years	396	63	69	78	51	129	6
5 to 9 years	292	87	63	55	29	57	1
10 years and over	690	332	161	124	15	52	6
Not reported	173	71	55	16	13	18	......
INDIANA.							
Total	805	161	153	158	66	252	15
Less than 1 year	92	5	3	11	15	53	5
1 year	73	2	4	12	8	46	1
2 to 4 years	158	16	18	23	23	73	5
5 to 9 years	112	16	29	24	5	37	1
10 years and over	282	91	78	76	12	23	2
Not reported	88	31	21	12	3	20	1
ILLINOIS.							
Total	1,425	284	286	219	227	391	18
Less than 1 year	135	5	10	17	37	62	4
1 year	150	9	13	13	38	75	2
2 to 4 years	317	27	43	33	83	127	4
5 to 9 years	244	41	59	57	29	55	3
10 years and over	426	146	109	85	26	57	3
Not reported	153	56	52	14	14	15	2
MICHIGAN.							
Total	946	378	290	117	38	114	9
Less than 1 year	76	6	19	14	8	26	3
1 year	75	14	17	13	9	21	1
2 to 4 years	159	41	58	22	7	30	1
5 to 9 years	152	62	51	22	3	12	2
10 years and over	416	224	120	44	8	18	2
Not reported	68	31	25	2	3	7	......
WISCONSIN.							
Total	591	378	106	65	25	13	4
Less than 1 year	45	24	5	4	7	5	......
1 year	40	26	5	5	2	1	1
2 to 4 years	118	65	26	16	7	3	1
5 to 9 years	89	55	24	8	1	1	......
10 years and over	256	181	38	28	7	1	1
Not reported	43	27	8	4	1	2	1
WEST NORTH CENTRAL.							
MINNESOTA.							
Total	293	140	33	21	77	20	2
Less than 1 year	28	6	4	5	5	7	1
1 year	17	8	2	2	2	3	......
2 to 4 years	50	17	7	3	15	7	1
5 to 9 years	50	20	6	4	19	1	......
10 years and over	90	41	13	4	30	2	......
Not reported	58	48	1	3	6	......	......
IOWA.							
Total	201	44	51	41	27	36	2
Less than 1 year	13	2	......	3	1	6	1
1 year	26	2	4	7	7	6	......
2 to 4 years	43	2	7	6	10	17	1
5 to 9 years	48	12	16	10	5	5	......
10 years and over	51	19	17	9	4	2	......
Not reported	20	7	7	6	......	......	......
MISSOURI.							
Total	3,666	798	691	620	443	1,073	41
Less than 1 year	510	31	35	48	94	288	14
1 year	296	20	24	32	68	144	8
2 to 4 years	741	68	97	108	141	317	10
5 to 9 years	528	97	118	106	64	138	5
10 years and over	1,322	490	355	295	57	122	3
Not reported	269	92	62	31	19	64	1

DIVISION, STATE, AND TERM OF OCCUPANCY.	Total.	Owners, free.	Owners, mortgaged.	Part owners.	Cash tenants.	Share tenants.	Managers.
WEST NORTH CENTRAL—Contd.							
NORTH DAKOTA.							
Total	743	686	31	10	7	7	2
Less than 1 year	7	6	......	......	......	1	......
1 year	26	21	......	2	......	2	1
2 to 4 years	171	161	3	......	2	4	1
5 to 9 years	127	117	6	2	2	......	......
10 years and over	242	224	12	4	2	......	......
Not reported	170	157	10	2	1	......	......
SOUTH DAKOTA.							
Total	2,808	2,644	28	64	43	22	7
Less than 1 year	64	54	......	1	3	5	1
1 year	56	41	3	4	4	3	1
2 to 4 years	251	214	4	15	14	3	1
5 to 9 years	212	189	7	11	4	1	......
10 years and over	515	478	9	22	3	2	1
Not reported	1,710	1,668	5	11	15	8	3
NEBRASKA.							
Total	462	336	17	16	55	37	1
Less than 1 year	51	18	1	3	16	13	......
1 year	38	23	2	2	4	7	......
2 to 4 years	108	75	2	4	17	10	......
5 to 9 years	78	63	2	1	7	4	1
10 years and over	116	100	6	4	5	1	......
Not reported	71	57	4	2	6	2	......
KANSAS.							
Total	1,691	503	286	309	199	373	21
Less than 1 year	233	20	14	24	60	108	7
1 year	144	30	14	16	30	51	3
2 to 4 years	360	102	42	61	56	96	3
5 to 9 years	278	75	40	66	32	60	5
10 years and over	498	206	137	109	13	32	1
Not reported	178	70	39	33	8	26	2
SOUTH ATLANTIC.							
DELAWARE.							
Total	922	198	149	59	75	425	16
Less than 1 year	143	6	5	1	15	111	5
1 year	110	7	10	4	12	75	2
2 to 4 years	235	19	32	16	31	132	5
5 to 9 years	162	42	38	13	10	57	2
10 years and over	230	110	54	24	4	36	2
Not reported	42	14	10	1	3	14	......
MARYLAND.							
Total	6,372	2,191	1,110	649	615	1,720	87
Less than 1 year	619	45	36	46	111	363	18
1 year	550	57	63	46	83	293	8
2 to 4 years	1,401	214	213	151	202	590	31
5 to 9 years	1,030	336	219	125	80	254	16
10 years and over	2,228	1,236	453	255	104	171	9
Not reported	544	303	126	26	35	49	5
DIST. OF COLUMBIA.							
Total	12	3	3	2	3	......	1
Less than 1 year	1	......	......	......	1	......	......
1 year	......	......	......	......	......	......	......
2 to 4 years	3	......	1	1	1	......	......
5 to 9 years	......	......	......	......	......	......	......
10 years and over	7	2	2	1	1	......	1
Not reported	1	1	......	......	......	......	......
VIRGINIA.							
Total	48,114	22,220	4,600	5,408	4,418	11,288	180
Less than 1 year	3,268	317	145	206	529	2,055	16
1 year	3,463	516	223	326	624	1,759	15
2 to 4 years	10,338	2,717	880	1,080	1,472	4,120	69
5 to 9 years	8,449	3,963	919	1,051	842	1,628	46
10 years and over	18,264	11,906	1,918	2,426	770	1,221	23
Not reported	4,332	2,801	515	319	181	505	11
WEST VIRGINIA.							
Total	708	417	70	71	63	80	7
Less than 1 year	41	13	4	5	9	10	......
1 year	57	19	7	3	10	16	2
2 to 4 years	147	65	25	13	15	27	2
5 to 9 years	131	70	17	18	14	11	1
10 years and over	288	222	14	31	10	10	1
Not reported	44	28	3	1	5	6	1

TABLE 70.—COLORED FARMS CLASSIFIED BY TENURE AND TERM OF OCCUPANCY, BY DIVISIONS AND STATES: 1910—Continued.

DIVISION, STATE, AND TERM OF OCCUPANCY.	COLORED FARMS: 1910.						
	Total.	Owners, free.	Owners, mortgaged.	Part owners.	Cash tenants.	Share tenants.	Managers.
SOUTH ATLANTIC—Continued.							
NORTH CAROLINA.							
Total	65,656	11,088	3,734	6,621	11,609	32,530	74
Less than 1 year	12,193	251	127	596	2,057	9,154	8
1 year	7,728	276	177	527	1,566	5,172	10
2 to 4 years	17,213	1,456	708	1,548	3,696	9,787	18
5 to 9 years	9,699	1,849	730	1,307	1,930	3,867	16
10 years and over	13,117	4,984	1,346	2,199	1,738	2,838	12
Not reported	5,706	2,272	646	444	622	1,712	10
SOUTH CAROLINA.							
Total	96,798	12,805	3,272	4,295	40,630	35,665	131
Less than 1 year	18,076	192	124	248	5,984	11,502	26
1 year	11,381	275	165	238	4,772	5,924	7
2 to 4 years	27,597	1,674	580	950	13,428	10,928	37
5 to 9 years	13,946	1,960	559	891	7,253	3,257	26
10 years and over	17,524	5,862	1,207	1,627	6,941	1,863	24
Not reported	8,274	2,842	637	341	2,252	2,191	11
GEORGIA.							
Total	122,559	9,649	3,210	2,839	50,479	56,259	123
Less than 1 year	31,523	253	215	296	9,680	21,060	19
1 year	17,015	289	192	230	6,861	9,430	13
2 to 4 years	35,281	1,588	687	674	16,863	15,439	30
5 to 9 years	16,224	1,800	595	572	8,579	4,654	24
10 years and over	14,241	3,871	936	820	6,209	2,382	23
Not reported	8,275	1,848	585	247	2,287	3,294	14
FLORIDA.							
Total	14,721	5,130	1,065	1,103	5,305	2,017	101
Less than 1 year	1,395	72	33	70	613	594	13
1 year	1,202	120	33	85	577	337	12
2 to 4 years	3,498	734	171	247	1,733	586	27
5 to 9 years	2,581	993	220	244	906	196	22
10 years and over	4,333	2,291	412	373	1,055	184	18
Not reported	1,712	920	196	84	383	120	9
EAST SOUTH CENTRAL.							
KENTUCKY.							
Total	11,730	3,488	978	1,463	602	5,159	40
Less than 1 year	2,378	74	60	164	174	1,899	7
1 year	1,262	92	48	119	80	921	2
2 to 4 years	2,425	488	167	296	178	1,283	13
5 to 9 years	1,514	582	200	280	71	373	8
10 years and over	2,969	1,745	347	492	66	311	8
Not reported	1,182	507	156	112	33	372	2
TENNESSEE.							
Total	38,308	5,826	1,914	2,960	11,801	15,756	51
Less than 1 year	8,974	124	115	278	2,415	6,028	14
1 year	4,823	215	136	237	1,612	2,618	5
2 to 4 years	9,731	762	441	720	3,744	4,049	15
5 to 9 years	5,272	1,068	392	614	1,875	1,314	9
10 years and over	6,834	2,947	596	959	1,417	909	6
Not reported	2,674	710	234	152	738	838	2
ALABAMA.							
Total	110,443	8,030	4,979	4,073	64,333	28,976	52
Less than 1 year	21,202	174	179	297	10,169	10,376	7
1 year	12,477	227	208	283	7,336	4,413	10
2 to 4 years	33,157	1,206	986	1,008	21,585	8,361	11
5 to 9 years	17,951	1,470	1,072	886	11,698	2,819	6
10 years and over	19,116	3,692	1,810	1,360	10,560	1,685	9
Not reported	6,540	1,261	724	239	2,985	1,322	9
MISSISSIPPI.							
Total	164,737	11,562	9,543	3,921	58,277	81,328	106
Less than 1 year	42,909	245	336	351	11,423	30,537	17
1 year	19,059	301	400	255	6,643	11,449	11
2 to 4 years	43,220	1,548	1,787	970	18,177	20,707	31
5 to 9 years	22,212	2,219	2,067	897	9,577	7,445	7
10 years and over	22,289	5,191	3,468	1,168	7,684	4,751	27
Not reported	15,048	2,058	1,485	280	4,773	6,439	13

DIVISION, STATE, AND TERM OF OCCUPANCY.	COLORED FARMS: 1910.						
	Total.	Owners, free.	Owners, mortgaged.	Part owners.	Cash tenants.	Share tenants.	Managers.
WEST SOUTH CENTRAL.							
ARKANSAS.							
Total	63,593	7,891	3,969	2,802	19,803	29,082	46
Less than 1 year	14,991	158	140	261	3,687	10,734	11
1 year	8,088	215	204	265	2,631	4,763	10
2 to 4 years	16,195	1,034	661	607	6,383	7,505	5
5 to 9 years	8,238	1,609	896	660	2,857	2,208	8
10 years and over	8,490	3,196	1,322	791	1,962	1,209	10
Not reported	7,591	1,679	746	218	2,283	2,663	2
LOUISIANA.							
Total	54,879	7,312	2,287	1,126	9,573	34,504	77
Less than 1 year	10,669	98	75	89	1,666	8,724	17
1 year	5,496	140	95	87	978	4,191	5
2 to 4 years	14,872	806	369	241	2,684	10,754	18
5 to 9 years	8,619	1,389	554	251	1,754	4,657	14
10 years and over	10,613	3,440	789	392	1,890	4,085	17
Not reported	4,610	1,439	405	66	601	2,093	6
OKLAHOMA.							
Total	20,671	7,713	2,206	1,231	1,997	7,497	27
Less than 1 year	4,681	463	133	185	634	3,254	12
1 year	2,433	376	129	152	368	1,407	1
2 to 4 years	4,005	1,135	353	285	599	1,630	3
5 to 9 years	2,594	1,377	434	229	139	411	4
10 years and over	3,127	2,050	588	232	76	179	2
Not reported	3,831	2,312	569	148	181	616	5
TEXAS.							
Total	69,918	13,034	3,644	4,554	6,367	42,238	81
Less than 1 year	16,261	323	201	417	1,454	13,849	17
1 year	8,570	299	224	331	858	6,848	10
2 to 4 years	17,789	1,375	843	997	1,976	12,579	19
5 to 9 years	8,964	2,043	727	950	975	4,252	17
10 years and over	12,883	6,796	1,165	1,503	800	2,612	7
Not reported	5,451	2,198	484	356	304	2,098	11
MOUNTAIN.							
MONTANA.							
Total	1,196	1,157	9	1	21	5	3
Less than 1 year	84	80	1		2	1	
1 year	18	15				3	
2 to 4 years	121	110	1	1	9		
5 to 9 years	142	138	2		2		
10 years and over	136	127	2		5	1	1
Not reported	695	687	3		3		2
IDAHO.							
Total	405	328	8	7	54	8	
Less than 1 year	15	1	2		10	2	
1 year	19	7	1		9	2	
2 to 4 years	56	32	1	2	18	3	
5 to 9 years	63	50	2	2	9		
10 years and over	164	154	2	2	6		
Not reported	88	84		1	2	1	
WYOMING.							
Total	65	56	4	1	1	2	1
Less than 1 year	8	5	1		1		1
1 year	2		2				
2 to 4 years	13	11		1	1		
5 to 9 years	6	6					
10 years and over	16	16					
Not reported	20	18	1			1	
COLORADO.							
Total	574	442	16	8	41	66	1
Less than 1 year	44	6	1		12	25	
1 year	35	6	2	1	14	11	1
2 to 4 years	54	17	3	2	10	22	
5 to 9 years	20	10	3	2	3	2	
10 years and over	32	23	5	3		1	
Not reported	389	380	2		2	5	
NEW MEXICO.							
Total	2,148	2,103	8	10	11	12	4
Less than 1 year	35	17	1	1	3	11	2
1 year	122	119		2		1	
2 to 4 years	156	151	2	2	1		
5 to 9 years	132	126	4	1			1
10 years and over	914	908		4	1		1
Not reported	789	782	1		6		

TABLE **70.**—COLORED FARMS CLASSIFIED BY TENURE AND TERM OF OCCUPANCY, BY DIVISIONS AND STATES: 1910—Continued.

DIVISION, STATE, AND TERM OF OCCUPANCY.	COLORED FARMS: 1910.							DIVISION, STATE, AND TERM OF OCCUPANCY.	COLORED FARMS: 1910.						
	Total.	Owners, free.	Owners, mortgaged.	Part owners.	Cash tenants.	Share tenants.	Managers.		Total.	Owners, free.	Owners, mortgaged.	Part owners.	Cash tenants.	Share tenants.	Managers.
MOUNTAIN—Contd.								PACIFIC.							
ARIZONA.								WASHINGTON.							
Total.............	3,203	3,147	2	....	41	2	11	Total.............	1,125	651	32	18	325	88	11
Less than 1 year......	31	26	1	....	4	....	......	Less than 1 year......	111	19	2	....	76	9	5
1 year...............	45	34	....	....	9	....	2	1 year...............	92	8	3	2	63	15	1
2 to 4 years..........	202	185	....	....	15	2	......	2 to 4 years..........	253	71	8	....	125	47	2
5 to 9 years..........	224	216	....	....	7	....	1	5 to 9 years..........	118	65	7	3	34	8	1
10 years and over.....	857	851	....	....	1	....	5	10 years and over......	322	279	9	17	17	4	2
Not reported..........	1,844	1,835	1	....	5	....	3	Not reported..........	229	209	3	2	10	5	......
UTAH.								OREGON.							
Total.............	276	207	2	7	54	5	1	Total.............	627	439	28	11	103	38	8
Less than 1 year......	14	2	....	....	11	1	......	Less than 1 year......	47	11	5	1	17	9	4
1 year...............	16	4	....	1	11	....	......	1 year...............	37	14	3	....	13	5	2
2 to 4 years..........	50	18	1	3	24	3	1	2 to 4 years..........	114	56	5	2	40	11	......
5 to 9 years..........	31	27	....	1	3	....	......	5 to 9 years..........	93	56	6	6	2	9	1
10 years and over.....	75	73	....	1	....	1	......	10 years and over......	269	249	7	4	6	3	......
Not reported..........	90	83	1	1	5	....	......	Not reported..........	67	53	2	2	8	1	1
NEVADA.								CALIFORNIA.							
Total.............	161	152	....	....	6	2	1	Total.............	3,078	684	195	59	1,646	432	62
Less than 1 year......	2	....	....	....	1	....	1	Less than 1 year......	451	13	18	4	289	114	13
1 year...............	....	....	....	....	....	....	......	1 year...............	374	26	22	5	257	59	5
2 to 4 years..........	20	18	....	....	2	....	......	2 to 4 years..........	1,238	120	96	18	803	177	24
5 to 9 years..........	13	12	....	....	1	....	......	5 to 9 years..........	358	107	31	8	156	44	12
10 years and over.....	62	61	....	....	1	....	......	10 years and over......	332	205	17	17	69	18	6
Not reported..........	64	61	....	....	1	2	......	Not reported..........	325	213	11	7	72	20	2

21857°—18——41

TABLE **71.**—FARMS OPERATED BY NEGROES—NUMBER, ACREAGE, AND VALUE OF LAND AND BUILDINGS, AND OF IMPLEMENTS AND MACHINERY, BY STATES AND COUNTIES: 1910.

[Counties in which no farms operated by Negroes were reported are omitted.]

STATE AND COUNTY.	Number of farms.	FARM ACREAGE.				VALUE OF FARM LAND, BUILDINGS, AND IMPLEMENTS AND MACHINERY.					
		Total.	Improved.	Woodland.	Other un-improved.	Total.	Land and buildings.			Implements and ma-chinery.
							Total.	Land.	Buildings.	

ALABAMA.

Total	110,387	5,083,552	3,561,674	1,208,660	313,218	$77,157,965	$73,834,072	$59,258,839	$14,575,233	$3,323,893
Autauga	2,111	77,319	56,954	18,642	1,723	1,136,806	1,099,440	849,326	250,114	37,366
Baldwin	325	11,869	4,637	6,140	1,092	245,440	235,991	153,808	82,183	9,449
Barbour	2,805	200,166	132,279	48,507	19,380	2,081,697	1,993,453	1,613,313	380,140	88,244
Bibb	647	29,218	17,014	10,891	1,313	512,064	499,535	403,166	96,369	12,529
Blount	90	5,496	2,402	2,818	276	66,369	63,960	46,315	17,645	2,409
Bullock	4,056	195,756	166,959	18,433	10,364	2,819,735	2,707,987	2,218,018	489,969	111,748
Butler	2,034	102,799	65,423	30,592	6,784	1,420,408	1,364,513	1,034,258	330,255	55,895
Calhoun	706	30,484	20,265	8,954	1,265	514,401	491,223	396,746	94,477	23,178
Chambers	2,771	156,935	104,541	35,303	17,091	2,713,203	2,599,234	2,060,101	539,133	113,969
Cherokee	355	16,072	10,896	4,486	690	268,946	258,184	210,199	47,985	10,762
Chilton	506	29,529	14,459	12,971	2,099	400,153	380,715	265,390	115,325	19,438
Choctaw	1,935	112,939	57,109	51,975	3,855	987,647	926,221	665,221	261,000	61,426
Clarke	2,673	130,581	67,787	49,443	13,351	1,261,505	1,199,291	887,129	312,162	62,214
Clay	351	15,293	9,455	4,888	950	200,044	190,681	145,417	45,264	9,363
Cleburne	97	4,009	2,353	1,620	36	113,295	107,315	46,570	60,745	5,980
Coffee	665	40,162	28,987	10,841	334	581,632	561,476	462,434	99,042	20,156
Colbert	931	48,130	37,817	8,654	1,659	1,022,718	981,750	845,417	136,333	40,968
Conecuh	1,568	66,845	40,777	23,358	2,710	1,028,930	974,192	735,428	238,764	54,738
Coosa	978	68,026	31,117	28,666	8,243	571,184	543,701	423,906	119,795	27,483
Covington	429	25,469	14,659	10,611	199	375,406	360,788	287,103	73,685	14,618
Crenshaw	1,006	54,731	36,997	12,940	4,794	743,711	718,170	570,507	147,663	25,541
Cullman	48	3,349	1,598	1,537	214	31,051	29,470	24,545	4,925	1,581
Dale	784	48,863	33,963	11,169	3,731	639,843	612,036	509,431	102,605	27,807
Dallas	7,419	230,128	198,899	25,405	5,824	3,948,153	3,724,731	2,875,020	849,711	223,422
Dekalb	73	2,821	1,742	1,055	24	59,589	56,893	44,733	12,160	2,696
Elmore	1,727	79,212	52,954	22,013	4,245	1,356,964	1,304,560	991,467	313,093	52,404
Escambia	267	11,623	4,851	4,737	2,035	189,055	179,013	123,198	55,815	10,042
Etowah	213	10,471	6,454	3,681	336	179,046	172,861	144,711	28,150	6,185
Fayette	309	17,711	8,909	8,008	794	178,386	171,434	136,113	35,321	6,952
Franklin	118	6,564	4,431	1,856	277	125,216	120,679	99,564	21,115	4,537
Geneva	365	21,313	13,768	5,742	1,803	372,367	359,137	298,242	60,895	13,230
Greene	3,536	149,827	108,986	33,446	7,395	1,928,535	1,825,388	1,481,900	343,488	103,147
Hale	3,553	144,646	102,239	28,539	13,868	2,493,068	2,407,295	1,973,358	433,937	85,773
Henry	1,574	107,379	75,730	27,363	4,286	1,299,329	1,241,407	1,021,413	219,994	57,922
Houston	853	42,785	32,321	10,139	325	751,804	716,895	589,795	127,100	34,909
Jackson	391	15,020	11,391	3,340	289	302,235	289,531	246,891	42,640	12,704
Jefferson	462	12,589	7,636	4,699	254	909,207	888,370	750,785	137,585	20,837
Lamar	520	38,001	15,825	17,460	4,716	325,352	309,667	245,732	63,935	15,685
Lauderdale	909	37,978	30,225	6,072	1,681	863,994	835,031	711,503	123,528	28,963
Lawrence	1,181	53,766	43,376	8,721	1,669	1,036,368	995,698	852,468	143,230	40,670
Lee	2,574	166,894	111,749	40,552	14,593	2,302,904	2,195,651	1,726,842	468,809	107,253
Limestone	1,780	66,897	55,855	10,282	760	1,466,245	1,415,958	1,166,488	249,470	50,287
Lowndes	5,755	182,545	149,984	18,586	13,975	2,899,485	2,785,363	2,218,171	567,192	114,122
Macon	3,842	169,163	130,719	34,145	4,299	2,971,032	2,838,121	2,162,538	675,583	132,911
Madison	2,595	117,569	92,162	20,865	4,542	2,656,683	2,571,932	2,173,925	398,007	84,751
Marengo	5,147	188,779	140,756	35,664	12,359	2,664,287	2,517,295	2,020,581	496,714	146,992
Marion	85	6,672	2,683	3,672	317	48,191	45,822	35,202	10,620	2,369
Marshall	145	6,612	4,480	1,601	531	88,095	84,640	69,205	15,435	3,455
Mobile	286	17,682	2,283	13,741	1,658	269,993	258,500	186,240	72,260	11,493
Monroe	2,623	111,740	69,862	37,435	4,443	1,247,585	1,180,760	886,305	294,455	66,825
Montgomery	5,578	230,780	194,590	22,919	13,271	5,639,324	5,451,041	4,667,796	783,245	188,283
Morgan	649	28,938	19,441	8,503	994	632,317	607,656	504,693	102,963	24,661
Perry	4,004	167,444	127,012	28,733	11,699	2,724,638	2,604,177	2,216,226	387,951	120,461
Pickens	2,190	118,450	73,997	33,857	10,596	1,293,836	1,233,008	967,048	265,960	60,828
Pike	1,820	108,631	80,910	22,046	5,675	1,654,193	1,613,513	1,391,987	221,526	40,680
Randolph	917	48,769	30,417	15,421	2,931	676,440	648,960	524,544	124,416	27,480
Russell	2,456	151,977	113,796	26,693	11,488	1,741,176	1,646,392	1,296,814	349,578	94,784
St. Clair	372	19,961	11,210	8,392	359	234,571	221,800	169,170	52,630	12,771
Shelby	601	41,302	18,062	20,633	2,607	449,096	430,110	310,369	119,741	18,986
Sumter	3,880	183,935	132,305	39,512	12,118	2,370,769	2,248,539	1,823,019	425,520	122,230
Talladega	2,197	97,011	67,892	25,761	3,358	1,594,858	1,521,111	1,222,181	298,930	73,747
Tallapoosa	1,660	94,362	59,645	23,840	10,877	1,399,382	1,350,944	1,078,859	272,085	48,438
Tuscaloosa	1,651	84,161	47,328	33,745	3,088	1,302,179	1,245,991	1,030,174	215,817	56,188
Walker	64	2,968	1,258	1,577	133	47,805	45,442	32,557	12,885	2,363
Washington	598	32,804	11,646	20,667	491	310,185	294,432	211,342	83,090	15,753
Wilcox	5,575	181,382	133,397	33,903	14,082	2,416,425	2,277,598	1,724,822	552,776	138,827
Winston	2	250	50	200	....	1,415	1,400	1,100	300	15

TABLE 71.—FARMS OPERATED BY NEGROES—NUMBER, ACREAGE, AND VALUE OF LAND AND BUILDINGS, AND OF IMPLEMENTS AND MACHINERY, BY STATES AND COUNTIES: 1910—Continued.

[Counties in which no farms operated by Negroes were reported are omitted.]

STATE AND COUNTY.	Number of farms.	FARM ACREAGE.				VALUE OF FARM LAND, BUILDINGS, AND IMPLEMENTS AND MACHINERY.					
		Total.	Improved.	Woodland.	Other un-improved.	Total.	Land and buildings.			Implements and machinery.
							Total.	Land.	Buildings.	
ARIZONA.										
Total	12	1,222	186	120	916	$32,021	$30,100	$23,500	$6,600	$1,921
Cochise	5	645	111	....	534	8,795	8,150	5,700	2,450	645
Gila	1	85	2	....	83	2,125	2,000	1,700	300	125
Graham	1	....	....	....	....	500	....	....	....	500
Maricopa	4	332	72	120	140	19,071	18,450	15,200	3,250	621
Yavapai	1	160	1	....	159	1,530	1,500	900	600	30
ARKANSAS.										
Total	63,578	2,652,684	1,772,702	797,566	82,416	$71,766,910	$68,978,464	$57,920,360	$11,058,104	$2,788,446
Arkansas	677	33,443	20,307	12,036	1,100	619,042	591,947	492,882	99,065	27,095
Ashley	1,964	66,040	52,249	12,531	1,260	2,029,814	1,911,099	1,550,868	360,231	118,715
Benton	1	20	18	2	....	3,540	3,500	3,200	300	40
Boone	1	31	31	....	....	750	600	600	....	150
Bradley	357	25,220	10,594	8,469	6,157	249,807	239,044	170,804	68,240	10,763
Calhoun	435	31,451	11,899	18,067	1,485	286,204	273,554	204,352	69,202	12,650
Carroll	3	212	177	30	5	3,325	3,000	2,350	650	325
Chicot	3,302	85,181	65,505	18,469	1,207	3,582,796	3,472,733	2,859,513	613,220	110,063
Clark	777	46,992	23,512	21,473	2,007	524,201	499,806	394,711	105,095	24,395
Cleveland	580	34,562	15,346	18,173	1,043	347,347	328,944	245,714	83,230	18,403
Columbia	1,441	108,398	55,356	42,919	10,123	1,242,417	1,184,147	950,351	233,796	58,270
Conway	1,520	75,993	48,422	25,922	1,649	1,853,384	1,773,711	1,482,918	290,793	79,673
Craighead	24	809	599	210	....	34,340	32,940	27,720	5,220	1,400
Crawford	212	8,277	6,638	1,517	122	267,745	259,390	224,395	34,995	8,355
Crittenden	3,380	117,060	98,314	16,214	2,532	5,619,482	5,361,362	4,642,220	719,142	258,120
Cross	939	35,738	26,029	7,978	1,731	872,854	825,353	669,328	156,025	47,501
Dallas	416	28,473	11,803	12,805	3,865	261,248	248,600	190,190	58,410	12,648
Desha	2,161	106,545	68,845	36,810	890	2,957,383	2,870,135	2,410,059	460,076	87,248
Drew	1,983	96,996	57,485	35,885	3,626	1,776,176	1,696,632	1,393,737	302,895	79,544
Faulkner	714	38,637	23,413	13,691	1,533	559,789	522,060	407,213	114,847	37,729
Franklin	43	2,506	1,790	535	181	43,635	41,225	33,190	8,035	2,410
Fulton	7	555	222	333	....	5,857	5,450	3,700	1,750	407
Garland	34	1,937	643	1,253	41	28,045	26,105	18,883	7,222	1,940
Grant	151	11,449	4,369	6,986	94	124,827	118,304	95,009	23,295	6,523
Greene	1	27	15	12	....	500	500	450	50	....
Hempstead	2,047	102,124	66,550	32,172	3,402	1,612,385	1,527,263	1,193,154	334,109	85,122
Hot Spring	101	4,620	2,524	2,075	21	88,142	82,855	57,755	25,100	5,287
Howard	537	25,149	17,501	6,997	651	402,342	386,346	317,423	68,923	15,996
Independence	83	4,185	2,519	1,586	80	87,115	83,255	72,800	10,455	3,860
Izard	47	3,249	1,275	1,945	29	22,941	21,490	17,576	3,914	1,451
Jackson	796	36,217	26,166	9,892	159	1,372,996	1,328,148	1,149,213	178,935	44,848
Jefferson	6,346	180,656	139,616	39,123	1,917	6,494,596	6,326,960	5,469,476	857,484	167,636
Johnson	46	1,172	1,112	58	2	37,261	36,305	32,780	3,525	956
Lafayette	738	39,688	23,695	15,763	230	695,602	666,898	539,020	127,878	28,704
Lawrence	69	2,780	1,993	787	....	54,029	51,681	43,176	8,505	2,348
Lee	3,351	128,230	95,665	31,776	789	4,047,589	3,767,717	2,931,154	836,563	279,872
Lincoln	2,053	71,004	47,046	23,289	669	1,745,069	1,668,435	1,431,798	236,637	76,634
Little River	975	46,973	29,125	17,152	696	822,592	794,884	688,654	106,230	27,708
Logan	74	3,399	2,702	692	5	120,626	116,505	100,810	15,695	4,121
Lonoke	2,296	64,966	53,623	11,192	151	2,594,527	2,522,996	2,183,681	339,315	71,531
Madison	10	864	336	528	....	5,050	4,755	3,840	915	295
Miller	545	27,736	16,683	10,258	795	502,868	488,233	418,970	69,263	14,635
Mississippi	1,872	53,854	48,574	4,983	297	3,145,960	3,059,323	2,726,190	333,133	86,637
Monroe	2,131	79,516	61,454	17,625	437	2,394,479	2,304,253	1,922,028	382,225	90,226
Montgomery	50	2,840	1,127	1,628	85	28,375	26,805	22,080	4,725	1,570
Nevada	840	60,600	32,405	22,894	5,301	522,628	491,481	378,670	112,811	31,147
Newton	1	120	25	....	95	525	500	475	25	25
Ouachita	1,296	109,687	48,558	48,515	12,614	1,024,064	982,476	783,297	199,179	41,588
Perry	141	5,893	3,715	1,871	307	113,945	108,240	92,200	16,040	5,705
Phillips	4,185	132,948	108,848	22,863	1,237	5,022,491	4,790,451	3,974,265	816,186	232,040
Pike	99	5,688	2,937	2,716	35	85,003	81,259	65,319	15,940	3,744
Poinsett	244	8,741	6,646	2,095	....	336,887	327,365	270,615	56,750	9,522
Polk	6	669	211	448	10	3,947	3,860	3,410	450	87
Pope	233	11,899	8,375	3,469	55	307,738	295,945	247,839	48,106	11,793
Prairie	620	26,503	18,852	7,284	367	888,320	864,150	726,843	137,307	24,170
Pulaski	3,002	90,992	68,479	21,149	1,364	4,634,098	4,531,219	4,011,459	519,760	102,879
Randolph	54	2,904	1,955	832	117	134,280	129,925	116,355	13,570	4,355
St. Francis	2,930	107,922	79,832	25,679	2,411	3,266,251	3,153,303	2,616,632	536,671	112,948
Saline	283	10,093	6,404	3,296	393	274,664	262,594	211,074	51,520	12,070
Scott	1	114	17	6	91	1,075	1,000	900	100	75
Searcy	2	186	29	157	....	1,400	1,300	1,175	125	100
Sebastian	106	4,280	2,848	1,312	120	237,628	233,260	211,835	21,425	4,368
Sevier	310	18,772	10,607	7,290	875	242,153	230,250	185,775	44,475	11,903

NEGRO POPULATION.

TABLE 71.—FARMS OPERATED BY NEGROES—NUMBER, ACREAGE, AND VALUE OF LAND AND BUILDINGS, AND OF IMPLEMENTS AND MACHINERY, BY STATES AND COUNTIES: 1910—Continued.

[Counties in which no farms operated by Negroes were reported are omitted.]

STATE AND COUNTY.	Number of farms.	FARM ACREAGE.				VALUE OF FARM LAND, BUILDINGS, AND IMPLEMENTS AND MACHINERY.				
		Total.	Improved.	Woodland.	Other un-improved.	Total.	Land and buildings.			Implements and machinery.
							Total.	Land.	Buildings.	
ARKANSAS—Continued.										
Sharp	13	504	335	159	10	$3,822	$3,650	$2,895	$755	$172
Stone	11	834	256	578	....	6,540	6,050	4,950	1,100	490
Union	1,319	108,208	47,916	58,347	1,945	873,901	832,662	658,902	173,760	41,239
Van Buren	38	3,862	1,397	2,465	....	33,043	30,398	22,448	7,950	2,645
Washington	20	1,477	732	683	62	29,458	28,570	24,650	3,920	888
White	160	9,205	5,161	3,960	84	140,783	132,745	102,310	30,435	8,038
Woodruff	2,173	85,293	67,071	14,586	3,636	3,781,315	3,677,021	3,225,395	451,626	104,294
Yell	191	9,516	6,224	3,071	221	231,899	223,542	184,737	38,805	8,357
CALIFORNIA.										
Total	159	52,930	40,836	4,198	7,896	$2,136,975	$2,100,935	$1,994,290	$106,645	$36,040
Butte	2	197	77	20	100	2,345	2,200	1,950	250	145
Colusa	1	240	240	....	....	9,675	9,600	8,100	1,500	75
Contra Costa	1	6	6	....	....	2,605	2,500	1,300	1,200	105
Eldorado	5	800	218	287	295	13,500	12,500	9,900	2,600	1,000
Fresno	22	664	542	50	72	417,825	412,800	406,785	6,015	5,025
Glenn	1	12	12	....	....	1,400	1,200	1,100	100	200
Imperial	1	150	150	....	....	30,150	30,000	29,000	1,000	150
Inyo	1	120	6	....	114	3,100	3,000	2,500	500	100
Kern	9	1,286	240	190	856	40,415	38,800	35,000	3,800	1,615
Kings	5	530	530	....	....	39,120	38,750	37,850	900	370
Los Angeles	20	257	203	38	16	124,190	121,800	107,370	14,430	2,390
Madera	4	30,400	30,300	....	100	675,600	671,000	659,600	11,400	4,600
Mariposa	6	1,935	870	45	1,020	27,080	24,880	20,880	4,000	2,200
Mendocino	1	22	12	....	10	2,050	2,000	1,000	1,000	50
Orange	2	44	37	7	....	13,900	13,600	13,100	500	300
Riverside	14	750	485	....	265	95,425	90,200	86,100	4,100	5,225
San Bernardino	4	97	82	....	15	28,135	27,800	25,440	2,360	335
San Diego	12	1,125	465	16	644	56,890	55,700	53,495	2,205	1,190
San Francisco	1	1	1	....	....	2,000	2,000	2,000	....	905
San Joaquin	6	966	374	....	592	45,965	45,060	33,300	11,760	905
San Luis Obispo	1	6	6	....	....	1,065	1,050	900	150	15
San Mateo	1	2	....	....	2	1,175	1,000	800	200	175
Santa Cruz	1	100	40	....	60	5,100	5,000	4,600	400	100
Shasta	1	20	8	....	12	825	800	700	100	25
Siskiyou	3	405	102	265	38	8,525	8,200	7,200	1,000	325
Solano	1	65	65	....	....	25,400	25,000	21,000	4,000	400
Sonoma	1	80	80	....	....	7,075	7,000	6,500	500	75
Stanislaus	1	8	8	....	....	5,100	5,000	2,000	3,000	100
Sutter	3	210	205	....	5	13,195	13,000	10,575	2,425	195
Tehama	5	574	474	....	100	35,150	33,700	29,600	4,100	1,450
Trinity	3	260	37	183	40	2,325	2,100	1,650	450	225
Tulare	11	6,890	785	2,565	3,540	130,270	128,345	122,145	6,200	1,925
Yolo	9	4,708	4,176	532	....	270,400	265,350	250,850	14,500	5,050
COLORADO.										
Total	81	32,003	4,776	816	26,411	$492,465	$477,520	$427,930	$49,590	$14,945
Adams	4	963	408	....	555	43,200	42,050	39,850	2,200	1,150
Arapahoe	10	18,190	455	322	17,413	115,385	114,070	110,820	3,250	1,315
Boulder	2	137	137	....	....	30,450	30,000	21,300	8,700	450
Conejos	2	109	107	....	2	4,250	4,150	3,400	750	100
El Paso	9	2,180	900	22	1,258	29,120	27,200	20,600	6,600	1,920
Fremont	2	128	8	120	....	4,350	4,300	4,000	300	50
Garfield	2	311	44	50	217	6,075	5,500	5,250	250	575
Grand	1	160	50	....	110	2,300	2,000	1,800	200	300
Gunnison	1	80	80	....	....	3,050	3,000	2,800	200	50
Huerfano	2	319	160	80	79	3,500	3,300	3,050	250	200
Jefferson	2	370	35	....	335	8,950	8,500	7,700	800	450
La Plata	3	480	124	220	136	13,300	12,500	11,600	900	800
Larimer	1	152	152	....	....	20,000	20,000	12,000	8,000	....
Mesa	4	152	30	....	122	17,090	16,700	14,900	1,800	390
Morgan	2	173	27	....	46	5,725	5,600	4,400	1,200	125
Otero	8	836	406	....	430	59,410	57,050	52,450	4,600	2,360
Prowers	1	320	50	....	270	3,215	3,200	3,140	60	15
Pueblo	10	755	509	2	444	32,610	31,300	28,480	2,820	1,310
Routt	1	160	20	....	140	1,150	1,000	940	60	150
San Miguel	1	160	30	....	130	4,200	4,000	3,300	700	200
Sedgwick	2	440	300	....	40	26,900	25,600	23,400	2,200	1,300
Washington	8	2,108	612	....	1,496	21,260	20,300	18,110	2,190	960
Weld	3	3,320	132	....	3,188	36,975	36,200	34,640	1,560	775

TABLE 71.—FARMS OPERATED BY NEGROES—NUMBER, ACREAGE, AND VALUE OF LAND AND BUILDINGS, AND OF IMPLEMENTS AND MACHINERY, BY STATES AND COUNTIES: 1910—Continued.

[Counties in which no farms operated by Negroes were reported are omitted.]

STATE AND COUNTY.	Number of farms.	FARM ACREAGE.				VALUE OF FARM LAND, BUILDINGS, AND IMPLEMENTS AND MACHINERY.					
		Total.	Improved.	Woodland.	Other un-improved.	Total.	Land and buildings.			Implements and machinery.
							Total.	Land.	Buildings.	

CONNECTICUT.

STATE AND COUNTY.	Number of farms.	Total.	Improved.	Woodland.	Other un-improved.	Total.	Total.	Land.	Buildings.	Implements and machinery.
Total	105	5,440	2,231	2,090	1,119	$357,444	$341,195	$192,770	$148,425	$16,249
Fairfield	24	600	322	169	109	100,159	96,200	45,550	50,650	3,959
Hartford	29	430	310	41	79	85,025	81,145	42,895	38,250	3,880
Litchfield	15	1,644	890	435	319	76,325	72,750	51,450	21,300	3,575
Middlesex	3	119	84	35	....	8,410	8,000	3,800	4,200	410
New Haven	7	154	63	56	35	11,280	11,100	8,275	2,825	180
New London	16	2,029	454	1,172	403	60,230	57,200	33,900	23,300	3,030
Tolland	3	99	25	24	50	3,625	3,300	1,700	1,600	325
Windham	8	365	83	158	124	12,390	11,500	5,200	6,300	890

DELAWARE.

STATE AND COUNTY.	Number of farms.	Total.	Improved.	Woodland.	Other un-improved.	Total.	Total.	Land.	Buildings.	Implements and machinery.
Total	922	56,973	37,076	16,268	3,629	$2,081,806	$1,981,716	$1,451,457	$530,259	$100,090
Kent	353	20,623	14,016	4,775	1,832	931,179	887,940	639,711	248,229	43,239
New Castle	98	4,679	3,692	604	383	221,765	208,600	142,050	66,550	13,165
Sussex	471	31,671	19,368	10,889	1,414	928,862	885,176	669,696	215,480	43,686

DISTRICT OF COLUMBIA.

STATE AND COUNTY.	Number of farms.	Total.	Improved.	Woodland.	Other un-improved.	Total.	Total.	Land.	Buildings.	Implements and machinery.
Total	12	95	95	....	....	$90,355	$89,400	$66,600	$22,800	$955

FLORIDA.

STATE AND COUNTY.	Number of farms.	Total.	Improved.	Woodland.	Other un-improved.	Total.	Total.	Land.	Buildings.	Implements and machinery.
Total	14,698	768,140	482,140	258,160	27,840	$12,475,410	$11,874,283	$9,264,332	$2,609,951	$601,127
Alachua	1,468	65,792	43,332	19,957	2,503	778,499	738,821	572,857	165,964	39,678
Baker	7	418	206	208	4	5,690	5,425	3,815	1,610	265
Bradford	296	12,365	6,550	5,669	146	217,286	207,970	151,960	56,010	9,316
Brevard	53	1,663	465	542	656	242,275	238,950	204,225	34,725	3,325
Calhoun	77	5,096	1,681	3,415	....	47,643	45,740	38,230	7,510	1,903
Citrus	10	1,058	284	736	38	11,430	10,900	8,700	2,200	530
Clay	31	1,603	430	1,153	20	49,990	48,075	31,650	16,425	1,915
Columbia	855	61,508	39,191	21,843	474	538,376	513,985	399,643	114,342	24,391
Dade	69	2,020	732	955	333	137,211	133,280	121,520	11,760	3,931
De Soto	12	484	124	215	145	45,806	45,000	41,350	3,650	806
Duval	299	5,438	1,821	2,961	656	420,856	409,085	297,777	111,308	11,773
Escambia	41	2,170	416	1,689	65	84,641	80,180	63,770	16,410	4,461
Franklin	1	13	8	1	4	140	130	130	....	10
Gadsden	985	55,416	28,626	21,765	5,025	915,909	867,378	665,436	201,942	48,531
Hamilton	430	28,798	20,496	8,081	221	366,453	351,090	281,670	69,420	15,363
Hernando	65	4,827	1,521	895	2,411	109,554	106,175	95,235	10,940	3,379
Hillsborough	115	3,688	1,509	2,011	108	252,429	244,900	209,214	35,686	7,529
Holmes	35	2,294	717	1,576	1	26,342	25,030	19,695	5,335	1,312
Jackson	1,895	107,808	78,287	28,224	1,297	1,454,025	1,389,503	1,128,594	260,909	64,522
Jefferson	1,610	76,861	64,445	9,599	2,817	995,101	925,716	712,555	213,161	69,388
Lafayette	20	1,324	808	456	60	10,395	9,985	7,180	2,805	410
Lake	121	4,856	2,042	2,266	548	151,647	147,200	114,890	32,310	4,447
Lee	7	263	61	23	179	34,735	34,500	31,735	2,765	235
Leon	1,649	79,560	62,125	15,778	1,657	1,318,640	1,236,396	979,884	256,512	82,244
Levy	175	11,649	5,053	6,400	196	135,491	130,105	101,260	28,845	5,386
Liberty	82	6,337	2,198	4,094	45	79,385	75,120	32,015	43,105	4,265
Madison	929	48,012	38,712	7,885	1,415	693,232	655,400	524,551	130,849	37,832
Manatee	54	310	299	11	....	90,788	89,265	83,848	5,417	1,523
Marion	1,097	45,563	22,500	22,575	488	728,473	679,349	472,254	207,095	49,124
Monroe	11	1,201	229	172	800	61,200	61,200	57,660	3,540	....
Nassau	88	4,890	752	3,140	998	88,343	83,730	66,420	17,310	4,613
Orange	141	5,511	1,649	3,610	261	482,651	467,800	370,140	97,660	14,851
Osceola	9	318	64	254	....	13,715	13,200	10,775	2,425	515
Palm Beach	86	2,294	589	1,588	117	124,210	122,365	95,250	27,115	1,845
Pasco	16	1,058	393	205	460	16,395	15,655	13,475	2,180	740
Polk	43	950	459	470	21	80,369	78,250	64,325	13,925	2,119
Putnam	294	11,319	3,877	6,629	813	275,272	263,134	163,529	99,605	12,138
St. Johns	34	1,131	460	649	22	83,536	79,875	68,420	11,455	3,661
St. Lucie	43	1,255	344	869	42	108,156	106,850	88,950	17,900	1,305
Santa Rosa	65	3,413	1,029	2,320	64	50,492	48,164	35,029	13,135	2,328
Sumter	143	4,017	2,187	1,761	69	97,728	92,880	73,147	19,683	4,898
Suwannee	697	52,124	30,977	19,721	1,426	539,697	508,861	388,809	120,052	30,836
Taylor	21	858	600	258	....	15,694	15,196	12,926	2,270	498
Volusia	111	2,041	1,021	958	62	134,747	131,780	97,585	34,195	2,967
Wakulla	87	7,062	3,444	3,157	461	48,492	43,744	32,848	10,896	4,755
Walton	129	8,985	2,831	6,137	17	88,928	79,516	59,441	20,075	4,412
Washington	282	22,519	6,545	15,279	695	28,332	217,480	169,960	47,520	10,852

TABLE 71.—FARMS OPERATED BY NEGROES—NUMBER, ACREAGE, AND VALUE OF LAND AND BUILDINGS, AND OF IMPLEMENTS AND MACHINERY, BY STATES AND COUNTIES: 1910—Continued.

[Counties in which no farms operated by Negroes were reported are omitted.]

STATE AND COUNTY.	Number of farms.	FARM ACREAGE.				VALUE OF FARM LAND, BUILDINGS, AND IMPLEMENTS AND MACHINERY.					
		Total.	Improved.	Woodland.	Other unimproved.	Total.	Land and buildings.				Implements and machinery.
							Total.	Land.	Buildings.	

GEORGIA.

STATE AND COUNTY.	Number of farms.	Total.	Improved.	Woodland.	Other unimproved.	Total.	Total.	Land.	Buildings.	Implements and machinery.
Total	122,554	7,091,949	4,791,460	1,944,721	355,768	$133,435,929	$128,877,032	$105,849,590	$23,027,442	$4,558,897
Appling	264	26,839	5,493	20,863	483	235,405	226,425	174,840	51,585	8,980
Baker	908	55,285	45,322	8,713	1,250	583,151	546,985	414,669	132,316	36,166
Baldwin	960	85,967	48,438	32,581	4,948	970,291	914,775	760,235	154,540	55,516
Banks	428	18,413	12,245	4,481	1,687	445,804	434,420	369,935	64,485	11,384
Bartow	529	23,752	18,358	4,878	516	546,222	533,256	455,309	77,947	12,966
Ben Hill	401	29,460	14,360	15,043	57	527,546	513,239	446,829	66,410	14,307
Berrien	368	25,689	12,212	13,160	317	473,354	456,728	378,428	78,300	16,626
Bibb	705	37,517	25,762	10,292	1,463	1,060,973	1,011,893	815,338	196,555	49,080
Brooks	1,369	72,071	48,719	22,108	1,244	1,393,765	1,346,922	1,113,922	233,050	46,793
Bryan	304	18,055	5,845	12,104	106	190,138	181,977	137,832	44,145	8,161
Bulloch	1,281	68,381	47,078	20,628	675	2,068,099	1,996,473	1,713,354	283,119	71,626
Burke	3,261	180,518	148,639	29,515	2,364	3,024,876	2,859,474	2,218,758	640,716	165,402
Butts	928	44,193	32,856	7,726	3,611	1,334,392	1,305,458	1,103,971	201,487	28,934
Calhoun	1,139	56,117	50,234	4,984	899	985,574	948,298	790,578	157,720	37,276
Camden	541	24,643	3,875	18,992	1,776	259,665	247,627	141,848	105,779	12,038
Campbell	524	25,584	15,721	7,298	2,565	572,814	560,442	464,707	95,735	12,372
Carroll	913	37,000	27,380	6,955	2,665	962,427	938,725	748,050	190,675	23,702
Catoosa	59	2,222	1,587	634	1	36,886	35,683	28,783	6,900	1,203
Charlton	36	4,240	468	3,765	7	23,269	22,270	15,070	7,200	999
Chatham	223	5,944	3,215	2,544	185	231,415	219,482	176,092	43,390	11,933
Chattahooche	479	49,845	23,680	21,884	4,281	457,373	441,480	357,108	84,372	15,893
Chattooga	336	18,867	11,557	6,858	452	311,422	302,015	244,881	57,134	9,407
Cherokee	117	5,685	2,937	2,457	291	88,335	85,783	68,043	17,740	2,552
Clarke	912	34,974	27,212	7,051	711	1,440,440	1,401,842	1,171,572	230,270	38,598
Clay	811	57,980	43,968	7,907	6,105	993,748	952,215	798,240	153,975	41,533
Clayton	677	31,013	22,262	6,332	2,419	1,028,914	1,002,560	778,885	223,675	26,354
Clinch	102	8,553	1,883	6,670	....	63,713	60,390	48,805	11,585	3,323
Cobb	700	27,838	19,136	6,962	1,740	709,410	690,154	549,079	141,075	19,256
Coffee	349	30,084	13,912	15,250	922	458,684	341,407	372,917	68,490	17,277
Colquitt	250	12,154	8,542	2,912	700	337,204	328,871	283,252	45,619	8,333
Columbia	1,387	71,152	51,237	18,393	1,522	1,061,088	1,010,193	787,605	222,588	50,895
Coweta	2,155	112,281	80,708	22,398	9,175	2,833,334	2,758,889	2,272,164	486,725	74,445
Crawford	604	53,950	27,519	22,561	3,870	472,929	451,397	338,997	112,400	21,532
Crisp	684	38,039	28,432	9,446	161	957,769	924,257	771,264	152,993	33,512
Dade	18	606	286	310	10	8,552	8,400	6,020	2,380	152
Dawson	32	1,695	844	769	82	19,478	18,975	15,665	3,310	503
Decatur	1,490	81,785	47,822	33,147	816	1,097,254	1,051,065	833,070	217,995	46,189
Dekalb	734	28,863	18,829	7,425	2,609	992,322	973,401	799,172	174,229	18,921
Dodge	1,069	64,226	49,047	15,005	174	1,107,373	1,042,611	813,651	228,960	64,762
Dooly	1,588	92,393	71,281	14,940	6,172	2,209,528	2,129,426	1,790,416	339,010	80,102
Dougherty	1,180	58,214	55,241	2,206	767	1,008,132	967,560	804,024	163,536	40,572
Douglas	344	19,545	11,896	6,993	656	335,039	324,415	262,075	62,340	10,624
Early	1,576	96,266	68,108	24,974	3,184	1,602,349	1,543,713	1,242,101	301,612	58,636
Echols	36	2,497	1,234	675	588	22,782	21,550	17,000	4,550	1,232
Effingham	315	34,315	6,312	28,003	....	284,952	276,940	230,015	46,925	8,012
Elbert	1,532	81,028	46,328	25,366	9,334	1,809,430	1,764,387	1,486,549	277,838	45,043
Emanuel	1,104	79,392	44,419	34,371	602	1,568,907	1,529,128	1,299,785	229,343	39,775
Fannin	7	240	136	104	....	3,184	3,120	2,505	615	64
Fayette	596	28,539	19,876	7,018	1,645	1,014,507	995,456	860,001	135,455	19,051
Floyd	764	44,090	25,369	17,059	1,662	838,904	802,562	651,533	151,029	36,342
Forsyth	172	7,539	4,565	2,428	546	144,826	139,660	111,307	28,353	5,166
Franklin	610	22,390	16,615	4,330	1,445	845,755	831,350	705,540	125,810	14,405
Fulton	263	8,281	5,256	2,685	340	787,872	774,166	695,171	78,995	13,706
Gilmer	5	517	101	416	....	2,623	2,560	1,400	1,160	63
Glascock	234	12,573	8,871	3,208	494	162,878	158,972	129,222	29,750	3,906
Glynn	100	14,072	1,035	12,748	289	64,417	61,105	41,037	20,068	3,312
Gordon	147	6,902	4,694	2,100	108	134,752	131,373	110,743	20,630	3,379
Grady	725	43,934	25,804	16,576	1,554	590,890	571,456	464,699	106,757	19,374
Greene	1,831	101,533	59,141	32,417	9,975	1,854,309	1,794,729	1,463,029	331,700	59,580
Gwinnett	501	24,057	15,507	7,060	1,490	622,900	608,837	492,405	116,432	14,063
Habersham	79	3,823	1,537	2,262	24	68,642	66,775	54,260	12,515	1,867
Hall	362	17,573	10,574	6,042	957	364,783	355,580	292,135	63,445	9,203
Hancock	2,032	123,626	78,644	37,082	7,900	1,799,065	1,728,602	1,355,061	373,541	70,463
Haralson	243	13,125	7,328	5,476	321	268,883	262,049	207,493	54,556	6,834
Harris	1,950	135,811	76,097	44,686	15,028	1,914,705	1,862,458	1,521,660	340,798	52,247
Hart	839	37,482	24,015	11,795	1,672	1,284,180	1,262,935	1,103,211	159,724	21,245
Heard	647	38,972	24,062	9,569	5,341	502,366	487,832	395,185	92,647	14,534
Henry	1,451	72,332	50,575	17,272	4,485	1,934,867	1,897,455	1,594,730	302,725	37,412
Houston	1,814	119,035	93,765	21,512	3,758	2,411,587	2,332,179	1,938,259	393,920	79,403
Irwin	406	25,180	16,435	7,655	1,090	761,031	732,760	651,260	81,500	28,271
Jackson	1,249	51,052	38,377	11,028	1,647	1,802,446	1,764,697	1,481,737	282,960	37,749
Jasper	1,802	100,652	71,411	23,495	5,746	2,030,258	1,961,975	1,607,036	354,939	68,283
Jeff Davis	130	20,305	3,570	16,684	51	188,231	184,490	163,285	21,205	3,741
Jefferson	1,667	91,235	75,966	14,272	997	1,743,888	1,659,379	1,292,692	366,687	84,509
Jenkins	818	41,739	34,349	7,230	160	731,670	706,647	580,657	125,990	25,023

TABLE 71.—FARMS OPERATED BY NEGROES—NUMBER, ACREAGE, AND VALUE OF LAND AND BUILDINGS, AND OF IMPLEMENTS AND MACHINERY, BY STATES AND COUNTIES: 1910—Continued.

[Counties in which no farms operated by Negroes were reported are omitted.]

STATE AND COUNTY.	Number of farms.	FARM ACREAGE.				VALUE OF FARM LAND, BUILDINGS, AND IMPLEMENTS AND MACHINERY.				
		Total.	Improved.	Woodland.	Other un-improved.	Total.	Land and buildings.			Imple-ments and ma-chinery.
							Total.	Land.	Buildings.	
GEORGIA—Continued.										
Johnson	633	33,023	28,475	4,345	203	$560,430	$532,599	$414,178	$118,421	$27,831
Jones	1,239	97,294	58,359	31,655	7,280	1,258,725	1,207,316	945,992	261,324	51,409
Laurens	2,266	118,641	95,662	19,724	3,255	2,351,808	2,269,601	1,926,389	343,212	82,207
Lee	1,520	86,952	76,529	9,233	1,190	1,564,746	1,475,396	1,183,506	291,890	89,350
Liberty	1,269	50,652	19,332	30,738	582	686,953	631,841	412,604	219,237	55,112
Lincoln	850	51,670	28,026	19,465	4,179	768,910	734,163	604,013	130,150	34,747
Lowndes	1,125	60,555	36,812	22,710	1,033	1,176,053	1,142,254	962,219	180,035	33,799
Lumpkin	41	2,757	1,055	1,672	30	21,218	20,600	16,935	3,665	618
McDuffie	883	54,249	35,131	16,412	2,706	765,565	719,838	555,858	163,980	45,727
McIntosh	169	10,650	2,218	8,021	411	228,646	212,417	155,787	56,630	16,229
Macon	1,193	82,241	61,511	18,570	2,160	1,256,894	1,216,742	1,021,141	195,601	40,152
Madison	855	38,153	26,305	10,392	1,456	1,023,091	997,060	842,380	154,680	26,031
Marion	733	63,982	41,928	14,336	7,718	556,334	535,154	418,349	116,805	21,180
Meriwether	2,126	117,308	85,436	24,595	7,337	2,717,612	2,632,102	2,118,268	513,834	85,510
Miller	337	23,020	14,574	6,970	1,476	252,819	243,100	201,992	41,108	9,719
Milton	105	4,393	3,066	778	549	116,786	113,525	95,678	17,847	3,261
Mitchell	1,523	86,611	68,740	17,327	544	1,594,448	1,540,366	1,276,106	264,260	54,082
Monroe	1,763	124,266	74,843	34,754	14,669	1,787,260	1,721,797	1,387,112	334,685	65,463
Montgomery	953	54,011	34,049	19,674	288	1,100,260	1,064,424	884,377	180,047	35,836
Morgan	1,999	92,953	71,277	17,418	4,258	2,312,901	2,239,509	1,908,030	331,479	73,392
Murray	55	1,955	1,580	296	79	41,243	39,920	34,790	5,130	1,323
Muscogee	593	39,073	24,805	11,595	2,673	470,259	452,623	363,783	88,840	17,636
Newton	1,391	65,070	50,676	11,706	2,688	1,771,409	1,732,462	1,465,035	267,427	38,947
Oconee	835	37,166	29,690	5,468	2,008	1,186,798	1,148,550	951,215	197,335	38,248
Oglethorpe	1,904	100,956	63,810	28,152	8,994	2,210,477	2,139,671	1,802,426	337,245	70,806
Paulding	244	13,091	8,311	3,415	1,365	238,076	230,934	183,244	47,690	7,142
Pickens	16	965	433	495	37	18,080	17,710	15,675	2,035	370
Pierce	203	9,602	4,217	4,327	1,058	171,759	164,955	127,234	37,721	6,804
Pike	1,289	71,703	50,779	14,640	6,284	1,442,046	1,403,807	1,130,568	273,239	38,239
Polk	650	29,962	19,861	9,055	1,046	558,178	531,420	421,642	109,778	26,758
Pulaski	1,573	91,765	71,129	19,861	775	2,043,941	1,952,432	1,647,002	305,430	91,509
Putnam	1,552	92,099	64,300	22,474	5,325	1,348,214	1,292,276	1,050,251	242,025	55,938
Quitman	523	35,102	25,510	4,727	4,865	425,175	409,790	339,500	70,290	15,385
Rabun	12	1,003	160	783	60	9,883	9,600	7,870	1,730	283
Randolph	1,563	101,926	77,969	18,269	5,688	1,794,683	1,734,323	1,456,828	277,495	60,360
Richmond	608	31,290	23,423	7,303	564	679,152	647,680	528,715	118,965	31,472
Rockdale	475	24,415	16,958	5,035	2,422	497,580	487,062	400,322	86,740	10,518
Schley	487	41,232	26,938	8,315	5,979	476,757	459,056	363,521	95,535	17,701
Screven	1,563	80,611	56,673	23,365	573	1,363,659	1,320,667	1,090,067	230,600	42,992
Spalding	927	43,892	33,225	7,475	3,192	1,077,914	1,050,624	841,889	208,735	27,290
Stephens	200	8,504	5,161	2,942	401	229,626	224,367	190,947	33,420	5,259
Stewart	1,235	111,340	73,846	30,438	7,056	1,257,773	1,204,324	1,010,399	193,925	53,449
Sumter	2,160	124,725	103,020	18,553	3,152	3,009,904	2,897,184	2,364,438	532,746	112,720
Talbot	1,159	89,437	47,413	30,233	11,791	897,734	865,049	682,952	182,097	32,685
Taliaferro	1,125	65,966	40,477	23,389	2,100	1,137,713	1,098,274	953,624	144,650	39,439
Tattnall	637	40,709	20,235	20,474	....	823,674	798,890	655,839	143,051	24,784
Taylor	637	43,423	26,140	17,135	148	457,650	440,674	357,599	83,075	16,976
Telfair	444	30,923	15,481	13,940	1,502	490,073	476,883	386,888	89,995	13,190
Terrell	2,098	110,749	97,395	10,496	2,858	3,066,285	3,002,190	2,526,358	475,832	64,095
Thomas	1,489	80,339	55,940	23,436	963	1,387,274	1,336,469	1,048,566	287,903	50,805
Tift	229	9,870	7,257	2,562	51	305,153	297,730	243,345	54,385	7,423
Toombs	350	19,083	11,783	7,300	....	376,608	364,892	300,777	64,115	11,716
Towns	3	57	57	....	....	1,858	1,850	1,685	165	8
Troup	1,978	122,602	77,106	29,759	15,737	2,056,809	1,990,437	1,624,737	365,700	66,372
Turner	374	17,447	14,903	2,518	26	477,015	465,983	394,533	71,450	11,032
Twiggs	1,063	64,712	46,421	15,745	2,546	862,454	828,072	655,692	172,380	34,382
Union	13	820	234	586		5,847	5,650	4,450	1,200	197
Upson	901	75,502	39,994	27,618	7,890	925,258	894,949	717,469	177,480	30,309
Walker	233	9,327	6,290	2,954	83	188,440	183,821	148,181	35,640	4,619
Walton	1,351	61,424	48,416	8,823	4,185	2,020,886	1,978,351	1,662,811	315,540	42,535
Ware	111	6,655	2,280	4,343	32	79,596	76,206	59,091	17,115	3,390
Warren	1,202	79,608	48,555	29,277	1,776	1,280,055	1,230,220	1,049,529	180,691	49,835
Washington	2,438	135,943	109,895	21,864	4,184	2,114,001	2,041,641	1,660,981	380,660	72,360
Wayne	148	23,779	2,516	20,587	676	145,058	139,505	112,105	27,400	5,553
Webster	596	44,008	32,994	7,859	3,155	540,909	519,845	415,945	103,900	21,064
White	53	3,412	1,224	1,907	281	52,217	50,925	41,990	8,935	1,292
Whitfield	127	5,907	3,671	2,089	147	110,151	105,619	79,999	25,620	4,532
Wilcox	605	41,804	25,216	15,725	863	796,769	769,384	631,419	137,965	27,385
Wilkes	2,453	120,501	81,411	30,559	8,531	2,566,495	2,465,349	2,085,143	380,206	101,146
Wilkinson	639	61,412	32,288	25,479	3,645	532,786	515,845	395,049	120,796	16,941
Worth	1,292	73,903	58,952	17,848	2,103	1,232,234	1,186,303	956,402	222,901	45,931

TABLE 71.—FARMS OPERATED BY NEGROES—NUMBER, ACREAGE, AND VALUE OF LAND AND BUILDINGS, AND OF IMPLEMENTS AND MACHINERY, BY STATES AND COUNTIES: 1910—Continued.

[Counties in which no farms operated by Negroes were reported are omitted.]

STATE AND COUNTY.	Number of farms.	FARM ACREAGE.				VALUE OF FARM LAND, BUILDINGS, AND IMPLEMENTS AND MACHINERY.					
		Total.	Improved.	Woodland.	Other un-improved.	Total.	Land and buildings.			Implements and machinery.
							Total.	Land.	Buildings.	

IDAHO.

Total................	13	1,043	346	503	194	$56,515	$54,250	$47,525	$6,725	$2,265
Bingham..............	3	109	91	....	18	10,900	10,300	9,350	950	660
Blaine...............	1	160	40	80	40	2,700	2,500	1,500	1,000	200
Canyon..............	2	45	45	....	....	19,575	19,000	16,500	2,500	575
Fremont.............	1	39	15	....	24	700	500	400	100	200
Kootenai............	2	50	15	35	....	2,450	2,450	2,150	300	....
Latah...............	1	160	18	100	42	6,300	6,000	5,000	1,000	300
Shoshone............	1	160	10	140	10	3,100	3,000	2,700	300	100
Washington..........	2	320	112	148	60	10,790	10,500	9,925	575	290

ILLINOIS.

Total................	1,422	87,784	68,299	17,145	2,340	$6,106,110	$5,972,592	$5,299,868	$672,724	$133,518
Adams...............	13	600	501	99	....	39,955	38,740	34,990	3,750	1,215
Alexander...........	107	7,361	4,382	2,806	173	340,513	327,960	292,111	35,849	12,553
Bond................	18	1,040	888	73	79	48,460	47,980	41,480	6,500	480
Bureau..............	1	240	240	....	....	36,500	36,000	32,000	4,000	500
Carroll..............	1	10	....	....	10	500	500	500	....	....
Champaign...........	6	1,259	1,232	27	....	256,700	254,290	241,690	12,600	2,410
Christian............	8	1,787	1,714	73	....	257,410	252,610	244,910	7,700	4,800
Clark...............	1	40	15	25	....	1,650	1,600	1,600	....	50
Clay................	2	60	60	....	....	2,830	2,580	1,780	800	250
Clinton.............	11	1,409	1,250	144	15	70,675	68,650	61,850	6,800	2,025
Coles...............	1	20	8	12	....	1,535	1,500	1,100	400	35
Cook................	10	222	187	12	23	81,820	80,900	68,300	12,600	920
Crawford............	1	63	63	....	....	3,350	3,150	2,150	1,000	200
Cumberland..........	1	185	130	55	....	7,600	7,400	6,800	600	200
Dekalb..............	2	32	15	17	....	2,375	2,300	1,850	450	75
Dewitt..............	1	220	180	40	....	22,000	22,000	21,000	1,000	....
Douglas.............	1	300	300	....	....	60,800	60,000	59,700	300	800
Dupage..............	1	75	55	....	20	8,200	8,000	8,000	....	200
Edgar...............	3	388	383	....	5	50,250	49,750	43,050	6,700	500
Edwards.............	3	82	66	16	....	7,560	7,400	5,850	1,550	160
Franklin............	1	30	30	....	....	518	450	450	....	68
Fulton..............	1	6	6	....	....	2,100	2,000	600	1,400	100
Gallatin............	26	1,955	1,705	250	....	73,210	71,140	63,440	7,700	2,070
Greene..............	5	286	205	81	....	26,390	26,080	23,630	2,450	310
Hancock.............	6	409	352	17	40	30,415	29,930	25,230	4,700	485
Hardin..............	8	418	223	195	....	9,192	9,040	7,240	1,800	152
Henderson...........	2	200	200	....	....	17,425	17,000	15,400	1,600	425
Iroquois............	5	762	752	10	....	88,625	86,825	68,825	18,000	1,800
Jackson.............	46	3,351	2,423	886	42	142,623	139,119	121,299	17,820	3,504
Jasper..............	14	767	720	25	22	48,240	46,055	37,730	8,325	2,185
Jefferson...........	8	331	244	87	....	12,810	12,615	10,955	1,660	195
Jersey..............	3	335	172	93	70	12,415	11,700	9,000	2,700	715
Jo Daviess..........	1	338	300	38	....	27,255	26,630	21,030	5,600	625
Johnson.............	3	338	248	90	....	10,075	9,900	9,000	900	175
Kane................	1	5	5	....	....	4,100	4,000	2,500	1,500	100
Kankakee............	7	810	280	530	....	31,875	31,600	27,000	4,600	275
Kendall.............	1	12	12	....	....	1,250	1,200	600	600	50
Knox................	2	147	127	20	....	16,150	15,800	12,000	3,800	350
La Salle............	5	248	186	62	....	37,825	37,300	35,000	2,300	525
Lake................	2	14	14	....	....	4,650	4,500	2,500	2,000	150
Lawrence............	20	1,389	1,348	39	2	101,915	100,850	88,775	12,075	1,065
Logan...............	5	445	445	....	....	66,125	64,800	59,900	4,900	1,325
McHenry.............	1	20	18	....	2	2,050	2,000	1,000	1,000	50
McLean..............	8	789	789	....	....	159,500	155,700	143,700	12,000	3,800
Macon...............	6	115	103	12	....	40,480	40,300	27,800	12,500	180
Macoupin............	20	2,522	2,118	198	206	175,330	172,595	157,530	15,065	2,735
Madison.............	50	4,592	3,088	634	870	309,375	301,115	263,590	37,525	8,260
Marion..............	10	480	367	108	5	33,730	32,900	27,200	5,700	830
Marshall............	3	538	526	12	....	68,040	67,480	61,580	5,900	560
Massac..............	128	6,413	4,177	2,182	54	232,398	226,005	187,705	38,300	6,393
Mercer..............	2	8	8	....	....	2,710	2,600	1,900	700	110
Monroe..............	2	325	225	....	100	19,130	19,000	18,450	550	130
Montgomery..........	3	103	80	23	....	4,830	4,700	3,870	830	130
Morgan..............	4	444	444	....	....	97,985	96,600	91,400	5,200	1,385
Ogle................	1	9	9	....	....	3,000	3,000	1,400	1,600	....
Peoria..............	3	181	159	22	....	22,675	22,300	19,500	2,800	375
Perry...............	12	1,028	735	293	....	38,305	37,300	31,345	5,955	1,005
Pike................	14	1,208	1,128	60	20	92,825	90,730	76,130	14,600	2,095
Pope................	55	3,549	2,315	1,234	....	92,822	88,890	78,585	10,305	3,932
Pulaski.............	450	17,887	13,217	4,559	111	824,693	793,725	662,710	131,015	30,968

TABLE 71.—FARMS OPERATED BY NEGROES—NUMBER, ACREAGE, AND VALUE OF LAND AND BUILDINGS, AND OF IMPLEMENTS AND MACHINERY, BY STATES AND COUNTIES: 1910—Continued.

[Counties in which no farms operated by Negroes were reported are omitted.]

STATE AND COUNTY.	Number of farms.	FARM ACREAGE.				VALUE OF FARM LAND, BUILDINGS, AND IMPLEMENTS AND MACHINERY.					
		Total.	Improved.	Woodland.	Other un-improved.	Total.	Land and buildings.			Implements and machinery.
							Total.	Land.	Buildings.	
ILLINOIS—Continued.										
Randolph	38	1,945	1,415	386	144	$83,582	$80,400	$64,460	$15,940	$3,182
St. Clair	51	2,443	2,199	170	74	338,595	335,055	312,905	22,150	3,540
Saline	70	4,386	3,810	570	6	215,438	212,130	183,985	28,145	3,308
Sangamon	38	3,406	3,333	48	25	601,573	596,380	562,080	34,300	5,193
Shelby	2	353	287	66	....	28,225	28,000	24,800	3,200	225
Tazewell	2	14	14	....	....	4,700	4,600	2,600	2,000	160
Union	3	160	105	55	....	6,715	6,500	6,000	500	215
Vermilion	6	399	333	24	42	48,025	47,000	44,600	2,400	1,025
Wabash	5	420	393	16	11	17,615	17,250	15,330	1,920	365
Warren	4	650	610	30	10	99,000	97,300	92,725	4,575	1,700
Washington	15	603	510	93	....	23,480	22,460	18,660	3,800	1,020
Wayne	1	40	40	....	....	1,420	1,400	1,300	100	20
White	18	2,006	1,913	47	46	159,910	157,120	145,995	11,125	2,790
Whiteside	1	4	4	....	....	2,525	2,500	1,500	1,000	25
Will	12	674	510	143	21	61,953	60,393	48,198	12,195	1,560
Williamson	14	1,316	1,119	167	30	38,770	38,100	30,600	7,500	670
Winnebago	2	74	33	6	35	6,140	6,000	4,300	1,700	140
Woodford	4	741	499	215	27	82,700	81,220	71,620	9,600	1,480
INDIANA.										
Total	785	43,627	36,865	4,713	2,049	$3,380,862	$3,317,747	$2,878,997	$438,750	$63,115
Allen	2	83	41	40	2	10,010	10,000	6,000	4,000	10
Bartholomew	3	299	224	50	25	18,950	18,200	17,000	1,200	750
Benton	1	80	80	....	....	10,100	10,000	9,500	500	100
Boone	4	223	203	20	....	28,400	27,675	25,175	2,500	725
Carroll	1	200	180	20	....	20,125	20,000	19,600	400	125
Clark	22	604	483	104	17	28,755	27,450	18,200	9,250	1,305
Clay	2	96	60	....	36	4,895	4,820	3,620	1,200	75
Daviess	13	986	928	33	25	97,680	94,800	86,060	8,740	2,880
Dearborn	16	1,021	745	160	116	61,755	60,525	54,775	5,750	1,230
Delaware	5	275	228	47	....	30,025	29,700	25,700	4,000	325
Dubois	1	147	115	32	....	3,625	3,500	2,800	700	125
Elkhart	1	149	117	22	10	3,630	3,600	3,000	600	30
Fayette	3	180	171	2	7	6,060	6,000	5,950	50	60
Floyd	14	513	311	175	27	20,450	19,600	15,450	4,150	850
Fulton	1	4	4	....	....	650	600	300	300	50
Gibson	92	7,964	7,134	722	108	466,950	457,545	414,320	43,225	9,405
Grant	40	1,729	1,653	76	....	191,695	187,675	161,250	26,425	4,020
Greene	8	454	439	11	4	45,850	44,950	41,400	3,550	900
Hamilton	33	2,107	1,806	280	21	229,735	226,165	198,965	27,200	3,570
Harrison	22	1,150	853	205	92	24,027	23,220	16,995	6,225	807
Hendricks	16	510	409	67	34	56,373	55,400	48,580	6,820	973
Henry	13	1,930	1,544	294	92	179,470	177,480	161,380	16,100	1,990
Howard	11	491	478	11	2	56,437	54,562	46,262	8,300	1,875
Jackson	1	10	10	....	....	625	600	600	....	25
Jay	2	13	13	....	....	4,610	4,600	1,700	2,900	10
Jefferson	20	691	515	103	73	26,390	25,675	18,315	7,360	715
Jennings	20	707	556	78	73	28,500	27,115	20,065	7,050	1,385
Johnson	2	78	53	....	25	19,280	19,250	3,630	15,620	30
Knox	10	418	402	6	10	32,350	31,600	28,400	3,200	750
Lake	1	100	80	20	....	10,200	10,000	9,100	900	200
Laporte	4	212	169	43	....	13,585	13,500	12,000	1,500	85
Lawrence	4	149	113	14	22	6,560	6,500	4,850	1,650	60
Madison	4	84	54	30	....	6,495	6,300	5,000	1,300	195
Marion	37	849	766	71	12	294,180	291,440	264,120	27,320	2,740
Miami	1	30	30	....	....	3,065	3,000	2,800	200	65
Monroe	7	187	131	30	26	18,905	18,600	14,800	3,800	305
Montgomery	1	67	64	3	....	6,775	6,700	5,300	1,400	75
Morgan	6	168	75	80	13	5,620	5,450	4,275	1,175	170
Newton	1	90	90	....	....	9,015	9,000	8,600	400	15
Ohio	10	306	256	50	....	15,975	15,475	13,375	2,100	500
Orange	2	235	120	115	....	11,525	11,200	7,500	3,700	325
Owen	2	133	83	42	8	4,590	4,500	4,000	500	90
Parke	6	362	197	79	86	28,105	27,600	24,200	3,400	505
Perry	6	141	139	....	2	9,520	9,060	5,610	3,450	460
Pike	2	18	18	....	....	935	900	800	100	35
Posey	13	1,041	877	109	55	35,395	34,080	29,955	4,125	1,315
Putnam	4	438	324	114	....	28,990	28,700	26,200	2,500	290
Randolph	36	1,733	1,636	93	4	146,107	143,450	122,830	20,620	2,657
Ripley	3	256	192	17	47	7,175	7,000	4,525	2,475	175
Rush	21	1,150	991	146	13	98,580	97,580	86,780	10,800	1,000

TABLE **71.**— FARMS OPERATED BY NEGROES—NUMBER, ACREAGE, AND VALUE OF LAND AND BUILDINGS, AND OF IMPLEMENTS AND MACHINERY, BY STATES AND COUNTIES: 1910—Continued.

[Counties in which no farms operated by Negroes were reported are omitted.]

STATE AND COUNTY.	Number of farms.	FARM ACREAGE.				VALUE OF FARM LAND, BUILDINGS, AND IMPLEMENTS AND MACHINERY.				
		Total.	Improved.	Woodland.	Other un-improved.	Total.	Land and buildings.			Implements and machinery.
							Total.	Land.	Buildings.	

INDIANA—Continued.

St. Joseph	2	28	25		3	$4,530	$4,500	$3,900	$600	$30
Shelby	5	365	365			41,800	41,300	39,300	2,000	500
Spencer	70	2,497	2,397	64	36	186,520	183,140	159,105	24,035	3,380
Starke	2	287	163	20	104	11,500	11,000	8,500	2,500	500
Steuben	1	32	30	2		1,050	1,000	850	150	50
Sullivan	10	683	642	36	5	46,765	46,155	42,035	4,120	610
Switzerland	4	292	235	19	38	12,240	12,100	9,600	2,500	140
Tippecanoe	1	240	200	40		24,000	24,000	20,000	4,000	
Vanderburg	24	1,128	876	156	96	81,455	80,250	71,400	8,850	1,205
Vermilion	1	15	15			603	600	400	200	3
Vigo	64	3,393	2,550	318	525	211,230	207,090	172,990	34,100	4,140
Wabash	2	426	267	38	121	28,880	28,380	25,380	3,000	500
Warren	2	228	185	43		9,670	9,120	8,420	700	550
Warrick	9	416	386	8	22	24,800	24,440	20,515	3,925	360
Wayne	34	1,383	1,219	152	12	127,930	124,890	96,200	28,690	3,040
Wells	1	160	142	18		18,100	17,600	15,600	2,000	500
White	2	760	635	125		45,850	45,200	41,700	3,500	650
Whitley	1	433	373	60		35,240	34,640	31,490	3,150	600

IOWA.

Total	187	13,617	10,647	2,015	955	$1,092,443	$1,054,495	$869,300	$185,195	$37,948
Allamakee	4	458	358	55	45	24,670	24,000	20,700	3,300	670
Appanoose	6	130	113	11	6	6,065	5,550	3,950	1,600	515
Blackhawk	1	43	40		3	4,075	4,000	3,400	600	75
Cedar	1	40	40			6,125	6,000	4,000	2,000	125
Clarke	3	772	453	254	65	39,195	38,420	36,020	2,400	775
Davis	1	20	20			1,825	1,800	1,300	500	25
Decatur	1	57	52	5		3,495	3,420	2,920	500	75
Dickinson	2	225	145		80	11,800	11,500	10,050	1,450	300
Fayette	16	1,978	1,480	354	144	121,680	115,380	96,180	19,200	6,300
Fremont	4	209	184		25	15,400	14,925	12,375	2,550	475
Greene	1	160	80		80	13,300	12,800	11,300	1,500	500
Hancock	2	240	230		10	18,800	18,350	15,850	2,500	450
Henry	3	90	66		24	7,490	7,160	5,760	1,400	330
Humboldt	1	80	80			8,400	6,400	6,400		2,000
Jasper	1	70	70			7,100	7,000	6,600	400	100
Jefferson	1	56	36	20		5,800	5,600	4,800	800	200
Kossuth	1	47	39		8	6,250	6,000	5,100	900	250
Lee	32	2,071	1,325	527	219	128,653	124,485	93,160	31,325	4,168
Linn	2	13	13			8,225	8,000	4,300	3,700	225
Lucas	3	336	233	103		17,565	17,240	14,340	2,900	325
Madison	1	52	50	2		4,360	3,960	2,760	1,200	400
Mahaska	5	248	228	15	5	22,660	21,600	14,450	7,150	1,060
Marion	2	77	65	12		5,050	4,700	4,400	300	350
Marshall	1	5	5			1,800	1,700	1,300	400	100
Mitchell	1	112	100	10	2	11,400	11,200	9,200	2,000	200
Monroe	43	1,023	873	139	11	118,940	112,515	72,965	39,550	6,425
Montgomery	1	240	240			30,300	30,000	28,800	1,200	300
Muscatine	4	92	92			13,220	12,650	8,650	4,000	570
Page	5	179	174	5		22,135	21,780	19,280	2,500	355
Polk	3	105	105			16,500	16,200	13,100	3,100	300
Pottawattamie	2	94	79	15		12,600	12,000	9,700	2,300	600
Scott	1	1	1			1,400	1,400	400	1,000	
Shelby	2	360	320	40		39,000	38,000	34,000	4,000	1,000
Taylor	2	145	102	43		13,800	13,400	11,100	2,300	400
Union	1	417	417			41,700	41,700	38,700	3,000	
Van Buren	2	29	23	6		2,675	2,660	2,060	600	15
Wapello	9	266	173	71	22	20,145	19,750	16,290	3,460	395
Warren	3	557	485	72		47,810	47,160	43,860	3,300	650
Washington	2	117	117			19,300	18,850	17,500	1,350	450
Wayne	1	80	70	10		5,250	5,200	5,140	60	50
Webster	2	560	530		30	51,450	49,600	44,600	5,000	1,850
Winneshiek	1	41	37	4		2,525	2,500	1,900	600	25
Woodbury	3	913	555	238	120	80,870	78,250	64,850	13,400	2,620
Worth	4	809	749	4	56	51,640	49,690	45,790	3,900	1,950

KANSAS.

Total	1,532	183,453	131,206	9,142	43,105	$7,507,827	$7,317,314	$6,468,294	$849,020	$190,513
Allen	20	976	906	43	27	40,880	40,060	33,760	6,300	820
Anderson	7	681	545	93	43	25,312	24,520	21,470	3,050	792
Atchison	56	3,602	2,649	745	208	227,840	220,720	191,600	29,120	7,120
Barber	4	833	793		40	29,645	29,120	27,320	1,800	525
Barton	25	5,994	5,616	85	293	315,990	309,250	292,790	16,460	6,740

TABLE 71.—FARMS OPERATED BY NEGROES—NUMBER, ACREAGE, AND VALUE OF LAND AND BUILDINGS, AND OF IMPLEMENTS AND MACHINERY, BY STATES AND COUNTIES: 1910—Continued.

[Counties in which no farms operated by Negroes were reported are omitted.]

STATE AND COUNTY.	Number of farms.	FARM ACREAGE.				VALUE OF FARM LAND, BUILDINGS, AND IMPLEMENTS AND MACHINERY.				
		Total.	Improved.	Woodland.	Other un-improved.	Total.	Land and buildings.			Implements and machinery.
							Total.	Land.	Buildings.	
KANSAS—Continued.										
Bourbon	37	3,166	2,197	410	559	$131,710	$129,655	$116,355	$13,300	$2,055
Brown	13	1,836	1,371	340	125	153,100	150,400	138,450	11,950	2,700
Butler	2	200	70		130	6,610	6,400	5,600	800	210
Chase	3	660	520	25	115	26,200	25,000	22,700	2,300	1,200
Chautauqua	13	1,537	628	703	206	30,160	29,415	25,415	4,000	745
Cherokee	47	3,056	2,641	232	183	102,890	99,110	84,465	14,645	3,780
Coffey	5	237	220	7	10	8,475	8,100	7,100	1,000	375
Cowley	9	854	798	50	6	60,686	59,320	55,395	3,925	1,366
Crawford	21	1,125	959	26	140	65,618	63,450	56,700	6,750	2,168
Dickinson	6	470	440		30	25,390	24,700	19,800	4,900	690
Doniphan	36	1,768	1,557	179	32	130,620	127,650	113,145	14,505	2,970
Douglas	88	4,158	3,395	548	215	257,763	248,760	203,355	45,405	9,003
Edwards	6	1,200	1,140		60	38,820	38,600	37,875	725	220
Elk	2	105	50	45	10	2,295	2,250	1,450	800	45
Ellsworth	6	1,331	771	65	495	68,670	68,000	64,000	4,000	670
Finney	10	1,038	673	10	355	29,240	27,800	23,875	3,925	1,440
Ford	1	160	40		120	2,450	2,400	2,300	100	50
Franklin	25	2,110	1,752	292	66	120,995	118,980	99,135	19,845	2,015
Geary	4	193	143		50	8,245	7,925	5,725	2,200	320
Gove	22	6,626	3,391		3,235	105,650	103,425	89,200	14,225	2,225
Graham	110	20,042	15,015	120	4,907	463,041	446,690	411,705	34,985	16,351
Grant	5	880	390		490	6,970	6,500	5,700	800	470
Gray	6	3,864	1,354		2,510	68,430	67,180	63,030	4,150	1,250
Greeley	1	160	4		156	1,000	1,000	975	25	
Greenwood	2	292	158		134	9,150	8,800	7,900	900	350
Hamilton	6	1,235	455		780	39,650	39,000	33,200	5,800	650
Harvey	9	852	847		5	56,315	54,475	46,125	8,350	1,840
Haskell	1	160	50		110	1,550	1,500	1,300	200	50
Hodgeman	16	3,385	1,062	57	2,266	64,750	62,200	57,400	4,800	2,550
Jackson	13	1,559	1,488	71		105,660	104,700	98,155	6,545	960
Jefferson	44	3,587	2,999	439	149	195,765	191,680	170,500	21,180	4,085
Johnson	35	2,546	1,734	623	189	193,065	191,230	177,945	13,285	1,835
Kearny	1	160	70		90	825	800	725	75	25
Kiowa	1	240	240			15,000	14,400	13,625	775	600
Labette	17	1,864	1,682	129	53	55,480	53,675	48,415	5,260	1,805
Leavenworth	101	7,538	5,972	1,431	135	391,510	378,200	338,025	40,175	13,310
Lincoln	6	968	968			34,732	33,800	30,700	3,100	932
Linn	21	1,430	839	181	410	39,450	38,240	28,990	9,250	1,210
Logan	68	17,370	7,551	2	9,817	182,352	175,949	160,639	15,310	6,403
Lyon	37	2,150	1,684	63	403	100,943	97,580	77,380	20,200	3,363
Marion	8	1,325	877	3	445	76,100	74,700	67,800	6,900	1,400
Marshall	19	4,308	3,047	96	1,165	253,340	249,320	231,370	17,950	4,020
Meade	5	2,180	1,980		200	39,375	38,400	35,100	3,300	975
Miami	26	3,245	2,852	238	155	181,325	177,200	160,900	16,300	4,125
Montgomery	32	2,851	2,158	417	276	105,193	102,790	90,520	12,270	2,403
Morris	27	1,798	1,539	12	247	66,215	64,050	55,375	8,675	2,165
Morton	7	1,120	1,020		100	9,370	8,850	7,490	1,360	520
Nemaha	3	430	387	20	23	33,475	33,000	30,350	2,650	475
Neosho	7	362	260	102		14,895	14,340	12,940	1,400	555
Norton	5	1,500	938	5	557	27,145	26,300	22,450	3,850	845
Osage	20	902	737	87	78	43,125	41,650	32,875	8,775	1,475
Osborne	8	1,365	1,205	10	150	21,325	20,600	18,475	2,125	725
Ottawa	2	305	305			23,800	23,500	23,500		300
Pawnee	10	2,354	1,933		421	122,609	118,000	108,425	9,575	4,609
Phillips	8	2,045	723	72	1,250	64,560	62,650	58,710	3,940	1,910
Pottawatomie	6	525	397	6	122	35,475	34,600	30,800	3,800	875
Pratt	23	6,528	5,968		560	310,245	300,525	278,795	21,730	9,720
Reno	10	1,286	1,261		25	71,875	70,350	62,800	7,550	1,525
Rice	4	635	589	25	21	46,450	44,600	41,100	3,500	1,850
Rooks	9	2,525	1,479		1,046	70,035	67,800	65,100	2,700	2,235
Rush	1	176	146		30	9,400	8,800	7,900	900	600
Russell	4	623	420		203	19,235	18,600	17,150	1,450	635
Saline	6	824	525		299	21,150	20,300	17,900	2,400	850
Sedgwick	14	1,585	1,504	1	80	126,350	123,950	110,300	13,650	2,400
Seward	1	160	90		70	3,275	3,200	2,800	400	75
Shawnee	80	3,938	3,387	287	264	279,717	271,700	232,405	39,295	8,017
Stafford	17	4,775	3,894	7	874	199,200	194,400	183,300	11,100	4,800
Stanton	1	160	14		146	1,025	1,000	900	100	25
Stevens	20	3,780	2,064		1,716	41,236	40,000	37,325	2,675	1,236
Sumner	9	2,010	1,909	20	81	107,500	105,550	100,850	4,700	1,950
Trego	1	160	100		60	2,300	2,000	1,400	600	300
Wabaunsee	61	6,192	4,692	250	1,250	308,035	299,000	258,475	40,525	9,035
Wallace	9	2,119	529		1,590	20,195	19,500	17,450	2,050	695
Washington	2	200	160	40		8,640	8,400	7,600	800	240
Woodson	3	1,415	1,322	83	10	27,715	27,340	25,140	2,200	375
Wyandotte	96	3,549	2,968	347	234	676,030	667,740	501,110	106,630	8,290

TABLE 71.—FARMS OPERATED BY NEGROES—NUMBER, ACREAGE, AND VALUE OF LAND AND BUILDINGS, AND OF IMPLEMENTS AND MACHINERY, BY STATES AND COUNTIES: 1910—Continued.

[Counties in which no farms operated by Negroes were reported are omitted.]

STATE AND COUNTY.	Number of farms.	FARM ACREAGE.				VALUE OF FARM LAND, BUILDINGS, AND IMPLEMENTS AND MACHINERY.					
		Total.	Improved.	Woodland.	Other un-improved.	Total.	Land and buildings.			Implements and machinery.
							Total.	Land.	Buildings.	
KENTUCKY.										
Total	11,709	439,657	342,895	81,357	15,405	$15,437,763	$15,017,228	$12,227,341	$2,789,887	$420,535
Adair	192	7,986	5,367	2,472	147	124,860	120,405	94,134	26,271	4,455
Allen	112	3,793	2,948	758	87	69,511	67,860	56,025	11,835	1,651
Anderson	29	486	405	23	58	20,000	19,390	14,505	4,885	610
Ballard	196	9,383	7,565	1,760	58	378,979	366,955	301,635	65,320	12,024
Barren	496	14,921	12,702	1,991	228	434,548	424,228	343,053	81,175	10,320
Bath	86	1,908	1,510	346	52	93,538	90,605	71,736	18,869	2,933
Bell	15	485	182	291	12	12,546	12,430	10,540	1,890	116
Boone	27	1,052	925	60	67	41,590	40,110	28,635	11,475	1,480
Bourbon	113	2,727	2,715	6	6	330,705	320,885	255,979	64,906	9,820
Boyd	8	88	76	12	....	5,115	4,850	3,470	1,380	265
Boyle	104	2,516	1,836	612	68	125,937	123,046	98,621	24,425	2,891
Bracken	19	963	931	32	....	37,419	36,650	30,100	6,550	769
Breathitt	26	5,692	532	5,155	5	79,917	79,320	76,385	2,935	597
Breckinridge	94	4,666	3,289	988	389	61,107	59,001	43,131	15,870	2,106
Bullitt	37	2,113	1,379	454	280	48,980	47,430	39,590	7,840	1,550
Butler	56	2,969	1,887	1,027	55	34,683	33,190	26,950	6,240	1,493
Caldwell	159	6,359	5,708	528	123	120,006	117,344	96,424	20,920	2,662
Calloway	78	4,675	2,589	1,914	172	65,017	62,465	49,310	13,155	2,552
Carlisle	16	574	495	76	3	14,325	13,595	11,075	2,520	730
Carroll	29	860	734	14	112	42,471	41,910	34,970	6,940	561
Carter	5	177	114	62	1	3,120	3,000	2,225	775	120
Casey	43	1,772	930	786	56	29,575	28,120	23,075	5,045	1,455
Christian	878	35,875	29,642	4,979	1,254	938,882	916,341	758,993	157,348	22,541
Clark	92	2,583	1,894	402	287	146,976	144,205	111,725	32,480	2,771
Clay	84	3,460	1,947	1,412	101	42,996	41,710	32,510	9,200	1,286
Clinton	21	477	309	168	....	6,639	6,325	4,645	1,680	314
Crittenden	56	3,069	2,320	726	23	35,738	34,455	25,985	8,470	1,283
Cumberland	84	3,275	1,691	1,505	79	67,788	66,536	55,605	10,931	1,252
Daviess	256	9,336	8,474	627	235	538,111	526,265	446,615	79,650	11,846
Edmonson	64	2,735	1,886	790	59	40,254	38,615	27,525	11,090	1,639
Estill	4	172	117	55	....	2,360	2,250	1,725	525	110
Fayette	107	4,569	4,295	229	45	636,074	617,231	494,731	122,500	18,843
Fleming	63	1,582	1,369	178	35	109,657	107,995	85,190	22,805	1,662
Floyd	17	926	332	569	25	15,106	14,735	12,550	2,185	371
Franklin	33	1,087	917	33	137	66,800	65,375	51,625	13,750	1,425
Fulton	228	8,068	7,707	359	2	436,007	425,397	386,532	38,865	10,610
Gallatin	25	786	703	51	32	26,782	25,735	20,945	4,790	1,047
Garrard	230	5,875	5,328	331	216	375,921	369,300	315,560	53,740	6,621
Grant	19	1,250	1,043	70	137	40,595	40,100	31,750	8,350	495
Graves	224	7,506	6,459	839	208	224,144	216,628	181,408	35,220	7,516
Grayson	14	1,190	758	427	5	12,778	12,500	9,815	2,685	278
Green	170	7,045	5,240	1,455	350	112,969	109,099	87,094	22,005	3,870
Greenup	6	69	60	9	....	3,113	3,050	1,465	1,585	63
Hancock	45	1,277	1,055	103	119	30,173	28,731	24,186	4,545	1,442
Hardin	67	3,356	2,541	661	154	102,172	98,185	76,565	21,620	3,987
Harlan	34	1,594	610	984	....	24,803	24,470	20,840	3,630	333
Harrison	107	2,991	2,855	71	65	190,106	185,100	144,005	41,095	5,006
Hart	236	7,466	5,884	1,521	61	270,846	263,553	219,683	43,870	7,293
Henderson	469	18,548	16,571	1,512	465	803,232	781,396	659,445	121,951	21,836
Henry	116	2,240	2,173	16	51	146,050	143,360	112,235	31,125	2,690
Hickman	77	4,999	4,010	944	45	187,210	182,064	163,279	18,785	5,146
Hopkins	150	6,713	5,102	1,211	400	248,470	240,395	197,715	42,680	8,075
Jackson	3	188	65	83	40	805	750	500	250	55
Jefferson	142	4,372	3,787	335	250	484,085	468,375	382,020	86,355	15,710
Jessamine	126	3,315	2,861	294	160	276,830	271,215	215,270	55,945	5,615
Johnson	10	382	251	131	....	6,378	6,250	4,685	1,565	128
Kenton	16	416	298	8	110	13,625	12,800	8,550	4,250	825
Knott	22	866	331	535	....	7,130	7,125	5,885	1,240	5
Knox	57	1,929	1,272	644	13	40,489	40,098	29,908	10,190	391
Larue	47	1,177	1,085	139	3	35,005	33,830	26,120	7,710	1,175
Laurel	32	523	323	200	....	16,189	15,785	8,670	7,115	404
Lawrence	3	178	98	80	....	1,615	1,500	1,200	300	115
Lee	10	415	164	247	4	3,807	3,722	2,967	755	85
Leslie	15	593	270	194	129	7,124	6,910	5,105	1,805	214
Letcher	3	34	29	5	....	555	550	350	200	5
Lewis	22	1,267	540	647	80	29,886	29,320	24,095	5,225	566
Lincoln	191	5,097	3,973	1,016	108	244,402	239,285	202,920	36,365	5,117
Livingston	44	2,172	1,543	574	55	29,452	28,550	23,525	5,025	902
Logan	503	17,936	14,222	3,283	431	489,163	477,510	380,839	96,671	11,653
Lyon	123	5,198	2,559	1,619	20	80,121	77,670	61,197	16,473	2,451
McCracken	186	6,300	5,322	889	89	280,497	270,815	216,950	53,865	9,682
McLean	46	2,091	1,706	380	5	63,437	60,805	50,405	10,400	2,632
Madison	580	14,528	13,133	963	432	860,939	839,865	693,388	146,477	21,074
Magoffin	5	411	241	170	....	5,781	5,750	5,100	650	31
Marion	93	3,562	2,487	923	152	103,789	98,565	72,720	25,845	5,224

TABLE 71.—FARMS OPERATED BY NEGROES—NUMBER, ACREAGE, AND VALUE OF LAND AND BUILDINGS, AND OF IMPLEMENTS AND MACHINERY, BY STATES AND COUNTIES: 1910—Continued.

[Counties in which no farms operated by Negroes were reported are omitted.]

STATE AND COUNTY.	Number of farms.	FARM ACREAGE.				VALUE OF FARM LAND, BUILDINGS, AND IMPLEMENTS AND MACHINERY.				
		Total.	Improved.	Woodland.	Other un-improved.	Total.	Land and buildings.			Implements and machinery.
							Total.	Land.	Buildings.	
KENTUCKY—Continued.										
Marshall	14	687	479	208	....	$17,510	$17,110	$15,585	$1,525	$400
Mason	77	2,640	2,489	75	76	194,749	191,060	149,760	41,300	3,689
Meade	79	4,896	3,590	957	349	71,782	68,046	49,927	18,119	3,736
Menifee	5	392	130	262	....	1,692	1,650	1,325	325	42
Mercer	73	2,610	2,243	145	222	128,542	124,965	98,895	26,070	3,577
Metcalfe	149	5,319	4,372	852	95	109,315	106,835	85,455	21,380	2,480
Monroe	77	2,991	1,811	1,086	94	36,224	35,005	26,385	8,620	1,219
Montgomery	103	2,962	1,913	1,016	33	155,042	149,775	116,050	33,725	5,267
Morgan	4	84	67	17	....	1,673	1,625	1,190	435	48
Muhlenberg	111	6,409	4,127	1,903	379	115,114	111,102	84,687	26,415	4,012
Nelson	125	6,529	4,386	1,956	187	202,076	196,800	160,885	35,915	5,276
Nicholas	40	1,126	1,068	48	10	74,970	73,270	60,670	12,600	1,700
Ohio	63	3,676	2,375	905	396	58,398	55,765	40,670	15,095	2,633
Oldham	29	1,185	826	187	172	42,242	41,155	30,405	10,750	1,087
Owen	105	3,934	3,212	218	504	144,580	140,825	106,780	34,045	3,755
Owsley	11	291	191	100	....	3,013	2,975	2,390	585	38
Pendleton	19	757	690	17	50	21,990	20,620	14,455	6,165	1,370
Perry	33	1,726	725	1,001	....	14,514	14,420	11,790	2,630	94
Pike	18	1,393	392	959	42	26,456	26,300	23,700	2,600	156
Powell	57	2,670	1,432	1,147	91	34,037	32,620	22,850	9,770	1,417
Pulaski	73	2,334	1,502	820	12	53,271	51,639	37,186	14,453	1,632
Robertson	12	296	272	2	22	12,500	12,180	9,145	3,035	320
Rockcastle	7	336	165	147	24	3,750	3,650	2,770	880	100
Russell	30	1,538	758	736	44	25,531	24,775	21,100	3,675	756
Scott	102	3,248	3,045	105	98	233,756	226,961	185,257	41,704	6,795
Shelby	140	3,579	3,341	108	130	284,076	277,645	217,580	60,065	6,431
Simpson	114	4,202	3,678	440	84	152,814	149,270	123,545	25,725	3,544
Spencer	61	1,319	1,129	48	142	54,280	53,230	42,275	10,955	1,050
Taylor	134	5,863	4,085	1,244	534	112,572	107,515	84,285	23,230	5,057
Todd	415	14,366	12,642	1,554	170	388,160	379,142	301,802	77,340	9,018
Trigg	371	18,180	13,341	3,711	1,128	237,787	228,391	180,087	48,304	9,396
Trimble	12	413	212	141	60	10,310	10,135	6,735	3,400	175
Union	87	2,571	2,378	134	59	121,900	118,560	96,680	21,880	3,340
Warren	295	11,326	9,130	1,529	667	359,535	348,598	278,043	70,555	10,937
Washington	149	4,594	3,966	152	476	222,370	213,094	169,769	43,325	9,276
Wayne	83	2,841	1,854	975	12	50,042	48,495	38,990	9,505	1,547
Webster	123	6,940	5,971	855	114	243,662	237,435	202,135	35,300	6,227
Whitley	20	949	454	445	50	14,076	13,690	10,340	3,350	386
Wolfe	6	135	125	10	....	1,510	1,500	1,250	250	10
Woodford	94	3,116	2,708	179	229	264,137	258,465	218,630	39,835	5,672
LOUISIANA.										
Total	54,819	2,121,258	1,465,775	570,454	85,029	$46,573,105	$44,891,918	$36,170,690	$8,721,228	$1,681,187
Acadia	400	15,792	14,721	939	132	542,737	524,839	466,739	58,100	17,898
Ascension	218	8,393	4,940	3,195	258	276,604	267,545	205,145	62,400	9,059
Assumption	17	511	423	88	....	30,633	29,120	23,720	5,400	1,513
Avoyelles	1,281	29,861	26,003	3,574	284	1,121,046	1,078,461	896,800	181,661	42,585
Bienville	1,209	77,803	40,886	35,018	1,899	795,748	760,568	564,814	195,754	35,180
Bossier	2,605	110,412	68,317	36,267	5,828	2,109,227	2,050,911	1,704,953	345,958	58,316
Caddo	3,846	156,848	119,533	28,782	8,533	3,450,428	3,346,362	2,864,226	482,136	104,066
Calcasieu	305	18,500	7,886	7,042	3,572	393,884	367,960	283,065	84,895	25,924
Caldwell	322	20,251	7,790	12,383	78	235,343	221,954	168,634	53,320	13,389
Cameron	76	4,457	2,689	22	1,746	67,312	65,700	54,465	11,235	1,612
Catahoula	710	17,777	13,969	3,640	168	395,058	381,086	290,822	90,264	13,972
Claiborne	2,285	169,469	104,830	54,905	9,734	1,372,616	1,318,472	1,008,808	309,664	54,144
Concordia	1,055	24,544	18,853	5,576	115	720,028	690,508	518,210	172,298	29,520
De Soto	3,033	165,027	104,234	55,398	5,395	1,510,484	1,431,118	1,101,014	330,104	79,367
East Baton Rouge	1,180	34,459	27,739	5,916	804	1,007,843	977,297	769,804	207,493	30,540
East Carroll	1,717	36,461	29,139	7,266	56	1,285,910	1,228,808	917,558	311,250	57,102
East Feliciana	1,820	65,426	49,765	12,629	3,032	997,252	943,566	693,623	249,943	53,686
Franklin	852	22,867	16,931	5,109	827	581,138	553,428	424,453	128,975	27,710
Grant	460	9,685	8,483	743	459	352,285	341,215	277,024	64,191	11,070
Iberia	549	26,171	23,615	801	1,755	1,254,306	1,222,350	1,085,250	137,100	31,956
Iberville	251	10,831	7,891	2,903	37	680,899	649,000	539,335	109,665	31,899
Jackson	508	38,794	18,571	19,718	505	287,140	273,542	211,623	61,919	13,598
Jefferson	35	970	803	152	15	78,600	74,700	62,670	12,030	3,900
La Salle	60	3,756	1,202	2,434	120	33,420	31,055	20,015	11,040	2,365
Lafayette	935	36,445	33,526	656	2,263	1,815,030	1,777,270	1,626,002	151,268	37,760
Lafourche	71	3,381	2,309	796	276	172,505	167,675	144,340	23,329	4,830
Lincoln	868	57,104	37,273	17,939	1,892	563,649	537,227	402,643	134,584	26,422
Livingston	104	4,063	1,772	1,955	336	55,794	53,795	40,735	13,060	1,999
Madison	1,652	39,174	29,788	8,684	702	1,269,592	1,250,206	986,287	263,919	19,386
Morehouse	2,411	67,909	56,718	10,651	540	1,808,438	1,734,287	1,373,059	361,228	74,151

TABLE 71.—FARMS OPERATED BY NEGROES—NUMBER, ACREAGE, AND VALUE OF LAND AND BUILDINGS, AND OF IMPLEMENTS AND MACHINERY, BY STATES AND COUNTIES: 1910—Continued.

[Counties in which no farms operated by Negroes were reported are omitted.]

STATE AND COUNTY.	Number of farms.	FARM ACREAGE.				VALUE OF FARM LAND, BUILDINGS, AND IMPLEMENTS AND MACHINERY.					
		Total.	Improved.	Woodland.	Other un-improved.	Total.	Land and buildings.			Imple-ments and ma-chinery.
							Total.	Land.	Buildings.	
LOUISIANA—Continued.										
Natchitoches	2,872	84,474	59,474	22,529	2,471	$2,172,071	$2,096,609	$1,749,410	$347,199	$75,462
Orleans	34	631	233	344	54	168,404	165,200	131,370	33,830	3,204
Ouachita	1,214	45,173	27,878	16,979	316	1,141,133	1,105,886	895,928	209,958	35,247
Plaquemines	199	8,772	3,916	838	4,018	269,080	251,152	191,072	60,080	17,928
Pointe Coupee	1,632	35,943	30,284	5,215	444	1,248,860	1,219,263	925,481	293,782	29,597
Rapides	1,001	25,643	19,903	5,482	257	1,118,328	1,074,479	905,604	168,875	43,849
Red River	1,002	30,541	22,589	7,385	567	610,733	596,174	470,905	125,269	14,559
Richland	1,615	43,427	36,815	6,238	374	1,105,267	1,069,131	814,631	254,500	36,136
Sabine	421	25,046	12,047	8,455	4,544	236,674	225,398	173,463	51,935	11,276
St. Bernard	12	445	251	144	50	30,825	29,300	23,345	5,955	1,525
St. Charles	92	2,590	1,939	615	36	131,235	123,565	87,265	36,300	7,670
St. Helena	648	30,826	18,081	7,552	5,193	329,072	309,738	211,023	98,715	19,334
St. James	63	3,949	3,540	346	63	173,787	165,220	133,772	31,448	8,567
St. John the Baptist	53	3,942	2,873	890	179	199,775	181,450	138,440	43,010	18,325
St. Landry	3,748	123,429	105,525	14,532	3,372	4,061,316	3,913,659	3,248,115	665,544	147,657
St. Martin	924	34,616	29,283	2,634	2,699	1,562,349	1,510,295	1,333,865	176,430	52,054
St. Mary	218	8,816	7,504	1,239	73	584,602	568,222	458,719	109,503	16,380
St. Tammany	69	5,773	1,295	4,381	97	100,947	97,370	73,385	23,985	3,577
Tangipahoa	436	16,591	7,144	9,049	398	282,905	271,307	181,967	89,340	11,598
Tensas	2,729	52,850	44,663	7,185	1,002	1,989,005	1,942,073	1,496,208	445,865	46,932
Terrebonne	76	4,789	2,135	1,630	1,024	147,817	140,615	114,295	26,320	7,202
Union	776	66,411	33,110	32,689	612	466,018	438,413	324,987	113,426	27,605
Vermilion	314	14,983	12,563	586	1,834	664,769	644,485	584,713	59,772	20,284
Vernon	47	2,312	764	1,469	79	28,646	27,550	17,350	10,200	1,096
Washington	426	24,044	11,976	11,665	403	375,510	357,235	251,390	105,845	18,275
Webster	1,033	73,335	37,944	33,271	2,120	706,149	671,119	492,459	178,660	35,030
West Baton Rouge	340	7,570	6,609	901	60	361,013	347,116	246,136	100,980	13,897
West Carroll	432	13,472	9,277	3,945	250	317,177	303,492	244,562	58,930	13,685
West Feliciana	1,281	35,125	28,610	5,819	696	583,242	561,881	427,361	134,520	21,361
Winn	268	18,599	6,951	11,265	383	141,446	134,496	97,627	36,869	6,950
MAINE.										
Total	28	1,280	624	442	214	$40,080	$36,850	$16,575	$20,275	$3,230
Aroostook	1	65	65	....	....	3,300	3,000	1,800	1,200	300
Cumberland	9	250	129	56	65	14,650	13,800	6,125	7,675	850
Kennebec	4	167	87	75	5	7,000	6,100	2,300	3,800	900
Lincoln	2	135	45	55	35	1,440	1,400	800	600	40
Oxford	1	60	9	51	....	550	450	300	150	100
Penobscot	5	328	210	43	75	8,925	8,300	4,000	4,300	625
Sagadahoc	2	50	23	27	....	1,900	1,800	400	1,400	100
Waldo	2	80	30	40	10	1,115	1,100	350	750	15
Washington	2	145	26	95	24	1,200	900	500	400	300
MARYLAND.										
Total	6,370	358,509	218,574	122,381	17,554	$10,704,224	$10,267,284	$7,096,892	$3,170,392	$436,940
Allegany	4	420	225	175	20	11,630	11,000	8,400	2,600	630
Anne Arundel	421	26,962	19,179	6,921	862	989,042	951,407	627,300	324,107	37,635
Baltimore	137	5,615	3,926	1,484	205	696,010	673,135	447,770	225,365	22,875
Calvert	424	33,992	20,825	10,992	2,175	446,975	434,079	286,077	148,002	12,896
Caroline	395	15,750	10,768	4,349	633	643,826	615,374	437,779	177,595	28,452
Carroll	28	999	751	197	51	44,140	41,530	29,010	12,520	2,610
Cecil	64	1,664	1,338	232	94	102,339	98,650	56,100	42,550	3,689
Charles	633	58,960	31,246	25,579	2,135	972,900	924,599	594,669	329,930	48,301
Dorchester	513	31,951	17,222	12,007	2,722	691,337	659,365	514,490	144,875	31,972
Frederick	75	3,572	2,860	601	111	183,776	174,690	118,175	56,515	9,086
Garrett	5	668	380	238	50	32,050	31,200	15,400	15,800	850
Harford	197	8,632	5,467	2,264	901	334,156	309,985	173,190	136,795	24,171
Howard	147	5,210	3,804	1,136	270	295,166	281,655	178,135	103,520	13,511
Kent	151	4,080	2,875	1,005	200	212,059	204,338	150,866	53,472	7,721
Montgomery	349	9,811	7,822	1,750	239	605,831	582,713	427,285	155,428	23,118
Prince Georges	479	35,685	22,461	11,965	1,259	1,140,333	1,098,413	795,773	302,640	41,920
Queen Annes	224	9,707	7,326	1,904	480	382,970	364,920	279,322	85,598	18,050
St. Marys	438	28,819	14,779	12,007	2,033	457,829	438,491	273,678	164,813	19,338
Somerset	574	13,158	8,784	3,762	612	603,315	577,508	392,533	184,975	25,807
Talbot	202	7,437	5,448	1,675	314	564,895	546,730	360,203	186,165	18,527
Washington	22	1,483	1,146	332	5	68,420	65,910	48,510	17,400	2,510
Wicomico	407	16,908	10,146	6,325	437	503,970	486,878	349,151	137,727	17,092
Worcester	481	37,026	19,799	15,481	1,746	721,255	695,076	533,076	162,000	26,179

TABLE 71.—FARMS OPERATED BY NEGROES—NUMBER, ACREAGE, AND VALUE OF LAND AND BUILDINGS, AND OF IMPLEMENTS AND MACHINERY, BY STATES AND COUNTIES: 1910—Continued.

[Counties in which no farms operated by Negroes were reported are omitted.]

STATE AND COUNTY.	Number of farms.	FARM ACREAGE.				VALUE OF FARM LAND, BUILDINGS, AND IMPLEMENTS AND MACHINERY.				
		Total.	Improved.	Woodland.	Other un-improved.	Total.	Land and buildings.			Implements and machinery.
							Total.	Land.	Buildings.	

MASSACHUSETTS.

STATE AND COUNTY.	Number of farms.	Total.	Improved.	Woodland.	Other un-improved.	Total.	Total.	Land.	Buildings.	Implements and machinery.
Total	103	3,535	1,305	1,511	719	$270,122	$258,065	$129,490	$128,575	$12,057
Barnstable	10	179	86	31	62	16,865	16,200	5,300	10,900	665
Berkshire	18	684	251	221	212	29,520	28,280	13,280	15,000	1,240
Bristol	10	247	108	84	55	18,875	17,800	8,400	9,400	1,075
Dukes	3	195	41	55	99	6,060	5,450	3,650	1,800	610
Essex	3	29	19	9	1	15,900	15,000	5,500	9,500	900
Franklin	7	195	85	59	51	8,375	7,775	3,375	4,400	600
Hampden	3	132	56	66	10	8,860	8,000	3,800	4,200	860
Hampshire	4	193	96	94	3	5,856	5,375	3,675	1,700	481
Middlesex	15	378	137	110	131	62,670	61,360	31,685	29,675	1,310
Norfolk	11	582	152	387	43	41,593	40,100	17,900	22,200	1,493
Plymouth	8	307	95	181	31	34,035	32,250	20,450	11,800	1,785
Worcester	11	414	179	214	21	21,513	20,475	12,475	8,000	1,038

MICHIGAN.

STATE AND COUNTY.	Number of farms.	Total.	Improved.	Woodland.	Other un-improved.	Total.	Total.	Land.	Buildings.	Implements and machinery.
Total	640	45,331	32,260	5,540	7,531	$2,113,942	$2,024,685	$1,490,450	$534,235	$89,257
Allegan	48	2,986	2,270	421	295	134,357	128,550	85,960	42,590	5,807
Antrim	3	268	185	10	73	9,135	8,900	7,150	1,750	235
Barry	4	340	250	27	63	13,975	13,050	10,250	2,800	925
Bay	3	145	131	10	4	12,100	11,400	6,900	4,500	700
Benzie	7	780	458	110	212	23,478	22,065	16,365	5,700	1,413
Berrien	23	1,313	1,137	64	112	106,165	103,450	77,750	25,700	2,715
Branch	3	149	121	15	13	7,460	7,250	4,900	2,350	210
Calhoun	11	554	430	17	107	20,020	18,950	12,750	6,200	1,070
Cass	171	13,515	10,420	1,647	1,448	661,808	637,775	496,190	141,585	24,033
Charlevoix	4	243	140	10	93	17,610	16,900	9,600	7,300	710
Cheboygan	2	80	50	10	20	2,050	1,800	1,225	575	250
Chippewa	1	80	20		60	2,050	2,000	1,900	100	50
Clinton	6	542	182	300	60	18,210	17,600	12,000	5,600	610
Crawford	1	120	48		72	3,150	3,000	2,900	100	150
Delta	1	10	3		7	700	700	500	200	
Eaton	3	276	180	23	73	13,400	13,000	6,700	6,300	400
Emmet	1	40	40			1,540	1,500	600	900	40
Genesee	2	80	80			3,400	3,100	1,900	1,200	300
Gladwin	4	380	141	10	229	7,250	7,000	6,450	550	250
Grand Traverse	2	224	64	40	120	2,225	2,100	1,500	600	125
Gratiot	11	729	569	77	83	36,630	35,400	26,450	8,950	1,230
Hillsdale	2	42	35	2	5	2,830	2,600	1,300	1,300	230
Huron	1	40	25		15	1,275	1,200	900	300	75
Ingham	5	419	337	50	32	22,715	21,300	16,800	4,500	1,415
Ionia	1	80	66	8	6	3,425	3,200	1,800	1,400	225
Iosco	1	120	30		90	210	200	125	75	10
Isabella	27	2,471	1,550	198	723	68,140	64,325	51,890	12,435	3,815
Jackson	5	202	180	7	15	16,775	16,100	10,200	5,900	675
Kalamazoo	5	245	222	10	13	21,450	20,800	14,500	6,300	650
Kalkaska	1	40	40			900	800	300	500	100
Kent	12	522	361	73	88	43,450	41,980	31,320	10,660	1,470
Lapeer	1	16	16			1,600	1,500	900	600	100
Leelanau	5	514	235	203	76	8,500	8,000	4,700	3,300	500
Lenawee	3	111	103	8		6,800	6,300	4,150	2,150	500
Livingston	1	7	7			2,200	2,000	1,200	800	200
Manistee	5	365	128	129	108	11,825	11,000	7,300	3,700	825
Mecosta	35	2,773	1,599	110	1,064	62,930	60,100	45,510	14,590	2,830
Midland	19	1,291	729	334	228	51,515	49,800	34,375	15,425	1,715
Missaukee	1	38	5		33	400	400	350	50	
Monroe	10	861	605	78	178	75,275	73,400	61,750	11,650	1,875
Montcalm	25	1,667	1,168	165	334	60,715	58,320	43,470	14,850	2,395
Muskegon	5	134	85	39	10	15,041	14,500	8,300	6,200	541
Newaygo	2	273	50	163	60	1,775	1,700	1,200	500	75
Oakland	3	29	29			3,670	3,500	2,200	1,300	170
Oceana	3	100	68	14	18	5,675	5,600	4,250	1,350	75
Ontonagon	1	80	8		72	1,600	1,500	1,000	500	100
Osceola	3	200	30		170	2,660	2,550	1,950	600	110
Oscoda	1	320	80	240		1,330	1,280	1,080	200	50
Ottawa	1	50	50			2,200	2,200	2,200		
Saginaw	1	5	5			600	500	200	300	100
St. Joseph	3	148	114	8	26	7,988	7,500	5,300	2,200	488
Sanilac	2	200	180	20		6,200	6,000	4,800	1,200	200
Shiawassee	1	10	10			650	600	550	50	50
Tuscola	2	60	36	24		1,750	1,600	1,200	400	150
Van Buren	78	4,990	4,000	529	461	287,725	273,915	198,065	75,850	13,810
Washtenaw	26	1,712	1,546	94	72	116,080	108,900	72,450	36,450	7,180
Wayne	30	1,757	1,499	218	40	95,245	90,300	59,800	30,500	4,945
Wexford	2	585	110	25	450	4,110	3,725	3,125	600	385

TABLE **71.**—FARMS OPERATED BY NEGROES—NUMBER, ACREAGE, AND VALUE OF LAND AND BUILDINGS, AND OF IMPLEMENTS AND MACHINERY, BY STATES AND COUNTIES: 1910—Continued.

[Counties in which no farms operated by Negroes were reported are omitted.]

STATE AND COUNTY.	Number of farms.	FARM ACREAGE.				VALUE OF FARM LAND, BUILDINGS, AND IMPLEMENTS AND MACHINERY.					
		Total.	Improved.	Woodland.	Other un-improved.	Total.	Land and buildings.			Implements and machinery.
							Total.	Land.	Buildings.	

MINNESOTA.

STATE AND COUNTY.	Number of farms.	Total.	Improved.	Woodland.	Other un-improved.	Total.	Total.	Land.	Buildings.	Implements and machinery.
Total	29	2,362	1,631	448	283	$128,910	$123,915	$94,815	$29,100	$4,995
Anoka	3	388	193	146	49	20,650	19,300	13,075	6,225	1,350
Dakota	2	250	212	2	36	8,930	8,500	6,375	2,125	430
Goodhue	2	40	24	1	15	5,175	5,000	1,500	3,500	175
Hennepin	5	77	67	1	9	22,550	21,800	15,100	6,700	750
Hubbard	1	40	4	36	....	800	800	700	100	....
Itasca	1	160	40	120	....	4,000	4,000	4,000	....	....
Kittson	2	310	240	70	....	13,950	13,400	11,100	2,300	550
Le Suer	2	95	75	20	....	3,770	3,500	2,600	900	270
McLeod	1	9	9	....	....	1,500	1,500	1,000	500	....
Otter Tail	1	40	1	5	34	1,020	1,000	850	150	20
Pennington	1	160	45	30	85	4,000	4,000	3,900	100	....
Redwood	2	130	120	....	10	7,625	7,500	6,200	1,300	125
Rice	2	126	101	9	16	7,700	7,375	5,675	1,700	325
St. Louis	1	8	5	3	....	850	800	400	400	50
Wabasha	1	18	18	....	....	5,300	5,000	4,000	1,000	300
Watonwan	1	280	275	5	....	11,600	11,200	9,700	1,500	400
Wilkin	1	231	202	....	29	9,490	9,240	8,640	600	250

MISSISSIPPI.

STATE AND COUNTY.	Number of farms.	Total.	Improved.	Woodland.	Other un-improved.	Total.	Total.	Land.	Buildings.	Implements and machinery.
Total	164,488	6,445,077	4,481,575	1,567,501	396,001	$153,994,866	$148,396,668	$120,288,410	$28,108,258	$5,598,198
Adams	1,706	68,438	39,287	21,951	7,200	1,102,961	1,040,311	734,690	305,621	62,650
Alcorn	441	20,099	13,451	5,572	1,076	316,502	300,457	236,437	64,020	16,045
Amite	1,787	82,404	53,516	26,119	2,769	1,062,151	1,005,297	725,257	280,040	56,854
Attala	2,181	115,034	64,409	38,291	12,334	1,557,663	1,490,590	1,171,925	318,665	67,073
Benton	943	70,061	37,700	18,295	14,066	713,514	682,221	538,386	143,835	31,293
Bolivar	9,823	224,812	204,365	19,121	1,326	12,578,947	12,249,233	10,389,076	1,860,157	329,714
Calhoun	682	33,189	18,390	11,572	3,227	474,497	454,324	368,279	86,045	20,173
Carroll	2,519	118,161	76,912	28,105	13,144	1,588,413	1,499,834	1,128,046	371,788	88,579
Chickasaw	1,901	92,980	63,455	20,157	9,368	1,951,309	1,855,145	1,560,255	294,890	96,164
Choctaw	667	39,250	21,590	14,283	3,377	483,495	452,712	353,354	99,358	30,783
Clairborne	2,133	93,396	58,500	27,832	7,064	1,214,635	1,151,465	836,888	314,577	63,170
Clarke	1,548	73,261	37,768	31,859	3,634	979,995	930,917	654,811	276,106	49,078
Clay	2,241	100,684	80,619	17,788	2,277	2,596,133	2,490,876	2,077,412	413,464	105,257
Coahoma	6,483	149,315	139,769	8,486	1,060	8,991,041	8,726,706	7,417,747	1,308,959	264,335
Copiah	3,059	134,925	88,439	36,777	9,709	1,928,630	1,828,745	1,252,674	576,071	99,885
Covington	506	30,207	13,476	11,097	5,634	400,429	382,231	285,154	97,077	18,198
De Soto	3,593	163,580	122,166	28,124	13,290	4,030,901	3,884,698	3,120,722	763,976	146,203
Forrest	264	17,544	5,582	11,187	775	273,963	259,945	194,170	65,775	14,018
Franklin	837	43,365	23,720	15,554	4,091	462,937	437,714	333,071	104,643	25,223
George	59	5,039	511	4,004	524	54,296	49,450	32,390	17,060	4,846
Greene	98	7,896	1,186	6,602	108	70,720	67,900	44,875	23,025	2,820
Grenada	1,784	111,626	63,443	36,127	12,056	1,699,830	1,627,615	1,259,065	368,550	72,215
Hancock	62	2,699	375	1,537	787	57,277	54,485	33,710	20,775	2,792
Harrison	134	9,815	1,566	6,853	1,396	266,997	259,805	148,240	111,565	7,192
Hinds	6,208	225,492	185,902	27,651	11,939	4,678,058	4,474,130	3,468,105	1,006,025	203,928
Holmes	5,437	232,091	170,438	43,277	18,376	5,732,884	5,497,126	4,379,079	1,118,047	235,758
Issaquena	2,154	49,826	41,673	8,117	36	2,258,135	2,193,685	1,774,621	419,064	64,450
Itawamba	202	11,803	5,721	5,447	635	135,512	130,138	107,728	22,410	5,374
Jackson	65	4,935	467	4,225	243	89,552	85,250	47,350	37,900	4,302
Jasper	1,489	93,225	44,199	41,238	7,788	968,252	926,462	703,290	223,172	41,790
Jefferson	2,235	84,018	60,672	19,861	3,485	1,205,557	1,140,906	839,674	301,232	64,651
Jefferson Davis	1,080	63,960	35,471	27,158	1,331	981,639	940,525	709,261	231,264	41,114
Jones	455	25,849	10,334	14,002	1,513	363,249	347,768	263,113	84,655	15,481
Kemper	1,934	116,677	70,064	40,083	6,530	1,349,852	1,273,140	988,258	284,882	76,712
Lafayette	1,796	110,640	53,635	44,347	12,658	1,126,058	1,063,325	865,000	198,325	62,733
Lamar	101	5,067	1,971	1,562	1,534	67,541	65,611	43,132	22,479	1,930
Lauderdale	1,781	103,679	58,150	40,321	5,208	1,311,438	1,256,098	952,781	303,317	55,340
Lawrence	783	47,534	22,764	21,730	3,040	594,742	568,055	415,726	152,329	26,687
Leake	1,166	68,860	34,541	27,876	6,443	711,067	679,233	526,030	153,203	31,834
Lee	1,839	57,769	46,571	8,276	2,922	1,906,231	1,836,421	1,555,876	280,545	69,810
Leflore	5,824	165,202	154,939	9,909	354	9,861,456	9,619,541	8,344,984	1,274,557	241,915
Lincoln	1,216	50,983	29,771	20,728	484	680,450	648,495	461,693	186,802	31,955
Lowndes	3,297	120,662	98,373	19,008	3,281	3,011,980	2,900,972	2,392,544	508,428	111,008
Madison	4,996	214,229	168,778	31,733	13,718	3,767,445	3,554,406	2,718,302	836,104	213,039
Marion	693	35,648	16,433	18,707	508	502,294	482,405	362,015	120,390	19,889
Marshall	3,480	206,061	115,635	45,895	44,531	2,550,580	2,434,982	1,906,946	528,036	115,598
Monroe	3,309	139,208	107,894	27,267	4,047	3,647,968	3,489,122	2,968,510	520,612	158,846
Montgomery	1,433	68,935	45,646	16,027	7,262	1,036,830	995,111	754,726	240,385	41,719
Neshoba	478	27,545	14,892	11,614	1,039	365,392	350,948	284,908	66,040	14,444
Newton	1,347	64,979	35,745	22,335	6,899	907,926	876,134	663,838	212,296	31,792

TABLE 71.—FARMS OPERATED BY NEGROES—NUMBER, ACREAGE, AND VALUE OF LAND AND BUILDINGS, AND OF IMPLEMENTS AND MACHINERY, BY STATES AND COUNTIES: 1910—Continued.

[Counties in which no farms operated by Negroes were reported are omitted.]

STATE AND COUNTY.	Number of farms.	FARM ACREAGE.				VALUE OF FARM LAND, BUILDINGS, AND IMPLEMENTS AND MACHINERY.					
		Total.	Improved.	Woodland.	Other un-improved.	Total.	Land and buildings.				Implements and machinery.
							Total.	Land.	Buildings.		

MISSISSIPPI—Continued.

STATE AND COUNTY.	Number of farms.	Total.	Improved.	Woodland.	Other un-improved.	Total.	Total.	Land.	Buildings.	Implements and machinery.
Noxubee	4,422	173,229	141,097	25,362	6,770	$3,858,218	$3,720,370	$3,183,102	$537,268	$137,848
Oktibbeha	2,218	95,951	65,117	28,276	2,558	1,341,044	1,270,796	984,471	286,325	70,248
Panola	4,215	174,641	120,931	32,707	21,003	3,455,689	3,301,391	2,634,566	666,825	154,298
Pearl River	93	7,827	1,818	5,824	185	95,744	92,176	61,851	30,325	3,568
Perry	170	15,784	3,031	12,741	12	251,869	239,600	170,585	69,015	12,269
Pike	1,811	94,199	50,416	35,894	7,889	1,366,900	1,304,953	890,948	414,005	61,947
Pontotoc	845	41,274	23,787	10,914	6,573	693,548	672,794	555,218	117,576	20,754
Prentiss	473	18,872	13,543	3,092	2,237	424,607	410,974	357,364	53,610	13,633
Quitman	1,966	47,702	41,834	5,548	320	2,470,167	2,394,993	2,072,331	322,662	75,174
Rankin	2,455	127,666	74,652	50,731	2,283	1,477,101	1,421,123	1,110,358	310,765	55,978
Scott	1,051	51,924	26,641	24,030	1,253	569,843	545,737	413,193	132,544	24,106
Sharkey	3,206	68,530	64,494	3,904	132	4,184,633	4,083,215	3,226,180	857,035	101,418
Simpson	1,004	49,444	26,926	21,734	784	619,753	593,019	424,507	168,512	26,734
Smith	432	26,121	11,701	13,662	758	285,547	273,334	208,489	64,845	12,213
Sunflower	4,662	111,674	105,129	6,006	539	5,776,613	5,624,890	4,849,782	775,108	151,723
Tallahatchie	3,872	106,803	91,012	11,598	4,193	3,830,192	3,729,145	3,078,195	650,950	101,047
Tate	2,541	105,391	76,406	18,148	10,837	1,927,490	1,856,920	1,468,392	388,528	70,570
Tippah	439	24,560	12,986	8,553	3,021	283,867	271,069	213,509	57,560	12,798
Tishomingo	131	8,651	3,300	5,110	241	78,151	75,216	56,326	18,890	2,935
Tunica	4,153	102,955	95,705	6,767	483	5,643,546	5,470,060	4,694,309	775,751	173,486
Union	659	27,488	19,111	6,445	1,932	541,794	523,965	419,749	104,216	17,829
Warren	2,669	64,538	47,109	15,471	1,958	1,479,676	1,424,505	1,041,639	382,866	55,171
Washington	7,969	167,608	152,673	13,764	1,261	8,248,681	8,074,090	6,750,830	1,323,260	174,591
Wayne	662	39,198	15,737	22,060	1,401	373,505	360,366	258,925	101,441	15,139
Webster	583	32,787	17,572	13,719	1,496	380,119	365,623	294,303	71,320	14,496
Wilkinson	1,979	74,631	50,175	18,214	6,242	918,826	875,834	658,148	217,686	42,992
Winston	1,142	70,009	37,349	30,435	2,225	795,941	756,889	584,589	172,300	39,052
Yalobusha	1,704	94,110	55,602	32,628	5,880	1,357,945	1,293,729	991,661	302,068	64,216
Yazoo	6,713	218,763	174,847	38,477	5,439	6,592,533	6,357,227	5,240,766	1,116,461	235,306

MISSOURI.

STATE AND COUNTY.	Number of farms.	Total.	Improved.	Woodland.	Other un-improved.	Total.	Total.	Land.	Buildings.	Implements and machinery.
Total	3,656	229,255	172,200	50,425	6,630	$12,322,243	$12,006,443	$10,556,515	$1,449,928	$315,800
Adair	2	108	98	10	....	6,010	5,760	5,110	650	250
Andrew	4	121	109	12	....	11,925	11,600	10,260	1,340	325
Audrain	42	3,133	2,704	264	165	220,228	216,120	182,100	34,020	4,108
Barton	2	113	113	....	....	3,690	3,390	3,190	200	300
Bates	1	85	55	25	5	3,450	3,400	3,150	250	50
Benton	9	632	474	144	14	28,240	27,470	24,220	3,250	770
Bollinger	2	37	37	....	....	1,486	1,480	1,360	120	6
Boone	58	11,111	8,437	2,450	224	587,915	573,410	499,480	73,930	14,505
Buchanan	11	484	447	35	2	166,583	165,710	151,710	14,000	873
Butler	48	2,646	1,619	1,022	5	95,355	92,290	79,615	12,675	3,065
Caldwell	9	341	310	27	4	21,497	20,790	16,750	4,040	707
Callaway	278	16,990	10,326	5,320	1,344	531,000	511,005	418,770	92,235	19,995
Camden	7	1,045	350	635	60	13,800	13,100	11,200	1,900	700
Cape Girardeau	71	4,069	2,944	1,102	23	158,846	152,370	129,380	22,990	6,476
Carroll	42	3,112	2,804	248	60	231,515	226,800	210,850	15,950	4,715
Carter	1	80	40	40	....	1,550	1,500	1,425	75	50
Cass	8	461	371	85	5	37,040	36,450	31,500	4,950	590
Cedar	3	213	95	18	100	6,805	6,620	5,620	1,000	185
Chariton	135	7,399	5,907	1,445	47	394,265	382,080	331,785	50,295	12,185
Christian	4	91	75	16	....	4,740	4,520	3,770	750	220
Clark	2	90	90	....	....	3,550	3,400	2,100	1,300	150
Clay	23	1,134	1,037	85	12	123,480	120,645	108,895	11,750	2,835
Clinton	30	1,821	1,388	402	31	112,610	109,050	94,775	14,275	3,560
Cole	16	1,162	777	357	28	41,775	40,200	34,100	6,100	1,575
Cooper	138	8,264	6,509	1,401	354	482,269	470,735	417,620	53,115	11,534
Crawford	5	440	215	225	....	7,345	7,200	5,900	1,300	145
Dade	13	667	467	200	....	25,950	24,970	23,470	1,500	980
Dallas	1	40	15	25	....	525	500	425	75	25
Daviess	5	539	498	39	2	17,725	17,325	12,700	4,625	400
Dekalb	10	984	919	65	....	99,235	97,250	83,550	13,700	1,985
Dent	1	115	53	52	10	2,475	2,400	2,000	400	75
Douglas	1	160	60	100	....	820	800	650	150	20
Dunklin	6	301	221	80	....	22,347	22,090	19,740	2,350	257
Franklin	83	5,180	3,235	1,896	49	207,522	200,746	167,160	33,586	6,776
Gasconade	5	1,212	340	828	44	14,800	14,200	10,100	4,100	600
Greene	69	2,881	2,337	465	79	172,045	168,255	148,375	19,880	3,790
Grundy	2	137	124	12	....	8,700	8,300	7,500	800	400
Harrison	2	103	88	....	15	10,625	10,400	8,900	1,500	225
Henry	38	2,404	2,138	266	....	127,795	124,140	112,190	11,950	3,655
Holt	6	678	659	19	....	48,900	48,000	43,600	4,400	900
Howard	118	8,853	7,183	1,530	140	475,524	462,120	406,790	55,330	13,404
Howell	10	887	418	469	....	13,160	12,960	10,660	2,300	200
Iron	2	14	10	4	....	1,760	1,700	1,200	500	60
Jackson	21	1,439	1,313	106	20	311,945	310,250	298,500	11,750	1,695
Jasper	1	24	14	10	....	5,900	5,800	5,200	600	100

TABLE 71.—FARMS OPERATED BY NEGROES—NUMBER, ACREAGE, AND VALUE OF LAND AND BUILDINGS, AND OF IMPLEMENTS AND MACHINERY, BY STATES AND COUNTIES: 1910—Continued.

[Counties in which no farms operated by Negroes were reported are omitted.]

STATE AND COUNTY.	Number of farms.	FARM ACREAGE.				VALUE OF FARM LAND, BUILDINGS, AND IMPLEMENTS AND MACHINERY.					Implements and machinery.
		Total.	Improved.	Woodland.	Other unimproved.	Total.	Land and buildings.				
							Total.	Land.	Buildings.		

MISSOURI—Continued.

STATE AND COUNTY.	Number of farms.	Total.	Improved.	Woodland.	Other unimproved.	Total.	Total.	Land.	Buildings.	Implements and machinery.
Jefferson	17	1,299	828	471	....	$43,540	$42,620	$31,120	$11,500	$920
Johnson	87	5,681	4,815	787	79	293,103	286,738	248,050	38,688	6,365
Knox	8	788	638	140	10	46,085	45,400	38,450	6,950	685
Laclede	19	2,272	681	1,017	574	36,162	35,200	32,540	2,660	962
Lafayette	52	2,613	2,081	481	51	207,262	199,045	176,380	22,665	8,217
Lawrence	5	768	679	89	....	32,235	30,850	26,450	4,400	1,385
Lewis	24	2,175	1,871	304	....	113,035	110,185	99,910	10,275	2,850
Lincoln	130	6,871	5,234	1,385	252	298,175	288,646	259,151	29,495	9,529
Linn	13	506	409	97	....	38,725	37,710	31,210	6,500	1,015
Livingston	23	1,254	1,025	205	24	85,135	82,620	71,995	10,625	2,515
Macon	27	1,499	1,210	285	4	60,302	58,085	48,710	9,375	2,217
Madison	5	550	211	339	....	9,670	9,240	7,600	1,640	430
Maries	1	70	60	10	....	1,010	1,030	850	150	10
Marion	52	3,189	2,100	1,010	79	162,095	157,785	134,405	23,380	4,310
Mercer	6	210	125	78	7	7,865	7,600	6,205	1,395	265
Miller	19	1,201	634	460	107	30,470	29,670	27,620	2,050	800
Mississippi	136	8,821	8,157	567	97	385,510	374,635	336,175	38,460	10,875
Moniteau	18	2,025	1,224	797	4	87,093	84,280	75,180	9,100	2,813
Monroe	91	5,406	4,474	700	232	291,430	280,205	238,995	41,210	11,225
Montgomery	86	6,997	3,890	2,702	405	219,010	208,630	182,900	25,730	10,380
Morgan	14	1,032	789	243	....	36,445	35,330	29,705	5,625	1,115
New Madrid	203	10,173	9,621	537	15	637,510	625,035	565,900	59,135	12,475
Newton	42	2,058	1,495	530	33	83,031	81,500	71,065	10,435	1,531
Nodaway	2	146	123	23	....	11,780	11,480	10,180	1,300	300
Osage	7	485	224	211	50	7,985	7,680	5,640	2,040	305
Ozark	1	160	40	120	....	1,060	1,000	900	100	60
Pemiscot	92	3,183	3,116	67	....	244,950	240,850	223,355	17,495	4,100
Perry	20	1,307	1,050	175	82	71,180	69,125	61,945	7,180	2,055
Pettis	77	3,142	2,701	427	14	192,665	188,550	163,570	24,980	4,115
Phelps	2	85	12	73	....	1,025	1,000	560	440	25
Pike	206	14,814	11,933	2,691	190	717,402	697,490	609,870	87,620	19,912
Platte	21	1,356	1,021	248	87	101,330	99,000	91,850	7,150	2,330
Polk	6	259	224	35	....	11,585	10,810	8,810	2,000	775
Pulaski	4	219	47	172	....	4,710	4,600	3,600	1,000	110
Putnam	2	192	142	30	20	8,450	8,300	5,900	2,400	150
Ralls	37	2,482	1,942	350	190	113,551	110,160	93,075	17,085	3,391
Randolph	104	5,989	4,337	1,493	159	293,770	283,205	221,735	61,470	10,565
Ray	30	1,698	1,423	234	41	12,088	96,663	82,963	13,700	2,425
St. Charles	61	3,931	3,269	543	119	196,277	191,415	164,220	27,195	4,862
St. Clair	11	434	297	132	5	9,827	9,300	6,700	2,600	527
St. Francois	4	496	310	132	54	24,050	23,800	22,200	1,600	250
St. Louis	83	5,566	2,924	2,461	181	929,745	921,775	837,780	83,995	7,970
St. Louis City	8	98	81	3	14	56,963	55,150	53,900	1,250	1,813
Ste. Genevieve	23	1,751	850	814	87	58,755	56,850	47,675	9,175	1,905
Saline	151	9,505	8,620	693	192	760,448	745,545	682,082	63,463	14,903
Scott	16	1,369	1,319	....	50	72,315	67,845	62,845	5,000	4,470
Shelby	37	1,498	1,138	360	....	72,915	69,880	58,680	11,200	3,035
Stoddard	1	60	60	....	....	1,900	1,800	1,400	400	100
Texas	1	60	50	10	....	920	900	800	100	20
Vernon	7	473	386	87	....	18,690	18,400	16,000	2,400	290
Warren	32	2,535	1,360	1,062	113	65,595	62,905	52,405	10,500	2,690
Washington	36	2,020	1,017	942	61	37,893	36,615	30,580	6,035	1,278
Wayne	2	244	124	120	....	6,510	6,200	3,400	2,800	310
Webster	2	146	128	18	....	4,230	3,980	3,180	800	250
Wright	47	4,294	2,258	1,930	106	55,059	52,860	40,804	12,056	2,199

MONTANA.

STATE AND COUNTY.	Number of farms.	Total.	Improved.	Woodland.	Other unimproved.	Total.	Total.	Land.	Buildings.	Implements and machinery.
Total	29	7,918	1,751	1,324	4,843	$129,255	$114,680	$97,255	$17,425	$14,575
Cascade	10	1,820	430	298	1,092	30,170	28,480	25,055	3,425	1,690
Chouteau	4	930	190	10	730	13,450	12,900	10,700	2,200	550
Dawson	1	160	160	....	....	4,000	4,000	3,950	50	....
Fergus	1	160	160	....	....	3,450	3,200	2,200	1,000	250
Granite	1	2,540	540	1,000	1,000	30,000	20,000	14,000	6,000	10,000
Lewis and Clark	1	40	12	....	28	2,545	2,500	1,600	900	45
Madison	1	120	40	....	80	3,600	3,500	3,000	500	100
Park	2	1,120	30	....	1,090	11,400	11,200	10,850	350	200
Rosebud	2	480	50	....	430	7,390	6,800	6,350	450	590
Sanders	1	287	75	....	212	10,200	10,000	9,200	800	200
Silver Bow	1	160	5	....	155	1,600	1,000	600	400	600
Yellowstone	4	101	59	16	26	11,450	11,100	9,750	1,350	350

TABLE 71.—FARMS OPERATED BY NEGROES—NUMBER, ACREAGE, AND VALUE OF LAND AND BUILDINGS, AND OF IMPLEMENTS AND MACHINERY, BY STATES AND COUNTIES: 1910—Continued.

[Counties in which no farms operated by Negroes were reported are omitted.]

STATE AND COUNTY.	Number of farms.	FARM ACREAGE.				VALUE OF FARM LAND, BUILDINGS, AND IMPLEMENTS AND MACHINERY.				
		Total.	Improved.	Woodland.	Other un-improved.	Total.	Land and buildings.			Implements and machinery.
							Total.	Land.	Buildings.	
NEBRASKA.										
Total	96	36,585	11,923	730	23,932	$524,640	$513,360	$459,350	$54,010	$11,280
Adams	5	162	159	3	....	28,400	27,500	21,300	6,200	900
Blaine	5	3,360	482	....	2,878	14,450	14,000	12,625	1,375	450
Boone	1	250	155	....	95	20,300	20,000	18,800	1,200	300
Box Butte	1	2,080	165	....	1,915	16,815	16,640	15,640	1,000	175
Brown	1	640	130	....	510	6,600	6,400	6,100	300	200
Cedar	1	40	12	28	....	1,250	1,200	1,150	50	50
Cherry	24	14,110	3,043	87	10,980	58,200	56,640	50,515	6,125	1,560
Cheyenne	2	960	35	....	925	4,750	4,700	4,350	350	50
Colfax	1	10	10	....	....	2,000	2,000	1,000	1,000	....
Custer	1	20	20	....	....	1,800	1,800	1,600	200	....
Douglas	4	93	88	5	....	36,135	35,700	34,150	1,550	435
Dundy	1	760	760	....	....	11,900	11,400	9,400	2,000	500
Fillmore	1	171	171	....	....	14,300	14,000	13,300	700	300
Furnas	1	560	105	....	455	14,200	14,000	13,925	75	200
Garfield	2	800	210	15	575	8,215	8,000	6,960	1,040	215
Greeley	1	85	51	....	34	2,675	2,600	1,800	800	75
Hall	1	95	70	....	25	4,950	4,750	3,750	1,000	200
Hamilton	3	252	252	....	....	31,050	30,250	26,750	3,500	800
Harlan	3	340	307	1	32	21,900	21,400	18,400	3,000	500
Holt	2	980	767	33	180	23,840	23,300	20,700	2,600	540
Howard	1	120	112	4	4	10,250	10,000	9,000	1,000	250
Knox	2	320	190	3	127	8,150	8,000	6,900	1,100	150
Lancaster	2	110	100	....	10	13,200	13,000	12,500	500	200
Lincoln	4	1,440	789	11	640	13,225	12,750	11,950	800	475
McPherson	1	640	400	....	240	1,240	1,200	1,050	150	40
Madison	1	160	160	....	....	5,200	5,000	3,500	1,500	200
Morrill	1	320	10	....	310	1,630	1,630	1,430	200	....
Saline	2	245	202	....	43	23,750	23,500	22,000	1,500	250
Sarpy	3	171	171	....	....	25,025	24,400	21,700	2,700	625
Saunders	1	80	80	....	....	8,150	8,000	6,500	1,500	150
Scotts Bluff	1	160	55	....	105	3,275	3,200	1,700	1,500	75
Seward	2	186	186	....	....	25,670	25,200	22,400	2,800	470
Sioux	5	2,785	1,301	525	959	24,125	23,800	21,850	1,950	325
Thomas	1	640	150	....	490	3,150	3,000	2,800	200	150
Wheeler	8	3,440	1,025	15	2,400	34,870	34,400	31,855	2,545	470
NEVADA.										
Total	6	2,280	1,115	1	1,164	$72,325	$70,500	$64,500	$6,000	$1,825
Douglas	2	1,640	880	....	760	56,200	55,500	51,100	4,400	700
Elko	1	120	85	1	34	2,100	1,500	1,000	500	600
Humboldt	1	160	40	....	120	3,575	3,500	3,400	100	75
Lincoln	2	360	110	....	250	10,450	10,000	9,000	1,000	450
NEW HAMPSHIRE.										
Total	14	923	293	249	381	$64,255	$61,300	$30,750	$30,550	$2,955
Belknap	5	460	101	104	255	45,295	42,900	21,300	21,600	2,395
Carroll	1	15	15	....	....	525	500	250	250	25
Grafton	3	303	113	110	80	3,900	3,800	1,600	2,200	100
Hillsborough	3	45	35	10	....	11,710	11,300	5,800	5,500	410
Merrimack	1	30	9	....	21	2,025	2,000	1,000	1,000	25
Sullivan	1	70	20	25	25	800	800	800	....	....
NEW JERSEY.										
Total	472	22,200	15,016	3,471	3,713	$1,773,883	$1,689,737	$1,025,917	$663,820	$84,146
Atlantic	14	260	105	121	34	38,200	37,050	24,000	13,050	1,150
Bergen	4	77	60	8	9	37,050	35,000	27,000	8,000	2,050
Burlington	43	1,852	1,301	376	175	178,106	170,347	129,847	40,500	7,759
Camden	20	462	342	70	50	60,778	57,800	29,600	28,200	2,978
Cape May	12	463	207	187	69	32,395	31,200	20,850	10,350	1,195
Cumberland	96	5,751	3,186	652	1,913	273,412	259,150	156,925	102,225	14,262
Essex	1	20	18	....	2	5,100	5,000	3,500	1,500	100
Gloucester	44	1,577	1,095	339	143	90,440	81,200	45,770	35,430	9,240
Hunterdon	5	216	180	29	7	10,295	9,900	3,965	5,935	395
Mercer	18	498	431	40	27	48,775	45,800	24,500	21,300	2,975
Middlesex	11	468	407	46	15	50,800	47,900	31,400	16,500	2,900
Monmouth	53	2,308	1,759	395	154	352,450	339,850	197,825	142,025	12,600
Morris	4	364	206	139	19	66,450	65,000	38,500	26,500	1,450
Ocean	1	86	36	50	....	4,000	3,500	2,000	1,500	500
Passaic	3	131	65	46	20	15,800	15,000	10,300	4,700	800
Salem	125	6,507	4,786	722	999	297,452	281,140	171,735	109,405	16,312
Somerset	13	818	693	113	12	164,855	158,400	78,700	79,700	6,455
Sussex	1	120	60	20	40	6,200	6,000	3,500	2,500	200
Union	3	72	54	18	....	39,825	39,000	25,000	14,000	825
Warren	1	150	25	100	25	1,500	1,500	1,000	500	....

TABLE 71.—FARMS OPERATED BY NEGROES—NUMBER, ACREAGE, AND VALUE OF LAND AND BUILDINGS, AND OF IMPLEMENTS AND MACHINERY, BY STATES AND COUNTIES: 1910—Continued.

[Counties in which no farms operated by Negroes were reported are omitted.]

| STATE AND COUNTY. | Number of farms. | FARM ACREAGE. | | | | VALUE OF FARM LAND, BUILDINGS, AND IMPLEMENTS AND MACHINERY. | | | | Implements and machinery. |
| | | Total. | Improved. | Woodland. | Other unimproved. | Total. | Land and buildings. | | | |
							Total.	Land.	Buildings.	
NEW MEXICO.										
Total	48	11,633	1,574	1,532	8,527	$207,228	$199,245	$181,175	$18,070	$7,983
Bernalillo	4	331	16		315	7,465	7,100	3,950	3,150	365
Chaves	11	1,970	681	200	1,089	70,855	66,880	61,850	5,030	3,975
Colfax	1	5,040	25	320	4,695	50,909	50,400	50,000	400	509
Dona Ana	3	232	192		40	43,611	42,625	40,175	2,450	986
Grant	3	360	113		247	3,300	3,000	2,250	750	300
Guadalupe	1	160		30	130	515	500	425	75	15
Lincoln	1	160	8	152		300	300	280	20	
Luna	1	10	8		2	2,000	1,800	1,300	500	200
McKinley	1	160	20	140		600	500	400	100	100
Otero	3	488	105	130	253	9,475	9,150	7,425	1,725	625
Quay	2	320	74		246	1,310	1,300	1,210	90	10
Rio Arriba	1	4	4			900	800	600	200	100
San Juan	2	340	40		300	4,550	4,500	4,185	315	50
San Miguel	3	480	54	129	297	3,250	3,000	2,400	600	250
Sandoval	3	290	29	181	80	3,325	3,200	1,550	1,650	125
Santa Fe	2	248	9	100	139	1,050	1,000	830	170	50
Torrance	1	160	6		154	402	400	390	10	2
Union	5	880	190	150	540	3,120	2,790	1,955	835	330
NEW YORK.										
Total	295	22,552	15,301	4,823	2,428	$1,306,623	$1,234,530	$752,365	$482,165	$72,093
Albany	5	343	291	46	6	58,650	57,000	13,900	43,100	1,650
Allegany	14	1,154	613	209	332	36,415	33,560	19,960	13,600	2,855
Broome	10	760	576	154	30	22,325	20,800	10,600	10,200	1,525
Cattaraugus	8	524	291	233		21,075	19,950	11,150	8,800	1,125
Cayuga	4	241	196	45		16,465	15,750	9,650	6,100	715
Chautauqua	2	52	43	8	1	3,115	3,000	1,900	1,100	115
Chemung	3	97	88	7	2	8,775	7,300	4,400	2,900	1,475
Chenango	3	91	71		20	5,265	5,000	2,400	2,600	265
Columbia	9	317	283	28	6	22,875	21,000	10,950	10,050	1,875
Cortland	1	4	2		2	360	300	50	250	60
Delaware	10	2,400	1,400	655	345	43,860	41,200	28,300	12,900	2,660
Dutchess	18	2,060	1,613	380	67	69,080	65,500	38,950	26,550	3,580
Erie	3	152	122	30		12,500	12,000	6,900	5,100	500
Franklin	3	170	47	78	45	3,390	3,300	2,750	550	90
Fulton	3	104	73	20	11	7,950	7,500	3,800	3,700	450
Genesee	5	110	84	20	6	13,625	12,900	3,900	9,000	725
Greene	9	577	436	46	95	45,785	43,500	18,300	25,200	2,285
Herkimer	1	66	66			3,300	2,800	600	2,200	500
Lewis	1	24	5		19	250	200	150	50	50
Livingston	10	914	789	64	61	58,745	54,920	37,220	17,700	3,825
Madison	4	343	228	31	84	12,050	11,000	8,000	3,000	1,050
Monroe	9	828	692	66	70	61,075	55,900	37,100	18,800	5,175
Nassau	4	89	82	7		74,900	73,000	64,000	9,000	1,900
Niagara	1	55	30	25		5,400	5,200	4,400	800	200
Oneida	11	847	676	102	69	27,025	25,350	16,740	8,610	1,675
Onondaga	9	531	469	19	43	27,090	25,500	14,500	11,000	1,590
Ontario	6	113	108	5		15,617	14,700	10,700	4,000	917
Orange	14	556	299	245	12	41,891	40,800	24,800	16,000	1,091
Orleans	2	250	244	6		24,600	22,000	16,000	6,000	2,600
Oswego	3	31	20	1	10	1,710	1,700	600	1,100	10
Otsego	4	199	149	50		2,135	2,000	1,175	825	135
Putnam	2	204	70	36	98	7,930	7,800	3,800	4,000	130
Queens	1	3	3			10,000	10,000	8,000	2,000	
Rensselaer	7	601	317	188	96	12,535	11,650	4,950	6,700	885
Rockland	7	269	161	86	22	29,650	29,000	18,100	10,900	560
Saratoga	6	878	606	143	129	15,125	13,200	5,500	7,700	1,925
Schenectady	1	33	23	10		1,000	900	700	200	100
Schoharie	2	111	91	20		5,880	4,800	2,300	2,500	1,080
Schuyler	9	601	495	76	30	20,400	18,050	8,300	9,750	2,350
Steuben	7	595	431	147	17	22,850	21,250	16,250	5,000	1,600
Suffolk	9	452	237	215		118,625	109,300	72,300	37,000	9,325
Sullivan	1	50	50			2,050	2,000	1,000	1,000	50
Tioga	7	696	548	130	18	10,900	10,200	5,300	4,900	700
Tompkins	7	585	462	123		29,985	28,350	11,650	16,700	1,635
Ulster	13	850	610	201	39	53,080	50,050	25,370	24,680	3,030
Washington	5	1,672	399	739	534	43,275	39,800	17,950	21,850	3,475
Wayne	9	387	352	12	23	24,410	23,400	14,200	9,200	1,010
Westchester	8	246	109	73	64	135,725	135,150	104,850	30,300	575
Wyoming	1	80	70	2	8	4,150	4,000	2,500	1,500	150
Yates	4	237	181	42	14	11,845	11,000	5,500	5,500	845

TABLE 71.—FARMS OPERATED BY NEGROES—NUMBER, ACREAGE, AND VALUE OF LAND AND BUILDINGS, AND OF IMPLEMENTS AND MACHINERY, BY STATES AND COUNTIES: 1910—Continued.

[Counties in which no farms operated by Negroes were reported are omitted.]

STATE AND COUNTY.	Number of farms.	FARM ACREAGE.				VALUE OF FARM LAND, BUILDINGS, AND IMPLEMENTS AND MACHINERY.					
		Total.	Improved.	Woodland.	Other un-improved.	Total.	Land and buildings.				Imple-ments and ma-chinery.
							Total.	Land.	Buildings.		

NORTH CAROLINA.

STATE AND COUNTY.	Number of farms.	Total.	Improved.	Woodland.	Other un-improved.	Total.	Total.	Land.	Buildings.	Imple-ments and ma-chinery.
Total............	64,456	3,121,827	1,700,102	1,286,037	135,688	$68,995,921	$66,793,591	$53,125,563	$13,668,028	$2,202,330
Alamance........	593	39,649	17,120	18,182	4,347	631,048	604,050	439,670	164,380	26,998
Alexander.......	125	4,970	2,878	1,757	335	102,139	99,110	81,804	17,306	3,029
Alleghany.......	59	2,162	1,429	728	5	51,964	51,015	44,474	6,541	949
Anson...........	1,648	87,391	47,807	36,419	3,165	1,592,142	1,536,873	1,221,118	315,755	55,269
Ashe............	75	4,481	2,161	2,306	14	106,616	105,606	94,101	11,505	1,010
Beaufort........	818	30,812	14,253	15,987	572	797,577	779,499	633,904	145,595	18,078
Bertie..........	1,665	79,587	46,990	30,327	2,270	1,742,984	1,669,998	1,286,317	383,681	72,986
Bladen..........	995	49,861	17,555	29,688	2,618	648,509	620,145	443,532	176,613	28,364
Brunswick.......	504	32,133	6,560	25,007	566	266,508	249,810	174,735	75,075	16,698
Buncombe........	180	5,558	3,224	2,142	192	193,725	189,120	147,505	41,615	4,605
Burke...........	240	8,948	3,674	4,945	329	149,779	145,946	114,976	30,970	3,833
Cabarrus........	557	30,959	18,866	8,598	3,495	771,654	751,211	631,261	119,950	20,443
Caldwell........	169	6,557	2,840	3,398	319	104,425	102,175	79,209	22,966	2,250
Camden..........	262	14,989	9,528	5,220	241	300,875	293,070	232,620	60,450	7,805
Carteret........	107	4,001	1,974	1,792	235	79,857	72,471	58,116	14,355	7,386
Caswell.........	791	69,922	29,325	32,357	8,240	707,822	679,773	482,218	197,555	28,049
Catawba.........	274	11,310	6,781	4,124	405	330,028	320,511	264,856	55,655	9,517
Chatham.........	1,059	67,796	26,758	35,970	5,068	787,931	757,511	552,773	204,738	30,420
Cherokee........	16	631	212	419	....	12,840	12,580	10,950	1,630	260
Chowan..........	382	14,500	9,032	5,372	96	442,373	423,835	327,960	95,875	18,538
Clay............	26	1,229	572	465	192	19,319	18,805	16,015	2,790	514
Cleveland.......	691	30,614	19,786	8,291	2,537	990,333	970,777	811,372	159,405	19,556
Columbus........	837	39,893	13,496	25,967	430	722,578	683,190	531,775	151,415	39,388
Craven..........	1,031	41,139	17,647	22,622	870	969,295	933,955	728,073	205,882	35,340
Cumberland......	1,337	69,967	31,698	37,241	1,028	1,470,560	1,425,511	1,151,090	274,421	45,049
Currituck.......	250	16,679	9,997	5,193	1,489	323,434	317,836	245,606	72,230	5,598
Dare............	10	292	107	179	6	9,715	9,600	5,700	3,900	115
Davidson........	212	10,684	6,421	3,950	313	243,684	234,865	193,340	41,525	8,819
Davie...........	256	11,361	7,237	3,178	946	237,768	230,885	183,785	47,100	6,883
Duplin..........	1,114	37,223	20,892	16,019	312	785,801	763,210	586,877	176,333	22,591
Durham..........	512	26,950	12,608	13,054	1,288	546,259	532,444	418,864	113,580	13,815
Edgecombe.......	1,612	75,704	59,806	14,323	1,575	2,188,884	2,091,256	1,611,459	479,797	97,628
Forsyth.........	289	12,719	6,794	5,185	740	381,932	370,476	298,821	71,655	11,456
Franklin........	1,398	64,744	38,666	22,953	3,125	1,288,714	1,246,888	939,213	307,675	41,826
Gaston..........	792	33,495	22,083	9,711	1,701	1,178,711	1,154,717	954,626	200,091	23,994
Gates...........	449	23,247	10,444	12,432	371	509,554	488,845	361,305	127,540	20,709
Graham..........	1	200	15	185	....	710	700	675	25	10
Granville.......	1,315	72,107	37,639	29,256	5,212	1,008,632	975,887	715,695	260,192	32,745
Greene..........	899	30,225	24,943	4,937	345	1,090,285	1,068,790	885,800	182,990	21,495
Guilford........	608	32,224	15,189	14,350	2,685	747,018	724,196	588,743	135,453	22,822
Halifax.........	2,901	131,810	83,111	44,566	4,133	2,276,745	2,154,771	1,603,126	551,645	121,974
Harnett.........	684	33,548	14,645	18,332	571	516,951	493,136	382,536	110,600	23,815
Haywood.........	17	759	443	256	60	30,995	30,330	25,310	5,020	665
Henderson.......	107	3,400	1,668	1,434	298	94,077	90,775	70,585	20,190	3,302
Hertford........	1,146	56,517	30,811	24,782	924	1,598,328	1,551,733	1,198,688	353,045	46,595
Hyde............	443	12,409	10,321	1,951	137	508,024	500,965	457,328	43,637	7,059
Iredell.........	642	30,842	17,431	11,102	2,309	744,659	724,945	609,711	115,234	19,714
Jackson.........	65	2,316	1,196	1,075	45	44,152	42,910	28,405	14,505	1,242
Johnston........	1,148	55,247	28,203	26,338	706	1,348,597	1,311,095	1,088,303	222,792	37,502
Jones...........	582	34,075	16,700	17,134	241	425,096	413,852	343,795	70,057	11,244
Lee.............	335	20,652	6,749	13,624	279	276,301	266,876	206,131	60,745	9,425
Lenoir..........	816	30,796	22,834	7,704	258	925,101	907,859	751,393	156,466	17,242
Lincoln.........	311	13,171	8,585	3,669	917	306,146	298,363	240,203	58,160	7,783
McDowell........	160	7,592	2,885	4,220	487	103,544	100,057	81,107	18,950	3,487
Macon...........	66	2,815	1,475	1,199	141	31,202	30,360	23,745	6,615	842
Madison.........	32	1,034	619	367	48	21,946	21,710	18,910	2,800	236
Martin..........	779	42,102	21,439	19,324	1,339	790,232	766,580	585,823	180,757	23,652
Mecklenburg.....	1,751	83,205	54,619	21,978	6,608	3,214,352	3,141,944	2,719,361	422,583	72,408
Mitchell........	30	1,059	597	442	20	27,136	25,937	21,012	4,925	1,199
Montgomery......	342	17,359	7,848	8,593	918	217,898	207,235	144,695	62,540	10,663
Moore...........	406	23,866	7,536	15,333	997	230,833	221,273	147,803	73,470	9,560
Nash............	1,538	68,628	41,665	26,151	812	1,786,810	1,731,533	1,369,091	362,442	55,277
New Hanover.....	171	7,826	2,918	4,727	181	211,147	204,759	162,045	42,714	6,388
Northampton.....	1,813	86,383	49,911	31,604	4,868	1,624,450	1,571,892	1,250,754	321,138	52,558
Onslow..........	474	20,499	11,434	8,555	510	327,946	318,850	245,827	73,023	9,096
Orange..........	494	32,637	14,394	16,635	1,608	397,737	379,375	265,119	114,256	18,362
Pamlico.........	244	10,959	5,611	5,063	285	383,499	377,634	330,754	46,880	5,865
Pasquotank......	514	21,102	15,095	5,660	347	611,791	595,581	481,524	114,057	16,210
Pender..........	764	32,261	9,754	21,288	1,219	502,544	481,070	335,652	145,418	21,474
Perquimans......	491	20,461	12,923	6,685	853	422,970	403,655	296,195	107,460	19,315
Person..........	861	65,445	31,520	30,463	3,462	858,913	833,075	632,990	200,085	25,838
Pitt............	1,948	76,253	50,889	23,612	1,752	2,214,075	2,167,757	1,771,734	396,023	46,318
Polk............	143	7,420	3,240	3,971	209	142,531	137,682	114,092	23,590	4,849
Randolph........	349	20,505	7,578	11,461	1,466	307,852	294,446	219,786	74,660	13,406
Richmond........	871	47,694	24,000	21,953	1,741	983,517	943,089	759,589	183,500	40,428

TABLE 71.—FARMS OPERATED BY NEGROES—NUMBER, ACREAGE, AND VALUE OF LAND AND BUILDINGS, AND OF IMPLEMENTS AND MACHINERY, BY STATES AND COUNTIES: 1910—Continued.

[Counties in which no farms operated by Negroes were reported are omitted.]

STATE AND COUNTY.	Number of farms.	FARM ACREAGE.				VALUE OF FARM LAND, BUILDINGS, AND IMPLEMENTS AND MACHINERY.				
		Total.	Improved.	Woodland.	Other un-improved.	Total.	Land and buildings.			Implements and machinery.
							Total.	Land.	Buildings.	
NORTH CAROLINA—Continued.										
Robeson	2,547	104,345	76,106	27,533	706	$3,273,014	$3,154,604	$2,528,400	$626,204	$118,410
Rockingham	742	51,576	21,678	22,842	7,056	679,435	661,804	509,428	152,376	17,631
Rowan	477	24,718	14,800	8,458	1,460	599,416	577,842	468,222	109,620	21,574
Rutherford	511	25,711	11,990	12,537	1,184	531,241	515,878	419,007	96,871	15,363
Sampson	1,202	63,887	28,057	34,800	1,030	1,172,356	1,138,034	913,837	224,197	34,322
Scotland	822	34,481	29,532	4,657	292	2,033,648	1,994,161	1,812,501	181,660	39,487
Stanly	234	10,748	5,469	4,456	823	186,946	181,315	145,015	36,300	5,631
Stokes	354	20,130	9,434	8,681	2,015	303,892	291,886	227,011	64,875	12,006
Surry	264	10,077	4,801	4,836	440	181,216	177,075	138,700	38,375	4,141
Swain	15	753	237	516		12,984	12,250	9,370	2,880	734
Transylvania	24	577	381	196		25,406	24,502	18,237	6,265	904
Tyrrell	145	5,129	2,703	2,403	23	95,237	92,480	77,690	14,790	2,757
Union	1,251	56,478	31,253	21,476	3,749	1,163,848	1,134,165	906,643	227,522	29,683
Vance	994	53,467	28,692	21,863	2,912	927,509	899,042	712,212	186,830	28,467
Wake	2,157	110,662	57,389	45,833	7,440	2,313,012	2,238,364	1,685,733	552,631	74,648
Warren	1,740	82,476	41,466	37,156	3,854	1,525,285	1,425,514	1,002,050	423,464	99,771
Washington	256	11,956	5,853	5,688	415	262,958	255,815	204,677	51,138	7,143
Watauga	30	1,265	607	658		18,916	18,550	15,085	3,465	366
Wayne	1,389	69,570	43,095	24,398	2,077	2,564,451	2,513,717	2,135,892	377,825	50,734
Wilkes	365	12,525	5,739	6,261	525	229,260	223,917	183,995	39,922	5,343
Wilson	1,142	45,693	31,567	13,291	835	1,712,260	1,674,885	1,369,460	305,425	37,375
Yadkin	153	4,611	2,819	1,404	388	112,677	109,205	85,403	23,802	3,472
Yancey	46	1,432	780	614	38	28,875	28,340	22,940	5,400	535
NORTH DAKOTA.										
Total	22	5,484	4,142	138	1,204	$163,550	$154,100	$139,100	$15,000	$9,450
Billings	1	160	140	20		4,100	4,000	3,600	400	100
Cass	2	1,280	1,280			58,400	56,000	52,500	3,500	2,400
Grand Forks	1	320	280		40	11,450	11,000	10,400	600	450
Kidder	1	320	202	118		8,500	8,000	7,300	700	500
McHenry	2	760	520		240	21,600	20,200	17,000	3,200	1,400
McKenzie	2	320	102		218	3,975	3,800	3,350	450	175
McLean	1	320	220		100	7,400	7,000	6,000	1,000	400
Morton	3	324	183		141	7,950	7,900	5,750	2,150	50
Pierce	2	400	350		50	11,400	10,000	9,000	1,000	1,400
Rolette	1	160	5		155	1,600	1,600	1,600		
Stark	1	160	75		85	5,350	5,000	4,000	1,000	350
Ward	3	640	640			15,600	14,000	13,650	350	1,600
Williams	2	320	145		175	6,225	5,600	4,950	650	625
OHIO.										
Total	1,948	106,742	83,311	15,043	8,388	$6,137,353	$5,989,075	$4,862,138	$1,126,937	$148,278
Adams	10	248	216	30	2	13,270	12,405	7,805	4,600	865
Allen	3	238	215	23		19,765	19,500	15,600	3,900	265
Ashtabula	6	208	123	48	37	10,395	10,100	6,690	3,410	295
Athens	34	2,095	1,371	588	136	42,775	41,325	33,160	8,165	1,450
Auglaize	1	23	23			2,025	2,000	1,500	500	25
Belmont	27	1,391	1,112	200	79	71,440	69,460	55,010	14,450	1,980
Brown	127	3,812	3,354	163	295	181,000	176,245	130,430	45,815	4,755
Butler	16	1,512	1,235	101	176	115,925	113,650	94,700	18,950	2,275
Carroll	4	278	187	73	18	8,975	8,700	7,450	1,250	275
Champaign	23	1,102	966	115	21	136,110	132,480	116,050	16,430	3,630
Clark	48	2,061	1,797	159	105	161,820	158,070	125,570	32,500	3,750
Clermont	64	2,794	2,015	249	530	119,617	115,880	79,700	36,180	3,737
Clinton	43	2,385	2,131	213	41	198,915	196,220	167,495	28,725	2,695
Columbiana	5	432	224	176	32	19,410	19,000	12,400	6,600	410
Cuyahoga	6	433	309	57	67	96,135	95,200	72,200	23,000	935
Darke	60	2,846	2,720	114	12	202,355	195,410	152,180	43,230	6,945
Delaware	11	530	383	97	50	34,260	33,300	25,700	7,600	960
Erie	6	280	247	28	5	28,000	27,500	21,800	5,700	500
Fairfield	3	42	42			9,700	9,400	9,200	200	300
Fayette	15	716	658	52	6	68,990	67,950	59,525	8,425	1,040
Franklin	42	1,678	1,521	120	37	197,689	193,875	168,225	25,650	3,814
Gallia	131	6,119	4,981	585	553	117,056	112,920	82,674	30,246	4,136
Greene	107	5,179	4,405	503	271	518,230	504,765	363,509	141,256	13,465
Guernsey	6	126	120	6		12,985	12,750	10,550	2,200	235
Hamilton	25	666	515	38	113	70,500	68,060	45,910	22,150	2,440
Hancock	6	507	452	55		41,210	40,560	35,610	4,950	650
Hardin	23	1,859	1,742	117		151,900	149,240	135,120	14,120	2,660
Harrison	23	1,085	949	77	59	57,077	55,615	42,815	12,800	1,462
Henry	3	175	175			12,700	12,400	7,075	5,325	300
Highland	49	1,738	1,567	128	43	100,533	98,268	73,958	24,310	2,265

TABLE **71.**—FARMS OPERATED BY NEGROES—NUMBER, ACREAGE, AND VALUE OF LAND AND BUILDINGS, AND OF IMPLEMENTS AND MACHINERY, BY STATES AND COUNTIES: 1910—Continued.

[Counties in which no farms operated by Negroes were reported are omitted.]

| STATE AND COUNTY. | Number of farms. | FARM ACREAGE. | | | | VALUE OF FARM LAND, BUILDINGS, AND IMPLEMENTS AND MACHINERY. | | | | |
| | | Total. | Improved. | Woodland. | Other unimproved. | Total. | Land and buildings. | | | Implements and machinery. |
							Total.	Land.	Buildings.	
OHIO—Continued.										
Hocking	5	559	397	117	45	$19,995	$19,500	$16,100	$3,400	$495
Huron	6	296	227	24	45	21,680	20,710	15,960	4,750	970
Jackson	75	4,159	3,122	728	309	64,110	61,615	40,110	21,505	2,495
Jefferson	39	3,029	2,199	551	279	132,048	128,350	100,415	27,935	3,698
Knox	2	14	12		2	1,510	1,400	1,300	100	110
Lake	5	124	104	19	1	30,700	30,200	21,600	8,600	500
Lawrence	73	2,506	1,606	561	339	67,462	65,623	49,423	16,200	1,839
Licking	2	45	44	1		2,000	1,900	1,300	600	100
Logan	45	2,732	2,374	237	121	189,910	185,180	151,830	33,350	4,730
Lorain	19	756	615	105	36	64,235	62,805	40,105	22,700	1,430
Lucas	3	93	88	5		17,875	17,800	15,100	2,700	75
Madison	28	3,328	3,044	253	31	276,890	273,450	251,950	21,500	3,440
Mahoning	4	380	270	22	88	20,912	20,412	17,412	3,000	500
Medina	1	42	42			4,150	4,000	2,500	1,500	150
Meigs	26	1,088	912	120	56	33,530	31,880	20,905	10,975	1,650
Mercer	17	1,035	833	177	25	77,900	76,340	61,230	15,110	1,560
Miami	14	629	588	14	27	63,065	61,300	48,550	12,750	1,765
Monroe	6	289	224	32	33	7,797	7,620	5,895	1,725	177
Montgomery	15	466	369	53	44	62,105	61,025	46,805	14,220	1,080
Morgan	21	1,162	1,017	135	10	31,185	30,320	20,320	10,000	865
Morrow	6	488	418	70		33,470	32,450	25,050	7,400	1,020
Muskingum	21	735	664	65	6	57,985	55,120	41,970	13,150	2,865
Noble	5	228	204	9	15	8,580	8,330	5,280	3,050	250
Ottawa	1	8	8			1,425	1,400	800	600	25
Paulding	57	3,399	2,816	445	138	334,565	325,560	299,100	26,460	9,005
Perry	7	484	316	98	70	11,502	11,220	9,070	2,150	282
Pickaway	14	2,185	2,090	64	31	199,000	196,680	187,330	9,350	2,320
Pike	100	7,000	2,685	2,114	2,201	79,914	76,628	65,313	11,315	3,286
Portage	4	235	164	21	50	19,245	19,000	11,400	7,600	245
Preble	30	1,482	1,277	150	55	109,145	106,700	84,745	21,955	2,445
Putnam	2	42	42			4,055	3,880	3,180	700	175
Ross	110	9,130	6,935	1,696	499	531,406	521,240	468,785	52,455	10,166
Sandusky	2	154	125	13	16	12,870	12,520	10,920	1,600	350
Scioto	11	772	250	467	55	13,738	13,380	11,505	1,875	358
Seneca	2	17	12	5		2,500	2,500	1,700	800	
Shelby	18	985	876	102	7	77,415	75,285	62,935	12,350	2,130
Stark	4	128	118	10		20,095	18,500	13,900	4,600	1,595
Summit	1	180	110	40	30	6,600	6,500	4,500	2,000	100
Trumbull	4	270	167	58	45	21,550	21,000	18,200	2,800	550
Union	11	693	679	2	12	70,005	68,500	57,700	10,800	1,505
Van Wert	22	1,389	1,211	148	30	128,921	126,484	101,864	24,620	2,437
Vinton	8	407	188	219		4,430	4,275	3,325	950	155
Warren	36	2,397	1,890	350	157	168,835	165,480	134,580	30,900	3,355
Washington	137	8,572	6,152	1,628	792	204,461	197,065	146,265	50,800	7,396
Wood	1	40	40			2,620	2,500	1,900	600	120
Wyandot	1	32	32			3,200	3,200	2,400	800	
OKLAHOMA.										
Total	13,209	1,066,863	664,434	288,741	113,688	$25,365,640	$24,552,515	$21,788,491	$2,764,024	$813,125
Adair	3	1,150	47	1,103		5,545	5,430	4,930	500	115
Alfalfa	1	160	100		60	18,150	18,000	17,600	400	150
Atoka	191	16,816	6,423	6,960	3,433	226,366	217,235	189,250	27,985	9,131
Beaver	3	480	260		220	4,775	4,500	4,150	350	275
Blaine	237	38,375	17,794	9,168	11,413	544,552	526,040	470,058	55,982	18,512
Bryan	282	19,829	14,532	4,318	979	394,466	379,795	336,340	43,455	14,671
Caddo	124	14,142	8,187	3,802	2,153	336,050	325,775	295,780	29,995	10,275
Canadian	27	3,995	2,645	316	1,034	127,075	122,100	109,750	12,350	4,975
Carter	423	31,659	18,304	11,795	1,560	541,876	520,837	462,182	58,655	21,039
Cherokee	109	9,016	3,661	4,131	1,224	95,031	91,690	76,020	15,670	3,341
Choctaw	472	28,048	15,349	12,028	671	369,393	349,874	301,930	47,944	19,519
Cleveland	58	7,603	3,353	4,130	120	111,122	107,300	93,810	13,490	3,822
Coal	51	3,257	2,021	803	433	32,585	30,690	25,340	5,350	1,895
Comanche	41	4,644	2,677	232	1,735	133,915	130,840	121,750	9,090	3,075
Craig	111	14,356	10,537	2,733	1,086	283,444	274,682	250,407	24,275	8,762
Creek	317	24,133	13,674	6,639	3,820	385,816	366,556	327,491	39,065	19,260
Custer	25	3,131	2,179	30	922	91,055	89,050	82,150	6,900	2,005
Delaware	3	490	185	305		8,055	7,900	6,970	930	155
Dewey	13	2,034	1,039	413	582	45,735	44,110	40,078	4,032	1,625
Ellis	2	455	210	1	244	7,130	7,000	6,425	575	130
Garfield	30	3,859	2,193	785	881	113,574	110,600	99,875	10,725	2,974
Garvin	265	17,121	13,102	2,524	1,495	396,599	369,875	322,386	47,489	26,724
Grady	38	4,081	2,728	690	663	136,322	133,190	121,965	11,225	3,132
Grant	4	820	390		430	25,150	22,500	21,350	1,150	2,650
Greer	9	1,123	953		170	39,575	38,750	36,000	2,750	825

TABLE **71.**—FARMS OPERATED BY NEGROES—NUMBER, ACREAGE, AND VALUE OF LAND AND BUILDINGS, AND OF IMPLEMENTS AND MACHINERY, BY STATES AND COUNTIES: 1910—Continued.

[Counties in which no farms operated by Negroes were reported are omitted.]

STATE AND COUNTY.	Number of farms.	FARM ACREAGE.				VALUE OF FARM LAND, BUILDINGS, AND IMPLEMENTS AND MACHINERY.				
		Total.	Improved.	Woodland.	Other un-improved.	Total.	Land and buildings.			Implements and machinery.
							Total.	Land.	Buildings.	

OKLAHOMA—Continued.

STATE AND COUNTY.	Number of farms.	Total.	Improved.	Woodland.	Other un-improved.	Total.	Total.	Land.	Buildings.	Implements and machinery.
Harper	1	168	168			$1.088	$1,008	$948	$60	$80
Haskell	45	2,171	1,669	350	152	38,170	36,256	27,111	9,145	1,914
Hughes	216	18,777	9,207	4,203	5,367	244,617	211,876	172,401	39,475	32,741
Jackson	1	65	65			2,500	2,500	2,350	150	
Jefferson	4	387	320		67	12,600	12,400	11,175	1,225	200
Johnston	101	6,018	3,442	2,260	316	77,124	74,122	66,027	8,095	3,002
Kay	1	320	315		5	16,300	16,000	15,000	1,000	300
Kingfisher	353	42,753	23,147	15,242	4,364	968,940	940,200	823,145	117,055	28,740
Kiowa	22	2,503	1,543		960	66,642	64,425	56,375	8,050	2,217
Latimer	12	682	251	426	5	8,240	7,795	5,945	1,850	445
Le Flore	216	9,376	5,939	2,871	566	212,818	205,511	179,358	26,153	7,307
Lincoln	606	59,019	31,458	24,852	2,709	1,202,361	1,172,205	1,012,305	159,900	30,156
Logan	814	83,861	51,757	23,900	8,204	1,953,601	1,883,671	1,597,799	285,872	69,930
Love	154	9,963	7,255	1,807	901	177,112	169,169	147,279	21,890	7,943
McClain	85	5,226	3,793	761	672	151,154	147,600	132,670	14,930	3,554
McCurtain	528	26,433	15,307	10,458	668	548,698	532,908	457,828	75,080	15,790
McIntosh	648	44,877	30,759	10,141	3,977	876,828	845,840	712,718	133,122	30,988
Major	21	3,172	1,983	98	1,091	68,460	65,650	59,825	5,825	2,810
Marshall	25	2,476	1,770	252	454	46,015	44,495	40,735	3,760	1,520
Mayes	116	10,335	5,732	3,119	1,484	219,140	210,810	179,135	31,675	8,330
Murray	27	2,169	883	1,095	191	52,327	51,452	48,397	3,055	875
Muskogee	940	70,310	51,777	11,013	7,520	3,427,247	3,348,744	2,991,606	357,138	78,503
Noble	49	5,970	3,725	739	1,506	137,687	134,170	118,320	15,850	3,517
Nowata	272	32,247	25,558	1,903	4,786	841,309	821,801	749,371	72,430	19,508
Okfuskee	939	67,717	44,309	21,002	2,406	1,095,166	1,045,068	927,708	117,360	50,098
Oklahoma	417	48,039	25,559	19,098	3,382	1,667,790	1,641,316	1,507,999	133,317	26,474
Okmulgee	720	52,549	32,483	12,199	7,867	1,608,341	1,552,500	1,424,140	128,360	56,341
Osage	26	1,874	1,571	253	50	32,030	30,885	27,725	3,160	1,145
Ottawa	4	150	128	22		109,820	109,600	109,300	300	220
Pawnee	89	6,614	4,754	828	1,032	139,732	136,525	124,365	12,160	3,207
Payne	167	11,307	8,418	1,101	1,788	378,385	368,970	328,890	40,080	9,415
Pittsburg	124	6,817	3,761	2,226	830	116,085	111,479	95,656	15,823	4,606
Pontotoc	116	10,601	5,940	4,004	657	187,190	182,240	167,646	14,594	4,950
Pottawatomie	167	12,783	8,125	3,992	666	290,473	281,835	251,030	30,805	8,638
Pushmataha	32	2,098	962	1,136		29,320	28,050	22,680	5,370	1,270
Rogers	38	4,638	1,928	725	1,985	98,664	94,914	82,974	11,940	3,750
Seminole	584	41,273	24,963	13,994	2,316	627,843	599,420	522,330	77,090	28,423
Sequoyah	389	19,396	13,112	5,533	751	484,463	469,086	412,866	56,220	15,377
Stephens	5	280	212	23	45	7,042	6,900	6,350	550	142
Texas	1	160	50		110	1,505	1,500	1,460	40	5
Tillman	15	2,095	1,642	40	413	57,475	55,300	50,755	4,545	2,175
Tulsa	107	8,102	5,719	1,514	869	278,939	272,305	254,925	17,380	6,634
Wagoner	1,152	76,260	59,237	12,285	4,738	2,275,018	2,215,895	1,987,432	228,463	59,123
Washington	16	3,385	917	170	2,298	46,700	45,600	42,750	2,850	1,100
Washita	2	190	150		40	5,200	5,000	4,800	200	200
Woodward	3	480	128	200	152	3,625	3,200	2,900	300	425

OREGON.

STATE AND COUNTY.	Number of farms.	Total.	Improved.	Woodland.	Other un-improved.	Total.	Total.	Land.	Buildings.	Implements and machinery.
Total	27	3,021	1,104	702	1,215	$156,865	$151,350	$129,878	$21,472	$5,515
Baker	2	360	125		235	8,700	8,000	5,578	2,422	700
Clackamas	1	160	80	25	55	32,800	32,000	30,000	2,000	800
Coos	1	160	6	120	34	8,040	8,000	6,800	1,200	40
Curry	1	113	20		93	3,100	3,000	2,500	500	100
Douglas	1	235	14	146	75	3,200	3,000	2,400	600	200
Grant	1	160	7	80	73	1,300	1,000	700	300	300
Jackson	5	242	88	78	76	15,700	15,600	12,800	2,800	100
Lake	1	320	100		220	1,700	1,600	1,450	150	100
Lincoln	1	160	20	140		3,025	3,000	2,800	200	25
Marion	4	155	83	35	37	11,600	10,950	9,250	1,700	650
Multnomah	4	35	30		5	34,200	33,500	29,100	4,400	700
Umatilla	1	480	400		80	9,920	9,000	7,500	1,500	920
Union	2	354	114	25	215	16,700	16,000	13,200	2,800	700
Washington	1	47	15	23	9	4,840	4,700	4,200	500	140
Yamhill	1	40	2	30	8	2,040	2,000	1,600	400	40

PENNSYLVANIA.

STATE AND COUNTY.	Number of farms.	Total.	Improved.	Woodland.	Other un-improved.	Total.	Total.	Land.	Buildings.	Implements and machinery.
Total	543	30,097	19,152	8,829	2,116	$2,469,100	$2,375,080	$1,654,195	$720,885	$94,020
Adams	2	14	13		1	2,540	2,500	700	1,800	40
Allegheny	18	878	487	362	29	295,145	287,400	269,400	18,000	7,745
Armstrong	3	3,563	540	3,021	2	108,900	107,900	104,500	3,400	1,000
Beaver	12	716	409	184	123	52,980	51,600	41,800	9,800	1,380
Bedford	7	451	197	224	30	12,075	11,300	7,150	4,150	775

TABLE 71.—FARMS OPERATED BY NEGROES—NUMBER, ACREAGE, AND VALUE OF LAND AND BUILDINGS, AND OF IMPLEMENTS AND MACHINERY, BY STATES AND COUNTIES: 1910—Continued.

[Counties in which no farms operated by Negroes were reported are omitted.]

STATE AND COUNTY.	Number of farms.	FARM ACREAGE.				VALUE OF FARM LAND, BUILDINGS, AND IMPLEMENTS AND MACHINERY.				
		Total.	Improved.	Woodland.	Other unimproved.	Total.	Land and buildings.			Implements and machinery.
							Total.	Land.	Buildings.	
PENNSYLVANIA—Continued.										
Berks	4	170	97	73	....	$7,285	$6,900	$2,700	$4,200	$385
Bradford	4	317	245	41	31	18,500	17,000	8,000	9,000	1,500
Bucks	20	653	612	31	10	78,827	74,800	29,720	45,080	4,027
Butler	4	390	294	70	26	19,950	18,800	14,300	4,500	1,150
Cambria	2	170	48	120	2	8,050	7,600	6,500	1,100	450
Center	1	44	21	23	....	1,400	1,300	500	800	100
Chester	112	3,886	3,270	485	131	397,329	378,835	198,015	180,820	18,494
Clearfield	2	187	42	145	....	2,510	2,340	1,115	1,225	170
Clinton	7	503	299	204	....	8,635	7,750	4,775	2,975	885
Columbia	1	8	8	....	....	500	500	200	300	....
Cumberland	6	88	61	19	8	22,460	22,040	17,690	4,350	420
Dauphin	8	664	420	243	1	68,515	66,360	33,260	33,100	2,155
Delaware	21	700	552	118	30	79,385	75,800	39,800	36,000	3,585
Erie	5	234	172	10	52	13,190	12,700	7,000	5,700	490
Fayette	29	1,819	988	459	372	164,700	161,400	113,575	47,825	3,300
Franklin	18	398	327	70	1	50,070	47,025	25,615	21,410	3,045
Greene	11	944	737	182	25	85,215	83,360	72,710	10,650	1,855
Huntingdon	2	98	46	52	....	3,025	2,900	1,600	1,300	125
Indiana	5	237	163	74	....	9,580	9,000	6,600	2,460	580
Jefferson	4	111	53	4	54	5,225	5,100	3,650	1,450	125
Juniata	16	1,587	990	507	90	46,865	43,500	27,500	16,000	3,365
Lackawanna	2	30	10	19	1	20,700	20,500	12,300	8,200	200
Lancaster	40	1,454	590	780	84	59,137	55,260	24,660	30,600	3,877
Lawrence	7	325	247	20	58	28,055	25,600	16,800	8,800	2,455
Luzerne	3	110	78	22	10	2,905	2,620	1,340	1,280	285
Lycoming	4	401	228	170	3	12,840	12,300	6,400	5,900	540
McKean	3	299	114	58	127	7,128	6,500	4,100	2,400	628
Mercer	9	356	294	55	7	17,700	16,695	9,295	7,400	1,005
Monroe	1	60	35	25	....	1,100	1,000	400	600	100
Montgomery	22	1,179	980	97	102	152,120	146,600	97,325	49,275	5,520
Montour	1	3	3	....	....	535	500	450	50	35
Northampton	1	175	115	10	50	2,050	2,000	1,000	1,000	50
Philadelphia	6	175	150	8	17	182,000	180,000	168,850	11,150	2,000
Potter	6	655	334	77	244	16,265	14,625	7,090	7,535	1,640
Somerset	1	81	51	10	20	1,230	1,200	500	700	30
Susquehanna	6	295	201	66	28	9,453	8,900	4,600	4,300	553
Tioga	6	595	525	55	15	37,485	35,800	22,000	13,800	1,685
Union	1	32	22	10	....	1,650	1,500	700	800	150
Venango	2	22	10	8	4	5,227	5,000	3,500	1,500	227
Warren	2	51	15	18	18	1,125	1,000	700	300	125
Washington	49	3,766	3,159	349	258	254,678	245,270	179,960	65,310	9,408
Westmoreland	8	310	264	40	6	30,410	28,500	21,750	6,750	1,910
Wyoming	1	16	8	....	8	1,000	1,000	500	500	....
York	38	877	628	211	38	61,451	57,000	31,600	25,400	4,451
RHODE ISLAND.										
Total	40	1,664	582	786	296	$67,920	$62,600	$37,950	$24,650	$5,320
Bristol	7	121	88	25	8	13,700	12,350	6,250	6,100	1,350
Kent	1	5	5	....	....	2,000	1,500	500	1,000	500
Newport	9	146	131	5	10	30,275	28,600	21,600	7,000	1,675
Providence	5	254	63	109	82	4,980	4,550	1,950	2,600	430
Washington	18	1,138	295	647	196	16,965	15,600	7,650	7,950	1,365
SOUTH CAROLINA.										
Total	96,772	3,939,592	2,597,497	1,096,175	245,920	$102,333,604	$98,966,444	$84,018,490	$14,947,954	$3,367,160
Abbeville	3,686	193,467	109,225	45,129	39,113	3,639,387	3,528,545	2,982,934	545,611	110,842
Aiken	2,357	139,056	91,589	42,556	4,911	2,624,197	2,518,136	2,048,006	470,130	106,061
Anderson	3,646	146,423	105,139	25,967	15,317	6,150,916	6,031,029	5,292,818	738,211	119,887
Bamberg	1,520	84,265	60,896	17,569	5,800	2,002,816	1,938,620	1,661,635	276,985	64,196
Barnwell	2,676	143,775	113,430	27,093	3,252	2,753,914	2,651,055	2,202,390	448,665	102,859
Beaufort	4,197	87,541	60,501	23,764	3,276	1,860,687	1,750,937	1,264,051	486,886	109,750
Berkeley	2,764	86,502	47,091	37,193	2,218	1,589,260	1,464,224	1,043,019	421,205	125,036
Calhoun	1,904	56,054	43,891	11,492	671	1,378,512	1,326,193	1,105,270	220,923	52,319
Charleston	3,071	48,355	29,946	16,990	1,419	1,666,829	1,579,134	1,177,058	402,076	87,695
Cherokee	981	43,391	27,394	13,262	2,735	1,097,843	1,061,235	896,500	164,735	36,603
Chester	2,440	135,861	81,269	35,037	19,555	2,234,579	2,144,626	1,733,598	411,028	89,953
Chesterfield	1,149	49,928	29,212	19,720	996	975,286	930,305	786,698	143,607	44,981
Clarendon	3,815	97,440	75,962	19,171	2,307	3,171,009	3,050,974	2,608,224	442,750	120,035
Colleton	2,506	77,847	42,862	33,771	1,214	1,271,437	1,198,912	909,540	289,372	72,525
Darlington	2,362	74,616	65,048	8,854	714	3,403,389	3,294,114	2,851,104	443,010	109,175

TABLE 71.—FARMS OPERATED BY NEGROES—NUMBER, ACREAGE, AND VALUE OF LAND AND BUILDINGS, AND OF IMPLEMENTS AND MACHINERY, BY STATES AND COUNTIES: 1910—Continued.

[Counties in which no farms operated by Negroes were reported are omitted.]

STATE AND COUNTY.	Number of farms.	FARM ACREAGE.				VALUE OF FARM LAND, BUILDINGS, AND IMPLEMENTS AND MACHINERY.				
		Total.	Improved.	Woodland.	Other unimproved.	Total.	Land and buildings.			Implements and machinery.
							Total.	Land.	Buildings.	

SOUTH CAROLINA—Continued.

Dillon	1,300	51,556	40,146	10,343	1,067	$3,239,991	$3,143,210	$2,825,945	$317,265	$96,781
Dorchester	1,211	45,735	24,216	20,255	1,264	791,748	756,939	564,230	192,709	34,809
Edgefield	3,118	137,883	96,709	27,927	13,247	2,950,320	2,825,064	2,363,886	461,178	125,256
Fairfield	2,796	194,286	104,749	67,338	22,199	2,212,825	2,112,020	1,751,831	360,189	100,805
Florence	2,044	74,514	50,258	23,216	1,040	2,408,429	2,320,292	2,012,647	307,645	88,137
Georgetown	519	19,223	5,198	13,434	591	207,476	194,670	144,709	49,961	12,806
Greenville	1,941	76,599	52,182	19,712	4,705	3,481,797	3,416,801	3,079,632	337,169	64,996
Greenwood	2,932	126,191	84,946	31,782	9,463	3,253,927	3,162,594	2,563,497	599,097	91,333
Hampton	2,073	94,004	59,284	32,875	1,845	1,506,819	1,428,255	1,091,816	336,439	78,564
Horry	666	24,597	9,208	14,973	416	367,493	354,387	285,174	69,213	13,106
Kershaw	1,770	90,916	48,921	38,826	3,169	1,082,959	1,024,131	833,970	190,161	58,828
Lancaster	1,847	77,431	50,040	21,759	5,632	1,472,656	1,423,511	1,178,120	245,391	49,145
Laurens	2,921	156,540	93,943	41,077	21,520	3,395,136	3,318,554	2,839,742	478,812	76,582
Lee	2,213	75,279	59,765	14,420	1,094	3,777,190	3,685,552	3,355,717	329,835	91,638
Lexington	1,348	60,160	36,992	20,992	2,176	1,347,954	1,302,300	1,099,216	203,084	45,654
Marion	1,037	38,930	24,467	13,243	1,220	1,059,670	1,023,652	888,869	134,783	36,018
Marlboro	2,333	93,852	76,097	17,234	521	6,689,555	6,551,289	6,013,694	537,595	138,266
Newberry	2,203	106,538	67,636	32,415	6,487	2,271,458	2,215,047	1,881,675	333,372	56,411
Oconee	833	42,735	21,626	18,914	2,195	797,976	778,916	635,921	142,995	19,060
Orangeburg	4,144	168,161	125,738	38,844	3,579	4,891,998	4,724,890	4,055,624	669,266	167,108
Pickens	690	25,459	16,708	7,288	1,463	1,046,717	1,027,730	911,830	115,900	18,987
Richland	1,872	58,778	44,993	12,912	873	1,580,143	1,519,241	1,272,898	246,343	60,902
Saluda	1,764	74,074	51,787	19,695	2,592	2,025,946	1,976,941	1,656,341	320,600	59,005
Spartanburg	2,508	100,478	68,102	26,150	6,226	4,020,574	3,948,647	3,514,382	434,265	71,927
Sumter	3,204	102,337	76,907	23,103	2,327	3,383,460	3,263,787	2,795,210	468,577	119,673
Union	1,833	99,316	58,792	29,245	11,279	1,395,153	1,341,637	1,080,712	260,925	53,516
Williamsburg	3,462	121,027	72,105	46,741	2,181	2,368,556	2,259,721	1,856,945	402,776	108,835
York	3,116	138,472	92,527	33,894	12,051	3,475,717	3,398,627	2,901,412	497,215	77,090

SOUTH DAKOTA.

Total	67	20,753	8,817	150	11,786	$526,169	$507,405	$467,935	$39,470	$18,764
Armstrong	1	640	10	20	610	1,900	1,600	1,480	120	300
Beadle	1	480	480			19,160	18,860	17,760	1,100	300
Brookings	3	1,040	945		95	45,255	44,200	40,700	3,500	1,055
Clark	1	80	80			3,400	3,200	2,700	500	200
Davison	1	10	10			4,150	4,000	2,000	2,000	150
Deuel	1	237	144		93	9,410	9,110	7,910	1,200	300
Dewey	1	320			320	2,100	2,000	2,000		100
Douglas	1	160	130		30	8,075	8,000	7,300	700	75
Edmunds	2	640	637		3	25,700	24,800	23,000	1,800	900
Fall River	2	320	5		315	2,500	2,400	2,275	125	100
Gregory	1	480	300		180	15,000	14,000	13,700	300	1,000
Hand	1	167	10		157	2,120	2,100	2,080	20	20
Hughes	2	1,700	1,660		40	68,883	67,400	63,300	4,100	1,483
Kingsbury	2	694	694			33,210	32,960	28,960	4,000	250
Lawrence	2	240	80		160	2,700	2,500	2,000	500	200
Lyman	6	2,181	529	20	1,632	35,782	34,020	30,540	3,480	1,762
Meade	7	1,120	23		1,097	11,000	11,000	10,635	365	
Minnehaha	1	135	125		10	12,050	12,050	11,050	1,000	
Pennington	3	1,289	402	110	777	21,879	20,900	18,825	2,075	979
Perkins	1	160	6		154	3,300	3,200	2,900	300	100
Stanley	8	1,490	592		898	24,490	24,000	22,860	1,140	490
Sterling	1	1,280			1,280	12,920	12,820	12,800	20	100
Sully	12	5,140	1,750		3,390	139,935	132,485	122,785	9,700	7,450
Todd	1	160	55		105	4,150	4,000	3,950	50	150
Tripp	2	320			320	5,600	5,600	5,400	200	
Union	1	10	10			1,200	1,000	500	500	200
Walworth	1	160	60		100	3,300	3,200	2,700	500	100
Yankton	1	100	80		20	7,000	6,000	5,825	175	1,000

TENNESSEE.

Total	38,300	1,605,694	1,161,985	338,863	104,846	$44,004,147	$42,183,226	$35,237,523	$6,945,703	$1,820,921
Anderson	72	2,166	1,215	840	111	47,986	45,106	30,871	14,235	2,880
Bedford	475	15,881	12,152	2,799	930	537,885	518,547	422,262	96,285	19,338
Benton	40	1,963	1,246	648	69	33,870	29,315	21,500	7,815	4,555
Bledsoe	45	2,334	1,379	939	16	46,911	45,340	36,955	8,385	1,571
Blount	75	5,440	3,583	1,725	132	135,417	129,035	100,760	28,275	6,382
Bradley	82	3,963	2,347	1,359	257	59,778	56,808	45,438	11,370	2,970
Campbell	17	416	318	98		9,888	9,625	5,675	3,950	263
Cannon	52	1,579	1,150	406	23	35,507	34,367	28,267	6,100	1,140
Carroll	703	35,771	21,418	9,232	5,121	556,237	527,631	428,197	99,434	28,606
Carter	55	1,320	822	339	159	40,833	39,380	28,165	11,215	1,453

TABLE 71.—FARMS OPERATED BY NEGROES—NUMBER, ACREAGE, AND VALUE OF LAND AND BUILDINGS, AND OF IMPLEMENTS AND MACHINERY, BY STATES AND COUNTIES: 1910—Continued.

[Counties in which no farms operated by Negroes were reported are omitted.]

STATE AND COUNTY.	Number of farms.	FARM ACREAGE.				VALUE OF FARM LAND, BUILDINGS, AND IMPLEMENTS AND MACHINERY.					
		Total.	Improved.	Woodland.	Other un-improved.	Total.	Land and buildings.			Imple-ments and ma-chinery.
							Total.	Land.	Buildings.	
TENNESSEE—Continued.										
Cheatham	124	5,530	3,141	1,922	467	$100,440	$95,721	$73,814	$21,907	$4,719
Chester	226	11,310	7,266	3,045	999	159,705	150,776	124,365	26,411	8,929
Claiborne	58	2,201	1,201	935	65	30,350	29,510	24,025	5,485	840
Clay	25	1,316	502	754	60	18,763	18,265	16,190	2,075	498
Cocke	99	2,550	1,939	601	10	69,085	66,205	52,450	13,755	2,880
Coffee	87	4,273	2,776	1,497	....	73,555	70,345	57,939	12,415	3,210
Crockett	612	18,895	16,131	2,478	286	609,499	580,440	475,975	104,465	29,059
Cumberland	3	165	45	120	....	1,939	1,800	1,000	800	139
Davidson	440	14,711	9,984	3,988	739	1,066,065	1,028,962	822,271	206,691	37,103
Decatur	137	5,326	3,051	1,957	318	75,959	72,781	60,486	12,295	3,178
Dekalb	59	1,570	1,014	510	46	45,485	44,200	36,550	7,650	1,285
Dickson	258	13,112	6,274	6,694	144	196,904	185,450	137,820	47,630	11,454
Dyer	544	16,083	13,456	1,373	1,254	669,510	648,675	557,043	91,632	20,835
Fayette	4,069	202,124	153,381	34,202	14,541	3,092,506	2,902,518	2,341,432	561,086	189,988
Fentress	3	120	110	10	....	680	600	450	150	80
Franklin	197	7,277	5,147	1,961	169	167,774	157,746	130,031	27,715	10,028
Gibson	1,076	37,450	30,590	5,627	1,233	1,141,109	1,100,116	915,235	184,881	40,993
Giles	1,326	44,826	35,979	6,792	2,055	1,396,790	1,352,515	1,135,947	216,568	44,275
Grainger	68	2,548	1,557	936	55	48,236	46,510	36,875	9,635	1,726
Greene	105	3,176	2,609	519	48	102,866	99,049	76,879	22,170	3,817
Hamblen	77	2,845	2,270	417	158	88,476	83,535	66,982	16,553	4,941
Hamilton	150	5,242	3,298	1,903	41	146,249	139,968	106,055	33,913	6,281
Hancock	60	2,457	1,205	1,223	29	24,695	24,157	19,805	4,352	538
Hardeman	1,544	91,594	55,999	26,518	9,077	1,098,260	1,045,886	823,020	222,866	52,374
Hardin	297	11,418	8,392	2,822	204	268,317	256,510	208,030	48,480	11,807
Hawkins	129	4,649	3,061	1,442	146	132,911	128,455	108,370	20,085	4,456
Haywood	3,137	136,538	109,551	24,746	2,241	3,334,200	3,138,221	2,556,928	581,293	195,979
Henderson	250	18,845	8,301	6,945	3,599	139,747	131,158	103,075	28,083	8,589
Henry	624	28,929	18,185	6,868	3,876	457,684	440,609	358,179	82,430	17,075
Hickman	154	8,125	4,390	3,448	287	152,510	143,414	112,650	30,764	9,096
Houston	67	3,199	1,643	1,482	74	36,405	35,185	28,070	7,115	1,220
Humphreys	57	3,397	1,469	1,831	97	62,103	59,850	52,120	7,730	2,253
Jackson	22	1,105	751	354	....	29,399	28,810	26,315	2,495	589
James	22	1,440	600	770	70	9,318	8,625	6,505	2,120	693
Jefferson	81	3,091	2,273	776	42	100,246	96,360	73,040	23,320	3,886
Johnson	13	277	71	206	....	6,219	6,050	4,150	1,900	169
Knox	196	6,198	4,226	1,775	197	246,442	235,677	176,577	59,100	10,765
Lake	189	7,731	7,451	280	....	408,033	398,340	352,550	45,790	9,693
Lauderdale	1,651	77,434	50,514	8,228	18,692	2,266,464	2,167,683	1,872,458	295,225	98,781
Lawrence	64	2,753	1,242	1,434	77	31,377	29,935	22,475	7,460	1,442
Lewis	29	2,177	648	1,506	23	15,183	14,125	11,568	2,557	1,058
Lincoln	574	21,219	17,115	2,904	1,200	743,881	724,455	641,387	83,068	19,426
Loudon	65	3,244	1,910	1,248	86	48,398	45,410	36,145	9,265	2,988
McMinn	134	5,583	3,155	2,067	361	65,639	61,785	47,975	13,810	3,854
McNairy	195	10,370	4,988	4,352	1,030	101,475	96,342	76,847	19,495	5,133
Macon	118	4,554	3,009	1,391	154	100,525	97,075	80,130	16,945	3,450
Madison	1,811	95,065	62,231	21,882	10,952	1,805,245	1,711,157	1,415,785	295,372	94,088
Marion	58	2,316	1,497	704	115	59,195	56,520	47,660	8,860	2,675
Marshall	320	10,720	7,904	2,213	603	318,467	308,831	259,241	49,590	9,636
Maury	811	26,085	18,848	5,022	2,215	1,043,481	1,002,271	829,887	172,384	41,210
Meigs	67	4,733	2,539	1,973	221	48,053	46,052	40,542	5,510	2,001
Monroe	103	5,509	3,924	1,542	43	117,915	111,440	89,155	22,285	6,475
Montgomery	1,108	45,177	33,258	8,506	3,413	881,735	846,901	651,931	194,970	34,834
Moore	28	1,597	1,166	310	121	35,755	34,190	28,885	5,305	1,565
Morgan	2	54	25	29	....	800	700	525	175	100
Obion	208	8,160	7,079	1,037	44	505,293	489,640	420,770	68,870	15,653
Overton	26	707	534	143	30	13,213	12,810	9,975	2,835	403
Perry	50	3,908	1,127	2,706	75	56,417	55,155	49,645	5,510	1,262
Pickett	1	80	40	40	....	420	400	300	100	20
Polk	18	1,995	1,088	664	243	42,406	41,060	36,865	4,195	1,346
Putnam	87	2,556	1,798	748	10	75,013	72,440	54,195	18,245	2,573
Rhea	38	1,495	927	558	10	29,213	27,835	21,895	5,940	1,378
Roane	86	3,551	1,781	1,696	74	43,887	41,380	29,135	12,245	2,507
Robertson	790	30,408	25,881	3,652	875	974,071	939,733	747,038	192,695	34,338
Rutherford	1,240	43,772	31,103	10,462	2,207	1,547,773	1,495,601	1,277,646	217,955	52,172
Scott	5	153	55	98	....	2,063	1,925	1,100	825	138
Sequatchie	3	68	43	25	....	792	777	647	130	15
Sevier	39	1,090	797	271	22	33,188	32,183	26,290	5,893	1,005
Shelby	5,469	195,020	164,031	24,732	6,257	9,876,104	9,564,582	8,389,761	1,174,821	311,522
Smith	178	5,988	4,440	1,214	334	226,602	222,960	195,595	27,365	3,642
Stewart	166	16,903	5,545	11,160	198	180,932	174,460	148,897	25,563	6,472
Sullivan	30	1,101	760	309	32	33,111	32,150	27,125	5,025	961
Sumner	342	11,954	8,268	3,223	463	313,190	301,880	230,199	71,681	11,310
Tipton	2,385	84,901	69,750	13,658	1,493	2,903,552	2,756,043	2,293,979	462,064	147,509
Trousdale	120	5,125	3,421	1,159	545	148,209	144,775	117,845	26,930	3,434
Unicoi	1	25	25	....	....	2,500	2,500	2,450	50	....
Union	4	172	141	31	....	1,807	1,700	975	725	107

TABLE **71.**—FARMS OPERATED BY NEGROES—NUMBER, ACREAGE, AND VALUE OF LAND AND BUILDINGS, AND OF IMPLEMENTS AND MACHINERY, BY STATES AND COUNTIES: 1910—Continued.

[Counties in which no farms operated by Negroes were reported are omitted.]

STATE AND COUNTY.	Number of farms.	FARM ACREAGE.				VALUE OF FARM LAND, BUILDINGS, AND IMPLEMENTS AND MACHINERY.				
		Total.	Improved.	Woodland.	Other un-improved.	Total.	Land and buildings.			Implements and machinery.
							Total.	Land.	Buildings.	
TENNESSEE—Continued.										
Van Buren	5	700	320	380	....	$6,925	$6,100	$4,475	$1,625	$825
Warren	136	6,294	4,341	1,935	18	113,106	108,054	86,703	21,351	5,052
Washington	54	1,276	993	231	52	60,861	59,055	46,220	12,835	1,806
Wayne	37	1,097	634	334	129	21,358	20,714	18,544	2,170	644
Weakley	271	11,179	8,282	2,640	257	326,391	314,448	253,678	60,770	11,943
White	78	3,653	2,530	1,078	45	101,570	98,370	89,110	9,260	3,200
Williamson	540	21,617	15,359	4,605	1,653	789,287	760,234	649,569	110,665	29,053
Wilson	554	19,680	12,000	6,651	1,029	578,559	561,242	447,022	114,220	17,317
TEXAS.										
Total	69,816	4,264,198	2,762,958	1,212,049	289,191	$93,820,233	$90,660,074	$77,899,003	$12,761,071	$3,160,159
Anderson	1,553	107,492	64,503	40,651	2,338	1,105,357	1,050,337	808,307	242,030	55,020
Angelina	63	3,189	1,614	1,554	21	36,552	34,115	24,565	9,550	2,437
Aransas	1	30	30	....	....	625	600	480	120	25
Atascosa	37	11,048	2,087	8,169	792	98,792	95,769	87,079	8,690	3,023
Austin	775	34,545	25,234	3,689	5,622	970,627	947,177	800,437	146,740	23,450
Bandera	4	1,757	126	....	1,631	8,545	8,160	7,570	590	385
Bastrop	1,191	79,731	54,499	21,579	3,653	1,769,545	1,708,011	1,483,776	224,235	61,534
Bee	24	4,174	1,406	1,738	1,030	99,980	98,065	92,940	5,125	1,915
Bell	196	12,839	10,499	807	1,533	841,870	819,575	758,815	60,760	22,295
Bexar	85	7,506	4,314	2,670	522	265,015	257,990	242,665	15,325	7,025
Blanco	33	7,206	1,374	....	5,832	61,793	59,393	52,623	6,770	2,400
Bosque	75	7,657	5,365	1,079	1,213	214,290	207,990	183,140	24,850	6,300
Bowie	1,654	69,371	50,109	18,624	638	1,476,146	1,430,443	1,148,161	282,282	45,703
Brazoria	783	32,456	19,706	10,722	2,028	1,009,282	1,041,161	912,133	129,028	28,121
Brazos	1,189	64,960	48,313	14,904	1,743	1,595,124	1,532,946	1,305,519	227,427	62,178
Brewster	4	65,920	....	....	65,920	131,349	131,324	130,324	1,000	25
Brown	3	349	138	211	....	7,240	6,890	6,140	750	350
Burleson	1,311	97,505	49,464	47,101	940	1,913,074	1,862,074	1,654,260	207,814	51,000
Burnet	15	1,256	785	163	308	27,089	25,630	21,780	3,850	1,459
Caldwell	623	42,483	28,580	12,631	1,272	1,464,028	1,414,651	1,279,376	135,275	49,377
Calhoun	12	878	476	....	402	34,460	33,420	30,845	2,575	1,040
Callahan	1	320	55	265	....	5,150	5,000	4,900	100	150
Camp	689	40,751	26,745	9,513	4,493	603,986	580,298	471,553	108,745	23,688
Cass	1,517	96,229	56,316	33,443	6,470	1,011,334	970,652	717,366	253,286	40,682
Chambers	128	12,712	1,717	1,687	9,308	160,543	156,535	129,855	26,680	4,008
Cherokee	1,046	64,673	42,830	20,449	1,394	898,871	852,214	681,978	170,236	46,657
Clay	6	830	657	50	123	32,805	31,850	29,450	2,400	955
Coleman	1	20	20	....	....	700	700	650	50	....
Collin	135	7,581	6,951	434	196	484,578	474,715	438,425	36,290	9,863
Colorado	692	33,900	24,007	6,899	2,994	1,020,172	987,011	846,716	140,295	33,161
Comal	12	612	544	30	38	46,225	44,910	39,960	4,950	1,315
Comanche	1	100	30	....	70	3,600	3,500	3,500	....	100
Cooke	64	5,189	3,799	742	648	183,575	177,450	157,590	19,860	6,125
Coryell	19	1,351	777	318	256	40,070	37,400	31,775	5,625	2,670
Dallas	554	28,757	25,341	2,243	1,173	1,828,704	1,793,645	1,653,707	139,938	35,059
De Witt	386	28,741	18,863	5,389	4,489	955,787	931,478	838,450	93,028	24,309
Delta	74	2,985	2,836	92	57	114,940	111,925	99,045	12,880	3,015
Denton	230	17,425	12,326	4,511	588	590,577	573,730	495,475	78,255	16,847
Dimmit	1	320	22	298	....	4,800	4,800	4,770	30	....
El Paso	1	11	11	....	....	1,140	1,100	800	300	40
Ellis	563	31,551	29,004	742	1,805	2,159,915	2,123,125	1,981,515	141,610	36,790
Erath	23	1,445	1,043	377	25	47,965	46,310	39,435	6,875	1,655
Falls	1,456	77,078	69,121	6,791	1,166	3,575,789	3,492,130	3,159,515	332,615	83,659
Fannin	502	30,203	24,577	4,290	1,336	966,390	933,707	813,247	120,460	32,683
Fayette	919	54,996	34,327	17,809	2,860	1,304,151	1,258,526	1,073,456	185,070	45,625
Fort Bend	1,636	69,737	50,034	7,470	12,233	2,621,776	2,553,955	2,267,985	285,970	67,821
Franklin	136	6,216	5,295	858	63	110,697	106,205	88,668	17,537	4,492
Freestone	1,512	103,134	64,474	32,784	5,876	1,408,861	1,346,453	1,058,245	288,208	62,408
Frio	15	3,983	1,200	2,753	30	62,710	58,300	54,310	3,990	4,410
Galveston	78	666	371	36	259	125,255	122,604	88,269	34,335	2,651
Gillespie	10	791	498	218	75	28,020	27,150	24,725	2,425	870
Goliad	115	22,440	5,448	16,528	464	324,363	314,407	285,617	28,790	9,956
Gonzales	1,103	76,472	48,848	25,476	2,148	1,769,873	1,710,010	1,499,497	210,513	59,863
Grayson	289	13,766	11,918	1,233	615	630,784	613,250	530,499	82,751	17,534
Gregg	1,056	62,584	38,588	23,022	974	812,534	775,723	576,085	199,638	36,811
Grimes	1,384	69,061	48,124	19,454	1,483	1,007,945	959,967	794,622	165,345	47,978
Guadalupe	654	52,021	31,735	19,065	1,221	1,572,833	1,531,877	1,387,733	144,144	40,956
Hamilton	1	230	20	50	160	1,525	1,500	1,450	50	25
Hardin	14	604	95	506	3	8,370	7,850	5,800	2,050	520
Harris	326	16,032	8,406	3,518	4,108	675,809	652,966	571,861	81,105	22,843
Harrison	3,306	217,825	145,030	69,128	3,667	2,503,788	2,389,783	1,841,073	548,710	114,005
Hartley	1	640	100	....	540	5,120	4,620	4,620	500	300
Haskell	2	117	82	35	....	4,375	4,225	3,900	325	150
Hayes	130	6,741	4,936	1,024	781	532,975	517,515	464,220	53,295	15,460

Table 71.—FARMS OPERATED BY NEGROES—NUMBER, ACREAGE, AND VALUE OF LAND AND BUILDINGS, AND OF IMPLEMENTS AND MACHINERY, BY STATES AND COUNTIES: 1910—Continued.

[Counties in which no farms operated by Negroes were reported are omitted.]

STATE AND COUNTY.	Number of farms.	FARM ACREAGE.				VALUE OF FARM LAND, BUILDINGS, AND IMPLEMENTS AND MACHINERY.				
		Total.	Improved.	Woodland.	Other un-improved.	Total.	Land and buildings.			Implements and machinery.
							Total.	Land.	Buildings.	
TEXAS—Continued.										
Henderson	646	45,017	25,577	19,167	273	$509,400	$484,325	$391,520	$92,805	$25,075
Hidalgo	2	2,050	145	65	1,840	4,945	4,800	4,340	460	145
Hill	251	15,924	13,291	1,366	1,267	799,547	779,495	717,675	61,820	20,052
Hood	32	1,304	1,063	79	162	49,060	47,835	42,045	5,790	1,225
Hopkins	366	19,792	14,994	4,248	550	369,895	352,850	284,425	68,425	17,045
Houston	1,780	103,821	63,789	36,915	3,117	1,179,305	1,126,751	919,211	207,540	52,554
Hunt	298	16,909	13,693	2,234	982	627,020	608,030	535,680	72,350	18,990
Jackson	254	40,926	13,576	24,473	2,877	918,418	902,255	843,620	58,635	16,163
Jasper	269	18,617	6,544	12,063	10	194,881	186,938	114,465	72,473	7,943
Jefferson	36	2,199	2,139	30	30	194,225	185,700	151,000	34,700	8,525
Johnson	65	3,870	3,527	153	190	219,926	216,020	199,720	16,300	3,906
Karnes	68	8,326	3,963	3,072	1,291	218,822	213,357	198,517	14,840	5,465
Kaufman	722	54,338	43,897	8,753	1,688	1,919,394	1,871,687	1,679,252	192,435	47,707
Kendall	9	2,868	246	369	2,253	23,474	22,740	21,420	1,320	734
Kerr	7	1,904	343	1,561	....	17,440	17,140	16,315	825	300
Kinney	1	2,000	250	500	1,250	20,900	20,000	19,000	1,000	900
La Salle	3	255	255	....	....	8,250	8,050	7,750	300	200
Lamar	1,127	57,048	49,219	6,862	967	2,028,339	1,970,567	1,721,062	249,505	57,772
Lampasas	11	685	305	364	16	18,130	17,600	13,400	4,200	530
Lavaca	531	34,948	17,821	14,658	2,469	727,705	708,829	603,710	105,119	18,876
Lee	667	53,899	25,136	24,881	3,882	784,632	742,437	607,698	134,739	42,195
Leon	1,176	73,017	43,821	18,863	10,333	854,991	822,082	673,432	148,650	32,909
Liberty	280	10,585	5,586	3,934	1,065	182,149	174,000	143,080	30,920	8,149
Limestone	1,033	63,643	50,619	9,735	3,289	2,111,128	2,037,819	1,823,556	214,263	73,309
Live Oak	5	8,096	361	7,735	....	31,075	30,675	28,875	1,800	400
Llano	1	1,300	12	1,288	....	13,300	13,150	13,000	150	150
McCulloch	14	1,348	1,058	290	....	46,995	45,670	44,290	1,380	1,325
McLennan	1,219	64,517	55,109	7,502	1,906	3,396,785	3,310,200	2,961,896	348,304	86,585
McMullen	2	6,807	107	....	6,700	32,300	32,000	31,650	350	300
Madison	476	33,513	20,142	12,924	447	390,129	378,503	320,793	57,710	11,626
Marion	916	69,746	35,845	31,324	2,577	913,005	840,589	617,685	222,904	72,416
Mason	3	83	82	....	1	9,150	9,000	8,080	920	150
Matagorda	384	14,680	8,956	4,724	1,000	559,768	541,525	475,140	66,385	18,243
Maverick	1	42	....	....	42	420	420	420	....	....
Medina	40	6,136	2,492	1,640	2,004	124,857	120,512	111,117	9,395	4,345
Milam	1,240	72,648	59,989	11,639	1,020	2,082,493	2,022,314	1,812,010	210,304	60,179
Mills	2	830	190	90	550	9,700	9,400	9,050	350	300
Mitchell	3	900	290	490	120	18,735	18,300	17,500	800	435
Montague	1	65	65	....	....	1,500	1,500	1,400	100	....
Montgomery	781	39,239	24,682	12,405	2,152	562,214	531,751	393,481	138,270	30,463
Morris	574	28,594	19,419	7,840	1,335	390,290	369,192	272,142	97,050	21,098
Nacogdoches	855	47,589	28,488	16,605	2,496	545,617	523,661	405,419	118,242	21,956
Navarro	986	68,864	54,730	10,677	3,457	2,451,174	2,381,648	2,133,644	248,004	69,526
Newton	333	22,125	7,502	11,716	2,907	230,411	217,685	142,165	75,520	12,726
Nolan	1	85	85	....	....	2,500	2,400	1,900	500	100
Nueces	6	518	316	182	20	22,990	22,490	20,300	2,190	500
Orange	7	583	91	482	10	8,680	8,260	6,910	1,350	420
Palo Pinto	1	40	10	30	....	825	800	400	400	25
Panola	1,406	92,623	60,321	29,081	3,221	851,192	808,826	647,327	161,499	42,366
Parker	24	2,101	1,320	398	383	48,795	47,200	41,150	6,050	1,595
Polk	597	28,387	14,611	12,817	959	348,293	330,692	242,170	88,522	17,601
Rains	121	7,088	4,214	2,699	175	144,776	137,475	114,720	22,755	7,301
Red River	1,342	67,180	51,052	15,506	622	1,560,349	1,500,992	1,268,776	232,216	59,357
Refugio	25	2,988	1,011	498	1,479	64,673	62,825	56,315	6,510	1,848
Robertson	2,363	123,982	98,634	20,764	4,584	3,248,200	3,156,154	2,707,659	448,495	92,046
Rockwall	27	1,517	1,462	55	....	81,805	79,960	72,644	7,316	1,845
Runnels	1	80	80	....	....	4,040	4,000	3,900	100	40
Rusk	1,983	135,452	82,123	51,632	1,697	1,282,889	1,213,546	933,286	280,260	69,343
Sabine	235	14,087	8,450	5,181	456	147,459	140,709	110,699	30,010	6,750
San Augustine	514	27,694	16,419	10,875	400	308,426	292,378	241,618	50,760	16,048
San Jacinto	867	37,713	20,436	15,738	1,539	383,061	367,340	287,606	79,734	15,721
San Patricio	2	130	130	....	....	7,400	7,300	6,450	850	100
San Saba	1	2,400	125	....	2,275	30,600	30,000	29,200	800	600
Shackelford	1	100	100	....	....	3,050	3,000	2,700	300	50
Shelby	582	33,293	21,117	11,919	257	423,924	403,707	309,032	94,675	20,217
Smith	2,602	165,493	113,418	48,376	3,699	2,052,928	1,954,769	1,563,254	391,515	98,159
Tarrant	126	7,264	5,278	1,450	533	390,042	383,245	339,845	43,400	6,797
Taylor	1	52	52	....	....	1,760	1,660	1,640	20	100
Throckmorton	1	240	240	....	....	7,050	7,000	6,850	150	50
Titus	368	17,716	11,862	5,299	555	254,024	243,478	194,266	49,212	10,546
Tom Green	2	351	171	....	180	16,225	16,000	15,000	1,000	225
Travis	787	48,157	39,803	6,070	2,284	2,787,740	2,722,945	2,508,024	214,921	64,795
Trinity	249	13,276	6,217	6,932	127	170,719	159,686	120,871	38,815	11,033
Tyler	184	11,972	3,401	8,172	399	96,747	91,160	66,170	25,090	5,587
Upshur	964	55,692	33,514	21,012	1,166	590,156	554,659	436,853	117,806	35,497
Uvalde	3	634	436	....	198	22,125	21,700	21,100	600	425
Van Zandt	228	17,308	10,019	6,750	539	265,455	254,544	194,864	59,680	10,911
Victoria	272	21,139	10,307	4,003	6,829	863,021	848,423	799,496	48,927	14,598
Walker	1,216	59,574	37,488	19,793	2,293	709,152	677,564	540,221	137,343	31,588

TABLE 71.—FARMS OPERATED BY NEGROES—NUMBER, ACREAGE, AND VALUE OF LAND AND BUILDINGS, AND OF IMPLEMENTS AND MACHINERY, BY STATES AND COUNTIES: 1910—Continued.

[Counties in which no farms operated by Negroes were reported are omitted.]

| STATE AND COUNTY. | Number of farms. | FARM ACREAGE. | | | | VALUE OF FARM LAND, BUILDINGS, AND IMPLEMENTS AND MACHINERY. | | | | |
| | | Total. | Improved. | Woodland. | Other un-improved. | Total. | Land and buildings. | | | Implements and machinery. |
							Total.	Land.	Buildings.	
TEXAS—Continued.										
Waller	1,114	45,376	37,238	5,676	2,462	$1,078,325	$1,033,515	$849,445	$184,070	$44,810
Washington	1,646	83,824	62,254	17,236	4,334	2,215,304	2,106,162	1,743,099	363,063	109,142
Wharton	1,190	45,329	36,160	6,028	3,141	2,246,582	2,187,892	1,945,926	241,966	58,690
Wichita	1	70	70			2,800	2,800	2,600	200	
Wilbarger	1	203	120		83	6,290	6,090	5,590	500	200
Williamson	260	21,315	14,673	5,168	1,474	1,292,757	1,264,948	1,190,234	74,714	27,809
Wilson	105	10,001	5,549	3,985	467	197,105	192,045	166,715	25,330	5,060
Wood	501	26,912	17,520	9,186	206	347,642	333,441	257,381	76,060	14,201
UTAH.										
Total	11	506	262	117	127	$81,615	$80,500	$70,500	$10,000	$1,115
Beaver	1	71	30	7	34	3,300	3,000	2,800	200	300
Iron	1	30	30			2,050	1,900	1,900		150
Millard	1	160	40	100	20	1,600	1,600	1,400	200	
Salt Lake	6	92	92			62,915	62,500	55,000	7,500	415
Sanpete	1	40	30		10	1,550	1,500	1,400	100	50
Utah	1	113	40	10	63	10,200	10,000	8,000	2,000	200
VERMONT.										
Total	20	1,917	634	469	814	$45,310	$42,350	$20,100	$22,250	$2,960
Addison	3	226	131	20	75	10,925	10,300	5,500	4,800	625
Bennington	1	5	5			1,000	1,000	500	500	
Chittenden	5	276	99	37	140	9,510	9,000	3,950	5,050	510
Orange	1	85	30	30	25	1,775	1,600	500	1,100	175
Orleans	1	80	30	25	25	1,650	1,500	1,000	500	150
Rutland	3	606	181	130	295	10,300	9,500	4,200	5,300	800
Windham	4	417	92	165	160	4,300	3,950	1,950	2,000	350
Windsor	2	222	66	62	94	5,850	5,500	2,500	3,000	350
VIRGINIA.										
Total	48,039	2,233,883	1,109,235	995,990	128,658	$46,993,076	$45,143,291	$32,497,542	$12,645,749	$1,849,785
Accomac	875	43,804	20,976	21,659	1,169	2,745,839	2,673,720	2,228,385	445,335	72,119
Albemarle	637	25,239	13,586	10,859	794	777,054	752,246	472,225	280,021	24,808
Alexandria	7	159	117	39	3	120,015	119,300	106,250	13,050	715
Alleghany	19	966	309	657		23,056	22,375	16,075	6,300	681
Amelia	720	45,515	19,052	23,253	3,210	554,325	526,997	347,352	179,645	27,328
Amherst	822	44,615	22,304	18,378	3,933	716,933	691,921	495,249	196,672	25,012
Appomattox	357	25,225	11,536	11,433	2,251	350,448	332,305	230,005	102,300	18,143
Augusta	164	5,988	4,476	1,364	148	274,164	265,615	196,820	68,795	8,549
Bath	23	879	297	525	57	15,895	15,400	10,955	4,445	495
Bedford	858	41,445	22,931	14,084	4,430	715,379	688,342	514,751	173,591	27,037
Bland	16	1,491	249	1,242		16,384	15,800	14,410	1,390	584
Botetourt	154	4,655	2,590	1,764	301	153,092	146,730	93,625	53,105	6,362
Brunswick	1,093	70,008	30,648	33,531	5,829	1,068,694	1,018,697	769,797	248,900	49,997
Buckingham	967	53,865	23,460	26,806	3,599	712,299	674,671	426,359	248,312	37,628
Campbell	808	40,086	20,736	18,073	1,277	686,105	657,632	453,934	203,698	28,473
Caroline	1,192	59,400	30,032	25,104	4,264	847,722	805,546	527,525	278,021	42,176
Carroll	26	770	471	280	19	18,791	17,934	14,235	3,699	857
Charles City	604	19,965	9,322	10,493	150	430,578	405,199	228,074	177,125	25,379
Charlotte	1,023	52,135	22,832	25,562	3,741	893,963	853,692	587,948	265,744	40,271
Chesterfield	594	18,558	7,286	10,399	873	547,435	526,936	389,524	137,412	20,499
Clarke	25	2,633	1,874	666	93	180,719	177,524	133,774	43,750	3,195
Craig	13	1,136	256	880		16,555	16,000	11,170	4,830	555
Culpeper	480	17,204	12,497	4,442	265	553,397	529,197	344,471	184,726	24,200
Cumberland	924	46,209	20,400	24,114	1,695	556,775	534,798	360,487	174,311	21,977
Dinwiddie	1,242	80,566	32,575	43,688	4,303	1,727,920	1,664,142	1,246,689	417,453	63,778
Elizabeth City	147	2,043	1,662	312	69	142,631	138,803	109,883	28,920	3,828
Essex	807	35,147	18,800	14,230	2,117	635,681	607,248	367,453	239,795	28,433
Fairfax	317	8,524	5,960	2,385	179	606,120	583,204	404,449	178,755	22,916
Fauquier	535	23,407	15,932	7,108	367	688,096	662,740	467,040	195,700	25,356
Floyd	102	4,861	3,407	1,339	115	114,003	112,090	93,720	18,370	1,913
Fluvanna	493	16,739	7,579	7,979	1,181	243,621	232,141	162,254	69,887	11,480
Franklin	773	41,119	18,447	16,708	5,964	463,067	440,035	337,870	102,165	23,032
Frederick	28	1,258	1,047	211		98,640	95,900	77,455	18,445	2,740
Giles	51	1,019	703	272	44	32,737	32,130	24,435	7,695	607
Gloucester	887	18,972	11,771	6,741	460	684,704	654,722	370,341	284,381	29,982
Goochland	609	28,751	12,223	12,328	4,200	397,975	371,408	239,203	132,205	26,567
Grayson	99	2,404	1,673	675	56	65,245	64,201	50,061	14,140	1,044
Greene	105	2,503	1,836	667		64,937	62,550	40,400	22,150	2,387
Greensville	725	40,458	20,518	17,898	2,042	676,556	640,192	465,800	174,392	36,364
Halifax	2,344	117,810	64,451	45,737	7,622	1,989,727	1,907,639	1,430,294	477,345	82,088

TABLE 71.—FARMS OPERATED BY NEGROES—NUMBER, ACREAGE, AND VALUE OF LAND AND BUILDINGS, AND OF IMPLEMENTS AND MACHINERY, BY STATES AND COUNTIES: 1910—Continued.

[Counties in which no farms operated by Negroes were reported are omitted.]

STATE AND COUNTY.	Number of farms.	FARM ACREAGE.				VALUE OF FARM LAND, BUILDINGS, AND IMPLEMENTS AND MACHINERY.					
		Total.	Improved.	Woodland.	Other un-improved.	Total.	Land and buildings.				Implements and machinery.
							Total.	Land.	Buildings.	

VIRGINIA—Continued.

STATE AND COUNTY.	Number of farms.	Total.	Improved.	Woodland.	Other un-improved.	Total.	Total.	Land.	Buildings.	Implements and machinery.
Hanover	832	32,072	15,585	15,274	1,213	$548,645	$521,325	$334,051	$187,274	$27,320
Henrico	332	8,905	3,614	4,912	379	444,883	430,470	329,985	100,485	14,413
Henry	774	45,714	22,739	18,966	4,009	506,007	487,750	376,940	110,810	18,257
Highland	19	1,971	798	1,011	162	27,828	26,580	21,120	5,460	1,248
Isle of Wight	548	22,942	11,472	11,273	197	516,722	498,668	379,753	118,915	18,054
James City	220	6,743	2,918	3,550	275	139,883	134,610	96,531	38,079	5,273
King and Queen	833	37,646	18,893	17,980	773	503,498	463,470	252,795	210,675	40,028
King George	369	14,991	9,730	4,811	450	427,427	414,060	306,840	107,220	13,367
King William	541	21,930	11,652	10,129	149	326,564	309,495	204,713	104,782	17,069
Lancaster	555	11,527	6,389	4,622	516	342,536	328,325	187,635	140,690	14,211
Lee	63	1,828	1,286	526	16	43,678	42,820	36,445	6,375	858
Loudoun	247	6,947	5,438	1,214	295	324,172	314,403	185,335	129,068	9,769
Louisa	978	48,572	20,972	25,278	2,322	762,503	725,662	455,057	270,605	36,841
Lunenburg	881	53,935	20,070	32,417	1,448	905,657	872,715	612,363	260,352	32,942
Madison	341	10,124	6,450	3,618	56	255,459	243,845	153,725	90,120	11,614
Mathews	245	2,833	2,032	755	46	219,007	211,650	123,870	87,780	7,357
Mecklenburg	1,876	90,493	44,255	40,506	5,732	1,513,742	1,461,421	1,038,219	423,202	52,321
Middlesex	772	16,136	8,851	7,102	183	547,382	526,815	298,600	228,215	20,567
Montgomery	146	4,043	2,569	1,421	53	177,839	171,815	127,825	43,990	6,024
Nansemond	926	33,870	16,752	16,610	508	937,042	905,635	655,839	249,796	31,407
Nelson	610	23,271	13,181	8,877	1,213	408,235	398,505	286,995	111,510	9,730
New Kent	374	15,731	7,026	8,235	470	235,557	224,349	157,319	67,030	11,208
Norfolk	543	15,718	11,077	3,724	917	792,273	772,460	646,908	125,552	19,813
Northampton	591	20,564	12,371	7,972	221	1,470,543	1,430,660	1,145,566	285,094	39,883
Northumberland	551	16,443	8,574	6,519	1,350	412,039	392,036	258,601	133,425	20,003
Nottoway	826	38,767	15,428	17,531	5,808	944,301	903,863	625,409	278,454	40,438
Orange	386	14,590	8,162	6,050	378	328,018	313,316	204,151	109,165	14,702
Page	39	1,140	607	420	113	46,328	45,050	32,545	12,505	1,278
Patrick	244	10,446	4,955	4,105	1,386	128,202	124,575	101,615	22,960	3,627
Pittsylvania	1,888	110,805	56,755	45,428	8,622	1,751,105	1,687,587	1,278,601	408,986	63,518
Powhatan	437	24,193	10,724	12,555	914	412,741	392,540	241,587	150,953	20,201
Prince Edward	924	52,140	20,458	26,880	4,802	725,028	691,957	473,211	218,746	33,071
Prince George	501	27,811	14,570	12,441	800	501,932	472,300	345,005	127,295	29,632
Prince William	196	9,854	6,247	3,400	207	272,068	260,470	171,569	88,901	11,598
Princess Anne	497	15,423	11,383	3,953	87	738,559	709,812	590,147	119,665	28,747
Pulaski	102	2,066	1,240	791	35	103,798	101,758	63,323	38,435	2,040
Rappahannock	175	7,247	5,728	1,351	168	155,975	149,155	96,420	52,735	6,820
Richmond	340	14,705	7,443	6,727	535	213,136	205,285	140,675	64,610	7,851
Roanoke	102	3,520	1,903	1,426	191	135,839	131,301	107,670	23,631	4,538
Rockbridge	99	3,847	2,520	922	405	144,376	139,565	98,315	41,250	4,811
Rockingham	69	1,433	892	408	133	61,683	58,185	38,195	19,990	3,498
Russell	38	1,663	971	655	37	48,973	48,015	42,810	5,205	958
Scott	51	1,557	723	774	60	26,876	26,430	22,670	3,760	446
Shenandoah	4	211	132	74	5	13,000	12,400	9,450	2,950	600
Smyth	39	1,671	594	1,027	50	35,921	35,290	27,290	8,000	631
Southampton	1,427	82,984	42,614	39,819	551	1,553,565	1,489,127	1,155,433	333,694	64,438
Spotsylvania	554	29,239	13,155	15,232	852	408,535	391,576	263,496	128,080	16,959
Stafford	167	8,219	4,321	3,709	189	121,621	116,919	70,579	46,340	4,702
Surry	573	30,302	11,058	13,263	5,981	716,022	689,947	527,087	162,860	26,075
Sussex	926	63,293	28,935	30,462	3,896	918,155	869,045	614,408	254,637	49,110
Tazewell	86	9,991	4,509	5,261	221	356,482	352,470	313,805	38,665	4,012
Warren	24	1,706	1,203	501	2	54,760	53,400	45,000	8,400	1,360
Warwick	193	4,061	2,310	1,515	236	447,690	441,625	390,015	51,610	6,065
Washington	67	2,107	1,488	457	162	84,332	82,735	66,450	16,285	1,597
Westmoreland	569	34,337	19,054	13,377	1,906	534,031	511,005	386,635	124,370	23,026
Wise	12	367	159	207	1	11,577	11,510	10,240	1,270	67
Wythe	58	1,435	997	416	22	75,492	69,290	51,185	18,105	6,202
York	571	10,034	6,254	3,650	130	465,857	449,012	315,014	133,998	16,845
INDEPENDENT CITIES:										
Charlottesville city	1	3	3	....	....	6,050	6,000	5,000	1,000	50
Danville city	2	35	35	....	....	14,100	14,000	13,200	800	100
Lynchburg city	1	18	15	3	....	4,550	4,500	4,100	400	50
Petersburg city	3	14	14	....	....	3,970	3,800	1,700	2,100	170
Radford city	10	69	66	3	....	14,375	13,800	8,200	5,600	575
Staunton city	3	20	20	....	....	14,290	14,160	8,660	5,500	130
Williamsburg city	2	70	65	5	....	1,350	1,250	900	350	100
Winchester city	1	10	10	....	....	2,015	2,000	2,000	....	15

WASHINGTON.

STATE AND COUNTY.	Number of farms.	Total.	Improved.	Woodland.	Other un-improved.	Total.	Total.	Land.	Buildings.	Implements and machinery.
Total	77	7,651	2,828	1,777	3,046	$481,794	$470,625	$427,170	$43,455	$11,169
Adams	1	160	25	135	....	1,050	1,000	950	50	50
Benton	1	160	160	....	....	3,290	3,200	2,900	300	90
Clarke	1	80	....	....	80	600	600	400	200	....
Cowlitz	1	120	4	116	....	1,125	1,000	700	300	125
Ferry	2	312	50	80	182	5,875	5,500	4,925	575	375

TABLE 71.—FARMS OPERATED BY NEGROES—NUMBER, ACREAGE, AND VALUE OF LAND AND BUILDINGS, AND OF IMPLEMENTS AND MACHINERY, BY STATES AND COUNTIES: 1910—Continued.

[Counties in which no farms operated by Negroes were reported are omitted.]

STATE AND COUNTY.	Number of farms.	FARM ACREAGE.				VALUE OF FARM LAND, BUILDINGS, AND IMPLEMENTS AND MACHINERY.				Implements and machinery.
		Total.	Improved.	Woodland.	Other unimproved.	Total.	Land and buildings.			
							Total.	Land.	Buildings.	
WASHINGTON—Continued.										
Garfield	1	960	800	....	160	$24,800	$24,000	$22,000	$2,000	$800
King	6	91	45	28	18	16,752	16,375	13,950	2,425	377
Kitsap	1	126	8	118	....	3,020	3,000	2,400	600	20
Kittitas	7	1,012	184	50	778	34,820	34,100	33,300	800	720
Klickitat	6	860	267	200	393	29,630	29,000	26,850	2,150	630
Lewis	7	372	86	126	160	17,320	17,000	14,325	2,675	320
Lincoln	1	160	25	....	135	1,300	1,200	1,100	100	100
Mason	4	214	37	165	12	10,650	10,350	7,650	2,700	300
Okanogan	5	720	365	40	315	87,675	87,000	85,620	1,380	675
Pierce	6	35	24	7	4	24,087	23,900	21,425	2,475	187
Skagit	1	100	50	50	....	17,500	17,000	16,000	1,000	500
Snohomish	2	97	75	10	12	20,750	20,000	17,800	2,200	750
Spokane	3	188	43	141	4	29,175	29,000	25,700	3,300	175
Stevens	3	426	50	376	....	25,910	25,500	24,150	1,350	410
Thurston	1	4	4	....	....	9,010	9,000	7,000	2,000	10
Whatcom	2	200	22	135	43	8,025	8,000	7,950	50	25
Yakima	15	1,254	504	....	750	109,430	104,900	90,075	14,825	4,530
WEST VIRGINIA.										
Total	707	34,520	20,236	12,516	1,768	$1,106,747	$1,075,204	$827,749	$247,455	$31,543
Barbour	93	4,044	2,549	703	792	104,540	99,950	77,995	21,955	4,590
Berkeley	34	1,502	1,170	329	3	59,064	57,335	43,160	14,175	1,729
Boone	18	1,267	472	728	67	31,498	30,890	26,635	4,255	608
Braxton	19	926	669	229	28	20,072	19,725	15,450	4,275	347
Brooke	1	58	45	8	5	3,500	3,500	3,000	500	....
Cabell	6	534	421	109	4	22,975	22,710	19,210	3,500	265
Calhoun	10	748	296	452	....	9,786	9,550	8,250	1,300	236
Fayette	44	1,190	576	576	38	67,763	66,869	41,545	25,324	894
Gilmer	1	58	55	3	....	1,525	1,500	1,200	300	25
Grant	12	957	301	590	66	6,664	6,330	5,565	765	334
Greenbrier	49	2,428	1,180	1,174	74	56,144	54,605	41,820	12,785	1,539
Hampshire	3	1,235	735	485	15	19,855	19,500	14,550	4,950	355
Hancock	2	98	73	20	5	14,110	14,000	7,500	6,500	110
Hardy	7	185	71	114	....	3,310	3,100	2,000	1,100	210
Harrison	9	282	244	33	5	15,175	14,820	12,490	2,330	355
Jackson	1	73	60	10	3	1,535	1,460	910	550	75
Jefferson	41	2,748	2,501	186	61	195,133	186,603	137,883	48,720	8,530
Kanawha	57	2,038	1,431	399	208	129,938	127,495	101,380	26,115	2,443
Lewis	1	53	41	10	2	875	800	600	200	75
Lincoln	1	8	8	....	....	150	150	100	50	....
Logan	4	236	59	177	....	2,170	2,050	1,600	450	120
McDowell	8	37	27	10	....	8,152	7,950	6,250	1,700	202
Marion	1	79	65	14	....	6,000	6,000	5,000	1,000	....
Marshall	2	66	58	....	8	1,870	1,810	1,560	250	60
Mason	5	382	338	44	....	13,275	13,100	11,325	1,775	175
Mercer	24	859	400	417	42	15,668	15,310	12,800	2,510	358
Mineral	8	702	446	256	....	13,452	13,150	10,100	3,050	302
Mingo	1	50	20	30	....	1,005	1,000	900	100	5
Monongalia	3	58	44	....	14	3,825	3,800	2,150	1,650	25
Monroe	59	2,365	1,170	1,053	142	67,562	64,900	51,790	13,110	2,662
Morgan	2	293	106	187	....	1,312	1,300	1,225	75	12
Nicholas	2	21	19	2	....	590	570	370	200	20
Ohio	2	26	15	8	3	3,825	3,800	2,400	1,400	25
Pendleton	8	383	122	224	37	3,362	3,279	2,819	460	83
Pleasants	1	235	35	200	....	4,500	4,500	4,200	300	....
Pocahontas	22	1,059	302	755	2	20,010	19,190	14,690	4,500	820
Preston	5	165	85	78	2	3,417	3,240	2,165	1,075	177
Putnam	9	288	129	159	....	5,241	5,125	3,870	1,255	116
Raleigh	10	424	239	184	1	16,380	15,800	9,650	6,150	580
Randolph	6	248	106	142	....	4,250	4,150	3,525	625	100
Ritchie	3	171	83	88	....	2,715	2,680	2,280	400	35
Roane	1	80	60	20	....	4,050	4,000	3,200	800	50
Summers	29	1,724	715	1,009	....	26,066	25,700	21,894	3,806	366
Taylor	37	2,212	1,595	529	88	58,785	57,645	47,480	10,165	1,140
Tucker	1	105	60	45	....	1,705	1,700	1,450	250	5
Upshur	4	140	99	41	....	3,110	2,950	1,900	1,050	160
Wayne	10	305	247	55	3	7,535	7,150	6,375	775	385
Webster	1	65	25	40	....	530	520	320	200	10
Wetzel	1	20	15	5	....	825	800	700	100	25
Wirt	7	519	298	221	....	9,133	8,958	4,433	4,525	175
Wood	11	285	203	36	46	21,650	21,120	17,770	3,350	530
Wyoming	11	486	153	329	4	11,165	11,065	10,315	750	100

TABLE 71.—FARMS OPERATED BY NEGROES—NUMBER, ACREAGE, AND VALUE OF LAND AND BUILDINGS, AND OF IMPLEMENTS AND MACHINERY, BY STATES AND COUNTIES: 1910—Concluded.

[Counties in which no farms operated by Negroes were reported are omitted.]

STATE AND COUNTY.	Number of farms.	FARM ACREAGE.				VALUE OF FARM LAND, BUILDINGS, AND IMPLEMENTS AND MACHINERY.					
		Total.	Improved.	Woodland.	Other unimproved.	Total.	Land and buildings.			Implements and machinery.
							Total.	Land.	Buildings.	
WISCONSIN.										
Total..................	48	4,029	2,039	1,501	489	$180,075	$173,550	$137,650	$35,900	$6,525
Adams...................	1	40	2	38	....	500	500	450	50	....
Calumet.................	1	12	12	....	....	1,250	1,200	1,000	200	50
Chippewa................	2	240	100	140	....	11,175	11,000	9,300	1,700	175
Clark...................	1	80	35	25	20	2,600	2,500	2,000	500	100
Dane....................	2	145	108	37	....	20,050	19,500	16,700	2,800	550
Douglas.................	1	120	30	....	90	1,800	1,200	1,000	200	600
Grant...................	3	314	183	111	20	16,525	16,150	13,950	2,200	375
Jefferson...............	1	80	25	....	55	3,800	3,500	1,500	2,000	300
Juneau..................	4	631	340	125	166	16,065	15,500	12,900	2,600	565
La Crosse...............	2	213	83	90	40	3,225	3,100	2,200	900	125
Manitowoc...............	1	80	50	12	18	7,010	7,000	6,700	300	10
Price...................	1	80	25	35	20	2,150	2,000	1,600	400	150
Rock....................	2	105	95	....	10	17,325	17,000	12,900	4,100	325
Sauk....................	1	40	35	....	5	2,600	2,500	1,600	900	100
Shawano.................	2	174	65	104	5	6,350	6,000	3,500	2,500	350
Vernon..................	18	1,415	634	778	3	42,325	40,300	32,600	7,700	2,025
Vilas...................	1	1	1	....	....	400	400	50	350	....
Walworth................	2	162	160	....	2	16,550	16,200	12,700	3,500	350
Waukesha................	1	57	20	2	35	4,075	4,000	3,000	1,000	75
Winnebago...............	1	40	36	4	....	4,300	4,000	2,000	2,000	300
WYOMING.										
Total..................	19	6,202	1,521	95	4,586	$132,135	$129,200	$121,145	$8,055	$2,935
Big Horn................	3	375	150	15	210	13,900	13,500	10,700	2,800	400
Carbon..................	1	1,120	341	....	779	56,200	56,000	55,620	380	200
Crook...................	1	320	6	....	314	1,525	1,500	1,100	400	25
Laramie.................	9	3,437	762	....	2,675	46,600	45,000	41,450	3,550	1,600
Sheridan................	3	560	192	....	368	9,960	9,400	8,800	600	560
Uinta...................	1	230	50	....	180	2,400	2,300	2,175	125	100
Weston..................	1	160	20	80	60	1,550	1,500	1,300	200	50

21857°—18——43

TABLE 72.—STATISTICS OF AGRICULTURE FOR COLORED AND WHITE

COUNTY	FARM ACREAGE: 1910.				ACREAGE AND YIELD OF COTTON: 1909.				ACREAGE AND YIELD OF CORN: 1909.			
	Total.		Improved.		Acreage.		Yield in bales.		Acreage.		Yield in bushels.	
	Colored farmers.	White farmers.	Colored farmers.	White farmers.	Colored farmers.	White farmers.	Colored farmers.	White farmers.	Colored farmers.	White farmers.	Colored farmers.	White farmers.
ALABAMA.												
Total	5,091,435	15,640,877	3,563,176	6,130,405	1,960,709	1,769,773	510,465	619,062	818,175	1,754,793	8,557,923	22,137,814
Autauga	77,319	168,349	56,954	57,897	32,291	18,466	8,475	6,070	13,002	15,275	110,720	167,642
Baldwin	11,869	141,069	4,637	28,226	1,561	4,682	452	1,735	1,207	7,356	15,667	122,478
Barbour	200,166	223,421	132,279	111,699	63,914	35,256	16,464	11,989	38,669	33,049	279,422	333,372
Bibb	29,218	151,995	17,014	47,051	7,783	11,285	2,487	3,868	4,404	15,700	45,304	196,335
Bullock	195,756	101,628	166,959	53,288	94,385	12,714	18,402	3,044	42,123	11,241	257,478	86,482
Butler	102,799	235,559	65,423	87,933	35,907	33,622	9,931	10,707	16,948	23,770	153,826	241,160
Calhoun	30,484	227,659	20,265	98,821	9,161	30,461	3,040	10,938	4,930	24,045	50,142	299,883
Chambers	156,935	177,062	104,541	83,310	64,461	34,818	20,625	13,810	21,816	20,444	212,839	253,473
Cherokee	16,072	267,247	10,896	118,175	4,785	33,598	1,645	13,175	2,980	31,264	34,061	417,167
Chilton	29,529	234,364	14,459	88,729	6,172	28,701	1,704	9,484	3,911	27,759	35,390	310,814
Choctaw	112,939	218,549	57,109	55,069	27,049	13,430	6,986	4,432	12,775	12,294	123,795	133,569
Clarke	130,631	356,025	67,837	87,586	32,059	23,826	8,304	7,680	15,479	20,318	146,779	205,890
Clay	15,293	240,037	9,455	99,835	3,622	30,068	1,344	11,835	2,674	28,258	32,013	374,082
Coffee	40,162	317,758	28,987	156,439	13,838	58,697	4,571	20,636	9,017	49,871	97,632	594,070
Colbert	48,130	185,230	37,817	83,774	17,685	19,957	4,303	5,517	12,547	26,972	163,031	427,360
Conecuh	66,845	202,934	40,777	63,868	19,688	22,712	6,300	8,533	13,959	21,834	122,026	235,119
Coosa	68,026	204,938	31,117	77,271	13,020	19,027	4,270	7,226	7,421	17,400	85,337	235,302
Covington	25,683	289,557	14,873	104,939	6,129	36,399	2,198	13,695	4,180	37,182	44,567	409,418
Crenshaw	54,731	255,105	36,997	112,300	18,627	41,206	5,476	13,984	11,507	37,971	104,002	393,152
Dale	48,863	266,011	33,963	125,319	16,599	44,457	5,607	16,621	9,341	36,466	100,556	432,407
Dallas	230,128	132,617	198,899	57,687	135,649	17,824	33,622	6,454	30,525	8,037	448,990	122,268
Elmore	79,212	217,542	52,954	96,762	27,372	33,185	7,938	11,774	10,847	21,908	124,539	285,923
Escambia	12,152	114,882	5,109	37,993	1,868	12,641	593	4,241	1,632	12,525	16,540	141,751
Etowah	10,471	238,897	6,454	105,669	2,544	27,820	869	9,857	1,821	28,761	18,732	310,491
Fayette	17,711	278,308	8,909	83,907	3,771	24,167	1,173	8,363	2,523	27,973	26,006	343,366
Franklin	6,564	250,263	4,431	86,395	1,299	20,860	381	7,018	1,779	32,687	19,931	479,609
Geneva	21,313	254,293	13,768	118,140	6,550	50,095	2,340	19,382	4,136	40,341	52,453	566,265
Greene	149,827	129,748	108,986	49,169	62,919	9,832	11,599	2,764	21,410	8,141	166,206	89,736
Hale	144,646	184,059	102,239	82,921	65,418	22,663	14,468	6,340	19,531	12,076	215,427	126,130
Henry	107,379	198,690	75,730	89,160	36,600	33,629	13,329	14,263	20,292	26,817	199,098	318,279
Houston	42,785	281,823	32,321	151,998	15,535	53,234	5,782	21,317	10,604	48,081	129,296	699,139
Jackson	15,383	427,906	11,464	158,426	3,519	23,274	1,260	8,342	4,880	66,146	58,576	905,286
Jefferson	12,589	223,231	7,636	88,220	1,649	11,523	674	4,364	2,716	29,035	40,114	434,071
Lamar	38,001	275,064	15,825	79,101	6,778	24,138	1,928	7,948	4,438	24,976	39,889	275,265
Lauderdale	37,978	307,524	30,225	133,568	15,295	28,596	3,535	9,171	8,713	47,537	134,373	847,276
Lawrence	53,766	257,715	43,376	118,646	22,061	29,474	5,875	9,073	12,772	35,921	151,795	509,716
Lee	166,894	151,305	111,749	79,786	53,415	25,846	15,420	8,991	19,866	14,369	180,815	171,184
Limestone	66,897	231,496	55,855	107,437	30,540	27,639	7,719	8,929	16,375	32,840	227,412	627,825
Lowndes	182,545	125,344	149,984	54,412	101,664	20,965	21,602	6,343	26,734	8,729	315,622	109,341
Macon	169,163	82,102	130,719	40,399	75,815	13,981	16,709	4,459	27,401	8,488	193,762	82,825
Madison	177,569	291,212	92,162	152,894	44,648	30,979	10,607	9,275	27,256	47,936	325,050	691,101
Marengo	189,0(?)	264,370	140,806	98,138	89,825	27,432	23,631	8,569	22,263	14,056	319,300	170,228
Marshall	6,822	323,520	4,480	148,366	1,547	46,844	448	17,156	1,388	50,622	17,650	593,370
Mobile	17,682	126,778	2,283	19,748	64	828	29	345	596	5,000	10,272	105,597
Monroe	118,217	321,072	70,710	94,055	38,316	27,638	11,005	10,353	16,802	18,514	171,860	213,416
Montgomery	230,780	152,906	194,590	91,271	129,589	27,412	29,871	8,614	33,476	13,293	469,205	180,298
Morgan	28,938	265,262	19,441	120,929	8,193	29,334	2,479	10,384	5,305	35,086	68,734	503,253
Perry	167,444	189,296	127,012	61,261	75,006	20,751	22,401	7,058	22,410	12,579	307,835	161,597
Pickens	118,450	251,841	73,997	77,347	40,611	21,573	8,471	6,029	17,342	21,512	128,323	195,091
Pike	108,631	256,213	80,910	139,913	42,105	54,435	12,172	17,462	22,924	42,341	183,374	414,111
Randolph	48,769	253,485	30,417	116,673	12,580	34,633	4,274	13,202	8,257	33,862	90,814	425,956
Russell	151,977	114,807	113,796	49,644	60,345	23,405	14,204	6,468	28,325	12,813	191,599	117,513
St. Clair	19,961	207,654	11,210	78,762	3,712	16,905	1,119	6,000	3,028	22,060	23,905	237,016
Shelby	41,312	237,807	18,071	81,628	6,483	19,128	2,168	6,821	5,049	23,263	47,725	277,102
Sumter	183,935	187,356	132,305	79,365	69,081	11,413	15,082	3,627	31,354	10,560	304,544	123,032
Talladega	97,011	186,073	67,892	97,043	31,680	32,667	10,328	12,671	17,855	24,910	178,984	332,109
Tallapoosa	94,362	305,831	59,645	128,067	27,763	43,019	9,333	16,154	13,597	31,800	146,695	385,452
Tuscaloosa	84,161	366,050	47,328	115,791	24,508	34,817	6,840	12,236	10,610	32,783	125,701	439,865
Washington	32,804	311,816	11,646	31,318	4,149	6,997	1,495	2,649	3,183	8,158	39,094	105,868
Wilcox	181,382	196,748	133,397	81,734	87,662	19,818	23,959	6,603	25,166	10,007	387,112	146,886
All other counties	25,565	2,003,474	12,086	705,133	3,845	174,977	1,149	63,014	4,104	249,781	45,984	3,004,032

FARMERS, BY COUNTIES, FOR SOUTHERN STATES: 1909–1910.

ALABAMA.

| VALUE OF LAND, BUILDINGS, IMPLEMENTS, AND MACHINERY: 1910. | | | | | | NUMBER OF DAIRY COWS, WORK HORSES, AND WORK MULES: 1910. | | | | | | |
| Land. | | Buildings. | | Implements and machinery. | | Dairy cows. | | Work horses. | | Work mules. | | COUNTY. |
Colored farmers.	White farmers.	Colored farmers.	White farmers.	Colored farmers.	White farmers.	Colored farmers.	White farmers.	Colored farmers.	White farmers.	Colored farmers.	White farmers.	
$59,324,679	$157,619,496	$14,594,048	$56,715,368	$3,332,509	$12,957,495	126,570	264,966	35,816	89,448	87,172	155,113	Total.
849,326	1,397,858	250,114	574,440	37,366	119,097	1,934	2,253	404	738	1,236	1,165	Autauga.
153,808	2,304,932	82,183	833,218	9,449	134,269	560	4,309	310	1,765	51	377	Baldwin.
1,613,313	1,878,789	380,140	724,733	88,244	172,322	2,748	2,463	329	546	2,554	2,048	Barbour.
403,166	1,463,615	96,369	546,846	12,529	99,433	656	2,656	146	799	562	1,632	Bibb.
2,218,018	1,069,771	489,969	375,735	111,748	93,297	4,547	1,522	901	600	3,454	823	Bullock.
1,034,258	2,067,535	330,255	913,930	55,895	166,977	1,950	3,606	466	1,101	1,532	2,129	Butler.
396,746	2,549,158	94,477	1,012,713	23,178	258,054	674	4,321	207	1,616	607	2,638	Calhoun.
2,060,101	2,547,105	539,133	1,221,511	113,969	295,221	2,887	3,464	751	1,469	2,586	2,020	Chambers.
210,199	2,733,670	47,985	1,010,569	10,762	269,336	353	4,222	81	1,352	318	3,387	Cherokee.
265,390	2,016,843	115,325	1,048,104	19,438	203,964	513	4,752	213	1,424	322	2,264	Chilton.
665,221	1,152,919	261,000	477,240	61,426	126,760	2,710	3,705	1,007	1,219	1,181	1,146	Choctaw.
887,529	1,990,566	312,262	923,291	62,234	161,566	3,181	5,808	1,231	1,659	1,385	1,765	Clarke.
145,417	1,973,450	45,264	839,478	9,363	205,879	312	4,160	73	1,203	213	2,767	Clay.
462,434	3,339,486	99,042	1,041,939	20,156	251,958	527	3,798	67	589	675	3,695	Coffee.
845,417	1,985,734	136,333	620,455	40,968	155,496	1,280	3,267	487	1,413	1,066	2,096	Colbert.
735,428	2,393,239	238,764	813,485	54,738	180,719	1,713	3,729	590	1,082	886	1,666	Conecuh.
423,906	1,127,354	119,795	565,791	27,483	149,005	1,085	3,111	284	844	749	1,819	Coosa.
292,028	2,971,366	75,300	982,455	14,962	204,144	459	4,952	86	832	370	3,091	Covington.
570,507	2,436,063	147,663	933,770	25,541	184,267	880	3,414	162	817	873	2,966	Crenshaw.
509,431	2,187,519	102,605	805,075	27,807	174,587	509	2,862	57	375	754	2,806	Dale.
2,875,020	1,563,426	849,711	698,525	223,422	184,046	8,746	2,207	2,240	1,090	5,288	1,173	Dallas.
991,467	2,564,454	313,093	941,850	52,404	205,523	1,570	3,746	532	1,311	1,231	2,424	Elmore.
133,098	1,280,077	58,915	549,371	10,607	102,440	536	3,932	190	995	88	776	Escambia.
144,711	2,676,099	28,150	835,361	6,185	213,443	229	4,105	96	1,382	161	2,715	Etowah.
136,113	1,676,965	35,321	625,901	6,952	143,104	272	3,649	100	1,355	267	2,647	Fayette.
99,564	1,849,989	21,115	595,723	4,537	144,831	171	4,110	77	1,502	136	2,600	Franklin.
298,242	3,147,501	60,895	944,146	13,230	213,605	329	4,588	57	616	340	3,105	Geneva.
1,481,900	1,288,744	343,488	463,111	103,147	85,755	5,187	1,744	1,371	778	2,704	1,289	Greene.
1,973,358	2,328,258	433,937	698,231	85,773	130,495	4,280	2,167	942	809	3,094	1,671	Hale.
1,021,413	1,862,842	219,994	609,689	57,922	173,688	1,303	2,248	155	440	1,628	2,309	Henry.
589,795	3,714,996	127,100	1,172,601	34,909	276,862	806	4,859	233	1,233	709	3,551	Houston.
250,611	4,087,527	43,040	1,111,090	12,854	259,021	364	6,807	180	2,889	404	5,403	Jackson.
750,785	9,237,304	137,585	2,069,721	20,837	355,480	614	10,754	275	2,483	203	2,696	Jefferson.
245,732	1,719,256	63,935	693,970	15,685	177,041	514	3,591	215	1,580	459	2,396	Lamar.
711,503	3,169,694	123,528	1,076,730	28,963	264,214	1,083	5,183	472	2,720	960	4,005	Lauderdale.
852,468	2,286,047	143,230	735,202	40,670	212,689	1,365	4,670	546	2,111	1,274	3,271	Lawrence.
1,726,842	1,702,632	468,809	874,547	107,253	188,863	2,803	2,800	774	865	2,183	1,386	Lee.
1,166,488	3,534,177	249,470	1,060,898	50,287	269,925	1,819	4,288	783	2,519	1,551	3,084	Limestone.
2,218,171	1,410,287	567,192	540,598	114,122	112,839	7,048	2,411	1,603	1,050	3,514	1,121	Lowndes.
2,162,538	974,448	675,583	486,558	132,911	91,251	3,999	1,176	1,146	622	2,597	623	Macon.
2,173,925	4,505,666	398,007	1,676,175	84,751	347,356	2,873	5,489	1,125	3,180	2,516	4,492	Madison.
2,026,881	2,264,889	496,914	723,133	147,067	151,756	5,639	3,838	1,528	1,403	4,149	1,945	Marengo.
69,205	3,855,954	15,435	1,318,452	3,455	329,598	165	6,060	48	1,918	131	4,691	Marshall.
186,240	2,041,044	72,260	902,430	11,493	118,132	509	4,084	223	1,441	52	352	Mobile.
926,700	2,389,966	307,455	937,011	74,137	224,114	2,939	4,601	1,075	1,369	1,490	1,682	Monroe.
4,667,796	3,173,669	783,245	907,800	188,283	216,598	6,927	3,335	1,873	1,004	5,853	1,813	Montgomery.
504,693	2,895,914	102,963	1,015,524	24,661	261,397	678	4,805	355	2,291	521	3,436	Morgan.
2,216,226	1,715,814	387,951	564,862	120,461	126,836	4,812	2,626	966	841	3,868	1,681	Perry.
967,048	1,649,374	265,960	728,068	60,828	148,240	2,818	3,411	1,141	1,749	1,946	2,111	Pickens.
1,391,987	3,004,445	221,526	1,037,581	40,680	223,908	1,585	3,573	179	726	1,593	3,094	Pike.
524,544	2,429,685	124,416	930,938	27,480	266,960	897	4,380	284	1,546	608	2,533	Randolph.
1,296,814	1,079,169	349,578	435,871	94,784	113,970	2,919	1,272	663	555	1,813	1,028	Russell.
169,170	1,651,253	52,630	685,148	12,771	160,590	448	3,850	114	1,222	293	1,991	St. Clair.
310,569	2,022,628	120,141	873,686	19,136	176,558	728	4,430	260	1,136	396	2,272	Shelby.
1,823,019	1,798,960	425,520	627,455	122,230	108,258	5,372	3,090	2,233	1,453	3,466	1,466	Sumter.
1,222,181	2,333,936	298,930	911,858	73,747	237,265	2,099	3,523	504	1,196	2,034	2,611	Talladega.
1,078,859	2,909,798	272,085	1,165,449	48,438	245,215	1,850	5,423	283	1,382	1,507	3,236	Tallapoosa.
1,030,174	3,702,884	215,817	1,111,312	56,188	290,916	1,816	5,860	444	1,687	1,584	3,513	Tuscaloosa.
211,342	1,447,121	83,090	478,948	15,753	144,760	909	4,034	396	1,128	242	536	Washington.
1,724,822	1,653,983	552,776	838,878	138,827	175,681	7,563	4,070	2,122	1,558	2,644	914	Wilcox.
231,022	15,431,649	119,280	5,795,688	17,413	1,477,921	508	31,803	161	10,870	301	19,171	All other counties.

NEGRO POPULATION.

TABLE 72.—STATISTICS OF AGRICULTURE FOR COLORED AND WHITE

COUNTY.	FARM ACREAGE: 1910.				ACREAGE AND YIELD OF COTTON: 1909.				ACREAGE AND YIELD OF CORN: 1909.			
	Total.		Improved.		Acreage.		Yield in bales.		Acreage.		Yield in bushels.	
	Colored farmers.	White farmers.	Colored farmers.	White farmers.	Colored farmers.	White farmers.	Colored farmers.	White farmers.	Colored farmers.	White farmers.	Colored farmers.	White farmers.
ARKANSAS.												
Total	2,653,323	14,762,752	1,773,206	6,303,048	949,734	1,203,486	348,635	428,244	386,913	1,890,203	6,107,452	31,502,092
Arkansas	33,443	266,974	20,307	153,151	9,129	6,077	1,881	1,688	4,410	10,855	45,959	132,650
Ashley	66,040	167,866	52,249	53,923	31,245	12,779	11,025	4,056	12,474	16,596	199,137	219,403
Bradley	25,220	116,191	10,594	37,050	3,719	9,223	878	2,823	3,072	12,032	34,245	160,985
Calhoun	31,471	103,896	11,914	33,225	4,138	7,997	1,032	2,448	3,815	11,397	44,301	153,015
Chicot	85,181	90,862	65,505	28,177	40,765	8,919	17,836	4,725	9,973	5,145	163,310	92,399
Clark	46,992	217,874	23,512	79,757	7,592	13,979	2,305	4,747	7,169	25,333	105,202	436,685
Cleveland	34,562	162,765	15,346	56,540	5,847	13,337	1,493	4,105	4,001	14,374	43,262	178,674
Columbia	108,398	238,592	55,356	89,517	23,011	30,412	5,986	9,700	15,187	26,696	164,414	359,324
Conway	75,993	174,619	48,422	94,664	24,776	31,175	8,237	9,919	12,759	27,211	172,069	392,915
Crawford	8,277	228,176	6,638	117,494	2,392	26,217	747	9,203	1,231	31,139	21,190	562,174
Crittenden	117,085	20,791	98,339	11,005	59,834	4,190	30,071	2,115	15,773	2,578	326,827	61,718
Cross	35,738	90,528	26,029	38,098	12,591	7,802	5,056	3,342	6,286	9,995	124,609	165,480
Dallas	28,473	136,067	11,803	38,229	3,274	7,173	896	2,260	3,825	12,979	41,727	168,551
Desha	106,545	70,624	68,845	18,478	30,208	5,622	10,853	2,577	7,849	3,496	120,278	72,008
Drew	96,996	206,150	57,485	71,016	23,210	15,488	5,856	4,540	13,403	15,743	154,460	205,894
Faulkner	38,637	260,977	23,413	129,618	10,314	38,849	3,419	11,506	5,899	37,337	79,695	501,966
Grant	11,449	110,685	4,369	39,295	1,273	9,216	376	3,324	1,277	14,122	15,769	190,437
Hempstead	102,124	202,211	66,550	103,119	28,282	23,800	5,729	5,876	21,120	29,372	336,280	471,879
Hot Spring	4,620	173,705	2,524	61,896	579	11,700	218	4,200	868	22,299	16,595	426,257
Howard	25,149	186,122	17,501	80,341	7,696	17,044	2,160	4,978	5,654	29,744	95,627	504,092
Jackson	36,217	177,033	26,166	86,567	15,951	39,900	6,585	18,913	5,063	26,822	92,857	602,046
Jefferson	180,656	174,505	139,616	52,829	93,515	17,285	37,602	8,755	19,099	8,621	328,657	157,770
Lafayette	39,688	111,695	23,695	43,339	8,271	9,732	2,299	2,669	7,405	15,746	100,878	234,172
Lee	128,290	78,282	95,725	34,372	58,762	10,098	23,608	4,242	21,848	7,376	445,064	146,851
Lincoln	71,022	145,219	47,064	51,048	28,184	16,324	9,388	6,452	9,543	11,134	144,562	159,259
Little River	47,018	117,600	29,170	46,408	11,738	8,498	3,358	2,258	9,784	15,128	171,694	276,374
Lonoke	64,986	222,705	53,643	128,215	31,936	34,170	11,378	11,656	8,404	25,390	129,912	391,120
Miller	27,736	153,900	16,683	57,999	5,891	12,709	1,622	3,475	5,763	22,754	78,312	344,675
Mississippi	53,854	125,893	48,574	80,298	33,250	34,454	20,641	22,030	8,784	25,572	278,573	829,791
Monroe	79,516	62,284	61,454	27,359	40,253	10,564	11,523	3,461	10,486	5,552	158,649	102,488
Nevada	60,600	219,473	32,405	96,879	11,408	20,712	2,851	5,773	9,112	28,388	100,381	379,013
Ouachita	109,687	150,028	48,558	49,513	15,734	10,014	3,554	2,852	14,537	15,188	141,401	181,563
Perry	5,893	83,790	3,715	37,771	1,865	12,017	705	3,914	1,020	12,706	15,358	196,825
Phillips	132,948	84,721	108,848	35,648	73,053	11,231	24,957	4,325	18,577	7,135	293,351	116,005
Poinsett	8,741	92,629	6,646	44,873	2,775	9,447	1,432	4,827	1,300	16,010	28,678	348,846
Pope	11,899	278,617	8,375	136,511	4,440	43,127	1,642	14,385	1,994	44,400	32,353	743,973
Prairie	26,503	162,968	18,852	90,066	11,916	10,557	3,143	2,641	3,926	12,804	46,202	146,426
Pulaski	90,992	148,025	68,479	59,033	46,104	13,999	21,340	4,797	11,415	16,664	212,164	266,014
St. Francis	107,922	69,936	79,832	33,787	48,815	11,125	20,082	4,206	19,051	8,456	361,997	159,510
Saline	10,093	213,117	6,404	69,631	3,312	11,759	1,050	4,133	1,156	24,890	17,927	419,668
Sebastian	4,315	217,872	2,878	131,183	881	26,503	244	7,509	876	36,338	12,340	589,175
Sevier	18,772	199,450	10,607	77,007	3,618	12,528	799	3,722	3,996	26,801	73,482	511,375
Union	108,208	307,709	47,916	102,078	13,965	21,348	2,635	4,887	12,837	30,725	111,048	311,304
White	9,205	319,923	5,161	150,019	1,944	34,747	573	10,164	1,494	41,594	19,228	589,188
Woodruff	85,293	70,814	67,071	34,527	41,994	14,348	15,852	6,412	13,548	9,427	235,603	217,017
Yell	9,516	273,232	6,224	137,729	2,445	43,886	848	16,454	1,830	46,891	28,489	840,060
All other counties	41,360	7,275,657	22,744	3,073,766	7,839	401,407	2,870	145,200	8,020	989,248	143,336	16,785,078
DELAWARE.												
Total	56,973	981,893	37,076	676,462					12,636	176,119	252,478	4,587,070
Kent	20,623	314,642	14,016	225,298					3,704	52,345	80,664	1,517,171
Sussex	31,671	437,507	19,368	269,011					8,149	92,495	154,038	2,027,694
All other counties	4,679	229,744	3,692	182,153					783	31,279	17,776	1,042,205
DISTRICT OF COLUMBIA.												
Total	95	5,968	95	5,038					2	424	50	12,617
FLORIDA.												
Total	768,705	4,484,833	482,353	1,323,055	121,905	141,549	28,324	36,732	191,400	414,371	2,065,082	4,958,685
Alachua	65,792	209,038	43,332	94,309	8,884	10,105	1,617	2,333	14,116	25,320	146,720	323,622
Bradford	12,370	122,514	6,555	47,700	2,134	10,661	384	2,614	2,394	18,587	27,295	221,848
Columbia	61,508	155,381	39,191	71,066	10,530	11,614	1,686	2,256	12,115	20,248	108,863	222,904
Duval	5,474	105,427	1,857	7,714		2		1	431	2,159	8,239	41,403
Gadsden	55,416	162,027	28,626	51,006	3,507	1,257	934	331	14,600	20,092	215,227	306,434
Hamilton	28,798	135,911	20,496	53,909	7,183	10,913	1,446	2,399	7,017	16,684	59,681	164,777
Hillsborough	3,688	110,249	1,569	29,683					551	6,282	5,955	87,493
Jackson	107,808	267,795	78,287	103,250	27,214	21,259	7,958	7,158	29,744	39,120	296,887	478,246
Jefferson	76,861	88,264	64,445	40,255	22,029	4,419	5,669	1,257	31,871	14,445	400,548	184,413
Lake	4,856	107,268	2,042	22,202	6	8	1	1	410	3,856	4,479	47,077

FARMERS, BY COUNTIES, FOR SOUTHERN STATES: 1909-1910—Continued.

| VALUE OF LAND, BUILDINGS, IMPLEMENTS, AND MACHINERY: 1910. | | | | | | NUMBER OF DAIRY COWS, WORK HORSES, AND WORK MULES: 1910. | | | | | | COUNTY. |
| Land. | | Buildings. | | Implements and machinery. | | Dairy cows. | | Work horses. | | Work mules. | | |
Colored farmers.	White farmers.	Colored farmers.	White farmers.	Colored farmers.	White farmers.	Colored farmers.	White farmers.	Colored farmers.	White farmers.	Colored farmers.	White farmers.	
ARKANSAS.												
$57,952,855	$188,068,595	$11,060,254	$52,085,109	$2,789,157	$14,075,041	81,122	344,671	36,948	191,531	52,772	153,680	Total.
492,882	7,844,089	99,065	1,100,900	27,095	772,734	1,510	7,096	752	3,895	483	2,611	Arkansas.
1,550,868	1,818,434	360,231	613,120	118,715	174,747	3,100	5,166	1,486	2,346	1,827	1,153	Ashley.
170,804	873,178	68,240	449,820	10,763	99,101	721	3,286	263	1,113	227	945	Bradley.
204,452	601,999	69,252	291,280	12,700	73,646	828	2,898	266	851	343	916	Calhoun.
2,859,513	1,742,974	613,220	451,435	110,063	223,943	2,668	1,208	2,272	955	2,135	1,222	Chicot.
394,711	1,559,961	105,095	595,294	24,395	152,989	1,511	5,727	592	2,554	617	1,880	Clark.
245,714	965,360	83,230	438,234	18,403	97,092	1,083	4,333	445	1,524	363	1,229	Cleveland.
950,351	1,990,175	233,796	855,828	58,270	196,318	1,942	4,776	709	1,622	1,195	2,435	Columbia.
1,482,918	2,269,772	290,793	654,798	79,673	175,801	2,009	3,970	1,072	2,506	1,494	2,387	Conway.
224,395	3,642,424	34,995	953,707	8,355	238,447	207	5,704	207	3,606	182	3,397	Crawford.
4,643,470	692,376	719,392	172,995	258,220	35,160	4,153	512	1,460	279	3,344	538	Crittenden.
669,328	1,502,704	156,025	314,385	47,501	123,382	1,030	2,182	437	1,190	1,000	1,050	Cross.
190,190	839,619	58,410	362,544	12,648	73,563	802	3,274	284	991	288	1,172	Dallas.
2,410,059	1,267,735	460,076	229,770	87,248	79,138	2,506	1,087	1,196	661	1,745	838	Desha.
1,393,737	1,909,723	302,895	643,865	79,544	149,649	2,792	4,558	1,056	2,202	1,802	1,655	Drew.
407,213	1,933,393	114,847	890,630	37,729	271,123	1,148	6,006	381	3,328	753	3,063	Faulkner.
95,009	741,285	23,295	371,157	6,523	88,695	369	3,542	128	1,178	124	1,178	Grant.
1,193,154	2,442,375	334,109	829,456	85,122	226,662	3,181	4,770	1,402	2,373	1,865	2,461	Hempstead.
57,755	1,430,513	25,100	574,455	5,287	143,509	154	4,515	88	1,698	85	1,821	Hot Spring.
317,423	1,480,331	68,923	588,405	15,996	145,082	803	5,362	357	2,131	474	2,163	Howard.
1,149,213	3,630,200	178,935	815,080	44,848	231,000	1,163	5,111	684	3,143	853	2,986	Jackson.
5,469,476	3,436,778	857,484	573,086	167,636	203,485	5,549	2,252	2,911	992	4,086	2,148	Jefferson.
539,020	1,185,671	127,878	350,015	28,704	100,980	1,416	2,604	535	1,177	595	1,151	Lafayette.
2,932,254	1,638,520	836,963	394,545	280,047	154,710	4,776	1,159	2,540	904	2,654	1,144	Lee.
1,432,418	1,531,963	236,737	337,780	76,669	103,949	2,254	2,734	1,154	1,339	1,409	1,346	Lincoln.
689,204	1,357,088	106,330	304,192	27,718	83,762	1,431	2,736	817	1,331	863	1,045	Little River.
2,185,381	4,457,053	339,615	1,113,423	71,571	427,560	2,059	7,178	756	3,214	1,991	3,688	Lonoke.
418,970	1,603,361	69,263	503,645	14,635	101,165	881	4,281	494	1,904	433	1,236	Miller.
2,726,190	5,255,537	333,133	962,802	86,637	253,117	2,037	3,632	833	1,702	1,923	3,978	Mississippi.
1,922,028	1,075,252	382,225	254,578	90,226	68,094	2,829	1,656	1,271	765	2,344	1,099	Monroe.
378,670	1,544,209	112,811	673,827	31,747	199,398	1,401	4,998	519	2,215	589	2,151	Nevada.
783,297	1,046,136	199,179	440,480	41,588	111,047	2,424	3,010	789	1,041	1,001	976	Ouachita.
92,200	804,279	16,040	259,316	5,705	68,806	230	2,917	91	1,042	129	1,122	Perry.
3,974,265	2,047,884	816,186	502,075	232,040	140,691	5,080	1,337	1,957	862	2,483	1,362	Phillips.
270,615	2,131,861	56,750	458,390	9,522	185,413	257	2,433	93	1,396	277	1,577	Poinsett.
247,839	3,170,840	48,106	1,010,567	11,793	236,261	286	5,709	208	3,620	268	3,829	Pope.
726,843	3,672,202	137,307	643,560	24,170	259,310	1,059	5,629	328	2,124	704	1,886	Prairie.
4,011,459	3,210,284	519,760	937,418	102,879	222,607	2,511	5,100	1,244	1,763	2,227	2,542	Pulaski.
2,616,632	1,291,352	536,671	360,320	112,948	122,286	3,408	1,918	1,205	1,026	2,973	1,111	St. Francis.
211,074	2,062,878	51,520	630,431	12,070	180,807	226	5,434	74	1,692	169	2,306	Saline.
214,135	5,823,240	21,525	1,248,991	4,368	267,776	131	7,952	136	5,355	42	2,171	Sebastian.
185,775	1,887,049	44,475	576,749	11,903	146,525	552	4,128	295	2,128	202	1,646	Sevier.
658,902	1,952,475	173,760	870,304	41,239	208,336	2,278	5,726	680	1,852	1,018	2,173	Union.
102,310	3,154,715	30,435	1,230,893	8,038	352,986	231	7,901	165	5,183	151	3,578	White.
3,225,395	1,655,800	451,626	351,270	104,294	109,489	2,814	2,112	1,457	1,216	2,187	1,438	Woodruff.
184,737	3,807,365	38,805	1,036,112	8,357	275,757	234	6,738	134	4,364	231	3,943	Yell.
650,607	86,686,183	115,746	23,863,184	34,155	5,718,943	1,088	158,314	725	101,178	624	65,934	All other counties.
DELAWARE.												
$1,451,457	$33,486,704	$530,259	$17,687,563	$100,090	$3,106,005	1,077	34,631	1,529	28,103	349	5,327	Total.
639,711	10,492,362	248,229	4,305,205	43,239	905,797	536	10,862	677	9,068	79	1,425	Kent.
669,696	10,800,172	215,480	4,979,158	43,686	986,139	336	7,487	637	9,271	260	3,429	Sussex.
142,050	12,194,170	66,550	8,403,200	13,165	1,214,069	205	16,282	215	9,764	10	473	All other counties.
DISTRICT OF COLUMBIA.												
$66,600	$7,127,350	$22,800	$1,014,593	$955	$91,395	11	846	18	545	1	52	Total.
FLORIDA.												
$9,297,717	$84,440,348	$2,617,851	$21,790,073	$602,531	$3,843,476	15,872	100,169	9,794	33,221	5,026	18,102	Total.
572,857	2,145,193	165,964	666,000	39,678	159,539	1,288	5,394	1,418	2,029	243	970	Alachua.
152,210	1,286,695	56,210	519,375	9,318	96,446	150	3,016	172	1,361	82	656	Bradford.
399,643	1,093,073	114,342	394,941	24,391	83,264	709	3,436	486	805	499	938	Columbia.
302,577	2,810,265	112,408	675,345	11,773	103,379	242	2,515	163	659	47	207	Duval.
665,436	3,777,052	201,942	1,791,759	48,531	156,183	1,397	1,996	935	884	228	1,029	Gadsden.
281,670	1,181,632	69,420	344,420	15,363	74,679	404	3,568	160	564	289	602	Hamilton.
209,214	6,996,910	35,686	1,250,205	7,529	239,986	59	3,008	105	1,882	14	386	Hillsborough.
1,128,594	2,322,337	260,909	766,140	64,522	169,414	1,757	5,691	1,007	2,070	1,219	1,498	Jackson.
712,555	817,232	213,161	241,980	69,388	63,668	2,687	1,132	627	405	761	567	Jefferson.
114,890	3,409,149	32,310	812,061	4,447	114,728	113	1,206	93	817	21	190	Lake.

TABLE **72.**—STATISTICS OF AGRICULTURE FOR COLORED AND WHITE

COUNTY.	FARM ACREAGE: 1910.				ACREAGE AND YIELD OF COTTON: 1909.				ACREAGE AND YIELD OF CORN: 1909.			
	Total.		Improved.		Acreage.		Yield in bales.		Acreage.		Yield in bushels.	
	Colored farmers.	White farmers.	Colored farmers.	White farmers.	Colored farmers.	White farmers.	Colored farmers.	White farmers.	Colored farmers.	White farmers.	Colored farmers.	White farmers.
FLORIDA—Continued.												
Leon	79,560	117,724	62,125	47,224	17,432	1,072	3,990	324	26,525	11,171	278,821	128,850
Levy	11,649	123,865	5,053	32,807	326	1,666	59	334	1,838	9,295	19,511	97,210
Madison	48,012	203,483	38,712	85,897	11,717	11,456	2,237	2,822	15,979	28,773	147,744	310,567
Marion	45,563	172,988	22,500	64,751	576	323	94	66	9,013	16,297	95,111	209,125
Orange	5,513	117,020	1,642	21,374	....	....	....	....	271	2,279	4,779	41,868
Putnam	11,319	65,524	3,877	15,412	198	199	41	49	1,296	3,918	13,882	52,527
Sumter	4,017	72,502	2,187	20,763	....	16	....	8	886	5,989	9,243	77,441
Suwannee	52,124	221,206	30,977	104,779	7,927	18,933	1,562	3,905	9,566	32,995	86,543	334,148
Volusia	2,156	70,819	1,041	12,742	5	8	1	2	347	2,248	4,029	34,113
Walton	8,985	104,039	2,831	25,230	387	3,457	110	1,110	1,688	14,563	13,890	137,333
Washington	22,519	119,059	6,545	27,269	481	2,624	150	901	3,863	13,412	34,711	155,194
All other counties	54,717	1,632,730	18,463	343,013	1,369	31,557	385	8,861	6,879	106,638	82,924	1,302,092
GEORGIA.												
Total	7,092,051	19,861,362	4,791,562	7,506,455	2,468,242	2,415,062	927,162	1,065,246	1,278,627	2,104,434	12,881,533	26,493,086
Appling	26,839	254,146	5,493	47,581	1,320	13,015	425	4,858	2,446	18,304	27,614	239,524
Baker	55,285	67,609	45,322	32,823	17,868	7,112	5,453	2,591	13,562	9,191	120,902	102,491
Baldwin	85,967	63,566	48,438	32,615	23,668	9,315	7,628	3,619	10,632	7,930	89,468	86,642
Banks	18,413	111,477	12,245	50,547	6,042	19,837	2,529	9,114	2,621	11,905	23,996	141,054
Bartow	23,752	197,090	18,358	102,629	9,906	36,740	3,010	12,721	3,454	19,818	38,278	247,926
Ben Hill	29,460	100,510	14,360	25,903	5,745	9,486	2,583	4,923	3,745	7,415	42,585	108,122
Berrien	25,689	342,118	12,212	78,651	5,519	23,734	2,362	11,021	3,604	23,671	53,680	375,061
Bibb	37,517	88,315	25,762	46,193	12,128	12,407	4,259	5,160	5,460	9,885	57,553	152,214
Brooks	72,071	210,035	48,719	72,658	18,444	15,621	7,135	6,842	16,855	23,266	217,167	329,593
Bryan	18,055	134,149	5,845	18,070	894	2,058	555	1,474	2,570	6,749	30,641	89,301
Bulloch	68,381	357,121	47,078	99,099	22,341	35,869	11,024	18,017	14,109	32,978	242,337	503,309
Burke	180,518	174,194	148,639	90,128	79,943	24,843	33,572	13,169	40,032	20,982	391,691	247,368
Butts	44,193	63,744	32,856	38,402	19,840	18,073	7,520	8,150	7,214	9,233	69,471	116,671
Calhoun	56,117	55,280	50,234	21,029	28,948	7,214	10,184	2,877	16,431	6,265	175,470	77,857
Camden	24,643	170,736	3,875	9,684	75	40	36	21	1,851	1,854	27,163	31,159
Campbell	25,584	90,064	15,721	42,572	8,542	15,803	2,853	6,169	2,839	9,248	27,742	104,284
Carroll	37,000	252,468	27,380	136,378	14,861	50,785	5,098	21,493	5,567	33,593	56,026	425,892
Chatham	5,985	43,265	3,256	9,146	74	72	47	42	742	1,709	16,892	43,174
Chattahoochee	49,845	68,969	23,680	21,906	11,588	6,141	3,624	2,376	7,628	5,712	59,818	55,595
Chattooga	18,867	135,795	11,557	61,101	5,281	14,191	1,860	5,707	3,210	16,560	31,930	209,790
Cherokee	5,685	204,138	2,937	75,242	1,243	19,263	529	9,029	596	23,394	10,641	337,859
Clarke	34,974	32,178	27,212	17,576	16,083	6,924	5,824	3,522	5,741	3,431	54,360	50,740
Clay	57,980	48,088	43,968	25,885	22,638	11,004	8,206	4,418	12,311	7,164	105,156	74,735
Clayton	31,013	56,645	22,262	30,387	12,728	11,550	4,831	5,288	3,788	6,323	44,271	85,388
Clinch	8,553	217,659	1,883	21,441	392	4,339	136	1,460	910	8,887	12,163	113,162
Cobb	27,838	166,481	19,136	85,036	8,243	24,636	3,508	12,470	5,382	23,159	52,753	303,713
Coffee	30,084	387,188	13,912	74,640	5,115	21,481	2,212	8,974	4,739	27,148	55,236	342,770
Colquitt	12,154	232,525	8,542	76,197	3,156	26,607	1,549	13,223	1,667	22,680	32,214	376,815
Columbia	71,152	65,538	51,237	30,946	27,827	10,111	10,896	4,755	12,037	6,480	116,167	81,604
Coweta	112,281	131,654	80,708	73,537	50,729	36,120	17,197	14,052	13,164	14,305	123,812	169,151
Crawford	53,950	109,618	27,519	42,485	12,559	10,452	4,096	4,328	6,521	10,294	61,490	114,676
Crisp	38,039	94,577	28,432	44,690	16,466	18,202	8,223	9,869	8,113	13,880	94,941	183,520
Decatur	81,785	318,089	47,822	82,213	14,968	14,248	4,828	5,225	18,567	31,094	207,391	424,081
Dekalb	28,863	114,378	18,829	53,217	9,465	15,960	3,816	7,452	4,931	15,516	51,274	204,248
Dodge	64,226	182,198	49,047	87,707	24,993	32,239	10,809	15,047	14,267	28,301	154,531	321,881
Dooly	92,393	114,543	71,281	60,834	43,063	28,333	20,238	15,127	20,673	18,757	219,141	247,626
Dougherty	58,214	76,021	55,241	33,580	24,190	10,080	8,790	4,374	12,277	5,718	109,922	73,663
Douglas	19,545	87,589	11,896	42,430	5,256	14,114	2,026	6,328	2,825	10,571	25,771	123,822
Early	96,266	95,061	68,108	43,006	36,511	16,058	12,429	6,302	22,529	15,187	226,490	184,514
Effingham	34,315	183,172	6,312	28,598	1,510	3,750	865	2,461	2,475	10,871	34,013	192,462
Elbert	81,028	118,338	46,328	53,697	26,620	24,445	10,338	11,088	9,491	12,349	93,065	151,463
Emanuel	79,392	305,842	44,419	98,583	21,838	37,426	9,290	17,805	16,022	37,618	176,444	462,961
Fayette	28,539	83,459	19,876	46,529	11,667	20,795	4,874	9,281	4,677	11,539	45,834	136,727
Floyd	44,110	208,036	25,389	95,993	10,860	27,290	3,504	10,451	5,623	21,668	52,592	252,839
Forsyth	7,539	138,945	4,565	62,259	2,021	21,405	865	10,344	1,373	19,894	17,131	268,012
Franklin	22,390	125,239	16,615	69,272	10,390	33,205	4,227	15,085	3,601	16,488	37,112	209,080
Fulton	8,281	51,138	5,256	22,188	1,518	3,011	555	1,401	1,068	5,515	14,905	80,255
Glascock	12,573	53,956	8,871	27,375	4,089	9,238	1,538	3,357	3,476	9,954	30,142	90,383
Glynn	14,072	48,710	1,035	3,147	14	43	7	30	589	751	7,817	12,383
Gordon	6,902	191,351	4,694	96,373	1,637	21,203	624	8,990	1,238	22,158	15,815	318,214
Grady	43,934	188,611	25,804	68,767	7,427	13,537	2,325	5,092	10,450	27,112	111,279	364,480
Greene	101,533	100,692	59,141	47,325	34,115	17,719	11,475	7,073	12,364	9,771	109,499	113,048
Gwinnett	24,057	261,491	15,507	134,827	7,322	47,020	2,855	21,437	4,234	38,702	43,344	453,956
Hall	17,573	222,882	10,574	89,366	3,500	28,461	1,678	11,795	2,774	25,840	29,738	335,134
Hancock	123,626	129,882	78,644	56,580	41,130	18,381	13,948	7,431	22,088	14,706	169,041	144,305
Haralson	13,125	135,727	7,328	52,317	3,859	17,979	1,068	6,281	1,640	14,872	14,130	156,197
Harris	135,811	108,753	76,097	41,909	45,287	16,577	13,533	6,152	16,684	9,296	154,844	107,259
Hart	37,482	109,873	24,015	60,110	14,727	30,331	5,419	13,203	4,866	13,248	49,737	165,643
Heard	38,972	122,840	24,062	61,265	11,963	21,113	4,007	8,514	5,411	16,590	49,138	185,965
Henry	72,332	119,677	50,575	64,681	31,760	32,139	11,765	14,368	10,570	16,118	109,669	214,904

FARMERS, BY COUNTIES, FOR SOUTHERN STATES: 1909-1910—Continued.

| VALUE OF LAND, BUILDINGS, IMPLEMENTS, AND MACHINERY: 1910. | | | | | | NUMBER OF DAIRY COWS, WORK HORSES, AND WORK MULES: 1910. | | | | | | COUNTY. |
| Land. | | Buildings. | | Implements and machinery. | | Dairy cows. | | Work horses. | | Work mules. | | |
Colored farmers.	White farmers.	Colored farmers.	White farmers.	Colored farmers.	White farmers.	Colored farmers.	White farmers.	Colored farmers.	White farmers.	Colored farmers.	White farmers.	
FLORIDA—Continued.												
$979,884	$1,151,795	$256,512	$513,790	$82,244	$85,006	1,946	2,764	1,172	508	512	439	Leon.
101,260	686,880	28,845	205,370	5,386	69,768	246	2,255	210	878	17	166	Levy.
524,551	1,611,054	130,849	420,376	37,832	118,472	978	4,578	513	792	342	998	Madison.
472,254	2,634,258	207,095	787,452	49,124	174,721	1,134	4,364	1,038	1,768	88	666	Marion.
370,240	5,934,505	98,410	1,612,745	14,851	237,711	86	1,500	88	1,189	29	388	Orange.
163,529	1,772,617	99,605	642,995	12,138	74,912	79	1,096	157	552	33	189	Putnam.
73,147	1,297,917	19,683	289,437	4,898	88,536	89	6,251	143	1,125	7	138	Sumter.
388,809	1,542,083	120,052	583,103	30,836	147,436	732	4,274	364	1,267	261	1,050	Suwannee.
101,585	2,523,330	35,195	689,000	3,117	66,710	29	697	63	658	13	156	Volusia.
59,441	842,788	20,075	292,140	4,412	64,978	195	2,523	90	466	28	600	Walton.
169,960	976,660	47,520	322,834	10,852	55,400	361	2,712	162	623	121	593	Washington.
1,353,411	37,626,923	291,658	7,968,605	51,901	1,398,540	1,191	36,193	628	11,919	172	5,676	All other counties.
GEORGIA.												
$105,855,590	$264,497,825	$23,028,142	$85,822,775	$4,559,962	$16,388,094	104,966	300,744	28,094	86,571	109,983	183,248	Total.
174,840	1,542,962	51,585	501,461	8,980	112,948	368	4,391	133	617	141	1,352	Appling.
414,669	658,026	132,316	153,525	36,166	37,680	842	1,102	185	180	802	427	Baker.
760,235	619,025	154,540	366,400	55,516	73,448	884	979	282	338	845	628	Baldwin.
370,035	2,059,636	64,485	531,086	11,384	104,468	347	1,912	54	498	320	1,704	Banks.
455,309	3,286,672	77,947	909,735	12,966	167,621	453	2,837	83	893	451	2,974	Bartow.
446,829	1,616,782	66,410	379,200	14,307	59,665	294	1,027	118	368	347	721	Ben Hill.
378,428	3,335,007	78,300	834,405	16,626	143,225	433	5,178	125	822	282	2,002	Berrien.
815,338	2,113,539	196,555	878,135	49,080	145,963	630	2,142	182	562	591	1,145	Bibb.
1,113,922	3,005,258	233,050	799,270	46,793	178,637	1,157	3,738	398	777	1,098	1,768	Brooks.
137,832	594,941	44,145	223,590	8,161	36,008	416	1,829	130	314	122	465	Bryan.
1,713,354	7,516,785	283,119	1,556,330	71,626	275,146	1,271	5,405	235	1,142	918	3,170	Bulloch.
2,218,758	2,146,722	640,716	591,200	165,402	176,919	2,378	728	842	521	3,128	1,372	Burke.
1,103,971	1,632,629	201,487	565,160	28,934	104,622	841	1,250	132	436	934	996	Butts.
790,578	659,387	157,720	206,390	37,276	50,355	823	415	158	158	1,354	529	Calhoun.
141,848	689,510	105,779	389,285	12,038	66,088	1,070	1,657	200	315	31	110	Camden.
464,707	1,918,676	95,735	602,114	12,372	110,381	508	2,083	70	440	388	1,214	Campbell.
748,050	4,344,322	190,675	1,876,621	23,702	310,851	636	4,667	149	1,939	773	3,392	Carroll.
181,492	1,036,980	43,690	354,565	12,933	35,007	169	1,108	99	196	85	250	Chatham.
357,108	476,822	84,372	145,785	15,893	44,427	486	596	57	121	494	354	Chattahoochee.
244,881	1,684,053	57,134	559,472	9,407	97,982	363	2,075	117	1,055	302	1,405	Chattooga.
68,043	1,994,585	17,740	686,130	2,552	158,553	96	2,902	17	797	56	2,187	Cherokee.
1,171,572	1,272,485	230,270	482,975	38,598	90,997	691	825	301	390	596	558	Clarke.
798,240	621,300	153,975	221,025	41,533	45,911	753	517	217	241	808	478	Clay.
778,885	1,687,751	223,675	749,725	26,354	107,077	515	1,384	84	332	555	1,072	Clayton.
48,805	737,345	11,585	220,010	3,323	71,956	104	3,251	33	281	58	604	Clinch.
549,079	3,308,611	141,075	1,459,670	19,256	184,237	583	3,733	172	1,340	403	2,317	Cobb.
372,917	3,194,146	68,490	672,005	17,277	128,178	314	3,082	85	712	351	1,810	Coffee.
283,252	3,354,161	45,619	757,095	8,333	160,550	215	5,344	27	784	239	2,340	Colquitt.
787,605	781,769	222,588	330,044	50,895	76,043	1,049	801	244	370	1,424	610	Columbia.
2,272,164	2,660,249	486,725	959,904	74,445	169,432	1,698	1,838	153	584	2,339	1,995	Coweta.
338,997	867,499	112,400	356,335	21,532	90,627	645	960	143	299	592	832	Crawford.
771,264	1,608,567	152,993	503,017	33,512	110,085	571	1,341	114	357	724	1,329	Crisp.
833,070	3,338,881	217,995	1,310,563	46,189	190,381	1,908	4,282	1,050	1,609	752	1,431	Decatur.
799,172	4,123,289	174,229	1,419,635	18,921	198,399	599	5,783	116	974	534	1,822	Dekalb.
813,651	2,321,471	228,960	707,175	64,762	173,184	1,017	3,127	168	486	1,278	2,373	Dodge.
1,790,416	2,076,873	339,010	667,160	80,102	148,852	1,067	1,227	311	542	1,945	1,612	Dooly.
804,024	1,074,085	163,536	183,250	40,572	71,005	934	295	155	72	982	561	Dougherty.
262,075	1,065,763	62,340	458,017	10,624	90,807	311	1,479	49	349	333	1,186	Douglas.
1,242,101	1,064,382	301,612	398,252	58,636	83,522	1,439	1,580	290	415	1,809	1,102	Early.
230,015	950,061	46,925	391,435	8,012	68,419	376	2,669	112	503	172	846	Effingham.
1,486,549	2,549,248	277,838	845,041	45,043	147,570	1,329	2,300	343	631	1,221	1,727	Elbert.
1,299,785	4,796,074	229,343	1,068,320	39,775	215,861	1,024	4,210	208	817	1,186	2,695	Emanuel.
860,001	2,109,558	135,455	730,531	19,051	109,548	481	1,575	58	392	604	1,384	Fayette.
651,633	2,820,249	151,129	1,112,710	36,342	234,786	875	3,903	191	1,233	843	2,792	Floyd.
111,307	2,020,571	28,353	596,655	5,166	140,141	160	2,709	41	601	116	2,151	Forsyth.
705,540	3,525,143	125,810	1,183,081	14,405	152,892	484	2,671	69	691	392	2,484	Franklin.
695,171	3,619,866	78,995	1,042,520	13,706	159,251	250	2,038	107	561	209	769	Fulton.
129,222	421,534	29,750	174,570	3,906	34,847	96	530	36	185	214	558	Glascock.
41,037	227,280	20,068	71,300	3,312	17,630	334	661	65	161	21	28	Glynn.
110,743	2,542,020	20,630	830,718	3,379	159,132	153	3,211	33	1,490	127	2,279	Gordon.
464,699	2,149,619	106,757	689,005	19,374	148,264	611	3,026	369	1,205	420	1,515	Grady.
1,463,029	1,657,614	331,700	856,800	59,580	118,069	1,456	2,393	831	1,075	1,293	805	Greene.
492,405	4,800,287	116,432	1,683,009	14,063	288,740	406	5,049	123	1,651	398	3,588	Gwinnett.
292,135	3,278,190	63,445	975,803	9,203	200,673	305	3,299	49	726	265	2,967	Hall.
1,355,061	1,246,763	373,541	539,548	70,463	108,674	1,746	1,805	665	812	1,909	1,123	Hancock.
207,493	1,314,359	54,556	550,347	6,834	102,883	189	2,144	90	734	125	1,375	Haralson.
1,521,660	1,212,405	340,798	553,070	52,247	110,111	1,840	1,522	213	496	1,788	1,127	Harris.
1,103,211	3,177,471	159,724	923,110	21,245	164,811	727	2,481	133	858	591	1,664	Hart.
395,185	1,370,974	92,647	506,505	14,534	123,178	549	1,736	97	565	546	1,403	Heard.
1,594,730	2,600,609	302,725	946,671	37,412	144,844	1,120	1,953	464	947	1,057	1,713	Henry.

TABLE 72.—STATISTICS OF AGRICULTURE FOR COLORED AND WHITE

COUNTY.	FARM ACREAGE: 1910.				ACREAGE AND YIELD OF COTTON: 1909.				ACREAGE AND YIELD OF CORN: 1909.			
	Total.		Improved.		Acreage.		Yield in bales.		Acreage.		Yield in bushels.	
	Colored farmers.	White farmers.	Colored farmers.	White farmers.	Colored farmers.	White farmers.	Colored farmers.	White farmers.	Colored farmers.	White farmers.	Colored farmers.	White farmers.
GEORGIA—Continued.												
Houston	119,035	171,543	93,765	94,023	49,520	28,441	16,815	12,607	28,185	24,675	276,009	316,798
Irwin	25,180	163,214	16,435	38,491	8,428	14,152	4,851	8,417	3,923	8,840	54,486	145,408
Jackson	51,052	204,649	38,377	119,935	23,874	59,019	9,457	27,310	7,126	25,280	62,533	298,332
Jasper	100,652	79,163	71,411	40,185	47,136	21,032	16,943	8,905	12,562	7,762	127,017	92,951
Jeff Davis	20,305	140,504	3,570	20,406	793	4,804	317	2,128	1,291	8,180	15,880	103,381
Jefferson	91,235	170,234	75,966	93,543	35,329	27,927	14,049	12,918	24,217	26,822	237,737	298,861
Jenkins	41,739	120,580	34,349	44,378	17,822	14,181	7,279	6,273	10,213	12,717	102,671	139,342
Johnson	33,023	111,170	28,475	56,267	14,421	23,261	5,164	9,022	8,935	19,823	84,852	195,813
Jones	97,294	118,859	58,359	50,513	31,345	17,175	10,479	6,912	13,122	11,950	131,403	130,305
Laurens	118,641	292,133	95,662	137,942	49,475	50,778	19,671	22,213	28,309	41,128	290,600	499,938
Lee	86,952	96,675	76,529	43,169	40,145	13,009	17,113	6,602	26,614	9,271	259,084	115,214
Liberty	50,652	180,877	19,332	20,470	2,290	2,514	968	1,186	7,948	7,809	124,843	103,607
Lincoln	51,670	82,928	28,026	28,028	15,055	10,110	5,949	4,984	6,145	7,031	66,576	99,760
Lowndes	60,555	223,669	36,812	63,684	12,407	15,370	4,411	5,676	9,843	18,624	117,075	237,858
McDuffie	54,249	63,053	35,131	26,930	17,230	10,627	6,013	4,271	7,707	7,465	72,346	78,832
McIntosh	10,650	20,890	2,218	1,734	11	5	6	4	668	420	15,656	10,143
Macon	82,241	116,414	61,511	51,568	31,454	14,301	12,168	6,739	19,974	16,605	163,309	175,282
Madison	38,153	118,270	26,305	61,369	15,697	30,463	5,948	13,496	6,523	16,098	51,604	166,913
Marion	63,982	122,501	41,928	47,897	17,542	12,634	5,265	4,533	12,690	14,250	97,076	128,321
Meriwether	117,368	147,898	85,436	82,792	53,894	38,431	17,565	14,653	18,697	18,705	167,405	211,188
Miller	23,020	86,000	14,574	33,760	4,777	7,684	1,562	2,927	4,574	11,609	49,589	137,894
Milton	4,393	77,250	3,066	41,903	1,552	14,793	700	7,556	772	11,664	9,665	159,710
Mitchell	86,611	191,582	68,740	83,407	30,562	26,350	13,229	12,400	22,168	26,861	257,034	364,797
Monroe	124,266	140,194	74,843	67,582	38,147	22,561	13,309	9,645	15,654	14,487	162,905	186,372
Montgomery	54,011	244,186	34,049	76,905	15,337	28,699	7,015	13,884	11,806	28,876	138,606	377,431
Morgan	92,953	89,302	71,277	52,620	46,723	29,051	16,415	12,881	12,256	9,841	114,609	125,849
Muscogee	39,073	67,881	24,805	28,705	12,277	7,081	3,615	2,810	5,498	5,540	47,230	74,680
Newton	65,070	87,146	50,676	51,493	31,456	23,613	10,281	9,237	8,096	9,153	69,099	113,403
Oconee	37,166	67,713	29,690	42,566	16,969	17,874	6,971	8,573	6,400	8,785	62,588	115,581
Oglethorpe	100,956	127,375	63,810	58,353	34,323	24,805	12,338	10,632	14,334	12,462	123,722	142,472
Paulding	13,091	155,305	8,311	70,827	4,017	24,037	1,452	10,288	1,998	17,736	17,474	194,167
Pierce	9,602	224,154	4,217	37,296	1,242	8,110	387	3,029	1,751	14,200	19,778	206,112
Pike	71,703	107,512	50,779	60,891	29,658	27,459	10,434	11,376	12,218	14,985	114,236	177,001
Polk	29,962	123,850	19,861	61,885	9,342	19,692	2,920	7,499	4,570	14,726	39,883	164,484
Pulaski	91,765	143,480	71,129	71,356	40,480	29,955	16,556	14,462	20,989	23,574	207,741	284,409
Putnam	92,099	85,753	64,300	37,116	31,538	9,515	11,331	4,249	13,290	6,204	112,029	74,544
Quitman	35,102	48,193	25,510	12,905	13,505	4,508	4,272	1,571	7,226	3,715	64,794	37,968
Randolph	101,926	126,662	77,969	60,790	39,541	20,268	15,169	8,225	22,742	15,532	223,025	171,087
Richmond	31,290	113,434	23,423	48,602	8,414	9,928	3,355	5,275	6,151	11,348	55,516	153,025
Rockdale	24,415	49,334	16,958	24,708	9,082	10,049	3,050	4,130	3,503	6,926	27,158	72,432
Schley	41,232	57,255	26,938	28,812	12,271	7,040	4,258	2,797	8,033	7,764	64,922	72,370
Screven	80,611	244,102	56,673	80,024	25,341	24,621	12,475	13,586	18,240	23,234	204,312	300,436
Spalding	43,892	73,111	33,225	41,953	18,999	17,668	7,439	8,145	6,424	8,516	63,900	109,519
Stephens	8,504	84,017	5,161	27,397	2,433	10,160	908	4,377	1,492	8,014	16,552	109,493
Stewart	111,340	103,162	73,846	48,407	32,576	11,186	10,982	4,558	20,430	11,026	183,056	117,861
Sumter	124,725	152,109	103,020	67,805	62,702	30,120	25,281	14,366	28,040	19,366	326,674	256,856
Talbot	89,437	91,252	47,413	30,835	24,411	11,513	7,397	4,294	12,523	7,891	109,480	85,385
Taliaferro	65,966	35,054	40,477	15,618	21,732	4,979	7,432	2,242	7,808	2,713	70,907	34,301
Tattnall	40,709	285,189	20,235	62,802	7,948	22,766	3,366	10,657	8,410	25,986	112,488	396,121
Taylor	43,423	163,936	26,140	50,835	11,932	15,165	4,547	6,576	8,268	16,903	78,612	187,979
Telfair	30,923	176,347	15,481	56,852	5,896	19,291	2,586	9,448	5,364	18,724	59,623	235,562
Terrell	110,749	67,058	97,395	34,373	60,800	14,325	28,527	7,458	26,809	9,905	317,790	133,247
Thomas	80,339	175,315	55,940	63,265	20,779	13,499	7,772	6,769	21,802	20,674	250,092	311,948
Tift	9,870	103,564	7,257	36,982	2,915	13,447	1,604	7,173	1,864	10,399	28,048	165,338
Toombs	19,083	156,235	11,783	41,312	5,036	13,875	2,587	7,661	4,631	15,772	57,463	215,694
Troup	122,602	97,728	77,106	47,871	46,785	20,730	15,938	8,673	15,529	10,198	148,873	130,011
Turner	17,447	112,642	14,903	39,561	8,961	16,545	4,187	8,403	3,756	10,748	47,860	153,839
Twiggs	64,712	107,600	46,421	38,334	24,802	14,827	8,250	5,844	14,925	11,707	114,523	116,471
Upson	75,502	94,686	39,994	40,183	19,017	16,310	6,175	7,125	10,420	11,436	98,136	133,001
Walker	9,327	205,466	6,290	87,992	1,502	9,486	494	3,825	1,872	21,075	22,068	313,320
Walton	61,424	139,185	48,416	80,956	27,437	42,161	9,704	17,150	8,164	19,712	70,224	215,142
Ware	6,655	158,074	2,280	26,141	442	3,577	121	1,130	1,115	11,006	13,785	149,726
Warren	79,608	78,656	48,555	40,002	27,118	15,474	9,163	6,218	11,668	9,958	102,190	100,777
Washington	135,943	206,009	109,895	100,267	51,411	32,467	18,351	13,523	33,438	29,595	293,969	314,042
Wayne	23,779	296,020	2,516	34,331	569	7,795	202	2,901	1,241	16,145	15,838	213,436
Webster	44,008	63,351	32,994	32,087	14,479	7,734	4,270	2,553	11,708	9,003	88,964	81,496
Whitfield	5,907	156,476	3,671	74,219	904	8,986	332	3,709	879	17,388	9,256	204,681
Wilcox	41,804	146,511	25,216	63,161	13,323	24,790	6,095	12,803	6,789	15,648	75,111	201,442
Wilkes	120,501	135,011	81,411	46,551	48,640	21,369	18,765	10,574	19,269	11,480	188,565	155,056
Wilkinson	61,412	157,760	32,288	61,272	12,349	14,209	3,741	4,743	11,220	19,413	84,421	174,365
Worth	73,903	129,244	53,952	58,774	27,926	22,221	12,058	11,008	15,030	17,676	156,482	243,836
All other counties	26,850	1,784,274	10,977	481,162	2,089	33,325	673	12,233	4,454	160,063	49,069	2,061,955

FARMERS, BY COUNTIES, FOR SOUTHERN STATES: 1909–1910—Continued.

| VALUE OF LAND, BUILDINGS, IMPLEMENTS, AND MACHINERY: 1910 | | | | | | NUMBER OF DAIRY COWS, WORK HORSES, AND WORK MULES: 1910 | | | | | | COUNTY. |
| Land. | | Buildings. | | Implements and machinery. | | Dairy cows. | | Work horses. | | Work mules. | | |
Colored farmers.	White farmers.	Colored farmers.	White farmers.	Colored farmers.	White farmers.	Colored farmers.	White farmers.	Colored farmers.	White farmers.	Colored farmers.	White farmers.	
						GEORGIA—Continued.						
$1,938,259	$3,112,022	$393,920	$1,066,524	$79,408	$211,716	1,304	1,172	490	702	2,039	2,042	Houston.
651,280	3,111,796	81,500	529,780	28,271	132,419	276	1,457	98	421	432	835	Irwin.
1,481,737	6,190,159	282,960	1,907,302	37,749	302,267	993	4,117	252	1,472	918	3,939	Jackson.
1,607,036	1,309,663	354,939	458,652	68,283	88,278	1,466	1,051	266	437	1,939	1,153	Jasper.
163,285	1,043,215	21,205	245,270	3,741	39,764	199	2,051	42	278	91	561	Jeff Davis.
1,292,692	2,395,821	366,687	786,538	84,509	135,496	1,100	1,365	522	764	1,383	1,954	Jefferson.
580,657	1,574,717	125,990	367,710	25,023	75,085	374	1,390	68	279	919	1,008	Jenkins.
414,178	1,371,928	118,421	460,552	27,831	106,456	297	1,367	91	394	645	1,124	Johnson.
945,992	1,029,242	261,324	444,576	51,409	80,201	1,246	1,351	178	299	1,231	910	Jones.
1,926,389	4,390,815	343,212	1,173,396	82,207	260,727	1,611	4,093	486	1,299	2,048	2,744	Laurens.
1,183,506	1,358,786	291,890	320,505	89,350	97,771	930	451	271	353	1,744	583	Lee.
412,604	1,031,192	219,237	264,190	55,112	49,177	2,989	2,338	682	481	166	381	Liberty.
604,013	996,246	130,150	399,908	34,747	97,126	856	1,163	156	345	900	817	Lincoln.
962,219	2,510,183	180,035	564,224	33,799	101,937	1,106	3,563	588	1,050	598	967	Lowndes.
555,858	627,437	163,980	230,714	45,727	36,730	708	815	179	319	722	666	McDuffie.
155,787	89,625	56,630	47,290	16,229	26,395	344	382	99	56	11	18	McIntosh.
1,021,141	1,296,309	195,601	443,749	40,152	100,973	758	923	170	356	1,390	1,050	Macon.
842,380	2,739,296	154,680	831,446	26,031	141,281	711	2,579	218	1,005	670	1,908	Madison.
418,349	531,811	116,805	290,329	21,180	59,302	606	1,169	154	457	609	770	Marion.
2,118,268	2,590,108	513,834	1,147,400	85,510	155,712	1,714	2,222	186	566	2,286	2,138	Meriwether.
201,992	755,977	41,108	203,221	9,719	49,511	430	2,419	119	471	113	260	Miller.
95,678	1,380,982	17,847	405,213	3,261	86,705	98	1,763	12	358	94	1,289	Milton.
1,276,106	3,210,404	264,260	683,924	54,082	143,817	1,397	3,786	647	1,435	1,283	1,519	Mitchell.
1,387,112	1,767,581	334,685	827,406	65,463	190,756	1,595	1,813	271	591	1,766	1,543	Monroe.
884,377	3,259,177	180,047	958,770	35,836	175,673	818	4,129	258	929	803	1,744	Montgomery.
1,908,030	1,949,032	331,479	754,431	73,392	152,770	1,416	1,244	378	543	1,771	1,449	Morgan.
363,783	1,066,957	88,840	531,540	17,636	76,559	572	1,375	89	329	620	627	Muscogee.
1,465,035	1,895,874	267,427	644,690	38,947	115,391	1,041	1,347	142	458	1,297	1,366	Newton.
951,215	1,876,232	197,335	697,560	38,248	141,593	757	1,573	400	829	563	943	Oconee.
1,802,426	2,178,330	337,245	787,610	70,806	136,960	1,580	1,978	804	947	1,331	1,362	Oglethorpe.
183,244	1,632,186	47,690	679,645	7,142	108,393	233	2,704	40	512	248	2,063	Paulding.
127,234	1,481,324	37,721	493,270	6,804	96,388	232	4,538	109	895	86	765	Pierce.
1,130,568	1,667,446	273,239	766,398	38,239	129,155	999	1,660	138	459	1,317	1,659	Pike.
421,642	1,755,896	109,778	688,213	26,758	146,216	589	2,238	182	857	532	1,391	Polk.
1,647,002	2,655,997	305,430	721,006	91,509	167,701	946	1,645	708	799	1,296	1,315	Pulaski.
1,050,251	949,891	242,025	425,940	55,938	101,980	1,650	1,515	219	386	1,649	765	Putnam.
339,500	374,861	70,290	114,345	15,385	31,111	436	306	57	107	605	222	Quitman.
1,456,828	1,588,863	277,495	452,116	60,360	101,599	1,182	1,092	216	439	1,770	1,132	Randolph.
528,715	1,930,687	118,965	750,945	31,472	131,709	334	1,485	176	570	535	1,004	Richmond.
400,322	828,580	86,740	384,345	10,518	60,017	344	838	42	250	392	802	Rockdale.
363,521	386,730	95,535	206,295	17,701	38,164	363	493	76	156	552	495	Schley.
1,090,067	3,117,501	230,600	867,651	42,992	206,908	1,439	3,266	280	743	1,170	2,003	Screven.
841,889	1,535,171	208,735	695,699	27,290	122,699	721	1,358	90	395	924	1,150	Spalding.
190,947	1,533,778	33,420	353,465	5,259	70,292	169	1,076	30	323	144	946	Stephens.
1,010,399	898,607	193,925	312,135	53,449	76,051	1,308	738	154	320	1,439	741	Stewart.
2,364,438	3,157,031	532,746	765,450	112,720	185,074	1,146	1,100	241	474	2,266	1,904	Sumter.
682,952	646,259	182,097	371,520	32,685	67,752	1,176	1,369	144	386	1,208	739	Talbot.
953,624	516,512	144,650	247,275	39,439	37,462	1,017	705	422	307	912	374	Taliaferro.
655,839	3,765,927	143,051	950,620	24,784	141,316	723	4,534	181	703	526	1,986	Tattnall.
357,599	1,073,413	83,075	407,325	16,976	103,769	475	1,452	96	493	604	1,076	Taylor.
386,888	1,771,820	89,995	536,978	13,190	98,101	463	2,594	248	783	219	1,031	Telfair.
2,526,358	1,306,624	475,832	505,400	64,095	88,904	1,300	724	319	381	2,210	1,080	Terrell.
1,048,566	2,328,074	287,903	934,255	50,805	164,209	1,581	3,541	521	870	1,303	1,456	Thomas.
243,345	1,785,273	54,385	435,305	7,423	86,312	170	1,889	66	587	177	899	Tift.
300,777	2,043,141	64,115	464,871	11,716	98,153	306	1,963	70	295	375	1,258	Toombs.
1,624,737	1,460,520	365,700	665,145	66,372	113,342	1,649	1,459	184	500	2,104	1,245	Troup.
394,533	1,934,976	71,450	434,242	11,032	77,716	227	1,553	61	304	343	1,152	Turner.
655,692	1,215,789	172,380	370,089	34,382	95,268	903	773	169	320	1,111	839	Twiggs.
717,469	988,516	177,480	462,625	30,309	88,842	861	1,372	95	339	928	1,011	Upson.
148,181	3,276,312	35,640	806,491	4,619	140,726	251	3,282	99	1,707	144	1,958	Walker.
1,662,711	3,868,077	315,540	1,243,015	42,535	240,107	1,027	2,583	160	1,280	1,212	2,270	Walton.
59,091	904,335	17,115	281,806	3,390	68,697	138	4,196	42	504	71	664	Ware.
1,049,529	913,620	180,691	355,375	49,835	52,852	978	822	424	398	833	774	Warren.
1,660,981	2,305,462	380,660	857,290	72,360	189,270	1,255	1,998	335	806	2,500	2,090	Washington.
112,105	1,616,496	27,400	454,749	5,553	89,741	236	4,833	73	794	55	886	Wayne.
415,945	474,582	103,900	207,995	21,064	57,718	568	483	260	284	353	470	Webster.
79,999	1,460,721	25,620	618,194	4,532	129,915	125	2,997	57	1,162	71	1,617	Whitfield.
631,419	2,175,770	137,965	492,249	27,385	108,919	706	2,128	106	432	706	1,636	Wilcox.
2,085,143	2,282,830	380,206	875,947	101,146	223,323	1,998	2,157	647	812	2,127	1,404	Wilkes.
395,049	850,736	120,796	387,410	16,941	73,794	422	1,136	61	253	662	963	Wilkinson.
956,402	1,742,741	229,901	548,545	45,931	122,805	1,098	2,935	273	945	983	1,089	Worth.
264,598	11,122,992	61,790	3,520,256	10,239	655,515	541	24,013	132	6,058	258	10,064	All other counties.

TABLE **72.**—STATISTICS OF AGRICULTURE FOR COLORED AND WHITE

COUNTY.	FARM ACREAGE: 1910.				ACREAGE AND YIELD OF COTTON: 1909.				ACREAGE AND YIELD OF CORN: 1909.			
	Total.		Improved.		Acreage.		Yield in bales.		Acreage.		Yield in bushels.	
	Colored farmers.	White farmers.	Colored farmers.	White farmers.	Colored farmers.	White farmers.	Colored farmers.	White farmers.	Colored farmers.	White farmers.	Colored farmers.	White farmers.

KENTUCKY.

COUNTY.	Total Colored	Total White	Improved Colored	Improved White	Cotton Acreage Colored	Cotton Acreage White	Cotton Yield Colored	Cotton Yield White	Corn Acreage Colored	Corn Acreage White	Corn Yield Colored	Corn Yield White
Total	440,777	21,748,350	343,694	14,010,777	2,937	4,874	1,478	1,991	104,055	3,332,285	2,442,054	80,905,970
Adair	7,986	216,924	5,367	126,617					1,916	35,403	29,712	639,800
Allen	3,7.8	200,888	2,948	129,154					1,022	33,877	23,045	710,092
Ballard	9,.3	135,802	7,565	104,004		6		1	2,017	35,310	55,385	1,028,421
Barren	14,921	282,972	12,702	224,201					3,341	50,098	60,904	1,071,916
Bourbon	2,727	187,069	2,715	179,839					757	28,793	30,556	1,171,986
Boyle	2,516	108,002	1,836	84,529					503	16,434	17,625	751,109
Caldwell	6,359	189,083	5,708	138,550					942	29,054	16,760	605,906
Christian	35,875	381,888	29,642	272,424					6,909	57,195	153,909	1,416,875
Daviess	9,336.	257,726	8,474	219,234					2,391	57,371	62,331	1,632,068
Fayette	4,569	160,972	4,295	149,359					1,838	26,642	87,510	1,139,847
Fulton	8,068	81,824	7,707	67,663	2,936	4,621	1,478	1,911	3,241	23,746	103,373	786,730
Garrard	5,875	121,913	5,328	106,157					1,474	22,969	50,410	897,958
Graves	7,506	328,324	6,459	253,481		30		10	2,146	68,113	53,115	1,663,843
Green	7,045	160,330	5,240	117,279					1,351	27,053	18,796	492,649
Harrison	2,991	189,858	2,855	172,309					528	22,946	20,220	891,712
Hart	7,466	238,941	5,884	163,150					1,196	36,245	19,285	664,554
Henderson	18,548	213,129	16,571	184,383					7,390	65,432	191,353	1,881,739
Henry	2,240	175,977	2,173	153,070					273	19,893	8,560	694,563
Hopkins	6,713	291,550	5,102	175,853		18		8	1,781	50,384	37,903	997,097
Jefferson	4,372	192,335	3,787	147,275					1,050	30,150	29,830	917,194
Jessamine	3,315	96,572	2,861	73,139					756	16,453	24,832	615,779
Lincoln	5,097	185,177	3,973	128,487					1,362	27,568	44,251	880,727
Logan	17,936	310,346	14,222	219,665					4,209	49,644	91,242	1,096,974
Lyon	5,198	105,107	3,559	67,489	1	(1)			1,623	20,085	36,848	480,258
McCracken	6,300	125,806	5,322	98,471					1,944	27,428	40,847	685,924
Madison	14,528	246,124	13,133	208,277					4,170	41,256	133,130	1,406,255
Metcalfe	5,319	160,514	4,372	97,738					1,074	22,520	15,906	379,382
Montgomery	2,962	113,703	1,913	91,318					562	16,327	20,387	565,247
Muhlenburg	6,429	238,781	4,147	130,891					1,579	38,391	21,657	592,018
Nelson	6,529	222,121	4,386	146,609					982	34,104	27,605	1,068,432
Owen	3,934	209,852	3,212	183,198					483	21,107	16,184	706,955
Scott	3,248	183,190	3,045	169,948					635	23,567	17,269	894,960
Shelby	3,579	235,306	3,341	213,255					599	30,985	20,075	1,113,810
Simpson	4,202	144,139	3,678	118,190					1,017	24,940	21,925	528,738
Taylor	5,863	153,308	4,085	88,953		4		1	1,146	24,047	16,756	440,425
Todd	14,386	210,349	12,662	153,221					3,348	33,215	69,832	748,003
Trigg	18,180	239,490	13,341	122,919					3,749	33,051	82,000	822,673
Warren	11,326	310,600	9,130	224,386					2,982	58,956	53,332	1,328,110
Washington	4,594	181,254	3,966	147,966		10		1	899	22,217	31,460	720,440
Webster	6,940	197,510	5,971	159,156					1,614	40,378	38,570	920,773
All other counties	122,623	13,763,594	81,017	7,998,970		185		59	27,256	1,988,938	547,364	44,854,028

LOUISIANA.

COUNTY.	Total Colored	Total White	Improved Colored	Improved White	Cotton Acreage Colored	Cotton Acreage White	Cotton Yield Colored	Cotton Yield White	Corn Acreage Colored	Corn Acreage White	Corn Yield Colored	Corn Yield White
Total	2,124,321	8,315,160	1,466,607	3,809,409	514,352	442,659	141,882	127,027	505,431	1,085,399	7,432,322	18,578,039
Acadia	15,792	258,140	14,721	225,872	2,265	7,298	680	2,446	5,468	33,760	94,801	632,159
Ascension	8,393	95,860	4,940	52,179	1,180	6,097	501	2,908	1,717	16,013	30,172	313,834
Avoyelles	29,940	178,043	26,082	100,358	7,696	18,938	2,089	6,128	11,905	46,942	184,061	881,158
Bienville	77,803	217,177	40,886	81,775	14,125	16,374	2,758	4,034	14,448	26,277	142,861	304,821
Bossier	110,412	138,502	68,317	59,736	24,737	11,026	7,397	3,166	17,565	22,051	239,917	340,367
Caddo	156,848	174,788	119,533	91,469	46,102	16,058	14,251	5,430	38,112	30,934	550,321	634,990
Calcasieu	20,000	470,594	8,175	266,085	203	1,699	61	550	2,050	18,742	31,240	313,763
Caldwell	20,251	103,765	7,790	29,288	1,108	1,511	333	332	2,606	8,642	37,008	121,920
Catahoula	17,777	95,388	13,969	34,149	3,086	1,824	918	502	6,103	13,201	98,952	209,180
Claiborne	169,469	231,246	104,830	110,849	36,603	20,778	7,199	5,090	27,292	26,289	243,297	296,168
Concordia	24,544	140,962	18,853	45,583	8,149	8,241	2,433	2,496	7,626	12,561	118,961	218,093
De Soto	165,027	204,622	104,234	83,044	40,628	17,469	9,793	5,258	30,133	18,036	331,170	235,920
East Baton Rouge	34,459	151,651	27,739	75,742	13,089	10,723	2,994	2,803	10,007	16,694	171,692	291,628
East Carroll	36,461	101,727	29,139	45,822	13,269	4,135	6,841	1,711	5,245	6,769	107,047	122,480
East Feliciana	65,426	129,552	49,765	70,803	22,093	11,258	3,446	1,928	19,346	15,405	230,439	224,455
Franklin	22,867	101,354	16,931	34,627	6,663	4,938	1,957	1,576	7,636	12,644	127,227	231,173
Grant	9,685	112,977	8,483	35,788	3,066	3,025	904	767	2,985	11,010	46,584	161,131
Iberia	26,171	144,890	23,615	97,821	1,649	1,603	119	189	10,893	33,583	211,404	681,036
Iberville	10,831	93,897	7,891	56,531	1,212	627	220	100	3,089	17,114	74,264	375,377
Jackson	38,794	150,833	18,571	46,162	3,867	5,374	586	920	6,611	16,132	55,440	159,235
Lafayette	36,445	125,884	33,526	108,236	7,923	12,006	2,206	3,449	17,595	49,722	309,110	920,673
Lincoln	57,104	181,608	37,273	92,594	9,460	13,442	1,566	2,668	10,464	23,611	100,632	275,475
Livingston	4,063	91,645	1,772	22,973	701	5,360	211	1,932	494	8,485	7,255	133,588
Madison	39,174	103,001	29,788	35,913	15,162	9,636	7,152	4,515	7,935	9,893	144,723	159,290
Morehouse	67,909	153,127	56,718	37,204	28,355	6,819	10,124	2,592	16,758	9,852	237,195	155,037
Natchitoches	84,489	193,490	59,489	68,114	27,541	15,479	9,648	4,820	19,275	23,073	293,052	348,234
Ouachita	45,173	167,832	27,878	64,143	11,987	13,905	3,152	3,835	8,674	17,779	116,262	260,412
Plaquemines	8,772	76,608	3,916	26,481					206	2,568	4,431	51,993
Pointe Coupee	35,943	167,648	30,284	85,545	6,693	11,471	1,059	1,799	19,710	33,361	338,736	647,694
Rapides	25,748	225,887	19,968	88,774	7,226	8,194	2,652	2,818	7,209	32,317	153,856	663,713

[1] Less than 1 bale.

FARMERS, BY COUNTIES, FOR SOUTHERN STATES: 1909–1910—Continued.

Land.		Buildings.		Implements and machinery.		Dairy cows.		Work horses.		Work mules.		COUNTY.
Colored farmers.	White farmers.	Colored farmers.	White farmers.	Colored farmers.	White farmers.	Colored farmers.	White farmers.	Colored farmers.	White farmers.	Colored farmers	White farmers.	

VALUE OF LAND, BUILDINGS, IMPLEMENTS, AND MACHINERY: 1910. — **NUMBER OF DAIRY COWS, WORK HORSES, AND WORK MULES: 1910.**

KENTUCKY.

Land Colored	Land White	Buildings Colored	Buildings White	Impl. Colored	Impl. White	Dairy Colored	Dairy White	Horses Colored	Horses White	Mules Colored	Mules White	County
$12,238,866	$472,225,751	$2,793,042	$148,201,713	$420,909	$20,430,937	9,882	399,952	10,362	377,433	6,157	189,518	Total.
94,134	2,224,986	26,271	925,823	4,455	143,299	144	3,418	164	3,770	89	1,847	Adair.
56,025	2,426,152	11,835	927,123	1,651	142,061	68	2,979	55	2,643	60	3,011	Allen.
301,635	4,256,872	65,320	1,127,905	12,024	190,521	158	2,413	224	3,366	136	2,437	Ballard.
343,053	6,226,043	81,175	2,362,036	10,320	300,950	393	5,071	306	4,900	236	4,375	Barren.
255,979	16,624,163	64,906	2,867,139	9,820	312,225	90	3,124	165	5,111	35	1,514	Bourbon.
98,621	6,071,580	24,425	1,593,225	2,891	155,097	74	2,176	94	2,596	25	1,010	Boyle.
96,424	2,128,970	20,920	790,836	2,662	124,749	122	2,826	83	2,656	101	2,304	Caldwell.
758,993	7,869,783	157,348	2,417,526	22,541	503,302	675	4,768	501	4,005	505	5,823	Christian.
446,615	10,620,222	79,650	3,028,860	11,846	424,437	194	5,122	269	7,320	134	3,471	Daviess.
494,731	17,214,533	122,500	4,913,170	18,843	613,782	179	5,010	360	6,433	76	2,376	Fayette.
386,532	3,538,062	38,865	840,675	10,610	163,134	229	1,804	179	1,931	315	1,796	Fulton.
315,560	6,181,154	53,740	1,467,845	6,621	183,158	155	2,562	218	3,539	56	1,381	Garrard.
181,408	6,779,917	35,220	2,378,858	7,516	417,433	196	6,046	180	8,542	129	5,191	Graves.
87,094	2,205,237	22,005	839,160	3,870	147,192	133	2,757	101	2,512	130	2,321	Green.
144,005	8,457,050	41,095	2,415,920	5,006	252,833	69	4,155	149	6,250	14	736	Harrison.
219,683	4,459,228	43,870	1,517,055	7,293	201,127	156	4,132	151	3,921	113	2,420	Hart.
659,445	7,698,923	121,951	1,909,115	21,836	282,303	387	3,548	439	4,403	438	4,218	Henderson.
112,235	6,497,022	31,125	2,257,950	2,690	214,404	25	3,155	65	4,953	6	1,181	Henry.
197,715	5,850,880	42,680	1,651,327	8,075	255,337	147	4,545	132	4,872	181	3,890	Hopkins.
382,020	17,400,684	86,355	5,846,515	15,710	785,660	101	7,493	209	6,395	101	2,495	Jefferson.
215,270	6,580,092	55,945	1,678,383	5,615	214,507	106	2,505	156	2,831	39	1,095	Jessamine.
202,920	5,886,175	36,365	1,749,875	5,117	221,028	173	4,011	168	4,339	56	1,496	Lincoln.
380,839	6,078,970	96,671	2,210,059	11,653	336,202	379	4,454	299	4,947	300	4,607	Logan.
61,197	1,128,726	16,473	422,025	2,451	74,332	130	1,977	79	1,389	101	1,510	Lyon.
216,950	3,728,308	53,865	1,244,821	9,682	223,411	215	3,083	230	3,605	139	1,871	McCracken.
693,388	10,155,460	146,477	2,394,993	21,074	233,467	531	5,265	605	6,247	143	2,223	Madison.
85,455	1,937,534	21,380	714,491	2,480	120,126	100	2,324	94	2,115	59	1,753	Metcalfe.
116,050	6,506,945	33,725	1,566,445	5,267	161,118	101	2,534	120	3,125	28	904	Montgomery.
84,787	2,788,414	26,515	1,135,727	4,057	170,118	114	3,687	80	3,001	103	2,788	Muhlenburg.
160,885	4,585,794	35,915	1,906,195	5,276	257,058	128	3,767	182	4,533	40	1,360	Nelson.
106,780	4,591,385	34,045	1,946,195	3,755	218,630	63	3,339	133	5,576	32	797	Owen.
185,257	10,308,102	41,704	2,255,825	6,795	238,873	127	3,582	106	4,829	16	1,212	Scott.
217,580	11,881,605	60,065	3,801,444	6,431	407,254	100	6,589	159	5,863	18	1,920	Shelby.
123,545	4,004,544	25,725	1,176,572	3,544	199,467	89	2,095	104	2,679	65	2,181	Simpson.
84,285	2,185,053	23,230	824,399	5,057	151,441	119	2,528	130	2,876	65	1,321	Taylor.
303,002	3,828,730	77,740	1,383,785	9,018	214,721	272	2,580	193	2,313	250	3,596	Todd.
180,087	2,034,777	48,304	711,567	9,396	128,477	315	2,622	203	2,199	302	3,092	Trigg.
278,043	8,083,413	70,555	2,483,110	10,937	357,643	250	5,247	219	5,139	218	4,311	Warren.
169,769	5,572,268	43,325	1,921,610	9,276	297,459	131	3,648	219	5,474	42	1,185	Washington.
202,135	4,761,459	35,300	1,335,168	6,227	202,208	102	2,777	123	4,294	88	2,137	Webster.
2,538,735	220,866,536	638,462	73,260,961	91,521	10,190,394	2,642	254,234	2,716	209,941	1,173	94,362	All other counties.

LOUISIANA.

Land Colored	Land White	Buildings Colored	Buildings White	Impl. Colored	Impl. White	Dairy Colored	Dairy White	Horses Colored	Horses White	Mules Colored	Mules White	County
$36,202,905	$151,600,372	$8,730,753	$41,010,420	$1,684,573	$17,292,480	64,204	214,893	47,589	117,015	35,760	92,907	Total.
466,739	7,543,247	58,100	1,002,477	17,898	719,954	528	8,086	972	7,872	241	3,600	Acadia.
205,145	2,944,725	62,400	821,925	9,059	402,084	286	3,590	311	1,524	134	1,371	Ascension.
898,290	4,266,877	182,271	1,104,445	42,637	367,723	898	6,389	1,317	5,927	402	1,819	Avoyelles.
564,814	1,532,510	195,754	809,835	35,180	164,655	1,627	3,888	639	1,530	855	1,770	Bienville.
1,704,953	1,889,893	345,958	605,793	58,316	181,044	2,839	2,922	925	1,079	1,829	1,914	Bossier.
2,864,226	3,652,371	482,136	817,754	104,066	223,316	5,008	4,610	2,005	1,522	3,273	2,190	Caddo.
295,440	8,045,937	88,620	1,605,030	27,704	945,638	732	14,393	705	8,703	75	4,099	Calcasieu.
168,634	685,215	53,320	276,560	13,389	83,182	663	3,184	273	906	160	602	Caldwell.
290,822	1,219,232	90,264	384,978	13,972	86,036	820	2,984	651	1,245	509	669	Catahoula.
1,008,808	1,626,736	309,664	794,881	54,144	152,758	3,017	4,354	1,111	1,554	1,932	1,958	Claiborne.
518,210	2,358,954	172,298	529,564	29,520	232,172	997	2,066	932	896	580	1,391	Concordia.
1,101,014	1,653,364	330,104	686,589	79,367	146,009	4,411	6,272	2,210	1,894	1,944	1,357	De Soto.
769,804	2,494,564	207,493	804,420	30,546	189,239	1,069	3,571	1,184	1,785	931	1,815	East Baton Rouge
917,558	1,854,803	311,250	338,635	57,402	185,791	1,121	416	1,040	421	881	1,379	East Carroll.
693,623	1,381,877	249,943	615,430	53,686	115,323	2,233	3,228	1,358	1,276	1,415	1,002	East Feliciana.
424,453	1,600,511	128,975	390,977	27,710	98,993	1,025	3,939	963	1,804	610	913	Franklin.
277,024	1,256,937	64,191	371,669	11,070	87,583	465	3,446	306	1,380	326	881	Grant.
1,085,250	5,360,194	137,100	1,113,770	31,956	351,603	579	3,072	720	2,072	1,076	3,808	Iberia.
539,335	3,828,625	109,665	1,031,022	31,899	789,692	191	684	333	1,468	376	2,623	Iberville.
211,623	826,330	61,919	334,759	13,598	72,864	763	3,191	310	1,020	416	1,137	Jackson.
1,626,002	5,791,100	151,268	999,398	37,760	265,355	1,064	6,088	1,827	6,087	886	2,644	Lafayette.
402,643	1,287,680	134,584	709,741	26,422	156,460	1,002	3,303	355	1,304	737	1,631	Lincoln.
40,735	863,224	13,060	305,678	1,999	67,375	134	3,030	73	1,350	30	402	Livingston.
986,287	1,775,408	263,919	387,790	19,386	177,925	1,333	585	911	665	769	1,310	Madison.
1,373,059	1,905,019	361,228	408,860	74,151	161,413	2,385	2,031	1,628	1,199	1,870	922	Morehouse.
1,749,735	2,296,928	347,239	689,654	75,462	176,232	2,874	5,761	3,150	3,243	1,569	1,826	Natchitoches.
895,928	2,502,870	209,958	745,520	35,247	234,901	1,662	3,417	701	1,212	908	1,377	Ouachita.
191,072	2,143,925	60,080	653,250	17,928	469,710	122	596	214	423	36	926	Plaquemines.
925,481	4,339,578	293,782	1,230,279	29,597	501,136	1,339	2,858	987	1,117	587	1,974	Pointe Coupee.
906,404	4,622,107	169,325	1,112,624	43,926	256,298	1,092	7,162	839	3,607	803	2,213	Rapides.

TABLE **72.**—STATISTICS OF AGRICULTURE FOR COLORED AND WHITE

COUNTY.	FARM ACREAGE: 1910.				ACREAGE AND YIELD OF COTTON: 1909.				ACREAGE AND YIELD OF CORN: 1909.			
	Total.		Improved.		Acreage.		Yield in bales.		Acreage.		Yield in bushels.	
	Colored farmers.	White farmers.	Colored farmers.	White farmers.	Colored farmers.	White farmers.	Colored farmers.	White farmers.	Colored farmers.	White farmers.	Colored farmers.	White farmers.
LOUISIANA—Continued.												
Red River	30,541	115,657	22,589	44,204	8,474	8,867	2,515	2,530	7,814	13,819	133,562	190,468
Richland	43,427	103,029	36,815	31,818	17,700	6,902	4,959	2,162	11,394	9,216	183,312	167,232
Sabine	25,053	209,810	12,054	72,149	3,933	17,298	1,060	5,110	4,039	22,606	39,574	279,593
St. Helena	30,826	73,375	18,081	21,217	8,079	6,873	1,890	2,065	6,239	6,878	68,297	88,199
St. Landry	123,631	344,192	105,680	221,943	27,169	28,000	7,099	9,208	48,611	77,646	843,724	1,335,960
St. Martin	34,616	83,935	29,283	58,037	6,650	8,049	1,214	1,635	14,142	23,758	307,467	483,449
St. Mary	8,816	153,826	7,504	95,434	....	6	....	1	3,071	24,365	56,939	590,162
Tangipahoa	16,591	123,465	7,144	33,964	2,646	7,040	753	2,263	2,100	8,841	25,902	137,593
Tensas	52,850	129,186	44,663	48,977	22,519	7,011	9,100	2,155	11,045	17,412	179,382	324,095
Union	66,411	297,701	33,110	115,616	10,306	24,174	1,499	4,050	10,180	33,119	95,527	365,314
Vermilion	14,983	243,729	12,563	165,261	2,231	13,502	554	3,741	5,089	47,986	90,110	860,577
Washington	24,044	126,295	11,976	40,995	5,775	13,728	2,047	5,839	4,272	15,288	46,377	214,045
Webster	73,335	153,944	37,944	59,113	12,215	12,055	2,652	3,423	11,367	17,962	114,734	224,582
West Baton Rouge	7,570	49,813	6,609	33,257	1,530	1,820	177	247	3,637	9,878	93,157	219,071
West Carroll	13,472	45,675	9,277	19,325	4,059	4,602	1,292	1,715	3,100	6,457	42,665	111,285
West Feliciana	35,125	110,435	28,610	49,060	12,827	7,127	1,145	752	11,506	9,039	146,124	157,199
Winn	18,599	162,164	6,951	45,917	970	3,499	167	675	2,554	16,135	20,527	167,511
All other parishes	38,661	1,006,231	20,678	379,462	1,431	6,794	509	2,694	6,114	111,534	112,832	2,296,707
MARYLAND.												
Total	358,517	4,698,623	218,582	3,136,185	....	....	....	....	52,139	594,873	985,310	16,926,126
Anne Arundel	26,967	181,278	19,184	119,943	....	....	....	....	3,853	18,848	63,633	388,771
Baltimore	5,615	320,867	3,926	226,545	....	....	....	....	723	35,582	15,370	1,172,204
Calvert	33,992	90,703	20,825	53,303	....	....	....	....	2,677	7,691	43,094	168,858
Caroline	15,750	171,128	10,768	117,438	....	....	....	....	2,917	27,282	58,585	796,728
Charles	58,960	173,377	31,222	90,375	....	....	....	....	6,068	14,909	99,906	280,950
Dorchester	31,951	203,034	17,222	106,457	....	....	....	....	4,368	23,004	80,068	614,668
Harford	8,632	238,514	5,467	166,006	....	....	....	....	1,062	26,629	26,820	1,030,512
Howard	5,210	143,842	3,804	110,223	....	....	....	....	837	19,072	24,264	610,287
Kent	4,080	168,743	2,875	136,911	....	....	....	....	627	27,159	10,019	682,548
Montgomery	9,811	263,459	7,822	201,331	....	....	....	....	1,751	37,527	51,251	1,328,998
Prince Georges	35,688	204,348	22,464	131,950	....	....	....	....	4,424	21,859	105,729	614,519
Queen Annes	9,707	209,365	7,323	164,291	....	....	....	....	1,758	33,365	39,849	927,933
St. Marys	28,819	163,968	14,779	83,468	....	....	....	....	3,621	17,387	63,788	378,224
Somerset	13,158	133,112	8,784	67,665	....	....	....	....	3,062	17,674	56,625	393,252
Talbot	7,437	155,601	5,448	112,280	....	....	....	....	1,170	21,011	34,066	739,935
Wicomico	16,908	180,913	10,146	98,946	....	....	....	....	3,708	33,234	54,091	558,145
Worcester	37,026	197,499	19,799	102,031	....	....	....	....	8,111	35,242	126,950	661,893
All other counties	8,806	1,498,872	6,700	1,047,022	....	....	....	....	1,402	177,398	31,202	5,577,701
MISSISSIPPI.												
Total	6,457,427	12,100,106	4,487,383	4,520,927	2,263,166	1,137,044	727,996	399,160	1,032,413	1,140,199	12,707,309	15,721,358
Adams	68,438	93,056	39,287	33,339	14,543	2,921	1,322	338	12,416	6,225	171,814	113,206
Alcorn	20,099	192,196	13,451	75,950	4,667	14,731	1,102	3,969	3,919	20,878	44,419	298,713
Amite	82,404	224,421	53,516	91,432	23,923	19,672	6,743	6,709	17,208	21,796	216,136	313,199
Attala	115,102	286,196	64,477	103,087	28,062	28,662	7,350	8,026	18,270	28,024	154,950	290,844
Benton	70,061	138,556	37,700	43,526	14,195	7,260	2,870	1,923	9,529	12,432	79,353	147,391
Bolivar	224,832	103,253	204,385	47,210	134,869	26,498	50,609	10,833	27,500	10,694	494,446	200,359
Calhoun	33,189	248,905	18,390	86,907	6,541	16,518	2,196	6,369	6,174	27,517	76,771	428,398
Carroll	118,161	200,275	76,912	74,824	37,512	20,121	10,413	6,430	22,326	19,675	234,770	248,081
Chickasaw	92,980	151,095	63,455	66,686	31,902	16,693	7,596	4,996	15,671	16,733	190,138	259,215
Choctaw	39,250	198,518	21,590	76,832	6,953	15,979	1,738	4,628	5,827	20,218	51,629	219,825
Claiborne	93,426	130,754	58,530	57,218	27,583	9,013	6,539	2,205	16,643	9,343	182,256	122,775
Clarke	73,296	176,443	37,803	57,204	14,488	16,335	4,142	5,390	8,597	12,814	71,209	137,142
Clay	100,684	120,292	80,619	61,974	44,490	12,309	10,465	3,062	17,061	10,881	197,140	117,381
Coahoma	149,315	62,072	139,769	32,620	85,172	13,280	40,113	6,856	17,996	7,774	408,150	171,872
Copiah	134,965	248,300	88,454	117,696	34,386	23,094	10,830	8,886	22,223	21,304	232,645	282,381
Covington	30,207	129,457	13,476	36,936	5,724	12,670	2,146	5,692	4,177	11,758	46,400	161,866
De Soto	163,580	105,977	122,516	55,708	60,568	10,275	22,076	3,955	25,362	11,852	367,280	216,249
Forrest	17,544	63,626	5,582	16,391	2,059	4,675	747	1,915	1,571	5,215	19,875	83,412
Franklin	43,400	178,017	23,755	61,661	9,923	14,162	2,084	3,767	7,273	15,686	88,921	226,951
Grenada	111,626	91,489	63,443	30,885	29,256	7,896	7,965	2,560	16,962	7,515	200,714	100,909
Harrison	9,815	108,034	1,566	12,537	129	349	45	133	530	4,168	8,140	81,344
Hinds	226,098	162,582	186,384	94,715	87,945	15,220	25,264	5,289	47,456	14,150	494,791	184,875
Holmes	232,091	149,211	170,438	65,172	81,453	17,074	24,887	4,988	39,627	14,291	457,460	169,477
Issaquena	49,826	28,420	41,673	12,480	28,966	4,024	14,212	2,067	6,737	3,602	133,050	68,478
Itawamba	11,803	263,857	5,721	89,457	2,187	21,768	660	7,080	1,867	30,336	17,869	395,684
Jasper	93,434	195,953	44,319	51,100	18,932	16,807	5,408	6,249	9,950	13,211	83,102	155,925
Jefferson	84,018	140,077	60,672	62,979	24,514	7,367	5,092	1,784	16,435	11,048	212,230	161,771
Jefferson Davis	63,960	93,628	35,471	38,251	15,617	10,765	6,209	5,211	10,620	10,368	123,131	154,299
Jones	25,869	199,012	10,354	56,949	4,604	20,513	1,642	8,867	2,859	15,675	27,768	199,718
Kemper	118,039	200,756	70,776	90,757	28,125	22,615	6,595	6,170	17,730	19,317	144,508	189,807

FARMERS, BY COUNTIES, FOR SOUTHERN STATES: 1909–1910—Continued.

| VALUE OF LAND, BUILDINGS, IMPLEMENTS, AND MACHINERY: 1910. | | | | | | NUMBER OF DAIRY COWS, WORK HORSES, AND WORK MULES: 1910. | | | | | | COUNTY. |
| Land. | | Buildings. | | Implements and machinery. | | Dairy cows. | | Work horses. | | Work mules. | | |
Colored farmers.	White farmers.	Colored farmers.	White farmers.	Colored farmers.	White farmers.	Colored farmers.	White farmers.	Colored farmers.	White farmers.	Colored farmers.	White farmers.	
						LOUISIANA—Continued.						
$470,905	$1,252,969	$125,269	$407,345	$14,559	$114,137	1,043	2,171	585	1,164	745	988	Red River.
814,631	1,477,811	254,500	446,023	36,136	77,081	1,992	3,871	1,301	1,388	861	770	Richland.
173,488	1,443,563	52,035	607,280	11,278	130,550	590	5,780	308	2,086	104	1,045	Sabine.
211,023	465,892	98,715	248,595	19,334	52,950	947	2,535	474	709	338	338	St. Helena.
3,252,765	7,560,524	666,694	2,091,547	147,902	573,147	4,570	13,412	6,393	12,016	1,370	3,163	St. Landry.
1,333,865	2,837,602	176,430	795,145	52,054	149,547	937	2,694	1,651	2,924	914	1,580	St. Martin.
458,719	5,583,796	109,503	1,495,967	16,380	1,278,927	163	1,114	213	1,117	365	4,948	St. Mary.
181,967	1,796,566	89,340	938,923	11,598	136,922	634	5,147	443	2,229	79	521	Tangipahoa.
1,496,208	2,455,081	445,865	599,675	46,932	218,322	1,989	836	1,701	496	978	1,868	Tensas.
324,987	1,673,316	113,426	511,474	27,605	152,898	1,189	4,557	432	1,882	684	2,140	Union.
584,713	6,884,683	59,772	952,422	20,284	320,790	463	8,484	805	8,110	263	2,769	Vermilion.
251,390	1,205,701	105,845	760,329	18,275	140,687	933	4,951	393	1,443	139	782	Washington.
492,459	1,062,343	178,660	544,207	35,030	115,029	1,851	3,873	931	1,495	579	1,022	Webster.
246,136	1,993,997	100,980	547,195	13,897	567,714	371	766	434	466	342	1,746	West Baton Rouge.
244,562	751,802	58,930	226,579	13,685	65,497	997	3,502	474	1,089	185	456	West Carroll.
427,361	1,496,377	134,520	490,972	21,361	122,694	1,368	1,525	1,087	783	745	648	West Feliciana.
97,627	923,485	36,869	469,362	6,950	102,265	561	5,045	196	1,507	147	968	Winn.
1,036,988	27,184,123	277,532	7,193,875	66,616	4,910,859	1,327	25,514	818	10,026	762	15,632	All other parishes.
						MARYLAND.						
$7,098,692	$156,352,922	$3,171,092	$75,114,417	$437,070	$11,422,701	6,339	160,520	9,169	128,109	1,178	20,320	Total.
627,600	10,614,788	324,307	3,624,132	37,665	412,080	433	3,122	790	4,042	82	1,080	Anne Arundel.
447,770	23,441,383	225,365	12,391,701	22,875	1,673,734	239	17,846	211	10,170	67	3,083	Baltimore.
286,077	1,036,549	148,002	670,255	12,896	66,925	491	1,542	655	1,794	....	23	Calvert.
437,779	5,042,010	177,595	1,874,010	28,452	384,274	282	4,219	578	4,919	128	1,186	Caroline.
594,669	1,679,359	329,930	1,134,697	48,301	166,538	960	2,938	1,106	2,796	53	193	Charles.
514,490	4,484,496	144,875	1,572,960	31,972	326,730	524	4,323	679	4,156	121	864	Dorchester.
173,190	5,762,645	136,795	5,110,951	24,171	727,723	320	11,985	279	6,306	67	1,674	Harford.
178,135	4,915,620	103,520	3,275,250	13,511	481,839	114	4,908	213	4,668	16	403	Howard.
150,866	6,214,658	53,472	1,966,205	7,721	385,926	76	6,124	233	6,726	15	549	Kent.
427,285	12,250,993	155,428	5,008,152	23,118	710,725	330	9,992	492	8,861	14	239	Montgomery.
797,273	7,074,224	303,140	3,304,047	42,020	446,606	523	4,182	968	5,252	25	412	Prince Georges.
279,322	7,210,185	85,598	2,068,485	18,050	454,424	256	7,191	440	5,831	50	2,142	Queen Annes.
273,678	2,195,644	164,813	1,208,579	19,338	201,165	445	2,930	572	3,115	7	154	St. Marys.
392,533	3,465,227	184,975	1,641,555	25,807	245,041	191	1,872	441	2,428	123	982	Somerset.
360,203	6,842,187	186,165	2,458,264	18,527	476,667	183	5,191	330	4,396	52	1,699	Talbot.
349,151	3,914,067	137,727	1,586,849	17,092	247,102	150	2,504	367	3,240	99	1,218	Wicomico.
533,076	3,541,870	162,000	1,422,939	26,179	222,823	492	3,408	467	2,891	253	1,534	Worcester.
275,595	46,667,017	147,385	24,795,386	19,375	3,792,379	330	66,243	348	46,518	6	2,885	All other counties.
						MISSISSIPPI.						
$120,393,484	$133,608,805	$28,131,073	$52,028,927	$5,602,295	$11,302,917	179,432	250,155	82,071	114,338	126,306	120,330	Total.
734,690	1,177,414	305,621	559,050	62,650	88,733	2,554	1,565	1,484	677	1,469	784	Adams.
236,437	1,617,136	64,020	609,423	16,045	163,043	528	3,215	303	2,041	335	1,836	Alcorn.
725,257	1,708,439	280,040	989,597	56,854	195,069	2,746	5,771	930	1,984	1,280	1,601	Amite.
1,172,580	2,314,123	318,915	1,008,434	67,138	241,711	2,767	5,182	1,065	2,472	1,447	2,955	Attala.
538,386	727,395	143,835	335,915	31,293	77,926	1,216	1,895	600	1,042	952	1,093	Benton.
10,390,276	3,336,500	1,860,157	569,125	329,714	180,988	4,992	1,452	2,600	758	7,915	2,098	Bolivar.
368,279	2,349,766	86,045	739,265	20,173	206,250	746	3,807	375	2,243	703	3,175	Calhoun.
1,128,046	1,683,830	371,788	711,711	88,579	169,959	3,097	3,788	1,032	1,810	2,463	2,032	Carroll.
1,560,255	1,899,071	294,890	663,340	96,164	144,220	2,722	3,237	1,085	1,683	1,893	2,007	Chickasaw.
353,354	1,560,691	99,358	725,616	30,783	163,441	658	3,008	478	1,664	330	1,766	Choctaw.
837,188	1,093,517	314,677	550,595	63,170	111,661	3,139	2,098	1,613	1,175	1,539	950	Claiborne.
655,216	1,185,393	276,231	667,743	49,078	105,472	2,089	3,924	803	1,229	587	1,373	Clarke.
2,077,412	1,769,417	413,464	506,611	105,257	149,534	3,085	2,108	1,396	1,340	2,104	1,134	Clay.
7,417,747	2,678,991	1,308,959	512,409	264,335	165,683	4,396	629	2,094	423	3,598	1,755	Coahoma.
1,252,774	2,351,417	576,371	1,493,238	99,930	282,188	3,545	5,573	1,575	2,450	2,412	2,391	Copiah.
285,154	1,137,019	97,077	688,478	18,198	102,536	690	3,411	330	1,225	234	811	Covington.
3,120,722	2,014,982	763,976	782,545	146,203	154,764	4,262	3,483	2,640	1,580	3,268	1,212	De Soto.
194,170	838,028	65,775	420,897	14,018	68,416	521	2,315	223	671	92	347	Forrest.
333,421	1,116,562	104,793	512,515	25,253	116,473	1,279	3,635	486	1,424	602	1,183	Franklin.
1,259,065	936,108	368,550	321,025	72,215	54,632	2,791	1,245	1,168	848	1,378	591	Grenada.
148,240	1,377,883	111,565	773,050	7,192	78,555	302	3,340	130	1,061	28	255	Harrison.
3,475,320	2,744,579	1,007,940	1,143,479	204,243	200,995	8,415	4,791	4,017	2,022	3,771	1,752	Hinds.
4,379,079	2,298,670	1,118,047	902,350	235,758	202,297	7,326	2,873	1,860	1,254	5,362	1,565	Holmes.
1,774,621	887,220	419,064	157,665	64,450	74,859	1,479	339	1,144	323	1,064	978	Issaquena.
107,728	1,874,521	22,410	677,110	5,374	163,509	279	4,247	127	2,290	130	2,401	Itawamba.
704,605	1,430,496	223,747	732,193	41,882	109,871	2,082	4,137	883	1,454	834	1,544	Jasper.
839,674	1,141,783	301,232	584,908	64,651	111,639	2,903	2,728	1,585	1,127	1,853	878	Jefferson.
709,261	898,333	231,264	414,647	41,114	92,813	1,516	2,157	928	752	741	768	Jefferson Davis.
263,313	1,901,829	84,755	882,347	15,491	167,836	665	5,077	255	1,448	253	1,713	Jones.
999,143	1,784,124	286,552	779,024	77,286	162,472	2,475	3,710	977	1,381	1,657	1,945	Kemper.

Table **72.**—STATISTICS OF AGRICULTURE FOR COLORED AND WHITE

COUNTY.	FARM ACREAGE: 1910.				ACREAGE AND YIELD OF COTTON: 1909.				ACREAGE AND YIELD OF CORN: 1909.			
	Total.		Improved.		Acreage.		Yield in bales.		Acreage.		Yield in bushels.	
	Colored farmers.	White farmers.	Colored farmers.	White farmers.	Colored farmers.	White farmers.	Colored farmers.	White farmers.	Colored farmers.	White farmers.	Colored farmers.	White farmers.

MISSISSIPPI—Continued.

Lafayette	110,640	237,145	53,635	79,455	20,742	17,512	6,882	6,913	16,720	26,506	200,979	416,500
Lamar	5,067	63,391	1,971	15,948	689	4,273	260	1,845	628	5,661	7,801	93,212
Lauderdale	103,679	194,744	58,150	75,459	27,289	24,373	6,835	7,837	10,126	15,373	88,612	176,679
Lawrence	47,534	105,830	22,764	32,689	9,164	11,242	3,337	5,181	6,735	11,438	69,572	150,669
Leake	72,545	215,709	35,633	84,618	14,447	21,330	3,631	6,274	10,181	22,832	87,614	238,483
Lee	57,781	202,069	46,583	119,385	24,090	36,230	8,053	12,691	12,037	28,415	180,075	455,268
Leflore	165,202	63,110	154,939	18,656	92,649	8,921	35,252	3,380	28,185	4,569	524,182	80,752
Lincoln	50,983	220,875	29,771	81,993	14,344	27,546	4,725	11,322	7,964	22,236	92,459	329,693
Lowndes	120,662	121,171	98,373	60,613	54,258	11,576	11,596	3,443	21,572	9,760	200,121	121,018
Madison	214,229	154,846	168,778	85,114	72,355	13,856	19,349	4,525	39,185	11,481	387,196	145,949
Marion	35,648	132,324	16,433	40,040	6,757	11,935	2,683	5,511	5,222	12,411	59,484	177,573
Marshall	206,061	144,840	115,635	54,902	55,969	12,009	13,957	3,470	32,045	15,535	331,869	211,752
Monroe	139,208	255,321	107,894	98,326	65,600	25,995	14,489	7,860	24,725	23,212	266,109	316,494
Montgomery	68,935	145,027	45,646	60,720	19,289	13,488	5,606	4,484	12,162	14,515	119,923	174,222
Neshoba	31,401	222,385	16,925	84,249	7,752	25,996	2,094	8,464	4,602	22,970	39,312	250,415
Newton	66,014	222,507	36,349	75,553	17,019	23,451	4,565	7,746	9,373	20,425	84,027	221,711
Noxubee	173,229	111,244	141,097	57,544	84,282	10,277	17,083	2,508	30,126	7,821	247,964	79,879
Oktibbeha	95,951	136,113	65,117	64,646	26,045	8,260	6,133	2,579	14,164	10,433	138,322	128,593
Panola	174,672	166,206	120,962	60,353	69,967	17,724	20,873	6,383	31,652	15,612	358,180	229,673
Perry	15,784	67,784	3,031	11,308	542	2,521	195	1,080	1,060	4,002	13,567	59,368
Pike	94,199	204,438	50,416	69,559	22,115	19,736	8,493	9,050	15,049	21,063	187,425	334,203
Pontotoc	41,304	226,517	23,817	86,857	9,926	23,272	2,913	8,425	6,554	29,332	84,567	460,382
Prentiss	18,872	215,025	13,543	88,142	6,312	25,553	1,551	7,517	3,868	27,699	48,613	392,723
Quitman	47,702	44,284	41,834	17,148	26,827	8,590	13,007	4,634	8,000	3,680	170,178	90,098
Rankin	127,729	227,129	74,715	92,122	28,004	14,645	8,459	5,544	15,829	15,022	147,528	189,572
Scott	53,002	163,119	26,981	58,643	10,078	13,995	2,678	4,661	6,599	14,373	52,281	150,178
Sharkey	68,530	38,558	64,494	18,079	39,804	10,573	17,863	4,556	9,915	6,059	194,858	113,762
Simpson	49,444	145,773	26,926	55,892	11,290	17,621	3,765	7,428	7,764	16,427	79,830	204,627
Smith	26,156	212,758	11,732	73,240	4,429	21,610	1,484	9,320	3,194	19,611	31,346	242,949
Sunflower	111,674	112,493	105,129	51,777	64,575	27,050	24,791	12,042	15,494	10,530	322,513	238,780
Tallahatchie	106,803	128,913	91,012	40,782	58,724	12,108	27,827	4,303	23,948	13,836	419,047	205,722
Tate	105,391	107,430	76,406	59,247	37,274	16,630	11,590	5,943	19,099	15,628	235,009	228,590
Tippah	24,560	234,865	12,986	72,949	4,514	16,173	1,119	4,474	3,732	23,933	40,311	311,079
Tishomingo	8,651	188,192	3,300	52,569	1,061	12,556	278	3,719	1,147	20,259	15,696	276,348
Tunica	102,955	49,059	95,705	16,258	63,657	6,667	29,601	3,367	13,232	5,139	280,792	125,940
Union	27,488	199,129	19,111	94,802	7,404	23,391	1,916	6,897	5,029	28,626	57,442	367,023
Warren	64,538	146,979	47,109	33,910	24,131	4,794	8,326	1,714	10,674	6,614	151,053	112,084
Washington	167,698	141,794	152,673	40,209	78,663	12,948	37,881	6,817	17,758	7,398	339,248	162,005
Wayne	39,198	146,274	15,737	34,517	6,134	10,843	1,660	4,010	4,410	10,384	38,056	130,388
Webster	32,787	206,112	17,572	85,174	6,285	19,327	1,836	6,550	5,215	22,312	60,641	305,356
Wilkinson	74,631	160,520	50,175	53,135	19,855	8,571	2,813	1,331	17,874	12,110	243,383	175,977
Winston	70,009	207,211	37,349	78,794	13,432	18,088	3,268	5,353	9,138	19,041	75,398	196,318
Yalobusha	94,110	165,437	55,602	60,847	23,199	13,204	6,672	5,026	15,968	16,842	163,585	233,862
Yazoo	218,778	224,046	174,862	79,856	102,260	18,001	31,336	5,226	42,359	19,487	520,025	268,444
All other counties	28,481	336,982	4,377	42,365	676	3,317	211	1,410	1,584	15,087	20,051	245,498

NORTH CAROLINA.

Total	3,185,804	19,253,325	1,730,712	7,082,344	474,889	799,515	232,536	432,596	535,037	1,924,420	5,876,253	28,187,278
Alamance	39,649	212,929	17,120	90,313	307	1,482	140	796	4,824	23,644	72,393	386,346
Alexander	4,970	154,974	2,878	63,709	261	2,484	75	797	1,003	18,388	12,382	256,982
Anson	87,416	202,574	47,832	68,547	24,467	22,235	11,366	12,119	10,815	16,002	105,512	216,647
Beaufort	30,812	218,288	14,253	56,256	3,693	11,447	1,954	6,964	5,189	20,875	89,681	441,288
Bertie	79,587	202,884	46,990	56,402	6,993	7,184	3,039	3,312	14,207	17,611	119,334	169,036
Bladen	49,917	237,856	17,595	49,379	3,294	6,296	1,619	3,738	8,580	18,870	85,822	224,833
Brunswick	32,133	235,969	6,560	26,036	365	1,585	148	736	2,291	6,596	25,004	98,629
Buncombe	5,558	414,224	3,224	154,234					1,057	32,335	15,742	609,632
Burke	8,948	213,934	3,674	67,866	34	390	6	125	1,766	24,757	20,833	373,262
Cabarrus	30,959	176,467	18,866	90,285	6,471	15,410	2,587	7,159	4,758	21,196	52,949	302,701
Caldwell	6,557	211,814	2,840	71,864		39		16	1,064	22,765	13,477	341,661
Camden	14,989	45,024	9,528	26,507	1,636	3,554	609	1,588	5,421	13,166	39,911	127,884
Carteret	4,001	73,180	1,974	18,201	426	1,917	225	1,146	550	5,017	6,766	70,338
Caswell	70,262	193,608	29,495	74,089		7		3	5,784	11,946	78,433	182,032
Catawba	11,310	229,727	6,781	118,883	1,741	14,119	594	5,750	2,048	28,888	23,612	425,243
Chatham	67,796	311,836	26,758	94,830	5,408	8,508	2,531	4,569	8,994	28,705	115,327	440,897
Chowan	14,500	60,063	9,032	24,761	2,337	3,831	934	1,667	2,659	7,574	23,479	84,398
Cleveland	30,614	232,274	19,786	110,093	8,160	30,716	2,833	12,735	6,249	35,222	67,312	497,137
Columbus	39,893	293,523	13,496	61,188	2,013	7,292	1,041	4,423	5,665	24,090	62,779	336,092
Craven	41,139	161,099	17,647	46,296	3,273	4,871	1,344	2,522	6,365	12,370	64,521	194,107
Cumberland	70,286	337,300	31,793	73,141	10,744	17,569	6,440	12,035	11,368	28,306	124,972	383,730
Currituck	16,679	70,674	9,997	28,329	590	1,040	143	404	4,954	12,181	33,848	142,329
Davidson	10,684	320,575	6,421	140,601	820	5,013	311	2,073	1,603	30,904	23,103	484,274
Davie	11,361	144,218	7,237	71,118	792	3,727	215	1,103	1,882	16,483	24,502	230,068
Duplin	37,223	355,412	20,892	97,472	2,946	8,511	1,402	4,906	8,998	31,433	96,407	432,629
Durham	26,950	110,427	12,608	36,217	756	1,279	293	595	3,964	9,765	48,771	152,530
Edgecombe	75,720	207,349	59,822	89,195	23,653	24,113	12,029	14,770	13,392	19,823	112,484	243,370
Forsyth	12,719	209,086	6,794	95,170	5	22	2	7	1,759	19,671	26,164	368,487
Franklin	64,744	193,376	38,666	83,115	12,611	16,656	5,103	7,946	11,078	21,151	98,045	235,616
Gaston	33,495	166,456	22,083	79,613	8,859	17,541	3,737	8,521	6,412	23,549	69,178	340,880

FARMERS, BY COUNTIES, FOR SOUTHERN STATES: 1909-1910—Continued.

VALUE OF LAND, BUILDINGS, IMPLEMENTS, AND MACHINERY: 1910.						NUMBER OF DAIRY COWS, WORK HORSES, AND WORK MULES: 1910.						
Land.		Buildings.		Implements and machinery.		Dairy cows.		Work horses.		Work mules.		COUNTY.
Colored farmers.	White farmers.	Colored farmers.	White farmers.	Colored farmers.	White farmers.	Colored farmers.	White farmers.	Colored farmers.	White farmers.	Colored farmers.	White farmers.	

MISSISSIPPI—Continued.

Land Colored	Land White	Bldg Colored	Bldg White	Impl Colored	Impl White	Dairy Colored	Dairy White	Horses Colored	Horses White	Mules Colored	Mules White	County
$865,000	$1,839,146	$198,325	$551,472	$62,733	$187,906	2,173	3,813	911	2,078	1,907	2,746	Lafayette.
43,132	486,636	22,479	279,915	1,930	40,993	157	2,787	78	671	15	339	Lamar.
952,781	2,146,298	303,317	1,228,578	55,340	222,987	2,053	4,254	795	1,497	1,400	1,921	Lauderdale.
415,726	848,366	152,329	448,013	26,687	88,053	1,115	2,408	529	1,134	441	683	Lawrence.
556,000	1,656,274	158,123	735,644	32,558	163,641	1,613	4,569	737	2,132	725	1,726	Leake.
1,556,476	4,015,340	280,545	1,313,221	69,810	287,699	1,871	5,203	722	2,934	1,662	3,831	Lee.
3,344,984	1,618,415	1,274,557	421,665	241,915	176,087	4,847	761	2,828	333	4,298	957	Leflore.
461,693	1,817,529	186,802	1,025,505	31,955	215,086	1,597	5,866	855	2,554	573	1,973	Lincoln.
2,392,544	2,508,469	508,428	820,095	111,008	183,336	3,517	2,250	1,593	1,485	2,822	1,548	Lowndes.
2,718,302	2,280,775	836,104	911,213	213,039	186,139	7,001	3,134	2,709	1,705	4,030	1,363	Madison.
362,015	1,258,630	120,390	589,285	19,889	105,848	1,206	4,071	620	1,136	202	909	Marion.
1,906,946	1,364,561	528,036	624,850	115,598	109,757	4,659	2,748	2,301	1,807	3,518	1,400	Marshall.
2,968,510	3,128,512	520,612	1,168,536	158,846	279,567	3,834	4,018	1,621	2,396	3,073	2,599	Monroe.
754,726	1,305,784	240,385	637,054	41,719	119,210	1,659	2,649	545	1,438	1,241	1,688	Montgomery.
317,147	2,037,981	74,930	865,337	15,657	165,474	639	4,128	274	1,761	371	2,364	Neshoba.
672,053	2,080,657	213,751	1,085,071	32,377	196,419	1,354	4,249	557	1,808	855	2,508	Newton.
3,183,102	1,629,689	537,268	561,090	137,848	124,659	5,484	2,440	2,503	1,689	3,323	1,228	Noxubee.
984,471	1,602,043	286,325	618,835	70,248	122,428	2,944	2,857	1,076	1,288	1,866	1,510	Oktibbeha.
2,635,151	1,804,003	667,025	589,747	154,318	151,482	4,899	2,992	3,004	2,253	3,516	1,644	Panola.
170,585	773,602	69,015	324,461	12,269	45,426	463	2,354	167	565	44	220	Perry.
890,948	1,862,053	414,005	1,114,000	61,947	212,647	2,905	5,146	1,834	2,421	725	1,134	Pike.
555,818	2,383,010	117,626	831,606	20,769	175,405	946	4,162	630	3,135	610	2,580	Pontotoc.
357,364	2,196,028	53,610	733,601	13,633	189,238	508	3,645	236	2,052	460	2,911	Prentiss.
2,072,331	1,370,132	322,662	252,755	75,174	66,302	1,857	963	638	400	1,779	728	Quitman.
1,110,693	2,140,421	310,980	892,476	56,003	150,804	3,352	4,469	1,315	1,859	1,577	1,752	Rankin.
421,698	1,261,809	133,894	582,317	24,360	116,029	1,247	3,293	505	1,494	637	1,486	Scott.
3,226,180	1,545,521	857,035	357,225	101,418	80,073	2,167	812	1,160	508	1,903	1,025	Sharkey.
424,507	1,167,676	168,512	694,763	26,734	125,076	1,327	3,995	453	1,215	639	1,536	Simpson.
208,739	1,814,624	64,945	834,506	12,253	154,402	691	5,663	181	1,518	318	2,254	Smith.
4,849,782	3,691,997	775,108	649,215	151,723	255,302	3,384	2,090	882	1,057	3,559	2,934	Sunflower.
3,078,195	2,004,908	650,950	574,890	101,047	177,051	3,331	2,468	1,550	1,309	4,012	1,575	Tallahatchie.
1,468,392	1,395,421	388,528	543,699	70,570	113,731	2,741	2,651	1,688	2,097	2,113	1,505	Tate.
213,509	1,581,411	57,560	619,765	12,798	157,870	523	3,394	237	2,060	330	2,475	Tippah.
56,326	1,098,054	18,890	448,839	2,935	97,073	144	2,776	79	1,335	103	1,561	Tishomingo.
4,694,309	1,709,027	775,751	305,000	173,486	146,675	2,535	462	1,569	546	3,115	1,054	Tunica.
419,749	2,436,640	104,216	826,421	17,829	173,871	811	4,541	373	2,769	557	2,915	Union.
1,041,639	1,675,235	382,866	550,967	55,171	116,243	2,746	2,349	1,498	843	1,830	922	Warren.
6,750,830	3,050,872	1,323,260	542,490	174,591	224,016	3,373	574	1,920	457	4,882	2,101	Washington.
258,925	1,038,573	101,441	508,037	15,139	79,928	941	4,284	441	1,189	222	538	Wayne.
294,303	1,601,911	71,320	686,117	14,496	155,019	670	3,388	322	2,055	531	2,087	Webster.
658,148	1,306,069	217,686	485,139	42,992	96,470	2,708	3,283	1,657	1,326	1,591	935	Wilkinson.
584,589	1,606,411	172,300	685,518	39,052	150,573	1,304	3,401	524	1,674	824	1,784	Winston.
991,661	1,618,006	302,068	661,528	64,216	127,043	2,562	2,803	1,068	1,806	1,693	1,576	Yalobusha.
5,240,916	2,835,356	1,116,611	946,196	235,356	265,049	7,403	5,871	2,371	1,957	6,665	2,146	Yazoo.
221,176	3,179,693	129,385	1,487,965	18,368	217,285	906	11,381	329	2,741	55	766	All other counties.

NORTH CAROLINA.

Land Colored	Land White	Bldg Colored	Bldg White	Impl Colored	Impl White	Dairy Colored	Dairy White	Horses Colored	Horses White	Mules Colored	Mules White	County
$55,362,178	$287,802,767	$13,904,038	$99,555,624	$2,261,470	$16,180,149	42,637	266,277	24,926	131,023	34,532	136,603	Total.
439,670	2,361,505	164,380	1,325,200	26,998	232,304	635	3,540	436	2,605	268	1,054	Alamance.
81,804	2,152,310	17,306	660,342	3,029	113,878	104	2,398	29	879	52	1,426	Alexander.
1,221,668	2,818,022	315,955	1,076,903	55,289	201,257	1,368	2,231	225	749	1,668	2,266	Anson.
633,904	3,329,726	145,595	944,894	18,078	156,378	289	2,143	324	1,664	217	1,102	Beaufort.
1,286,317	2,204,274	383,681	924,645	72,986	154,360	1,103	1,707	1,021	1,495	436	1,086	Bertie.
445,032	1,764,270	177,113	762,853	28,439	121,121	389	1,466	220	493	445	1,251	Bladen.
174,735	1,047,655	75,075	432,625	16,698	77,110	371	1,293	127	432	139	590	Brunswick.
147,505	9,760,353	41,615	2,313,553	4,605	277,346	207	8,799	60	2,973	61	1,910	Buncombe.
114,976	2,966,000	30,970	1,066,582	3,833	144,545	168	3,072	32	1,005	133	1,822	Burke.
631,261	3,275,573	119,950	1,078,459	20,443	220,068	548	3,208	255	2,110	501	1,688	Cabarrus.
79,209	3,162,467	22,966	1,061,368	2,250	136,400	137	3,336	20	1,061	59	1,527	Caldwell.
232,620	787,220	60,450	356,745	7,805	41,371	175	871	243	847	66	232	Camden.
58,116	781,405	14,355	375,170	7,386	53,034	49	1,121	38	962	19	155	Carteret.
485,418	1,343,371	198,355	960,969	28,149	121,980	765	1,813	527	1,532	354	675	Caswell.
264,856	5,326,288	55,655	1,677,505	9,517	316,980	246	4,645	100	2,605	130	1,875	Catawba.
552,773	2,387,715	204,738	1,254,859	30,420	234,424	1,024	4,208	353	1,522	642	2,484	Chatham.
327,960	1,226,382	95,875	438,910	18,538	74,456	208	352	137	625	191	580	Chowan.
811,372	6,073,581	159,405	1,855,707	19,556	271,654	674	4,867	111	1,164	428	3,516	Cleveland.
531,775	3,271,500	151,415	1,123,240	39,388	170,836	312	1,647	179	761	398	1,929	Columbus.
728,073	2,324,719	205,882	562,943	35,340	106,048	510	1,424	349	774	193	640	Craven.
1,156,040	4,820,999	276,171	1,468,293	45,164	215,403	623	2,323	232	856	906	2,199	Cumberland.
245,606	1,324,842	72,230	589,130	5,598	55,402	193	1,148	232	904	86	183	Currituck.
193,340	5,999,073	41,525	1,873,795	8,819	436,830	189	5,137	101	3,559	126	2,114	Davidson.
183,785	2,208,902	47,100	751,067	6,883	148,551	211	2,324	110	1,393	117	1,247	Davie.
586,877	3,822,295	176,333	1,414,235	22,591	179,022	497	3,012	382	1,724	273	1,866	Duplin.
418,864	1,755,400	113,580	797,930	13,815	90,873	517	1,801	270	997	214	698	Durham.
1,611,699	3,859,678	479,997	1,427,068	97,678	261,749	366	1,355	475	1,453	1,388	2,251	Edgecombe.
298,821	5,137,371	71,655	1,603,705	11,456	307,830	250	4,373	128	2,108	114	1,776	Forsyth.
939,213	2,418,013	307,675	1,020,797	41,826	172,069	998	2,446	824	1,757	451	1,244	Franklin.
954,626	4,796,915	200,091	1,653,237	23,994	226,206	761	3,431	176	1,385	530	2,258	Gaston.

NEGRO POPULATION.

TABLE 72.—STATISTICS OF AGRICULTURE FOR COLORED AND WHITE

COUNTY.	FARM ACREAGE: 1910.				ACREAGE AND YIELD OF COTTON: 1909.				ACREAGE AND YIELD OF CORN: 1909.			
	Total.		Improved.		Acreage.		Yield in bales.		Acreage.		Yield in bushels.	
	Colored farmers.	White farmers.	Colored farmers.	White farmers.	Colored farmers.	White farmers.	Colored farmers.	White farmers.	Colored farmers.	White farmers.	Colored farmers.	White farmers.
NORTH CAROLINA—Continued.												
Gates	23,247	113,501	10,444	41,165	1,349	4,001	497	1,929	3,727	14,600	27,804	141,652
Granville	72,107	241,945	37,639	105,781	959	2,266	438	1,155	8,116	15,838	122,406	284,715
Greene	30,225	101,897	24,943	48,296	8,469	9,815	3,503	4,744	9,125	15,969	96,298	202,614
Guilford	32,520	334,308	15,429	141,695	93	985	28	373	5,400	36,108	69,526	554,501
Halifax	131,810	219,976	83,111	101,827	23,974	21,557	10,712	12,700	21,156	20,830	179,673	247,092
Harnett	34,136	211,900	14,796	61,772	4,892	15,202	2,464	9,357	6,351	24,774	62,299	341,119
Henderson	3,400	183,276	1,668	61,448					882	18,281	9,501	254,704
Hertford	56,517	127,480	30,811	38,145	4,571	4,315	1,684	2,057	8,486	10,807	62,748	112,196
Hyde	12,409	73,272	10,321	27,016	2,471	4,311	1,076	2,714	4,627	14,013	72,503	301,462
Iredell	30,842	320,922	17,431	141,928	4,935	21,729	1,575	7,726	5,516	37,172	65,463	534,970
Johnston	55,247	394,485	28,203	146,315	10,678	42,359	6,451	28,344	9,264	52,375	122,726	828,715
Jones	34,075	136,786	16,700	37,039	4,823	5,495	2,167	2,826	7,050	11,132	71,969	136,153
Lee	20,652	99,006	6,749	28,573	1,910	5,929	891	3,388	2,418	10,164	24,442	137,003
Lenoir	30,796	184,278	22,834	76,548	6,490	10,307	2,795	5,002	8,778	23,414	101,492	301,033
Lincoln	13,171	159,935	8,585	80,297	2,807	13,834	898	5,548	2,631	20,428	24,022	281,108
McDowell	7,592	166,895	2,885	42,616		13		6	1,391	15,086	17,164	215,575
Martin	42,102	165,109	21,439	56,759	4,052	7,783	1,590	4,187	5,960	15,042	49,852	185,333
Mecklenburg	83,205	235,077	54,619	123,593	24,903	38,317	9,573	17,893	12,542	29,270	114,065	363,820
Montgomery	17,380	186,632	7,858	41,522	2,494	5,730	1,019	2,707	2,202	12,670	20,406	177,096
Moore	23,866	210,730	7,536	44,256	1,155	2,745	433	1,261	2,916	14,844	30,653	198,929
Nash	68,638	213,896	41,674	85,404	11,877	19,625	6,385	11,452	11,063	25,242	122,236	345,794
New Hanover	7,937	27,790	2,974	6,701	15	83	8	64	711	1,331	10,446	25,807
Northampton	86,413	190,029	49,936	76,333	12,895	11,544	4,947	5,834	15,630	17,996	112,921	186,567
Onslow	20,499	235,593	11,434	55,711	1,585	4,458	771	2,517	4,294	16,496	40,362	181,447
Orange	32,677	178,152	14,424	62,556	819	2,129	377	1,053	4,552	17,662	62,252	276,817
Pamlico	10,959	79,049	5,611	21,822	2,176	5,802	1,274	3,668	2,116	8,752	49,658	189,834
Pasquotank	21,102	61,143	15,095	35,593	2,690	4,607	913	1,985	7,863	16,775	61,275	192,328
Pender	32,261	234,713	9,754	42,131	484	1,749	239	1,032	3,901	11,391	44,787	153,138
Perquimans	20,461	80,670	12,923	40,272	3,501	5,987	1,238	2,501	4,886	13,255	32,599	113,741
Person	65,445	172,236	31,520	73,314					6,088	14,809	84,664	225,855
Pitt	76,253	267,221	50,889	98,757	16,176	22,624	7,407	10,647	17,514	30,223	200,629	438,303
Polk	7,420	104,232	3,240	28,033	752	3,691	255	1,480	1,575	10,591	17,512	142,856
Randolph	20,505	412,535	7,578	137,334	252	1,540	85	673	2,675	38,792	34,123	587,681
Richmond	47,694	127,894	24,000	32,354	11,816	10,325	6,855	6,478	6,227	9,931	74,909	134,642
Robeson	147,201	326,722	99,297	118,154	51,729	42,592	34,552	31,271	30,302	40,865	406,356	635,704
Rockingham	51,576	276,939	21,678	103,441					5,215	23,501	69,198	376,025
Rowan	24,718	264,412	14,800	128,201	3,410	16,369	1,206	6,753	4,482	31,946	58,610	494,881
Rutherford	25,711	249,983	11,990	89,119	2,576	14,908	914	6,057	4,826	31,548	53,563	429,592
Sampson	65,127	426,542	28,898	122,587	5,849	22,909	2,873	13,294	13,672	48,413	142,425	634,915
Scotland	35,228	89,645	30,077	32,669	18,843	16,964	14,251	14,346	6,778	8,728	101,663	185,948
Stanley	10,748	211,021	5,469	81,940	1,348	11,701	556	5,836	1,479	21,959	16,928	319,048
Stokes	20,130	254,079	9,434	98,259		3		(¹)	2,388	19,446	34,602	318,539
Surry	10,077	291,936	4,801	115,422					1,322	30,594	17,560	480,500
Tyrrell	5,129	51,246	2,703	19,564	532	1,089	131	506	1,168	6,192	11,414	83,404
Union	56,478	303,478	31,253	120,143	13,256	34,430	5,494	17,032	7,048	31,265	80,559	441,324
Vance	53,467	103,269	28,692	44,341	3,937	2,942	1,411	1,345	7,028	9,248	74,428	132,712
Wake	110,662	370,360	57,389	134,475	19,828	28,836	9,980	17,478	16,124	35,762	175,921	511,070
Warren	83,046	129,345	41,591	48,395	14,112	6,486	6,027	3,594	14,536	10,694	155,066	148,635
Washington	11,956	72,388	5,853	28,117	833	3,127	313	1,343	2,081	10,451	19,672	113,830
Wayne	69,570	252,572	43,095	111,249	16,061	28,094	8,399	16,153	15,633	35,767	180,022	465,570
Wilkes	12,525	398,705	5,739	142,933		32		6	2,343	41,938	31,317	577,349
Wilson	45,693	151,510	31,567	67,227	13,856	19,235	7,160	11,732	9,696	20,675	113,870	319,705
Yadkin	4,611	203,590	2,819	81,822	1	92	1	19	1,070	24,464	15,275	363,648
All other counties	37,717	2,375,900	15,872	987,670		11		5	5,514	191,618	71,676	3,367,211

OKLAHOMA.

COUNTY.	Colored	White	Colored	White	Colored	White	Colored	White	Colored	White	Colored	White
Total	2,276,711	26,582,642	1,172,819	16,378,518	217,231	1,759,704	70,738	485,004	369,818	5,544,251	5,949,363	88,334,044
Atoka	44,225	148,944	11,255	62,616	1,445	11,753	320	2,638	4,090	28,035	57,988	381,055
Blaine	41,992	469,802	19,305	318,193	2,629	4,531	521	1,069	7,074	100,059	44,195	1,133,233
Bryan	65,894	270,835	32,498	203,813	5,334	41,060	1,187	10,270	10,392	95,183	155,267	1,372,258
Caddo	36,307	790,671	16,795	491,360	2,476	56,433	474	12,446	6,455	255,665	87,271	3,412,184
Carter	42,436	202,059	22,477	125,378	7,117	35,247	1,680	8,341	8,138	52,040	117,363	790,669
Cherokee	60,022	104,209	19,487	55,597	2,575	11,455	727	3,774	7,226	21,083	92,779	340,307
Choctaw	59,435	104,735	23,766	63,907	5,323	12,134	1,064	3,103	8,486	30,086	126,215	559,508
Craig	60,765	297,630	42,711	209,254	3	58	1	12	14,248	90,743	232,322	1,572,737
Creek	34,933	266,120	17,854	97,534	6,252	17,921	2,505	7,852	4,923	32,734	99,430	731,586
Garvin	43,193	298,978	25,290	217,908	4,873	47,240	1,485	14,849	6,456	102,444	102,388	1,919,588
Hughes	35,098	216,900	15,441	129,909	4,410	36,982	1,750	14,522	5,277	53,488	91,719	1,027,606
Johnston	31,080	216,034	11,254	113,753	577	16,492	133	4,100	2,570	57,805	33,550	863,386
Kingfisher	43,862	487,767	24,046	329,104	4,837	9,815	1,376	2,584	8,616	119,384	104,241	1,572,155
Le Flore	24,617	155,971	12,369	107,888	2,586	33,699	859	10,704	2,738	37,967	46,210	741,632
Lincoln	61,469	535,458	32,395	290,051	13,393	86,537	3,496	25,406	7,345	95,808	86,756	1,391,741
Logan	83,901	365,580	51,797	230,416	18,144	27,347	4,857	8,255	12,661	76,833	193,427	1,260,218
Love	21,027	131,806	12,389	85,708	3,482	24,427	672	5,742	4,126	33,770	55,675	501,774
McCurtain	71,420	66,403	22,810	38,192	3,731	3,686	840	929	9,791	19,582	175,895	389,847
McIntosh	69,753	165,134	42,560	109,826	13,992	27,942	4,907	10,921	15,661	62,551	268,551	1,002,949
Mayes	49,917	177,529	24,997	125,175	437	1,928	126	653	10,856	52,576	158,565	793,873

¹ Less than 1 bale.

FARMERS, BY COUNTIES, FOR SOUTHERN STATES: 1909–1910—Continued.

VALUE OF LAND, BUILDINGS, IMPLEMENTS, AND MACHINERY: 1910.						NUMBER OF DAIRY COWS, WORK HORSES, AND WORK MULES: 1910.						COUNTY.
Land.		Buildings.		Implements and machinery.		Dairy cows.		Work horses.		Work mules.		
Colored farmers.	White farmers.	Colored farmers.	Whits farmer.	Colored farmers.	White farmers.	Colored farmers.	White farmers.	Colored farmers.	White farmers.	Colored farmers.	White farmers.	
NORTH CAROLINA—Continued.												
$361,305	$1,515,665	$127,540	$711,450	$20,709	$84,762	367	1,701	336	1,284	123	454	Gates.
715,695	2,413,975	260,192	1,518,641	32,745	164,882	1,169	2,795	786	2,471	328	903	Granville.
885,800	2,549,232	182,990	797,057	21,495	108,920	197	661	229	867	645	1,312	Greene.
593,443	5,841,739	136,253	2,305,911	23,972	388,852	685	6,804	349	3,652	269	2,184	Guilford.
1,603,126	3,077,345	551,645	1,028,278	121,974	230,429	1,627	1,600	1,466	2,014	1,334	1,403	Halifax.
385,656	2,610,153	110,835	1,029,130	23,900	156,584	522	2,264	132	557	486	2,022	Harnett.
70,585	3,092,778	20,190	1,218,477	3,302	139,779	98	3,366	33	877	18	799	Henderson.
1,198,688	1,965,317	353,045	829,406	46,595	112,240	616	1,287	607	1,258	379	564	Hertford.
457,328	1,424,255	43,637	399,705	7,059	58,581	311	2,162	218	1,125	64	308	Hyde.
609,711	5,697,998	115,234	1,974,630	19,714	399,142	617	5,565	222	2,654	374	3,391	Iredell.
1,088,303	7,806,413	222,792	2,467,556	37,502	446,695	480	3,980	175	1,505	906	5,067	Johnston.
343,795	1,046,980	70,057	347,157	11,244	60,920	214	825	163	492	310	660	Jones.
206,131	1,034,033	60,745	528,345	9,425	77,937	293	1,239	71	432	213	928	Lee.
751,393	3,404,878	156,466	1,046,810	17,242	133,934	179	1,234	195	1,088	424	1,481	Lenoir.
240,203	2,956,575	58,160	1,035,131	7,783	218,231	287	2,996	83	1,432	178	1,920	Lincoln.
81,107	1,732,223	18,950	549,481	3,487	68,208	128	2,093	30	411	57	1,021	McDowell.
585,823	2,097,645	180,757	816,555	23,652	133,426	335	1,310	338	804	373	1,209	Martin.
2,719,361	7,692,154	422,583	2,330,750	72,408	384,720	1,920	5,897	596	2,453	1,370	3,446	Mecklenburg.
144,945	1,306,827	62,690	643,288	10,713	134,364	276	1,746	73	550	276	1,315	Montgomery.
147,803	1,404,143	73,470	680,830	9,560	111,403	310	2,214	109	765	199	1,149	Moore.
1,369,591	3,888,480	362,442	1,580,410	55,277	233,613	567	1,811	483	1,527	1,034	2,360	Nash.
179,851	508,328	43,414	265,729	6,712	35,796	24	302	59	201	118	210	New Hanover.
1,251,029	2,268,958	321,163	1,016,025	52,563	149,077	1,043	1,918	936	1,624	599	1,251	Northampton.
245,827	1,374,930	73,023	611,455	9,096	75,646	100	749	120	802	211	895	Onslow.
265,519	1,456,419	114,356	765,020	18,402	134,573	534	2,579	345	1,704	182	869	Orange.
330,754	1,538,565	46,880	397,990	5,865	51,093	70	755	94	604	108	449	Pamlico.
481,524	1,347,094	114,057	535,568	16,210	75,506	418	1,529	415	1,238	105	258	Pasquotank.
335,652	1,747,136	145,418	760,295	21,474	106,051	346	1,327	201	622	212	826	Pender.
296,195	1,106,856	107,460	488,906	19,315	76,876	273	1,258	354	1,246	215	374	Perquimans.
632,990	1,673,007	200,085	879,635	25,838	116,401	878	2,080	617	1,800	300	827	Person.
1,771,734	5,808,654	396,023	1,715,125	46,318	247,259	458	2,248	601	2,548	887	1,757	Pitt.
114,092	1,378,236	23,590	496,376	4,849	72,541	152	1,486	30	221	66	750	Polk.
219,786	4,162,302	74,660	1,852,955	13,406	357,952	354	5,617	161	2,524	198	3,579	Randolph.
759,589	1,457,085	183,500	511,965	40,428	102,471	622	960	117	368	830	945	Richmond.
4,563,730	8,524,861	817,424	2,257,711	166,669	429,254	1,203	1,738	768	1,389	3,105	3,638	Robeson.
509,428	3,035,982	152,376	1,278,685	17,631	217,951	729	3,728	298	2,246	309	1,610	Rockingham.
468,222	4,569,593	109,620	1,761,132	21,574	365,519	509	5,238	291	3,473	244	2,078	Rowan.
419,007	4,104,451	96,871	1,224,995	15,363	197,928	534	4,201	100	1,150	318	2,641	Rutherford.
940,377	5,416,112	231,257	1,869,841	35,551	291,854	636	3,644	375	1,204	547	3,102	Sampson.
1,834,076	3,762,664	186,650	621,495	41,407	205,605	367	551	192	454	891	1,198	Scotland.
145,015	2,536,151	36,300	984,325	5,631	232,156	192	2,973	103	1,680	121	1,978	Stanley.
227,011	3,111,215	64,875	1,194,674	12,006	239,762	345	3,757	82	1,068	196	2,680	Stokes.
138,700	3,851,490	38,375	1,437,674	4,141	238,949	216	4,926	86	1,969	50	2,194	Surry.
77,690	653,175	14,790	210,240	2,757	28,730	137	1,216	41	500	22	83	Tyrrell.
906,643	4,363,717	227,522	1,719,968	29,683	308,554	1,049	4,668	232	1,789	989	3,884	Union.
712,212	1,550,730	186,830	695,050	28,467	113,323	914	1,441	648	1,197	118	379	Vance.
1,685,733	5,274,514	552,631	2,512,942	74,648	363,315	1,795	5,297	698	2,719	1,259	3,075	Wake.
1,009,495	1,429,731	423,964	728,106	99,956	128,649	1,625	1,791	1,191	1,403	193	347	Warren.
204,677	1,042,937	51,138	432,368	7,143	87,476	147	1,006	112	575	51	495	Washington.
2,135,892	5,873,787	377,825	1,535,955	50,734	263,727	436	2,083	633	2,011	917	2,181	Wayne.
183,995	4,132,778	39,922	1,286,364	5,343	215,905	236	6,497	69	1,552	71	1,906	Wilkes.
1,369,460	4,061,442	305,425	1,386,170	37,375	186,761	129	668	242	1,135	943	2,188	Wilson.
85,403	3,083,853	23,802	901,155	3,472	182,702	131	3,219	54	1,339	56	1,686	Yadkin.
463,163	32,529,382	105,046	8,528,003	15,114	1,113,680	950	49,786	251	15,756	136	8,730	All other counties.
OKLAHOMA.												
$40,971,750	$608,094,918	$6,250,043	$83,360,513	$1,637,769	$25,451,097	40,874	489,922	51,953	591,465	17,854	202,136	Total.
433,711	1,414,734	67,985	288,997	22,265	95,184	952	4,327	941	3,213	246	1,402	Atoka.
550,073	10,480,108	68,267	1,435,894	23,788	449,010	501	8,220	776	10,675	175	2,038	Blaine.
1,017,066	5,267,681	196,745	881,681	41,561	275,050	1,097	6,588	1,209	6,004	617	4,062	Bryan.
946,473	20,324,932	98,462	2,524,650	29,056	771,831	312	14,661	1,041	18,587	188	6,209	Caddo.
607,352	3,048,842	93,145	501,576	28,846	192,802	1,113	6,217	1,188	5,270	535	2,740	Carter.
503,850	1,442,125	156,480	293,740	40,928	84,921	1,262	3,304	1,359	3,140	348	1,212	Cherokee.
636,980	1,631,199	116,639	288,578	31,697	89,141	1,466	3,712	1,371	2,527	475	1,588	Choctaw.
1,072,212	5,692,041	161,040	644,040	45,415	256,124	1,109	5,758	1,474	7,412	315	2,498	Craig.
508,795	2,960,305	70,071	321,256	23,738	137,349	492	3,874	865	4,818	271	1,603	Creek.
727,406	6,730,547	142,299	841,650	35,219	310,342	573	6,604	914	6,872	353	4,712	Garvin.
417,050	2,987,054	100,100	512,491	49,080	191,391	681	6,089	912	5,189	347	2,777	Hughes.
375,898	3,149,646	63,735	408,994	12,878	140,863	411	5,199	576	4,123	102	2,422	Johnston.
872,800	14,343,952	120,585	2,123,935	29,932	568,916	605	9,703	1,086	12,552	217	2,175	Kingfisher.
369,623	2,190,082	89,020	576,069	24,392	165,910	672	7,960	720	5,575	253	2,616	Le Flore.
1,065,970	10,734,767	172,760	2,385,311	34,211	457,919	755	12,063	1,062	13,236	480	3,734	Lincoln.
1,599,099	10,144,546	286,172	1,871,248	70,031	439,105	1,258	8,533	1,508	9,965	689	2,077	Logan.
311,226	1,851,442	67,375	272,789	13,717	101,826	446	2,974	482	2,708	150	1,684	Love.
810,812	669,833	127,847	177,169	31,761	60,238	2,202	3,375	1,681	1,732	516	1,030	McCurtain.
1,074,915	2,974,795	223,312	593,795	53,240	153,023	1,602	4,248	2,018	4,213	734	2,091	McIntosh
916,158	4,012,396	144,449	492,289	35,462	163,522	1,181	3,673	1,356	5,069	309	1,866	Mayes.

TABLE **72.**—STATISTICS OF AGRICULTURE FOR COLORED AND WHITE

COUNTY.	FARM ACREAGE: 1910.				ACREAGE AND YIELD OF COTTON: 1909.				ACREAGE AND YIELD OF CORN: 1909.			
	Total.		Improved.		Acreage.		Yield in bales.		Acreage.		Yield in bushels.	
	Colored farmers.	White farmers.	Colored farmers.	White farmers.	Colored farmers.	White farmers.	Colored farmers.	White farmers.	Colored farmers.	White farmers.	Colored farmers.	White farmers.
OKLAHOMA—Continued.												
Muskogee	102,804	218,087	71,275	146,247	10,973	17,045	3,705	7,018	27,303	57,232	412,352	1,099,234
Nowata	60,870	188,322	45,630	120,336					16,087	40,330	249,171	714,876
Okfuskee	77,047	155,781	47,819	84,012	18,341	23,402	7,450	10,206	10,801	27,899	225,738	548,714
Oklahoma	48,429	347,346	25,849	231,336	10,117	17,143	2,596	5,724	5,567	78,168	78,902	1,351,371
Okmulgee	67,396	267,473	38,681	93,824	9,760	6,907	3,958	2,977	13,188	44,633	225,507	783,928
Payne	11,982	412,030	8,663	253,435	4,180	44,754	1,669	16,698	3,032	91,359	68,552	1,785,292
Pittsburg	51,022	198,450	17,558	118,265	1,724	21,833	475	6,811	3,522	40,696	56,352	729,592
Pontotoc	23,441	217,714	11,409	135,983	1,834	28,309	492	8,986	2,688	50,969	41,067	847,371
Pottawatomie	23,283	424,090	12,964	248,830	4,931	70,762	1,778	25,536	4,236	88,727	81,430	1,718,302
Seminole	59,776	180,344	30,498	105,847	10,209	34,603	3,826	13,257	8,479	37,279	139,616	703,463
Sequoyah	48,257	142,642	27,815	105,663	8,459	37,524	2,956	11,871	8,350	35,629	178,185	715,278
Tulsa	26,043	238,582	15,819	148,851	766	3,632	344	1,633	6,881	83,516	148,990	1,830,230
Wagoner	94,138	176,333	71,590	127,974	17,150	11,555	8,249	5,641	12,985	60,967	213,591	984,076
All other counties	600,877	17,942,882	265,753	11,052,333	15,171	935,548	4,260	220,476	89,570	3,389,011	1,500,103	52,764,011
SOUTH CAROLINA.												
Total	3,940,476	9,571,552	2,598,224	3,499,775	1,364,375	1,192,092	612,953	666,913	653,856	911,976	7,309,064	13,562,882
Abbeville	193,467	184,777	109,225	76,413	66,325	30,767	22,153	12,787	18,427	14,508	161,276	180,875
Aiken	139,056	319,475	91,589	131,560	39,230	39,728	18,529	22,879	28,975	38,120	255,204	417,570
Anderson	146,423	298,183	105,139	155,407	65,630	67,713	25,199	30,682	19,830	34,659	198,723	464,541
Bamberg	84,265	108,186	60,896	50,123	31,503	14,390	15,907	7,954	18,676	13,085	220,360	172,308
Barnwell	143,775	264,922	113,430	147,166	53,163	45,213	23,430	24,548	33,635	36,522	315,847	450,774
Beaufort	87,541	101,373	60,501	27,676	16,747	3,298	6,343	1,939	18,117	4,944	241,691	98,501
Berkeley	86,502	262,014	47,091	40,079	21,086	9,663	11,132	6,283	14,976	9,061	239,614	151,581
Calhoun	56,654	120,360	43,891	55,187	23,224	19,154	12,043	13,893	12,264	13,070	131,839	258,119
Charleston	48,395	129,261	29,966	36,496	12,781	6,575	6,044	4,417	6,151	4,333	112,482	104,165
Cherokee	43,391	173,215	27,394	71,138	13,940	25,376	5,323	10,946	6,545	19,442	72,425	290,550
Chester	135,861	176,890	81,269	74,864	41,813	20,082	14,978	9,271	19,771	14,159	150,093	159,067
Chesterfield	49,928	321,771	29,212	79,988	14,533	30,247	8,545	20,110	8,138	27,359	93,153	350,985
Clarendon	97,440	158,496	75,962	69,068	39,560	24,644	20,030	16,974	21,283	18,493	291,736	349,222
Colleton	77,847	393,166	42,862	107,635	16,162	21,752	7,094	12,306	15,572	31,188	205,668	505,579
Darlington	74,616	180,817	65,048	79,565	36,909	37,367	20,802	25,610	14,890	20,436	242,761	500,281
Dillon	51,805	123,671	40,348	50,448	26,419	23,841	22,237	19,465	7,650	12,738	161,477	299,970
Dorchester	45,735	150,556	24,216	41,486	9,970	13,364	4,677	8,259	7,977	12,217	100,970	197,737
Edgefield	137,883	158,474	96,709	65,499	51,692	21,998	20,364	11,759	21,711	15,003	205,058	202,272
Fairfield	194,286	203,599	104,749	76,200	52,865	22,762	15,897	9,486	20,908	14,208	153,784	173,247
Florence	74,514	229,785	50,258	78,011	25,662	30,928	13,619	22,443	12,678	20,834	166,338	419,123
Georgetown	19,223	207,650	5,198	18,175	1,074	3,616	469	1,943	2,064	6,189	28,134	93,524
Greenville	76,599	339,196	52,182	143,624	26,073	46,401	9,469	20,810	14,572	42,609	130,672	511,093
Greenwood	126,191	162,758	84,946	65,548	53,100	24,195	19,151	11,140	16,728	14,334	168,602	208,805
Hampton	94,004	304,250	59,284	100,319	20,916	20,540	10,343	12,678	20,912	27,063	260,551	400,356
Horry	24,597	402,725	9,208	79,041	2,457	15,315	1,210	8,303	3,342	29,381	44,450	413,407
Kershaw	90,916	224,597	48,921	66,152	26,516	25,642	9,982	14,192	12,960	18,379	120,682	262,397
Lancaster	77,457	195,999	50,066	76,611	26,729	25,385	10,907	13,302	11,378	17,298	115,951	236,199
Laurens	156,540	223,823	93,943	103,817	57,394	44,435	20,275	18,291	16,691	20,378	147,251	258,942
Lee	75,279	143,899	59,765	62,371	38,671	31,384	20,778	21,462	13,215	15,646	191,489	320,407
Lexington	60,160	391,560	36,992	121,768	16,694	29,643	7,696	17,094	10,122	38,708	102,815	467,366
Marion	38,930	162,229	24,467	54,818	11,892	20,003	7,842	15,015	6,635	13,462	89,329	247,643
Marlboro	93,852	136,500	76,097	51,877	55,459	30,560	47,315	27,257	14,682	13,869	309,127	345,475
Newberry	106,538	209,817	67,636	86,480	41,124	34,538	15,432	16,529	13,898	19,445	114,192	227,230
Oconee	42,735	295,143	21,626	84,300	10,658	26,165	3,877	11,395	6,056	27,513	60,015	356,273
Orangeburg	168,161	359,200	125,738	163,752	67,194	61,859	31,949	39,143	34,001	42,952	396,283	716,580
Pickens	25,459	224,684	16,708	89,563	7,802	26,419	3,027	11,833	5,342	27,595	52,546	334,485
Richland	58,778	148,783	44,993	54,062	23,247	14,012	9,097	8,379	12,061	15,250	126,044	240,239
Saluda	74,074	180,175	51,787	75,912	27,516	25,807	12,770	14,763	12,457	19,018	132,609	251,569
Spartanburg	100,478	344,799	68,102	174,389	34,976	64,879	14,405	30,633	17,045	45,845	184,579	672,026
Sumter	102,723	165,767	77,209	72,654	40,399	27,328	16,575	16,064	20,320	17,791	227,635	327,161
Union	99,316	152,000	58,792	52,289	30,540	17,710	9,778	7,175	16,269	14,785	126,900	151,499
Williamsburg	121,027	294,885	72,105	84,495	34,027	31,567	15,611	19,740	22,674	25,380	255,365	429,316
York	138,655	242,122	92,704	103,749	50,703	35,827	20,649	17,831	22,258	24,707	203,344	344,423
All other counties												
TENNESSEE.												
Total	1,606,078	18,435,579	1,162,276	9,728,208	387,527	399,989	116,874	147,688	354,996	2,791,352	6,331,010	61,351,479
Bedford	15,881	275,792	12,152	188,155	176	634	62	242	4,548	54,641	94,570	1,221,315
Carroll	35,771	303,148	21,418	135,901	7,569	22,066	2,525	7,431	7,185	45,653	132,531	916,228
Cheatham	5,530	138,229	3,141	60,610		6		5	1,221	19,680	30,167	536,954
Chester	11,310	146,757	7,266	57,970	2,344	9,326	652	2,859	2,233	18,024	28,781	277,911
Crockett	18,895	126,718	16,131	93,491	5,673	16,633	2,067	6,367	5,022	27,019	113,264	645,474
Davidson	14,711	274,694	9,984	154,985	3	125	2	37	3,702	36,570	88,293	1,072,279
Decatur	5,326	169,611	3,051	58,859	768	7,212	290	2,578	1,350	22,750	26,550	448,674
Dickson	13,112	235,934	6,274	101,726					2,577	29,224	56,181	704,061
Dyer	16,083	186,634	13,456	137,359	5,001	28,411	2,305	13,968	4,938	45,797	124,587	1,479,809
Fayette	202,124	155,893	153,381	93,491	71,658	15,836	15,423	3,951	41,576	17,854	387,011	231,315

FARMERS, BY COUNTIES, FOR SOUTHERN STATES: 1909–1910—Continued.

| VALUE OF LAND, BUILDINGS, IMPLEMENTS, AND MACHINERY: 1910. | | | | | | NUMBER OF DAIRY COWS, WORK HORSES, AND WORK MULES: 1910. | | | | | | COUNTY. |
| Land. | | Buildings. | | Implements and machinery. | | Dairy cows. | | Work horses. | | Work mules. | | |
Colored farmers.	White farmers.	Colored farmers.	White farmers.	Colored farmers.	White farmers.	Colored farmers.	White farmers.	Colored farmers.	White farmers.	Colored farmers.	White farmers.	
						OKLAHOMA—Continued.						
$3,730,558	$6,232,282	$515,143	$702,233	$107,507	$191,687	3,522	5,086	3,301	4,990	1,324	2,836	Muskogee.
1,297,976	3,060,487	181,900	380,283	40,405	92,910	1,159	3,216	1,845	4,313	371	1,227	Nowata.
1,054,218	2,113,636	140,335	277,963	57,658	112,135	1,300	3,130	1,730	3,690	1,132	1,469	Okfuskee.
1,521,649	22,415,226	135,867	2,202,394	26,734	475,103	580	8,269	835	9,127	354	2,351	Oklahoma.
1,721,690	4,173,383	180,973	328,657	70,143	126,775	1,156	3,309	1,572	3,677	979	1,452	Okmulgee.
347,790	10,302,456	42,680	1,766,080	10,165	445,712	146	11,271	266	11,966	85	2,703	Payne.
539,275	3,223,941	95,360	643,026	22,550	187,188	708	7,966	753	6,280	230	2,484	Pittsburg.
314,276	3,192,343	59,159	571,906	11,617	197,870	345	6,618	442	5,236	109	2,857	Pontotoc.
554,289	10,753,495	86,286	1,973,740	21,539	433,903	270	9,133	524	9,952	296	4,667	Pottawatomie.
691,855	2,049,118	119,835	318,278	40,512	149,340	1,418	5,150	1,855	4,471	579	2,280	Seminole.
805,975	2,163,378	182,710	472,210	42,276	140,689	1,405	5,323	1,306	3,852	711	2,658	Sequoyah.
894,847	6,158,767	109,287	562,690	27,756	205,060	569	4,454	899	5,696	177	2,191	Tulsa.
2,367,157	4,375,206	208,443	413,137	74,782	165,112	1,689	3,168	2,168	3,980	1,258	2,108	Wagoner.
10,312,726	415,830,173	1,535,577	55,311,764	406,908	17,422,546	7,917	286,747	11,918	381,355	2,929	120,317	All other counties.
						SOUTH CAROLINA.						
$84,046,645	$184,728,209	$14,953,109	$49,160,118	$3,368,463	$10,740,390	70,886	109,956	27,075	49,896	61,761	93,045	Total.
2,982,934	3,305,522	545,611	1,199,050	110,842	219,469	3,344	3,025	747	1,164	2,711	2,005	Abbeville.
2,048,006	4,572,632	470,130	1,423,745	106,061	352,485	1,603	2,343	564	1,388	2,139	2,893	Aiken.
5,292,818	11,843,576	738,211	3,547,720	119,887	644,800	3,061	6,521	586	2,404	2,348	5,273	Anderson.
1,661,635	1,864,469	276,985	458,802	64,196	129,882	892	819	345	576	1,504	1,089	Bamberg.
2,202,390	4,025,380	448,665	1,133,130	102,859	291,347	1,842	1,587	778	1,789	2,016	2,175	Barnwell.
1,264,051	852,759	486,886	209,593	109,750	66,444	3,840	2,144	2,095	478	285	446	Beaufort.
1,043,019	1,842,678	421,205	430,613	125,036	100,345	3,031	2,380	1,039	736	827	758	Berkeley.
1,105,270	2,605,809	220,923	580,108	52,319	174,931	666	799	381	690	932	1,234	Calhoun.
1,183,028	2,373,913	402,106	486,110	87,695	129,487	1,695	1,333	1,803	612	535	640	Charleston.
896,500	3,440,453	164,735	868,371	36,608	182,169	1,163	3,325	137	645	987	2,535	Cherokee.
1,733,598	2,380,599	411,028	986,250	89,953	170,955	2,690	2,287	381	779	2,458	1,463	Chester.
786,698	3,663,458	143,607	796,239	44,981	226,021	684	2,169	249	824	994	2,757	Chesterfield.
2,608,224	3,816,415	442,750	947,853	120,035	193,560	2,006	1,439	879	946	1,623	1,801	Clarendon.
909,540	3,929,652	289,372	1,024,913	72,525	327,409	1,953	4,597	1,050	1,962	713	2,134	Colleton.
2,851,104	5,662,289	443,010	1,259,755	109,175	296,912	917	1,646	809	1,397	1,684	2,424	Darlington.
2,832,845	4,978,966	319,145	1,012,535	97,516	257,281	437	785	308	744	1,073	1,836	Dillon.
564,230	1,603,528	192,709	553,566	34,809	107,499	855	1,328	515	772	572	957	Dorchester.
2,363,886	2,928,399	461,178	1,181,070	125,256	274,025	2,686	2,429	917	1,226	2,473	1,589	Edgefield.
1,751,831	2,104,662	360,189	797,075	100,805	172,962	2,856	2,355	354	713	2,777	1,557	Fairfield.
2,012,647	6,227,197	307,645	1,383,916	88,137	280,002	959	1,730	722	1,253	1,330	2,287	Florence.
144,709	1,142,339	49,961	320,190	12,806	88,252	418	1,414	76	459	43	433	Georgetown.
3,079,632	10,578,778	337,169	2,497,345	64,996	531,540	1,875	7,012	456	2,519	1,249	3,912	Greenville.
2,563,497	3,437,517	599,097	1,356,625	91,333	230,753	2,412	2,505	673	1,173	2,156	2,023	Greenwood.
1,091,816	2,830,425	336,439	851,292	78,564	193,430	1,359	1,861	934	1,259	1,011	1,550	Hampton.
285,174	3,564,636	69,213	812,096	13,106	187,058	339	2,966	103	617	282	2,837	Horry.
833,970	2,224,993	190,161	619,420	58,828	167,913	1,380	1,906	593	900	1,148	1,695	Kershaw.
1,178,770	3,231,394	245,491	772,193	49,145	195,340	1,502	2,311	348	876	1,445	2,143	Lancaster.
2,839,742	4,671,434	478,812	1,625,375	76,582	292,453	2,489	3,522	414	1,464	2,750	3,013	Laurens.
3,355,717	5,353,481	329,835	1,162,421	91,638	226,313	866	1,108	485	940	1,639	2,011	Lee.
1,099,216	5,939,596	203,084	1,814,986	45,654	374,284	684	3,269	292	1,733	941	3,352	Lexington.
888,869	3,341,403	134,783	635,859	36,018	151,281	369	1,193	430	654	544	1,535	Marion.
6,013,694	6,139,937	537,595	1,505,640	138,266	332,041	912	1,026	802	1,160	2,175	2,132	Marlboro.
1,881,675	3,892,408	333,372	1,302,208	56,411	246,169	1,515	2,220	226	832	1,698	2,608	Newberry.
635,921	4,337,317	142,995	1,119,012	19,060	204,346	833	4,172	176	1,335	579	2,430	Oconee.
4,055,624	8,173,147	689,266	2,057,521	167,108	527,733	2,406	3,166	1,802	2,920	2,377	2,889	Orangeburg.
911,830	6,134,371	115,900	1,299,667	18,987	251,348	617	3,699	118	1,238	390	2,658	Pickens.
1,272,898	3,145,691	246,343	815,733	60,902	178,027	1,128	1,587	485	689	895	1,239	Richland.
1,656,341	3,685,564	320,600	1,264,666	59,005	274,857	1,401	2,462	383	1,276	1,429	2,250	Saluda.
3,514,382	12,531,952	434,265	2,722,800	71,927	572,882	2,308	7,373	386	2,187	1,807	5,682	Spartanburg.
2,806,110	4,871,482	470,377	1,012,245	120,123	209,592	1,759	1,233	989	1,032	1,534	1,675	Sumter.
1,080,712	1,936,203	260,925	607,365	53,516	142,252	1,792	2,123	292	581	1,629	1,347	Union.
1,856,945	4,417,630	402,776	1,156,747	108,835	252,890	1,926	2,667	1,377	1,583	1,289	2,264	Williamsburg.
2,905,147	5,124,155	498,560	1,548,298	77,208	311,655	3,416	4,120	576	1,371	2,770	3,514	York.
....	....	....	....	....	....	....	....	....	....	....	....	All other counties.
						TENNESSEE.						
$35,244,393	$336,171,390	$6,948,173	$102,158,631	$1,821,238	$19,470,933	42,522	354,582	30,097	270,230	28,526	211,756	Total.
422,262	7,649,438	96,285	2,540,144	19,338	433,233	382	5,583	411	6,802	213	4,016	Bedford.
428,197	3,006,482	99,434	1,268,175	28,606	287,366	701	4,531	553	4,438	535	3,537	Carroll.
73,814	1,678,332	21,907	646,010	4,719	124,231	109	1,635	83	1,353	88	1,643	Cheatham.
124,365	1,008,576	26,411	404,302	8,929	97,799	234	2,021	151	1,818	226	1,221	Chester.
475,975	2,962,155	104,465	1,192,261	29,059	249,997	612	3,433	633	4,193	356	2,200	Crockett.
822,271	15,938,360	206,691	4,932,010	37,103	717,028	628	10,862	552	6,688	282	3,396	Davidson.
60,486	1,252,657	12,295	438,045	3,178	95,258	118	1,942	44	1,152	99	1,905	Decatur.
137,820	2,159,761	47,630	952,170	11,454	178,144	245	3,278	141	1,949	229	2,359	Dickson.
557,043	6,892,046	91,632	1,573,137	20,835	369,692	477	5,119	403	4,647	396	4,591	Dyer.
2,341,432	1,748,875	561,086	733,026	189,988	164,439	5,688	2,992	3,305	2,406	3,578	1,669	Fayette.

TABLE **72.**—STATISTICS OF AGRICULTURE FOR COLORED AND WHITE

COUNTY.	FARM ACREAGE: 1910.				ACREAGE AND YIELD OF COTTON: 1909.				ACREAGE AND YIELD OF CORN: 1909.			
	Total.		Improved.		Acreage.		Yield in bales.		Acreage.		Yield in bushels.	
	Colored farmers.	White farmers.	Colored farmers.	White farmers.	Colored farmers.	White farmers.	Colored farmers.	White farmers.	Colored farmers.	White farmers.	Colored farmers.	White farmers.

TENNESSEE—Continued.

Franklin	7,277	219,211	5,147	124,747	118	608	25	159	1,991	40,122	29,335	738,968
Gibson	37,450	303,855	30,590	214,671	10,177	32,079	3,393	12,477	9,022	62,697	188,654	1,609,867
Giles	44,826	312,896	35,979	207,245	8,142	10,826	2,279	3,473	14,696	63,715	328,661	1,535,162
Greene	3,176	351,245	2,609	248,425					745	50,387	18,208	1,013,489
Hamilton	5,242	117,667	3,298	64,417	67	119	12	35	1,250	17,676	14,278	298,081
Hardeman	91,594	254,834	55,999	90,762	23,762	16,613	4,998	4,323	15,800	26,656	183,125	346,011
Hardin	11,418	264,731	8,392	100,032	2,215	15,943	694	4,690	3,899	39,890	84,571	814,053
Hawkins	4,649	292,783	3,061	173,407					1,101	35,014	19,429	761,919
Haywood	136,538	113,077	109,551	73,880	48,551	12,560	14,669	4,370	30,053	16,808	451,181	344,756
Henderson	18,845	287,066	8,301	115,776	2,250	17,673	617	5,882	2,828	37,969	41,988	671,472
Henry	28,929	313,654	18,185	163,559	2,487	6,673	574	1,780	5,966	43,151	125,650	963,249
Hickman	8,125	242,682	4,390	86,409	9	3	2	1	1,961	31,848	48,369	849,869
Knox	6,198	279,146	4,226	186,625					1,288	36,521	19,302	737,431
Lake	7,731	50,678	7,451	40,748	5,816	24,418	3,346	13,531	1,273	11,325	35,660	347,080
Lauderdale	77,434	137,268	50,514	69,923	26,421	19,500	10,650	9,105	13,626	20,337	324,697	557,140
Lincoln	21,219	301,594	17,115	178,744	2,398	8,701	714	2,739	7,682	61,040	187,774	1,478,690
McMinn	5,583	257,878	3,155	142,923	157	3,407	38	905	1,020	31,842	10,412	456,411
McNairy	10,370	269,384	4,988	88,502	1,538	17,650	345	4,644	1,980	35,162	21,199	523,529
Macon	4,554	180,409	3,009	91,076					825	28,275	18,730	595,723
Madison	95,065	213,592	62,231	106,001	25,031	16,463	6,738	5,157	18,659	30,804	285,448	584,292
Marshall	10,720	216,819	7,904	129,249	103	61	28	17	3,743	40,180	80,596	969,415
Maury	26,085	339,236	18,818	220,807	160	342	43	90	8,663	66,035	203,280	1,750,716
Monroe	5,509	249,738	3,924	128,511		424		90	1,180	33,507	17,745	534,082
Montgomery	45,177	279,534	33,258	180,200					9,889	41,195	199,387	1,003,026
Obion	8,160	299,461	7,079	209,406	382	8,075	152	3,262	3,649	83,343	125,166	2,879,991
Robertson	30,408	265,243	25,881	196,681					6,697	36,744	142,428	816,431
Rutherford	43,872	319,951	31,118	190,094	9,297	10,016	3,635	3,966	12,558	60,190	227,053	1,384,674
Shelby	195,020	149,650	164,031	97,454	87,778	19,321	26,004	6,849	38,352	21,946	538,214	404,303
Smith	5,988	196,940	4,440	117,070					1,892	37,753	53,123	1,067,536
Stewart	16,903	182,736	5,545	86,088					1,772	29,519	36,410	720,279
Sumner	11,954	313,136	8,268	208,834					2,879	49,345	76,980	1,373,142
Tipton	84,921	152,957	69,770	96,186	36,309	33,225	14,244	14,499	17,656	26,380	387,097	680,642
Trousdale	5,125	63,977	3,421	39,159					1,224	12,528	28,917	325,061
Warren	6,294	234,581	4,341	126,858		12		3	1,805	39,464	30,131	709,090
Weakley	11,179	321,630	8,282	215,868	673	11,372	220	3,894	2,957	65,745	67,421	1,571,892
Williamson	21,617	301,551	15,359	172,023	47	7	19	3	6,239	45,380	149,079	1,197,997
Wilson	19,680	334,962	12,000	179,820	16	68	2	26	4,404	50,585	102,798	1,329,882
All other counties	92,500	7,436,417	54,362	3,493,481	431	13,581	107	4,280	19,420	1,013,062	346,579	19,872,108

TEXAS.

Total	4,283,663	108,151,404	2,776,513	24,584,153	1,358,209	8,571,970	341,884	2,113,290	738,924	4,391,128	10,906,429	64,592,266
Anderson	107,492	268,437	64,503	107,583	22,727	25,946	5,931	7,754	18,181	28,314	211,202	393,256
Austin	34,545	305,476	25,234	139,214	13,762	35,970	3,173	10,939	6,462	27,358	133,918	641,106
Bastrop	79,731	316,027	54,499	102,729	36,401	48,408	7,291	10,722	11,549	26,690	113,344	323,274
Bell	12,839	555,464	10,499	338,012	6,501	183,716	2,004	56,046	2,394	75,782	32,903	1,120,461
Bowie	69,371	264,794	50,109	111,007	19,896	31,411	5,273	8,358	15,179	37,555	268,554	661,400
Brazoria	32,525	215,987	19,771	51,850	5,344	1,929	385	193	9,174	7,230	133,888	130,186
Brazos	64,960	223,767	48,313	89,573	29,858	42,417	8,041	13,412	11,577	22,444	222,665	468,137
Burleson	97,505	244,465	49,464	81,091	28,872	37,916	9,136	9,558	12,392	20,924	269,750	363,003
Caldwell	42,483	244,095	28,580	139,061	19,101	93,746	4,795	30,978	4,793	24,278	46,292	331,667
Camp	40,751	67,228	26,745	36,297	11,873	12,161	3,300	3,678	8,078	11,018	113,243	173,619
Cass	96,229	301,503	56,316	129,377	23,139	33,387	5,048	8,649	18,524	39,416	200,278	541,835
Chambers	12,712	167,854	1,717	52,108	3	162	2	61	503	2,373	9,166	49,863
Cherokee	64,673	280,221	42,830	142,358	13,993	24,968	3,645	7,128	13,246	42,702	186,242	680,656
Collin	7,581	494,274	6,951	420,630	3,184	161,772	1,018	55,237	2,738	142,918	41,182	2,697,945
Colorado	33,900	350,019	24,007	143,859	12,264	29,934	1,268	4,065	6,796	25,936	126,733	540,522
Dallas	29,010	463,878	25,531	327,770	14,191	136,173	3,555	34,157	5,606	67,574	73,193	886,504
De Witt	28,741	517,114	18,863	145,050	11,045	71,105	2,905	23,543	5,103	39,873	84,190	856,935
Denton	17,425	522,955	12,326	331,139	6,058	107,496	1,310	24,173	3,165	88,179	32,963	905,657
Ellis	31,551	507,588	29,004	417,190	21,853	252,813	6,831	70,310	3,691	58,882	57,461	857,806
Falls	77,143	329,915	69,186	221,030	40,312	118,657	11,336	39,686	14,678	52,283	274,364	1,055,783
Fannin	30,203	447,593	24,577	346,079	13,025	142,873	3,215	44,163	7,284	113,722	133,667	2,432,805
Fayette	54,996	466,133	34,327	165,362	19,068	70,736	3,261	15,288	8,583	48,075	154,769	1,011,468
Fort Bend	69,737	239,917	50,034	90,721	25,760	22,323	4,877	4,411	14,927	22,944	305,965	573,404
Franklin	6,216	135,631	5,295	70,730	2,119	19,790	610	5,528	1,563	19,105	24,672	339,847
Freestone	108,134	215,872	64,474	87,103	31,874	34,227	6,941	7,970	17,902	24,213	218,415	333,505
Goliad	22,440	366,328	5,448	72,535	2,541	32,493	638	8,725	1,634	18,988	21,915	293,930
Gonzales	76,472	545,731	48,848	169,409	29,932	87,746	6,561	22,344	10,131	44,914	132,092	685,392
Grayson	13,766	539,761	11,918	390,907	4,774	104,588	1,439	29,449	3,555	128,348	62,995	2,311,270
Gregg	62,584	71,802	38,588	31,650	16,042	7,943	3,872	2,134	10,862	6,565	95,702	69,007
Grimes	69,061	251,318	48,124	107,185	24,833	32,535	5,654	8,330	14,383	22,856	234,772	388,089
Guadalupe	52,021	325,086	31,735	169,664	17,284	82,983	3,809	31,457	7,080	41,744	68,308	570,107
Harris	19,624	381,025	11,268	136,904	1,526	7,162	318	1,937	2,120	18,702	33,784	406,446
Harrison	217,825	220,732	145,030	113,551	54,253	18,407	13,373	4,789	34,318	17,260	353,748	210,411
Hays	6,741	344,085	4,936	87,341	3,365	50,410	196	17,906	936	16,221	23,646	309,607
Henderson	45,017	315,202	25,577	129,553	9,734	37,691	2,269	9,893	7,760	38,346	01,388	571,557

FARMERS, BY COUNTIES, FOR SOUTHERN STATES: 1909–1910—Continued.

VALUE OF LAND, BUILDINGS, IMPLEMENTS, AND MACHINERY: 1910.						NUMBER OF DAIRY COWS, WORK HORSES, AND WORK MULES: 1910.						
Land.		Buildings.		Implements and machinery.		Dairy cows.		Work horses.		Work mules.		COUNTY.
Colored farmers.	White farmers.	Colored farmers.	White farmers.	Colored farmers.	White farmers.	Colored farmers.	White farmers.	Colored farmers.	White farmers.	Colored farmers.	White farmers.	

TENNESSEE—Continued.

$130,031	$3,124,529	$27,715	$1,028,687	$10,028	$252,108	188	4,060	187	3,430	94	2,422	Franklin.
915,235	7,695,082	184,881	2,688,478	40,993	499,078	951	6,799	914	8,460	718	5,282	Gibson.
1,135,947	7,246,200	216,568	2,337,089	44,275	365,732	1,190	6,042	1,029	6,402	816	4,409	Giles.
76,879	8,099,400	22,170	2,292,100	3,817	410,359	105	8,557	85	7,521	30	2,474	Greene.
106,055	3,252,990	33,913	924,625	6,281	150,980	194	3,751	96	1,646	68	1,135	Hamilton.
823,020	1,756,906	222,866	748,946	52,374	191,342	2,130	4,120	1,187	2,825	1,058	2,136	Hardeman.
208,030	2,399,664	48,480	743,912	11,807	186,442	258	3,827	138	2,500	292	3,630	Hardin.
108,370	5,516,280	20,085	1,278,066	4,456	230,796	120	5,943	77	4,510	38	1,683	Hawkins.
2,556,928	1,936,214	581,293	918,131	195,979	185,078	3,733	2,644	3,223	2,595	2,669	1,509	Haywood.
103,075	1,744,156	28,083	667,101	8,589	178,872	255	3,536	117	2,404	249	3,379	Henderson.
358,179	4,042,450	82,430	1,407,708	17,075	282,811	596	4,337	497	4,626	459	3,922	Henry.
112,650	2,621,261	30,764	749,410	9,096	156,423	170	2,921	94	1,784	170	2,830	Hickman.
176,577	8,926,582	59,100	3,084,969	10,765	562,713	184	9,617	121	4,994	74	2,802	Knox.
352,550	2,101,293	45,790	407,020	9,693	74,606	156	1,142	52	722	280	1,869	Lake.
1,872,458	3,391,013	295,225	1,077,637	98,781	233,163	1,723	2,857	1,288	2,538	1,450	2,210	Lauderdale.
641,387	7,351,159	83,068	1,849,481	19,426	345,302	511	5,713	426	5,237	415	4,909	Lincoln.
47,975	2,726,406	13,810	926,485	3,854	220,117	149	5,896	68	2,413	64	2,286	McMinn.
76,847	1,410,712	19,495	607,934	5,133	175,247	210	3,844	132	3,039	113	2,448	McNairy.
80,130	2,258,628	16,945	822,680	3,450	148,120	77	2,742	41	2,282	96	2,559	Macon.
1,415,785	3,201,159	295,372	1,196,993	94,088	256,836	2,293	4,205	1,566	3,591	1,578	2,260	Madison.
259,241	5,559,046	49,590	1,644,318	9,636	285,320	307	4,876	262	5,822	160	3,611	Marshall.
829,887	12,302,240	172,384	3,247,110	41,210	584,464	795	6,850	759	7,018	588	5,921	Maury.
89,155	3,217,716	22,285	1,008,905	6,475	236,244	149	5,088	72	2,510	77	1,960	Monroe.
651,931	4,412,012	194,970	1,883,629	34,834	305,881	903	3,982	502	2,954	880	4,564	Montgomery.
420,770	10,504,278	68,870	2,473,497	15,653	486,778	197	5,422	193	6,659	164	5,202	Obion.
747,038	5,681,613	192,695	2,294,351	34,338	436,120	571	3,478	381	3,604	535	3,775	Robertson.
1,278,196	8,187,444	218,105	2,558,715	52,222	440,947	1,305	7,483	1,122	7,306	577	4,594	Rutherford.
8,389,761	11,281,034	1,174,821	2,595,980	311,522	422,809	6,618	8,644	3,638	3,816	4,487	2,688	Shelby.
195,595	5,615,179	27,365	1,499,600	3,642	212,811	131	3,884	127	4,567	115	3,680	Smith.
148,897	1,794,350	25,563	619,325	6,472	141,034	214	2,954	88	1,528	189	3,039	Stewart.
230,199	7,651,459	71,681	2,408,022	11,310	372,232	371	6,221	345	6,507	216	3,622	Sumner.
2,294,579	3,999,596	462,264	1,385,164	147,590	321,239	2,534	4,149	2,077	3,535	1,593	3,078	Tipton.
117,845	1,597,787	26,930	508,740	3,434	76,197	130	1,268	109	1,559	126	1,080	Trousdale.
86,703	2,719,727	21,351	910,582	5,052	211,397	154	3,382	107	3,176	82	2,231	Warren.
253,678	6,579,945	60,770	2,224,307	11,943	431,602	235	5,912	268	8,073	204	5,262	Weakley.
649,569	8,940,851	110,665	2,364,730	29,053	432,860	658	5,660	576	5,283	422	4,575	Williamson.
447,022	7,825,042	114,220	2,368,468	17,317	373,704	696	7,633	558	7,694	242	4,323	Wilson.
1,412,554	103,166,305	337,755	29,726,447	76,447	5,875,982	2,167	133,747	1,299	79,654	1,136	65,860	All other counties.

TEXAS.

$78,742,082	$1,554,465,053	$12,846,866	$197,154,394	$3,273,931	$53,516,329	100,136	913,731	73,857	947,304	69,079	548,077	Total.
808,307	2,207,422	242,030	731,635	55,020	173,569	2,470	5,882	1,126	2,887	1,393	1,987	Anderson.
800,437	5,006,603	146,740	1,614,704	23,450	303,283	1,078	10,190	1,095	5,657	715	2,880	Austin.
1,483,776	4,745,616	224,235	882,744	61,534	206,918	1,822	5,899	1,469	3,788	1,698	3,364	Bastrop.
758,815	27,669,218	60,760	3,375,768	22,295	862,503	199	9,371	266	8,950	314	10,008	Bell.
1,148,161	2,974,356	282,282	1,013,167	45,703	189,216	2,041	6,851	1,222	3,780	1,310	2,292	Bowie.
915,088	5,203,820	129,228	825,218	28,196	224,445	1,160	3,184	1,419	3,057	690	1,541	Brazoria.
1,305,519	4,362,300	227,427	802,918	62,178	266,544	1,326	4,937	958	2,663	1,428	2,461	Brazos.
1,654,260	3,811,777	207,814	678,759	51,000	222,292	1,456	4,561	975	2,605	1,449	1,746	Burleson.
1,279,376	10,432,029	135,275	1,407,705	49,377	422,832	946	5,231	778	4,044	934	5,335	Caldwell.
471,553	796,472	108,745	375,512	23,688	63,296	800	1,723	476	1,026	716	806	Camp.
717,366	2,212,308	253,286	1,074,581	40,682	225,690	2,155	5,954	919	3,231	1,110	2,316	Cass.
129,855	2,134,993	26,680	329,015	4,008	131,394	166	791	304	1,688	54	963	Chambers
681,978	3,833,224	170,236	1,110,807	46,657	286,384	1,915	8,251	863	3,389	941	2,993	Cherokee.
438,425	25,035,798	36,290	3,554,392	9,863	884,874	103	8,160	122	9,595	143	10,883	Collin.
846,716	5,648,111	140,295	1,174,155	33,161	341,561	853	7,485	871	5,253	802	3,181	Colorado.
1,663,407	27,555,726	142,238	3,615,166	35,384	712,937	456	11,216	573	9,202	810	8,732	Dallas.
838,450	13,906,869	93,028	1,571,545	24,309	337,602	693	11,006	681	7,618	484	4,241	De Witt.
495,475	17,673,503	78,255	2,841,376	16,847	627,426	247	7,907	308	9,839	311	6,762	Denton.
1,981,515	30,320,017	141,610	3,781,472	36,790	862,986	311	7,743	347	8,424	1,026	12,797	Ellis.
3,163,515	15,224,857	333,015	2,086,790	83,809	503,843	1,407	6,392	1,659	6,943	1,829	6,419	Falls.
813,247	14,675,552	120,460	3,054,592	32,683	763,152	488	8,092	514	8,700	666	8,524	Fannin.
1,073,456	8,885,629	185,070	2,232,244	45,625	486,709	1,405	15,801	1,173	8,933	903	4,208	Fayette.
2,267,985	6,978,210	285,970	981,133	67,821	476,182	2,022	3,992	2,844	3,036	2,082	3,429	Fort Bend.
88,668	1,520,220	17,537	586,971	4,492	131,183	145	3,210	109	2,365	115	1,184	Franklin.
1,058,245	2,161,845	288,208	709,709	62,498	134,084	2,272	4,583	1,437	2,881	1,379	1,800	Freestone.
285,617	5,991,116	28,790	548,623	9,956	145,962	300	4,386	366	4,201	176	2,394	Goliad.
1,499,497	11,648,872	210,513	1,638,050	59,863	378,135	1,597	11,053	1,712	7,854	970	4,940	Gonzales.
530,499	19,476,914	82,751	3,856,732	17,534	804,597	250	11,387	317	9,782	270	8,598	Grayson.
576,085	697,265	199,638	349,959	36,811	58,475	1,368	1,495	694	656	793	533	Gregg.
794,622	2,466,380	165,345	620,747	47,978	202,562	2,086	5,998	1,312	3,423	1,026	1,566	Grimes.
1,387,733	13,747,138	144,144	2,293,288	40,956	397,037	990	7,651	986	5,942	1,018	5,537	Guadalupe.
784,761	12,424,048	92,205	1,918,330	58,183	471,541	473	8,239	789	8,279	265	2,696	Harris.
1,841,073	2,076,663	548,710	710,718	114,005	155,065	5,749	4,232	2,595	1,537	2,682	1,415	Harrison.
464,220	7,634,393	53,295	937,261	15,460	245,251	149	3,691	201	3,812	228	3,555	Hays.
391,520	3,030,610	92,805	1,029,098	25,075	265,148	1,071	7,699	611	4,035	553	2,425	Henderson.

TABLE **72.**—STATISTICS OF AGRICULTURE FOR COLORED AND WHITE

COUNTY.	FARM ACREAGE: 1910.				ACREAGE AND YIELD OF COTTON: 1909.				ACREAGE AND YIELD OF CORN: 1909.			
	Total.		Improved.		Acreage.		Yield in bales.		Acreage.		Yield in bushels.	
	Colored farmers.	White farmers.	Colored farmers.	White farmers.	Colored farmers.	White farmers.	Colored farmers.	White farmers.	Colored farmers.	White farmers.	Colored farmers.	White farmers.
TEXAS—Continued.												
Hill	16,044	526,745	13,391	394,795	9,116	238,030	2,344	64,390	2,632	75,142	34,190	968,619
Hopkins	19,792	422,236	14,994	238,516	6,983	86,863	1,975	22,145	4,314	68,611	66,873	1,021,873
Houston	103,821	299,414	63,789	129,582	25,241	40,123	7,224	12,235	17,234	32,446	214,825	461,770
Hunt	16,909	447,889	13,693	330,234	9,164	181,503	2,301	53,595	3,095	91,347	44,482	1,507,584
Jackson	40,926	948,641	13,576	244,494	3,416	4,401	460	748	3,733	7,394	57,481	114,712
Jasper	18,617	82,293	6,544	15,688	805	766	144	203	3,089	5,814	32,651	94,581
Kaufman	54,728	399,661	44,062	226,146	29,965	119,370	7,670	33,553	6,881	50,749	91,129	731,389
Lamar	57,048	411,628	49,219	264,560	27,780	114,314	8,154	37,154	14,871	82,470	324,976	1,790,224
Lavaca	34,948	460,025	17,821	142,932	8,897	72,058	1,085	16,714	5,386	43,293	85,195	983,266
Lee	53,899	230,483	25,136	70,641	14,526	30,109	2,847	7,260	6,052	19,003	78,658	263,441
Leon	73,017	281,596	43,821	94,604	18,723	25,664	5,307	7,697	12,201	20,345	166,418	314,265
Liberty	10,615	92,565	5,616	29,871	730	1,355	189	461	2,852	8,945	49,611	179,260
Limestone	63,643	422,407	50,619	264,450	32,337	162,756	8,928	49,389	11,543	54,423	203,310	1,272,835
McLennan	64,517	532,837	55,109	388,434	37,310	202,130	11,061	57,714	11,302	71,721	215,981	1,168,326
Madison	33,513	195,943	20,142	68,643	9,832	25,887	2,303	6,778	5,862	18,952	83,667	319,650
Marion	69,851	69,574	35,883	21,073	14,108	4,776	3,300	1,365	10,717	5,160	109,590	68,949
Matagorda	16,580	248,763	10,856	143,998	749	899	34	80	6,662	5,264	54,008	65,716
Milam	72,648	428,810	59,989	233,150	37,432	125,346	10,584	35,706	13,972	61,150	297,743	1,326,878
Montgomery	39,239	131,367	24,682	37,552	9,772	7,109	2,207	1,842	7,715	12,086	112,786	196,151
Morris	28,594	83,551	19,419	33,249	8,891	12,587	2,168	3,537	6,212	11,959	84,152	195,072
Nacogdoches	47,589	293,195	28,488	123,395	10,274	30,047	2,759	8,412	10,076	38,381	126,874	541,044
Navarro	68,864	492,651	54,730	322,984	35,782	183,710	9,172	49,984	12,642	78,449	218,117	1,259,350
Newton	22,125	79,478	7,502	12,963	937	596	277	173	3,540	5,592	42,237	82,499
Panola	92,653	220,168	60,336	104,265	24,094	29,086	5,962	8,458	16,053	24,957	163,571	322,005
Polk	29,632	166,175	14,943	31,525	5,412	4,305	1,847	1,466	5,766	12,095	88,997	182,159
Rains	7,088	96,443	4,214	50,255	1,837	19,800	464	4,255	1,272	14,340	19,095	173,522
Red River	67,180	340,544	51,052	172,594	21,388	51,741	5,086	15,400	19,910	55,290	397,041	1,104,575
Robertson	124,015	233,760	98,667	102,365	67,729	49,115	19,616	13,746	19,864	30,184	359,399	528,171
Rusk	135,452	316,174	82,123	157,601	29,440	35,188	7,150	9,225	23,570	37,218	241,718	460,465
Sabine	14,087	91,442	8,450	30,830	3,269	6,501	677	1,479	2,648	8,711	28,651	112,233
San Augustine	27,694	110,074	16,419	42,090	5,873	10,225	1,625	2,851	5,974	13,315	70,875	178,541
San Jacinto	37,713	79,263	20,436	23,300	6,702	3,398	2,476	1,366	7,638	7,253	109,133	105,527
Shelby	33,293	269,336	21,117	123,236	7,957	34,703	2,224	10,257	6,432	36,150	78,014	501,502
Smith	165,493	281,685	113,418	153,389	48,159	38,964	12,522	11,632	30,849	37,203	316,456	505,923
Tarrant	7,264	460,147	5,278	256,950	2,206	73,732	336	11,244	981	40,569	7,981	364,620
Titus	17,716	188,203	11,862	93,139	5,495	30,190	1,404	8,463	3,964	29,883	62,586	545,536
Travis	48,157	455,119	39,803	194,270	27,266	112,305	8,963	42,958	6,391	35,978	108,578	706,780
Trinity	13,276	107,296	6,217	36,967	2,079	9,793	564	2,934	2,094	11,819	23,818	174,048
Tyler	11,972	113,154	3,401	24,347	461	2,744	108	750	1,528	10,837	16,998	162,321
Upshur	55,692	194,461	33,514	93,923	14,429	29,136	4,063	9,692	9,868	26,132	106,398	360,069
Van Zandt	17,408	413,986	10,119	213,183	4,075	79,452	926	18,812	2,795	60,091	35,403	850,643
Victoria	21,139	421,838	10,307	72,997	4,554	27,213	1,324	8,747	3,411	18,902	66,810	396,548
Walker	59,574	123,077	37,488	44,221	17,212	13,886	4,310	3,663	9,428	9,870	120,329	153,160
Waller	45,376	147,651	37,238	70,922	17,214	12,834	3,797	3,102	10,558	16,013	233,293	342,875
Washington	83,824	260,458	62,254	116,697	33,267	47,275	8,656	13,864	15,574	29,461	336,528	747,958
Wharton	48,386	306,689	38,397	175,239	15,807	18,397	1,174	1,500	15,748	26,026	322,769	638,031
Williamson	21,315	640,331	14,673	348,593	10,200	209,346	3,141	65,580	1,959	60,232	28,682	1,005,358
Wilson	10,001	391,296	5,549	134,422	2,444	60,097	568	13,229	1,236	31,052	9,830	270,048
Wood	26,972	247,504	17,560	128,416	6,876	38,036	1,800	12,330	5,586	37,240	64,693	535,324
All other counties	202,760	82,386,101	57,970	12,060,841	23,487	3,652,095	4,328	712,181	8,377	1,377,879	96,480	14,070,410
VIRGINIA.												
Total	2,238,220	17,257,416	1,111,208	8,758,850	13,362	11,785	5,051	5,429	338,378	1,521,981	4,966,904	33,328,237
Accomac	43,804	141,734	20,976	62,140	....	....	....	....	8,212	24,115	138,928	504,510
Albemarle	25,239	361,252	13,586	213,244	....	....	....	....	3,465	27,742	53,966	655,615
Amelia	45,515	143,527	19,052	46,979	....	....	....	....	5,303	8,026	66,293	138,641
Amherst	44,691	213,682	22,330	100,977	....	....	....	....	4,373	12,960	91,175	317,388
Appomattox	25,225	149,116	11,536	62,713	....	....	....	....	1,886	8,166	29,291	143,467
Augusta	5,988	385,754	4,476	280,771	....	....	....	....	897	37,198	20,496	1,150,019
Bedford	41,445	385,266	22,931	213,916	....	....	....	....	4,367	26,898	81,553	627,404
Botetourt	4,655	194,248	2,590	109,235	....	....	....	....	604	12,834	11,026	354,197
Brunswick	70,008	212,012	30,648	74,438	2,926	3,418	1,136	1,506	8,356	13,852	103,932	241,421
Buckingham	53,865	229,950	23,460	86,676	....	....	....	....	5,439	13,691	68,908	248,941
Campbell	40,086	234,653	20,736	106,989	....	....	....	....	4,296	16,489	64,123	320,364
Caroline	59,400	248,899	30,032	111,214	....	....	....	....	12,387	24,681	143,311	372,714
Charles City	21,700	58,849	9,977	24,446	....	....	....	....	5,094	6,536	77,449	129,779
Charlotte	52,135	209,086	22,832	71,877	....	....	....	....	7,061	13,225	107,018	264,879
Chesterfield	18,558	166,174	7,286	57,761	10	....	2	....	2,680	12,864	38,552	275,285
Culpeper	17,204	200,733	12,497	142,253	....	....	....	....	3,323	22,036	56,539	476,470
Cumberland	46,209	116,215	20,400	46,495	....	....	....	....	5,846	8,611	60,028	130,959
Dinwiddie	80,566	184,007	32,575	66,815	77	97	45	55	8,391	11,660	124,223	214,066
Elizabeth City	2,043	16,872	1,662	11,678	....	....	....	....	718	2,888	9,386	55,015
Essex	35,147	109,452	18,800	49,700	....	....	....	....	7,253	12,302	91,325	208,661
Fairfax	8,524	182,471	5,960	110,266	....	....	....	....	1,563	21,091	28,644	526,519
Fauquier	23,407	358,675	15,932	266,085	....	....	....	....	3,778	41,245	62,250	930,151
Floyd	4,861	232,267	3,407	156,184	....	....	....	....	527	16,220	9,932	352,487
Fluvanna	16,739	134,815	7,579	55,832	....	....	....	....	2,318	9,499	29,402	165,314
Franklin	41,119	370,403	18,447	157,161	....	....	....	....	4,336	26,071	70,272	534,093

FARMERS, BY COUNTIES, FOR SOUTHERN STATES: 1909-1910—Continued.

VALUE OF LAND, BUILDINGS, IMPLEMENTS, AND MACHINERY: 1910.						NUMBER OF DAIRY COWS, WORK HORSES, AND WORK MULES: 1910.						COUNTY.
Land.		Buildings.		Implements and machinery.		Dairy cows.		Work horses.		Work mules.		
Colored farmers.	White farmers.	Colored farmers.	White farmers.	Colored farmers.	White farmers.	Colored farmers.	White farmers.	Colored farmers.	White farmers.	Colored farmers.	White farmers.	

TEXAS—Continued.

$726,875	$25,737,348	$63,420	$3,679,681	$20,452	$869,552	231	8,665	284	9,300	421	11,519	Hill.
284,425	6,549,070	68,425	2,002,021	17,045	415,619	443	8,802	416	8,400	253	4,021	Hopkins.
919,211	2,402,526	207,540	933,886	52,554	200,412	3,277	8,439	1,267	3,386	994	2,114	Houston.
535,680	15,120,707	72,350	3,166,930	18,990	782,911	295	7,876	352	9,211	380	8,387	Hunt.
843,620	12,151,920	58,635	510,285	16,163	292,453	538	2,117	767	2,991	153	1,235	Jackson.
114,465	672,290	72,473	407,275	7,943	54,405	520	3,167	291	971	127	232	Jasper.
1,684,877	11,328,330	192,935	1,946,811	47,982	463,230	727	6,803	601	6,334	1,284	6,059	Kaufman.
1,721,062	10,592,664	249,505	2,570,194	57,772	563,454	1,075	7,772	919	6,554	1,359	8,117	Lamar.
603,710	11,287,290	105,119	1,866,008	18,876	410,661	895	13,895	737	9,497	226	2,998	Lavaca.
607,698	2,056,129	134,739	584,390	42,195	165,416	1,428	6,684	773	2,816	398	1,730	Lee.
673,432	2,120,541	148,650	580,429	32,909	125,151	1,888	6,190	944	2,777	979	1,470	Leon.
143,780	1,244,892	30,970	263,970	8,224	89,809	527	2,779	674	3,200	84	661	Liberty.
1,823,556	13,233,732	214,263	2,219,512	73,309	642,774	969	7,760	1,162	7,615	1,449	7,858	Limestone.
2,961,896	25,404,878	348,304	3,636,060	86,585	960,100	1,084	9,351	1,033	8,456	1,806	11,848	McLennan.
320,793	1,753,697	57,710	413,814	11,626	88,582	915	3,962	507	2,395	357	1,142	Madison.
618,410	508,651	223,004	170,720	72,429	39,741	1,986	1,151	843	544	711	385	Marion.
541,890	6,899,976	70,635	703,495	30,293	351,846	640	1,616	750	2,025	580	3,144	Matagorda.
1,812,010	11,029,238	210,304	1,742,642	60,179	502,481	1,078	8,835	1,125	6,970	1,954	6,905	Milam.
393,481	1,041,983	138,270	382,425	30,463	88,568	1,337	4,291	947	1,976	535	688	Montgomery.
272,142	825,719	97,050	417,116	21,098	88,902	684	2,086	469	1,234	390	823	Morris.
405,419	2,424,298	118,242	1,118,070	22,956	207,714	1,104	6,980	695	3,467	566	2,580	Nacogdoches.
2,133,644	16,581,917	248,004	2,481,541	69,526	695,144	1,066	8,347	1,608	10,083	1,446	8,000	Navarro.
142,165	531,019	75,520	217,110	12,726	36,216	614	1,647	403	761	117	206	Newton.
647,427	1,457,254	161,549	608,854	42,366	144,397	2,542	6,903	1,011	2,284	1,040	1,615	Panola.
252,420	922,073	93,522	383,422	18,002	86,903	1,429	3,706	853	1,875	327	513	Polk.
114,720	1,172,455	22,755	326,265	7,301	97,092	167	2,087	132	1,804	105	896	Rains.
1,268,776	5,017,934	232,216	1,326,521	59,357	332,167	2,075	7,525	1,562	5,436	1,095	4,120	Red River.
2,708,449	2,880,690	448,695	799,795	92,061	251,335	2,275	6,949	1,485	3,357	2,736	2,976	Robertson.
933,286	2,158,639	280,260	961,819	69,343	273,791	3,371	8,093	1,452	3,341	1,667	2,923	Rusk.
110,699	660,199	30,010	243,530	6,750	53,148	467	2,773	207	869	142	602	Sabine.
241,618	791,469	50,760	272,426	16,048	80,980	832	3,339	459	1,491	286	841	San Augustine.
287,606	541,918	79,734	143,509	15,721	35,072	1,621	2,964	1,184	1,245	381	413	San Jacinto.
309,032	2,044,704	94,675	965,755	20,217	211,190	1,330	8,650	474	2,909	353	2,305	Shelby.
1,563,254	3,365,034	391,515	1,364,286	98,159	299,374	3,745	7,638	1,924	4,019	2,344	2,722	Smith.
339,845	19,813,138	43,400	2,602,703	6,797	545,580	132	8,844	168	7,619	170	5,909	Tarrant.
194,266	1,964,854	49,212	735,913	10,546	159,790	431	4,902	268	2,927	278	1,865	Titus.
2,508,024	16,995,752	214,921	2,616,467	64,795	640,141	981	8,857	1,039	6,729	1,397	7,042	Travis.
120,871	731,810	38,815	354,770	11,033	85,865	480	3,920	223	1,746	146	615	Trinity.
66,070	646,257	25,090	307,121	5,587	60,002	312	2,845	152	1,209	77	563	Tyler.
436,853	1,432,436	117,806	693,302	35,497	184,795	1,540	5,476	558	2,314	774	2,051	Upshur.
198,864	4,941,296	60,180	1,460,649	11,011	391,951	401	8,926	218	6,767	190	3,488	Van Zandt.
799,496	11,153,575	48,927	768,352	14,598	218,059	472	5,587	602	4,662	417	2,710	Victoria.
540,221	914,953	137,343	297,771	31,588	73,799	2,108	3,765	1,306	1,678	511	798	Walker.
849,445	2,203,805	184,070	527,904	44,810	171,990	1,532	3,498	1,840	3,072	963	1,317	Waller.
1,743,099	5,281,458	363,063	1,576,161	109,142	389,736	2,117	8,338	1,965	4,711	1,627	2,919	Washington.
2,090,706	10,622,988	254,016	1,239,812	103,330	805,243	1,501	5,025	1,901	4,171	1,810	5,450	Wharton.
1,190,234	32,787,458	74,714	3,530,694	27,809	934,455	299	11,196	389	10,319	452	10,353	Williamson.
166,715	6,855,935	25,330	998,694	5,060	203,927	171	5,623	198	5,612	88	2,698	Wilson.
258,081	2,265,874	76,360	999,606	14,251	203,381	740	6,590	440	3,594	314	2,205	Wood.
3,078,542	909,172,406	346,951	84,719,024	107,656	25,482,347	1,775	385,784	2,189	561,054	1,537	241,535	All other counties.

VIRGINIA.

$32,553,640	$362,105,272	$12,670,864	$124,728,286	$1,852,503	$16,263,380	42,242	314,042	38,905	249,954	8,783	47,233	Total.
2,228,385	6,428,634	445,335	2,063,516	72,119	310,325	499	2,172	1,422	3,918	248	944	Accomac.
472,225	7,960,739	280,021	4,307,115	24,808	388,931	653	6,782	608	5,426	63	964	Albemarle.
347,352	1,403,862	179,645	614,145	27,328	82,524	741	1,487	551	946	191	429	Amelia.
495,659	2,643,029	196,812	1,272,183	25,012	157,965	987	3,383	794	3,027	21	129	Amherst.
230,005	1,145,707	102,300	657,439	18,143	109,944	385	1,855	308	1,548	34	181	Appomattox.
196,820	15,575,481	68,795	5,200,985	8,549	750,928	167	8,178	209	10,186	5	298	Augusta.
514,751	5,526,459	173,591	2,200,647	27,037	299,902	1,012	7,444	827	6,038	114	660	Bedford.
93,625	4,630,696	53,105	1,634,710	6,362	248,918	138	4,178	141	3,516	5	209	Botetourt.
769,797	1,535,805	248,900	715,566	49,997	104,831	1,135	2,397	824	1,498	221	659	Brunswick.
426,359	1,961,499	248,312	877,438	37,628	114,794	832	2,255	654	1,895	166	466	Buckingham.
453,934	2,841,469	203,698	1,489,613	28,473	182,424	885	3,891	584	2,664	160	734	Campbell.
527,525	2,613,028	278,021	1,215,753	42,176	179,862	1,148	3,079	880	2,156	316	1,094	Caroline.
241,807	614,218	183,435	316,894	26,191	42,458	433	740	177	400	199	417	Charles City.
587,948	1,863,542	265,744	934,555	40,271	115,265	842	2,305	709	1,784	126	576	Charlotte.
389,524	4,390,372	137,412	1,812,915	20,499	195,596	529	3,196	347	1,985	132	841	Chesterfield.
344,471	5,216,547	184,726	1,787,685	24,200	230,322	705	5,347	636	3,564	55	642	Culpeper.
360,487	1,131,799	174,311	680,481	21,977	80,884	708	1,478	515	1,045	166	440	Cumberland.
1,246,689	2,513,107	417,453	1,070,360	63,778	142,773	1,308	2,711	733	1,678	207	618	Dinwiddie.
109,883	1,328,297	28,920	452,325	3,828	41,450	59	787	103	385	9	141	Elizabeth City.
367,453	1,096,839	239,795	510,770	28,433	63,806	706	1,706	770	1,243	67	452	Essex.
404,449	7,364,292	178,755	3,693,662	22,916	464,435	336	7,115	406	4,677	8	198	Fairfax.
467,040	9,697,164	195,700	3,301,349	25,356	383,913	773	7,136	865	7,814	13	323	Fauquier.
93,720	4,723,970	18,370	1,123,191	1,913	159,492	147	5,893	64	3,065	9	229	Floyd.
162,254	1,320,426	69,887	783,166	11,480	83,851	424	2,117	241	1,330	69	540	Fluvanna.
337,870	3,520,630	102,165	1,505,038	23,032	251,221	781	6,626	404	3,997	225	1,205	Franklin.

TABLE **72.**—STATISTICS OF AGRICULTURE FOR COLORED AND WHITE

COUNTY.	FARM ACREAGE: 1910.				ACREAGE AND YIELD OF COTTON: 1909.				ACREAGE AND YIELD OF CORN: 1909.			
	Total.		Improved.		Acreage.		Yield in bales.		Acreage.		Yield in bushels.	
	Colored farmers.	White farmers.	Colored farmers.	White farmers.	Colored farmers.	White farmers.	Colored farmers.	White farmers.	Colored farmers.	White farmers.	Colored farmers.	White farmers.
VIRGINIA—Continued.												
Gloucester	18,972	94,761	11,771	43,934					6,096	13,070	85,642	236,213
Goochland	28,751	114,413	12,223	47,434					3,735	9,949	40,789	192,529
Greene	2,503	85,022	1,836	47,902					565	8,114	14,678	222,484
Greensville	40,458	88,339	20,518	27,410	3,214	1,824	1,098	827	6,344	5,376	52,462	61,673
Halifax	117,810	380,663	64,451	172,090					13,157	26,207	236,913	545,653
Hanover	32,072	209,564	15,585	97,330		1			5,392	23,639	71,783	399,190
Henrico	8,905	101,818	3,614	53,697					1,142	11,588	15,246	264,184
Henry	45,714	173,913	22,739	75,465					4,382	11,716	80,432	231,342
Isle of Wight	22,942	131,043	11,472	51,517	27	154	7	72	4,312	17,160	65,121	317,265
James City	6,743	48,696	2,918	17,823					1,598	4,374	19,023	99,486
King and Queen	37,646	116,656	18,893	46,929					7,172	13,078	98,514	188,931
King George	14,991	89,433	9,730	53,027					5,176	14,938	85,434	296,096
King William	23,023	110,217	12,218	49,030					6,261	12,141	76,057	182,441
Lancaster	11,527	44,353	6,389	22,192					2,582	6,766	47,257	142,166
Loudoun	6,947	302,787	5,438	246,179					1,370	40,534	23,342	1,096,042
Louisa	48,572	186,798	20,972	80,573					5,957	14,747	70,366	234,085
Lunenburg	53,935	156,399	20,070	54,158		1		1	5,715	10,497	93,149	199,251
Madison	10,124	160,741	6,450	98,432					1,746	15,824	33,796	444,358
Mathews	2,833	40,372	2,032	23,103					948	8,586	17,426	184,130
Mecklenburg	90,493	272,129	44,255	97,016	1,558	997	592	525	11,287	19,561	166,558	358,528
Middlesex	16,136	54,261	8,851	25,521					3,862	7,589	53,384	157,037
Montgomery	4,043	206,760	2,569	121,097					588	13,897	11,699	397,474
Nansemond	33,870	145,294	16,752	57,576	698	1,300	312	578	5,763	18,553	89,073	342,027
Nelson	23,271	217,553	13,181	100,661					3,500	14,081	69,642	341,431
New Kent	16,783	88,763	7,471	23,096					3,448	6,034	42,615	105,536
Norfolk	15,870	103,660	11,177	56,206	504	829	136	313	6,944	22,165	85,018	403,004
Northampton	20,564	62,872	12,371	33,288					5,694	12,693	111,126	360,288
Northumberland	16,443	79,192	8,574	43,021					3,251	11,738	55,109	278,862
Nottoway	38,767	112,097	15,428	38,246					5,627	7,674	82,897	149,429
Orange	14,590	176,452	8,162	101,324					2,399	17,116	40,003	394,327
Patrick	10,446	260,701	4,955	98,648					1,508	19,303	22,446	319,647
Pittsylvania	110,805	490,007	56,755	223,975					10,521	34,516	178,633	663,426
Powhatan	24,193	107,913	10,724	41,295					3,880	8,130	55,984	146,703
Prince Edward	52,140	128,521	20,458	45,719					5,276	8,233	69,323	149,337
Prince George	27,811	101,452	14,570	47,820	2	2	(1)	1	4,149	10,492	52,049	175,104
Prince William	9,854	160,377	6,247	93,933					1,644	17,282	26,039	323,612
Princess Anne	15,423	86,697	11,383	51,849	53	75	13	45	7,198	26,994	86,728	346,581
Pulaski	2,066	139,915	1,240	97,567					359	11,736	8,474	415,614
Rappahannock	7,247	148,785	5,728	96,176					1,413	11,610	26,112	300,320
Richmond	14,705	79,893	7,443	35,596					2,745	9,518	37,270	193,416
Roanoke	3,520	127,485	1,903	72,952					524	11,059	10,462	286,497
Southampton	82,984	250,721	42,614	85,042	3,402	2,726	1,410	1,314	14,277	22,079	159,334	312,974
Spotsylvania	29,239	157,866	13,155	66,458					4,568	14,237	53,593	248,917
Stafford	8,219	113,266	4,321	55,508					1,533	12,969	19,892	236,845
Surry	30,302	84,876	11,058	28,411					5,257	7,481	71,923	135,947
Sussex	63,293	139,200	28,935	47,352	891	361	300	192	8,048	9,270	96,819	146,440
Warwick	4,061	17,886	2,310	6,684					1,161	2,215	24,561	49,568
Westmoreland	34,337	84,198	19,054	42,408					6,233	10,578	108,559	250,931
York	10,034	40,557	6,254	16,973					4,106	6,065	66,159	94,626
All other counties	44,110	5,141,962	24,284						5,492	417,909	119,968	10,367,911
WEST VIRGINIA.												
Total	34,541	9,991,901	20,257	5,501,500					4,421	671,890	105,814	17,013,283

[1] Less than 1 bale.

FARMERS, BY COUNTIES, FOR SOUTHERN STATES: 1909–1910—Continued.

VALUE OF LAND, BUILDINGS, IMPLEMENTS, AND MACHINERY: 1910.						NUMBER OF DAIRY COWS, WORK HORSES, AND WORK MULES: 1910.						COUNTY.
Land.		Buildings.		Implements and machinery.		Dairy cows.		Work horses.		Work mules.		
Colored farmers.	White farmers.	Colored farmers.	White farmers.	Colored farmers.	White farmers.	Colored farmers.	White farmers.	Colored farmers.	White farmers.	Colored farmers.	White farmers.	
						VIRGINIA—Continued.						
$370,341	$2,104,917	$284,381	$1,256,045	$29,982	$132,457	629	1,890	855	1,890	17	292	Gloucester.
239,203	1,384,720	132,205	615,816	26,567	95,238	757	1,933	434	1,205	118	493	Goochland.
40,400	1,049,945	22,150	459,825	2,387	78,786	102	1,882	81	1,512	3	239	Greene.
465,800	810,743	174,392	271,160	36,364	46,279	529	702	416	625	229	178	Greensville.
1,430,294	4,650,602	477,345	1,988,714	82,088	288,228	2,065	5,035	1,691	4,025	428	1,466	Halifax.
334,051	2,606,740	187,274	1,401,950	27,320	208,014	794	3,710	651	2,543	209	1,296	Hanover.
329,985	7,469,114	100,485	2,079,060	14,413	285,451	273	4,558	239	1,984	102	897	Henrico.
376,940	1,643,880	110,810	641,300	18,257	106,201	684	2,323	258	1,170	225	908	Henry.
379,753	2,004,476	118,915	929,351	18,054	107,567	234	1,530	488	1,702	161	677	Isle of Wight.
96,531	1,253,189	38,079	253,530	5,273	30,455	121	536	160	503	16	213	James City.
252,795	851,022	210,675	462,200	40,028	57,703	729	1,909	813	1,373	66	350	King and Queen.
306,840	1,577,755	107,220	565,675	13,367	73,908	370	1,781	435	1,419	38	345	King George.
212,718	1,207,722	113,397	518,880	18,245	64,333	557	1,520	596	1,165	106	515	King William.
187,635	752,115	140,690	605,115	14,211	54,335	300	876	496	1,145	8	31	Lancaster.
185,335	9,874,749	129,068	4,587,810	9,769	505,172	276	8,824	329	8,745	2	151	Loudoun.
455,057	2,134,822	270,605	1,241,939	36,841	138,098	1,130	3,225	721	1,895	235	716	Louisa.
612,363	1,437,390	260,352	821,090	32,942	94,329	874	1,797	549	1,154	266	619	Lunenburg.
153,725	2,528,902	90,120	1,074,023	11,614	159,867	394	3,681	302	2,758	13	264	Madison.
123,870	1,738,889	87,780	1,150,823	7,357	98,452	121	1,299	148	1,308	2	64	Mathews.
1,038,219	2,671,194	423,202	1,411,550	52,321	146,841	1,667	3,556	1,223	2,620	353	1,101	Mecklenburg.
298,600	1,258,866	228,215	688,325	20,567	80,020	436	1,034	569	1,142	25	149	Middlesex.
127,825	5,592,413	43,990	1,337,171	6,024	156,233	194	4,109	112	2,991	12	155	Montgomery.
655,839	2,696,010	249,796	1,167,370	31,407	168,548	331	1,689	684	1,941	154	861	Nansemond.
286,995	2,400,304	111,510	1,059,035	9,730	121,809	512	2,990	450	2,610	36	302	Nelson.
177,044	1,070,377	73,805	254,665	11,448	36,412	394	828	308	575	90	233	New Kent.
652,558	6,467,833	126,802	1,285,360	20,193	200,349	243	2,074	333	1,333	244	1,279	Norfolk.
1,145,566	3,357,978	285,094	1,198,976	39,883	165,481	213	822	1,071	2,152	68	441	Northampton.
258,601	1,352,679	133,435	888,865	20,003	105,245	267	1,779	525	1,943	6	95	Northumberland.
625,409	1,350,159	278,454	595,255	40,438	77,794	699	1,671	568	995	88	345	Nottoway.
204,151	3,692,676	109,165	1,603,799	14,702	218,202	453	3,778	487	2,803	42	732	Orange.
101,615	2,816,979	22,960	871,189	3,627	139,835	224	4,342	88	1,811	48	768	Patrick.
1,278,601	6,168,274	408,986	3,061,941	63,518	445,608	1,566	6,582	1,059	5,220	566	1,843	Pittsylvania.
241,587	1,513,405	150,953	845,435	20,201	196,873	519	1,368	389	924	137	367	Powhatan.
473,211	1,468,441	218,746	876,034	33,071	94,989	752	1,637	660	1,229	113	360	Prince Edward.
345,005	1,350,285	127,295	565,300	29,632	99,212	350	1,089	404	1,055	249	654	Prince George.
171,569	3,141,719	88,901	1,434,255	11,598	187,425	283	3,559	325	3,165	13	136	Prince William.
590,147	2,484,054	119,665	960,225	28,747	136,163	229	1,132	386	1,948	228	274	Princess Anne.
63,323	6,421,750	38,435	1,262,735	2,040	141,568	86	2,191	53	2,258	8	161	Pulaski.
96,420	2,504,987	52,735	846,578	6,820	124,356	269	2,551	206	2,281	25	346	Rappahannock.
140,675	743,391	64,610	481,155	7,851	62,966	287	1,437	280	1,318	8	62	Richmond.
107,670	4,924,652	23,631	1,412,479	4,538	192,838	137	3,313	95	2,426	7	279	Roanoke.
1,155,433	2,621,164	333,694	1,218,840	64,438	148,482	860	1,684	863	1,507	536	729	Southampton.
263,496	2,151,915	128,080	949,907	16,959	140,688	659	3,174	598	2,001	137	652	Spotsylvania.
70,579	1,381,007	46,340	712,016	4,702	103,021	177	2,383	166	1,754	17	319	Stafford.
527,087	1,128,078	162,860	596,277	26,075	79,444	359	788	599	920	59	279	Surry.
614,408	1,493,860	254,637	602,180	49,110	113,088	571	1,080	774	1,279	277	332	Sussex.
390,015	454,050	51,610	253,850	6,065	28,490	194	511	168	357	16	78	Warwick.
386,635	931,178	124,370	542,465	23,026	71,721	579	1,743	679	1,595	19	84	Westmoreland.
315,014	1,056,359	133,998	409,725	16,845	52,376	312	1,112	408	794	20	72	York.
1,326,675	139,309,932	323,739	34,189,522	40,339	4,415,616	1,148	104,767	941	81,101	109	10,642	All other counties.
						WEST VIRGINIA.						
$828,589	$206,247,170	$247,805	$57,067,390	$31,693	$6,979,820	1,111	238,428	888	158,669	81	10,719	Total.

TABLE 73.—STATISTICS OF SIZE OF FARMS AND FOR TENURE CLASSES OF FARMS

ALABAMA.

		The state.	Autauga.	Baldwin.	Barbour.	Bibb.	Bullock.	Butler.	Calhoun.	Chambers.	Cherokee.
1	Number of farms	110,443	2,111	325	2,805	647	4,056	2,034	706	2,771	355
	FARMS CLASSIFIED BY SIZE.										
2	Under 3 acres	22						1			
3	3 to 9 acres	9,229	623	56	50	32	102	157	36	36	5
4	10 to 19 acres	13,410	164	83	85	115	210	231	91	95	63
5	20 to 49 acres	57,766	851	127	1,359	335	2,428	1,019	404	1,551	190
6	50 to 99 acres	19,679	337	31	782	101	1,012	381	116	690	63
7	100 to 174 acres	7,288	100	24	357	50	228	162	45	318	28
8	175 to 259 acres	1,755	21	3	97	8	47	50	12	51	5
9	260 to 499 acres	1,086	12	1	54	5	27	31	1	27	
10	500 to 999 acres	173	3		16	1	2	2	1	3	1
11	1,000 acres and over	35			5						
	FARMERS CLASSIFIED BY TENURE.										
12	Owners, free	8,030	161	157	133	95	92	140	75	97	45
13	Owners, mortgaged	4,979	94	23	101	36	49	179	26	47	8
14	Part owners	4,073	49	55	66	38	25	57	63	26	30
15	Cash tenants	61,235	1,648	57	1,493	82	2,369	916	129	874	11
16	Share tenants	27,687	131	30	955	372	1,316	687	406	1,400	247
17	Share-cash tenants	1,289	8		17	9	132	37	1	201	2
18	Tenure not specified	3,098	19	3	40	15	72	18	5	126	12
19	Managers	52	1				1		1		
	FARMS OPERATED BY OWNERS, FREE.										
20	Total acreage	660,075	12,339	6,413	13,919	6,224	9,729	9,788	4,541	10,324	3,345
21	Improved acreage	283,558	5,817	1,784	7,806	2,552	6,142	4,392	1,781	5,147	1,402
22	Value of land	$5,924,448	$83,604	$88,677	$88,067	$41,040	$88,685	$90,695	$35,286	$112,027	$22,245
23	Value of buildings	$1,948,083	$28,526	$51,272	$24,385	$18,975	$22,905	$35,800	$12,850	$38,640	$6,945
24	Value of implements and machinery	$436,991	$5,352	$5,586	$9,768	$3,364	$6,860	$6,605	$2,996	$12,869	$1,815
25	Number of dairy cows	13,821	244	299	217	137	181	180	94	180	61
26	Number of work horses	4,673	65	150	28	43	63	63	28	60	16
27	Number of work mules	6,552	104	10	99	68	99	101	60	131	43
28	Acreage in cotton	110,385	2,043	434	2,685	777	2,112	1,846	751	2,266	554
29	Bales of cotton grown in 1909	31,263	501	127	734	214	429	501	243	798	174
30	Acreage in corn	71,442	1,762	540	2,124	777	1,515	1,257	502	1,205	375
31	Bushels of corn grown in 1909	733,340	11,785	7,600	17,501	7,442	9,062	10,566	4,772	12,127	3,589
	FARMS OPERATED BY OWNERS, MORTGAGED.										
32	Total acreage	498,567	9,399	994	14,078	2,804	4,320	16,150	2,233	5,613	910
33	Improved acreage	222,641	3,526	332	7,265	1,165	2,821	7,249	874	2,943	321
34	Value of land	$4,165,183	$67,321	$10,600	$99,404	$53,755	$41,675	$126,515	$18,650	$62,635	$6,355
35	Value of buildings	$1,184,847	$17,450	$4,900	$17,260	$8,655	$12,240	$51,490	$5,850	$23,675	$1,495
36	Value of implements and machinery	$293,036	$3,419	$814	$5,672	$1,362	$4,453	$12,423	$1,333	$6,215	$350
37	Number of dairy cows	8,420	125	53	163	51	108	281	38	98	11
38	Number of work horses	2,665	28	24	27	13	31	108	8	31	2
39	Number of work mules	5,236	74	6	127	30	49	136	30	71	10
40	Acreage in cotton	95,110	1,270	98	2,754	401	1,119	3,324	385	1,522	164
41	Bales of cotton grown in 1909	25,166	301	30	726	109	200	767	137	496	41
42	Acreage in corn	50,565	1,019	93	1,942	296	837	1,848	203	565	94
43	Bushels of corn grown in 1909	471,930	7,201	1,031	13,055	2,366	3,449	12,954	1,675	6,085	943
	FARMS OPERATED BY PART OWNERS.										
44	Total acreage	308,077	3,967	2,427	8,768	2,610	1,729	4,173	2,729	2,541	1,785
45	Owned acreage	184,120	2,526	1,690	5,405	1,670	765	2,854	1,434	1,046	1,095
46	Improved acreage	169,620	2,217	1,091	4,571	1,223	1,312	2,024	1,918	1,299	928
47	Owned improved acreage	79,751	1,211	464	2,316	524	575	1,093	649	469	334
48	Value of land	$3,217,875	$27,813	$23,209	$54,234	$29,165	$24,828	$40,510	$41,365	$35,810	$23,851
49	Value of buildings	$845,066	$9,225	$10,641	$12,015	$6,600	$4,875	$16,235	$10,750	$7,540	$4,670
50	Value of land and buildings owned	$2,371,987	$24,736	$24,242	$38,451	$21,325	$11,862	$38,537	$26,805	$19,180	$13,765
51	Value of implements and machinery	$206,535	$1,824	$1,651	$4,256	$1,102	$1,192	$2,909	$2,065	$1,390	$1,095
52	Number of dairy cows	6,922	78	116	104	62	44	79	62	37	38
53	Number of work horses	2,503	24	69	24	14	9	22	24	10	9
54	Number of work mules	4,345	48	11	81	55	19	55	65	40	28
55	Acreage in cotton	77,113	945	429	1,669	577	509	1,058	806	659	367
56	Bales of cotton grown in 1909	20,707	222	132	404	172	121	297	267	190	111
57	Acreage in corn	39,573	520	248	1,093	279	344	629	440	243	235
58	Bushels of corn grown in 1909	419,772	4,226	2,844	7,787	2,670	2,067	4,466	4,237	2,365	2,010
	FARMS OPERATED BY CASH TENANTS, INCLUDING TENURE NOT SPECIFIED.										
59	Total acreage	2,611,447	46,541	1,467	112,358	5,901	126,338	48,420	6,327	60,106	1,087
60	Improved acreage	2,037,433	40,833	899	72,300	2,574	106,790	31,717	4,090	40,280	726
61	Value of land	$32,106,811	$598,190	$20,512	$890,940	$65,399	$1,446,499	$499,150	$82,303	$813,131	$16,610
62	Value of buildings	$7,325,794	$174,088	$10,875	$215,190	$16,420	$299,146	$138,868	$16,757	$203,080	$3,325
63	Value of implements and machinery	$1,901,064	$24,429	$740	$53,351	$2,033	$80,663	$24,868	$6,015	$45,056	$940
64	Number of dairy cows	75,410	1,402	63	1,671	126	3,158	952	122	1,165	15
65	Number of work horses	21,292	273	47	207	27	695	195	38	258	9
66	Number of work mules	52,780	910	13	1,430	84	2,411	793	120	1,065	18
67	Acreage in cotton	1,208,159	25,788	371	36,171	1,085	60,611	17,562	1,772	23,829	392
68	Bales of cotton grown in 1909	296,807	6,767	103	8,498	329	11,557	4,746	578	7,410	135
69	Acreage in corn	444,842	8,919	192	21,375	721	27,614	7,893	972	8,627	208
70	Bushels of corn grown in 1909	4,657,492	80,830	2,382	141,555	6,550	167,618	71,938	8,884	82,354	1,925
	FARMS OPERATED BY SHARE AND SHARE-CASH TENANTS.										
71	Total acreage	995,787	4,588	568	51,043	11,679	53,180	24,268	14,574	78,351	8,945
72	Improved acreage	844,912	4,261	531	40,337	9,500	49,834	20,041	11,562	54,872	7,519
73	Value of land	$13,655,798	$67,448	$10,810	$480,668	$213,807	$611,731	$277,388	$218,542	$1,036,498	$141,138
74	Value of buildings	$3,130,093	$20,425	$4,495	$111,290	$45,719	$149,793	$87,862	$48,170	$266,198	$31,550
75	Value of implements and machinery	$479,126	$2,292	$658	$15,197	$4,668	$18,380	$9,090	$10,754	$48,439	$6,562
76	Number of dairy cows	21,741	83	29	593	280	1,054	458	357	1,407	228
77	Number of work horses	4,603	14	20	43	49	102	78	109	392	45
78	Number of work mules	18,073	98	11	817	325	874	447	331	1,279	219
79	Acreage in cotton	469,520	2,222	229	20,635	4,943	29,984	12,117	5,442	36,185	3,308
80	Bales of cotton grown in 1909	135,818	677	60	6,102	1,663	6,082	3,620	1,813	11,731	1,184
81	Acreage in corn	210,752	769	134	12,135	2,331	11,803	5,321	2,803	11,176	2,068
82	Bushels of corn grown in 1909	2,261,117	6,598	1,810	99,524	26,276	75,132	53,902	30,499	109,908	25,594

OPERATED BY COLORED FARMERS, BY COUNTIES, FOR SOUTHERN STATES: 1910.

ALABAMA—continued.

Chilton.	Choctaw.	Clarke.	Clay.	Coffee.	Colbert.	Conecuh.	Coosa.	Covington.	Crenshaw.	Dale.	Dallas.	Elmore.	Escambia.	Etowah.	
506	1,935	2,675	351	665	931	1,568	978	435	1,006	784	7,419	1,727	282	213	1
		1										1	1		2
20	109	368	14	18	21	197	25	16	39	16	1,180	119	30	21	3
61	346	591	73	32	85	200	86	27	53	50	1,220	278	60	25	4
242	901	1,070	177	357	477	789	389	223	576	418	3,832	883	118	87	5
108	264	338	52	156	252	249	249	102	214	164	928	285	47	53	6
57	194	183	28	74	75	92	166	54	83	91	186	110	22	24	7
13	62	65	6	20	9	31	40	9	29	29	47	29	2	2	8
3	49	46	1	8	12	9	22	4	11	15	20	19	2	1	9
2	10	9				1	1		1	1	3	2			10
		4									3	1			11
84	171	377	35	64	76	292	117	95	73	57	246	115	123	33	12
82	238	174	24	43	40	242	81	57	93	44	101	180	48	16	13
30	158	333	17	21	71	143	27	45	43	26	88	105	28	21	14
181	978	1,283	21	202	413	513	287	66	350	259	6,381	745	49	19	15
119	347	432	224	315	312	367	407	168	433	374	247	432	31	121	16
9	8	41	4	10	12	3	7	4	9	18	14	47		1	17
1	33	34	26	10	7	8	52		5	6	339	103	3	2	18
	2	1							4		3				19
5,925	20,200	41,785	2,635	6,262	4,787	17,560	12,893	7,467	7,552	5,704	15,867	10,938	5,811	2,423	20
2,247	6,182	13,082	1,128	3,200	2,883	8,104	4,359	2,625	2,976	2,789	8,636	4,708	1,868	945	21
$46,370	$102,635	$224,413	$15,835	$69,600	$75,850	$186,452	$64,375	$73,120	$67,228	$47,485	$185,446	$96,284	$51,420	$20,427	22
$24,140	$40,880	$83,713	$6,465	$14,295	$18,882	$69,500	$20,465	$21,400	$18,815	$9,625	$60,017	$32,505	$29,575	$7,615	23
$3,908	$7,011	$19,838	$1,747	$3,406	$4,756	$15,680	$6,460	$3,584	$3,509	$3,288	$13,716	$7,057	$4,590	$1,632	24
106	426	721	46	84	141	461	187	136	95	53	419	182	325	49	25
51	130	262	8	9	56	151	56	27	27	7	153	58	93	21	26
45	138	244	30	78	104	171	114	64	80	55	194	136	28	29	27
793	2,253	4,414	325	1,450	1,128	3,352	1,505	928	1,231	1,028	4,513	1,825	605	280	28
212	681	1,226	120	472	287	1,129	533	320	374	341	1,288	550	203	113	29
690	1,470	2,888	323	1,225	998	2,848	1,070	915	1,105	828	1,404	878	744	314	30
6,337	15,109	26,757	4,050	13,702	12,590	25,683	11,586	8,721	10,145	7,963	20,076	9,844	7,673	3,067	31
6,020	32,360	19,356	1,806	4,963	4,059	17,454	9,052	5,157	9,762	5,806	8,714	15,944	2,553	1,358	32
2,656	11,307	6,649	819	2,451	2,220	7,803	3,824	2,041	4,472	2,781	4,167	7,677	874	615	33
$49,155	$168,959	$111,767	$11,460	$49,515	$57,570	$177,596	$46,546	$50,882	$92,470	$37,330	$65,340	$149,607	$22,150	$15,285	34
$21,515	$53,405	$56,940	$4,550	$8,575	$12,550	$56,030	$14,750	$15,440	$22,225	$11,830	$17,370	$46,773	$9,690	$2,575	35
$6,089	$12,278	$7,967	$1,030	$2,490	$3,010	$13,699	$3,737	$2,688	$5,626	$3,970	$5,064	$10,360	$2,057	$895	36
117	490	342	35	50	82	348	134	78	126	47	176	227	85	21	37
45	174	121	8	4	29	111	34	12	20	5	51	69	29	7	38
53	241	127	26	61	60	180	99	53	137	51	112	182	27	24	39
1,015	4,238	2,678	315	1,224	912	3,528	1,604	792	1,928	1,227	2,164	3,254	317	172	40
268	1,105	705	108	414	205	1,102	468	264	567	425	507	929	112	48	41
743	2,238	1,351	246	731	669	2,460	823	575	1,344	711	716	1,457	303	151	42
6,537	22,155	12,706	2,324	7,435	7,758	21,336	8,052	4,815	12,492	7,601	9,963	15,651	2,894	1,730	43
2,396	14,763	34,662	1,038	1,917	5,029	8,634	2,858	3,373	3,145	2,121	4,677	7,200	1,265	971	44
1,684	10,133	16,332	580	1,099	2,669	5,259	1,950	2,372	1,781	1,388	2,598	3,342	926	634	45
1,159	5,673	11,548	536	1,357	3,534	5,108	1,191	1,787	1,975	1,282	3,545	4,182	734	556	46
610	2,482	5,577	249	652	1,618	2,215	744	1,007	952	621	1,621	1,683	399	249	47
$26,890	$89,739	$154,432	$11,255	$22,040	$69,085	$97,995	$14,965	$38,825	$30,459	$20,855	$61,868	$94,326	$20,280	$11,930	48
$6,375	$31,910	$53,230	$2,235	$4,150	$14,580	$29,895	$4,125	$9,110	$9,455	$3,950	$19,910	$33,060	$7,870	$2,150	49
$25,200	$83,240	$138,364	$6,515	$13,270	$48,265	$80,929	$12,490	$33,330	$24,905	$13,930	$51,439	$65,541	$16,043	$7,945	50
$1,145	$8,999	$11,351	$863	$1,225	$4,213	$7,922	$1,425	$2,195	$2,012	$1,980	$4,798	$5,368	$1,481	547	51
32	341	571	24	31	141	245	42	60	49	24	168	122	41	22	52
11	120	228	4	6	65	63	9	16	17	2	78	71	20	12	53
27	132	248	19	35	102	126	41	47	46	28	84	96	10	15	54
572	2,635	5,267		609	1,484	2,304	400	728	919	739	2,146	1,827	237	199	55
163	669	1,316		219	372	738	140	268	259	246	628	507	74	71	56
258	1,250	2,576	141	465	1,133	1,731	288	447	572	413	494	800	178	128	57
2,360	12,105	21,410	1,365	4,450	14,605	15,433	3,160	4,867	4,959	3,585	7,863	10,668	1,765	1,250	58
9,789	37,019	33,800	2,267	12,624	23,187	13,592	25,044	2,930	18,924	16,589	193,454	30,064	1,521	848	59
4,986	26,387	27,043	1,166	9,527	19,057	11,656	11,035	2,169	13,262	11,533	175,395	23,843	858	579	60
$87,905	$242,357	$290,988	$14,360	$141,453	$451,368	$157,377	$171,330	$33,045	$189,165	$173,953	$2,425,736	$443,302	$21,848	$15,355	61
$43,465	$106,398	$97,078	$4,955	$31,365	$59,355	$46,799	$40,865	$8,540	$48,455	$34,780	$721,034	$140,165	$7,715	$2,325	62
$5,903	$30,405	$20,023	$814	$7,105	$20,710	$11,235	$10,250	$2,043	$9,172	$9,922	$196,284	$22,711	$1,474	$656	63
190	1,203	1,166	44	167	617	409	413	70	348	187	7,804	744	52	16	64
72	492	518	12	24	276	175	113	14	77	28	1,932	267	34	12	65
119	574	589	23	225	559	254	285	61	334	275	4,800	583	12	15	66
2,157	14,294	14,809	448	4,610	8,788	5,585	4,877	998	6,749	5,703	122,796	14,123	390	197	67
592	3,589	3,828	163	1,486	2,156	1,734	1,621	336	1,862	1,949	30,045	4,050	111	62	68
1,342	6,037	6,452	352	2,910	6,301	4,050	2,656	589	4,018	3,270	27,068	4,954	244	127	69
11,687	57,268	66,627	3,960	28,924	80,176	33,376	31,163	6,335	33,555	35,411	398,936	59,111	2,528	1,153	70
5,399	7,797	11,022	7,547	14,396	11,068	9,605	18,179	6,756	15,348	18,643	6,203	15,066	1,002	4,871	71
3,411	7,365	9,509	5,806	12,452	10,123	8,106	10,708	6,251	14,312	15,573	6,051	12,544	775	3,759	72
$55,070	$58,731	$105,869	$92,507	$179,826	$191,544	$118,008	$126,690	$96,156	$191,185	$209,808	$102,835	$207,948	$17,400	$81,714	73
$19,830	$26,207	$41,301	$27,059	$40,657	$30,966	$36,540	$39,590	$20,810	$48,713	$42,420	$29,155	$60,590	$4,005	$13,485	74
$2,393	$2,333	$3,055	$4,909	$5,930	$8,279	$6,202	$5,611	$4,452	$5,222	$8,647	$3,130	$6,908	$1,005	$2,455	75
68	242	381	163	195	299	250	309	115	262	198	169	295	33	121	76
34	91	102	41	24	61	90	72	17	21	15	21	67	14	44	77
78	89	177	115	276	241	155	210	145	276	345	87	234	11	78	78
1,635	3,598	5,818	2,534	5,945	5,373	4,919	4,634	2,683	7,800	7,902	3,950	6,343	319	1,696	79
469	932	1,228	953	1,980	1,283	1,597	1,508	1,010	2,414	2,646	1,126	1,902	93	575	80
878	1,749	2,212	1,612	3,686	3,446	2,870	2,584	1,654	4,468	4,119	825	2,758	163	1,101	81
8,469	16,683	19,279	20,314	43,121	47,902	26,198	31,376	19,829	42,851	45,996	11,627	29,265	1,680	11,532	82

TABLE **73.**—STATISTICS OF SIZE OF FARMS AND FOR TENURE CLASSES OF FARMS

ALABAMA—continued.

		Fayette.	Franklin.	Geneva.	Greene.	Hale.	Henry.	Houston.	Jackson.	Jefferson.	Lamar.
1	Number of farms	309	118	365	3,536	3,553	1,574	853	394	462	520
	FARMS CLASSIFIED BY SIZE.										
2	Under 3 acres									5	
3	3 to 9 acres				336	301	29	30	17	119	7
4	10 to 19 acres	4	5	6	620	615	39	47	71	122	72
5	20 to 49 acres	63	13	13	1,816	1,950	886	522	224	158	220
6	50 to 99 acres	152	63	216	501	464	367	181	60	44	100
7	100 to 174 acres	39	20	80	148	146	147	54	14	10	83
8	175 to 259 acres	31	11	41	60	44	51	10	5	3	22
9	260 to 499 acres	10	4	4	47	26	46	7	3		12
10	500 to 999 acres	10	2	1	6	3	9	2		1	3
11	1,000 acres and over				2	4					1
	FARMERS CLASSIFIED BY TENURE.										
12	Owners, free	43	12	54	163	224	64	73	38	175	103
13	Owners, mortgaged	26		38	106	164	81	50	22	25	85
14	Part owners	20	4	21	64	146	58	24	50	51	37
15	Cash tenants	8	35	71	2,676	1,941	737	367	19	102	63
16	Share tenants	211	65	176	395	994	610	320	263	83	228
17	Share-cash tenants	1	2	2	47	22	9	3		8	1
18	Tenure not specified			3	83	59	15	16	2	16	3
19	Managers				2	3				2	
	FARMS OPERATED BY OWNERS, FREE.										
20	Total acreage	5,378	1,349	4,096	15,929	16,670	8,172	6,105	3,143	4,955	13,243
21	Improved acreage	1,560	711	2,035	7,719	8,218	3,892	3,450	1,151	2,578	4,247
22	Value of land	$29,515	$16,150	$52,450	$147,864	$200,436	$59,781	$78,555	$32,440	$221,405	$69,015
23	Value of buildings	$7,285	$4,750	$11,620	$47,325	$70,486	$16,200	$18,060	$6,090	$52,325	$19,035
24	Value of implements and machinery	$1,786	$1,240	$2,601	$12,781	$11,631	$3,858	$6,098	$1,661	$8,516	$5,934
25	Number of dairy cows	61	26	78	399	385	91	105	51	260	154
26	Number of work horses	27	14	9	100	104	24	33	29	107	55
27	Number of work mules	44	19	48	203	223	94	76	39	71	143
28	Acreage in cotton	469	148	850	3,155	3,462	1,450	1,380	247	443	1,383
29	Bales of cotton grown in 1909	127	39	287	635	864	541	567	95	188	454
30	Acreage in corn	503	210	605	1,645	1,419	1,138	1,308	392	942	1,350
31	Bushels of corn grown in 1909	5,331	2,155	7,778	13,082	15,612	10,490	15,466	4,140	14,477	12,215
	FARMS OPERATED BY OWNERS, MORTGAGED.										
32	Total acreage	4,139		3,649	13,758	14,388	10,189	4,331	1,529	639	8,426
33	Improved acreage	1,173		1,563	6,193	7,128	5,300	2,048	861	349	2,916
34	Value of land	$18,625		$38,175	$120,564	$151,399	$92,875	$51,545	$20,870	$35,190	$43,658
35	Value of buildings	$5,950		$8,175	$31,230	$46,310	$22,850	$10,880	$5,040	$7,410	$12,185
36	Value of implements and machinery	$1,088		$2,087	$7,409	$10,332	$6,058	$3,815	$1,437	$625	$3,616
37	Number of dairy cows	44		57	235	294	116	102	29	31	109
38	Number of work horses	18		8	52	77	17	27	12	11	46
39	Number of work mules	33		44	175	181	132	53	31	13	89
40	Acreage in cotton	425		750	2,912	3,286	2,625	972	220	61	1,211
41	Bales of cotton grown in 1909	98		243	511	683	890	347	84	22	330
42	Acreage in corn	303		545	1,212	1,220	1,277	652	262	142	827
43	Bushels of corn grown in 1909	2,405		6,625	8,485	11,126	13,525	8,657	3,035	1,180	7,177
	FARMS OPERATED BY PART OWNERS.										
44	Total acreage	1,893	324	2,040	5,341	12,051	5,874	1,535	2,193	1,270	2,580
45	Owned acreage	1,512	55	1,329	3,297	7,124	4,031	912	867	620	1,677
46	Improved acreage	762	227	1,081	3,126	6,614	3,574	1,114	1,654	873	1,198
47	Owned improved acreage	419	48	561	1,725	3,190	1,951	501	444	348	694
48	Value of land	$12,330	$5,350	$23,450	$47,707	$140,519	$57,149	$19,965	$33,585	$66,185	$21,982
49	Value of buildings	$2,530	$1,100	$4,300	$11,910	$34,183	$11,615	$5,410	$9,375	$17,425	$6,070
50	Value of land and buildings owned	$8,755	$2,150	$18,065	$36,807	$102,298	$46,115	$16,200	$20,280	$38,700	$17,610
51	Value of implements and machinery	$575	$90	$1,091	$3,910	$6,010	$7,140	$1,137	$2,021	$2,564	$1,083
52	Number of dairy cows	27	11	30	152	261	71	43	52	81	42
53	Number of work horses	11	3	7	53	73	12	17	37	34	26
54	Number of work mules	23	9	27	70	194	90	20	57	32	26
55	Acreage in cotton	247	83	516	1,568	3,705	1,764	480	421	166	479
56	Bales of cotton grown in 1909	72	19	157	275	796	639	166	139	69	141
57	Acreage in corn	289	89	286	521	1,124	1,014	352	694	338	341
58	Bushels of corn grown in 1909	2,690	650	3,300	5,317	11,507	9,280	3,935	6,725	4,870	3,045
	FARMS OPERATED BY CASH TENANTS, INCLUDING TENURE NOT SPECIFIED.										
59	Total acreage	499	2,603	4,328	99,941	72,664	58,172	17,308	699	2,615	3,861
60	Improved acreage	209	1,507	2,625	80,427	58,148	39,405	13,688	507	1,942	1,753
61	Value of land	$2,765	$32,775	$58,132	$1,019,681	$1,051,379	$499,807	$215,279	$11,765	$268,680	$27,518
62	Value of buildings	$1,445	$7,275	$10,175	$216,788	$205,240	$109,961	$47,135	$950	$29,300	$5,185
63	Value of implements and machinery	$275	$1,470	$2,624	$72,068	$45,689	$31,020	$15,161	$716	$4,780	$1,538
64	Number of dairy cows	8	60	57	3,927	2,404	753	385	23	127	51
65	Number of work horses	5	22	16	1,025	578	87	115	7	84	35
66	Number of work mules	5	53	63	2,062	1,833	909	317	17	35	51
67	Acreage in cotton	83	448	1,270	48,943	39,542	18,630	6,887	174	511	884
68	Bales of cotton grown in 1909	26	133	413	8,834	8,433	6,585	2,404	58	203	227
69	Acreage in corn	69	592	726	15,608	11,125	10,739	4,776	239	582	497
70	Bushels of corn grown in 1909	770	7,111	9,042	123,168	124,816	97,051	54,952	3,120	8,465	3,533
	FARMS OPERATED BY SHARE AND SHARE-CASH TENANTS.										
71	Total acreage	5,802	2,288	7,200	14,736	23,961	24,972	13,506	7,819	2,435	9,891
72	Improved acreage	5,205	1,986	6,464	11,489	21,958	23,559	12,021	7,291	1,789	5,711
73	Value of land	$72,878	$45,289	$126,035	$144,573	$413,635	$311,801	$224,451	$151,951	$151,825	$83,559
74	Value of buildings	$18,111	$7,990	$26,625	$34,035	$74,718	$59,368	$45,615	$21,585	$28,625	$21,460
75	Value of implements and machinery	$3,228	$1,737	$4,827	$6,979	$9,266	$9,846	$8,698	$7,019	$3,952	$3,514
76	Number of dairy cows	132	74	107	471	925	272	171	209	112	158
77	Number of work horses	39	38	17	139	107	15	41	95	38	53
78	Number of work mules	162	55	158	194	654	403	243	260	50	150
79	Acreage in cotton	2,547	620	3,164	6,321	15,376	12,131	5,816	2,457	468	2,821
80	Bales of cotton grown in 1909	850	190	1,240	1,341	3,669	4,674	2,298	884	192	776
81	Acres in corn	1,359	838	1,974	2,418	4,593	6,124	3,516	3,293	654	1,423
82	Bushels of corn grown in 1909	14,810	10,015	25,708	16,114	51,516	68,752	46,286	41,556	10,862	13,919

OPERATED BY COLORED FARMERS, BY COUNTIES, FOR SOUTHERN STATES: 1910—Continued.

ALABAMA—continued.

Lauderdale.	Lawrence.	Lee.	Limestone.	Lowndes.	Macon.	Madison.	Marengo.	Marshall.	Mobile.	Monroe.	Montgomery.	Morgan.	Perry.	Pickens.	
909	1,181	2,574	1,780	5,755	3,842	2,595	5,149	145	286	2,650	5,578	649	4,004	2,190	1
		1							1	2					2
29	19	101	27	1,274	410	33	561	1	80	269	271	38	340	51	3
85	94	123	190	656	316	189	1,105	20	42	527	523	104	456	156	4
551	687	1,160	1,096	2,852	2,119	1,599	2,584	85	73	1,309	3,239	334	2,187	1,219	5
183	278	642	400	783	704	560	573	27	34	289	1,215	116	737	513	6
47	73	432	60	130	216	175	225	9	46	158	252	46	198	176	7
12	20	76	6	27	29	25	61	2	3	48	52	7	49	38	8
2	10	36	1	25	38	12	32	1	3	38	23	2	30	33	9
		3		4	8	2	6		4	8	3	2	7	4	10
				3	1		2			2					11
84	68	144	90	187	178	153	257	19	236	268	200	74	177	151	12
44	45	105	77	84	176	112	199	5	10	186	76	34	129	101	13
93	86	69	69	97	76	160	193	20	5	178	56	75	158	15	14
424	584	1,325	595	4,253	2,528	899	3,543	4	18	1,536	4,123	139	2,692	1,259	15
256	389	704	930	652	662	1,225	669	95	2	308	963	287	782	564	16
3	2	14	10	14	88	20	148	1		9	98	30	4	10	17
4	7	212	9	467	122	24	137	1	14	165	59	10	61	90	18
1		1		1	12	2	3		1		3		1		19
5,147	5,568	13,248	5,583	12,436	14,207	10,678	23,051	1,426	15,459	28,772	10,564	4,378	13,849	15,371	20
2,834	3,222	7,784	2,555	5,785	7,901	10,013	6,388	478	1,764	9,684	7,400	2,108	5,855	5,896	21
$62,014	$62,579	$113,620	$82,205	$128,709	$172,300	$161,111	$186,969	$5,140	$132,985	$170,839	$272,943	$47,395	$141,638	$86,112	22
$23,430	$20,285	$52,055	$21,015	$47,157	$68,629	$51,035	$53,530	$1,845	$54,275	$63,405	$61,576	$19,180	$37,200	$28,235	23
$3,469	$4,837	$11,330	$4,337	$7,531	$15,443	$10,672	$43,115	$370	$8,838	$18,999	$13,234	$3,897	$9,408	$7,047	24
117	109	261	109	327	307	275	467	22	464	457	316	92	298	291	25
58	56	86	64	103	111	140	144	10	190	167	147	41	77	123	26
92	88	126	81	147	175	196	233	8	36	130	224	58	174	163	27
875	1,186	3,036	1,055	3,476	3,675	2,140	4,317	117	55	3,478	4,246	691	3,073	2,538	28
258	326	926	283	672	913	577	1,192	30	24	1,039	1,039	230	826	570	29
810	900	1,480	723	1,061	1,877	1,889	1,645	122	525	2,321	1,241	595	1,202	1,574	30
12,738	10,263	14,035	9,863	10,969	13,520	22,896	20,761	1,030	8,749	23,847	19,084	7,493	15,247	11,645	31
3,090	4,899	11,264	5,808	8,118	17,943	9,368	18,349	537	779	20,820	5,713	3,247	14,795	9,961	32
1,793	2,570	6,246	2,606	3,708	9,470	5,315	8,634	232	201	7,352	3,951	1,356	5,420	4,161	33
$37,735	$57,620	$101,928	$71,395	$62,817	$197,064	$118,348	$6,335	$2,555	$15,335	$114,675	$104,863	$31,015	$111,153	$54,938	34
$10,600	$12,530	$33,700	$19,030	$27,342	$58,370	$30,277	$36,558	$410	$4,865	$38,895	$26,457	$7,640	$24,020	$14,880	35
$2,033	$3,905	$9,138	$4,406	$3,101	$14,484	$6,296	$11,093	$215	$1,215	$8,917	$5,141	$2,067	$6,252	$4,260	36
79	69	194	136	175	286	173	350	6	12	330	143	48	240	161	37
46	37	73	65	59	89	97	110	1	10	102	53	33	53	66	38
48	69	113	90	72	193	158	229		5	99	120	24	157	120	39
657	992	2,549	1,249	2,083	4,239	1,970	4,222	36		3,130	2,065	544	2,748	1,890	40
160	247	774	317	358	1,022	454	1,155	9		825	583	135	667	419	41
475	618	1,166	645	576	2,060	1,326	1,457	21	7	1,758	681	324	1,046	978	42
6,934	5,732	10,468	7,297	5,618	15,530	13,043	17,391	260	128	15,766	8,895	3,571	11,111	7,150	43
5,433	6,624	6,693	3,563	7,129	6,573	12,634	15,537	1,662	50	13,714	2,947	4,673	14,687	1,244	44
2,838	4,300	3,352	2,128	3,772	3,282	7,777	7,871	1,017	19	9,711	1,225	2,676	8,129	572	45
3,662	4,297	3,742	2,349	4,768	3,969	7,986	8,511	967	50	6,390	2,516	2,682	6,706	679	46
1,435	2,293	1,772	1,095	2,118	1,856	4,173	3,498	360	19	3,157	974	1,180	3,229	226	47
$80,085	$85,966	$60,334	$61,503	$80,669	$81,265	$179,917	$129,031	$15,300	$5,300	$120,637	$57,590	$58,962	$147,627	$10,447	48
$19,810	$22,252	$18,360	$13,240	$18,305	$26,020	$37,955	$32,208	$3,160	$3,300	$33,079	$18,603	$15,896	$33,401	$2,830	49
$53,181	$72,733	$41,601	$37,566	$54,722	$60,986	$129,570	$88,070	$9,250	$6,100	$103,209	$38,913	$42,065	$100,374	$6,562	50
$4,181	$8,079	$4,533	$3,651	$6,347	$5,315	$9,849	$10,045	$868	$60	$7,044	$3,334	$4,039	$8,792	$501	51
149	171	116	86	222	129	287	398	30	14	309	112	99	298	38	52
84	91	23	61	81	46	135	123	6	4	121	41	68	79	19	53
124	118	92	69	96	74	247	232	31	1	130	60	72	215	19	54
1,352	1,639	1,927	913	2,373	1,941	3,263	4,948	350	6	2,877	1,430	958	3,760	354	55
349	484	500	264	463	503	716	1,242	104	4	892	364	303	947	78	56
1,157	1,257	737	715	684	841	2,141	1,155	173	14	1,507	434	750	1,197	185	57
18,205	15,835	5,203	11,489	6,817	6,121	25,005	16,873	2,542	485	15,785	4,764	9,946	15,326	1,505	58
16,736	25,936	106,132	24,850	133,951	105,486	46,051	114,028	242	1,342	47,464	175,676	6,446	106,464	71,393	59
15,060	23,042	70,352	22,591	116,749	86,550	36,125	97,080	125	228	40,103	149,015	4,762	91,768	47,319	60
$379,056	$460,741	$1,097,903	$456,745	$1,682,021	$1,297,151	$920,657	$1,354,938	$2,280	$26,800	$434,998	$3,535,028	$179,386	$1,531,358	$595,521	61
$48,178	$60,707	$271,950	$95,690	$407,815	$387,547	$140,233	$308,880	$560	$7,520	$148,228	$545,029	$24,875	$241,505	$161,810	62
$14,989	$18,228	$71,327	$23,346	$84,978	$87,042	$38,274	$101,358	$17	$1,070	$36,106	$150,650	$5,782	$88,901	$41,147	63
536	732	1,797	840	5,622	2,676	1,210	3,912	6	18	1,653	5,519	168	3,505	1,818	64
221	296	529	399	1,282	780	549	1,074	2	15	636	1,470	95	716	768	65
539	758	1,362	714	2,911	1,756	1,121	3,068	2	10	987	4,649	137	3,005	1,260	66
8,863	12,784	32,483	13,074	80,840	53,748	17,922	65,765	41	3	24,355	100,715	2,083	53,317	27,043	67
1,915	3,387	9,108	3,036	17,292	11,222	3,975	17,216	9	1	6,767	22,517	592	16,226	5,551	68
3,997	6,905	12,127	7,259	20,930	17,804	11,075	15,367	33	40	9,439	25,585	1,191	15,974	10,747	69
60,847	81,683	108,039	91,927	254,537	118,965	125,090	229,754	205	710	98,291	366,438	14,115	223,275	79,555	70
7,552	10,739	29,521	27,093	19,597	22,946	38,448	16,820	2,745	32	7,447	35,601	10,194	17,549	20,481	71
6,856	10,245	23,601	25,754	18,874	21,533	36,158	16,468	2,678	30	7,181	31,549	8,533	17,163	15,942	72
$152,113	$185,562	$349,457	$494,640	$248,465	$329,438	$788,352	$192,138	$43,930	$2,400	$85,551	$685,422	$187,935	$283,550	$220,030	73
$19,510	$27,456	$90,744	$100,495	$65,823	$85,767	$136,547	$62,938	$9,460	$800	$23,848	$121,130	$35,372	$51,225	$58,205	74
$4,276	$5,621	$10,625	$14,547	$12,065	$9,750	$19,445	$10,656	$1,985	$10	$3,071	$13,889	$8,876	$4,608	$7,837	75
200	284	433	648	700	444	923	506	101		190	826	271	467	510	76
62	66	62	194	78	80	202	75	29	3	49	160	118	37	165	77
157	241	489	597	282	292	790	380	84		144	795	230	309	384	78
3,548	5,460	13,420	14,249	12,792	12,176	19,324	10,453	1,003		4,476	21,118	3,467	12,008	8,786	79
853	1,431	4,112	3,819	2,787	3,041	4,876	2,806	296		1,482	5,366	1,096	3,680	1,853	80
2,266	3,092	4,350	7,033	3,483	4,293	10,788	2,609	1,039	8	1,777	5,526	2,445	2,966	3,858	81
35,524	38,282	42,970	106,836	37,681	32,010	138,366	34,301	13,613	160	18,171	69,934	33,609	42,406	28,468	82

TABLE **73.**—STATISTICS OF SIZE OF FARMS AND FOR TENURE CLASSES OF FARMS

				ALABAMA—continued						
		Pike.	Randolph.	Russell.	St. Clair.	Shelby.	Sumter.	Talladega.	Talla-poosa.	Tusca-loosa.	Wash-ington.
1	Number of farms	1,820	917	2,456	372	602	3,880	2,197	1,660	1,651	598
	FARMS CLASSIFIED BY SIZE.										
2	Under 3 acres						1	1			
3	3 to 9 acres	64	27	58	20	54	164	78	78	129	75
4	10 to 19 acres	69	95	84	52	75	462	195	161	299	115
5	20 to 49 acres	996	487	1,376	151	274	2,180	1,339	816	779	234
6	50 to 99 acres	424	199	595	93	112	721	417	348	238	67
7	100 to 174 acres	191	72	236	48	53	232	125	181	133	73
8	175 to 259 acres	54	24	60	5	15	61	30	46	35	18
9	260 to 499 acres	20	12	39	3	6	53	9	28	33	15
10	500 to 999 acres	2	1	8		9	5	3	2	4	1
11	1,000 acres and over					4	1			1	
	FARMERS CLASSIFIED BY TENURE.										
12	Owners, free	70	123	166	90	122	183	293	109	157	188
13	Owners, mortgaged	65	45	64	32	53	125	143	107	138	61
14	Part owners	36	34	44	37	49	75	78	48	135	34
15	Cash tenants	698	187	1,577	36	185	2,802	852	492	739	214
16	Share tenants	920	488	377	166	190	621	797	842	390	90
17	Share-cash tenants	6	5	61	9		10	12	9	23	
18	Tenure not specified	22	35	166	2	2	64	22	53	67	11
19	Managers	3		1		1				2	
	FARMS OPERATED BY OWNERS, FREE.										
20	Total acreage	6,753	9,124	15,585	6,375	9,687	23,850	18,418	10,527	12,936	16,600
21	Improved acreage	3,285	4,519	8,369	2,589	3,236	9,173	8,488	5,564	4,371	3,463
22	Value of land	$73,325	$77,640	$105,807	$41,475	$63,860	$165,589	$165,936	$106,188	$122,253	$85,645
23	Value of buildings	$13,265	$19,325	$40,770	$16,445	$29,625	$38,035	$55,530	$34,835	$40,485	$37,915
24	Value of implements and machinery	$2,654	$6,796	$10,968	$4,149	$5,110	$9,502	$14,087	$7,384	$7,582	$7,833
25	Number of dairy cows	82	152	296	129	179	438	373	181	220	419
26	Number of work horses	17	54	83	31	60	178	92	40	68	162
27	Number of work mules	70	83	143	67	78	189	256	119	151	60
28	Acreage in cotton	1,335	1,508	4,391	677	681	3,341	3,314	1,640	1,670	925
29	Bales of cotton grown in 1909	356	494	1,064	206	219	782	1,079	636	519	333
30	Acreage in corn	1,071	1,233	2,231	699	889	1,704	2,478	1,136	1,089	1,127
31	Bushels of corn grown in 1909	8,035	13,452	15,654	5,908	8,743	15,548	24,118	11,675	12,916	13,424
	FARMS OPERATED BY OWNERS, MORTGAGED.										
32	Total acreage	7,719	5,338	8,117	2,543	3,315	17,805	10,026	11,606	15,839	5,837
33	Improved acreage	4,304	2,073	4,101	1,120	1,740	7,533	5,167	6,083	5,409	1,602
34	Value of land	$62,763	$42,375	$64,634	$15,265	$25,445	$118,051	$83,800	$98,775	$110,815	$34,745
35	Value of buildings	$12,900	$8,325	$16,295	$4,935	$12,650	$32,360	$22,730	$31,950	$26,500	$13,575
36	Value of implements and machinery	$2,654	$2,795	$5,632	$1,405	$2,886	$6,628	$5,898	$5,975	$8,280	$2,751
37	Number of dairy cows	89	56	126	46	83	282	189	185	234	120
38	Number of work horses	16	30	23	14	30	123	53	31	47	50
39	Number of work mules	83	38	73	37	46	160	157	136	145	39
40	Acreage in cotton	1,652	737	2,121	355	522	2,652	2,157	2,278	2,288	626
41	Bales of cotton grown in 1909	456	249	511	79	150	591	627	725	621	206
42	Acreage in corn	946	544	1,112	276	488	1,098	1,214	1,230	1,271	425
43	Bushels of corn grown in 1909	7,219	5,210	7,400	1,803	4,953	10,290	10,437	10,968	12,711	4,693
	FARMS OPERATED BY PART OWNERS.										
44	Total acreage	3,385	3,030	4,018	2,258	1,965	9,182	5,476	5,393	12,245	1,385
45	Owned acreage	1,507	1,642	1,931	1,467	1,015	5,843	2,934	3,097	8,634	912
46	Improved acreage	2,092	1,581	2,578	1,215	1,004	4,656	3,273	2,841	5,602	733
47	Owned improved acreage	904	773	1,066	659	417	2,438	1,497	1,563	2,955	309
48	Value of land	$37,151	$33,250	$39,172	$17,545	$23,351	$68,601	$52,705	$58,622	$144,508	$11,216
49	Value of buildings	$6,045	$5,320	$12,290	$5,215	$9,702	$11,025	$15,505	$13,225	$20,941	$5,620
50	Value of land and buildings owned	$21,287	$20,385	$27,946	$14,082	$19,305	$43,275	$36,960	$42,393	$101,410	$12,273
51	Value of implements and machinery	$1,559	$1,903	$2,482	$1,710	$1,759	$3,383	$3,170	$3,423	$5,380	$1,126
52	Number of dairy cows	47	41	68	59	58	163	115	95	222	52
53	Number of work horses	7	12	30	18	19	48	33	15	55	22
54	Number of work mules	50	38	42	36	31	103	93	72	181	18
55	Acreage in cotton	888	578	1,222	382	347	1,740	1,322	1,190	2,693	268
56	Bales of cotton grown in 1909	255	190	336	130	120	355	406	379	691	72
57	Acreage in corn	561	463	651	329	321	787	790	599	1,159	140
58	Bushels of corn grown in 1909	4,444	5,125	5,359	2,510	3,574	6,904	7,527	6,550	14,023	1,441
	FARMS OPERATED BY CASH TENANTS, INCLUDING TENURE NOT SPECIFIED.										
59	Total acreage	46,474	13,351	105,937	1,967	19,417	114,950	38,555	35,731	28,042	6,635
60	Improved acreage	33,885	8,122	82,604	1,045	7,080	94,132	29,348	20,619	20,547	3,927
61	Value of land	$539,659	$144,060	$895,679	$18,935	$116,063	$1,280,407	$534,035	$416,572	$422,119	$56,686
62	Value of buildings	$85,841	$37,705	$237,506	$3,685	$37,635	$290,060	$116,255	$91,960	$78,094	$18,790
63	Value of implements and machinery	$20,755	$7,505	$68,519	$1,654	$5,232	$92,089	$31,625	$18,530	$25,778	$3,087
64	Number of dairy cows	757	229	2,149	62	237	3,952	877	650	816	243
65	Number of work horses	118	90	485	24	103	1,698	232	115	209	140
66	Number of work mules	743	163	1,398	28	129	2,622	896	581	757	85
67	Acreage in cotton	16,907	3,231	44,761	322	2,684	52,419	13,839	9,811	12,003	1,678
68	Bales of cotton grown in 1909	4,580	1,073	10,076	97	912	11,229	4,422	3,239	3,249	634
69	Acreage in corn	9,649	2,058	20,803	387	1,970	23,694	7,490	4,646	4,527	1,031
70	Bushels of corn grown in 1909	70,615	21,888	136,404	2,595	16,560	231,161	70,740	50,306	54,721	13,650
	FARMS OPERATED BY SHARE AND SHARE-CASH TENANTS.										
71	Total acreage	44,030	17,926	18,260	6,818	6,879	18,148	24,536	31,105	14,541	2,347
72	Improved acreage	37,222	14,122	16,124	5,241	4,979	16,811	21,616	24,538	11,093	1,921
73	Value of land	$673,719	$227,219	$190,922	$75,950	$80,150	$190,371	$385,705	$398,702	$213,779	$23,050
74	Value of buildings	$103,245	$53,741	$42,617	$22,350	$29,729	$54,040	$88,910	$100,115	$49,297	$7,190
75	Value of implements and machinery	$13,023	$8,481	$7,153	$3,853	$4,064	$10,628	$18,967	$13,126	$8,968	$956
76	Number of dairy cows	600	419	280	152	169	537	545	739	320	75
77	Number of work horses	21	98	42	27	47	186	94	82	63	22
78	Number of work mules	646	286	156	125	112	392	632	599	346	40
79	Acreage in cotton	21,270	6,526	7,840	1,976	2,239	8,929	11,048	12,844	5,814	652
80	Bales of cotton grown in 1909	6,516	2,268	2,217	607	764	2,125	3,794	4,354	1,740	250
81	Acreage in corn	10,669	3,959	3,526	1,337	1,373	4,071	5,883	5,986	2,540	460
82	Bushels of corn grown in 1909	92,786	45,139	26,776	11,089	13,795	40,641	66,162	67,196	30,755	5,886

OPERATED BY COLORED FARMERS, BY COUNTIES, FOR SOUTHERN STATES: 1910—Continued.

ALABAMA—cont'd.		ARKANSAS.													
Wilcox.	All other counties.	The state.	Arkansas.	Ashley.	Bradley.	Calhoun.	Chicot.	Clark.	Cleveland.	Columbia.	Conway.	Crawford.	Crittenden.	Cross.	
5,575	459	63,593	677	1,964	357	436	3,302	777	580	1,441	1,520	212	3,381	939	1
5		15					1	1						1	2
805	29	2,716	19	57	2	8	449	16	31	23	90	12	74	23	3
1,137	81	16,273	153	496	37	30	1,354	132	76	98	245	41	926	251	4
2,841	189	31,156	289	1,144	162	186	1,252	316	262	650	654	112	1,941	499	5
506	75	8,191	137	194	75	113	166	174	106	321	353	38	295	107	6
199	66	3,798	59	53	56	73	56	95	75	231	134	5	104	45	7
36	16	909	16	12	18	19	12	28	20	62	36	4	19	4	8
41	3	450	4	8	7	7	10	15	10	53	8		15	1	9
4		72								3			4		10
1		13					2						3		11
238	103	7,891	105	213	156	183	186	193	153	355	239	21	217	70	12
110	30	3,969	74	71	52	85	159	61	85	200	135	12	66	27	13
61	52	2,802	43	46	40	39	63	161	73	119	224	20	57	13	14
4,163	23	17,104	195	610	4	22	993	11	44	19	321	14	1,534	323	15
859	241	27,582	246	898	96	106	1,507	300	196	640	568	127	866	395	16
9	5	1,500	4	24	1		302	8	6	28		2	72	81	17
133	3	2,699	10	102	8	1	91	42	26	102	5	3	566	30	18
2	2	46					1	1					3		19
18,650	8,362	636,899	9,173	12,909	14,281	13,768	11,062	15,579	12,398	41,204	20,821	1,869	13,339	5,823	20
9,836	2,882	275,226	4,140	6,589	4,848	4,743	4,664	5,991	9,401	16,612	9,401	1,341	7,550	2,504	21
$145,505	$59,789	$8,563,203	$102,426	$265,135	$82,325	$84,270	$352,450	$106,206	$78,790	$346,811	$179,484	$41,175	$537,699	$73,785	22
$49,075	$18,560	$2,187,548	$22,140	$78,580	$38,235	$33,760	$62,930	$36,010	$30,950	$94,625	$66,325	$10,835	$90,620	$21,920	23
$12,134	$4,762	$629,102	$8,171	$23,370	$5,110	$6,793	$20,513	$8,794	$7,903	$28,759	$17,040	$2,015	$33,099	$5,908	24
656	150	19,793	369	716	403	379	424	461	440	749	497	55	572	144	25
199	45	7,920	189	278	117	122	334	195	156	271	271	51	228	63	26
138	82	8,633	100	203	113	157	160	150	93	461	249	36	326	97	27
4,187	673	106,502	1,392	2,817	1,659	1,543	2,470	1,784	1,273	6,360	3,533	395	3,998	862	28
1,091	212	32,483	313	926	375	379	1,011	529	326	1,613	783	118	2,096	293	29
1,530	1,021	75,729	967	1,783	1,536	1,626	1,170	1,951	1,139	4,788	2,777	276	1,565	698	30
23,676	9,558	1,030,439	11,570	25,949	16,530	18,219	18,415	26,089	11,465	50,877	29,970	4,605	33,118	13,565	31
10,630	3,188	353,283	5,530	5,821	4,258	7,673	10,617	6,410	7,980	20,881	13,349	939	8,604	2,322	32
5,059	1,052	152,155	2,601	2,593	1,598	2,364	4,491	2,364	2,629	9,479	5,916	564	4,853	878	33
$71,944	$17,410	$4,853,616	$83,827	$73,295	$33,135	$41,365	$302,557	$47,695	$56,960	$171,761	$141,787	$13,770	$352,520	$24,150	34
$25,150	$4,640	$1,087,951	$14,805	$21,330	$12,750	$16,230	$57,145	$14,565	$16,780	$45,826	$41,930	$3,050	$44,865	$5,775	35
$11,079	$1,062	$319,677	$4,087	$4,891	$2,195	$2,735	$14,222	$3,428	$4,037	$12,449	$14,128	$460	$27,752	$2,179	36
256	39	9,563	296	207	112	181	381	206	223	350	308	15	208	37	37
80	15	3,719	100	87	48	63	263	63	76	140	112	21	69	14	38
79	23	4,917	77	75	45	67	188	69	75	250	181	7	162	38	39
2,289	301	65,333	1,169	960	580	780	2,685	839	995	3,778	2,534	133	2,867	348	40
534	80	18,297	219	271	135	180	1,114	231	220	986	497	33	1,315	142	41
614	354	39,434	604	714	472	772	952	693	712	2,413	1,633	87	935	258	42
9,541	3,388	484,971	5,717	7,087	5,270	8,335	13,714	8,434	7,145	24,557	17,963	977	19,492	4,275	43
3,173	3,525	213,932	3,566	2,912	2,899	3,297	4,308	12,697	4,701	12,696	15,388	1,035	6,215	723	44
1,638	2,629	137,983	2,236	1,165	1,752	2,643	2,335	8,350	3,142	8,588	10,557	633	3,326	406	45
2,069	1,729	113,884	1,797	1,407	1,341	1,303	2,310	6,198	2,248	5,439	9,438	743	4,031	494	46
850	994	56,941	286	668	729	729	1,256	3,067	1,181	2,750	5,384	361	1,663	212	47
$30,738	$32,432	$3,300,608	$53,615	$45,275	$20,935	$20,564	$131,680	$109,805	$36,650	$100,705	$243,945	$26,792	$244,675	$13,925	48
$12,235	$11,050	$701,289	$8,270	$11,285	$5,745	$4,925	$20,038	$26,800	$11,245	$20,710	$66,965	$4,188	$36,335	$5,100	49
$22,890	$27,330	$2,318,381	$38,440	$13,985	$16,390	$20,030	$93,155	$78,730	$32,480	$81,656	$179,094	$16,605	$147,760	$12,305	50
$3,179	$2,194	$188,104	$2,810	$4,478	$1,847	$906	$5,742	$6,978	$2,278	$4,447	$17,952	$1,055	$12,345	$1,235	51
154	87	6,410	196	106	47	91	170	420	150	197	460	26	156	27	52
33	29	2,808	63	47	47	27	96	159	78	73	226	23	65	7	53
59	36	3,464	50	49	21	33	135	141	45	141	286	30	140	22	54
1,421	457	46,474	834	655	485	441	1,444	1,707	873	2,224	4,161	226	2,632	227	55
375	125	14,333	143	225	112	116	563	496	198	473	1,215	83	1,226	71	56
378	495	28,018	352	344	358	406	410	1,847	556	1,484	2,463	103	838	91	57
6,262	6,316	393,191	2,987	5,500	3,665	5,444	6,911	26,837	5,625	14,184	32,676	1,920	13,863	1,980	58
124,151	1,153	695,584	8,038	22,625	915	2,151	29,252	2,988	3,211	6,522	12,146	584	68,595	13,055	59
95,869	470	577,603	5,636	20,898	406	690	24,576	1,597	1,682	3,816	10,013	459	62,283	10,765	60
$1,236,991	$10,965	$20,969,618	$122,754	$632,598	$9,105	$14,570	$912,984	$27,200	$21,114	$72,578	$422,407	$13,773	$3,047,693	$279,480	61
$368,764	$4,475	$3,557,215	$26,426	$129,211	$2,950	$3,975	$202,937	$4,905	$7,805	$13,202	$53,863	$1,317	$414,184	$68,335	62
$100,413	$519	$1,078,927	$5,952	$55,608	$389	$628	$40,058	$1,572	$1,464	$2,129	$17,421	$438	$165,544	$25,149	63
5,503	24	26,655	378	1,320	17	34	1,033	91	72	108	366	13	2,779	457	64
1,468	9	13,987	255	669	13	12	1,032	31	55	47	235	17	989	203	65
2,187	15	20,717	121	762	5	24	793	61	32	79	371	12	2,451	495	66
65,858	133	350,665	2,933	13,154	196	275	15,274	656	667	1,647	6,211	182	40,166	5,265	67
17,715	40	140,683	639	4,847	53	65	6,496	198	156	385	2,669	44	20,422	2,164	68
18,103	167	115,962	1,220	5,141	120	178	3,979	497	383	1,107	2,445	93	10,375	2,556	69
286,927	2,220	2,096,104	12,106	87,121	1,613	2,200	63,711	8,825	4,080	10,740	39,958	765	218,992	48,085	70
22,601	9,123	747,532	7,136	21,773	2,867	4,582	29,928	9,218	6,272	27,095	14,289	3,745	19,685	13,815	71
20,137	5,863	651,270	6,133	20,762	2,401	2,814	29,460	7,332	4,654	20,010	13,654	3,426	19,240	11,388	72
$227,504	$102,426	$20,057,895	$130,260	$534,565	$25,304	$43,683	$1,158,342	$102,655	$52,200	$258,496	$495,295	$126,035	$436,233	$277,988	73
$75,252	$28,555	$3,495,251	$27,555	$119,825	$8,560	$10,362	$270,170	$22,775	$16,450	$59,433	$61,710	$14,755	$130,688	$54,895	74
$11,597	$5,376	$557,888	$6,075	$30,368	$1,222	$1,658	$29,528	$3,548	$2,721	$10,486	$13,132	$4,102	$16,830	$13,030	75
980	202	18,590	271	751	89	143	660	331	198	538	378	96	423	365	76
333	60	8,469	145	405	38	42	547	143	80	178	228	89	107	150	77
174	144	14,920	135	738	43	62	859	195	118	264	407	94	262	150	78
13,886	2,281	379,863	2,801	13,659	799	1,099	18,892	2,601	2,039	9,002	8,337	1,380	10,006	5,889	79
4,231	692	142,507	567	4,756	203	292	8,652	849	583	2,529	3,073	443	4,879	2,386	80
4,481	2,027	127,121	1,267	4,492	586	833	3,462	2,161	1,211	5,395	3,441	659	1,993	2,683	81
59,956	23,702	2,091,192	13,579	73,480	7,167	10,103	60,559	34,317	14,947	64,056	51,502	12,603	40,162	56,704	82

TABLE **73.**—STATISTICS OF SIZE OF FARMS AND FOR TENURE CLASSES OF FARMS

ARKANSAS—continued.

		Dallas.	Desha.	Drew.	Faulkner.	Grant.	Hempstead.	Hot Spring.	Howard.	Jackson.	Jefferson.
1	Number of farms	416	2,161	1,983	714	151	2,047	101	537	796	6,346
	FARMS CLASSIFIED BY SIZE.										
2	Under 3 acres										2
3	3 to 9 acres	17	143	95	17		47	3	6	20	411
4	10 to 19 acres	46	697	484	105	23	322	19	74	111	2,397
5	20 to 49 acres	155	935	832	333	55	1,068	47	304	486	2,920
6	50 to 99 acres	106	184	263	157	32	375	25	104	111	434
7	100 to 174 acres	72	103	183	87	29	174	6	38	50	141
8	175 to 259 acres	13	49	47	11	8	42		8	10	22
9	260 to 499 acres	6	25	24	4	3	18	1	3	7	14
10	500 to 999 acres	1	22	4		1	1			1	4
11	1,000 acres and over		3	1		1					1
	FARMERS CLASSIFIED BY TENURE.										
12	Owners, free	168	176	234	142	53	403	37	104	47	502
13	Owners, mortgaged	44	47	233	87	25	195	7	40	52	245
14	Part owners	54	25	67	53	31	120	25	38	15	119
15	Cash tenants	9	650	454	130	10	89	2	11	279	1,946
16	Share tenants	129	672	938	279	29	1,177	20	331	388	3,060
17	Share-cash tenants	10	3	29	5	1	18	1	2	7	296
18	Tenure not specified	2	587	26	18	1	43	9	11	8	168
19	Managers		1	2		1	2				10
	FARMS OPERATED BY OWNERS, FREE.										
20	Total acreage	14,224	13,940	23,753	12,140	5,137	32,304	2,177	8,404	4,707	32,295
21	Improved acreage	5,276	5,228	8,967	6,069	1,737	16,504	994	4,371	1,698	12,278
22	Value of land	$99,940	$264,425	$245,052	$91,034	$30,306	$347,534	$22,575	$77,231	$80,893	$591,167
23	Value of buildings	$32,800	$74,342	$62,230	$34,186	$10,230	$113,675	$11,125	$24,605	$17,485	$118,230
24	Value of implements and machinery	$7,959	$13,053	$15,696	$11,730	$2,906	$28,121	$2,319	$6,152	$9,795	$28,468
25	Number of dairy cows	422	575	613	374	167	1,033	63	260	153	1,029
26	Number of work horses	150	229	233	118	53	458	39	114	70	413
27	Number of work mules	165	220	290	188	51	489	31	143	78	465
28	Acreage in cotton	1,406	2,718	3,065	2,393	483	5,664	183	1,591	655	6,124
29	Bales of cotton grown in 1909	395	968	764	609	131	1,160	62	419	219	2,128
30	Acreage in corn	1,689	1,010	2,133	1,678	502	5,376	258	1,539	519	2,588
31	Bushels of corn grown in 1909	19,289	16,467	22,549	20,652	5,425	82,058	4,625	24,930	7,020	37,981
	FARMS OPERATED BY OWNERS, MORTGAGED.										
32	Total acreage	4,341	5,036	26,432	7,001	3,356	17,244	389	2,990	6,090	16,163
33	Improved acreage	1,461	1,904	10,181	3,332	903	8,842	110	1,516	2,223	6,963
34	Value of land	$22,487	$111,420	$228,274	$51,690	$35,005	$179,907	$3,700	$33,705	$101,440	$382,602
35	Value of buildings	$7,550	$21,275	$58,840	$22,010	$5,410	$55,255	$1,350	$6,415	$18,295	$62,595
36	Value of implements and machinery	$1,490	$6,106	$17,240	$6,212	$1,652	$15,757	$175	$1,825	$5,930	$19,313
37	Number of dairy cows	97	160	625	200	61	441	10	84	155	456
38	Number of work horses	30	44	227	66	21	161	5	36	70	209
39	Number of work mules	35	90	345	104	30	261	3	42	98	334
40	Acreage in cotton	391	945	3,976	1,476	240	3,116	13	535	1,031	4,071
41	Bales of cotton grown in 1909	103	312	889	358	72	536	11	122	304	1,466
42	Acreage in corn	462	365	2,497	868	279	2,484	32	466	572	1,246
43	Bushels of corn grown in 1909	4,035	5,178	25,625	9,092	2,930	34,213	310	6,795	7,258	22,065
	FARMS OPERATED BY PART OWNERS.										
44	Total acreage	3,894	1,480	5,093	4,508	1,719	9,183	1,169	2,308	1,689	7,331
45	Owned acreage	2,817	1,058	3,843	2,878	1,295	5,698	757	1,364	1,012	4,657
46	Improved acreage	1,475	782	2,255	2,694	852	5,244	701	1,477	861	4,034
47	Owned improved acreage	768	420	1,189	1,442	464	2,846	289	717	434	1,611
48	Value of land	$26,860	$30,395	$44,034	$41,075	$19,156	$90,562	$16,915	$31,420	$47,705	$170,474
49	Value of buildings	$7,405	$7,770	$10,770	$10,590	$5,200	$22,865	$6,450	$6,835	$7,150	$25,855
50	Value of land and buildings owned	$24,390	$25,430	$37,655	$25,440	$18,170	$65,583	$11,950	$20,095	$37,300	$117,128
51	Value of implements and machinery	$1,956	$1,450	$2,197	$3,765	$1,330	$6,247	$1,390	$1,704	$1,375	$8,120
52	Number of dairy cows	122	44	112	115	81	270	49	80	40	210
53	Number of work horses	44	35	48	54	32	99	26	45	29	121
54	Number of work mules	43	33	60	76	26	168	26	52	33	137
55	Acreage in cotton	387	369	888		211	2,354	154	573	438	1,986
56	Bales of cotton grown in 1909	98	130	214		68	423	71	143	130	779
57	Acreage in corn	468	147	536	642	249	1,489	282	511	86	538
58	Bushels of corn grown in 1909	5,002	1,881	4,994	7,085	3,792	22,417	6,160	7,755	1,380	8,556
	FARMS OPERATED BY CASH TENANTS, INCLUDING TENURE NOT SPECIFIED.										
59	Total acreage	382	59,763	17,710	6,781	506	5,736	248	845	12,523	59,314
60	Improved acreage	231	40,133	14,613	4,589	214	4,158	194	648	11,046	53,058
61	Value of land	$1,978	$1,348,824	$341,984	$99,375	$3,025	$62,561	$3,760	$11,830	$505,730	$1,927,574
62	Value of buildings	$770	$241,914	$66,514	$20,570	$625	$22,302	$1,050	$2,050	$71,055	$290,782
63	Value of implements and machinery	$124	$49,790	$21,386	$8,397	$220	$5,868	$383	$697	$18,933	$77,164
64	Number of dairy cows	22	1,445	733	254	13	266	13	29	517	2,354
65	Number of work horses	4	793	317	85	12	93	5	12	373	1,474
66	Number of work mules	5	1,119	518	179	3	117	10	22	395	2,083
67	Acreage in cotton	73	18,579	6,049	2,676	81	1,827	74	274	6,853	37,579
68	Bales of cotton grown in 1909	18	6,935	1,581	1,074	20	380	26	65	2,992	14,781
69	Acreage in corn	71	4,700	3,338	1,101	68	1,545	112	202	2,409	8,514
70	Bushels of corn grown in 1909	630	73,021	41,138	19,047	607	28,948	1,840	3,240	48,209	148,094
	FARMS OPERATED BY SHARE AND SHARE-CASH TENANTS.										
71	Total acreage	5,632	26,296	22,288	8,207	601	37,397	637	10,602	11,208	64,058
72	Improved acreage	3,360	20,768	20,389	6,729	638	31,597	525	9,489	10,338	63,085
73	Value of land	$38,925	$654,695	$451,373	$124,039	$7,487	$509,790	$10,805	$163,237	$413,445	$2,345,916
74	Value of buildings	$9,885	$114,475	$86,966	$27,491	$1,780	$119,212	$5,125	$29,018	$64,950	$357,157
75	Value of implements and machinery	$1,119	$16,749	$14,351	$7,625	$410	$28,954	$1,020	$5,618	$8,815	$33,406
76	Number of dairy cows	139	277	668	205	47	1,168	19	350	298	1,490
77	Number of work horses	56	95	225	58	9	588	13	150	142	689
78	Number of work mules	40	281	558	206	14	827	15	215	249	1,051
79	Acreage in cotton	1,017	7,597	9,183	3,769	252	15,242	155	4,723	6,974	43,609
80	Bales of cotton grown in 1909	282	2,508	2,400	1,378	85	3,213	48	1,411	2,940	18,406
81	Acreage in corn	1,135	1,611	4,769	1,610	179	10,116	184	2,936	1,477	6,139
82	Bushels of corn grown in 1909	12,771	23,531	57,604	23,819	3,015	165,944	3,660	52,907	28,990	110,941

OPERATED BY COLORED FARMERS, BY COUNTIES, FOR SOUTHERN STATES: 1910—Continued.

ARKANSAS—continued.

Lafayette.	Lee.	Lincoln.	Little River.	Lonoke.	Miller.	Mississippi.	Monroe.	Nevada.	Ouachita.	Perry.	Phillips.	Poinsett.	Pope.	Prairie.	
738	3,353	2,054	977	2,297	545	1,872	2,131	840	1,296	141	4,185	244	233	620	1
.....	2	.....	.....	.....	.....	.....	.....	.....	.....	.....	1	1	.....	.....	2
23	37	189	44	112	17	64	33	8	42	18	112	6	5	15	3
103	752	776	192	891	91	639	383	78	89	21	1,415	57	31	93	4
370	1,917	788	481	1,075	281	970	1,313	349	437	66	2,164	144	114	366	5
129	423	171	157	161	98	159	310	208	355	26	342	21	55	101	6
79	151	92	76	46	40	29	78	139	249	8	116	14	22	37	7
22	22	32	18	11	11	8	13	33	75	2	19	1	6	4	8
7	16	13	8	1	6	2	1	24	39	.....	14	.....	.....	4	9
.....	3	2	.....	.....	1	1	.....	1	10	.....	1	.....	.....	.....	10
.....	.....	.....	1	.....	.....	.....	.....	.....	.....	.....	1	.....	.....	.....	11
168	331	206	142	133	102	45	183	160	488	22	378	13	23	76	12
78	268	89	60	93	42	53	67	106	205	11	159	12	17	25	13
67	103	44	32	44	39	20	82	65	85	20	50	1	38	27	14
71	1,489	587	50	602	103	954	848	41	129	69	1,778	109	85	194	15
317	1,039	923	658	1,287	257	772	878	460	329	16	1,689	100	64	274	16
8	63	18	21	66	1	7	11	11	52	3	36	.....	3	7	17
29	60	183	14	66	1	11	62	6	8	.....	93	9	3	16	18
.....	.....	4	.....	6	.....	.....	.....	2	.....	.....	2	.....	.....	1	19
13,045	23,085	16,951	13,600	9,436	7,377	3,392	12,458	17,670	49,951	1,173	25,300	992	2,044	5,043	20
5,907	11,733	6,630	5,785	4,538	3,397	1,395	5,359	7,925	20,218	597	13,885	470	917	2,484	21
$118,365	$192,265	$279,925	$152,750	$170,922	$69,001	$110,089	$199,383	$93,631	$315,105	$16,015	$627,977	$18,500	$18,740	$74,005	22
$12,350	$143,206	$49,272	$31,825	$37,585	$19,289	$17,115	$51,415	$30,940	$97,022	$3,625	$142,020	$2,800	$7,375	$24,055	23
$9,870	$79,540	$18,684	$6,472	$9,912	$4,852	$4,905	$12,239	$9,220	$23,094	$2,305	$18,072	$560	$2,175	$5,297	24
571	860	542	384	353	311	176	384	410	1,210	50	1,067	26	44	235	25
166	384	219	178	108	146	50	190	145	348	21	342	12	27	90	26
111	377	264	166	235	94	83	218	172	469	23	397	14	33	86	27
1,528	6,015	3,005	1,629	2,161	982	711	2,909	2,355	6,054	265	7,379	173	379	1,214	28
325	2,423	908	392	596	208	442	713	542	1,389	88	2,497	58	100	354	29
1,696	3,261	1,318	1,660	1,098	1,338	408	1,244	2,255	6,185	203	2,890	133	268	563	30
20,051	68,341	19,499	27,678	13,279	16,655	13,471	16,585	22,409	63,453	2,520	49,397	2,300	3,163	6,227	31
7,193	19,696	7,710	6,720	6,463	3,687	3,601	4,207	11,312	20,402	913	12,198	1,128	1,266	1,863	32
2,898	9,768	2,944	2,753	1,475	1,894	2,256		4,991	8,173	428	6,218	388	715	778	33
$63,600	$372,321	$157,440	$70,063	$126,647	$48,539	$137,125	$71,910	$64,780	$135,637	$12,975	$310,513	$20,440	$11,700	$26,335	34
$19,575	$104,785	$27,435	$14,350	$25,365	$8,125	$19,755	$18,090	$20,491	$38,265	$3,775	$51,615	$5,510	$1,820	$4,065	35
$4,122	$31,696	$12,950	$3,910	$6,742	$1,978	$5,134	$1,770	$5,972	$8,178	$665	$15,970	$890	$1,063	$1,020	36
204	622	249	218	261	113	163	142	252	485	22	408	29	20	56	37
70	304	98	84	79	48	57	64	95	131	11	138	12	22	21	38
60	293	170	92	158	36	106	92	101	179	13	149	20	14	32	39
895	5,426	1,593	885	1,568	458	1,062	1,151	1,669	2,822	189	3,118	107	285	403	40
200	1,933	462	174	432	93	535	294	376	594	56	943	55	75	70	41
797	2,464	700	808	712	438	398	355	1,368	2,726	100	1,150	97	153	176	42
8,526	42,521	9,145	11,069	8,269	4,755	10,595	4,040	13,744	24,752	1,060	15,742	1,725	2,160	1,500	43
6,101	7,955	4,883	3,405	3,340	2,790	2,337	5,562	6,913	6,788	1,445	4,324	80	3,088	2,227	44
4,217	4,148	3,805	2,117	1,960	1,829	1,165	3,551	4,638	5,248	1,057	2,238	40	2,075	1,251	45
3,138	5,323	1,961	1,594	2,133	1,479	1,586	3,266	3,179	3,217	708	2,802	40	1,933	1,126	46
1,433	2,352	1,050	833	1,037	689	846	1,613	2,037	1,918	325	1,427	20	1,142	550	47
$84,649	$191,300	$54,041	$40,832	$86,677	$27,274	$83,522	$110,924	$38,626	$43,607	$14,055	$109,645	$2,600	$50,180	$31,925	48
$21,041	$48,900	$6,400	$5,590	$10,915	$5,868	$11,870	$20,390	$12,325	$11,480	$3,185	$18,725	$400	$11,800	$7,350	49
$60,725	$121,593	$37,655	$29,515	$52,100	$20,130	$53,670	$78,029	$31,770	$41,675	$9,400	$68,650	$1,500	$35,255	$22,750	50
$6,094	$12,527	$3,025	$1,430	$3,312	$1,656	$3,512	$6,043	$4,365	$3,257	$725	$6,940	$100	$3,125	$1,335	51
176	251	123	88	137	131	162	183	173	197	54	114	2	76	69	52
65	207	44	43	44	43	52	92	56	53	24	44	.....	43	21	53
78	86	69	39	82	39	46	120	75	83	20	84	2	61	40	54
919	2,260	876	559	860	290	914	1,810	1,075	1,103	348	1,279	.....	986	600	55
267	802	297	115	248	43	517	481	256	239	108	496	.....	290	134	56
885	1,058	389	441	352	615	359	605	854	1,028	167	410	.....	436	262	57
11,158	17,052	5,947	6,384	4,604	7,797	11,965	9,331	8,310	8,743	2,605	7,844	.....	6,525	2,530	58
3,757	51,676	22,981	3,329	20,092	4,417	29,689	32,681	3,552	9,771	1,927	58,027	3,936	3,521	7,984	59
2,924	44,661	19,117	1,885	18,620	3,406	28,968	28,409	1,683	4,481	1,620	53,645	3,645	2,988	6,579	60
$87,859	$1,251,363	$547,429	$35,979	$687,650	$113,500	$1,490,324	$875,664	$22,119	$63,467	$40,830	$1,911,641	$139,065	$105,799	$208,235	61
$11,004	$348,708	$79,805	$7,570	$108,365	$12,760	$164,452	$154,912	$6,610	$13,678	$4,205	$397,638	$29,915	$16,336	$49,775	62
$2,599	$113,418	$27,782	$1,977	$34,427	$2,140	$55,641	$45,061	$1,272	$2,420	$1,830	$130,568	$5,760	$3,717	$8,911	63
121	2,219	943	136	823	100	1,268	1,473	71	180	96	2,723	148	99	394	64
72	1,242	619	79	346	96	619	699	30	92	29	1,214	59	70	114	65
81	1,338	671	54	1,016	105	1,172	1,151	29	77	63	1,630	183	110	283	66
1,134	28,392	11,895	765	11,517	1,528	19,604	18,511	597	1,660	915	36,910	1,561	1,671	4,276	67
352	11,997	4,069	186	4,090	513	11,806	5,410	142	366	402	12,658	795	707	1,261	68
854	10,274	4,021	619	3,640	1,052	6,076	5,299	413	1,393	453	10,052	723	633	1,452	69
12,341	221,246	64,431	10,506	61,082	17,926	189,311	81,961	4,401	12,682	7,948	159,110	17,178	12,706	17,035	70
9,592	25,878	18,172	19,964	25,377	9,465	14,835	24,608	21,153	22,775	435	32,913	2,605	1,980	9,339	71
8,828	21,240	16,301	17,152	24,850	6,926	11,731	22,164	11,627	12,469	362	32,178	2,103	1,822	7,870	72
$184,547	$622,005	$387,013	$389,580	$1,101,885	$160,605	$905,139	$664,117	$159,514	$225,481	$8,325	$1,009,864	$90,010	$61,420	$386,003	73
$30,908	$191,364	$72,925	$46,995	$155,985	$22,230	$116,941	$137,418	$12,445	$38,734	$1,250	$205,113	$18,125	$7,775	$52,002	74
$6,019	$42,866	$13,503	$13,929	$16,528	$4,009	$17,445	$22,310	$9,318	$4,639	$180	$30,260	$2,212	$1,713	$7,582	75
344	824	391	605	469	226	268	647	495	352	8	764	52	47	301	76
162	403	166	433	173	161	55	226	193	165	6	218	10	46	80	77
265	560	221	512	472	159	516	733	212	193	10	219	58	50	263	78
3,795	16,669	10,734	7,800	15,697	2,627	10,959	15,782	5,712	4,095	148	24,351	934	1,119	5,387	79
1,155	6,453	3,534	2,491	5,958	763	7,341	4,625	1,535	966	51	8,359	524	470	1,323	80
3,163	4,791	3,069	6,256	2,510	2,320	1,543	2,983	4,222	3,205	97	4,065	347	504	1,470	81
48,802	95,904	44,840	116,057	41,458	31,179	53,231	46,732	51,517	31,771	1,225	61,043	7,475	7,799	18,830	82

TABLE 73.—STATISTICS OF SIZE OF FARMS AND FOR TENURE CLASSES OF FARMS

		ARKANSAS—continued.									
		Pulaski.	St. Francis.	Saline.	Sebastian.	Sevier.	Union.	White.	Woodruff.	Yell.	All other counties.
1	Number of farms	3,002	2,930	283	107	310	1,319	160	2,173	191	754
	FARMS CLASSIFIED BY SIZE.										
2	Under 3 acres	3		3							
3	3 to 9 acres	186	72	26	9	7	32	5	46	5	44
4	10 to 19 acres	1,115	684	91	23	47	113	23	319	25	105
5	20 to 49 acres	1,317	1,656	113	55	154	483	70	1,364	93	334
6	50 to 99 acres	276	361	35	12	52	316	35	323	50	145
7	100 to 174 acres	83	132	10	4	30	251	20	98	15	110
8	175 to 259 acres	15	18	2	3	12	81	5	17	3	12
9	260 to 499 acres	6	5	3	1	8	36	•2	4		4
10	500 to 999 acres	1	2				6		2		
11	1,000 acres and over						1				
	FARMERS CLASSIFIED BY TENURE.										
12	Owners, free	392	242	51	15	95	262	42	127	34	194
13	Owners, mortgaged	95	147	11	5	21	250	16	66	17	54
14	Part owners	123	89	81	10	25	118	11	55	22	96
15	Cash tenants	601	801	30	16	3	119	20	612	44	79
16	Share tenants	1,653	1,532	92	52	145	544	69	1,098	62	304
17	Share-cash tenants	90	4	17	4	3	4		159		14
18	Tenure not specified	46	114	1	5	18	19	2	56	10	12
19	Managers	2	1				3			2	1
	FARMS OPERATED BY OWNERS, FREE.										
20	Total acreage	22,419	16,974	2,836	1,330	9,298	29,638	3,245	9,581	2,194	16,560
21	Improved acreage	10,456	8,331	919	667	4,385	10,794	1,374	4,473	1,119	5,829
22	Value of land	$615,427	$364,782	$44,775	$27,675	$82,246	$161,086	$27,315	$217,655	$29,890	$134,975
23	Value of buildings	$122,816	$86,525	$13,400	$3,725	$19,620	$50,634	$10,570	$47,590	$9,510	$37,435
24	Value of implements and machinery	$29,885	$21,764	$3,660	$730	$4,767	$12,189	$2,967	$9,108	$2,047	$11,194
25	Number of dairy cows	714	668	59	30	245	699	73	346	57	381
26	Number of work horses	315	238	19	23	123	200	43	150	36	195
27	Number of work mules	475	306	23	7	76	261	45	208	41	154
28	Acreage in cotton	4,488	4,086	321	101	1,103	2,990	443	2,039	442	1,272
29	Bales of cotton grown in 1909	1,922	1,675	69	24	202	578	109	670	141	351
30	Acreage in corn	2,514	2,450	183	171	1,256	3,263	376	1,091	354	1,983
31	Bushels of corn grown in 1909	37,448	45,015	2,164	1,935	21,187	28,618	4,000	15,847	5,020	22,809
	FARMS OPERATED BY OWNERS, MORTGAGED.										
32	Total acreage	5,450	11,927	612	101	2,393	28,429	1,548	4,839	1,278	4,921
33	Improved acreage	2,300	5,187	231	66	920	11,559	510	1,999	647	2,068
34	Value of land	$126,132	$179,740	$4,790	$32,100	$20,545	$161,622	$12,060	$98,386	$22,295	$72,830
35	Value of buildings	$30,615	$40,306	$950	$6,600	$4,350	$48,078	$3,350	$16,195	$5,625	$11,875
36	Value of implements and machinery	$7,282	$11,569	$341	$825	$1,130	$14,250	$920	$3,847	$1,405	$3,785
37	Number of dairy cows	156	304	14	8	44	640	24	174	31	111
38	Number of work horses	80	116	6	21	17	172	9	53	17	69
39	Number of work mules	94	192	5		25	291	19	120	25	55
40	Acreage in cotton	1,143	2,756	65	7	313	3,893	142	1,113	239	569
41	Bales of cotton grown in 1909	354	812	12	3	65	670	35	292	79	157
42	Acreage in corn	648	1,427	63	15	333	3,549	155	487	182	617
43	Bushels of corn grown in 1909	6,713	21,123	500	550	6,375	29,149	1,360	6,048	3,305	9,778
	FARMS OPERATED BY PART OWNERS.										
44	Total acreage	7,731	6,838	3,035	498	1,655	11,307	807	4,267	1,640	6,105
45	Owned acreage	4,509	4,545	1,552	169	1,109	8,049	602	2,669	1,215	3,713
46	Improved acreage	4,604	3,969	2,108	418	575	4,502	440	2,165	940	3,554
47	Owned improved acreage	1,814	2,047	634	119	234	2,663	239	1,077	515	1,613
48	Value of land	$206,068	$139,239	$66,465	$25,920	$11,925	$57,350	$10,300	$120,099	$28,322	$94,901
49	Value of buildings	$41,310	$33,935	$19,660	$2,130	$2,750	$15,610	$3,400	$24,790	$5,900	$20,069
50	Value of land and buildings owned	$128,124	$110,955	$42,395	$10,530	$8,705	$52,825	$9,800	$84,974	$24,433	$61,452
51	Value of implements and machinery	$7,579	$9,483	$4,551	$625	$481	$3,896	$918	$5,490	$980	$5,048
52	Number of dairy cows	207	233	81	21	41	271	33	138	37	190
53	Number of work horses	107	95	19	16	21	82	10	60	19	104
54	Number of work mules	210	113	68	10	10	129	17	93	30	113
55	Acreage in cotton	2,233	1,740	1,097	112	247	1,413	170	1,319		965
56	Bales of cotton grown in 1909	989	481	386	30	48	264	49	469		347
57	Acreage in corn	794	896	375	143	237	1,313	113	476	265	1,345
58	Bushels of corn grown in 1909	15,980	13,261	6,553	2,055	3,985	10,909	1,204	8,315	5,030	24,490
	FARMS OPERATED BY CASH TENANTS, INCLUDING TENURE NOT SPECIFIED.										
59	Total acreage	20,702	31,924	1,192	763	737	11,663	1,152	30,202	2,392	3,627
60	Improved acreage	17,603	27,483	962	448	666	4,739	833	25,661	1,913	2,959
61	Value of land	$1,054,333	$834,234	$29,460	$53,135	$12,455	$82,358	$14,265	$1,255,672	$61,595	$108,290
62	Value of buildings	$112,448	$163,110	$4,640	$3,285	$2,275	$16,030	$4,915	$167,638	$11,540	$14,990
63	Value of implements and machinery	$30,328	$44,132	$1,980	$828	$595	$3,951	$1,286	$52,108	$2,215	$4,667
64	Number of dairy cows	651	1,302	29	15	28	144	41	1,167	56	109
65	Number of work horses	388	511	10	24	15	56	44	685	35	113
66	Number of work mules	828	1,000	40	8	10	89	19	939	72	92
67	Acreage in cotton	11,697	16,124	502	126	281	1,095	310	16,160	1,131	1,582
68	Bales of cotton grown in 1909	5,266	6,775	178	38	74	196	99	6,214	426	653
69	Acreage in corn	3,377	6,805	107	111	308	918	207	5,543	504	964
70	Bushels of corn grown in 1909	66,719	128,648	2,253	1,425	4,314	7,425	3,233	95,993	7,635	25,625
	FARMS OPERATED BY SHARE AND SHARE-CASH TENANTS.										
71	Total acreage	34,660	40,185	2,418	1,623	4,689	26,771	2,453	36,404	1,830	9,987
72	Improved acreage	33,487	34,823	2,184	1,279	4,061	16,071	2,004	32,773	1,457	8,316
73	Value of land	$2,003,499	$1,098,257	$65,584	$75,305	$58,604	$190,861	$38,370	$1,533,583	$38,735	$238,761
74	Value of buildings	$212,071	$212,495	$12,870	$5,785	$15,480	$42,633	$8,200	$195,413	$5,630	$31,227
75	Value of implements and machinery	$27,755	$25,800	$1,538	$1,360	$4,930	$6,843	$1,947	$33,741	$1,485	$9,436
76	Number of dairy cows	782	901	43	57	194	518	60	989	52	297
77	Number of work horses	354	245	20	52	119	168	59	509	27	242
78	Number of work mules	618	1,362	33	17	81	245	51	827	52	210
79	Acreage in cotton	26,528	24,089	1,327	535	1,674	4,562	879	21,363	621	3,451
80	Bales of cotton grown in 1909	12,804	10,334	405	149	410	925	281	8,207	199	1,362
81	Acreage in corn	4,080	7,463	428	436	1,862	3,774	643	5,951	499	3,101
82	Bushels of corn grown in 1909	85,204	153,940	6,457	6,375	37,621	34,807	9,431	109,400	7,199	60,534

OPERATED BY COLORED FARMERS, BY COUNTIES, FOR SOUTHERN STATES: 1910—Continued.

DELAWARE				DISTRICT OF COLUMBIA	FLORIDA										No.
The state.	Kent.	Sussex.	All other counties.		The state.	Alachua.	Bradford.	Columbia.	Duval.	Gadsden.	Hamilton.	Hillsborough.	Jackson.	Jefferson.	
922	353	471	98	12	14,721	1,468	297	855	303	985	430	115	1,895	1,610	1
3			3	4	66		5		6	1		29	1		2
125	59	36	30	4	1,334	87	41	41	158	59		25	111	28	3
165	84	63	18	2	1,665	255	60	46	66	145	2	43	137	103	4
221	82	122	17	2	7,139	731	131	367	50	466	10	12	1,011	1,071	5
195	52	129	14		2,743	257	31	216	13	183	226	5	389	273	6
153	54	90	9		1,284	119	24	125	8	78	121		166	103	7
42	13	24	5		305	11	3	39	1	32	50	1	51	22	8
14	6	6	2		158	7	1	17	1	18	11		27	9	9
4	3	1			23	1	1	4		3	8		1	1	10
				1	4						2		1		11
198	68	98	32	3	5,130	644	112	233	233	352	69	81	389	241	12
149	75	51	23	3	1,065	171	39	121	18	71	36	10	161	35	13
59	20	33	6	2	1,103	211	17	86	3	111	25	6	111	69	14
55	34	11	10	3	4,259	248	32	143	21	327	130	4	887	594	15
421	128	271	22		1,871	177	75	233	1	97	146	4	190	377	16
4	2	2			146	6	5			14	10	1	9	5	17
20	16	3	1		1,046	10	1	34	22	10	14	3	145	289	18
16	10	2	4	1	101	1	1	1	5	3		6	3		19
6,439	1,639	4,162	638	15	308,559	32,563	3,839	23,243	4,220	25,416	8,071	3,164	30,508	18,869	20
4,070	1,184	2,455	431	15	146,833	19,020	1,866	12,987	1,428	10,972	3,827	1,170	17,209	12,042	21
$161,370	$58,290	$87,030	$16,050	$11,900	$3,577,891	$290,970	$58,020	$148,355	$193,300	$347,700	$64,890	$105,244	$319,161	$165,421	22
$84,625	$23,955	$49,970	$10,700	$6,500	$1,241,209	$91,506	$23,180	$51,835	$84,675	$95,790	$17,150	$19,006	$80,810	$63,150	23
$18,673	$4,491	$12,312	$1,870	$300	$256,666	$21,347	$4,431	$10,253	$8,831	$27,545	$3,940	$4,278	$17,285	$18,095	24
148	50	77	21	8	7,378	733	62	321	216	792	225	46	650	642	25
276	94	136	46	4	4,291	677	79	161	126	414	43	76	302	126	26
53	2	51			1,315	98	17	174	33	119	54	12	257	84	27
					24,894	3,606	316	2,773		1,483	1,142		4,992	2,778	28
					6,008	666	54	445		466	201		1,570	872	29
1,532	364	1,054	114		58,001	6,651	691	3,985	339	5,385	1,346	443	6,806	5,852	30
32,260	7,870	22,040	2,350		676,720	67,159	8,830	35,999	7,258	121,402	10,977	4,235	68,969	81,627	31
4,999	2,073	2,325	601	3	85,775	9,142	2,220	13,004	199	4,794	3,685	133	16,134	3,360	32
3,458	1,497	1,490	471	3	43,639	5,890	999	7,142	105	2,328	1,782	69	8,316	1,831	33
$137,615	$66,745	$54,445	$16,425	$5,900	$895,948	$75,419	$24,475	$78,853	$37,375	$44,216	$31,155	$52,950	$133,181	$24,280	34
$77,385	$43,455	$21,705	$12,225	$6,100	$236,597	$21,025	$10,225	$19,817	$12,925	$18,350	$6,425	$4,650	$31,960	$6,460	35
$16,299	$9,209	$4,530	$2,560	$375	$54,888	$4,557	$1,784	$5,553	$1,290	$3,829	$1,520	$216	$7,644	$2,510	36
139	68	40	31		1,347	196	39	131	15	106	53	3	218	69	37
238	117	87	34	2	853	178	39	93	9	86	17	7	126	13	38
35	10	24	1		465	30	14	87	7	18	29		118	20	39
					10,147	1,570	354	1,902		284	547		2,302	443	40
					2,066	276	55	263		58	88		660	122	41
1,232	523	585	124		15,373	1,922	402	2,395	51	1,553	611	8	2,635	871	42
23,007	9,200	11,620	2,187		153,329	19,252	4,210	19,772	316	16,033	4,895	70	28,344	12,500	43
2,177	401	1,518	258	40	64,109	8,135	722	6,296	48	6,242	2,087	108	8,860	4,555	44
1,128	176	833	119	10	38,844	4,730	441	4,498	11	3,782	1,370	58	5,420	2,144	45
1,746	386	1,118	242	40	39,389	5,915	422	4,041	29	3,388	1,405	77	6,661	3,234	46
829	164	549	116	10	18,496	2,982	171	2,365	5	1,382	748	32	3,426	1,006	47
$63,606	$20,690	$36,116	$6,800	$14,000	$621,910	$60,289	$9,530	$37,629	$4,450	$67,300	$18,400	$6,655	$100,511	$32,822	48
$22,950	$6,950	$11,000	$5,000	$4,000	$213,255	$21,749	$2,325	$10,890	$400	$28,720	$3,950	$1,445	$29,824	$13,557	49
$49,080	$15,920	$26,180	$6,980	$10,000	$520,077	$53,134	$5,800	$35,209	$2,050	$59,190	$14,575	$4,025	$88,031	$21,942	50
$6,133	$2,965	$2,283	$885	$75	$46,489	$5,729	$547	$2,524	$25	$4,383	$1,440	$295	$5,390	$3,711	51
42	11	19	12	1	1,253	198	13	96		137	41	1	129	122	52
99	37	46	16	8	967	225	9	66	5	108	5	8	69	54	53
12	1	11			418	28	9	52		32	33		90	26	54
					8,160	983	129	1,248		311	493		2,225	964	55
					1,893	185	17	190		69	104		720	215	56
746	105	581	60	2	15,605	2,045	187	1,282	12	1,743	475	39	2,087	1,459	57
14,544	2,330	10,990	1,224	50	158,565	21,901	2,063	11,345	150	18,743	3,972	305	21,188	17,036	58
4,112	2,858	945	309	33	219,906	8,378	1,560	9,273	607	14,046	7,727	102	44,027	35,623	59
2,647	1,945	523	179	33	180,349	6,478	768	6,437	239	8,851	6,582	96	38,654	33,136	60
$99,810	$76,175	$15,185	$8,450	$28,000	$2,605,491	$73,935	$18,925	$60,254	$51,802	$150,370	$76,080	$10,290	$481,211	$335,360	61
$32,690	$24,675	$4,065	$3,950	$5,000	$626,017	$17,392	$7,225	$15,490	$11,308	$40,162	$18,740	$1,860	$99,807	$105,019	62
$6,413	$4,393	$745	$1,275	$155	$183,958	$4,237	$911	$3,418	$1,242	$10,984	$4,727	$885	$29,780	$33,761	63
69	59	4	6	2	4,818	98	11	92	7	305	53	4	655	1,459	64
105	78	9	18	3	2,908	228	15	106	19	275	59	5	472	241	65
16	10	6		1	2,049	18	10	72	7	47	89	2	584	523	66
					58,198	1,567	300	2,182		1,174	2,672		14,780	12,159	67
					13,508	276	49	329		279	540		4,085	2,969	68
754	499	210	45		77,396	2,032	285	2,104	27	4,732	2,293	20	16,068	16,453	69
15,510	10,300	4,325	885		799,283	21,351	3,280	18,779	485	46,657	19,171	645	153,250	198,657	70
36,851	12,295	22,273	2,283		80,382	7,454	4,017	9,667	7	4,451	7,228	114	8,079	14,454	71
23,121	7,824	13,343	1,954		67,891	5,949	2,500	8,559	5	2,910	6,900	90	7,282	14,202	72
$889,156	$350,011	$466,420	$72,725		$957,312	$71,144	$39,760	$73,952	$1,150	$53,100	$91,145	$9,375	$92,205	$154,672	73
$266,709	$113,694	$127,240	$25,775		$201,048	$14,192	$11,755	$15,910	$100	$18,120	$23,155	$1,425	$18,083	$24,975	74
$47,082	$18,241	$23,016	$5,825		$45,124	$3,758	$1,620	$2,493	$50	$1,740	$3,736	$280	$4,378	$11,311	75
615	302	192	121		1,021	61	24	69		56	32	5	100	395	76
750	313	358	79		719	109	29	60	1	50	36	5	38	193	77
213	43	161	9		737	68	32	113		12	84		167	108	78
					20,338	1,131	1,035	2,421		237	2,329		2,898	5,685	79
					4,823	212	209	458		57	513		919	1,491	80
7,943	1,943	5,619	381		23,897	1,446	821	2,343	2	1,153	2,292	41	2,128	7,236	81
154,872	42,204	103,113	9,555		261,685	16,857	8,832	22,868	30	12,087	20,666	700	24,036	90,728	82

Table 73.—STATISTICS OF SIZE OF FARMS AND FOR TENURE CLASSES OF FARMS

FLORIDA—continued.

	Lake.	Leon.	Levy.	Madison.	Marion.	Orange.	Putnam.	Sumter.	Suwannee.	Volusia.
1 Number of farms	121	1,649	175	929	1,007	142	294	143	697	112
FARMS CLASSIFIED BY SIZE.										
2 Under 3 acres		1	1	1	2	9	8			2
3 3 to 9 acres	32	65	14	23	140	43	87	31	28	54
4 10 to 19 acres	31	117	18	71	194	19	57	31	48	24
5 20 to 49 acres	30	1,054	63	555	387	40	79	61	293	22
6 50 to 99 acres	15	275	43	188	202	14	35	19	176	8
7 100 to 174 acres	8	100	29	63	63	12	18	1	106	2
8 175 to 259 acres	3	25	4	17	9	3	6		24	
9 260 to 499 acres	2	11	3	10	6	2	4		19	
10 500 to 999 acres		1		1	3				3	
11 1,000 acres and over					1					
FARMERS CLASSIFIED BY TENURE.										
12 Owners, free	83	223	112	99	673	105	213	98	261	74
13 Owners, mortgaged	7	26	11	35	34	14	8	8	109	11
14 Part owners	11	55	7	31	155		44	7	31	6
15 Cash tenants	9	961	27	538	94	2	7		125	8
16 Share tenants	2	54	15	112	37	2	10	10	148	1
17 Share-cash tenants		34		16	6		2	4	16	2
18 Tenure not specified	2	295	3	94	4	11	6	16	5	1
19 Managers	7	1		4	4	8	4		2	9
FARMS OPERATED BY OWNERS, FREE.										
20 Total acreage	3,038	15,472	7,903	8,147	31,074	3,263	6,369	3,099	23,499	1,541
21 Improved acreage	1,367	9,447	3,235	4,625	15,133	948	2,025	1,614	12,549	699
22 Value of land	$55,395	$166,675	$65,850	$88,965	$333,237	$116,800	$100,040	$51,432	$166,875	$55,915
23 Value of buildings	$18,585	$63,535	$21,700	$24,865	$160,959	$52,900	$67,120	$13,883	$57,905	$19,645
24 Value of implements and machinery	$2,418	$17,853	$3,901	$7,469	$35,566	$7,711	$8,371	$3,718	$13,603	$2,467
25 Number of dairy cows	77	445	194	191	868	68	36	86	381	23
26 Number of work horses	67	201	139	74	761	59	101	105	165	44
27 Number of work mules	5	61	13	41	46	14	19	4	92	8
28 Acreage in cotton		2,042	180	1,080	450		79		2,889	5
29 Bales of cotton grown in 1909		472	39	218	76		14		568	1
30 Acreage in corn	257	3,987	1,196	1,705	6,069	207	688	693	4,184	209
31 Bushels of corn grown in 1909	2,294	41,256	12,581	15,895	64,221	3,924	7,828	7,215	36,153	2,054
FARMS OPERATED BY OWNERS, MORTGAGED.										
32 Total acreage	533	2,115	894	5,093	2,622	590	122	241	12,159	216
33 Improved acreage	150	1,387	346	2,691	1,344	129	64	129	6,161	106
34 Value of land	$5,275	$22,430	$9,500	$43,960	$27,285	$19,390	$5,500	$4,135	$91,720	$11,200
35 Value of buildings	$1,350	$7,360	$1,500	$13,940	$8,470	$7,410	$1,350	$865	$25,475	$4,400
36 Value of implements and machinery	$199	$2,562	$390	$2,480	$3,830	$635	$235	$195	$8,700	$235
37 Number of dairy cows	3	25	16	100	45	8		1	169	4
38 Number of work horses	8	22	17	28	33	11	1	7	83	5
39 Number of work mules	4	8	1	30	7	3	2		47	1
40 Acreage in cotton		298	39	564	13				1,586	
41 Bales of cotton grown in 1909		56	4	120	2				305	
42 Acreage in corn	25	423	122	840	465	35	22	49	1,990	21
43 Bushels of corn grown in 1909	155	4,131	1,005	8,010	5,419	570	400	430	18,144	240
FARMS OPERATED BY PART OWNERS.										
44 Total acreage	504	3,571	630	2,874	5,779		3,920	176	3,123	50
45 Owned acreage	125	1,674	350	1,846	3,517		3,053	10	2,098	24
46 Improved acreage	222	2,646	308	1,764	3,309		1,272	115	1,688	45
47 Owned improved acreage	109	903	143	917	1,477		602	10	922	22
48 Value of land	$14,295	$33,115	$3,430	$27,287	$55,249		$33,684	$3,360	$21,065	$2,870
49 Value of buildings	$3,925	$10,895	$1,750	$6,828	$20,920		$19,290	$1,115	$5,747	$1,450
50 Value of land and buildings owned	$9,351	$21,705	$2,580	$24,260	$48,040		$39,594	$600	$16,327	$2,570
51 Value of implements and machinery	$710	$3,692	$115	$1,930	$5,811		$2,547	$285	$1,276	$115
52 Number of dairy cows	13	90	8	47	170		38		42	
53 Number of work horses	7	46	13	38	163		42	9	17	4
54 Number of work mules	7	39	1	11	19		8	1	19	1
55 Acreage in cotton	4	616	34	439	80		68		360	
56 Bales of cotton grown in 1909	1	167	6	79	11		11		64	
57 Acreage in corn	44	1,388	91	721	1,548		468	51	457	23
58 Bushels of corn grown in 1909	550	15,210	1,160	6,605	15,147		4,393	460	3,940	325
FARMS OPERATED BY CASH TENANTS, INCLUDING TENURE NOT SPECIFIED.										
59 Total acreage	370	53,907	1,558	25,792	2,563	683	421	324	6,116	123
60 Improved acreage	148	45,160	818	23,867	1,349	263	165	189	4,448	113
61 Value of land	$9,725	$680,489	$15,115	$301,534	$23,112	$105,300	$3,915	$9,700	$49,974	$9,600
62 Value of buildings	$2,250	$155,717	$2,360	$74,416	$7,321	$16,300	$4,425	$2,300	$14,105	$1,500
63 Value of implements and machinery	$460	$53,341	$645	$24,111	$2,071	$1,940	$395	$395	$4,559	$185
64 Number of dairy cows	15	1,291	14	603	33	3	3	2	93	2
65 Number of work horses	5	880	28	351	58	7	3	9	63	6
66 Number of work mules	3	363		237	6	7	3	2	43	
67 Acreage in cotton	2	13,676	59	8,215	29		15		1,138	
68 Bales of cotton grown in 1909		3,137	9	1,542	3		7		221	
69 Acreage in corn	48	19,514	309	10,379	444	26	36	33	1,376	81
70 Bushels of corn grown in 1909	390	205,325	2,995	97,363	4,423	225	416	483	13,116	1,260
FARMS OPERATED BY SHARE AND SHARE-CASH TENANTS.										
71 Total acreage	80	4,315	664	4,649	2,014	24	317	177	7,177	45
72 Improved acreage	15	3,423	346	4,428	1,104	24	233	140	6,081	20
73 Value of land	$550	$75,175	$7,365	$49,865	$22,321	$1,200	$3,240	$4,520	$58,325	$1,100
74 Value of buildings	$150	$17,505	$1,535	$10,050	$5,775	$50	$1,970	$1,520	$15,970	$400
75 Value of implements and machinery	$60	$3,643	$335	$1,542	$1,096	$5	$445	$305	$2,696	$65
76 Number of dairy cows	4	81	14	33	17		1		46	
77 Number of work horses	3	20	13	20	20		9	13	36	
78 Number of work mules		36	2	18	4	1			60	1
79 Acreage in cotton		800	14	1,350	4		36		1,928	
80 Bales of cotton grown in 1909		158	1	268	2		9		401	
81 Acreage in corn	12	1,193	120	1,764	412	3	62	60	1,552	13
82 Bushels of corn grown in 1909	440	12,689	1,770	17,771	4,066	60	645	655	15,110	150

OPERATED BY COLORED FARMERS, BY COUNTIES, FOR SOUTHERN STATES: 1910—Continued.

| FLORIDA—continued. | | | GEORGIA. | | | | | | | | | | | | |
Walton.	Washington.	All other counties.	The state.	Appling.	Baker.	Baldwin.	Banks.	Bartow.	Ben Hill.	Berrien.	Bibb.	Brooks.	Bryan.	Bulloch.	
129	282	1,083	122,559	264	908	960	428	529	401	368	705	1,369	304	1,281	1
6	13	29	16												2
16	18	242	3,770	30	8	5	33	15	23	12	31	59	48	17	3
53	101	174	7,780	29	22	25	62	76	26	28	50	93	50	44	4
22	68	205	65,410	76	601	427	215	288	200	184	368	750	118	790	5
25	67	183	27,811	53	171	229	77	109	80	78	174	296	40	271	6
4	12	112	12,117	28	58	149	35	30	36	38	57	125	21	113	7
3	3	28	3,704	21	36	57	4	5	13	16	17	28	11	30	8
		6	1,579	20	6	47	1	5	17	9	6	16	14	15	9
		2	320	7	5	19	1		5	2	2	2	14	1	10
		2	52		1	2			1		1				11
97	159	579	9,649	117	66	46	26	37	55	60	76	191	155	118	12
13	13	114	3,210	39	24	2	15	15	38	12	25	106	7	25	13
	44	73	2,839	7		9	2	28	54	12	16	35	15	60	14
5	20	77	46,451	42	350	632	54	42	109	77	261	478	51	186	15
14	14	152	54,464	51	239	162	326	401	139	194	295	516	76	860	16
		12	1,795	6	47	104	4	4	4	12	4	16		29	17
	30	36	4,028	2	182	4		1	1	1	22	27		3	18
	2	40	123			1	1	1			6				19
7,186	14,265	33,810	785,895	11,411	8,469	6,802	2,059	2,461	6,415	4,575	5,311	15,018	8,953	10,771	20
1,938	3,574	9,158	352,940	2,238	5,317	3,493	1,085	1,248	1,702	1,736	2,957	7,051	2,464	4,293	21
$40,456	$101,375	$541,815	$8,885,677	$82,135	$61,039	$54,610	$40,765	$23,238	$68,205	$64,120	$89,944	$202,383	$61,825	$195,895	22
$15,250	$30,675	$167,085	$2,750,531	$25,705	$14,240	$19,175	$7,785	$7,532	$12,420	$17,260	$37,200	$57,700	$24,400	$48,810	23
$3,482	$6,671	$27,431	$623,825	$4,977	$9,535	$4,395	$1,670	$1,665	$2,890	$3,773	$12,069	$12,617	$4,603	$11,744	24
152	234	936	16,342	245	191	86	30	37	74	77	121	353	255	266	25
72	92	407	4,864	69	31	49	5	8	24	30	24	82	74	36	26
18	71	75	7,947	64	66	55	42	34	44	47	89	208	40	97	27
207	276	596	132,891	418	1,500	1,604	429	448	668	805	1,463	2,581	258	1,893	28
55	90	201	51,803	132	580	476	180	119	269	329	573	1,147	141	931	29
1,266	2,181	3,861	109,368	1,095	1,401	1,029	325	273	510	536	871	2,527	1,018	1,697	30
10,325	19,039	47,479	1,196,061	12,542	12,995	7,495	3,400	1,931	5,413	7,270	8,490	34,230	11,689	24,135	31
945	1,340	6,234	346,221	4,996	5,978	140	1,457	1,091	3,758	1,218	1,833	8,658	593	2,426	32
280	349	2,041	163,893	905	2,987	105	768	527	1,490	336	902	4,447	134	1,085	33
$7,320	$10,820	$135,509	$3,890,860	$32,355	$41,735	$1,300	$27,000	$11,200	$54,795	$12,425	$30,816	$105,490	$3,380	$44,025	34
$1,630	$1,780	$29,230	$1,038,598	$8,665	$10,385	$100	$5,990	$3,350	$10,240	$2,925	$11,555	$27,875	$1,110	$8,425	35
$530	$425	$5,569	$230,483	$1,656	$1,840	$75	$1,527	$640	$2,413	$775	$2,565	$7,076	$225	$1,855	36
24	23	99	4,869	62	34	3	22	16	45	18	29	134	13	39	37
8	7	55	1,595	25	5	1	9	3	22	10	12	69	1	10	38
5	8	26	3,836	17	38	3	20	25	40	7	21	100	5	29	39
45	19	181	70,006	249	859	40	228	239	611	165	459	1,736	7	434	40
15	3	39	25,412	73	255	30	118	78	259	68	166	704	4	206	41
153	154	626	43,827	425	581	28	139	93	402	96	221	1,441	38	323	42
1,365	1,180	6,888	418,028	4,580	5,140	162	1,035	795	3,908	1,165	1,946	17,905	375	4,140	43
	3,265	3,164	217,387	284		615	133	1,578	4,074	884	836	1,719	1,317	4,752	44
	1,634	2,059	113,118	43		228	96	687	2,200	639	352	999	1,033	3,099	45
	1,213	1,635	127,563	134		424	86	1,214	2,380	481	609	1,111	431	2,630	46
	483	791	54,975	16		129	49	419	898	248	194	494	210	1,443	47
	$28,415	$61,554	$3,181,540	$4,150		$5,400	$2,000	$25,917	$66,975	$10,800	$17,000	$27,015	$9,442	$113,340	48
	$7,525	$20,950	$793,704	$1,550		$2,440	$500	$7,360	$12,575	$2,660	$1,905	$6,800	$2,520	$15,590	49
	$18,200	$52,894	$2,116,774	$1,950		$3,100	$1,750	$14,689	$41,140	$8,510	$7,033	$21,915	$7,470	$83,995	50
	$2,250	$3,714	$165,075	$290		$1,035	$50	$1,410	$2,900	$760	$370	$1,525	$757	$5,852	51
	71	37	3,791	6		12	2	35	59	23	14	19	41	94	52
	34	45	1,454	6		5		13	19	3	6	20	9	14	53
	22	20	3,028	4		4	4	30	63	15	11	20	9	33	54
	87	119	54,790	4		231	60	411	911	250	244	319	87	1,107	55
	29	25	20,504	2		96	24	120	399	97	87	127	45	570	56
	771	714	34,028	65		133	21	210	496	94	139	277	165	833	57
	7,387	6,685	341,985	648		1,165	125	2,453	5,658	1,780	1,205	4,030	1,860	12,079	58
230	2,844	3,632	3,272,972	5,040	27,907	62,729	3,283	2,557	7,903	8,183	15,216	26,138	2,378	9,990	59
135	1,073	1,380	2,189,038	796	25,218	34,538	1,917	1,907	3,580	2,776	10,163	18,558	600	6,910	60
$4,510	$23,475	$110,815	$45,961,551	$22,545	$201,325	$547,450	$62,080	$41,710	$106,969	$102,220	$314,413	$399,774	$15,400	$238,020	61
$1,400	$5,940	$20,980	$9,526,559	$5,730	$78,581	$101,055	$9,125	$6,545	$13,360	$16,380	$53,775	$73,895	$4,035	$39,300	62
$185	$1,174	$4,552	$2,232,637	$758	$18,842	$41,379	$1,825	$1,775	$3,045	$4,005	$11,014	$17,698	$836	$12,789	63
7	27	41	47,808	24	433	656	61	42	56	106	228	425	45	186	64
4	24	50	13,617	13	115	207	12	3	32	228	56	171	18	40	65
3	12	18	53,151	20	432	611	58	62	91	64	278	447	20	116	66
59	71	100	1,157,314	296	10,857	17,350	935	945	1,491	1,262	4,971	6,865	79	3,100	67
14	21	27	411,521	102	3,161	5,539	383	289	646	556	1,583	2,353	37	1,485	68
71	604	461	585,814	285	8,063	7,561	372	365	881	701	2,188	6,481	315	2,305	69
610	5,790	4,612	5,470,722	3,349	71,029	64,379	3,225	3,837	9,065	10,704	21,348	77,178	3,137	32,071	70
624	725	4,100	2,442,025	5,108	12,931	15,531	11,481	15,927	7,310	10,829	13,129	20,538	4,814	40,442	71
478	298	2,904	1,946,912	1,420	11,800	9,798	8,389	13,392	5,208	6,883	10,279	17,552	2,216	32,160	72
$7,155	$5,175	$134,818	$43,338,970	$33,655	$110,570	$148,825	$238,090	$351,864	$149,885	$188,863	$297,315	$379,260	$47,785	$1,122,074	73
$1,795	$1,400	$15,213	$8,757,705	$9,935	$29,110	$31,420	$41,085	$52,960	$17,815	$39,075	$74,470	$66,780	$12,080	$170,994	74
$215	$307	$5,044	$1,281,741	$1,299	$5,949	$8,482	$6,312	$7,416	$3,059	$7,313	$21,722	$7,877	$1,740	$39,386	75
12	6	65	31,950	31	184	124	232	321	60	209	200	226	62	686	76
6	4	54	6,458	20	34	20	28	56	21	50	78	56	28	135	77
2	7	22	41,687	36	266	170	196	298	109	149	178	323	48	643	78
76	28	366	1,050,103	353	4,652	4,441	4,390	7,847	2,064	3,037	4,891	6,943	463	15,807	79
26	7	92	416,390	116	1,457	1,486	1,824	2,400	1,010	1,312	1,803	2,804	328	7,832	80
198	151	895	502,728	576	3,517	1,873	1,764	2,505	1,456	2,177	1,891	6,129	1,034	8,951	81
1,590	1,295	8,640	5,417,633	6,495	31,738	16,207	16,211	29,187	18,541	32,761	19,269	83,824	13,580	169,912	82

TABLE **73.**—STATISTICS OF SIZE OF FARMS AND FOR TENURE CLASSES OF FARMS

GEORGIA—continued.

		Burke.	Butts.	Calhoun.	Camden.	Campbell.	Carroll.	Chatham.	Chatta-hoochee.	Chat-tooga.	Chero-kee.
1	Number of farms	3,261	928	1,139	541	524	913	225	479	336	117
	FARMS CLASSIFIED BY SIZE.										
2	Under 3 acres				1			2			
3	3 to 9 acres	19	9	7	89	31	24	111	9	15	8
4	10 to 19 acres	38	48	17	136	73	106	64	6	45	20
5	20 to 49 acres	2,128	520	802	158	241	529	33	162	145	59
6	50 to 99 acres	748	258	241	85	99	179	5	145	67	16
7	100 to 174 acres	238	81	56	49	62	64	3	73	53	9
8	175 to 259 acres	58	8	11	15	15	11	4	39	8	3
9	260 to 499 acres	22	4	3	8	2			38	3	2
10	500 to 999 acres	9		2		1		2	6		
11	1,000 acres and over	1						1	1		
	FARMERS CLASSIFIED BY TENURE.										
12	Owners, free	123	21	39	439	12	50	86	17	26	13
13	Owners, mortgaged	31	8	10	20	8	13	7	12	16	2
14	Part owners	23	9	15	11	20	17	22	12	12	3
15	Cash tenants	1,720	435	554	31	98	94	100	196	8	3
16	Share tenants	1,219	363	516	31	336	730	5	234	246	95
17	Share-cash tenants	29	61		1	5	5		2		1
18	Tenure not specified	114	29	3	8	45	4	3	6	28	
19	Managers	2	2	2				2			
	FARMS OPERATED BY OWNERS, FREE.										
20	Total acreage	16,604	928	3,234	18,329	549	4,024	1,447	4,144	2,660	1,038
21	Improved acreage	8,668	651	1,757	2,801	334	2,044	834	1,396	1,293	315
22	Value of land	$163,774	$24,895	$41,332	$99,691	$11,867	$50,905	$36,067	$20,775	$24,400	$6,395
23	Value of buildings	$50,121	$7,550	$9,120	$81,772	$4,050	$16,095	$13,665	$10,975	$5,650	$3,005
24	Value of implements and machinery	$13,012	$1,230	$2,459	$10,335	$605	$2,111	$4,814	$1,745	$1,436	$350
25	Number of dairy cows	110	21	49	912	15	52	57	29	37	13
26	Number of work horses	84	9	16	167	4	15	35	4	19	4
27	Number of work mules	139	18	52	23	10	57	53	28	36	4
28	Acreage in cotton	3,085	349	902	52	106	958	39	568	522	69
29	Bales of cotton grown in 1909	1,281	160	328	23	39	327	22	178	171	26
30	Acreage in corn	2,316	164	621	1,477	50	432	285	414	322	94
31	Bushels of corn grown in 1909	22,635	1,625	6,975	21,932	630	4,080	6,161	3,100	2,745	1,206
	FARMS OPERATED BY OWNERS, MORTGAGED.										
32	Total acreage	5,879	617	1,115	1,761	1,002	962	100	2,244	1,757	280
33	Improved acreage	3,429	482	593	237	470	471	66	723	716	72
34	Value of land	$46,655	$12,200	$15,415	$12,935	$9,340	$14,665	$4,970	$8,180	$16,600	$1,050
35	Value of buildings	$23,000	$5,985	$2,450	$5,825	$2,600	$4,685	$1,190	$2,190	$3,750	$325
36	Value of implements and machinery	$4,030	$905	$647	$625	$620	$382	$505	$400	$1,138	$154
37	Number of dairy cows	34	13	9	30	15	11	7	21	21	1
38	Number of work horses	24	1	3	7	4	4	2		10	
39	Number of work mules	61	12	18	3	14	13		19	21	2
40	Acreage in cotton	1,188	233	282		173	252	3	265	334	18
41	Bales of cotton grown in 1909	487	115	78		70	72	2	67	110	7
42	Acreage in corn	800	131	154	94	73	102	21	259	151	15
43	Bushels of corn grown in 1909	6,650	1,060	1,475	1,211	775	955	456	1,590	1,202	150
	FARMS OPERATED BY PART OWNERS.										
44	Total acreage	4,361	669	2,088	244	1,455	1,049	474	1,898	747	531
45	Owned acreage	1,833	338	1,273	62	838	585	136	1,352	384	221
46	Improved acreage	3,135	429	1,063	89	930	719	241	721	480	135
47	Owned improved acreage	1,063	206	471	29	405	302	100	456	181	90
48	Value of land	$47,720	$15,915	$18,414	$2,010	$22,362	$12,941	$18,905	$15,200	$16,795	$4,000
49	Value of buildings	$10,795	$3,850	$3,975	$4,777	$6,470	$4,635	$7,200	$2,850	$5,000	$400
50	Value of land and buildings owned	$24,870	$10,465	$13,775	$3,995	$18,355	$11,155	$15,155	$10,570	$9,440	$1,500
51	Value of implements and machinery	$3,950	$615	$865	$202	$1,413	$719	$1,100	$495	$520	$135
52	Number of dairy cows	27	18	26	13	29	19	23	20	13	3
53	Number of work horses	20	2	11	3	3	3	13	7	7	
54	Number of work mules	48	14	23	1	28	22	12	11	11	4
55	Acreage in cotton	1,191	176	503		480	330	1	284	206	49
56	Bales of cotton grown in 1909	515	65	205		157	121	1	77	64	17
57	Acreage in corn	703	102	316	27	192	190	74	173	127	42
58	Bushels of corn grown in 1909	6,193	875	3,630	540	1,855	1,770	2,071	1,460	1,235	500
	FARMS OPERATED BY CASH TENANTS, INCLUDING TENURE NOT TPECIFIED.										
59	Total acreage	103,296	25,636	27,983	2,637	8,847	5,685	3,779	23,710	3,079	225
60	Improved acreage	87,060	18,158	25,630	558	4,886	3,610	1,973	10,744	1,678	65
61	Value of land	$1,229,555	$624,569	$404,587	$18,327	$165,773	$89,314	$104,460	$152,038	$39,600	$2,095
62	Value of buildings	$354,214	$115,266	$81,550	$8,900	$32,060	$21,075	$15,150	$35,417	$7,425	$255
63	Value of implements and machinery	$112,698	$18,888	$21,319	$520	$3,710	$3,692	$5,594	$7,728	$918	$20
64	Number of dairy cows	1,842	504	477	60	151	79	72	231	47	2
65	Number of work horses	535	82	103	15	24	27	45	35	12	
66	Number of work mules	2,006	565	689	3	156	106	36	229	27	3
67	Acreage in cotton	48,507	10,687	14,231	22	2,592	1,801	17	5,090	946	31
68	Bales of cotton grown in 1909	19,507	3,999	4,804	13	844	601	14	1,580	317	12
69	Acreage in corn	24,565	4,097	8,324	159	903	692	304	3,700	549	19
70	Bushels of corn grown in 1909	236,017	38,264	84,531	2,255	8,759	7,145	6,709	27,555	3,927	100
	FARMS OPERATED BY SHARE AND SHARE-CASH TENANTS.										
71	Total acreage	50,305	16,269	21,527	1,672	13,731	25,280	110	17,849	10,624	3,611
72	Improved acreage	46,285	13,081	21,067	190	9,101	20,536	71	10,096	7,390	2,350
73	Value of land	$730,184	$423,692	$308,830	$8,885	$255,365	$580,225	$3,590	$160,915	$156,486	$54,503
74	Value of buildings	$196,986	$68,036	$60,075	$4,505	$50,555	$144,185	$585	$32,940	$35,309	$13,755
75	Value of implements and machinery	$31,612	$7,221	$11,887	$356	$6,024	$16,798	$145	$5,525	$5,395	$1,893
76	Number of dairy cows	364	283	261	55	298	475	3	185	245	77
77	Number of work horses	177	37	25	8	35	100	2	11	69	13
78	Number of work mules	873	324	569	1	180	575	2	207	207	43
79	Acreage in cotton	25,948	8,350	12,972	1	5,191	11,520	12	5,381	3,273	1,076
80	Bales of cotton grown in 1909	11,777	3,162	4,744	(1)	1,713	3,977	6	1,722	1,198	467
81	Acreage in corn	11,633	2,708	6,986	94	1,621	4,151	27	3,082	2,061	426
82	Bushels of corn grown in 1909	120,046	27,347	78,559	1,225	15,723	42,076	715	26,113	22,821	8,685

[1] Less than 1 bale.

OPERATED BY COLORED FARMERS, BY COUNTIES, FOR SOUTHERN STATES: 1910—Continued.

GEORGIA—continued.

Clarke.	Clay.	Clayton.	Clinch.	Cobb.	Coffee.	Colquitt.	Columbia.	Coweta.	Crawford.	Crisp.	Decatur.	Dekalb.	Dodge.	Dooly.	No.
912	811	677	102	700	349	250	1,387	2,155	604	684	1,490	734	1,069	1,588	1
1															2
90	2	11	13	45	9	7	47	57	11	4	79	50	15	22	3
152	6	69	19	125	30	20	107	143	15	11	168	127	19	31	4
447	454	342	32	364	160	169	782	1,130	267	387	748	365	537	906	5
157	175	177	11	109	82	36	306	533	103	197	290	135	340	383	6
53	120	73	11	48	26	9	102	228	109	65	132	47	100	188	7
10	35	4	9	7	19	5	30	43	73	16	54	7	49	45	8
2	14	1	7	2	15	3	8	19	21	2	13	2	7	10	9
	4				8	1	5	5	5	2	4	1		3	10
	1										2				11
88	32	13	51	64	62	9	89	49	48	24	284	43	125	72	12
40	33	11	12	58	22	6	22	20	34	12	117	16	59	32	13
70	5	2		57	15	2	54	11	15	6	103	23	22	7	14
336	161	244	20	76	79	48	704	681	332	255	569	216	315	681	15
374	367	394	18	433	110	174	439	1,380	167	369	373	422	482	765	16
1	64	3		8	6	2	36		4	3	19	3	9	1	17
3	148	10	1	3	55	9	43	14	3	11	22	9	54	30	18
	1														19
2,953	4,426	1,080	4,252	3,413	10,755	648	8,121	4,465	8,028	1,539	24,532	2,024	10,751	5,114	20
2,040	2,462	589	988	1,880	2,697	288	4,129	2,881	2,841	814	9,356	1,052	6,274	3,078	21
$94,735	$84,230	$17,760	$23,265	$50,510	$101,090	$9,621	$104,150	$82,130	$32,990	$29,555	$197,326	$48,380	$133,320	$66,957	22
$36,300	$9,955	$9,900	$5,710	$18,355	$22,770	$2,175	$31,925	$17,880	$14,025	$5,315	$55,283	$14,175	$38,495	$19,005	23
$4,930	$1,515	$1,510	$2,110	$2,954	$4,596	$320	$6,247	$3,861	$3,260	$1,390	$12,822	$2,028	$12,362	$4,366	24
91	49	16	63	77	113	13	122	60	99	38	577	53	219	91	25
49	23	9	15	27	30	2	21	21	24	12	292	14	39	28	26
54	34	13	34	69	79	11	94	65	71	23	99	39	134	98	27
1,011		253	193	698	881	82	1,634	1,454	1,090	414	2,969	423	2,768	1,572	28
380		106	58	295	369	32	616	478	349	205	936	165	1,187	681	29
532	749	139	503	517	1,017	89	856	361	750	264	4,027	298	2,023	978	30
5,594	5,088	1,640	6,813	5,194	10,510	1,105	9,215	3,774	6,522	2,800	46,193	3,460	19,407	10,152	31
1,759	5,477	997	865	3,096	4,198	166	2,397	2,163	5,328	1,428	9,558	1,086	5,583	3,292	32
1,284	3,327	572	152	1,686	1,072	95	1,332	1,985	778		4,179	524	3,099	1,958	33
$50,620	$53,225	$11,200	$5,375	$52,500	$44,245	$4,100	$30,875	$31,675	$26,307	$30,010	$95,805	$16,275	$68,630	$44,750	34
$17,350	$15,150	$9,950	$2,150	$16,505	$8,320	$1,100	$10,530	$6,555	$8,475	$5,400	$25,895	$6,200	$22,410	$14,875	35
$3,397	$2,097	$1,960	$343	$1,835	$1,797	$225	$1,762	$1,237	$3,130	$1,600	$5,140	$833	$5,495	$2,738	36
47	60	21	26	58	40	6	34	30	60	21	224	27	112	35	37
17	13	5	5	29	10	2	8	5	15	8	92	5	18	19	38
48	67	20	5	51	27	4	27	29	52	19	77	22	91	52	39
759	1,547	281	18	604	354	50	570	563	1,033	293	1,274	190	1,592	1,164	40
272	512	122	6	299	157	15	237	206	321	132	370	82	679	454	41
277	931	109	87	502	397	18	250	222	570	188	1,497	167	1,023	630	42
2,495	6,510	1,435	1,130	5,263	4,145	245	2,415	2,165	5,074	1,790	15,315	2,110	13,865	5,440	43
2,509	1,790	147		2,265	1,804	715	4,851	714	1,574	371	5,020	1,133	1,749	536	44
1,056	1,361	105		1,183	1,501	702	2,748	222	1,135	165	2,763	502	1,019	217	45
2,125	1,544	102		1,501	518	132	3,169	450	846	251	3,220	712	1,144	457	46
765	1,130	75		604	238	122	1,636	160	502	70	1,298	274	418	163	47
$97,010	$18,050	$4,110		$57,805	$19,652	$6,075	$56,365	$12,437	$12,425	$5,915	$55,347	$24,445	$24,525	$9,055	48
$20,100	$4,650	$150		$15,255	$2,430	$1,425	$15,195	$3,295	$6,185	$825	$16,822	$7,625	$3,325	$3,250	49
$51,855	$17,160	$3,200		$41,250	$12,014	$7,000	$44,794	$7,162	$14,662	$2,650	$42,283	$18,035	$15,010	$5,040	50
$3,816	$450	$25		$1,893	$870	$210	$4,331	$645	$780	$341	$3,798	$1,150	$1,050	$680	51
77	8	2		52	23	4	77	13	16	6	172	36	29	10	52
33	3	2		25	1		22	3	9	4	109	12	4	5	53
65	18	2		50	20	4	79	14	15	5	32	24	29	10	54
1,233	702	58		651	198	7	1,440	291	329	127	1,007	265	464	227	55
460	156	14		264	82	1	502	102	102	48	345	123	180	122	56
481	204	17		441	210	8	796	92	226	77	1,250	199	292	164	57
4,690	3,800	120		4,455	2,498	150	6,715	813	2,235	655	13,177	2,155	3,110	1,575	58
16,619	23,055	15,034	2,178	3,409	7,426	2,084	37,657	45,560	30,844	16,331	24,087	10,859	21,355	47,895	59
12,447	17,042	9,618	270	2,013	5,147	1,780	28,339	30,711	15,567	11,908	17,916	6,361	17,092	34,668	60
$537,977	$289,600	$331,990	$7,265	$74,335	$111,980	$52,130	$380,408	$881,538	$197,715	$315,943	$245,076	$268,045	$311,286	$914,536	61
$91,910	$54,985	$101,775	$1,525	$16,845	$18,040	$10,425	$107,623	$187,645	$58,680	$55,183	$62,730	$60,140	$79,755	$155,830	62
$21,382	$14,055	$15,483	$495	$2,632	$5,619	$1,955	$30,394	$32,506	$11,680	$15,838	$12,245	$7,333	$23,665	$45,794	63
293	338	260	10	58	69	56	634	719	378	289	638	219	366	586	64
155	99	41	10	25	24	7	169	92	84	68	398	54	67	180	65
313	296	314	7	58	129	58	832	866	331	317	223	224	468	926	66
7,148	9,391	5,514	23	855	1,817	748	15,902	18,265	7,097	6,834	5,895	3,124	9,110	20,561	67
2,396	3,222	2,009	7	333	786	361	5,917	6,014	2,284	3,154	1,875	1,226	3,858	9,397	68
2,545	5,027	1,837	124	537	1,692	217	7,069	5,566	3,565	3,457	6,885	1,866	4,950	10,088	69
22,536	36,593	20,890	1,935	5,404	21,039	5,995	64,624	51,018	33,276	37,803	72,146	18,206	50,873	102,980	70
11,134	23,202	13,755	1,268	15,635	5,901	8,541	18,126	59,379	8,006	17,949	17,389	13,460	24,163	35,556	71
9,316	19,563	11,381	473	12,038	4,478	6,247	14,268	45,383	6,250	14,435	12,576	10,090	21,141	31,120	72
$391,330	$352,735	$413,825	$12,900	$313,429	$95,950	$211,326	$215,807	$1,264,384	$68,960	$372,041	$209,816	$387,327	$264,140	$755,118	73
$64,610	$69,135	$101,900	$2,200	$72,615	$16,930	$30,494	$57,315	$271,350	$24,635	$83,070	$54,965	$83,589	$81,825	$146,050	74
$5,072	$23,416	$7,376	$375	$9,912	$4,395	$5,623	$8,161	$36,196	$2,632	$13,668	$9,074	$7,227	$21,730	$26,524	75
183	298	216	5	337	69	136	182	876	87	215	295	261	288	345	76
47	78	27	3	66	20	16	24	32	11	20	158	30	39	79	77
116	393	206	12	174	96	162	392	1,365	122	351	243	223	499	859	78
5,932	10,935	6,622	158	1,865	1,865	2,269	8,281	30,156	2,997	8,709	3,817	5,446	10,934	19,539	79
2,316	4,306	2,580	65	2,314	818	1,140	3,624	10,397	1,037	4,617	1,300	2,212	4,842	9,584	80
1,906	5,385	1,686	196	3,375	1,423	1,335	3,066	6,923	1,400	4,062	4,696	2,389	5,901	8,813	81
10,045	52,990	20,186	2,285	32,387	17,044	24,719	33,198	66,042	14,283	51,043	58,455	25,093	66,451	98,994	82

TABLE **73.**—STATISTICS OF SIZE OF FARMS AND FOR TENURE CLASSES OF FARMS

		GEORGIA—continued.								
		Dough-erty.	Douglas.	Early.	Effing-ham.	Elbert.	Emanuel.	Fayette.	Floyd.	Forsyth.	Franklin.
1	Number of farms	1,180	344	1,576	315	1,532	1,104	596	765	172	610
	FARMS CLASSIFIED BY SIZE.										
2	Under 3 acres	1									
3	3 to 9 acres	112	11	17	41	41	8	15	15	6	33
4	10 to 19 acres	25	33	43	75	199	28	46	76	25	107
5	20 to 49 acres	733	152	850	119	727	595	317	350	85	334
6	50 to 99 acres	234	96	425	41	353	250	152	217	38	112
7	100 to 174 acres	47	39	-180	26	159	128	53	79	18	22
8	175 to 259 acres	21	10	44	4	33	56	12	19		2
9	260 to 499 acres	7	2	12	6	18	31	1	7		
10	500 to 999 acres		1	5	2	2	6		2		
11	1,000 acres and over				1		2				
	FARMERS CLASSIFIED BY TENURE.										
12	Owners, free	26	48	96	111	47	107	10	96	14	23
13	Owners, mortgaged	17	10	55	26	49	27	3	63	10	7
14	Part owners	4	12	51	47	22	28	6	38	9	22
15	Cash tenants	616	62	697	73	597	212	261	63	2	66
16	Share tenants	353	209	520	54	747	662	273	492	132	487
17	Share-cash tenants	3	3	7	3	12	14	5	3		1
18	Tenure not specified	161		150	1	58	53	35	7	5	4
19	Managers						1	3	2		
	FARMS OPERATED BY OWNERS, FREE.										
20	Total acreage	3,802	3,719	9,207	5,038	4,640	12,283	634	6,602	626	1,251
21	Improved acreage	3,199	1,713	4,565	1,709	2,052	4,415	380	3,371	309	787
22	Value of land	$49,570	$38,175	$97,270	$42,100	$84,650	$154,552	$18,550	$65,455	$7,825	$33,655
23	Value of buildings	$17,105	$12,765	$37,870	$15,905	$17,725	$31,155	$3,450	$21,960	$2,225	$6,975
24	Value of implements and machinery	$5,890	$2,190	$7,865	$2,508	$5,702	$5,682	$550	$6,516	$623	$1,085
25	Number of dairy cows	54	54	180	106	72	243	11	149	16	26
26	Number of work horses	16	8	53	47	23	47	1	48	6	11
27	Number of work mules	58	56	114	49	61	128	13	110	12	32
28	Acreage in cotton	1,216	545	1,938	310	1,078	1,729	178	1,321	110	379
29	Bales of cotton grown in 1909	583	203	734	149	457	617	79	464	52	158
30	Acreage in corn	743	470	1,572	678	497	1,723	81	818	111	177
31	Bushels of corn grown in 1909	9,231	3,822	16,620	9,119	4,837	16,977	975	8,394	1,388	1,831
	FARMS OPERATED BY OWNERS, MORTGAGED.										
32	Total acreage	3,278	1,009	4,910	2,452	3,383	3,875	265	5,446	527	354
33	Improved acreage	2,298	443	2,560	646	1,635	1,379	174	2,512	321	220
34	Value of land	$40,080	$11,460	$47,295	$14,655	$64,805	$35,415	$9,910	$55,405	$7,660	$6,210
35	Value of buildings	$15,340	$4,000	$12,030	$4,995	$16,050	$11,920	$650	$13,440	$2,000	$2,850
36	Value of implements and machinery	$4,907	$865	$2,910	$787	$3,330	$1,356	$225	$4,876	$530	$183
37	Number of dairy cows	36	11	92	34	75	78	10	93	12	6
38	Number of work horses	12	2	26	19	37	7	2	22	6	1
39	Number of work mules	38	11	66	16	49	47	10	79	9	7
40	Acreage in cotton	815	200	1,164	119	844	742	85	943	135	116
41	Bales of cotton grown in 1909	318	67	387	66	362	198	35	365	59	46
42	Acreage in corn	501	105	892	219	346	442	34	550	98	50
43	Bushels of corn grown in 1909	4,405	826	8,301	3,180	3,248	3,682	395	4,111	1,065	315
	FARMS OPERATED BY PART OWNERS.										
44	Total acreage	251	936	3,440	2,447	2,045	2,280	685	2,208	380	1,106
45	Owned acreage	107	775	1,012	1,742	975	1,330	261	1,422	244	646
46	Improved acreage	178	442	2,442	1,093	1,313	1,341	326	1,220	219	756
47	Owned improved acreage	101	313	644	457	681	616	87	742	131	374
48	Value of land	$4,800	$8,670	$45,045	$20,180	$39,585	$30,505	$22,730	$20,140	$5,550	$27,545
49	Value of buildings	$1,300	$2,900	$11,690	$7,195	$10,275	$5,950	$3,100	$9,470	$1,450	$7,085
50	Value of land and buildings owned	$2,900	$8,976	$21,405	$19,810	$24,160	$21,670	$8,722	$18,979	$4,500	$20,770
51	Value of implements and machinery	$311	$480	$2,630	$1,390	$1,790	$1,373	$435	$3,100	$218	$753
52	Number of dairy cows	8	12	73	45	36	45	9	62	9	26
53	Number of work horses	2	4	24	15	10	5	2	15	4	3
54	Number of work mules	5	13	62	32	33	40	12	53	7	26
55	Acreage in cotton	55	196	1,231	307	879	764	173	530	110	430
56	Bales of cotton grown in 1909	18	56	354	175	284	246	76	153	42	149
57	Acreage in corn	58	68	739	484	207	474	83	349	75	200
58	Bushels of corn grown in 1909	515	695	7,231	6,005	1,995	4,309	925	2,359	870	1,925
	FARMS OPERATED BY CASH TENANTS INCLUDING TENURE NOT SPECIFIED.										
59	Total acreage	35,191	4,090	53,326	2,185	42,398	21,206	17,553	4,986	240	4,287
60	Improved acreage	34,087	2,603	37,057	1,500	22,108	11,693	11,380	2,911	181	2,691
61	Value of land	$465,762	$56,290	$669,370	$27,485	$669,388	$327,582	$517,196	$129,412	$3,499	$117,235
62	Value of buildings	$89,692	$10,495	$150,417	$7,155	$123,310	$58,660	$78,375	$24,230	$725	$21,250
63	Value of implements and machinery	$22,687	$2,639	$32,924	$1,392	$23,207	$10,685	$13,440	$6,793	$355	$3,700
64	Number of dairy cows	618	64	817	58	712	257	315	121	7	88
65	Number of work horses	117	10	148	26	220	78	36	25	4	17
66	Number of work mules	663	77	972	37	685	295	356	100	4	108
67	Acreage in cotton	15,494	990	19,578	330	12,540	5,684	6,468	1,252	100	1,612
68	Bales of cotton grown in 1909	5,447	413	6,406	168	4,897	2,234	2,695	366	45	604
69	Acreage in corn	8,304	626	12,746	531	4,815	4,121	2,668	537	70	643
70	Bushels of corn grown in 1909	70,595	5,377	123,347	6,644	46,729	41,113	25,536	4,904	821	6,295
	FARMS OPERATED BY SHARE AND SHARE-CASH TENANTS.										
71	Total acreage	15,692	9,791	25,383	22,193	28,562	39,323	8,936	24,537	5,766	15,392
72	Improved acreage	15,479	6,695	21,484	1,364	19,220	25,466	7,475	15,220	3,535	12,161
73	Value of land	$243,812	$147,480	$383,121	$125,595	$628,121	$748,731	$288,615	$377,571	$86,773	$520,895
74	Value of buildings	$40,099	$32,180	$89,605	$11,675	$110,478	$120,658	$49,430	$75,729	$21,953	$87,650
75	Value of implements and machinery	$6,777	$4,450	$12,307	$1,935	$11,014	$18,679	$4,101	$14,452	$3,440	$8,664
76	Number of dairy cows	218	170	277	133	434	381	135	438	116	338
77	Number of work horses	8	25	39	14	53	69	17	77	21	37
78	Number of work mules	218	176	595	38	393	670	203	491	84	219
79	Acreage in cotton	6,610	3,325	12,600	444	11,279	12,884	4,700	6,806	1,566	7,853
80	Bales of cotton grown in 1909	2,424	1,287	4,548	307	4,338	5,975	1,964	2,153	667	3,270
81	Acreage in corn	2,671	1,556	6,580	563	3,626	9,187	1,768	3,285	1,019	2,531
82	Bushels of corn grown in 1909	25,176	15,051	70,991	9,065	36,256	109,363	17,613	32,464	12,987	26,746

OPERATED BY COLORED FARMERS, BY COUNTIES, FOR SOUTHERN STATES: 1910—Continued.

GEORGIA—continued.

Fulton.	Glascock.	Glynn.	Gordon.	Grady.	Greene.	Gwinnett.	Hall.	Hancock.	Haralson.	Harris.	Hart.	Heard.	Henry.	Houston.	
263	234	100	147	725	1,831	501	362	2,032	243	1,950	839	647	1,451	1,814	1
1						1		1		1					2
41	5	14	9	34	82	14	13	50	14	33	28	13	32	13	3
72	15	31	25	60	155	73	70	102	31	68	128	62	98	36	4
109	139	28	72	364	883	234	164	1,039	82	892	416	312	747	872	5
26	48	11	25	134	420	116	67	483	80	482	212	128	386	589	6
9	20	8	12	83	216	54	37	259	26	321	48	85	153	228	7
5	2		2	37	51	8	5	69	9	114	3	37	33	47	8
	5	5	2	12	20	1	6	21	1	34	3	10	2	23	9
		1		1		4		8		5				5	10
		2									1			1	11
14	7	86	15	83	70	36	27	119	40	90	24	32	64	80	12
6	1	5	10	41	42	18	18	35	21	29	26	13	25	34	13
25	1	8	16	49	35	19	9	78	25	26	12	17	12	15	14
124	69		4	281	938	69	26	1,054	41	994	187	193	387	1,169	15
84	153	1	102	224	705	358	274	652	111	793	580	374	892	437	16
3	1			6	7	1	2	34	1	1	4	1	39	7	17
3				41	34		5	58	3	16	5	17	31	64	18
4	2					1		2	1	1	1		1	8	19
458	698	6,477	1,122	7,796	5,092	2,454	2,241	9,180	2,550	10,711	1,220	2,670	4,366	8,095	20
262	328	856	449	2,135	1,272		962	4,523	1,306	4,206	1,416	2,523		5,290	21
$35,600	$5,710	$26,777	$9,030	$73,552	$67,335	$35,968	$24,570	$108,728	$34,885	$78,484	$35,990	$23,525	$86,370	$102,985	22
$5,200	$1,400	$14,303	$4,610	$25,117	$22,395	$10,876	$5,400	$40,215	$11,135	$26,525	$8,900	$7,985	$23,535	$28,325	23
$2,680	$261	$2,757	$470	$3,826	$4,360	$1,608	$1,162	$10,106	$2,084	$4,704	$1,082	$1,556	$2,730	$5,625	24
13	8	288	21	121	88	38	28	155	42	145	30	37	55	77	25
4	1	56	5	70	53	10	13	78	40	34	6	6	44	36	26
21	7	13	16	52	59	42	36	121	13	117	23	31	51	115	27
24	126	14	102	798	1,220	449	451	2,214	657	2,029	310	720	1,345	2,412	28
11	48	7	44	276	479	199	160	843	202	613	139	232	527	909	29
66	128	496	155	1,438	572	371	305	1,152	348	1,021	149	362	585	1,535	30
570	945	6,621	1,435	16,183	5,182	4,116	3,200	9,593	3,433	9,629	1,645	3,430	5,855	17,890	31
95	84	7,429	814	3,840	3,361	1,818	1,205	3,559	1,371	3,671	1,680	1,333	1,915	3,663	32
66	30	95	505	1,519	1,491	801	659	1,770	692	1,531	1,025	690	1,155	2,203	33
$15,800	$200	$12,250	$6,925	$36,779	$44,505	$31,232	$16,985	$41,538	$18,212	$33,673	$49,125	$9,510	$34,720	$52,310	34
$3,000	$50	$4,700	$1,605	$8,303	$15,300	$6,390	$3,065	$10,600	$6,350	$8,660	$13,400	$3,100	$9,450	$12,800	35
$540		$450	$345	$1,994	$2,744	$975	$670	$2,838	$810	$1,702	$1,780	$643	$1,535	$2,193	36
6		28	13	60	54	24	21	55	26	47	45	17	31	33	37
4	1	2	3	38	49	4	3	24	5	10	5	14		17	38
2		7	15	22	24	26	22	36	24	36	24	18	29	46	39
14	15		123	466	778	348	312	949	346	852	529	307	644	1,058	40
5	6		46	145	280	134	112	335	97	247	193	97	232	345	41
14	15	39	105	547	380	211	135	460	156	374	226	164	281	658	42
235	75	690	1,060	5,615	3,052	2,241	1,260	3,234	1,070	3,510	2,447	1,405	2,605	5,220	43
724	35	150	1,425	3,885	2,589	825	620	5,036	1,616	3,389	688	2,026	934	1,999	44
284	17	26	860	2,200	990	475	413	2,069	755	1,850	409	1,145	371	1,022	45
570	35	80	649	2,042	1,548	643	324	2,816	890	1,120	419	920	574	1,583	46
199	17	20	395	854	589	300	152	1,082	327	383	227	456	239	788	47
$43,220	$300	$1,950	$10,960	$38,830	$37,490	$20,010	$10,190	$77,345	$27,627	$26,250	$23,045	$19,052	$22,920	$28,180	48
$6,525	$100	$1,050	$2,995	$8,915	$14,305	$4,180	$2,829	$31,050	$6,865	$5,830	$3,475	$3,350	$4,210	$7,675	49
$19,880	$200	$1,380	$8,875	$29,718	$24,445	$14,460	$8,307	$51,295	$17,275	$13,415	$14,745	$13,760	$11,880	$19,005	50
$1,045	$10	$105	$710	$2,615	$1,940	$866	$430	$4,210	$1,142	$1,247	$630	$819	$529	$1,630	51
31	1	18	20	68	52	20	13	89	26	38	19	23	14	17	52
9		6	4	42	40	11	2	43	14	7	2	7	12	9	53
33	1	1	21	49	31	19	13	75	22	31	16	19	14	29	54
136	14		197	583	975	275	103	1,497	413	556	291	364	334	672	55
49	6		75	197	346	116	43	504	116	170	115	131	160	209	56
148	15	44	171	762	335	197	89	891	181	184	96	180	156	374	57
2,898	100	426	1,900	7,512	2,545	1,980	1,015	6,677	1,912	1,430	958	1,759	1,507	3,650	58
4,459	5,150		306	15,273	62,794	4,310	2,291	75,657	2,750	78,505	10,289	16,724	25,522	83,469	59
2,476	3,088		164	10,287	35,284	2,342	1,188	46,864	1,276	42,003	6,405	8,826	16,274	64,934	60
$373,680	$49,519		$6,000	$145,093	$890,965	$81,666	$38,281	$783,249	$46,300	$863,157	$292,250	$152,315	$557,146	$1,381,369	61
$36,540	$10,615		$1,800	$30,842	$188,225	$19,255	$11,155	$208,248	$10,870	$184,730	$42,565	$33,277	$92,280	$265,795	62
$3,673	$1,700		$245	$6,518	$38,669	$2,682	$1,123	$42,065	$1,123	$32,649	$7,483	$5,471	$14,671	$60,714	63
101	43		8	212	965	60	30	1,041	26	1,132	232	211	389	987	64
60	20		1	171	511	26	8	346	15	142	48	50	84	401	65
85	65		9	153	874	79	30	1,182	21	1,135	176	50	471	1,379	66
744	1,330		37	2,819	20,255	1,316	441	24,723	634	24,733	3,882	4,503	10,152	34,539	67
280	483		21	776	6,782	476	150	8,117	179	7,261	1,347	1,432	3,683	11,396	68
517	1,178		76	4,561	7,459	586	269	13,649	243	9,405	1,375	1,949	3,498	19,620	69
6,199	9,722		1,300	43,666	66,702	5,445	2,465	101,119	2,170	85,910	13,354	15,926	36,191	189,185	70
2,265	6,395	16	3,235	13,140	27,697	14,650	11,176	29,974	4,803	39,135	23,585	16,219	39,540	20,734	71
1,684	5,277	4	2,927	8,552	18,683	10,449	7,401	22,606	3,134	27,037	15,546	12,210	29,994	18,975	72
$193,971	$72,084	$60	$77,828	$170,445	$422,734	$323,529	$200,809	$342,076	$80,169	$515,096	$701,801	$190,783	$891,274	$349,840	73
$19,130	$17,310	$15	$9,620	$33,580	$91,475	$75,731	$40,705	$83,153	$19,236	$114,053	$91,384	$44,935	$173,050	$69,475	74
$4,518	$1,852		$1,609	$4,421	$11,867	$7,842	$5,793	$11,204	$1,670	$11,795	$10,270	$6,045	$17,947	$7,696	75
82	43		91	150	297	264	213	404	68	475	400	261	631	182	76
23	15	1	20	48	178	72	22	173	15	21	67	29	310	23	77
63	138		66	144	305	232	164	493	45	469	352	302	490	445	78
595	2,567		1,121	2,761	10,887	4,934	2,193	11,712	1,807	16,987	9,699	6,069	19,285	10,565	79
238	980		416	931	3,588	1,930	1,213	4,125	474	5,172	3,622	2,115	7,163	3,837	80
288	2,104	10	731	3,142	3,618	2,869	1,968	5,920	708	5,650	3,016	2,756	6,050	5,714	81
4,373	18,940	80	10,120	38,313	32,018	29,562	21,673	48,258	5,505	53,865	31,318	26,618	63,511	57,264	82

TABLE **73.**—STATISTICS OF SIZE OF FARMS AND FOR TENURE CLASSES OF FARMS

GEORGIA—continued.

		Irwin.	Jackson.	Jasper.	Jeff Davis.	Jefferson.	Jenkins.	Johnson.	Jones.	Laurens.	Lee.
1	Number of farms	406	1,249	1,802	130	1,667	818	633	1,239	2,266	1,520
	FARMS CLASSIFIED BY SIZE.										
2	Under 3 acres		1			2				1	
3	3 to 9 acres	11	43	27	9	14	2	4	14	32	7
4	10 to 19 acres	13	169	77	8	37	9	14	29	65	12
5	20 to 49 acres	233	715	990	38	1,039	583	404	502	1,463	1,017
6	50 to 99 acres	105	240	490	32	414	160	152	359	475	329
7	100 to 174 acres	25	66	144	16	115	37	43	214	144	113
8	175 to 259 acres	5	9	44	10	32	16	11	83	59	30
9	260 to 499 acres	11	5	26	12	13	9	5	30	24	11
10	500 to 999 acres	2	1	3	2	1	2		7	3	1
11	1,000 acres and over	1		1	3				1		
	FARMERS CLASSIFIED BY TENURE.										
12	Owners, free	22	40	65	48	78	37	18	48	120	76
13	Owners, mortgaged	14	32	26	13	30	2	8	37	81	21
14	Part owners	6	49	17	4	43	7		12	36	23
15	Cash tenants	42	315	1,076	18	566	333	205	739	830	893
16	Share tenants	311	732	586	38	791	428	258	251	953	490
17	Share-cash tenants	8	7	18		41	2	60	28	153	
18	Tenure not specified	3	74	14	9	117	9	84	124	93	13
19	Managers					1					4
	FARMS OPERATED BY OWNERS, FREE.										
20	Total acreage	3,632	2,776	7,543	6,651	8,581	4,564	1,280	5,688	11,746	7,251
21	Improved acreage	807	1,739	3,805	1,195	5,106	2,285	939	2,688	5,927	3,982
22	Value of land	$52,180	$71,845	$87,705	$39,775	$122,150	$51,245	$13,125	$39,462	$163,560	$93,683
23	Value of buildings	$11,225	$22,320	$31,360	$7,975	$37,425	$13,600	$7,405	$15,395	$34,220	$22,575
24	Value of implements and machinery	$1,776	$2,336	$4,736	$1,516	$12,608	$2,740	$2,098	$2,480	$8,504	$7,115
25	Number of dairy cows	35	58	100	103	95	42	14	80	185	74
26	Number of work horses	15	21	43	20	42	11	4	11	48	35
27	Number of work mules	14	57	105	28	107	52	23	48	126	84
28	Acreage in cotton	324	752	1,986	247	1,883	847	424	1,049	2,784	1,900
29	Bales of cotton grown in 1909	144	318	826	84	756	287	155	372	1,057	846
30	Acreage in corn	238	324	721	501	1,417	741	325	582	1,853	1,329
31	Bushels of corn grown in 1909	2,920	3,058	9,187	5,145	13,786	7,190	2,975	5,829	19,544	13,060
	FARMS OPERATED BY OWNERS, MORTGAGED.										
32	Total acreage	842	2,004	2,091	2,824	3,401	506	972	6,386	11,158	3,198
33	Improved acreage	502	1,236	1,020	364	1,846	180	687	2,998	5,763	1,605
34	Value of land	$19,700	$55,195	$29,795	$26,465	$37,040	$4,700	$9,625	$43,230	$135,340	$30,298
35	Value of buildings	$4,000	$12,530	$8,700	$2,385	$11,570	$1,100	$1,675	$17,425	$29,400	$8,830
36	Value of implements and machinery	$1,368	$1,150	$1,922	$599	$1,850	$60	$520	$3,630	$7,652	$2,160
37	Number of dairy cows	14	37	25	23	34	7	5	63	120	20
38	Number of work horses	5	16	12	5	14	2	4	9	27	14
39	Number of work mules	16	35	39	12	33	4	14	55	119	22
40	Acreage in cotton	143	701	611	121	782	80	300	1,064	2,466	754
41	Bales of cotton grown in 1909	71	262	231	49	274	37	90	355	1,004	265
42	Acreage in corn	97	208	236	171	675	50	165	475	1,507	448
43	Bushels of corn grown in 1909	1,355	1,435	2,191	1,755	5,000	480	1,340	4,565	16,186	3,795
	FARMS OPERATED BY PART OWNERS.										
44	Total acreage	716	2,645	2,076	389	2,742	697		1,914	2,681	2,196
45	Owned acreage	147	1,424	899	258	1,303	334		1,159	1,307	1,441
46	Improved acreage	225	1,926	1,196	169	2,217	361		1,066	1,794	1,488
47	Owned improved acreage	87	968	477	52	869	155		586	645	753
48	Value of land	$4,765	$71,882	$30,351	$4,875	$47,521	$6,920		$18,040	$46,055	$34,623
49	Value of buildings	$1,025	$18,510	$6,325	$575	$10,225	$1,415		$5,000	$7,495	$13,925
50	Value of land and buildings owned	$2,710	$52,270	$14,621	$2,200	$30,287	$4,300		$15,890	$22,430	$37,923
51	Value of implements and machinery	$185	$3,221	$1,816	$53	$2,338	$345		$995	$3,110	$2,995
52	Number of dairy cows	8	52	27	5	25	7		20	55	23
53	Number of work horses	4	21	13		26	2		3	8	16
54	Number of work mules	6	62	44	4	41	10		19	50	35
55	Acreage in cotton	112	945	624	28	875	103		288	799	860
56	Bales of cotton grown in 1909	53	365	294	8	334	29		115	316	332
57	Acreage in corn	56	388	199	27	634	108		197	582	484
58	Bushels of corn grown in 1909	730	3,605	2,195	280	5,306	1,115		2,210	6,043	5,065
	FARMS OPERATED BY CASH TENANTS, INCLUDING TENURE NOT SPECIFIED.										
59	Total acreage	3,530	19,097	67,007	4,755	39,949	19,682	17,150	70,382	49,493	52,194
60	Improved acreage	2,039	13,067	46,822	651	33,238	15,812	14,400	42,058	40,511	48,533
61	Value of land	$86,460	$518,239	$1,062,839	$26,440	$542,265	$254,380	$208,109	$695,309	$786,252	$706,177
62	Value of buildings	$8,120	$96,365	$229,680	$2,295	$154,933	$52,780	$61,546	$182,329	$134,675	$170,795
63	Value of implements and machinery	$3,322	$16,492	$50,037	$559	$39,855	$13,421	$15,803	$39,278	$40,782	$59,222
64	Number of dairy cows	53	374	1,058	48	565	197	186	910	788	655
65	Number of work horses	20	126	173	14	300	42	58	62	300	186
66	Number of work mules	58	404	1,405	16	581	429	324	960	955	1,106
67	Acreage in cotton	1,173	8,157	31,438	145	15,646	8,264	7,363	23,668	21,556	25,098
68	Bales of cotton grown in 1909	660	3,170	11,187	58	6,121	3,165	2,566	7,733	8,009	10,413
69	Acreage in corn	488	2,654	8,692	212	10,663	4,664	4,503	9,656	12,622	16,972
70	Bushels of corn grown in 1909	6,416	22,872	87,170	2,730	101,950	44,973	42,377	94,017	122,047	161,783
	FARMS OPERATED BY SHARE AND SHARE-CASH TENANTS.										
71	Total acreage	16,460	24,530	21,935	5,686	36,318	16,290	13,621	12,924	43,563	21,359
72	Improved acreage	12,862	20,409	18,568	1,191	33,465	15,711	12,449	9,549	41,667	20,534
73	Value of land	$488,155	$764,576	$396,346	$65,730	$540,788	$263,412	$183,319	$149,951	$795,182	$305,665
74	Value of buildings	$57,130	$133,235	$78,874	$7,975	$151,659	$57,095	$47,795	$41,175	$137,422	$70,965
75	Value of implements and machinery	$21,620	$14,550	$9,772	$1,014	$27,658	$8,457	$9,410	$5,026	$22,159	$16,773
76	Number of dairy cows	166	472	256	20	378	121	92	173	463	157
77	Number of work horses	54	68	25	3	140	11	25	93	103	18
78	Number of work mules	338	360	346	31	614	424	284	149	798	495
79	Acreage in cotton	6,676	13,319	12,477	252	16,098	8,528	6,334	5,276	21,870	11,443
80	Bales of cotton grown in 1909	3,923	5,342	4,405	118	6,540	3,761	2,353	1,904	9,285	5,233
81	Acreage in corn	3,044	3,552	2,714	380	10,783	4,650	3,942	2,212	11,745	7,311
82	Bushels of corn grown in 1909	43,065	31,563	26,274	5,970	111,195	48,913	38,160	24,782	126,780	74,621

OPERATED BY COLORED FARMERS, BY COUNTIES, FOR SOUTHERN STATES: 1910—Continued.

GEORGIA—continued.

Liberty.	Lincoln.	Lowndes.	McDuffie.	McIntosh.	Macon.	Madison.	Marion.	Meri-wether.	Miller.	Milton.	Mitchell.	Monroe.	Montgomery.	Morgan.	
1,269	850	1,125	883	169	1,193	855	733	2,126	337	105	1,523	1,763	953	1,999	1
															2
278	21	60	3	40	7	26	9	42	4	3	9	14	22	46	3
384	69	122	26	31	16	112	10	80	5	21	43	47	73	196	4
345	467	585	484	55	652	433	335	1,124	182	53	951	871	530	1,106	5
155	140	205	253	22	281	214	141	571	74	22	349	433	201	467	6
62	92	95	71	13	170	59	148	254	48	2	102	260	75	148	7
19	40	38	24	2	40	8	53	43	18	4	46	91	37	22	8
20	17	16	19	4	21	2	32	8	6		20	36	10	13	9
5	4	4	3	1	6	1	5	3			3	10	4	1	10
1				1				1				1	1		11
1,065	25	213	18	147	41	34	44	54	41	7	91	75	159	34	12
12	8	68	13		12	18	25	19	12	3	57	70	42	19	13
71	12	85	2		15	17	16	54	3	1	9	42	52	28	14
47	500	248	297	1	437	306	243	888	72	4	464	767	180	940	15
61	299	361	391	13	656	472	392	1,090	57	90	806	548	492	884	16
2	1	9	34		8	4	2	12	21		60	28	15	3	17
11	4	139	128	5	22	4	7	8	131		35	233	13	91	18
	1	2		3	2		4	1			1				19
37,044	3,655	19,026	1,124	6,766	4,976	2,187	7,026	5,018	4,022	386	10,845	8,282	11,156	2,660	20
14,463	1,393	6,742	565	1,768	2,689	1,124	3,832	3,147	2,041	204	5,827	4,164	4,490	1,454	21
$312,166	$40,939	$209,544	$11,262	$136,782	$43,960	$44,076	$36,951	$84,345	$32,166	$8,650	$118,073	$79,544	$163,690	$47,990	22
$179,111	$11,845	$44,020	$3,599	$51,080	$9,935	$11,950	$10,870	$28,975	$7,600	$3,200	$34,385	$27,173	$38,510	$14,130	23
$47,390	$3,610	$9,737	$1,318	$15,935	$3,115	$2,185	$2,431	$4,303	$2,288	$425	$8,650	$5,152	$7,499	$3,268	24
2,599	54	333	18	340	46	47	59	73	126	10	233	98	233	49	25
580	20	147	8	81	12	21	24	16	16	4	98	34	62	11	26
93	42	106	7	10	64	43	59	84	15	7	109	96	135	48	27
1,294	670	2,026	316	8	988	554	1,453	1,576	605	104	2,060	1,545	1,929	937	28
592	306	722	104	5	394	239	432	585	181	63	846	594	865	372	29
6,041	393	1,911	163	576	837	323	1,071	748	818	76	1,930	912	1,859	292	30
98,786	4,000	23,545	1,542	14,371	5,568	2,978	8,108	6,502	9,213	1,220	21,340	8,957	20,998	3,558	31
484	1,185	6,498	1,343		1,996	1,514	4,625	2,478	1,457	140	9,453	10,151	3,193	1,901	32
168	440	2,376	551		995	701	2,264	1,345	642	115	5,435	4,648	1,337	1,030	33
$3,575	$10,960	$84,685	$13,249		$16,295	$30,067	$27,810	$44,945	$13,670	$2,000	$97,852	$95,438	$47,805	$34,260	34
$1,625	$2,320	$17,690	$4,350		$2,955	$6,625	$7,010	$14,875	$2,900	$400	$20,465	$24,400	$9,075	$13,295	35
$382	$460	$3,458	$1,350		$770	$1,580	$1,535	$2,944	$450	$120	$4,455	$7,340	$2,546	$2,115	36
26	14	120	14		15	26	34	25	45	1	149	122	55	25	37
4	2	52	5		4	8	15	6	6	1	57	34	13	4	38
4	14	43	9		19	29	37	22	6	3	81	115	35	35	39
21	204	827	272		450	355	929	550	152	40	1,617	2,174	549	674	40
10	82	312	104		126	139	242	202	49	11	617	767	233	261	41
93	81	704	145		336	144	684	233	266	15	1,210	987	501	230	42
1,010	770	7,834	1,265		2,280	1,262	4,765	1,765	3,355	180	12,478	9,472	5,404	2,698	43
3,970	1,324	4,966	181		987	932	1,658	4,428	194	43	974	3,559	4,557	1,949	44
2,305	662	3,182	101		298	610	766	1,981	131	3	317	1,644	2,443	845	45
1,811	559	2,962	140		665	671	1,013	2,671	99	43	568	2,038	2,220	1,532	46
877	207	1,205	60		222	369	332	1,104	65	3	139	795	917	593	47
$32,906	$11,750	$88,870	$3,660		$12,469	$23,590	$9,100	$74,771	$2,550	$3,400	$14,095	$40,710	$61,370	$55,130	48
$14,263	$3,535	$19,805	$240		$1,991	$4,450	$2,310	$20,605	$800	$600	$1,780	$7,627	$13,815	$11,425	49
$32,796	$7,556	$65,318	$1,700		$6,557	$19,595	$5,150	$50,086	$2,880	$1,000	$3,675	$24,632	$40,775	$29,700	50
$4,077	$1,385	$3,447	$305		$542	$430	$418	$3,757	$150	$75	$590	$2,034	$3,105	$1,857	51
203	23	117	4		10	20	7	67	7	2	14	51	68	30	52
40	4	68	4		7	18	5	17	6	1	12	13	20	20	53
36	22	51	1		15	17	17	74		1	10	51	47	35	54
460	233	1,029	70		323	328	314	1,609	34	30	232	917	983	778	55
181	119	380	22		118	139	86	555	13	10	101	386	427	269	56
748	145	941	60		201	191	234	657	42	10	156	427	689	229	57
10,310	1,730	10,354	325		1,992	1,455	1,593	4,636	440	300	2,087	4,570	7,315	2,429	58
5,033	36,537	15,249	31,143	213	38,607	17,427	25,275	55,708	14,122	250	28,078	76,435	12,155	59,520	59
938	18,168	11,925	19,096	106	26,261	11,364	15,464	38,489	8,961	198	23,398	43,804	7,372	43,589	60
$33,760	$419,503	$241,894	$309,386	$1,465	$425,906	$383,731	$148,480	$962,393	$120,676	$3,250	$444,980	$828,050	$174,710	$1,135,874	61
$5,905	$83,530	$47,845	$87,264	$650	$88,575	$67,245	$42,420	$214,145	$20,988	$900	$81,085	$192,205	$34,735	$195,782	62
$1,325	$25,461	$9,763	$29,363	$107	$22,031	$14,902	$9,391	$44,879	$4,997	$145	$24,028	$42,146	$8,299	$53,679	63
45	603	295	438	2	389	326	248	874	205	7	583	1,038	197	962	64
30	119	192	116	5	99	115	49	98	65		232	159	56	291	65
4	605	192	395	1	600	339	273	1,118	60	6	469	1,132	152	1,220	66
93	10,143	4,167	10,079	3	12,857	6,659	6,419	25,111	2,771	69	11,242	22,936	3,523	28,188	67
31	3,879	1,374	3,541	1	4,554	2,438	1,769	7,925	906	28	4,318	7,824	1,534	9,791	68
395	4,167	3,180	4,742	67	8,735	2,766	4,531	8,577	2,607	40	8,600	8,983	2,414	8,384	69
5,271	45,005	35,118	43,834	690	67,295	20,815	31,371	75,106	26,601	470	89,912	91,580	26,142	77,245	70
4,121	8,963	14,346	20,458	1,254	34,740	16,093	24,013	48,586	3,225	3,574	36,550	25,839	22,950	26,923	71
1,952	7,460	12,630	14,779	314	30,566	12,445	18,565	39,484	2,831	2,506	33,472	20,189	18,630	23,672	72
$30,197	$120,741	$322,626	$218,301	$8,370	$517,811	$360,916	$176,808	$927,814	$32,930	$78,378	$599,506	$343,370	$436,802	$634,776	73
$18,333	$28,920	$49,475	$68,527	$1,600	$91,745	$64,410	$50,695	$229,234	$8,820	$12,747	$125,745	$83,280	$83,912	$96,847	74
$1,938	$3,826	$7,194	$13,391	$110	$13,659	$6,934	$6,855	$29,627	$1,834	$2,496	$16,059	$8,791	$14,387	$12,473	75
116	162	239	234		296	292	254	675	47	78	418	286	265	350	76
28	11	127	46		48	56	61	41	26	6	248	31	107	52	77
29	216	203	310		689	242	204	988	32	77	612	372	434	433	78
422	3,805	4,353	6,493		16,813	7,801	8,087	25,048	1,215	1,309	15,411	10,575	8,353	16,146	79
154	1,563	1,621	2,242		6,965	2,993	2,564	8,298	413	588	7,347	3,738	3,956	5,722	80
671	1,359	3,072	2,597	5	9,821	3,099	5,943	8,457	841	631	10,272	4,345	6,343	3,121	81
9,466	15,071	39,674	25,380	135	85,799	25,094	48,189	79,096	9,980	7,495	131,217	48,326	78,747	28,679	82

Table **73.**—STATISTICS OF SIZE OF FARMS AND FOR TENURE CLASSES OF FARMS

		Muscogee.	Newton.	Oconee.	Oglethorpe.	Paulding.	Pierce.	Pike.	Polk.	Pulaski.	Putnam.
					GEORGIA—continued.						
1	Number of farms	593	1,391	835	1,904	244	203	1,289	650	1,573	1,552
	FARMS CLASSIFIED BY SIZE.										
2	Under 3 acres										
3	3 to 9 acres	7	55	27	167	5	33	24	27	32	20
4	10 to 19 acres	20	135	79	91	30	49	63	82	33	71
5	20 to 49 acres	266	763	475	936	111	60	658	345	906	885
6	50 to 99 acres	163	311	173	415	66	34	340	142	386	303
7	100 to 174 acres	98	94	66	228	27	20	164	43	150	190
8	175 to 259 acres	33	26	14	47	3	3	33	7	30	48
9	260 to 499 acres	6	7	1	19	2	3	7	3	26	31
10	500 to 999 acres				1		1			3	3
11	1,000 acres and over								1	2	1
	FARMERS CLASSIFIED BY TENURE.										
12	Owners, free	29	56	24	68	33	91	34	96	85	23
13	Owners, mortgaged	14	28	12	32	20	19	19	17	35	21
14	Part owners	4	34	19	20	9	14	25	37	27	12
15	Cash tenants	374	498	321	1,047	49	28	547	68	916	985
16	Share tenants	163	660	422	707	125	45	618	388	474	480
17	Share-cash tenants	4	99	11	3	1	1	29	5	2	19
18	Tenure not specified	2	16	25	26	7	5	18	13	34	11
19	Managers	3		1	1			1			1
	FARMS OPERATED BY OWNERS, FREE.										
20	Total acreage	2,435	3,866	2,582	5,642	2,086	5,396	2,652	6,908	9,150	3,342
21	Improved acreage	1,310	2,069	1,508	3,343	1,085	1,707	1,605	3,168	4,578	1,816
22	Value of land	$17,680	$64,225	$56,065	$108,076	$29,730	$55,825	$57,250	$65,325	$147,447	$30,630
23	Value of buildings	$4,790	$25,325	$17,100	$27,520	$12,500	$17,685	$17,710	$24,540	$39,557	$9,030
24	Value of implements and machinery	$1,152	$4,345	$8,640	$7,133	$1,738	$2,903	$3,072	$5,772	$9,470	$2,457
25	Number of dairy cows	37	55	45	108	36	148	42	115	113	56
26	Number of work horses	8	13	33	46	4	62	16	51	67	15
27	Number of work mules	29	78	26	95	41	28	46	83	66	36
28	Acreage in cotton	447	1,006	602	1,353	449	442	768	1,340	2,173	610
29	Bales of cotton grown in 1909	117	388	328	581	164	160	288	415	958	268
30	Acreage in corn	346	492	391	754	308	764	481	963	1,487	324
31	Bushels of corn grown in 1909	2,480	4,519	3,630	7,010	2,845	8,565	4,753	7,561	15,041	2,973
	FARMS OPERATED BY OWNERS, MORTGAGED.										
32	Total acreage	1,908	2,270	859	3,299	1,966	1,475	1,511	2,958	4,179	2,789
33	Improved acreage	973	1,371	581	1,681	985	522	840	1,555	2,269	1,553
34	Value of land	$15,650	$36,862	$17,040	$59,461	$21,389	$14,360	$19,749	$24,955	$69,082	$27,005
35	Value of buildings	$3,350	$10,175	$5,050	$19,295	$6,025	$4,450	$5,225	$9,250	$13,325	$8,575
36	Value of implements and machinery	$674	$2,303	$950	$2,602	$883	$1,731	$1,385	$3,250	$2,894	$2,177
37	Number of dairy cows	22	34	18	61	31	38	18	51	43	42
38	Number of work horses	6	7	23	24	9	13	2	13	19	14
39	Number of work mules	19	48	14	42	25	18	29	43	54	34
40	Acreage in cotton	320	706	338	826	452	192	527	687	1,000	618
41	Bales of cotton grown in 1909	75	264	144	316	148	54	232	180	394	210
42	Acreage in corn	206	274	155	376	207	192	231	313	562	261
43	Bushels of corn grown in 1909	1,430	2,280	2,390	3,175	1,925	2,175	2,235	2,399	5,407	2,520
	FARMS OPERATED BY PART OWNERS.										
44	Total acreage	254	1,919	1,784	2,104	1,021	556	1,626	2,102	2,165	1,722
45	Owned acreage	120	1,022	1,082	959	539	364	790	1,143	1,161	457
46	Improved acreage	211	1,124	1,187	1,223	655	323	1,225	1,422	1,654	743
47	Owned improved acreage	79	495	563	499	365	153	580	590	692	311
48	Value of land	$1,983	$30,801	$35,470	$37,511	$15,300	$9,430	$23,340	$37,230	$38,680	$17,345
49	Value of buildings	$775	$6,305	$15,650	$11,544	$3,200	$2,950	$8,550	$9,895	$7,640	$3,950
50	Value of land and buildings owned	$1,372	$18,111	$33,540	$25,346	$11,210	$5,820	$17,177	$23,910	$25,645	$6,590
51	Value of implements and machinery	$142	$1,123	$2,205	$1,595	$562	$374	$1,060	$1,810	$2,866	$570
52	Number of dairy cows	5	23	26	33	16	7	29	44	34	13
53	Number of work horses	3	7	13	8	5	5	8	17	30	3
54	Number of work mules	4	36	29	32	16	10	36	34	26	17
55	Acreage in cotton	38	613	478	589	269	97	663	558	885	280
56	Bales of cotton grown in 1909	13	205	229	204	75	30	244	193	343	107
57	Acreage in corn	41	169	237	251	120	103	255	230	552	147
58	Bushels of corn grown in 1909	295	1,526	2,220	2,235	970	1,395	2,075	2,145	4,998	1,390
	FARMS OPERATED BY CASH TENANTS, INCLUDING TENURE NOT SPECIFIED.										
59	Total acreage	26,912	31,167	18,633	66,128	3,960	759	37,540	4,054	56,259	65,596
60	Improved acreage	15,860	23,518	14,259	39,193	2,261	514	24,178	2,614	45,038	44,037
61	Value of land	$261,633	$708,772	$478,971	$1,114,023	$51,980	$16,419	$572,230	$55,237	$1,001,288	$732,046
62	Value of buildings	$59,095	$113,587	$91,410	$196,710	$12,630	$5,406	$130,920	$10,995	$182,293	$164,220
63	Value of implements and machinery	$12,412	$21,194	$18,217	$49,155	$2,080	$549	$23,311	$2,617	$63,155	$43,246
64	Number of dairy cows	414	521	391	1,030	50	9	555	78	620	1,252
65	Number of work horses	55	83	260	569	8	12	81	39	492	167
66	Number of work mules	428	739	322	840	70	9	710	59	763	1,228
67	Acreage in cotton	8,071	14,410	8,112	21,191	1,139	110	14,180	1,164	25,913	21,647
68	Bales of cotton grown in 1909	2,265	4,587	3,179	7,473	417	27	4,884	351	10,168	7,657
69	Acreage in corn	3,342	4,132	3,025	9,051	496	154	6,107	554	13,285	9,593
70	Bushels of corn grown in 1909	27,922	33,775	27,784	77,794	3,592	1,860	54,846	4,704	125,976	78,095
	FARMS OPERATED BY SHARE AND SHARE-CASH TENANTS.										
71	Total acreage	7,157	25,848	13,188	23,623	4,058	1,416	28,204	13,940	20,012	18,375
72	Improved acreage	6,264	22,594	12,075	18,270	3,325	1,151	22,891	11,102	17,590	16,006
73	Value of land	$59,162	$624,375	$361,069	$481,655	$64,845	$31,200	$455,299	$238,895	$390,505	$239,110
74	Value of buildings	$17,105	$112,035	$67,125	$89,676	$13,335	$7,230	$110,534	$55,098	$62,615	$55,500
75	Value of implements and machinery	$2,746	$9,982	$8,236	$10,221	$1,879	$1,217	$9,311	$13,309	$13,124	$7,288
76	Number of dairy cows	91	408	276	347	100	30	353	301	136	284
77	Number of work horses	15	32	63	156	14	17	31	62	100	19
78	Number of work mules	136	396	172	319	96	21	495	313	387	332
79	Acreage in cotton	3,360	14,721	7,409	10,319	1,708	401	13,500	5,593	10,509	8,348
80	Bales of cotton grown in 1909	1,119	4,837	3,078	3,752	648	116	4,777	1,781	4,693	3,067
81	Acreage in corn	1,528	3,029	2,582	3,887	867	538	5,134	2,510	5,103	2,944
82	Bushels of corn grown in 1909	14,703	26,999	26,489	33,358	8,142	5,783	50,227	23,074	56,319	26,826

OPERATED BY COLORED FARMERS, BY COUNTIES, FOR SOUTHERN STATES: 1910—Continued.

GEORGIA—continued.

Quitman.	Randolph.	Richmond.	Rockdale.	Schley.	Screven.	Spalding.	Stephens.	Stewart.	Sumter.	Talbot.	Talia-ferro.	Tattnall.	Taylor.	Telfair.	
523	1,563	608	475	487	1,563	927	200	1,235	2,160	1,159	1,125	637	637	444	1
	13	61	13		60	28	4	7	10	31	41	1	8	24	2
5	28	55	36	11	85	67	32	13	33	28	76	7	14	39	3
360	768	315	239	226	1,018	499	112	628	1,414	427	543	35	330	198	4
91	489	104	131	95	256	235	37	258	434	298	258	337	158	77	5
31	177	51	47	96	87	80	12	156	173	257	157	136	67	51	6
17	62	14	8	40	29	16	2	100	69	91	34	79	46	45	7
9	21	3		17	18	2		59	25	26	15	27	12	10	8
5	5	5	1	2	7		1	10	1	1	1	14	2		9
1					3			4	1			1			10
		7													11
10	52	59	27	17	130	46	21	63	99	75	49	140	48	118	12
7	43	8	11	9	42	22	11	27	32	16	19	22	26	27	13
3	20	35	13	6	41	21	6	8	7	16	38	30	5	40	14
220	359	351	100	203	537	326	11	429	701	728	647	43	309	53	15
274	1,008	105	313	243	786	498	149	635	1,199	313	351	391	235	129	16
3	30	29	2		20	2	2	6	67	3	6	2	6	17	17
5	51	14	9	9	7	11		64	50	8	15	8	7	58	18
1		7				1		3	5			1	1	2	19
2,428	5,803	3,860	2,193	3,965	12,283	2,632	1,313	11,268	9,883	7,782	4,618	12,536	5,790	7,589	20
584	3,376	1,689	1,211	2,110	5,210	1,814	529	6,278	7,034	2,672	2,845	4,097	2,183	3,178	21
$13,574	$52,285	$40,687	$29,698	$26,115	$135,847	$49,203	$20,377	$72,195	$148,374	$45,565	$73,485	$142,945	$24,595	$99,300	22
$3,300	$19,850	$13,155	$9,560	$8,000	$31,435	$20,575	$4,690	$22,885	$59,575	$14,980	$20,800	$38,910	$8,200	$27,280	23
$835	$3,280	$2,825	$1,800	$1,523	$8,415	$2,550	$725	$5,245	$18,899	$3,883	$7,115	$7,280	$1,893	$3,785	24
22	61	34	32	26	292	64	24	117	111	113	93	272	53	172	25
3	25	17	5	7	45	7	4	25	47	23	48	55	11	74	26
11	65	25	44	26	122	61	21	100	166	76	38	125	64	57	27
255	1,209	392	613	591	1,812	914	245	2,288	3,727	1,353	1,120	1,429	789	1,260	28
79	438	156	250	203	833	342	95	676	1,666	432	504	538	273	541	29
144	931	438	383	534	1,542	403	135	1,571	2,174	848	586	1,722	774	1,382	30
946	7,475	4,338	2,843	3,665	16,603	3,844	1,355	14,786	37,165	6,947	5,835	21,486	6,805	15,714	31
984	5,634	782	928	1,690	5,220	1,722	1,172	4,835	3,673	2,637	1,703	2,040	4,330	2,386	32
400	3,507	437	821	2,263	2,263	1,048	350	2,800	2,553	987	963	736	1,397	922	33
$7,330	$47,131	$7,130	$13,590	$6,925	$54,894	$26,465	$26,825	$34,350	$62,635	$11,137	$24,920	$18,600	$16,054	$20,554	34
$2,575	$14,760	$2,150	$3,800	$2,325	$11,590	$8,575	$3,475	$6,650	$13,250	$3,825	$8,900	$6,200	$4,470	$5,235	35
$647	$3,295	$695	$605	$525	$2,749	$1,480	$670	$2,590	$3,990	$702	$3,835	$955	$758	$913	36
7	61	7	12	11	86	34	15	51	37	23	38	48	21	50	37
4	23	4	2	3	19	10	6	10	9	2	21	8	7	20	38
10	51	9	18	11	48	33	12	46	66	29	16	28	34	10	39
168	1,429	165	276	264	884	525	178	992	1,475	534	546	264	503	267	40
44	423	39	107	65	382	207	66	312	544	139	216	106	166	114	41
103	898	150	153	207	671	183	91	663	735	275	195	275	423	300	42
930	7,568	1,058	1,010	1,535	5,586	1,565	850	5,415	7,625	2,198	1,370	3,180	3,521	3,007	43
1,423	2,343	1,824	1,432	820	3,879	1,303	269	1,912	581	2,068	2,941	1,893	547	3,410	44
305	954	1,091	772	223	2,884	669	75	1,337	101	847	1,101	1,301	166	1,877	45
144	1,511	1,273	886	495	1,911	746	138	1,076	383	1,005	1,688	1,132	363	1,583	46
47	624	595	465	121	962	323	21	731	60	515	563	595	157	706	47
$4,370	$25,955	$26,935	$21,240	$7,111	$54,667	$18,573	$5,825	$11,740	$8,650	$14,550	$44,140	$24,330	$5,330	$40,475	48
$330	$8,450	$8,350	$5,050	$2,190	$10,750	$6,625	$925	$2,500	$2,650	$3,775	$13,685	$5,565	$805	$8,740	49
$1,300	$18,043	$17,090	$15,385	$4,140	$47,002	$13,550	$1,000	$9,465	$2,455	$8,415	$26,220	$18,400	$1,960	$27,445	50
$1,075	$1,880	$2,292	$805	$165	$2,331	$973	$200	$830	$655	$875	$2,279	$1,253	$422	$1,892	51
2	21	26	17	6	71	21	6	13	5	37	50	53	9	43	52
1	11	15	4	5	22	9		4	1	6	33	9		44	53
3	24	32	24	8	53	25	6	21	11	24	31	32	9	12	54
40	542	366	414	200	922	373	75	314	144	447	708	376	166	587	55
10	194	147	142	57	434	145	21	109	51	133	249	150	56	237	56
23	446	382	191	86	654	156	38	239	72	223	277	405	135	612	57
220	3,535	3,552	1,357	740	6,799	1,450	275	1,920	860	1,839	2,526	4,409	1,367	5,585	58
17,340	33,273	18,218	7,252	21,410	29,643	19,774	469	56,717	52,701	61,814	43,599	2,842	21,550	7,321	59
12,073	23,519	14,420	4,551	12,584	20,284	13,412	268	32,701	40,523	31,899	25,241	1,365	13,270	3,897	60
$158,519	$375,655	$319,228	$116,265	$187,425	$343,329	$349,608	$10,125	$448,242	$943,354	$471,199	$615,826	$52,030	$200,325	$79,590	61
$33,650	$71,920	$67,219	$21,080	$45,705	$71,696	$81,250	$2,275	$72,860	$179,117	$118,707	$74,035	$10,850	$44,300	$17,375	62
$8,367	$19,023	$18,393	$3,562	$10,738	$18,518	$14,251	$335	$21,492	$46,753	$22,877	$22,575	$1,845	$10,795	$2,705	63
256	419	224	100	41	517	316	8	558	505	823	678	60	263	105	64
33	100	109	13	41	135	50	1	79	131	97	274	22	65	57	65
280	479	323	136	259	508	424	8	645	965	853	581	37	329	67	66
6,243	11,007	5,514	2,322	5,726	8,802	7,562	117	12,948	25,348	16,358	13,756	555	6,466	1,733	67
2,044	3,715	2,077	739	1,911	4,093	2,791	47	3,916	9,249	4,884	4,577	232	2,493	736	68
3,579	6,822	3,841	987	3,713	6,316	2,795	106	8,865	10,753	7,980	5,057	525	4,202	1,155	69
31,994	57,814	31,410	6,850	28,708	66,831	27,277	1,265	70,197	112,667	68,679	45,153	6,761	39,791	12,615	70
12,377	54,873	5,118	12,610	13,347	29,586	18,326	5,281	35,128	57,290	15,136	13,105	21,144	10,606	10,182	71
12,109	46,056	4,652	9,869	10,928	27,005	16,105	3,876	30,061	52,100	10,850	9,740	12,855	8,787	5,866	72
$148,207	$955,802	$92,035	$219,529	$135,945	$501,330	$391,740	$127,795	$437,872	$1,157,625	$140,501	$195,253	$416,034	$109,595	$146,719	73
$29,685	$162,515	$19,391	$47,250	$37,315	$105,129	$91,010	$22,055	$88,030	$244,454	$40,810	$27,230	$80,426	$25,000	$31,165	74
$4,361	$32,882	$3,652	$3,746	$4,750	$10,979	$7,986	$3,329	$23,087	$39,158	$4,348	$3,635	$13,406	$3,078	$3,895	75
149	620	38	183	136	473	285	116	559	481	180	158	290	129	93	76
16	57	22	18	20	59	14	19	35	48	16	46	87	13	53	77
297	1,151	113	170	248	439	379	97	612	1,048	226	246	302	165	72	78
6,784	25,354	1,554	5,457	5,490	12,921	9,611	1,818	15,844	31,805	5,719	5,602	5,299	4,008	2,039	79
2,090	10,399	646	1,812	2,022	6,733	3,945	679	5,915	13,664	1,809	1,886	2,334	1,559	953	80
3,242	13,645	1,066	1,789	3,493	9,057	2,872	1,122	8,971	14,202	3,197	1,693	5,458	2,734	1,905	81
29,354	146,633	11,718	15,098	30,274	108,493	29,689	12,807	89,283	166,477	29,817	16,023	76,452	27,128	22,602	82

NEGRO POPULATION.

TABLE **73.**—STATISTICS OF SIZE OF FARMS AND FOR TENURE CLASSES OF FARMS

		GEORGIA—continued.									
		Terrell.	Thomas.	Tift.	Toombs.	Troup.	Turner.	Twiggs.	Upson.	Walker.	Walton.
1	Number of farms	2,098	1,489	229	350	1,978	374	1,063	901	233	1,351
	FARMS CLASSIFIED BY SIZE.										
2	Under 3 acres		1								
3	3 to 9 acres	23	58	14	8	47	5	48	14	18	38
4	10 to 19 acres	38	106	29	31	90	14	29	46	49	115
5	20 to 49 acres	1,321	897	129	200	927	241	594	352	106	761
6	50 to 99 acres	522	265	40	67	515	89	231	216	43	325
7	100 to 174 acres	143	109	12	27	297	18	105	168	15	95
8	175 to 259 acres	37	30	3	15	70	5	31	69	2	13
9	260 to 499 acres	11	16	2		28	2	22	25		4
10	500 to 999 acres	3	4		1	4		3	10		
11	1,000 acres and over		3		1				1		
	FARMERS CLASSIFIED BY TENURE.										
12	Owners, free	55	243	23	37	75	13	68	44	29	49
13	Owners, mortgaged	24	93	6	14	32	12	17	24	22	12
14	Part owners	13	59	15	12	14	5	12	14	21	18
15	Cash tenants	533	603	39	73	988	109	835	519	4	391
16	Share tenants	1,452	454	110	209	841	224	119	288	144	837
17	Share-cash tenants	7	10	22	2	14	4		4	7	15
18	Tenure not specified	13	26	13	3	12	6	12	8	6	29
19	Managers	1	1	1		2	1				
	FARMS OPERATED BY OWNERS, FREE.										
20	Total acreage	5,018	19,854	619	2,203	6,819	504	7,135	7,122	1,674	4,540
21	Improved acreage	3,141	10,055	342	934	3,505	282	3,954	2,731	884	2,374
22	Value of land	$74,180	$230,114	$14,470	$32,285	$67,900	$13,175	$62,620	$57,209	$17,843	$113,454
23	Value of buildings	$20,225	$67,095	$2,840	$8,350	$23,405	$3,075	$25,675	$16,802	$7,450	$24,825
24	Value of implements and machinery	$3,810	$14,787	$515	$1,455	$4,961	$838	$5,027	$4,940	$1,136	$5,693
25	Number of dairy cows	52	489	26	55	112	11	96	68	37	62
26	Number of work horses	26	125	9	14	19	3	37	19	31	12
27	Number of work mules	75	253	13	32	100	10	80	53	19	95
28	Acreage in cotton	1,313	3,158	137	353	1,878	153	1,724	1,103	243	962
29	Bales of cotton grown in 1909	609	1,338	68	167	671	73	596	353	37	416
30	Acreage in corn	850	3,466	147	400	889	75	1,237	570	216	374
31	Bushels of corn grown in 1909	8,690	40,764	1,754	4,699	7,510	905	9,515	5,175	2,210	3,671
	FARMS OPERATED BY OWNERS, MORTGAGED.										
32	Total acreage	3,097	7,476	310	1,283	4,149	771	1,988	3,022	871	1,118
33	Improved acreage	1,694	4,211	161	506	2,274	381	898	1,478	483	758
34	Value of land	$37,331	$89,615	$6,900	$15,485	$47,180	$12,375	$17,900	$21,314	$12,538	$33,775
35	Value of buildings	$8,075	$24,660	$1,050	$2,425	$10,180	$4,225	$3,800	$6,310	$4,270	$7,275
36	Value of implements and machinery	$1,510	$6,015	$272	$770	$2,085	$1,117	$1,640	$1,508	$590	$1,700
37	Number of dairy cows	25	163	5	16	60	20	20	43	31	20
38	Number of work horses	17	47	3	3	9	5	7	4	10	6
39	Number of work mules	38	91	6	17	58	24	21	31	15	28
40	Acreage in cotton	767	1,540	50	207	1,229	149	519	654	205	420
41	Bales of cotton grown in 1909	301	582	26	93	362	63	156	213	64	168
42	Acreage in corn	465	1,368	47	199	408	95	314	360	141	128
43	Bushels of corn grown in 1909	4,525	16,248	645	2,230	2,835	803	2,290	3,120	1,435	1,310
	FARMS OPERATED BY PART OWNERS.										
44	Total acreage	1,292	4,321	571	1,199	808	229	1,998	1,422	1,059	1,573
45	Owned acreage	469	1,357	245	510	462	36	861	756	616	716
46	Improved acreage	841	2,114	469	476	646	193	808	898	615	939
47	Owned improved acreage	340	625	167	202	311	25	345	360	237	400
48	Value of land	$20,780	$50,227	$14,820	$14,605	$11,680	$9,950	$18,420	$13,610	$8,247	$40,700
49	Value of buildings	$9,310	$11,300	$2,620	$3,660	$2,845	$2,600	$4,350	$3,920	$2,450	$8,775
50	Value of land and buildings owned	$15,380	$19,219	$7,390	$9,215	$9,375	$5,000	$11,440	$11,185	$5,192	$21,455
51	Value of implements and machinery	$2,155	$2,550	$775	$765	$551	$330	$932	$860	$398	$1,612
52	Number of dairy cows	18	105	19	28	14	6	18	23	22	25
53	Number of work horses	6	27	7	1	5	1	2	1	14	7
54	Number of work mules	18	55	12	16	16	7	22	20	15	26
55	Acreage in cotton	495	696	197	241	371	90	597	416	125	493
56	Bales of cotton grown in 1909	223	280	103	125	112	51	142	142	34	191
57	Acreage in corn	223	728	161	208	112	40	340	180	205	148
58	Bushels of corn grown in 1909	2,670	8,209	2,065	2,765	965	500	2,205	1,685	1,663	975
	FARMS OPERATED BY CASH TENANTS, INCLUDING TENURE NOT SPECIFIED.										
59	Total acreage	36,144	29,941	3,113	3,100	71,941	6,367	48,080	49,260	245	24,682
60	Improved acreage	29,447	23,236	1,697	2,661	42,342	5,024	36,137	25,075	190	18,076
61	Value of land	$711,223	$387,096	$53,990	$58,197	$929,129	$127,605	$485,687	$457,620	$4,580	$707,434
62	Value of buildings	$140,161	$127,286	$9,640	$14,975	$206,670	$23,060	$124,265	$106,908	$1,540	$121,570
63	Value of implements and machinery	$24,568	$19,587	$2,065	$2,665	$40,404	$5,442	$24,597	$17,437	$205	$23,986
64	Number of dairy cows	491	592	40	75	993	100	721	550	7	420
65	Number of work horses	162	254	17	32	115	24	119	62	5	84
66	Number of work mules	781	515	42	77	1,159	142	907	571	3	570
67	Acreage in cotton	17,552	8,698	648	1,160	25,407	2,861	19,804	11,724	54	10,957
68	Bales of cotton grown in 1909	7,124	2,965	352	555	8,402	1,309	6,501	3,726	22	3,755
69	Acreage in corn	8,260	9,730	529	910	8,656	1,431	11,636	6,402	42	3,592
70	Bushels of corn grown in 1909	87,250	105,625	6,994	11,400	81,447	14,390	88,528	58,708	585	30,789
	FARMS OPERATED BY SHARE AND SHARE-CASH TENANTS.										
71	Total acreage	64,723	18,592	4,767	11,298	38,067	9,326	5,511	14,676	5,478	29,511
72	Improved acreage	62,097	16,289	4,478	7,206	28,281	8,898	4,624	9,812	4,118	26,269
73	Value of land	$1,674,344	$290,114	$141,935	$180,205	$563,748	$208,128	$71,065	$167,716	$104,973	$767,348
74	Value of buildings	$297,061	$56,962	$34,765	$34,705	$122,500	$37,290	$14,290	$43,540	$19,930	$153,095
75	Value of implements and machinery	$31,802	$7,846	$3,496	$6,061	$18,056	$3,055	$2,186	$5,564	$2,290	$9,544
76	Number of dairy cows	713	231	80	132	468	87	48	177	154	500
77	Number of work horses	107	68	28	20	36	25	4	9	39	51
78	Number of work mules	1,288	387	102	233	770	156	81	253	92	493
79	Acreage in cotton	40,585	6,683	1,853	3,075	17,894	5,657	2,358	5,120	875	14,605
80	Bales of cotton grown in 1909	20,222	2,604	1,035	1,647	6,388	2,659	855	1,741	337	5,174
81	Acreage in corn	16,944	6,486	970	2,914	5,452	2,080	1,398	2,908	1,268	3,922
82	Bushels of corn grown in 1909	214,155	78,746	16,490	36,369	55,916	30,562	11,985	29,448	16,175	33,479

OPERATED BY COLORED FARMERS, BY COUNTIES, FOR SOUTHERN STATES: 1910—Continued.

	GEORGIA—continued.											KENTUCKY.				
Ware.	Warren.	Washington.	Wayne.	Webster.	Whitfield.	Wilcox.	Wilkes.	Wilkinson.	Worth.	All other counties.	The state.	Adair.	Allen.	Ballard.	
111	1,202	2,438	148	596	127	605	2,453	639	1,292	467	11,730	192	112	196	1
		1									28			2	2
11	7	67	22	5	10	13	78	5	20	45	2,202	24	15	29	3
29	55	72	15	3	30	24	197	9	38	95	2,945	45	33	51	4
35	559	1,485	40	323	48	303	1,398	288	760	168	3,970	65	42	63	5
16	345	537	25	139	24	142	496	133	296	91	1,565	38	14	22	6
9	157	184	22	76	10	71	225	104	116	38	756	17	7	14	7
8	54	61	10	33	5	39	39	57	41	15	182	3		10	8
3	22	27	10	14		11	14	37	20	12	69		1	5	9
	3	4	2	2		2	6	3	1	3	12				10
			2	1				3			1				11
43	30	60	70	29	36	85	118	36	80	142	3,488	84	24	25	12
6	2	26	9	18	3	38	34	11	58	24	978	14	10	13	13
3	22	25	12	7	13	31	33	2	20	34	1,463	28	8	24	14
18	431	703	15	170	10	149	1,505	322	329	21	473	3	1	18	15
37	619	1,458	34	327	61	299	714	237	629	240	5,013	60	67	115	16
	61	27	1	33	3	2	26	17	3	1	146	3	1		17
4	37	133	7	12			22	13	172	5	129		1	1	18
		6				1		1	1	1	40				19
2,172	2,818	5,689	7,009	5,631	2,415	7,941	10,356	5,628	7,188	11,438	143,507	3,940	825	1,779	20
689	1,753	3,038	823	2,819	1,082	3,853	4,985	2,662	3,616	2,965	98,385	2,530	449	1,380	21
$15,345	$27,084	$52,369	$33,950	$36,020	$28,640	$101,693	$156,090	$37,590	$92,135	$68,615	$2,567,926	$37,105	$10,155	$42,255	22
$5,430	$8,070	$19,540	$9,950	$9,440	$7,120	$33,170	$40,960	$13,135	$22,805	$23,780	$878,219	$11,710	$3,210	$11,225	23
$1,358	$1,926	$3,912	$2,970	$3,305	$1,526	$7,005	$11,072	$2,826	$5,022	$3,743	$135,096	$2,307	$468	$2,707	24
92	42	71	120	47	40	192	190	42	145	240	3,595	63	16	37	25
21	31	34	38	16	17	31	76	6	46	47	3,545	79	14	62	26
24	10	66	20	51	19	106	140	50	64	73	1,888	40	21	34	27
103	728	1,168	138	839	181	1,689	2,585	953	1,914	287	5				28
25	246	444	33	252	67	736	1,092	332	843	93	1				29
425	407	1,148	440	829	233	1,008	1,214	919	1,276	1,274	27,302	802	130		30
4,353	4,039	9,802	4,961	5,422	2,365	11,440	12,637	6,135	13,570	12,813	530,453	11,637	2,388		31
537	360	2,491	1,034	2,949	105	3,378	3,647	1,804	5,236	1,250	51,080	935	521	905	32
128	140	1,370	130	1,530	85	1,391	1,696	665	2,542	478	36,681	524	351	549	33
$5,610	$3,450	$22,081	$5,220	$18,732	$1,050	$37,195	$53,495	$11,565	$62,435	$8,740	$959,173	$10,825	$6,780	$26,350	34
$1,390	$1,150	$8,010	$1,330	$4,500	$600	$9,215	$15,600	$4,345	$14,945	$2,610	$293,497	$2,975	$3,260	$3,750	35
$504	$125	$1,628	$298	$1,420	$35	$1,912	$6,865	$420	$2,860	$705	$53,858	$775	$110	$945	36
2	4	26	14	25	3	52	64	10	73	30	1,045	16	8	23	37
3	2	11	1	11	1	15	24	5	26	7	1,146	27	9	27	38
6	3	26	6	19	3	44	49	13	50	15	781	9	11	23	39
24	53	580	18	438	10	717	907	240	1,239	97	18				40
9	11	193	7	102	4	337	411	72	465	23	6				41
94	22	451	71	494	17	361	466	206	697	206	9,349	147	85	202	42
1,290	90	3,591	680	2,945	160	3,792	4,720	1,905	7,691	1,410	186,133	2,080	1,459	5,090	43
38	2,958	3,707	335	1,029	437	2,776	2,743	417	2,505	1,689	60,776	1,505	424	588	44
16	1,255	1,254	180	643	289	1,729	1,321	207	1,775	1,044	29,964	1,072	151	167	45
24	1,778	2,341	233	666	298	1,428	1,616	197	1,431	861	50,723	1,015	334	549	46
7	700	790	78	433	168	649	605	97	716	382	22,322	614	106	156	47
$1,050	$54,900	$49,690	$5,160	$6,485	$4,095	$31,451	$47,244	$3,001	$26,195	$17,210	$2,005,785	$20,215	$4,185	$20,035	48
$850	$8,125	$8,525	$2,280	$1,950	$1,915	$7,720	$12,070	$800	$6,575	$4,330	$449,568	$6,245	$905	$6,360	49
$740	$33,791	$20,726	$3,475	$6,030	$4,090	$22,436	$27,650	$2,121	$22,292	$10,290	$1,088,813	$17,685	$2,050	$10,380	50
$105	$1,793	$2,210	$475	$278	$455	$1,252	$2,488	$175	$1,435	$607	$75,106	$1,034	$320	$1,567	51
3	49	32	12	8	17	39	38	2	22	41	1,451	27	5	20	52
2	26	9	7	4	9	10	16		9	12	1,736	31	6	31	53
1	15	43	3	7	10	36	48	4	39	21	1,021	26	9	20	54
2	763	749	65	190	76	636	841	47	734	120	18				55
	262	280	25	60	27	264	327	19	289	38	6				56
17	390	542	96	173	101	306	332	65	427	389	16,415	477	91	263	57
225	2,993	4,400	1,374	1,430	1,190	3,135	3,625	400	3,837	3,528	409,277	7,845	1,413	7,325	58
2,472	38,820	55,663	9,533	14,996	555	11,764	81,641	36,450	29,284	1,444	25,139	25	45	429	59
506	21,511	42,675	505	10,620	365	6,493	54,133	17,831	22,295	647	18,795	12	23	424	60
$14,856	$477,293	$617,070	$29,980	$140,783	$8,100	$174,705	$1,368,757	$222,713	$346,364	$17,265	$802,471	$465	$400	$14,465	61
$3,900	$84,520	$143,210	$4,225	$36,140	$2,250	$31,225	$232,600	$65,396	$71,371	$2,860	$145,658	$85	$25	$3,650	62
$720	$27,763	$34,481	$515	$7,771	$325	$6,368	$70,055	$8,901	$19,979	$594	$27,222	$5	$75	$690	63
6	529	590	57	204	8	167	1,435	264	426	17	531	1	1	12	64
8	252	179	14	87	7	28	487	41	138	8	587	1	1	24	65
10	401	967	5	125	4	177	1,505	356	443	12	516			16	66
111	12,296	20,834	82	4,833	108	3,299	32,985	6,564	11,527	133	754				67
32	3,900	7,052	30	1,372	34	1,429	12,461	2,001	4,649	21	359				68
169	5,718	13,732	255	3,664	61	1,861	13,115	5,927	6,431	244	6,899	14	6	323	69
2,141	47,049	113,702	3,008	26,564	535	19,665	125,410	44,693	62,033	2,439	174,438	50	180	8,690	70
1,436	34,652	67,393	5,868	19,403	2,290	15,545	21,892	16,113	29,683	11,029	155,957	1,581	1,978	5,682	71
933	23,373	60,117	825	17,359	1,781	11,951	18,901	10,883	24,063	6,026	135,533	1,286	1,791	4,663	72
$22,230	$486,802	$911,321	$37,795	$213,925	$33,114	$281,735	$456,447	$116,305	$428,623	$152,768	$5,615,851	$25,524	$34,505	$198,530	73
$5,545	$78,826	$200,425	$9,615	$51,870	$8,735	$56,335	$77,976	$36,995	$114,055	$28,210	$936,305	$5,256	$4,435	$40,335	74
$703	$18,228	$29,847	$1,295	$8,290	$1,691	$10,748	$10,466	$4,614	$16,610	$4,590	$121,890	$334	$678	$6,115	75
35	354	532	33	284	54	254	265	104	431	213	3,155	37	38	66	76
8	113	99	13	142	21	22	43	9	53	58	3,120	26	25	80	77
30	404	1,389	21	151	34	339	384	239	387	137	1,883	14	19	43	78
202	13,278	27,921	266	8,179	529	6,952	11,287	4,545	12,512	1,452	2,142				79
55	4,744	10,331	107	2,484	200	3,315	4,456	1,317	5,812	498	1,106				80
410	5,131	17,460	379	6,548	467	3,233	4,132	4,063	6,196	2,341	43,291	476	710	1,229	81
5,776	48,019	161,425	5,815	52,603	5,006	36,779	42,073	30,788	69,321	28,879	1,116,418	8,100	17,605	34,280	82

NEGRO POPULATION.

Table 73.—STATISTICS OF SIZE OF FARMS AND FOR TENURE CLASSES OF FARMS

KENTUCKY—continued.

		Barren.	Bourbon.	Boyle.	Caldwell.	Christian.	Daviess.	Fayette.	Fulton.	Garrard.	Graves.
1	Number of farms	436	113	104	159	878	256	107	228	230	224
	FARMS CLASSIFIED BY SIZE.										
2	Under 3 acres	1	1			4	1			2	
3	3 to 9 acres	74	39	38	10	84	42	25	10	66	14
4	10 to 19 acres	132	29	33	48	236	81	26	30	70	67
5	20 to 49 acres	203	34	16	65	353	70	34	149	71	102
6	50 to 99 acres	70	4	12	19	106	38	13	32	16	31
7	100 to 174 acres	14	5	5	15	68	19	4	6	3	9
8	175 to 259 acres	2	1		2	20	4	3		1	
9	260 to 499 acres					7	1		1		1
10	500 to 999 acres								2	1	
11	1,000 acres and over										
	FARMERS CLASSIFIED BY TENURE.										
12	Owners, free	182	19	62	28	171	58	20	4	63	35
13	Owners, mortgaged	37	5	5	8	60	18	9	5	31	14
14	Part owners	60	32	16	15	73	27	42	2	35	17
15	Cash tenants	4	7	1	3	66	6	5	46	1	5
16	Share tenants	208	41	17	103	499	143	26	164	92	147
17	Share-cash tenants	2	7		2		2		1	6	1
18	Tenure not specified	3	1	1		6	1	2	4	2	5
19	Managers		1	2		3	1	3	2		
	FARMS OPERATED BY OWNERS, FREE.										
20	Total acreage	6,505	384	1,127	1,979	7,734	4,000	191	92	1,163	1,807
21	Improved, acreage	5,105	378	570	1,719	5,741	3,667	183	85	838	1,340
22	Value of land	$105,848	$31,625	$21,575	$21,230	$88,925	$125,415	$20,912	$3,250	$43,510	$29,430
23	Value of buildings	$36,575	$14,975	$9,425	$6,095	$33,780	$39,445	$16,525	$550	$13,990	$8,740
24	Value of implements and machinery	$5,458	$1,080	$942	$1,245	$5,400	$6,631	$2,675	$115	$1,557	$1,867
25	Number of dairy cows	183	10	39	35	177	82	27	3	47	43
26	Number of work horses	160	22	49	32	133	88	32	4	53	53
27	Number of work mules	110	7	9	34	149	65	4	4	4	34
28	Acreage in cotton								5		
29	Bales of cotton grown in 1909								1		
30	Acreage in corn	1,503	102	162	359	1,471	828	205	26	230	426
31	Bushels of corn grown in 1909	24,619	3,500	5,201	5,620	25,360	19,169	11,305	600	6,145	8,665
	FARMS OPERATED BY OWNERS, MORTGAGED.										
32	Total acreage	1,547	44	75	601	3,994	1,281	175	125	772	669
33	Improved acreage	1,274	44		532	2,718	1,022	169	110	680	502
34	Value of land	$24,260	$4,100	$5,830	$4,875	$51,598	$43,605	$14,545	$8,110	$46,465	$10,765
35	Value of buildings	$7,570	$1,600	$4,550	$2,125	$16,100	$6,915	$6,990	$475	$9,025	$2,910
36	Value of implements and machinery	$1,370	$200	$439	$420	$3,084	$1,415	$1,676	$210	$1,600	$481
37	Number of dairy cows	38	4	4	11	67	18	19	9	19	15
38	Number of work horses	35	9	7	9	64	25	12	8	39	18
39	Number of work mules	30		1	11	82	14	3	4	15	17
40	Acreage in cotton								18		
41	Bales of cotton grown in 1909								6		
42	Acreage in corn	287	11	29	101	726	237	35	36	250	170
43	Bushels of corn grown in 1909	4,304	400	459	1,460	11,315	4,750	1,212	1,225	8,335	3,405
	FARMS OPERATED BY PART OWNERS.										
44	Total acreage	1,939	777	692	556	3,596	947	2,210	95	1,324	935
45	Owned acreage	1,077	208	258	423	1,696	380	190	75	742	560
46	Improved acreage	1,621	777	656	501	3,078	855	2,123	72	1,194	714
47	Owned improved acreage	827	208	222	368	1,364	338	163	52	614	401
48	Value of land	$44,900	$74,384	$40,638	$6,855	$93,655	$36,585	$192,791	$3,230	$73,510	$18,390
49	Value of buildings	$9,235	$22,501	$7,725	$2,325	$22,009	$6,975	$36,827	$250	$12,250	$2,515
50	Value of land and buildings owned	$24,885	$34,200	$19,820	$6,085	$64,459	$20,565	$52,243	$2,500	$46,730	$11,425
51	Value of implements and machinery	$1,089	$5,295	$980	$185	$3,045	$1,057	$8,258	$160	$1,840	$685
52	Number of dairy cows	51	33	20	12	64	22	65	6	44	18
53	Number of work horses	41	64	23	8	45	50	97	6	45	20
54	Number of work mules	36	12	11	16	60	18	39	3	21	22
55	Acreage in cotton								18		
56	Bales of cotton grown in 1909								6		
57	Acreage in corn	379	175	172	102	669	327	1,032	37	482	216
58	Bushels of corn grown in 1909	7,475	7,285	7,925	1,810	15,110	7,400	47,688	950	16,635	5,760
	FARMS OPERATED BY CASH TENANTS, INCLUDING TENURE NOT SPECIFIED.										
59	Total acreage	87	184	26	122	4,040	197	234	2,037	44	384
60	Improved acreage	87	178	26	92	3,254	172	188	1,904	44	331
61	Value of land	$2,625	$16,000	$1,460	$775	$79,275	$5,790	$38,739	$92,322	$2,250	$6,000
62	Value of buildings	$775	$2,700	$300	$325	$11,705	$785	$7,308	$10,485	$350	$950
63	Value of implements and machinery	$70	$860		$50	$3,045	$163	$1,300	$4,370	$35	$120
64	Number of dairy cows	6	13		2	69	9	16	55	1	9
65	Number of work horses	3	9		2	63	9	11	41	2	8
66	Number of work mules	2	6		4	48	5	1	113		1
67	Acreage in cotton								754		
68	Bales of cotton grown in 1909								359		
69	Acreage in corn	34	85		10	677	55	64	820	15	106
70	Bushels of corn grown in 1909	650	3,160		100	14,160	520	3,620	24,529	300	3,025
	FARMS OPERATED BY SHARE AND SHARE-CASH TENANTS.										
71	Total acreage	4,843	1,178	584	3,101	16,272	2,829	1,004	5,416	2,572	3,711
72	Improved acreage	4,615	1,178	504	2,864	14,672	2,684	1,002	5,233	2,572	3,572
73	Value of land	$165,420	$113,870	$28,818	$62,689	$443,110	$233,920	$109,244	$262,670	$149,825	$116,823
74	Value of buildings	$27,020	$19,130	$2,175	$10,050	$72,604	$25,230	$8,850	$26,405	$18,125	$20,105
75	Value of implements and machinery	$2,333	$2,235	$530	$762	$7,807	$2,430	$1,584	$5,655	$1,589	$4,363
76	Number of dairy cows	115	20	11	62	292	66	23	140	44	111
77	Number of work horses	67	57	15	32	193	95	37	116	79	81
78	Number of work mules	58	6	4	36	160	31	18	180	16	55
79	Acreage in cotton								2,141		
80	Bales of cotton grown in 1909								1,106		
81	Acreage in corn	1,138	351	139	370	3,326	934	462	2,236	497	1,228
82	Bushels of corn grown in 1909	23,856	14,561	4,015	7,770	87,064	30,392	22,085	72,469	18,995	32,260

OPERATED BY COLORED FARMERS, BY COUNTIES, FOR SOUTHERN STATES: 1910—Continued.

KENTUCKY—continued.

Green.	Harrison.	Hart.	Henderson.	Henry.	Hopkins.	Jefferson.	Jessamine.	Lincoln.	Logan.	Lyon.	McCracken.	Madison.	Metcalfe.	Montgomery.	
170	107	236	469	116	150	142	126	191	503	123	186	580	149	103	1
						1			5					4	2
23	20	55	57	47	10	55	42	74	59	9	29	194	15	37	3
44	30	52	136	43	38	36	36	35	138	39	47	128	39	20	4
59	43	81	164	19	56	30	33	60	194	39	71	184	61	28	5
27	10	32	65	3	28	12	9	15	70	23	28	53	27	8	6
12	4	16	34	3	15	4	3	5	31	12	9	16	6	3	7
5			12	1	3	1	3		3	1	2	4	1	3	8
			1			2		1	3			1			9
						1		1							10
															11
57	13	65	51	14	28	59	37	108	140	34	44	264	27	50	12
26	6	23	29	1	6	8	13	9	57	5	26	41	21	12	13
20	26	29	47	4	15	21	23	30	27	22	55	82	28	6	14
2	2	4	37	2	3	32	5	5	10	7	15	21	1	2	15
53	34	112	293	94	96	15	42	29	268	54	41	142	69	29	16
	25		5			3	6	4	1	1	4	25	1	2	17
11		3	7	1	1			6				3	2	2	18
1	1				1	4					1	2			19
2,868	547	2,863	2,282	303	1,925	1,015	603	1,886	6,392	2,286	1,627	5,467	1,368	1,772	20
1,920	531	1,841	2,070	292	1,251	916	375	1,247	4,087	1,332	1,349	4,612	1,071	978	21
$35,352	$13,010	$40,865	$74,390	$10,400	$41,500	$87,735	$25,200	$50,745	$72,410	$24,580	$51,125	$200,965	$19,235	$54,600	22
$9,865	$6,570	$14,040	$17,200	$3,550	$10,710	$25,630	$18,555	$15,250	$31,915	$6,055	$14,745	$71,290	$5,270	$14,725	23
$1,800	$1,055	$2,421	$4,014	$510	$2,360	$4,695	$1,475	$1,600	$4,376	$1,158	$2,453	$8,777	$749	$3,149	24
57	17	55	73	6	44	35	36	92	126	56	48	270	22	51	25
45	23	58	73	17	43	62	50	80	108	36	55	284	23	58	26
61	1	38	62	1	36	26	13	18	101	43	30	56	14	10	27
															28
															29
550	68	484	708	44	358	270	144	456	1,116	456	366	1,392	234	211	30
8,085	2,600	6,360	16,250	1,170	6,815	8,420	3,465	12,375	20,967	9,410	6,590	39,270	2,531	6,230	31
1,266	379	1,243	1,527	15	210	151	380	262	2,862	476	1,044	1,445	1,033	519	32
1,065	359	862	1,264	15	151	106	276	142	2,350	224	820	1,279	800	274	33
$12,745	$10,400	$19,600	$37,190	$450	$4,420	$12,150	$18,300	$5,625	$48,810	$4,125	$26,910	$46,433	$11,795	$17,300	34
$4,085	$3,600	$5,500	$10,650	$300	$1,320	$5,200	$7,515	$2,650	$14,715	$700	$6,785	$13,372	$3,505	$5,100	35
$705	$265	$877	$1,856	$50	$195	$2,380	$903	$415	$2,525	$235	$1,360	$4,216	$528	$515	36
23	10	23	33		6	4	13	8	46	9	28	49	20	12	37
14	16	21	35	2	2	11	17	12	44	4	37	51	15	19	38
28		17	40		6	4	4	3	59	11	21	16	10	5	39
															40
															41
250	46	212	358	5	48	17	130	44	544	88	221	306	179	97	42
3,456	1,320	2,970	7,435	125	595	345	3,640	850	8,665	1,510	3,380	6,860	1,705	2,825	43
1,205	755	1,069	3,102	59	707	382	897	1,529	1,041	909	1,812	2,297	1,224	152	44
479	303	574	1,413	25	449	113	277	559	412	618	1,038	969	748	87	45
845	712	941	2,765	59	628	362	832	1,261	798	676	1,591	2,154	954	86	46
368	263	477	1,218	25	370	107	217	317	255	385	853	884	511	65	47
$16,018	$43,240	$39,330	$101,830	$4,065	$19,680	$38,275	$70,840	$64,870	$21,000	$10,665	$72,035	$107,190	$19,660	$8,000	48
$4,080	$11,675	$7,500	$17,680	$2,400	$4,950	$10,500	$9,425	$5,315	$5,026	$3,970	$18,245	$21,750	$4,005	$2,075	49
$8,466	$22,650	$24,310	$55,245	$3,350	$15,940	$23,500	$19,935	$14,605	$9,056	$7,942	$52,550	$59,085	$12,950	$5,800	50
$877	$1,380	$1,210	$3,315	$170	$740	$2,330	$1,499	$682	$617	$398	$3,487	$3,825	$691	$565	51
25	14	23	60	2	16	9	20	28	17	30	86	80	22	9	52
20	38	23	83	5	17	18	34	35	25	19	81	98	21	10	53
29	2	20	64		19	24	10	13	20	18	61	33	21		54
															55
															56
235	145	164	1,095	12	157	240	250	435	202	346	718	681	269	27	57
2,330	5,345	3,355	29,920	400	2,830	8,815	9,077	14,735	4,530	6,990	17,009	19,690	3,050	1,200	58
399	191	168	2,713	98	250	1,245	76	282	521	360	260	575	145	48	59
195	136	165	2,074	98	182	1,029	46	257	350	252	259	455	133	40	60
$4,940	$3,575	$5,508	$99,090	$4,200	$5,200	$103,825	$4,560	$15,530	$9,530	$3,450	$15,930	$22,340	$2,660	$1,700	61
$630	$500	$690	$17,790	$350	$700	$10,775	$5,650	$2,450	$2,520	$1,350	$4,810	$4,185	$450	$1,125	62
$45	$225	$80	$2,653	$20	$155	$2,580	$65	$305	$410	$170	$807	$423	$75	$30	63
5	4	6	45	2	8	25	6	12	7	8	19	11	2	3	64
10	8	11	58	1	3	54	3	11	7	4	16	16	3	3	65
1	2	4	74		6	16	2	7	12	7	7	9	3		66
															67
															68
41	35	60	1,261	31	25	251	9	93	118	109	97	107	5	5	69
465	1,050	770	41,340	1,210	480	5,165	320	3,500	2,210	2,580	3,075	2,787	50	150	70
1,259	1,079	2,123	8,924	1,765	3,589	1,031	1,359	1,138	7,120	1,167	1,417	4,550	1,549	471	71
1,187	1,077	2,075	8,398	1,709	2,866	946	1,332	1,066	6,637	1,075	1,183	4,449	1,414	470	72
$17,439	$69,780	$114,380	$346,945	$93,120	$123,415	$92,035	$96,370	$66,150	$223,089	$18,377	$41,950	$309,630	$32,105	$34,450	73
$3,245	$18,750	$16,140	$58,631	$24,525	$23,500	$10,650	$14,800	$10,700	$42,495	$4,398	$8,280	$34,730	$8,150	$10,700	74
$368	$2,081	$2,705	$9,998	$1,940	$4,525	$1,525	$1,673	$2,115	$3,725	$490	$1,575	$3,733	$437	$1,008	75
21	22	49	176	15	73	21	31	33	183	27	33	119	34	26	76
11	63	38	190	40	67	52	52	30	115	16	37	152	32	30	77
8	9	34	198	5	113	26	10	15	108	22	17	29	11	13	78
										1					79
										(1)					80
265	214	276	3,968	181	1,183	131	223	334	2,229	624	502	1,628	387	222	81
4,410	9,305	5,830	96,408	5,655	26,883	3,585	8,330	12,791	54,870	16,358	9,593	62,703	8,570	9,982	82

¹ Less than 1 bale.

TABLE **73.**—STATISTICS OF SIZE OF FARMS AND FOR TENURE CLASSES OF FARMS

		Muhlenburg.	Nelson.	Owen.	Scott.	Shelby.	Simpson.	Taylor.	Todd.	Trigg.	Warren.
						KENTUCKY—continued.					
1	Number of farms	112	125	105	102	140	114	134	416	371	295
	FARMS CLASSIFIED BY SIZE.										
2	Under 3 acres										
3	3 to 9 acres	9	34	14	46	52	22	17	56	21	59
4	10 to 19 acres	15	29	36	26	36	15	25	106	106	54
5	20 to 49 acres	41	26	32	14	37	51	50	181	134	106
6	50 to 99 acres	30	16	10	7	10	17	29	46	54	53
7	100 to 174 acres	12	10	12	6	2	8	11	21	40	18
8	175 to 259 acres	4	5			2	1	1	4	13	4
9	260 to 499 acres		5	1	3	1		1	2	2	1
10	500 to 999 acres	1								1	
11	1,000 acres and over										
	FARMERS CLASSIFIED BY TENURE.										
12	Owners, free	55	61	27	37	24	25	60	82	77	131
13	Owners, mortgaged	4	15	7	8	9	18	32	51	27	37
14	Part owners	12	10	7	11	19	8	10	42	36	21
15	Cash tenants	4	4		5	6	5	4	13	8	10
16	Share tenants	35	34	63	35	79	54	27	218	222	92
17	Share-cash tenants				5	3		1	3	1	2
18	Tenure not specified	2	1	1			4		6		2
19	Managers				1				1		
	FARMS OPERATED BY OWNERS, FREE.										
20	Total acreage	3,708	2,886	1,331	1,157	462	590	2,215	2,844	5,902	4,431
21	Improved acreage	2,410	1,804	1,028	1,090	392	480	1,534	2,188	3,624	3,419
22	Value of land	$39,705	$54,235	$28,735	$48,115	$16,310	$16,875	$26,775	$34,815	$36,795	$81,365
23	Value of buildings	$15 920	$15,080	$14,920	$14,670	$6,690	$4,325	$10,770	$17,480	$11,585	$26,725
24	Value of implements and machinery	$2,826	$3,389	$1,645	$2,158	$827	$810	$2,602	$2,100	$3,455	$4,428
25	Number of dairy cows	63	77	26	56	18	22	63	57	94	125
26	Number of work horses	45	102	53	41	24	21	70	43	56	106
27	Number of work mules	62	12	2	5	1	13	25	63	124	86
28	Acreage in cotton										
29	Bales of cotton grown in 1909										
30	Acreage in corn	713	430	168	173	87	81	502	589	938	1,033
31	Bushels of corn grown in 1909	9,357	10,691	5,723	4,415	2,440	1,690	7,081	8,972	17,480	14,855
	FARMS OPERATED BY OWNERS, MORTGAGED.										
32	Total acreage	461	664	337	206	424	676	1,690	2,812	2,265	1,926
33	Improved acreage	185	428	222	184	343	512	1,001	2,316	1,452	1,358
34	Value of land	$2,550	$19,660	$6,290	$8,876	$12,030	$15,665	$17,400	$38,035	$17,960	$35,020
35	Value of buildings	$900	$5,140	$1,750	$4,000	$6,650	$4,725	$4,830	$15,150	$7,020	$12,215
36	Value of implements and machinery	$100	$515	$315	$450	$860	$773	$1,185	$2,233	$1,195	$2,350
37	Number of dairy cows	5	14	4	10	28	13	25	46	34	42
38	Number of work horses	3	22	11	11	13	19	33	34	26	34
39	Number of work mules	4	3		2	2	6	18	71	46	43
40	Acreage in cotton										
41	Bales of cotton grown in 1909										
42	Acreage in corn	66	113	36	98	34	115	275	391	276	530
43	Bushels of corn grown in 1909	865	2,710	986	2,634	775	1,950	3,495	7,470	5,665	9,485
	FARMS OPERATED BY PART OWNERS.										
44	Total acreage	491	891	239	94	235	261	510	2,309	2,215	1,124
45	Owned acreage	271	554	111	21	86	117	285	1,257	1,455	508
46	Improved acreage	420	614	237	94	225	242	345	2,197	1,849	1,051
47	Owned improved acreage	202	295	109	21	76	99	206	1,168	1,094	457
48	Value of land	$9,215	$15,400	$4,345	$4,050	$15,950	$7,970	$6,875	$56,915	$27,930	$36,530
49	Value of buildings	$4,250	$2,500	$1,675	$3,900	$7,100	$2,500	$1,725	$16,085	$8,470	$8,950
50	Value of land and buildings owned	$8,205	$9,300	$2,350	$3,750	$11,800	$6,700	$5,325	$39,083	$21,904	$20,985
51	Value of implements and machinery	$525	$360	$230	$250	$683	$325	$515	$2,610	$1,321	$1,500
52	Number of dairy cows	12	10	7	2	6	7	12	40	44	23
53	Number of work horses	15	19	9	7	20	7	10	39	33	28
54	Number of work mules	12	11	2		1	11	10	44	50	27
55	Acreage in cotton										
56	Bales of cotton grown in 1909										
57	Acreage in corn	220	141	43	8	72	91	88	465	463	359
58	Bushels of corn grown in 1909	2,410	4,245	865	200	2,320	1,800	925	8,425	10,565	6,290
	FARMS OPERATED BY CASH TENANTS, INCLUDING TENURE NOT SPECIFIED.										
59	Total acreage	145	522	10	43	644	338	184	496	703	810
60	Improved acreage	108	61	10	43	642	309	138	462	575	525
61	Value of land	$2,300	$2,680	$800	$1,510	$55,225	$8,885	$2,175	$9,920	$4,045	$19,380
62	Value of buildings	$600	$220		$790	$7,125	$2,500	$425	$2,925	$775	$4,190
63	Value of implements and machinery	$12	$32		$80	$935	$280	$60	$267	$186	$420
64	Number of dairy cows	7	3		2	2	9	3	15	6	8
65	Number of work horses	4	7		6	9	13	3	8	5	9
66	Number of work mules		1			9	8		17	11	15
67	Acreage in cotton										
68	Bales of cotton grown in 1909										
69	Acreage in corn	66	21		11	38	74	20	235	99	211
70	Bushels of corn grown in 1909	965	214		290	1,600	1,450	500	4,338	2,155	4,165
	FARMS OPERATED BY SHARE AND SHARE-CASH TENANTS.										
71	Total acreage	1,624	1,566	2,017	1,732	1,814	2,337	1,264	5,743	7,095	3,035
72	Improved acreage	1,024	1,479	1,715	1,618	1,739	2,135	1,067	5,327	5,841	2,777
73	Value of land	$31,017	$68,910	$66,610	$121,981	$118,065	$74,150	$31,060	$160,417	$93,357	$105,748
74	Value of buildings	$4,845	$12,975	$15,700	$18,269	$32,500	$11,675	$5,480	$26,000	$20,454	$18,475
75	Value of implements and machinery	$594	$980	$1,565	$3,857	$3,126	$1,356	$695	$1,783	$3,239	$2,239
76	Number of dairy cows	27	24	26	57	46	38	16	112	137	52
77	Number of work horses	13	32	60	41	93	44	14	69	83	42
78	Number of work mules	25	13	28	9	5	27	12	52	71	47
79	Acreage in cotton										
80	Bales of cotton grown in 1909										
81	Acreage in corn	514	277	236	332	368	656	261	1,653	1,973	849
82	Bushels of corn grown in 1909	8,060	9,745	8,610	9,580	12,940	15,035	4,755	40,377	46,135	18,537

OPERATED BY COLORED FARMERS, BY COUNTIES, FOR SOUTHERN STATES: 1910—Continued.

KENTUCKY—continued.			LOUISIANA.												
Washington.	Webster.	All other counties.	The state.	Acadia.	Ascension.	Avoyelles.	Bienville.	Bossier.	Caddo.	Calcasieu.	Caldwell.	Catahoula.	Claiborne.	Concordia.	
149	123	2,898	54,879	400	218	1,287	1,209	2,605	3,846	340	322	710	2,285	1,055	1
		7	33					1	1	2			1		2
25	11	640	4,335	9	31	169	28	202	192	55	18	73	18	181	3
42	29	684	15,353	66	42	448	101	657	1,026	39	94	316	108	561	4
59	34	816	25,161	244	91	587	595	1,144	1,902	149	97	278	1,112	271	5
12	29	427	6,041	60	40	64	247	368	460	49	49	26	528	23	6
11	15	231	2,753	14	13	15	189	177	178	31	46	10	323	7	7
	3	60	694	4	1	4	28	37	44	5	9	3	116	2	8
	2	27	384	3			18	15	27	7	6	2	66	4	9
		5	89				3	4	11	2	3	1	11	4	10
		1	36						5	5		1	2	2	11
53	27	1,063	7,312	61	129	111	325	445	401	216	116	27	321	51	12
15	12	231	2,287	12	26	37	67	108	82	12	14	14	147	3	13
24	11	438	1,126	10	9	42	63	77	58	11	3	6	31		14
2	2	96	8,723	6	22	227	139	291	991	15	9	97	172	72	15
48	66	987	33,596	310	7	854	578	1,668	2,243	50	168	501	1,589	898	16
2		27	908	1		8	32	9	14	3		55	10	7	17
3	5	42	850		25	7	5	7	48		12	10	13	20	18
2		14	77			1			9				2	4	19
1,675	2,732	48,844	567,301	3,135	5,359	4,556	34,012	36,004	37,003	12,072	12,559	1,997	43,890	3,640	20
1,326	2,228	29,005	259,152	2,669	2,974	2,812	13,746	14,704	19,669	3,460	3,117	964	22,539	1,597	21
$47,365	$81,605	$671,884	$6,195,618	$88,509	$114,270	$86,960	$206,898	$191,827	$400,349	$142,255	$57,290	$21,595	$253,608	$55,930	22
$16,380	$14,475	$237,584	$1,866,784	$12,475	$38,425	$27,025	$71,079	$74,359	$96,250	$57,030	$22,155	$9,030	$83,978	$14,920	23
$3,784	$2,517	$31,511	$422,801	$3,785	$5,092	$5,849	$15,196	$17,570	$28,207	$12,998	$3,628	$1,220	$17,547	$5,715	24
63	35	1,146	17,928	132	172	177	647	1,082	1,322	548	340	96	770	104	25
97	54	1,037	9,923	222	182	191	239	296	382	475	145	62	307	64	26
19	37	414	5,992	45	69	42	342	416	496	21	40	19	455	89	27
			67,705	306	702	625	3,833	3,982	5,940	127	148	131	6,406	614	28
			16,024	90	307	170	723	714	1,476	37	22	39	1,321	229	29
275	619	8,593	82,090	932	1,086	1,201	4,687	4,191	4,361	1,355	1,070	393	5,456	410	30
8,520	12,030	152,452	1,044,197	16,018	18,227	19,140	41,302	40,355	51,549	20,017	13,091	6,535	48,542	8,980	31
633	1,032	13,498	188,352	768	1,013	1,968	6,203	9,741	8,402	1,238	2,300	1,156	19,049	712	32
516	860	8,288	92,766	690	623	1,158	2,783	3,984	4,926	356	854	458	9,591	293	33
$18,845	$25,700	$206,781	$2,362,012	$23,970	$27,625	$43,590	$41,960	$67,735	$127,220	$14,555	$21,400	$17,100	$125,698	$14,720	34
$4,350	$4,750	$68,775	$605,314	$2,925	$6,925	$10,185	$14,750	$20,670	$25,660	$2,695	$5,600	$4,450	$31,465	$1,500	35
$1,082	$1,185	$11,865	$145,322	$1,200	$1,058	$2,685	$3,160	$5,239	$7,891	$860	$5,515	$1,250	$7,217	$550	36
15	19	255	5,152	26	47	65	154	251	284	29	71	44	297	14	37
22	21	308	3,027	64	41	63	46	78	77	28	19	21	136	5	38
6	13	123	2,240	16	14	26	73	97	146	8	20	13	170	9	39
			26,783	132	115	260	948	1,088	1,683		16	97	2,911	120	40
			5,864	54	48	62	168	208	462		2	19	526	28	41
118	229	2,207	29,631	197	181	424	915	944	1,371	58	176	210	2,306	108	42
4,755	5,770	48,398	404,649	3,070	3,710	6,825	8,522	10,123	22,076	801	2,260	2,915	20,488	2,680	43
697	717	18,265	79,042	599	301	1,506	4,798	5,291	4,456	1,678	149	266	3,763		44
379	304	9,553	49,436	273	164	887	3,577	3,927	2,105	1,196	120	183	1,975		45
621	664	13,618	47,732	562	214	1,162	2,288	2,897	2,464	926	47	198	1,965		46
304	286	6,257	24,162	236	86		1,338	1,576	1,028	572	18	115	952		47
$27,565	$20,845	$506,124	$1,444,130	$20,610	$7,200	$32,525	$42,534	$43,892	$63,085	$28,975	$655	$5,662	$27,288		48
$5,725	$4,735	$117,235	$305,712	$2,900	$5,250	$7,900	$13,645	$11,715	$14,610	$4,650	$100	$2,575	$6,525		49
$14,565	$11,195	$285,240	$1,015,338	$12,630	$8,710	$24,180	$41,338	$33,220	$29,985	$25,620	$600	$5,692	$17,598		50
$1,640	$435	$17,411	$73,926	$640	$825	$2,292	$2,087	$2,535	$3,128	$4,440	$35	$535	$1,815		51
17	9	434	2,158	21	11	49	114	126	160	13	4	18	58		52
32	12	511	1,569	33	13	72	48	61	69	37	2	16	22		53
2	15	209	1,396	11	11	17	60	78	81	11		4	45		54
			11,147	61	71	360	701	794	1,055			70	748		55
			2,355	23	27	80	120	126	230			19	139		56
114	191	4,762	16,865	241	98	412	900	786	850	45	17	94	531		57
3,685	4,630	99,020	246,752	4,290	1,660	6,131	8,490	10,932	10,349	543	140	1,345	4,410		58
221	311	5,527	323,641	593	1,120	5,892	8,460	16,719	46,728	1,738	1,009	3,775	16,765	2,745	59
171	214	3,091	243,487	468	910	5,584	4,553	8,744	37,678	1,210	418	2,157	9,215	2,009	60
$4,400	$5,620	$122,927	$5,718,760	$13,950	$42,000	$210,695	$57,095	$152,284	$579,881	$39,540	$11,045	$59,328	$112,178	$43,300	61
$1,000	$1,100	$30,590	$1,440,786	$5,400	$9,950	$38,690	$23,655	$30,391	$103,610	$9,900	$3,675	$14,153	$21,685	$14,420	62
$765	$425	$4,934	$329,616	$2,132	$1,879	$12,290	$3,889	$9,520	$28,378	$4,056	$371	$2,529	$4,120	$3,066	63
3	4	116	12,117	1	41	181	188	424	1,783	60	30	161	287	63	64
9	2	130	9,113	8	68	357	103	141	772	73	27	140	107	111	65
	2	107	6,548	8	34	113	95	245	920	11	9	80	161	39	66
			92,814	26	241	1,971	1,792	2,529	14,032	23	93	554	3,263	518	67
			26,141	5	100	554	294	528	3,222	11	34	171	639	97	68
12	75	1,581	79,709	66	269	2,609	1,802	2,676	8,625	264	142	929	2,370	1,071	69
350	2,250	32,025	1,172,072	1,436	4,935	41,534	17,942	30,476	104,940	4,495	1,840	14,968	19,805	13,425	70
1,190	2,148	35,100	945,009	10,697	600	15,958	24,330	42,657	57,221	2,954	4,234	10,583	85,727	15,496	71
1,181	2,005	24,925	815,423	10,332	219	15,366	17,516	37,988	53,509	1,903	3,354	10,192	61,400	14,453	72
$65,244	$68,365	$980,744	$19,966,339	$319,700	$14,050	$523,520	$216,327	$1,249,215	$1,630,691	$61,515	$78,244	$187,137	$488,296	$372,495	73
$13,920	$10,240	$176,358	$4,424,132	$34,400	$1,850	$98,471	$72,625	$208,823	$233,156	$13,345	$21,790	$60,056	$165,711	$137,583	74
$1,855	$1,665	$24,623	$692,224	$10,141	$205	$19,521	$10,848	$23,452	$33,587	$3,350	$3,840	$8,438	$23,395	$19,939	75
28	35	669	26,613	348	15	426	524	956	1,372	81	218	501	1,603	784	76
51	34	716	23,824	645	7	632	203	349	699	90	80	412	539	745	77
13	21	302	19,370	161	6	204	285	993	1,591	20	91	393	1,099	436	78
			314,855	1,740	51	4,480	6,851	16,282	23,192	53	851	2,234	23,219	6,825	79
			91,150	508	19	1,223	1,453	5,799	8,794	13	275	670	4,566	2,071	80
355	500	9,854	294,888	4,032	83	7,259	6,144	8,968	22,071	328	1,201	4,477	16,629	5,887	81
13,550	13,890	206,479	4,530,152	69,987	1,640	110,431	66,605	148,031	349,707	5,384	19,677	73,189	150,052	92,176	82

TABLE 73.—STATISTICS OF SIZE OF FARMS AND FOR TENURE CLASSES OF FARMS

LOUISIANA—continued.

		De Soto.	East Baton Rouge.	East Carroll.	East Feliciana.	Franklin.	Grant.	Iberia.	Iberville.	Jackson.	Lafayette.
1	Number of farms	3,033	1,189	1,717	1,820	852	460	549	251	508	935
	FARMS CLASSIFIED BY SIZE.										
2	Under 3 acres		5	1				29	31	12	1
3	3 to 9 acres	75	85	500	123	39	36	68	71	49	23
4	10 to 19 acres	472	378	755	368	350	227	257	110	202	67
5	20 to 49 acres	1,682	597	409	1,036	406	176	144	22	130	603
6	50 to 99 acres	469	85	29	183	39	17	44	10	69	218
7	100 to 174 acres	212	29	11	76	11	2	6	4	29	23
8	175 to 259 acres	65	4	5	17	1	2	1	2	13	
9	260 to 499 acres	44	5	3	15	5				4	
10	500 to 999 acres	6	1	1	2	1			1		
11	1,000 acres and over	8		3							
	FARMERS CLASSIFIED BY TENURE.										
12	Owners, free	558	107	29	133	64	23	115	53	169	112
13	Owners, mortgaged	194	30	12	79	34	12	56	19	38	34
14	Part owners	76	11	7	14		3	79	16	47	36
15	Cash tenants	752	338	870	333	156	154	51	105	26	3
16	Share tenants	1,307	672	752	1,163	593	261	238	53	225	712
17	Share-cash tenants	123	12	7	64			6	2		3
18	Tenure not specified	20	19	35	33	5	7	2	2	3	7
19	Managers	3		5	1			2	1		
	FARMS OPERATED BY OWNERS, FREE.										
20	Total acreage	51,022	7,001	931	10,670	4,863	1,191	4,029	2,293	17,576	4,575
21	Improved acreage	25,091	4,065	726	5,119	2,023	532	3,387	1,261	7,030	3,925
22	Value of land	$411,979	$134,735	$27,825	$104,884	$78,305	$17,785	$165,775	$73,920	$88,103	$182,615
23	Value of buildings	$103,320	$42,070	$12,930	$41,875	$18,235	$5,925	$28,755	$24,680	$28,925	$20,015
24	Value of implements and machinery	$31,897	$6,070	$2,350	$8,390	$5,323	$1,340	$6,094	$4,600	$7,652	$6,515
25	Number of dairy cows	1,723	261	36	366	162	77	157	78	347	203
26	Number of work horses	640	179	44	179	119	30	160	87	125	301
27	Number of work mules	481	149	34	140	84	21	161	49	170	92
28	Acreage in cotton	8,638	1,139	272	1,801	666	112	236	194	1,198	895
29	Bales of cotton grown in 1909	1,987	281	169	275	172	26	17	35	181	304
30	Acreage in corn	7,141	1,198	178	1,563	775	267	1,558	494	2,498	1,867
31	Bushels of corn grown in 1909	76,141	21,504	3,127	19,313	13,600	3,685	30,231	11,882	20,178	37,497
	FARMS OPERATED BY OWNERS, MORTGAGED.										
32	Total acreage	14,578	1,982	1,222	7,949	2,515	768	2,727	1,001	3,756	1,443
33	Improved acreage	7,496	986	502	4,433	1,019	444	2,341	504	1,698	1,144
34	Value of land	$113,113	$27,130	$29,655	$75,735	$43,525	$14,175	$109,975	$30,585	$19,885	$50,315
35	Value of buildings	$28,462	$8,375	$7,150	$28,734	$8,925	$4,375	$17,305	$8,175	$5,200	$3,535
36	Value of implements and machinery	$8,277	$1,715	$2,214	$4,856	$2,100	$530	$4,296	$1,290	$1,290	$1,210
37	Number of dairy cows	463	50	29	217	79	41	65	27	79	63
38	Number of work horses	200	41	10	89	61	20	91	29	27	87
39	Number of work mules	145	40	30	83	39	10	126	16	43	23
40	Acreage in cotton	3,221	408	158	1,397	270	118	163	77	457	354
41	Bales of cotton grown in 1909	789	85	67	258	80	17	12	14	60	95
42	Acreage in corn	2,273	334	147	1,193	519	187	1,078	198	683	538
43	Bushels of corn grown in 1909	23,131	5,380	2,315	14,836	9,671	2,655	20,929	4,753	5,612	10,643
	FARMS OPERATED BY PART OWNERS.										
44	Total acreage	6,447	738	674	840		147	5,167	368	4,191	1,792
45	Owned acreage	4,288	325	412	625		99	2,459	146	2,479	739
46	Improved acreage	3,557	466	281	400		114	4,603	325	2,440	1,622
47	Owned improved acreage	1,748	210	172	205		66	2,210	107	1,318	664
48	Value of land	$41,909	$21,810	$15,490	$8,849		$5,780	$223,865	$13,510	$22,131	$98,390
49	Value of buildings	$11,245	$6,440	$3,300	$1,595		$850	$31,405	$4,955	$4,703	$11,480
50	Value of land and buildings owned	$33,750	$13,130	$13,540	$7,919		$4,230	$130,025	$9,825	$17,520	$52,660
51	Value of implements and machinery	$3,763	$1,185	$683	$789		$240	$6,732	$791	$1,569	$2,920
52	Number of dairy cows	218	24	15	34		10	115	10	84	56
53	Number of work horses	80	23	8	18		4	132	21	33	113
54	Number of work mules	77	14	10	11		5	205	18	57	50
55	Acreage in cotton	1,353	138	143	157		44	322	50	434	258
56	Bales of cotton grown in 1909	330	34	72	31		9	23	9	59	92
57	Acreage in corn	984	140	46	160		60	2,124	127	793	805
58	Bushels of corn grown in 1909	11,228	2,395	1,140	2,030		1,050	41,224	3,045	6,159	14,867
	FARMS OPERATED BY CASH TENANTS, INCLUDING TENURE NOT SPECIFIED.										
59	Total acreage	30,264	10,198	20,861	11,275	3,689	3,241	2,543	5,305	1,888	1,121
60	Improved acreage	23,443	8,197	16,408	8,887	3,131	3,113	2,354	4,185	841	1,024
61	Value of land	$114,426	$296,653	$503,723	$116,193	$62,300	$121,850	$92,765	$309,155	$11,000	$56,275
62	Value of buildings	$69,268	$67,690	$150,295	$45,093	$23,165	$24,250	$9,560	$54,430	$4,475	$4,985
63	Value of implements and machinery	$14,397	$9,458	$34,961	$8,841	$6,615	$6,950	$2,570	$20,803	$568	$1,167
64	Number of dairy cows	964	299	624	465	289	195	46	54	37	35
65	Number of work horses	602	411	701	312	235	174	64	143	20	69
66	Number of work mules	466	290	548	222	96	168	107	232	17	19
67	Acreage in cotton	10,877	3,933	8,401	4,069	1,445	1,431	165	643	200	194
68	Bales of cotton grown in 1909	2,633	944	4,569	622	406	392	12	117	34	62
69	Acreage in corn	7,777	2,623	3,179	3,386	1,394	1,283	1,089	1,637	329	536
70	Bushels of corn grown in 1909	79,945	47,260	66,259	38,056	20,093	19,278	21,140	39,360	2,391	9,898
	FARMS OPERATED BY SHARE AND SHARE-CASH TENANTS.										
71	Total acreage	62,605	14,540	10,365	34,663	11,800	4,338	11,705	1,662	11,383	27,514
72	Improved acreage	44,536	14,025	10,265	30,897	10,758	4,280	10,930	1,414	6,562	25,811
73	Value of land	$418,621	$289,476	$299,590	$385,962	$240,323	$117,434	$492,870	$98,025	$18,616	$111,253
74	Value of buildings	$117,459	$82,918	$127,925	$129,646	$78,650	$28,791	$50,075	$17,425	$2,519	$25,948
75	Value of implements and machinery	$20,969	$12,118	$11,475	$30,760	$13,672	$2,010	$12,264	$4,415	$216	$707
76	Number of dairy cows	1,042	435	411	1,148	495	142	196	22	105	1,257
77	Number of work horses	688	530	270	755	548	78	273	52	129	702
78	Number of work mules	770	438	224	959	391	122	477	54		
79	Acreage in cotton	16,525	7,471	4,272	14,662	4,282	1,361	763	217	1,578	6,222
80	Bales of cotton grown in 1909	4,049	1,650	1,952	2,258	1,299	460	55	39	252	1,653
81	Acreage in corn	11,908	5,712	1,632	13,030	4,918	1,188	5,044	553	2,308	13,849
82	Bushels of corn grown in 1909	140,365	95,153	33,006	156,029	83,863	19,916	97,880	13,293	21,100	236,205

OPERATED BY COLORED FARMERS, BY COUNTIES, FOR SOUTHERN STATES: 1910—Continued.

LOUISIANA—continued.

Lincoln.	Living-ston.	Madison.	More-house.	Natchi-toches.	Ouachita.	Plaque-mines.	Pointe Coupee.	Rapides.	Red River.	Rich-land.	Sabine.	St. Helena.	St. Landry.	St. Martin.	
868	104	1,652	2,411	2,873	1,214	199	1,632	1,004	1,002	1,615	422	648	3,755	924	1
4													1		2
11	11	223	67	171	113	17	178	145	71	74	20	26	195	30	3
50	24	813	779	1,172	398	32	884	340	336	550	51	119	683	109	4
393	50	567	1,381	1,215	530	112	477	431	469	877	199	338	2,345	590	5
237	12	27	126	194	91	29	61	64	92	81	86	84	428	159	6
130	5	9	44	95	58	7	17	16	22	23	50	50	81	30	7
34		4	7	18	14	1	9	6	9	6	9	20	12	4	8
9	1	2	6	7	7		4	2	2	4	5	11	7	2	9
	1	3	1				2		1		2		2		10
		4		1	1	1							1		11
197	43	27	185	343	168	90	79	123	98	99	133	85	448	155	12
52	5	8	26	63	60	20	40	21	67	29	37	43	163	92	13
16	1	1	21	63	5	10	7	3	10	4	18	7	37	51	14
18	4	234	405	179	160	55	327	70	114	13	110	73		15	15
572	50	1,337	1,631	2,169	685	17	1,135	512	674	1,343	214	242	2,918	601	16
	1	23	115	46	90		10	3	82	13	5	91	9	6	17
10		18	26	8	44	4	21	13	1	13	2	70	99	3	18
3		4	2	2	2	3	6	2					8	1	19
19,831	1,327	3,028	13,521	24,400	13,569	3,364	6,213	5,736	7,550	6,564	12,088	9,980	21,856	6,452	20
11,374	483	668	5,045	8,921	5,170	1,376	2,936	2,281	3,363	2,913	4,169	3,750	14,314	4,959	21
$129,103	$12,930	$49,260	$184,614	$237,481	$119,870	$78,995	$135,428	$86,671	$48,565	$89,180	$70,635	$63,400	$517,329	$241,800	22
$44,350	$6,900	$6,440	$50,015	$66,817	$41,510	$30,875	$44,675	$29,900	$16,540	$35,370	$21,265	$27,700	$124,045	$33,635	23
$9,281	$1,027	$1,821	$12,863	$17,685	$9,568	$4,884	$3,778	$6,070	$2,871	$7,446	$5,683	$5,035	$32,211	$10,884	24
338	87	55	407	695	382	70	169	319	207	414	267	267	1,338	247	25
115	29	40	244	514	154	114	66	165	112	193	126	87	1,238	339	26
247	9	33	177	265	146	22	45	59	63	46	32	60	260	149	27
2,288	103	260	2,032	2,687	1,305		540	463	950	1,252	1,081	1,269	3,025	974	28
346	26	68	760	685	269		75	159	209	296	285	295	901	156	29
2,830	137	174	1,410	3,102	1,775	110	1,062	989	1,109	944	1,449	1,064	6,068	2,353	30
25,917	1,562	2,320	18,717	34,643	17,597	2,467	17,335	15,370	11,158	13,411	12,922	12,205	113,456	43,629	31
5,244	385	2,080	1,594	4,452	5,550	789	3,070	1,696	4,339	2,804	2,519	4,270	8,600	4,070	32
2,842	75	730	904	1,936	1,985	303	1,486	832	2,149	1,152	1,052	1,543	6,014	3,035	33
$32,417	$2,575	$32,290	$28,450	$68,780	$61,287	$28,750	$66,215	$43,295	$37,010	$45,140	$18,660	$28,850	$220,120	$133,025	34
$11,245	$600	$3,340	$7,810	$16,300	$16,818	$7,400	$20,250	$6,765	$12,520	$11,440	$6,095	$10,650	$36,195	$25,615	35
$2,333	$103	$1,240	$2,025	$5,277	$3,555	$728	$3,174	$1,511	$1,182	$2,095	$1,082	$1,662	$10,528	$7,062	36
81	7	34	63	148	120	12	48	67	140	148	57	127	429	133	37
31	4	21	22	111	62	23	55	29	71	58	23	34	448	218	38
67	2	29	28	54	62	5	32	23	48	30	12	28	92	105	39
665	34	276	357	698	667		308	135	598	468	368	670	1,392	772	40
92	7	118	132	197	126		44	38	162	125	93	152	350	116	41
840	20	332	181	622	650	27	607	262	700	318	297	470	2,419	1,469	42
7,365	190	5,560	2,535	9,195	7,931	445	8,600	5,020	7,956	5,850	3,127	4,865	40,313	31,606	43
988	55	200	1,656	3,528	271	767	267	81	909	265	1,359	619	2,039	2,306	44
602	40	180	888	2,916	202	388	164	34	675	209	1,009	472	1,235	1,221	45
653	21	100	788	1,731	169	289	221	74	345	176	674	257	1,403	1,810	46
349	7	100	317	1,141	100	128	131	27	191	120	429	160	701	883	47
$7,144	$640	$2,800	$25,315	$33,469	$2,462	$11,470	$15,475	$2,340	$6,655	$4,033	$8,681	$4,188	$47,815	$85,830	48
$3,505	$30	$1,200	$5,335	$8,538	$650	$4,030	$2,175	$400	$2,375	$575	$3,965	$1,525	$9,385	$13,050	49
$6,391	$500	$3,940	$15,235	$32,850	$1,860	$7,980	$13,310	$1,060	$7,055	$3,456	$9,874	$4,710	$33,619	$56,410	50
$545	$20	$200	$1,477	$2,069	$160	$448	$456	$110	$355	$90	$687	$432	$2,097	$4,312	51
21	2	1	54	142	18	7	23	7	28	19	44	13	95	65	52
4	1	1	23	92	11	13	11	7	10	8	14	6	95	114	53
21		1	30	51	1	2	7		11	9	11	1	31	53	54
187	8	10	320	573	75		33	26	92	90	276	179	301	398	55
32	3	1	105	147	12		5	11	15	30	79	25	70	62	56
258	10	8	220	552	57	23	127	30	80	48	200	95	669	816	57
2,506	4	40	3,223	6,164	660	499	1,570	285	845	1,070	2,220	1,070	8,955	16,522	58
1,339	588	6,506	10,311	4,465	5,086	2,888	6,850	8,836	2,123	3,172	521	5,547	5,964	1,104	59
1,007	170	4,891	10,030	4,131	4,084	1,317	6,514	7,589	1,774	2,795	421	4,432	5,232	1,001	60
$13,240	$3,970	$167,897	$206,772	$114,966	$172,809	$47,302	$208,147	$344,921	$34,288	$60,626	$3,690	$44,000	$194,565	$46,070	61
$5,445	$180	$43,615	$63,865	$21,215	$33,820	$12,830	$48,095	$69,405	$7,225	$19,070	$1,315	$18,425	$28,975	$7,340	62
$706	$152	$2,122	$22,120	$5,245	$4,707	$10,678	$6,432	$22,497	$1,260	$5,050	$208	$6,493	$6,242	$1,777	63
24	11	337	439	331	309	20	458	438	103	269	26	236	208	16	64
15	2	202	372	352	139	32	271	372	62	176	6	146	328	53	65
14	3	101	347	97	136	6	195	320	45	41	1	98	73	20	66
258	5	2,963	5,020	2,074	1,778		588	2,616	421	1,232	86	2,117	1,090	49	67
40	2	1,274	1,869	772	493		113	905	94	335	17	514	280	3	68
235	20	1,401	2,489	1,198	1,124	43	4,815	2,685	525	905	157	1,696	2,471	260	69
2,260	220	26,572	33,218	20,940	16,819	940	95,539	59,350	7,267	13,608	875	18,142	39,608	4,410	70
29,639	1,708	22,727	40,600	47,260	20,297	635	19,158	9,224	15,620	30,622	8,566	10,410	83,076	20,649	71
21,341	1,023	22,722	39,764	42,551	16,145	510	18,879	9,017	14,958	29,779	5,738	8,099	77,633	18,453	72
$214,239	$20,620	$679,190	$921,448	$1,287,619	$522,500	$11,555	$490,566	$427,277	$844,387	$615,652	$71,822	$70,585	$2,239,966	$825,740	73
$66,739	$5,350	$199,874	$233,853	$233,919	$110,660	$3,445	$174,537	$62,055	$86,609	$188,045	$19,395	$40,415	$463,294	$95,790	74
$13,357	$697	$13,093	$35,626	$44,871	$16,707	$890	$15,657	$13,813	$8,891	$21,455	$3,618	$5,712	$96,569	$27,869	75
534	27	897	1,421	1,556	811	13	635	239	565	1,142	196	304	2,472	469	76
189	37	642	964	2,078	330	28	574	260	330	866	139	201	4,264	926	77
387	16	566	1,284	1,093	563		305	399	578	735	48	151	903	585	78
6,062	551	11,415	20,598	21,418	8,124		5,209	3,986	6,413	14,658	2,122	3,844	21,325	4,449	79
1,056	173	5,482	7,250	7,814	2,236		822	1,539	2,035	4,178	586	904	5,493	873	80
6,300	307	5,770	12,446	13,676	5,024	3	13,078	3,209	5,400	9,179	1,936	2,914	36,915	9,228	81
62,559	5,279	105,231	179,322	219,860	72,725	80	215,242	73,231	106,336	149,373	20,430	32,015	640,572	210,993	82

TABLE **73.**—STATISTICS OF SIZE OF FARMS AND FOR TENURE CLASSES OF FARMS

LOUISIANA—continued.

		St. Mary.	Tangi-pahoa.	Tensas.	Union.	Vermilion.	Wash-ington.	Webster.	West Baton Rouge.	West Carroll.	West Feliciana.
1	Number of farms	218	436	2,729	776	314	426	1,033	340	432	1,281
	FARMS CLASSIFIED BY SIZE.										
2	Under 3 acres		2								
3	3 to 9 acres	53	86	482	20	22	7	24	44	28	177
4	10 to 19 acres	39	122	1,542	31	31	44	87	155	187	374
5	20 to 49 acres	67	130	618	285	148	239	471	117	155	634
6	50 to 99 acres	43	53	53	199	86	69	209	20	37	60
7	100 to 174 acres	13	37	20	171	22	46	170	3	17	20
8	175 to 259 acres	2	3	4	45	3	14	41	1	6	7
9	260 to 499 acres		2	3	22	2	6	28		2	6
10	500 to 999 acres	1	1	6	2		1	3			2
11	1,000 acres and over			1	1						1
	FARMERS CLASSIFIED BY TENURE.										
12	Owners, free	74	175	46	173	67	149	233	32	56	34
13	Owners, mortgaged	17	45	14	130	23	36	98	27	23	17
14	Part owners	57	6	8	44	39	4	42	3	2	4
15	Cash tenants	6	113	392	67	4	92	226	187	108	415
16	Share tenants	52	84	2,166	351	164	125	423	71	226	792
17	Share-cash tenants			14	3	4		3	18		2
18	Tenure not specified	7	11	88	7	13	20	8	1	17	17
19	Managers	5	2	1	1				1		
	FARMS OPERATED BY OWNERS, FREE.										
20	Total acreage	1,021	7,307	5,057	20,672	3,149	12,678	26,079	734	3,940	5,106
21	Improved acreage	878	2,377	1,783	9,034	2,378	4,800	11,062	574	1,720	2,013
22	Value of land	$56,315	$80,410	$116,793	$99,691	$112,328	$117,530	$158,842	$29,810	$67,140	$48,825
23	Value of buildings	$34,525	$40,290	$26,295	$41,395	$14,797	$54,875	$71,525	$16,800	$18,350	$8,140
24	Value of implements and machinery	$3,422	$5,524	$8,545	$8,888	$6,482	$10,261	$15,620	$1,515	$3,645	$1,690
25	Number of dairy cows	49	308	148	395	146	502	683	67	333	105
26	Number of work horses	67	193	92	169	244	187	289	47	124	57
27	Number of work mules	38	28	106	165	39	71	172	34	30	42
28	Acreage in cotton		711	895	2,173	282	2,469	2,866	121	634	496
29	Bales of cotton grown in 1909		194	383	332	91	789	658	17	206	39
30	Acreage in corn	426	751	532	2,639	880	1,862	2,937	317	505	505
31	Bushels of corn grown in 1909	8,228	8,941	10,111	24,616	15,343	19,665	29,685	8,180	6,280	5,870
	FARMS OPERATED BY OWNERS, MORTGAGED.										
32	Total acreage	493	2,261	948	16,217	861	2,996	10,852	1,383	2,351	1,750
33	Improved acreage	479	773	575	6,721	681	1,103	4,483	891	894	800
34	Value of land	$19,670	$20,417	$19,015	$68,520	$25,365	$27,135	$59,985	$41,385	$46,670	$17,780
35	Value of buildings	$7,980	$9,590	$6,615	$24,450	$5,435	$10,765	$22,940	$15,735	$8,750	$3,800
36	Value of implements and machinery	$1,196	$1,509	$710	$6,961	$2,375	$1,471	$5,130	$2,453	$2,105	$671
37	Number of dairy cows	12	65	31	258	40	80	242	67	167	40
38	Number of work horses	11	52	22	88	46	42	117	35	56	22
39	Number of work mules	22	5	16	154	20	16	67	49	19	17
40	Acreage in cotton		252	232	2,064	73	477	1,399	162	315	233
41	Bales of cotton grown in 1909		53	104	261	22	166	296	10	95	12
42	Acreage in corn	204	210	136	2,007	221	388	1,264	488	272	196
43	Bushels of corn grown in 1909	3,454	1,939	2,255	19,112	3,788	3,990	12,393	12,280	3,720	2,205
	FARMS OPERATED BY PART OWNERS.										
44	Total acreage	3,164	832	561	4,377	2,326	93	3,570	195	332	540
45	Owned acreage	1,359	684	140	3,532	1,351	53	2,853	120	292	357
46	Improved acreage	3,001	140	350	1,858	1,834	88	2,011	190	70	270
47	Owned improved acreage	1,208	87	102	1,123	888	48	1,304	115	60	147
48	Value of land	$161,617	$5,160	$11,490	$20,170	$112,670	$1,650	$26,485	$7,750	$10,250	$3,216
49	Value of buildings	$40,318	$1,100	$2,650	$6,145	$11,050	$1,100	$6,725	$2,800	$1,400	$500
50	Value of land and buildings owned	$112,595	$4,700	$3,840	$21,105	$76,205	$2,200	$26,680	$6,800	$10,500	$2,436
51	Value of implements and machinery	$6,764	$215	$1,197	$1,511	$3,067	$125	$1,410	$450	$350	$240
52	Number of dairy cows	57	19	31	89	67	9	81	11	14	8
53	Number of work horses	76	10	19	28	108	5	39	6	3	2
54	Number of work mules	146		20	45	29	2	40	11	3	3
55	Acreage in cotton		77	95	504	272	38	552	25	35	79
56	Bales of cotton grown in 1909		17	25	67	70	14	90	1	14	8
57	Acreage in corn	1,213	41	179	614	781	18	522	130	22	75
58	Bushels of corn grown in 1909	22,213	615	3,220	4,815	13,690	280	5,675	3,100	475	940
	FARMS OPERATED BY CASH TENANTS, INCLUDING TENURE NOT SPECIFIED.										
59	Total acreage	412	4,177	11,499	3,765	624	4,050	13,522	3,511	2,455	10,214
60	Improved acreage	365	2,271	8,807	1,733	504	2,824	7,230	3,286	2,316	9,277
61	Value of land	$25,335	$45,235	$285,540	$18,258	$25,300	$43,065	$90,033	$106,066	$55,325	$118,250
62	Value of buildings	$7,280	$24,860	$88,295	$7,622	$2,650	$18,345	$29,760	$42,705	$10,555	$46,555
63	Value of implements and machinery	$720	$2,625	$10,935	$1,136	$565	$3,012	$5,797	$6,047	$3,790	$7,410
64	Number of dairy cows	6	179	566	99	27	198	417	144	189	556
65	Number of work horses	11	108	457	45	40	101	223	235	124	447
66	Number of work mules	14	27	241	24	1	28	96	168	76	231
67	Acreage in cotton		903	4,631	606	115	1,261	2,436	669	1,207	4,189
68	Bales of cotton grown in 1909		277	1,607	77	31	507	522	73	431	331
69	Acreage in corn	179	615	2,251	798	224	1,019	2,309	1,842	804	4,025
70	Bushels of corn grown in 1909	4,390	6,773	36,986	7,000	4,590	10,755	21,491	46,514	11,663	51,513
	FARMS OPERATED BY SHARE AND SHARE-CASH TENANTS.										
71	Total acreage	2,630	1,852	33,613	21,260	8,023	4,227	19,312	1,727	4,394	17,515
72	Improved acreage	2,543	1,521	32,848	13,704	7,166	3,161	13,158	1,648	4,277	16,250
73	Value of land	$133,587	$28,570	$1,039,930	$117,248	$309,050	$62,010	$157,114	$69,985	$65,177	$239,290
74	Value of buildings	$16,100	$12,000	$319,310	$33,714	$25,840	$20,760	$47,710	$22,140	$19,875	$75,525
75	Value of implements and machinery	$3,372	$1,550	$22,045	$9,069	$7,795	$3,406	$7,073	$3,332	$3,795	$11,350
76	Number of dairy cows	32	61	1,211	346	183	144	428	82	294	659
77	Number of work horses	42	63	1,103	102	367	58	263	109	167	559
78	Number of work mules	131	14	580	293	174	22	204	80	57	452
79	Acreage in cotton		692	16,566	4,944	1,489	1,530	4,962	553	1,868	7,830
80	Bales of cotton grown in 1909		209	6,946	760	340	571	1,086	76	546	755
81	Acreage in corn	926	472	7,700	4,107	2,983	985	4,335	860	1,497	6,705
82	Bushels of corn grown in 1909	16,164	7,414	124,810	39,834	52,699	11,687	45,490	23,083	20,527	85,596

OPERATED BY COLORED FARMERS, BY COUNTIES, FOR SOUTHERN STATES: 1910—Continued.

LOUISIANA—contd.		MARYLAND.													
Winn.	All other parishes.	The state.	Anne Arundel.	Baltimore.	Calvert.	Caroline.	Charles.	Dorchester.	Harford.	Howard.	Kent.	Montgomery.	Prince Georges.	Queen Annes.	
268	712	6,372	422	137	424	395	633	513	197	147	151	349	480	224	1
......	14	7	......	......	......	1	2	......	......	......	......	......	3	......	2
11	100	1,608	69	35	50	81	73	102	52	65	83	172	114	76	3
28	110	1,327	81	44	67	108	97	99	61	29	35	70	81	51	4
109	266	1,386	105	32	101	113	139	126	41	27	17	56	91	46	5
60	131	767	51	11	67	54	106	78	19	11	7	23	52	18	6
45	62	780	82	11	89	24	109	66	12	11	5	19	72	20	7
11	18	311	29	......	30	8	62	31	8	1	2	6	37	6	8
4	4	146	5	3	17	5	34	6	1	2	1	3	25	7	9
......	5	35	......	1	3	1	8	4	3	1	1	......	5	......	10
......	2	5	......	......	......	......	3	1	......	......	......	......	......	......	11
122	312	2,191	135	37	183	120	255	182	61	47	69	167	200	86	12
30	71	1,110	61	45	53	100	54	88	78	48	26	84	42	44	13
18	44	649	42	12	16	47	33	38	11	18	18	26	33	12	14
18	127	405	35	26	10	21	34	40	12	11	12	28	31	16	15
77	123	1,685	130	8	158	91	231	156	29	3	19	29	77	42	16
......	15	35	1	......	......	6	......	5	......	1	1	2	3	4	17
3	13	210	9	1	3	6	23	1	......	13	......	8	86	11	18
......	7	87	9	8	1	4	3	3	6	6	6	5	8	9	19
11,411	16,290	58,733	3,655	508	6,733	2,393	10,304	5,809	1,150	689	635	2,292	6,309	1,408	20
3,607	5,794	35,176	2,608	402	4,135	1,581	5,494	3,047	770	500	509	1,743	4,152	999	21
$56,850	$280,406	$1,132,183	$92,045	$41,960	$59,365	$54,575	$94,688	$92,160	$32,125	$27,115	$25,490	$95,235	$149,373	$38,792	22
$22,690	$103,609	$724,503	$54,552	$31,215	$48,452	$36,345	$89,980	$41,700	$23,075	$20,485	$17,770	$58,165	$81,550	$18,553	23
$4,504	$24,560	$109,946	$9,677	$4,450	$4,192	$5,296	$14,008	$8,226	$4,648	$2,380	$2,990	$6,793	$16,080	$3,792	24
364	766	1,554	79	33	145	59	331	144	67	22	19	121	138	32	25
115	374	2,387	148	40	168	141	346	194	64	35	80	163	290	117	26
71	168	183	20	9	......	7	10	24	9	2	......	5	11	......	27
321	543	......													28
42	168	......													29
1,311	2,168	8,937	542	80	719	516	1,110	988	184	150	151	397	922	304	30
9,619	34,036	162,419	6,943	1,420	10,146	7,446	18,069	18,474	4,498	4,405	2,115	12,005	19,431	4,633	31
2,509	3,778	39,195	2,082	1,203	4,224	2,674	4,228	3,244	1,607	1,354	455	1,825	2,601	1,355	32
885	2,160	24,125	1,505	772	2,263	1,838	2,183	1,779	1,175	977	301	1,305	1,554	1,024	33
$10,425	$119,115	$814,566	$60,585	$78,150	$28,660	$74,905	$32,171	$53,880	$36,965	$36,055	$12,278	$68,427	$57,350	$34,555	34
$3,845	$45,305	$441,188	$35,625	$33,300	$15,115	$41,125	$21,200	$21,195	$33,070	$25,435	$10,930	$31,998	$22,780	$14,995	35
$868	$11,918	$67,744	$4,984	$4,460	$1,862	$6,628	$2,765	$4,302	$7,626	$3,700	$880	$6,103	$3,547	$2,373	36
59	82	906	51	55	63	54	74	58	92	42	7	79	58	24	37
30	63	1,402	74	60	77	141	90	102	81	75	29	108	78	72	38
14	77	131	14	9	......	15	5	10	7	5	2	2	1	6	39
114	61	......													40
17	22	......													41
324	667	5,901	284	169	301	547	492	487	269	234	57	362	336	264	42
2,455	13,105	106,705	4,294	4,470	3,970	10,441	7,819	7,629	6,401	6,979	672	10,276	8,042	4,402	43
1,246	3,325	24,111	1,824	753	1,640	1,457	1,674	1,065	575	422	322	1,737	2,002	470	44
853	1,628	9,964	710	329	485	799	665	501	193	211	70	533	580	139	45
437	2,241	17,263	1,442	635	927	1,128	1,094	843	436	353	257	1,464	1,394	415	46
213	894	6,173	481	281	228	518	315	303	148	155	56	416	437	126	47
$6,793	$94,402	$563,931	$55,580	$27,210	$14,370	$34,944	$21,415	$22,060	$11,140	$15,515	$8,813	$52,185	$37,210	$19,100	48
$2,420	$26,923	$248,402	$21,400	$18,500	$4,375	$16,765	$14,355	$10,290	$8,100	$10,250	$6,067	$13,230	$13,450	$4,025	49
$6,290	$61,565	$431,696	$35,265	$22,290	$6,451	$34,020	$20,978	$18,945	$7,770	$15,245	$7,485	$27,245	$24,325	$9,175	50
$419	$7,716	$39,825	$4,776	$1,640	$424	$2,908	$1,379	$2,265	$1,265	$1,652	$687	$3,005	$2,675	$3,488	51
37	56	492	29	46	19	41	47	25	33	6	4	50	33	11	52
10	48	941	71	29	30	73	66	48	21	28	30	72	70	23	53
14	89	87	12	3	......	3	4	2	5	4	......	5	2	4	54
69	74	......													55
9	20	......													56
179	685	5,459	445	104	174	392	385	291	108	81	68	310	318	104	57
1,487	13,181	102,088	6,840	2,423	2,075	7,380	5,583	5,502	2,010	1,645	1,078	8,245	9,506	2,175	58
1,222	6,961	41,820	2,634	1,667	1,060	1,245	7,118	1,952	907	2,036	163	956	13,605	488	59
390	4,567	23,463	1,777	1,235	642	785	2,970	1,008	362	1,393	88	670	7,859	349	60
$5,969	$231,545	$1,005,089	$134,540	$169,650	$6,935	$25,025	$62,210	$27,540	$9,600	$67,500	$6,285	$57,101	$263,270	$15,045	61
$2,714	$49,885	$309,060	$31,150	$32,900	$4,615	$10,325	$30,425	$9,320	$8,050	$20,400	$2,780	$17,030	$77,580	$5,575	62
$301	$13,029	$42,793	$5,125	$4,075	$211	$1,475	$5,302	$1,612	$982	$4,339	$346	$1,400	$8,752	$757	63
33	225	522	27	49	13	18	86	14	10	31	2	20	133	4	64
11	145	856	50	38	17	35	100	41	15	53	11	36	252	29	65
9	256	115	24	29	......	7	4	9	1	2	......	4	......	......	66
14	86	......													67
2	26	......													68
123	1,440	4,607	290	180	37	209	548	285	46	281	34	131	1,286	104	69
815	30,338	92,115	4,917	4,012	910	5,013	7,250	4,154	841	9,030	649	2,815	35,981	1,369	70
2,211	7,022	181,297	15,129	1,224	20,185	6,936	34,801	18,841	3,925	85	1,650	2,412	10,603	3,889	71
1,632	5,193	109,540	10,873	745	12,788	4,536	19,085	10,090	2,408	78	1,180	2,121	7,204	2,938	72
$17,590	$200,220	$2,816,093	$241,950	$31,800	$176,047	$193,830	$369,925	$275,550	$63,960	$3,550	$34,800	$87,537	$218,170	$90,630	73
$5,200	$31,410	$1,042,219	$131,360	$20,450	$74,645	$57,535	$159,770	$59,670	$51,100	$2,350	$8,825	$25,005	$85,580	$23,650	74
$858	$7,388	$135,556	$8,483	$1,850	$6,187	$9,245	$19,647	$14,157	$7,100	$241	$1,693	$4,340	$8,826	$4,530	75
68	182	2,611	230	38	250	103	418	271	105	......	23	46	154	129	76
30	176	3,297	419	23	360	182	494	289	91	7	56	97	266	128	77
39	166	521	8	12	......	51	25	64	36	......	4	......	7	24	78
452	664	......													79
97	270	......													80
617	1,065	25,915	2,128	175	1,433	1,199	3,483	2,282	393	18	234	473	1,500	711	81
6,151	19,760	467,006	37,009	2,475	25,743	26,095	60,185	41,309	11,050	435	3,180	13,330	30,514	17,370	82

TABLE **73.**—STATISTICS OF SIZE OF FARMS AND FOR TENURE CLASSES OF FARMS

		MARYLAND—continued.						MISSISSIPPI			
		St. Marys.	Somerset.	Talbot.	Wicomico.	Worcester.	All other counties.	The state.	Adams.	Alcorn.	Amite.
1	Number of farms	438	574	202	407	481	198	164,737	1,706	441	1,787
	FARMS CLASSIFIED BY SIZE.										
2	Under 3 acres		1					65			
3	3 to 9 acres	81	233	90	97	66	69	7,947	255	24	91
4	10 to 19 acres	69	165	54	103	75	38	40,875	518	97	296
5	20 to 49 acres	100	109	28	103	117	35	83,840	707	195	934
6	50 to 99 acres	70	37	7	51	82	23	19,951	136	78	263
7	100 to 174 acres	81	23	13	38	86	19	8,705	46	39	147
8	175 to 259 acres	26	3	3	12	34	13	2,095	12	3	39
9	260 to 499 acres	10	3	6	3	14	1	1,035	17	5	16
10	500 to 999 acres	1		1		6		184	10		1
11	1,000 acres and over					1		40	5		
	FARMERS CLASSIFIED BY TENURE.										
12	Owners, free	143	178	79	76	98	75	11,562	102	52	211
13	Owners, mortgaged	53	114	45	73	41	61	9,543	75	46	113
14	Part owners	40	127	8	122	36	10	3,921	3	27	14
15	Cash tenants	23	20	24	13	27	22	54,222	613	20	719
16	Share tenants	159	114	30	108	275	26	78,272	862	292	516
17	Share-cash tenants	2	5	1	1	3		3,056	13	1	70
18	Tenure not specified	18	14		14	1	2	4,055	27	3	143
19	Managers		2	15			2	106	11		1
	FARMS OPERATED BY OWNERS, FREE.										
20	Total acreage	5,517	3,097	1,239	2,544	3,258	1,193	1,038,452	9,897	3,737	20,225
21	Improved acreage	2,585	1,746	985	1,343	1,709	868	437,548	3,162	2,006	9,811
22	Value of land	$43,987	$95,910	$54,645	$44,067	$48,941	$41,710	$11,645,675	$93,515	$40,150	$167,036
23	Value of buildings	$37,398	$53,615	$24,555	$26,583	$24,685	$35,825	$3,848,707	$36,605	$16 670	$69,785
24	Value of implements and machinery	$4,989	$7,270	$4,232	$3,754	$3,152	$4,017	$851,163	$6,668	$3,798	$14,706
25	Number of dairy cows	119	60	41	33	53	58	24,499	273	77	600
26	Number of work horses	157	126	103	54	82	79	11,733	128	65	206
27	Number of work mules	1	34	6	20	24	1	11,705	121	55	206
28	Acreage in cotton							149,357	635	507	3,066
29	Bales of cotton grown in 1909							46,129	90	119	950
30	Acreage in corn	614	586	269	466	707	232	108,570	844	524	2,531
31	Bushels of corn grown in 1909	9,890	11,204	8,065	7,216	11,961	4,498	1,255,356	10,953	6,066	33,189
	FARMS OPERATED BY OWNERS, MORTGAGED.										
32	Total acreage	3,010	2,051	657	1,797	2,487	2,341	881,445	8,652	3,727	9,909
33	Improved acreage	1,347	1,348	554	1,127	1,354	1,716	402,434	3,462	1,954	5,289
34	Value of land	$23,890	$55,650	$33,195	$38,985	$31,095	$57,770	$10,358,260	$79,619	$32,649	$86,145
35	Value of buildings	$16,915	$33,425	$13,235	$22,690	$10,925	$37,230	$2,898,984	$34,153	$7,855	$31,992
36	Value of implements and machinery	$1,902	$3,789	$2,385	$2,746	$1,991	$5,701	$743,111	$6,056	$3,137	$7,742
37	Number of dairy cows	48	33	16	23	35	94	19,399	216	79	293
38	Number of work horses	68	95	56	59	42	95	8,957	110	41	101
39	Number of work mules		20	1	11	22	1	11,073	118	48	121
40	Acreage in cotton							153,213	1,087	613	1,998
41	Bales of cotton grown in 1909							43,078	82	138	490
42	Acreage in corn	396	382	135	400	417	369	93,697	900	504	1,497
43	Bushels of corn grown in 1909	5,324	7,381	2,581	5,565	7,205	7,656	994,785	12,120	4,930	18,246
	FARMS OPERATED BY PART OWNERS.										
44	Total acreage	3,204	1,925	94	3,112	1,385	450	307,297	830	2,262	1,094
45	Owned acreage	1,762	746	38	1,224	807	172	181,802	748	1,179	751
46	Improved acreage	1,526	1,652	83	2,375	905	334	162,363	159	1,199	636
47	Owned improved acreage	662	515	30	868	492	142	80,254	78	574	358
48	Value of land	$29,276	$79,458	$4,345	$88,920	$24,405	$17,985	$4,447,256	$12,760	$27,195	$11,720
49	Value of buildings	$15,825	$37,830	$2,875	$38,290	$8,800	$3,976	$1,118,882	$5,200	$5,930	$2,650
50	Value of land and buildings owned	$28,475	$70,688	$3,950	$69,094	$21,275	$9,020	$3,164,732	$14,750	$16,318	$11,135
51	Value of implements and machinery	$2,085	$3,875	$505	$4,578	$1,643	$975	$274,482	$310	$1.321	$1,090
52	Number of dairy cows	47	31	2	30	27	11	7,489	5	37	39
53	Number of work horses	69	106	9	131	45	20	3,632	9	23	15
54	Number of work mules		14		12	15	2	4,628	7	31	21
55	Acreage in cotton							66,196	14	356	300
56	Bales of cotton grown in 1909							18,921	4	81	76
57	Acreage in corn	360	709	25	1,033	454	98	36,184	55	246	203
58	Bushels of corn grown in 1909	5,870	13,710	480	16,512	8,235	2,819	399,966	1,278	2,575	2,430
	FARMS OPERATED BY CASH TENANTS, INCLUDING TENURE NOT SPECIFIED.										
59	Total acreage	2,722	1,319	379	1,206	1,507	856	2,186,589	19,363	1,103	31,948
60	Improved acreage	1,291	606	279	624	787	738	1,716,899	13,771	604	23,312
61	Value of land	$23,610	$32,435	$15,833	$20,685	$32,875	$24,900	$47,017,608	$209,499	$11,970	$295,048
62	Value of buildings	$13,595	$8,525	$5,275	$7,385	$9,925	$14,205	$9,747,188	$95,869	$2,230	$105,109
63	Value of implements and machinery	$2,014	$1,020	$890	$983	$1,480	$2,030	$2,461,805	$22,049	$790	$24,015
64	Number of dairy cows	44	19	7	6	16	23	73,553	981	26	1,249
65	Number of work horses	45	25	28	21	28	32	36,157	560	17	409
66	Number of work mules		11	2	11	11		57,521	582	15	659
67	Acreage in cotton							949,232	4,915	212	11,129
68	Bales of cotton grown in 1909							304,657	474	44	3,140
69	Acreage in corn	310	247	87	208	245	79	397,326	4,146	158	7,838
70	Bushels of corn grown in 1909	4,709	3,520	1,855	2,740	4,630	2,350	5,014,157	57,281	1,611	98,274
	FARMS OPERATED BY SHARE AND SHARE-CASH TENANTS.										
71	Total acreage	14,366	4,619	2,333	8,249	28,389	3,661	2,006,766	21,063	9,270	19,088
72	Improved acreage	8,039	3,303	1,644	4,677	15,044	2,796	1,757,269	16,378	7,688	14,353
73	Value of land	$152,915	$125,780	$86,685	$156,494	$395,760	$110,730	$46,172,079	$223,421	$124,473	$164,108
74	Value of buildings	$81,080	$36,280	$33,725	$42,779	$107,665	$40,650	$10,294,337	$102,654	$31,335	$70,204
75	Value of implements and machinery	$8,348	$6,828	$5,035	$5,631	$17,913	$6,102	$1,229,319	$21,092	$6,999	$9,301
76	Number of dairy cows	187	42	60	58	361	136	54,225	1,026	309	565
77	Number of work horses	233	88	78	102	270	114	21,424	645	157	199
78	Number of work mules	6	38	18	45	181	2	41,080	598	186	273
79	Acreage in cotton							939,063	7,606	2,979	7,430
80	Bales of cotton grown in 1909							314,528	652	720	2,087
81	Acreage in corn	1,941	1,127	336	1,601	6,288	595	394,835	6,019	2,487	5,104
82	Bushels of corn grown in 1909	37,995	20,655	9,855	22,058	94,919	12,829	5,018,087	82,739	29,237	63,797

OPERATED BY COLORED FARMERS, BY COUNTIES, FOR SOUTHERN STATES: 1910—Continued.

MISSISSIPPI—continued.

	Attala.	Benton.	Bolivar.	Calhoun.	Carroll.	Chickasaw.	Choctaw.	Claiborne.	Clarke.	Clay.	Coahoma.	Copiah.	Covington.	De Soto.	Forrest.
1	2,184	943	9,824	682	2,519	1,901	667	2,134	1,551	2,241	6,483	3,060	506	3,593	264
2	56	3	790	3	34	32	17	1	197	83	4	2	3	24	19
3	387	58	4,277	15	435	325	129	156	255	291	370	118	21	575	44
4	1,055	409	4,243	173	1,448	983	284	501	655	1,252	2,592	646	67	2,002	94
5	368	231	422	313	313	346	130	1,094	270	418	3,230	1,601	236	674	54
6	227	180	74	87	199	158	71	186	129	147	238	395	98	235	38
7	62	40	15	64	61	35	26	111	33	34	40	192	54	48	7
8	27	17	3	17	27	19	9	36	10	15	4	68	17	31	7
9	2	4		10	2	3	1	34	2	1	5	31	9	4	1
10		1						13				6	1		
11								2				1			
12	221	49	264	56	137	156	96	67	381	178	152	227	107	203	106
13	224	32	402	30	243	132	96	112	203	124	142	313	100	126	32
14	102	19	138	38	21	65	48	37	141	159	97	77	33	63	14
15	349	468	3,637	84	713	593	39	820	569	868	1,307	779	66	1,884	42
16	1,066	354	4,770	435	1,343	866	341	1,053	247	718	4,323	1,590	194	1,193	64
17	107	2	245	26	13	67	46	10	1	7	168	5	3	74	1
18	115	9	368	10	49	22	1	32		187	290	64	3	50	5
19		10		3				3			4	5			
20	20,803	7,268	11,778	7,691	18,159	14,424	10,145	9,029	27,075	14,083	7,760	19,209	9,417	18,615	9,000
21	8,500	2,580	7,134	2,059	6,905	7,050	4,438	3,605	10,186	7,544	4,951	9,293	3,165	10,781	2,257
22	$215,473	$42,202	$514,370	$56,975	$137,305	$188,839	$79,945	$62,522	$221,198	$229,689	$378,993	$154,525	$84,374	$273,435	$82,620
23	$60,735	$15,400	$137,890	$13,575	$44,225	$46,585	$25,810	$32,015	$99,445	$61,991	$73,427	$78,739	$31,000	$88,335	$35,280
24	$17,516	$4,985	$31,289	$3,828	$11,297	$15,946	$6,636	$4,082	$17,579	$13,718	$20,254	$14,039	$5,978	$17,662	$7,739
25	388	113	200	399	275	365	115	224	659	382	282	406	202	468	323
26	175	66	61	61	122	176	101	99	261	204	148	204	101	256	101
27	208	79	405	80	173	213	85	57	133	212	220	207	61	263	40
28	3,022	669	3,908	488	2,044	2,600	1,053	809	2,963	3,426	2,777	2,270	1,079	3,419	717
29	720	169	1,575	167	546	660	260	206	838	866	1,274	717	451	1,136	264
30	2,497	758	1,435	617	1,753	1,674	1,083	693	2,348	1,621	1,030	1,880	1,050	2,114	681
31	20,815	7,210	29,375	8,270	17,915	20,540	9,901	7,853	19,467	18,785	22,061	22,355	11,449	28,733	9,411
32	23,758	6,332	20,971	3,604	31,064	13,015	10,737	18,654	15,630	11,060	7,772	29,689	8,281	12,197	2,665
33	9,669	2,241	12,641	1,226	13,106	7,176	4,725	7,362	6,268	6,579	4,620	14,319	2,822	7,179	686
34	$195,281	$23,850	$923,025	$24,030	$225,279	$202,748	$83,948	$136,885	$136,876	$200,620	$363,788	$220,364	$72,804	$140,763	$28,540
35	$60,840	$7,310	$210,835	$6,570	$71,200	$49,140	$22,202	$44,795	$59,474	$40,410	$59,417	$102,340	$25,575	$44,821	$8,685
36	$14,268	$1,668	$43,972	$2,168	$18,433	$19,144	$6,135	$12,967	$11,736	$13,092	$55,665	$22,353	$5,082	$7,885	$1,722
37	416	69	613	45	498	334	134	386	388	270	279	624	169	268	77
38	206	35	282	33	217	173	119	172	131	145	98	257	91	157	31
39	243	46	719	40	343	244	69	172	112	147	254	339	67	197	10
40	3,466	547	6,870	316	4,175	3,164	1,303	2,282	1,862	3,013	2,654	4,278	1,212	2,317	251
41	736	112	2,543	108	1,124	737	309	477	519	781	1,120	1,271	403	717	89
42	2,559	451	2,227	292	3,046	1,471	1,134	1,536	1,199	1,155	921	3,109	939	1,401	179
43	19,604	3,693	41,644	3,750	30,879	19,647	9,330	15,689	9,379	17,609	17,500	31,453	10,125	18,607	2,360
44	10,674	2,597	8,809	4,372	2,438	5,927	3,946	4,040	7,990	11,006	4,636	4,657	2,894	6,408	759
45	6,968	1,921	4,771	3,463	1,573	3,543	2,834	2,723	4,644	5,995	1,285	2,567	1,759	3,718	585
46	4,025	1,132	6,142	1,576	1,551	3,335	1,910	1,853	4,766	7,922	3,314	2,655	1,193	4,343	318
47	2,452	615	2,973	907	1,019	1,772	1,237	937	1,982	3,832	770	1,157	584	2,395	144
48	$93,416	$17,555	$370,535	$33,365	$24,488	$89,855	$36,255	$34,762	$82,117	$230,505	$211,071	$47,255	$26,285	$92,210	$8,300
49	$22,440	$3,550	$83,420	$7,820	$5,100	$17,765	$7,855	$12,450	$36,310	$44,500	$24,070	$26,450	$7,485	$24,160	$2,860
50	$76,789	$14,235	$245,435	$30,955	$19,923	$61,444	$30,795	$33,265	$76,900	$166,529	$64,126	$45,820	$20,215	$67,855	$8,560
51	$5,714	$1,103	$19,859	$2,325	$1,278	$5,937	$2,230	$3,635	$7,335	$12,647	$9,020	$4,155	$1,890	$7,025	$505
52	170	42	247	57	40	140	63	145	261	321	126	133	64	139	17
53	76	26	100	38	24	56	52	63	113	138	41	71	40	74	14
54	122	29	303	61	42	116	30	49	96	171	132	65	26	84	5
55	1,587	510	2,621	479	408	1,530	561	790	1,916	3,836	2,113	827	412	1,408	138
56	362	83	1,030	135	96	334	149	173	516	894	755	275	171	420	51
57	1,152	361	925	477	380	838	548	518	1,074	1,502	534	507	355	725	111
58	9,460	2,410	15,485	5,078	2,837	10,330	4,495	6,169	10,511	21,372	8,197	5,514	4,192	10,343	1,176
59	23,523	36,786	100,709	4,061	29,183	33,024	2,510	30,915	17,098	43,980	42,770	36,048	3,273	88,298	2,566
60	13,879	20,250	96,728	2,436	21,779	23,169	1,149	22,691	11,433	38,669	41,172	24,946	1,608	67,885	968
61	$260,312	$293,655	$4,728,895	$47,765	$318,612	$579,571	$24,585	$262,840	$156,374	$984,000	$2,091,503	$316,761	$31,805	$1,887,324	$32,505
62	$66,815	$70,220	$746,257	$11,535	$106,005	$93,151	$5,595	$102,199	$55,488	$168,138	$366,384	$124,730	$7,375	$412,329	$8,705
63	$15,014	$17,128	$190,049	$2,019	$36,143	$36,534	$1,358	$26,909	$10,577	$51,621	$96,994	$23,883	$1,150	$95,109	$1,405
64	662	669	2,636	119	1,046	985	46	1,348	640	1,495	1,602	1,168	96	2,619	47
65	281	368	1,615	54	348	459	42	812	254	734	966	600	36	1,777	33
66	306	478	4,572	108	775	792	10	797	185	1,134	1,633	694	34	1,841	17
67	6,367	7,998	66,608	973	12,145	11,803	363	12,237	5,398	22,527	25,909	10,413	761	35,676	328
68	1,447	1,554	24,769	325	3,450	2,670	106	3,022	1,513	4,897	12,310	3,165	259	13,674	121
69	3,905	4,976	14,833	825	6,660	5,582	373	7,153	2,883	8,214	6,244	6,650	455	14,103	183
70	30,729	41,149	259,966	10,036	72,439	65,084	3,210	76,764	23,315	86,698	147,831	66,453	4,895	209,412	1,832
71	36,344	14,608	82,565	13,405	37,317	26,590	11,912	29,053	5,503	20,555	86,164	43,051	6,342	38,062	2,554
72	28,404	10,957	81,740	11,040	33,571	22,725	9,368	22,544	5,150	19,915	85,499	36,194	4,688	31,978	1,353
73	$408,098	$140,694	$3,853,451	$205,564	$422,362	$498,242	$128,621	$272,749	$58,651	$432,598	$4,364,292	$482,019	$69,886	$726,990	$42,205
74	$108,085	$41,230	$681,755	$46,275	$145,258	$88,249	$37,896	$116,043	$25,514	$98,425	$782,071	$210,362	$25,642	$194,331	$10,245
75	$14,626	$5,129	$44,545	$9,833	$27,428	$18,603	$14,424	$14,277	$1,851	$14,179	$79,552	$25,240	$4,098	$18,522	$2,647
76	1,131	300	1,097	427	1,238	898	300	1,003	141	617	2,105	1,198	159	768	57
77	327	85	403	189	321	221	164	459	44	175	840	437	62	376	44
78	568	303	1,916	414	1,130	528	136	444	61	440	1,349	1,097	46	883	20
79	13,620	4,263	54,862	4,285	18,740	12,805	3,673	11,405	2,349	11,688	51,661	16,562	2,260	17,748	625
80	4,085	899	20,692	1,461	5,197	3,195	914	2,648	756	3,027	24,628	5,393	862	6,129	222
81	8,157	2,799	8,080	3,955	10,487	6,106	2,689	6,533	1,093	4,569	9,434	10,022	1,378	7,019	417
82	74,342	23,297	147,976	49,587	110,700	74,537	24,693	73,281	8,537	52,676	211,701	106,003	15,739	100,185	5,096

TABLE 73.—STATISTICS OF SIZE OF FARMS AND FOR TENURE CLASSES OF FARMS

MISSISSIPPI—continued.

		Franklin.	Grenada.	Harrison.	Hinds.	Holmes.	Issaquena.	Ita-wamba.	Jasper.	Jefferson.	Jefferson Davis.
1	Number of farms	838	1,784	134	6,224	5,437	2,154	202	1,496	2,235	1,080
	FARMS, CLASSIFIED BY SIZE.										
2	Under 3 acres		1	1	7			4			
3	3 to 9 acres	63	10	22	251	159	295		78	142	10
4	10 to 19 acres	176	148	18	982	1,016	1,004	19	243	578	146
5	20 to 49 acres	346	981	30	3,937	3,200	745	85	614	1,148	550
6	50 to 99 acres	120	342	25	709	639	70	60	271	196	206
7	100 to 174 acres	95	211	33	269	278	25	30	194	107	116
8	175 to 259 acres	26	49	4	47	72	7	3	60	41	35
9	260 to 499 acres	10	36		17	53	5	1	28	20	14
10	500 to 999 acres	2	4	1	4	15	3		8	3	2
11	1,000 acres and over		2		1	5					1
	FARMERS, CLASSIFIED BY TENURE.										
12	Owners, free	71	166	98	359	352	122	32	179	126	254
13	Owners, mortgaged	72	97	5	236	348	32	26	252	95	215
14	Part owners	15	20	6	132	70	12	13	133	16	26
15	Cash tenants	280	420	7	1,866	1,672	549	10	406	531	115
16	Share tenants	388	938	5	3,113	2,657	976	120	508	1,323	448
17	Share-cash tenants		33	1	45	138	389		12	9	17
18	Tenure not specified	12	109		470	197	72	1	6	135	4
19	Managers		1	12	3	3	2				1
	FARMS OPERATED BY OWNERS, FREE.										
20	Total acreage	7,655	24,202	7,325	31,849	41,378	7,848	2,827	19,477	13,402	24,520
21	Improved acreage	2,815	9,632	1,028	19,556	22,470	3,830	1,087	6,334	6,783	11,562
22	Value of land	$65,384	$226,465	$70,860	$463,197	$525,647	$234,691	$23,515	$131,246	$109,218	$246,716
23	Value of buildings	$19,503	$80,255	$39,815	$160,315	$161,410	$54,425	$5,385	$48,360	$49,120	$96,664
24	Value of implements and machinery	$4,752	$17,553	$4,392	$32,840	$36,000	$11,708	$1,412	$9,078	$10,971	$17,626
25	Number of dairy cows	188	418	215	976	806	225	62	338	406	528
26	Number of work horses	81	205	99	534	287	153	38	170	195	303
27	Number of work mules	76	196	22	377	433	135	25	137	157	208
28	Acreage in cotton	868	2,908	79	5,410	7,165	2,313	335	2,540	1,688	3,895
29	Bales of cotton grown in 1909	176	820	29	1,541	1,871	1,042	97	761	334	1,608
30	Acreage in corn	908	2,118	390	3,900	4,772	739	426	1,683	1,412	3,331
31	Bushels of corn grown in 1909	11,532	23,797	6,300	8,330	47,822	14,946	4,007	14,545	17,227	39,013
	FARMS OPERATED BY OWNERS, MORTGAGED.										
32	Total acreage	9,670	15,238	893	21,116	36,028	1,965	2,273	25,129	10,116	15,818
33	Improved acreage	3,840	7,098	83	13,121	18,770	935	855	9,813	5,357	7,826
34	Value of land	$64,185	$171,863	$5,350	$284,241	$495,189	$64,067	$17,335	$178,144	$81,160	$173,065
35	Value of buildings	$20,595	$47,217	$2,850	$105,835	$152,030	$17,016	$4,040	$52,807	$32,165	$51,075
36	Value of implements and machinery	$4,945	$11,152	$435	$24,472	$38,251	$3,293	$1,117	$13,418	$6,516	$10,636
37	Number of dairy cows	178	277	19	658	776	45	42	486	252	396
38	Number of work horses	63	111	4	364	263	31	23	226	103	196
39	Number of work mules	101	151	2	291	480	44	30	215	126	182
40	Acreage in cotton	1,060	2,023	11	4,157	7,377	591	302	3,905	1,286	3,474
41	Bales of cotton grown in 1909	216	579	5	1,222	1,893	220	86	1,041	240	1,340
42	Acreage in corn	802	1,331	26	2,835	4,409	193	301	2,213	1,004	2,457
43	Bushels of corn grown in 1909	9,529	16,929	460	32,405	42,855	3,338	2,645	16,849	12,545	27,619
	FARMS OPERATED BY PART OWNERS.										
44	Total acreage	1,452	1,929	405	6,516	7,045	640	814	12,329	1,082	2,352
45	Owned acreage	1,059	1,150	326	3,114	3,102	236	581	8,018	328	1,518
46	Improved acreage	688	984	135	4,770	3,778	457	400	5,403	573	1,317
47	Owned improved acreage	376	445	56	2,108	1,897	170	233	3,179	195	728
48	Value of land	$12,280	$22,320	$3,905	$143,100	$126,709	$33,218	$6,420	$91,089	$11,375	$25,460
49	Value of buildings	$3,280	$5,750	$2,225	$50,085	$27,615	$7,150	$1,495	$26,184	$4,165	$6,720
50	Value of land and buildings owned	$11,550	$16,805	$4,870	$100,340	$71,684	$13,859	$4,980	$75,905	$6,070	$21,205
51	Value of implements and machinery	$685	$1,498	$470	$8,645	$12,332	$2,563	$441	$5,474	$667	$805
52	Number of dairy cows	41	45	28	309	154	14	17	279	35	46
53	Number of work horses	11	23	8	156	70	12	7	120	27	35
54	Number of work mules	17	15		105	108	21	14	104	12	19
55	Acreage in cotton	253	407	12	1,777	1,370	266	135	2,271	132	477
56	Bales of cotton grown in 1909	68	97	3	483	315	165	40	637	30	213
57	Acreage in corn	161	248	37	1,023	840	89	118	1,144	159	278
58	Bushels of corn grown in 1909	1,885	3,115	490	11,490	9,097	1,721	955	9,381	2,520	3,266
	FARMS OPERATED BY CASH TENANTS, INCLUDING TENURE NOT SPECIFIED.										
59	Total acreage	10,710	31,051	167	84,107	79,604	15,461	1,117	20,986	25,257	4,355
60	Improved acreage	7,230	18,100	45	73,964	61,160	13,783	292	10,417	18,107	3,016
61	Value of land	$74,571	$334,823	$4,200	$1,309,864	$1,546,422	$544,055	$7,350	$146,910	$253,555	$47,905
62	Value of buildings	$25,710	$95,264	$1,425	$387,411	$373,061	$107,870	$1,300	$50,216	$87,012	$15,730
63	Value of implements and machinery	$6,503	$20,341	$95	$87,363	$88,427	$24,162	$522	$8,151	$22,960	$2,917
64	Number of dairy cows	363	940	5	3,762	3,206	441	15	460	914	155
65	Number of work horses	178	293	2	2,050	825	404	4	248	525	96
66	Number of work mules	195	541		1,935	2,144	514	12	239	530	60
67	Acreage in cotton	3,258	8,740		37,175	31,302	9,381	132	5,168	7,583	1,621
68	Bales of cotton grown in 1909	693	2,461		10,830	9,375	5,169	34	1,454	1,531	634
69	Acreage in corn	2,278	5,031	12	19,879	15,112	2,413	106	2,364	4,530	1,008
70	Bushels of corn grown in 1909	25,353	58,281	175	220,524	172,030	53,097	765	18,284	54,579	11,938
	FARMS OPERATED BY SHARE AND SHARE-CASH TENANTS.										
71	Total acreage	13,913	38,996	499	82,320	66,884	22,800	4,772	15,513	34,161	16,850
72	Improved acreage	9,182	27,529	87	74,316	64,115	22,544	3,087	12,352	29,852	11,705
73	Value of land	$117,001	$501,894	$3,975	$1,259,118	$1,634,412	$855,771	$53,108	$157,216	$384,366	$214,615
74	Value of buildings	$35,705	$139,064	$2,800	$299,094	$403,331	$231,303	$10,190	$46,180	$128,770	$57,575
75	Value of implements and machinery	$8,368	$21,471	$200	$50,698	$60,573	$21,424	$1,882	$5,761	$23,537	$9,105
76	Number of dairy cows	509	1,107	12	2,707	2,380	753	143	519	1,296	391
77	Number of work horses	153	534	5	912	414	539	55	119	735	298
78	Number of work mules	213	473	1	1,059	2,191	344	49	139	1,028	272
79	Acreage in cotton	4,484	15,143	27	39,423	34,213	16,378	1,283	5,048	13,825	6,150
80	Bales of cotton grown in 1909	931	3,997	8	11,187	11,426	7,589	403	1,515	2,957	2,414
81	Acreage in corn	3,124	8,206	49	19,803	14,484	3,279	916	2,546	9,330	3,536
82	Bushels of corn grown in 1909	40,622	98,292	605	186,902	185,591	59,668	9,497	24,043	125,359	41,195

OPERATED BY COLORED FARMERS, BY COUNTIES, FOR SOUTHERN STATES: 1910—Continued.

MISSISSIPPI—continued.

Jones.	Kemper.	Lafayette.	Lamar.	Lauderdale.	Lawrence.	Leake.	Lee.	Leflore.	Lincoln.	Lowndes.	Madison.	Marion.	Marshall.	Monroe.	
456	1,956	1,796	101	1,781	783	1,215	1,840	5,824	1,216	3,297	4,996	693	3,480	3,309	1
							4					1		1	2
29	43	23	13	46	18	37	64	104	63	131	233	40	41	80	3
93	220	279	14	197	116	234	487	1,325	263	484	680	118	305	401	4
185	925	806	46	901	339	491	1,027	3,936	613	2,073	2,908	342	1,704	2,030	5
82	430	366	10	358	165	236	193	386	174	463	827	105	860	605	6
41	238	223	16	196	110	156	53	55	77	105	248	65	430	137	7
15	76	60	2	54	23	38	10	7	17	29	55	11	100	35	8
10	23	37		29	9	21	2	8	8	10	36	6	37	15	9
1	1	2				3	2			2	8	5	2	5	10
								3			1				11
85	265	225	29	294	131	174	99	55	161	148	219	219	292	190	12
85	219	126	8	221	170	215	76	67	183	133	246	152	137	194	13
41	49	26	15	94	37	82	70	26	31	78	137	41	81	115	14
98	629	424	21	553	121	97	90	2,901	232	2,052	2,687	74	1,639	1,764	15
125	747	975	23	604	309	628	1,480	2,696	588	860	1,597	193	1,300	948	16
3	33	5		9		9	6	16	5	5	26	7	7	61	17
18	14	15	5	6	15	10	19	60	16	21	81	7	22	36	18
1								3			3		2		19
8,469	28,235	28,324	1,927	25,238	11,548	15,970	6,327	3,531	10,869	9,863	20,961	13,737	33,562	15,420	20
2,311	13,028	9,472	503	11,205	4,348	6,120	3,194	2,085	4,311	5,218	10,685	5,198	13,054	7,550	21
$75,590	$226,001	$166,661	$13,920	$202,829	$88,246	$111,780	$130,090	$160,360	$89,035	$139,972	$233,570	$124,995	$280,600	$214,410	22
$27,970	$65,209	$43,345	$6,291	$72,153	$37,719	$39,200	$32,800	$33,050	$40,675	$52,463	$87,523	$45,075	$100,900	$56,400	23
$5,659	$14,773	$15,495	$950	$15,826	$8,842	$7,727	$7,212	$5,517	$7,374	$11,888	$22,018	$8,273	$21,240	$21,217	24
184	501	376	59	473	293	331	156	162	335	230	589	505	631	323	25
64	182	195	28	177	138	157	77	85	171	150	240	232	387	179	26
61	300	316	4	278	98	137	144	55	96	143	261	68	382	228	27
744	4,565	2,646	164	4,088	1,630	1,976	1,268	1,109	1,849	2,300	3,410	1,919	4,470	3,111	28
322	1,133	845	72	1,034	656	575	376	414	668	500	970	798	1,159	729	29
812	3,019	2,721	179	2,222	1,389	1,771	739	432	1,308	1,222	2,385	1,802	3,546	1,614	30
8,423	24,612	31,980	2,159	18,792	16,231	16,069	10,891	8,020	16,058	12,431	26,165	20,732	38,359	19,111	31
7,269	23,916	15,935	728	21,403	15,423	22,716	5,952	4,673	12,328	9,444	26,528	12,267	15,764	14,488	32
2,232	11,474	5,307	197	9,563	6,062	8,849	3,501	2,846	5,476	4,822	13,916	4,382	6,261	7,920	33
$59,121	$192,610	$90,242	$4,662	$168,365	$130,705	$174,089	$125,590	$220,885	$106,432	$119,856	$260,550	$116,000	$121,445	$216,374	34
$18,812	$51,675	$20,810	$1,183	$54,455	$48,815	$47,200	$27,705	$38,025	$40,917	$39,615	$81,643	$35,945	$36,670	$51,705	35
$3,997	$11,036	$7,894	$120	$11,484	$9,265	$10,979	$6,508	$12,382	$7,995	$13,235	$20,558	$6,248	$7,616	$15,101	36
162	426	193	17	400	349	415	144	128	316	214	658	415	278	347	37
59	159	84	7	134	147	184	84	132	192	131	252	162	147	186	38
69	279	191		238	126	203	125	41	113	137	314	62	161	266	39
1,016	4,204	1,667	35	3,891	2,303	3,274	1,222	1,425	2,582	2,100	4,713	2,122	2,425	4,017	40
340	993	503	16	931	821	812	372	337	732	437	1,165	819	586	876	41
636	2,762	1,392	43	1,780	1,751	2,247	702	475	1,692	1,003	2,984	1,302	1,620	1,603	42
5,516	21,496	15,456	470	15,128	16,506	17,999	10,060	5,423	17,539	7,337	27,888	13,756	17,057	17,926	43
2,877	4,485	4,579	535	8,585	2,936	7,802	2,542	4,268	1,626	5,713	10,010	1,773	9,634	7,292	44
1,946	2,822	3,092	331	4,918	2,155	6,131	1,190	1,512	989	3,191	4,698	1,074	5,726	4,716	45
1,172	2,375	1,295	263	4,123	1,334	3,236	1,936	2,894	886	3,351	6,358	992	4,168	4,837	46
592	1,247	658	113	2,025	713	2,102	760	833	383	1,438	2,745	433	2,317	2,648	47
$29,835	$35,807	$23,087	$6,420	$75,649	$26,925	$51,075	$66,625	$190,995	$14,978	$94,346	$136,151	$21,980	$77,408	$135,555	48
$7,570	$11,883	$5,235	$2,590	$23,845	$8,355	$13,535	$15,705	$30,600	$6,345	$25,639	$41,673	$7,730	$24,400	$31,459	49
$24,390	$34,282	$18,709	$6,055	$58,605	$25,430	$51,300	$37,095	$93,280	$14,308	$65,387	$97,762	$18,275	$65,286	$108,350	50
$1,544	$3,087	$2,217	$365	$4,615	$1,352	$2,956	$3,508	$5,670	$1,156	$5,063	$8,089	$1,288	$7,486	$10,208	51
82	94	54	26	166	61	139	45	75	49	145	307	61	174	202	52
22	42	38	17	60	38	54	45	56	42	69	147	48	88	128	53
38	71	52	2	88	27	97	82	29	15	88	141	12	110	157	54
531	900	410	91	1,757	511	1,353	878	1,322	432	1,177	2,398	445	1,471	2,411	55
183	205	134	34	414	162	289	281	503	164	252	667	175	340	581	56
274	582	444	114	758	371	891	472	378	252	510	1,279	332	1,008	1,010	57
2,610	5,060	5,110	1,235	6,012	3,535	7,122	7,197	4,290	3,035	4,399	14,002	3,380	9,768	12,017	58
4,246	30,808	23,428	1,104	28,868	7,798	5,753	4,183	92,849	9,877	74,769	114,543	2,579	102,567	74,763	59
2,149	21,777	13,730	480	17,742	3,659	3,030	2,982	87,852	5,665	64,939	97,995	1,533	59,321	63,148	60
$54,591	$268,581	$203,394	$9,080	$262,233	$71,105	$43,014	$111,680	$4,667,560	$90,810	$1,543,186	$1,485,779	$27,350	$961,323	$1,752,869	61
$16,354	$96,508	$45,814	$7,515	$80,749	$23,355	$8,625	$16,025	$661,525	$35,995	$293,403	$446,042	$7,515	$249,926	$270,768	62
$2,402	$37,757	$16,347	$260	$15,094	$2,564	$2,316	$3,620	$163,370	$6,000	$74,302	$142,200	$1,194	$63,316	$97,543	63
139	735	616	31	625	143	140	129	3,332	329	2,489	4,572	103	2,610	2,275	64
65	396	251	20	288	92	75	76	1,735	179	1,143	1,851	71	1,298	906	65
39	636	515	4	425	80	62	99	2,769	127	2,218	2,715	14	1,798	2,075	66
1,176	8,531	5,748	142	8,449	1,397	1,366	1,481	55,471	2,639	37,662	45,046	588	29,304	41,469	67
395	1,962	2,006	55	2,033	530	320	446	21,644	847	7,943	11,874	198	7,218	8,928	68
542	6,139	4,356	118	2,925	1,033	884	701	17,477	1,489	14,644	23,924	442	16,218	15,165	69
4,626	53,180	53,923	1,587	25,242	10,481	7,093	9,466	337,663	16,864	135,465	234,266	4,797	166,068	154,628	70
2,994	30,595	38,374	773	19,585	9,829	20,304	38,777	59,433	16,283	20,873	40,698	5,292	44,407	26,864	71
2,477	22,122	23,831	528	15,517	7,361	14,398	34,970	59,024	13,433	20,043	39,035	4,328	32,716	24,358	72
$43,476	$276,144	$381,616	$9,050	$243,705	$98,745	$176,042	$1,122,491	$3,095,924	$160,438	$495,184	$584,037	$71,690	$460,840	$634,052	73
$13,749	$61,277	$83,121	$4,900	$72,115	$34,085	$49,563	$188,310	$510,357	$62,870	$97,308	$177,118	$24,125	$115,190	$108,480	74
$1,884	$10,633	$20,780	$235	$8,321	$4,664	$8,580	$48,962	$54,696	$9,430	$6,520	$18,953	$2,886	$15,465	$14,202	75
98	719	934	24	389	269	588	1,339	1,148	568	439	859	122	954	685	76
45	198	343	6	136	114	267	440	820	271	100	212	107	377	214	77
46	371	833	5	371	226	226	1,212	1,398	222	236	591	46	1,065	339	78
1,135	9,925	10,271	257	9,104	3,323	6,478	19,241	33,270	6,842	11,019	16,784	1,683	18,229	14,577	79
402	2,302	3,394	83	2,423	1,168	1,635	6,578	12,341	2,314	2,464	4,671	693	4,654	3,372	80
588	5,228	7,807	174	2,441	2,191	4,388	9,423	9,411	3,223	4,193	8,530	1,344	9,630	5,328	81
6,498	40,160	94,510	2,350	23,438	22,819	39,331	142,461	168,674	38,963	40,489	83,275	16,819	100,392	62,337	82

Table **73.**—STATISTICS OF SIZE OF FARMS AND TENURE CLASSES OF FARMS

MISSISSIPPI—continued.

		Mont-gomery.	Neshoba.	Newton.	Noxubee.	Oktib-beha.	Panola.	Perry.	Pike.	Pontotoc.	Prentiss.
1	Number of farms	1,433	559	1,370	4,422	2,218	4,217	170	1,811	846	473
	FARMS CLASSIFIED BY SIZE.										
2	Under 3 acres							1			
3	3 to 9 acres	36	8	57	140	82	35	5	43	29	20
4	10 to 19 acres	231	101	303	747	487	660	12	229	187	112
5	20 to 49 acres	751	266	599	2,483	1,078	2,443	49	945	350	238
6	50 to 99 acres	247	97	240	817	363	756	39	375	175	69
7	100 to 174 acres	126	61	124	175	167	264	50	166	88	26
8	175 to 259 acres	30	18	30	44	28	44	10	42	12	6
9	260 to 499 acres	10	8	17	13	11	14	4	11	5	2
10	500 to 999 acres	2			3	2	1				
11	1,000 acres and over										
	FARMERS CLASSIFIED BY TENURE.										
12	Owners, free	99	91	163	201	199	228	125	446	93	22
13	Owners, mortgaged	105	76	184	111	183	194	18	267	65	19
14	Part owners	67	21	124	87	124	38	6	47	55	21
15	Cash tenants	158	26	209	1,989	774	1,631	7	391	110	6
16	Share tenants	970	341	679	1,856	722	2,083	7	599	506	400
17	Share-cash tenants	15	4	2	131	177	7		27	9	5
18	Tenure not specified	18		8	46	39	35	7	34	8	
19	Managers	1		1	1		1				
	FARMS OPERATED BY OWNERS, FREE.										
20	Total acreage	10,932	10,383	11,555	15,415	16,537	22,560	12,408	33,426	7,911	2,124
21	Improved acreage	4,602	3,655	4,980	6,875	8,046	9,097	2,083	14,702	3,332	854
22	Value of land	$76,920	$96,005	$109,337	$184,231	$148,237	$232,934	$127,785	$293,990	$80,482	$21,335
23	Value of buildings	$34,490	$25,775	$37,785	$49,127	$57,070	$74,705	$57,040	$152,035	$18,275	$4,275
24	Value of implements and machinery	$6,567	$6,637	$7,956	$12,393	$13,438	$19,884	$10,479	$25,782	$3,729	$2,032
25	Number of dairy cows	175	151	231	433	464	482	361	1,080	151	36
26	Number of work horses	85	70	92	239	198	338	128	579	129	21
27	Number of work mules	131	108	176	204	227	262	34	251	99	37
28	Acreage in cotton	1,266	1,419	1,959	3,003	2,217	4,037	321	5,848	1,103	254
29	Bales of cotton grown in 1909	387	404	582	589	523	1,211	123	2,331	340	58
30	Acreage in corn	1,168	1,066	1,349	1,471	1,515	2,469	783	4,666	881	197
31	Bushels of corn grown in 1909	11,796	9,659	12,153	11,199	15,832	30,025	10,260	58,354	11,469	1,712
	FARMS OPERATED BY OWNERS, MORTGAGED.										
32	Total acreage	11,357	6,179	16,456	10,543	13,863	17,428	1,893	20,179	6,244	1,496
33	Improved acreage	5,376	2,769	6,310	5,749	7,023	8,318	420	9,152	2,411	762
34	Value of land	$84,432	$58,965	$134,106	$125,876	$129,915	$196,607	$16,290	$175,840	$65,486	$19,770
35	Value of buildings	$28,300	$13,785	$46,605	$26,365	$35,905	$53,505	$7,360	$79,800	$13,784	$3,190
36	Value of implements and machinery	$5,490	$3,280	$8,985	$8,680	$9,539	$15,975	$950	$14,438	$2,872	$1,015
37	Number of dairy cows	176	111	281	236	347	373	53	577	101	36
38	Number of work horses	51	61	128	143	151	217	22	342	75	18
39	Number of work mules	160	71	183	137	205	230	3	159	76	30
40	Acreage in cotton	1,756	1,192	2,679	2,221	2,335	3,829	91	3,697	923	276
41	Bales of cotton grown in 1909	462	316	662	410	507	1,117	33	1,361	248	68
42	Acreage in corn	1,228	1,014	1,621	1,054	1,243	1,979	130	2,838	654	206
43	Bushels of corn grown in 1909	10,765	5,898	11,658	6,744	11,923	23,247	1,540	33,486	8,326	2,475
	FARMS OPERATED BY PART OWNERS.										
44	Total acreage	5,246	1,375	8,294	5,154	9,172	3,685	306	3,522	4,843	1,762
45	Owned acreage	3,575	913	5,869	2,601	5,400	2,647	182	1,245	2,855	1,185
46	Improved acreage	2,564	700	4,204	3,269	5,660	1,720	143	1,696	2,036	893
47	Owned improved acreage	1,282	413	2,510	1,293	2,878	1,007	91	575	1,103	551
48	Value of land	$50,937	$13,747	$82,734	$86,791	$99,666	$45,135	$3,450	$32,900	$44,539	$22,180
49	Value of buildings	$15,925	$3,155	$27,395	$19,895	$27,555	$8,355	$1,500	$14,600	$13,635	$4,055
50	Value of land and buildings owned	$42,792	$11,760	$76,668	$56,582	$72,662	$36,940	$2,990	$19,110	$36,907	$16,370
51	Value of implements and machinery	$2,650	$637	$4,709	$5,060	$8,799	$3,102	$230	$2,706	$3,057	$1,140
52	Number of dairy cows	102	32	162	134	249	68	12	94	90	35
53	Number of work horses	44	14	68	76	113	34	3	63	62	18
54	Number of work mules	75	20	153	84	171	60	1	24	55	31
55	Acreage in cotton	1,039	312	1,896	1,743	2,051	825	9	782	826	323
56	Bales of cotton grown in 1909	260	82	482	376	475	256	3	285	210	83
57	Acreage in corn	667	231	1,016	616	1,095	443	26	461	572	277
58	Bushels of corn grown in 1909	5,480	2,062	8,727	4,301	11,174	4,592	307	5,105	7,503	3,040
	FARMS OPERATED BY CASH TENANTS, INCLUDING TENURE NOT SPECIFIED.										
59	Total acreage	8,364	2,533	10,382	91,635	35,271	73,475	580	16,079	6,688	485
60	Improved acreage	5,918	817	5,833	76,504	25,729	51,823	280	10,117	3,929	312
61	Value of land	$93,920	$25,025	$115,622	$1,665,800	$331,149	$1,150,444	$17,850	$172,175	$100,645	$5,900
62	Value of buildings	$27,960	$5,225	$30,780	$266,535	$93,795	$286,765	$1,850	$77,655	$17,885	$950
63	Value of implements and machinery	$6,362	$684	$5,419	$85,694	$28,331	$76,968	$310	$10,116	$4,093	$265
64	Number of dairy cows	235	46	242	3,148	1,208	2,463	24	565	146	10
65	Number of work horses	78	17	111	1,569	485	1,589	12	394	111	6
66	Number of work mules	163	23	167	2,114	882	1,584	4	138	96	12
67	Acreage in cotton	2,390	413	2,757	48,865	11,114	30,363	88	4,858	1,527	189
68	Bales of cotton grown in 1909	636	98	732	9,568	2,521	9,135	23	1,682	404	48
69	Acreage in corn	1,477	205	1,473	16,993	5,843	13,908	82	3,081	935	83
70	Bushels of corn grown in 1909	14,039	1,519	12,172	136,255	55,573	161,153	820	35,695	10,590	545
	FARMS OPERATED BY SHARE AND SHARE-CASH TENANTS.										
71	Total acreage	33,030	10,931	19,272	49,519	21,108	57,511	597	20,993	15,618	13,005
72	Improved acreage	27,181	8,984	15,002	48,237	18,659	49,991	195	14,749	12,109	10,722
73	Value of land	$447,517	$123,405	$229,254	$1,106,144	$275,504	$1,009,231	$5,210	$216,043	$264,666	$288,179
74	Value of buildings	$131,710	$26,990	$71,186	$170,346	$72,000	$243,645	$1,265	$89,915	$54,047	$41,140
75	Value of implements and machinery	$20,475	$4,419	$5,298	$25,621	$10,141	$38,384	$300	$8,905	$7,018	$9,181
76	Number of dairy cows	971	299	438	1,521	676	1,513	13	589	458	391
77	Number of work horses	287	112	158	474	129	826	2	456	253	173
78	Number of work mules	712	149	175	776	381	1,379	2	153	284	350
79	Acreage in cotton	12,838	4,416	7,708	27,510	8,328	30,900	33	6,930	1,947	5,216
80	Bales of cotton grown in 1909	3,861	1,194	2,100	5,938	2,107	9,148	13	2,834	1,711	1,284
81	Acreage in corn	7,617	2,086	3,914	9,972	4,468	12,853	39	4,003	3,512	3,105
82	Bushels of corn grown in 1909	77,803	20,174	39,317	89,265	43,820	139,163	640	54,785	46,679	40,841

OPERATED BY COLORED FARMERS, BY COUNTIES, FOR SOUTHERN STATES: 1910—Continued.

MISSISSIPPI—continued.

Quitman.	Rankin.	Scott.	Sharkey.	Simpson.	Smith.	Sunflower.	Talla-hatchie.	Tate.	Tippah.	Tisho-mingo.	Tunica.	Union.	Warren.	Wash-ington.	
1,966	2,457	1,080	3,206	1,004	433	4,662	3,872	2,541	439	131	4,153	659	2,669	7,969	1
			9				2				2		5		2
89	92	76	314	23	24	275	71	61	12	4	152	15	486	853	3
822	504	296	1,340	221	97	1,740	1,291	527	105	27	1,512	148	1,076	3,907	4
949	1,168	397	1,423	468	154	2,407	2,187	1,307	179	45	2,234	328	935	2,976	5
87	400	168	98	164	77	204	235	436	72	31	209	112	96	177	6
13	199	107	18	94	52	30	66	179	49	16	35	49	50	37	7
2	54	27	3	27	19	5	14	22	9	6	5	5	9	3	8
4	24	8		5	9	1	6	9	13	2	4	2	8	7	9
	14	1	1	2	1								2	6	10
	2												2	3	11
60	287	164	37	153	43	73	98	90	49	33	109	34	188	156	12
87	344	143	37	187	70	91	101	48	33	12	71	31	48	85	13
30	100	56	36	28	37	27	31	35	9	18	66	26	28	50	14
562	736	90	932	156	46	1,268	883	993	45	3	1,800	131	1,527	2,813	15
1,191	954	606	2,055	452	215	2,346	2,654	1,362	292	63	1,882	420	685	4,709	16
10	8	12	11	7	6	578	14	6	10	1	30	6	156	69	17
26	22	9	95	20	16	279	91	7		1	195	11	37	77	18
	6		3	1					1					10	19
3,183	25,943	13,050	1,689	14,188	4,545	4,199	7,065	8,952	7,283	3,554	6,293	2,703	12,071	12,378	20
1,730	11,664	4,936	813	4,994	1,475	2,391	2,831	4,856	1,995	933	3,534	1,374	4,037	5,972	21
126,160	208,904	92,985	71,759	107,848	30,867	164,915	108,562	104,935	37,430	17,929	231,292	28,539	156,854	357,547	22
$27,350	$63,840	$33,350	$22,915	$47,170	$13,730	$30,915	$26,385	$40,090	$12,590	$5,205	$58,462	$8,621	$56,778	$64,790	23
$6,667	$14,364	$7,670	$4,710	$9,002	$2,801	$9,551	$7,667	$11,485	$3,227	$949	$13,919	$2,291	$12,604	$15,203	24
176	650	281	96	317	112	174	202	196	94	52	174	58	427	182	25
57	281	116	56	108	35	70	109	159	54	24	105	29	212	79	26
108	258	166	40	150	45	122	113	147	69	25	167	34	191	309	27
1,105	3,084	1,500	490	1,883	364	1,105	1,302	1,566	548	254	1,921	312	1,368	2,592	28
504	1,004	417	220	694	133	423	442	517	136	61	852	88	375	1,144	29
430	2,186	1,275	199	1,511	387	523	953	1,131	653	390	684	302	950	1,132	30
8,377	22,444	10,096	4,760	17,143	3,625	12,501	12,647	14,049	6,599	3,371	13,585	3,267	12,356	22,050	31
5,129	27,753	11,345	2,123	14,831	6,976	5,570	7,741	4,486	4,104	1,217	3,839	2,506	3,819	5,479	32
2,675	13,860	4,595	944	6,106	2,613	2,962	3,549	2,349	1,463	339	2,241	1,136	1,618	2,915	33
201,425	217,035	84,622	77,743	117,395	47,945	195,198	130,782	46,688	22,736	7,695	172,331	19,240	52,040	227,490	34
$43,032	$53,845	$24,035	$21,630	$43,555	$14,395	$37,919	$30,300	$15,355	$6,260	$3,355	$32,585	$6,100	$13,726	$35,415	35
$15,765	$13,578	$5,789	$4,784	$8,652	$4,206	$13,704	$7,120	$3,270	$2,225	$336	$8,379	$1,132	$4,431	$9,582	36
236	656	240	98	388	174	195	232	91	55	15	114	53	92	114	37
86	292	99	36	130	50	65	108	67	45	11	79	39	43	57	38
156	309	138	39	182	71	164	161	55	38	5	94	26	56	188	39
1,661	4,451	1,706	658	2,631	896	1,568	1,556	807	407	109	1,418	325	455	1,732	40
729	1,281	445	251	819	277	481	529	271	82	27	596	71	127	707	41
615	2,704	1,164	209	1,858	713	524	996	518	350	90	444	280	268	659	42
13,057	23,410	8,074	4,251	16,867	5,791	9,060	12,565	7,320	3,070	1,394	9,082	2,640	3,836	12,192	43
1,428	10,967	5,352	1,735	1,905	2,773	1,533	2,468	2,464	1,048	1,337	4,130	1,799	1,408	2,725	44
648	4,926	3,203	811	1,208	2,019	739	1,550	1,163	661	1,171	2,438	1,223	858	1,584	45
925	5,009	1,920	1,135	1,004	1,130	1,122	1,182	1,408	336	463	2,745	1,117	664	1,669	46
281	2,043	917	319	531	690	442	591	542	196	302	1,268	638	273	686	47
$55,090	$99,559	$42,740	$77,280	$15,600	$19,561	$61,785	$46,569	$37,813	$5,571	$8,075	$179,492	$26,885	$27,505	$103,350	48
$9,385	$19,194	$9,475	$16,200	$7,550	$7,095	$10,500	$7,025	$10,624	$890	$2,165	$44,945	$7,555	$9,635	$18,100	49
$27,435	$56,321	$32,815	$41,295	$16,485	$18,326	$32,500	$29,829	$27,777	$3,615	$8,500	$132,055	$22,240	$27,375	$70,615	50
$3,101	$4,308	$2,375	$5,598	$1,308	$1,305	$3,684	$1,710	$1,403	$305	$511	$12,376	$1,883	$1,413	$4,209	51
65	255	101	59	49	79	69	70	46	16	28	138	44	42	88	52
17	80	35	30	22	26	26	31	47	5	12	138	29	24	22	53
69	124	64	53	15	34	71	43	33	18	20	150	39	26	84	54
508	1,396	693	731	368	480	571	571	572	129	183	1,283	396	236	1,105	55
233	434	201	367	111	171	200	202	171	27	51	501	98	75	536	56
166	822	502	263	245	293	178	321	341	134	152	567	242	129	364	57
3,382	7,742	3,669	4,597	2,543	2,931	3,208	4,958	4,364	950	2,320	12,191	3,250	1,810	6,855	58
15,634	33,671	5,653	26,225	6,099	3,324	41,910	28,980	51,365	2,229	184	54,650	7,150	32,760	68,618	59
14,385	21,442	2,554	25,699	4,189	1,584	40,788	25,980	35,818	1,365	99	53,266	4,903	27,727	67,286	60
$677,038	$319,190	$44,894	$1,286,111	$59,227	$27,302	$1,891,926	$936,721	$713,002	$20,876	$1,360	$2,475,091	$111,080	$541,955	$2,789,759	61
$100,900	$86,202	$11,886	$286,499	$21,860	$7,948	$275,221	$177,735	$190,510	$5,940	$600	$388,213	$25,510	$196,367	$541,744	62
$29,844	$14,589	$2,030	$60,471	$2,413	$1,348	$72,704	$38,740	$39,294	$1,368	$110	$118,622	$4,497	$27,279	$116,362	63
805	1,059	126	1,125	207	83	1,496	1,177	1,462	65	5	1,677	224	1,689	2,031	64
299	427	52	658	83	18	302	655	942	32	2	1,122	123	985	1,259	65
658	521	54	1,114	52	52	1,661	1,040	1,092	43	4	2,245	160	1,188	3,482	66
9,116	8,887	799	16,413	1,729	610	25,699	17,587	17,261	474	16	37,956	1,954	15,206	39,423	67
4,630	2,505	209	7,806	551	208	10,303	8,919	5,316	119	4	18,107	462	4,814	19,186	68
2,820	4,930	570	4,739	1,110	415	6,340	6,460	9,009	436	18	8,591	1,106	6,879	10,071	69
62,848	42,975	4,494	97,410	11,764	4,730	146,494	124,519	109,853	4,042	230	187,602	11,795	95,590	192,647	70
22,328	25,462	17,602	35,598	12,401	8,538	58,462	60,549	38,124	9,876	2,359	34,043	13,330	14,480	73,808	71
22,119	22,235	12,976	35,493	10,623	4,930	57,866	57,470	31,975	7,807	1,466	33,919	10,581	13,063	73,476	72
$1,012,618	$241,692	$156,457	$1,701,799	$124,237	$83,064	$2,535,958	$1,855,561	$565,954	$126,796	$21,267	$1,636,103	$234,005	$263,285	$3,141,984	73
$141,995	$86,789	$55,148	$493,636	$47,577	$21,777	$420,553	$409,505	$131,949	$31,780	$7,565	$251,546	$56,430	$106,360	$649,581	74
$19,797	$8,879	$6,496	$20,685	$5,259	$2,593	$52,080	$45,810	$15,118	$5,623	$1,029	$20,190	$8,026	$9,444	$24,996	75
575	716	499	781	365	243	1,450	1,650	946	292	44	432	432	496	946	76
179	232	203	370	109	52	419	647	473	99	30	125	153	234	472	77
788	358	215	639	207	116	1,541	2,655	786	162	49	459	298	369	736	78
14,437	10,127	5,380	21,471	4,676	2,079	35,632	37,701	17,068	2,953	499	21,079	4,417	6,866	33,551	79
6,911	3,223	1,406	9,210	1,588	695	13,384	17,735	5,315	753	135	9,545	1,197	2,935	16,117	80
3,969	5,130	3,088	4,261	3,036	1,386	7,929	15,218	8,100	2,156	497	2,946	3,099	2,448	5,385	81
82,514	50,307	25,948	79,558	31,463	14,269	155,250	264,358	99,423	25,590	8,381	58,332	36,490	37,461	103,309	82

TABLE 73.—STATISTICS OF SIZE OF FARMS AND FOR TENURE CLASSES OF FARMS

		MISSISSIPPI—continued.						NORTH CAROLINA.		
		Wayne.	Webster.	Wilkinson.	Winston.	Yalo-busha.	Yazoo.	All other counties.	The state.	Alamance.	Alex-ander.
1	Number of farms	662	583	1,979	1,142	1,704	6,714	380	65,656	593	125
	FARMS CLASSIFIED BY SIZE.										
2	Under 3 acres	1	.....	1	.....	.....	2	13	32	1	.....
3	3 to 9 acres	64	11	158	32	18	298	60	5,296	52	13
4	10 to 19 acres	95	117	499	182	273	1,775	40	10,920	75	37
5	20 to 49 acres	275	252	1,024	479	849	3,790	115	29,250	157	42
6	50 to 99 acres	119	98	173	243	325	582	62	12,197	152	23
7	100 to 174 acres	75	79	83	147	175	178	68	5,668	114	9
8	175 to 259 acres	20	21	22	36	34	45	10	1,447	37	1
9	260 to 499 acres	10	5	10	22	25	32	7	677	5	.....
10	500 to 999 acres	2	.....	4	1	4	10	4	139	.....	.....
11	1,000 acres and over	1	.....	5	.....	1	2	1	30	.....	.....
	FARMERS CLASSIFIED BY TENURE.										
12	Owners, free	192	79	125	133	154	220	308	11,088	141	26
13	Owners, mortgaged	105	57	65	235	103	199	14	3,734	57	15
14	Part owners	68	36	13	91	28	47	9	6,621	81	34
15	Cash tenants	179	58	105	90	410	3,278	8	10,110	7	1
16	Share tenants	98	339	1,641	589	890	2,875	23	31,609	304	49
17	Share-cash tenants	2	8	3	2	26	18	15	921	1	.....
18	Tenure not specified	18	6	26	2	93	68	1	1,499	2	.....
19	Managers	.....	.....	1	.....	.....	9	2	74	.....	.....
	FARMS OPERATED BY OWNERS, FREE.										
20	Total acreage	14,686	8,459	14,156	14,969	17,960	21,730	23,366	604,292	5,486	1,007
21	Improved acreage	4,130	3,060	4,004	6,568	8,123	8,007	3,089	236,163	2,719	435
22	Value of land	$89,463	$52,700	$88,474	$111,427	$154,160	$387,455	$166,050	$7,944,466	$69,240	$11,234
23	Value of buildings	$43,109	$13,860	$23,083	$42,355	$60,520	$124,035	$95,440	$3,007,544	$42,560	$2,316
24	Value of implements and machinery	$5,767	$3,278	$4,827	$11,205	$15,628	$27,092	$14,296	$511,087	$5,354	$468
25	Number of dairy cows	334	123	325	214	366	611	813	9,448	151	26
26	Number of work horses	156	76	164	127	188	167	281	5,073	91	5
27	Number of work mules	72	67	126	140	245	389	38	5,058	53	7
28	Acreage in cotton	1,388	841	1,046	1,653	2,185	3,100	421	43,194	44	21
29	Bales of cotton grown in 1909	393	241	118	437	664	1,054	126	20,770	19	4
30	Acreage in corn	1,338	817	1,176	1,419	2,009	2,254	1,313	82,350	898	146
31	Bushels of corn grown in 1909	11,757	9,056	16,636	12,270	21,465	31,660	16,283	881,768	11,401	1,685
	FARMS OPERATED BY OWNERS, MORTGAGED.										
32	Total acreage	10,334	6,506	9,273	23,161	14,511	19,490	817	257,037	3,223	434
33	Improved acreage	3,190	2,226	3,494	10,498	5,835	7,496	210	105,115	1,363	240
34	Value of land	$54,939	$38,350	$55,879	$181,519	$114,710	$456,212	$9,260	$3,586,871	$37,030	$7,235
35	Value of buildings	$19,934	$11,500	$20,130	$51,365	$33,905	$98,735	$4,890	$1,122,318	$19,045	$2,005
36	Value of implements and machinery	$3,181	$2,300	$4,512	$13,262	$12,022	$21,334	$445	$210,657	$2,472	$149
37	Number of dairy cows	181	96	225	365	213	500	26	3,289	67	9
38	Number of work horses	104	54	98	151	111	169	12	2,315	46	6
39	Number of work mules	45	55	97	251	136	316	1	2,223	29	3
40	Acreage in cotton	1,336	755	1,199	2,936	1,728	3,217	73	21,884	25	15
41	Bales of cotton grown in 1909	316	209	147	718	469	989	15	9,205	8	2
42	Acreage in corn	885	626	973	2,391	1,384	1,926	70	32,021	420	89
43	Bushels of corn grown in 1909	7,199	6,100	12,207	18,509	14,688	25,170	945	322,079	5,620	985
	FARMS OPERATED BY PART OWNERS.										
44	Total acreage	6,015	3,311	1,245	8,620	3,009	3,771	335	336,167	3,993	1,654
45	Owned acreage	3,693	2,376	829	5,186	1,995	1,836	263	[1]179,677	1,628	767
46	Improved acreage	2,514	1,608	287	3,668	1,721	1,964	133	171,289	1,940	996
47	Owned improved acreage	1,396	940	169	2,113	1,143	865	61	[1]69,977	808	407
48	Value of land	$41,353	$25,225	$7,382	$61,188	$32,717	$73,390	$4,686	$5,532,251	$46,543	$24,425
49	Value of buildings	$15,451	$6,070	$2,960	$16,395	$9,280	$19,200	$1,870	$1,616,639	$21,570	$6,965
50	Value of land and buildings owned	$36,840	$20,780	$7,345	$49,390	$27,862	$47,320	$4,400	[1]$4,012,066	$39,140	$15,425
51	Value of implements and machinery	$3,211	$1,573	$520	$5,309	$2,484	$4,123	$300	$267,498	$4,338	$1,445
52	Number of dairy cows	149	64	48	136	66	122	25	5,022	90	34
53	Number of work horses	67	37	19	64	31	34	5	3,241	64	14
54	Number of work mules	23	30	11	103	38	90	2	3,795	32	26
55	Acreage in cotton	782	442	123	1,486	637	689	16	36,905	82	123
56	Bales of cotton grown in 1909	187	126	17	307	150	199	5	16,573	36	37
57	Acreage in corn	614	322	138	840	435	390	39	60,963	653	380
58	Bushels of corn grown in 1909	4,683	3,850	2,145	6,610	3,416	5,182	475	655,927	8,500	4,476
	FARMS OPERATED BY CASH TENANTS, INCLUDING TENURE NOT SPECIFIED.										
59	Total acreage	5,616	3,727	4,400	5,241	27,514	114,749	3,290	601,283	775	140
60	Improved acreage	3,531	2,011	3,075	2,641	16,780	101,202	860	326,085	249	15
61	Value of land	$43,341	$36,459	$39,647	$53,549	$310,311	$2,578,205	$26,800	$9,892,373	$7,430	$2,100
62	Value of buildings	$16,107	$9,490	$14,040	$11,880	$83,024	$525,575	$7,285	$2,140,264	$2,370	$400
63	Value of implements and machinery	$2,050	$1,838	$1,956	$2,255	$16,822	$151,291	$1,207	$425,032	$265	$10
64	Number of dairy cows	206	82	148	107	903	4,801	25	7,972	10	1
65	Number of work horses	90	41	100	48	400	1,694	17	5,249	4	.....
66	Number of work mules	60	61	56	79	540	3,756	9	6,577	10	.....
67	Acreage in cotton	1,573	755	1,140	1,148	7,700	60,500	131	111,208	15	2
68	Bales of cotton grown in 1909	455	233	210	240	2,144	17,819	50	50,543	7	1
69	Acreage in corn	1,003	560	1,020	755	5,016	27,315	112	93,554	64	7
70	Bushels of corn grown in 1909	8,687	6,773	10,938	5,130	50,393	317,950	1,578	901,088	845	50
	FARMS OPERATED BY SHARE AND SHARE-CASH TENANTS.										
71	Total acreage	2,547	10,784	44,312	18,018	31,116	55,565	645	1,368,033	26,172	1,735
72	Improved acreage	2,372	8,667	38,970	13,974	23,143	55,277	173	886,816	10,849	1,192
73	Value of land	$29,829	$141,569	$454,816	$176,906	$379,763	$1,661,049	$8,880	$28,038,967	$279,427	$36,810
74	Value of buildings	$6,840	$30,400	$156,973	$50,305	$115,339	$342,491	$5,400	$5,827,523	$78,835	$5,620
75	Value of implements and machinery	$930	$5,507	$31,097	$7,021	$17,260	$29,791	$370	$830,301	$14,614	$957
76	Number of dairy cows	71	305	1,961	482	1,014	1,350	15	16,740	317	34
77	Number of work horses	24	114	1,275	134	338	297	13	8,985	231	4
78	Number of work mules	22	318	1,299	251	734	1,481	4	16,765	144	16
79	Acreage in cotton	1,055	3,492	16,347	6,209	10,949	34,541	35	261,524	141	100
80	Bales of cotton grown in 1909	309	1,027	2,321	1,566	3,245	11,218	15	134,969	70	31
81	Acreage in corn	570	2,890	14,532	3,733	7,124	10,199	50	264,909	2,789	381
82	Bushels of corn grown in 1909	5,730	34,862	200,957	32,879	73,623	135,718	770	3,088,814	46,027	5,186

[1] Total for the state excepting figures for Catawba County, which are not available.

OPERATED BY COLORED FARMERS, BY COUNTIES, FOR SOUTHERN STATES: 1910—Continued.

NORTH CAROLINA—continued.

Anson.	Beaufort.	Bertie.	Bladen.	Brunswick.	Buncombe.	Burke.	Cabarrus.	Caldwell.	Camden.	Carteret.	Caswell.	Catawba.	Chatham.	Chowan.	
1,649	818	1,665	996	504	180	240	557	169	262	107	792	274	1,059	382	1
							1								2
57	130	44	139	89	55	37	23	36	16	17	27	48	76	34	3
233	235	217	217	109	40	65	69	28	22	27	82	57	159	75	4
833	283	937	371	123	51	80	223	56	107	39	195	105	368	194	5
310	111	267	161	74	22	40	144	35	80	15	210	37	204	56	6
150	36	142	69	70	9	13	85	11	25	7	160	19	188	17	7
39	11	38	18	23	3	4	10	1	8	1	78	5	39	5	8
22	9	17	14	11		1	1	2	3	1	39	3	23	1	9
4	3	3	6	4			1		1		1		2		10
1			1	1			1								11
101	244	262	406	278	87	110	38	120	30	30	73	62	194	63	12
59	84	198	50	24	5	12	17	8	26	8	39	25	44	64	13
93	163	183	306	83	37	59	20	6	15	12	55	53	159	66	14
602	21	415	7	11	4		45	2	4	6	12	4	131	60	15
768	274	410	213	106	42	49	417	31	185	44	596	127	506	125	16
10	5	65	5	2	1	1	2		1	2	13	1	13	2	17
16	25	131	9		3	9	17	2	1	4	4	1	9	2	18
	2	1			1		1		1	1		1	3		19
8,092	9,536	19,616	22,749	18,629	2,738	4,266	1,556	5,215	1,607	1,550	4,856	1,482	11,726	2,046	20
3,394	3,337	7,920	6,779	3,390	1,332	1,558	972	2,196	782	436	2,148	868	4,460	1,144	21
$109,817	$176,525	$285,879	$186,784	$89,265	$68,845	$43,430	$21,250	$52,520	$21,935	$15,125	$33,400	$35,555	$85,150	$44,295	22
$34,815	$55,326	$84,910	$102,110	$48,140	$23,935	$15,615	$9,200	$17,890	$7,325	$5,925	$20,730	$13,520	$41,880	$16,875	23
$5,325	$6,153	$16,941	$15,896	$8,914	$2,379	$1,906	$2,447	$1,692	$1,475	$1,221	$3,565	$1,819	$7,340	$2,570	24
117	116	353	172	261	108	84	47	100	32	21	78	51	211	48	25
34	112	192	140	81	29	19	29	18	27	10	58	23	79	21	26
109	53	43	174	83	25	61	20	41	5	6	33	20	131	22	27
1,412	911	964	1,458	133		10	264		122	85		163	752	253	28
617	433	411	785	66		1	122		55	44		65	339	100	29
858	1,131	2,411	3,705	1,153	445	749	235	788	300	162	491	294	1,503	428	30
7,400	18,066	21,944	39,320	13,651	6,605	8,624	2,965	9,425	2,190	1,860	6,510	3,142	18,889	3,480	31
5,146	3,837	16,236	3,751	2,905	79	272	969	262	1,829	375	4,383	855	3,005	2,784	32
2,334	1,491	6,676	861	422	46	143	564	105	1,088	181	1,741	479	1,143	1,453	33
$72,505	$67,380	$248,345	$25,470	$13,755	$3,650	$2,140	$15,325	$2,475	$23,675	$5,225	$33,837	$17,250	$25,005	$67,565	34
$16,635	$16,030	$71,110	$7,420	$7,145	$2,150	$1,060	$4,390	$925	$7,525	$1,975	$13,765	$5,460	$13,860	$20,525	35
$3,120	$2,889	$18,230	$1,709	$3,324	$135	$29	$880	$172	$939	$5,205	$2,689	$1,303	$2,135	$3,343	36
80	38	165	17	23	4	4	21	8	19	6	51	19	59	61	37
14	41	154	16	6	1		14		31	5	38	13	15	30	38
80	29	42	18	13	2	1	13	9	8	1	26	14	38	18	39
1,227	411	817	128	35		2	196		170	31		122	235	329	40
495	208	324	50	6			73		46	17		48	98	145	41
525	522	1,912	446	80	10	65	151	44	505	39	354	134	376	386	42
4,935	9,007	14,440	3,790	941	160	400	1,217	530	1,930	340	5,540	1,319	4,420	4,140	43
7,377	6,647	9,355	15,405	4,360	1,152	2,035	1,037	92	569	561	3,358	2,313	10,968	3,027	44
4,139	4,192	5,651	8,140	3,056	617	1,207	472	55	186	324	1,819	(²)	5,596	1,581	45
3,498	3,171	5,299	5,821	1,174	796	1,023	655	68	432	229	1,653	1,423	4,346	1,810	46
1,733	1,362	2,313	2,168	395	284	472	287	35	138	69	785	(²)	2,060	532	47
$108,345	$133,942	$170,717	$143,215	$30,075	$32,350	$32,310	$18,055	$3,010	$9,830	$6,080	$26,495	$45,031	$79,769	$77,525	48
$29,025	$33,285	$58,375	$44,984	$8,980	$9,120	$8,775	$3,825	$420	$2,570	$1,690	$10,420	$12,310	$42,846	$23,515	49
$79,435	$96,705	$151,456	$114,959	$23,740	$19,070	$26,140	$9,890	$1,000	$5,115	$4,005	$19,955	(²)	$71,550	$57,560	50
$5,388	$4,833	$8,623	$8,048	$1,887	$1,136	$956	$798	$52	$378	$287	$2,060	$2,424	$6,420	$3,222	51
106	61	113	133	63	41	45	22	3	13	9	54	58	174	16	52
26	85	128	43	18	13	10	16		14	8	43	25	83	22	53
126	60	83	169	25	17	45	12		5	3	29	36	121	36	54
1,566	665	643	891	97		14	200		56	51		371	841	424	55
703	349	245	414	41		2	77		23	31		116	387	130	56
868	1,154	1,788	2,646	478	311	493	201	37	322	68	377	470	1,490	563	57
8,133	19,295	11,011	26,585	4,969	4,727	5,801	2,195	407	2,340	1,370	6,145	5,532	18,521	4,123	58
37,591	2,285	20,487	1,073	2,102	139	569	4,451	66	134	364	1,433	198	14,204	2,336	59
18,992	642	15,337	337	256	114	185	2,309	41	84	154	655	114	3,842	1,794	60
$487,128	$21,270	$322,392	$6,830	$11,850	$3,055	$4,555	$82,660	$914	$1,850	$3,550	$9,435	$2,470	$119,054	$39,520	61
$118,680	$6,945	$100,371	$1,855	$1,450	$545	$795	$15,740	$401	$575	$900	$4,125	$560	$24,800	$11,200	62
$24,878	$437	$20,699	$270	$290	$120	$178	$3,094	$34	$47	$213	$500	$85	$3,958	$3,339	63
564	12	335	6	6	7	8	71	4	1	5	16	3	149	45	64
99	21	391	5	4	3		41	1	1	9	12	1	46	27	65
681	5	86	3	5	2	7	48		1		9	3	119	35	66
9,817	136	2,413	76	8			778		10	9		32	825	506	67
4,257	65	1,129	35	6			282		3	4		12	377	208	68
4,260	204	4,865	147	69	33	77	602	11	53	53	137	21	1,227	518	69
39,371	2,653	43,439	1,275	820	635	720	6,051	210	270	590	1,670	190	14,688	4,725	70
29,210	8,242	13,858	6,939	4,137	1,390	1,806	22,231	922	10,850	1,051	56,232	6,387	27,368	4,307	71
19,614	5,397	11,723	3,797	1,318	921	765	14,331	430	7,142	929	23,298	3,857	12,913	2,831	72
$443,873	$214,587	$258,384	$82,733	$29,790	$36,405	$32,541	$487,071	$20,290	$175,330	$24,336	$382,251	$162,050	$242,120	$99,055	73
$116,800	$32,215	$68,515	$20,744	$9,360	$5,065	$4,725	$86,545	$3,330	$42,455	$3,665	$149,315	$23,305	$80,677	$23,760	74
$16,578	$3,166	$8,393	$2,516	$2,283	$735	$764	$13,149	$300	$4,966	$360	$19,335	$3,786	$10,497	$6,064	75
501	47	137	61	18	46	27	386	22	110	7	566	113	427	38	76
52	61	154	16	18	14	3	153	1	170	6	376	38	128	37	77
672	61	182	81	13	13	19	408	9	47	8	257	55	229	80	78
10,445	1,500	2,145	741	92		8	5,031		1,278	240		1,045	2,752	825	79
5,294	839	921	335	29		3	2,031		482	127		349	1,329	351	80
4,204	2,153	3,220	1,636	511	250	382	3,564	184	4,241	218	4,425	1,119	4,380	764	81
45,673	39,885	28,280	14,852	5,223	3,535	5,288	40,421	2,905	33,181	2,481	58,568	13,229	58,659	7,011	82

² Data not available.

TABLE **73.**—STATISTICS OF SIZE OF FARMS AND FOR TENURE CLASSES OF FARMS

NORTH CAROLINA—continued.

		Cleveland.	Columbus.	Craven.	Cumberland.	Currituck.	Davidson.	Davie.	Duplin.	Durham.	Edgecombe.
1	Number of farms	691	837	1,031	1,343	250	212	256	1,114	512	1,613
	FARMS CLASSIFIED BY SIZE.										
2	Under 3 acres				1					1	
3	3 to 9 acres	26	155	238	120	15	21	27	218	49	36
4	10 to 19 acres	102	211	247	213	21	52	56	319	98	99
5	20 to 49 acres	361	257	315	623	103	71	101	378	168	999
6	50 to 99 acres	129	124	132	236	70	36	46	131	106	364
7	100 to 174 acres	62	51	58	81	27	22	15	45	70	76
8	175 to 259 acres	7	15	29	36	8	8	11	14	15	23
9	260 to 499 acres	4	18	9	21	3	2		4	5	12
10	500 to 999 acres		4	2	9	2			5		3
11	1,000 acres and over		2	1	3	1					1
	FARMERS CLASSIFIED BY TENURE.										
12	Owners, free	48	416	375	337	43	28	28	202	45	67
13	Owners, mortgaged	26	78	71	41	28	25	20	83	18	37
14	Part owners	38	168	135	216	11	30	70	268	42	19
15	Cash tenants	73	29	108	161	12	1		49	56	229
16	Share tenants	495	125	328	512	153	128	137	461	348	1,157
17	Share-cash tenants	3	14	1	23	2			11	3	71
18	Tenure not specified	8	6	11	48	1		1	40		28
19	Managers		1	2	5						5
	FARMS OPERATED BY OWNERS, FREE.										
20	Total acreage	2,868	22,403	18,888	19,354	4,914	917	986	8,443	2,385	4,391
21	Improved acreage	1,429	5,976	5,756	6,015	2,345	523	677	3,134	1,036	2,434
22	Value of land	$76,580	$247,515	$275,932	$216,600	$44,061	$18,050	$13,250	$135,234	$45,075	$90,415
23	Value of buildings	$18,940	$90,970	$105,935	$76,360	$20,725	$6,560	$5,175	$42,275	$18,080	$37,800
24	Value of implements and machinery	$2,869	$13,205	$19,661	$12,029	$1,771	$1,438	$984	$5,308	$1,966	$12,055
25	Number of dairy cows	69	218	295	234	43	33	28	122	57	51
26	Number of work horses	13	110	148	72	45	18	11	90	29	51
27	Number of work mules	59	171	45	180	15	10	17	54	28	72
28	Acreage in cotton	523	633	802	1,319	61	26	29	384	89	942
29	Bales of cotton grown in 1909	220	336	327	725	20	10	7	176	37	488
30	Acreage in corn	462	2,778	2,177	2,516	463	141	166	1,458	391	724
31	Bushels of corn grown in 1909	5,598	29,079	22,564	22,502	4,517	2,245	2,116	14,488	4,315	6,755
	FARMS OPERATED BY OWNERS, MORTGAGED.										
32	Total acreage	1,702	3,235	5,671	3,249	2,083	1,017	688	3,285	1,360	4,916
33	Improved acreage	813	981	1,706	976	899	628	471	1,435	482	2,198
34	Value of land	$32,215	$52,120	$82,715	$39,215	$20,350	$16,405	$9,060	$55,627	$16,203	$71,185
35	Value of buildings	$9,010	$11,105	$17,330	$12,215	$5,875	$5,155	$2,625	$21,250	$3,925	$16,570
36	Value of implements and machinery	$1,285	$2,599	$3,725	$1,809	$830	$1,025	$729	$4,654	$692	$3,826
37	Number of dairy cows	33	20	30	22	29	22	24	55	18	28
38	Number of work horses	7	17	38	8	26	18	13	39	16	37
39	Number of work mules	31	40	29	40	15	21	10	30	7	45
40	Acreage in cotton	273	143	271	285	49	71	34	219	27	697
41	Bales of cotton grown in 1909	92	77	100	146	14	24	6	92	12	319
42	Acreage in corn	255	415	536	328	379	130	128	661	148	491
43	Bushels of corn grown in 1909	2,315	4,576	4,532	3,205	2,353	2,024	1,525	6,382	1,760	3,342
	FARMS OPERATED BY PART OWNERS.										
44	Total acreage	1,772	7,036	4,493	11,543	498	1,378	2,831	9,115	2,189	1,471
45	Owned acreage	978	5,056	2,586	7,203	305	663	946	5,387	1,100	732
46	Improved acreage	1,160	3,267	2,369	5,614	287	891	1,765	5,131	1,171	791
47	Owned improved acreage	555	1,479	890	2,187	122	480	500	1,801	487	317
48	Value of land	$46,780	$115,945	$128,889	$190,150	$8,570	$25,130	$42,010	$132,584	$51,940	$28,922
49	Value of buildings	$10,075	$23,780	$34,385	$57,855	$1,695	$6,370	$10,845	$44,870	$10,745	$9,360
50	Value of land and buildings owned	$30,515	$84,805	$88,692	$140,245	$6,139	$19,705	$23,255	$98,407	$31,330	$20,255
51	Value of implements and machinery	$1,506	$4,633	$4,245	$9,228	$165	$1,815	$2,308	$5,540	$1,142	$4,058
52	Number of dairy cows	46	38	72	109	6	35	55	127	48	10
53	Number of work horses	9	27	46	45	11	20	40	114	27	13
54	Number of work mules	39	110	41	160	6	19	38	71	27	23
55	Acreage in cotton	448	589	408	1,626	15	95	256	561	136	325
56	Bales of cotton grown in 1909	157	285	174	912	6	45	63	282	45	158
57	Acreage in corn	375	1,326	826	2,302	221	214	467	2,086	402	209
58	Bushels of corn grown in 1909	3,689	14,401	11,022	25,445	1,765	2,735	5,705	21,711	5,175	1,924
	FARMS OPERATED BY CASH TENANTS, INCLUDING TENURE NOT SPECIFIED.										
59	Total acreage	3,609	2,270	2,508	12,619	595	22	80	5,218	5,223	15,108
60	Improved acreage	2,320	828	1,672	5,810	352	10	80	2,976	1,832	10,570
61	Value of land	$87,840	$27,375	$74,173	$188,685	$10,635	$350	$1,600	$65,780	$77,050	$290,356
62	Value of buildings	$20,900	$5,155	$12,471	$39,656	$3,225	$50	$100	$16,775	$15,200	$65,475
63	Value of implements and machinery	$2,200	$4,729	$2,395	$7,372	$273	$10		$2,501	$2,338	$20,975
64	Number of dairy cows	95	9	26	122	15		3	44	72	86
65	Number of work horses	18	9	42	48	14			39	43	158
66	Number of work mules	76	19	24	163	5			37	33	235
67	Acreage in cotton	1,046	260	368	2,258	16			564	172	3,733
68	Bales of cotton grown in 1909	305	142	129	1,197	6			221	53	1,793
69	Acreage in corn	748	247	660	1,794	113			1,253	547	2,240
70	Bushels of corn grown in 1909	6,980	3,395	6,459	18,094	1,165			10,897	5,623	16,892
	FARMS OPERATED BY SHARE AND SHARE-CASH TENANTS.										
71	Total acreage	20,663	4,860	7,892	19,631	8,589	7,350	6,776	11,162	15,793	46,659
72	Improved acreage	14,064	2,364	5,798	13,193	6,114	4,369	4,244	8,216	8,087	42,385
73	Value of land	$567,957	$82,820	$157,829	$583,540	$161,990	$133,405	$117,865	$197,652	$228,596	$1,045,781
74	Value of buildings	$100,480	$16,405	$34,991	$86,886	$40,710	$23,390	$28,355	$51,163	$65,630	$246,942
75	Value of implements and machinery	$11,696	$13,972	$5,254	$14,411	$2,559	$4,531	$2,862	$4,588	$7,677	$50,514
76	Number of dairy cows	431	24	87	135	100	99	101	149	322	175
77	Number of work horses	64	14	75	58	136	45	46	100	155	210
78	Number of work mules	223	57	54	358	45	76	52	81	119	997
79	Acreage in cotton	5,870	373	1,424	5,250	449	628	473	1,218	332	17,779
80	Bales of cotton grown in 1909	2,059	194	614	3,456	97	232	139	631	146	9,174
81	Acreage in corn	4,409	859	2,161	4,402	3,778	1,118	1,121	3,540	2,476	9,568
82	Bushels of corn grown in 1909	48,730	10,528	19,919	55,206	24,048	16,099	15,156	42,929	31,898	82,271

OPERATED BY COLORED FARMERS, BY COUNTIES, FOR SOUTHERN STATES: 1910—Continued.

NORTH CAROLINA—continued.

Forsyth.	Franklin.	Gaston.	Gates.	Granville.	Greene.	Guilford.	Halifax.	Harnett.	Henderson.	Hertford.	Hyde.	Iredell.	Johnston.	Jones.	
289	1,398	792	449	1,315	899	610	2,901	691	107	1,146	443	642	1,148	582	1
					6							1			2
53	94	41	43	81	68	75	269	49	24	96	69	26	83	41	3
72	233	151	85	224	146	111	487	120	28	183	111	123	220	86	4
88	632	413	148	532	533	197	1,412	307	33	531	200	285	519	335	5
42	266	122	108	244	101	137	437	135	17	189	54	132	184	63	6
19	136	44	49	172	32	53	192	58	4	99	8	59	100	29	7
11	29	13	10	42	13	30	54	13	1	31	1	10	25	4	8
4	7	7	5	17		7	37	7		15		4	14	10	9
	1	1	1	2			13	1		2		2	3	9	10
				1										5	11
51	121	52	144	178	29	134	307	236	53	188	32	82	97	41	12
31	49	25	110	99	30	61	122	29	17	100	14	32	64	24	13
82	84	101	14	53	34	131	313	46	11	123	49	124	107	27	14
5	589	111	45	67	45	9	1,476	203		262		13	312	40	15
113	528	487	104	833	671	248	591	166	22	429	346	361	545	446	16
1	6	11	5	65	40	1	47	7	3	25	2	2	16	4	17
1	20	4	27	18	50	20	44	4	1	16		28	6		18
5	1	1		2		6	1			3			1		19
1,902	8,149	2,165	6,261	9,651	1,670	5,254	22,119	13,352	1,737	13,709	903	3,443	5,849	3,649	20
898	4,040	1,230	2,838	4,754	963	2,403	10,847	4,106	704	5,326	553	1,929	2,258	1,062	21
$42,121	$110,554	$54,790	$113,000	$104,805	$36,370	$77,275	$252,467	$109,160	$28,270	$232,413	$24,015	$66,954	$98,969	$28,375	22
$15,515	$40,041	$19,295	$49,500	$61,740	$9,050	$29,785	$114,195	$40,740	$12,780	$92,565	$3,460	$19,545	$25,250	$9,840	23
$2,633	$10,507	$2,680	$7,409	$8,569	$1,120	$4,646	$28,201	$9,424	$1,934	$12,713	$436	$3,924	$4,400	$1,071	24
43	129	55	151	194	14	161	244	241	47	158	29	76	65	24	25
28	117	23	103	143	18	84	229	49	22	112	19	39	23	15	26
18	33	39	41	58	28	59	153	125	9	50	2	62	90	23	27
	1,061	338	310	97	191	22	2,562	879		538	171	529	856	194	28
	480	156	110	39	70	5	1,218	383		218	76	168	510	81	29
229	1,171	339	1,003	974	325	836	2,695	2,065	439	1,737	231	526	811	450	30
3,005	10,655	3,924	8,254	14,942	3,680	11,526	24,358	17,810	4,614	11,387	3,257	5,851	11,463	4,358	31
1,740	4,213	1,904	5,828	6,350	2,361	2,343	12,889	1,869	510	7,709	418	1,850	4,790	3,697	32
785	1,855	897	2,420	2,713	1,308	1,114	5,589	531	242	3,154	308	790	2,053	1,060	33
$37,420	$83,165	$40,162	$79,995	$60,520	$51,165	$66,214	$147,938	$13,920	$7,525	$110,845	$14,430	$21,615	$74,673	$21,440	34
$10,745	$25,340	$9,490	$30,325	$27,605	$11,100	$17,603	$42,841	$7,065	$3,050	$43,020	$2,800	$4,460	$13,350	$3,915	35
$1,906	$3,877	$1,325	$5,600	$3,952	$1,355	$3,115	$11,712	$1,003	$461	$5,374	$389	$1,385	$3,106	$945	36
33	82	36	82	98	11	62	108	23	16	64	17	32	40	13	37
22	60	13	80	89	23	35	83	5	5	94	7	13	14	7	38
16	32	36	34	41	31	26	86	22	3	48	1	25	72	22	39
	561	193	273	73	274	11	1,232	150		393	113	163	698	242	40
	265	78	106	44	102	3	603	65		133	44	48	369	110	41
178	574	193	745	618	439	433	1,123	298	118	831	126	235	680	377	42
2,204	6,428	2,449	5,537	9,797	4,154	5,450	10,545	1,993	1,423	5,277	2,165	2,694	7,077	2,865	43
3,212	4,514	4,811	1,109	3,551	2,495	5,979	18,091	2,243	434	7,730	2,352	5,045	6,478	3,387	44
1,517	1,993	2,174	724	1,865	1,569	2,700	8,693	1,567	267	4,346	1,217	2,271	4,276	2,482	45
1,909	2,571	3,076	547	1,685	1,540	3,368	10,383	1,257	291	3,649	1,425	3,131	3,024	1,151	46
847	936	1,154	254	781	752	1,239	4,102	583	174	1,396	426	1,286	1,552	512	47
$80,955	$69,945	$138,272	$15,725	$39,322	$66,325	$108,937	$246,795	$28,745	$7,885	$160,625	$69,665	$95,359	$111,115	$22,750	48
$15,910	$25,270	$44,670	$4,500	$10,495	$12,360	$29,600	$121,276	$8,860	$1,685	$46,440	$7,275	$20,954	$25,927	$5,165	49
$48,985	$49,880	$93,122	$11,150	$26,562	$51,350	$69,182	$223,337	$23,700	$4,945	$107,885	$32,440	$59,170	$86,096	$18,975	50
$3,045	$3,015	$6,551	$795	$2,261	$1,902	$4,312	$18,254	$1,725	$385	$7,518	$1,521	$4,307	$5,238	$961	51
86	72	111	14	51	17	158	223	44	15	75	66	118	71	28	52
37	72	42	14	54	15	78	252	14	4	91	43	51	20	11	53
39	33	80	7	21	41	69	153	44	4	39	8	91	115	24	54
	840	863	74	44	458	20	2,724	414		405	467	795	1,141	286	55
	309	391	34	15	183	8	1,187	208		149	187	242	661	139	56
520	758	917	168	428	502	1,311	2,940	547	132	996	635	1,057	962	382	57
7,775	6,632	9,251	1,040	4,890	4,292	15,820	24,859	4,952	1,473	6,636	11,710	12,506	12,627	3,665	58
194	29,053	6,529	3,870	5,693	2,790	1,503	57,910	7,768	14	12,709		1,839	20,137	6,899	59
97	17,338	3,672	1,509	3,065	2,274	730	37,634	5,166	14	7,554		1,105	8,550	1,299	60
$7,000	$364,207	$196,290	$61,570	$58,753	$74,580	$24,385	$646,487	$126,390	$700	$301,805		$45,254	$373,188	$42,540	61
$650	$112,610	$30,960	$15,740	$16,075	$20,280	$5,165	$175,867	$28,165		$72,695		$6,075	$60,315	$6,070	62
$70	$16,896	$3,675	$2,354	$3,021	$1,775	$1,003	$46,661	$7,524		$8,908		$911	$12,116	$1,045	63
3	482	120	48	87	20	36	838	124		140		40	153	31	64
4	419	25	55	74	18	19	766	39		173		14	62	22	65
1	166	126	17	24	62	5	455	189		99		29	291	29	66
	5,789	1,427	254	118	766	14	11,073	2,193		1,362		490	3,154	307	67
	2,191	577	76	45	306	5	4,537	1,135		502		161	1,724	121	68
43	4,867	994	597	629	1,004	226	10,290	1,878		1,763		333	2,753	541	69
540	40,864	10,054	3,873	9,070	10,679	2,425	85,133	19,939		12,808		3,517	34,064	4,765	70
5,526	18,755	18,076	6,179	45,873	20,909	16,820	20,698	8,904	705	14,520	8,736	18,665	11,987	16,443	71
2,986	12,846	13,198	3,130	25,252	18,858	7,484	18,608	3,736	417	11,043	8,035	10,476	12,312	12,128	72
$113,275	$271,342	$524,612	$91,015	$438,295	$657,360	$279,482	$307,364	$107,441	$26,205	$387,700	$349,218	$380,529	$430,263	$228,690	73
$20,085	$84,414	$95,626	$27,475	$133,277	$130,200	$49,750	$96,966	$26,005	$2,675	$96,225	$30,102	$64,200	$97,925	$45,067	74
$3,252	$7,471	$9,743	$4,551	$14,142	$15,343	$8,849	$17,096	$4,224	$522	$11,507	$4,713	$9,187	$12,632	$7,222	75
81	233	439	72	734	135	245	214	90	20	179	199	351	151	118	76
32	156	73	84	421	155	125	136	25	2	136	149	105	55	108	77
40	187	248	24	182	483	104	484	106	2	141	53	167	338	212	78
5	4,360	6,038	438	607	6,775	26	6,348	1,256		1,865	1,720	2,958	4,829	3,794	79
2	1,858	2,535	171	289	2,842	7	3,149	673		677	769	956	3,187	1,716	80
759	3,696	3,969	1,214	5,407	6,855	2,516	4,092	1,563	193	3,109	3,635	3,365	4,058	5,300	81
11,920	33,291	43,500	9,100	82,757	73,493	32,955	34,528	17,605	1,991	25,807	55,371	40,895	57,490	56,316	82

TABLE 73.—STATISTICS OF SIZE OF FARMS AND FOR TENURE CLASSES OF FARMS

NORTH CAROLINA—continued.

		Lee.	Lenoir.	Lincoln.	Mc-Dowell.	Martin.	Mecklen-burg.	Mont-gomery.	Moore.	Nash.	New Hanover.
1	Number of farms	335	816	311	160	779	1,751	343	406	1,539	174
	FARMS CLASSIFIED BY SIZE.										
2	Under 3 acres						1		1		
3	3 to 9 acres	32	75	21	29	34	54	33	62	83	40
4	10 to 19 acres	55	127	57	21	119	218	54	91	268	41
5	20 to 49 acres	106	456	134	59	354	874	141	110	752	58
6	50 to 99 acres	79	109	72	32	166	401	70	68	283	17
7	100 to 174 acres	39	35	23	13	74	179	28	41	123	11
8	175 to 259 acres	15	8	3	4	18	19	10	21	17	4
9	260 to 499 acres	6	3	1	2	10	5	6	7	10	1
10	500 to 999 acres	3	3			4		1	5	1	1
11	1,000 acres and over									2	1
	FARMERS CLASSIFIED BY TENURE.										
12	Owners, free	70	24	43	78	148	89	59	131	120	75
13	Owners, mortgaged	13	12	12	4	101	33	19	23	65	7
14	Part owners	47	18	52	28	59	44	54	62	50	36
15	Cash tenants	112	77	7	1	54	328	64	54	327	24
16	Share tenants	86	664	192	49	325	1,196	146	127	952	16
17	Share-cash tenants	4	12	1		22	40	1	6	12	13
18	Tenure not specified	3	8	4		68	19		2	11	1
19	Managers		1			2	2		1	2	2
	FARMS OPERATED BY OWNERS, FREE.										
20	Total acreage	3,334	1,518	1,533	3,306	11,047	4,630	2,100	6,681	7,449	3,532
21	Improved acreage	1,168	778	812	1,118	4,482	2,833	832	2,233	3,474	985
22	Value of land	$35,760	$25,610	$26,546	$18,810	$119,173	$151,485	$21,170	$48,010	$145,470	$60,065
23	Value of buildings	$15,975	$5,935	$9,940	$10,195	$48,615	$48,340	$9,740	$27,025	$45,615	$22,100
24	Value of implements and machinery	$2,418	$1,071	$1,167	$2,050	$7,529	$8,999	$1,791	$3,842	$8,258	$2,598
25	Number of dairy cows	54	13	38	50	123	150	52	115	77	14
26	Number of work horses	10	15	14	12	78	45	16	37	60	29
27	Number of work mules	46	12	21	20	80	100	31	82	86	44
28	Acreage in cotton	306	85	228		616	1,090	202	241	972	6
29	Bales of cotton grown in 1909	150	33	64		231	498	92	98	505	5
30	Acreage in corn	475	288	238	479	1,207	735	277	893	1,042	204
31	Bushels of corn grown in 1909	5,080	3,085	1,849	4,804	8,896	6,388	2,368	9,518	11,185	4,432
	FARMS OPERATED BY OWNERS, MORTGAGED.										
32	Total acreage	866	1,140	473	154	7,157	2,368	1,825	1,613	5,177	273
33	Improved acreage	282	530	297	77	2,829	1,310	395	397	2,284	91
34	Value of land	$6,895	$14,300	$10,635	$550	$81,468	$59,100	$13,470	$8,380	$88,543	$8,425
35	Value of buildings	$2,695	$5,400	$4,625	$400	$29,457	$12,725	$6,550	$7,715	$24,282	$2,775
36	Value of implements and machinery	$384	$248	$628	$85	$4,992	$2,273	$1,001	$922	$4,974	$205
37	Number of dairy cows	17	12	10	4	55	65	20	19	43	
38	Number of work horses	4	8	2	2	60	26	6	7	33	2
39	Number of work mules	13	11	13		59	46	18	13	70	6
40	Acreage in cotton	81	64	94		543	518	74	60	635	
41	Bales of cotton grown in 1909	40	23	29		159	206	34	21	309	
42	Acreage in corn	116	202	78	28	849	333	136	124	670	26
43	Bushels of corn grown in 1909	1,061	1,660	975	215	6,211	3,049	1,167	1,020	6,665	470
	FARMS OPERATED BY PART OWNERS.										
44	Total acreage	2,427	1,485	2,065	1,475	2,898	2,507	2,764	3,926	2,547	1,390
45	Owned acreage	1,305	1,051	1,053	1,072	1,731	1,235	1,276	1,605	1,576	727
46	Improved acreage	1,035	549	1,435	617	1,294	1,714	1,460	1,266	1,421	862
47	Owned improved acreage	541	278	650	239	491	742	565	473	703	230
48	Value of land	$26,585	$55,250	$33,262	$17,432	$42,565	$95,264	$19,020	$18,483	$51,328	$34,440
49	Value of buildings	$9,710	$11,475	$13,575	$3,055	$12,560	$18,342	$9,735	$11,130	$13,510	$7,375
50	Value of land and buildings owned	$22,915	$54,675	$26,361	$12,767	$35,135	$57,385	$16,791	$18,425	$42,820	$18,660
51	Value of implements and machinery	$1,664	$803	$1,869	$785	$1,568	$2,937	$2,047	$1,678	$3,042	$2,185
52	Number of dairy cows	48	9	54	30	32	68	49	59	24	2
53	Number of work horses	18	8	24	10	27	22	12	24	25	12
54	Number of work mules	38	18	44	20	26	59	49	39	41	31
55	Acreage in cotton	265	96	464		134	714	437	238	426	
56	Bales of cotton grown in 1909	126	44	150		66	281	167	91	204	
57	Acreage in corn	401	244	479	345	411	401	441	550	348	207
58	Bushels of corn grown in 1909	4,250	2,229	3,729	4,330	3,123	3,072	4,209	5,993	3,615	2,060
	FARMS OPERATED BY CASH TENANTS, INCLUDING TENURE NOT SPECIFIED.										
59	Total acreage	10,064	4,581	553	20	7,037	22,341	3,593	3,836	17,655	1,629
60	Improved acreage	2,561	2,773	258	10	3,719	12,936	1,798	1,143	9,080	343
61	Value of land	$97,620	$88,930	$10,090	$150	$84,907	$810,667	$28,681	$25,915	$293,140	$43,000
62	Value of buildings	$20,450	$19,175	$1,725	$50	$21,045	$86,253	$12,270	$11,215	$66,790	$3,015
63	Value of implements and machinery	$3,724	$2,307	$168	$2	$2,383	$20,813	$2,133	$1,038	$12,558	$535
64	Number of dairy cows	110	32	6	1	57	439	60	34	162	4
65	Number of work horses	31	41	2		47	281	12	12	159	10
66	Number of work mules	83	63	8		39	329	62	25	196	13
67	Acreage in cotton	731	753	117		743	5,402	684	176	3,187	3
68	Bales of cotton grown in 1909	323	267	30		317	1,938	267	64	1,590	1
69	Acreage in corn	851	912	91	5	698	2,943	466	403	2,538	101
70	Bushels of corn grown in 1909	7,853	9,900	490	75	4,589	24,361	4,369	4,690	26,423	1,250
	FARMS OPERATED BY SHARE AND SHARE-CASH TENANTS.										
71	Total acreage	3,961	22,028	8,547	2,637	13,712	51,337	7,098	7,760	33,875	755
72	Improved acreage	1,703	18,174	5,783	1,063	8,993	35,804	3,373	2,462	24,855	560
73	Value of land	$39,271	$566,453	$159,670	$44,165	$253,210	$1,601,045	$62,604	$43,315	$754,610	$21,046
74	Value of buildings	$11,915	$114,331	$28,295	$5,250	$68,580	$249,723	$24,395	$16,085	$207,245	$4,024
75	Value of implements and machinery	$1,235	$12,763	$3,951	$565	$7,050	$36,836	$3,741	$1,930	$25,370	$850
76	Number of dairy cows	64	113	179	43	64	1,148	95	83	257	4
77	Number of work horses	8	123	41	6	124	221	27	27	203	6
78	Number of work mules	33	319	92	17	167	835	116	40	615	21
79	Acreage in cotton	527	5,484	1,904		1,948	17,178	1,097	440	6,482	6
80	Bales of cotton grown in 1909	252	2,426	625		811	6,649	459	159	3,664	2
81	Acreage in corn	575	7,122	1,745	534	2,756	8,087	882	946	6,352	160
82	Bushels of corn grown in 1909	6,198	84,518	16,979	7,740	26,783	76,775	8,293	9,522	73,068	1,734

OPERATED BY COLORED FARMERS, BY COUNTIES, FOR SOUTHERN STATES: 1910—Continued.

NORTH CAROLINA—continued.

North-ampton.	Onslow.	Orange.	Pamlico.	Pasquo-tank.	Pender.	Perqui-mans.	Person.	Pitt.	Polk.	Ran-dolph.	Rich-mond.	Robeson.	Rocking-ham.	Rowan.	
1,814	474	495	244	514	764	491	861	1,948	143	349	871	3,368	742	477	1
					14		1								2
57	36	28	18	47	186	28	20	88	4	50	40	131	42	22	3
228	84	60	49	97	194	105	63	330	30	60	107	320	113	78	4
998	253	155	111	234	212	214	254	1,130	59	98	418	2,013	217	200	5
340	54	127	38	98	74	101	262	271	27	69	184	632	176	105	6
143	31	94	24	29	46	38	194	91	14	50	94	195	135	62	7
35	11	24	2	6	22	5	46	26	8	14	12	49	38	7	8
10	4	7	1	3	11		19	10	1	8	11	23	21		9
1	1			1		5		2	2		5		3		10
2												2			11
189	133	109	50	73	400	78	100	93	25	123	171	581	108	49	12
105	20	30	24	33	84	70	47	73	11	45	33	75	38	35	13
148	61	55	58	103	125	45	14	64	4	72	44	305	34	78	14
599	16	16		18	17	21	2	74	3	4	159	517	22	15	15
662	242	275	109	277	128	274	669	1,501	52	105	447	1,681	533	279	16
34	1	2	1	6	5	2		26	17		11	73	2	1	17
76	1	8	2	3	5	1	28	115	31		6	136	4	20	18
1				1			1	2					1		19
14,257	7,095	6,226	3,256	3,087	16,916	4,020	7,492	6,489	1,341	6,295	9,285	31,844	6,873	1,754	20
5,628	2,705	2,711	944	1,686	4,138	1,995	3,303	2,359	521	2,245	3,322	13,915	2,630	1,141	21
$166,530	$59,770	$43,365	$56,855	$68,828	$169,756	$46,560	$67,995	$121,520	$18,970	$56,100	$94,120	$701,299	$60,960	$57,685	22
$67,020	$23,865	$26,740	$14,295	$19,592	$87,613	$23,725	$28,750	$40,475	$8,850	$27,360	$47,615	$190,748	$31,620	$16,110	23
$11,024	$3,333	$5,122	$1,852	$2,747	$9,711	$4,573	$3,775	$4,247	$1,110	$4,249	$7,448	$45,014	$3,808	$3,594	24
184	46	142	22	60	206	70	109	60	34	125	121	309	128	66	25
164	44	102	23	57	110	65	80	70	6	52	39	160	71	41	26
69	65	42	29	17	95	37	43	44	8	58	130	576	44	24	27
1,109	283	158	261	348	203	481		671	102	39	1,294	5,935		246	28
418	124	69	142	110	103	179		294	36	13	604	3,627		101	29
1,851	908	898	318	844	1,654	797	817	1,002	261	766	1,243	5,612	651	402	30
13,857	7,789	12,887	6,682	5,795	20,298	5,581	9,595	9,734	3,080	1,524	12,424	71,687	8,407	5,405	31
8,049	1,497	2,494	1,984	1,287	4,206	3,978	4,125	5,803	335	2,002	3,306	4,906	2,678	1,751	32
3,226	528	966	749	699	1,089	2,211	1,762	2,308	187	848	845	1,875	1,000	994	33
$106,310	$10,550	$18,885	$54,150	$26,285	$55,827	$50,770	$35,835	$111,110	$6,330	$17,315	$21,770	$99,685	$25,631	$23,100	34
$35,850	$3,850	$8,625	$7,525	$8,700	$22,315	$19,275	$17,445	$27,240	$2,000	$8,415	$9,975	$22,305	$8,755	$9,465	35
$4,568	$490	$2,121	$965	$1,155	$5,884	$3,259	$1,991	$3,748	$500	$1,558	$1,187	$4,353	$1,599	$1,791	36
89	9	35	7	27	29	68	59	59	9	39	32	39	39	53	37
95	5	24	11	17	37	69	61	60	3	22	6	22	28	40	38
49	10	23	20	8	34	41	14	39	7	27	30	78	19	16	39
592	78	68	275	145	55	471		533	32	27	260	874		243	40
214	39	31	155	51	27	153		197	13	10	112	481		77	41
1,000	204	310	263	411	319	766	340	786	88	275	210	708	245	260	42
5,720	1,853	4,165	6,155	2,917	3,956	5,048	4,644	7,879	1,090	3,018	2,159	8,840	3,035	3,270	43
10,005	2,723	2,375	2,704	4,089	5,240	2,058	667	3,214	340	3,462	2,963	15,433	1,736	2,825	44
4,436	1,587	968	1,725	1,944	3,179	1,227	259	1,823	95	2,023	1,075	9,251	664	1,453	45
4,289	1,427	1,153	1,466	3,293	1,975	1,166	366	1,474	94	1,670	1,110	9,019	829	1,992	46
1,594	158	407	608	1,250	601	505	113	644	22	731	352	3,771	268	915	47
$154,820	$38,590	$20,755	$82,345	$110,449	$52,233	$24,480	$8,600	$61,840	$3,555	$37,646	$30,335	$353,260	$17,595	$51,837	48
$36,815	$13,080	$10,660	$12,035	$24,060	$18,238	$8,171	$4,180	$16,340	$875	$14,175	$7,955	$87,820	$7,795	$17,955	49
$95,650	$30,255	$17,645	$54,025	$74,255	$41,055	$19,325	$3,580	$46,200	$1,500	$31,407	$17,130	$264,758	$10,400	$38,680	50
$5,791	$1,115	$1,588	$1,296	$3,625	$3,125	$1,198	$397	$1,853	$60	$2,987	$1,739	$17,510	$765	$4,127	51
114	17	59	25	102	65	26	14	29	6	77	29	127	36	90	52
122	22	34	20	97	31	42	12	37		34	9	54	9	56	53
44	24	25	29	35	46	11	4	24	2	53	36	345	23	48	54
775	207	47	583	660	90	183		520	26	96	366	4,100		375	55
282	101	17	320	208	46	49		221	14	29	189	2,348		140	56
1,230	592	503	568	1,927	935	417	88	629	34	674	378	3,209	233	736	57
7,806	5,035	6,945	12,826	14,228	10,226	2,207	1,270	6,191	395	8,574	4,123	39,295	3,231	9,452	58
29,007	1,087	1,976	47	1,263	1,165	1,255	1,836	7,913	1,266	141	10,411	31,932	2,097	2,068	59
17,743	602	734	47	650	318	699	916	4,339	574	70	4,744	22,893	886	1,269	60
$385,092	$13,535	$12,565	$2,500	$30,440	$8,780	$18,610	$21,895	$160,527	$28,000	$1,425	$122,946	$1,044,908	$16,935	$46,460	61
$85,380	$2,760	$3,475		$5,000	$2,345	$5,590	$5,580	$33,643	$4,400	$525	$27,000	$157,455	$5,215	$7,010	62
$19,827	$413	$672	$20	$869	$617	$802	$833	$4,876	$1,360	$150	$6,526	$41,433	$810	$1,022	63
440	2	25		8	8	9	34	67	31	4	158	276	23	35	64
396	12	19		19	4	22	23	65	5	1	21	184	12	18	65
209	4	10	1	4	7	13	8	59	10	2	179	769	11	20	66
5,598	57	83	20	95	19	208		1,441	111	7	2,363	13,272		273	67
1,957	19	39	14	31	14	72		568	41	2	1,075	8,567		101	68
6,071	192	285	23	229	104	261	196	1,614	348	36	1,180	6,442	178	302	69
42,311	1,960	3,558	650	1,990	1,029	1,900	2,738	16,363	4,025	350	12,464	83,721	1,905	3,990	70
23,108	8,097	19,606	2,968	11,331	4,734	9,150	51,298	52,711	4,138	8,605	21,729	63,086	37,932	16,320	71
18,763	6,172	8,860	2,405	8,732	2,234	6,852	25,148	40,309	1,864	2,745	13,979	51,595	16,283	9,404	72
$432,317	$123,382	$169,949	$134,904	$243,322	$49,056	$155,775	$498,165	$1,314,737	$57,237	$107,300	$490,418	$2,364,578	$385,707	$289,140	73
$94,798	$29,468	$64,856	$13,025	$55,905	$14,907	$50,700	$143,630	$278,125	$7,465	$24,185	$90,955	$359,096	$98,991	$59,080	74
$10,403	$3,745	$8,899	$1,732	$7,739	$2,137	$9,483	$18,792	$31,524	$1,819	$4,462	$23,528	$58,359	$10,540	$11,040	75
213	26	273	16	219	38	100	661	243	72	109	282	452	503	265	76
156	37	166	40	223	19	156	440	369	16	52	42	348	178	136	77
217	108	82	29	41	30	113	231	718	39	58	455	1,337	212	136	78
4,741	960	463	1,037	1,434	117	2,158		12,987	481	83	7,533	27,548		2,273	79
2,016	488	221	643	509	49	785		6,118	151	31	4,875	19,529		787	80
5,403	2,398	2,556	944	4,427	889	2,645	4,642	13,447	844	924	3,216	14,331	3,908	2,782	81
43,152	23,725	34,697	23,345	35,845	9,238	17,863	66,317	160,147	8,922	12,657	43,739	202,813	52,620	36,493	82

TABLE 73.—STATISTICS OF SIZE OF FARMS AND FOR TENURE CLASSES OF FARMS

NORTH CAROLINA—continued.

		Rutherford.	Sampson.	Scotland.	Stanly.	Stokes.	Surry.	Tyrrell.	Union.	Vance.	Wake.
1	Number of farms	511	1,234	831	234	354	264	145	1,251	994	2,157
	FARMS CLASSIFIED BY SIZE.										
2	Under 3 acres	26	95	3	14	21	47	20	106	89	131
3	3 to 9 acres	110	253	31	47	38	81	40	225	210	343
4	10 to 19 acres	184	551	563	98	129	85	60	502	346	922
5	20 to 49 acres	126	186	192	46	95	36	15	291	179	432
6	50 to 99 acres	50	100	29	22	62	11	7	102	113	255
7	100 to 174 acres	10	17	6	6	8	2	1	14	41	53
8	175 to 259 acres	4	23	7	1		1	2	11	15	21
9	260 to 499 acres	1	8			1				1	
10	500 to 999 acres		1				1				
11	1,000 acres and over										
	FARMERS CLASSIFIED BY TENURE.										
12	Owners, free	87	304	49	57	41	88	24	80	128	307
13	Owners, mortgaged	24	84	15	11	22	26	20	44	58	127
14	Part owners	83	219	3	25	33	38	26	25	120	143
15	Cash tenants	22	50	83	11	5		3	443	180	634
16	Share tenants	292	517	654	112	250	110	68	647	502	887
17	Share-cash tenants	1	21	11			1	1	4	5	28
18	Tenure not specified	2	35	16	18	3	1	3	6	1	27
19	Managers		4						2		4
	FARMS OPERATED BY OWNERS, FREE.										
20	Total acreage	5,318	16,744	3,153	2,886	2,795	2,782	1,317	5,326	7,182	16,220
21	Improved acreage	1,802	5,465	1,687	1,252	1,186	1,377	417	2,398	3,603	7,583
22	Value of land	$69,920	$198,796	$70,290	$29,050	$28,355	$32,725	$10,635	$67,745	$92,223	$252,033
23	Value of buildings	$21,535	$72,015	$14,760	$10,725	$11,935	$12,085	$2,915	$22,825	$39,030	$96,782
24	Value of implements and machinery	$4,323	$11,755	$4,620	$1,752	$2,161	$1,537	$367	$3,540	$5,542	$15,890
25	Number of dairy cows	101	195	43	49	46	78	24	95	142	329
26	Number of work horses	25	122	25	17	11	21	7	26	113	141
27	Number of work mules	72	107	64	43	40	19	2	102	15	193
28	Acreage in cotton	335	740	893	209			35	831	453	2,197
29	Bales of cotton grown in 1909	125	357	537	84			10	350	156	1,088
30	Acreage in corn	775	2,719	617	332	267	412	168	619	834	2,344
31	Bushels of corn grown in 1909	8,470	28,531	6,025	3,459	3,810	4,707	946	7,939	10,101	26,966
	FARMS OPERATED BY OWNERS, MORTGAGED.										
32	Total acreage	2,145	6,731	1,435	599	1,599	1,209	1,437	3,216	4,182	7,972
33	Improved acreage	743	2,190	634	169	483	491	626	1,425	1,856	3,838
34	Value of land	$21,535	$73,518	$23,750	$6,340	$16,603	$14,850	$15,915	$45,345	$45,709	$106,105
35	Value of buildings	$12,025	$22,670	$6,040	$1,285	$4,005	$6,950	$3,500	$11,270	$18,780	$50,905
36	Value of implements and machinery	$1,490	$3,857	$1,970	$175	$1,005	$925	$696	$1,933	$2,916	$7,133
37	Number of dairy cows	35	65	13	10	26	29	29	50	74	152
38	Number of work horses	4	31	8	6	3	30	11	17	53	59
39	Number of work mules	35	54	28	5	23	2	9	40	15	106
40	Acreage in cotton	102	352	367	32			142	499	243	1,201
41	Bales of cotton grown in 1909	32	169	200	15			26	202	88	575
42	Acreage in corn	268	960	191	57	143	141	220	281	453	1,071
43	Bushels of corn grown in 1909	2,755	10,350	1,705	590	2,125	2,013	1,508	2,983	4,664	11,419
	FARMS OPERATED BY PART OWNERS.										
44	Total acreage	4,835	13,153	140	943	1,720	3,149	981	1,421	4,499	7,768
45	Owned acreage	2,469	6,760	73	391	969	893	397	718	1,685	3,969
46	Improved acreage	2,205	5,698	125	604	809	1,206	440	757	2,781	3,743
47	Owned improved acreage	909	2,118	58	215	385	320	123	372	1,010	1,745
48	Value of land	$72,959	$196,217	$4,545	$18,695	$18,580	$45,280	$14,280	$23,920	$71,622	$128,765
49	Value of buildings	$20,600	$47,012	$325	$3,665	$7,950	$6,620	$2,610	$4,210	$22,855	$47,090
50	Value of land and buildings owned	$49,339	$131,495	$2,370	$8,725	$16,790	$17,575	$8,255	$16,200	$49,676	$106,335
51	Value of implements and machinery	$3,491	$7,795	$200	$940	$1,603	$813	$1,090	$1,542	$3,298	$7,767
52	Number of dairy cows	91	131	2	23	34	34	30	28	113	142
53	Number of work horses	24	105		20	15	15	6	12	88	66
54	Number of work mules	74	104	5	13	21	20	6	20	16	107
55	Acreage in cotton	422	925	60	180			129	267	582	1,230
56	Bales of cotton grown in 1909	137	454	45	72			27	111	188	611
57	Acreage in corn	949	2,725	43	199	207	227	217	164	869	1,157
58	Bushels of corn grown in 1909	9,994	26,755	750	2,075	3,158	2,945	2,795	1,815	8,823	12,828
	FARMS OPERATED BY CASH TENANTS, INCLUDING TENURE NOT SPECIFIED.										
59	Total acreage	1,900	6,628	4,292	1,470	622	7	161	26,485	11,727	42,585
60	Improved acreage	622	2,493	3,584	789	285	7	86	12,862	6,147	20,259
61	Value of land	$28,755	$87,748	$185,671	$19,330	$6,325	$70	$3,775	$414,652	$147,195	$572,058
62	Value of buildings	$4,435	$13,330	$23,060	$5,235	$1,375	$30	$1,275	$104,067	$26,510	$156,685
63	Value of implements and machinery	$760	$2,057	$5,723	$554	$265		$144	$13,117	$4,474	$21,682
64	Number of dairy cows	24	34	58	25	11		10	445	159	608
65	Number of work horses	11	24	33	12	4			104	118	226
66	Number of work mules	12	39	120	19	5		1	469	20	428
67	Acreage in cotton	200	490	2,337	153				5,873	928	7,152
68	Bales of cotton grown in 1909	64	257	1,578	60				2,338	322	3,293
69	Acreage in corn	282	813	902	199	87		42	2,847	1,352	5,527
70	Bushels of corn grown in 1909	2,575	7,783	12,520	2,485	985		135	30,787	12,384	50,677
	FARMS OPERATED BY SHARE AND SHARE-CASH TENANTS.										
71	Total acreage	11,513	21,619	26,208	4,850	13,394	2,930	1,233	19,960	25,877	35,939
72	Improved acreage	6,618	12,980	24,047	2,655	6,671	1,720	1,134	13,751	14,305	21,848
73	Value of land	$225,938	$378,648	$1,549,820	$71,600	$157,148	$45,775	$33,085	$353,581	$355,463	$621,472
74	Value of buildings	$38,276	$74,830	$142,465	$15,390	$39,610	$12,690	$4,490	$84,720	$79,655	$199,369
75	Value of implements and machinery	$5,299	$9,832	$28,894	$2,210	$6,972	$866	$460	$9,476	$12,237	$21,851
76	Number of dairy cows	283	209	251	85	228	75	44	428	426	551
77	Number of work horses	36	90	126	48	49	20	17	73	276	203
78	Number of work mules	125	242	674	41	107	9	4	354	52	421
79	Acreage in cotton	1,517	3,324	15,186	774			226	5,755	1,731	8,021
80	Bales of cotton grown in 1909	556	1,624	11,961	325			68	2,475	657	4,385
81	Acreage in corn	2,552	6,398	5,025	692	1,684	542	521	3,111	3,520	5,977
82	Bushels of corn grown in 1909	29,769	68,166	80,663	8,319	24,524	7,895	6,030	36,710	38,456	73,306

OPERATED BY COLORED FARMERS, BY COUNTIES, FOR SOUTHERN STATES: 1910—Continued.

| | NORTH CAROLINA—continued. | | | | | | OKLAHOMA. | | | | | | | | |
Warren.	Washington.	Wayne.	Wilkes.	Wilson.	Yadkin.	All other counties.	The state.	Atoka.	Blaine.	Bryan.	Caddo.	Carter.	Cherokee.	Choctaw.	
1,743	256	1,389	365	1,142	153	821	20,671	327	270	466	288	506	526	638	1
3		1		72	31	124	15		6	1		11	11	6	2
126	28	92	101	168	37	161	430	17	6	11	2	23	46	38	3
374	55	152	81	595	57	265	1,171	28	21	24	9	189	118	336	4
681	115	685	97	241	22	183	6,328	103	63	146	49	162	145	116	5
348	36	311	57	54	6	68	5,436	61	133	110	54	79	101	76	6
155	17	103	23	9		13	4,904	67	20	84	152	26	55	21	7
29	3	33	4	3		6	1,096	17	18	35	10	10	35	29	8
23	1	10	2				870	17	2	23	9	4	15	11	9
4		1				1	318	13	1	23	3	2		5	10
	1	1					103	4		9					11
330	79	86	130	50	38	492	7,713	157	89	173	136	152	354	308	12
113	46	65	30	29	11	28	2,206	22	51	61	53	70	50	50	13
193	6	107	56	20	40	103	1,231	10	52	23	10	67	22	22	14
717	18	107	5	61	1	12	1,398	12	19	8	24	12	3	10	15
238	50	986	140	973	63	153	7,249	102	56	186	53	187	94	243	16
46	1	14	2	4		3	248		1	3	2	7			17
104	56	24	2	5		27	599	23	1	12	9	9	2	5	18
2						3	27	1	1		1	2	1		19
18,569	5,148	4,252	4,815	3,286	1,227	24,393	1,100,167	27,566	14,742	38,434	17,542	16,008	43,350	41,703	20
8,416	1,157	2,165	1,923	1,264	612	8,792	459,420	4,975	4,966	14,955	6,664	6,292	12,904	12,560	21
$236,553	$56,560	$92,591	$43,802	$91,485	$19,845	$216,947	$17,964,631	$253,976	$160,505	$544,485	$503,493	$212,860	$304,195	$426,688	22
$138,476	$13,600	$32,530	$17,723	$23,200	$8,710	$61,353	$3,209,644	$41,970	$25,540	$115,585	$56,817	$40,975	$109,245	$81,987	23
$29,820	$3,062	$4,324	$2,312	$2,377	$1,005	$8,952	$764,892	$12,249	$8,438	$20,965	$15,356	$10,639	$28,660	$15,887	24
381	46	41	106	13	31	603	21,191	686	146	574	108	452	922	958	25
276	36	58	21	24	20	151	25,645	612	289	658	605	462	959	850	26
48	8	45	34	40	16	80	6,272	108	58	279	42	167	239	262	27
2,226	105	681		464	1		43,364	526	383	1,542	420	1,710	1,565	2,173	28
1,049	39	328		229	1		13,468	118	86	359	85	391	464	421	29
2,685	475	889	616	501	226	3,205	148,033	1,798	1,973	3,980	2,567	2,577	4,732	3,936	30
32,974	3,483	10,145	6,664	5,275	3,205	36,893	2,385,346	22,888	15,234	62,960	36,002	34,387	61,987	58,834	31
7,883	2,489	5,024	1,616	2,113	437	1,481	289,952	3,117	7,325	10,085	6,769	8,785	6,908	3,625	32
2,964	1,181	2,704	514	975	207	598	156,867	1,239	3,581	4,330	3,129	3,320	2,546	1,758	33
$107,037	$43,657	$121,736	$15,323	$53,550	$4,935	$21,755	$5,634,485	$50,915	$110,570	$160,664	$148,580	$127,870	$94,610	$39,650	34
$44,815	$6,558	$30,280	$5,147	$13,650	$1,965	$5,315	$1,020,704	$5,050	$11,480	$38,785	$14,520	$21,965	$18,900	$9,295	35
$11,503	$2,421	$5,356	$605	$1,625	$178	$631	$244,304	$1,507	$4,421	$6,630	$5,700	$5,083	$5,844	$4,104	36
153	44	41	25	11	10	35	5,699	48	107	216	110	206	162	117	37
111	34	52	13	14	6	14	6,641	62	150	191	153	245	145	99	38
14	14	60	5	33	5	4	2,205	17	39	59	65	64	44	29	39
1,068	152	868		348			24,739	83	424	580	658	786	378	470	40
473	42	465		165			6,782	14	86	138	131	165	89	71	41
1,005	380	915	172	303	74	143	53,367	365	1,192	1,602	1,417	1,078	765	624	42
11,960	2,835	11,110	1,790	3,415	981	1,848	846,467	3,780	6,859	22,135	14,168	12,496	10,710	7,265	43
11,956	188	6,099	2,288	1,254	1,055	3,741	209,536	3,351	10,332	3,720	2,322	6,201	4,141	2,627	44
6,760	50	3,213	1,336	768	436	2,403	106,684	410	6,571	1,862	1,050	3,851	1,872	1,496	45
5,529	135	3,751	1,227	580	807	2,129	118,307	512	5,491	2,335	1,212	3,551	1,633	1,228	46
2,591	45	1,523	511	299	291	1,031	59,866	160	2,834	1,467	420	1,860	538	453	47
$139,250	$5,070	$173,635	$42,541	$28,360	$23,825	$61,681	$3,924,485	$26,425	$147,263	$47,942	$58,900	$89,984	$47,200	$35,825	48
$66,265	$1,000	$49,125	$8,207	$8,080	$5,825	$15,508	$571,399	$4,310	$16,877	$9,255	$7,750	$10,115	$16,140	$4,960	49
$137,576	$1,000	$124,350	$22,565	$25,430	$13,920	$43,394	$2,417,076	$5,420	$102,705	$25,644	$16,090	$63,150	$23,540	$20,230	50
$13,807	$80	$5,124	$1,228	$1,242	$690	$2,309	$151,003	$1,656	$5,762	$3,337	$1,490	$4,122	$1,950	$2,283	51
202	3	52	52	9	33	122	3,550	17	134	49	27	194	61	53	52
191	3	89	22	10	14	38	4,535	35	176	51	38	190	63	43	53
31	2	63	17	17	15	23	1,526	9	33	37	24	78	14	28	54
1,922	10	1,118		193			13,868	31	835	246	163	1,194	157	205	55
808	3	501		92			4,190	5	169	51	27	286	37	43	56
2,068	29	1,384	527	166	281	789	37,132	158	1,897	468	534	1,174	601	384	57
18,949	205	15,580	8,298	2,240	3,744	10,729	589,732	1,950	8,721	5,970	11,415	17,005	6,855	5,590	58
33,884	2,569	7,353	51	3,225	13	1,031	203,293	2,800	3,675	1,092	4,453	1,406	166	585	59
17,842	2,029	4,061	49	1,748	5	535	102,533	1,446	1,824	873	2,542	868	146	510	60
$406,422	$53,790	$199,268	$3,250	$80,110	$150	$13,030	$3,123,160	$35,560	$44,260	$21,160	$118,735	$19,780	$2,085	$7,067	61
$126,723	$17,500	$31,508	$200	$16,450	$50	$3,080	$338,403	$6,315	$5,390	$2,865	$9,665	$1,830	$500	$940	62
$34,607	$665	$4,663	$8	$2,923	$5	$325	$119,324	$2,991	$2,311	$886	$3,200	$1,230	$125	$446	63
625	40	37		12		21	2,836	58	36	19	28	24	5	25	64
463	32	57		35		8	3,846	64	53	39	111	27	10	25	65
68	12	111	1	48		1	1,942	33	22	20	15	22	1	12	66
6,257	279	1,599		606			29,795	256	504	97	319	382	23	196	67
2,552	113	749		308			10,276	72	91	16	60	82	7	49	68
6,320	574	1,396	20	560		296	29,417	696	932	387	1,021	284	25	190	69
63,418	3,977	15,205	210	5,760		3,885	505,606	12,665	6,831	4,390	13,695	4,610	400	2,720	70
10,232	1,562	46,842	3,755	35,815	1,879	6,894	467,468	4,391	5,838	12,563	5,061	9,791	4,977	10,895	71
6,680	1,351	30,414	2,026	27,000	1,188	3,663	334,208	3,082	3,433	10,005	3,223	8,341	2,238	7,710	72
$116,483	$45,600	$1,548,662	$79,079	$1,115,955	$36,648	$145,355	$10,207,267	$56,885	$86,925	$242,815	$111,565	$151,608	$55,260	$127,750	73
$46,935	$12,480	$234,082	$8,645	$244,045	$7,252	$17,685	$1,091,153	$10,290	$8,930	$30,255	$8,910	$18,060	$11,195	$19,457	74
$10,169	$915	$31,267	$1,190	$29,208	$1,594	$2,394	$355,074	$3,837	$2,856	$9,743	$3,110	$7,497	$4,249	$8,977	75
263	14	265	53	84	57	161	7,566	139	78	239	39	236	112	313	76
149	7	377	13	159	14	37	11,181	165	108	270	111	263	180	354	77
32	15	638	14	805	20	24	5,887	79	23	222	42	200	50	144	78
2,624	287	11,795		12,245			105,294	549	473	2,869	916	3,045	452	2,279	79
1,137	116	6,356		6,366			35,953	111	87	623	171	756	130	480	80
2,440	623	11,049	1,008	8,166	489	1,013	101,283	1,073	1,068	3,955	901	3,025	1,088	3,352	81
27,455	9,172	127,982	14,355	97,180	7,345	14,067	1,615,437	16,705	6,490	59,812	11,491	48,865	12,627	51,806	82

NEGRO POPULATION.

TABLE **73.**—STATISTICS OF SIZE OF FARMS AND FOR TENURE CLASSES OF FARMS

		OKLAHOMA—continued.									
		Craig.	Creek.	Garvin.	Hughes.	Johnston.	Kingfisher.	Le Flore.	Lincoln.	Logan.	Love.
1	Number of farms..................	383	381	354	397	178	364	346	636	815	206
	FARMS CLASSIFIED BY SIZE.										
2	Under 3 acres....................			1	4		1	23	9	18	1
3	3 to 9 acres.....................		1	7	15	7	4	65	21	40	5
4	10 to 19 acres...................	9	17	18	32	10	44	139	142	168	76
5	20 to 49 acres...................	35	144	135	131	65	119	55	213	220	70
6	50 to 99 acres...................	110	102	111	98	33	168	30	220	328	31
7	100 to 174 acres.................	110	104	44	91	32	17	17	21	27	8
8	175 to 259 acres.................	60	6	23	13	9	17	11	10	13	9
9	260 to 499 acres.................	45	3	7	9	6	10	11	10	13	4
10	500 to 999 acres.................	13	3	5	2	10	1	5		1	2
11	1,000 acres and over.............	1	1	3	2	6		1			
	FARMERS CLASSIFIED BY TENURE.										
12	Owners, free.....................	200	81	143	155	86	105	148	84	150	41
13	Owners, mortgaged...............	51	19	44	24	31	111	23	106	162	31
14	Part owners.....................	56	6	23	14	12	33	14	42	51	32
15	Cash tenants....................	9	44	6	29	5	7	43	71	59	2
16	Share tenants...................	64	202	134	159	43	69	110	270	313	78
17	Share-cash tenants..............	2	2	2	15	1	1	5	8	53	1
18	Tenure not specified............	1	27	2	1		38	3	52	24	21
19	Managers........................								3	3	
	FARMS OPERATED BY OWNERS, FREE.										
20	Total acreage....................	33,344	12,962	24,797	15,033	18,928	12,228	14,942	7,830	14,933	5,136
21	Improved acreage................	23,358	5,337	10,661	5,700	6,810	6,421	5,143	3,415	7,733	2,518
22	Value of land....................	$599,582	$213,920	$402,310	$119,829	$233,758	$246,480	$167,453	$144,865	$260,826	$75,765
23	Value of buildings...............	$90,455	$34,730	$96,805	$51,090	$35,240	$35,760	$56,957	$32,600	$67,327	$21,830
24	Value of implements and machinery.	$24,943	$9,105	$15,778	$14,214	$6,204	$8,242	$9,963	$7,033	$17,117	$4,094
25	Number of dairy cows.............	614	189	281	304	229	183	429	134	309	90
26	Number of work horses...........	799	282	501	480	276	310	403	213	306	123
27	Number of work mules............	164	72	153	98	36	63	102	64	148	25
28	Acreage in cotton................	3	873	1,586	983	269	1,219	783	1,107	2,866	599
29	Bales of cotton grown in 1909.....	1	345	500	324	60	331	217	306	884	109
30	Acreage in corn..................	7,469	1,455	2,243	2,084	1,220	2,619	1,156	1,162	2,112	912
31	Bushels of corn grown in 1909.....	119,981	28,017	39,827	32,137	15,355	28,460	16,745	15,036	30,618	11,852
	FARMS OPERATED BY OWNERS, MORTGAGED.										
32	Total acreage....................	7,417	1,348	4,536	3,911	5,896	13,324	2,473	11,906	20,462	5,199
33	Improved acreage................	5,156	700	2,978	1,193	2,327	7,447	1,034	6,140	11,891	2,693
34	Value of land....................	$126,680	$23,505	$106,165	$60,090	$84,941	$261,000	$25,575	$200,485	$337,715	$79,030
35	Value of buildings...............	$19,500	$7,045	$18,285	$20,820	$16,525	$41,750	$4,125	$39,270	$74,280	$27,365
36	Value of implements and machinery.	$5,515	$1,760	$9,150	$3,612	$3,398	$9,883	$7,200	$9,300	$20,657	$4,148
37	Number of dairy cows.............	161	42	83	83	78	229	42	183	401	84
38	Number of work horses...........	172	70	114	84	101	345	72	231	378	69
39	Number of work mules............	52	6	45	41	12	92	13	135	221	26
40	Acreage in cotton................		314	480	252	30	1,608	165	2,871	5,132	529
41	Bales of cotton grown in 1909.....		151	146	95	13	463	47	726	1,255	94
42	Acreage in corn..................	1,637	315	1,112	544	455	2,709	159	1,531	2,777	676
43	Bushels of corn grown in 1909.....	25,755	7,525	17,010	14,040	7,265	37,162	2,105	15,326	48,592	10,688
	FARMS OPERATED BY PART OWNERS.										
44	Total acreage....................	12,248	827	1,916	3,371	3,924	6,149	2,400	6,166	5,284	4,392
45	Owned acreage................	6,960	262	908	1,583	1,292	3,609	1,112	2,614	2,793	2,642
46	Improved acreage................	8,220	406	1,394	539	577	3,579	1,811	3,095	4,009	2,200
47	Owned improved acreage.......	4,602	91	638	333	317	2,048	741	1,423	2,081	1,210
48	Value of land....................	$224,710	$6,385	$45,487	$45,229	$29,847	$128,500	$51,117	$94,855	$121,935	$74,680
49	Value of buildings...............	$35,770	$1,095	$7,788	$7,325	$8,725	$16,000	$12,460	$14,515	$23,760	$5,295
50	Value of land and buildings owned.	$153,345	$3,130	$31,175	$29,130	$17,060	$90,700	$29,955	$50,815	$80,665	$45,485
51	Value of implements and machinery.	$9,443	$440	$2,247	$1,455	$1,665	$4,635	$1,923	$3,850	$4,845	$1,655
52	Number of dairy cows.............	256	9	50	72	23	83	34	86	111	72
53	Number of work horses...........	234	10	70	69	119	126	38	94	104	108
54	Number of work mules............	60	9	39	28	19	24	9	48	52	21
55	Acreage in cotton................		90	386	134	45	525	77	1,401	1,065	623
56	Bales of cotton grown in 1909.....		39	121	81	10	177	20	352	238	125
57	Acreage in corn..................	2,445	93	748	154	274	1,093	58	574	1,127	546
58	Bushels of corn grown in 1909.....	43,935	1,980	11,025	1,750	4,208	14,275	964	6,148	16,731	8,030
	FARMS OPERATED BY CASH TENANTS, INCLUDING TENURE NOT SPECIFIED.										
59	Total acreage....................	1,050	6,847	3,837	2,588	266	4,986	1,777	11,601	9,020	1,276
60	Improved acreage................	568	3,183	3,735	949	227	2,607	1,476	5,921	5,508	1,038
61	Value of land....................	$15,315	$78,334	$30,175	$35,147	$4,140	$97,625	$34,385	$201,005	$163,435	$18,500
62	Value of buildings...............	$3,335	$8,221	$700	$3,470	$210	$10,875	$4,606	$24,175	$26,740	$4,400
63	Value of implements and machinery.	$835	$4,639	$345	$1,780	$267	$2,680	$2,088	$3,238	$6,818	$810
64	Number of dairy cows.............	9	95	11	53	20	51	67	112	105	28
65	Number of work horses...........	31	148	13	70	15	132	83	140	166	32
66	Number of work mules............	12	62	3	19	3	20	39	63	74	20
67	Acreage in cotton................		1,326	127	282	25	529	473	2,130	1,819	315
68	Bales of cotton grown in 1909.....		592	32	123	4	175	157	593	494	56
69	Acreage in corn..................	192	767	85	355	45	900	388	923	1,314	338
70	Bushels of corn grown in 1909.....	3,400	13,710	1,325	6,790	655	13,323	7,340	9,650	19,884	4,055
	FARMS OPERATED BY SHARE AND SHARE-CASH TENANTS.										
71	Total acreage....................	6,706	12,949	8,107	10,195	2,066	7,175	3,025	23,716	33,642	5,024
72	Improved acreage................	5,409	8,228	6,522	7,060	1,313	3,992	2,905	13,744	22,184	3,940
73	Value of land....................	$105,925	$186,651	$143,269	$156,755	$23,212	$139,195	$91,093	$422,135	$696,226	$63,249
74	Value of buildings...............	$11,980	$18,980	$18,721	$17,395	$3,035	$16,200	$10,872	$62,050	$89,590	$8,485
75	Value of implements and machinery.	$4,679	$7,794	$7,699	$28,019	$1,344	$4,492	$3,218	$10,790	$19,872	$3,010
76	Number of dairy cows.............	69	157	148	169	61	59	100	240	326	172
77	Number of work horses...........	188	355	216	209	65	173	124	384	542	150
78	Number of work mules............	27	122	113	161	32	18	90	170	188	58
79	Acreage in cotton................		3,649	2,294	2,759	208	956	1,088	5,881	7,262	1,416
80	Bales of cotton grown in 1909.....		1,378	685	1,127	46	230	418	1,518	1,987	288
81	Acreage in corn..................	2,505	2,293	2,268	2,140	576	1,295	977	3145	5,197	1,654
82	Bushels of corn grown in 1909.....	39,251	48,198	33,201	37,002	6,067	11,021	19,056	40,446	74,722	21,050

OPERATED BY COLORED FARMERS, BY COUNTIES, FOR SOUTHERN STATES: 1910—Continued.

OKLAHOMA—continued.

	McCurtain	McIntosh	Mayes	Muskogee	Nowata	Okfuskee	Oklahoma	Okmulgee	Payne	Pittsburg	Pontotoc	Pottawatomie	Seminole	Sequoyah	Tulsa	
	801	896	411	1,206	436	1,031	421	833	174	280	185	301	803	717	239	1
		3	1	1		6	5	15		1	4	6	2	21	5	2
	43	20	8	34	3	52	10	41		17	5	8	12	92	10	3
	84	42	21	84	11	414	73	326	6	33	71	100	44	321	71	4
	341	357	63	431	66	309	100	251	64	81	32	123	327	165	65	5
	140	251	142	377	149	224	197	160	74	42	36	51	221	62	57	6
	122	173	100	190	96	15	28	23	27	32	25	9	165	27	13	7
	25	31	33	30	49	10	8	10	3	25	6	3	21	23	15	8
	29	16	33	40	54	1		6		24	4	1	6	6	3	9
	10	3	10	12	7			1		15	2		4			10
	7			7	1					10			1			11
	392	261	260	388	208	132	56	164	26	131	84	99	289	281	91	12
	58	50	48	115	65	41	72	32	6	37	28	35	33	66	29	13
	26	30	32	86	60	10	33	24		8	19	23	11	50	14	14
	24	38	6	59	6	225	75	107	18	21	8	22	138	45	20	15
	207	484	58	518	88	556	167	463	124	79	40	116	296	249	76	16
	4	8	1	12	3	10	2	22				2	13	9	3	17
	90	25	6	21	6	57	14	20		4	6	4	23	17	6	18
				7			2	1								19
	51,017	25,319	36,063	46,548	31,473	14,735	6,811	19,099	2,633	34,616	15,919	8,388	27,699	26,814	12,329	20
	10,619	12,322	15,820	29,036	22,149	6,589	3,052	7,871	1,332	9,140	6,473	3,618	9,740	12,217	7,001	21
	$482,796	$367,612	$633,315	$1,547,592	$739,054	$195,965	$190,415	$436,230	$73,550	$339,570	$201,350	$249,020	$308,465	$359,214	$500,514	22
	$73,490	$92,830	$94,450	$247,326	$118,035	$44,125	$24,995	$70,378	$14,380	$55,805	$37,220	$43,930	$63,620	$100,740	$61,645	23
	$19,562	$22,429	$20,730	$55,563	$24,729	$12,208	$5,895	$20,156	$2,598	$11,839	$7,152	$10,793	$16,907	$19,833	$15,352	24
	1,371	751	805	2,328	629	259	120	410	52	390	210	93	668	787	261	25
	1,002	856	918	1,567	896	405	142	521	93	443	246	257	962	684	424	26
	273	249	172	582	174	121	70	173	9	100	54	77	152	252	61	27
	1,501	3,164	290	2,867		2,115	1,118	715	427	510	777	836	1,897	2,923	140	28
	330	1,106	86	1,009		963	326	297	232	131	215	308	675	933	54	29
	4,939	4,576	6,258	9,328	7,537	1,735	746	3,038	524	1,410	1,259	1,828	2,503	3,336	2,425	30
	80,302	80,170	93,190	150,954	120,823	38,729	8,375	52,940	11,720	22,462	19,410	35,425	43,515	68,171	54,085	31
	4,837	5,226	6,136	11,802	10,867	4,502	9,426	4,225	832	8,566	2,539	3,547	2,940	5,703	3,377	32
	1,756	2,918	3,622	7,029	8,874	2,499	4,304	2,266	414	2,320	1,375	1,934	1,601	3,130	2,233	33
	$74,133	$79,032	$131,827	$350,315	$201,965	$79,175	$179,083	$125,645	$15,425	$111,835	$40,315	$73,134	$45,685	$90,685	$94,808	34
	$11,402	$26,105	$23,075	$65,510	$27,345	$13,925	$22,092	$19,250	$3,775	$21,855	$8,045	$19,001	$8,440	$30,170	$20,137	35
	$2,288	$4,870	$5,380	$10,425	$6,164	$3,282	$5,261	$6,455	$775	$598	$1,385	$3,683	$3,084	$4,387	$3,580	36
	145	132	146	284	222	121	138	82	10	171	50	59	57	184	107	37
	126	156	162	409	257	94	169	133	13	132	57	81	112	119	121	38
	28	43	58	129	45	71	59	41	11	63	12	52	14	72	21	39
	273	600	24	709		790	1,562	346	293	195	217	774	457	643	9	40
	41	181	7	243		281	405	112	87	51	65	282	141	182	5	41
	707	1,218	1,807	2,556	3,799	632	1,010	898	75	752	355	615	474	973	964	42
	11,305	19,318	30,330	41,556	56,816	11,820	12,450	16,320	1,360	9,351	5,580	12,905	9,145	20,670	21,965	43
	2,671	3,300	3,827	9,608	8,668	1,040	5,631	3,062		2,664	2,267	2,745	953	4,528	2,958	44
	1,353	1,746	1,981	3,969	4,480	540	3,370	1,381		1,959	1,087	1,595	620	2,431	1,837	45
	1,324	2,134	2,956	6,896	7,016	620	3,082	2,197		1,954	1,602	1,527	708	2,786	1,399	46
	689	857	1,349	2,070	3,698	310	1,702	932		1,331	722	823	1,247		908	47
	$34,745	$48,567	$81,579	$341,888	$164,035	$15,675	$110,890	$84,870		$12,025	$31,730	$49,205	$15,375	$97,885	$69,280	48
	$8,875	$10,803	$12,326	$54,475	$21,945	$3,025	$16,785	$11,750		$6,210	$9,925	$5,625	$4,350	$21,265	$13,850	49
	$27,040	$27,624	$49,880	$180,735	$97,750	$9,550	$83,146	$47,580		$13,995	$19,890	$32,710	$12,950	$62,040	$51,395	50
	$2,080	$3,125	$4,120	$11,451	$4,334	$765	$3,422	$2,914		$1,380	$1,175	$1,717	$845	$8,252	$2,230	51
	151	78	119	178	160	27	83	59		34	30	40	33	89	72	52
	75	76	103	311	339	17	95	68		30	53	44	33	108	99	53
	47	32	32	83	71	20	41	28		8	7	46	21	112	13	54
	216	478	36	680		167	1,256	173		40	132	640	264	769		55
	51	142	13	241		58	282	80		6	39	212	115	289		56
	691	783	1,061	2,399	1,950	105	695	625	418	118	410	424	119	955	614	57
	15,155	11,727	16,200	40,820	29,615	2,470	11,487	7,905	8,910	1,800	6,555	7,425	2,250	24,995	10,500	58
	5,001	4,576	706	4,674	733	24,799	10,014	11,067	1,550	1,093	915	2,061	11,585	2,602	2,523	59
	3,643	2,963	447	3,367	653	14,435	6,561	6,785	1,040	827	680	1,103	7,253	2,131	1,612	60
	$110,736	$73,050	$14,485	$179,195	$16,190	$305,015	$174,356	$286,670	$39,020	$8,105	$11,996	$42,035	$128,623	$61,990	$85,835	61
	$13,235	$11,170	$2,865	$23,385	$1,195	$33,825	$28,815	$19,990	$4,200	$2,550	$734	$3,315	$16,317	$6,200	$3,245	62
	$2,668	$3,410	$1,037	$4,174	$595	$18,070	$4,806	$10,493	$1,345	$1,410	$275	$1,270	$8,569	$3,512	$1,882	63
	227	81	24	134	18	385	97	177	16	51	16	20	329	93	38	64
	208	146	29	146	35	501	162	235	39	40	20	44	315	87	67	65
	76	38	17	81	2	382	64	176	12	10	10	25	175	77	20	66
	725	1,162	25	403		5,418	2,591	2,181	418	162	214	515	2,913	779	99	67
	177	460	6	141		2,112	579	769	144	50	56	178	1,119	358	49	68
	1,207	1,135	224	1,461	224	2,904	1,011	1,912	5	255	226	330	2,066	735	851	69
	22,763	23,595	3,850	17,265	2,900	59,803	16,924	34,334	200	4,459	3,005	5,585	34,635	19,724	19,805	70
	7,894	31,332	3,185	29,667	9,129	31,971	16,292	29,783	6,967	4,083	1,801	6,542	16,599	8,610	4,856	71
	5,468	22,223	2,152	24,585	6,938	23,676	8,756	20,395	5,877	3,317	1,279	4,782	11,196	7,551	3,574	72
	$108,402	$506,654	$54,952	$1,285,068	$176,732	$458,388	$835,920	$786,475	$219,795	$67,740	$28,885	$140,895	$193,707	$196,201	$144,410	73
	$20,845	$82,404	$11,733	$120,947	$13,380	$45,435	$41,165	$59,405	$20,325	$8,920	$3,235	$14,415	$27,108	$24,335	$10,410	74
	$5,163	$19,406	$4,195	$25,649	$4,583	$23,333	$7,035	$29,850	$5,447	$2,723	$1,630	$4,076	$11,107	$6,292	$4,712	75
	308	560	87	591	130	508	140	428	68	62	39	58	331	252	91	76
	270	784	144	849	318	713	264	607	121	108	66	98	433	308	188	77
	92	372	30	443	79	538	118	559	53	49	26	96	217	198	62	78
	1,016	8,588	62	6,244		9,851	3,586	6,342	3,042	817	494	2,166	4,678	3,345	518	79
	241	3,018	14	2,047		4,036	1,002	2,699	1,206	237	117	799	1,776	1,194	236	80
	2,247	7,949	1,506	11,469	2,577	5,425	2,060	6,705	2,010	987	438	1,039	3,317	2,351	2,027	81
	46,370	133,741	14,995	160,157	39,017	112,916	29,316	113,958	46,362	18,280	6,517	20,090	50,071	44,625	42,635	82

TABLE **73.**—STATISTICS OF SIZE OF FARMS AND FOR TENURE CLASSES OF FARMS

#		OKLAHOMA—contd.		SOUTH CAROLINA.								
		Wagoner.	All other counties.	The state.	Abbeville.	Aiken.	Anderson.	Bamberg.	Barnwell.	Beaufort.	Berkeley.
1	Number of farms	1,286	3,551	96,798	3,686	2,357	3,646	1,520	2,676	4,197	2,764
	FARMS CLASSIFIED BY SIZE.										
2	Under 3 acres	1	....	157	....	1	4	....	....		1
3	3 to 9 acres	21	58	11,592	125	139	136	30	162	1,010	580
4	10 to 19 acres	90	137	17,537	338	169	597	50	113	2,043	865
5	20 to 49 acres	591	586	45,848	1,681	1,280	1,908	892	1,550	968	948
6	50 to 99 acres	329	824	14,037	1,045	408	754	363	557	126	252
7	100 to 174 acres	178	1,184	5,398	404	225	216	124	196	26	78
8	175 to 259 acres	38	315	1,318	67	69	28	36	56	4	18
9	260 to 499 acres	25	304	693	23	50	3	20	28	5	10
10	500 to 999 acres	10	111	164	3	14	....	5	11	7	9
11	1,000 acres and over	3	32	54	....	2	....	....	3	8	3
	FARMERS CLASSIFIED BY TENURE.										
12	Owners, free	222	2,067	12,805	131	236	119	124	142	2,494	1,447
13	Owners, mortgaged	85	447	3,272	86	168	128	50	89	41	50
14	Part owners	41	275	4,295	84	167	49	41	53	446	291
15	Cash tenants	125	98	36,658	1,595	818	696	271	1,003	1,016	754
16	Share tenants	752	613	34,169	1,718	785	2,481	918	884	6	129
17	Share-cash tenants	47	11	1,496	13	40	7	15	114	5	16
18	Tenure not specified	13	57	3,972	59	142	165	99	384	172	75
19	Managers	1	4	131	....	1	1	2	7	17	2
	FARMS OPERATED BY OWNERS, FREE.										
20	Total acreage	25,919	357,940	607,767	8,788	22,690	7,870	12,113	16,674	46,188	55,392
21	Improved acreage	16,628	134,485	286,275	4,466	9,564	3,806	5,825	8,991	34,435	27,437
22	Value of land	$568,400	$5,900,577	$9,102,777	$153,695	$211,766	$221,705	$131,729	$165,424	$528,146	$678,207
23	Value of buildings	$109,905	$961,857	$2,698,142	$48,122	$68,020	$59,915	$29,175	$50,860	$306,382	$272,404
24	Value of implements and machinery	$23,140	$247,119	$635,774	$10,427	$19,316	$11,261	$9,895	$10,010	$64,554	$86,138
25	Number of dairy cows	581	4,846	13,211	191	221	174	74	171	2,644	2,205
26	Number of work horses	734	7,367	6,135	76	102	60	64	110	1,267	678
27	Number of work mules	201	1,533	5,659	144	218	112	124	143	120	426
28	Acreage in cotton	1,802	3,675	111,040	2,244	3,324	2,138	2,438	3,100	9,132	11,191
29	Bales of cotton grown in 1909	936	863	51,549	858	1,491	940	1,060	1,308	3,263	6,515
30	Acreage in corn	6,097	46,499	83,749	884	3,363	875	1,611	2,757	10,142	8,469
31	Bushels of corn grown in 1909	102,555	772,135	1,063,687	8,660	28,152	10,701	15,965	23,865	138,383	153,634
	FARMS OPERATED BY OWNERS, MORTGAGED.										
32	Total acreage	10,534	71,807	271,588	6,796	20,473	8,970	4,908	10,491	1,505	2,547
33	Improved acreage	7,404	41,726	123,158	3,407	8,946	4,848	2,592	6,116	732	1,014
34	Value of land	$279,435	$1,623,943	$4,377,557	$95,977	$225,920	$246,170	$57,935	$124,495	$19,203	$40,415
35	Value of buildings	$41,545	$270,072	$975,145	$30,165	$53,310	$61,525	$14,750	$34,450	$10,130	$11,230
36	Value of implements and machinery	$8,646	$61,529	$245,422	$6,554	$13,936	$12,585	$4,111	$8,509	$2,533	$2,228
37	Number of dairy cows	233	1,206	3,659	142	167	208	37	88	51	64
38	Number of work horses	256	1,908	1,556	60	80	54	25	42	30	16
39	Number of work mules	80	463	3,265	90	205	171	65	104	7	26
40	Acreage in cotton	699	2,388	55,378	1,995	3,104	2,791	1,227	2,443	173	478
41	Bales of cotton grown in 1909	368	654	22,855	676	1,345	1,077	524	1,004	67	259
42	Acreage in corn	2,506	15,068	30,930	621	2,702	1,052	803	1,791	177	320
43	Bushels of corn grown in 1909	36,850	265,645	317,304	5,095	20,723	10,918	7,232	14,605	2,302	4,150
	FARMS OPERATED BY PART OWNERS.										
44	Total acreage	5,113	71,130	218,689	6,673	13,903	3,299	4,456	5,010	8,304	7,658
45	Owned acreage	2,015	35,433	[1] 122,842	3,544	7,969	1,894	1,517	2,356	3,865	4,248
46	Improved acreage	3,909	36,405	129,914	3,556	8,340	2,014	2,029	3,515	6,833	5,088
47	Owned improved acreage	1,583	19,962	[1] 59,020	1,542	3,795	1,044	839	1,304	3,029	2,094
48	Value of land	$111,815	$1,378,637	$4,062,509	$102,259	$170,892	$107,310	$63,820	$117,375	$95,248	$93,630
49	Value of buildings	$18,975	$149,075	$896,161	$22,415	$45,165	$20,065	$12,485	$18,515	$67,180	$32,345
50	Value of land and buildings owned	$57,110	$855,442	[1] $2,866,073	$70,595	$124,209	$73,655	$32,325	$60,285	$106,905	$77,821
51	Value of implements and machinery	$3,588	$46,847	$218,952	$5,359	$11,947	$4,429	$1,955	$4,186	$14,024	$7,468
52	Number of dairy cows	81	955	4,073	126	151	69	39	58	436	239
53	Number of work horses	119	1,347	2,062	41	60	24	29	30	221	105
54	Number of work mules	56	377	3,242	92	216	61	41	81	76	123
55	Acreage in cotton	535	1,305	59,771	1,813	3,015	930	945	1,789	2,190	2,472
56	Bales of cotton grown in 1909	514	361	26,674	610	1,316	378	390	882	861	1,203
57	Acreage in corn	1,311	12,126	35,746	566	2,457	356	546	1,097	2,057	1,669
58	Bushels of corn grown in 1909	19,630	205,736	401,425	5,497	19,360	4,033	5,203	11,324	25,090	19,704
	FARMS OPERATED BY CASH TENANTS, INCLUDING TENURE NOT SPECIFIED.										
59	Total acreage	9,793	52,176	1,595,244	108,590	50,152	45,737	24,014	69,987	18,416	13,134
60	Improved acreage	7,748	8,722	1,073,124	56,239	36,286	29,534	15,324	56,743	14,162	11,001
61	Value of land	$276,826	$382,329	$30,946,365	$1,560,571	$669,373	$1,576,538	$382,457	$948,458	$163,420	$187,827
62	Value of buildings	$20,640	$32,065	$5,358,123	$253,247	$160,290	$189,720	$66,185	$194,993	$79,404	$88,882
63	Value of implements and machinery	$9,031	$12,088	$1,394,511	$68,299	$38,320	$38,951	$18,400	$54,299	$21,053	$25,213
64	Number of dairy cows	179	190	29,241	1,949	684	931	237	1,023	641	407
65	Number of workhorses	217	390	12,106	471	222	232	132	424	558	180
66	Number of work mules	192	145	26,864	1,627	850	846	351	1,094	77	227
67	Acreage in cotton	2,343	1,042	568,212	33,856	15,478	17,867	7,238	25,536	5,163	5,467
68	Bales of cotton grown in 1909	1,170	292	231,593	11,107	6,540	6,173	3,168	10,427	2,110	2,486
69	Acreage in corn	2,611	3,418	275,023	10,346	11,999	6,260	4,572	17,757	5,596	3,746
70	Bushels of corn grown in 1909	49,976	61,340	2,829,720	86,922	96,423	56,850	46,067	156,248	73,779	45,941
	FARMS OPERATED BY SHARE AND SHARE-CASH TENANTS.										
71	Total acreage	42,739	49,897	1,204,734	62,620	31,558	80,402	38,574	39,134	1,349	2,731
72	Improved acreage	35,861	33,249	970,879	41,757	28,353	64,917	34,926	37,240	937	2,491
73	Value of land	$1,129,481	$1,013,044	$34,670,128	$1,070,432	$769,055	$3,139,595	$1,019,144	$810,563	$17,580	$36,440
74	Value of buildings	$104,378	$118,308	$4,931,953	$191,662	$141,345	$406,986	$154,140	$135,647	$2,790	$12,344
75	Value of implements and machinery	$30,227	$75,640	$845,150	$20,203	$22,412	$52,651	$29,635	$23,675	$226	$3,864
76	Number of dairy cows	612	639	20,531	936	378	1,679	504	492	21	113
77	Number of work horses	838	1,159	5,132	99	100	215	95	164	12	58
78	Number of work mules	729	478	22,539	758	646	1,157	917	568	....	21
79	Acreage in cotton	11,771	6,678	567,166	26,417	14,303	41,894	19,618	19,970	40	1,467
80	Bales of cotton grown in 1909	5,261	2,042	278,661	8,902	7,833	16,628	10,744	9,612	21	664
81	Acreage in corn	460	12,204	226,480	6,010	8,489	11,277	11,088	10,015	59	758
82	Bushels of corn grown in 1909	4,580	193,997	2,663,488	55,102	90,246	116,101	145,193	107,135	715	15,970

[1] Total for the state excepting figures for Georgetown County, which are not available.

OPERATED BY COLORED FARMERS, BY COUNTIES, FOR SOUTHERN STATES: 1910—Continued.

SOUTH CAROLINA—continued.

Calhoun.	Charleston.	Cherokee.	Chester.	Chesterfield.	Clarendon.	Colleton.	Darlington.	Dillon.	Dorchester	Edgefield.	Fairfield.	Florence.	Georgetown.	Greenville.	
1,904	3,072	981	2,440	1,149	3,815	2,506	2,362	1,305	1,211	3,118	2,796	2,044	519	1.941	1
	4				3			1							2
713	1,779	31	38	62	1,194	617	192	39	190	85	67	206	147	111	3
154	729	133	117	205	854	667	389	143	343	285	158	471	150	355	4
761	446	576	1,404	601	1,330	830	1,420	795	475	1,916	1,445	1,026	126	1,002	5
191	76	153	493	181	295	246	298	236	118	561	522	213	51	338	6
53	18	58	288	70	98	103	48	79	57	203	390	86	30	114	7
12	8	23	62	15	25	21	10	11	11	48	121	27	4	15	8
16	7	6	35	14	14	17	4	1	13	18	69	8	8	6	9
4	3	1	2		1	5	1		2	2	20	4	2		10
	2		1	1	1				2		4	3	1		11
64	1,138	43	84	160	288	932	118	73	400	98	182	135	365	107	12
21	72	25	98	63	104	120	34	19	52	112	105	48	11	84	13
53	110	34	71	96	130	252	85	24	181	21	62	123	18	106	14
1,328	1,340	112	1,136	244	3,038	793	897	183	386	1,718	1,266	1,185	77	344	15
390	20	751	1,031	562	82	294	1,175	940	136	962	1,037	430	47	1,257	16
26	11	7	2	9	57	55	34	11	35	7	39	27		16	17
17	378	9	18	13	111	60	18	55	20	197	98	94	1	24	18
5	3			2	5		1		1	3	7	2		3	19
6,782	22,333	2,682	8,596	12,001	13,962	36,551	4,743	3,615	17,941	9,692	18,840	7,781	15,760	5,557	20
3,427	14,637	1,386	3,826	3,857	8,316	14,368	3,025	1,878	7,072	4,309	7,571	3,370	3,520	2,829	21
$107,547	$561,867	$45,317	$113,935	$114,240	$363,912	$378,087	$172,534	$136,775	$222,835	$118,680	$175,520	$186,770	$112,775	$190,510	22
$21,490	$218,070	$11,350	$35,645	$27,065	$78,275	$124,721	$34,600	$21,795	$86,015	$36,830	$46,285	$39,960	$39,146	$34,695	23
$6,211	$43,359	$2,705	$8,570	$9,016	$18,498	$29,624	$9,119	$7,218	$15,317	$9,468	$13,346	$9,189	$9,206	$7,920	24
39	801	62	138	126	233	964	69	35	347	161	269	100	335	150	25
31	785	17	27	50	101	450	65	24	191	61	54	62	48	42	26
63	192	45	105	120	196	196	92	67	162	118	203	101	27	97	27
1,413	5,363	475	1,387	1,605	3,777	4,361	1,509	895	2,785	1,840	3,379	1,602	720	1,110	28
762	2,571	188	504	892	2,217	1,859	832	602	1,234	751	1,085	891	313	453	29
899	2,700	344	864	1,228	2,527	5,278	768	579	2,414	1,048	1,711	956	1,407	985	30
12,172	39,726	4,375	7,014	12,972	40,249	70,561	12,108	10,040	30,318	10,060	15,157	14,373	19,482	10,644	31
1,418	2,866	1,557	11,425	4,427	8,280	7,289	2,288	1,294	4,444	10,954	14,350	3,831	925	4,316	32
794	1,158	782	5,199	1,817	4,466	3,089	1,196	612	1,642	5,316	5,341	1,437	159	2,514	33
$22,910	$52,665	$31,980	$100,266	$44,135	$162,215	$71,000	$66,275	$39,500	$42,258	$130,439	$119,259	$91,158	$5,385	$129,718	34
$6,050	$14,695	$8,510	$26,280	$8,995	$29,145	$20,965	$13,740	$4,820	$12,375	$34,000	$35,085	$13,812	$1,915	$20,605	35
$1,440	$3,111	$1,792	$6,818	$3,216	$7,002	$4,800	$3,037	$1,190	$1,981	$11,719	$10,042	$3,603	$350	$4,932	36
13	44	37	167	50	97	115	25	10	54	159	171	28	6	121	37
14	42	5	39	21	37	54	19	9	24	67	28	26	2	36	38
14	13	30	129	66	107	52	31	18	32	143	143	48	2	83	39
295	412	306	2,031	821	1,891	973	567	277	565	2,491	2,643	723	43	1,259	40
147	184	113	656	419	1,020	400	299	162	230	896	769	341	18	418	41
227	192	380	1,032	484	1,209	878	238	179	402	1,047	1,191	427	59	656	42
2,131	3,081	2,050	6,621	4,613	15,694	11,592	3,761	2,253	4,612	9,525	9,326	5,424	625	5,783	43
4,768	2,458	2,314	2,902	5,674	7,429	8,371	3,767	940	6,240	2,002	8,690	6,043	525	5,925	44
2,481	1,290	1,622	1,181	3,238	3,313	5,520	1,763	470	4,015	985	4,018	3,817	(2)	3,779	45
2,894	1,334	1,233	2,192	2,734	4,342	4,911	2,825	678	3,619	1,103	3,363	3,363	194	3,674	46
1,375	633	701	742	1,223	1,954	2,229	1,062	257	1,581	518	1,629	1,583	(2)	1,929	47
$69,440	$46,624	$37,057	$56,925	$81,117	$166,027	$105,970	$153,832	$25,830	$68,380	$22,666	$103,258	$150,753	$3,975	$204,587	48
$11,565	$26,520	$11,320	$16,544	$15,040	$23,060	$33,269	$27,535	$2,450	$24,729	$6,270	$18,600	$29,985	$1,945	$31,820	49
$42,757	$50,580	$31,993	$41,515	$53,854	$101,673	$97,858	$87,009	$14,900	$65,152	$15,974	$59,036	$114,203	(2)	$146,652	50
$3,193	$4,547	$2,740	$2,672	$4,637	$6,237	$10,407	$5,197	$1,555	$5,070	$2,573	$4,948	$6,899	$637	$7,048	51
49	115	62	95	60	121	175	48	12	152	35	112	98	5	152	52
21	56	12	22	35	48	159	55	7	89	21	18	62	1	47	53
69	24	45	69	84	83	100	62	29	83	26	100	91	1	118	54
1,129	579	676	1,041	1,190	1,944	1,752	1,461	261	1,432	528	1,684	1,528	21	1,676	55
586	256	237	360	633	1,016	803	866	167	657	232	495	776	11	616	56
763	350	363	561	818	1,135	1,814	638	199	1,296	284	752	902	82	1,109	57
6,858	5,630	3,758	3,708	8,670	15,982	23,877	11,577	2,985	15,793	2,535	5,564	12,063	1,100	9,457	58
29,985	18,252	7,273	73,303	10,044	64,480	14,238	29,695	13,107	11,891	88,403	105,135	44,208	1,209	18,200	59
24,662	12,357	4,262	40,809	5,931	55,708	11,252	25,007	9,203	7,628	61,642	54,270	30,227	714	11,954	60
$553,324	$486,963	$174,560	$867,868	$150,241	$1,824,238	$198,696	$1,058,721	$696,011	$145,282	$1,241,708	$897,404	$1,118,230	$10,248	$684,090	61
$129,566	$138,841	$26,575	$199,680	$23,602	$296,242	$66,752	$164,370	$80,730	$45,710	$251,930	$172,826	$156,984	$4,180	$66,990	62
$25,736	$35,716	$7,008	$54,853	$8,126	$84,148	$16,812	$42,341	$24,885	$9,269	$87,724	$55,029	$52,297	$1,471	$16,114	63
393	729	162	1,521	171	1,496	554	420	119	212	1,928	1,583	593	42	424	64
249	914	28	188	52	662	308	421	87	177	645	193	460	15	127	65
550	302	146	1,272	207	1,156	177	589	265	186	1,727	1,405	796	5	333	66
13,591	6,282	2,141	21,086	2,955	30,437	4,766	13,740	5,663	3,218	32,915	26,546	15,150	176	6,011	67
6,584	2,966	841	7,290	1,473	14,964	1,961	6,887	4,454	1,515	11,526	7,509	7,301	77	2,076	68
7,057	2,850	1,150	9,897	1,898	15,530	4,194	6,052	1,762	2,603	13,968	10,287	7,603	292	3,009	69
72,892	63,181	13,682	71,295	17,777	208,017	56,948	86,735	35,494	32,657	123,137	70,935	90,386	3,878	25,523	70
12,716	329	29,565	39,635	17,671	3,220	11,398	34,023	32,849	5,196	26,422	44,731	12,541	804	42,272	71
11,829	224	19,731	29,243	14,798	3,074	9,242	32,935	27,977	4,243	24,104	33,322	11,806	611	31,046	72
$344,149	$10,484	$607,586	$594,604	$394,865	$91,197	$155,787	$1,392,742	$1,934,729	$85,265	$846,543	$429,040	$459,636	$12,326	$1,835,227	73
$50,852	$3,180	$106,980	$132,879	$67,855	$15,753	$43,665	$202,265	$209,350	$23,780	$131,138	$84,693	$65,504	$2,775	$181,359	74
$12,409	$648	$22,363	$17,040	$19,786	$3,880	$10,882	$49,360	$62,668	$3,165	$13,447	$16,365	$15,799	$1,142	$28,082	75
172	3	840	769	276	57	145	346	261	90	399	714	140	30	1,019	76
62	5	75	105	91	31	79	243	181	34	122	59	112	10	199	77
231	2	721	883	515	78	195	910	694	109	450	906	291	8	613	78
6,691	114	10,342	16,268	7,929	1,497	4,310	19,620	19,323	1,969	13,893	18,344	6,630	114	15,990	79
3,925	47	3,944	6,168	5,107	809	2,071	11,910	16,852	1,040	6,950	5,878	4,273	50	5,888	80
3,238	48	4,308	7,417	3,695	862	3,408	7,174	4,931	1,260	5,350	6,837	2,774	224	8,758	81
37,051	724	48,560	61,455	48,931	11,369	42,690	128,180	110,705	17,555	59,651	49,530	43,342	3,049	78,855	82

2 Data not available.

TABLE **73.**—STATISTICS OF SIZE OF FARMS AND FOR TENURE CLASSES OF FARMS

SOUTH CAROLINA—continued.

		Green-wood.	Hamp-ton.	Horry.	Kershaw.	Lancas-ter.	Laurens.	Lee.	Lexing-ton.	Marion.	Marlboro.
1	Number of farms	2,932	2,073	666	1,770	1,848	2,921	2,213	1,348	1,037	2,333
	FARMS CLASSIFIED BY SIZE.										
2	Under 3 acres			1				1			
3	3 to 9 acres	127	178	150	66	130	69	318	80	119	45
4	10 to 19 acres	296	397	178	251	262	333	258	244	240	206
5	20 to 49 acres	1,773	1,033	188	935	1,073	1,502	1,221	722	495	1,553
6	50 to 99 acres	470	294	90	300	228	598	324	168	105	421
7	100 to 174 acres	197	108	44	145	97	296	68	87	51	79
8	175 to 259 acres	46	29	7	38	35	86	14	25	11	18
9	260 to 499 acres	21	23	7	26	19	29	6	18	13	7
10	500 to 999 acres	1	5	1	7	3	8	2	2	3	3
11	1,000 acres and over	1	6		2	1		1	2		1
	FARMERS CLASSIFIED BY TENURE.										
12	Owners, free	112	664	312	286	57	54	109	126	86	89
13	Owners, mortgaged	95	56	56	81	31	66	70	55	54	33
14	Part owners	68	109	46	52	39	31	80	45	68	43
15	Cash tenants	1,230	916	25	751	704	826	1,009	348	317	501
16	Share tenants	1,295	95	211	569	908	1,837	718	689	442	1,500
17	Share-cash tenants	43	73	7	14	35	11	73	29	58	158
18	Tenure not specified	89	130	9	12	72	96	152	55	12	8
19	Managers		30		5	2		2	1		1
	FARMS OPERATED BY OWNERS, FREE.										
20	Total acreage	7,478	35,262	13,026	24,072	5,766	3,892	5,849	9,076	5,848	5,867
21	Improved acreage	3,419	16,483	4,001	8,120	1,956	1,952	3,095	3,943	2,137	2,661
22	Value of land	$137,178	$372,066	$137,061	$204,943	$83,252	$77,050	$183,400	$114,055	$95,958	$215,560
23	Value of buildings	$52,112	$173,829	$37,580	$41,011	$13,800	$20,270	$36,865	$41,185	$15,020	$41,575
24	Value of implements and machinery	$8,115	$30,073	$7,865	$14,718	$3,434	$3,820	$9,298	$8,862	$3,537	$10,954
25	Number of dairy cows	150	647	217	284	70	89	58	108	56	70
26	Number of work horses	56	402	61	115	16	16	49	49	30	65
27	Number of work mules	77	229	137	176	64	69	83	91	67	79
28	Acreage in cotton	1,716	4,957	961	3,788	863	1,005	1,684	1,158	896	1,387
29	Bales of cotton grown in 1909	663	2,319	412	1,460	374	380	814	535	534	1,044
30	Acreage in corn	760	6,329	1,281	2,432	468	411	729	1,074	672	640
31	Bushels of corn grown in 1909	8,173	83,583	16,831	23,453	5,142	4,074	9,882	10,819	7,983	11,734
	FARMS OPERATED BY OWNERS, MORTGAGED.										
32	Total acreage	8,113	3,138	3,772	10,287	3,247	6,684	5,332	4,037	4,431	2,501
33	Improved acreage	3,758	1,662	1,026	3,221	1,232	2,836	2,395	1,602	1,375	1,087
34	Value of land	$132,795	$36,275	$31,210	$89,255	$36,425	$105,415	$146,395	$56,005	$82,390	$78,030
35	Value of buildings	$62,415	$12,390	$6,910	$18,740	$6,975	$21,640	$16,805	$15,190	$8,315	$13,665
36	Value of implements and machinery	$8,382	$4,115	$1,484	$5,208	$1,668	$4,760	$6,120	$4,970	$3,249	$3,530
37	Number of dairy cows	134	86	39	94	41	107	46	49	42	29
38	Number of work horses	64	27	11	43	10	34	33	20	28	28
39	Number of work mules	81	32	48	72	42	98	71	62	37	34
40	Acreage in cotton	1,825	526	268	1,366	548	1,305	1,412	697	540	583
41	Bales of cotton grown in 1909	665	263	108	585	204	448	648	333	294	425
42	Acreage in corn	744	599	385	911	257	479	670	482	435	290
43	Bushels of corn grown in 1909	7,587	7,117	4,497	8,149	2,430	4,624	7,896	6,416	4,268	4,747
	FARMS OPERATED BY PART OWNERS.										
44	Total acreage	3,888	5,732	2,606	5,683	2,999	2,261	4,438	2,917	4,504	2,863
45	Owned acreage	1,310	3,958	1,723	3,175	2,057	1,677	2,700	1,624	2,988	1,483
46	Improved acreage	2,233	3,394	879	2,366	1,341	1,110	2,689	1,788	1,700	2,007
47	Owned improved acreage	705	1,732	391	971	694	632	1,290	764	780	772
48	Value of land	$87,855	$66,494	$26,836	$66,922	$57,411	$40,395	$105,349	$60,991	$74,172	$97,770
49	Value of buildings	$27,240	$17,250	$5,240	$15,465	$10,925	$8,740	$19,440	$10,240	$13,490	$16,075
50	Value of land and buildings owned	$46,405	$58,738	$19,632	$43,757	$39,306	$33,607	$68,389	$39,428	$48,910	$56,030
51	Value of implements and machinery	$4,253	$5,271	$1,117	$3,275	$2,915	$1,058	$4,705	$2,285	$4,146	$5,085
52	Number of dairy cows	71	113	19	61	47	42	47	31	50	39
53	Number of work horses	32	54	10	15	11	9	32	22	46	30
54	Number of work mules	50	72	34	67	47	37	73	50	32	69
55	Acreage in cotton	1,237	999	219	1,157	640	634	1,529	724	708	1,026
56	Bales of cotton grown in 1909	454	471	118	413	270	235	654	297	397	760
57	Acreage in corn	424	1,152	330	539	341	256	602	534	555	379
58	Bushels of corn grown in 1909	4,464	13,635	4,325	4,932	3,033	1,997	6,840	5,060	6,509	6,115
	FARMS OPERATED BY CASH TENANTS, INCLUDING TENURE NOT SPECIFIED.										
59	Total acreage	69,217	31,873	1,634	29,110	40,283	70,354	33,632	20,582	10,446	24,907
60	Improved acreage	43,947	27,055	422	19,936	24,579	35,353	27,558	12,382	6,891	19,094
61	Value of land	$1,331,817	$395,317	$14,480	$295,870	$566,308	$1,108,056	$1,439,828	$403,251	$227,790	$1,477,530
62	Value of buildings	$266,515	$100,105	$6,080	$73,655	$110,844	$177,775	$147,470	$52,670	$36,828	$129,290
63	Value of implements and machinery	$54,393	$32,176	$509	$22,472	$27,505	$34,067	$42,731	$14,932	$10,444	$42,509
64	Number of dairy cows	1,398	452	12	556	840	1,077	500	213	113	263
65	Number of work horses	417	392	2	139	212	200	271	108	128	360
66	Number of work mules	1,259	515	11	574	748	1,138	733	358	155	547
67	Acreage in cotton	26,939	11,779	129	11,116	12,442	21,000	17,528	5,817	3,229	13,215
68	Bales of cotton grown in 1909	9,167	5,828	56	3,863	4,746	6,837	8,334	2,531	1,894	10,269
69	Acreage in corn	8,850	10,539	148	4,915	5,348	6,853	6,262	2,564	2,051	3,854
70	Bushels of corn grown in 1909	84,922	124,571	1,950	39,476	53,617	53,915	85,574	33,179	23,250	69,569
	FARMS OPERATED BY SHARE AND SHARE-CASH TENANTS.										
71	Total acreage	37,495	8,196	3,559	21,075	24,288	73,349	25,676	23,523	13,701	57,681
72	Improved acreage	31,589	5,553	2,880	14,894	20,691	52,692	23,868	17,265	12,364	51,223
73	Value of land	$873,852	$87,489	$75,587	$170,720	$423,439	$1,508,826	$1,460,025	$463,914	$408,559	$4,139,604
74	Value of buildings	$190,815	$18,990	$13,303	$39,900	$101,747	$250,387	$107,255	$81,799	$61,130	$336,690
75	Value of implements and machinery	$16,190	$5,249	$2,131	$12,870	$13,318	$32,877	$26,634	$14,555	$14,642	$75,988
76	Number of dairy cows	659	45	52	381	502	1,174	212	282	108	511
77	Number of work horses	104	43	19	275	98	155	98	92	198	318
78	Number of work mules	689	139	52	255	539	1,408	671	380	253	1,446
79	Acreage in cotton	21,383	1,964	866	9,007	12,086	33,390	16,373	8,298	6,519	39,228
80	Bales of cotton grown in 1909	8,202	1,057	502	3,611	5,246	12,375	10,202	4,000	4,723	34,804
81	Acreage in corn	5,950	1,868	1,198	4,058	4,912	8,692	4,895	4,463	2,922	9,514
82	Bushels of corn grown in 1909	63,456	25,755	16,847	43,362	50,999	82,641	79,217	47,316	47,319	216,887

OPERATED BY COLORED FARMERS, BY COUNTIES, FOR SOUTHERN STATES: 1910—Continued.

	SOUTH CAROLINA—continued.												TENNESSEE.			
	Newberry.	Oconee.	Orangeburg.	Pickens.	Richland.	Saluda.	Spartanburg.	Sumter.	Union.	Williamsburg.	York.	All other counties.	The state.	Bedford.	Carroll.	
	2,203	833	4,144	690	1,872	1,764	2,508	3,211	1,833	3,462	3,128	.....	38,308	475	703	1
	.....	.....	.....	.....	2	.....	.....	1	.....	.....	138	.....	7	.....	.....	2
	72	42	456	49	275	51	92	579	37	642	362	.....	2,391	67	17	3
	265	147	490	161	458	234	405	580	182	875	1,747	.....	6,883	133	129	4
	1,275	361	2,232	343	903	1,032	1,348	1,521	1,102	1,311	545	.....	19,063	187	306	5
	358	168	678	106	155	304	513	381	223	398	278	.....	6,866	65	162	6
	152	91	200	18	43	107	127	105	214	162	43	.....	2,369	18	66	7
	43	13	54	8	23	26	18	26	39	53	15	.....	490	2	16	8
	31	9	25	3	10	8	5	17	27	14	.....	.....	196	3	7	9
	7	1	6	2	2	2	.....	.....	6	7	.....	.....	34	.....	.....	10
	.....	1	1	.....	1	.....	.....	1	3	.....	.....	.....	9	.....	.....	11
	117	63	402	52	166	102	147	240	94	553	94	.....	5,826	132	101	12
	59	66	249	25	60	62	82	208	35	165	84	.....	1,914	32	58	13
	53	33	249	27	92	38	53	161	22	438	51	.....	2,960	80	74	14
	833	73	1,558	13	1,241	570	126	2,095	427	1,997	898	.....	11,038	9	79	15
	1,064	579	1,069	564	194	880	2,017	336	1,029	224	1,914	.....	15,257	217	382	16
	12	10	283	.....	4	30	15	14	9	33	39	.....	499	3	8	17
	63	9	330	9	110	82	66	151	215	50	43	.....	763	.....	1	18
	2	.....	4	.....	5	.....	.....	2	2	2	5	.....	51	2	.....	19
	8,655	4,020	27,494	2,947	12,410	8,112	7,783	13,243	10,462	34,220	5,734	.....	307,399	3,819	8,434	20
	4,214	1,737	13,996	1,199	5,054	4,604	4,196	5,992	3,278	13,739	2,586	.....	168,597	2,473	3,656	21
	$167,632	$86,155	$561,943	$69,370	$142,328	$133,373	$231,488	$325,352	$100,606	$481,657	$90,374	.....	$4,557,480	$61,750	$69,489	22
	$37,528	$19,470	$108,031	$14,630	$38,494	$42,420	$51,790	$64,414	$29,370	$104,293	$23,635	.....	$1,468,333	$28,485	$20,490	23
	$7,101	$3,750	$27,407	$2,695	$13,294	$10,558	$8,850	$12,321	$6,595	$27,138	$5,022	.....	$370,173	$5,657	$7,552	24
	117	80	329	53	134	138	180	175	124	467	156	.....	8,010	120	133	25
	20	22	226	16	48	52	53	112	34	268	60	.....	6,009	121	112	26
	107	75	301	36	118	159	158	113	97	273	86	.....	4,485	47	101	27
	1,928	818	6,714	350	2,011	1,908	1,910	2,731	1,440	5,873	1,154	.....	26,316	12	790	28
	839	365	3,408	154	792	1,025	883	1,170	511	2,820	458	.....	7,815	5	256	29
	797	518	3,803	356	1,600	1,065	1,159	1,813	1,012	4,328	693	.....	50,490	785	1,048	30
	7,400	5,524	48,431	3,652	15,630	11,352	14,039	22,134	7,960	50,956	6,324	.....	868,410	10,995	18,990	31
	4,655	4,211	23,475	1,738	4,784	4,349	4,182	12,402	3,618	14,195	7,083	.....	125,686	1,263	4,947	32
	2,397	1,770	11,798	765	2,330	2,318	2,430	6,588	1,287	4,818	3,286	.....	74,137	805	2,181	33
	$77,427	$88,291	$530,383	$46,260	$71,737	$62,900	$137,990	$318,356	$34,836	$190,445	$105,459	.....	$1,828,198	$16,733	$36,770	34
	$19,183	$19,160	$90,010	$6,570	$18,685	$18,110	$24,315	$61,750	$6,375	$33,920	$27,410	.....	$479,928	$7,475	$12,065	35
	$4,669	$2,926	$26,707	$1,200	$5,525	$4,410	$5,106	$17,088	$2,490	$8,572	$7,747	.....	$136,434	$1,887	$2,525	36
	64	94	251	38	52	74	95	139	54	130	147	.....	2,868	29	76	37
	12	31	162	6	31	27	30	102	9	76	42	.....	2,165	34	46	38
	83	79	269	33	59	81	87	132	50	122	114	.....	2,035	13	94	39
	1,301	947	5,263	333	1,023	1,072	1,245	3,267	627	2,208	1,514	.....	16,792	7	739	40
	462	381	2,486	110	432	487	459	1,292	177	973	599	.....	4,844	2	242	41
	478	481	2,707	230	581	548	495	1,567	306	1,425	793	.....	19,850	251	650	42
	3,918	5,345	30,800	1,950	8,034	5,718	6,331	18,150	2.635	17,557	7,019	.....	329,506	2,580	11,800	43
	4,051	1,709	14,169	1,202	4,040	3,255	1,839	8,659	1,258	20,230	3,035	.....	157,591	3,660	5,685	44
	1,757	879	8,468	622	2,268	2,095	866	4,714	365	13,309	1,919	.....	91,717	1,651	4,006	45
	2,034	1,069	9,443	727	3,108	1,789	1,491	6,409	669	12,099	1,935	.....	106,958	2,937	2,842	46
	768	493	4,636	268	1,414	923	617	2,947	201	5,940	1,029	.....	50,498	1,017	1,688	47
	$73,156	$41,438	$308,971	$46,895	$85,547	$50,840	$80,902	$226,035	$34,670	$326,705	$56,180	.....	$3,145,363	$90,774	$60,129	48
	$14,305	$10,100	$49,905	$7,990	$22,385	$10,150	$13,620	$45,402	$5,740	$59,747	$13,790	.....	$700,478	$18,170	$14,660	49
	$40,430	$27,683	$219,250	$27,280	$67,965	$42,190	$44,587	$156,380	$17,205	$258,067	$41,883	.....	$2,091,817	$43,199	$45,619	50
	$3,015	$1,136	$14,859	$1,345	$5,482	$2,305	$2,458	$11,732	$1,300	$21,116	$2,366	.....	$193,300	$4,818	$4,387	51
	62	49	225	36	78	56	63	143	21	336	75	.....	3,963	83	104	52
	14	13	167	10	46	16	17	76	3	260	16	.....	3,342	106	90	53
	73	28	236	25	85	65	50	140	17	251	66	.....	3,026	60	87	54
	1,081	517	5,162	348	1,729	801	769	3,258	320	5,898	959	.....	20,343	83	879	55
	367	191	2,417	137	839	345	302	1,379	105	2,779	393	.....	6,409	28	274	56
	417	246	2,540	284	770	395	354	1,644	172	3,563	435	.....	35,148	952	961	57
	3,615	2,228	30,141	2,800	10,381	3,565	3,590	21,044	1,748	41,161	4,474	.....	683,161	19,407	16,255	58
	57,766	6,011	59,854	1,537	31,039	31,944	10,780	57,449	45,783	44,815	56,775	.....	525,125	230	4,529	59
	31,688	2,625	49,520	629	28,342	20,684	6,021	48,038	24,862	35,413	33,170	.....	397,328	56	2,695	60
	$915,655	$136,184	$1,446,490	$42,770	$795,505	$669,730	$304,654	$1,525,798	$409,030	$715,498	$1,128,576	.....	$12,836,927	$2,695	$63,291	61
	$150,709	$12,834	$245,595	$4,600	$142,483	$117,785	$29,875	$247,391	$100,260	$174,969	$172,690	.....	$2,138,002	$1,250	$12,420	62
	$29,124	$2,722	$59,036	$547	$33,022	$25,672	$5,804	$65,144	$25,848	$46,368	$33,422	.....	$740,943	$166	$4,667	63
	800	87	1,007	1	771	594	205	1,126	767	919	1,296	.....	16,079	4	99	64
	151	24	688	1	337	202	52	618	100	681	278	.....	11,354	5	101	65
	934	96	994	18	558	659	161	892	697	528	1,101	.....	11,619	2	60	66
	18,588	1,260	27,530	332	15,569	10,875	2,891	25,303	13,049	17,053	17,226	.....	191,006	5	1,125	67
	6,507	413	12,705	139	5,762	4,551	1,076	9,717	3,749	7,464	6,550	.....	56,039	1	317	68
	6,807	596	13,706	161	7,658	4,822	1,542	13,113	6,578	11,573	7,725	.....	110,677	15	917	69
	51,419	5,447	157,079	1,615	76,489	47,924	15,502	136,843	46,798	121,222	64,592	.....	1,634,949	250	16,155	70
	31,311	26,784	42,544	18,035	6,015	26,414	75,713	10,723	36,368	7,079	65,465	.....	472,595	6,427	12,176	71
	27,213	14,427	40,656	13,388	5,694	22,392	53,874	9,995	28,244	5,821	51,350	.....	408,478	5,726	10,044	72
	$641,165	$283,853	$1,195,662	$706,535	$161,831	$739,498	$2,754,418	$396,034	$482,450	$132,720	$1,506,958	.....	$12,189,490	$229,210	$198,518	73
	$110,447	$81,430	$169,250	$82,110	$20,196	$132,135	$314,065	$49,280	$118,900	$28,747	$256,435	.....	$2,043,862	$38,505	$39,799	74
	$12,292	$8,526	$34,400	$13,200	$3,249	$16,060	$49,534	$13,263	$17,078	$5,001	$28,391	.....	$368,019	$6,360	$9,475	75
	470	523	565	464	91	539	1,762	171	825	74	1,737	.....	11,454	142	289	76
	29	86	552	85	17	86	234	79	143	91	179	.....	7,117	141	204	77
	497	301	562	278	71	465	1,350	250	763	107	1,390	.....	7,173	84	193	78
	18,158	7,116	22,506	6,439	2,704	12,860	28,131	5,756	15,073	2,895	29,671	.....	132,886	69	4,036	79
	7,237	2,527	10,908	2,487	1,191	6,362	11,672	2,953	5,225	1,478	12,583	.....	41,728	26	1,436	80
	5,377	4,215	11,125	4,311	1,356	5,627	13,458	2,088	8,190	1,732	12,549	.....	137,501	2,480	3,609	81
	47,680	41,471	124,357	42,529	14,615	64,050	144,877	27,423	67,669	22,749	120,160	.....	2,782,172	59,538	69,331	82

TABLE 73.—STATISTICS OF SIZE OF FARMS AND FOR TENURE CLASSES OF FARMS

TENNESSEE—continued.

		Cheatham.	Chester.	Crockett.	Davidson.	Decatur.	Dickson.	Dyer.	Fayette.	Franklin.	Gibson.
1	Number of farms	124	226	612	440	137	258	544	4,070	197	1,076
	FARMS CLASSIFIED BY SIZE.										
2	Under 3 acres										
3	3 to 9 acres	4	8	30	90	16	17	23	46	31	59
4	10 to 19 acres	26	61	179	107	40	48	182	219	52	253
5	20 to 49 acres	56	90	319	148	52	94	287	2,378	76	547
6	50 to 99 acres	27	31	66	70	20	63	42	969	26	173
7	100 to 174 acres	9	24	16	20	6	29	6	336	9	41
8	175 to 259 acres	2	9	....	2	1	6	2	83	2	3
9	260 to 499 acres	....	3	1	3	1	1	1	35	....	....
10	500 to 999 acres	....	....	1	....	....	1	....	4	1	....
11	1,000 acres and over	....	....	....	....	....	....	1	....	....	....
	FARMERS CLASSIFIED BY TENURE.										
12	Owners, free	36	27	41	148	29	126	31	201	80	94
13	Owners, mortgaged	17	7	22	22	1	41	12	123	7	76
14	Part owners	28	24	31	77	22	46	34	58	53	98
15	Cash tenants	7	9	228	46	3	3	131	2,215	2	191
16	Share tenants	36	152	263	118	79	41	325	1,311	55	573
17	Share-cash tenants	....	....	21	17	3	1	10	49	....	37
18	Tenure not specified	....	7	6	8	....	....	1	112	....	7
19	Managers	....	....	....	4	....	....	....	1	....	....
	FARMS OPERATED BY OWNERS, FREE.										
20	Total acreage	1,859	1,989	1,717	4,223	2,494	6,854	1,238	21,198	1,855	4,866
21	Improved acreage	830	1,104	1,359	2,638	731	3,051	893	12,073	1,168	3,381
22	Value of land	$20,405	$14,280	$45,010	$170,676	$13,430	$53,775	$30,480	$225,380	$26,894	$95,310
23	Value of buildings	$8,455	$4,540	$13,735	$70,589	$4,095	$24,425	$8,025	$54,778	$12,365	$26,755
24	Value of implements and machinery	$1,868	$1,740	$3,227	$14,509	$1,208	$5,901	$1,806	$27,929	$2,752	$6,353
25	Number of dairy cows	48	37	64	246	38	128	48	461	78	117
26	Number of work horses	31	27	66	191	15	81	38	328	62	141
27	Number of work mules	26	29	29	79	23	106	40	302	32	98
28	Acreage in cotton	....	318	315	....	96	....	295	3,396	15	703
29	Bales of cotton grown in 1909	....	87	120	....	37	....	120	854	3	223
30	Acreage in corn	285	333	420	890	215	1,199	307	2,537	386	865
31	Bushels of corn grown in 1909	7,575	4,525	9,955	20,225	3,800	24,639	7,905	28,136	5,039	15,985
	FARMS OPERATED BY OWNERS, MORTGAGED.										
32	Total acreage	845	463	856	850	6	2,210	373	13,665	283	4,033
33	Improved acreage	454	328	713	468	6	970	231	8,490	168	2,838
34	Value of land	$7,750	$4,750	$20,690	$27,100	$150	$20,295	$8,810	$148,357	$4,335	$75,751
35	Value of buildings	$2,800	$1,750	$5,550	$8,800	$50	$7,235	$2,750	$34,196	$815	$18,565
36	Value of implements and machinery	$770	$638	$1,455	$1,924	$10	$1,271	$1,227	$14,380	$316	$4,709
37	Number of dairy cows	15	12	30	29	....	43	7	318	3	95
38	Number of work horses	12	7	39	22	....	18	14	218	7	105
39	Number of work mules	12	12	11	18	....	32	14	179	2	64
40	Acreage in cotton	....	135	249	....	4	....	81	2,965	7	789
41	Bales of cotton grown in 1909	....	35	79	....	....	....	27	648	1	228
42	Acreage in corn	117	106	214	95	....	327	81	1,680	41	693
43	Bushels of corn grown in 1909	2,129	1,185	3,660	2,390	....	6,082	2,030	17,052	610	14,145
	FARMS OPERATED BY PART OWNERS.										
44	Total acreage	1,458	2,589	1,625	2,763	986	2,055	1,060	5,339	1,997	5,240
45	Owned acreage	946	1,724	804	1,324	537	1,310	506	3,582	1,070	3,367
46	Improved acreage	859	1,235	1,235	2,090	571	1,169	862	3,478	1,578	4,004
47	Owned improved acreage	436	621	579	749	143	514	310	2,142	667	2,301
48	Value of land	$20,349	$19,960	$37,305	$122,705	$10,425	$25,350	$30,330	$62,767	$34,282	$105,527
49	Value of buildings	$4,947	$3,630	$9,575	$25,737	$2,190	$8,560	$10,450	$17,019	$7,535	$23,770
50	Value of land and buildings owned	$15,635	$13,087	$24,990	$70,181	$4,480	$17,030	$19,320	$55,816	$21,597	$80,535
51	Value of implements and machinery	$1,070	$1,645	$2,095	$6,867	$402	$2,490	$1,795	$5,477	$2,492	$6,256
52	Number of dairy cows	22	49	49	97	25	44	40	132	63	124
53	Number of work horses	21	19	63	108	11	23	31	86	71	126
54	Number of work mules	26	37	30	70	19	52	31	93	29	127
55	Acreage in cotton	....	312	381	....	102	....	424	1,294	37	1,482
56	Bales of cotton grown in 1909	....	87	130	....	34	....	149	282	8	460
57	Acreage in corn	334	331	368	825	251	499	282	858	764	1,101
58	Bushels of corn grown in 1909	8,100	4,985	8,760	19,374	3,975	11,985	7,020	8,421	11,561	24,091
	FARMS OPERATED BY CASH TENANTS, INCLUDING TENURE NOT SPECIFIED										
59	Total acreage	419	781	8,796	2,239	69	417	5,356	118,389	26	7,446
60	Improved acreage	182	450	7,041	1,339	39	27	3,600	90,925	26	5,919
61	Value of land	$9,025	$7,470	$205,030	$191,920	$465	$1,935	$148,275	$1,367,748	$235	$185,690
62	Value of buildings	$875	$1,740	$43,285	$30,780	$85	$265	$23,780	$326,692	$215	$33,980
63	Value of implements and machinery	$280	$415	$16,202	$7,322	$30	$5	$7,281	$127,565	$40	$10,133
64	Number of dairy cows	10	18	296	119	....	1	164	3,778	1	210
65	Number of work horses	6	16	307	109	....	....	152	2,366	3	210
66	Number of work mules	9	11	216	28	1	1	152	2,485	....	204
67	Acreage in cotton	....	215	2,882	....	1	....	1,558	43,784	....	2,175
68	Bales of cotton grown in 1909	....	53	931	....	....	....	599	9,337	....	690
69	Acreage in corn	102	169	2,131	525	20	....	1,447	25,984	18	1,762
70	Bushels of corn grown in 1909	3,155	1,770	45,150	13,751	130	....	35,160	232,583	140	35,767
	FARMS OPERATED BY SHARE AND SHARE-CASH TENANTS.										
71	Total acreage	949	5,488	5,901	4,273	1,771	1,576	8,056	43,063	3,116	15,865
72	Improved acreage	816	4,149	5,783	3,155	1,704	1,057	7,870	38,103	2,207	14,448
73	Value of land	$16,285	$77,905	$167,940	$197,470	$36,016	$36,465	$339,148	$532,480	$64,285	$452,957
74	Value of buildings	$4,830	$14,751	$32,320	$25,285	$5,875	$7,145	$46,627	$126,801	$6,785	$81,811
75	Value of implements and machinery	$731	$4,491	$6,080	$5,881	$1,528	$1,787	$8,726	$14,577	$4,428	$13,542
76	Number of dairy cows	14	126	173	131	55	29	218	999	43	405
77	Number of work horses	13	82	158	110	18	19	168	307	44	332
78	Number of work mules	15	137	70	80	56	38	159	511	31	225
79	Acreage in cotton	....	1,364	1,846	3	565	....	2,643	20,219	59	5,028
80	Bales of cotton grown in 1909	....	390	807	2	219	....	1,410	4,302	13	1,792
81	Acreage in corn	383	1,294	1,889	1,350	864	552	2,821	10,497	782	4,601
82	Bushels of corn grown in 1909	9,208	16,316	45,739	32,133	13,645	13,475	72,472	100,719	11,985	98,666

[1] Less than 1 bale.

OPERATED BY COLORED FARMERS, BY COUNTIES, FOR SOUTHERN STATES: 1910—Continued.

TENNESSEE—continued.

Giles.	Greene.	Hamilton.	Harde-man.	Hardin.	Hawkins.	Haywood.	Hender-son.	Henry.	Hick-man.	Knox.	Lake.	Lauder-dale.	Lincoln.	McMinn.	
1,326	105	150	1,544	297	129	3,137	250	624	154	196	189	1,651	574	134	1
1	...	...	...	...	...	...	...	...	...	2	...	...	...	...	2
85	28	29	14	11	29	46	8	43	11	70	31	35	23	14	3
358	24	33	121	78	23	354	52	144	21	45	5	300	141	31	4
631	37	52	793	148	48	1,752	75	247	54	39	98	952	291	51	5
201	10	27	339	39	20	733	40	105	46	24	46	248	89	24	6
43	5	9	194	15	7	217	44	73	18	13	8	71	23	12	7
7	...	...	56	3	1	27	22	7	4	2	1	9	4	2	8
...	1	...	24	3	1	7	9	5	...	1	...	17	3	...	9
...	...	...	3	...	...	1	...	...	...	...	...	15	...	...	10
...	...	...	...	...	...	...	...	...	...	...	...	4	...	...	11
166	40	60	147	29	59	192	52	128	90	121	2	76	54	91	12
70	8	8	54	3	4	199	22	70	16	14	...	93	22	8	13
168	20	38	36	49	31	170	20	66	16	27	2	72	52	11	14
90	...	13	493	12	...	1,589	25	57	6	10	100	671	7	2	15
803	37	30	733	189	35	962	128	300	25	23	78	699	435	21	16
20	...	...	4	11	...	13	...	2	...	...	5	5	2	...	17
6	...	...	77	4	...	12	2	1	1	1	2	35	1	1	18
3	...	1	...	...	...	...	1	...	...	...	...	...	1	1	19
7,921	1,066	2,365	17,498	2,967	1,905	14,229	7,820	8,296	5,097	3,724	13	5,312	2,949	3,882	20
4,975	728	1,218	7,211	1,094	1,171	9,279	2,504	4,227	2,418	2,302	13	3,369	1,502	2,016	21
$153,445	$27,270	$30,485	$95,894	$26,745	$35,935	$236,645	$28,661	$79,250	$47,825	$85,670	$1,050	$104,550	$52,077	$29,895	22
$50,180	$11,480	$15,335	$35,111	$9,530	$9,915	$75,995	$9,281	$22,975	$17,639	$34,425	$3,400	$24,125	$13,445	$8,960	23
$9,268	$2,294	$2,552	$9,530	$2,273	$2,235	$29,170	$3,827	$5,840	$6,049	$6,206	$50	$9,262	$2,950	$2,689	24
209	38	74	320	44	54	420	75	167	107	115	3	123	72	98	25
204	34	41	213	36	34	357	35	143	56	81	...	135	74	47	26
119	9	19	143	46	17	247	74	133	83	34	1	104	49	40	27
850	...	8	2,028	137	...	3,010	503	548	2	...	9	991	154	38	28
226	...	1	423	40	...	970	129	119	(1)	...	5	365	39	8	29
1,707	182	430	2,056	509	357	2,335	774	1,292	1,038	671	...	720	591	640	30
37,220	4,400	4,835	23,168	7,515	4,880	38,405	11,330	23,650	19,509	8,384	...	15,305	11,627	6,257	31
3,909	395	132	6,225	379	131	15,258	2,322	4,719	906	462	...	6,508	1,129	334	32
2,414	304	104	2,794	180	53	10,483	925	2,608	498	289	...	4,084	682	172	33
$67,756	$7,100	$3,350	$40,520	$4,000	$1,810	$263,927	$9,895	$39,323	$13,525	$11,700	...	$162,161	$24,075	$2,825	34
$18,230	$2,000	$2,600	$11,940	$1,500	$150	$53,865	$3,490	$11,945	$5,125	$3,350	...	$32,415	$4,055	$1,285	35
$4,903	$350	$463	$4,140	$500	$45	$19,056	$1,168	$3,051	$1,100	$863	...	$12,186	$1,196	$180	36
83	10	34	126	4	2	356	34	82	21	15	...	202	27	9	37
83	8	5	86	6	...	303	15	72	14	9	...	127	26	3	38
71	3	2	61	6	...	246	36	88	22	6	...	159	21	5	39
476	...	...	938	24	...	4,236	242	288	2	...	...	1,791	63	23	40
124	...	...	193	7	...	1,315	55	61	1	...	...	704	16	7	41
831	50	50	742	79	25	2,342	267	716	217	61	...	1,140	281	63	42
17,520	1,078	478	7,910	1,950	230	34,308	3,390	14,205	6,135	650	...	25,317	4,980	710	43
7,287	559	1,410	3,025	2,421	1,522	12,566	1,763	3,980	879	647	58	5,481	3,072	668	44
3,720	327	840	1,515	1,362	762	8,148	1,401	2,685	617	235	12	3,480	1,833	383	45
5,657	480	969	1,709	1,710	980	9,066	752	2,251	476	570	58	3,811	2,154	481	46
2,296	252	450	757	659	417	5,121	432	1,181	217	190	12	2,064	1,038	274	47
$172,620	$13,424	$22,603	$31,330	$40,765	$36,920	$258,404	$7,469	$43,928	$18,575	$30,772	$3,400	$144,735	$75,435	$6,545	48
$35,185	$3,310	$8,450	$11,750	$8,525	$5,845	$56,186	$2,515	$8,865	$4,075	$7,050	$280	$21,585	$11,755	$1,820	49
$95,819	$10,090	$17,903	$20,760	$21,255	$16,135	$205,795	$6,460	$32,353	$11,257	$17,925	$960	$102,147	$50,850	$4,460	50
$9,133	$555	$1,580	$3,437	$3,102	$1,005	$18,691	$473	$2,370	$945	$1,961	$40	$7,875	$3,345	$485	51
198	26	47	76	52	39	308	25	80	14	32	1	142	72	16	52
186	17	25	57	36	30	293	13	72	13	20	1	99	60	10	53
146	9	26	34	61	16	206	21	72	18	18	3	108	67	9	54
1,026	...	18	598	509	...	3,830	179	303	...	...	52	1,646	225	37	55
274	...	2	139	150	...	1,273	51	70	...	...	35	600	72	9	56
2,058	212	355	468	717	449	2,009	233	908	236	260	4	942	915	153	57
43,460	5,730	3,895	6,062	14,150	8,899	31,122	3,555	16,390	7,800	3,910	110	17,650	22,885	1,605	58
3,725	...	329	37,302	533	...	67,778	1,845	3,162	208	233	4,296	38,568	714	60	59
2,929	...	199	22,963	432	...	56,243	786	1,748	167	162	4,024	21,774	380	40	60
$93,047	...	$14,192	$356,379	$11,220	...	$1,271,260	$12,785	$33,315	$3,375	$7,440	$187,195	$825,708	$16,350	$775	61
$14,707	...	$3,278	$88,890	$3,025	...	$280,160	$3,865	$9,040	$1,075	$2,860	$26,695	$120,174	$1,500	$125	62
$3,707	...	$435	$25,986	$650	...	$107,356	$729	$1,870	$220	$750	$6,110	$51,134	$465	$100	63
92	...	17	913	16	...	2,039	21	49	7	4	108	794	8	3	64
112	...	5	587	8	...	1,735	13	55	4	4	35	653	8	...	65
69	...	5	594	24	...	1,462	28	56	6	4	183	714	10	...	66
637	...	...	10,306	92	...	25,988	265	343	...	...	2,940	11,632	38	7	67
153	...	...	2,119	29	...	7,718	67	75	...	...	1,541	4,811	9	2	68
1,393	...	84	6,507	203	...	16,266	333	568	84	33	789	6,353	157	12	69
26,538	...	870	72,152	4,370	...	231,243	3,866	9,709	2,100	425	20,030	157,231	4,825	80	70
21,582	1,156	956	27,544	5,118	1,091	26,707	5,089	8,772	1,035	1,132	3,364	21,565	13,217	614	71
19,714	1,097	758	21,322	4,976	857	24,480	3,328	7,351	831	903	3,356	17,476	12,259	426	72
$638,579	$29,085	$30,725	$298,897	$125,300	$33,705	$526,692	$44,190	$162,363	$29,350	$40,995	$160,905	$635,304	$470,866	$7,785	73
$95,641	$5,380	$3,050	$75,175	$25,900	$4,175	$115,087	$8,932	$29,605	$2,850	$11,405	$15,415	$96,926	$52,313	$1,570	74
$16,905	$618	$1,161	$9,281	$5,282	$1,171	$21,706	$2,392	$3,944	$782	$985	$3,493	$18,324	$11,450	$400	75
600	31	22	695	142	25	610	100	218	21	18	44	462	332	23	76
435	26	20	244	52	13	535	41	155	7	7	16	274	258	8	77
402	9	14	226	155	5	508	90	110	41	12	93	365	268	10	78
5,151	...	41	9,892	1,453	...	11,487	1,061	1,005	5	...	2,815	10,361	1,898	52	79
1,502	...	9	2,124	468	...	3,393	315	249	1	...	1,765	4,170	572	12	80
8,607	301	331	6,027	2,391	270	7,101	1,221	2,482	386	263	480	4,471	5,718	152	81
202,648	7,000	4,200	73,833	56,586	5,420	116,103	19,847	61,696	12,825	5,933	15,520	109,194	143,207	1,760	82

TABLE **73.**—STATISTICS OF SIZE OF FARMS AND FOR TENURE CLASSES OF FARMS

		McNairy.	Macon.	Madison.	Marshall.	Maury.	Monroe.	Montgomery.	Obion.	Robertson.	Rutherford.
							TENNESSEE—continued.				
1	Number of farms	195	118	1,811	320	811	103	1,108	208	790	1,241
	FARMS CLASSIFIED BY SIZE.										
2	Under 3 acres									68	96
3	3 to 9 acres	11	13	24	44	169	3	108	11	238	269
4	10 to 19 acres	47	23	187	79	208	16	335	51	305	621
5	20 to 49 acres	70	56	978	140	296	49	378	100	117	206
6	50 to 99 acres	40	20	367	41	101	23	162	33	45	42
7	100 to 174 acres	17	5	192	13	25	10	101	7	12	6
8	175 to 259 acres	6	1	55	1	7	1	19	4	5	1
9	260 to 499 acres	4		6	2	4		5	2		
10	500 to 999 acres			2			1				
11	1,000 acres and over						1				
	FARMERS CLASSIFIED BY TENURE.										
12	Owners, free	47	43	197	78	242	46	180	22	68	332
13	Owners, mortgaged	10	6	87	29	56	5	142	10	58	42
14	Part owners	10	9	99	35	148	22	139	12	79	165
15	Cash tenants	6	8	561	16	47		54	13	10	80
16	Share tenants	119	52	834	157	304	29	532	149	546	611
17	Share-cash tenants	2		6	4	9		49		4	8
18	Tenure not specified	1		25	1	2	1	11	1	24	2
19	Managers			2		3	1	1	1	1	1
	FARMS OPERATED BY OWNERS, FREE.										
20	Total acreage	4,235	1,643	20,175	1,958	7,159	1,835	9,432	877	3,910	12,569
21	Improved acreage	1,187	1,015	9,468	1,182	4,163	1,255	5,866	533	2,808	6,770
22	Value of land	$14,440	$21,955	$196,613	$38,775	$151,135	$24,975	$106,206	$18,775	$63,765	$252,745
23	Value of buildings	$7,560	$7,860	$57,790	$11,915	$55,590	$7,225	$42,085	$7,075	$26,685	$69,815
24	Value of implements and machinery	$2,003	$1,667	$18,285	$2,217	$12,458	$2,351	$10,762	$1,198	$4,777	$17,373
25	Number of dairy cows	63	33	426	77	266	48	186	30	66	424
26	Number of work horses	58	22	276	70	268	31	120	19	52	342
27	Number of work mules	21	42	247	38	162	23	214	14	78	146
28	Acreage in cotton	352		2,912	5	28			22		1,596
29	Bales of cotton grown in 1909	78		744	1	10			8		615
30	Acreage in corn	489	279	2,575	513	1,815	366	1,629	189	561	2,652
31	Bushels of corn grown in 1909	5,289	5,800	36,986	10,322	37,602	4,725	30,008	5,065	9,595	51,607
	FARMS OPERATED BY OWNERS, MORTGAGED.										
32	Total acreage	1,323	241	8,262	1,161	1,759	143	8,994	365	3,679	2,339
33	Improved acreage	366	114	4,217	696	1,053	99	6,035	290	2,765	1,318
34	Value of land	$5,080	$2,725	$94,285	$18,440	$40,650	$2,175	$86,271	$11,090	$65,424	$41,925
35	Value of buildings	$1,700	$775	$23,420	$6,670	$12,729	$975	$26,650	$2,850	$19,865	$9,210
36	Value of implements and machinery	$441	$157	$7,601	$1,765	$3,130	$145	$6,428	$600	$4,519	$2,535
37	Number of dairy cows	12	6	179	31	54	4	146	14	56	54
38	Number of work horses	7	1	118	26	50	2	103	13	42	54
39	Number of work mules	10	7	99	26	52		181	12	76	27
40	Acreage in cotton	82		1,393	17	36			12		282
41	Bales of cotton grown in 1909	18		344	7	10			4		83
42	Acreage in corn	95	35	1,055	362	441	50	1,505	132	567	389
43	Bushels of corn grown in 1909	670	1,020	14,368	6,265	8,665	375	23,319	3,750	9,810	7,413
	FARMS OPERATED BY PART OWNERS.										
44	Total acreage	561	351	7,202	1,993	5,435	1,231	8,796	703	4,265	6,995
45	Owned acreage	379	265	4,453	985	2,443	520	5,840	370	2,585	3,544
46	Improved acreage	304	263	4,519	1,274	4,015	899	6,057	639	3,431	4,800
47	Owned improved acreage	142	183	2,394	487	1,371	360	3,531	328	2,049	1,634
48	Value of land	$4,645	$3,920	$102,427	$38,998	$166,947	$19,205	$106,049	$41,950	$88,870	$175,617
49	Value of buildings	$1,625	$1,250	$26,230	$5,530	$41,035	$6,525	$29,545	$6,300	$29,310	$32,130
50	Value of land and buildings owned	$3,460	$3,990	$81,951	$18,764	$99,395	$13,620	$85,373	$29,110	$73,040	$90,709
51	Value of implements and machinery	$260	$352	$7,584	$1,732	$9,698	$1,495	$6,648	$1,560	$6,242	$8,707
52	Number of dairy cows	14	7	204	47	161	32	149	21	80	225
53	Number of work horses	5	2	130	49	170	15	79	18	58	225
54	Number of work mules	12	14	104	37	145	24	197	18	96	102
55	Acreage in cotton	100		1,461	21	17			23		1,083
56	Bales of cotton grown in 1909	23		385	5	3			8		407
57	Acreage in corn	142	67	1,213	571	1,859	240	1,546	269	743	2,001
58	Bushels of corn grown in 1909	1,355	975	18,485	10,545	45,401	3,635	31,015	10,350	12,973	37,550
	FARMS OPERATED BY CASH TENANTS, INCLUDING TENURE NOT SPECIFIED.										
59	Total acreage	517	468	30,808	482	1,227		3,506	643	1,382	3,633
60	Improved acreage	200	251	20,348	331	905		2,226	507	1,135	2,575
61	Value of land	$2,350	$7,035	$502,268	$9,220	$35,425		$57,068	$25,090	$28,530	$120,090
62	Value of buildings	$600	$1,315	$94,105	$2,300	$8,595		$21,120	$4,165	$7,940	$15,460
63	Value of implements and machinery	$65	$288	$36,498	$445	$1,518		$2,452	$940	$1,835	$4,040
64	Number of dairy cows	9	5	842	17	39		52	14	25	109
65	Number of work horses	4	2	573	23	37		39	19	19	88
66	Number of work mules	7	10	594	10	29		59	20	26	46
67	Acreage in cotton	45		8,468	10	18			53		824
68	Bales of cotton grown in 1909	11		2,290	3	3			20		294
69	Acreage in corn	74	114	6,149	206	482		641	301	296	944
70	Bushels of corn grown in 1909	815	2,395	94,641	3,569	11,083		11,143	9,120	5,315	13,510
	FARMS OPERATED BY SHARE AND SHARE-CASH TENANTS.										
71	Total acreage	3,734	1,851	27,798	5,126	8,895	2,235	14,444	5,244	16,898	18,086
72	Improved acreage	2,931	1,366	23,575	4,421	7,402	1,606	13,069	4,860	15,503	15,652
73	Value of land	$50,332	$44,495	$513,092	$153,808	$323,730	$41,700	$295,337	$290,515	$491,489	$685,469
74	Value of buildings	$8,010	$5,745	$91,927	$23,175	$46,435	$7,460	$72,570	$48,030	$107,895	$91,340
75	Value of implements and machinery	$2,364	$986	$23,545	$3,477	$11,606	$2,444	$8,494	$9,855	$16,815	$19,542
76	Number of dairy cows	112	26	638	135	236	64	370	116	342	493
77	Number of work horses	58	14	466	94	227	24	161	123	203	413
78	Number of work mules	63	23	531	49	173	28	228	92	255	256
79	Acreage in cotton	959		10,756	50	61			272		5,512
80	Bales of cotton grown in 1909	215		2,965	12	17			112		2,236
81	Acreage in corn	1,180	330	7,633	2,091	3,811	516	4,566	2,648	4,500	6,572
82	Bushels of corn grown in 1909	13,070	8,540	120,713	49,895	92,279	8,930	103,857	91,881	103,735	116,973

OPERATED BY COLORED FARMERS, BY COUNTIES, FOR SOUTHERN STATES: 1910—Continued.

TENNESSEE—continued.											TEXAS.				
Shelby.	Smith.	Stewart.	Sumner.	Tipton.	Trousdale.	Warren.	Weakley.	Williamson.	Wilson.	All other counties.	The state.	Anderson.	Austin.	Bastrop.	
5,469	178	166	342	2,386	120	136	271	540	554	2,119	69,918	1,553	775	1,191	1
2									1	1	23		1		2
179	21	17	81	71	8	12	13	58	109	390	2,082	26	45	17	3
832	54	36	72	456	32	30	72	122	115	450	6,755	125	76	53	4
3,347	64	32	110	1,401	49	49	111	213	205	681	32,176	683	441	525	5
889	34	46	60	361	23	32	46	102	85	373	17,666	370	147	357	6
180	5	27	15	79	6	10	23	35	31	169	8,168	238	50	169	7
30		6	2	13		1	5	8	7	33	1,927	77	11	56	8
9		1	2	3	2	2	1	2	1	18	865	24	4	10	9
1				2						2	202	9		4	10
		1								2	54	1			11
307	42	55	196	180	50	59	44	139	238	908	13,034	394	74	174	12
52	9	25	23	45	12	8	22	37	50	177	3,644	74	45	110	13
104	15	11	58	125	17	28	33	72	73	303	4,554	113	60	26	14
3,018	6	9	12	1,074	3	2	19	29	13	60	5,109	13	114	43	15
1,522	95	62	49	893	34	38	146	247	148	640	40,447	867	390	704	16
100	3	1	1	39	4		5	10	25	18	1,791	3	70	67	17
354	8	1		30			1	6	6	6	1,258	88	21	62	18
12		2	3			1	1		1	7	81	1		5	19
18,582	1,624	4,914	6,144	9,847	1,948	2,736	2,777	5,832	6,574	37,038	1,101,166	40,196	4,825	16,643	20
12,700	957	2,484	3,882	6,790	1,166	1,670	1,886	3,244	3,345	18,833	530,642	19,300	2,571	8,615	21
$672,885	$38,825	$34,920	$93,604	$220,275	$27,165	$22,715	$43,639	$114,097	$129,432	$408,263	$13,962,952	$273,920	$93,270	$216,069	22
$152,550	$8,300	$12,230	$37,836	$65,892	$8,770	$7,480	$18,390	$36,995	$52,580	$155,167	$3,438,433	$88,835	$20,450	$44,380	23
$36,073	$1,262	$2,800	$6,381	$20,674	$1,564	$2,004	$3,540	$9,687	$7,806	$30,594	$849,606	$25,085	$2,720	$12,521	24
688	40	100	199	295	54	75	52	210	298	943	32,491	999	183	421	25
385	55	44	160	312	40	38	63	164	231	556	18,862	410	160	314	26
370	26	67	103	167	42	27	50	126	106	386	13,860	457	88	248	27
4,414				2,545			83	22	4	115	200,928	6,238	1,152	5,167	28
1,354				905			27	12	1	30	48,434	1,698	254	1,004	29
2,829	323	701	1,397	1,401	376	593	435	1,101	1,464	6,230	159,609	5,804	613	2,302	30
42,727	7,802	13,383	35,324	31,175	5,970	7,935	8,905	22,840	29,958	91,143	2,036,412	68,255	11,585	22,339	31
3,828	385	1,721	1,008	3,514	314	603	1,245	2,068	1,832	8,299	372,044	7,768	3,761	11,170	32
2,589	254	822	671	1,903	243	732	1,070	914		4,578	181,706	3,534	1,751	5,517	33
$92,079	$7,600	$13,950	$17,555	$93,818	$5,230	$3,675	$19,235	$39,360	$32,690	$111,483	$5,049,586	$55,810	$77,618	$138,154	34
$21,550	$2,950	$3,950	$5,815	$21,320	$2,270	$2,475	$5,400	$8,740	$12,620	$33,993	$951,489	$16,350	$9,220	$28,172	35
$5,545	$325	$1,311	$645	$6,123	$250	$390	$1,157	$3,480	$2,157	$7,417	$306,611	$3,833	$2,338	$9,388	36
115	12	33	23	76	9	10	23	56	86	207	9,316	204	149	313	37
76	12	13	25	58	6	5	37	47	47	144	5,775	77	104	190	38
56	15	39	15	64	7	9	20	30	23	90	5,059	107	72	215	39
904				873			83	14		37	86,326	1,675	1,090	3,549	40
254				345			25	2		7	20,046	385	226	643	41
511	77	297	190	421	71	116	241	392	297	1,487	48,237	1,139	472	1,266	42
6,508	1,255	5,580	4,595	8,510	1,392	1,310	4,870	7,980	5,990	23,337	642,275	12,760	9,315	14,286	43
4,629	867	768	2,095	7,156	778	1,196	1,646	3,034	3,317	14,778	393,532	14,319	3,305	3,031	44
2,112	339	614	1,037	4,209	441	686	1,176	1,317	1,671	8,584	227,702	8,488	2,265	1,745	45
3,722	448	451	1,504	5,036	411	929	1,218	2,397	2,124	8,533	233,670	6,241	2,290	2,024	46
1,543	160	317	600	2,474	193	444	822	778	751		112,767	3,219	1,321	1,026	47
$172,532	$21,710	$6,720	$41,635	$188,665	$13,325	$13,638	$32,819	$79,157	$64,380	$235,326	$6,211,202	$91,759	$79,704	$45,438	48
$39,550	$4,040	$1,800	$12,390	$34,210	$4,725	$4,276	$12,295	$14,315	$12,495	$47,463	$1,073,610	$24,740	$13,200	$7,560	49
$113,617	$9,610	$6,045	$26,150	$141,895	$10,855	$10,546	$34,034	$39,335	$33,540	$141,100	$4,046,314	$73,770	$58,085	$27,719	50
$10,412	$718	$585	$2,165	$15,181	$540	$945	$2,264	$4,300	$2,896	$14,225	$348,468	$6,027	$2,857	$2,214	51
176	18	17	60	198	19	29	40	90	103	321	10,792	317	144	54	52
121	18	9	77	196	18	31	49	87	95	203	7,107	109	134	41	53
114	22	12	42	171	24	22	41	77	53	224	6,042	155	69	74	54
1,706				2,323			122		12	58	104,108	2,443	1,429	1,257	55
513				888			36		1	13	24,394	593	314	242	56
824	251	174	541	1,303	186	389	419	950	812	3,203	60,688	1,752	556	409	57
12,198	6,690	3,457	14,556	29,434	4,010	5,735	9,005	20,665	18,655	55,315	866,375	20,273	12,345	3,375	58
126,152	396	676	157	41,729	185	24	762	1,262	803	2,863	323,587	5,073	6,115	8,501	59
105,691	348	409	119	34,520	77	14	499	845	387	1,795	223,237	3,639	4,093	4,292	60
$5,778,185	$13,750	$7,275	$5,650	$1,095,821	$5,000	$285	$16,480	$42,040	$14,245	$54,300	$6,087,479	$43,345	$126,283	$86,340	61
$705,644	$1,390	$1,325	$2,060	$219,717	$900	$40	$1,700	$5,925	$3,385	$9,555	$938,300	$12,675	$27,795	$17,565	62
$226,325	$240	$366	$215	$86,212	$165	$125	$1,182	$1,295	$442	$2,677	$242,817	$2,510	$3,661	$3,909	63
4,662	13	15	18	1,351	3	2	16	36	16	64	8,169	103	180	127	64
2,698	5	6	17	1,186	6	3	31	37	18	49	7,436	70	212	112	65
3,391	8	15	10	992			13	23	4	38	5,674	51	80	127	66
58,357				19,154			67			17	107,844	1,236	2,056	2,544	67
17,248				7,594			19			5	26,649	314	476	453	68
24,664	179	166	78	9,142	40	5	199	329	116	680	60,851	962	1,046	945	69
337,361	4,400	2,425	2,500	193,156	900	90	3,860	7,107	1,905	12,206	941,262	11,168	19,230	8,177	70
40,317	2,716	1,399	2,008	22,675	1,900	1,335	4,649	9,421	6,990	27,271	1,998,650	39,918	16,523	40,008	71
38,293	2,433	1,224	1,611	21,512	1,601	1,160	3,865	7,803	5,140	19,255	1,599,132	31,771	14,513	33,806	72
$1,468,330	$113,710	$26,282	$59,655	$696,000	$67,125	$28,390	$140,255	$374,915	$201,075	$540,366	$46,418,528	$340,473	$423,162	$992,925	73
$215,677	$10,685	$5,508	$9,880	$121,125	$10,265	$5,080	$22,735	$44,690	$32,340	$89,332	$6,364,819	$99,160	$75,875	$125,158	74
$31,002	$1,097	$1,215	$1,279	$19,319	$915	$838	$3,730	$10,291	$3,916	$19,789	$1,498,621	$17,315	$11,874	$33,362	75
954	48	45	46	614	45	35	102	266	191	609	39,100	847	422	872	76
339	37	14	48	325	39	21	88	241	152	343	34,186	460	485	809	77
500	44	51	39	199	53	14	78	166	54	370	38,169	621	404	1,025	78
22,276				11,414			318	11		204	857,222	11,135	8,035	23,719	79
6,512				4,512			13	5		52	221,853	2,881	1,903	4,906	80
9,189	1,062	395	671	5,389	551	662	1,645	3,467	1,700	7,600	408,075	8,524	3,775	6,572	81
133,745	32,976	10,965	19,945	124,822	16,645	13,461	40,381	90,487	45,915	158,958	6,368,715	98,746	81,443	64,607	82

TABLE **73.**—STATISTICS OF SIZE OF FARMS AND FOR TENURE CLASSES OF FARMS

TEXAS—continued.

		Bell.	Bowie.	Brazoria.	Brazos.	Burleson.	Caldwell.	Camp.	Cass.	Chambers.	Cherokee.
1	Number of farms	196	1,654	786	1,189	1,311	623	689	1,517	128	1,046
	FARMS CLASSIFIED BY SIZE.										
2	Under 3 acres			3		3					
3	3 to 9 acres	4	48	75	11	48	13	7	26	33	20
4	10 to 19 acres	10	304	221	68	112	26	50	128	47	92
5	20 to 49 acres	75	876	359	672	644	238	320	617	28	488
6	50 to 99 acres	64	281	80	300	274	221	198	424	7	261
7	100 to 174 acres	40	115	34	104	147	95	84	247	8	123
8	175 to 259 acres	1	21	7	19	40	21	25	55	3	42
9	260 to 499 acres	2	8	4	12	24	9	4	18		18
10	500 to 999 acres		1	1	2	10		1	2	1	2
11	1,000 acres and over			2	1	9				1	
	FARMERS CLASSIFIED BY TENURE.										
12	Owners, free	24	272	212	175	148	105	143	403	96	206
13	Owners, mortgaged	12	50	19	22	45	64	57	130	3	66
14	Part owners	10	87	83	47	75	35	57	79	2	83
15	Cash tenants	1	181	153	240	210	3	6	28	3	28
16	Share tenants	147	982	312	682	714	387	354	833	21	655
17	Share-cash tenants	2	8	1	11	100	8	2	2		6
18	Tenure not specified		74	6	11	18	20	70	42	3	2
19	Managers					1	1	1			
	FARMS OPERATED BY OWNERS, FREE.										
20	Total acreage	1,318	19,377	10,066	12,471	19,357	7,094	12,002	40,129	11,462	20,164
21	Improved acreage	963	10,189	4,812	7,093	6,003	4,049	6,384	18,447	868	9,934
22	Value of land	$72,000	$283,970	$305,648	$218,687	$223,029	$140,411	$123,375	$282,323	$105,565	$188,316
23	Value of buildings	$7,800	$83,642	$45,940	$49,117	$33,490	$25,490	$45,150	$107,310	$18,910	$58,188
24	Value of implements and machinery	$2,865	$13,546	$9,385	$14,111	$11,900	$7,315	$9,577	$18,027	$2,845	$16,078
25	Number of dairy cows	28	750	466	378	313	254	254	981	134	595
26	Number of work horses	43	381	481	214	223	169	133	371	243	257
27	Number of work mules	36	247	169	256	208	149	192	366	35	233
28	Acreage in cotton	578	3,444	1,264	4,100	2,999	2,303	2,507	7,164	3	2,695
29	Bales of cotton grown in 1909	223	717	101	1,129	702	495	781	1,589	2	659
30	Acreage in corn	248	3,354	2,250	1,886	1,699	884	2,115	6,226	379	3,055
31	Bushels of corn grown in 1909	4,150	48,208	33,837	33,946	26,429	7,570	30,590	65,659	7,016	41,443
	FARMS OPERATED BY OWNERS, MORTGAGED.										
32	Total acreage	1,055	3,165	1,142	2,116	6,022	5,990	4,341	12,141	265	6,990
33	Improved acreage	679	1,641	512	1,142	2,403	3,282	2,708	5,991	153	3,699
34	Value of land	$51,810	$60,065	$22,630	$39,950	$74,759	$122,620	$49,050	$88,128	$4,400	$50,410
35	Value of buildings	$4,925	$12,575	$2,655	$6,650	$10,385	$17,490	$14,385	$25,985	$1,200	$14,625
36	Value of implements and machinery	$1,905	$2,187	$953	$2,149	$3,247	$6,830	$3,510	$5,872	$175	$5,075
37	Number of dairy cows	22	106	45	89	101	153	118	246	5	178
38	Number of work horses	28	61	46	36	44	117	68	96	4	88
39	Number of work mules	21	30	25	49	48	116	75	140	5	72
40	Acreage in cotton	446	743	124	738	1,304	2,183	1,307	2,385		1,152
41	Bales of cotton grown in 1909	149	146	7	183	376	417	397	480		281
42	Acreage in corn	156	531	224	347	585	624	873	1,960	5	959
43	Bushels of corn grown in 1909	2,250	7,923	4,560	6,435	11,050	6,392	11,495	20,065	55	15,065
	FARMS OPERATED BY PART OWNERS.										
44	Total acreage	980	6,147	4,050	4,219	7,483	3,056	4,348	5,711	258	7,905
45	Owned acreage	368	3,971	2,236	2,291	4,909	1,568	2,871	3,423	54	4,803
46	Improved acreage	842	3,553	2,250	2,819	4,743	1,835	2,889	3,143	220	4,935
47	Owned improved acreage	308	1,586	868	1,431	2,537	801	1,680	1,413	16	2,855
48	Value of land	$67,690	$86,604	$109,301	$73,047	$165,244	$51,950	$51,230	$42,764	$5,210	$72,264
49	Value of buildings	$3,950	$21,329	$18,135	$15,870	$18,215	$7,655	$9,125	$15,643	$240	$18,646
50	Value of land and buildings owned	$27,040	$62,402	$76,315	$51,718	$114,958	$25,239	$41,675	$34,694	$1,100	$57,220
51	Value of implements and machinery	$2,180	$4,365	$5,647	$4,484	$6,638	$2,496	$2,737	$3,602	$315	$5,558
52	Number of dairy cows	21	219	210	90	142	75	83	152	2	236
53	Number of work horses	21	94	210	46	106	60	55	81	6	94
54	Number of work mules	24	98	100	88	165	51	77	68	8	113
55	Acreage in cotton	491	1,326	516	1,655	2,677	1,070	1,312	1,629		1,660
56	Bales of cotton grown in 1909	139	326	36	414	752	227	341	362		413
57	Acreage in corn	154	1,083	1,112	655	1,008	449	796	1,102	3	1,296
58	Bushels of corn grown in 1909	1,425	19,070	18,408	12,807	22,650	3,986	10,415	11,771	5	16,912
	FARMS OPERATED BY CASH TENANTS, INCLUDING TENURE NOT SPECIFIED.										
59	Total acreage	5	9,464	4,168	13,867	10,608	1,811	3,275	3,479	221	2,018
60	Improved acreage	5	7,702	3,441	10,732	9,004	966	2,353	2,523	69	1,156
61	Value of land	$200	$209,300	$131,737	$339,334	$289,008	$55,910	$32,015	$24,815	$5,220	$28,685
62	Value of buildings	$100	$38,295	$20,823	$46,620	$28,475	$5,575	$6,435	$10,090	$420	$4,325
63	Value of implements and machinery	$40	$7,527	$5,233	$15,955	$8,357	$845	$1,152	$1,313	$70	$1,327
64	Number of dairy cows		276	242	254	223	36	58	65	2	68
65	Number of work horses	2	246	280	226	167	23	56	54	10	25
66	Number of work mules		206	128	337	354	40	43	27	1	35
67	Acreage in cotton	4	2,832	1,202	6,835	5,573	576	1,093	999		297
68	Bales of cotton grown in 1909	2	858	69	1,955	1,837	121	294	231		76
69	Acreage in corn		2,299	1,780	2,384	2,197	147	727	805	44	384
70	Bushels of corn grown in 1909		46,335	27,240	48,000	56,591	1,219	10,140	9,215	635	4,663
	FARMS OPERATED BY SHARE AND SHARE-CASH TENANTS.										
71	Total acreage	9,481	31,218	13,099	31,785	53,625	24,472	16,785	34,769	506	27,596
72	Improved acreage	8,010	27,024	8,756	26,309	27,201	18,403	12,411	26,212	407	23,106
73	Value of land	$567,115	$508,222	$345,772	$620,071	$894,520	$904,235	$215,883	$279,336	$9,460	$342,303
74	Value of buildings	$43,985	$126,441	$41,675	$108,540	$116,749	$78,815	$33,650	$94,258	$5,910	$74,452
75	Value of implements and machinery	$15,305	$18,078	$6,978	$24,479	$20,658	$31,641	$6,712	$11,868	$603	$18,619
76	Number of dairy cows	128	690	197	515	665	427	287	711	23	838
77	Number of work horses	172	440	402	433	433	406	164	317	41	399
78	Number of work mules	233	729	268	642	668	576	329	509	5	488
79	Acreage in cotton	4,982	11,551	2,238	16,437	16,309	12,939	5,654	10,962		8,189
80	Bales of cotton grown in 1909	1,491	3,226	172	4,329	5,466	3,524	1,487	2,386		2,216
81	Acreage in corn	1,836	7,912	3,808	6,180	6,828	2,674	3,567	8,431	72	7,552
82	Bushels of corn grown in 1909	25,078	147,018	49,843	120,937	151,030	26,825	50,603	93,568	1,455	108,159

OPERATED BY COLORED FARMERS, BY COUNTIES, FOR SOUTHERN STATES: 1910—Continued.

TEXAS—continued.

Collin.	Colorado.	Dallas.	De Witt.	Denton.	Ellis.	Falls.	Fannin.	Fayette.	Fort Bend.	Franklin.	Free-stone.	Goliad.	Gonzales.	Grayson.	
135	692	556	386	230	563	1,457	502	919	1,636	136	1,512	115	1,103	289	1
													1		2
8	23	14	11	5	10	25	16	22	85	2	40	1	26	14	3
11	71	49	24	9	60	57	39	59	283	11	112	18	43	34	4
60	380	248	145	84	205	758	183	432	906	83	607	32	460	129	5
36	138	188	129	78	205	489	181	268	258	26	463	30	347	82	6
14	62	49	51	39	75	106	74	100	77	12	206	26	158	26	7
3	13	7	13	10	7	15	7	28	19	2	49	3	49	3	8
3	4	1	10	4	1	5	1	9	5		25	3	17		9
	1		2	1		2	1	1	2		9	1	2		10
			1						1		1	1	1		11
19	83	64	74	37	18	164	71	97	307	21	262	53	161	47	12
6	26	15	17	17	13	64	19	48	41	2	111		53	17	13
3	41	18	32	11	6	77	23	64	127	5	127	11	74	27	14
4	38	6	20	1	48	64	1	69	336	1	56	3	42	10	15
101	427	446	233	158	470	927	365	464	797	106	910	47	745	185	16
	72	2	8	1	3	117	3	176	15		6		24		17
2	3	2	1	5	5	43	19	1	10	1	40		2	3	18
	2	3	1	1		1	1	1	3			1	2		19
517	5,909	3,571	5,561	2,829	927	9,200	4,680	8,097	16,623	1,409	24,782	3,847	16,214	2,040	20
466	2,860	2,779	2,618	1,637	802	6,893	3,360	3,415	9,355	963	11,472	1,868	6,357	1,669	21
$22,975	$119,171	$220,757	$123,270	$57,275	$48,570	$301,285	$99,893	$125,091	$456,185	$18,460	$213,359	$91,540	$249,257	$80,365	22
$6,850	$25,035	$21,813	$20,990	$12,605	$6,500	$52,980	$24,780	$25,825	$87,465	$4,800	$67,834	$12,670	$47,626	$17,235	23
$1,151	$4,399	$4,579	$4,740	$2,780	$1,660	$12,983	$9,305	$7,124	$14,710	$1,155	$14,165	$3,380	$12,887	$3,885	24
14	180	91	187	58	18	322	121	205	715	31	629	186	506	52	25
22	144	119	138	52	23	265	114	137	741	19	296	117	340	68	26
16	89	100	81	58	37	215	123	113	378	23	246	75	218	56	27
253	1,038	1,148	1,179	834	581	3,662	1,737	1,468	3,788	304	5,188	990	3,569	616	28
76	112	270	235	140	154	964	414	244	571	87	1,197	268	714	186	29
209	891	755	912	488	148	1,787	1,143	956	3,283	235	3,252	633	1,800	525	30
3,385	15,647	9,809	12,759	4,490	1,835	31,136	19,632	16,843	63,130	4,250	37,527	8,000	21,691	11,115	31
443	2,611	939	1,662	2,678	1,063	4,436	1,528	4,036	2,831	99	12,734		6,016	875	32
382	1,411	777	723	1,328	911	3,123	1,135	1,382	1,685	69	6,044		2,597	775	33
$15,800	$52,034	$59,620	$36,690	$63,275	$74,495	$159,983	$39,925	$54,701	$96,307	$900	$103,507		$84,875	$28,895	34
$2,750	$7,725	$8,100	$5,125	$10,300	$6,925	$20,635	$7,325	$9,250	$12,770	$250	$29,583		$12,980	$7,025	35
$535	$2,066	$2,470	$1,240	$3,125	$1,400	$7,283	$1,562	$2,231	$3,828	$70	$6,883		$4,600	$1,590	36
10	73	28	59	53	17	125	27	137	74	3	291		155	22	37
11	68	30	48	63	28	152	28	79	104	3	154		137	33	38
9	53	32	28	38	32	93	37	51	77	1	155		67	24	39
135	713	431	330	817	675	1,897	715	935	884	44	2,951		1,306	296	40
43	106	109	59	185	247	517	139	134	143	14	646		271	104	41
109	316	147	202	301	182	852	322	572	548	22	1,663		513	293	42
1,876	6,625	2,000	2,125	2,547	1,105	17,395	6,250	8,601	11,520	175	19,046		4,886	4,855	43
95	2,706	1,093	4,413	1,262	451	6,699	2,235	6,145	7,628	540	11,954	734	7,515	1,756	44
28	1,743	525	2,146	616	212	2,554	973	3,576	4,817	165	6,460	472	4,299	745	45
93	1,715	918	1,970	927	439	5,000	1,737	2,940	5,323	381	6,526	508	4,269	1,603	46
28	863	408	914	452	200	1,632	726	1,340	2,763	156	2,925	256	1,740	675	47
$7,620	$58,670	$65,975	$147,970	$34,460	$33,850	$249,766	$51,970	$100,246	$224,491	$11,150	$111,024	$15,154	$128,354	$68,110	48
$300	$12,930	$5,195	$8,885	$4,350	$4,500	$36,285	$6,745	$18,220	$29,125	$550	$27,895	$1,500	$18,162	$12,350	49
$1,550	$40,750	$31,880	$61,289	$19,650	$15,850	$115,611	$25,190	$68,432	$160,251	$2,600	$81,129	$11,416	$79,671	$36,315	50
$105	$2,810	$815	$2,850	$705	$590	$8,635	$1,450	$4,565	$6,171	$295	$9,762	$670	$6,207	$3,568	51
2	109	31	112	27	4	139	37	162	318	11	290	16	179	34	52
4	81	31	73	18	11	189	40	123	343	7	181	32	188	56	53
1	54	30	54	32	16	128	41	83	224	7	119	10	86	34	54
45	998	521	1,127	428	361	2,847	851	1,523	2,947	177	3,254	262	2,681	561	55
18	97	116	255	89	111	767	142	280	560	49	731	55	504	207	56
38	586	277	504	285	77	1,029	505	736	1,441	85	1,689	153	899	484	57
760	9,065	2,650	7,950	3,030	560	17,681	9,135	13,487	27,088	1,290	20,293	2,315	9,968	9,150	58
893	2,213	372	1,112	315	2,807	4,930	1,041	3,979	12,448	60	5,034	755	4,081	837	59
893	1,863	248	790	270	2,455	4,368	846	2,098	10,494	32	3,312	202	2,071	515	60
$50,380	$70,895	$34,250	$31,970	$11,050	$112,270	$180,844	$29,705	$71,255	$413,520	$550	$43,620	$28,660	$92,335	$27,195	61
$2,000	$9,000	$3,250	$6,560	$1,260	$10,380	$18,165	$5,125	$10,310	$46,255	$50	$13,570	$590	$9,635	$2,675	62
$805	$2,562	$755	$1,161	$125	$2,705	$6,743	$995	$2,158	$15,160	$25	$2,576	$530	$3,065	$505	63
5	71	6	42	2	37	87	17	81	373	1	129	4	75	23	64
2	62	8	50	6	33	97	10	93	644	2	103	11	89	10	65
20	61	9	19		90	103	22	36	388	1	64	5	44	15	66
293	841	81	528	108	1,614	2,639	472	1,140	5,427	20	1,588	35	1,320	98	67
75	69	14	132	23	524	773	138	169	1,215	5	386	12	299	22	68
407	729	30	165	65	351	860	197	499	3,333	13	883	118	397	161	69
6,140	17,700	300	2,745	800	5,107	17,805	3,590	7,814	73,206	160	10,076	3,230	6,017	1,640	70
5,633	20,291	22,866	15,243	10,341	26,303	51,845	20,586	32,659	29,563	4,108	48,630	3,466	41,992	8,258	71
5,117	16,137	20,740	12,747	8,164	24,397	49,769	17,392	23,932	22,626	3,850	37,120	2,745	33,384	7,356	72
$341,650	$544,346	$1,271,655	$491,250	$329,325	$1,712,230	$2,270,537	$588,554	$716,163	$1,053,612	$57,608	$586,735	$72,063	$932,651	$325,934	73
$24,390	$84,405	$103,330	$51,268	$49,740	$113,305	$204,850	$71,685	$119,465	$108,205	$11,887	$149,326	$8,430	$121,595	$43,466	74
$7,267	$21,284	$26,130	$14,268	$10,112	$30,435	$48,165	$19,021	$29,347	$27,567	$2,947	$29,022	$3,376	$32,889	$7,986	75
72	402	293	288	107	235	734	281	818	542	99	933	83	677	119	76
83	516	380	369	169	252	955	321	739	1,007	78	703	110	953	150	77
97	545	637	302	183	851	1,290	439	617	985	83	795	46	555	141	78
2,458	8,674	11,987	7,881	3,871	18,622	29,242	9,227	13,971	12,514	1,574	18,896	1,254	20,691	3,203	79
806	884	3,039	2,224	873	5,795	8,309	2,377	2,428	2,350	455	3,981	303	4,755	920	80
1,975	4,272	4,366	3,305	2,026	2,933	10,142	5,097	5,780	6,182	1,208	10,415	715	6,467	2,092	81
29,021	77,686	58,049	58,461	22,096	48,854	190,097	94,760	107,224	125,421	18,797	131,473	7,620	88,010	36,235	82

TABLE **73.**—STATISTICS OF SIZE OF FARMS AND FOR TENURE CLASSES OF FARMS

TEXAS—continued.

		Gregg.	Grimes.	Guadalupe.	Harris.	Harrison.	Hays.	Henderson.	Hill.	Hopkins.	Houston.
1	Number of farms	1,056	1,384	654	335	3,306	130	646	252	366	1,780
	FARMS CLASSIFIED BY SIZE.										
2	Under 3 acres										1
3	3 to 9 acres	33	15	3	51	58	11	11	4	10	52
4	10 to 19 acres	97	141	22	65	315	10	53	9	39	182
5	20 to 49 acres	472	773	218	131	1,486	59	269	99	155	853
6	50 to 99 acres	268	289	223	44	741	38	194	95	109	401
7	100 to 174 acres	132	125	143	25	471	9	85	37	47	197
8	175 to 259 acres	40	32	31	7	154	2	25	8	5	62
9	260 to 499 acres	13	9	13	3	71	1	5		1	27
10	500 to 999 acres	1		1	9	10		3			5
11	1,000 acres and over							1			
	FARMERS CLASSIFIED BY TENURE.										
12	Owners, free	261	221	111	147	924	42	99	29	67	342
13	Owners, mortgaged	55	54	92	17	185	12	67	11	16	106
14	Part owners	96	34	26	12	199	2	57	12	30	138
15	Cash tenants	60	198	9	63	974	2	6	2	3	38
16	Share tenants	570	845	403	88	1,007	55	387	174	226	1,114
17	Share-cash tenants	10	26	7		5	14		5		20
18	Tenure not specified	4	6	6	6	10	2	30	19	24	18
19	Managers				2	2	1				4
	FARMS OPERATED BY OWNERS, FREE.										
20	Total acreage	24,753	15,536	10,786	5,660	89,732	1,850	9,007	2,141	5,219	32,543
21	Improved acreage	11,983	7,248	5,130	2,645	51,764	995	3,968	1,270	3,368	13,727
22	Value of land	$201,903	$132,740	$227,373	$163,970	$753,582	$92,385	$62,023	$76,535	$64,534	$253,297
23	Value of buildings	$87,220	$37,400	$39,505	$36,275	$239,948	$20,150	$21,490	$10,205	$18,530	$69,248
24	Value of implements and machinery	$17,208	$12,468	$11,890	$8,305	$56,186	$5,155	$5,911	$3,205	$5,125	$17,510
25	Number of dairy cows	591	560	302	252	2,745	67	237	46	131	1,091
26	Number of work horses	256	295	231	347	946	91	112	49	103	312
27	Number of work mules	264	161	239	72	984	69	97	49	73	235
28	Acreage in cotton	4,535	2,942	2,797	429	17,033	651	1,352	688	1,357	4,941
29	Bales of cotton grown in 1909	1,114	581	580	78	4,301	182	333	184	365	1,397
30	Acreage in corn	3,498	2,357	1,608	834	12,325	241	1,331	346	899	4,157
31	Bushels of corn grown in 1909	29,563	31,865	17,099	13,636	127,729	4,511	16,260	3,460	13,690	45,904
	FARMS OPERATED BY OWNERS, MORTGAGED.										
32	Total acreage	4,442	5,273	9,203	1,793	19,483	896	6,819	1,269	1,238	10,069
33	Improved acreage	2,473	2,400	4,869	1,422	11,007	436	3,058	786	772	4,576
34	Value of land	$38,035	$38,977	$200,414	$74,820	$160,491	$37,575	$44,700	$35,495	$14,100	$77,374
35	Value of buildings	$14,100	$8,750	$23,270	$5,650	$40,951	$5,550	$12,980	$3,300	$3,700	$15,229
36	Value of implements and machinery	$3,303	$3,280	$7,454	$17,975	$9,934	$2,180	$5,289	$1,250	$1,240	$4,481
37	Number of dairy cows	104	162	204	23	513	27	201	22	28	310
38	Number of work horses	61	71	181	26	196	28	94	27	25	108
39	Number of work mules	48	57	176	35	224	28	67	24	14	94
40	Acreage in cotton	922	1,155	2,806	43	3,988	280	1,164	477	387	1,882
41	Bales of cotton grown in 1909	217	208	576	6	1,046	89	279	121	110	489
42	Acreage in corn	656	581	1,217	119	2,564	137	942	222	241	1,292
43	Bushels of corn grown in 1909	4,940	8,037	12,303	1,625	27,822	3,215	11,940	3,219	3,350	15,169
	FARMS OPERATED BY PART OWNERS.										
44	Total acreage	7,783	3,116	2,872	2,106	18,440	75	5,276	1,119	2,525	12,210
45	Owned acreage	5,143	1,678	1,824	960	11,624	27	3,453	473	1,528	8,067
46	Improved acreage	4,470	1,893	1,525	1,834	12,444	75	2,696	811	1,754	5,967
47	Owned improved acreage	2,425	789	847	874	6,451	27	1,286	273	939	3,180
48	Value of land	$68,095	$28,292	$43,585	$131,770	$170,863	$4,750	$41,755	$36,185	$37,490	$107,022
49	Value of buildings	$21,405	$4,990	$4,045	$6,900	$51,791	$1,250	$9,715	$3,850	$8,425	$22,650
50	Value of land and buildings owned	$61,197	$16,311	$30,025	$63,726	$146,693	$2,100	$29,510	$11,860	$28,225	$87,634
51	Value of implements and machinery	$4,105	$2,016	$1,666	$15,960	$11,445	$300	$2,785	$1,455	$2,785	$7,807
52	Number of dairy cows	201	93	63	17	559	3	127	17	71	465
53	Number of work horses	89	59	53	30	222		68	18	51	170
54	Number of work mules	104	27	44	50	224	4	60	32	35	144
55	Acreage in cotton	1,841	820	698	94	4,487	31	1,098	557	712	2,522
56	Bales of cotton grown in 1909	437	151	155	11	1,180	10	273	124	202	704
57	Acreage in corn	1,400	535	355	59	2,579	9	753	155	525	1,871
58	Bushels of corn grown in 1909	10,762	6,685	2,480	683	29,789	300	9,595	2,295	8,110	22,140
	FARMS OPERATED BY CASH TENANTS, INCLUDING TENURE NOT SPECIFIED.										
59	Total acreage	3,247	10,758	1,415	4,552	46,529	237	2,533	1,144	1,515	3,422
60	Improved acreage	2,089	6,909	707	1,585	35,442	220	1,628	1,018	967	2,000
61	Value of land	$29,309	$130,046	$29,585	$248,425	$404,286	$19,750	$28,840	$32,450	$23,730	$25,632
62	Value of buildings	$11,865	$23,930	$4,865	$22,440	$108,792	$2,250	$5,600	$4,100	$4,285	$5,235
63	Value of implements and machinery	$1,681	$7,812	$650	$5,733	$23,381	$525	$1,421	$770	$707	$1,612
64	Number of dairy cows	91	356	27	83	1,336	6	65	20	31	73
65	Number of work horses	54	285	22	190	820	5	29	20	22	44
66	Number of work mules	33	141	26	42	712	9	34	42	15	43
67	Acreage in cotton	847	3,743	357	264	15,647	186	624	705	418	834
68	Bales of cotton grown in 1909	175	786	56	66	3,741	61	137	126	121	219
69	Acreage in corn	544	2,124	160	450	9,132	23	455	115	252	473
70	Bushels of corn grown in 1909	5,055	34,832	1,245	7,163	89,643	880	6,120	1,455	2,973	6,624
	FARMS OPERATED BY SHARE AND SHARE-CASH TENANTS.										
71	Total acreage	22,359	34,378	27,745	5,394	43,341	3,283	21,382	10,371	9,295	45,043
72	Improved acreage	17,573	29,674	19,504	3,696	34,234	3,110	14,227	9,506	8,133	37,295
73	Value of land	$238,743	$464,207	$886,796	$162,676	$349,166	$259,760	$214,202	$546,210	$144,571	$450,796
74	Value of buildings	$65,048	$90,275	$72,459	$20,140	$107,053	$20,595	$43,020	$41,765	$33,485	$94,628
75	Value of implements and machinery	$10,514	$22,402	$19,296	$9,710	$13,037	$7,050	$9,669	$13,772	$7,188	$20,799
76	Number of dairy cows	381	915	394	98	596	45	441	126	182	1,333
77	Number of work horses	234	602	499	164	409	57	308	170	215	628
78	Number of work mules	344	640	533	66	518	107	295	274	116	478
79	Acreage in cotton	7,897	16,173	10,623	696	13,081	2,217	5,496	6,689	4,109	14,967
80	Bales of cotton grown in 1909	1,929	3,928	2,441	157	3,102	854	1,247	1,789	1,177	* 4,374
81	Acreage in corn	4,764	8,816	3,740	658	7,708	446	4,279	1,794	2,397	9,365
82	Bushels of corn grown in 1909	45,382	153,353	35,181	10,677	78,590	11,940	57,453	23,761	38,750	123,453

OPERATED BY COLORED FARMERS, BY COUNTIES, FOR SOUTHERN STATES: 1910—Continued.

TEXAS—continued.

Hunt.	Jackson.	Jasper.	Kaufman.	Lamar.	Lavaca.	Lee.	Leon.	Liberty.	Lime-stone.	McLen-nan.	Madison.	Marion.	Mata-gorda.	Milam.	
298	254	269	724	1,127	531	667	1,176	281	1,033	1,219	476	918	387	1,240	1
7													1		2
24	6	12	10	27	17	10	11	43	21	38	5	10	32	20	3
109	10	37	21	92	41	48	105	75	45	99	31	70	109	42	4
129	70	110	226	511	211	255	600	104	455	557	231	337	181	615	5
23	68	54	293	387	164	164	251	38	352	395	112	236	33	382	6
4	37	32	134	102	77	131	140	13	123	112	59	191	20	145	7
1	17	18	28	5	11	31	42	5	27	10	23	45	5	28	8
1	26	4	11	2	7	23	23	2	9	7	12	24	2	7	9
	16	2		1	2	4	4	1	1	1	3	4	2	1	10
	4		1		1	1						1		5	11
43	77	141	44	154	56	100	185	92	127	173	72	394	76	110	12
7	10	5	29	24	64	84	57	5	62	73	30	57	4	25	13
16	17	40	40	67	30	21	95	19	58	44	63	60	13	43	14
6	4	11	11	20	42	22	41	34	6	10	9	86	97	29	15
220	133	72	594	797	296	420	703	123	762	874	300	248	196	990	16
3	3		1	22	43	6	89	1	11	22				31	17
3	6		5	42		12	6	6	7	21	2	48	1	7	18
	4		1			2		1		2		4		5	19
3,119	8,313	11,440	2,387	8,900	4,021	12,847	18,900	4,870	9,154	7,977	8,622	40,845	3,667	8,149	20
1,860	3,143	3,420	1,540	5,944	1,505	4,040	7,732	2,015	5,463	5,768	4,092	19,029	1,407	4,872	21
$79,980	$158,520	$71,980	$40,470	$169,365	$65,661	$133,810	$140,248	$60,110	$197,647	$316,959	$69,597	$350,114	$86,800	$202,897	22
$16,750	$17,485	$47,403	$11,420	$42,890	$14,066	$28,865	$29,980	$15,050	$33,240	$73,645	$13,290	$135,418	$17,940	$34,095	23
$3,375	$5,087	$4,814	$2,750	$9,137	$2,639	$11,104	$8,029	$3,790	$9,657	$17,425	$2,867	$47,930	$5,285	$8,488	24
86	215	333	66	251	112	387	527	313	211	224	238	1,214	191	166	25
80	258	162	64	202	93	152	231	314	229	200	127	455	174	171	26
55	49	80	60	220	36	100	173	52	193	297	80	399	136	181	27
1,051	960	404	851	2,594	615	1,911	2,853	183	3,007	3,422	1,653	6,634	132	2,774	28
231	106	71	170	645	72	407	812	49	823	985	395	1,601	5	689	29
496	1,061	1,651	490	1,917	567	1,065	2,091	1,048	1,502	1,722	1,086	5,419	1,124	1,418	30
5,680	15,766	16,081	6,160	34,314	7,924	13,729	26,240	18,496	27,595	32,154	14,395	56,108	8,369	25,900	31
637	973	248	2,554	1,994	6,606	11,209	7,080	263	8,097	4,685	4,012	7,211	210	2,140	32
497	394	119	1,598	1,189	2,401	4,123	3,014	76	4,685	3,253	1,621	2,531	78	1,316	33
$16,145	$21,970	$1,400	$48,325	$37,125	$80,437	$139,556	$41,855	$2,495	$179,325	$153,545	$36,596	$66,182	$3,575	$27,325	34
$2,880	$1,940	$2,400	$6,500	$12,635	$16,425	$28,495	$10,030	$525	$19,085	$24,910	$5,360	$19,674	$2,175	$5,240	35
$1,630	$855	$170	$2,182	$3,520	$3,740	$12,105	$2,131	$109	$6,505	$7,522	$1,015	$6,622	$375	$1,207	36
14	34	10	44	52	197	328	175	6	134	110	95	163	12	56	37
16	35	7	45	43	144	157	68	17	133	101	45	55	5	34	38
13	15	4	57	41	44	107	68	1	133	128	38	79	6	58	39
277	169	26	1,258	458	1,218	2,684	1,054	23	2,776	2,085	821	1,215		879	40
93	20	4	309	133	119	514	302	3	722	538	187	263		246	41
137	126	64	318	357	799	1,009	705	44	1,107	648	422	809	90	343	42
2,120	1,425	770	5,103	7,775	11,408	14,942	9,420	770	17,045	11,390	6,360	8,062	307	5,605	43
949	4,894	2,397	3,243	4,072	3,153	2,163	9,503	1,026	4,366	3,401	7,224	4,546	618	4,813	44
518	1,485	1,741	1,801	2,079	1,883	1,558	6,852	603	1,958	1,855	5,135	2,114	179	2,672	45
820	3,243	1,219	2,358	3,210	1,033	1,087	5,050	490	3,274	2,544	3,422	2,308	375	3,067	46
423	1,191	608	1,110	1,356	508	644	2,845	263	1,276	1,255	1,940	975	117	1,633	47
$24,010	$125,490	$17,100	$61,381	$105,985	$47,370	$15,669	$82,280	$9,905	$91,630	$132,666	$66,573	$45,360	$11,385	$61,046	48
$5,150	$5,650	$8,305	$14,540	$17,170	$6,493	$4,765	$15,470	$2,480	$15,120	$18,420	$11,860	$12,914	$2,955	$11,100	49
$16,320	$50,580	$18,590	$36,856	$57,695	$32,944	$13,991	$67,370	$7,920	$51,780	$83,413	$56,018	$30,890	$5,820	$43,270	50
$1,500	$1,062	$1,720	$3,401	$3,709	$998	$1,320	$5,284	$495	$5,550	$4,370	$2,292	$5,417	$641	$2,978	51
19	57	77	78	81	53	67	253	53	87	105	176	113	36	101	52
27	72	47	64	95	40	33	126	69	96	60	90	59	29	62	53
12	16	25	60	93	18	20	119	3	91	87	78	47	26	90	54
512	253	163	1,470	1,408	560	660	2,016	98	1,891	1,299	1,667	897	22	1,589	55
116	31	28	322	395	52	119	547	25	460	309	370	225	2	380	56
219	211	547	490	1,089	296	251	1,268	234	702	468	984	585	209	596	57
2,570	3,265	6,181	4,879	23,895	4,630	2,760	16,145	3,990	12,435	6,615	13,080	6,315	1,217	10,165	58
304	1,361	1,767	1,088	2,876	2,518	2,126	2,627	1,475	771	1,918	782	6,271	3,967	2,337	59
257	416	176	805	2,705	1,338	1,064	1,745	652	607	1,260	657	3,904	2,791	1,700	60
$15,430	$14,420	$4,575	$27,085	$93,135	$53,655	$21,030	$18,535	$22,225	$22,825	$77,670	$6,326	$52,241	$139,375	$39,550	61
$850	$1,330	$3,575	$2,800	$14,405	$8,320	$4,440	$5,230	$3,865	$2,500	$6,775	$1,300	$17,695	$14,835	$6,390	62
$158	$165	$220	$1,410	$3,880	$2,133	$1,133	$1,250	$1,254	$1,265	$2,166	$215	$4,471	$4,845	$1,593	63
7	10	20	18	49	73	40	83	46	10	28	9	208	176	29	64
7	24	14	19	59	79	39	50	78	15	26	10	112	200	31	65
3	3	1	21	46	22	10	36	8	10	39	39	70	139	46	66
192	81	13	491	1,569	677	524	754	100	351	797	282	1,945	232	916	67
46	15	3	111	475	97	99	190	26	105	213	51	413	11	257	68
71	53	70	95	733	408	209	511	290	98	226	132	1,303	1,846	360	69
1,557	700	860	1,325	15,767	6,638	2,410	5,700	5,025	1,610	4,275	1,825	12,950	16,855	4,598	70
11,900	24,195	2,765	45,456	39,126	18,650	25,124	34,907	2,956	41,255	45,746	12,873	10,646	8,118	54,518	71
10,259	6,060	1,610	37,761	36,091	11,544	14,687	26,280	2,371	36,535	41,759	10,350	7,919	6,205	48,628	72
$400,115	$494,170	$19,410	$1,507,616	$1,312,252	$356,592	$290,383	$390,514	$47,470	$1,332,129	$2,237,116	$141,701	$101,693	$300,755	$1,465,222	73
$46,720	$29,230	$10,790	$157,675	$162,405	$59,815	$67,124	$87,940	$9,025	$144,318	$219,554	$25,900	$36,888	$32,730	$150,619	74
$12,327	$8,519	$1,019	$38,239	$37,526	$9,366	$16,383	$16,215	$2,559	$50,332	$53,902	$5,237	$7,881	$19,147	$44,192	75
169	209	80	521	642	460	589	850	109	527	614	397	278	225	711	76
222	341	61	409	520	381	384	469	196	689	613	235	159	342	808	77
297	66	17	1,086	959	106	159	583	20	1,022	1,250	157	116	273	1,535	78
7,132	1,883	199	25,895	21,751	5,827	8,747	12,046	326	24,312	29,407	5,409	3,355	363	31,020	79
1,515	282	38	6,758	6,506	745	1,708	3,456	86	6,818	8,931	1,300	786	16	8,913	80
2,172	2,130	757	5,488	10,695	3,316	3,518	7,626	1,236	8,134	8,098	3,238	2,562	3,393	11,156	81
32,555	34,029	8,759	73,662	241,625	54,595	44,817	108,913	21,330	144,625	158,747	48,007	25,861	27,260	248,795	82

TABLE 73.—STATISTICS OF SIZE OF FARMS AND FOR TENURE CLASSES OF FARMS

TEXAS—continued.

		Mont-gomery.	Morris.	Nacogdo-ches.	Navarro.	Newton.	Panola.	Polk.	Rains.	Red River.	Robertson.
1	Number of farms	781	574	855	986	333	1,407	619	121	1,342	2,365
	FARMS CLASSIFIED BY SIZE.										
2	Under 3 acres										
3	3 to 9 acres	32	6	25	15	12	9	38	1	29	24
4	10 to 19 acres	101	57	125	42	47	85	131	17	138	96
5	20 to 49 acres	401	315	388	383	138	641	277	53	734	1,418
6	50 to 99 acres	132	124	181	352	63	369	100	33	320	617
7	100 to 174 acres	96	61	100	141	52	213	50	12	90	156
8	175 to 259 acres	14	6	22	35	12	64	18	1	19	32
9	260 to 499 acres	4	5	11	16	6	22	3	3	7	18
10	500 to 999 acres	1		3	2	2	4	2	1	5	3
11	1,000 acres and over					1					1
	FARMERS CLASSIFIED BY TENURE.										
12	Owners, free	160	68	171	97	267	330	192	20	166	180
13	Owners, mortgaged	41	43	52	43	12	92	22	5	44	59
14	Part owners	40	39	31	58	8	52	81	21	72	90
15	Cash tenants	82	4	19	11		59	24		44	188
16	Share tenants	403	417	574	765	46	862	285	46	968	1,756
17	Share-cash tenants	53	1	6	2		4	11		7	83
18	Tenure not specified	2	2	2	10		8	4	29	41	7
19	Managers										2
	FARMS OPERATED BY OWNERS, FREE.										
20	Total acreage	11,253	5,858	14,795	7,418	19,938	35,034	13,629	2,408	12,539	13,758
21	Improved acreage	4,623	2,411	6,688	4,527	6,286	18,336	4,659	777	7,077	7,220
22	Value of land	$100,056	$51,480	$108,984	$212,650	$125,220	$243,345	$97,048	$36,700	$171,836	$143,936
23	Value of buildings	$39,825	$21,640	$36,256	$34,675	$62,020	$62,790	$40,950	$8,950	$44,180	$49,910
24	Value of implements and machinery	$8,048	$4,663	$7,146	$8,602	$10,961	$18,496	$6,731	$2,305	$11,927	$12,588
25	Number of dairy cows	441	153	349	161	524	1,064	576	46	423	461
26	Number of work horses	234	87	196	254	336	378	288	42	279	227
27	Number of work mules	118	64	167	131	100	302	110	23	167	240
28	Acreage in cotton	1,608	1,034	1,813	2,820	780	6,394	1,013	295	2,166	4,247
29	Bales of cotton grown in 1909	343	274	460	686	224	1,634	284	77	469	1,105
30	Acreage in corn	1,680	877	2,250	1,287	3,022	4,802	1,837	191	2,359	2,234
31	Bushels of corn grown in 1909	24,188	12,041	26,825	20,035	34,921	46,692	24,694	3,650	43,615	34,834
	FARMS OPERATED BY OWNERS, MORTGAGED.										
32	Total acreage	3,145	4,095	4,857	6,254	609	9,359	1,700	330	4,688	6,694
33	Improved acreage	1,506	1,802	2,243	3,486	231	5,174	517	200	1,867	2,987
34	Value of land	$28,305	$31,605	$30,189	$189,221	$5,450	$54,387	$11,994	$3,350	$45,346	$71,636
35	Value of buildings	$10,920	$12,340	$9,095	$18,650	$3,200	$14,290	$5,135	$1,650	$10,290	$16,347
36	Value of implements and machinery	$2,195	$3,180	$2,105	$6,592	$530	$6,155	$775	$600	$2,566	$4,923
37	Number of dairy cows	97	101	101	86	22	276	75	13	125	181
38	Number of work horses	61	56	67	148	14	97	31	10	88	84
39	Number of work mules	53	39	65	82	5	101	13	7	27	99
40	Acreage in cotton	528	878	775	2,068	22	2,027	185	60	690	2,069
41	Bales of cotton grown in 1909	129	231	191	542	9	489	52	19	184	506
42	Acreage in corn	531	665	770	739	110	1,315	210	31	780	797
43	Bushels of corn grown in 1909	7,260	8,430	7,730	11,605	1,989	13,736	3,300	500	13,645	13,561
	FARMS OPERATED BY PART OWNERS.										
44	Total acreage	3,208	2,995	2,217	4,786	311	4,632	4,602	1,439	5,632	7,967
45	Owned acreage	1,797	1,814	1,576	2,277	208	3,131	3,047	927	3,353	4,564
46	Improved acreage	1,822	1,822	1,394	3,617	198	2,634	2,122	924	3,857	4,974
47	Owned improved acreage	886	968	797	1,477	96	1,375	1,034	481	1,724	2,271
48	Value of land	$26,970	$27,205	$14,305	$144,410	$2,510	$30,144	$36,857	$24,675	$92,316	$102,014
49	Value of buildings	$8,495	$8,540	$3,965	$22,270	$1,125	$7,095	$12,647	$4,650	$17,489	$23,310
50	Value of land and buildings owned	$21,335	$23,665	$12,020	$79,110	$2,690	$26,458	$31,655	$17,840	$60,110	$65,930
51	Value of implements and machinery	$5,427	$1,848	$755	$5,158	$120	$1,748	$2,356	$1,790	$5,364	$5,965
52	Number of dairy cows	135	69	67	76	18	129	206	41	212	217
53	Number of work horses	67	49	27	135	11	42	121	30	128	109
54	Number of work mules	51	37	36	101	1	62	38	27	105	144
55	Acreage in cotton	736	847	552	2,131	32	1,166	721	382	1,307	3,186
56	Bales of cotton grown in 1909	167	210	119	616	11	252	196	103	299	800
57	Acreage in corn	536	522	495	812	81	678	747	295	1,373	1,148
58	Bushels of corn grown in 1909	8,635	7,340	5,068	14,460	997	7,040	11,094	4,560	23,510	20,345
	FARMS OPERATED BY CASH TENANTS, INCLUDING TENURE NOT SPECIFIED.										
59	Total acreage	3,501	499	1,782	1,079		4,913	1,505	772	4,262	11,603
60	Improved acreage	2,734	153	719	666		3,082	648	717	3,283	9,956
61	Value of land	$38,160	$2,750	$12,295	$41,750		$34,836	$11,095	$11,730	$81,765	$404,630
62	Value of buildings	$13,020	$1,150	$3,670	$4,125		$5,945	$2,425	$2,270	$17,965	$27,785
63	Value of implements and machinery	$2,965	$155	$2,173	$1,058		$1,999	$738	$725	$3,486	$9,847
64	Number of dairy cows	137	7	33	14		140	52	33	135	156
65	Number of work horses	129	7	18	37		53	45	26	120	121
66	Number of work mules	52	6	13	11		64	10	11	70	351
67	Acreage in cotton	1,079	68	236	362		1,220	187	293	1,685	7,470
68	Bales of cotton grown in 1909	241	13	59	87		246	58	79	372	2,446
69	Acreage in corn	822	63	301	170		827	236	217	1,177	1,738
70	Bushels of corn grown in 1909	12,650	1,112	3,169	2,229		7,305	3,182	3,315	23,146	33,315
	FARMS OPERATED BY SHARE AND SHARE-CASH TENANTS.										
71	Total acreage	18,132	15,147	23,938	49,327	1,267	38,715	8,196	2,139	40,059	79,574
72	Improved acreage	13,997	13,201	17,444	42,434	787	31,110	6,997	1,596	34,968	73,260
73	Value of land	$199,990	$159,102	$239,646	$1,545,613	$8,985	$284,715	$95,426	$38,265	$877,513	$1,885,253
74	Value of buildings	$66,010	$53,380	$65,256	$168,284	$9,175	$71,429	$32,365	$5,235	$142,292	$328,343
75	Value of implements and machinery	$11,828	$11,252	$10,777	$48,116	$1,115	$13,968	$7,402	$1,881	$1,180	$1,255
76	Number of dairy cows	527	354	554	729	50	933	520	34	947	909
77	Number of work horses	456	270	387	1,034	42	441	368	24	726	1,897
78	Number of work mules	261	244	285	1,121	11	511	156	37	726	1,897
79	Acreage in cotton	5,821	6,064	6,898	28,491	103	13,287	3,306	807	15,540	50,742
80	Bales of cotton grown in 1909	1,327	1,440	1,930	7,241	33	3,341	1,256	186	3,812	14,754
81	Acreage in corn	4,146	4,085	6,260	9,634	327	8,431	2,736	538	14,221	13,872
82	Bushels of corn grown in 1909	60,053	55,229	84,082	169,788	4,330	88,798	46,727	7,070	293,125	255,844

OPERATED BY COLORED FARMERS, BY COUNTIES, FOR SOUTHERN STATES: 1910—Continued.

TEXAS—continued.

Rusk.	Sabine.	San Augustine.	San Jacinto.	Shelby.	Smith.	Tarrant.	Titus.	Travis.	Trinity.	Tyler.	Upshur.	Van Zandt.	Victoria.	Walker.	
1,983	235	514	867	582	2,602	126	368	787	249	184	964	229	272	1,216	1
			1					1							2
26	4	10	89	7	32	5	18	27	17	18	58	1	11	37	3
139	25	69	209	53	185	11	38	43	43	37	119	13	33	202	4
803	105	254	343	292	1,146	51	203	302	87	52	423	94	117	596	5
588	69	102	116	129	739	36	69	287	59	30	191	60	72	218	6
321	18	59	84	77	388	18	32	104	36	38	122	43	18	130	7
68	6	14	16	18	64	5	4	19	5	6	34	9	7	22	8
33	7	5	8	5	42		3	3	2	2	16	9	9	10	9
4	1	1	1	1	5		1	1	1		1	1	3	1	10
1					1								2		11
431	54	91	250	141	431	49	64	102	95	91	220	61	61	231	12
175	6	19	25	36	178	6	21	33	14	6	44	8	7	57	13
153	32	26	90	25	274	8	24	43	14	11	36	33	70	78	14
31	4	12	28	10	88	2	14	21	18	23	1	7	13	274	15
1,075	136	362	440	367	1,558	58	234	497	107	52	643	120	116	562	16
5	3	1	3	1	51			84	1	1	2		2	9	17
113		3	31	2	20	3	11	6			17			5	18
					2			1			1		3		19
42,518	5,778	10,015	17,484	12,694	43,835	2,865	5,872	6,297	7,170	8,100	21,761	6,353	4,004	17,038	20
23,697	2,448	3,527	6,438	6,651	24,575	1,852	2,589	3,805	2,103	1,740	10,299	2,634	1,703	7,691	21
$282,053	$41,517	$61,114	$118,963	$107,729	$396,746	$129,175	$59,468	$240,554	$49,530	$40,505	$163,702	$58,850	$143,412	$145,354	22
$96,780	$9,860	$16,265	$32,240	$39,305	$113,345	$15,460	$16,307	$39,750	$22,970	$15,435	$46,315	$19,830	$11,870	$43,890	23
$26,967	$2,255	$4,330	$6,954	$8,913	$34,723	$3,225	$3,895	$10,744	$5,409	$3,697	$20,562	$3,244	$2,834	$9,292	24
1,191	183	223	667	550	1,048	65	147	195	263	205	660	146	132	716	25
450	56	102	384	161	476	85	76	177	117	97	211	75	121	371	26
469	40	73	111	108	526	63	71	168	61	41	291	73	97	151	27
6,983	647	881	1,650	2,339	8,340	524	929	1,990	578	147	4,071	1,040	675	3,032	28
1,771	135	223	536	621	2,292	92	248	602	132	34	1,156	266	209	783	29
6,581	681	1,058	2,301	1,994	6,521	426	776	827	820	783	3,032	874	585	2,256	30
66,942	6,335	11,528	29,521	24,163	66,384	3,840	12,816	13,281	9,460	9,136	30,917	12,355	10,140	28,036	31
16,472	426	1,290	2,169	3,140	17,864	383	1,432	3,768	886	516	4,113	1,049	698	6,927	32
8,477	190	666	684	1,582	9,454	284	2,145	2,145	377	192	2,015	448	264	2,791	33
$102,897	$3,200	$8,792	$17,310	$22,710	$148,395	$11,940	$13,975	$130,790	$8,010	$3,692	$29,250	$6,410	$17,590	$59,432	34
$34,685	$500	$1,990	$3,415	$8,805	$32,705	$1,180	$3,815	$20,840	$2,290	$1,350	$7,625	$1,300	$1,400	$10,138	35
$12,280	$250	$695	$1,104	$2,045	$12,700	$295	$1,282	$6,065	$746	$355	$2,549	$300	$505	$4,994	36
429	17	64	79	107	458	9	46	68	40	16	109	31	15	165	37
167	7	20	47	35	202	9	20	87	15	7	35	22	19	115	38
212	3	18	29	28	252	9	20	108	12	5	52	5	13	39	39
3,039	64	206	183	554	4,146	91	273	1,544	156	29	833	152	158	1,548	40
801	11	63	64	153	1,634	16	72	448	37	6	211	33	42	322	41
2,628	70	217	280	469	2,760	50	247	354	154	56	542	135	89	662	42
27,439	690	2,210	4,075	4,295	28,463	300	5,040	6,270	1,645	640	5,520	1,240	1,475	9,130	43
14,277	2,618	1,720	6,128	1,645	25,943	561	1,301	3,058	803	606	2,947	2,846	6,519	6,682	44
8,773	1,539	1,132	3,985	939	15,254	185	924	1,680	451	548	2,210	1,745	3,730	3,409	45
8,368	1,410	845	2,797	1,073	16,423	382	996	2,386	401	211	1,507	1,826	3,187	3,514	46
4,572	648	364	1,133	525	8,748	96	629	1,163	188	153	895	876	1,447	1,227	47
$94,219	$21,573	$14,417	$40,713	$18,055	$209,048	$13,800	$15,875	$135,730	$5,835	$3,875	$21,225	$39,494	$243,399	$51,600	48
$26,285	$5,475	$2,430	$7,954	$4,700	$54,095	$1,500	$5,010	$18,250	$2,025	$1,450	$4,525	$6,340	$14,522	$12,190	49
$80,476	$16,453	$10,441	$28,845	$13,200	$162,331	$4,350	$15,415	$89,540	$4,765	$4,095	$19,838	$22,250	$128,756	$36,088	50
$7,086	$1,275	$817	$1,901	$993	$13,696	$440	$1,455	$5,802	$750	$319	$1,468	$2,070	$4,510	$3,516	51
403	78	58	296	61	589	9	42	102	43	18	115	72	169	241	52
145	36	33	163	24	246	13	29	86	16	7	25	36	184	101	53
184	29	16	70	23	390	11	21	74	15	5	51	37	131	61	54
2,980	583	322	943	535	6,636	171	388	1,271	134	26	800	700	1,487	1,389	55
682	124	66	299	120	1,691	27	109	590	37	9	218	143	404	319	56
2,226	467	282	978	306	3,945	58	303	394	128	79	448	434	973	843	57
20,867	4,650	3,135	12,034	3,540	39,272	537	5,015	5,789	1,375	1,004	5,305	5,283	18,995	11,440	58
8,537	305	671	2,211	679	8,512	368	463	1,256	705	597	691	378	1,199	10,880	59
5,388	128	400	1,387	376	4,420	141	441	1,082	414	275	604	225	398	8,267	60
$59,729	$2,450	$3,399	$17,645	$7,530	$80,362	$32,140	$7,191	$72,185	$6,550	$3,463	$5,124	$4,850	$30,575	$91,616	61
$16,885	$700	$780	$6,305	$1,675	$18,020	$2,300	$800	$7,100	$1,775	$1,630	$1,765	$2,150	$2,235	$27,245	62
$3,352	$215	$260	$947	$370	$3,412	$285	$135	$1,608	$673	$465	$221	$305	$395	$6,884	63
151	8	34	79	26	163	7	13	37	22	22	21	18	27	489	64
80	6	13	83	11	79	5	17	48	20	13	7	10	22	327	65
130	3	4	12	5	100	6	7	35	6	6	16	5	20	121	66
2,053	58	131	351	128	1,823	93	227	604	89	40	295	59	178	3,887	67
520	11	24	133	34	431	18	67	190	19	6	54	12	47	950	68
1,263	36	134	532	128	1,232	12	107	162	105	136	143		161	2,069	69
12,570	480	1,535	6,240	1,600	13,016	80	1,730	2,880	830	1,487	1,240		2,945	24,116	70
53,648	4,960	13,998	9,721	15,135	69,094	3,087	8,648	33,678	3,712	2,153	26,018	6,782	6,827	18,047	71
36,193	4,274	10,981	9,130	11,435	58,385	2,619	7,142	30,355	2,922	983	19,049	4,986	4,650	15,225	72
$394,388	$41,959	$153,896	$92,975	$153,008	$720,903	$152,790	$97,757	$1,870,265	$50,946	$14,535	$216,552	$89,260	$299,020	$192,219	73
$105,625	$13,475	$29,295	$29,820	$40,190	$163,150	$22,960	$23,280	$127,481	$9,755	$5,225	$54,576	$30,560	$16,600	$43,880	74
$19,658	$2,755	$9,946	$4,815	$7,896	$33,068	$2,552	$3,779	$40,376	$3,455	$751	$10,597	$5,092	$6,179	$6,902	75
1,197	181	453	500	586	1,482	42	183	563	112	51	629	134	116	497	76
610	102	291	507	243	918	56	126	639	55	28	277	75	245	392	77
672	67	175	159	189	1,074	81	159	1,010	52	20	361	70	152	139	78
14,385	1,917	4,333	3,575	4,401	27,174	1,327	3,678	21,857	1,122	219	8,430	2,124	2,033	7,356	79
3,376	396	1,249	1,444	1,296	7,065	183	908	7,133	339	53	2,424	472	617	1,936	80
10,872	1,394	4,283	3,547	3,535	16,336	435	2,531	4,654	887	474	5,688	58	1,546	3,598	81
113,900	16,496	52,467	57,263	44,416	168,761	3,224	37,985	80,358	10,508	4,731	63,296	705	31,105	47,607	82

TABLE 73.—STATISTICS OF SIZE OF FARMS AND FOR TENURE CLASSES OF FARMS

		TEXAS—continued.							VIRGINIA.	
		Waller.	Washington.	Wharton.	Williamson.	Wilson.	Wood.	All other counties.	The state.	Accomac.
1	Number of farms	1,114	1,646	1,199	260	105	502	1,133	48,114	875
	FARMS CLASSIFIED BY SIZE.									
2	Under 3 acres							11	44	
3	3 to 9 acres	53	69	86	3	5	14	109	6,979	49
4	10 to 19 acres	159	139	230	19	4	58	114	10,079	82
5	20 to 49 acres	653	889	628	72	19	232	302	16,431	363
6	50 to 99 acres	187	367	174	92	36	117	275	8,685	283
7	100 to 174 acres	45	131	60	50	32	66	186	4,166	91
8	175 to 259 acres	12	32	12	12	5	13	49	1,070	4
9	260 to 499 acres	3	16	6	11	3	2	46	530	3
10	500 to 999 acres	1	3	2	1	1		23	112	
11	1,000 acres and over	1		1				18	18	
	FARMERS CLASSIFIED BY TENURE.									
12	Owners, free	161	201	169	39	33	118	299	22,220	64
13	Owners, mortgaged	45	74	33	19	7	36	85	4,600	71
14	Part owners	122	124	97	13	6	57	91	5,408	10
15	Cash tenants	238	194	130			7	58	3,661	329
16	Share tenants	521	809	613	178	59	270	522	10,906	396
17	Share-cash tenants	23	219	153	4		1	14	382	2
18	Tenure not specified	2	25	3	7		13	48	757	2
19	Managers	2		1				16	180	1
	FARMS OPERATED BY OWNERS, FREE.									
20	Total acreage	9,265	12,510	9,300	4,568	3,834	10,160	31,367	889,297	2,251
21	Improved acreage	5,010	7,895	4,747	2,094	1,656	4,961	10,253	421,031	1,111
22	Value of land	$147,233	$254,094	$353,254	$182,755	$58,685	$77,690	$632,778	$11,885,058	$96,560
23	Value of buildings	$35,330	$61,996	$63,346	$16,175	$8,475	$29,390	$107,685	$6,290,120	$38,240
24	Value of implements and machinery	$7,476	$18,542	$12,970	$5,675	$1,700	$6,296	$28,218	$882,939	$5,750
25	Number of dairy cows	385	405	404	81	90	303	607	21,264	41
26	Number of work horses	348	254	357	101	65	140	669	18,290	94
27	Number of work mules	127	219	297	78	40	118	350	3,351	22
28	Acreage in cotton	1,505	3,144	1,480	1,252	660	1,868	3,280	2,888	
29	Bales of cotton grown in 1909	304	756	117	303	148	468	520	1,149	
30	Acreage in corn	1,589	1,839	2,160	430	347	1,628	3,477	128,589	499
31	Bushels of corn grown in 1909	30,670	38,560	42,469	3,915	2,830	18,376	18,339	1,881,621	8,592
	FARMS OPERATED BY OWNERS, MORTGAGED.									
32	Total acreage	3,241	6,598	2,513	2,616	1,046	2,780	24,105	243,224	3,201
33	Improved acreage	1,983	3,783	1,434	1,047	406	1,470	6,724	108,228	1,533
34	Value of land	$62,313	$137,464	$96,453	$87,015	$8,745	$31,285	$286,187	$3,215,804	$109,190
35	Value of buildings	$10,595	$29,485	$11,450	$6,625	$1,505	$4,775	$55,785	$1,403,484	$38,410
36	Value of implements and machinery	$3,230	$9,180	$3,795	$2,105	$405	$1,057	$18,634	$212,431	$6,405
37	Number of dairy cows	121	176	112	48	8	77	217	4,154	48
38	Number of work horses	107	134	107	43	11	49	242	4,120	128
39	Number of work mules	53	106	78	42	5	28	220	938	26
40	Acreage in cotton	700	1,667	537	679	165	683	2,445	1,558	
41	Bales of cotton grown in 1909	140	481	42	163	36	178	389	558	
42	Acreage in corn	488	846	652	191	97	465	735	31,343	564
43	Bushels of corn grown in 1909	10,140	19,440	13,603	2,195	750	5,195	5,985	428,601	10,703
	FARMS OPERATED BY PART OWNERS.									
44	Total acreage	6,115	11,128	7,432	1,162	305	3,827	16,192	248,702	288
45	Owned acreage	3,119	6,585	4,046	643	127	2,086	6,365	[1]136,134	(2)
46	Improved acreage	4,952	7,240	5,152	582	273	2,422	5,257	140,099	159
47	Owned improved acreage	2,259	3,643	2,120	176	95	1,018	2,564	[1]62,426	(2)
48	Value of land	$121,722	$212,704	$306,052	$25,970	$5,340	$39,436	$251,072	$3,759,469	$17,620
49	Value of buildings	$22,935	$41,585	$41,755	$2,940	$1,090	$11,825	$26,430	$1,505,599	$4,750
50	Value of land and buildings owned	$78,659	$149,663	$203,556	$12,070	$3,490	$28,191	$138,772	[1]$3,147,802	(2)
51	Value of implements and machinery	$6,318	$16,717	$47,947	$835	$215	$2,025	$8,403	$232,705	$510
52	Number of dairy cows	285	252	293	25	7	108	168	5,434	6
53	Number of work horses	271	219	224	27	12	70	258	5,621	12
54	Number of work mules	113	180	272	20	4	44	151	1,269	3
55	Acreage in cotton	2,205	3,174	2,252	288	91	1,052	2,208	948	
56	Bales of cotton grown in 1909	428	710	156	49	23	266	383	352	
57	Acreage in corn	1,415	1,615	1,757	123	41	835	800	53,650	55
58	Bushels of corn grown in 1909	32,347	35,785	38,436	1,050	420	9,430	8,772	759,081	985
	FARMS OPERATED BY CASH TENANTS, INCLUDING TENURE NOT SPECIFIED.									
59	Total acreage	7,822	10,097	4,491	653		683	15,451	244,343	14,904
60	Improved acreage	7,214	7,790	4,021	613		521	4,070	104,938	7,166
61	Value of land	$133,071	$216,543	$218,000	$31,100		$7,775	$254,869	$4,169,564	$794,850
62	Value of buildings	$33,135	$38,805	$22,090	$2,200		$2,675	$23,985	$939,244	$129,825
63	Value of implements and machinery	$8,833	$13,179	$6,725	$1,460		$548	$7,180	$148,392	$24,261
64	Number of dairy cows	303	247	163	6		26	109	2,900	180
65	Number of work horses	467	318	234	15		9	139	3,123	512
66	Number of work mules	122	203	204	11		5	154	835	91
67	Acreage in cotton	3,236	4,135	1,680	427		216	1,534	3,817	
68	Bales of cotton grown in 1909	675	1,101	132	120		55	298	1,352	
69	Acreage in corn	2,183	2,042	2,178	85		126	403	31,322	2,887
70	Bushels of corn grown in 1909	45,332	41,930	49,775	1,735		1,617	3,673	414,226	49,343
	FARMS OPERATED BY SHARE AND SHARE-CASH TENANTS.									
71	Total acreage	18,663	43,491	24,580	12,316	4,816	9,522	50,865	582,669	22,943
72	Improved acreage	17,809	35,546	22,988	10,337	3,214	8,186	28,513	322,866	10,932
73	Value of land	$381,806	$922,294	$1,113,447	$863,394	$93,945	$101,895	$1,214,611	$8,492,620	$1,198,165
74	Value of buildings	$78,375	$191,192	$115,125	$46,774	$14,260	$27,695	$114,541	$2,232,727	$231,110
75	Value of implements and machinery	$18,553	$51,524	$31,743	$17,734	$2,740	$4,325	$34,701	$347,178	$34,693
76	Number of dairy cows	403	1,037	528	139	66	226	1,348	8,042	223
77	Number of work horses	644	1,040	978	203	110	172	705	7,401	673
78	Number of work mules	535	919	957	301	39	119	590	2,234	106
79	Acreage in cotton	9,556	21,147	9,833	7,554	1,528	3,057	13,815	4,113	
80	Bales of cotton grown in 1909	2,247	5,608	725	2,506	361	833	2,720	1,631	
81	Acreage in corn	4,778	9,232	8,992	1,130	751	2,534	4,378	91,026	4,196
82	Bushels of corn grown in 1909	112,004	200,813	178,206	19,787	5,830	30,075	58,896	1,436,161	68,805

[1] Total for the state excepting figures for Accomac and Madison Counties, which are not available

OPERATED BY COLORED FARMERS, BY COUNTIES, FOR SOUTHERN STATES: 1910—Continued.

VIRGINIA—continued.

Albemarle.	Amelia.	Amherst.	Appomattox.	Augusta.	Bedford.	Botetourt.	Brunswick.	Buckingham	Campbell.	Caroline.	Charles City.	Charlotte.	Chesterfield.	Culpeper.	
637	720	824	357	164	858	154	1,093	967	808	1,192	622	1,023	594	480	1
	1								1						2
162	50	72	25	60	102	54	60	71	101	78	117	126	176	117	3
171	147	139	58	38	167	33	159	186	186	212	190	202	176	120	4
179	235	311	106	35	273	38	423	380	235	492	204	338	164	143	5
79	162	168	78	13	200	20	232	188	153	274	67	189	46	68	6
22	76	100	59	13	94	6	143	99	97	91	30	130	20	18	7
11	23	22	17	1	15	2	44	19	26	30	10	27	4	8	8
8	17	11	13	4	6	1	27	19	9	12	2	9	4	5	9
4	9		1		1		4	4		3	2	2	3	1	10
1		1					1	1					1		11
491	376	386	155	90	368	116	415	611	375	577	446	352	428	321	12
22	89	57	35	36	86	5	133	34	88	117	12	88	22	51	13
68	95	57	14	23	125	19	96	121	86	235	112	165	58	75	14
9	57	50	14	2	53	2	165	30	23	20	37	44	46	15	15
30	77	264	133	9	216	6	244	166	233	198	14	364	21	7	16
	2	5	1	1	7		21		1	3	1	7	5	2	17
5	20	3	5		1	5	19	5	1	39		1	11	5	18
12	4	2		3	2	1			1	3		2	3	4	19
14,923	19,003	16,906	10,430	2,099	16,127	3,214	29,325	30,911	15,803	26,213	14,349	17,145	9,918	8,879	20
8,356	8,760	8,793	4,642	1,511	8,632	1,501	11,407	13,342	7,881	12,171	6,224	6,666	3,975	6,117	21
$278,649	$165,545	$200,605	$113,285	$67,755	$204,929	$57,885	$351,085	$213,340	$204,354	$220,035	$158,102	$198,555	$218,896	$185,568	22
$180,956	$101,530	$105,005	$48,130	$34,425	$79,241	$36,410	$131,679	$152,587	$112,593	$148,600	$133,821	$102,180	$90,920	$118,720	23
$18,311	$14,688	$13,639	$6,534	$3,080	$12,924	$4,065	$25,249	$24,284	$15,103	$19,704	$18,325	$15,831	$11,486	$14,521	24
492	376	461	181	88	470	102	527	527	454	566	294	313	381	434	25
406	288	392	158	90	379	95	381	417	302	405	126	240	226	382	26
42	104	10	19	2	38	5	87	89	55	167	126	33	70	17	27
							871						3		28
							344				1				29
2,045	2,552	1,612	836	313	1,580	338	3,186	2,822	1,598	4,316	2,785	1,850	1,507	1,646	30
31,609	34,328	33,783	11,986	6,571	29,774	6,307	38,442	35,966	21,084	46,458	44,294	27,138	21,651	26,629	31
766	5,751	3,543	2,282	1,110	4,692	104	9,358	2,345	6,571	6,362	290	5,722	550	2,238	32
439	2,484	1,539	847	805	2,621	30	3,601	1,068	2,445	3,165	108	1,968	195	1,403	33
$12,630	$40,110	$32,263	$16,700	$27,815	$52,295	$2,750	$109,611	$18,520	$58,835	$59,955	$2,793	$64,728	$5,798	$38,760	34
$8,450	$20,750	$12,292	$8,150	$12,020	$24,335	$1,650	$34,888	$10,975	$22,045	$29,605	$2,369	$26,215	$4,472	$18,905	35
$818	$3,918	$1,925	$1,135	$1,712	$4,250	$105	$7,330	$1,897	$3,167	$6,292	$472	$3,746	$542	$2,345	36
18	92	71	34	34	118	3	158	27	84	129	5	76	16	83	37
22	75	71	35	36	94	3	102	22	66	81	1	61	11	68	38
3	25	4			15		34	12	23	30	3	13	5	9	39
							268								40
							94						7		41
90	713	340	180	140	446	16	1,110	235	390	1,059	53	498	48	368	42
1,490	7,780	6,713	1,870	3,285	8,301	188	13,712	2,553	4,476	11,035	855	6,614	572	6,085	43
2,488	5,661	2,281	1,164	1,082	5,163	708	6,298	6,032	6,715	13,254	4,309	9,105	1,789	3,771	44
974	2,626	1,046	850	459	2,845	357	4,216	3,347	4,430	6,564	2,321	5,249	886	1,764	45
1,964	2,717	1,606	542	841	3,378	520	2,999	2,852	3,001	7,124	2,714	4,338	1,021	3,174	46
612	1,192	740	528	306	1,642	169	1,510	1,366	1,756	3,142	921	2,173	397	1,382	47
$49,763	$44,759	$39,125	$8,020	$40,290	$76,276	$13,560	$83,274	$52,039	$65,895	$129,121	$50,445	$117,471	$70,000	$73,636	48
$26,185	$23,315	$14,860	$4,120	$9,200	$22,410	$5,025	$25,780	$32,710	$32,560	$56,870	$35,630	$56,210	$10,535	$31,233	49
$48,070	$40,415	$31,650	$9,380	$26,590	$59,350	$10,008	$77,036	$57,267	$68,625	$116,954	$62,536	$124,434	$37,200	$56,285	50
$2,833	$4,871	$2,282	$515	$2,197	$3,257	$727	$6,365	$4,979	$4,669	$10,059	$6,379	$9,226	$3,729	$5,347	51
76	107	72	16	26	142	21	98	114	114	263	110	173	57	133	52
104	87	67	16	47	133	26	82	98	85	242	40	170	60	143	53
6	34	2	2	3	33		27	20	41	66	64	21	21	15	54
							196						7		55
							76				1				56
853	1,003	401	93	242	854	171	808	949	692	3,676	1,895	1,492	442	969	57
13,107	11,888	8,321	1,365	5,110	14,527	2,401	10,575	13,064	8,954	40,168	27,435	20,785	7,808	16,890	58
1,538	5,838	5,406	1,372	18	2,228	374	12,319	4,480	1,504	2,662	2,378	2,582	3,062	436	59
324	1,945	1,345	514	17	996	317	5,214	1,284	807	1,322	629	788	986	325	60
$12,830	$33,780	$30,206	$14,115	$460	$24,415	$12,430	$100,664	$70,535	$13,875	$22,220	$24,620	$24,474	$54,430	$5,375	61
$3,100	$14,455	$7,990	$4,440	$300	$6,710	$3,020	$22,400	$7,155	$5,500	$10,370	$8,890	$10,611	$11,060	$4,650	62
$216	$1,504	$999	$270	$75	$1,148	$960	$4,734	$1,283	$460	$1,659	$520	$1,145	$1,299	$605	63
8	59	74	14	1	54	8	151	32	20	40	13	29	36	20	64
14	44	49	6	2	34	8	124	22	16	36	4	27	22	7	65
1	10	4	2		1		33	1	3	4	5	3	15		66
							569								67
							193								68
58	452	241	90	9	272	43	1,294	254	106	512	178	345	252	76	69
910	5,355	4,495	1,520	185	4,039	1,370	15,052	2,804	1,970	5,603	2,115	4,005	3,555	1,190	70
2,063	7,750	16,400	9,977	1,363	13,118	235	12,708	12,097	9,477	10,531	374	16,551	2,689	727	71
1,264	2,746	8,939	4,991	1,021	7,247	206	7,427	4,914	6,594	6,075	302	8,614	894	609	72
$26,978	$51,058	$187,710	$265,595	$50,400	$153,336	$5,000	$125,163	$71,925	$105,975	$93,894	$5,847	$172,895	$24,900	$18,832	73
$6,265	$17,695	$54,515	$37,460	$10,000	$37,895	$1,000	$34,153	$44,885	$30,000	$30,376	$2,725	$69,378	$11,930	$2,518	74
$930	$1,797	$5,867	$9,689	$1,205	$5,413	$305	$6,319	$5,185	$4,974	$4,212	$495	$10,048	$743	$622	75
17	68	309	140	13	225	4	201	132	208	142	11	242	33	13	76
25	53	213	93	28	184	5	135	95	114	112	6	201	20	23	77
4	14	1	11		127		40	44	38	49	1	51	11		78
							1,022								79
							429								80
296	539	1,769	687	167	1,208	39	1,958	1,179	1,503	2,782	183	2,851	303	139	81
5,025	5,767	37,648	12,550	4,825	24,712	760	26,151	14,521	27,489	39,657	2,750	47,561	3,560	2,375	82

² Data not available.

TABLE **73.**—STATISTICS OF SIZE OF FARMS AND TENURE CLASSES OF FARMS

VIRGINIA—continued.

		Cumberland.	Dinwiddie.	Elizabeth City.	Essex.	Fairfax.	Fauquier.	Floyd.	Fluvanna.	Franklin.	Gloucester.
1	Number of farms	924	1,242	147	807	317	535	102	493	773	887
	FARMS CLASSIFIED BY SIZE.										
2	Under 3 acres			1		6					
3	3 to 9 acres	73	80	77	149	128	127	14	86	65	247
4	10 to 19 acres	221	169	44	206	78	138	20	132	135	324
5	20 to 49 acres	334	445	19	239	62	153	33	173	276	259
6	50 to 99 acres	165	292	6	133	24	57	21	69	186	39
7	100 to 174 acres	93	171		50	12	34	11	25	84	11
8	175 to 259 acres	21	55		17	4	16	3	6	18	5
9	260 to 499 acres	14	23		6	3	7		2	8	2
10	500 to 999 acres	3	6		7		3			1	
11	1,000 acres and over		1								
	FARMERS CLASSIFIED BY TENURE.										
12	Owners, free	459	528	61	527	216	380	51	315	300	414
13	Owners, mortgaged	104	112	15	68	22	64	11	27	61	181
14	Part owners	60	132	27	111	34	54	26	78	77	258
15	Cash tenants	81	192	20	18	26	16	1	19	30	12
16	Share tenants	190	236	2	75	8	17	8	50	298	5
17	Share-cash tenants	27	25		1	1	1	1	3	2	15
18	Tenure not specified	2	16	19	5	7	1	4	1	5	2
19	Managers	1	1	3	2	3	2				
	FARMS OPERATED BY OWNERS, FREE.										
20	Total acreage	23,609	31,634	870	18,583	4,822	12,085	2,607	9,571	18,575	8,703
21	Improved acreage	9,929	12,893	676	9,654	3,233	8,184	1,818	4,222	7,512	5,026
22	Value of land	$175,551	$681,812	$28,633	$205,627	$185,084	$246,720	$49,200	$92,815	$147,035	$159,285
23	Value of buildings	$98,665	$200,138	$14,275	$145,335	$112,530	$115,480	$9,285	$41,762	$52,508	$128,445
24	Value of implements and machinery	$13,920	$34,755	$110	$16,213	$15,358	$15,140	$863	$7,326	$11,757	$14,783
25	Number of dairy cows	397	637	32	426	248	514	85	279	366	308
26	Number of work horses	288	388	31	472	267	544	31	154	200	374
27	Number of work mules	104	113	5	33	3	9	3	41	101	7
28	Acreage in cotton		46								
29	Bales of cotton grown in 1909		32								
30	Acreage in corn	2,882	3,560	286	3,631	890	1,958	231	1,198	1,589	2,363
31	Bushels of corn grown in 1909	30,375	54,214	4,055	45,325	18,574	30,480	4,256	11,901	25,077	38,114
	FARMS OPERATED BY OWNERS, MORTGAGED.										
32	Total acreage	5,631	8,014	206	3,056	844	2,386	802	1,154	3,897	4,771
33	Improved acreage	2,378	2,862	161	1,527	656	1,650	470	451	1,515	2,716
34	Value of land	$42,635	$100,260	$15,090	$35,735	$34,350	$46,005	$13,310	$9,250	$27,624	$103,171
35	Value of buildings	$23,790	$40,780	$3,925	$24,260	$18,750	$18,265	$2,260	$3,750	$6,780	$76,211
36	Value of implements and machinery	$2,629	$5,498	$1,185	$3,897	$2,033	$2,821	$277	$715	$1,976	$7,670
37	Number of dairy cows	88	134	6	64	18	81	13	16	66	126
38	Number of work horses	63	80	7	77	28	84	8	10	27	180
39	Number of work mules	15	15	1	6	1	2	1	1	26	5
40	Acreage in cotton		9								
41	Bales of cotton grown in 1909		4								
42	Acreage in corn	673	758	72	516	106	367	72	103	317	1,167
43	Bushels of corn grown in 1909	6,513	12,275	570	6,342	1,725	5,105	1,645	1,020	4,920	15,779
	FARMS OPERATED BY PART OWNERS.										
44	Total acreage	2,297	9,958	355	4,047	1,118	3,540	1,068	2,847	4,057	4,706
45	Owned acreage	1,530	6,457	112	1,739	347	1,690	700	1,738	2,569	2,774
46	Improved acreage	1,237	4,296	285	2,469	863	2,714	787	1,616	1,890	3,500
47	Owned improved acreage	644	2,445	79	969	248	1,236	424	879	1,109	1,611
48	Value of land	$24,010	$112,808	$10,180	$54,902	$52,640	$76,667	$22,670	$35,094	$38,950	$93,875
49	Value of buildings	$11,285	$50,341	$4,385	$32,085	$17,000	$29,205	$4,820	$12,600	$12,330	$64,085
50	Value of land and buildings owned	$27,335	$127,567	$6,243	$43,338	$31,150	$56,155	$18,925	$27,040	$32,285	$121,503
51	Value of implements and machinery	$1,498	$7,396	$512	$4,010	$2,770	$3,515	$629	$2,686	$2,100	$6,731
52	Number of dairy cows	45	138	8	92	34	106	34	81	85	173
53	Number of work horses	54	82	26	139	49	144	21	56	40	276
54	Number of work mules	8	37	1	4	1		4	21	26	2
55	Acreage in cotton										
56	Bales of cotton grown in 1909										
57	Acreage in corn	466	1,106	167	1,319	323	933	165	610	528	2,324
58	Bushels of corn grown in 1909	4,667	11,596	2,542	15,785	4,710	16,995	2,988	11,057	8,776	28,311
	FARMS OPERATED BY CASH TENANTS, INCLUDING TENURE NOT SPECIFIED.										
59	Total acreage	5,232	14,486	452	1,022	1,056	1,211	60	1,337	2,153	411
60	Improved acreage	1,940	5,133	420	494	584	889	43	294	850	327
61	Value of land	$31,576	$173,374	$48,955	$9,020	$62,975	$30,790	$1,145	$7,855	$15,390	$8,125
62	Value of buildings	$9,505	$36,839	$3,435	$4,755	$13,475	$5,800	$335	$4,185	$4,110	$12,775
63	Value of implements and machinery	$1,072	$6,135	$1,691	$270	$1,085	$285	$8	$172	$600	$423
64	Number of dairy cows	52	169	8	12	20	11	3	11	33	12
65	Number of work horses	27	102	35	10	30	17	1	6	22	17
66	Number of work mules	7	16	1	2	1	2		1	9	
67	Acreage in cotton		3								
68	Bales of cotton grown in 1909		2								
69	Acreage in corn	435	1,070	173	121	158	173	11	78	219	140
70	Bushels of corn grown in 1909	3,734	17,032	2,024	1,465	2,335	3,355	155	614	2,560	2,105
	FARMS OPERATED BY SHARE AND SHARE-CASH TENANTS.										
71	Total acreage	9,358	16,234	25	7,815	326	3,875	324	1,830	12,437	381
72	Improved acreage	4,909	7,291	25	4,416	278	2,203	289	996	6,680	202
73	Value of land	$86,015	$173,435	$625	$59,669	$10,900	$58,858	$7,395	$17,240	$108,871	$5,885
74	Value of buildings	$30,966	$49,355	$225	$28,360	$4,500	$14,450	$1,670	$7,590	$26,437	$2,865
75	Value of implements and machinery	$2,858	$9,694	$90	$3,591	$1,060	$2,565	$136	$581	$6,599	$375
76	Number of dairy cows	126	227	2	108	9	47	12	37	231	10
77	Number of work horses	83	79	2	66	16	56	3	15	115	8
78	Number of work mules	32	24		22			1	5	63	3
79	Acreage in cotton		19								
80	Bales of cotton grown in 1909		7								
81	Acreage in corn	1,390	1,887		1,575	47	316	48	329	1,683	102
82	Bushels of corn grown in 1909	14,739	28,936		20,358	560	5,550	888	4,810	28,939	1,333

OPERATED BY COLORED FARMERS, BY COUNTIES, FOR SOUTHERN STATES: 1910—Continued.

VIRGINIA—continued.

Goochland.	Greene.	Greensville.	Halifax.	Hanover.	Henrico.	Henry.	Isle of Wight.	James City.	King and Queen.	King George.	King William.	Lancaster.	Loudoun.	Louisa.	
609	105	725	2,344	832	332	774	548	220	833	369	573	555	247	978	1
				8	7										2
61	30	42	186	151	117	56	71	49	68	26	70	188	122	78	3
130	30	89	485	202	117	128	111	72	182	88	144	179	58	175	4
215	34	309	824	270	62	246	198	68	321	172	223	139	29	402	5
134	10	165	511	133	16	184	108	20	155	61	82	32	23	203	6
48		83	244	56	8	121	48	8	84	13	35	14	7	86	7
14	1	24	67	7	2	28	11	2	17	6	13	3	4	20	8
7		12	24	3		9	1		5	2	6		4	11	9
		1	3		2	2			1	1				3	10
				2	1										11
435	62	189	559	548	240	156	184	137	513	196	384	409	160	740	12
38	13	112	156	77	18	28	82	24	98	43	33	99	34	69	13
73	16	69	194	52	22	73	31	22	130	52	92	11	19	70	14
25		156	37	65	28	51	69	18	20	6	24	25	23	20	15
31	13	121	1,387	58	9	442	169	16	66	71	17	10	9	78	16
	1	27	5	1		7	9	2	4		3		1		17
7		50	4	27	13	16	4	1	2	1	19	1		1	18
		1	2	4	2	1		1			1		1	1	19
19,488	1,525	11,894	28,037	16,232	5,707	9,624	7,931	2,958	23,777	6,589	13,455	7,724	2,663	33,638	20
8,766	1,030	5,266	13,877	8,206	2,462	4,263	3,734	1,405	11,758	4,052	6,673	4,357	1,929	14,546	21
$163,000	$24,680	$137,695	$337,609	$192,905	$195,760	$71,693	$121,085	$48,496	$157,705	$104,490	$119,415	$129,595	$72,050	$325,150	22
$109,925	$13,200	$64,685	$152,960	$123,979	$67,260	$29,915	$42,105	$22,059	$144,555	$54,515	$76,270	$104,095	$65,018	$208,450	23
$18,602	$1,543	$15,861	$24,436	$16,268	$8,782	$5,357	$6,716	$2,932	$28,160	$7,504	$11,737	$10,937	$4,548	$28,224	24
559	56	180	608	501	206	153	99	65	508	201	368	237	163	856	25
327	47	112	400	420	169	81	166	96	561	231	371	381	164	552	26
84	1	39	133	119	70	55	63	8	38	16	52	5		167	27
		788					5								28
		296					1								29
2,639	239	1,700	2,680	2,940	797	819	1,368	774	4,211	2,022	3,351	1,881	557	4,153	30
30,069	6,023	14,933	47,793	39,065	9,868	12,938	21,313	9,288	62,872	32,340	40,746	35,280	8,262	49,691	31
2,393	313	8,094	10,674	3,315	344	1,987	3,814	1,250	5,001	2,072	1,576	2,091	1,524	4,428	32
808	216	3,475	5,697	1,605	181	764	1,555	433	2,342	1,183	727	1,135	1,214	1,609	33
$18,930	$5,265	$98,405	$129,455	$37,085	$11,850	$14,479	$61,220	$16,225	$31,265	$31,835	$13,775	$33,465	$34,925	$36,951	34
$8,370	$3,025	$39,090	$52,095	$17,360	$5,700	$3,940	$21,860	$6,490	$25,275	$12,870	$7,600	$26,245	$24,050	$19,315	35
$1,743	$285	$6,544	$13,025	$2,715	$555	$307	$2,573	$1,050	$4,503	$1,645	$1,045	$2,364	$1,590	$3,371	36
48	10	95	181	80	12	21	28	18	74	39	38	49	43	74	37
30	13	76	176	59	13	6	73	23	84	56	32	80	42	51	38
7	1	47	44	23	6	8	27	7	15	2	1		1	13	39
		649					12								40
		203					2								41
245	53	1,096	971	533	68	96	568	276	774	492	300	419	210	438	42
2,316	990	8,097	16,929	7,600	655	1,407	8,071	3,365	9,436	7,022	3,432	7,512	2,995	4,910	43
3,034	356	3,707	8,481	1,761	1,208	4,800	1,264	733	4,790	1,980	4,205	558	838	4,482	44
1,475	125	2,222	4,783	1,004	394	2,723	857	226	3,081	957	2,461	194	267	2,508	45
1,325	333	2,021	5,094	1,262	351	2,697	605	346	2,686	1,521	2,863	350	753	2,366	46
526	104	1,025	2,596	573	133	1,116	241	101	1,200	608	1,176	120	203	1,203	47
$30,430	$6,950	$48,579	$125,983	$25,603	$44,295	$40,066	$19,337	$12,415	$32,750	$58,005	$39,565	$6,400	$30,760	$42,611	48
$11,730	$3,650	$17,005	$43,940	$13,525	$12,265	$17,220	$7,445	$3,855	$27,420	$17,115	$17,850	$2,275	$12,050	$18,665	49
$22,445	$6,160	$45,660	$109,511	$28,578	$27,110	$33,725	$16,896	$7,650	$46,180	$38,875	$36,920	$4,545	$19,830	$39,291	50
$1,660	$370	$4,516	$6,780	$2,825	$3,907	$2,059	$712	$466	$4,723	$2,045	$4,135	$373	$1,665	$3,224	51
97	16	45	205	57	26	92	18	16	105	53	94	5	26	115	52
53	14	53	166	53	19	33	26	19	124	75	133	15	55	68	53
23		27	33	25	14	43	8	1	8	12	43	1		36	54
		312					1								55
		109					1								56
513	134	686	1,232	636	115	545	255	239	1,436	1,016	1,677	107	238	688	57
4,928	2,835	5,968	19,883	7,980	2,090	11,610	3,235	2,595	16,721	17,725	21,153	1,720	5,045	8,999	58
1,785		9,056	3,066	3,472	1,221	2,802	3,141	542	1,751	170	2,648	561	319	976	59
601		5,306	1,183	1,818	345	1,422	1,530	280	621	103	1,274	246	216	273	60
$10,340		$102,580	$31,300	$33,638	$58,840	$25,535	$62,272	$8,225	$16,010	$4,445	$33,900	$8,475	$5,675	$4,550	61
$5,570		$34,797	$6,705	$12,910	$8,910	$6,505	$14,775	$2,705	$4,390	$1,895	$6,585	$4,525	$6,975	$3,245	62
$366		$5,283	$1,225	$2,114	$669	$624	$2,507	$265	$666	$140	$915	$197	$541	$230	63
30		126	40	77	20	44	29	5	10	6	37	3	15	11	64
8		105	40	65	20	14	71	10	7	5	48	11	11	7	65
2		55	8	19	9	14	16		1		8			2	66
		865					5								67
		279					1								68
142		1,709	206	616	77	321	547	133	119	89	651	114	118	68	69
1,005		12,949	3,217	5,973	1,023	4,703	8,490	2,020	1,585	1,235	7,475	1,815	1,650	613	70
2,051	309	6,807	67,310	5,306	377	26,111	6,792	1,260	2,327	4,180	939	593	1,349	4,918	71
723	257	4,400	38,505	1,815	236	13,428	4,048	454	1,486	2,871	581	301	1,082	2,128	72
$16,503	$3,505	$69,541	$802,267	$30,420	$9,740	$221,317	$115,839	$11,170	$15,065	$108,065	$14,063	$9,700	$31,925	$44,315	73
$5,610	$2,275	$18,615	$218,575	$9,800	$2,350	$53,180	$32,730	$2,970	$9,035	$20,825	$2,092	$3,550	$10,975	$20,430	74
$4,196	$189	$4,115	$36,302	$1,478	$375	$9,760	$5,546	$560	$1,976	$2,033	$413	$340	$925	$1,767	75
23	20	82	1,027	62	7	374	60	17	32	71	15	6	28	74	76
16	7	69	908	49	11	124	152	12	37	68	12	9	48	41	77
2	1	61	210	11	3	105	47		4	8	2	2	1	17	78
		596					4								79
		209					2								80
196	139	1,143	8,010	505	70	2,595	1,574	176	632	1,557	279	61	205	610	81
2,471	4,830	10,440	148,516	7,965	1,210	49,699	24,012	1,755	7,900	27,112	3,235	930	4,290	6,153	82

TABLE 73.—STATISTICS OF SIZE OF FARMS AND FOR TENURE CLASSES OF FARMS

VIRGINIA—continued.

		Lunenburg.	Madison.	Mathews.	Mecklenburg.	Middlesex.	Montgomery.	Nansemond.	Nelson.	New Kent.	Norfolk.
1	Number of farms	881	341	245	1,876	772	146	926	610	385	547
	FARMS CLASSIFIED BY SIZE.										
2	Under 3 acres	1	....	3	....	....	....	9	1	....	1
3	3 to 9 acres	55	91	143	214	217	30	177	138	86	162
4	10 to 19 acres	155	101	65	372	278	50	203	155	79	108
5	20 to 49 acres	269	91	26	658	218	42	336	183	122	181
6	50 to 99 acres	232	36	6	386	50	20	126	64	52	64
7	100 to 174 acres	110	18	2	185	7	3	57	53	33	23
8	175 to 259 acres	39	3	....	38	2	1	12	7	7	6
9	260 to 499 acres	16	1	....	19	....	....	3	9	5	2
10	500 to 999 acres	4	....	....	4	....	....	3	....	....	....
11	1,000 acres and over	....	....	....	....	....	....	....	....	1	....
	FARMERS CLASSIFIED BY TENURE.										
12	Owners, free	424	259	195	618	398	121	389	321	225	126
13	Owners, mortgaged	99	37	10	152	210	7	150	25	10	38
14	Part owners	62	29	29	159	118	13	43	30	66	72
15	Cash tenants	68	7	....	170	33	....	189	21	57	91
16	Share tenants	178	8	2	709	8	4	143	206	15	178
17	Share-cash tenants	2	....	....	3	2	....	6	3	3	12
18	Tenure not specified	48	....	8	62	3	....	4	4	7	18
19	Managers	....	1	1	3	....	1	2	....	2	12
	FARMS OPERATED BY OWNERS, FREE.										
20	Total acreage	26,239	6,809	2,029	28,455	8,507	3,040	13,044	11,175	7,361	2,523
21	Improved acreage	9,995	4,264	1,496	12,465	4,573	1,820	5,728	5,951	3,041	1,484
22	Value of land	$323,115	$100,780	$88,475	$355,301	$153,815	$69,300	$245,409	$136,893	$70,045	$82,258
23	Value of buildings	$160,255	$67,795	$68,325	$192,414	$123,945	$36,610	$110,191	$70,200	$39,345	$25,757
24	Value of implements and machinery	$21,535	$7,881	$5,389	$21,969	$11,110	$2,504	$14,119	$6,553	$5,744	$3,283
25	Number of dairy cows	488	283	89	629	236	152	173	276	210	41
26	Number of work horses	341	211	113	448	308	95	273	266	174	82
27	Number of work mules	140	13	2	108	10	10	63	24	25	39
28	Acreage in cotton	....	....	....	327	....	....	306	....	....	58
29	Bales of cotton grown, 1909	....	....	....	139	....	....	140	....	....	19
30	Acreage in corn	2,648	1,185	707	3,380	1,854	431	2,042	1,650	1,583	817
31	Bushels of corn grown in 1909	45,710	22,592	13,151	48,308	27,605	8,249	31,558	27,757	19,220	12,081
	FARMS OPERATED BY OWNERS, MORTGAGED.										
32	Total acreage	6,571	1,834	156	8,149	4,420	165	5,374	1,122	480	755
33	Improved acreage	2,428	1,139	116	3,351	2,241	120	2,390	547	132	525
34	Value of land	$70,590	$33,350	$9,650	$95,313	$80,820	$2,510	$109,575	$17,615	$5,150	$30,405
35	Value of buildings	$30,380	$9,500	$4,325	$40,705	$60,120	$1,425	$37,420	$6,375	$1,650	$8,730
36	Value of implements and machinery	$3,938	$1,790	$390	$5,439	$5,639	$65	$7,104	$491	$227	$1,045
37	Number of dairy cows	101	56	7	184	14	8	57	33	7	20
38	Number of work horses	55	44	7	121	128	1	124	21	6	18
39	Number of work mules	40	....	....	31	6	....	20	4	3	21
40	Acreage in cotton	....	....	....	85	....	....	80	....	....	40
41	Bales of cotton grown, 1909	....	....	....	25	....	....	39	....	....	19
42	Acreage in corn	619	262	38	881	916	14	853	141	63	201
43	Bushels of corn grown in 1909	9,410	5,483	1,120	12,620	12,759	270	13,660	2,905	655	2,915
	FARMS OPERATED BY PART OWNERS.										
44	Total acreage	4,054	1,130	496	7,141	2,545	494	2,176	1,382	4,324	1,680
45	Owned acreage	2,680	[2]	197	4,362	1,571	235	1,346	384	2,278	739
46	Improved acreage	1,480	803	303	3,550	1,630	377	1,213	792	2,332	1,306
47	Owned improved acreage	821	[2]	121	1,803	800	149	587	154	807	443
48	Value of land	$42,756	$15,020	$18,495	$91,353	$52,625	$10,685	$41,180	$16,665	$36,439	$79,510
49	Value of buildings	$16,730	$9,300	$9,205	$48,588	$36,965	$2,085	$13,360	$6,215	$14,985	$20,325
50	Value of land and buildings owned	$42,372	[2]	$16,600	$96,881	$68,396	$5,450	$35,365	$7,750	$32,170	$46,250
51	Value of implements and machinery	$2,659	$1,703	$978	$5,575	$3,142	$450	$1,694	$527	$3,742	$2,812
52	Number of dairy cows	58	44	19	158	75	18	33	35	102	23
53	Number of work horses	51	44	22	139	115	10	47	28	80	43
54	Number of work mules	26	....	....	53	7	....	19	1	37	30
55	Acreage in cotton	....	....	....	107	....	....	6	....	....	34
56	Bales of cotton grown, 1909	....	....	....	41	....	....	2	....	....	9
57	Acreage in corn	537	251	175	1,190	871	102	440	200	985	863
58	Bushels of corn grown in 1909	8,162	4,966	2,460	17,531	10,119	1,840	5,522	3,865	11,845	9,141
	FARMS OPERATED BY CASH TENANTS, INCLUDING TENURE NOT SPECIFIED.										
59	Total acreage	8,620	131	42	14,966	509	....	7,737	1,601	3,700	3,363
60	Improved acreage	2,369	108	41	6,831	279	....	3,859	611	1,579	1,942
61	Value of land	$81,194	$1,875	$1,350	$137,727	$8,675	....	$142,490	$12,835	$58,525	$208,165
62	Value of buildings	$22,465	$1,875	$2,325	$34,275	$5,640	....	$55,725	$2,975	$16,310	$24,905
63	Value of implements and machinery	$1,973	$80	$100	$6,012	$505	....	$5,263	$262	$1,195	$4,828
64	Number of dairy cows	97	9	1	190	10	....	43	18	52	39
65	Number of work horses	52	....	....	142	14	....	148	18	36	88
66	Number of work mules	26	....	....	42	....	....	24	3	17	53
67	Acreage in cotton	....	....	....	648	....	....	178	....	....	18
68	Bales of cotton grown in 1909	....	....	....	208	....	....	80	....	....	7
69	Acreage in corn	734	21	2	1,507	129	....	1,205	128	655	683
70	Bushels of corn grown in 1909	10,765	395	45	19,580	1,551	....	17,615	1,910	8,868	10,929
	FARMS OPERATED BY SHARE AND SHARE-CASH TENANTS.										
71	Total acreage	8,451	206	60	31,175	155	159	5,196	7,991	468	6,807
72	Improved acreage	3,798	124	46	17,883	128	92	3,962	5,280	335	5,484
73	Value of land	$94,708	$2,450	$2,900	$348,025	$2,665	$3,830	$113,185	$102,987	$4,660	$171,730
74	Value of buildings	$30,522	$1,500	$600	$99,720	$1,545	$370	$32,100	$25,745	$990	$28,575
75	Value of implements and machinery	$2,837	$160	$100	$12,826	$171	$5	$2,947	$1,897	$340	$6,750
76	Number of dairy cows	130	2	3	502	1	5	25	150	16	71
77	Number of work horses	50	3	4	370	4	1	83	117	10	89
78	Number of work mules	34	....	....	115	2	....	28	4	6	82
79	Acreage in cotton	....	....	....	391	....	....	128	....	....	353
80	Bales of cotton grown in 1909	....	....	....	179	....	....	51	....	....	82
81	Acreage in corn	1,177	27	20	4,241	92	25	1,183	1,381	127	4,281
82	Bushels of corn grown in 1909	19,102	360	500	67,469	1,350	800	19,968	33,205	1,377	46,377

[1] Less than 1 bale.

OPERATED BY COLORED FARMERS, BY COUNTIES, FOR SOUTHERN STATES: 1910—Continued.

VIRGINIA—continued.

North-ampton.	North-umberland.	Notto-way.	Orange.	Patrick.	Pittsyl-vania.	Pow-hatan.	Prince Edward.	Prince George.	Prince William.	Princess Anne.	Pulaski.	Rappa-hannock.	Rich-mond.	Roanoke.	
591	551	826	386	244	1,888	437	924	501	196	497	102	175	340	102	1
1					2										2
149	130	95	69	31	131	51	64	40	23	87	44	31	45	20	3
111	157	199	101	51	258	79	170	75	40	106	29	36	86	29	4
189	181	284	144	92	612	166	317	191	69	219	18	57	135	33	5
96	62	153	45	47	483	74	220	121	38	63	7	33	43	11	6
37	16	57	18	17	321	40	111	49	16	17	4	14	20	7	7
5	1	20	5	3	64	18	24	18	7	4		4	3	2	8
3	2	16	3	3	16	6	14	6	3	1			7		9
	2	2			1	3	3	1							10
			1												11
63	306	496	256	65	411	200	444	183	101	136	60	94	185	59	12
106	61	55	60	18	112	28	97	69	15	74	15	14	10	5	13
46	120	39	49	37	69	111	121	95	56	63	15	42	54	14	14
74	19	85	2	6	43	23	45	59	5	38	1	15	10	4	15
296	31	115	14	116	1,110	68	206	89	11	117	9	6	67	18	16
3	3	3		1	7	3	4	1	2	14		3	4	1	17
3	11	31	3		136	1	6	2	3	47		1	7		18
			2							8	2		3		19
1,339	7,159	20,530	7,324	3,353	20,947	9,829	21,917	9,253	4,214	3,734	1,370	3,414	6,173	2,042	20
737	3,757	8,355	4,413	1,355	9,463	4,270	8,932	4,752	2,531	1,971	690	2,646	3,231	1,034	21
$82,870	$117,318	$398,147	$114,100	$27,735	$213,226	$102,288	$203,518	$123,777	$59,687	$104,985	$34,785	$40,880	$60,695	$52,525	22
$33,930	$78,360	$203,209	$68,740	$9,945	$107,066	$75,405	$115,840	$53,175	$41,338	$33,180	$28,625	$29,720	$37,115	$14,441	23
$3,975	$11,912	$28,810	$8,909	$1,304	$14,421	$10,823	$20,354	$13,961	$5,127	$12,329	$1,485	$3,517	$4,481	$2,309	24
24	126	457	274	66	389	236	381	137	139	59	56	140	144	88	25
98	295	394	302	29	302	164	336	153	132	113	36	103	153	55	26
4		43	19	17	129	56	37	74	5	42	4	6	3	3	27
								2		8					28
								(1)		2					29
379	1,459	3,267	1,302	346	1,859	1,473	2,377	1,315	589	1,212	189	547	1,274	250	30
8,235	25,112	47,829	22,917	5,146	29,921	19,992	31,599	17,747	8,901	16,151	3,998	9,830	16,282	5,015	31
3,130	1,888	3,077	2,430	997	8,077	1,969	6,942	5,181	844	2,291	123	761	798	155	32
1,709	876	1,053	1,297	333	3,575	835	2,433	2,367	329	1,396	94	564	386	82	33
$150,789	$28,855	$39,215	$32,900	$9,050	$76,435	$17,784	$55,255	$70,055	$15,925	$86,772	$6,255	$8,630	$4,740	$2,960	34
$61,481	$15,150	$16,240	$18,265	$2,500	$26,275	$11,136	$25,080	$25,925	$6,425	$20,230	$4,570	$2,770	$1,560	$980	35
$7,743	$2,411	$3,269	$3,011	$260	$4,901	$1,243	$3,705	$5,743	$775	$3,337	$109	$420	$435	$194	36
42	36	51	65	10	116	37	89	52	12	39	12	22	7	11	37
193	45	47	85	10	96	28	88	54	18	79	1	15	9	7	38
13	3	12	6	6	40	8	18	54		30	2				39
										18					40
										7					41
785	259	336	380	94	615	278	621	617	64	782	8	80	95	35	42
14,937	5,332	5,173	5,541	1,055	9,835	3,182	6,825	8,338	1,045	8,202	220	1,136	1,824	683	43
1,022	3,943	2,373	2,820	1,476	3,554	6,029	5,519	5,079	2,562	1,603	281	1,726	1,854	466	44
243	2,258	1,088	1,039	915	1,565	3,932	3,086	3,395	1,521	582	92	978	948	212	45
851	2,297	865	1,305	735	2,073	3,031	2,712	3,224	1,800	1,447	235	1,506	1,150	371	46
196	258	477	612	362	860	1,590	1,419	1,717	854	429	72	786	474	132	47
$91,385	$63,208	$37,197	$30,186	$14,320	$47,345	$77,062	$60,499	$55,633	$45,687	$96,990	$9,123	$27,890	$26,960	$20,185	48
$21,580	$29,180	$14,100	$10,935	$3,310	$16,915	$41,747	$22,585	$21,500	$21,288	$19,240	$3,390	$12,375	$13,910	$3,790	49
$44,830	$60,019	$25,620	$22,476	$10,365	$32,705	$85,281	$51,638	$56,521	$45,030	$49,270	$7,025	$21,773	$24,145	$12,590	50
$2,846	$3,883	$1,627	$2,020	$522	$2,560	$5,170	$3,535	$5,053	$2,579	$2,749	$239	$1,875	$1,513	$1,175	51
15	71	37	63	34	69	149	110	70	72	30	13	72	65	13	52
84	132	31	76	10	54	146	117	89	119	42	7	59	48	16	53
	3	9	13	5	27	50	15	64	5	34	2	12		3	54
															55
															56
523	1,022	320	513	210	466	1,252	786	947	654	990	111	580	525	109	57
10,285	16,199	4,955	8,625	3,077	7,704	18,323	9,038	10,216	10,358	8,905	2,917	11,701	7,046	2,086	58
2,116	1,087	7,134	153	128	10,969	1,997	4,973	4,330	150	2,615	30	840	927	132	59
1,325	402	2,366	122	91	5,087	549	1,095	1,604	97	2,165	30	622	253	41	60
$116,432	$15,310	$89,490	$2,090	$1,835	$130,391	$10,995	$30,380	$36,970	$2,450	$87,965	$3,000	$12,900	$6,190	$1,575	61
$30,968	$4,045	$25,870	$2,200	$295	$42,669	$4,825	$12,900	$13,590	$1,150	$17,985		$5,200	$1,595	$650	62
$4,150	$397	$4,188	$10	$30	$6,976	$670	$885	$2,012	$276	$5,558	$100	$575	$339	$146	63
25	8	85	4	4	141	22	36	33	8	42		18	6	1	64
114	14	57	3	1	90	13	24	41	6	91	4	18	8		65
7		12		1	38	5	1	23	1	19		7	1		66
															67
															68
602	148	860	23	51	956	197	227	414	26	1,316	5	114	113	9	69
10,838	1,586	11,746	130	695	17,429	2,680	2,248	4,368	330	19,765	300	1,870	1,436	150	70
12,957	2,366	5,606	1,495	4,092	67,258	4,159	12,683	3,529	1,061	4,168	111	506	4,796	660	71
7,749	1,242	2,769	819	2,191	36,557	1,914	5,236	2,338	884	3,673	103	390	2,365	320	72
$704,090	$33,860	$60,010	$19,250	$41,675	$811,204	$31,988	$123,159	$38,570	$28,020	$119,655	$4,910	$6,120	$39,990	$16,425	73
$137,135	$6,700	$18,085	$8,350	$5,910	$216,061	$15,890	$42,041	$10,605	$8,700	$24,210	$800	$2,670	$7,280	$2,770	74
$21,169	$1,400	$2,484	$637	$1,161	$34,660	$2,185	$4,567	$2,338	$1,591	$3,481	$107	$433	$948	$214	75
107	26	26	22	105	851	69	135	45	22	57	4	17	61	17	76
582	39	38	18	31	517	34	94	62	30	58	4	11	57	16	77
44		12	2	17	332	18	42	26		65			3	1	78
															79
															80
3,405	363	838	178	787	6,625	649	1,257	777	217	2,803	42	92	703	111	81
66,831	6,880	13,109	2,770	11,948	113,744	11,542	19,583	9,130	4,320	32,055	939	1,575	10,182	2,128	82

² Data not available.

TABLE 73.—STATISTICS OF SIZE OF FARMS AND FOR TENURE CLASSES OF FARMS OPERATED BY COLORED FARMERS, BY COUNTIES, FOR SOUTHERN STATES: 1910—Continued.

				VIRGINIA—continued.						WEST VIRGINIA.
	Southampton.	Spotsylvania.	Stafford.	Surry.	Sussex.	Warwick.	Westmoreland.	York.	All other counties.	The state.
1 Number of farms	1,427	554	167	573	926	193	569	571	1,006	708
FARMS CLASSIFIED BY SIZE.										
2 Under 3 acres									5	3
3 3 to 9 acres	48	48	3	37	36	97	51	231	321	137
4 10 to 19 acres	144	102	33	112	110	55	86	217	204	139
5 20 to 49 acres	708	214	72	229	377	32	201	96	245	191
6 50 to 99 acres	305	132	42	124	209	5	135	20	132	147
7 100 to 174 acres	144	38	9	48	129	1	62	1	64	57
8 175 to 259 acres	47	8	6	12	35	1	21	2	18	21
9 260 to 499 acres	28	7	2	8	24	1	9	3	14	12
10 500 to 999 acres	3	3		1	6	1	3	1	2	
11 1,000 acres and over		2		2			1		1	1
FARMERS CLASSIFIED BY TENURE.										
12 Owners, free	242	318	106	169	230	133	283	363	507	417
13 Owners, mortgaged	123	102	28	105	100	10	35	25	60	70
14 Part owners	50	73	11	76	137	14	95	85	173	71
15 Cash tenants	385	19	4	41	143	31	27	27	41	62
16 Share tenants	600	38	17	123	295	2	125	25	193	78
17 Share-cash tenants	17	2		57	19		2		11	2
18 Tenure not specified	10	1	1	2		2	2		8	1
19 Managers		1			2	1		46	13	7
FARMS OPERATED BY OWNERS, FREE.										
20 Total acreage	18,953	12,523	5,409	9,021	14,935	1,580	11,690	5,500	18,109	19,894
21 Improved acreage	7,115	6,133	2,836	3,484	6,597	1,133	6,120	3,245	8,854	10,521
22 Value of land	$218,183	$115,221	$46,665	$160,555	$150,088	$29,195	$133,115	$171,341	$428,965	$397,117
23 Value of buildings	$84,520	$65,050	$30,675	$77,760	$80,386	$33,305	$64,005	$78,763	$147,279	$126,715
24 Value of implements and machinery	$14,996	$8,530	$3,209	$11,502	$12,050	$2,817	$12,525	$10,724	$17,456	$15,804
25 Number of dairy cows	222	356	126	157	174	137	273	171	596	637
26 Number of work horses	210	313	98	187	204	103	320	259	412	472
27 Number of work mules	78	64	15	25	68	3	3	16	48	45
28 Acreage in cotton	333				141					
29 Bales of cotton grown in 1909	126				49					
30 Acreage in corn	2,490	2,243	841	1,529	1,996	668	2,089	2,458	1,936	2,054
31 Bushels of corn grown in 1909	29,234	25,981	11,061	24,655	28,532	15,093	35,399	39,174	40,122	49,254
FARMS OPERATED BY OWNERS, MORTGAGED.										
32 Total acreage	12,596	5,276	1,500	6,717	10,483	229	1,908	359	1,945	3,040
33 Improved acreage	4,714	2,490	665	2,290	4,087	121	835	218	909	2,007
34 Value of land	$138,150	$53,905	$11,024	$101,675	$111,214	$3,650	$19,825	$10,670	$49,780	$95,520
35 Value of buildings	$46,635	$24,700	$8,730	$37,575	$45,150	$3,150	$7,800	$3,795	$19,145	$33,989
36 Value of implements and machinery	$7,113	$3,160	$690	$5,528	$10,256	$290	$1,285	$391	$1,929	$3,336
37 Number of dairy cows	126	132	30	77	98	6	28	6	45	125
38 Number of work horses	95	119	32	109	102	11	45	12	41	96
39 Number of work mules	41	28	2	23	48				2	7
40 Acreage in cotton	267				130					
41 Bales of cotton grown in 1909	117				48					
42 Acreage in corn	1,535	874	239	968	1,047	70	273	138	225	482
43 Bushels of corn grown in 1909	17,185	10,460	3,070	12,858	15,059	1,200	4,470	1,760	3,551	11,975
FARMS OPERATED BY PART OWNERS.										
44 Total acreage	2,977	3,919	402	4,437	7,604	550	7,710	1,469	7,607	3,023
45 Owned acreage	1,696	2,671	237	2,690	4,429	172	2,928	651	4,147	1,881
46 Improved acreage	1,767	1,892	289	1,605	3,842	253	3,927	1,104	4,852	1,994
47 Owned improved acreage	563	1,035	136	735	1,603	101	1,069	411	1,987	1,063
48 Value of land	$33,680	$34,039	$4,675	$85,240	$81,594	$43,140	$89,780	$59,498	$202,531	$68,125
49 Value of buildings	$11,865	$17,060	$1,850	$20,577	$33,710	$5,900	$27,935	$20,145	$72,420	$16,795
50 Value of land and buildings owned	$27,910	$39,574	$4,840	$64,373	$80,734	$18,950	$52,515	$38,733	$118,934	$52,100
51 Value of implements and machinery	$2,491	$3,572	$278	$3,989	$7,984	$630	$4,686	$2,214	$6,981	$2,755
52 Number of dairy cows	40	98	9	48	81	13	110	74	219	119
53 Number of work horses	20	103	15	114	124	25	139	75	192	90
54 Number of work mules	13	29		5	44	2		1	22	8
55 Acreage in cotton	155				130					
56 Bales of cotton grown in 1909	65				48					
57 Acreage in corn	588	629	166	852	1,129	165	1,421	783	1,242	487
58 Bushels of corn grown in 1909	5,969	8,162	2,030	9,946	11,756	3,155	24,882	11,852	31,146	13,017
FARMS OPERATED BY CASH TENANTS, INCLUDING TENURE NOT SPECIFIED.										
59 Total acreage	21,843	2,178	200	3,251	14,569	399	1,801	382	1,439	2,190
60 Improved acreage	12,324	213	116	756	5,589	343	987	280	691	1,166
61 Value of land	$363,705	$13,885	$1,500	$69,285	$112,851	$300,170	$16,705	$13,110	$52,965	$75,960
62 Value of buildings	$77,095	$1,675	$1,100	$8,395	$34,970	$5,055	$3,215	$3,510	$7,610	$17,405
63 Value of implements and machinery	$20,283	$192	$335	$1,693	$7,647	$1,168	$503	$526	$892	$1,400
64 Number of dairy cows	267	12	4	16	75	12	25	14	60	75
65 Number of work horses	241	7	4	46	138	22	20	10	39	59
66 Number of work mules	163			1	38	3			4	9
67 Acreage in cotton	1,282				249					
68 Bales of cotton grown in 1909	506				76					
69 Acreage in corn	3,917	76	37	346	1,344	153	281	202	284	387
70 Bushels of corn grown in 1909	42,682	755	500	4,322	11,812	2,963	2,890	3,326	5,104	8,946
FARMS OPERATED BY SHARE AND SHARE-CASH TENANTS.										
71 Total acreage	26,615	5,307	708	6,876	15,617	403	11,228	1,154	8,509	5,739
72 Improved acreage	16,694	2,397	415	2,923	8,770	260	7,185	624	6,077	3,967
73 Value of land	$401,710	$46,086	$6,715	$110,332	$158,011	$6,560	$127,210	$15,530	$344,674	$166,167
74 Value of buildings	$113,579	$19,345	$3,985	$18,553	$60,071	$1,200	$21,415	$8,245	$56,125	$42,906
75 Value of implements and machinery	$19,555	$1,505	$190	$3,363	$11,023	$160	$4,027	$1,016	$10,810	$7,650
76 Number of dairy cows	205	60	8	61	141	8	143	18	201	135
77 Number of work horses	297	54	17	143	204	5	155	20	198	149
78 Number of work mules	241	16		5	79	2	16	2	19	12
79 Acreage in cotton	1,365				235					
80 Bales of cotton grown in 1909	596				76					
81 Acreage in corn	5,747	716	250	1,562	2,519	70	2,169	204	1,460	963
82 Bushels of corn grown in 1909	64,264	8,085	3,231	20,142	29,490	1,650	40,918	4,130	36,220	21,407

PART VII.—GENERAL TABLES.

GENERAL TABLES.

TABLE I.—STATISTICS OF NEGRO POPULATION FOR CITIES AND TOWNS OF 2,500 INHABITANTS OR MORE: 1910.

[Cities or towns having less than 100 Negro inhabitants in 1910 are not shown.]

CITY, TOWN, VILLAGE, AND BOROUGH.	Total population: 1910.	NEGRO POPULATION: 1910.					
		Total.	Males 21 years of age and over.	Persons 10 years of age and over. Total.	Persons 10 years of age and over. Illiterate.	Persons 6 to 14 years of age. Total.	Persons 6 to 14 years of age. Number attending school.
ALABAMA.							
Anniston	12,794	4,570	1,229	3,569	868	874	515
Attalla	2,513	896	225	672	159	201	131
Bessemer	10,864	6,210	2,038	5,080	1,455	944	632
Birmingham	132,685	52,305	16,441	43,194	9,528	7,982	5,807
Decatur	4,228	2,499	725	2,021	663	407	264
Dothan	7,016	3,483	777	2,435	208	891	403
Eufaula	4,259	2,155	513	1,725	651	395	242
Florence	6,689	1,798	432	1,443	388	358	234
Gadsden	10,557	3,435	1,124	2,707	771	590	340
Girard	4,214	1,472	304	1,098	639	327	119
Greenville	3,377	1,918	450	1,454	115	401	240
Huntsville	7,611	3,309	819	2,752	817	556	364
Jasper	2,509	609	155	435	91	137	68
Lanett	3,820	832	201	647	240	169	115
Mobile	51,521	22,763	6,578	18,943	4,913	3,451	2,361
Montgomery	38,136	19,322	4,988	16,150	4,059	3,105	2,064
New Decatur	6,118	902	260	714	232	129	64
Opelika	4,734	2,228	534	1,750	868	418	270
Phenix City	4,555	612	120	446	111	137	30
Selma	13,649	7,863	1,925	6,536	1,867	1,281	956
Sheffield	4,865	1,766	522	1,391	475	318	154
Talladega	5,854	2,793	629	2,171	519	602	334
Troy	4,961	2,543	602	1,911	776	526	280
Tuscaloosa	8,407	4,148	1,124	3,297	1,021	773	489
Tuscumbia	3,324	1,259	323	975	359	254	123
Tuskegee	2,803	2,137	552	1,684	355	426	285
Union Springs	4,055	2,719	542	1,934	902	657	264
ARIZONA.							
Bisbee	9,019	195	70	173	8	14	13
Douglas	6,437	158	50	139	7	21	16
Globe	7,083	188	68	167	23	19	16
Phoenix	11,134	328	115	274	16	43	34
Prescott	5,093	113	41	95	5	8	8
Tucson	13,193	222	69	183	3	30	26
ARKANSAS.							
Argenta	11,138	4,210	1,407	3,429	807	579	444
Arkadelphia	2,745	744	167	542	237	158	109
Batesville	3,399	673	177	561	168	108	77
Blytheville	3,849	691	266	549	159	95	58
Camden	3,995	1,980	449	1,521	183	439	344
Conway	2,794	568	125	425	98	119	108
El Dorado	4,202	1,455	350	1,045	155	300	221
Fayetteville	4,471	278	73	219	67	50	44
Fordyce	2,794	1,239	275	888	135	299	233
Fort Smith	23,975	4,456	1,323	3,667	602	747	576
Helena	8,772	5,596	1,836	4,794	859	732	396
Hope	3,639	1,275	300	963	94	240	140
Hot Springs	14,434	3,827	1,212	3,321	415	515	432
Jonesboro	7,123	979	298	786	191	158	128
Little Rock	45,941	14,539	4,592	12,317	1,943	1,941	1,504
Malvern	2,778	939	282	726	80	191	159
Marianna	4,810	2,991	793	2,309	155	638	602
Newport	3,557	1,544	506	1,286	243	218	196
Pine Bluff	15,102	6,124	1,749	5,058	856	945	682
Prescott	2,705	1,187	291	908	265	248	190
Russellville	2,936	378	90	281	59	73	62
Stuttgart	2,740	533	161	419	88	111	91
Texarkana (part)	5,655	2,101	508	1,716	463	408	297
Texarkana (total)[1]	15,445	5,319	1,403	4,240	1,004	998	707
Van Buren	3,878	735	180	585	137	171	149
CALIFORNIA.							
Alameda	23,383	211	50	170	22	41	36
Bakersfield	12,727	262	93	227	14	26	24
Berkeley	40,434	247	56	211	8	41	36
Fresno	24,892	250	74	223	20	45	40
Hanford	4,829	128	39	101	11	28	27
Long Beach	17,809	100	32	80	10	13	12
Los Angeles	319,198	7,599	2,571	6,528	389	933	868
Marysville	5,430	188	68	161	3	18	16
Monrovia	3,576	121	25	97	14	31	30
Oakland	150,174	3,055	1,238	2,656	87	280	247

CITY, TOWN, VILLAGE, AND BOROUGH.	Total population: 1910.	NEGRO POPULATION: 1910.					
		Total.	Males 21 years of age and over.	Persons 10 years of age and over. Total.	Persons 10 years of age and over. Illiterate.	Persons 6 to 14 years of age. Total.	Persons 6 to 14 years of age. Number attending school.
CALIFORNIA—Continued.							
Pasadena	30,291	744	227	632	38	93	82
Redding	3,572	114	43	97	7	19	19
Redlands	10,449	130	47	113	7	13	12
Riverside	15,212	421	107	319	26	84	79
Sacramento	44,696	486	207	433	24	46	35
San Bernardino	12,779	177	54	157	16	27	23
San Diego	39,578	597	232	541	52	53	49
San Francisco	416,912	1,642	831	1,480	76	108	87
San Jose	28,946	182	66	157	4	14	12
Santa Monica	7,847	191	49	153	12	34	29
Stockton	23,253	196	71	170	8	23	17
Vallejo	11,340	224	102	207	6	24	20
COLORADO.							
Boulder	9,539	166	36	125	14	37	30
Canon City	5,162	168	98	156	7	15	15
Colorado Springs	29,078	1,107	338	943	65	182	166
Denver	213,381	5,426	1,999	4,814	291	579	513
Grand Junction	7,754	106	39	89	5	12	9
La Junta	4,154	110	42	93	5	15	14
Pueblo	44,395	1,498	581	1,290	137	192	150
Trinidad	10,204	180	70	162	20	17	14
CONNECTICUT.							
Ansonia	15,152	413	112	328	13	88	81
Bridgeport	102,054	1,332	471	1,108	58	162	141
Danbury town	23,502	230	66	186	13	36	30
Danbury city	*20,234*	*197*	*58*	*162*	*7*	*29*	*24*
Greenwich town	16,463	429	107	362	23	62	50
Greenwich borough	*3,886*	*115*	*27*	*111*	*5*	*9*	*7*
Hamden	5,850	190	59	153	16	37	34
Hartford	98,915	1,745	501	1,449	70	276	251
Meriden town	32,066	133	29	110	3	27	27
Meriden city	*27,265*	*133*	*29*	*110*	*3*	*27*	*27*
Middletown town	20,749	177	57	167	17	19	18
Milford	4,366	143	29	118	10	29	26
New Haven	133,605	3,561	1,191	3,044	137	436	400
New London	19,659	379	126	317	23	60	52
New Milford	5,010	144	34	122	6	30	29
Norwalk town	24,211	497	150	409	19	84	67
Norwalk city	*6,954*	*185*	*62*	*164*	*7*	*24*	*24*
South Norwalk city	*8,968*	*184*	*60*	*152*	*5*	*30*	*22*
Norwich town	28,219	627	191	546	67	83	80
Norwich city	*20,367*	*528*	*165*	*463*	*49*	*67*	*65*
Orange	11,272	113	27	89	7	28	27
Plainville	2,882	153	49	126	11	23	23
South Norwalk city. [See Norwalk town.]							
Stamford town	28,836	343	96	290	13	33	31
Stamford city	*25,138*	*332*	*93*	*279*	*11*	*33*	*31*
Stonington	9,154	127	39	106	5	20	20
Stratford	5,712	133	32	114	13	24	24
Waterbury	73,141	775	252	613	32	117	105
Windsor	4,178	166	38	121	1	43	39
DELAWARE.							
Dover	3,720	978	256	798	68	192	155
Milford	2,603	546	159	447	147	97	84
New Castle	3,351	552	178	462	115	88	65
Wilmington	87,411	9,081	2,981	7,798	1,457	1,362	1,134
DISTRICT OF COLUMBIA.							
Washington	331,069	94,446	27,621	79,964	10,814	12,910	10,807
FLORIDA.							
Apalachicola	3,065	1,525	475	1,261	298	257	193
Bartow	2,662	1,137	295	807	74	249	195
Daytona	3,082	1,605	450	1,295	150	329	293
De Land	2,812	1,107	347	895	165	200	96
Fernandina	3,482	2,407	719	1,912	443	441	312
Gainesville	6,183	3,079	849	2,479	534	558	410
Jacksonville	57,699	29,293	9,652	24,786	3,654	4,125	2,996
Key West	19,945	5,515	1,380	4,152	568	1,188	963
Lake City	5,032	1,564	412	1,210	160	326	221
Lakeland	3,719	1,048	319	833	134	188	143

[1] Joint population of Texarkana city, Miller County, Ark., and Texarkana city, Bowie County, Tex.

TABLE I.—STATISTICS OF NEGRO POPULATION FOR CITIES AND TOWNS OF 2,500 INHABITANTS OR MORE: 1910—Con.

[Cities or towns having less than 100 Negro inhabitants in 1910 are not shown.]

CITY, TOWN, VILLAGE, AND BOROUGH.	NEGRO POPULATION: 1910.							CITY, TOWN, VILLAGE, AND BOROUGH.	NEGRO POPULATION: 1910.						
	Total population: 1910.	Total.	Males 21 years of age and over.	Persons 10 years of age and over.		Persons 6 to 14 years of age.			Total population: 1910.	Total.	Males 21 years of age and over.	Persons 10 years of age and over.		Persons 6 to 14 years of age.	
				Total.	Illiterate.	Total.	Number attending school.					Total.	Illiterate.	Total.	Number attending school.
FLORIDA—Continued.								ILLINOIS—Continued.							
Live Oak	3,450	1,768	392	1,340	318	418	139	Canton	10,453	103	32	79	12	15	14
Miami	5,471	2,258	790	1,883	235	281	221	Carbondale	5,411	1,140	383	947	156	169	149
Ocala	4,370	2,179	632	1,828	91	402	274	Carmi	2,883	250	69	184	32	52	42
Orlando	3,894	1,416	396	1,119	139	251	169	Centralia	9,680	593	153	462	12	128	107
Palatka	3,779	2,239	706	1,858	197	435	330	Champaign	12,421	759	243	624	55	114	104
Pensacola	22,982	10,214	2,905	8,198	1,361	1,817	1,179	Chester	2,747	165	52	120	31	24	18
Quincy	3,204	2,150	386	1,770	763	659	383	Chicago	2,185,283	44,103	17,845	39,484	1,595	3,840	3,424
St. Augustine	5,494	2,116	619	1,804	154	318	188	Chicago Heights	14,525	104	54	93	6	9	6
St. Petersburg	4,127	1,100	364	882	161	181	160	Collinsville	7,478	250	80	182	11	44	29
								Danville	27,871	1,465	526	1,233	166	183	167
Sanford	3,570	1,592	498	1,248	174	316	247	Decatur	31,140	776	260	663	57	108	91
Tallahassee	5,018	3,237	1,546	2,832	413	389	286	Duquoin	5,454	584	158	443	40	113	95
Tampa	37,782	8,951	2,926	7,396	850	1,289	984	East St. Louis	58,547	5,882	2,286	4,893	715	752	603
West Tampa	8,258	1,086	322	845	145	194	103	Edwardsville	5,014	368	102	277	21	78	70
								Elgin	25,976	171	56	147	24	19	16
GEORGIA.								Evanston	24,978	1,160	378	941	47	170	145
Albany	8,190	4,812	1,208	3,816	1,453	899	522	Galesburg	22,089	701	245	599	42	94	68
Americus	8,063	4,574	1,148	3,616	840	890	680	Harrisburg	5,309	262	91	221	38	48	45
Athens	1,913	6,316	1,483	4,962	1,600	1,209	870	Harvey	7,227	215	62	164	7	47	46
Atlanta	154,839	51,902	13,865	42,996	9,005	8,011	5,685	Jacksonville	15,326	1,245	397	1,039	170	178	159
Augusta	41,040	18,344	5,067	15,634	3,110	2,740	1,867	Joliet	34,670	497	195	436	46	65	60
Bainbridge	4,217	2,314	646	1,935	661	472	328	Kankakee	13,986	204	82	172	41	21	18
Barnesville	3,068	1,158	252	911	337	244	155	Lake Forest	3,349	145	49	120	13	21	18
Brunswick	10,182	5,567	1,651	4,510	1,002	1,008	598	Lincoln	10,892	278	75	217	29	43	34
Carrollton	3,297	684	145	499	135	179	107	Litchfield	5,971	106	34	87	13	17	15
Cartersville	4,067	1,577	359	1,188	291	351	279	Macomb	5,774	109	32	91	16	15	15
Cedartown	3,551	978	242	724	228	176	94	Madison	5,046	381	140	307	35	49	39
Columbus	20,554	7,644	1,792	6,184	1,699	1,401	952	Marion	7,093	263	84	214	35	38	32
Cordele	5,883	3,209	838	2,513	639	622	473	Mattoon	11,456	166	56	142	20	20	10
Covington	2,697	1,040	254	839	266	204	147	Metropolis	4,655	926	288	751	136	128	119
Cuthbert	3,210	2,113	501	1,643	599	422	277	Moline	24,199	281	104	229	24	35	32
Dalton	5,324	952	199	710	163	227	149	Monmouth	9,128	537	183	454	71	67	61
Dawson	3,827	2,216	551	1,769	982	462	247	Mound City	2,837	1,065	310	858	212	178	157
Douglas	3,550	1,515	497	1,218	321	255	156	Mount Vernon	8,007	328	93	269	29	55	45
Dublin	5,795	2,769	669	2,075	611	563	369	Murphysboro	7,485	692	223	575	91	114	89
East Point	3,682	903	247	700	197	151	63	Normal	4,024	204	58	168	17	46	20
Elberton	6,483	2,919	678	2,142	774	665	452	Oak Park	19,444	116	41	110	8	5	5
Fitzgerald	5,795	2,151	643	1,703	397	356	274	Paris	7,664	289	88	239	29	34	31
Fort Valley	2,697	1,370	333	1,077	290	297	194	Peoria	66,950	1,569	644	1,372	99	187	152
Gainesville	5,925	1,629	374	1,273	372	340	267	Pontiac	6,090	301	113	273	28	28	25
Griffin	7,478	3,425	798	2,681	623	716	533	Quincy	36,587	1,596	555	1,305	191	210	179
Hawkinsville	3,420	1,846	457	1,433	238	387	256	Rock Island	24,335	397	159	335	30	53	44
La Grange	5,587	2,063	508	1,654	505	453	291	Rockford	45,401	197	74	178	9	17	14
Macon	40,665	18,150	4,988	15,009	2,938	3,036	1,963	Sparta	3,081	437	126	357	40	90	77
Marietta	5,949	2,192	515	1,715	434	423	281	Springfield	51,678	2,961	1,021	2,521	350	437	380
Milledgeville	4,385	2,560	541	1,957	622	547	417	Streator	14,253	196	66	165	17	40	35
Monroe	3,029	951	248	728	244	203	168	Upper Alton	2,918	218	62	167	20	41	31
Moultrie	3,349	1,329	385	1,070	244	255	131	Urbana	8,245	117	34	93	12	16	11
Newnan	5,548	2,180	513	1,693	623	459	343	Venice	3,718	229	81	178	9	43	39
Quitman	3,915	1,801	478	1,385	429	346	253	Waukegan	16,069	101	43	89	5	11	11
Rome	12,099	3,758	965	2,975	771	657	446	Zion City	4,789	108	19	82	8	24	19
Sandersville	2,641	1,391	298	1,072	16	299	203	INDIANA.							
Savannah	65,064	33,246	9,962	27,842	7,387	4,917	3,262	Alexandria	5,096	125	41	111	18	19	16
Statesboro	2,529	871	205	639	174	200	54	Anderson	22,476	532	183	455	45	70	63
Summerville	4,361	1,586	387	1,315	312	283	228	Bloomington	8,838	402	119	323	59	56	50
Thomasville	6,727	3,789	898	3,038	928	686	379	Boonville	3,934	155	51	127	22	30	29
Toccoa	3,120	888	201	638	5	199	58	Brazil	9,340	212	59	169	32	37	30
Valdosta	7,656	3,844	1,051	2,993	529	772	476	Clarksville	2,743	264	182	260	17	4	2
Washington	3,065	1,865	438	1,478	623	410	255	Clinton	6,229	103	33	78	8	18	16
Waycross	14,485	6,729	2,232	5,208	1,285	1,226	729	Columbus	3,448	217	75	187	16	27	25
Waynesboro	2,729	1,706	405	1,404	539	305	217	Connersville	7,738	423	124	348	47	79	68
								Crawfordsville	9,371	238	75	197	13	39	36
IDAHO.								Evansville	69,647	6,266	2,242	5,389	1,010	891	776
Boise	17,358	135	50	119	9	10	7	Fort Wayne	63,933	572	215	502	35	72	68
Pocatello	9,110	127	92	123	1	2	1	Franklin	4,502	270	68	223	18	54	42
								Gary	16,802	383	206	352	34	20	19
ILLINOIS.								Greencastle	3,790	191	56	159	19	22	21
Alton	17,528	1,160	389	954	128	181	162	Indianapolis	233,650	21,816	7,556	18,736	2,316	2,759	2,496
Aurora	29,807	293	100	251	22	49	35	Jeffersonville	10,412	1,535	446	1,255	157	246	200
Belleville	21,122	216	86	184	18	27	25	Kokomo	17,010	388	141	339	16	50	43
Bloomington	25,768	809	272	678	60	116	103	Lafayette	20,081	338	110	272	29	43	30
Cairo	14,548	5,434	1,832	4,684	855	735	592	Logansport	19,050	177	82	158	14	13	11

TABLE **I.**—STATISTICS OF NEGRO POPULATION FOR CITIES AND TOWNS OF 2,500 INHABITANTS OR MORE: 1910—Con.

[Cities or towns having less than 100 Negro inhabitants in 1910 are not shown.]

CITY, TOWN, VILLAGE, AND BOROUGH.	Total population: 1910.	NEGRO POPULATION: 1910.					
		Total.	Males 21 years of age and over.	Persons 10 years of age and over.		Persons 6 to 14 years of age.	
				Total.	Illiterate.	Total.	Number attending school.
INDIANA—Continued.							
Madison	6,934	413	127	340	39	70	61
Marion	19,359	836	265	728	63	116	102
Michigan City	19,027	285	247	279	65	6	6
Mitchell	3,438	204	89	169	28	27	26
Mount Vernon	5,563	761	237	634	168	132	128
Muncie	24,005	1,005	355	859	114	141	114
New Albany	20,629	1,583	526	1,321	264	244	218
New Castle	9,446	213	66	172	13	43	37
Noblesville	5,073	294	90	237	29	57	52
North Vernon	2,915	134	34	99	12	27	26
Portland	5,130	111	31	88	5	19	15
Princeton	6,448	683	178	540	99	130	114
Richmond	22,324	1,191	397	994	72	178	162
Rockport	2,736	359	113	295	78	55	51
Rushville	4,925	206	69	173	44	25	22
Seymour	6,305	124	38	100	19	24	23
Shelbyville	9,500	386	111	317	44	71	65
South Bend	53,684	604	225	515	18	76	65
Terre Haute	58,157	2,593	906	2,193	152	363	301
Vincennes	14,895	413	124	336	51	57	47
Wabash	8,687	152	55	120	11	28	25
Washington	7,854	129	29	108	13	23	19
IOWA.							
Albia	4,969	131	54	105	8	22	20
Burlington	24,324	398	150	342	38	49	41
Cedar Rapids	32,811	213	93	184	12	28	23
Centerville	6,936	285	89	217	50	53	48
Clarinda	3,832	175	56	144	21	29	24
Clinton	25,577	432	142	302	27	74	70
Colfax	2,524	117	45	103	11	25	20
Council Bluffs	29,292	320	160	290	36	37	33
Davenport	43,028	569	224	493	56	92	79
Des Moines	86,368	2,930	1,043	2,469	217	374	331
Fort Madison	8,900	290	146	251	14	43	39
Keokuk	14,008	1,016	345	878	135	139	127
Marshalltown	13,374	128	38	105	9	25	20
Mason City	11,230	142	53	117	8	23	22
Mount Pleasant	3,874	217	66	188	28	30	28
Muscatine	16,178	122	44	101	9	17	15
Oskaloosa	9,466	254	87	210	31	34	30
Ottumwa	22,012	533	185	441	57	85	81
Sioux City	47,828	305	122	258	1	39	38
KANSAS.							
Abilene	4,118	110	23	91	7	29	27
Arkansas City	7,508	297	95	245	32	50	43
Atchison	16,429	2,618	837	2,211	219	390	308
Chanute	9,272	255	78	188	19	42	36
Cherryvale	4,304	312	78	223	26	81	76
Clay Center	3,438	103	34	79	13	21	20
Coffeyville	12,687	1,309	399	1,046	51	207	163
Columbus	3,064	110	28	80	15	23	23
Emporia	9,058	533	145	436	62	83	74
Fort Scott	10,463	1,047	300	854	111	185	165
Galena	6,096	239	65	193	31	47	43
Garden City	3,171	158	51	137	8	24	24
Great Bend	4,622	255	86	209	30	50	42
Hiawatha	2,974	190	53	152	15	38	34
Horton	3,600	106	30	85	11	25	24
Hutchinson	16,364	840	277	722	47	119	105
Independence	10,480	733	225	591	61	119	104
Iola	9,032	573	173	447	38	88	77
Junction	5,598	389	101	315	23	64	59
Kansas City	82,331	9,286	3,088	7,772	775	1,334	1,134
Lawrence	12,374	1,764	538	1,503	209	267	237
Leavenworth	19,363	2,477	769	2,112	306	395	315
Manhattan	5,722	303	100	249	34	42	38
Newton	7,862	383	129	305	34	62	54
Olathe	3,272	179	51	150	30	37	32
Osawatomie	4,046	255	96	227	67	32	30
Ottawa	7,650	363	109	298	70	59	49
Paola	3,207	449	150	371	60	79	69
Parsons	12,463	999	327	838	123	185	167

CITY, TOWN, VILLAGE, AND BOROUGH.	Total population: 1910.	NEGRO POPULATION: 1910.					
		Total.	Males 21 years of age and over.	Persons 10 years of age and over.		Persons 6 to 14 years of age.	
				Total.	Illiterate.	Total.	Number attending school.
KANSAS—Continued.							
Pittsburg	14,755	500	147	406	27	94	81
Pratt	3,302	118	44	101	10	19	18
Rosedale	5,960	497	158	420	94	85	76
Salina	9,688	484	171	406	55	66	56
Topeka	43,684	4,538	1,364	3,809	395	682	572
Wellington	7,034	185	73	156	7	27	13
Wichita	52,450	2,457	880	2,043	149	354	291
Winfield	6,700	172	58	151	24	24	20
KENTUCKY.							
Ashland	8,688	505	181	434	52	86	77
Bowling Green	9,173	2,486	656	2,104	631	372	317
Catlettsburg	3,520	186	58	146	27	38	36
Central City	2,545	256	75	195	52	48	35
Covington	53,270	2,899	961	2,513	520	337	274
Cynthiana	3,603	851	269	718	210	122	114
Danville	5,420	1,991	566	1,667	445	314	228
Earlington	3,931	1,393	429	1,064	126	274	206
Frankfort	10,465	2,851	1,263	2,575	806	284	254
Franklin	3,063	964	260	780	276	180	96
Fulton	2,575	427	128	353	80	71	53
Georgetown	4,533	1,624	526	1,410	380	210	156
Harrodsburg	3,147	1,074	279	900	307	184	107
Henderson	11,452	3,016	867	2,524	713	523	454
Hickman	2,736	893	272	721	274	147	54
Hopkinsville	9,419	4,187	1,034	3,444	799	788	509
Lebanon	3,077	899	227	721	339	153	109
Lexington	35,099	11,011	3,379	9,590	2,743	1,445	1,168
Louisville	223,928	40,522	13,687	35,544	6,662	4,902	4,240
Madisonville	4,966	1,860	525	1,538	427	338	271
Mayfield	5,916	1,233	309	951	254	216	129
Maysville	6,141	1,167	325	1,006	342	176	155
Middlesboro	7,305	1,441	408	1,122	175	311	178
Morganfield	2,725	487	156	402	4	78	37
Mount Sterling	3,932	1,264	365	1,092	353	209	149
Newport	30,309	569	167	477	58	80	72
Nicholasville	2,935	975	339	852	217	138	111
Owensboro	16,011	3,115	900	2,654	591	527	450
Paducah	22,760	6,047	1,895	5,149	1,088	877	641
Paris	5,859	1,764	570	1,538	323	251	232
Princeton	3,015	1,003	251	814	241	193	160
Richmond	5,340	1,917	486	1,528	362	344	280
Russellville	3,111	1,031	253	846	230	182	146
Shelbyville	3,412	1,366	415	1,163	400	229	167
Somerset	4,491	519	152	420	91	76	61
Winchester	7,156	2,688	876	2,286	669	355	312
LOUISIANA.							
Abbeville	2,907	1,198	221	855	556	325	78
Alexandria	11,213	5,854	1,425	4,534	1,404	1,255	788
Baton Rouge	14,897	7,899	2,016	6,456	1,584	1,377	727
Covington	2,601	729	169	556	133	163	101
Crowley	5,099	1,963	447	1,492	881	427	226
Donaldsonville	4,090	1,813	463	1,453	546	335	183
Franklin	3,857	1,717	493	1,401	469	315	159
Hammond	2,942	962	262	753	253	178	106
Houma	5,024	1,794	480	1,428	416	355	236
Jennings	3,925	1,197	280	870	448	248	88
Kentwood	3,609	1,181	371	946	416	191	95
Lafayette	6,392	2,792	587	2,092	1,282	700	230
Lake Charles	11,449	4,437	1,107	3,369	972	922	586
Minden	3,002	1,562	404	1,183	392	322	151
Monroe	10,209	5,320	1,364	4,237	1,160	906	582
Morgan City	5,477	2,351	690	1,841	903	441	231
Natchitoches	2,532	1,226	254	948	340	273	173
New Iberia	7,499	3,480	779	2,646	1,274	741	313
New Orleans	339,075	89,262	25,269	73,814	13,541	13,990	9,446
Opelousas	4,623	2,491	519	1,807	928	558	255
Patterson	2,998	1,810	488	1,417	466	351	243
Plaquemine	4,955	2,673	705	2,142	929	430	230
Ruston	3,377	1,095	221	803	278	239	116
Shreveport	28,015	13,896	3,704	11,314	3,362	2,353	1,502
Thibodaux	3,824	1,281	327	1,027	313	236	155
Winnfield	2,925	862	248	683	263	150	92

TABLE I.—STATISTICS OF NEGRO POPULATION FOR CITIES AND TOWNS OF 2,500 INHABITANTS OR MORE: 1910—Con.

[Cities or towns having less than 100 Negro inhabitants in 1910 are not shown.]

CITY, TOWN, VILLAGE, AND BOROUGH.	Total population: 1910.	NEGRO POPULATION: 1910.					
		Total.	Males 21 years of age and over.	Persons 10 years of age and over.		Persons 6 to 14 years of age.	
				Total.	Illiterate.	Total.	Number attending school.
MAINE.							
Bangor	24,803	205	54	149	10	35	35
Portland	58,571	273	80	241	7	33	32
MARYLAND.							
Annapolis	8,609	3,184	863	2,533	613	524	364
Baltimore	558,485	84,749	26,214	71,705	9,438	11,265	8,509
Brunswick	3,721	192	42	140	23	45	26
Cambridge	6,407	2,000	585	1,694	451	348	288
Chestertown	2,735	988	295	817	261	152	117
Crisfield	3,468	870	250	672	231	191	137
Cumberland	21,839	1,067	315	844	166	214	141
Easton	3,083	872	232	738	324	149	118
Frederick	10,411	1,468	398	1,169	326	273	176
Frostburg	6,028	237	63	186	28	54	43
Hagerstown	16,507	1,125	354	953	104	167	123
Havre de Grace	4,212	680	199	552	89	119	82
Salisbury	6,690	1,404	378	1,113	349	250	189
Westminster	3,295	336	93	274	37	67	58
MASSACHUSETTS.							
Amherst	5,112	146	34	118	1	34	30
Andover	7,301	144	47	110	12	29	27
Attleborough	16,215	138	45	113	4	18	15
Barnstable	4,676	138	51	108	20	24	20
Boston	670,585	13,564	5,070	11,880	420	1,430	1,337
Bridgewater	7,688	126	81	120	38	3	3
Brockton	56,878	531	151	416	16	92	83
Brookline	27,792	221	50	213	1	8	7
Cambridge	104,839	4,707	1,384	3,822	213	752	715
Chelsea	32,452	242	66	203	9	41	34
Everett	33,484	795	204	627	17	167	162
Fall River	119,295	355	133	308	25	37	36
Falmouth	3,144	160	61	121	33	30	27
Great Barrington	5,926	104	26	83	6	14	13
Haverhill	44,115	397	120	331	16	56	50
Lawrence	85,892	265	128	224	62	23	22
Lowell	106,294	133	44	113	3	12	10
Lynn	89,336	700	218	577	36	110	100
Malden	44,404	486	119	382	30	94	89
Medford	23,150	431	97	338	5	88	83
Melrose	15,715	110	23	86	5	22	18
Middleborough	8,214	100	57	87	36	9	8
New Bedford	96,652	2,885	934	2,247	532	367	327
Newton	39,806	467	100	394	35	60	57
Pittsfield	32,121	320	103	257	8	50	44
Plymouth	12,141	145	56	127	13	13	13
Salem	43,697	163	53	143	4	19	16
Somerville	77,236	217	54	181	12	43	40
Springfield	88,926	1,475	450	1,253	58	204	197
Taunton	34,259	297	91	216	72	47	44
Wareham	4,102	440	185	308	125	57	43
Williamstown	3,708	122	33	100	3	16	15
Winchester	9,309	281	59	237	1	60	55
Woburn	15,308	242	57	181	12	59	55
Worcester	145,986	1,241	384	1,031	36	170	159
MICHIGAN.							
Adrian	10,763	164	48	145	10	26	25
Ann Arbor	14,817	515	170	445	14	61	57
Battle Creek	25,267	575	197	484	20	52	47
Bay City	45,166	160	62	135	5	15	14
Benton Harbor	9,185	302	106	263	8	44	41
Detroit	465,766	5,741	2,224	5,068	176	615	536
Dowagiac	5,088	159	53	119	10	25	25
Flint	38,550	397	147	338	3	54	45
Grand Rapids	112,571	665	264	584	28	65	58
Jackson	31,433	354	155	323	28	37	32
Kalamazoo	39,437	685	254	585	29	86	75
Lansing	31,229	354	113	300	21	60	57
Niles	5,156	152	58	133	14	17	16
Pontiac	14,532	192	55	151	8	36	29
Saginaw	50,510	313	127	281	16	29	23
Ypsilanti	6,230	434	122	366	14	85	71

CITY, TOWN, VILLAGE, AND BOROUGH.	Total population: 1910.	NEGRO POPULATION: 1910.					
		Total.	Males 21 years of age and over.	Persons 10 years of age and over.		Persons 6 to 14 years of age.	
				Total.	Illiterate.	Total.	Number attending school.
MINNESOTA.							
Duluth	78,466	410	198	376	3	34	29
Minneapolis	301,408	2,592	1,227	2,364	69	225	197
St. Paul	214,744	3,144	1,573	2,840	66	261	243
MISSISSIPPI.							
Aberdeen	3,708	1,960	498	1,578	613	300	247
Bay St. Louis	3,388	1,014	228	784	211	232	152
Biloxi	8,049	1,436	364	1,171	248	247	163
Brookhaven	5,293	2,732	619	2,086	543	571	439
Canton	3,929	2,398	593	1,956	410	427	324
Clarksdale	4,079	2,478	783	2,124	188	321	267
Collins	2,581	1,036	336	807	170	185	132
Columbus	8,988	4,401	1,081	3,519	1,149	793	599
Corinth	5,020	1,563	379	1,243	331	267	144
Greenville	9,610	6,010	1,765	5,098	1,377	855	672
Greenwood	5,836	3,062	900	2,556	125	471	324
Grenada	2,814	1,227	286	981	264	217	157
Gulfport	6,386	1,703	600	1,444	348	209	130
Hattiesburg	11,733	4,357	1,143	3,390	811	797	454
Jackson	21,262	10,554	2,818	8,517	2,484	1,715	1,265
Laurel	8,465	3,103	834	2,356	478	589	462
McComb	6,237	1,140	260	882	277	221	163
Meridian	23,285	9,321	2,399	7,385	2,248	1,670	1,125
Moss Point	3,054	1,591	501	1,270	446	261	211
Natchez	11,791	6,700	1,476	5,459	1,794	1,192	885
Okolona	2,584	1,386	319	1,056	168	258	217
Pascagoula	3,379	1,220	331	957	220	199	161
Starkville	2,698	1,438	290	1,064	666	335	242
Tupelo	3,881	1,883	469	1,448	348	381	312
Vicksburg	20,814	12,053	3,190	10,054	2,155	1,977	1,442
Water Valley	4,275	1,460	393	1,123	206	291	236
West Point	4,864	2,772	612	2,129	619	584	439
Winona	2,512	1,205	277	892	272	227	152
Yazoo	6,796	4,154	981	3,345	568	804	604
MISSOURI.							
Boonville	4,252	910	249	797	124	155	126
Brookfield	5,749	261	93	230	34	28	5
Butler	2,894	205	57	161	27	37	36
Cameron	2,980	114	28	99	32	21	19
Cape Girardeau	8,475	875	273	721	138	126	109
Carrollton	3,452	565	154	460	98	94	86
Carthage	9,483	454	128	354	56	93	79
Caruthersville	3,655	697	231	584	159	101	55
Charleston	3,144	719	200	583	159	125	100
Chillicothe	6,265	444	145	393	81	73	66
Clinton	4,992	374	104	306	71	54	49
Columbia	9,662	2,246	671	1,878	471	346	294
De Soto	4,721	339	74	253	43	74	46
Excelsior Springs	3,900	222	78	202	19	27	22
Farmington	2,613	340	78	252	43	75	69
Fayette	2,586	855	263	722	278	148	82
Festus	2,556	253	87	200	47	48	30
Fredericktown	2,632	246	46	159	32	72	27
Fulton	5,228	1,134	368	949	160	182	147
Hannibal	18,341	1,846	632	1,612	362	234	191
Higginsville	2,628	434	139	355	94	85	71
Independence	9,859	1,031	350	888	171	156	123
Jefferson City	11,850	1,924	1,030	1,733	299	197	163
Joplin	32,073	801	282	699	82	89	73
Kansas City	248,381	23,566	9,101	21,166	2,038	2,251	1,910
Kirksville	6,347	190	58	170	36	23	18
Kirkwood	4,171	690	184	572	107	116	96
Lexington	5,242	1,319	410	1,106	174	226	179
Liberty	2,980	475	125	386	108	86	65
Louisiana	4,454	705	219	625	126	79	74
Macon	3,584	544	149	462	94	83	82
Marceline	3,920	137	35	105	11	35	20
Marshall	4,869	698	214	582	145	125	105
Maryville	4,762	138	40	121	10	25	25
Mexico	5,939	853	253	725	183	117	94

TABLE I.—STATISTICS OF NEGRO POPULATION FOR CITIES AND TOWNS OF 2,500 INHABITANTS OR MORE: 1910—Con.

[Cities or towns having less than 100 Negro inhabitants in 1910 are not shown.]

CITY, TOWN, VILLAGE, AND BOROUGH.	Total population: 1910	NEGRO POPULATION: 1910.					
		Total.	Males 21 years of age and over.	Persons 10 years of age and over. Total.	Persons 10 years of age and over. Illiterate.	Persons 6 to 14 years of age. Total.	Persons 6 to 14 years of age. Number attending school.
MISSOURI—Contd.							
Moberly	10,923	988	303	841	100	137	84
Neosho	3,661	204	59	166	40	40	36
Poplar Bluff	6,916	858	262	680	18	135	108
Richmond	3,664	633	162	490	98	139	123
St. Charles	9,437	708	222	571	96	135	118
St. Joseph	77,403	4,249	1,598	3,720	480	493	425
St. Louis	687,029	43,960	16,381	38,687	4,799	4,725	3,941
Sedalia	17,822	1,871	599	1,644	280	270	250
Slater	3,238	491	166	404	38	94	64
Springfield	35,201	1,995	583	1,668	250	337	264
Trenton	5,656	147	47	131	35	15	14
Warrensburg	4,689	411	130	350	92	64	55
Washington	3,670	191	49	145	18	51	42
Webster Groves	7,080	413	114	351	58	52	48
Wellston	7,312	376	118	292	34	51	37
MONTANA.							
Anaconda	10,134	124	63	110	2	11	11
Billings	10,031	144	67	136	9	12	9
Butte	39,165	240	117	224	10	23	21
Great Falls	13,948	116	41	103	7	11	10
Helena	12,515	420	198	367	18	38	30
Missoula	12,869	120	48	98	4	15	12
NEBRASKA.							
Grand Island	10,326	117	44	97	13	8	8
Lincoln	43,973	733	302	643	36	83	73
Omaha	124,096	4,426	1,885	3,944	249	382	343
South Omaha	26,259	717	313	605	46	92	79
NEW HAMPSHIRE.							
Portsmouth	11,269	117	33	97	15	15	13
NEW JERSEY.							
Asbury Park	10,150	1,934	608	1,696	68	208	174
Atlantic City	46,150	9,834	3,756	8,793	670	902	704
Bayonne	55,545	561	166	434	34	86	72
Bloomfield	15,070	490	139	390	15	79	73
Bordentown	4,250	213	70	174	16	25	20
Bridgeton	14,209	801	217	651	84	148	128
Burlington	8,336	538	162	453	55	74	60
Camden	94,538	6,076	1,945	4,998	701	877	715
East Orange	34,371	1,907	422	1,576	117	263	230
East Rutherford	4,275	147	40	111	3	31	29
Elizabeth	73,409	1,391	400	1,102	93	224	176
Englewood	9,924	777	213	618	81	105	93
Freehold	3,233	139	30	117	5	22	20
Glen Ridge	3,260	165	27	159	7	12	7
Hackensack	14,050	773	218	625	51	129	97
Haddonfield	4,142	352	78	300	34	36	27
Hoboken	70,324	120	39	108	1	23	20
Jersey City	267,779	5,960	2,104	4,948	240	774	674
Keyport	3,554	152	48	126	10	25	21
Lambertville	4,657	110	24	92	11	23	21
Long Branch	13,298	1,248	376	1,010	86	211	200
Madison	4,658	393	106	311	27	67	61
Millville	12,451	116	39	96	13	13	13
Montclair	21,550	2,485	635	2,090	125	307	279
Morristown	12,507	991	266	817	87	165	145
New Brunswick	23,388	690	188	545	49	124	112
Newark	347,469	9,475	3,015	7,888	589	1,184	1,076
North Plainfield	6,117	212	53	180	26	37	27
Nutley	6,009	126	36	112	12	11	11
Orange	29,630	2,479	720	2,044	155	364	331
Passaic	54,773	535	156	452	54	67	56
Paterson	125,600	1,539	453	1,287	146	217	192
Perth Amboy	32,121	165	50	129	9	23	19
Plainfield	20,550	1,833	504	1,553	143	249	233
Pleasantville	4,390	619	196	573	65	93	89
Princeton	5,136	1,148	397	981	94	147	141
Rahway	9,337	393	115	336	26	75	66
Red Bank	7,398	844	259	703	102	139	128
Ridgewood	5,416	247	62	226	14	14	11
NEW JERSEY—Contd.							
Roselle	2,725	157	42	124	7	12	12
Rutherford	7,045	149	36	132	13	13	13
Salem	6,614	1,015	324	825	146	163	139
Somerville	5,060	434	110	333	34	76	73
South Orange	6,014	253	61	214	16	26	24
Summit	7,500	273	71	260	14	5	5
Trenton	96,815	2,581	1,124	2,272	244	242	213
Vineland	5,282	197	53	154	26	30	26
Washington	3,567	157	46	131	29	23	20
West New York	13,560	147	37	105	......	35	29
Westfield	6,420	466	107	391	22	63	60
Woodbury	4,642	564	157	462	43	76	67
NEW MEXICO.							
Albuquerque	11,020	244	90	206	12	17	13
Rosewell	6,172	165	64	143	19	18	16
NEW YORK.							
Albany	100,253	1,037	379	924	39	125	113
Amsterdam	31,267	118	33	97	4	14	13
Auburn	34,668	527	213	454	13	54	50
Binghamton	48,443	635	244	571	21	59	57
Buffalo	423,715	1,773	740	1,596	65	176	157
Catskill	5,296	226	72	186	22	26	23
Cornwall	2,658	287	156	258	29	20	19
Elmira	37,176	513	183	464	44	44	42
Fishkill Landing	3,902	108	25	85	3	24	19
Freeport	4,836	219	53	193	......	25	25
Geneva	12,446	153	41	127	7	22	18
Gloversville	20,642	194	54	159	17	32	25
Goshen	3,081	299	79	246	36	54	45
Haverstraw	5,669	315	187	292	10	22	18
Hempstead	4,964	242	68	200	32	38	28
Hudson	11,417	417	133	379	63	52	45
Ithaca	14,802	470	151	410	27	52	47
Jamestown	31,297	108	39	96	1	16	15
Johnstown	10,447	101	33	91	11	7	7
Kingston	25,908	630	197	502	45	105	87
Lackawanna	14,549	197	77	156	3	37	31
Lockport	17,970	126	46	113	15	17	12
Mamaroneck	5,699	231	59	176	4	45	42
Middletown	15,313	317	92	274	4	55	52
Mount Vernon	30,919	896	236	749	46	106	87
New Rochelle	28,867	1,754	445	1,438	134	218	198
New York City	4,766,883	91,709	30,855	79,919	2,893	8,864	7,783
Manhattan Borough	*2,331,542*	*60,534*	*21,279*	*53,571*	*1,711*	*4,993*	*4,345*
Bronx Borough	*430,980*	*4,117*	*1,269*	*3,415*	*181*	*512*	*457*
Brooklyn Borough	*1,634,351*	*22,708*	*7,011*	*19,335*	*806*	*2,764*	*2,441*
Queens Borough	*284,041*	*3,198*	*959*	*2,655*	*135*	*418*	*382*
Richmond Borough	*85,969*	*1,152*	*337*	*943*	*60*	*177*	*158*
Newburgh	27,805	604	189	526	19	78	57
Niagara Falls	30,445	266	118	239	25	21	19
North Tarrytown	5,421	268	91	216	14	38	37
Norwich	7,442	133	44	115	3	19	16
Nyack	4,619	332	83	250	18	58	54
Olean	14,743	161	51	137	10	29	28
Ossining	11,480	631	326	555	18	55	49
Oswego	23,368	364	273	353	4	6	4
Owego	4,633	144	45	121	14	25	25
Peekskill	15,245	346	110	276	16	48	42
Port Chester	12,809	237	67	188	13	47	43
Poughkeepsie	27,936	699	211	599	19	78	69
Rochester	218,149	879	305	769	11	96	90
Rome	20,497	136	50	124	24	19	14
Rye	3,964	283	33	211	8	148	108
Sag Harbor	3,408	119	27	91	8	22	19
Saratoga Springs	12,693	555	163	495	39	63	59
Schenectady	72,826	274	85	242	8	32	26
Syracuse	137,249	1,124	437	972	50	126	112
Tarrytown	5,600	237	63	204	9	35	31
Troy	76,813	651	226	579	26	72	68
Utica	74,419	357	135	306	23	54	47
White Plains	15,949	858	264	711	43	96	86
Yonkers	79,803	1,549	501	1,294	90	179	164

TABLE I.—STATISTICS OF NEGRO POPULATION FOR CITIES AND TOWNS OF 2,500 INHABITANTS OR MORE: 1910—Con.

[Cities or towns having less than 100 Negro inhabitants in 1910 are not shown.]

CITY, TOWN, VILLAGE, AND BOROUGH.	Total population: 1910.	NEGRO POPULATION: 1910.					
		Total.	Males 21 years of age and over.	Persons 10 years of age and over. Total.	Illiterate.	Persons 6 to 14 years of age. Total.	Number attending school.
NORTH CAROLINA.							
Asheville	18,762	5,359	1,277	4,267	685	924	764
Belhaven	2,863	1,439	404	1,066	341	271	201
Burlington	4,808	491	104	363	96	104	42
Charlotte	34,014	11,752	2,801	9,309	2,269	2,135	1,354
Concord	8,715	1,831	392	1,368	350	386	287
Durham	18,241	6,869	1,634	5,497	1,494	1,308	867
Edenton	2,789	1,669	389	1,268	237	338	318
Elizabeth City	8,412	3,977	970	2,991	563	828	554
Fayetteville	7,045	3,293	725	2,503	694	672	430
Gastonia	5,759	1,320	270	1,002	289	272	214
Goldsboro	6,107	2,521	580	1,937	388	481	324
Graham	2,504	464	91	333	94	119	66
Greensboro	15,895	5,710	1,323	4,415	951	1,032	754
Greenville	4,101	2,221	465	1,720	442	442	259
Henderson	4,503	2,484	538	1,852	529	587	342
Hendersonville	2,818	737	163	556	147	170	106
Hickory	3,716	907	190	659	249	196	132
High Point	9,525	2,099	547	1,615	358	385	284
Kinston	6,995	3,027	688	2,262	394	596	442
Lenoir	3,364	819	156	579	147	209	149
Lexington	4,163	858	208	668	169	147	118
Monroe	4,082	1,264	336	984	387	245	126
Mooresville	3,400	543	107	385	117	121	69
Morganton	2,712	802	144	597	149	177	140
Mount Airy	3,844	625	127	487	194	148	96
Newbern	9,961	5,649	1,388	4,429	1,353	980	734
Oxford	3,018	1,392	273	1,040	293	320	248
Raleigh	19,218	7,372	1,787	5,920	1,280	1,425	944
Reidsville	4,828	1,903	388	1,459	453	433	282
Rocky Mount	8,051	3,069	759	2,301	607	541	332
Salem	5,533	1,259	298	964	168	241	186
Salisbury	7,153	2,432	598	2,001	469	399	285
Shelby	3,127	743	174	578	202	118	87
Statesville	4,599	805	162	624	141	169	127
Tarboro	4,129	1,569	361	1,196	218	308	228
Thomasville	3,877	696	197	517	144	141	105
Washington	6,211	3,072	692	2,321	565	660	423
Wilmington	25,748	12,107	3,066	9,628	2,717	2,067	1,480
Wilson	6,717	2,998	763	2,309	730	521	321
Winston	17,167	7,828	2,065	6,359	1,959	1,354	776
OHIO.							
Akron	69,067	657	238	559	50	99	83
Alliance	15,083	116	40	94	3	21	20
Athens	5,463	245	79	214	22	38	29
Barnesville	4,233	232	59	191	23	45	41
Bellaire	12,946	355	119	303	25	62	58
Bellefontaine	8,238	355	110	299	21	48	43
Bridgeport	3,974	206	65	172	17	31	29
Cambridge	11,327	343	87	247	24	64	53
Canton	50,217	291	129	256	5	41	31
Carthage	3,618	305	22	270	8	122	103
Chillicothe	14,508	948	280	774	82	135	120
Cincinnati	363,591	19,639	7,387	17,462	2,503	2,024	1,807
Circleville	6,744	376	137	320	59	59	57
Cleveland	560,663	8,448	3,298	7,476	306	838	775
Columbus	181,511	12,739	5,028	11,119	962	1,396	1,210
Dayton	116,577	4,842	1,781	4,143	392	556	486
Delaware	9,076	485	163	410	24	76	72
East Liverpool	20,387	315	100	260	16	52	46
Elmwood Place	3,423	119	37	95	8	24	24
Elyria	14,825	235	85	202	19	27	26
Findlay	14,858	193	59	160	5	33	29
Fostoria	9,597	128	47	111	9	21	19
Franklin	2,659	111	43	99	11	16	15
Fremont	9,939	119	41	98	6	14	13
Gallipolis	5,560	684	223	580	70	85	77
Glouster	2,527	207	56	160	10	39	34
Greenfield	4,228	247	75	204	28	43	40
Hamilton	35,279	725	297	607	62	92	85
Hartwell	2,823	217	87	186	34	27	23
Hillsboro	4,296	696	202	573	72	136	122

CITY, TOWN, VILLAGE, AND BOROUGH.	Total population: 1910.	NEGRO POPULATION: 1910.					
		Total.	Males 21 years of age and over.	Persons 10 years of age and over. Total.	Illiterate.	Persons 6 to 14 years of age. Total.	Number attending school.
OHIO—Continued.							
Ironton	13,147	1,046	358	844	176	172	153
Jackson	5,468	126	46	100	9	21	19
Kenton	7,185	263	81	216	21	43	38
Lancaster	13,093	223	66	185	12	29	24
Lebanon	2,698	274	86	224	32	38	36
Lima	30,508	978	329	803	45	146	129
Lockland	3,439	853	287	704	157	128	123
London	3,530	326	103	260	39	52	45
Lorain	28,883	375	121	298	7	56	43
Madisonville	5,193	375	105	304	28	71	66
Mansfield	20,768	105	33	96	5	14	14
Marietta	12,923	270	71	233	9	45	39
Marion	18,232	193	65	157	20	32	29
Martins Ferry	9,133	227	86	189	21	31	23
Massillon	13,879	197	72	158	7	36	32
Middleport	3,194	241	76	194	22	42	40
Middletown	13,152	405	150	353	31	42	41
Mount Vernon	9,087	289	91	236	18	39	36
Nelsonville	6,082	160	50	128	14	34	28
Newark	25,404	346	117	297	21	40	32
Norwalk	7,858	109	39	92	13	10	10
Oberlin	4,365	789	235	674	56	120	110
Painesville	5,501	165	63	149	10	21	15
Piqua	13,388	527	202	454	46	52	40
Pomeroy	4,023	191	57	162	26	29	27
Portsmouth	23,481	772	279	668	91	109	98
Ravenna	5,310	152	47	125	5	24	21
Salem	8,943	235	81	202	8	33	31
Sandusky	19,989	172	57	150	12	18	17
Sidney	6,607	106	24	84	4	23	23
Springfield	46,921	4,933	1,735	4,144	352	715	616
Steubenville	22,391	677	236	576	30	87	75
Toledo	168,497	1,877	719	1,649	71	191	173
Troy	6,122	353	107	291	32	59	50
Urbana	7,739	851	264	704	36	140	118
Van Wert	7,157	146	41	124	20	9	8
Washington C. H.	7,277	704	218	577	62	112	91
Wellsville	7,769	204	73	157	8	27	25
Wilmington	4,491	465	154	386	40	72	62
Xenia	8,706	2,052	637	1,730	236	305	288
Youngstown	79,066	1,936	785	1,623	94	233	174
Zanesville	28,026	1,384	424	1,126	98	200	166
OKLAHOMA.							
Ada	4,349	159	61	133	21	20	17
Altus	4,821	104	60	97	17	3	1
Anadarko	3,439	323	137	276	54	49	47
Ardmore	8,618	1,628	437	1,287	236	335	247
Bartlesville	6,181	212	104	203	22	7	7
Chickasha	10,320	1,265	419	996	139	223	197
Claremore	2,866	316	116	268	14	38	36
Coalgate	3,255	221	85	166	38	35	30
El Reno	7,872	688	246	563	58	115	93
Enid	13,799	661	220	527	30	110	76
Frederick	3,027	142	57	119	22	21	20
Guthrie	11,654	2,976	807	2,271	271	618	559
Hartshorn	2,963	517	153	382	52	108	83
Hugo	4,582	512	157	417	144	87	57
Kingfisher	2,538	410	107	318	55	82	69
Krebs	2,884	101	29	73	8	23	9
Lawton	7,788	542	208	449	62	76	59
McAlester	12,954	2,997	1,225	2,437	442	429	357
Muskogee	25,278	7,831	2,464	6,320	763	1,370	1,007
Nowata	3,672	456	145	385	117	77	70
Oklahoma City	64,205	6,546	2,392	5,433	363	897	746
Okmulgee	4,176	1,376	430	1,106	131	250	229
Pauls Valley	2,689	330	89	247	48	67	40
Perry	3,133	347	102	272	61	62	55
Purcell	2,740	422	107	304	49	105	98
Sapulpa	8,283	406	161	342	28	37	31
Shawnee	12,474	828	267	649	48	156	130
Stillwater	3,444	105	32	81	13	21	12
Sulphur	3,684	164	41	135	19	28	21
Tahlequah	2,891	316	71	241	58	61	48

TABLE I.—STATISTICS OF NEGRO POPULATION FOR CITIES AND TOWNS OF 2,500 INHABITANTS OR MORE: 1910—Con.

[Cities or towns having less than 100 Negro inhabitants in 1910 are not shown.]

CITY, TOWN, VILLAGE, AND BOROUGH.	Total population: 1910.	Total.	Males 21 years of age and over.	Persons 10 years of age and over. Total.	Persons 10 years of age and over. Illiterate.	Persons 6 to 14 years of age. Total.	Persons 6 to 14 years of age. Number attending school.
OKLAHOMA—Contd.							
Tulsa	18,182	1,959	636	1,612	91	294	232
Vinita	4,082	518	144	388	46	96	80
Wagoner	4,018	1,038	318	820	100	169	123
Waurika	2,928	300	111	236	50	54	48
OREGON.							
Portland	207,214	1,045	525	958	18	63	48
PENNSYLVANIA.							
Allentown	51,913	134	47	114	3	13	12
Altoona	52,127	453	165	390	15	67	60
Ambler	2,649	266	85	214	6	41	38
Beaver Falls	12,191	161	58	126	17	25	20
Bellefonte	4,145	136	34	120	15	24	20
Belleview	6,323	251	64	190	13	46	41
Bethlehem	12,837	100	39	83	9	19	16
Braddock	19,357	421	172	356	32	51	48
Bradford	14,544	135	36	110	4	15	10
Bristol	9,256	286	94	244	31	42	37
Butler	20,728	159	67	139	11	20	20
Canonsburg	3,891	240	80	195	14	48	33
Carlisle	10,303	1,119	293	889	145	220	192
Carnegie	10,009	310	94	240	31	54	42
Chambersburg	11,800	744	209	594	69	125	104
Charleroi	9,615	220	71	173	9	38	33
Chester	38,537	4,795	1,615	3,993	552	719	585
Coatesville	11,084	1,520	558	1,213	175	220	186
Columbia	11,454	417	135	332	63	70	64
Connellsville	12,845	558	198	460	41	83	74
Coraopolis	5,252	292	102	240	15	47	42
Darby	6,305	676	188	549	13	124	97
Derry	2,954	115	59	89	60	8	4
Donora	8,174	359	129	285	12	54	53
Downingtown	3,326	264	73	205	7	58	40
Duquesne	15,727	246	74	179	17	52	48
Easton	28,523	284	95	238	9	43	28
Erie	66,525	340	134	300	18	41	34
Franklin	9,767	288	79	233	6	38	27
Gettysburg	4,030	259	97	216	23	32	23
Greensburg	13,012	180	74	162	9	21	19
Harrisburg	64,186	4,535	1,550	3,872	444	580	513
Hollidaysburg	3,734	109	42	90	9	19	14
Homestead	18,713	867	317	704	86	129	109
Huntingdon	6,861	102	32	85	8	14	12
Jeannette	8,077	109	37	91	11	18	13
Jenkintown	2,968	246	60	220	18	29	28
Johnstown	55,482	442	185	381	19	46	34
Kittanning	4,311	116	44	91	7	13	13
Lancaster	47,227	803	275	704	92	123	104
Lansdown	4,066	214	37	207	7	12	8
Lewistown	8,166	145	46	119	10	27	23
McDonald	2,543	133	35	95	5	25	23
McKeesport	42,694	799	248	638	43	144	121
Meadville	12,780	187	70	164	10	22	20
Media	3,562	542	169	439	68	81	61
Meyersdale	2,741	119	30	90	6	27	26
Middletown	5,374	244	67	177	26	57	49
Monessen	11,775	232	90	181	26	31	27
Monongahela	7,598	463	143	377	47	93	80
Mount Pleasant	5,812	144	42	115	16	25	23
New Brighton	8,329	175	45	136	7	27	24
New Castle	36,280	529	189	444	48	67	59
Norristown	27,875	1,015	311	812	128	176	132
North Braddock	11,824	287	93	238	33	48	43
Oil City	15,657	187	50	147	3	37	31
Parkersburg	2,522	161	44	121	3	33	25
Philadelphia	1,549,008	84,459	28,120	71,973	5,595	9,604	8,051
Phoenixville	10,743	191	47	147	21	44	36
Pittsburgh	533,905	25,623	9,362	21,441	1,409	3,371	2,833
Pottstown	15,599	341	99	273	29	63	44
Rankin	6,043	443	151	337	35	59	48
Reading	96,071	787	295	667	23	109	95
Rochester	5,903	225	78	175	11	31	24
Scottdale	5,456	119	49	102	16	14	11
PENNSYLVANIA—Con.							
Scranton	129,867	567	216	482	16	80	73
Sewickley	4,479	428	121	348	24	63	57
Sharon	15,270	194	72	157	14	31	24
Sharpsburg	8,153	209	79	174	6	32	27
Shippensburg	3,457	183	60	151	32	19	18
South Bethlehem	19,973	128	43	113	5	19	18
South Brownsville	3,943	332	112	275	35	53	43
South Sharon	10,190	185	90	152	32	21	14
Steelton	14,246	1,234	442	1,018	163	197	182
Stroudsburg	4,379	120	31	94	17	30	24
Tyrone	7,176	121	31	98	5	24	22
Uniontown	13,344	1,280	427	1,024	123	203	160
Washington	18,778	1,471	446	1,158	125	264	223
Waynesboro	7,199	119	41	99	22	14	12
Waynesburg	3,545	190	57	142	12	45	39
West Chester	11,767	1,868	559	1,565	88	317	262
West Pittston	6,848	101	35	85	7	15	14
Wilkes-Barre	67,105	673	246	570	46	107	96
Wilkinsburg	18,924	428	112	339	28	93	79
Williamsport	31,860	957	259	784	55	158	142
York	44,750	1,231	373	991	115	183	139
RHODE ISLAND.							
Cranston	21,107	245	101	220	27	31	29
East Providence	15,808	435	111	313	51	100	84
Newport	27,149	1,600	480	1,339	78	212	187
North Kingstown	4,048	106	28	86	6	21	18
Pawtucket	51,622	234	68	189	11	42	40
Providence	224,326	5,316	1,765	4,486	434	679	603
South Kingstown	5,176	267	72	202	11	45	40
Warwick	26,629	173	58	144	13	28	24
Westerly	8,696	193	50	152	8	30	25
SOUTH CAROLINA.							
Abbeville	4,459	2,122	488	1,668	402	459	398
Aiken	3,911	2,289	558	1,832	291	443	313
Anderson	9,654	3,370	797	2,614	830	671	427
Bennettsville	2,646	1,133	247	858	253	231	123
Camden	3,569	1,858	381	1,429	524	410	312
Charleston	58,833	31,056	7,881	25,082	6,988	5,329	3,470
Cheraw	2,873	1,546	381	1,165	390	294	165
Chester	4,754	2,041	475	1,629	706	436	311
Clinton	3,272	1,033	229	760	296	218	126
Columbia	26,319	11,546	3,076	9,481	3,050	1,884	1,247
Darlington	3,789	1,720	405	1,336	324	350	274
Easley	2,983	599	132	440	165	122	74
Florence	7,057	3,536	874	2,710	638	671	408
Gaffney	4,767	1,152	243	870	252	264	93
Georgetown	5,530	3,650	917	2,876	1,239	652	412
Greenville	15,741	6,319	1,500	4,965	1,453	1,194	790
Greenwood	6,614	2,943	696	2,282	496	646	530
Laurens	4,818	1,923	416	1,489	602	424	226
Marion	3,844	1,959	466	1,461	399	387	236
Newberry	5,028	1,698	373	1,297	297	358	333
Orangeburg	5,906	3,017	669	2,389	579	612	490
Rock Hill	7,216	2,167	531	1,718	519	423	171
Spartanburg	17,517	6,873	1,568	5,311	1,773	1,367	893
Sumter	8,109	4,125	986	3,326	889	806	511
Union	5,623	2,027	439	1,530	442	464	262
SOUTH DAKOTA.							
Deadwood	3,653	100	41	85	5	10	8
TENNESSEE.							
Bristol (part)	7,148	1,073	264	852	166	197	158
Bristol (total)[1]	13,395	2,217	568	1,756	356	418	312
Brownsville	2,882	1,286	309	1,023	250	252	126
Chattanooga	44,604	17,942	5,700	15,008	3,104	2,486	1,856
Clarksville	8,548	4,285	1,041	3,483	787	815	599
Cleveland	5,549	846	190	666	136	162	146
Columbia	5,754	2,336	590	1,908	553	413	311
Covington	2,990	1,132	298	884	289	212	146
Dyersburg	4,149	1,756	466	1,357	376	317	218
Fayetteville	3,439	1,213	287	981	334	235	174

[1] Joint population of Bristol town, Sullivan County, Tenn., and Bristol city, Va.

NEGRO POPULATION.

TABLE I.—STATISTICS OF NEGRO POPULATION FOR CITIES AND TOWNS OF 2,500 INHABITANTS OR MORE: 1910—Con.

[Cities or towns having less than 100 Negro inhabitants in 1910 are not shown.]

CITY, TOWN, VILLAGE, AND BOROUGH.	Total population: 1910	NEGRO POPULATION: 1910.					
		Total.	Males 21 years of age and over.	Persons 10 years of age and over.		Persons 6 to 14 years of age.	
				Total.	Illiterate.	Total.	Number attending school.
TENNESSEE—Contd.							
Franklin	2,924	1,417	345	1,185	425	241	152
Harriman	3,061	521	130	393	81	123	110
Humboldt	3,446	1,448	351	1,141	209	281	189
Jackson	15,779	5,719	1,483	4,661	975	965	569
Johnson City	8,502	1,441	362	1,115	256	282	231
Knoxville	36,346	7,638	2,297	6,553	932	1,032	703
La Follette	2,816	453	171	375	230	66	23
Lebanon	3,659	1,195	294	955	228	210	149
Memphis	131,105	52,441	17,238	44,976	7,932	6,440	4,317
Morristown	4,007	771	162	600	129	155	126
Murfreesboro	4,679	2,030	504	1,672	521	314	197
Nashville	110,364	36,523	9,713	30,918	6,810	5,538	4,098
Paris	3,881	1,405	337	1,087	329	274	169
Park City	5,126	531	135	429	57	92	79
Pulaski	2,928	1,242	291	1,005	356	240	191
Rockwood	3,660	718	196	533	127	149	119
Shelbyville	2,869	901	238	759	211	148	111
Tullahoma	3,049	640	148	489	140	135	104
Union City	4,389	1,583	350	1,290	222	299	236
TEXAS.							
Abilene	9,204	602	190	516	73	107	79
Amarillo	9,957	123	44	111	19	6	2
Austin	29,860	7,478	1,929	6,023	1,131	1,389	1,093
Bay City	3,156	852	205	658	108	167	121
Beaumont	20,640	6,896	1,996	5,626	910	1,070	804
Beeville	3,269	346	77	269	53	68	39
Belton	4,164	842	190	646	112	181	142
Bonham	4,844	903	239	734	173	165	138
Brady	2,669	101	32	80	12	12	4
Brenham	4,718	2,129	521	1,733	368	435	330
Brownwood	6,967	500	136	382	76	98	74
Bryan	4,132	1,701	431	1,409	276	354	275
Calvert	2,579	1,461	359	1,168	302	305	253
Cameron	3,263	1,043	222	792	182	229	164
Cleburne	10,364	891	215	687	106	182	119
Commerce	2,818	154	31	106	10	37	18
Corpus Christi	8,222	436	103	336	55	68	59
Corsicana	9,749	2,842	714	2,271	528	541	393
Crockett	3,947	2,254	451	1,381	272	494	277
Cuero	3,109	704	143	575	119	141	105
Dallas	92,104	18,024	5,830	15,413	2,370	2,393	1,738
Denison	13,632	2,799	780	2,232	523	531	423
Denton	4,732	556	152	450	111	102	73
El Paso	39,279	1,452	486	1,226	116	192	136
Ennis	5,669	1,557	389	1,192	194	332	247
Fort Worth	73,312	13,280	4,513	11,035	1,329	1,956	1,289
Gainesville	7,624	1,269	352	1,052	164	226	176
Galveston	36,981	8,036	2,654	6,905	845	1,064	816
Georgetown	3,096	712	173	546	117	154	128
Gonzales	3,139	755	173	599	192	150	113
Greenville	8,850	1,887	468	1,447	312	409	295
Hillsboro	6,115	1,084	279	858	180	216	165
Houston	78,800	23,929	7,240	20,180	3,318	3,569	2,656
Houston Heights	6,984	719	193	590	92	135	94
Jacksonville	2,875	741	217	584	186	141	90
Jefferson	2,515	1,336	302	972	278	296	223
Lockhart	2,945	540	117	412	89	116	83
Longview	5,155	2,253	570	1,779	575	436	333
Lufkin	2,749	521	134	402	122	100	69
McKinney	4,714	762	210	602	154	143	105
Marlin	3,878	1,511	407	1,234	255	279	192
Marshall	11,452	4,997	1,184	3,899	873	1,013	774
Mart	2,939	708	197	561	143	137	66
Mexia	2,694	972	225	716	98	219	172
Mineral Wells	3,950	489	150	409	51	53	39
Mount Pleasant	3,137	1,133	383	861	284	221	129
Nacogdoches	3,369	1,076	214	773	229	278	168
Navasota	3,284	1,588	357	1,236	389	353	246
New Braunfels	3,165	121	39	93	5	14	7
Orange	5,527	1,519	459	1,187	265	292	215
TEXAS—Continued.							
Palestine	10,482	3,554	925	2,848	668	628	439
Paris	11,269	3,131	756	2,435	556	718	450
Port Arthur	7,663	1,493	739	1,311	76	140	102
San Angelo	10,321	652	194	552	70	99	53
San Antonio	96,614	10,716	2,917	8,893	1,174	1,717	1,238
San Marcos	4,071	892	197	698	127	169	118
Seguin	3,116	876	196	684	128	182	139
Sherman	12,412	2,220	635	1,818	342	397	308
Smithville	3,167	713	173	550	127	147	110
Stamford	3,902	150	63	136	30	17	4
Stephenville	2,561	166	31	119	8	41	29
Sulphur Springs	5,151	1,449	313	1,085	401	370	232
Taylor	5,314	1,878	449	1,448	311	421	324
Teague	3,288	564	161	437	30	100	65
Temple	10,993	2,814	767	2,201	294	565	419
Terrell	7,050	1,617	439	1,321	300	288	200
Texarkana (part)[1]	9,790	3,218	895	2,524	541	590	410
Tyler	10,400	2,954	712	2,267	480	593	406
Uvalde	3,998	178	34	122	17	48	23
Victoria	3,673	742	163	585	139	144	100
Waco	26,425	6,067	1,636	5,023	844	1,056	711
Waxahachie	6,205	1,592	434	1,253	214	294	241
Weatherford	5,074	512	112	406	43	116	76
Wichita Falls	8,200	578	223	481	74	88	67
Yoakum	4,657	984	227	748	174	210	157
UTAH.							
Ogden	25,580	203	110	186	5	18	16
Salt Lake City	92,777	737	369	674	31	52	43
VERMONT.							
Burlington	20,468	115	34	93	3	14	14
Colchester	6,450	653	516	622	6	15	11
Essex	2,714	317	244	304	1	6	4
VIRGINIA.							
Alexandria	15,329	4,188	1,246	3,481	628	658	457
Bedford City	2,508	851	177	667	118	186	98
Big Stone Gap	2,590	396	91	300	79	91	66
Bristol (part)[2]	6,247	1,144	304	904	190	221	154
Buena Vista	3,245	416	89	311	71	83	48
Charlottesville	6,765	2,524	550	2,038	514	500	378
Clifton Forge	5,748	1,092	357	891	141	168	119
Covington	4,234	1,000	303	792	180	201	152
Danville	19,020	6,207	1,380	5,015	1,868	1,144	748
Farmville	2,971	1,598	347	1,243	322	354	200
Fredericksburg	5,874	1,480	353	1,193	238	270	172
Hampton	5,505	2,182	621	1,795	326	381	285
Harrisonburg	4,879	941	228	756	211	187	156
Lexington	2,931	1,173	279	943	236	221	172
Lynchburg	29,494	9,466	2,232	7,753	1,964	1,519	1,059
Marion	2,727	324	64	239	46	72	39
Martinsville	3,368	1,475	276	1,071	429	346	215
Newport News	20,205	7,259	2,478	5,922	708	1,133	783
Norfolk	67,452	25,039	7,864	21,059	4,148	3,423	2,401
Petersburg	24,127	11,014	2,595	8,797	2,303	2,126	1,384
Portsmouth	33,190	11,617	3,394	9,445	2,317	1,849	1,225
Pulaski	4,807	1,221	301	951	199	277	179
Radford	4,202	665	148	509	141	160	75
Richmond	127,628	46,733	13,279	38,876	7,615	6,927	4,514
Roanoke	34,874	7,924	2,066	6,402	1,451	1,403	1,025
Salem	3,849	849	228	722	136	143	114
South Boston	3,516	1,441	297	1,111	345	300	169
Staunton	10,604	2,476	640	2,067	405	419	304
Suffolk	7,008	2,806	687	2,221	563	531	293
Williamsburg	2,714	897	218	706	290	149	73
Winchester	5,864	1,038	269	860	251	172	126
Wytheville	3,054	782	187	633	202	162	88

[1] For Texarkana (total), see Arkansas.

[2] For Bristol (total), see Tennessee.

TABLE **I.**—STATISTICS OF NEGRO POPULATION FOR CITIES AND TOWNS OF 2,500 INHABITANTS OR MORE: 1910—Con.

[Cities or towns having less than 100 Negro inhabitants in 1910 are not shown.]

CITY, TOWN, VILLAGE, AND BOROUGH.	Total population: 1910.	NEGRO POPULATION: 1910.						CITY, TOWN, VILLAGE, AND BOROUGH.	Total population: 1910.	NEGRO POPULATION: 1910.					
		Total.	Males 21 years of age and over.	Persons 10 years of age and over.		Persons 6 to 14 years of age.				Total.	Males 21 years of age and over.	Persons 10 years of age and over.		Persons 6 to 14 years of age.	
				Total.	Illiterate.	Total.	Number attending school.					Total.	Illiterate.	Total.	Number attending school.
WASHINGTON.								WEST VIRGINIA—Con.							
Everett	24,814	185	74	165	13	18	15	Huntington	31,161	2,140	752	1,809	240	327	269
North Yakima	14,082	176	90	160	11	16	10	Martinsburg	10,698	992	290	812	131	139	113
Roslyn	3,126	111	51	101	7	14	13	Morgantown	9,150	214	55	162	8	49	41
Seattle	237,194	2,296	1,204	2,125	57	153	127	Moundsville	8,918	544	421	523	90	21	19
Spokane	104,402	723	305	659	16	61	54								
Tacoma	83,743	778	351	702	25	66	51	Parkersburg	17,842	869	275	743	76	122	102
Walla Walla	19,364	114	60	101	4	10	9	Princeton	3,027	389	116	301	94	82	57
								Wheeling	41,641	1,201	461	1,053	95	97	91
WEST VIRGINIA.								Williamson	3,561	466	225	413	115	38	36
Bluefield	11,188	2,238	721	1,797	267	351	282	WISCONSIN.							
Charles Town	2,662	883	198	711	158	189	138	Madison	25,531	143	47	116	6	20	16
Charleston	22,996	3,086	936	2,549	275	451	387	Milwaukee	373,857	980	396	890	26	72	58
Clarksburg	9,201	847	267	703	98	118	92	Racine	38,002	112	42	102	4	13	12
								Superior	40,384	182	68	165	2	10	7
Elkins	5,260	215	71	165	15	24	21	WYOMING.							
Fairmont	9,711	458	163	392	25	51	36								
Grafton	7,563	166	57	142	19	29	26	Cheyenne	11,320	653	242	552	71	63	52
Hinton	3,656	274	91	230	43	43	35	Sheridan	8,408	153	63	138	1	11	9

TABLE II.—NEGRO POPULATION, 1910, 1900, 1890, 1880, DECENNIAL INCREASES, PROPORTION NEGRO, LAND AREA, AND NEGRO POPULATION PER SQUARE MILE, BY COUNTIES, FOR SOUTHERN STATES.

[A minus sign (−) denotes decrease.]

STATE AND COUNTY.	NEGRO POPULATION.				INCREASE.						PERCENTAGE NEGRO IN TOTAL POPULATION.				Negroes per 1,000 whites, 1910	Land area, square miles, 1910	Negroes per square mile, 1910
					Number.			Per cent.									
	1910	1900	1890	1880	1900–1910	1890–1900	1880–1890	1900–1910	1890–1900	1880–1890	1910	1900	1890	1880			
ALABAMA	908,282	827,307	678,489	600,103	80,975	148,818	78,386	9.8	21.9	13.1	42.5	45.2	44.8	47.5	739	51,279	17.7
Autauga	11,717	11,173	8,418	8,710	544	2,755	−292	4.9	32.7	−3.4	58.5	62.4	63.2	66.4	1,408	584	20.1
Baldwin	5,110	4,179	3,263	3,675	931	916	−412	22.3	28.1	−11.2	28.1	31.7	36.5	42.7	391	1,595	3.2
Barbour	20,456	22,371	21,442	20,884	−1,915	929	558	−8.6	4.3	2.7	62.5	63.6	61.4	61.5	1,667	912	22.4
Bibb	7,710	6,213	4,744	3,600	1,497	1,469	1,144	24.1	31.0	31.8	33.8	33.6	34.3	37.9	511	634	12.2
Blount [1]	1,181	1,781	1,770	1,159	−600	11	611	−33.7	0.6	52.7	5.5	7.7	8.1	7.5	58	649	1.8
Bullock	25,362	26,097	21,005	22,119	−735	5,092	−1,114	−2.8	24.2	−5.0	84.0	81.7	77.6	76.1	5,248	610	41.6
Butler	15,373	13,246	10,315	8,965	2,127	2,931	1,350	16.1	28.4	15.1	53.0	51.4	47.7	45.6	1,126	763	20.1
Calhoun [1]	10,757	10,626	9,879	5,457	131	747	4,422	1.2	7.6	81.0	27.5	30.5	29.2	27.9	379	630	17.1
Chambers	18,660	17,415	13,858	12,075	1,245	3,557	1,783	7.1	25.7	14.8	51.8	53.5	52.7	51.5	1,073	588	31.7
Cherokee	2,606	3,016	2,803	2,690	−410	213	113	−13.6	7.6	4.2	12.9	14.3	13.7	14.1	148	577	4.5
Chilton	4,759	3,264	3,066	2,142	1,495	198	924	45.8	6.5	43.1	20.5	19.8	21.1	19.8	258	729	6.5
Choctaw	11,503	10,277	9,313	8,341	1,226	964	972	11.9	10.4	11.7	62.2	56.7	53.1	53.0	1,648	932	12.3
Clarke	17,311	15,829	12,939	10,086	1,482	2,890	2,853	9.4	22.3	28.3	55.9	57.0	57.2	56.6	1,267	1,216	14.2
Clay [1]	2,648	1,884	1,704	1,068	764	180	636	40.6	10.6	59.6	12.6	11.0	10.8	8.3	144	614	4.3
Cleburne [1]	711	881	791	668	−170	90	123	−19.3	11.4	18.4	5.3	6.7	6.0	6.1	56	568	1.3
Coffee	5,782	4,233	1,933	1,288	1,549	2,300	645	36.6	119.0	50.1	22.1	20.2	15.9	15.9	284	678	8.5
Colbert [1]	9,449	9,546	7,828	6,950	−97	1,718	878	−1.0	21.9	12.6	38.1	42.7	38.8	43.0	615	618	15.3
Conecuh	10,079	7,793	6,606	6,380	2,286	1,187	226	29.3	18.0	3.5	47.0	44.5	45.3	50.6	888	849	11.9
Coosa	6,256	5,288	5,354	5,059	968	−66	295	18.3	−1.2	5.8	37.6	32.8	33.7	33.5	603	655	9.6
Covington	8,001	2,434	841	671	5,567	1,593	170	228.7	189.4	25.3	24.9	15.9	11.2	11.9	333	1,042	7.7
Crenshaw	7,514	5,601	3,679	2,608	1,913	1,922	1,071	34.2	52.2	41.1	32.2	28.5	23.9	22.2	476	618	12.2
Cullman [1]	533	21	38	43	512	−17	−5	(2)	(2)	(2)	1.9	0.1	0.3	0.7	19	763	0.7
Dale [1]	5,810	4,869	3,358	2,122	941	1,511	1,236	19.3	45.0	58.2	26.9	23.0	19.5	16.7	368	563	10.3
Dallas	43,511	45,372	41,329	40,007	−1,861	4,043	1,322	−4.1	9.8	3.3	81.5	83.0	83.7	82.6	4,399	957	45.5
Dekalb	854	972	1,204	682	−118	−232	522	−12.1	−19.3	76.5	3.0	4.1	5.7	5.4	31	786	1.1
Elmore	13,246	12,051	10,288	8,755	1,195	1,763	1,533	9.9	17.1	17.5	46.9	46.2	47.3	50.0	883	622	21.3
Escambia	5,569	3,515	2,650	1,590	2,054	865	1,060	58.4	32.6	66.7	29.5	31.0	30.6	27.8	423	957	5.8
Etowah	6,804	4,366	3,755	2,502	2,438	611	1,253	55.8	16.3	50.1	17.4	16.0	17.1	16.2	211	542	12.6
Fayette	1,866	1,701	1,682	1,262	165	19	420	9.7	1.1	33.3	11.5	12.0	13.1	12.5	130	643	2.9
Franklin [1]	1,842	2,158	1,160	1,076	−316	998	84	−14.6	86.0	7.8	9.5	13.1	10.9	11.8	105	647	2.8
Geneva [1]	4,305	3,218	1,026	513	1,087	2,192	513	33.8	213.6	100.0	16.4	16.9	9.6	11.8	196	578	7.4
Greene	19,705	20,875	18,771	18,165	−1,170	2,104	606	−5.6	11.2	3.3	86.7	86.3	85.3	82.8	6,542	635	31.0
Hale	21,987	25,347	22,321	21,650	−3,360	3,026	671	−13.3	13.6	3.1	78.9	81.7	81.2	81.5	3,730	646	34.0
Henry [1]	10,150	13,604	8,809	6,767	−3,454	4,795	2,042	−25.4	54.4	30.2	48.5	37.6	35.5	36.1	944	560	18.1
Houston [1]	9,597				9,597						29.6				421	579	16.6
Jackson	3,136	3,642	3,840	4,033	−506	−198	−193	−13.9	−5.2	−4.8	9.5	11.9	13.7	16.1	106	1,140	2.8
Jefferson [1]	90,617	56,917	32,142	5,053	33,700	24,775	27,089	59.2	77.1	536.1	40.0	40.5	36.3	21.7	667	1,135	79.8
Lamar	3,180	3,069	2,748	2,173	111	321	575	3.6	11.7	26.5	18.2	19.1	19.4	17.9	222	601	5.3
Lauderdale	7,096	7,390	7,091	6,860	−294	299	231	−4.0	4.2	3.4	22.9	27.8	29.9	32.6	298	694	10.2
Lawrence [1]	6,933	7,156	8,171	8,750	−223	−1,015	−579	−3.1	−12.4	−6.6	31.5	35.6	39.4	40.9	461	700	9.9
Lee	19,643	19,067	16,497	15,041	576	2,570	1,456	3.0	15.6	9.7	59.8	59.9	57.5	55.2	1,485	632	31.1
Limestone	10,255	9,828	9,002	9,963	427	826	−961	4.3	9.2	−9.6	38.2	43.9	42.5	46.1	617	596	17.2
Lowndes	28,125	30,889	26,985	25,528	−2,764	3,904	1,457	−8.9	14.5	5.7	88.2	86.6	85.5	81.9	7,462	739	38.1
Macon	22,039	18,874	14,188	12,784	3,165	4,686	1,404	16.8	33.0	11.0	84.6	81.6	76.9	73.6	5,500	614	35.9
Madison	18,894	19,875	18,769	19,034	−981	1,106	−265	−4.9	5.9	−1.4	40.2	45.5	49.2	50.6	671	811	23.3
Marengo	30,846	29,473	25,149	23,612	1,373	4,324	1,537	4.7	17.2	6.5	77.3	76.9	76.0	76.4	3,401	966	31.9
Marion	520	778	578	520	−258	200	58	−33.2	34.6	11.2	3.0	5.4	5.1	5.6	31	743	0.7
Marshall	1,365	1,500	1,279	1,496	−135	221	−217	−9.0	17.3	−14.5	4.8	6.4	6.8	10.3	50	602	2.3
Mobile	34,719	28,409	22,804	21,443	6,310	5,605	1,361	22.2	24.6	6.3	42.9	45.3	44.2	44.1	753	1,226	28.3
Monroe	15,727	13,116	10,608	9,234	2,611	2,508	1,374	19.9	23.6	14.9	57.9	55.4	55.9	54.0	1,412	1,012	15.5
Montgomery	56,867	52,207	41,485	38,899	4,660	10,722	2,586	8.9	25.8	6.6	69.2	72.5	73.9	74.3	2,248	801	71.0
Morgan	8,198	7,378	6,073	4,670	820	1,305	1,403	11.1	21.5	30.0	24.3	25.6	25.2	28.4	320	587	14.0
Perry	24,494	24,962	22,516	23,591	−468	2,446	−1,075	−1.9	10.9	−4.6	78.5	78.5	76.8	76.7	3,641	737	33.2
Pickens	12,951	13,921	13,185	12,347	−970	736	838	−7.0	5.6	6.8	51.7	57.0	58.7	57.5	1,070	875	14.8
Pike	14,437	12,474	9,070	6,272	1,963	3,404	2,798	15.7	37.5	44.6	46.9	42.8	37.1	30.4	882	671	21.5
Randolph	5,717	5,178	3,305	3,420	539	1,873	−115	10.4	56.7	−3.4	23.2	23.9	19.2	20.6	302	590	9.7
Russell	20,198	21,152	18,279	18,655	−954	2,873	−376	−4.5	15.7	−2.0	77.9	78.1	75.9	75.1	3,523	655	30.8
St. Clair	3,632	3,442	3,050	2,834	190	392	216	5.5	12.9	7.6	17.5	17.7	17.6	19.6	213	645	5.6
Shelby [1]	7,641	7,004	6,596	4,983	637	408	1,613	9.1	6.2	32.4	28.4	29.6	31.6	28.9	396	806	9.5
Sumter	23,322	27,038	23,631	22,277	−3,716	3,407	1,354	−13.7	14.4	6.1	81.3	82.7	79.9	77.5	4,337	908	25.7
Talladega [1]	18,265	18,223	13,944	12,504	42	4,279	1,440	0.2	30.7	11.5	48.1	50.9	47.5	53.5	929	755	24.2
Tallapoosa	11,457	10,688	8,508	7,293	769	2,180	1,215	7.2	25.6	16.7	36.9	36.0	33.4	31.2	585	763	15.0
Tuscaloosa	19,026	14,638	12,091	9,741	4,388	2,547	2,350	30.0	21.1	24.1	40.0	40.5	39.8	39.0	667	1,346	14.1
Walker [1]	6,538	4,116	1,656	501	2,422	2,460	1,155	58.8	148.6	230.5	17.7	16.4	10.3	5.3	215	777	8.4
Washington	6,064	5,028	3,249	1,729	1,036	1,779	1,520	20.6	54.8	87.9	42.0	45.2	40.9	38.1	738	1,087	5.6
Wilcox	27,602	28,652	24,022	25,117	−1,050	4,630	−1,095	−3.7	19.3	−4.4	81.6	80.4	78.0	78.9	4,446	896	30.8
Winston	54	7	36	17	47	−29	19	(2)	(2)	(2)	0.4	0.1	0.5	0.4	4	630	0.1

[1] For changes in boundaries, see note at end of table.   [2] Per cent not shown where base is less than 100.

TABLE II.—NEGRO POPULATION, 1910, 1900, 1890, 1880, DECENNIAL INCREASES, PROPORTION NEGRO, LAND AREA, AND NEGRO POPULATION PER SQUARE MILE, BY COUNTIES, FOR SOUTHERN STATES—Continued.

[A minus sign (−) denotes decrease.]

STATE AND COUNTY.	NEGRO POPULATION.				INCREASE.						PERCENTAGE NEGRO IN TOTAL POPULATION.				Negroes per 1,000 whites, 1910	Land area, square miles, 1910	Negroes per square mile, 1910
					Number.			Per cent.									
	1910	1900	1890	1880	1900–1910	1890–1900	1880–1890	1900–1910	1890–1900	1880–1890	1910	1900	1890	1880			
ARKANSAS......	442,891	366,856	309,117	210,666	76,035	57,739	98,451	20.7	18.7	46.7	28.1	28.0	27.4	26.3	392	52,525	8.4
Arkansas [1]	4,269	4,058	3,532	3,067	211	526	465	5.2	14.9	15.2	26.5	31.3	30.9	38.2	361	1,000	4.3
Ashley	13,276	10,599	6,868	5,130	2,677	3,731	1,738	25.3	54.3	33.9	52.5	53.7	51.7	50.5	1,107	940	14.1
Baxter	7	5	18	45	2	−13	−27	(2)	(2)	(2)	0.1	0.1	0.2	0.7	(3)	586	(4)
Benton	110	112	92	128	−2	20	−36	−1.8	(2)	−28.1	0.3	0.4	0.3	0.6	3	876	0.1
Boone	7	142	91	88	−135	51	3	−95.1	(2)	(2)	(3)	0.9	0.6	0.7	(5)	608	(4)
Bradley	4,641	3,340	2,864	2,210	1,301	476	654	39.0	16.6	29.6	32.0	34.6	35.9	35.2	470	659	7.0
Calhoun	3,413	3,285	2,720	2,088	128	565	632	3.9	20.8	30.3	34.5	38.5	37.4	36.8	527	629	5.4
Carroll	66	166	82	60	−100	84	22	−60.2	(2)	(2)	0.4	0.9	0.5	0.4	4	641	0.1
Chicot	17,682	12,650	10,023	8,495	5,032	2,627	1,528	39.8	26.2	18.0	80.4	87.1	87.8	84.0	4,124	607	29.1
Clark	7,367	7,267	6,785	5,203	100	482	1,582	1.4	7.1	30.4	31.1	34.1	32.3	33.0	451	882	8.4
Clay [1]	10	9	43	22	1	−34	21	(2)	(2)	(2)	(3)	0.1	0.4	0.3	(3)	654	(4)
Cleburne [1]	7	11	49	....	−4	−38	49	(2)	(2)	....	0.1	0.1	0.6	....	(5)	596	(4)
Cleveland [1]	4,334	3,514	3,327	2,329	820	187	998	23.3	5.6	42.9	32.1	30.2	29.3	27.8	475	603	7.2
Columbia [1]	10,869	9,467	7,312	5,503	1,402	2,155	1,809	14.8	29.5	32.9	45.6	42.9	36.8	39.1	839	785	13.8
Conway	8,298	7,622	7,671	3,206	676	−49	4,465	8.9	−0.6	139.3	36.5	38.5	39.4	25.1	575	563	14.7
Craighead	1,328	1,203	519	261	125	684	258	10.4	131.8	98.9	4.8	6.2	4.3	3.7	51	687	1.9
Crawford [1]	2,063	2,224	2,296	1,392	−161	−72	904	−7.2	−3.1	64.9	8.6	10.5	10.6	9.4	94	593	3.5
Crittenden	19,000	12,290	11,890	7,516	6,710	400	4,374	54.6	3.4	58.2	84.6	84.6	85.3	79.8	5,520	582	32.6
Cross	6,127	4,863	2,890	1,789	1,264	1,973	1,101	26.0	68.3	61.5	43.6	44.0	37.6	35.4	774	619	9.9
Dallas	4,657	4,583	3,265	2,206	74	1,318	1,059	1.6	40.4	48.0	36.9	39.8	35.1	33.9	585	679	6.9
Desha [1]	12,129	9,405	8,198	6,514	2,724	1,207	1,684	29.0	14.7	25.9	79.4	81.7	79.4	72.6	3,862	747	16.2
Drew	11,789	10,289	9,865	5,759	1,500	424	4,106	14.6	4.3	71.3	53.7	52.9	56.9	47.1	1,159	847	13.9
Faulkner [1]	4,460	4,440	3,348	1,418	20	1,092	1,930	0.5	32.6	136.1	18.8	21.4	18.3	11.1	232	651	6.9
Franklin [1]	382	587	677	493	−205	−90	184	−34.9	−13.3	37.3	1.9	3.4	3.4	3.3	19	606	0.6
Fulton	44	79	85	36	−35	−6	49	(2)	(2)	(2)	0.4	0.6	0.8	0.5	4	625	0.1
Garland	4,665	3,674	2,774	1,562	991	900	1,212	27.0	32.4	77.6	17.1	19.6	18.1	17.3	208	631	7.4
Grant	994	846	1,035	556	148	−189	479	17.5	−18.3	86.2	10.5	11.0	13.3	9.0	118	637	1.6
Greene [1]	40	81	161	75	−41	−80	86	(2)	−49.7	(2)	0.2	0.5	1.2	1.0	2	561	0.1
Hempstead	14,100	11,990	10,968	9,421	2,110	1,022	1,547	17.6	9.3	16.4	49.8	49.7	48.1	49.5	994	727	19.4
Hot Spring	1,960	1,485	1,249	745	475	236	504	32.0	18.9	67.7	13.0	11.6	10.8	9.6	150	613	3.2
Howard [1]	3,498	3,098	3,054	2,508	400	44	546	12.9	1.4	21.8	20.7	22.0	22.1	25.3	261	602	5.8
Independence [1]	1,264	1,483	1,568	1,382	−219	−85	186	−14.8	−5.4	13.5	5.1	6.6	7.1	7.6	54	762	1.7
Izard	242	285	262	222	−43	23	40	−15.1	8.8	18.0	1.7	2.1	2.0	2.0	17	583	0.4
Jackson	6,203	5,290	4,329	2,763	913	961	1,566	17.3	22.2	56.7	26.4	28.8	28.5	25.4	359	634	9.8
Jefferson [1]	37,692	29,812	29,908	17,011	7,880	−96	12,897	26.4	−0.3	75.8	71.5	72.8	73.2	76.0	2,506	903	41.7
Johnson	517	619	631	491	−102	−12	140	−16.5	−1.9	28.5	2.6	3.5	3.8	4.2	27	675	0.8
Lafayette [1]	7,181	6,486	4,543	3,614	695	1,943	929	10.7	42.8	25.7	52.3	61.2	59.0	63.1	1,095	525	13.7
Lawrence	750	1,051	833	467	−301	218	366	−28.6	26.2	78.4	3.7	6.4	6.4	5.3	39	592	1.3
Lee	19,003	15,105	14,187	9,150	3,898	918	5,037	25.8	6.5	55.0	78.4	77.8	75.1	68.9	3,634	601	31.6
Lincoln	9,967	8,451	6,469	5,040	1,516	1,982	1,429	17.9	30.6	28.4	65.9	63.1	63.1	54.5	1,935	571	17.5
Little River	5,698	5,749	4,001	3,335	−51	1,748	666	−0.9	43.7	20.0	41.9	41.9	44.9	52.1	722	546	10.4
Logan [1]	640	779	1,124	984	−139	−345	140	−17.8	−30.7	14.2	2.4	3.8	5.4	6.6	25	726	0.9
Lonoke [1]	11,268	9,294	7,981	4,003	1,974	1,313	3,978	21.2	16.5	99.4	40.3	41.2	41.4	33.0	674	794	14.2
Madison [1]	45	44	58	124	1	−14	−66	(2)	(2)	−53.2	0.3	0.2	0.3	1.1	3	836	0.1
Marion		38	32	43		6	−11		(2)	(2)		0.3	0.3	0.5		646	
Miller	7,163	7,619	6,565	4,595	−456	1,054	1,970	−6.0	16.1	42.9	36.6	43.4	44.6	46.3	578	623	11.5
Mississippi [1]	13,472	8,321	5,884	2,654	5,151	2,437	3,230	61.9	41.4	121.7	44.2	50.8	50.6	36.2	793	792	17.0
Monroe [1]	12,526	10,995	9,203	5,209	1,531	1,792	3,994	13.9	19.5	76.7	62.9	65.4	60.0	54.4	1,697	603	20.8
Montgomery	304	319	302	258	−15	17	44	−4.7	5.6	17.1	2.4	3.4	3.8	4.5	25	891	0.3
Nevada	6,790	5,833	4,304	3,722	957	1,529	582	16.4	35.5	15.6	35.1	35.1	29.0	23.7	541	620	11.0
Newton	10	7	6	5	3	1	1	(2)	(2)	(2)	0.1	0.1	0.1	0.1	(3)	846	(4)
Ouachita	12,333	11,634	8,954	6,253	699	2,680	2,701	6.0	29.9	43.2	56.6	55.7	52.6	53.2	1,306	733	16.8
Perry	910	810	941	800	100	−131	141	12.3	−13.9	17.6	9.7	11.1	17.0	20.7	107	552	1.6
Phillips	26,354	20,877	19,640	15,809	5,477	1,237	3,831	26.2	6.3	24.2	78.6	78.6	77.5	74.4	3,673	692	38.1
Pike	918	596	484	392	322	112	92	54.0	23.1	23.5	7.3	5.8	5.7	6.2	79	601	1.5
Poinsett	2,121	1,031	546	290	1,090	485	256	105.7	88.8	88.3	16.6	14.7	12.8	13.2	199	721	2.9
Polk	46	177	46	61	−131	131	−15	−74.0	(2)	(2)	0.3	1.0	0.5	1.0	3	846	0.1
Pope	1,867	1,865	1,621	909	2	244	712	0.1	15.1	78.3	7.6	8.6	8.3	6.3	82	828	2.3
Prairie [1]	4,481	4,191	4,363	2,734	290	−172	1,629	6.9	−3.9	59.6	32.3	35.3	38.4	32.4	478	675	6.6
Pulaski	35,462	29,116	21,935	14,921	6,346	7,181	7,014	21.8	32.7	47.0	40.9	46.1	46.3	45.7	692	747	47.5
Randolph	515	606	595	627	−91	11	−32	−15.0	1.8	−5.1	2.7	3.5	4.1	5.3	28	654	0.8
St. Francis	15,508	11,005	8,000	3,467	4,503	3,005	4,533	40.9	37.6	130.7	68.8	64.1	59.1	41.3	2,203	628	24.7
Saline	1,833	1,920	1,484	1,366	−87	436	118	−4.5	29.4	8.6	11.0	14.6	13.1	15.3	124	775	2.4
Scott [1]	22	102	31	83	−80	71	−52	−78.4	(2)	(2)	0.2	0.8	0.2	0.9	2	970	(4)
Searcy	104	16	28	16	88	−12	12	(2)	(2)	(2)	0.7	0.1	0.3	0.2	7	673	0.2
Sebastian [1]	5,410	4,407	3,740	1,541	1,003	667	2,199	22.8	17.8	142.7	10.3	11.9	11.3	7.9	115	531	10.2
Sevier [1]	2,296	2,041	1,453	1,096	255	588	357	12.5	40.5	32.6	13.8	12.5	14.4	17.7	160	572	4.0
Sharp	83	212	177	176	−129	35	1	−60.8	19.8	0.6	0.7	1.7	1.7	1.9	7	609	0.1
Stone	94	79	113	99	15	−34	14	(2)	−30.1	(2)	1.1	1.0	1.6	1.9	11	611	0.2
Union	13,747	9,720	6,372	6,434	4,027	3,348	−62	41.4	52.5	−1.0	44.7	43.2	42.5	47.9	810	1,048	13.1
Van Buren [1]	220	326	162	118	−106	164	44	−32.5	101.2	37.3	1.6	2.9	1.9	1.2	17	730	0.3
Washington	614	888	1,010	944	−274	−122	66	−30.9	−12.1	7.0	1.8	2.6	3.2	4.0	18	955	0.6
White [1]	2,162	2,656	2,563	2,032	−494	93	531	−18.6	3.6	26.1	7.6	10.7	11.2	11.4	82	1,037	2.1
Woodruff	11,705	9,947	7,556	4,483	1,758	2,391	3,073	17.7	31.6	68.5	58.4	61.0	53.9	51.9	1,403	577	20.3
Yell	1,759	1,670	1,362	1,118	89	308	244	5.3	22.6	21.8	6.7	7.3	7.6	8.1	72	955	1.8

[1] For changes in boundaries, see note at end of table.
[2] Per cent not shown where base is less than 100.
[3] Less than 1 per 1,000 whites.
[4] Less than one-tenth of 1 per cent.

TABLE II.—NEGRO POPULATION, 1910, 1900, 1890, 1880, DECENNIAL INCREASES, PROPORTION NEGRO, LAND AREA, AND NEGRO POPULATION PER SQUARE MILE, BY COUNTIES, FOR SOUTHERN STATES—Continued.

[A minus sign (−) denotes decrease.]

STATE AND COUNTY.	NEGRO POPULATION.				INCREASE. Number.			INCREASE. Per cent.			PERCENTAGE NEGRO IN TOTAL POPULATION.				Negroes per 1,000 whites, 1910	Land area, square miles, 1910	Negroes per square mile, 1910
	1910	1900	1890	1880	1900–1910	1890–1900	1880–1890	1900–1910	1890–1900	1880–1890	1910	1900	1890	1880			
DELAWARE	31,181	30,697	28,386	26,442	484	2,311	1,944	1.6	8.1	7.4	15.4	16.6	16.8	18.0	182	1,965	15.9
Kent	7,561	7,738	8,036	8,114	−177	−298	−78	−2.3	−3.7	−1.0	23.1	23.6	24.6	24.7	301	617	12.3
New Castle	15,682	16,197	14,365	12,636	−515	1,832	1,729	−3.2	12.8	13.7	12.7	14.8	14.8	16.3	146	435	36.1
Sussex	7,938	6,762	5,985	5,692	1,176	777	293	17.4	13.0	5.1	17.1	16.0	15.5	15.8	206	913	8.7
DIST. OF COLUMBIA	94,446	86,702	75,572	59,596	7,744	11,130	15,976	8.9	14.7	26.8	28.5	31.1	32.8	33.6	400	60	1,574.1
FLORIDA	308,669	230,730	166,180	126,690	77,939	64,550	39,490	33.8	38.8	31.2	41.0	43.7	42.5	47.0	696	54,861	5.6
Alachua	19,092	18,965	13,260	10,016	127	5,705	3,244	0.7	43.0	32.4	55.7	58.8	57.8	60.8	1,255	1,262	15.1
Baker	1,159	1,191	745	643	−32	446	102	−2.7	59.9	15.9	24.1	26.4	22.4	27.9	318	587	2.0
Bradford	3,987	2,727	1,555	1,290	1,260	1,172	265	46.2	75.4	20.5	28.3	26.5	20.7	21.1	395	539	2.4
Brevard	1,399	1,074	541	84	325	533	457	30.3	98.5	(2)	29.7	20.8	15.9	5.7	423	1,025	1.4
Calhoun	2,140	2,040	549	396	100	1,491	153	4.9	271.6	38.6	28.7	39.8	32.7	25.1	402	1,192	1.8
Citrus[1]	3,635	2,637	304	......	998	2,333	304	37.8	767.4	......	54.0	48.9	12.7	......	1,174	620	5.9
Clay	2,453	1,832	1,521	573	621	311	948	33.9	20.4	165.4	40.1	32.5	29.5	20.2	670	617	4.0
Columbia	8,411	9,321	6,484	4,769	−910	2,837	1,715	−9.8	43.8	36.0	47.5	54.5	50.4	49.7	907	792	10.6
Dade[1]	4,194	1,293	87	67	2,901	1,206	20	224.4	(2)	(2)	35.1	26.1	10.1	26.1	542	2,733	1.5
De Soto[1]	2,351	672	139	......	1,679	533	139	249.9	383.5	......	16.6	8.4	2.8	......	199	3,754	0.6
Duval	37,270	22,417	14,802	10,850	14,853	7,615	3,952	66.3	51.4	36.4	49.6	56.4	55.2	55.8	986	786	47.4
Escambia	15,111	11,925	8,706	5,302	3,186	3,219	3,404	26.7	37.0	64.2	39.7	42.1	43.1	43.6	660	657	23.0
Franklin	2,487	2,242	1,358	592	245	884	766	10.9	65.1	129.4	47.8	45.8	41.1	33.1	917	541	4.6
Gadsden	14,965	9,856	7,448	8,055	5,109	2,408	−607	51.8	32.3	−7.5	67.4	64.4	62.6	66.2	2,070	540	27.7
Hamilton	5,533	5,376	3,170	2,318	157	2,206	852	2.9	69.6	36.8	46.8	45.2	37.3	34.1	879	528	10.5
Hernando[1]	2,781	1,815	892	929	966	923	−37	53.2	103.5	−4.0	55.7	49.9	36.0	21.9	1,255	497	5.6
Hillsborough	16,445	8,449	2,917	915	7,996	5,532	2,002	94.6	189.6	218.8	21.0	23.5	19.5	15.7	266	1,329	12.4
Holmes	1,194	1,281	184	106	−87	1,097	78	−6.8	596.2	73.6	10.3	16.5	4.2	4.9	115	458	2.6
Jackson	14,254	12,276	11,211	8,735	1,978	1,065	2,476	16.1	9.5	28.3	47.8	52.5	63.9	60.8	916	965	14.8
Jefferson	13,114	12,620	12,199	12,668	494	421	−469	3.9	3.5	−3.7	76.2	77.9	77.4	78.9	3,202	585	22.4
Lafayette	1,361	763	239	173	598	524	66	78.4	219.2	38.2	20.3	15.3	6.5	7.1	254	1,244	1.1
Lake[1]	3,627	2,636	1,844	......	991	792	1,844	37.6	43.0	......	38.1	35.3	23.0	......	617	1,047	3.5
Lee[1]	937	188	80	......	749	108	80	398.4	(2)	......	14.9	6.1	5.7	......	175	4,031	0.2
Leon	14,726	15,999	14,631	16,840	−1,273	1,368	−2,209	−8.0	9.4	−13.1	75.8	80.4	82.4	85.6	3,135	715	20.6
Levy	4,727	3,282	2,129	2,035	1,445	1,153	94	44.0	54.2	4.6	45.6	38.1	32.3	35.3	839	1,143	4.1
Liberty	2,111	1,497	634	548	614	863	86	41.0	136.1	15.7	44.9	50.6	43.7	40.2	815	823	2.6
Madison	9,410	8,904	8,760	9,184	506	144	−424	5.7	1.6	−4.6	55.6	57.6	61.2	62.1	1,253	719	13.1
Manatee[1]	2,346	458	181	135	1,888	277	46	412.2	153.0	34.1	24.0	9.8	6.3	3.8	326	1,337	1.8
Marion	16,376	15,047	11,485	8,305	1,329	3,562	3,180	8.8	31.0	38.3	60.8	61.7	55.2	63.7	1,550	1,647	9.9
Monroe[1]	5,842	5,788	5,935	3,197	54	−147	2,738	0.9	−2.5	85.6	27.1	32.1	31.6	29.2	372	1,100	5.3
Nassau	5,553	5,092	4,338	3,547	461	754	791	9.1	17.4	22.3	52.8	52.7	52.3	53.5	1,117	630	8.8
Orange[1]	7,604	4,027	3,536	1,023	3,577	491	2,513	88.8	13.9	245.7	39.8	35.4	28.1	15.5	661	1,250	6.1
Osceola[1]	927	431	476	......	496	−45	476	115.1	−9.5	......	16.8	12.5	15.2	......	202	1,773	0.5
Palm Beach[1]	2,220	......	......	......	2,220						39.8				670	3,048	0.7
Pasco[1]	2,456	1,679	376	......	777	1,303	376	46.9	346.5	......	32.7	27.7	8.8	......	487	767	3.2
Polk[1]	7,419	2,948	784	122	4,471	2,164	662	151.7	276.0	542.6	30.7	23.6	9.9	3.8	444	1,907	3.9
Putnam	6,804	5,621	4,778	2,416	1,183	843	2,362	21.0	17.6	97.8	52.0	48.3	42.7	38.6	1,082	752	9.0
St. John	5,454	3,621	3,195	1,363	1,833	426	1,832	50.6	13.3	134.4	41.3	39.5	36.7	30.1	686	966	5.6
St. Lucie[1]	865	......	......	......	865						21.2				269	1,395	0.6
Santa Rosa	4,234	2,466	2,192	1,872	1,768	274	320	71.7	12.5	17.1	28.4	24.0	27.5	28.2	397	1,546	2.7
Sumter[1]	2,255	2,280	1,498	1,185	−25	782	313	−1.1	52.2	26.4	33.7	36.9	27.9	25.3	508	583	3.9
Suwannee	7,813	6,577	4,943	3,140	1,236	1,634	1,803	18.8	33.1	57.4	42.0	45.2	47.0	43.8	724	692	11.3
Taylor	2,689	438	151	165	2,251	287	−14	513.9	190.1	−8.5	37.9	11.0	7.1	7.2	609	1,064	2.5
Volusia	6,592	3,464	2,462	538	3,128	1,002	1,924	89.4	40.7	357.6	39.9	34.6	29.1	16.3	665	1,256	5.2
Wakulla	2,384	2,790	1,379	1,160	−406	1,411	219	−14.6	102.3	18.9	49.6	54.2	44.2	42.6	986	602	4.0
Walton	4,997	2,039	743	516	2,958	1,296	227	145.1	174.4	44.0	30.4	21.8	15.4	12.3	436	1,382	3.6
Washington	4,965	2,686	1,339	918	2,279	1,347	421	84.8	100.6	45.9	30.3	26.5	20.8	22.5	434	1,435	3.5
GEORGIA	1,176,987	1,034,813	858,815	725,133	142,174	175,998	133,682	13.7	20.5	18.4	45.1	46.7	46.7	47.0	822	58,725	20.0
Appling[1]	2,863	3,513	2,462	1,192	−650	1,051	1,270	−18.5	42.7	106.5	23.2	28.5	28.4	22.6	303	604	4.7
Baker	5,718	4,770	4,549	5,565	948	221	−1,016	19.9	4.9	−18.3	71.7	71.2	74.0	76.2	2,536	357	16.0
Baldwin	11,005	11,256	9,343	9,294	−251	1,913	49	−2.2	20.5	0.5	60.0	63.3	64.0	67.3	1,498	307	35.8
Banks	2,321	2,097	1,563	1,507	224	534	56	10.7	34.2	3.7	20.6	19.9	18.3	20.5	260	222	10.5
Bartow	6,348	6,187	6,041	6,271	161	146	−230	2.6	2.4	−3.7	25.0	29.7	29.3	33.6	333	471	13.5
Ben Hill[1]	4,901	......	......	......	4,901						41.3				704	256	19.1
Berrien[1]	6,263	5,937	2,417	836	326	3,520	1,581	5.5	145.6	189.1	27.5	30.5	22.6	12.6	380	735	8.5
Bibb	27,481	27,384	23,336	15,700	97	4,048	7,636	0.4	17.3	48.6	48.5	54.3	55.1	57.8	942	277	99.2
Brooks	14,086	10,904	7,637	6,057	3,182	3,267	1,580	29.2	42.8	26.1	59.1	58.6	54.6	51.7	1,445	514	27.4
Bryan	3,337	3,153	2,687	2,561	184	466	126	5.8	17.3	4.9	49.8	51.5	48.7	52.0	992	431	7.7
Bulloch[1]	10,591	9,164	4,689	2,256	1,427	4,475	2,433	15.6	95.4	107.8	40.0	42.9	34.2	28.0	668	887	11.9
Burke[1]	22,462	24,643	22,680	21,031	−2,181	1,963	1,649	−8.9	8.7	7.8	82.4	81.7	79.6	77.5	4,675	956	23.5
Butts	7,200	6,807	5,398	4,034	393	1,409	1,364	5.8	26.1	33.8	52.8	53.2	51.1	48.5	1,121	203	35.5
Calhoun	8,361	6,875	6,199	4,670	1,486	676	1,529	21.6	10.9	32.7	73.8	74.1	73.5	66.5	2,812	284	29.4
Camden	5,113	5,246	4,137	4,092	−133	1,109	45	−2.5	26.8	1.1	66.5	68.4	67.0	66.2	1,984	711	7.2

[1] For changes in boundaries, see note at end of table.   [2] Per cent not shown where base is less than 100.

TABLE II.—NEGRO POPULATION, 1910, 1900, 1890, 1880, DECENNIAL INCREASES, PROPORTION NEGRO, LAND AREA, AND NEGRO POPULATION PER SQUARE MILE, BY COUNTIES, FOR SOUTHERN STATES—Continued.

[A minus sign (−) denotes decrease.]

STATE AND COUNTY.	NEGRO POPULATION.				INCREASE. Number.			INCREASE. Per cent.			PERCENTAGE NEGRO IN TOTAL POPULATION.				Negroes per 1,000 whites, 1910	Land area, square miles, 1910	Negroes per square mile, 1910
	1910	1900	1890	1880	1900–1910	1890–1900	1880–1890	1900–1910	1890–1900	1880–1890	1910	1900	1890	1880			
GEORGIA—Con.																	
Campbell	3,616	3,168	3,493	3,885	448	−325	−392	14.1	−9.3	−10.1	33.3	33.3	38.3	39.0	498	213	17.0
Carroll	6,383	5,036	3,851	2,310	1,347	1,185	1,541	26.7	30.8	66.7	20.7	18.9	17.3	13.7	261	492	13.0
Catoosa	476	482	636	612	−6	−154	24	−1.2	−24.2	3.9	6.6	8.3	11.7	12.9	71	169	2.8
Charlton	1,189	743	870	360	446	−127	510	60.0	−14.6	141.7	25.2	20.7	26.1	16.7	337	905	1.3
Chatham	43,981	41,257	34,757	27,515	2,724	6,500	7,242	6.6	18.7	26.3	55.2	57.9	60.2	61.1	1,233	370	118.9
Chattahoochee	3,864	3,938	3,065	3,540	−74	873	−475	−1.9	28.5	−13.4	69.2	68.0	62.5	62.4	2,244	218	17.7
Chattooga	2,454	2,238	1,998	2,040	216	240	−42	9.7	12.0	−2.1	18.0	17.3	17.8	20.4	220	328	7.5
Cherokee	1,168	1,285	1,508	1,626	−117	−223	−118	−9.1	−14.8	−7.3	7.0	8.4	9.8	11.4	75	429	2.7
Clarke[1]	11,767	9,476	8,111	6,388	2,291	1,365	1,723	24.2	16.8	27.0	50.6	53.5	53.4	54.6	1,023	114	103.2
Clay	6,569	5,703	4,815	3,852	866	888	963	15.2	18.4	25.0	73.3	66.6	61.6	57.9	2,747	203	32.4
Clayton[1]	4,632	4,026	3,075	3,089	606	951	−14	15.1	30.9	−0.5	44.3	41.9	37.1	38.5	796	142	32.6
Clinch	3,378	3,590	2,360	838	−212	1,230	1,522	−5.9	52.1	181.6	40.1	41.1	35.5	20.3	669	961	3.5
Cobb	7,418	7,328	6,774	6,012	90	554	762	1.2	8.2	12.7	26.1	29.7	30.4	29.0	354	353	21.0
Coffee[1]	7,734	6,611	3,858	1,042	1,123	2,753	2,816	17.0	71.4	270.2	35.2	40.9	36.8	20.6	544	901	8.6
Colquitt	4,617	3,602	477	105	1,015	3,125	372	28.2	655.1	354.3	23.3	26.4	9.9	4.2	304	529	8.7
Columbia	9,198	7,753	8,038	7,435	1,445	−285	603	18.6	−3.5	8.1	74.6	72.8	71.3	71.0	2,944	350	26.3
Coweta	16,267	14,220	12,612	11,797	2,047	1,608	815	14.4	12.7	6.9	56.5	56.9	56.4	55.9	1,298	470	34.6
Crawford	4,922	5,818	5,156	4,716	−896	662	440	−15.4	12.8	9.3	59.2	56.1	55.3	54.5	1,453	319	15.4
Crisp[1]	8,616	...	...	...	8,616	...	...	...	...	...	52.5	...	...	...	1,104	277	31.1
Dade	291	438	1,093	1,084	−147	−655	9	−33.6	−59.9	0.8	7.0	9.6	19.2	23.1	76	186	1.6
Dawson	152	171	259	356	−19	−88	−97	−11.1	−34.0	−27.2	3.2	3.1	4.6	6.1	34	216	0.7
Decatur[1]	16,738	15,778	10,811	10,183	960	4,967	628	6.1	45.9	6.2	57.6	53.6	54.2	53.4	1,360	823	20.3
Dekalb	8,362	7,044	5,974	4,543	1,318	1,070	1,431	18.7	17.9	31.5	30.0	33.4	34.8	31.3	428	272	30.7
Dodge	8,460	5,705	5,309	1,852	2,755	396	3,457	48.3	7.5	186.7	42.0	40.8	46.4	34.6	725	431	19.6
Dooly[1]	12,728	14,684	8,914	5,828	−1,956	5,770	3,086	−13.3	64.7	53.0	61.9	55.3	49.1	46.9	1,626	397	32.1
Dougherty	12,049	11,228	10,231	10,670	821	997	−439	7.3	9.7	−4.1	75.1	82.1	83.8	84.5	3,025	342	35.2
Douglas	2,171	2,155	1,801	1,471	16	354	330	0.7	19.7	22.4	24.2	24.6	23.1	21.2	320	208	10.4
Early	11,273	8,965	6,122	4,596	2,308	2,843	1,526	25.7	46.4	33.2	62.2	60.5	62.5	60.4	1,646	524	21.5
Echols	990	991	1,020	500	−1	−29	520	−0.1	−2.8	104.0	29.9	30.9	33.1	19.6	427	362	2.7
Effingham	4,278	3,704	2,210	2,751	574	1,494	−541	15.5	67.6	−19.7	42.9	44.4	39.5	46.0	751	448	9.5
Elbert	12,082	9,792	7,884	6,872	2,290	1,908	1,012	23.4	24.2	14.7	50.1	49.6	51.3	53.0	1,003	361	33.5
Emanuel[1]	9,990	8,406	5,306	3,085	1,584	3,100	2,221	18.8	58.4	72.0	39.7	39.5	36.1	31.6	659	935	10.7
Fannin	162	296	112	133	−134	184	−21	−45.3	164.3	−15.8	1.3	2.6	1.3	1.8	13	401	0.4
Fayette	3,815	3,561	3,074	2,863	254	487	211	7.1	15.8	7.4	34.8	35.2	35.2	33.3	533	234	16.3
Floyd	10,482	11,476	10,414	9,460	−994	1,062	954	−8.7	10.2	10.1	28.5	34.7	36.7	38.7	399	502	20.9
Forsyth	1,098	1,083	1,288	1,487	15	−205	−199	1.4	−15.9	−13.4	9.2	9.4	11.5	14.1	101	247	4.4
Franklin[1]	3,974	4,204	3,298	2,547	−230	906	751	−5.5	27.5	29.5	22.2	23.8	22.5	22.2	285	279	14.2
Fulton[1]	57,985	45,532	35,397	20,842	12,453	10,135	14,555	27.3	28.6	69.8	32.6	38.8	41.8	42.4	485	183	316.9
Gilmer	71	77	69	126	−6	8	−57	(2)	(2)	−45.2	0.8	0.8	0.8	1.5	8	440	0.2
Glascock	1,507	1,515	1,168	1,071	−8	347	97	−0.5	29.7	9.1	32.3	33.5	31.4	29.9	477	170	8.9
Glynn	9,774	9,104	7,741	4,300	670	1,363	3,441	7.4	17.6	80.0	62.2	63.6	57.7	66.2	1,646	439	22.3
Gordon	1,356	1,631	1,727	1,820	−275	−96	−93	−16.9	−5.6	−5.1	8.5	11.6	13.5	16.3	93	375	3.6
Grady[1]	7,403	...	...	...	7,403	...	...	...	...	...	40.1	...	...	...	670	444	16.7
Greene	11,636	11,217	11,719	11,974	419	−502	−255	3.7	−4.3	−2.1	62.9	67.8	68.7	68.2	1,693	416	28.0
Gwinnett	4,431	4,143	2,996	3,515	288	1,147	−519	7.0	38.3	−14.8	15.4	16.2	15.1	18.0	182	491	9.0
Habersham[1]	711	1,792	1,589	1,361	−1,081	203	228	−60.3	12.8	16.8	7.0	13.2	13.7	15.6	75	290	2.5
Hall	4,030	3,272	2,767	2,258	758	505	509	23.2	18.3	22.5	15.7	15.8	15.3	14.8	186	437	9.2
Hancock	14,268	13,628	12,410	11,943	640	1,218	467	4.7	9.8	3.9	74.4	74.6	72.4	70.3	2,902	530	26.9
Haralson	2,027	1,639	1,117	153	388	522	964	23.7	46.7	630.1	15.0	13.7	9.9	2.6	176	284	7.1
Harris	12,865	12,186	10,797	9,286	679	1,389	1,511	5.6	12.9	16.3	71.9	67.7	64.3	58.9	2,562	501	25.7
Hart	5,080	4,025	2,957	2,882	1,055	1,068	75	26.2	36.1	2.6	31.3	27.8	27.2	31.7	456	261	19.5
Heard	3,756	4,014	3,342	3,095	−258	672	247	−6.4	20.1	8.0	33.6	35.9	35.0	35.3	505	258	14.6
Henry	10,184	9,389	7,591	6,229	795	1,798	1,362	8.5	23.7	21.9	51.1	50.5	48.8	43.9	1,045	324	31.4
Houston	17,388	17,006	16,341	16,390	382	665	−49	2.2	4.1	−0.3	73.6	75.1	75.6	73.1	2,795	585	29.7
Irwin[1]	4,916	4,680	2,075	535	236	2,605	1,540	5.0	125.5	287.9	47.0	34.3	32.9	19.8	887	378	13.0
Jackson	8,613	7,606	5,396	5,157	1,007	2,210	239	13.2	41.0	4.6	28.5	31.6	28.1	31.6	400	433	19.9
Jasper	11,484	9,645	8,487	7,593	1,839	1,158	894	19.1	13.6	11.8	69.4	64.2	61.1	64.1	2,266	321	35.8
Jeff Davis[1]	1,593	...	...	...	1,593	...	...	...	...	...	26.3	...	...	...	357	300	5.3
Jefferson	12,979	11,578	10,763	10,090	1,401	815	673	12.1	7.6	6.7	60.7	63.6	62.5	64.4	1,545	720	18.0
Jenkins[1]	7,296	...	...	...	7,296	...	...	...	...	...	63.3	...	...	...	1,727	342	21.3
Johnson	5,557	4,531	1,456	1,345	1,026	3,075	111	22.6	211.2	8.3	43.1	39.7	23.8	28.0	757	292	19.0
Jones	9,288	9,450	8,778	7,860	−162	672	918	−1.7	7.7	11.7	70.9	70.7	69.1	67.7	2,435	377	24.6
Laurens	17,544	11,338	6,093	4,351	6,206	5,245	1,742	54.7	86.1	40.0	49.4	43.8	44.3	43.3	977	806	21.8
Lee	9,992	8,837	7,642	8,837	1,155	1,195	−1,195	13.1	15.6	−13.5	85.6	85.4	84.2	83.5	5,923	326	30.7
Liberty	8,355	8,614	8,673	7,061	−259	−59	1,612	−3.0	−0.7	22.8	64.6	65.8	67.3	66.3	1,829	936	8.9
Lincoln	5,175	4,273	3,673	4,158	902	600	−485	21.1	16.3	−11.7	59.4	59.7	59.8	64.8	1,462	291	17.8
Lowndes	12,955	10,688	7,974	5,637	2,267	2,714	2,337	21.2	34.0	41.5	53.0	53.3	52.8	51.0	1,128	482	26.9
Lumpkin	320	482	414	451	−162	68	−37	−33.6	16.4	−8.2	5.9	6.5	6.0	6.9	62	280	1.1
McDuffie	5,985	6,143	5,522	6,019	−158	621	−497	−2.6	11.2	−8.3	58.0	62.7	62.8	63.7	1,380	287	20.9
McIntosh	4,978	5,081	5,212	4,695	−103	−131	517	−2.0	−2.5	11.0	77.3	77.7	80.6	75.2	3,400	470	10.6
Macon	10,581	9,791	9,181	7,387	790	610	1,794	8.1	6.6	24.3	70.5	69.5	69.6	63.3	2,386	369	28.7
Madison	5,149	3,885	3,662	2,586	1,264	223	1,076	32.5	6.1	41.6	30.6	29.4	33.2	32.4	440	284	18.1
Marion	5,364	5,849	4,261	4,304	−485	1,588	−43	−8.3	37.3	−1.0	58.6	58.0	55.1	50.1	1,418	360	14.9
Meriwether	14,730	13,817	11,538	9,854	913	2,279	1,684	6.6	19.8	17.1	58.5	59.2	55.6	55.8	1,410	496	29.7
Miller	3,257	2,708	1,574	1,393	549	1,134	181	20.3	72.0	13.0	40.8	42.9	36.8	37.4	690	253	12.9
Milton	718	763	672	777	−45	91	−105	−5.9	13.5	−13.5	9.9	11.3	10.8	12.4	110	145	5.0
Mitchell	11,649	7,989	6,106	5,203	3,660	1,883	903	45.8	30.8	17.4	52.7	54.1	56.0	55.4	1,113	548	21.3
Monroe	13,656	13,865	12,516	12,115	−209	1,349	401	−1.5	10.8	3.3	66.8	67.0	65.4	64.4	2,010	584	23.4
Montgomery[1]	7,310	6,706	3,658	1,871	604	3,048	1,787	9.0	83.3	95.5	37.2	41.0	39.6	34.8	593	591	12.4
Morgan	13,414	10,606	10,997	9,782	2,808	−391	1,215	26.5	−3.6	12.4	68.0	67.1	68.6	69.7	2,128	390	34.4

[1] For changes in boundaries, see note at end of table.   [2] Per cent not shown where base is less than 100.

TABLE **II.**—NEGRO POPULATION, 1910, 1900, 1890, 1880, DECENNIAL INCREASES, PROPORTION NEGRO, LAND AREA, AND NEGRO POPULATION PER SQUARE MILE, BY COUNTIES, FOR SOUTHERN STATES—Continued.

[A minus sign (−) denotes decrease.]

STATE AND COUNTY.	NEGRO POPULATION.				INCREASE.						PERCENTAGE NEGRO IN TOTAL POPULATION.				Negroes per 1,000 whites, 1910	Land area, square miles, 1910	Negroes per square mile, 1910
					Number.			Per cent.									
	1910	1900	1890	1880	1900–1910	1890–1900	1880–1890	1900–1910	1890–1900	1880–1890	1910	1900	1890	1880			
GEORGIA—Con.																	
Murray	402	521	484	906	−119	37	−422	−22.8	7.6	−46.6	4.1	6.0	5.7	11.0	43	342	1.2
Muscogee	16,747	15,597	15,362	10,327	1,150	235	5,035	7.4	1.5	48.8	46.2	52.3	55.3	53.4	860	235	71.3
Newton	9,458	8,144	7,164	6,883	1,314	980	281	16.1	13.7	4.1	51.3	48.7	50.1	50.5	1,052	262	36.1
Oconee	5,162	4,413	3,832	3,024	749	581	808	17.0	15.2	26.7	46.5	51.3	49.7	47.6	869	172	30.0
Oglethorpe [1]	11,338	12,243	11,264	9,931	−905	979	1,333	−7.4	8.7	13.4	60.7	68.5	66.5	64.5	1,544	504	22.5
Paulding	1,588	1,345	1,505	984	243	−160	521	18.1	−10.6	52.9	11.2	10.4	12.6	9.0	127	324	4.9
Pickens	440	415	349	145	25	66	204	6.0	18.9	140.7	4.9	4.8	4.3	2.1	51	231	1.9
Pierce	2,742	2,184	1,983	1,472	558	201	511	25.5	10.1	34.7	25.5	27.0	31.1	32.4	342	605	4.5
Pike	10,159	9,602	8,077	8,069	557	1,525	8	5.8	18.9	0.1	52.1	51.2	49.6	50.9	1,088	307	33.1
Polk	5,697	4,916	4,654	4,147	781	262	507	15.9	5.6	12.2	28.2	27.5	31.1	34.7	393	317	18.0
Pulaski	13,504	11,029	10,001	8,225	2,475	1,028	1,776	22.4	10.3	21.6	59.1	59.7	60.4	58.5	1,448	463	29.2
Putnam	10,178	10,057	10,903	11,021	121	−846	−118	1.2	−7.8	−1.1	73.3	74.9	73.5	75.8	2,753	361	28.2
Quitman	3,588	3,447	3,050	2,619	141	397	431	4.1	13.0	16.5	78.1	73.3	68.2	59.6	3,610	144	24.9
Rabun	156	181	166	197	−25	15	−31	−13.8	9.0	−15.7	2.8	2.9	3.0	4.3	29	377	0.4
Randolph	12,986	11,297	9,473	7,796	1,689	1,824	1,677	15.0	19.3	21.5	68.9	67.1	62.0	58.4	2,218	412	31.5
Richmond	28,390	26,255	22,818	17,464	2,135	3,437	5,354	8.4	15.1	30.7	48.2	48.9	50.5	50.4	932	319	89.0
Rockdale	3,592	3,096	2,686	2,689	496	410	−3	16.0	15.3	−0.1	40.3	41.2	39.4	39.3	675	119	30.2
Schley	3,291	3,583	3,205	3,073	−292	378	132	−8.1	11.8	4.3	.63.1	65.2	58.9	58.0	1,712	154	21.4
Screven [1]	12,165	10,946	7,507	6,613	1,219	3,439	894	11.1	45.8	13.5	60.2	56.9	52.0	51.7	1,514	794	15.3
Spalding	10,060	9,154	7,281	7,146	906	1,873	135	9.9	25.7	1.9	51.0	52.0	55.5	56.8	1,039	209	48.1
Stephens [1]	2,222				2,222						22.8				296	166	13.4
Stewart	10,381	11,837	11,484	9,622	−1,456	353	1,862	−12.3	3.1	19.4	77.3	74.7	73.2	68.7	3,397	411	25.3
Sumter	21,243	18,813	15,098	12,189	2,430	3,715	2,909	12.9	24.6	23.9	73.0	71.8	68.3	66.8	2,707	456	46.6
Talbot	8,230	8,539	9,239	9,667	−309	−700	−428	−3.6	−7.6	−4.4	70.4	70.0	69.7	68.5	2,374	312	26.4
Taliaferro	6,450	5,521	4,827	4,722	929	694	105	16.8	14.4	2.2	73.6	69.8	66.2	67.1	2,785	212	30.4
Tattnall [1]	5,841	7,113	3,115	1,974	−1,272	3,998	1,141	−17.9	128.3	57.8	31.5	34.8	30.4	28.2	459	642	9.1
Taylor	5,379	5,026	4,068	3,827	353	958	241	7.0	23.5	6.3	49.6	51.0	46.9	44.5	985	340	15.8
Telfair	4,761	4,126	2,335	2,161	635	1,791	174	15.4	76.7	8.1	35.8	40.9	42.6	44.8	558	373	12.8
Terrell	16,607	13,349	9,169	6,183	3,258	4,180	2,986	24.4	45.6	48.3	75.5	70.2	63.2	59.2	3,078	322	51.6
Thomas [1]	17,086	17,450	15,028	12,213	−364	2,422	2,815	−2.1	16.1	23.0	58.8	56.2	57.5	59.3	1,426	530	32.2
Tift [1]	3,777				3,777						32.9				490	243	15.5
Toombs [1]	3,411				3,411						30.4				438	393	8.7
Towns	15	71	74	104	−56	−3	−30	(2)	(2)	−28.8	0.4	1.5	1.8	3.2	4	181	0.1
Troup	15,399	15,332	13,661	13,970	67	1,671	−309	0.4	12.2	−2.2	58.7	63.9	65.9	67.9	1,422	435	35.4
Turner [1]	4,018				4,018						39.9				664	231	17.4
Twiggs	7,396	5,805	5,447	6,074	1,591	358	−627	27.4	6.6	−10.3	68.9	66.6	66.5	68.1	2,214	314	23.6
Union	64	128	165	110	−64	−37	55	−50.0	−22.4	50.0	0.9	1.5	2.1	1.7	9	324	0.2
Upson	6,998	7,481	6,123	6,267	−483	1,358	−144	−6.5	22.2	−2.3	54.9	54.7	50.2	50.5	1,215	317	22.1
Walker	2,451	2,464	1,932	1,563	−13	532	369	−0.5	27.5	23.6	13.1	15.7	14.5	14.1	151	432	5.7
Walton	10,070	8,341	7,155	6,301	1,729	1,186	854	20.7	16.6	13.6	39.7	39.8	41.0	40.3	657	370	27.2
Ware	8,914	5,109	3,619	1,144	3,805	1,490	2,475	74.5	41.2	216.3	38.8	37.1	41.1	27.5	635	804	11.1
Warren	8,132	7,621	6,756	6,846	511	865	−90	6.7	12.8	−1.3	68.6	66.5	61.7	62.9	2,181	404	20.1
Washington	17,393	17,422	14,925	12,515	−29	2,497	2,410	−0.2	16.7	19.3	61.7	61.7	59.1	57.0	1,613	669	26.0
Wayne	3,309	2,227	2,195	1,920	1,082	32	275	48.6	1.5	14.3	25.3	23.6	29.3	32.1	339	764	4.3
Webster	4,182	4,114	3,272	2,570	68	842	702	1.7	25.7	27.3	68.0	62.2	57.5	49.1	2,124	302	13.8
White	397	600	662	590	−203	−62	72	−33.8	−9.4	12.2	7.8	10.1	10.8	11.0	84	245	1.6
Whitfield	1,719	1,824	1,930	2,210	−105	−106	−280	−5.8	−5.5	−12.7	10.8	12.6	14.9	18.6	121	283	6.1
Wilcox [1]	5,505	4,204	3,155	698	1,301	1,049	2,457	30.9	33.2	352.0	40.8	37.9	39.5	22.5	690	403	13.7
Wilkes	16,598	14,442	12,464	10,812	2,156	1,978	1,652	14.9	15.9	15.3	70.8	69.2	68.9	67.6	2,426	458	36.2
Wilkinson	5,155	6,031	5,214	5,511	−876	817	−297	−14.5	15.7	−5.4	51.2	52.7	48.4	45.7	1,047	472	10.9
Worth [1]	9,517	8,412	4,176	1,824	1,105	4,236	2,352	13.1	101.4	128.9	49.7	45.1	41.6	31.0	988	651	14.6
KENTUCKY	261,656	284,706	268,071	271,451	−23,050	16,635	−3,380	−8.1	6.2	−1.2	11.4	13.3	14.4	16.5	129	40,181	6.5
Adair	1,475	1,594	1,828	2,171	−119	−234	−343	−7.5	−12.8	−15.8	8.9	10.7	13.3	16.6	98	400	3.7
Allen	910	1,098	1,042	1,069	−188	56	−27	−17.1	5.4	−2.5	6.1	7.5	7.6	8.8	65	394	2.3
Anderson [1]	734	994	1,063	1,069	−260	−69	−6	−26.2	−6.5	−0.6	7.2	9.9	10.0	11.4	78	201	3.7
Ballard [1]	1,585	1,502	1,412	1,725	83	90	−313	5.5	6.4	−18.1	12.5	14.0	16.8	12.0	143	252	6.3
Barren	3,590	3,787	3,724	4,941	−197	63	−1,217	−5.2	1.7	−24.6	14.2	16.3	17.3	22.1	165	485	7.4
Bath	1,336	1,692	1,578	2,017	−356	114	−439	−21.0	7.2	−21.8	9.6	11.5	12.3	16.8	106	270	4.9
Bell	2,920	1,754	740	181	1,166	1,014	559	66.5	137.0	308.8	10.3	11.2	7.2	3.0	114	384	7.6
Boone	478	810	1,112	1,232	−332	−302	−120	−41.0	−27.2	−9.7	5.1	7.3	9.1	10.3	53	251	1.9
Bourbon	5,642	6,792	6,797	7,314	−1,150	−5	−517	−16.9	−0.1	−7.1	32.3	37.6	40.0	45.8	477	304	18.6
Boyd	822	771	705	556	51	66	149	6.6	9.4	26.8	3.5	4.1	5.0	4.6	36	159	5.2
Boyle	4,153	4,781	4,809	4,737	−628	−28	72	−13.1	−0.6	1.5	28.3	34.6	37.1	39.7	395	186	22.3
Bracken	339	572	646	816	−233	−74	−170	−40.7	−11.5	−20.8	3.3	4.7	5.2	6.0	34	204	1.7
Breathitt [1]	260	299	169	185	−39	130	−16	−13.0	76.9	−8.6	1.5	2.1	1.9	2.4	15	483	0.5
Breckinridge	1,581	2,096	2,080	2,204	−515	16	−124	−24.6	0.8	−5.6	7.5	10.2	11.0	12.6	81	568	2.8
Bullitt	679	1,094	1,048	1,307	−415	46	−259	−37.9	4.4	−19.8	7.2	11.4	12.6	15.3	77	308	2.2
Butler	561	725	773	820	−164	−48	−47	−22.6	−6.2	−5.7	3.5	4.6	5.5	6.7	37	417	1.3
Caldwell	2,520	2,775	2,736	2,187	−255	39	549	−9.2	1.4	25.1	17.9	19.1	20.7	19.4	218	322	7.8
Calloway	1,069	1,258	1,092	1,215	−189	166	−123	−15.0	15.2	−10.1	5.4	7.1	7.4	9.1	57	412	2.6
Campbell	735	580	686	441	155	−106	245	26.7	−15.5	55.6	1.2	1.1	1.6	1.2	13	145	5.1
Carlisle [1]	393	638	389		−245	249	389	−38.4	64.0		4.3	6.3	5.1		45	198	2.0
Carroll	530	804	757	771	−274	47	−14	−34.1	6.2	−1.8	6.5	8.2	8.2	8.6	70	132	4.0
Carter	110	143	137	371	−33	6	−234	−23.1	4.4	−63.1	0.5	0.7	0.8	3.0	5	413	0.3
Casey	278	504	516	608	−226	−12	−92	−44.8	−2.3	−15.1	1.8	3.3	4.4	5.5	18	379	0.7
Christian	15,956	16,597	15,231	14,639	−641	1,366	592	−3.9	9.0	4.0	41.1	43.7	44.6	46.2	697	725	22.0
Clark	4,462	5,177	4,826	4,186	−715	351	640	−13.8	7.3	15.3	24.8	31.0	31.3	34.6	330	265	16.8

[1] For changes in boundaries, see note at end of table.   [2] Per cent not shown where base is less than 100.

TABLE **II.**—NEGRO POPULATION, 1910, 1900, 1890, 1880, DECENNIAL INCREASES, PROPORTION NEGRO, LAND AREA, AND NEGRO POPULATION PER SQUARE MILE, BY COUNTIES, FOR SOUTHERN STATES—Continued.

[A minus sign (−) denotes decrease.]

STATE AND COUNTY.	NEGRO POPULATION.				INCREASE.						PERCENTAGE NEGRO IN TOTAL POPULATION.				Negroes per 1,000 whites, 1910	Land area, square miles, 1910	Negroes per square mile, 1910
					Number.			Per cent.									
	1910	1900	1890	1880	1900–1910	1890–1900	1880–1890	1900–1910	1890–1900	1880–1890	1910	1900	1890	1880			
KENTUCKY—Continued.																	
Clay	494	564	413	706	−70	151	−293	−12.4	36.6	−41.5	2.8	3.7	3.3	6.9	29	478	1.0
Clinton	94	175	188	311	−81	−13	−123	−46.3	−6.9	−39.5	1.2	2.2	2.7	4.3	12	233	0.4
Crittenden	588	876	930	1,151	−288	−54	−221	−32.9	−5.8	−19.2	4.4	5.8	7.1	9.8	46	391	1.5
Cumberland	1,024	922	996	1,567	102	−74	−571	11.1	−7.4	−36.4	10.4	10.3	11.8	17.6	116	387	2.6
Daviess	5,195	5,554	5,367	4,854	−359	187	513	−6.5	3.5	10.6	12.7	14.4	16.2	17.5	145	478	10.9
Edmonson	439	452	458	555	−13	−6	−97	−2.9	−1.3	−17.5	4.2	4.5	5.7	7.7	44	308	1.4
Elliott	1	2	27	43	−1	−25	−16	(1)	(1)	−37.2	(2)	(2)	0.3	0.7	(2)	263	(2)
Estill[4]	106	223	581	511	−117	−358	70	−52.5	−61.6	13.7	0.9	1.9	5.4	5.2	9	254	0.4
Fayette	14,879	15,409	13,625	12,974	−530	1,784	651	−3.4	13.1	−5.0	31.2	36.6	38.2	44.7	453	269	55.3
Fleming	1,027	1,585	1,625	1,575	−558	−40	50	−35.2	−2.5	3.2	6.4	9.3	10.1	10.3	68	325	3.2
Floyd[4]	99	136	136	199	−37	....	−63	−27.2	....	−31.7	0.5	0.9	1.2	2.0	5	399	0.2
Franklin	3,746	4,348	4,757	4,860	−602	−409	−103	−13.8	−8.6	−2.1	17.7	20.9	22.4	26.0	215	199	18.8
Fulton	3,356	2,838	2,208	1,605	518	630	603	18.3	28.5	37.6	23.8	24.6	22.1	20.1	312	193	17.4
Gallatin	274	565	497	647	−291	68	−150	−51.5	13.7	−23.2	5.8	10.9	10.8	13.4	62	109	2.5
Garrard	2,284	2,946	3,024	3,695	−662	−78	−671	−22.5	−2.6	−18.2	19.2	24.5	27.2	31.6	238	237	9.6
Grant	292	427	483	733	−135	−56	−250	−31.6	−11.6	−34.1	2.8	3.2	3.8	5.6	28	264	1.1
Graves	2,899	3,345	3,154	2,851	−446	191	303	−13.3	6.1	10.6	8.6	10.1	11.1	11.8	95	551	5.3
Grayson	333	428	489	407	−95	−61	82	−22.2	−12.5	20.1	1.7	2.2	2.6	2.6	17	497	0.7
Green	1,343	1,739	1,891	2,408	−396	−152	−517	−22.8	−8.0	−21.5	11.3	14.2	16.5	20.3	128	279	4.8
Greenup	257	272	338	439	−15	−66	−101	−5.5	−19.5	−23.0	1.4	1.8	2.8	3.3	14	346	0.7
Hancock	566	644	758	803	−78	−114	−45	−12.1	−15.0	−5.6	6.6	7.2	8.2	9.4	71	193	2.9
Hardin	1,826	2,071	2,347	3,282	−245	−276	−935	−11.8	−11.8	−28.5	8.0	9.0	11.0	14.5	87	606	3.0
Harlan	564	226	154	114	338	72	40	149.6	46.8	35.1	5.3	2.3	2.5	2.2	56	478	1.2
Harrison	1,750	2,421	2,467	2,932	−671	−46	−465	−27.7	−1.9	−15.9	10.4	13.0	14.6	17.8	116	311	5.6
Hart	1,991	2,220	2,002	2,839	−229	218	−837	−10.3	10.9	−29.5	11.0	12.1	12.2	16.6	123	430	4.6
Henderson	6,818	8,804	8,219	7,572	−1,986	585	647	−22.6	7.1	8.5	23.2	26.8	27.8	30.9	303	435	15.7
Henry	1,792	1,930	2,365	2,869	−138	−435	−504	−7.2	−18.4	−17.6	13.1	13.2	16.7	19.8	150	303	5.9
Hickman	1,766	2,123	1,768	1,964	−357	355	−196	−16.8	20.1	−10.0	15.0	18.1	15.2	18.4	177	225	7.8
Hopkins	6,573	5,118	3,433	2,710	1,455	1,685	723	−28.4	49.1	26.7	19.2	16.5	14.6	14.2	237	546	12.0
Jackson	22	19	54	45	3	−35	9	(1)	(1)	20.0	0.2	0.2	0.7	0.7	2	333	0.1
Jefferson	45,794	43,916	33,595	25,595	1,878	10,321	8,000	4.3	30.7	31.3	17.4	18.9	17.8	17.5	211	387	118.3
Jessamine	2,962	3,349	3,706	4,401	−387	−357	−695	−11.6	−9.6	−15.8	23.5	28.1	32.9	40.5	307	172	17.2
Johnson	47	1	84	103	46	−83	−19	(1)	(2)	−18.4	0.3	(2)	0.8	1.1	3	268	0.2
Kenton	3,228	3,282	2,667	2,528	−54	615	139	−1.6	23.1	5.5	4.6	5.2	4.9	5.7	48	163	19.8
Knott[4]	157	169	73	....	−12	96	73	−7.1	(1)	(1)	1.5	1.9	1.3	....	15	348	0.5
Knox	1,059	754	778	662	305	−24	116	40.5	−3.1	17.5	4.8	4.3	5.7	6.3	50	356	3.0
Larue	785	782	791	1,047	3	−9	−256	0.4	−1.1	−24.5	7.3	7.3	8.4	10.7	79	288	2.7
Laurel	657	654	555	267	3	99	288	0.5	17.8	107.9	3.3	3.7	4.0	2.9	34	447	1.5
Lawrence	163	185	176	241	−22	9	−65	−11.9	5.1	−27.0	0.8	0.9	1.0	1.8	8	422	0.4
Lee	234	271	459	230	−37	−188	229	−13.7	−41.0	100.0	2.5	3.4	7.4	5.4	25	199	1.2
Leslie	132	75	32	28	57	43	4	(1)	(1)	14.3	1.5	1.1	0.8	0.7	15	373	0.4
Letcher[4]	17	46	75	142	−29	−29	−67	(1)	(1)	−47.2	0.2	0.5	1.1	2.2	2	355	(2)
Lewis	141	175	177	229	−34	−2	−52	−19.4	−1.1	−22.7	0.8	1.0	1.2	1.7	8	491	0.3
Lincoln	2,955	3,512	3,574	3,908	−557	−62	−334	−15.9	−1.7	−8.5	16.5	20.6	22.4	25.9	198	338	8.7
Livingston	670	778	741	1,034	−108	37	−293	−13.9	5.0	−28.3	6.3	6.9	7.8	11.3	67	392	1.7
Logan	5,349	6,738	6,560	7,381	−1,389	178	−821	−20.6	2.7	−11.1	21.4	25.9	27.5	30.3	273	643	8.3
Lyon	1,799	1,932	1,317	1,488	−133	615	−171	−6.9	46.7	−11.5	19.1	20.7	17.3	22.0	236	277	6.5
McCracken	7,934	7,283	5,703	4,383	651	1,580	1,320	8.9	27.7	30.1	22.6	25.3	27.1	27.0	292	239	33.2
McLean	750	874	786	848	−124	88	−62	−14.2	11.2	−7.3	5.7	7.0	7.9	9.1	60	253	3.0
Madison	5,698	6,690	7,399	7,288	−992	−709	111	−14.8	−9.6	1.5	21.1	26.1	30.4	33.0	268	446	12.8
Magoffin[4]	54	136	160	150	−82	−24	10	−60.3	−15.0	6.7	0.4	1.1	1.7	2.2	4	302	0.2
Marion	2,266	2,811	3,148	3,504	−545	−337	−356	−19.4	−10.7	−10.2	13.9	17.3	20.1	23.8	161	345	6.6
Marshall	135	348	342	440	−213	6	−98	−61.2	1.8	−22.3	0.9	2.5	3.0	4.6	9	327	0.4
Martin	4	15	23	32	−11	−8	−9	(1)	(1)	(1)	0.1	0.3	0.5	1.0	(3)	227	(2)
Mason	2,868	3,768	4,168	4,392	−900	−400	−224	−23.9	−9.6	−5.1	15.4	18.4	20.1	21.5	182	227	12.6
Meade	655	890	769	1,274	−235	121	−505	−26.4	15.7	−39.6	6.7	8.4	8.1	12.3	72	301	2.2
Menifee[4]	40	41	27	48	−1	14	−21	(1)	(1)	(1)	0.7	0.6	0.6	1.3	7	203	0.2
Mercer	2,171	2,468	3,075	3,148	−297	−607	−73	−12.0	−19.7	−2.3	15.4	17.1	20.5	22.3	183	253	8.6
Metcalfe	794	999	900	1,036	−205	99	−136	−20.5	11.0	−13.1	7.6	10.0	9.1	11.0	82	303	2.6
Monroe	705	682	540	661	23	142	−121	3.4	26.3	−18.3	5.2	5.2	4.9	6.2	54	441	1.6
Montgomery	3,192	3,483	3,643	3,566	−291	−160	77	−8.4	−4.4	2.2	24.8	27.1	29.5	33.7	330	198	16.1
Morgan	34	53	49	33	−19	4	16	(1)	(1)	(1)	0.2	0.4	0.4	0.4	2	365	0.1
Muhlenberg	2,911	2,157	2,359	2,078	754	−202	281	35.0	−8.6	13.5	10.2	10.4	13.1	13.8	113	472	6.2
Nelson	2,935	3,442	3,821	4,716	−507	−379	−895	−14.7	−9.9	−19.0	17.4	20.8	23.3	28.4	211	411	7.1
Nicholas	896	1,332	1,316	1,750	−436	16	−434	−32.7	1.2	−24.8	8.5	11.1	12.2	14.7	92	208	4.3
Ohio	1,288	1,393	1,346	1,464	−105	47	−118	−7.5	3.5	−8.1	4.7	5.1	5.9	7.4	49	584	2.2
Oldham	1,078	1,620	1,647	2,211	−542	−27	−564	−33.5	−1.6	−25.5	14.9	22.9	24.4	28.8	175	180	6.0
Owen	943	1,470	1,427	1,503	−527	43	−76	−35.9	3.0	−5.1	6.6	8.4	8.1	8.6	71	367	2.6
Owsley	75	73	84	89	2	−11	−5	(1)	(1)	(1)	0.9	1.1	1.4	1.8	9	216	0.3
Pendleton	261	488	507	780	−227	−19	−273	−46.5	−3.7	−35.0	2.2	3.3	3.1	4.7	22	279	0.9
Perry[4]	214	161	160	139	53	1	21	32.9	0.6	15.1	1.9	1.9	2.5	2.5	19	335	0.6
Pike	332	190	166	174	142	24	−8	74.7	14.5	−4.6	1.0	0.8	1.0	1.3	11	779	0.4
Powell[4]	337	375	379	287	−38	−4	92	−10.1	−1.1	32.1	5.4	5.8	8.1	7.9	57	181	1.9
Pulaski	1,187	1,336	1,291	1,196	−149	45	95	−11.2	3.5	7.9	3.3	4.3	5.0	5.6	34	779	1.5
Robertson	70	128	155	283	−58	−27	−128	−45.3	−17.4	−45.2	1.7	2.6	3.3	4.9	17	109	0.6

[1] Per cent not shown where base is less than 100.
[2] Less than one-tenth of 1 per cent.
[3] Less than 1 per 1,000 whites.
[4] For changes in boundaries, see note at end of table.

TABLE **II.**—NEGRO POPULATION, 1910, 1900, 1890, 1880, DECENNIAL INCREASES, PROPORTION NEGRO, LAND AREA, AND NEGRO POPULATION PER SQUARE MILE, BY COUNTIES, FOR SOUTHERN STATES—Continued.

[A minus sign (−) denotes decrease.]

STATE AND COUNTY.	NEGRO POPULATION.				INCREASE.						PERCENTAGE NEGRO IN TOTAL POPULATION.				Negroes per 1,000 whites, 1910	Land area, square miles, 1910	Negroes per square mile, 1910
					Number.			Per cent.									
	1910	1900	1890	1880	1900–1910	1890–1900	1880–1890	1900–1910	1890–1900	1880–1890	1910	1900	1890	1880			
KENTUCKY—Continued.																	
Rockcastle	125	157	155	437	−32	2	−282	−20.4	1.3	−64.5	0.9	1.3	1.6	4.5	9	310	0.4
Rowan	59	54	106	106	5	−52	....	(1)	−49.1	....	0.6	0.7	1.7	2.4	6	272	0.2
Russell	207	294	266	354	−87	28	−88	−29.6	10.5	−24.9	1.9	3.0	3.3	4.7	19	329	0.6
Scott	4,044	5,062	5,063	5,002	−1,018	−1	61	−20.1	(1)	1.2	23.9	28.0	30.6	33.4	313	289	14.0
Shelby	3,991	4,698	4,776	5,555	−707	−78	−779	−15.0	−1.6	−14.0	22.1	25.6	28.9	33.0	284	427	9.3
Simpson	2,165	2,550	2,374	2,797	−385	176	−423	−15.1	7.4	−15.1	18.9	21.9	21.8	26.3	233	216	10.0
Spencer	758	1,251	1,250	1,626	−493	1	−376	−39.4	0.1	−23.1	10.0	16.9	18.5	23.1	111	186	4.1
Taylor	1,429	1,643	1,474	1,899	−214	169	−425	−13.0	11.5	−22.4	11.9	14.8	15.8	20.5	136	279	5.1
Todd	5,343	6,169	6,301	6,567	−826	−132	−266	−13.4	−2.1	−4.1	32.4	35.5	37.5	41.1	479	367	14.6
Trigg	3,322	3,497	3,652	4,040	−175	−155	−388	−5.0	−4.2	−9.6	22.8	24.8	26.3	27.9	296	428	7.8
Trimble	142	201	321	577	−59	−120	−256	−29.4	−37.4	−44.4	2.2	2.8	4.5	8.0	22	154	0.9
Union	2,414	3,113	2,656	3,163	−699	457	−507	−22.5	17.2	−16.0	12.1	14.6	14.6	17.8	138	325	7.4
Warren	6,113	6,992	7,926	7,639	−879	−934	287	−12.6	−11.8	3.8	20.0	23.3	26.3	27.7	250	530	11.5
Washington [2]	1,779	1,899	2,094	2,430	−120	−195	−336	−6.3	−9.3	−13.8	12.8	13.4	15.4	16.9	146	299	5.9
Wayne	739	608	618	899	131	−10	−281	21.5	−1.6	−31.2	4.2	4.1	4.8	7.2	44	590	1.3
Webster	2,643	2,389	1,912	1,666	254	477	246	10.6	24.9	14.8	12.6	11.9	11.1	11.7	144	344	7.7
Whitley	1,111	769	752	237	342	17	515	44.5	2.3	217.3	3.5	3.1	4.3	2.0	36	585	1.9
Wolfe [2]	56	97	122	75	−41	−25	47	−42.3	−20.5	(1)	0.6	1.1	1.7	1.3	6	230	0.2
Woodford	3,724	4,719	4,853	5,642	−995	−134	−789	−21.1	−2.8	−14.0	29.6	35.9	39.2	47.8	421	195	19.1
LOUISIANA	713,874	650,804	559,193	483,655	63,070	91,611	75,538	9.7	16.4	15.6	43.1	47.1	50.0	51.5	759	45,409	15.7
Acadia [2]	6,546	4,820	1,629	....	1,726	3,191	1,629	35.8	195.9	....	20.6	20.5	12.3	....	259	647	10.1
Ascension	11,255	12,081	11,270	10,855	−826	811	415	−6.8	7.2	3.8	47.1	50.0	57.7	64.2	891	291	38.7
Assumption	10,105	9,438	8,890	8,067	667	548	823	7.1	6.2	10.2	41.9	43.7	45.3	47.4	721	484	20.9
Avoyelles	12,039	11,891	12,161	8,213	148	−270	3,948	1.2	−2.2	48.1	35.3	40.0	48.4	49.0	547	847	14.2
Bienville	9,464	8,240	6,268	4,987	1,224	1,972	1,281	14.9	31.5	25.7	43.5	46.9	44.4	47.8	769	848	11.2
Bossier	16,735	18,890	16,225	12,786	−2,155	2,665	3,439	−11.4	16.4	26.9	77.0	78.2	79.8	79.7	3,345	863	19.4
Caddo	36,142	30,662	23,541	19,368	5,480	7,121	4,173	17.9	30.2	21.5	62.1	68.9	74.6	73.7	1,640	880	41.1
Calcasieu	16,562	5,966	3,194	2,407	10,596	2,772	787	1,776	86.8	32.7	24.6	19.6	15.8	19.3	361	3,650	4.5
Caldwell	3,465	3,076	3,106	2,896	389	−30	210	12.6	−1.0	7.3	40.3	44.5	53.4	50.2	676	531	6.5
Cameron	538	577	426	324	−39	151	102	−6.8	35.4	31.5	12.5	14.6	15.1	13.4	143	1,501	0.4
Catahoula [2]	5,195	6,793	4,976	4,527	−1,598	1,817	449	−23.5	36.5	9.9	49.9	41.5	41.5	44.0	998	718	7.2
Claiborne	14,938	13,827	13,512	10,295	1,111	315	3,217	8.0	2.3	31.2	59.6	60.0	58.0	54.7	1,477	778	19.2
Concordia	11,941	11,845	13,112	13,594	96	−1,267	−482	0.8	−9.7	−3.5	83.6	87.4	88.2	91.1	5,110	714	16.7
De Soto	17,932	16,903	13,220	10,487	1,029	3,683	2,733	6.1	27.9	26.1	64.8	67.4	66.6	67.2	1,838	872	20.6
East Baton Rouge	21,342	20,578	16,420	12,863	764	4,158	3,557	3.7	25.3	27.7	61.7	66.1	63.3	64.4	1,615	455	46.9
East Carroll	10,390	10,412	11,360	11,090	−22	−948	270	−0.2	−8.3	2.4	89.3	91.6	91.9	91.4	8,366	420	24.7
East Feliciana	14,536	14,871	12,707	10,635	−335	2,164	2,072	−2.3	17.0	19.5	72.5	72.7	71.0	70.3	2,634	464	31.3
Franklin	5,264	5,020	4,040	3,793	244	980	247	4.9	24.3	6.5	43.9	56.5	58.6	58.4	783	630	8.4
Grant	4,869	3,665	3,416	2,862	1,204	249	554	32.9	7.3	19.4	30.5	28.4	41.3	46.3	439	683	7.1
Iberia	14,474	14,282	10,477	8,575	192	3,805	1,902	1.3	36.3	22.2	46.3	49.2	49.9	51.4	862	589	24.6
Iberville	19,145	17,159	15,142	12,759	1,986	2,017	2,383	11.6	13.3	18.7	61.8	63.5	69.3	72.7	1,622	584	32.8
Jackson	3,996	3,204	2,608	2,403	792	596	205	24.7	22.9	8.5	28.9	35.1	35.0	45.1	407	578	6.9
Jefferson	6,785	6,279	6,484	7,290	506	−205	−806	8.1	−3.2	−11.1	37.2	41.0	49.0	59.9	596	425	16.0
La Salle [2]	1,953				1,953	....	....				20.8				263	640	3.1
Lafayette	10,734	9,516	6,884	5,541	1,218	2,632	1,343	12.8	38.2	24.2	37.4	41.7	43.1	41.9	597	279	38.5
Lafourche	7,973	8,184	7,819	7,806	−211	365	13	−2.6	4.7	0.2	24.1	28.3	35.4	40.8	317	991	8.0
Lincoln	7,289	6,759	6,269	4,898	530	490	1,371	7.8	7.8	28.0	39.4	42.5	42.5	44.2	651	472	15.4
Livingston	1,377	1,144	871	993	233	273	−122	20.4	31.3	−12.3	13.0	14.1	15.1	18.9	149	662	2.1
Madison	9,455	11,422	13,204	12,645	−1,967	−1,782	559	−17.2	−13.5	4.4	88.6	92.7	93.4	90.9	7,750	650	14.5
Morehouse	13,971	12,722	13,267	10,659	1,249	−545	2,608	9.8	−4.1	24.5	74.4	76.5	79.0	75.0	2,902	831	16.8
Natchitoches	20,334	19,544	15,551	12,020	790	3,993	3,531	4.0	25.7	29.4	55.8	58.8	60.2	61.0	1,262	1,289	15.8
Orleans	89,262	77,714	64,491	57,617	11,548	13,223	6,874	14.9	20.5	11.9	26.3	27.1	26.6	26.7	358	200	446.3
Ouachita	14,153	13,098	12,344	10,180	1,055	754	2,164	8.1	6.1	21.3	54.8	62.5	68.6	69.3	1,213	642	22.0
Plaquemines	6,847	7,276	7,258	7,214	−429	18	44	−5.9	0.2	0.6	54.7	55.8	57.9	62.3	1,206	1,005	6.8
Pointe Coupee	17,147	19,174	14,917	12,999	−2,027	4,257	1,918	−10.6	28.5	14.8	67.8	74.4	76.1	73.1	2,106	576	29.8
Rapides	21,445	21,210	15,800	13,942	235	5,410	1,858	1.1	34.2	13.3	48.1	53.6	57.2	59.2	933	1,370	15.7
Red River	6,212	7,471	7,760	6,066	−1,259	−289	1,694	−16.9	−3.7	27.9	54.5	64.7	68.6	70.8	1,197	400	15.5
Richland	10,463	7,892	7,213	5,279	2,571	679	1,934	32.6	9.4	36.6	66.4	71.0	70.5	62.5	1,973	565	18.5
Sabine	4,164	3,002	2,067	1,847	1,162	935	220	38.7	45.2	11.9	21.0	19.5	22.0	25.1	265	1,020	4.1
St. Bernard	1,933	2,197	1,977	2,288	−264	220	−311	−12.0	11.1	−13.6	36.6	43.7	45.7	51.9	578	616	3.1
St. Charles	6,720	6,102	5,751	5,746	618	351	5	10.0	6.1	0.1	60.0	67.3	74.3	80.2	1,498	295	22.8
St. Helena	4,573	4,583	4,589	4,176	−10	−6	413	−0.2	−0.1	9.9	49.9	54.1	56.9	55.7	994	420	10.9
St. James	13,164	11,356	9,997	9,862	1,808	1,359	135	15.9	13.6	1.4	57.2	56.2	63.6	67.0	1,337	254	51.8
St. John the Baptist	8,126	7,184	6,637	5,792	942	547	845	13.1	8.2	14.6	56.7	58.3	58.4	59.8	1,309	231	35.2
St. Landry [2]	31,234	26,658	22,274	19,399	4,576	4,384	2,875	17.2	19.7	14.8	46.9	50.4	55.3	48.5	883	1,645	19.0
St. Martin	9,836	8,883	7,821	6,876	953	1,062	945	10.7	13.6	13.7	42.6	46.9	52.5	54.3	743	525	18.7
St. Mary	21,266	20,264	14,395	13,115	1,002	5,869	1,280	4.9	40.8	9.8	54.0	59.3	64.2	65.9	1,179	632	33.6
St. Tammany	6,731	4,889	3,702	2,595	1,842	1,187	1,107	37.7	32.1	42.7	35.6	36.7	36.4	37.7	553	906	7.4
Tangipahoa	9,135	5,375	4,698	4,014	3,760	677	684	70.0	14.4	17.0	31.3	30.5	37.1	41.6	456	790	11.6
Tensas	15,613	17,839	15,492	16,237	−2,226	2,347	−745	−12.5	15.1	−4.6	91.5	93.5	93.1	91.1	10,797	632	24.7

[1] Per cent not shown where base is less than 100.   [2] For changes in boundaries, see note at end of table.

TABLE **II.**—NEGRO POPULATION, 1910, 1900, 1890, 1880, DECENNIAL INCREASES, PROPORTION NEGRO, LAND AREA, AND NEGRO POPULATION PER SQUARE MILE, BY COUNTIES, FOR SOUTHERN STATES—Continued.

[A minus sign (−) denotes decrease.]

STATE AND COUNTY.	NEGRO POPULATION.				INCREASE.						PERCENTAGE NEGRO IN TOTAL POPULATION.				Negroes per 1,000 whites, 1910	Land area, square miles, 1910	Negroes per square mile, 1910
					Number.			Per cent.									
	1910	1900	1890	1880	1900–1910	1890–1900	1880–1890	1900–1910	1890–1900	1880–1890	1910	1900	1890	1880			
LOUISIANA— Continued.																	
Terrebonne	11,194	10,312	9,699	9,111	882	613	588	8.6	6.3	6.5	39.5	42.2	48.1	50.7	659	1,756	6.4
Union	7,448	6,967	7,403	5,512	481	−436	1,891	6.9	−5.9	34.3	36.4	37.6	42.8	40.8	573	918	8.1
Vermilion	4,500	3,747	2,899	1,957	753	848	942	20.1	29.3	48.1	17.1	18.1	20.4	22.4	206	1,213	3.7
Vernon	3,716	1,279	540	377	2,437	739	163	190.5	136.9	43.2	21.4	12.4	9.1	7.3	272	1,367	2.7
Washington	5,458	2,776	2,062	1,712	2,682	714	350	96.6	34.6	20.4	28.9	28.8	30.8	33.0	407	655	8.3
Webster	9,900	8,262	7,289	5,683	1,638	973	1,606	19.8	13.3	28.3	51.6	54.6	58.5	56.8	1,066	609	16.3
West Baton Rouge	9,223	7,934	5,964	5,415	1,289	1,970	549	16.2	33.0	10.1	73.0	77.1	71.3	70.6	2,703	214	43.1
West Carroll	2,724	2,128	2,310	1,437	596	−182	873	28.0	−7.9	60.8	43.6	57.7	61.6	51.8	773	366	7.4
West Feliciana	11,012	13,781	12,785	10,522	−2,769	996	2,263	−20.1	7.8	21.5	81.9	86.2	84.9	82.1	4,521	352	31.3
Winn	3,931	1,681	1,010	1,047	2,250	671	−37	133.8	66.4	−3.5	21.4	17.4	14.3	17.9	273	969	4.1
MARYLAND	232,250	235,064	215,657	210,230	−2,814	19,407	5,427	−1.2	9.0	2.6	17.9	19.8	20.7	22.5	219	9,941	23.4
Allegany	1,517	1,669	1,431	1,549	−152	238	−118	−9.1	16.6	−7.6	2.4	3.1	3.4	4.1	25	443	3.4
Anne Arundel	14,136	15,367	14,509	13,877	−1,231	858	632	−8.0	5.9	4.6	35.7	38.8	42.6	48.6	557	432	32.7
Baltimore	12,601	11,618	10,230	10,565	983	1,388	−335	8.5	13.6	−3.2	10.3	12.8	14.0	12.7	115	650	19.4
Baltimore city	84,749	79,258	67,104	53,716	5,491	12,154	13,388	6.9	18.1	24.9	15.2	15.6	15.4	16.2	179	30	2,825.0
Calvert	5,046	5,143	5,064	5,696	−97	79	−632	−1.9	1.6	−11.1	48.9	50.3	51.4	54.1	956	218	23.1
Caroline	4,787	4,237	3,811	4,166	550	426	−355	13.0	11.2	−8.5	24.9	26.1	27.4	30.3	332	319	15.0
Carroll	2,006	2,143	2,133	2,286	−137	10	−153	−6.4	0.5	−6.7	5.9	6.3	6.6	7.4	63	447	4.5
Cecil	3,315	3,805	3,978	4,464	−490	−173	−486	−12.9	−4.3	−10.9	14.0	15.4	15.4	16.5	162	377	8.8
Charles	8,572	9,648	8,136	10,848	−1,076	1,512	−2,712	−11.2	18.6	−25.0	52.3	54.6	53.6	58.5	1,097	464	18.5
Dorchester	9,421	9,484	8,709	8,476	−63	775	233	−0.7	8.9	2.7	32.9	33.9	35.1	36.7	489	576	16.4
Frederick	5,399	6,012	6,528	7,520	−613	−516	−992	−10.2	−7.9	−13.2	10.3	11.6	13.2	14.9	114	663	8.1
Garrett	107	126	185	112	−19	−59	73	−15.1	−31.9	65.2	0.5	0.7	1.3	0.9	5	685	0.2
Harford	5,116	5,854	6,376	6,657	−738	−522	−281	−12.6	−8.2	−4.2	18.3	20.7	22.0	23.7	224	442	11.6
Howard	3,772	4,405	4,110	4,399	−633	295	−289	−14.4	7.2	−6.6	23.4	26.4	25.3	27.3	306	250	15.1
Kent	6,162	7,442	6,807	7,205	−1,280	635	−398	−17.2	9.3	−5.5	36.3	39.6	39.0	40.9	571	282	21.9
Montgomery	9,235	10,054	9,685	9,150	−819	369	535	−8.1	3.8	5.8	28.8	33.0	35.6	37.0	404	521	17.7
Prince Georges	11,493	11,985	11,210	12,486	−492	775	−1,276	−4.1	6.9	−10.2	31.8	40.1	43.0	47.2	466	482	23.8
Queen Annes	5,814	6,372	6,557	7,189	−558	−185	−632	−8.8	−2.8	−8.8	34.5	34.7	35.5	37.3	527	365	15.9
St. Marys	7,304	8,256	7,666	8,690	−952	590	−1,024	−11.5	7.7	−11.8	42.9	48.1	48.5	51.3	751	371	19.7
Somerset	9,476	9,533	9,505	8,694	−57	28	811	−0.6	0.3	9.3	35.8	36.8	39.4	40.1	558	331	28.6
Talbot	6,774	7,466	7,483	7,329	−692	−17	154	−9.3	−0.2	2.1	34.5	36.7	37.9	38.4	528	268	25.3
Washington	2,113	2,488	2,507	3,066	−375	−19	−559	−15.1	−0.8	−18.2	4.3	5.5	6.3	8.0	44	459	4.6
Wicomico	6,310	5,828	5,199	5,073	482	629	126	8.3	12.1	2.5	23.5	25.5	26.1	28.2	308	371	17.0
Worcester	7,025	6,871	6,734	7,017	154	137	−283	2.2	2.0	−4.0	32.2	32.9	34.1	35.9	474	495	14.2
MISSISSIPPI	1,009,487	907,630	742,559	650,291	101,857	165,071	92,268	11.2	22.2	14.2	56.2	58.5	57.6	57.5	1,284	46,362	21.8
Adams	18,908	23,668	19,895	17,847	−4,760	3,773	2,048	−20.1	19.0	11.5	74.8	78.6	76.4	78.8	2,976	426	44.4
Alcorn	4,275	3,825	3,510	4,409	450	315	−899	11.8	9.0	−20.4	23.5	25.5	26.8	30.9	308	386	11.1
Amite	12,590	12,308	10,597	8,510	282	1,711	2,087	2.3	16.1	24.5	54.8	59.4	58.2	60.8	1,215	714	17.6
Attala	13,219	12,350	9,444	8,260	869	2,906	1,184	7.0	30.8	14.3	45.8	47.1	42.5	41.3	846	715	18.5
Benton	5,037	5,200	4,919	5,246	−163	281	−327	−3.1	5.7	−6.2	49.2	49.5	46.5	47.6	967	396	12.7
Bolivar	42,763	31,197	26,737	15,958	11,566	4,460	10,779	37.1	16.7	67.5	87.4	88.1	89.2	85.6	7,013	879	48.6
Calhoun	3,812	4,097	3,412	3,300	−285	685	112	−7.0	20.1	3.4	21.5	24.8	23.2	24.5	274	579	6.6
Carroll	13,475	12,919	10,611	9,961	556	2,308	650	4.3	21.8	6.5	58.2	58.4	56.5	56.0	1,394	624	21.6
Chickasaw	12,714	11,744	11,400	10,209	970	344	1,191	8.3	3.0	11.7	55.7	59.0	57.3	57.0	1,255	501	25.4
Choctaw	4,169	3,585	2,638	2,498	584	947	140	16.3	35.9	5.6	29.0	27.5	24.3	27.6	409	414	10.1
Claiborne	13,608	16,213	10,980	12,858	−2,605	5,233	−1,878	−16.1	47.7	−14.6	78.2	78.0	75.6	76.7	3,594	489	27.8
Clarke	10,262	8,493	8,104	7,828	1,769	389	276	20.8	4.8	3.5	47.4	47.9	51.2	52.1	904	675	15.2
Clay	14,105	13,633	12,982	12,110	472	651	872	3.5	5.0	7.2	69.8	69.7	69.8	69.7	2,314	408	34.6
Coahoma	30,382	23,183	16,069	11,155	7,199	7,114	4,914	31.1	44.3	44.1	88.8	88.2	87.6	82.2	7,983	530	57.3
Copiah	19,981	18,036	15,600	14,442	1,945	2,436	1,158	10.8	15.6	8.0	55.6	52.4	51.6	52.4	1,255	769	26.0
Covington [1]	5,224	4,605	2,971	1,958	619	1,634	1,013	13.4	55.0	51.7	30.9	35.2	35.8	32.7	447	410	12.7
De Soto	17,572	18,513	17,224	15,343	−941	1,289	1,881	−5.1	7.5	12.3	76.0	74.8	71.2	66.9	3,163	475	37.0
Forrest [1]	7,683				7,683						37.1				589	462	16.6
Franklin	6,823	6,799	4,934	4,871	24	1,865	63	0.4	37.8	1.3	44.9	49.7	47.3	50.1	816	547	12.5
George [1]	1,827				1,827						27.7				383	475	3.8
Greene [1]	1,347	1,778	933	785	−431	845	148	−24.3	90.6	18.9	22.3	26.2	23.9	24.6	287	710	1.9
Grenada	11,161	10,281	11,076	8,831	880	−795	2,245	8.6	−7.2	25.4	71.0	72.9	74.0	73.2	2,445	442	25.3
Hancock [1]	4,339	3,469	2,509	1,764	870	960	745	25.1	38.3	42.2	38.7	29.2	30.2	27.4	636	469	9.3
Harrison	10,643	6,367	3,314	2,146	4,276	3,053	1,168	67.2	92.1	54.4	30.7	30.3	26.6	27.2	443	1,013	10.5
Hinds	45,407	39,531	28,368	32,279	5,876	11,163	−3,911	14.9	39.4	−12.1	71.3	75.2	72.2	73.4	2,479	858	52.9
Holmes	31,197	28,707	23,883	20,233	2,490	4,824	3,650	8.7	20.2	18.0	79.8	77.9	77.1	74.5	3,954	834	37.4
Issaquena	9,946	9,771	11,579	9,174	175	−1,808	2,405	1.8	−15.6	26.2	94.2	94.0	94.0	91.7	16,278	406	24.5
Itawamba	1,198	1,342	985	1,108	−144	357	−123	−10.7	36.2	−11.1	8.2	9.9	8.4	10.4	899	529	2.3
Jackson [1]	5,467	5,815	3,436	2,482	−348	2,379	954	−6.0	69.2	38.4	35.4	35.2	30.5	32.6	548	710	7.7
Jasper	9,013	7,474	7,238	5,631	1,539	236	1,607	20.6	3.3	28.5	48.7	48.6	49.0	46.4	954	667	13.5
Jefferson	14,287	17,270	15,356	13,051	−2,983	1,914	2,305	−17.3	12.5	17.7	78.4	81.1	81.0	75.4	3,632	507	28.2
Jefferson Davis [1]	6,757				6,757						52.5				1,107	404	16.7
Jones	8,417	4,670	1,246	359	3,747	3,424	887	80.2	274.8	247.1	28.2	26.2	15.0	9.4	392	696	12.1
Kemper	11,691	11,645	10,058	8,537	46	1,587	1,521	0.4	15.8	17.8	57.5	56.8	56.0	54.3	1,367	752	15.5
Lafayette	9,904	9,730	8,853	10,286	174	877	−1,433	1.8	9.9	−13.9	45.3	44.0	43.1	47.5	827	664	14.9

[1] For changes in boundaries, see note at end of table.

TABLE **II.**—NEGRO POPULATION, 1910, 1900, 1890, 1880, DECENNIAL INCREASES, PROPORTION NEGRO, LAND AREA, AND NEGRO POPULATION PER SQUARE MILE, BY COUNTIES, FOR SOUTHERN STATES—Continued.

[A minus sign (−) denotes decrease.]

STATE AND COUNTY.	NEGRO POPULATION.				INCREASE. Number.			INCREASE. Per cent.			PERCENTAGE NEGRO IN TOTAL POPULATION.				Negroes per 1,000 whites, 1910	Land area, square miles, 1910	Negroes per square mile, 1910
	1910	1900	1890	1880	1900–1910	1890–1900	1880–1890	1900–1910	1890–1900	1880–1890	1910	1900	1890	1880			
MISSISSIPPI—Con.																	
Lamar [1]	3,619				3,619	3,986	3,434		26.6	29.8	30.8				446	495	7.3
Lauderdale	21,875	18,958	14,972	11,538	2,917	1,490	1,605	15.4	24.5	35.9	46.6	49.7	50.5	53.7	874	700	31.2
Lawrence [1]	5,147	7,568	6,078	4,473	−2,421	1,213	358	−32.0	24.2	7.7	39.4	50.1	49.3	47.5	649	418	12.3
Leake	6,171	6,231	5,018	4,660	−60	1,128	−284	−1.0	15.0	−3.6	33.7	35.9	33.9	35.4	520	576	10.7
Lee	10,667	8,658	7,530	7,814	2,009			23.2			36.9	39.4	37.6	38.2	585	448	23.8
Leflore	30,628	21,031	14,267	7,997	9,597	6,764	6,270	45.6	47.4	78.4	84.4	88.2	84.6	78.1	5,422	572	53.5
Lincoln	12,054	9,209	7,587	5,842	2,845	1,622	1,745	30.9	21.4	29.9	42.2	42.7	42.4	43.1	729	578	20.9
Lowndes	21,784	21,972	21,036	22,656	−188	936	−1,620	−0.9	4.4	−7.2	71.0	75.5	77.8	80.2	2,442	499	43.7
Madison	27,298	25,918	21,290	19,907	1,380	4,628	1,383	5.3	21.7	6.9	81.5	79.8	77.9	77.0	4,406	725	37.7
Marion [1]	6,063	4,323	3,002	2,451	1,740	1,321	551	40.2	44.0	22.5	38.9	32.0	31.5	35.5	636	624	9.7
Marshall	19,342	18,708	16,306	18,338	634	2,402	−2,032	3.4	14.7	−11.1	72.2	67.6	62.6	62.5	2,595	689	28.1
Monroe	19,535	18,656	18,619	18,001	879	37	618	4.7	0.2	3.4	55.5	59.8	60.6	63.0	1,017	398	22.4
Montgomery	8,927	8,573	7,009	6,677	354	1,564	332	4.1	22.3	5.0	50.4	51.8	48.5	50.0	203	561	5.3
Neshoba	2,949	2,279	2,172	1,768	670	107	404	29.4	4.9	22.9	16.4	17.9	19.5	20.2	639	568	15.8
Newton	8,950	7,614	6,156	4,686	1,336	1,458	1,470	17.5	23.7	31.4	38.8	38.6	37.0	34.9			
Noxubee	23,947	26,146	22,629	24,572	−2,199	3,517	−1,943	−8.4	15.5	−7.9	84.0	84.8	82.8	82.3	5,257	682	35.1
Oktibbeha	12,675	13,819	11,934	10,869	−1,144	1,885	1,065	−8.3	15.8	9.8	64.4	68.5	67.4	68.0	1,811	457	27.7
Panola	21,224	19,366	17,729	18,830	1,858	1,637	−1,101	9.6	9.2	−5.8	67.9	66.7	65.7	66.4	2,112	696	30.5
Pearl River [1]	2,422	1,792	656	....	630	1,136	656	35.2	173.2	...	22.9	26.8	22.2	...	296	797	3.0
Perry [1]	2,581	4,822	1,874	1,070	−2,241	2,948	804	−46.5	157.3	75.1	33.6	32.8	28.9	31.2	506	644	4.0
Pike	17,597	13,713	10,620	8,112	3,884	3,093	2,508	28.3	29.1	30.9	47.2	49.8	50.1	48.6	895	707	24.9
Pontotoc	4,727	4,827	4,355	4,249	−100	472	106	−2.1	10.8	2.5	24.0	26.4	29.1	30.7	316	494	9.6
Prentiss	2,875	3,131	2,845	2,421	−256	286	424	−8.2	10.1	17.5	17.0	19.8	20.8	19.9	205	409	7.0
Quitman	8,864	4,177	2,392	815	4,687	1,785	1,577	112.2	74.6	193.5	76.5	76.9	72.8	57.9	3,253	395	22.4
Rankin	14,249	12,269	10,413	9,559	1,980	1,856	854	16.1	17.8	8.9	59.5	58.5	58.1	57.1	1,470	791	18.0
Scott	6,896	6,065	4,616	4,132	831	1,449	484	13.7	31.4	11.7	41.2	42.4	39.3	38.1	711	597	11.6
Sharkey	13,967	10,723	7,141	4,893	3,244	3,582	2,248	30.3	50.2	45.9	89.0	88.1	85.2	77.6	8,116	444	31.5
Simpson	5,969	4,954	3,909	3,014	1,015	1,045	895	20.5	26.7	29.7	34.7	38.7	38.6	37.6	531	575	10.4
Smith	2,899	2,360	1,711	1,636	539	649	75	22.8	37.9	4.6	17.5	18.1	16.1	20.2	212	626	4.6
Sunflower	23,281	12,070	6,850	2,897	11,211	5,220	3,953	92.9	76.2	136.5	80.9	75.0	73.0	62.2	4,237	690	33.7
Tallahatchie	20,180	13,281	9,207	6,757	6,899	4,074	2,450	51.9	44.2	36.3	69.4	67.8	64.1	61.8	2,269	629	32.1
Tate	11,535	12,179	10,756	9,627	−644	1,423	1,129	−5.3	13.2	11.7	58.5	59.1	55.9	51.4	1,410	400	28.8
Tippah	2,801	2,903	2,925	3,065	−102	−22	−140	−3.5	−0.8	4.6	19.1	22.4	22.6	23.8	237	446	6.3
Tishomingo	1,089	1,051	991	1,163	38	60	−172	3.6	6.1	−14.8	8.3	10.4	10.7	13.3	91	428	2.5
Tunica	16,910	14,914	10,895	7,205	1,996	4,019	3,690	13.4	36.9	51.2	90.7	90.5	89.6	85.2	9,786	418	40.5
Union	4,216	4,142	3,998	3,098	74	144	900	1.8	3.6	29.1	22.2	25.1	25.6	23.8	285	412	10.2
Warren	26,191	30,554	24,356	22,516	−4,363	6,198	1,840	−14.3	25.4	8.2	69.9	74.7	73.4	72.1	2,320	572	45.8
Washington	41,600	44,143	35,530	21,861	−2,543	8,613	13,669	−5.8	24.2	62.5	85.0	89.7	87.9	86.2	5,706	877	47.4
Wayne	5,843	5,058	4,011	3,770	785	1,047	241	15.5	26.1	6.4	39.7	40.3	40.9	43.1	659	812	7.2
Webster [1]	3,286	3,925	2,980	2,295	−639	945	685	−16.3	31.7	29.8	22.1	28.8	24.7	24.1	284	416	7.9
Wilkinson	13,904	17,069	13,626	14,243	−3,165	3,443	−617	−18.5	25.3	−4.3	76.9	79.6	77.5	79.9	3,333	667	20.8
Winston	6,863	5,901	5,061	3,927	962	840	1,134	16.3	16.6	28.9	40.0	41.8	41.9	38.9	668	597	11.5
Yalobusha	11,182	10,458	8,945	8,116	724	1,513	829	6.9	16.9	10.2	52.0	53.0	53.8	51.9	1,082	490	22.8
Yazoo	35,502	33,902	27,701	25,342	1,600	6,201	2,359	4.7	22.4	9.3	76.1	77.1	76.1	74.9	3,182	1,038	34.2
NORTH CAROLINA	697,843	624,469	561,018	531,277	73,374	63,451	29,741	11.7	11.3	5.6	31.6	33.0	34.7	38.0	465	48,740	14.3
Alamance	7,173	6,723	5,583	4,613	450	1,140	970	6.7	20.4	21.0	25.0	26.2	30.6	31.6	333	492	14.6
Alexander	910	856	842	897	54	14	−55	6.3	1.7	−6.1	7.9	7.8	8.9	10.7	85	289	3.1
Alleghany	340	466	460	519	−126	6	−59	−27.0	1.3	−11.4	4.4	6.0	7.1	9.5	46	234	1.5
Anson	13,326	11,674	9,789	9,204	1,652	1,885	585	14.2	19.3	6.4	52.3	53.4	48.9	51.2	1,098	556	24.0
Ashe	550	684	595	963	−134	89	−368	−19.6	15.0	−38.2	2.9	3.5	3.8	6.7	30	427	1.3
Beaufort	12,941	11,336	9,203	7,452	1,605	2,133	1,751	14.2	23.2	23.5	41.9	42.9	43.7	42.6	722	840	15.4
Bertie	13,503	11,821	11,291	9,584	1,682	530	1,707	14.2	4.7	17.8	58.6	57.6	58.9	58.4	1,416	703	19.2
Bladen	8,392	8,223	8,117	8,560	169	106	−443	2.1	1.3	−5.2	46.6	46.5	48.4	53.0	876	1,004	8.4
Brunswick	5,406	5,044	4,761	4,052	362	283	709	7.2	5.9	17.5	37.5	39.9	43.7	43.2	599	790	6.8
Buncombe	7,982	8,120	6,626	3,476	−138	1,494	3,150	−1.7	22.5	90.6	16.0	18.3	18.8	15.9	191	639	12.5
Burke	2,570	2,676	2,561	2,721	−106	115	−160	−4.0	4.5	−5.9	12.0	15.1	17.1	21.2	136	534	4.8
Cabarrus	6,095	6,101	5,459	5,115	−6	642	344	(²)	11.8	6.7	23.2	27.2	30.1	34.2	303	390	15.6
Caldwell	2,416	1,931	1,554	1,599	485	377	−45	25.1	24.3	−2.8	11.7	12.3	12.6	15.5	133	512	4.7
Camden	2,213	2,191	2,320	2,471	22	−129	−151	1.0	−5.6	−6.1	39.2	40.0	40.9	39.4	646	220	10.1
Carteret [1]	2,292	2,127	2,297	2,676	165	−170	−379	7.8	−7.4	−14.2	16.6	18.0	21.2	27.4	158	573	4.0
Caswell	7,651	8,199	9,389	10,656	−548	−1,190	−1,267	−6.7	−12.7	−11.9	51.5	54.6	58.6	59.8	1,062	402	19.0
Catawba	3,471	2,985	2,616	2,477	486	369	139	16.3	14.1	5.6	12.4	13.5	14.0	16.6	142	408	8.5
Chatham [1]	7,668	8,339	8,199	7,953	−671	140	246	−8.0	1.7	3.1	33.9	34.9	32.3	33.9	513	696	11.0
Cherokee	503	432	274	288	71	158	−14	16.4	57.7	−4.9	3.6	3.6	2.7	3.5	39	454	1.1
Chowan	6,159	5,850	5,156	4,267	309	694	889	5.3	13.5	20.8	54.5	57.0	56.2	54.0	1,197	165	37.3
Clay	158	134	142	141	24	−8	1	17.9	−5.6	0.7	4.0	3.0	3.4	4.3	42	220	0.7
Cleveland	5,779	4,820	3,093	2,871	959	1,727	222	19.9	55.8	7.7	19.6	19.2	15.2	17.3	244	488	11.8
Columbus	8,955	6,476	6,052	5,513	2,479	424	539	38.3	7.0	9.8	32.0	30.4	33.9	38.2	470	933	9.6
Craven [1]	14,310	14,543	13,358	13,064	−233	1,185	294	−1.6	8.9	2.3	55.9	60.2	65.1	66.2	1,269	660	21.7
Cumberland	15,353	12,571	12,341	11,241	2,782	230	1,100	22.1	1.9	9.8	43.5	43.0	45.2	47.2	772	1,013	15.2
Currituck	2,598	1,777	2,016	1,981	821	−239	35	46.2	−11.9	1.8	33.8	27.2	29.9	30.6	510	292	8.9
Dare	495	574	406	368	−79	168	38	−13.8	41.4	10.3	10.2	12.1	10.8	11.3	114	377	1.3
Davidson [1]	3,744	3,174	3,528	3,992	570	−354	−464	18.0	−10.0	−11.6	12.7	13.6	16.3	19.6	146	569	6.6
Davie	2,350	2,635	2,852	3,326	−285	−217	−474	−10.8	−7.6	−14.3	17.5	21.7	24.5	30.0	213	258	9.1
Duplin	9,281	8,528	7,087	8,186	753	1,441	−1,099	8.8	20.3	−13.4	36.5	38.1	37.9	43.6	574	783	11.9

[1] For changes in boundaries, see note at end of table.   [2] Less than one-tenth of 1 per cent.

TABLE II.—NEGRO POPULATION, 1910, 1900, 1890, 1880, DECENNIAL INCREASES, PROPORTION NEGRO, LAND AREA, AND NEGRO POPULATION PER SQUARE MILE, BY COUNTIES, FOR SOUTHERN STATES—Continued.

[A minus sign (−) denotes decrease.]

| STATE AND COUNTY. | NEGRO POPULATION. | | | | INCREASE. | | | | | | PERCENTAGE NEGRO IN TOTAL POPULATION. | | | | Negroes per 1,000 whites, 1910 | Land area, square miles, 1910 | Negroes per square mile, 1910 |
| | | | | | Number. | | | Per cent. | | | | | | | | | |
	1910	1900	1890	1880	1900–1910	1890–1900	1880–1890	1900–1910	1890–1900	1880–1890	1910	1900	1890	1880			
NORTH CAROLINA—Continued.																	
Durham[1]	12,383	9,749	7,329	......	2,634	2,420	7,329	27.0	33.0	......	35.1	37.2	40.6	......	541	291	42.6
Edgecombe	19,453	16,584	15,599	18,213	2,869	985	−2,614	17.3	6.3	14.4	60.8	62.4	64.7	69.6	1,549	509	38.2
Forsyth[1]	14,027	10,541	8,999	4,629	3,486	1,542	4,370	33.1	17.1	94.4	29.6	29.9	31.6	25.6	421	376	37.3
Franklin[1]	11,564	12,438	10,335	11,353	−874	2,103	−1,018	−7.0	20.3	−9.0	46.8	49.5	49.0	54.5	881	468	24.7
Gaston	8,502	7,242	4,836	4,066	1,260	2,406	770	17.4	49.8	18.9	22.9	26.0	27.2	28.5	298	371	22.9
Gates	4,693	4,804	4,713	3,924	−111	91	789	−2.3	1.9	20.1	44.9	46.1	46.0	44.1	814	359	13.1
Graham	......	26	25	23	−26	1	2	(2)	(2)	(2)	......	0.6	0.8	1.0	......	298	......
Granville[1]	12,239	11,887	12,360	17,679	352	−473	−5,319	3.0	−3.8	−30.1	48.8	51.1	50.5	56.5	952	503	24.3
Greene	6,096	5,778	4,758	5,385	318	1,020	−627	5.5	21.4	−11.6	46.6	48.0	47.4	53.7	872	252	24.2
Guilford	15,379	11,103	8,223	6,700	4,276	2,880	1,523	38.5	35.0	22.7	25.4	28.4	29.3	28.4	341	691	22.3
Halifax	24,328	19,733	19,293	21,162	4,595	440	−1,869	23.3	2.3	−8.8	64.6	64.1	66.7	69.8	1,827	676	36.0
Harnett	6,442	5,058	4,220	3,770	1,384	838	450	27.4	19.9	11.9	29.1	31.6	30.8	34.7	410	595	10.8
Haywood	567	613	517	484	−46	96	33	−7.5	18.6	6.8	2.7	3.8	3.9	4.7	28	546	1.0
Henderson	1,815	1,759	1,378	1,388	56	381	−10	3.2	27.6	−0.7	11.2	12.5	10.9	13.5	126	358	5.1
Hertford	9,098	8,391	7,944	6,721	707	447	1,223	8.4	5.6	18.2	58.9	58.7	57.4	56.8	1,435	341	26.7
Hyde	3,701	4,014	3,941	3,341	−313	73	600	−7.8	1.9	18.0	41.9	43.3	44.3	43.0	720	617	6.0
Iredell	7,456	7,332	5,939	5,913	124	1,393	26	1.7	23.5	0.4	21.7	25.2	23.3	26.1	278	588	12.7
Jackson	603	591	518	375	12	73	143	2.0	14.1	38.1	4.6	5.0	5.4	5.1	50	494	1.2
Johnston	10,169	8,171	7,322	7,465	1,998	849	−143	24.5	11.6	−1.9	24.6	25.3	26.9	31.8	326	694	14.7
Jones	4,096	3,760	3,518	4,279	336	242	−761	8.9	6.9	−17.8	47.0	45.7	47.5	57.1	886	417	9.8
Lee[1]	3,526				3,526						31.0				449	261	13.5
Lenoir	10,225	8,046	6,362	8,067	2,179	1,684	−1,705	27.1	26.5	−21.1	44.9	43.2	42.8	52.6	815	397	25.8
Lincoln	2,797	2,961	2,558	2,881	−164	403	−323	−5.5	15.8	−11.2	16.3	19.1	20.3	26.0	195	299	9.4
McDowell	2,080	1,893	1,825	1,897	187	68	−72	9.9	3.7	−3.8	15.4	15.1	16.7	19.3	182	443	4.7
Macon	576	673	665	656	−97	8	9	−14.4	1.2	1.4	4.7	5.6	6.6	8.1	50	513	1.1
Madison	432	551	710	459	−119	−159	251	−21.6	−22.4	54.7	2.1	2.7	4.0	3.6	22	436	1.0
Martin	8,838	7,327	7,383	6,479	1,511	−56	904	20.6	−0.8	14.0	49.7	47.6	48.5	49.3	986	438	20.2
Mecklenburg	25,481	23,873	19,526	16,241	1,608	4,347	3,285	6.7	22.3	20.2	38.0	43.2	45.8	47.5	613	597	42.7
Mitchell	343	536	553	503	−193	−17	50	−36.0	−3.1	9.9	2.0	3.5	4.3	5.3	20	371	0.9
Montgomery	3,660	3,682	2,257	2,517	−22	1,425	−260	−0.6	63.1	−10.3	24.5	25.9	20.1	26.9	324	498	7.3
Moore[1]	5,637	7,849	6,479	5,332	−2,212	1,370	1,147	−28.2	21.1	21.5	33.1	33.2	31.6	31.7	496	639	8.8
Nash	14,104	10,619	8,521	8,314	3,485	2,098	207	32.8	24.6	2.5	41.8	41.7	41.2	46.9	719	586	24.1
New Hanover	15,302	13,109	13,935	13,217	2,193	−826	718	16.7	−5.9	5.4	47.8	50.8	58.0	61.8	916	216	70.8
Northampton	13,062	12,118	12,018	12,045	944	100	−27	7.8	0.8	−0.2	58.5	57.3	56.6	60.1	1,410	504	25.9
Onslow	4,238	3,610	2,911	3,229	628	699	−318	17.4	24.0	−9.8	30.0	30.2	28.3	32.9	429	743	5.7
Orange[1]	4,926	5,261	5,242	9,143	−335	19	−3,901	−6.4	0.4	−42.8	32.7	35.8	35.1	38.6	486	390	12.6
Pamlico	3,773	2,637	2,379	2,116	1,136	258	263	43.1	10.8	12.4	37.9	32.8	33.3	33.5	609	350	10.8
Pasquotank	8,357	7,027	5,546	5,514	1,330	1,481	32	18.9	26.7	0.6	50.1	51.4	51.6	53.2	1,003	223	37.5
Pender	7,620	6,909	6,546	6,957	711	363	−411	10.3	5.5	−5.9	49.3	51.6	52.3	55.8	971	815	9.3
Perquimans	5,589	5,003	4,574	4,671	586	429	−97	11.7	9.4	−2.1	50.6	49.6	49.2	49.3	1,023	252	22.2
Person	7,474	7,023	6,899	6,513	451	124	386	6.4	1.8	5.9	43.1	42.1	45.5	47.5	756	391	19.1
Pitt	18,106	15,492	12,327	11,088	2,614	3,165	1,239	16.9	25.7	11.2	49.8	50.2	48.3	50.9	993	627	28.9
Polk	1,094	1,207	1,093	1,144	−113	114	−51	−9.4	10.4	−4.5	14.3	17.2	18.5	22.6	167	251	4.4
Randolph	3,421	3,672	3,347	3,078	−251	325	269	−6.8	9.7	8.7	11.6	13.0	13.3	14.8	131	803	4.3
Richmond[1]	9,225	7,763	12,959	10,104	1,462	−5,196	2,855	18.8	−40.1	28.3	44.0	49.0	54.1	55.4	883	521	17.7
Robeson	22,518	16,917	14,672	11,938	5,601	2,245	2,734	33.1	15.3	22.9	43.3	41.9	46.6	50.0	957	1,051	21.4
Rockingham	10,474	11,617	10,164	9,313	−1,143	1,453	851	−9.8	14.3	9.1	28.7	35.0	40.1	42.8	403	579	18.1
Rowan	9,074	8,115	6,980	6,339	959	1,135	641	11.8	16.3	10.1	24.2	26.1	28.9	31.8	319	489	18.6
Rutherford	4,288	4,441	3,692	3,255	−153	749	437	−3.4	20.3	13.4	15.1	17.7	19.7	21.4	178	544	7.9
Sampson	10,043	9,130	9,136	9,540	913	−6	−404	10.0	−0.1	−4.2	33.5	34.6	36.4	41.7	509	922	10.9
Scotland[1]	8,473	6,710	......	......	1,763	6,710	......	26.3			55.2	53.5			1,243	349	24.3
Stanly	2,132	1,799	1,507	1,339	333	292	168	18.5	19.4	12.5	10.7	11.8	12.4	12.7	120	416	5.1
Stokes	2,569	2,991	2,813	3,623	−422	178	−810	−14.1	6.3	−22.4	12.7	15.1	16.4	23.6	146	480	5.4
Surry	2,632	2,904	2,348	2,075	−272	556	273	−9.4	23.7	13.2	8.9	11.4	12.2	13.6	97	520	5.1
Swain	185	174	225	109	11	−51	116	6.3	−22.7	106.4	1.8	2.1	3.4	2.9	20	553	0.3
Transylvania	638	615	513	517	23	102	−4	3.7	19.9	−0.8	8.9	9.3	8.7	9.7	97	379	1.7
Tyrrell	1,642	1,462	1,225	1,435	180	237	−210	12.3	19.3	−14.6	31.5	29.4	29.0	31.6	459	390	4.2
Union	9,337	7,999	5,547	4,536	1,338	2,452	1,011	16.7	44.2	22.3	28.1	29.5	26.1	25.1	390	565	16.5
Vance[1]	10,004	9,755	11,143	......	249	−1,388	11,143	2.6	−12.5	......	51.5	58.5	63.4	......	1,062	279	35.9
Wake[1]	25,870	24,358	23,109	23,650	1,512	1,249	−541	6.2	5.4	−2.3	40.9	44.6	47.0	49.3	692	845	30.6
Warren[1]	13,207	13,069	13,480	16,233	138	−411	−2,753	1.1	−3.0	−17.0	65.2	68.2	69.6	71.8	1,877	425	31.1
Washington	5,503	5,366	5,238	4,374	137	128	864	2.6	2.4	19.8	49.7	50.6	51.4	49.0	990	327	16.8
Watauga	246	391	431	414	−145	−40	17	−37.1	−9.3	4.1	1.8	2.9	4.1	5.1	19	342	0.7
Wayne	15,579	13,419	10,984	12,124	2,160	2,435	−1,140	16.1	22.2	−9.4	43.6	42.8	42.1	48.6	774	615	25.3
Wilkes	2,591	2,437	2,042	1,924	154	395	118	6.3	19.3	6.1	8.6	9.1	9.0	10.0	94	735	3.5
Wilson	12,350	9,905	7,760	7,409	2,445	2,145	351	24.7	27.6	4.7	43.7	42.0	41.6	46.1	776	384	32.2
Yadkin	1,174	1,187	1,368	1,544	−13	−181	−176	−1.1	−13.2	−11.4	7.6	8.4	9.9	12.4	82	324	3.6
Yancey	233	283	292	325	−50	−9	−33	−17.7	−3.1	−10.2	1.9	2.5	3.1	4.2	20	298	0.8
SOUTH CAROLINA	835,843	782,321	688,934	604,332	53,522	93,387	84,602	6.8	13.6	14.0	55.2	58.4	59.8	60.7	1,231	30,495	27.4
Abbeville[1]	22,522	22,069	31,705	27,637	453	−9,636	4,068	2.1	−30.4	14.7	64.7	66.1	67.7	67.7	1,834	678	33.2
Aiken	22,850	21,640	18,059	15,170	1,210	3,581	2,889	5.6	19.8	19.0	54.6	55.4	56.8	54.0	1,203	1,100	20.8
Anderson	26,335	23,496	18,428	14,865	2,839	5,068	3,563	12.1	27.5	24.0	37.9	42.2	42.2	44.2	609	758	34.7
Bamberg[1]	12,874	11,638			1,236	11,638		10.6			69.4	67.3			2,271	371	34.7
Barnwell[1]	24,647	25,416	30,416	26,003	−769	−5,000	4,413	−3.0	−16.4	17.0	72.0	71.6	68.2	65.2	2,578	890	27.7

[1] For changes in boundaries, see note at end of table.   [2] Per cent not shown where base is less than 100.

TABLE **II.**—NEGRO POPULATION, 1910, 1900, 1890, 1880, DECENNIAL INCREASES, PROPORTION NEGRO, LAND AREA, AND NEGRO POPULATION PER SQUARE MILE, BY COUNTIES, FOR SOUTHERN STATES—Continued.

[A minus sign (−) denotes decrease.]

STATE AND COUNTY.	NEGRO POPULATION.				INCREASE.						PERCENTAGE NEGRO IN TOTAL POPULATION.				Negroes per 1,000 whites, 1910	Land area, square miles, 1910	Negroes per square mile, 1910
					Number.			Per cent.									
	1910	1900	1890	1880	1900–1910	1890–1900	1880–1890	1900–1910	1890–1900	1880–1890	1910	1900	1890	1880			
SOUTH CAROLINA Continued.																	
Beaufort	26,376	32,137	31,421	27,732	−5,761	716	3,689	−17.9	2.3	13.3	86.9	90.5	92.0	91.9	6,656	920	28.7
Berkeley [1]	18,231	23,973	47,739		−5,742	−23,766	47,739	−24.0	−49.8		77.6	78.7	86.1		3,469	1,238	14.7
Calhoun [1]	12,739				12,739						76.6				3,271	391	32.6
Charleston [1]	56,033	60,312	35,073	71,868	−4,279	25,239	−36,795	−7.1	72.0	−51.2	63.2	68.5	58.5	69.9	1,722	685	81.8
Cherokee [1]	8,510	7,396			1,114	7,396		15.1			32.5	34.6			482	373	22.8
Chester	19,140	19,372	18,178	16,517	−232	1,194	1,661	−1.2	6.6	10.1	65.0	67.7	68.2	68.4	1,861	592	32.3
Chesterfield	10,557	8,145	7,479	6,847	2,412	666	632	29.6	8.9	9.2	40.1	39.9	40.5	41.9	671	837	12.6
Clarendon [1]	23,393	20,151	16,246	12,908	3,242	3,905	3,338	16.1	24.0	25.9	72.7	71.5	69.5	67.3	2,660	717	32.6
Colleton [1]	22,296	22,265	26,245	24,181	31	−3,980	2,064	0.1	−15.2	8.5	63.0	66.6	65.1	66.5	1,703	1,333	16.7
Darlington [1]	21,283	19,304	17,384	21,556	1,979	1,920	−4,172	10.3	11.0	−19.4	59.1	59.6	59.7	62.5	1,444	605	35.2
Dillon [1]	11,539				11,539						51.0				1,049	471	24.5
Dorchester [1]	10,982	10,089			893	10,089		8.9			61.4	61.9			1,590	613	17.9
Edgefield [1]	20,114	18,131	31,916	29,826	1,983	−13,785	2,090	10.9	−43.2	7.0	71.1	71.2	64.8	65.1	2,463	700	28.7
Fairfield	22,377	22,375	21,460	20,880	2	915	580	(2)	4.3	2.8	76.0	76.0	75.0	75.2	3,167	792	28.3
Florence [1]	20,340	16,654	14,554		3,686	2,100	14,554	22.1	14.4		57.0	58.5	58.2		1,327	607	33.5
Georgetown	16,110	17,507	16,804	16,146	−1,397	703	658	−8.0	4.2	4.1	72.3	76.6	80.6	82.3	2,616	828	19.5
Greenville	20,861	19,488	16,789	14,511	1,373	2,699	2,278	7.0	16.1	15.7	30.5	36.4	37.9	38.7	439	761	27.4
Greenwood [1]	21,302	18,906			2,396	18,906		12.7			62.2	66.7			1,648	508	41.9
Hampton	16,120	15,502	13,717	12,453	618	1,785	1,264	4.0	13.0	10.2	64.2	65.3	66.8	66.4	1,790	958	16.8
Horry	6,668	6,320	5,550	4,942	348	770	608	5.5	13.9	12.3	24.7	27.1	28.8	31.7	328	1,158	5.8
Kershaw [1]	16,444	14,693	13,810	13,646	1,751	883	164	11.9	6.4	1.2	60.7	59.5	61.8	63.4	1,544	673	24.4
Lancaster	13,115	12,110	10,349	8,957	1,005	1,761	1,392	8.3	17.0	15.5	49.2	49.8	49.8	53.0	970	515	25.5
Laurens	22,753	22,177	18,441	17,688	576	3,736	753	2.6	20.3	4.3	54.8	59.3	58.3	60.1	1,211	690	33.0
Lee [1]	17,251				17,251						68.1				2,139	407	42.4
Lexington [1]	11,638	10,303	8,411	7,467	1,335	1,892	944	13.0	22.5	12.6	36.3	37.8	37.9	40.2	570	833	14.0
Marion [1]	11,208	18,160	15,436	18,226	−6,952	2,724	−2,790	−38.3	17.6	−15.3	54.4	51.6	51.5	53.4	1,194	529	21.2
Marlboro	18,928	16,413	14,435	12,571	2,515	1,978	1,864	15.3	13.7	14.8	60.7	59.4	61.4	61.0	1,544	519	36.5
Newberry [1]	22,040	19,831	17,468	18,261	2,209	2,363	−793	11.1	13.5	−4.3	63.7	65.7	66.1	68.9	1,757	601	36.7
Oconee	6,848	6,104	5,008	4,301	744	1,096	707	12.2	21.9	16.4	25.1	25.8	26.8	26.5	334	650	10.5
Orangeburg [1]	36,794	41,442	33,738	28,453	−4,648	7,704	5,285	−11.2	22.8	18.6	65.8	69.5	68.3	68.7	1,927	1,131	32.5
Pickens	5,430	4,801	4,136	3,716	629	665	420	13.1	16.1	11.3	21.4	24.8	25.2	25.8	272	529	10.3
Richland	29,533	28,070	24,885	19,388	1,463	3,185	5,497	5.2	12.8	28.4	53.6	61.6	67.6	67.9	1,153	611	48.3
Saluda [1]	11,189	10,147			1,042	10,147		10.3			53.4	53.5			1,147	435	25.7
Spartanburg [1]	26,410	21,167	18,527	14,035	5,243	2,640	4,492	24.8	14.2	32.0	31.6	32.3	33.5	34.7	463	765	34.5
Sumter [1]	28,103	38,353	31,792	27,058	−10,250	6,561	4,734	−26.7	20.6	17.5	73.0	74.9	72.9	73.1	2,743	574	49.0
Union [1]	15,471	14,558	14,390	13,551	913	168	839	6.3	1.2	6.2	51.7	57.1	56.3	56.3	1,071	492	31.4
Williamsburg [1]	23,214	19,867	18,420	16,352	3,347	1,447	2,068	16.8	7.9	12.6	61.7	62.7	66.3	67.8	1,611	1,006	23.1
York [1]	25,275	21,839	20,525	16,620	3,436	1,314	3,905	15.7	6.4	23.5	53.0	52.4	52.9	54.1	1,132	651	38.8
OKLAHOMA	137,612	[3] 55,684	[4] 21,609		81,928	34,075		147.1	157.7		8.3	7.0	3.8		95	69,414	2.0
Adair	22										0.2				3	584	
Alfalfa	5										(2)				(5)	867	
Atoka	2,109										15.3				196	997	2.1
Beaver	12	18			−6	18		(6)			0.1	0.6	(2)		(5)	1,813	
Beckham	2										(2)				(5)	917	
Blaine	1,434	1,106			328	1,106		29.7			8.0	10.4			92	931	1.5
Bryan	2,184										7.3				85	928	2.4
Caddo	1,178										3.3				36	1,377	0.9
Canadian	823	363	189		460	174		126.7	92.1		3.5	2.3	2.6		37	891	0.9
Carter	4,315										17.0				215	831	5.2
Cherokee	995										5.9				87	791	1.3
Choctaw	4,303										19.7				265	790	5.4
Cimarron	2										(2)				(5)	1,849	
Cleveland	456	475	8		−19	467		−4.0	(6)		2.4	2.9	0.1		25	554	0.8
Coal	976										6.2				69	525	1.9
Comanche	962										2.3				25	1,726	0.6
Craig	1,175										6.8				91	757	1.6
Creek	2,778										10.6				100	962	2.9
Custer	291	190			101	190		53.2			1.3	1.5			13	998	0.3
Delaware	38										0.3				5	794	
Dewey	52	74			−22	74		(6)			0.4	0.8			4	989	0.1
Ellis	2										(2)				(5)	1,218	
Garfield	822	368			454	368		123.4			2.5	1.7			26	1,061	0.8
Garvin	2,318										8.7				100	821	2.8
Grady	1,731										5.7				63	1,024	1.7
Grant	14	92			−78	92		(6)	(6)		0.1	0.5			(5)	994	
Greer	146	9	2		137	7		(6)	(6)		0.9	0.1	(2)		9	644	0.2
Harmon																548	
Harper	4										(2)				(5)	1,033	
Haskell	385										2.0				22	615	0.6

[1] For changes in boundaries, see note at end of table.
[2] Less than one-tenth of 1 per cent.
[3] State total includes population of Kaw, Osage, Wichita, and Kiowa, Comache, and Apache Indian Reeservations; population Day County, part taken to form part of Ellis in 1907 and part annexed to Roger Mills County since 1900; population Indian Territory returned by nations and reservations in 1900—Negroes 36,965
[4] State total includes 18,636 Negroes in Indian Territory specially enumerated, not distributed by counties.
[5] Less than 1 per 1,000 whites.
[6] Per cent not shown where base is less than 100.

TABLE II.—NEGRO POPULATION, 1910, 1900, 1890, 1880, DECENNIAL INCREASES, PROPORTION NEGRO, LAND AREA, AND NEGRO POPULATION PER SQUARE MILE, BY COUNTIES, FOR SOUTHERN STATES—Continued.

[A minus sign (−) denotes decrease.]

STATE AND COUNTY.	NEGRO POPULATION.				INCREASE. Number.			INCREASE. Per cent.			PERCENTAGE NEGRO IN TOTAL POPULATION.				Negroes per 1,000 whites, 1910	Land area, square miles, 1910	Negroes per square mile, 1910
	1910	1900	1890	1880	1900-1910	1890-1900	1880-1890	1900-1910	1890-1900	1880-1890	1910	1900	1890	1880			
OKLAHOMA—Con.																	
Hughes	1,737										7.2				83	855	2.0
Jackson	114										0.5				5	778	0.1
Jefferson	397										2.3				24	767	0.5
Johnston	884										5.3				53	658	1.3
Kay	109	276			−167	276		−60.5			0.4	1.2			4	934	0.1
Kingfisher	2,392	2,453	1,300		−61	1,153		−2.5	88.7		12.7	13.3	15.6		147	890	2.7
Kiowa	317										1.2				12	1,179	0.3
Latimer	618										5.5				61	735	0.8
Le Flore	1,781										6.1				69	1,614	1.1
Lincoln	3,945	2,158			1,787	2,158		82.8			11.3	8.0			129	959	4.1
Logan	8,196	6,102	724		2,094	5,378		34.3	742.8		25.8	23.0	5.7		349	739	11.1
Love	1,021										10.0				118	496	2.1
McClain	1,081										6.9				76	562	1.9
McCurtain	4,576										22.1				337	1,897	2.4
McIntosh	5,283										25.2				398	661	8.0
Major	90										0.6				6	937	0.1
Marshall	319										2.7				30	419	0.8
Mayes	799										5.9				83	676	1.2
Murray	423										3.3				36	424	1.0
Muskogee	16,454										31.2				493	814	20.2
Noble	642	448			194	448		43.3			4.3	3.2			46	734	0.9
Nowata	1,954										13.7				185	586	3.3
Okfuskee	8,073										40.4				722	623	13.0
Oklahoma	9,227	2,944	650		6,283	2,294		213.4	352.9		10.8	11.4	5.5		122	717	12.9
Okmulgee	5,933										28.1				423	679	8.7
Osage	391										1.9				21	2,277	0.2
Ottawa	11										0.1				(3)	477	......
Pawnee	806	192			614	192		319.8			4.7	1.6			51	584	1.4
Payne	1,456	450	100		1,006	350		223.6	350.0		6.1	2.2	1.4		66	678	2.1
Pittsburg	5,244										11.0				128	1,370	3.8
Pontotoc	1,009										4.1				45	728	1.4
Pottawatomie	2,017	815			1,202	815		147.5			4.6	3.1			50	793	2.5
Pushmataha	385										3.8				44	1,430	0.3
Roger Mills	......	2			−2	2		(1)			......	(2)			......	1,135	......
Rogers	620										3.5				44	730	0.8
Seminole	4,081										20.4				286	633	6.4
Sequoyah	3,178										12.7				168	693	4.6
Stephens	96										0.4				4	897	0.1
Texas	1										(2)				(3)	2,065	......
Tillman	432										2.3				24	733	0.6
Tulsa	2,754										7.9				89	565	4.9
Wagoner	8,761										39.7				710	545	16.1
Washington	434										2.5				27	425	1.0
Washita	25	7			18	7		(1)			0.1	(2)			1	1,006	......
Woods	3	167			−164	167		−98.2			(2)	0.5			(3)	1,255	......
Woodward	9	10			−1	10		(1)			1.	0.1			(3)	1,233	......
TENNESSEE [4]	473,088	480,243	430,678	403,151	−7,155	49,565	27,527	−1.5	11.5	6.8	21.7	23.8	24.4	26.1	276	41,687	11.3
Anderson	921	1,118	1,184	903	−197	−66	281	−17.6	−5.6	31.1	5.2	6.3	7.8	8.3	55	337	2.7
Bedford	5,486	6,268	6,196	7,489	−782	72	−1,293	−12.5	1.2	−17.3	24.2	26.3	25.0	28.8	319	514	10.7
Benton	340	540	617	633	−200	−77	−16	−37.0	−12.5	−2.5	2.7	4.5	5.5	6.5	28	456	0.7
Bledsoe	391	475	500	747	−84	−25	−247	−17.7	−5.0	−33.1	6.2	7.2	8.2	13.3	66	391	1.0
Blount	1,221	1,607	1,577	1,705	−386	30	−128	−24.0	1.9	−7.5	5.9	8.4	9.0	10.7	62	571	2.1
Bradley	1,717	2,085	1,771	1,845	−368	314	−74	−17.6	17.7	−4.0	10.5	13.2	13.0	15.2	118	336	5.1
Campbell	1,887	616	559	432	1,271	57	127	206.3	10.2	29.4	6.9	3.6	4.1	4.3	74	464	4.1
Cannon	580	827	952	1,116	−247	−125	−164	−29.9	−13.1	−14.7	5.4	6.8	7.8	9.4	57	268	2.2
Carroll	5,051	5,581	5,664	5,579	−530	−83	85	−9.5	−1.5	1.5	21.1	23.0	24.0	25.2	267	619	8.2
Carter	660	661	697	628	−1	−36	69	−0.2	−5.2	11.0	3.3	4.0	5.2	6.3	34	353	1.9
Cheatham	1,593	1,662	1,528	1,661	−69	134	−133	−4.2	8.8	−8.0	15.1	16.4	17.3	20.9	178	314	5.1
Chester [5]	1,571	2,026	1,776		−455	250	1,776	−22.5	14.1		17.3	20.5	19.6		209	313	5.0
Claiborne	819	729	518	789	90	211	−271	12.3	40.7	−34.3	3.5	3.5	3.4	5.9	36	468	1.8
Clay	289	368	374	399	−79	−6	−25	−21.5	−1.6	−6.3	3.2	4.4	5.2	5.7	33	254	1.1
Cocke	1,051	1,261	1,307	1,447	−210	−46	−140	−16.7	−3.5	−9.7	5.4	6.6	7.9	9.8	57	427	2.5
Coffee	1,624	1,802	1,723	1,723	−178	79	......	−9.9	4.6	......	10.4	11.6	12.5	13.4	116	443	3.7
Crockett	3,611	4,046	4,186	3,612	−435	−140	574	−10.8	−3.3	15.9	22.5	25.5	27.6	25.6	290	267	13.5
Cumberland	63	572	51	42	−509	521	9	−89.0	(1)	(1)	0.7	6.9	0.9	0.9	7	655	0.1
Davidson	46,710	43,902	41,315	31,331	2,808	2,587	9,984	6.4	6.3	31.9	31.2	35.7	38.2	39.6	455	511	91.4
Decatur	1,019	1,220	1,304	1,222	−201	−84	82	−16.5	−6.4	6.7	10.1	11.7	14.5	14.4	112	288	3.5

[1] Per cent not shown where base is less than 100.
[2] Less than one-tenth of 1 per cent.
[3] Less than 1 per 1,000 whites.

[4] Island No. 25 ceded to Mississippi County, Ark., in 1905. Total population 115 in 1900.
[5] For changes in boundaries, see note at end of table.

TABLE **II.**—NEGRO POPULATION, 1910, 1900, 1890, 1880, DECENNIAL INCREASES, PROPORTION NEGRO, LAND AREA, AND NEGRO POPULATION PER SQUARE MILE, BY COUNTIES, FOR SOUTHERN STATES—Continued.

[A minus sign (−) denotes decrease.]

STATE AND COUNTY.	NEGRO POPULATION.				INCREASE. — Number.			INCREASE. — Per cent.			PERCENTAGE NEGRO IN TOTAL POPULATION.				Negroes per 1,000 whites, 1910	Land area, square miles, 1910	Negroes per square mile, 1910
	1910	1900	1890	1880	1900–1910	1890–1900	1880–1890	1900–1910	1890–1900	1880–1890	1910	1900	1890	1880			
TENNESSEE— Continued.																	
Dekalb	835	1,108	1,159	1,151	−273	−51	8	−24.6	−4.4	0.7	5.4	6.7	7.4	7.8	57	311	2.7
Dickson	3,079	2,919	2,101	2,231	160	818	−130	5.5	38.9	−5.8	15.4	15.7	15.4	17.9	183	549	5.6
Dyer	5,685	5,742	4,690	3,912	−57	1,052	778	−1.0	22.4	19.9	20.5	24.2	23.6	25.9	258	500	11.4
Fayette	22,702	21,682	20,492	22,238	1,020	1,190	−1,746	4.7	5.8	−7.9	75.0	73.0	71.0	69.8	3,010	618	36.7
Fentress [1]	98	25	46	103	73	−21	−57	(2)	(2)	−55.3	1.3	0.4	0.9	1.7	13	486	0.2
Franklin	3,126	3,439	3,570	3,530	−313	−131	40	−9.1	3.7	1.1	15.3	16.9	18.9	20.5	180	575	5.4
Gibson	9,547	10,313	9,337	9,145	−766	976	192	−7.4	10.5	2.1	22.9	26.2	26.0	28.0	298	633	15.1
Giles	10,867	11,406	12,320	14,189	−539	−914	−1,869	−4.7	−7.4	−13.2	33.3	34.5	35.2	39.4	499	628	17.3
Grainger	483	650	685	829	−167	−35	−144	−25.7	−5.1	−17.4	3.5	4.2	5.2	6.7	36	307	1.6
Greene	1,369	1,569	1,519	2,152	−200	50	−633	−12.7	3.3	−29.4	4.4	5.1	5.7	9.0	46	613	2.2
Grundy	143	315	438	438	−172	−123	....	−54.6	−28.1	....	1.7	4.0	6.9	9.5	18	375	0.4
Hamblen	1,610	1,791	1,520	1,706	−181	271	−186	−10.1	17.8	−10.9	11.8	14.1	13.3	16.7	134	158	10.2
Hamilton	26,026	19,490	17,717	7,399	6,536	1,773	10,318	33.5	10.0	139.5	29.2	31.6	33.1	31.3	412	409	63.6
Hancock	481	273	727	482	208	−454	245	76.2	62.4	50.8	4.5	2.4	7.0	5.3	47	228	2.1
Hardeman [1]	10,098	10,205	8,787	9,608	−107	1,418	−821	−1.0	16.1	−8.5	43.9	44.4	41.8	41.9	782	697	14.5
Hardin	2,170	2,678	2,401	2,016	−508	277	385	−19.0	11.5	19.1	12.4	13.9	13.6	13.6	141	582	3.7
Hawkins	1,805	2,154	2,268	2,641	−349	−114	−373	−16.2	−5.0	−14.1	7.7	8.9	10.2	12.8	83	482	3.7
Haywood	17,710	17,080	15,569	17,556	630	1,511	−1,987	3.7	9.7	−11.3	68.4	67.8	66.1	67.4	2,160	508	34.9
Henderson [1]	1,918	2,637	2,365	3,016	−719	272	−651	−27.3	11.5	−21.6	11.3	14.6	14.5	17.3	127	536	3.6
Henry	5,921	5,999	5,853	6,654	−78	146	−801	−1.3	2.5	−12.0	23.3	24.8	27.8	30.1	303	626	9.5
Hickman [1]	2,430	2,611	2,744	2,246	−181	−133	498	−6.9	−4.8	22.2	14.7	16.0	18.9	18.6	172	570	4.3
Houston	910	1,056	827	808	−146	229	19	−13.8	27.7	2.4	14.6	16.3	15.3	18.8	171	197	4.6
Humphreys	1,201	1,515	1,562	1,671	−314	−47	−109	−20.8	−3.0	−6.5	8.6	11.3	13.3	14.7	95	451	2.7
Jackson	302	470	479	433	−168	−9	46	−35.7	−1.9	10.6	2.0	3.1	3.6	3.6	20	301	1.0
James	492	506	535	667	−14	−29	−132	−2.8	−5.4	−19.8	9.4	9.4	10.9	12.9	104	165	3.0
Jefferson	1,639	2,174	2,153	2,500	−535	21	−347	−24.6	1.0	−13.9	9.2	11.7	13.1	15.8	102	312	5.3
Johnson	377	368	350	470	9	18	−120	2.4	5.1	−25.5	2.9	3.5	4.0	6.1	29	294	1.3
Knox	12,709	11,777	10,940	7,244	932	837	3,696	7.9	7.7	51.0	13.5	15.9	18.4	18.5	156	504	25.2
Lake	3,268	1,984	1,075	691	1,284	909	384	64.7	84.6	55.6	37.5	26.9	20.3	17.4	601	122	26.8
Lauderdale [1]	9,554	10,169	7,810	5,837	−615	2,359	1,973	−6.0	30.2	33.8	45.3	46.3	41.6	39.1	827	456	21.0
Lawrence	969	967	779	784	2	188	−5	0.2	24.1	−0.6	5.5	6.3	6.3	7.6	58	611	1.6
Lewis [1]	854	392	252	218	462	140	34	117.9	55.6	15.6	14.2	8.8	9.9	10.0	165	286	3.0
Lincoln	5,502	6,084	6,259	6,310	−582	−175	−51	−9.6	−2.8	−0.8	21.2	23.1	22.9	23.4	270	587	9.4
Loudon	964	1,360	1,436	1,758	−396	−76	−322	−29.1	−5.3	−18.3	7.1	12.5	15.5	19.2	76	219	4.4
McMinn	1,892	1,997	2,128	2,325	−105	−131	−197	−5.3	−6.2	−8.5	9.0	10.4	11.9	15.4	99	432	4.4
McNairy [1]	1,557	2,442	1,881	2,426	−885	561	−545	−36.2	29.8	−22.5	9.5	13.8	12.1	14.0	105	588	2.6
Macon	732	874	781	890	−142	93	−109	−16.2	11.9	−12.2	5.0	6.8	7.2	9.5	53	286	2.6
Madison [1]	16,167	16,754	14,669	15,467	−587	2,085	−798	−3.5	14.2	−5.2	41.1	46.1	48.1	50.1	697	552	29.3
Marion	2,289	2,105	2,379	1,369	184	−274	1,010	8.7	−11.5	73.8	12.2	12.2	15.4	12.5	138	504	4.5
Marshall	3,414	4,260	4,494	4,830	−846	−234	−336	−19.9	−5.2	−7.0	20.2	22.7	23.8	25.1	254	378	9.0
Maury	16,169	18,164	15,910	18,171	−1,995	2,254	−2,261	−11.0	14.2	−12.4	40.0	42.5	41.7	45.5	666	582	27.8
Meigs	566	663	698	814	−97	−35	−116	−14.6	−5.0	−14.3	9.2	8.9	10.1	11.4	102	199	2.8
Monroe	1,167	1,222	1,247	1,292	−55	−25	−45	−4.5	−2.0	−3.5	5.6	6.6	8.1	9.0	60	673	1.7
Montgomery	13,430	16,158	13,814	13,694	−2,728	2,344	120	−16.9	17.0	0.9	39.9	44.9	46.5	48.1	664	516	26.0
Moore	334	469	540	785	−135	−71	−245	−28.8	−13.1	−31.2	7.0	8.2	9.0	12.6	75	141	2.4
Morgan	691	600	333	289	91	267	44	15.2	80.2	15.2	6.0	6.3	4.4	5.6	64	529	1.3
Obion	5,293	4,840	4,333	4,069	453	507	264	9.4	11.7	6.5	17.7	17.1	15.9	17.8	215	552	9.6
Overton [1]	299	273	264	342	26	9	−78	9.5	3.4	−22.8	1.9	2.0	2.2	2.8	19	446	0.7
Perry [1]	633	665	670	565	−32	−5	105	−4.8	−0.7	18.6	7.2	7.6	8.6	7.9	77	487	1.3
Pickett [1]	11	11	12	....	....	−1	12	....	(2)	....	0.2	0.2	0.3	....	2	162	0.1
Polk	284	303	566	344	−19	−263	222	−6.3	−46.5	64.5	2.0	2.7	6.8	4.7	21	432	0.7
Putnam	892	768	622	598	124	146	24	16.1	23.5	4.0	4.5	4.5	4.5	5.2	47	404	2.2
Rhea	1,316	1,878	1,721	773	−562	157	948	−29.9	9.1	122.6	8.5	13.1	13.6	10.9	94	365	3.6
Roane	2,366	2,625	1,937	1,906	−259	688	31	−9.9	35.5	1.6	10.3	11.5	11.1	12.5	115	388	6.1
Robertson	6,492	6,822	5,525	5,618	−330	1,297	−93	−4.8	23.5	−1.7	25.5	27.3	27.5	29.8	342	455	14.3
Rutherford	11,357	12,965	14,415	16,493	−1,608	−1,450	−2,078	−12.4	−10.1	−12.6	34.2	38.7	41.1	44.9	520	614	18.5
Scott	97	335	366	157	−238	−31	209	−71.0	−8.5	133.1	0.7	3.0	3.7	2.6	8	550	0.2
Sequatchie	139	37	70	56	102	−33	14	(2)	(2)	(2)	3.3	1.1	2.3	2.2	34	264	0.5
Sevier	378	565	599	693	−187	−34	−94	−33.1	−5.7	−13.6	1.7	2.6	3.2	4.5	17	587	0.6
Shelby	91,719	84,773	61,613	43,903	6,946	23,160	17,710	8.2	37.6	40.3	47.9	55.2	54.7	56.0	921	801	114.5
Smith	2,325	3,008	2,979	3,578	−683	29	−599	−22.7	1.0	−16.7	12.5	15.8	16.2	20.1	143	296	7.9
Stewart	1,806	2,352	2,177	2,757	−546	175	−580	−23.2	8.0	−21.0	12.2	15.4	17.9	21.7	138	449	4.0
Sullivan	1,535	1,565	1,400	1,305	−30	165	95	−1.9	11.8	7.3	5.5	6.3	6.7	7.1	58	436	3.5
Sumner	5,386	6,677	6,354	7,331	−1,291	323	−977	−19.3	5.1	−13.3	21.0	25.6	26.8	31.0	266	558	9.7
Tipton	13,353	13,965	11,770	10,543	−612	2,195	1,227	−4.4	18.6	11.6	45.3	47.7	48.5	50.1	829	442	30.2
Trousdale	1,781	2,033	1,827	2,141	−252	206	−314	−12.4	11.3	−14.7	30.3	33.9	31.2	32.2	435	106	16.8
Unicoi	131	130	219	119	1	−89	100	0.8	−40.6	84.0	1.8	2.2	4.7	3.3	19	201	0.7
Union	30	79	103	218	−49	−24	−115	(2)	23.3	−52.8	0.3	0.6	0.9	2.1	3	235	0.1
Van Buren	48	55	67	186	−7	−12	−119	(2)	(2)	−64.0	1.7	1.8	2.3	6.3	18	293	0.2
Warren	1,949	2,074	2,011	2,276	−125	63	−265	−6.0	3.1	−11.6	11.8	12.6	14.0	16.2	134	423	4.6
Washington	2,267	2,147	1,945	1,577	120	202	368	5.6	10.4	23.3	7.8	9.5	9.6	9.7	85	325	7.0
Wayne [1]	845	1,144	884	1,069	−299	260	−185	−26.1	29.4	−17.3	7.0	8.8	7.7	9.5	75	749	1.1
Weakley	3,470	4,228	4,520	4,413	−758	−292	107	−17.9	−6.5	2.4	10.9	13.0	15.6	18.0	122	580	6.0
White	899	1,024	849	985	−125	175	−139	−12.2	20.6	−14.1	5.8	7.2	6.9	8.8	62	363	2.5
Williamson	7,828	9,664	10,084	12,390	−1,836	−420	−2,306	−19.0	−4.2	−18.6	32.3	36.6	38.3	43.8	478	586	13.4
Wilson	6,303	7,256	7,338	8,455	−953	−82	−1,117	−13.1	−1.1	−13.2	24.8	26.8	27.0	29.4	330	613	10.3

[1] For changes in boundaries, see note at end of table.   [2] Per cent not shown where base is less than 100.

TABLE II.—NEGRO POPULATION, 1910, 1900, 1890, 1880, DECENNIAL INCREASES, PROPORTION NEGRO, LAND AREA, AND NEGRO POPULATION PER SQUARE MILE, BY COUNTIES, FOR SOUTHERN STATES—Continued.

[A minus sign (−) denotes decrease.]

State and county	Negro population 1910	1900	1890	1880	Increase Number 1900–1910	Number 1890–1900	Number 1880–1890	Increase Per cent 1900–1910	Per cent 1890–1900	Per cent 1880–1890	Percentage negro 1910	1900	1890	1880	Negroes per 1,000 whites, 1910	Land area, sq. miles, 1910	Negroes per sq. mile, 1910
TEXAS	690,049	620,722	¹488,171	²393,384	69,327	132,551	94,787	11.2	27.2	24.1	17.7	20.4	21.8	24.7	215	262,398	2.6
Anderson	11,323	11,615	9,502	7,775	−292	2,113	1,727	−25	22.2	22.2	38.2	41.5	45.4	44.7	618	938	12.1
Andrews³	1				1						0.1				1	1,565	(4)
Angelina	2,435	2,156	601	834	279	1,555	−233	12.9	258.7	−27.9	13.8	16.0	9.5	15.9	159	940	2.6
Aransas	136	189	137	79	−53	52	58	−28.0	38.0	(5)	6.5	11.0	7.5	7.9	69	240	0.6
Archer	3	2	12	7	1	−10	5	(5)	(5)	(5)	(4)	0.1	0.6	1.2	(6)	872	(4)
Armstrong		2			−2	2		(5)				0.2				903	
Atascosa	228	277	285	279	−49	−8	6	−17.7	−2.8	2.2	2.3	3.9	4.4	6.6	23	1,358	0.2
Austin	5,018	6,193	5,185	3,939	−1,175	1,008	1,246	−19.0	19.4	31.6	28.4	30.9	29.0	27.3	396	728	6.9
Bailey																1,030	
Bandera	34	89	126	31	−55	−37	95	(5)	−29.4	(5)	0.7	1.7	3.3	1.4	7	983	(4)
Bastrop	9,428	10,369	8,898	7,306	−941	1,471	1,592	−9.1	16.5	21.8	37.2	38.6	42.9	42.4	592	867	10.9
Baylor	3	16	6	6	−13	10		(5)	(5)	(5)	(4)	0.5	0.2	0.8	(6)	880	(4)
Bee	568	476	317	153	92	159	164	19.3	50.2	107.2	4.7	6.2	8.5	6.7	49	856	0.7
Bell	6,302	3,812	2,650	1,734	2,490	1,162	916	65.3	43.8	52.8	12.8	8.4	7.9	8.5	147	1,083	5.8
Bexar	11,642	8,530	5,504	3,867	3,112	3,026	1,637	36.5	55.0	42.3	9.7	12.3	11.2	12.7	108	1,263	9.2
Blanco	350	224	210	168	126	14	42	56.3	6.7	25.0	8.1	4.8	4.5	4.7	88	750	0.5
Borden		2	5		−2	−3	5	(5)	(5)			0.3	2.3			895	
Bosque	848	845	641	498	3	204	143	0.4	31.8	28.7	4.5	4.9	4.5	4.4	47	975	0.9
Bowie	12,734	10,199	7,591	4,331	2,535	2,608	3,260	24.9	34.4	75.3	36.6	38.2	37.5	39.5	576	873	14.6
Brazoria	6,237	8,219	8,523	7,524	−1,982	−304	999	−24.1	−3.6	13.3	46.9	55.3	74.1	77.0	885	1,340	4.7
Brazos	8,827	8,845	8,433	6,250	−18	412	2,183	−0.2	4.9	34.9	46.7	46.9	50.6	46.0	875	597	14.8
Brewster³	71	80	13		−9	67	13	(5)	(5)		1.4	3.4	1.8		14	5,935	(4)
Briscoe																903	
Brown³	525	206	73	114	319	133	−41	154.9	(5)	−36.0	2.3	1.3	0.6	1.4	23	956	0.5
Burleson	8,587	8,321	5,727	3,886	266	2,594	1,841	3.2	45.3	47.4	46.0	45.3	44.1	42.0	850	684	12.6
Burnet	292	264	307	248	28	−43	59	10.6	−14.0	2.4	2.7	2.5	2.9	3.6	28	974	0.3
Caldwell	5,378	5,687	4,878	4,034	−309	809	844	−5.4	16.6	20.9	22.2	26.1	30.9	34.3	285	511	10.5
Calhoun	491	271	168	547	220	103	−379	81.2	61.3	−69.3	13.5	11.3	20.6	31.5	156	563	0.9
Callahan	4	25	31	24	−21	−6	7	(5)	(5)	(5)	(4)	0.3	0.6	0.7	(6)	854	(4)
Cameron	74	177	108	117	−103	69	−9	−58.2	63.9	−7.7	0.3	1.1	0.7	0.8	3	2,434	(4)
Camp	4,415	4,354	3,296	2,845	61	1,058	451	1.4	32.1	15.9	46.2	47.6	49.8	48.0	860	207	21.3
Carson		2	1		−2	1	1	(5)	(5)			0.4	0.3			893	
Cass	9,952	8,908	8,512	6,444	1,044	396	2,068	11.7	4.7	32.1	36.1	39.0	37.7	38.5	564	951	10.5
Castro																896	
Chambers	1,032	829	757	693	203	72	64	24.5	9.5	9.2	24.4	27.2	33.8	31.7	323	618	1.7
Cherokee	7,641	8,196	7,705	5,708	−555	491	1,997	−6.8	6.4	35.0	26.3	32.6	33.5	34.1	357	1,049	7.3
Childress		1	2	1	−1	−1	1	(5)	(5)	(5)		(4)	0.2	(5)		733	
Clay	101	44	102	26	57	−58	76	(5)	−56.9	(5)	0.6	0.5	1.4	0.5	6	1,158	0.1
Cochran																869	
Coke³		2			−2	2		(5)				0.1				931	
Coleman	253	90	69	35	163	21	34	(5)	(5)	(5)	1.1	0.9	1.1	1.0	11	1,290	0.2
Collin	2,206	2,456	2,525	1,979	−250	−69	546	−10.2	−2.7	27.6	4.5	4.9	6.9	7.6	471	878	2.5
Collingsworth	3	2		3	1	2	−3	(5)	(5)	(5)	0.1	0.2		(5)	(6)	898	(4)
Colorado	7,074	9,633	8,845	7,686	−2,559	788	1,159	−26.6	8.9	15.1	37.4	43.4	45.3	46.1	598	972	7.3
Comal	232	259	180	270	−27	79	−90	−10.4	43.9	−33.3	2.8	3.7	2.8	4.9	28	559	0.4
Comanche³	12		8	79	12	−8	−71	(5)	(5)	(5)	(4)		0.1	0.9	(6)	948	(4)
Concho	7	14	14	17	−7		−3	(5)	(5)	(5)	0.1	1.0	1.3	2.1	1	918	(4)
Cooke	1,688	1,875	1,351	814	−187	524	537	−10.0	38.8	66.0	6.3	6.8	5.5	4.0	68	902	1.9
Coryell	488	570	459	385	−82	111	74	−14.4	24.2	19.2	2.2	2.7	2.7	3.5	23	1,085	0.4
Cottle	1				1			(5)			(4)				(6)	1,012	(4)
Crane³																878	
Crockett³	4	8			−4	8		(5)	(5)		0.3	0.5			3	3,215	(4)
Crosby		3	1	1	−3	2		(5)	(5)	(5)		0.4	0.3	(5)		870	
Dallam	6				6			(5)			0.1				2	1,532	(4)
Dallas	24,355	13,646	11,177	4,947	10,709	2,469	6,230	78.5	22.1	125.9	17.9	16.5	16.7	14.8	219	859	28.4
Dawson³	2		1	1	2	−1		(5)	(5)		0.1		(5)	(5)	(6)	903	(4)
De Witt	4,753	4,940	3,995	2,938	−187	945	1,057	−3.8	23.7	36.0	20.2	23.2	27.9	29.1	254	879	5.4
Deaf Smith	68	1		1	67	1	−1	(5)	(5)		1.7	0.1		(5)	18	1,549	(4)
Delta	809	967	728	598	−158	239	130	−16.3	32.8	21.7	5.6	6.3	8.0	10.7	59	261	3.1
Denton	2,210	2,067	1,707	1,070	143	360	637	6.9	21.1	59.5	7.1	7.3	8.0	5.9	76	952	2.3
Dickens	2				2			(5)			0.1				(6)	881	(4)
Dimmit	29	41	37	16	−12	4	21	(5)	(5)	(5)	0.8	3.7	3.5	2.4	8	1,360	(4)
Donley	38	49	40		−11	9	40	(5)	(5)		0.7	1.8	3.8		7	906	(4)
Duval	8	12	7	37	−4	5	−30	(5)	(5)	(5)	0.1	0.1	0.1	0.6	(6)	1,825	(4)
Eastland	57	51	25	18	6	26	7	(5)	(5)	(5)	0.2	0.3	0.2	0.4	2	925	0.1
Ector³		3	1		−3	2	1	(5)	(5)			0.8	0.4			892	
Edwards	4	11	6	1	−7	5	5	(5)	(5)	(5)	0.1	0.4	0.3	0.4	1	2,352	(4)
El Paso	1,562	620	377	47	942	243	330	151.9	64.5	(5)	3.0	2.5	2.4	1.2	31	9,331	0.2
Ellis	9,623	4,841	3,376	2,539	4,782	1,465	837	98.8	43.4	33.0	17.9	9.7	10.6	11.9	219	975	9.9
Erath	589	579	723	257	10	−144	466	1.7	−19.9	181.3	1.8	1.9	3.3	2.2	19	1,083	0.5
Falls	12,612	11,985	7,961	6,673	627	4,024	1,288	5.2	50.5	19.3	35.4	35.9	38.4	41.1	548	745	16.9
Fannin	5,366	5,465	4,241	3,416	−99	1,224	825	−1.8	28.9	24.2	12.0	10.6	11.0	13.4	136	838	6.4
Fayette	7,361	10,394	8,446	8,763	−3,033	1,948	−317	−29.2	23.1	−3.6	24.7	28.4	26.8	31.3	328	968	7.6
Fisher	9	3	15	1	6	−12	14	(5)	(5)	(5)	0.1	0.1	0.5	0.7	(6)	885	(4)
Floyd					−8	8		(5)	(5)							1,011	

¹ 1890: Includes 34 persons in Buchel, Encinal, and Foley Counties.
² 1880: Includes 1 person in Encinal County.
³ For changes in boundaries, see note at end of table.
⁴ Less than one-tenth of 1 per cent.
⁵ Per cent not shown where base is less than 100.
⁶ Less than 1 per 1,000 whites.

TABLE II.—NEGRO POPULATION, 1910, 1900, 1890, 1880, DECENNIAL INCREASES, PROPORTION NEGRO, LAND AREA, AND NEGRO POPULATION PER SQUARE MILE, BY COUNTIES, FOR SOUTHERN STATES—Continued.

[A minus sign (−) denotes decrease.]

STATE AND COUNTY.	NEGRO POPULATION.				INCREASE. Number.			INCREASE. Per cent.			PERCENTAGE NEGRO IN TOTAL POPULATION.				Negroes per 1,000 whites, 1910	Land area, square miles, 1910	Negroes per square mile, 1910
	1910	1900	1890	1880	1900-1910	1890-1900	1880-1890	1900-1910	1890-1900	1880-1890	1910	1900	1890	1880			
TEXAS—Con.																	
Foard [1]	6				6						0.1				1	612	(²)
Fort Bend	11,422	10,814	8,981	7,508	608	1,833	1,473	5.6	20.4	19.6	62.9	65.4	84.8	80.0	1,693	792	14.4
Franklin	735	929	819	614	−194	110	205	−20.9	13.4	33.4	7.9	10.7	12.6	11.6	86	289	2.5
Freestone	8,772	8,302	6,675	6,652	470	1,627	23	5.7	24.4	0.3	42.7	43.9	41.8	44.6	744	882	9.9
Frio	151	163	102	65	−12	61	37	−7.4	59.8	(³)	1.7	3.9	3.3	3.1	17	1,124	0.1
Gaines [1]																1,540	
Galveston	8,747	8,798	7,009	5,651	−51	1,789	1,358	−0.6	25.5	24.0	19.7	19.9	22.3	23.4	245	395	22.1
Garza [1]	36	2		1	34	2	−1	(³)	1.1		1.8	1.1		(³)	18	870	(²)
Gillespie	116	105	108	132	11	−3	−24	10.5	−2.8	−18.2	1.2	1.3	1.5	2.5	12	1,109	0.1
Glasscock [1]	5	1			4	1		(³)			0.4	0.3			4	866	(²)
Goliad	1,501	1,806	1,644	1,666	−305	162	−22	−16.9	9.9	−1.3	15.1	21.7	27.8	28.6	179	799	1.9
Gonzales	8,212	8,642	5,869	4,861	−430	2,773	1,008	−5.0	47.2	20.7	29.3	29.9	32.6	32.8	414	1,020	8.1
Gray [1]	2	13	1	1	−11	12		(³)	(³)	(³)	0.1	2.7	0.5	(³)	(⁴)	899	(²)
Grayson	7,753	7,742	6,712	4,548	11	1,030	2,164	0.1	15.3	47.6	11.7	12.2	12.6	11.9	133	942	8.2
Gregg	7,781	6,898	5,349	4,711	883	1,549	638	12.8	29.0	13.5	55.0	55.9	56.9	55.2	1,227	312	24.9
Grimes	9,858	14,327	11,664	10,276	−4,469	2,663	1,388	−31.2	22.8	13.5	46.5	54.9	54.7	55.2	869	812	12.1
Guadalupe	5,681	5,187	4,415	3,455	494	772	960	9.5	17.5	27.8	22.8	24.3	29.0	28.3	296	703	8.1
Hale	5	3	3		2		3	(³)			0.1	0.2	0.4		(⁴)	1,036	(z)
Hall	2		1	1	2	−1		(²)		(³)	(²)		0.1	(³)	(⁴)	901	(⁷)
Hamilton [1]	8	7	13	24	1	−6	−11	(³)	(³)	(³)	0.1	0.1	0.1	0.4	(⁴)	833	(²)
Hansford		1			−1	1		(³)				0.6				882	
Hardeman [1]	40	18	21	1	22	−3	20	(³)	(³)	(³)	0.4	0.5	0.5	(³)	4	761	0.1
Hardin	2,550	948	967	236	1,602	−19	731	169.0	−2.0	309.7	19.7	18.8	24.4	12.6	245	862	3.0
Harris	30,950	19,894	13,522	10,816	11,056	6,372	2,706	55.6	47.1	25.0	26.8	31.2	36.3	38.6	366	1,654	18.7
Harrison	23,698	21,697	18,191	17,196	2,001	3,506	995	9.2	19.3	5.8	63.6	68.1	68.1	68.3	1,750	872	27.2
Hartley	3	1	1		2		1	(³)	(³)	(³)	0.2	0.3	0.4		(⁴)	1,507	(²)
Haskell	84	5	6	2	79	−1	4	(³)	(³)	(³)	0.5	0.2	0.4	(³)	5	923	0.1
Hays	2,165	2,132	2,171	1,475	33	−39	696	1.5	−1.8	47.2	14.0	15.1	19.1	19.5	162	623	3.5
Hemphill		2	9	3	−2	−7	6	(³)	(³)	(³)		0.2	1.7	2.0		873	
Henderson	4,177	4,347	2,988	2,094	−170	1,359	894	−3.9	45.5	42.7	20.7	21.8	24.3	21.5	262	946	4.4
Hidalgo	62	110	76	114	−48	34	−38	−43.7	(³)	−33.3	0.5	1.6	1.2	2.6	5	2,276	(²)
Hill	4,856	2,973	2,096	1,298	1,883	877	798	63.3	41.8	61.5	10.4	7.2	7.6	7.8	116	966	5.0
Hockley																867	
Hood	212	241	274	198	−29	−33	76	−12.0	−12.0	38.4	2.1	2.6	3.6	3.2	22	405	0.5
Hopkins	3,283	3,808	2,838	2,153	−525	970	685	−13.8	34.2	31.8	10.6	13.6	13.8	13.9	118	813	4.0
Houston	12,548	10,342	8,467	7,233	2,206	1,875	1,234	21.3	22.1	17.1	42.4	40.6	43.7	43.3	737	1,231	10.2
Howard	4	86	34	2	−82	52	32	(³)	(³)	(³)	(²)	3.4	2.8	(³)	(⁴)	891	(²)
Hunt	4,579	4,340	2,953	1,211	239	1,387	1,742	5.5	47.0	143.8	9.5	9.2	9.3	7.0	105	893	5.1
Hutchinson [1]	1		2		1	−2	2	(³)		(³)	0.1		(³)		1	879	(²)
Irion [1]	1	4	2		−3	2	2	(³)	(³)		0.1	0.5	0.2		(⁴)	998	(²)
Jack	118	115	97	118	3	18	−21	2.6	(³)	−17.8	1.0	1.1	1.0	1.8	10	962	0.1
Jackson	2,114	2,189	1,822	1,412	−75	367	410	−3.4	20.1	29.0	32.7	35.9	55.5	51.9	485	893	2.4
Jasper	4,731	2,996	2,378	2,538	1,735	618	−160	57.9	26.0	−6.3	33.8	42.0	42.5	46.9	510	978	4.8
Jeff Davis [1]	47	42	37		5	5	37	(³)	(³)		2.8	3.7	2.7		29	2,263	(²)
Jefferson	10,676	3,945	2,218	1,199	6,731	1,727	1,019	170.6	77.9	85.0	28.0	27.7	37.9	34.4	388	920	11.6
Johnson	1,637	1,147	852	574	490	295	278	42.7	34.6	48.4	4.8	3.4	3.8	3.2	50	740	2.2
Jones	259	4	7	4	255	−3	3	(³)	(³)	(³)	1.1	0.1	0.2	0.7	11	922	0.3
Karnes	793	633	544	489	160	89	55	25.3	16.4	11.2	5.3	7.3	15.0	15.0	56	692	1.1
Kaufman	8,374	6,092	3,176	1,974	2,282	2,916	1,202	37.5	91.8	60.9	23.7	18.3	14.7	12.8	311	834	10.0
Kendall	253	235	216	175	18	19	41	7.7	8.8	23.4	5.6	5.7	5.6	6.3	59	598	0.4
Kent	1				1			(²)							(⁴)	875	(²)
Kerr	248	148	106	92	100	42	14	67.6	39.6	(³)	4.5	3.0	2.4	4.2	47	1,197	0.2
Kimble		6	5	8	−6	1	−3	(³)	(³)	(³)		0.2	0.2	0.6		1,301	
King	8		2	1	8	−2	1	(³)	(³)	(³)	1.0		1.2	(³)	10	867	(²)
Kinney [1]	158	349	253	475	−191	96	−222	−54.7	37.9	−46.7	4.6	14.3	6.7	10.6	52	1,312	0.1
Knox [1]	17			3	17		−3	(³)		(³)	0.2			(³)	2	862	(²)
La Salle	93	63	67	14	30	−4	53	(³)	(³)	(³)	2.0	2.7	3.1	1.8	20	1,561	0.1
Lamar	10,993	11,007	9,378	6,729	−14	1,629	2,649	−0.1	17.4	39.4	23.6	22.6	25.1	24.7	309	945	11.6
Lamb [1]	1				1			(³)			0.2				2	1,022	(³)
Lampasas [1]	436	370	262	172	66	108	90	17.8	41.2	52.3	4.6	4.3	3.5	3.2	48	740	0.6
Lavaca	4,384	4,890	4,253	3,420	−506	637	833	−10.3	15.0	24.4	16.6	17.4	19.4	25.1	199	950	4.6
Lee	4,039	4,343	3,102	1,956	−304	1,241	1,146	−7.0	40.0	58.6	30.8	29.8	26.0	21.9	444	562	7.2
Leon	6,878	6,937	5,377	5,102	−59	1,560	275	−0.9	29.0	5.4	41.5	38.4	38.8	39.8	709	1,101	6.2
Liberty	3,401	2,366	1,715	2,433	1,035	651	−718	43.7	38.0	−29.5	31.8	29.2	40.5	48.7	467	1,160	2.9
Limestone	9,247	6,354	4,459	3,171	2,893	1,895	1,288	45.5	42.5	40.6	26.7	19.5	20.6	19.5	365	974	9.5
Lipscomb	3			2	3		−2	(³)		(³)	0.1			(³)	1	888	(²)
Live Oak	36	73	49	76	−37	24	−27	(³)	(³)	(³)	1.0	3.2	2.4	3.8	11	1,116	(⁷)
Llano	62	39	52	66	23	−13	−14	(³)	(³)	(³)	1.0	0.5	0.8	1.3	10	971	0.1
Loving [1]	1				1			(³)			0.4				4	753	(²)
Lubbock	5		2		5	−2	2	(³)		(³)	0.1		(³)		1	868	(²)
Lynn [1]																864	
McCulloch	189	31	12	22	158	19	−10	(³)	(³)	(³)	1.4	0.8	0.4	1.4	14	1,073	0.2
McLennan	17,234	14,405	10,381	7,643	2,829	4,024	2,738	19.6	38.8	35.8	23.5	24.1	26.5	28.4	308	1,049	16.4
McMullen	58	33	44	47	25	−11	−3	(³)	(³)	(³)	5.3	3.2	4.2	6.7	56	1,302	(²)
Madison	2,757	2,458	2,070	1,702	299	388	368	12.2	18.7	21.6	26.7	23.6	24.3	31.5	365	495	5.6

[1] For changes in boundaries, see note at end of table.
[2] Less than one-tenth of 1 per cent.
[3] Per cent not shown where base is less than 100.
[4] Less than 1 per 1,000 whites.

TABLE II.—NEGRO POPULATION, 1910, 1900, 1890, 1880, DECENNIAL INCREASES, PROPORTION NEGRO, LAND AREA, AND NEGRO POPULATION PER SQUARE MILE, BY COUNTIES, FOR SOUTHERN STATES—Continued.

[A minus sign (−) denotes decrease.]

| STATE AND COUNTY. | NEGRO POPULATION. | | | | INCREASE. | | | | | | PERCENTAGE NEGRO IN TOTAL POPULATION. | | | | Negroes per 1,000 whites, 1910 | Land area, square miles, 1910 | Negroes per square mile, 1910 |
| | | | | | Number. | | | Per cent. | | | | | | | | | |
	1910	1900	1890	1880	1900-1910	1890-1900	1880-1890	1900-1910	1890-1900	1880-1890	1910	1900	1890	1880			
TEXAS—Con.																	
Marion	6,725	7,147	6,989	7,210	−422	158	−221	−5.9	2.3	−3.1	64.2	66.5	64.4	65.6	1,796	391	17.2
Martin	1	2			−1	2		(1)			0.1	0.6			(2)	904	(3)
Mason	70	54	31	41	16	23	−10	(1)	(1)	(1)	1.2	1.0	0.6	1.5	12	969	0.1
Matagorda	4,457	3,791	2,621	2,524	666	1,170	97	17.6	44.6	3.8	32.8	62.2	65.8	64.1	490	1,136	3.9
Maverick	96	195	142	94	−99	53	48	−50.8	37.3	(1)	1.9	4.8	3.8	3.2	19	1,251	0.1
Medina	449	356	283	277	93	73	6	26.1	25.8	2.2	3.3	4.6	4.9	6.2	35	1,353	0.3
Menard	24	20	23	37	4	−3	−14	(1)	(1)	(1)	0.9	1.0	1.9	3.0	9	914	(3)
Midland[4]	26	56	3		−30	53	3	(1)	(1)		0.8	3.2	0.3		8	887	(3)
Milam	9,485	10,473	6,220	3,934	−988	4,253	2,286	−9.4	68.4	58.1	25.8	26.4	25.1	21.1	348	959	9.9
Mills[4]	7	13	57		−6	−44	57	(1)	(1)		0.1	0.2	1.0		(2)	696	(3)
Mitchell	192	140	99	5	52	41	94	37.1	(1)	(1)	2.1	4.9	4.8	4.3	22	885	0.2
Montague	27	26	87	47	1	−61	40	(1)	(1)	(1)	0.1	0.1	0.5	0.4	1	929	(3)
Montgomery	7,104	6,619	5,488	5,220	485	1,131	268	7.3	20.6	5.1	45.3	38.8	46.6	51.4	828	1,017	7.0
Moore																921	
Morris	3,706	3,342	2,610	2,043	364	732	567	10.9	28.0	27.8	35.5	40.7	39.7	40.6	550	259	14.3
Motley			3			−3	3		(1)				2.2			1,030	
Nacogdoches	7,030	6,677	4,257	3,040	353	2,420	1,217	5.3	56.8	40.0	25.7	27.1	26.6	26.2	345	1,059	6.6
Navarro	10,968	9,072	6,266	5,344	1,896	2,806	922	20.9	44.8	17.3	23.3	20.9	23.8	24.6	304	1,060	10.3
Newton	3,864	2,485	1,558	1,507	1,379	927	51	55.5	59.5	3.4	35.6	34.1	33.5	34.6	553	889	4.3
Nolan	111	20	32	5	91	−12	27	(1)	(1)	(1)	0.9	0.8	2.0	0.8	9	880	0.1
Nueces	742	577	707	629	165	−130	78	28.6	−18.4	12.4	3.4	5.5	8.7	8.2	35	2,275	0.3
Ochiltree																891	
Oldham		1	3		−1	−2	3	(1)	(1)			0.3	1.1			1,543	
Orange	1,898	1,018	829	463	880	189	366	86.4	22.8	79.0	19.9	17.2	17.4	15.8	250	363	5.2
Palo Pinto	528	292	67	85	236	225	−18	80.8	(1)	(1)	2.7	2.4	0.8	1.4	28	958	0.6
Panola	8,842	9,204	6,350	4,924	−362	2,854	1,426	−3.9	44.9	29.0	43.3	43.0	44.3	40.3	763	842	10.5
Parker	693	865	671	615	−172	194	56	−19.9	28.9	9.1	2.6	3.3	3.1	3.9	27	875	0.8
Parmer[4]																902	
Pecos[4]	2	22	8	127	−20	14	−119	(1)	(1)	−93.7	0.1	0.9	0.6	7.0	(2)	4,134	(3)
Polk	6,594	4,849	3,837	2,611	1,745	1,012	1,226	36.0	26.4	47.0	37.8	33.6	37.1	36.3	618	1,217	5.4
Potter	149	15	14	2	134	1	12	(1)	(1)	(1)	1.2	0.8	1.6	(1)	12	934	0.2
Presidio[4]	31	53	26	429	−22	27	−403	(1)	(1)	−93.9	0.6	1.4	1.5	14.9	6	3,812	(3)
Rains	616	539	415	250	77	124	165	14.3	29.9	66.0	9.1	8.8	10.6	8.2	100	267	2.3
Randall		1			−1	1		(1)				0.1				937	
Reagan[4]	2				2						0.5				5	1,071	
Red River	8,673	8,422	6,628	6,242	251	1,794	386	3.0	27.1	6.2	30.4	28.2	30.9	36.3	436	1,039	8.3
Reeves[4]	82	12	7		70	5	7	(1)	(1)		1.9	0.6	0.6		19	2,781	(3)
Refugio	481	461	324	336	20	137	−12	4.3	42.3	−3.6	17.1	28.1	26.2	21.2	206	740	0.6
Roberts	3	9	2		−6	7	2	(1)	(1)		0.3	1.5	0.6		3	882	(3)
Robertson	14,571	16,747	14,142	10,925	−2,176	2,605	3,217	−13.0	18.4	29.4	53.1	53.2	53.4	48.8	1,131	872	16.7
Rockwall	731	402	216	83	329	186	133	81.8	86.1	(1)	9.1	4.7	3.6	2.8	100	149	4.9
Runnels	133	33	31	13	100	2	18	(1)	(1)	(1)	0.6	0.6	1.0	1.3	6	1,083	0.1
Rusk	11,314	11,039	7,624	8,169	275	3,415	−545	2.5	44.8	−6.7	42.0	42.3	41.1	43.0	724	983	11.5
Sabine	1,679	1,752	1,084	993	−73	668	91	−4.2	61.6	9.2	19.6	27.4	21.8	23.9	244	589	2.9
San Augustine	3,453	2,921	2,131	1,915	532	790	216	18.2	37.1	11.3	30.7	34.6	31.9	37.7	442	622	5.6
San Jacinto	5,193	5,531	4,328	3,293	−338	1,203	1,035	−6.1	27.8	31.4	54.4	53.8	58.8	53.2	1,194	602	8.6
San Patricio	79	36	25	74	43	11	−49	(1)	(1)	(1)	1.1	1.5	1.9	7.3	11	676	0.1
San Saba	103	61	53	140	42	8	−87	(1)	(1)	−62.2	0.9	0.8	0.8	2.6	9	1,116	0.1
Schleicher[4]	44	13	4		31	9	4	(1)	(1)		2.3	2.5	2.6		24	1,387	(3)
Scurry	1		2	8	1	−2	−6			(1)	(3)		0.1	7.8	(2)	887	(3)
Shackelford	126	134	167	135	−8	−33	32	−6.0	−19.8	23.7	3.0	5.4	8.3	6.6	31	947	0.1
Shelby	5,274	4,117	2,954	2,154	1,157	1,163	800	28.1	39.4	37.1	20.0	20.1	20.6	22.6	249	833	6.3
Sherman	2	3	1		−1	2	1	(1)	(1)		0.1	2.9	(1)		1	935	(3)
Smith	17,246	16,043	12,690	10,357	1,203	3,353	2,333	7.5	26.4	22.5	41.3	42.9	44.8	47.4	704	920	18.7
Somervell	1	6	6	24	−5		−18	(1)		(1)	(3)	0.2	0.2	0.9	(2)	184	(3)
Starr	21	141	10	211	−120	131	−201	−85.1	(1)	−95.3	0.2	1.2	0.1	2.5	2	2,675	(3)
Stephens	4	5	5	25	−1		−20	(1)		(1)	0.1	0.1	0.1	0.5	(2)	925	(3)
Sterling[4]	1	2			−1	2		(1)			0.1	0.2			(2)	948	(3)
Stonewall	3		2	10	3	−2	−8	(1)	(1)	(1)	0.1		0.2	9.6	(2)	852	(3)
Sutton[4]	3	5	1		−2	4	1	(1)	(1)		0.2	0.3	0.2		2	1,521	(3)
Swisher																898	
Tarrant	15,418	5,756	4,316	2,160	9,662	1,440	2,156	167.9	33.4	99.8	14.2	11.0	10.5	8.8	166	903	17.1
Taylor	639	178	174	8	461	4	166	259.0	2.3	(1)	2.4	1.7	2.5	0.5	25	908	0.7
Terrell[4]	4				4						0.3				3	2,635	(3)
Terry[4]	1				1						0.1				(2)	870	(3)
Throckmorton	11	2	11	12	9	−9	−1	(1)	(1)	(1)	0.2	0.1	1.2	1.7	2	879	(3)
Titus	3,118	2,148	1,760	1,346	970	388	414	45.2	22.0	30.8	19.0	17.5	21.5	22.6	234	398	7.8
Tom Green[4]	716	898	202	645	−182	696	−443	−20.3	344.6	−68.7	4.0	13.2	3.9	17.8	42	1,454	0.5
Travis	15,473	13,299	10,090	8,599	2,174	3,209	1,491	16.3	31.8	17.3	27.8	28.1	27.8	31.8	386	1,004	15.4
Trinity	3,195	2,813	1,903	1,162	382	910	741	13.6	47.8	63.8	25.0	25.6	24.9	23.6	334	716	4.5
Tyler	2,207	2,389	2,392	1,502	−182	−3	890	−7.6	−0.1	59.3	21.5	20.1	22.0	25.8	274	908	2.4
Upshur	5,649	4,957	3,929	3,381	692	1,028	548	14.0	26.2	16.2	28.3	30.5	30.9	32.9	395	600	9.4
Upton[4]	12		1		12	−1	1	(1)			2.4		(1)		25	1,195	(3)
Uvalde	262	129	84	63	133	45	21	103.1	(1)	(1)	2.3	2.8	2.2	2.5	24	1,589	0.2
Val Verde[4]	153	156	108		−3	48	108	−1.9	44.4		1.8	3.0	3.8		18	3,083	(3)

[1] Per cent not shown where base is less than 100.
[2] Less than 1 per 1,000 whites.
[3] Less than one-tenth of 1 per cent.
[4] For changes in boundaries, see note at end of table.

TABLE II.—NEGRO POPULATION, 1910, 1900, 1890, 1880, DECENNIAL INCREASES, PROPORTION NEGRO, LAND AREA, AND NEGRO POPULATION PER SQUARE MILE, BY COUNTIES, FOR SOUTHERN STATES—Continued.

[A minus sign (−) denotes decrease.]

STATE AND COUNTY.	NEGRO POPULATION.				INCREASE.						PERCENTAGE NEGRO IN TOTAL POPULATION.				Negroes per 1,000 whites, 1910	Land area, square miles, 1910	Negroes per square mile, 1910
					Number.			Per cent.									
	1910	1900	1890	1880	1900-1910	1890-1900	1880-1890	1900-1910	1890-1900	1880-1890	1910	1900	1890	1880			
TEXAS—Con.																	
Van Zandt	1,534	1,365	1,098	1,163	169	267	−65	12.4	24.3	−5.6	6.0	5.4	6.8	9.2	64	831	1.8
Victoria	3,600	3,787	3,519	2,406	−187	268	1,113	−4.9	7.6	46.3	24.0	27.7	40.3	38.3	316	890	4.0
Walker	8,362	8,319	7,232	6,766	43	1,087	466	0.5	15.0	6.9	52.1	52.6	56.2	56.3	1,086	791	10.6
Waller	6,712	7,871	6,703	5,830	−1,159	1,168	873	−14.7	17.4	15.0	55.3	55.3	61.6	64.6	1,237	519	12.9
Ward [1]	3	3	3				3				0.1	0.2	[2]		1	827	[3]
Washington	12,017	16,039	15,200	14,719	−4,022	839	481	−25.1	5.5	3.3	47.0	48.7	52.1	53.4	887	628	19.1
Webb [1]	38	205	214	184	−167	−9	30	−81.5	−4.2	16.3	0.2	0.9	1.4	3.5	2	3,219	[3]
Wharton	8,889	8,717	6,119	3,631	172	2,598	2,488	2.0	42.5	68.5	42.1	51.5	80.7	79.8	729	1,112	8.0
Wheeler	2	14	16	35	−12	−2	−19	[2]	[2]	[2]	[3]	2.2	2.1	6.8	[4]	895	[3]
Wichita	612	204	128	17	408	76	111	200.0	59.4	[2]	3.8	3.5	2.6	3.9	40	604	1.0
Wilbarger	70	43	26		27	17	26	[2]	[2]		0.6	0.7	0.4		6	928	0.1
Williamson	7,370	4,332	2,755	1,631	3,038	1,577	1,124	70.1	57.2	68.9	17.5	11.4	10.6	10.8	211	1,129	6.5
Wilson	956	1,114	1,053	921	−158	61	132	−14.2	5.8	14.3	5.6	8.0	9.9	12.9	59	813	1.2
Winkler [1]	1				1				[2]		0.2				2	844	[2]
Wise	67	167	161	165	−100	6	−4	−59.9	3.7	−2.4	0.3	0.6	0.7	1.0	3	863	0.1
Wood	3,926	4,012	3,249	2,558	−86	763	691	−2.1	23.5	27.0	16.8	19.1	23.3	22.8	201	657	6.0
Yoakum [1]																879	
Young	3	7	15	17	−4	−8	−2	[2]	[2]	[2]	[3]	0.1	0.3	0.4	[4]	875	[3]
Zapata				7			−7			[2]				0.2		1,288	
Zavalla	1	1	3	10		−2	−7		[2]	[2]	0.1	0.1	0.3	2.4	[4]	1,348	[3]
VIRGINIA	671,096	660,722	635,438	631,616	10,374	25,284	3,822	1.6	4.0	0.6	32.6	35.6	38.4	41.8	483	40,262	16.7
Accomac	13,273	11,825	9,730	9,393	1,448	2,095	337	12.2	21.5	3.6	36.2	36.3	35.7	38.5	568	502	26.4
Albemarle [1]	9,673	10,337	11,598	16,659	−664	−1,261	−5,061	−6.4	−10.9	−30.4	32.4	36.3	43.8	51.1	479	750	16.2
Alexandria	2,645	2,467	2,123	2,194	178	344	−71	7.2	16.2	−3.2	25.9	38.4	49.9	56.4	349	31	213.5
Alleghany [1]	2,945	4,013	2,328	1,132	−1,068	1,685	1,196	−26.6	72.4	105.7	21.8	25.1	20.3	21.2	262	457	7.2
Amelia	5,490	5,985	6,045	7,340	−495	−60	−1,295	−8.3	−1.0	−17.6	63.0	66.2	66.7	70.7	1,700	371	14.8
Amherst	7,465	7,057	7,628	8,702	408	−571	−1,074	5.8	−7.5	−12.3	39.4	39.5	43.5	46.5	651	470	15.9
Appomatox	3,089	3,931	4,335	4,927	−842	−404	−592	−21.4	−9.3	−12.0	34.7	40.7	45.2	48.9	531	342	9.0
Augusta [1]	4,541	5,700	6,112	7,085	−1,159	−412	−973	−20.3	−6.7	−13.7	14.0	17.6	20.4	24.4	163	1,003	7.0
Bath	1,176	1,006	761	961	170	245	−200	16.9	32.2	−20.8	18.0	18.0	16.6	21.4	219	545	2.2
Bedford	8,455	9,739	11,149	12,677	−1,284	−1,410	−1,528	−13.2	−12.6	−12.1	28.6	32.1	35.7	40.6	401	791	10.7
Bland	133	212	241	254	−79	−29	−13	−37.3	−12.0	−5.1	2.6	3.9	4.7	5.1	26	360	0.4
Botetourt	3,495	3,877	3,732	4,650	−382	145	−918	−9.9	−3.9	−19.7	19.7	22.6	25.1	31.4	246	548	6.4
Brunswick	11,366	10,842	10,584	10,685	524	258	−101	4.8	2.4	−0.9	59.1	59.5	61.4	64.0	1,443	557	20.4
Buchanan [1]	4	5	24	33	−1	−19	−9	−20.0	[2]	[2]	[3]	0.1	0.4	0.6	[4]	514	
Buckingham	7,570	7,851	7,597	8,773	−281	254	−1,176	−3.6	3.3	−13.4	49.8	51.4	52.8	56.5	992	584	13.0
Campbell [1]	9,002	9,615	9,998	10,479	−613	−383	−481	−6.4	−3.8	−4.6	39.1	41.3	46.8	51.6	641	552	33.2
Caroline	8,750	9,042	9,322	9,628	−292	−280	−306	−3.2	−3.0	−3.2	52.7	54.1	55.9	55.8	1,115	529	16.5
Carroll	268	339	358	346	−71	−19	12	−20.9	−5.3	3.5	1.3	1.8	2.3	2.6	13	458	0.6
Charles City	3,765	3,696	3,717	3,751	69	−21	−34	1.9	−0.6	−0.9	71.7	73.3	73.4	68.1	2,738	188	20.0
Charlotte	8,335	8,545	9,361	10,949	−210	−816	−1,588	−2.5	−8.7	−14.5	52.8	55.7	62.1	65.7	1,119	496	16.8
Chesterfield [1]	7,527	11,037	10,811	11,521	−3,510	226	−710	−31.8	2.1	−6.2	35.3	40.9	41.2	45.9	547	471	16.0
Clarke	1,900	2,231	2,454	2,537	−331	−223	−83	−14.8	−9.1	−3.3	25.4	28.1	30.4	33.0	341	171	11.1
Craig	207	261	149	236	−54	112	−87	−20.7	75.2	−36.9	4.4	6.1	3.9	6.2	46	333	0.6
Culpeper	5,262	6,053	6,085	6,623	−791	−32	−538	−13.1	−0.5	−8.1	39.1	42.9	46.0	49.4	641	384	13.7
Cumberland	6,053	6,205	6,622	7,417	−152	−417	−795	−2.4	−6.3	−10.7	65.8	69.0	69.8	70.4	1,926	293	20.7
Dickenson	7		26		7	−26	26		[2]		0.1		0.5		[4]	325	
Dinwiddie	9,368	9,500	8,394	6,727	−132	1,106	1,667	−1.4	13.2	24.8	60.7	61.8	62.1	60.0	1,542	518	39.1
Elizabeth City	7,992	8,582	7,774	6,531	−590	808	1,243	−6.9	10.4	19.0	37.7	44.1	48.1	61.1	604	54	148.0
Essex	5,315	6,125	6,462	7,569	−810	−337	−1,107	−13.2	−5.2	−14.6	58.4	63.1	64.3	68.6	1,402	258	20.6
Fairfax	4,864	5,003	5,069	5,264	−139	−66	−195	−2.8	−1.3	−3.7	23.7	26.9	30.4	32.8	310	417	11.7
Fauquier	7,486	8,298	7,904	9,305	−812	394	−1,401	−9.8	5.0	−15.1	33.2	35.5	35.0	40.5	498	666	11.2
Floyd	837	1,075	1,175	1,274	−238	−100	−99	−22.1	−8.5	−7.8	5.9	7.0	8.2	9.6	63	376	2.2
Fluvanna	3,374	4,011	4,457	5,290	−637	−446	−833	−15.9	−10.0	−15.7	40.5	44.3	46.9	49.0	682	285	11.8
Franklin	5,435	5,947	6,248	8,015	−512	−301	−1,767	−8.6	−4.8	−22.0	20.5	22.9	25.0	32.0	258	697	7.8
Frederick	694	753	805	1,039	−59	−52	−234	−7.8	−6.5	−22.5	5.4	5.7	6.3	8.2	57	434	4.0
Giles	755	799	837	1,109	−44	−38	−272	−5.5	−4.5	−24.5	6.7	7.4	9.2	12.6	69	369	2.0
Gloucester	5,907	6,608	6,216	6,533	−701	392	−317	−10.6	6.3	−4.9	47.3	51.5	53.3	55.0	899	223	26.5
Goochland	5,230	5,558	5,874	6,234	−328	−316	−360	−5.9	−5.4	−5.8	56.6	58.4	59.0	60.6	1,305	287	18.2
Grayson	939	959	920	997	−20	39	−77	−2.1	4.2	−7.7	4.7	5.7	6.4	7.6	50	425	2.2
Greene	1,339	1,431	1,508	1,825	−92	−77	−317	−6.4	−5.1	−17.4	19.3	23.0	26.8	31.3	239	155	8.6
Greensville	7,393	6,356	5,311	5,650	1,037	1,045	−339	16.3	19.7	−6.0	62.2	65.1	64.5	67.2	1,644	307	24.1
Halifax	20,013	19,275	19,416	20,295	738	−141	−879	3.8	−0.7	−4.3	50.0	51.8	56.4	60.4	999	814	24.6
Hanover	7,040	7,898	8,211	9,282	−858	−313	−1,071	−10.9	−3.8	−11.5	40.9	44.8	47.2	49.9	693	512	13.8
Henrico [1]	6,837	12,816	11,265	10,046	−5,979	1,551	1,219	−46.7	13.8	12.1	29.2	42.6	51.2	52.6	412	266	193.4
Henry	7,462	8,383	8,283	7,395	−921	100	888	−11.0	1.2	12.0	40.4	43.5	45.5	46.2	679	444	16.8
Highland	260	378	422	449	−118	−44	−27	−31.2	−10.4	−6.0	4.9	6.7	7.9	8.7	51	422	0.6
Isle of Wight	7,512	6,268	5,144	4,555	1,244	1,124	589	19.8	21.9	12.9	50.3	47.8	45.5	43.1	1,013	314	23.9
James City	3,034	3,020	3,326	3,195	14	−306	131	0.5	−9.2	4.1	47.9	52.7	58.9	58.9	919	164	18.5
King and Queen	5,373	5,259	5,430	6,078	114	−171	−648	2.2	−3.1	−10.7	56.1	56.8	56.2	57.9	1,278	320	16.8
King George	2,913	3,322	3,208	3,235	−409	114	−27	−12.3	3.6	−0.8	45.7	48.0	48.3	50.6	841	180	16.2

[1] For changes in boundaries, see note at end of table.   [3] Less than one-tenth of 1 per cent.
[2] Per cent not shown where base is less than 100.   [4] Less than 1 per 1,000 whites.

TABLE II.—NEGRO POPULATION, 1910, 1900, 1890, 1880, DECENNIAL INCREASES, PROPORTION NEGRO, LAND AREA, AND NEGRO POPULATION PER SQUARE MILE, BY COUNTIES, FOR SOUTHERN STATES—Continued.

[A minus sign (−) denotes decrease.]

| STATE AND COUNTY. | NEGRO POPULATION. | | | | INCREASE. | | | | | | PERCENTAGE NEGRO IN TOTAL POPULATION. | | | | Negroes per 1,000 whites, 1910 | Land area, square miles, 1910 | Negroes per square mile, 1910 |
| | | | | | Number. | | | Per cent. | | | | | | | | | |
	1910	1900	1890	1880	1900–1910	1890–1900	1880–1890	1900–1910	1890–1900	1880–1890	1910	1900	1890	1880			
VIRGINIA—Con.																	
King William	4,855	4,962	5,685	5,464	−107	−723	221	−2.2	−12.7	4.0	56.8	59.2	59.2	62.4	1,382	263	18.5
Lancaster	5,139	4,891	4,020	3,534	248	871	486	5.1	21.7	13.8	52.7	54.7	55.9	57.4	1,114	130	39.5
Lee	952	740	1,213	922	212	−473	291	28.6	−39.0	31.6	4.0	3.7	6.7	6.1	42	446	2.1
Loudoun	5,221	5,868	6,578	7,243	−647	−710	−665	−11.0	−10.8	−9.2	24.7	26.7	28.3	30.6	327	519	10.1
Louisa	7,883	8,621	9,805	11,531	−738	−1,184	−1,726	−8.6	−12.1	−15.0	47.6	52.2	57.7	60.9	907	516	15.3
Lunenburg	6,811	6,572	6,736	6,924	239	−164	−188	3.6	−2.4	−2.7	53.3	56.1	59.2	60.0	1,141	430	15.8
Madison	3,264	3,521	3,965	4,556	−257	−444	−591	−7.3	−11.2	−13.0	32.5	34.5	38.8	43.1	481	324	10.1
Mathews	2,513	2,395	2,137	2,459	118	258	−322	4.9	12.1	−13.1	28.2	29.1	28.2	32.8	392	94	26.7
Mecklenburg	16,394	16,198	16,030	16,388	196	168	−358	1.2	1.0	−2.2	56.6	61.0	63.2	66.6	1,305	669	24.5
Middlesex	4,636	4,536	4,317	3,634	100	219	683	2.2	5.1	18.8	52.4	55.2	57.9	58.1	1,100	146	31.8
Montgomery[1]	2,323	2,925	3,515	4,227	−602	−590	−712	−20.6	−16.8	−16.8	13.5	18.5	19.8	25.3	155	396	7.5
Nansemond	15,536	12,962	10,765	8,175	2,574	2,197	2,590	19.9	20.4	31.7	57.8	56.2	54.7	51.4	1,369	423	36.7
Nelson	5,263	5,672	6,303	7,508	−409	−631	−1,205	−7.2	−10.0	−16.0	31.3	33.5	41.1	45.4	455	473	11.1
New Kent	2,791	3,204	3,545	3,232	−413	−341	313	−12.9	−9.6	9.7	59.6	65.9	64.3	58.6	1,569	191	14.6
Norfolk[1]	31,791	31,600	19,216	15,556	191	12,384	3,660	0.6	64.4	23.5	60.3	62.2	66.5	61.5	1,520	404	165.3
Northampton	9,314	7,627	5,479	5,263	1,687	2,148	216	22.1	39.2	4.1	55.9	55.4	53.1	57.5	1,266	239	39.0
Northumberland	4,267	4,166	3,090	3,483	101	1,076	−393	2.4	34.8	−11.3	39.6	42.3	39.2	43.9	655	205	20.8
Nottoway	7,347	7,400	7,623	8,144	−53	−223	−521	−0.7	−2.9	−6.4	54.6	59.8	65.8	73.0	1,201	310	23.7
Orange	5,526	5,519	6,241	6,842	7	−722	−601	0.1	−11.6	−8.8	41.0	43.9	48.7	52.4	694	359	15.4
Page	1,166	1,440	1,772	1,119	−274	−332	653	−19.0	−18.7	58.4	8.2	10.4	13.5	11.2	90	322	3.6
Patrick	1,618	1,624	2,068	2,734	−6	−444	−666	−0.4	−21.5	−24.4	9.4	10.5	14.6	21.3	104	485	3.3
Pittsylvania[1]	20,163	21,289	23,553	22,803	−1,126	−2,264	750	−5.3	−9.6	3.3	39.8	45.4	47.5	50.6	660	1,012	26.0
Powhatan	3,633	4,481	4,433	5,091	−848	48	−658	−18.9	1.1	12.9	59.6	65.7	65.3	65.1	1,473	273	13.3
Prince Edward	8,458	9,769	9,924	9,914	−1,311	−155	10	−13.4	−1.6	0.1	59.3	64.9	67.5	67.6	1,456	356	23.8
Prince George	4,551	4,858	5,132	6,799	−307	−274	−1,667	−6.3	−5.3	−24.5	58.0	62.7	65.2	67.6	1,380	294	15.5
Prince William	2,825	2,871	2,595	2,600	−46	276	−5	−1.6	10.6	−0.2	23.5	25.8	26.5	28.3	307	345	8.2
Princess Anne	5,818	5,687	4,130	4,262	131	1,557	−132	2.3	37.7	−3.1	50.5	50.8	43.4	45.4	1,019	279	20.9
Pulaski	2,930	3,237	3,120	2,452	−307	117	668	−9.5	3.8	27.2	17.0	22.2	24.4	28.0	205	333	8.8
Rappahannock	2,148	2,722	2,815	3,536	−574	−93	−721	−21.1	−3.3	−20.4	26.7	30.8	32.4	38.1	364	274	7.8
Richmond	3,071	2,929	3,148	3,389	142	−219	−241	4.8	−7.0	−7.1	41.4	41.3	44.1	47.1	707	204	15.1
Roanoke[1]	3,525	3,845	4,076	4,828	−320	−231	−752	−8.3	−5.7	−15.6	18.0	24.3	29.2	36.8	219	300	37.5
Rockbridge[1]	3,528	4,084	5,131	5,343	−556	−1,047	−212	−13.6	−20.4	−4.0	16.7	18.7	22.2	26.7	200	613	6.4
Rockingham	2,335	2,632	2,814	3,433	−297	−182	−619	−11.3	−6.5	−18.0	6.7	7.9	9.0	11.6	72	876	2.7
Russell[1]	1,025	764	1,203	1,272	261	−439	−69	34.2	−36.5	−5.4	4.4	4.2	7.5	9.1	46	496	2.1
Scott	503	627	968	676	−124	−341	292	−19.8	−35.2	43.2	2.1	2.8	4.5	3.9	22	543	0.9
Shenandoah	493	649	842	1,006	−156	−193	−164	−24.0	−22.9	−16.3	2.4	3.2	4.3	5.5	24	510	1.0
Smyth	981	1,170	1,224	1,640	−189	−54	−416	−16.2	−4.4	−25.4	4.8	6.8	9.2	13.5	51	435	2.3
Southampton	16,091	13,683	11,782	10,565	2,408	1,901	1,217	17.6	16.1	11.5	61.2	59.9	58.7	58.7	1,576	604	26.6
Spotsylvania	3,593	3,886	4,395	4,547	−293	−509	−152	−7.5	−11.6	−3.3	36.2	42.1	45.3	46.3	567	412	12.3
Stafford	1,720	1,608	1,469	1,653	112	139	−184	7.0	9.5	−11.1	21.3	19.9	20.0	22.9	271	274	6.3
Surry	6,005	5,183	5,017	4,559	822	166	458	15.9	3.3	10.0	61.8	61.0	60.8	61.7	1,619	278	21.6
Sussex	8,962	7,961	7,576	6,701	1,001	385	875	12.6	5.1	13.1	65.6	65.9	68.3	66.6	1,906	515	17.4
Tazewell	2,820	3,582	3,504	1,914	−762	78	1,590	−21.3	2.2	83.1	11.3	15.3	17.6	14.9	127	531	5.3
Warren	1,131	1,463	1,264	1,441	−332	199	−177	−22.7	15.7	−12.3	13.2	16.6	15.3	19.5	152	216	5.2
Warwick[1]	4,334	3,729	1,320	1,479	605	2,409	−159	16.2	182.5	−10.8	71.7	76.3	60.0	65.5	2,539	67	168.0
Washington[1]	2,312	2,555	2,965	4,086	−243	−410	−1,121	−9.5	−13.8	−27.4	7.0	8.8	11.4	16.2	76	602	5.7
Westmoreland	4,668	4,861	4,737	5,100	−193	124	−363	−4.0	2.6	−7.1	50.1	52.6	56.4	57.7	1,005	252	18.5
Wise[1]	2,861	1,965	582	101	896	1,383	481	45.6	237.6	476.2	8.4	10.0	6.2	1.3	91	420	6.8
Wythe	2,188	2,783	3,170	2,850	−595	−387	320	−21.4	−12.2	11.2	10.7	13.6	17.6	19.9	120	479	4.6
York	3,764	4,081	4,395	4,512	−317	−314	−117	−7.8	−7.1	−2.6	48.5	54.5	57.9	61.4	943	136	27.7
Independent cities.[2]																	
Alexandria city	4,188	4,533	5,113	5,380	−345	−580	−267	−7.6	−11.3	−5.0	27.3	31.2	35.7	39.4	376	1	4,188.0
Bristol city[1]	1,144	1,027	833	....	117	194	833	11.4	23.3	......	18.3	22.4	28.7	......	224	2	572.0
Buena Vista city	416	410	....	....	6	410	....	1.5	......	......	12.8	17.2	......	......	147	3	138.7
Charlottesville city[1]	2,524	2,613	2,528	....	−89	85	2,528	−3.4	3.4	......	37.3	40.5	45.2	......	596	1	2,524.0
Clifton Forge city[1]	1,092	....	....	....	1,092	....	....	......	......	......	19.0	......	......	......	235	1	1,092.0
Danville city[1]	6,207	6,515	5,538	4,397	−308	977	1,141	−4.7	17.6	25.9	32.6	39.4	53.7	58.4	485	3	2,069.0
Fredericksburg city	1,480	1,621	1,682	1,859	−141	−61	−177	−8.7	−3.6	−9.5	25.2	32.0	37.1	37.1	337	1	1,480.0
Lynchburg city[1]	9,466	8,254	9,802	8,474	1,212	−1,548	1,328	14.7	−15.8	15.7	32.1	43.7	49.7	53.1	473	5	1,893.2
Newport News city[1]	7,259	6,798	2,546	....	461	4,252	2,546	6.8	167.0	......	35.9	34.6	57.2	......	561	2	3,629.5
Norfolk city[1]	25,039	20,230	16,244	10,068	4,809	3,986	6,176	23.8	24.5	61.3	37.1	43.4	46.6	45.8	591	7	3,577.0
Petersburg city	11,014	10,751	12,221	11,701	263	−1,470	520	2.4	−12.0	4.4	45.7	49.3	53.9	54.0	840	3	3,671.3
Portsmouth city[1]	11,617	5,625	4,018	3,829	5,992	1,607	189	106.5	40.0	4.9	35.0	32.3	30.3	33.6	539	3	3,872.3
Radford city[1]	665	456	....	....	209	456	....	45.8	......	......	15.8	13.6	......	......	188	5	133.0
Richmond city[1]	46,733	32,230	32,330	27,832	14,503	−100	4,498	45.0	−0.3	16.2	36.6	37.9	39.7	43.8	578	11	4,248.5
Roanoke city[1]	7,924	5,834	4,929	....	2,090	905	4,929	35.8	18.4	......	22.7	27.1	30.5	......	294	5	1,584.8
Staunton city[1]	2,476	1,828	2,295	2,225	648	−467	70	35.4	−20.3	3.1	23.3	25.1	32.9	33.4	305	3	825.3
Winchester city	1,038	1,105	1,423	1,517	−67	−318	−94	−6.1	−22.3	−6.2	17.7	21.4	27.4	30.6	215	1	1,038.0

[1] For changes in boundaries, see note at end of table.   [2] The population of the independent cities is not included in the population given for counties.

TABLE **II.**—NEGRO POPULATION, 1910, 1900, 1890, 1880, DECENNIAL INCREASES, PROPORTION NEGRO, LAND AREA, AND NEGRO POPULATION PER SQUARE MILE, BY COUNTIES, FOR SOUTHERN STATES—Continued.

[A minus sign (−) denotes decrease.]

STATE AND COUNTY.	NEGRO POPULATION.				INCREASE. Number.			INCREASE. Per cent.			PERCENTAGE NEGRO IN TOTAL POPULATION.				Negroes per 1,000 whites, 1910	Land area, square miles, 1910	Negroes per square mile, 1910
	1910	1900	1890	1880	1900–1910	1890–1900	1880–1890	1900–1910	1890–1900	1880–1890	1910	1900	1890	1880			
WEST VIRGINIA.	64,173	43,499	32,690	25,886	20,674	10,809	6,804	47.5	33.1	26.3	5.3	4.5	4.3	4.2	55	24,022	2.7
Barbour	920	808	498	457	112	310	41	13.9	62.2	9.0	5.8	5.7	3.9	3.9	62	348	2.6
Berkeley	1,801	1,765	1,694	1,928	36	71	−234	2.0	4.2	−12.1	8.2	9.1	9.1	11.1	89	325	5.5
Boone	164	135	170	189	29	−35	−19	21.5	−20.6	−10.1	1.6	1.6	2.5	3.2	16	506	0.3
Braxton	221	187	134	104	34	53	30	18.2	39.6	28.8	1.0	1.0	1.0	1.1	10	517	0.4
Brooke	151	139	114	85	12	25	29	8.6	21.9	(1)	1.4	1.9	1.7	1.4	14	89	1.7
Cabell	2,447	1,537	1,493	902	910	44	591	59.2	2.9	65.5	5.2	5.3	6.3	6.6	55	261	9.4
Calhoun	80	83	81	74	−3	2	7	(1)	(1)	(1)	0.7	0.8	1.0	1.2	7	286	0.3
Clay	5	18	....	....	−13	18	....	(1)	....	....	(2)	0.2	(2)	(2)	(3)	332	(2)
Doddridge	8	25	131	54	−17	−106	77	(1)	−80.9	(1)	0.1	0.2	1.1	0.5	(3)	317	(2)
Fayette	9,311	5,857	3,054	1,122	3,454	2,803	1,932	59.0	91.8	172.2	17.9	18.3	14.9	9.7	219	667	14.0
Gilmer	17	36	50	47	−19	−14	3	(1)	(1)	(1)	0.1	0.3	0.5	0.7	1	331	0.1
Grant	253	252	379	503	1	−127	−124	0.4	−33.5	−24.7	3.2	3.5	5.6	9.1	33	461	0.5
Greenbrier	1,779	1,829	1,993	1,981	−50	−164	12	−2.7	−8.2	0.6	7.2	8.8	11.1	13.2	78	998	1.8
Hampshire	303	461	567	652	−158	−106	−85	−34.3	−18.7	−13.0	2.6	3.9	5.0	6.3	27	648	0.5
Hancock	37	46	21	24	−9	25	−3	(1)	(1)	(1)	0.4	0.7	0.3	0.5	4	83	0.4
Hardy	387	457	590	752	−70	−133	−162	−15.3	−22.5	−21.5	4.2	5.4	7.8	11.1	44	574	0.7
Harrison	1,359	1,252	760	889	107	492	−129	8.5	64.7	−14.5	2.8	4.5	3.5	4.4	29	416	3.3
Jackson	26	115	87	103	−89	28	−16	−77.4	(1)	−15.5	0.1	0.5	0.5	0.6	1	461	0.1
Jefferson	3,499	3,941	4,116	4,045	−442	−175	71	−11.2	−4.3	1.8	22.0	24.7	26.5	27.0	282	211	16.6
Kanawha	6,476	3,983	3,402	2,870	2,493	581	532	62.6	17.1	18.5	8.0	7.3	8.0	8.8	86	860	7.5
Lewis	239	178	261	323	61	−83	−62	34.3	−31.8	−19.2	1.3	1.0	1.6	2.4	13	393	0.6
Lincoln	30	63	211	52	−33	−148	159	(1)	−70.1	(1)	0.1	0.4	1.9	0.6	1	418	0.1
Logan ⁴	532	61	685	109	471	−624	576	(1)	−91.1	528.4	3.7	0.9	6.2	1.5	38	438	1.2
McDowell	14,667	5,969	1,591	3	8,698	4,378	1,588	145.7	275.2	(1)	30.6	31.8	21.8	0.1	442	533	27.5
Marion	851	482	104	155	369	378	−51	76.6	363.5	−32.9	2.0	1.5	0.5	0.9	20	315	2.7
Marshall	575	499	236	223	76	263	13	15.2	111.4	5.8	1.8	1.9	1.1	1.2	18	310	1.9
Mason	349	537	759	859	−188	−222	−100	−35.0	−29.2	−11.6	1.5	2.2	3.3	3.9	15	475	0.7
Mercer	5,960	2,902	2,022	366	3,058	880	1,656	105.4	43.5	452.5	15.5	12.6	12.6	4.9	184	419	14.2
Mineral	601	665	481	489	−64	184	−8	−9.6	38.3	−1.6	3.6	5.2	4.0	5.7	37	349	1.7
Mingo ⁴	1,236	309	....	....	927	309	....	300.0	....	....	6.4	2.7	....	....	68	416	3.0
Monongalia	294	299	227	317	−5	72	−90	−1.7	31.7	−28.4	1.2	1.6	1.4	2.1	12	358	0.8
Monroe	673	830	979	1,129	−157	−149	−150	−18.9	−15.2	−13.3	5.2	6.3	7.9	9.8	54	457	1.5
Morgan	177	220	275	197	−43	−55	78	−19.5	−20.0	39.6	2.3	3.0	4.1	3.4	23	233	0.8
Nicholas	48	19	21	58	29	−2	−37	(1)	(1)	(1)	0.3	0.2	0.2	0.8	3	680	0.1
Ohio	1,389	1,251	1,098	870	138	153	228	11.0	13.9	26.2	2.4	2.6	2.6	2.3	25	107	13.0
Pendleton	132	123	126	99	9	−3	27	7.3	−2.4	(1)	1.4	1.3	1.4	1.2	14	699	0.2
Pleasants	9	6	9	26	3	−3	−17	(1)	(1)	(1)	0.1	0.1	0.1	0.4	1	132	0.1
Pocahontas	445	625	353	334	−180	272	19	−28.8	77.1	5.7	3.0	7.3	5.2	6.0	31	904	0.5
Preston	151	162	134	206	−11	28	−72	−6.8	20.9	−35.0	0.6	0.7	0.7	1.1	6	650	0.2
Putnam	435	378	237	355	57	141	−118	15.1	59.5	−33.2	2.3	2.2	1.7	3.1	24	336	1.3
Raleigh	2,052	360	79	71	1,692	281	8	470.0	(1)	(1)	8.0	2.9	0.8	1.0	87	597	3.4
Randolph	376	519	262	112	−143	257	150	−27.6	98.1	133.9	1.4	2.9	2.3	1.4	15	1,036	0.4
Ritchie	26	26	36	64	....	−10	−28	(1)	(1)	(1)	0.1	0.1	0.2	0.5	1	453	0.1
Roane	18	32	29	39	−14	3	−10	(1)	(1)	(1)	0.1	0.2	0.2	0.3	(3)	522	(2)
Summers	1,130	1,115	1,127	771	15	−12	356	1.3	−1.1	46.2	6.1	6.9	8.6	8.5	65	369	3.1
Taylor	527	423	362	399	104	61	−37	24.6	16.9	−9.3	3.2	2.8	3.0	3.5	33	175	3.0
Tucker	344	353	183	26	−9	170	157	−2.5	92.9	(1)	1.8	2.6	2.8	0.8	19	405	0.8
Tyler	115	94	2	6	21	92	−4	(1)	(1)	(1)	0.7	0.5	(2)	0.1	7	260	0.4
Upshur	226	221	256	201	5	−35	55	2.3	−13.7	27.4	1.4	1.5	2.0	2.0	14	351	0.6
Wayne	169	321	160	220	−152	161	−60	−47.4	100.6	−27.3	0.7	1.4	0.9	1.5	7	517	0.3
Webster	8	12	11	2	−4	1	9	(1)	(1)	(1)	0.1	0.1	0.2	0.1	(3)	583	(2)
Wetzel	57	439	36	22	−382	403	14	−87.0	(1)	(1)	0.2	1.9	0.2	0.2	2	357	0.2
Wirt	40	64	24	13	−24	40	11	(1)	(1)	(1)	0.4	0.6	0.3	0.2	4	218	0.2
Wood	943	922	910	925	21	12	−15	2.3	1.3	−1.6	2.5	2.7	3.2	3.7	25	364	2.6
Wyoming	105	94	70	64	11	24	6	(1)	(1)	(1)	1.0	1.1	1.1	1.5	10	502	0.2

¹ Per cent not shown where base is less than 100.
² Less than one-tenth of 1 per cent.
³ Less than 1 per 1,000 whites.
⁴ For changes in boundaries, see note at end of table.

NOTES REGARDING CHANGES IN COUNTY AND CITY BOUNDARIES: 1880-1910.

ALABAMA.
Counties.

BLOUNT.—Parts annexed to Cullman between 1880 and 1890 and in 1901.
CALHOUN.—Part of Cleburne annexed in 1907; part annexed to Cleburne in 1907.
CLAY.—Part of Talladega annexed in 1895.
CLEBURNE.—Part of Calhoun annexed in 1907; part annexed to Calhoun in 1907.
COLBERT.—Part annexed to Franklin between 1890 and 1900; part of Lawrence annexed between 1890 and 1900.
CULLMAN.—Parts of Blount annexed between 1880 and 1890 and in 1901.
DALE.—Part taken to form part of Houston in 1903. (See also note.)
FRANKLIN.—Part of Colbert annexed between 1890 and 1900.
GENEVA.—Part taken to form part of Houston in 1903. (See also note.)
HENRY.—Part taken to form part of Houston in 1903. (See also note.)
HOUSTON.—Organized from parts of Dale, Geneva, and Henry in 1903. (See also note.)
JEFFERSON.—Part of Shelby annexed between 1880 and 1890; part annexed to Walker between 1890 and 1900.
LAWRENCE.—Part annexed to Colbert between 1890 and 1900.
SHELBY.—Part annexed to Jefferson between 1880 and 1890.
TALLADEGA.—Part annexed to Clay in 1895.
WALKER.—Part of Jefferson annexed between 1890 and 1900.

Note.—Dale, Geneva, Henry, and Houston Counties combined—Total Negro population: 1910, 29,862; 1900, 21,691; increase, 1900-1910, 8,171; per cent of increase 37.7.

ARKANSAS.
Counties.

ARKANSAS.—Part annexed to Jefferson between 1880 and 1890; part of Desha annexed between 1880 and 1890.
CLAY.—Part of Greene annexed between 1890 and 1900.
CLEBURNE.—Organized from parts of Independence, Van Buren, and White in 1883.
CLEVELAND.—Name changed in 1885.
COLUMBIA.—Part annexed to Lafayette in 1901.
CRAWFORD.—Part of Franklin annexed between 1890 and 1900.
DESHA.—Part annexed to Arkansas County between 1880 and 1890.
FRANKLIN.—Part of Madison annexed in 1885; part annexed to Crawford between 1890 and 1900.
GREENE.—Part annexed to Clay between 1890 and 1900.
HOWARD.—Part annexed to Sevier between 1890 and 1900.
INDEPENDENCE.—Part taken to form part of Cleburne in 1883.
JEFFERSON.—Part of Arkansas County annexed between 1880 and 1890.
LAFAYETTE.—Part of Columbia annexed in 1901.
LOGAN.—Part of Scott annexed in 1903.
LONOKE.—Part of Prairie annexed between 1880 and 1890.
MADISON.—Part annexed to Franklin in 1885.
MISSISSIPPI.—Island No. 25 ceded from Lauderdale, Tenn. (total population 115 in 1900), and annexed in 1905.
MONROE.—Part of Prairie annexed between 1880 and 1890.
PRAIRIE.—Parts annexed to Lonoke and Monroe between 1880 and 1890
SCOTT.—Part annexed to Logan in 1903.
SEBASTIAN.—Part of Indian Territory annexed in 1905.
SEVIER.—Part of Howard annexed between 1890 and 1900.
VAN BUREN.—Part taken to form part of Cleburne in 1883.
WHITE.—Part taken to form part of Cleburne in 1883.

FLORIDA.
Counties.

BREVARD.—Part taken to form part of Osceola in 1887; part taken to form St. Lucie in 1905. (See also Note 1.)
CITRUS.—Organized from part of Hernando in 1887.
DADE.—Part taken to form Palm Beach in 1909. (See also Note 2.)
DE SOTO.—Organized from part of Manatee in 1887.
HERNANDO.—Parts taken to form Citrus and Pasco in 1887.
LAKE.—Organized from parts of Orange and Sumter in 1887.
LEE.—Organized from part of Monroe in 1887.
MANATEE.—Part taken to form De Soto in 1887.
MONROE.—Part taken to form Lee in 1887.
ORANGE.—Parts taken to form parts of Lake and Osceola in 1887.
OSCEOLA.—Organized from parts of Brevard and Orange in 1887.
PALM BEACH.—Organized from part of Dade in 1909. (See also Note 2.)
PASCO.—Organized from part of Hernando in 1887; part annexed to Polk between 1890 and 1900.
POLK.—Part of Pasco annexed between 1890 and 1900.
ST. LUCIE.—Organized from part of Brevard in 1905. (See also Note 1.)
SUMTER.—Part taken to form part of Lake in 1887.

Note 1.—Brevard and St. Lucie Counties combined—Total Negro population: 1910, 2,264; 1900, 1,074; increase, 1900-1910, 1,190; per cent of increase, 110.8.

Note 2.—Dade and Palm Beach Counties combined—Total Negro population: 1910, 6,414; 1900, 1,293; increase, 1900-1910, 5,121; per cent of increase, 396.1.

GEORGIA.
Counties.

APPLING.—Part taken to form part of Jeff Davis in 1905. (See also Note 1.)
BEN HILL.—Organized from parts of Irwin and Wilcox in 1906. (See also Note 2.)
BERRIEN.—Part taken to form part of Tift in 1905. (See also Note 2.)
BULLOCH.—Part taken to form part of Jenkins in 1905. (See also Note 3.)
BURKE.—Part taken to form part of Jenkins in 1905. (See also Note 3.)
CLARKE.—Part of Oglethorpe annexed in 1906.
CLAYTON.—Part annexed to Fulton in 1908.
COFFEE.—Part taken to form part of Jeff Davis in 1905. (See also Note 1.)
CRISP.—Organized from part of Dooly in 1905. (See also Note 2.)
DECATUR.—Part taken to form part of Grady in 1905. (See also Note 4.)
DOOLY.—Parts taken to form Crisp and part of Turner in 1905. (See also Note 2.)
EMANUEL.—Parts taken to form parts of Jenkins and Toombs in 1905. (See also Note 3.)
FRANKLIN.—Part taken to form part of Stephens in 1905. (See also Note 5.)
FULTON.—Part of Clayton annexed in 1908.
GRADY.—Organized from parts of Decatur and Thomas in 1905. (See also Note 4.)
HABERSHAM.—Part taken to form part of Stephens in 1905. (See also Note 5.)
IRWIN.—Parts taken to form parts of Tift and Turner in 1905, and part of Ben Hill in 1906. (See also Note 2.)

JEFF DAVIS.—Organized from parts of Appling and Coffee in 1905. (See also Note 1.)
JENKINS.—Organized from parts of Bulloch, Burke, Emanuel, and Screven in 1905. (See also Note 3.)
MONTGOMERY.—Part taken to form part of Toombs in 1905. (See also Note 3.)
OGLETHORPE.—Part annexed to Clarke in 1906.
SCREVEN.—Part taken to form part of Jenkins in 1905. (See also Note 3.)
STEPHENS.—Organized from parts of Franklin and Habersham in 1905. (See also Note 5.)
TATTNALL.—Part taken to form part of Toombs in 1905. (See also Note 3.)
THOMAS.—Part taken to form part of Grady in 1905. (See also Note 4.)
TIFT.—Organized from parts of Berrien, Irwin, and Worth in 1905. (See also Note 2.)
TOOMBS.—Organized from parts of Emanuel, Montgomery, and Tattnall in 1905. (See also Note 3.)
TURNER.—Organized from parts of Dooly, Irwin, Wilcox, and Worth in 1905. (See also Note 2.)
WILCOX.—Parts taken to form part of Turner in 1905 and part of Ben Hill in 1906. (See also Note 2.)
WORTH.—Parts taken to form parts of Tift and Turner in 1905. (See also Note 2.)

Note 1.—Appling, Coffee, and Jeff Davis Counties combined—Total Negro population: 1910, 12,190; 1900, 10,124; increase, 1900-1910, 2,066; per cent of increase, 20.4.

Note 2.—Ben Hill, Berrien, Crisp, Dooly, Irwin, Tift, Turner, Wilcox, and Worth Counties combined—Total Negro population: 1910, 60,241; 1900, 37,917; increase, 1900-1910, 22,324; per cent of increase, 58.9.

Note 3.—Bulloch, Burke, Emanuel, Jenkins, Montgomery, Screven, Tattnall, and Toombs Counties combined—Total Negro population: 1910, 79,066; 1900, 66,978; increase, 1900-1910, 12,088; per cent of increase, 18.0.

Note 4.—Decatur, Grady, and Thomas Counties combined—Total Negro population: 1910, 41,227; 1900, 33,228; increase, 1900-1910, 7,999; per cent increase, 24.1.

Note 5.—Franklin, Habersham, and Stephens Counties combined—Total Negro population: 1910, 6,907; 1900, 5,996; increase, 1900-1910, 911; per cent of increase, 15.2.

KENTUCKY.
Counties.

ANDERSON.—Part of Washington annexed between 1880 and 1890.
BALLARD.—Part taken to form Carlisle in 1886.
BREATHITT.—Part taken to form part of Knott in 1884.
CARLISLE.—Organized from part of Ballard in 1886.
ESTILL.—Part annexed to Powell between 1890 and 1900.
FLOYD.—Part taken to form part of Knott in 1884.
KNOTT.—Organized from parts of Breathitt, Floyd, Letcher, Magoffin, and Perry in 1884.
LETCHER.—Part taken to form part of Knott in 1884.
MAGOFFIN.—Part taken to form part of Knott in 1884.
MENIFEE.—Parts of Powell and Wolfe annexed in 1880.
PERRY.—Part taken to form part of Knott in 1884.
POWELL.—Part annexed to Menifee in 1880; part of Estill annexed between 1890 and 1900.
WASHINGTON.—Part annexed to Anderson between 1880 and 1890.
WOLFE.—Part annexed to Menifee in 1880.

LOUISIANA.
Parishes.

ACADIA.—Organized from part of St. Landry in 1886.
CATAHOULA.—Part taken to form La Salle in 1910. (See also note.)
LA SALLE.—Organized from part of Catahoula in 1910. (See also note.)
ST. LANDRY.—Part taken to form Acadia in 1886.

NOTE.—Catahoula and La Salle Parishes combined—Total Negro population: 1910, 7,148; 1900, 6,793; increase, 1900-1910, 355; per cent of increase, 5.2.

MISSISSIPPI.
Counties.

COVINGTON.—Part taken to form part of Jefferson Davis in 1906. (See also Note 1.)
FORREST.—Organized from part of Perry in 1908. (See also Note 2.)
GEORGE.—Organized from parts of Greene and Jackson in 1910. (See also Note 3.)
GREENE.—Part taken to form part of George in 1910. (See also Note 3.)
HANCOCK.—Part taken to form part of Pearl River in 1890 and part annexed to Pearl River in 1908.
JACKSON.—Part taken to form part of George in 1910. (See also Note 3.)
JEFFERSON DAVIS.—Organized from parts of Covington and Lawrence in 1906. (See also Note 1.)
LAMAR.—Organized from parts of Marion and Pearl River in 1904. (See also Note 4.)
LAWRENCE.—Part taken to form part of Jefferson Davis in 1906. (See also Note 1.)
MARION.—Parts taken to form part of Pearl River in 1890 and part of Lamar in 1904. (See also Note 4.)
PEARL RIVER.—Organized from parts of Hancock and Marion in 1890; part taken to form part of Lamar in 1904; part of Hancock annexed in 1908. (See also Note 4.)
PERRY.—Part taken to form Forrest in 1908. (See also Note 2.)
WEBSTER.—Name changed from Sumner in 1882.

Note 1.—Covington, Jefferson Davis, and Lawrence Counties combined—Total Negro population: 1910, 17,128; 1900, 12,173; increase, 1900-1910, 4,955; per cent of increase, 40.7.

Note 2.—Forrest and Perry Counties combined—Total Negro population: 1910, 10,264; 1900, 4,822; increase, 1900-1910, 5,442; per cent of increase, 112.9.

Note 3.—George, Greene, and Jackson Counties combined—Total Negro population: 1910, 8,641; 1900, 7,593; increase, 1900-1910, 1,048; per cent of increase, 13.8.

Note 4.—Lamar, Marion, and Pearl River Counties combined—Total Negro population: 1910, 12,104; 1900, 6,115; increase, 1900-1910, 5,989; per cent of increase, 97.9.

NORTH CAROLINA.
Counties.

CARTERET.—Part of Craven annexed between 1880 and 1890.
CHATHAM.—Part taken to form part of Lee in 1908. (See also note.)
CRAVEN.—Part annexed to Carteret between 1880 and 1890.

NOTES REGARDING CHANGES IN COUNTY AND CITY BOUNDARIES: 1880–1910—Continued.

NORTH CAROLINA—continued.

Counties—Continued.

DAVIDSON.—Part annexed to Forsyth between 1880 and 1890.

DURHAM.—Organized from parts of Orange and Wake in 1881.

FORSYTH.—Part of Davidson annexed between 1880 and 1890.

FRANKLIN.—Part taken to form part of Vance in 1881.

GRANVILLE.—Part taken to form part of Vance in 1881.

LEE.—Organized from parts of Chatham and Moore in 1908. (See also note.)

MOORE.—Part taken to form part of Lee in 1908. (See also note.)

ORANGE.—Part taken to form part of Durham in 1881.

RICHMOND.—Part taken to form Scotland in 1900.

SCOTLAND.—Organized from part of Richmond in 1900.

VANCE.—Organized from parts of Franklin, Granville, and Warren in 1881.

WAKE.—Part taken to form part of Durham in 1881.

WARREN.—Part taken to form part of Vance in 1881.

Note.—Chatham, Lee, and Moore Counties combined—Total Negro population: 1910, 16,831; 1900, 16,188; increase, 1900–1910, 643; per cent of increase, 4.0.

OKLAHOMA.

Counties.

ADAIR.—Organized from part of Cherokee Nation in 1907.

ALFALFA.—Organized from part of Woods in 1907.

ATOKA.—Organized from part of Choctaw Nation in 1907.

BEAVER.—Parts taken to form Cimarron and Texas in 1907.

BECKHAM.—Organized from parts of Greer and Roger Mills in 1907; part annexed to Greer in 1910.

BLAINE.—Organized from Indian lands between 1890 and 1900 and part of Wichita Indian Reservation annexed in 1901.

BRYAN.—Organized from parts of Chickasaw and Choctaw Nations in 1907.

CADDO.—Organized from parts of Wichita and Kiowa, Comanche, and Apache Indian Reservations in 1901; part taken to form part of Grady in 1907.

CANADIAN.—Part of Wichita Indian Reservation annexed in 1901.

CARTER.—Organized from part of Chickasaw Nation in 1907.

CHEROKEE.—Organized from part of Cherokee Nation in 1907.

CHOCTAW.—Organized from part of Choctaw Nation in 1907.

CIMARRON.—Organized from part of Beaver in 1907.

COAL.—Organized from parts of Chickasaw and Choctaw Nations in 1907.

COMANCHE.—Organized from part of Kiowa, Comanche, and Apache Indian Reservation in 1901; parts taken to form Tillman and parts of Grady, Jefferson, and Stephens in 1907; part taken to form part of Swanson in 1910, but by a decision of the Supreme Court of Oklahoma, August 9, 1911, the creation of Swanson County was declared illegal, and the territory embraced in said county has reverted to the parent counties, Comanche and Kiowa.

CRAIG.—Organized from part of Cherokee Nation in 1907.

CREEK.—Organized from part of Creek Nation in 1907.

CUSTER.—Organized from Indian lands between 1890 and 1900 and part of Wichita Indian Reservation annexed in 1901.

DELAWARE.—Organized from parts of Cherokee Nation and Seneca Indian Reservation in 1907.

DEWEY.—Organized from Indian lands between 1890 and 1900.

ELLIS.—Organized from parts of Day and Woodward in 1907.

GARFIELD.—Organized from Indian lands between 1890 and 1900.

GARVIN.—Organized from part of Chickasaw Nation in 1907.

GRADY.—Organized from parts of Chickasaw Nation and Caddo and Comanche Counties in 1907.

GRANT.—Organized from Indian lands between 1890 and 1900.

GREER.—Formerly Greer County, Tex.; first returned as part of Oklahoma in 1890; parts taken to form Jackson and part of Beckham in 1907 and Harmon in 1909; part of Beckham annexed in 1910.

HARMON.—Organized from part of Greer in 1909.

HARPER.—Organized from part of Woodward in 1907.

HASKELL.—Organized from part of Choctaw Nation in 1907.

HUGHES.—Organized from part of Creek Nation in 1907.

JACKSON.—Organized from part of Greer in 1907.

JEFFERSON.—Organized from parts of Chickasaw Nation and Comanche County in 1907.

JOHNSTON.—Organized from parts of Chickasaw and Choctaw Nations in 1907.

KAY.—Organized from Indian lands between 1890 and 1900, and Kansas (Kaw) Indian Reservation and part of Ponca Indian Reservation annexed in 1904.

KIOWA.—Organized from part of Kiowa, Comanche, and Apache Indian Reservation in 1901; part taken to form part of Swanson in 1910, but by a decision of the Supreme Court of Oklahoma, August 9, 1911, the creation of Swanson County was declared illegal, and the territory embraced in said county has reverted to the parent counties, Comanche and Kiowa.

LATIMER.—Organized from part of Choctaw Nation in 1907.

LE FLORE.—Organized from part of Choctaw Nation in 1907.

LINCOLN.—Organized from Indian lands between 1890 and 1900.

LOVE.—Organized from part of Chickasaw Nation in 1907.

McCLAIN.—Organized from part of Chickasaw Nation in 1907.

McCURTAIN.—Organized from part of Choctaw Nation in 1907.

McINTOSH.—Organized from parts of Cherokee and Creek Nations in 1907.

MAJOR.—Organized from part of Woods in 1907.

MARSHALL.—Organized from part of Chickasaw Nation in 1907.

MAYES.—Organized from parts of Cherokee and Creek Nations in 1907.

MURRAY.—Organized from part of Chickasaw Nation in 1907.

MUSKOGEE.—Organized from parts of Cherokee and Creek Nations in 1907.

NOBLE.—Organized from Indian lands between 1890 and 1900; parts of Otoe and Missouri, and Ponca Indian Reservations annexed in 1904 and part of Payne County annexed in 1907.

NOWATA.—Organized from part of Cherokee Nation in 1907.

OKFUSKEE.—Organized from part of Creek Nation in 1907.

OKMULGEE.—Organized from part of Creek Nation in 1907.

OSAGE.—Organized from Osage Indian Reservation in 1907.

OTTAWA.—Organized from Modoc, Ottawa, Peoria, Quapaw, Shawnee, and Wyandotte Indian Reservations and parts of Cherokee Nation and Seneca Indian Reservation in 1907.

PAWNEE.—Organized from Indian lands between 1890 and 1900, and part of Otoe and Missouri Indian Reservation annexed in 1904.

PAYNE.—Part annexed to Noble in 1907.

PITTSBURG.—Organized from part of Choctaw Nation in 1907.

PONTOTOC.—Organized from parts of Chickasaw and Choctaw Nations in 1907.

POTTAWATOMIE.—Organized from Indian lands between 1890 and 1900.

PUSHMATAHA.—Organized from part of Choctaw Nation in 1907.

ROGER MILLS.—Organized from Indian lands between 1890 and 1900; part of Day annexed since 1900 and part of Kiowa, Comanche, and Apache Indian Reservation annexed in 1901; part taken to form part of Beckham in 1907.

OKLAHOMA—continued.

Counties—Continued.

ROGERS.—Organized from parts of Cherokee and Creek Nations in 1907.

SEMINOLE.—Organized from Seminole Nation and part of Creek Nation in 1907.

SEQUOYAH.—Organized from part of Cherokee Nation in 1907.

STEPHENS.—Organized from parts of Chickasaw Nation and Comanche County in 1907.

TEXAS.—Organized from part of Beaver in 1907.

TILLMAN.—Organized from part of Comanche in 1907.

TULSA.—Organized from parts of Cherokee and Creek Nations in 1907 and part of Wagoner, annexed in 1909.

WAGONER.—Organized from parts of Cherokee and Creek Nations in 1907 and part annexed to Tulsa in 1909.

WASHINGTON.—Organized from part of Cherokee Nation in 1907.

WASHITA.—Organized from Indian lands between 1890 and 1900 and part of Wichita Indian Reservation annexed in 1901.

WOODS.—Organized from Indian lands between 1890 and 1900 and part of Woodward annexed since 1900; parts taken to form Alfalfa and Major in 1907.

WOODWARD.—Organized from Indian lands between 1890 and 1900; part annexed to Woods since 1900 and parts taken to form Harper and part of Ellis in 1907.

Note.—Greer and Harmon Counties combined—Total Negro population: 1910, 146; 1900, 9; increase, 1900–1910, 137.

Cities.

ADA.—Incorporated since 1900.

ALTUS.—Incorporated in 1901.

CLINTON.—Incorporated in 1904.

ELK CITY.—Incorporated since 1900.

FREDERICK.—Incorporated since 1900.

GUTHRIE.—Parts of Guthrie township annexed in 1906 and 1909.

HUGO.—Incorporated since 1900.

LAWTON.—Incorporated in 1901.

McALESTER.—Consolidated with South McAlester town in 1907.

MANGUM.—Incorporated in 1900.

OKLAHOMA CITY.—Part of Greeley township annexed in 1905, part (including Capitol Hill town) annexed in 1910, parts of Oklahoma township annexed in 1905, 1906, and 1908, and part of Council Grove township annexed in 1910

OKMULGEE.—Incorporated since 1900.

PAWHUSKA.—Incorporated in 1907.

TULSA.—West Tulsa town annexed in 1909.

WAURIKA.—Incorporated in 1903.

WOODWARD.—Incorporated since 1900.

SOUTH CAROLINA.

Counties.

ABBEVILLE.—Part taken to form part of Greenwood in 1897.

BAMBERG.—Organized from part of Barnwell in 1897.

BARNWELL.—Part taken to form Bamberg in 1897.

BERKELEY.—Organized from part of Charleston in 1882; part taken to form part of Dorchester in 1897, part annexed to Charleston between 1890 and 1900, and part annexed to Orangeburg in 1910.

CALHOUN.—Organized from parts of Lexington and Orangeburg in 1908.

CHARLESTON.—Part taken to form Berkeley in 1882; part of Berkeley annexed between 1890 and 1900.

CHEROKEE.—Organized from parts of Spartanburg, Union, and York in 1897.

CLARENDON.—Part taken to form part of Florence in 1888.

COLLETON.—Part taken to form part of Dorchester in 1897.

DARLINGTON.—Parts taken to form parts of Florence and Lee in 1888 and 1902, respectively, and part annexed to Florence between 1890 and 1900.

DILLON.—Organized from part of Marion in 1910.

DORCHESTER.—Organized from parts of Berkeley and Colleton in 1897.

EDGEFIELD.—Part taken to form part of Greenwood in 1897 and part taken to form Saluda in 1896.

FLORENCE.—Organized from parts of Clarendon, Darlington, Marion, and Williamsburg in 1888, part of Darlington annexed between 1890 and 1900, and part of Williamsburg annexed in 1905.

GREENWOOD.—Organized from parts of Abbeville and Edgefield in 1897.

KERSHAW.—Part taken to form part of Lee in 1902.

LEE.—Organized from parts of Darlington, Kershaw, and Sumter in 1902.

LEXINGTON.—Part taken to form part of Calhoun in 1908, and part annexed to Newberry in 1901.

MARION.—Part taken to form part of Florence in 1888; part taken to form Dillon in 1910.

NEWBERRY.—Part of Lexington annexed in 1901.

ORANGEBURG.—Part taken to form part of Calhoun in 1908; part of Berkeley annexed in 1910.

SALUDA.—Organized from part of Edgefield in 1896.

SPARTANBURG.—Part taken to form part of Cherokee in 1897.

SUMTER.—Part taken to form part of Lee in 1902.

UNION.—Part taken to form part of Cherokee in 1897.

WILLIAMSBURG.—Part taken to form part of Florence in 1888 and part annexed to Florence in 1905.

YORK.—Part taken to form part of Cherokee in 1897.

Note 1.—Berkeley, Calhoun, Lexington, and Orangeburg Counties combined—Total Negro population: 1910, 79,402; 1900, 75,718; increase, 1900–1910, 3,684; per cent of increase, 4.9.

Note 2.—Darlington, Kershaw, Lee, and Sumter Counties combined—Total Negro population: 1910, 83,081; 1900, 72,350; increase, 1900–1910, 10,731; per cent of increase, 14.8.

Note 3.—Dillon and Marion Counties combined—Total Negro population: 1910, 22,747; 1900, 18,160; increase, 1900–1910, 4,587; per cent of increase, 25.3.

TENNESSEE.

The state.

Island No. 25 ceded to Arkansas in 1905.

Counties.

CHESTER.—Organized from parts of Hardeman, Henderson, McNairy, and Madison in 1882 and parts of Henderson and McNairy annexed in 1886 and 1887, respectively.

FENTRESS.—Part taken to form part of Pickett in 1881.

HARDEMAN.—Part taken to form part of Chester in 1882.

HENDERSON.—Part taken to form part of Chester in 1882 and part annexed to Chester in 1886.

HICKMAN.—Part annexed to Lewis in 1897.

LAUDERDALE.—Island No. 25 ceded to Arkansas in 1905.

NOTES REGARDING CHANGES IN COUNTY AND CITY BOUNDARIES: 1880–1910—Continued.

TENNESSEE—continued.

Counties—Continued.

LEWIS.—Parts of Hickman and Wayne annexed in 1897.
MCNAIRY.—Part taken to form part of Chester in 1882 and part annexed to Chester in 1887.
MADISON.—Part taken to form part of Chester in 1882.
OVERTON.—Part taken to form part of Pickett in 1881.
PERRY.—Part of Wayne annexed in 1909.
PICKETT.—Organized from parts of Fentress and Overton in 1881.
WAYNE.—Part annexed to Lewis in 1897 and part to Perry in 1909.

TEXAS.

Counties.

ANDREWS.—Organized from unorganized county of Andrews in 1910.
BREWSTER.—Organized from part of Presidio in 1887 and Buchel and Foley annexed in 1897.
BROWN.—Part taken to form part of Mills in 1887.
COKE.—Organized from part of Tom Green in 1889.
COMANCHE.—Part taken to form part of Mills in 1887.
CRANE.—Formed from part of Tom Green in 1887.
CROCKETT.—Parts taken to form Schleicher and Sutton in 1887 and part of Val Verde in 1885.
DAWSON.—Organized from unorganized county of Dawson in 1905.
ECTOR.—Formed from part of Tom Green in 1887.
FOARD.—Organized from parts of Hardeman and Knox in 1891.
GAINES.—Organized from unorganized county of Gaines in 1905.
GARZA.—Organized from unorganized county of Garza in 1907.
GLASSCOCK.—Formed from part of Tom Green in 1887.
GRAY.—Organized from unorganized county of Gray in 1902.
HAMILTON.—Part taken to form part of Mills in 1887.
HARDEMAN.—Part taken to form part of Foard in 1891.
HUTCHINSON.—Organized from unorganized county of Hutchinson in 1901.
IRION.—Organized from part of Tom Green in 1889.
JEFF DAVIS.—Organized from part of Presidio in 1887.
KINNEY.—Part taken to form part of Val Verde in 1885.
KNOX.—Part taken to form part of Foard in 1891.
LAMB.—Organized from unorganized county of Lamb in 1908.
LAMPASAS.—Part taken to form part of Mills in 1887.
LOVING.—Formed from part of Tom Green in 1887.
LYNN.—Organized from unorganized county of Lynn in 1903.
MIDLAND.—Organized from part of Tom Green in 1885.
MILLS.—Organized from parts of Brown, Comanche, Hamilton, and Lampasas in 1887.
PARMER.—Organized from unorganized county of Parmer in 1907.
PECOS.—Parts taken to form Reeves and Terrell in 1883 and 1905, respectively; part taken to form part of Val Verde in 1885. (See also Note 1.)
PRESIDIO.—Parts taken to form Brewster, Buchel, Foley, and Jeff Davis in 1887.
REAGAN.—Organized from part of Tom Green in 1903. (See also Note 2.)
REEVES.—Organized from part of Pecos in 1883.
SCHLEICHER.—Formed from part of Crockett in 1887; organized from unorganized county of Schleicher in 1901.
STERLING.—Organized from part of Tom Green in 1891.
SUTTON.—Formed from part of Crockett in 1887.
TERRELL.—Organized from part of Pecos in 1905. (See also Note 1.)
TERRY.—Organized from unorganized county of Terry in 1904.
TOM GREEN.—Parts taken to form Midland in 1885; Crane, Ector, Glasscock, Loving, Upton, Ward, and Winkler in 1887; Coke and Irion in 1889; Sterling in 1891; and Reagan in 1903. (See also Note 2.)
UPTON.—Formed from part of Tom Green in 1887; organized from unorganized county of Upton in 1910.
VAL VERDE.—Organized from parts of Crockett, Kinney, and Pecos in 1885.
WARD.—Formed from part of Tom Green in 1887.

TEXAS—continued.

Counties—Continued.

WEBB.—Encinal annexed in 1899.
WINKLER.—Formed from part of Tom Green in 1887; organized from unorganized county of Winkler in 1910.
YOAKUM.—Organized from unorganized county of Yoakum in 1909.

Note 1.—Pecos and Terrell Counties combined—Total Negro population: 1910, 6; 1900, 22; decrease, 1900–1910, 16.

Note 2.—Reagan and Tom Green Counties combined—Total Negro population: 1910, 718; 1900, 898; decrease, 1900–1910, 180; per cent of decrease, 20.0.

VIRGINIA.

Counties.

ALBEMARLE.—Formerly included Charlottesville city, which was made independent in 1888.
ALLEGHANY.—Formerly included Clifton Forge city, which was made independent in 1906.
AUGUSTA.—Part of Augusta County annexed to Staunton city in 1905.
BUCHANAN.—Part taken to form Dickenson in 1880.
CAMPBELL.—Parts of Campbell County annexed to Lynchburg city in 1901 and 1908.
CHESTERFIELD.—Formerly included Manchester city, which was made independent in 1874 and annexed to Richmond city in 1910, and part of Petersburg city, which was made independent prior to 1870.
DICKENSON.—Organized from parts of Buchanan, Russell, and Wise in 1880.
HENRICO.—Part of Henrico County and Manchester city annexed to Richmond city in 1906 and 1910, respectively.
MONTGOMERY.—Formerly included Radford city, which was made independent in 1892.
NORFOLK.—Part of Norfolk County annexed to Portsmouth city between 1890 and 1900 and in 1909, and parts annexed to Norfolk city in 1902 and 1906.
PITTSYLVANIA.—Parts of Pittsylvania County annexed to Danville city between 1890 and 1900 and in 1907.
ROANOKE.—Formerly included Roanoke city, which was made independent in 1884; part of Roanoke County annexed to Roanoke city between 1890 and 1900.
ROCKBRIDGE.—Formerly included Buena Vista city, which was made independent in 1892.
RUSSELL.—Part taken to form Dickenson in 1880.
WARWICK.—Formerly included Newport News city, which was made independent in 1896.
WASHINGTON.—Formerly included Bristol city, which was made independent in 1890.
WISE.—Part taken to form Dickenson in 1880.

Cities.

CLIFTON FORGE.—Incorporated as a city from Clifton Forge and West Clifton Forge towns, Alleghany County, and made independent in 1906.
DANVILLE.—Part of Pittsylvania County annexed in 1907.
LYNCHBURG.—Parts of Campbell County annexed in 1901 and 1908.
NORFOLK.—Part of Norfolk County annexed in 1902 and part (Berkley town) annexed in 1906.
PORTSMOUTH.—Part of Norfolk County annexed in 1909.
RICHMOND.—Manchester city and part of Henrico County (including Fairmount town) annexed in 1910 and 1906, respectively.
STAUNTON.—Part of Augusta County annexed in 1905.

WEST VIRGINIA.

Counties.

LOGAN.—Part taken to form Mingo in 1895.
MINGO.—Organized from part of Logan in 1895.

TABLE **III.**—GENERAL STATISTICS OF THE NEGRO POPULATION OF THE UNITED STATES, BY COUNTIES: 1910.

[Counties in which no Negroes were reported are omitted.]

COUNTY.	Total.	Per cent of total population.	Color.		Sex.		Males 21 years of age and over.				Persons 10 years of age and over.			Persons 6 to 14 years of age.		
			Black.	Mulatto.	Male.	Female.	Number.	Per cent of total.	Illiterate.		Total.	Illiterate.		Total.	Attending school.	
									Number.	Per cent.		Number.	Per cent.		Number.	Per cent.

ALABAMA.

COUNTY.	Total.	Per cent	Black.	Mulatto.	Male.	Female.	Number.	Per cent	Illit. No.	Illit. Pct.	Total.	Illit. No.	Illit. Pct.	Total.	Att. No.	Att. Pct.
Total	908,282	42.5	756,872	151,410	447,794	460,488	213,923	41.7	92,744	43.4	662,356	265,628	40.1	208,548	102,813	49.3
Autauga	11,717	58.5	9,848	1,869	5,690	6,027	2,670	56.9	1,149	43.0	8,561	3,372	39.4	2,877	1,304	45.3
Baldwin	5,110	28.1	3,503	1,607	2,596	2,514	1,299	26.3	491	37.8	3,718	1,316	35.4	1,137	569	50.0
Barbour	20,456	62.5	18,023	2,433	9,724	10,732	4,044	57.7	1,990	49.2	14,257	6,595	46.3	5,325	2,515	47.2
Bibb	7,710	33.8	7,184	526	4,211	3,499	2,209	37.3	716	32.4	5,664	1,655	29.2	1,710	982	57.4
Blount	1,181	5.5	717	464	628	553	319	6.7	147	46.1	857	329	38.4	270	103	38.1
Bullock	25,362	84.0	22,078	3,284	12,322	13,040	5,019	79.8	2,391	47.6	17,587	7,492	42.6	6,430	3,114	48.4
Butler	15,373	53.0	13,367	2,006	7,560	7,813	3,249	50.2	1,534	47.2	10,748	4,530	42.1	3,805	1,786	46.9
Calhoun	10,757	27.5	8,240	2,517	5,256	5,501	2,649	28.4	910	34.4	7,999	2,492	31.2	2,385	1,229	51.5
Chambers	18,660	51.8	15,193	3,467	9,180	9,480	3,825	48.4	1,721	45.0	12,999	5,095	39.2	4,786	2,201	46.0
Cherokee	2,606	12.9	2,077	529	1,316	1,290	562	12.2	252	44.8	1,800	682	37.9	672	327	48.7
Chilton	4,759	20.5	4,132	627	2,452	2,307	1,132	21.0	424	37.5	3,340	1,159	34.7	1,147	568	49.5
Choctaw	11,503	62.2	9,693	1,810	5,681	5,822	2,194	57.2	1,010	46.0	7,755	3,414	44.0	3,014	1,343	44.6
Clarke	17,311	55.9	14,667	2,644	8,631	8,680	3,724	52.3	1,680	45.1	12,178	5,130	42.1	4,344	2,010	46.3
Clay	2,648	12.6	2,374	274	1,337	1,311	597	12.7	245	41.0	1,842	680	36.9	622	280	45.0
Cleburne	711	5.3	552	159	349	362	138	4.7	55	39.9	497	202	40.6	162	57	35.2
Coffee	5,782	22.1	4,782	1,000	3,019	2,763	1,353	22.1	661	48.9	4,028	1,816	45.1	1,422	683	48.0
Colbert	9,449	38.1	7,267	2,182	4,646	4,803	2,189	36.4	886	40.5	6,877	2,581	37.5	2,205	956	43.4
Conecuh	10,079	47.0	8,280	1,799	5,000	5,079	2,151	44.2	946	44.0	7,036	2,832	40.3	2,548	1,395	54.7
Coosa	6,256	37.6	5,721	535	3,120	3,136	1,195	33.1	526	44.0	4,185	1,722	41.1	1,722	561	32.6
Covington	8,001	24.9	7,185	816	4,378	3,623	2,487	30.2	934	37.6	5,990	2,344	39.1	1,552	534	34.4
Crenshaw	7,514	32.2	6,323	1,191	3,743	3,771	1,653	30.5	608	36.8	5,122	1,712	33.4	1,873	785	41.9
Cullman	533	1.9	333	200	295	238	151	2.4	41	27.2	388	124	32.0	119	67	56.3
Dale	5,810	26.9	4,783	1,027	2,903	2,907	1,228	25.4	500	40.7	3,981	1,632	41.0	1,557	620	39.8
Dallas	43,511	81.5	38,093	5,418	20,701	22,810	9,997	78.0	5,189	51.9	32,638	15,386	47.1	9,717	4,951	51.0
Dekalb	854	3.0	681	173	421	433	184	2.9	70	38.0	603	183	30.3	222	127	57.2
Elmore	13,246	46.9	11,287	1,959	6,684	6,562	3,146	47.0	1,347	42.8	9,612	3,774	39.3	3,128	1,392	44.5
Escambia	5,569	29.5	5,151	418	2,842	2,727	1,428	32.4	553	38.7	4,014	1,396	34.8	1,203	525	43.6
Etowah	6,804	17.4	4,496	2,308	3,652	3,152	2,012	20.1	688	34.2	5,152	1,575	30.6	1,350	733	54.3
Fayette	1,866	11.5	1,380	486	959	907	400	11.2	159	39.8	1,275	470	36.9	447	229	51.2
Franklin	1,842	9.5	1,202	640	929	913	498	11.5	202	40.6	1,385	508	36.7	354	170	48.0
Geneva	4,305	16.4	3,805	500	2,245	2,060	1,033	17.6	441	42.7	2,944	1,251	42.5	1,063	456	42.9
Greene	19,705	86.7	18,169	1,536	9,391	10,314	4,108	83.1	2,472	60.2	13,935	6,965	50.0	4,873	2,622	53.8
Hale	21,987	78.9	17,887	4,100	10,692	11,295	4,715	75.2	2,453	52.0	15,571	7,114	45.7	5,558	2,928	52.7
Henry	10,150	48.5	8,549	1,601	5,008	5,142	1,933	43.7	879	45.5	6,692	2,769	41.4	2,676	1,183	44.2
Houston	9,597	29.6	8,139	1,458	4,903	4,694	2,180	29.2	756	34.7	6,651	2,292	34.5	2,415	875	36.2
Jackson	3,136	9.5	2,210	926	1,519	1,617	658	8.7	247	37.5	2,186	769	35.2	750	293	39.1
Jefferson	90,617	40.0	73,704	16,913	46,761	43,856	29,623	43.6	8,215	27.7	73,480	18,681	25.4	14,391	9,711	67.5
Lamar	3,180	18.2	2,668	512	1,578	1,602	640	16.8	264	41.3	2,125	802	37.7	801	414	51.7
Lauderdale	7,096	22.9	5,380	1,716	3,445	3,651	1,600	22.8	615	38.4	5,146	1,846	35.9	1,593	739	46.4
Lawrence	6,933	31.5	5,613	1,320	3,382	3,551	1,496	31.0	605	40.4	4,999	1,860	37.2	1,624	898	55.3
Lee	19,643	59.8	15,653	3,990	9,404	10,239	3,946	54.5	2,093	53.0	13,691	6,494	47.4	5,049	2,386	47.3
Limestone	10,255	38.2	8,884	1,371	5,050	5,205	2,208	35.9	1,221	55.3	7,329	4,011	54.7	2,454	526	21.4
Lowndes	28,125	88.2	25,549	2,576	13,704	14,421	6,053	86.0	3,541	58.5	20,135	10,280	51.1	6,786	3,142	46.3
Macon	22,039	84.6	19,183	2,856	10,581	11,458	4,648	81.5	2,037	43.8	15,666	5,690	36.3	5,465	3,721	68.1
Madison	18,894	40.2	12,553	6,341	9,143	9,751	4,326	38.9	1,910	44.2	13,925	5,566	40.0	4,273	1,990	46.6
Marengo	30,846	77.3	25,540	5,306	14,996	15,850	6,906	74.7	4,003	58.0	22,209	12,265	55.2	7,387	2,753	37.3
Marion	520	3.0	296	224	263	257	104	2.9	38	36.5	341	116	34.0	118	51	43.2
Marshall	1,365	4.8	1,107	258	660	705	318	5.1	129	40.6	972	372	38.3	299	130	43.5
Mobile	34,719	42.9	25,977	8,742	16,367	18,352	9,859	43.2	2,984	30.3	28,027	8,105	28.9	5,833	3,705	63.5
Monroe	15,727	57.9	12,412	3,315	7,764	7,963	3,294	54.9	1,795	54.5	10,832	5,244	48.4	4,008	1,416	35.3
Montgomery	56,867	69.2	46,253	10,614	26,812	30,055	13,571	64.4	5,306	39.1	43,554	15,432	35.4	12,113	6,951	57.4
Morgan	8,198	24.3	6,299	1,899	4,022	4,176	2,074	24.1	806	38.9	6,192	2,073	33.5	1,691	947	56.0
Perry	24,494	78.5	21,604	2,890	11,912	12,582	5,304	76.4	2,788	52.6	17,513	7,642	43.6	5,835	3,488	59.8
Pickens	12,951	51.7	11,367	1,584	6,328	6,623	2,799	49.0	1,888	67.5	9,209	5,434	59.0	3,243	1,161	35.8
Pike	14,437	46.9	11,201	3,236	7,116	7,321	3,201	45.1	1,568	49.0	10,119	4,508	44.5	3,423	1,526	44.6
Randolph	5,717	23.2	4,627	1,090	2,877	2,840	1,179	22.1	402	34.1	3,899	1,175	30.1	1,490	744	49.9
Russell	20,198	77.9	17,383	2,815	9,741	10,457	3,882	72.1	1,895	49.1	14,058	6,433	45.8	5,474	2,095	38.3
St. Clair	3,632	17.5	3,147	485	1,893	1,739	897	18.7	243	27.1	2,645	725	27.4	901	387	43.0
Shelby	7,641	28.4	7,015	626	3,979	3,662	2,007	30.8	895	44.6	5,579	2,188	39.2	1,671	882	52.8
Sumter	23,322	81.3	20,807	2,515	11,177	12,145	4,810	77.1	2,748	57.1	16,676	8,895	53.3	5,931	2,245	37.9
Talladega	18,265	48.1	15,417	2,848	9,016	9,249	3,780	44.8	1,687	44.6	12,668	4,763	37.6	4,703	2,443	51.9
Tallapoosa	11,457	36.9	8,614	2,843	5,686	5,771	2,347	34.2	1,207	51.4	7,859	3,636	46.0	2,941	1,309	44.5
Tuscaloosa	19,026	40.0	15,687	3,339	9,693	9,333	4,976	40.4	2,222	44.7	14,082	5,856	41.6	4,083	2,047	50.1
Walker	6,538	17.7	5,771	767	3,657	2,881	2,192	23.6	664	30.3	5,029	1,528	30.4	1,166	720	61.7
Washington	6,064	42.0	4,688	1,376	3,138	2,926	1,442	41.1	618	42.9	4,273	1,756	41.1	1,477	656	44.4
Wilcox	27,602	81.6	25,050	2,552	13,629	13,973	6,104	78.3	3,078	50.4	20,010	8,900	44.5	6,880	3,155	45.9
Winston	54	0.4	52	2	37	17	28	1.0	6	(1)	47	14	(1)	5	2	(1)

[1] Per cent not shown where base is less than 100.

TABLE III.—GENERAL STATISTICS OF THE NEGRO POPULATION OF THE UNITED STATES, BY COUNTIES: 1910—Con.

[Counties in which no Negroes were reported are omitted.]

COUNTY	Total	Per cent of total population	Color		Sex		Males 21 years of age and over				Persons 10 years of age and over			Persons 6 to 14 years of age		
			Black	Mulatto	Male	Female	Number	Per cent of total	Illiterate Number	Illiterate Per cent	Total	Illiterate Number	Illiterate Per cent	Total	Attending school Number	Attending school Per cent
ARIZONA.																
Total	2,009	1.0	1,561	448	1,054	955	764	1.0	64	8.4	1,691	122	7.2	254	207	81.5
Apache	8	0.1	3	5	6	2	3	0.1			5			1		(1)
Cochise	478	1.4	442	36	230	248	173	1.3	11	6.4	423	29	6.9	50	42	(1)
Coconino	35	0.4	23	12	21	14	15	0.5	1	(1)	29	2	(1)	5	5	(1)
Gila	226	1.4	208	18	117	109	88	1.3	18	(1)	201	28	13.9	23	19	(1)
Graham	112	0.5	65	47	59	53	43	0.6	2	(1)	88	4	(1)	15	15	(1)
Maricopa	469	1.4	276	193	228	241	161	1.4	16	9.9	387	32	8.3	67	55	(1)
Mohave	10	0.3	2	8	8	2	6	0.3			9			2	2	(1)
Navajo	38	0.3	22	16	31	7	25	0.7			35			5	3	(1)
Pima	295	1.3	247	48	148	147	100	1.4	3	3.0	241	5	2.1	43	37	(1)
Pinal	48	0.5	40	8	42	6	40	1.2	4	(1)	47	4	(1)	1		
Santa Cruz	34	0.5	28	6	19	15	14	0.7	1	(1)	26	3	(1)	4	3	(1)
Yavapai	148	0.9	108	40	79	69	60	0.8	4	(1)	127	9	7.1	10	8	(1)
Yuma	108	1.4	97	11	66	42	36	1.1	4	(1)	73	6	(1)	28	18	(1)
ARKANSAS.																
Total	442,891	28.1	361,520	81,371	223,323	219,568	111,365	28.1	32,013	28.7	327,009	86,398	26.4	99,383	57,872	58.2
Arkansas	4,269	26.5	2,960	1,209	2,181	2,088	1,026	23.4	269	26.2	3,074	730	23.7	1,005	479	47.7
Ashley	13,276	52.5	11,202	2,074	6,742	6,534	3,253	52.0	726	22.3	9,718	2,100	21.6	3,094	1,266	40.9
Baxter	7	0.1	7		3	4	3	0.1			6			2	2	(1)
Benton	110	0.3	67	43	49	61	24	0.3	9	(1)	86	27	(1)	24	15	(1)
Boone	7	(1)	2	5	2	5	1	(2)			4	2	(1)	1	1	(1)
Bradley	4,641	32.0	3,854	787	2,276	2,365	1,021	29.9	316	31.0	3,175	1,002	31.6	1,107	568	51.3
Calhoun	3,413	34.5	2,859	554	1,735	1,678	715	31.1	276	38.6	2,366	924	39.1	871	316	36.3
Carroll	66	0.4	38	28	32	34	20	0.5	3	(1)	50	9	(1)	13	10	(1)
Chicot	17,682	80.4	14,457	3,225	8,885	8,797	4,735	78.2	1,726	36.5	13,464	4,577	34.0	3,829	2,095	54.7
Clark	7,367	31.1	5,425	1,942	3,704	3,663	1,573	28.6	480	30.5	5,106	1,332	26.1	1,855	985	53.1
Clay	10	(2)	9	1	6	4	6	0.1	3	(1)	9	5	(1)	1	1	(1)
Cleburne	7	0.1	7		6	1	5	0.2	1	(1)	7	1	(1)			
Cleveland	4,334	32.1	3,753	581	2,261	2,073	969	31.1	340	35.1	2,852	1,006	35.3	1,054	434	41.2
Columbia	10,869	45.6	9,303	1,566	5,325	5,544	2,104	40.4	810	38.5	7,313	2,443	33.4	2,935	1,474	50.2
Conway	8,298	36.5	7,421	877	4,102	4,196	1,740	35.0	440	25.3	5,820	1,248	21.4	2,054	1,429	69.6
Craighead	1,328	4.8	1,212	116	627	701	399	5.6	98	24.6	1,057	266	25.2	227	184	81.1
Crawford	2,063	8.6	2,012	51	1,067	996	551	9.5	154	27.9	1,577	394	25.0	464	325	70.0
Crittenden	19,000	84.6	17,022	1,978	9,809	9,191	5,255	81.2	1,252	23.8	14,565	3,078	21.1	4,078	2,819	69.1
Cross	6,127	43.6	2,817	3,310	3,129	2,998	1,592	42.4	425	26.7	4,507	1,143	25.4	1,382	706	51.1
Dallas	4,657	36.9	3,565	1,092	2,272	2,385	974	32.0	266	27.3	3,156	811	25.7	1,205	602	50.0
Desha	12,129	79.4	11,255	874	6,245	5,884	3,440	75.2	1,367	39.7	9,224	3,494	37.9	2,616	1,497	57.2
Drew	11,789	53.7	8,963	2,826	5,848	5,941	2,627	51.7	886	33.7	8,355	2,738	32.8	2,875	1,262	43.9
Faulkner	4,460	18.8	3,129	1,331	2,242	2,218	909	17.6	221	24.3	3,108	650	20.9	1,186	867	73.1
Franklin	382	1.9	194	188	181	201	83	1.8	22	(1)	281	58	20.6	92	77	(1)
Fulton	44	0.4	11	33	26	18	14	0.5	4	(1)	33	9	(1)	10	5	(1)
Garland	4,665	17.1	2,947	1,718	2,199	2,466	1,459	17.3	229	15.7	3,994	628	15.7	662	538	81.3
Grant	994	10.5	773	221	530	464	225	10.1	50	22.2	680	149	21.9	246	134	54.5
Greene	40	0.2	39	1	17	23	12	0.2	1	(1)	34	3	(1)	7	2	(1)
Hempstead	14,100	49.8	10,887	3,213	6,984	7,116	2,818	44.2	965	34.2	9,739	2,570	26.4	3,814	2,169	56.9
Hot Springs	1,960	13.0	1,851	109	1,041	919	530	14.9	110	20.0	1,460	277	19.0	434	290	66.8
Howard	3,498	20.7	2,731	767	1,770	1,728	753	19.2	221	29.3	2,395	612	25.6	855	445	52.0
Independence	1,264	5.1	614	650	608	656	304	5.3	83	27.3	984	225	22.9	261	138	52.9
Izard	242	1.7	217	25	121	121	56	1.7	13	(1)	159	51	32.1	44	15	(1)
Jackson	6,203	26.4	5,519	684	3,070	3,133	1,605	26.1	375	23.4	4,638	1,039	22.4	1,297	821	63.3
Jefferson	37,692	71.5	30,269	7,423	18,731	18,961	9,747	68.2	2,768	28.4	28,509	7,376	25.9	8,063	5,168	64.1
Johnson	517	2.6	364	153	258	259	129	2.9	40	31.0	377	119	31.6	116	81	69.8
Lafayette	7,181	52.3	5,817	1,364	3,637	3,544	1,752	50.9	440	25.1	5,256	1,275	24.3	1,693	844	49.9
Lawrence	750	3.7	652	98	382	368	193	3.9	71	36.8	570	175	30.7	153	87	56.9
Lee	19,003	78.4	15,353	3,650	9,861	9,142	5,071	76.7	1,097	21.6	14,281	2,440	17.1	4,172	3,240	77.7
Lincoln	9,967	65.9	6,879	3,088	5,253	4,714	2,702	68.2	700	25.9	7,434	1,946	26.2	2,151	1,055	49.0
Little River	5,698	41.9	4,970	728	2,886	2,812	1,276	38.7	460	36.1	4,086	1,381	33.8	1,391	590	42.4
Logan	640	2.4	543	97	320	320	141	2.3	24	17.0	448	97	21.7	168	71	42.3
Lonoke	11,268	40.3	10,409	859	5,693	5,575	2,755	39.6	932	33.8	8,105	2,516	31.0	2,615	1,488	56.9
Madison	45	0.3	10	35	23	22	14	0.4	3	(1)	32	12	(1)	10		
Miller	7,163	36.6	5,482	1,681	3,414	3,749	1,708	35.3	682	39.9	5,428	1,852	34.1	1,664	1,071	64.4
Mississippi	13,472	44.2	10,071	3,401	7,114	6,358	4,083	45.8	1,360	33.3	10,441	3,478	33.3	2,615	1,208	46.2
Monroe	12,526	62.9	10,408	2,118	6,408	6,118	3,208	59.9	997	31.1	9,305	2,574	27.7	2,900	1,627	56.1
Montgomery	304	2.4	215	89	162	142	66	2.3	21	(1)	206	50	24.3	91	52	(1)
Nevada	6,790	35.1	5,149	1,641	3,340	3,450	1,286	30.5	499	38.8	4,518	1,667	36.9	1,838	912	49.6
Newton	10	0.1	9	1	7	3	2	0.1	2	(1)	6	5	(1)	4		
Ouachita	12,333	56.6	9,958	2,375	5,992	6,341	2,480	50.6	600	24.2	8,543	1,832	21.4	3,283	1,807	55.0
Perry	910	9.7	812	98	465	445	230	10.3	58	25.2	651	166	25.5	206	129	62.6
Phillips	26,354	78.6	23,654	2,700	13,497	12,857	7,449	76.0	1,969	26.3	20,255	4,741	23.4	5,311	3,700	69.7
Pike	918	7.3	771	147	489	429	239	8.0	63	26.4	663	163	24.6	208	110	52.9
Poinsett	2,121	16.6	2,032	89	1,147	974	669	18.2	103	15.4	1,642	290	17.7	416	203	48.8

¹ Per cent not shown where base is less than 100. ² Less than one-tenth of 1 per cent.

TABLE III.—GENERAL STATISTICS OF THE NEGRO POPULATION OF THE UNITED STATES, BY COUNTIES: 1910—Con.

[Counties in which no Negroes were reported are omitted.]

COUNTY.	NEGRO POPULATION: 1910.															
	Total.	Per cent of total population.	Color.		Sex.		Males 21 years of age and over.				Persons 10 years of age and over.			Persons 6 to 14 years of age.		
			Black.	Mu-latto.	Male.	Fe-male.	Num-ber.	Per cent of total.	Illiterate.		Total.	Illiterate.		Total.	Attending school.	
									Num-ber.	Per cent.		Num-ber.	Per cent.		Num-ber.	Per cent.
ARKANSAS—Continued.																
Polk	46	0.3	21	25	24	22	11	0.3	6	(1)	31	10	(1)	13	4	(1)
Pope	1,867	7.6	1,568	299	913	954	393	7.2	99	25.2	1,331	278	20.9	441	237	65.1
Prairie	4,481	32.3	4,037	444	2,242	2,239	1,076	30.9	315	29.3	3,206	730	22.8	1,060	787	74.2
Pulaski	35,462	40.9	28,457	7,005	17,767	17,695	10,412	39.2	2,393	23.0	28,273	6,005	21.2	6,178	4,780	77.4
Randolph	515	2.7	449	66	260	255	135	3.0	54	40.0	396	125	31.6	111	40	36.0
St. Francis	15,508	68.8	13,624	1,884	7,835	7,673	3,810	65.3	1,141	29.9	11,388	3,035	26.7	3,648	2,012	55.2
Saline	1,833	11.0	1,737	96	967	866	502	12.2	157	31.3	1,400	363	25.9	407	271	66.6
Scott	22	0.2	21	1	11	11	6	0.2	3	(1)	17	6	(1)	4	4	(1)
Searcy	104	0.7	99	5	71	33	51	1.5	18	(1)	98	29	(1)	9	7	(1)
Sebastian	5,410	10.3	4,390	1,020	2,651	2,759	1,581	11.1	290	18.3	4,363	776	17.8	959	731	76.2
Sevier	2,296	13.8	2,031	265	1,125	1,171	452	11.7	131	29.0	1,548	415	26.8	537	259	48.2
Sharp	83	0.7	74	9	42	41	17	0.6	6	(1)	62	21	(1)	29	17	(1)
Stone	94	1.1	94	......	46	48	22	1.1	11	(1)	57	32	(1)	22	......	......
Union	13,747	44.7	11,450	2,297	6,894	6,853	2,860	39.6	1,198	41.9	9,195	3,737	40.6	3,499	1,280	36.6
Van Buren	220	1.6	167	53	105	115	43	1.5	17	(1)	149	34	22.8	54	46	(1)
Washington	614	1.8	453	161	295	319	154	1.8	55	35.7	464	124	26.7	125	86	68.8
White	2,162	7.6	1,522	640	1,117	1,045	554	7.9	162	29.2	1,567	389	24.8	464	250	53.9
Woodruff	11,705	58.4	9,124	2,581	5,901	5,804	2,808	55.0	795	28.3	8,435	2,177	25.8	2,739	1,325	48.4
Yell	1,759	6.7	1,253	506	883	876	427	6.8	132	30.9	1,277	356	27.9	416	272	65.4
CALIFORNIA.																
Total	21,645	0.9	13,787	7,858	11,303	10,342	8,143	0.9	556	6.8	18,699	1,329	7.1	2,579	2,281	88.4
Alameda	3,634	1.5	1,753	1,881	1,896	1,738	1,413	1.6	53	3.8	3,153	133	4.2	370	327	88.4
Amador	2	(2)	......	2	1	1	1	(2)	......	......	2	......	......	......	......	......
Butte	122	0.4	95	27	66	56	48	0.4	8	(1)	106	15	14.2	20	18	(1)
Calaveras	17	0.2	16	1	8	9	6	0.2	1	(1)	15	2	(1)	3	3	(1)
Colusa	50	0.6	7	43	31	19	21	0.7	1	(1)	44	2	(1)	8	7	(1)
Contra Costa	67	0.2	40	27	39	28	27	0.2	2	(1)	55	3	(1)	11	10	(1)
Del Norte	1	(2)	1	......	......	1	......	......	......	......	1	......	(1)	......	......	......
Eldorado	28	0.4	24	4	22	6	19	0.6	3	(1)	28	3	(1)	2	2	(1)
Fresno	474	0.6	377	97	228	246	148	0.5	14	9.5	390	37	9.5	88	65	(1)
Glenn	15	0.2	12	3	9	6	9	0.3	2	(1)	14	2	(1)	1	......	......
Humboldt	40	0.1	28	12	14	26	10	0.1	1	(1)	34	4	(1)	6	5	(1)
Imperial	65	0.5	51	14	46	19	46	0.7	5	(1)	63	6	(1)	2	1	(1)
Inyo	21	0.3	10	11	13	8	10	0.3	3	(1)	18	4	(1)	2	1	(1)
Kern	369	1.0	286	83	185	184	132	0.7	8	6.1	311	24	7.7	45	41	(1)
Kings	172	1.1	106	66	89	83	53	0.9	5	(1)	134	12	9.0	40	39	(1)
Lake	11	0.2	10	1	6	5	4	0.2	1	(1)	10	1	(1)	1	1	(1)
Lassen	1	(2)	......	1	......	1	......	......	......	......	1	......	......	......	......	......
Los Angeles	9,424	1.9	6,462	2,962	4,555	4,869	3,115	1.7	153	4.9	8,063	523	6.5	1,207	1,115	92.4
Madera	56	0.7	50	6	40	16	22	0.6	......	......	41	1	(1)	8	5	(1)
Marin	145	0.6	100	45	117	28	99	0.9	6	(1)	141	11	7.8	12	11	(1)
Mariposa	18	0.5	......	18	9	9	8	0.4	......	......	17	2	(1)	......	......	......
Mendocino	31	0.1	20	11	18	13	16	0.2	......	......	31	2	(1)	2	1	(1)
Merced	75	0.5	50	25	41	34	28	0.5	5	(1)	63	9	(1)	14	11	(1)
Modoc	4	0.1	3	1	3	1	3	0.1	......	......	3	......	......	1	1	(1)
Monterey	107	0.4	74	33	57	50	38	0.4	1	(1)	93	10	(1)	15	12	(1)
Napa	48	0.2	36	12	25	23	23	0.3	5	(1)	47	6	(1)	2	2	(1)
Nevada	14	0.1	9	5	11	3	10	0.2	3	(1)	14	5	(1)	......	......	......
Orange	97	0.3	68	29	45	52	29	0.3	1	(1)	78	6	(1)	12	8	(1)
Placer	55	0.3	43	12	40	15	37	0.4	5	(1)	52	6	(1)	4	4	(1)
Plumas	5	0.1	1	4	2	3	2	0.1	......	......	4	1	(1)	1	1	(1)
Riverside	518	1.5	284	234	242	276	139	1.1	16	11.5	384	39	10.2	107	97	90.7
Sacramento	631	0.9	400	231	379	252	299	1.0	31	10.4	560	49	8.8	60	44	(1)
San Benito	26	0.3	17	9	13	13	7	0.2	......	......	25	......	......	2	2	(1)
San Bernardino	642	1.1	506	136	368	274	279	1.3	64	22.9	580	105	18.1	64	56	(1)
San Diego	684	1.1	457	227	356	328	277	1.2	27	9.7	623	59	9.5	60	54	(1)
San Francisco	1,642	0.4	881	761	1,025	617	831	0.5	43	5.2	1,480	76	5.1	108	87	80.6
San Joaquin	307	0.6	198	109	164	143	108	0.5	7	6.5	262	19	7.3	45	34	(1)
San Luis Obispo	77	0.4	72	5	48	29	33	0.5	4	(1)	64	14	(1)	13	12	(1)
San Mateo	67	0.3	45	22	33	34	17	0.2	......	......	56	1	(1)	12	11	(1)
Santa Barbara	108	0.4	63	45	53	55	39	0.4	1	(1)	90	4	(1)	12	10	(1)
Santa Clara	262	0.3	175	87	121	141	96	0.3	6	(1)	230	13	5.7	25	23	(1)
Santa Cruz	83	0.3	37	46	52	31	31	0.3	3	(1)	71	3	(1)	13	13	(1)
Shasta	159	0.8	61	98	92	67	71	0.9	2	(1)	140	8	5.7	24	24	(1)
Siskiyou	29	0.2	20	9	20	9	18	0.2	2	(1)	29	3	(1)	1	1	(1)
Solano	250	0.9	205	45	140	110	113	0.9	4	3.5	229	13	5.7	26	21	(1)
Sonoma	43	0.1	28	15	25	18	15	0.1	......	......	41	3	(1)	4	3	(1)
Stanislaus	89	0.4	62	27	53	36	34	0.4	2	(1)	74	3	(1)	12	8	(1)
Sutter	10	0.2	9	1	4	6	4	0.2	1	(1)	10	3	(1)	2	2	(1)
Tehama	91	0.8	52	39	40	51	28	0.6	3	(1)	76	5	(1)	23	21	(1)
Trinity	8	0.2	3	5	5	3	3	0.2	1	(1)	6	1	(1)	2	1	(1)
Tulare	190	0.5	99	91	118	72	81	0.7	13	(1)	161	28	17.4	25	15	(1)
Tuolumne	14	0.1	12	2	13	1	11	0.3	1	(1)	14	2	(1)	......	......	......
Ventura	64	0.3	48	16	32	32	20	0.3	1	(1)	52	3	(1)	10	8	(1)
Yolo	280	2.0	136	144	188	92	134	2.3	33	24.6	240	39	16.3	34	27	(1)
Yuba	203	2.0	184	19	103	100	78	1.6	5	(1)	176	6	3.4	18	16	(1)

1 Per cent not shown where base is less than 100.   2 Less than one-tenth of 1 per cent.

TABLE III.—GENERAL STATISTICS OF THE NEGRO POPULATION OF THE UNITED STATES, BY COUNTIES: 1910—Con.

[Counties in which no Negroes were reported are omitted.]

COUNTY.	NEGRO POPULATION: 1910.															
	Total.	Per cent of total population.	Color.		Sex.		Males 21 years of age and over.				Persons 10 years of age and over.			Persons 6 to 14 years of age.		
			Black.	Mulatto.	Male.	Female.	Number.	Per cent of total.	Illiterate.		Total.	Illiterate.		Total.	Attending school.	
									Number.	Per cent.		Number.	Per cent.		Number.	Per cent.
COLORADO.																
Total	11,453	1.4	7,815	3,638	5,867	5,586	4,283	1.6	373	8.7	9,990	856	8.6	1,429	1,220	85.4
Adams	49	0.6	32	17	28	21	17	0.5	3	(1)	41	5	(1)	13	12	(1)
Arapahoe	131	1.3	68	63	60	71	41	1.1	3	(1)	111	8	7.2	18	18	(1)
Archuleta	7	0.2	1	6	3	4	2	0.2			6			1		
Baca	2	0.1	2		1	1	1	0.1			2					
Bent	51	1.0	18	33	32	19	22	1.2	15	(1)	40	22	(1)	7	7	(1)
Boulder	186	0.6	122	64	84	102	42	0.5	7	(1)	141	17	12.1	38	31	(1)
Chaffee	60	0.8	27	33	46	14	28	1.0	3	(1)	56	3	(1)	6	6	(1)
Cheyenne	27	0.7	27		23	4	17	1.3			25			1	1	(1)
Clear Creek	43	0.9	41	2	24	19	24	1.3	3	(1)	42	5	(1)	2	2	(1)
Conejos	49	0.4	48	1	28	21	18	0.6	2	(1)	46	5	(1)	8	7	(1)
Costilla	22	0.4	22		12	10	12	0.8	1	(1)	21	1	(1)	3	2	(1)
Custer	1	0.1	1		1		1	0.1			1					
Delta	9	0.1	9		4	5	4	0.1	2	(1)	8	3	(1)	1	1	(1)
Denver	5,426	2.5	3,297	2,129	2,652	2,774	1,999	2.8	100	5.0	4,814	291	6.0	579	513	88.6
Dolores	1	0.2		1	1		1	0.4			1					
Douglas	8	0.3	8		5	3	2	0.2			5			1	1	(1)
Eagle	1	(2)	1		1		1	0.1			1					
El Paso	1,330	3.1	941	389	630	700	432	3.1	25	5.8	1,140	79	6.9	209	186	89.0
Fremont	339	1.9	285	54	212	127	161	2.5	9	5.6	295	16	5.4	45	42	(1)
Garfield	64	0.6	35	29	28	36	24	0.6	6	(1)	55	10	(1)	8	8	(1)
Gilpin	18	0.4	8	10	9	9	6	0.4			17			2	2	(1)
Grand	9	0.5	5	4	3	6	3	0.4			7	1	(1)	1	1	(1)
Gunnison	44	0.7	24	20	31	13	26	1.1	1	(1)	44	3	(1)	4	4	(1)
Hinsdale	6	0.9		6	2	4	2	0.7			6	1	(1)			
Huerfano	323	2.4	303	20	185	138	144	3.4	16	11.1	279	34	12.2	47	29	(1)
Jefferson	134	0.9	87	47	93	41	39	0.8	9	(1)	126	16	12.7	30	30	(1)
Kiowa	1	(2)	1		1		1	0.1	1	(1)	1	1	(1)			
Kit Carson	5	0.1	5		5		4	0.2			4			1		
La Plata	63	0.6	57	6	37	26	25	0.7	3	(1)	53	6	(1)	7	7	(1)
Lake	71	0.7	56	15	36	35	30	0.7	6	(1)	62	12	(1)	6	6	(1)
Larimer	33	0.1	22	11	15	18	13	0.2	2	(1)	27	3	(1)	3	3	(1)
Las Animas	379	1.1	300	79	211	168	174	1.5	26	14.9	344	57	16.6	36	30	(1)
Lincoln	8	0.1	8		6	2	2	0.1			7			1	1	(1)
Logan	23	0.2	21	2	20	3	17	0.5	1	(1)	20	1	(1)	2	1	(1)
Mesa	130	0.6	93	37	63	67	46	0.6	6	(1)	110	8	7.3	15	12	(1)
Mineral	2	0.2	2		1	1	1	0.2			2					
Montezuma	3	0.1	1	2	2	1	2	0.1			3					
Montrose	9	0.1	4	5	5	4	2	0.1			8			1		
Morgan	17	0.2	17		8	9	7	0.2	2	(1)	17	2	(1)	3	3	(1)
Otero	247	1.2	199	48	138	109	81	1.3	7	(1)	199	15	7.5	46	39	(1)
Ouray	22	0.6	21	1	13	9	10	0.6	1	(1)	20	2	(1)	2	2	(1)
Park	1	(2)	1		1		1	0.1			1					
Phillips	1	(2)	1			1					1					
Pitkin	15	0.3	14	1	9	6	6	0.4	2	(1)	14	3	(1)	3	3	(1)
Prowers	38	0.4	37	1	23	15	20	0.7	3	(1)	34	3	(1)	3	3	(1)
Pueblo	1,689	3.2	1,284	405	883	806	629	3.2	92	14.6	1,426	193	13.5	223	170	76.2
Rio Blanco	7	0.3	7		3	4	3	0.4			7			1		
Rio Grande	5	0.1	1	4	3	2	2	0.1			5					
Routt	28	0.4	28		17	11	14	0.5	5	(1)	22	8	(1)	4	2	(1)
Saguache	5	0.1	2	3	3	2	1	0.1			4	1	(1)	3	3	(1)
San Juan	16	0.5	8	8	8	8	5	0.3	1	(1)	13	1	(1)	4	4	(1)
San Miguel	16	0.3	12	4	9	7	8	0.3			15					
Sedgwick	15	0.5	3	12	9	6	3	0.3			10			5	5	(1)
Summit	2	0.1	2		2		2	0.2			2					
Teller	139	1.0	102	37	69	70	58	1.1	2	(1)	125	6	4.8	19	12	(1)
Washington	31	0.5	24	7	16	15	14	0.7	2	(1)	30	4	(1)	4	3	(1)
Weld	92	0.2	70	22	53	39	33	0.3	6	(1)	74	10	(1)	13	8	(1)
CONNECTICUT.																
Total	15,174	1.4	11,428	3,746	7,229	7,945	4,765	1.4	314	6.6	12,598	792	6.3	2,274	2,057	90.5
Fairfield	3,516	1.4	2,814	702	1,633	1,883	1,101	1.4	69	6.3	2,920	183	6.3	487	417	85.6
Hartford	2,934	1.2	2,047	887	1,426	1,508	889	1.1	54	6.1	2,380	133	5.6	499	458	91.8
Litchfield	758	1.1	621	137	375	383	238	1.1	18	7.6	615	39	6.3	143	133	93.0
Middlesex	367	0.8	282	85	157	210	115	0.8	17	14.8	316	35	11.1	53	47	(1)
New Haven	5,634	1.7	4,244	1,390	2,716	2,918	1,799	1.7	84	4.7	4,724	241	5.1	801	735	91.8
New London	1,431	1.6	1,040	391	667	764	460	1.6	51	11.1	1,213	120	9.9	199	182	91.5
Tolland	109	0.4	68	41	65	44	41	0.5	6	(1)	84	8	(1)	21	20	(1)
Windham	425	0.9	312	113	190	235	122	0.8	15	12.3	346	33	9.5	71	65	(1)

[1] Per cent not shown where base is less than 100.   [2] Less than one-tenth of 1 per cent.

TABLE **III.**—GENERAL STATISTICS OF THE NEGRO POPULATION OF THE UNITED STATES, BY COUNTIES: 1910—Con.

[Counties in which no Negroes were reported are omitted.]

COUNTY.	NEGRO POPULATION: 1910.															
	Total.	Per cent of total population.	Color.		Sex.		Males 21 years of age and over.				Persons 10 years of age and over.			Persons 6 to 14 years of age.		
			Black.	Mulatto.	Male.	Female.	Number.	Per cent of total.	Illiterate.		Total.	Illiterate.		Total.	Attending school.	
									Number.	Per cent.		Number.	Per cent.		Number.	Per cent.

DELAWARE.

COUNTY.	Total.	Per cent	Black.	Mulatto.	Male.	Female.	Number.	Per cent	Illit. No.	Illit. Pct.	Total.	Illit. No.	Illit. Pct.	Total.	Att. No.	Att. Pct.
Total	31,181	15.4	27,475	3,706	16,011	15,170	9,050	14.6	2,829	31.3	24,777	6,345	25.6	6,172	4,689	76.0
Kent	7,561	23.1	6,276	1,285	3,905	3,656	1,962	20.6	721	36.7	5,773	1,637	28.4	1,731	1,265	73.1
New Castle	15,682	12.7	14,476	1,206	8,035	7,647	5,134	13.0	1,312	25.6	13,089	2,926	22.4	2,572	2,041	79.4
Sussex	7,938	17.1	6,723	1,215	4,071	3,867	1,954	15.0	796	40.7	5,915	1,782	30.1	1,869	1,383	74.0

DISTRICT OF COLUMBIA.

COUNTY.	Total.	Per cent	Black.	Mulatto.	Male.	Female.	Number.	Per cent	Illit. No.	Illit. Pct.	Total.	Illit. No.	Illit. Pct.	Total.	Att. No.	Att. Pct.
Total	94,446	28.5	61,494	32,952	42,615	51,831	27,621	26.6	3,801	13.8	79,964	10,814	13.5	12,910	10,807	83.7
District of Columbia	94,446	28.5	61,494	32,952	42,615	51,831	27,621	26.6	3,801	13.8	79,964	10,814	13.5	12,910	10,807	83.7

FLORIDA.

COUNTY.	Total.	Per cent	Black.	Mulatto.	Male.	Female.	Number.	Per cent	Illit. No.	Illit. Pct.	Total.	Illit. No.	Illit. Pct.	Total.	Att. No.	Att. Pct.
Total	308,669	41.0	259,158	49,511	161,362	147,307	89,659	41.9	23,219	25.9	233,744	59,503	25.5	63,486	36,278	57.1
Alachua	19,092	55.7	15,472	3,620	9,838	9,254	5,116	55.7	1,524	29.8	14,096	3,803	27.0	4,329	2,527	58.4
Baker	1,159	24.1	1,116	43	655	504	333	30.1	105	31.5	817	289	35.4	246	72	29.3
Bradford	3,987	28.3	3,287	700	2,099	1,888	1,048	30.5	272	26.0	2,839	704	24.8	971	528	54.4
Brevard	1,399	29.7	977	422	812	587	532	34.1	112	21.1	1,114	191	17.1	240	176	73.3
Calhoun	2,140	28.7	1,923	217	1,168	972	602	32.6	163	27.1	1,480	421	28.4	468	157	33.5
Citrus	3,635	54.0	2,869	766	2,142	1,493	1,383	60.9	447	32.3	2,879	996	34.6	629	235	37.4
Clay	2,453	40.1	1,950	503	1,339	1,114	755	45.2	162	21.5	1,818	433	23.8	488	238	48.8
Columbia	8,411	47.5	7,074	1,337	4,347	4,064	1,977	47.1	625	31.6	5,979	1,638	27.4	2,117	1,312	62.0
Dade	4,194	35.1	3,817	377	2,285	1,909	1,586	36.6	176	41.1	3,426	362	10.6	568	442	77.8
De Soto	2,351	16.6	2,187	164	1,393	958	953	23.6	179	18.8	1,827	323	17.7	397	199	50.1
Duval	37,270	49.6	31,012	6,258	18,827	18,443	12,061	48.9	1,811	15.0	30,835	4,821	15.6	5,722	4,135	72.3
Escambia	15,111	39.7	13,035	2,076	7,469	7,642	4,283	40.4	937	21.9	11,941	2,403	20.1	2,820	1,840	65.2
Franklin	2,487	47.8	2,192	295	1,305	1,182	847	51.9	303	35.8	2,049	670	32.7	399	254	63.7
Gadsden	14,965	67.4	13,033	1,932	7,251	7,714	3,096	61.2	1,382	44.6	10,679	4,307	40.3	3,949	2,312	58.5
Hamilton	5,533	46.8	5,020	513	2,816	2,717	1,286	46.2	447	34.8	3,863	1,445	37.4	1,413	418	29.6
Hernando	2,781	55.7	2,288	493	1,568	1,213	923	59.5	256	27.7	2,046	532	26.0	589	302	51.3
Hillsboro	16,445	21.0	12,322	4,123	8,513	7,932	5,465	22.4	873	16.0	13,340	1,964	14.7	2,638	1,925	73.0
Holmes	1,194	10.3	1,043	151	666	528	379	14.3	152	40.7	899	366	40.7	221	88	39.8
Jackson	14,254	47.8	12,593	1,661	6,931	7,323	2,990	46.3	1,230	41.1	10,020	4,112	41.0	3,557	1,705	47.9
Jefferson	13,114	76.2	11,919	1,195	6,587	6,527	2,689	70.4	867	32.2	9,309	2,618	28.1	3,495	1,586	45.4
Lafayette	1,361	20.3	1,216	145	803	558	464	26.6	122	26.3	992	315	31.8	278	35	12.6
Lake	3,627	38.1	2,865	762	2,046	1,581	1,204	40.8	409	34.0	2,823	850	30.1	717	520	72.5
Lee	937	14.9	642	295	589	348	423	20.4	34	8.0	764	49	6.4	131	46	35.1
Leon	14,726	75.8	12,224	2,502	7,572	7,154	4,130	75.6	1,193	28.9	11,109	3,544	31.9	3,171	2,006	63.3
Levy	4,727	45.6	4,342	385	2,643	2,084	1,531	50.8	432	28.2	3,486	916	26.3	968	658	68.0
Liberty	2,111	44.9	1,906	205	1,215	896	639	50.7	202	31.6	1,502	447	29.8	565	368	65.1
Madison	9,410	55.6	8,729	681	4,725	4,685	2,054	53.3	756	36.8	6,390	2,485	38.9	2,397	667	27.8
Manatee	2,346	24.6	2,103	243	1,387	959	958	32.0	213	22.2	1,904	415	21.8	337	232	68.8
Marion	16,376	60.8	13,923	2,453	8,477	7,899	4,497	59.0	1,165	25.9	12,146	2,777	22.9	3,727	2,563	68.8
Monroe	5,842	27.1	4,207	1,635	2,834	3,008	1,566	24.3	255	16.3	4,440	644	14.5	1,221	980	80.3
Nassau	5,553	52.8	4,972	581	2,979	2,574	1,665	56.2	517	31.1	4,185	1,123	26.8	1,077	683	63.4
Orange	7,604	39.8	7,116	488	4,006	3,598	2,256	38.5	478	21.2	5,758	1,127	19.6	1,539	911	59.2
Osceola	927	16.8	892	35	551	376	367	20.3	118	32.2	728	212	29.1	164	115	70.1
Palm Beach	2,220	39.8	2,066	154	1,261	959	867	43.1	125	14.4	1,812	216	11.9	339	294	86.7
Pasco	2,456	32.7	2,070	386	1,491	965	995	40.9	413	41.5	1,960	718	36.6	415	170	41.0
Polk	7,419	30.7	4,779	2,640	4,428	2,991	2,932	37.5	512	17.5	5,835	983	16.8	1,127	651	57.8
Putman	6,804	52.0	4,700	2,104	3,584	3,220	2,062	52.1	418	20.3	5,243	963	18.4	1,419	969	68.3
St. Johns	5,454	41.3	4,390	1,064	2,887	2,567	1,869	45.0	437	23.4	4,423	958	21.7	887	438	49.4
St. Lucie	865	21.2	808	57	491	374	335	25.8	67	20.0	684	129	18.9	128	83	64.8
Santa Rosa	4,234	28.4	3,414	820	2,338	1,896	1,416	35.9	477	33.7	3,178	1,077	33.9	746	343	46.0
Sumter	2,255	33.7	2,190	65	1,246	1,009	694	37.4	190	27.4	1,635	440	26.9	480	244	50.8
Suwannee	7,813	42.0	5,291	2,522	3,901	3,912	1,709	40.3	571	33.4	5,502	1,933	35.1	1,990	582	29.2
Taylor	2,689	37.9	2,051	638	1,688	1,001	1,091	49.1	364	33.4	2,098	799	38.1	412	79	19.2
Volusia	6,592	39.9	5,999	593	3,537	3,055	2,113	40.9	572	27.1	5,164	1,182	22.9	1,266	901	71.2
Wakulla	2,384	49.6	2,208	176	1,278	1,106	589	50.6	176	29.9	1,679	502	29.9	589	305	51.8
Walton	4,997	30.4	4,439	558	2,705	2,292	1,482	34.1	589	39.7	3,542	1,331	37.6	1,076	464	43.1
Washington	4,965	30.3	4,487	478	2,689	2,276	1,447	34.2	391	27.0	3,506	970	27.7	1,064	520	48.9

TABLE III.—GENERAL STATISTICS OF THE NEGRO POPULATION OF THE UNITED STATES, BY COUNTIES: 1910—Con.

[Counties in which no Negroes were reported are omitted.]

GEORGIA.

COUNTY.	Total.	Per cent of total population.	Color. Black.	Color. Mulatto.	Sex. Male.	Sex. Female.	Males 21 years of age and over. Number.	Males 21 years of age and over. Per cent of total.	Males 21 years of age and over. Illiterate. Number.	Males 21 years of age and over. Illiterate. Per cent.	Persons 10 years of age and over. Total.	Persons 10 years of age and over. Illiterate. Number.	Persons 10 years of age and over. Illiterate. Per cent.	Persons 6 to 14 years of age. Total.	Persons 6 to 14 years of age. Attending school. Number.	Persons 6 to 14 years of age. Attending school. Per cent.
Total	1,176,987	45.1	972,782	204,205	580,263	596,724	266,814	43.0	111,037	41.6	846,195	308,639	36.5	282,070	156,258	55.4
Appling	2,863	23.2	2,117	746	1,535	1,328	752	26.6	282	37.5	2,008	660	32.9	649	287	44.2
Baker	5,718	71.7	5,128	590	2,859	2,859	1,295	70.8	780	60.2	4,075	2,281	56.0	1,497	994	66.4
Baldwin	11,005	60.0	9,226	1,779	5,390	5,615	2,619	52.9	1,398	53.4	8,090	3,426	42.3	2,470	1,554	62.9
Banks	2,321	20.6	2,074	247	1,157	1,164	468	19.1	207	44.2	1,538	513	33.4	587	406	69.2
Bartow	6,348	25.0	5,316	1,032	3,224	3,124	1,469	25.1	587	40.0	4,568	1,499	32.8	1,599	923	57.7
Ben Hill	4,901	41.3	3,489	1,412	2,526	2,375	1,265	39.9	394	31.1	3,611	1,054	29.2	1,054	624	59.2
Berrien	6,263	27.5	5,640	623	3,240	3,023	1,577	30.0	594	37.7	4,387	1,565	35.7	1,490	667	44.8
Bibb	27,481	48.5	23,987	3,494	12,979	14,502	7,145	46.5	1,675	23.4	21,840	4,760	21.8	5,288	3,400	64.3
Brooks	14,086	59.1	12,122	1,964	7,111	6,975	3,051	56.4	1,316	43.1	9,614	3,688	38.4	3,578	1,776	49.6
Bryan	3,337	49.8	2,531	806	1,763	1,574	838	50.7	302	36.0	2,328	883	37.9	837	347	41.5
Bulloch	10,591	40.0	8,472	2,119	5,460	5,131	2,192	38.4	726	33.1	7,046	2,061	29.3	2,927	1,343	45.9
Burke	22,462	82.4	18,039	4,423	10,922	11,540	4,920	79.1	2,133	43.4	16,092	6,143	38.2	5,524	3,064	55.5
Butts	7,200	52.8	5,752	1,448	3,627	3,573	1,577	48.7	639	40.5	4,990	1,734	34.7	1,807	706	39.1
Calhoun	8,361	73.8	6,529	1,832	4,123	4,238	1,852	71.4	1,100	59.4	5,840	3,169	54.3	2,093	1,073	51.3
Camden	5,113	66.5	4,836	277	2,664	2,449	1,222	65.3	415	34.0	3,633	1,162	32.0	1,316	712	54.1
Campbell	3,616	33.3	3,333	283	1,907	1,709	823	31.8	351	42.6	2,515	907	36.1	912	422	46.3
Carroll	6,383	20.7	5,213	1,170	3,232	3,151	1,387	19.9	536	38.6	4,369	1,470	33.6	1,675	830	49.6
Catoosa	476	6.6	265	211	242	234	117	5.2	30	25.6	346	82	26.7	92	50	......
Charlton	1,189	25.2	1,092	97	684	505	401	32.5	183	45.6	908	430	47.4	216	68	31.5
Chatham	43,981	55.2	34,109	9,872	20,656	23,325	12,929	53.9	3,634	28.1	35,977	10,581	29.4	7,162	4,654	65.0
Chattahoochee	3,864	69.2	3,181	683	1,858	2,006	736	63.0	382	51.9	2,624	1,053	40.1	1,042	647	62.1
Chatooga	2,454	18.0	1,932	522	1,291	1,163	550	17.8	199	36.2	1,746	469	26.9	626	412	65.8
Cherokee	1,168	7.0	947	221	574	594	252	6.7	104	41.3	803	304	37.9	284	141	49.6
Clarke	11,767	50.6	9,823	1,944	5,585	6,182	2,593	45.3	1,061	40.9	8,725	2,906	33.3	2,610	1,788	68.5
Clay	6,569	73.3	6,003	566	3,183	3,386	1,349	69.3	550	40.8	4,522	1,842	40.7	1,609	738	45.9
Clayton	4,632	44.3	3,872	760	2,360	2,272	958	40.9	415	43.3	3,299	1,197	36.3	1,225	571	46.6
Clinch	3,378	40.1	3,276	102	1,896	1,482	1,065	46.4	311	29.2	2,467	805	32.6	678	294	43.4
Cobb	7,418	26.1	5,824	1,594	3,594	3,824	1,694	25.0	545	32.2	5,419	1,505	27.8	1,744	1,053	60.4
Coffee	7,734	35.2	7,128	606	4,091	3,643	2,032	38.9	757	37.3	5,540	2,056	37.1	1,779	775	43.6
Colquitt	4,617	23.3	4,064	553	2,383	2,234	1,261	27.0	441	35.0	3,349	1,145	34.2	1,019	441	43.3
Columbia	9,198	74.6	5,604	3,594	4,575	4,623	1,959	70.6	969	49.5	6,438	2,557	39.7	2,359	1,315	55.7
Coweta	16,267	56.5	13,800	2,467	8,005	8,262	3,414	52.3	1,517	44.4	11,420	4,273	37.4	4,223	2,433	57.6
Crawford	4,922	59.2	3,995	927	2,449	2,473	917	52.7	475	51.8	3,289	1,346	40.9	1,379	808	58.6
Crisp	8,616	52.5	8,297	319	4,251	4,365	2,044	51.6	754	36.9	6,317	2,100	33.2	1,969	1,334	67.8
Dade	291	7.0	230	61	148	143	27	7.6	27	(1)	199	71	35.7	76	23	(1)
Dawson	152	3.2	129	23	72	80	32	3.1	15	(1)	104	59	56.7	40	4	(1)
Decatur	16,738	57.6	14,169	2,569	8,330	8,408	3,835	56.5	1,508	39.3	11,836	4,477	37.8	4,163	2,360	56.7
Dekalb	8,362	30.0	7,078	1,284	4,285	4,077	2,065	30.0	909	44.0	6,150	2,307	37.5	1,902	1,021	53.7
Dodge	8,460	42.0	7,679	781	4,306	4,154	1,772	41.3	855	48.3	5,826	2,435	41.8	2,217	1,045	47.1
Dooly	12,728	61.9	11,400	1,328	6,415	6,313	2,680	58.7	1,485	55.4	8,790	4,069	46.3	3,502	2,240	64.0
Dougherty	12,049	75.1	10,446	1,603	5,793	6,256	3,053	71.0	1,905	62.4	9,254	5,587	60.4	2,526	1,009	39.9
Douglas	2,171	24.2	1,713	458	1,102	1,069	460	22.2	145	31.5	1,525	394	25.8	617	313	50.7
Early	11,273	62.2	9,782	1,492	5,652	5,621	2,412	59.9	1,013	42.0	7,710	2,964	38.4	2,918	1,220	41.8
Echols	990	29.9	947	43	577	413	309	35.2	101	32.7	735	235	32.0	211	59	28.0
Effingham	4,278	42.9	3,250	1,028	2,170	2,108	1,010	42.1	486	48.1	3,021	1,315	43.5	990	484	48.9
Elbert	12,082	50.1	10,371	1,711	6,100	5,982	2,499	46.5	1,157	46.3	8,283	3,170	38.3	3,220	1,835	57.0
Emanuel	9,990	39.7	7,671	2,319	5,175	4,815	2,303	41.0	1,078	46.8	6,853	3,001	43.8	2,494	1,280	51.3
Fannin	162	1.3	114	48	76	86	32	1.2	15	(1)	123	53	43.1	42	11	(1)
Fayette	3,815	34.8	2,453	1,362	1,901	1,914	813	32.7	374	46.0	2,599	974	37.5	983	439	44.7
Floyd	10,482	28.5	7,440	3,042	5,180	5,302	2,508	27.9	867	34.6	7,750	2,251	29.0	2,353	1,319	56.1
Forsyth	1,098	9.2	658	440	552	546	243	16.5	97	39.9	749	293	39.1	266	94	35.3
Franklin	3,974	22.2	3,385	589	2,017	1,957	832	21.4	370	44.5	2,742	1,021	37.2	1,038	652	62.8
Fulton	57,985	32.6	39,838	18,147	26,513	31,472	15,739	30.5	3,662	23.3	47,744	10,503	22.0	9,192	6,334	68.9
Gilmer	71	0.8	49	22	36	35	17	0.8	3	(1)	44	11	(1)	18	1	(1)
Glascock	1,507	32.3	1,432	75	725	782	312	30.2	153	49.0	1,022	451	44.1	359	201	56.0
Glynn	9,774	62.2	7,585	2,189	4,988	4,786	2,724	60.6	920	33.8	7,410	2,171	29.3	2,041	1,121	54.9
Gordon	1,356	8.5	1,008	348	699	657	311	8.4	145	46.6	995	344	34.6	301	165	54.8
Grady	7,403	40.1	6,147	1,256	3,707	3,696	1,510	37.8	640	42.4	4,971	1,979	39.8	1,920	978	50.9
Greene	11,636	62.9	9,559	2,077	5,725	5,911	2,445	58.6	1,415	57.9	8,358	3,964	47.4	2,843	1,507	53.0
Gwinnett	4,431	15.4	3,441	990	2,237	2,194	1,008	15.3	447	44.3	3,102	1,202	38.7	1,123	578	51.5
Habersham	711	7.0	477	234	337	374	144	6.3	58	40.3	524	135	25.8	183	119	65.0
Hall	4,030	15.7	2,856	1,174	1,946	2,084	867	14.9	349	40.3	2,891	1,003	34.7	974	585	60.1
Hancock	14,268	74.4	11,970	2,298	7,114	7,154	2,831	69.6	1,197	42.3	9,794	3,407	34.8	3,940	2,154	54.7
Haralson	2,027	15.0	1,777	250	952	1,075	410	13.8	110	26.8	1,437	374	26.0	533	289	54.2
Harris	12,865	71.9	11,087	1,778	6,295	6,570	2,518	65.9	1,147	45.6	8,869	3,521	39.7	3,451	1,765	51.1
Hart	5,080	31.3	4,727	353	2,522	2,558	1,150	32.3	520	45.2	3,536	1,355	38.3	1,285	742	57.7
Heard	3,756	33.6	2,969	787	1,899	1,857	776	32.3	330	42.5	2,586	959	37.1	964	555	57.6
Henry	10,184	51.1	7,840	2,344	5,048	5,136	2,212	48.6	967	43.7	7,232	2,686	37.1	2,629	1,082	41.2
Houston	17,388	73.6	14,328	3,060	8,496	8,892	3,615	68.8	1,839	50.9	12,106	4,911	40.6	4,515	2,938	65.1
Irwin	4,916	47.0	4,276	640	2,532	2,384	1,185	48.5	520	43.9	3,432	1,293	37.7	1,201	718	59.8

[1] Per cent not shown where base is less than 100.

TABLE III.—GENERAL STATISTICS OF THE NEGRO POPULATION OF THE UNITED STATES, BY COUNTIES: 1910—Con.

[Counties in which no Negroes were reported are omitted.]

COUNTY.	Total.	Per cent of total population.	Color.		Sex.		Males 21 years of age and over.				Persons 10 years of age and over.			Persons 6 to 14 years of age.		
									Illiterate.			Illiterate.			Attending school.	
			Black.	Mulatto.	Male.	Female.	Number.	Per cent of total.	Number.	Per cent.	Total.	Number.	Per cent.	Total.	Number.	Per cent.

GEORGIA—Continued.

Jackson	8,613	28.5	6,935	1,678	4,335	4,278	1,847	27.0	781	42.3	5,906	2,082	35.3	2,169	1,077	49.7
Jasper	11,484	69.4	9,908	1,576	5,738	5,746	2,326	64.1	1,313	56.4	7,998	3,564	44.6	3,010	1,631	54.2
Jeff Davis	1,593	26.3	1,376	217	821	772	399	28.2	160	40.1	1,128	405	35.9	367	141	38.4
Jefferson	12,979	60.7	11,500	1,479	6,273	6,706	2,502	56.4	900	36.0	8,839	2,525	28.4	3,502	1,887	53.9
Jenkins	7,296	63.3	6,229	1,067	3,632	3,664	1,739	63.3	821	47.2	5,270	2,337	44.3	1,675	926	55.3
Johnson	5,557	43.1	5,072	485	2,755	2,802	1,120	39.6	424	37.9	3,793	1,330	35.1	1,448	602	41.6
Jones	9,288	70.9	8,259	1,029	4,598	4,690	1,794	65.3	897	50.0	6,350	2,512	39.6	2,588	1,287	49.7
Laurens	17,544	49.4	14,774	2,770	8,624	8,920	3,656	47.4	1,603	43.8	12,026	4,611	38.3	4,568	2,370	51.9
Lee	9,992	85.6	8,436	1,556	5,058	4,934	2,388	83.8	1,394	58.4	7,281	3,570	49.0	2,400	1,649	68.7
Liberty	8,355	64.6	7,219	1,136	4,271	4,084	1,968	63.8	623	31.7	5,978	1,551	25.9	2,218	1,059	47.7
Lincoln	5,175	59.4	4,302	873	2,588	2,587	1,027	55.6	522	50.8	3,542	1,485	41.9	1,398	653	46.7
Lowndes	12,955	53.0	10,442	2,513	6,615	6,340	3,097	51.2	903	29.2	9,213	2,491	27.0	3,161	1,697	53.7
Lumpkin	320	5.9	284	36	157	163	61	4.8	31	(1)	223	71	31.8	86	43	(1)
McDuffie	5,985	58.0	3,786	2,199	2,966	3,019	1,348	56.0	466	34.6	4,396	1,258	28.6	1,458	626	42.9
McIntosh	4,978	77.3	4,198	780	2,382	2,596	1,110	73.0	318	28.6	3,561	849	23.8	1,284	773	60.2
Macon	10,581	70.5	9,122	1,459	5,093	5,488	2,207	65.4	1,212	54.9	7,371	3,186	43.2	2,629	1,861	70.8
Madison	5,149	30.6	4,346	803	2,524	2,625	1,019	27.7	541	53.1	3,457	1,515	43.8	1,443	774	53.6
Marion	5,364	58.6	4,705	659	2,581	2,783	1,033	53.1	622	60.2	3,620	1,922	53.1	1,391	545	39.2
Meriwether	14,730	58.5	11,652	3,078	7,307	7,423	3,039	53.7	1,681	55.3	10,089	4,379	43.4	3,806	2,448	64.3
Miller	3,257	40.8	2,466	791	1,724	1,533	728	40.7	401	55.1	2,157	1,226	56.8	864	199	23.0
Milton	718	9.9	598	120	377	341	139	8.4	40	28.8	463	116	25.1	217	67	30.9
Mitchell	11,649	52.7	10,539	1,110	5,735	5,914	2,577	52.2	1,305	50.6	8,286	3,802	45.9	2,950	1,518	51.5
Monroe	13,656	66.8	10,857	2,799	6,600	7,056	2,698	61.9	1,388	51.4	9,274	3,774	40.7	3,586	2,049	57.1
Montgomery	7,310	37.2	6,314	996	3,722	3,588	1,586	36.3	489	30.8	4,954	1,413	28.5	1,916	883	46.1
Morgan	13,414	68.0	11,464	1,950	6,658	6,756	3,074	66.3	1,723	56.1	9,671	4,387	45.4	3,313	1,920	58.0
Murray	402	4.1	401	1	219	183	86	3.9	37	(1)	284	83	29.2	93	69	(1)
Muscogee	16,747	46.2	12,044	4,703	7,688	9,059	3,858	42.9	1,421	36.8	12,856	4,119	32.0	3,605	2,246	62.3
Newton	9,458	51.3	7,371	2,087	4,621	4,837	2,003	47.9	836	41.7	6,663	2,288	34.3	2,388	1,227	51.4
Oconee	5,162	46.5	4,389	773	2,654	2,508	1,095	43.3	587	53.6	3,544	1,538	43.4	1,318	614	46.6
Oglethorpe	11,338	60.7	9,650	1,688	5,712	5,626	2,426	57.8	1,318	54.3	7,839	3,389	43.2	2,920	1,749	59.9
Paulding	1,588	11.2	1,291	297	804	784	335	11.1	111	33.1	1,063	299	28.1	399	227	56.9
Pickens	440	4.9	397	43	225	215	96	.4.8	31	(1)	320	77	24.1	98	68	(1)
Pierce	2,742	25.5	2,227	515	1,542	1,200	761	30.6	255	33.5	2,008	595	29.6	603	361	59.9
Pike	10,159	52.1	9,225	934	4,951	5,208	2,062	47.7	1,073	52.0	7,109	3,082	43.4	2,756	1,393	50.5
Polk	5,697	28.2	4,408	1,289	2,849	2,848	1,305	28.1	482	36.9	4,042	1,227	30.4	1,360	755	55.5
Pulaski	13,504	59.1	10,758	2,746	6,611	6,893	2,873	56.6	1,523	53.0	9,514	4,452	46.8	3,325	1,670	50.2
Putnam	10,178	73.3	8,691	1,487	5,015	5,163	2,201	68.9	1,311	59.6	7,138	3,560	49.9	2,600	1,355	52.1
Quitman	3,588	78.1	2,593	995	1,762	1,826	698	72.0	357	51.1	2,388	1,052	44.1	932	557	59.8
Rabun	156	2.8	55	101	75	81	30	2.4	10	(1)	111	27	24.3	46	36	(1)
Randolph	12,986	68.9	11,361	1,625	6,315	6,671	2,672	63.7	1,382	51.7	8,921	4,136	46.4	3,229	1,542	47.8
Richmond	28,390	48.2	22,206	6,184	13,110	15,280	7,709	46.4	1,783	23.1	23,491	5,316	22.6	4,792	3,220	67.2
Rockdale	3,592	40.3	2,808	784	1,775	1,817	761	36.9	289	38.0	2,476	774	31.3	882	592	67.1
Schley	3,291	63.1	2,809	482	1,593	1,698	613	55.1	247	40.3	2,263	699	30.9	936	700	74.8
Screven	12,165	60.2	10,853	1,312	6,132	6,033	2,461	55.9	1,218	49.5	8,140	3,737	45.9	3,267	1,517	46.4
Spalding	10,060	51.0	7,619	2,441	4,953	5,107	2,205	46.9	990	44.9	7,265	2,728	37.5	2,393	1,213	50.7
Stephens	2,222	22.8	2,174	48	1,085	1,137	477	21.8	122	25.6	1,541	303	19.7	559	308	55.1
Stewart	10,381	77.3	8,717	1,664	5,131	5,250	2,029	71.3	699	34.5	7,078	2,155	30.4	2,849	1,600	56.2
Sumter	21,243	73.0	19,311	1,932	10,524	10,719	4,623	68.9	1,827	39.5	15,278	5,129	33.6	5,067	3,346	66.0
Talbot	8,230	70.4	7,062	1,168	4,033	4,197	1,610	63.9	807	50.1	5,611	2,413	43.0	2,146	987	46.0
Taliaferro	6,450	.73.6	5,642	808	3,161	3,289	1,312	68.9	610	46.5	4,530	1,678	37.0	1,674	905	54.1
Tattnall	5,841	31.5	4,698	1,143	2,999	2,842	1,306	31.8	465	35.6	3,968	1,254	31.6	1,549	778	50.2
Taylor	5,379	49.6	4,398	981	2,612	2,767	1,045	44.1	540	51.7	3,615	1,611	44.6	1,390	815	58.6
Telfair	4,761	35.8	4,245	516	2,414	2,347	1,044	34.1	372	35.6	3,312	1,080	32.6	1,181	488	41.3
Terrell	16,607	75.5	14,237	2,370	8,117	8,490	3,496	71.3	2,020	57.8	11,716	5,889	50.3	4,233	2,264	52.9
Thomas	17,086	58.8	14,714	2,372	8,267	8,819	3,707	54.9	1,516	40.9	12,333	4,536	36.8	4,130	2,151	52.1
Tift	3,777	32.9	3,282	495	1,960	1,817	996	35.2	404	40.6	2,710	993	36.6	853	483	56.6
Toombs	3,411	30.4	3,020	391	1,777	1,634	840	32.4	416	49.5	2,431	1,187	48.8	842	405	48.1
Towns	15	0.4	15	....	7	8	3	0.4	1	(1)	11	6	(1)	3	3	(1)
Troup	15,399	58.7	12,377	3,022	7,548	7,851	3,298	54.3	1,472	44.6	11,065	4,167	37.7	3,913	2,314	59.1
Turner	4,018	39.9	3,471	547	2,055	1,963	957	40.2	447	46.7	2,781	1,226	44.1	929	359	38.6
Twiggs	7,396	68.9	6,722	674	3,629	3,767	1,499	64.9	762	50.8	5,132	1,968	38.3	1,962	1,306	66.6
Union	64	0.9	53	11	33	31	15	1.0	3	(1)	50	9	(1)	10	5	(1)
Upson	6,998	54.9	6,236	762	3,467	3,531	1,402	49.7	581	41.4	4,872	1,647	33.8	1,848	1,069	57.8
Walker	2,451	13.1	2,004	447	1,289	1,162	597	13.1	159	26.6	1,786	399	22.3	559	327	58.5
Walton	10,070	39.7	8,093	1,977	4,942	5,128	2,110	36.9	1,079	51.1	6,954	2,867	41.2	2,560	1,371	53.6
Ware	8,914	38.8	6,450	2,464	4,966	3,948	2,830	42.5	852	30.1	6,754	1,826	27.0	1,755	813	46.3
Warren	8,132	68.6	7,363	769	3,923	4,209	1,679	63.0	709	42.2	5,645	1,823	32.3	2,060	1,159	56.3
Washington	17,393	61.7	16,109	1,284	8,391	9,002	3,521	57.7	1,506	42.8	12,171	4,393	36.1	4,496	2,628	58.5
Wayne	3,309	25.3	2,668	641	1,725	1,584	888	29.2	311	35.0	2,369	738	31.2	741	393	53.0
Webster	4,182	68.0	3,705	477	2,015	2,167	808	63.6	409	50.6	2,833	1,091	38.5	1,118	646	57.8
White	397	7.8	323	74	215	182	76	6.8	26	(1)	262	66	25.2	108	76	70.4
Whitfield	1,719	10.8	1,119	600	829	890	349	9.5	111	31.8	1,226	316	25.8	442	289	65.4
Wilcox	5,505	40.8	4,525	980	2,788	2,717	1,271	41.1	595	46.8	3,874	1,610	41.6	1,375	796	57.9
Wilkes	16,598	70.8	13,714	2,884	8,186	8,412	3,581	68.0	2,279	63.6	11,744	6,147	52.3	4,207	2,419	57.5
Wilkinson	5,155	51.2	4,474	681	2,577	2,578	1,087	46.3	602	55.4	3,534	1,514	42.8	1,371	848	61.9
Worth	9,517	49.7	8,625	892	4,840	4,677	2,198	50.0	924	42.0	6,643	2,488	37.5	2,352	1,221	51.9

1 Per cent not shown where base is less than 100.

TABLE III.—GENERAL STATISTICS OF THE NEGRO POPULATION OF THE UNITED STATES, BY COUNTIES: 1910—Con.

[Counties in which no Negroes were reported are omitted.]

COUNTY.	Total.	Per cent of total population.	Color.		Sex.		Males 21 years of age and over.				Persons 10 years of age and over.			Persons 6 to 14 years of age.		
			Black.	Mulatto.	Male.	Female.	Number.	Per cent of total.	Illiterate. Number.	Illiterate. Per cent.	Total.	Illiterate. Number.	Illiterate. Per cent.	Total.	Attending school. Number.	Attending school. Per cent.

IDAHO.

COUNTY.	Total.	Per cent	Black.	Mulatto.	Male.	Female.	Number.	Per cent	Illit. No.	Illit. Pct.	Total.	Illit. No.	Illit. Pct.	Total.	Att. No.	Att. Pct.
Total	651	0.2	425	226	398	253	328	0.3	16	4.9	578	37	6.4	45	33	(1)
Ada	168	0.6	91	77	100	68	72	0.7	3	(1)	147	10	6.8	15	11	(1)
Bannock	129	0.7	84	45	96	33	93	1.3	1	(1)	125	1	0.8	2	1	(1)
Bear Lake	1	(2)	1		1		1	0.1			1					
Bingham	44	0.2	43	1	25	19	21	0.3	2	(1)	40	3	(1)			
Blaine	10	0.1	4	6	7	3	4	0.1			8			2	2	(1)
Boise	3	0.1	1	2	2	1	2	0.1	1	(1)	3	1	(1)			
Bonner	16	0.1	11	5	8	8	6	0.1			14	3	(1)			
Canyon	33	0.1	21	12	16	17	11	0.1			25	1	(1)	5	3	(1)
Cassia	1	(2)		1	1		1	(2)			1					
Custer	1	(2)	1		1		1	0.1			1					
Elmore	1	(2)	1		1		1	(2)	1	(1)	1	1	(1)			
Fremont	20	0.1	12	8	11	9	7	0.1	2	(1)	15	3	(1)	3	2	(1)
Idaho	5	(2)	2	3	2	3	2	(2)	1	(1)	4	1	(1)			
Kootenai	44	0.2	18	26	22	22	17	0.2	1	(1)	34	4	(1)	6	5	(1)
Latah	28	0.1	26	2	15	13	9	0.2			26			5	5	(1)
Lemhi	5	0.1	5		3	2	2	0.1	1	(1)	4	1	(1)			
Lincoln	28	0.2	28		17	11	16	0.3	1	(1)	24	2	(1)	2	1	(1)
Nez Perce	48	0.2	29	19	29	19	25	0.3			42			3	2	(1)
Oneida	2	(2)	1	1	1	1	1	(2)			2					
Owyhee	3	0.1	2	1		3					3					
Shoshone	18	0.1	12	6	10	8	10	0.2	1	(1)	18	5	(1)			
Twin Falls	31	0.2	22	9	20	11	17	0.3			30					
Washington	12	0.1	10	2	10	2	9	0.2	1	(1)	10	1	(1)	2	1	(1)

ILLINOIS.

COUNTY.	Total.	Per cent	Black.	Mulatto.	Male.	Female.	Number.	Per cent	Illit. No.	Illit. Pct.	Total.	Illit. No.	Illit. Pct.	Total.	Att. No.	Att. Pct.
Total	109,049	1.9	72,221	36,828	56,909	52,140	39,983	2.3	4,349	10.9	92,928	9,713	10.5	14,020	11,636	83.0
Adams	1,880	2.9	1,335	545	975	905	692	3.3	132	19.1	1,639	268	16.4	241	204	84.6
Alexander	7,775	34.2	5,322	2,453	3,983	3,792	2,583	35.6	567	22.0	6,492	1,235	19.0	1,201	875	72.9
Bond	160	0.9	93	67	78	82	56	1.2	14	(1)	131	25	19.1	27	23	(1)
Boone	43	0.3	17	26	20	23	13	0.3	1	(1)	33	2	(1)	7	5	(1)
Brown	6	0.1	1	5	5	1	2	0.1			4			2	2	(1)
Bureau	223	0.5	216	7	114	109	72	0.5	14	(1)	176	24	13.6	37	32	(1)
Carroll	13	0.1	13		8	5	6	0.1			12	2	(1)	1	1	(1)
Cass	4	(2)	4		2	2	1	(2)			3			1	1	(1)
Champaign	950	1.8	774	176	476	474	304	2.0	33	10.9	775	70	9.0	139	122	87.8
Christian	181	0.5	119	62	94	87	57	0.6	12	(1)	154	24	15.6	32	29	(1)
Clark	74	0.3	62	12	37	37	17	0.3	1	(1)	59	8	(1)	19	16	(1)
Clay	26	0.1	23	3	10	16	9	0.2			25	1	(1)	4	4	(1)
Clinton	285	1.2	226	59	147	138	66	1.1	4	(1)	196	9	4.6	74	64	(1)
Coles	201	0.6	127	74	93	108	67	0.7	10	(1)	167	20	12.0	25	15	(1)
Cook	46,627	1.9	27,511	19,116	23,915	22,712	18,694	2.4	586	3.1	41,602	1,713	4.1	4,179	3,724	89.1
Crawford	38	0.1	38		22	16	18	0.2			37	1	(1)	3	1	(1)
Cumberland	7	(2)	1	6	5	2	3	0.1			6			1	1	(1)
Dekalb	151	0.5	125	26	85	66	56	0.5	8	(1)	123	13	10.6	25	23	(1)
Dewitt	65	0.3	55	10	34	31	26	0.5	3	(1)	51	5	(1)	12	11	(1)
Douglas	58	0.3	42	16	29	29	21	0.4	2	(1)	46	6	(1)	7	6	(1)
Dupage	171	0.5	130	41	75	96	41	0.4	3	(1)	146	10	6.8	31	20	(1)
Edgar	312	1.1	227	85	143	169	96	1.2	16	(1)	255	34	13.3	38	33	(1)
Edwards	86	0.9	61	25	54	32	30	1.1	3	(1)	73	7	(1)	13	11	(1)
Effingham	23	0.1	14	9	13	10	8	0.1			19			7	6	(1)
Fayette	19	0.1	9	10	11	8	8	0.1	2	(1)	18	2	(1)	3	3	(1)
Ford	87	0.5	60	27	43	44	30	0.6	6	(1)	73	9	(1)	9	6	(1)
Franklin	19	0.1	6	13	10	9	5	0.1			16	2	(1)	6	4	(1)
Fulton	248	0.5	141	107	131	117	94	0.6	19	(1)	199	32	16.1	35	34	(1)
Gallatin	606	4.1	482	124	314	292	175	4.6	67	38.3	494	135	27.3	118	80	67.8
Greene	62	0.3	57	5	33	29	25	0.4	1	(1)	55	4	(1)	8	8	(1)
Grundy	78	0.3	65	13	46	32	34	0.5	11	(1)	64	14	(1)	13	13	(1)
Hamilton	3	(2)	3		2	1					1					
Hancock	59	0.2	43	16	31	28	20	0.2	4	(1)	51	9	(1)	12	8	(1)
Hardin	140	2.0	116	24	75	65	36	2.0	11	(1)	108	35	34.0	41	25	(1)
Henderson	15	0.2	9	6	11	4	5	0.2	3	(1)	11	3	(1)	2	2	(1)
Henry	175	0.4	119	56	94	81	68	0.5	4	(1)	156	15	9.6	24	21	(1)
Iroquois	172	0.5	161	11	89	83	55	0.5	9	(1)	140	18	12.9	28	24	(1)
Jackson	2,696	7.7	2,008	688	1,358	1,338	864	9.1	179	20.7	2,195	385	17.5	444	367	82.7
Jasper	69	0.4	16	53	35	34	19	0.4	4	(1)	44	6	(1)	15	14	(1)
Jefferson	378	1.3	333	45	179	199	166	1.4	21	19.8	310	45	14.5	66	52	(1)
Jersey	89	0.6	77	12	46	43	30	0.7	6	(1)	80	17	(1)	17	16	(1)
Jo Daviess	20	0.1	14	6	8	12	6	0.1			18	2	(1)	3	3	(1)
Johnson	164	1.1	110	54	96	68	50	1.4	13	(1)	135	31	23.0	25	20	(1)
Kane	760	0.8	556	204	374	386	223	0.8	27	12.1	659	51	7.7	139	118	84.9
Kankakee	315	0.8	232	83	166	149	125	1.0	24	19.2	266	49	18.4	34	29	(1)

1 Per cent not shown where base is less than 100.　　　　2 Less than one-tenth of 1 per cent.

TABLE III.—GENERAL STATISTICS OF THE NEGRO POPULATION OF THE UNITED STATES, BY COUNTIES: 1910—Con.

[Counties in which no Negroes were reported are omitted.]

COUNTY.	NEGRO POPULATION; 1910.															
	Total.	Per cent of total population.	Color.		Sex.		Males 21 years of age and over.				Persons 10 years of age and over.			Persons 6 to 14 years of age.		
			Black.	Mu-latto.	Male.	Fe-male.	Num-ber.	Per cent of total.	Illiterate.		Total.	Illiterate.		Total.	Attending school.	
									Num-ber.	Per cent.		Num-ber.	Per cent.		Num-ber.	Per cent.

ILLINOIS—Continued.

COUNTY.	Total.	Per cent	Black.	Mulatto.	Male.	Female.	Number.	Per cent	Illit. No.	Illit. Pct.	Total.	Illit. No.	Illit. Pct.	Total.	Att. No.	Att. Pct.
Kendall	51	0.5	44	7	29	22	19	0.6	3	(1)	44	3	(1)	7	7	(1)
Knox	770	1.7	510	260	386	384	270	1.8	20	7.4	659	51	7.7	101	73	72.3
La Salle	311	0.3	281	30	159	152	104	0.4	14	13.5	257	28	10.9	59	52	(1)
Lake	491	0.9	339	152	230	261	164	0.9	12	7.3	419	37	8.8	63	52	(1)
Lawrence	289	1.3	229	60	137	152	93	1.4	10	(1)	219	17	7.8	44	30	(1)
Lee	62	0.2	56	6	31	31	24	0.3	4	(1)	54	8	(1)	7	5	(1)
Livingston	397	1.0	323	74	283	114	148	1.2	25	16.9	354	42	11.9	46	42	(1)
Logan	377	1.2	325	52	192	185	108	1.2	19	17.6	301	44	14.6	53	44	(1)
McDonough	123	0.5	72	51	62	61	39	0.5	10	(1)	105	17	16.2	15	15	(1)
McHenry	29	0.1	20	9	17	12	13	0.1	1	(1)	26	2	(1)	1		
McLean	1,118	1.6	848	270	566	552	358	1.7	31	8.7	925	83	9.0	182	138	75.8
Macon	906	1.7	588	318	458	448	295	1.8	37	12.5	772	78	10.1	130	109	83.8
Macoupin	186	0.4	165	21	82	104	53	0.4	13	(1)	159	30	18.9	40	35	(1)
Madison	3,146	3.5	2,648	498	1,683	1,463	1,046	3.6	117	11.2	2,499	284	11.4	540	459	85.0
Marion	651	1.9	326	325	330	321	170	1.7	12	7.1	508	21	4.1	142	116	81.7
Marshall	41	0.3	18	23	23	18	13	0.3	2	(1)	31	5	(1)	9	7	(1)
Mason	10	0.1	10		7	3	4	0.1			10			1	1	(1)
Massac	2,584	18.2	1,440	1,144	1,324	1,260	779	19.5	199	25.5	2,033	432	21.2	437	351	80.3
Menard	107	0.8	77	30	55	52	34	0.9	6	(1)	95	16	(1)	16	14	(1)
Mercer	34	0.2	29	5	17	17	14	1	1	(1)	30	3	(1)	4	2	(1)
Monroe	13	0.1	2	11	5	8	2	0.1			11	1	(1)	3	2	(1)
Montgomery	238	0.7	193	45	123	115	71	0.7	15	(1)	198	34	17.2	35	32	(1)
Morgan	1,361	4.0	800	561	679	682	445	4.3	85	19.1	1,136	181	15.9	193	172	89.1
Moultrie	4	(1)	4		2	2	2	(2)	1	(1)	4	1	(1)			
Ogle	33	0.1	32	1	17	16	12	0.1	1	(1)	28	5	(1)	4	4	(1)
Peoria	1,737	1.7	1,131	606	969	768	725	2.1	60	8.3	1,523	118	7.7	203	166	81.8
Perry	814	3.7	659	155	410	404	219	3.7	29	13.2	615	83	13.5	161	122	75.8
Piatt	12	0.1	12		5	7	5	0.1			12			1	1	(1)
Pike	162	0.6	147	15	77	85	49	0.6	7	(1)	138	17	12.3	27	27	(1)
Pope	523	4.7	321	202	280	243	139	4.9	29	20.9	402	85	21.1	125	93	74.4
Pulaski	5,911	37.8	3,863	2,048	3,017	2,894	1,575	37.3	456	29.0	4,484	1,017	22.7	1,214	941	77.5
Putnam	10	0.1	2	8	7	3	4	0.2	1	(1)	8	2	(1)	1	1	(1)
Randolph	1,525	5.2	1,261	264	984	541	720	8.1	170	23.6	1,288	268	20.8	226	179	79.2
Richland	15	0.1	8	7	4	11	1	(2)			10			3	2	(1)
Rock Island	822	1.2	603	219	465	357	337	1.4	41	12.2	696	79	11.4	101	88	87.1
St. Clair	8,110	6.8	6,135	1,975	4,465	3,645	3,087	8.0	450	14.6	6,763	956	14.1	1,095	867	79.2
Saline	918	3.0	534	384	519	399	299	3.6	64	21.4	713	116	16.3	180	120	66.7
Sangamon	3,633	4.0	2,336	1,297	1,869	1,764	1,228	4.4	185	15.1	3,052	441	14.4	588	507	86.2
Schuyler	6	(2)	4	2	3	3	2	(2)			6					
Scott	15	0.1	3	12	5	10	4	0.1	1	(1)	12	2	(1)	3		
Shelby	75	0.2	51	24	39	36	23	0.3	2	(1)	58	2	(1)	16	11	(1)
Stark	9	0.1	9		7	2	6	0.2	1	(1)	9	1	(1)	1	1	(1)
Stephenson	82	0.2	74	8	47	35	30	0.3	11	(1)	72	15	(1)	7	7	(1)
Tazewell	25	0.1	17	8	8	17	7	0.1	2	(1)	20	3	(1)	2	2	(1)
Union	211	1.0	98	113	107	104	77	1.3	29	(1)	190	67	35.3	18	9	(1)
Vermilion	2,038	2.6	1,784	254	1,173	865	866	3.4	135	15.6	1,723	262	15.2	249	224	90.0
Wabash	45	0.3	42	3	24	21	18	0.4	4	(1)	39	5	(1)	6	6	(1)
Warren	576	2.5	514	62	296	280	197	2.7	34	17.3	487	77	15.8	70	63	(1)
Washington	73	0.4	40	33	40	33	29	0.6	7	(1)	63	15	(1)	13	9	(1)
Wayne	11	(2)	5	6	5	6	2	(2)	1	(1)	10	2	(1)	3	3	(1)
White	470	2.0	362	108	243	227	128	2.1	27	21.1	351	56	16.0	105	77	73.3
Whiteside	62	0.2	42	20	35	27	25	0.2	3	(1)	50	3	(1)	8	8	(1)
Will	1,134	1.3	756	378	704	430	579	2.1	60	10.4	1,005	101	10.0	131	113	86.3
Williamson	866	1.9	633	233	489	377	297	2.4	70	23.6	680	134	19.7	133	115	86.5
Winnebago	257	0.4	213	44	127	130	99	0.5	12	(1)	231	19	8.2	25	22	(1)
Woodford	37	0.2	30	7	20	17	10	0.2			29	2	(1)	5	5	(1)

INDIANA.

COUNTY.	Total.	Per cent	Black.	Mulatto.	Male.	Female.	Number.	Per cent	Illit. No.	Illit. Pct.	Total.	Illit. No.	Illit. Pct.	Total.	Att. No.	Att. Pct.
Total	60,320	2.2	45,767	14,553	31,044	29,276	20,651	2.5	3,312	16.0	50,650	6,959	13.7	8,931	7,832	87.7
Adams	2	(2)	2		2		2	(2)			2					
Allen	601	0.6	438	163	315	286	226	0.8	13	5.8	523	37	7.1	77	72	(1)
Bartholomew	319	1.3	252	67	165	154	101	1.4	13	12.9	262	28	10.7	46	42	(1)
Benton	71	0.6	9	62	42	29	24	0.6	2	(1)	55	4	(1)	14	14	(1)
Blackford	40	0.3	37	3	25	15	20	0.4	1	(1)	34	1	(1)	5	3	(1)
Boone	123	0.5	68	55	58	65	35	0.5	3	(1)	102	12	11.8	28	21	(1)
Brown	1	(2)	1			1					1					
Carroll	7	(2)	7		5	2	5	0.1	1	(1)	7	1	(1)	1	1	(1)
Cass	240	0.7	181	59	148	92	117	1.0	12	10.3	211	20	9.5	26	20	(1)
Clark	2,745	9.1	2,381	364	1,436	1,309	871	9.3	122	14.0	2,220	306	13.8	473	402	85.0
Clay	227	0.7	142	85	108	119	66	0.7	19	(1)	182	34	18.7	38	31	(1)
Clinton	84	0.3	56	28	45	39	31	0.4	1	(1)	71	2	(1)	16	14	(1)
Daviess	210	0.8	137	73	104	106	59	0.8	8	(1)	180	18	10.0	36	32	(1)
Dearborn	180	0.8	62	118	94	86	50	0.8	17	(1)	138	30	21.7	39	34	(1)
Decatur	89	0.5	52	37	35	54	20	0.4	5	(1)	64	12	(1)	21	16	(1)

¹ Per cent not shown where base is less than 100.　　　² Less than one-tenth of 1 per cent.

TABLE **III.**—GENERAL STATISTICS OF THE NEGRO POPULATION OF THE UNITED STATES, BY COUNTIES: 1910—Con.

[Counties in which no Negroes were reported are omitted.]

	NEGRO POPULATION: 1910.															
COUNTY.	Total.	Per cent of total popula-tion.	Color.		Sex.		Males 21 years of age and over.				Persons 10 years of age and over.			Persons 6 to 14 years of age.		
			Black.	Mu-latto.	Male.	Fe-male.	Num-ber.	Per cent of total.	Illiterate.		Total.	Illiterate.		Total.	Attending school.	
									Num-ber.	Per cent.		Num-ber.	Per cent.		Num-ber.	Per cent.
INDIANA—Continued.																
Dekalb	21	0.1	15	6	10	11	7	0.1	......	......	17	......	......	4	2	(1)
Delaware	1,460	2.8	1,115	345	739	721	488	3.1	78	16.0	1,204	160	13.3	234	193	82.5
Dubois	9	(2)	7	2	5	4	3	0.1	......	......	9	1	(1)	1	1	(1)
Elkhart	91	0.2	57	34	50	41	39	0.3	......	......	81	......	......	12	12	(1)
Fayette	440	3.1	293	147	210	230	129	2.8	25	19.4	362	54	14.9	81	69	(1)
Floyd	1,749	5.8	730	1,019	892	857	577	6.5	139	24.1	1,442	290	20.1	280	251	89.6
Fountain	30	0.1	24	6	20	10	14	0.2	2	(1)	27	7	(1)	1	1	(1)
Franklin	6	(2)	6	......	3	3	3	0.1	......	......	5	......	......	......	......	......
Fulton	6	(2)	6	......	5	1	5	0.1	1	(1)	6	2	(1)	......	......	......
Gibson	1,445	4.8	961	484	750	695	404	4.8	87	21.5	1,105	169	15.3	295	264	89.5
Grant	1,528	3.0	646	882	829	699	559	3.3	128	22.9	1,274	199	15.6	230	200	87.0
Greene	85	0.2	77	8	43	42	25	0.2	5	(1)	65	11	(1)	15	13	(1)
Hamilton	555	2.1	99	456	291	264	190	2.4	30	15.8	459	59	12.9	96	89	(1)
Hancock	125	0.7	124	1	68	57	42	0.7	2	(1)	98	4	(1)	18	10	(1)
Harrison	293	1.4	230	63	142	151	79	1.5	14	(1)	230	30	13.0	60	52	(1)
Hendricks	301	1.4	246	55	225	76	54	0.9	7	(1)	273	21	7.7	80	78	(1)
Henry	415	1.4	277	138	216	199	146	1.4	21	14.4	338	41	12.1	78	64	(1)
Howard	490	1.5	154	336	253	237	176	1.7	12	6.8	421	27	6.4	70	61	(1)
Huntington	16	0.1	13	3	3	13	2	(2)	......	......	10	1	(1)	3	3	(1)
Jackson	136	0.6	85	51	69	67	44	0.6	8	(1)	110	19	17.3	26	25	(1)
Jasper	6	(2)	6	......	2	4	2	0.1	......	......	6	1	......	......	......	......
Jay	171	0.7	147	24	87	84	52	0.7	3	(1)	139	7	5.0	31	24	(1)
Jefferson	604	2.9	351	253	297	307	189	3.1	40	21.2	498	77	15.5	113	96	85.0
Jennings	295	2.1	212	83	152	143	82	2.0	12	(1)	220	25	11.4	62	55	(1)
Johnson	360	1.8	293	67	162	198	92	1.5	17	(1)	296	41	13.9	72	59	(1)
Knox	572	1.5	342	230	279	293	163	1.5	31	19.0	441	69	15.6	101	86	85.1
Kosciusko	28	0.1	18	10	17	11	9	0.1	1	(1)	23	1	(1)	6	6	(1)
Lagrange	10	0.1	8	2	6	4	6	0.1	1	(1)	9	1	(1)	......	......	......
Lake	493	0.6	455	38	298	195	253	0.8	23	9.1	448	38	8.5	38	34	(1)
Laporte	338	0.7	226	112	277	61	264	1.7	58	22.0	328	69	21.0	16	12	(1)
Lawrence	345	1.1	189	156	197	148	131	1.5	26	19.8	287	49	17.1	52	47	(1)
Madison	690	1.1	468	222	355	335	239	1.2	33	13.8	599	77	12.9	92	82	(1)
Marion	23,256	8.8	19,434	3,822	11,546	11,710	7,987	9.2	1,113	13.9	19,886	2,517	12.7	3,028	2,729	90.1
Marshall	71	0.3	34	37	49	22	29	0.4	......	......	55	1	(1)	15	15	(1)
Martin	18	0.1	16	2	17	1	15	0.4	......	......	18	......	......	......	......	......
Miami	109	0.4	84	25	58	51	36	0.4	5	(1)	96	13	(1)	16	12	(1)
Monroe	438	1.9	187	251	226	212	132	2.0	34	25.8	351	70	19.9	62	55	(1)
Montgomery	246	0.8	193	53	125	121	77	0.9	7	(1)	204	15	7.4	40	37	(1)
Morgan	94	0.4	67	27	50	44	29	0.5	2	(1)	72	4	(1)	19	14	(1)
Newton	20	0.2	12	8	12	8	10	0.3	4	(1)	17	7	(1)	3	3	(1)
Noble	26	0.1	17	9	14	12	8	0.1	......	......	24	......	......	4	4	(1)
Ohio	144	3.3	139	5	76	68	40	3.0	20	(1)	111	29	26.1	28	21	(1)
Orange	363	2.1	281	82	222	141	192	4.0	7	3.6	332	13	3.9	26	24	(1)
Owen	89	0.6	87	2	50	39	28	0.7	4	(1)	72	11	(1)	13	12	(1)
Parke	160	0.7	147	13	69	91	53	0.8	14	(1)	143	23	16.1	26	23	(1)
Perry	193	1.1	119	74	86	107	59	1.3	22	(1)	154	40	26.0	36	30	(1)
Pike	133	0.7	116	17	73	60	37	0.7	7	(1)	104	18	17.3	25	21	(1)
Porter	8	(2)	7	1	3	5	2	(1)	1	(1)	8	1	(1)	1	1	(1)
Posey	963	4.4	930	33	517	446	313	5.0	106	33.9	788	217	27.5	163	150	92.0
Pulaski	2	(2)	2	......	1	1	1	(2)	......	......	2	......	......	......	......	......
Putnam	221	1.1	205	16	103	118	65	1.0	12	(1)	187	23	12.3	27	25	(1)
Randolph	235	0.8	142	93	137	98	80	0.9	8	(1)	193	12	6.2	39	35	(1)
Ripley	31	0.2	20	11	16	15	9	0.2	......	......	23	......	......	4	4	(1)
Rush	418	2.2	310	108	220	198	141	2.4	30	21.3	351	60	17.1	60	53	(1)
St. Joseph	722	0.9	474	248	419	303	316	1.2	56	17.7	629	64	10.2	81	70	(1)
Scott	1	(2)	1	......	1	......	......	......	......	......	1	......	......	1	1	(1)
Shelby	483	1.8	442	41	228	255	139	1.7	25	18.0	387	50	12.9	95	84	(1)
Spencer	837	4.0	565	272	421	416	243	4.2	63	25.9	657	140	21.3	154	145	94.2
Starke	14	0.1	14	......	8	6	8	0.3	2	(1)	14	4	(1)	......	......	......
Steuben	22	0.2	8	14	16	6	14	0.3	1	(1)	20	2	(1)	2	1	(1)
Sullivan	120	0.4	39	81	65	55	47	0.5	10	(1)	98	18	(1)	11	10	(1)
Switzerland	48	0.5	30	18	25	23	14	0.5	6	(1)	43	12	(1)	8	4	(1)
Tippecanoe	387	1.0	324	63	206	181	130	1.0	17	13.1	316	44	13.9	48	35	(1)
Tipton	9	0.1	3	6	6	3	4	0.1	1	(1)	9	1	(1)	2	1	(1)
Union	101	1.6	53	48	55	46	34	1.7	9	(4)	83	17	(1)	19	15	(1)
Vanderburg	6,548	8.5	5,164	1,384	3,407	3,141	2,364	10.0	522	22.1	5,625	1,060	18.8	933	805	86.3
Vermilion	121	0.6	92	29	73	48	40	0.7	3	(1)	94	8	(1)	22	20	(1)
Vigo	3,323	3.8	2,648	675	1,715	1,608	1,110	4.1	86	7.7	2,731	199	7.3	544	444	81.6
Wabash	167	0.6	84	83	97	70	60	0.8	7	(1)	133	14	10.5	34	31	(1)
Warren	18	0.2	3	15	14	4	6	0.2	......	......	16	......	......	5	5	(1)
Warrick	456	2.1	425	31	244	212	139	2.3	30	21.6	365	77	21.1	83	64	(1)
Washington	8	(2)	3	5	4	4	1	(2)	......	......	5	1	(1)	2	1	(1)
Wayne	1,591	3.6	1,114	477	809	782	527	3.6	57	10.8	1,304	119	9.1	253	228	90.1
Wells	3	(2)	3	......	2	1	2	(2)	......	......	2	......	......	1	1	(1)
White	11	0.1	11	......	4	7	2	(2)	......	......	9	......	......	3	3	(1)
Whitley	40	0.2	13	27	21	19	13	0.3	......	......	36	......	......	8	7	(1)

¹ Per cent not shown where base is less than 100. ² Less than one-tenth of 1 per cent.

TABLE **III.**—GENERAL STATISTICS OF THE NEGRO POPULATION OF THE UNITED STATES, BY COUNTIES: 1910—Con.

[Counties in which no Negroes were reported are omitted.]

COUNTY.	Total.	Per cent of total population.	Color.		Sex.		Males 21 years of age and over.				Persons 10 years of age and over.			Persons 6 to 14 years of age.		
			Black.	Mu-latto.	Male.	Fe-male.	Num-ber.	Per cent of total.	Illiterate.		Total.	Illiterate.		Total.	Attending school.	
									Num-ber.	Per cent.		Num-ber.	Per cent.		Num-ber.	Per cent.

IOWA.

COUNTY.	Total.	Per cent of total population.	Black.	Mu-latto.	Male.	Fe-male.	Num-ber.	Per cent of total.	Num-ber.	Per cent.	Total.	Num-ber.	Per cent.	Total.	Num-ber.	Per cent.
Total	14,973	0.7	11,329	3,644	8,120	6,853	5,443	0.8	626	11.5	12,380	1,272	10.3	2,268	2,026	89.3
Adair	21	0.1	16	5	9	12	5	0.1	1	(¹)	16	1	(¹)	6	6	(¹)
Adams	13	0.1	13		5	8	3	0.1			12	3	(¹)			
Allamakee	19	0.1	3	16	12	7	5	0.1	1	(¹)	11	1	(¹)	5	5	(¹)
Appanoose	486	1.7	406	80	256	230	153	1.9	41	26.8	370	75	20.3	100	90	90.0
Audubon	5	(²)	3	2	1	4	1	(²)			3					
Benton	9	(²)	9		3	6	2	(²)	1	(¹)	5	1	(¹)	2	2	(¹)
Blackhawk	29	0.1	23	6	18	11	17	0.1	2	(¹)	29	3	(¹)			
Boone	105	0.4	62	43	62	43	36	0.4	4	(¹)	87	7	(¹)	22	21	(¹)
Bremer	6	(²)	6		3	3	3	0.1			6					
Buchanan	18	0.1	13	5	9	9	7	0.1	1	(¹)	17	2	(¹)	4	4	(¹)
Butler	1	(²)		1	1						1			1	1	(¹)
Calhoun	11	0.1	11		4	7	4	0.1			9			2	2	(¹)
Carroll	31	0.2	28	3	17	14	11	0.2	1	(¹)	28	3	(¹)	8	6	(¹)
Cass	22	0.1	5	17	12	10	11	0.2			20			1	1	(¹)
Cedar	21	0.1	19	2	12	9	9	0.2	4	(¹)	18	7	(¹)	1	1	(¹)
Cerro Gordo	148	0.6	123	25	87	61	56	0.7	5	(¹)	123	9	7.3	23	22	(¹)
Cherokee	5	(²)	3	2	3	2	3	0.1			5					
Clarke	43	0.4	33	10	21	22	16	0.5	6	(¹)	39	9	(¹)	3	3	(¹)
Clayton	26	0.1	20	6	7	19	5	0.1			21			7	7	(¹)
Clinton	436	1.0	308	128	255	181	144	1.0	12	8.3	305	28	9.2	74	70	(¹)
Crawford	25	0.1	23	2	17	8	15	0.3	1	(¹)	22	1	(¹)	4	4	(¹)
Dallas	131	0.6	93	38	83	48	67	0.9	13	(¹)	112	19	17.0	13	10	(¹)
Davis	43	0.3	9	34	24	19	15	0.4	3	(¹)	37	7	(¹)	8	7	(¹)
Decatur	34	0.2	34		17	17	13	0.3	6	(¹)	31	8	(¹)	4	4	(¹)
Delaware	2	(²)	2			2					1					
Des Moines	429	1.2	306	123	238	191	172	1.5	17	9.9	369	41	11.1	51	43	(¹)
Dickinson	5	0.1	2	3	2	3	1	(²)			5			1	1	(¹)
Dubuque	96	0.2	68	28	60	36	47	0.3			83	1	(¹)	13	12	(¹)
Emmet	19	0.2	17	2	9	10	7	0.2			15	1	(¹)	4	4	(¹)
Fayette	107	0.4	13	94	63	44	28	0.3	2	(¹)	74	5	(¹)	25	24	(¹)
Floyd	17	0.1	17		8	9	5	0.1			16			4	4	(¹)
Franklin	10	0.1	9	1	4	6	4	0.1			10	1	(¹)	1	1	(¹)
Fremont	39	0.2	35	4	17	22	8	0.2	1	(¹)	26	6	(¹)	9	7	(¹)
Greene	1	(²)		1	1		1	(²)			1					
Grundy	11	0.1	10	1	10	1	6	0.2			8			2	1	(¹)
Guthrie	2	(²)	2			2					2			1	1	(¹)
Hamilton	37	0.2	16	21	30	7	22	0.4	1	(¹)	31	1	(¹)	3	3	(¹)
Hancock	11	0.1	11		4	7	3	0.1			9					
Hardin	46	0.2	26	20	40	6	2	(²)			45	1	(¹)	13	13	(¹)
Harrison	15	0.1	12	3	12	3	11	0.2	2	(¹)	15	2	(¹)			
Henry	264	1.4	237	27	123	141	92	1.6	23	(¹)	235	47	20.0	31	28	(¹)
Howard	12	0.1	3	9	6	6	5	0.1			9					
Humboldt	4	(²)	4		3	1	3	0.1	1	(¹)	4	1	(¹)			
Ida	2	(²)	2			2					1					
Iowa	5	(²)	5		3	2	2	(²)	1	(¹)	5	1	(¹)			
Jasper	182	0.7	153	29	104	78	75	0.9	7	(¹)	161	16	9.9	32	24	(¹)
Jefferson	79	0.5	53	26	45	34	27	0.6	3	(¹)	61	6	(¹)	12	12	(¹)
Johnson	65	0.3	52	13	39	26	29	0.4			59	2	(¹)	7	5	(¹)
Jones	83	0.4	65	18	63	20	53	0.9	1	(¹)	83	1	(¹)			
Keokuk	17	0.1	9	8	10	7	7	0.1	1	(¹)	15	2	(¹)			
Kossuth	6	(²)	6		2	4	1	(²)			6			2	2	(¹)
Lee	1,471	4.0	1,026	445	765	706	851	4.8	74	13.4	1,269	164	12.9	208	188	90.4
Linn	258	0.4	168	90	149	109	118	0.6	13	11.0	225	22	9.8	31	26	(¹)
Louisa	17	0.1	17		10	7	4	0.1	1	(¹)	13	2	(¹)	2	1	(¹)
Lucas	83	0.6	75	8	41	42	25	0.7	7	(¹)	64	14	(¹)	14	13	(¹)
Lyon	4	(²)	4		2	2	2	0.1			4					
Madison	5	(²)	1	4	3	2	3	0.1			5					
Mahaska	677	2.3	464	213	373	304	221	2.5	33	14.9	537	63	11.7	126	107	84.9
Marion	93	0.4	76	17	79	14	47	0.7	16	(¹)	74	18	(¹)	13	9	(¹)
Marshall	148	0.5	92	56	77	71	56	0.6	6	(¹)	125	11	8.8	25	20	(¹)
Mills	47	0.3	46	1	25	22	14	0.3	5	(¹)	42	18	(¹)	10	6	(¹)
Mitchell	5	(²)	1	4	1	4	1	(²)			4			2	2	(¹)
Monroe	2,371	9.3	1,977	394	1,292	1,079	764	10.4	34	4.5	1,850	62	3.4	413	378	91.5
Montgomery	48	0.3	46	2	27	21	23	0.5	4	(¹)	44	9	(¹)	4	3	(¹)
Muscatine	137	0.5	76	61	75	62	53	0.6	5	(¹)	116	11	9.5	17	15	(¹)
O'Brien	2	(²)	2			2								2	1	(¹)
Osceola	6	0.1	6			6					6		(¹)			
Page	262	1.1	236	26	137	125	94	1.3	18	(¹)	224	39	17.4	36	31	(¹)
Palo Alto	4	(²)	3	1	2	2	2	0.1	1	(¹)	3	1	(¹)	1	1	(¹)
Plymouth	10	(²)	9	1	7	3	6	0.1	1	(¹)	9	1	(¹)	1	1	(¹)
Pocahontas	3	(²)	3		2	1	1	(²)			2					
Polk	3,591	3.3	2,804	787	1,845	1,746	1,258	3.6	141	11.2	2,970	296	10.0	492	435	88.4
Pottawattamie	353	0.6	296	57	222	131	171	1.0	24	14.0	314	37	11.8	46	41	(¹)
Poweshiek	55	0.3	34	21	32	23	25	0.4	2	(¹)	48	5	(¹)	8	8	(¹)
Ringgold	1	(²)	1			1					1					

¹ Per cent not shown where base is less than 100.   ² Less than one-tenth of 1 per cent.

TABLE III.—GENERAL STATISTICS OF THE NEGRO POPULATION OF THE UNITED STATES, BY COUNTIES: 1910—Con.

[Counties in which no Negroes were reported are omitted.]

COUNTY.	NEGRO POPULATION: 1910.															
	Total.	Per cent of total population.	Color.		Sex.		Males 21 years of age and over.				Persons 10 years of age and over.			Persons 6 to 14 years of age.		
			Black.	Mulatto.	Male.	Female.	Number.	Per cent of total.	Illiterate.		Total.	Illiterate.		Total.	Attending school.	
									Number.	Per cent.		Number.	Per cent.		Number.	Per cent.
IOWA—Continued.																
Sac	30	0.2	19	11	30	......	18	0.4	2	(¹)	30	6	(¹)	......	......	......
Scott	572	1.0	459	113	318	254	227	1.2	23	10.1	496	56	11.3	92	79	(¹)
Shelby	7	(²)	6	1	3	4	3	0.1			6					
Sioux	2	(²)	2			2					1			2	2	(¹)
Story	8	(²)	8		4	4	4	0.1			7			1	1	(¹)
Tama	33	0.1	17	16	20	13	14	0.2	1	(¹)	25	2	(¹)	7	7	(¹)
Taylor	61	0.4	29	32	30	31	20	0.4	3	(¹)	49	6	(¹)	13	11	(¹)
Union	70	0.4	60	10	38	32	27	0.6	5	(¹)	62	13	(¹)	9	7	(¹)
Van Buren	60	0.4	44	16	26	34	18	0.4	1	(¹)	57	10	(¹)	11	11	(¹)
Wapello	624	1.7	413	211	321	303	223	2.0	36	16.1	517	71	13.7	96	88	(¹)
Warren	47	0.3	14	33	25	22	15	0.3	2	(¹)	40	5	(¹)	9	8	(¹)
Washington	104	0.5	86	18	56	48	39	0.7	2	(¹)	85	4	(¹)	18	16	(¹)
Wayne	9	0.1	9		1	8	1	(²)	1	(¹)	9	3	(¹)			
Webster	84	0.2	78	6	53	41	43	0.4	2	(¹)	74	3	(¹)	9	9	(¹)
Winnebago	2	(²)	2		1	1	1	(²)			2					
Winneshiek	18	0.1	3	15	9	9	4	0.1			11			5	5	(¹)
Woodbury	317	0.5	201	116	174	143	126	0.6	1	0.8	265	1	0.4	42	41	(¹)
Worth	16	0.2	15	1	9	7	7	0.3			15			2	2	(¹)
Wright	4	(²)	3	1	2	2	2	(²)			4			1	1	(¹)
KANSAS.																
Total	54,030	3.2	37,889	16,141	27,964	26,066	17,588	3.5	2,380	13.5	44,542	5,341	12.0	8,855	7,495	84.6
Allen	1,047	3.8	724	323	562	485	367	4.5	44	12.0	842	85	10.1	148	126	85.1
Anderson	161	1.2	143	18	76	85	58	1.4	9	(¹)	143	22	15.4	27	27	(¹)
Atchison	2,992	10.6	2,468	524	1,544	1,448	952	11.2	113	11.9	2,514	257	10.2	468	374	79.9
Barber	72	0.7	34	38	44	28	17	0.6	2	(¹)	56	4	(¹)	20	16	(¹)
Barton	388	2.2	237	151	219	169	136	2.5	19	14.0	306	37	12.1	73	62	(¹)
Bourbon	1,215	5.1	929	286	605	610	357	5.1	55	15.4	990	143	14.4	224	195	87.1
Brown	457	2.1	194	263	236	221	126	2.0	16	12.7	349	40	11.5	96	86	(¹)
Butler	149	0.6	119	30	80	69	53	0.8	11	(¹)	124	25	20.2	19	13	(¹)
Chase	103	1.4	94	9	56	47	31	1.4	9	(¹)	84	12	(¹)	19	19	(¹)
Chautauqua	118	1.0	104	14	58	60	26	0.8	5	(¹)	93	9	(¹)	29	23	(¹)
Cherokee	1,181	3.1	836	345	574	607	336	3.2	52	15.5	926	138	14.9	237	220	92.8
Clark	21	0.5	20	1	6	15	5	0.4			16			3	3	(¹)
Clay	111	0.7	78	33	52	59	37	0.8	5	(¹)	86	13	(¹)	22	21	(¹)
Cloud	58	0.3	49	9	31	27	20	0.4	1	(¹)	47	4	(¹)	11	11	(¹)
Coffey	75	0.5	68	7	37	38	26	0.6	6	(¹)	67	14	(¹)	8	5	(¹)
Cowley	571	1.8	436	135	302	269	184	1.9	34	18.5	480	82	17.1	92	74	(¹)
Crawford	1,563	3.1	1,132	431	797	766	474	3.2	58	12.2	1,217	129	10.6	313	237	75.7
Decatur	17	0.2	15	2	5	12	2	0.1	1	(¹)	13	1	(¹)	8	7	(¹)
Dickinson	162	0.7	108	54	81	81	37	0.5	2	(¹)	131	8	6.1	40	36	(¹)
Doniphan	683	4.7	521	162	358	325	209	4.9	48	23.0	534	104	19.5	126	106	84.1
Douglas	2,281	9.2	1,596	685	1,097	1,184	692	9.6	112	16.2	1,932	295	15.3	375	330	88.0
Edwards	50	0.7	46	4	27	23	12	0.6	2	(¹)	42	5	(¹)	12	12	(¹)
Elk	6	0.1	5	1	2	4	2	0.1	1	(¹)	6	1	(¹)			
Ellis	69	0.6	58	11	38	31	22	0.7	2	(¹)	60	4	(¹)	11	9	(¹)
Ellsworth	113	1.1	43	70	68	45	51	1.6	5	(¹)	103	12	11.7	8	6	(¹)
Finney	189	2.7	187	2	98	91	64	3.0	2	(¹)	163	9	5.5	30	29	(¹)
Ford	93	0.8	54	39	54	39	39	1.1	1	(¹)	83	3	(¹)	11	10	(¹)
Franklin	490	2.3	349	141	255	235	144	2.3	31	21.5	392	82	20.9	77	64	(¹)
Geary	587	4.6	456	131	339	248	250	4.9	11	4.4	509	31	6.1	68	61	(¹)
Gove	55	0.9	43	12	31	24	22	1.3	1	(¹)	45	3	(¹)	6	6	(¹)
Graham	595	6.8	239	356	304	291	161	7.1	16	9.9	461	33	7.2	123	96	78.0
Grant	21	1.9		21	15	6	10	3.1			17			5		
Gray	14	0.4	1	13	10	4	3	0.3			11			4	4	(¹)
Greeley	2	0.1	2		2		2	0.5			2					
Greenwood	32	0.2	27	5	15	17	10	0.2	1	(¹)	27	3	(¹)	7	7	(¹)
Hamilton	25	0.7	13	12	18	7	9	0.9			18			5	2	(¹)
Harper	37	0.3	24	13	20	17	13	0.3	2	(¹)	31	4	(¹)	2	1	(¹)
Harvey	415	2.2	329	86	216	199	135	2.3	14	10.4	329	36	10.9	74	65	(¹)
Haskell	9	0.9		9	6	3	2	0.7			4			3	2	(¹)
Hodgeman	67	2.3	67		33	34	19	2.2	2	(¹)	53	4	(¹)	11	10	(¹)
Jackson	153	0.9	139	14	72	81	42	0.9			123	16	13.0	30	24	(¹)
Jefferson	451	2.8	287	164	254	197	140	3.0	33	23.6	347	63	18.2	80	63	(¹)
Johnson	611	3.3	432	179	298	313	183	3.3	44	24.0	496	99	20.0	118	102	86.4
Kearny	1	(²)	1		1		1	0.1								
Kingman	32	0.2	32		19	13	12	0.3	2	(¹)	31	5	(¹)	4	2	(¹)
Kiowa	8	0.1	8		3	5	2	0.1	1	(¹)	7	2	(¹)	2	2	(¹)
Labette	1,756	5.6	1,340	416	899	857	510	5.5	105	20.6	1,416	237	16.7	352	313	88.9
Lane	1	(²)	1			1										
Leavenworth	4,071	9.9	3,182	889	2,385	1,686	1,758	10.7	277	15.8	2,550	493	13.9	564	447	79.3
Lincoln	27	0.3	27		13	14	7	0.2			21	4	(¹)	9	8	(¹)

¹ Per cent not shown where base is less than 100.   ² Less than one-tenth of 1 per cent.

TABLE III.—GENERAL STATISTICS OF THE NEGRO POPULATION OF THE UNITED STATES, BY COUNTIES: 1910—Con.

[Counties in which no Negroes were reported are omitted.]

COUNTY.	NEGRO POPULATION: 1910.															
	Total.	Per cent of total population.	Color.		Sex.		Males 21 years of age and over.				Persons 10 years of age and over.			Persons 6 to 14 years of age.		
			Black.	Mu-latto.	Male.	Fe-male.	Number.	Per cent of total.	Illiterate.		Total.	Illiterate.		Total.	Attending school.	
									Num-ber.	Per cent.		Num-ber.	Per cent.		Num-ber.	Per cent.

KANSAS—Continued.

COUNTY.	Total.	Per cent	Black.	Mu-latto.	Male.	Fe-male.	Number.	Per cent	Num-ber.	Per cent.	Total.	Num-ber.	Per cent.	Total.	Num-ber.	Per cent.
Linn	323	2.2	235	88	174	149	106	2.5	19	17.9	263	35	13.3	47	40	(1)
Logan	298	7.0	31	267	145	153	84	6.6	2	(1)	208	8	3.8	56	44	(1)
Lyon	786	3.2	474	312	381	405	225	3.1	44	19.6	635	87	13.7	135	120	88.9
McPherson	3	(2)	3		1	2	1	(2)			2					
Marion	132	0.6	116	16	75	57	53	0.9	4	(1)	115	14	12.2	17	15	(1)
Marshall	244	1.0	222	22	122	122	71	1.0	7	(1)	202	20	9.9	37	34	(1)
Meade	32	0.6	27	5	17	15	10	0.7			23	2	(1)	5	2	(1)
Miami	873	4.4	726	147	462	411	295	4.7	78	26.4	732	152	20.8	144	127	88.2
Mitchell	46	0.3	43	3	4	42	2	(2)			45			19	19	(1)
Montgomery	2,966	6.0	2,329	637	1,523	1,443	939	6.1	96	10.2	2,369	219	9.2	507	435	85.8
Morris	317	2.6	258	59	170	147	91	2.5	16	(1)	239	39	16.3	59	53	(1)
Morton	20	1.5	4	16	10	10	8	1.7			13			2	2	(1)
Nemaha	164	0.9	153	11	83	81	49	0.9	12	(1)	140	25	17.9	29	28	(1)
Neosho	376	1.6	128	248	212	164	119	1.7	23	19.3	283	34	12.0	71	57	(1)
Norton	28	0.2	6	22	15	13	8	0.3	1	(1)	24	5	(1)	3	2	(1)
Osage	362	1.8	187	175	191	171	103	1.8	30	29.1	293	55	18.8	80	74	(1)
Osborne	69	0.5	53	16	42	27	25	0.7	3	(1)	56	8	(1)	11	9	(1)
Ottawa	42	0.4	42		24	18	16	0.5	6	(1)	39	7	(1)	5	5	(1)
Pawnee	81	0.9	64	17	41	40	32	1.2			69	4	(1)	15	13	(1)
Phillips	67	0.5	56	11	36	31	23	0.6			49	1	(1)	6	5	(1)
Pottawatomie	132	0.8	62	70	73	59	42	0.8	17	(1)	107	32	29.9	31	28	(1)
Pratt	218	2.0	129	89	112	106	73	2.2	7	(1)	182	19	10.4	37	31	(1)
Reno	904	2.4	647	257	503	401	295	2.5	24	8.1	774	51	6.6	133	119	89.5
Republic	8	(2)	6	2	4	4	4	0.1			6					
Rice	132	0.9	87	45	62	70	35	0.8	1	(1)	108	3	2.8	28	27	(1)
Riley	311	2.0	238	73	160	151	104	2.2	22	21.2	255	35	13.7	42	38	(1)
Rooks	79	0.7	58	21	41	38	28	0.9	2	(1)	72	5	(1)	15	13	(1)
Rush	14	0.2	1	13	7	7	3	0.1			11			2	1	(1)
Russell	54	0.5	22	32	32	22	17	0.6	1	(1)	42	2	(1)	9	9	(1)
Saline	509	2.5	399	110	271	238	184	2.9	27	14.7	429	59	13.8	69	59	(1)
Scott	2	0.1	2				1	0.1			2					
Sedgwick	2,652	3.6	1,471	1,181	1,439	1,213	950	3.9	90	9.5	2,198	177	8.1	383	315	82.2
Seward	2	(2)	2		1	1	1	0.1			2					
Shawnee	5,722	9.2	3,856	1,866	2,807	2,915	1,644	8.5	196	11.9	4,756	477	10.0	935	798	85.3
Sheridan	29	0.5	9	20	17	12	11	0.7			23			4	3	(1)
Sherman	16	0.4	10	6	6	10	5	0.4			11	2	(1)	1		
Smith	5	(2)	5		3	2	3	0.1			5					
Stafford	127	1.0	118	9	66	61	38	1.0	3	(1)	107	5	4.7	23	17	(1)
Stanton	2	0.2	2		1	1	1	0.3			1					
Stevens	81	3.3	28	53	51	30	28	3.8	4	(1)	66	7	(1)	18	17	(1)
Sumner	328	1.1	248	80	177	151	125	1.3	14	11.2	275	26	9.5	53	33	(1)
Thomas	7	0.1	7		2	5	1	0.1			4					
Trego	26	0.5	26		15	11	6	0.4			21			3	2	(1)
Wabaunsee	708	5.6	445	263	396	312	202	5.4	31	15.3	543	66	12.2	154	128	83.1
Wallace	36	1.3	34	2	21	15	16	1.8	3	(1)	29	4	(1)	6	3	(1)
Washington	8	(2)	8		4	4	2	(2)			6					
Wichita	3	0.1	3		2	1	2	0.3			3					
Wilson	85	0.4	85		53	32	41	0.7	3	(1)	74	5	(1)	10	5	(1)
Woodson	24	0.3	24		12	12	7	0.3			19			5	5	(1)
Wyandotte	11,172	11.2	7,403	3,769	5,581	5,591	3,689	11.5	432	11.7	9,314	1,080	11.6	1,672	1,424	85.2

KENTUCKY.

COUNTY.	Total.	Per cent	Black.	Mu-latto.	Male.	Fe-male.	Number.	Per cent	Num-ber.	Per cent.	Total.	Num-ber.	Per cent.	Total.	Num-ber.	Per cent.
Total	261,656	11.4	195,713	65,943	131,492	130,164	75,694	12.5	25,958	34.3	210,028	57,900	27.6	48,039	33,761	70.3
Adair	1,475	8.9	1,207	268	704	771	334	8.5	153	45.8	1,075	422	39.3	346	189	54.6
Allen	910	6.1	632	278	452	458	223	5.8	94	42.2	668	236	34.9	173	71	41.0
Anderson	734	7.2	415	319	377	357	230	5.8	67	29.1	610	143	23.4	149	109	73.2
Ballard	1,585	12.5	1,341	244	837	748	442	12.8	173	39.1	1,182	346	29.3	329	243	73.9
Barren	3,590	14.2	2,907	683	1,813	1,777	853	13.2	370	43.4	2,665	907	34.0	829	538	64.9
Bath	1,336	9.6	893	443	679	657	365	10.0	146	40.0	1,032	342	33.1	275	171	62.2
Bell	2,920	10.3	2,559	361	1,652	1,268	982	13.5	262	26.7	2,318	566	24.4	507	299	59.0
Boone	478	5.1	425	53	248	230	134	4.5	41	30.6	378	87	23.0	83	47	(1)
Bourbon	5,642	22.3	4,843	799	2,763	2,879	1,746	32.3	638	36.5	4,635	1,395	30.1	951	706	74.2
Boyd	822	3.5	612	210	461	361	289	4.7	54	18.7	686	114	16.6	141	123	87.2
Boyle	4,153	28.3	3,288	865	2,048	2,105	1,169	28.8	436	37.3	3,357	985	29.3	747	491	65.7
Bracken	339	3.3	259	80	185	154	100	3.2	37	37.0	264	81	30.7	80	65	(1)
Breathitt	260	1.5	199	61	142	118	73	2.0	30	(1)	205	79	38.5	61	26	(1)
Breckinridge	1,581	7.5	1,141	440	839	742	441	8.1	144	32.7	1,228	287	23.4	361	252	69.8
Bullitt	679	7.2	497	182	335	344	169	6.4	70	41.4	505	161	31.9	167	103	61.7
Butler	561	3.5	495	66	279	282	152	3.9	51	33.6	424	108	25.5	124	90	72.6
Caldwell	2,520	17.9	1,530	990	1,206	1,314	617	16.9	225	36.5	1,941	522	26.9	547	419	76.6
Calloway	1,069	5.4	895	174	528	541	251	5.1	101	40.2	805	238	29.6	235	181	77.0
Campbell	735	1.2	557	178	360	375	230	1.3	44	19.1	625	105	16.8	96	75	(1)
Carlisle	393	4.3	297	96	193	200	115	4.8	42	36.5	311	84	27.0	71	58	(2)

1 Per cent not shown where base is less than 100. 2 Less than one-tenth of 1 per cent.

TABLE III.—GENERAL STATISTICS OF THE NEGRO POPULATION OF THE UNITED STATES, BY COUNTIES: 1910—Con.

[Counties in which no Negroes were reported are omitted.]

COUNTY.	NEGRO POPULATION: 1910.															
	Total.	Per cent of total population.	Color.		Sex.		Males 21 years of age and over.				Persons 10 years of age and over.			Persons 6 to 14 years of age.		
			Black.	Mulatto.	Male.	Female.	Number.	Per cent of total.	Illiterate.		Total.	Illiterate.		Total.	Attending school.	
									Number.	Per cent.		Number.	Per cent.		Number.	Per cent.
						KENTUCKY—Continued.										
Carroll	530	6.5	416	114	284	246	153	6.4	57	37.3	406	113	27.8	121	90	74.4
Carter	110	0.5	97	13	57	53	34	0.7	13	(1)	87	22	(1)	21	17	(1)
Casey	278	1.8	183	95	137	141	75	2.1	30	(1)	222	67	30.2	60	30	(1)
Christian	15,956	41.1	12,914	3,042	7,859	8,097	3,928	36.7	1,718	43.7	12,237	3,926	32.1	3,490	2,299	65.9
Clark	4,462	24.8	3,786	676	2,234	2,228	1,362	26.3	457	33.6	3,638	984	27.0	697	520	74.6
Clay	494	2.8	313	181	255	239	110	3.1	33	30.0	332	100	30.1	113	68	60.2
Clinton	94	1.2	92	2	50	44	25	1.4	14	(1)	81	38	(1)	26	15	(1)
Crittenden	588	4.4	454	134	311	277	165	4.8	46	27.9	462	111	24.0	117	83	70.9
Cumberland	1,024	10.4	960	64	496	528	236	10.5	90	38.1	761	218	28.6	261	137	52.5
Daviess	5,195	12.7	4,182	1,013	2,598	2,597	1,491	13.3	462	31.0	4,238	1,029	24.3	962	721	74.9
Edmonson	439	4.2	292	147	231	208	97	4.1	34	(1)	304	68	22.4	123	117	95.1
Elliott	1	(2)	1		1		1	0.1	1	(1)	1	1	(1)			
Estill	106	0.9	79	27	49	57	34	1.3	14	(1)	86	30	(1)	20	11	(1)
Fayette	14,879	31.2	12,593	2,286	7,221	7,658	4,559	30.7	1,612	35.4	12,729	3,633	28.5	2,212	1,831	82.8
Fleming	1,027	6.4	603	424	526	501	280	6.3	120	42.9	800	261	32.6	227	157	69.2
Floyd	99	0.5	26	73	45	54	25	0.6	11	(1)	71	34	(1)	25	6	(1)
Franklin	3,746	17.7	2,149	1,597	2,124	1,622	1,522	22.4	559	36.7	3,290	1,049	31.9	445	381	85.6
Fulton	3,356	23.8	2,809	547	1,729	1,627	910	23.1	344	37.8	2,561	872	34.0	685	348	50.8
Gallatin	274	5.8	131	143	141	133	76	5.3	34	(1)	216	70	32.4	49	36	(1)
Garrard	2,284	19.2	1,668	616	1,167	1,117	625	20.3	166	26.6	1,781	363	20.4	472	300	63.6
Grant	292	2.8	258	34	149	143	85	2.8	35	(1)	232	78	33.6	60	40	(1)
Graves	2,899	8.6	2,145	753	1,439	1,460	705	8.5	233	33.0	2,119	551	26.0	659	437	66.3
Grayson	333	1.7	332	1	161	172	91	1.9	28	(1)	255	71	27.8	60	44	(1)
Green	1,343	11.3	1,190	153	705	638	291	10.0	150	51.5	983	333	33.9	326	197	60.4
Greenup	257	1.4	206	51	167	90	89	2.0	35	(1)	217	68	31.3	39	33	(1)
Hancock	566	6.6	417	149	290	276	143	6.3	71	49.7	446	142	31.8	126	91	72.2
Hardin	1,826	8.0	1,522	304	921	905	478	8.0	183	38.3	1,396	397	28.4	406	286	70.4
Harlan	564	5.3	145	419	390	174	264	11.5	157	59.5	508	273	53.7	65	40	(1)
Harrison	1,750	10.4	1,177	573	884	866	532	11.0	175	32.9	1,428	397	27.8	303	236	77.9
Hart	1,991	11.0	1,868	123	997	994	452	9.9	169	37.4	1,426	376	26.4	509	293	57.6
Henderson	6,818	23.2	5,548	1,270	3,437	3,381	1,891	24.2	685	36.2	5,356	1,489	27.8	1,388	1,137	81.9
Henry	1,792	12.6	1,448	344	893	899	502	12.6	240	47.8	1,450	569	39.2	363	187	51.5
Hickman	1,766	15.0	1,438	328	889	877	480	15.4	203	42.3	1,305	446	34.2	388	218	56.9
Hopkins	6,573	19.2	5,512	1,061	3,451	3,122	1,946	20.5	647	33.2	5,184	1,320	25.5	1,225	927	75.7
Jackson	22	0.2	5	17	13	9	3	0.1	1	(1)	12	5	(1)	6		
Jefferson	45,794	17.4	29,499	16,295	22,407	23,387	15,447	19.4	3,399	22.0	39,815	7,830	19.7	5,757	4,893	85.0
Jessamine	2,962	23.5	1,994	968	1,591	1,371	941	25.0	341	36.2	2,419	716	29.6	529	299	56.5
Johnson	47	0.3	5	42	22	25	10	0.3	4	(1)	34	14	(1)	11	3	(1)
Kenton	3,228	4.6	2,335	893	1,578	1,650	1,069	5.2	251	23.5	2,787	583	20.9	407	327	80.3
Knott	157	1.5	146	11	84	73	27	1.3	1	(1)	94	4	(1)	49	20	(1)
Knox	1,059	4.8	613	446	557	502	276	5.7	85	30.8	784	195	24.9	237	194	81.9
Larue	785	7.3	620	165	400	385	191	7.1	97	50.8	553	189	34.2	208	151	72.6
Laurel	657	3.3	369	288	339	318	156	3.5	49	31.4	469	110	23.5	154	117	76.0
Lawrence	163	0.8	133	30	89	74	43	1.0	18	(1)	123	39	31.7	27	17	(1)
Lee	234	2.5	109	125	122	112	71	3.3	22	(1)	179	47	26.3	54	31	(1)
Leslie	132	1.5	15	117	72	60	28	1.6	17	(1)	89	51	(1)	40	14	(1)
Letcher	17	0.2	10	7	11	6	4	0.2	3	(1)	11	10	(1)	4		
Lewis	141	0.8	110	31	75	66	48	1.1	24	(1)	116	47	40.5	23	14	(1)
Lincoln	2,955	16.5	2,427	528	1,462	1,493	784	16.9	277	35.3	2,271	624	27.5	569	356	62.6
Livingston	670	6.3	559	111	337	333	163	6.0	72	44.2	484	136	28.1	169	129	76.3
Logan	5,349	21.4	4,468	881	2,684	2,665	1,350	20.2	592	43.9	4,127	1,319	32.0	1,162	820	70.6
Lyon	1,799	19.1	1,461	338	1,143	656	714	26.3	271	38.0	1,452	451	31.1	354	266	75.1
McCracken	7,934	22.6	4,852	3,082	3,844	4,090	2,376	23.4	644	27.1	6,542	1,500	22.9	1,282	861	69.5
McLean	750	5.7	562	188	392	358	214	6.1	95	44.4	563	189	33.6	143	85	59.4
Madison	5,698	21.1	4,340	1,358	2,846	2,852	1,425	20.5	448	31.4	4,354	1,070	24.6	1,251	817	65.3
Magoffin	54	0.4	31	23	27	27	14	0.5	8	(1)	43	23	(1)	12	3	(1)
Marion	2,266	13.9	1,734	532	1,141	1,125	549	13.6	294	53.6	1,696	708	41.7	503	296	58.8
Marshall	135	0.9	114	21	78	57	32	0.8	14	(1)	95	32	(1)	38	23	(1)
Martin	4	0.1	2	2	2	2	2	0.1			4	2	(1)			
Mason	2,868	15.4	2,035	833	1,373	1,495	831	15.0	297	35.7	2,361	699	29.6	501	366	73.1
Meade	655	6.7	483	172	362	293	179	7.1	67	37.4	514	137	26.7	151	113	74.8
Menifee	40	0.7	40		24	16	10	0.7	8	(1)	27	11	(1)	15	13	(1)
Mercer	2,171	15.4	1,776	395	1,055	1,116	584	15.3	248	42.5	1,746	524	30.0	408	250	61.3
Metcalf	794	7.6	597	197	409	385	183	7.2	88	48.1	561	210	37.4	211	127	60.2
Monroe	705	5.2	431	274	350	355	151	4.7	53	35.1	477	171	35.8	152	65	42.8
Montgomery	3,192	24.8	2,593	599	1,573	1,619	923	25.2	358	38.8	2,616	790	30.2	610	405	66.4
Morgan	34	0.2	32	2	21	13	11	0.3	5	(1)	23	8	(1)	5	4	(1)
Muhlenberg	2,911	10.2	1,895	1,016	1,549	1,362	815	11.0	287	35.2	2,217	580	26.2	563	449	79.8
Nelson	2,935	17.4	2,562	373	1,485	1,450	767	17.8	295	38.5	2,249	668	29.7	645	301	46.7
Nicholas	896	8.5	653	243	429	467	270	8.8	112	41.5	740	269	36.4	121	80	66.1
Ohio	1,288	4.7	649	639	654	634	399	5.5	150	37.6	1,009	288	28.5	230	180	78.3
Oldham	1,078	14.9	835	243	547	531	328	14.1	145	44.2	897	298	33.2	204	144	70.6
Owen	943	6.6	725	218	485	458	256	6.4	133	52.0	724	261	36.0	212	147	69.3
Owsley	75	0.9	72	3	40	35	17	1.0	9	(1)	52	23	(1)	19	11	(1)
Pendleton	261	2.2	123	138	138	123	76	2.3	33	(1)	205	73	35.6	51	33	(1)

[1] Per cent not shown where base is less than 100. [2] Less than one-tenth of 1 per cent.

TABLE **III.**—GENERAL STATISTICS OF THE NEGRO POPULATION OF THE UNITED STATES, BY COUNTIES: 1910—Con.

[Counties in which no Negroes were reported are omitted.]

COUNTY.	Total.	Per cent of total population.	Color.		Sex.		Males 21 years of age and over.				Persons 10 years of age and over.			Persons 6 to 14 years of age.		
									Illiterate.			Illiterate.			Attending school.	
			Black.	Mulatto.	Male.	Female.	Number.	Per cent of total.	Number.	Per cent.	Total.	Number.	Per cent.	Total.	Number.	Per cent.

KENTUCKY—Continued.

COUNTY.	Total.	Per cent	Black.	Mulatto.	Male.	Female.	Number.	Per cent	Illit. No.	Illit. Pct.	Total.	Illit. No.	Illit. Pct.	Total.	Attend No.	Attend Pct.
Perry	214	1.9	111	103	114	100	50	2.2	14	(1)	141	33	23.4	51	31	(1)
Pike	332	1.0	225	107	182	150	103	1.5	45	43.7	258	101	39.1	73	40	(1)
Powell	337	5.4	295	42	176	161	113	7.3	42	37.2	272	86	31.6	61	42	(1)
Pulaski	1,187	3.3	800	387	569	618	329	3.9	96	29.2	929	199	21.4	220	170	77.3
Robertson	70	1.7	54	16	44	26	19	1.6	11	(1)	51	25	(1)	19	6	(1)
Rockcastle	125	0.9	95	30	59	66	34	1.0	18	(1)	89	35	(1)	23	12	(1)
Rowan	59	0.6	45	14	33	26	21	1.0	8	(1)	42	16	(1)	10	----	----
Russell	207	1.9	86	121	103	104	42	1.7	16	(1)	151	41	27.2	52	31	(1)
Scott	4,044	23.9	2,519	1,525	2,082	1,962	1,274	25.0	466	36.6	3,365	982	29.2	634	426	67.2
Shelby	3,991	22.1	3,118	873	2,024	1,967	1,176	22.0	579	49.2	3,204	1,239	38.7	785	463	59.0
Simpson	2,165	18.9	1,794	371	1,083	1,082	534	16.8	263	49.3	1,632	580	35.5	494	275	55.7
Spencer	758	10.0	427	331	398	360	197	10.0	106	53.8	579	211	36.4	190	93	48.9
Taylor	1,429	11.9	1,151	278	697	732	335	11.2	134	40.0	1,086	315	29.0	298	215	72.1
Todd	5,343	32.4	4,059	1,284	2,708	2,635	1,322	30.0	591	44.7	4,060	1,321	32.5	1,225	812	66.3
Trigg	3,322	22.8	2,677	645	1,644	1,678	733	20.8	242	33.0	2,382	564	23.7	809	523	64.6
Trimble	142	2.2	112	30	76	66	35	1.9	14	(1)	110	33	30.0	27	8	(1)
Union	2,414	12.1	2,184	230	1,289	1,125	718	13.5	258	35.9	1,915	508	26.5	459	304	66.2
Warren	6,113	20.0	5,023	1,090	2,936	3,177	1,579	19.1	727	46.0	4,877	1,787	36.6	1,135	755	66.5
Washington	1,779	12.8	1,245	534	903	876	441	12.4	183	41.5	1,322	416	31.5	437	266	60.9
Wayne	739	4.2	643	96	352	387	193	4.9	72	37.3	550	177	32.2	154	112	72.7
Webster	2,643	12.6	1,698	945	1,361	1,282	715	13.3	199	27.8	2,090	434	20.8	563	443	78.7
Whitley	1,111	3.5	785	326	575	536	304	4.2	71	23.4	815	160	19.6	227	156	68.7
Wolfe	56	0.6	35	21	25	31	11	0.5	1	(1)	35	5	(1)	18	10	(1)
Woodford	3,724	29.6	2,571	1,153	1,860	1,864	1,107	30.6	483	43.6	3,017	1,024	33.9	678	525	77.4

LOUISIANA.

COUNTY.	Total.	Per cent	Black.	Mulatto.	Male.	Female.	Number.	Per cent	Illit. No.	Illit. Pct.	Total.	Illit. No.	Illit. Pct.	Total.	Attend No.	Attend Pct.
Total	713,874	43.1	561,297	152,577	353,824	360,050	174,211	42.0	84,176	48.3	525,450	254,148	48.4	161,969	60,654	37.4
Acadia	6,546	20.6	3,707	2,839	3,242	3,304	1,360	19.9	1,029	75.7	4,468	3,226	72.2	1,670	423	25.3
Ascension	11,255	47.1	8,996	2,259	5,568	5,687	2,909	50.6	1,603	55.1	8,535	4,368	51.2	2,382	1,017	42.7
Assumption	10,105	41.9	9,392	713	5,126	4,979	2,588	44.9	1,417	54.8	7,596	3,857	50.8	2,217	992	44.7
Avoyelles	12,039	35.3	9,795	2,244	6,024	6,015	2,627	36.1	1,596	60.8	8,375	4,742	56.6	3,117	1,131	36.3
Bienville	9,464	43.5	6,724	2,740	4,716	4,748	1,816	38.4	962	53.0	6,267	3,356	53.6	2,591	683	26.4
Bossier	16,735	77.0	14,109	2,626	8,264	8,471	3,766	73.9	2,266	60.2	12,103	6,842	56.5	4,250	1,839	43.3
Caddo	36,142	62.1	32,077	4,065	17,435	18,707	8,752	54.7	3,885	44.4	27,397	11,808	43.1	8,042	4,339	54.0
Calcasieu	16,562	26.4	12,779	3,783	8,812	7,750	4,975	28.9	1,965	39.5	12,868	4,925	39.8	3,211	1,442	44.9
Caldwell	3,465	40.3	2,870	595	1,737	1,728	716	36.1	272	38.0	2,401	928	38.7	901	226	25.1
Cameron	538	12.5	299	239	290	248	122	12.6	80	65.6	357	218	61.1	129	3	2.3
Catahoula	5,195	49.9	4,081	1,114	2,605	2,590	1,039	46.2	738	71.0	3,566	2,486	69.7	1,479	350	23.7
Claiborne	14,938	59.6	13,703	1,235	7,256	7,682	2,645	51.4	1,492	56.4	9,750	5,218	53.5	4,175	1,120	26.8
Concordia	11,941	83.6	10,523	1,418	6,131	5,810	3,419	82.7	2,124	62.1	9,191	5,822	63.3	2,377	537	22.6
De Soto	17,932	64.8	16,018	1,914	8,843	9,089	3,760	59.8	1,961	52.2	12,401	6,455	52.1	4,750	1,553	32.7
East Baton Rouge	21,342	61.7	15,280	6,062	10,065	11,277	5,070	58.5	2,244	44.3	15,991	7,125	44.6	4,682	1,403	30.0
East Carroll	10,390	89.3	9,339	1,051	5,152	5,238	2,765	86.8	1,432	51.8	8,087	4,167	51.5	2,162	1,109	51.3
East Feliciana	14,536	72.5	12,561	1,975	7,077	7,459	2,800	62.1	1,628	58.5	9,749	5,242	53.8	3,871	1,651	42.7
Franklin	5,264	43.9	4,879	385	2,673	2,591	1,195	43.0	729	61.0	3,788	2,574	68.0	1,361	454	33.4
Grant	4,869	30.5	4,179	690	2,508	2,361	1,244	32.2	617	49.6	3,526	2,080	59.0	1,078	253	23.5
Iberia	14,474	46.3	10,431	4,043	7,253	7,221	3,446	46.9	1,967	57.1	10,479	5,776	55.1	3,424	944	27.6
Iberville	19,145	61.8	15,746	3,399	9,691	9,454	5,300	65.4	3,061	57.8	14,824	8,565	57.8	3,768	1,096	29.1
Jackson	3,996	28.9	3,658	338	1,991	2,005	796	25.4	322	40.5	2,639	1,156	43.8	1,013	389	38.4
Jefferson	6,785	37.2	5,821	964	3,536	3,249	2,079	40.5	986	47.4	5,251	2,508	46.9	1,264	675	53.4
La Salle	1,953	20.8	1,016	937	1,083	870	588	24.7	178	30.3	1,891	452	32.9	396	152	38.4
Lafayette	10,734	37.4	7,403	3,331	5,327	5,407	2,106	35.2	1,692	80.3	7,291	5,824	79.9	2,915	383	13.1
Lafourche	7,973	24.1	6,859	1,114	4,240	3,733	2,319	30.1	1,273	54.9	6,169	3,169	51.4	1,664	754	45.6
Lincoln	7,289	39.4	5,831	1,458	3,469	3,820	1,387	34.5	711	51.3	4,886	2,414	49.4	1,996	763	38.2
Livingston	1,377	13.0	1,095	282	714	663	342	13.4	168	49.1	959	450	46.9	308	97	31.5
Madison	9,455	88.6	8,626	829	4,728	4,727	2,593	85.7	1,543	59.5	7,366	4,117	55.9	1,912	934	48.8
Morehouse	13,971	74.7	12,159	1,812	6,978	6,993	3,161	71.2	2,036	64.4	10,068	6,001	59.6	3,436	1,355	39.4
Natchitoches	20,334	55.8	16,153	4,181	9,885	10,449	4,239	53.2	2,561	60.4	14,149	8,516	60.2	5,292	1,494	28.2
Orleans	89,262	26.3	58,782	30,480	40,946	48,316	25,269	26.1	4,330	17.1	73,814	13,541	18.3	13,990	9,446	67.5
Ouachita	14,153	54.8	11,859	2,294	6,734	7,419	3,394	50.1	1,376	40.5	10,549	4,152	39.4	3,115	1,460	46.9
Plaquemines	6,847	54.7	4,814	2,033	3,570	3,277	1,668	47.7	1,007	60.4	4,802	3,045	63.4	1,615	334	20.7
Pointe Coupee	17,147	67.8	13,822	3,325	8,637	8,510	3,976	67.5	2,422	60.9	12,515	8,239	65.8	4,348	649	14.9
Rapides	21,445	48.1	19,042	2,403	10,480	10,965	4,947	46.0	2,358	47.7	15,695	7,326	46.7	5,258	2,207	42.0
Red River	6,212	54.5	5,788	424	3,048	3,164	1,348	52.9	850	63.1	4,248	2,743	64.6	1,637	445	27.2
Richland	10,463	66.4	9,189	1,274	5,208	5,255	2,382	63.3	1,427	59.9	7,450	4,763	63.9	2,631	512	19.5
Sabine	4,164	21.0	3,447	717	2,134	2,030	997	21.6	432	43.3	2,948	1,158	39.3	1,014	564	55.6
St. Bernard	1,933	36.6	1,524	409	986	947	513	37.3	254	49.5	1,435	775	54.0	410	147	35.9
St. Charles	6,720	60.0	4,219	2,501	3,685	3,035	1,892	65.0	960	50.7	4,882	2,491	51.0	1,615	382	23.7
St. Helena	4,573	49.9	4,130	443	2,247	2,326	894	44.7	434	48.5	2,992	1,411	47.2	1,242	136	11.0
St. James	13,164	57.2	9,259	3,905	6,795	6,369	3,589	60.8	1,796	50.0	9,903	4,836	48.8	2,821	1,337	47.4
St. John the Baptist	8,126	56.7	6,625	1,501	4,328	3,798	2,339	60.2	1,275	54.5	5,970	3,286	55.0	1,611	615	38.2
St. Landry	31,234	46.9	21,568	9,666	15,529	15,705	6,197	45.3	4,483	72.3	21,092	15,049	71.3	8,423	1,475	17.5

¹ Per cent not shown where base is less than 100.

TABLE III.—GENERAL STATISTICS OF THE NEGRO POPULATION OF THE UNITED STATES, BY COUNTIES: 1910—Con.

[Counties in which no Negroes were reported are omitted.]

COUNTY.	NEGRO POPULATION: 1910.															
	Total.	Per cent of total popula-tion.	Color.		Sex.		Males 21 years of age and over.				Persons 10 years of age and over.			Persons 6 to 14 years of age.		
			Black.	Mu-latto.	Male.	Fe-male.	Num-ber.	Per cent of total.	Illiterate.		Total.	Illiterate.		Total.	Attending school.	
									Num-ber.	Per cent.		Num-ber.	Per cent.		Num-ber.	Per cent.
LOUISIANA—Continued.																
St. Martin	9,836	42.6	5,392	4,444	4,905	4,931	1,963	40.8	1,254	63.9	6,693	4,216	63.0	2,636	598	22.7
St. Mary	21,266	54.0	14,400	6,866	10,806	10,460	5,629	55.5	2,882	51.2	15,988	7,778	48.6	4,546	2,135	47.0
St. Tammany	6,731	35.6	3,948	2,783	3,403	3,328	1,769	36.2	642	36.3	4,886	1,702	34.8	1,502	759	50.5
Tangipahoa	9,135	31.3	7,180	1,955	4,969	4,166	2,580	33.0	1,055	40.9	6,822	2,898	42.5	1,915	721	37.7
Tensas	15,613	91.5	13,333	2,280	7,709	7,909	4,016	89.4	2,644	65.8	11,969	7,754	64.8	3,440	1,760	51.2
Terrebonne	11,194	39.5	9,337	1,857	5,698	5,496	2,915	42.7	1,325	45.5	8,317	3,749	45.1	2,528	1,081	42.8
Union	7,448	36.4	6,902	546	3,678	3,770	1,369	31.1	476	34.8	4,813	1,425	29.6	2,097	619	29.5
Vermilion	4,500	17.1	2,935	1,565	2,283	2,217	920	16.7	587	63.8	3,067	1,893	61.7	1,214	222	18.3
Vernon	3,716	21.1	2,850	866	2,118	1,598	1,306	28.1	394	30.2	2,894	765	26.4	625	378	60.5
Washington	5,458	28.9	4,346	1,112	3,039	2,419	1,613	31.8	561	34.8	3,913	1,384	35.4	1,196	463	38.7
Webster	9,900	51.6	8,057	1,843	4,924	4,976	2,081	46.1	911	43.8	6,668	2,950	44.2	2,526	916	36.3
West Baton Rouge	9,223	73.0	7,582	1,641	4,593	4,630	2,448	73.2	1,406	57.4	6,894	4,179	60.6	1,986	554	27.9
West Carroll	2,724	43.6	2,465	259	1,396	1,328	707	41.9	173	24.5	1,963	413	21.0	577	74	12.8
West Feliciana	11,012	81.9	9,204	1,808	5,439	5,573	2,428	72.8	1,454	59.9	7,860	4,691	59.7	2,842	636	22.4
Winn	3,931	21.4	3,189	742	2,118	1,813	1,138	24.2	463	40.7	2,920	1,149	39.3	776	464	59.8
MAINE.																
Total	1,363	0.2	737	626	700	663	476	0.2	55	11.6	1,166	93	8.0	183	166	90.7
Androscoggin	73	0.1	61	12	40	33	27	0.2	6	(1)	67	8	(1)	9	8	(1)
Aroostook	51	0.1	44	7	32	19	19	0.1	2	(1)	46	2	(1)	8	6	(1)
Cumberland	428	0.4	206	222	201	227	134	0.4	7	5.2	373	15	4.0	62	60	(1)
Franklin	17	0.1	10	7	11	6	8	0.1	2	(1)	15	2	(1)	3	3	(1)
Hancock	33	0.1	21	12	20	13	16	0.1	1	(1)	30	1	(1)	1	1	(1)
Kennebec	139	0.2	101	38	72	67	60	0.3	10	(1)	125	13	10.4	15	15	(1)
Knox	73	0.3	41	32	36	37	30	0.3	1	(1)	70	4	(1)	9	9	(1)
Lincoln	18	0.1	9	9	13	5	7	0.1	1	(1)	14	1	(1)	4	2	(1)
Oxford	30	0.1	4	26	17	13	10	0.1	1	(1)	23	1	(1)	4	3	(1)
Penobscot	246	0.3	123	123	120	126	69	0.3	7	(1)	188	13	6.9	41	40	(1)
Piscataquis	7	(2)	2	5	6	1	6	0.1	2	(1)	7	2	(1)			
Sagadahoc	103	0.6	27	76	52	51	37	0.6	11	(1)	82	25	(1)	12	6	(1)
Somerset	19	0.1	17	2	9	10	7	0.1	....	....	17	....	....	2	2	(1)
Waldo	15	0.1	14	1	10	5	8	0.1	....	....	15	....	....	2	2	(1)
Washington	59	0.1	21	38	37	22	19	0.2	3	(1)	49	5	(1)	7	6	(1)
York	52	0.1	36	16	24	28	19	0.1	1	(1)	45	1	(1)	4	3	(1)
MARYLAND.																
Total	232,250	17.9	189,098	43,152	114,749	117,501	63,963	17.4	17,484	27.3	180,454	42,289	23.4	45,233	31,968	70.7
Allegany	1,517	2.4	1,089	428	733	784	439	2.7	96	21.9	1,183	221	18.7	306	211	69.0
Anne Arundel	14,136	35.7	11,344	2,792	7,203	6,933	3,518	31.9	1,230	35.0	10,319	3,066	29.7	3,215	2,034	63.3
Baltimore	12,601	16.3	10,539	2,062	6,692	5,909	4,245	11.6	1,008	23.7	10,336	2,246	21.7	1,977	1,468	74.3
Baltimore City	84,749	15.2	66,508	18,241	39,054	45,695	26,214	16.0	3,509	13.4	71,705	9,438	13.2	11,265	8,509	75.5
Calvert	5,046	48.9	4,271	775	2,563	2,483	1,112	44.2	464	41.7	3,531	1,152	32.6	1,358	961	70.8
Caroline	4,787	24.9	3,944	843	2,487	2,300	1,174	22.7	428	36.5	3,450	995	28.8	1,186	850	71.7
Carroll	2,006	5.9	1,194	812	951	1,055	482	5.0	128	26.6	1,483	309	20.8	471	349	74.1
Cecil	3,315	14.0	2,906	409	1,699	1,616	955	13.6	331	34.7	2,546	731	28.7	677	433	64.0
Charles	8,572	52.3	6,471	2,101	4,485	4,087	1,859	47.2	972	52.3	5,798	2,378	41.0	2,333	1,280	53.7
Dorchester	9,421	32.9	7,854	1,567	4,834	4,587	2,320	30.1	792	34.1	6,960	1,907	27.4	2,271	1,792	78.9
Frederick	5,399	10.3	4,228	1,171	2,659	2,740	1,365	9.6	437	32.0	4,017	997	24.8	1,177	869	73.8
Garrett	107	0.5	52	55	60	47	39	0.7	10	(1)	88	24	(1)	18	6	(1)
Harford	5,116	18.3	4,279	837	2,642	2,474	1,422	17.1	417	29.3	3,978	975	24.5	1,082	778	71.9
Howard	3,772	23.4	2,618	1,154	1,957	1,815	930	21.1	282	30.3	2,741	653	23.8	902	565	62.6
Kent	6,162	36.3	5,806	356	3,198	2,964	1,714	34.5	688	40.1	4,718	1,469	31.1	1,379	1,114	80.8
Montgomery	9,235	28.8	7,836	1,399	4,727	4,508	2,311	26.2	879	38.0	6,753	1,859	27.5	2,103	1,454	69.1
Prince Georges	11,493	31.8	8,520	2,973	5,902	5,591	2,698	27.1	1,015	37.6	8,083	2,466	30.5	2,862	1,879	65.7
Queen Annes	5,814	34.5	5,234	580	3,002	2,812	1,556	33.4	673	43.3	4,334	1,579	36.4	1,260	877	69.6
St. Marys	7,304	42.9	5,924	1,380	3,791	3,513	1,600	40.6	864	54.0	4,978	2,091	42.0	1,089	1,248	62.7
Somerset	9,476	35.8	8,101	1,375	4,905	4,571	2,391	33.4	1,015	42.5	6,923	2,396	34.6	2,250	1,538	68.4
Talbot	6,774	34.5	6,282	492	3,448	3,326	1,765	32.1	713	40.4	5,153	1,718	33.3	1,522	1,064	69.9
Washington	2,113	4.3	1,702	411	1,043	1,070	644	4.7	111	17.2	1,736	259	14.9	358	256	71.5
Wicomico	6,310	23.5	5,703	607	3,129	3,181	1,529	20.9	554	36.2	4,590	1,311	28.6	1,496	1,190	79.5
Worcester	7,025	32.2	6,693	332	3,585	3,440	1,681	28.5	868	51.6	5,048	2,049	40.6	1,726	1,243	72.0

1 Per cent not shown where base is less than 100.   2 Less than one-tenth of 1 per cent.

TABLE **III.**—GENERAL STATISTICS OF THE NEGRO POPULATION OF THE UNITED STATES, BY COUNTIES: 1910--Con.

[Counties in which no Negroes were reported are omitted.]

COUNTY.	NEGRO POPULATION: 1910.																
	Total.	Per cent of total popula- tion.	Color.		Sex.		Males 21 years of age and over.				Persons 10 years of age and over.			Persons 6 to 14 years of age.		
			Black.	Mu- latto.	Male.	Fe- male.	Num- ber.	Per cent of total.	Illiterate.		Total.	Illiterate.		Total.	Attending school.	
									Num- ber.	Per cent.		Num- ber.	Per cent.		Num- ber.	Per cent.

MASSACHUSETTS.

COUNTY.	Total.	Per cent	Black.	Mulatto.	Male.	Female.	Number.	Per cent	Illit. Number.	Illit. Per cent.	Total.	Illit. Number.	Illit. Per cent.	Total.	Att. Number.	Att. Per cent.
Total	38,055	1.1	24,100	13,955	18,748	19,307	12,591	1.2	1,186	9.4	31,718	2,584	8.1	5,223	4,806	92.0
Barnstable	897	3.3	260	637	507	390	276	3.1	83	30.1	662	185	27.9	201	172	85.6
Berkshire	1,149	1.1	843	306	563	586	344	1.1	37	10.8	927	63	6.8	191	175	91.6
Bristol	4,003	1.3	1,494	2,509	2,052	1,951	1,307	1.4	290	22.2	3,154	672	21.3	525	467	89.0
Dukes	193	4.3	130	63	101	92	64	4.3	12	(1)	151	26	17.2	18	15	(1)
Essex	2,024	0.5	1,415	609	1,004	1,020	670	0.5	87	13.0	1,700	154	9.1	284	259	91.2
Franklin	119	0.3	90	29	71	48	41	0.3	6	(1)	103	7	6.8	23	19	(1)
Hampden	1,757	0.8	1,338	419	808	949	524	0.8	37	7.1	1,464	78	5.3	259	247	95.4
Hampshire	281	0.4	171	110	134	147	77	0.4	4	(1)	238	8	3.4	61	55	(1)
Middlesex	8,583	1.3	6,455	2,128	3,963	4,620	2,328	1.2	129	5.5	6,981	368	5.3	1,455	1,375	94.5
Nantucket	35	1.2	8	27	13	22	8	0.9	1	(1)	34	1	(1)	4	4	(1)
Norfolk	797	0.4	593	204	338	459	232	0.4	13	5.6	692	32	4.6	109	104	95.4
Plymouth	2,484	1.7	838	1,646	1,505	979	1,001	2.1	332	33.2	1,919	499	26.0	329	277	84.2
Suffolk	13,886	1.9	9,076	4,810	6,802	7,084	5,160	2.3	137	2.7	12,152	431	3.5	1,476	1,376	93.2
Worcester	1,847	0.5	1,389	458	887	960	559	0.5	18	3.2	1,541	60	3.9	288	261	90.6

MICHIGAN.

COUNTY.	Total.	Per cent	Black.	Mulatto.	Male.	Female.	Number.	Per cent	Illit. Number.	Illit. Per cent.	Total.	Illit. Number.	Illit. Per cent.	Total.	Att. Number.	Att. Per cent.
Total	17,115	0.6	9,079	8,036	9,007	8,108	6,266	0.7	397	6.3	14,557	826	5.7	2,297	2,053	89.4
Alcona	9	0.2	2	7	7	2	2	0.1	1	(1)	7	3	(1)	2	1	(1)
Alger	12	0.2	1	11	6	6	4	0.1			8			2	1	(1)
Allegan	241	0.6	91	150	136	105	93	0.8	12	(1)	200	22	11.0	30	28	(1)
Alpena	3	(2)	2	1	2	1	2	(2)			3					
Antrim	35	0.2	17	18	20	15	12	0.2			27	1	(1)	4	4	(1)
Arenac	6	0.1	6		3	3	3	0.1			6			1	1	(1)
Baraga	2	(2)	1	1	1	1	1	0.1			2					
Barry	23	0.1	1	22	14	9	7	0.1			16			4	3	(1)
Bay	188	0.3	71	117	97	91	73	0.4	4	(1)	155	5	3.2	24	22	(1)
Benzie	89	0.8	29	60	53	36	22	0.7			61	1	(1)	28	27	(1)
Berrien	713	1.3	213	500	363	350	247	1.5	21	8.5	611	39	6.4	93	87	(1)
Branch	50	0.2	34	16	30	20	15	0.2	2	(1)	38	2	(1)	13	12	(1)
Calhoun	690	1.2	347	343	345	345	232	1.2	14	6.0	583	24	4.1	75	70	(1)
Cass	1,444	7.0	333	1,111	768	676	502	7.3	62	12.4	1,154	140	12.1	231	218	94.4
Charlevoix	89	0.5	15	74	50	39	32	0.6	2	(1)	63	2	(1)	15	14	(1)
Cheboygan	34	0.2	11	23	17	17	12	0.2	1	(1)	27	3	(1)	5	5	(1)
Chippewa	43	0.2	34	9	25	18	20	0.3	1	(1)	40	3	(1)	7	7	(1)
Clare	3	(2)	2	1	1	2	1	(2)			3					
Clinton	38	0.2	18	20	18	20	14	0.2			34	1	(1)	3	3	(1)
Crawford	2	0.1	2		2		2	0.2			2					
Delta	34	0.1	16	18	19	15	14	0.2	1	(1)	30	1	(1)	7	7	(1)
Dickinson	9	(2)	1	8	6	3	5	0.1			6					
Eaton	74	0.2	52	22	40	34	31	0.3	1	(1)	65	1	(1)	8	8	(1)
Emmet	44	0.2	7	37	22	22	16	0.3	3	(1)	36	3	(1)	8	8	(1)
Genesee	416	0.6	367	49	224	192	152	0.6	2	1.3	357	7	2.0	56	47	(1)
Gladwin	37	0.4	33	4	21	16	12	0.5	2	(1)	28	3	(1)	9	6	(1)
Gogebic	6	(2)	4	2	3	3	2	(2)			6			1	1	(1)
Grand Traverse	32	0.1	12	20	13	19	11	0.1	2	(1)	23	4	(1)	3	3	(1)
Gratiot	92	0.3	28	64	54	38	30	0.3	1	(1)	72	3	(1)	17	17	(1)
Hillsdale	22	0.1	13	9	13	9	9	0.1			19	1	(1)	2	2	(1)
Houghton	61	0.1	48	13	29	32	24	0.1	1	(1)	53	2	(1)	4	4	(1)
Huron	8	(2)	3	5	6	2	6	0.1			8					
Ingham	404	0.8	195	209	203	201	133	0.7	13	9.8	347	31	8.9	65	62	(1)
Ionia	90	0.3	55	35	57	33	48	0.4	3	(1)	85	6	(1)	7	5	(1)
Iosco	5	0.1	2	3	2	3	2	0.1			5					
Iron	8	0.1	5	3	6	2	6	0.1	1	(1)	8	1	(1)			
Isabella	135	0.6	53	82	70	65	37	0.6	9	(1)	106	15	14.2	29	26	(1)
Jackson	399	0.7	314	85	216	183	176	1.0	15	8.5	357	29	8.1	41	34	(1)
Kalamazoo	790	1.3	464	326	425	365	292	1.5	7	2.4	665	31	4.7	106	91	85.8
Kalkaska	23	0.3	10	13	15	8	8	0.3	2	(1)	18	3	(1)	3	3	(1)
Kent	729	0.5	506	223	390	339	304	0.6	15	4.9	644	35	5.4	68	61	(1)
Keweenaw	3	(2)	3		3		3	0.1			3					
Lake	5	0.1	5		1	4	1	0.1			5			2	2	(1)
Lapeer	28	0.1	15	13	17	11	11	0.1	3	(1)	26	9	(1)	4	3	(1)
Leelanau	22	0.2	11	11	10	12	6	0.2			17			4	4	(1)
Lenawee	245	0.5	80	165	110	135	75	0.5	10	(1)	215	16	7.4	37	34	(1)
Livingston	35	0.2	21	14	17	18	14	0.2	1	(1)	31	2	(1)	4	4	(1)
Luce	3	0.1	3		3		3	0.2	1	(1)	3	1	(1)			
Mackinac	11	0.1	7	4	7	4	6	0.2			11					
Macomb	102	0.3	62	40	47	55	31	0.3	1	(1)	87	2	(1)	19	17	(1)
Manistee	20	0.1	5	15	9	11	7	0.1			15	1	(1)	2	1	(1)
Marquette	83	0.2	24	59	54	29	37	0.3	2	(1)	68	2	(1)	17	17	(1)
Mason	6	(2)		6	4	2	1	(2)			3					
Mecosta	237	1.2	53	184	122	115	60	1.0	8	(1)	178	13	7.3	61	59	(1)
Menominee	7	(2)	5	2	4	3	2	(2)			4			4	4	(1)

[1] Per cent not shown where base is less than 100.　　　　[2] Less than one-tenth of 1 per cent.

TABLE III.—GENERAL STATISTICS OF THE NEGRO POPULATION OF THE UNITED STATES, BY COUNTIES: 1910—Con.

[Counties in which no Negroes were reported are omitted.]

	NEGRO POPULATION: 1910.																
			Color.		Sex.		Males 21 years of age and over.				Persons 10 years of age and over.			Persons 6 to 14 years of age.		
COUNTY.	Total.	Per cent of total population.	Black.	Mulatto.	Male.	Female.	Number.	Per cent of total.	Illiterate.		Total.	Illiterate.		Total.	Attending school.	
									Number.	Per cent.		Number.	Per cent.		Number.	Per cent.

MICHIGAN—Continued.

COUNTY.	Total.	Per cent	Black.	Mulatto.	Male.	Female.	Number.	Per cent	Illit. No.	Illit. Pct.	Total.	Illit. No.	Illit. Pct.	Total.	Att. No.	Att. Pct.
Midland	119	0.8	15	104	63	56	36	0.9	5	(1)	94	8	(1)	27	27	(1)
Missaukee	15	0.1	6	9	5	10	3	0.1	1	(1)	10	1	(1)	4	4	(1)
Monroe	88	0.3	51	37	44	44	26	0.3	8	(1)	68	14	(1)	16	13	(1)
Montcalm	105	0.3	26	79	65	40	43	0.4	4	(1)	88	6	(1)	17	15	(1)
Montmorency	1	(2)	1			1										
Muskegon	79	0.2	48	31	41	38	27	0.2	2	(1)	62	3	(1)	14	6	(1)
Newaygo	19	0.1	15	4	12	7	7	0.1			16			4	4	(1)
Oakland	251	0.5	176	75	122	129	80	0.5	7	(1)	207	13	6.3	43	36	(1)
Oceana	25	0.1	18	7	16	9	11	0.2	2	(1)	22	2	(1)	4	4	(1)
Ogemaw	2	(2)	1	1	1	1	1	(2)			2					
Ontonagon	2	(2)	2		1	1	1	(2)	1	(1)	2	1	(1)			
Osceola	39	0.2	12	27	24	15	8	0.2	1	(1)	22	2	(1)	13	11	(1)
Oscoda	4	0.2	4		1	3	1	0.2			3					
Otsego	1	(2)	1			1								1	1	(1)
Ottawa	42	0.1	31	11	23	19	20	0.2	4	(1)	40	6	(1)	3	3	(1)
Presque Isle	3	(2)	3		3		3	0.1			3					
Roscommon	2	0.1	2		1	1	1	0.1			2					
Saginaw	343	0.4	257	86	183	160	139	0.5	10	7.2	306	18	5.9	33	27	(1)
St. Clair	65	0.1	42	23	34	31	18	0.1			58	1	(1)	4	2	(1)
St. Joseph	88	0.3	58	30	53	35	34	0.4	1	(1)	69	2	(1)	16	16	(1)
Sanilac	8	(2)	4	4	6	2	5	0.1			7					
Schoolcraft	5	0.1	2	3	4	1	2	0.1			3			2	2	(1)
Shiawassee	39	0.1	26	13	23	16	14	0.1	1	(1)	26	1	(1)	8	8	(1)
Tuscola	21	0.1	3	18	7	14	5	(2)	1	(1)	18	1	(1)	5	5	(1)
Van Buren	535	1.6	133	402	292	243	183	1.8	17	9.3	429	33	7.7	92	82	(1)
Washtenaw	1,130	2.5	742	388	555	575	344	2.5	16	4.7	958	39	4.1	179	160	89.4
Wayne	6,085	1.1	3,672	2,413	3,196	2,889	2,367	1.4	89	3.8	5,362	203	3.8	670	584	87.2
Wexford	60	0.3	16	44	32	28	16	0.3	3	(1)	36	4	(1)	17	10	(1)

MINNESOTA.

COUNTY.	Total.	Per cent	Black.	Mulatto.	Male.	Female.	Number.	Per cent	Illit. No.	Illit. Pct.	Total.	Illit. No.	Illit. Pct.	Total.	Att. No.	Att. Pct.
Total	7,084	0.3	4,468	2,616	4,183	2,901	3,390	0.5	123	3.6	6,366	215	3.4	649	584	90.0
Aitkin	46	0.4	28	18	26	20	12	0.4	4	(1)	28	5	(1)	10	7	(1)
Anoka	41	0.3	19	22	21	20	18	0.5	4	(1)	38	7	(1)	7	6	(1)
Becker	4	(2)	4		4		4	0.1			4					
Beltrami	11	0.1	9	2	5	6	5	0.1			11					
Benton	2	(2)	2		1	1	1	(2)			2					
Big Stone	3	(2)	2	1	2	1	2	0.1			3					
Blue Earth	8	(2)	8		5	3	4	(2)	1	(1)	8	1	(1)	1		
Brown	2	(2)	2		1	1	1	(2)			2					
Carver	4	(2)	4		4		3	0.1			4					
Cass	36	0.3	35	1	23	13	19	0.5			33			7	7	(1)
Chippewa	5	(2)	2	3	3	2	3	0.1			5					
Chisago	4	(2)	2	2	2	2	2	0.1			3			1	1	(1)
Clay	15	0.1	8	7	8	7	8	0.1			13	1	(1)	1		
Cottonwood	2	(2)	2			2								1	1	(1)
Crow Wing	2	(2)	1	1	2		2	(2)			2					
Dakota	40	0.2	29	11	24	16	20	0.3	2	(1)	37	2	(1)	5	5	(1)
Dodge	27	0.2	2	25	27		27	0.8	26	(1)	27	26	(1)			
Douglas	5	(2)	4	1	2	3	2	(2)	1	(1)	4	1	(1)	2	2	(1)
Faribault	9	(2)	4	5	5	4	5	0.1			9					
Fillmore	11	(2)	6	5	4	7	2	(2)	1	(1)	8	2	(1)			
Freeborn	7	(2)	1	6	4	3	4	0.1	1	(1)	7	1	(1)			
Goodhue	45	0.1	29	16	32	13	9	0.1			39	1	(1)	9	9	(1)
Hennepin	2,646	0.8	1,679	967	1,525	1,121	1,246	1.1	41	3.3	404	74	3.1	231	203	87.9
Houston	1	(2)	1		1		1	(2)			1					
Hubbard	15	0.2	12	3	9	6	4	0.1			10			3	3	(1)
Isanti	4	(2)		4	3	1					4					
Itasca	12	0.1	7	5	7	5	6	0.1			10			1	1	(1)
Jackson	2	(2)	2		2											
Kandiyohi	5	(2)	4	1	3	2	2	(2)			4			1	1	(1)
Kittson	2	(2)	2			2					2					
Koochiching	10	0.2	10		7	3	6	0.2			9			3	3	(1)
Lac qui Parle	5	(2)	5		2	3	2	(2)			3			1	1	(1)
Le Sueur	23	0.1	4	19	15	8	9	0.2	1	(1)	21	1	(1)	3	2	(1)
Lincoln	1	(2)	1			1					1					
Lyon	5	(2)	5		1	4					3			1	1	(1)
McLeod	12	0.1	11	1	7	5	6	0.1			9					
Marshall	3	(2)	2	1	2	1	1	(2)			2			1	1	(1)
Martin	4	(2)	4		2	2	1	(2)			2					
Meeker	3	(2)	2	1	2	1	1	(2)			3	1	(1)			
Mille Lacs	6	0.1	5	4	2						3	1	(1)	3	3	(1)

[1] Per cent not shewn where base is less than 100.   [2] Less than one-tenth of 1 per cent.

Table III.—GENERAL STATISTICS OF THE NEGRO POPULATION OF THE UNITED STATES, BY COUNTIES: 1910—Con.

[Counties in which no Negroes were reported are omitted.]

COUNTY.	Total.	Per cent of total population.	Color.		Sex.		Males 21 years of age and over.				Persons 10 years of age and over.			Persons 6 to 14 years of age.		
			Black.	Mulatto.	Male.	Female.	Number.	Per cent of total.	Illiterate Number.	Illiterate Per cent.	Total.	Illiterate Number.	Illiterate Per cent.	Total.	Attending school Number.	Attending school Per cent.
MINNESOTA—Continued.																
Morrison	6	(1)	6	......	4	2	4	0.1	......	......	5	......	......	1	1	(2)
Mower	21	0.1	16	5	16	5	12	0.2	1	(2)	16	1	(2)	2	1	(2)
Murray	1	(1)	1	......	1	......	1	(1)	......	......	1	......	......	......	......	......
Nicollet	11	0.1	3	8	7	4	5	0.1	......	......	8	......	......	4	3	(2)
Norman	2	(1)	2	......	1	1	......	......	......	......	1	......	......	1	1	(2)
Olmsted	33	0.1	25	8	18	15	14	0.2	1	(2)	27	3	(2)	3	3	(2)
Otter Tail	52	0.1	36	16	26	26	11	0.1	2	(2)	36	3	(2)	11	10	(2)
Pennington	7	0.1	2	5	2	5	2	0.1	......	......	4	......	......	3	3	(2)
Pine	11	0.1	6	5	6	5	4	0.1	......	......	8	......	......	3	3	(2)
Pipestone	1	(1)	1	......	1	......	1	(1)	......	......	1	......	......	......	......	......
Polk	27	0.1	6	21	9	18	4	(1)	......	......	25	......	......	4	4	(2)
Pope	3	(1)	2	1	1	2	1	(1)	......	......	2	......	......	1	1	(2)
Ramsey	3,154	1.4	1,958	1,196	1,910	1,244	1,579	2.1	27	1.7	2,850	68	2.4	261	243	93.1
Redwood	11	0.1	5	6	4	7	4	0.1	......	......	9	......	......	1	1	(2)
Renville	1	(1)	1	......	1	......	1	(1)	......	......	1	......	......	......	......	......
Rice	21	0.1	17	4	13	8	8	0.1	......	......	19	2	(2)	3	1	(2)
Rock	3	(1)	3	......	1	2	1	(1)	......	......	3	......	......	1	......	......
Roseau	2	(1)	2	......	......	2	......	......	......	......	......	......	......	......	......	......
St. Louis	439	0.3	291	148	251	188	209	0.3	4	1.9	400	7	1.8	36	31	(2)
Scott	1	(1)	1	......	1	......	1	(1)	1	(2)	1	1	(2)	......	......	......
Sherburne	9	0.1	9	......	6	3	4	0.2	......	......	8	......	......	......	......	......
Sibley	6	(1)	6	......	......	6	......	......	......	......	6	1	(2)	......	......	......
Stearns	14	(1)	13	1	8	6	7	0.1	......	......	14	......	......	1	1	(2)
Steele	20	0.1	16	4	14	6	2	(1)	1	(2)	15	1	(2)	13	13	(2)
Stevens	2	(1)	2	......	1	1	1	(1)	......	......	1	......	......	1	1	(2)
Swift	1	(1)	1	......	1	......	1	(1)	......	......	1	......	......	......	......	......
Todd	2	(1)	2	......	......	2	......	......	......	......	1	......	......	1	1	(2)
Traverse	2	(1)	1	1	2	......	2	0.1	......	......	2	......	......	......	......	......
Wabasha	11	0.1	10	1	6	5	6	0.1	1	(2)	8	1	(2)	1	1	(2)
Wadena	1	(1)	......	1	1	......	1	(1)	......	......	1	......	......	......	......	......
Waseca	5	(1)	3	2	3	2	1	(1)	......	......	3	......	......	1	1	(2)
Washington	71	0.3	37	34	47	24	43	0.5	2	(2)	69	2	(2)	......	......	......
Watonwan	1	(1)	1	......	......	1	......	......	......	......	1	......	......	......	......	......
Wilkin	3	(1)	2	1	2	1	2	0.1	......	......	3	......	......	......	......	......
Winona	22	0.1	9	13	15	7	13	0.1	1	(2)	21	1	(2)	1	1	(2)
Wright	18	0.1	17	1	6	12	6	0.1	......	......	15	......	......	3	2	(2)
Yellow Medicine	1	(1)	......	1	1	......	1	(1)	......	......	1	......	......	......	......	......
MISSISSIPPI.																
Total	1,009,487	56.2	838,482	171,005	502,796	506,691	233,701	54.7	95,702	41.0	727,851	259,438	35.6	238,101	151,581	63.7
Adams	18,908	74.8	14,938	3,970	8,648	10,260	4,247	71.5	1,954	46.0	14,344	5,780	40.3	4,144	2,931	70.7
Alcorn	4,275	23.5	2,850	1,425	2,039	2,236	958	22.0	260	27.1	3,169	727	22.9	980	609	62.1
Amite	12,590	54.8	10,285	2,305	6,214	6,376	2,289	49.4	1,123	49.1	8,395	3,437	40.9	3,517	2,294	65.2
Attala	13,219	45.8	10,479	2,740	6,549	6,670	2,598	41.7	1,112	42.8	8,949	2,962	33.1	3,439	2,304	67.0
Benton	5,037	49.2	3,983	1,054	2,496	2,541	1,049	45.7	337	32.1	3,485	928	26.6	1,241	730	58.8
Bolivar	42,763	87.4	36,099	6,664	21,748	21,015	11,864	86.5	4,409	37.2	33,360	12,017	36.0	8,819	4,979	56.5
Calhoun	3,812	21.5	2,890	922	1,887	1,925	793	20.3	317	40.0	2,528	882	34.9	924	517	56.0
Carroll	13,475	58.2	11,678	1,797	6,848	6,627	2,779	54.7	1,100	39.6	9,169	3,126	34.1	3,503	2,227	63.6
Chickasaw	12,714	55.7	10,378	2,336	6,271	6,443	2,610	51.3	934	35.8	8,604	2,366	27.5	3,111	2,282	73.4
Choctaw	4,169	29.0	3,645	524	2,002	2,167	772	24.8	276	35.8	2,771	879	31.7	1,141	616	54.0
Claiborne	13,608	78.2	8,876	4,732	6,547	7,061	2,931	74.4	1,338	45.6	9,784	3,501	35.8	3,238	2,513	77.6
Clarke	10,262	47.4	9,037	1,225	5,098	5,164	2,029	43.3	714	35.2	7,052	1,900	26.9	2,732	1,817	66.5
Clay	14,105	69.8	11,004	3,101	6,787	7,318	2,961	65.0	1,220	41.2	10,118	3,228	31.9	3,393	2,573	75.8
Coahoma	30,382	88.8	26,030	4,352	15,475	14,907	8,482	86.0	2,905	34.2	23,206	7,488	32.3	6,190	3,748	60.5
Copiah	19,981	55.6	16,365	3,616	9,743	10,238	3,942	51.3	1,874	47.5	13,633	5,170	37.9	5,207	3,338	64.1
Covington	5,224	30.9	3,918	1,306	2,801	2,423	1,301	32.8	412	31.7	3,680	1,030	28.0	1,191	844	70.9
De Soto	17,572	76.0	14,933	2,639	8,835	8,737	4,008	73.8	1,648	41.1	12,645	4,641	36.7	4,320	2,816	65.2
Forrest	7,683	37.1	6,724	959	3,847	3,836	2,034	37.7	627	30.8	5,766	1,681	29.2	1,545	928	60.1
Franklin	6,823	44.9	4,969	1,854	3,428	3,395	1,308	40.7	735	56.2	4,523	2,329	51.5	1,904	1,015	53.3
George	1,827	27.7	1,618	209	968	859	518	31.6	146	28.2	1,327	370	27.9	386	247	64.0
Greene	1,347	22.3	998	349	719	628	370	25.4	103	27.8	997	257	25.8	303	195	64.4
Grenada	11,161	71.0	8,865	2,296	5,472	5,689	2,405	67.0	818	34.0	7,858	2,189	27.9	2,789	1,925	69.0
Hancock	4,339	38.7	2,791	1,548	2,349	1,990	1,293	43.6	364	28.2	3,260	887	27.2	870	508	58.4
Harrison	10,643	30.7	7,881	2,762	5,376	5,267	3,109	33.1	944	30.4	8,321	2,343	28.2	1,933	1,199	62.0
Hinds	45,407	71.3	36,858	8,549	22,016	23,391	9,993	65.3	3,838	38.4	32,834	10,419	31.7	10,816	7,357	68.0
Holmes	31,197	79.8	25,052	6,145	15,465	15,732	6,858	76.7	2,804	40.9	22,334	7,238	32.4	7,780	5,780	74.3
Issaquena	9,946	94.2	8,848	1,098	5,097	4,849	2,655	92.3	1,195	45.0	7,530	3,196	42.4	2,138	1,176	55.0
Itawamba	1,198	8.2	723	475	591	607	232	7.3	88	37.9	837	231	27.6	327	219	67.0
Jackson	5,467	35.4	3,712	1,755	2,845	2,622	1,622	38.1	536	33.0	4,209	1,238	29.4	1,020	614	60.2
Jasper	9,013	48.7	7,139	1,874	4,508	4,505	1,730	44.4	718	41.5	6,005	1,898	31.6	2,446	1,823	74.5

1 Less than one-tenth of 1 per cent. 2 Per cent not shown where base is less than 100.

TABLE III.—GENERAL STATISTICS OF THE NEGRO POPULATION OF THE UNITED STATES, BY COUNTIES: 1910—Con.

[Counties in which no Negroes were reported are omitted.]

COUNTY.	NEGRO POPULATION: 1910.															
	Total.	Per cent of total population.	Color.		Sex.		Males 21 years of age and over.				Persons 10 years of age and over.			Persons 6 to 14 years of age.		
			Black.	Mulatto.	Male.	Female.	Number.	Per cent of total.	Illiterate.		Total.	Illiterate.		Total.	Attending school.	
									Number.	Per cent.		Number.	Per cent.		Number.	Per cent.

MISSISSIPPI—Continued.

COUNTY.	Total.	%	Black.	Mulatto.	Male.	Female.	Number.	% total.	Illit. No.	Illit. %	Total.	Illit. No.	Illit. %	Total.	Att. No.	Att. %
Jefferson	14,287	78.4	12,083	2,204	6,910	7,377	2,912	74.2	1,419	48.7	10,005	4,018	40.2	3,726	2,384	64.0
Jefferson Davis	6,757	52.5	5,688	1,069	3,506	3,251	1,454	51.5	573	39.4	4,402	1,500	34.1	1,717	1,188	69.2
Jones	8,417	28.2	7,054	1,363	4,164	4,253	2,033	29.7	691	34.0	6,072	1,832	30.2	1,911	1,273	66.6
Kemper	11,691	57.5	10,182	1,509	5,884	5,807	2,302	52.7	994	43.2	7,952	2,670	33.6	3,084	1,995	64.7
Lafayette	9,904	45.3	8,142	1,762	4,904	5,000	2,074	30.6	635	30.6	6,794	1,821	26.8	2,413	1,647	68.3
Lamar	3,619	30.8	3,184	435	2,072	1,547	1,174	37.9	520	44.3	2,714	1,041	38.4	686	425	62.0
Lauderdale	21,875	46.6	19,284	2,591	10,594	11,281	4,956	42.3	2,015	40.7	15,954	5,754	36.1	4,996	3,160	63.3
Lawrence	5,147	39.4	4,162	985	2,627	2,520	1,134	38.6	440	38.8	3,505	1,179	33.6	1,267	804	63.5
Leake	6,171	33.7	4,885	1,286	3,070	3,101	1,181	30.4	435	36.8	3,999	1,264	31.6	1,584	1,033	65.2
Lee	10,667	36.9	8,106	2,561	5,255	5,412	2,383	35.6	913	38.3	7,630	2,364	31.0	2,665	1,887	70.8
Leflore	30,628	84.4	27,603	3,025	15,750	14,878	7,915	80.9	3,403	43.0	22,770	8,654	38.0	6,706	4,157	62.0
Lincoln	12,054	42.2	10,099	1,955	5,790	6,264	2,499	39.5	1,063	42.5	8,339	3,154	37.8	2,978	2,010	67.5
Lowndes	21,784	71.0	17,762	4,022	10,403	11,381	4,987	67.3	2,313	46.4	15,971	6,242	39.1	4,894	3,246	66.3
Madison	27,298	81.5	23,741	3,557	13,258	14,040	5,730	77.2	2,371	41.4	19,514	6,603	33.8	6,692	4,293	64.2
Marion	6,063	38.9	5,233	830	3,301	2,762	1,623	41.7	511	31.5	4,240	1,196	28.2	1,405	957	68.1
Marshall	19,342	72.2	13,781	5,561	9,537	9,805	3,911	66.8	1,708	43.7	13,434	4,788	35.6	4,965	3,328	67.0
Monroe	19,535	55.5	17,176	2,359	9,661	9,874	4,388	52.4	1,729	39.4	14,033	4,537	32.3	4,666	3,270	70.1
Montgomery	8,927	50.4	7,682	1,245	4,471	4,456	1,851	46.7	806	43.5	6,091	2,100	34.5	2,260	1,307	57.8
Neshoba	2,949	16.4	2,328	621	1,502	1,447	586	15.1	261	44.5	1,957	761	38.9	805	510	63.4
Newton	8,950	38.8	7,574	1,376	4,510	4,440	1,854	36.4	779	42.0	6,041	2,036	33.7	2,331	1,645	70.6
Noxubee	23,947	84.0	20,279	3,668	11,676	12,271	4,939	79.9	2,467	49.9	17,076	6,852	40.1	6,138	4,486	73.1
Oktibbeha	12,675	64.4	11,005	1,670	6,042	6,633	2,552	59.7	1,179	46.2	8,784	3,460	39.4	3,187	1,763	55.3
Panola	21,224	67.9	18,101	3,123	10,611	10,613	4,599	64.4	1,963	42.7	14,912	6,467	43.4	5,282	2,110	39.9
Pearl River	2,422	22.9	1,991	431	1,295	1,127	679	27.1	224	33.0	1,732	521	30.1	546	358	65.6
Perry	2,581	33.6	2,261	320	1,449	1,132	736	37.4	260	35.3	1,931	581	30.1	604	303	50.2
Pike	17,597	47.2	13,195	4,402	8,910	8,687	3,760	43.9	1,665	44.3	12,211	4,484	36.7	4,413	2,807	63.6
Pontotoc	4,727	24.0	2,663	2,064	2,418	2,309	1,060	23.6	383	36.1	3,335	921	27.6	1,088	737	67.7
Prentiss	2,875	17.0	2,253	622	1,453	1,422	628	16.5	251	40.0	2,039	678	33.3	707	490	69.3
Quitman	8,864	76.5	8,186	678	4,693	4,171	2,576	75.8	968	37.6	6,740	2,466	36.6	1,813	939	51.8
Rankin	14,249	59.5	11,624	2,625	7,031	7,218	2,802	53.8	1,429	51.0	9,640	3,763	39.0	3,755	2,743	73.0
Scott	6,896	41.2	6,115	781	3,455	3,441	1,384	37.1	564	40.8	4,593	1,664	36.2	1,808	778	43.0
Sharkey	13,967	89.0	13,327	640	7,043	6,924	3,696	88.2	1,379	37.3	10,612	3,624	34.2	2,915	1,886	64.7
Simpson	5,969	34.7	4,853	1,116	2,952	3,017	1,233	33.9	561	45.5	4,015	1,566	39.0	1,510	947	62.7
Smith	2,899	17.5	2,124	775	1,535	1,364	608	17.3	253	41.6	1,940	700	36.1	763	492	64.5
Sunflower	23,281	80.9	20,934	2,347	12,487	10,794	6,761	80.9	2,805	41.5	17,590	6,745	38.3	4,813	1,976	41.1
Tallahatchie	20,180	69.4	18,246	1,934	10,404	9,776	5,046	68.5	2,425	48.1	14,833	6,632	44.7	4,789	2,519	52.6
Tate	11,535	58.5	10,268	1,267	5,739	5,796	2,465	55.6	1,101	44.7	8,158	3,097	38.0	2,992	1,986	66.4
Tappah	2,801	19.1	2,205	596	1,389	1,412	531	16.5	198	37.3	1,827	562	30.8	760	505	66.4
Tishomingo	1,089	8.3	708	381	513	576	246	8.4	94	38.2	808	292	36.1	280	139	49.6
Tunica	16,910	90.7	13,699	3,211	8,664	8,246	4,754	89.5	2,043	43.0	13,140	5,611	42.7	3,458	1,537	44.4
Union	4,216	22.2	3,342	874	2,089	2,127	924	21.0	395	42.7	2,922	1,002	34.3	965	665	68.9
Warren	26,191	69.9	20,973	5,218	12,289	13,902	6,679	65.9	2,355	35.3	20,610	6,551	31.8	5,246	3,665	69.9
Washington	41,600	85.0	36,431	5,169	20,622	20,978	11,844	82.8	5,264	44.4	32,497	13,432	41.3	8,010	5,387	67.3
Wayne	5,843	39.7	4,517	1,326	2,986	2,857	1,263	38.9	539	42.7	4,090	1,453	35.5	1,486	825	55.5
Webster	3,286	22.1	2,498	788	1,641	1,645	679	20.5	261	38.4	2,215	721	32.6	856	452	52.8
Wilkinson	13,904	76.9	11,246	2,658	6,808	7,096	2,671	73.1	1,563	58.5	9,457	5,029	53.2	3,743	2,000	53.4
Winston	6,863	40.0	5,814	1,049	3,381	3,482	1,280	34.9	531	41.5	4,419	1,708	38.7	1,825	1,000	54.8
Yalobusha	11,182	52.0	9,898	1,284	5,615	5,567	2,401	47.6	889	37.0	7,773	2,346	30.2	2,831	1,918	67.7
Yazoo	35,502	76.1	30,411	5,091	17,768	17,734	8,218	73.8	3,265	39.7	25,824	8,658	33.5	8,420	5,525	65.6

MISSOURI.

COUNTY.	Total.	%	Black.	Mulatto.	Male.	Female.	Number.	% total.	Illit. No.	Illit. %	Total.	Illit. No.	Illit. %	Total.	Att. No.	Att. %
Total	157,452	4.8	112,762	44,690	80,489	76,963	52,921	5.4	10,068	19.0	132,385	23,062	17.4	23,465	17,811	75.9
Adair	216	1.0	123	93	103	113	69	1.1	18	(1)	192	42	21.9	25	20	(1)
Andrew	130	0.9	86	44	72	58	52	1.2	7	(1)	115	21	18.3	24	15	(1)
Atchison	14	0.1	12	2	9	5	8	0.2	1	(1)	12	1	(1)	1	1	(1)
Audrain	1,617	7.5	1,329	288	798	819	477	7.4	155	32.5	1,298	337	26.0	284	210	73.9
Barry	6	(2)	6	....	1	5	1	(2)			6			1	1	(1)
Barton	24	0.1	16	8	13	11	10	0.2	4	(1)	20	7	(1)	2	1	(1)
Bates	238	0.9	167	71	114	124	71	0.9	17	(1)	186	36	19.4	40	36	(1)
Benton	136	0.9	101	35	68	68	31	0.8	11	(1)	102	27	26.5	39	22	(1)
Bollinger	30	0.2	....	30	13	17	2	0.1	2	(1)	18	12	(1)	7	3	(1)
Boone	4,185	13.7	2,026	2,159	2,072	2,113	1,232	13.9	417	33.8	3,369	943	28.0	741	555	74.9
Buchanan	4,457	4.8	3,620	837	2,386	2,071	1,711	4.8	293	17.1	3,902	570	14.6	513	432	84.2
Butler	1,372	6.7	1,231	141	683	689	392	7.0	50	12.8	1,037	118	11.4	264	202	76.5
Caldwell	278	1.9	180	98	148	130	77	1.8	11	(1)	220	22	10.0	72	66	(1)
Callaway	3,514	14.4	2,616	898	1,867	1,647	1,034	13.9	289	27.9	2,752	619	22.5	697	431	61.8
Camden	46	0.4	38	8	23	23	12	0.4	4	(1)	36	18	(1)	9	2	(1)
Cape Girardeau	1,990	7.2	976	1,014	1,026	964	568	7.7	155	27.3	1,543	349	22.6	381	289	75.9
Carroll	1,019	4.4	562	457	484	535	299	4.4	74	24.7	812	177	21.8	172	139	80.8
Carter	2	(2)	2	....		2	2	0.2	1	(1)	2	1	(1)			(1)
Cass	510	2.2	397	113	275	235	157	2.3	31	19.7	414	70	16.9	82	68	(1)
Cedar	13	0.1	8	5	8	5	7	0.2	3	(1)	11	1	(1)	1		

[1] Per cent not shown where base is less than 100. [2] Less than one-tenth of 1 per cent.

TABLE III.—GENERAL STATISTICS OF THE NEGRO POPULATION OF THE UNITED STATES, BY COUNTIES: 1910—Con.

[Counties in which no Negroes were reported are omitted.]

COUNTY.	Total.	Per cent of total population.	Color.		Sex.		Males 21 years of age and over.				Persons 10 years of age and over.			Persons 6 to 14 years of age.		
			Black.	Mulatto.	Male.	Female.	Number.	Per cent of total.	Illiterate.		Total.	Illiterate.		Total.	Attending school.	
									Number.	Per cent.		Number.	Per cent.		Number.	Per cent.

MISSOURI—Continued.

COUNTY.	Total.	Per cent	Black.	Mulatto.	Male.	Female.	Number.	Per cent	Illit. No.	Illit. Pct.	Total.	Illit. No.	Illit. Pct.	Total.	Att. No.	Att. Pct.
Chariton	2,232	9.5	1,753	479	1,132	1,100	602	8.9	185	30.7	1,765	420	23.8	491	362	73.
Christian	51	0.3	27	24	23	28	13	0.3	2	(1)	47	11	(1)	8	8	(1)
Clark	50	0.4	43	7	25	25	22	0.6	7	(1)	45	12	(1)	3	3	(1)
Clay	1,052	5.2	939	113	536	516	336	5.3	95	28.3	875	214	24.5	163	109	66.9
Clinton	769	5.0	602	167	392	377	218	4.9	78	35.8	604	149	24.7	144	117	81.3
Cole	2,157	9.8	1,620	537	1,449	708	1,105	14.8	216	19.5	1,925	334	17.4	241	186	77.2
Cooper	2,878	14.2	2,235	643	1,505	1,373	790	13.8	215	27.2	2,306	460	19.9	585	423	72.3
Crawford	35	0.3	28	7	15	20	9	0.3	3	(1)	30	9	(1)	6	....	....
Dade	235	1.5	223	12	109	126	66	1.6	12	(1)	190	32	16.8	57	54	(1)
Dallas	2	(2)	2	....	2	....	2	0.1	1	(1)	2	1	(1)	....	....	....
Daviess	258	1.5	90	168	132	126	84	1.6	28	(1)	219	50	22.8	45	43	(1)
Dekalb	64	0.5	64	....	37	27	29	0.8	3	(1)	58	10	(1)	10	8	(1)
Dent	18	0.1	1	17	9	9	3	0.1	1	(1)	11	4	(1)	5	3	(1)
Douglas	8	(2)	6	2	6	2	4	0.1	3	(1)	8	5	(1)	....	....	....
Dunklin	96	0.3	76	20	46	50	23	0.3	12	(1)	85	45	(1)	18	4	(1)
Franklin	1,365	4.6	988	377	696	669	332	4.0	85	25.6	997	216	21.7	348	264	75.9
Gasconade	41	0.3	6	35	18	23	13	0.4	3	(1)	30	4	(1)	7	7	(1)
Gentry	11	0.1	7	4	5	6	5	0.1			10	1	(1)	1		
Greene	2,625	4.1	2,022	603	1,317	1,308	760	4.2	140	18.4	2,141	337	15.7	483	342	70.8
Grundy	159	0.9	134	25	70	89	50	1.9	16	(1)	139	38	27.3	16	15	(1)
Harrison	28	0.1	11	17	14	14	10	0.2	1	(1)	26	2	(1)	3		
Henry	842	3.1	668	174	422	420	233	3.0	81	34.8	675	190	28.1	155	103	66.5
Hickory	7	0.1	7	....	4	3	2	0.1	2	(1)	7	5	(1)			
Holt	118	0.8	66	52	62	56	41	1.0	17	(1)	97	32	(1)	17	12	(1)
Howard	3,152	20.1	2,516	636	1,661	1,491	951	20.4	412	43.3	2,557	886	34.6	656	404	61.6
Howell	127	0.6	61	66	75	52	37	0.7	15	(1)	94	33	(1)	32	23	(1)
Iron	179	2.1	162	17	88	91	52	2.5	14	(1)	138	36	26.1	25	12	(1)
Jackson	24,936	8.8	16,620	8,316	12,604	12,332	9,592	9.7	904	9.4	22,350	2,299	10.3	2,449	2,056	84.0
Jasper	1,368	1.5	830	538	692	676	448	1.7	62	13.8	1,132	155	13.7	263	165	81.3
Jefferson	1,565	5.6	1,327	238	880	685	479	6.0	142	29.6	1,243	273	22.0	318	229	72.0
Johnson	1,251	4.8	982	269	650	601	393	5.1	139	35.4	1,029	273	26.5	215	168	78.1
Knox	168	1.4	148	20	86	82	47	1.3	8	(1)	128	16	12.5	27	21	(1)
Laclede	216	1.2	99	117	104	112	56	1.3	15	(1)	161	44	27.3	47	32	(1)
Lafayette	2,809	9.5	2,487	382	1,511	1,358	910	10.1	237	26.0	2,368	482	20.4	517	387	74.9
Lawrence	91	0.3	49	42	45	46	29	0.4	12	(1)	69	18	(1)	14	12	(1)
Lewis	776	5.0	372	404	385	391	212	4.6	59	27.8	597	166	27.8	150	87	58.0
Lincoln	1,362	8.0	989	373	714	648	376	7.7	122	32.4	1,049	290	27.6	291	196	67.4
Linn	668	2.6	520	148	339	329	215	2.9	61	28.4	558	121	21.7	103	56	54.4
Livingston	596	3.1	473	123	302	294	197	3.5	41	20.8	522	110	21.1	102	89	87.3
McDonald	2	(2)	....	2	....	2					1			1	1	(1)
Macon	1,004	3.3	804	200	488	516	291	3.2	84	28.9	824	176	21.4	172	160	93.0
Madison	280	2.5	222	58	132	148	54	2.0	12	(1)	184	36	19.6	79	29	(1)
Maries	8	0.1	4	4	4	4	1	(2)			7	1	(1)	2	2	(1)
Marion	2,894	9.5	2,460	434	1,427	1,467	957	10.1	250	26.1	2,479	570	23.0	444	365	82.2
Mercer	33	0.3	23	10	19	14	14	0.4	4	(1)	28	8	(1)	3		
Miller	96	0.6	83	13	49	47	23	0.5	4	(1)	77	12	(1)	19	13	(1)
Mississippi	2,006	13.8	1,788	218	1,057	949	592	15.1	145	24.5	1,564	343	21.9	395	304	77.0
Moniteau	503	3.5	435	68	244	259	126	3.1	27	21.4	385	64	16.6	104	82	78.8
Monroe	1,223	6.7	870	353	637	586	356	6.5	127	35.7	989	268	27.1	223	148	66.4
Montgomery	1,176	7.5	822	354	595	581	329	7.3	113	34.3	910	249	27.4	252	162	64.3
Morgan	410	3.2	290	120	206	204	112	3.2	25	22.3	325	72	22.2	86	61	(1)
New Madrid	2,097	10.8	1,809	288	1,103	994	616	11.3	277	45.0	1,640	567	34.6	404	297	73.5
Newton	539	2.0	457	82	260	279	136	1.9	38	27.9	411	89	21.7	115	96	83.5
Nodaway	155	0.5	135	20	77	78	47	0.6	7	(1)	136	15	11.0	26	26	(1)
Oregon	9	0.1	9	....	2	7	1	(2)			7	1	(1)	2	1	(1)
Osage	149	1.0	58	91	76	73	40	1.1	8	(1)	119	26	21.8	32	16	(1)
Ozark	16	0.1	4	12	4	12	1	(2)			8			3	3	(1)
Pemiscot	1,533	7.8	1,389	144	818	715	507	9.3	118	23.3	1,246	287	23.0	243	97	39.9
Perry	228	1.5	203	25	130	98	70	1.9	13	(1)	170	31	18.2	45	25	(1)
Pettis	2,715	8.0	1,954	761	1,371	1,344	870	8.4	198	22.8	2,308	467	20.2	445	331	74.4
Phelps	136	0.9	60	76	66	70	37	0.9	6	(1)	112	19	17.0	23	21	(1)
Pike	3,350	14.9	2,880	470	1,728	1,622	986	14.3	277	28.1	2,694	601	22.3	588	456	77.6
Platte	719	5.0	595	124	372	347	209	4.7	46	22.0	585	113	19.3	149	99	66.4
Polk	138	0.6	111	27	72	66	37	0.7	12	(1)	103	27	26.2	32	27	(1)
Pulaski	22	0.2	22	....	9	13	7	0.2	6	(1)	21	14	(1)	1		
Putnam	20	0.1	15	5	6	14	5	0.1	1	(1)	17	1	(1)	5	3	(1)
Ralls	610	4.7	480	130	324	286	186	4.3	61	32.8	467	125	26.8	118	49	41.5
Randolph	2,458	9.4	1,233	1,225	1,258	1,200	726	9.0	159	21.9	1,980	368	18.6	438	288	65.8
Ray	1,215	5.7	991	224	626	589	330	5.4	88	26.7	937	193	20.6	257	200	81.3
Reynolds	2	(2)	2	....	1	1					1			1	1	(1)
Ripley	5	(2)	5	....	1	4	1	(2)			4			1		
St. Charles	1,718	7.0	1,343	375	891	827	475	6.7	131	27.6	1,323	285	21.5	410	315	76.8
St. Clair	184	1.1	139	45	89	95	50	1.1	9	(1)	143	21	14.7	32	21	
St. Francois	556	1.6	550	6	271	285	132	1.3	35	26.5	410	86	21.0	118	105	89.0
St. Louis	4,253	5.2	3,775	478	2,061	2,192	1,260	5.1	300	23.8	3,408	700	20.5	771	583	75.6

¹ Per cent not shown where base is less than 100.   ² Less than one-tenth of 1 per cent.

TABLE III.—GENERAL STATISTICS OF THE NEGRO POPULATION OF THE UNITED STATES, BY COUNTIES: 1910—Con.

[Counties in which no Negroes were reported are omitted.]

COUNTY.	Total.	Per cent of total population.	Color.		Sex.		Males 21 years of age and over.				Persons 10 years of age and over.			Persons 6 to 14 years of age.		
			Black.	Mu-latto.	Male.	Fe-male.	Num-ber.	Per cent of total.	Illiterate.		Total.	Illiterate.		Total.	Attending school.	
									Num-ber.	Per cent.		Num-ber.	Per cent.		Num-ber.	Per cent.
MISSOURI—Continued.																
St. Louis City	43,960	6.4	29,004	14,956	22,168	21,792	16,381	7.4	1,875	11.4	38,687	4,799	12.4	4,725	3,941	83.4
Ste. Genevieve	386	3.6	321	65	193	193	92	3.4	26	(1)	278	60	21.6	99	71	(1)
Saline	3,784	12.8	2,782	1,002	1,945	1,839	1,107	12.7	287	25.9	2,970	596	20.1	776	565	72.8
Schuyler	4	(2)	4			4					3	1	(1)			
Scotland	45	0.4	45		20	25	16	0.4	2	(1)	41	4	(1)	5		
Scott	545	2.4	391	154	309	236	224	3.6	126	56.3	464	208	44.8	74	45	(1)
Shelby	558	3.8	457	101	280	278	157	3.6	31	19.7	450	78	17.3	122	94	77.0
Stoddard	24	0.1	19	5	14	10	14	0.2	6	(1)	23	8	(1)	1	1	(1)
Stone	1	(2)	1		1											
Sullivan	93	0.5	93		49	44	28	0.6	4	(1)	77	5	(1)	19	18	(1)
Taney	1	(2)	1			1								1		
Texas	2	(2)	1	1	1	1	1	(2)			2	1	(1)			
Vernon	138	0.5	92	46	63	75	45	0.5	11	(1)	108	16	14.8	19	11	(1)
Warren	478	5.2	407	71	262	216	124	4.8	53	42.7	371	119	32.1	109	64	58.7
Washington	403	3.0	278	125	197	206	106	3.1	50	47.2	295	114	38.6	87	44	(1)
Wayne	23	0.2	21	2	12	11	5	0.1	1	(1)	16	5	(1)	3	2	(1)
Webster	87	0.5	56	31	40	47	12	0.3	3	(1)	60	15	(1)	25	19	(1)
Wright	236	1.3	23	213	134	102	67	1.5	20	(1)	183	40	21.9	51	47	(1)
MONTANA.																
Total	1,834	0.5	1,223	611	1,058	776	851	0.5	75	8.8	1,633	114	7.0	166	138	83.1
Beaverhead	26	0.4	25	1	19	7	17	0.6			26			1	1	(1)
Broadwater	19	0.5	9	10	6	13	3	0.2			15			9	9	(1)
Carbon	5	(2)	4	1	2	3	2	(2)	1	(1)	5	1	(1)			
Cascade	145	0.5	111	34	78	67	54	0.5	7	(1)	128	10	7.8	15	14	(1)
Chouteau	56	0.3	47	9	27	29	18	0.2	1	(1)	45	1	(1)	7	3	(1)
Custer	94	0.7	76	18	54	40	41	0.7	13	(1)	84	15	(1)	9	6	(1)
Dawson	12	0.1	11	1	6	6	5	0.1			11			1	1	(1)
Deer Lodge	130	1.0	81	49	78	52	67	1.3	1	(1)	116	2	1.7	11	11	(1)
Fergus	64	0.4	58	6	30	34	25	0.4	2	(1)	58	7	(1)	2	2	(1)
Flathead	27	0.1	26	1	17	10	14	0.2			24			2	2	(1)
Gallatin	49	0.3	35	14	27	22	18	0.4	2	(1)	42	4	(1)	3	3	(1)
Granite	10	0.3	10		2	8	2	0.2	1	(1)	8	2	(1)			
Jefferson	12	0.2	5	7	7	5	7	0.3			11					
Lewis and Clark	430	2.0	150	280	250	180	206	2.1	16	7.8	376	21	5.6	38	30	(1)
Lincoln	1	(2)	1		1		1	0.1			1					
Madison	27	0.4	15	12	16	11	13	0.5	4	(1)	19	4	(1)	3	3	(1)
Meagher	30	0.7	23	7	13	17	12	0.6	3	(1)	29	5	(1)	1	1	(1)
Missoula	133	0.6	78	55	76	57	56	0.5	3	(1)	111	4	3.6	15	12	(1)
Park	21	0.2	14	7	13	8	9	0.2			20			1	1	(1)
Powell	43	0.7	34	9	36	7	36	1.3	11	(1)	43	11	(1)			
Ravalli	13	0.1	11	2	7	6	6	0.1			13			1	1	(1)
Rosebud	18	0.2	18		10	8	6	0.2			12			6	5	(1)
Sanders	19	0.5	16	3	11	8	8	0.5	2	(1)	16	4	(1)	1	1	(1)
Silver Bow	260	0.5	185	75	155	105	127	0.6	3	2.4	243	10	4.1	24	22	(1)
Sweet Grass	1	(2)		1	1		1	0.1			1					
Teton	7	0.1	7		7		7	0.2			7					
Valley	15	0.1	15		13	2	11	0.2	1	(1)	13	1	(1)	1		
Yellowstone	167	0.7	158	9	96	71	79	0.8	4	(1)	156	12	7.7	15	10	(1)
NEBRASKA.																
Total	7,689	0.6	5,602	2,087	4,259	3,430	3,225	0.9	231	7.2	6,725	482	7.2	819	720	87.9
Adams	97	0.5	83	14	52	45	31	0.5	4		82	7	(1)	16	16	(1)
Antelope	9	0.1	6	3	5	4	5	0.1			9					
Blaine	14	0.8	12	2	8	6	7	1.4	2		11	3	(1)	1	1	(1)
Boone	5	(2)	4	1	4	1	3	0.1			4			1	1	(1)
Box Butte	55	0.9	34	21	31	24	23	1.2			49	2	(1)	5	5	(1)
Boyd	3	(2)	1	2	2	1	1	(2)			3					
Brown	5	0.1	4	1	4	1	4	0.2			5					
Buffalo	58	0.3	30	28	39	19	11	0.2	2	(1)	46	4	(1)	19	17	(1)
Burt	5	(2)	5		2	3	2	0.1			5			1	1	(1)
Butler	12	0.1	12		4	8	2	(2)			11			4	4	(1)
Cass	30	0.2	14	16	12	18	7	0.1	1	(1)	24	4	(1)	1	1	(1)
Cedar	2	(2)	2		2		2	(2)			2					
Cherry	80	0.8	25	55	43	37	30	0.9	2	(1)	64	4	(1)	14	11	(1)
Cheyenne	4	0.1	3	1	4		4	0.3			4					
Clay	9	0.1	8	1	6	3	4	0.1			9			1	1	(1)

[1] Per cent not shown where base is less than 100.   [2] Less than one-tenth of 1 per cent.

TABLE III.—GENERAL STATISTICS OF THE NEGRO POPULATION OF THE UNITED STATES, BY COUNTIES: 1910—Con.

[Counties in which no Negroes were reported are omitted.]

COUNTY.	NEGRO POPULATION: 1910.															
	Total.	Per cent of total population.	Color.		Sex.		Males 21 years of age and over.				Persons 10 years of age and over.			Persons 6 to 14 years of age.		
			Black.	Mulatto.	Male.	Female.	Number.	Per cent of total.	Illiterate.		Total.	Illiterate.		Total.	Attending school.	
									Number.	Per cent.		Number.	Per cent.		Number.	Per cent.

NEBRASKA—Continued.

COUNTY.	Total.	Per cent	Black.	Mulatto.	Male.	Female.	Num.	Per cent	Ill. Num.	Ill. Pct.	Total.	Ill. Num.	Ill. Pct.	Total.	Att. Num.	Att. Pct.
Colfax	12	0.1	12		5	7	4	0.1			9	1	(1)			
Cuming	1	(2)	1		1		1	(2)			1					
Custer	54	0.2	19	35	29	25	17	0.2	3	(1)	43	10	(1)	10	9	(1)
Dakota	12	0.2	7	5	4	8	2	0.1			10	1	(1)			
Dawes	105	1.3	100	5	61	44	53	1.8	6	(1)	95	8	(1)	14	6	(1)
Dawson	11	0.1	9	2	9	2	6	0.1			10			1	1	(1)
Dodge	56	0.3	51	5	27	29	16	0.2	1	(1)	39	2	(1)	9	9	(1)
Douglas	5,208	3.1	3,811	1,397	2,841	2,367	2,217	3.9	144	6.5	4,604	306	6.6	484	431	89.0
Dundy	8	0.2	6	2	2	6	2	0.2			5					
Fillmore	8	0.1	8		4	4	3	0.1	1	(1)	7	1	(1)	1	1	(1)
Franklin	2	(2)	2		1	1	1	(2)			2					
Frontier	1	(2)	1		1		1	(2)			1					
Furnas	7	0.1	2	5	3	4	3	0.1			5					
Gage	58	0.2	28	30	29	29	18	0.2	1	(1)	53	2	(1)	13	12	(1)
Garden	4	0.1	1	3	2	2	1	0.1			4			1		
Garfield	14	0.4	1	13	8	6	2	0.2			9			8	3	(1)
Gosper	1	(2)	1			1										
Grant	15	1.4	8	7	7	8	5	1.4			9			1		
Greeley	5	0.1	4	1	3	2	3	0.1	1	(1)	5	2	(1)	1	1	(1)
Hall	129	0.6	100	29	71	58	54	0.8	8	(1)	109	15	13.8	8	8	(1)
Hamilton	29	0.2	21	8	16	13	13	0.3	1	(1)	23	1	(1)	3	3	(1)
Harlan	24	0.3	17	7	14	10	7	0.3	1	(1)	17	2	(1)	4	4	(1)
Hayes	4	0.1	4		3	1	2	0.3			4	1	(1)	1	1	(1)
Hitchcock	1	(2)	1			1					1					
Holt	10	0.1		10	5	5	3	0.1			7			2	2	(1)
Howard	3	(2)	3		1	2	1	(2)			3					
Jefferson	33	0.2	33		19	14	11	0.2			30			7	7	(1)
Johnson	1	(2)	1		1		1	(2)	1	(1)	1	1	(1)			
Kearney	15	0.2	15		14	1	12	0.5			15					
Keyapaha	7	0.2		7	6	1	5	0.5	1	(1)	6	2	(1)			
Kimball	2	0.1	1	1	2		2	0.3			2					
Knox	8	(2)	5	3	5	3	5	0.1	1	(1)	8	1	(1)	1	1	(1)
Lancaster	870	1.2	626	244	525	345	406	1.8	23	5.7	780	52	6.7	85	75	(1)
Lincoln	25	0.2	15	10	15	10	10	0.2			21	1	(1)	1	1	(1)
Loup	4	0.2		4	2	2					1			3	3	(1)
McPherson	3	0.1	2	1	2	1	2	0.3			3					
Madison	61	0.3	55	6	31	30	23	0.4	1	(1)	51	2	(1)	11	11	(1)
Merrick	28	0.3	21	7	12	16	8	0.3			20	1	(1)	6	3	(1)
Morrill	6	0.1	6		5	1	4	0.3			5					
Nance	12	0.1	12		7	5	6	0.3			12			2	2	(1)
Nemaha	19	0.1	12	7	8	11	6	0.2	1	(1)	18	3	(1)	1	1	(1)
Nuckolls	4	(2)		4	1	3	1	(2)			4					
Otoe	81	0.4	64	17	39	42	26	0.5	4	(1)	72	9	(1)	13	12	(1)
Phelps	8	0.1	6	2	3	5	3	0.1			5					
Platte	15	0.1	14	1	11	4	5	0.1			11			4	4	(1)
Polk	6	0.1	6		3	3	2	0.1			5			2	2	(1)
Redwillow	4	(2)	4		3	1	3	0.1			4					
Richardson	83	0.5	76	7	49	34	31	0.6	7	(1)	72	10	(1)	19	16	(1)
Rock	1	(2)	1		1		1	0.1			1					
Saline	23	0.1	14	9	13	10	9	0.2	1	(1)	19	1	(1)	6	6	(1)
Sarpy	36	0.4	24	12	19	17	10	0.3	2	(1)	28	3	(1)	9	8	(1)
Saunders	21	0.1	18	3	8	13	7	0.1	2	(1)	18	4	(1)	2	1	(1)
Scotts Bluff	16	0.2	15	1	12	4	5	0.2			11			4	4	(1)
Seward	8	0.1	7	1	5	3	5	0.1	1	(1)	7	3	(1)	1	1	(1)
Sheridan	1	(2)		1	1		1	(2)	1	(1)	1	1	(1)			
Sherman	5	0.1		5	5		4	0.2			5					
Sioux	14	0.3	11	3	10	4	9	0.5	1	(1)	13	1	(1)	1	1	(1)
Stanton	1	(2)		1	1		1	(2)								
Thayer	2	(2)	1	1	1	1	1	(2)			2					
Thomas	11	0.9	11		3	8	1	0.3	1	(1)	7	2	(1)	4	3	(1)
Thurston	13	0.1	11	2	11	2	4	0.2			6			2		
Valley	2	(2)	1	1	1	1	1	(2)			2					
Washington	2	(2)	2		1	1					2					
Wayne	1	(2)	1			1										
Webster	6	(2)	6		3	3	3	0.1			6					
Wheeler	33	1.4	33		19	14	10	1.6	4	(1)	24	5	(1)	7	5	(1)
York	28	0.1	11	17	17	11	11	0.2	1	(1)	23	4	(1)	4	4	(1)

1 Per cent not shown where base is less than 100.   2 Less than one-tenth of 1 per cent.

TABLE III.—GENERAL STATISTICS OF THE NEGRO POPULATION OF THE UNITED STATES, BY COUNTIES: 1910—Con.

[Counties in which no Negroes were reported are omitted.]

COUNTY.	NEGRO POPULATION: 1910.															
	Total.	Per cent of total population.	Color.		Sex.		Males 21 years of age and over.				Persons 10 years of age and over.			Persons 6 to 14 years of age.		
			Black.	Mulatto.	Male.	Female.	Number.	Per cent of total.	Illiterate.		Total.	Illiterate.		Total.	Attending school.	
									Number.	Per cent.		Number.	Per cent.		Number.	Per cent.
NEVADA.																
Total	513	0.6	323	190	263	250	229	0.6	15	6.6	469	26	5.5	32	27	(1)
Churchill	1	(2)	1	......	......	1	......	......	......	......	......	......	......	1	1	(1)
Clark	12	0.4	12	......	5	7	5	0.3	......	......	12	......	......	......	......	......
Douglas	7	0.4	5	2	3	4	3	0.4	......	......	7	......	......	......	......	......
Elko	38	0.5	23	15	16	22	14	0.3	2	(1)	29	2	(1)	4	4	(1)
Esmeralda	99	1.1	50	49	44	55	38	0.8	3	(1)	93	9	(1)	7	7	(1)
Eureka	1	0.1	1	......	......	1	......	......	......	......	1	......	......	......	......	......
Humboldt	36	0.5	25	11	16	20	12	0.3	......	......	32	1	(1)	5	4	(1)
Lander	7	0.4	1	6	3	4	3	0.3	......	......	5	......	......	......	......	......
Lincoln	7	0.2	6	1	6	1	6	0.3	2	(1)	7	2	(1)	1	......	......
Lyon	4	0.1	4	......	2	2	2	0.1	......	......	4	......	......	......	......	......
Nye	74	1.0	44	30	39	35	33	0.8	......	......	70	......	......	2	2	(1)
Ormsby	56	1.6	53	3	38	18	34	2.5	3	(1)	52	5	(1)	2	1	(1)
Storey	10	0.3	9	1	3	7	3	0.2	1	(1)	10	2	(1)	......	......	......
Washoe	115	0.7	70	45	67	48	59	0.8	4	(1)	107	5	4.7	6	5	(1)
White Pine	46	0.6	19	27	21	25	17	0.4	......	......	40	......	......	4	3	(1)
NEW HAMPSHIRE.																
Total	564	0.1	356	208	288	276	200	0.1	29	14.5	480	51	10.6	74	62	(1)
Belknap	41	0.2	13	28	20	21	16	0.2	6	(1)	35	10	(1)	3	3	(1)
Carroll	13	0.1	9	4	11	2	8	0.1	1	(1)	11	1	(1)	2	2	(1)
Cheshire	26	0.1	16	10	16	10	14	0.1	2	(1)	23	2	(1)	3	2	(1)
Coos	31	0.1	27	4	20	11	13	0.1	2	(1)	23	3	(1)	4	3	(1)
Grafton	44	0.1	18	26	27	17	15	0.1	2	(1)	28	4	(1)	6	4	(1)
Hillsborough	77	0.1	48	29	38	39	29	0.1	1	(1)	68	2	(1)	6	5	(1)
Merrimack	122	0.2	53	69	68	54	41	0.2	5	(1)	103	9	8.7	25	24	(1)
Rockingham	158	0.3	128	30	64	94	48	2.3	6	(1)	132	15	11.4	20	15	(1)
Strafford	25	0.1	20	5	13	12	9	0.1	3	(1)	21	3	(1)	2	1	(1)
Sullivan	27	0.1	24	3	11	16	7	0.1	1	(1)	26	2	(1)	3	3	(1)
NEW JERSEY.																
Total	89,760	3.5	75,553	14,207	43,602	46,158	28,601	3.7	3,052	10.7	74,577	7,405	9.9	12,600	10,796	85.7
Atlantic	10,782	15.0	9,237	1,545	5,327	5,455	4,058	17.5	267	6.6	9,576	770	8.0	1,038	824	79.4
Bergen	3,295	2.4	2,950	345	1,482	1,813	909	2.3	145	16.0	2,660	354	13.3	499	387	77.6
Burlington	3,454	5.2	3,356	98	1,740	1,714	1,092	5.2	188	17.2	2,829	392	13.9	550	440	80.0
Camden	9,402	6.6	8,025	1,377	4,612	4,790	2,938	6.8	472	16.1	7,680	1,108	14.4	1,421	1,152	81.1
Cape May	1,444	7.3	1,300	144	751	693	472	7.3	52	11.0	1,174	118	10.1	240	197	82.1
Cumberland	2,641	4.8	1,451	1,190	1,344	1,297	775	4.6	139	17.9	2,081	292	14.0	496	410	82.7
Essex	18,104	3.5	14,870	3,234	8,102	10,002	5,276	3.5	366	6.9	15,065	1,087	7.2	2,347	2,120	90.3
Gloucester	2,375	6.4	2,072	303	1,359	1,016	846	7.0	76	9.0	1,896	163	8.6	365	298	81.6
Hudson	7,173	1.3	6,275	898	3,637	3,536	2,499	1.5	107	4.3	5,920	316	5.3	976	843	86.4
Hunterdon	438	1.3	408	30	191	247	114	1.0	19	16.7	342	38	11.1	107	98	91.6
Mercer	5,125	4.1	4,447	678	2,749	2,376	1,978	4.9	265	13.4	4,350	515	11.8	628	564	89.8
Middlesex	1,846	1.6	1,669	177	992	854	562	1.5	66	11.7	1,484	134	9.0	322	273	84.8
Monmouth	8,279	8.7	6,016	2,263	3,937	4,342	2,551	8.5	278	10.9	6,883	682	9.9	1,271	1,138	80.5
Morris	1,940	2.6	1,807	133	901	1,039	554	2.3	79	14.3	1,594	167	10.5	298	265	88.9
Ocean	438	2.1	416	22	179	259	114	1.7	4	3.5	380	18	4.7	60	54	......
Passaic	2,401	1.1	2,112	289	1,131	1,270	714	1.1	78	10.9	1,996	219	11.0	337	297	88.1
Salem	3,324	12.3	2,566	758	1,803	1,521	1,095	12.8	213	19.5	2,660	415	15.6	533	458	85.9
Somerset	1,414	3.6	1,345	69	707	707	410	3.3	66	16.1	1,149	160	13.9	254	219	86.2
Sussex	168	0.6	153	15	88	80	60	0.6	13	(1)	141	26	18.4	15	10	......
Union	5,353	3.8	4,742	611	2,379	2,974	1,475	3.5	141	9.6	4,425	380	8.6	778	690	88.7
Warren	364	0.8	336	28	191	173	109	0.8	18	16.5	292	51	17.5	65	59	......
NEW MEXICO.																
Total	1,628	0.5	1,189	439	891	737	644	0.7	88	13.7	1,344	191	14.2	210	155	73.8
Bernalillo	311	1.3	260	51	154	157	113	1.7	7	6.2	266	19	7.1	29	27	(1)
Chaves	233	1.4	181	52	125	108	86	1.7	13	(1)	191	29	15.2	30	23	(1)
Colfax	225	1.4	177	48	118	107	87	1.4	15	(1)	174	36	20.7	30	20	(1)
Curry	6	0.1	6	......	2	4	1	(2)	......	......	6	......	......	2	2	(1)
Dona Ana	65	0.5	58	7	38	27	26	0.8	2	(1)	58	9	(1)	6	2	(1)
Eddy	56	0.5	45	11	27	29	20	0.6	2	(1)	50	3	(1)	6	5	(1)
Grant	164	1.1	106	58	97	67	72	1.5	10	(1)	135	21	15.6	17	12	(1)
Guadalupe	10	0.1	8	2	7	3	4	0.1	......	......	6	......	......	1	1	(1)
Lincoln	27	0.3	15	12	21	6	16	0.6	7	(1)	25	9	(1)	3	3	(1)
Luna	11	0.3	11	......	7	4	5	0.4	......	......	11	......	......	3	3	(1)

[1] Per cent not shown where base is less than 100.   [2] Less than one-tenth of 1 per cent.

TABLE III.—GENERAL STATISTICS OF THE NEGRO POPULATION OF THE UNITED STATES, BY COUNTIES: 1910—Con.

[Counties in which no Negroes were reported are omitted.]

COUNTY.	NEGRO POPULATION: 1910.															
	Total.	Per cent of total population.	Color.		Sex.		Males 21 years of age and over.				Persons 10 years of age and over.			Persons 6 to 14 years of age.		
			Black.	Mulatto.	Male.	Female.	Number.	Per cent of total.	Illiterate.		Total.	Illiterate.		Total.	Attending school.	
									Number.	Per cent.		Number.	Per cent.		Number.	Per cent.

NEW MEXICO—Continued.

McKinley	66	0.5	47	19	48	18	44	1.2	6	(1)	63	13	(1)	2	.1	(1)
Mora	5	(2)	3	2	2	3	2	0.1	.....	.....	4	.....	.....	1	.....	.....
Otero	24	0.3	14	10	16	8	11	0.6	4	(1)	23	7	(1)	3	3	(1)
Quay	25	0.2	19	6	15	10	12	0.3	.....	.....	21	.....	.....	2	1	(1)
Rio Arriba	2	(2)	2	.....	.....	2	.....	.....	.....	.....	1	.....	.....	1	1	(1)
Roosevelt	4	(2)	4	.....	3	1	3	0.1	1	(1)	4	1	(1)	1	.....	.....
San Juan	7	0.1	1	6	4	3	3	0.1	.....	.....	5	.....	.....	2	2	(1)
San Miguel	122	0.5	53	69	55	67	40	0.7	8	(1)	90	16	(1)	25	21	(1)
Sandoval	7	0.1	4	3	5	2	3	0.1	.....	.....	6	.....	.....	4	4	(1)
Santa Fe	128	0.9	101	27	72	56	51	1.2	.....	.....	97	2	(1)	22	19	(1)
Sierra	8	0.2	4	4	6	2	4	0.4	.....	.....	8	1	(1)	1	1	(1)
Socorro	45	0.3	26	19	29	16	17	0.4	6	(1)	38	12	(1)	7	5	(1)
Taos	5	(2)	4	1	2	3	2	0.1	2	(1)	5	3	(1)	1	1	(1)
Torrance	8	0.1	5	3	3	5	3	0.1	2	(1)	8	3	(1)	1	1	(1)
Union	42	0.4	30	12	20	22	11	0.3	1	(1)	32	3	(1)	8	.....	.....
Valencia	22	0.2	9	13	15	7	8	0.2	2	(1)	17	4	(1)	4	3	(1)

NEW YORK.

Total	134,191	1.5	103,583	30,608*	64,034	70,157	45,877	1.6	2,295	5.0	115,843	5,768	5.0	14,456	12,596	87.1
Albany	1,222	0.7	930	292	577	645	434	0.8	27	6.2	1,075	53	4.9	152	139	91.4
Allegany	325	0.8	158	167	172	153	108	0.8	2	1.9	258	6	2.3	53	46	(1)
Broome	725	0.9	502	223	360	365	275	1.1	8	2.9	641	24	3.7	75	69	(1)
Cattaraugus	333	0.5	168	165	177	156	107	0.5	10	9.3	266	16	6.0	65	62	(1)
Cayuga	661	1.0	548	113	346	315	257	1.1	20	7.8	568	35	6.2	81	74	(1)
Chautauqua	169	0.2	94	75	92	77	59	0.2	1	(1)	144	1	0.7	30	25	(1)
Chemung	593	1.1	396	197	326	267	220	1.2	28	12.7	536	49	9.1	54	52	(1)
Chenango	196	0.6	162	34	93	103	67	0.5	4	(1)	173	7	4.0	26	22	(1)
Clinton	251	0.5	106	145	219	32	200	1.3	17	8.5	230	23	10.0	11	8	(1)
Columbia	1,103	2.5	1,045	58	583	520	419	2.8	58	13.8	961	125	13.0	144	124	86.1
Cortland	71	0.2	53	18	42	29	20	0.2	1	(1)	50	1	(1)	15	14	(1)
Delaware	226	0.5	96	130	124	102	78	0.5	10	10.8	186	20	10.8	38	34	(1)
Dutchess	2,367	2.7	2,122	245	1,253	1,114	803	2.7	107	13.3	1,925	193	10.0	346	285	82.4
Erie	2,059	0.4	1,259	800	1,090	969	851	0.5	46	5.4	1,824	80	4.4	222	196	88.3
Essex	82	0.2	50	32	42	40	23	0.2	4	(1)	63	8	(1)	17	11	(1)
Franklin	53	0.1	29	24	23	30	12	0.1	3	(1)	42	7	(1)	8	6	(1)
Fulton	317	0.7	250	67	142	175	95	0.7	13	(1)	270	30	11.1	40	33	(1)
Genesee	162	0.4	127	35	85	77	53	0.4	6	(1)	126	9	7.1	28	25	(1)
Greene	513	1.7	440	73	263	250	172	1.7	33	19.2	429	58	13.5	71	57	(1)
Herkimer	196	0.3	166	30	91	105	60	0.3	1	(1)	151	8	5.3	31	22	(1)
Jefferson	244	0.3	73	171	100	144	63	0.2	4	(1)	213	6	2.8	31	27	(1)
Kings	22,708	1.4	17,682	5,026	10,245	12,463	7,011	1.5	241	3.4	19,335	806	4.2	2,764	2,441	88.3
Lewis	13	0.1	6	7	7	6	6	0.1	2	(1)	12	2	(1)	.....	.....	.....
Livingston	344	0.9	297	47	192	152	124	1.0	16	12.9	283	26	9.2	46	40	(1)
Madison	296	0.8	233	63	161	135	94	0.7	10	(1)	242	24	9.9	55	44	(1)
Monroe	1,224	0.4	893	331	632	592	421	0.5	28	6.7	1,056	45	4.3	149	136	91.3
Montgomery	213	0.4	164	49	115	98	79	0.4	6	(1)	186	9	4.8	22	21	(1)
Nassau	2,317	2.8	2,231	86	1,119	1,198	668	2.6	72	10.8	1,886	191	10.1	348	292	83.9
New York	64,651	2.3	47,727	16,924	29,935	34,716	22,548	2.6	571	2.5	56,986	1,892	3.3	5,505	4,802	87.2
Niagara	435	0.5	356	79	233	202	181	0.6	24	13.3	386	45	11.7	42	32	(1)
Oneida	632	0.4	481	151	328	304	229	0.5	28	12.2	547	49	9.0	93	80	(1)
Onondaga	1,296	0.6	878	418	677	619	507	0.8	34	6.7	1,117	59	5.3	151	135	89.4
Ontario	365	0.7	289	76	175	190	100	0.6	6	6.0	291	17	5.8	72	62	(1)
Orange	3,081	2.7	2,795	286	1,680	1,401	1,112	2.9	113	10.2	2,568	222	8.6	437	356	81.5
Orleans	147	0.5	117	30	66	81	44	0.4	7	(1)	119	14	11.8	23	14	(1)
Oswego	437	0.6	387	50	325	112	298	1.3	3	1.0	418	8	1.9	23	21	(1)
Otsego	104	0.2	83	21	44	60	38	0.2	4	(1)	99	11	(1)	5	5	(1)
Putnam	190	1.3	170	20	133	57	108	1.9	12	11.1	176	20	11.4	15	12	(1)
Queens	3,198	1.1	2,445	753	1,440	1,758	959	1.2	54	5.6	2,655	135	5.1	418	382	91.4
Rensselaer	798	0.7	694	104	362	436	268	0.7	15	5.6	693	40	5.8	102	94	92.2
Richmond	1,152	1.3	1,060	92	523	629	337	1.3	25	7.4	943	60	6.4	177	158	89.3
Rockland	1,534	3.3	1,161	373	840	694	550	3.8	52	9.5	1,240	105	8.5	207	178	86.0
St. Lawrence	56	0.1	39	17	25	31	19	0.1	5	(1)	53	16	(1)	4	4	(1)
Saratoga	697	1.1	497	200	314	383	216	1.1	16	7.4	613	50	8.2	81	75	(1)
Schenectady	288	0.3	240	48	131	157	93	0.3	3	(1)	256	10	3.9	32	26	(1)
Schoharie	224	0.9	183	41	121	103	71	0.9	12	(1)	169	20	11.8	39	34	(1)
Schuyler	184	1.3	138	46	94	90	62	1.3	8	(1)	153	13	8.5	29	26	(1)
Seneca	122	0.5	108	14	56	66	41	0.4	7	(1)	105	22	21.0	10	7	(1)
Steuben	357	0.4	244	113	190	167	144	0.5	22	15.3	310	33	10.6	39	33	(1)
Suffolk	2,771	2.9	2,608	163	1,342	1,429	851	2.7	83	9.8	2,288	184	8.0	414	363	87.7

1 Per cent not shown where base is less than 100.   2 Less than one-tenth of 1 per cent.

TABLE III.—GENERAL STATISTICS OF THE NEGRO POPULATION OF THE UNITED STATES, BY COUNTIES: 1910—Con.

[Counties in which no Negroes were reported are omitted.]

COUNTY	NEGRO POPULATION: 1910.															
	Total.	Per cent of total population.	Color.		Sex.		Males 21 years of age and over.				Persons 10 years of age and over.			Persons 6 to 14 years of age.		
			Black.	Mu-latto.	Male.	Fe-male.	Num-ber.	Per cent of total.	Illiterate.		Total.	Illiterate.		Total.	Attending school.	
									Num-ber.	Per cent.		Num-ber.	Per cent.		Num-ber.	Per cent.
NEW YORK—Continued.																
Sullivan	64	0.2	56	8	31	33	19	0.2	......	..	47	2	(1)	16	15	(1)
Tioga	212	0.9	198	44	124	118	79	0.9	8	(1)	205	20	9.8	44	42	(1)
Tompkins	513	1.6	387	146	223	310	173	1.6	11	6.4	464	31	6.7	62	55	(1)
Ulster	2,026	2.2	1,806	220	1,359	667	997	3.2	165	16.5	1,784	274	15.4	218	178	81.7
Warren	25	0.1	23	2	7	18	5	(2)	......	..	20	......	..	2	2	(1)
Washington	197	0.4	153	44	106	91	77	0.5	15	(1)	165	21	12.7	26	24	(1)
Wayne	194	0.4	168	26	109	85	71	0.4	10	(1)	157	19	12.1	23	16	(1)
Westchester	8,986	3.2	7,644	1,342	4,255	4,731	2,827	3.2	197	7.0	7,515	502	6.7	1,190	1,032	86.7
Wyoming	88	0.3	54	34	47	41	35	0.3	5	(1)	74	8	(1)	8	4	(1)
Yates	134	0.7	114	20	68	66	39	0.6	2	(1)	96	4	(1)	27	24	(1)
NORTH CAROLINA.																
Total	697,843	31.6	553,720	144,123	339,581	358,262	146,752	29.0	56,669	38.6	490,395	156,303	31.9	169,034	108,200	64.0
Alamance	7,173	25.0	5,145	2,028	3,533	3,640	1,487	22.3	629	42.3	5,037	1,680	33.4	1,832	1,153	62.9
Alexander	910	7.9	661	249	418	492	177	7.2	68	38.4	618	204	33.0	228	150	65.8
Alleghany	340	4.4	263	77	162	178	69	4.1	26	(1)	242	79	32.6	83	39	(1)
Anson	13,326	52.3	11,136	2,190	6,482	6,844	2,532	45.7	1,055	41.7	9,134	3,123	34.2	3,526	2,119	60.1
Ashe	550	2.9	411	139	272	278	118	2.9	52	44.1	413	147	35.6	133	85	63.9
Beaufort	12,941	41.9	10,952	1,989	6,326	6,615	2,928	39.4	1,082	37.0	9,193	3,112	33.9	3,039	1,857	61.1
Bertie	13,503	58.6	10,191	3,312	5,989	6,914	2,686	52.9	930	34.6	9,222	2,547	27.6	3,435	2,369	69.0
Bladen	8,392	46.6	6,514	1,878	4,048	4,344	1,599	21.0	821	51.3	5,783	2,365	40.9	2,202	1,346	61.1
Brunswick	5,406	37.5	4,521	885	2,645	2,761	1,129	32.6	404	35.8	3,696	1,335	36.1	1,335	903	67.6
Buncombe	7,982	16.0	5,182	2,800	3,633	4,349	1,837	15.4	409	22.3	6,150	1,069	17.4	1,553	1,146	73.8
Burke	2,570	12.0	1,569	1,001	1,196	1,374	479	10.3	206	43.0	1,838	606	33.0	628	397	63.2
Cabarrus	6,095	23.2	5,303	792	2,933	3,162	1,264	21.2	521	41.2	4,315	1,285	29.8	1,480	1,031	69.7
Caldwell	2,416	11.7	1,349	1,067	1,209	1,207	472	10.5	202	42.8	1,657	559	33.7	622	375	60.3
Camden	2,213	39.2	2,099	114	1,149	1,064	494	36.5	222	44.9	1,531	522	34.1	582	435	74.7
Carteret	2,292	16.6	1,605	687	1,108	1,184	506	14.5	193	38.1	1,683	548	32.6	515	374	72.6
Caswell	7,651	51.5	6,551	1,100	3,739	3,912	1,533	45.9	828	54.0	5,236	2,145	41.0	2,027	1,084	53.5
Catawba	3,471	12.4	3,088	383	1,603	1,868	663	11.1	196	29.6	2,364	482	20.4	904	617	68.3
Chatham	7,668	33.9	6,286	1,382	3,812	3,856	1,537	29.7	710	46.2	5,300	1,698	32.0	2,000	1,415	70.8
Cherokee	503	3.6	302	201	250	253	112	3.6	53	47.3	356	138	38.8	128	82	64.1
Chowan	6,159	54.5	5,676	483	3,006	3,153	1,307	51.3	483	37.0	4,358	1,111	25.5	1,509	1,158	76.7
Clay	158	4.0	79	79	80	78	31	3.5	15	(1)	100	36	36.0	43	15	(1)
Cleveland	5,779	19.6	4,719	1,060	2,858	2,921	1,145	17.7	481	42.0	3,956	1,347	34.0	1,434	768	53.6
Columbus	8,955	32.0	6,312	2,643	4,425	4,530	1,895	29.6	640	33.8	6,160	1,918	31.1	2,093	1,477	70.6
Craven	14,310	55.9	11,478	2,832	6,817	7,493	3,345	52.5	1,094	32.7	10,547	3,306	31.3	2,956	2,167	73.3
Cumberland	15,353	43.5	12,346	3,007	7,360	7,993	3,016	38.0	1,113	36.9	10,710	3,300	30.8	3,824	2,418	63.2
Currituck	2,598	33.8	2,350	248	1,370	1,228	591	30.8	217	36.7	1,783	504	28.3	666	455	68.3
Dare	495	10.2	366	129	245	250	134	11.0	17	12.7	369	41	11.1	106	89	84.0
Davidson	3,744	12.7	3,146	598	1,955	1,789	947	13.6	375	39.6	2,766	898	32.5	817	539	66.0
Davie	2,350	17.5	1,479	871	1,131	1,219	445	14.7	211	47.4	1,614	555	34.4	658	468	71.1
Duplin	9,281	36.5	7,737	1,544	4,450	4,831	1,787	31.3	713	39.9	6,309	1,918	30.4	2,191	1,403	64.0
Durham	12,383	35.1	8,439	3,944	5,888	6,495	2,864	33.5	1,020	35.6	9,438	2,942	31.2	2,662	1,619	60.8
Edgecombe	19,453	60.8	17,458	1,995	9,532	9,921	4,105	55.9	1,865	45.4	13,482	5,197	38.5	4,618	2,849	61.7
Forsyth	14,027	29.6	10,930	3,097	6,976	7,051	3,586	29.8	1,229	34.3	10,929	3,355	30.7	2,754	1,759	63.9
Franklin	11,564	46.8	8,625	2,939	5,743	5,821	2,389	42.0	995	41.6	8,016	2,636	32.9	2,975	1,881	63.2
Gaston	8,502	22.9	7,364	1,138	4,110	4,392	1,673	20.9	670	40.0	5,884	1,960	33.3	2,172	1,323	60.9
Gates	4,693	44.9	3,682	1,011	2,280	2,413	943	40.0	260	27.6	3,278	683	20.8	1,179	739	62.7
Granville	12,239	48.8	8,833	3,406	6,053	6,186	2,364	43.9	1,097	46.4	8,393	2,856	34.0	3,329	2,142	64.3
Greene	6,096	46.6	5,619	477	3,047	3,049	1,284	43.0	524	40.8	4,083	1,348	33.0	1,488	967	65.0
Guilford	15,379	25.4	11,482	3,897	7,366	8,013	3,468	23.3	1,035	29.8	11,328	2,741	24.2	3,334	2,394	71.8
Halifax	24,328	64.6	14,197	10,131	11,880	12,448	5,144	58.9	2,123	41.3	16,727	5,652	33.8	5,878	3,695	62.9
Harnett	6,442	29.1	5,078	1,364	3,104	3,338	1,230	24.8	448	36.4	4,263	1,385	32.5	1,671	918	54.9
Haywood	567	2.7	415	152	283	284	129	2.6	27	20.9	422	64	15.2	128	68	53.1
Henderson	1,815	11.2	1,390	425	877	938	405	10.6	137	33.8	1,364	390	28.6	451	254	56.3
Hertford	9,098	58.9	5,313	3,785	4,559	4,539	1,857	53.4	782	42.1	6,264	1,937	30.9	2,336	1,535	65.7
Hyde	3,701	41.9	3,301	400	1,818	1,883	750	35.2	356	47.5	2,484	1,138	45.8	988	337	34.1
Iredell	7,456	21.7	6,022	1,434	3,582	3,874	1,501	19.9	544	36.2	5,210	1,455	27.9	1,895	1,190	62.8
Jackson	603	4.6	294	309	300	303	137	4.7	37	27.0	429	98	22.8	152	115	75.7
Johnston	10,169	24.6	8,656	1,513	5,025	5,144	2,190	23.3	828	37.8	7,017	2,248	32.0	2,404	1,682	70.0
Jones	4,096	47.0	3,808	288	1,998	2,098	798	41.3	336	42.1	2,668	841	31.5	1,056	761	72.1
Lee	3,526	31.0	2,321	1,205	1,675	1,851	684	26.6	257	37.6	2,492	700	28.1	830	612	73.7
Lenoir	10,225	44.9	8,932	1,293	4,887	5,338	2,114	40.6	828	39.2	7,058	2,222	31.5	2,423	1,680	69.3
Lincoln	2,797	16.3	2,327	470	1,332	1,465	537	14.6	159	29.6	1,940	435	22.4	721	529	73.4
McDowell	2,080	15.4	1,238	842	1,021	1,059	474	15.4	160	33.8	1,498	401	26.8	466	269	57.7
Macon	576	4.7	472	104	277	299	121	4.5	46	38.0	400	119	29.8	148	102	68.9
Madison	432	2.1	354	78	245	187	114	2.6	53	46.5	311	115	37.0	95	52	(1)
Martin	8,838	49.7	7,317	1,521	4,310	4,528	1,822	44.9	832	45.7	6,053	2,405	39.7	2,129	1,245	58.5
Mecklenburg	25,481	38.0	22,015	3,466	12,070	13,411	5,604	34.5	1,873	33.4	18,941	5,462	28.8	5,726	3,288	57.4
Mitchell	343	2.0	185	158	183	160	72	1.9	39	(1)	261	110	42.1	86	52	(1)
Montgomery	3,660	24.5	2,844	816	1,748	1,912	696	21.5	317	45.5	2,471	889	36.0	921	578	62.8

1 Per cent not shown where base is less than 100.　　　　2 Less than one-tenth of 1 per cent.

TABLE **III.**—GENERAL STATISTICS OF THE NEGRO POPULATION OF THE UNITED STATES, BY COUNTIES: 1910—Con.

[Counties in which no Negroes were reported are omitted.]

COUNTY.	NEGRO POPULATION: 1910.																
	Total.	Per cent of total population.	Color.		Sex.		Males 21 years of age and over.				Persons 10 years of age and over.			Persons 6 to 14 years of age.		
			Black.	Mulatto.	Male.	Female.	Number.	Per cent of total.	Illiterate.		Total.	Illiterate.		Total.	Attending school.	
									Number.	Per cent.		Number.	Per cent.		Number.	Per cent.

NORTH CAROLINA—Continued.

COUNTY.	Total.	Per cent	Black.	Mulatto.	Male.	Female.	Number.	Per cent	Illit. Num.	Illit. Per cent	Total.	Illit. Num.	Illit. Per cent	Total.	Att. Num.	Att. Per cent
Moore	5,637	33.1	4,600	1,037	2,723	2,914	1,122	29.4	430	38.3	3,892	1,157	29.7	1,403	860	61.3
Nash	14,104	41.8	9,051	5,053	7,070	7,034	3,100	38.6	1,235	39.8	9,625	3,472	36.1	3,415	2,035	59.6
New Hanover	15,302	47.8	11,314	3,988	7,106	8,196	3,881	44.4	1,066	27.5	11,969	3,361	28.1	2,771	2,020	72.9
Northampton	13,062	58.5	9,732	3,330	6,307	6,755	2,623	52.5	1,188	45.3	8,972	3,183	35.5	3,339	2,077	62.2
Onslow	4,238	30.1	3,635	603	2,142	2,096	877	26.6	310	35.3	2,820	829	29.4	1,076	735	68.3
Orange	4,926	32.7	3,819	1,107	2,413	2,513	1,024	28.3	337	32.9	3,431	822	24.0	1,263	752	59.5
Pamlico	3,773	37.9	2,967	806	1,915	1,858	803	34.6	251	31.3	2,528	704	27.8	919	675	73.4
Pasquotank	8,357	50.1	7,120	1,237	4,132	4,225	1,904	48.0	625	32.8	5,952	1,613	27.1	1,939	1,196	61.7
Pender	7,620	49.3	6,584	1,036	3,714	3,906	1,598	43.6	608	38.0	5,232	1,747	33.4	1,898	1,101	58.0
Perquimans	5,589	50.6	4,752	837	2,803	2,786	1,192	46.7	337	28.3	3,812	829	21.7	1,341	942	70.2
Person	7,474	43.1	6,033	1,441	3,663	3,811	1,475	38.6	806	54.6	5,110	2,044	40.0	1,920	1,020	53.1
Pitt	18,106	49.8	15,564	2,542	8,749	9,357	3,527	44.0	1,715	48.6	12,143	5,047	41.6	4,715	2,913	61.8
Polk	1,094	14.3	921	173	530	564	232	13.4	70	30.2	789	208	26.4	271	157	57.9
Randolph	3,421	11.6	2,332	1,089	1,646	1,775	713	10.4	248	34.8	2,330	610	26.2	894	607	67.9
Richmond	9,225	46.9	8,682	543	4,479	4,746	1,887	41.9	683	36.2	6,406	1,841	28.7	2,374	1,532	64.5
Robeson	22,518	43.3	20,822	1,696	11,083	11,435	4,522	39.1	1,874	41.4	15,454	5,653	36.6	5,539	3,561	64.3
Rockingham	10,474	28.7	7,282	3,192	4,972	5,502	1,990	25.2	948	47.6	7,380	2,548	34.5	2,786	1,616	58.0
Rowan	9,074	24.2	6,627	2,447	4,413	4,661	2,064	23.1	700	33.9	6,782	1,824	26.9	2,050	1,413	68.9
Rutherford	4,288	15.1	3,037	1,251	2,067	2,221	829	13.5	331	39.9	2,953	917	31.1	1,079	607	56.3
Sampson	10,043	33.5	8,255	1,788	4,804	5,239	1,864	28.0	719	38.6	6,802	1,963	28.9	2,519	1,570	62.3
Scotland	8,473	55.2	7,514	959	4,129	4,344	1,648	45.9	757	45.9	5,778	2,307	39.9	2,115	1,354	64.0
Stanly	2,132	10.7	1,949	183	1,129	1,003	537	12.1	233	43.4	1,561	630	40.4	483	256	53.0
Stokes	2,569	12.7	1,825	744	1,282	1,287	518	12.1	279	53.9	1,764	724	41.0	725	384	53.0
Surry	2,632	8.9	2,204	428	1,292	1,340	594	9.0	335	56.4	1,908	777	40.7	640	420	65.6
Swain	185	1.8	159	26	95	90	39	1.6	13	(1)	135	37	27.4	54	43	(1)
Transylvania	638	8.9	472	166	324	314	135	7.8	50	37.0	457	131	28.7	171	105	61.4
Tyrrell	1,642	31.5	1,335	307	829	813	366	28.9	148	40.4	1,123	377	33.6	405	248	61.2
Union	9,337	28.1	7,831	1,506	4,596	4,741	1,893	26.3	835	44.1	6,391	2,367	37.0	2,368	1,529	64.6
Vance	10,004	51.5	7,967	2,037	4,815	5,189	1,968	46.0	777	39.5	6,987	2,084	29.8	2,707	1,660	61.3
Wake	25,870	40.9	22,011	3,859	12,570	13,300	5,733	36.8	1,848	32.2	18,780	5,052	26.9	5,973	3,964	66.4
Warren	13,207	65.2	9,266	3,941	6,513	6,694	2,689	60.4	956	35.6	9,103	2,354	25.9	3,412	2,453	71.9
Washington	5,503	49.7	5,010	493	2,685	2,818	1,190	46.1	327	27.5	3,870	872	22.5	1,390	852	61.3
Watauga	246	1.8	105	141	138	108	49	1.7	15	(1)	177	56	31.6	68	37	(1)
Wayne	15,579	43.6	12,577	3,002	7,425	8,154	3,371	40.7	1,293	38.4	11,008	3,574	32.5	3,518	2,368	67.3
Wilkes	2,591	8.6	1,413	1,178	1,229	1,362	491	7.6	127	25.9	1,818	396	21.8	669	505	75.5
Wilson	12,350	43.7	10,029	2,321	6,107	6,243	2,686	39.9	1,205	44.9	8,664	3,468	40.0	2,907	1,845	63.5
Yadkin	1,174	7.6	1,022	152	592	582	245	7.3	124	50.6	780	298	38.2	295	191	64.7
Yancey	233	1.9	175	58	127	106	53	2.0	23	(1)	165	65	39.4	59	28	(1)

NORTH DAKOTA.

COUNTY.	Total.	Per cent	Black.	Mulatto.	Male.	Female.	Number.	Per cent	Illit. Num.	Illit. Per cent	Total.	Illit. Num.	Illit. Per cent	Total.	Att. Num.	Att. Per cent
Total	617	0.1	460	157	381	236	311	0.2	16	5.1	546	26	4.8	56	43	(1)
Barnes	2	(2)	2		2		2	(2)			2					
Benson	9	0.1	1	8	2	7	2	0.1			7			2	1	(1)
Billings	6	0.1	5	1	3	3	2	0.1			4					
Bottineau	10	0.1	10		6	4	1	(2)			5			5	5	(1)
Bowman	1	(2)	1		1		1	0.1			1					
Burke	4	(2)	4		2	2	2	0.1			4			1	1	(1)
Burleigh	54	0.4	42	12	49	5	42	0.9	1	(1)	51	1	(1)	5		
Cass	120	0.4	109	11	67	53	62	0.6	1	(1)	118	3	2.5	2	2	(1)
Cavalier	14	0.1	7	7	9	5	8	0.2			9			2	2	(1)
Dickey	6	0.1	6		2	4	2	0.1			3			1	1	(1)
Divide	3	(2)	2	1	2	1	2	0.1	1	(1)	3	1	(1)			
Eddy	2	(2)	2		2		2	0.1			2					
Emmons	9	0.1	9		6	3	3	0.1			7					
Foster	3	0.1	3		1	2	1	0.1			2					
Grand Forks	60	0.2	23	37	35	25	26	0.3			55			8	8	(1)
Griggs	15	0.2	2	13	7	8	4	0.2			11			4	4	(1)
Hettinger	8	0.1	8		4	4	3	0.1			7					
Kidder	11	0.2	11		2	9	2	0.1			8			1	1	(1)
Lamoure	5	(2)	5		5		4	0.1			4			1	1	(1)
Logan	1	(2)	1		1		1	0.1			1					
McHenry	14	0.1	5	9	8	6	5	0.1	1	(1)	12	2	(1)	5	2	(1)
McIntosh	3	(2)	3		2	1	2	0.1	2	(1)	3	2	(1)			
McKenzie	2	(2)		2	1	1	1	(2)			2					
McLean	4	(2)	4		4		3	0.1			3					
Morton	12	(2)	9	3	9	3	5	0.1	1	(1)	12	1	(1)			
Mountrail	1	(2)	1		1	1										
Nelson	1	(2)	1				1	(2)			1					
Pembina	5	(2)	2	3	3	2	2	0.1			5					
Pierce	25	0.3	20	5	12	13	7	0.3	1	(1)	17	2	(1)	1	1	(1)
Ramsey	44	0.3	24	20	27	17	20	0.4			38			6	5	(1)

[1] Per cent not shown where base is less than 100.　　　[2] Less than one-tenth of 1 per cent.

TABLE III.—GENERAL STATISTICS OF THE NEGRO POPULATION OF THE UNITED STATES, BY COUNTIES: 1910—Con.

[Counties in which no Negroes were reported are omitted.]

COUNTY.	Total.	Per cent of total population.	Color.		Sex.		Males 21 years of age and over.				Persons 10 years of age and over.			Persons 6 to 14 years of age.		
			Black.	Mulatto.	Male.	Female.	Number.	Per cent of total.	Illiterate. Number.	Illiterate. Per cent.	Total.	Illiterate. Number.	Illiterate. Per cent.	Total.	Attending school. Number.	Attending school. Per cent.

NORTH DAKOTA—Continued.

COUNTY.	Total.	Per cent	Black.	Mulatto.	Male.	Female.	Number.	Per cent	Ill. Num.	Ill. Per cent	Total.	Ill. Num.	Ill. Per cent	Total.	Att. Num.	Att. Per cent
Ransom	8	0.1	8	....	7	1	6	0.2	1	[1]	8	1	[1]	......	......	......
Richland	11	0.1	9	2	6	5	5	0.1	......	......	9	......	......	2	2	[1]
Rolette	6	0.1	2	4	3	3	2	0.1	1	[1]	4	1	[1]			
Sargent	1	[2]	1	....	......	1					1					
Stark	6	[2]	6	....	2	4	2	0.1			5	......	......	1		
Steele	3	[2]	3	....	3	....	3	0.1			3					
Stutsman	8	[2]	8	....	6	2	6	0.1	1	[1]	7	1	[1]			
Towner	19	0.2	18	1	13	6	11	0.4	......	......	17	1	[1]			
Traill	2	[2]	1	1	2	....	1	[2]			2					
Walsh	5	[2]	5	....	2	3	2	[2]	......	......	5	......	......	1	1	[1]
Ward	67	0.3	60	7	45	22	41	0.5	3	[1]	63	6	[1]	2	2	[1]
Wells	3	[2]	3	....	2	1	2	0.1			3					
Williams	24	0.2	14	10	14	10	12	0.2	2	[1]	22	4	[1]			

OHIO.

COUNTY.	Total.	Per cent	Black.	Mulatto.	Male.	Female.	Number.	Per cent	Ill. Num.	Ill. Per cent	Total.	Ill. Num.	Ill. Per cent	Total.	Att. Num.	Att. Per cent
Total	111,452	2.3	72,203	39,249	57,995	53,457	39,188	2.6	5,169	13.2	93,910	10,460	11.1	15,755	13,742	87.2
Adams	184	0.7	166	18	88	96	56	0.8	15	[1]	156	28	17.9	35	30	[1]
Allen	1,030	1.8	787	243	564	466	349	2.1	24	6.9	848	47	5.5	153	135	88.2
Ashland	25	0.1	20	5	14	11	11	0.2	1	[1]	23	1	[1]	2	2	[1]
Ashtabula	217	0.4	195	22	113	104	79	0.4	6	[1]	190	11	5.8	33	29	[1]
Athens	1,240	2.6	603	637	686	554	371	2.7	82	22.1	960	157	16.4	259	194	74.9
Auglaize	36	0.1	20	16	17	19	13	0.1	2	[1]	28	2	[1]	5	5	[1]
Belmont	1,782	2.3	1,352	430	954	828	563	2.4	90	16.0	1,437	177	12.3	304	254	83.6
Brown	1,288	5.2	1,071	217	674	614	392	5.3	85	21.7	1,061	191	18.0	231	196	84.8
Butler	1,781	2.5	1,004	777	929	852	664	3.0	78	11.7	1,498	167	11.1	229	207	90.4
Carroll	25	0.2	25	....	10	15	8	0.2	......	......	19	......	......	2	2	[1]
Champaign	1,410	5.4	1,059	351	708	702	461	5.5	43	9.3	1,170	78	6.7	223	197	88.3
Clark	5,583	8.4	2,724	2,859	2,937	2,646	1,921	9.0	204	10.6	4,654	418	9.0	867	745	85.9
Clermont	865	2.9	580	285	435	430	258	2.9	44	17.1	693	92	13.3	174	155	89.1
Clinton	939	4.0	524	415	479	460	300	4.2	55	18.3	772	99	12.8	146	132	90.4
Columbiana	967	1.3	569	398	499	468	317	1.4	26	8.2	789	47	6.0	154	142	92.2
Coshocton	97	0.3	60	37	44	53	33	0.4	3	[1]	76	11	[1]	13	13	[1]
Crawford	77	0.2	53	24	52	25	42	0.4	2	[1]	67	4	[1]	5	5	[1]
Cuyahoga	8,763	1.4	6,127	2,636	4,519	4,244	3,436	1.7	139	4.0	7,752	329	4.2	868	803	92.5
Darke	376	0.9	25	351	192	184	111	0.9	14	12.6	304	22	7.2	82	79	[1]
Defiance	23	0.1	9	14	14	9	12	0.2	3	[1]	21	3	[1]	4	3	[1]
Delaware	671	2.5	338	333	291	380	207	2.5	17	8.2	580	32	5.5	118	111	94.1
Erie	311	0.8	201	110	173	138	125	0.9	28	22.4	270	43	15.9	38	33	[1]
Fairfield	449	1.1	255	194	307	142	83	0.7	8	[1]	395	25	6.3	111	105	94.6
Fayette	1,231	5.7	658	573	647	584	383	5.9	80	20.9	985	141	14.3	222	185	83.3
Franklin	14,006	6.3	9,379	4,627	7,483	6,523	5,487	7.5	545	9.9	12,163	1,111	9.1	1,603	1,393	86.9
Fulton	6	[2]	4	2	2	4	2	[2]	......	......	6					
Gallia	1,875	7.3	945	930	983	892	552	7.5	108	19.6	1,468	218	14.9	378	332	87.8
Geauga	9	0.1	8	1	8	1	8	0.2	2	[1]	9	2	[1]			
Greene	3,970	13.4	2,465	1,505	1,997	1,973	1,221	13.5	218	17.9	3,268	418	12.8	673	632	93.9
Guernsey	489	1.1	271	218	257	232	143	1.1	17	11.9	367	34	9.5	83	68	[1]
Hamilton	24,300	5.3	16,963	7,337	12,167	12,133	8,802	6.1	1,474	16.7	21,246	3,112	14.6	2,869	2,564	89.4
Hancock	249	0.7	141	108	125	124	77	0.7	4	[1]	206	8	3.9	43	36	[1]
Hardin	556	1.8	353	203	299	257	167	1.8	34	20.4	436	51	11.7	111	98	88.3
Harrison	612	3.2	527	85	284	328	151	2.6	19	12.6	471	48	10.2	124	83	66.9
Henry	8	[2]	6	2	4	4	3	[2]	......	......	6	1	[1]	1	1	[1]
Highland	1,379	4.8	850	529	708	671	422	4.9	69	16.4	1,113	154	13.8	268	237	88.4
Hocking	143	0.6	88	55	80	63	53	0.8	13	[1]	121	23	19.0	25	23	[1]
Holmes	8	[2]	2	6	3	5	1	[2]	......	......	4	3	[1]	4	......	......
Huron	284	0.8	181	103	158	126	101	0.9	16	15.8	236	33	14.0	47	42	[1]
Jackson	708	2.3	268	440	369	339	196	2.4	33	16.8	518	91	17.6	158	129	81.6
Jefferson	1,647	2.5	1,442	205	826	821	511	2.4	43	8.4	1,296	93	7.2	287	233	81.2
Knox	323	1.1	233	90	166	157	105	1.1	7	6.7	267	19	7.1	43	38	[1]
Lake	237	1.0	167	70	124	113	87	1.2	8	[1]	199	13	6.5	38	30	[1]
Lawrence	1,789	4.5	752	1,037	957	832	599	5.9	137	22.9	1,388	288	20.7	331	292	88.2
Licking	432	0.8	275	157	219	213	151	0.9	11	7.3	367	24	6.5	47	38	[1]
Logan	777	2.6	400	377	401	376	252	2.7	28	11.1	635	48	7.6	129	113	87.6
Lorain	1,521	2.0	593	928	740	781	479	1.9	36	7.5	1,277	86	6.7	229	205	89.5
Lucas	1,918	1.0	1,288	630	958	960	733	1.2	32	4.4	1,687	74	4.4	198	180	90.9
Madison	745	3.7	577	168	410	335	250	4.1	45	18.0	593	79	13.3	124	106	85.5
Mahoning	2,083	1.8	1,612	471	1,148	935	845	2.1	61	7.2	1,751	107	6.1	252	190	75.4
Marion	232	0.7	161	71	124	108	79	0.8	12	[1]	187	23	12.3	35	30	[1]
Medina	114	0.5	101	13	60	54	36	0.5	7	[1]	94	17	[1]	22	22	[1]
Meigs	690	2.7	433	257	353	337	222	3.0	35	15.8	556	79	14.2	111	104	93.7
Mercer	115	0.4	84	31	66	49	40	0.5	2	[1]	89	2	[1]	20	20	[1]
Miami	1,109	2.5	734	375	563	546	386	2.8	61	15.8	932	122	13.1	164	141	86.0

[1] Per cent not shown where base is less than 100. [2] Less than one-tenth of 1 per cent.

TABLE III.—GENERAL STATISTICS OF THE NEGRO POPULATION OF THE UNITED STATES, BY COUNTIES: 1910—Con.

[Counties in which no Negroes were reported are omitted.]

COUNTY.	Total.	Per cent of total population.	Color. Black.	Mulatto.	Sex. Male.	Female.	Males 21 yrs+ Number.	Per cent of total.	Illiterate Number.	Illiterate Per cent.	Persons 10 yrs+ Total.	Illiterate Number.	Illiterate Per cent.	Persons 6-14 Total.	Attending school Number.	Attending school Per cent.
OHIO—Continued.																
Monroe	90	0.4	40	50	45	45	20	0.3	2	(1)	63	8	(1)	24	23	(1)
Montgomery	5,481	3.3	4,033	1,448	2,929	2,552	2,180	3.9	409	18.8	4,736	655	13.8	603	530	87.9
Morgan	147	0.9	69	78	84	63	45	0.9	6	(1)	108	14	13.0	26	22	(1)
Morrow	56	0.3	30	26	27	29	17	0.3	1	(1)	43	1	(1)	4	3	(1)
Muskingum	1,686	2.9	1,012	674	820	866	504	2.9	60	11.9	1,346	127	9.4	259	213	82.2
Noble	44	0.2	24	20	20	24	11	0.2	1	(1)	28	1	(1)	10	9	(1)
Ottawa	31	0.1	23	8	22	9	17	0.2	1	(1)	25	2	(1)	.....	.....	.....
Paulding	502	2.2	149	353	274	228	147	2.3	23	15.6	382	42	11.0	105	95	90.5
Perry	563	1.6	468	95	298	265	176	1.7	21	11.9	424	40	9.4	107	81	75.7
Pickaway	695	2.7	497	198	415	280	272	3.3	56	20.6	591	98	16.6	106	95	89.6
Pike	717	4.6	381	336	435	282	264	5.9	57	21.6	549	117	21.3	134	101	75.4
Portage	192	0.6	47	145	100	92	60	0.6	2	(1)	159	8	5.0	34	29	(1)
Preble	265	1.1	83	182	149	116	107	1.4	18	16.8	225	30	13.3	40	39	(1)
Putnam	26	0.1	25	1	12	14	9	0.1	.....	.....	22	3	(1)	6	6	(1)
Richland	253	0.5	188	65	184	69	139	0.9	5	3.6	239	9	3.8	18	18	(1)
Ross	2,382	5.9	1,458	924	1,230	1,152	688	6.0	93	13.5	1,860	222	11.9	420	340	81.0
Sandusky	146	0.4	83	63	72	74	51	0.5	1	(1)	119	7	5.9	21	20	(1)
Scioto	1,016	2.1	685	331	603	413	415	3.0	74	17.8	892	137	15.4	131	114	87.0
Seneca	157	0.4	55	102	82	75	59	0.4	7	(1)	136	14	10.3	25	24	(1)
Shelby	231	0.9	220	11	114	117	63	0.9	7	(1)	194	12	6.2	50	49	(1)
Stark	752	0.6	563	189	416	336	301	0.7	22	7.3	630	34	5.4	118	98	83.1
Summit	757	0.7	579	178	417	340	263	0.7	29	11.0	629	54	8.6	123	103	83.7
Trumbull	208	0.4	121	87	110	98	78	0.5	12	(1)	176	18	10.2	35	29	(1)
Tuscarawas	194	0.3	140	54	108	86	54	0.3	15	(1)	145	25	17.2	39	35	(1)
Union	264	1.2	183	81	141	123	85	1.3	5	(1)	217	11	5.1	45	37	(1)
Van Wert	327	1.1	189	138	166	161	85	1.0	13	(1)	261	31	11.9	60	37	(1)
Vinton	213	1.6	16	197	117	96	56	1.6	14	(1)	151	20	13.2	51	39	(1)
Warren	729	3.0	402	327	385	344	246	3.2	25	10.2	601	69	11.5	118	111	94.1
Washington	1,378	3.0	546	832	702	676	350	2.7	53	15.1	1,073	123	11.5	308	265	86.0
Wayne	70	0.2	70	.....	40	30	16	0.1	4	(1)	51	7	(1)	17	15	(1)
Williams	5	(2)	1	4	1	4	1	(2)	.....	.....	4	1	(1)	.....	.....	.....
Wood	150	0.3	85	65	77	73	43	0.3	6	(1)	108	13	12.0	22	19	(1)
Wyandot	21	0.1	10	11	12	9	10	0.2	1	(1)	19	1	(1)	1	1	(1)
OKLAHOMA.																
Total	137,612	8.3	98,269	39,343	71,937	65,675	36,841	8.2	7,396	20.1	101,157	17,858	17.7	30,818	23,581	76.5
Adair	22	0.2	18	4	16	6	4	0.2	1	(1)	16	2	(1)	5	4	(1)
Alfalfa	5	(2)	.....	5	3	2	1	(2)	.....	.....	3	.....	.....	1	1	(1)
Atoka	2,109	15.3	1,204	905	1,161	948	624	17.1	208	33.3	1,562	409	26.2	426	281	66.0
Beaver	12	0.1	5	7	7	5	4	0.1	.....	.....	11	.....	.....	1	.....	.....
Beckham	2	(2)	2	.....	.....	2	.....	.....	.....	.....	2	.....	.....	.....	.....	.....
Blaine	1,434	8.0	973	461	729	705	376	7.7	82	21.8	1,077	202	18.8	356	284	79.8
Bryan	2,184	7.3	1,743	441	1,177	1,007	577	7.8	207	35.9	1,563	470	30.1	529	359	67.9
Caddo	1,178	3.3	879	299	637	541	358	3.8	89	24.9	881	166	18.8	249	159	63.9
Canadian	823	3.5	783	40	452	371	290	4.1	34	11.7	659	73	11.1	141	107	75.9
Carter	4,315	17.0	2,921	1,394	2,195	2,120	991	16.1	293	29.6	3,071	708	23.1	1,046	841	80.4
Cherokee	995	5.9	930	65	499	496	246	6.1	55	22.4	740	149	20.1	224	165	73.7
Choctaw	4,303	19.7	3,296	1,007	2,163	2,140	1,050	18.7	319	30.4	3,078	858	27.9	1,004	721	71.8
Cimarron	2	(2)	2	.....	1	1	1	0.1	.....	.....	2	.....	.....	.....	.....	.....
Cleveland	456	2.4	442	14	219	237	113	2.4	44	38.9	325	88	27.1	103	84	81.6
Coal	976	6.2	651	325	508	468	263	6.5	67	25.5	693	164	23.7	228	157	68.9
Comanche	962	2.3	655	307	521	441	308	2.6	57	18.5	753	127	16.9	189	118	62.4
Craig	1,175	6.8	794	381	609	566	313	6.8	47	15.0	882	117	13.3	260	215	82.7
Creek	2,778	10.6	1,991	787	1,485	1,293	731	9.3	139	19.0	1,985	315	15.9	638	447	70.1
Custer	291	1.3	225	66	153	138	80	1.3	13	(1)	209	29	13.9	64	53	(1)
Delaware	38	0.3	37	1	17	21	8	0.3	2	(1)	27	5	(1)	11	3	(1)
Dewey	52	0.4	45	7	31	21	17	0.5	3	(1)	46	5	(1)	10	10	(1)
Ellis	2	(2)	2	.....	1	1	1	(2)	1	(1)	2	1	(1)	.....	.....	.....
Garfield	822	2.5	560	262	423	399	259	2.8	17	6.6	633	35	5.5	153	118	77.1
Garvin	2,318	8.7	1,869	449	1,150	1,168	484	7.6	137	28.3	1,547	351	22.7	594	461	77.6
Grady	1,731	5.7	1,200	531	918	813	540	6.5	92	17.0	1,346	182	13.5	336	289	86.0
Grant	14	0.1	14	.....	6	8	3	0.1	1	(1)	12	4	(1)	3	3	(1)
Greer	146	0.9	123	23	80	66	42	1.1	6	(1)	107	13	12.1	34	1	(1)
Harper	4	(2)	4	.....	2	2	2	0.1	1	(1)	3	1	(1)	.....	.....	.....
Haskell	385	2.0	358	27	204	181	102	2.3	30	29.4	276	59	21.4	86	69	(1)
Hughes	1,737	7.2	1,411	326	900	837	400	6.8	122	30.5	1,171	288	24.6	399	254	63.7
Jackson	114	0.5	88	26	70	44	64	1.0	13	(1)	105	19	18.1	6	1	(1)
Jefferson	397	2.3	378	19	228	169	147	3.1	41	27.9	317	76	24.0	73	60	(1)
Johnston	884	5.3	572	312	451	433	219	5.5	85	38.8	662	214	32.3	203	153	75.4
Kay	109	0.4	69	40	54	55	42	0.5	4	(1)	96	4	(1)	16	14	(1)
Kingfisher	2,392	12.7	1,840	552	1,215	1,177	619	12.4	110	17.8	1,813	266	14.7	545	416	76.3

1 Per cent not shown where base is less than 100.   2 Less than one-tenth of 1 per cent.

TABLE III.—GENERAL STATISTICS OF THE NEGRO POPULATION OF THE UNITED STATES, BY COUNTIES: 1910—Con.

[Counties in which no Negroes were reported are omitted.]

NEGRO POPULATION: 1910.

COUNTY	Total	Per cent of total population	Color: Black	Color: Mulatto	Sex: Male	Sex: Female	Males 21 years of age and over: Number	Males 21: Per cent of total	Males 21 Illiterate: Number	Males 21 Illiterate: Per cent	Persons 10 years of age and over: Total	Persons 10+ Illiterate: Number	Persons 10+ Illiterate: Per cent	Persons 6 to 14 years of age: Total	Persons 6–14 Attending school: Number	Per cent
OKLAHOMA—Continued.																
Kiowa	317	1.2	276	41	183	134	107	1.5	20	18.7	229	44	19.2	60	7	[1]
Latimer	618	5.5	541	77	358	260	201	6.7	39	19.4	445	84	18.9	110	95	86.4
Le Flore	1,781	6.1	1,413	368	964	817	504	7.1	131	26.0	1,311	278	21.2	390	296	75.9
Lincoln	3,945	11.3	2,921	1,024	2,031	1,914	899	10.5	166	18.5	2,670	385	14.4	1,038	869	83.7
Logan	8,196	25.8	5,679	2,517	4,107	4,089	1,984	22.5	289	14.6	5,957	1,004	16.9	1,976	1,604	81.2
Love	1,021	10.0	728	293	535	486	215	9.1	84	39.1	663	173	26.1	274	191	69.7
McClain	1,081	6.9	984	97	573	508	264	6.8	62	23.5	780	149	19.1	290	255	87.9
McCurtain	4,576	22.1	3,072	1,504	2,383	2,193	1,122	21.5	357	31.8	3,266	920	28.2	1,125	725	64.4
McIntosh	5,283	25.2	3,409	1,874	2,739	2,544	1,213	24.4	233	19.2	3,683	651	17.7	1,328	1,095	82.5
Major	90	0.6	71	19	57	33	22	0.6	4	[1]	64	6	[1]	21	18	[1]
Marshall	319	2.7	296	23	156	163	76	2.8	22	[1]	217	52	24.0	73	51	[1]
Mayes	799	5.9	597	202	410	389	197	5.7	69	35.0	562	140	24.9	177	134	75.7
Murray	423	3.3	368	55	199	224	110	3.4	30	27.3	323	59	18.3	84	67	[1]
Muskogee	16,454	31.2	11,550	4,904	8,375	8,079	4,524	28.7	630	13.9	12,569	1,517	12.1	3,482	2,571	73.8
Noble	642	4.3	527	115	339	303	181	4.4	44	24.3	469	94	20.0	126	105	83.3
Nowata	1,954	13.7	1,108	846	989	965	375		163	28.3	1,537	326	21.2	391	340	87.0
Okfuskee	8,073	40.4	4,332	3,741	4,177	3,896	1,824	38.5	331	18.1	5,677	932	16.4	2,063	1,455	70.5
Oklahoma	9,227	10.8	7,429	1,798	4,931	4,296	3,068	10.0	286	9.3	7,348	687	9.3	1,546	1,314	85.0
Okmulgee	5,933	28.1	3,411	2,522	3,115	2,818	1,507	25.8	321	21.3	4,260	793	18.6	1,428	1,125	78.8
Osage	391	1.9	384	7	234	157	161	2.6	14	8.7	320	37	11.6	49	24	[1]
Ottawa	11	0.1	5	6	6	5	6	0.1	3	[1]	11	3	[1]	2	2	[1]
Pawnee	806	4.7	621	185	445	361	223	4.7	44	19.7	591	100	16.9	176	142	80.7
Payne	1,456	6.1	1,147	309	785	671	394	6.4	55	14.0	1,045	143	13.7	349	208	59.6
Pittsburg	5,244	11.0	3,303	1,941	3,122	2,122	1,900	13.6	397	20.9	4,096	796	19.4	920	752	81.7
Pontotoc	1,009	4.1	683	326	569	440	295	5.0	86	29.2	744	205	27.6	212	183	86.3
Pottawatomie	2,017	4.6	1,719	298	1,081	936	555	4.9	62	11.2	1,487	142	9.5	480	379	79.0
Pushmataha	385	3.8	239	146	192	193	91	3.5	20	[1]	263	46	17.5	109	82	75.2
Rogers	620	3.5	272	348	339	281	202	4.2	20	9.9	509	65	12.8	109	89	81.7
Seminole	4,081	20.4	3,396	685	2,106	1,975	955	20.0	299	31.3	2,800	699	25.0	1,028	809	78.7
Sequoyah	3,178	12.7	1,971	1,207	1,619	1,559	793	13.4	218	27.5	2,288	539	23.6	730	570	78.1
Stephens	96	0.4	72	24	51	45	22	0.4	7	[1]	63	16	[1]	21	6	[1]
Texas	1	[2]	1		1		1	[2]			1					
Tillman	432	2.3	359	73	236	196	127	2.6	26	20.5	306	67	21.9	98	40	[1]
Tulsa	2,754	7.9	2,502	252	1,425	1,329	903	8.1	76	8.4	2,218	183	8.3	459	364	79.3
Wagoner	8,761	39.7	6,379	2,382	4,556	4,205	2,149	38.2	437	20.3	6,307	1,045	16.6	2,105	1,723	81.9
Washington	434	2.5	396	38	240	194	180	3.2	34	18.9	372	71	19.1	49	39	[1]
Washita	25	0.1	12	13	15	10	5	0.1			20	6	[1]	6	3	[1]
Woods	3	[2]	3		3		1	[2]			3	1	[1]			
Woodward	9	0.1	9		6	3	6	0.1			8			1	1	[1]
OREGON.																
Total	1,492	0.2	1,058	434	907	585	766	0.3	24	3.1	1,359	46	3.4	102	79	77.5
Baker	27	0.1	20	7	16	11	12	0.2	1	[1]	24	2	[1]	3	2	[1]
Benton	1	[2]	1		1		1	[2]			1					
Clackamas	11	[2]	6	5	9	2	5	0.1			8			2	2	[1]
Clatsop	25	0.2	20	5	13	12	10	0.1	2	[1]	20	2	[1]			
Columbia	1	[2]	1			1					1					
Coos	17	0.1	7	10	11	6	8	0.1	1	[1]	15	1	[1]	5	5	[1]
Crook	8	0.1	8		6	2	6	0.2			8			1	1	[1]
Curry	1	[2]	1			1	1	0.1			1					
Douglas	11	0.1	7	4	11		9	0.1	1	[1]	11	1	[1]			
Gilliam	1	[2]	1		1		1	0.1			1					
Grant	3	0.1		3	2	1	2	0.1			3					
Harney	2	[2]	2		2		2	0.1			2					
Hood River	8	0.1	4	4	2	6	2	0.1			8	1	[1]			
Jackson	41	0.2	12	29	30	11	21	0.2	2	[1]	33	2	[1]	9	6	[1]
Josephine	14	0.1	3	11	3	11	3	0.1			4			1		
Klamath	21	0.2	20	1	14	7	12	0.3	2	[1]	20	2	[1]	1	1	[1]
Lake	8	0.2	2	6	6	2	6	0.3			8					
Lane	13	[2]	7	6	13		10	0.1	1	[1]	13	1	[1]			
Lincoln	2	[2]	2		2		2	0.1			2					
Linn	2	[2]	2		1	1	1	[2]			2					
Malheur	14	0.2	9	5	7	7	4	0.1			10	1	[1]			
Marion	58	0.1	36	22	45	13	37	0.3	4	[1]	56	8	[1]	4	2	[1]
Morrow	5	0.1	5			5					5					
Multnomah	1,081	0.5	794	287	629	452	544	0.6	7	1.3	990	18	1.8	68	52	[1]
Polk	2	[2]	1	1	1	1	1	[2]			2					
Sherman	1	[2]	1			1					1					
Tillamook	1	[2]	1		1						1					
Umatilla	55	0.3	39	16	35	20	31	0.4	1	[1]	49	3	[1]	1	1	[1]
Union	21	0.1	9	12	12	9	8	0.2			19	1	[1]	3	3	[1]
Wallowa	1	[2]	1			1					1					
Wasco	31	0.2	27	4	23	8	18	0.2	2	[1]	26	2	[1]	3	3	[1]
Washington	7	[2]	3	4	5	2	5	0.1			7	1	[1]			
Wheeler	2	0.1	2		1	1					1			1	1	[1]
Yamhill	6	[2]	4	2	5	1	4	0.1			6					

[1] Per cent not shown where base is less than 100.   [2] Less than one-tenth of 1 per cent.

TABLE **III.**—GENERAL STATISTICS OF THE NEGRO POPULATION OF THE UNITED STATES, BY COUNTIES: 1910—Con.

[Counties in which no Negroes were reported are omitted.]

COUNTY.	NEGRO POPULATION: 1910.																
	Total.	Per cent of total population.	Color.		Sex.		Males 21 years of age and over.				Persons 10 years of age and over.				Persons 6 to 14 years of age.		
			Black.	Mulatto.	Male.	Female.	Number.	Per cent of total.	Illiterate.		Total.	Illiterate.		Total.	Attending school.	
									Number.	Per cent.		Number.	Per cent.		Number.	Per cent.

PENNSYLVANIA.

COUNTY.	Total.	Per cent	Black	Mulatto	Male	Female	Number	Per cent	Illit. No.	Illit. Pct	Total	Illit. No.	Illit. Pct	Total	Att. No.	Att. Pct
Total	193,919	2.5	156,765	37,154	95,830	98,089	64,272	2.8	6,479	10.1	161,126	14,638	9.1	27,105	22,475	82.9
Adams	325	0.9	282	43	174	151	123	1.3	19	15.4	273	34	12.5	45	33	(1)
Allegheny	34,217	3.4	26,527	7,690	17,906	16,311	12,282	3.8	999	8.1	28,305	2,093	7.4	4,745	4,001	84.3
Armstrong	495	0.7	289	206	273	222	182	0.9	12	6.6	389	30	7.7	63	57	(1)
Beaver	1,235	1.6	986	249	640	595	395	1.5	44	11.1	978	95	9.7	212	167	78.8
Bedford	365	0.9	247	118	188	177	101	1.0	14	13.9	273	33	12.1	70	52	(1)
Berks	1,007	0.5	845	162	543	464	386	0.7	28	7.3	853	58	6.8	140	120	85.7
Blair	786	0.7	564	222	408	378	274	0.9	19	6.9	662	42	6.3	131	114	87.0
Bradford	234	0.4	161	73	116	118	70	0.4	7	(1)	189	10	5.3	40	34	(1)
Bucks	1,832	2.4	1,444	388	909	923	532	2.3	67	12.6	1,485	136	9.2	383	312	81.5
Butler	217	0.3	150	67	117	100	87	0.4	9	(1)	187	15	8.0	28	27	(1)
Cambria	640	0.4	528	112	362	278	289	0.6	19	6.6	563	42	7.5	53	40	(1)
Cameron	31	0.4	27	4	17	14	10	0.4	2	(1)	26	5	(1)	5	5	(1)
Carbon	27	0.1	21	6	14	13	10	0.1			20			7	7	(1)
Center	265	0.6	247	18	128	137	85	0.7	18	(1)	228	33	14.5	42	35	(1)
Chester	10,622	9.7	8,779	1,843	5,590	5,032	3,250	9.6	450	13.8	8,353	882	10.6	2,087	1,634	78.3
Clarion	24	0.1	20	4	7	17	7	0.1			22	2	(1)			
Clearfield	315	0.3	132	183	153	162	94	0.4	14	(1)	238	27	11.3	62	48	(1)
Clinton	209	0.7	85	124	104	105	70	0.8	20	(1)	177	37	20.9	32	25	(1)
Columbia	119	0.2	108	11	62	57	39	0.3	7	(1)	98	11	(1)	28	28	(1)
Crawford	355	0.6	280	75	182	173	123	0.6	13	10.6	299	26	8.7	52	45	(1)
Cumberland	1,788	3.3	1,389	399	851	937	501	3.2	103	20.6	1,436	234	16.3	336	301	89.6
Dauphin	6,536	4.8	5,359	1,177	3,340	3,196	2,277	5.4	351	15.4	5,496	713	13.0	920	818	88.9
Delaware	11,897	10.1	10,278	1,619	5,741	6,156	3,568	9.9	502	14.1	9,795	1,133	11.6	1,941	1,567	80.7
Elk	34	0.1	29	5	22	12	18	0.2	1	(1)	30	1	(1)	3		
Erie	392	0.3	334	58	203	189	156	0.4	15	9.6	349	23	6.6	46	39	(1)
Fayette	5,852	3.5	4,318	1,534	3,150	2,702	1,920	3.5	381	19.8	4,491	710	15.8	1,067	862	80.8
Forest	8	0.1	6	2	3	5	3	0.1		(1)	8	1	(1)	1	1	(1)
Franklin	1,716	2.9	1,015	701	851	865	491	3.1	109	22.2	1,359	241	17.7	300	247	82.3
Fulton	94	1.0	94		45	49	19	0.7	8	(1)	65	24	(1)	28	12	(1)
Greene	389	1.3	199	190	210	179	121	1.5	21	17.4	293	41	14.0	75	60	(1)
Huntingdon	305	0.8	244	61	198	107	97	0.9	12	(1)	261	15	5.7	22	17	(1)
Indiana	183	0.3	117	66	96	87	66	0.3	12	(1)	158	20	12.7	27	24	(1)
Jefferson	105	0.2	84	21	65	40	47	0.3	8	(1)	86	9	(1)	21	15	(1)
Juniata	171	1.1	63	108	91	80	42	1.1	4	(1)	135	7	5.2	46	42	(1)
Lackawanna	696	0.3	636	60	364	332	253	0.3	9	3.6	578	23	4.0	106	96	90.6
Lancaster	2,299	1.4	1,708	591	1,198	1,101	721	1.5	120	16.6	1,882	294	15.6	422	343	81.3
Lawrence	699	1.0	575	124	376	323	248	1.1	41	16.5	573	68	11.9	99	87	(1)
Lebanon	215	0.4	178	37	126	89	79	0.4	17	(1)	176	32	18.2	36	33	(1)
Lehigh	247	0.2	190	57	123	124	89	0.3	5	(1)	211	17	8.1	35	33	(1)
Luzerne	924	0.3	742	182	504	420	349	0.4	31	8.9	785	67	8.5	145	127	87.6
Lycoming	1,182	1.5	943	239	557	625	331	1.4	31	9.4	970	79	8.1	196	174	88.8
McKean	251	0.5	178	73	125	126	70	0.5	6	(1)	191	9	4.7	41	33	(1)
Mercer	621	0.8	362	259	361	260	255	1.0	42	16.5	500	60	12.0	89	72	(1)
Mifflin	172	0.6	132	40	96	76	55	0.7	5	(1)	139	13	9.4	32	27	(1)
Monroe	185	0.8	130	55	92	93	57	0.8	11	(1)	149	19	12.8	42	34	(1)
Montgomery	6,021	3.6	5,571	450	2,729	3,292	1,686	3.3	152	9.0	4,968	370	7.4	874	683	78.1
Montour	77	0.5	58	19	46	31	32	0.7	5	(1)	67	11	(1)	9	7	(1)
Northampton	615	0.5	512	103	332	283	208	0.5	3	1.4	516	22	4.3	109	84	77.1
Northumberland	237	0.2	172	65	121	116	75	0.2	7	(1)	198	16	8.1	43	37	(1)
Perry	73	0.3	46	27	37	36	23	0.3	3	(1)	51	8	(1)	13	5	(1)
Philadelphia	84,459	5.5	70,479	13,980	39,431	45,028	28,120	6.0	2,108	7.5	71,973	5,595	7.8	9,604	8,051	83.8
Pike	72	0.9	55	17	34	38	21	0.9	6	(1)	59	8	(1)	12	12	(1)
Potter	54	0.2	15	39	27	27	21	0.2	4	(1)	46	4	(1)	7	7	(1)
Schuylkill	242	0.1	151	91	130	112	87	0.1	12	(1)	190	25	13.2	37	31	(1)
Snyder	4	(2)	4		2	2	2	(2)			4	1	(1)			
Somerset	246	0.4	198	48	141	105	85	0.4	13	(1)	196	22	11.2	44	38	(1)
Sullivan	2	(2)	2		1	1	1	(2)			2					
Susquehanna	114	0.3	107	7	56	58	45	0.4	5	(1)	103	7	6.8	13	10	(1)
Tioga	73	0.2	66	7	42	31	29	0.2	5	(1)	61	9	(1)	6	6	(1)
Union	59	0.4	42	17	25	34	18	0.4	1	(1)	48	2	(1)	7	4	(1)
Venango	541	1.0	286	255	279	262	154	0.9	9	5.8	436	21	4.8	93	71	(1)
Warren	75	0.2	30	45	32	43	22	0.2	2	(1)	58	6	(1)	12	10	(1)
Washington	5,888	4.1	4,174	1,714	3,155	2,733	1,816	4.0	263	14.5	4,598	504	11.0	1,094	917	83.8
Wayne	20	0.1	19	1	12	8	11	0.1	2	(1)	18	2	(1)	1	1	(1)
Westmoreland	2,641	1.1	2,081	560	1,483	1,158	988	1.4	201	20.3	2,148	353	16.4	432	330	76.4
Wyoming	12	0.1	6	6	6	6	4	0.1			10			1	1	(1)
York	2,113	1.5	1,666	447	1,028	1,085	582	1.5	72	12.4	1,642	188	11.4	393	322	81.9

[1] Per cent not shown where base is less than 100.   [2] Less than one-tenth of 1 per cent.

TABLE III.—GENERAL STATISTICS OF THE NEGRO POPULATION OF THE UNITED STATES, BY COUNTIES: 1910—Con.

[Counties in which no Negroes were reported are omitted.]

COUNTY.	NEGRO POPULATION: 1910.																
	Total.	Per cent of total popula-tion.	Color.		Sex.		Males 21 years of age and over.				Persons 10 years of age and over.				Persons 6 to 14 years of age.		
			Black.	Mu-latto.	Male.	Fe-male.	Num-ber.	Per cent of total.	Illiterate.		Total.	Illiterate.		Total.	Attending school.	
									Num-ber.	Per cent.		Num-ber.	Per cent.		Num-ber.	Per cent.

RHODE ISLAND.

COUNTY.	Total.	Per cent	Black.	Mu-latto.	Male.	Fe-male.	Num-ber.	Per cent	Num-ber.	Per cent.	Total.	Num-ber.	Per cent.	Total.	Num-ber.	Per cent.
Total	9,529	1.8	6,350	3,179	4,645	4,884	3,067	1.9	345	11.2	7,913	752	9.5	1,323	1,160	87.7
Bristol	153	0.9	47	106	66	87	39	0.7	14	(1)	121	33	27.3	24	18	(1)
Kent	266	0.7	199	67	138	128	93	0.9	9	(1)	222	17	7.7	40	36	(1)
Newport	1,881	4.8	1,433	448	881	1,000	578	4.6	47	8.1	1,570	99	6.3	253	226	89.3
Providence	6,391	1.5	4,140	2,251	3,141	3,250	2,121	1.7	255	12.0	5,346	554	10.4	867	764	88.1
Washington	838	3.4	531	307	419	419	236	2.9	20	8.5	654	49	7.5	139	116	83.5

SOUTH CAROLINA.

COUNTY.	Total.	Per cent	Black.	Mu-latto.	Male.	Fe-male.	Num-ber.	Per cent	Num-ber.	Per cent.	Total.	Num-ber.	Per cent.	Total.	Num-ber.	Per cent.
Total	835,843	55.2	701,462	134,381	408,078	427,765	169,155	50.5	72,857	43.1	584,064	226,242	38.7	212,125	118,981	56.1
Abbeville	22,522	64.7	19,232	3,290	11,157	11,365	4,556	59.9	1,977	43.4	15,718	5,343	34.0	5,975	3,877	64.9
Aiken	22,850	54.6	17,841	5,009	11,138	11,712	4,812	50.5	1,901	39.5	16,165	5,793	35.8	5,576	2,989	53.6
Anderson	26,335	37.9	21,695	4,640	13,101	13,234	5,417	35.7	2,277	42.0	18,427	6,791	36.9	6,675	3,636	54.5
Bamberg	12,874	69.4	12,120	754	6,328	6,546	2,331	62.1	794	34.1	8,723	2,878	33.0	3,506	1,915	54.6
Barnwell	24,647	72.0	21,889	2,758	11,989	12,658	4,842	66.3	2,081	43.0	17,245	7,034	40.8	6,451	3,467	53.7
Beaufort	26,376	86.9	25,146	1,230	12,630	13,746	5,634	80.1	2,585	45.9	19,345	8,315	43.0	6,667	3,292	49.4
Berkeley	18,231	77.6	17,445	786	8,989	9,242	3,835	75.5	1,835	47.8	13,030	5,687	43.6	4,675	1,935	41.4
Calhoun	12,739	76.6	11,395	1,344	6,159	6,580	2,460	71.5	929	37.8	8,601	2,999	34.9	3,367	2,258	67.1
Charleston	56,033	63.2	46,967	9,066	25,810	30,223	13,631	58.0	4,544	33.3	43,261	14,143	32.7	11,086	6,610	59.6
Cherokee	8,510	32.5	7,117	1,393	4,267	4,243	1,637	28.9	764	46.7	5,797	2,352	40.6	2,276	1,142	50.2
Chester	19,140	65.0	16,071	3,069	9,248	9,892	3,790	59.3	1,976	52.1	13,419	5,921	44.1	4,987	2,431	48.7
Chesterfield	10,557	40.1	7,768	2,789	5,306	5,251	2,128	36.4	957	45.0	7,207	3,138	43.5	2,650	1,310	49.4
Clarendon	23,393	72.9	19,600	3,793	11,646	11,747	4,490	68.9	1,807	40.2	15,646	5,624	35.9	6,274	3,615	57.6
Colleton	22,296	63.6	19,290	3,006	10,884	11,412	4,552	59.0	2,610	57.3	15,706	9,144	58.2	5,719	1,860	32.5
Darlington	21,283	59.1	15,312	5,971	10,490	10,793	4,302	53.7	1,787	41.5	14,553	5,292	36.4	5,442	3,730	68.5
Dillon	11,539	51.0	10,474	1,065	5,723	5,816	2,318	47.0	834	36.0	7,916	2,590	32.7	2,900	1,771	61.1
Dorchester	10,982	61.4	9,645	1,337	5,273	5,709	2,152	56.5	914	42.5	7,672	2,983	38.9	2,857	1,418	49.6
Edgefield	20,114	71.1	16,196	3,918	10,071	10,043	3,876	65.0	2,038	52.6	13,670	5,601	41.0	5,457	3,525	64.6
Fairfield	22,377	76.0	17,865	4,512	11,041	11,336	4,108	69.5	2,135	52.0	15,174	6,784	44.7	6,029	3,063	50.8
Florence	20,340	57.0	16,411	3,929	9,945	10,395	4,040	50.7	1,558	38.6	13,946	5,007	35.9	5,119	3,080	60.2
Georgetown	16,110	72.3	14,611	1,499	7,766	8,344	3,571	68.5	1,725	48.3	11,602	5,838	50.3	3,700	2,073	56.0
Greenville	20,861	30.5	15,131	5,730	10,115	10,746	4,391	28.0	1,707	38.9	14,852	4,952	33.3	5,087	3,065	60.3
Greenwood	21,302	62.2	16,927	4,375	10,626	10,676	4,413	58.0	1,969	44.6	14,949	5,010	33.5	5,548	4,052	73.0
Hampton	16,120	64.2	14,161	1,959	8,014	8,106	3,193	64.0	1,492	46.7	11,056	5,025	45.5	4,223	2,077	49.2
Horry	6,668	24.7	5,636	1,032	3,258	3,410	1,217	21.2	477	39.2	4,483	1,843	41.1	1,744	856	49.1
Kershaw	16,444	60.7	13,135	3,309	8,079	8,365	3,129	55.8	1,629	52.1	11,176	5,504	49.2	4,343	2,043	47.0
Lancaster	13,115	49.2	10,968	2,147	6,405	6,710	2,466	45.0	1,272	51.6	8,905	4,163	46.7	3,454	1,603	46.4
Laurens	22,753	54.8	20,133	2,620	11,161	11,592	4,528	49.7	2,408	53.2	15,889	6,602	41.6	5,969	3,394	56.9
Lee	17,251	68.1	15,117	2,134	8,539	8,712	3,203	61.6	1,734	54.1	11,378	5,908	51.9	4,647	2,036	43.8
Lexington	11,638	36.3	10,359	1,279	5,864	5,774	2,358	31.0	1,051	44.6	8,034	3,148	39.2	3,060	1,567	51.2
Marion	11,208	54.4	9,111	2,097	5,604	5,604	2,288	49.8	625	27.3	7,678	2,016	26.3	2,738	1,612	58.9
Marlboro	18,928	60.7	17,029	1,899	9,240	9,688	3,648	54.5	1,686	46.2	12,834	5,422	42.2	4,779	2,816	58.9
Newberry	22,040	63.7	20,037	2,003	10,859	11,181	4,356	58.0	1,676	38.5	15,127	4,631	30.6	5,784	3,993	69.0
Oconee	6,848	25.1	5,114	1,734	3,372	3,476	1,357	22.9	535	30.4	4,783	1,478	30.9	1,854	1,012	54.6
Orangeburg	36,794	65.8	31,114	5,680	17,994	18,800	7,134	60.2	2,591	36.3	25,286	8,261	32.7	9,651	5,488	56.9
Pickens	5,430	21.4	4,460	970	2,713	2,717	1,147	20.5	462	40.3	3,769	1,452	38.0	1,432	679	47.4
Richland	29,533	33.6	21,101	8,432	13,907	15,626	6,829	48.5	2,272	33.3	22,060	6,857	31.1	6,393	4,323	67.6
Saluda	11,189	53.4	8,747	2,442	5,640	5,549	2,189	48.8	1,061	48.5	7,406	2,811	37.5	2,973	1,934	65.1
Spartanburg	26,410	31.6	21,944	4,466	12,958	13,452	5,425	29.2	2,426	44.7	18,619	6,831	36.7	6,613	3,964	59.9
Sumter	28,103	73.0	23,299	4,804	13,549	14,554	5,499	67.2	1,975	25.9	19,451	6,236	32.1	7,252	4,521	62.3
Union	15,471	51.7	12,489	2,982	7,683	7,788	2,876	45.8	1,287	44.7	10,381	4,126	39.7	4,265	1,955	45.8
Williamsburg	23,214	61.7	20,051	3,163	11,164	12,050	4,093	55.0	1,996	48.8	15,446	7,012	45.4	6,326	3,670	58.0
York	25,275	53.0	21,309	3,966	12,373	12,902	4,934	48.0	2,498	50.6	17,589	7,697	43.8	6,602	3,324	50.3

SOUTH DAKOTA.

COUNTY.	Total.	Per cent	Black.	Mu-latto.	Male.	Fe-male.	Num-ber.	Per cent	Num-ber.	Per cent.	Total.	Num-ber.	Per cent.	Total.	Num-ber.	Per cent.
Total	817	0.1	521	296	468	349	341	0.2	24	7.0	697	38	5.5	110	95	86.4
Armstrong	1	0.2	1			1	1	0.6			1					
Aurora	1	(2)		1		1	1	0.1			1					
Beadle	39	0.2	27	12	17	22	12	0.2	1	(1)	29	1	(1)	2	2	(1)
Bon Homme	1	(2)	1			1	1	(2)			1					
Brookings	21	0.1	11	10	11	10	4	0.1			18			4	4	(1)
Brown	74	0.3	39	35	50	24	48	0.6	1	(1)	72	1	(1)	2	2	(1)
Brule	2	(2)	2		2		2	0.1			2					
Buffalo	1	0.1		1		1					1					
Clark	4	(2)	2	2	4		3	0.1			3					
Codington	25	0.2	25		17	8	10	0.2	2	(1)	21	2	(1)	4	4	(1)

¹ Per cent not shown where base is less than 100.   ² Less than one-tenth of 1 per cent.

TABLE **III.**—GENERAL STATISTICS OF THE NEGRO POPULATION OF THE UNITED STATES, BY COUNTIES: 1910—Con.

[Counties in which no Negroes were reported are omitted.]

COUNTY.	NEGRO POPULATION: 1910.															
	Total.	Per cent of total population.	Color.		Sex.		Males 21 years of age and over.				Persons 10 years of age and over.			Persons 6 to 14 years of age.		
			Black.	Mulatto.	Male.	Female.	Number.	Per cent of total.	Illiterate.		Total.	Illiterate.		Total.	Attending school.	
									Number.	Per cent.		Number.	Per cent.		Number.	Per cent.

SOUTH DAKOTA—Continued.

COUNTY.	Total	%tot	Black	Mulatto	Male	Female	No.	%tot	Ill.No.	Ill.%	Total	Ill.No.	Ill.%	Total	Att.No.	Att.%
Corson	3	0.1	3		1	2	1	0.1			3					
Custer	4	0.1	4		3	1	2	0.1			4					
Davison	18	0.2	11	7	12	6	11	0.3			17			1		
Day	1	(1)	1		1		1	0.1			1					
Deuel	5	0.1	2	3	2	3	1	(1)	1	(2)	3	1	(2)	3	3	(2)
Douglas	2	(1)	1	1	2		1	0.1			1			1	1	(2)
Edmunds	5	0.1	1	4	2	3	2	0.1			4					
Fall River	20	0.3	13	7	12	8	11	0.4	4	(2)	18	5	(2)			
Faulk	3	(1)	3		1	2					1			1	1	(2)
Gregory	20	0.2	4	16	16	4	16	0.5			20					
Hand	2	(1)		2	2		2	0.1			2					
Hanson	1	(1)		1		1	1	0.1			1					
Hughes	13	0.2	7	6	8	5	6	0.3			13					
Hutchinson	3	(1)	1	2	2	1	2	0.1	2	(2)	2	2	(2)	1	1	(2)
Hyde	1	(1)		1	1		1	0.1			1					
Kingsbury	13	0.1	12	1	9	4	7	0.2	1	(2)	10	1	(2)	1	1	(2)
Lake	1	(1)	1		1		1	(1)			1					
Lawrence	177	0.9	131	46	93	84	54	0.7	2	(2)	144	7	4.9	33	29	(2)
Lincoln	2	(1)		2	2		2	0.1			2					
Lyman	27	0.2	9	18	14	13	7	0.2	1	(2)	24	1	(2)	2	2	(2)
McCook	5	0.1	5		4	1	2	0.1			5			2	2	(2)
Marshall	6	0.1		6	4	2	3	0.1			5					
Meade	30	0.2	29	1	14	16	11	0.2	1	(2)	27	2	(2)	5	2	(2)
Minnehaha	72	0.2	41	31	32	40	28	0.3			65	1	(2)	6	6	(2)
Moody	2	(1)	2		2		2	0.1			2					
Pennington	33	0.3	28	5	18	15	14	0.3	3	(2)	30	4	(2)	8	8	(2)
Perkins	2	(1)	2		1	1	1	(1)			2					
Roberts	3	(1)	1	2	3		3	0.1			3					
Sanborn	3	(1)	1	2	3		3	0.2	1	(2)	3	1	(2)			
Stanley	38	0.3	32	6	17	21	13	0.3	1	(2)	32	2	(2)	6	4	(2)
Sterling	1	0.4	1			1								1		
Sully	49	2.0	6	43	29	20	19	2.1	2	(2)	39	4	(2)	11	10	(2)
Todd	5	0.2	5		5		3	0.5			4			2	2	(2)
Tripp	5	0.1	4	1	2	3	2	0.1			5					
Union	2	(1)	2				1	(1)			2			1	1	(2)
Yankton	61	0.5	39	22	34	27	16	0.4			42	2	(2)	13	10	(2)
Pine Ridge Indian Reservation	10	0.2	10		9	1	9	0.5	1	(2)	10	1	(2)			

TENNESSEE.

COUNTY.	Total	%tot	Black	Mulatto	Male	Female	No.	%tot	Ill.No.	Ill.%	Total	Ill.No.	Ill.%	Total	Att.No.	Att.%
Total	473,088	21.7	354,391	118,697	233,710	239,378	119,142	21.6	38,273	32.1	360,663	98,541	37.3	97,927	58,895	60.1
Anderson	921	5.2	729	192	510	411	269	6.6	90	33.5	711	155	21.8	201	171	85.1
Bedford	5,486	24.2	3,924	1,562	2,650	2,636	1,310	22.5	443	33.8	4,193	1,085	25.9	1,138	801	70.4
Benton	340	2.7	304	36	162	178	80	2.7	18	(2)	244	54	22.1	73	41	(2)
Bledsoe	391	6.2	280	111	203	188	90	5.9	42	(2)	280	86	30.7	86	60	(2)
Blount	1,221	5.9	933	288	631	590	297	6.1	84	28.3	921	188	20.4	265	218	82.3
Bradley	1,717	10.5	1,141	576	825	892	388	10.1	119	30.7	1,280	326	25.5	403	294	73.0
Campbell	1,887	6.9	1,584	303	1,064	823	641	9.8	188	29.3	1,495	404	27.0	312	197	63.1
Cannon	580	5.4	361	219	292	288	144	5.5	67	46.5	427	193	45.2	118	49	41.5
Carroll	5,051	21.1	3,851	1,200	2,592	2,522	1,114	18.8	427	38.3	3,699	1,071	29.2	1,237	875	70.7
Carter	660	3.3	580	80	335	325	153	3.4	35	22.9	459	97	21.1	158	91	57.6
Cheatham	1,593	15.1	1,245	348	777	816	351	13.5	115	32.8	1,131	281	24.8	407	270	66.3
Chester	1,571	17.3	1,353	218	770	801	327	15.2	145	44.3	1,120	405	36.2	394	153	38.8
Claiborne	819	3.5	706	113	459	360	232	4.3	99	42.7	578	234	40.5	186	60	32.3
Clay	289	3.2	88	201	143	146	64	3.2	28	(2)	201	83	41.3	67	37	(2)
Cocke	1,051	5.4	828	223	543	508	233	5.5	91	39.1	760	211	27.8	276	227	82.2
Coffee	1,624	10.4	988	636	756	868	359	9.2	161	44.8	1,190	384	32.3	385	276	71.7
Crockett	3,611	22.5	3,214	397	1,815	1,796	777	20.4	320	41.2	2,564	880	34.3	839	400	47.7
Cumberland	63	0.7	6	57	28	35	13	0.6	7	(2)	43	12	(2)	17	15	(2)
Davidson	46,710	31.2	32,435	14,275	21,683	25,027	12,666	30.4	3,712	29.3	38,984	9,348	24.0	7,634	5,453	71.4
Decatur	1,019	10.1	700	319	521	498	231	9.9	68	29.4	717	186	25.9	253	121	47.8
Dekalb	835	5.4	770	65	401	434	194	5.3	83	42.8	624	200	32.1	198	116	58.6
Dickson	3,079	15.4	2,483	596	1,547	1,532	687	14.6	221	32.2	2,172	556	25.6	765	429	56.1
Dyer	5,685	20.5	4,220	1,465	2,868	2,817	1,378	19.9	509	36.9	4,181	1,276	30.5	1,263	706	55.9
Fayette	22,702	75.0	18,454	4,248	11,373	11,329	4,503	69.3	1,928	42.8	15,428	6,021	39.0	5,789	2,410	41.6
Fentress	98	1.3	76	22	60	38	35	2.1	9	(2)	75	18	(2)	15	5	(2)
Franklin	3,126	15.3	2,333	793	1,540	1,586	739	14.8	282	38.2	2,322	704	30.3	712	384	53.9
Gibson	9,547	22.9	7,911	1,636	4,766	4,781	2,169	20.9	742	34.2	7,060	1,862	26.4	2,222	1,456	65.5
Giles	10,867	33.3	8,710	2,157	5,353	5,514	2,313	29.5	964	41.7	7,758	2,698	34.8	2,657	1,262	47.5
Grainger	483	3.5	317	166	250	233	103	3.1	28	27.2	328	67	20.4	127	81	63.8
Greene	1,369	4.4	891	478	674	695	350	4.8	153	43.7	1,027	322	31.4	321	228	71.0

[1] Less than one-tenth of 1 per cent.　　　　[2] Per cent not shown where base is less than 100.

TABLE **III.**—GENERAL STATISTICS OF THE NEGRO POPULATION OF THE UNITED STATES, BY COUNTIES: 1910—Con.

[Counties in which no Negroes were reported are omitted.]

COUNTY.	Total.	Per cent of total popula- tion.	Color.		Sex.		Males 21 years of age and over.				Persons 10 years of age and over.			Persons 6 to 14 years of age.		
			Black.	Mu- latto.	Male.	Fe- male.	Num- ber.	Per cent of total.	Illiterate.		Total.	Illiterate.		Total.	Attending school.	
									Num- ber.	Per cent.		Num- ber.	Per cent.		Num- ber.	Per cent.

TENNESSEE—Continued.

COUNTY.	Total.	Per cent	Black.	Mulatto.	Male.	Female.	Number.	Per cent	Illit. No.	Illit. %	Total.	Illit. No.	Illit. %	Total.	Att. No.	Att. %
Grundy	143	1.7	116	27	80	63	39	2.1	9	(1)	112	27	24.1	38	29	(1)
Hamblen	1,610	11.8	1,225	385	766	844	367	10.7	140	38.1	1,218	299	24.5	360	294	81.7
Hamilton	26,026	29.2	16,069	9,957	12,868	13,158	7,812	30.8	1,710	21.9	21,198	4,197	19.8	4,120	3,126	75.9
Hancock	481	4.5	105	376	234	247	91	4.0	61	(1)	330	175	53.0	108	59	54.6
Hardeman	10,098	43.9	8,455	1,643	5,070	5,028	2,113	39.4	971	46.0	7,160	2,841	39.7	2,548	1,264	49.6
Hardin	2,170	12.4	1,621	549	1,096	1,074	475	11.6	128	26.9	1,540	365	23.7	529	363	68.6
Hawkins	1,805	7.7	1,174	631	914	891	450	8.4	192	42.7	1,421	462	32.5	413	282	68.3
Haywood	17,710	68.4	12,248	5,462	8,737	8,973	3,726	63.8	1,252	33.6	12,509	3,510	28.1	4,409	1,880	42.6
Henderson	1,918	11.3	1,372	546	957	961	417	10.2	126	30.2	1,369	340	24.8	481	261	54.3
Henry	5,921	23.3	5,065	856	2,971	2,950	1,351	21.2	511	37.8	4,308	1,350	31.3	1,402	858	61.2
Hickman	2,430	14.7	1,774	656	1,230	1,200	551	14.3	203	36.8	1,710	521	30.5	565	329	58.2
Houston	910	14.6	589	321	443	467	210	13.6	43	20.5	674	103	15.3	225	137	60.9
Humphreys	1,201	8.6	1,108	93	603	598	272	8.2	123	45.2	864	316	36.6	285	150	52.6
Jackson	302	2.0	88	214	166	136	65	2.0	31	(1)	217	89	41.0	74	44	(1)
James	492	9.4	313	179	254	238	137	10.7	72	52.6	362	159	43.9	115	81	70.4
Jefferson	1,639	9.2	1,257	382	803	836	382	9.1	160	41.9	1,214	365	30.1	373	263	70.5
Johnson	377	2.9	121	256	191	186	78	2.8	30	(1)	248	68	27.4	97	80	(1)
Knox	12,709	13.5	10,195	2,514	6,128	6,581	3,559	14.4	733	20.6	10,453	1,754	16.8	2,100	1,551	73.9
Lake	3,268	37.5	3,005	263	1,760	1,508	972	41.2	373	38.4	2,512	943	37.5	607	186	30.6
Lauderdale	9,554	45.3	8,184	1,370	4,844	4,710	2,187	42.9	799	36.5	6,913	2,111	30.5	2,259	1,129	50.6
Lawrence	969	5.5	689	280	498	471	226	5.4	98	43.4	702	228	32.5	234	158	67.5
Lewis	854	14.2	595	259	467	387	268	18.1	93	34.7	634	178	28.1	174	108	62.1
Lincoln	5,502	21.2	4,410	1,092	2,731	2,771	1,190	18.9	485	40.8	3,996	1,228	30.7	1,318	837	63.5
Loudon	964	7.1	804	160	482	482	222	7.0	64	28.8	720	143	19.9	231	168	72.7
McMinn	1,892	9.0	1,419	473	942	950	439	9.0	148	33.7	1,400	394	28.1	451	334	74.1
McNairy	1,557	9.7	1,103	454	778	779	321	8.3	114	35.5	1,097	295	26.9	357	211	59.1
Macon	732	5.0	535	197	376	356	161	4.7	60	37.3	513	153	29.8	166	111	66.9
Madison	16,167	41.1	12,595	3,572	7,739	8,428	3,653	36.4	1,052	28.8	11,932	3,015	25.3	3,610	2,212	61.3
Marion	2,289	12.2	1,613	676	1,256	1,033	707	14.8	168	23.8	1,781	379	21.3	391	301	77.0
Marshall	3,414	20.2	2,517	897	1,680	1,734	736	16.6	276	37.5	2,491	728	29.2	819	507	61.9
Maury	16,169	40.0	11,369	4,800	8,046	8,123	4,087	38.2	1,699	41.6	12,159	4,133	34.0	3,414	1,956	57.3
Meigs	566	9.2	324	242	280	286	109	7.9	41	37.6	366	100	27.3	159	131	82.4
Monroe	1,167	5.6	658	509	567	600	246	5.0	82	33.3	834	205	24.6	307	215	70.0
Montgomery	13,430	39.9	9,402	4,028	6,473	6,957	3,067	37.4	1,214	39.6	10,087	2,903	28.8	3,064	2,169	70.8
Moore	334	7.0	293	41	180	154	84	6.9	26	(1)	246	74	30.1	84	46	(1)
Morgan	691	6.0	628	63	653	38	515	16.3	178	34.6	668	232	34.7	13	12	(1)
Obion	5,293	17.7	3,891	1,402	2,631	2,662	1,292	16.6	371	28.7	4,053	930	22.9	1,118	714	63.9
Overton	299	1.9	154	145	155	144	79	2.2	22	(1)	219	50	22.8	55	35	(1)
Perry	633	7.2	448	185	312	321	140	6.8	47	33.6	423	107	25.3	140	55	39.3
Pickett	11	0.2	11	....	5	6	3	0.3	3	(1)	9	5	(1)	2	....	....
Polk	284	2.0	148	136	144	140	87	2.4	45	(1)	219	81	37.0	48	21	(1)
Putnam	892	4.5	488	404	448	444	203	4.5	88	43.3	657	204	31.1	203	135	66.5
Rhea	1,316	8.5	955	361	698	618	331	9.2	107	32.3	972	247	25.4	278	199	71.6
Roane	2,366	10.3	1,200	1,166	1,228	1,138	612	11.3	203	33.2	1,724	416	24.1	532	423	79.5
Robertson	6,492	25.5	4,723	1,769	3,313	3,179	1,598	24.0	756	47.3	4,868	1,593	32.7	1,510	1,065	70.5
Rutherford	11,357	34.2	7,671	3,686	5,496	5,861	2,548	31.5	1,053	41.3	8,487	2,797	33.0	2,519	1,627	64.6
Scott	97	0.7	78	19	75	22	62	2.2	48	(1)	87	64	(1)	10	4	(1)
Sequatchie	139	3.3	75	64	74	65	42	4.3	11	(1)	103	25	24.3	28	20	(1)
Sevier	378	1.7	197	181	199	179	84	1.8	29	(1)	261	69	26.4	96	50	(1)
Shelby	91,719	47.9	72,047	19,672	45,192	46,527	26,964	44.9	5,922	22.0	73,859	15,973	21.6	15,338	9,257	60.4
Smith	2,325	12.5	1,642	683	1,143	1,182	500	11.2	216	43.2	1,636	549	33.6	604	284	47.0
Stewart	1,806	12.2	1,527	279	901	905	390	11.3	194	49.7	1,256	445	35.4	422	285	67.5
Sullivan	1,535	5.5	928	607	738	797	401	5.9	122	30.4	1,209	309	25.6	284	198	69.7
Sumner	5,386	21.0	4,370	1,016	2,648	2,738	1,212	18.4	556	45.9	4,049	1,368	33.8	1,307	734	56.2
Tipton	13,353	45.3	10,639	2,714	6,864	6,489	3,069	43.5	1,271	41.4	9,540	3,254	34.1	3,237	1,638	50.6
Trousdale	1,781	30.3	1,406	375	883	898	381	26.3	183	48.0	1,297	413	31.8	433	263	60.7
Unicoi	131	1.8	93	38	85	46	59	3.5	20	(1)	111	40	36.0	17	....	....
Union	30	0.3	5	25	14	16	5	0.2	2	(1)	22	10	(1)	9	1	(1)
Van Buren	48	1.7	48	....	27	21	12	1.9	6	(1)	33	10	(1)	15	15	(1)
Warren	1,949	11.8	1,190	759	979	970	464	11.1	175	37.7	1,463	453	31.0	447	328	73.4
Washington	2,267	7.8	1,553	714	1,118	1,149	632	7.3	217	34.3	1,778	467	26.3	444	348	78.4
Wayne	845	7.0	603	242	412	433	205	7.3	71	34.6	631	183	29.0	189	142	75.1
Weakley	3,470	10.9	2,642	828	1,744	1,726	834	10.2	288	34.5	2,583	657	25.4	756	485	64.2
White	899	5.8	487	412	460	439	229	6.3	111	48.5	674	252	37.4	186	89	47.8
Williamson	7,828	32.3	6,390	1,438	3,880	3,948	1,747	29.3	897	51.3	5,832	2,265	38.8	1,858	1,010	54.4
Wilson	6,303	24.8	4,329	1,974	3,053	3,250	1,462	21.9	596	40.8	4,708	1,515	32.2	1,424	742	52.1

TEXAS.

COUNTY.	Total.	Per cent	Black.	Mulatto.	Male.	Female.	Number.	Per cent	Illit. No.	Illit. %	Total.	Illit. No.	Illit. %	Total.	Att. No.	Att. %
Total	690,049	17.7	565,354	124,695	344,941	345,108	166,398	16.6	49,699	29.9	507,089	124,618	24.6	159,597	103,014	64.5
Anderson	11,323	38.2	9,893	1,430	5,515	5,808	2,550	35.2	827	32.4	8,240	2,184	26.5	2,689	1,483	55.2
Andrews	1	0.1	....	1	....	1	....	....	....	....	1	....	....	....	....	....
Angelina	2,435	13.8	2,195	240	1,277	1,158	688	15.6	216	31.4	1,811	509	28.1	531	338	63.7
Aransas	136	6.5	97	39	70	66	38	6.0	10	(1)	115	21	18.3	21	12	(1)
Archer	3	(2)	....	3	3	....	3	0.2	1	(1)	3	1	(1)	....	....	....

¹ Per cent not shown where base is less than 100.   ² Less than one-tenth of 1 per cent.

TABLE **III.**—GENERAL STATISTICS OF THE NEGRO POPULATION OF THE UNITED STATES, BY COUNTIES: 1910—Con.

[Counties in which no Negroes were reported are omitted.]

	NEGRO POPULATION: 1910.															
			Color.		Sex.		Males 21 years of age and over.				Persons 10 years of age and over.			Persons 6 to 14 years of age.		
COUNTY.	Total.	Per cent of total popula-tion.	Black.	Mu-latto.	Male.	Fe-male.	Num-ber.	Per cent of total.	Illiterate.		Total.	Illiterate.		Total.	Attending school.	
									Num-ber.	Per cent.		Num-ber.	Per cent.		Num-ber.	Per cent.
TEXAS—Continued.																
Atascosa	228	2.3	197	31	121	107	56	2.3	21	(1)	161	49	30.4	65	47	(1)
Austin	5,018	28.4	4,309	709	2,426	2,592	1,068	25.2	412	38.6	3,556	991	27.9	1,320	835	63.3
Bandera	34	0.7	32	2	19	15	8	0.7	1	(1)	27	6	(1)	10	6	(1)
Bastrop	9,428	37.2	8,693	735	4,665	4,763	1,999	22.0	667	33.4	6,726	1,625	24.2	2,413	1,693	70.2
Baylor	3	(2)		3		1	2	1	(2)			3				
Bee	568	4.7	474	94	281	287	125	4.2	25	20.0	416	87	20.9	130	63	48.5
Bell	6,302	12.8	5,115	1,187	3,190	3,112	1,634	13.1	346	21.2	4,754	898	18.9	1,302	794	61.0
Bexar	11,642	9.7	8,889	2,753	5,391	6,251	3,132	14.0	437	14.0	9,572	1,298	13.6	1,953	1,369	70.1
Blanco	350	8.1	197	153	170	180	74	6.9	31	(1)	250	87	34.8	87	41	(1)
Bosque	848	4.5	662	186	447	401	189	4.0	43	22.8	619	113	18.3	219	157	71.7
Bowie	12,734	36.6	10,340	2,394	6,263	6,471	2,965	34.1	985	33.2	9,211	2,594	28.2	3,016	1,795	59.5
Brazoria	6,237	46.9	5,008	1,229	3,481	2,756	1,809	43.9	711	39.3	4,721	1,601	33.9	1,420	884	62.3
Brazos	8,827	46.7	7,748	1,079	4,369	4,458	2,229	46.2	851	38.2	6,525	1,891	29.0	1,991	1,381	69.4
Brewster	71	1.4	38	33	37	34	21	1.6	3	(1)	56	10	(1)	15	5	(1)
Brown	525	2.3	386	139	251	274	141	2.5	25	17.7	403	83	20.6	106	74	69.8
Burleson	8,587	46.0	6,366	2,221	4,392	4,195	2,127	45.0	762	35.8	6,273	1,648	26.3	1,979	1,330	67.2
Burnet	292	2.7	196	96	155	137	68	2.6	28	(1)	211	54	25.6	63	49	(1)
Caldwell	5,378	22.2	4,081	1,297	2,647	2,731	1,103	19.2	344	31.2	3,739	892	23.9	1,373	908	66.1
Calhoun	491	13.5	286	205	245	246	127	12.3	22	17.3	361	47	13.0	110	86	78.2
Callahan	4	(2)	2	2	1	3	1	(2)			4			1		
Cameron	74	0.3	67	7	40	34	27	0.4	6	(1)	63	15	(1)	5	2	(1)
Camp	4,415	46.2	2,758	1,657	2,192	2,223	879	41.3	356	40.5	3,054	883	28.9	1,231	804	65.3
Cass	9,952	36.1	6,137	3,815	4,957	4,995	1,961	32.0	800	40.8	6,667	2,097	31.5	2,716	1,749	64.4
Chambers	1,032	24.4	797	235	551	481	276	23.2	76	27.5	766	156	20.4	233	146	62.7
Cherokee	7,641	26.3	6,914	727	3,909	3,732	1,664	23.8	552	33.2	5,328	1,370	25.7	2,004	1,254	62.6
Clay	101	0.6	48	53	61	40	32	0.8	9	(1)	84	20	(1)	16	7	(1)
Coleman	253	1.1	214	39	164	89	118	2.1	18	15.3	228	33	14.5	18	11	(1)
Collin	2,206	4.5	1,685	521	1,133	1,073	587	5.0	179	30.5	1,686	423	25.1	467	302	64.7
Collingsworth	3	0.1	2	1	1	2	1	0.1	1	(1)	2	1	(1)			
Colorado	7,074	37.4	5,986	1,088	3,478	3,596	1,601	33.5	638	39.9	5,239	1,581	30.2	1,792	1,269	70.3
Comal	232	2.8	219	13	117	115	63	2.6	11	(1)	174	26	14.9	43	27	(1)
Comanche	12	(2)	2	10	6	6	5	0.1	1	(1)	8	3	(1)	2	1	(1)
Concho	7	0.1	7		6	1	5	0.3	2	(1)	6	2	(1)			
Cooke	1,688	6.3	1,423	265	830	858	457	6.8	105	23.0	1,357	252	18.6	323	238	73.7
Coryell	488	2.2	387	101	269	219	104	2.0	13	12.5	376	29	7.7	115	70	60.9
Cottle	1	(2)	1		1		1	0.1			1					
Crockett	4	0.3	4		4		3	0.7	2	(1)	4	3	(1)			
Dallam	6	0.1	6		3	3	3	0.2			6			1	1	(1)
Dallas	24,355	17.9	20,828	3,527	12,100	12,255	7,560	18.3	1,387	18.3	20,048	3,539	17.7	3,840	2,634	68.6
Dawson	2	0.1	2			2	2	0.4			2					
De Witt	4,753	20.2	4,015	738	2,236	2,517	1,020	18.3	292	28.6	3,544	789	22.3	1,188	775	65.2
Deaf Smith	68	1.7	55	13	55	13	30	2.7	4	(1)	59	6	(1)	10	7	(1)
Delta	809	5.6	672	137	418	391	173	5.2	47	27.2	569	119	20.9	203	146	71.9
Denton	2,210	7.1	1,407	803	1,115	1,095	540	7.0	192	35.6	1,627	402	24.7	524	332	63.4
Dickens	2	0.1	2			2					2					
Dimmit	29	0.8	7	22	12	17	6	0.6	1	(1)	20	6	(1)	7	2	(1)
Donley	38	0.7	27	11	15	23	8	0.6	1	(1)	30	4	(1)	7	2	(1)
Duval	8	0.1	7	1	2	6	2	0.1	1	(1)	5	1	(1)			
Eastland	57	0.2	52	5	27	30	18	0.3	2	(1)	47	8	(1)	8	2	(1)
Edwards	4	0.1	1	3	4		2	0.2			4	1	(1)	1	1	(1)
El Paso	1,562	3.0	1,196	366	768	794	526	3.4	48	9.1	1,315	123	9.4	203	143	70.4
Ellis	9,623	17.9	7,554	2,069	4,940	4,683	2,428	18.4	591	24.3	7,053	1,476	20.9	2,138	1,289	60.3
Erath	589	1.8	498	91	318	271	186	2.4	52	28.0	465	98	21.1	111	82	73.9
Falls	12,612	35.4	11,509	1,103	6,267	6,345	2,842	33.9	866	30.5	9,077	2,180	24.0	3,091	1,843	59.6
Fannin	5,366	12.0	4,500	866	2,738	2,628	1,301	11.9	446	34.3	3,964	1,020	25.7	1,232	852	69.2
Fayette	7,361	24.7	6,012	1,349	3,655	3,706	1,521	21.7	469	30.8	5,161	1,186	23.0	1,884	1,292	68.6
Fisher	9	0.1	5	4	7	2	2	0.1	1	(1)	7	3	(1)	4	1	(1)
Foard	6	0.1	6		2	4	2	0.1			5	1	(1)			
Fort Bend	11,422	62.9	9,884	1,538	6,266	5,156	3,433	62.7	1,816	52.9	8,748	3,668	41.9	2,473	1,417	57.3
Franklin	735	7.9	444	291	378	357	180	8.4	83	46.1	541	210	38.8	175	124	70.9
Freestone	8,772	42.7	7,846	926	4,344	4,428	1,875	38.1	538	28.7	6,088	1,456	23.9	2,237	1,544	69.0
Frio	151	1.7	146	5	85	66	36	1.6	6	(1)	114	10	8.8	38	28	(1)
Galveston	8,747	19.7	5,187	3,560	4,270	4,477	2,872	18.6	365	12.7	7,441	972	13.1	1,221	914	74.9
Garza	36	1.8	36		27	9	20	2.6	8	(1)	34	15	(1)			
Gillespie	116	1.2	66	50	64	52	31	1.3	7	(1)	86	24	(1)	25	14	(1)
Glasscock	5	0.4	5		4	1	2	0.7			3			2		
Goliad	1,501	15.1	1,339	162	738	763	335	14.1	80	23.9	1,070	232	21.7	371	236	63.6
Gonzales	8,212	29.3	6,806	1,406	4,125	4,087	1,677	25.9	614	36.6	5,707	1,504	26.4	2,149	1,485	69.1
Gray	2	0.1	1	1	2		2	0.2			2					
Grayson	7,753	11.7	6,347	1,406	3,859	3,894	2,123	12.0	581	27.4	6,070	1,373	22.6	1,547	1,153	74.5
Gregg	7,781	55.0	5,331	2,450	3,770	4,011	1,700	49.6	572	33.6	5,597	1,532	27.4	1,932	1,368	70.8
Grimes	9,858	46.5	9,252	606	4,802	5,056	2,118	43.2	897	42.4	7,048	2,212	31.4	2,540	1,471	57.9
Guadalupe	5,681	22.8	5,099	582	2,829	2,852	1,163	19.4	394	33.9	3,960	920	23.2	1,486	1,048	70.5
Hale	5	0.1	5		3	2	2	0.1	1	(1)	5	1	(1)	1	1	(1)
Hall	2	(2)	2		2		2	0.1			2					

[1] Per cent not shown where base is less than 100.   [2] Less than one-tenth of 1 per cent.

TABLE III.—GENERAL STATISTICS OF THE NEGRO POPULATION OF THE UNITED STATES, BY COUNTIES: 1910—Con.

[Counties in which no Negroes were reported are omitted.]

NEGRO POPULATION: 1910.

TEXAS—Continued.

COUNTY	Total	Per cent of total population	Black	Mulatto	Male	Female	Males 21+ Number	Males 21+ Per cent of total	Males 21+ Illiterate Number	Males 21+ Illiterate Per cent	Persons 10+ Total	Persons 10+ Illiterate Number	Persons 10+ Illiterate Per cent	Persons 6–14 Total	Persons 6–14 Attending Number	Persons 6–14 Attending Per cent
Hamilton	8	0.1	8		3	5	2	0.1	2	(1)	8	5	(1)	7	2	(1)
Hardeman	40	0.4	27	13	25	15	15	0.5	1	(1)	32	5	(1)	5		
Hardin	2,550	19.7	2,037	513	1,439	1,111	882	22.5	193	21.9	2,023	399	19.7	446	328	73.5
Harris	30,950	26.8	26,180	4,770	14,935	16,015	9,270	25.2	1,719	18.5	25,553	4,610	18.0	5,045	3,546	70.3
Harrison	23,698	63.6	18,674	5,024	11,554	12,144	4,851	56.5	1,791	36.9	16,709	4,647	27.8	6,189	3,987	64.4
Hartley	3	0.2	3	1	1	2	1	0.3	1	(1)	3	1	(1)	1		
Haskell	84	0.5	75	9	56	28	43	1.1	10	(1)	77	17	(1)	5	2	(1)
Hays	2,165	14.0	1,416	749	1,029	1,136	438	11.5	91	20.8	1,618	310	19.2	532	327	61.5
Henderson	4,177	20.7	3,476	701	2,150	2,027	910	19.3	316	34.7	2,926	777	26.6	1,081	773	71.5
Hidalgo	62	0.5	12	50	33	29	15	0.4	6	(1)	45	12	(1)	20	11	(1)
Hill	4,856	10.4	3,797	1,059	2,450	2,406	1,229	10.9	351	28.6	3,583	893	24.9	1,077	585	54.3
Hood	212	2.1	171	41	103	109	65	2.7	26	(1)	159	58	36.5	34	17	(1)
Hopkins	3,283	10.6	2,879	404	1,670	1,613	688	9.6	278	40.4	2,324	720	31.0	846	538	63.6
Houston	12,548	42.4	10,325	2,223	6,347	6,201	2,631	38.7	678	25.8	8,529	1,839	21.6	3,201	1,779	55.6
Howard	4	(2)	2	2	3	1	2	0.1			4			1		
Hunt	4,579	9.5	3,559	1,020	2,245	2,334	1,030	8.9	325	31.6	3,360	839	25.0	1,106	716	64.7
Hutchinson	1	0.1	1			1					1	1	(1)	1	1	(1)
Irion	1	0.1	1		1						1	1	(1)	1	1	(1)
Jack	118	1.0	111	7	58	60	27	0.9	6	(1)	81	8	(1)	31	27	(1)
Jackson	2,114	32.7	1,260	854	1,020	1,094	439	26.4	151	34.4	1,504	369	24.5	561	344	61.3
Jasper	4,731	33.8	3,693	1,038	2,520	2,211	1,222	32.6	393	32.2	3,418	912	26.7	1,060	657	62.0
Jeff Davis	47	2.8	12	35	29	18	19	4.3	1	(1)	35	1	(1)	7	5	(1)
Jefferson	10,676	28.0	9,144	1,532	5,551	5,125	3,525	26.8	594	16.9	8,701	1,521	17.5	1,619	1,205	74.4
Johnson	1,637	4.8	1,276	361	787	850	407	4.8	83	20.4	1,257	235	18.7	342	214	62.6
Jones	259	1.1	200	59	146	113	104	1.7	19	18.3	224	65	29.0	35	9	(1)
Karnes	793	5.3	650	143	389	404	178	5.0	53	29.8	582	141	24.2	192	116	60.4
Kaufman	8,374	23.7	5,945	2,429	4,233	4,141	2,001	21.9	672	33.6	6,142	1,685	27.4	2,057	1,213	59.0
Kendall	253	5.6	241	12	112	141	62	5.0	9	(1)	177	19	10.7	57	31	(1)
Kent	1	(2)	1			1					1			1	1	(1)
Kerr	248	4.5	127	121	131	117	53	3.7	16	(1)	165	32	19.4	76	60	(1)
King	8	1.0	8		7	1	4	1.8	2	(1)	8	3	(1)			
Kinney	158	4.6	87	71	73	85	28	2.5	3	(1)	114	18	15.8	30	14	(1)
Knox	17	0.2	17		13	4	7	0.3	3	(1)	17	7	(1)	2	1	(1)
La Salle	93	2.0	93		47	46	21	1.7	6	(1)	75	16	(1)	23	15	(1)
Lamar	10,993	23.6	8,262	2,731	5,420	5,573	2,447	21.8	824	33.7	7,812	2,198	28.1	2,794	1,635	58.5
Lamb	1	0.2	1			1								1		
Lampasas	436	4.6	315	121	214	222	121	4.9	52	43.0	349	115	33.0	90	71	(1)
Lavaca	4,384	16.6	3,518	866	2,163	2,221	868	14.1	294	33.9	3,062	737	24.1	1,207	855	70.8
Lee	4,039	30.8	3,315	724	2,001	2,038	862	29.2	238	27.6	2,793	605	21.7	998	715	71.6
Leon	6,878	41.5	6,089	789	3,512	3,366	1,413	37.3	607	43.0	4,678	1,470	31.4	1,889	1,261	66.8
Liberty	3,401	31.8	2,669	732	1,827	1,574	961	30.7	436	45.4	2,549	1,017	39.9	709	389	54.9
Limestone	9,247	26.7	7,835	1,412	4,858	4,389	2,271	27.6	524	23.1	6,684	1,426	21.3	2,177	1,242	57.1
Lipscomb	3	0.1	3		1	2					2			1		
Live Oak	36	1.0	30	6	21	15	10	1.1	1	(1)	23	3	(1)	6	2	(1)
Llano	62	1.0	20	42	35	27	20	1.2	7	(1)	46	21	(1)	9		
Loving	1	0.4	1			1	1	(1)			1					
Lubbock	5	0.1	5		4	1	1	(1)			2			1	1	(1)
McCulloch	189	1.4	173	16	108	81	76	2.3	19	(1)	159	44	27.7	19	4	(1)
McLennan	17,234	23.5	15,041	2,193	8,492	8,742	4,335	23.0	1,015	23.4	13,124	2,563	19.5	3,753	2,437	64.9
McMullen	58	5.3	31	27	29	29	17	5.4	9	(1)	42	15	(1)	9	5	(1)
Madison	2,757	26.7	2,542	215	1,378	1,379	545	22.9	223	40.9	1,873	572	30.5	732	422	57.7
Marion	6,725	64.2	5,486	1,239	3,299	3,426	1,418	58.1	430	30.3	4,684	1,152	24.6	1,655	1,168	70.6
Martin	1	0.1	1								1			1		
Mason	70	1.2	69	1	35	35	9	0.6	1	(1)	46	7	(1)	27	18	(1)
Matagorda	4,457	32.8	2,887	1,570	2,311	2,146	1,092	27.9	316	28.9	3,315	740	22.3	1,035	777	75.1
Maverick	96	1.9	82	14	51	45	29	2.2	5	(1)	72	16	(1)	21	12	(1)
Medina	449	3.3	428	21	227	222	105	3.2	28	26.7	331	76	23.0	112	69	61.6
Menard	24	0.9	21	3	15	9	8	1.2	2	(1)	14	4	(1)	4	2	(1)
Midland	26	0.8	17	9	8	18	8	0.9	1	(1)	25	1	(1)	5	1	(1)
Milam	9,485	25.8	7,922	1,563	4,706	4,779	2,128	23.9	666	31.3	6,687	1,615	24.2	2,317	1,546	66.7
Mills	7	0.1	6	1	5	2	3	0.1	1	(1)	7	2	(1)	2	1	(1)
Mitchell	192	2.1	113	79	97	95	47	2.2	13	(1)	155	27	17.4	38	30	(1)
Montague	27	0.1	27		11	16	6	0.1	3	(1)	13	4	(1)	6	4	(1)
Montgomery	7,104	45.3	6,424	680	3,530	3,574	1,608	41.5	614	38.2	5,023	1,531	30.5	1,778	1,118	62.9
Morris	3,706	35.5	3,186	520	1,847	1,859	731	30.7	221	30.2	2,493	627	25.2	991	615	62.1
Nacogdoches	7,030	25.7	5,629	1,401	3,512	3,518	1,422	22.8	597	35.7	4,770	1,426	29.9	1,871	1,175	62.8
Navarro	10,968	23.3	8,811	2,157	5,605	5,363	2,593	22.6	754	29.1	8,093	1,975	24.4	2,651	1,599	60.3
Newton	3,864	35.6	3,409	455	2,008	1,856	912	31.7	201	22.0	2,606	525	20.1	925	521	56.3
Nolan	111	0.9	105	6	70	41	48	1.4	5	(1)	90	12	(1)	16	7	(1)
Nueces	742	3.4	630	112	370	372	233	3.9	29	12.4	585	79	13.5	110	73	66.4
Orange	1,898	19.9	1,556	342	1,015	883	629	22.6	173	27.5	1,500	370	24.7	341	237	69.5
Palo Pinto	528	2.7	501	27	248	280	167	3.4	19	11.4	446	60	13.5	57	41	(1)
Panola	8,842	43.3	7,402	1,440	4,354	4,488	1,670	38.1	630	37.7	5,868	1,713	29.2	2,452	1,622	66.2
Parker	693	2.6	320	373	335	358	151	2.4	28	18.5	526	73	13.9	175	120	68.6
Pecos	2	0.1			1	1		0.2			2			1		

[1] Per cent not shown where base is less than 100.   [2] Less than one-tenth of 1 per cent.

TABLE III.—GENERAL STATISTICS OF THE NEGRO POPULATION OF THE UNITED STATES, BY COUNTIES: 1910—Con.

[Counties in which no Negroes were reported are omitted.]

COUNTY.	Total.	Per cent of total population.	Color.		Sex.		Males 21 years of age and over.				Persons 10 years of age and over.			Persons 6 to 14 years of age.		
			Black.	Mulatto.	Male.	Female.	Number.	Per cent of total.	Illiterate. Number.	Illiterate. Per cent.	Total.	Illiterate. Number.	Illiterate. Per cent.	Total.	Attending school. Number.	Attending school. Per cent.
TEXAS—Continued.																
Polk	6,594	37.8	5,146	1,448	3,408	3,186	1,594	36.5	558	35.0	4,735	1,435	30.3	1,626	1,026	63.1
Potter	149	1.2	137	12	69	80	57	1.3	9	(1)	136	26	19.1	7		
Presidio	31	0.6	22	9	27	4	14	1.2	2	(1)	27	4	(1)	6	3	(1)
Rains	616	9.1	562	54	321	295	135	8.7	58	43.0	435	122	28.0	152	122	80.3
Reagan	2	0.5	2			2					2					
Red River	8,673	30.4	6,380	2,293	4,359	4,314	1,859	28.1	696	37.4	6,008	1,699	28.3	2,300	1,513	65.8
Reeves	82	1.9	82		51	31	35	2.6	12	(1)	71	21	(1)	6	3	(1)
Refugio	481	17.1	357	124	234	247	112	15.6	50	44.6	341	119	34.9	112	45	40.2
Roberts	3	0.3	3		1	2	1	0.4			3			1	1	(1)
Robertson	14,571	53.1	12,599	1,972	7,260	7,311	3,495	52.1	1,341	38.4	10,758	3,269	30.4	3,403	2,350	69.1
Rockwall	731	9.1	598	133	397	334	223	11.0	96	43.0	559	204	36.5	131	52	39.7
Runnels	133	0.6	67	66	67	66	49	1.0	6	(1)	110	19	17.3	18	7	(1)
Rusk	11,314	42.0	9,772	1,542	5,641	5,673	2,231	37.7	848	38.0	7,616	2,119	27.8	3,117	2,164	69.4
Sabine	1,679	19.6	1,237	442	849	830	326	16.6	92	28.2	1,094	279	25.5	444	245	55.2
San Augustine	3,453	30.7	3,103	350	1,732	1,721	688	27.2	307	44.6	2,315	789	34.1	920	573	62.3
San Jacinto	5,193	54.4	4,176	1,017	2,585	2,608	1,103	51.1	205	18.6	3,612	586	16.2	1,381	698	50.5
San Patricio	79	1.1	72	7	48	31	26	1.2	8	(1)	62	18	(1)	15	1	(1)
San Saba	103	0.9	92	11	48	55	27	1.0	4	(1)	73	15	(1)	19	7	(1)
Schleicher	44	2.3	44		30	14	28	4.9	5	(1)	41	10	(1)			
Scurry	1	(2)	1			1										
Shackelford	126	3.0	61	65	67	59	38	3.6	6	(1)	95	17	(1)	27	15	(1)
Shelby	5,274	20.0	4,181	1,093	2,649	2,625	1,046	17.7	419	40.1	3,588	1,113	31.0	1,425	890	62.5
Sherman	2	0.1	2		2						2					
Smith	17,246	41.3	14,169	3,077	8,426	8,820	3,574	36.5	1,246	34.9	12,051	3,204	26.6	4,464	2,774	62.1
Somervell	1	(2)	1			1					1					
Starr	21	0.2	19	2	13	8	7	0.2			18	1	(1)	4		
Stephens	4	0.1	4		1	3	1	0.1			4			1	1	(1)
Sterling	1	0.1	1		1		1	0.2			1					
Stonewall	3	0.1	3		3						1			2	1	(1)
Sutton	3	0.2	3		3		2	0.5			3					
Tarrant	15,418	14.2	12,868	2,550	7,899	7,519	5,116	14.9	685	13.4	12,646	1,686	13.3	2,388	1,552	65.0
Taylor	639	2.4	538	101	328	311	206	3.1	33	16.0	548	78	14.2	114	84	73.7
Terrell	4	0.3	4		3	1	3	0.6	1	(1)	4	2	(1)			
Terry	1	0.1	1			1					1					
Throckmorton	11	0.2	11		4	7	2	0.2	1	(1)	8	4	(1)	3		
Titus	3,118	19.0	2,639	479	1,639	1,479	805	19.6	297	36.9	2,213	768	34.7	725	408	56.3
Tom Green	716	4.0	410	306	349	367	242	4.8	55	22.7	615	105	17.1	101	53	52.5
Travis	15,473	27.8	13,031	2,442	7,351	8,122	3,652	24.5	986	27.0	11,719	2,468	21.1	3,486	2,377	68.2
Trinity	3,195	25.0	2,557	638	1,621	1,574	784	25.6	182	23.2	2,277	432	19.0	806	478	59.3
Tyler	2,207	21.5	1,593	614	1,121	1,086	487	20.2	170	34.9	1,521	448	29.5	584	360	61.6
Upshur	5,649	28.3	5,048	601	2,794	2,855	1,100	24.2	435	39.5	3,835	1,232	32.1	1,530	946	61.8
Upton	12	2.4	12		6	6	4	2.5	4	(1)	8	6	(1)	2		
Uvalde	262	2.3	251	11	126	136	56	2.0	11	(1)	183	25	13.7	63	26	(1)
Val Verde	153	1.8	96	57	72	81	40	1.7	7	(1)	122	24	19.7	31	20	(1)
Van Zandt	1,534	6.0	1,251	283	796	738	350	5.9	103	29.4	1,072	234	21.8	383	243	63.4
Victoria	3,600	24.0	2,862	738	1,742	1,858	820	21.3	320	39.0	2,675	788	29.5	847	532	62.8
Walker	8,362	52.1	7,394	968	4,192	4,170	1,834	45.5	652	35.6	5,881	1,584	26.9	2,116	1,271	60.1
Waller	6,712	55.3	5,941	771	3,311	3,401	1,520	51.0	577	38.0	4,881	1,572	32.2	1,632	938	57.5
Ward	3	0.1	1	2	1	2	1	0.2			3	1	(1)			
Washington	12,017	47.0	10,375	1,642	5,750	6,267	2,583	44.3	865	33.5	8,661	2,035	23.5	2,964	2,313	78.0
Webb	38	0.2	19	19	17	21	11	0.2	2	(1)	32	6	(1)	10	9	(1)
Wharton	8,889	42.1	5,787	3,102	4,563	4,326	2,188	38.7	775	35.4	6,615	1,852	28.0	2,048	1,354	66.1
Wheeler	2	(2)	2		2						2					
Wichita	612	3.8	367	245	327	285	232	4.9	35	15.1	506	79	15.6	100	71	71.0
Wilbarger	70	0.6	63	7	39	31	31	1.0	7	(1)	65	15	(1)	6	1	(1)
Williamson	7,370	17.5	6,215	1,155	3,820	3,550	1,764	16.8	554	31.4	5,373	1,502	28.0	1,718	936	54.5
Wilson	956	5.6	895	61	468	488	184	4.5	61	33.2	670	148	22.1	281	189	67.3
Winkler	1	0.2		1	1		1	0.7			1					
Wise	67	0.3	54	13	33	34	17	0.3	3	(1)	58	11	(1)	13	9	(1)
Wood	3,926	16.8	3,762	164	2,002	1,924	875	16.0	317	36.2	2,795	781	27.9	972	608	62.6
Young	3	(2)	3			3					3					
Zavalla	1	0.1		1		1					1	1	(1)			
UTAH.																
Total	1,144	0.3	854	290	691	453	568	0.5	26	4.6	1,026	49	4.8	106	86	81.1
Beaver	13	0.3	13		9	4	6	0.4	2	(1)	10	4	(1)	1		
Box Elder	7	0.1	5	2	7		6	0.2			7					
Cache	7	(2)		7	5	2					5			2	2	(1)
Carbon	6	0.1	5	1	5	1	5	0.1			6					
Emery	1	(2)	1		1		1	0.1			1					

1 Per cent not shown where base is less than 100.　　2 Less than one-tenth of 1 per cent.

TABLE III.—GENERAL STATISTICS OF THE NEGRO POPULATION OF THE UNITED STATES, BY COUNTIES: 1910—Con.

[Counties in which no Negroes were reported are omitted.]

COUNTY.	NEGRO POPULATION: 1910.															
	Total.	Per cent of total population.	Color.		Sex.		Males 21 years of age and over.				Persons 10 years of age and over.			Persons 6 to 14 years of age.		
			Black.	Mulatto.	Male.	Female.	Number.	Per cent of total.	Illiterate.		Total.	Illiterate.		Total.	Attending school.	
									Number.	Per cent.		Number.	Per cent.		Number.	Per cent.

UTAH—Continued.

COUNTY.	Total.	Per cent	Black.	Mulatto.	Male.	Female.	Number.	Per cent	Number.	Per cent.	Total.	Number.	Per cent.	Total.	Number.	Per cent.
Grand	1	0.1		1	1		1	0.2			1					
Iron	2	0.1	1	1	1	1	1	0.1			2					
Juab	4	(1)	2	2	3	1	3	0.1			4					
Millard	22	0.4	22		14	8	10	0.7			19			6	6	(2)
Piute	1	0.1	1		1		1	0.3			1					
Salt Lake	827	0.6	611	216	479	348	392	0.9	19	4.8	741	35	4.7	75	61	(2)
San Juan	17	0.7	17		17		17	2.7	3	(2)	17	3	(2)			
Sanpete	18	0.1	17	1	12	6	5	0.1			12			3		
Summit	1	(1)	1			1					1					
Tooele	7	0.1	7		6	1	5	0.2			7			1	1	(2)
Uinta	3	(1)	2	1	3		3	0.2	1	(2)	3	1	(2)			
Utah	2	(1)	2			2					1	1	(2)			
Wasatch	1	(1)	1		1		1	(1)			1					
Weber	204	0.6	146	58	126	78	111	1.1	1	0.9	187	5	2.7	18	16	(2)

VERMONT.

COUNTY.	Total.	Per cent	Black.	Mulatto.	Male.	Female.	Number.	Per cent	Number.	Per cent.	Total.	Number.	Per cent.	Total.	Number.	Per cent.
Total	1,621	0.5	1,185	436	1,173	448	975	0.9	38	3.9	1,446	69	4.8	129	113	87.6
Addison	45	0.2	22	23	22	23	12	0.2	4	(2)	32	6	(2)	9	8	(2)
Bennington	92	0.4	49	43	46	46	28	0.4	6	(2)	72	12	(2)	17	16	(2)
Caledonia	10	(1)	4	6	4	6	2	(1)			6			1	1	(2)
Chittenden	1,114	2.6	908	206	898	216	804	6.4	3	0.4	1,043	11	1.1	45	37	(2)
Essex	5	0.1	5		4	1	3	0.1			5			1	1	(2)
Franklin	59	0.2	36	23	34	25	21	0.2	4	(2)	46	8	(2)	13	13	(2)
Lamoille	3	(1)	1	2	3		3	0.1			3					
Orange	12	0.1	4	8	8	4	7	0.1	2	(2)	11	2	(2)			
Orleans	20	0.1	7	13	13	7	6	0.1			13			4	4	(2)
Rutland	108	0.2	61	47	67	41	40	0.3	6	(2)	86	12	(2)	17	14	(2)
Washington	41	0.1	29	12	19	22	15	0.1	4	(2)	34	5	(2)	5	5	(2)
Windham	45	0.2	26	19	25	20	16	0.2	4	(2)	39	5	(2)	5	4	(2)
Windsor	67	0.2	33	34	30	37	18	0.2	5	(2)	56	8	(2)	12	10	(2)

VIRGINIA.

COUNTY.	Total.	Per cent	Black.	Mulatto.	Male.	Female.	Number.	Per cent	Number.	Per cent.	Total.	Number.	Per cent.	Total.	Number.	Per cent.
Total	671,096	32.6	488,186	222,910	330,542	340,554	159,593	30.5	57,867	36.3	496,418	148,950	30.0	153,827	90,367	58.7
Accomac	13,273	36.2	10,619	2,654	6,728	6,545	2,811	30.2	1,211	43.1	9,166	3,137	34.2	3,606	1,974	54.7
Albemarle	9,673	32.4	6,685	2,988	4,663	5,010	2,073	29.8	893	43.1	7,066	2,279	32.3	2,502	1,575	62.9
Alexandria	2,645	25.9	2,470	175	1,366	1,279	806	23.1	182	22.6	2,125	415	19.5	502	363	72.3
Alexandria city	4,188	27.3	2,556	1,632	1,970	2,218	1,246	26.8	213	17.1	3,481	628	18.0	658	457	69.5
Alleghany	2,945	20.8	2,351	594	1,660	1,285	911	23.7	322	35.3	2,262	640	28.3	593	399	67.3
Amelia	5,490	63.0	4,264	1,226	2,832	2,658	1,264	58.4	586	46.4	3,978	1,493	37.5	1,445	804	55.6
Amherst	7,465	39.4	5,606	1,859	3,743	3,722	1,581	36.1	818	51.7	5,176	2,186	42.2	1,969	919	46.7
Appomattox	3,089	34.7	2,074	1,015	1,503	1,586	630	30.9	160	25.4	2,202	441	20.0	845	221	26.2
Augusta	4,541	14.0	3,294	1,247	2,245	2,296	1,129	13.8	426	37.7	3,384	933	27.6	1,044	602	57.7
Bath	1,176	18.0	900	276	695	481	403	22.2	83	20.6	944	206	21.8	211	100	47.4
Bedford	8,455	28.6	5,810	2,645	4,209	4,246	1,791	25.8	904	50.5	6,049	2,228	36.8	2,221	1,317	59.3
Bland	133	2.6	61	72	69	64	29	2.3	17		93	32	(2)	39	22	(2)
Botetourt	3,495	19.7	2,128	1,367	1,768	1,727	821	19.2	262	31.9	2,550	607	23.8	819	480	58.6
Bristol city	1,144	18.3	978	166	537	607	304	18.0	72	23.7	904	190	21.0	221	154	69.7
Brunswick	11,366	59.1	6,659	4,707	5,817	5,549	2,479	54.4	989	39.9	7,824	2,272	29.0	2,948	1,853	62.9
Buchanan	4	(1)	2	2	1	3					4	1	(2)	2	1	(2)
Buckingham	7,570	49.8	5,087	2,483	3,689	3,881	1,621	45.4	675	41.6	5,446	1,796	33.0	1,982	842	42.5
Buena Vista city	416	12.8	374	42	188	228	89	11.8	25		311	71	22.8	83	48	(2)
Campbell	9,002	39.1	5,182	3,820	4,385	4,617	1,879	35.5	886	47.2	6,286	2,243	35.7	2,407	1,476	61.3
Caroline	8,750	52.7	4,792	3,958	4,436	4,314	1,785	47.1	834	46.7	6,132	2,181	35.6	2,324	1,288	55.4
Carroll	268	1.3	177	91	129	139	46	1.0	18	(2)	184	66	35.9	64	22	(2)
Charles City	3,765	71.7	1,861	1,904	1,948	1,817	844	64.7	336	39.8	2,614	773	29.6	963	527	54.7
Charlotte	8,335	52.8	4,785	3,550	4,068	4,267	1,696	47.0	843	49.7	5,900	2,070	35.1	2,206	1,389	63.0
Charlottesville city	2,524	37.3	1,734	790	1,069	1,455	550	31.6	158	28.7	2,038	514	25.2	500	373	74.6
Chesterfield	7,527	35.3	6,631	896	3,793	3,734	1,832	33.6	772	42.1	5,419	1,815	33.5	1,775	1,129	63.6
Clarke	1,900	25.4	1,388	512	961	939	472	24.1	185	39.2	1,415	432	30.5	470	298	63.4
Clifton Forge city	1,092	19.0	513	579	573	519	357	20.7	63	17.6	891	141	15.8	168	119	70.8
Craig	207	4.4	188	19	130	77	73	6.0	1	(2)	168	9	5.4	35	2	(2)
Culpeper	5,262	39.1	2,957	2,305	2,586	2,676	1,102	34.2	514	46.6	3,785	1,186	31.3	1,435	843	58.7
Cumberland	6,053	65.8	3,583	2,470	3,087	2,966	1,249	59.8	651	52.1	4,143	1,550	37.4	1,630	769	47.2
Danville city	6,207	32.6	3,971	2,236	2,683	3,524	1,380	28.8	540	39.1	5,015	1,868	37.2	1,144	748	65.4
Dickenson	7	0.1		7	3	4					7			4		
Dinwiddie	9,368	60.7	7,065	2,303	4,749	4,619	2,120	56.0	767	36.2	6,593	1,970	29.9	2,403	1,174	48.9
Elizabeth City	7,992	37.7	5,045	2,947	3,928	4,064	2,327	26.7	644	27.7	6,447	1,440	22.3	1,506	1,111	73.8
Essex	5,315	58.4	4,143	1,172	2,697	2,618	1,166	54.0	433	37.1	3,793	1,036	27.3	1,400	890	63.6

[1] Less than one-tenth of 1 per cent. [2] Per cent not shown where base is less than 100.

TABLE III.—GENERAL STATISTICS OF THE NEGRO POPULATION OF THE UNITED STATES, BY COUNTIES: 1910—Con.

[Counties in which no Negroes were reported are omitted.]

	NEGRO POPULATION: 1910.																
COUNTY.	Total.	Per cent of total population.	Color.		Sex.		Males 21 years of age and over.				Persons 10 years of age and over.			Persons 6 to 14 years of age.			
			Black.	Mulatto.	Male.	Female.	Number.	Per cent of total.	Illiterate.		Total.	Illiterate.		Total.	Attending school.	
									Number.	Per cent.		Number.	Per cent.		Number.	Per cent.

VIRGINIA—Continued.

COUNTY.	Total.	Per cent	Black.	Mulatto.	Male.	Female.	Number.	Per cent	Illit. No.	Illit. %	Total.	Illit. No.	Illit. %	Total.	Att. No.	Att. %
Fairfax	4,864	23.7	2,392	2,472	2,474	2,390	1,225	21.4	369	30.1	3,629	836	23.0	1,152	781	67.8
Fauquier	7,486	33.2	4,593	2,893	3,756	3,730	1,659	30.1	614	37.0	5,441	1,591	29.2	1,857	1,049	56.5
Floyd	837	5.9	556	281	423	414	166	5.5	76	45.8	598	184	30.8	215	164	76.3
Fluvanna	3,374	40.5	2,354	1,020	1,632	1,742	722	36.0	394	54.6	2,426	1,016	41.9	847	381	45.0
Franklin	5,435	20.5	4,030	1,405	2,636	2,799	1,052	18.8	615	58.5	3,831	1,641	42.8	1,533	719	46.9
Frederick	694	5.4	540	154	375	319	178	5.2	70	39.3	514	144	28.0	168	117	69.6
Fredericksburg city	1,480	25.2	457	1,023	667	813	353	23.4	79	22.4	1,193	238	19.9	270	172	63.7
Giles	755	6.5	548	207	389	366	188	6.9	88	46.8	534	206	38.6	158	70	44.3
Gloucester	5,907	47.3	5,084	823	2,994	2,913	1,366	43.8	569	41.7	4,189	1,147	27.4	1,556	1,192	76.6
Goochland	5,230	56.6	3,512	1,718	2,645	2,585	1,218	51.6	545	44.7	3,735	1,368	36.6	1,324	636	48.0
Grayson	939	4.7	446	493	448	491	177	4.1	76	42.9	651	251	38.6	258	160	62.0
Greene	1,339	19.3	931	408	645	694	279	18.3	140	50.2	921	365	39.6	385	222	57.7
Greensville	7,393	62.2	4,941	2,452	3,673	3,720	1,585	56.7	715	45.1	5,144	1,905	37.0	1,900	966	50.8
Halifax	20,013	50.0	11,348	8,665	9,683	10,330	4,064	46.1	1,869	46.0	14,097	4,796	34.0	5,029	3,225	64.1
Hanover	7,040	40.9	6,219	821	3,607	3,433	1,513	35.6	681	45.0	5,091	1,678	33.0	1,851	1,049	56.7
Henrico	6,837	29.2	5,364	1,473	3,388	3,449	1,701	28.0	590	34.7	5,174	1,431	27.7	1,426	904	63.4
Henry	7,462	40.4	3,938	3,524	3,566	3,896	1,410	34.9	750	53.2	5,147	2,023	39.3	1,951	1,200	61.5
Highland	260	4.9	135	125	128	132	59	4.1	31	(1)	190	76	40.0	61	22	(1)
Isle of Wight	7,512	50.3	6,357	1,155	3,782	3,730	1,652	45.8	815	49.3	5,205	2,218	42.6	1,924	869	45.2
James City	3,034	47.9	2,593	441	1,555	1,479	776	41.9	349	45.0	2,268	914	40.3	644	278	43.2
King and Queen	5,373	56.1	3,659	1,714	2,738	2,635	1,121	50.6	466	41.6	3,808	1,262	33.1	1,420	849	59.8
King George	2,913	45.7	1,985	928	1,500	1,413	618	41.1	288	46.6	2,126	752	35.4	789	433	54.9
King William	4,855	56.8	3,753	1,102	2,446	2,409	1,076	51.7	356	33.1	3,451	871	25.2	1,273	799	62.8
Lancaster	5,139	52.7	3,487	1,652	2,608	2,531	1,204	48.5	669	55.6	3,688	1,474	40.0	1,257	720	57.3
Lee	952	4.0	645	307	512	440	267	5.0	85	31.8	690	198	28.7	178	96	53.9
Loudoun	5,221	24.7	2,900	2,321	2,624	2,597	1,269	22.3	528	41.6	3,873	1,246	32.2	1,216	703	57.8
Louisa	7,883	47.6	5,303	2,580	3,801	4,082	1,638	42.0	621	37.9	5,602	1,652	29.5	2,056	1,324	64.4
Lunenburg	6,811	53.3	4,816	1,995	3,473	3,338	1,423	46.2	618	43.4	4,783	1,537	32.1	1,794	929	51.8
Lynchburg city	9,466	32.1	5,875	3,591	4,029	5,437	2,232	28.4	629	28.2	7,753	1,964	25.3	1,519	1,059	69.7
Madison	3,264	32.5	2,466	798	1,643	1,621	669	29.3	353	52.8	2,293	821	35.8	881	612	69.5
Mathews	2,513	28.2	1,836	677	1,284	1,229	611	26.1	210	34.4	1,854	455	24.5	594	359	60.4
Mecklenburg	16,394	56.6	11,531	4,863	8,114	8,280	3,369	51.9	1,344	39.9	11,571	3,529	30.5	4,239	2,397	56.5
Middlesex	4,636	52.4	3,750	886	2,488	2,148	1,151	50.1	413	35.9	3,374	881	26.1	1,163	749	64.4
Montgomery	2,323	13.5	1,180	1,143	1,129	1,194	558	13.7	204	36.6	1,788	516	28.9	543	406	74.8
Nansemond	15,536	57.8	10,397	5,139	7,689	7,847	3,623	54.4	1,516	41.8	11,345	4,135	36.4	3,651	2,029	55.6
Nelson	5,263	31.3	4,271	992	2,623	2,640	1,068	27.9	542	50.7	3,621	1,502	41.5	1,402	668	47.6
New Kent	2,791	59.6	2,220	571	1,474	1,317	657	54.3	312	47.5	2,014	725	36.0	684	374	54.7
Newport News city	7,259	35.9	6,226	1,033	3,714	3,545	2,478	36.8	276	11.1	5,922	708	12.0	1,133	783	69.1
Norfolk	31,791	60.3	20,069	11,722	15,855	15,936	8,485	58.4	2,532	29.8	23,623	6,284	26.6	6,691	4,714	70.5
Norfolk city	25,039	37.1	12,839	12,200	11,887	13,152	7,864	31.6	1,463	18.6	21,059	4,148	19.7	3,423	2,401	70.1
Northampton	9,314	55.9	6,696	2,618	4,727	4,587	2,175	49.9	771	35.4	6,536	1,783	27.3	2,267	1,263	55.7
Northumberland	4,267	39.6	3,260	1,007	2,271	1,996	1,009	35.2	359	35.6	2,990	820	27.4	1,133	748	66.0
Nottoway	7,347	54.6	5,218	2,129	3,632	3,715	1,640	49.6	528	32.2	5,352	1,285	24.0	1,863	1,167	62.6
Orange	5,526	41.0	4,025	1,501	2,715	2,811	1,143	35.9	474	41.5	3,964	1,197	30.2	1,458	818	56.1
Page	1,166	8.2	842	324	553	613	267	7.7	97	36.3	862	273	31.7	266	155	58.3
Patrick	1,618	9.4	1,069	549	792	826	308	8.6	119	38.6	1,109	301	27.1	420	199	47.4
Petersburg city	11,014	45.7	5,704	5,310	4,831	6,183	2,595	40.9	712	27.4	8,797	2,303	26.2	2,126	1,384	65.1
Pittsylvania	20,163	39.8	15,646	4,517	9,794	10,369	4,020	35.9	1,990	49.5	14,045	5,983	42.6	5,188	2,375	45.8
Portsmouth city	11,617	35.0	5,865	5,752	5,542	6,075	3,394	31.9	783	23.1	9,445	2,317	24.5	1,849	1,225	66.3
Powhatan	3,633	59.6	2,714	919	1,815	1,818	819	53.1	396	48.4	2,576	900	34.9	986	496	50.3
Prince Edward	8,458	59.3	5,472	2,986	4,091	4,367	1,819	54.0	578	31.8	6,145	1,592	25.9	2,196	1,198	54.6
Prince George	4,551	58.0	3,363	1,188	2,294	2,257	1,040	53.6	485	46.6	3,209	1,129	35.2	1,121	674	60.1
Prince William	2,825	23.5	1,290	1,535	1,457	1,368	658	21.0	257	39.1	1,995	581	29.1	688	453	65.8
Princess Anne	5,818	50.5	5,519	299	2,935	2,883	1,415	45.6	576	40.7	4,148	1,385	33.4	1,392	955	68.6
Pulaski	2,930	17.0	2,330	600	1,460	1,470	711	17.5	248	34.9	2,241	676	30.2	690	389	56.4
Radford city	665	15.8	623	42	313	352	148	13.7	51	34.5	509	141	27.7	160	75	46.9
Rappahannock	2,148	26.7	1,339	809	1,090	1,058	443	23.4	182	41.1	1,553	474	30.5	600	360	60.0
Richmond	3,071	41.4	2,091	980	1,557	1,514	636	37.1	415	65.3	2,193	1,238	56.5	823	277	33.7
Richmond city	46,733	36.6	28,088	18,645	21,472	25,261	13,279	35.7	2,765	20.8	38,876	7,615	19.6	6,927	4,514	65.2
Roanoke	3,525	18.0	2,105	1,420	1,703	1,822	842	18.0	299	35.5	2,711	703	25.9	805	567	70.4
Roanoke city	7,924	22.7	5,265	2,659	3,650	4,274	2,066	20.4	534	25.8	6,402	1,451	22.7	1,403	1,025	73.1
Rockbridge	3,528	16.7	2,308	1,220	1,689	1,839	843	16.3	320	38.0	2,709	777	28.7	782	545	69.7
Rockingham	2,335	6.7	1,954	381	1,120	1,215	572	6.6	252	44.1	1,755	555	31.6	523	383	73.2
Russell	1,025	4.4	817	208	605	420	349	6.0	113	32.4	785	239	30.4	190	86	45.3
Scott	503	2.1	222	281	238	265	102	1.9	48	47.1	353	143	40.5	126	73	57.9
Shenandoah	493	2.4	277	216	261	232	137	2.5	54	39.4	386	111	28.8	95	77	(1)
Smyth	981	4.8	515	466	486	495	217	4.5	67	30.9	716	172	24.0	218	117	53.7
Southampton	16,091	61.2	11,916	4,175	8,086	8,005	3,453	56.6	1,550	44.9	11,026	4,347	39.4	4,120	2,160	52.4
Spotsylvania	3,593	35.2	2,181	1,412	1,793	1,800	780	32.6	375	48.1	2,533	875	34.5	894	549	61.4
Stafford	1,720	21.3	1,163	557	934	786	464	21.5	174	37.5	1,262	395	31.3	425	215	50.6
Staunton city	2,476	23.3	2,050	426	1,053	1,423	640	20.6	149	23.3	2,067	405	19.6	419	304	72.6
Surry	6,005	61.8	4,309	1,696	3,201	2,804	1,511	58.0	617	40.8	4,236	1,412	33.3	1,462	528	36.1
Sussex	8,962	65.6	4,567	4,395	4,504	4,458	1,964	60.0	937	47.7	6,258	2,374	37.9	2,268	1,213	53.5
Tazewell	2,320	11.3	1,697	1,123	1,409	1,411	788	12.8	230	29.2	2,136	523	24.5	574	310	54.0

1 Per cent not shown where base is less than 100.

TABLE III.—GENERAL STATISTICS OF THE NEGRO POPULATION OF THE UNITED STATES, BY COUNTIES: 1910—Con.

[Counties in which no Negroes were reported are omitted.]

COUNTY.	NEGRO POPULATION: 1910.															
	Total.	Per cent of total population.	Color.		Sex.		Males 21 years of age and over.				Persons 10 years of age and over.			Persons 6 to 14 years of age.		
			Black.	Mulatto.	Male.	Female.	Number.	Per cent of total.	Illiterate.		Total.	Illiterate.		Total.	Attending school.	
									Number.	Per cent.		Number.	Per cent.		Number.	Per cent.
VIRGINIA—Continued.																
Warren	1,131	13.2	816	315	564	567	250	11.3	106	42.4	813	267	32.8	268	168	62.7
Warwick	4,334	71.7	3,108	1,226	2,281	2,053	1,228	71.8	436	35.5	3,190	1,065	33.4	817	455	55.7
Washington	2,312	7.0	1,441	871	1,149	1,163	538	7.0	163	30.3	1,711	416	24.3	487	225	46.2
Westmoreland	4,668	50.1	2,502	2,166	2,389	2,279	992	43.7	488	49.2	3,258	1,295	39.7	1,216	637	52.4
Winchester city	1,038	17.7	627	411	448	590	269	16.3	94	34.9	860	251	29.2	172	126	73.3
Wise	2,861	8.4	2,222	639	1,624	1,237	1,049	12.0	357	34.0	2,256	698	30.9	462	265	57.4
Wythe	2,188	10.7	1,264	924	1,065	1,123	511	10.9	182	35.6	1,672	447	26.7	507	314	61.9
York	3,764	48.5	2,227	1,537	1,944	1,820	919	45.2	193	21.0	2,760	495	17.9	902	431	47.8
WASHINGTON.																
Total	6,058	0.5	4,218	1,840	3,736	2,322	3,120	0.7	121	3.9	5,517	239	4.3	480	390	81.3
Adams	9	0.1	2	7	7	2	4	0.1	2	(1)	6	3	......	3	1	(1)
Asotin	1	(2)	1			1					1					
Benton	6	0.1	4	2	4	2	4	0.1			6					
Chehalis	60	0.2	56	4	32	28	31	0.2	10	(1)	59	10	(1)	1	1	(1)
Chelan	8	0.1	7	1	6	2	5	0.1			7			1	1	(1)
Clallam	2	(2)	2			2	1	(2)			2					
Clarke	47	0.2	40	7	32	15	25	0.3	3	(1)	40	6	(1)	5	4	(1)
Columbia	2	(2)		2		2					1					
Cowlitz	9	0.1	5	4	7	2	5	0.1			7			1	1	(1)
Douglas	11	0.1	11		5	6	3	0.1	1	(1)	11	1	(1)	1	1	(1)
Ferry	10	0.2	6	4	3	7	2	0.1			9	1	(1)	2	2	(1)
Franklin	19	0.4	8	11	13	6	11	0.5			19			4	4	(1)
Garfield	7	0.2	7		4	3	3	0.2			7			1	1	(1)
Grant	3	(2)	2	1	2	1	2	0.1			3					
Jefferson	11	0.1	9	2	6	5	6	0.1			11					
King	2,487	0.9	1,507	980	1,506	981	1,278	1.1	31	2.4	2,279	73	3.2	182	150	82.4
Kitsap	43	0.2	29	14	30	13	27	0.4	1	(1)	43	2	(1)	1	1	(1)
Kittitas	247	1.3	163	84	139	108	116	1.5	10	8.6	219	19	8.7	6	4	(1)
Klickitat	33	0.3	12	21	19	14	10	0.3			22	1	(1)	6	4	(1)
Lewis	79	0.3	48	31	47	32	26	0.2	3	(1)	56	7	(1)	16	15	(1)
Lincoln	13	0.1	13		10	3	5	0.1			9			3	3	(1)
Mason	6	0.1	2	4	4	2	4	0.2			5	1	(1)			
Okanogan	19	0.2	16	3	11	8	10	0.2			17			3	1	(1)
Pacific	3	(2)	3		2	1	2	(2)			3					
Pierce	889	0.7	643	246	514	375	424	0.9	24	5.7	806	40	5.0	71	54	(1)
Skagit	30	0.1	27	3	23	7	20	0.2	3	(1)	30	5	(1)			
Skamania	3	0.1	3		1	2	1	0.1			2			1		
Snohomish	219	0.4	186	33	115	104	93	0.4	6	(1)	198	17	8.6	19	16	(1)
Spokane	1,170	0.8	926	244	808	362	701	1.3	9	1.3	1,097	22	2.0	64	57	(1)
Stevens	12	(2)	7	5	11	1	11	0.1			12					
Thurston	24	0.1	13	11	13	11	12	0.2	1	(1)	23	2	(1)			
Wahkiakum	2	0.1	2		2		2	0.1			2					
Walla Walla	152	0.5	124	28	104	48	88	0.7	2	(1)	138	6	4.3	11	10	(1)
Whatcom	56	0.1	34	22	30	26	23	0.1	1	(1)	48	3	(1)	6	3	(1)
Whitman	12	(2)	11	1	10	2	9	0.1	2	(1)	12	2	(1)	1	1	(1)
Yakima	354	0.8	289	65	214	140	156	1.0	12	7.7	307	18	5.9	47	31	(1)
WEST VIRGINIA.																
Total	64,173	5.3	43,294	20,879	36,607	27,566	22,757	6.7	5,457	24.0	50,925	10,347	20.3	10,404	7,927	76.2
Barbour	920	5.8	71	849	508	412	247	5.7	67	27.1	652	161	24.7	212	137	64.6
Berkeley	1,801	8.2	1,479	322	932	869	531	8.6	149	28.1	1,443	320	22.2	313	215	68.7
Boone	164	1.6	62	102	91	73	48	2.0	12	(1)	110	21	19.1	35	26	(1)
Braxton	221	1.0	41	180	117	104	64	1.1	13	(1)	165	36	21.8	49	40	(1)
Brooke	151	1.4	121	30	81	70	51	1.4	2	(1)	129	8	6.2	25	18	(1)
Cabell	2,447	5.2	1,623	824	1,351	1,096	868	6.6	135	15.6	2,058	288	14.0	371	306	82.5
Calhoun	80	0.7	17	63	44	36	17	0.7			56			22	22	(1)
Clay	5	(2)	5		5		1	(2)			3			1	1	(1)
Doddridge	8	0.1	7	1	6	2	5	0.2			8					
Fayette	9,311	17.9	6,755	2,556	5,540	3,771	3,488	22.3	847	24.3	7,208	1,413	19.6	1,528	1,206	78.9
Gilmer	17	0.1	17		10	7	5	0.2	1	(1)	10	2	(1)			
Grant	253	3.2	99	154	135	118	64	3.0	26	(1)	187	62	33.2	63	48	(1)
Greenbrier	1,779	7.2	1,263	516	901	878	467	7.4	151	32.3	1,341	329	24.5	367	263	71.7
Hampshire	303	2.6	240	63	152	151	82	2.7	33	(1)	238	84	35.3	75	42	(1)
Hancock	37	0.4	37		24	13	13	0.4	3	(1)	30	4	(1)	6	5	(1)
Hardy	387	4.2	187	200	221	166	101	4.4	32	31.7	286	89	31.1	90	47	(1)
Harrison	1,359	2.8	846	513	720	639	458	3.1	81	17.7	1,124	202	18.0	184	129	70.1
Jackson	26	0.1	22	4	17	9	6	0.1	3	(1)	25	5	(1)	6	1	(1)
Jefferson	3,499	22.0	2,904		1,724	1,775	859	20.2	207	24.1	2,650	518	19.5	773	530	68.6
Kanawha	6,476	8.0	4,227	2,249	3,438	3,038	2,120	9.8	384	18.1	5,181	762	14.7	1,067	886	83.0

[1] Per cent not shown where base is less than 100. [2] Less than one-tenth of 1 per cent.

NEGRO POPULATION.

TABLE III.—GENERAL STATISTICS OF THE NEGRO POPULATION OF THE UNITED STATES, BY COUNTIES: 1910—Con.

[Counties in which no Negroes were reported are omitted.]

COUNTY.	NEGRO POPULATION: 1910.															
	Total.	Per cent of total population.	Color.		Sex.		Males 21 years of age and over.				Persons 10 years of age and over.			Persons 6 to 14 years of age.		
			Black.	Mulatto.	Male.	Female.	Number.	Per cent of total.	Illiterate.		Total.	Illiterate.		Total.	Attending school.	
									Number.	Per cent.		Number.	Per cent.		Number.	Per cent.

WEST VIRGINIA—Continued.

COUNTY.	Total.	Per cent pop.	Black.	Mulatto.	Male.	Female.	M21 No.	M21 %.	M21 Ill. No.	M21 Ill. %.	P10 Total.	P10 Ill. No.	P10 Ill. %.	P6-14 Total.	Attend No.	Attend %.
Lewis	239	1.3	150	89	127	112	108	2.1	16	14.8	228	60	26.3	9	8	[1]
Lincoln	30	0.1	22	8	17	13	12	0.3	3	[1]	27	8	[1]	5	3	[1]
Logan	532	3.7	464	68	363	169	237	5.9	53	22.4	433	102	23.6	62	32	[1]
McDowell	14,667	30.6	10,032	4,635	9,120	5,547	5,883	34.1	1,618	27.5	11,754	2,830	24.1	2,067	1,639	79.3
Marion	851	2.0	638	213	468	383	326	2.5	43	13.2	699	80	11.4	112	88	78.6
Marshall	575	1.8	431	144	494	81	433	4.2	77	17.8	548	94	17.2	27	20	[1]
Mason	349	1.5	233	116	186	163	123	2.1	28	22.8	296	55	18.6	63	58	[1]
Mercer	5,960	15.5	3,929	2,031	3,268	2,692	2,009	18.5	548	27.3	4,647	1,054	22.7	962	763	79.3
Mineral	601	3.6	423	178	304	297	169	3.6	44	26.0	464	91	19.6	125	100	80.0
Mingo	1,236	6.4	876	360	867	369	643	11.2	242	37.6	1,087	377	34.7	105	55	52.4
Monongalia	294	1.2	262	32	146	148	85	1.2	11	[1]	225	25	11.1	67	49	[1]
Monroe	673	5.2	291	382	328	345	161	4.9	54	33.5	497	118	23.7	151	116	76.8
Morgan	177	2.3	50	127	95	82	54	2.6	9	[1]	142	17	12.0	37	31	[1]
Nicholas	48	0.3	43	5	17	31	10	0.2			35	5	[1]	9	2	[1]
Ohio	1,389	2.4	660	729	712	677	543	3.1	50	9.2	1,222	120	9.8	114	100	87.7
Pendleton	132	1.4	80	52	72	60	33	1.4	10	[1]	96	19	[1]	29	10	[1]
Pleasant	9	0.1	1	8	4	5	3	0.1	1	[1]	9	1	[1]	2	2	[1]
Pocahontas	445	3.0	367	78	250	195	131	2.9	41	31.3	323	74	22.9	101	78	77.2
Preston	151	0.6	113	38	101	50	70	0.9	15	[1]	122	23	18.9	21	18	[1]
Putnam	435	2.3	365	70	226	209	125	2.8	32	25.6	310	56	18.1	109	86	78.9
Raleigh	2,052	8.0	1,852	200	1,280	772	866	11.9	189	21.8	1,624	330	20.3	264	188	71.2
Randolph	376	1.4	245	131	200	176	113	1.4	26	23.0	280	52	18.6	76	49	[1]
Ritchie	26	0.1	7	19	11	15	9	0.2	3	[1]	24	3	[1]	5	3	[1]
Roane	18	0.1	8	10	11	7	6	0.1	2	[1]	14	6	[1]	3		
Summers	1,130	6.1	293	837	577	553	310	6.8	53	17.1	887	147	16.6	235	159	67.7
Taylor	527	3.2	250	277	300	227	136	3.0	33	24.3	399	69	17.3	126	111	88.1
Tucker	344	1.8	263	81	202	142	126	2.1	15	11.9	269	31	11.5	58	43	[1]
Tyler	115	0.7	64	51	61	54	44	1.1	6	[1]	98	13	[1]	16	12	[1]
Upshur	226	1.4	131	95	99	127	62	1.4	19	[1]	166	33	19.9	49	38	[1]
Wayne	169	0.7	99	70	94	75	57	1.0	14	[1]	124	22	17.7	30	17	[1]
Webster	8	0.1	4	4	4	4	4	0.2			8			1		
Wetzel	57	0.2	48	9	33	24	25	0.4	1	[1]	41	1	[1]	9	3	[1]
Wirt	40	0.4	39	1	27	13	9	0.4			34	1	[1]	10	10	[1]
Wood	943	2.5	459	484	466	477	304	2.8	40	13.2	806	91	11.3	134	111	82.8
Wyoming	105	1.0	79	26	60	45	33	1.4	15	[1]	83	35	[1]	24	3	[1]

WISCONSIN.

COUNTY.	Total.	Per cent pop.	Black.	Mulatto.	Male.	Female.	M21 No.	M21 %.	M21 Ill. No.	M21 Ill. %.	P10 Total.	P10 Ill. No.	P10 Ill. %.	P6-14 Total.	Attend No.	Attend %.
Total	2,900	0.1	1,757	1,143	1,476	1,424	1,082	0.2	58	5.4	2,500	113	4.5	341	303	88.9
Adams	4	[2]	4		3	1	2	0.1			4			1	1	[1]
Ashland	8	[2]	7	1	6	2	2	[2]			7			3	3	[1]
Barron	18	0.1	4	14	10	8	3	[2]			15			3	3	[1]
Bayfield	8	0.1	6	2	4	4	3	0.1	1	[1]	7	2	[1]	1		
Brown	69	0.1	33	36	32	37	19	0.1			54	2	[1]	9	9	[1]
Buffalo	1	[2]	1			1								1	1	[1]
Burnett	6	0.1	2	4	3	3	1	[2]			3			1	1	[1]
Calumet	3	[2]	2	1	2	1	2	[2]			3					
Chippewa	7	[2]	3	4	6	1	4	[2]	1	[1]	6	1	[1]	3	3	[1]
Clark	15	[2]	3	12	11	4	4	[2]			12			3	3	[1]
Columbia	18	0.1	9	9	11	7	8	0.1			16			3	2	[1]
Crawford	3	[2]	3			3					2					
Dane	173	0.2	89	84	87	86	61	0.3	2	[1]	142	7	4.9	24	19	[1]
Dodge	43	0.1	33	10	35	8	29	0.2	2	[1]	39	4	[1]	5	5	[1]
Door	3	[2]	1	2	2	1	2	[2]			2			1		
Douglas	184	0.4	171	13	80	104	69	0.4			167	3	1.8	10	7	[1]
Dunn	12	[2]	11	1	2	10	1	[2]			8			4	4	[1]
Eau Claire	33	0.1	20	13	12	21	9	0.1			24					
Fond du Lac	54	0.1	29	25	27	27	22	0.1	4		50	7	[1]	6	6	[1]
Forest	2	[2]	2			2	1	[2]			2					
Grant	55	0.1	30	25	23	32	15	0.1			44	1	[1]	8	7	[1]
Green	6	[2]	3	3	3	3	3	[2]	1		6	2	[1]			
Green Lake	8	0.1	7	1	2	6	1	[2]			5			2	2	[1]
Iowa	20	0.1	13	7	11	9	4	0.1	1		14	1	[1]	5	4	[1]
Iron	3	[2]	3			3					2					
Jackson	2	[2]	1	1	2		2	[2]			2					
Jefferson	22	0.1	19	3	12	10	12	0.1			22			1	1	[1]
Juneau	13	0.1	2	11	8	5	5	0.1			11					
Kenosha	40	0.1	24	16	23	17	20	0.2	1		39	1	[1]	4	4	[1]
La Crosse	74	0.2	29	45	38	36	26	0.2	1		66	2	[1]	19	19	[1]
Lafayette	5	[2]	5		1	4	1	[2]			4			1	1	[1]
Langlade	10	0.1	4	6	4	6	1	[2]			6			4	4	[1]
Lincoln	12	0.1	5	7	10	2	3	0.1			12			2	2	[1]
Manitowoc	16	[2]	3	13	8	8	7	0.1	1	[1]	14	1	[1]	2	2	[1]
Marathon	12	[2]	7	5	4	8	3	[2]			11			2	2	[1]

[1] Per cent not shown where base is less than 100.　　　[2] Less than one-tenth of 1 per cent.

TABLE III.—GENERAL STATISTICS OF THE NEGRO POPULATION OF THE UNITED STATES, BY COUNTIES: 1910—Con.

[Counties in which no Negroes were reported are omitted.]

COUNTY.	NEGRO POPULATION: 1910.															
	Total.	Per cent of total population.	Color.		Sex.		Males 21 years of age and over.				Persons 10 years of age and over.			Persons 6 to 14 years of age.		
			Black.	Mulatto.	Male.	Female.	Number.	Per cent of total.	Illiterate.		Total.	Illiterate.		Total.	Attending school.	
									Number.	Per cent.		Number.	Per cent.		Number.	Per cent.
WISCONSIN—Continued.																
Marinette	11	(1)	3	8	5	6	3	(1)	2	(2)	6	2	(2)	2	2	(2)
Marquette	9	0.1	8	1	7	2	7	0.2			9					
Milwaukee	996	0.2	619	377	494	502	410	0.3	13	3.2	905	30	3.3	74	60	(2)
Monroe	36	0.1	14	22	18	18	8	0.1			28			10	8	(2)
Oconto	2	(1)	2		1	1	1	(1)	1	(2)	2	1	(2)	1	1	(2)
Oneida	3	(1)	2	1	3		3	0.1	2	(2)	3	2	(2)			
Outagamie	28	0.1	13	15	9	19	6	(1)	1	(2)	24	2	(2)	3	3	(2)
Ozaukee	7	(1)	5	2	4	3	1	(1)			5			3	3	(2)
Pepin	1	(1)	1		1		1	(1)			1					
Pierce	15	0.1	10	5	11	4	9	0.1	2	(2)	13	2	(2)	1	1	(2)
Polk	5	(1)	4	1	3	2	3	0.1	1	(2)	5	2	(2)			
Portage	5	(1)	4	1	3	2	1	(1)			5			1	1	(2)
Price	6	(1)	2	4	2	4	1	(1)			3					
Racine	115	0.2	94	21	55	60	43	0.2	2	(2)	105	4	3.8	13	12	(2)
Richland	13	0.1	11	2	5	8	3	0.1			9			1	1	(2)
Rock	157	0.3	98	59	76	81	60	0.3	5	(2)	138	10	7.2	17	16	(2)
Rusk	2	(1)	2			2					2					
St. Croix	3	(1)	3		2	1	2	(1)	1	(2)	3	1	(2)			
Sauk	30	0.1	19	11	25	5	17	0.2	4	(2)	30	7	(2)	1	1	(2)
Shawano	31	0.1	9	22	17	14	9	0.1	1	(2)	24	1	(2)	4	4	(2)
Sheboygan	19	(1)	15	4	8	11	4	(1)			15			2	2	(2)
Taylor	24	0.2	7	17	12	12	7	0.2	1	(2)	18	1	(2)	3	2	(2)
Trempealeau	2	(1)	2		1	1	1	(1)			2	1	(2)			
Vernon	116	0.4	41	75	74	42	35	0.4	2	(2)	77	2	(2)	33	31	(2)
Vilas	10	0.2	9	1	8	2	7	0.3			9			1	1	(2)
Walworth	64	0.2	47	17	36	28	25	0.3			57	2	(2)	11	11	(2)
Washburn	3	(1)	2	1	2	1	1	(1)			2			1		
Washington	6	(1)	6		3	3	3	(1)			5					
Waukesha	74	0.2	50	24	39	35	21	0.2	1	(2)	55	3	(2)	16	15	(2)
Waupaca	18	0.1	6	12	11	7	10	0.1	2	(2)	17	2	(2)	1	1	(2)
Waushara	11	0.1	7	4	3	8	3	0.1			10			1		
Winnebago	110	0.2	50	60	51	59	31	0.2	2	(2)	87	4	(2)	13	12	(2)
Wood	6	(1)	4	2	3	3	2	(1)			5					
WYOMING.																
Total	2,235	1.5	1,942	293	1,544	691	1,325	2.1	50	3.8	2,024	102	5.0	137	116	84.7
Albany	59	0.5	56	3	31	28	27	0.5	1	(2)	52	2	(2)	4	4	(2)
Big Horn	9	0.1	7	2	6	3	4	0.1			9					
Carbon	146	1.3	102	44	95	51	77	1.4	7	(2)	129	15	11.6	11	8	(2)
Converse	24	0.4	23	1	18	6	16	0.6	1	(2)	24	2	(2)			
Crook	5	0.1	3	2	3	2	3	0.1			5					
Fremont	32	0.3	31	1	15	17	14	0.2			29			2	2	(2)
Johnson	2	0.1	2		2		2	0.1			2					
Laramie	1,607	6.2	1,432	175	1,183	424	1,045	8.9	37	3.5	1,484	74	5.0	82	69	(2)
Natrona	19	0.4	18	1	10	9	8	0.3			18					
Park	13	0.3	7	6	8	5	5	0.3			9					
Sheridan	183	1.1	148	35	97	86	72	1.0			158	2	1.3	15	13	(2)
Sweetwater	101	0.9	84	17	56	45	37	0.6	3	(2)	79	6	(2)	15	13	(2)
Uinta	26	0.2	22	4	16	10	11	0.2	1	(2)	18	1	(2)	7	7	(2)
Weston	5	0.1	5		3	2	3	0.1			4			1		
Yellowstone National Park	4	0.8	2	2	1	3	1	0.3			4					

[1] Less than one-tenth of 1 per cent.   [2] Per cent not shown where base is less than 100.

TABLE **IV.**—TOTAL POPULATION AT EACH CENSUS, BY DIVISIONS AND STATES: 1790–1910.

DIVISION AND STATE.	TOTAL POPULATION.												
	1910	1900	1890 [1]	1880	1870	1860	1850	1840	1830	1820	1810	1800	1790
UNITED STATES....	91,972,266	75,994,575	62,947,714	50,155,783	38,558,371	31,443,321	23,191,876	[2]17,069,453	[2]12,866,020	9,638,453	7,239,881	5,308,483	3,929,214
GEOGRAPHIC DIVISIONS:													
New England.......	6,552,681	5,592,017	4,700,749	4,010,529	3,487,924	3,135,283	2,728,116	2,234,822	1,954,717	1,660,071	1,471,973	1,233,011	1,009,408
Middle Atlantic.....	19,315,892	15,454,678	12,706,220	10,496,878	8,810,806	7,458,985	5,898,735	4,526,260	3,587,664	2,699,845	2,014,702	1,402,565	958,632
East North Central..	18,250,621	15,985,581	13,478,305	11,206,668	9,124,517	6,926,884	4,523,260	2,924,728	1,470,018	792,719	272,324	51,006	....
West North Central .	11,637,921	10,347,423	8,932,112	6,157,443	3,856,594	2,169,832	880,335	426,814	140,455	66,586	19,783	....	....
South Atlantic.......	12,194,895	10,443,480	8,857,922	7,597,197	5,853,610	5,364,703	4,679,090	3,925,299	3,645,752	3,061,063	2,674,891	2,286,494	1,851,806
East South Central..	8,409,901	7,547,757	6,429,154	5,585,151	4,404,445	4,020,991	3,363,271	2,575,445	1,815,969	1,190,489	708,590	335,407	109,368
West South Central..	8,784,534	6,532,290	4,740,983	3,334,220	2,029,965	1,747,667	940,251	449,985	246,127	167,680	77,618	....	....
Mountain.............	2,633,517	1,674,657	1,213,935	653,119	315,385	174,923	72,927	....	....	....	....	....	....
Pacific..............	4,192,304	2,416,692	1,888,334	1,114,578	675,125	444,053	105,891	....	....	....	....	....	....
NEW ENGLAND:													
Maine...............	742,371	694,466	661,086	648,936	626,915	628,279	583,169	501,793	399,455	298,335	228,705	151,719	96,540
New Hampshire.....	430,572	411,588	376,530	346,991	318,300	326,073	317,976	284,574	269,328	244,161	214,460	183,858	141,885
Vermont............	355,956	343,641	332,422	332,286	330,551	315,098	314,120	291,948	280,652	235,981	217,895	154,465	85,425
Massachusetts.......	3,366,416	2,805,346	2,238,947	1,783,085	1,457,351	1,231,066	994,514	737,699	610,408	523,287	472,040	422,845	378,787
Rhode Island........	542,610	428,556	345,506	276,531	217,353	174,620	147,545	108,830	97,199	83,059	76,931	69,122	68,825
Connecticut.........	1,114,756	908,420	746,258	622,700	537,454	460,147	370,792	309,978	297,675	275,248	261,942	251,002	237,946
MIDDLE ATLANTIC:													
New York..........	9,113,614	7,268,894	6,003,174	5,082,871	4,382,759	3,880,735	3,097,394	2,428,921	1,918,608	1,372,812	959,049	589,051	340,120
New Jersey.........	2,537,167	1,883,669	1,444,933	1,131,116	906,096	672,035	489,555	373,306	320,823	277,575	245,562	211,149	184,139
Pennsylvania.......	7,665,111	6,302,115	5,258,113	4,282,891	3,521,951	2,906,215	2,311,786	1,724,033	1,348,233	1,049,458	810,091	602,365	434,373
EAST NORTH CENTRAL:													
Ohio................	4,767,121	4,157,545	3,672,329	3,198,062	2,665,260	2,339,511	1,980,329	1,519,467	937,903	581,434	230,760	45,365	....
Indiana.............	2,700,876	2,516,462	2,192,404	1,978,301	1,680,637	1,350,428	988,416	685,866	343,031	147,178	24,520	5,641	....
Illinois.............	5,638,591	4,821,550	3,826,352	3,077,871	2,539,891	1,711,951	851,470	476,183	157,445	55,211	12,282	....	....
Michigan............	2,810,173	2,420,982	2,093,890	1,636,937	1,184,059	749,113	397,654	212,267	31,639	8,896	4,762	....	....
Wisconsin...........	2,333,860	2,069,042	1,693,330	1,315,497	1,054,670	775,881	305,391	30,945	....	....	....	....	....
WEST NORTH CENTRAL:													
Minnesota..........	2,075,708	1,751,394	1,310,283	780,773	439,706	172,023	6,077	....	....	....	....	....	....
Iowa...............	2,224,771	2,231,853	1,912,297	1,624,615	1,194,020	674,913	192,214	43,112	....	....	....	....	....
Missouri...........	3,293,335	3,106,665	2,679,185	2,168,380	1,721,295	1,182,012	682,044	383,702	140,455	66,586	19,783	....	....
North Dakota......	577,056	319,146	190,983 }	[3]135,177	[3]14,181	[4]4,837	....	....	....	....	....	....	....
South Dakota......	583,888	401,570	348,600 }				....	....	....	....	....	....	....
Nebraska...........	1,192,214	1,066,300	1,062,656	452,402	122,993	28,841	....	....	....	....	....	....	....
Kansas.............	1,690,949	1,470,495	1,428,108	996,096	364,399	107,206	....	....	....	....	....	....	....
SOUTH ATLANTIC:													
Delaware...........	202,322	184,735	168,493	146,608	125,015	112,216	91,532	78,085	76,748	72,749	72,674	64,273	59,096
Maryland...........	1,295,346	1,188,044	1,042,390	934,943	780,894	687,049	583,034	470,019	447,040	407,350	380,546	341,548	319,728
District of Columbia.	331,069	278,718	230,392	177,624	131,700	75,080	51,687	43,712	39,834	33,039	24,023	14,093	....
Virginia............	2,061,612	1,854,184	1,655,980	1,512,565	1,225,163	1,596,318	1,421,661	1,239,797	1,211,405	1,065,366	974,600	880,200	747,610
West Virginia.......	1,221,119	958,800	762,794	618,457	442,014	....	....	....	....	....	....	....	....
North Carolina.....	2,206,287	1,893,810	1,617,949	1,399,750	1,071,361	992,622	869,039	753,419	737,987	638,829	555,500	478,103	393,751
South Carolina.....	1,515,400	1,340,316	1,151,149	995,577	705,606	703,708	668,507	594,398	581,185	502,741	415,115	345,591	249,073
Georgia............	2,609,121	2,216,331	1,837,353	1,542,180	1,184,109	1,057,286	906,185	691,392	516,823	340,989	252,433	162,686	82,548
Florida............	752,619	528,542	391,422	269,493	187,748	140,424	87,445	54,477	34,730	....	....	....	....
EAST SOUTH CENTRAL:													
Kentucky..........	2,289,905	2,147,174	1,858,635	1,648,690	1,321,011	1,155,684	982,405	779,828	687,917	564,317	406,511	220,955	73,677
Tennessee.........	2,184,789	2,020,616	1,767,518	1,542,359	1,258,520	1,109,801	1,002,717	829,210	681,904	422,823	261,727	105,602	35,691
Alabama...........	2,138,093	1,828,697	1,513,401	1,262,505	996,992	964,201	771,623	590,756	309,527	127,901	....	....	....
Mississippi........	1,797,114	1,551,270	1,289,600	1,131,597	827,922	791,305	606,526	375,651	136,621	75,448	40,352	8,850	....
WEST SOUTH CENTRAL:													
Arkansas...........	1,574,449	1,311,564	1,128,211	802,525	484,471	435,450	209,897	97,574	30,388	14,273	1,062	....	....
Louisiana..........	1,656,388	1,381,625	1,118,588	939,946	726,915	708,002	517,762	352,411	215,739	153,407	76,556	....	....
Oklahoma..........	1,657,155	[5]790,391	[5]258,657	....	....	....	....	....	....	....	....	....	....
Texas..............	3,896,542	3,048,710	2,235,527	1,591,749	818,579	604,215	212,592	....	....	....	....	....	....
MOUNTAIN:													
Montana...........	376,053	243,329	142,924	39,159	20,595	....	....	....	....	....	....	....	....
Idaho..............	325,594	161,772	88,548	32,610	14,999	....	....	....	....	....	....	....	....
Wyoming...........	145,965	92,531	62,555	20,789	9,118	....	....	....	....	....	....	....	....
Colorado...........	799,024	539,700	413,249	194,327	39,864	34,277	....	....	....	....	....	....	....
New Mexico........	327,301	195,310	160,282	119,565	91,874	93,516	61,547	....	....	....	....	....	....
Arizona............	204,354	122,931	88,243	40,440	9,658	....	....	....	....	....	....	....	....
Utah...............	373,351	276,749	210,779	143,963	86,786	40,273	11,380	....	....	....	....	....	....
Nevada.............	81,875	42,335	47,355	62,266	42,491	6,857	....	....	....	....	....	....	....
PACIFIC:													
Washington........	1,141,990	518,103	357,232	75,116	23,955	11,594	....	....	....	....	....	....	....
Oregon............	672,765	413,536	317,704	174,768	90,923	52,465	13,294	....	....	....	....	....	....
California..........	2,377,549	1,485,053	1,213,398	864,694	560,247	379,994	92,597	....	....	....	....	....	....

[1] Includes population (325,464) of Indian Territory and Indian reservations, specially enumerated in 1890, but not included in the general report on population in 1890.
[2] Includes persons (6,100 in 1840 and 5,318 in 1830) on public ships in the service of the United States, not credited to any division or state.
[3] Population for that part of Dakota territory taken to form North Dakota, in 1880, 36,909; and in 1870, 2,405; and for that part taken to form South Dakota, in 1880, 98,268; and in 1870, 11,776.
[4] Dakota territory.
[5] Includes population of Indian Territory as follows: 1900, 392,060; 1890, 180,182.

INDEX.

○